WISDEN

CRICKETERS' ALMANACK

2022

EDITED BY LAWRENCE BOOTH

WISDEN

CRICKETERS' ALMANACK

2022

159th EDITION

John Wisden & Co

An imprint of Bloomsbury Publishing Plc

WISDEN
Bloomsbury Publishing Plc
50 Bedford Square, London, WC1B 3DP, UK
29 Earlsfort Terrace, Dublin 2, Ireland

BLOOMSBURY, WISDEN and the wood-engraving device are trademarks of
Bloomsbury Publishing Plc

First published in Great Britain 2022

WISDEN CRICKETERS' ALMANACK

Editor **Lawrence Booth**

Co-editor **Hugh Chevallier**

International editor **Steven Lynch**

Statistical editor **Harriet Monkhouse**

Assistant editor **Kit Harris**

Production co-ordinator **Matt Boulton**

Statisticians **Philip Bailey** and **Andrew Samson**

Proofreader **Charles Barr**

Database and typesetting **James Parsisson**

Publisher **Katy McAdam**

Consultant publisher **Christopher Lane**

Reader feedback: almanack@wisdenalmanack.com

www.wisdenalmanack.com

www.wisdenrecords.com

Follow Wisden on Twitter @WisdenAlmanack

and on Facebook at Wisden Sports

A catalogue record for this book is available from the British Library

Library of Congress Cataloguing-in-Publication data has been applied for

Hardback 978-1-4729-9110-2   £57

Soft cover 978-1-4729-9111-9   £57

Large format 978-1-4729-9109-6   £80

Leatherbound 978-1-3994-0289-7   £300

The Shorter Wisden (ePDF) 978-1-4729-9089-1   £15

The Shorter Wisden (ePub) 978-1-3994-0433-4   £15

2 4 6 8 10 9 7 5 3 1

A Taste of Wisden 2022

I was disappointed there were so few voices in women's cricket highlighting our plight. I thought they would all speak out. Without cricket, the only headlines Afghanistan can make are negative.
Afghanistan and the Taliban, page 54

* * *

Not all the sledging was poetic: in one saga, the hero calls his opponent a "cesspool pig"; in another, a player breaks a spectator's neck after being barracked.
Cricket and knattleikr, page 83

* * *

At one in the morning just before the Lord's Test, he was enjoying a night at the Embassy Club in Bond Street when the message arrived. "If the selectors had informed me a bit earlier, I should have gone to bed at a timely hour and knocked off a cigar or two."
A history of selection, page 93

* * *

A gambling addiction led to embezzlement, a spell in prison and the end of his first marriage. More recently, he had a leg amputated.
Cricket books, page 141

* * *

Sri Lanka's coach, Mickey Arthur, was incensed, and complained to the match referee, but he was unaware of Law 33.2.2.2.
The Laws of the game, page 186

* * *

Kohli's face, always a picture, recalled Munch's *The Scream*.
India v England, page 340

* * *

If Robinson's pace was visibly down, the Burnley express had become the Burnley rail-replacement bus service.
England v India, page 403

* * *

The ice cream queues routinely outstripped those for beer.
The women's Hundred, page 1200

LIST OF CONTRIBUTORS

Cartoons by Nick Newman. Contributors to the **Round the World** section are listed after their articles.

The editor also acknowledges with gratitude assistance from the following: Robin Abrahams, Clare Adams, Anna Ash, Colin Bateman, Trevor Bedells, Martin Bicknell, John Bryant, Andrew Burgess-Tupling, Derek Carlaw, Mike Coward, Prakash Dahatonde, Nigel Davies, Isabelle Duncan, Gulu Ezekiel, M. L. Fernando, Ric Finlay, Alan Fordham, David Frith, Peter Gibbs, Alexander Goldie, David Graveney, Nigel Hancock, Richard Heller, Clive Hitchcock, John Jackson, David Kendix, Rajesh Kumar, John Leather, Edward Liddle, Mahendra Mapagunaratne, Robin Marlar, Peter Martin, Colin Maynard, Ashu Mitra, Caroline Nyamande, Michael Owen-Smith, Rachel Pagan, Francis Payne, Peter Pollock, Mick Pope, Qamar Ahmed, Clive Radley, Chris Smith, Steven Stern, Bob Thomas, John Treleven, Gordon Vince, Iain Wakefield, Chris Walmsley, Keith Walmsley.

The production of *Wisden* would not be possible without the support and co-operation of many other cricket officials, county scorers, writers and lovers of the game. To them all, many thanks.

PREFACE

John Woodcock, who died last year aged 94 – on W. G. Grace's birthday, and three days before the start of The Hundred – was the first of the modern-era *Wisden* editors, and an inimitable cricket correspondent of *The Times*. A few years ago, in spidery script on headed notepaper ("The Old Curacy, Longparish"), he good-naturedly berated me for tweaks to a piece he had written for the Almanack. After recalling how telephone copytakers would occasionally mangle his prose – "beautiful for dutiful, rarely for really, cedar fences for sea defences" – he said how much he had enjoyed the latest edition. It was typical Wooders: both forthright and charming.

Wisden lost other friends. David Foot wrote lyrically for us, often about Somerset, always with an eye on the person behind the scorecard, while for many years Geoffrey Wheeler was our Gloucestershire correspondent. We were saddened, too, by the sudden death of Douglas Henderson, who had diligently compiled the schools section since 2006; a full obituary will appear next year.

Three long-serving county correspondents have stepped down: Mark Pennell covered Kent for 17 editions, Mark Eklid Derbyshire for 12, and Andy Stockhausen Gloucestershire for nine. We also say goodbye to Abid Ali Kazi, who had supplied reports from Pakistan since 1986.

After much consideration, the Almanack has aligned its figures with those of the Association of Cricket Statisticians and Historians, with repercussions – outlined in these pages – for W. G. Grace, Wilfred Rhodes and others. (If you thought it agonising that Jack Hobbs had finished with 197 first-class centuries, things just got worse.)

The editorial team handled another busy year with their usual verve. Co-editor Hugh Chevallier kept the show on the road, and Harriet Monkhouse remained the last word on accuracy. In his 36th year as a Wisden employee, Steven Lynch settled into semi-retirement, but will remain indispensable. Kit Harris has arrived as assistant editor, and made an instant impact. Thanks, too, to Matt Boulton, our production co-ordinator, to Christopher Lane, our consultant publisher (and much more), to Richard Whitehead, one of our chief obituarists, to Charles Barr for his proofreading, James Parsisson for his typesetting, and Philip Bailey and Andrew Samson for their statistics.

At Bloomsbury, Katy McAdam was a generous boss, and we're grateful for the hard work of Lizzy Ewer and Katherine Macpherson. My colleagues at the *Daily Mail* and *The Mail on Sunday* – Marc Padgett, Paul Newman, Richard Gibson and Mike Richards – were understanding about my other job.

Heartfelt thanks go to my wife, Anjali, after a winter like no other. One moment, we were set to spend most of it together; the next, I was answering a late call to cover the Ashes. Fortunately, and despite my new grey hairs brought on by England's performance, she and our daughters, Aleya and Anoushka, still recognised me.

LAWRENCE BOOTH
Barnes, February 2022

8

CONTENTS

Part One – Comment

Part Two – The Wisden Review

Part Three – English International Cricket

Part Four – English Domestic Cricket

STATISTICS

LV= COUNTY CHAMPIONSHIP

LIMITED-OVERS COMPETITIONS

OTHER ENGLISH CRICKET

Part Five – Overseas Cricket

Part Eight – Records and Registers

Part Nine – The Almanack

SYMBOLS AND ABBREVIATIONS

*	In full scorecards and lists of tour parties signifies the captain. In short scorecards, averages and records signifies not out.
†	In full scorecards signifies the designated wicketkeeper. In averages signifies a left-handed batsman.
‡	In short scorecards signifies the team who won the toss.
DLS	Signifies where the result of a curtailed match has been determined under the Duckworth/Lewis/Stern method.

Other uses of symbols are explained in notes where they appear.

First-class matches Men's matches of three or more days are first-class unless otherwise stated. All other matches are not first-class, including one-day and T20 internationals.

Scorecards Where full scorecards are not provided in this book, they can be found at Cricket Archive (www.cricketarchive.co.uk) or ESPNcricinfo (www.cricinfo.com). Full scorecards from matches played overseas can also be found in the relevant *ACS Overseas First-Class Annuals*. In Twenty20 scorecards, the first figure in a bowling analysis refers to balls bowled, not overs, and the second to dot balls, not maidens (as in first-class or List A games).

Records The Records section (pages 926–1076) is online at www.wisdenrecords.com. The database is regularly updated and, in many instances, more detailed than in *Wisden 2021*.

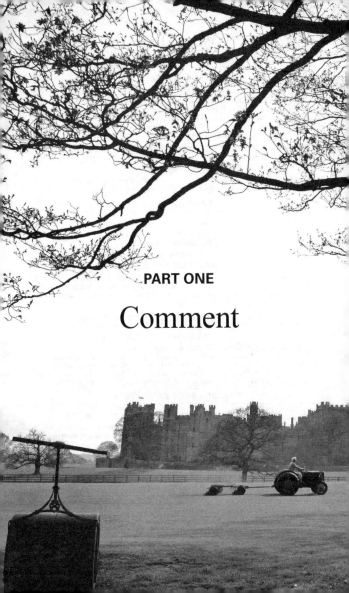

PART ONE

Comment

Wisden Honours

THE LEADING CRICKETERS IN THE WORLD

Joe Root (page 98)
Lizelle Lee (page 97)

The Leading Cricketers in the World are chosen by the editor of *Wisden* in consultation with some of the world's most experienced writers and commentators. Selection is based on a player's class and form shown in all cricket during the calendar year, and is guided by statistics rather than governed by them. Players may be chosen more than once. A list of past winners can be found on pages 97 and 99. A list of notional past winners, backdated to 1900, appeared on page 35 of *Wisden 2007*.

THE LEADING TWENTY20 CRICKETER IN THE WORLD

Mohammad Rizwan (page 1114)

This award exactly mirrors those above, but is based solely on performances in Twenty20 cricket, both international and domestic – and may be won by a male or female player.

FIVE CRICKETERS OF THE YEAR

Jasprit Bumrah (page 65)
Devon Conway (page 67)
Ollie Robinson (page 69)
Rohit Sharma (page 71)
Dane van Niekerk (page 73)

The Five Cricketers of the Year are chosen by the editor of *Wisden*, and represent a tradition that dates back to 1889, making this the oldest individual award in cricket. Excellence in and/or influence on the previous English summer are the major criteria for inclusion. No one can be chosen more than once. A list of past winners can be found on page 1454.

WISDEN SCHOOLS CRICKETER OF THE YEAR

Jacob Bethell (page 790)

The Schools Cricketer of the Year, based on first-team performances during the previous English summer, is chosen by *Wisden's* schools correspondent in consultation with the editor and other experienced observers. The winner's school must be in the UK, play cricket to a standard approved by *Wisden* and provide reports to this Almanack. A list of past winners can be found on page 790. A list of notional past winners, backdated to 1900, appeared on page 128 of *Wisden 2021*.

WISDEN BOOK OF THE YEAR

Who Only Cricket Know by David Woodhouse (page 145)

The Book of the Year is selected by *Wisden's* guest reviewer; all cricket books published in the previous calendar year and submitted to *Wisden* for possible review are eligible. A list of past winners can be found on page 147.

WISDEN CRICKET PHOTOGRAPH OF THE YEAR

was won by David Gray (whose entry appears opposite page 64)

The Wisden Cricket Photograph of the Year is chosen by a panel of independent experts; all images on a cricket theme photographed in the previous calendar year are eligible.

WISDEN'S WRITING COMPETITION

was won by Peter Hobday (page 116)

Wisden's Writing Competition is open to anyone (other than previous winners) who has not been commissioned to write for, or has a working relationship with, the Almanack. Full details on page 117.

Full details of past winners of all these honours can be found at www.wisdenalmanack.com

NOTES BY THE EDITOR

Can there ever have been a bigger gap between what English cricket hoped to be, and what it was – between reality and fantasy? Early in 2022, a long-planned assault on the Ashes ended with all-out surrender: Hobart was England's tenth defeat in 14 Tests, their most abject sequence in nearly 30 years. Before that, a racism scandal brought to light by the courage of Azeem Rafiq made the game look unwelcoming, and worse. There was little to cherish.

Hammerings in Australia are nothing new, but the latest felt especially futile. The players were sent out with one hand tied behind their back, by a domestic structure that takes the red-ball game for granted – 12 weeks between June 7 and August 29 found room for eight days of first-class county cricket – and by an international schedule that reduces athletes to husks. For all the talk of the pandemic, both issues long pre-dated Covid. Did the ECB really expect anything other than an Ashes thrashing, or imagine it was sensible to allow Yorkshire to mark their own homework on Rafiq? Delusion ran through the game like the Australian attack through the English batting.

Only when Joe Root's side lost 4–0, and only when public opinion turned against Yorkshire – and by extension the ECB – were reports promised and 12-point plans devised. The damage, though, had been done. Early in the new year, the Test team were deep in crisis, while old white administrators peddled racial stereotypes. It might have been the 1980s.

In one respect, times *had* changed. For overseeing the launch of The Hundred, ECB chief executive Tom Harrison and a few lucky colleagues stood to share a bonus of £2.1m. As the *annus horribilis* took shape, this felt more and more wrong. Harrison, remember, had presided over 62 job losses; he had used procedural excuses to defend his failure to intervene at Yorkshire; and, the Ashes up in smoke, he had blamed the domestic structure on the (usefully anonymous) Professional Game Group, and the international calendar on administrators in faraway lands. Of his own shortcomings, he had less to say.

Shocked by what they had learned about racism in cricket, the parliamentary Digital, Culture, Media and Sport select committee threatened to withhold public funds unless the English game "cleaned up its act", and ordered Harrison to appear before them every three months. It was one thing that – after a pay cut to prove we were all in it together – his basic salary topped half a million. But an attempt to justify the bonus as a fact of corporate life was the soulless logic of the suiterati, who regard cricket as a business, not a sport, measured in pounds and rupees, not runs and wickets.

In early February, Harrison – bonus not yet banked – insisted he would not be "running away from the challenges", as if taking one for the team. And though those challenges occurred on his watch, it was others who paid for them: Ashley Giles was sacked as the men's team's managing director, Chris Silverwood as head coach, Graham Thorpe as his assistant. Eight members of the Ashes squad were dropped for the Test series in the Caribbean, including James Anderson and Stuart Broad. The ECB had no full-time chairman, after Ian Watmore came up short; the acting-MD, Andrew Strauss, was passing through. We were down to the bare bones.

The ethics of the bonus scandal were as bad as the optics. But there was an exit strategy, if only Harrison would recognise it: the bonus should either be returned, allowing the ECB to re-employ some of the staff whose work still had to be done, or used to broaden the game's diversity. If, by now, he has resigned or refused the money, we applaud. If not, the African-Caribbean Engagement programme is doing vital work on behalf of the very demographics the ECB say they care about. There is still time to undo at least part of the damage.

Sorry, not sorry

On the second morning of the summer's first Test, against New Zealand at Lord's in June, Ollie Robinson returned to fine leg, earning applause from spectators in the Mound Stand: less than rapturous, more than polite, it sounded like a show of support. The previous evening, he had read out an apology after old tweets surfaced in which he insulted Muslims, women and Asians. And a few hours before *that*, he and other England players had lined up on the outfield wearing anti-discrimination T-shirts. For the ECB, scrambling to be on the right side of history, the timing was horrific.

Yet this wasn't about the ECB, and it shouldn't have been about Robinson. Because if your first instinct was to wail about freedom of speech, or bemoan the excavation of tweets, rather than appreciate their impact on those they mocked, then you were – unconsciously or otherwise – part of the problem. The applause was as revealing as it was disquieting.

His apology and suspension ought to have been the end of it. But others saw their chance to co-opt cricket into their own battles. They called the suspension a ban – a cancellation by the woke mob. Culture secretary Oliver Dowden said the ECB had gone over the top; prime minister Boris Johnson agreed. The Establishment were rumbling into action. It showed why English cricket's race relations would deteriorate before they could improve.

As Yorkshire's mishandling of the Rafiq affair went from bad to abysmal, the scale of the crisis became clear not through solecisms from the past, but clumsy attempts to navigate the present. Gary Ballance, a former friend and county team-mate, apologised for calling Rafiq a "Paki", then suggested he might feel just as bad "about some of the things he said to me". Ryan Sidebottom – hired as an interim coach at Headingley – said the club should "try and forget", and never mind "all the politics". The problem was not confined to Yorkshire. Middlesex chairman Mike O'Farrell told the DCMS committee in January that diversification of the dressing-room had been hampered by an Anglo-Caribbean love of football, and Anglo-Asian preference for education. Both Sidebottom and O'Farrell said sorry. There were a lot of apologies in 2021; a few were heartfelt.

The effect of all these comments was insidious, and the message to those on the game's margins unambiguous: cricket's mainstream remained tone-deaf, even after Black Lives Matter, Michael Holding, Ebony Rainford-Brent, Rafiq and countless others who had been emboldened to speak out. And if they weren't paying attention on a subject as important as this, what else had they missed? With Mehmooda Duke, until November the only non-white county chair, leaving Leicestershire, and Vikram Solanki, the only non-white head coach, leaving Surrey, the need for diversity – a collection of different perspectives, not the tokenism some imagine – has never felt more urgent.

Weasel words

In "You Guys Are History", a Sky Sports documentary, the former England and Gloucestershire fast bowler Syd Lawrence mentioned the banana skin left outside his hotel room by a county team-mate. Gloucestershire contacted him straight away, issued a statement in which they "apologised unreservedly", and thanked him for going public. It wasn't difficult.

Yorkshire – under pressure to release the findings of a law firm's investigation into Rafiq's claims – showed the world how not to do it. On the day the media were swamped by the cancellation of the Old Trafford Test, Headingley smuggled out a press release. It offered both an olive twig ("Azeem Rafiq was the victim of racial harassment") and a slap in the face (his sacking was not for "anything other than cricketing reasons"). It admitted to instances of racist language and jokes about religion, but said there was not enough evidence to say Yorkshire was institutionally racist. It was a game of semantics, the work of a club passing judgment on themselves.

In October, Yorkshire were still trying to brazen it out, and issued another press release in which the seventh word was "pleased". No one, it said, warranted disciplinary action; the issues raised by Rafiq had become part of the club's "continuing journey". Despite all this, chief executive Mark Arthur soon resigned, after "eight fantastic years". Second on his valedictory list of achievements was a "new contract giving YCCC a 50% share of catering" at Headingley. Fifth was a "six-year South Asian engagement programme".

Five days later, Rafiq spoke from the heart in front of the DCMS committee. Poignantly, he said he didn't want his son "to go anywhere near cricket". Roger Hutton, having stepped down as chairman 11 days earlier, said he feared Yorkshire were indeed institutionally racist. More accusations followed, at other counties too. The situation was made messier by the alleged involvement of Michael Vaughan, who denied making a racist remark before a county game in 2009, even as Naved-ul-Hasan and Adil Rashid supported Rafiq's claim that he had. (Ajmal Shahzad said he could not remember.)

Rafiq experienced the fate of many a whistle-blower: canonised by friends, then castigated by foes. Stories emerged of his own tainted past, to the delight of those who believed they invalidated his testimony. If anything, the mud-slinging helped prove a more profound point: this wasn't about one man – it was about a sport's response to a social problem. And while cricket couldn't solve racism, it could at least get its own house in order.

Thanks to Rafiq's determination, the support of sections of the media, the scrutiny of politicians, and the resolve of Kamlesh Patel, Yorkshire's new chairman, to break with a toxic past, there is hope. But it has taken some shameful kicking and screaming – and suffering – to get there.

Bubble, bubble, toil and trouble

Before the New Zealand series, it was still just about possible to blame England's implosion in India a few months earlier on minefields masquerading as pitches. The past, after all, was a foreign country – and Joe Root had fixed his gaze on a greater prize. The best preparation for the Ashes, he said, was to win seven home Tests out of seven against New Zealand and India. No matter that these teams would soon contest the World Test Championship final, or that England's Ashes obsession was blinding them to the task under their nose, or that it was all completely delusional.

It didn't take long for actions to speak louder than words, when England declined to chase 273 in 75 overs on the last afternoon at Lord's. Their feebleness set the tone: of the summer's six Tests before India's early departure, they won one. Again, no matter: in Australia, Root repeatedly insisted, England could "do something special".

Once there, rather than treat the Ashes like the climax they had depicted, they kept preparing for a future that never arrived. From Brisbane to Hobart, no tactic was too ill-conceived, no plan too half-baked. Stuart Broad, terroriser of David Warner in 2019, was left out at the Gabba, where Root batted in glorious conditions for bowling (and Warner made 94). James Anderson was absent, too, which meant both new-ball veterans were missing for the first time since October 2016 at Mirpur. That was also the last time Chris Woakes had bowled England's first over: sure enough, he did so again now. Spinner Jack Leach was ignored all summer, then picked for a Gabba greentop, and mauled for eight an over. Mark Wood, a menace at Brisbane, was rested at Adelaide to ensure readiness for Melbourne, by which time it was 2–0. And at Adelaide, as four years earlier, England picked a bunch of right-arm seamers of similar speed, perhaps keen for a second opinion on a terminal diagnosis. Their only draw, nine wickets down at Sydney, was rain-assisted.

In a crowded field, this was one of England's most hapless tours. Even the few successes were qualified: Ollie Robinson averaged 25 with the ball, only he was not fit enough; Jonny Bairstow scored a century at Sydney, only to miss Hobart with a busted thumb; Dawid Malan began well, only to fade away; Root scored three half-centuries in his first five innings, only to make none in his second five.

Yet even a well-rested team, full of high-quality players and afforded a better warm-up than two rainy weeks in a biosecure bubble, would have struggled. England ticked none of those boxes. Between the start of the Test series in South Africa in December 2019 and the end of the Ashes, their all-format schedule included 187 days of cricket – 37 more than India, who were next on the list, and 83 ahead of Australia, who had not played an overseas Test since September 2019 at The Oval. In the same period, England had played 17 abroad. They were knackered.

The administrators knew this, said the right things about mental health and duties of care, and ploughed on. Before the Sydney Test, Ashley Giles admitted the priority during the pandemic had been to keep the show on the road, an uninspiring ambition that betrayed the ECB's primary goal – the need to protect their income. It left the cricketers feeling like pawns. By the end, they were almost too exhausted to mouth sound bites about putting pride in the badge or throwing punches at the bowlers. These were the exhortations of the school field, not a strategy to regain the Ashes.

Things won't get any quieter. England were due to play a three-Test series in the Caribbean in March. After seven Tests this summer, plus the usual white-ball games, they will embark on another winter apparently designed to break spirits. We may look back on 2021 as the glory days, when they kept the show on the road.

Barely a leg to stand on

For Root, it was a disorientating time. In August, he had become England's most victorious Test captain, in December their most defeated. His batting was often sublime, though it couldn't make up for his team-mates' inadequacies, or his own as a tactician (to choose the worst of many examples, India won at Lord's because he sanctioned some witless bowling to the tourists' tail). He had been mainly calm, occasionally angry. He had defended Silverwood, against his better judgment. Now, in a corner of Hobart's Bellerive Oval, a field regarded as foreign even by some Australians, he was trying to solve English cricket.

Asked what changes to the domestic structure might benefit the Test team, he replied: "How long have you got?" The points he made – about a lack of batsmen capable of long innings, and of genuinely fast bowlers or world-class spinners – were hardly controversial. But one deficiency couldn't be laid at county cricket's door. Like England's Ashes points haul for the World Test Championship – minus four, thanks to a terrible over-rate at Brisbane – many of their batsmen had gone backwards.

Dom Sibley, after averaging 47 the previous year, became a sitting duck. Zak Crawley hit 267 against Pakistan, then averaged under 11. Haseeb Hameed scored two sixties against India on his comeback, then suffered six single-figure dismissals in a row at the Ashes. Rory Burns was Player of the Series against New Zealand, a flurry of nerves and limbs thereafter. Ollie Pope shone in South Africa in early 2020, then flopped in Australia.

Since Jonathan Trott's debut in 2009, the only newcomer to average over 40 has been Root, which helps explain England's results on the toughest tours: from the start of the 2013-14 Ashes, they have won one Test out of 28 in Australia, New Zealand and India, and lost 22.

An absence of quality in the county game was compounded by the England set-up: the sight of Burns and Hameed batting on one leg in the Melbourne nets was not immediately reassuring. It was right that Silverwood went, and not simply because of the coaching. He lost the faith of the players, and his public utterances invited ridicule. He is a good man, but he was out of his depth, thrown into the open sea with a deflated lifebelt. It was right, too, that Giles went with him, having lumbered Silverwood with the extra burden of selection in an era of multi-format cricket – and Covid. The further England moved from Ed Smith, sacked as national selector in April, the cosier the dressing-room became. He had not been to everyone's taste, but he was bright and – crucially – independent. Root and Silverwood, whose shared placidity deprived the selection process of creative tension, allowed things to drift.

It said little for the county game that there was no obvious successor to Root, and no Englishman crying out to replace Silverwood. 'Twas ever thus: the men's sides' greatest achievements in the era of coaching have all come under a foreigner – the 2005 Ashes (Duncan Fletcher), the No. 1 Test ranking in 2011, sandwiched by wins in Australia and India (Andy Flower), and the 2019 World Cup (Trevor Bayliss). Can England really succeed only when an outsider, unencumbered by the English way of doing things, comes in and shakes things up?

Most importantly, it was time to end the fiction that one man could do it all. Not only is there too much cricket, but England's teams have become different beasts. While the Test side are light years adrift of their main competitors, the white-ball teams have led the way. The case for separate coaches has never been stronger.

Who did you say they dropped?

If saving the Sydney Test proves the last thing James Anderson and Stuart Broad do together on an England tour, it will be a symbolic exit – two old bowlers bailing out their batsmen one final time. Of those dropped for the West Indies, they alone had good reason to question the selectors' sanity. Andrew Strauss has got much right during his career, but this smacked of England's favourite mistake: they wanted a glimpse of the future before the present had run its course.

Anderson, in particular, has reached the point where an opponent's first thought is survival. In 2021, his Test economy-rate was 2.12, his lowest in a calendar year since he started in 2003. Only one other Test regular was meaner, by a fraction – Indian spinner Akshar Patel, who played only at home.

Broad is less of a natural athlete, but even more of a competitor. Left out at Brisbane and Melbourne, he responded with a five-for at Sydney (in a total of 416 for eight) and six wickets at Hobart. He reads the game more instinctively than Root, and talks about it with passion, not in platitudes.

If these two were dropped with one eye on the next Ashes tour, in 2025-26, more fool England: injuries last year to Jofra Archer and Olly Stone confirmed how easily circumstance can scupper the best-laid plans. But they can't have been dropped for performance reasons, and it's a nonsense to punish them for their age, since younger team-mates aren't nearly as fit. Yet again, England placed a vague vision of the future over the needs of the here and now.

The people's champions

Things seem so much simpler for New Zealand – fewer players, less cricket, a domestic structure not drawn up by a sadist. And, with a fraction of the resources available to the English game, their men's team keep reaching finals. After the 2015 and 2019 one-day World Cups came two more last year: the

World Test Championship, where they won a seam-bowling shootout against India at the Rose Bowl, and the T20 World Cup, where they lost a vital toss to Australia in Dubai. With a scintilla of luck, they might now be champions in all three formats, and their captain, Kane Williamson, even more loved. They won friends in defeat, too. At Mumbai in December, India beat them by 372 runs, though not before New Zealand's left-arm spinner Ajaz Patel became the third – after Jim Laker and Anil Kumble – to take all ten in a Test innings. He wasn't picked for their next game, which barely raised a murmur. New Zealand have cricket in perspective. There's a lesson in there somewhere.

You say "jump", we say "how high?"

England stayed in India during a Covid spike, and never considered leaving Australia, where the virus was a constant threat. But a white-ball trip to Bangladesh was easily ditched, and so was a goodwill tour of Pakistan. In both cases, the reasoning was hazy.

The Pakistan fiasco generated plenty of heat, since England were snubbing a team who had visited them twice during the pandemic, and had just seen New Zealand cry off at the last minute because of unspecified security concerns. England's decision was one of the most ungrateful they have ever made. Ramiz Raja, the energetic new chairman of the Pakistan board, gave them both barrels, and didn't waste a shot.

The Bangladesh decision had shed light on England's kowtowing to India. Their tour of Bangladesh clashed with the delayed second half of the IPL – a problem for the BCCI and so for the ECB, who didn't want to jeopardize a treasured scenario: the participation of India's male stars in The Hundred.

It would not be the last time England fell into line. A month later, Virat Kohli's Indians pulled out of the Fifth Test at Manchester only hours before the start, ostensibly because of a Covid scare. It just happened to be a game they never fancied playing in the first place, since its scheduled finish was only a few days before the restart of the IPL. According to Dinesh Karthik, the former Indian wicketkeeper whose ear was close to the ground, they were "tired". Then, as if on their behalf: "How many more bubbles can they do?" And so India left for another six-day spell in isolation in the UAE, just in time for the IPL.

Economists shrugged: the IPL was reckoned to be worth £400m to the BCCI, a lone Test £40m to the ECB. Tom Harrison said he did not believe "for a second" that the IPL was behind the cancellation. If he fooled anyone, it was himself. And when Sunrisers Hyderabad were soon struck by a Covid outburst, everything carried on as normal – because of course it did.

Spheres of influence

It used to be said you could walk between Oxford and Cambridge on land owned by their universities. Now that the IPL has expanded to ten teams, it won't be long before franchise cricket can plot an unbroken path from January to December – with devastating consequences for the international game.

Harrison's reluctance to analyse Manchester was not the only symptom. In the West Indies, three Caribbean Premier League franchises have been subsumed by IPL teams – the cricket equivalent of the Belt and Road Initiative, China's global land grab. Trinidad & Tobago Red Steel became Trinbago Knight Riders after investment in 2015 from Red Chillies Entertainment (parent company of Kolkata Knight Riders). Last year, St Lucia Zouks became St Lucia Kings (after Punjab Kings), and Barbados Tridents became Barbados Royals (after Rajasthan Royals).

This is where cricket's cutting edge now resides, where the money circulates. Rashid Khan, the Afghanistan leg-spinner, earned almost £1m for 56 overs in last year's IPL; for nearly 100 in the Second Test against Zimbabwe at Abu Dhabi in March, he picked up roughly £1,000. Unless you receive a handsome central contract from one of the richer boards, there is no reason beyond loyalty or pride to make the international game your priority. The schedule tells a similar story: in this year's *Wisden*, only one Test series not involving England (South Africa v India) comprises more than two matches. Remember that, next time an administrator stresses the sanctity of Test cricket.

Yes, she can

For those in search of good news, it helped to be at The Oval on July 21. Admittedly, the first ball of the women's Hundred did not bode well: Oval Invincibles' Marizanne Kapp sent down a wide which wicketkeeper Sarah Bryce fumbled; in between, Manchester Originals opener Lizelle Lee fell over. After that – all the way to the final a month later – the ECB hit the jackpot.

Fears that spectators might be unmoved by the contrivances of the new competition gave way to something rather wonderful: girls in the crowd, told for so long that women were cricket's second-class citizens, could watch their heroines on the big stage. By the end of the evening, they were jumping around – for a home win, yes, but also for the realisation that someone had taken them seriously.

Covid restrictions encouraged double-headers, which brought the men's and women's events closer together, and drew bigger crowds. New faces embraced the spotlight: 16-year-old Alice Capsey blazed a fifty at Lord's while she awaited her GCSE results; peroxide-blonde Isabelle Eleanor Chih Ming Wong charged in for Birmingham Phoenix; team-mate Abtaha Maqsood, the Scotland leg-spinner, wore the hijab with pride. It felt like a game for everyone.

Similar claims had been made four years earlier when England won the women's World Cup, but the impact of that victory, obscured by the satellite paywall, dribbled away. The recent Ashes series was a reminder of how far England's women have fallen behind Australia: Heather Knight's team came close to victory only once, after a generous declaration by Meg Lanning.

But The Hundred showed what was possible, and research by the Women's Sports Trust highlighted the benefit of even part-time free-to-air coverage. All domestic women's sport in the UK last year was watched by nearly 33m, of which free-to-air TV accounted for 19m; cricket alone made up 41% of viewing hours. And a quarter of those who watched the women's Hundred did not watch any men's cricket: the competition can help the women's game achieve autonomy. Then again, the revelation in December that The Hundred's best-paid female cricketer would only now earn more than the worst-paid male underlined how far there is to go.

Another truth from the opening night at The Oval was even simpler: cricket is a damn good game, more so when staged at the height of summer, backed by expensive marketing and cheap tickets, and broadcast freely. Of the Royal London Cup, which began next day, not a peep was heard. And that's why some of the claims made on behalf of the *men's* Hundred, mainly by commentators and executives with vested interests, wouldn't have been out of place in North Korea.

Shots routinely seen in the T20 Blast were hailed as groundbreaking, players nurtured by the counties as unearthed gems. There was little attempt to attract newcomers to other domestic competitions. On the day of the final, the tournament's Twitter handle posted a photo of a couple of players languishing in a dugout, and the comment: "When #TheHundred is over and you don't know what to do with yourself for the next year." Still to come was the climax to the England–India Test series and the County Championship, the men's and women's T20 finals day and the second half of the Rachael Heyhoe Flint Trophy. So much for the gateway drug.

The Hundred's appointment-to-view format, with a game per gender per night, certainly encouraged a narrative stronger than an 18-team county competition can manage. But instead of working out how better to present the Blast to the public, the ECB tried on the emperor's new clothes: why say "over" when you can say "set of five"? And, at a stroke, they compromised the first-class, 50-over and T20 formats. They believe The Hundred will one day be sold abroad, protecting them from a collapse in broadcast rights for international cricket. By the time anyone is daft enough to cough up, the impact on our men's game could be incalculable.

Not forgotten

Last year's Almanack was 1,248 pages, roughly 20% down on the norm – because of Covid. This year's edition is its usual chunky self, though that doesn't tell the whole story. The obituary section in *Wisden 2021* included at least 16 who died, as far as we know, because of coronavirus. In *Wisden 2022*, that figure rises to 24 (and probably more). Cricket and many of the countries who play it did their best to move on, but the pandemic wasn't for budging.

Jargon neutral

In 2003, *Wisden* put a photo on the cover. This upset a few, then became a talking point, and finally an honour. Its unveiling on social media is part of the Almanack's cycle. That's the thing about change: it's ensconced before you can remember why you objected. Language evolves more quickly. Some felt replacing Man of the Match with Player of the Match was, well, political correctness gone mad; now, it seems normal to use a phrase that works for both genders, and harms no one. The same outrage has greeted batter, even though it is the perfect linguistic companion to bowler and fielder. Nightwatcher has already been road-tested; third man may be for the scrapheap; Sussex and Gloucestershire recently advertised for a groundsperson. There'll be spluttering. But the game will go on, and future generations will wonder what the fuss was about.

The odds couple

William Goldman had the film industry in mind when he said "nobody knows anything". But the County Championship can make mugs of us, too. On page 454 comes a reminder that bookies offered 16-1 on both Warwickshire and Sussex. Warwickshire won the title, Sussex the wooden spoon.

And having writ, they moved on

It's hard to imagine three more contrasting cricket writers than David Foot, Martin Johnson and John Woodcock, who all died last year – and were masters of their genre. Foot explored the human condition, Johnson cracked high-class jokes, Woodcock watched the game with a discerning eye, and reported in 24-carat prose. Asked if *The Times* troubled him during the long boat trips to Australia, he would reply: "They wanted 200 words by Ceylon."

How might they have fared if starting out today? Rolling deadlines and shrinking budgets have created a breed of cricket journalist expected to write match reports, features and news stories, for paper and web, while tweeting and podcasting. It is the age of the all-rounder – and homogeneity. Thank goodness Footy, Jonno and Wooders could play to their strengths.

CRICKET'S RACISM SCANDAL

Who do you think you are?

AZEEM RAFIQ

When I first spoke, in the summer of 2020, about the racial abuse I received during my time at Yorkshire, I didn't for a moment imagine I'd end up talking about my experiences in front of a parliamentary committee, or cause a once-proud club to internally combust, or force English cricket to examine its conscience. I didn't think the chief executive of the ECB would be told he had to update politicians every three months on cricket's fight against racism, or that the game would be warned its funding might come under threat. I didn't think I'd be any kind of catalyst at all.

Even now, my emotions are mixed. I'm hugely grateful that Julian Knight and his colleagues on the Digital, Culture, Media and Sport select committee gave me the chance in November to release some of the pain I'd been carrying around for so long. And I was happy to see the changes made at Yorkshire by Kamlesh Patel, who is the kind of leader English cricket badly needs. I'm hopeful plenty of good can come from all this.

But, deep down, I'd rather have quit the game aged 18 than carry the mental scars I do now. They'll stay with me for the rest of my life. I never thought being a whistle-blower would be easy, but nothing prepared me for the reality. Ever since I went public, other players have rung me and said they want to speak out about their own treatment, and I've had to tell them how challenging it is. At the same time, I know I can't walk away: I want to be there for anyone who needs to talk.

I've struggled with my mental health since 2013 – and I've considered suicide. The toll on my family, too, has been huge. We recently received death threats and, although we can get someone to our place at a moment's notice if we feel in danger, I have two young kids and ageing parents to think about. Of course you ask yourself if it's worth it.

My wife, Faryal, has been amazing, and completely gets the mixed emotions. She said she could see the

Amends: Azeem Rafiq lights a candle on Holocaust Memorial Day, January 2022.

difference I was making to others, as well as the hell I've gone through myself. It's exhausting, and yet I've come to accept that this is my life. Other members of my family have told me I'm an idiot. The trouble is, I can't bear injustice. I've been incredibly lucky my voice has been heard. But I have to keep putting people under pressure so that, one day, cricket will truly be a game for everyone.

Until the start of 2021, I didn't want anyone at Yorkshire to lose their jobs. I just wanted an acknowledgment that I had been treated dreadfully. But it was becoming obvious the club didn't want to listen to my grievances. When that happened, it was clear to me that guys like chief executive Mark Arthur and director of cricket Martyn Moxon had to go. We are where we are now because Yorkshire wanted a fight. They could have handled things so much better.

A lot of mud has been thrown my way since then, including the claim that I'm in it for the money. That isn't true. When I left Yorkshire in 2018, I had five months to go on my contract. They encouraged me to take a payout and sign a confidentiality form. And that five-figure sum would have been useful in the months ahead as I struggled to put food on my family's table. But I turned it down because I wanted to be able to talk about my experiences. If it had been about money, believe me, I could have earned a lot more in recent years with a fraction of the stress.

Another common accusation is that I should have complained earlier. A lot of the upsetting stuff at Yorkshire happened during my second stint there. The truth is I didn't want to believe it was racism. It's draining when you do, and you wonder if it's your fault, so initially I reported it as bullying. But that changed when we lost our son after a horrible pregnancy. I chose not to go on a pre-season tour, and I was treated awfully. I decided enough was enough: I could no longer put their behaviour down to anything other than the colour of my skin or my religion. I was fed up telling myself it was bullying.

Others have said I was sacked for cricketing reasons. Again, not true. When I came back to Yorkshire in 2016, we had been struggling in T20, but that year we reached finals day. I was joint-second in the club's T20 wicket-taking charts – and the only guy above me, Tim Bresnan, had played four more matches. Our attack included several England internationals. In 2017, only one other bowler in the country took more wickets than I did in the Royal London Cup. So, no, it wasn't about cricket.

The more I spoke, the more I was depicted as a troublemaker, which happens easily to people of colour. The implication is clear. Who do you think you are? Get back in your box. An age-group coach at Yorkshire said to me he was told to pick "two or three of those Pakis", but no more. We're allowed to reach a certain station, but if we strive beyond that, we're labelled difficult, opinionated, selfish. Worst of all, we don't play for the team.

I fully accept I've done things in my past I'm not proud of. I never said I was perfect. In some cases, I drank to fit in, and was more easily accepted by others as a result; when I stopped, so did the acceptance. More recently, some old messages of mine resurfaced in which I'd made anti-Semitic remarks. It made me sick to my stomach. It's something I regret massively, and I am continuing to try to educate myself. Anti-Semitism is the same as racism. I should have been able to see that then, and I can certainly see it now.

What came naturally: Azeem Rafiq bowls for Yorkshire's Twenty20 team in 2013.

Despite everything, there are positive signs. At Yorkshire, I'm shocked but pleasantly surprised how quickly things can move. It shows what happens when you have a leader who gets it. I'm hopeful they're on the right path, even if some of the old guard have been obstructive. But I've seen a shift in momentum: a lot of people now want the changes at Yorkshire to be a blueprint for others to follow. The key is that we continue to scrutinise every county. We've seen promises made before, only for things to go back to the way they were.

It's also important that institutions accept their own failings. The ECB have got this horribly wrong. They said they couldn't step in at Headingley because they doubled up as the game's regulators and promoters. For that reason, I'd like to see independent regulators given powers along the lines of anti-doping bodies: they can drop in at a club whenever they want, and check measures are in place to encourage diversity, and people are being treated fairly. The key is to act *before* the car crash happens, not after – which is partly why the Yorkshire situation became such a mess. And if the independent regulators are granted wide-ranging powers, such as stripping a venue of its international status, so be it. If cricket is serious about tackling racism, it needs serious sanctions up its sleeve.

I know many will regard this kind of scenario as extreme. I know those in the game won't want to give up power. I know this will hurt egos. But the time for waffle and anti-discrimination T-shirts and action plans that never get acted on is over.

It's clearly a good thing that the ECB will be held accountable by politicians every three months. As we've seen at Yorkshire, once sponsors start to leave,

HOW IT UNFOLDED

Jun 17	Yorkshire say they have failed to reach a mediated resolution with Azeem Rafiq, after his claim against them under the Equality Act in December 2020.
Aug 18	Yorkshire confirm they have received the investigation report, conducted by the law firm Squire Patton Boggs, former employers of club chairman Roger Hutton, into Rafiq's allegations of racism. ECB chairman Ian Watmore asks to see it, and commends him for his bravery.
Aug 19	Yorkshire apologise to Rafiq, calling him the "victim of inappropriate behaviour", while noting that "many of the allegations were not upheld".
Sep 8	Julian Knight MP, chairman of the House of Commons Digital, Culture, Media and Sport committee, tells Yorkshire to publish the report.
Sep 10	Yorkshire publish a heavily redacted version, accepting Rafiq was the victim of "racial harassment and bullying". Since only seven of 43 allegations have been upheld, they claim there is "insufficient evidence to prove or disprove institutional racism".
Oct 28	Yorkshire issue a statement concluding: "There is no conduct or action taken by any of its employees, players or executives that warrants disciplinary action."
Nov 1	ESPNcricinfo publish details of the report, including an admission by a senior player that he called Rafiq a "Paki". The report says Rafiq called a white Zimbabwean player "Zimbo"; Yorkshire consider that "a racist, derogatory term", for which Rafiq would have been disciplined had he still been on the staff.
Nov 2	Sajid Javid MP, the Health Secretary, says: "Heads should roll at Yorkshire". Hutton is called to appear before the DCMS committee.
Nov 3	*MailOnline* identify Gary Ballance as the player who said "Paki". He expresses regret, and calls Rafiq "my closest friend in cricket". Emerald, Yorkshire Tea, Tetley's and Anchor Butter end their sponsorship of Yorkshire. Nike follow suit the next day.
Nov 4	The ECB suspend Yorkshire from hosting international matches. Michael Vaughan identifies himself as the player accused by Rafiq of telling him and three other players of Asian heritage in 2009: "There's too many of you lot – we need to do something about it." Vaughan denies the claim.
Nov 5	Hutton resigns, and calls on the Yorkshire board to do likewise. He is replaced by Lord Kamlesh Patel. Rana Naved-ul-Hasan corroborates Rafiq's 2009 claim about Vaughan, who is suspended from his BBC radio show, but retained by Australia's Fox Sports for the Ashes.
Nov 6	An unnamed former Yorkshire player of South Asian heritage – later confirmed as Tabassum Bhatti – claims to have been urinated upon by a team-mate.
Nov 7	Liz Neto, Yorkshire's head of human resources, accuses Khalid Akram – who had made a complaint about racist abuse from fellow spectators in 2018 – of a "campaign being waged by such as you and Azeem Rafiq on social media". She calls him a "coward", and writes: "I do hope you are proud."
Nov 8	Lord Patel announces that Yorkshire has settled its legal case with Rafiq.
Nov 9	A former Yorkshire Academy player, Irfan Amjad, says a coach accused him of getting out to a "typical Paki shot". Chris Philp MP, the sports and culture minister, tells parliament it is "unacceptable" that Yorkshire have taken no disciplinary action. Yorkshire suspend coach Andrew Gale for tweeting "Button it yid!" to Paul Dews, former Leeds United FC head of media, in 2010. Gale said he had no idea the word was offensive and, after being told it was, deleted the tweet immediately.
Nov 11	Yorkshire CEO Mark Arthur resigns. The club open a "whistleblowing hotline". England captain Joe Root says he has never witnessed racism at Yorkshire, but calls it "intolerable"; the club must "make sure this never happens again".

Nov 12	Essex chairman John Faragher resigns after an allegation he used the "n-word" in a 2017 meeting, which he denies.
Nov 13	Former Essex player Zoheb Sharif says he was nicknamed "Bomber" the day after the 9/11 attacks, called a "curry muncher", and asked not to pray on the outfield because it "looks bad".
Nov 15	Maurice Chambers says jokes were routinely made about bananas while he was at Essex, citing an occasion when a drunken team-mate threw one down the stairs, and said: "Climb for it, you fucking monkey." He also accuses a senior Northamptonshire player of singing songs featuring the "n-word". Essex announce an investigation. Adil Rashid corroborates Rafiq's claim regarding Vaughan, though Ajmal Shahzad – also there – has already said he does not remember the incident.
Nov 16	The DCMS committee hold their hearing, and interview Rafiq, Hutton and the ECB's Tom Harrison. Rafiq claims black players were called "Kevin", as Alex Hales named his (black) dog; Hales denies any racial connotation. Hutton says he believes Yorkshire are an institutionally racist club.
Nov 17	Ebony Rainford-Brent publishes a racist hate letter she has received: "We found you naked in Africa Ebony! Naked! Illiterate, primitive! Leave our country bitch!" Majid Haq, the Scotland international, tells the BBC that reports of racism in Scottish cricket have "fallen on deaf ears".
Nov 18	*The Times* report Facebook messages, sent by Rafiq in 2011, calling a thrifty acquaintance a "Jew". Rafiq apologises. Jack Brooks apologises for tweeting "Cheers Negro" to Tymal Mills in 2012, during his time at Northamptonshire. He also apologises to Cheteshwar Pujara for calling him "Steve" – supposedly because he couldn't pronounce Cheteshwar – while at Yorkshire in 2015.
Nov 19	Pictures emerge of Hales attending a 2009 party in blackface. He apologises.
Nov 23	A third former Essex player, Jahid Ahmed, says he was asked if he was "going to bomb" the club, and was routinely mimicked by other staff. He concludes that cricket is a "white man's world, where brown people were outsiders".
Nov 24	The Independent Commission for Equity in Cricket say they have received racism complaints about all 18 counties in the last two weeks. Seetec, a senior sponsor of Essex, suspend their ties with the club.
Nov 25	Mehmooda Duke, the Leicestershire chair, resigns, saying "cricket has been torn apart" by racism, and calling for "fresh leadership at national level".
Nov 26	The ECB publish a 12-point plan to tackle discrimination.
Nov 27	Vaughan tells BBC Breakfast he is "sorry for the hurt [Rafiq] has gone through". He adds: "I was proud as punch we had four Asian players."
Nov 28	Monty Panesar, the former England spinner, tells *The Guardian* "British Asians should focus on cricket", and avoid "conversations about fitting in and diversity".
Dec 3	Yorkshire announce the dismissal of 16 staff, including director of cricket Martyn Moxon, Gale, batting coach Paul Grayson, bowling coach Richard Pyrah, Second XI coach Ian Dews and Neto.
Dec 6	Darren Gough is appointed director of cricket at Yorkshire.
Dec 8	Sport Scotland announce an independent review of racism in Scottish cricket.
Dec 21	Referring to the Yorkshire affair, the UK's Equality and Human Rights Commission say "we consider it likely that an unlawful act has taken place".
2022	
Jan 3	Yorkshire hire Ryan Sidebottom and Steve Harmison as interim coaches.
Jan 11	Sidebottom tells Sky Sports News that people should "try and forget about" the racism scandal. He later apologises.

clubs and governing bodies take matters more seriously. But there is a long way to go, as some of the county chairmen demonstrated when they went in front of the DCMS committee in January. It was one thing to hear the Middlesex chair speak in stereotypes about black and Asian players – another to hear him say his club didn't get enough credit for the work they've done on diversity. His Hampshire counterpart, meanwhile, said his club had "over-achieved".

All that really triggered me, because it was the language used by Yorkshire to defend themselves – always citing the work they had done in the community. My argument is that a lot of that work happens because it ensures funding; it shouldn't be used as a method of protection. So while I'm hopeful about the way ahead, there needs to be a diagnosis everywhere – not only at Yorkshire. We can't just have administrators sitting there in front of politicians, saying everything's great.

I would also like to make a plea for forgiveness. This isn't about sacking people who have had the courage to apologise for mistakes from the past. The last thing I wanted, for instance, was for David Lloyd – Bumble – to lose his job at Sky because of comments he made. He rang me to say sorry, and that was good enough for me. We all need to show love and compassion.

I used to think my post-playing career would consist of two of my passions: coaching and media. But if anyone wanted me back in the game as a coach or a pundit, it would have to be on my terms. I won't be quietened by the system any more, and I don't care if you call me difficult. Besides, I've got a third passion now, and it's the most important one: I want kids from all backgrounds to see cricket as a chance to have the time of their life. And I'm not interested in tokenism: I want an England team who are properly representative of their country, with players who fully deserve their place.

One thing is for certain: if the ECB don't learn from this, we'll be sitting here in 20 years with another racism scandal on our hands. If that happens, I hope whoever is involved survives the experience – because I nearly didn't.

Azeem Rafiq played 35 first-class and 125 white-ball matches for Yorkshire in two stints between 2009 and 2018. He was talking to Lawrence Booth.

AZEEM RAFIQ v YORKSHIRE

Arms folded, eyes shut

DAVID HOPPS

It had to be Yorkshire. When the dam finally broke, and the history of racism in English professional cricket began to flood into the nation's consciousness, it was always likely to be Yorkshire who bore the brunt; Yorkshire who would symbolise the prejudice and inequality, both within our game and the nation at large; and Yorkshire who would surrender to rancour and division as demands grew that change – long-overdue change – had to occur.

The story of racism in English cricket is not solely about Yorkshire. How could it be? But some of the county's least endearing traits meant that, when the dam did break, holed by the initially accidental, then increasingly obsessive, campaign of a cricketer who said "enough is enough", it was White Rose intransigence, insensitivity and inability to see the bigger picture that led to the torrent of condemnation. Other counties kept their heads down; racism elsewhere is often more insidious. In Yorkshire, very little is hidden for long.

It took some doing for a player once seen as *proof* that the club were changing, that they were capable of developing young Asian talent, to become evidence of precisely the opposite – that their culture had become so toxic, so awash with institutional racism, that it had driven their former all-rounder Azeem Rafiq to a state of near mental collapse, during which he says he

Old guard: Yorkshire's former chief executive Mark Arthur and chair Roger Hutton.

contemplated suicide. But Yorkshire – as much as they had sought to address his mental-health issues – somehow pulled it off.

During a year-long independent inquiry into his allegations against them, their PR was non-existent. Behind the scenes, arguments raged. And when the report finally emerged, accepting seven of Rafiq's 43 charges, including one that he was bullied for being overweight, the fact that it could not be published in full for legal reasons was condemned as evasion. An apology from the Yorkshire chairman, Roger Hutton, had come far too late. He had become an isolated figure, and he resigned, castigating senior management for "lacking contrition".

The management saw in Rafiq only a disruptive, high-maintenance cricketer; they folded their arms, and refused to consider whether they might share the blame. Yorkshire's previous coach, the Australian Jason Gillespie, had departed in 2016 with his reputation high, having narrowly missed a hat-trick of Championship titles, and softened the club's harder edges. His replacement, Andrew Gale, was more abrasive, as stereotypically Yorkshire as they come, and Gale's relationship with Rafiq soon deteriorated; at Rafiq's employment tribunal in Leeds for racial discrimination and harrassment, he alleged Gale was hostile to Asian players. And there was the sorry business of the soured friendship with Zimbabwe-raised Gary Ballance, who for so long could not see what he described as "banter" – calling Rafiq a "Paki" – might have been a throwback to white colonial supremacy.

Foreign players were given English names, their status as outsiders dunder-headedly underlined. Overseeing all this, Martyn Moxon – a popular and comparatively gentle director of cricket – appeared too unaware of his wider responsibilities, a man who just wanted to coach cricketers. Eventually, he was too worn down by the whole thing to intervene, and took sick leave. If he had sinned, it was sins of omission. Coaches, captains, senior professionals and a head of HR who knew whose side she was on – every person of influence contributed to the mess. We haven't yet mentioned the chief executive, which is apt: one wonders exactly what Mark Arthur was doing.

Arguably, Yorkshire's fault arose in the main from unconscious bias, a propensity for social stereotypes, and unquestioning faith in the status quo. Even when they finally abandoned their policy, in 1992, of fielding only Yorkshire-born cricketers – a policy that mass mobility had made preposterous – they did so not out of enlightened recognition of the plight of immigrant Asians, but because of defeats on the field and a worsening balance sheet. "Yorkshireness", that heavily loaded word, was culpable, because Yorkshire traditionally prefers forthrightness to evasion, certainty to nuance, conservatism to progressive ideals. "Yorkshire plain speaking can be merely a cover for racism," came the cry from south of the Trent. Well, yes, but there is ample evidence that metropolitan disingenuousness is not the answer, either. When the comedian Harry Enfield's "Yorkshireman" sketch began to do the rounds again, however, no one could really complain.

On social media, identity politics held sway. Many adopted views based on how they felt, not what they knew. Sides were taken as an article of faith. Individuals on both sides were traduced. It became part of the narrative, for instance, that Yorkshire had defended racist terms as banter. They had done nothing of the sort. In fact, it was the independent inquiry, which was summed up by Hutton in the county's statement as follows: "The Panel concluded that Azeem Rafiq and his team-mate's language towards each other was unacceptable and was racist and derogatory, and the Panel did not condone the language… The Panel found that this highlighted the importance of YCCC monitoring the use of such language and taking appropriate action against those individuals who engage in such comments, even if it is in the context of 'banter', or 'friendly'." But social media preferred emotion to facts.

It all came to a head on November 16. Rafiq's moving televised testimony to a Digital, Culture, Media and Sport select committee shone a

Coach: Martyn Moxon.

light on Yorkshire cricket's failure to embrace a multicultural society fully 60 years after mass immigration and post-industrial decline had begun to change many of the county's towns and cities. Yorkshire's response, such as it was, was left to Hutton, yet his internal investigation only heightened tensions: it dragged on for over a year, and was conducted by the Leeds branch of Squire Patton Boggs, a law firm he had once worked for.

By the time Hutton faced the select committee, he was prepared to concede Yorkshire were institutionally racist, and ran for the hills, pausing only to pen a pertinent follow-up letter in which he castigated the ECB for refusing to get involved in the investigation. The ECB's chief executive, Tom Harrison, instead contributed some corporate squirming which could not hide the board's own historic failures. A week later, they released a 12-point plan to "tackle racism and promote inclusion and diversity at all levels going forward". But most people were tired of high-sounding policy statements. They wanted action. There was a sense that, this time, the ECB would also be held to account.

Rafiq, predictably, suffered a media examination of his own character defects. He never said he was a saint, and perhaps it was just as well. An anti-Semitic post was unearthed, suggesting that he, too, was not free of racism; full of remorse, he met a Holocaust survivor. There were other allegations. But not every campaigner for social justice can be a Nelson Mandela. To a large extent, it didn't matter: Rafiq, however flawed, was a catalyst for change.

Once Yorkshire's new chairman, Lord Patel, was appointed in November, that change came quickly. Born Kamlesh Patel in Kenya to a family of Gujarati descent, and raised in Bradford, he was a big hitter: a member of the House of Lords and the first British Asian to become a senior independent director of the ECB. He had also chaired the Mental Health Commission, before assuming a similar role with Social Care England. "What's with the woke diversity appointment?" asked someone below the line on the *Huddersfield Daily Examiner's* website, as if to encapsulate the size of his task.

Lord Patel promised "seismic and urgent changes". He settled out of court Rafiq's compensation claim at the Leeds tribunal. He introduced a whistle-blowing hotline, commissioned an independent review into the county's diversity and inclusion policies, and praised Rafiq for his "phenomenal cricketing intelligence", hinting there might one day be a job for him. "If anyone here thinks that Paki, or any other such word, is banter, then the door is there," he added. Lord Patel didn't release the report either, but escaped censure.

The biggest jolt, though, was still to come, when Patel's Yorkshire sacked 16 members of staff – not just Gale and Moxon (Arthur had already gone), but signatories of a letter to the old board in October, in which they had doubled down on criticism of Rafiq, accusing him of being "a complete liability off the field", and "on a one-man mission to bring down the club". The allegations, the letter said, were having "a profound effect on us all, physically, emotionally and psychologically".

That hurt was deepened: the letter was seen as uncompliant, and they were summarily sacked in December. Legal advice was taken, and many felt hard done by. In Lord Patel's Yorkshire, there were to be no concessions; indeed, when it came to uncompromising traits, he seemed to have as many as anyone. He wooed Yorkshire traditionalists by persuading Darren Gough, who had a good relationship with Rafiq, to suspend a lucrative career on TalkSport radio, and accept a temporary role as director-of-cricket-cum-cheerer-upper.

That serious issues existed beyond individual antagonism was clear, since Yorkshire's development pathways were no longer producing players from minority-ethnic communities. Talk of bias and unofficial quota systems was disturbing, although proof was not in the public domain. In that failure, Yorkshire are not unique. When an estimated 35% of recreational cricketers in England are of Asian heritage, yet barely 20% fill county Academies, and that figure drops to 6% among county professionals, there is a deep-seated national malaise. Many non-white players who do make it come oven-ready from private schools, already culturally integrated and well-coached, full of aspiration and confident of their place in the system. In the backstreets of Bradford, Dewsbury or Rotherham, there are few off-the-shelf products. Poverty grinds down expectation and ambition.

Too many make light of this challenge. Official studies tell how, in inner-city Bradford – the home of Adil Rashid, who did beat the system – different communities remain largely apart. Ted Cantle, an advocate of interculturalism, was invited in 2001 to compile a Home Office report into race riots in the city. He wrote: "Separate educational arrangements, community and voluntary bodies, employment, places of worship, language, social and cultural networks, mean that many communities operate on the basis of a series of parallel lives. They do not touch at any point, let alone overlap and promote any meaningful interchange."

Bradford's suburbs have since become even more monoethnic, and mistrust, especially in working-class areas, is entrenched. Bradford is not alone.

New broom: Lord Patel – appointed Yorkshire chairman in November 2021 – had previously been chair of the ECB's South Asian Advisory Group.

Recreational cricket in Yorkshire has been one of the most successful touching points and, despite uneven progress and a level of white flight, as clubs on the fringes of the cities have retreated to more rural leagues, cultural understanding has improved – in defiance of those on the far right who deemed it impossible.

For many amateur clubs, change has not come easily. These clubs have no diversity training, no professional ethos, no authority figures; they have managed to find a way. No wonder so many recreational cricketers of all races in Yorkshire look at the failures of their county, and wonder why they have not had the aptitude or determination to take on the challenge.

And it is in amateur clubs, especially in the North, that integration has been more complex. To grasp the most obvious nettle, post-match socialising in the club bar has been seen not just as a key component after a day's cricket, but a financial necessity. Muslim players, entirely blamelessly, find that culture problematic. David Lloyd, a former England coach steeped in northern club cricket himself, had to apologise on Twitter for his trenchant observations about such tensions; far from coincidentally, a 22-year commentary stint on Sky TV soon ended with his abrupt "retirement", any consideration of an individual's soul having long given way to demands for linguistic purity. Another high-profile media figure, the former England captain Michael Vaughan, was dragged into the mire, for allegedly remarking to four non-white players (Rafiq among them) when taking the field before a county game in 2009: "There's too many of you lot. We need to do something about that." At worst, it would be hostile and racist; at best, an appallingly misjudged attempt at humour belonging to another age. Vaughan denied it, and the BBC agonised about his future.

How different it all was from the optimism 15 years earlier, when Rashid, a Bradford-born leg-spinner of Pakistani heritage, bowled out Warwickshire on Championship debut. That day, some of Yorkshire's stoutest supporters really did march up and down the concourse at Scarborough as if years had fallen off them. Afterwards, David Byas, the county's coach and one of the hardest men to don a Yorkshire sweater, saw no romanticism in a historic moment, and shunned interviews. The same Byas was to be condemned many years later for racist language in Rafiq's testimony to the employment tribunal.

Where does this leave Yorkshire? There remains a pressing need for cultural education for people of all races the moment they enter the club's system, no matter how young; for a new code of "White Rose values" that goes beyond hard work and straight talking; and for the introduction of systems and processes to ensure Yorkshire – forever cast as prejudiced and outdated – can be reinvented as a force for good.

As the year turned, though, the talk was more about recrimination than education. Rafiq's testimony had left the need to build something better. But if Yorkshire don't find what Martin Luther King called "a common humanity", then the wreckage could be irreparable for another generation.

David Hopps is a Yorkshire-based freelance cricket writer.

THE PITCH DEBATE

Surface tension

Andy Bull

It all started with an argument. Perhaps the oldest surviving account of a cricket game is a Latin poem written over 300 years ago by William Goldwyn, a Cambridge scholar. It opens with a description of England in spring, and the players arriving at the ground: they greet each other, and almost immediately start to bicker. There were no laws nor lawnmowers, so compromise was required before the match could start. Where, for instance, to pitch the wickets? Soon, as Goldwyn puts it, the teams "are mingling quarrels and mutual rage as each want to impose their own rules on the game".

In *The Cricketers of My Time*, published in 1832, Hambledon's John Nyren hints at the nature of the argument. First, he wrote, you needed to consider the wind: "If you have one slow and one fast bowler, pitch your wickets right, and down the wind – a slow bowler can never bowl well with the wind in his face. If your bowling is all fast, and the opponents have a slow bowler, pitch your wickets with a cross wind, that you may in some degree destroy the effect of slow bowling."

Then came topography. "If either of your bowlers twists his balls, favour such twist as much as possible by taking care to choose the ground at that spot where the ball should pitch its proper length, a little sloping inwards." And this was just the rudimentary stuff: the great bowlers turned the process into a proper study. Hambledon's champion, David Harris, "became so well acquainted with the science of the game of cricket that he could take a very great advantage in pitching the wickets". He would be out pacing the field at dawn on the day of a match, picking out the best patch of ground. It was, suggested Nyren, his greatest strength.

Harris's great rival, Edward "Lumpy" Stevens of Surrey, preferred a pitch with a brow, causing his deliveries to scuttle at the stumps. "Nothing delighted the old man like bowling a wicket down with a shooting ball," wrote Nyren. "When by this forethought and contrivance the old man would prove successful in bowling his men out, he would turn round to his party with a little grin of triumph." Harris, on the other hand, would choose a "rising ground to pitch the ball against", so his bowling tended to spit at the batsman. "Consequently more players would be caught out from Harris than Lumpy, and not half the number of runs got from his bowling."

Already the pitch was disputed territory, and not, as you might think, the home side's prerogative. For a time, Nyren said, it was the custom in Hambledon for the side "going away from home to pitch their own wickets". In Goldwyn's poem, the dispute is settled by a wise man in the crowd, "a Daniel come to judgment", in one translation. He persuades the teams to compromise, and mark out a pitch "where the level surface stretches flat all around".

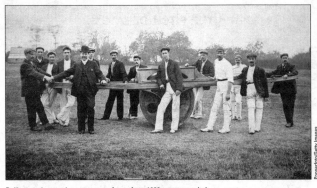

Popperfoto/Getty Images

Rolling stock: an unknown group of men from 1906 prepare a pitch.

These were not simple sporting disagreements. In those days, huge sums were wagered on some games, and it was not unusual for teams to sue each other if they reneged on bets. In September 1718, the *Saturday Post* reported on a match between London and Kent at White Conduit Fields. The purse was half a guinea a man, but three Kent players absconded before they batted because they knew their team would lose. They blamed the coming rain, and proposed a rematch for double the stakes. The case went to court: the judge ordered a replay the following year.

The first set of known written rules are the "articles of agreement" drawn up in 1727 for two home-and-away matches between teams representing the Duke of Richmond and Viscount Middleton. They specified that the home umpires, selected by the noblemen captains, should choose where to pitch the wickets, but obliged them to pick "a fair and even place". This ambiguity allowed home advantage, so long as no one tried to take it too far. Since it depended on the definition of "fair", this was a grey area. It wasn't just a practical issue – a matter of finding and preparing a fit, flat patch of ground – but a moral one.

This idea still exists. Cricket is strange that way: pitch conditions mean the home side have a greater advantage than in almost any other sport, despite the implication that it would be unfair to exploit it too obviously. Then again, some exploitation is more equal than others: witness the punishments handed out to Northamptonshire for producing spinning surfaces a couple of decades ago, and to Somerset more recently, but the general shrug of shoulders when other counties routinely prepare greentops.

A newcomer to cricket may ask why the home team shouldn't be allowed to do everything in their power to improve their chances. After all, other sports employ plenty of ruses. In 2018, Norwich City painted the away dressing-room at Carrow Road bright pink to "lower the testosterone levels" of opponents. At Turf Moor, Burnley installed a small door, obliging visiting teams to stoop on their way out. Rugby union sides arriving at Edinburgh's

Murrayfield have complained for years about being held up by a funeral marching band, who pace ahead of the team bus on the way into the stadium. Ryder Cup sides both set up home courses to suit their style of golf. In cricket, the situation is complicated by debate about the national team's interests, although anyone arguing that Somerset's pitches have been detrimental to England's prospects may also concede that the two spinners in last winter's Ashes squad, Jack Leach and Dom Bess, both grew up playing there.

There is something else going on – and it has its roots in those early disputes at Hambledon, and the notion of a "fair" surface. As soon as the characteristics of the pitch skew too far in favour of the hosts, a row breaks out.

In 1905, Yorkshire's F. S. Jackson gave a speech damning the "Southern counties" for preparing wickets so that "it was almost impossible for any bowler, however good, to get even the slightest work on the ball". This practice, he said, was unknown in his county, "where they always tried to play the game as it was meant to be played, on natural turf". And in the 1950s, Jim Laker and Tony Lock bowled England to Ashes victory on pitches that the Australians insisted had been "specially doctored" under orders from the selectors; Gubby Allen, the chairman in 1956, always claimed innocence.

On it went. In 1975, John Arlott wrote "no one can seriously deny the fact that the Test pitches in England were deliberately made sluggish to reduce the effectiveness, perhaps even the danger, of the Australian fast bowlers. Similarly in the previous season the spinners who were India's main strength were denied any bounce or turn. Too many touring sides of recent years have returned home convinced that a perfidious Albion had doctored its soil to its own advantage."

Thirteen years later, the English authorities were in the middle of a crackdown on pitch-manipulation in county cricket, which didn't stop them asking the Old Trafford groundsman, Peter Marron, to prepare a spinning surface for the Third Test against West Indies, in the hope of hobbling their quicks. England picked two slow bowlers: John Childs and the one-off captain, John Emburey, who took the new ball. They managed one for 145 between them. Malcolm Marshall, meanwhile, dropped his pace, and returned match figures of nine for 41; West Indies won by an innings and 156. "Don't ever try that again," Viv Richards is supposed to have told England.

There are echoes of all this in the row that broke out during the tour of India in 2020-21. After a handsome victory at Chennai, England were badly beaten on spinning pitches in the next three matches. The low point came in the Third Test at Ahmedabad, where India won inside five sessions, and five spinners took 28 of the 30 wickets. England's players kept their own counsel, though Joe Root hinted at his feelings when he said India would face "really good pitches" on their return tour a few months later. Some of his predecessors as captain were blunter. "Tough to watch," said Alastair Cook; "awful", said Michael Vaughan; "a lottery", said Andrew Strauss.

India's response was led by India's off-spinner Ravichandran Ashwin, who had taken seven of those 28. When an English journalist asked him if it had been "a good pitch for Test cricket", and whether he wanted "a similar surface in the next match", Ashwin replied with questions of his own: "What is a good

Hard graft: Vic Demain prepares a pitch at Durham's Riverside.

cricket surface? Who defines it?" The journalist suggested a balance between bat and ball. Ashwin agreed, then repeated his questions.

Of course, they were rhetorical: it is the ICC who define the quality of a pitch, on a scale ranging from "very good" to "unfit". And Ashwin was familiar with their criteria. As he put it: "Seam on the first day, then bat well, then spin on the last two days?" It wasn't far off: the ICC's pitch-monitoring tool defines a "very good" pitch as one which offers "good carry, limited seam movement and consistent bounce throughout, little or no turn on the first two days, but natural wear sufficient to be responsive to spin later in the game". A "poor" pitch offers either "excessive seam movement or unevenness of bounce at any stage, excessive assistance to spin, especially early in the match, or no or little seam movement, spin, bounce or carry".

The idea is to provide "a balanced contest between bat and ball over the course of the match, allowing all the individual skills of the game to be demonstrated at various stages". In short, a pitch should do a little of everything, and not too much of anything.

How much is too much? It depends what we understand by "excessive" – which means the regulations are, in effect, a more complicated version of that single word used in 1727: "fair". The interpretation is so loose that only one international pitch in the last four years has been rated poor: the Wanderers at Johannesburg in January 2018, when the umpires ended play 20 minutes early on the third evening after South African opener Dean Elgar was hit under the grille by India's Jasprit Bumrah. Even South Africa didn't try to defend it. The Ahmedabad pitch, on the other hand, was rated average.

If the regulations read like an attempt to please everyone, it may be because everyone wants something different. Fast bowlers want pitches to be hard and green, slow bowlers dry and dusty, batsmen true, chief executives durable, spectators entertaining, and coaches whatever gives their team the best chance. Groundstaff, you suspect, simply want the critics off their back.

And that's what Ashwin seemed to be getting at. There was a lot to unpick in his exchange with the journalist, since the question implied India had fixed the pitch to suit their strengths, produced a surface so tricky for batting it resulted in a game of chance, and robbed spectators of over three days of cricket. His answer came across as a challenge to the moral authority of the English, and tapped into old charges of arrogance, exceptionalism and hypocrisy. Simmering beneath was the idea of fairness: how far it stretches, who defines it. John Nyren might have chuckled at the familiarity of it all.

Andy Bull is a senior sportswriter for The Guardian.

CRICKET AND LANGUAGE

Changing the subject

EMMA JOHN

The fact you're reading *Wisden* at all means I can be fairly certain that, whatever your gender, you winced the first time you heard "batter" – at least in reference to cricket, rather than baseball or Yorkshire pudding.

I certainly did. Whether my lips formed a moue, I can't remember; I do know that the moment the word registered, some region of my brain automatically rejected it without stopping to ask why. Reasons followed later: batter was an egregious Americanism, it sounded ugly and unrefined, and it was, just, you know, unnecessary. If forced to boil my reaction down, I'd have said the word simply didn't belong in the game.

Which shows how little I know. Thanks to the internet, not to mention *Wisden's* own archives and its *Dictionary of Cricket*, it's a mere hop, click and jump to discover that batter was in regular use in cricket from at least 1773 and, until the mid-19th century, was preferred to batsman. The pioneering cricket writer and chronicler of the Georgian game, John Nyren, employed it freely: it was a fundamentally British word, whose country of origin took against it only when it travelled across the Atlantic – just like all that "Americanized" spelling and grammar, which can actually be traced back to the Elizabethan era.

That's the annoying thing about language, isn't it? It changes, whether we like it or not. We use words to describe the world we live in; as that world evolves, so does our vocabulary. Obsolescence, modernisation and coinage are part of the evolution of any sport that sticks around as long as ours. No cricket lover wants the game to lose its charming linguistic quirks, yet it has shed plenty without us noticing or feeling bereft, probably because it's constantly adding more in their place. Goodbye "lobster", hello "flipper"; see ya "draw shot", wassup "ramp".

We recently lost batsman for batter – not just in the conversation of the female players who have been using it for years, but in the Laws of the game, as written by MCC. Some commentators are beginning to drop the "man" from third man; it's reasonable to imagine that nightwatchman and twelfth man will also be rendered gender-neutral in time to come.

You can argue that the -man suffix is neutral (much easier if you're a man, and determined to ignore the millennia of patriarchal society that forged it). You can wilfully discount cricket's male-dominated history and the fact that female players were frequently designated batswomen (or even "batsmen", complete with quotation marks). You can say that having a masculine term is harmless. Plenty of women, me included, have no difficulty falling for a game with archaic terminology and a chauvinist history. So where's the problem?

MCC TO USE THE TERM "BATTERS" THROUGHOUT THE LAWS OF CRICKET

POSTED: 22 September 2021

MCC HAS TODAY ANNOUNCED AMENDMENTS TO THE LAWS OF CRICKET TO USE THE GENDER-NEUTRAL TERMS "BATTER" AND "BATTERS", RATHER THAN "BATSMAN" OR "BATSMEN".

One giant leap for womankind: how MCC broke the news.

The problem is our inability – perhaps refusal – to see the problem. We don't notice gendered language because we're used to it, and we don't worry about it if we're part of the subset it favours. We feel bound to protect cricket's unique lexicon because it's our heritage, without stopping to wonder whether an inheritance that encodes and assumes male priority and authority is desirable. How easy to mock the idea that batsman is an exclusive term when you're not the one it excludes.

Why do we get defensive when we're encouraged to change our language? Because we're uncomfortable with the idea that we need to, and because such a request calls our attention to societal systems that benefit us at the expense of others, or to the possibility we have hurt others without realising. For decades, our cricketing jargon retained "Chinaman", a word born of racist abuse, without qualm. *Wisden* and others stopped using it not because it suddenly became taboo, but because thoughtful editors listened to concerns, considered its origins, and recognised that it enshrined rancid racial stereotypes.

No one's arguing that third man is offensive to women, by the way. No one's demanding we cease using it, on pain of excommunication from Lord's. If you're the kind of soul who is happier celebrating a "sixer" when Liam Livingstone tonks one out of the ground, you do you. What changed my own mind about gender-neutral language was this: if I can use a word that makes the game more inclusive for everyone, and offers cricket a chance to redeem just the tiniest bit of its sexist past, why wouldn't I?

Most of us would celebrate the steps cricket has made towards gender equality. The fact that it took two centuries for females to be considered worthy of a place in the game left an imbalance we have only begun to address. We can't be blamed because the generations before us didn't want women around; nor is it our fault that cricket's language, along with pretty much every power structure we inherited, prioritises men. The likelihood is that you, along with most *Wisden* readers, are doing your best to make the women you know and love feel cricket is their game too. But it is hard to tackle systemic inequality. It will take years and years.

It is, however, easy to say "batter"; it takes no time at all. The word has the same number of syllables as batsman, making it a simple substitute, and mirrors one you already use liberally. Think about it: is batter really a discordant aberration? Or is it a much neater and more harmonious complement to "bowler" than the one we have unthinkingly employed all these years?

As for the horror-cum-outrage of renaming a fielding position, all I can say is that it has happened plenty, and no one, so far, has died. "Point" used to be "bat's end". "Gully" was known as "box". "Third man" is itself a contraction of "third man up", so further shortening is hardly a crime; it may not yet sound right to hear that someone is fielding "at third", but it's linguistically consistent with a player standing at slip, and you might even draw a distinction between "short third" and "deep third".

Tradition is one of cricket's most highly valued characteristics, which is why we guard it so fiercely, and react so emotionally to what we see as needless change. But tradition should never be an excuse for not doing things better. There's a reason we don't subject ourselves to Victorian dentistry, and abandoned the idea that women were men's property.

Maybe you reckon you're too old, too set in your ways, to adopt new vocabulary, in which case you clearly haven't googled Covid to doomscroll about the Omicron variant, or WhatsApped your family when you were self-isolating. Maybe you think this entire article is virtue-signalling, if only you could find a phrase for that.

Does language wield power, or not? If it doesn't, then using alternative (and less ambiguous) terms for things that already exist can't hurt. I'm guessing that you believe words matter. In which case, why not use them for good?

Emma John is author of Following On, *the Wisden Book of the Year in 2016.*

Last man in?

Alex Massie

Just as good ideas may have unwelcome consequences, so it should be allowed that disagreeable innovations can spawn cheerful developments. Even critics of The Hundred must concede it did wonders for the status and profile of women's cricket. That this might have been achieved by other means matters less than it has been achieved at all. From there, other things follow. On the previous occasion cricket contemplated what is now known as "gendered language" – a review conducted as long ago as 2017 – MCC concluded there was nothing worth seeing here, and certainly nothing which needed changing. Times move on.

And so "batsmen" are out, "batters" are in. "Third man" is quietly transitioning to "third", and "Man of the Match" awards have ceased to be, since these baubles are now handed to the "Player of the Match". Wokeism, it seems, has conquered cricket.

In truth, most of these are changes of no great import. The game has always evolved, and cricket's genius lies in its adaptability. There is nothing sacrosanct about the six-ball over; nothing which says the sport's only proper form is played in white clothing, with a red ball. Even so, "batter" is an ugly replacement for "batsman". For some of us, anyway, batsman encompasses greater possibilities – a measure of artistry, perhaps, or certainly of craftsmanship, now reduced to the simplicity of brute force and slugging. If batsman had to go, bat might have been better.

Mystery is a part of the game too, and for that reason the death of "Chinaman" as an acceptable term for left-arm wrist-spin is also worth a small tear. Cricket has no shortage of racial baggage – and class baggage, for that matter – but few in 2022 can think Chinaman a term freighted with racial, or orientalist, connotations. It is merely one example of cricket's arcane lingo. (One assumes Australians will still be allowed to refer to the "wrong'un"?)

De-gendering the game's language is not really the point, either. Whatever MCC recommend, many people will continue to refer to batsmen; at least in Test cricket, that out-of-fashion station will remain third man. These linguistic changes may allow cricket to argue it is marching in step with the times, but no great claims should be made for them. The things which limit cricket's appeal are the things which make cricket, well, cricket.

It is a complex game demanding time and attention. In its purest – which is to say its least contrived – form, it is a sporting equivalent of the "Slow Food" movement. Test cricket is valued *because* the drama unfolds over 30 hours of play, not *in spite* of doing so. On one level this makes it inaccessible, but that is the point. It is not feasible to render it accessible without destroying the very thing the game's authorities must nourish and protect.

And this, not cricket's language, is where the true fault line between modernist and traditionalist lies. At root, it is a division between those who think cricket must always be thrusting forward, seeking new worlds to conquer, and those for whom bigger and faster does not inherently mean better; the difference between those who think a "maximum" the most exciting thing, and those who would never refer that way to a six. Perhaps most of all, it is a division between those thoroughly focused on the game's future and those worried this risks losing sight of both the present and the qualities which make cricket worth protecting in the first place.

Inclusivity is, for sure, welcome, but the ECB – in common with other custodial bodies – sometimes give the impression they think people who do not like cricket are more important than those who do. The customer you don't have may be more appealing to marketing folk than the loyal supporters you do, but cricket's authorities might reflect that the latter are the base from which you build, not an obstacle blocking the road to a glitzier future.

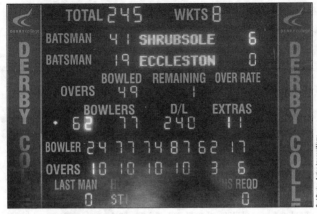

No cause for alarm: three men appear on the Derby scoreboard during a women's ODI between England and New Zealand, September 2021.

Cricket can be many things, and accepting that is its greatest diversity. There is a place for the contrivances of the shorter forms of the game, but not – at least, we must hope, not yet – at the expense of its subtler treats. It is hard to banish the suspicion that red-ball cricket is increasingly seen as a hindrance, getting in the way of making cricket a vastly more profitable business. Life would be simpler without it.

Doubtless it would be, but much would be lost on this march to modernity. Until now, the game has balanced change with continuity: unlike other sports, such as football or rugby, it has changed utterly, while remaining recognisably the same. This is both unusual and precious, for it fashions a kind of golden thread by which Joe Root is connected to W. G. Grace, and back, way back, even before Grace, to the pioneers gambolling in the field at Broadhalfpenny Down. For those who appreciate such things, this matters.

Change is not so much necessary as unavoidable, but the happier forms of change are incremental, not revolutionary. Few reasonable people can really believe "batter" is a reform worth going to the stake for, but there remains something mildly absurd about ECB press releases updating us with the latest developments at "The Men's Ashes". It is possible to see, and even accept, their intentions, while still thinking them faddish.

Of course language matters. It is a form of signifying, after all. But it matters a little less than the bigger struggle which, all too often, takes the form of protecting cricket from those who are themselves charged with protecting cricket. That is a task for batsmen and batters alike.

Alex Massie writes about politics for The Times *and* The Sunday Times.

THREE PHOTOGRAPHS OF THE 1960s

Memory game

HUGH CHEVALLIER

For modern-day photographers, there is no meaningful limit to the number of pictures that can be taken in a session. The capacity of memory cards, once measured in megabytes, then gigabytes, is now in terabyte territory: a tiny bit of plastic the size of a fingernail can hold hundreds of thousands of high-resolution images. Battery power may be more of a concern, yet it's easy enough to pack a spare; shutter-happy photographers have been known to take as many as 10,000 digital pictures in a day. Captioning and labelling them in a coherent and informative fashion, however, presents a separate problem.

Things were different in the analogue world. For example, the lens used in 1960 by Ron Lovitt for the photograph on the next page was 1010mm (39 inches) long, and may have seen action on a German reconnaissance aircraft – perhaps even a Zeppelin – during the First World War. British-made equivalents from the same era would be an imperial 48 inches (about 1200mm). Whatever the precise length of the wartime equipment, they were enormously heavy, and it usually needed two people simply to move the combination of lens and camera.

WINNERS OF THE WISDEN PHOTOGRAPH OF THE YEAR

2010	Scott Barbour	2016	Saqib Majeed
2011	S. L. Shanth Kumar (amateur)	2017	Stu Forster
2012	Anthony Au-Yeung	2018	Phil Hillyard
2013	Atul Kamble	2019	Gareth Copley
2014	Matthew Lewis	2020	Steve Waugh (amateur)
2015	Robert Cianflone	**2021**	**David Gray**

The other major difference between the 2020s and the 1960s lies in the capture and storage of images. Film was neither easy to handle, nor cheap. Lovitt and his colleagues would start the day with perhaps two magazines, each containing 12 negatives: having just 24 exposures at his disposal, he had to choose his moment with care. While concentration has always been a *sine qua non* for cricket photographers, the 1960s fraternity (and there were vanishingly few women) also had to show judgment. If the weather looked iffy, it might be wise to take a few images early on in case rain swept in. If the day was set fair, it made sense to keep a few plates back in case the denouement got exciting. Inevitably, plans did not always work out, and drama went unrecorded.

It didn't help that reloading the camera after an exposure was a tiresome business. Part of the skill of the job was minimising downtime, though even the most dextrous would take ten or 12 seconds. And much can happen in those lost moments – indeed the modern-day photographer might have taken another 50 or 60 images.

THE PHOTOGRAPHS

Patrick Eagar

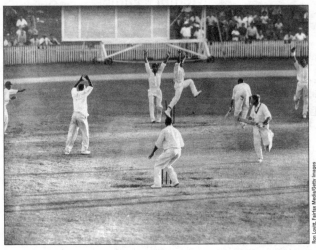

This picture, of the exact moment Test cricket gained its first tie, is a great image. Played at Brisbane in December 1960, the match was seemingly in the bag for West Indies after Australia slipped to 57 for five in pursuit of 233 – and the prospect of a home defeat persuaded many to leave early. Accounts vary, but agree there were just two photographers left for the final eight-ball over: Ron Lovitt of *The Age* and Bob Barnes of Brisbane's *Courier-Mail*.

Judging from the pictures in *The Greatest Test of All*, Jack Fingleton's account of the game, the pair were sitting next to each other, and decided to collaborate. With the few remaining plates they had, Barnes would take the action – the moment ball reached bat – while Lovitt would see what unfolded before pressing the shutter.

Lovitt timed it to perfection: Joe Solomon, on the far left and with one stump to aim at, has run out the sprinting Ian Meckiff, and the West Indians celebrate as though they have won, not tied. But, for Lovitt, there was one more layer of tension. He had exhausted his usual supply of film, and in desperation had loaded a double slide, one half of which was already exposed. He had no means of knowing which half was which, and only later did his good fortune become clear. Barnes, who was also processing his negatives in a nearby darkroom at *The Courier-Mail*, said Lovitt's shout of glee was deafening. Had he been unlucky, the image would have been unusable.

Dennis Oulds, Central Press/Getty Images

How often can you take a photograph with the faces of an entire team visible? Dennis Oulds has done exactly that at The Oval in August 1968, and again it's Australia batting. And once again their opponents are jubilant. Torrential rain had threatened to ruin England's charge towards victory, but the crowd helped the groundstaff make the pitch playable. Derek Underwood found the drying surface perfect for his left-arm spin, and caused all manner of problems.

Opener John Inverarity, though, had held out for more than four hours. With just six minutes to go and the last pair at the crease, Colin Cowdrey's field could not have been more attacking. To widespread disbelief, Inverarity played no shot, prompting an enormous appeal. Like Lovitt eight years earlier, Oulds knew when to press the shutter: just as Charlie Elliott raises his finger. There's something wonderful, too, about the shape of the non-striker, Alan Connolly.

On the technical side, Oulds is using a 28-inch lens, allowing a little more width, and so can capture all 11 England players. And they're all (with the possible exception of Colin Milburn) looking at Elliott, and at the camera.

In 1968, Central Press were the only agency allowed to cover Tests at The Oval. The monopoly may have served them well, but it heaped extra pressure on the three photographers they sent. They could rely on Oulds.

And now for something completely different. There's an otherworldliness to this gentle picture of John Lennon, taken in October 1966. It's by Zdenko Hirschler, an Austrian more used to photographing swinging Londoners than swinging deliveries. Lennon took time away from the Beatles to star in *How I Won the War*, a dark comedy directed by Richard Lester. The scenes set in North Africa were shot in Almería, Spain, where Hirschler took this image, which was originally in colour. (See also Cricket Round the World, page 1102.)

It's a simple composition, probably taken on a $2\frac{1}{4}$-inch square camera such as a Hasselblad, with the horizon almost exactly in the middle. And it's remarkable for what's not there: no extras from the film, no adoring fans, no vegetation, not even a wicketkeeper or bowler. There's nothing more than Lennon, who's clearly concentrating, an upturned chair and a wooden crate. But it ticks boxes: an excellent subject and an arresting situation. In fact, it's distinctly better than the film, which bombed.

Patrick Eagar began his career as a professional photographer in 1965. He was talking to Hugh Chevallier.

AFGHANISTAN AND THE TALIBAN

A love that dare not speak its name

Tuba Sangar

First came the anonymous phone calls. The Taliban had just arrived in Kabul, despite everyone saying they would not take the city, and the voices at the end of the line told me they knew I worked for the Afghanistan Cricket Board. I had been in the role of development manager since 2014, and it had not always been easy: not all Afghan families want their female members doing such jobs. But now I felt threatened. My father told me to change location to stay safe, so I went to different relatives' homes and switched off my phone. It stayed off, and I changed location many times, before eventually resigning from my job on August 31, and heading for Toronto, Canada.

That was the first reason I left Afghanistan. The second was because I wanted to be able to speak out about the plight of our country's women cricketers. The world should know what has happened to us since the Taliban returned to power last year – and I could not have spoken out if I had remained at home.

The Taliban have told the world they have changed since they were last in power. They are saying they will give women equal rights. This is not true. Twenty years ago, when Afghanistan was full of bomb blasts, suicide attacks and murder, we still had hope that one day it would become a better place. Now, it feels as if there is no hope.

When I came to Canada, as part of a scheme for women journalists – I am studying sports journalism – I was full of sadness for the country I left behind. One of the most poignant differences was seeing the children here, busy with their toys. In Afghanistan, parents are worried about how they are going to get their children out of the country.

A lot of our female cricketers are stuck there, too. One or two managed to escape to Canada, and another to the UK. But the rest are in hiding. Even I can't contact them. They have already gone through so much, and now they have had their dream of playing cricket taken away.

Like many, I made a lot of sacrifices for Afghanistan cricket. I left university only one year into a master's degree because I wanted to fulfil my dream: that, one day, our women's team would play international cricket. The players made similar sacrifices, which in our country is not easy. If you are an unmarried 20-year-old woman, people say bad things about you. So you have to convince your family that cricket is a career path: first your father, then your brother, then your uncle's family, and so on. You give up a lot, emotionally, financially, educationally. But the dream spurs you on.

And it was all beginning to take shape. Back in 2014, when I started work for the ACB, we spread the word around the country that cricket was a sport for women and girls, as well as men and boys. We visited different provinces, and chose players for the national team. At the end of that year, the ACB

THE FALL OF KABUL

Last flight out of Afghanistan

SHADI KHAN

If you have ever seen a glass object shatter, that is how it felt on August 15 for the long-cherished dreams of so many Afghans. I was among them. Writing these words a few weeks later in a spookily quiet hostel in Islamabad, the capital city of neighbouring Pakistan, I was anxiously awaiting a safe migration onwards to the UK, the European Union or Australia. But my heart and soul remained in Kabul, at the moment everything fell apart.

My dangerous exit from our nation's fallen capital seemed like a never-ending nightmare, as I failed to make sense of all the questions surrounding Afghanistan's collapse – and the return of the Taliban regime, after two decades of international engagement which had witnessed the transformation of the country.

The first clear sign of the impending storm came around noon: loud and terrifying sounds of gunshot fired by guards at a private bank to disperse thousands of panicked customers in downtown Kabul. My local office set off an alarm, and asked all the staff to rush to their homes. The word was that the Taliban were marching on the city. From that moment, it felt as if we were living in a ghost town, in which everyone feared each other, even each other's shadows.

The Taliban had promised not to enter Kabul following the withdrawal of Western troops. But, as I headed home, I passed through many of their checkpoints, and held my breath. I was grappling with many thoughts, about my family, their security and aspirations, my own career as a journalist, and my belief in equal rights, which I knew would be upended by the new regime. Out of desperation and fear, I had to leave my family behind, since they had no travel documents. They were upset, but they understood. Though I knew little about the mayhem at the airport, I headed there next morning, hoping to take the first available flight out.

When I arrived, I saw terrified people climbing walls and scattering to escape beatings by the Taliban. I was convinced there would be much worse to come. It seemed as if men, women and children from across the country wanted to flee such an apocalyptic moment. Holding each other's hands, they were carrying small bags on their back, and broken dreams in their heart. For me, an immediate escape was not possible.

Thanks to the Thomson Reuters Foundation – an organisation I had been associated with for more than two years – and other friends and news outlets, an evacuation plan was formed for a group of journalists. I rushed to nearby accommodation to evade imminent threats to my life and my family.

There, I fearfully hid for a week, and made multiple life-threatening attempts to reach the airport, both by day and night, as Taliban fighters pushed us back, firing shots in the air and near our feet. Finally, on August 22, I received a tip-off that I should be ready to enter the airport at 10am. After a sleepless night, I reached close by, and waited for almost 12 hours. Eventually, the Taliban allowed us access. We were disguised in stained clothes, our faces covered by the traditional scarf. No one realised we were journalists.

It felt like an escape from hell. But the moment the plane left the devastated airport, a yearning for my homeland overwhelmed me in tears of hopelessness.

Shadi Khan has written for Wisden *on Afghanistan, and had been a journalist there for nearly 15 years.*

Girls allowed: a cricket camp in Herat in 2019.

chairman changed, and our activities were stopped. But in 2018, we started again, and we had a couple of really good years.

Recently, we awarded 25 national contracts to women players, and received help on a development project from UNICEF. We were planning a camp abroad, and chose Oman, because we thought it would be easier to begin in another Muslim country. We were planning to go after the men's T20 World Cup last year. The players were arranging their passports. We were all excited. Then the Taliban came back into our lives, and everything changed.

The whole world knows what the Taliban means. The first thing that comes to mind is that they are against women's rights, and produce reasons why women can't do this or that. In my view, they know nothing about Islam. They are unable to read a line of the Quran, or pray, in the right way. They are not just against women's rights: they are against human rights. They are using a twisted interpretation of Islam against the true version of Islam.

But I am not afraid to say I love cricket. It is a passion that started when I became the biggest fan of Afghanistan's headband-wearing all-rounder, Hamid Hassan. I used to dream of meeting him face to face. Isn't that normal, when you're young, to be attracted to a beautiful man, a hero? I'm a Pashtun, and our people are the biggest cricket lovers in the country. But when I went to other provinces, everyone was talking about the game and Hamid Hassan. When I joined the ACB, I just had to tell him: I'm your greatest fan. After that, I did a lot of courses – umpiring, coaching, scoring. Others were better on the technical side of the game, but I was the only one who understood the administrative issues. We achieved a lot.

It helped that our men's team were making headlines. Guys like Rashid Khan and Mujeeb Zadran were an inspiration. Until then, Afghan girls didn't know much about cricket. But when Rashid started playing in the IPL in 2017, the whole nation went crazy. And when the Afghanistan men's team win a game, people cry tears of joy. Everyone uses Facebook there, and everyone has an opinion on cricket – even on subjects like a change in personnel on the national board. In our country, it is more than a game of bat and ball: it is a game of hope and inspiration.

That is why I had mixed feelings when Australia cancelled the men's Test against Afghanistan in November because the Taliban said women could no longer play cricket. On the one hand, I was happy that others were speaking out on our behalf: I wish more had. On the other hand, Afghanistan's men have done a lot for cricket in our country. They're the reason we developed a women's team. And if the men play no games, people at home will have less cricket to get excited about. If that happens, women's cricket suffers too. If you refuse to play our men's team, then there is no hope the Taliban will suddenly recognise the women's.

I would like to see other teams coming together and offering our women the chance to play cricket in their countries. That would be one way of offering us hope. I was disappointed there were so few voices in women's cricket highlighting our plight. I thought they would all speak out on our behalf. Without cricket, the only headlines Afghanistan can make are negative. Cricket is our way of portraying ourselves in a positive light.

The young people in Afghanistan will fight for their country. Sometimes, my friends ask me on Facebook why I left. They think I should have stayed. I tell them it is my choice – but I will not leave my people to their fate. I want to go back, but they might arrest me, or even kill me. One day, if the situation improves, I will return. When I came to Canada, every night I dreamed I was back in my office in Kabul, or playing with the girls at the ground. In whatever way I can, I will help the Afghan people and make them proud, and tell the world they are talented and can do what they want. Please, do not forget us.

Tuba Sangar was talking to Lawrence Booth.

PHILIP LARKIN

Between the lines

CHARLES BARR

"If only Larkin were here now," laments Duncan Hamilton in *One Long and Beautiful Summer*. Michael Henderson also invokes him in *That Will Be England Gone: The Last Summer of Cricket*, the main title a quotation from Philip Larkin. Published in 2020, both books focus, in an elegiac spirit, on the summer of 2019, which would have been the last pre-Hundred season had Covid not intervened; Henderson ends with the claim that Larkin "would have been rude about the Hundred".

Larkin died in 1985, leaving almost no reference to cricket in his collected poetry. What is it, then, that makes him, decades later, such a tempting reference point? Born in 1922 – his centenary is now being celebrated – he is described by his biographer James Booth as "by common consent, the best-loved British poet of the last century". Booth's claim becomes stronger if one calls him the best-loved *English* poet of the century, his chief rival then being the more prolific, less disciplined John Betjeman, whose game was golf.

Larkin disliked abroad, venturing outside these islands only once in his adult life, to collect a prize in Germany. After five years in Belfast, early in his career as a librarian, he reflected in a 1955 poem on the experience of being "Lonely in Ireland, since it was not home". Back on English turf, settling into 30 years of living and working in Hull, he affirmed that "these are my customs and establishments", now re-embraced for life.

Getting to grips with line and length: Philip Larkin bats; a friend of his sister, Kitty, joins in.

One of his English customs was indeed cricket, and in time he joined the game's Establishment, becoming an MCC member in 1974, his candidacy seconded by Harold Pinter. Their friendship, based on love of the game and respect for each other's writings, crossed a political divide: Pinter was a man of the left, Larkin of the right, verging, as he grew older, on the far right – with worrying implications for any project that might today invoke him as a spokesman for the Spirit of Cricket.

Pinter played the game, wrote about it, and earned a generous *Wisden* obituary in 2009. In contrast, it was only after Larkin's death that the extent of his absorption in cricket became visible, through a succession of biographies, memoirs and, especially, letters. Living mostly on his own, he was one of the last of the great letter-writers of the pre-digital era. We now have three volumes drawn from a much larger archive, adding up to around 2,000 pages: *Letters Home* (mostly to his widowed mother), *Letters to Monica* (to his long-term lover in Leicester, Monica Jones) and *Selected Letters* (to a wider range of contacts).

These volumes are rich in cricket references, if you look for them. But none of Larkin's editors or biographers shows much interest. When a cricket passage does slip through, it is seldom annotated or collated with other references. Authors, colleagues and friends are identified in footnotes, cricketers hardly ever: Hobbs, Sutcliffe, Miller, Hassett, Graveney, Pelham Warner are left as names on the page. But there is enough to help us trace his involvement in cricket, from his youth to MCC membership and beyond.

Apart from childhood games in the back garden, and a bit at school, Larkin never really played. But he went on to a lifetime of devotion: as a radio listener, a TV viewer, a reader, and a spectator, notably at Lord's, both before and after

his membership came through. His journey becomes vividly typical of that generation of followers.

In his Belfast exile, he tracks the 1950-51 tour of Australia by Freddie Brown's team, woken by his alarm clock to listen to the crackly commentary on the day's last session. Back in England, he welcomes the great advance of 1957, the start of ball-by-ball coverage of home Tests, writing to Monica of "listening to the endless cricket commentary… I took my portable wireless in yesterday and had it muttering among the shelves as I checked art books". On a country cycle ride, he tells her of making a detour to find an evening paper to check the scores. When he belatedly buys a TV set, he makes full use of it for the cricket.

Major partnership: Philip Larkin and Monica Jones in 1984.

Daily Express/Hulton Archive/Getty Images

By now, they are going together each year to the Lord's Test, initially with tickets supplied by an MCC friend, and cricket has become a way for her to measure their complicated relationship: "Do you realise that you and I have known each other ten years… three Australian tours [1948, 1953 and 1956], three General Elections? I wonder for how many more decades we shall know each other." Working in 1948 in the Leicester library, Larkin had taken care to book ahead for the county's match against Bradman's side. Several more tours – Ashes and

Player's players: the young Larkin was a keen collector of cigarette cards.

otherwise – lie ahead. For Lord's, they stay each year at Durrants Hotel, east of Baker Street, and their typical packed lunch is dutifully recorded for his mother: pork pies, lettuce, tomatoes, bananas and cherries – better to bring your own food than risk the queues. In 1975, the David Steele series, he reports to mother on the cascade of Australian wickets on the second day: "We were all grinning like Cheshire cats, everyone friends with everyone else."

It is tempting to go on quoting, and there is scope for a modest anthology, *Larkin and Cricket*, that draws further on the archives at Hull. Yet why is there so little cricket in his work written for publication? Reviewing a biography of Francis Thompson, author of arguably the greatest cricket poem, *At Lord's* – "O my Hornby and my Barlow long ago" – Larkin makes no mention of it. In his own poems, there are just three references. One compares the crowds lining up to enlist in 1914 to the queues "Standing as patiently | As if they were stretched outside | The Oval or Villa Park." A second recalls how, during childhood trips to the beach, "I searched the sand for Famous Cricketers", a cryptic reference to the John Player cigarette cards of the 1930s which he hoarded carefully.

The last is more direct and memorable. In one of his best-loved poems, *The Whitsun Weddings*, published in 1964, a succession of views from the window of a train heading from Hull to London includes that of "someone running up to bowl". No cricketer could fail to embrace that image, the glimpse of a moment of action cut tantalisingly short as the train moves on.

And that is it. Booth notes the pattern by which Larkin's poems regularly give us, with scrupulous calculation, only one instance, across his work, from among a range of possibilities, in genre, topic and vocabulary – for example, the verb in a famous first line, "They fuck you up, your mum and dad." Just the one time. Cricket, too, has one vivid image – part of the control, the discipline, that helps make Larkin special. "Running up to bowl" is the tip of a cricketing iceberg, and we might now explore the mass that floats beneath.

But there is an elephant in the room. In a letter of 1978, Larkin explains his avoidance of the Lord's Test against Pakistan: there will be too many non-white faces among the crowd. In fact, he uses an utterly repugnant combination of adjective and noun. There is a lot more where that came from.

Lovers of Larkin and his work either focus – like Henderson and Hamilton – entirely on the poems, or they scramble to explain: this was decades ago, and it comes from a private letter, written to a friend he knew would be far from offended, the right-wing author Robert Conquest. Larkin, with the same tight control as in his poems, famously presented a very different self to different lovers, friends, correspondents. The racism surfaces in letters to a small set of individuals, most consistently to Monica, who days later accompanied him to the Oxford–Cambridge match at Lord's – where they drank non-stop – rather than to the Test.

Yet the bile would not surface if it were not there. Larkin scholars have played it down, partly because it erupts mainly within cricket, a strand of his life they see as marginal. But cricket was not really so marginal; nor do cricket people have this excuse. *Wisden 2021* contained, along with a books review by Emma John that started with the two pro-Larkin titles, a mass of clinical analysis of the structures of racism in cricket, historical and current. Since then, we have had the scandal of systemic racism at Yorkshire – Larkin's adopted county. His centenary year, far from being a good time to follow those two fine authors by enlisting him in a romantic spirit to defend the game's traditions, is a spectacularly bad time.

The idea of that collection, *Larkin and Cricket,* has great appeal. But it will need to come with a health warning.

Charles Barr is professor emeritus of film studies at the University of East Anglia.

WOMEN'S CRICKET DURING THE WAR

Military advance

Raf Nicholson

On October 14, 1948, Joan "Wilkie" Wilkinson boarded the RMS *Orion* to Australia – one of a party of 17 women selected for England on their first postwar tour. The next few months would prove an all-embracing experience: meeting high commissioners, visiting koala sanctuaries, and hobnobbing with Don Bradman at the MCG, where in January she would make her England debut. At a time when long-distance travel was reserved for a few, a tour Down Under was always special. For Wilkinson, it represented something more fundamental.

A decade earlier, she had been a weaver in a cotton mill in Lancashire, having left school at 14 – a typical 1930s working-class girl. She loathed every minute. Then war was declared on Germany and, for the first time in the country's history, women were conscripted into the armed forces: in 1941, Wilkinson was called up into the newly formed Women's Auxiliary Air Force. After learning cricket in the backstreets of her village, and appearing for Burnley, she was handed the chance to train and play as part of her everyday duties in the WAAF. She became the captain of an inter-services XI, remained in the Air Force after the war ended, and caught the eye of the selectors. Wilkinson would go on to play in 13 Tests between 1949 and 1958 – the mill long forgotten. In short, the Second World War transformed her life by offering her cricketing opportunities that were scarcely conceivable to working-class women before 1939.

Middlesex off-spinner Cecily Mawer was killed in an air raid in 1941, but for Joan Wilkinson the conflict helped foster a fulfilling cricket career.

Inevitably, the war was disruptive for the women's game – as it was for the men's. At the AGM of the Women's Cricket Association, held at Devonshire Street in London on October 13, 1945, it was announced that during the war the number of women's clubs in England had fallen from 105 to 18, and affiliated colleges and schools from 103 to 12. Clubs found their members scattered all over the world, called up to serve their country; many disbanded. The WCA at least continued to function, setting up a war emergency committee in 1942 and raising over £300 for the Red Cross through charity matches. By contrast, the English Women's Cricket Federation, which had run thriving leagues in Yorkshire and Lancashire in the 1930s, attracting a playing membership of over 3,000 and crowds of up to 8,000, ceased activity altogether, and never re-formed.

War also delayed the 1939-40 tour of Australia and New Zealand by almost a decade. In September 1939, the players had already been selected, and were weeks away from setting sail. Audrey Collins, who later served as WCA president, had spent two years saving £115 for the boat fare, and handed in her notice as a teacher. Another tour would not take place until 1948-49, by which time Collins had been deselected: her chance of an overseas Test had vanished for ever. It haunted her for decades. "The disappointment at not going was intense," she wrote in 1985.

Despite the disruption, the war threw up opportunities for women to participate in cricket, as Wilkinson soon discovered. Women's cricket had previously been a minority, middle-class sport – difficult to access if you had not played at a fee-paying school, with travel to matches and equipment expensive, and no prospect of it being a career, unlike the men's game. There had also been entrenched opposition to women participating: one correspondent wrote to the WCA's Marjorie Pollard in May 1930, insisting that the women's game was "a sacrilege… a direct insult at the heads of those who call themselves men".

The pressures of total war, though, meant such attitudes were no longer sustainable. The conscription of women into the armed forces, essential industrial work, or the Women's Land Army, left the government concerned about female morale. Actively promoting women's sport was one solution: organised team games between women war workers would prevent boredom and promote *esprit de corps*. An anonymous article in *Women's Cricket* magazine in May 1939 declared:

> If the British Empire is to survive as the greatest barrier in the world against despotism, she must be upheld by the trained service of all her peoples… The team-games player learns discipline through games, so that this comes naturally to her; she will fall into the ways of an organised service all the more easily.

With 950,000 women taking up work in munitions, many factories were encouraged by the government to open their on-site recreation facilities to women for the first time. Barbara Blaker, the daughter of Kent CCC's Dick Blaker and another member of the 1948-49 tour party, worked on the production of Wellington bombers at the Vickers Armstrong plant in Weybridge, Surrey. She joined a works team that used the factory ground. One government report

Services with a smile: the WRNS side before a game against the ATS at Sudbury Hill, August 1943.

from 1943 suggested female workers showed "a great improvement in bearing and appearance… there is a definite desire for camping and outdoor exercise, which certainly was not the case before".

Other WCA members followed the 1939 call to "fall into the ways of an organised service" by participating in the war effort. Kathleen Doman, who had originally proposed the formation of a "central association for women's cricket" at a meeting in October 1926, was put in charge of clothing in the WLA, a civilian organisation which sent women to farms to replace conscripted men. They were often lodged together in hostels, and encouraged by local welfare officers to set up sports teams as a way to spend their free time "productively"; Doman's influence meant cricket was particularly popular. Intriguingly, while she had earlier overseen the introduction of a rule making skirts and stockings compulsory in women's cricket, she now helped push for breeches and dungarees for the Land Girls. As a result, WLA cricket was played in trousers.

Among others, Dorothy Broadbent of Yorkshire and Cecily Mawer of Middlesex both contributed thousands of hours to civil defence; Mawer became an ARP ambulance driver. The physical fitness required to cope with demanding conditions during air raids meant the government encouraged physical recreation for civil defence workers via their Fitness for Service scheme. Broadbent recalled several cricket matches with fellow volunteers: "On the first occasion, I was the only woman. I suppose all the spectators thought I was a brazen hussy, but what did it matter? I enjoyed myself enormously." Mawer, an off-spinner, continued playing for the London-based Wagtails club. On January 5, 1941, she was killed in Harrow during an air raid.

Away from the home front, cricket thrived within the women's armed forces – the WAAF, the Women's Royal Naval Service and the Auxiliary Territorial Service, all formed in 1938-39. By 1945, some 445,000 women were serving in them, and their day-to-day lives involved compulsory physical training and team games. A battle had been fought to ensure this was possible: Dame Leslie Whateley, director of the ATS, described "resentment" among male officers at the idea that women should be permitted to do PT in their working hours; another struggle was "convincing the Treasury that money was necessary for [female] PT kit". But with support from leading officers, the battle was won, and thousands of working-class women gained access to cricket. As Peggy Scott, a war chronicler, wrote in 1944:

> Never has the average girl had the opportunity of playing games as boys have always done. Netball and rounders have been the extent of her games experience. A new world of sport has opened out before her, and she finds everybody in it anxious that she should have a place. The hockey player will coach her, although she has never before played hockey. She learns to play lacrosse and tennis. She plays in the cricket team. The airmen teach the girls cricket, using their left hands or some other handicap… The aim in the unit is not only to do the best for the unit, but to spread the ability to play games to those who have never before had the opportunity.

As elsewhere, WCA members led the way. Betty Archdale, who had captained England in 1934-35 and been due to do so again in 1939-40, signed up for the WRNS and was stationed in Singapore and Colombo, starting teams in both (Colombo Cricket Club made her an honorary member). Nancy Joy, one of the 1948-49 England team who travelled to Australia, served as a member of the First Aid Nursing Yeomanry. Future chair of the WCA, Sylvia Swinburne joined the WAAF, became a squadron officer, and started cricket at every station to which she was posted; she also set up an inter-station competition. Seventy teams entered in 1945, when the winners were RAF Weeton, thanks to the performances of Corporal "Wilkie" Wilkinson, who averaged 58 with the bat and below six with the ball.

The ATS, though, outshone the other services thanks to their three established England players: Joy Liebert, Muriel Lowe and Myrtle Maclagan. In 1943, when inter-service matches began, the ATS – with Maclagan as captain – thrashed both the WRNS (bowling them out for 41 after scoring 252 for two), and the WAAF (by 131 runs). The ATS also took part in games against male officers' teams, including one in 1940 against a side featuring Colonel Alexander Johnston, a former first-class cricketer for Hampshire. Maclagan hit a century, before declaring with the total on 140, "leaving, I considered, defeat impossible. Our opponents had 140 to make in 70 minutes… [but] one brigadier employed a golf swing to such use that they passed our total on time."

By 1942, Maclagan's prowess had become so well known within the army she was asked to play in an otherwise all-male Officers v Sergeants match. She recalled congratulations from her senior commander "on being in natty white…

The Joys of the game: an ATS match in 1943, the batter is Nancy Joy, and the keeper Joy Liebert, who played for England in 1934-35.

while the men were mostly in khaki or grey flannels. I was in such a dither that I can remember nothing else about the match!" In general, though, mixed cricket had been frowned on before the war; Marjorie Pollard described it as "a waste of time", and argued it was important women were not seen to be trying to "play like men". Wartime, it seemed, helped break down gender divisions.

But what would happen when hostilities ended? The first post-war gathering of women cricketers came with the revival of the WCA's Cricket Week at Colwall, Herefordshire, from August 26 to September 1, 1945. All told, 68 players showed up, though the absence of Archdale and Maclagan (still waiting for demobilisation) was keenly felt. Club numbers were way down, and Pollard struck a note of despair in the first post-war edition of *Women's Cricket*, in May 1946. "Now where are we?" she wrote. "Almost where we began in 1926."

That proved pessimistic. By 1950, the WCA reported that they had exceeded pre-war affiliation figures, with active clubs rising to 200 in 1953. This included the three women's services, who maintained their enthusiasm for the sport. Audrey Disbury, who would play for England between 1957 and 1973, signed up for the WRNS as a mechanic in the 1950s because of the cricketing opportunities. "I met someone who persuaded me to join," she recalled. "She said I could play as much cricket as I liked."

The WCA were quick to clamp down on some wartime innovations: skirts would remain the uniform of the Association until the 1990s, while the pre-war ban on mixed cricket was hastily reinstated. But England captain Molly

Hide wrote in 1950 that "the number of women and girls wishing to learn and play cricket [has] increased enormously, and there has been a great demand for coaches". Presumably some of the women exposed to cricket for the first time during the war were keen to continue.

The men played a series of Victory Tests to celebrate the coming of peacetime; the WCA could not afford to. It would take six years of fundraising before they could welcome the Australians again, in 1951. But it was worth the wait. The Oval Test, played in late July, saw England triumph by 137 runs, and was attended by a record 15,000 spectators. The war, it seemed, had helped shift any remaining public opposition to women playing cricket. Like the victory against Hitler, it was not to be taken for granted.

Raf Nicholson is a women's cricket writer, the author of Ladies and Lords: A History of Women's Cricket in Britain*, and editor of CRICKETher.com.*

The 12th Wisden Cricket Photograph of the Year competition attracted almost 400 entries. First prize was £1,000, and the two runners-up received £400. Any image with a cricket theme taken during 2021 was eligible. The independent judging panel, chaired by former *Sunday Times* chief photographer Chris Smith, comprised award-winning photographer Patrick Eagar, former art director of *The Cricketer* Nigel Davies, and Clare Adams, MCC's former filming and photography manager. For more details, go to wisden.com/photographoftheyear

THE WISDEN CRICKET PHOTOGRAPH OF 2021 David Gray, of Associated Australia Press, wins the award for his picture of Jos Buttler leaping over Steve Smith during the England v Australia game at the T20 World Cup in Dubai on October 30.

David Gray, AAP Images

THE WISDEN CRICKET PHOTOGRAPH OF 2021   Chris Strickland is one of two runners-up, for his image of a scene familiar to most recreational players. These intrepid hunters are from the Wooler Cricket Club in Northumberland, June 5.

Chris Strickland

THE WISDEN CRICKET PHOTOGRAPH OF 2021   The other runner-up is Nathan Stirk, who captured Finn Allen (of Birmingham Phoenix) making a meal of a chance in the game against Trent Rockets, Nottingham, August 13.

Nathan Stirk, Getty Images

FIVE CRICKETERS OF THE YEAR   Jasprit Bumrah

FIVE CRICKETERS OF THE YEAR   Devon Conway

FIVE CRICKETERS OF THE YEAR   Ollie Robinson

FIVE CRICKETERS OF THE YEAR   Rohit Sharma

FIVE CRICKETERS OF THE YEAR   Dane van Niekerk

FIVE CRICKETERS OF THE YEAR

The Five Cricketers of the Year represent a tradition that dates back in Wisden *to 1889, making this the oldest individual award in cricket. The Five are picked by the editor, and the selection is based, primarily but not exclusively, on the players' influence on the previous English season. No one can be chosen more than once. A list of past Cricketers of the Year appears on page 1454.*

Jasprit Bumrah

Nagraj Gollapudi

Anger, says Jasprit Bumrah with a smile, used to come naturally to him – and on the last morning of the Second Test at Lord's, he was angry. On the third evening, India's fielders had exchanged words with James Anderson. Bumrah had just bowled him a ten-ball over, including four no-balls and plenty of short stuff. Anderson was unimpressed, India unrepentant.

On the final morning, as Bumrah walked out to bat with the Test tantalisingly poised, he knew his arrival would stir things up. But instead of facing the forensic Anderson, he was confronted by the ferocious Mark Wood, who sent three bouncers his way. And instead of breaking through, England lost control. Despite having reached double figures only once in 30 Test innings before this series, Bumrah added an unbroken 89 for India's ninth wicket with Mohammed Shami, not much of a batsman either. The momentum had shifted.

Bumrah is just happy that, unlike England, he kept his emotions in check. "I don't get intimidated," he says. "When I started playing cricket, I used to be ready for a fight. So this was like playing a game when I was a child. I just wanted to be in the moment, and not forget I had a job to do. It's not a wrestling competition. So, yeah, emotion got the better of them."

But his batting, important though it was, was a bonus: it was his bowling that unsettled England. At Trent Bridge, his match haul of nine wickets might have led to victory had rain not washed out the last day. Now, at Lord's, where England needed to survive 60 overs, Bumrah and Shami picked up a wicket each in the first two. Bumrah removed Root in the first over of the final session, but Jos Buttler and Ollie Robinson knuckled down. Bumrah put his T20 thinking cap on, and went round the wicket to Robinson. "I thought he was expecting the yorker, so I kept in mind that he will not be expecting a slower ball." He was hit on the pad and, after a review, out lbw. "That opened the door," says Bumrah. Next over, Mohammed Siraj charged through it, sealing a memorable win.

Fast forward to the last afternoon of the Fourth Test at The Oval. With the series all square, Bumrah turned it in India's favour with another unforgettable spell. England had begun resolutely in pursuit of 368; the sun was out, the pitch a road. But he pushed himself to counter the conditions. His key weapon, other than high pace, was the reverse swing he had learned during long spells for Gujarat in the Ranji Trophy. Now, in successive overs, he burst through the defences of Ollie Pope – making Bumrah the fastest Indian seamer to 100 Test wickets, in his 24th game – and Jonny Bairstow. Once again, he had opened the door to victory.

JASPRIT JASBIRSINGH BUMRAH was born on December 6, 1993, in Ahmedabad, the capital of Gujarat, on India's western flank. When he was eight, his father, Jasbir, passed away following a sudden illness; Jasbir's family immediately cut ties with Bumrah's mother, Daljit. A teacher, she stretched her schedule to fit in one-on-one tuition, and make ends meet for Jasprit and his sister, Juhika. At 13, Bumrah asked Daljit to allow him to pursue his cricketing dream. She was uncertain, but had seen her son watching the game, transfixed, on television, and endlessly hurling tennis balls against the wall in their small apartment. Knowing his greatest strength was his self-belief, Daljit crossed her fingers – and agreed.

In 2010, Bumrah was spotted by a local Gujarat Cricket Association administrator, Anil Patel, who encouraged him to join the state Under-19 side; the following year, five days before he turned 18, he was playing for them. Team-mates, coaches and selectors wondered who this stick-thin fast bowler was, with speed and an action they could barely comprehend. In 2013, he made his debut – a T20 game – for Gujarat's senior team. Watching his second match was former New Zealand captain John Wright, then head coach at Mumbai Indians. "Real wheels," he told ESPNcricinfo.

Bumrah joined Mumbai Indians that season. Hit for three boundaries in his first four balls on IPL debut by Virat Kohli, he trapped him with the fifth, on his way to three for 32. He produced yorkers at will, and flummoxed batters with his underwhelming, though unique, approach to the crease – described by one writer last summer as resembling a "dressage horse being put through its paces" – his sleights of hand, changes of pace and ramrod-straight arm. He soon became one of the world's best death-over specialists, often unhittable. Above all, he turned himself into a lethal fast bowler.

He has also played a crucial part in India's improved record abroad. Between his Test debut at Cape Town in January 2018 and the premature end of the series in England, no bowler in the world had come close to his 97 wickets away from home (Shami was next, with 76). Indeed, until he was selected against England at Chennai in February 2021, he had not even played a Test in India, the result of rest and rotation, plus a back problem; by then, he had earned 17 caps away from home. But an average of 22 suggested he has relished the various challenges posed by overseas conditions, with five-fors in Johannesburg, Nottingham (twice), Melbourne, Antigua and Jamaica. And like all great fast men, Bumrah creates a buzz, a sense of an impending event. In his own words, he enjoys conjuring "something when there is nothing".

V. V. S. Laxman has compared his variations to those of Wasim Akram, but Bumrah says: "My biggest strength is not any skill I possess. My biggest strength, I feel, is my mind: if I am in control of everything – of what I'm thinking and how I'm evaluating a situation – then I feel I am in a very good space. Nobody can enter that bubble, and nobody can cause any trouble."

Devon Conway

Mark Geenty

Devon Conway's patience had already been tested when he strode through the Lord's Long Room to make his Test debut on a sun-drenched June morning: only a few weeks short of his 30th birthday, he was playing his 109th first-class match, having qualified for New Zealand nine months earlier. And he was opening the batting, which he had rarely done before.

More suspense ensued as Conway – calm on the outside, a bundle of nervous energy within – watched Tom Latham face the first 18 balls of the series, from James Anderson and Stuart Broad. Conway recalls: "The over before, Broady said really loud, 'Is this going to be the longest someone has not faced a ball on debut?' My biggest memory is him running in – he swung it away and I let it go by. Then I thought: 'I can see the ball, it's not too unfamiliar.'"

Over the next day and a half, the left-handed Conway did not simply announce himself to the cricketing world: he shouted through a megaphone. It came as no surprise to those who had watched him gorge on runs ever since arriving in Wellington from Johannesburg in September 2017. A checked drive off Broad soon fizzed through extra cover, the first of 22 fours in almost ten hours. Watertight defence and clinical accumulation occasionally gave way to flamboyance, notably when Conway swatted Ollie Robinson through square leg to raise his century. Next day, he pulled Mark Wood for his only six of the innings to bring up the first double-hundred by a Test debutant in England. Four balls later, he was last to go, run out by Joe Root at the second attempt, for exactly 200.

But he was not done. A knock of 80 helped set up New Zealand's first Test win at Edgbaston, and a first series victory in England in 22 years. Then, in the inaugural World Test Championship final, against India at the Rose Bowl, Conway's first-innings 54 proved the game's highest score in tricky conditions, and paved the way for a historic New Zealand triumph. At Taunton, Somerset unfurled the red carpet for their new import, who had previously played six seasons of league cricket in England for five different teams, including Taunton Deane. He averaged 61 from eight T20 Blast innings, and 40 from three in the Championship.

Not everything, it's true, went his way. Back at Lord's, this time for Southern Brave in The Hundred, Conway broke a finger, which meant eight weeks without gripping a bat, including 14 days in an isolation hotel back in New Zealand. Then, in the T20 World Cup semi-final at Abu Dhabi in November, after tormenting England once more, he instinctively punched his bat in frustration when he was stumped for 46. Next day, in an emotional address to team-mates, he revealed he had fractured a bone in his right hand. He was out of the final against Australia, and the subsequent two-Test tour of India.

It meant another gloomy flight home, though Conway soon lifted his spirits by writing a summary of the 12 months since his international debut, a home

T20 against West Indies. By the end of 2021, that format alone had brought him an average of 50 and a strike-rate of 139 (in three ODIs, all against Bangladesh, he averaged 75). "I jotted down all these really cool things that had happened – the first time in my life I'd written things down. Along with that, there are the lows that balance things out. But it was nice to take that moment to reflect on everything."

DEVON PHILIP CONWAY was born in Johannesburg on July 8, 1991, the youngest of Denton and Sandy Conway's three children. His parents ran an office-products store, and Devon and his sisters, Candice and Charne, grew up on a plot of land near the airport. Among the farm animals, he played cricket and football, hit golf balls and rode quad bikes. Denton's sporting passions were kart-racing and football, but he coached Devon's cricket team; his first representative side were Gauteng Under-13. At King Edward VII Preparatory School, he was one year ahead of the future South African wicketkeeper Quinton de Kock, still a close friend, but they parted ways when Conway earned a sporting bursary to nearby St John's College. "That was probably the best decision my parents made for me," he says.

At 14, he chose cricket ahead of a potential career as a central midfielder; at 17, he made his first-class debut for Gauteng in March 2009, against Easterns at the Wanderers (he was out for a duck). It was there, eight years later, that he signed off from South African cricket with a double-century against Border. Conway had made up his mind to leave, having raised the prospect during a round of golf with his partner, Kim. She urged him to chase his dream, and they agreed to start a new life in New Zealand. The young couple sold their car and three-bedroom house in Bedfordview, a well-to-do suburb of Johannesburg, and booked the flight.

"It was two things," he says. "A better opportunity to play international cricket, and a better lifestyle in a different country. We had really good feedback from friends, who said New Zealand was a safe and beautiful place to live, so we thought let's give it a go."

Wellington had seen a few South Africans come and go, but Conway was on a different level. His new team-mates at Victoria University Cricket Club were struck by his humility and good nature, and watched open-mouthed as he batted in the nets. In October 2019, he plundered 327 not out off 352 balls against Canterbury in a Plunket Shield match – the highest score both for Wellington and at the Basin Reserve. That summer, he topped the domestic run-charts in all three formats, and murmurs grew louder around the city of a Test-cricketer-in-waiting – three years of waiting, in fact, to satisfy the ICC's residency rules.

The New Zealand coach, Gary Stead, had seen enough. In May 2020, three months before he became eligible, Conway was named among the country's 20 contracted players. He made his debut, at Auckland, then won the public's hearts with a whirlwind 99 not out off 59 balls at Christchurch to help secure a T20 win over Australia. After being bafflingly passed over for home Tests against West Indies and Pakistan, he made up for lost time at Lord's – one of cricket's all-time memorable debuts.

Ollie Robinson

VITHUSHAN EHANTHARAJAH

Ollie Robinson was sitting on the edge of a bath in the Lord's dressing-room at the end of his first day as a Test cricketer. It had begun with the presentation of his cap by England bowling coach Jon Lewis, a guiding influence at Sussex, as his family leaned over the advertising boards to get as close as Covid protocols allowed. Now alone, staring at a wall, he wondered if his international career was already over.

A few hours earlier, while taking the first two of his 37 Test wickets in 2021, a series of offensive tweets he had sent between the ages of 18 and 20 were catching fire. Only at stumps was he informed: head coach Chris Silverwood and media manager Danny Reuben gave him five minutes, then told his team-mates, who that morning had – like Robinson – worn anti-discrimination T-shirts on the outfield. The Cricket Discipline Committee called the tweets "racist, sexist, disablist, Islamophobic and offensive", and banned him for eight matches (three already served, five suspended). He was fined £3,200, and had to undergo training from the Professional Cricketers' Association.

Robinson returned against India, and took 21 wickets, the most on either side. It was a nod to a future beyond James Anderson and Stuart Broad. Yet the stain of those tweets feels indelible. "I know it is always going to be there," he says.

OLIVER EDWARD ROBINSON was born in Margate, on December 1, 1993. As a two-year-old, he was gifted a bat and ball by his grandfather Rex, who along with his father, Ian, form a generational lineage at the local club. At five, Robinson was representing Thanet District Under-10. "There's a cutting I have, and the ball looks humongous in my hand," he laughs, pretending to hold a beach ball. The reason for the press coverage? He had taken a hat-trick. A childhood infatuation became an adolescent's dream when, aged 13, he joined the Kent Academy. He started as an off-spinner, and turned to pace only at 16, after a growth spurt (he is now 6ft 5in). Still, a handful of his 320 first-class scalps are from off-breaks, and he even twirled a few overs during the Second Ashes Test at Adelaide in December. But he relished the aggression of speed. "I like to get in the battle. As a spin bowler, I found it quite hard. You can't bowl bouncers, can you?"

Kent decided against a full-time deal, but his stepfather, Paul Farbrace, then a coach at Headingley, engineered a move to Yorkshire. Jason Gillespie, who later oversaw Robinson's progress at Hove too, handed him a one-day debut in 2013, but he was sacked in 2014 for what the club described as "a number of unprofessional actions". Essex offered a route back, but Sussex head coach Mark Robinson called with a better one. His first-class debut came at Durham in April 2015: he scored 110 from No. 9 and took four for 71. The joy of 46 wickets that summer, however, was tempered by an operation to alleviate compartment syndrome in his shins. He spent two seasons recovering, before taking 74 Championship wickets in 2018, and 63 in 2019.

Robinson's craft relies more on manipulation than miles per hour. "People started calling me 'Glenn' [McGrath]. I was thinking, lads, I don't feel I'm that good. And they were saying: 'Well, you don't miss.'" Gillespie and team-mate Steve Magoffin reinforced an appetite for off stump; Lewis and Sussex bowling coach James Kirtley polished the mechanics. In early 2021, his reputation grew on the tour of Sri Lanka and India. By the summer, Joe Root knew exactly the qualities Robinson would bring.

Underpinning it all was self-sufficiency. He developed a fascination with South Africa's Vernon Philander: "He's not very tall, he doesn't get a lot of bounce – how is he doing it?!" Between the Third and Fourth Ashes Tests – by which time he was England's leading wicket-taker, with nine at 26 – Robinson watched India's Mohammed Shami against South Africa, and tried to mimic aspects of his action in the nets.

But back to that day at Lord's. Robinson collected his thoughts, emerged from the bathroom, and said sorry to team-mates. "That was the hardest thing. I stood up and got that choked feeling straightaway. I said I hoped they'd all forgive me." By then, the ECB had drafted a statement for him to read out. "In hindsight, I probably should have gone off the cuff, and apologised from the heart."

The crowd gave him a generous reception next day. He finished the match with seven wickets, before going dark to avoid the storm. It soon arrived at his door: journalists showed up at his father's house, then at the home of his girlfriend's parents, while he was inside. Robinson even had to message a family WhatsApp group to plead calm, following arguments on social media.

"Two days after the match, I was watching the news, and the first thing was comments about me from Oliver Dowden [the culture secretary]. I realised I can't get away." He was the epicentre of a culture war; some even championed him for the tweets. "I was living a bit of a drunk life back then," he says. "My parents had divorced, and I was going out three or four times a week with my mates, joy-riding at night, living a different life to that person I feel I am now. I understand why people were shocked.

"When the tweets resurfaced, I felt like I was different already. But I looked at myself and thought: 'Do I still have those views? Am I still that person?' I might have turned a corner four or five years ago, but have I really got better? Are there bits of those tweets that are still in me?" Reassurance came from team-mates and friends, some from backgrounds he had mocked. "It was nice I had their support. They told me that's not who I am. I was having doubts – that I was the worst human ever."

Following a break, he took five for 85 against India at Trent Bridge, then five for 65 at Headingley. The Ashes reinforced his worth, but also highlighted issues. "I know I need to be fitter to maintain spells at my ideal pace of 82, 83mph. I get that little bit more off the wicket. If I can do that consistently for five days, instead of being 80, 81 the first two days, then 78 the last few, it would mean batters don't feel they are getting as much relief."

The introspection and desire for self-improvement are in keeping with the main themes, painfully learned, from Robinson's first year as a Test cricketer.

Rohit Sharma

ANAND VASU

A man who has every shot in the book, and plays three – pull, cover-drive, back-foot punch – to perfection, put them away last summer in single-minded pursuit of one of Test cricket's toughest challenges: opening the batting in England, a job he had never done. The results were a triumph. In four matches, Rohit Sharma faced 866 balls, scored 368 runs at 52, and helped India to a 2–1 lead before the Covid-related postponement of the final game.

He had set the scene in the Second Test at Lord's, where he batted beautifully for more than three hours to make 83 in an opening stand of 126 with K. L. Rahul. But his defining hand came in the second innings of the Fourth at The Oval. India, who had just been thrashed at Headingley to make it 1–1, had conceded a first-innings lead of 99, but Rohit refused to buckle, facing 256 balls for 127. Set 368, England got nowhere near.

His consistency was all the more remarkable because his record had been skewed so heavily towards performances at home. He had begun in November 2013 with 177 and 111 not out from No. 6 against a weak West Indies – Sachin Tendulkar's final series. He then went 19 Tests and four years without another century, even as his limited-overs stock rose, both at international level and in the IPL with the all-powerful Mumbai Indians, whom he led to all five of their titles. In Tests, though, he was often the subject of cruel memes, some dubbing him "No-hit."

But when he turned himself into a Test opener for the visit of South Africa in October 2019, his fortunes rocketed: he made 176, 127 and 212. Late last year, he replaced Virat Kohli as India's white-ball captain, recognition not just of his success in 50- and 20-over cricket – he holds the world record for the highest score in one-day internationals (264), and has three of the format's eight double-centuries – but also a hat-tip to his reading of the game and management of players. In February 2022, his ascendancy was complete, when he was appointed Test captain.

Throughout, a question remained: could he replicate his home Test numbers in overseas conditions? England, with its early swing and seam, presented a particular challenge. But Rohit had his eye on the ball. "I've always thought about how I can be effective and produce results, rather than whether I can establish myself in the team," he says. "That thought I left behind a long time ago. If I think about establishing myself, that is an additional pressure."

He puts his performance in England down to preparation. "Luckily, we had about 25 days to get ready after the World Test Championship. I focused on what I would be facing from Anderson and Broad. I wanted to prepare very specifically. I never thought about what would happen after 20 overs: my first goal was to *bat* 20 overs. I asked the throwdown guys to bowl up to me, swing the ball away from me in front of my pads, and occasionally bring it in."

The Indian team had for a while travelled with at least two throwdown specialists: Raghavindraa, a right-hander, and Nuwan Seneviratne, a left-hander. Rohit used them extensively. "What I've seen in England is that people get out more to the fuller ball than the short ball or back of a length. My front-foot defence would be challenged." He knuckled down, looking at the clock not the scoreboard. "I wanted to play time, bat as long as possible, and get the bowlers tired. The trick is to be there when they are in their third spell, when they will give you balls you can pounce on. The first two spells are for them, and in the third I will take my chances."

This was not an easy adjustment, but Rohit says it is one for which all senior players should be ready. Working out the opposition bowlers' plans was crucial. "I know, with the ability I have, I can get runs, but I never felt at any stage that I needed to score more quickly. In England, bowlers think: 'Just bowl maidens, frustrate the batsman, force a mistake.' So I wanted to think alike, and transfer the pressure back on to them."

It was not only in England that Rohit tormented them. When Joe Root's side toured India earlier in the year, and won the First Test in Chennai, they were served up a rank turner in the Second. Batsmen on both teams struggled to survive, but Rohit batted as though on another surface, making 161 off 231 balls in India's first-innings 329. "Scoring runs on that pitch was tough," he says. "In the last few years, conditions in India have been extreme. It's often more challenging to play there than abroad."

ROHIT GURUNATH SHARMA was born on April 30, 1987, in Bansod, near the central Indian city of Nagpur. He spent his infancy in Dombivli, an eastern suburb of Mumbai. The first child of Gurunath, who did odd jobs, and Purnima, a home-maker, Rohit spent much of his childhood with his grandparents and uncle in Borivali, a western suburb of the city, and occasional weekends with his parents. He has a younger brother, Vishal, who did not follow him into cricket.

Aged 12, he was playing in a summer-camp tournament, where his team were thrashed by Swami Vivekanand International School. But Dinesh Lad, Swami's coach, saw something in Rohit – who had been bowling off-spin – and asked him to report for trials.

When he did, accompanied by his uncle Ravi, they were dismayed to learn that the monthly fee was Rs275, which they could not afford. But Lad prevailed upon a trustee to waive the charge, allowing Rohit to enrol in an institution that took cricket seriously. Even then, he continued mainly to bowl spin, and when Lad, some months later, saw an unusually correct batsman knocking up in the outfield, he wondered who the kid was. He was taken aback; young Rohit had been too modest to tell his coach that he batted, as well.

He first played for India Under-19 at the age of 17, and for Mumbai at 19. His ODI debut, at Belfast of all places, followed soon after. But then came a long wait before his first Test cap: six years, encompassing 108 one-day and 36 T20 internationals, still a record for someone who has gone on to play Test cricket. From shy kid in Mumbai to elder statesman in England, Rohit's throwdown story had come full circle.

Dane van Niekerk

TANYA ALDRED

Dane van Niekerk arrived in England dubious about The Hundred. Sitting in her quarantine hotel, she pondered the new rules. After months of rehabilitation because of a lower back injury, she was low on confidence and momentum. She needn't have worried.

On a steamy night in south London, in front of a crowd fizzing with young families, the competition was launched with cheering swagger by two women's teams. Van Niekerk lost the toss, but won everything else, making fifty and edging the winning runs for Oval Invincibles against Manchester Originals with two balls to spare. "I was pretty lucky," she says. "I should have been out twice, but it was special to start a tournament like that, and it put me in the right frame of mind."

The Invincibles powered on, watched by thousands, despite the pandemic. It felt like a giant leap for the women's game, as unknowns made headlines. "After the second game I was like, yes, I can do this. From not knowing what to expect, to it being such a success, and me enjoying every moment, was amazing. The support the tournament got was incredible."

A veteran of Australia's Big Bash and England's Kia Super League, van Niekerk ended up intrigued by The Hundred's quirks. "It challenged me as a captain. In T20, you have your plans, but with The Hundred you have the ten balls, and with its fast pace you have to think on your feet."

She hadn't been the Invincibles' first choice as captain. Australia's Rachael Haynes withdrew because of Covid restrictions, but coach Jonathan Batty had no regrets about his late signing, regarding her as a deeply underrated cricketer whose excellent fielding and shrewd leadership complement her leg-spin and fireworks with the bat. "She's really up there with the best," he says. "The word to use is 'warrior'. She sets high standards on the field, she's happy to take on the difficult bowling, and she trusts her players. She's also passionate. She tries to keep a lid on that, but you can see how much it means to her. Some of the girls were worried she was shouting at them – I had to reassure them it was her way of communicating. I don't think there's a poker face in her."

And there was no hiding van Niekerk's delight when the Invincibles went on to win the tournament: tears flowed as she lifted the trophy, even if she was a little surprised. "Southern Brave really set the tone, but we had a special group who didn't take ourselves too seriously." Not just the winning captain, she was the competition's MVP, having top-scored with 259 runs at 43, and taken eight wickets at 20. She was planning to be back for season two.

DANE VAN NIEKERK was born on May 14, 1993, in Pretoria. Her brother, Gerrit, a year older to the day and unusually obliging, always let her bat in the backyard – knowing she would otherwise walk away – while their parents, Andri, who played korfball for South Africa, and Pieter, were very encouraging. Little Dane was rather naughty and not a fan of school, but trudged along because of the sport. She played cricket with the boys, and by nine had been drafted into Northerns' girls age-groups side. She caught the eye of the South African set-up, and in 2009 made her debut, at just 15, during the World Cup in Australia.

Two days later, 19-year-old Marizanne Kapp also made her debut. "I was actually very, very afraid of her," says van Niekerk. "I'll never forget in 2008, when we both made South Africa's Under-19s, she bowled her first ball, and it went straight up in the air. I dropped it. She had a laugh; I almost wanted to cry." A few months later, they were in a relationship. In July 2018, they married.

It has had its complications. The day van Niekerk was made South African captain, in June 2016, the pair sat down and chatted about how they were going to navigate the situation. "I hope the team have seen over time that I have tried very hard, sometimes to the detriment of my relationship, to make sure they come first," she says.

The relationship also ran contrary to her parents', and her own, deeply held Christian values. "It was a big shock for them, because it is frowned upon. And I contradict myself, because both Marizanne and I say we don't think it is right, but we can't help that we love one another. I'm not going to give up my beliefs or my relationship because of what people say, because it is between me and God, and no one else." Her parents came round, and are now very close to Marizanne, while van Niekerk is quietly proud to be a role model to young gay South African women.

Although valued around the franchise world as an all-rounder, she says her heart lies with leg-spin. She doesn't turn the ball hugely, but is skiddy and quick through the air, and has been working on her googly: after a dozen years of international cricket, "you've got to change something". She's always had the ability to rattle through line-ups, becoming – at 19 – the first South African woman to take an international hat-trick, against West Indies in St Kitts; the second was Kapp, eight months later, in a T20 against Bangladesh. Van Niekerk also picked up four for none against West Indies and at Leicester in the 2017 World Cup. She hit her first international century against Sri Lanka at Potchefstroom in February 2019 – a long time coming – but next day was diagnosed with a stress fracture of the hip, the start of an unlucky run of injuries.

A career that began in the amateur age, and spanned the semi-pro era, is now fully professional – and the profile of the South African women's game has risen in tandem. The team reached the semi-finals of the T20 World Cup in 2014 and 2020; in between, they got to the last four of the 2017 one-day World Cup, where they lost, heartbreakingly, to England. Van Niekerk was the tournament's leading wicket-taker, with 15 at ten.

She dreams of that World Cup win. Otherwise, she'll be happy "to leave a legacy, as part of an era that really put women's cricket on the map – if I can bow out saying I've done that, I'll be very happy." Mission, already, accomplished.

ENGLAND'S REBEL TOURS

Without a cause

ANDREW MILLER

Forty years ago, in the final week of February, 12 English cricketers slipped out of Heathrow, and into the eye of an international storm. The "Dirty Dozen", as the tabloids called them, included five who had returned only the previous week from England's Test trip to India and Sri Lanka. As they embarked on a month-long rebel tour of South Africa, they stood accused in the House of Commons of "selling themselves for blood-covered Krugerrands".

In petitioning for an emergency debate, Labour MP Gerald Kaufman claimed the team's contravention of the 1977 Gleneagles Agreement – signed by Commonwealth leaders to discourage sporting links with South Africa's apartheid regime – was "jeopardising this country's place in international Test cricket, and could affect the future of both the Commonwealth and the Olympic Games". Conservative MP John Carlisle condemned Kaufman's rhetoric as a "scurrilous attack" on the players' integrity, while the Speaker turned to a more pressing matter: the draft safety regulations for filament lamps in vehicles.

The indifference went well beyond Westminster. "I didn't think I was doing anything wrong," says Graham Gooch. "I just took up an offer to play cricket." He now admits it was a "schoolboy error" to accept the captaincy, "because then you become the focal point of the team". Dennis Amiss had defected to Kerry Packer's World Series Cricket in 1977, almost losing his Warwickshire contract, and believes the South Africa trip was a minor inconvenience by comparison: "For me, the Packer fallout was toughest. You go in with your eyes open, and accept there will be repercussions. But we went to South Africa for what we felt were the right reasons."

Those reasons, Amiss still insists, were broader than the financial lure of WSC. "There was some money in it, obviously, but I loved South Africa. It was sold to us that we were going to go around schools – black and white – and coach. So that was good, because I was not an apartheid person. I felt very sorry that the country was in the situation it was, but we played some really good cricket, and I hope we helped a country that was in turmoil."

Fundamentally, though, it was the rands wot won it: South Africa's authorities offered upwards of £45,000 for a few weeks' work, a windfall for players who, pre-Packer, had been earning around £200 per Test. And as Peter Willey could confirm, after being overlooked for the tour of India where much of the rebel recruitment took place, Test opportunities were often fleeting.

"Look, the people who wrote all this 'Dirty Dozen' stuff... put them in the same position," he says. "You've got a family, and a six-month job which could end any time. Go out there for six weeks and be guaranteed two or three years' living wage? What would they do? I have no regrets about going. You'd

Bob Thomas Sports Photography/Getty Images

Rebel, rebel… Standing: Wayne Larkins, Bob Woolmer, Tiger Lance (liaison officer), Les Taylor, Chris Old, Mike Hendrick, Peter Willey, John Lever. Sitting: Geoff Humpage, Derek Underwood, Geoff Boycott, Graham Gooch, Peter Cooke (tour organiser), Dennis Amiss, Alan Knott. Johannesburg, 1982.

soon get dropped from the England set-up, or kicked out of a county side. In this world, you look after your own. I found that out."

South Africa's price was so right for so many that, eight years later – and in spite of the three-year international bans imposed on the original squad by the TCCB – history repeated itself. During England's dismal 1989 Ashes campaign, word got out of a second rebel tour, planned for the following spring. The captain would be the man who had led England to victory in Australia three years earlier. "Do I really want to talk about that again?" says Mike Gatting.

Something had shifted in the meantime, an impression confirmed by John Emburey, who alone went on both tours: "You look back now… was it a mistake going? In 1982, I was disenchanted, so I'd say, no, it wasn't a mistake. Was it a mistake going on the second tour? Yes, it was. If that one hadn't taken place, I'd be happy as Larry."

In January 1983, almost a year after Gooch's squad had touched down, 15 West Indian cricketers made the same journey through immigration at Jan Smuts Airport in Johannesburg. (Rebel Sri Lankans had visited in late 1982, while an Australian side would come twice in the mid-1980s.) The reaction in the Caribbean was rather different from the British Establishment's collective shrug. Among the politicians who lined up in condemnation was Roy Fredericks, once a Packer signatory, then a government minister in Guyana. "They should not cause further discomfort to the West Indian population by attempting to live among us," he declared. And so it proved. As told recently by Ashley Gray in *The Unforgiven*, his powerful book on those tours, the fate of those players was sealed the moment they put pens to apartheid paper; a litany of sanctions included life bans.

Lawrence Rowe, the captain and star batter whose name might otherwise sit alongside Viv Richards and Clive Lloyd, now lives in exile in Florida, unknown in his native Jamaica to anyone under the age of 50. David Murray, son of Everton Weekes, peddles drugs to tourists in Bridgetown. Richard Austin – "Danny Germs" to the few who stayed in contact – died in 2015 aged 60 after decades of addiction to crack cocaine. "I mean, you do feel sorry for these blokes in a roundabout way when, like me, they were probably just earning a crust," says Willey. "But I haven't lost a minute's sleep over it. Am I allowed to say that? I don't know what I'm allowed to say these days."

In all, 30 players spanned the two English tours. They include 12 who represented their country after the bans were lifted, of whom three made Test debuts and two became captain: Gooch and Emburey would both play their final Tests in 1995, long after turning 40. Gooch, Geoff (now Sir Geoffrey) Boycott, Alan Knott and Derek Underwood are in the ICC Hall of Fame. Gatting and Underwood have served as MCC president. Amiss has been the ECB's deputy chairman, and David Graveney the chairman of selectors and chief executive of the PCA. Others, notably Bob Woolmer, became international coaches. A long-time ICC match referee, Chris Broad, and a pair of Test umpires – Willey and Tim Robinson – complete a set of forgiven individuals.

Meanwhile, Everton Mattis, who was 25 and had played only four Tests, says in *The Unforgiven*: "We thought, 'OK, we are going to get a little two- or three-year ban'. But oh boy…" In 1987, fearing for his life in his native Jamaica, he fled to New York, where he now walks with a limp after his femur was shattered by a bullet. He dreads deportation. "If I could do it all over again, I wouldn't go. I am still suffering from South Africa."

Michael Holding's book on race, *Why We Kneel, How We Rise*, excoriates the double standards: "There is certainly something depressing about the English reaction, as I can't remember hearing too many apologies being issued, but maybe they see no need to apologise. All manner of cushy jobs handed out. The arrogance, the hypocrisy, the… let me think… there must be a phrase for it? Oh yes. White privilege."

This sits uncomfortably with Graveney, player–manager on the second tour, and Gatting, who says: "I would hate to think Mikey thought I was racist, if that's what he's saying." Graveney adds: "I'm very fortunate to have been involved in cricket for the whole of my adult life. If people feel I've been let off, that's their view. I've tried to serve the game to the best of my ability. Maybe in hindsight going on a rebel tour wasn't the right thing to do. That's the only thing I can say. I've often apologised when I speak at dinners – it's often the first point I make. I let a lot of people down by going."

Gooch, though, sees no reason to deviate from the line he has held for four decades. "I don't look at that," he says. "Every board had to make their own decision. We made ours, and got banned for three years. We accepted the ban. What are you asking me? Should it be a life sentence?" As he points out, the West Indies board rescinded the ban on their players in 1989, and one of the rebels inflicted a blow that would prove crucial during England's tour of the Caribbean a few months later. "Ezra Moseley definitely came back, because he's the one who broke my hand!"

English cricket spent much of 2021 assessing the impact of historic wrongs, but the original batch of rebels believe they were the ones hard done by. At the

Fielding questions: Mike Gatting, David Graveney and John Emburey at Heathrow, January 1990.

time, it was not an uncommon view, either. In his Notes by the Editor for *Wisden 1983*, John Woodcock – who had covered the tour as a strictly sporting venture for *The Times* – denounced the criticism as "hysterical". The players, he felt, had become "pawns in a fiercely political game", driven by the governments of India and Pakistan, who had both threatened to cancel their 1982 tours of England unless action was taken. In late 1988, India refused visas to several England tourists, including Gooch, the captain, because of their South African connections; the trip was called off.

"I was never not wanting to play for England," says Gooch, who successfully sued *The Sun* in 1984 for claiming he no longer cared about his Test career. "I didn't ever not love my country. If they had imposed the same ban on trade, then maybe they've got an argument. But, in politics, anything goes. We see the same things now, where human rights are concerned, with Russia and China. But we're not going to stop buying their products. I wouldn't say we thought as deeply as that back in 1982. That's the reality of the situation."

The woolly wording of the Gleneagles Agreement (what constitutes "sporting contacts of any significance"?) was another reason to think that the ambiguously named "South African Breweries XI" could, in theory, have escaped anyone's notice – much as Derrick Robins's XI and the International Wanderers had provided South Africa with a glut of county tourists between 1973 and 1976. But that notion was scotched on the morning of the first match in Pretoria, when each rebel received a telegram warning of a ban. "We'd already started playing," says Emburey, "so that was irrelevant."

The fact that several tourists, including Gooch, Emburey, Willey and Wayne Larkins, spent the winters of their ban playing for South African provincial sides was a further twist. Heading in the opposite direction, though, and straight into a Test debut against India – who had just threatened to cancel their visit – was England's newest South African import, Allan Lamb. "It was a bit annoying," says Willey of his long-time Northamptonshire team-mate. "Somebody who was brought up in the system was allowed to play. We hadn't upset anybody, or we didn't think we had. So, yeah, we did feel it was odd."

On the tour of India a month earlier, England's prospective rebels had spoken in code – including references to chess moves – to ensure their manoeuvrings were not disclosed. Ian Botham and David Gower, England's most marketable stars, had in principle agreed to take part, but were persuaded it would be an unwise career move; Botham's solicitor, Alan Herd, even dashed to India to explain the issues face to face. Botham's official reason for not going was that he would have been unable to "look Viv [Richards] in the eye". Boycott dismissed this as "puke-making".

Matthew Engel, the former *Wisden* editor who covered the tour for *The Guardian*, says: "What the South Africans got from the major cricketing countries were the fringe players, the ageing players, and the pissed-off players, without exception. On the whole, they were all making a logical decision. It would have been absolute folly for Botham or Gower to have gone, because even in those days they were making more money than the South Africans could stump up."

The ageing process couldn't exactly be held against the TCCB and yet, throughout the 1980s, the number of pissed-off players kept mounting, starting with a bleak tour of India, where England lost the First Test before being bored into submission during five dull draws. "When we made the decision, Test cricket was at a low ebb, and there was disenchantment among the players," says Emburey. "It was quite easy to accept the contract." Gooch agrees. "It's probably the most boring tour I've ever been on. They were bowling nine overs an hour, with Dilip Doshi on at one end, then walking to long-off at the other."

On August 1, 1989, the final morning of the Fourth Ashes Test at Old Trafford, news broke of the second English rebel tour. Emburey, not out overnight, was one of nine in Gatting's rebel squad who had already played for England that summer, though only he, Neil Foster and Robinson were still in the side. Emburey had also been the rebels' go-between with Dr Ali Bacher, who was pulling the strings in South Africa. "When it broke, I was batting with Jack Russell and we managed to get a partnership going," he says. "Having gone through that before, I was a little more hardened to it, and I more or less knew what to expect. I knew we were about to be banned. But it affected Neil Foster a lot. He was crying as he ran in."

The announcement was the culmination of arguably the most shambolic two-year period in English cricket history. And it stemmed from Gatting's row with Pakistani umpire Shakoor Rana at Faisalabad in December 1987. His sacking the following June had precipitated the season of four Test captains during a 4–0 trouncing by West Indies. Now, England chewed through 29 players in six Ashes Tests. "They were horrible times," says Gatting. "I hadn't known anything about the tour. I was told: 'This is the team, will you captain it?' The players were totally disenchanted with the people running the game."

Emburey shares the view. "That era was a shambles, a disgrace," he says. "You can understand why the side performed poorly. You'd turn up at a pre-Test dinner in 1988, and the chairman of selectors would repeat the same speech for the first three or four matches against West Indies: 'You're the best 11 in the country. Go out and play.' We picked 28 that summer!"

Among them was Phil DeFreitas, who had featured in the first four Tests of the 1986-87 Ashes as a 20-year-old, but had been dropped after eight of his next nine appearances, including the first Test of the 1989 summer. When he failed to regain his place in the next three, a meeting with Bacher at a

Simon Bruty, Allsport/Getty Images

Window dressing: Chris Broad (visible through glass), Greg Thomas, John Embury, Paul Jarvis and Mike Gatting in Kimberley, February 1990.

Manchester railway station led to him becoming one of two black players in the rebel party, alongside Middlesex's Roland Butcher. After feeling the full heat of the backlash, both withdrew.

"I was a young lad, very naive, and I signed up through anger, to have a go at the system for treating me this way, because I felt England were messing me around," says DeFreitas. "Not because, deep down, I wanted to go. It was the disappointment of being dropped all the time. There was a horrible reaction towards me. But I was never going to go – and I didn't."

Butcher, whose entire Test career took place in the winter of 1980-81, was 36 when South Africa came calling. But he knew his reputation might never recover: "There's no forgiveness in the Caribbean. Two black guys going to South Africa would have been seen as selling out – two guys not in tune with their African brothers. So it was natural for both black and white to identify us as the ones to pick out. They wouldn't pick out Embers and Gatt for those reasons."

Had DeFreitas and Butcher travelled to South Africa, they would – like their West Indies forebears – have had to accept "honorary white" status to obtain the same privileges their team-mates would have taken for granted. "It would have been a coup for South Africa if they had got one of the black players to visit," says Embury. "It would have been the first multiracial rebel team." DeFreitas is sure his card would have been marked for ever had he gone – unlike so many England rebels, Embury included, who strolled back into the system after their bans. "Everything I fought for, and everything about how I wanted to be as a professional cricketer... I would have just thrown it away," says DeFreitas.

THE REBEL SQUADS

1981-82	1989-90
*G. A. Gooch (*Essex*)	*M. W. Gatting (*Middlesex*)
D. L. Amiss (*Warwickshire*)	C. W. J. Athey (*Gloucestershire*)
G. Boycott (*Yorkshire*)	K. J. Barnett (*Derbyshire*)
J. E. Emburey (*Middlesex*)	B. C. Broad (*Nottinghamshire*)
M. Hendrick (*Derbyshire*)	C. S. Cowdrey (*Kent*)
G. W. Humpage (*Warwickshire*)	G. R. Dilley (*Worcestershire*)
A. P. E. Knott (*Kent*)	R. M. Ellison (*Kent*)
W. Larkins (*Northamptonshire*)	J. E. Emburey (*Middlesex*)
J. K. Lever (*Essex*)	N. A. Foster (*Essex*)
C. M. Old (*Yorkshire*)	B. N. French (*Nottinghamshire*)
A. Sidebottom (*Yorkshire*)	D. A. Graveney (*Gloucestershire*)
L. B. Taylor (*Leicestershire*)	P. W. Jarvis (*Yorkshire*)
D. L. Underwood (*Kent*)	M. P. Maynard (*Glamorgan*)
P. Willey (*Northamptonshire*)	R. T. Robinson (*Nottinghamshire*)
R. A. Woolmer (*Kent*)	J. G. Thomas (*Northamptonshire*)
	A. P. Wells (*Sussex*)

Humpage (who appeared in three one-day internationals) and Graveney never played Test cricket. Sidebottom, Taylor and Wells made their England debuts after completing their bans.

As it transpired, the 1990 tour – which coincided with the release of Nelson Mandela and the legalisation of protests that, at Pietermaritzburg, led Bacher to fear Gatting would be killed – meant the rebels returned with their preconceptions transformed. "It was the magnitude of the events," says Graveney. "I've been involved in the selection of England teams, and the immediate tension that creates. But this was a world event, and it had media interest way beyond anything I'd encountered. That made a vast impression." As with many others, Graveney admits his involvement fractured several close relationships, including one within his own family that would never be resolved. But it is an encounter in the Gloucestershire dressing-room that still sits most awkwardly with him.

"Courtney Walsh was a team-mate, and is still a friend. But once the team had been declared, there was an interesting conversation with him. I think he would have wanted me, as a friend, to explain why I was going, before it got in the public domain. As he put it: 'At least Lawrence Rowe had the courtesy to tell me.' I failed, which was completely insensitive of me. We all have regrets. That's probably one of my biggest."

And what of Gatting? "At the end of the day, you make decisions in your life, and it's history," he says. "There's nothing you can do about it once it's been done. Sometimes you make good decisions, sometimes you make bad decisions. To be perfectly honest, it was probably a mistake to go on that trip."

Andrew Miller is UK editor of ESPNcricinfo.

THE VIKINGS AND KNATTLEIKR

Cricket's 1,111th anniversary?

KIT HARRIS

The Vikings are back. It may have taken a millennium, but they're in fashion again: *Ragnarok* is on Netflix, *Loki* on Disney+, *Norsemen* had three television series, and the fourth *Thor* film is out this year. None depicted cricket, but they might have done, for buried away in the Icelandic sagas are numerous references to a pastime called *knattleikr* – "the ball game" – which bears a passing resemblance to our summer sport.

Eight sagas can be mined for details of *knattleikr*, and three – *Egil's saga*, *Grettir's saga* and *Gísli's saga* – allow the historian to figure out the specifics. Admittedly, this exercise has not been undertaken often, nor with much enthusiasm; the study of Norse recreation usually plays second fiddle to tales of marauding, exploring or pillaging. But to a cricket enthusiast, an attempt to reconstruct the game's history and characteristics bears unexpected fruit.

There is, of course, no Viking *Wisden* (but then there isn't a W in the Norse alphabet). Indeed, it is likely there were no scores at all: these games were played

YOU CAN'T BEAT A GAME OF PILLAGE CRICKET!

for honour, as a show of strength, to settle – or start – a feud. You won simply by being judged a better man. Dr Terry Gunnell, Iceland's foremost – and only – expert in Norse pastimes, views *knattleikr* primarily as a means of developing a narrative. "It's a way of fighting without fighting," he says. "The game focuses on upsets; it's never described as an end in itself, more a way of advancing the story of the men involved."

Men played against men, though there were secondary games for the juniors; there is no mention of women, though it is by no means unlikely that they did play. They were strong, occupied key roles in society, and feature prominently throughout the sagas, even if there is little mention of them in tales of law, war or sport. It is possible they were above such coarse and acrimonious competition.

Players faced each other in pairs. One hurled a ball at his opponent, who wielded a bat and could strike the ball, which could be chased or caught by the bowler. Very hard hits could put the ball beyond the boundary of the playing area. Intimidation was common, if not integral. The bowler was embarrassed if the batter struck the ball back over his head, forcing him to chase it, and the ball was hard enough to fell the batter. Dr Bev Thurber, a scholar of winter sports from Illinois, says a Norse ball was found "during an excavation in York. It was made from several pieces of leather, sewn together and tightly stuffed. It was probably pretty hard." Physical fights frequently ensued, and sledging was highly esteemed, especially in traditional Skaldic verse.

Knattleikr was popular among spectators, too. Tournaments drew huge crowds from all over Iceland, and many would camp near the field of play, since the game took place from dawn until dusk over several days. The participants represented their homesteads: teams were often divided not only geographically but along family lines. Each had a captain, usually a senior member of the family rather than the best player; however, the stories in the sagas focus on the sporting prowess of their eponymous hero.

The earliest dateable reference to the game comes from *Egil's saga*, set in west Iceland. Egil was born in 904 and is one of the great antiheroes of the Viking sagas; his contest against Grím is *knattleikr*'s most famous. Grím intimidates Egil, who retaliates by hitting him with the bat. Grím pins him to the ground, before Egil skulks away, jeered by the crowd. Shortly after, Grím takes a catch and runs around in celebration, whereupon Egil seizes an axe and drives it into Grím's head, "right down to the brain". This precipitates a battle in which seven men are killed. Grím is 11, and Egil seven.

Grettir's saga tells the tale of a typically hot-tempered outlaw from Norway. When he is 14, Grettir is invited to play in a tournament in north Iceland. The captain nominates him to bowl to Auðun, the opposing team's strongest player; Auðun, much older than Grettir, hits the ball back, far over his head, across the ice (Thurber says the game would have been played on frozen lakes, since they would have been the only flat surfaces, and the players wore studded shoes). Grettir is so incensed that he hurls the next ball straight at the batter's head, drawing blood. A fight ensues. Auðun tries to hit Grettir with the bat, and they wrestle; the spectators are impressed at how Grettir can hold his own, at which point Auðun knees him in the groin. The fight is broken up, since nobody wants it to develop into a full-blown feud; wars within extended Viking families make the Middle East look like a Punch and Judy show. The saga baldly reports that "the game went on and nothing else caused friction".

Another account, in *Gísli's saga*, describes a game in the rocky and windswept fjords, pitting two Norwegian fugitives – Gísli and Þorgrím – against each other. Initially, Gísli is criticised by his team-mates for not giving his all; he ups his game and brings "Þorgrím down so that the ball went out of play". This doesn't necessarily imply bodily contact. One interpretation is that Gísli knocked Þorgrím over with a short-pitched delivery, and the ball ran away to the boundary. Þorgrím rises and sees, beyond the field, the burial mound of Gísli's brother, whom he had killed in a feud a few months previously. Gaining confidence, he recalls, in verse: *"The spear screeched his wound sorely / I cannot be sorry."* But Gísli sticks to Bodyline, and fells Þorgrím again, saying: *"The ball smashed his shoulders broadly / I cannot be sorry either."* Gísli is unanimously declared the winner – surely the first occasion a sporting contest was won not by strength but by stanza.

The ICC disciplinary committee would have had their hands full. Not all the sledging was poetic: in one saga, the hero calls his opponent a "cesspool pig"; in another, a player breaks a spectator's neck after being barracked. In a third, a team win by slaying six rivals. But there was a governing body: the Norse parliament, no less, which had their own version of Law 42: "Whenever a man goes to play a game, let him stay no longer at it than he pleases. Then he is responsible for whatever harm may come to him."

And we have all known a Norseman on the cricket field, for the traits of the players are timeless: here is Blíg, dropped from his team on account of his aggressive temperament; there is Gull-þórir, an accomplished player, but an unpopular captain. Everyone knows an Ingólfur, who quits a game so he can flirt with a female spectator. Numerous shady figures have played Kolgrímur, who fixes the outcome. And every club cricketer has rolled their eyes at a Kjartan, who says he hasn't played for ages, but proves the best of the lot.

It is not easy to draw a conclusive link between *knattleikr* and cricket. Gunnell believes that, given the link between the Norse and the Gaelic, hurling may be a more likely descendant, though cricket has more in common with the Viking

game. The trouble, Gunnell points out, is that there is no literary reference to *knattleikr* after Iceland's Norse era ends in 1262. There is a missing link to bridge the game across the ocean to its first proven appearance in England, at Guildford in the mid-16th century. But Gunnell is not a cricket historian. He does not know that the etymology of "cricket" hints at an origin in France or Belgium. Suppose we wanted to find a connection, even for fancy's sake? With a little artistic licence we could construct a Piltdown Man, and adorn it with barely believable bones.

There is a Danish saga which tells of two famous and unbeatable *knattleikr* players from Flanders. Imagine if the Viking game reached Belgium! And then there is French cricket, in which the batter has to repel attacks on his legs by the bowler, with no method of scoring. Is it a sanitised *knattleikr* that children still play in the gardens or on the beaches of Britain?

If *knattleikr* really is the forerunner of the great game, then bloodthirsty Egil is the godfather – the Norse would call him a *freyr* – since his contest is the oldest. He was born in 904, and as he was seven when he slayed his opponent, it follows that cricket celebrates its 1,111th birthday this year: a Nelson of sorts. And Egil, also a great poet, might say: *My claim as the freyr of krikket shall stand / and that of Broadhalfpenny Down be damned*!

TIMELINE OF A PANDEMIC – YEAR TWO

Testing, testing…

Jan 2 A video posted on Twitter shows India's Rohit Sharma, Rishabh Pant, Shubman Gill, Prithvi Shaw and Navdeep Saini breaking biosecurity protocols by dining inside a Melbourne restaurant. Cricket Australia say "the BCCI and CA are investigating the matter… the players have been placed in isolation as a precaution". However, a BCCI official claims there has been no breach, and that the affair is "a malicious spin by a section of Australian media after their humiliating defeat [in the Second Test]".

Jan 4 Further videos appear, purportedly from December, showing Virat Kohli and Hardik Pandya going maskless in a Sydney shop, and other players doing likewise in Adelaide. All the Indian players and support staff test negative.

Moeen Ali tests positive at the start of England's tour of Sri Lanka. He begins ten days' quarantine; Chris Woakes, considered a close contact, has to quarantine for seven.

Jan 6 Thousands of fans who attended the Boxing Day Test at Melbourne are instructed to undergo testing after a single spectator has contracted Covid.

Jan 8 Lord's opens as a vaccination centre; about 1,000 are injected on the first day.

Jan 9 Ireland's ODI series in Abu Dhabi is suspended after three UAE players test positive. Four more test positive three days later.

Jan 13 After their first night in Brisbane, India players complain they have no access to the hotel gym, pool or lifts, no room service, and have to clean their own toilets.

Nineteen are arrested for playing cricket, in breach of social-distancing rules, in Gujarat.

Jan 18 The UAE and Ireland finally complete an ODI in Abu Dhabi.

Jan 22 The BCCI decide the first two Tests against England will be behind closed doors.

Former Indian spinner Harbhajan Singh apologises after sharing an anti-vaccination hoax news story with his 11m followers on Twitter. He says he "didn't check the facts".

Jan 26 Greg Dyer, the chairman of the Australian Cricketers' Association, says it would not be "morally defensible" for international players to receive vaccinations before more vulnerable members of the public.

Jan 30 The BCCI announce that the Ranji Trophy will not be held in 2020-21, the first time it has been cancelled in its 87-year history.

Feb 2 CA announce that Australia will not travel to South Africa later in the month. The host board's director of cricket, Graeme Smith, says he is "extremely disappointed".

Feb 5 India hosts its first international match for 330 days – the First Test against England at Chennai. No spectators are allowed. England's players wear black armbands in memory of war veteran and fundraiser Captain Sir Tom Moore, who has died of Covid aged 100.

Melbourne Renegades all-rounder Will Sutherland is fined $A5,000 for playing golf with friends outside his bubble during the Big Bash.

Feb 11 Pakistan's women abort their tour of Zimbabwe after a single match when Emirates announce they are suspending flights in two days' time.

Feb 13 Some 15,000 spectators are allowed in to watch the Second Test in Chennai. The *Hindustan Times* report there is scant observation of health measures. "How will Ashwin hear us if we wear masks?" asks one supporter.

David Gray, AFP/Getty Images

And for his neck's trick… With saliva outlawed, Matthew Wade uses sweat from Josh Hazlewood to shine the ball; with them is Tim Paine.

Feb 17   Cricket South Africa submit a formal complaint to the ICC over Australia's withdrawal.

Feb 24   Ahmedabad's Narendra Modi Stadium welcomes 40,000 people for the Third Test. One invades the pitch, trying to shake hands with Virat Kohli.

The UK government say recreational cricket can resume in England from March 29.

Feb 27   In response to a lockdown in Auckland, New Zealand Cricket move the men's and women's T20s – against Australia and England respectively – to Wellington.

Mar 2   NZC move the final T20 against Australia from Tauranga to Wellington, and bring it forward to enable the tourists to return home early. Chief executive David White says the ban on spectators in Wellington has cost at least $NZ1.4m.

Mar 4   The Pakistan Super League is suspended after cases among players rise to seven.

Mar 8   The Pakistan Cricket Board's office in Lahore is closed after an official tests positive.

Mar 12   Ahmedabad hosts 57,000 spectators at the first T20 between India and England, the highest attendance at a cricket match since the start of the pandemic.

Amid a third wave, police in Gujarat launch an investigation after a member of the public calls a senior officer at the stadium, and threatens to immolate himself if the T20 series is not cancelled.

Mar 14   The Bangladesh Premier League is cancelled.

Mar 17   India's Covid-19 cases are at their highest for four months. The BCCI suspend children's cricket, and the remaining matches of the England tour are played in empty stadiums.

Mar 20   Imran Khan, Pakistan's prime minister and former national captain, tests positive.

Mar 27   Sachin Tendulkar tests positive and quarantines at home.

Mar 30   Harmanpreet Kaur, India's T20 captain, tweets that she has tested positive.

The ECB's managing director of county cricket, Neil Snowball, says government guidance will allow spectators to attend domestic matches from May 17, but they may need to show proof of vaccination.

Apr 2   ICC set up a $5m fund to help members who are struggling to stage international cricket during the pandemic.

Apr 7   BCCI president Sourav Ganguly, referring to players' concerns over bubble life, says many England, Australia and West Indies cricketers "just give up on mental health". He adds: "I feel we Indians are a bit more tolerant… all of us have to train ourselves mentally so that only good will happen."

Apr 13   Five of the South African women's team remain in Bangladesh, after being diagnosed with Covid, while the rest of the party return home.

Apr 25   In India, 349,691 people contract Covid in a day, a global record; 17m people there now have the virus. *The New Indian Express* suspend coverage of the IPL: continuing is "commercialism gone crass". Ravichandran Ashwin returns home, while Australian Andrew Tye is the first overseas player to withdraw.

Apr 26   Adam Zampa and Kane Richardson quit the IPL, but the Australian government ban arrivals from India. Pat Cummins donates $50,000 to India's relief effort.

Apr 27   The ICC are reported to be drawing up plans to relocate the T20 World Cup from India to the UAE.

Hemang Amin, the BCCI's interim chief executive, emails all IPL players: "You are totally safe within the bubble… you have nothing to worry about." He tells them they are "playing for humanity."

Apr 28   The BCCI defend their stance, telling Reuters the IPL "spreads positivity", and pointing out that it keeps millions of people at home and provides them with entertainment. However, they cancel the Women's T20 Challenge.

The ACA say around 40 Australian players, coaches, officials and commentators are now stuck in India. The Australian government refuse to make special arrangements for their repatriation. Scott Morrison, the prime minister, says: "They travelled there privately."

May 1   Zampa and Richardson travel home via Doha, whereupon the Australian government ban all travel from India via other countries; 38 Australians remain in India.

May 2   Jack Brooks becomes county cricket's first Covid substitute, when Lewis Gregory is forced to isolate after two days of Somerset's match against Middlesex at Taunton.

May 3   CA donate $50,000 to India's coronavirus recovery programme.

The IPL game between Royal Challengers Bangalore and Kolkata Knight Riders is postponed after KKR's Varun Chakravarthy and Sandeep Warrier test positive.

May 4   The BCCI suspend the IPL indefinitely.

May 5   India's second wave of infections peaks at 414,433 new cases.

May 6   All but one of the stranded Australians leave India for the Maldives. Michael Hussey, Chennai Super Kings' batting coach, remains behind to be treated for Covid.

May 11   The ECB report a loss of £16.1m for the financial year 2020-21.

May 17   County grounds open their gates to spectators, though at a reduced capacity.

May 20   The Pakistan board announce the PSL will resume on June 9, in Abu Dhabi.

May 24	The BCCI donate 2,000 oxygen concentrators to India's medical services.
May 25	Naseem Shah (Quetta Gladiators) is banned from the PSL after submitting an outdated test result, before departure for the UAE. Team-mate Anwar Ali tests positive, and misses the flight.
May 29	The BCCI say the IPL will resume on September 19, in the UAE.
Jun 8	An expanded squad of 29 players are announced for Australia's tours of the West Indies and Bangladesh, with CA citing the need for wellbeing in the face of "bubble fatigue".
Jun 19	India wear black armbands during the World Test Championship final in Southampton, in honour of Milkha Singh, the former Olympic athlete, who died from Covid.
Jun 27	ICC referee Phil Whitticase tests positive after the second England v Sri Lanka T20.
Jun 28	Niroshan Dickwella, Dhanushka Gunathilleke and Kusal Mendis are sent home from Sri Lanka's tour of England, after being seen out in public in Durham.
Jun 29	Tom Clark (Sussex) tests positive; seven team-mates are put into isolation.
June 30	ICC confirm the T20 World Cup will be played in Oman and the UAE, rather than India.
Jul 6	Three England players, and four support staff, test positive. The whole squad are sent into isolation, forcing the ECB to name a new squad for the ODI series against Pakistan.
Jul 10	Sam Billings tests positive after a T20 Blast game against Surrey; Kent's squad are obliged to isolate.
Jul 11	Kent field five debutants against Sussex in the Championship at Canterbury. A sixth is added the following day, after Nathan Gilchrist is pinged by the NHS app.
Jul 12	An unnamed Derbyshire player contracts Covid, forcing the abandonment of their match with Essex after the first day. Two days later, their Blast games against Northamptonshire and Yorkshire are cancelled.
Jul 19	The UK's pandemic controls are relaxed, allowing spectators to attend professional cricket matches without restrictions.
Jul 23	The second ODI between West Indies and Australia is postponed after the toss, when it is learned that one of the touring party has tested positive.
	Zimbabwe delay their tour of Ireland (due to start on August 6) as they are on the UK's red list (most of the games are to be played in Northern Ireland).
Jul 26	Cricket West Indies remove a T20 from the series against Pakistan, to accommodate the postponed Australia ODI.
	Andy Flower, head coach of Trent Rockets in The Hundred, tests positive, as do two of his staff.
Jul 27	The second T20 between Sri Lanka and India in Colombo is postponed for 24 hours after India's Krunal Pandya is diagnosed with Covid.
	It is reported that several England players are considering making themselves unavailable for the Ashes, if their families are not allowed to accompany them.
Jul 28	India fulfil their match in Colombo, despite having only 11 players available, and just five specialist batsmen.
Aug 1	Shane Warne, head coach of London Spirit in The Hundred, tests positive.

Kai Schwoerer, Getty Images

Sign of the times: a men's Super Smash game at Hagley Oval in Christchurch, New Zealand.

Aug 2   England's captain Joe Root refuses to rule out the cancellation of the Ashes: "We don't think this is a sustainable way of living and playing."

Aug 3   The BCB and ECB agree to postpone England's white-ball tour of Bangladesh, scheduled for September and October.

Aug 7   Middlesex's Royal London Cup match against Gloucestershire is abandoned after a Covid outbreak in the visitors' squad. The ECB decide their group will be decided on average points per game, all but ending Middlesex's qualification hopes.

Aug 9   Two unnamed Northern Superchargers players test positive, the first Covid cases among cricketers in The Hundred.

Aug 15   An ODI series between Afghanistan and Australia, set for October, is postponed, leaving players free to perform in the rescheduled IPL.

Aug 25   After Pakistan's tour of the West Indies, head coach Misbah-ul-Haq tests positive and remains in Jamaica under quarantine.

Aug 28   Maia Bouchier and Charlie Dean are pinged, and withdraw from England's women's T20 squad to face New Zealand.

Aug 30   The Championship match between Durham and Surrey at Chester-le-Street is cancelled after a Surrey player tests positive.

Aug 31   India's head coach Ravi Shastri attends a launch party for his new book, accompanied by players, support staff and 150 maskless members of the public. The ECB are said to be "furious" the event has taken place; chief executive Tom Harrison attended.

Sep 3   Shastri tests positive on the second day of the Oval Test and enters isolation.

Sep 6   India's bowling coach Bharat Arun and fielding coach Ramakrishnan Sridhar test positive; Nitin Patel, the physiotherapist, enters isolation.

Sep 7   A senior BCCI official tells *The Times of India* the board are "embarrassed" that the team attended a book launch without seeking clearance: "The incident is all the more unsettling, because [BCCI secretary] Jay Shah had written to every team member before the series, asking them to be cautious and refrain from attending crowded events."

South Africa's John Watkins, the world's oldest male Test cricketer, dies of Covid complications in Durban, aged 98.

Sep 8   Yogesh Parmer, India's assistant physiotherapist, tests positive.

Sep 10   On the scheduled first morning of the Fifth Test, India announce their withdrawal owing to "fears of a further increase in the number of Covid cases inside the camp". The ECB say that the match has been "forfeited", but change this to "cancelled".

Australian journalist Malcolm Conn, who was working for the board the previous season, says Shastri refused to wear a mask while in Australia, and was "railing every day against health protocols designed to protect him and everyone else".

Sep 16   India postpone their tour of New Zealand until 2022.

Sep 17   Shastri tells *The Guardian*: "Once you're double-jabbed, it's a bloody ten-day flu. That's it." He says it is impossible he caught the virus at his book launch, and adds: "I have absolutely no regrets because the people I met at that function were fabulous, and it was good for the boys to get out and meet different people."

Sep 19   The IPL resumes in the UAE.

Sep 22   T. Natarajan (Sunrisers Hyderabad) tests positive in Dubai; two players and six support staff are isolated.

Sep 23   Australian prime minister Scott Morrison tells his British counterpart, Boris Johnson, there will be no deals regarding the quarantining of players before the Ashes.

Sep 28   Brisbane's first match of the Sheffield Shield season, between Queensland and Tasmania, is called off an hour before play, after four new cases of Covid in Queensland.

Sep 30   Health authorities in South Australia refuse to let the New South Wales and Victoria teams enter the state, following outbreaks in Sydney and Melbourne.

Oct 10   CSA report a R221m (£10.9m) loss over the last year. "We have been unable to escape the effects of Covid-19," says Mark Rayner, chair of their finance committee.

Oct 11   England announce a full-strength Ashes squad.

Oct 14   CA report a small annual deficit of $A151,000 – better than expected, thanks to the home Test series with India, which produced around $A400m.

Oct 19   Ten South Australia players are thrown out of an Adelaide nightclub for breaching Covid regulations; local police confirm a "disturbance".

Oct 28   Umpire Michael Gough begins a six-day suspension from the T20 World Cup following a breach of biosecurity protocols; he later returns to England.

Nov 17   At the first T20 between India and New Zealand at Jaipur, pandemic protocols are ignored: spectators are not asked for proof of vaccination or a negative test result, nor required to wear masks.

Nov 18   CA confirm no limit on attendance for the Boxing Day Test at the MCG, after Victoria lifts its state restrictions.

Nov 26   The Netherlands abort their series in South Africa after one game, due to Omicron.

Nov 27   ICC cancel the women's World Cup Qualifier in Zimbabwe mid-tournament.

Dec 6   CA say the Fifth Test will not be held in Perth; four days later, they move it to Hobart.

Dec 10   Andre Russell, newly arrived from the West Indies, makes his debut for Melbourne Stars in the BBL – but is forbidden from touching any team-mates, or using the same facilities.

Dec 11   West Indies players Roston Chase, Sheldon Cottrell and Kyle Mayers test positive on arrival in Pakistan for a white-ball tour, as does a member of the support staff.

Dec 16   Australia captain Pat Cummins is forced to isolate, missing the Second Ashes Test at Adelaide, after coming into contact with a Covid case.

              CA move all Perth's remaining BBL games away from Western Australia.

              Five more members of the West Indies tour party test positive. The tour of Pakistan is cut short after the T20s, with the ODIs postponed until June 2022.

Dec 19   Two members of the media test positive during the Adelaide Test. *Test Match Special* is forced off the air, and the Channel 7 TV commentary team are obliged to isolate.

Dec 21   Four USA players test positive.

Dec 26   The first ODI between the USA and Ireland is cancelled after three officials test positive.

Dec 27   After three England coaches and three family members test positive, the second day of the Third Test at Melbourne is delayed by 30 minutes.

Dec 28   Ireland's series in the USA is off, after Paul Stirling and Shane Getkate test positive.

              BCCI president Sourav Ganguly is hospitalised with Covid.

Dec 30   Referee David Boon is withdrawn from the Fourth Test at Sydney, suffering from Covid; England's coach Chris Silverwood isolates after a family member tests positive.

Dec 31   Australian batsman Travis Head tests positive and misses the Fourth Test; his replacement, Usman Khawaja, scores a century in each innings.

A HISTORY OF SELECTION

Sins of commission

RICHARD HOBSON

With his side stumbling through the Ashes summer of 1989, captain David Gower looked ahead to another forlorn selection meeting. "I'm going down to London," he said, "to help pick a few names out of the hat for England." It was typically flippant – black comedy with an edge. And it sprang to mind last year when Ashley Giles, then ECB managing director of men's cricket, abolished Ed Smith's role as national selector.

For over a century, selection had been governed by instinct and hunch – or, as the more cynical might put it, by guesswork and hope. Now, gigabytes of data and footage were said to be turning a haphazard art into a well-honed science, the technology backed by a scouting system of "multiple eyes, multiple times", to quote the ECB's performance director, Mo Bobat. Across 2018 alone, some 209 players were scrutinised in 1,213 reports. Instead of plucking the name of the next bowler from a topper, Gower would have had to highlight them in an Excel spreadsheet.

The one that got away? National selector Ed Smith in 2018.

Philip Brown, Getty Images

By transferring Smith's work to head coach Chris Silverwood, Giles oversaw the most radical shift in selection since a national committee first met in 1899. The intervening 122 years had witnessed changing numbers and personnel, the recycling of ideas (and players), brainwaves and bra<i>fades</i>, inspiration and desperation. What never altered was the need for a thick skin, or – better – results.

Until 1899, home teams were chosen by the host venue, and overseas teams by tour organisers. Bias, prejudice and vested interest were not unknown. In 1901, Lord Hawke, the first chairman, left out George Hirst and Wilfred Rhodes from an Ashes tour because he wanted them fit for Yorkshire the following summer. In *Sins of Omission*, a study of the selectors up to 1990, Allen

Synge wondered how "this man of manifestly divided loyalties ever got the job, or contrived to retain it for a decade".

Hawke's fractious relationship with captain Archie MacLaren reached a nadir in 1902. For the Old Trafford Test against Australia, his panel spitefully omitted three apparent certainties in C. B. Fry, Gilbert Jessop and S. F. Barnes, after MacLaren had independently summoned Barnes, his Lancashire teammate, for the previous Test, at Sheffield. When MacLaren saw the squad for Manchester, he famously exclaimed: "My God, look what they've given me." In protest, he blindsided Hawke, omitting Hirst from the final XI, and choosing the inferior Fred Tate. The pawn in a private squabble, Tate dropped a crucial catch and was last out, with England needing four to win.

Captains since have generally held their tongue – unlike the media and public who, as Silverwood knows after the latest Ashes horror, are happy to pile in. Selection, well... we may not play international cricket, but we can all scribble 11 names on the back of an envelope. And some of the harshest words have been written in these pages. When the panel (led, in the temporary absence of Hawke, by Henry Leveson Gower) picked only one fast bowler for The Oval in 1909, *Wisden* editor Sydney Pardon accused them of touching "the confines of lunacy". The phrase has been much cited since.

"Experts," as Pardon wrote, "occasionally do strange things." Perhaps Fry's experience of such whims – and not, as was thought, his love of the Romans – tipped him towards autocracy in 1912. At his insistence as captain, the committee met just once all summer. "This did not provide much fodder for the scribes, pharisees and dramatists," Fry recalled, "but it worked." To a point, yes. England did win an underwhelming triangular series against Australia and South Africa, but a dispute had left the Australians without key players, Victor Trumper among them. Fry had discovered one of the secrets of selection: pick a summer when the opposition are weak.

Immediately after the First World War, they were anything but. Australia arrived in 1921 after whitewashing England 5–0 the previous winter, provoking panic in Henry Foster's panel. Thirty players represented England, still a record, and nothing spoke of chaos better than the choice of Lionel Tennyson. At one in the morning just before the Lord's Test, he was enjoying a night at the Embassy Club in Bond Street when the message arrived. "If the selectors had informed me a bit earlier," he said, "I should have gone to bed at a timely hour and knocked off a cigar or two." Although England lost their seventh Test in a row, Tennyson saw through his fug to score 74 not out, and was made captain.

By now, selection was a national pastime. "The business has become almost as exciting as the match itself," wrote the *News Chronicle* in 1930, amid debate around Percy Chapman's future as captain. And if the public thought they could do a better job than the selectors, occasionally the selectors thought they could do a better job than the players. In 1926, after more than five years away from Test cricket, committee member Rhodes agreed to a comeback, aged 48. Match figures of six for 79 in the decisive Ashes game at The Oval vindicated him: England won by 289 runs.

Freddie Brown went further in 1953, when he became the only chairman ever to pick himself. Despite his eminence, Brown, an amateur, played under

Services with a smile: a wartime gathering at Lord's includes (standing) Captain Billy Griffith, Lieutenant Greville Stevens, Flight-Lieutenant Walter Robins, Major Gubby Allen, Pilot Officer Reginald Taylor, Sergeant-Instructor Len Hutton, and (sitting) George Heane, Cadet Bryan Valentine, Lieutenant Freddie Brown and Learie Constantine.

Len Hutton, who had become England's first full-time professional captain the previous year. There was a sense of an old social battle being refought, and the pair took the unusual step of issuing a joint statement to say they were happy with the decision, which only increased the suspicion they were not.

Two years later, Gubby Allen, another Establishment figure, took the chair, and cultivating a good relationship with the press became a priority. "He learned the technique of dropping the occasional deliberate leak," recalled E. W. Swanton, the *Daily Telegraph's* cricket correspondent. Quite how much to reveal has proved a continuing challenge. But Doug Insole probably went too far in 1967, after Colin Cowdrey pipped Brian Close to the Test captaincy. Insole let slip not only that Cowdrey had won "by the narrowest possible majority", but admitted personally plumping for Close.

Alec Bedser proved as resilient a selector as he had been a seamer. He served 23 years in all, ending in 1985, and 12 as chairman, both records, and could claim perhaps the most inspired pick of all time: 33-year-old David Steele, the grey-haired batsman who made such an impression repelling Lillee and Thomson in 1975 that he became the BBC Sports Personality of the Year. Bedser's successor, Peter May, cut an aloof figure. Frank Keating called him "the wintry-faced mandarin", while Ian Botham described his panel as "gin-swilling dodderers". In 1988, May got through four captains, including Chris Cowdrey, his godson, and 23 players in total. Robin "Snarler" Marlar evoked

Oliver Cromwell when he told the selectors: "In the name of God, go." Like the Rump Parliament, May went.

Yet this was a model of stability compared with what came next. Ted Dexter was now at the helm and, with news of a rebel South Africa tour breaking midway through the 1989 summer, England picked 29 men to face Australia. For someone who worked in PR, Dexter was comically accident-prone. Trying to dredge positives from an innings defeat at Trent Bridge, he said: "Who can forget Malcolm Devon?" Devon Malcolm was not alone in his bemusement. In *The Independent*, Martin Johnson asked: "Who can forget Ted Lord?"

Public desire to play selector took its ultimate course in 1993, when MCC members pushed for a vote of no confidence after Gower, Jack Russell and Ian Salisbury were overlooked for a tour of India. No matter that MCC had ceded power as appointing authority in 1969, or that tours had not been held under their auspices since 1976-77. Of the special meeting, Dexter noted: "There must be better ways of spending £17,000." Costs were largely defrayed, as the 10,776 returned ballots included a donation of £1.50 towards the room hire, though his point remained. The motion was defeated, but he resigned later that year. "He stood there with a very English, if slightly batty, heroism as shot and shell flew about him," wrote Matthew Engel of his final days.

Where the dreamy Dexter enjoyed flights of fancy, Ray Illingworth was the canny Yorkshireman. Asked by *The Cricketer* around the time of his appointment to name the current players he admired, he replied: "None." Nothing during his reign suggested a change of heart, yet the game had evolved since he led England to the 1970-71 Ashes. Disagreements with captain Mike Atherton became a trans-Pennine soap opera, echoing the relationship between Hawke and MacLaren 90 years earlier. Where Atherton sought a long-term strategy based around youth, Illingworth chopped, changed, and said "no". Atherton wrote: "It was clear to me from the start that, whatever vision I had, and whatever plans I made, would be cast aside."

When he absorbed the role of cricket manager, Illingworth became the nearest thing before Silverwood to a supremo. The problem was that fellow selectors Fred Titmus and Brian Bolus were of a similar, detached generation. "Why," asked Botham, "are people too old, at 37, to play Test cricket, but too young to select the team until they are collecting their pension?" Botham tried to change that, one of nine men standing for two places in 1996. *Romeo and Juliet* had less rancour. Titmus pulled out, describing the election as "a rat race", while Botham claimed he had been victim of a dirty tricks campaign. David Graveney and Graham Gooch emerged as relatively youthful winners. But, from then on, selectors would be appointed, rather than voted in and out.

Graveney proved approachable and conciliatory when he replaced Illingworth as chair. He was happy – and shrewd – enough to allow Nasser Hussain and Duncan Fletcher to call the shots, and the early years of the millennium embraced continuity and consistency, helped by central contracts. In 2005, England used only 12 players to reclaim the Ashes, including Marcus Trescothick and Michael Vaughan, blooded a few years earlier despite limited county returns. Graveney's 11-year stint was largely successful, until a 5–0 defeat by Australia in 2006-07 prompted a review by Ken Schofield, previously

A cunning plan: David Graveney, Ray Illingworth and a head-scratching Mike Atherton, The Oval, 1995.

a long-standing executive director of golf's European Tour. On his recommendation, the full-time job of national selector was born.

For Geoff Miller, then James Whitaker and finally Smith, the growing influence of white-ball cricket was problematic. As the IPL became king, England's attitude to the one-day game remained stubbornly analogue, until the dreadful 2015 World Cup campaign persuaded them to go digital. No longer was it a given that Test players could adapt to the shorter formats. But could the old belief work in reverse? Evidence suggested not, as bashers such as Jason Roy and Alex Hales were exposed in Tests. Balancing the formats, while keeping the different captains happy, became a game within a game.

Breaking team news is strong currency for the media. Alan Smith, as head of the old Test and County Cricket Board, was known to get on his hands and knees to sweep meeting rooms for bugs. Paranoia, you might think, but journalists covering a county game at Trent Bridge in 2009 discovered that Jonathan Trott would make his debut in the Ashes decider. After the selectors had met in a nearby room, one threw a torn sheet bearing the squad names into a waste paper basket – an easy jigsaw for the hacks to reassemble. It ended well: Trott scored 119, and England regained the Ashes.

And yet – as always – the player received more plaudits than the men who gave him his chance. "Selectors," Bedser wrote, "are the anvil for the hammer of every critic… there are occasions when [they] are human enough to pause for self-congratulation when they get it right – even if no one else notices." Maybe Pardon was only half-right: the lunacy is not in the selectors' choices, but their decision to put their heads on the block to make them.

Richard Hobson is a freelance cricket writer. He covered the game for more than 20 years at The Times, *and now gives guided tours of Oxford.*

LEEDS STORY Azeem Rafiq gives a moving account of the abuse he suffered at Yorkshire to the Digital, Culture, Media and Sport select committee in November. A few days earlier, Lord (Kamlesh) Patel joins the club as their new chair.

FROM FIRST TO LAST   While Rory Burns departs to the opening delivery of the men's Ashes, in Brisbane, the England women show more fight in Canberra, where No. 11 Kate Cross survives the last ball of their one-off Test. Neither team won a single game.

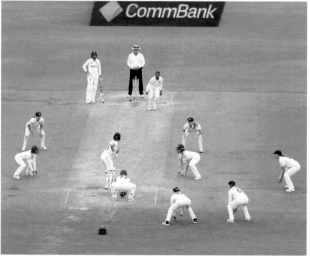

SIDEWAYS MOVEMENT   Kane Williamson hurls himself into the action at Southampton, where he led New Zealand to victory in the World Test Championship final; at Old Trafford, Lancashire's Jimmy Anderson dismisses Kent's Heino Kuhn, his 1,000th first-class wicket.

FACIAL STARE Alice Capsey of Oval Invincibles appears to have a WG-like beard; India's Smriti Mandhana locks her gaze on the ball during the Test at Bristol.

Irfan Nabi Dar

THE PEAK OF THE CROP   Harmukh, a 5,142m (16,870ft) Himalayan mountain in India's Jammu and Kashmir region, rises above a game of cricket, while boys play in a field of mustard in Gobindaganj, north-western Bangladesh.

Abdul Momin

Sajid Hasan Shahid

OUTDOOR PURSUIT Beside the Gorai river, Kushtia, Bangladesh; and in Kolkata's morning haze.

Rajesh Dhar

ANYWHERE WILL DO   For these lads in Chittagong, Bangladesh, the pitch is on the third floor, and fielders leave the leg side unguarded. At the Hagley Oval in Christchurch, New Zealand, children prefer their own game to the professional entertainment nearby.

THE LEADING CRICKETERS IN THE WORLD   Joe Root and Lizelle Lee

LEADING WOMAN CRICKETER IN THE WORLD IN 2021

Lizelle Lee

RAF NICHOLSON

Since Lizelle Lee made her debut for South Africa in 2013, her calling card has been slogging huge sixes, but last year her focus shifted. "I didn't like the tag saying I was only a big hitter," she says. "So I invested a bit more in my ODI game." The numbers suggest those efforts paid off: she averaged 90 in the format, and scored 632 runs, over 100 more than anyone else. In March, after a career-best 132 not out against India at Lucknow, she moved top of the ICC rankings.

But, for Lee, 2021 had another story. "It was probably one of my toughest years as a cricketer, mentally," she says. "I'm one of those players who, when I wake up in the morning, I want to do everything – I want to go and train, I want to play. But at points last year, I didn't even want to go to bed, because I didn't want to wake up."

Her breaking point came at the end of a tour of the West Indies in September. It had been an intense few months following the trip to India, where South Africa won the ODIs 4–1, and Lee was the leading run-scorer, averaging 144. Then came a two-week quarantine period in Croatia en route to England for The Hundred. During that fortnight, her parents both caught severe Covid: "My dad nearly died." But there was no question of travelling home to be with them. Instead, from England, she went straight to the Caribbean, and into yet another bubble.

On the pitch, everything was great. Playing for Manchester Originals, she was the seventh-leading run-scorer in The Hundred; then, against West Indies, she hit 91 not out, 18, 78 not out and 61, helping South Africa to another ODI series win. But a crisis was brewing: the return home was delayed because of a lack of flights, meaning even less time with her wife, Tanja, before Lee was supposed to dash off to the Big Bash League in Australia. "I cried the whole day," she says. She decided she needed a break, opted out of the Big Bash and spent several weeks at her parents' with Tanja. Lee had learned cricket in the backyard from her dad but, for the final three months of 2021, she did not pick up a bat.

The break worked. "I can't wait to play again," she says. "I'm feeling very happy." Yet Lee – who quit her teaching degree after she was offered a full-time contract by Cricket South Africa in 2014 – is a reminder of the strain Covid has placed on professional cricketers. Even as we celebrate her, we shouldn't forget the need to nurture players off the field, as well as on it.

THE LEADING WOMAN CRICKETER IN THE WORLD

2014	Meg Lanning (Aus)	2017	Mithali Raj (Ind)	2020	Beth Mooney (Aus)
2015	Suzie Bates (NZ)	2018	Smriti Mandhana (Ind)	**2021**	**Lizelle Lee (SA)**
2016	Ellyse Perry (Aus)	2019	Ellyse Perry (Aus)		

THE LEADING CRICKETER IN THE WORLD IN 2021

Joe Root

Scyld Berry

Don Bradman had Bill Woodfull and Bill Ponsford to pave the way, Wally Hammond had Jack Hobbs and Herbert Sutcliffe, Viv Richards had Desmond Haynes and Gordon Greenidge. In 2021, Joe Root kept coming in at 20 for two, and yet he scored 1,708 Test runs, only 80 short of Mohammad Yousuf's record for a calendar year. Root, in the fifth year of his captaincy, when previous England captains have either wilted or resigned, touched the heights of English batsmanship; he even raised them to a new level in Asia.

The list of great Test batsmen in weak batting sides, which Root joined, is short and select. Others include West Indies' George Headley before the Second World War, Martin Crowe of New Zealand, Allan Border in the Australian team of the mid-1980s, Zimbabwe's Andy Flower. These Atlases are rare. Off his own bat, Root in 2021 scored more than three times as many as the next batsman in England's Test side – Rory Burns, with 530. And he averaged 61, when nobody else reached 30, except Dawid Malan, from just five Tests. Amid all the difficulties of leading a struggling team in and out of biobubbles (England lost nine out of 15), Root was perfectly balanced at the crease.

Once the ECB had decided to press ahead through Covid with a never-ceasing schedule, Root was able to find his rhythm and, by playing 29 Test innings, to stay there. He even had time for a bad streak, going 11 innings without a fifty: this was partly due to the pitches which India produced after England had won the opening Test, and which turned so much that Root's own off-spin took five for eight at Ahmedabad; and partly due to the mediocrity of his team which faced New Zealand, when England's selectors ignored players who had participated in the IPL. Even he was dragged down in that two-Test series. Either side, he flourished, in the first three Tests of the year, in Asia, then in the home series against India.

Every version of the sweep shot was the basis of Root's brilliance in Galle, and to a lesser extent in Chennai, where India's taller and bouncier spinners were more likely to take a top edge. He had been adept against spin from the moment he scored ten runs off his first ten balls in Tests, on debut at Nagpur in December 2012, but now he attacked it in a way no England batsman had ever done on the subcontinent. He scored at 71 runs per 100 balls in his 228 in Galle, when his team-mates mustered 180 between them. And such was his reach – the elasticity of his arms – that he had a sweep or reverse sweep or slog-sweep for any length Sri Lanka bowled, opening up an area of more than 180 degrees from deep midwicket round to what he could turn into deep square leg on the other side. Sri Lanka were powerless. When Root followed with 186 in the Second Test at Galle, then another double-hundred at Chennai, his sweep promised to become England's signature shot of the decade, the successor to Kevin Pietersen's flamingo drive of the 2010s, and Michael Vaughan's pull that set the tone for the 2000s.

After the lowlights, Root scored three centuries in consecutive Tests at home against India's splendid attack. And these masterpieces, notably his unbeaten 180 at Trent Bridge, propelled him to the top of another list. Hitherto he had been the least of the quartet competing for the unofficial title of the world's

HIGHEST PERCENTAGE OF A TEST TEAM'S RUNS IN A YEAR

				T	*Runs*	*Team runs*
28.47	D. G. Bradman	Australia	1930	6	978	3,434
27.80	D. G. Bradman	Australia	1931	7	783	2,816
26.38	G. S. Sobers	West Indies	1960	7	855	3,241
26.21	**J. E. Root**	**England**	**2021**	**15**	**1,708**	**6,516**
25.84	K. F. Barrington	England	1967	6	750	2,902
25.57	R. B. Richardson	West Indies	1989	6	797	3,116
25.33	I. V. A. Richards	West Indies	1976	12	1,710	6,750
25.10	A. Flower	Zimbabwe	2000	9	1,045	4,162

Note: minimum 6 Tests.

best batsman. But in 2021, Virat Kohli's fire burned less intensely; Kane Williamson's right elbow did not allow him to grip a bat at times; and Steve Smith had too much on his plate, in the wake of Sandpapergate, to focus entirely on his unique technique. Root purred past them.

Before this string of masterpieces, his best Test innings had been his 254 against Pakistan at Old Trafford in 2016, when he restrained himself to three main strokes, hour after hour, without his impishness tempting him to score behind point with the open face of an almost vertical bat. For most of 2021, he found batting so easy that he dabbed and steered with impunity, until Australia, where he was dismissed three times in 11 balls by Scott Boland banging out a length on fourth or fifth stump. Desperate to inject quick runs into England's innings, Root succumbed to his Achilles heel. He did not leave the ball and make the bowler come to him, or square cut with a horizontal bat: he tried something speculative in between. But as he did not turn 31 until the end of 2021, Root the batsman, if not the captain, had time on his side. Combining the best of both worlds – the defensive technique of the ancients with the novel strokes of the moderns – he could yet become England's finest.

THE LEADING CRICKETER IN THE WORLD

2003	Ricky Ponting (Australia)	2013	Dale Steyn (South Africa)
2004	Shane Warne (Australia)	2014	Kumar Sangakkara (Sri Lanka)
2005	Andrew Flintoff (England)	2015	Kane Williamson (New Zealand)
2006	Muttiah Muralitharan (Sri Lanka)	2016	Virat Kohli (India)
2007	Jacques Kallis (South Africa)	2017	Virat Kohli (India)
2008	Virender Sehwag (India)	2018	Virat Kohli (India)
2009	Virender Sehwag (India)	2019	Ben Stokes (England)
2010	Sachin Tendulkar (India)	2020	Ben Stokes (England)
2011	Kumar Sangakkara (Sri Lanka)	**2021**	**Joe Root (England)**
2012	Michael Clarke (Australia)		

Boundary writer: John Woodcock and a phalanx of photographers, Lahore, 1987.

JOHN WOODCOCK 1926–2021

The Sage of Longparish

MIKE ATHERTON

There is an intriguing image of John Woodcock. Taken by Adrian Murrell during the Lahore Test between Pakistan and England in November 1987, it shows Woodcock from a distance, sitting in a low-slung chair near the boundary watching the game – close to, but a little apart from, a line of photographers. About 20 yards away, over his right shoulder, you can just spot the shoes of a player prowling the rope.

Woodcock looks utterly relaxed and content: striped shirt, sleeves rolled halfway up, legs crossed, notepad and binoculars at the ready, his chair at an angle. It is how I imagine he would have liked to watch Test cricket if conditions allowed: outside the press box to get a sense of the smells, sights and sounds of the game; away from other writers and close to cricketers, so he could watch intently, pass judgment, and hone a finely crafted piece for the following day's paper.

The photograph shows why there will never be another Woodcock. That can be a cliché when someone of significance dies, but in his case it is true: not so much because of his own qualities – there were good cricket writers before Woodcock, and there will be again – but because of the time in which he operated. Principally, that is to say, before television became ubiquitous, rendering the role of the match reporter in print increasingly superfluous, and reducing the proximity between players and journalists.

What cricket writer could now wander to the boundary during a Test match, and plonk himself in a deckchair for the day? There would be all kinds of obstacles – security, mainly, and a growing feeling that cricket writers must know their place, and that place is nowhere near players, for heaven's sake. When Woodcock operated, cricket writers mattered to the game's authorities more than today, when they are perceived as a nuisance to be tolerated.

> "If I was good at anything, I could write a decent match report."

More likely, were you to come by cricket writers now, they would be tethered to their desks like goats, simultaneously checking Twitter, watching television, listening to the commentary and keeping half an eye on the game. A non-stop whirl of information to take in, action to follow, instant judgment to make – all before the thoughts turn to the match report. Not that such engagement leads to greater profundity. There are exceptions, but only a few.

Woodcock was, above all, a match reporter. No correspondent today could afford to ignore or refuse to write comment pieces, interviews and features. He did. He travelled, he watched the game and he reported on it, no more, no less. Along with the likes of E. W. Swanton and John Arlott, he operated in an era where newspapers were ascendant, and the words of these giants of sports journalism were awaited eagerly.

To get a sense of why Woodcock was such a good writer, you have to read these match reports in the round. They are mostly hidden away now in the archive of *The Times*, for whom he was the cricket correspondent for a little more than three decades, and a contributor for twice as long. His prose was clear, concise, rhythmical. He was a stylist, but not a show-off: a lovely writer.

When he died, an editor on the newspaper said we should reproduce some of his best lines, but that wasn't easy. He wasn't a flashy writer, concocting memorable phrases or lines; rather his strength was giving an overview of the day, a sense of the ebb and flow of the game. "If I was good at anything, I could write a decent match report," he told me on his 90th birthday. "I was a decent reader of a match."

Informing all that was a deep love and knowledge of cricket. He watched his first Test at Lord's in 1936, and filed his last piece for *The Times* in 2020, on the occasion of Everton Weekes's passing. He had seen Weekes play, as he had many of the greats of the 20th century, and could give context and balance from first-hand experience. And he did so fairly: he was not an "in my day" kind of writer. He enjoyed the modern game, although he lamented the loss of variety that covered pitches have encouraged.

Not only had he seen the greats play, he knew them well. He corresponded with Don Bradman, went duck shooting with Harold Larwood, batted in a friendly with Wally Hammond, played golf with Len Hutton, Herbert Sutcliffe and Geoff Boycott. When he travelled by boat on the 1954-55 tour of Australia, he was the same age as many of the players. They became lifelong friends.

JOHN WOODCOCK AND WISDEN

Pub lunch, choc ice, dog walk

GRAEME WRIGHT

It's well enough documented how John Woodcock came to be *Wisden* editor after chatting to Kirsty Ennever, managing editor of the Almanack's publisher, Queen Anne Press, at a wedding reception in the Long Room at Lord's. Less known is that some years earlier, when managing editor of QAP myself, I gave Kirsty her first job out of university. Fate or not, the coincidence was certainly serendipitous.

John and I weren't starting from scratch when it came to putting a book together. John (always John, never "Wooders") had just finished a stint as assistant editor on Jim Swanton's authoritative *Barclays World of Cricket*. "His hand was everywhere," EWS wrote appreciatively in his introduction. And the evidence was everywhere on my first visit to The Old Curacy in Longparish, with proofs and photos spread across the dining-room table, soon to be replaced by *Wisden* articles, match reports and printers' proofs. Editing and producing books was what I did, and I had worked with Norman Preston on two *Wisdens* before his death in March 1980. Christine Forrest, a neighbour, had helped with these, and was into the swing of the Almanack's idiosyncrasies, style and work cycle.

I would sometimes describe my early relationship with John as resembling that between cabinet minister and departmental civil servant, only more complicated. My first responsibility was to QAP, and later John Wisden, keeping the book within budget, to its page extent and on schedule. But with John's prime commitment being to *The Times*, he had asked that I also be his assistant editor. In that sense, I had a responsibility to him and the Almanack's content. We, including Christine, had to be a team. It helped that we all became the best of friends.

Given the three of us had work ties other than *Wisden*, we needed a division of duties, and trust in each other's abilities. John would give the book its authority, and be *Wisden's* man-at-large. He commissioned and edited the main articles, Test reports and the county and tour reviews. He chose the Five Cricketers of the Year, and of course he wrote the Notes. Christine and I handled the rest: the subbing and checking, the proofreading and, on a rolling basis, passing pages for press.

Neither John nor I had the ego to impose ourselves on the book's structure, but we agreed we wanted to improve its literary quality. He came into his own here. A wonderful writer himself, he was also a fine judge of a writer; it was all the same to him whether that person appeared in tabloids or broadsheets. Younger journalists were chuffed to be asked to write for *Wisden*.

What is surprising now is how infrequently Christine and I met up with John: three times a year on average. Otherwise, in that pre-internet age, we got by on phone and post. But those visits to Longparish became special: the ritual of a pub lunch at John's local, the choc ice back at The Old Curacy and, work over for the day, walking his dog, Yorker mostly, along the river bank. Amazing we got any *Wisden* done, but we did, and had fun doing it. There was good gossip as well, not that any made it into *Wisden*.

After John died, a friend sent me an email of sympathy: "He was someone you always mentioned as a good friend you respected and admired." And when I recollect the years we worked together, that sums it up.

Graeme Wright edited eight editions of Wisden, *in two stints, between 1987 and 2002.*

He was closest to Colin Cowdrey. He told me, rather wistfully, that he could no longer see in his mind's eye the way Cowdrey played on that tour while making a hundred in the Melbourne Test – Woodcock's favourite innings of all he had seen – but he still remembered the way he *felt* during it. As a result of knowing them so well, he wondered whether he was too close to be objective – not a worry for many current writers.

Before television, social media, and the decline of print, he knew he had the best of journalism, and was grateful for it. It afforded him a modestly comfortable but fun life. At Woodcock's memorial service, Henry Blofeld recalled the 1976 journey the two had taken to India in a 1921 Rolls-Royce. Nowadays, entire tours are often shorter than the overland journey these old friends enjoyed, one that gave them memories to last a lifetime.

Back then, the less frenetic nature of the sport allowed observers to take in far more than the cricket, and their journalism was better informed for it: rounded, with a sense of hinterland that encouraged them to keep the game in proper perspective. Woodcock's contemporaries at Oxford had been through the war, and they and he knew what sport meant in the grand scheme of things.

The requirements of travel and time can often play havoc with a cricket journalist's private life, but underpinning everything was Woodcock's sense of place, which anchored him throughout. He lived all his life in Longparish, a quiet Hampshire village on the river Test, and returned there happily whenever cricket was done. He knew everyone in the village; they knew him. He came to be indelibly associated with it through the name given him by Alan Gibson, a fellow scribe on *The Times*: The Sage of Longparish.

It was there, in St Nicholas's church – a place of worship with which his family had been associated for more than 250 years – that we gathered last August. Cricketers, journalists, administrators, friends, family and villagers turned out in their hundreds, with overflow areas laid out in the local school and pub, to say goodbye to a remarkable and very lovely man. In the small and relatively insignificant world of cricket writing, a giant had passed from the page.

Mike Atherton is cricket correspondent of The Times.

TRAVELS WITH JOHN WOODCOCK

The extra mile

HENRY BLOFELD

In December 1975, John Woodcock and I were in Perth for an extraordinary Test between Australia and West Indies. We were staying at the Weld Club, and one evening I said to him that in a year's time we would be with England in India. "The last time we went," he replied, "Brian Johnston, Michael Melford and I decided to drive. We didn't in the end, because the wives didn't think it was a good idea. But that doesn't apply to either of us at the present time, Blowers, so why don't we do it now?"

By the time dinner was over, we had already selected our first travelling companion, Judy Casey, a mutual friend who lived in Sydney and exactly the ebullient extrovert this sort of adventure needed. When we returned to England, Wooders persuaded a farming friend in Hampshire, Adrian (Ady) Liddell, who collected old cars, to join the party, along with his lovely claret-coloured 1921 Rolls-Royce. Michael Bennett, a drinking companion of mine, was the fifth member of the party, and brought along his new yellow three-litre Rover.

The two cars left an underground garage near the Albert Hall in the rain at 6.30am on October 6, 1976. The Rolls had luggage and spare tyres piled on the roof and running boards, and both cars were plastered with stickers from our sponsors, who included a celebrated maker of Scotch whisky.

John Woodcock

For flock's sake: Ady Liddell investigates a little local difficulty.

Ady, in his cap, drove the Rolls every inch of the way to Bombay, and without blemish. I sat beside him in the assistant chauffeur's seat, which was lumpy and uncomfortable. When it rained, the top of the windscreen leaked plentifully. Wooders sat like an off-duty maharajah in the ample back seat, protected by the window which separated the passengers from the chauffeurs. Michael drove the Rover peering over the top of his horn-rimmed, half-moon glasses, while Judy encouraged, and sometimes spelled, him.

Our journey through Europe was circuitous, owing to the demands of sponsors, but without problem. We took in Paris and Frankfurt, then drove through Austria into what was still Yugoslavia, and on to Thessaloniki in Greece. We went across the top of the Aegean to Istanbul, the Bosporus and Asia, where we entered a different world. Driving became increasingly difficult, with huge, speeding, long-distance lorries, a lot of rather curious local traffic, much hooting and fearsome potholes.

The racing line? The Rolls-Royce picks up speed on the open road.

We made for Ankara, where the Turkish political parties were having their annual conferences. Hotels were full, but at a petrol station Wooders fell into conversation with some students, one of them the son of the Turkish judge advocate general. We spent the night on a plush carpet in the drawing-room of his parents' luxurious apartment. Our eminent host and Wooders might have been sailors on shore leave. The next night, in Sivas, in the most spartan hotel of all, was a great contrast, and marked by a lively discussion. The occupants of the two cars disagreed as to whether the purpose of our journey was to have a look around, or simply to get there. It was partly Wooders's sure diplomatic touch which patched things up.

We stayed in Tehran with a friend of Ady, who was also the Shah's personal solicitor. He put us up in a magnificent house just outside his boss's Sa'dabad Palace. We spent four days there, while Ady fully serviced the Rolls; we saw the Iranian crown jewels, and watched a game of cricket put on by the British embassy at Tehran airport, which began at half past six in the morning. Wooders said a few words at dinner one night in the embassy and, by the end, when he was talking to our ambassador, we were not entirely certain who was who. Still in Iran, we ate caviar at Babolsar on the Caspian, from a barbecue on a roundabout in Bojnord, and discovered an unlikely cache of champagne in the holy city of Mashhad – all orchestrated by Wooders.

Next day, the crossing from Iran into Afghanistan, accompanied by hangovers, was much the most difficult of the trip. The border post was run by a teenager, a budding dictator who met his match in Wooders. After a slight problem with his deafness, they quickly became great friends; when Wooders slid him a bottle of whisky, it might have been a gold bar.

JOHN WOODCOCK'S NOTES BY THE EDITOR

Never what it was

Wisden 1981

I do enjoin umpires to keep a close eye on over-rates, especially in Test matches. For fear of being fined, as now happens, for dropping below 19 overs an hour, English county sides are conscious of the need to keep moving. Unfortunately the International Cricket Conference allowed their annual meeting at Lord's last August to pass without giving more than a shadowy undertaking to keep an eye on what is becoming a cause for serious concern in the Test game. Meeting as they did immediately after a Test series in which England and West Indies had seldom bowled more than 15 overs an hour and sometimes as few as 12, the time was ripe for taking firm action. But nothing positive was done.

New to the English scene in 1980 was night cricket, played on football grounds. Though the cricket itself was of no consequence, a germ has been implanted. There are, in cricketing administration today, marketing men whose desire to bring money into the game causes them to trifle with its origins and gamble with its charm… Should it ever catch on, it may have to be given another name, which is not to dismiss it as being of no threat to the present game.

Last year was the first in which helmets, or reinforced caps, became standard wear in first-class cricket. When, as more often than not, they have a visor attached, they reduce the batsman, or short-leg fielder, to wretched anonymity. I find it sartorially and aesthetically an objectionable trend. It has, furthermore, detracted from the artistry of batting. As you would expect, old players deplore the sight of a helmeted batsman. Yet if their use saves cricketers from serious injury, they must be allowed.

Wisden 1982

No one, I believe, can ever have played a finer Test innings *of its type* than Botham's at Old Trafford. I have been told that Australia's attack was by no means one of their strongest, and that by the time Botham came in the best of their bowlers, Lillee and Alderman, were on their last legs. To which I will say only that you would never have known it from the way they were bowling.

It seemed an absurdity when young members of the Yorkshire team, unfit in terms of cricketing ability and commitment so much as to tie up Boycott's bootlaces, were asked to vote on whether or not they wanted to play with him any more, let alone when their feelings were made public. It is to England's cost that Yorkshire insist upon tearing at each other's throats.

Wisden 1983

Trapped in the maelstrom, the TCCB, by imposing a three-year ban [on England's South African rebels] – to preserve international multi-racial cricket – bowed to political pressures to the consternation not only of the players concerned but also of the average cricket follower.

The game is never quite the same from one season to the next. As has been said before now, it never has been what it was. To those who love it, though, it remains… an incomparable pastime.

Wisden 1984

The World Cup was a great success, and India's victory a splendid surprise. They brought warmth and excitement in the place of dampness and depression. In the early years of limited-overs cricket no one, themselves included, took India seriously.

Sir Donald Bradman, no less, thinks the time has come for electronic assistance to be made available to umpires in Test matches, for use in certain types of dismissal (run-outs, stumpings and occasionally catches). If it had been, an absurdly bad run-out decision, in the first over of the match, would not have cast a shadow across the Fifth Test in January between England and Australia in Sydney. On the other hand, the tempo of the game would be further slowed down and the umpire's supremacy undermined. Umpires themselves, while acknowledging their fallibility, prefer things as they are. So, for the moment, do I.

Wisden 1985

It was hard to watch the West Indian, Marshall, bowling at Pocock in last season's Fifth Test match at The Oval without recoiling. Pocock was the nightwatchman from the previous day. As such, he could expect few favours. However, the Laws of Cricket make it abundantly clear that the relative skill of the striker must be taken into consideration by an umpire when deciding whether the bowling of fast, short-pitched balls amounts to "intimidation" and is therefore unfair. That Marshall, a superb bowler, should have kept bouncing the ball at so inept a batsman as Pocock was unwarrantable; that Lloyd should have condoned his doing so was disconcerting; that Constant, the umpire at Marshall's end, should have stood passively by was unaccountable. It was a woeful piece of cricket, entirely lacking in chivalry.

For those at the top there is a lot of money in today's game – too much, I am inclined to think, for the results which a good many of them produce. For the boots, bats and other cricketing equipment that he endorses, Botham receives something in the region of £40,000 a year. A county cricketer, capped and in mid-career, receives the comparatively modest minimum wage of £7,250 for his season's labours.

In purely technical terms the standard of English batsmanship can seldom, if ever, have been so low. Even among the Test side there is an absence of basic, orthodox footwork, while the bat, time and again, comes through across the line of the ball. Why? Because four competitions out of five, from the cradle to the grave, are now played on a limited-overs basis, culminating in a slog.

A friend trekking in the Himalayas came upon a cluster of Kashmiris glued to their transistor sets, listening to a Test match commentary. That was near Ladakh, at nearly 14,000 feet. So in all manner of places the heart of the game beats strongly.

Wisden 1986

I doubt whether the 1985 Australians would have finished in the first four in the County Championship. As a consequence of playing so much one-day cricket – they did nothing else for the first nine weeks of last year – they seemed to have lost the knack of taking wickets themselves and of selling their own wickets dearly.

Botham was never out of the news for long. Not since W. G. Grace can a cricketer, by his physical presence and remarkable exploits, have so caught the attention of the sporting world. Bradman's feats were, of course, more phenomenal, Sobers's more effortlessly versatile; but off the field they maintained a lower, more urbane profile than Botham.

Nearly there: in Delhi, John Woodcock and Henry Blofeld drink coconut milk with Renu, whose husband, Ashwini Kumar, was an old friend of Wooders.

We were through, beating infuriated lorry drivers, some of whom had already been kept waiting for at least four days. In Kandahar, we were greeted by a bearded rogue who insisted on selling us cigarettes most certainly not filled with tobacco. Wooders was all for giving them a go, and we had a headache for three days. We then drove through the Kabul Gorge, more impressive than the Khyber Pass, on the way to the still beautiful and unspoiled Kabul, where we saw Curzon's magnificent embassy, admired the architecture and bought sheepskin coats on Chicken Street.

After leaving Afghanistan, we rolled into Dean's Hotel in Peshawar, where one of the bearers greeted Wooders, who had stayed there once before, with great warmth. There was much hugging. We then went to Islamabad, and into India. In Delhi, Wooders met up with an old friend, Ashwini Kumar, a former Indian hockey player who was now their representative on the International Olympic Committee. He was also the head of India's border security force, and arranged for us to spend two fascinating days at their base in Tekanpur, south of Delhi.

Finally, we passed through Rajasthan, then spent one night with the Maharajah of Baroda at his palace. Two days later, soon after one o'clock on November 22, Ady drove the Rolls into the small, semi-circular courtyard of the Taj Mahal Hotel in Bombay. It was 46 days after we had left the Albert Hall. Wooders and I were in time for the start of Tony Greig's victorious tour. The cars, once again good friends, caught a ship home.

Henry Blofeld, who is 82, began commentating for Test Match Special *in 1972, and retired 45 years later.*

HOW TO MEASURE A CAPTAIN

Turn on the ratio

TIM DE LISLE

It was the best of years, it was the worst of years. For Joe Root, 2021 was an *annus mirabilis* and *horribilis* at the same time. Those twin impostors, triumph and disaster, turned out to be conjoined. It wasn't just that he was often triumphant at the crease and disastrous at the helm: his captaincy alone kept contradicting itself. He ended the Ashes as the most successful captain England had ever had – and the most unsuccessful. When his team hammered India at Headingley in August, Root surpassed Michael Vaughan as the England captain with most Test victories – 27. As they left Adelaide in December, he had dislodged Alastair Cook as the England captain with most Test defeats – 23. By the end of the series, at Hobart, it was 25. Was he England's biggest winner, or their biggest loser, or both?

Actually, he was neither. Career aggregates are a poor guide to a captain's calibre: they have less to say about excellence than about longevity and fixture lists. At Sydney, he collected yet another record, outlasting Cook and becoming the first England captain to reach 60 Tests; Hobart was Root's 61st Test as captain in 55 months.

Modern sport is steeped in statistics. In cricket, it's no longer just the scores on the board – it's runs per 100 balls, percentage of dots, average against seam, average against this bowler. There's a flood of numbers coming at us all day long, and even flowing back into history. We can be told now that John Crawley's Test average against spin was 74. If the England selectors of the 1990s had known that, they might have given him a go in the subcontinent. When it comes to batting and bowling, we are far better informed than ever before. The statisticians are getting there with fielding, too, and can show us that, in men's Tests, New Zealand have the best slips.

But there is one department where the stats are still primitive: captaincy. In the 50 years I've been following the game, nothing has changed. A captain's record pops up on the screen only when a landmark comes along. We end up applauding them for avoiding the sack. Captaincy is cricket's most cerebral element, the most analytical, and yet it is barely analysed. Well, you may say, it's impossible to pin down – it's about feel, instinct and inspiring the troops to run through a brick wall. The answer to that is: up to a point, Lord Botham.

Of course it's not all measurable, but neither is batting or bowling. Statistics still struggle to do justice to the unplayable over that spreads fear through a team, or the doughty 20 in dodgy light that sees off the new ball. The central stat remains the average, which tends to be worn like a badge, or a medal. We all know Bradman's Test batting average is 99.94, a figure so resonant it's almost a brand. We know a few others have finished on 60 (Graeme Pollock,

George Headley, Herbert Sutcliffe). Bowling averages are less famous, because of the age-old bias towards the bat, but the well-informed *Wisden* reader may recognise a few: ten is George Lohmann, 16 S. F. Barnes, 18 Frank Tyson, and just under 21 means Malcolm Marshall, Joel Garner or Curtly Ambrose. In the women's game, there are some formidable figures waiting to be memorised: batting averages of 75 for Ellyse Perry and 59 for Enid Bakewell, bowling averages of 11 for Betty Wilson and 13 for Mary Duggan, who, like Garry Sobers, was both a fast left-armer and a slow one.

Averages force players to lug their career around, but they still have some use, which is why they have survived as a yardstick. We need something similar for captaincy. But what, in a captain's record, might resemble an average? It needs to be clear, clean and reasonably fair. It ought to shed light and ring true. And it should be inclusive, able to be worked out by a ten-year-old.

First, let's look at percentage of matches won, with a minimum of ten Tests as captain. Here's the top ten:

MOST SUCCESSFUL TEST CAPTAINS BY WIN PERCENTAGE

		P	W	%				P	W	%
1	W. W. Armstrong (A) ...	10	8	**80.0**	6	D. R. Jardine (E)	15	9	**60.0**
2	S. R. Waugh (A).	57	41	**71.9**		F. M. M. Worrell (WI)...	15	9	**60.0**
3	D. G. Bradman (A)......	24	15	**62.5**	8	V. Kohli (I)	68	40	**58.8**
4	R. T. Ponting (A)	77	48	**62.3**		Waqar Younis (P)	17	10	**58.8**
5	W. G. Grace (E)	13	8	**61.5**	10	A. L. Hassett (A)	24	14	**58.3**
						Salim Malik (P)	12	7	**58.3**

Minimum: 10 Tests.   *All statistics are correct at February 8, 2022.*

As in batting, several get close to 60, but not many climb higher. So hats off to Warwick Armstrong, the greatest of all time by this measure, even if he was a captain for only eight months in 1920 and 1921; to Steve Waugh, the greatest of the past century; and to Virat Kohli, the greatest of the past decade. But hang on a minute – the top four are all Australians, which makes you wonder: is there a reason Aussies dominate? Yes, and it's not just that they're good at cricket. Of the ten nations and one region to have hosted more than one Test, Australia has the lowest incidence of draws, partly because all Tests there between 1882-83 and 1936-37 were played to a finish.

The draw, much like hair, was big in the 1980s, before being trimmed to reasonable proportions. It accounted for 45% of all Tests in the 1980s, and only 19% in the 2010s. Going by win percentage, you find a giant of old, such as Clive Lloyd of West Indies (48% – 36 wins in 74 Tests), being felled by a medium-sized figure from the 21st century, such as Faf du Plessis of South Africa (50% – 18 wins in 36), which doesn't seem right.

So I tried putting the draw in a drawer, and looking at wins divided by losses. I raised the qualification too, to 25 Tests, because longevity does count for something, and heavier fixture lists bring more robust samples (Bradman's win/loss ratio was five, but his 24 Tests in charge came at the rate of two a year, and against only two opponents). The top ten now looked like this:

MOST SUCCESSFUL TEST CAPTAINS BY WIN/LOSS RATIO (1)

		P	W	L	W/L			P	W	L	W/L
1	S. R. Waugh (A). . . .	57	41	9	**4.55**	8	S. M. Pollock (SA). .	26	14	5	**2.80**
2	J. M. Brearley (E). . .	31	18	4	**4.50**	9	K. S. Williamson (NZ)	38	22	8	**2.75**
3	I. V. A. Richards (WI)	50	27	8	**3.37**	10	W. J. Cronje (SA). . .	53	27	11	**2.45**
4	R. Benaud (A)	28	12	4	**3.00**						
	I. M. Chappell (A) . .	30	15	5	**3.00**						
	C. H. Lloyd (WI) . . .	74	36	12	**3.00**						
	R. T. Ponting (A) . . .	77	48	16	**3.00**			*Minimum: 25 Tests.*				

Again, there's a cluster. Several captains can manage three wins for every defeat, but only two can reach four: Waugh and Mike Brearley. This is not the last word on captaincy – Waugh had Glenn McGrath and Shane Warne, Brearley never led England against West Indies, and there's still a bias towards the land of few draws – but it sure beats win percentage. The list rings true, with Kohli toppled by Kane Williamson. And it sheds some light: who knew the only seamer would be Shaun Pollock, rather than Imran Khan?

If you stretch to a top 20, the Aussie dominance is diluted. There are seven Australians, six Englishmen, two South Africans, two West Indians, one New Zealander, one Indian and one Pakistani, who is still not the one you might expect. Root, by the way, is 41st out of 62, above Mohammad Azharuddin and Inzamam-ul-Haq, but below Rahul Dravid.

MOST SUCCESSFUL TEST CAPTAINS BY WIN/LOSS RATIO (2)

		P	W	L	W/L			P	W	L	W/L
11	R. Illingworth (E) . .	31	12	5	**2.40**	16	W. M. Woodfull (A)	25	14	7	**2.00**
12	M. P. Vaughan (E) . .	51	26	11	**2.36**		P. B. H. May (E). . .	41	20	10	**2.00**
13	V. Kohli (I)	68	40	17	**2.35**		M. C. Cowdrey (E) .	27	8	4	**2.00**
14	Javed Miandad (P) . .	34	14	6	**2.33**		M. A. Taylor (A). . .	50	26	13	**2.00**
15	A. J. Strauss (E). . . .	50	24	11	**2.18**	20	S. P. D. Smith (A). .	35	19	10	**1.90**

Minimum: 25 Tests.

So, of the 62 men who have been in charge for at least 25 Tests, only 19 have managed two wins for every defeat. If we get used to the win/loss ratio, this could become a marker, like averaging 50 with the bat or under 25 with the ball: a sign of success. Tests are not enough. This measure is going to have to work for white-ball cricket too.

MOST SUCCESSFUL ODI CAPTAINS BY WIN/LOSS RATIO

		P	W	L	W/L			P	W	L	W/L
1	C. H. Lloyd (WI) .	84	64	18	**3.55**	6	S. R. Waugh (A) . .	106	67	35	**1.91**
2	R. T. Ponting (A)†	230	165	51	**3.23**	7	E. J. G. Morgan (E)	124	75	40	**1.87**
3	W. J. Cronje (SA) .	138	99	35	**2.82**	8	I. V. A. Richards (WI)	105	67	36	**1.86**
4	V. Kohli (I)	95	65	27	**2.40**	9	S. M. Pollock (SA)†	97	60	33	**1.81**
5	M. J. Clarke (A) . .	75	50	21	**2.38**	10	G. C. Smith (SA)†	150	92	51	**1.80**

Minimum: 50 ODIs.

† *Ponting captained an ICC World XI in one match, Pollock in two. Pollock also captained an Africa XI in two matches, Smith in one.*

Leading from the front: Mike Brearley at Melbourne with England's 1979-80 tour party.

In an era when no other one-day captain stood tall, Lloyd comes top. Ricky Ponting overtakes Waugh, or builds on his success. Kohli is well ahead of Eoin Morgan. South Africa have as many entries in the top ten as Australia, and again Pollock shines.

As before, there's a cluster: 1.80 is very good going, but won't get you near the top five. The full list is 60-strong and, at No. 54, rubbing shoulders with Zimbabweans and latter-day West Indians, is an unexpected name: Sachin Tendulkar, on 0.53. Again, the list is plausible, even if Hansie Cronje's appearance is hard to stomach. If only yardsticks came with a moral compass.

MOST SUCCESSFUL T20I CAPTAINS BY WIN/LOSS RATIO

		P	W	L	W/L			P	W	L	W/L
1	Asghar Afghan (Afg)	52	42	10	**4.20**	7	M. S. Dhoni (I)	72	42	28	**1.50**
2	Babar Azam (P)	40	26	9	**2.88**	8	A. J. Finch (A)	59	32	25	**1.28**
3	V. Kohli (I)	50	32	16	**2.00**	9	K. S. Williamson (NZ)	56	27	26	**1.03**
4	F. du Plessis (SA)†	40	25	15	**1.66**	10	K. J. Coetzer (Sco)	41	20	20	**1.00**
5	D. J. G. Sammy (WI)	47	28	17	**1.64**		W. T. S. Porterfield (Ire)	56	26	26	**1.00**
6	E. J. G. Morgan (E)	72	44	27	**1.62**						

Minimum: 40 T20Is.

† *Du Plessis captained an ICC World XI in three matches.*

Let's hear it for the minnows. In T20 cricket, Asghar Afghan is way out in front of the big fish and, if that's partly because he often faces even smaller fry, the same can be said of some more famous captains down the decades.

For Twenty20, a format that is often 50–50, Asghar's record is phenomenal. To make this top ten, you just have to win as many as you lose, as Kyle Coetzer and William Porterfield have done, and Shahid Afridi has not. Kohli and Morgan are the only captains to shine in both T20s and ODIs, and nobody makes all three top tens.

Our yardstick also has to work for the women's game. Women's Tests are a challenge because they are so few; and three of the contenders are unbeaten.

MOST SUCCESSFUL TEST CAPTAINS BY WIN/LOSS RATIO

		P	W	L	W/L
1	L. A. Larsen (A)	10	5	0	–
2	R. Heyhoe Flint (E)	12	2	0	–
3	K. Smithies (E)	10	1	0	–
4	B. J. Clark (A)	11	3	1	3.00
5	M. E. Hide (E)	11	4	2	2.00

Minimum: 10 Tests.

Lyn Larsen is a worthy winner, but the two Englishwomen below her, admirable as they were, get too much credit for avoiding defeat. As in football, 3–1 is a better score than 1–0. But this is still a tough club to join, with Clare Connor and Charlotte Edwards among those missing out. And the solution is obvious: more women's Tests. The white-ball game works far better.

MOST SUCCESSFUL ODI CAPTAINS BY WIN/LOSS RATIO

		P	W	L	W/L			P	W	L	W/L
1	M. M. Lanning (A)	66	57	8	7.12	6	H. C. Knight (E)	60	40	19	2.10
2	B. J. Clark (A)	102	84	17	4.94	7	C. M. Edwards (E)	117	72	38	1.89
3	L. A. Larsen (A)	41	28	11	2.54	8	D. van Niekerk (SA)	50	29	19	1.52
4	E. C. Drumm (NZ)	41	28	12	2.33	9	M. Raj (I)	144	85	56	1.51
5	K. L. Rolton (A)	43	30	13	2.30	10	M. du Preez (SA)	44	23	18	1.27

Minimum: 40 ODIs.

Meg Lanning, take a bow. That score of 7.12 is beyond the wildest dreams of any other captain so far. And if Australians dominate this list, Lanning stands out even among her compatriots. I wonder if she'll do it again in T20...

MOST SUCCESSFUL T20I CAPTAINS BY WIN/LOSS RATIO

		P	W	L	W/L			P	W	L	W/L
1	M. Musonda (Zim)	21	19	2	9.50	6	S. Tippoch (Tha)	39	25	13	1.92
2	R. C. Belbashi (Nep)	22	17	5	3.40	7	A. L. Watkins (NZ)	29	19	10	1.90
3	M. M. Lanning (A)	83	61	19	3.21	8	H. Kaur (Ind)	65	39	23	1.69
4	H. C. Knight (E)	54	40	13	3.07	9	S. W. Bates (NZ)	64	39	24	1.62
5	C. M. Edwards (E)	93	68	24	2.83	10	J. M. Fields (A)	26	16	10	1.60

Minimum: 20 T20Is.

Shining light: Australia captain Meg Lanning celebrates winning the 2020 T20 World Cup.

Lanning is still there or thereabouts, but Mary-Anne Musonda is in a league of her own. On Twitter, she describes herself as a "tall glass of awesomeness", and this table backs her up. It also shows T20 doing its job, and promoting the smaller nations: Lanning is the last Aussie standing.

So win/loss ratio seems to work for everything except women's Tests. It's time to see what happens if we compare captains from the same country: England, for instance.

MOST SUCCESSFUL ENGLAND TEST CAPTAINS BY WIN/LOSS RATIO

		P	W	L	W/L			P	W	L	W/L
1	J. M. Brearley	31	18	4	**4.50**	8	E. R. Dexter	30	9	7	**1.28**
2	R. Illingworth	31	12	5	**2.40**	9	N. Hussain	45	17	15	**1.13**
3	M. P. Vaughan	51	26	11	**2.36**	10	A. N. Cook	59	24	22	**1.09**
4	A. J. Strauss	50	24	11	**2.18**	11	J. E. Root	61	27	25	**1.08**
5	M. C. Cowdrey	27	8	4	**2.00**	12	G. A. Gooch	34	10	12	**0.83**
	P. B. H. May	41	20	10	**2.00**	13	M. A. Atherton	54	13	21	**0.61**
7	M. J. K. Smith	25	5	3	**1.66**	14	D. I. Gower	32	5	18	**0.27**

Minimum: 25 Tests.

The effect is to make Brearley look even better, and to confirm Ray Illingworth, Michael Vaughan and Andrew Strauss as all-time greats. Graham Gooch is low down, but higher than his successor (Mike Atherton) and his immediate predecessor (David Gower). Captains from Essex stick close together (three between nine and 12), and Nasser Hussain gets some of the credit for Vaughan's success. And Root? On February 10, 2021, he was seventh with 26 wins, 15 losses and a score of 1.73. Then came ten defeats in 14 Tests. He suffered from bad luck, with injuries and illness and Covid bubbles, but also from bad judgment – playing four seamers on a turning pitch at Ahmedabad, disdaining a chase against New Zealand at Lord's, picking neither Stuart Broad nor James Anderson at Brisbane.

What changed, early in 2021? After the Indian tour, Ashley Giles decided England didn't need a national selector any more, and laid off Ed Smith. Selectors, perhaps even more than captains, lend themselves to win/loss ratios.

ENGLAND IN TESTS SINCE MAY 2018

	P	W	L	W/L
Selected by Ed Smith	37	21	12	**1.75**
Selected by Chris Silverwood	11	1	7	**0.14**

Smith didn't appoint Root, but they made a good team. Since Smith's defenestration, England have been eighth in the world, behind Bangladesh (from, admittedly, a small sample). During his time, even after losing in India, England were third, ahead of Australia. The top two were New Zealand and India, in that order. If you have a win/loss ratio, you don't need a World Test Championship.

Tim de Lisle is a cricket writer for The Guardian *and former editor of* Wisden.

WISDEN WRITING COMPETITION IN 2021

The old kit bag

Peter Hobday

During lockdown, and contemplating moving house in a couple of years' time, I look under the bed for items to get rid of, and find a large black bag labelled Gunn & Moore, long forgotten. I pull it out. The layer of dust betrays my infrequent cleaning, and its lack of use. My last match was when my elder daughter was a year old; she is about to go to university. Suddenly, the years roll back as I slide the zip open, and once-familiar smells escape their long confinement. Leather. Sweat. Linseed oil. Dressing-room. I breathe it in, and close my eyes; my mind drifts away and recalls old sounds – the clatter of studs on the concrete floor, the laughter of team-mates' mickey-taking, the silence of the changing-room when alone after dismissal.

Carefully folded on top of a pair of worn whites is a cream cable-knit sweater, ready for use in an April that never came again. As a young club cricketer, fed up with yet another edged boundary sailing unhindered between a pair of statuesque slips, I vowed to stop playing when my own lack of mobility made me a liability in the field. In what turned out to be my final season, I threw my shoulder out in August and, sticking with my decision, retired when I found it hadn't recovered the following spring.

Back to the contents of the bag. Bat: a Gray-Nicolls Powerspot, well taped, the one that scored my only century, in 1998. Mostly off the edge, according to my more talented brother. In my hand, it still feels familiar: light and nicely balanced. I shape up, and imagine the opening bowler running in at me. I move back and across and, in my mind's eye, that's another push through the covers to the boundary. Helmet: worn at my wife's insistence after the day I top-edged into my face, leaving blood on the pitch, and retired hurt for a visit to the minor injuries unit and stitches above my eye; inside the helmet are gloves, shiny with soaked-in sweat. Pads: still quite firm and new, the last kit I bought. Boots: marked with specks of mud from my last game in that final September. Rummaging around, I find other oddments: a ball, some extra studs, and of course the vital box. From my spare shirt flutters an envelope with ten other names making up the team when I last stood in as captain. I can still remember nine of them: probably a Saturday Third XI, and a bit short of batting, by the look of it.

I replace everything as neatly as I found it, and slide the bag back under the bed. I may yet come out of retirement for one last hurrah. I'm only 54, and still fit, even if I can't throw. I may even field in the slips.

Peter Hobday is an IT Consultant and former adhesive Second XI opening batsman for clubs in Surrey and Essex, whose team-mates preferred to read their newspapers than watch him bat.

THE COMPETITION

Wisden received more than 100 entries for its tenth writing competition. Entries arrived from far afield: Australia, Canada, Ireland, the Netherlands, Pakistan and Spain. The standard was very high, and every entry was read by the editorial team. Wisden much appreciates the imagination and hard work of all entrants. The first prize is publication, adulation, and invitation to the launch dinner, held at Lord's in April. The winner, as well as the five runners-up, receives a year's subscription to *The Nightwatchman* (which will also publish the shortlisted entries). Please note that circumstances beyond Wisden's control may force cancellation of the dinner, as happened in 2020 and 2021.

The rules are unchanged. Anyone who has never been commissioned by Wisden can take part. Entries, which should not have been submitted before (and are restricted to a maximum of two per person), must be:

1. the entrant's own work
2. unpublished in any medium
3. received by the end of October 2022
4. between 480 and 500 words (excluding the title)
5. neither libellous nor offensive
6. related to cricket, but not a match report

Articles should be sent to competitions@wisdenalmanack.com, with "Writing Competition 2022" as the subject line. Those without access to email may post their entry to Writing Competition 2022, John Wisden & Co, 13 Old Aylesfield, Golden Pot, Alton, Hampshire GU34 4BY, *though email is much preferred*. Please provide your name, address and telephone number. All entrants will be contacted by the end of November 2022. Please contact Wisden if your entry has not been acknowledged by the start of December. The winner will be informed by the end of January 2023. Past winners of this competition, Bloomsbury staff and those who in the editor's opinion have a working relationship with Wisden are ineligible. The editor's decision is final. We look forward to receiving your contributions.

THE 2021 ENTRANTS

Thomas Barclay, Christopher Barker, Mike Bechley, Jamie Beer, Luke Bennett, Ian Bickerstaffe, Rob Blackhall, Jordi Blake, David Bown, Martin Briggs, Brenda Brown, Lee Burman, James Butler, Scott Campbell, Andrew Carr, Donal Casey, Paul Caswell, Mark Catley, Colin Cessford, Michael Claughton, Norman Crampton, Keith Cundale, John Daniels, Nicholas Davey, Pagen Davis, Rupert Dean, John Dinnis, Somya Ehsan, Rory Ffoulkes, Anna Forsyth, Jonathan Forwood, David Fraser, Alex Furneaux, Mark Gannaway, Simon Gayler, Ian Gent, Ken Gibb, Ian Gray, Steve Green, Mike Harfield, Richard Hepburn, Peter Hobday, Jack Howes, Richard Hunter, Marco Jackson, Ian Jones, Philip Keenan, E. U. Khokar, Howard Lowe, Philip Lowthian, Tom Marsh, Tim Maynard, Robert Meakings, Tim Mickleburgh, Rhodri Morgan, Alex Morris, Michael Norman, Stephen Pickles, Richard Pierce, Joe Pinkstone, David Potter, Gordon Price, Peter Quinn, Rajiv Radhakrishnan, Richard Reardon, John Rigg, Kenneth Rignall, Wasi Rizvi, Philip Robins, Michael Sanders, Terry Sanderson, Andrew Scott, David Shervington, John Sleigh, Shastri Sookdeo, Peter Stone, Seth Thomas, David Thornley, David Thornton, Bill Udy, Willem van Denderen, Dave Vine, Matthew Waghorn, George Walker, David Walsh, Jeremy Waxman, Simon Wellings, Martin Wheatley, David Windram, Tim Wye.

WISDEN QUIZ

At the beginning of January 2022, the Wisden blog published a 100-question cricket quiz. The top mark was 100 by Roger Lyon, who wins £100 worth of books from Bloomsbury. Two runners-up scored 99: Nilesh Jain and Ian Oakhill, who each receive a copy of *Wisden on the Ashes*. The Wisden blog, which publishes a new article every month, is at wisdenblog.wordpress.com. The next Wisden Quiz will be published in December 2022.

WISDEN ALIGNS WITH THE ACS

The Great Accord

LAWRENCE BOOTH

In late September 1873, W. G. Grace helped knock off the runs against Kent at Gravesend's Bat and Ball Ground. It was his last innings of the summer in a so-called "great or important match". At 25, he was already a celebrity – his team's name was "W. G. Grace's XI" – and there would be more special treatment to come.

WG finished the season with 1,805 runs at 72 in great or important matches (the term "first-class" did not become established until about 1880). It was, in the language of the time, an uncommonly good haul. But it also presented a problem. Two seasons earlier, he had notched up 2,739 – an eye-watering 1,671 clear of the field – and attained stardom. It suited everyone in cricket, maybe even his opponents, to keep him there. And it might help if he topped 2,000 again. Would anyone object if those extra runs somehow materialised? The fixture list was so messy – and the County Championship still 17 years from a settled structure – that a spot of creative accountancy might slip through unnoticed.

A-listers: W. G. Grace and James Southerton pose for a *carte de visite*, 1871.

And slip through it did, thanks to *James Lillywhite's Cricketers' Annual*, which added six more innings from four more games: 47 and 26 for MCC against Hertfordshire at Chorleywood; 67 for MCC against Staffordshire at Lord's; 152 and five for the Gentlemen to Canada Touring Team against MCC at Lord's; and 37 not out for South v North at The Oval. WG's aggregate was now 2,139. He had done it again! (Better still, an extra 31 wickets lifted his haul to 106: *doubly* good.)

Until now – and with the exception of *Wisden 1981* – those four games have been included in the Almanack's tally of Grace's first-class runs. But there have always been elephants in the dressing-room: Hertfordshire and Staffordshire have never been first-class counties; the MCC XI who took on the touring team to Canada were actually a XV, including so many weak players they felt the need to be bolstered by a professional, Arnold Rylott; and the game at The Oval was a one-innings affair, tagged on to the end of a match that had finished early. To make matters more dubious, WG was the only player in those four games whose runs were recorded as first-class. Not for the first time, it was one rule for W. G. Grace, another for everyone else.

In all, the Association of Cricket Statisticians and Historians – founded in 1973, partly to bring clarity to the sport's rich and varied numerical past – believe Grace's figures in the Almanack include ten matches unworthy of first-class status. So while *Wisden* has said 54,896 runs and 2,876 wickets, the ACS have gone with 54,211 and 2,809. Drops in the ocean, maybe, but enough to cause ripples.

In 1981, *Wisden's* statistician, Michael Fordham, brought the Almanack's records into line with the ACS; in 1982, *Wisden's* editor, John Woodcock, explained this had been done "because Mr Fordham thought, mistakenly, that he had cleared them with me", and changed the numbers back again. In a typically eloquent piece, Woodcock said he preferred "to leave the great man's figures as they have been for as long as anyone cares to remember". He added: "Then, as now, contemporary opinion was the best criterion." Hence the impasse: *Wisden* in one corner, deferring to the WG exceptionalism of Victorian England; the ACS in the other, preferring rigour.

But *Wisden* has crossed the ring, and aligned with the ACS. It has always been faintly ludicrous that a player of Grace's standing did not possess universally accepted figures, and the ACS have done more than anyone to determine which games should and should not be first-class. However wedded *Wisden* might have become to its own version, there remained a simple choice: massaged reputation or statistical coherence. The time has come to accept that the Almanack should be more concerned with record than romance.

This will not please everyone. Among WG's lost 685 runs are two hundreds – that 152 at Lord's, and 113 for Gloucestershire against Somerset at Clifton in 1879 (Somerset are regarded as first-class from 1882 to 1885, then from 1891). That means his haul of centuries falls to 124, though he remains 11th in the all-time list, between Graham Gooch (128) and Denis Compton (123); he also retains fifth place in the list of leading run-scorers. The effect on Grace the bowler is more pronounced: he slips from sixth to tenth, beneath Alex Kennedy, Derek Shackleton, Tony Lock and Fred Titmus.

Some may feel all this diminishes the occasion of, say, WG's 100th hundred, celebrated at Bristol in 1895, when Somerset's captain Sammy Woods had, in his own words, "the satisfaction of giving him a full pitch to get to his hundred, not that he wanted any help". Grace went on to make 288. But history is full of tweaks, and most are more significant. Nor does it dilute WG's essence: he was, and still is, a giant.

Alignment with the ACS brings other changes. Jack Hobbs gains two hundreds, taking him to 199, because the ACS give first-class status to matches played on a tour of India and Sri Lanka by the Maharaj Kumar of Vizianagram's XI: either side of Christmas 1930, Hobbs made centuries in Colombo against Dr J. Rockwood's Ceylon XI. (Hobbs, it must be said, disagreed, and felt those

CRICKET'S FIRST-CLASS DEBUT

Kit Harris

This year marks the 250th anniversary of the oldest game deemed first-class by the Association of Cricket Statisticians and Historians, between Hampshire and England at Broadhalfpenny Down, Hambledon, on June 24 and 25, 1772. The England team comprised players from Kent and Surrey; Hampshire recruited two Surrey players, William Yalden and John Edmeads. *The Salisbury and Winchester Journal* considered Minchin the "best batsman in the world", but he was substantially outscored by Hampshire's John Small, "to the surprise of all present". Hampshire won by 53 runs.

Hampshire

T. Brett	11	–		2
W. Yalden	5	–		9
J. Small, snr	78	–	(4)	34
T. Sueter	2	–	(3)	9
R. Nyren	9	–		4
G. Leer	1	–		0
J. Edmeads	0	–		6
P. Stewart	12	–	(9)	11
E. Aburrow	27	–	(8)	0
W. Hogsflesh	0	–		4
W. Barber	1	–		0
	146			79

England

T. White	35	–		6
J. Fuggles	5	–	(5)	12
J. Minchin	16	–		1
Miller	11	–		0
Gill	5	–	(11)	2
W. Palmer	13	–		8
T. May	15	–		18
Childs	2	–	(2)	0
J. Frame	2	–	(10)	4
E. Stevens	5	–	(8)	7
R. May	0	–	(9)	5
	109			63

NOTES ON THE TEAMS

Hampshire   John Nyren, 12 years old on the day of this match, described Tom Brett in *The Cricketers of My Time* as "the fastest and straitest bowler that ever was known". William Yalden was one of the earliest genuine wicketkeeper-batsmen; the following year, on the same ground, he surpassed John Small's 78, with 88 for Surrey against Hampshire. Nyren credited Small as the pioneer of the quick single, and carpenter Tom Sueter as one of the first "who departed from the custom of the old players, who deemed it a heresy to leave the crease for the ball". The captain was Dick Nyren (John's father), who with Brett did the bulk of the bowling. "Little" George Leer's principal role was specialist long stop. John Edmeads, a farmer, was reckoned a superb fielder; Peter "Buck" Stewart, an innkeeper, was the prankster of the team. Edward "Curry" Aburrow was the son of a smuggler, and had a strong throw. The first-change bowler was William Hogsflesh, whose "high delivery" action was as high as the underarm law of the day would allow. William Barber, a cobbler, later took over from Dick Nyren as innkeeper of the Bat and Ball at Hambledon.

England   Two of their five Surrey men were catalysts for change. Opener Thomas "Daddy" White had, the previous year, batted for Chertsey against Hambledon with a bat as wide as the wicket. The bowler, Brett, objected – and the bat's width was limited to $4\frac{1}{4}$ inches in 1774. Edward "Lumpy" Stevens, meanwhile, was bowling against Hambledon at Chertsey in 1775, when a delivery passed through Small's two-stump wicket; Stevens's protests led to the introduction of a middle stump. John Frame was a remarkable bowler: short, fat and fast. William Palmer was a good batsman from Coulsdon; details of Childs, another batsman, are scant. Kent's John Minchin, an employee of the Duke of Dorset, had an agricultural style, and in 1769 had struck the earliest known century: 107 for the Duke's XI against Wrotham. In 1773, he became the first recorded as out hit wicket. Miller is almost certainly Joseph (the Nyren book describes him and Minchin as "the only two batsmen the Hambledon men were afraid of"). Arthur Haygarth wrote of the brothers Tom and Richard May: "Tom was for batting, Dick for bowling famed." Not much is known of James Fuggles, except he was a noted batsman. The wicketkeeper, Gill, was probably a Buckinghamshire man who occasionally played in Dartford.

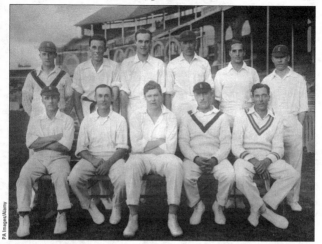

Give and take: the England team for the Fifth Test of the 1926 Ashes gather at The Oval. Herbert Sutcliffe, standing second right, gains two hundreds, as does Jack Hobbs, seated second left. Wilfred Rhodes, the other side of captain Percy Chapman, has his averages slightly revised – not to his advantage.

two innings shouldn't count.) Herbert Sutcliffe was on the same tour, and scored two hundreds, taking him to 151, equal fifth on the all-time list, with Geoff Boycott.

The record of another Yorkshireman, Wilfred Rhodes, has a net gain of three matches. He adds two each in Bombay and Lahore in 1922-23, when he turned out three times for the Europeans and once, intriguingly, for the Hindus & Muslims *against* the Europeans & Parsees. And he loses one from a tour of South Africa in 1909-10. It's perhaps a good thing he's no longer around to learn that his bowling average has been adjusted from 16.71 to 16.72, and his batting average from 30.83 to 30.81.

One long-standing team record has changed. For years, *Wisden* decreed that the lowest total in first-class cricket was 12, an ignominy shared by Oxford University and Northamptonshire. Now, what was once a footnote to the table you can find on page 1262 gains importance. In 1810, at Lord's Old Ground in Marylebone, The Bs were bowled out in their second innings by England for six. There were three scoring shots, including a four by John Wells, one of two players whose surname did not begin with the appropriate letter.

That game is one of over 300 to have taken place between 1772 and 1815 reckoned to be first-class by the ACS. The Almanack's cut-off point had been 1815, "after the Napoleonic War". We hope readers will agree *Wisden* hasn't reinvented the wheel, but tightened a few nuts. With any luck, the whole thing will proceed more smoothly.

MCC COWDREY LECTURE

Lead piping in the House of Cricket

STEPHEN FRY

This is an abridged version of the MCC Cowdrey Spirit of Cricket Lecture given at Lord's on November 16, 2021.

Now, while being asked to deliver this lecture is a terrific honour, fate has seen to it that it is an honour that comes with a venomous sting in its tail. How characteristic of what Thomas Hardy called "life's little ironies" it is that I address you at a time when we *should* be happily caught between the celebration of a mesmerising men's T20 World Cup and the mouth-watering promise of the 72nd men's Ashes.

Instead, I find myself giving this talk from inside the choking miasma of one of those unsavoury scandals that regularly seem to engulf the game we love. The mephitic stink that arose from Yorkshire two weeks ago is being smelled around the world, and has done no favours to that club, to the reputation of cricket, or this country? In the midst of this stench, do we need another ageing white male from the heart of the Establishment to lecture us in plummy tones on the spirit of cricket? I seriously considered recusing myself from this gig, and dashing this poisoned chalice from my lips. However, I may not be a cricketer, but I know an incoming batter doesn't turn tail and creep back to the pavilion because the ball is swinging; a bowler doesn't throw the ball back to the captain because the pitch isn't to their liking.

So here I stand – uniquely *un*qualified to deliver this lecture. Even if we overlook the awkward truth that I come from exactly the cultural, social pool whose embarrassing legacy cricket – especially cricket in this country – most needs to shake off, I am a *non*-cricketer. As *non* as there can be. *Nonner* than an Italian grandmother. Who invites a eunuch to teach the harem how to hump?

Well, in some regards the old phrase is true, the spectator sees more of the game. Perhaps my experiences and observations may be of use.

I grew up a decidedly unathletic child, lanky, gawky, uncoordinated – you know the boy, the one who when trying to catch a ball claps his hands at it, who can't run in a straight line without colliding with trees or goalposts, who trips over the football field's white lines. Every morning was spent trying to induce an asthma attack to win what I believed to be my young life's highest prize, a chit to declare me officially Off Games. Whatever I might have thought of cricket, I loathed all other sport with a passion I could barely express.

Life was a battle – no a *war*, a total war between the aesthetic and the athletic, between sport and thought, brain and brawn, the philosopher and the philistine, the bohemian and the barbarian, and never, never, never the twain could meet. I learned how to mock. My technique against bullying was exemplary. If someone couldn't take the lash of my tongue and leapt forward

Address sense: 20 years after Richie Benaud's inaugural lecture, Stephen Fry takes to the stage.

to attack me physically, I would throw up my hands and cry, "No, no, don't hit me – it'll give me an erection!" A ploy I recommend to anyone who hides in fear of bullies.

I'm sorry. To return to our theme. Through the stories of P. G. Wodehouse, and his depiction of a game of extraordinary subtlety, beauty and drama, I decided cricket would be exempt from my passionate loathing of sport, and I fell on cricket writing like a lion on an antelope – everything by Neville Cardus and the great C. L. R. James, Jack Fingleton's *Brightly Fades The Don* and *Masters of Cricket,* and my all-too-distant kinsman C. B. Fry's *Life Worth Living*. And that's how I came to watch the game. And *game* it was to me, not that hated thing: sport.

I yearned to be a bowler. As a boy I would practise all summer long, using a child's swing in the garden as the wicket, and apples for balls. If I made the swing swing, I reckoned I had hit the top of the stumps. I attempted to emulate the style of my hero, Gloucestershire's Mike Procter. In aping his chest-on style, I bowled off the wrong foot. That sounds like a euphemism for something else, doesn't it? "They say he bowls off the wrong foot – know what I mean? He enters stage left… Let me put it this way, he poles from the Cambridge end of the punt." And indeed, I had known from an early age that, in every sense, I did bowl off the wrong foot. Manly cricket and the manly world of manly men didn't accept people like me. Except perhaps as the licensed clown in the corner. When I suggest I'd known from an early age that I was gay, I like to say it was the moment I was born. I looked back up and thought, "That's the last time I'm going up one of *those*."

But, extraordinarily, it turned out I was not condemned by social convention to the furtive life of criminality, secrecy, exclusion, contempt and shame that had been the fate of generations before me. I found that – painfully glacial and incremental as it was – things changed. Yes, in the teeth of virulent opposition from many, but within my lifetime, the law and, more importantly, the generality of my fellow citizens have moved in the direction of acceptance, understanding and equity. From police sirens to wedding bells. And here I am, six years married.

In the 50 years that I have followed the game, have I seen it change! The balance of bat and ball, essential for cricket to make any sense as a sporting spectacle, became threatened, all agreed, by the covering of wickets, which would surely favour the bat, and spoil everything. The one-day game appeared, shyly at first. Only 60 overs an innings? It'll kill the game. The look and style of cricketers were apparently for ever compromised by helmets, visors and elastic-waisted trouserings, hideous to behold. The rise and mutation of one-day cricket caused panic from Windermere to Woking, as white balls and black sightscreens threatened the sanity of *Telegraph* readers everywhere.

Cameras and microphones got closer to the action, to overhear the insults and demystify the bowling actions. The art of spin was lost, some believed. Clever 3D images appeared on the outfield, promoting power-generation and insurance companies no one had ever heard of. The county game was rent asunder into leagues and divisions no one understood; day/night matches, coloured pyjamas, pink balls and flashing LED bails. Colonel and Mrs Buckinghamshire bridled and bristled. Is this cricket, or some kind of gay disco?

The politics and structure of the game, with its contracts and coaches, its bloated fixture list and auctions of broadcasting rights, caused hand-wringing too, though some would rather it had been neck-wringing.

South Africa returned to the fold. Zimbabwe, Bangladesh and, glory be, Afghanistan joined the first rank of cricket-playing nations. Governance of the game had been taken away from MCC. The years of white Anglocentric control of cricket seemed to be over. *Seemed.*

Meanwhile, drugs, drinking binges, nightclub fights, lurid and disloyal text messages and other embarrassments continued to erupt like acne on a teenager. Allegations of systematic cheating and spot-fixing grew commonplace. And always the cancer of racism failing to respond to each new round of treatment.

Change hurts. The *Daily Telegraph's* E. W. "Jim" Swanton once burst out of the committee room here at Lord's, exclaiming in a hoarse and outraged whisper, "There's a *woman* in there!" "Yes, Jim, of course there is," it was explained. "It's the Saturday of the Ashes Test. It's the Queen." Jim absorbed this for a second, before coming back with "*Nevertheless…*"

What would the old boy have thought of a female MCC president and the rise of the women's game? Would he have been able to hold his pen and write – without a vein popping – phrases like spin vision, slog-sweep and paddle-scoop? How in hell, he might have wondered, did Warwickshire become Birmingham Phoenix, or Lancashire Manchester Originals? As for pop music blaring from speakers, flames shooting up with each boundary, fireworks, beer snakes, radio mikes on fielders – it is surely the End of Days.

Striking the right note: Stephen Fry sounds the bell before play in the Lord's Test, July 2014.

Now, it would be grossly unfair to use Jim Swanton as an Aunt Sally, depicting him as a stereotypical old buffer standing in the way of change and progress. He was a remarkable man: three years in a Japanese prisoner-of-war camp slaving on the Burma railway. This is not someone mockingly to disparage. He came from the time he came from. As a baby in a pram, he was there when W. G. Grace scored a century for London County; he died a couple of weeks into the new millennium.

If Jim has been watching cricket from the bar of heaven, I do not think he will have tut-tutted. He loved the game with a profound passion and knowledge. And under it all – I had the privilege of sitting by his side for several full days of play – he knew the game is not, and never has been, a frozen entity. Cricket is not a noun, it is a verb.

Whoever had the idea, back in the late 18th century, that catching the ball in a top hat to dismiss a batsman might be replaced with catching the ball in your hands, was surely denounced as a wild radical. What anarchistic troublemaker first straightened out the hockey-stick curve of early bats? Blasphemy and abomination. And as for roundarm bowling – which history relates to have been the invention of Christina Willes – it was repeatedly no-balled. Yet eventually the mode of delivery was accepted. Which, as we know, utterly destroyed the game.

The ghost of Jim Swanton would see that none of these changes or evolutions – professionalism, covered wickets, helmets, day/night games – confirmed the dire prognostications of those who believed each one might hammer a stump into cricket's fragile heart. This same period of my cricket-watching life saw some of the great matches, as well as the advent of a new aggression and bold, inventive strokeplay that no one could disapprove of. And to keep the game balanced, spin bowling – far from being dead – is supremely alive, even producing new manifestations in the doosra, knuckle and carrom ball. Levels of fitness and standards of fielding have rocketed. And, most importantly of all, this is now a game equally for men and women. Schoolgirls match and often exceed schoolboys in their skill, commitment and ambition. Triumphant Tests, tours and T20 tournaments in the women's game have frequently trumped and topped the men's game for quality and suspense.

The beginning of a lifelong love affair with the culture, food, comedy, music and people…

But great as all this is, it still only describes the structural, outward nature and appearance of cricket, its Laws, its evolution of formatting, franchising and financing. Inside, for the players, for administrators and for us followers, many questions arise, often grim and distressing. The length of a cricket pitch is based on the old English land measurement, the 22-yard chain, and a chain is only as strong as its weakest link.

One way of looking at cricket is to call it just a game, a kind of island. Ball versus bat. The spirit of cricket means fair play, applauding the opponent with a smile on your face, being a good loser. End of story. Cricket's spirit has nothing to do with politics. Nothing to do with the rainbow of social, cultural, racial, sexual, personal elements that colour our world. Indeed, it's an escape from all those.

Or you could search deeper.

For many, cricket comes into its own on the international stage. To have the visiting fans assemble here at Lord's, to sit alongside West Indian steel drums at The Oval, or Indian tabla players at Edgbaston. Or amidst the Barmy Army in Eden Gardens and the Gabba. For cricketers and fans, an overseas tour is often the beginning of a lifelong love affair with the culture, food, comedy, music and people of the nation visited. The friendships forged in the fierce fires of foreign fixtures can be imperishable. Which makes the revelations to have emerged from Yorkshire and the rest of the country all the more terrible, all the less defensible, entirely less forgivable.

We must remind ourselves: how did cricket get to the West Indies in the first place, and why do we find it in Kenya, Sri Lanka and Afghanistan, in Uganda, Pakistan, South Africa, India and New Zealand? It is a game on which the sun never sets, like the empire of administrators, soldiers and privateers who took it to those countries, along with trains, taxes, slavery, laws, segregation, guns, governors and garrisons.

"Must we go there?" some still ask. "We all know the footprint of cricket around the world is a colonial one," they groan. "But come on, Stephen, we're no longer in control of those countries, for all that our monarch may still be on a few currency notes. I haven't come here to be lectured—Oh, well, all right, yes, I have, but not *this* kind of lecturing. Are you going to go all woke on us?"

Well, you can call it wokeness if you think that wins an argument or proves a point. I'm old enough to have attended, had I wished, the last Gentlemen v Players match in 1962, about the time George Martin and the Beatles first recorded in Abbey Road. Public-school and Oxbridge, Mr M. J. K. Smith captained a gentlemen's team defeated by a professional side including Trueman, F. S., Edrich, J. H., and Barrington, K. F. That's how they were listed: Mike Smith, the gentleman amateur, was Mr; the non-gentlemen were surname only.

That year, the fixture – and the distinction – was finally abolished. Was that wokeness? The word didn't exist, but there were many who flooded letters pages with outrage and lamentation at the ushering in of modern ideas and progressive liberal nonsense: phrases that preceded woke, but meant the same. Was it sanctimonious virtue-signalling that pressured the cricket world to bar apartheid South Africa from playing, in the teeth of dogged opposition from many running the game here? Was it wokeness that finally brought the age of women's cricket? Or was it not a frozen, deferential blindness and ignorance, and a disastrously complacent lack of imagination, that had allowed such snobbery, inequity and injustice to persist unchallenged for so long? The main emotion when contemplating such grotesqueries as the Gentlemen v Players match is not outrage so much as the English signature emotion: embarrassment. And maybe shame. Yes, shame.

There *may* be those who think we should go back to gentlemen amateurs travelling in a different class from the pros, go back to apartheid, go back to men-only cricket and men-only commentators and administrators. There may be, but while they were a large vocal minority, and even perhaps a majority decades ago, surely today all save the most demented and malign are now converted. In decades to come, much of what we do and say here today will look as archaic and embarrassing as what was done and said here yesterday.

While it would be grotesquely slimy to apologise for the circumstances of my birth, ethnicity and education, it is just as slimy and grotesque not to recognise how relatively easy it has been for people like me to acquire and afford membership of this club, MCC; to travel and watch the game; to sit here in boxes meeting players past and present; to have our love of cricket enriched by so much access and ease – and that's just talentless non-players like me. Transfer that ease of access across to being supported in junior cricket through to the professional level. Like coins whose impress has been rubbed away by overuse, so the currency of those P-words, privilege and patriarchy, has been all but debased. But it is surely true that the gap between what people like me desire, and what we can have, is so much narrower than it is for most, and if we don't see that, we are wilfully looking away.

Think of cricket as a house. The water from the mains may be pure and clean, but what if the plumbing and pipework are made of lead? The old mansion may receive a coat of paint every now and then; it may have ultrafast broadband and a kitchenful of mod cons. But if the lagging in the cavity walls is asbestos…?

Fry's delight: the 2021 lecture ends with a standing ovation.

That is what is meant by phrases like structural or institutional racism. The old toxins in the system are so insidious many haven't noticed them, or have even refused to accept they are there. *I* never really saw it; I suspect most of us here never really did, until it was shown to us. But the poisons will continue to do their deadly work unless we have the courage to make deep structural changes that do more than prettify the exterior.

Films like *Fire in Babylon*, the passionate eloquence of Michael Holding and Ebony Rainford-Brent, for example, and more recently the courage, conviction and clarity of Azeem Rafiq, must be harnessed to make a difference. I know from my own experience in gay rights and mental health advocacy that progress comes at a maddening pace, but meaningful structural change *can* happen.

Taking the knee is one outward and visible sign of an inward faith. It's not a solution, but a message – a prayer, perhaps. A commitment to something more than sighing and shrugging the shoulders, or parroting the fatuous and wicked lie that politics has nothing to do with sport. Where a national anthem is an expression of loyalty and belonging, so taking the knee is an expression of a *wider* loyalty and belonging.

But the commitment is not the deed. We have scotched the snake, not killed it. There are plenty of boils on the body of cricket, and when – as in the Yorkshire case – they erupt and burst their noxious matter over the front pages, it behoves us to understand what is going on, what it means, and how it can be addressed. It astounds me that there can still be administrators, governors and board members in professional cricket who have not understood the history and the pain, and prefer dogged denial to open scrutiny. Cleansing the Augean stables of Headingley has been a horribly necessary experience, but it will count for nothing if we fail to own it, learn from it and act upon it.

There has of late been a recalibration in human affairs, as we come to grips in the West with the legacy of empire and subjugation – which gave the world cricket, but also raped the riches and resources of peoples around the globe, stole the dignity and rights of more than a billion, and created an imbalance that had seemed permanent, immutable and unquestionable.

But questioning the unquestionable is what drives our species forward, and it propels and energises cricket too. After all, who could question the gentleman amateur, or the prerogative of MCC to govern cricket? For 200 years, who could question the exclusion of one sex from the male sanctuary of Lord's, unless cleaning or serving – or, at a push, visiting as a reigning monarch?

All our lives, old men have grumbled about change, sneering at the ideals, hopes and beliefs of the young – in the wider world, no less than in cricket. I pray I'll never to succumb to the easy, rancid, better-in-my-day, young-people-nowadays rubbish. When embittered and rancorous old men today say it was better back then, what they really mean is it was better *for them*.

> Great players, now legends, summoned to the committee room by pompous prefect types

I'm proud and pleased to be a patron of the MCC Foundation, which among other aims seeks to arrange ways for private schools to open their facilities to all the girls and boys in their area. But it's typically, Britishly slow progress, and there are plenty of old and not-so-old farts whose veins start out on their foreheads at the sound of words like inclusion or diversity, finding it easier to dismiss them as woke jargon, or anything that might excuse them from helping enrich the game they profess to love.

Over the years, players have been treated abysmally by the rulers of the game – "the Cricketing Lords", they were called, partly because they governed from this place, Thomas Lord's Cricket Ground, but also because so many *were* lords. Post-war, they may have been slightly less aristocratic than Lord Hawke and his fellow blue bloods, but for decades they were Oxbridge and public-school almost to a man, and treated cricketers with paternalistic condescension: great players, now legends, summoned to the committee room by pompous prefect types, like school fags brought for a beating. Those of us who experienced such degrading humiliation as children know the school experience exemplifies the self-sustaining wickedness of this kind of power structure. Victims would often visit punishment and abuse on the next generation: "I had it tough; so should you." Cricket long suffered from the vicious cycle of bullying dressing-rooms, hard men humbling the softer, more sensitive players, and an atmosphere of unforgiving cruelty called "manliness".

At its darkest, cricket has a tragic trail of misery, addiction, despair and suicide. We all know examples of the lost. In times of war, they would have been called fallen comrades, and been mourned and commemorated on walls and plaques. To honour those whom cricket cruelly emptied and threw away, this needs to change, and is changing. Thanks to the courage and candour of leading players like Jonathan Trott, Sarah Taylor and Marcus Trescothick, this is a subject at last being understood and addressed. Freddie Flintoff, Ben Stokes and many others represent scores of less celebrated figures who have had the courage and sense to value their mental fitness as highly as their physical.

At the summit of the game, as we see from all the televised tournaments around the world, cricket is flourishing. Those at the top are enjoying new-found rewards, fame, success and fulfilment. Thanks to the Big Bash, the IPL and other franchise competitions, they are bonding with players from varying nations, religions, cultures and ethnicities like never before, finding respect, understanding and friendship, and their mental health can be addressed without embarrassment or stigma. Wonderful as this is, important as their example can be, the spirit of cricket can't be expected to trickle down only from the top. I speak in the most famous nursery in cricket, but every school, every village, every town team, every league, every county is a nursery too.

When speaking to the parliamentary subcommittee this morning, Azeem Rafiq mentioned the game's grassroots. Cricket is played on grass. The international stars may be the top dressing for the pitch, but the true spirit of cricket is fed, sown and nourished beneath the surface. This is one reason why these racism revelations must be understood and dealt with. The thought that so many potential players are put off the game because their cries of pain at this exclusion are not heard – this creates a bare, sparse, hostile and ultimately unplayable surface.

Like my befuddled, bewildered, benighted and bedevilled homeland, cricket is beautiful and brutal, fair and foul, glorious and ghastly, decent and degraded. And as with my homeland, my love and belief in cricket and its ability to change are strong enough and deep enough for me to believe that all is not lost.

But not until those lead pipes and that asbestos lagging are torn out can the House of Cricket stand proud. Cricket and the wider culture owe Azeem Rafiq an enormous debt, as well as an enormous apology. When he said he didn't want his son to go anywhere near cricket, my heart sank. But actually, that simple statement crystallises everything: it gives us a clear human image. It is a rallying cry. Unless all our nation's sons and daughters, with the talent and desire to have a life in cricket, are confident that cricket will want to have a life with them, the spirit of cricket, its very flame, will flicker and go out. Let's dedicate ourselves to ensuring that will never happen.

Stephen Fry is an actor, writer and presenter.

PART TWO

The Wisden Review

CRICKET BOOKS IN 2021

Life-streaming

Vic Marks

There have been many dark clouds for cricket in the wake of the pandemic, but a sliver of silver has been visible in the world of publishing. New authors have locked themselves away in front of a laptop; new readers have been eager for respite.

Ed Faulkner, a publisher at Allen & Unwin, reported that "non-fiction book sales soared, despite the pandemic, with readers having more time on their hands and searching for escapism. The sale of cricket books certainly benefited from this trend. With bookshops so often closed, over two-thirds of sales were through online channels, which helped smaller publishers to keep trading, provided people knew what book to search for."

So here are some books from 2021 worth searching for. As ever, there are plenty of biographies and autobiographies from a variety of sources: a pop star, a self-confessed also-ran, a cricketing badger, a Vietnam war veteran, a peerless historian, an anonymous pro, an MCC president or two, a professional ballroom dancer of the pre-*Strictly* era, a member of the Australian SAS, a Welsh administrator, a teak-tough Scot and one of England's most prolific batsmen of half a century ago.

Let's start with the last, Dennis Amiss, whose autobiography, **Not Out at Close of Play**, is as rock-solid as his batting. He was assisted by James Graham-Brown, once an all-rounder for Kent and Derbyshire, who has written plays as Dougie Blaxland; two have been inspired by the lives of supremely gifted, troubled cricketers, Colin Milburn and Chris Lewis. Now Graham-Brown turns his hand to ghostwriting, and he does it deftly.

Amiss was a prodigious run-scorer with a broad bat, but here is confirmation of the self-doubt that can still plague the best cricketers: there were moments when he wondered whether he would ever excel, having hit just one fifty in his first 21 Test innings. Eventually the doubt gave way to relentless determination. In his first Test as Geoffrey Boycott's opening partner, there was a famous run-out. Amiss had been warned about his running between the wickets by his county captain at Edgbaston, M. J. K. Smith, and against New Zealand in 1973 there was a nasty misunderstanding. To the surprise of many, the victim was Boycott.

Amiss explains how, after hitting the ball towards Vic Pollard at cover, he changed his mind about a single, and yelled "Go back!" Too late, it seems. "Geoffrey kept on coming and, just as he was about to overtake me, MJK's cautionary advice came flooding back. I instantly turned and grounded my bat behind the crease, and poor Geoffrey was the man run out." Before the next match, the England captain, Ray Illingworth, had to oversee a meeting between his openers, when Boycott, initially reluctant to attend, "grudgingly agreed to a ceasefire. 'All right then, I promise,' he said. 'I won't run him out – not on purpose anyway.'"

This is a faithful autobiography recalling Amiss's trials and triumphs with England and Warwickshire. An unlikely rebel, he is more illuminating – and convincing – about his reasons for joining Packer than going on the first unauthorised tour of South Africa. He returned to the game as a successful chief executive of Warwickshire and as deputy chairman of the ECB. Boycott, by the way, contributes the foreword and makes no mention of the run-out, which does not mean he has forgotten it.

Harry Altham was another stalwart, in a different guise. Amiss was a run-hungry professional; Altham played as an amateur for Surrey and Hampshire, and spent most of his working life teaching and running the cricket at Winchester College. His greatest contributions, though, came as an administrator, selector and historian. **The Altham–Bradman Letters**, edited by Altham's grandson, Robin Brodhurst, gives an insight into how the game

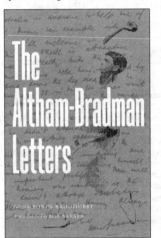

was run in the early 1960s (basically by MCC and an Australian Board of Control prompted by Don Bradman).

At the start of their correspondence, Altham had just been appointed president of MCC, which meant he was also chairman of the Imperial Cricket Conference. Bradman was one of South Australia's delegates to the Australian board between 1945 and 1980, acting as chairman for two terms. He was a prolific writer of letters – always a source of fascination since they offer clues about an impenetrable man (and batsman). There's no doubt he enjoyed being in charge. Brodhurst tells how as the senior selector in 1963, Bradman invited four of the five state captains to dinner, imploring them not to bowl Ian Meckiff or others with a dubious action. He then selected Meckiff for

the First Test against South Africa, in Brisbane; he was no-balled several times, and never played for Australia again. Bradman liked to win, to have his own way, and – though a decorous writer – this is reflected in his letters. To the exasperation of Altham, he seems to have regarded the lbw and no-ball laws as more important than the issue of throwing.

Pitch Publishing have become a prolific source of books, often providing relatively unknown – or anonymous – cricket lovers the chance to get into print. **Bowler's Name?** is a fine title for a book which describes "The Life of a Cricketing Also-Ran". It is written by Tom Hicks who, in the grand scheme of things, is a cricketer way above average ability. He played 19 first-class university matches, and captained Oxford six times; he also appeared for Dorset and MCC, as well as in club cricket for over two decades, whereupon he retired… unsuccessfully. Hicks's love of a game which brought him countless friendships and several unlikely escapades shines through. He finally admits, almost sheepishly, that after five years of refraining from bowling his off-breaks, his abstinence ended once he had moved to Hong Kong. If nothing else, this document will intrigue the grandchildren.

I suspect Rob Harris was never such a good cricketer as Hicks, but he is equally consumed by the sport. His **Won't You Dance for Virat Kohli?** reveals "The Secret Life and Thoughts of a Cricketing Badger" who has been a village player for four decades. It is a tough undertaking to write beguilingly about characters of whom readers have never heard, but Harris succeeds. There are poignant moments when he writes about his dad and their shared love of a game that has enchanted them from Headingley 1981 to Headingley 2019: "We still communicate in a code of our own, full of long pauses with things left unsaid, and cricket chat full of hidden extra meanings." The same applies when he is watching England play a T20 international at Edgbaston with his new wife, which is where Kohli pops up. There is also humour, farcical and dark. Check out Oscar's flipper.

Beyond a few tight circles, Harris and Hicks are anonymous figures. **The Secret Cricketer** would be well known to many as a player who reached the fringes of the England side during two decades as a professional, except he is determined to maintain his anonymity. He says at the outset that he welcomes this device, because he does not want to worry about upsetting anyone while outlining the realities of life as a county player. In fact, he is rarely indiscreet or overly cynical because – in a different way from Hicks and Harris – he loves the game too. He is good on The Hundred ("a risk we don't need to be taking"), and laments its absence of home-grown coaches. He mentions one consultant coach with the ECB who "in one week managed to ruin about five players' careers for the next five years", but does not give us a name. Part of the fun of this book, though, is trying to work out the secret cricketer's own identity.

David Frith's **Paddington Boy** is an updated version of an earlier work. In 2020, he told his publisher: "If I have one more book left in me it might be my autobiography, which seemed to have been blanked by much of the cricket world in 1997." Here Frith seizes the opportunity to

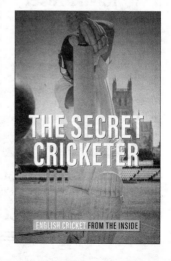

THE SECRET CRICKETER

ENGLISH CRICKET FROM THE INSIDE

give his side of the argument – and he had a few of those in the 53 years since his first book. He remains a cricket historian without parallel and, like many, kept diaries that would later prove invaluable. We learn how, on June 20, 1958, he wrote the entry "Douglas Jardine died". Then he adds: "How could I have known that one distant day I'd write the definitive book on Bodyline [*Bodyline Autopsy*, 2002]?"

Later, Frith highlights the rigour of the true historian as he prepared for this project. "I had spoken to quite a few survivors of that sensational 1932-33 Ashes series over the years, which enriched the research, but now the intensive reading of books, cuttings and magazines resulted in a huge mound of material before the first words could be written." He explains how he laid out hundreds of reference pieces across the lounge carpet, and was close to panic at the scale of the task ahead. But after some reassurance from his wife, Debbie, he managed it all right.

The Bodyline story remains mesmeric, and has prompted another biography of Jardine, this time from the graceful, busy pen of Mark Peel. **Never Surrender** may not contain much fresh material, but it offers an intriguing view of his subject: "Any reappraisal of Jardine's life and character cannot erase the trauma of Bodyline, but it can allow him to take his rightful place in the pantheon of great England cricketers and, quite possibly, its greatest captain." It is a view seldom expressed on the other side of the globe. Frith might argue.

Patrick Ferriday's new biography is entitled **The Triumphal Arch**, partly because his subject, Wilfred Rhodes, bowled to W. G. Grace on his first-class debut, while in his last match Don Bradman was among the opposition. The life of this legendary all-rounder (just the 4,204 wickets and 39,969 runs) is meticulously researched, and ends with Rhodes's own assessment: "Ah were never a star; Ah always considered myself a good utility cricketer." Despite the absence of laptops and video cameras, he was surely one of the game's greatest analysts. Roy Kilner once compared him to the other giant from Kirkheaton, George Hirst: "When George got you out, you were out. When Wilfred got you out, you were out twice, because he knew by then how to get you out in the second innings too."

Rhodes is supposed to have said: "We don't play this game for fun." I'm not sure whether Mike Fatkin ever took this to heart. His autobiography, **Bingo Comes Back Down Again**, does not take itself too seriously. Fatkin worked for Glamorgan for 22 years, ending up as chief executive before being shown the door in September 2008. The introduction hints at the style and fun that lie ahead: "This book isn't going to sell thousands, probably not even hundreds. It contains few revelations. It has a very niche target audience. And its prose won't win any literary prizes: it doesn't half ramble – why use three words when you can use ten?"

He promises a different kind of autobiography, and he delivers – although he does, like many (including Frith), begin with the traumatic moment in his professional life, when he felt betrayed and confused: his sudden sacking by Glamorgan. But Fatkin possesses bouncebackability (my attempt to use one word when three or four may do better): "I refuse to allow one bad day at the office, orchestrated by one person working to his personal agenda, to cast a shadow over the other 8,000-odd I enjoyed at the club." He signs off in characteristic style: "Right then. That's your lot. Bingo's done. Over and out."

Roger Knight delivers **Boundaries**, a more sober, conventional memoir. It reflects his measured view of the world. Early on, he makes an unfashionable observation: "I was aware of boundaries from an early age. This desire to conform has always remained. Perhaps becoming a schoolmaster, a county cricket captain and a Secretary at MCC contributed to the necessity of wanting to wear the right clothes, say the right things and make the right impression." In fact, such an admission is rather non-conformist in an autobiography. Moreover, Knight can be proud of so much, from helping to restore Surrey's fortunes back in the 1980s to being in harness at Lord's when MCC finally allowed women to become members.

Some autobiographies may have cricket only in the periphery, yet for the writers the game has been a constant presence, and often a haven. Anthony "Harry" Moffitt is an Australian who worked for over 20 years for his country's SAS. In **Eleven Bats**, he recalls how he organised matches in

mountains of East Timor, the backstreets of Baghdad and the hills of Afghanistan. His impromptu games built important bridges, and provided much-needed relief.

Meanwhile, Timothy Abraham and James Coyne take us on an entertaining odyssey through Latin America in **Evita Burned Down Our Pavilion**. Inevitably, it has a foreword from Tim Rice, who regrets not being aware of this act of arson when writing his musical.

Anthony Gibson has roamed the more tranquil surroundings of the West Country for decades. For most of his working life, he was employed by the National Farmers' Union, ending up as a much-lauded regional director during several crises. But in **Westcountryman**, his connections with cricket are never far away, which is not so surprising since he is the

son of the inimitable broadcaster and writer, Alan, about whom he writes with warmth and candour. Since 2013, Anthony has been commentating, ball by ball, hour after hour, on Somerset cricket for the BBC. With the advent of live-streamed county matches using local radio commentary, Gibson's voice has become ever more familiar to the county's supporters. But you do not have to be a westcountryman to enjoy his book.

And Bring the Darkness Home, a biography of Tony Dell by Greg Milam, is a rather more harrowing story. Dell, who won the first of two caps for

Australia in the final match of the 1970-71 Ashes, is the only Test cricketer to have fought in the Vietnam War. After his sudden retirement from the game, his life fell apart, and it was not until his mid-sixties that Dell, living in his mother's garage, learned he was suffering from post-traumatic stress disorder – a realisation that jolted him into rebuilding his life and campaigning vigorously on behalf of veterans who had endured similar hardships.

For a happier tale, go to **Punchy's Hampshire Years**, a book about cricket and dancing from Alan Rayment, assisted by the tireless Stephen Chalke. Throughout the 1950s, Rayment, who died aged 92 in October 2020, played for Hampshire in the summer and taught ballroom in Southampton in the winter – for which he was much better remunerated. That was just the beginning of a remarkable life more frequently punctuated by love and laughter than most.

Those who do not have the stomach for full-blown biographies might turn to **Cricketing Lives** by Richard H. Thomas. This history of the game is told through those who played it. The format works, rather brilliantly. Thomas has researched extensively – there are 60 pages of references at the back of the book – yet this is no dry tome. The pages are laced with humour and lovely vignettes, highlighting the character of his subjects. They range from Lumpy Stevens and Lord Botham to the not so lumpy or lordly Ben Stokes, who also appears in Geoff Lemon's latest offering.

Lemon does not know how to write a dull sentence. His *Steve Smith's Men* mopped up most of the prizes in 2019, and **The Comeback Summer** is a sort of sequel, charting the resurgence of Smith, David Warner and Stokes after their contrasting falls from grace. Quite how Lemon finds the time to do this is a puzzle. In one chapter he explains how he and his fellow Australian Adam Collins, an equally voracious cricket nut who is not quite so softly spoken, formed a partnership which found them writing, podcasting and broadcasting in every cricketing nook and cranny on the planet, often without any guarantee of equipment, recompense or accommodation. Or sleep. So we can forgive Lemon for describing Bristol and the nightclub Mbargo – "the place that's missing a vowel", which attracted Stokes and Alex Hales in September 2017 – as being "on England's south coast". Now, justifiably, the work of Lemon and Collins is much admired and sought after.

Lemon writes piercingly well about Smith, who "still relates to cricket like a seven-year-old", and spends a surprisingly long time dissecting how it was that Warner, and not Smith, won the Allan Border Medal in February 2020 at the glitzy annual black-tie awards ceremony in Melbourne, an occasion Australians take very seriously. He describes this decision as the "most interesting in the event's uninspiring history". It is not necessarily the most interesting segment of another fine book from Lemon.

The Covers Are Off: Civil War at Lord's comes from the potent pen of Charles Sale, who recently retired after 40 years as a sports journalist. Sale's diary column in the *Daily Mail* was always eagerly anticipated in the press box, and often enjoyed – if not by those he happened to be targeting. He never seemed bothered about upsetting anybody. Ian Chappell was one of many to march into the press box demanding to know: "Which one's Sale?" This book will upset a few people at Lord's, though if they want to seek

out the author, they will probably do so more discreetly than Chappell.

In the foreword, Matthew Engel refers to the 19th-century territorial dispute known as the Schleswig-Holstein Question. "Only three ever people understood it," Lord Palmerston said. "One's dead and one went mad. I'm the third, and I've forgotten." Engel suggests the Lord's tunnels are the modern equivalent. This is, indeed, an arcane tale, but one thing becomes clear: life would have been much simpler if MCC had found the money to buy the old railway tunnels under the Nursery Ground in 1999. But they didn't, and the property developer Charles Rifkind did.

Here was the seed of a dark dungeon of a saga that stretches over two decades, and Sale is prepared to

delve deep and tenaciously into the detail. For most of us, the interest stems more from his picture of how one of the great old institutions grinds into action – or inaction – with cast members including former prime ministers and England captains. In his acknowledgments, Sale thanks those who have generously granted him time to discuss the affair; then, unusually, he lists those who declined to talk to him, or did not respond to his requests. It is quite a long list.

Thomas Blow's **Kings in Waiting** charts Somerset's superlative performances throughout the 2010s, which rarely led to silverware. Like me, he takes a positive view of the decade, when they finished runners-up in the Championship – a competition they are yet to win – five times. Ten years ago, "Somerset were a club that wanted to win every competition. Today they are a club that can win every competition," concludes Blow. Not in 2021, however.

Contrasting offerings come from New Zealand. **'Tails' to Tell** is the story of Bruce Taylor, who died in February 2021 at the age of 77, a few months before the publication of this delightful small book by Bill Francis. Taylor is the only person to hit a century and bag a five-wicket haul on his Test debut, at Calcutta in March 1965. He was a dynamic all-rounder, a left-handed batsman who could hit the ball vast distances, and a natural, right-arm pace bowler. Giving little thought to tomorrow, he inspired a generation of Kiwi cricketers. Former New Zealand wicketkeeper Warren Lees recalls how "Tails would give you the shirt off his back."

His on-field triumphs are eagerly recorded by Francis, who sympathetically charts the lows endured by Taylor after he finished playing. A gambling addiction led to embezzlement, a spell in prison in 1993-94 and the end of his first marriage. More recently, he had a leg amputated. Yet Taylor enjoyed a second wind in his later years, with help from the close-knit community that is New Zealand cricket. It tickles me that Francis quotes both Henry Blofeld and Henry Calthorpe (of *The Daily Telegraph*) when recounting Taylor's Herculean efforts in the Caribbean in 1971-72. They are, of course, one and the same, the indefatigable Blofeld, who is still going strong. **Ten to Win… and the Last Man In** is his latest bubbly offering, which will delight his fan club. Henry does not know how to decelerate.

'Tails' to Tell reminds us that, in the world of cricket publishing, small can sometimes be beautiful. By contrast, **The Warm Sun on My Face** is nearly 700 pages long and decorated by intriguing old photographs, charting the story

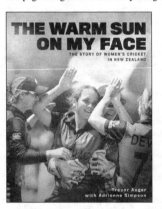

of women's cricket in New Zealand. The project took 25 years to bear fruit, and Trevor Auger is quick to acknowledge the huge contribution of Adrienne Simpson, who died in 2010, but whose research lives on. Like most cricket books, it is more labour of love than commercial undertaking; it is also a significant historical document.

This book could easily reside on a coffee table, provided it's sturdy, and could be placed alongside **The Colours of Cricket**. Philip Brown's book is reminiscent of Patrick Eagar's wonderful collection of photographs in *An Eye for Cricket*, published in 1979, when most of the pictures were black and white. Eagar was the

pioneer, who demonstrated what a photogenic sport cricket is. Brown, in his trademark tan-coloured boots, is following in his footsteps. An irrepressible Aussie based in England for three decades, he has travelled the world with his cameras. He has taken many thousands of photographs, and 340 of his best are here. As with Eagar's publication, once you start flicking through the pages it's hard to put it down.

Hitting Against the Spin is a very good title for a very good book by Nathan Leamon, England's analyst, and Ben Jones. The subtitle, provocative to sensitive curmudgeons of a certain age, is *How Cricket Really Works*. So the old-timers have got it wrong for years, have they? Actually, I do not think the authors are quite suggesting that, but they do debunk some of the clichés that have inhabited commentary boxes. "Win the toss and bat nine times out of ten; on the tenth, think about bowling… and bat." This was always nonsense, especially after the abandonment of uncovered pitches, but the authors dig into the data to prove their point. They even contrive to cheer up Nasser Hussain by explaining that his decision to insert Australia (364 for two at the close) at Brisbane in 2002-03 contained plenty of logic, while reminding us that Steve Waugh, Australia's captain, would have made the same decision if he had won the toss.

Another perennial groan from the boxes is that the new-ball bowlers are bowling too short. This can be true, but what does the data tell us? The authors give one example involving Stuart Broad who, along with Jimmy Anderson, was slammed for that very reason during the First Test against Pakistan in 2018 (when England lost by nine wickets). They compare Broad's lengths in that game with those when he took eight for 15 to win the Ashes at Trent Bridge in 2015. And they are almost identical.

Leamon and Jones explain the paucity of left-handed Indian Test batsmen, and the welcome and unexpected resurgence of wrist-spinners in short-form cricket. Most of the time, they reach conclusions that would have had an old sage such as Ray Illingworth nodding in agreement, even though they had no recourse to the charts and graphs that decorate and, occasionally, overwhelm the narrative. The authors acknowledge that their studies of the data are not all-encompassing – at least, not yet – which is a relief. "For all our advances in understanding, cricket will always keep her secrets, there will always be a level of mystery she won't let us penetrate. We will never know it all." It is a useful thought for the ever-increasing phalanx of infallible, laptop-hugging analysts to bear in mind.

Rock guitarist Felix White's **It's Always Summer Somewhere**, I'm pleased to say, prompted me to introduce myself to the music of the Maccabees, which had not been one of my New Year's resolutions. This is an extraordinary book, a memoir that dwells on White's twin passions, music and cricket, as he deals with the loss of his mother when he was 17. He does not pretend to be good at cricket, but he tries to bowl "lovely, loopy stuff", like his first hero, Phil Tufnell, whom he describes thus: "A befuddled and underused genius, he was a strange lone presence, an odd anomaly, whom team-mates and opponents alike were unsure whether to treat with mystical awe or alien suspicion."

Somehow, White identifies with the chaos that occasionally surrounded the young Tufnell, alongside his virtuosity as a left-arm spinner. Such chaos also seemed to be a feature of English cricket throughout the 1990s, when new calamities might be punctuated by the odd triumph. White forever sneaks off to a corner of some recording studio to check on the Test score. Cricket becomes not only a passion but a refuge.

In the end, it is also a little part of his working life, on the Radio 5 Live show *Tailenders*, which he co-presents with Greg James and Jimmy Anderson. This role has enabled him to meet so many of his heroes; oddly, despite the warnings about such an undertaking, he never seems disappointed. This is White's first book. It is funny, tragic, candid and heartfelt; it would be remarkable if he ever wrote a better one.

Scyld Berry has been writing about cricket for over four and a half decades. He has probably watched more Tests than anyone, so may be considered fortunate to have hit upon his calling straight away. I have not come across anyone who loves the game so much. When he withdrew as the *Telegraph's*

cricket correspondent in 2020, he said it was to enable him to play more often for Hinton Charterhouse – before his leg-breaks lost their zip.

In **Beyond the Boundaries**, he seeks to justify his existence: "I have consumed far too much of the Earth's resources, flown too many air miles, wasted piles of plastic, and it is only by communicating happy or interesting experiences to others that I can justify this parasitism. Besides, I could not have done much else." Well, judging from this, he could have been a brilliant travel writer (though the problem of air miles remains), more Jan Morris than John Morris, despite John's odd memorable flight. Berry invites us on a trip around the cricketing nations, and his unique curiosity often takes us to places and stories tourists miss.

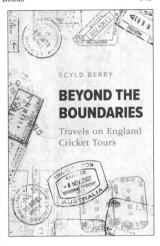

His first tour was to Australia in 1978-79, and he tells of his arrival on the circuit:

> John Woodcock of *The Times*, who had been touring Australia since 1950-51, kindly introduced this whippersnapper to the veterans… This left me the tricky task of explaining the name Scyld. Any stuck-up Pom in Australia was going to be bracketed with Douglas Jardine, still a national hate-figure for devising Bodyline to beat Bradman.
>
> "Hi, I was born in Yorkshire, in Sheffield," I said brightly, then with a surge of inspiration, "So I'm Sheffield Scyld!" Cricket's strongest domestic competition was still called the Sheffield Shield…
>
> "G'day mate! How are yer?"

Since then, Scyld has introduced quite a few whippersnappers to the press corps. Unsurprisingly, *Beyond the Boundaries* is a delight.

Three prominent cricketers – Michael Holding (**Why We Kneel, How We Rise**), Ravi Shastri (**Star Gazing**) and Tufnell (**How Not To Be A Cricketer**) – have burst into print with the assistance of capable ghosts, whom we should recognise: Ed Hawkins, Ayaz Memon and John Woodhouse. Holding shares experiences of racism with Usain Bolt, Michael Johnson and Thierry Henry, among others. The book is less about cricket than racism in sport, but it is undoubtedly the most significant of the trio.

The topic is also addressed by David Woodhouse. He has written a tour book, which has become an unfashionable undertaking in the 21st century. **Who Only Cricket Know** covers England's passage through the West Indies under Len Hutton in the winter of 1953-54 – and much else besides. That trip has been dubbed "the second most controversial tour in cricket", after Bodyline. But, unlike Jardine's expedition, it has attracted little attention – until now.

We all acknowledge that timing is everything in cricket, and the publication of this book, almost 70 years after the trip, is unwittingly appropriate. Cricket's racism crisis had reached fever pitch as *Who Only Cricket Know* appeared on the shelves last autumn, when Yorkshire seemed to be in self-inflicted freefall. Issues of racism – and class – were prevalent in both camps during the tour, and perhaps today we can learn something from Woodhouse's all-encompassing account. "Cricket," he concludes, "is one of the activities where our different backgrounds and characters can come to life in a way which allows us to respect, and gently celebrate, what Arlott once called 'the essential humanity of the difference'."

England and West Indies were arguably the best teams in the world back then, and the cast was stellar. Hutton – flanked by Compton, Bailey and Evans – was the first professional captain to lead England on a major tour, and he had just overseen victory against the Australians after the Coronation. West Indies had their Three Ws, two spinners enshrined by calypsonians (Ramadhin and Valentine), and Sobers, who would make his Test debut in the last match of the series.

The divisions were deep and plentiful. At parties thrown for the tourists by the white elite, "they kept telling the players that beating West Indies was a matter of life and death". Some of the hosts thought it was a humiliation for England to have a professional captain and, as the campaign faltered, similar thoughts emanated from "the inner circle" back at Lord's. There were more familiar cricketing controversies – umpiring, throwing, dissent, sledging, allegations of too much revelling among the tourists – plus the odd riot. After two Tests, England were 2–0 down. Moreover, the travelling journalists were not universally welcomed. One local wrote that "a more biased set of typewriter-punchers than the English press could only be found in the offices of the late Dr Goebbels".

Meanwhile, there was rising political tension at venues where a craving for independence was advancing rapidly. British Guiana was under a state of emergency imposed by Winston Churchill's government, which had shipped in a battalion of Argyll and Sutherland Highlanders to maintain order. In cricketing circles, the absurdity of insisting on a white captain of the West Indies team was becoming ever more apparent. This was some Caribbean cauldron, especially for first-time tourists such as Fred Trueman, who lost his good-conduct bonus; he would not tour with England again for five years.

The characters and the plot – England came back to draw the series, which cannot be a spoiler for anyone who has got this far – make for a fascinating tale. But Woodhouse achieves far more than the standard tour book by placing the series in its historical context in a scholarly, yet accessible way. *Who Only Cricket Know* is a tour de force, and *Wisden's* Book of the Year.

Vic Marks's latest book, Late Cuts, *was published by Allen & Unwin in 2021; he was persuaded not to choose it as the Almanack's Book of the Year.*

All new cricket books received by *Wisden* will be listed in the next edition of the Almanack, considered for review and eligible for Wisden Book of the Year. Please send review copies to:

Wisden Cricketers' Almanack, 13 Old Aylesfield, Froyle Road, Golden Pot, Alton, Hampshire GU34 4BY.

WISDEN BOOK OF THE YEAR

Since 2002, *Wisden's* reviewer has selected a Book of the Year. The winners have been:

2002 *Bodyline Autopsy* by David Frith
2003 *No Coward Soul* by Stephen Chalke and Derek Hodgson
2004 *On and Off the Field* by Ed Smith
2005 *Ashes 2005* by Gideon Haigh
2006 *Brim Full of Passion* by Wasim Khan
2007 *Tom Cartwright: The Flame Still Burns* by Stephen Chalke
2008 *Sweet Summers: The Classic Cricket Writing of J. M. Kilburn* edited by Duncan Hamilton
2009 *Harold Larwood: The Authorised Biography of the World's Fastest Bowler* by Duncan Hamilton
2010 *The Cricketer's Progress: Meadowland to Mumbai* by Eric Midwinter
2011 *Fred Trueman: The Authorised Biography* by Chris Waters
2012 *Bookie Gambler Fixer Spy: A Journey to the Heart of Cricket's Underworld* by Ed Hawkins
2013 *Driving Ambition* by Andrew Strauss
2014 *Wounded Tiger: A History of Cricket in Pakistan* by Peter Oborne
2015 *The Test: My Life, and the Inside Story of the Greatest Ashes Series* by Simon Jones and Jon Hotten
2016 *Following On: A Memoir of Teenage Obsession and Terrible Cricket* by Emma John
2017 *A Clear Blue Sky* by Jonny Bairstow and Duncan Hamilton
2018 *Steve Smith's Men* by Geoff Lemon
2019 *Cricket 2.0: Inside the T20 Revolution* by Tim Wigmore and Freddie Wilde
2020 *This is Cricket: In the Spirit of the Game* by Daniel Melamud
2021 *Who Only Cricket Know: Hutton's Men in the West Indies 1953-54* by David Woodhouse

OTHER AWARDS

In September, Ashley Gray won the cricket category at the British Sports Book Awards for **The Unforgiven: Mercenaries or Missionaries? The untold stories of the rebel West Indian cricketers who toured apartheid South Africa** (Pitch).

The Cricket Society Literary Award has been presented since 1970 to the author of the cricket book judged best of the year. The 2021 award, made in October by the Cricket Society in association with MCC, was also won by Ashley Gray for **The Unforgiven**.

BOOKS RECEIVED IN 2021

GENERAL

Abraham, Timothy and Coyne, James **Evita Burned Down Our Pavilion** A Cricket Odyssey Through Latin America Foreword by Sir Tim Rice (Constable, £20)

Auger, Trevor, with Simpson, Adrienne **The Warm Sun on My Face** The Story of Women's Cricket in New Zealand (Upstart Press, \$NZ69.99)

Berry, Scyld **Beyond the Boundaries** Travels on England Cricket Tours (Fairfield Books, £22)

Blofeld, Henry **Ten to Win… and the Last Man In** My Pick of Test Match Cliffhangers (Hodder & Stoughton, £20)

Blow, Thomas **Kings in Waiting** Somerset's Quest to Win the County Championship (Pitch, £16.99)

Brodhurst, Robin, ed. **The Altham–Bradman Letters** Foreword by Bob Barber (Christopher Saunders, paperback, £12)

Broom, John **Cricket in the Second World War** The Grim Test Foreword by David Frith (Pen & Sword, £25)

Curry, Guy **A Tour but for The War** The story of the cancelled MCC tour to India in 1939-40 and those due to participate in it Foreword by Mike Griffith (privately published, £45 + p&p; details from guycurry87@gmail.com)

Ezekiel, Gulu **Myth-Busting** Indian Cricket Behind the Headlines Foreword by Anil Kumble (Rupa Publications, paperback, Rs295)

Hilton, Bob and Masey, David, ed. **Cardus in an Australian Light** The Neville Cardus Archive Foreword by Gideon Haigh (limited edition of 250, from max-books.co.uk, paperback, £18)

Holding, Michael, with Hawkins, Ed **Why We Kneel, How We Rise** (Simon & Schuster, £20)

Leamon, Nathan and Jones, Ben **Hitting Against the Spin** How Cricket Really Works (Constable, £20)

Lemon, Geoff **The Comeback Summer** When Smith and Stokes got the magic back (Hardie Grant, paperback, £12.99)

Marks, Vic **Late Cuts** Musings on Cricket (Allen & Unwin, £16.99)

Midwinter, Eric **Cricket's Four Epochs** How cricket reflects civil society (ACS, paperback, £16)

Morgan, Roy **Cricket in a Multiracial Society** A history of cricket in Malaysia (ACS, paperback, £15)

Mukherjee, Abhishek and Sengupta, Arunabha **Sachin and Azhar at Cape Town** Indian and South African Cricket Through the Prism of a Partnership   Foreword by Harsha Bhogle (Pitch, £16.99)

Pai Vaidya, Nishad, and Bajaj, Sachin **Twice Upon a Time** India's Fairytale Cricket Victories of 1971   Foreword by Sir Clive Lloyd (Notion Press, paperback, Rs399)

Sale, Charles **The Covers Are Off** Civil War at Lord's   Foreword by Matthew Engel (Mensch, paperback, £25)

Shastri, Ravi, with Memon, Ayaz **Star Gazing** The Players in My Life (HarperCollins India, Rs 699)

Thomas, Richard H., **Cricketing Lives** A Characterful History from Pitch to Page   Foreword by Daniel Norcross (Reaktion Books, £20)

Townsend, David **Do They Play Cricket in Ireland?** The 25-year journey to a Test match at Lord's (Pitch, £16.99)

Tufnell, Phil, with Woodhouse, John **How Not To Be A Cricketer** (Simon & Schuster, £20)

Woodhouse, David **Who Only Cricket Know** Hutton's Men in the West Indies 1953-54 (Fairfield Books, £25)

BIOGRAPHY

Battersby, David **An appreciation of Jack Phillipps** New Zealand Cricket Administrator (limited-edition paperback, £7.50; details from dave@talbot.force9.co.uk)

Battersby, David **The Cricketing Career of the Colourful Peter Douglas Swart** (limited-edition paperback, £7.50; details from dave@talbot.force9.co.uk)

Bradbury, Anthony **Frank Gillingham** Clerical Cricketer or Cricketing Clergyman? (ACS, paperback, £15)

Ferriday, Patrick **Wilfred Rhodes** The Triumphal Arch   Foreword by David Frith (Von Krumm, £25)

Francis, Bill **'Tails' to Tell** The Bruce Taylor Story (Cricket Press, Pty, paperback, $NZ40)

Harte, Wesley **Glenn Turner** A Professional Cricketer (privately published, paperback, £15.99; details from robbierobbo@gmail.com)

Hignell, Andrew **Fly at a higher game** The story of T. A. L. Whittington and the elevation of Glamorgan CCC into the County Championship (ACS, paperback, £15)

Milam, Greg **And Bring the Darkness Home** The Tony Dell Story (Pitch, £19.99)

Peel, Mark **Never Surrender** The Life of Douglas Jardine (Pitch, £19.99)

Pope, Mick **Bill Bestwick** Rough Diamond (ACS, paperback, £16)

Rogers, Martin **Invincible** The Life & Times of Sam Loxton   Foreword by Neil Harvey (Cricketbooks.com.au, $A50)

Wilcock, Giles **George Macaulay** The Road to Sullom Voe (ACS, paperback, £16)

AUTOBIOGRAPHY

Amiss, Dennis, with Graham-Brown, James **Not Out at Close of Play** A Life in Cricket   Foreword by Sir Geoffrey Boycott (The History Press, £20)

Anonymous **The Secret Cricketer** English Cricket from the Inside (Pitch, £16.99)

Fatkin, Mike **Bingo Comes Back Down Again** A Life on the Periphery of Sport (privately published, paperback, £16; details from mike.fatkin@outlook.com)

Gibson, Anthony **Westcountryman** A life in farming, countryside, cricket and cider (Charlcombe Books, £20)

Harris, Rob **Won't You Dance for Virat Kohli?** The Secret Life and Thoughts of a Cricketing Badger (Pitch, paperback, £12.99)

Hicks, Tom **Bowler's Name?** The Life of a Cricketing Also-Ran (Pitch, £16.99)

Knight, Roger **Boundaries** A memoir   Forewords by Sir Tim Rice and Mike Brearley (J. W. McKenzie, £20)

Moffitt, Anthony "Harry", **Eleven Bats** A story of combat, cricket and the SAS (Allen & Unwin, paperback, £14.99)

Nash, David **Bails and Boardrooms** How Cricket Changed My Life   Foreword by Sir Andrew Strauss (Pitch, £19.99)

Rayment, Alan with Chalke, Stephen **Punchy's Hampshire Years** Cricket and Dancing (Charlcombe Books, £15)

White, Felix **It's Always Summer Somewhere** A matter of life & cricket (Cassell, £20)

ILLUSTRATED

Brown, Philip **The Colours of Cricket** Foreword by Stuart Broad (Pitch, £25)

FICTION

Richardson, Mark **A Century, Not Out** A cricketing tale (Charles Porter Books, paperback, £6.99; details from mrbooks@btinternet.com)

STATISTICAL

Bryant, John, ed. **First-Class Matches: Pakistan 1984-85 to 1986-87** (ACS, paperback, £27)
Walmsley, Keith, ed. **First-Class Matches: West Indies 1999-2000 to 2006-07** (ACS, paperback, £27)

HANDBOOKS AND ANNUALS

Bailey, Philip, ed. **ACS International Cricket Year Book 2021** (ACS, paperback, £34)
Bryant, John, ed. **ACS Overseas First-Class Annual 2021** (ACS, paperback, £27)
 Full scorecards for first-class matches outside England in 2020-21.
Colliver, Lawrie, ed. **Australian Cricket Digest 2021-22** (paperback, $A35; details from AustCricketDigest@gmail.com)
Marshall, Ian, ed. **Playfair Cricket Annual 2021** (Headline, paperback, £9.99)
Moorehead, Benj, ed. **The Cricketers' Who's Who 2021** Foreword by Darren Stevens (TriNorth, £19.99)
Payne, Francis and Smith, Ian, ed. **2021 New Zealand Cricket Almanack** (Upstart Press, $NZ55)
Piesse, Ken, ed. **Pavilion 2021** (Australian Cricket Society/Cricketbooks.com.au, paperback, $A10)

REPRINTS AND UPDATES

Battersby, David **The Tours of the Pakistan Eaglets to the United Kingdom in the 1950s**
 Additional Findings & Reflections (limited-edition paperback, £10; details
from dave@talbot.force9.co.uk)
Frith, David **Paddington Boy** (CricketMASH Publications, £17.95)
Heavens, Roger comp. **Arthur Haygarth: Cricket Scores and Biographies (Volume XXII)** (from Roger Heavens, roger.heavens@btinternet.com, booksoncricket.net, £125) *More than 700 scores from 1885.*
Heavens, Roger comp. **An Index to Arthur Haygarth's Cricket Scores and Biographies for 1885 (Volume XXII)** (from Roger Heavens, details as above, £5)
Lloyd, David "Bumble" **Simply The Best** The Great Characters of Cricket from The Don to The Ben (Simon & Schuster, paperback, £9.99)

PERIODICALS

The Cricketer (monthly) ed. Huw Turbervill (The Cricketer Publishing, £6.50; £49.99 for 12 print issues, £49.99 digital, £54.99 print & digital, thecricketer.com)
The Cricket Paper (weekly) ed. Jon Couch (Greenways Publishing, £2; £20 for ten issues inc p&p, £49.99 for one year digital, thecricketpaper.com)
The Cricket Statistician (quarterly) ed. Simon Sweetman (ACS, £3.50 to non-members)
The Journal of the Cricket Society ed. Nigel Hancock (twice yearly) (from D. Seymour, 13 Ewhurst Road, Crofton Park, London SE4 1AG, £5 to non-members, cricketsociety.com, details from nigelhancock@cricketsociety.com)
The Nightwatchman The Wisden Cricket Quarterly ed. Tanya Aldred, Jon Hotten and Benj Moorehead (TriNorth, £10 print, £5 digital; from £29.95 for four print issues exc p&p, from £15 digital, thenightwatchman.net)
Wisden Cricket Monthly ed. Phil Walker (editor-in-chief) (TriNorth, £4.95; from £35.99 for 12 print issues, £23.99 digital, wisden.com/wisden-cricket-monthly)

CRICKET AND THE MEDIA IN 2021

Screen shots

JON HOTTEN

There's nothing like writing a media review to make you realise a) how much media there actually is, and b) how its physical element, the paper and print, has retreated almost entirely behind a screen. Last year, I felt as if I knew almost everything, almost as soon as it happened (or at least almost as soon as it was reported), and I barely held a newspaper in my hands. Whoever writes this piece in a decade may have to explain what a newspaper actually was.

This is an unoriginal observation, but the meaning of media has changed. If it exists on a screen, it exists in a state of flux – always evolving, changing, being re-contextualised. Every event may have multiple and immediate interpretations, each adding its own inflection and agenda, each subject to change in its own way.

In *The Times* (or should we now say "on" *The Times*?) James Marriott wrote about the tenth anniversary of the death of the journalist Christopher Hitchens, who "stood between two worlds: the old world, in which serious political and cultural debate was conducted at length and in print, and our new world, in which it is conducted glibly and furiously on screens". Not about our game, sure, but pertinent to it. The year in cricket was urgent and demanding, and the major stories and themes began long before January 2021. We are in the midst of them still, and do not know how – or if – they will end.

How does it feel in the eye of the storm? Ask Michael Vaughan, who seemed right at home in this multiverse, with berths on *Test Match Special* and BBC television as a pundit, in *The Daily Telegraph* as a columnist, and on Twitter as a knowingly divisive presence, his habit being to follow his more didactic pronouncements with "#OnOn", as if he could somehow leave his views behind and not be torched by the blowback. "What Vaughan grasped above all was the essential disposability of opinions in the digital era," wrote Jonathan Liew in *The Guardian*. "People wanted them; he supplied them; they reacted. Tomorrow, the game starts all over again."

But behind Vaughan, a furore had been gathering. Where had it begun? Perhaps it was in 2009 at a game between Yorkshire and Nottinghamshire, when – as he wrote in *The Telegraph* on November 4 – it was alleged that "I had said to [Azeem] Rafiq and two [*sic*] other Asian players as we walked on to the field together that there are 'too many of you lot, we need to do something about it'". Those words – words he says were never spoken, but three other players say they heard – would appear again and again beside his name, and may for ever more.

Or maybe it started in August 2020, when Taha Hashim published a piece on Wisden.com headlined "The Extraordinary Life of Azeem Rafiq". This had started out as a feelgood story about his catering business giving free meals to

Out of the Ashes... Michael Vaughan, dropped from coverage of the Australia–England Tests, finds work at the Big Bash League.

NHS workers but, as Rafiq later told George Dobell at ESPNcricinfo, he "got emotional", and "a lot more came out".

In 2021, Dobell reported on the story in March, April, June, August (four times), September, October and November (twice). You could feel the vice tightening. These articles, based on Rafiq's experiences but not confined to them, were about a culture of institutional racism at Yorkshire that ran wide, deep and a long way back. With help from the "Cricket Badger" podcast by James Buttler, a story that the sport's Establishment had controlled and subjugated became live at last. Yorkshire's intransigence was another factor but, in the new media, intransigence is less effective. A report the club did not want to commission, then went to great lengths not to publish, was forced into the light.

Like Sherman McCoy, the Master of the Universe character in Tom Wolfe's *The Bonfire of the Vanities*, Vaughan was supposed impregnable, kept safe by his station in life. And yet no one is, not any more. The tipping point came in early November. With the names contained in the report now likely to leak, Vaughan stood on the precipice as *The Telegraph* published his partial mea culpa (again, the story was on the website several hours before it reached print). Did they wonder whether the standard grinning byline picture might look incongruous next to a headline that read "I totally deny any accusation of racism"? It ran nonetheless. "The allegation hit me over the head like a brick," Vaughan went on, with his usual subtlety. "But I have nothing to hide."

He had, he wrote, long admired Rafiq as a player: "I was a massive fan... he thought out of the box... but the 'you lot' comment never happened." All that Vaughan, or anyone in his position, could do next was wait. How would the world react, how would all the tweets, stories and comment pieces coalesce? For or against? Cancelled or alive?

It would take a writer as audacious as Wolfe to imagine what did happen. On November 16, Rafiq sat at Portcullis House in Westminster to testify in front of the Digital, Culture, Media and Sport select committee. Parliamentary privilege meant he could speak freely. He wore a plain blue shirt, his physique suggesting the cricketer he still should be. It was his moment, one he must have thought about so often. Here was the sport's reality check, on a dim morning, out of season. The story Rafiq had to tell was full of piercing truth. As he spoke, it was striking how rarely we had heard what he had to say, and yet it was universal, lived experience for so many cricketers, amateur and pro. It felt like politics as true public service. Rafiq was deeply impressive. When he could have pointed a gun, he held out a hand. He accepted apologies from Gary Ballance and Matthew Hoggard. They were, he said, what he had wanted most of all.

> Being a whistle-blower, of course, involves an element of the circular firing squad

Three weeks later, having appeared in print, (wisely) left Twitter alone, and been stood down from radio by the BBC, Vaughan opted for TV, where he could look his public in the eye, and they could look back. "Society is a different place," he told a whey-faced Dan Walker on BBC Breakfast. "We all know things back then were wrong, and now things are right and getting better." Liew said his interview "bore all the hallmarks of reputation laundry. Vaughan apologised for some of his more reprehensible older tweets, including one suggesting that Moeen Ali should spend his time in between Test matches asking Muslims if they are terrorists. But it also felt like an attempt to move on, rebuild his reputation, launch the comeback."

BT Sport found a way of excluding Vaughan from their Ashes coverage, despite his being part of the Fox commentary team whose feed they had planned to use: the interconnectedness of global broadcasting contracts needed unpicking to avoid the voice of one man. Sky were not covering the series, which is perhaps why the departure of David "Bumble" Lloyd was announced during the white noise of England's Second Test defeat at Adelaide. He had been named by Rafiq at the DCMS session, after sending direct messages about South Asian players to a "third party". He apologised, immediately and profusely.

"It does not take the combined talents of Hercule Poirot and Inspector Morse to work this one out," wrote Paul Newman in the *Daily Mail*. "One of the very best sporting commentators and one of the great men of cricket has been 'cancelled' by Sky because he was dragged into the Azeem Rafiq affair."

Player, umpire, coach, broadcaster – Lloyd had spent his life in the game. Rafiq had been in touch with him, Newman reported, as soon as the news broke. "[He] does not want to scapegoat Bumble, so who does?"

But being a whistle-blower, of course, involves an element of the circular firing squad, and Rafiq quickly faced a reckoning of his own: older posts, anti-Semitic in nature. At least he responded as he had wanted to be responded to, by apologising sincerely and taking responsibility. Sky's decision to let Lloyd

go had more subtle implications for Rafiq, along with the consequences for Lloyd. Who decides how these are weighed, and who are the scapegoats now?

Truth and reconciliation had become a theme. Ollie Robinson was busted for some unpleasant historical tweets, Tim Paine lost the Australian captaincy over some similarly historic "sexting". The ECB's response to Robinson was measured and appropriate, Cricket Australia's to Paine a pearl-clutching horror. "The broader question here may be why governing bodies find it hard right now to strike the right note in their decision-making and public statements," wrote Mike Atherton in *The Times*. "My guess is that, corporate interests to the fore, they are constantly fearful of a backlash, but that they misunderstand general sentiment. They think they know what the public think, but the very nature of public discourse creates an illusion."

Dobell asked: "So where does all this leave us? With a mess, no doubt. Construction sites often look that way." If *Wisden* named a Leading Cricket Writer in the World, it would have been Dobell. He has the gentle face of a post-war clergyman, but his pulpit rains evangelical fire. He became the conscience of the game, not just with Rafiq and Yorkshire, but with the launch of The Hundred ("smoke, mirrors and gimmickry") and the ECB's last-ditch abandonment of the Pakistan tour ("put simply, England, and all the England players not obliged to take pay cuts, owe them"). Together with *The Guardian*, he also broke the news of Moeen Ali's retirement from Test cricket, and grabbed the first interview ("I was wasted, but in a good way"). Dobell landed the year's best backhanded compliment, too: when it was announced he was leaving ESPNcricinfo, the ECB – where he has long been Public Frenemy No. 1 – invited him to apply for a job. He went to *The Cricketer* instead, but it's the thought that counts.

It was easy to forget that the summer's major bone to be picked was supposed to be The Hundred, a concocted jamboree hyped with enforced jollity from the ECB and their "media partners". Inevitably, cricket's crossover everyman Andrew "Freddie" Flintoff was to be one of the commentators. (Were they still called commentators? Or were they part of the new language of "sets" and "outs"?) Freddie is a rare phenomenon, a laddish yet married presence who once pedalled out to sea in despair but now drives cars, makes stunt-based travel shows, and has terrible books written under his name. He is much more famous than, say, the current England captain(s).

The Hundred's hoped-for audience of people who didn't like cricket – or at least didn't know that they did like cricket – would at least like Freddie. Ultimately, it was a cheery competition, and offered some of the summer's least offensive moments. The players threw themselves into the fray, and the pairing of women's and men's fixtures was its outstanding achievement. "Maybe the surest sign of success will be if someone eventually pops their head above the parapet and claims ownership of the idea," noted Atherton.

The sting in the tail was the £2.1m bonus pot awarded to ECB executives, a story broken by Ali Martin in *The Guardian*. As his colleague Barney Ronay

| Wisden India | | | | | **WISDEN** |

MATCH CENTRE   STORIES   PLAY & WIN   SHOP   WISDEN

THE ADRIAN SHANKAR FILES

The Adrian Shankar files, part one: What we know & what we don't know... yet

The Adrian Shankar Files, part one, by Scott Oliver.

by Scott Oliver
🐦 @reverse_sweeper

In The Adrian Shankar Files, a six-part series, Scott Oliver delves deep into new material about a player who, in May 2011, was fired just 16 days after signing for Worcestershire when it was discovered that his age and the tournaments he claimed to have played in had been fabricated. We will see in detail how Shankar attempted to land an IPL

Wisden.com

The unbelievable truth: Scott Oliver teases out the Adrian Shankar story.

put it, this was "in return, basically, for delivering The Hundred". Ronay went on: "Look up from all this, and there are profound, delicately poised existential questions here about the future of cricket, about what can be saved, about how the national summer sport can continue to inform and delight and console. Do you trust this current crew to oversee that balancing act?"

If there is one entity that can survive the media that surrounds it, it is the BCCI. Their men's team left the UK before a Fifth Test they had long wanted to cancel. (And could you blame them? Home was a distant memory, and the next flight landed in another bubble in the UAE for the resumption of the interrupted IPL.) The ECB waved them on their way, acquiescing to a higher power. The closest to an inside account came from Dinesh Karthik, the former Indian wicketkeeper commentating for Sky. "I spoke to a few of the guys," he said. "The general feeling is that after the Fourth Test, the players [said] this is tiring. Almost all of the games have gone to the wire, they're tired, and they're down to one physio. How many more bubbles can they do?"

A Test match and series pushed aside so the players could move on. Virat Kohli had driven his team to the World Test Championship final. He had driven them to a series lead in England. He is the most examined, written-about, filmed, photographed and broadcast cricketer of the year, maybe ever.

He loves Test cricket, when he doesn't have to. And yet here even he was, forced away by the endless demands made on him and his team. In the *Daily Mail*, Lawrence Booth unpicked the chaos that had rained down overnight. "It left the ECB fighting to avoid potential losses of £40m, haggling with their Indian counterparts over the result of the match and, in private, furious at the tourists' lax approach to Covid precautions. Chief executive Tom Harrison admitted: 'We're absolutely gutted.'"

Amid the seriousness, there was strangeness, too. Over at Wisden.com, Scott Oliver began an Ahab-like pursuit. His whale was Adrian Shankar, a mysterious figure who had once tried to fashion a career as a professional cricketer from the threads of YouTube, Twitter and some distant websites that carried reports of matches that may or may not have happened, in which Shankar may or may not have starred. In reality, he played at Worcestershire for a total of 16 days.

It was a story that could have existed only in this time and place: Shankar had catfished cricket. And as Oliver's online serial stretched into seven parts, it became a story of obsession, the hunter now hunted by his vision of what did or did not take place. "The Adrian Shankar Files" were odd, compulsive and sad, a tale that somehow fitted with the year. Shankar himself was last seen working in the film industry, slipping behind another kind of screen. Like Christopher Hitchens, like all of us, he exists now between these two worlds.

Jon Hotten is the author of five books, including The Meaning of Cricket.

CRICKET PODCASTS IN 2021

Morality tales

JAMES GINGELL

After the Taliban retook Afghanistan in August, Australia swiftly cancelled the visit of the men's Test team, scheduled for the end of November. The Australian board presented this as a straightforward protest against abhorrent treatment of women. But it meant abandoning Afghanistan to extremists, stalling one of cricket's greatest success stories, and punishing innocent people with no involvement in the regime. Here was a subtle dilemma, the kind ill suited to modern broadcast media. Neither the schedule nor attention spans seem to tolerate nuance; even when debate is permitted, few can resist the urge to block their ears and shout, or grope for the viral clip. But podcasts, less subject to convention, bucked the trend.

On **The Final Word**, Adam Collins and Geoff Lemon asked the big questions. Is boycott more effective than engagement? Should nations play nice with those from different moral galaxies? When they lacked firm answers, it never felt like a dodge, more an acknowledgment of complexity. F. Scott Fitzgerald said first-class minds could hold opposing views at the same time; here were two men passing the test.

A common comparison was apartheid. If South Africa were excommunicated from cricket for oppression of their own people, surely Afghanistan deserved the same. On **Cricket, Et Cetera**, Gideon Haigh disagreed. "South Africa's government was a bastion of the white minority," he said, "and sport was explicitly a demonstration of the government's view." By contrast, the Taliban merely tolerate cricket, and "hold the odd mass execution in cricket grounds". Haigh believed Australia's decision would have no impact on Afghanistan's unequal gender structures; playing their men, he argued, might be the least bad option. Meanwhile, Peter Lalor, his partner on the show, worried about legitimising Taliban ambassadors, and the symbolism of raising their flag at Bellerive Oval. Tuffers and Vaughan this was not.

It wasn't all white men opining from comfort. On **The Emerging Cricket Podcast**, former Afghanistan Cricket Board CEO Shafiq Stanikzai expanded on the Taliban's complex relationship with the sport. He explained that some of the tolerance arose from self-interest: they recognised that the game elevates Afghanistan on the international stage. But he stressed not all Talibs are cynics. One of them, said at the time to be the most wanted man in the country, posed for a selfie with all-rounder Mohammad Nabi, piquing the interest of Afghan intelligence. Nabi laughed it off: the selfie was only one of a thousand that day.

Less measured was Barney Ronay on **The Grade Cricketer**. Asked to weigh the success of The Hundred, he monstered the ECB. "There hasn't been a game of cricket in Kent for a month, counties have been laying people off, and we now hear that Tom Harrison and his executives are due a £2.1m payout." This is what happens, he said, when sport is left to marketers; no one in South London, where he lives, knows what the game is. The presenters give Ronay room to swing. "The sport should be run by ten deeply religious headmasters and headmistresses who don't care about money. Or the kind of freaks who run your local club for nothing." He ended by urging the board back to their financial-sector sinecures.

Since they began in 2016, **The Grade Cricketer's** Iain Higgins and Sam Perry have gained myriad fans for their satire of the macho Australian. In 2021, they remained more regularly hilarious than anyone else, particularly when lamenting the death of Anglospheric dominance. But they discovered new depth, exemplified by the hour given to Michael Holding to discuss his book, *Why We Kneel, How We Rise*. Perry and Higgins had no pretension to Pulitzers. The interview began with: "Here we are, two idiots from the internet learning about human rights from an ornament to the game." But their respect for Holding was genuine, their questions on racism subtle and probing.

Elsewhere, they discussed Tom Wills, the icon who co-founded Australian Rules, and led the first Australian touring cricket team. He was also discovered to have participated in a massacre of Aboriginals – motivated, apparently, by vengeance for his father. "Australians would do well to learn about these stories," said Perry. "Land was stolen. People were murdered. It's a dark secret that permeates the psyche." As followings grow, the temptation is to shrink the field of inquiry, away from difficulty or controversy. Higgins and Perry are models for how to broaden appeal and interest at the same time.

In their episode on racism in modern South African cricket, **Oborne & Heller** show they are serious journalists used to serious subjects. With Mo Allie and Aslam Khota, they touched on the poison that remains – white gatekeepers to elite schools, and the torment of Makhaya Ntini running from hotel to ground to avoid his team-mates on the bus. When Oborne exclaimed that a form of apartheid is still operational, it felt thunderous, but not hyperbolic.

Still, the solemn podcasts were merely the most memorable, not the most common. Of the lighter ones, Brian Murgatroyd's **One Test Wonders** stood out. Perhaps only the more contented subjects make themselves available, but these mayflies seemed an affable bunch. Just before opening the batting for England, Alan Butcher was collared in the changing-room by Alec Bedser: "Don't do anything bloody stupid." He thought it might have dampened his usual free scoring (that, and Geoffrey Boycott's refusal of several easy singles). His late mum kept a photo of him on her mantelpiece, showing his score after 30 overs: 14 not out. To this day, he is unsure if it symbolised unconditional love or extraordinary cruelty.

James Gingell is a civil servant whose only partiality is to Somerset CCC.

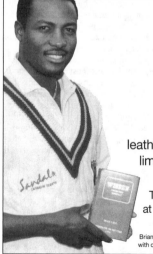

CRICKET AND SOCIAL MEDIA IN 2021

Like, really?

DAVE TICKNER

It was the year cricket was dragged – inevitably and irreversibly – into the culture wars. At the most serious end of the scale was the Yorkshire racism scandal, and its grim, shambolic fallout. And while social media was a front in that battle, it was not the major one: the Azeem Rafiq affair was a controversy too big for Twitter to do it justice.

Then there was the case of Ollie Robinson, whose otherwise impressive Test debut against New Zealand at Lord's was overshadowed by the unearthing of some dreadful tweets he had written several years earlier. It forced him to apologise on live television, and the ECB to suspend him while they carried out an investigation.

Robinson will remain an important case study, a member of the only generation vulnerable to this kind of sting – to have social media available in their teens, but with no idea of the power it would one day hold. He had nobody to blame but himself, of course, for the content of those tweets. But, for the ECB, the timing was excruciating: that morning, they had launched their strategy for tackling racism – and indeed all inequality – via T-shirt slogans.

Another battle on #CricketTwitter involved sexism and misogyny. There were two key skirmishes, one deeply unpleasant and highlighting the worst of Twitter's cesspit tendencies, the other quite funny.

The unpleasantness had come back in February, when England's men were losing a Test in India inside five sessions. Alex Hartley – once an international spinner, now a broadcaster – turned to black humour, as England supporters do in such times. "Nice of the England boys to get this Test match finished just before England Women play tonight," she tweeted. To further signpost the joke, even to the dim-witted – many of whom can be found among those who reply to any tweet by any woman about anything – she followed her comment with some clapping emojis.

Rory Burns, though, was not laughing. Taking a break from setting a calendar-year record for ducks by a Test opener, he fired off a reply: "Very disappointing attitude considering all the 'boys' do to support the Women's game." His tweet was liked by Ben Stokes and James Anderson, then deleted. The ECB took the view that mistakes had been made on both sides, with Burns "reminded of his social-media responsibilities". It was an unsatisfactory outcome, with predictable after-effects.

Hartley, needless to say, received waves of abuse. As she put it on the "No Balls" podcast hosted with her close friend, England international Kate Cross: "I've done a tweet that was meant to be funny, and it's been taken as not funny, and people are giving me grief, like I still play for England. It's been really weird, because the tweet went down really, really well – until Rory

CRICKET AND BLOGS IN 2021

Old virtues in the new normal

BRIAN CARPENTER

Time and its passing are disorientating beasts. Covid has simultaneously lengthened and foreshortened memory: things which happened in 2019 seem to belong to another universe, while daily events rush at you like asteroids. So it is with cricket. If the English summer saw the start of The Hundred, a glowing but truncated Test series, and later the fall of Yorkshire, the year's early months were not exactly quiet.

In January, India recovered from being skittled for 36 at Adelaide to win in Australia, and Siddhartha Vaidyanathan, at **81allout.com**, wrote of falling in love, "the elasticity of a Test match", and the dreamy quality of one of the year's outstanding cricketers, Rishabh Pant. And in March, Venkatraman Ganesan, at **blogternator.com**, deconstructed Pant's reverse sweep off Jimmy Anderson during his century in the Fourth Test against England at Ahmedabad, and paid tribute to his sheer nerve: "This is the irreverence that instils hope when one is down in the depths of despair. This is the irreverence that is revered by so many ordinary mortals." Pant also had his part to play during the return series in England, but the bowling of Jasprit Bumrah and his compatriots on the last afternoon at Lord's led Vaidyanathan to write of "something visceral yet cerebral, raw yet refined. A spectacle but also an art form. Thrilling to watch yet difficult to explain… a bowling performance for the ages."

After a gestation which spanned two British prime ministers, two American presidents and the biggest pandemic for a century, The Hundred finally took physical form. Everyone, it seemed, had expressed their view on how it would look and what it would mean, so it was a relief to find that, when the women's teams of Oval Invincibles and Manchester Originals took the field in late July, the world did not stop turning.

As so often, the blog which reflected the debates in the English game was **beingoutsidecricket.com**. Chris Crampton saluted veterans and paid homage to the peerless Joe Root; Danny Frankland skewered the ECB media machine with inspired satirical hoaxes; and Dmitri Old ranted as only he can. The most splenetic of his pieces was, as usual, framed by a song lyric, which spoke of "lies and deceit" gaining "a little more power". It is impossible to distil the breadth of Old's disdain into a few quotations, but he cares deeply, speaks for many and needs to be read.

It may seem a tasteless observation during a pandemic, but the retirement of cricketers has sometimes been viewed as analogous to death – confirmation that their youth, hopes and dreams are at an end. John Rigg, at **anordinaryspectator.com**, focused on the fact that the absence of crowds in 2020 and early 2021 deprived many players of the farewells they deserved. "When we enter the post-restrictive 'new normal' of watching live sport, a number of constituents of that universe will have been permanently removed," he wrote. "There will be a new 'now', which will be devoid of some of the participants of the previous 'then', whose departures we will only be able to mark long after they occurred."

For the second year running, the future was shrouded in uncertainty. But cricket's propensity for regeneration and controversy meant that, for the present, its ability to inspire fine writing would endure.

In 2013, Brian Carpenter was the inaugural winner of Wisden's *writing competition.*

quoted it, and then it went down like a sack of shit. I just felt like I was getting attacked from all angles over something that genuinely was meant to be a bit of humour. The messages of slating women's cricket, and saying that the men fund women's cricket, blah, blah, blah – I can deal with that. But it's when people are telling you to go and die in a hole. Like, really?"

In September, MCC announced the Laws would use the gender-neutral "batter" rather than "batsman". Now, there are objections, especially since the word comes out as "badder" when pronounced by nearly all television commentators. But it's hardly a big deal. Some were quick, though not

> ♥ James Anderson and Ben Stokes liked
>
> **Rory Burns** ✓
> @roryburns17
>
> Very disappointing attitude considering all the "boys" do to support the Women's game.
>
> > 🏏 **Alexandra Hartley** ✓ @AlexHartley...
> > Nice of the England boys to get this test match finished just before England Women play tonight 👏👏👏👏
> >
> > Catch them on @btsportcricket ...
>
> 19:19 · 25/02/2021 · Twitter for iPhone
>
> **222** Retweets **90** Quote Tweets **3,022** Likes

quick enough, to point out that this apparent affront to tradition had been around for centuries, in both formal and informal cricket writing. Wasn't there also uniformity in having batter join bowler and fielder as the default terminology?

But it was too late. MCC had fallen to the online woke brigade. Political correctness had gone mad yet again. You can't say anything these days, can you? Leading the race to take offence was Piers Morgan, who desperately sought – and got – our attention with a perfect slice of Twitter, combining indignation with nonsense. "OK," he began, before warming to his theme. "If we're going all PC with cricket terminology, what happens to maidens, third man, bunny rabbit, Chinaman, duck, flat-track bully, jockstrap, Michelle (5-for), Nelson, Nightwatchman, Dropped a Dolly, Twelfth Man, whites, & full toss in the crease?"

There was so much going on in his tweet. Sneaking "Chinaman" – a term that has already been widely discredited – into the middle of his list was bad enough; so was the apparent suggestion that worries over making cricket more accessible to women will lead to everyone having to consider the feelings of ducks, rabbits and Michelle Pfeiffer. It was the last of his phrases, though, that really caught the eye. Has anyone ever said "full toss in the crease"? Not even the satirical-tea-towel industry, which for decades has been hell-bent on bringing cricket to its knees. Yet the phrase, it seems, must be protected at all costs. Sorry, ladies.

Dave Tickner is editor of Cricket365.com, and can generally be found posting the same three or four tired jokes on Twitter as @tickerscricket.

RETIREMENTS IN 2021

The last of a breed

JACK SHANTRY

The zenith of **Tim Bresnan's** career surely came during England's 2010-11 Ashes victory, when he came in for the final two Tests, at Melbourne and Sydney, and picked up 11 wickets at 19 in a pair of innings wins. A strong, dependable action, a yeoman work ethic, and useful lower-order runs would have made him a fixture in the England side for more than 23 Tests, were it not for recurrent elbow injuries. He had played 60 List A games for his beloved Yorkshire before turning 20, and was on the winning side in each of his first 13 Tests, two behind Adam Gilchrist's record. Bresnan won Championships with Yorkshire in 2014 and 2015, before moving to Warwickshire in 2020. Last season, he added a final Championship winner's medal to his tally.

    Gareth Batty was a combative cricketer, with a fast bowler's temperament trapped in an off-spinner's body. In his final season, at 43, he could still be heard chuntering "age is just a number", as the ball fizzed past the outside edge. An engaging character, he was a master of his craft during a county career spanning 25 seasons. He had a long apprenticeship in the professional game. From 16, he played regular Second XI cricket for Yorkshire, as well as England age-groups, before moving to Surrey at the age of 20. By 24, however,

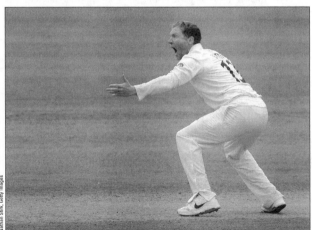

Live wire: Gareth Batty bowls another appeal.

he had made only one Championship appearance, mainly because of Saqlain Mushtaq's presence at The Oval. Remarkably, at least by modern standards, Batty had played 82 Second XI matches before that Championship debut. (In comparison, England's two spinners in Australia over the winter – Jack Leach and Dom Bess – had played barely a dozen before theirs.)

Batty's longevity – he retired with nearly 1,100 wickets in all formats – surely owed something to this period of development. As English cricket navel-gazes once again, it may consider whether a burgeoning off-spinner in 2022 would be given eight seasons of second-team cricket to hone his craft. And Batty repaid English cricket in spades. A move from The Oval to New Road in 2002 properly kickstarted his career. Successive 50-wicket summers earned him a Test call-up for the tours of Bangladesh and Sri Lanka in 2003-04, when he formed a spin pairing with Ashley Giles. A few months later, in the West Indies, Batty was bowling when Brian Lara broke Matthew Hayden's Test-record 380, and again when he moved to 400.

He was a mainstay of the Worcestershire side, winning the NatWest Pro40 in 2007, and worked with a young Moeen Ali. In 2010, Batty moved back to Surrey, part of an exodus from New Road that included Simon Jones, Kabir Ali and Steven Davies. He became an important part of the dressing-room, and was widely praised for his empathetic leadership following the death of Tom Maynard in 2012. More trophies followed, as well as a belated England recall at the age of 39 for the 2016-17 tour of Bangladesh and India, where he played two more Tests. Batty retired as Surrey's joint-leading T20 wicket-taker (with Jade Dernbach, on 114), and became their interim coach.

Daryl Mitchell was unfortunate that his most prolific years coincided with the era of Andrew Strauss and Alastair Cook. A batting average hovering around 40 might otherwise have earned him higher honours. As it was, Mitchell had the satisfaction of being a one-county man, known among his peers as a gritty run-scorer: he passed 1,000 in a season six times. He is the only batsman in first-class cricket to be dismissed for 298, against Somerset at Taunton in 2009.

Mitchell had made his Championship debut as Worcestershire's first substitute, replacing Batty after a Test call-up in 2005. He often found a way to succeed. In T20 cricket, he was not a natural power hitter, so he developed his bowling – a mixture of fast off-cutters, cross-seamers and back-of-the-hand deliveries. He called his style "hybrid", and became increasingly effective, especially on used wickets; he finished as Worcestershire's leading T20 wicket-taker, with 101. Mitchell served two terms as chairman of the Professional Cricketers' Association, captained his club to two promotions, and won the Blast in 2018. He takes up a full-time role with the PCA.

Rikki Clarke was one of the county game's most prolific all-rounders, mainly at Surrey and Warwickshire, with a brief spell at Derbyshire; he won three Championships and two one-day titles. He broke into international cricket early, after prospering for Surrey in 2002, but his England career was modest: two Tests in Bangladesh in 2003-04, plus 20 ODIs, the last in 2006. This was unfortunate, as Clarke's seamers got better with age; Graeme Welch, his bowling coach at Edgbaston, was credited with the improvement. Had he been

Top order: Varun Chopra and the 2017 Championship trophy.

able to marry his late-career experience with his 20-year-old body, he might have enjoyed a longer international career. He became director of cricket at King Edward's School in Witley.

Ryan ten Doeschate captained Essex to Championship wins in 2017 and 2019, and was an integral part of their success. Born in South Africa, and a Dutch international, Tendo was an attractive batsman, highly popular and well regarded. On his retirement, his ODI batting average from 33 games for the Netherlands was 67 – higher than anyone to have played at least 20 innings. He joined Kent as their batting coach.

Peter Trego was an ebullient all-rounder, incapable of a backwards step. A brief time out of cricket as a youngster might have helped fuel the fire and, after spells at Kent and Middlesex, it was at Somerset that he first made his name. A fans' favourite because of his explosive hitting, Trego moved to Nottinghamshire late in his career, helping them win the Blast in 2020. A gifted sportsman, he excelled at football, and hoped to forge a career in golf.

When **Stuart Meaker** – first of Surrey, later of Sussex – burst on the scene, he soon developed a reputation as one of the fastest men on the circuit. He was a regular in England performance squads, and his rare pace meant he was earmarked early for an international career, though it never fully materialised. Two stellar years in 2011 and 2012 promised much, but injuries limited him to four white-ball games for his country, even if he did remove Virat Kohli in both his T20 internationals, at Pune and Mumbai.

Opening batsman **Varun Chopra** started and finished at Essex, and in between – in 2014 – captained Warwickshire to T20 glory. A product of the

A. B. de VILLIERS RETIRES

Mr 360, 24/7

Daniel Gallan

Which Abraham Benjamin de Villiers will you remember? The swashbuckling, reverse-scooping virtuoso, who decimated attacks with gumption and grace? Or the immovable, textbook-perfect stoic, who batted for days on a foundation of granite and grit? In January 2015, he cracked 149 off 44 balls in an ODI against West Indies at Johannesburg. That December, he faced 297 deliveries for 43 in a futile effort to save a Test in Delhi. Among innings of 20 balls or more, the difference in strike-rate of 324 – between his fastest ODI knock and his slowest in Tests – is a record.

He was a Test debutant at 20, registering a maiden century in his inaugural series, against England in 2004-05. In 2008, he averaged 58 in Tests in a year that included tours of India, England and Australia. That same year the IPL began, and the tournament is stamped with de Villiers's mark. He has the most match awards (25), two of the five highest innings (133 and 129, both unbeaten), the fourth-highest number of scores of 50-plus (43), and the second-most sixes (250).

Yet he never lifted the trophy, nor reached a final in eight World Cups. Though he helped South Africa attain the No. 1 Test ranking in 2012 and 2014, his brilliance could not shake the chokers tag. He captained his country in 126 white-ball games, but only three Tests, stepping down in 2017 after a series of injuries and a loss of motivation. Despite averaging 71 against Australia in his final Test series, he retired from international cricket in May 2018.

He remained a force on the T20 circuit, and had demigod status in Bangalore. But his presence hung heavy over the South African game. Rumours of a return dogged his school-mate and new captain Faf du Plessis; a last-ditch attempt by de Villiers to join the 2019 World Cup was rejected.

For many, the final chapter of his career left a sour taste. CSA's Social Justice and Nation Building Hearings – aimed at dealing with the sport's racist past – implicated de Villiers for elbowing out wicketkeeper Thami Tsolekile, and sidelining batter Khaya Zondo. He denied the suggestions.

But his contribution to the sport has no caveat. He earned the moniker "Mr 360" for his range of strokes. He could hit the same ball almost anywhere. His records – the fastest ODI fifty, hundred and 150, and one of the highest Test averages from No. 5 (62) – are easily measured. Less quantifiable is the awe he inspired every time he took guard.

	M	I	NO	R	HS	100	Avge	SR	Ct/St
Tests	114	191	18	8,765	278*	22	50.66	54.51	222/5
ODIs	228	218	39	9,577	176	25	53.50	101.09	176/5
T20Is	78	75	11	1,672	79*	0	26.12	135.16	65/7
First-class	141	238	23	10,689	278*	25	49.71	56.18	275/6

De Villiers also took two wickets in Tests, and seven in ODIs; he never bowled in T20Is.

DALE STEYN RETIRES

Milk snatcher – and cream of the crop

TELFORD VICE

Even stripped down to his numbers, Dale Steyn was a bowler among bowlers, in any era. His Test strike-rate was 42, not far behind S. F. Barnes. And of those who have delivered at least 2,000 balls in Tests, it was better than Fred Spofforth, Fred Trueman, Dennis Lillee, Malcolm Marshall and Waqar Younis. His average, just under 23, puts him ahead of Ray Lindwall, Shaun Pollock, Wasim Akram and Michael Holding.

No South Africa bowler has taken more Test wickets than Steyn's 439. Seven from other countries have more, but from many more Tests. And, for 263 weeks, between 2008 and 2014, no one could dislodge him from the top of the Test rankings.

But it is as a complete person, walking among us, that Steyn truly stood out. As a young unknown, he would arrive extra early at Centurion to raid the dressing-room supplies: he couldn't afford milk for his breakfast cereal. At the same ground in November 2007, his bouncer broke New Zealander Craig Cumming's facial bones in 23 places. With Steyn, contrasts were stark.

He was at once a thoroughly modern exponent of the game, and a throwback to a time when players behaved like everyone else. You could engage with him as you would with mortals. "How do you manage to have fun and look so angry at the same time," a little girl once asked him at a sponsor's do. It remains the best of the thousands of questions directed his way. How indeed? She was never given a proper answer. Maybe Steyn didn't know. Perhaps it would have required him to think too much about the tightrope he walked.

For many he was too short, at 1.79m, and too slight to be a proper fast bowler, at least for long enough to make a lasting impact. He got ahead of that curve by training so hard that not even his penchant for late-night junk food could dent his conditioning. You might say he needed after-hours calorie bombs just to keep his body going.

He made his debut in December 2004, bowling Marcus Trescothick for his first Test wicket, and in the second innings bowling Michael Vaughan too. Only in November 2015, when he suffered a significant groin injury in India, did he fall off the high wire. In the next two years, there were two broken shoulders and a torn tendon in his heel. He would never really get back to those heights. But he will always be up there in other senses. And with us.

	M	Balls	R	W	BB	5I	10M	Avge	SR
Tests	93	18,608	10,077	439	7-51	26	5	22.95	42.38
ODIs	125	6,256	5,087	196	6-39	3	–	25.95	31.91
T20Is	47	1,015	1,175	64	4-9	0	–	18.35	15.85
First-class	141	27,183	14,569	618	8-41	35	7	23.57	43.98

Steyn also scored 1,251 runs (13.59) in Tests, 365 (9.35) in ODIs, and 21 (3.50) in T20Is.

Chelmsford Academy, he scored almost 18,000 runs in all formats; on his Championship debut in 2006, aged 18, he became Essex's youngest centurion. **Alex Wakely**, once England Under-19 captain, led Northamptonshire to three T20 finals between 2013 and 2016, winning two. His side captured the heart of many cricket fans, helped by the inclusion of several players who seemed to have avoided the strength and conditioning coach. "Big bellies, bigger sixes" was their unofficial motto, though Wakely himself was fit as a flea.

Tim Groenewald was a skilful swing bowler who made his name at Warwickshire, before moving to Derbyshire, Somerset and finally Kent. Educated, like Kevin Pietersen, at Maritzburg College in Natal, Groenewald qualified as a non-overseas player through his English mother, and led the Derbyshire attack in their promotion year of 2012.

Nottinghamshire left-arm seamer **Harry Gurney** played ten one-day and two T20 internationals, all in the space of seven months in 2014. An excellent yorker and well-disguised slower ball served him well in the death overs. As his career developed, so did his variety of white-ball deliveries, and he became a T20 gun for hire, helping win the CPL and Big Bash, and often defending the franchise system to outraged traditionalists on Twitter. He owns a pub with Stuart Broad.

Over a 17-year career, Australian-born seamer **Mitchell Claydon** represented Yorkshire, Durham, Kent and Sussex. He played over 370 matches, and was known as a big-hearted performer. Leg-spinner **Josh Poysden** first came on the radar with Cambridge MCCU and the Unicorns. He started at Warwickshire, before seeking regular cricket at Yorkshire. Seen as a limited-overs specialist, he played two one-day games for England Lions in Sri Lanka in 2016-17. Two years later, he suffered a fractured skull while giving throwdowns to Dom Bess, though this did not affect his decision to leave the game at the age of 29. However, Derbyshire wicketkeeper **Harvey Hosein** did retire, at 25, because of complications arising from a series of head injuries. He took 11 catches on first-class debut at The Oval, and was improving as a middle-order batsman, making two first-class centuries. **Gareth Harte** returned to his native South Africa after four years at Durham, having scored three hundreds in 25 first-class appearances.

Charlie Hemphrey took the road less travelled to county cricket. Part of the Kent Academy system as an off-spinning all-rounder, he made his Second XI debut in 2005, but couldn't break into the first team. Thinking his chance had gone, he moved to Queensland, played grade cricket and earned a call-up to the state team in 2015. Four years later, he was signed by Glamorgan, but his decision to represent Queensland as a local meant he was not England-qualified, reducing Glamorgan's income from fielding home-grown players. Hemphrey petitioned the ECB to make an exception, to no avail, and did not feature for the county in 2021. He had made 13 first-class appearances for them, with a best of 75.

Jack Shantry made 255 appearances in a ten-year career for Worcestershire. He retired in 2018, aged 30, and has taken up umpiring.

CAREER FIGURES

Players not expected to appear in county cricket in 2022

(minimum 25 first-class appearances)

BATTING

	M	I	NO	R	HS	100	Avge	1,000r/ season
G. J. Batty	261	389	68	7,399	133	3	23.04	–
T. T. Bresnan	213	294	45	7,128	169*	7	28.62	–
J. T. A. Burnham......	52	87	7	2,045	135	2	25.56	–
V. Chopra	192	317	20	10,243	233*	20	34.48	3
R. Clarke..............	267	403	49	11,387	214	17	32.16	1
M. E. Claydon.........	113	146	36	1,710	77	–	15.54	–
J. W. Dernbach........	113	139	47	871	56*	–	9.46	–
T. D. Groenewald	139	200	66	2,375	78	–	17.72	–
H. F. Gurney..........	103	131	63	424	42*	–	6.23	–
G. T. Hankins	38	60	3	1,211	116	1	21.24	–
H. R. Hosein	59	100	20	2,580	138*	2	32.25	–
D. Klein.............	71	100	19	1,455	94	–	17.96	–
R. E. Levi	106	176	18	5,722	168	10	36.21	–
S. C. Meaker	98	132	26	1,664	94	–	15.69	–
D. K. H. Mitchell	225	403	40	13,920	298	39	38.34	6
L. E. Plunkett	158	216	39	4,378	126	3	24.73	–
S. W. Poynter	47	73	4	1,522	170	2	22.05	–
N. J. Selman	61	113	6	2,863	150	7	26.75	–
R. N. ten Doeschate	203	294	39	11,298	259*	29	44.30	1
P. D. Trego	223	332	38	9,644	154*	15	32.80	1
A. G. Wakely	148	236	16	6,880	123	9	31.27	–
M. H. Wessels.........	224	369	31	11,701	202*	23	34.61	2

BOWLING AND FIELDING

	R	W	BB	Avge	5I	10M	Ct/St
G. J. Batty	22,356	682	8-64	32.78	27	4	163
T. T. Bresnan	17,820	575	5-28	30.99	9	–	125
J. T. A. Burnham	17	0	0-0	–	–	–	17
V. Chopra	128	0	0-1	–	–	–	228
R. Clarke	16,296	534	7-55	30.51	8	–	391
M. E. Claydon	9,943	312	6-104	31.86	9	–	11
J. W. Dernbach........	10,139	311	6-47	32.60	10	–	17
T. D. Groenewald......	11,904	403	6-50	29.53	16	–	45
H. F. Gurney	9,472	310	6-25	30.55	8	–	12
G. T. Hankins.........	13	0	0-13	–	–	–	42
H. R. Hosein	–	–	–	–	–	–	132/5
D. Klein	6,626	225	8-72	29.44	10	1	19
R. E. Levi	–	–	–	–	–	–	89
S. C. Meaker	9,451	290	8-52	32.58	11	2	22
D. K. H. Mitchell	1,649	33	4-49	49.96	–	–	301
L. E. Plunkett	14,433	453	6-33	31.86	11	1	86
S. W. Poynter	21	0	0-21	–	–	–	139/4
N. J. Selman	36	1	1-22	36.00	–	–	67
R. N. ten Doeschate	7,242	214	6-20	33.84	7	–	127
P. D. Trego	14,359	395	7-84	36.35	5	1	90
A. G. Wakely	426	6	2-62	71.00	–	–	98
M. H. Wessels	130	3	1-10	43.33	–	–	339/16

CRICKETANA IN 2021

From four cents to a small fortune

MARCUS WILLIAMS

Just as England's Ashes campaign was coming off the rails at the end of the year, a reminder arrived of past Australian dominance. At an auction Down Under, the bat with which Don Bradman scored 758 runs in the 1934 series sold for just over \$A245,500 (£132,000), a record for a bat.

The back of it has an inscription in Bradman's own hand: "This is the bat with which I scored 304 at Leeds and 244 at The Oval against England, 1934". The Australian buyer, who fought off competition from overseas, agreed it should remain on display at the Bradman Museum in Bowral. Earlier in the year, Bradman's bat from the 1931-32 series against South Africa, which had been in private hands, realised a previous high of \$A183,305.

Further evidence of history repeating itself came at a sale in England. Pitches, weather, umpiring issues, travel problems, months away from home, the early departure of a team member, and extracurricular activities: all are part of the modern tour. But they were also features of the first by an English team to the West Indies more than 125 years ago.

These details were brought to light in a vivid, detailed diary compiled by Legh Barratt, who played cricket for Norfolk, and was a member of R. S. Lucas's ground-breaking team that visited the Caribbean between January and April 1895. Barratt went back with Arthur Priestley's side, two years later, when he again wrote a diary. The two handwritten volumes were bequeathed by Barratt to his grandson. Together with two locally published and rare books relating to the tours, as well as some of Barratt's other cricketing possessions, they came up for auction at Knights, and fetched £58,180 (hammer price plus buyer's premium), well ahead of estimate.

Oddly, Barratt is listed in *Wisden's* accounts of the tours as R. Leigh-Barratt, although he appears correctly in the Norfolk sections of the Almanack as L. Barratt; birth and other official records, and a note in the first diary, confirm Legh was his only forename. He had never left Britain before, so his journals have a freshness and sense of wonder. The first opens with the team's departure from Waterloo Station: "I feel as though I am going away for years instead of three months." The voyage from Southampton was anything but smooth – "shipped 500 tons of water, 700 plates smashed" – but the welcome in Bridgetown, Barbados, like the weather, was warm.

Barratt records that "several thousand people thronged on the landing place and cheered us. We are taken in private carriages and driven to our hotel, where a most delicious breakfast was provided. In the afternoon we went to practice… the hospitality of the people is unbounded. The strangeness and beauty of the place is unlike anything I have seen before. Everything is provided for us free of charge."

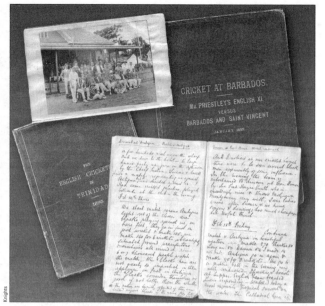

Tourist class: Legh Barratt and his fellow amateurs had everything laid on for them.

As for the cricket, the all-amateur team played 16 matches in various Caribbean islands, as well as Demerara (now Guyana), winning ten and losing four. The highlight was a 25-run victory in a five-day game against Barbados, which produced more than 1,350 runs. The quality of the opposition – who were predominantly white, except in Antigua – varied, as did the pitches: St Vincent ("very awful pitch, like a gravel road, absolutely no grass"); St Lucia ("good wicket, pretty little ground"); and Demerara ("by far the best ground in the West Indies. It exactly resembles a good, fast English wicket like Lord's.").

When Barratt reached Trinidad – in a precursor to the Tiger Moth escapade of David Gower and John Morris in Australia in 1990-91 – he took his life in his hands on what he described as an "eventful day… We all go to the Gymkhana race meeting… I rode in a race and jolly nearly got killed. I shall not be able to play cricket for some time." He was, however, fit enough to play against West Jamaica, when he scored 20 "and then was umpired out".

Meanwhile, another player, Harry Smith-Turberville, decided on the spur of the moment to return home early. The only person he informed was Lucas, his captain. Maybe he'd been put off by the local wildlife. "We found a scorpion in one of the cricket bags," says Barratt. "I got it put into a jar which I still retain."

Despite a note indicating that Barratt's journal might be published, it never was. Consisting of 146 pages and running to nearly 20,000 words, it went under the hammer for £23,560. The journal from his second tour was less comprehensive, and concludes abruptly, without explanation, with six matches remaining. It realised £3,720.

Both tours involved cricket of a decent quality, though Priestley's, which contained nine first-class matches to Lucas's eight, was probably of a higher standard; a member of the party was England captain A. E. Stoddart. In a non-first-class game against Antigua, Barratt – who made 96 – shared a big partnership with Stoddart (107), and commented that it was "indeed a pleasure and an experience to be opposite such a batsman". The pair had struck up a rapport on the voyage out and, during several long talks with Stoddart on his cricket life and Australian experiences, Barratt observes "it is still true that real greatness and modesty always go together".

Two of Barratt's other possessions – short but extremely rare books relating to the tours – attracted fierce competition from cricket bibliophiles; few collectors or dealers had seen them before. *The English Cricketers in Trinidad: Details of the Matches Played, 1895*, published in Port-of-Spain, made £16,120, while *Cricket at Barbados: Mr Priestley's English XI versus Barbados and Saint Vincent, January 1897*, published in Bridgetown (and on sale for a mere four cents) reached £13,640.

Another collection of unique handwritten material with cricketing links also came to auction. In May 1953, the First World War poet Siegfried Sassoon had been in Cambridge to receive an award, and was asked by a friend to look up Dennis Silk, then an opening bat for the University XI (and a future chairman of the Test and County Cricket Board). Silk's widow recalls her late husband telling of a gaunt, handsome stranger who approached the Fenner's pavilion with a long, forked hazel staff in his hand. He looked up at the rows of seated spectators and asked, a little tentatively: "Dennis Silk?" When Silk identified himself, the visitor simply said: "Siegfried Sassoon". Over the next 13 years, the pair met frequently and exchanged correspondence. The 85 letters

---

OTHER NOTABLE LOTS SOLD IN 2021

- A printed silk scorecard of Kent v All England, 1839 (John Nicholson's, Haslemere, £1,105)

- Three photographs from Cambridge University v Australians, 1886 (Gorringe's of Lewes, £3,062, nearly ten times estimate, despite poor condition)

- A presentation scorebook for the 1921 Australian tour of England, compiled by W. H. Ferguson, the Australians' official scorer, and signed by their team (Knights, £8,060)

- The ball used by Ken Cranston to take four wickets in an over for England against South Africa at Headingley in 1947 (Knights, £2,728)

- A complete set of 33 trade cards produced by Hoadley's Chocolates in 1928, featuring Australian Test and state cricketers (Loddon, £2,800)

- A complete set of 50 of the Wills 1896 Cricketers cigarette cards (Loddon, £2,700)

Special delivery: some of the 85 letters sent between Siegfried Sassoon and Dennis Silk.

– mainly on literary matters, but with a sprinkling of cricket – and autographed copies of Sassoon's poems, were offered by Lawrences of Crewkerne, and fetched £14,300.

While the contents of the envelopes were the main attraction, it was an envelope itself that generated intense competition on eBay from collectors of cricket-themed stamps. The target had been sent during the 1971 UK postal strike, the first full national walkout in the history of the Post Office, and bears two stamps titled "The Ashes Return", depicting a batsman sweeping, as well as a non-striker, umpire and fielders.

The stamps were produced by London Express, created by Mark Purnell, and one of many private enterprises that sprang up during the 44-day stoppage to carry mail. Three other services produced stamps with a cricket theme, but London Express have always been the most elusive, as a winning bid of £2,650 testifies – not bad for two items of, literally, postage-stamp dimensions and a face value of 25p. It is believed to be the highest price for any philatelic item produced during the strike.

CRICKET AND THE WEATHER IN 2021

September to the rescue after grim May days

ANDREW HIGNELL

With the county season starting as early as April 8, there was always a chance of the weather interfering. Yet few expected Old Trafford, Trent Bridge, Headingley or Northampton to join Buxton on the list of venues where snow has stopped play in the Championship. A fortnight later, an area of high pressure – a blocking anticyclone – was established over the British Isles and, under cloudless skies, the third round suffered no interruption at all.

In fact, April was both the sunniest and frostiest on record and, by the completion of the fourth round on May 2, not a single Championship day had been washed out. That soon changed, though, when Saturday May 8 saw a deep area of low pressure move east across the country: six games had no play and, in the two that did, at Lord's and the Rose Bowl, there was a total of 68 overs. Disturbance of the jet streams in the upper atmosphere continued, making it – at least for some parts of the UK – the wettest May since the 19th century. Three rounds of Championship matches were badly affected.

The weather was much kinder when first-class games resumed at the end of August, with high pressure bringing warm, dry, continental air. It was the country's second-warmest September (and average temperatures were barely lower than for August). In the second week, the mercury soared towards 30°C and, on the few occasions play was lost, it was usually because of the gloom, despite many grounds using floodlights.

But by the penultimate round of Championship games, low pressure was back in charge, and rain swept in. On the third day, Cardiff was alone in having no interruptions; six games had no cricket at all.

HOURS LOST TO THE WEATHER IN THE 2021 CHAMPIONSHIP

	Home	Away	2021	2019	Difference
Derbyshire	21.75	23.50	45.25	33.00	12.25
Durham	9.00	37.00	46.00	40.50	5.50
Essex	35.00	13.00	48.00	42.50	5.50
Glamorgan	24.25	40.00	64.25	47.50	16.75
Gloucestershire	32.00	2.50	34.50	48.25	–13.75
Hampshire	31.75	14.75	46.50	56.00	–9.50
Kent	32.50	51.25	83.75	54.75	29.00
Lancashire	31.50	39.00	70.50	56.00	14.50
Leicestershire	20.25	28.00	48.25	62.00	–13.75
Middlesex	24.00	14.25	38.25	65.25	–27.00
Northamptonshire	43.25	23.25	66.50	47.50	19.00
Nottinghamshire	23.25	20.25	43.50	41.50	2.00
Somerset	35.25	28.75	64.00	48.00	16.00
Surrey	21.25	40.25	61.50	51.25	10.25
Sussex	16.25	30.00	46.25	50.75	–4.50
Warwickshire	30.75	24.25	55.00	29.50	25.50
Worcestershire	5.25	31.00	36.25	52.75	–16.50
Yorkshire	40.50	16.75	57.25	50.50	6.75

CRICKET PEOPLE IN 2021

Generation game

KIT HARRIS

To keep the children occupied, a busy mother took her young son and daughter to the local club to try cricket. But the boy refused to get out of the car, and the girl went alone.

So began the inspirational journey of **Beth Barrett-Wild**, once the only girl at Kelvedon & Fearing CC in Essex, and now a senior administrator at the ECB, where she runs the women's Hundred. When she debuted in adult men's cricket, an opponent groaned: "Oh God, they've turned up with a girl. They must be useless." The rejoinder from a Kelvedon team-mate was swift. "That's not a girl. That's Beth."

She scored a men's league hundred, was the first girl to join the Essex Academy, and made her first county century at 13. By the time she was at Oxford University – where she was the first woman selected for their MCCU programme – she had played for England Under-21. "I dreamed of being a professional," she says. "I was desperate to play in a World Cup. I hit balls every day. But by the time I graduated, I knew I hadn't made it."

After taking a communications role with MCC, she was appointed media manager for the England women's team. Then came the 2017 World Cup, for which she was the ECB's project lead. "The final was when I realised how big it was. Someone said: 'Look at the queues!' I said: 'What do you mean? There are queues?' And they were around the block."

She claims she was "just in the right place at the right time" to oversee the women's Hundred. There were difficulties: as the pandemic surged, high-profile players withdrew. "I had an almost overwhelming feeling of nervousness and fear. But when the pyros went off for the opening game, I felt so proud. And a little bit smug about all the haters."

Beth married her partner, Eliza, in the Long Room at Lord's. They have a young son, and now it is her turn to be the busy mother. "He threw a toy car at the telly the other day," she says. "I know he shouldn't have done it… but he's got a good arm." She took him down to Kelvedon for the ECB's All-Stars programme. He got out of the car.

An unlikely dream came true for 22-year-old medical student **Anna Harris** when she stood in the second women's ODI between England and New Zealand at Worcester – and became the youngest umpire in international cricket. She, too, had club cricket to thank for her rapid rise, beginning at Chesham and earning selection, aged 13, for Buckinghamshire. After scoring three hundreds for her county, she attracted the interest of England Under-15. She also bowled leg-spin. "I could rip it, even though I have tiny hands," she says. Her mother was supportive, gaining her ECB Level 1 umpiring certificate, and encouraged Anna to do likewise.

Harris went to Australia for her gap year and, to earn her keep, umpired for Melbourne CC. Soon after she started at Cardiff University, she was standing in the South Wales Premier League, and became fully qualified through the ECB's Young Officials Pathway. Then came the call, from down the road in Bristol: an official had to isolate, so could she be fourth umpire for the first ODI? She made a good impression, and was asked to stand at Worcester. But the moment proved too much: "I felt sick with nerves. By the break, I was panicking. Someone called a paramedic, and I was stood down for the second innings." Harris thought that would spell the end of her umpiring career, but she was retained for the fourth ODI. There was a lot less attention, and she made it through.

Then came a call-up for The Hundred. "I was nervous," she says. "Steve O'Shaughnessy told me to enjoy it – and remember to smile, because we were on national television." In the London derby, she gave Heather Knight out lbw. The England captain reviewed it. Harris recounts: "Graham Lloyd was at square leg, and said she was quite far forward. Then the replay came on the screen. It was plumb. I thought, I've smashed that! One in the bag…"

It is December 2015, in the first season of the women's Big Bash, and Brisbane Heat need 79 from 8.2 overs to beat Melbourne Stars. Their No. 6 strides to the middle: on debut, no pressure. Though Heat lose by 20 runs, she strikes 39 off 27, and is last out. She had received no formal cricket coaching.

Ash Barty might have played only that one senior cricket season, having taken a break from professional tennis in 2014, but it was a watershed moment: she realised where her true love lay. "I chatted to my good friend and doubles partner Casey Dellacqua, and decided to give tennis another go," she says.

Cricket appears to have acted as a breather, maybe even a sporting reset. "I loved being part of Brisbane Heat, and the camaraderie. I formed some great friendships, and I still keep in touch with the girls now." But her passion for tennis had been rekindled. In 2017, she qualified for all four Grand Slams, and was ranked 17th in the world. Within two years, she was No. 1.

Through her great-grandmother, she is a member of the aboriginal Ngaragu people of Queensland. Like all Australian children, she played backyard cricket; she still has a hit. "My team and I have a game of cricket most days when we warm up. It's a great way to disconnect from tennis. And I have an English trainer, so we give him plenty of stick." And there can surely be no giving it back – Barty won Wimbledon in 2021, her second Slam after the French Open in 2019. She was WTA Player of the Year in both years, and has been No. 1 for more than 100 weeks, adding the Australian Open in January 2022. Only Chris Evert, Martina Navratilova, Steffi Graf and Serena Williams have had longer unbroken reigns.

"It's been amazing to see the growth of women's cricket," she says. "There's so much talent in Australia. I love watching Meg Lanning. She's the complete player, and has set the standard in the women's game for a long time." Coming from Barty, that is some compliment.

CRICKET AND THE LAW OF THE LAND IN 2021

Caught by a bouncer

On a peaceful July afternoon at Stanton Harcourt, in Oxfordshire, word spread that a thief had been spotted rifling through the pavilion till, as well as wallets in the dressing-room. Fielders noticed a suspicious figure on a bench, and moved towards him; he legged it, but was caught beside a barbed-wire fence by home captain Ryan Wastie. The visiting team, Wolvercote, included a professional bouncer, who held the suspect until police arrived.

At Oxford Crown Court in September, Raymond Starkings pleaded guilty to a string of thefts and burglaries in the area, going back to December 2020. He stole from a church, a pub on Christmas Day, Oxford City FC – and £200 from Stanton Harcourt. He was jailed for two years. After the excitement, and all the time spent dealing with the police, the match was abandoned. "It was a huge shame," said Wastie, whose team had Wolvercote in trouble at 92 for six, "but we couldn't just let him go."

STAND COLLAPSE: DURHAM FINED

On December 10, Durham County Cricket Club were ordered to pay around £100,000 for an incident at the Riverside ground in Chester-le-Street in 2017, when part of the North-East Terrace stand collapsed. It happened near the end of a Twenty20 international between England and West Indies; four people were hurt, including a woman who broke her leg. She had stood up to let someone past and, as one eyewitness said, the board beneath her gave way "like a trap door".

The stand had previously been used at the beach volleyball tournament at the 2012 London Olympics, but James Hill, prosecuting, said it was unclear whether Durham officials realised the company that sold the stand had not been contracted to maintain it. Simon Antrobus, for the club, read out a statement from the chairman, Lord Botham, explaining the safety checks that had been carried out, and adding: "The club wholeheartedly apologises for this enormously embarrassing incident."

Judge H. K. Crowther told Teesside Crown Court it was clear the club did have "the safety of the spectators at heart", and said he did not need to impose an exemplary punishment. But he fined Durham £18,000 for "failing to discharge a duty to a person other than an employee", and ordered them to pay £94,000 costs.

SOME YOU WIN...

Westow CC, near Malton in Yorkshire, defeated Her Majesty's Revenue and Customs in April, after a nine-year battle against a £20,000 penalty for not paying VAT on their new pavilion – which the club said was done on HMRC's advice. Westow were originally told the project appeared to qualify for zero-rating, because the money came entirely from donations. However, the Revenue pursued them because the club were not a registered charity. Westow lost at the original hearing, but a tribunal ruled in their favour, accepting the argument that they not only had a reasonable excuse, but that the penalty was a breach of human rights on grounds of "proportionality". HMRC said they were "disappointed", but would not pursue the case further. By way of celebration, the club's tax lawyers were promised lemon drizzle cake.

... SOME YOU DON'T

In February, Eynsham CC, from Oxfordshire, lost their third legal case over a £35,000 VAT bill for a new pavilion destroyed by suspected arson in 2012. Like Westow, the club argued that, as a community amateur sports club, they should be treated as charity. But they did not claim they had been offered wrong advice, and the appeal court agreed with the tribunals that had ruled against them.

MAD MAGPIES MAYHEM

In a dispute about whether a ball was a wide, wicketkeeper William John Campbell, 39, shoved the batsman and punched a player-umpire in the head. It was in theory a game of "social cricket", and his team were the Mad Magpies, from Dunedin, New Zealand. Campbell was banned by the Otago Cricket Association for three and a half years, and pleaded guilty to two charges of assault at Dunedin District Court in May. Judge Michael Turner sentenced Campbell to nine months' supervision, plus 60 hours' community work. His lawyer claimed "social anxiety" prevented him from carrying out the work. "He was playing social cricket," the judge replied. "He didn't seem to have any social anxiety then."

CRICKETERS PUNISHED FOR SEX OFFENCES

David Hymers, 29, was arrested in dramatic circumstances after members of an anti-paedophile group, Guardians of the North, interrupted a training session at Tynemouth CC. They explained their accusations to Hymers in front of his dumbfounded team-mates, and the police soon arrived. The Guardians had set up fake online profiles, and duped him into believing he was talking to girls in their early teens.

At Newcastle Crown Court in July, Hymers pleaded guilty to two charges of attempting to engage in sexual communication with a child, was given a three-year community order, and obliged to undergo a sex-offenders' programme. Recorder Ben Nolan noted his willingness to undergo therapy, and the support given him by the cricket club. He hinted at reservations about the Guardians' entrapment. It was perfectly legal, he said, before adding: "Whether or not that is to be approved of, I'm not going to make any comment."

A coach formerly employed by Essex was jailed in September after admitting he had surreptitiously filmed underage girls in changing-rooms. Matthew Hyam, 48, was charged with 12 counts of offences relating to voyeurism and indecent images of children. None of the charges involved Essex themselves. He was imprisoned for 28 months.

Aaron Summers, 25, who played one Big Bash match for Hobart Hurricanes and three List A games for Tasmania, was jailed by a court in Darwin for four years. He admitted possession of sexual images of children, and grooming. It was alleged Summers used social media to gain images for potential blackmail; his victims included two boys, aged 12 and 13, whom he had met through cricket.

BEN STOKES AND THE SUN

The Sun apologised (and paid damages) to Ben Stokes two years after they reprinted the story of a family tragedy that had taken place in New Zealand in 1988, before Stokes was born. The newspaper argued the story was in the public domain, since it had been widely reported in New Zealand at the time. But they acknowledged that reviving it, and doorstepping the family, constituted an invasion of privacy.

THE LAWS OF THE GAME

Too short is two short

FRASER STEWART

There was no lack of conundrums in 2021, with several incidents leaving players and even umpires unsure as to the correct answer. In a men's Big Bash League game on Christmas Eve, Hobart Hurricanes' Tim David seemed unaware of Law 18.5 (deliberate short runs) in the final over of the innings against Melbourne Stars. With his team batting first, and two balls to go, David had 18 off nine deliveries, while his partner, No. 8 Nathan Ellis, was yet to face. David struck Brody Couch to long-on, and was keen to run two and keep the strike. As he approached the non-striker's end, he realised two would be tight, so turned for the second while still a metre short of the popping crease. He narrowly avoided being run out at the striker's end, but that was where his luck stopped. The umpires spotted the ruse, and applied the Law: while the Hurricanes received no runs, the Stars were awarded five penalty runs, and began their reply on five without loss.

This was different from the more common accidental short run, where the batters (last year, MCC replaced "batsman" in the Laws) only marginally fail to ground their bat beyond the crease. In those circumstances, Law 18.3 (short runs) decrees that, although both runs are technically short, only one is deemed as such. David probably felt he could turn short of his ground, get back to the other end, collect a run and retain the strike – it is a mistake he's unlikely to repeat.

In the Vitality Blast final at Edgbaston in September, Somerset's Will Smeed hit the ball in the air towards the square-leg boundary, where two Kent fielders converged for the catch. Jordan Cox held on, and remained wholly within the field of play, but collided with team-mate Daniel Bell-Drummond, who tumbled to the ground. Part of Bell-Drummond's body was clearly over the boundary, but his legs were within the field of play while also in contact with the legs of Cox, who had already caught the ball. Did this chain of contact mean Cox should also be deemed beyond the boundary?

After reviewing the footage, the TV umpire clearly thought so: he ruled Smeed not out, and awarded six runs. But this failed to take into account that MCC had amended the Law in 2017, to cater for just this eventuality. Law 19.5 states that "a fielder is grounded beyond the boundary if some part of his/her person is in contact with… another fielder who is grounded beyond the boundary, if the umpire considers that it was the intention of either fielder that the contact should assist in the fielding of the ball". Therefore, if the fielders make accidental contact, as they did here, the one within the boundary is not deemed to be beyond it. If, however, the fielder beyond the boundary is doing something to assist his/her team-mate, such as supporting or lifting them, then both fielders are deemed to be beyond the boundary.

In an ODI at Malahide in July, South Africa's Keshav Maharaj hit a borderline waist-high full toss to deep midwicket, where Ireland's Curtis Campher held on. It was not called a no-ball, but Campher thought it might be: seeing both batters standing mid-pitch, he threw the ball to the wicketkeeper, who took off the bails, with the non-striker, Kagiso Rabada, closer to that end. After a TV replay did confirm a no-ball, Rabada was given run out. MCC felt the wrong decision had been reached, since the ball should have been dead once the catch was taken. Furthermore, both umpires had left their positions to consult each other by the time the throw had come in; before they do this, they are supposed to call dead ball, if the ball is not already dead.

In the Second Test against Afghanistan at Abu Dhabi in March, Zimbabwe were 281 for eight in their first innings, with Sikandar Raza on 79 and Blessing Muzarabani yet to score. Raza struck the ball – the last of an over – through point, but it stopped centimetres short of the rope. The batters sauntered a single, meaning Raza would keep the strike, but the fielder, Hashmatullah Shahidi, deliberately placed one leg over the boundary before picking up the ball, hoping four runs would be awarded, and Muzarabani on strike. He was unaware of Law 19.8: the wilful act of a fielder causing a boundary sees not only the runs for the boundary credited, but also any runs completed, which includes when the batters have crossed. In this case, that meant five runs, with Raza on strike for the next delivery.

Two months earlier, in the First Test between Sri Lanka and England at Galle, Joe Root was correctly given not out for a close catch. After he had defended the ball into the ground, it bounced back up, hit his glove and ballooned to a fielder. Sri Lanka's coach, Mickey Arthur, was incensed by the decision and complained to the match referee, but he was unaware of Law 33.2.2.2. Although it states that a batter can indeed be out caught after a lawful second strike (such as inadvertent contact with the glove), it is out only if the ball has not been grounded since the first strike. The reason is simple: to avoid being caught, a batter needs to hit the ball into the ground. Once this has happened, it would not be fair for an involuntary second strike to reopen the possibility of being caught. As with other examples listed above, it highlights the importance of players, officials and coaches having a sound knowledge of the Laws.

Fraser Stewart is Laws manager at MCC.

CRICKET IN FILM AND TELEVISION IN 2021

Delighted of Tunbridge Wells

GARY NAYLOR

India's victory over West Indies in the 1983 World Cup final was, said *Wisden*, "an absorbing game of increasing drama and finally of much emotion". Drama and emotion, surely the raw materials for any Bollywood blockbuster, are exactly what Kabir Khan delivers in his outrageously entertaining *83*.

If failure is an orphan, success has many parents. India's current status in the game might be traced back to Joginder Sharma's dismissal of Misbah-ul-Haq to win the World T20, to Sourav Ganguly's shirt-twirling, or to V. V. S. Laxman's 281 in the Miracle of Kolkata. But one might delve still further into history, to Tunbridge Wells, where a quiet man, lacking the English to impress his team-mates, let alone a patronising press pack, looked up at a scoreboard reading 17 for five. At that moment, Kapil Dev was the only Indian – of nearly a billion – who believed the World Cup could still be won. Their match against Zimbabwe was not televised, and only a smattering of spectators were at the Nevill Ground to watch him enter cricketing lore. At Manchester, where England were getting all the attention, the announcement of Kapil's world-record 175 earned a standing ovation.

If that innings is the pivotal dramatic moment in *83*, there is emotion to burn as we get to know the Indian players. Mohinder "Jimmy" Amarnath, living in the shadow cast by his father, the legendary Lala (played by Mohinder himself), finds validation in his Player of the Match performances in the semi-final and final. The Anglo-Indian Roger Binny, nicknamed "Brit", struggles with the national anthem, then realises his potential. P. R. Man Singh, the team manager, indulges his boys, blinks back the insults, and finds resolve.

For all the vivid cameos – a gum-chewing Viv Richards, a Kevin Curran blonder than his IPL-star sons, and a mad-eyed Bob Willis – it's Ranveer Singh who anchors the film as Kapil Dev. A Bollywood superstar, he draws on his charisma to invest Kapil with a kind of noble heroism that should be cheesy, but somehow isn't.

If there are a few anachronisms – fun to spot, rather than a distraction – and CGI work that feels more 1990s than 2020s, that can be excused because so much else is dead right. Malcolm Marshall's slanting run-up and little skip of celebration? Check. Dickie Bird's white cap, and bellow ("Out!") that sends a nation into ecstasy? Check. Officious Lord's gateman? Check.

The last ten minutes of metaphorical (and literal) flag-waving may not please everyone, but what comes before is as entertaining as what came after. The likes of Sachin Tendulkar, M. S. Dhoni and Virat Kohli have captured the Kapil magic ever since.

Reliance Entertainment

Class of *83*: the ensemble cast, including Saqib Saleem as Mohinder Amarnath (middle row, left), Ranveer Singh as Kapil Dev (middle row, centre) and Tahir Raj Bhasin as Sunil Gavaskar (middle row, right).

It isn't easy making history. Just ask Nick Hockley, the new chief executive of Cricket Australia, whose goal to fill the Melbourne Cricket Ground for the 2020 women's T20 World Cup final is the focus of *The Record*, made for Amazon Prime by Nicole Minchin and Angela Pippos. The record in question is the highest attendance for a standalone women's sports event, though the narrative arc of the film is Australia's progress from nervous net sessions to raucous celebrations with the trophy (and Katy Perry).

The story is told through the now-familiar format of behind-the-scenes footage, supplemented by studio interviews. For the cricket fan, it's frustrating to see so little of the shape of the matches: the ebb and flow of Australia's route to the final is told largely through close-ups of players looking joyful, anxious or disappointed, depending on the (unseen) score, and images of fans correspondingly singing and dancing, gnawing their fingernails, or slumping in their seats.

There are some engaging interviewees, and the best is Beth Mooney, who top-scored in the tournament, and F-bombs in the documentary. That earthiness alone takes us beyond the predictability of post-match press conferences, but the relentless positive vibe, the dedication to the group ethos, and the hard sell of professional women's cricket as a sporting enterprise mean we never get to the acid drops and score-settling found in the best (and worst) autobiographies. While *The Record* may inspire young women, at long last, to be what they can see, it's hard to sustain two hour-long episodes on a man's quest to action one of his key performance indicators.

Gary Naylor writes The Final Over of the Week at The Guardian, *and reviews theatre for* Broadway World *and* The Arts Desk.

CRICKET AND TECHNOLOGY IN 2021

All you have to do is stream

LIAM CROMAR

Was it the comedy moment a fielder missed the ball, and was then hit by his team-mate's wayward return? Was it, instead, the one where the batsman simultaneously smashed a six and his own car window? Or perhaps it was the unscriptable masterpiece of yes–no–remonstrance, in which the disgruntled run-out victim accidentally took out his comrade with a flying bat. Whichever was your favourite, you had to see it to believe it – and with modern advancements, you and thousands probably have.

Slapstick has always been a staple of club cricket, but only in recent years has technology made live video streaming a realistic possibility in the recreational game. Now that high-quality digital video cameras, 4G and 5G internet speeds, large data allowances, wifi connectivity and computers are all widely available, many clubs have seen the potential to bring their game to the people – mishaps and all.

Throw in the pandemic, and more serious benefits become obvious. Matt Pickering of New Zealand tech outfit NV Play observed that video streaming has "turned a corner". He said he was "undecided whether it's because of, or in spite of, Covid", but added: "The restrictions to spectators have forced a rethink in terms of investment and effort to engage with fans at club level."

For NV Play, this involved extending new video-streaming functionality – rolled out for the county game in 2020 in what Pickering called "trial by fire" – down to the grassroots level via their Play-Cricket Scorer Pro software. Since it was used for Sky Sports' broadcast of the Bob Willis Trophy, this meant the recreational game had access to high-pedigree technology. However, software is only the second half of the picture – or strictly speaking, not the picture at all: obtaining usable footage in the first place is a major challenge. "If you don't understand it, video is hard," said Pickering.

To lower the hardware barrier, NV Play provided hundreds of live-streaming kits to ECB clubs, with prices ranging from £200 to £2,000. Similarly, Melbourne's InteractSport offered the Australian and UK markets the all-in-one solution FrogBox, a bright green case with camcorder, mast, video encoder and accessories (for £1,300, plus £500 annually for a streaming licence). DIY remains an option for those with the technical knowhow, time and patience; Philip Wolski, a video scorer for Colchester & East Essex CC, ticks those boxes, but recognises this can be challenging, and recommends the kit route.

Increasing the reach is the primary reward, but there are ancillary benefits. Wolski points to greater bar revenue (at least in non-Covid times), since players are more likely to hang around to review the highlights, or to watch the end of a concurrent match. And eyeballs translate into sponsorship opportunities: PCS Pro and FrogBox both offer built-in options to display logos.

Then there is the on-field impact. Wolski – also chairman of the Essex adult participation group for live streaming of cricket – believes "video has improved culture, etiquette and player discipline, and also the relationships between players and officials". It's much harder for a batsman to maintain he was sawn off when replays show him being hit on the toe in front of middle. As a scorer, Wolski has also found umpires learning how to make their signals clearer. Although some have been hesitant at the thought of video scrutiny, many have also sought out replays after the game, and acknowledged obvious misjudgments to the players.

It is no accident that both PCS Pro and FrogBox pair video with electronic scoring, so opening up opportunities for analysis – with no extra in-match burden on the scorers. Players or coaches can more easily identify and address technical weaknesses. On a broader level, live streaming provides a valuable talent-identification tool for representative cricket. But challenges remain.

First, streamed cricket brings the danger of corruption, as glimpsed in the amateur European Cricket Series: *Wisden 2021* reported on the suspension of one ECS team after suspicious betting. With their limited resources, recreational clubs may struggle to identify, let alone combat, such activity.

Second, as videoing becomes more common, expect pressure from players to review umpiring decisions (Seattle-based Fulltrack AI offer an iPhone ball-tracking system). The game's lawmakers might want to affirm that, unless permitted by competition regulations, decision-making is handled on the field, unaided by electronic technology. Players need to understand that a DRS-like system is neither realistic nor appropriate in a recreational context.

Third, there are privacy concerns, particularly in junior and open-age cricket. Even adults may object to their every blunder being exposed and recorded for posterity. Others may not wish to be filmed – either out of self-consciousness, because of their religious or cultural beliefs, or to preserve anonymity.

Participants have some legal safeguards, since such video footage is typically classed as personal information under data-protection legislation. But there is work to do to promote compliance. The ECB provided a videoing guidance document in 2019, but it lacked clarity (misspelling "GDPR" as "DGPR" was an inauspicious start), focusing on obtaining consent but failing to suggest how to proceed without it. Clubs that attempt to solve the problem by mandating consent will likely find themselves at odds with the GDPR, which requires it to be "freely given". A technological solution, such as automatic anonymisation and face-blurring, may be required, to avoid having to cut the feed entirely.

Assuming these challenges can be overcome, however, there is every reason to suppose that live video will play an ever-expanding role in refreshing even the parched corners of the game. Less stream, more flood.

Liam Cromar freelances in cricket at @LiamCromar, and in code at @Spinnerwebs.

CRICKET AND THE ENVIRONMENT IN 2021

Good COP, bad COP

Tanya Aldred

As the 21st century slips beyond young adulthood, cricketers have started finding their voice. Players raise topics once talked about only behind closed doors – racism, misogyny, abuse, depression. And as the scale of the emergency becomes clearer, a small but growing number want to talk about climate change.

The year dawned with the news that 2021 had been the fifth-hottest on record, despite La Niña's cooling effect. And it maintained a trend: 21 of the 22 hottest years have come since the turn of the century. The amount of carbon dioxide and methane in the atmosphere surged to record levels. Europe suffered its hottest summer, New Zealand its hottest year. In India, 1,750 people died because of extreme weather events, taking the number of climate-related deaths there to nearly 35,000 since 2010.

Perhaps because of COP26, the UN climate summit held in Glasgow in November 2021, sports broadcasters stepped up. Jonathan Overend's "Emergency on Planet Sport" podcast was joined by the BBC's "Sport 2050" project and Sky's "Summer of Sustainability". Ebony Rainford-Brent fronted a 13-minute Sky documentary, "Cricket's Climate Crisis", which discussed how the sport is being affected, what has been – and what needs to be – done, and the difficulty of trying to balance international cricket with its carbon footprint.

Several players made an appearance, including Shane Warne, Rohit Sharma, Katherine Brunt, Tammy Beaumont and Glamorgan's Joe Cooke. "I think about our future generations: what will they have?" said Rohit. "They'll have nothing if the world continues the way it is right now. They won't have fresh air to breathe, they won't have oceans to go and watch the marine life – that's something you think about every day."

Brunt recalled the time she spent in Australia during the bush fires of 2019-20 and, in typical no-nonsense style, said: "It comes down to making a sustainable change in your life, and not being lazy. We've created a lazy environment – people don't want to make an extra effort." The England women's team have been unusually proactive, and on their Ashes 2021-22 tour aimed to raise money to offset their flights through an Australian cricket climate-crisis initiative. The England and Australian boards hope it will become reciprocal.

Mady Villiers, England's young off-spinner, remembers when she first started worrying about the climate. Stuck in her bedroom around the time of the 2018 "Game Changer" report because of a stress fracture, she ended up in a vortex of videos and documentaries. She felt overwhelmed. "It really opened my eyes. Sometimes you feel very helpless. What can I actually do that will make a difference?" Her own answer was going vegan – team-mates bombarded her with questions – and she has also started a degree in

Joe Cooke

Friend of the Earth: Joe Cooke arrives at Glasgow.

environmental science at the Open University. After a visit to Loughborough from the ECB's sustainability manager, Kathy Gibbs, the whole team began to engage properly with the issues.

Before she headed to Australia for the Ashes, Villiers worried about her carbon footprint. "Flying stresses me out. It's not like football, where they're European flights: these are long-haul. I think longer tours are great – putting the Ashes and a World Cup in New Zealand in a single year avoids some unnecessary travel. But Covid has been a bit of a nightmare – a lot of single-use plastics, and we couldn't get coaches anywhere, so there has been a lot of driving around the UK, which we shouldn't be doing. It is about balance, and making sacrifices elsewhere, taking ownership for what we do outside cricket."

Australia's vice-captain Rachael Haynes was – like Brunt – shocked by the bush fires. "We were playing a game of club cricket very close to the harbour, which we actually couldn't see, even though it was the other side of the field. The game was stopped because of the smoke. There was ash coming from the sky, which was a really deep red – not uncommon in Sydney that summer. You would wake up, and the smoke would be in your lungs straight away. It was just so visual, it was undeniable. We need to make changes."

Motherhood has intensified those feelings. "I think you've got an obligation to leave things in a better place than when you inherited them. You hear a lot of players talking about a legacy in terms of the game – I can't help think that climate is more important, not just in maintaining an existence but in having a full life. I have an opportunity to shine a light on these type of issues: I've got a profile and a voice."

Haynes has been in contact with the Australian men's captain, Pat Cummins, and they both signed an open letter organised by David Pocock, the former captain of the Wallabies, the national rugby union team. It called on Australians to work towards reducing carbon emissions, and "safeguard the games we love". And in early February 2022, when Cummins launched his Cricket for Climate movement to great acclaim, Haynes was one of 13 players signed up. His goal is for cricket clubs across Australia to achieve net-zero emissions in the next ten years. This involves the players putting their hands in their pockets to drive practical change: the first initiative was placing solar panels on the roofs of 15 local clubs. Cummins also took an important stance by stating he would not accept personal sponsorship by a fossil fuel company. Rarely has an Australian cricket captain worn his Baggy Green with such metaphorical class. And he was supported by the Australian Cricketers' Association, who shortly afterwards announced they had signed up to the UN's Sports for Climate Action declaration.

"We are passionate as a playing cohort that it is not just something we are saying," said Haynes, "but that we are acting on at grassroots level." She is quietly scathing about the lack of leadership from the ICC: "I think, in all honesty, cricket is a little bit like that. I don't know if that's because they want to appeal to the masses, but we're beginning to see that what you stand for is really important, and advocating really strongly is not just for the good of the game, but the state of the earth. People are looking for guidance on what they can do. The ICC have a really important role to play here."

Back in the UK, Joe Cooke, a star of Glamorgan's trophy-winning Royal London Cup campaign, has been a leading voice. Already a volunteer at Friends of the Earth Cymru, he has been part of a campaign to urge supermarkets to put doors on their fridges, and in the autumn took on a role as his club's sustainability champion. He also attended COP26, and spoke on various athletes' panels. Cooke is encouraged by the number of cricketers now approaching him to discuss climate issues. "I go through waves of feeling," he says. "Before COP, I was very optimistic. After it, I had some very dark days, but I think it was a step in the right direction."

At 78, former Australian captain Ian Chappell is 54 years older than Cooke, but he's long been aware of the climate crisis: he has been married for 40 years to an activist who has been issuing warnings for over half that time. "I worry like hell about where we are going," he says. "You always like to see a good young cricketer coming along, but you worry now what their future is going to be. Cricket cannot be separated from the environment: it is all intertwined. It is a huge worry, and you wonder what you can do – probably very little."

Tanya Aldred is a freelance writer and editor, and founder of @TheNextTest.

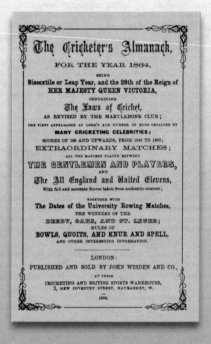

OBITUARIES

A'COURT, DENNIS GEORGE, who died on May 23, aged 83, was a brisk seamer who made an eye-opening start to his first-class career in 1960. In only his fifth match, he took six for 25 as Gloucestershire skittled the South African tourists for 49 on a helpful Bristol surface. "He kept his head, bowled a length along the line of the off stump, and left his natural swing and the pitch to do the rest," wrote John Arlott. *Wisden* went further: "He shocked the South Africans with his accuracy, liveliness, and disconcerting swing and movement." Gloucestershire made heavy weather of a target of 85, but crept home by three wickets. Less than a fortnight later, against eventual champions Yorkshire, A'Court took six for 69, five in quick succession with the second new ball. He finished that first season with 53 wickets, and added 71 in 1961, including a hat-trick to reduce Derbyshire to 43 for six at the Wagon Works ground in Gloucester. That brought his county cap – but, bothered by injuries, he made only seven more appearances before leaving the staff, and starting a successful electronics company in Bristol. "He was quite small in stature, but quicker than he looked," said David Graveney.

ALDRIDGE, BRIAN LESLIE, who died on December 9, aged 81, was an umpire from Christchurch who stood in 26 Tests and 45 one-day internationals, including the World Cup final between Pakistan and England at Melbourne in March 1992. "That was the pinnacle of his career," said fellow official Steve Dunne. "I believe his enthusiasm waned a little towards the end." After retiring in 1995, Aldridge became New Zealand's umpiring manager and – initially at least – was against the idea of video reviews, calling them "sanctioned dissent".

AMMAR MAHMOOD, who died of stomach cancer on October 29, aged 42, hit two centuries in Pakistan domestic cricket for Faisalabad. In 2007-08, in only his third match, he made 87 and 106 against WAPDA, and finished with 760 runs that season; in December 2013, by now captain, he scored 147 against Hyderabad. He also played club cricket in England, latterly for Cleckheaton in the Bradford League. "Life is so unpredictable," lamented Misbah-ul-Haq, who captained Ammar at Faisalabad Wolves.

AMONKAR, PRASAD ATMARAM, who died of Covid-19 complications on June 9, aged 56, was an opening batsman who played 22 Ranji Trophy matches for Goa, without surpassing the 74 he made on debut in January 1989 against Tamil Nadu, who had piled up 912 for six. He scored three other half-centuries, although his best innings was probably a battling 42, in three and a half hours, against Karnataka's Test new-ball pair of Javagal Srinath and Venkatesh Prasad on a green Bangalore pitch in December 1993.

ANDERSON, DALE THOMAS, who died on September 29, aged 90, played six matches for Tasmania over a decade from 1952-53 as a fast-medium bowler who could swing and cut the ball. His most satisfying effort was to have the future Test batsman Ian Redpath caught behind in both innings against Victoria at Geelong in 1961-62.

APTED, MICHAEL DAVID, CMG, who died on January 7, aged 79, was a distinguished film and TV director, probably best known for the *Seven Up* series of documentaries which followed a group of seven-year-olds in 1963. The concept proved so successful it has been revisited every seven years, with the subjects now in their sixties. Apted's bulging CV included award-winning movies, several episodes of *Coronation Street*, and the James Bond film *The World Is Not Enough*. Before all this, he opened the batting for the City of London School First XI with the future England captain Mike Brearley. They once put on 120 – of which, said Apted, he made three.

ARMSTRONG, WESLEY THOMAS, died on June 10, aged 88. Wes Armstrong was the head groundsman at the Basin Reserve in Wellington from September 1971 to March 1994. In that time, New Zealand won five and lost only one of 18 Tests there, on pitches he prepared using clay soil from Wairarapa. No shrinking violet, Armstrong crossed swords with Geoff Boycott, England's captain in 1977-78. "He was a bit of an arrogant guy. I came out with a fork in my hand, and he asked me what I was going to do with it. And I told him, before one of the umpires broke us up." The groundsmen's quarters were refurbished and named after him in 2015.

ARNOLD, ARNOLD PETER, died on September 6, aged 94. Peter Arnold sailed from his native New Zealand in 1950 with one aim in mind: professional cricket in England. He succeeded. Signed by Northamptonshire after a brief trial, he played for a decade, becoming a regular in 1954 – usually opening with the seemingly ageless Dennis Brookes – and receiving his county cap the following year. That season, his best, "Kiwi" Arnold scored 1,699 runs, with three of his five county centuries, including the highest – 122 against Somerset, when he and Brookes put on 230. Arnold also scored two hundreds for Canterbury, back in New Zealand in 1953-54. He retired after a subdued summer in 1960 to concentrate on his engineering business. Later, he served on Northamptonshire's committees, and was president from 1996 to 2000.

ASH, EILEEN MAY (*née* Whelan), who died on December 3, aged 110, was the longest-lived Test cricketer of all, having made her debut for England against Australia at Northampton in 1937. A seam bowler from north London, she took four wickets, including Australia's top-scorer Nell McLarty in the second innings. She played all three Tests that summer, and four more in Australia and New Zealand in 1948-49; she finished with ten wickets at 23. On that tour, though she did little in the Tests, she followed a century against a Victoria Country XI at Ballarat with a spell of five for ten. "We were pretty fit," she recalled. "I probably bowled at 60 or 70mph, and could bowl 16 to 18 overs in a spell."

Women's cricket was in its infancy when she started. Much later, she told ESPNcricinfo: "They treat women as cricketers now, whereas before they treated them as… you know… odd!" The game was certainly frowned upon at her convent school in Ilford, where she was forced to play hockey. "The Mother Superior is the only person who's ever scared me," said Ash. "She was so frightfully strict." But, having been given a bat when she was five, she did manage some cricket: "I used to play for my father's team because I was quite a good fielder – if they were one short, I'd play."

Women cricketers, even internationals, had to pay their own way back then: while playing at home was open to most, long overseas tours meant big sacrifices (or private means). The cricketers largely stayed with host families on tour, and Ash's luggage for Australia included a ball gown and posh frocks for functions. At such an event in Sydney in 1949, Don Bradman signed one of her bats. Years later, she kept it by her bed in case of burglars – and, past 100 years of age, confronted an intruder with it in her garage. Such exploits appeared to come naturally: she was seconded into MI6 during the war, and remained in military intelligence for 11 years; she refused to divulge details. Ash had started with the Civil Service: "They gave you time off if you played for England or your county. I thought it was a jolly good way of getting a couple of days off!"

She remained active after giving up cricket, taking up golf, squash, boules – and yoga, which she practised regularly almost until her death; she showed the England captain Heather Knight a few moves in 2016. "I've met teenagers who have a lot less energy," said Knight. "My pride – and a number of my muscle groups – are in tatters after being put to shame by a 105-year-old."

As the cricket world realised it had a remarkable centenarian in the ranks, Ash's renown grew. Behind the wheel of her trademark Mini ("I had four – I like a small car and it's quite speedy, the acceleration is good"), she appeared on a TV show about elderly drivers, and celebrated her 106th birthday in 2017 with a flight in a Tiger Moth, not long after ringing the pre-match bell for the women's World Cup final at Lord's, where she had been awarded life membership on reaching her century. Her portrait resides in the museum there. Ash had long since surpassed South Africa's Norman Gordon, who died aged 103 in 2014, as the oldest Test player. "Her energy was incredible," remembered

Ash and willow: Don Bradman signs a bat on New Year's Day, 1949, while Eileen Ash, its owner, looks down.

Isabelle Duncan, the author of a history of women's cricket, who sat alongside her as England beat India in that final. "She was drinking champagne in the president's box, and flirting with John Major."

The England men's team wore black armbands in her honour on the first day of the opening Ashes Test in Brisbane.

BAKER, DAVID WILLIAM, died on December 26, aged 86. A prolific leg-spinner for the Honor Oak club, "Doughie" Baker had four seasons on the Kent staff from 1960. He took a lot of wickets for the Second XI, but found the step up harder, although he did claim 40 in 14 first-team games in 1961, and two years later added five for 90 against Somerset at Taunton. Baker joined Nottinghamshire in 1964, and again did well for the Seconds – he took 12 wickets in one game against Lincolnshire – but made only seven appearances for the Firsts.

Another time, another time: Lucy Baldwin outside Lord's, 1923.

Trinity Mirror/Mirrorpix/Alamy

THE WOMEN WISDEN MISSED

Tea at No. 10

BALDWIN, LUCY, COUNTESS BALDWIN OF BEWDLEY, GBE, died on June 17, 1945, two days before her 76th birthday. Amid the national emergency of the General Strike in May 1926, the wife of the prime minister might have been too distracted to worry about sport. Not Lucy Baldwin. While husband Stanley grappled with the crisis, she welcomed fellow members of the White Heather Club, one of England's oldest women's cricket clubs, to No. 10 Downing Street for a meeting. It was a sign of her deep commitment to her favourite sport.

Born Lucy Ridsdale, she was brought up in the East Sussex village of Rottingdean, where she met Baldwin, then working in his family's iron and steel business. While visiting his uncle, the artist Edward Burne-Jones, he would sometimes watch the Rottingdean women's team, for whom Ridsdale played. Burne-Jones introduced them in September 1891; the following spring, they were engaged. The relationship transformed her cricket. "I was frightfully nervous when I went in," she told Australian captain Herbie Collins in 1926. "But when I became engaged to Mr Baldwin, I lost all my nervousness." They were married in September 1892; Rudyard Kipling was a guest. "It was the year I was married that I made my best batting average, 62 runs for the season," she said.

Baldwin became a member of the White Heather Club in 1890, and remained one for the rest of her life. The club were enjoying a boom: by 1891, they had 50 members, "all of gentle birth". In 1930, she wrote to Marjorie Pollard (see *Wisden 2021*, page 272) with congratulations on the first issue of *Women's Cricket* magazine. "The crack of the bat against the ball amid the humming and buzzing of summer sounds is still a note of pure joy," she wrote. She invited the 1937 Australian women's team to tea at No. 10.

After her first child was stillborn in 1894, Baldwin became a campaigner for improvements in maternity care. She persuaded the cricket-loving philanthropist Sir Julien Cahn to fund a maternity hospital at Bewdley in Worcestershire. It was named after her, and he installed a plaque placed over the entrance: "What she wanted most in the world."

For too long, these obituaries largely ignored women's cricket. In the coming years, Wisden will publish details of significant figures whose death was overlooked.

BANERJEE, RABI, who died on June 9, aged 70, was a seamer who played ten Ranji Trophy matches for Bengal in the 1970s, never taking more than two wickets in an innings. He also had an excellent memory. "We did a number of sports-quiz programmes," said broadcaster Gautam Roy, "and I was amazed to realise his depth of knowledge."

BANSAL, SUMIT, died of a heart attack on October 10, a few days after being hit in the face by a deflected straight-drive while umpiring a club match in Delhi. Bansal, who was 46, stood in 19 List A games, and a Ranji Trophy match in 2009-10. His father, Shyam Kumar Bansal, umpired six Tests and 30 one-day internationals.

BAROT, AVI ARUNBHAI, who died of a heart attack on October 15, aged 29, was a capable all-rounder who was part of the Saurashtra side that reached three Ranji Trophy finals, suffering two defeats before they won the competition for the first time in 2019-20. Barot also played for Gujarat, and for India's Under-19 team (he was the BCCI's Young Player of the Year in 2011). He made one first-class century – 130 for Saurashtra against Rajasthan at Jaipur in 2017-18 – and flayed 122 from 53 balls in a T20 match against Goa in January 2021. His captain in that match, the Indian left-arm seamer Jaydev Unadkat, remembered: "Right from our Under-19 days to the Ranji title, and our synchronised clap routine (which you invented), we've shared it all, my friend."

BASCOME, OSAGI, died after being stabbed outside a restaurant on St David's Island, Bermuda, on December 18. He was 23. A footballer who had been on the books of Aston Villa, Bristol City and Darlington, he won 19 international caps. His brothers Okera, Onias and Oronde all played cricket for Bermuda, as did their father, Herbert; Osagi himself had been prominent in local cricket with the St George's club.

BASSON, DR WILLIAM, died on July 19, aged 80. A long-serving administrator from the Northerns Cricket Union (formerly North Eastern Transvaal), Willie Basson was their president from 1980 to 1990, and in 2012 had a spell as acting-president of Cricket South Africa. He was also involved with the national Olympic committee, around the time of reintegration. "Few people have made a bigger contribution to sport in South Africa," said CSA chair Lawson Naidoo, "particularly during the difficult period of unifying sport here." Basson was also professor of chemistry at Pretoria University.

BENDRE, VIVEK, who died of Covid-19 on April 25, aged 59, was an Indian photographer specialising in sport – particularly cricket – for *The Hindu* newspaper and *Sportstar* magazine.

BENJAMIN, JOSEPH EMMANUEL, died of a heart attack on March 8, aged 60. Fast bowler Joey Benjamin came late to first-class cricket, but quickly made up for lost time. In 1994, aged 33, he made his Test debut in the final match of the series against South Africa at The Oval, his home ground. He had an outstanding first day, walking off with four for 42, including Hansie Cronje and Kepler Wessels. "Bowling an admirably tight off-stump line and taking his wickets with balls of full length, he took his haul of first-class wickets for the season to 75," wrote Christopher Martin-Jenkins in *The Daily Telegraph*. "I seriously thought I was dreaming," said Benjamin.

But with South Africa eight down, he was not given the ball next morning, and missed out on a five-for. In the second innings, he bowled 11 wicketless overs, as a rampaging Devon Malcolm took nine for 57. Still, Benjamin had done enough to earn a place on that winter's Ashes tour – a fitting end to his best season. With the Surrey seam attack beset by injuries, he bowled nearly 600 overs – "ploughing his lone furrow," said *Wisden* – and took 80 wickets at 20, finishing sixth in the first-class averages. "He carried our attack that summer," said fellow Surrey seamer Martin Bicknell. "He was outstanding."

In Australia, though, he had a miserable time. Benjamin and Malcolm, his room-mate, contracted chickenpox 48 hours before the First Test. He had played in three of England's four warm-up matches, but modest returns meant he probably wouldn't have been selected, and the management seemed to lose faith. He went two months without a first-class game,

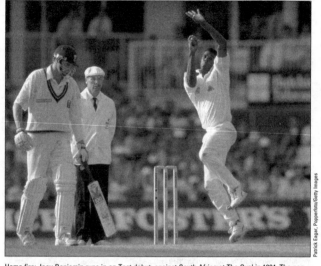

Patrick Eagar, Popperfoto/Getty Images

Home fire: Joey Benjamin runs in on Test debut, against South Africa at The Oval in 1994. The non-striker is Fanie de Villiers, the umpire Steve Dunne.

and a couple of one-day appearances, against Australia and Zimbabwe, were scant consolation. Angus Fraser and Chris Lewis, who had both been flown out to bolster an injury-ravaged squad, were chosen ahead of him later in the series, and Benjamin returned angry and disillusioned. "I felt like I had been picked just to give our batsmen practice in the nets," he said. "By the end of the tour I was embarrassed to be there – people back home thought I had chickenpox for three months."

Born in St Kitts, Benjamin moved to the Midlands in the early 1970s. He played for Dudley in the Birmingham League, where he was coached by Ron Headley, who quickly spotted his potential. Headley's son, Dean, remembered picking up Benjamin at the family's sixth-floor flat; he would put his kit in the rubbish chute to avoid carrying it down the stairs. He first played for Staffordshire in 1986, and was offered a contract by Warwickshire two years later, making his first-class debut aged 27. In 1990, he managed 43 wickets, but had limited opportunities the following season, and turned down a two-year contract to seek regular first-team cricket elsewhere. Five counties were interested, but Benjamin chose Surrey.

He settled in straight away, although a sponsored car, newly emblazoned with his name, was quickly returned when the club discovered he couldn't drive. Off a run of 25 yards, he bowled at about 85mph. "He was such a skilful bowler," said Bicknell. "He had a great wrist position that helped him move the ball away from right-handers." Benjamin was a member of the team that won the Sunday League in 1996, and the Benson and Hedges Cup the following year, although he did not play in the semi-final or final. Regardless, he was enormously popular in the dressing-room. "He treated everyone with respect," recalled Surrey captain Adam Hollioake. "Whether you were the prime minister, a security guard, a Surrey fan or a junior or senior player, he took people at face value."

Benjamin was a film buff with an encyclopaedic knowledge of cinema, and an avid reader. Although he eventually learned to drive, his team-mates usually found an excuse if offered a lift. He later played for Bromley, and Reigate Priory, and coached at Reigate Grammar School for over a decade. After his dream introduction to Test cricket, Benjamin was asked if he had any advice for players starting their career at 27. "If you're a bowler, don't," he said. "At that age, come in as a batsman."

BHAMJEE, ABDUL, who died on January 18, aged 82, was an opening batsman who played 15 matches now considered first-class for Transvaal's non-racial team in the 1970s, making 89 against Eastern Province on New Year's Eve in 1973. After his club, College Old Boys, won the local league in 1963, he persuaded them – along with two other teams – to apply for membership of the (white) Transvaal Cricket Association; none received a reply. Although his first love was cricket, Bhamjee was long linked with South African football, earning the nickname "Mr Soccer" – but that came to an end when he was charged with fraud over missing funds, which he claimed were due to him as compensation for time spent away from his own business. Bhamjee remained popular, with colleagues praising his "oratory skills and chutzpah as a sporting promoter".

BHAMJEE, EBRAHIM AHMED, died on March 24, aged 69. "Chicken" Bhamjee was a wicketkeeper who played 22 first-class matches for Transvaal's non-racial team in the 1970s, making 14 stumpings to go with 49 catches. He was, wrote Donald Woods in *Wisden 1993*, "regarded by some sound judges as being at least as good as [his] counterparts in the white cricket world". Bhamjee later moved to Botswana, and chaired their national cricket association for many years.

BOHRA, SANJAY, who died of Covid-19 on March 2, aged 50, was an Indian journalist and broadcaster who covered cricket for various English and Hindi outlets. He was part of the Sky commentary team when England toured India in 1992-93.

BOKHARI, SYED IFTIKHAR ALI, died on November 10, aged 86. A member of an influential Punjab family, "Iffy" Bokhari was close to selection for Pakistan during a varied first-class career. While studying in England, he averaged 72 for Cambridgeshire in 1956, winning the Wilfred Rhodes Trophy as the leading Minor Counties batsman, but made only one appearance the following year for a strong Cambridge University side captained by Ted Dexter. Back home, Bokhari hit 203 for Lahore against Punjab University in 1960-61 before retiring hurt, and ended the season with an average of 178; he was irked that *Wisden 1962* overlooked the fact that his big innings was unfinished, denying him a place at the top of their averages. He later became a politician, serving in the senate and as minister for finance. His brother, Zulfiqar Bokhari, was chairman of the Pakistan board from 1995 to 1998.

BORDE, RAMESH GULABRAO, who died on July 8, aged 69, was a leg-spinning all-rounder who played 36 Ranji Trophy matches for Maharashtra. His first, in 1972-73, was one of the last in the distinguished career of his brother Chandu – his senior by 18 years – who won 55 Test caps. In 1981-82, Ramesh claimed his best figures of five for 30 against Baroda; in the next match, against Saurashtra, he made a career-best 124. He also played for West Zone against the 1983-84 West Indian tourists, when his three wickets included Richie Richardson and Larry Gomes. Latterly he worked as the head groundsman at the international ground in Pune, where England played three ODIs in March 2021.

BOWDEN, DOUGLAS WILLIAM, died on January 20, aged 93. Doug Bowden was a left-hander from Manawatu who hammered 234 against Hawke's Bay in the Hawke Cup, for New Zealand's minor associations, in March 1954. Bowden played for Central Districts when they made their debut in the Plunket Shield in 1950-51, and was part of the side that won the Shield for the first time three years later. In the last match that season, he made 60 – his highest first-class score – in the title-clinching victory over Canterbury.

Graham Barclay, Bloomberg/Getty Images

Lord's of all he surveys: Keith Bradshaw in 2007.

BRADSHAW, KEITH, who died of cancer on November 8, aged 58, was a left-field choice as MCC's chief executive in 2006. A chartered accountant from Tasmania, for whom he played 25 first-class matches in the 1980s – his two centuries included one against a Queensland attack led by Jeff Thomson – he was recommended to throw his hat into the ring, and originally thought he was applying to run the Melbourne Cricket Club. Instead he found himself in Marylebone, and became the first man chosen by head-hunters to get the top job at Lord's. Christopher Martin-Jenkins joked that having an Australian in charge made him "the enemy within", but a sunny personality won over the doubters, and Bradshaw set about making Lord's a more approachable place. He tried to telephone two members every day, and regularly chatted to those queuing outside the gates before big matches. While embracing the traditions, he remained proudly Australian, installing a barbecue in his grace-and-favour house behind the Pavilion (which he thought might be haunted), and raised a few eyebrows with a colourful personal life.

Bradshaw will be best remembered for championing the pink ball for use in first-class and Test matches under floodlights; he later took over the South Australian Cricket Association in Adelaide, and was instrumental in the first pink-ball Test being played there, against New Zealand in November 2015. He also came up with the idea of asking celebrities to ring the five-minute bell before big matches at Lord's; the tradition has spread to Adelaide Oval, where they ring the newly cast Bradshaw Bell.

He had left Lord's in 2011 after his mother died suddenly, but admitted he might have been forced out anyway because of his support for the controversial Nursery End redevelopment scheme, which was eventually rejected by the MCC committee (and, in due course, by an overwhelming majority of members). While at Lord's, he had his first skirmish with multiple myeloma; he went into remission twice, but knew it was incurable. "He uniquely embodied and enhanced the personalities of both Lord's and Adelaide Oval – no mean feat," said fellow player-turned-administrator Tony Dodemaide. Darren Lehmann, who worked alongside Bradshaw in South Australia, called him "a brilliant administrator and cricketer, but more importantly a great man and friend".

BRANCKER, RAWLE CECIL, who died on July 27, aged 83, was a left-handed all-rounder from Barbados who came close to appearing for West Indies: he toured England in 1966 without playing a Test, after being controversially selected ahead of the uncapped Clive Lloyd. Brancker followed six wickets with his left-arm spin against Gloucestershire with a career-best seven for 78 against Kent. He had been an outstanding schoolboy batsman, and scored five first-class centuries – one against the 1964-65 Australian tourists – but failed to fire in England, managing a best of 33; with Lance Gibbs ensconced in the Test side, any other spin was provided by Garry Sobers and the leg-breaks of David Holford. Brancker had been part of the Barbados team that won the inaugural Shell Shield in 1965-66, and retained it the following season. He played for them until 1970, then carved out a successful business career. Former Test fast bowler Wes Hall gave the eulogy at his funeral. He recalled their first conversation about cricket, 75 years previously in front of the gates of Combermere School – and their last, four days before his death, when he was "so vibrant, so happy".

BROOKS, GORDON FRANKSHOT DELISLE, who died on June 29, aged 81, was an award-winning photographer from Barbados, who ran his own agency and was a director of the island's *Nation* newspaper. He produced a book, *Caught in Action: 20 Years of West Indies Cricket Photography*, in 2003. Brooks was particularly proud during a visit to Lord's to discover several of his photos on display. "He made a name for himself and for Barbados with some of the finest photography to be found anywhere," said the island's prime minister, Mia Mottley. Brooks's son, Randy, also a photographer, was highly commended in the MCC–Wisden Photograph of the Year awards in 2016.

BROUWERS, NIGEL GRANT, died of Covid-related complications on July 3, aged 44. His mother died the same day, and his father later that week; all three were buried together. Brouwers was a well-built, left-handed all-rounder, and good slip fielder, who played for South Western Districts, based in Oudtshoorn in South Africa's Western Cape. He also appeared a few times for Eastern Province and Northerns. A clean hitter, he smashed 94 from 47 balls, with seven sixes, in a one-day game against Kei in 2006-07, after taking three for 17 with his slow left-armers. His best first-class figures were six for 57 against Griqualand West B in February 1999. "He was one of the most talented cricketers I have known," said the former Test opener Alviro Petersen, who emerged from the same club in Gelvandale, Port Elizabeth.

BROWN, DAVID WYNDHAM JAMES, who died on August 17, aged 79, turned out regularly for Gloucestershire between 1964 and 1967. A batsman from Cheltenham, he came close to 1,000 runs twice: 900 in 1965, and 952 in 1966. But, with opposing fast bowlers sensing unease against pace, he was released after averaging 18 the following season. His only century – "driving grandly" in what *Wisden* called "a dashing innings of 142" – came against Glamorgan at Bristol in 1965, when a fourth-wicket stand of 186 with the unrelated Tony Brown ensured Gloucestershire saved the match after following on. Another highlight came at Cheltenham College in 1967, when Brown made 60 against the Pakistan tourists. "Being a local boy, I knew a lot of people, and it was lovely to walk off to a local crowd, getting a lot of applause and cheers."

BUCKINGHAM, PROFESSOR AMYAND DAVID, CBE, FRS, died on February 4, aged 91. Sydney-born David Buckingham was a distinguished and decorated chemist, who was a professorial fellow at Pembroke College, Cambridge, from 1970 to 1997. "A brilliant scientist, responsible for a number of ground-breaking discoveries in the field of chemical physics and molecular science," said Lord Smith, the Master of Pembroke. "He had a scientific unit of measurement named after him [the unit of electric quadrupole], a signal honour in tribute to his towering status." While studying at Cambridge in 1955, he had played four first-class matches, missing out on a Blue despite scoring 43 against Yorkshire ("Buckingham dealt competently and carefully with Trueman," said *The Times*) and 52 not out against Essex. He later played six first-class games for Free Foresters against the universities, making 61 – and sharing a century stand with the Australian Test batsman Ian Craig – at Fenner's in 1957. Buckingham was the only man to have been treasurer of both Oxford and Cambridge's cricket clubs, and was the Cambridge president for 19 years from 1990.

BURGESS, ALAN THOMAS, who died on January 6, aged 100, was a left-arm spinner who took nine wickets on his first-class debut, for Canterbury against Otago at Lancaster Park in Christchurch over Christmas 1940. His career was derailed by the war, which he spent as a tank driver in Egypt and Italy, where he was involved in the Battle of Monte Cassino. In the summer of 1945, he turned out for a New Zealand Services team in England, making his highest first-class score of 61 not out at Scarborough; he treasured memories of playing alongside Martin Donnelly, perhaps his country's most graceful batsman, and fast bowler Tom Pritchard, one of only three other New Zealand first-class cricketers to make it to the age of 100. Back home, by now playing more as a batsman, Burgess resumed with Canterbury until 1951-52.

His father, Tom Burgess, umpired the First Test against England at Lancaster Park early in 1933, when Herbert Sutcliffe was dismissed by the first ball of the match, and opening partner Eddie Paynter also went without scoring (Wally Hammond redressed the balance with 227). Alan had succeeded another 100-year-old, the Indian Vasant Raiji, as the world's oldest male first-class cricketer in 2020. He spent what turned out to be his last day watching coverage of Kane Williamson's double-century against Pakistan at Christchurch's Hagley Oval; there was a minute's silence in his honour before the start of the fourth day.

BUTTSWORTH, FREDERICK JAMES, died on May 11, aged 93. A stylish batsman, capable of exhilaratingly powerful driving, Fred Buttsworth played for Western Australia in their early seasons of Sheffield Shield cricket. His most valuable contribution was 60 against Queensland at the Gabba in 1947-48, when he and Dave Watt put on 125 to lay the foundations of a victory that ensured the newcomers would win the Shield at their first attempt. He was also a superb Australian Rules footballer: a Perth newspaper headlined one interstate game as "Buttsworth beat Victoria". His father, also Fred, played for WA in the 1920s, his fast bowling being overshadowed by a rapid 100 from No. 10 against Victoria. An older brother, Wally, played twice for WA in 1937-38, before moving to Melbourne, where he excelled at Aussie Rules for Essendon.

CASSIEM, MOEGAMAT GIELMIE, died on September 16, aged 67. An unlikely hero at Newlands in Cape Town, "Boeta" Cassiem sold ice cream around the ground for some 55 years, dispensing cheery rhymes such as "a lolly to make you jolly", and advising customers to "keep the change" he gave them. A plaque recognising his long association was unveiled at Newlands in March 2021, and Ashwell Prince and J-P. Duminy were among prominent local players who paid tribute.

CHALLIS, JOHN SPURLEY, who died on September 19, aged 79, was an actor best known for portraying dodgy car dealer Boycie in the long-running TV comedy *Only Fools and Horses*. He was a lifelong cricket fan, supporting Somerset. He played as well, as he told *The Cricketer* in 2017: "I used to be obdurate yet elegant. It was all to do with style. The nearest I got to a century was 96 at school. I have a great memory of it. I was given a full toss outside leg stump. I swung wildly, it came off the edge, hit the wicketkeeper on the head and I was caught at slip. A ridiculous comedy moment."

CHANDORKAR, RAGHUNATH RAMACHANDRA, who died on September 3, aged 100, played seven first-class matches in India. His debut, for Maharashtra in 1943-44, started promisingly: Bombay slipped to 90 for five, before Vijay Merchant (359) put on 371 with Rusi Modi. Bombay eventually reached 735. Chandorkar, who sometimes kept wicket, had a highest score of 37, against Sind in 1945-46. Some sources have his year of birth as 1922, but his passport said 1920, which would make him the third Indian first-class cricketer to reach 100 years of age.

CHIKANE, SUBHASH, who died of Covid-related complications on September 22, aged 59, was an all-rounder from Mumbai – known for big hitting, despite only one hand. He captained India's Disabled team against England in 2002-03. His 96-year-old mother also succumbed to Covid, the day before his death.

CLIFFE, DESMA NOELINE, died on September 7, aged 94. Noeline Cliffe was an early stalwart of women's cricket in New Zealand, playing 51 matches for Auckland over a quarter of a century from her debut in December 1944. Initially more of a bowler, she took five for 28 against Canterbury at Hagley Oval in Christchurch in 1945-46; two decades later, she hit 81 against Otago. In her last senior game, against the 1968-69 England tourists captained by Rachael Heyhoe, she scored 38. Cliffe was the oldest Auckland player – man or woman – at the time of her death.

COLEMAN, BERNARD, OBE, died on November 13, aged 97. A shrewd businessman who ran a chain of pubs in south London, cricket-loving Bernie Coleman helped drag the game into the commercial era. His portfolio included the Dog and Fox in Wimbledon Village, and the Castle in Tooting Broadway, from where Coleman would nip to The Oval during quiet times. He was courted by several players to help with their benefits, and was eventually elected to the Surrey committee, despite murmurings from members more used to retired military types.

Raman Subba Row, the former Surrey and England batsman who had become a forward-thinking administrator, spotted a like mind. Between them (and helped by Derek Newton, who also died in 2021) they transformed a cash-strapped county with innovative sponsorships. Gubby Allen, then the *éminence grise* of Lord's, turned even greyer when he saw an advertising board at The Oval in 1968: "What on earth is that?" Coleman explained: "That, Mr Allen, is £500, and we're skint." Two decades later, Allen was similarly unimpressed by a million-pound contract for the ground to be renamed the Foster's Oval after sponsorship from the Australian beer company. "I brought all sports into the 20th century," said Coleman, whose other initiatives included a pop concert in 1971, which attracted 40,000 people (and was overseen by one policeman). "Until then, nobody had named a ground, or thought of marketing. They were all very backward."

Subba Row was also a big wheel over the river at the Test and County Cricket Board, the forerunner of the ECB, and recruited Coleman to their marketing committee; he later took over as chairman, and stayed for 18 years. One notable change came in the county

Drinking it in: Bernie Coleman (far right), Doug Insole, Elton John and Alan Smith celebrate an England victory at the MCG, December 1986.

knockout competition, which had been sponsored by the same company since its inception in 1963. "I sacked Gillette!" laughed Coleman. He had discovered they had offered just £30,000 to renew their contract in 1981, whereas the NatWest Bank had put up £100,000. And he was an early advocate of paid-for television, which eventually arrived in the shape of Sky: "Let us have a channel where people have the opportunity to buy the best."

After stepping down from day-to-day involvement, Coleman was Surrey's president in 1991, when the Queen opened the redeveloped pavilion and Bedser Stand. He spent several winters in Sydney, where he would play golf with Richie Benaud. In his time, Coleman also owned Wimbledon FC, and inaugurated a charitable foundation that supported young cricketers and journalists, and funded medical research. Surrey's chairman, Richard Thompson, said: "Without ego or malice, Bernie did more for Surrey than people will ever know. Never wanting the limelight or attention, he just wanted to help in any way he could. His contribution to English cricket was profound across an extraordinary 78 years of continuous membership of his beloved Surrey CCC."

COLLINS, JOHN RICHARD, died on June 18, aged 88. Jack Collins was a Melbourne umpire who stood in 40 first-class matches, including five Tests, in the decade up to 1975-76. After the last, against West Indies at the MCG, Clive Lloyd said he was "nervous and made too many errors", and insisted that Australia's best two umpires – Robin Bailhache and Tom Brooks – should officiate in the remaining Tests, which they did. Incensed at what he viewed as the Australian board hanging him out to dry, Collins resigned. He subsequently stood in six Super Tests in World Series Cricket.

COOK, DAVID ROLAND, who died on December 20, aged 85, was a left-arm seamer who had fleeting success for Warwickshire. In August 1967, he followed a career-best four for 66 against Yorkshire – including Geoff Boycott, Phil Sharpe and John Hampshire – with six wickets in the match against Kent. But he faded away the following season, after three games produced only three wickets. Cook, whose brother Michael also played briefly for Warwickshire, remained a prolific wicket-taker for Stratford-upon-Avon, and claimed nine for 22 for the Midlands Club Cricket Conference against I Zingari Australia in a tour match in Sydney in February 1977. He was also a talented rugby player.

CORNELL, JOHN SYDNEY, who died on July 23, aged 80, first entered the Australian consciousness as "Strop", the ineptly lecherous companion – never parted from his lifesaver's cap – to the eponymous eponymous chancer in the popular *Paul Hogan Show*. Unlike Strop, Cornell was a shrewd businessman: he produced and co-wrote the screenplay for Hogan's hugely successful film *Crocodile Dundee*, and its sequel.

Cornell also recognised the changing nature of Australian society, and its implications for cricket. By November 1976, he was co-managing Dennis Lillee and Rod Marsh, with agent Austin Robertson. The Test captain Ian Chappell had raised concerns about player remuneration after series against England and West Indies that attracted 1.5m spectators, but the Australian board, still dominated by Don Bradman, curtly rejected his requests for a pay review. Not long afterwards, following a discussion with Lillee, Cornell approached the TV magnate Kerry Packer and asked: "How would you like some cricket on Channel Nine? By next week, we can sign up the entire Test team. They earn a pittance. There isn't a cricketer in the world who wouldn't be in it." Packer liked the idea, and World Series Cricket was born.

Cornell was also in at the start of floodlit white-ball cricket, but eventually left the sports business to others. He lived in picturesque Byron Bay in northern New South Wales, where he bought acres of land in a popular holiday area, and lovingly restored an old beachside hotel. Like many of his ventures, it turned to gold: he sold it in 2007 for $A44m.

CRAIG, DENISE, who died on July 5, aged 79, chaired the New Zealand Women's Cricket Association at a difficult time in the 1990s: they were often short of money, before the merger of the men's and women's boards. Craig helped set up the Central Districts women's team, and was their first coach; she also managed the national side when England toured in 1991-92. A former wicketkeeper, she had a long career with Wellington, scoring 68 not out against Otago in January 1973.

CURTIS, ALAN VICTOR, who died on February 18, aged 90, was an adaptable actor and theatre director whose voice was familiar in cricket: from 1967, he was the man behind the public-address microphone for major matches at Lord's and elsewhere. He was a fixture as the master of ceremonies at the Players' Theatre near Charing Cross, often dashing there by taxi after stumps in a Test, and was a pantomime regular from the early 1950s, when he played the Sheriff of Nottingham opposite the young Morecambe and Wise. "He was one of the great panto villains, by all accounts the definitive Abanazar," remembered his friend Martin Milnes. Curtis brought a grand theatrical flourish to his cricket announcements, invariably beginning with a jaunty "Good morning, ladies and gentlemen, boys and girls…" He suffered a stroke in 1995, and stepped back from the microphone – temporarily, he assumed. But the cricket authorities stuck with his replacement, Johnny Dennis, as they were worried about Curtis's health; he outlived Dennis by more than four years.

DAVIDSON, ALAN KEITH, AM, MBE, who died on October 30, aged 92, was – with his long-time friend and captain Richie Benaud – one of Australia's last genuine all-rounders. A hard-hitting left-hander and an excellent close fielder nicknamed "The Claw", Davidson was also a versatile left-arm bowler, who pounded in off an economical run-up: his autobiography was called *Fifteen Paces*. Once he established himself as Australia's new-ball spearhead, in 1957-58 – more than four years after his Test debut – he took 170 wickets at 19. And in the historic tie against West Indies at Brisbane in 1960-61, he became the first to score 100 runs and take ten wickets in the same Test. "He could have been a Test batsman alone, because he had all the strokes and good technique," said Ted Dexter. "Not the man you wanted to see coming in at No. 8 when the bowlers were tired."

Davidson personified one of Australia's favourite stories, the boy from the bush made good. He grew up among the orange trees of Gosford, 50 miles north of Sydney, and in school cricket had his first jousts with Benaud, who recalled: "We were both spin bowlers, attacking batsmen and keen in the field. Davo was a left-arm spinner – not orthodox but over the wrist. He was very good, but had to give that away when the skipper of the Gosford area team found his opening bowler hadn't arrived, and gave the new ball to Alan."

The 20-year-old Davidson was tipped for stardom after a promising debut season for New South Wales in 1949-50 brought him 26 wickets, and a trip with an Australia B-Team to New Zealand, where he took all ten Wairarapa wickets for 29, then smashed 157 not out. But he faced a battle at NSW: Ray Lindwall and Keith Miller shared the new ball when not terrorising Test opponents, and Bill Johnston was also an Australian regular. To complicate matters, Queenslander Ron Archer had emerged as a promising all-rounder: he, Davidson and Benaud all toured England in 1953. Davidson played in each of the five Tests, hitting a bright 76 at Lord's, but an injury (and selectorial dithering as Frank Tyson sliced through the batting) restricted him to three appearances in the 1954-55 Ashes; he then sprained an ankle early on a tour of the West Indies. In England in 1956, he broke his thumb against MCC at Lord's, before chipping a bone in his ankle in the First Test. On that tour, with Lindwall and Miller still ruling the roost, Davidson often bowled left-arm spin, including 44 overs in an innings against Surrey.

When Australia arrived in South Africa in 1957-58, he had a modest record from 12 Tests: 317 runs at 18, and 16 wickets at 34. But now, usually opening the bowling, he turned the corner dramatically. Swinging the ball both ways, often late, he took 72 wickets on the tour, 25 in the Tests. His batting developed too: he hit four centuries in all games, and an important 62 in the Fourth Test at Johannesburg. "On the sun-drenched veld, I became a matured Test cricketer," he wrote.

England arrived for the 1958-59 Ashes with what looked an excellent side. But Australia, now captained by Benaud, upset them 4–0. Davidson and Ian Meckiff – a more controversial left-armer, with a dubious action – harried the tourists from the start. Davidson's second over in the Second Test at Melbourne was a devastating demonstration of new-ball virtuosity: Peter Richardson nibbled outside off, then Willie Watson and Tom Graveney were beaten for pace. Davidson also had his first brushes with the man

Central Press/Getty Images

Spearhead: Alan Davidson in 1961.

who would captain England on the next tour. Dexter analysed him in typically forensic fashion: "Unlike the moderns who rush through the crease, Davo made a full turn, getting his front foot close to the stumps and then making a full body rotation. Swing and cut were a natural result. So he had good control, which accounts for his excellent career stats – details of which he always had readily available for anyone willing to listen."

Davidson's purple patch continued in the subcontinent in 1959-60. He got through 393 overs in the eight Tests (only Benaud bowled more), and reverted to brisk left-arm spin against India at Kanpur, where he took seven for 93. Then, at Brisbane in 1960, against Frank Worrell's West Indians, he followed 11 wickets with a commanding 80, which took Australia to the brink of victory, only to be run out after what he thought was a poor call from Benaud. The match ended in Test cricket's first tie.

A regular sight around this time was Davidson rubbing ruefully away at a niggle, and Benaud imploring his old mate for one more over. He usually responded. "We never knew if his injuries were imaginary or real," recalled team-mate Ken Mackay. "He would look and act as if he was dead on his feet, then bowl some unsuspecting batsman with a purler." Despite missing the Fourth Test with hamstring trouble, Davidson finished that 1960-61 series with 33 wickets, then undertook a third tour of England, where he turned the tide – and helped seal the Ashes – in the Fourth Test at Old Trafford. He hit a defiant undefeated 77, mostly in a last-wicket stand of 98 with Graham McKenzie that included 20 in an over of David Allen's off-spin. "These were not a wild slogger's swings," observed John Arlott, "but superbly made, measured strokes of immense power and timing." He was named as one of *Wisden's* Five Cricketers of the Year, with the accompanying essay written by Benaud, who was also chosen.

Davidson called a halt after one more Ashes series, in 1962-63, signing off with 24 wickets at 20, including one (Alan Smith) with his final delivery in Test and first-class cricket. Though greying at the temples, he was only 33, and still a considerable force. "His inswinger was often so pronounced as to be in the cartwheel category, and he retained the ability to slant the ball across," wrote local journalist Tom Goodman. "In a deadly spell in the Third Test in Sydney, Davidson resorted to fast-medium leg-cutters, and was well-nigh unplayable."

He became a respected administrator, a frequent sight at the SCG, with several trips to Lord's thrown in. In 1970, he started a 33-year stint as president of the New South Wales Cricket Association, an honorary post which involved criss-crossing the state promoting the game with unquenched enthusiasm; he was a Test selector from 1979 to 1984. His name was attached to NSW's schools' knockout competition. Lee Germon, the former New Zealand captain who is now chief executive of the NSWCA, paid tribute: "He was a wonderful player, administrator, mentor and benefactor, but most of all he was a gentleman of the game." A few years before, Benaud had pronounced: "There is no question Alan Davidson was one of the greatest all-rounders in history."

DEXTER, EDWARD RALPH, CBE, died on August 25, aged 86. The most charismatic English cricketer of his generation, Ted Dexter was, along with Garry Sobers, the most exciting batsman in the world in the early 1960s. Tall and correct, he rolled out cover-drives to delight the purists, while in defence, even against high pace, the ball usually hit the middle of the bat. "He seems to find time to play the fastest of bowling and still retain dignity, something near majesty, as he does it," said John Arlott.

Dexter packed 62 Tests into a relatively short career, captaining in 30, and hit nine centuries – although two of his best-remembered innings were shorter show-stoppers. At Old Trafford in 1961, he seemed to be hauling England to an Ashes victory with 76 – "the finest short innings I have seen in a Test," wrote Richie Benaud, who ended the fun with a magical bowling spell. Then at Lord's in 1963, Dexter took on the fearsome West Indian fast bowlers Wes Hall and Charlie Griffith in a rapid 70. "The earth itself seemingly stood still as he played one of the truly great innings of our time," eulogised Ian Wooldridge, who described the atmosphere when he walked off: "Anyone who did not feel some tiny tingle down the spine must have been soulless or very, very cynical."

Cricket was lucky to have had him. Dexter was adept at most sports, particularly golf, which he played to an advanced age. In the early 1960s, Jack Nicklaus and Gary Player admired his swing, and suggested he could become a tour professional. He also loved horse racing, once declaring Sussex's innings closed by phone from a local meeting; he later owned horses and greyhounds, and admitted to a bad gambling habit. A roving mind was rarely still. He wrote newspaper columns and commentated on television, ran a PR company, stood for Parliament, drove fast cars (or sometimes arrived at meetings in motorbike leathers) and piloted his own light plane: in 1970-71, he flew his family to Australia to cover the Ashes. His former England team-mate Fred Trueman quipped: "He had more theories than Darwin."

Perhaps his most lasting contribution to cricket was devising the rankings for batsmen and bowlers, now widely quoted in the media, in 1987. He wanted a better system than the conventional runs-divided-by-dismissals – adding, only half-jokingly, that he was "pissed off with Geoff Boycott always being top of the averages".

But then little about Dexter was conventional. He was born in Italy, where his father was an insurance underwriter in Milan. When he was later mulling over prospective jobs, Dexter wondered about following him into the business, because it had "clearly provided him with a comfortable life and enough leisure time to play as much golf as he wanted." At Radley College, he acquired his lifelong nickname, after forgetting to notify the local paper about the teams' results and – otherwise engaged at dinner – ringing the cricket master, Ivor Gilliat, and asking him to do it. "He referred to me as 'Lord Edward' from then on. And it stuck."

After national service, he went up to Cambridge, although he rarely attended lectures: he left during his finals, without a degree. Cricket was another matter. His maiden first-class hundred came at Fenner's, against Sussex in 1956, with one straight six off his bowling persuading their captain, Robin Marlar, that they should sign him up (the joke was that he qualified for Sussex because it was the nearest county to Milan). The following year, Dexter spanked an

Triple top: Ted Dexter during his 180 against Australia at Edgbaston, 1961. Wally Grout is the keeper, and Alan Davidson is at slip.

imperious 185 against Lancashire, whose influential captain Cyril Washbrook – a Test selector – thought he had rarely seen the ball hit harder. Dexter might have appeared for England that season, but picked up an injury and played little after the end of July.

The first cap was not long delayed. July 1958 was a heady month: Dexter led Cambridge to victory over Oxford, stayed at Lord's to play for the Gentlemen, and made his Test debut a week later at Old Trafford. He made 52, but the opposition were a weak New Zealand team, and he was omitted from that winter's Ashes tour before receiving a late call after some injuries. Pausing only to propose to Susan Longfield, his model girlfriend – "in order to deter predators in my absence" – he went to Australia, but managed only 18 runs in two Tests. Things perked up in New Zealand, with a boundary-studded maiden century at Christchurch. He also took three wickets with his waspish seamers.

A subdued summer saw him play only twice against India in 1959, but Dexter really blossomed as a Test cricketer in the West Indies early the following year. He hit 136 not out in the First Test, at Bridgetown, where E. W. Swanton observed: "He showed us some fine cricket, flicking the short ones to the midwicket fence with the least possible effort, and forcing off the back foot into the covers and past mid-off in a way that reminded the older school of Walter Hammond." He added 110 at Georgetown, and in all scored 526 runs at 65, his best series return. "In Dexter," declared Alan Ross, "we had found a successor to the luckless Peter May."

May, who had undergone an abdominal operation, missed the whole of the 1960 season, and Dexter – newly installed as captain of Sussex – was a contender to replace him. But Colin Cowdrey was the man in possession, and Dexter did not sparkle at home against the South Africans, although his Caribbean exploits may have helped in his being named one of *Wisden's* Five in the 1961 Almanack. But the return of the Australians that year brought renewed riches: Dexter applied himself for almost a day to save the First Test at Edgbaston, finishing with 180. That winter, with May virtually retired and Cowdrey unavailable, Dexter took over for an enervating tour of the subcontinent. "Travelling by road and staying in somewhat rudimentary guest houses was exhausting," he recalled, "although our hosts did their best to look after us, often in the most primitive conditions."

An England team lacking several senior players went down 2–0 in India, but won 1–0 to record a rare series victory in Pakistan. It was sealed in the drawn Third Test at Karachi, where Dexter made 205, his highest first-class score, and the joint-highest at the time by an England captain overseas. Leslie Smith delivered a mixed verdict in *Wisden*: "He played many fine innings… As a captain he learned as he went along, but never seemed to possess the inspiration which a leader needs to make ordinary players do so much better." It might have helped if he had won the toss more than once in eight attempts.

The Test captaincy was a season-long soap opera in 1962, with the choice between Dexter and Cowdrey complicated by the return of David Sheppard, briefly available again on sabbatical from the Church. Dexter eventually won the day for the Ashes tour, and many looked forward to him doing battle with the equally dashing Benaud. But the series was a disappointment, its attritional nature contrasting with Australia's recent games

HIGHEST TEST SCORES BY AN ENGLAND CAPTAIN ABROAD

263	A. N. Cook	v Pakistan at Abu Dhabi	2015-16
228	J. E. Root	v Sri Lanka at Galle	2020-21
226	J. E. Root	v New Zealand at Hamilton	2019-20
218	J. E. Root	v India at Chennai	2020-21
205	L. Hutton	v West Indies at Kingston	1953-54
205	**E. R. Dexter**	**v Pakistan at Karachi**	**1961-62**
193	M. E. Trescothick	v Pakistan at Multan	2005-06
190	A. N. Cook	v India at Kolkata	2012-13
188	M. H. Denness	v Australia at Melbourne	1974-75
186	J. E. Root	v Sri Lanka at Galle	2020-21
185*	M. A. Atherton	v South Africa at Johannesburg	1995-96

All smiles: former England captains Ray Illingworth and Ted Dexter after Leicestershire win the 1975 Benson and Hedges Cup at Lord's.

against West Indies. Dexter did well with the bat, though: his 481 runs (with a best of 99 at Brisbane) remains the most by an England captain in a series Down Under.

He kept the reins for the visit of West Indies in 1963 – the highlight that 70 in the exciting draw at Lord's – and for the 1964 Ashes. In that series, he responded to his opposite number Bob Simpson's 311 at Old Trafford with a studied 174; with Ken Barrington contributing 256, both sides topped 600, and there was barely time for Australia to start their second innings.

It was uninspiring stuff, and Mike Smith took over when Dexter initially made himself unavailable for the tour of South Africa. He had decided to stand as a Conservative candidate in the General Election, but had a tough opponent in his bid to win Cardiff South East: Labour heavyweight Jim Callaghan, later prime minister, increased a slim majority of 868 to a more comfortable 7,841, and became chancellor of the exchequer when Harold Wilson appointed his new administration. Dexter decamped to South Africa, where he revelled in the freedom back in the ranks: "It allowed me to relax and enjoy some spectacular tourism." In a series England squeaked 1–0, he hit 172 in the Second Test at Johannesburg, the last of his nine hundreds. It completed his set against the six available opponents.

Dexter missed much of the 1965 season – and that winter's Ashes tour – after breaking his leg in a freak accident, when his Jaguar broke down and he lost control while pushing it. The *Evening Standard's* John Clarke observed: "'Retired, ran himself over', the entry should have gone down in *Wisden*."

He never led England again, and the consensus was that his approach had erred on the defensive. Ray Illingworth – who, like Trueman, had an uneasy time under Dexter in Australia in 1962-63 – summed up: "I don't think he was ever a great captain, because he hadn't the powers of concentration that captaincy requires… Quite often he would be miles away playing a quite marvellous eight-iron shot to the green, while the ball was on its way to him in the gully. A good bloke, Ted, but not a great captain, in my opinion."

Dexter had greater success at county level, even if Sussex's first Championship title was still nearly 40 years off. But they did win the first two editions of the Gillette Cup, professional cricket's inaugural one-day competition, in 1963 and 1964. While other teams were playing it like a three-day game, he had twigged that the best way to keep scores down was to tell his seamers to bowl slightly short of a length, with the field spread wide. "He was the first to do this, and it wasn't very attractive," admitted county colleague Jim Parks. "He pushed the field back, and took second slip out, putting him in front of the wicket to stop the singles." In the first final, against Worcestershire at Lord's in September 1963, Sussex successfully defended a total of 168, with tactics Parks admitted were "unashamedly defensive and insidiously effective".

Dexter made a brief comeback to international cricket in 1968. A week before the Fourth Test against Australia, he played for Sussex against Kent at Hastings. Entering at six for two, he caned Derek Underwood and friends for a superb 203. The following day, he warned his *Sunday Mirror* readers they were unlikely to read his usual Test report the following week: "I've been asked if I'm prepared to play for England if selected. I've said 'Yes'." It wasn't a great success: he made ten and 38 at Headingley, then 21 and 28 in the Oval victory made famous by Basil D'Oliveira's 158.

That really was it at international level, after 62 Tests and 4,502 runs at 47. He played only one more first-class match, but appeared regularly in benefit and charity games, and also for Sussex in the Sunday League in 1971 and 1972. To prepare for those games, he once turned up to the practice nets on the Nursery ground at Lord's, and asked the bowlers – youngsters from the groundstaff, who disliked the task, as they had to stay late – to pitch it up so he could hone his cover-drive. According to legend, the first lad didn't think much of this instruction from a "jazz hat", so let him have his quickest bouncer. Dexter hooked it over the wall into Wellington Road, tucked his bat under his arm and – satisfied he still had it – strolled off, thanking Ian Botham for his efforts.

After he had finally finished playing, Dexter remained in the public eye, particularly when he became the first paid chairman of selectors in 1989. He kept the tabloids amused with more theories – one defeat was put down to Venus being "in juxtaposition to somewhere else" – and memorably asked everyone "not to forget about Malcolm Devon". Mike Atherton wrote in *The Times*: "He appointed me as England captain [in 1993]. I was always grateful for the faith and trust placed in me – even if he resigned midway through the first game I captained. I was very fond of him, and we stayed in touch until near the end."

Others tried to sum up a complex character. "Ted was a man of moods, keen when the action was hot, uninterested when the game was dull," said John Snow, a similarly mercurial performer for Sussex and England. But no one was in much doubt about his batting. "You had to have seen this guy to understand how good he was," said the broadcaster Mark Nicholas.

Dexter produced a lively second autobiography, *85 Not Out*, which came out in 2020, a few months before he succumbed to cancer. It followed *Ted Dexter Declares*, 54 years previously. He also wrote books on coaching and other subjects, and with Clifford Makins co-wrote two detective novels – *Testkill* and *Deadly Putter* – which featured a golf-loving England cricket captain.

He remained a stylish dresser – like his wife, he occasionally modelled clothes – and had a reputation for elegance into old age. A prominent chain of London estate agents was named after him by its cricket-loving founder, and he even made it into the Beatles' consciousness. Early in their famous Savile Row rooftop concert in 1969, the first number was received with a smattering of polite, cricket-style applause, as people in the street below were only just starting to realise what was unfolding above them. Paul McCartney quipped: "Ted Dexter's scored another."

DOLLEY, RICHARD BERTRAM, who died of Covid-19 on June 30, aged 61, was an all-rounder from a prominent sporting family in Port Elizabeth. He played 36 first-class matches for Eastern Province's non-racial team, being marooned three short of a century against Natal in 1987-88. Entering at No. 7, with his side 97 for five, Dolley shared substantial stands with Andre Peters and Allister Coetzee, and EP reached 311. He took exactly 100 wickets with his seamers, including six for 65 (nine for 90 in the match) against Transvaal in 1988-89. A deputy headmaster, he coached cricket and hockey. "He was a gentleman and a giant, an advocate for non-racial sport, and a dedicated teacher," said a colleague.

DORMER, MICHAEL EDMUND FRANCIS, died on April 19, three days before his 84th birthday; the family funeral notice said he had been "bowled by an inswinger". He kept wicket in four matches for Auckland, marking his debut by stumping the Test batsman Matt Poore on Christmas Day, 1961. Dormer founded The Willows CC, just outside Christchurch, and played a big part in it until his death. Many recalled his coaching mantra: "Always play in the V."

DOWNIE, JOSHUA, died of an apparent heart attack while practising in the nets in Birkenhead on May 6. He was 24, and held the record for the highest individual score – 137 not out – for the Nottinghamshire club Burton Joyce. His sisters, Becky and Ellie, are both Olympic gymnasts.

DUTTA, NILAYANANDA, died on September 19, aged 68. A senior lawyer who became the advocate-general of Arunachal Pradesh, Nilay Dutta was one of four members of the independent commission that investigated allegations of corruption in the 2013 IPL. He was also president of the Assam Cricket Association, and an umpire who stood in 15 first-class matches, plus a one-day international between India and Sri Lanka at Pune in December 1990.

EDINBURGH, THE PRINCE PHILIP, DUKE OF, KG, KT, OM, GBE, AC, QSO, PC, died on April 9, two months short of his 100th birthday. Lieutenant Philip Mountbatten married the then Princess Elizabeth in November 1947 and, after King George VI's death from cancer in 1952, spent the rest of his life as the Queen's consort, rarely far from her side. He performed myriad royal duties, but arguably those he enjoyed most involved sport – particularly cricket.

One half of a successful partnership: the Duke of Edinburgh at Dean Park, Bournemouth, 1949.

A useful off-spinner and attacking batsman, he had captained the school XI at Gordonstoun, and later occasionally raised his own team for special matches. In one, in 1949, his side against Hampshire at Bournemouth included England captains past and present in Gubby Allen, Walter Robins and Freddie Brown, as well as Denis and Leslie Compton; the wicket of Gilbert Dawson is recorded on the scorecard as "c Brown b Edinburgh".

He was president of MCC in 1949-50, when only 27, and had a second term in 1975, during which he presented the trophy after the first World Cup final. He was only the third person, after two 19th-century noblemen, to do the job twice. He also contributed an article – "The Pleasures of Cricket" – to the 1975 *Wisden*. It reads like an affectionate personal remembrance, and it seems doubtful any ghost was involved in its preparation. After pointing out that "Watching cricket without *Wisden* is almost as unthinkable as batting without pads", he enthused: "I enjoy everything about cricket. I suppose I must have played the game off and on from the age of eight until about 48, and I am sure I will go on watching it as long as I can."

Royal visits to Lord's – with or without the Queen – were a regular feature. David Dunbar, whose father was an MCC assistant secretary at the time, recalled one solo trip to meet the Australian touring team. Prince Philip drove himself, and the royal MG was expected at the Grace Gates. But time passed, and the assembled bigwigs began to fidget, worried he had had an accident, been kidnapped, or – worse still – gone to The Oval by mistake. It turned out the reception committee was not necessary: "Everyone was looking in the wrong direction. He had come in by the North Gate, found the far end of the line, and begun introducing himself, as it were backwards."

One of his final official engagements, before retiring from public life in 2017, was opening the new Warner Stand at Lord's. "You are watching the world's most experienced plaque-unveiler," said the Duke. Almost 96, he robustly declined the offer of using the lift to reach the restaurant high in the new stand.

FERNANDO, UPHEKA ASHANTHA, who died of a heart attack on October 26, aged 41, was a hard-hitting batsman from St Thomas' College who played alongside Kumar Sangakkara and Rangana Herath for Sri Lanka Under-19. He seemed destined for great things, and scored five centuries for Sinhalese Sports Club in Colombo, the highest 128 against Panadura in February 2001. But his first-class career was over before he turned 24: he ran into health problems, not helped by a fondness for alcohol, and developed diabetes.

FIELDEN, SIDNEY, died on December 15, aged 88. A detective sergeant in the police force and a Methodist lay preacher, Sid Fielden was a lifelong follower of Yorkshire cricket. He came to prominence as one of the leading lights in the Reform Group mobilised following the decision to strip Geoff Boycott of the county captaincy late in 1978, and later campaigned successfully to have him reinstated after he was sacked in 1983. But the pair eventually fell out when Boycott joined him on Yorkshire's committee while still a player, a conflict of interest of which Fielden disapproved. "Geoff Boycott is a very great cricketer," he later said. "I have known him for many years, through sadness and elation. But now I wish I had never met him." Boycott hit back at "Judas" in his 1987 autobiography: "He saw himself as the champion of Boycott the underdog, and he enjoyed the public notoriety that went with it. When I could make out my own case on the committee, Fielden may have felt he had lost some sort of starring role."

The *Yorkshire Post* cricket writer Chris Waters had a long friendship with Fielden, who kept detailed notes on cricket matters. "On one occasion, the cricket and the police work got comically mixed up," he recalled. "Sid was preparing to give evidence during an important trial when he suddenly realised he had brought along his cricket notebook by mistake. Consequently, he had plenty of info concerning the lack of soap in the Headingley toilets but rather less gen on the defendant. Sid winged it – and no one was any the wiser."

FITCHETT, MICHAEL KING, died on April 1, aged 93. After captaining Victoria in two matches against Tasmania in 1950-51, Mike Fitchett made an impressive start to his Sheffield Shield career the following season: 108 against Western Australia in Perth, then two games later an undefeated 97 off a Test-strength New South Wales attack led by Ray Lindwall and Keith Miller at the MCG. Melbourne journalist Hec de Lacy said Fitchett "drove, pulled and glanced in confident fashion, showing that big names meant nothing to him". He finished that season with 523 runs at 47 but, in the next, facing intense competition, he played only twice. He became one of Melbourne's leading amateur golfers.

FLAWS, THOMAS, died on June 24, aged 89. A tidy wicketkeeper from Dunedin, Tom Flaws appeared 27 times for Otago over a decade from 1952-53, making 29 stumpings – many off the Test leg-spinner Alex Moir – and holding 44 catches. There was general surprise when Artie Dick was selected as reserve keeper for New Zealand's 1961-62 tour of South Africa – where he played the first of his 17 Tests – as Flaws kept for both Dick's province and his club, Kaikorai.

FLEMING, ROBERT ATHOLL, who died on February 26, aged 87, had a successful career as a TV producer and director before, in retirement, becoming honorary secretary of the Primary Club, the charity for visually impaired cricketers. He served eight years, plus four as chairman and – with his wife, Marion – brought, in one colleague's words, "energy, wisdom and innovation" to the small operation. His TV credits ranged from the pioneering pop programme *Ready Steady Go!* and the talent show *Opportunity Knocks* to a profile of Cardinal Basil Hume. He later founded his own production company, and directed a ground-breaking series, *Flying Squad*, which included a wages snatch in which the police killed a robber. Fleming was a keen cricketer, purveying inswing for a light-hearted team called the Jolly Rogers. He was born and brought up in Australia, and exemplified traditional Aussie congeniality. He did lose his accent, though – except, according to his friend Frank Keating, when appealing for lbw.

FOOT, DAVID GEORGE, who died on May 25, aged 92, was one of the best-loved cricket writers of his generation. The affection came both from his colleagues, who delighted in his kind and gentle company, and from his readers, who sensed the warmth behind the graceful, sympathetic prose. Footy rarely went near a Test match, and most unusually had a highly successful career in journalism without venturing much from his West Country base. But he wrote for *The Guardian* for 40 years until 2011, and his fascination with interesting and often difficult characters made him the ideal chronicler of the years when the Somerset of Beefy and Viv were the most talked-about team in the country.

Foot was Somerset to the core. The son of an estate worker, he made his way to grammar school, weekly journalism and the *Evening World* in Bristol. When the *World* closed in 1962, he had a young family, and spurned the chance of Fleet Street. He remained in Bristol, working all hours as a jobbing freelance covering anything and everything, both for radio (he had a lovely voice) and print. In time, he was able to pick and choose, and he proved a classic *Guardian* man, writing provincial theatre reviews as well as epitomising a golden age of county cricket and the reporting of it. In 1985, having missed the tour of India, Ian Botham was back captaining Somerset – with dyed hair and renewed zest. He scored a 76-ball century against Malcolm Marshall and all, rescuing Somerset from 108 for six, and was still game for more. "The blond hair tops a face of buoyant challenge," wrote Foot. "The sheer strength of the man is remarkable. Here he was, in the evening, opening the bowling again, as if he'd been strolling round the Quantock hedgerows with his 12-bore all day."

Throughout, Foot wrote books – quickie local numbers and ghost-writing jobs at first to make ends meet, though even these produced something exotic: *Ladies' Mile*, the ghosted memoirs of a lavatory attendant in Bristol's twilight zone. He graduated to write two of cricket's most remarkable biographies, sweeping aside the conventions of genteel reticence to cover the subject's off-field flaws, and conducting a search for the truth about two of his boyhood heroes. *Harold Gimblett: Tormented Genius of Cricket* and *Wally Hammond: The Reasons Why* were compassionate as well as honest. The first was informed by very

Compassionate and honest: David Foot at Worcester in 2003.

personal tapes which Gimblett recorded and handed over to him before he committed suicide; it was a sign of the trust Footy inspired. And his vignettes of cricketing characters collected in *Beyond Bat & Ball* and the more eclectic *Fragments of Idolatry* comprised clusters of diamonds, often funny, usually poignant, all meticulously observed and beautifully written.

His work for *Wisden* included stints as the Almanack's correspondent for both Gloucestershire and Somerset. The esteem of his colleagues was marked in 2002 by the Cricket Writers' Club's Peter Smith Award "for the presentation of cricket to the public", the only time in its 30-year history that the prize has been won by a journalist outside the Test circuit. Part of that golden age was Footy's reporting of it, and the warmth he spread wherever he went.

GALLAWAY, IAIN WATSON, OBE, who died on April 18, aged 98, combined a career as a New Zealand lawyer with sports commentary for radio and TV. He covered rugby for 26 years and cricket for 40, giving up after the 1992 World Cup as he feared failing eyesight might cause mistakes. He was known as the "Voice of Carisbrook", since much of his work was carried out at the famous old Dunedin ground: he was upset when it was supplanted as the city's Test venue by the University Oval. He had seen every rugby international there, bar one: as president of the national cricket board, he was in England in 1999, watching New Zealand achieve their only Test win at Lord's. Shortly before, he had written *Not a Cloud in the Sky*, a lively autobiography. Much earlier, he kept wicket for Otago in three first-class matches, stumping Denis Compton in MCC's tour game at Carisbrook early in 1947.

GANNON, JOHN BRYANT, OAM, died on February 5, three days before his 74th birthday. A strongly built left-arm seamer, "Sam" Gannon had two bites at first-class cricket. He made his debut for Western Australia in 1966-67, taking six for 107 – his best figures – in his fourth match, against South Australia at the WACA. The following summer, he claimed 14 wickets at 18 as WA won the Sheffield Shield. But he stepped down after one game in 1972-73, sensing opportunities would be few in a side boasting the Test new-ball pair of Dennis Lillee and Bob Massie.

He kept fit in grade cricket for Scarborough and, when Lillee was among those who joined World Series Cricket in 1977-78, Gannon returned to the Shield side. He followed seven wickets in the match against South Australia with five against the Indian tourists, and was whistled up for the Second Test. On home turf in Perth, he took the last three wickets in India's first innings, and did well again in the second, with four in 29 balls transforming figures of none for 63. "Gannon cut a swath through the middle order and the tail – a wonderful, wholehearted debut," wrote Bob Simpson, recalled as captain aged 39. Gannon was equally delighted: "I got seven wickets, and my good mate Tony Mann got a century. To do it in front of our home crowd was fantastic."

He could not repeat the magic in the next two Tests, collecting four wickets – including Sunil Gavaskar for 118 at Melbourne – and was dropped for the decider. He was part of another Shield-winning side, but missed the West Indian tour. Next season, Test selector Neil Harvey suggested "the left-arm fastie from Western Australia could fill the bill" for the 1978-79 Ashes but, with Rodney Hogg running into contention, it did not happen; Gannon played only four Shield matches that summer before, still 31, retiring for good.

He carved out a highly successful career in the financial world – some estimated he was the richest former wearer of a Baggy Green – and played a part in cricket administration, serving terms on the board of Cricket Australia and as president of the WACA. He retained a sharp sense of humour, often recalling the time when, during his playing career, he was stopped for speeding. His attempts to talk his way out of a ticket provoked some sage advice from the traffic cop: "Concentrate on bowling faster and driving slower."

GHOSH, SUNIT KUMAR, who died on November 7, aged 87, was an umpire from Calcutta who stood in 37 first-class matches between 1972 and 1990, including two Tests against New Zealand in 1988-89. He also oversaw seven one-day internationals, notably the final of the Nehru Cup (a tournament involving six Test teams) at Eden Gardens in November 1989. Although West Indies lost the final to Pakistan, their manager Clive Lloyd and ICC chairman Colin Cowdrey congratulated Ghosh and his colleague Piloo Reporter on their performance, leaving them hugging each other and reflecting on "a red-letter day for Indian umpiring".

GIBBONS, GEORGE HENRY DENNIS, died on September 3, the eve of his 97th birthday. Wicketkeeper Dennis Gibbons played for Huntingdonshire throughout the 1950s, latterly captaining them. His club cricket was for Godmanchester and Huntingdon.

GILLAN, DAME CHERYL ELISE KENDALL, who died on April 4, aged 68, had been the Conservative MP for Amersham and Chesham since 1992. Born in Cardiff, she was Secretary of State for Wales from 2010 to 2012. She was a lifelong cricket enthusiast, and one of the first female MPs to play for Lords and Commons, the parliamentary team.

GLOVER, ED, was killed in a car accident in Kent on July 13, while returning home from a cricket match in Bexley which he had won with his beloved reverse sweep. He was 18. Also a good tennis player, Glover was a popular all-rounder for Simon Langton Grammar School, Street End CC and Canterbury Under-19. A celebration of his life was attended by over 500 people.

GOOD, DENNIS CUNLIFFE, who died on June 26, aged 94, had been Worcestershire's oldest surviving player: he appeared once for them in 1946, aged 19, against the Combined Services at New Road. Good opened the bowling and took one wicket – the future England batsman John Dewes – but had to watch Don Kenyon, soon to become a Worcestershire regular, make a century. He also had three games for Glamorgan in 1947, again claiming a distinguished maiden scalp, South Africa's Alan Melville. On his Championship debut, he removed Surrey's openers, then took four more wickets against Derbyshire before injuring his Achilles tendon. Good, who was born in Yorkshire and played as a professional in the leagues there, had been a prominent schoolboy cricketer for Denstone College. After studying at Leeds University, he emigrated to Canada for work in 1952.

GOODALL, FREDERICK ROBERT, ONZM, died on October 19, aged 83. An umpire who started young – he stood in his first Test, against Pakistan at Wellington in February 1965, not long after his 27th birthday – Fred Goodall officiated in 39 men's internationals, including 24 Tests, and the women's World Cup final in February 1982. He was best remembered for his part in an ill-tempered series against West Indies in 1979-80. New Zealand pinched the First Test at Dunedin by one wicket, with seven lbws for Richard Hadlee – all given by Goodall. In the next Test, at Christchurch, incensed by what they saw as more one-eyed umpiring, the West Indians first refused to restart for 12 minutes after tea on the third day, then were petulant on the resumption: at one point, Colin Croft ran in to bowl and barged into Goodall, knocking him sideways. Croft maintained it was not deliberate – "I'm six foot six and 230 pounds. If I'd meant to hit him, he wouldn't have got up" – but others weren't so sure. "It was a calculated attack," said Hadlee, the non-striker. Geoff Howarth, New Zealand's captain, was equally unconvinced: "Croft tried to pretend he'd lost his run-up. It was disgraceful. He should have been banned for life." Even Clive Lloyd, West Indies' captain, admitted the situation had got out of hand: "I wish those things hadn't happened, and no one wants black marks on his record. But it's a lucky man who gets through life without the odd confrontation." He added: "The officials were telling me the umpires were not accustomed to such fast bowling. 'What you really mean,' I replied, 'is that they're unable to umpire at this level.'" Goodall carried on, in 14 more Tests until 1987-88 with no such drama, although he had courted controversy by including what some construed as racist remarks in after-dinner speeches about the West Indians. In all, he stood in 102 first-class matches in over a quarter of a century until February 1989; that included a season in England in 1978 which, thought Hadlee, improved his umpiring immeasurably. His wife, Di Malthus, played for Wellington.

Avid scorer: Jimmy Greaves heads off in search of runs, 1958.

GREAVES, JAMES PETER, MBE, died on September 19, aged 81. Probably the greatest goal-scorer English football has ever produced, Jimmy Greaves hit the net a record 357 times in the First Division. He was equally prolific for England, with 44 goals in 57 matches, although he is remembered more for a game he missed – the 1966 World Cup final, when he was left out after an injury earlier in the tournament had given an opportunity to Geoff Hurst. A dry sense of humour later helped Greaves become a familiar face on television. Once, sympathising with a player experiencing a goal drought, he nodded and said: "All strikers go through barren spells. I had one. Worst 15 minutes of my life." Greaves was a keen follower of cricket, particularly Essex, and played occasionally. His son Danny recalled an incident in the garden: "I bowled him a ball, and he whips it off his legs – a hell of a cricket shot – straight into the greenhouse window, about 20 minutes before we were due to go on holiday to Portugal." He had been in poor health for some time after a stroke, and spent his last day surrounded by his family, watching coverage of T20 finals day.

GREEN, AARON, who died on July 12, aged 26, had been a popular captain of Sussex's Disability side. An opening batsman and left-arm bowler, he joined Middlesex in 2019, but various health complications, following a heart and lung transplant, meant he never played for his new side.

GREENWOOD, PETER, who died on November 30, aged 97, was a versatile all-round sportsman from Todmorden, who mixed off-spin with medium-pace in 75 matches for Lancashire between football commitments for Burnley and Chester. "I was on £5 a week when I signed for Burnley after leaving the navy in 1946," he said. "That was more than I would have got in the cotton mill, so I took it." After making his debut for Lancashire in 1948, Greenwood claimed five for 24 in his first Championship match, as Kent were skittled for 80 at Gillingham; next season, he was awarded his county cap, allying 572 runs to 75 wickets. That included a career-best six for 35 (and ten in the match) after taking the new ball against Northamptonshire at Old Trafford, "bowling off-breaks into a stiff breeze," according to *Wisden*. In 1950, he was part of the Lancashire team that shared the Championship with Surrey. The following year, he made his only century, 113 against Kent (plus five for 66), but his batting fell away: bothered by an arm injury, he averaged less than nine in 1952, his final season. He dismissed Len Hutton four times in Roses matches, including twice in the same game in 1948, and ran him out for a duck from the fourth ball of the match at Leeds in 1949. Greenwood, who lived to a greater age than any other Lancashire player, always remembered the silence that fell over Headingley as Yorkshire's talisman returned to the pavilion.

GUNN, TERRY, who died on April 5, aged 85, was a wicketkeeper from Barnsley who joined Sussex in 1960 after a few matches for Yorkshire's Second XI. Signed mainly to cover the absences of Jim Parks with England, Gunn played 41 first-class games over seven seasons. He was an excellent keeper, but in 54 attempts he never reached 20. He did, though, play a part in a spot of Sussex history, at his home club Worthing in 1964, when seamer Ian Thomson (who also died in 2021) took all ten wickets for 49, and credited Gunn with creating pressure by standing up to the stumps, which brought lbws into play. Afterwards, Thomson told county captain Ted Dexter that Gunn should be capped, which he was in 1965.

GUPTE, DINAR, who died of Covid-19 on May 6, aged 76, was a long-serving scorer and statistician for the Saurashtra Cricket Association, All India Radio and (for 15 years) the Indian board; he was the national team's scorer at the 1999 World Cup.

GURPREET SINGH, who died of Covid-19 on May 6, aged 38, was the video analyst for the Chhattisgarh Cricket Association. "Very prompt, helpful and precise in his job," said the Indian umpire Gautam Gavankar.

HAMMOND, JOHN ARTHUR, who died on December 20, aged 84, was a popular commentator for the telephone service Cricketcall. He covered Northamptonshire for three seasons from 1988, and was also one of the main trio – with Neville Scott and the late Pete Hardy – who provided ball-by-ball coverage of England games for 14 years. Hammond was raised in Ipswich, and captained his school at cricket and hockey; his future wife, Margaret, led the hockey team. He played club cricket for King's Lynn and Saffron Walden, keeping a mental tally of every team-mate who ran him out. Uncharacteristically, he once reacted to a poor decision by flinging his bat over the pavilion. "A gust of wind took it," he assured his grandson decades later.

HARKNESS, DONALD PETER, died on September 2, aged 90. Left-hander Don Harkness had one great day for Worcestershire, hammering 163 against a strong Cambridge University side at New Road in 1954, after reaching his century in two hours. In a dozen other matches that season, his highest was 53, against Hampshire. Also a lively seamer, at the end of the season he returned to his native Sydney, where he played for the St George club, among others.

HARMON, EVELYN, who died of cancer on July 10, aged 58, was a long-standing committee member at Malahide CC, and instrumental in developing it as Ireland's premier ground – the stage for their first official men's Test, against Pakistan in 2018.

HEDGCOCK, MURRAY BERTRAM, who died on May 6, aged 90, was an Australian journalist who spent most of his adult life in London, and became a welcome regular in English press boxes; he was also a leading light in the Council of Cricket Societies. Hedgcock (pronounced "Hedge-coe", which is how he habitually answered the phone) first came to the UK in 1953, then went back to work for the *Adelaide News*, an evening paper with a sparky proprietor his own age, Rupert Murdoch. The two became friends, and in 1966 Murdoch sent him back to London as correspondent, a job that turned – as the empire grew – into being head of a substantial bureau serving News Corporation's outlets. And this time Murray stayed for good.

He was hardly a typical Australian: he did not drink, smoke, gamble, swear, drive or swim, though his friend David Frith insisted: "His heart was always in the bush." And he certainly never switched his cricketing allegiance. The young Murray was much influenced by Bill Woodfull, the high-minded former Australian captain who was his headmaster in Upwey, Victoria, and he turned into a serious man himself. But he was kindly, with a humour so wry and understated it was not always easy to discern.

In summer, Murray would lay off the London office administration, and disappear to write astute and readable columns from Lord's, The Oval and Wimbledon. He had a huge library at his home in Mortlake, much of it devoted to cricket and plenty more to his hero, P. G. Wodehouse. He combined the two enthusiasms in his book *Wodehouse at the Wicket*, and wrote the rules governing the Wodehouse Society's fixture against the Sherlock Holmes Society, based on the laws and customs of 1895: five-ball overs, leg-side hits permitted but considered vulgar, an underarm lob bowler on each side. There was a sense he would have preferred it had the game stayed that way. Generations of newspapermen revered him as a mentor, including his former boss. "Murray was a great and wise friend and adviser for many years," said Murdoch.

HENDRICK, MICHAEL, died on July 26, aged 72. It became a familiar sight on English Test grounds in the 1970s: Mike Hendrick approaching the wicket with his loose-limbed, rhythmic run-up and, deploying a classical sideways action and textbook high arm, leaving batsmen groping outside off stump. Oohs and aahs from the crowd would be followed by looks of frustration between wicketkeeper and slips: it seemed Hendrick never reaped the rewards he deserved. The consensus among coaches and commentators was that he bowled fractionally too short to find the edge, sacrificing incision for economy. "He was a mean bowler, and in some ways he preferred to have two or three for 50 off 30 overs than taking more wickets but going for more runs," said wicketkeeper Bob Taylor, a team-mate for Derbyshire and England. In 30 Tests, Hendrick took 87 wickets at 25 and went for two an over; no one has taken more Test wickets without a five-for (though he was the first England bowler to take five wickets in an ODI, against Australia at The Oval in 1980).

Theories and statistics should not obscure his class. "He was very clever," said Taylor. "He bowled a line which made batsmen play at balls they could have left." Hendrick played a significant role in two Ashes triumphs. In three Tests in 1977, he took 14 wickets at 20 – including eight in the series-clinching win at Headingley – and 19 at 15 in Australia in 1978-79. His parsimony also made him an ideal one-day performer. In star-studded company, he was the leading wicket-taker at the 1979 World Cup. Had Viv Richards, only 22 runs into his eventual 138, been given out lbw to the first ball of Hendrick's second spell – as Hendrick always believed he should – England might not have needed to wait 40 years to lift the trophy.

At Derbyshire, he was heir to a proud seam-bowling tradition. Although he took fewer wickets than Billy Bestwick, Bill Copson, Cliff Gladwin or Les Jackson, Hendrick earned the extended international recognition they were denied. Even so, he felt that being at an unfashionable county was a hindrance. "I probably played for England *despite* playing for

MOST TEST WICKETS WITHOUT FIVE IN AN INNINGS

		T	Balls	Runs	BB	Avge
87	**M. Hendrick (England)**	30	6,208	2,248	4-28	25.83
78	Mashrafe bin Mortaza (Bangladesh)	36	5,990	3,239	4-60	41.52
75	B. M. McMillan (South Africa)	38	6,048	2,537	4-65	33.82
71	D. R. Hadlee (New Zealand)	26	4,883	2,389	4-30	33.64
70	B. R. Knight (England)	29	5,377	2,223	4-38	31.75
66	**E. R. Dexter (England)**	62	5,317	2,306	4-10	34.93
61	W. K. M. Benjamin (West Indies)	21	3,694	1,648	4-46	27.01
60	J. D. P. Oram (New Zealand)	33	4,964	1,983	4-41	33.05
57	R. M. S. Eranga (Sri Lanka)	19	3,891	2,138	4-49	37.50
53	Mohammad Hafeez (Pakistan)	55	4,067	1,808	4-16	34.11
51	N. J. Astle (New Zealand)	81	5,688	2,143	3-27	42.01
51	Wasim Raja (Pakistan)	57	4,082	1,826	4-50	35.80
51	G. J. Whittall (Zimbabwe)	46	4,686	2,088	4-18	40.94

Derbyshire," he said. He was born in the county, but took a roundabout route to a first-class debut in 1969. His father was a feared fast bowler for Darley Dale – and also a tax inspector. "They used to say that if he didn't get you on Saturday afternoon, he'd get you on Monday morning," said Hendrick. But the family moved to the North-East, and his first exposure to cricket was at Darlington. When his father was transferred to Leicester, Hendrick was in his teens, and began to take wickets for the county youth teams. A few Second XI appearances encouraged him to give up a loathed job with the electricity board, but he was left unemployed when a contract never materialised. Fortunately, an old friend of his father was running Derbyshire Colts, and he was invited to a trial in the spring of 1968.

His first exposure to the spartan County Ground was eye-opening: "The dressing-rooms should have been condemned as unfit for human habitation." After a trial came a contract, as well as the job of bowling at members in the nets. "Myself and Alan Ward used to bowl bouncers, so they wouldn't want to come back the next week." Technical guidance was limited to Second XI coach Denis Smith occasionally calling: "Showder!" Hendrick asked one of the senior bowlers what this meant. "He wants you to get your shoulder round when you bowl." Hendrick agreed this was sound advice, but noted that Smith shouted the same instruction to the batsmen.

Injuries hampered his progress. When he broke his ankle at Derby, there was no stretcher, so a dressing-room door had to be unscrewed from its hinges to carry him off. At the end of his third season, in 1971, he was worrying about a new contract. But it turned up, and he worked as a labourer through the winter to build up his chest and shoulder muscles. He was rewarded with 58 wickets at 23, including eight for 50 against Northamptonshire at Chesterfield. His reputation for accuracy was cemented by figures of six for seven in a Sunday League game against Nottinghamshire.

Hendrick played his first one-day international against West Indies in 1973, and at the end of the season was voted the Cricket Writers' Club's Young Cricketer of the Year. Shortly afterwards, he was named in Mike Denness's squad for the Caribbean, though he didn't play a Test. "I learned a lot about myself on that tour – not least that I was not as good as I thought." His Test debut came in the summer of 1974: three matches against India, two against Pakistan. Twenty wickets at 20 was an encouraging start, but he felt he underperformed: "I became very uptight, and just could not let the ball go." In Australia in 1974-75, more injury problems limited him to two Tests.

A career-defining moment was the appointment of the ebullient South African Eddie Barlow as Derbyshire captain in 1976. He told Hendrick and Ward they were not fit enough for county cricket, let alone Test matches – and, after being left out of the tour of India, Hendrick pounded the hills around his home. In 1977, the benefits were obvious: 67 wickets at 15, and an England recall. Late on the second day of the Fourth Test at Headingley, he tore into Australia's top order. "On a hazy evening, the batsmen were always likely to have

Patrick Eagar, Popperfoto/Getty Images

Letting go: Mike Hendrick flies in against India at The Oval, 1979.

trouble with Hendrick, whose ability to move the ball about with a high degree of accuracy, and to make it bounce more than most, allowed few errors," wrote Michael Melford in *The Daily Telegraph*. Australia slumped to 67 for five, and the Ashes were almost secured. He was one of *Wisden's* Five in 1978.

When England thrashed an understrength Australia in 1978-79, he was even more effective. He was left out for the First Test, but eight wickets against Western Australia at the WACA before the Second presented an unanswerable case. "We almost missed selecting him for the Perth Test because of preconceptions about the kind of bowler he was – English for English conditions," said captain Mike Brearley, who had been told over lunch by WA captain John Inverarity that Hendrick was England's most threatening seamer. Early on the tour, he had asked Brearley and assistant manager Ken Barrington why he so regularly beat the bat without taking wickets. Barrington urged him to pitch the ball up a little more; the extra bounce on Australian pitches added to his new potency. But his economy remained a prime asset. "We had two attacking bowlers in Botham and Willis," said Brearley, "so it was usually just what we needed to have Mike bowl his way, going at two runs an eight-ball over and getting good players out too."

He had a moderately successful summer against India in 1979, but his career was winding down: his final Tests were at the start and end of the 1981 Ashes. At loggerheads with Barlow's successor, Barry Wood, he also left Derbyshire; his last game for them was the NatWest Trophy final win over Northamptonshire. That winter, he joined the rebel tour of South Africa. He then spent three seasons with Nottinghamshire, before retiring in

1984 with 770 wickets at 20. He was a genuine rabbit as a batsman, but 176 catches were testament to his ability close to the wicket.

After a brief spell as an umpire, Hendrick moved into coaching. He was cricket manager at Nottinghamshire, and later returned there as bowling coach. In 1995, he was appointed coach of Ireland and spent four years in the role, moving to Belfast and immersing himself in the challenge of making the team more competitive. He set up programmes to identify emerging talent, and ended the policy of selecting older players who offered safety over flair. Nor was he afraid of taking on the Irish Cricket Union. Before one overseas tournament, he demanded that the travelling party be restricted to players and coaching staff; officials could pay their own way.

His dry sense of humour and love of chat over a pint made him a popular dressing-room figure. His final years were blighted by bowel and liver cancer. In July 2021, Mike Atherton contacted him for a *Times* feature marking the 40th anniversary of the 1981 Ashes. "I'm in the departure lounge," said Hendrick. "But the flight has not quite left yet." He died just over a fortnight later.

HILL, ALAN, who died on February 5, aged 92, was a journalist who moved down from his native Yorkshire to join Hayter's Sports Agency in London, where he wrote about football and, particularly, cricket. After ghosting Bill Alley's 1969 autobiography, *My Incredible Innings*, Hill started writing cricket books under his own name. The eventual list of his biographical subjects forms an impressive England line-up: Herbert Sutcliffe, Bill Edrich, Peter May, Brian Close, Trevor Bailey, Les Ames, Jim Laker, Johnny Wardle, Tony Lock, Hedley Verity and the Bedser twins. In *Wisden 2003*, Frank Keating observed that "down the years, the diligent cuttings-librarian Hill has been a productive cottage industry, doing the game proud with a succession of fond and important studies". His cottage was, for over 50 years, in the Sussex village of Lindfield, where he lived with his schoolteacher wife, Betty, who died a few days before him. Hill's books, while notable for their accuracy, were somewhat dry – perhaps because most of his subjects were already dead – and he could be prickly. "He was always moaning about how his research had been filched by other writers," remembered David Frith.

HOWARD, KEITH, OBE, who died on August 12, aged 89, was a successful publisher, whose company Emerald Press specialised in academic research. He built up a substantial fortune and, always a cricket lover, donated £10m to Yorkshire CCC when he heard they might lose the right to stage Test matches because of substandard facilities. The ground was until 2021 known as Emerald Headingley. Many years earlier, he had dismissed Herbert Sutcliffe for a duck in a club game; Sutcliffe's attempts to procure him a trial were scotched when Howard admitted he had been born in Lancashire.

HUTCHINSON, GEOFFREY, who died on July 3, aged 87, was a prolific batsman for the Carlton club in Bridgetown. He played two first-class matches for Barbados in March 1956, against a strong touring team assembled by E. W. Swanton. Hutchinson opened with Conrad Hunte, and made 35 in the first game, before falling to Frank Tyson.

IFTIKHAR AHMED, who died on May 3, aged 66, had been a Hindi cricket commentator on Indian radio for almost 40 years, known by his nickname, "Papu"; his last assignments came during England's tour early in 2021.

IGGLESDEN, ALAN PAUL, died of complications caused by a brain tumour on November 1, aged 57. Beset by injuries and defections to a rebel tour of South Africa, England were desperately seeking a new-ball bowler for the Sixth Test of their shambolic 1989 Ashes campaign. Team manager Micky Stewart called the Kent seamer Alan Igglesden: he was delighted, but had to wait for a neighbour to fix his washing machine before he could travel to The Oval with clean kit. Matters did not improve when Stewart appeared to suggest at a press conference that he was England's 17th choice. He was making a point about the length of the injury list, not Igglesden's credentials, but even his endorsement contained a caveat: "He is tall, strong and quick, and has the ability to move the ball away from the bat – if he is not too tired." It was unfortunate for Igglesden that he came to be remembered as one of the last of the 29 players used by England that summer. Between 1986 and 1998, he took more than 500 first-class wickets.

Igglesden stood 6ft 6in, and used his height to great effect. "Iggy had everything when he was fit and well," said his Kent captain Chris Cowdrey. "He swung the ball out, had real pace, and bounce off a full length." Igglesden came to Kent's attention while playing for Holmesdale in Sevenoaks, and joined the staff in 1985, making his debut the following summer. In his second match, against Surrey at The Oval, he took six wickets, but a month later suffered a side strain and missed the rest of the season. Injuries bedevilled his career, as he acknowledged: "Discs slip out at a moment's notice." He started the 1987 season with 23 wickets in four matches, including a five-for against the Pakistanis, but managed only ten more games after another injury setback.

Kent were runners-up in the Championship in 1988, with Igglesden taking 37 wickets in just seven matches. "We would have won the Championship comfortably if he had stayed fit for a few more," said Cowdrey. "It was so frustrating for him and all of us that he was so unlucky with injuries." In 1989 he did stay fit, making 20 first-class appearances and finishing as Kent's leading wicket-taker with 53. "Iggy Stardust" was a headline in *The Sun* after one eye-catching performance. He was considered for the Fifth Test at Trent

Pace and bounce: Alan Igglesden at Sabina Park, Jamaica, in 1994. Ian Robinson keeps watch.

David Munden, Popperfoto/Getty Images

Bridge, but there were concerns about his workload, and Greg Thomas was preferred. When Australia batted first at The Oval, he was thrust into the action, taking the new ball with Gladstone Small. He later said: "When the umpire says play, stop for a moment, have a look around, take it all in. You only bowl your first ball in an Ashes Test once." He took three wickets in the match, including Mark Taylor and Steve Waugh in the first innings.

Igglesden spent several winters in South Africa, playing for the multi-racial Cape Town club Avendale, and Western Province. In 1992-93, he enjoyed a successful season with Boland, taking 39 wickets at 11, including a career-best seven for 28 (and 12 in the match) against Griqualand West at Kimberley. The England selectors took note, and named him in the squad for the First Test of the 1993 Ashes at Old Trafford, but he suffered a groin strain the day before the game. He was chosen again for the Third Test at Trent Bridge, but this time was scuppered by a back injury. His Kent new-ball partner Martin McCague made his debut, raising a possibility that had long tantalised Canterbury regulars: on paper they made a formidable pair, but seldom appeared side by side. Some members joked that they were so rarely seen together they must be the same player.

Igglesden's 54 wickets in 1993 earned him a place on the tour of the Caribbean. He played in the First and Second Tests, as well as four ODIs, but made little impact. His appearances for Kent dwindled – he missed the entire season in 1996 – and he left in 1998. He intended to play Minor Counties cricket for Berkshire, but suffered an epileptic fit in his second match; doctors discovered a brain tumour the size of a junior cricket ball. An experimental drug treatment reduced its size, and he was able to take up teaching jobs in Kent and Yorkshire. Ten years after the diagnosis, the tumour erupted and he had life-saving surgery. He suffered strokes in 2018 and 2020, which left him partially paralysed.

He received help from the Professional Cricketers' Trust, and became a patron and fundraiser for the Brain Tumour Charity. He raised more than £300,000 by holding golf days supported by former cricketers. "It was a privilege to have known him, and he has been a real inspiration to our supporters living with brain tumours," said the charity's co-founders, Neil and Angela Dickson. Not long before he died, a group of his old Kent colleagues visited him at home. "If I could pick a team of the nicest guys I played with," said Cowdrey, "Iggy would be inked in very early."

ILLINGWORTH, RAYMOND, CBE, died on December 25, aged 89. The moment that changed Ray Illingworth's life was witnessed live by millions on television – not that he knew anything about it. On May 25, 1969, England captain Colin Cowdrey was batting for Kent in a Sunday League game against Glamorgan when he snapped an Achilles tendon. With the First Test against West Indies less than three weeks away, England needed a new leader. Blissfully unaware, Illingworth was busy steering his new county Leicestershire to victory over Nottinghamshire. Cowdrey's injury was front-page news. "I expect the selectors will look no further than their senior man Tom Graveney," wrote E. W. Swanton in *The Daily Telegraph*. John Woodcock in *The Times* believed the choice lay between Graveney and Roger Prideaux, "with Ray Illingworth holding an outsider's chance". John Arlott in *The Guardian* saw significance in Prideaux's selection to lead MCC against the touring team.

In the first week of June, chairman of selectors Alec Bedser appointed Illingworth. The news came late in the day. Bedser had failed to contact the new captain, who was driving between Leeds and Hove. En route, he called in to the Northampton hospital where Colin Milburn was recovering from a car crash in which he lost an eye. With Illingworth out of reach for seven hours, Bedser eventually had to break the news; when he arrived on the south coast, he was greeted by a posse of journalists. "I wondered what the hell was going on."

He was 37 on the day his first squad was announced. As an off-spinning all-rounder, usually batting at No. 7 or 8, he had played 30 Tests, taking 71 wickets and scoring 548 runs – hardly compelling. And after leaving Yorkshire for Leicestershire, he was only seven Championship matches into his career as a county captain. Yet Illingworth became one of England's greatest leaders, losing only five of his 31 Tests in charge, and regaining the Ashes in Australia in 1970-71. Tough, shrewd, an unrivalled reader of pitches and conditions, a canny motivator and a brilliant tactician, he moulded a team in his own image: uncompromising and hard to beat. "He enjoyed the challenge of the game," said his Leicestershire team-mate Jack Birkenshaw. "Generally, he defended – but he knew exactly the right moment to go in for the kill." Ian Chappell, his Ashes opposite number in 1972, recalled: "I learned from him how to captain the side when the opposition is starting to get on top and you know that you have got to save some runs, but you don't want to totally hand over control to the batting side." Mike Brearley added: "I always learned things from him, got ideas and ways of thinking."

Illingworth was born in the cricket nursery of Pudsey, six miles from Leeds, the son of a joiner and cabinet-maker. He excelled at cricket and football. As captain of the school cricket team, he averaged 100 with the bat and two with the ball, and was a seamer until an umpire saw him bowl an experimental off-break. "If you can spin it like that, lad, I'd forget the seamers." He was invited for football trials by Aston Villa, Huddersfield Town and Bradford City, but in his mid-teens decided to focus on cricket. At 15, he was in Farsley's first team in the Bradford League, and soon scored a century in a cup final.

He made his Yorkshire debut in 1951 during his national service, making a fifty against Hampshire, but not until 1953 did he have a run of games. It was a tough apprenticeship. A dropped catch off Bob Appleyard was met with a withering put-down. "No word of encouragement, no helpful tips, no pat on the back," he said. "There was no mitigation, no excuse accepted, no allowances made. You either swallowed the insults and gritted your teeth, or you went to pieces."

But he was good enough to survive, then thrive. He hit his maiden century against Essex at Hull in 1953, passed 100 wickets in 1956, and achieved the first of six doubles in 1957. That season, he claimed a career-best nine for 42 against Worcestershire, taking particular satisfaction from the fact that Johnny Wardle was bowling at the other end. In 1959, Ronnie Burnet took over as Yorkshire captain, creating a more harmonious dressing-room and leading them to their first Championship in 10 years. Illingworth imbibed lessons in man-management, and responded to the improved atmosphere with 1,726 runs at 46 and 110 wickets at 21. In the title-clinching win against Sussex at Hove, he made a crucial century and took seven wickets. He was named a Wisden Cricketer of the Year.

Rosy prospect: Ray Illingworth in 1957.

Allsport/Hulton Archive/Getty Images

He had made an unspectacular Test debut against a weak New Zealand the previous summer, but two tidy performances against India in 1959 earned him a winter tour of the Caribbean, where he played in all five Tests, though with modest returns. The end of Jim Laker's international career after the 1958-59 Ashes led to a beauty contest for the job of England's frontline off-spinner involving Illingworth, David Allen, John Mortimore and Fred Titmus. "I thought he was the best of them," said Birkenshaw, an off-spinner himself. "Starting as a seamer meant he had a lovely side-on action, and it was only when you batted against him in the nets that you realised how subtly he varied his length." The hot competition meant Illingworth's appearances were sporadic. On his first Ashes tour in 1962-63, he played in just two Tests, and lost £50 from his tour bonus for failing to contribute to team spirit. Not until he became captain did he play a full home summer of Tests.

Compensation came at county level. Yorkshire were champions seven times in ten seasons, with Illingworth usually making a telling contribution. When his great friend Brian Close was appointed captain in 1962, he became a loyal deputy, to whom other players turned when Close's mind was drifting towards the racing results. In a profile, the journalist Norman Harris asked a friend of both to imagine them as First World War officers. Close, he guessed, would lead his men out of the trenches into the teeth of the battle. "Illy would call for a full intelligence report on the enemy's strength and positions, a detailed survey of the terrain between us, an up-to-date report from the Met Office, a final check on the men and weapons of his own forces, and then would probably decide against going because the odds were wrong."

In 1968, aged 36, Illingworth asked for the security of a three-year contract. But Yorkshire handed out only one-year deals, and would not budge. Illingworth resigned. Five counties were interested; Nottinghamshire offered the best salary, but not the captaincy. Leicestershire had never won a trophy, but Illingworth was impressed by the ambition of secretary Mike Turner. Fed up with getting splinters in his feet after using the Headingley showers, he also liked Grace Road's new dressing-rooms.

He set about recruiting players who were not inured to defeat, improving fielding, and focusing, initially, on one-day matches, where victories were easier to achieve. But England duty meant progress was slow. A breakthrough came in 1972, when Leicestershire won the first Benson and Hedges Cup, beating Yorkshire at Lord's. Illingworth said he had never been more nervous before a match. They added the John Player League two

MOST TESTS AS CAPTAIN BEFORE FIRST DEFEAT

T	W	D		First Test	First defeat
19	8	11	**R. Illingworth (England)**	**1969**	**1971**
18	6	12	S. M. Gavaskar (India)	1975-76	1979-80
15	10	5	J. M. Brearley (England)	1977	1978-79
14	4	10	M. J. K. Smith (England)	1963-64	1965
11	7	4	I. V. A. Richards (West Indies)	1980	1985-86
11	8	3	M. S. Dhoni (India)	2007-08	2009-10
11	7	4	S. P. D. Smith (Australia)	2014-15	2015-16
10	5	5	M. C. Cowdrey (England)	1959	1961
10	2	8	N. J. Contractor (India)	1960-61	1961-62

W. W. Armstrong captained Australia in ten Tests (1920-21 to 1921), winning eight and drawing two.

years later, and in 1975 were crowned county champions for the first time. They lost only once, and pipped Yorkshire by 16 points. Illingworth was outstanding. "As captain he was supreme, always leading by example," said *Wisden*. They had already lifted a second B&H Cup, to become the first county to win the Championship and a one-day trophy in the same season. "He turned Grace Road into a fortress," said Birkenshaw. "The wickets didn't always look great, but we knew how to play on them."

It helped that he was no longer a Test cricketer. Having led England to 2–0 wins over West Indies and New Zealand in 1969, he kept the job the following summer when South Africa's abandoned tour was replaced by a series against a Rest of the World team packed with galacticos. England lost 4–1, but Illingworth again led the team astutely and had a superb series with the bat: only his opposite number, Garry Sobers, bettered his aggregate of 476. Although Cowdrey was short of form and fitness, there was still debate about who would captain England in Australia that winter. At the end of the fourth match at Headingley, it was announced Illingworth had got the job. "He is a shop steward rather than a cavalier, a sergeant-major not a brigadier: the personification in fact of the modern game," wrote Woodcock. Cowdrey was offered the vice-captaincy, but asked for time to

On top of the world: Ray Illingworth is chaired off the field after victory at Sydney in the Seventh Test won England the Ashes, February 1971.

think it over, even though Illingworth gave encouragement: "Colin is one of the best batsmen in the world and the best in England." Cowdrey eventually said yes.

It was an attritional tour. In expectation of Cowdrey being captain, MCC had chosen David Clark, a former Kent player and gentleman farmer, as manager. His relationship with Illingworth was fractious. At one point, Clark told the English press he would prefer an Australian victory to a string of stalemates. Illingworth's tactics were criticised by Don Bradman before the series had started, and the Australian media dubbed England "Dad's Army". "The other side of that was it meant everyone had a lot of experience," said fast bowler John Snow. Much to Illingworth's irritation, Cowdrey was a distant figure. "He did not carry out his duties in the way I had hoped and, indeed, expected," he later wrote. It confirmed his opinion that Cowdrey's affable public persona was fake: "He was generally not liked by cricketers." Yet adversity glued the team together. "Illingworth did a magnificent job," wrote E. M. Wellings in *Wisden*. "Under severe provocation, he remained cool off the field and courteously approachable by friend and foe alike."

England went 1–0 up after winning the Fourth Test at Sydney, and had been astonished when Clark agreed to play a seventh match to replace the abandoned New Year Test in Melbourne (where the teams ended up playing cricket's first one-day international). "The first we knew about it was when Don Bradman poked his head around the door and thanked us for agreeing to play," said Snow. "We knew the Australians were being paid and there was a fee for the umpires, but there was no mention of money for us." Snow thought the consensus of an angry team meeting was that the players would refuse to play, but a cable from Lord's reassured them they would be paid. In unpromising circumstances – injury ruled out Geoffrey Boycott – they eventually forced a backs-to-the-wall victory to secure the Ashes.

In the first innings, a ball from Snow hit Terry Jenner on the head. When umpire Lou Rowan warned Snow, Illingworth stepped in angrily to indicate it had been his first short ball of the over. Snow went to field on the boundary, and was greeted by a hail of missiles, then grabbed by a spectator. Illingworth was calm and decisive: when debris continued to rain down, he led the players off. Clark demanded they go back out, while Rowan said England were in danger of forfeiting the match. "Ray said to him, 'We'll go back out when it's safe,'" Snow recalled. In the second innings, Snow broke a finger trying to take a catch on the boundary, and could not bowl. Their chances of winning the Ashes were slipping away, but England fought tenaciously and, with Illingworth taking three key wickets and directing operations superbly, won by 62 runs. They took the series without a single lbw decision from the home umpires. Illingworth was chaired off. "No victory has ever given me so much satisfaction," he said.

Back in England, they beat Pakistan 1–0, then lost a home series to India for the first time. After a drawn Ashes in 1972, he elected not to tour the subcontinent, before regaining the captaincy from Tony Lewis. New Zealand were beaten in 1973, but Illingworth was 41 by the time West Indies won 2–0 later that summer. His time was up. During the final Test, at Lord's, Mike Denness was appointed captain for the tour of the Caribbean. Illingworth sensed an Establishment plot led by Gubby Allen.

He returned to Yorkshire in 1979 as cricket manager, but failed to heal the rifts in a dressing-room divided by the appointment of John Hampshire as captain after Boycott's sacking. In June 1982 – two weeks after his 50th birthday and almost four years since his previous first-class appearance – Illingworth took over the captaincy from Chris Old. "One of the most controversial moves of even Yorkshire's trouble-strewn recent history," wrote John Callaghan in *Wisden*. There was no improvement. In 1983, they won the John Player League but finished bottom of the Championship. His 787th and final first-class appearance, 32 years after his first, came at Chelmsford, for the first and only time. He scored 24,134 runs at 28 and took 2,072 wickets at 20. Asked whether DRS might have made a difference, he declared that he would have had 520 more wickets. He was sacked as manager in 1984,

HOME COMFORTS

Highest percentage of Test wickets (minimum 100) in home matches:

%		Overall (avge)	Home	Away
89.38	P. P. Ojha (India)	113 (30.26)	101 (27.51)	12 (53.41)
83.60	**R. Illingworth (England)**	**122 (31.20)**	**102 (27.14)**	**20 (51.90)**
79.86	Taijul Islam (Bangladesh)	144 (32.61)	115 (27.11)	29 (54.44)
79.67	R. M. Hogg (Australia)	123 (28.47)	98 (24.30)	25 (44.84)
77.09	D. G. Cork (England)	131 (29.81)	101 (29.26)	30 (31.66)
75.49	N. S. Yadav (India)	102 (35.09)	77 (34.10)	25 (38.16)
75.20	C. R. Woakes (England)	125 (30.01)	94 (22.63)	31 (52.38)
74.59	F. S. Trueman (England)	307 (21.57)	229 (20.04)	78 (26.08)
74.33	B. A. Reid (Australia)	113 (24.63)	84 (20.05)	29 (37.89)
71.87	D. K. Morrison (New Zealand)	160 (34.68)	115 (27.12)	45 (54.00)

As at January 18, 2022. J. J. Bumrah (India) had taken 113 Test wickets – 109 overseas, and only four at home (3.54%).

and began a decade-long career in the media which combined commentary for BBC television with trenchant punditry in the *Daily Express*.

He was tempted away from those roles by the chance to become chairman of selectors in 1994. A year later, Keith Fletcher was dismissed as England coach, and Illingworth became their first football-style manager. It proved an unhappy time. He was in his early sixties, and plainly out of touch with the modern game. He appointed men of his generation to key positions – Fred Titmus and Brian Bolus as selectors, Peter Lever and John Edrich as coaches. His relationship with captain Mike Atherton was often uneasy. Several players grumbled about his manner, including Robin Smith, Graeme Hick, Darren Gough and Devon Malcolm, with whom he had a highly publicised falling-out after the tour of South Africa in 1995-96. After a shambolic World Cup in 1996, Illingworth resigned. Later, he was fined by the TCCB for bringing the game into disrepute after his account of the Malcolm dispute appeared in a newspaper.

It was not the end of his involvement with the game. For many years, he was groundsman at Farsley, using decades of wisdom to tend the square. Two weeks before his death, he spoke movingly in favour of assisted dying after his wife of 63 years, Shirley, died of breast cancer earlier in 2021; Illingworth revealed he was being treated for oesophageal cancer. After his death was announced on Christmas Day, the England players wore black armbands on Boxing Day at Melbourne. "I had a lot of respect for him," said Snow. "You can't argue with his record. He was down to earth, an old-school professional, not flashy. He was the shrewdest captain I played under."

ILLINGWORTH, THOMAS RICHARD, died on July 8, aged 80. A much-travelled farmer, Richard Illingworth helped revitalise cricket in Costa Rica, setting up their national body in the early 1990s, and pushing for membership of the ICC. His initiatives included a proper league, plus development programmes for women, youngsters and local black players. He last appeared for the national team aged 69. He contributed to *Wisden's* Cricket Round the World section.

IRANI, MEHLI DINSHAW, who died on April 2, aged 90, was a left-hand batsman and wicketkeeper who played in the Kanga League (a long-running competition in Mumbai's monsoon season) for a record 57 seasons. As late as 1991, when he was 60, he stumped Sachin Tendulkar. While at Bombay University in 1952-53, Irani had captained a side containing five future Test players: one of them, Nari Contractor, remembered a game in which they dropped five catches in the first over. He said of Irani: "He was a good batsman, but in those days you were considered lucky if you got to play for Bombay, as there were some seven or eight Test players in the team. That's the reason I played for Gujarat!" Irani did manage four first-class matches, only one in the Ranji Trophy, and scored 68 against the Commonwealth XI at the Brabourne Stadium in 1953-54.

IRFAN HABIB QURESHI, who died of a brain haemorrhage on September 15, aged 53, was a medium-pacer who took 19 wickets in ten first-class matches for various sides in Pakistan. His best figures, five for 78, came in the BCCP Patron's Trophy final in 1989-90, and helped Karachi Whites win by one wicket. He later became an umpire.

JADEJA, RAJENDRA RAISINH, died of Covid-19 on May 16, aged 65. A lively seamer and useful batsman, Raju Jadeja played for Saurashtra and – for two heady seasons – alongside a host of Test stars for Bombay. One of them, Sunil Gavaskar, said: "Today, players like him would have been superstars in the IPL." Jadeja's highest score of 97 came during a partnership of 192 with Gavaskar, for West Zone in the Duleep Trophy final at Delhi in March 1979, after Kapil Dev had taken a hat-trick for North Zone. His best figures were seven for 58 for Saurashtra against Gujarat at Rajkot in 1977-78; the previous season, Gavaskar had fallen for a duck on a matting pitch in Surendranagar, when Jadeja took six for 27 as Bombay were demolished for 79. "He was a fine all-rounder – he could generate pace and bounce," said Dilip Vengsarkar. "He was unlucky to not have played for India." Jadeja had toured England with an Indian Schools team in 1973; his brother, Dharmaraj, also played for Saurashtra.

JAGGANADHA RAO, K., who died on April 18, aged 78, was a seasoned journalist, latterly sports editor of the Press Trust of India, who covered World Cups and other international matches, as well as several Olympics. Outside sport, in 1971 he broke the news that Pakistan forces had surrendered to the Indian army, which led to the formation of Bangladesh. "He never liked us calling him 'Boss'," remembered another veteran sportswriter, G. Rajaraman. "He'd insist: 'I am your colleague.'"

JOHN, LEO, who died on May 13, aged 84, was a batsman and occasional off-spinner from Trinidad who played 25 first-class matches in the 1960s. His only century came for South against North Trinidad in 1967-68 in the Beaumont Cup, which had first-class status. For the full Trinidad & Tobago side, John never bettered the 85 he made on debut, against Barbados – batting for five hours against Hall, Griffith and all – at Port-of-Spain in March 1964. Trinidad's Over-40s competition was named after him.

JOHNSON, IVAN NICHOLAS, who died on October 4, aged 68, was the first Bahamian to play county cricket when he appeared for Worcestershire in 1972, after studying at Malvern College. A slow left-armer and useful batsman, he went on to play 33 first-class matches for them, taking five for 74 against Oxford University in 1974, when his victims included Imran Khan and Vic Marks. A fine fielder, he featured prominently in Worcestershire's one-day side, which reached the Benson and Hedges Cup final in 1973; the following year, he was part of the squad that won the County Championship. "He was very popular," said his captain Norman Gifford. "He made some excellent contributions, although I suppose if you'd asked him he might have said he underachieved a little with bat and ball." Johnson later worked as a journalist in England, Australia and the Bahamas, eventually starting up a tabloid newspaper – *The Punch* – in Nassau.

JOHNSON, MARTIN STEPHEN, who died on March 13, aged 71, began his career as a Fleet Street cricket writer with the journalistic equivalent of a triple-century on debut. It was not a world exclusive: it was a joke. Johnson had been plucked from obscurity by the newly established *Independent*, and flown out to cover the 1986-87 Ashes, which England began with a series of sloppy and dismal warm-ups. After they had been mashed by Western Australia, avoiding defeat only through rare Perth rain, Johnson trumped the routine condemnations dealt out in the other papers. He said there were only three things wrong with England: "They can't bat, they can't bowl and they can't field." The fact that England went on to beat a much-vaunted Australian team who turned out to be paper tigers only made the quote and its writer ever more famous. In London, his editors were thrilled, not just by the publicity that followed but by a whole tour's worth of reports that often read more like a music-hall turn by an old-style northern comedian. Non-cricket readers were drawn in by his byline, and he returned to the office months later to a hero's welcome.

Any other novice writer who had written something like that might have ended up behind the pavilion with a bail up his nostril. But players and colleagues alike found something so endearing about Jonno's nature that he could get away with anything. He totally lacked malice or even ambition (his nickname was Scoop, because he never got one). It helped that the cricketers knew him: he had already been on the county circuit for 13 years, covering Leicestershire home and away, long enough to become a character in his own right – and anyone who played at Grace Road might well have picked up a zinger. He could be truculent, especially to players who objected, but his greatest gift was to ensure that any argument would end with gales of laughter and another pint. Despite being a writer of rare natural gifts, he never seemed to get pleasure from his craft. He would far rather be playing golf or in the pub.

He was born and brought up in Monmouthshire, and cut his journalistic teeth on the Newport *Evening Argus*, which – so the story went – he left hurriedly just ahead of the brother of a girlfriend who was beyond placating with a joke. He fetched up in Leicester, and might have had to leave there abruptly when the *Mercury* editor rang his Newport counterpart for a reference. Fortunately, the Newport editor thought he was talking about

MARTIN JOHNSON 1949–2021

Scooping the best lines

"There are only three things wrong with this England team: they can't bat, they can't bowl and they can't field." *Before the 1986-87 Ashes*

"There is no more vibrant form of the game than Test cricket, and neither does it need ridiculous gimmicks to fool you into thinking you're getting something you're not. If it did, the match just ended in Birmingham – quite possibly the best in history – would doubtless have been marketed as the Australian Aardvarks versus the English Electrics."
After Edgbaston 2005

"Michael Atherton is one of the few people capable of looking more dishevelled at the start of a six-hour century than at the end of it."

"While Australian fast bowlers were resting up before a Test last summer, England's were contemplating another late-night journey drawn up by a computer programmed by a direct descendant of the Marquis de Sade."

"It would be a surprise if the mirrors in Kevin Pietersen's house totalled anything less than the entire stock at one of the larger branches of B&Q."

"Wayne Larkins's form has been so bad that he might have considered turning up to the Christmas fancy-dress party disguised as a batsman."

"It's the eyes – barely visible through two narrow slits, and as cold and unblinking as anything you'll see on a fishmonger's slab – that let the bowler know exactly what he's up against. If they'd belonged to a baddie at the OK Corral, Wyatt Earp would not so much have reached for his six-gun as the lavatory paper." *On Steve Waugh*

"How anyone can spin a ball the width of Mike Gatting boggles the mind."
On Shane Warne's 1993 Ball of the Century

"If he's not talking about the flipper it's the zooter, the slider, or the wrong'un. He'll shortly start working on a ball that loops the loop, disappears down his trouser leg, and whistles *Waltzing Matilda* before rattling into the stumps." *Warne again*

"His mincing run-up resembles someone in high heels and a panty girdle chasing after a bus." *On Merv Hughes*

"He swings it both ways through the air (and that's just his stomach)… his coiffure appears to have been entrusted to an inebriated sheepshearer somewhere in the outback." *Hughes again*

"If, in cricket's imagery, David Gower was the silk-scarved boy racer bombing around the country lanes, Chris Tavaré was the Ford Fiesta with the boiling radiator in an M25 tailback."

"He looked like a man who had got his braces caught on the sightscreen." *Angus Fraser's run-up*

"Even the Australians have embraced Darren Gough's exuberant brand of cricket. While their perception of the Poms is of trying to take Australia's castle by swimming the moat (and mostly drowning), Gough bursts through the front door and swings from the chandeliers. Some of the others would not enjoy the Errol Flynn approach for fear of laddering their tights."

"History was made yesterday, when Geoff Boycott made his 150th first-class century. Now I can die happy – pausing only, before I go, to give grateful thanks for having missed the other 149."

"Andy Caddick's other problem is that when a batsman gets after him, he has the body language of a failed soufflé."

"He hunches over the bowling stumps with the screwed-up grimace of a man who is sitting on the wrong end of a shooting-stick with a couple of thousand volts running through it." *Dickie Bird*

Ever the joker: Martin Johnson (second right) joins in Christmas Day celebrations in 1986, along with (back row) Paul Weaver, Graham Morris, Chris Lander, Dominic Allan and (front row) Graham Otway, Mike Gatting, David Norrie and David Gower.

another Martin. Soon enough he was covering both cricket and rugby, and he might have spent his life on the *Mercury* had the *Independent* not started up with a sports editor, Charlie Burgess, who knew his worth, and tapped him up as rugby writer.

Before the paper's launch, Johnson was switched to cricket, much to the alarm of the editor, Andreas Whittam Smith, who was hoping for a high-profile name. He soon recanted, and Johnson would remain one of his star writers for the next nine years. It is true that he was at his best when England were at their most mockable, and in that era they obliged more often than not. And underneath the gags, he knew his cricket – another reason for players to tolerate his barbs. *The Daily Telegraph*, where the sports editor was an old Leicester friend, were keen to land him, and their blandishments became too much to resist: Johnson had a long stint there as a sports-columnist-cum-sketchwriter, including cricket, rugby and much else besides. Later, he had a less happy stay on *The Sunday Times*.

Away from his comfort zone, his unworldliness could let him down: at the *Telegraph* he managed to get himself safely to Las Vegas for a Lennox Lewis title fight. It just happened to be taking place 3,000 miles away in New York. His final illness was difficult, and left him unable to speak, but he kept tapping out texts to friends, jokes included. He grew a little weary of being greeted by strangers with his most famous line, but it was true enough when he said it and, as he reflected later: "Right quote, wrong team."

JOYNT, HARTLEY KELLY, who died on May 12, aged 82, was unable to nail down a place in a strong Western Australian Sheffield Shield side, despite obvious talent and 17 appearances in the first half of the 1960s. His big moment came for a Combined XI against the touring South Africans at Perth in 1963-64; with four sessions to survive, Joynt made 81 in a sixth-wicket stand of 182 with Bob Simpson, saving the match. He later became a respected journalist with the *West Australian* newspaper, before managing a large group of suburban papers in Perth.

KAMAL ZIAUL ISLAM, who died on May 3, aged 86, was the president of the Bangladesh Cricket Board from January 1983 to February 1987, during which time he introduced a tournament for schools, sponsored by his company Nirman International.

KANOJIA, SHYAMJI, collapsed and died during a veterans' match in Virar, near Mumbai, on January 3. He was 65. A useful batsman and good fielder, he played four first-class matches for Indian Railways in 1976-77, without reaching double figures.

KEMP, DAVID STEPHEN, who died on September 22, aged 92, was chairman of Kent between 1994 and 1998, after being president in 1992; his tenure was bedevilled by financial problems. He had a long association with Tonbridge School, where he was in the XI at the same time as Colin Cowdrey; in 1947, Kemp had the higher batting average. He gave up a career in the law to return to the school in 1956, later serving as a housemaster, second master and, in 1989-90, acting-headmaster. He remained a close confidant of Cowdrey, who entrusted his three sons to Kemp's care; his own son, Nick, was Chris Cowdrey's vice-captain in the school XI, and later played with him for Kent before moving to Middlesex.

KHAN, ABDUL QADEER, who died on October 10, aged 85, was the founder of Pakistan's nuclear programme. A decorated and dedicated scientist, he was either the saviour of the nation (the general perception in Pakistan), or "the most dangerous man in the world", according to former CIA director George Tenet, who added that Khan was "at least as dangerous as Osama bin Laden". In 1976, he founded Khan Research Laboratories, which fielded a team – based at the company's ground in Rawalpindi – in Pakistan's first-class cricket competitions from 1997-98 to 2018-19.

KHAN, IMRAN, who died of Covid-19 on September 28, aged 43, worked in the media department of the West Indian cricket board for several years, where he proved popular with the press, and rose to become head of marketing and communications. More recently, he had performed a similar role for the Alliance for Change, Guyana's parliamentary opposition coalition.

KHAN, KHALID H., who died of a brain haemorrhage on November 23, aged 58, was the senior sports reporter of Pakistan's *Dawn* newspaper. He was particularly known for his coverage of the country's domestic cricket, an otherwise neglected area. "He was an extremely nice person and a hard-working reporter," said former Test captain Rashid Latif.

KIDDEY, JOHN WILLIAM FRANCIS, who died on November 13, aged 92, was an accurate left-arm seamer who took 141 wickets at 20 for the New Zealand province of Canterbury, despite not making his debut until he was 27, in January 1957. At Hamilton four years later, he bowled the top four Northern Districts batsmen as they lurched to 13 for six, and finished with career-best figures of 21–11–24–7 in a total of 59. Kiddey recalled: "The humidity was high that day, and the ball moved considerably. At one stage, keeper John Ward told me he had never kept to a banana before." Noted for his economy – he conceded less than two an over across his career – Kiddey added three for 35 in 25 overs in the second innings. He was unlucky New Zealand had no Tests that season, and was overlooked for the 1961-62 tour of South Africa, but he did represent New Zealand at hockey. Outside first-class cricket, Kiddey took 862 wickets in the Christchurch senior club competition, mainly for Riccarton. He and his wife, Betty, were married for 70 years.

KIRBY, DAVID, who died on October 7, aged 82, was a brilliant schoolboy batsman who captained Cambridge University in 1961 – his side included future England captains Mike Brearley and Tony Lewis – and the following year took charge of Leicestershire, not long after turning 23. The captaincy proved a millstone, and his average – over 30 in 1961 – dipped below 20, though he did pass 1,000 runs in the season, helped by centuries against Somerset and Kent. Some enjoyed his leadership: one team-mate, Jack van Geloven, called Kirby "the best amateur captain I ever played under – he gave up far too soon".

Kirby had been a prolific scorer for St Peter's School, York, making more than 2,000 runs during six years in the First XI; he captained the Public Schools at Lord's in 1958.

LOWEST AVERAGE WHEN HITTING 1,000 RUNS IN A SEASON

	M	I	NO	R	HS	100	50	Year
17.70 A. H. H. Gilligan (Sussex)	37	70	3	1,186	68	0	7	1923
17.74 J. J. Lyons (Australians)	33	59	1	1,029	99	0	5	1890
18.37 G. H. S. Trott (Australians)	36	61	2	1,084	73	0	3	1888
18.73 A. W. Wellard (Somerset/England) ..	32	60	4	1,049	91*	0	6	1937
19.00 D. Kirby (Leicestershire)	**31**	**53**	**0**	**1,007**	**118**	**2**	**3**	**1962**
19.11 J. E. Timms (Northamptonshire)	30	55	1	1,032	97	0	7	1932
19.25 W. E. Bates (Glamorgan)	30	52	0	1,001	74	0	4	1931
19.25 A. F. T. White (Worcestershire)	30	54	2	1,001	79	0	4	1947
19.32 G. Ulyett (Yorkshire/England)	30	52	0	1,005	78	0	4	1886
19.71 J. T. Murray (Middlesex)	33	57	5	1,025	120	1	3	1957

Only main team shown.

The following season – his first in first-class cricket – he scored 1,102 runs, mostly for Cambridge, before joining Leicestershire. He won Blues in the next two years as well, his off-breaks bringing four for 41 in the 1961 Varsity Match; he also tormented his county team-mates with five for 76 at Loughborough. Overall, that season proved his most successful: 46 wickets and 1,158 runs, including – for the county – 62 and 91 in a big win over Yorkshire, and four sixes in a rapid chase against Nottinghamshire.

After leaving university, he was employed as cricket secretary at Grace Road, which allowed him to retain his amateur status, and was soon appointed captain, ahead of the more experienced Maurice Hallam (who took over the following year). The distinction between amateurs and professionals was abolished late in 1962, and around that time Kirby accepted a teaching post at his old school. His first-class career was effectively over, although he returned for two matches in 1964 (and bagged a pair against Worcestershire in the first). He taught French and German, and ran the cricket at St Peter's for 44 years. The best player to emerge in that time was Jonny Bairstow, who remembered: "David was experienced and kind, good at sharpening my skills and pushing me along. He was the sort of man you instantly respected."

KNIGHT, GEORGE WILLIAM, who died on May 7, aged 100, collected 1,250 runs and 59 wickets for Victoria College, Jersey, in 1939, which led to his being retrospectively named in *Wisden 2021* as a Schools Cricketer of the Year. Later that summer, with war looming, he took the last wicket to secure a two-run win for Young Amateurs over the Young Professionals at Lord's in a two-day game that started on his 19th birthday. He remained in Jersey, where his brisk off-spinners brought him ten for 24 in one innings, and two hat-tricks; the *Jersey Evening Post* called him "the most outstanding all-round cricketer this island has produced". Knight turned 100 a few months before his award was announced; his son, Michael, said he was "visibly overwhelmed by the news". Not long afterwards, George "died peacefully with a copy of *Wisden 2021* on one bedside cabinet, and *Wisden 1940* on the other".

KRAMER, DIRK EVERT JOHANNES, died on January 7, aged 76. Dick Kramer was a leg-spinning all-rounder who played for Quick CC in The Hague from 1959 – when he was 15 – to 1980, and helped them win their first domestic title, in 1965. He also made several appearances for the Dutch national side, taking three wickets in each innings against Denmark in 1977.

KUNDAN SINGH RAJPUT, who died of kidney failure on January 10, aged 25, had been a promising cricketer for Janakpur in Nepal before falling ill. Fellow players, and their clubs, helped raise money for his treatment. Hobart Hurricanes, whose squad for the Australian Big Bash included Nepali leg-spinner Sandeep Lamichhane, observed a minute's silence before a match in January in Kundan's memory.

Cloud 19: Jim and Lilly Laker leave their hotel after the 1956 Old Trafford Test.

LAKER, LILLY, who died on September 30, aged 102, was the widow of the Surrey and England off-spinner Jim Laker, who died in 1986. They first met when Corporal Laker was serving in the army in Egypt, and then again at a reunion in London eight years later. Born in Austria, Lilly had little idea about cricket. One day in 1954, Jim returned home from The Oval and announced he had got 113. Thinking he meant no wicket for 113, she kept quiet – only to read in next morning's paper that he had scored a career-best.

LARKIN, THOMAS CEDRIC, ONZM, who died on August 17, aged 103, shared a stand of 234 in 1936 with the future New Zealand Test batsman Martin Donnelly, while both were at New Plymouth High School. Larkin represented Taranaki in the Hawke Cup, and against an MCC touring team in 1935-36; later he made a double-century at university. He played a few minor matches for Wellington after the war, before embarking on a long diplomatic career; he was New Zealand's ambassador to Japan from 1972 to 1976.

LATTY-SCOTT, VIVALYN, who died on January 9, aged 81, appeared in ten of West Indies' first 11 women's Tests, between 1975-76 and 1979 (they have played only one since, in 2004). An off-spinning all-rounder for Jamaica, she took five for 48 in 41 overs on her debut, against Australia at Montego Bay in May 1976, and scored an unbeaten 51 against

---

BEST BOWLING ON DEBUT IN WOMEN'S TESTS

7-10	M. E. Maclagan	England v Australia at Brisbane (Exhibition)	1934-35
7-18	A. Palmer	Australia v England at Brisbane (Exhibition)	1934-35
7-24	L. J. Johnston	Australia v New Zealand at Melbourne (St Kilda)	1971-72
6-21	I. M. H. C. Joyce	Ireland v Pakistan at Dublin (College Park)	2000
6-28	B. R. Wilson	Australia v New Zealand at Wellington	1947-48
6-42	G. P. Gooder	New Zealand v England at Auckland	1948-49
5-15	M. F. Spear	England v Australia at Brisbane (Exhibition)	1934-35
5-28	L. I. Bayliss	New Zealand v Australia at Dunedin (Carisbrook)	1960-61
5-31	C. R. Seneviratne	Sri Lanka v Pakistan at Colombo (Colts)	1997-98
5-37	S. Loubser	South Africa v Netherlands at Rotterdam	2007
5-48	**V. Latty-Scott**	**West Indies v Australia at Montego Bay**	**1975-76**
5-48	S. Kulkarni	India v West Indies at Bangalore	1976-77
5-79	R. J. Steele	New Zealand v India at Vapi	2003-04

India at Jammu that November. She also represented Jamaica in the first women's World Cup, in England in 1973, making 61 in a victory over Young England, and remains the only cricketer to win Jamaica's Sportswoman of the Year award. She later coached and umpired, before moving to the United States. Former team-mate Ann Browne-John, now West Indies' chief selector, said: "Vivalyn was always a fierce competitor, and took her cricket very seriously. She was truly one of the stalwarts of women's cricket in the Caribbean."

LAWRENCE, KENNETH DOUGLAS, died on June 25, aged 90. Ken Lawrence was a long-standing sports editor on the *Daily* and later *Sunday Express*. His most significant intervention in cricket came after he had retired from print and, in 1992, was appointed public relations officer for the then Test and County Cricket Board following the sudden death of Peter Smith. Lawrence, however, had some trouble adjusting his focus from a sometimes ramped-up newspaper truth to the obfuscation demanded of PR men. After a one-day international at The Oval, Ian Botham got into a sweary off-field contretemps with the Pakistan captain Javed Miandad, which Ken – supposedly in charge of the official, sanitised message – recounted with relish round the press box. He did not last long in the job, and some of his successors were so differently inclined they would have regarded MI6 as blabby. Lawrence was successful at just about everything else. He was a much-admired, hard-driving sports editor, and deeply involved in *pro bono* work, especially for Surrey and the Lord's Taverners. His huge contacts book and persuasive tongue enabled him to raise a lot of money, especially for youth sport. And, like most sports editors of his generation, he adored cricket and ensured it was reported prominently – arguably a more effective form of PR than anything devised at Lord's.

LAXMAN, BOCKAPATNA, who died on April 28, aged 75, was a legendary figure in senior Bombay cricket, playing swashbuckling innings for the State Bank of India and the Karnatak club, where he was an early role model for Ravi Shastri, then 16: "He was the Viv Richards of our team, playing shots I'd yet to see." Contemporaries remembered an innings of 141 in an inter-banks final that lasted less than two hours; at one point, the game was held up while a new ball was found, after Laxman hit the original into Marine Drive. He was apparently invited to play for Mysore in 1980, after outscoring Test batsmen Ajit Wadekar and Hanumant Singh for the State Bank in the Times Shield, but chose to concentrate on his studies.

LEE, CHRISTOPHER ROBIN JAMES, who died of Covid-19 complications on February 14, aged 79, was a much-travelled journalist and author – and, for ten years from 1976, the BBC's defence correspondent. That entailed living in Moscow, where he co-founded a cricket club. Later, he was a research fellow at Cambridge, wrote scripts for *The Archers*, and kept fit by riding an exercise bike, although he offset the health benefits by smoking cigars in the saddle. Lee's main legacy was *This Sceptred Isle*, a history of Britain for the radio, covering 2,000 years from the Roman invasion: he wrote all 396 episodes himself. Among his many books were *Nicely Nurdled, Sir!*, about village cricket, and *From the Sea End*, a lively history of Sussex CCC, on whose committee he sat for a while. "A story told with humour and warmth, immensely readable," wrote John Arlott in *Wisden 1990*.

LEKA, API KUNE, who died on July 13, aged 69, was a pillar of cricket in Papua New Guinea, playing for the national team in four ICC Trophy tournaments between 1979 and 1994, captaining in three. He hit 69 as they racked up 455 in their 60 overs against Gibraltar in 1986. Leka later coached the national team, and was a selector. "PNG is what it is today thanks to the efforts of players like Api," said a board spokesman.

LIHOU, JACK, who died on January 6, aged 90, was a tall leg-spinner from Brisbane who played 26 matches for Queensland spread over a decade from 1955-56, taking 50 wickets at 50 apiece. He claimed some notable scalps – Neil Harvey (his first victim) and Bob Simpson, plus Garry Sobers and Hanif Mohammad (for 95) in tour games – but quick-footed batsmen often feasted on his tossed-up deliveries.

LIVINGSTON, NEVILLE O'REILLY, died on March 2, aged 73. A Jamaican reggae singer better known as Bunny Wailer, he was the last survivor of Bob Marley's backing group. According to *The Times*, their "ska and dancehall sound had been refined into the slower rhythms of reggae, with Wailer's sweet tenor voice harmonising beautifully with Marley's, while Wailer added percussive beats on the drums". Bunny, who carved out an impressive solo career after leaving the group, was also an avid cricket fan, and featured in the acclaimed 2011 documentary *Fire in Babylon*, which charted the rise of the

West Indian team that dominated world cricket in the 1980s. He insisted on wearing white for the filming. "The Caribbean people have some sort of knowledge of how to hold a bat or how to bowl a ball," he said, before using the local patois to shoo off a dog which had interrupted the interview. Returning to the task at hand, he described West Indies' 1984 blackwash of England as "like slaves whipping the asses of masters".

LODHGAR, MURTAZA YAKUBBHAI, died of a heart attack on September 17, aged 45, shortly after having dinner in Visakhapatnam with the Mizoram Under-19 side he was coaching in India's Vinoo Mankad Trophy. A slow left-armer, Lodhgar played nine matches for Bengal, taking 11 for 117 in a victory over Karnataka in his second match, at Kolkata in 2004-05.

LORING, KEITH, who died on December 4, aged 76, was Derbyshire's chief executive from 2008 to 2012, having joined their commercial department in 2002. He arrived soon after a long spell at Derby County FC, during which he oversaw their move from the Baseball Ground to Pride Park. Don Arnott, Derbyshire's chairman, said: "I feel like I've lost my right arm."

LUSH, NORMAN HAROLD, who died on October 10, aged 100, was the master in charge of cricket at St Columba's College in Dublin for around 30 years. A staunch supporter of local cricket, he was president of the short-lived Irish Cricket Society, and of the Leprechauns, a wandering side. He retired to Somerset, and was a regular visitor to Lord's, most recently for Ireland's first Test there, in 2019.

McCAW, PETER MALCOLM, died on July 28, aged 91. Malcolm McCaw was given a chance by Wellington after scoring 120 against them for New Zealand Universities at the Basin Reserve in April 1952 (team-mates included future Test players Jack Alabaster and Zin Harris). He played three Plunket Shield matches the following season, making 51 on debut against Auckland on Christmas Day 1952. A chartered accountant, he was treasurer of the Wellington Cricket Association from 1970 to 1976, and later their president.

McDONALD, COLIN CAMPBELL, AM, who died on January 8, aged 92, opened in 47 Tests for Australia for a decade from 1951-52. He was not an eye-catching batsman, but durable and calm under pressure. When he made his debut, alongside his Victoria and Melbourne University club team-mate George Thoms in the last Test against West Indies at Sydney, the local *Daily Mirror* dubbed them "Stodge" and "Splodge". McDonald recalled: "We never did ask who was Stodge and who was Splodge. We were just happy to be there."

Thoms chose to concentrate on his medical career, and never played another Test. But McDonald, who started with 32 and 62 as Australia won easily, became a fixture, alongside the third debutant in that match, Richie Benaud; they undertook three Ashes tours together. "He was one of the most courageous cricketers I saw," said Benaud.

Jack Fingleton, the former Test-opener-turned-journalist, wrote: "He is no stylist. He plays a lot with his bottom hand and doesn't move on the balls of his feet, so his footwork is not as deft as others, but there is no mistaking his capacity or temperament… He reminded me of Herbert Sutcliffe, and that must be pretty high praise." McDonald's ability to cut and hook allowed him to deal with short-pitched bowling and, despite Fingleton's misgivings, he developed into a successful player of spin.

He was born into a cricket family: his mother's cousin Keith Rigg won eight Test caps in the 1930s, while his brother Ian also played for Victoria, and accompanied the national team to India and Pakistan in 1959-60 as their medical officer. Colin made his debut for Victoria in 1947-48, and leapt into the Test reckoning four years later with 207 at the SCG against a New South Wales attack including Benaud, Keith Miller and Alan Davidson. He ensured a first Ashes tour with 154 against South Africa at Adelaide in January 1953, when he put on 275 with Australia's captain Lindsay Hassett, but had an underwhelming time in England, failing to make the Test side. Back home, though, McDonald quickly recovered his touch, making his highest first-class score, a chanceless 229 against South Australia at Adelaide.

After Frank Tyson's searing pace brought two big England victories in the 1954-55 Ashes, McDonald was recalled for the Fourth Test. Even though Australia lost again, his 48 and 29 were glimmers of resistance amid the carnage, before 72 and 37 in the final match kept England at bay. Heavy rain had prevented any play until the fourth afternoon, but McDonald's composure against left-arm spinner Johnny Wardle, who reaped eight of the 16 wickets to fall, helped avert another defeat.

The Australians were able to breathe more easily on their inaugural tour of the West Indies. McDonald's 449 runs included three century opening partnerships, and a memorable 127 in the last Test, in Jamaica, where he and Neil Harvey added 295 after Australia had been seven for two. McDonald called it "the tour of a lifetime", and matched his distinguished partner, Arthur Morris, run for run; in four opening stands together, they put on 102, 191, 71 and 70. "It would be absolutely wrong to draw conclusions," said McDonald of Morris, who was in awe of him. "I was in awe of him."

His second tour of England, in 1956, proved more rewarding than the first, although the series was overshadowed by the feats of Jim Laker. McDonald's 89 in 337 minutes in the second innings at Old Trafford was more than 50 ahead of any other Australian, as Laker claimed 19 wickets. In the Second Test, at Lord's, McDonald and his new opening partner, Jim Burke, had shared a stand of 137, which paved the way for Australia's only victory of the summer. There was much discussion about the pitches being tailored to suit England's strengths but, in an interview with Gideon Haigh half a century later, McDonald admitted that the side "were poor at playing off-spin on slow, turning wickets. They bowled well. We batted very badly."

The 1958-59 Ashes series found McDonald at the peak of his powers. He contributed 519 runs at 64, with a four-hour 47 in the Second Test, while in the Fourth he amassed 170 – his highest Test score – and an opening stand of 171 with Burke, after a narrow escape first ball, from Brian Statham: "It beat me all ends up and flew about one inch over the top of my middle stump." He shifted up a gear in the final Test, on home turf at Melbourne, hitting a first-innings 133 out of 209 while he was at the crease, then attacking Fred Trueman to make 51 of a target of 69.

There was a reminder of the Laker nightmare in India in 1959-60, when off-spinner Jasu Patel took 14 wickets on a dusty track in Kanpur. McDonald top-scored in both innings, with 53 and 34, but could not stop India recording their first Test victory over Australia. He adopted a more pugnacious approach against the extreme pace of Wes Hall during the memorable 1960-61 series, which began with the historic tie at Brisbane. In the final Test at Melbourne, which Australia won by two wickets to pinch the series 2–1, he and Bob Simpson kicked off with a stand of 146 in 166 minutes early on the second day; McDonald's 91 represented one for each thousand of a then-record crowd. He and Hall, after a high-intensity summer-long duel, exchanged sweaters, and remained friends for life.

Victoria plum: Colin McDonald in 1955.

Fairfax Media/Getty Images

DOUBLING UP

Most innings before first single-figure dismissal in Tests:

		Debut			Debut
23	C. C. McDonald (A)	1951-52	14	D. I. Gower (E).........	1978
17	G. Pullar (E)	1959	13	K. R. Miller (A)	1945-46
17	P. J. L. Dujon (WI)	1981-82	13	G. S. Sobers (WI).......	1953-54
15	S. G. Barnes (A)........	1938	13	A. P. Gurusinha (SL)	1985-86
14	F. M. M. Worrell (WI) ...	1947-48	13	P. S. P. Handscomb (A) ..	2016-17
14	E. D. Weekes (WI)	1947-48	12	C. E. Pellew (A)........	1920-21

J. B. Bolus (E, debut 1963) was not dismissed in single figures in any of his 12 Test innings.

Later in 1961 came a third tour of England, but a half-century in the Third Test at Headingley proved McDonald's international swansong: his trip was virtually ended by a freak wrist injury, caused by the stiff gearstick of a minivan he had bought to ferry his family around the country. "I had determined that it was time to earn a living away from cricket," he wrote. "It was wonderful to view, even if from the dressing-room, the most remarkable Fourth Test victory at Manchester, the scene of the 1956 debacle."

After a spell as a teacher, he moved into insurance, and did some cricket commentary. His style reflected his character: undramatic, insightful and nuanced. He decried sledging as "an abomination". McDonald was executive director of the national Lawn Tennis Association from 1976 to 1987, overseeing the construction of the shiny new venue for the Australian Open in Flinders Park, across the railway from the MCG. He had also been a Melbourne city councillor for a decade from 1963.

He remained a familiar face around the MCG and, after much prompting, produced an autobiography in 2009. "He was an asset to Australian cricket, whose courage was of the highest order," said Neil Harvey, who first met McDonald when they were 14-year-old school cricketers. "He was a pleasure to bat with, because he was so supportive and read the game so well."

McKAIG, WILLIAM, died on April 25, aged 72. A cricket-loving minister in the Church of Scotland, Bill McKaig was a keen follower of both Greenock CC and the national team, often travelling to their away games. A fount of general knowledge, he was the only contestant to reach the maximum possible score (433) on the TV quiz show *Fifteen to One*.

McKECHNIE, DONALD ERNEST CAMERON, died on August 10, aged 77. A left-arm spinner from Dunedin, Don McKechnie played 14 first-class matches for Otago, his highlight coming when his nine wickets in the match helped earn a ten-run victory over Auckland in 1975-76; his haul included four Test players. He later became an umpire, and stood in eight first-class games.

McKNIGHT, STEWART GEMMELL, who died on January 8, the day before his 86th birthday, was a good all-round sportsman who played seven matches for Otago in 1958-59 and 1966-67, usually opening the batting, although his highest score was 23. Against the MCC tourists during his first season, he was bowled by Frank Tyson in the first innings, and Fred Trueman in the second. In 1964, McKnight undertook a three-month world tour with a New Zealand Cricket Council team, playing in 11 different countries. "There were three of us who scored 1,000 runs," he remembered. "I think I celebrated fairly well." He later took up bowls, and represented New Zealand at curling. His son, Ken, also played for Otago.

MAINS, GEOFFREY, MBE, died on April 16, aged 87. Seamer Geoff Mains played six matches for Gloucestershire in the early 1950s, starting against the touring South Africans in 1951, when he realised – as he prepared to face the speedy Cuan McCarthy – that he had forgotten to put on a box. He never managed more than two wickets in a first-class innings, but did take seven for 28 for the Second XI against Wiltshire in 1954. A brewery representative, Mains later undertook charity work, recognised by an MBE.

MALLETT, ASHLEY ALEXANDER, who died on October 29, aged 76, was Australia's best off-spinner in the long period between Hugh Trumble's retirement in 1903-04 and the recent emergence of Nathan Lyon. Tall and accurate, Mallett had a delicate, spidery approach to the crease, and delivered the ball with a precise action that suggested he was placing it on the desired spot, coupled with a clear turn of the wrist, as if closing a door. He was also a superb fielder, despite short-sightedness and a reputation for pratfalls. According to Ian Chappell, his long-time captain, he "might just have been the clumsiest man ever to take a hundred Test wickets and a slew of blinding catches in the gully".

Mallett had a circuitous route to the top. Born in Sydney but brought up in Perth, he took up off-spin after reading of Jim Laker's exploits in 1956. He was twelfth man in two matches for Western Australia in 1966-67 but, frustrated by the WACA's pace-friendly pitches, he (and future Test team-mate Terry Jenner) moved to Adelaide, not long after getting a lesson in slow bowling from the old Australian leg-spinner Clarrie Grimmett. "It was all about getting hard-spun deliveries above the level of the eyes of the batsman," remembered Mallett, who would later write a biography of Grimmett. "He always said the secret to spin bowling was not where the ball landed but how it arrived."

Things started moving more quickly: Mallett took 32 wickets at 25 in his first season for South Australia, including six for 75 in a satisfying victory in Perth. "I could play you till the cows come home," WA's captain Tony Lock had informed Mallett the night before – but he was the last to fall, offering no shot to a big turner that knocked back leg stump. "The cows have arrived early," announced Mallett.

He also acquired his lifelong nickname. "I was twelfth man for the first match," he recalled. "Not a word did I utter unless I was answering a question from one of the players. After pouring the drinks at the close of play on day three, the keeper, Barry Jarman, walked past me, stopped abruptly, turned and yelled: 'Shut up, you rowdy bugger!'" Thus was born "Rowdy" Mallett.

That first season won Mallett a place on the 1968 England tour but, with the cautious Bill Lawry no great admirer, he received few opportunities until the final Test at The Oval. He claimed a distinguished maiden scalp, Colin Cowdrey, with his fifth ball, and finished with five wickets, all from the top seven – including Basil D'Oliveira after his historic 158 – plus a three-hour unbeaten 43, the highest score of his 38 Tests.

Mallett had a stellar tour of India in 1969-70. "I regard Erapalli Prasanna as the best off-spinner I played against," said Chappell, "and Rowdy matched him wicket for wicket – he ended up taking 28, two more than Prasanna." Even so, he was jettisoned after one Test in South Africa soon after, despite taking five for 126 in the first innings at Cape Town, which earned him a "Well bowled, bird-brain!" from his skipper. "Lawry, a renowned bird-fancier, probably meant it as a term of endearment, although he could have been kinder," reflected Mallett.

Things changed once Chappell became captain. After a subdued second tour of England, he bowled Australia to victory over Pakistan at Adelaide in December 1972 with a career-best eight for 59. "Pakistan fell victim to Mallett's improved guile and accuracy," wrote Phil Wilkins in *Wisden*. A burgeoning career as a journalist

Rowdy: Ashley Mallett at the MCG, 1980.

meant he missed the West Indian tour that followed, but he elbowed his way back into the side for the 1974-75 Ashes, when his gully fielding came to the fore as England's helmetless batsmen fidgeted and flinched against Dennis Lillee and Jeff Thomson.

After a quiet time at the inaugural World Cup in 1975 in England – Mallett played in Australia's three group games, but not the knockouts – and in the four Ashes Tests that followed, he lost his regular place. He eventually signed for World Series Cricket – against the wishes of Kerry Packer, who thought he was just a "straight-breaker". Ian Chappell insisted on his inclusion, and Packer agreed, initially stipulating that he would sign Mallett only if he could get him out twice in an over in the nets. It's thought this confrontation never took place.

Increasingly troubled by arthritis, which affected his high action, Mallett played only three more Tests after peace was brokered. He went out in style, with the Centenary Test at Lord's in 1980, when he was preferred to Thomson, and claimed David Gower as his 132nd and last wicket. "He had the capacity to bowl sides out and contain batsmen when the situation arose," said Chappell. "Added to this was a good temperament and the ability to bowl his best at the better players."

He took up coaching, refusing to teach off-spinners the doosra because he was convinced it was impossible without throwing, and turned full-time to journalism. He produced two dozen books, the best probably the studies of his contemporaries Chappell, Thomson and Doug Walters. His last, a biography of Neil Harvey, was published a few months before Mallett's death from cancer. Left-arm spinner Brad Hogg, one of many who benefited from his wise counsel, summed him up: "Drift through the wonders of life, drop on the lives of many, and put a spin on a great story."

MAQSOOD ANWAR, who was 44, collapsed and died of an apparent heart attack on July 17, while playing for Sully Centurions in a club match in Glamorgan. A fund was set up in his memory, aimed at providing defibrillators for local teams.

MARISA, NATASHA HANNAH (*née* Raine), who died of breast cancer on September 7, aged 29, had a long involvement with Hampshire cricket. From the Cove club near Farnborough, she played for the county Under-13s (whom she would later coach) and upwards to the senior team, captaining them for a time. In 2009, she made 97 not out at Tiverton for Hampshire against Devon (the future England captain Heather Knight replied with 161). She was married to Stanley Marisa, a left-handed all-rounder who played first-class cricket in Zimbabwe, and for their youth team in the Under-19 World Cup.

MATIER, ROBERT BOYD, died on March 30, aged 85. A left-handed all-rounder who played three times for Ireland in 1963, Bobby Matier was unlucky that two of his appearances came against the West Indian tourists; he had to face Charlie Griffith and Lester King on a sporting pitch in Dublin's College Park. "I was sitting behind the bowler's arm that day," recalled the Irish historian Edward Liddle. "It was terrifying even from 70 yards away. How Griffith didn't seriously injure someone I will never know." In club cricket, Matier captained Queen's University, Woodvale and Lurgan, and played for Ulster Country in the inter-provincial competition. A teacher, he became headmaster of Limavady Grammar School.

MISHRA, RUCHIR, who died of Covid-19 on May 4, aged 42, was a writer from Nagpur who covered cricket for *The Times of India*. "He was one of the nicest journalists," said the former Test opener Wasim Jaffer.

MOHAN SINGH, who committed suicide on November 7, aged 45, had been a groundsman at the Sheikh Zayed Stadium in Abu Dhabi for 17 years, after moving from Mohali in India. He was found at home shortly before the T20 World Cup match between Afghanistan and New Zealand, which went ahead as planned after consultation with Mohan's family.

MOHAPATRA, PRASANTA RAGHUNATH, died of Covid-19 on May 19, aged 47, ten days after his father – an MP in the Rajya Sabha – also succumbed. The son scored five centuries in 57 matches for Orissa, whom he often captained. His highest score, an eight-hour unbeaten 157 against Bihar at Ranchi, came on his debut, aged 17, in December 1990. He later became a BCCI match referee.

MOORE, EDWARD ROBERT, committed suicide on February 6, aged 50. A left-arm opening bowler from Dublin, Eddie Moore made 25 appearances for Ireland between 1992 and 1995, achieving good pace, although his 22 wickets came at over 53 apiece. He first caught the eye for Irish Schools in 1986, when he dismissed the 16-year-old Mark Ramprakash. After being dropped by Ireland, Moore seemingly lost his love for cricket, and rarely played again.

MOORE, CAPTAIN SIR THOMAS, died on February 2, aged 100. "Captain Tom" captured the attention and admiration of Covid-ravaged Britain during 2020, when news filtered out of his attempts to raise money for NHS charities by walking 100 lengths of his back garden as his 100th birthday loomed in April. Footage of Moore undertaking his daily task, complete with walking frame, soon featured on every news channel, and he achieved astonishing celebrity – and astonishing success, as donations rocketed him far beyond the original target of £1,000; the final figure was around £33m. Captain Tom and his twinkling smile were everywhere: he was knighted by the Queen at Windsor Castle, collaborated on a No. 1 hit single, was honoured with an RAF fly-past, released an autobiography, and had buses and trains named after him. Moore, who had a lifelong interest in cricket, was made an honorary member of the England team, fulfilled a cherished ambition by visiting Barbados (where he met Garry Sobers), and received life membership from MCC, who invited him to ring the bell at a Test in 2021. It never happened: already suffering from pneumonia, which prevented him being vaccinated, he contracted Covid.

MOSELEY, EZRA ALPHONSA, died after a road accident in Barbados on February 6, aged 63. When he was called up by West Indies for the Third Test against England in Trinidad in 1989-90, debate over Moseley's selection centred on politics rather than cricket. What perturbed many was not a 32-year-old debutant replacing Malcolm Marshall, but Moseley's participation, seven years earlier, in a rebel tour of apartheid South Africa. As Jamaican politician A. J. Nicholson pointed out in a letter to *The Gleaner*, the timing was especially sensitive: "To my mind there is something utterly wrong in witnessing the jubilation of the release in February of Nelson Mandela after 27 years in bondage, and the inclusion of Moseley in March."

Of the 20 players who took part in the two tours of South Africa, Moseley alone went on to represent West Indies after their life bans were rescinded in 1989. He played in just two Tests, but made a decisive contribution in his first, when a spiteful delivery broke the hand of England captain Graham Gooch. In Gooch's absence, West Indies came from behind to win 2–1. Moseley kept his place for the Fourth Test on his home ground at Bridgetown, but there was talk of a supporter boycott if he was selected for the Fifth, in Antigua. He withdrew, citing a – possibly diplomatic – hamstring strain. His two Tests brought six wickets at 43, though Alec Stewart rated him the fastest bowler in the series.

The ball to Gooch summed up Moseley's threat. Like Marshall, he had a chest-on action and a comparatively short run-up, but – from only 5ft 10in, and despite a skiddy trajectory – could produce disconcerting bounce at high speed. Robin Smith believed he generated more pace off the pitch than any bowler he faced. At Newlands against South Africa on the first rebel tour in 1983, he forced Jimmy Cook into desperate evasive action. Barry Richards, Cook's opening partner, said: "Ezra was very deceptive. He bowled James the quickest bouncer. I'll never forget that look on his face when he looked down the other end."

Moseley had been working as a waiter at Grantley Adams Airport in Barbados, and playing club cricket, when he was spotted by Trevor Bailey. Essex had no vacancy, but

Adrian Murrell, Getty Images

Quite a handful: Ezra Moseley in 1990.

Bailey recommended him to Glamorgan. He must have regretted his generosity: on a freezing opening day of the 1980 season at Swansea, Moseley marked his first-class debut with six for 102 – against Essex. His victims included Mike Denness, Ken McEwan, Keith Fletcher and Brian Hardie. "Six wickets on a plate as Moseley the waiter puts poor Essex in the soup," said the *Daily Express*.

He finished the season with 51 wickets at 26, and returned in 1981 to take 52 at 18. "He was unknown when he came to us, but he had that extra pace from a very short run-up," said the Glamorgan opener Alan Jones. Moseley's 1981 tally included a career-best six for 23 against the Australians at Swansea. Nine days earlier, he had taken a hat-trick against Kent in the Benson and Hedges Cup. "He made a big difference to our side, because we'd always lacked genuine pace," said Jones. "I faced him in the nets a lot, and he helped me prepare for the other West Indian bowlers on the circuit." Moseley finally made his Barbados debut in 1981-82, but suffered a stress fracture in his lower back. Uncertainty over his future prompted his decision to go to South Africa. He played little on the first tour but, when the rebels returned in 1983-84, took 24 wickets at 24 in the first-class matches; only Sylvester Clarke had more. Moseley was also the leading wicket-taker in the one-day games. It led to a contract with Eastern Province.

He returned briefly to Glamorgan in 1986, but otherwise found employment in the Central Lancashire League. In 2007, the journalist Les Barlow named him ahead of Andy Roberts in an all-time CLL professionals XI. Able to play at home again in 1989-90, he took 24 wickets in the Shell Shield to earn his Test call-up when Marshall injured a finger. He retired after a successful season with Northern Transvaal in 1991-92.

Moseley became a coach and selector in Barbados, and was assistant coach to West Indies women when they won the 2016 World T20. All-rounder Deandra Dottin said: "He did a fantastic job for the players and the game." At St Michael's School, he worked with the future Test captain Jason Holder. Moseley was reluctant to revisit the rebel tours, and the writer Ashley Gray found him elusive when researching his book, *The Unforgiven*. He died after his bicycle was in collision with a car.

MOSSOP, BRIAN CAMPBELL, who died on May 12, aged 82, was a South African-born journalist who arrived in Australia as a stowaway and began work as a farmhand before finding a newspaper job and, under an amnesty, officially becoming a fair-dinkum Aussie. He spent a decade as the cricket correspondent of *The Sydney Morning Herald*, covering the Ashes tours of 1977 and 1981. "Brian was an unpretentious and versatile journalist, greatly admired by his peers," said his friend Mike Coward. Mossop was big and bearded, and looked like an old sea-dog. He had a great sense of fun, and finished his career as food critic of the *Gold Coast Bulletin*, which suited him fine.

MURDEN, KRISTIAN JOHN, who died of cancer on December 31, aged 50, did not pick up a bat until he was 15, but became a destructive Nottinghamshire club cricketer, hitting 20 centuries – and almost 600 sixes – for Clifton Village CC. "His mantra was to dominate," said team-mate Richard Harrison. "Once, he hit a flat pull shot into a dry stone wall on the boundary, and the ball was buried that deep we couldn't extricate it."

NADIR SHAH, who died of cancer on September 10, aged 57, was a long-serving umpire from Bangladesh who officiated in 76 first-class games and 43 white-ball internationals. He also featured in nine Tests as a reserve or TV umpire. His career at international level was ended by a ten-year ban in 2012 after he was implicated in a match-fixing sting by an Indian TV programme. He was allowed to return at domestic level when the ban was lifted in 2016. His brother, Jahangir Shah, played five ODIs before Bangladesh attained Test status.

NANAN, NIRMAL, who died on December 4, aged 70, was a middle-order batsman from Trinidad who tried his luck in England after touring with West Indies Young Cricketers in 1970. He spent a decade on the Nottinghamshire staff, hinting at promise with an early century for the Second XI, but 32 first-class matches brought a highest score of 72, against Oxford University in 1971; his other two half-centuries also came in the Parks, in the same fixture in 1977. He played three first-class games in Trinidad, and eventually returned there to live. Although there was less than two years between them, the off-spinner Rangy Nanan – a prolific wicket-taker for Trinidad who played once for West Indies, in 1980-81 – was his nephew.

NASEER SAHAK, who was killed in a bomb attack near Kabul airport on August 26, was a 20-year-old all-rounder who played for the youth teams of Afghanistan's Laghman province.

NAYUDU, CHANDRA, who died on April 4, aged 88, was thought to be the first woman to commentate on cricket for Indian radio, during the 1976-77 England tour. A keen cricketer in her youth, and later a professor of English in Indore for over 30 years, she was the youngest daughter of C. K. Nayudu, India's first Test captain, and wrote a biography of him in 1995. She recalled his eye for neatness, fondness for dogs, and dislike of laziness: "The moment the horn of his car was heard, we would jump out of bed and get busy."

NEWTON, DEREK HENRY, who died on October 7, aged 88, was one of a quartet of progressive administrators who turned Surrey's finances around in the 1970s; they were nicknamed the Gang of Four by a disgruntled secretary who moaned that they wanted to run the club as a business. An insurance broker who captained Old Emanuel CC, Newton had been instrumental in setting up the Surrey Championship in 1968. Together with Bernie Coleman (who also died in 2021), Raman Subba Row and Peter Wreford, he put the county back on a secure financial footing thanks to canny investment and innovative sponsorships; the sale of the ground-naming rights to Foster's in 1988 netted £1m alone. "Although today Surrey is the wealthiest club in the country, in the early 1980s we were the one closest to going to the wall," Newton recalled. "We had the same crowds as, say, Derby and Northants, but we had enormous expenses." Later, when Surrey's chairman, he oversaw the redevelopment of the rickety old west wing of the pavilion, which became the cavernous Bedser Stand, opened in 1991. Surrey faced ruin if it was not replaced, as the ground looked likely to be deemed unfit for international matches. A "Save The Oval" fund was falling short before Newton roped in a recently retired banker with a bulging contacts book: "We were told we'd do well to get £250,000 in a year. Michael Sandberg took charge of the appeal and passed a million within six months. It was an astonishing achievement." Newton was Surrey's chairman from 1979 to 1994, and president in 2004.

OGILVIE, JOHN EDWARD, who died on April 17, aged 89, was a tall New Zealander who had an unusual first-class career: three matches for Wellington in 1953-54, scoring 54 against Auckland, and two more ten years later, making 50 against Northern Districts. In between, he became the first Hutt Valley player to score 5,000 runs in senior cricket.

OLTON, MALCOLM FRANCIS, died on April 10, aged 82. "Mike" Olton arrived in Kent in the early 1960s from Trinidad, where he had played two first-class matches, one against the 1959-60 England tourists. A hard-hitting batsman, off-spinner and excellent slip fielder, he appeared frequently for Kent's Second XI, taking six for five – 16-year-old

Derek Underwood claimed the other four – as Hampshire were bundled out for 48 in Beckenham in May 1962. His only first-team appearance came later that season, against the Pakistan tourists at Canterbury, where he dismissed Ijaz Butt and Wallis Mathias. By the time he was qualified to play in the Championship, Olton had a good job in the motor trade, and he concentrated on club cricket, mainly with Blackheath. They lifted the Kent League twice in his time, and reached two national club finals at Lord's, winning in 1971 but losing ten years later.

PANDA, RABI NARAYAN, who died of Covid-19 on May 7, aged 62, was a batsman who played 30 first-class matches for Orissa from 1976-77: his highest score was 77 against a strong Bengal attack at Eden Gardens in December 1978. He captained East Zone against the 1979-80 Australian tourists, and became a state selector.

PARANJAPE, VASUDEV JAGANNATH, who died on August 30, aged 82, played 29 first-class matches, mostly for Bombay, winning two Ranji Trophy finals. The higher of his two centuries was 127 against Baroda in November 1964, and the other followed a few weeks later against Ceylon. But he became far better known as a coach and mentor to up-and-coming cricketers, many from the Dadar Union club in Bombay, where generations awaited the pronouncements of "Vasoo Sir". His son, Jatin Paranjape, also played for Bombay, and won four one-day caps for India 1998; years later, he and journalist Anand Vasu assembled a book of tributes to his father, which included contributions from several Test players. "A gem of a man with a fantastic eye for spotting talent," said Sachin Tendulkar. Yuvraj Singh recalled: "He made me feel so comfortable. He had a way of disarming you, making you feel like you had known him all your life." As Rahul Dravid put it: "He was truly, deeply in love with the game. He inspired me first as a cricketer and inspires me now in my coaching career." The Indian team wore black armbands in Paranjape's memory on the first day of the Oval Test in September.

PARIDA, KANHU CHARAN, collapsed and died on December 19 after sending down the last ball of an evening game in Pattamundai, in rural Odisha in India. A 19-year-old nicknamed "Super Express", Parida had taken three wickets in his first five balls.

PARMAR, PRABHUDESAI M., died of Covid-19 on May 25, aged 76; his wife had also died from it, the previous day. An all-rounder, Parmar played four Ranji Trophy matches for Saurashtra in 1968-69, taking three for 33 against Gujarat in the last.

PEPPIATT, DEREK ROBIN, died on September 18, aged 91. A bowler of brisk inswingers off the wrong foot, Robin Peppiatt made his debut for Buckinghamshire in 1948, aged 18, not long after taking five for 49 to help Winchester College to victory in their annual game against Eton. Peppiatt remained connected to Buckinghamshire cricket for more than 50 years, playing for them until 1965, as a committee member from 1952, then became president in 1996. He captained Beaconsfield for a dozen seasons, and also served on MCC subcommittees. His father, Sir Kenneth Peppiatt, was chief cashier of the Bank of England from 1934 to 1949; his signature appeared on all English banknotes during that time.

PERERA, PETER CHANDRISHAN MANILLA, died of complications from Parkinson's disease on October 24, aged 59. A qualified lawyer, Shan Perera was the Sri Lankan board's first media officer, after a spell as the national team's trainer. While studying at Exeter in 1987, he played for Combined Universities in the Benson and Hedges Cup, and dismissed Hampshire's David Turner and Malcolm Marshall. He moved on to rugby, playing for Harlequins and Rosslyn Park and captaining Sri Lanka, before becoming a sports trainer; he whipped his country's cricketers into shape in 1992. "He did a damn good job in an era when not many had an idea about fitness," said journalist Rex Clementine.

PERVEZ AKHTAR, MIAN MOHAMMAD, who died of Covid-related problems on April 27, aged 68, made over 2,000 runs in first-class matches in Pakistan, with a best of 120 for Lahore B in 1971-72. His younger brother, Mian Aslam, was an umpire who stood in eight Tests, while his nephew, Taufeeq Umar, opened the batting for Pakistan.

PHILPOTT, PETER IAN, OAM, who died on October 31, aged 86, was a leg-spinning all-rounder whose opportunities – for New South Wales and Australia – might have been far greater but for the presence of Richie Benaud. Philpott finally seemed to have a clear run when Benaud retired in 1963-64, only for finger injuries to force early retirement.

Philpott ended up with only eight Test caps, although even that many would have seemed improbable when, as a child, he was diagnosed with a heart condition; medical advances enabled him to live to a good age. Short and energetic, he played first-grade cricket in Sydney at 15, with journalist Ray Robinson noting "signs of a first-class spin bowler" after Philpott caught the eye of Denis Compton and the Bedser twins during England's 1950-51 tour. He made his NSW debut on a peppery SCG pitch in 1954-55, and scored a composed 71 – soon followed by his first wicket, the future Test batsman Peter Burge – to set up victory over Queensland. He flitted up and down the order, sometimes as high as No. 3, and made four centuries – the highest 156 at the SCG in January 1964, also against Queensland, when he put on 176 with the 18-year-old Doug Walters.

"Percy" Philpott had subtle variations of flight, an ability to turn the ball, and a well-disguised wrong'un; he was also an agile fielder. His career-best figures, seven for 52, came in an innings victory over Western Australia at Perth in 1960-61, while three summers later he reaped seven for 71 – and ten in the match – against Victoria. Before that 1963-64 season, Philpott had played only 25 first-class matches in nearly a decade, so 543 runs and 30 wickets were a revelation – but South Australia's Rex Sellers had 46 scalps, and pinched the leg-spinner's spot for the first post-Benaud Ashes tour, in 1964.

Another strong season (and a career-ending injury for Sellers, who won a solitary cap) meant a trip to the Caribbean early in 1965. Philpott played in all five Tests, taking 18 wickets at 34, but did little with the bat. Benaud, by now in the media box, wrote early in the tour: "Just after his 30th birthday, Peter Philpott has come of age as Australia's No. 1 spin bowler". Benaud later sympathised that, in every Test bar the last, West Indies "got away to a good start, which meant Philpott always seemed to be coming on first change to bowl at the openers". Still, he was the man in possession, and took five for 90 in the First Test of the 1965-66 Ashes at Brisbane. But, hampered by torpid pitches and a nagging finger injury, he was discarded after the Third, and missed the following year's tour of South Africa; at the end of the 1966-67 season, still only 32, he retired.

Philpott, who had earlier enjoyed four productive seasons in the Lancashire Leagues, trained as a teacher of English and history. But he was soon in demand as a coach, working in England, New Zealand, South Africa and Sri Lanka, as well as Australia for the best part of half a century. "Peter had the generosity and wisdom to share his knowledge across the globe, and

Central Press/Hulton Archive/Getty Images

In demand: Peter Philpott in 1965.

helped shape the careers of countless cricketers," said Cricket Australia's chairman Richard Freudenstein.

In 1981, Philpott coached Australia's Ashes team in England, although the trip was soured by a lack of support for Kim Hughes, the captain, from some of the senior players. At Headingley, before the antics of Ian Botham and Bob Willis, Philpott was interviewed on *Test Match Special*, and asked whether Hughes was likely to enforce the follow-on. "The English batting is so shattered, with confidence so low, that I don't think Australia can ignore the psychological advantage," he replied. "But I wouldn't like to be batting last on that wicket with more than 100–120 to get…" Set 130, Australia were skittled for 111. "I regret my accuracy," sighed Philpott in his 1990 autobiography *A Spinner's Yarn*. In the foreword, Benaud acknowledged the competition Philpott had faced during his playing career. "Peter and I, Johnny Martin, Bob Simpson and Norm O'Neill all bowled over-the-wrist spin for NSW in those days, and all of us bowled in completely different styles… Peter gave the ball plenty of air and spun it hard – he gave it a really big tweak, far more than I did."

PICKLES, LEWIS, who died on June 11, aged 88, was a Yorkshireman who briefly found a home at Somerset, before being squeezed out when the arrival of Bill Alley increased the competition for batting places. "When I was in the army, I was stationed local to Taunton," said Pickles. "On the recommendation of Johnny Lawrence, I was invited to play for Somerset – I'd been to Johnny's indoor school some winters before." Pickles made 1,136 runs in 1956, including his highest score, a four-hour 87 after opening against Lancashire at Old Trafford. Following his release in 1958, he played for a while in Scotland, but returned to league cricket in Yorkshire, for Len Hutton's old club Pudsey St Lawrence, then for Lightcliffe in the Bradford League.

PILOWSKI, RONALD T., died on August 2, aged 78. An umpire from Cape Town, Ronnie Pilowski stood in ten men's first-class matches, and a women's Test against New Zealand at Newlands in February 1972. He had a vivid memory of South Africa's return to the international fold in 1991: "I was umpiring a club game. Brian McMillan was at slip, and there were other big names playing. Someone ran out of the clubhouse to advise that South Africa had been readmitted to Test cricket, and it was as if the internationals had received an electric shock – like a puppet suddenly coming to life after pulling the strings."

PRESLAND, EDWARD ROBERT, died on August 1, aged 78, Eddie Presland made 30 first-class and 24 one-day appearances for Essex between 1962 and 1970 without ever hitting the heights. He made one fifty – at Northampton in 1967 – but his best year was 1970, when ten appearances brought him 300 runs. He was a more regular performer for the Second XI. Presland enjoyed a dual career as a footballer. A full-back, he made a sensational debut for West Ham in February 1965, scoring the equaliser in a 2–1 win over Liverpool at Upton Park. Also playing were three who would soon help England win the World Cup: Bobby Moore, Martin Peters and Geoff Hurst, his Essex Second XI team-mate. A year earlier, Presland had been best man at Hurst's wedding. He went on to make 65 first-team appearances for Crystal Palace, and become a successful manager in non-league football, steering Dagenham to the FA Trophy at Wembley in 1980. Between 2001 and 2003, he was chief scout of Tottenham Hotspur.

RAJAH, GOOLAM, who died of complications from Covid-19 on June 29, aged 74, was a cricket administrator from Gauteng who was the South African team manager for 20 years – from soon after their readmission to international cricket until the 2011 World Cup, overseeing more than 650 matches, including 179 Tests. "When Ali Bacher offered me the job," Rajah told ESPNcricinfo, "I told him I didn't intend making this a profession: 'I'm already a pharmacist – I've got a reasonable practice, and enjoy what I do.' He said: 'Fine, I will give you a week to think about it.' And that week turned out to be 20 years." Former captain Graeme Smith recalled: "He was a true father figure who looked after the players like his own. He took care of everything with such detail that the players were able to focus totally on the cricket." The South African team wore black armbands in his memory during the third T20 against West Indies in Grenada.

RAJAMAHENDRAN, RAJENDRA, who died on July 25, aged 78, was a media magnate dubbed "the Sri Lankan Kerry Packer", and a philanthropist who supported local cricket in thin pre-Test times. He was the board's vice-president for a time in the 1980s, and helped prepare them for their first Test in England, at Lord's in 1984, by contracting expert advisers, including Ted Dexter. He also provided several prominent cricketers with jobs in his company, among them Duleep Mendis and Arjuna Ranatunga. "I came under his wing from school in 1972-73," said Mendis. "His contribution towards cricket was immense – he used to employ boys from all over, especially from the rural areas, and gave them jobs so they could concentrate on playing cricket." Rajamahendran headed up the Capital Maharaja media conglomerate for almost 30 years, and was credited with modernising television and other media in Sri Lanka. The day he died, the teams observed a minute's silence in his memory before a T20 international against India in Colombo.

RAMACHANDRAN, RAJANGAM THYAGARAJAN, who died on February 4, aged 73, was an umpire from Nagpur who stood in 36 first-class matches in India in a career stretching over more than 20 years. He also umpired four one-day internationals, including West Indies' victory against Sri Lanka in Bombay in the five-nation Hero Cup in 1993-94.

RANE, RANJITA, who died of cancer on May 26, aged 43, was a medium-paced all-rounder who played 44 matches for the Mumbai women's team between 1995 and 2003, before becoming a scorer.

RATCLIFFE, DAVID PHILIP, who died on April 30, aged 81, was a Birmingham-born batsman who played occasionally for Warwickshire, starting in 1957. Although he scored three centuries for the Second XI, he never quite translated that into consistent runs for the first team: he hit 79 against Scotland in May 1961, but 62 against Somerset a few days later remained his only Championship score above 28. His first-class career seemed over after 1962, but he continued to play for the Seconds, and made one final first-team appearance, against Scotland in 1968. His son, Jason, had a longer career with Warwickshire, before moving to Surrey.

RATTRAY, PETER JOHN, who died of cancer on February 22, aged 62, was a batsman from Christchurch who made one hundred in 22 appearances for Canterbury, a superb boundary-filled 133 against a strong Central Districts attack at Nelson in February 1983. He followed that with half-centuries in the next two matches, but faded after two more modest seasons. Rattray had a few games for Nottinghamshire's Second XI in 1984, scoring 82 against Northamptonshire. His sister, Sue, played nine Tests and 15 one-day games for New Zealand.

REHMAN DYER, ABDUR, who died on July 13, aged 84, was a Gujarat-born batsman who played 18 first-class matches in Pakistan. He had a best of 77 not out for Karachi Whites against Sind in 1956-57, sharing a ninth-wicket stand of 140 with the 13-year-old debutant Mushtaq Mohammad, who made 87 before being dismissed by the future cricket writer Qamar Ahmed. Dyer, who was born in Gujarat, rebuilt the family textile business, and invested heavily in sport: his Pakistan Textile Mills club had what Dyer claimed to be the country's first turf pitch, and sumptuous practice facilities for prominent locals. "There is no team or player in Pakistan that didn't practise at my place," Dyer told journalist Osman Samiuddin.

ROBERTS, JAMES BROWN, who died on April 15, aged 87, was a seamer who played the first of his ten first-class matches for Scotland in 1956, taking three Yorkshire wickets, including Ray Illingworth for a duck. In a two-day game against MCC at Lord's in 1958, he claimed five for 54. Initially from the East of Scotland club, he moved to Clydesdale CC when his work in the finance industry took him to Glasgow, and remained a staunch supporter; he also had a spell as a national selector.

Frank Burke, Fairfax Media/Getty Images

Preparing for battle: Cecilia Robinson (left) and England team-mate Edna Barker during a tour of Australasia, January 1958.

ROBINSON, MARY CECILIA, died on November 8, aged 97. The first Test player born in Canterbury, Kent, Cecilia Robinson made two centuries against Australia – 105 at Scarborough in 1951, and 102 at Adelaide in 1957-58, when she batted for more than a day. She captained in the following Test, at Perth (Mary Duggan was unfit), and carried her bat for 96 in the second innings to help England escape with a draw. Robinson taught at Roedean for 32 years, running the sport; latterly she was head of the Junior House. In 2014, she told the historian Raf Nicholson about a schoolmaster who had taught her two older brothers: "I was about five or six, and had been playing with the boys. And he said to my mother: 'She's going to be the best cricketer.'" Robinson made over 1,000 runs for Kent at an average above 50 – and finally received her county cap in September 2021, although she was too infirm to attend the ceremony before England women's one-day international against New Zealand.

CARRYING BAT THROUGH WOMEN'S TEST INNINGS

M. C. Robinson	96* (188)	England v Australia at Perth	1957-58
E. Bakewell	112* (164)	England v West Indies at Birmingham .	1979

RODRIGOPULLE, ELMO MICHAEL, who died on July 20, the day after his 80th birthday, was a Sri Lankan sportswriter with a lively turn of phrase, mainly for Colombo's *Daily News*. He covered cricket in all the Test nations and, until days before his death, was contributing a weekly column to the *Sunday Observer*. In his youth, he had been a handy leg-spinner, and played for the Ceylon Board President's XI against Hong Kong in March 1971. "He was a lovely man," remembered press-box colleague Rex Clementine. "In the 1990s, the skipper Arjuna Ranatunga made sure he travelled in the team bus during overseas tours. Some of the senior players didn't like it, but none dared tell that to Arjuna."

RUNGTA, KISHAN MAHABIRPRASAD, who died of Covid-related issues on May 1, aged 88, was India's chief selector in 1998. He had a long career with Rajasthan, playing in five Ranji Trophy finals, all lost to Bombay. In the 1962-63 final, he scored 64 and 80, hitting the West Indian fast bowler Charlie Stayers for four successive sixes; *Indian Cricket* named Rungta as one of their players of the year. But he missed out on international selection, despite scoring five centuries in all, the highest 130 against a Services attack containing four Test players, in 1960-61. His family were the power in Rajasthan cricket for almost 50 years – his brother, Purushottam Rungta, was the BCCI's treasurer during the 1970s – before the IPL founder Lalit Modi supplanted them.

SAID SHAH, MIAN AHMED, who died on February 5, aged 80, umpired 94 first-class matches in Pakistan between 1972 and 2000, when his last involved the Sri Lankan tourists. A professor of history at Government College, he stood in one Test, against West Indies in his native Peshawar in 1997-98, and five one-day internationals.

SAINSBURY, Dr ERICA JANE, who died on December 24, aged 62, kept wicket for New South Wales in the 1970s before becoming the scorer and statistician for the Australian women's team, a role she performed from 1987 to 2003. She was also an announcer at the SCG. Sainsbury was credited with writing an early version of the official song for the national team. According to former captain Mel Jones, now a commentator, she was "in every way, a really lovely woman".

SALMON, JOHN LIONEL, who died on May 22, aged 87, was a tall seamer who opened the bowling for Victoria in a dozen matches in the 1950s. A stalwart of the Hawthorn–East Melbourne club, he took seven wickets in an innings victory over Queensland at the MCG in 1957-58. But, perhaps lacking a yard of pace, he found his opportunities limited when Ian Meckiff returned to the state side after touring South Africa.

SATHYAJI RAO, BADAMI, who died on September 28, aged 91, was an umpire from Bangalore who officiated in 79 first-class matches over a 25-year period from December 1956. That included 17 Tests, starting with Pakistan's visit in 1960-61 and concluding with two matches of India's 1978-79 series against West Indies. He also stood in five Ranji and four Duleep Trophy finals, and eight games in the County Championship in 1978. He had a spell as assistant secretary of the Karnataka Cricket Association.

SCHONEGEVEL, DESMOND JOHN, died on July 6, aged 86. A hard-hitting batsman from Bloemfontein, Des Schonegevel played 100 first-class matches, including 49 apiece for Orange Free State and Griqualand West, often as captain. He hit ten centuries. He made the highest 151 for OFS against Border at East London in January 1964; he had made 115 against Transvaal B at the Wanderers in 1959-60, sharing a third-wicket stand of 280 with his captain, Clive Richardson, a Currie Cup record at the time. Schonegevel was also a serviceable off-spinner, who took six for 29 against Border in 1967-68. He had 24 wickets that season for Griqualand West, to go with 432 runs, and was one of the *South African Cricket Annual's* cricketers of the year in 1968, alongside soon-to-be Test players Barry Richards and Lee Irvine. When the Australians visited Kimberley in 1969-70, he top-scored twice, with 49 and 85. "Uncle Des" ran a sports shop in the town, and did a lot of coaching: "A bowling tip he gave me when I was 15, I still use 30 years later," said one satisfied customer. He moved into cricket administration: the first chairman of the non-racial Griqualand West board in 1991, he oversaw the unification process for the various governing bodies in the Northern Cape. Schonegevel's son, Wayne, also had a long career for Griqualand West.

SELWOOD, TIMOTHY, died on February 10, aged 76. Tim Selwood looked a good prospect when, aged 18, he scored 55 in his first match for Middlesex's Second XI in 1963. He remained on the fringes of the county side – and made 89 and 130, both not out, for the Seconds against Warwickshire in 1969 – but never cemented a regular first-team place. After failing to pass 35 in nine matches spread over seven seasons from 1966, Selwood played in New Zealand for Central Districts, making his highest first-class score of 89 against the 1972-73 Pakistan tourists at Wanganui. Perhaps boosted by this, he was chosen for nine Championship matches at home in 1973, but again failed to manage a half-century. "He was a good, organised batter, but struggled to hold a place in what was a pretty strong batting side," remembered Clive Radley. "He was a top bloke, great sense of humour. Sometimes he needed it: we sailed to South Africa together a few times, to play and coach, and our cabin was about three decks below the water line." Released by Middlesex, Selwood remained prolific at club level, winning a Scottish cup in 1980 while Stenhousemuir's professional, and the English national knockout two years later with his childhood club Finchley. He also taught and coached. Back in 1972, he had captained a Middlesex side containing Graham Barlow, Phil Edmonds, John Emburey and Mike Selvey to win the county Under-25 competition. His son, Steve, played for Derbyshire.

SHAW, SUSAN WINIFRED, who died on February 3, aged 70, was a glamour model, dubbed the "British Brigitte Bardot", who earned brief notoriety by appearing naked on the TVR car company's stand at the London Motor Show in 1971. Four years later, she featured in just about the only promotional material for the first World Cup in England: more modestly clad in a Jiminy Cricket T-shirt and hot pants, she posed with a bat and stumps on a chilly day at The Oval (Lord's was considered off-limits).

SHUTTLEWORTH, GUY MITCHELL, who died on January 21, aged 94, was a batsman and good cover fielder who made 25 appearances for Cambridge University in the first three years after the war. In 1948, he batted alongside four future England players – Trevor Bailey, John Dewes, Hubert Doggart and Doug Insole (they still lost the Varsity Match). Shuttleworth had made his highest score a fortnight before, against Sussex at Hove, where he put on 171 in two hours with Insole; they both made 96. He scored three centuries for Lancashire's Second XI, and later played a lot of club cricket, including several matches for MCC. Shuttleworth became a teacher, first at Mill Hill School, then at St Peter's in York, where a cup now bearing his name is awarded for sport. He was a noted footballer, appearing once for the England amateur team, and in the 1956 Amateur Cup final for Corinthian-Casuals, where a team-mate was the future England batsman Micky Stewart. He remembered "a very good marker, more defensive than attacking, and a 100% hard worker". Shuttleworth's grandson, the Leicester City and Chelsea fullback Ben Chilwell, made his England debut in 2018.

SILVA, CHANAKA, who died of a heart attack on September 9, aged 40, was an industrious media officer for Sri Lanka Cricket who was thought not to have missed an international match at home for almost 20 years. Affable and approachable, he was especially popular with the press. This eventually counted against him, as the board suspected he was briefing journalists, and transferred him outside Colombo. Rex Clementine denied this: "He was a friend and a brother. But despite our friendship, he never leaked information."

SMITH, DAVID HENRY KILNER, who died on December 17, aged 81, was an obdurate Yorkshire-born left-hander who did well for Derbyshire between 1967 and 1970, reaching 1,000 runs each year bar one (1969, when he made 882). He formed an effective opening partnership with Peter Gibbs, the former Oxford Blue, although their techniques led them to be dubbed "Nick and Block" by journalist Michael Carey; another local writer, Neil Hallam, recalled that not many of their runs came in front of square. The combination worked, though: in 1970, their average partnership was over 50, more than Geoff Boycott and Phil Sharpe (47 for Yorkshire) or Mike Denness and Brian Luckhurst (40 for Kent).

Gibbs recalled: "Determined and gritty, David took opening seriously, which involved seeing off both the shine and the new-ball bowlers, even if it meant a modest tally on the board by lunchtime. Derbyshire's traditional strength in seam bowling on green uncovered wickets meant that, despite relatively low totals, we were rarely out of a match." There was also a whiff of exoticism about the pairing. "And of course – important to cricket anoraks – we had six initials between us. Both of us were North/Midlands state-school boys, a sort of parody of the jazz hats of yesteryear."

Smith's cautious style sometimes had a cavalier side. Gibbs remembered a Sunday League game in 1970. "Hampshire posted 154 on a very slow wicket, and David and I set off at a funeral pace. I met him in between overs and made a disparaging remark about his batting. His response was like that of a horse stung by a bee. Next over, he smashed Derek Shackleton for six into the car park, and continued furiously. We ended up winning with ten overs to spare. David was out for 85, having looked on course for the fastest Sunday League ton. Shackleton, who had gone for an unheard-of six an over, threw his boots into our changing-room in mock resignation."

Obituaries 253

Derbyshire, May 1969. Standing: Bob Taylor, David Smith, John Harvey, Mike Page, Alan Ward, Peter Eyre, Peter Gibbs. Sitting: Ian Hall, Ian Buxton, Derek Morgan, Edwin Smith, Harold Rhodes.

That remained Smith's highest one-day score, but his four first-class centuries included 136 in a ten-wicket win over Lancashire at Derby in 1970, when he shared successive stands of 168 with Gibbs and 175 with Mike Page. Two years earlier, against Essex at Colchester in 1968, Gibbs was stumped for 90 and Smith run out for 99 after an opening partnership of 143. He was capped that season.

Smith emigrated to South Africa, where he played a few games for Orange Free State, although he eventually returned to England. Hallam recalled: "He had worked as a rep in the textile industry, and during his cricket career he had a sideline in flogging cheap bolts of cloth to team-mates for making up into suits." One son, Lawrence, played a few matches for Worcestershire, while another, Jason, appeared for Gloucestershire's Second XI.

SMITH, DONALD VICTOR, who died on January 10, aged 97, had just turned 34 when he was selected for England against West Indies in 1957. He celebrated his call-up with a century against the touring team at Hove, but – opening with Peter Richardson – he could not carry the momentum into the Tests. In three matches, he managed a best of 16 not out, and was not selected again. His confidence, though, was undented: he finished the summer with 2,088 runs at 42, comfortably his most prolific year, and 39 wickets.

Born in Broadwater, Worthing, Smith served as a Lancaster pilot during the Second World War, and made his debut for Sussex in 1946. Initially, his slow left-arm was his stronger suit, but he worked hard to become an attractive left-handed opener. In 1950, he passed 1,500 runs, including a career-best undefeated 206 against Nottinghamshire at Trent Bridge. "Don makes the grade" read the headline in the *Daily Express*. Except he hadn't. Partly because of the presence of David Sheppard, his career was becalmed, until Robin Marlar was made captain in 1955. That summer, Smith topped 1,000 runs, and was persuaded to become a medium-pacer. "He was no good as a left-arm spinner because he didn't spin it," said Marlar. "But I admired the role Trevor Goddard played for South Africa, and I thought Don could do the same for us. I had seen him in the nets, and I knew he could do it."

Smith became a valued member of the Sussex attack for the next six seasons. He was just as effective in 1956, when he combined 1,685 runs and 72 wickets, including a career-best seven for 40 for MCC against Oxford University at Lord's. But it was just a warm-up act for his golden summer in 1957. In the Championship opener against Gloucestershire at Hove, he led a pursuit of 267 with an explosive 166 in just under three hours. Exploiting a 40-yard boundary on the pavilion side, Smith treated off-spinners Bomber Wells and Derek Hawkins savagely. One spectator ran on with an umbrella pleading for an end to the bombardment; another suffered a fractured jaw after being hit by one of his nine sixes. When Smith visited him in hospital, he found his apology was not necessary. "It was a marvellous innings," the patient said. The *Daily Mirror* called him a "cricketing superman". Marlar said: "His batting improved tremendously because of the confidence he gained from his bowling success. He had been a nearly man, but suddenly he was performing."

Smith hit further hundreds against Glamorgan, Middlesex and the West Indians – carrying his bat for 147 out of Sussex's 256 – to earn selection for the Second Test at Lord's. "I suppose they thought, 'Well, this fella's in good nick, we might as well let him have a go,'" he said. But Test cricket was different, and in four innings he was dismissed three times – for eight, one and nought – by Frank Worrell. In his second match, at Trent

---

OLDEST DEBUTANT TEST OPENERS SINCE SECOND WORLD WAR

Yrs	Days			
39	231	E. C. Joyce	Ireland v Pakistan at Malahide	2018
39	105	S. J. Cook	South Africa v India at Durban	1992-93
39	102	Amir Elahi†	India v Australia at Sydney	1947-48
36	317	R. W. G. Emery	New Zealand v West Indies at Christchurch	1951-52
36	174	N. S. Asgarali	West Indies v England at Lord's	1957
35	219	G. M. Emmett	England v Australia at Manchester	1948
35	81	K. H. Eastwood	Australia v England at Sydney	1970-71
34	295	S. G. Gedye	New Zealand v South Africa at Wellington	1963-64
34	36	J. M. Brearley	England v West Indies at Nottingham	1976
34	27	R. G. A. Headley	West Indies v England at The Oval	1973
34	**6**	**D. V. Smith**	**England v West Indies at Lord's**	**1957**

Asgarali and Smith were in the same match.   † In second innings.

Bridge, he walked after edging Worrell to Rohan Kanhai, prompting a frosty dressing-room reception from captain Peter May: "You don't walk in Test matches." Recalling the incident with journalist Paul Hayward in 2017, Smith remembered: "I said, 'Sorry Peter, but this is a cricket match, it's what I do.'" After talking to the umpires, May told him he would have been given not out had he stood his ground. "I thought, 'This really isn't me.'"

In county cricket, he was never so successful again, but passed 1,000 runs for the next four summers, and enjoyed another productive year in 1961, with 1,527 runs and 58 wickets. Early the following season, he suffered a hairline fracture of the skull after being hit by Derbyshire's Harold Rhodes. He was out for only a couple of weeks, but retired at the end of the summer, aged 39.

Smith had started a rose-growing business, though gave it up for a post as coach and groundsman at Lancing College, where he stayed until 1986. In 1984, he coached Sri Lanka on their first Test tour of England, which led to a two-year spell in the role. Meanwhile, on a trip to Australia with Lancing, he reconnected with a former girlfriend. They had first met when he spotted her in the crowd while fielding at Lord's, but the relationship petered out, and she moved to Adelaide, marrying a policeman. When Smith was in the city, he found her in the phone book, discovered she was now divorced, and decided to emigrate. She soon became his second wife. He attended matches at Adelaide Oval before the crowd noise became too much. But he was happy to have had a career in

A cold and golden summer: Don Smith and Len Hutton open the batting for MCC against Lancashire at Old Trafford, June 1957. Smith made 49 and 55.

the 1950s: "I played towards the end of the great days of cricket." He was England's oldest surviving Test player when he died, a mantle that passed briefly to his old team-mate Ian Thomson, and then to another Sussex stalwart, Jim Parks.

STEPHENS, VIVIEN SHERILL (*née* Sexton), who died on September 5, aged 67, was a co-founder of the Central Districts women's team in New Zealand, and scored their first century – 135 against Auckland in December 1980, not long after moving from Wellington. She had played three one-day internationals at the 1977-78 World Cup in India.

STEVENS, GODFREY CYRIL, who died on August 30, aged 35, after contracting Covid-19, was a left-handed all-rounder who had a useful record for Boland in South Africa – 1,675 runs and 50 wickets in 50 matches, with a highest score of 82 after opening against Eastern Province at Port Elizabeth in 2012-13. Four seasons previously, he took three wickets, then made 40 not out, as Boland defeated KwaZulu-Natal in the final of the provincial one-day tournament at Paarl. Stevens had played in the Under-19 World Cup early in 2004, alongside Vernon Philander and Roelof van der Merwe. Latterly he had joined the Boland coaching staff.

STEWART, DAVID PURCELL, OBE, who died on March 16, aged 79, was the only man to hold Surrey's three main administrative posts: he became treasurer in 1997, chairman in 2003 – overseeing the completion of The Oval's huge OCS Stand at the Vauxhall End – and president in 2017. After a long career with financial giants Coopers & Lybrand, he became chairman of a charity providing homes for ex-servicemen. "I used to call him 'Solomon', because he was the wisest man I ever met," said Richard Thompson, who succeeded Stewart as chairman in 2010. "But beyond all his contributions, he just loved watching Surrey play cricket."

STUGER, WAYNE BERNHARDT, who died on January 18, aged 74, was highly thought of as a young cricketer in British Guiana (later Guyana), where his cousin John Trim had made his Test debut. A move to the United States stymied any chance of a long first-class career, but he became a feared opponent in New York league games, and represented the USA in the first two ICC Trophy tournaments, top-scoring with 48 against eventual champions Sri Lanka in the first, in 1979. "He had great hand–eye co-ordination, and a mind uncluttered with anxieties about proper batting technique," said club-mate Keith Lawrence. In 1974, Stuger hit 66 in the annual match against Canada.

SUTCLIFFE, PETER WILFRED, who died on January 10, three days before his 89th birthday, became in 1971 the first director of coaching for the National Cricket Association, the body responsible for recreational cricket (much later subsumed into the ECB). Sutcliffe had never played first-class cricket – but proved an inspired choice, setting up coaching courses and writing instructional books.

He had been a useful off-spinner, taking 54 wickets at 14 in the Minor Counties Championship in 1951 for Yorkshire's Second XI. Jobs in teaching (and teacher training) took him around the country. Eight years later, he claimed eight for 54 for Hertfordshire against Bedfordshire; in 1966, he turned out for Lancashire Seconds, and picked up six for 43 against a Yorkshire team including three future Test players. In 1974, aged 42, he took 11 wickets in three matches for Cumberland. He had been playing for the Staffordshire club Bignall End when the NCA job became available.

One of his sons, Simon, was an Oxford Blue, and played for Warwickshire as an off-spinner. The 2021 Yorkshire yearbook revealed that Sutcliffe senior – born in Halifax – had been approached by the legendary county coach Arthur "Ticker" Mitchell about the possibility of Simon playing for them. Sutcliffe explained that his son was ineligible, as he had not been able to persuade his wife to travel 150 miles so their baby would be born in Yorkshire. Mitchell tutted: "Nay lad, I'd have thought better o'thee than that."

TAHIR MUGHAL, who died of gall-bladder cancer on January 10, aged 43, was a seam-bowling all-rounder who turned out for eight different teams over 14 seasons in Pakistan's domestic competitions; he also made one appearance for Durham in 2004. During his long career he shared the new ball with Waqar Younis and Mohammad Asif, and collected more than 500 wickets, including 83 at 15 during 2001-02. His best figures were seven for 50 for Sialkot against Peshawar in December 2004, which included a hat-trick, with Test batsman Wajahatullah Wasti the middle victim. In 2011-12, now playing for United Bank, Mughal hit 130 not out, his only first-class century, against Quetta. Eight seasons previously, he had smashed 110 from 83 balls in a one-day game to haul Sialkot past United Bank's lofty total of 342 – including seven sixes against an attack led by three Test fast bowlers in Waqar, Mohammad Sami and Shabbir Ahmed. A fellow player thought that, while Test cricket might have been beyond Mughal's compass, he could have been tried in Pakistan's white-ball teams. "He was a brilliant all-rounder, rather unlucky not to play any internationals," agreed Waqar. The Test leg-spinner Imran Tahir, another former team-mate, paid tribute by revealing a shirt bearing a picture of his friend after taking a wicket in a PSL game in Karachi in March.

TARAK SINHA, who died on November 6, aged 71, was a highly respected coach, whose CV included a Ranji Trophy title with Delhi (1985-86) and the first Test series win abroad for India's women (in South Africa in 2001-02). He also churned out first-class cricketers from Sonnet, the club he established in Delhi in 1969: around 100, including 11 who went on to play for India, among them Shikhar Dhawan and Rishabh Pant. Another graduate, the recent Test player Ashish Nehra, bought Sinha a flat in Delhi when he encountered financial problems. Pant paid tribute to "My mentor, coach, motivator – my biggest critic and my greatest fan."

TAYLOR, BRUCE RICHARD, who died on February 6, aged 77, made a still-unmatched entry into Test cricket, hitting a century and taking five wickets for New Zealand against India at Calcutta in 1964-65. "Tails" had been a surprise choice for the tour, after just three first-class matches, and stepped in for the Second Test only when Barry Sinclair fell ill. He memorably filled the breach, sharing a seventh-wicket stand of 163 with his childhood hero Bert Sutcliffe, who kept telling him: "Keep your bloody head, don't slog." The next ball would disappear to the fence, and Sutcliffe gave up. After his 105, which included 74 in boundaries, Taylor took the new ball and claimed five for 86, although a masterly 153 from the Nawab of Pataudi, India's captain, ensured a draw.

Taylor seemed destined for stardom, but rarely approached such batting heights again – though he remained a regular choice until his retirement in 1973. An exception was his other Test century, against West Indies at Auckland in 1968-69, when he hurtled to three figures in 86 minutes, New Zealand's fastest at the time (since bettered by Brendon McCullum in 2015-16). Taylor reached 50 with two straight sixes off Garry Sobers, and 100 with another off Richard Edwards. Journalist Dick Brittenden called it "one of the finest strokemaking assaults I have ever seen". Tall and accurate, Taylor was more consistent with the ball, again reserving his best for West Indies. In the Caribbean in

"Tails, I win": Bruce Taylor hits out for the New Zealanders against Surrey at The Oval, 1965. Arnold Long is behind the stumps.

1971-72, despite being overlooked for the First Test, he took 27 wickets at 17, including a career-best seven for 74 in the Third at Bridgetown. "He made the best use of his height and upper part of his body to swing and cut the ball," said team-mate Mark Burgess. "When it came to batting, he was very balanced – a very big arc when he attacked, and timed it off the middle of the bat."

Another blitz followed at home. After Wellington slipped to 42 for four against Otago at Dunedin in January 1973, Taylor added 255 with 20-year-old Jeremy Coney, hitting 173 despite a knee injury. His hard-pressed runner was John Morrison, soon to be a Test player himself. "He was definitely more tired than I was," said Taylor.

His last Tests came in England soon after; he finished with 111 wickets, then a national record, quickly swamped by Richard Hadlee. Taylor retired after one more domestic season, bothered by back trouble – but returned in 1978-79, aged 35, when the problem turned out to have been an ulcer. He took 20 wickets at 21, prompting suggestions of an international recall. It didn't happen, and he retired for good after the following season, ending up with more than 4,500 runs and 400 wickets. Some felt his overall figures should have been even better. "He was never completely dedicated, and too easy-going to reach the top," wrote John Reid, his first Test captain. "The pity was he had a ton of ability. That's what makes me mad. When they don't have the talent, you can't do much about it. But when they do and don't use it, that's frustrating."

Taylor was a Test selector for a while, but his later years were tough. While working as a school bursar he was jailed for embezzling money to fund a gambling addiction, which ended his first marriage and left him estranged from his children. Later health troubles included the amputation of his right leg because of gangrene, several heart attacks, and bowel cancer. He was helped by his second wife, Annie, and the New Zealand Players' Association. When a fourth heart attack proved fatal, he had just finished collaborating on a book about his eventful life.

THAKUR, DEE, who died of Covid-19 on July 14, aged 54, was Namibia's high-performance manager; he had enjoyed a spell as the national team's coach, after starting as a development officer taking cricket to outlying areas. He played in the Over-50 World

Cup in South Africa early in 2020, taking three for 19 from nine overs against Pakistan. "Friend of many, enemy of none," said Rudie van Vuuren, the double cricket/rugby international who is now president of Cricket Namibia.

THOMSON, NORMAN IAN, died on August 1, aged 92. Ian Thomson looked destined to be remembered as a stalwart Sussex seamer, who collected 100 wickets a season for a dozen years from 1953. His only hint of international recognition had come when he was called up as a replacement for the 1955-56 MCC A-tour of Pakistan, after an injury to Yorkshire fast bowler Mick Cowan. But that changed in 1964. First, Thomson took all ten wickets for 49 against Warwickshire, on a helpful pitch at Worthing. He finished the match with 15 for 75, but Sussex lost after being skittled for 23. "Big Ian ambled shyly in as car horns sounded off a raucous fanfare," reported the *Daily Express* of his ten-for. "Now those silly rumours about me retiring should stop," Thomson said.

Soon after, he received a Test call-up. England were touring South Africa, and looking to move on from the new-ball partnership of Fred Trueman and Brian Statham. Trueman's county colleague Tony Nicholson was originally selected, but withdrew with back trouble, and Thomson again replaced a Yorkshire seamer. He played in all five Tests despite being,

MOST FIRST-CLASS WICKETS BEFORE TEST DEBUT

		M	Avge	Debut
1,527	J. Southerton	249	14.36	1876-77
1,504	W. E. Astill	424	22.74	1927-28
1,497	**N. I. Thomson**	**385**	**20.32**	**1964-65**
1,445	W. G. Grace	279	14.38	1880
1,252	R. D. Jackman	351	22.39	1980-81
1,215	A. S. Kennedy	269	20.28	1922-23
1,143	F. W. Tate	265	21.23	1902
1,089	T. P. B. Smith	313	25.69	1946
1,084	F. Barratt	295	21.47	1929
1,045	A. Shaw	214	12.85	1876-77

All played for England. The most for another team is 712 by T. J. Murtagh, before his Ireland debut in 2018. Shaw's figures include one innings for which the exact analysis is not known.

at 35, older than the pensioned-off pair. Trueman, 33, went on a private tour to Jamaica instead, sponsored by Rothmans, and was unamused to discover that, when injuries forced England to call up a replacement for the final Test, it was another gentle county seamer. "Look who's opening the bowling for England," he fumed. "Ian Thomson and Kenny bleeding Palmer. And here am I bowling for bloody cigarette coupons."

Thomson took nine Test wickets, including Eddie Barlow and Dennis Lindsay twice, but his exertions in South Africa affected him, and he retired at the end of the following summer, after missing out on his traditional 100 wickets. He was tempted back occasionally for one-day games – he had been an important cog in the side that won the first two Gillette Cups – then for two seasons in 1971 and 1972, by which time he was past 40. He had won the match award in the second Gillette final, in 1964. Ted Dexter, Sussex's captain, recalled: "There was dampness in the air, greenness in the wicket, and the redoubtable Thomson wrecked Warwickshire's innings – and the final – in about three overs." He ended with figures of 13–5–23–4 as Warwickshire were skittled for 127.

He finished his career with almost 1,600 first-class wickets at not much over 20. Thomson returned to the family garage business in east London, before teaching geography and coaching at Brighton College, and later at nearby Bevendean Primary School.

Thomson usually bowled within himself, letting the ball go from a high action after an unprepossessing shuffle to the crease. Robin Marlar, another of his captains, remembered:

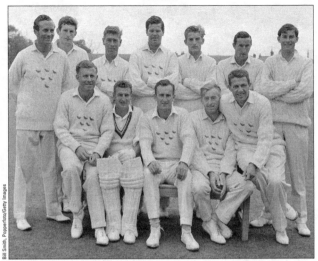

Sussex, August 1963. Standing: Les Lenham, John Snow, Ronnie Bell, Don Bates, Tony Buss, Graham Cooper, Richard Langridge. Sitting: Ken Suttle, Jim Parks, Ted Dexter, Alan Oakman, Ian Thomson.

"His consistent ability to swing the ball in and cut it away, while varying his pace from medium to distinctly sharp, meant his keeper had to hop about." That keeper was often Jim Parks, who succeeded Thomson as England's oldest living Test player. "I remember Ian's first over in Test cricket," said Parks. "He bowled two or three nipping in, then knocked Eddie Barlow's off stump out with a magnificent delivery which pitched middle and hit the top of off. He was a very, very high-class bowler."

TORRENS, ROBERT, OBE, died of complications from Covid-19 on January 23, aged 72. A key figure in Ireland's rise to Test-playing nation, Roy Torrens was an almost permanent presence in the dressing-room, latterly as manager for the World Cup wins over Pakistan in 2007, England in 2011 and West Indies in 2015. Also a useful footballer, Torrens started as a tearaway quick bowler – Ireland's fastest, if he was to be believed – and took 77 wickets in 18 years in the national team from 1966. His best performance was seven for 40 against Scotland at Ayr in 1972, but he missed the famous game in 1969 when West Indies were skittled for 25. He liked to joke: "Do you really think they'd have got that many if I'd been playing?" At club level, he and his two brothers helped Brigade win Ulster's North West Cup seven times, and he once smote 177 in an hour in an evening game.

After finally retiring, Torrens helped select the team, and was president of the Irish Cricket Union in 2000 before, five years later, becoming the team's manager/general factotum; he stepped down in 2015. "He did everything," said former Ireland off-spinner Kyle McCallan. "World Cups, Intercontinental Cups, awards nights or tucking your socks into your trousers." Opener Paul Stirling was particularly close to the man he called "Uncle Roy", and hit an emotional 128 against Afghanistan at Abu Dhabi the day after his death. "Crushing news," he said. "Irish cricket to the core – but an even better man."

Perks of the job... Roy Torrens and Archbishop Desmond Tutu show off their honours: an OBE (2009) and a personalised South Africa shirt (2006).

A tribute match was played in June between Brigade and an XI who had all appeared more than 100 times for Ireland. Former national captain William Porterfield said: "There was no trouble raising a team – everyone accepted straight away. They wanted to celebrate the life of a true friend."

TUTU, ARCHBISHOP DESMOND MPILO, CH, who died on December 26, aged 90, was a South African clergyman who played a major role in the anti-apartheid movement, and helped smooth the path to unity after the release of Nelson Mandela in 1990. He was credited with coming up with the term "Rainbow Nation" to encapsulate his vision of post-apartheid South Africa. In recognition of his efforts, Tutu had been awarded the Nobel Peace Prize in 1984. He was appointed Bishop of Johannesburg the following year, and in 1986 became the Archbishop of Cape Town; no black man had held either position.

In 2008, he was the first non-cricketer to deliver MCC's Cowdrey Lecture at Lord's (Stephen Fry in 2021 was the second). He related how, as a youngster ill with tuberculosis, he had been cheered up by radio commentary on Tests; he linked the "spirit of cricket" with humanity's respect for decency, and condemned the "pariah" regime in Zimbabwe. He also remembered visiting Lord's for South Africa's first post-admission Test there, in 1994: "I seem to recall a captain with dirt in his pockets, and an archbishop who was thought to be improperly dressed for the Pavilion." Fortunately for Anglo-South African relations, the story goes, the stewards were persuaded that an ecclesiastical dog-collar was an acceptable substitute for a tie.

Tutu retired from public life in 2010. "The time has now come to slow down, to sip rooibos tea with my beloved wife in the afternoons, to watch cricket, to travel to visit my children and grandchildren."

UFTON, DEREK GILBERT, died on March 27, aged 92. In the final summer of cricket before the Second World War, Sally Ufton gave in to her 11-year-old son's pleas to watch his beloved Kent, and took him to the Bat and Ball Ground in Gravesend. When Derbyshire opener Robin Buckston fell to a spectacular leg-side catch by Godfrey Evans, his first in first-class cricket, young Derek Ufton glimpsed his own future. "I wouldn't mind doing things like that," he told his mother.

Ten years later, Ufton became Evans's understudy, a role he filled uncomplainingly for a decade. However, Evans's Test career meant Ufton had more opportunities than many

WISDEN SCHOOLS CRICKETERS OF THE YEAR

Filling the gaps

Six of the players named as Schools Cricketers of the Year in the 2021 Almanack were not given obituaries in *Wisden* when they died:

BOWER, MICHAEL JOSEPH DYSON, died on October 24, 2009, aged 79. His 788 runs for Radley College in 1948 included 207 not out – a school record at the time – against St Edward's, Oxford; three days later, he carried his bat for 111 against Stowe. That year, he also reached three figures against the Free Foresters, took 40 wickets with his off-breaks, and captained the Public Schools at Lord's. The *Radleian* magazine warned of "a certain weakness outside off stump, especially to fast bowling", and Bower never did play first-class cricket. He had a few matches for Surrey's Second XI, and turned out for Lensbury, the house team of Shell Oil, based near Twickenham.

FARRELLY, FRANCIS JAMES, died on August 21, 1965, aged 69. A left-arm opening bowler, in 1913 he took 134 wickets at 5.39 for Stonyhurst College in Lancashire, the highest number recorded for a school season in *Wisden* (a team-mate, Roderick Riley, claimed 103). On returning to his native South Africa, Farrelly played for Griqualand West for around a decade, turning into more of a batsman. He made 94 after opening against a strong Western Province side at Kimberley in January 1926, and finished with more than 1,000 first-class runs, and 25 wickets.

FRANCIS, GODFREY HERBERT, died in January 1912, aged 21. In 1907, he took 123 wickets at 7.23 for Chatham House School in Kent, the second-highest number recorded for a school season in *Wisden*. By the time of the 1911 census, he was living with his widowed mother – and a sister who was an actress – in Loughton, Essex, and working in "the coaling trade". But he died early the following year, of an undisclosed illness.

LAY, ARTHUR TRADESCANT, died on October 1, 1947, aged 46. In 1919, he scored 1,259 runs at 57, and also claimed 49 wickets, for Fettes College; only one other winner of the Wisden award went to a Scottish school (Preston Mommsen of Gordonstoun in 2006). Lay became a silk inspector in Hong Kong, and was interned by the Chinese during the Second World War; he became ill and, by some reports, died while imprisoned there (others suggest he died in Surrey shortly after returning home). In addition to all-round sporting skills – he was in the school teams for rugby, hockey and fives – Lay was also an accomplished pianist; *The Fettesian* magazine records that he once produced "a startling new version of the hymn tune at House prayers".

SALMON, LAWRENCE ROBERT WILLIAM, died on April 29, 2001, aged 93. A left-arm opening bowler, in 1927 he took exactly 100 wickets for Allhallows School in Somerset. That included nine for 26 against Exeter School, eight for 45 against Newton College, and seven for 57 against Kelly College. The school magazine lauded his "meritorious feat", but cautioned that, when batting, he "should learn to keep his legs straight and knees unbent". Salmon never played first-class cricket, not helping his cause by going to live in the United States in the late 1930s.

TRICK, STANLEY ARTHUR, died on February 11, 1958, aged 73. In 1902, he scored 759 runs at 58 for Merchant Taylors' School (then based in central London, before moving out to Northwood in 1933), and took 55 wickets; his runs included 157 against Epsom College. He became a colliery agent, and captained the Old Merchant Taylors' club. He played five matches for Essex between 1905 and 1919, with a highest score of 26 against the 1907 South African tourists. His nephew, Stan Trick, had a few games for Glamorgan as a left-arm spinner after the Second World War.

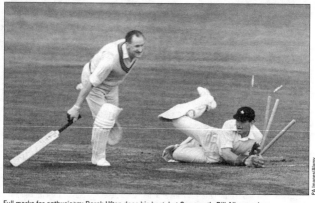

Full marks for enthusiasm: Derek Ufton does his best, but Somerset's Bill Alley survives.

reserve wicketkeepers: he finished with 260 catches, Kent's ninth-highest, and 44 stumpings, and also served as Second XI captain and coach, chairman of the cricket committee, and president in 2001. In the winter, he played football for Charlton Athletic, making 277 appearances, mainly at centre-half, and won an England cap against the Rest of Europe in 1953. At the time of his death, he was England's oldest international. But he said: "Though it's treasured, I'd swap my England football cap for an England cricket one."

As a boy in Crayford, he did not play cricket regularly until a scholarship to Dartford Grammar School, where he was encouraged by PE teacher Joe Jagger, father of Mick. Ufton worked in a shipping office in London, and in August 1944 received a call from his father. His mother had been caught in a V1 flying-bomb strike on Crayford High Street. They hurried to hospital, where a nurse said offhandedly: "Oh, she's dead."

After a trial at Canterbury in 1946, he joined the staff before his national service. Although Evans had succeeded Les Ames, Kent were short of wicketkeeping cover. Ufton had barely performed the role, but was desperate for a break. He gave up his job, and spent the summer playing for various Kent sides, scoring an unbeaten 131 for the Seconds against Sussex. Once in the army, he found more opportunities to play football, and his cricket was sporadic until he left the service in 1949. He was offered terms, but only after George Downton – father of the future Kent and England keeper Paul – had turned the county down. That summer, with Evans on Test duty, Ufton finally made his first-class debut, against Warwickshire at Maidstone.

It ended in a draw, with Warwickshire nine down, and two short of victory. Tom Dollery looked set to win the game, until he was brilliantly caught by Ufton down the leg side, though the press also took him to task for a missed stumping in the final over. He made 14 appearances in 1950, and 13 in 1953 and 1955, before an extended run the following season: 20 matches, sometimes as a batsman while Evans kept wicket. His only first-class hundred came against Sussex at Hastings in 1952. And, from 1954, the arrival of Tony Catt meant he also had a rival for the deputy's role. Ufton admitted he was not a natural behind the stumps, but Kent batsman Bob Wilson said: "I always felt he was a very competent keeper, not flashy like Godfrey or as energetic as Alan Knott. But if you were a bowler, and Derek was keeping, you could be confident he was going to catch anything that came to him."

He became good friends with Evans, though like many of his team-mates was dismayed by some of his county performances. "What time are we on TV?" Evans once asked during a Bank Holiday fixture. "He was keeping badly," said Ufton, "but when he found out we were on TV between 12.30 and one o'clock, he pulled off two marvellous catches. After one o'clock, he was terrible again. That was Godfrey."

Under Doug Wright's captaincy in 1956, Ufton performed well in a victory over Middlesex at Maidstone, but was told Evans would be returning next game, at Hove. Wright admitted: "But we're much better when you're playing." Ufton replied: "If that's so, Doug, pick me – you're the captain." Wright: "I daren't do that. The committee would lynch me." Wright arranged for Ufton to be given his county cap during the Sussex match; it arrived, without ceremony, in a plain envelope. When the team returned to Canterbury, there was a committee inquiry: the award had been made without their knowledge.

After Evans's retirement, Catt began the summer of 1960 as first choice. But he lost form with the bat, and Ufton took over, carrying the momentum into 1961, his best season: 90 dismissals and 668 runs. "He was certainly good enough to have been the first-choice keeper for about half the sides in the Championship," said Wilson. Ufton rejected approaches from Leicestershire, Somerset and Sussex.

Having played with Ames and deputised for Evans, he now helped mentor the young Alan Knott, as Second XI captain. "He was the greatest keeper England has ever had," said Ufton. "And he performed to the same levels for Kent."

Into his eighties, Ufton worked in the sports entertainment and hospitality business. He often organised cricket tickets for Mick Jagger, who became a friend: "He asked for my autograph before I asked for his." For historians and obituarists, Ufton was often a first port of call. His memory of team-mates, opponents and long-ago matches remained pin sharp. It usually took one question to set him off: "Well, we played them at Tunbridge Wells in 1956, and in the first hour it really moved around…"

VAIDYANATHAN, KARATHOLUVU SUBRAMANYAM, who died on March 8, 2020, aged 79, was a left-handed all-rounder who played three first-class matches for Madras. He took four for four in the second, as Kerala were skittled for 51 at Chepauk in December 1965, but made only one more appearance; his continued non-selection was put down to big-city bias against a country boy from near Coimbatore, in the west of the state. He had played for Madras University alongside Nasser Hussain's father, Joe, and in December 1960 slammed 183 for them against an attack containing the young Asif Iqbal. In the state squad, "Vaidy" rubbed shoulders with Abid Ali, Bhagwat Chandrasekhar and Srinivas Venkataraghavan. His father, K. G. Subramanyam, was a noted Indian lawyer, credited with helping remove the stigma of "untouchability", while his daughter, Nirupama, was one of the first Indian women tennis players to make an impression on the world stage. In her autobiography, *The Moon Baller*, she recalled: "There was constant friction between the city's best and the small-town prodigies. My father was a victim of petty politics; also, a knee injury prevented him from aspiring for top-level cricket."

VAN DOK, PHILIP, died on October 14, aged 86. "Flip" van Dok gave a lifetime of service to Dutch cricket. Initially a purveyor of wily, flighted leg-breaks for many celebrated clubs, especially Haarlem, De Flamingos (which he chaired for ten years) and Bloemendaal, he later became an administrator, and was a board member of the Royal Dutch Cricket Association from 1971 to 1980. He made many friends in English cricket, particularly through the annual contest between the Dutch and British Parliaments. He took part in each one, first as player then as scorer, from its foundation in 1977; the trophy now bears his name. His collection of cricket ties was one of the largest in private hands.

VARNALS, GEORGE DEREK, died on September 9, 2019, aged 84. After breaking through for Eastern Province in 1957-58 with 519 runs at 51, including carrying his bat for 157 against Border, Derek Varnals endured several thin seasons. He did not manage another first-class century until a purple patch in 1964-65, when hundreds for Natal against Transvaal, MCC and Rhodesia – plus another in a two-day Test trial – catapulted him into the South African side for the First Test against Mike Smith's England tourists, ahead of Ali Bacher and Barry Richards. He was a "compact and correct player with a good range of shots that come more of timing than of power", according to the broadcaster Charles Fortune. But team-mate Peter Pollock recalled: "He was one of those classic cases of a form guy forcing his way in, though everyone knew he was never going to make the grade. Derek was a nice guy who had to be admired for his application, guts and determination in getting a cap." Varnals struggled, managing a highest score of 23, and was dropped after three games. He missed the tour of England that followed, and never played again: his Test appearances were the last three matches of his first-class career. He later moved to Australia to join his children.

VASANTH KUMAR, RAMANATHAN CHANDRASEKARAN, died of a heart attack on October 16, aged 45. He had spent the previous evening watching the IPL final on television with his father; both had played for Tamil Nadu. The son made two centuries for them in 1997-98, following a match-saving unbeaten 103 against a strong Karnataka attack with 151 against Goa, before moving to Saurashtra, for whom he scored 482 runs in 1999-2000. "He was a terrific bat – superb timer, and had a lazy elegance for a right-hander," said a team-mate.

VIJAYAKRISHNA, BHARANIAH, who died on June 17, aged 71, was a slow left-armer and handy batsman who played 79 matches for Mysore (later Karnataka) and one for West Zone in a career that stretched over 16 seasons from 1968-69. Despite playing second fiddle early on to local greats Bhagwat Chandrasekhar and Erapalli Prasanna, Vijayakrishna took nearly 200 wickets, including seven for 85 and five for 28 against Andhra at Bangalore in 1982-83. He was probably more proud of his five for 63 against the Rest of India in the Irani Cup match at Rajkot in September 1983, as all his victims were Test players – Kris Srikkanth, Dilip Vengsarkar, Mohinder Amarnath, Yashpal Sharma and Shivlal Yadav. A clean hitter, he crunched 71 not out against Rajasthan in 1971-72, despite a leg injury that meant his team-mates had to carry him off, while his maiden century, against Maharashtra in 1975-76, was the fastest in that season's Ranji Trophy. He played in six Ranji finals, winning three, and took nine wickets as Karnataka defeated the 1978-79 West Indian tourists by 11 runs in Ahmedabad. "He was one of the stalwarts of Karnataka cricket," said Anil Kumble.

WALKER, CECIL, MBE, who died on November 15, aged 89, was a long-standing member of the Lisburn club in Northern Ireland. He captained them to four regional titles, and persuaded Ian Botham to attend their centenary celebrations in 1979. As an administrator, Walker pushed for a full-time national coach – Mike Hendrick was appointed in 1995 – and was president of the Irish Cricket Union in 1999, when they staged a match in the World Cup.

WALTERS, JOSEPH ARTHUR, died on May 16, aged 81. Leg-spinner Joe Walters was the youngest player ever signed by Nottinghamshire, at 14 in 1954. "I used to live near a cricket field in Creswell, and practise at the nets," he told Lincolnshire Live shortly before his 60th wedding anniversary early in 2021. "I moved into the first team at the age of 13. One day we had a game in Nottingham – Stapleford, I think – and Notts had two coaches who came to see me play. Before I knew it, I was given a letter to go to Trent Bridge to sign up. I was still at school, but as you can imagine for the last six months I did not give a damn about anything else!" Walters made his first-class debut four years later, sending down 18 wicketless overs at Northampton. He started 1959 with six for 139 against Oxford University, but managed just four wickets in three Championship appearances. His first-class career was over before he turned 20: he injured his back in a fall at the local Steetley Works, and was eventually forced to retire.

WARD, JOHN THOMAS, who died on January 12, aged 83, was an excellent wicketkeeper who was restricted to eight Test caps for New Zealand because his batting was less convincing; he was not helped by fragile fingers, and placed copper pipes in his gloves for protection. According to John Reid, his first Test captain, he was "easily the best wicketkeeper in New Zealand in his time, but was plagued by injury".

c Ward b Motz... but Ken Barrington has made 163, England are 382 for two, and John Edrich is en route to 310 not out against New Zealand at Headingley in 1965.

Ward was picked for the 1958 tour of England after only two first-class matches, neither for his province, Canterbury. Sam Guillen had the gloves there, but the Test selectors sometimes seemed reluctant to choose him, as he was born in Trinidad – though that hadn't stopped him playing the home Tests against his former West Indian team-mates in 1955-56. Ward shadowed Eric Petrie in England, and returned home to find Canterbury sticking with Guillen; he did not keep in the Plunket Shield until December 1959.

In 1961-62, Ward was the first-choice for the tour of South Africa – but another broken finger meant Artie Dick, a better batsman but a novice keeper, took the gloves instead. Ward eventually made his Test debut against South Africa at Wellington early in 1964 but, in a familiar tale, Dick returned for the rest of the series. Ward finally got a run in the side in India in 1964-65, keeping in all four Tests – but another damaged finger restored Dick to favour when they moved on to Pakistan. In England afterwards, after yet more finger trouble, Ward played the final Test at Headingley, but had little to do as John Edrich sprayed a record number of boundaries (68) during his unbeaten 310. "He kept wicket beautifully, [but] had both hands damaged while batting, and did not keep again on the tour," reported Dick Brittenden, who called Ward "a magnificent team man".

The selectors continued to chop and change. Petrie, now 38, returned for the home series against England in 1965-66, then Ray Harford was picked against India two years later. Ward made one last appearance in the final Test at Auckland, and played on for Canterbury until 1970-71. "He had marvellous hands," said seamer Harvey King. "When I first played for South Canterbury he was about 40, but still keeping wicket in his own effortless and nimble way." Ward liked to recall the pre-planned move, in 1966-67, when he stood up to Dick Motz, New Zealand's fastest bowler, and pulled off a slick stumping to send back Northern Districts' Gary Giles. "Usually things like that never work out," said Ward. His son, Barry, kept wicket for Canterbury in 1986-87.

WARNAPURA, BANDULA, who died on October 18, aged 68, captained Sri Lanka in four of their first five Tests, against England, Pakistan and India (he missed one because of injury), before effectively ending his international career by joining a rebel tour of

South Africa. The players were originally banned for 25 years; during his exile Warnapura coached in the Netherlands, before returning to Sri Lankan cricket with the Bloomfield club when the suspensions were lifted. Forgiven, he later coached the national team and worked for the board. An attractive opener born in Rambukkana, near Kandy, Warnapura scored a century in January 1972 for Ceylon Schools against a touring Australian youth side containing Graham Yallop and Ray Bright; he soon hammered 294 against Malaysia, putting on 426 with Anura Tennekoon. The following season, Warnapura played against Pakistan and England in Colombo, and in 1974-75 made 154 – his highest first-class score – against Pakistan Under-25 in Colombo. His first official one-day international came during the 1975 World Cup in England, and he hit 77 against Pakistan at Karachi in 1981-82. "He was an excellent cricketer, administrator, coach, commentator – and, above all, a good person," said Shammi Silva, the president of Sri Lanka Cricket. His nephew, Malinda Warnapura, later played 14 Tests.

WATKINS, JOHN CECIL, who died of Covid-related complications on September 3, aged 98, was a combative all-rounder from Natal – aggressive batsman and accurate swing bowler – who won 15 Test caps for South Africa. He was first chosen in 1949-50 after only five first-class matches, and his opening two deliveries at Johannesburg's Ellis Park were wides (he settled down to take two wickets, including Australia's captain Lindsay Hassett for 112). "Eric Rowan ran across from cover," Watkins told ESPNcricinfo in 2017. "He said: 'They haven't scored a run off the bat, so you've nothing to worry about. Hold the ball across the seam: it'll offer you better control.' Which I did – my third delivery landed, and after that I was away." Watkins added 36 with the bat, and 35 in the next Test.

Happiest when attacking, he made his highest score of 169 for Natal against Orange Free State at Durban in 1950-51, but was unavailable for the tour of England that followed, because of his job in the motor trade (he also missed the 1955 trip). However, Watkins was one of the unsung heroes – and the last survivor – of the 1952-53 tour of Australia. It had been in doubt, as the home board worried whether the South Africans would put up much opposition, but they fought tenaciously, twice coming from behind to square a series notable for their superb fielding; Watkins was a key part, usually in the slips. He took six wickets in the First Test at Brisbane, and made his highest Test score in the Fifth at Melbourne, although he always regretted chopping Ron Archer into his stumps, just short of the century he never made. "I'd been batting at No. 7, and Jack Cheetham [the captain] said we weren't getting off to good enough starts, so how about batting at three? I said fine, and scored 92. I never hooked – I didn't like hitting the ball in the air. I was more of an off-side player and a driver, but when I was on seven I hooked one down Colin McDonald's throat at fine leg and he dropped me, thank goodness." His second-innings 50, however, helped South Africa chase down 295 to level the series at 2–2.

When the team moved on to New Zealand, Watkins took four for 22 from 23.5 overs to seal an innings victory in the First Test at Wellington (his match figures were 50.5–31–51–5). He appeared in the first two Tests against England at home in 1956-57, before being cast aside. Watkins finished with 612 runs, and 29 wickets with an economy-rate of 1.74; only five others who sent down at least 2,000 balls in Tests did so more economically. "He was useful as a foiler of ambitions," said the Australian commentator Johnnie Moyes. "He could keep just short of a length, forcing any but the really gifted to remain quiescent."

After he finished playing, he underwent five operations to correct hip and back problems which had affected him since birth. During the Second World War, he had been training as a Spitfire pilot, until it was discovered that he was colour-blind. He was the oldest surviving Test cricketer, a mantle that passed to his compatriot, Ron Draper.

WATTS, CHARLES ROBERT, died on August 24, aged 80. For almost 60 years, Charlie Watts was the quiet man of the Rolling Stones. With a drumming style influenced by an early love of jazz, he joined the band in 1963, just as they were about to vault to stardom. And he stayed, despite not enjoying touring, and shunning the flamboyant lifestyle of his

Patrick Eagar, Popperfoto/Getty Images

All in a day's work: Charlie Watts (stripy blazer) sits with Dilip Doshi, Bob Willis and Mick Jagger, Lord's, 1984.

colleagues: on one early trip, he spent more than he was paid on calls home to his wife, Shirley. According to the entertainment trade paper *Variety*, the "wiry, ferret-faced" Watts looked like "the mild-mannered banker who no one in the heist movie realises is the guy actually blowing up the vault". Away from the hectic music scene, collecting became a passion. He had a barn full of classic cars on his Devon farm, although he never learned to drive, and masses of American Civil War memorabilia. He was also keen on cricket: he and Stones frontman Mick Jagger attended Tests all round the world, including Ireland's first, in 2018. When Watts appeared on radio's *Desert Island Discs*, one of his chosen tracks was John Arlott's commentary from Jim Laker's 19-wicket Ashes Test at Old Trafford in 1956. The farm also housed a sizeable collection of cricketana. The historian David Frith occasionally advised him on his purchases, and recalled helping to buy Don Bradman's 1934 Australian tour blazer. "I got an excited call that evening to say 'I've tried it on, and it fits!'"

WESTRAADT, BAREND DANIEL ALBERTUS, died on December 14, 2020, aged 63. An umpire originally from Durban, "Wessie" Westraadt stood in 64 first-class matches in South Africa between 1988 and 2014.

WHEELER, GEOFFREY JOHN, who died on May 1, aged 86, was destined to be a cricket lover from the moment he was lifted from the crowd as a toddler by Learie Constantine during the West Indians' match against Gloucestershire at Cheltenham in 1939. The College Ground remained close to his heart. Geoff Wheeler was cricket correspondent and sports editor of the Exchange Telegraph agency, which provided scores and updates via a teleprinter. He was *Wisden's* Gloucestershire correspondent from 1978 until 1992, and contributed several Test reports. After a period as a freelance, he joined *The Times*, and for many years crafted the round-up of matches where the paper did not have a journalist present. He was a member of the Tring club in Hertfordshire, and instrumental in persuading Northamptonshire to play Sunday League games there. One year, when he was manning the beer tent, local rowdies pulled out the guy ropes, and it collapsed around his head. He had a standard catchphrase for when things went awry on the *Times* sports desk: "It's the biggest cock-up since Mons."

WHITING, STEPHEN JOHN, died on July 29, aged 82. In the rough-and-tumble world of popular journalism in the late 1970s and '80s, Steve Whiting, cricket correspondent of *The Sun*, cut an unusual figure. He was a thoroughly competent journalist, and a good club cricketer who opened the batting for several top-flight clubs in Surrey. But he was never quite at home on the companionable evenings that were part of a long tour. On the 1982-83 trip to Australia, after a familiar defeat in Adelaide left England 2–0 down, Whiting claimed a drinking culture was part of the team's downfall. In the short term, the manager Doug Insole imposed a midnight curfew, without much impact. The longer-term effect was that the report infuriated the players (not to mention fellow pressmen), and most particularly Ian Botham, leader of the pack on the field and off it, and never quick to forgive. When *The Sun* later signed Botham as their star columnist, he refused to work with Whiting, who was expected to turn his musings into a readable column. There was only one loser – and Whiting went. He was not lucky thereafter. In 1987, he became cricket correspondent of the *London Daily News*, which its erratic owner Robert Maxwell closed after five months, in the middle of the Edgbaston Test. As Whiting trudged out of the press box, he invited allcomers to use the Maxwell-owned landline on his desk. He later returned to cricket writing for the *Sunday Mirror*. However, his second wife, Viv – a troubled soul he met in Australia – died young, leaving him in charge of a baby daughter. Steve himself was diagnosed with multiple sclerosis. He found solace in evangelical Christianity but, as he became more immobile, getting to matches grew more difficult. It was a sad fate for a kind and gifted man. On the 1981-82 tour of India, *Test Match Special* were short of a commentator, and he volunteered. The BBC view was that his voice, tone, eye and knowledge were all up to scratch; however, it was felt he was inclined to wander a little off-piste.

WILLIAMS, GLENYS ANN, who died of a brain tumour on December 4, aged 58, worked in the Lord's museum from 1988 to 2010, latterly as deputy curator of the MCC Collection. She undertook extensive research on the origin of the Ashes urn, and helped escort it on one of its rare trips outside the Pavilion, around Australia during the 2006-07 series. A friendly face in the library, she assisted several writers with their research, and wrote a thesis on the development of cricket from a social perspective.

WOODCOCK, JOHN CHARLES, OBE, died on July 18, aged 94. He never played first-class cricket, but John Woodcock left a lasting imprint on the game. He almost made it, missing out on selection for Oxford University against Gloucestershire just after the war, despite top-scoring in both innings of the final trial. "I must have come quite close to getting a pair against Tom Goddard," he joked. Instead, it was as one of cricket's greatest chroniclers that he left an indelible impression. Woodcock, cricket correspondent of *The Times* from 1954 to 1987, and editor of *Wisden* between 1981 and 1986, wrote elegantly, incisively – seldom short of an opinion, though never caustic – and with a deep affection for, and knowledge of, the game. His store of anecdotes and reminiscences included names from the distant past: he had known C. B. Fry and Neville Cardus, Harold Larwood and Len Hutton, Don Bradman and Jack Fingleton. Yet his eminence derived not just from longevity: his reputation rested on the quality of his work.

Woodcock was born in the pretty Hampshire village of Longparish. Apart from a brief spell in Oxford, he never left; Alan Gibson, a *Times* colleague, dubbed him "The Sage of Longparish". He had a remarkable family tree. His grandfather, also John, was born in 1813, two years before the Battle of Waterloo; his father, Parry, in 1856. Parry became rector of Longparish in 1906, and later married a widow, Nora Dunsford. John was born when his father was 70. "How nice to see your grandfather," people would remark when he appeared in early school matches. Though he shared his faith, he was unlikely to follow his father into the clergy: he was too smitten with cricket.

He attended the Dragon School in Oxford, then moved on to St Edward's, where – aged 15 – he contracted septic arthritis. The prognosis was grim, and prayers were said in the school chapel. After being attached to a frame that kept him motionless for four months,

Graham Morris

Natural habitat (1): John Woodcock, a glass of wine and his photograph albums, The Old Curacy, Longparish, 2016.

he gradually recovered. But there was lasting damage: he walked with a limp for the rest of his life (he had numerous hip operations), and was often in pain. It also ended his chances of a cricket career, though at Oxford he played for the Authentics, the university's Second XI, and earned a Blue as a hockey goalkeeper. After taking a fourth in geography, he briefly became a teacher, completing two terms at a secondary modern in Basingstoke. But while at Oxford, he met *Daily Telegraph* cricket correspondent Jim Swanton, who had brought his Arabs XI to the university. Swanton offered him the chance to become the television scorer for the 1948 Ashes, then tour Australia as his secretary – Woodcock preferred dogsbody – in 1950-51.

His main job was recording highlights and off-field moments on a huge 35mm cine-camera, and sending rolls of film back each week to the BBC. Some footage was lost, but a film called *Elusive Victory* was assembled, providing a fascinating glimpse the mid-20th-century touring experience. It gave him a taste of an enviable lifestyle, and the chance to cover the home Tests against India in 1952 for *The Manchester Guardian*. He was appointed their London sports editor, and reported on county cricket in the Ashes summer of 1953. It brought him to the attention of *The Times*, who were looking for a new cricket correspondent in 1954, when Geoffrey Green, who had been doubling up on football, became sports editor.

Woodcock fought off competition from rugby writer U. A. Titley to land the job at a salary of £900. Within weeks, he was off to Australia with Len Hutton's team for a tour that remained etched in his memory. Inspired by the pace of Frank Tyson, England fought back from a calamitous First Test at Brisbane to retain the Ashes. Woodcock was recovering from a duodenal ulcer during the decisive match at Adelaide, but was invited by Hutton to witness the moment of victory from the dressing-room. He wrote about the tour often, never more poignantly than in 2015, when the death of Tom Graveney left him the only survivor of the players, management or press corps. He settled into an agreeable routine, and was seldom at home for an English winter. As a bachelor, he relished touring life and the leisurely sea trips of another age.

Nor was there much pressure from the *Times* sports desk. Woodcock wrote previews and match reports: no interviews, news stories, features or follow-ups. But his reporting was peerless. "Nobody has better summed up a day's play in 800 or 900 words," said Scyld Berry, one of his successors as *Wisden* editor. He often sat a little apart from the press-box chatter, watching the play intently through his binoculars. Tight deadlines mean morning newspaper reporters have to begin their articles well before the close, deciding on the order of the day's events as they write. "Pieces often end up as a dog's dinner," said Berry. "But with Wooders, you would read his reports and never see the joins. His great skill was the structure of the piece." Henry Blofeld said: "He was the most thorough watcher of a day's cricket I have ever known."

But his work was never austere. On a rare six by Trevor Bailey at Brisbane in 1954-55, he wrote that Bailey "looked so ashamed that the umpire had a word with him, as though assuring him that he was within the law and inquiring whether he required the attention of a doctor". After Colin Cowdrey was summoned to bolster England's batting in 1974-75: "If he plays it will be as though he dreamt that he was batting against Australia at Perth and woke up to find that he was." Or on an out-of-form Derek Randall: "he has played two Championship matches at Trent Bridge this season. He made nought and one in the first, against Northamptonshire, but was less successful in the second, against Middlesex."

Woodcock was cheerfully frank about his lack of formal training. "You're a cricket writer, old son, not a journalist," the *Daily Mail's* Alex Bannister would tease him. It meant he was not at his best when cricket hit the front pages. He admitted he could have covered the D'Oliveira affair and the Packer schism with more authority. He was standing next to Blofeld at the SCG when he was handed a writ from Packer's lawyers: "I thought, 'If I'd have been doing my job properly, I'd have got one of those.'" Later, he expressed regret that he had ignored apartheid when reporting from South Africa. After retiring as cricket correspondent, he remained on the *Times* staff, and continued to cover Tests around the world, sometimes providing colour pieces alongside his successor, Alan Lee, or independently at series not involving England. He contributed to the paper until well into his nineties, celebrating Ben Stokes's epic Headingley innings in 2019 and, in his final article, marking the death of Everton Weekes in 2020.

He did not achieve the same fame as John Arlott or Swanton because he did no radio or television work; and until January 1967, when *The Times* changed their policy on bylines, he was just "Our Cricket Correspondent". Woodcock did not write books either, except for a list of his top 100 players, originally published in the *Times Magazine*. In 2019, a leading publisher approached him about an autobiography; he wavered, then courteously declined. This, though, did not lessen the deep respect in which he was held by cricket writers. "Some of the cricket correspondents of his generation were more celebrated, but he was the best," tweeted Simon Wilde of *The Sunday Times*, speaking for many.

WYNNE-THOMAS, PETER, BEM, who died on July 15, aged 86, was a leading historian and archivist of the game. His natural habitat was the library at Trent Bridge, which he founded in 1979. As it grew to become England's second-biggest cricket library after Lord's, it was almost an extension of his personality; in 2015, Nottinghamshire named it after him. He was appointed the club's president the following year, having served two decades on their committee.

He was born in Manchester and educated in Sussex, but the decisive event of his life came in 1942, when his family moved to Nottinghamshire. After the war, he was drawn to Trent Bridge, where Joe Hardstaff junior was his favourite player, and he began to compile county averages. This led to researching the lives of Nottinghamshire cricketers, going back to the 19th century, from which his interest spread into the history of the game in England and beyond.

Like his father, Wynne-Thomas became an architect. While working in London, he met the eccentric historian Rowland Bowen, who taught him to research with greater discrimination, and he contributed to Bowen's scholarly *Cricket Quarterly*; he expected to succeed him as editor, but Bowen closed the magazine when he retired in 1971. That

Frank Coppi, Popperfoto/Getty Images

Natural habitat (2): Peter Wynne-Thomas in the Trent Bridge library, 2003.

year, Wynne-Thomas published *Nottinghamshire Cricketers 1821–1914*, which won the Cricket Society book award. At the same time, he effectively gave up architecture, and returned home for good. In later life, when invited to London to discuss a project, he responded: "I never go. If you want to talk to me, you can come to Nottingham."

In 1973, he was one of the founder members of the Association of Cricket Statisticians, and served as their secretary from 1974 to 2006. He also set up a bookshop, Sport in Print, on the Radcliffe Road, and turned out more than 50 books – to say nothing of articles and the Nottinghamshire yearbooks. There were county histories, biographies, encyclopaedias, a massive *Who's Who of Cricketers* (detailing every player who had appeared in a first-class match in the British Isles), and *The History of Cricket: From the Weald to the World.* He argued that cricket had developed not among shepherds, but around 17th-century iron foundries in Sussex.

Wynne-Thomas was generous in his support for fellow researchers, welcoming them with a cry of "Hullo, my friend!" and always reminding them to return to the primary sources; in the 1980s, he rebuked *Wisden* for publishing fanciful claims about early cricket and, arguing from the original texts, dismantled them line by line.

A tall man, usually dressed in shirtsleeves and braces, with a walrus moustache that gradually turned white, Wynne-Thomas never took to the internet. Given a Twitter account, he composed a stock of tweets on the small manual typewriter he had used for decades.

YADAV, ASHWIN DHANNULAL, who died of a heart attack on April 24, aged 33, was a seamer whose 14 first-class matches for Hyderabad produced a best of six for 52 against Delhi in the 2008-09 Ranji Trophy; his victims included Shikhar Dhawan. "He had a good outswinger, and was nippy off the wicket," said one of his coaches.

YADAV, VIVEK, who died on May 5, aged 36, was an Indian leg-spinner who played 29 matches in all formats for Rajasthan, and was part of their Ranji Trophy-winning sides in 2010-11 and 2011-12, when his career-best return – six for 134 against Railways in Delhi

– was immediately followed by his other five-for, against Uttar Pradesh. He took up coaching, but had been suffering from stomach cancer, then contracted Covid-19.

YASHPAL SHARMA, who suffered a heart attack on July 13, aged 66, was an unsung member of India's first World Cup-winning team, and the first to die. Stocky and strong-armed, he also did well in Tests – once batting a whole day alongside Gundappa Viswanath – but was best remembered at home for his exploits in 1983, which were commemorated in a film about India's win that premiered a few months after his death.

He started that tournament with 89 at Old Trafford, which led to West Indies' first defeat at any World Cup. "That set the tone for us," said Dilip Vengsarkar. Yashpal then top-scored as Australia were crushed at Chelmsford, before returning to Manchester for the semi against England, where 61 helped book India's place in the final. "Yash was a very methodical, copybook, old-school Test player," recalled team-mate Kirti Azad. "But that day he did a Viv Richards: he shuffled towards off stump and flicked Bob Willis for six. And how can I forget his Ravi Jadeja-like throw from short leg to the non-striker's end to get Allan Lamb when I was bowling?"

Yashpal made only 11 at Lord's, but West Indies' collapse handed victory to India. "He didn't get the credit he deserved," said opening bowler Balwinder Singh Sandhu. "He scored runs and fielded well, effecting run-outs and taking good catches. He used to smash the ball a long way – I named it the *badam* shot because he used to eat a lot of *badams* [almonds]. He was a very strongly built guy."

Born in Ludhiana, north of Delhi, Yashpal served his time in domestic cricket. He first hit the headlines in 1972, with a rapid 260 for Punjab Schools, and made his Ranji Trophy debut for Punjab the following year: he scored 60 not out against Services, and shared a stand of 169 with Mohinder Amarnath, who would win the match award in the 1983 final. In 1977-78, Yashpal extended his maiden first-class century to 173, for North Zone in the Duleep Trophy against South Zone's Indian spin trio of Chandrasekhar, Prasanna and Venkataraghavan. He made his one-day international debut in Pakistan in September 1978, before another hundred, against the West Indian tourists – spearheaded by the young Malcolm Marshall – ensured a place on the 1979 trip to England.

Yashpal made his Test debut at Lord's, and was soon an important part of the middle order. "India's crisis man," said Sunil Gavaskar. "A fierce fighter, a loyal team-mate and a caring friend." He scored his first Test hundred that winter, against Australia at Delhi, after bagging a pair in the previous match. His other century was an eight-hour epic: dropped after an indifferent tour of Australasia, he was recalled for the Fifth Test against England at Madras in 1981-82, and joined Viswanath late on the first day, when Vengsarkar retired hurt after being hit on the head by Willis. They batted serenely through the second, and added 316, still India's highest for any wicket against England. Yashpal finished with 140, in "492 minutes of stolid accumulation", according to *Wisden*. "I never expected myself to bat for a whole day in Test cricket, because of my temperament," said Viswanath, whose 222 was also a career-best. "Yashpal played a magnificent and authoritative innings. He was a very good cricketer – a team man to the core."

His international career came to an end after England's next tour, in 1984-85, but he remained closely involved with cricket. He played on in the Ranji Trophy for eight seasons, latterly for Haryana and Railways, coached Uttar Pradesh, had two spells as a national selector, and even did a spot of umpiring – eight first-class matches, plus two in the 1997-98 women's World Cup. The Indian seamer Chetan Sharma (now a selector too) was Yashpal's nephew. They played together in two one-day internationals, and combined to dismiss England's Graeme Fowler at Pune in December 1984.

The obituaries section includes those who died, or whose deaths were notified, in 2021. Wisden always welcomes information about those who might be included: please send details to almanack@wisden.com, or to John Wisden & Co, 13 Old Aylesfield, Golden Pot, Alton, Hampshire GU34 4BY.

BRIEFLY NOTED

The following, whose deaths were noted during 2021, played or umpired in a small number of first-class (fc) matches.

	Died	*Age*	*Main team(s)*
AFZALUR RAHMAN	10.3.2021	54	Umpire

Stood in 26 fc matches – and one women's ODI – in Bangladesh.

ALWYN, Nicholas	16.6.2021	83	Cambridge University

Opened in five fc matches in 1961; 41 v Essex on debut. Hampstead CC stalwart.

BANDIWADEKAR, Vilas Manohar	5.4.2021	63	Umpire

Born in Bombay; stood in six fc matches and 26 one-day games.

BHATT, Janak Dinkarrai	27.11.2021	64	Vidarbha

Slow left-armer: seven wickets in eight fc matches; 2-33 against Railways in 1982-83.

BUTLER, Keith Owen	29.9.2020	86	Auckland

Seamer whose only fc match was against a Fijian touring team in 1953-54.

DAVEY, John Richard	26.3.2021	63	South Australia

Wicketkeeper: one fc match in 1981-82 (ct 4, st 2); his son, Tim, also played for South Australia.

DELLOW, Harold Noel	1.9.2021	92	Canterbury

Outswing bowler: five fc matches, 3-84 against Auckland in 1955-56.

PAYNE, Elrick Colin	21.8.2020	74	Barbados

Fast bowler: two wickets in two fc matches; the first was Glenn Turner of New Zealand in 1971-72.

PLUMMER, Basil Arthur John	6.2.2021	96/97	Europeans

Opened the bowling against Indians in the Madras Presidency match in 1945-46.

RAEESUDDIN Ahmed	20.1.2021	81	Dacca University

Leg-spinner; one fc match against East Pakistan (now Bangladesh) in 1957-58, but did not bowl.

SADASHIVAN, N.	29.4.2021	80	Mysore

Batsman who played six fc matches; 58 against Kerala in the last, in January 1965.*

SIGLEY, Ernest John	25.6.2021	89	Wellington

Off-spinner: five fc matches, 44 and 2-63 v Northern Districts in 1959-60.

SPRING, Michael Maurice	22.2.2021	78	Umpire

Wellington official who stood in eight fc matches, and one in the 1981-82 women's World Cup.

A LIFE IN NUMBERS

	Runs	Avge	Wkts	Avge		Runs	Avge	Wkts	Avge
A'Court, D. G.	420	11.35	145	26.82	Burgess, A. T.	466	22.19	16	30.68
Alwyn, N.	141	14.10	–	–	Butler, K. O.	24	24.00	0	–
Ammar Mahmood	2,381	30.92	8	59.50	Buttsworth, F. J.	343	22.86	–	–
Amonkar, P. A.	778	19.45	0	–	Chandorkar, R. R.	155	15.50	2	8.00
Anderson, D. T.	123	15.37	14	40.35	Cook, D. R.	108	13.50	23	23.21
Arnold, A. P.	8,013	27.53	3	28.33	Davey, J. R.	–	–	–	–
Ash, E. M.	**180**	**11.25**	**32**	**20.50**	Davidson, A. K.	**6,804**	32.86	**672**	**20.90**
Baker, D. W.	101	4.20	78	36.61	Dellow, H. N.	37	5.28	11	33.36
Banerjee, R.	113	12.55	11	33.45	**Dexter, E. R.**	**21,150**	**40.75**	**419**	**29.92**
Barot, A. A.	1,547	24.95	0	–	Dolley, R. B.	1,150	23.00	100	22.55
Benjamin, J. E.	**1,161**	**11.38**	**387**	**29.94**	Dormer, M. E. F.	48	12.00	–	–
Bhamjee, A.	532	23.13	0	–	Fernando, U. A.	2,328	33.73	14	26.92
Bhamjee, E.	371	18.55	0	–	Fitchett, M. K.	589	32.72	9	40.66
Bhatt, J. D.	164	12.61	7	49.71	Flaws, T.	438	10.18	–	–
Bokhari, S. I. A.	959	36.88	0	–	Gallaway, I. W.	26	8.66	–	–
Borde, R. G.	1,326	25.50	42	34.92	**Gannon, J. B.**	**141**	**6.40**	**117**	**30.47**
Bowden, D. W.	475	16.96	–	–	Good, D. C.	54	13.50	8	37.50
Bradshaw, K.	1,083	25.78	9	48.77	Greenwood, P.	1,270	16.49	208	24.47
Brancker, R. C.	1,666	27.31	106	27.32	Gunn, T.	179	5.11	–	–
Brouwers, N. G.	955	18.72	75	26.09	Harkness, D. P.	488	25.68	6	45.66
Brown, D. W. J.	2,863	20.16	3	28.00	**Hendrick, M.**	**1,601**	**10.13**	**770**	**20.50**
Buckingham, A. D.	349	18.36	0	–	Hutchinson, G.	63	21.00	0	–

	Runs	Avge	Wkts	Avge		Runs	Avge	Wkts	Avge
Igglesden, A. P.	876	8.34	503	26.81	Presland, E. R.	625	16.89	13	58.53
Illingworth, R.	24,134	28.06	2,072	20.27	Raeesuddin	7	3.50	–	–
Irani, M. D.	99	19.80	0	–	Ratcliffe, D. P.	603	19.45	–	–
Irfan Habib	78	9.75	19	34.36	Rattray, P. J.	909	22.72	0	–
Jadeja, R. R.	1,532	24.31	134	26.24	Rehman Dyer	428	21.40	4	15.25
John, L.	1,053	23.40	21	17.14	Roberts, J. B.	154	12.83	13	33.38
Johnson, I. N.	716	21.69	37	41.43	**Robinson, M. C.**	2,809	35.11	1	27.00
Joynt, H. K.	525	16.93	1	33.00	Rungta, K. M.	2,717	32.73	9	20.22
Kanojia, S.	23	7.66	0	–	Sadashivan, S.	119	23.80	1	18.00
Kiddey, J. W. F.	683	11.98	141	20.17	Salmon, J. L.	92	7.07	41	28.51
Kirby, D.	4,105	19.64	113	37.61	Schonegevel, D. J.	5,168	31.51	118	29.34
Latty-Scott, V.	287	16.88	43	15.25	Selwood, T.	603	19.45	–	–
Lihou, J.	115	5.22	50	50.34	Shuttleworth, G. M.	786	23.11	–	–
Lodhgar, M. Y.	113	9.41	34	24.55	Sigley, E. J.	140	15.55	4	43.75
McCaw, P. M.	115	19.16	–	–	Smith, D. H. K.	4,995	26.56	1	23.00
McDonald, C. C.	11,375	40.48	3	64.00	**Smith, D. V.**	16,960	30.33	340	28.44
McKechnie, D. E. C.	278	11.12	37	24.35	Stevens, G. C.	1,675	20.42	50	39.74
McKnight, S. G.	123	9.46	–	–	Tahir Mughal	3,263	21.05	503	21.66
Mains, G.	19	2.11	6	50.83	**Taylor, B. R.**	4,579	24.75	422	25.13
Mallett, A. A.	2,326	13.60	693	26.27	**Thomson, N. I.**	7,120	14.74	1,597	20.58
Mohapatra, P. R.	2,196	30.08	–	–	Torrens, R.	42	6.00	26	15.46
Moore, E. R.	–	–	1	168.00	Ufton, D. G.	3,919	19.99	–	–
Moseley, E. A.	1,431	17.45	279	23.31	Vaidyanathan, K. S.	40	20.00	4	12.50
Nanan, N.	925	15.67	9	35.77	**Varnals, G. D.**	2,628	30.20	0	–
Ogilvie, J. E.	244	24.40	–	–	Vasanth Kumar, R. C.	1,097	32.26	–	–
Olton, M. F.	98	19.60	2	99.50	Vijayakrishna, B.	2,297	25.80	195	27.16
Panda, R. N.	971	20.65	2	3.00	Walters, J. A.	64	64.00	10	46.40
Paranjape, J. V.	785	23.78	9	36.00	**Ward, J. T.**	1,117	12.41	0	–
Parmar, P. M.	85	21.25	6	21.16	**Warnapura, B.**	2,280	25.05	13	48.30
Payne, E. C.	14	7.00	2	71.00	Watkins, J. C.	2,158	24.80	96	28.52
Pervez Akhtar	2,277	27.43	4	32.25	Yadav, A. D.	120	9.23	34	32.70
Philpott, P. I.	2,886	31.36	245	30.31	Yadav, V.	349	15.17	57	30.87
Pickles, L.	1,702	20.50	1	65.00	**Yashpal Sharma**	8,933	44.88	47	33.70
Plummer, B. A. J.	0	0.00	0	–					

*Test players are in **bold**.*

Wicketkeepers: Barot took 50 catches and two stumpings; E. Bhamjee 46 and 14; Chandorkar three and two; Davey four and two; Dormer five and three; Flaws 44 and 29; Gallaway seven and one; Gunn 109 and five; McDonald 55 and two; Ufton 270 and 44; Ward 227 and 27; Yashpal Sharma 90 and two.

PART THREE

English
International
Cricket

THE ENGLAND TEAM IN 2021

The year the roof fell in

TIM WIGMORE

"How did you go bankrupt?" asks a character in Ernest Hemingway's *The Sun Also Rises*. "Two ways," comes the reply. "Gradually and then suddenly."

So it was for England in Test cricket in 2021. After years of incremental decline, concealed by the excellence of their seam bowlers at home and moments of freakish brilliance, this was the year the extent of their Test malaise became undeniable. It had begun with a trio of fine victories in Sri Lanka and India, but after that they managed just one more win and nine defeats – ten, if you include the final Ashes Test, at Hobart, early in 2022.

"The summer of Test cricket will be fascinating," said head coach Chris Silverwood in May. "Playing the top two teams in the world, in New Zealand and India, is perfect preparation for us, as we continue to improve and progress towards an Ashes series in Australia."

In one sense, Silverwood was right: the summer did provide a glimpse of what awaited England. They lost the series to New Zealand, ending their

ENGLAND IN 2021

	Played	Won	Lost	Drawn/No result
Tests	15	4	9	2
One-day internationals	9	6	2	1
Twenty20 internationals	17	11	6	–

seven-year undefeated run at home, and were 2–1 down against India when the final Test was postponed because of fears about Covid-19 in the tourists' camp. Even in the annals of their ignominious history Down Under, losing the urn in the equivalent of under ten days' playing time – four fewer than their pre-series quarantine on the Gold Coast – was among England's meekest showings in Australia.

Seldom can a more productive individual year in Test cricket have been so poorly rewarded as Joe Root's. In 2020, for the first time since his debut in late 2012, he had not scored a Test century in a calendar year. He resolved to become more selfish, and compartmentalise his batting and captaincy. He worked hard on his fitness, to improve his stamina for long innings, and made technical adjustments, becoming more compact and side-on against pace. After consulting with England's analysts, he also aimed to be more decisive in his footwork against spin, going well forward or back, and avoiding the danger zone in between.

The results were spectacular. Particularly adroit in his use of the sweep to disturb bowlers' lengths, he began with 228, 186 and 218 in successive matches at Galle and Chennai, arguably the greatest run by an England batsman against spin. While his returns dipped in the final three Tests in India on pitches that turned prodigiously, and at home against New Zealand's seamers, Root then unfurled three centuries in consecutive Tests against India. He ended 2021 with 1,708 Test runs, the third-highest annual tally, below Mohammad Yousuf (1,788 in 2006) and Viv Richards (1,710 in 1976).

His fate, however, was to stand out like a rose in a dung heap, such was the haplessness of England's batting. Like illicit government parties, everyone could pick their most egregious example. While Root averaged 61, the rest of the top seven averaged 21. Overall, England made only 24 runs per wicket, their lowest in a calendar year since 1950. They scored a record-equalling 54 ducks – and were bowled out for under 200 on 13 occasions, culminating in 68 at Melbourne to confirm their Ashes defeat.

A combination of the rest-and-rotation policy designed to protect player welfare, and the struggles of their top order, meant England picked 25 different players in Tests. Besides Root, only Dawid Malan, who was recalled against India after three years out of the side, and scored three half-centuries in his first five Tests, threatened to enhance his reputation with the bat, before fading in Australia. Rory Burns, England's second-highest run-scorer – 1,178 runs behind Root – was their Player of the Series against New Zealand, but dropped after the Second Ashes Test (then run out for a duck on his recall in the Fifth). And none of Zak Crawley, Dom Sibley, Ollie Pope or Haseeb Hameed, at various points considered the coming men of English Test batting, averaged over 22; Crawley followed his 267 against Pakistan in England's last Test of 2020 by averaging under 11. At least Root received reliable support from one source: Extras were his team's third-highest scorer.

It was disorientating merely to watch players shuffle in and out of the side, and up and down the order. Jonny Bairstow started the year with a recall as a specialist No. 3, and fared well in Sri Lanka. He returned to the UK, under pre-arranged plans, then flew back to India, where he made three ducks in

Last hurrah? After bowling well in Australia, Stuart Broad and James Anderson were dropped for the Test series in the Caribbean in March 2022.

four innings. Like all those with IPL contracts, he missed the New Zealand series. He was at No. 5 for the home series with India – taking the gloves for one Test when Jos Buttler was on paternity leave – but dropped for the first two games in Australia. With England 2–0 down, Bairstow was then recalled at No. 6 on Boxing Day.

The toil exerted by the schedule on the players, amplified by almost two years of biosecure conditions, was intolerable. While Bairstow – until his cathartic century in the first Test of 2022, at Sydney – and Buttler struggled for rhythm in Test cricket, three of England's other leading multi-format players had time away, for differing reasons. Ben Stokes took several months off to prioritise his mental health, missing the summer Tests against India. Jofra Archer – whose mismanagement could arguably be traced back to bowling 42 overs in an innings at Mount Maunganui in 2019-20 – played in only two Tests, and had remedial work on his elbow. Moeen Ali, who had to isolate in Sri Lanka after contracting Covid, ended the summer standing in as vice-captain, before announcing his Test retirement.

Just as a floundering batting line-up was nothing new, the same was true of England's confused use of spin. After usurping the inconsistent Dom Bess, Jack Leach finished with 28 wickets in six Tests in Asia. Yet he didn't play a single Test at home, before being picked at the Gabba, a graveyard for overseas finger-spin. After England were bundled out for 147, Australia ruthlessly

ENGLAND'S LOWEST RUNS PER WICKET IN A CALENDAR YEAR

19.06	1882	22.80	1950	25.36	1972
19.25	1906	**24.13**	**2021**	25.97	1958
21.18	1909	24.25	1999	26.15	2019
22.14	1902	24.74	1896	26.33	1998

Minimum: 5 Tests.

targeted him, and he haemorrhaged 102 in 13 overs, though he improved as the series went on. At least he got on the field: leg-spinner Matt Parkinson was the only player to stay in Sri Lanka and India for the entire three months without appearing once.

England's seam bowling was a reassuring constant – skilful and reliable, if often one-dimensional, with Archer, Mark Wood and Olly Stone playing only 11 of the 15 Tests between them, and Sam Curran fading before suffering injury himself. Jimmy Anderson's haul of wickets matched his age – 39, at 21 apiece – and he sent down one of England's greatest Test overs, a double-wicket maiden to dismiss Shubman Gill and Ajinkya Rahane at Chennai. That helped set up India's first home defeat for four years, and emphasised Anderson's evolution abroad. He played 12 Tests, and was more frugal than ever. There was widespread outrage when both he and Stuart Broad were left out of the West Indies tour in March 2022.

Broad managed just 12 wickets in seven Tests, though he began 2022 with a five-for at Sydney. But his role as steepling metronome was under threat from Ollie Robinson, who showed mastery of line and length, generated ample swing and seam, and subtly varied his release points. Snaring 37 wickets at 21 in his debut year, he looked like Broad's successor, and a cricketer who had been Test-ready for years. Only his fitness was a concern.

His debut, though, proved part of a wider crisis. The first day of the English Test summer had begun with the players lining up in front of the Lord's Pavilion in anti-discrimination T-shirts. A few hours later, with Robinson thriving on the field, tweets emerged – of a racist, sexist and Islamophobic nature – that he had written years earlier. He ended the day with a contrite apology, and was later suspended. It highlighted an unpalatable truth: the England team were not immune to the wider racism scandals that affected the sport.

While they left the ECB answering unwanted questions, the administrators also faced scrutiny over the management of the Test side. Not until their ninth game of the year, against India in August, were England able to pick their strongest available XI, without any players being rotated. Their Ashes planning – trumpeted in "Project Ashes", a six-part podcast series on the BBC – came to look absurd. While a combination of Covid-19 and the Gold Coast rain that decimated the intra-squad warm-up games contributed to England's challenge, a series of selection errors exacerbated it.

The decision to play Leach at Brisbane meant Broad – who had a good record at the Gabba, and had thrived against David Warner and Marcus Harris in the 2019 Ashes – was omitted. Haseeb Hameed, despite analysis suggesting he was ill suited to Australian conditions, played the first four Tests. After impressing in the First, Wood was omitted for the Second, so he could be selected for the Third – by which time England were 2–0 behind. After four years vowing to return Down Under with a more varied attack, England once again united Anderson, Broad and Chris Woakes in the pink-ball Test in Adelaide. In 2017-18 there, the trio had combined first-innings figures of 88–20–230–4. Four years on, it was almost identical: 78.4–22–234–4.

You could easily imagine Silverwood falling for a scam email, such was his penchant for being conned. In England's other day/night Test of the year, at

Parting glance: Joe Root and Chris Silverwood at training in Australia.

Ahmedabad, the allure of the swinging ball persuaded him to select four seamers and a solitary frontline spinner; while Root took five for eight with his off-breaks, the quartet of quicks managed one for 79 between them. England lost by ten wickets.

Silverwood was elevated to selector in April, when Ed Smith's role as national selector was made redundant. But Silverwood's new all-powerful position immediately seemed too much for one man. Perhaps the problem wasn't so much combining the two roles, but doing so while simultaneously being red- and white-ball coach: in 2021, Silverwood spent more than 300 days on the road. In February 2022, he was sacked, along with the team's managing director, Ashley Giles – who was replaced on a temporary basis by Andrew Strauss – and assistant coach Graham Thorpe.

The burden on Silverwood had been even greater than originally envisaged: in July, he left a family holiday early to take control of a completely new England ODI squad, hastily assembled when Covid-19 swept through the first-choice side before the series with Pakistan. England still waltzed to a 3–0 victory, illustrating the extraordinary depth of the white-ball stocks.

That was also in evidence in the UAE, where England hoped to add the T20 World Cup to the one-day trophy won in 2019. For much of the tournament – never more than when crushing Australia by eight wickets with 50 balls to spare – they looked joint-favourites with Pakistan, even in the absence of Stokes and Archer. Further injuries, to Tymal Mills and Jason Roy, undermined them before the semi-final. Even then, with New Zealand needing 57 from four overs, England were on course to reach the final. But they got the runs in only three, exposing England's weakness at the death.

The notion that the Test team had been sacrificed at the altar of the limited-overs game was exaggerated. Indeed, only in two white-ball series all year – the five T20s in India, and the World Cup – did England pick the strongest squad available. By the end of that tournament, they were missing five first-choice players.

With a far shallower talent pool – the result of other factors, such as the gap between the domestic and international game, and the lack of spin and high pace in the County Championship – England's Test side were simply less equipped to cope with the schedule. New Zealand, with one-tenth of the ECB's budget and the UK's population, were a model for how to sustain all-format excellence. Among the lessons were an emphasis on the quality of domestic pitches, the A-Team programme and a schedule designed to allow players to peak when it mattered.

The central irony of England's year, perhaps, was that the need to bankroll the board coincided with the team appearing bankrupt on the pitch. The ECB chief executive, Tom Harrison, admitted as much when the final Test against India in September was postponed: "The reality is, we're playing too much domestic cricket and international cricket, and we need to address both."

Whatever else English cricket needed to address, Harrison at least had one problem to look forward to: how to spend the £2.1m bonus that he and five other executives would share, largely for delivering the inaugural edition of The Hundred.

ENGLAND PLAYERS IN 2021

LAWRENCE BOOTH

The following 42 players (there were 31 in 2020, and 38 in 2019) appeared in 2021, when England played 15 Tests, nine one-day internationals and 17 Twenty20 internationals. Statistics refer to the full year, not the 2021 season.

MOEEN ALI
Worcestershire

Few were surprised when Ali retired from Test cricket in September. He admitted he had struggled to concentrate after returning to the side at Chennai in February, following a 19-month absence. It was not a good few weeks: having tested positive for Covid on arrival in Sri Lanka in January, he was limited to one Test in India because of rest and rotation, then ignored altogether during the five-match T20 series in Ahmedabad. Stokes's absence in the summer meant the selectors – who were not planning to take Ali to the Ashes – eventually conceded they needed the balance he provided, and even handed him the vice-captaincy. He overtook Jim Laker's haul of 193 Test wickets; among England spinners, only Derek Underwood and Graeme Swann finished with more than his 195. But it was not until the T20 World Cup in the UAE that he began to feel at home again, opening the bowling with his miserly off-breaks, and batting up the order. He later moved to the BT Sport sofa, where his jousts with Alastair Cook delighted social media.

4 Tests: 132 runs @ 18.85; 14 wickets @ 37.50.
6 ODIs: 87 runs @ 29.00, SR 73.10; 2 wickets @ 59.50, ER 5.40.
10 T20Is: 137 runs @ 22.83, SR 137.00; 11 wickets @ 11.90, ER 6.00.

JAMES ANDERSON
Lancashire

Anderson both confirmed cliches (he really was like a fine wine, improving with age), and undermined them. While six home Tests brought him 18 wickets at 32, six away – on surfaces that were supposed to neuter him – produced 21 at under 13. He began with six for 40 at Galle, sent down one of the overs of the year to remove Shubman Gill and Ajinkya Rahane at Chennai, and finished with four for 33 from 23 overs at Melbourne; in between, and now 39, he moved third on the all-time Test list ahead of Anil Kumble, and served up a masterful opening burst of 8–5–6–3 against India at Headingley. As batsmen concluded there was little to be gained from taking him on, they tried instead to see him off: Anderson's economy-rate of 2.12 was his lowest in a calendar year. When he removed Marcus Harris at Sydney in January 2022, he became the first to take a Test wicket in 20 different years, beating 19 by Sobers and Muralitharan. For good measure, he helped save the game by blocking out a last-over maiden.

12 Tests: 41 runs @ 4.10; 39 wickets @ 21.74.

JOFRA ARCHER
Sussex

Instead of lighting up the World Cup and the Ashes, Archer spent most of the year recovering from ailments. The tour of India provided flashes of his fire, but in March surgeons discovered a fragment of glass in his right middle finger

– he had dropped a fish tank in his bath two months earlier. In May, after a brief return for Sussex, he underwent an operation to remove an impingement on his troublesome right elbow. Another comeback, in July, ended with more bad news: the elbow had suffered a recurrence of the stress fracture that ended his tour of South Africa in 2019-20. Amid concerns about his long-term future, it meant more surgery, more rest, and no cricket until the new summer.

2 Tests: 16 runs @ 4.00; 4 wickets @ 30.50.

5 T20Is: 19 runs @ 19.00, SR 190.00; 7 wickets @ 22.14, ER 7.75.

JONNY BAIRSTOW   Yorkshire

A pair of blistering one-day knocks at Pune in March – 94 off 66, then 124 off 112, with a total of 14 sixes – underlined his power. But it was an otherwise patchy year. After batting well in Sri Lanka, he was rested-and-rotated out of the first two Tests in India, and on his return made three ducks in four innings at Ahmedabad. Demoted two places from No. 3 for the summer, he kept threatening substance without delivering it. By the end of the year, and a mid-Ashes recall, he had fallen between 28 and 37 eight times, a stat he improved with a stirring – and possibly career-saving – century in the new year at Sydney. In T20 cricket, he batted everywhere in the top six bar No. 5, and struggled at the World Cup. Asked to open in the semi-final against New Zealand in place of the injured Roy, he made 13 off 17. Like much of the rest of his year, it was slightly off the pace – until the SCG.

9 Tests: 391 runs @ 24.43; 5 catches as wicketkeeper.

6 ODIs: 291 runs @ 58.20, SR 121.75; 5 catches and 1 stumping as wicketkeeper.

17 T20Is: 258 runs @ 21.50, SR 124.03; 4 catches and 1 stumping as wicketkeeper.

DOM BESS   Yorkshire

The numbers barely hint at the turmoil. His winter in Asia began with a fortuitous five-for at Galle, and ended in disarray at Ahmedabad; in between, Bess lost his length, his confidence and the trust of his captain. Things began to unravel in the second innings of the First Test in India, when he looked overwhelmed, and bowled eight overs for 50. It was a surprise that he returned for the Fourth – less so when 17 wicketless overs cost 71. He didn't play for England again (though he was part of the Ashes squad), and attempted to rebuild his game during a mainly modest summer with Yorkshire.

4 Tests: 96 runs @ 16.00; 17 wickets @ 26.58.

STUART BROAD   Nottinghamshire

A year that started with a cheap three-for in Galle did not turn out as planned. Between dismissing Sri Lanka's Angelo Mathews in January, and New Zealand's Tom Latham at Lord's in June, Broad went more than 81 overs without a Test wicket, including the tour of India. A four-for against the New Zealanders at Edgbaston felt like a point well made, but the emergence of Robinson brought his future into sharper focus. Come the Ashes, he wasn't trusted in English-style conditions at Brisbane or Melbourne, and did his best to take it on the chin; a five-for at Sydney was another characteristic riposte. Even so, a future in the commentary box looked enticing.

7 Tests: 53 runs @ 6.62; 12 wickets @ 39.50.

RORY BURNS
Surrey

It spoke volumes for England's travails that Burns – who made six ducks, a Test record in a calendar year for a top-seven batsman – was their next-highest run-scorer after Root. After a difficult tour of India, he was England's Player of the Series against New Zealand, then managed two fifties and a 49 against India. But pundits were never far away from tearing apart his technique, which finally cracked in Australia. His golden duck at Brisbane was the most potent symbol of a hapless tour, and he was dropped for the Third Test at Melbourne, then recalled for the Fifth at Hobart, where he was run out for another duck. After 32 caps, England had hoped for better.

10 Tests: 530 runs @ 27.89.

JOS BUTTLER
Lancashire

For much of the year, Buttler embodied the debate about English cricket's priorities. He sat out five successive Tests – in India and at home to New Zealand – because of a mixture of rest-and-rotation and the IPL, and couldn't get going in the Ashes, despite an ultimately futile rearguard at Adelaide. When a finger injury ruled him out of the series finale at Hobart, some wondered if he had played his last Test, though he said he wanted more. In T20 cricket, he was a different beast, destroying Australia at the World Cup, and producing the innings of the tournament, against Sri Lanka. His Test glovework, though, never silenced the clamour for Foakes, not least when – moving to his right for regulation catches – he inexplicably dropped Labuschagne and Smith at Adelaide.

9 Tests: 353 runs @ 25.21; 41 catches, 1 stumping.
3 ODIs: 17 runs @ 5.66, SR 68.00; 4 catches.
14 T20Is: 589 runs @ 65.44, SR 143.30; 8 catches, 5 stumpings.

ZAK CRAWLEY
Kent

Crawley made the painful transition from next great thing to also-ran, as difficult tours of Sri Lanka and India were followed by a desperate summer. Eight innings in Asia, all as opener – and all at sea against spin – brought one score above 13. Back home, now at No. 3, he seemed unsure whether to attack or defend, and managed a best of 27 in six Test innings before the selectors stepped in. Since his apparently breakthrough 267 against Pakistan in 2020, he had averaged 11. Brief respite came on his one-day debut, as part of England's emergency squad against Pakistan, when an unbeaten 58 off 50 balls at Cardiff provided a reminder of his talents against pace. At Test level, it was back to the drawing board, though a fluent 77 at Sydney in January hinted at better things to come.

8 Tests: 173 runs @ 10.81.
3 ODIs: 97 runs @ 48.50, SR 114.11.

SAM CURRAN
Surrey

Not for the first time, Curran did a bit of this and a bit of that, without really doing much of anything. He dismissed Virat Kohli in the Lord's Test, where he also made a king pair; he made an unbeaten 95 from No. 8 in an ODI at Pune, but finished on the losing side; and he took a five-for against Sri Lanka at The Oval, but only two other one-day wickets. A stress fracture of the back then ruled him out of the T20 World Cup and the Ashes, unsatisfactorily rounding off another year in which he awaited his calling.

5 Tests: 87 runs @ 14.50, 6 wickets @ 58.66.

6 ODIs: 116 runs @ 116.00, SR 103.57; 7 wickets @ 37.28, ER 5.71.

8 T20Is: 48 runs @ 48.00, SR 184.61; 7 wickets @ 17.85, ER 6.57.

HASEEB HAMEED   Nottinghamshire

Over four years after his previous Test cap, Hameed returned, first as a replacement No. 3 for Crawley, then – after Sibley was dropped too – as opener. He began with a Bambi-fragile golden duck at Lord's against India, but found success partnering Burns: hundred stands at Headingley and The Oval were riches for England's first wicket in the post-Cook era. A pair of gutsy twenties at Brisbane seemed to bode well, before old concerns about low hands on bouncy Australian pitches returned to the fore, and were compounded by a new trigger movement that took him deep in his crease. He suffered six single-figure dismissals in a row, and was dropped for Hobart.

6 Tests: 205 runs @ 18.63.

CHRIS JORDAN   Sussex

Still considered central to England's T20 strategy, Jordan endured an up-and-down year, going at ten an over in India, then a run a ball at home to Sri Lanka. At the World Cup, his influence waned: Player of the Match in the thumping of Australia, he was himself thumped by New Zealand's Jimmy Neesham in the semi-final at Abu Dhabi, when he seemed unable to summon his trademark yorkers and slower balls. In October, it was announced Jordan would be rejoining Surrey, where he would captain the T20 side.

16 T20Is: 49 runs @ 12.25, SR 153.12; 13 wickets @ 34.07, ER 8.07.

DAN LAWRENCE   Essex

A stylish 73 on Test debut at Galle encouraged understandable excitement, but Lawrence often seemed too keen to make an impression. His talent was not in doubt: having been overly promoted in India to No. 3, he made a chutzpah-filled 46 and 50 from No. 7 in the Fourth Test at Ahmedabad, and it was a pity he ran out of partners against New Zealand at Edgbaston. But there were four ducks, too, and a sense that some fatal act of bravado was around the corner.

8 Tests: 354 runs @ 27.23; 1 wicket @ 33.00.

JACK LEACH   Somerset

He began the year as England's main weapon in Sri Lanka and India, and finished it in Australia as the symbol of a national malaise. In between taking 28 wickets with his left-arm spin in South Asia, including five hauls of four or more, and a pummelling at Brisbane, where 13 overs cost 102, Leach was ignored altogether during the home summer. Thrown in on a Gabba greentop, he was given little protection by Root's field placings, and spent the rest of the series trying to recover his poise. But his captain appeared to have lost faith, and Leach opted for a negative leg-stump line, reigniting age-old questions about county cricket's ability to produce world-class spinners.

8 Tests: 68 runs @ 6.80; 30 wickets @ 34.00.

LIAM LIVINGSTONE Lancashire

A white-ball star was born. With his T20 strike-rate of 177 – better than anyone among the major nations bar New Zealand's Finn Allen – Livingstone shot to the top of a crowded list: he was now England's biggest hitter. If a 42-ball century against Pakistan at Trent Bridge was not proof enough, two days later he hit Haris Rauf out of the ground at Headingley – the summer's most memorable shot. Then, after dominating The Hundred, three successive sixes off South Africa's Kagiso Rabada at the World Cup confirmed his prowess. His streetwise bowling proved a different kind of treat: off-breaks to left-handers, leg-breaks to right-handers, and a spell that ought to have been match-winning in the semi-final against New Zealand.

  3 ODIs: 72 runs @ 36.00, SR 112.50; 1 wicket @ 20.00, ER 6.66.
  12 T20Is: 236 runs @ 33.71, SR 177.44; 8 wickets @ 19.75, ER 6.32.

SAQIB MAHMOOD Lancashire

His reputation soared during a single new-ball spell in the first one-dayer against Pakistan at Cardiff, when he removed Imam-ul-Haq with his first delivery and Babar Azam with his third, en route to four wickets in the game and nine in the series. Offering pace, accuracy and reverse swing, he might have made his Test debut, against India – only for the selectors to prefer Overton's extra height at Headingley and The Oval. But they had taken note.

  3 ODIs: 8 runs @ 8.00, SR 50.00; 9 wickets @ 13.66, ER 4.39.
  3 T20Is: 3 runs without dismissal, SR 60.00; 4 wickets @ 28.00, ER 10.18.

DAWID MALAN Yorkshire

After briefly losing his No. 1 T20 ranking to Pakistan's Babar Azam, Malan finished 2021 back on top, though it was in Test cricket that – briefly – he made bigger strides. Ignored for three years by the selectors, he answered England's latest SOS for top-order solidity, making 70 against India at The Oval, then eighties at Brisbane and Adelaide, where he kept Root company. But his Ashes form dwindled, and he was left out of the Test tour of the Caribbean. The T20 World Cup had brought a top score of 41, and grumbles about his strike-rate on slow pitches.

  5 Tests: 308 runs @ 34.22; 2 wickets @ 16.50.
  5 ODIs: 134 runs @ 44.66, SR 89.33.
  17 T20Is: 384 runs @ 27.42, SR 116.01.

EOIN MORGAN Middlesex

Hopes of becoming the first captain to simultaneously hold the one-day and T20 World Cups were scuppered in a few minutes by New Zealand's Jimmy Neesham, triggering speculation that the Morgan white-ball era was at an end. Not so, he said, but his own numbers hardly helped his cause. Other than an unbeaten 75 against Sri Lanka at The Oval, there was little to shout about, though a World Cup 40 against the same opponents was full of guts and nous. Overall, the explosiveness had vanished. His IPL was a more extreme version of his experiences with England: he averaged 11 while captaining Kolkata Knight Riders to the final, where they lost.

  4 ODIs: 103 runs @ 51.50, SR 79.23.
  16 T20Is: 150 runs @ 16.66, SR 120.00.

OLLIE POPE   Surrey

After two years in which his stock rose, Pope's value crashed. His problem, until he reached Australia, was not playing himself in, but hanging around. He reached double figures 13 times, but only once passed 35. Batting experts questioned his new off-stump guard, a move designed to mitigate the risk of an outside edge, but which opened him up to being beaten on the inside. Twice, New Zealand's bowlers trapped him leg-before. At The Oval, he reverted to middle stump, and made 81 against India. But Nathan Lyon worked him over at Brisbane and Adelaide, and a recall at Hobart proved hapless.

  9 Tests: 368 runs @ 21.64.

ADIL RASHID   Yorkshire

If it was not quite a vintage year for England's leading white-ball spinner, then more than anything that was a reflection of his high standards. His 23 wickets in T20s were still ten clear of his next-best team-mate (Jordan), and figures of four for two against West Indies in the first game of the World Cup a national record. No England bowler looked more likely to take a wicket – he struck every 15 balls – which made his struggles in the 50-over game perplexing. In November, he made a different kind of headline, when he corroborated Azeem Rafiq's claim that he had heard Michael Vaughan making a racist remark before a county game in 2009.

  6 ODIs: 19 runs @ 9.50, SR 70.37; 4 wickets @ 85.50, ER 6.45.
  16 T20Is: 4 runs @ 4.00, SR 66.66; 23 wickets @ 17.78, ER 7.01.

OLLIE ROBINSON   Sussex

Fleetingly, it seemed the high and low of his career would be condensed into a few hours, when a Test debut four-for against New Zealand at Lord's unfolded as racist and sexist tweets emerged from his teenage years. He apologised, was suspended while the ECB investigated, and returned with a five-wicket haul against India at Trent Bridge, soon followed by another, at Headingley. He had it all: bounce, accuracy, movement and attitude. Or perhaps not quite all: England were unimpressed by his fitness, and his pace dropped after a promising start to the Ashes. His batting, too, fell away, but in the main it had been a high-class beginning.

  8 Tests: 125 runs @ 9.61; 37 wickets @ 21.16.

JOE ROOT   Yorkshire

Perhaps the most astonishing aspect of a year which brought him 1,708 Test runs and six hundreds (the first breaking the England record, the second equalling it), was the lack of support: Burns, next in the list, was 1,178 adrift. Scores of 228, 186 and 218 in two wins at Galle and one at Chennai showed off Root's mastery of the sweep, and he was soon hitting India for three more hundreds in four innings in the summer (in between, he took five for eight at Ahmedabad: even his off-breaks seemed blessed). Only a century in Australia, where he had now led England to a pair of 4–0 hammerings, continued to elude him. With little or no help from his team-mates, it was a matter of time before results suffered. Those three South Asian victories gave way to a run of one win in 14, and questions over his tactical acumen.

15 Tests: 1,708 runs @ 61.00; 14 wickets @ 30.50.
3 ODIs: 147 runs without dismissal, SR 84.48.

JASON ROY   Surrey

It was a measure of Roy's importance to the T20 team that his calf injury in England's final group game at the World Cup seemed instantly to diminish their prospects. Only Buttler, his opening partner, and Livingstone cut more destructive figures in the 20-over side. More often than not, Roy provided early electricity: three forties in the March T20s against India in Ahmedabad, 64 off 36 against Pakistan at Old Trafford, 61 off 38 against Bangladesh at Abu Dhabi. In his handful of ODIs, he was consistently powerful. His year deserved a better conclusion than hobbling off in tears at Sharjah.

5 ODIs: 175 runs @ 43.75, SR 120.68.
15 T20Is: 426 runs @ 30.42, SR 146.89.

DOMINIC SIBLEY   Warwickshire

Hopes that England had found a top-order rock turned to dust as Sibley became unselectable. Alarm bells first rang in India, where he followed a painstaking 87 on a flat first-day pitch in Chennai with 47 runs in seven innings against the turning ball. When he compiled a dreary 60 not out on the last day against New Zealand at Lord's, he seemed to sum up his team's lack of ambition. He had grown strokeless, a consequence of his desire to open up the off side, costing him his scoring shots to leg. After two Tests against India – and two lame chips to short midwicket – he was packed off to county cricket. Determined to rebuild his game, he turned down a Lions tour of Australia in favour of a winter in the Edgbaston nets.

10 Tests: 356 runs @ 19.77.

BEN STOKES   Durham

Soon after captaining an emergency one-day team to a 3–0 win over Pakistan, Stokes opted for time away from cricket, to look after his mental health and a finger badly broken during the IPL. For a while, he went to ground, inaccessible even to team-mates; the T20 World Cup came and went. But the injury healed and, almost from nowhere, he declared himself ready for the Ashes. Reality fell short of expectation: he averaged 23 with the bat and 71 with the ball, before a side strain – sustained, true to form, during a spell of bouncers at Sydney – limited him to batting at Hobart. Meanwhile, he claimed he didn't want to replace Root as captain, which was just as well: he had too much on his plate already.

7 Tests: 304 runs @ 21.71; 9 wickets @ 44.66.
6 ODIs: 189 runs @ 37.80, SR 121.15; 4 wickets @ 39.50, ER 6.32.
5 T20Is: 84 runs @ 28.00, SR 150.00; 3 wickets @ 35.00, ER 8.83.

CHRIS WOAKES   Warwickshire

Fortune deserted him. His tour of Sri Lanka and India never got going after he had to isolate on arrival because he had shared a taxi to Heathrow with Moeen Ali, who tested positive for Covid. Then, after asphyxiating Sri Lanka's batsmen with figures of 20–8–46–6 in two ODIs, he slipped on the stairs at home, injuring his heel and ruling him out until the last Test of the summer. That game, plus three in Australia, were a small sample size, but seven wickets against India at The Oval cost seven each, while six at Brisbane, where he opened the bowling, Adelaide and Hobart came at 55. In between, he had his moments at the T20 World Cup, but was asked to bowl at the death, which didn't suit him. As ever, he did it all uncomplainingly.

  3 Tests: 173 runs @ 28.83; 10 wickets @ 36.60.
  2 ODIs: did not bat; 6 wickets @ 7.66, ER 2.30.
  8 T20Is: 7 runs @ 7.00, SR 233.33; 8 wickets @ 21.75, ER 6.32.

MARK WOOD   Durham

The sight of Wood charging in on Australian pitches was one of the few to gladden English hearts during the Ashes – especially at Hobart in the new year, where he collected a career-best six for 37 in the second innings, and nine in the match. Having usually struggled with his ankle, it was perverse that a jarred shoulder – sustained in the field against India at Lord's – should disrupt his summer. And when he stepped in for the injured Mills during the T20 World Cup, eight rusty overs against South Africa and New Zealand cost 81. In Australia, he troubled the best batsmen – especially Marnus Labuschagne – more often than any team-mate, and endeared himself to the crowds.

  7 Tests: 98 runs @ 9.80; 19 wickets @ 34.78.
  4 ODIs: 16 runs @ 16.00, SR 57.14; 5 wickets @ 32.60, ER 4.79.
  8 T20Is: 1 run without dismissal, SR 100.00; 8 wickets @ 32.62, ER 8.15.

AND THE REST...

Ben Foakes (Surrey; 3 Tests) got his chance in India after Buttler was rested, and kept impeccably, but followed an unbeaten 42 with 36 runs in five innings. His summer was ruined when he slipped in the Oval dressing-room and injured a hamstring. **Craig Overton** (Somerset; 2 Tests, 3 ODIs) played a big part in England's only Test win at home, with six for 61 against India at Headingley, but was less effective – two for 107 – at The Oval. **Olly Stone** (Warwickshire; 2 Tests) troubled India's top order at Chennai in February, and was being lined up to hit Australia with pace, until he suffered a stress fracture of the back in June. **James Bracey** (Gloucestershire; 2 Tests) began with a first-baller on Test debut, against New Zealand at Lord's, then added another duck – and eight – at Edgbaston. He was equally unconvincing with the gloves. **Sam Billings** (Kent; 4 ODIs, 3 T20Is) couldn't build on a promising 2020, never passing 24, and not getting a bat in the T20 World Cup semi-final, his only game of the tournament. Injuries meant an unlikely Test debut at Hobart in January 2022. For **Tom Curran** (Surrey; 4 ODIs, 3 T20Is), four wickets in a rain-ruined ODI against Sri Lanka at Bristol were the highlight of a quiet year, in which he slipped down the white-ball pecking-order, and snaffled a place in the T20 World Cup squad only after brother Sam went down injured. **David Willey** (Yorkshire; 3 ODIs, 4 T20Is) took his chances when they came along, picking up nine wickets in three ODIs against Sri Lanka. **Matt Parkinson** (Lancashire; 3 ODIs, 2 T20Is) had his moments as Rashid's white-ball leg-spinning deputy, not least a big-turning delivery to bowl Pakistan's Imam-ul-Haq at Edgbaston. **Lewis Gregory** (Somerset; 3 ODIs, 1 T20I) was central to England's ODI whitewash of Pakistan, with 40 and three wickets at Lord's, then 77 off 69 at Edgbaston in partnership with Vince. **Brydon Carse** (Durham; 3 ODIs) burgled a late five-for against Pakistan at Edgbaston, where he also scored useful runs. **Phil Salt** (Sussex; 3 ODIs) typified England's top-order strength in depth in one-day cricket, cracking 60 off 54 in his second ODI, against Pakistan at Lord's. **John Simpson** (Middlesex; 3 ODIs) got his chance behind the stumps in the 50-over series against Pakistan, aged nearly 33, and held five catches at Lord's, his home ground. **James Vince** (Hampshire; 3 ODIs) finally ticked off an England hundred, at the 50th attempt, to marshal the Edgbaston chase, but was still among the second tier of white-ball batsmen. **Reece Topley** (Surrey; 2 ODIs) removed India's Shikhar Dhawan in only his second international appearance for five years, and was later added to the T20 World Cup squad as cover. **Tymal Mills** (Sussex; 4 T20Is) made a popular return to international cricket after more than four and a half years away, and offered England death-overs expertise at the T20 World Cup – only for a thigh injury to intervene.

ENGLAND TEST AVERAGES
IN CALENDAR YEAR 2021

BATTING AND FIELDING

		T	I	NO	R	HS	100	50	Avge	SR	Ct/St
1	J. E. Root	15	29	1	1,708	228	6	4	61.00	56.85	21
2	†D. J. Malan	5	9	0	308	82	0	3	34.22	43.50	1
3	C. R. Woakes	3	6	0	173	50	0	1	28.83	54.92	1
4	†R. J. Burns.	10	19	0	530	132	1	3	27.89	41.34	7
5	D. W. Lawrence	8	15	2	354	81*	0	3	27.23	49.03	1
6	J. C. Buttler.	9	16	2	353	55	0	2	25.21	42.78	41/1
7	J. M. Bairstow.	9	17	1	391	57	0	1	24.43	48.45	11
8	†B. A. Stokes	7	14	0	304	82	0	2	21.71	41.98	8
9	O. J. D. Pope.	9	18	1	368	81	0	1	21.64	48.04	8
10	D. P. Sibley.	10	20	2	356	87	0	3	19.77	30.29	5
11	†M. M. Ali	4	7	0	132	43	0	0	18.85	51.76	8
12	H. Hameed	6	11	0	205	68	0	2	18.63	31.68	3
13	D. M. Bess	4	6	0	96	34	0	0	16.00	34.16	0
14	B. T. Foakes	3	6	1	78	42*	0	0	15.60	30.00	4/3
15	†S. M. Curran	5	7	1	87	32	0	0	14.50	55.06	2
16	C. Overton	2	3	0	43	32	0	0	14.33	51.80	3
17	Z. Crawley	8	16	0	173	53	0	1	10.81	42.92	11
18	M. A. Wood	7	11	1	98	41	0	0	9.80	47.57	1
19	O. E. Robinson	8	14	1	125	42	0	0	9.61	39.06	3
20	O. P. Stone	2	4	0	36	20	0	0	9.00	31.30	1
21	†M. J. Leach	8	14	4	68	14*	0	0	6.80	26.15	4
22	†S. C. J. Broad	7	12	4	53	11*	0	0	6.62	36.80	4
23	†J. M. Anderson	12	21	11	41	10*	0	0	4.10	25.62	4
24	J. C. Archer	2	4	0	16	11	0	0	4.00	51.61	0
25	†J. R. Bracey.	2	3	0	8	8	0	0	2.66	29.62	6

BOWLING

		Style	O	M	R	W	BB	5I	Avge	SR	ER
1	C. Overton	RFM	62.3	16	168	8	3-14	0	21.00	46.87	2.68
2	O. E. Robinson ...	RFM/OB	295.4	85	783	37	5-65	2	21.16	47.94	2.64
3	J. M. Anderson ...	RFM	399.5	141	848	39	6-40	2	21.74	61.51	2.12
4	O. P. Stone	RF	47.4	11	165	7	3-47	0	23.57	40.85	3.46
5	D. M. Bess	OB	136.1	16	452	17	5-30	1	26.58	48.05	3.31
6	J. E. Root	RF	139.3	18	427	14	5-8	1	30.50	59.78	3.06
6	J. C. Archer......	OB	35.1	9	122	4	2-75	0	30.50	52.75	3.46
8	M. J. Leach	SLA	299.5	40	1,020	30	5-122	1	34.00	59.96	3.40
9	M. A. Wood	RF	202.3	33	661	19	3-51	0	34.78	63.94	3.26
10	C. R. Woakes	RFM	109.4	31	366	10	4-55	0	36.60	65.80	3.33
11	M. M. Ali	OB	147	13	525	14	4-98	0	37.50	63.00	3.57
12	S. C. J. Broad	RFM	179.1	48	474	12	4-48	0	39.50	89.58	2.64
13	B. A. Stokes	RFM	92.2	11	402	9	4-89	0	44.66	61.55	4.35
14	S. M. Curran	LFM	109.3	16	352	6	2-27	0	58.66	109.50	3.21

Also bowled: D. W. Lawrence (OB) 6–0–33–1; D. J. Malan (LB) 6–0–33–2.

> **"**
> Their 103-9 was weak, but the Spirit were willing."
> The women's Hundred, page 1207

ENGLAND ONE-DAY INTERNATIONAL AVERAGES IN CALENDAR YEAR 2021

BATTING AND FIELDING

		M	I	NO	R	HS	100	50	Avge	SR	Ct/St
1	†S. M. Curran	6	3	2	116	95*	0	1	116.00	103.57	2
2	J. M. Vince	3	2	0	158	102	1	1	79.00	107.48	2
3	L. Gregory	3	2	0	117	77	0	1	58.50	100.86	0
4	J. M. Bairstow	6	5	0	291	124	1	1	58.20	121.75	6/1
5	†E. J. G. Morgan	4	3	1	103	75*	0	1	51.50	79.23	1
6	Z. Crawley	3	3	1	97	58*	0	1	48.50	114.11	4
7	†D. J. Malan	5	5	2	134	68*	0	2	44.66	89.33	3
8	J. J. Roy	5	4	0	175	60	0	1	43.75	120.68	3
9	B. A. Carse	3	2	1	43	31	0	0	43.00	82.69	0
10	†B. A. Stokes	6	5	0	189	99	0	1	37.80	121.15	2
11	L. S. Livingstone	3	3	1	72	36	0	0	36.00	112.50	1
12	P. D. Salt	3	3	0	104	60	0	1	34.66	116.85	0
13	†M. M. Ali	6	3	0	87	30	0	0	29.00	73.10	4
14	C. Overton	3	2	1	18	18*	0	0	18.00	100.00	2
15	M. A. Wood	4	2	1	16	14	0	0	16.00	57.14	0
16	S. W. Billings	4	2	0	21	18	0	0	10.50	70.00	2
17	†J. A. Simpson	3	2	0	20	17	0	0	10.00	64.51	9
18	A. U. Rashid	6	2	0	19	19	0	0	9.50	70.37	4
19	J. C. Buttler	3	3	0	17	15	0	0	5.66	68.00	4
20	J. E. Root	3	2	2	147	79*	0	2	–	84.48	3

Played in four matches: T. K. Curran 11. Played in three matches: S. Mahmood 8; M. W. Parkinson 7* (1ct); †D. J. Willey did not bat (1ct). Played in two matches: R. J. W. Topley 1* (1ct); C. R. Woakes did not bat (1ct).

BOWLING

		Style	O	M	R	W	BB	4I	Avge	SR	ER
1	C. R. Woakes	RFM	20	8	46	6	4-18	1	7.66	2.30	20.00
2	S. Mahmood	RFM	28	3	123	9	4-42	1	13.66	4.39	18.66
3	D. J. Willey	LFM	27	2	144	9	4-64	1	16.00	5.33	18.00
4	B. A. Carse	RF	25	0	136	6	5-61	1	22.66	5.44	25.00
5	L. Gregory	RFM	19	1	97	4	3-44	0	24.25	5.10	28.50
6	M. W. Parkinson	LB	24	0	140	5	2-28	0	28.00	5.83	28.80
7	C. Overton	RFM	25.2	2	126	4	2-23	0	31.50	4.97	38.00
8	M. A. Wood	RF	34	3	163	5	3-34	0	32.60	4.79	40.80
9	S. M. Curran	LFM	45.4	3	261	7	5-48	1	37.28	5.71	39.14
10	T. K. Curran	RFM	40	0	224	6	4-35	1	37.33	5.60	40.00
11	R. J. W. Topley	LFM	17.2	0	116	3	2-50	0	38.66	6.69	34.66
12	B. A. Stokes	RFM	25	1	158	4	3-34	0	39.50	6.32	37.50
13	A. U. Rashid	LB	53	0	342	4	2-81	0	85.50	6.45	79.50

Also bowled: M. M. Ali (OB) 22–0–119–2; L. S. Livingstone (LB/OB) 3–0–20–1.

> ❝The travelling journalists were not universally welcomed. One local wrote that 'a more biased set of typewriter-punchers than the English press could only be found in the offices of the late Dr Goebbels'.❞
> Cricket books, page 146

ENGLAND TWENTY20 INTERNATIONAL AVERAGES IN CALENDAR YEAR 2021

BATTING AND FIELDING

		M	I	NO	R	HS	50	Avge	SR	4	6	Ct/St
1	J. C. Archer	5	2	1	19	18*	0	19.00	**190.00**	2	1	4
2	†S. M. Curran	8	5	4	48	16*	0	48.00	**184.61**	3	3	0
3	L. S. Livingstone	12	8	1	236	103	1	33.71	**177.44**	12	18	6
4	C. J. Jordan	16	7	3	49	14	0	12.25	**153.12**	4	2	8
5	†B. A. Stokes	5	3	0	84	46	0	28.00	**150.00**	7	3	1
6	J. J. Roy	15	15	1	426	64	2	30.42	**146.89**	48	17	9
7	†D. J. Willey	4	2	1	16	16	0	16.00	**145.45**	2	1	3
8	J. C. Buttler	14	14	5	589	101*	6	65.44	**143.30**	49	26	8/5
9	†M. M. Ali	10	8	2	137	51*	1	22.83	**137.00**	13	5	4
10	J. M. Bairstow	17	17	5	258	51	0	21.50	**124.03**	24	9	11/1
11	†E. J. G. Morgan	16	11	2	150	40	0	16.66	**120.00**	12	6	5
12	†D. J. Malan	17	16	2	384	76	2	27.42	**116.01**	35	11	10
13	T. K. Curran	3	2	0	10	9	0	5.00	**111.11**	1	0	0
14	M. W. Parkinson	2	2	0	5	5	0	2.50	**83.33**	1	0	0
15	S. W. Billings	3	2	0	26	24	0	13.00	**81.25**	2	0	1
16	A. U. Rashid	16	4	3	4	2*	0	4.00	**66.66**	0	0	5
17	S. Mahmood	3	2	2	3	3*	0	–	**60.00**	0	0	0

Played in eight matches: C. R. Woakes 7 (4ct); M. A. Wood 1*. Played in four matches: T. S. Mills did not bat. Played in one match: L. Gregory 10.

BOWLING

		Style	Balls	Dots	R	W	BB	4I	Avge	SR	ER
1	M. M. Ali	OB	131	58	131	11	2-15	0	11.90	11.90	**6.00**
2	L. S. Livingstone	LB/OB	150	55	158	8	2-15	0	19.75	18.75	**6.32**
3	C. R. Woakes	RFM	165	88	174	8	2-23	0	21.75	20.62	**6.32**
4	S. M. Curran	LFM	114	44	125	7	2-14	0	17.85	16.28	**6.57**
5	D. J. Willey	LFM	84	43	93	4	3-27	0	23.25	21.00	**6.64**
6	A. U. Rashid	LB	350	131	409	23	4-2	2	17.78	15.21	**7.01**
7	J. C. Archer	RF	120	54	155	7	4-33	1	22.14	17.14	**7.75**
8	T. S. Mills	LF	81	33	108	7	3-27	0	15.42	11.57	**8.00**
9	C. J. Jordan	RFM	329	128	443	13	3-17	0	34.07	25.30	**8.07**
10	M. A. Wood	RF	192	74	261	8	3-31	0	32.62	24.00	**8.15**
11	B. A. Stokes	RFM	72	21	106	3	1-25	0	35.33	24.00	**8.83**
12	T. K. Curran	RFM	60	22	95	3	2-47	0	31.66	20.00	**9.50**
13	S. Mahmood	RFM	66	21	112	4	3-33	0	28.00	16.50	**10.18**

Also bowled: L. Gregory (RFM) 12–2–25–1; M. W. Parkinson (LB) 48–10–72–1.

SRI LANKA v ENGLAND IN 2020-21

REVIEW BY RORY DOLLARD

Test matches (2): Sri Lanka 0 (0pts), England 2 (120pts)

At the end of December, a couple of weeks before England's first assignment of a busy 2021, their fresh-faced captain Joe Root turned 30. With Covid restrictions in force in the UK, he celebrated in the customary style: at home, with his wife, Carrie, and his children, Alfie and Isabella – plus "a nice bottle of wine". While some were trying to come to terms with the news that the bright young debutant of Nagpur in 2012 was easing into cricketing middle age, Root was facing his own moment of introspection.

For the first time since his maiden Test hundred, in 2013, he had gone a calendar year without adding another. With Marnus Labuschagne and Babar Azam lurking, there were rumblings that his membership of the Fab Four – alongside Steve Smith, Virat Kohli and Kane Williamson – might not be renewed. Instead, Root established himself in Sri Lanka as the series' undisputed centre of gravity, and England headed to India with a 2–0 win in the bag. His drought had ended in a deluge: sweeping relentlessly during masterful innings of 228 and 186, he finished with 426 runs in four innings – exactly twice as many as the next-highest, Angelo Mathews. Root also threw in seven catches, two cheap wickets and smart captaincy: this was a contest that carried his imprint at every turn, and guaranteed a chair at the top table.

The tour had actually begun ten months earlier, in March 2020, but England abandoned it once a fraught day of calls in Colombo confirmed the growing reach of coronavirus. Now, in an era of quarantine, restricted movement and biosecure bubbles, the ECB decided that the all-format players should not take part in every leg of the winter programme, for the sake of their long-term wellbeing. Absent were Ben Stokes and Jofra Archer, yet those two – as well as Jos Buttler, Sam Curran and Jonny Bairstow – had been promised breaks

---

RISING TO THE ISLAND CHALLENGE

Successful fourth-innings chases by Test teams visiting Sri Lanka:

382-3	Pakistan won by seven wickets at Pallekele	2015
264-3	India won by seven wickets at Kandy.	2001
258-5	India won by five wickets at Colombo (PSO).	2010
191-6	Bangladesh won by four wickets at Colombo (PSO)	2016-17
183-2	Pakistan won by eight wickets at Kandy.	2005-06
171-3	England won by seven wickets at Colombo (PSO).	1981-82
164-4	**England won by six wickets at Galle**	**2020-21**
161-7	England won by three wickets at Kandy.	2000-01
131-5	Pakistan won by five wickets at Colombo (SSC)	2000
97-2	England won by eight wickets at Colombo (PSO)	2011-12
92-0	Pakistan won by ten wickets at Galle	2015
76-3	**England won by seven wickets at Galle**	**2020-21**
74-6	England won by four wickets at Colombo (SSC)	2000-01

Sri Lanka Cricket

Reverse charge: Joe Root connects sweetly during the First Test.

from the England schedule, rather than during either of the IPLs which sandwiched the trip to Sri Lanka and India. This was met with a shrug of acceptance by the England camp, and a hint of distaste from purists. Rory Burns was also missing, because of paternity leave.

There were a couple of new faces among a tour party of 44 on the charter flight to Hambantota, where England spent the first ten days in biosecure isolation, and both owed their role to the pandemic. Phil Davies, a former policeman with counter-terrorism experience, was the team's Covid compliance officer; Dr James Bickley, a clinical psychologist, was in charge of the squad's mental health. Both must have been busy from the start, when Moeen Ali, having tested negative before departure, tested positive on arrival. He was hoping to make his Test comeback in a country where he had claimed 18 wickets in three matches in 2018-19, but endured isolation for 13 days, with no chance of being fit in time for either game. Chris Woakes, who shared a car with Ali from Birmingham to Heathrow, was confined to his room for a week. Though he tested negative, his chance of action was compromised too.

Medical teams were assigned to both squads, and there were seven rounds of screening in less than three weeks. No one else tested positive on either side, though there was a minor scare when two employees at England's hotel did. Galle International Stadium, which hosted both games, remained shut to spectators, and the media centres closed for business (except for the host broadcasters). At least the cricket could take its rightful place: in a return to some kind of normality, the results that mattered were determined on the pitch, not in the laboratory.

Neither team had ideal preparation. Sri Lanka arrived home straight from a two-match drubbing in South Africa, with plummeting confidence and a rising injury toll. Moving swiftly between the high veld and Galle, they were being asked to paint on canvas and brick with the same brushes. England, meanwhile, had not played Test cricket in nearly five months, and were reduced – by mandatory restrictions and poor weather – to a single day of intra-squad match practice. The entire trip allowed them just six days' full training, in contrast to their original pre-Covid itinerary, which had room for seven days of competitive cricket against strong opposition.

If ever there was an excuse for England to live down to their tag as slow starters, this was it. Instead, they bowled Sri Lanka out before tea on the first

---

FIVE STATS YOU MAY HAVE MISSED

BENEDICT BERMANGE

- James Anderson became the fifth-oldest seamer to take a five-wicket haul in Test cricket:

Years	Days			
40	304	S. F. Barnes	England v South Africa at Durban	1913-14
40	86	G. W. A. Chubb . .	South Africa v England at Manchester	1951
39	231	F. J. Laver	Australia v England at Manchester	1909
39	6	R. J. Hadlee	New Zealand v England at Birmingham	1990
38	**177**	**J. M. Anderson . .**	**England v Sri Lanka at Galle . . . .**	**2020-21**
38	141	C. A. Walsh	West Indies v South Africa at Port-of-Spain . .	2000-01

- In the first innings of the Second Test, all ten Sri Lankan wickets fell to seam. That had not happened in a Test innings in Sri Lanka since 2000-01, when England's Darren Gough, Andy Caddick and Craig White shared ten at Kandy.

- Only once before had a team dismissed their opponents without at least one bowler taking a wicket in both innings:

England v Australia at The Oval, 2019
First innings: J. C. Archer (6), S. M. Curran (3), C. R. Woakes (1).
Second innings: S. C. J. Broad (4), M. J. Leach (4), J. E. Root (2).

England v Sri Lanka at Galle, 2020-21
First innings: J. M. Anderson (6), M. A. Wood (3), S. M. Curran (1).
Second innings: D. M. Bess (4), M. J. Leach (4), J. E. Root (2).

- In the second innings of the Second Test, Joe Root took two wickets for no runs – the first instance of such Test figures. (However, against India at Delhi in 1959-60, Richie Benaud took three for none for Australia.) Against Pakistan at Manchester in 2016, Root had taken one for none, making him only the second bowler to have twice claimed wickets without conceding a run; Pakistan's Wasim Raja twice had figures of one for none.

- By the end of the tour, England had won six consecutive Tests in Sri Lanka, their second-longest winning streak away from home against one opponent:

8	v South Africa	from 1888-89 to 1898-99
6*	**v Sri Lanka . . . .**	**from 2011-12**
5	v Australia	from 1932-33 to 1936-37
5	v Bangladesh	from 2003-04 to 2016-17

* *Unbroken.*

Benedict Bermange is the cricket statistician for Sky Sports.

Same difference: seamer Jimmy Anderson and spinner Lasith Embuldeniya were both destructive with the new ball.

day, and never relinquished the advantage. For fans, the spectacle unfolded almost exclusively on screen, though one man – Rob Lewis – represented the Barmy Army in person. He stood vigil on the walls of the nearby fort, belted out "Jerusalem", and lapped up salutations from the players.

There were several threads common to the two games – perhaps unsurprisingly, given they took place at the same ground, a handful of days apart. This was a tour in the most minimal sense. On each occasion, Sri Lanka produced a woeful batting display, 135 in the First Test followed by 126 in the Second. In between, they batted with enough resolve and application to suggest things ought to have been closer. They were hampered by the last-minute withdrawal of their captain, Dimuth Karunaratne, with a fractured thumb. Even so, in a squad that boasted several former captains – Dinesh Chandimal, Suranga Lakmal, Mathews and Lahiru Thirimanne – a lack of on-field leadership was surprising. In the passages of play which shaped the games, there was too much hitting out, too little digging in. In a further reminder of the peculiar rhythms that can govern cricket in this part of the world, the match that started with an innings lasting 46 overs went to the fifth day, while the one in which Sri Lanka ground through almost 140 overs ended on the fourth.

For England, the tone was established by a statesman seamer – first Stuart Broad, then James Anderson. On the previous tour, they had managed one wicket between them, with Anderson declaring himself "a bit of a spare part".

This time, Broad set the standard with three wickets and a magnificent economy-rate, before Anderson – replacing him for the Second Test – raised the bar with a six-for. The idea of permanently rotating the pair to make room for younger, quicker alternatives had long been mooted; but they stubbornly refused to be anything short of brilliant.

Things were different in the spin department, where the Taunton-trained double act of Jack Leach and Dom Bess were outbowled by Lasith Embuldeniya. The England duo shared 22 wickets, but laboured for long periods. Embuldeniya, meanwhile, boasted less experience than off-spinner Dilruwan Perera, and less buzz than leggie Wanindu Hasaranga de Silva. But his left-arm spin led the Sri Lankan charge, and he gave Dom Sibley and Zak Crawley a crash course on the perils of subcontinental batting.

Not that Embuldeniya had an answer to Root. Where others pushed with hard hands or sat paralysed on the back foot, he neutered Sri Lanka's only real threat with the ball. His sweeping was so good and so varied – traditional or reverse, in front or behind square, dabbed or slogged – that even the home

HOWZAT FOR OPENERS?

Bowlers dismissing the top two for single figures in both innings of a Test:

M. D. Marshall	West Indies v India at Kanpur.	1983-84
R. A. S. Lakmal.	Sri Lanka v West Indies at Bridgetown.	2018
K. M. Jarvis	Zimbabwe v Bangladesh at Mirpur.	2018-19
L. Embuldeniya	**Sri Lanka v England at Galle**.	**2020-21**

batters were advised by Mathews to watch the boy from Sheffield for tips. Among visitors to Sri Lanka, only Brian Lara (688) and Mike Hussey (463) have scored more runs in a series, and both played in three matches. They were not the only names Root had in his sights. He overtook Geoffrey Boycott's Test haul of 8,114, before speeding past Kevin Pietersen (8,181) and David Gower (8,231). Victory in the Second Test, meanwhile, meant Root was just one behind Michael Vaughan's England record of 26.

As well as 120 World Test Championship points, which gave England an outside chance of reaching the final, they took ownership of the newly sponsored Moose Cup – in one sense, at least, a bigger prize than the Ashes urn. Root had enough boyish humour to pose with the trophy's antlers poking out from behind his head, but he had never been a more mature cricketing talent.

ENGLAND TOURING PARTY

*J. E. Root (Yorkshire), M. M. Ali (Worcestershire), J. M. Anderson (Lancashire), J. M. Bairstow (Yorkshire), D. M. Bess (Yorkshire), S. C. J. Broad (Nottinghamshire), J. C. Buttler (Lancashire), Z. Crawley (Kent), S. M. Curran (Surrey), B. T. Foakes (Surrey), D. W. Lawrence (Essex), M. J. Leach (Somerset), D. P. Sibley (Warwickshire), O. P. Stone (Warwickshire), C. R. Woakes (Warwickshire), M. A. Wood (Durham).

J. R. Bracey (Gloucestershire), M. S. Crane (Hampshire), S. Mahmood (Lancashire), C. Overton (Somerset), M. W. Parkinson (Lancashire), O. E. Robinson (Sussex) and G. S. Virdi (Surrey) travelled as reserve players. O. J. D. Pope (Surrey), not in the official party, was in Sri Lanka as part of his rehabilitation from injury, and played in the warm-up game.

Managing director, England men's cricket: A. F. Giles. *Head coach:* C. E. W. Silverwood. *Assistant coach:* P. D. Collingwood. *Batting consultant:* J. H. Kallis. *Bowling coach:* J. Lewis. *Spin-bowling consultant:* J. S. Patel. *Wicketkeeping consultant:* J. S. Foster. *Fielding coach:* C. D. Hopkinson. *Team manager:* A. W. Bentley. *Analyst:* G. Lindsay. *Doctors:* R. Young, N. Peirce. *Physiotherapists:* C. A. de Weymarn, B. Davies. *Nutritionist:* E. Gardner. *Strength and conditioning:* P. C. F. Scott. *Psychologist:* J. Bickley. *Security manager:* W. Carr. *Head of team communications:* D. M. Reuben. *Covid operations officer:* P. Davies.

At Hambantota, January 8–9, 2021 (not first-class). **Drawn. J. E. Root's XI 184-2 dec** (50 overs) (J. E. Root 74*); **J. C. Buttler's XI 120-6** (38 overs) (O. J. D. Pope 58*). *The second day of this intra-squad match was washed out, so the 88 overs on the first represented the entirety of England's competitive practice. Joe Root's team batted first by agreement, and there were runs for Zak Crawley (46) and Dan Lawrence (46*); in a hint of things to come, Root top-scored. Dom Bess was given 16 overs – twice as many as anyone else – and he removed James Bracey for 16. When Jos Buttler's team replied, Ollie Robinson and Jimmy Anderson reduced them to 31-4, with Anderson bowling Buttler first ball. Jack Leach made it 48-6, before Ollie Pope and Dom Sibley (18*) steadied the ship. Sibley was allowed to bat a second time after falling cheaply, and Ben Foakes played for both sides.*

SRI LANKA v ENGLAND

First Test

VITHUSHAN EHANTHARAJAH

At Galle, January 14–18, 2021. England won by seven wickets. England 60pts. Toss: Sri Lanka. Test debut: D. W. Lawrence.

Rarely have England begun a year with such authority. Professional and controlled from the first day, they handsomely won the first of their 17 Tests scheduled for 2021. The

Off and away: Dan Lawrence strikes out on debut.

Sri Lanka Cricket

result suggested there could be plenty of longer-term gains to follow. This series was the beginning of the ECB's rest-and-rotation policy, with Ben Stokes and Jofra Archer allowed to stay at home. The absence of Moeen Ali, who had tested positive for Covid-19, was not part of the plan, but that opened the door for Bess. Thrown into action on the first morning, he was soon basking in the glow of a five-wicket haul.

As ever, the expectation at Galle was for a turning pitch, so Chandimal – deputising for the injured Dimuth Karunaratne – chose to bat. What followed, though, was a surprise. The first two interventions came from Broad, who had Thirimanne caught at leg gully, then inflicted a fourth successive duck on Kusal Mendis with a neat leg-cutter that trimmed the edge.

Test cricket has seen few more fortuitous five-fors than the one Bess now collected. Kusal Perera's disregard for his off-breaks led to a reverse sweep that nestled in Root's hands at slip; Dickwella flailed a long hop to Sibley at point; Shanaka blazed a sweep into Bairstow's ankle at short leg, and Buttler collected the ricochet; Dilruwan Perera was bowled attempting an ambitious drive; Wanindu Hasaranga de Silva reverse-swept, as if it were a dare. From nowhere, Bess had five for 30.

With Broad accounting for Mathews, and Leach removing Chandimal and running out Embuldeniya, Sri Lanka were all out for 135 – the lowest first innings in a Galle Test, below their 181 against Pakistan in 2000. For Broad, figures of three for 20 were not par for the course either: three previous tours of Sri Lanka had produced three wickets at 83. For Grant Flower, Sri Lanka's batting coach, there was incredulity. "I've been with the team for a year," he said. "It's the worst batting I've seen… I'm at a loss for words."

Embuldeniya's left-arm spin quickly saw off Sibley and Crawley, but Bairstow and Root helped England to 127 for two by stumps. Twenty-four hours later, after a day

TEST DOUBLE-HUNDREDS BY AN ENGLAND CAPTAIN

333	G. A. Gooch	v India at Lord's	1990
285*	P. B. H. May	v West Indies at Birmingham	1957
263	A. N. Cook	v Pakistan at Abu Dhabi	2015-16
240	W. R. Hammond	v Australia at Lord's	1938
228	**J. E. Root**	**v Sri Lanka at Galle**	**2020-21**
226	J. E. Root	v New Zealand at Hamilton	2019-20
218	**J. E. Root**	**v India at Chennai**	**2020-21**
215	D. I. Gower	v Australia at Birmingham	1985
205	L. Hutton	v West Indies at Kingston	1953-54
205	E. R. Dexter	v Pakistan at Karachi	1961-62

limited by rain and bad light to 53 overs, they led by 185, with Root making a sweep-heavy 168 not out, his 18th Test century after a barren 2020. There was also a debut knock of immense maturity from Dan Lawrence, who had benefited from Stokes's rest and Ollie Pope's convalescence from shoulder surgery. He and Root added 173 in 43 overs, an England record for any wicket in Sri Lanka, beating 167 for the third by Nasser Hussain and Graham Thorpe at Kandy in 2000-01. Lawrence fell on the second afternoon, having made 73 – Root's score in his own debut Test innings, in India in 2012-13.

On the third morning, Root cracked on, and was last out for 228 in a total of 421, as the final six fell for 49, including Buttler and Curran to successive balls from Fernando. It was his fourth double-century, and the highest for England against Sri Lanka, beating Jonathan Trott's 203 at Cardiff in 2011 (by the end of the series, Root had three of the top four in that list). Only Alastair Cook, with 263 against Pakistan at Abu Dhabi in 2015-16, had hit more in a Test innings for England in Asia. Root also became the seventh England player to reach 8,000 runs and, from 178 innings, the second-quickest, behind Kevin Pietersen's 176.

He had batted for four minutes short of eight hours, and hit 18 fours and a six. It was a masterpiece.

Toiling for 117 overs in the heat had given Sri Lanka time to consider their first-innings wastefulness, and they now began a mission to save face and – they hoped – the match. Kusal Perera started slowly, before accelerating towards a typically punchy fifty. His partnership with Thirimanne was worth 101 when he carved a wide long hop from Curran towards deep point, where Leach had been positioned as little more than a boundary saver. When he held on, Curran celebrated sheepishly, and Perera was gone for 62. Soon after, Sibley at backward point dropped Thirimanne on 51 off Curran, and Mendis avoided equalling the Test record of five successive ducks. At 155 for one, Sri Lanka were making England sweat, but shortly before stumps Buttler held a sharp catch off Leach to end Mendis's stodgy resistance. The hosts closed on 156 for two, a deficit of 130.

Embuldeniya, the nightwatchman, fell early to Bess next morning, but Sri Lanka fought on. Thirimanne notched his second Test century – nearly eight years after his first, also at Galle, against Bangladesh – and Mathews helped him bring up the third fifty stand of the innings. But the run-rate had been gentle, and the second new ball did the trick, as Curran clipped Thirimanne's inside edge, and a diving Buttler clung on. Mathews batted doggedly, reaching the boundary just once in his first 151 balls, but Leach and Bess nibbled away at his support. Broad, meanwhile, finished with impeccable figures: 17–11–14–0.

With Sri Lanka nine down, an attempt by Mathews to retain the strike turned into a dab to Root at slip, handing Leach his second Test five-for, after Pallekele in 2018-19. It meant he and Bess became the first pair of England spinners to take a five-wicket haul in the same game since Derek Underwood and John Emburey in 1981-82, during Sri Lanka's inaugural Test, in Colombo. Buttler, meanwhile, pulled off his first Test stumping, as Dilruwan Perera played and missed at Leach; it had taken him 48 Tests (though this was his 28th behind the stumps). The only Test player to hold more catches than Buttler's 114 before his first stumping was South Africa's David Richardson, with 119. Mathews, though, had hung around for five and three-quarter hours over his 71, and the ball was turning.

England needed 74, and had plenty of time to get them. After six overs, they were 14 for three: Embuldeniya became the first spinner in history to snare the openers for single figures twice in the same Test, while Root was run out by Dickwella, having bumped into Dilruwan Perera, the bowler. But Bairstow and Lawrence fought their way to stumps: 36 needed next day.

A night's kip calmed nerves, and they knocked off the runs in 9.2 overs with little alarm – though Lawrence would have been lbw to Dilruwan Perera on nine had Sri Lanka asked for a review. Fittingly, victory came via a swept four, as Bairstow added 35 to his first-innings 47, and Lawrence 21 to his 73.

Soon after, the team wandered over towards their travelling support, which consisted of one man on top of the fort.

Long time coming: Lahiru Thirimanne reaches his second hundred, 28 Tests after his first.

Sri Lanka Cricket

Rob Lewis, a web designer from Surrey, had flown to Sri Lanka in March 2020 to watch the Test series that was called off because of Covid-19. He found work, stayed on, and became the Barmy Army's lone representative. He was acknowledged throughout, notably when Root moved to 200, and earned a round of applause at the conclusion. Root followed up with a thank-you call. It was a nod to what was missing, and an indication, perhaps, that better times lay ahead.

Player of the Match: J. E. Root.

Close of play: first day, England 127-2 (Bairstow 47, Root 66); second day, England 320-4 (Root 168, Buttler 7); third day, Sri Lanka 156-2 (Thirimanne 76, Embuldeniya 0); fourth day, England 38-3 (Bairstow 11, Lawrence 7).

Sri Lanka

H. D. R. L. Thirimanne c Bairstow b Broad	4	– (2) c Buttler b Curran	111
M. D. K. J. Perera c Root b Bess	20	– (1) c Leach b Curran	62
B. K. G. Mendis c Buttler b Broad	0	– (5) c Buttler b Leach	15
A. D. Mathews c Root b Broad	27	– (5) c Root b Leach	71
*L. D. Chandimal c Curran b Leach	28	– (6) c Root b Bess	20
†D. P. D. N. Dickwella c Sibley b Bess	12	– (7) c Buttler b Bess	29
M. D. Shanaka c Buttler b Bess	23	– (8) b Leach	4
P. W. H. de Silva b Bess	19	– (9) c Root b Leach	12
M. D. K. Perera b Bess	0	– (10) st Buttler b Leach	24
L. Embuldeniya run out (Leach)	0	– (4) c Sibley b Bess	0
A. M. Fernando not out	0	– not out	0
Lb 1, nb 1	2	B 7, lb 1, nb 3	11

1/16 (1) 2/16 (3) 3/25 (2)   (46.1 overs) 135   1/101 (1) 2/155 (3)   (136.5 overs) 359
4/81 (4) 5/81 (5) 6/105 (6)   3/158 (4) 4/210 (2)
7/126 (7) 8/126 (9) 9/130 (10) 10/135 (8)   5/243 (6) 6/291 (7) 7/296 (8)
                                      8/314 (9) 9/352 (10) 10/359 (5)

Broad 9–3–20–3; Curran 4–2–8–0; Wood 6–1–21–0; Bess 10.1–3–30–5; Leach 17–2–55–1. *Second innings*—Broad 17–11–14–0; Curran 11–1–37–2; Bess 33–4–100–3; Wood 21–5–49–0; Leach 41.5–6–122–5; Root 11–1–19–0; Lawrence 2–0–10–0.

England

Z. Crawley c de Silva b Embuldeniya	9	– c Mendis b Embuldeniya	8
D. P. Sibley c Thirimanne b Embuldeniya	4	– b Embuldeniya	2
J. M. Bairstow c Mendis b Embuldeniya	47	– not out	35
*J. E. Root c Embuldeniya b M. D. K. Perera	228	– run out (Dickwella)	1
D. W. Lawrence c Mendis b M. D. K. Perera	73	– not out	21
†J. C. Buttler c Dickwella b Fernando	30		
S. M. Curran b Fernando	0		
D. M. Bess run out (Thirimanne/Dickwella)	0		
M. J. Leach lbw b M. D. K. Perera	4		
M. A. Wood c Dickwella b M. D. K. Perera	2		
S. C. J. Broad not out	11		
B 7, nb 6	13	B 4, lb 5	9

1/10 (2) 2/17 (1) 3/131 (3)   (117.1 overs) 421   1/3 (2)   (3 wkts, 24.2 overs) 76
4/304 (5) 5/372 (6) 6/372 (7)   2/12 (1) 3/14 (4)
7/382 (8) 8/398 (9) 9/406 (10) 10/421 (4)

Embuldeniya 45–4–176–3; Fernando 14–1–44–2; de Silva 15–1–63–0; M. D. K. Perera 36.1–2–109–4; Shanaka 7–1–22–0. *Second innings*—Embuldeniya 12–3–29–2; M. D. K. Perera 11.2–2–34–0; de Silva 1–0–4–0.

Umpires: H. D. P. K. Dharmasena and R. S. A. Palliyaguruge.   Third umpire: L. E. Hannibal.
Referee: R. S. Madugalle.

SRI LANKA v ENGLAND

Second Test

JOHN ETHERIDGE

At Galle, January 22–25, 2021. England won by six wickets. England 60pts. Toss: Sri Lanka. Test debut: R. T. M. Wanigamuni.

Root completed his triumphant mini-tour of Sri Lanka with another huge century, and another victory in gruelling conditions after losing the toss. England's winning sequence away from home over Sri Lanka was extended to six Tests spread across three series, and this was their fifth overseas Test win on the trot, following three in South Africa in early 2020. It was their best run abroad since winning the final four Tests of the 1911-12 Ashes and the first three in South Africa in 1913-14.

Root's near-flawless 186, following 228 in the previous Test, was the bedrock of England's win. His footwork was exemplary – either right forward or, mainly, right back in his crease, allowing him time and space to play the turning ball off the surface. And, once more, he swept to devastating effect. There were reverse sweeps, too, as well as countless nudges and deflections for ones and twos. Few England batsmen have ever played spin more commandingly. In their first two Tests of 2021, he had piled up 426 of England's total of 1,005 runs. His four dismissals comprised two run-outs, holing out to deep midwicket with No. 11 at the other end, and bowled round his legs. He alone kept England in the game after Mathews scored 110, and three others passed 50, in Sri Lanka's first-innings 381.

The match was transformed on day four, when Sri Lanka – apparently unsure how to build on a lead of 37 – tossed wickets away with wild swings and a lack of application against England's spinners. Their coach, Mickey Arthur, put it down to batsmen feeling the need to attack because they did not trust their defence. Sri Lanka plummeted from 19 without loss to 78 for eight, then 126 all out. England required 164 which, after a wobble, they managed thanks to Sibley and Buttler. Only Pakistan, in 2000, had previously beaten Sri Lanka at Galle after losing the toss; England had done so twice inside a fortnight.

Bess, Leach and Root himself shared all ten wickets, after Anderson, Wood and Curran had taken all ten in Sri Lanka's first innings. It was the first time in Test history that all ten wickets had been claimed by seamers in one innings, and by spinners in the other. In the

---

MOST RUNS FOR ENGLAND IN A SERIES OF THREE TESTS OR FEWER

	M	I	NO	R	HS	100	Avge		
G. A. Gooch........	3	6	0	752	333	3	125.33	v India	1990
W. R. Hammond	2	2	1	563	336*	2	563.00	v New Zealand....	1932-33
L. Hutton	3	6	1	480	196	2	96.00	v West Indies.....	1939
A. N. Cook	3	5	0	450	263	1	90.00	v Pakistan (in UAE)	2015-16
D. I. Gower	3	5	1	449	173*	2	112.25	v Pakistan.........	1983-84
K. F. Barrington.....	3	5	2	426	148	3	142.00	v Pakistan.........	1967
J. E. Root	**2**	**4**	**0**	**426**	**228**	**2**	**106.50**	**v Sri Lanka......**	**2020-21**
D. L. Amiss	3	6	1	406	158	2	81.20	v Pakistan.........	1972-73
I. T. Botham	3	3	0	403	208	2	134.33	v India	1982
A. J. Stewart	3	5	0	396	170	1	79.20	v Pakistan.........	1996
A. N. Cook	3	4	0	390	133	2	97.50	v Sri Lanka	2011
W. R. Hammond	2	3	1	389	217	2	194.50	v India	1936

Against India in 1936, Hammond played in two of the three Tests. In three Tests against Australia in 1938, Hutton hit 473 (with a highest score of 364 and an average of 118.25), and in three against Australia in 1977, G. Boycott hit 442 (191 and 147.33); both were five-Test series.

Smother superior: Dom Sibley gets well forward.

first, Leach and Bess had bowled poorly, while Anderson had produced a masterclass of control and skill, returning figures of 29–13–40–6. Aged 38 years and 177 days, he became the oldest seamer to take a five-for in Asia. He also established the longest span for a seamer between his first and most recent Test five-for – a gap of 17 years and 244 days after he picked up five for 73 on debut against Zimbabwe at Lord's in May 2003. It was his 30th Test five-for; among quick bowlers, only Richard Hadlee (36) had more.

Sri Lanka had made three changes, bringing in Oshada Fernando for the struggling Kusal Mendis, as well as experienced seamer Suranga Lakmal and debutant off-spinning all-rounder Ramesh Mendis Wanigamuni; Dasun Shanaka and Wanindu Hasaranga de Silva were dropped. Anderson replaced Stuart Broad, who had been outstanding and economical – but Anderson was better still. Playing his first competitive match since August, he suggested his ability to manipulate a ball at around 82mph – and his determination to improve – was undiminished. He also revealed he was aiming to make his running style more efficient to reduce injury. That meant scouring YouTube for footage of Carl Lewis, the prolific American sprinter and long jumper regarded as having one of the purest running actions. Even on this pitch and in this heat, Anderson gained swing and seam movement, coupled with variation of pace, line and angle. His accuracy was unerring.

By contrast, Leach and Bess struggled, together conceding 195 runs without success. Mathews hit his 11th Test century, with composure and patience, while the chatty, combative Dickwella scored 92, equalling former India batsman Chetan Chauhan's record of 16 Test fifties without a hundred. Chandimal and Dilruwan Perera also managed half-centuries. Wood, wicketless in the previous Test, took three – reward for maintaining his speed.

When England began their reply after tea on the second day, Sibley and Crawley departed quickly, making Embuldeniya the first spinner to dismiss both openers for single figures in three consecutive innings. Entering at five for two, Root looked in no trouble, picking off runs at a rate that never allowed the bowlers to settle. This was the first time he had scored centuries in back-to-back Tests, and he was the first England player since Marcus Trescothick against Bangladesh in 2005 to make 150-plus in successive matches. (The last to do so away from home was David Gower, in Pakistan in 1983-84.)

During his innings, Root shot from seventh to fourth in England's all-time list, leaving only Alastair Cook, Graham Gooch and Alec Stewart above him. He offered one half-chance: on 172, an edge flew close to Thirimanne at slip. In extreme heat, the challenge was as much physical as technical or mental. Root suffered cramp and a back spasm, and took energy gels and bananas every 45 minutes between lunch and stumps on the third day, as well as guzzling litres of water and isotonic drinks. So, yes, there were aches and pains and fatigue – but pride and satisfaction, too.

Root, who put on 111 with Bairstow, 97 with Buttler and 81 with Bess, still wanted more. But he clipped a ball to short leg, where Oshada Fernando gathered it neatly and flicked it on to the stumps; Root, ninth out in the day's last over, could not disguise his annoyance. While Embuldeniya took 15 wickets in the series at 27, his head-to-head duel with Root brought none for 200 from 247 balls. Five catches by Thirimanne were a record for an outfielder off one bowler in a Test innings.

Sri Lanka extended a useful advantage to 56, before Kusal Perera missed a swipe against Leach. It began a clatter of wickets. Crawley clung on to two sharp chances at short leg, before Bess bowled Mathews on the sweep; then Chandimal hoicked horrendously, and was superbly caught by Anderson, back-pedalling at mid-on. Dickwella was held at cover, Dilruwan Perera gave Crawley a third, and Ramesh Mendis Wanigamuni departed when a sweep bounced off his boot. (Buttler, who held the chance, had already been caught off his own boot to give Wanigamuni his maiden Test wicket.) Sri Lanka would probably have been dismissed for under 100 had Embuldeniya not whacked 40, his highest score in senior cricket.

Although again struggling to find the right length, Leach and Bess finished with four wickets each. Crawley failed once more – he hit 35 runs in four innings – but Sibley, after scores of four, two and nought, piloted England home with 56 not out. He needed some fortune – three umpire's-call reviews for lbw went in his favour – but he played the turning ball with a straighter bat, rather than aiming towards midwicket. Chandimal's spreading of the field also meant he could pick off singles. Sibley admitted to a "bit of a stinker at the start of the series", and had worried he was not up to the challenge of playing spin in the subcontinent. England had been 89 for four when Lawrence was caught behind, but Buttler, who scored 46 not out from 48 balls, removed any doubt.

A 2–0 victory was a notable achievement, even if Sri Lanka's batting lacked nous, and – with the exception of Embuldeniya – their slow bowling was surprisingly short of potency. Root, Player of the Match in both Tests, was a happy man as he held up the sponsors' Moose Cup, antlers and all.

Player of the Match: J. E. Root.   *Player of the Series:* J. E. Root.
Close of play: first day, Sri Lanka 229-4 (Mathews 107, Dickwella 19); second day, England 98-2 (Bairstow 24, Root 67); third day, England 339-9 (Leach 0).

Sri Lanka

H. D. R. L. Thirimanne c Buttler b Anderson	43	– (2) c Crawley b Leach	13
M. D. K. J. Perera c Root b Anderson	6	– (1) lbw b Leach	14
B. O. P. Fernando b Anderson	0	– c Crawley b Bess	3
A. D. Mathews c Buttler b Anderson	110	– b Bess	5
*L. D. Chandimal lbw b Wood	52	– c Anderson b Leach	9
†D. P. D. N. Dickwella c Leach b Anderson	92	– c Lawrence b Bess	7
R. T. M. Wanigamuni c Buttler b Wood	0	– c Buttler b Leach	16
M. D. K. Perera c Leach b Curran	67	– c Crawley b Bess	4
R. A. S. Lakmal c Crawley b Anderson	0	– not out	11
L. Embuldeniya c Root b Wood	7	– c Bairstow b Root	40
A. M. Fernando not out	0	– b Root	0
Lb 2, w 1, nb 1	4	B 3, nb 1	4
	381		126

1/7 (2) 2/7 (3) 3/76 (1)   (139.3 overs) 381
4/193 (5) 5/232 (4) 6/243 (7)
7/332 (6) 8/332 (9) 9/364 (10) 10/381 (8)

1/19 (1) 2/29 (3)   (35.5 overs) 126
3/37 (2) 4/37 (4)
5/47 (5) 6/66 (6) 7/70 (8)
8/78 (7) 9/126 (10) 10/126 (11)

Anderson 29–13–40–6; Curran 18.3–3–60–1; Leach 38–5–119–0; Wood 28–4–84–3; Bess 26–2–76–0. *Second innings*—Anderson 2–0–6–0; Curran 2–0–9–0; Bess 16–1–49–4; Leach 14–1–59–4; Root 1.5–1–0–2.

England

Z. Crawley c Thirimanne b Embuldeniya	5	– c B. O. P. Fernando b Embuldeniya	.	13
D. P. Sibley lbw b Embuldeniya	0	– not out		56
J. M. Bairstow c B. O. P. Fernando b Embuldeniya	28	– lbw b Embuldeniya		29
*J. E. Root run out (B. O. P. Fernando)	186	– b Wanigamuni		11
D. W. Lawrence c Thirimanne b Embuldeniya	3	– c Dickwella b Embuldeniya		2
†J. C. Buttler c B. O. P. Fernando b Wanigamuni	55	– not out		46
S. M. Curran c Thirimanne b Embuldeniya	13			
D. M. Bess c Thirimanne b Embuldeniya	32			
M. A. Wood c Thirimanne b Embuldeniya	1			
M. J. Leach lbw b M. D. K. Perera	1			
J. M. Anderson not out	4			
B 8, lb 3, nb 5	16	Lb 4, nb 3		7

1/4 (2) 2/5 (1) 3/116 (3) (116.1 overs) 344 1/17 (1) (4 wkts, 43.3 overs) 164
4/132 (5) 5/229 (6) 6/252 (7) 2/62 (3) 3/84 (4)
7/333 (8) 8/337 (9) 9/339 (4) 10/344 (10) 4/89 (5)

Lakmal 16–7–31–0; Embuldeniya 42–6–137–7; A. M. Fernando 10–2–31–0; M. D. K. Perera 32.1–4–86–1; Wanigamuni 16–1–48–1. *Second innings*—Embuldeniya 20–3–73–3; M. D. K. Perera 13.3–1–39–0; Wanigamuni 10–0–48–1.

Umpires: H. D. P. K. Dharmasena and R. S. A. Palliyaguruge.   Third umpire: L. E. Hannibal.
Referee: R. S. Madugalle.

INDIA v ENGLAND IN 2020-21

REVIEW BY GEORGE DOBELL

Test matches (4): India 3 (90pts), England 1 (30pts)
Twenty20 internationals (5): India 3, England 2
One-day internationals (3): India 2 (20pts), England 1 (10pts)

There was a moment, about two weeks into the tour, when all – well, nearly all – seemed rosy in the garden of English cricket. The team had just won their sixth away Test in a row – for the first time since before the First World War – and their sixth in succession in Asia, too. They even had an outside chance of reaching the World Test Championship final in June. Joe Root had equalled the record for most wins as an England captain, and taken his Test average back above 50 for the first time in more than two years.

But the mood changed quickly. Defeats in the next three games – and the scale of those defeats – forced a reappraisal, and reopened old wounds. By the time England left India, they had lost series in all three formats, and debates thought to have been consigned to the past were raging once more. They included questions about the sustainability of a schedule which required too much of the participants; doubts about the ability of the County Championship to prepare players for such challenges; and concerns over the apparent prioritising of T20 – especially the IPL – over Test cricket.

Striding on: at Chennai, Joe Root passes 180 for the third Test in a row.

SHORTEST COMPLETED TEST MATCHES

Balls

656	Australia (153) beat South Africa (36 and 45) at Melbourne	1931-32
672	England (81-7 dec and 75-6) beat W. Indies (102 and 51-6 dec) at Bridgetown .	1934-35
788	England (172) beat Australia (81 and 70) at Manchester	1888
792	Australia (116 and 60) beat England (53 and 62) at Lord's	1888
796	England (292) beat South Africa (47 and 43) at Cape Town	1888-89
815	England (176 and 14-0) beat South Africa (95 and 93) at The Oval	1912
842	**India (145 and 49-0) beat England (112 and 81) at Ahmedabad**	**2020-21**
872	Australia (199-8 dec) beat New Zealand (42 and 54) at Wellington	1945-46
883	England (0-0 dec and 251-8) beat South Africa (248-8 dec) at Centurion	1999-2000
893	Australia (310) beat Pakistan (59 and 53) at Sharjah	2002-03

South Africa forfeited their second innings at Centurion.

A core issue was the management's decision to rest and rotate players. The intention was no doubt good. It recognised the strain of living inside a bio-bubble, and the absence of family support. Had the policy not been in place, it is entirely possible some of the squad would have opted out altogether. All-format players involved in both the Sri Lankan and Indian tours were likely to be away from home for three months – five, if they had an IPL deal. That might once have been acceptable; not any more.

But, on a tour already lacking warm-up games, the execution of the policy was flawed. Jonny Bairstow, for example, was sent home after looking in good touch in Sri Lanka, and returned looking all at sea: he made three ducks in his four Test innings. Jos Buttler was available for only the First Test, but came back to India for the white-ball series. But it was Moeen Ali who exemplified how England were hamstrung by their own strategy. Having contracted Covid-19, he had spent much of the Sri Lanka tour in his hotel room, but was recalled for the Second Test in India – his first first-class match for 17 months. He performed well, taking wickets and crashing 43 in 18 balls, even if England hurtled to defeat, and would have been an automatic pick for the next Test. Instead, he flew home as part of a prearranged rotation plan, returning only for the limited-overs games.

Explaining the move in a post-match media conference, Root said Ali had "chosen to go home". It wasn't a phrase used to describe the departure of any other player, nor Root's own absence on paternity leave a few months earlier, and gave the impression Ali had turned his back on the team. Root, to his credit, made a swift apology. But it transpired that Ed Smith, then the

---

ENGLAND'S TEST DOUBLE-HUNDREDS IN ASIA

263	A. N. Cook	v Pakistan at Abu Dhabi	2015-16
228	**J. E. Root**	**v Sri Lanka at Galle**	**2020-21**
218	**J. E. Root**	**v India at Chennai**	**2020-21**
207	M. W. Gatting	v India at Madras	1984-85
205	E. R. Dexter	v Pakistan at Karachi	1961-62
201	G. Fowler	v India at Madras	1984-85

Chennai was known as Madras until 1996.

Saikat Das, Sportpics/BCCI

Gripping: Ravichandran Ashwin and Akshar Patel turned the series India's way.

national selector, had made a late plea for Ali to stay on, putting him in an invidious position.

At the heart of it all was the understanding that no player would be asked to miss the IPL that followed the tour. With a T20 World Cup scheduled for India later in the year, this had some logic. But it went largely unspoken that, if the ECB forced the players into deciding between international cricket and the T20 leagues, the administrators might not like the answer. So England had to juggle their resources. Combined with illness and injury, it meant they were rarely, if ever, at full strength. The management insisted they still prioritised Test cricket, yet only the T20 team could pick from a first-choice group of players. It felt at times as if the ECB had accepted this was a Test series they could never win. So long as the domestic schedule continues to place T20 in prime summer, and pushes the Championship into the margins, they may be right.

In winning one Test, England fared better than many expected. And while there was much to admire in that game – Root recorded his third score in excess of 180 in three Tests, Jofra Archer made vital new-ball incisions, and James Anderson dazzled with his skill – England also won a disproportionately important toss on a pitch that started ideal for batting and deteriorated sharply. That result pulled the tiger's tail. Responding to the defeat, the BCCI produced a series of pitches which sought to maximise their superiority, in both bowling and facing spin. Having made 578 in the first innings of the series, England never again passed 205; on four occasions, they failed to reach 150.

FIVE STATS YOU MAY HAVE MISSED

BENEDICT BERMANGE

- In the first match, Joe Root became the second batsman to pass 180 in three successive Tests, after Kumar Sangakkara, who scored 200 and 222 (both not out) for Sri Lanka against Bangladesh, then 57 and 192 against Australia, between July and November 2007.

- Ravichandran Ashwin was called for the first no-balls of his Test career, after 20,614 deliveries. The record reverted to England's Graeme Swann, who sent down 15,349 deliveries without a no-ball, though he did bowl one wide. The most deliveries without a no-ball or a wide in a Test career is 14,513, by Clarrie Grimmett of Australia (in his first-class career of more than 73,000 deliveries he never bowled a no-ball, and only five wides).

- In the next game, Ashwin became the first to dismiss 200 left-handers in Tests when he bowled Stuart Broad. He ended the series with 207 left-handers among his 409 wickets; the only other man with more than 100 Test wickets to have dismissed more left-handers than right-handers was the Sri Lankan off-spinner Dilruwan Perera (91 out of 161).

- In 144 years of Test cricket before 2020-21, the only spinner to take a wicket with the first ball of an innings was England slow left-armer Bobby Peel, against Australia at Manchester in 1888. Both Ashwin and Akshar Patel did it in this series. (At The Oval in 1907, South Africa's Bert Vogler dismissed Tom Hayward with the first ball of the match; Vogler was by then primarily a leg-spinner, but *The Times* report says he "began with a few fast overs".)

- Patel reached 20 Test wickets after conceding just 174 runs. The only man to reach 20 for fewer is Australia's Bob Massie (167) in 1972.

Their frailty against the turning ball was brutally exposed. While Jack Leach performed admirably, dismissing Rohit Sharma and Cheteshwar Pujara four times each, and Root enjoyed one freakish spell on a surface offering copious assistance, Dom Bess's travails grew painful to watch. Having enjoyed some fortune in taking four for 76 in the first innings of the First Test (one wicket came from a full toss, another when a long hop deflected to midwicket via short leg's back), he declined to the point where full tosses became alarmingly regular. With Ali at home, it left England under-resourced. It was hard to avoid the suspicion that years of playing the Championship at either end of the home summer, when spin bowling is often of little relevance, had eroded their depth.

The batting was little better. In conditions few had experienced, they struggled to play not just the turning ball, but the one that skidded on. Highlights packages showed a succession of England batsmen missing straight deliveries. In truth, it was hard to imagine any era of English batting which would have flourished. And while players of a previous age might have prospered with a large stride and judicious use of the pad, DRS has removed such options. Against off-spinner Ravichandran Ashwin and slow left-armer Akshar Patel, who between them took 59 wickets at 12, batting was as hard as is imaginable.

It wasn't just England who struggled. Players as good as Virat Kohli, Pujara and Ajinkya Rahane averaged 28, 22 and 18 respectively. Only Rohit, who had the advantage of settling against the seamers, and Rishabh Pant, who

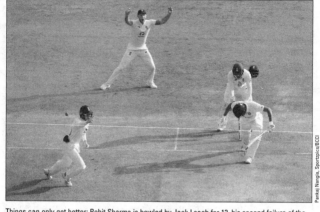

Things can only get better: Rohit Sharma is bowled by Jack Leach for 12, his second failure of the opening Test. Over the next three, he hit 327 runs.

confirmed his vast potential, regularly shone. Had India's batters been up against India's spinners, they might have fared no better.

There were tactical errors from England, though. They crammed their side with four seamers for the Third Test – a day/night encounter – in the expectation the pink ball would provide help. As it transpired, the quartet claimed one wicket between them, and England lost in two days, as Patel thrived on the confusion caused by his natural variation. With England preferring the seam of Stuart Broad (who finished the series without a wicket) to the all-round skills of Chris Woakes (who played none of the six winter Tests), they had a tail that would have impressed a diplodocus. Given his plight, playing Bess in the final Test seemed recklessly optimistic. It meant that, having reduced India to 146 for six in their first innings, England could not sustain the pressure. The next two wickets added a match-defining 219.

Were the pitches good enough? Certainly they turned from, if not the first session, very soon afterwards. And certainly batting became fiendish as surfaces broke up, sometimes unusually early, and the bounce grew more irregular. Some made the point that there are few complaints when England benefit from the Dukes ball and seaming, swinging conditions at home. Others argued that, though the ball in England may move laterally, the bounce is predictable. That was not the case here. Although desperate not to be seen to be whingeing, England also felt the net area in Ahmedabad was unfit for purpose, while the groundsman for the First Test was moved to other duties after their victory. At times, it really did feel as if winning had become a little bit too important.

The official rating of the pitches for the Second and Third Tests was "average", which seemed generous. But long before the end, it had become apparent there was little inclination from the ICC to censure the BCCI on any issue. Some of Kohli's interactions with the umpires (who, like the match referees, were Indian, as a result of Covid travel restrictions) pushed the limits of what was acceptable. Most of the on-field umpiring was impressive, though on one occasion, the officials called for a review of a Kohli dismissal after he had been clean bowled; on another, the TV umpire did not watch a delivery to its conclusion when declining an England review. Few seriously claimed bias, but this was a reminder that the presence of neutral umpires tends to quell such disputes before they can begin.

England had a good chance of winning the T20 series, having gone 2–1 up with two to play. But they barely experimented with their side – they did at least try Adil Rashid as an opening bowler – while India explored their bench

---

DOUBLE-CENTURY AND A FIVE-FOR IN THE SAME TEST SERIES

W. R. Hammond (231*, 5-57)......	England v Australia in Australia.........	1936-37
D. S. Atkinson (219, 5-56†).......	West Indies v Australia in West Indies....	1954-55
Mushtaq Mohammad (201, 5-49†)..	Pakistan v New Zealand in New Zealand..	1972-73
I. T. Botham (208, 5-46).........	England v India in England.............	1982
J. C. Adams (208*, 5-17).........	West Indies v New Zealand in West Indies.	1995-96
Wasim Akram (257*, 6-48)........	Pakistan v Zimbabwe in Pakistan........	1996-97
J. E. Root (218, 5-8).............	**England v India in India**.............	**2020-21**

† *Same match.*

---

options. Ishan Kishan was Player of the Match in the second game on his T20I debut, and Suryakumar Yadav in the fourth, after his first international innings; England used only 12 players, learned little and still lost.

While India's 2–1 win in the one-day series looked a close contest – the decider was settled by seven runs – the truth was less romantic. Reduced to 200 for seven chasing 330, England needed a remarkable innings from Sam Curran to take them anywhere close. Having not lost a bilateral ODI series since January 2017, also in India, England had lost two in a row. A failure to find an adequate replacement for Liam Plunkett (dropped after the World Cup), or Jofra Archer (rested), was costly; the absence of Root (also rested) was felt deeply.

They clung on to their No. 1 ranking in both formats, but the implications were clear: in Indian conditions, where the next T20 and 50-over World Cups were due to be played, the hosts were desperately tough to beat. An away Ashes remains the yardstick by which English cricket judges itself, but a Test series in India may have become the ultimate challenge.

❝
A gambling addiction led to embezzlement, a spell in prison in 1993-94 and the end of his first marriage. More recently, he had a leg amputated."
Cricket books, page 141

Helping hand: in the last T20 match, Chris Jordan athletically intercepts the ball on the boundary, before tossing it to Jason Roy to complete the catch.

ENGLAND TOURING PARTY

*J. E. Root (Yorkshire; T), M. M. Ali (Worcestershire; T/50/20), J. M. Anderson (Lancashire; T), J. C. Archer (Sussex; T/20), J. M. Bairstow (Yorkshire; T/50/20), D. M. Bess (Yorkshire; T), S. W. Billings (Kent; 50/20), S. C. J. Broad (Nottinghamshire; T), R. J. Burns (Surrey; T), J. C. Buttler (Lancashire; T/50/20), Z. Crawley (Kent; T), S. M. Curran (Surrey; 50/20), T. K. Curran (Surrey; 50/20), B. T. Foakes (Surrey; T), C. J. Jordan (Sussex; 20), D. W. Lawrence (Essex; T), M. J. Leach (Somerset; T), L. S. Livingstone (Lancashire; 50/20), D. J. Malan (Yorkshire; 50/20), E. J. G. Morgan (Middlesex; 50/20), M. W. Parkinson (Lancashire; 50), O. J. D. Pope (Surrey; T), A. U. Rashid (Yorkshire; 50/20), J. J. Roy (Surrey; 50/20), D. P. Sibley (Warwickshire; T), B. A. Stokes (Durham; T/50/20), O. P. Stone (Warwickshire; T), R. J. W. Topley (Surrey; 50/20), C. R. Woakes (Warwickshire; T), M. A. Wood (Durham (T/50/20).

Managing director, England men's cricket: A. F. Giles (50/20). *Head coach:* C. E. W. Silverwood (T/50/20). *Assistant coaches:* P. D. Collingwood (T/50/20), G. P. Thorpe (T). *Batting consultant:* I. J. L. Trott (T/50/20). *Bowling coaches:* J. Lewis (T), G. Welch (T). *Spin-bowling consultant:* J. S. Patel (T/50/20). *Wicketkeeping consultant:* J. S. Foster (50/20), C. M. W. Read (T). *Fielding coach:* C. D. Hopkinson (50/20). *Team manager:* A. W. Bentley (T), R. C. Dickason (50/20). *Analyst:* G. Lindsay (T), N. A. Leamon (T). *Doctors:* Moiz Moghal (T), J. D. Williams (T), R. Young (50/20). *Physiotherapists:* C. A. de Weymarn (T), B. Langley (T), S. Griffin (T/50/20), A. Tysoe (50/20). *Nutritionist:* E. Gardner (T/50/20). *Strength and conditioning:* P. C. F. Scott (T), D. Veness (T), R. Ahmun (50/20). *Psychologist:* M. Thompson (T), T. Goodall (50/20). *Massage therapist:* M. Saxby (T). *Security manager:* W. Carr. *Head of team communications:* D. M. Reuben (T), B. H. Murgatroyd (T/50/20). *Covid operations officer:* P. Davies (T/50/20).

Morgan and Buttler captained in the white-ball matches. Because of rotation, Bairstow and Wood joined the Test squad late, and Ali, Buttler and Woakes left during the tour. S. M. Curran was originally supposed to join in time for the Third Test, but travel restrictions meant he eventually arrived with the white-ball squad. The following also travelled as standby players: J. T. Ball (Nottinghamshire; 20), J. R. Bracey (Gloucestershire; T), M. S. Crane (Hampshire; T), S. Mahmood (Lancashire; T), M. W. Parkinson (Lancashire; T/20), O. E. Robinson (Sussex; T), G. S. Virdi (Surrey; T). Ball, Jordan and Malan stayed on as reserves for the 50-over matches; Malan was added to the squad after injuries to Billings and Morgan.

TEST MATCH AVERAGES

INDIA – BATTING AND FIELDING

	T	I	NO	R	HS	100	50	Avge	Ct/St
†M. S. Washington Sundar	3	4	2	181	96*	0	2	90.50	0
R. G. Sharma	4	7	1	345	161	1	1	57.50	5
†R. R. Pant.................	4	6	1	270	101	1	2	54.00	8/5
R. Ashwin	4	6	0	189	106	1	0	31.50	2
V. Kohli...................	4	6	0	172	72	0	2	28.66	4
C. A. Pujara...............	4	6	0	133	73	0	1	22.16	3
S. Gill....................	4	7	1	119	50	0	1	19.83	2
A. M. Rahane..............	4	6	0	112	67	0	1	18.66	8
†A. R. Patel	3	4	0	55	43	0	0	13.75	1
M. Siraj..................	2	3	1	20	16*	0	0	10.00	1
I. Sharma	4	6	2	26	10*	0	0	6.50	1
J. J. Bumrah	2	3	0	5	4	0	0	1.66	1

Played in one Test: S. Nadeem 0, 0; †K. Yadav 0, 3.

BOWLING

	Style	O	M	R	W	BB	5I	Avge
A. R. Patel	SLA	127.4	27	286	27	6-38	4	10.59
R. Ashwin	OB	188.1	33	471	32	6-61	3	14.71
M. Siraj...................	RFM	26	7	68	3	2-45	0	22.66
I. Sharma	RFM	59	15	160	6	2-22	0	26.66
J. J. Bumrah	RFM	48	10	129	4	3-84	0	32.25
S. Nadeem	SLA	59	6	233	4	2-66	0	58.25

Also bowled: R. G. Sharma (OB) 2–0–7–0; M. S. Washington Sundar (OB) 38.4–3–130–2; K. Yadav (SLW) 12.2–2–41–2.

ENGLAND – BATTING AND FIELDING

	T	I	NO	R	HS	100	50	Avge	Ct/St
J. E. Root	4	8	0	368	218	1	0	46.00	3
†B. A. Stokes................	4	8	0	203	82	0	2	25.37	5
D. W. Lawrence............	3	6	0	149	50	0	1	24.83	0
O. J. D. Pope	4	8	0	153	34	0	0	19.12	5
D. P. Sibley	4	8	0	134	87	0	1	16.75	1
Z. Crawley	2	4	0	67	53	0	1	16.75	2
D. M. Bess	2	4	0	64	34	0	0	16.00	0
B. T. Foakes...............	3	6	1	78	42*	0	0	15.60	4/3
†R. J. Burns	2	4	0	58	33	0	0	14.50	3
†M. J. Leach...............	4	8	2	48	14*	0	0	8.00	1
J. M. Bairstow.............	2	4	0	28	28	0	0	7.00	0
†S. C. J. Broad.............	2	4	2	9	5*	0	0	4.50	0
J. C. Archer	2	4	0	16	11	0	0	4.00	0
†J. M. Anderson.............	3	6	3	12	10*	0	0	4.00	1

Played in one Test: †M. M. Ali 6, 43 (1 ct); J. C. Buttler 30, 24 (5 ct); O. P. Stone 1, 0 (1 ct).

BOWLING

	Style	O	M	R	W	BB	5I	Avge
J. M. Anderson	RFM	65.5	31	127	8	3-17	0	15.87
O. P. Stone	RF	22.4	6	68	4	3-47	0	17.00
J. E. Root	OB	45	7	141	6	5-8	1	23.50
M. M. Ali	OB	61	10	226	8	4-98	0	28.25
M. J. Leach	SLA	161	26	517	18	4-54	0	28.72
J. C. Archer	RF	35.1	9	122	4	2-75	0	30.50
B. A. Stokes	RFM	42.4	8	153	5	4-89	0	30.60
D. M. Bess	OB	51	6	197	5	4-76	0	39.40

Also bowled: S. C. J. Broad (RFM) 26–6–78–0; D. W. Lawrence (OB) 1–0–7–0.

INDIA v ENGLAND

First Test

ALI MARTIN

At Chennai, February 5–9, 2021. England won by 227 runs. England 30pts. Toss: England.

Joe Root was presented with a silver cap before his 100th Test, but everything else he touched turned to gold. Becoming the first to mark the milestone with a double-century was one thing; it was quite another to see his innings form the foundation of England's biggest victory by runs in India.

This was Root's 26th Test win as captain, equalling Michael Vaughan's England record. And by mercilessly compiling 218 in his team's 578, he was scarcely offstage. Anderson twice sent stumps cartwheeling during a reverse-swing clinic on the final day, when India were bowled out for 192, and there were four-wicket hauls for Bess and Leach. But whether sweeping the spinners to distraction, nimbly marshalling his attack, or producing a collector's-item catch, Root's name ran through this match like Brighton through a stick of rock.

Not that there were many at the M. A. Chidambaram Stadium to watch: the pandemic meant the stands and the press box were empty throughout. There was, however, an increased audience among those enduring the winter lockdown back in the UK: after a

MARKING THE CENTURY IN STYLE

Batsmen who scored hundreds in their 100th Test match:

M. C. Cowdrey (104)	England v Australia at Birmingham	1968
Javed Miandad (145)	Pakistan v India at Lahore	1989-90
C. G. Greenidge (149)	West Indies v England at St John's	1989-90
A. J. Stewart (105)	England v West Indies at Manchester	2000
Inzamam-ul-Haq (184)	Pakistan v India at Bangalore	2004-05
R. T. Ponting (120 and 143*)	Australia v South Africa at Sydney	2005-06
G. C. Smith (131)	South Africa v England at The Oval	2012
H. M. Amla (134)	South Africa v Sri Lanka at Johannesburg	2016-17
J. E. Root (218)	**England v India at Chennai**	**2020-21**

J. H. Kallis hit 100 runs (38 and 62) in his 100th Test, for South Africa v New Zealand at Centurion in 2005-06.

Scurrying ahead: Ollie Pope extends England's lead on the fourth day.

near 16-year absence, Test cricket had returned to Channel 4, and thus free-to-air television. Studio production was pared back, thanks to the 11th-hour deal and a punishing time difference, but the action needed few accoutrements: unfancied England had inflicted on India only their second home defeat in 36 Tests, and so soon after their almighty felling of Australia.

That landmark result, in Brisbane a little over a fortnight earlier, was achieved with Kohli on paternity leave, and Rahane a calm stand-in. Yet while Kohli's return offered a frisson of intrigue, it was smothered by the rolling drums for Root, the 15th member of England's 100-cap club. It meant a raft of media appearances, all met with the smile and good grace of a man fresh from scores of 228 and 186 in Sri Lanka.

England had lost Zak Crawley to a sprained wrist, sustained when he slipped on a marble floor in spikes outside the dressing-room, but they had better fortune at the toss. Batting first on the red-soil of the Madras Cricket Club was an advantage, no question, but one squandered by plenty of visitors down the years; here in December 2016, England themselves had begun with 477, only to lose by an innings. Yet Root dominated from the moment he strode out shortly before lunch at 63 for two, following the demise in quick succession of Burns, who messed up a reverse sweep off Ashwin, and Lawrence, trapped by Bumrah. Of the eventual total, 414 came during Root's 128 overs at the crease.

He and the patient Sibley had put on 200, and reached the day's last over, when Bumrah – playing his first home Test after 17 abroad – lasered a yorker into Sibley's pads. It was galling for Sibley, who had demonstrated a defensive method against spin grooved during his final innings in Sri Lanka. Root had also been circumspect at first, adjusting to the new lengths posed by new opposition: he made 12 runs in 54 balls, before slipping into gear and requiring only 110 more to reach his 20th Test century.

The celebrations spoke of a player not remotely sated and, after Root suffered cramp from the heat that evening – Kohli helped him stretch – he emerged next morning on 128. With him was Stokes, who despite sitting out the Sri Lanka tour and having no match practice, responded to some spitting cobras out of the rough from Shahbaz Nadeem by going on the offensive in a stand of 124; Stokes's share was 82. Nadeem, playing because of injuries to fellow left-arm spinners Ravindra Jadeja and Akshar Patel, later drew the ire of Kohli, along with off-spinner Washington Sundar; between them, they took two for 265.

Root found another sidekick in Pope, back after shoulder surgery in September. When Root drilled Ashwin over long-on for six to reach his fifth Test double-century, he was unaware of the milestone, before noticing the applause from the pavilion balcony; not until he had spent almost nine hours at the crease did India get rid of him, trapped by Nadeem. In an innings based on gimlet-eyed reading of length, he had scored just 88 in

ENGLAND'S HIGHEST TEST TOTALS IN INDIA

652-7 dec	Madras	1984-85	497-5	Kanpur	1961-62
578	**Chennai**	**2020-21**	480	Bombay (Brabourne)	1972-73
559-8 dec	Kanpur	1963-64	477	Chennai	2016-17
537	Rajkot	2016-17	476-9 dec	Delhi	1981-82
523	Kolkata	2012-13	456	Bombay (Brabourne)	1951-52
500-8 dec	Bombay (Brabourne)	1961-62	451	Delhi	1963-64

boundaries. Having started the winter seventh in England's all-time Test run chart, he was now third. And he had made the highest Test score for England in India, beating Mike Gatting's 207 at the same venue, 36 years earlier.

England were finally snuffed out by the third new ball on the third morning. Once Archer had wiped out the openers, Bess produced a bold attacking line to take care of India's middle order. England's catching was immaculate, with Root's flying effort to remove Rahane at cover the pick. Rahane had pushed out to a Bess full toss – there would be plenty as the game wore on – after similar dip had teased a more classical inside edge from Kohli. At 73 for four, 505 behind, India were struggling.

Yet for two hours on a frantic afternoon, Pant – swaggering in after his Gabba heroics – made the stage his own. Like Stokes the day before, here was a left-hander taking calculated risks with devastating hand–eye elan. Leach was despatched for five sixes, and 48 runs, in a 21-ball rout, while Pant added 119 with the rock-steady Pujara. Five was the most by an Indian batsman off an England bowler in a Test innings, beating Kapil Dev's four in four balls off Eddie Hemmings at Lord's in 1990. Only when Bess had both men caught on the attack did England truly pin India down, at 225 for six: Pujara was caught by Burns at midwicket for 73 – after the ball ricocheted off Pope's back at short leg – and

You can't keep a good man down: Jimmy Anderson removes Shubman Gill, and England take another step towards victory.

Pant on 91 picked out a relieved Leach in the deep. Sundar's mature unbeaten 85 cut the deficit to 241 but, with five sessions left and the pitch on the wane, England did not consider the follow-on.

Instead, their batsmen had to take an Indian victory off the table, yet leave their bowlers time to take ten wickets. Root alone transcended the crumbling surface with a wing-heeled 40, as Ashwin profited from the urgency, and Ishant Sharma became the third Indian seamer to 300 Test wickets. There was much chatter about the declaration, not least when England slowed down towards the end. But, with the bounce now hugely variable, Root wanted his bowlers to have a hard ball both that evening and next morning. England were eventually rolled for 178. The lead was 419, and they had 103 overs to bowl India out. In the 13 before the close, Leach eased nerves by tickling Rohit Sharma's off stump.

It said much about Leach that he recovered from Pant's assault. His first eight overs had yielded none for 77, but thereafter he claimed six for 104, including three on the final day, starting with an early breakthrough when he found the shoulder of Pujara's bat en route to slip. Root had held Anderson back initially but, once the ball was 26 overs old and deemed ripe for reverse swing, he turned to his attack leader, with devastating results.

If Leach's early success had made India's task look sizeable, Anderson rendered it insurmountable, bowling Gill and Rahane in four balls with near-identical booming inswingers; in between, Rahane survived a tight lbw. Only Kohli offered any resistance, before a shooter from Stokes rattled his off stump on 72. Archer roughed up Ashwin, and completed the win when Bumrah provided a fifth catch in the game for the impressive Buttler, playing his only Test before an allocated rest period.

Kohli bemoaned the pitch and the SG ball's lack of hardiness, while Root compared Anderson's defining over to Andrew Flintoff's removal of Justin Langer and Ricky Ponting at Edgbaston in 2005. But, as good as it was, this was a victory forged by Root's own blade, and his Midas touch in Madras.

Player of the Match: J. E. Root.

Close of play: first day, England 263-3 (Root 128); second day, England 555-8 (Bess 28, Leach 6); third day, India 257-6 (Washington Sundar 33, Ashwin 8); fourth day, India 39-1 (Gill 15, Pujara 12).

England

R. J. Burns c Pant b Ashwin	33	– c Rahane b Ashwin	0
D. P. Sibley lbw b Bumrah	87	– c Pujara b Ashwin	16
D. W. Lawrence lbw b Bumrah	0	– lbw b I. Sharma	18
*J. E. Root lbw b Nadeem	218	– lbw b Bumrah	40
B. A. Stokes c Pujara b Nadeem	82	– c Pant b Ashwin	7
O. J. D. Pope lbw b Ashwin	34	– c R. G. Sharma b Nadeem	28
†J. C. Buttler b I. Sharma	30	– st Pant b Nadeem	24
D. M. Bess lbw b Bumrah	34	– lbw b Ashwin	25
J. C. Archer b I. Sharma	0	– b Ashwin	5
M. J. Leach not out	14	– not out	8
J. M. Anderson b Ashwin	1	– c and b Ashwin	0
B 7, lb 17, w 1, nb 20	45	Nb 7	7

1/63 (1) 2/63 (3) 3/263 (2)   (190.1 overs) 578   1/0 (1) 2/32 (2)   (46.3 overs) 178
4/387 (5) 5/473 (6) 6/477 (4)   3/58 (3) 4/71 (5)
7/525 (7) 8/525 (9) 9/567 (8) 10/578 (11)   5/101 (4) 6/130 (6) 7/165 (7)
                                         8/167 (8) 9/178 (9) 10/178 (11)

I. Sharma 27-7-52-2; Bumrah 36-7-84-3; Ashwin 55.1-5-146-3; Nadeem 44-4-167-2; Washington Sundar 26-2-98-0; R. G. Sharma 2-0-7-0. *Second innings*—Ashwin 17.3-2-61-6; Nadeem 15-2-66-2; I. Sharma 7-1-24-1; Bumrah 6-0-26-1; Washington Sundar 1-0-1-0.

India

R. G. Sharma c Buttler b Archer	6	– b Leach	12
S. Gill c Anderson b Archer	29	– b Anderson	50
C. A. Pujara c Burns b Bess	73	– c Stokes b Leach	15
*V. Kohli c Pope b Bess	11	– b Stokes	72
A. M. Rahane c Root b Bess	1	– b Anderson	0
†R. R. Pant c Leach b Bess	91	– c Root b Anderson	11
M. S. Washington Sundar not out	85	– c Buttler b Bess	0
R. Ashwin c Buttler b Leach	31	– c Buttler b Leach	9
S. Nadeem c Stokes b Leach	0	– c Burns b Leach	0
I. Sharma c Pope b Anderson	4	– not out	5
J. J. Bumrah c Stokes b Anderson	0	– c Buttler b Archer	4
B 4, lb 1, nb 1	6	B 8, lb 5, nb 1	14

1/19 (1) 2/44 (2) 3/71 (4)   (95.5 overs) 337   1/25 (1) 2/58 (3)   (58.1 overs) 192
4/73 (5) 5/192 (5) 6/225 (6)   3/92 (2) 4/92 (5)
7/305 (8) 8/312 (9) 9/323 (10) 10/337 (11)   5/110 (6) 6/117 (4) 7/171 (8)
                                         8/179 (4) 9/179 (9) 10/192 (11)

Anderson 16.5-5-46-2; Archer 21-3-75-2; Stokes 6-1-16-0; Leach 24.5-5-105-2; Bess 26-5-76-4; Root 2-0-14-0. *Second innings*—Archer 9.1-4-23-1; Leach 26-4-76-4; Anderson 11-4-17-3; Bess 8-0-50-1; Stokes 4-1-13-1.

Umpires: A. K. Chaudhary and N. N. Menon.   Third umpire: C. Shamshuddin.
Referee: J. Srinath.

INDIA v ENGLAND

Second Test

Anand Vasu

At Chennai, February 13–16, 2021. India won by 317 runs. India 30pts. Toss: India. Test debut: A. R. Patel.

India bounced back in emphatic fashion. The chief architect of their win was Ashwin, with match figures of eight for 96 and a second-innings century on a pitch already taking

Saikat Das, Sportspics/BCCI

Miss – and hit: Virat Kohli is bowled by Moeen Ali for a duck, but Kohli would have the last laugh.

significant turn. Equally, India's victory would have been less likely without Rohit Sharma, who scored 161 of their first-innings 329; England managed 134 and 164.

India went in with three specialist spinners, as debutant left-armer Akshar Patel and left-arm wrist-spinner Kuldeep Yadav replaced Shahbaz Nadeem, listless during the first game, and Washington Sundar. Jasprit Bumrah was rested, giving Mohammed Siraj a chance. England settled for two spinners, as Ali – ousting Dom Bess for his only Test of the winter – accompanied Leach, while Foakes took the gloves from Jos Buttler, who had flown home. Jofra Archer suffered a recurrence of his right elbow injury, allowing Olly Stone to win his second cap, more than 18 months after his first. Broad was swapped in for James Anderson.

Not long after Kohli won the toss, it was clear the pitch would take considerably more spin than the one for the First Test. Before that, though, Stone – running in with vigour and generating serious pace – removed Gill with a peach in the game's second over. Rohit was in glorious form, but lost two more colleagues before lunch. Pujara edged Leach to Stokes at slip, then Kohli aimed enthusiastically towards cover off Ali, creating a big gap between bat and pad, and was bowled for a duck – a classic off-spinner's dismissal. Kohli looked back at his stumps in bewilderment, prompting the on-field officials to turn to the third umpire for confirmation.

ALL-ROUND EXCELLENCE

A century and a five-for in the same Test on most occasions:

5	I. T. Botham (England)		2	Mushtaq Mohammad (Pakistan)
3	**R. Ashwin (India)**		2	Shakib Al Hasan (Bangladesh)
2	J. H. Kallis (South Africa)		2	G. S. Sobers (West Indies)

A further 17 have achieved the feat once.

At lunch, Rohit had 80 of India's 106 for three. After it, he was even better, seemingly batting on a different surface from the rest. When he was finally fourth out, sweeping Leach to deep square leg, he had made 161 from 231 balls in a total of 248, and taken his tally to 1,504 runs in his 16th Test in India, at an average of 83.

Rohit had survived a perilously close stumping off Leach shortly before his dismissal, and England's mood was not improved by a more glaring reprieve for Rahane, who had contributed to a match-changing fourth-wicket stand of 162. On 66, he tried to sweep Leach; ball missed bat, went up off pad, and kissed glove on the way to short leg. England's appeal was ruled not out by Virender Sharma, but Root asked for a review. Anil Chaudhary, the third umpire, correctly adjudged that ball had not touched bat, and ruled not out. He then belatedly checked for an lbw, though it had clearly pitched outside leg, but did not allow the video to play to its conclusion. The host broadcaster did not show the complete replay until the former England batsman Mark Butcher, part of the commentary team, repeatedly asked for it. Only then was the error – and the reason for Root's dismay – spotted. Eventually, match referee Javagal Srinath reinstated England's lost review. Rahane added only a single before he missed a sweep off Ali, but the incident sparked a debate about the need for neutral third umpires.

Root added Ashwin before stumps, and next morning Pant pushed the score to 329, the highest Test total without an extra, beating 328 (in 187.5 overs) in Pakistan's first innings against India at Lahore in 1954-55. India felt they were 50 runs light – their last seven had contributed 81 – but their fears were allayed when Burns fell to Ishant Sharma for a duck. Before long, the spinners took over. Ashwin, given the new ball, had already found his mojo, beating Sibley's premeditated sweep with extra bounce, while the in-form Root perished to the same stroke, a maiden Test wicket for Patel. Lawrence pressed forward at Ashwin with hard hands, and lobbed a catch to short leg, before Stokes was bowled playing across the line to a full one from Ashwin that dipped. England were 52 for five.

None of these wickets fell to a delivery that did anything dramatic, but the surface seemed to be weighing heavily on the batsmen's minds: shot selection was muddled, execution poor. Only Foakes, exemplary behind the stumps, showed any kind of calm, top-scoring with an unbeaten 42 in 107 balls as England slumped to 134. Broad registered his 36th Test duck, drawing level with New Zealand rabbit Chris Martin (only West

BEST FIGURES ON TEST DEBUT FOR INDIA

8-61	N. D. Hirwani......	v West Indies at Madras (*1st inns*)	1987-88
8-75	N. D. Hirwani......	v West Indies at Madras (*2nd inns*).....	1987-88
6-47	R. Ashwin.......	v West Indies at Delhi...............	2011-12
6-55	S. Abid Ali........	v Australia at Adelaide	1967-68
6-103	D. R. Doshi........	v Australia at Madras	1979-80
5-47	Mohammed Shami..	v West Indies at Kolkata.............	2013-14
5-60	**A. R. Patel........**	**v England at Chennai**	**2020-21**
5-64	V. V. Kumar.......	v Pakistan at Delhi	1960-61
5-71	A. Mishra	v Australia at Mohali................	2008-09
5-93	M. Nissar	v England at Lord's.................	1932

The lowdown: Rohit Sharma middles another sweep.

Indies' Courtney Walsh, with 43, lay ahead). Ashwin ended with five for 43 from 23.5 overs of high-quality off-spin.

In their second innings, India threatened to undo their good work when they slid from 42 without loss to 106 for six, including three wickets for Leach; two were stumpings by Foakes, who – on his 28th birthday – became the first England wicketkeeper to stump three in a Test since Alan Knott against Australia at Headingley in 1968. India were comforted by their first-innings lead of 195, but the top-order collapse seemed to back up the former England cricketers who had criticised the pitch. They sounded less convincing after Ashwin arrived. A hard, flat sweep for four off Ali got him going second ball, and a reverse sweep later in the over confirmed run-making really was possible.

Ashwin's tactical nous is normally more evident in his bowling, but now he applied it to his batting. Using a straight bat when needed, and sweeping only when safe – he had all but dispensed with the shot years earlier, after being dropped from an age-group team for playing it – he brought up his fifth Test hundred. It was his first both against a team other than West Indies, and at his home ground. His eventual 106 came off only 148 balls, and propelled India to 286, leaving England a notional target of 482.

England had clearly erred in selection: Leach and Ali sent down a combined 65 overs and, with Root and Lawrence contributing five more, the quick men had a workload of only 15.5. Their batsmen did better in the second innings, but only marginally: strangled at one end by Patel's accuracy, foxed at the other by Ashwin's guile. Root provided the only real fight among the top seven, but got a spiteful ball from Patel that leapt from a length and caught the glove. At the end, Ali provided breezy respite in a counter-attacking 43 from 27 balls that included five sixes, and did his chances at the upcoming IPL auction no harm. England were bowled out for 164, with Patel taking five for 60.

Much was made of the return of crowds. With Covid-19 restrictions in place, and the stadium allowed 50% capacity, 15,000 tickets had been made available; a little over 12,000 turned up on the first day. Kohli had spoken about how his team had been flat in the First Test, and how the lack of a crowd had lowered their intensity; in truth, India were jaded from a long tour of Australia, and still coming to terms with home conditions. Now that they had reacclimatised, on a pitch entirely to their tastes, they looked formidable once more.

Player of the Match: R. Ashwin.
Close of play: first day, India 300-6 (Pant 33, Patel 5); second day, India 54-1 (R. G. Sharma 25, Pujara 7); third day, England 53-3 (Lawrence 19, Root 2).

India

R. G. Sharma c Ali b Leach	161	– st Foakes b Leach	26
S. Gill lbw b Stone	0	– lbw b Leach	14
C. A. Pujara c Stokes b Leach	21	– run out (Pope/Foakes)	7
*V. Kohli b Ali	0	– lbw b Ali	62
A. M. Rahane b Ali	67	– (6) c Pope b Ali	10
†R. R. Pant not out	58	– (5) st Foakes b Leach	8
R. Ashwin c Pope b Root	13	– (8) b Stone	106
A. R. Patel st Foakes b Ali	5	– (7) lbw b Ali	7
I. Sharma c Burns b Ali	0	– (10) c Stone b Leach	7
K. Yadav c Foakes b Stone	0	– (9) lbw b Ali	3
M. Siraj c Foakes b Stone	4	– not out	16
		B 5, lb 15	20

1/0 (2) 2/85 (3) 3/86 (4)   (95.5 overs) 329   1/42 (2) 2/55 (3)   (85.5 overs) 286
4/248 (1) 5/249 (5) 6/284 (7)   3/55 (1) 4/65 (5)
7/301 (8) 8/301 (9) 9/325 (10) 10/329 (11)   5/86 (6) 6/106 (7) 7/202 (4)
                                     8/210 (9) 9/237 (10) 10/286 (8)

Broad 11–2–37–0; Stone 15.5–5–47–3; Leach 27–3–78–2; Stokes 2–0–16–0; Ali 29–3–128–4; Root 11–3–23–1. *Second innings*—Stone 6.5–1–21–1; Leach 33–6–100–4; Ali 32–7–98–4; Root 4–0–15–0; Broad 9–3–25–0; Lawrence 1–0–7–0.

England

R. J. Burns lbw b I. Sharma	0	– c Kohli b Ashwin	25
D. P. Sibley c Kohli b Ashwin	16	– lbw b Patel	3
D. W. Lawrence c Gill b Ashwin	9	– st Pant b Ashwin	26
*J. E. Root c Ashwin b Patel	17	– (5) c Rahane b Patel	33
B. A. Stokes b Ashwin	18	– (6) c Kohli b Ashwin	8
O. J. D. Pope c Pant b Siraj	22	– (7) c I. Sharma b Patel	12
†B. T. Foakes not out	42	– (8) c Patel b Yadav	2
M. M. Ali c Rahane b Patel	6	– (9) st Pant b Yadav	43
O. P. Stone c R. G. Sharma b Ashwin	1	– (10) lbw b Patel	0
M. J. Leach c Pant b I. Sharma	5	– (4) c R. G. Sharma b Patel	0
S. C. J. Broad b Ashwin	0	– not out	5
B 4, lb 4, nb 1	9	B 6, lb 1	7

1/0 (1) 2/16 (2) 3/23 (4)   (59.5 overs) 134   1/17 (2) 2/49 (1)   (54.2 overs) 164
4/39 (3) 5/52 (5) 6/87 (6)   3/50 (4) 4/66 (3)
7/105 (8) 8/106 (9) 9/131 (10) 10/134 (11)   5/90 (6) 6/110 (7) 7/116 (8)
                                       8/116 (5) 9/126 (10) 10/164 (9)

I. Sharma 5–1–22–2; Ashwin 23.5–4–43–5; Patel 20–3–40–2; Yadav 6–1–16–0; Siraj 5–4–5–1. *Second innings*—I. Sharma 6–3–13–0; Patel 21.5–5–60–5; Ashwin 18–5–53–3; Siraj 3–1–6–0; Yadav 6.2–1–25–2.

Umpires: N. N. Menon and V. K. Sharma.   Third umpire: A. K. Chaudhary.
Referee: J. Srinath.

INDIA v ENGLAND

Third Test

LAWRENCE BOOTH

At Ahmedabad, February 24–25, 2021 (day/night). India won by ten wickets. India 30pts. Toss: England.

For six overs, life felt vaguely normal. England won what seemed an important toss, lost Sibley early, and reached 27 for one thanks to some flowing drives from Crawley.

Then Kohli tossed the ball to Patel, fresh from seven wickets on debut. His first delivery skidded into Bairstow's pads, and triggered the briefest Test match in the era of covered wickets: 134 overs later, Patel had 11 for 70, and India a 2–1 lead. Analysis of how they got there depended on whether you thought the pitch was unworthy of the name (a mainly English perspective) or a function of home advantage (by and large the Indian view).

A few matters were less contentious. For a start, both sides had picked the wrong team. England were seduced by the only previous day/night Test in India, at Kolkata in 2019-20, when all the Bangladeshi wickets fell to seam. Equally excited by the behaviour of the pink ball in the nets, they went in with four quicks, including Stokes, and a lone frontline spinner – Leach, since Dom Bess still wasn't trusted. The four quicks took one wicket between them. India picked three slow bowlers, though Washington Sundar sent down just four deliveries. In the event, six seamers on either side took two at 62 each, and five spinners 28 at under nine.

It was also clear that, on a surface where some balls turned lavishly and others went straight on, India had the skill to exploit the conditions, while England lacked the nous to resist. Time and again, their batsmen played for spin that never came, making the arm-ball a hand grenade: 14 English wickets were bowled or lbw. Root claimed, plausibly, that the lacquer on the pink ball meant it hurried through: for batsmen reared on DRS, with pad play *verboten* and ball-tracking technology persuading umpires that more deliveries are hitting the stumps than once imagined, this added to the dilemma. Afraid to use their feet to the fast, accurate left-arm spin of Patel, or to the endlessly varied off-breaks of Ashwin, England were rabbits in headlights, lambs to the slaughter.

They were all out inside 49 overs in their first innings, and skittled in a session in their second – their fifth such collapse since 2016 (having previously endured none since 1938). Eighty-one was their lowest score against India, undercutting 101 at The Oval in 1971; only South Africa had fared worse against them, making 79 at Nagpur in 2015-16. Records littered the stadium like bodies on a battlefield.

Not that India were immune. Root, who in 101 Tests had only once taken more than a two-for, soon had figures of 3–3–0–3, and finished with five for eight – the cheapest five-

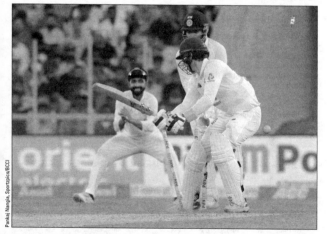

Sixes and sevens: Ben Foakes is flummoxed by Akshar Patel.

Pankaj Nangia, Sportpics/BCCI

BARGAIN HUNTING

Cheapest five-fors by an England spinner in Asia:

5-8	**J. E. Root**	**v India at Ahmedabad**	**2020-21**
5-18	N. G. B. Cook	v Pakistan at Karachi	1983-84
5-28	D. L. Underwood	v Sri Lanka at Colombo (PSS)	1981-82
5-30	D. A. Allen	v Pakistan at Dacca	1961-62
5-30	**D. M. Bess**	**v Sri Lanka at Galle**	**2020-21**
6-33	J. E. Emburey	v Sri Lanka at Colombo (PSS)	1981-82
6-48	R. Tattersall	v India at Kanpur	1951-52
7-49	H. Verity	v India at Chennai	1933-34
5-49	A. U. Rashid.	v Sri Lanka at Colombo (SSC)	2018-19

wicket haul in Tests by an off-spinner, beating Australia's Tim May, against West Indies
at Adelaide in 1992-93, by one run. On a less obliging surface, the ball that ripped the left-
handed Washington asunder – pitching middle and leg, hitting off – would have been a
hall-of-famer. Only when Rohit Sharma and Gill knocked off a target of 49 on the second
evening was batting anything other than a lottery. But by then England had lost heart, as
well as the chance of reaching the final of the World Test Championship; for India to get
there, all they needed from the Fourth Test was a draw.

At 842 balls, this was the shortest completed Test since England beat West Indies at
Bridgetown in 1934-35, when the captains traded tactical declarations on a sticky dog.
And it left the refurbished Motera – now the world's biggest cricket stadium, after its
capacity was doubled to 110,000 – without any play for almost ten of the 15 sessions. In
most Tests during the pandemic, this would have upset only the broadcasters. But India's
approach to Covid-19 had been erratic, and the authorities let in around 40,000 on both
days; social distancing and mask-wearing both appeared optional. This was the venue's
first Test for over eight years. For the locals, it was just as well Ahmedabad was staging
the next game, too.

England's batting, went the joke, was the worst performance at the ground since the
visit of US president Donald Trump a year earlier, when he made a mess of pronouncing
Virat Kohli and Sachin Tendulkar. Now, on the morning of the game, it was revealed that
the stadium had been renamed in honour of Indian prime minister Narendra Modi, formerly
chief minister of Gujarat, as well as president of the state's cricket association. But any
meaningful debate about the growing politicisation of Indian cricket was overshadowed
by a pitch squabble. Trying, but not quite managing, to sound diplomatic, Root suggested
a bowler of his capabilities should not have been gifted a five-for, though England later
thought better of complaining to match referee Javagal Srinath. Kohli described the surface
as "very good", while conceding that both sides had batted poorly; only one of those
claims rang true.

Both teams had made changes. Crawley was fit again, and replaced the struggling
Burns. Bairstow, back from rest and rotation, came in for Lawrence, while Ali and Stone
made way for Archer and Anderson, who was paired with Broad for the only time in

BEST MATCH FIGURES FOR INDIA AGAINST ENGLAND

12-108	M. H. Mankad (8-55 and 4-53)	Madras	1951-52
12-167	R. Ashwin (6-112 and 6-55)	Mumbai	2016-17
12-181	L. Sivaramakrishnan (6-64 and 6-117)	Bombay	1984-85
11-70	**A. R. Patel (6-38 and 5-32)**	**Ahmedabad**	**2020-21**
10-154	R. A. Jadeja (3-106 and 7-48)	Chennai	2016-17
10-177	S. A. Durani (6-105 and 4-72)	Madras	1961-62
10-188	C. Sharma (4-130 and 6-58)	Birmingham	1986
10-233	A. Kumble (7-115 and 3-118)	Ahmedabad	2001-02

In the pink: Joe Root and the ball that has just taken the last five Indian wickets.

England's winter, but for the 121st time in all (uniquely, neither would take a wicket). India brought back Sundar and Bumrah for Kuldeep Yadav and Mohammed Siraj.

But it was Ishant, in his 100th Test, who struck the first blow, Sibley edging to second slip for a duck. Bairstow also went without scoring, before Crawley purred to a 68-ball fifty, hitting ten fours; at 74 for two, they were 15 minutes from a decent first session. Then Ashwin, round the wicket, pinned Root, and Patel speared one into Crawley's pads. After the break, England disintegrated. With Archer the start of a long tail, their last eight fell for 38 in 27 overs. Patel, with six for 38, became a new face in an old story: like Mankad, Chandrasekhar, Bedi, Sivaramakrishnan, Kumble, Jadeja and Ashwin before him, he was the latest Indian spinner to wreak havoc on England's batsmen.

Their bowlers were now operating under lights, but 24 hours earlier than they had hoped. England thought they had Gill caught in the slips off Broad on nought, but Stokes dragged the ball along the turf. Archer eventually bounced Gill out – the game's final wicket for a fast bowler – and Leach quickly did a Patel on Pujara, hurrying one through. But the seamers couldn't nail their lengths, and Rohit tucked in. Just before the close, Leach persuaded Kohli to chop on: at 98 for three, India were not quite in the clear. England, meanwhile, had grown infuriated with TV umpire Chettithody Shamshuddin, who reached his conclusions more swiftly than they would have liked; a stumping appeal when Rohit had 53 deserved another look. Root and Chris Silverwood took their grievances to Srinath, who acknowledged their point. But the complaint had the air of deckchair rearrangement as an iceberg neared.

The first day felt manic, but it had nothing on the second. Moments after India took the lead, Leach won tight lbw shouts against Rahane and Rohit, before Root had Pant caught behind with his first ball – a lavish off-break that invited the drive, and kissed the edge. India's lower order proved almost as inept as England's: as Root put paid to the notion that Bess should have been picked, India's collapse extended to eight for 47, though Ishant had time to hit his first Test six. They led by 33. In theory, it was anyone's game… but now, only four sessions in, England had to bat again.

Things unravelled immediately. Crawley played back to the first ball, from Patel, and was bowled. Bairstow tried to sweep the second, and was given lbw. Since Patel had dismissed

ENGLAND'S LOWEST AGGREGATES IN TEST DEFEATS

115	53 and 62 v Australia at Lord's	1888
137	65 and 72 v Australia at Sydney	1894-95
162	61 and 101 v Australia at Melbourne	1903-04
175	82 and 93 v New Zealand at Christchurch	1983-84
178	101 and 77 v Australia at The Oval†	1882
190	68-7 dec and 122 v Australia at Brisbane	1950-51
193	**112 and 81 v India at Ahmedabad**	**2020-21**
197	71 and 126 v West Indies at Manchester	1976

† *The match that spawned the Ashes.*

Foakes with the last delivery of England's first innings, he began to celebrate a hat-trick. But Bairstow reviewed, and technology had it going over. There was no rest for the wicket: next ball, he played down the wrong line, and was bowled, for a gruesome pair.

Sibley edged a leg-side hack to Pant, though for a while Root and Stokes gave England hope, taking them 17 in front, until Ashwin got Stokes for the 11th time in Tests. Root fell next over. Before long, Ashwin was removing Archer, his 400th wicket in his 77th Test (only Muttiah Muralitharan, in 72, needed fewer), and 50 for three had morphed into 81 all out. For the first time since the 19th century, England had been dismissed for under 200 in five successive innings.

When India's openers took 11 runs from two overs before the day's second interval, it was evident there would be no final twist. Shortly after the break, Rohit polished things off with six over midwicket off Root, inflicting on England their first two-day defeat since Trent Bridge in 1921 against Australia. Only once had a Test team won by ten wickets after scoring fewer in their first innings than India's 145: England beat Australia at Edgbaston in 1909 after starting with 121, in the days when the art and science of pitch preparation was uncertain. India had spent millions on a new venue, but produced a surface that left batsmen on both sides with little chance, and too many bowlers as bystanders. In its own way, the entertainment on the second day, when 17 wickets fell, was gripping. But so is the spin of a roulette wheel.

Player of the Match: A. R. Patel.
Close of play: first day, India 99-3 (R. G. Sharma 57, Rahane 1).

England

Z. Crawley lbw b Patel	53	– b Patel	0
D. P. Sibley c R. G. Sharma b I. Sharma	0	– c Pant b Patel	7
J. M. Bairstow lbw b Patel	0	– b Patel	0
*J. E. Root lbw b Ashwin	17	– lbw b Patel	19
B. A. Stokes lbw b Patel	6	– lbw b Ashwin	25
O. J. D. Pope b Ashwin	1	– b Ashwin	12
†B. T. Foakes b Patel	12	– lbw b Patel	8
J. C. Archer b Patel	11	– lbw b Ashwin	0
M. J. Leach c Pujara b Ashwin	3	– c Rahane b Ashwin	9
S. C. J. Broad c Bumrah b Patel	3	– not out	1
J. M. Anderson not out	0	– c Pant b Washington Sundar	0
B 1, lb 2, nb 3	6		

1/2 (2) 2/27 (3) 3/74 (4)	(48.4 overs) 112	1/0 (1) 2/0 (3)	(30.4 overs) 81
4/80 (1) 5/81 (6) 6/81 (5)		3/19 (2) 4/50 (5)	
7/93 (8) 8/98 (9) 9/105 (10) 10/112 (7)		5/56 (4) 6/66 (6) 7/68 (8)	
		8/80 (7) 9/80 (9) 10/81 (11)	

I. Sharma 5–1–26–1; Bumrah 6–3–19–0; Patel 21.4–6–38–6; Ashwin 16–6–26–3. *Second innings*—Patel 15–0–32–5; Ashwin 15–3–48–4; Washington Sundar 0.4–0–1–1.

India

R. G. Sharma lbw b Leach	66	– not out	25
S. Gill c Crawley b Archer	11	– not out	15
C. A. Pujara lbw b Leach	0		
*V. Kohli b Leach	27		
A. M. Rahane lbw b Leach	7		
†R. R. Pant c Foakes b Root	1		
R. Ashwin c Crawley b Root	17		
M. S. Washington Sundar b Root	0		
A. R. Patel c Sibley b Root	0		
I. Sharma not out	10		
J. J. Bumrah lbw b Root	1		
B 2, lb 2, w 1	5	B 8, lb 1	9

1/33 (2) 2/34 (3) 3/98 (4)   (53.2 overs) 145   (no wkt, 7.4 overs) 49
4/114 (5) 5/115 (1) 6/117 (6)
7/125 (8) 8/125 (9) 9/134 (7) 10/145 (11)

Anderson 13–8–20–0; Broad 6–1–16–0; Archer 5–2–24–1; Leach 20–2–54–4; Stokes 3–0–19–0; Root 6.2–3–8–5. *Second innings*—Leach 4–1–15–0; Root 3.4–0–25–0.

Umpires: A. K. Chaudhary and N. N. Menon.   Third umpire: C. Shamshuddin.
Referee: J. Srinath.

INDIA v ENGLAND

Fourth Test

ANDREW MILLER

At Ahmedabad, March 4–6, 2021. India won by an innings and 25 runs. India 30pts. Toss: England.

It was, as England's young batsmen were used to saying by the end of an arduous series, an incredible learning experience. An Indian odyssey that had begun with such optimism

Fighting back: two feisty innings from Dan Lawrence brought England a little cheer.

in Chennai came to a tangled conclusion in Ahmedabad, where the team's shortcomings against spin were exposed for the fourth time in the space of five days' play.

India's innings victory completed a 3–1 win that accurately reflected the gulf between the teams. After winning the toss for the third time in four matches, England made 205, their highest total in six attempts. Even allowing for a range of surfaces that brought into question the balance between bat and ball, this was a damning statistic.

And yet, if learning was the aim of England's game, what could they hope to glean from the performance that ripped the contest from their grasp? In ransacking his way to a third Test hundred – his first at home – Pant transcended both the conditions and a tricky match situation to propel India to an insurmountable lead of 160. In so doing, he made a persuasive argument that genius cannot be taught.

After all, no coach would encourage the stroke he executed on a game-changing second evening. The outstanding Anderson had kept England competitive with another immaculate performance, claiming two for 19 in his first 17 overs across three spells – each negotiated with a respect granted to few visiting seamers in India. Pant had other plans. India's lead was a fragile 18, with four wickets left, as he climbed on to the front foot to flog consecutive fours from Anderson's first two deliveries with the new ball. Then, after he and Sundar had taken three fours off an over from Stokes, Pant unfurled the series' most startling stroke – a premeditated reverse lap that sailed high over the slips. It elicited a shrug of bewilderment from Anderson; even in his 19th year of Test cricket, he clearly hadn't seen it all before. But Pant wasn't done. He launched the first ball from Root – basking in figures of five for eight in the Third Test – high over square leg for six, to bring up a thrilling century from 115 deliveries.

Anderson exacted a measure of revenge one over later, when Pant heaved him to short midwicket, but India's lead had stretched beyond 50, priceless in a game of tight margins. And, the fabric of their defence torn apart, England's ill-balanced attack had no further answers, as Sundar and Patel put the contest out of reach in an eighth-wicket stand of 106.

Pant had laid the groundwork during an uncharacteristically measured first 50 runs spanning 82 balls – a broadly risk-free opening gambit that had begun straight after lunch, with India on their guard at 80 for four. It continued through the loss of two more wickets, as England briefly contemplated a first-innings lead, at 146 for six. It's feasible they might have got there, had it not been for a sliding-doors moment in the final over before tea, when the desperately off-colour Bess rapped Pant's pads, but failed to extract the on-field decision that would have sent him on his way for 35.

A wicket might have revitalised Bess, whose selection seemed as much a reaction to the hyper-spinning surface on which England had been routed in the Third Test, as a conviction that he was the man to partner the steadfast Leach. Bess bowled 17 wicketless overs for 71 – including 24 from 11 full tosses – and his lack of control gave Root no option but to turn, time and again, to Anderson and Stokes. The response of Stokes to his new-ball promotion, for the first time in his Test career, was four hard-earned wickets,

MOST WICKETS IN FIRST THREE TESTS

W	Avge		Debut
31	13.93	N. D. Hirwani (India)...............	1987-88
29	8.55	C. T. B. Turner (Australia)..........	1886-87
27	**10.59**	**A. R. Patel (India)**.................	**2020-21**
27	11.00	R. M. Hogg (Australia).............	1978-79
26	18.07	H. V. Hordern (Australia)..........	1910-11
26	18.38	B. A. W. Mendis (Sri Lanka)........	2008
24	12.37	V. D. Philander (South Africa)......	2011-12
24	12.41	A. V. Bedser (England).............	1946
24	14.08	F. S. Trueman (England)............	1952
24	14.41	J. J. Ferris (Australia)...............	1886-87

On fire: Rishabh Pant cuts loose after a circumspect start.

after just 15 overs in the first three Tests. Two of his scalps came in India's collapse of three for none in five deliveries at the end of their innings – instigated by Patel's run-out for 43 – as Sundar was stranded four short of a deserved maiden hundred.

England's rest and rotation policy attracted predictable scrutiny as their hopes slipped away, but it was hard to escape the conclusion that their available resources had simply been misdeployed on two very different Ahmedabad surfaces. Between them, Stuart Broad and Jofra Archer had bowled 11 overs for a solitary wicket in the Third Test; now, with Broad omitted and Archer unavailable because of his elbow, England were left with insufficient firepower to exploit a pitch offering two-paced bounce from the outset.

India, by contrast, had every weapon they needed, even in the absence of their own spearhead, Jasprit Bumrah, who was preparing for his wedding. In particular, they had Patel, after five-fors in each of the previous three innings of his debut series. Within the first half-hour, he had taken his tally to 20 wickets at under nine, once again bagging the England openers. Sibley played for turn, and was bowled via an inside edge by the one that slid on; Crawley followed a four off his first ball from Patel with a fifth-ball sucker punch, wafting airily to mid-off in a bid to disrupt his unwavering length. And when Root was nailed by a nipbacker from Siraj, any thoughts of a challenging total had gone. Stokes hit back in the manner that had earned him his only other fifty of the series, in the first innings at Chennai. But just as he was beginning to rise to a battle of wills with the spinners, Sundar pinned him in anticlimactic fashion from round the wicket.

After that it was a race to the bottom. Lawrence, recalled at No. 7 after starting the series at No. 3, traded his blows with more success than most in his first act of a personally rewarding series finale – although the shot that brought his demise for 46, stumped by three yards as he rushed past a length ball, was inelegant.

A subplot was the World Test Championship. England's ambitions had been ended by their Third Test defeat, although victory here would have allowed Australia to vault ahead of India into the final against New Zealand. Anderson's removal of Gill for a third-ball duck – the 104th Test batsman he had dismissed without scoring, equalling Glenn McGrath's record – suggested England weren't about to go quietly. Stokes's lifter to remove Kohli, also without scoring, confirmed it. In between, Leach extracted Pujara for the fourth time in the series and, when Stokes returned to dislodge Rohit for 49, India's conventional routes to the ascendancy had been cut off. Happily for their hopes of reaching June's final, Pant had no interest in the conventional.

The contest's final act was little more than an exercise in form-filling. England shipped four more wickets in the first hour on the final afternoon – two apiece to Patel and Ashwin, whose two in two balls included the hapless Bairstow for his third duck in four innings since his mid-tour break, and his sixth in his last nine against India. Pope concluded a chastening trip with an undignified stumping, while Root – his reading of length infallible in the early weeks of England's winter – found Ashwin's hang-time too tricksy for his back-foot game, and fell for 30. It was the sixth time in the series he had been lbw, one short of Kim Hughes's Test record, for Australia in the 1981 Ashes.

Only Lawrence made much headway, last out for 50, but his rustic slog ensured England's final innings of the tour was split, five wickets apiece, between the two men who had done most to defeat them. A combined haul of 59 wickets at 12 for Ashwin and Patel was one more than all the visiting bowlers had totalled. That, in essence, was the story of the series.

Player of the Match: R. R. Pant. *Player of the Series:* R. Ashwin.

Close of play: first day, India 24-1 (R. G. Sharma 8, Pujara 15); second day, India 294-7 (Washington Sundar 60, Patel 11).

England

Z. Crawley c Siraj b Patel	9	– c Rahane b Ashwin	5
D. P. Sibley b Patel	2	– c Pant b Patel	3
J. M. Bairstow lbw b Siraj	28	– c R. G. Sharma b Ashwin	0
*J. E. Root lbw b Siraj	5	– lbw b Ashwin	30
B. A. Stokes lbw b Washington Sundar	55	– c Kohli b Patel	2
O. J. D. Pope c Gill b Ashwin	29	– st Pant b Patel	15
D. W. Lawrence st Pant b Patel	46	– b Ashwin	50
†B. T. Foakes c Rahane b Ashwin	1	– c Pant b Patel	13
D. M. Bess lbw b Patel	3	– c Pant b Patel	2
M. J. Leach lbw b Ashwin	7	– c Rahane b Ashwin	2
J. M. Anderson not out	10	– not out	1
B 3, lb 5, w 1, nb 1	10	B 4, lb 8	12

1/10 (2) 2/15 (1) 3/30 (4) (75.5 overs) 205
4/78 (3) 5/121 (5) 6/166 (6)
7/170 (8) 8/188 (7) 9/189 (9) 10/205 (10)

1/10 (1) 2/10 (3) (54.5 overs) 135
3/20 (2) 4/30 (5)
5/65 (4) 6/65 (4) 7/109 (8)
8/111 (9) 9/134 (10) 10/135 (7)

I. Sharma 9–2–23–0; Siraj 14–2–45–2; Patel 26–7–68–4; Ashwin 19.5–4–47–3; Washington Sundar 7–1–14–1. *Second innings*—Siraj 4–0–12–0; Patel 24–6–48–5; Ashwin 22.5–4–47–5; Washington Sundar 4–0–16–0.

India

S. Gill lbw b Anderson	0	A. R. Patel run out (Bairstow/Root)	43
R. G. Sharma lbw b Stokes	49	I. Sharma lbw b Stokes	0
C. A. Pujara lbw b Leach	17	M. Siraj lbw b Stokes	0
*V. Kohli c Foakes b Stokes	0	B 10, lb 6, nb 3	19
A. M. Rahane c Stokes b Anderson	27		
†R. R. Pant c Root b Anderson	101	1/0 (1) 2/40 (3) 3/41 (4) (114.4 overs) 365
R. Ashwin c Pope b Leach	13	4/80 (5) 5/121 (2) 6/146 (7)
M. S. Washington Sundar not out	96	7/259 (6) 8/365 (9) 9/365 (10) 10/365 (11)

Anderson 25–14–44–3; Stokes 27.4–6–89–4; Leach 27–5–89–2; Bess 17–1–71–0; Root 18–1–56–0.

Umpires: N. N. Menon and V. K. Sharma. Third umpire: A. K. Chaudhary.
Referee: J. Srinath.

LIMITED-OVERS INTERNATIONAL REPORTS BY STEVEN LYNCH

INDIA v ENGLAND

First Twenty20 International

At Ahmedabad, March 12, 2021 (floodlit). England won by eight wickets. Toss: England.

Morgan established what, for three matches at least, seemed a template for success: win the toss, field – and later watch the opposition bowlers struggle with the dew. Archer's first over (the second of the innings) was a wicket-maiden, and in the next Kohli chipped Rashid, who had opened the bowling for the first time in internationals, to mid-off; after nought in the previous week's Test, it was the first time he had collected consecutive ducks for India. With the faster bowlers finding crisp bounce – and Wood frequently touching 95mph – Pant somehow reverse-swept Archer for six but, when he holed out to the last ball of the tenth, India looked sunk at 48 for four. Iyer repaired some of the damage, hitting Archer for successive fours, reaching a 36-ball fifty, then carving Jordan for six, but the eventual total was inadequate. Archer's figures of three for 23 were his best in T20 internationals. Roy lived dangerously, but added 72 with Buttler in eight overs, before Malan sealed a comfortable victory with a straight six off Sundar. England wore black armbands following the death of former Test seamer Joey Benjamin.

Player of the Match: J. C. Archer.

India

		B	4/6
1 S. Dhawan *b 11*	4	12	0
2 K. L. Rahul *b 10*	1	4	0
3 *V. Kohli *c 8 b 9*	0	5	0
4 †R. R. Pant *c 4 b 6*	21	23	2/1
5 S. S. Iyer *c 3 b 8*	67	48	8/1
6 H. H. Pandya *c 8 b 10*	19	21	1/1
7 S. N. Thakur *c 3 b 10*	0	3	0
8 M. S. Washington Sundar *not out*	3	3	0
9 A. R. Patel *not out*	7	3	1
W 2	2		
6 overs: 22-3	(20 overs)	124-7	

1/2 2/3 3/20 4/48 5/102 6/102 7/117

10 Bhuvneshwar Kumar and 11 Y. S. Chahal did not bat.

Rashid 18–11–14–1; Archer 24–16–23–3; Wood 24–11–20–1; Jordan 24–7–27–1; Stokes 18–5–25–1; Curran 12–4–15–0.

England

		B	4/6
1 J. J. Roy *lbw b 8*	49	32	4/3
2 †J. C. Buttler *lbw b 11*	28	24	2/1
3 D. J. Malan *not out*	24	20	2/1
4 J. M. Bairstow *not out*	26	17	1/2
W 3	3		
6 overs: 50-0	(15.3 overs)	130-2	

1/72 2/89

5 *E. J. G. Morgan, 6 B. A. Stokes, 7 S. M. Curran, 8 C. J. Jordan, 9 A. U. Rashid, 10 J. C. Archer and 11 M. A. Wood did not bat.

Patel 18–9–22–0; Bhuvneshwar Kumar 12–6–15–0; Chahal 24–7–44–1; Thakur 12–3–16–0; Pandya 12–5–13–0; Washington Sundar 15–5–18–1.

Umpires: K. N. Ananthapadmanabhan and N. N. Menon.   Third umpire: V. K. Sharma.
Referee: J. Srinath.

INDIA v ENGLAND

Second Twenty20 International

At Ahmedabad, March 14, 2021 (floodlit). India won by seven wickets. Toss: India. Twenty20 international debuts: I. P. Kishan, S. A. Yadav.

Put in after Kohli won his only toss of the white-ball games, England were up against it from the start: Buttler fell to his first ball, and Malan made a sedate 24 before Chahal's review proved positive. Roy again used most of his bat on the way to the forties, though none of the bowlers was really collared. England had 83 after ten overs, but failed to match that in the second half on a sluggish

Soaking it up: Ishan Kishan – and a crowd unconcerned with social distancing.

pitch. India also began poorly – Sam Curran opened with a wicket-maiden – before the debutant left-hander Ishan Kishan flourished. Just 22, but battle-hardened in the IPL, he lifted Tom Curran and Stokes for six, then took two off successive balls from Rashid, before misjudging a skidder; he did have a lucky escape at 40, when Stokes put down a sitter at long-on. Kohli – who was dropped on ten by Buttler down the leg side off Jordan's first ball – reached his half-century from 35 deliveries, and finished the match with a four and a six, becoming the first to reach 3,000 runs in T20 internationals. Victory was enjoyed by a large crowd – the last of the tour, because of a rise in Covid cases.

Player of the Match: I. P. Kishan.

England

		B	4/6
1 J. J. Roy *c 10 b 9*	46	35	4/2
2 †J. C. Buttler *lbw b 10*	0	1	0
3 D. J. Malan *lbw b 11*	24	23	4
4 J. M. Bairstow *c 6 b 9*	20	15	1/1
5 *E. J. G. Morgan *c 4 b 8*	28	20	4
6 B. A. Stokes *c 7 b 8*	24	21	1
7 S. M. Curran *not out*	6	5	1
8 C. J. Jordan *not out*	0	0	0
B 1, lb 10, w 5	16		

6 overs: 44-1   (20 overs) 164-6

1/1 2/64 3/91 4/119 5/142 6/160

9 T. K. Curran, 10 A. U. Rashid and 11 J. C. Archer did not bat.

Bhuvneshwar Kumar 24–10–28–1; Washington Sundar 24–11–29–2; Thakur 24–10–29–2; Pandya 24–4–33–0; Chahal 24–9–34–1.

India

		B	4/6
1 K. L. Rahul *c 2 b 7*	0	6	0
2 I. P. Kishan *lbw b 10*	56	32	5/4
3 *V. Kohli *not out*	73	49	5/3
4 †R. R. Pant *c 4 b 8*	26	13	2/2
5 S. S. Iyer *not out*	8	8	0
Lb 1, w 1, nb 1	3		

6 overs: 50-1   (17.5 overs) 166-3

1/0 2/94 3/130

6 S. A. Yadav, 7 H. H. Pandya, 8 S. N. Thakur, 9 M. S. Washington Sundar, 10 Bhuvneshwar Kumar and 11 Y. S. Chahal did not bat.

S. M. Curran 24–8–22–1; Archer 24–11–24–0; Jordan 17–3–38–1; T. K. Curran 12–2–26–0; Stokes 6–1–17–0; Rashid 24–7–38–1.

Umpires: K. N. Ananthapadmanabhan and A. K. Chaudhary.   Third umpire: V. K. Sharma.
Referee: J. Srinath.

INDIA v ENGLAND

Third Twenty20 International

At Ahmedabad, March 16, 2021 (floodlit). England won by eight wickets. Toss: England.

In his 100th T20 international, Morgan won the toss on a red pitch he had described in advance as "looking like Ayers Rock", and did not even have to bat as England steamed home, thanks to a typically destructive display from Buttler. India had made another poor start: Rahul collected a second successive duck during a rapid spell from Wood, who also shook up Kishan, the hero of the previous match. Returning after missing the second game with a bruised ankle, Wood grabbed three for 14 in his first three overs. From 86 for five in the 15th, Kohli at least made a game of it: he and Pandya piled on 70 in the last 33 balls. But it never looked enough once Buttler found his range by spanking Chahal for two huge straight sixes in the fourth over, then took 14 in four balls off Thakur in the fifth. His unbeaten 83 was a T20 international career-best.

Player of the Match: J. C. Buttler.

India

		B	4/6
1 R. G. Sharma *c 9 b 11*	15	17	2
2 K. L. Rahul *b 11*	0	4	0
3 I. P. Kishan *c 2 b 8*	4	9	0
4 *V. Kohli *not out*	77	46	8/4
5 †R. R. Pant *run out (2/7)*	25	20	3
6 S. S. Iyer *c 3 b 11*	9	9	1
7 H. H. Pandya *c 9 b 8*	17	15	0/2
B 1, lb 5, w 3	9		

6 overs: 24-3   (20 overs) 156-6

1/7 2/20 3/24 4/64 5/86 6/156

8 S. N. Thakur, 9 M. S. Washington Sundar, 10 Bhuvneshwar Kumar and 11 Y. S. Chahal did not bat.

Rashid 24–9–26–0; Archer 24–13–32–0; Wood 24–13–31–3; Jordan 24–11–35–2; Stokes 12–4–12–0; Curran 12–3–14–0.

England

		B	4/6
1 J. J. Roy *c 1 b 11*	9	13	2
2 †J. C. Buttler *not out*	83	52	5/4
3 D. J. Malan *st 5 b 9*	18	17	0/1
4 J. M. Bairstow *not out*	40	28	5
B 4, lb 2, w 2	8		

6 overs: 57-1   (18.2 overs) 158-2

1/23 2/81

5 *E. J. G. Morgan, 6 B. A. Stokes, 7 S. M. Curran, 8 C. J. Jordan, 9 J. C. Archer, 10 A. U. Rashid and 11 M. A. Wood did not bat.

Bhuvneshwar Kumar 24–10–27–0; Thakur 20–7–36–0; Chahal 24–6–41–1; Pandya 18–3–22–0; Washington Sundar 24–7–26–1.

Umpires: A. K. Chaudhary and V. K. Sharma.   Third umpire: N. N. Menon.
Referee: J. Srinath.

INDIA v ENGLAND

Fourth Twenty20 International

At Ahmedabad, March 18, 2021 (floodlit). India won by eight runs. Toss: England.

Despite again being asked to bat, India broke serve to square the series. After another sketchy start – the out-of-form Rahul fell for 14 in the eighth over, and Kohli soon followed, stumped off Rashid – they were rescued by another new face: the 30-year-old Suryakumar Yadav, who had made his debut in the second match but did not bat, pulled his first delivery, from Archer, for six, and cruised to a 31-ball 57. He fell to an outfield catch by Malan which replays indicated might have brushed the ground; this led to suggestions the umpires' soft signal for such distant catches should be discontinued. Sixes for Pandya and Iyer in a Jordan over that cost 18 helped swell the total to 185; Archer collected four for 33, his second career-best haul of the series. Roy crashed another adventurous 40, but Malan again found it hard to get going. Stokes led the recovery, and England were slight favourites at 131 for three in the 15th – but then four wickets tumbled, including Stokes and Morgan to successive balls from Thakur. Archer, batting for the first time in his 11th T20 international, thumped three boundaries, but India's victory was sealed when Jordan holed out.

Player of the Match: S. A. Yadav.

India

	B	4/6
1 R. G. Sharma c and b 9	12	12 1/1
2 K. L. Rahul c 9 b 5...........	14	17 2
3 S. A. Yadav c 3 b 7	57	31 6/3
4 *V. Kohli st 2 b 10..........	1	5 0
5 †R. R. Pant b 9	30	23 4
6 S. S. Iyer c 3 b 9...........	37	18 5/1
7 H. H. Pandya c 5 b 11	11	8 0/1
8 S. N. Thakur not out.........	10	4 2
9 M. S. Washington Sundar c 10 b	4	2 1
9.		
10 Bhuvneshwar Kumar not out ..	0	0 0
Lb 5, w 4	9	

6 overs: 45-1   (20 overs) 185-8

1/21 2/63 3/70 4/110 5/144 6/170 7/174 8/179

11 R. D. Chahar did not bat.

Rashid 24–8–39–1; Archer 24–10–33–4;
Wood 24–14–25–1; Jordan 24–6–41–0; Stokes
18–5–26–1; Curran 6–1–16–1.

England

	B	4/6
1 J. J. Roy c 3 b 7.............	40	27 6/1
2 †J. C. Buttler c 2 b 10	9	6 0/1
3 D. J. Malan b 11	14	17 0/1
4 J. M. Bairstow c 9 b 11	25	19 2/1
5 B. A. Stokes c 3 b 8..........	46	23 4/3
6 *E. J. G. Morgan c 9 b 8	4	6 0
7 S. M. Curran b 7	3	5 0
8 C. J. Jordan c 7 b 8	12	9 1
9 J. C. Archer not out	18	8 2/1
10 A. U. Rashid not out	0	0 0
Lb 2, w 4..................	6	

6 overs: 48-1   (20 overs) 177-8

1/15 2/60 3/66 4/131 5/140 6/140 7/153 8/177

11 M. A. Wood did not bat.

Bhuvneshwar Kumar 24–12–30–1; Pandya
24–13–16–2; Thakur 24–9–42–3; Washington
Sundar 24–5–52–0; Chahar 24–7–35–2.

Umpires: K. N. Ananthapadmanabhan and N. N. Menon.   Third umpire: V. K. Sharma.
Referee: J. Srinath.

INDIA v ENGLAND

Fifth Twenty20 International

At Ahmedabad, March 20, 2021 (floodlit). India won by 36 runs. Toss: England.
  India pinched the series the hard way, after being put in for the fourth time out of five. With Rahul dropped, Kohli moved up to open – and piled on 94 in nine overs with the equally feisty Rohit. This time there was no let-up. Yadav's rapid 32 was cut short by an astonishing one-handed grab from Jordan, running at full tilt around the long-on boundary and lobbing the ball nonchalantly to a delighted Roy just before he crossed the rope. But Pandya also pummelled a quick thirty, while

FASTEST TO 1,000 RUNS IN TWENTY20 INTERNATIONALS

I		100	50	I		100	50
24	D. J. Malan (England)	1	10	32	A. D. Hales (England)	1	7
26	Babar Azam (Pakistan).......	0	8	32	K. P. Pietersen (England)	0	5
27	V. Kohli (India)	0	9	34	C. H. Gayle (West Indies)......	1	10
29	A. J. Finch (Australia).........	1	6	34	M. D. K. J. Perera (Sri Lanka) ..	0	10
29	K. L. Rahul (India)..........	2	7	34	K. S. Williamson (New Zealand)	0	6
32	F. du Plessis (South Africa)	1	7	35	B. B. McCullum (New Zealand)	1	6

Kohli made an effortless 80 from 52 balls, taking his series tally to 231 (for twice out) from 157. With Wood and Jordan expensive, India scorched to 224, their highest total against England, beating 218 for four at Durban in 2007-08, when Yuvraj Singh hit Stuart Broad for six sixes in an over. England needed a sound start – but Roy fell second ball to the relentless Bhuvneshwar Kumar. Buttler and Malan repaired the damage with a stand of 130, only to be separated when Bhuvneshwar returned. Thakur bounced back from a costly first over with two wickets in his third, and England did not get close, as the middle order misfired again. It was their first T20 series defeat since losing at home to India in 2018 (India themselves were still unbeaten since 2018-19), and Morgan admitted: "They outplayed us in the big moments."

Player of the Match: Bhuvneshwar Kumar. *Player of the Series:* V. Kohli.

India

	B	4/6
1 R. G. Sharma *b* 6	64	34 4/5
2 *V. Kohli *not out*	80	52 7/2
3 S. A. Yadav *c 1 b* 10	32	17 3/2
4 H. H. Pandya *not out*	39	17 4/2
Lb 3, w 6	9	

6 overs: 60-0   (20 overs) 224-2

1/94 2/143

5 †R. R. Pant, 6 S. S. Iyer, 7 S. N. Thakur, 8 M. S. Washington Sundar, 9 Bhuvneshwar Kumar and 10 R. D. Chahar and 11 T. Natarajan did not bat.

12th man: K. L. Rahul.

Rashid 24–8–31–1; Archer 24–4–43–0; Wood 24–5–53–0; Jordan 24–4–57–0; Curran 6–1–11–0; Stokes 18–6–26–1.

England

	B	4/6
1 J. J. Roy *b* 9	0	2 0
2 †J. C. Buttler *c 4 b* 9	52	34 2/4
3 D. J. Malan *b* 7	68	46 9/2
4 J. M. Bairstow *c 3 b* 7	7	7 1
5 *E. J. G. Morgan *c 12 b* 4	1	4 0
6 B. A. Stokes *c 5 b* 11	14	12 2
7 C. J. Jordan *c 3 b* 7	11	10 0/1
8 J. C. Archer *run out (3/5)*	1	2 0
9 S. M. Curran *not out*	14	3 0/2
10 A. U. Rashid *not out*	0	0 0
Lb 9, w 11	20	

6 overs: 62-1   (20 overs) 188-8

1/0 2/130 3/140 4/142 5/142 6/165 7/168 8/174

11 M. A. Wood did not bat.

Bhuvneshwar Kumar 24–17–15–2; Pandya 24–9–34–1; Washington Sundar 6–0–13–0; Thakur 24–10–45–3; Natarajan 24–7–39–1; Chahar 18–4–33–0.

Umpires: A. K. Chaudhary and N. N. Menon.   Third umpire: K. N. Ananthapadmanabhan.
Referee: J. Srinath.

INDIA v ENGLAND

First One-Day International

At Pune, March 23, 2021 (day/night). India won by 66 runs. India 10pts. Toss: England. One-day international debuts: P. M. Krishna, K. H. Pandya.

As England's openers were hurtling along in pursuit of 318, spraying sixes galore – Bairstow alone smashed seven – a quick finish looked possible. And indeed the match did end almost eight overs early: but the winners were India, after all ten wickets folded for 116. Prasidh Krishna, a seamer from Bangalore, had watched his first three overs in international cricket disappear for 37; he

FASTEST FIFTIES ON ONE-DAY INTERNATIONAL DEBUT

Balls

26	**K. H. Pandya (58*)**	**India v England at Pune**	**2020-21**
35	R. O. Butcher (52)	England v Australia at Birmingham	1980
35	J. E. Morris (63*)	England v New Zealand at Adelaide.	1990-91
37	B. C. Hollioake (63)	England v Australia at Lord's	1997
38	A. R. Khurasiya (57)	India v Sri Lanka at Pune (Nehru) . . .	1998-99
38	L. J. Wright (50)	England v India at The Oval	2007
38	**Rahmanullah Gurbaz (127)**	**Afghanistan v Ireland at Abu Dhabi** . . .	**2020-21**
39	R. Mutumbami (64)	Zimbabwe v Afghanistan at Bulawayo . . .	2014
40	Nasir Jamshed (61)	Pakistan v Zimbabwe at Karachi	2007-08

Shahid Afridi (102) reached 50 in 18 balls for Pakistan v Sri Lanka in Nairobi in 1996-97; it was his second ODI, but he did not bat in the first. R. Lamba made 64 from 53 balls on debut for India v Australia at Jaipur in 1986-87; it is not known how many he needed to reach 50.

returned undaunted to finish with four for 54. It certainly seemed a different game once Roy lobbed a catch to backward point, held at the second attempt by the substitute Suryakumar Yadav. A Rootless England had Stokes – in his first ODI since the World Cup final – at No. 3, but he drove tamely to extra cover. When Bairstow fell for a 66-ball 94, the wheels were working loose. Morgan did not make the most of being dropped first ball by Kohli at slip, and England ground to a halt: only a brief stand between Billings and Ali held up India. Earlier, the hosts had used up 15 overs in an opening stand of 64. Dhawan carried on serenely to 98 before chipping to midwicket and, though Kohli hit another half-century, they were soon wobbling at 205 for five in the 41st. But Hardik Pandya's brother, Krunal, India's latest nerveless newcomer, spanked a half-century from 26 balls. He and Rahul – preferred to Rishabh Pant behind the stumps, despite a poor run with the bat in the T20s – thumped 112 in 9.3 overs. Rohit did not field after being hit on the elbow by Wood, and Iyer dislocated his shoulder diving in the field; for England, Morgan (four stitches in split webbing) and Billings (shoulder sprain) batted, despite knocks while fielding, and did not feature again in the series. Perhaps the biggest injury, though, was to England's pride.

Player of the Match: S. Dhawan.

India

R. G. Sharma c Buttler b Stokes	28		K. H. Pandya not out		58
S. Dhawan c Morgan b Stokes	98		Lb 3, w 5		8
*V. Kohli c Ali b Wood	56				
S. S. Iyer c sub (L. S. Livingstone) b Wood	6		1/64 (1) 2/169 (3) (5 wkts, 50 overs)		317
†K. L. Rahul not out	62		3/187 (4) 4/197 (2)		
H. H. Pandya c Bairstow b Stokes	1		5/205 (6)		
			10 overs: 39-0		

S. N. Thakur, Bhuvneshwar Kumar, K. Yadav and P. M. Krishna did not bat.

Wood 10–1–75–2; S. M. Curran 10–1–48–0; T. K. Curran 10–0–63–0; Stokes 8–1–34–3; Rashid 9–0–66–0; Ali 3–0–28–0.

England

J. J. Roy c sub (S. A. Yadav) b Krishna	46		A. U. Rashid c Rahul b Bhuvneshwar Kumar		0
J. M. Bairstow c Yadav b Thakur	94		M. A. Wood not out		2
B. A. Stokes c sub (S. Gill) b Krishna	1				
*E. J. G. Morgan c Rahul b Thakur	22				
†J. C. Buttler lbw b Thakur	2		Lb 3, w 10		13
S. W. Billings c Kohli b Krishna	18				
M. M. Ali c Rahul b Bhuvneshwar Kumar	30		1/135 (1) 2/137 (3) (42.1 overs)		251
S. M. Curran c sub (S. Gill) b K. H. Pandya	12		3/169 (2) 4/175 (4) 5/176 (5)		
T. K. Curran c Bhuvneshwar Kumar			6/217 (6) 7/237 (7) 8/239 (8)		
b Krishna	11		9/241 (10) 10/251 (9)		10 overs: 89-0

Bhuvneshwar Kumar 9–0–30–2; Krishna 8.1–1–54–4; Thakur 6–0–37–3; K. H. Pandya 10–0–59–1; Yadav 9–0–68–0.

Umpires: K. N. Ananthapadmanabhan and N. N. Menon.   Third umpire: A. K. Chaudhary.
Referee: J. Srinath.

INDIA v ENGLAND

Second One-Day International

At Pune, March 26, 2021 (day/night). England won by six wickets. England 10pts. Toss: England. One-day international debut: L. S. Livingstone.

This game followed the pattern of the first – until a stunning assault by Stokes. Chasing an imposing 337, England were well placed at halfway, with 167 for one. In the next over, Stokes survived when he lazily ran his bat in ahead of Yadav's direct hit from the deep: no more than a millimetre could have been over the line, but the TV umpire decided there was not enough evidence to give it out. Perhaps it woke him up: after reaching 50 from 40 deliveries, Stokes hurtled to 99 from his next 11, hitting ten sixes in all – six off Krunal Pandya, and four off the unfortunate Yadav, including three in succession – before edging his 52nd ball down the leg side. Bairstow had been scarcely less potent in a stand of 175 in 19 overs. He lofted seven sixes in a superb 124 and, although he and Buttler soon fell to Krishna, England waltzed home thanks to Malan, in only his second ODI, and Liam Livingstone, in his first. Earlier, India had built steadily after being put in by Buttler, deputising for the injured Morgan. Kohli and Rahul added 121 for the third wicket, with Rahul gliding to his fifth ODI century. The recalled Pant (in for the injured Shreyas Iyer) scattergunned 77

OUT FOR 99 IN AN ODI FOR ENGLAND

Balls			
52	B. A. Stokes ..	v India at Pune	**2020-21**
84	J. C. Buttler ...	v West Indies at North Sound	2013-14
93	A. Flintoff	v India at The Oval	2004
109	A. J. Lamb	v India at The Oval	1982
124	A. D. Hales ...	v South Africa at Port Elizabeth	2015-16
159	G. Boycott	v Australia at The Oval...............	1980
168	B. C. Broad ...	v Pakistan at The Oval	1987

Stokes's was the fastest 99 for any country; M. N. Waller made 99* from 74 balls for Zimbabwe v New Zealand at Bulawayo in 2011-12.

from 40 balls, with seven sixes, and Hardik Pandya clubbed four; the total might have been higher had India attacked Ali, who whistled through his ten overs, and conceded a solitary four. In all, England's spinners sent down 20 overs for 112, while India's 16 cost 156. Even though Roy finally escaped the flighty forties, and put on 110 with Bairstow – their 13th century stand in ODIs, a national record – England still had a lot to do. But when Stokes lit the blue touch paper, all Kohli could do was admire: "That was some of the most amazing batting while chasing a total that you're going to see." England had never previously knocked off more than 266, at Leeds in 1974, to win an ODI against India.

Player of the Match: J. M. Bairstow.

India

R. G. Sharma c Rashid b S. M. Curran	25	S. N. Thakur not out	0
S. Dhawan c Stokes b Topley	4		
*V. Kohli c Buttler b Rashid.............	66	Lb 2, w 7	9
K. L. Rahul c Topley b T. K. Curran......	108		—
†R. R. Pant c Roy b T. K. Curran	77	1/9 (2) 2/37 (1) (6 wkts, 50 overs) 336	
H. H. Pandya c Roy b Topley	35	3/158 (3) 4/271 (4)	
K. H. Pandya not out	12	5/308 (5) 6/334 (6) 10 overs: 41-2	

Bhuvneshwar Kumar, K. Yadav and P. M. Krishna did not bat.

S. M. Curran 7–0–47–1; Topley 8–0–50–2; T. K. Curran 10–0–83–2; Stokes 5–0–42–0; Ali 10–0–47–0; Rashid 10–0–65–1.

England

J. J. Roy run out (Sharma/Pant)..........	55	L. S. Livingstone not out..............	27
J. M. Bairstow c Kohli b Krishna	124	B 4, lb 2, w 8, nb 2	16
B. A. Stokes c Pant b Bhuvneshwar Kumar	99		—
D. J. Malan not out	16	1/110 (1) 2/285 (3) (4 wkts, 43.3 overs) 337	
*†J. C. Buttler b Krishna	0	3/287 (2) 4/287 (5) 10 overs: 59-0	

M. M. Ali, S. M. Curran, T. K. Curran, A. U. Rashid and R. J. W. Topley did not bat.

Bhuvneshwar Kumar 10–0–63–1; Krishna 10–0–58–2; Thakur 7.3–0–54–0; Yadav 10–0–84–0;
K. H. Pandya 6–0–72–0.

Umpires: N. N. Menon and V. K. Sharma.   Third umpire: A. K. Chaudhary.
Referee: J. Srinath.

INDIA v ENGLAND

Third One-Day International

At Pune, March 28, 2021 (day/night). India won by seven runs. India 10pts. Toss: England.

A high-octane one-day series bubbled to a classic conclusion, with both sides having periods of control. After being put in for the sixth time running, India's openers raised 100 in the 14th over, before a Rashid googly breached Rohit's defences. Dhawan popped a return catch to Rashid, then

---

SEVEN BOWLERS TAKING A WICKET IN AN ODI INNINGS

New Zealand v India (156) at Auckland	1975-76
New Zealand v Sri Lanka (165) at Dunedin	1990-91
Netherlands v Bermuda (115) at Rotterdam	2007
Australia v Scotland (156) at Edinburgh	2009
England v India (329) at Pune	**2020-21**

Kohli stepped back to cut Ali, and missed. And when Rahul cracked Livingstone's second ball in international cricket, a big full toss, straight to backward square, England were on top. After 30 overs, though, India had 206, with Pant and Hardik Pandya in full flow. They put on 99 in all, but back surged England, with four wickets in the last 15 deliveries. Roy then clattered 14 off the first five of the reply, from Bhuvneshwar Kumar, before being bowled by the sixth; Bairstow also fell cheaply. Hardik dropped a sitter at long-on when Stokes had 15, then breathed again when he slapped a full toss to square leg. Buttler reached double figures for the first time in six ODI innings since the 2019 World Cup final, but got little further. Malan and Livingstone added 60 but, when Ali lobbed a low chance to mid-off, England were 200 for seven. However, this engrossing tour had one final twist. Sam Curran, reprieved by another Hardik howler when 22, put on 57 with Rashid, and began to spook the Indians. He took 18 off Thakur's last over then, with 18 needed from ten balls, Thakur badly dropped Wood, and Natarajan misjudged a spiralling edge from Curran. Kohli's face, always a picture, recalled Munch's *The Scream*. In the final over, though, Hardik redeemed himself with a laser from long-off to run out Wood after a knockabout stand of 60, and Curran could not find enough boundaries off Natarajan's yorkers. It was the 27th time in an ODI that a team that had been bowled out beat one that hadn't, but England's total was the highest involved. India clinched a clean sweep of all three series. "This win has been sweet," said Kohli, "because it's against the top team in the world."

Player of the Match: S. M. Curran.   *Player of the Series:* J. M. Bairstow.

HIGHEST SCORE FROM No. 8 IN ODIs

95*	C. R. Woakes	England v Sri Lanka at Nottingham	2016
95*	**S. M. Curran**	**England v India at Pune**	**2020-21**
92	N. M. Coulter-Nile	Australia v West Indies at Nottingham	2019
84	T. M. Odoyo	Kenya v Bangladesh at Nairobi (Gymkhana)	2006
83	L. Klusener	South Africa v Australia at Johannesburg	2001-02
83	D. L. Vettori	New Zealand v Australia at Christchurch	2004-05
83	J. D. P. Oram	New Zealand v Bangladesh at Napier	2009-10
80*	**P. W. H. de Silva**	**Sri Lanka v West Indies at North Sound**	**2020-21**
80	T. T. Bresnan	England v Australia at Centurion	2009-10

India

R. G. Sharma b Rashid	37	P. M. Krishna b Wood	0
S. Dhawan c and b Rashid	67	T. Natarajan not out	0
*V. Kohli b Ali	7		
†R. R. Pant c Buttler b Curran	78	Lb 1, w 10	11
K. L. Rahul c Ali b Livingstone	7		
H. H. Pandya b Stokes	64	1/103 (1) 2/117 (2)	(48.2 overs) 329
K. H. Pandya c Roy b Wood	25	3/121 (3) 4/157 (5) 5/256 (4)	
S. N. Thakur c Buttler b Wood	30	6/276 (6) 7/321 (8) 8/328 (7)	
Bhuvneshwar Kumar c Curran b Topley	3	9/329 (10) 10/329 (9)	10 overs: 65-0

Curran 5–0–43–1; Topley 9.2–0–66–1; Wood 7–1–34–3; Stokes 7–0–45–1; Rashid 10–0–81–2; Ali 7–0–39–1; Livingstone 3–0–20–1.

England

J. J. Roy b Bhuvneshwar Kumar	14	A. U. Rashid c Kohli b Thakur	19
J. M. Bairstow lbw b Bhuvneshwar Kumar	1	M. A. Wood run out (Pandya/Pant)	14
B. A. Stokes c Dhawan b Natarajan	35	R. J. W. Topley not out	1
D. J. Malan c Sharma b Thakur	50	Lb 1, w 12	13
*†J. C. Buttler lbw b Thakur	15		
L. S. Livingstone c and b Thakur	36	1/14 (1) 2/28 (2)	(9 wkts, 50 overs) 322
M. M. Ali c H. H. Pandya		3/68 (3) 4/95 (5)	
b Bhuvneshwar Kumar	29	5/155 (6) 6/168 (4) 7/200 (7)	
S. M. Curran not out	95	8/257 (9) 9/317 (10)	10 overs: 66-2

Bhuvneshwar Kumar 10–0–42–3; Natarajan 10–0–73–1; Krishna 7–0–62–0; Thakur 10–0–67–4; H. H. Pandya 9–0–48–0; K. H. Pandya 4–0–29–0.

Umpires: A. K. Chaudhary and N. N. Menon. Third umpire: V. K. Sharma.
Referee: J. Srinath.

ENGLAND v NEW ZEALAND IN 2021

Review by Simon Wilde

Test matches (2): England 0, New Zealand 1

Two-Test series are rarely satisfactory. The better ones tend to leave everyone wanting more; many lack a narrative. In this instance, the storyline was writ large. New Zealand were among the best drilled and most organised teams to visit this country for years, while England were incoherent, disjointed and muddled – more so than in any home series since they fell prey to infighting during South Africa's visit in 2012. It was an unimpressive start for a streamlined management team, operating for the first time since the dismantling of Ed Smith's role as national selector, and the passing of the reins to head coach Chris Silverwood.

The games were a late addition to the schedule, and not part of the World Test Championship. They were designed to boost ECB coffers after the financial losses caused by the pandemic, and capitalise on the public's hunger for live sport. As it turned out, the government were not ready to permit full houses: the First Test at Lord's operated at 25% capacity, although the Second at Edgbaston rose to 70%, since it was designated as a "return to crowds" test event. Spectators had to provide evidence of a recent negative lateral-flow test, and agree to undergo a follow-up PCR test. Even so, this was heady stuff for

Mixed messages: at the start of the First Test, England players and staff state their principles; within hours, the resurrection of old tweets threatens to undermine the campaign.

players and public after the empty terraces of 2020. For the first three days, Edgbaston was at its vibrant best. It was a pity, then, that the home side gave their fans so little to cheer.

For New Zealand, the purpose of the Tests was clear: to win a series in England for the first time since 1999, and to prepare for the World Test Championship final against India. That was scheduled to start four days after Edgbaston, although New Zealand completed a stunning victory at a venue regarded as an English fortress with almost two days to spare. It was England's first home Test-series defeat since Sri Lanka prevailed in 2014, when they won with a ball to spare in Leeds after escaping defeat at Lord's by the skin of their teeth. This time, it was the hosts who wriggled free at Lord's, thanks in part to a third-day washout. Otherwise, New Zealand would probably have won both games, and secured their most decisive result in England in the 90 years since their first Test tour.

England had neither Jofra Archer nor Ben Stokes, both recovering from injury. But they grew obsessed with managing players through a packed schedule so they might peak for the Ashes at the end of the year. The most controversial move was to rest all those involved in the IPL, even though it had been suspended on May 4, four weeks before the Lord's Test, because of the pandemic. While it was true the returnees had to serve a period of quarantine, and fast bowlers need to build up workloads before playing a Test, the approach looked unnecessarily rigid, and was surely self-defeating. Those who might have featured, but did not, were first-choice keeper-batsman Jos Buttler, and Chris Woakes and Sam Curran, potent bowlers in English conditions. Woakes was even asked if he wanted to play the Second Test, at his home ground, but declined. This was a player who had spent much of the winter inside the team bubble without any game-time; offered a chance, he passed it up. Like a few others, he appeared in the Vitality Blast the day the Test finished.

To complicate matters further, two potential replacements for Buttler were ruled out: Jonny Bairstow was part of the IPL group, while Ben Foakes, named in the original squad, slipped in his socks during a county match at The Oval, and tore a hamstring, sidelining him for three months. The upshot was that Gloucestershire's James Bracey, who had spent much of the previous year in the bubble as a batting reserve, made his debut. He had kept wicket in six Championship matches earlier in the season, but only 17 times in all first-class cricket; his inexperience showed in some of his glovework, while his batting was a disaster.

The cricket was only part of England's problems. The players had committed to an anti-discrimination campaign, having undergone pre-season training workshops. But their decision to wear slogan-laden T-shirts before play on the opening day at Lord's backfired when historical racist and sexist tweets by Ollie Robinson, making his debut, resurfaced that afternoon. He performed with commendable focus during the Test – taking seven wickets, and justifying his claim that he knew how to trap Kane Williamson – but was compelled to make a public apology on the first evening; it was clear further action would follow.

England captain Joe Root called the tweets "not acceptable", and said Robinson had made a "huge mistake"; ECB chief executive Tom Harrison said

Gareth Copley, ECB/Getty Images

Debut debacle: James Bracey is bowled by Tim Southee on an unhappy foray into Test cricket.

he did "not have the words to express" his disappointment. After the game, the board suspended Robinson from international cricket while they investigated the matter. When questionable tweets from other England players emerged before the Second Test, the ECB said they would also look at the broader issue of how to deal with historical social-media material. Three weeks later, the Cricket Discipline Commission handed Robinson an eight-match ban, five of which were suspended for two years, and a fine of £3,200. (Since he had already missed three games – one for England, two for Sussex – he was free to play again.) The CDC also recommended he participate in social-media and anti-discrimination training programmes.

New Zealand took their own challenges in their stride. Some of their leading players had also been at the IPL, and most spent time in the Maldives rather than return home, in order to minimise quarantine time. Trent Boult did go back to see his family, and missed the First Test, but joined the tour in time to take the new ball in the Second (and claim six wickets). Everyone quarantined on arrival in the UK, and New Zealand had to make do with intra-squad training at their Rose Bowl base. They shuffled their XI in order to give players match time ahead of the World Test Championship final, and also had to deal with injuries to Williamson, Mitchell Santner and B-J. Watling, on his final tour before retirement. As a result, they made six changes between games – only Neil Wagner was a member of both attacks – and picked more players (17) in a two-Test series than any touring team in history. But the transition appeared seamless, and they pushed on for their first series win in Australia, England, India or South Africa in 21 attempts dating back 22 years.

The Tests were played on pitches less green and more dry than usual for early June, in an attempt by England to hone the art of taking 20 wickets on unhelpful surfaces. If they wanted to make their bowlers work harder, they got their wish, in part because even James Anderson, who had a quiet series, was unable to swing the ball as consistently as the New Zealanders. The overthinking did not stop there. Without Stokes, Woakes or Curran to balance the side, England decided they could not afford the luxury of picking first-choice spinner Jack Leach and, for the first time since 2001 against Pakistan, they eschewed a specialist slow bowler in a home series. New Zealand, by contrast, deployed a spinner in both games, and left-arm Ajaz Patel's four wickets proved crucial at Edgbaston.

The relative experience of the sides was telling. New Zealand contained a large group who had reached cricketing maturity: seven had played over 50 Tests, and Henry Nicholls had 40 by the end of the tour. And in 29-year-old Devon Conway, they found a newcomer ready-made for top-class action. He had learned the game in southern Africa (like Colin de Grandhomme, Wagner and Watling), and played more than 100 times at first-class level.

FIVE STATS YOU MAY HAVE MISSED

BENEDICT BERMANGE

- James Bracey had kept wicket in only 17 first-class matches before the First Test. Just three men had done so in fewer games before keeping for England:

0	L. Hone	v Australia at Melbourne	1878-79
4	R. A. Young	v Australia at Sydney	1907-08
5	O. J. D. Pope	v New Zealand at Hamilton	2019-20
17	**J. R. Bracey**	**v New Zealand at Lord's**	**2021**

Dublin-born Leland Hone had played only two first-class matches before the Australian tour, both for MCC, and made one more appearance for them after the trip.

- At Lord's, Devon Conway became the 12th South African-born man to score a century on Test debut. Six did so for a different country:

K. C. Wessels (162)	Australia v England at Brisbane	1982-83
A. J. Strauss (112)	England v New Zealand at Lord's.............	2004
M. J. Prior (126*).........	England v West Indies at Lord's..............	2007
I. J. L. Trott (119)........	England v Australia at The Oval..............	2009
K. K. Jennings (112)	England v India at Mumbai..................	2016-17
D. P. Conway (200)......	**New Zealand v England at Lord's**..........	**2021**

- Conway was the first to score a double-century on Test debut in England. Only three others had reached 200 in their first Test in England, having made their debut elsewhere:

Zaheer Abbas (274)	Pakistan v England at Birmingham	1971
I. V. A. Richards (232).....	West Indies v England at Nottingham	1976
G. C. Smith (277).........	South Africa v England at Birmingham	2003

- The First Test provided the second instance of an opener from each side batting with the No. 11 in the same match. At Adelaide in 1950-51, Arthur Morris was last out for 206 in Australia's first innings of 371, before Len Hutton carried his bat for 156* in England's first innings of 272.

- Bracey became the fourth wicketkeeper to start his Test career with two ducks. At Manchester in 1912, Tommy Ward of South Africa made a king pair, being the final victim of both leg-spinner Jimmy Matthews's hat-tricks; Ward made another duck in his next innings. The others were Ken James, for New Zealand against England at Christchurch in 1929-30, and Gary Wilson, in his only Test as Ireland's keeper, against England at Lord's in 2019.

Lord's a-leaping: Tim Southee dismisses Ollie Pope – the start of a streak of three for none.

His painstaking double-century on debut at Lord's broke records and English spirits, and set the tone for the tour. By contrast, England possessed three with over 100 Tests – at Edgbaston, Anderson passed Alastair Cook as the country's most-capped player – but no else had more than 25. They were unlucky that a low catch by Zak Crawley early in Conway's first-innings 80 at Edgbaston was ruled not out, though their fielding lacked sharpness. New Zealand caught practically everything.

England's batting attracted severe criticism. Rory Burns scored 132 and 81 in the two first innings, but received little support, and the temperament and technique of the younger guard came under scrutiny. Bracey began with two ducks, while Dan Lawrence also made two, either side of an attractive unbeaten 81; Ollie Pope reached 19 in each of his four innings without passing 23. In private, Root seemed to share the doubts of the former England captains who piled in. Beforehand, he had talked about winning all seven Tests of the summer but, when Williamson set a generous target of 273 in 75 overs at Lord's, Root was content for his side to block for the draw, and take the brickbats that followed.

It all raised the familiar question of whether county cricket was producing Test-class players, although Will Young, who replaced the injured Williamson for the second game (and played the longest innings of the match), had tuned up with two Championship centuries for Durham. England's collective batting average of 24 was their lowest in a home series of more than one match since 2000. While New Zealand headed for glory on the south coast, the direction of Root's side was less clear.

NEW ZEALAND TOURING PARTY

*K. S. Williamson, T. A. Blundell, T. A. Boult, D. A. J. Bracewell, D. P. Conway, C. de Grandhomme, J. A. Duffy, M. J. Henry, K. A. Jamieson, T. W. M. Latham, D. J. Mitchell, H. M. Nicholls, A. Y. Patel, R. Ravindra, M. J. Santner, T. G. Southee, L. R. P. L. Taylor, N. Wagner, B-J. Watling, W. A. Young.

Head coach: G. R. Stead. *Batting coach:* L. Ronchi. *Bowling coach:* S. J. Jurgensen. *Assistant coach:* H. Malan. *Doctor:* J. Cameron. *Trainer:* C. Donaldson. *Physiotherapists:* T. Simsek, V. Vallabh. *Manager:* M. Sandle. *Logistics manager:* R. Muller. *Media officers:* B. Mackey, W. Nicholls.

ENGLAND v NEW ZEALAND

First LV= Insurance Test

ANDY BULL

At Lord's, June 2–6. Drawn. Toss: New Zealand. Test debuts: J. R. Bracey, O. E. Robinson; D. P. Conway.

This should have been one of the summer's great events. It wasn't just the first Test, but the first at Lord's for nearly two years, and the first in front of a crowd anywhere in England for almost as long. After 15 gruelling months of on–off lockdown, the opening morning felt bright with sunshine and promise. Despite the face masks, one-way systems and social-distancing rules which limited daily attendance to around 6,500, Lord's provided familiar comforts. The place thrummed with delight, and even the oldest members seemed giddy with excitement. It did not last the week.

By stumps on Sunday, the end of the game came almost as a relief, not simply because it washed up in a stultifying draw, but because the match had been overshadowed by a crisis caused by a series of abusive tweets posted in 2012 and 2013 by one of England's debutants, Ollie Robinson. On the fifth evening, the ECB announced they were suspending him from international cricket pending an investigation, but the incident became a flashpoint in a broader culture war. Next morning, Oliver Dowden, secretary of state for digital, culture, media and sport, described the ECB's decision as "over the top"; he was soon supported by the prime minister, Boris Johnson.

Debut double: Devon Conway, in his first Test, reaches a hundred (left), then presses on.

OLLIE ROBINSON'S STATEMENT

"My actions were inexcusable"

On the biggest day of my career so far, I am embarrassed by the racist and sexist tweets that I posted over eight years ago, which have today become public. I want to make it clear that I'm not racist and I'm not sexist.

I deeply regret my actions, and I am ashamed of making such remarks. I was thoughtless and irresponsible, and regardless of my state of mind at the time, my actions were inexcusable. Since that period, I have matured as a person and fully regret the tweets.

Today should be about my efforts on the field, and the pride of making my Test debut for England, but my thoughtless behaviour in the past has tarnished this.

Over the past few years, I have worked hard to turn my life around. I have considerably matured as an adult. The work and education I have gained personally from the PCA, my county Sussex and the England cricket team have helped me to come to terms with, and gain a deep understanding of, being a responsible professional cricketer.

I would like to unreservedly apologise to anyone I have offended, my team-mates and the game as a whole in what has been a day of action and awareness in combating discrimination from our sport.

I don't want something that happened eight years ago to diminish the efforts of my team-mates and the ECB as they continue to build meaningful action with their comprehensive initiatives and efforts, which I fully endorse and support.

I will continue to educate myself, look for advice and work with the support network that is available to me to learn more about getting better in this area. I am sorry, and I have certainly learned my lesson today.

The tweets had come to light midway through the first day, when Robinson had embarked on one of the more successful, and controversial, debuts in recent history. Without a group of players who had not long returned from the postponed IPL, England had picked Robinson, whose performances for Sussex over the previous four seasons had made him one of county cricket's leading bowlers, and Gloucestershire's James Bracey, handed the gloves after Ben Foakes tore a hamstring slipping in the Oval dressing-room.

They also chose one of the youngest batting line-ups in their history, alongside one of their older bowling attacks. Robinson, at 27, was the junior member, but outbowled Anderson and Broad. He dismissed Latham, playing on, in his first spell, and Taylor, leg-before, in his second. By then his tweets, written in his late teens, were circulating on social media, apparently dug up by a journalism student after a hint dropped by an Australian blogger. The ECB should have been so diligent.

Hours earlier, Robinson and his team-mates had lined up in front of the Pavilion before play for what was described as "a moment of unity". They wore black T-shirts with "Cricket is a Game for Everyone" on the front, and "We Stand Together Against" every conceivable variety of discrimination on the back: racism, religious intolerance, sexism, transphobia, homophobia, ableism, ageism. It was well meant, part of a campaign to make amends for old offences, and to open the sport up to new audiences, but it all looked facile now. Robinson had no idea about the unfolding scandal until the close, which meant many spectators knew more about the story than he did, and had the uncomfortable experience of watching him revel in his first day of Test cricket.

England's head coach, Chris Silverwood, and captain, Root, told Robinson as soon as play was over. By Silverwood's account, Robinson immediately gave a full and sincere apology to his team-mates, which he expanded on during a TV interview and press conference. He spoke of his regret and shame. He explained how immature he had been

DOUBLE-HUNDRED ON TEST DEBUT

287	R. E. Foster	England v Australia at Sydney	1903-04
222*	J. A. Rudolph	South Africa v Bangladesh at Chittagong	2003
214	L. G. Rowe	West Indies v New Zealand at Kingston	1971-72
214	M. S. Sinclair	New Zealand v West Indies at Wellington	1999-2000
210*	**K. R. Mayers**	**West Indies v Bangladesh at Chittagong**	**2020-21**
201*	D. S. B. P. Kuruppu	Sri Lanka v New Zealand at Colombo (CCC)	1986-87
200	**D. P. Conway**	**New Zealand v England at Lord's**	**2021**

when he made the remarks, but didn't try to excuse them. He had his say. Now everyone else had theirs, in print, and on radio, TV and Twitter. Those on either side of a social, political and cultural divide used the story for their own ends. Some said they would give up on cricket if Robinson were allowed to play again; others insisted they would do the same if he faced any sort of punishment.

Out in the middle, New Zealand were trying to win a Test. They had picked a debutant of their own, Devon Conway, who had a different kind of past. Now 29, he had been born and raised in South Africa, and made his first-class debut for Gauteng in 2008-09. Good judges thought him one of the country's brightest prospects. Ray White, former president of the South African board, said: "If he is not a future star of international cricket, something will have gone seriously wrong." White was right, in the end, if perhaps not as he envisaged. For the next eight years, Conway knocked around the outskirts of the professional game – franchise and provincial cricket in South Africa, league and county Second XI cricket in England. It was only after he sold his house and car, and moved to New Zealand in 2017, that he made good on his promise.

Now, he batted with quiet competence and unobtrusive authority, the equal of everything England tried, including a ferocious spell from Wood, who hit him twice. A left-hander,

English International Cricket

Look back in anguish: Tom Latham is undone by Ollie Robinson, who by the end of the day also has cause to regret his actions.

Conway raised his fifty with a drive through extra cover off Broad, and his century with a whip over square leg off Robinson. Nicholls was a steady second fiddle. At stumps, Conway had more runs (136) on his first day of Test cricket than anyone since 1983-84, when Australia's Wayne Phillips smacked 159 against Pakistan at Perth.

Wood and Robinson dovetailed well on the second morning: from 288 for three, they collected four for six in 52 balls. If anything, Robinson bowled even better than the previous day; he would have had a fifth wicket, and a place on the honours board, had Broad caught Southee at mid-off. The crowd applauded before each spell, and after each wicket. Even that show of support made some uncomfortable: earlier in the week, the England football team had been booed for taking a knee before a friendly against Austria.

Conway pressed on. He had already ticked off the highest score by a Test debutant at Lord's (beating Sourav Ganguly's 131 for India in 1996). Now he went past K. S. Ranjitsinhji's unbeaten 154, against Australia at Manchester in 1896, to record the highest by a debutant in England. New Zealand's last man, Wagner, was in when he reached 200 by pulling Wood for his only six. Next over, he was run out by the barest of margins, having dominated a total of 378. After waiting so long for his opportunity, Conway had batted as though he knew how precious it was, for 578 minutes in all. (Only Sri Lanka's Brendon Kuruppu had managed longer on Test debut: 777 minutes against New Zealand in Colombo in 1986-87.)

His attitude felt all the more conspicuous when England batted, and Crawley became the first to give away his wicket, aiming a loose drive at Southee. As Root said later, the innings included "a number of dismissals that weren't good enough for Test cricket". The demise of Lawrence, who fiddled Southee to third slip, was another.

Those mishaps came either side of a Friday washout, which made the match a race against time. On Saturday, England resumed on 111 for two, but Root fell first ball that morning, to Jamieson, and the game lurched forward again. Southee bowled artfully from the Pavilion End, and took three wickets in successive overs as 140 for three became 140 for six. When Bracey was clean bowled by one that came back up the slope, England were

HIGHEST PERCENTAGE OF ALL-OUT TOTAL ON TEST DEBUT

67.34	C. Bannerman (165*/245)	Australia v England at Melbourne	1876-77
55.69	P. F. Warner (132*/237)	England v South Africa at Johannesburg	1898-99
55.61	A. B. Barath (104/187)	West Indies v Australia at Brisbane	2009-10
52.91	**D. P. Conway (200/378)**	**New Zealand v England at Lord's**	**2021**
52.50	Fawad Alam (168/320)	Pakistan v Sri Lanka at Colombo (PSO)	2009
50.59	Javed Omar (85*/168)	Bangladesh v Zimbabwe at Bulawayo	2000-01
50.49	K. S. Ranjitsinhji (154*/305)	England v Australia at Manchester	1896

Bannerman's percentage, in the first Test of all, remains the record for any completed innings.

39 short of avoiding the follow-on. But Burns and Robinson rallied in a 63-run partnership. Burns was dogged: his second fifty took 177 balls, though he raced through the nineties in just seven, because he was running out of partners. His third Test century in the bag, he walloped another 32 from his final 30, including his first six in Tests, a slog-sweep off an incredulous Wagner, and was last out after a tenth-wicket stand of 52 with Anderson. Southee finished with six for 43, his best Test figures since 2012 – and New Zealand's best at Lord's, beating his own six for 50 in 2013. They led by 103.

England bowled well in the third innings, and Robinson – putting his off-field troubles to one side – especially so during a spell of 9–4–8–2 on the fourth evening. But New Zealand were in control. Next morning, which included Broad's first Test wicket in 488 balls, rain meant a slightly early lunch, and Williamson declared, setting 273 in 75 overs.

It was bold captaincy, but England had other ideas. To the despair of their more romantic supporters, they chose to bat out the day, just to show they could. Sibley made a particularly gritty 60 from 207 balls. There have been plenty of times when many would have been delighted to see him play that way. This wasn't one of them, and there were ironic cheers when the England fifty came up in the 27th over. Crawley fell cheaply again, and New Zealand pressed on long into the last hour, as Wagner tried to flog life into a game everyone else thought dead. Cricket featured prominently on the evening news, but not because of the result. For the English, a match that started with such sweet promise left a rather sour taste.

Player of the Match: D. P. Conway.   *Attendance:* 32,500.

Close of play: first day, New Zealand 246-3 (Conway 136, Nicholls 46); second day, England 111-2 (Burns 59, Root 42); third day, no play; fourth day, New Zealand 62-2 (Latham 30, Wagner 2).

New Zealand

T. W. M. Latham b Robinson	23	– lbw b Broad	36
D. P. Conway run out (Pope/Root)	200	– b Robinson	23
*K. S. Williamson b Anderson	13	– lbw b Robinson	1
L. R. P. L. Taylor lbw b Robinson	14	– (5) c Bracey b Wood	33
H. M. Nicholls c Robinson b Wood	61	– (6) c Burns b Root	23
†B-J. Watling c Sibley b Wood	1	– (7) not out	15
C. de Grandhomme lbw b Robinson	0	– (8) not out	9
M. J. Santner c Anderson b Wood	0		
K. A. Jamieson c Crawley b Robinson	9		
T. G. Southee c Bracey b Anderson	8		
N. Wagner not out	25	– (4) c Bracey b Robinson	10
B 7, lb 15, nb 2	24	B 6, lb 12, nb 1	19

1/58 (1) 2/86 (3) 3/114 (4)   (122.4 overs) 378   1/39 (2)   (6 wkts dec, 52.3 overs) 169
4/288 (5) 5/292 (6) 6/293 (7)   2/57 (3) 3/74 (4)
7/294 (8) 8/317 (9) 9/338 (10) 10/378 (2)   4/105 (1) 5/133 (5) 6/159 (6)

Anderson 28–7–83–2; Broad 27.5–79–0; Robinson 28–6–75–4; Wood 27–8–81–3; Root 12.4–1–38–0. *Second innings*—Anderson 15.3–3–44–0; Broad 12–1–34–1; Robinson 14–5–26–3; Wood 7–0–31–1; Root 4–0–16–1.

England

R. J. Burns c Watling b Southee	132	– c Southee b Wagner	25
D. P. Sibley lbw b Jamieson	0	– not out	60
Z. Crawley c Watling b Southee	2	– c Nicholls b Southee	2
*J. E. Root c Taylor b Jamieson	42	– lbw b Wagner	40
O. J. D. Pope lbw b Southee	22	– not out	20
D. W. Lawrence c de Grandhomme b Southee	0		
†J. R. Bracey b Southee	0		
O. E. Robinson c Jamieson b Southee	42		
M. A. Wood c Watling b Jamieson	0		
S. C. J. Broad b Wagner	10		
J. M. Anderson not out	8		
B 4, lb 4, w 1, nb 8	17	B 8, lb 10, nb 5	23

1/4 (2) 2/18 (3) 3/111 (4)   (101.1 overs) 275   1/49 (1)   (3 wkts, 70 overs) 170
4/140 (5) 5/140 (6) 6/140 (7)   2/56 (3) 3/136 (4)
7/203 (8) 8/207 (9) 9/223 (10) 10/275 (1)

Southee 25.1–8–43–6; Jamieson 26–8–85–3; de Grandhomme 15–5–24–0; Wagner 24–3–83–1; Santner 10–4–30–0; Williamson 1–0–2–0. *Second innings*—Southee 17–1–37–1; Jamieson 15–6–28–0; de Grandhomme 7–3–12–0; Santner 13–3–38–0; Wagner 16–7–27–2; Williamson 2–0–10–0.

Umpires: M. A. Gough and R. A. Kettleborough.   Third umpire: R. K. Illingworth.
Referee: B. C. Broad.

ENGLAND v NEW ZEALAND

Second LV= Insurance Test

Phil Walker

At Birmingham, June 10–13. New Zealand won by eight wickets. Toss: England.

Against a backdrop of cheery renewal and fanfare, England surrendered their home record in a defeat utterly out of step with a raucous Edgbaston. Only on the third evening, when the chorus had run short of songs to shroud the home side's ineptitude, the beer snakes had slithered under the Hollies Stand, and the nuns, Lionhearts and WGs had begun to feel sticky under all their clobber, did the crowd fall quiet.

With 18,000 spectators, though no under-16s, allowed each day – 70% of capacity – a certain feverishness was always likely to accompany this trial event, among the first of its kind in the UK. Reminders of Covid-19 were hard to avoid. Volunteers dispensed lateral-flow test kits at New Street station, while Edgbaston rolled out a new smartphone app, featuring mobile ticketing, a queue time-checker, and a click-and-collect option for food and drink (during the game, the app received 314,344 views). The media box, meanwhile, was an empty shell, many of its regulars forced to isolate after being pinged by the NHS app at Lord's.

It was comforting then, amid the strangeness, that this new version of an old ceremony should be soundtracked by sweaty revivals of the Barmy Army's back catalogue – beery splurges of optimism given fresh juice by a sense of communion between the watched and the watchers which has rarely felt so essential, and at times moving, as it did here.

Twenty minutes before tea on the third day, they were still singing. England were hanging in – 85 behind on first innings, but with hopes of setting a target. Barely two hours later

As you were: Edgbaston welcomes back spectators, who busy themselves with traditional tasks. Will Young, meanwhile, makes a decent fist of standing in for Kane Williamson.

they were effectively done, with Root the last recognised batsman to go, making it 76 for seven. His 61-ball 11 was as doleful an innings as he has played for his country, and he traipsed out of Birmingham averaging 32 in home Tests since the start of 2018.

Survival to the close, nine down, merely triggered a mood of sarky resignation next morning: those who did turn up were reduced to laughter when Boult bounced out Stone with the first ball of the day, leaving New Zealand 38 to win. The crowd, such as they were, did at least have the option to watch another sport that afternoon, after Edgbaston chiefs, desperate for trade, agreed to show England's first match of the European football championship on the big screen. It felt apt. We had come to Birmingham to celebrate the return of sport, to glory in the resumption of frivolities; just as one game folded, another rolled around.

Indeed an awkward truth about this series, totalling seven and a bit days of cricket, was its comparative absence of tension or jeopardy. New Zealand, keeping their stocks fresh for a bigger Test to come, made six changes from Lord's, but maintained their quality; by contrast, England's timidity on that dreary final day there seeped into their work here.

They had actually started well, as Burns and Sibley became their first opening pair for almost a decade to reach lunch unscathed on the first day of a home Test. Sibley's quixotic stylings were in full evidence, though he accessed the off-side boundary a couple of times; Burns, following a hundred at Lord's, looked fluent. He is an oompah band of an opening batsman, with plenty going on, but when it clicks, there is a crispness to his strokeplay. Throughout the series, he also showed a new willingness to go on the pull and the hook.

That England, 67 without loss at lunch on a flat pitch, should stumble to the close seven down spoke not just of their fleshy underbelly, but of the relentless probing of New Zealand's enviably deep seam attack. With Kyle Jamieson and Tim Southee rested ahead of the World Test Championship final against India, they brought in Boult, newly available after quarantine, and Henry, a fine limited-overs quick (and a favourite at Kent) who had never come close to cracking Test cricket. It told its own story that he would be Player of the Match.

The top order fell in a heap after lunch. Wagner bowled full and fast, and got the crowd onside. Henry kept coming in hard. Boult, feeling his way back, flung down the occasional booming inducker. Mitchell was watertight with the ageing ball, and the left-arm spinner Patel nipped in to claim the wicket of Pope, frantically searching for composure. His edged cut brought Lawrence to the crease, and a skittish start gave way to a series of mini-marvels, the first punched through extra cover off the back foot, his body darting well wide of leg stump to make the angle. He is compulsively watchable.

After cruising to 81, Burns threw his hands at Boult, and nicked to Latham. This New Zealand side rarely drop slip catches: since the start of 2019, they had snaffled 91% of catchable edges (England had grassed one chance in four). Bracey followed a debut duck at Lord's with a first-baller, driving wildly at Boult, then slumping on his bat handle. But Lawrence enjoyed the new ball in the evening sunshine, and resumed next morning on 67. Wood, though, was the more inclined to have a whack, dominating a stand of 66. Lawrence, after a brace of lofted off-drives, ran out of partners – Anderson became Boult's 500th international victim – and strolled off with 81 to his name.

For much of the second day, Conway seemed assured of becoming the first to score a double and single century in his first two Tests (West Indies' Lawrence Rowe, in 1971-72, did both on debut). From an open-chested stance, he produced a technical clinic against

STARTING ENGLAND TEST CAREER WITH TWO DUCKS

G. F. Grace	v Australia at The Oval	1880
C. I. J. Smith	v West Indies at Bridgetown	1934-35
D. B. Close	v NZ at Manchester, v Australia at Melbourne . .	1949 to 1950-51
D. R. Smith	v India at Kanpur and Calcutta	1961-62
D. W. White	v Pakistan at Lahore and Karachi	1961-62
G. A. Gooch	v Australia at Birmingham	1975
G. M. Hamilton	v South Africa at Johannesburg	1999-2000
C. T. Tremlett	v India at Lord's	2007
J. R. Bracey	**v New Zealand at Lord's and Birmingham** . . .	**2021**

Grace and Hamilton were playing their only Tests; White never batted again.

pace, leaving on length, playing late, helping himself to a flurry of minimalist square-drives in Wood's first over, and rocking back to swivel-pull. Balls on the stumps were guided straight of midwicket; anything wide was ignored.

His control of mind and method was near-absolute. He had one scare, edging Broad to Crawley at third slip on 22. England claimed the catch but, after a soft signal of not out from Richard Kettleborough, his TV colleague Michael Gough agreed. Replays were inconclusive; Broad and Crawley were ticking, Conway unmoved. For a player with such a studied method, it was ironic that a one-day shot – on 80, he flicked a half-volley straight to deep backward square – should be his downfall. The wicket was Broad's 520th in Tests, one clear of Courtney Walsh; only five bowlers had more.

This was a game of inconclusive eighties. Previously, no more than two players in any Test had scored between 80 and 82. In this match, there were five. The last two played contrasting innings, at contrasting points in their careers. Young, in as cover for Kane Williamson, who was resting a troublesome elbow, survived a bad drop on seven by Root at slip off Stone, who had replaced Ollie Robinson. But he grafted his way to the final over of the second day, when he succumbed to the gangly trickery of Lawrence's occasional

Hooray, Henry: Zak Crawley is the third of Matt Henry's three second-innings wickets.

off-breaks. Next morning, after top-edging – and surviving – a relatively easy chance to substitute fielder Sam Billings on 68, Taylor got to 82, when Stone had him caught behind. For Bracey, mobbed by relieved team-mates, it was the briefest of respites: moments later, he put down Blundell before he had scored.

And so to England's fall. Henry roared in to claim the first three, including Burns second ball, and Crawley, who now had 123 runs in 12 Test innings since his 267 against Pakistan the previous summer. Wagner swerved a killer into Pope's pads, and got Lawrence prodding minutes later. Bracey, having avoided a third duck, was bowled round his legs trying to sweep Patel, as Root watched aghast. When Root edged a cut, also off Patel, the top seven were in tatters – and so was England's unbeaten home series record, dating back to 2014. Their 122 was their lowest at home against New Zealand, beneath the 126 they made here in 1999.

On the outfield after the massacre, Nasser Hussain took a deep breath, before launching into England's technical issues. "There seems to be a reinvention of the wheel out there with batting," he said. "It seems that everyone who has played the game before is wrong, and we are right. Viv Richards, you were wrong! Everyone else, you were wrong! And we are right! Because I'm not seeing 'We are right' at the moment. Please just get back to playing normally." For inspiration, Hussain pointed to the other dressing-room.

New Zealand didn't milk their first series win in England in 22 years. The celebrations were muted, the trophy-hoisting vaguely apologetic. No triumphalism, no histrionics. There was, after all, a game to play in a few days – a rather important one, for a quietly majestic team.

Player of the Match: M. J. Henry.   *Attendance:* 60,032.

Players of the Series: England – R. J. Burns; New Zealand – D. P. Conway.

Close of play: first day, England 258-7 (Lawrence 67, Wood 16); second day, New Zealand 229-3 (Taylor 46); third day, England 122-9 (Stone 15, Anderson 0).

England

R. J. Burns c Latham b Boult	81	– c Latham b Henry	0
D. P. Sibley c Blundell b Henry	35	– c Mitchell b Henry	8
Z. Crawley c Mitchell b Wagner	0	– lbw b Henry	17
*J. E. Root c Blundell b Henry	4	– c Blundell b Patel	11
O. J. D. Pope c Blundell b Patel	19	– lbw b Wagner	23
D. W. Lawrence not out	81	– c Blundell b Wagner	0
†J. R. Bracey c Mitchell b Boult	0	– b Patel	8
O. P. Stone lbw b Patel	20	– c Blundell b Boult	15
M. A. Wood b Henry	41	– c Blundell b Wagner	29
S. C. J. Broad c Blundell b Boult	0	– b Boult	1
J. M. Anderson lbw b Boult	4	– not out	0
B 5, lb 10, w 1, nb 2	18	B 5, lb 4, nb 1	10

1/72 (2) 2/73 (3) 3/85 (4)   (101 overs) 303   1/0 (1) 2/17 (2)   (41.1 overs) 122
4/127 (5) 5/169 (1) 6/175 (7)   3/30 (3) 4/58 (5)
7/222 (8) 8/288 (9) 9/289 (10) 10/303 (11)   5/58 (6) 6/71 (7) 7/76 (4)
                                                        8/120 (9) 9/121 (10) 10/122 (8)

Boult 29–6–85–4; Henry 26–7–78–3; Wagner 21–6–68–1; Mitchell 11–2–23–0; Patel 14–4–34–2. *Second innings*—Henry 12–2–36–3; Boult 10.1–2–34–2; Wagner 10–1–18–3; Patel 9–4–25–2.

New Zealand

*T. W. M. Latham lbw b Broad	6	– not out	23
D. P. Conway c Crawley b Broad	80	– c Bracey b Broad	3
W. A. Young c Pope b Lawrence	82	– b Stone	8
L. R. P. L. Taylor c Bracey b Stone	80	– not out	0
H. M. Nicholls c Bracey b Wood	21		
†T. A. Blundell c Root b Wood	34		
D. J. Mitchell c Crawley b Stone	6		
N. Wagner b Anderson	0		
M. J. Henry lbw b Wood	12		
A. Y. Patel lbw b Broad	20		
T. A. Boult not out	12		
B 13, lb 21, nb 1	35	B 4, w 1, nb 2	7

1/15 (1) 2/137 (2) 3/229 (3)   (119.1 overs) 388   1/6 (2)   (2 wkts, 10.5 overs) 41
4/292 (4) 5/312 (5) 6/335 (7)   2/33 (3)
7/336 (8) 8/353 (9) 9/361 (6) 10/388 (10)

Anderson 29–9–68–1; Broad 23.1–8–48–4; Wood 25–3–85–2; Stone 24–5–92–2; Root 15–3–45–0; Lawrence 3–0–16–1. *Second innings*—Anderson 5–1–11–0; Broad 4–1–13–1; Stone 1–0–5–1; Wood 0.5–0–8–0.

Umpires: R. K. Illingworth and R. A. Kettleborough.   Third umpire: M. A. Gough.
Referee: B. C. Broad.

For the World Test Championship final, see page 823.

ENGLAND v SRI LANKA IN 2021

WILL MACPHERSON

Twenty20 internationals (3): England 3, Sri Lanka 0
One-day internationals (3): England 2 (25pts), Sri Lanka 0 (5pts)

From long before they arrived to well after they left, Sri Lanka endured a horrible few weeks. Problems began with a pay dispute that reached a partial solution just a couple of days before they flew to London. They were then whitewashed in the three T20s in the space of four days, and had a sniff only in the second match, when England threatened to fluff their lines in a rain-affected chase. They lost the one-day internationals, too, and were spared another 3–0 defeat only by more rain in Bristol. That worsened their position in the ODI Super League, harming their chances of automatic qualification for the 2023 World Cup.

As if all that were not enough, the Sri Lankans sent home three players – vice-captain Kusal Mendis, Niroshan Dickwella and Dhanushka Gunathilleke – for breaching biosecurity conditions, after footage emerged of them out late in Durham, then a hotbed of Covid-19. They were later handed one-year bans. And when the rest of the touring party arrived home, the ECB passed on the news that seven members of their own dressing-room had just tested positive. There had been some mingling between the teams; soon, Grant Flower, Sri Lanka's batting coach, and G. G. T. Niroshan, their analyst, returned positive tests too. As a result, their two white-ball series at home against India were put back by five days.

Ramping up: Liam Livingstone marches on at Southampton.

Harry Trump, Getty Images

Top of the crops: Wanindu Hasaranga de Silva was the sole Sri Lankan highlight.

Ian Kington, AFP/Getty Images

England had treated their visitors – who had beaten them in their most recent white-ball meeting, at the 2019 World Cup – with respect. Their much-discussed rest and rotation policy, which had weakened them for the Tests against New Zealand, now left them with a strong side, a strength some argued was wasted on their opponents. Of the big-ticket players, Jofra Archer was still recovering from elbow trouble, and Ben Stokes up at Durham, returning from injury; Jos Buttler, meanwhile, picked up a calf strain after one match, having sat out five Tests. Even so, England fielded fearsome combinations.

But they did not get the examination they desired ahead of autumn's T20 World Cup, which – it was confirmed shortly after these 20-over games ended – would be moved from India to the Gulf because of the Covid crisis. Sri Lanka were outclassed, and competitive only for fleeting periods, almost exclusively with the ball: four overs for 12 from leg-spinner Wanindu Hasaranga de Silva in the first match; England's stumble to 36 for four in the second; and, unsettled by Dushmantha Chameera, another stumble in the third, from 143 for one to 162 for six. In each case, it was too little, too late, mainly because Sri Lanka's batting was so awful. They managed 129 for seven, 111 for seven and 91 (and later made 200 only once in the ODIs). Only Dasun Shanaka passed 40, while the three matches brought them a combined total of just 15 fours and eight sixes.

Any experimentation by England involved looking back. Chris Woakes, who had not played a T20 international since November 2015, returned after missing 19 matches in all formats for a variety of reasons, while David Willey played his first T20 international for over two years. Both did well: Woakes bowled seven overs for 23, and Willey collected three wickets in eight. But Moeen Ali, after sitting out ten T20s, had to wait until the third match to get a go; he batted at No. 6, and bowled five balls.

England preferred Liam Livingstone as their spin-bowling all-rounder, and he thrived. He was tricky to get away, often bowling off-breaks to the left-handers and leg-breaks to the right-handers. In the second match, his unbeaten 29 guided them to victory either side of a rain break. He did not fire when promoted to No. 3 in the third, but his all-round versatility, plus a bullet arm in the deep, made for an alluring package.

It seemed slightly odd that, when others were injured or rested (Jason Roy sat out the third game), England asked first-choice players – such as

Jonny Bairstow and Dawid Malan – to open, rather than try their hand at more challenging roles in the middle order. Even this paid off, however, when they added 105 – a return to form for Malan, who remained top of the T20 batting rankings.

The ODIs followed a similar pattern, which did not provide much entertainment for the larger crowds allowed in as part of government trials for the return of spectators to live events. And at Bristol, they had to endure the additional disappointment of losing half the match to the weather. By now, Sri Lanka were fatally undermanned after the bio-breach in Durham. England, on the other hand, welcomed back Joe Root, who marshalled their run-chases in the first two games, while Woakes, Willey (Player of the Series) and Sam Curran were in fine fettle again. England kept winning the toss, and all but settling the outcome inside the powerplay, taking three wickets in the first game, and four in both the second and third.

Yet, in the shadow of the national football team's run to the European championship final, an entertaining Wimbledon, and the early days of a chaotic British and Irish Lions rugby tour of South Africa, rarely had an England men's cricket team playing in high summer slipped under the radar.

SRI LANKAN TOURING TEAM

*M. D. K. J. Perera, K. I. C. Asalanka, P. V. D. Chameera, A. Dananjaya, D. M. de Silva, P. W. H. de Silva, D. P. D. N. Dickwella, A. M. Fernando, A. N. P. R. Fernando, B. O. P. Fernando, K. B. U. Fernando, S. A. Fernando, W. I. A. Fernando, M. D. Gunathilleke, H. I. A. Jayaratne, P. A. K. P. Jayawickrama, C. Karunaratne, P. A. D. Lakshan, B. K. G. Mendis, P. Nissanka, P. A. D. L. R. Sandakan, M. D. Shanaka, I. Udana, R. T. M. Wanigamuni.

Dickwella, Gunathilleke and Mendis were sent home for breaching biosecure protocols in Durham before the first ODI.

Coach: J. M. Arthur. *Director:* T. M. Moody. *Manager:* M. Kariyapperuma. *Selector:* R. S. Kaluwitharana. *Batting coach:* G. W. Flower. *Bowling coach:* W. P. U. J. C. Vaas. *Support coach:* M. K. Abeywickrama. *Trainer:* D. C. Fonseka. *Physiotherapist:* B. D. Harrop. *Doctor:* K. D. Dewapriya. *Masseur:* R. P. Wijeweera. *Analyst:* G. G. T. Niroshan.

ENGLAND v SRI LANKA

First Twenty20 International

At Cardiff, June 23 (floodlit). England won by eight wickets. Toss: Sri Lanka.

For England, this was a cruise – and a taste of things to come. After opting to bat, Sri Lanka limped to 129 for seven, and even that needed Shanaka to scramble 25 from the final two overs. They had been unsettled by Wood's pace, and stifled by spin: between them, Livingstone – switching between off- and leg-breaks – and Rashid did not concede a boundary in six overs, while there were just ten in all, of which Shanaka managed five. Sri Lanka also had the unhappy knack of picking out Jordan, the safest hands in the land. Roy and Buttler matched their boundary tally by the end of the powerplay, and took a controlled, clinical stand to 80 in nine overs, all but finishing the game as a contest. Roy, the aggressor, was well caught at mid-off, before Udana's nibble ended an uncomfortable innings from Malan. But Buttler forged ahead, reaching his 13th half-century in the format, while showing respect to Hasaranga de Silva, whose four boundary-free overs contained 14 dots. Even so, the hosts ambled home with 17 balls to spare. Sue Redfern, the reserve umpire, became the first woman to officiate in an England men's home international.

Player of the Match: J. C. Buttler.

Sri Lanka

			B	4/6
1 M. D. Gunathilleke c 2 b 8		19	16	3
2 W. I. A. Fernando c 8 b 7		0	4	0
3 *†M. D. K. J. Perera c 8 b 10		30	26	1/1
4 B. K. G. Mendis lbw b 6		9	12	0
5 D. M. de Silva c 10 b 11		3	4	0
6 M. D. Shanaka c 2 b 7		50	44	3/2
7 P. W. H. de Silva c 8 b 10		5	7	0
8 I. Udana not out		6	7	0
Lb 2, w 5		7		

6 overs: 39-2   (20 overs) 129-7

1/3 2/31 3/49 4/52 5/79 6/96 7/129

9 A. Dananjaya, 10 P. V. D. Chameera and 11 A. N. P. R. Fernando did not bat.

Woakes 18–11–14–0; Curran 18–6–25–2; Wood 24–10–33–1; Jordan 24–7–29–1; Livingstone 12–4–9–1; Rashid 24–9–17–2.

England

			B	4/6
1 J. J. Roy c 1 b 10		36	22	4/1
2 †J. C. Buttler not out		68	55	8/1
3 D. J. Malan b 8		7	14	0
4 J. M. Bairstow not out		13	12	1/1
Lb 1, w 5		6		

6 overs: 61-0   (17.1 overs) 130-2

1/80 2/112

5 *E. J. G. Morgan, 6 L. S. Livingstone, 7 S. M. Curran, 8 C. J. Jordan, 9 C. R. Woakes, 10 A. U. Rashid and 11 M. A. Wood did not bat.

Chameera 19–9–24–1; A. N. P. R. Fernando 12–3–23–0; Dananjaya 24–6–40–0; Udana 24–8–30–1; P. W. H. de Silva 24–14–12–0.

Umpires: D. J. Millns and M. J. Saggers.   Third umpire: M. Burns.
Referee: P. Whitticase.

ENGLAND v SRI LANKA

Second Twenty20 International

At Cardiff, June 24 (floodlit). England won by five wickets (DLS). Toss: Sri Lanka.

A rare appearance for England outside Sky's paywall was broadcast on BBC2, but was not the sort of game to draw in a new audience. Things got off to a bad start when it emerged that Buttler had torn a calf muscle in the first game. Then, on the same tired pitch, Sri Lanka's batsmen put on an even wearier performance, scraping together 111 for seven. It took them 46 balls to register a boundary: never before in their 133 T20s had they failed to score one in the powerplay, while England had never failed to concede one in *their* 133. In all, only Mendis and Udana reached the rope. Sam Curran had sparked the collapse with a neat side-footed run-out, before Rashid and Wood reasserted their grip. But England's top order were not much better: when Roy picked out long-on, it was 36 for four. Billings and Livingstone regrouped and, when rain fell, England were 69 for four from 12, just ahead on DLS. Nearly 40 minutes, but only two overs, were lost, which left them needing a further 34 off six. Livingstone ramped Chameera for six, before Billings was bowled by one that kept low from Hasaranga de Silva, but Curran sealed the series with a straight six.

Player of the Match: L. S. Livingstone.

Sri Lanka

		B	4/6
1 M. D. Gunathilleke *run out (7)* .	3	4	0
2 W. I. A. Fernando *c 6 b 7*......	6	10	0
3 *M. D. K. J. Perera *c 4 b 10*....	21	25	0
4 B. K. G. Mendis *c 2 b 11*......	39	39	3/1
5 †D. P. D. N. Dickwella *c 4 b 11*	3	3	0
6 M. D. Shanaka *c 8 b 9*........	8	14	0
7 P. W. H. de Silva *st 2 b 10*.....	3	7	0
8 I. Udana *not out*...........	19	14	1/1
9 A. Dananjaya *not out*.........	2	4	0
Lb 3, w 4.................	7		

6 overs: 26-2   (20 overs) 111-7

1/6 2/18 3/68 4/76 5/76 6/87 7/90

10 K. B. U. Fernando and 11 P. V. D. Chameera
did not bat.

Willey 24–12–17–0; Curran 12–6–8–1; Jordan
24–11–31–1; Livingstone 12–6–10–0; Wood
24–12–18–2; Rashid 24–5–24–2.

England

		B	4/6
1 J. J. Roy *c 6 b 7*	17	17	2
2 †J. M. Bairstow *b 10*	0	3	0
3 D. J. Malan *lbw b 11*	4	5	1
4 *E. J. G. Morgan *c 7 b 8*	11	9	2
5 S. W. Billings *b 7*...........	24	29	2
6 L. S. Livingstone *not out*	29	26	0/1
7 S. M. Curran *not out*	16	8	1/1
Lb 4, w 3.................	7		

6 overs: 31-3   (16.1 overs) 108-5

1/2 2/8 3/30 4/36 5/90

8 D. J. Willey, 9 C. J. Jordan, 10 A. U. Rashid
and 11 M. A. Wood did not bat.

Chameera 24–12–29–1; K. B. U. Fernando
18–9–17–1; Udana 24–7–25–1; de Silva
24–11–20–2; Dananjaya 7–0–13–0.

Umpires: M. Burns and A. G. Wharf.   Third umpire: M. J. Saggers.
Referee: P. Whitticase.

ENGLAND v SRI LANKA

Third Twenty20 International

At Southampton, June 26. England won by 89 runs. Toss: Sri Lanka.

With the series in the bag, England rested Roy (who had a hamstring issue) and Wood. But, after Perera won his third toss, and this time chose to bowl, a new opening pair of Bairstow and Malan put on 105 inside 12 overs; Malan quietened some doubters by hitting 34 in ten balls from Hasaranga de Silva. From 143 for one after 15, however, the loss of Livingstone, tamely plopping to cover, sparked a collapse. With Chameera making good use of his slower ball to finish with a career-best, England

LOWEST ALL-OUT T20 TOTALS AGAINST ENGLAND

45	West Indies at Basseterre.......	2018-19	91	**Sri Lanka at Southampton** .	**2021**
71	West Indies at Basseterre.......	2018-19	112	Pakistan at Dubai	2011-12
79	Australia at Southampton.......	2005	125	West Indies at The Oval.....	2011
80	Afghanistan at Colombo (RPS)..	2012-13	129	South Africa at Bridgetown ..	2010
89	Pakistan at Cardiff...........	2010	135	New Zealand at Manchester..	2015

lost five for 19 – only for the last over, from Udana, to cost 17. Set 181, Sri Lanka managed barely half. Two early wickets for Willey and one for Woakes got England going, before Curran chipped in, and a stunning direct hit from Billings in the deep did for Shanaka. That came in the final over, from Woakes, who conceded just nine runs – the fewest in a four-over spell by an England bowler.

Player of the Match: D. J. Malan.   *Player of the Series*: S. M. Curran.

England

		B	4/6
1 †J. M. Bairstow *b 8*	51	43	5/1
2 D. J. Malan *c 6 b 11*	76	48	5/4
3 L. S. Livingstone *c 6 b 9*	14	10	2
4 S. W. Billings *c 6 b 11*	2	3	0
5 *E. J. G. Morgan *c 1 b 11*	1	2	0
6 M. M. Ali *c 7 b 11*	7	7	1
7 S. M. Curran *not out*	9	5	1
8 C. J. Jordan *not out*	8	2	2
Lb 3, w 9	12		

6 overs: 48-0   (20 overs)   180-6

1/105 2/143 3/148 4/151 5/162 6/162

9 C. R. Woakes, 10 D. J. Willey and 11 A. U. Rashid did not bat.

Chameera 24–11–17–4; K. B. U. Fernando 24–10–26–1; Udana 24–8–55–1; Sandakan 24–9–28–0; de Silva 18–1–42–0; Shanaka 6–2–9–0.

Sri Lanka

		B	4/6
1 M. D. Gunathilleke *c 2 b 10*	4	2	1
2 *M. D. K. J. Perera *c 3 b 9*	3	6	0
3 B. O. P. Fernando *c 10 b 7*	19	27	0/1
4 B. K. G. Mendis *c 1 b 10*	6	4	0/1
5 †D. P. D. N. Dickwella *c 8 b 7*	11	19	1
6 M. D. Shanaka *run out (4)*	7	15	1
7 P. W. H. de Silva *c 2 b 8*	1	8	0
8 I. Udana *c 6 b 10*	0	4	0
9 K. B. U. Fernando *b 3*	20	14	1/1
10 P. A. D. L. R. Sandakan *not out*	3	11	0
11 P. V. D. Chameera *lbw b 6*	1	4	0
B 1, lb 7, w 7, nb 1	16		

6 overs: 39-3   (18.5 overs)   91

1/4 2/23 3/29 4/46 5/61 6/64 7/64 8/64 9/88

Willey 24–15–27–3; Woakes 24–17–9–1; Jordan 24–20–13–1; Curran 24–15–14–2; Rashid 6–2–9–0; Livingstone 6–3–8–1; Ali 5–2–3–1.

Umpires: M. J. Saggers and A. G. Wharf.   Third umpire: D. J. Millns.
Referee: P. Whitticase.

ENGLAND v SRI LANKA

First One-Day International

At Chester-le-Street, June 29. England won by five wickets. England 10pts. Toss: England. One-day international debuts: K. I. C. Asalanka, P. A. K. P. Jayawickrama, P. A. D. Lakshan.

It's the economy, stupid: Chris Woakes bowled England's cheapest ten overs against Sri Lanka.

This fixture took place in the shadow of England's European football championship match against Germany at Wembley. The cricketers were unable to see off Sri Lanka before the 5pm kick-off, but gave it a good try. Woakes, the Player of the Match, held his post-game press conference (via Zoom) at half-time in the football, before rejoining his team-mates to watch the other England complete a 2–0 win. Some hours earlier, he had put the outcome of the cricket beyond doubt. With Sri Lanka's batting already undermined by injury and a biosecurity breach that led to three players – Mendis, Dickwella and Gunathilleke – being sent home, he proved unplayable, picking up two wickets in each of his first two spells, and sending down five maidens, more than any England bowler in an ODI since James Anderson managed six against Australia at Adelaide in 2002-03. Willey, playing his 50th ODI, provided superb support. Sri Lanka's only period of stability was a partnership of 99 between the counter-attacking captain Perera and Hasaranga de Silva, promoted to No. 5. Once Woakes separated them, a second collapse ensued – seven for 40 – capped by a pair of run-outs by Billings. Bairstow flew out of the blocks with a 21-ball 43 but, at 80 for four, England had work to do. In his 150th ODI, Root unobtrusively chalked up his first half-century since the 2019

World Cup (also against Sri Lanka), and received help from the lesser-spotted Ali. One of Sri Lanka's replacements, Charith Asalanka, made his international debut on his 24th birthday – and bagged a duck, only the second to receive such an unwelcome present in ODIs after Pakistan's Asif Mujtaba, against West Indies at Gujranwala in 1986-87.

Player of the Match: C. R. Woakes.

Sri Lanka

P. Nissanka c Ali b Woakes	5		P. V. D. Chameera run out (Billings/Curran)		7
*†M. D. K. J. Perera c Billings b Willey	73		P. A. K. P. Jayawickrama run out (Billings)		4
K. I. C. Asalanka c Root b Willey	0				
M. D. Shanaka c Bairstow b Woakes	1		Lb 9, w 7, nb 1		17
P. W. H. de Silva c Livingstone b Woakes	54				
P. A. D. Lakshan c Root b Woakes	2		1/23 (1) 2/24 (3) (42.3 overs)		185
R. T. M. Wanigamuni lbw b Ali	1		3/46 (4) 4/145 (5) 5/149 (6)		
C. Karunaratne not out	19		6/152 (7) 7/152 (8) 8/160 (9)		
K. B. U. Fernando c Ali b Willey	2		9/170 (10) 10/185 (11) 10 overs: 47-3		

Woakes 10–5–18–4; Willey 10–1–44–3; Wood 7–0–19–0; Curran 7.3–0–45–0; Rashid 6–0–45–0; Ali 2–0–5–1.

England

†J. M. Bairstow b Fernando	43		S. M. Curran not out		9
L. S. Livingstone c Chameera b Karunaratne	9		Lb 5, w 5, nb 2		12
J. E. Root not out	79				
*E. J. G. Morgan c Perera b Chameera	6		1/54 (2) 2/59 (1) (5 wkts, 34.5 overs)		189
S. W. Billings c de Silva b Chameera	3		3/74 (4) 4/80 (5)		
M. M. Ali b Chameera	28		5/171 (6) 10 overs: 74-3		

C. R. Woakes, D. J. Willey, A. U. Rashid and M. A. Wood did not bat.

Chameera 8–0–50–3; Fernando 9.5–0–50–1; Karunaratne 7–0–39–1; de Silva 7–0–26–0; Lakshan 2–0–12–0; Jayawickrama 1–0–7–0.

Umpires: M. A. Gough and R. T. Robinson.   Third umpire: R. A. Kettleborough.
Referee: B. C. Broad.

ENGLAND v SRI LANKA

Second One-Day International

At The Oval, July 1 (day/night). England won by eight wickets. England 10pts. Toss: England.

By now, the pattern was set: Sri Lanka were put in, and started horribly. With Woakes rested again, Sam Curran inherited the role of new-ball destroyer, striking with his second, fourth and ninth deliveries on the way to a maiden international five-for. When Asalanka pulled Willey – who finished with four, making it nine in all for England's two Northampton-born left-armers – to midwicket, Sri Lanka were 21 for four, and many in a 14,000-strong crowd were not yet in their seats. And all this after Sri Lanka had bolstered their batting. One of those brought in, Dhananjaya de Silva, struck the ball crisply, and added 65 with the lively Hasaranga de Silva as the going grew easier against Rashid and Tom Curran. After Hasaranga was bounced out, Shanaka took over; and while Dhananjaya fell to the short ball, too, for a career-best 91, a total of 241 was a strong recovery. But with Bairstow and the fit-again Roy reunited, it still felt inadequate. Roy led the way in their run-a-ball stand of 76, before Hasaranga bowled Bairstow, and Roy popped Karunaratne to midwicket. Root carried on where he had left off in Durham, and Morgan, scratchy at first, scored his first international half-century in 16 innings in an unbroken stand of 140, to seal another series win.

Player of the Match: S. M. Curran.

Sri Lanka

P. Nissanka b S. M. Curran	5	K. B. U. Fernando c Rashid b Willey	17
*†M. D. K. J. Perera lbw b S. M. Curran	0	P. V. D. Chameera not out	14
W. I. A. Fernando lbw b S. M. Curran	2	A. M. Fernando not out	1
D. M. de Silva c Root b Willey	91	Lb 1, w 13	14
K. I. C. Asalanka c sub (G. H. S. Garton)			
b Willey	3	1/4 (2) 2/6 (3) (9 wkts, 50 overs) 241
P. W. H. de Silva c Billings b S. M. Curran	26	3/12 (1) 4/21 (5)
M. D. Shanaka c S. M. Curran b Willey	47	5/86 (6) 6/164 (4) 7/206 (7)
C. Karunaratne c Bairstow b S. M. Curran	21	8/217 (8) 9/229 (9) 10 overs: 47-4

Willey 10–1–64–4; S. M. Curran 10–1–48–5; T. K. Curran 10–0–43–0; Wood 10–1–35–0; Rashid 10–0–50–0.

England

J. J. Roy c D. M. de Silva b Karunaratne	60
†J. M. Bairstow b P. W. H. de Silva	29
J. E. Root not out	68
*E. J. G. Morgan not out	75
B 1, w 11	12
1/76 (2) 2/104 (1)   (2 wkts, 43 overs) 244
10 overs: 65-0

S. W. Billings, M. M. Ali, S. M. Curran, T. K. Curran, D. J. Willey, A. U. Rashid and M. A. Wood did not bat.

Chameera 9–0–46–0; K. B. U. Fernando 9–0–53–0; A. M. Fernando 10–0–54–0; P. W. H. de Silva 7–0–46–1; Karunaratne 6–0–34–1; D. M. de Silva 2–0–10–0.

Umpires: R. J. Bailey and R. A. Kettleborough.   Third umpire: M. A. Gough.
Referee: B. C. Broad.

ENGLAND v SRI LANKA

Third One-Day International

At Bristol, July 4. No result. England 5pts, Sri Lanka 5pts. Toss: England.

This was a dead rubber, but Morgan was in an uncompromising mood. With Woakes's return for the rested Wood the only change, it meant no debut for Sussex fast bowler George Garton, or first chance of the summer for Banton, a last-minute call-up thanks to outstanding form for Somerset. But Morgan cited the need for Super League points, and a desire to give new players more than just a game here or there. His decision to bowl in helpful conditions also lacked romance: England fans were itching to see their batters unleashed. Instead, Sri Lanka were skittled for 166, with Woakes and Willey in electric form once more, before Tom Curran – following three wickets in his last 11 ODIs – dismissed Oshada Fernando to make it 63 for five. Shanaka led the fightback again, but Curran finished with four for 35. It all proved academic. Rain that had first appeared shortly after the fall of the eighth wicket returned with vigour at the innings break. It cleared by late afternoon, but by then large puddles on the outfield had sealed the game's fate, and England had to settle for a share of the points.

Player of the Series: D. J. Willey.

Sri Lanka

W. I. A. Fernando lbw b Willey	14		P. V. D. Chameera st Bairstow b Rashid	16	

W. I. A. Fernando lbw b Willey 14
*†M. D. K. J. Perera b Woakes 9
P. Nissanka c Bairstow b Willey 6
D. M. de Silva c Rashid b Woakes 4
B. O. P. Fernando c Woakes b T. K. Curran 18
P. W. H. de Silva c Willey b T. K. Curran . 20
M. D. Shanaka not out 48
C. Karunaratne c Bairstow b T. K. Curran . 11
K. B. U. Fernando c Bairstow b T. K. Curran 7

P. V. D. Chameera st Bairstow b Rashid . . . 16
A. M. Fernando run out (Billings/
                S. M. Curran/Bairstow) . 0
    B 1, lb 1, w 11 13
                                  ——

1/19 (2) 2/29 (1)   (41.1 overs) 166
3/33 (3) 4/42 (4) 5/63 (5)
6/87 (6) 7/116 (8) 8/124 (9)
9/152 (10) 10/166 (11)   10 overs: 45-4

Woakes 10–3–28–2; Willey 7–0–36–2; S. M. Curran 6.1–1–30–0; T. K. Curran 10–0–35–4; Rashid 8–0–35–1.

England

J. J. Roy, †J. M. Bairstow, J. E. Root, *E. J. G. Morgan, S. W. Billings, M. M. Ali, S. M. Curran, C. R. Woakes, T. K. Curran, D. J. Willey, A. U. Rashid.

Umpires: M. A. Gough and D. J. Millns.   Third umpire: R. A. Kettleborough.
Referee: B. C. Broad.

ENGLAND v PAKISTAN IN 2021

Julian Guyer

One-day internationals (3): England 3 (30pts), Pakistan 0 (0pts)
Twenty20 internationals (3): England 2, Pakistan 1

That the one-day series went ahead, after England were forced to name an entirely new squad following a coronavirus outbreak, was a remarkable achievement in itself. That they won it so well against a Pakistan side who had lost only two of their previous 12 one-day internationals – and one of those defeats came in a super over – was testament to their strength in depth in white-ball cricket.

Two days before the first game in Cardiff, the ECB announced that PCR tests administered in Bristol after the series against Sri Lanka revealed three players and four support staff had Covid-19. With the rest of the squad deemed close contacts, England hastily assembled a new 18-man party – most pulled out of County Championship matches – nine of whom who had never played a one-day international.

Not since the fallout from the first rebel tour of South Africa in 1982 had they known upheaval quite like it. But there was, perhaps, a silver lining. One complaint during the series against a weak Sri Lanka was that England had been insufficiently adventurous in selection, a consequence of the ICC's aim of making all matches count as part of the qualifying process for the 2023 World Cup. Now, though, the likes of Test batsmen Zak Crawley and Dan Lawrence had a chance to make their 50-over debuts, and they were joined by several international newcomers: Durham fast bowler Brydon Carse, the Middlesex duo of seamer Tom Helm and wicketkeeper John Simpson, Surrey batsman Will Jacks, Gloucestershire left-armer David Payne, and opener Phil Salt of Sussex. Meanwhile, there were recalls for James Vince, Craig Overton, Jake Ball, Danny Briggs, Ben Duckett and Lewis Gregory, some of whom may have thought their England careers were behind them.

With Eoin Morgan among those ruled out, the decision to hand the captaincy to Ben Stokes, one of the few senior white-ball players available, seemed to make sense, given he had recently resumed playing for Durham after breaking a finger at the Indian Premier League. The ECB had originally planned to keep him away from the England team in a bid to help him back to full fitness. "It was the last call I was expecting, late in the evening," said Stokes. "After the call, my wife sent me a screenshot of an article saying: 'England aren't going to rush Ben Stokes back.' It's one of these situations where if you don't laugh, you'll cry. But it was like when I came back for Durham a bit earlier: my job needed me to do something, so I had to stand up and do it." Those words would sound poignant a few weeks later, when Stokes opted to take an indefinite break from all cricket to "prioritise his mental well-being", and recuperate properly from his finger injury. It was impossible to know how much the extra strain of the captaincy had been a factor.

Wham, bam, thank you Azam: Babar blasts his 14th ODI century, at Edgbaston.

Pakistan, who the previous season had visited England at the height of the pandemic, deserved praise for quarantining and remaining in the country in difficult circumstances, particularly given the outbreak in their opponents' camp. Asked if they had thought of calling off the tour, their captain, Babar Azam, was unequivocal: "It didn't come into our minds at any time."

Cynics recalled England's abandonment of their one-day tour of South Africa in December 2020 because of Covid concerns. It wasn't just in South Africa where eyebrows were raised by the speed with which the ECB insisted the Pakistan series had to go ahead. But Ashley Giles, the managing director of men's cricket, defended England's approach, saying: "We have identified the issue, we have shut it down, we are looking after our people and we are trying to keep cricket on for us, for the spectators, for the broadcasters, for all our partners." The cynicism seemed justified in September, when England pulled out of their two-match T20 tour of Pakistan, citing security concerns – but also Covid.

Giles was rather less forthcoming about the continued exclusion of top-order batsman Alex Hales. His exile, sparked by two failed drugs tests in the run-up to England's World Cup triumph in 2019, could easily be explained while Morgan was at the helm, but it was hard to maintain that Hales was not among the best 30-odd white-ball cricketers in the country. Giles insisted England had "never questioned Alex's ability", but added: "They're not things for us to get into now."

And yet England kept winning. It is a truism that county cricket gets most of the blame when they lose, and little of the credit when they win. And the impending arrival of The Hundred, as well as the increasingly polarised debate over the future of the domestic game, gave an edge to some of the rejoicing in the shires. After all, this was not so much an A-Team as, on paper at least, a C-Team. Going into the first match, Stokes had 98 ODI caps to his team-mates' combined 26, making it England's least-experienced one-day side since 1985.

From the moment Saqib Mahmood took a wicket with the first ball at Cardiff – then dismissed Babar, the world's top-ranked 50-over batsman, for a duck two balls later – England dominated the one-day series en route to 30 Super League points. Mahmood was especially potent, finishing the series with nine wickets at 13, and conceding just 4.39 an over (he added four wickets in the T20s). Overton (4.97) and Gregory (5.10) were thrifty too, while Carse collected a chaotic five-for in a run-filled third ODI at Edgbaston.

Once more, there was sympathy for a touring team denied meaningful warm-up games before being thrust into the fray. And it was perhaps no surprise that Pakistan's form mirrored that of Babar, whose one-day scores were nought, 19 and a career-best 158. But he, alone among the tourists, totalled 100 in the one-dayers, and an impressive attack led by the skilled Shaheen Shah Afridi were too often let down by lack of runs.

When Morgan returned to lead the T20 side, several of the stand-ins departed the scene, although by then Vince had delighted his many admirers by ending a long wait for a maiden international hundred to clinch the ODI whitewash at Edgbaston. But that innings was soon overshadowed by the gloriously clean striking of Liam Livingstone, who hit his way into England's T20 World Cup squad with a national-record 42-ball hundred, albeit in a 31-run defeat – Pakistan's lone victory – in Nottingham. He followed that with arguably the shot of the summer, a monstrous straight six off Haris Rauf over Headingley's new stand. In all, his 147 T20 runs at 49 came at a strike-rate of 216, and included 12 other sixes. For Pakistan, Mohammad Rizwan outscored Livingstone, with 176 runs at 88, but couldn't match his ferocity.

Another enduring image was the sight of wicketkeeper Simpson taking the field for a one-day international at Lord's, his home ground, in front of the first capacity crowd for a cricket match in England since the start of the pandemic. To paraphrase the reaction of Eric Russell, himself a Middlesex stalwart, to his Test debut 60 years earlier, no one could take it away from him now: it would always be John Simpson, Middlesex *and* England.

PAKISTAN TOURING PARTY

*Babar Azam (50/20), Abdullah Shafiq (50), Agha Salman (50), Arshad Iqbal (20), Azam Khan (20), Fahim Ashraf (50/20), Fakhar Zaman (50/20), Haris Rauf (50/20), Hasan Ali (50/20), Imad Wasim (20), Imam-ul-Haq (50), Mohammad Hafeez (50), Mohammad Hasnain (50/20), Mohammad Nawaz (50/20), Mohammad Rizwan (50/20), Mohammad Wasim (20), Sarfraz Ahmed (50/20), Saud Shakil (50), Shadab Khan (50/20), Shaheen Shah Afridi (50/20), Sharjeel Khan (20), Sohaib Maqsood (50/20), Usman Qadir (50/20).

Haider Ali was originally selected, but was withdrawn after breaking biosecurity protocols during the Pakistan Super League, and replaced by Sohaib Maqsood. Haris Sohail was selected for the ODI series, but flew home after tearing a hamstring in training.

Coach: Misbah-ul-Haq. *Manager:* Mansoor Rana. *Bowling coach:* Waqar Younis. *Fielding coach:* Abdul Majeed. *Strength and conditioning coach:* Mohammad Yasir Malik. *Assistant coach:* Shahid Aslam. *Physiotherapist:* W. A. Deacon. *Doctor:* Riaz Ahmed. *Masseur:* Malang Ali. *Security manager:* Lt-Col Mukarram. *Media manager:* Ibrahim Badees. *Analyst:* Talha Ejaz.

ENGLAND v PAKISTAN

First One-Day International

At Cardiff, July 8 (day/night). England won by nine wickets. England 10pts. Toss: England. One-day international debuts: B. A. Carse, Z. Crawley, L. Gregory, P. D. Salt, J. A. Simpson; Saud Shakil.

At the toss, Stokes struggled to recall the names of his five debutants – "Can someone help me out?" – yet that appeared to be his lone concern as England brushed aside Pakistan in 57 overs. Not since March 1985, and the plate final of the Rothmans Cup in Sharjah, also against Pakistan, had an

---

MOST ENGLAND DEBUTANTS IN AN ODI

6	v West Indies at Leeds	1973	5	v Ireland at Malahide	2015
5	v Australia at Manchester	1972	**5**	**v Pakistan at Cardiff**	**2021**
5	v West Indies at Scarborough	1976	4	v Pakistan at Sahiwal	1977-78
5	v Pakistan at Manchester	1996	4	v Zimbabwe at Harare	2001-02

* *There were 11 debutants in their first ODI, against Australia at Melbourne in 1970-71.*

England team boasted so few caps: 70 then, 124 now, of which Stokes had 98. Inevitably, his team became known as "Ben's Babes". Mahmood gave them a dream start, having Imam-ul-Haq lbw on review with the first delivery of the match. Two balls later, he added Pakistan's prize wicket, as their captain, Babar Azam, edged to second slip. Gregory removed Mohammad Rizwan and, when Mahmood trapped debutant Saud Shakil, it was 26 for four. Fakhar Zaman counter-attacked, but a promising innings of 47 ended tamely when he miscued Parkinson to backward point. Shadab Khan's 30 was the only other show of resistance. Sussex opener Phil Salt, the first Welsh-born player (Bodelwyddan, near the north coast) to appear for England in an international in Wales, went cheaply. But that paved the way for an unbroken stand of 120 in 17 overs between Malan, who made a run-a-ball 68, and Crawley, who shook off a bad few months in Test cricket to mark his first ODI with 58 from 50. So completely in control were England that Stokes bowled one over, and didn't bat. Welsh government social-distancing restrictions, stricter than those across the border, limited the size of the crowd in a day/night game that finished in bright sunshine.

Player of the Match: S. Mahmood.

Pakistan

Imam-ul-Haq lbw b Mahmood	0	Shaheen Shah Afridi c Stokes b Overton		12
Fakhar Zaman c Crawley b Parkinson	47	Haris Rauf not out		0
*Babar Azam c Crawley b Mahmood	0			
†Mohammad Rizwan c Simpson b Gregory	13	W 3, nb 1		4
Saud Shakil lbw b Mahmood	5			
Sohaib Maqsood run out (Vince)	19	1/0 (1) 2/0 (3) 3/17 (4)	(35.2 overs)	141
Shadab Khan c Malan b Overton	30	4/26 (5) 5/79 (6) 6/90 (2)		
Fahim Ashraf c Simpson b Mahmood	5	7/101 (8) 8/123 (9) 9/134 (7)		
Hasan Ali c Malan b Parkinson	6	10/141 (10)	10 overs: 46-4	

Mahmood 10–1–42–4; Gregory 4–1–11–1; Overton 6.2–0–23–2; Carse 7–0–31–0; Parkinson 7–0–28–2; Stokes 1–0–6–0.

England

P. D. Salt c Sohaib Maqsood
b Shaheen Shah Afridi . 7
D. J. Malan not out 68
Z. Crawley not out 58
Lb 1, w 7, nb 1 9

1/22 (1)   (1 wkt, 21.5 overs) 142
                               10 overs: 61-1

J. M. Vince, *B. A. Stokes, †J. A. Simpson, L. Gregory, C. Overton, B. A. Carse, S. Mahmood and M. W. Parkinson did not bat.

Shaheen Shah Afridi 5–0–22–1; Hasan Ali 4–0–33–0; Haris Rauf 4–0–28–0; Fahim Ashraf 5–0–33–0; Shadab Khan 3–0–22–0; Saud Shakil 0.5–0–3–0.

Umpires: R. A. Kettleborough and A. G. Wharf.   Third umpire: R. K. Illingworth.
Referee: B. C. Broad.

ENGLAND v PAKISTAN

Second One-Day International

At Lord's, July 10. England won by 52 runs. England 10pts. Toss: Pakistan.

The first one-day international at Lord's since the 2019 World Cup final may not have been quite as gripping, but an encounter reduced by rain to 47 overs a side still had ebb and flow. England were set for a commanding total while Salt and Vince were sharing a third-wicket stand of 97 in 13 overs, after Malan and Crawley had fallen for ducks. But from 118 for two they lost five for 42, including Salt, for a maiden international half-century that contained ten fours; Vince, whose second ODI fifty had taken just 36 balls; and Stokes, who in his 100th one-day game for England inexplicably charged at Hasan Ali, and was bowled. But Gregory and Brydon Carse, each playing his maiden ODI innings, frustrated Pakistan by putting on 69, an eighth-wicket record for a Lord's white-ball international. It needed Hasan, bowling with the fiery skill he had displayed during Pakistan's victorious 2017 Champions Trophy campaign, to wrap up the innings, and complete his country's best figures against England at Lord's. Gregory then struck with his first delivery, having Imam caught behind, before Mahmood took care of Babar and Rizwan. Hasan hit Parkinson for 22 in four balls but, when he holed out for 31, Pakistan were 152 for eight. Shakil's admirable first international fifty could only limit the damage, as England took the series. A crowd of 23,000 produced chants of "Football's coming home" on the eve of the European Championship final between England and Italy at Wembley.

Player of the Match: L. Gregory.

England

P. D. Salt b Saud Shakil	60		B. A. Carse b Haris Rauf	31
D. J. Malan c Shadab Khan b Hasan Ali . .	0		S. Mahmood c Haris Rauf b Hasan Ali	8
Z. Crawley b Shaheen Shah Afridi	0		M. W. Parkinson not out	7
J. M. Vince b Shadab Khan	56		W 5, nb 1	6
*B. A. Stokes b Hasan Ali	22			
†J. A. Simpson b Hasan Ali	17		1/9 (2) 2/21 (3) 3/118 (1) (45.2 overs)	247
L. Gregory c Fakhar Zaman b Haris Rauf . .	40		4/134 (4) 5/156 (5) 6/160 (6)	
C. Overton c Mohammad Rizwan			7/160 (8) 8/229 (7) 9/233 (9)	
b Hasan Ali .	0		10/247 (10) 10 overs: 72-2	

Shaheen Shah Afridi 8–0–37–1; Hasan Ali 9.2–0–51–5; Fahim Ashraf 6–0–45–0; Haris Rauf 9–0–54–2; Shadab Khan 10–1–46–1; Saud Shakil 3–0–14–1.

Pakistan

Imam-ul-Haq c Simpson b Gregory	1	Shaheen Shah Afridi not out	18
Fakhar Zaman b Overton	10	Haris Rauf c Simpson b Gregory	1
*Babar Azam lbw b Mahmood	19		
†Mohammad Rizwan c Simpson b Mahmood	5	Lb 5, w 6, nb 2	13
Saud Shakil c Overton b Parkinson	56		
Sohaib Maqsood c Simpson b Overton	19	1/1 (1) 2/25 (3) 3/36 (4) (41 overs)	195
Shadab Khan c Parkinson b Gregory	21	4/53 (2) 5/86 (6) 6/115 (7)	
Fahim Ashraf c Simpson b Parkinson	1	7/118 (8) 8/152 (9) 9/192 (5)	
Hasan Ali c Overton b Carse	31	10/195 (11) 10 overs: 38-3	

Mahmood 8–0–21–2; Gregory 8–0–44–3; Overton 9–2–39–2; Carse 8–0–44–1; Parkinson 8–0–42–2.

Umpires: R. K. Illingworth and A. G. Wharf.   Third umpire: M. A. Gough.

Referee: B. C. Broad.

ENGLAND v PAKISTAN

Third One-Day International

At Birmingham, July 13 (day/night). England won by three wickets. England 10pts. Toss: England. Six years after his international debut, Vince finally scored a century for England, in his 50th innings in all formats. Even better, his 102 helped them complete the highest successful run-chase in an Edgbaston ODI – surpassing Australia's 280 for four in 1993 – and a 3–0 whitewash. They had been faltering at 165 for five in pursuit of 332, before Vince and Gregory, with a 69-ball 77, wrested back the initiative in a stand of 129 – England's best for the sixth wicket in a victorious chase. Haris Rauf removed both in quick succession, but the hosts still won with two overs to spare, when Carse drove Shaheen Shah Afridi down the ground to cap a composed late stand with Overton. Earlier, Babar had struck a masterful career-best 158 from 139 balls, having spent 14 on nought, and brought up his half-century from 72. A cut for four off Mahmood, later named Player of the Series, took him to a 104-ball century, and he extended a brutal 20-over partnership with Rizwan to 179 – Pakistan's highest for any wicket against England. From 292 for two, they lost seven for 37, as Carse collected five for 17 in 12 deliveries. Malan fell for another duck, but Salt's 37 from 22 and a cameo from Crawley helped bring up three figures in just 12.1 overs. Shadab Khan got rid of Stokes and Simpson, but England were still ahead of the rate, and Vince and Gregory were in the mood. Edgbaston turned #BlueforBob, in honour of the former England and Warwickshire fast bowler Bob Willis, who died in December 2019, and to promote fund-raising for research into prostate cancer.

Player of the Match: J. M. Vince.   *Player of the Series:* S. Mahmood.

Pakistan

Imam-ul-Haq b Parkinson	56	Shaheen Shah Afridi c Vince b Carse	0
Fakhar Zaman c Crawley b Mahmood	6	Haris Rauf not out	0
*Babar Azam c Malan b Carse	158		
†Mohammad Rizwan c Simpson b Carse	74	Lb 3, w 9	12
Sohaib Maqsood c Vince b Carse	8		
Hasan Ali c Crawley b Carse	4	1/21 (2) 2/113 (1) (9 wkts, 50 overs)	331
Fahim Ashraf b Mahmood	10	3/292 (4) 4/305 (5)	
Shadab Khan c Simpson b Mahmood	0	5/309 (6) 6/324 (7) 7/324 (8)	
Saud Shakil not out	3	8/328 (3) 9/329 (10) 10 overs: 35-1	

Mahmood 10–2–60–3; Gregory 7–0–42–0; Overton 10–0–64–0; Carse 10–0–61–5; Stokes 4–0–31–0; Parkinson 9–0–70–1.

England

P. D. Salt c Fakhar Zaman b Haris Rauf . . . 37	L. Gregory c Shadab Khan b Haris Rauf. . . 77
D. J. Malan c Mohammad Rizwan	C. Overton not out 18
b Hasan Ali . 0	B. A. Carse not out 12
Z. Crawley b Haris Rauf 39	Lb 5, w 7 12
J. M. Vince c Babar Azam b Haris Rauf . . . 102	
*B. A. Stokes c Mohammad Rizwan	1/19 (2) 2/53 (1) (7 wkts, 48 overs) 332
b Shadab Khan . 32	3/104 (3) 4/151 (5)
†J. A. Simpson lbw b Shadab Khan 3	5/165 (6) 6/294 (4) 7/303 (7) 10 overs: 84-2

S. Mahmood and M. W. Parkinson did not bat.

Shaheen Shah Afridi 10–0–78–0; Hasan Ali 9–0–69–1; Haris Rauf 9–0–65–4; Fahim Ashraf 6–0–34–0; Shadab Khan 10–0–61–2; Saud Shakil 4–0–20–0.

Umpires: R. K. Illingworth and D. J. Millns.   Third umpire: R. A. Kettleborough.
Referee: B. C. Broad.

ENGLAND v PAKISTAN

First Twenty20 International

At Nottingham, July 16 (floodlit). Pakistan won by 31 runs. Toss: England. Twenty20 international debut: Azam Khan.

The England players forced to sit out the ODI series because of Covid were available once more, though Stokes was rested, and Buttler still nursing an injured calf. But Pakistan were undaunted. Carrying on from where he left off in Birmingham, Babar made a punishing 85, and shared an opening stand of 150 inside 15 overs with Rizwan in a national-record T20 total of 232 for six

It takes two to tangle: Haris Rauf catches Moeen Ali, despite colliding with Sohaib Maqsood.

(beating 205 for three against West Indies at Karachi in 2017-18). After no sixes in the first 11 overs, Pakistan ended up hitting 12, equalling their record; that included three each from Babar, Fakhar and Mohammad Hafeez, as 152 came off the last ten overs. Roy set off in a hurry but, when he fell in the seventh, England were 82 for four. It was the cue for an astonishing innings from Livingstone, who reached a maiden international fifty in 17 balls (beating Eoin Morgan's national record of 21, against

MOST SIXES IN A T20 INNINGS FOR ENGLAND

9	**L. S. Livingstone (103)** .	**v Pakistan at Nottingham**	**2021**
7	R. S. Bopara (65*)	v Australia at Hobart	2013-14
7	E. J. G. Morgan (71)	v India at Birmingham	2014
7	E. J. G. Morgan (74)	v Australia at Cardiff	2015
7	J. J. Roy (67)	v India at Bristol	2018
7	E. J. G. Morgan (91)	v New Zealand at Napier	2019-20
7	E. J. G. Morgan (57*) ...	v South Africa at Centurion	2019-20
6	L. J. Wright (99*)	v Afghanistan at Colombo (RPS).	2012-13
6	A. D. Hales (116*)	v Sri Lanka at Chittagong......	2013-14
6	E. J. G. Morgan (80*) ...	v New Zealand at Hamilton	2017-18
6	J. J. Roy (69)	v Sri Lanka at Colombo (RPS)..	2018-19
6	D. J. Malan (103*)	v New Zealand at Napier	2019-20
6	**J. C. Buttler (101*)**	**v Sri Lanka at Sharjah**.......	**2021-22**

The overall record is 16 sixes by Hazratullah Zazai for Afghanistan v Ireland at Dehradun in 2018-19.

New Zealand and South Africa, both in 2019-20), and a maiden international hundred in 42 (beating Malan's 48, against New Zealand in 2019-20). He also hit an England-record nine sixes, including five off Shadab, while the 15 team sixes equalled their best. But no one else could stay with him. Afridi held his nerve, having earlier taken a brilliant return catch to see off Malan, and Pakistan ran out comfortable winners, inflicting on England their only white-ball defeat of the summer.

Player of the Match: Shaheen Shah Afridi.

Pakistan

	B	4/6
1 †Mohammad Rizwan *c 3 b 7* ...	63	41 8/1
2 *Babar Azam *c 3 b 8*	85	49 8/3
3 Sohaib Maqsood *c 8 b 9*.......	19	7 1/2
4 Fakhar Zaman *c 2 b 10*........	26	8 1/3
5 Mohammad Hafeez *b 9*	24	10 1/3
6 Azam Khan *not out*	5	3 1
7 Imad Wasim *run out (2/3)*	3	2 0
Lb 4, w 3	7	

6 overs: 49-0   (20 overs) 232-6

1/150 2/169 3/175 4/221 5/221 6/232

8 Shadab Khan, 9 Shaheen Shah Afridi, 10 Haris Rauf and 11 Mohammad Hasnain did not bat.

Willey 24–8–39–1; Mahmood 24–5–46–1; Curran 24–10–47–2; Gregory 12–2–25–1; Parkinson 24–2–47–0; Livingstone 12–2–24–0.

England

	B	4/6
1 D. J. Malan *c and b 9*........	1	6 0
2 J. J. Roy *c 2 b 8*...........	32	13 2/3
3 †J. M. Bairstow *c 7 b 9*......	11	7 1/1
4 M. M. Ali *c 10 b 11*........	1	4 0
5 L. S. Livingstone *c 9 b 8*.....	103	43 6/9
6 *E. J. G. Morgan *c 10 b 7*	16	15 0/1
7 L. Gregory *c 9 b 8*.........	10	11 0
8 D. J. Willey *c 8 b 10*	16	11 2/1
9 T. K. Curran *run out (8)*	1	2 0
10 S. Mahmood *not out*	0	2 0
11 M. W. Parkinson *b 9*	0	2 0
Lb 1, w 9.................	10	

6 overs: 69-3   (19.2 overs) 201

1/12 2/42 3/48 4/82 5/133 6/177 7/183 8/191 9/201

Imad Wasim 24–6–46–1; Shaheen Shah Afridi 20–11–30–3; Mohammad Hasnain 24–8–28–1; Haris Rauf 24–7–44–1; Shadab Khan 24–8–52–3.

Umpires: D. J. Millns and M. J. Saggers.   Third umpire: A. G. Wharf.
Referee: W. M. Noon.

ENGLAND v PAKISTAN

Second Twenty20 International

At Leeds, July 18. England won by 45 runs. Toss: Pakistan.

In years to come, the result of this match may fade from memory, but Livingstone's 122m straight six off Rauf, sailing over the canopy of the redeveloped Football Stand, is unlikely to suffer a similar fate. The blow, arguably the biggest ever seen at Headingley, came from the first ball of the 16th over, as England responded to defeat at Trent Bridge by racking up 200. That included a typically watchable half-century from Buttler, deputising as captain for the rested Morgan in his first game since tearing his calf against Sri Lanka on June 23. England's series-levelling win also owed much to their spinners: between them, Rashid, Parkinson and Ali took five for 87 in 11 overs, with both Maqsood and Azam Khan stumped. There were also three wickets for Mahmood. Rizwan and Babar had begun well once more, putting on 50 inside six overs, but of the rest only Shadab passed 20.

Player of the Match: M. M. Ali.

England		B	4/6
1 J. J. Roy *c 4 b 7*	10	4	1/1
2 *†J. C. Buttler *c 2 b 11*	59	39	7/2
3 D. J. Malan *c 6 b 7*	1	5	0
4 M. M. Ali *c 2 b 11*	36	16	6/1
5 L. S. Livingstone *run out (6/10)*	38	23	2/3
6 J. M. Bairstow *c 5 b 8*	13	7	2
7 T. K. Curran *c 3 b 11*	9	7	1
8 C. J. Jordan *c 8 b 10*	14	8	1/1
9 A. U. Rashid *b 10*	2	4	0
10 S. Mahmood *not out*	3	3	0
11 M. W. Parkinson *b 9*	5	4	1
Lb 3, w 6, nb 1	10		

6 overs: 66-2 (19.5 overs) 200

1/11 2/18 3/85 4/137 5/153 6/164 7/182 8/191 9/191

Imad Wasim 24–11–37–2; Shaheen Shah Afridi 23–10–28–1; Mohammad Hasnain 24–4–51–3; Haris Rauf 24–8–48–2; Shadab Khan 24–7–33–1.

Pakistan		B	4/6
1 †Mohammad Rizwan *c and b 9*	37	29	3/1
2 *Babar Azam *c 3 b 10*	22	16	3
3 Sohaib Maqsood *st 2 b 9*	15	10	1/1
4 Mohammad Hafeez *c 6 b 4*	10	12	0
5 Fakhar Zaman *b 4*	8	8	1
6 Azam Khan *st 2 b 11*	1	4	0
7 Imad Wasim *c 1 b 7*	20	13	1/1
8 Shadab Khan *not out*	36	22	2/3
9 Shaheen Shah Afridi *c 8 b 10*	2	4	0
10 Haris Rauf *b 10*	0	1	0
11 Mohammad Hasnain *not out*	0	1	0
Lb 1, w 3	4		

6 overs: 51-1 (20 overs) 155-9

1/50 2/71 3/82 4/93 5/95 6/105 7/142 8/147 9/154

Rashid 24–7–30–2; Jordan 6–3–12–0; Curran 24–10–22–1; Mahmood 24–11–33–3; Ali 18–3–32–2; Parkinson 24–8–25–1.

Umpires: M. J. Saggers and A. G. Wharf.   Third umpire: D. J. Millns.
Referee: W. M. Noon.

ENGLAND v PAKISTAN

Third Twenty20 International

At Manchester, July 20 (floodlit). England won by three wickets. Toss: Pakistan.

England won a tense affair on a turning pitch with two balls to spare, after a career-best four for 35 from Rashid limited Pakistan to 154 for six. Rashid removed four of the top six and, despite the in-form Rizwan batting through the innings for 76, the tourists could never quite up the rate, with Ali sending down four tight overs for 19. Roy then made a typically dashing 64, hitting four fours in Afridi's only over. Yet Pakistan's spinners, to the delight of their loyal army of fans who, once again, made it seem England were the away side in Manchester, dragged them back into the game, especially when Hafeez was belatedly brought into the attack. Morgan hit two sixes off Hasan in the 18th over, but there was still time for England to lose three more wickets – including Livingstone, caught second ball for six – before Jordan sprinted the winning two to seal the series. An elated Morgan said: "This was the worst possible pitch for the way we play, so I am very proud."

Player of the Match: J. J. Roy.   *Player of the Series:* L. S. Livingstone.

Pakistan

		B	4/6
1 †Mohammad Rizwan *not out*	76	57	5/3
2 *Babar Azam *st 2 b 10*	11	13	1
3 Sohaib Maqsood *c 1 b 10*	13	12	2
4 Mohammad Hafeez *c 4 b 10*	1	2	0
5 Fakhar Zaman *lbw b 5*	24	20	1/1
6 Shadab Khan *c 7 b 10*	2	5	0
7 Imad Wasim *run out (4/8)*	3	2	0
8 Hasan Ali *not out*	15	9	1/1
B 4, lb 2, w 3	9		

6 overs: 50-1   (20 overs) 154-6

1/42 2/67 3/69 4/114 5/125 6/129

9 Shaheen Shah Afridi, 10 Usman Qadir and 11 Mohammad Hasnain did not bat.

Willey 12–8–10–0; Mahmood 18–5–33–0; Jordan 24–5–30–0; Rashid 24–10–35–4; Livingstone 18–4–21–0; Ali 24–8–19–1.

England

		B	4/6
1 J. J. Roy *c 5 b 10*	64	36	12/1
2 †J. C. Buttler *c 2 b 6*	21	22	3
3 D. J. Malan *b 4*	31	33	2
4 J. M. Bairstow *c 3 b 7*	5	8	0
5 M. M. Ali *b 4*	1	3	0
6 *E. J. G. Morgan *c 6 b 8*	21	12	1/2
7 L. S. Livingstone *c 3 b 4*	6	2	0/1
8 C. J. Jordan *not out*	4	2	0
9 D. J. Willey *not out*	0	0	0
Lb 1, w 1	2		

6 overs: 45-0   (19.4 overs) 155-7

1/67 2/92 3/104 4/112 5/143 6/149 7/151

10 A. U. Rashid and 11 S. Mahmood did not bat.

Imad Wasim 24–13–25–1; Shaheen Shah Afridi 6–2–16–0; Hasan Ali 22–12–28–1; Usman Qadir 24–7–35–1; Shadab Khan 24–8–28–3.

Umpires: D. J. Millns and A. G. Wharf.   Third umpire: M. J. Saggers.
Referee: W. M. Noon.

ENGLAND v INDIA IN 2021

JONATHAN LIEW

Test matches (4): England 1 (14pts), India 2 (26pts)

It was a series that crept up on you. Wedged into an overcrowded summer, forced to compete with the multimedia blizzard of The Hundred, and foisted on a public already engorged on sport, it seemed to arrive with a minimum of fanfare, advance billing or phoney war.

India landed two months earlier, and played so little cricket it was easy to forget they were still in the country. England, disjointed and distracted, were slaloming through an assault course of Covid outbreaks, format switches, eclectic selection and their own screaming tiredness. Ticket sales were strong, as one might have expected after the shutouts of 2020. But as the teams headed for the First Test in Nottingham, there was little sense of event, little idea of the epic, operatic, exhausting, baffling tussle about to be laid before us.

Actually, that's not quite true: India had an inkling. What quickly became clear was that those long weeks of confinement, the endless nasal swabs, the days and nights spent staring at hotel ceilings, had hardened something within. For most of the 41 days between their defeat by New Zealand in the World Test Championship final at the Rose Bowl and the start of play at Trent Bridge, they had been plotting, smouldering, straining at the leash, thirsting for the battle. Never was that more evident than in their electric final-day win in the Second Test at Lord's: a snarling, ill-tempered triumph in front of a partisan diasporic crowd. That sense of purpose, which fed into some of the most

Blowing his own trumpet: Virat Kohli barracks the Barmy Army at The Oval.

Christopher Lee, Getty Images

intense cricket ever played by an Indian team on these shores, was perhaps the single biggest difference between the sides.

And yet the hasty cancellation of the Fifth Test at Manchester after a Covid outbreak in the tourists' camp left the series in a contested space, with India 2–1 up and on the brink of their first victory in England since 2007 – an outcome that would advance their claim as one of the finest teams of the 21st century. The game was later scheduled for Edgbaston in July 2022. But even if England win, only the most one-eyed supporter would claim the spoils had genuinely been shared. Over these four Tests, when the contest burned white-hot and the pressure was at its fiercest, India proved their greatness, despite the administrative asterisk.

As in Australia several months earlier, they succeeded not through individual acts of brilliance but a collective resolve borne of solitude and adversity. Unlike their previous tour of England in 2018, a 4–1 defeat gilded by the supreme form of Virat Kohli, the glory was shared between at least half a dozen. Indeed, India had clearly learned the lessons from that visit, building in serious preparation time that gave many of their all-format players – the likes of Rohit Sharma, K. L. Rahul, Shardul Thakur, Jasprit Bumrah – the chance to hone their red-ball skills. The upshot was a top order capable of batting time (never had Sharma faced nearly as many balls as the 866 in this series) and a bowling unit that hunted in a rapacious, disciplined pack. Kohli endured a relatively modest time with the bat, yet his team's controlled, brazen aggression – from the relentless pace battery via the sparkling fielding to the ceaseless sledging – had his fingerprints all over it.

England, who lost Ben Stokes shortly before the series began, as he took an indefinite break to look after his mental well-being and nurse his injured finger, had moments of promise. Their sole victory, a romp at Headingley, offered a glimpse of their potential. Their defiance in the second innings at Trent Bridge and the first at The Oval offered a glimpse of their resilience. They had the highest wicket-taker in Ollie Robinson, and the highest run-scorer in the formidable Joe Root; at times, Jimmy Anderson, 39 now, was unplayable. They put together competent passages of play, and rarely let their heads drop.

And yet, over the series, they did little to counter the long-standing charge that they remained a bits-and-pieces side with a wildly inconsistent streak, a worrying reliance on a small coterie of champion players, and a board that seemed hell-bent on flinging obstacles in their path. On the basis of numbers and scorecards alone, an observer might conclude this was a close encounter

---

THERE'S LIFE IN THE OLD DOG YET

Oldest seamers to take a five-wicket haul in Tests:

40 years 304 days	*S. F. Barnes (7-88)	England v South Africa at Durban	1913-14
40 years 86 days	G. W. A. Chubb (6-51)	South Africa v England at Manchester	1951
39 years 231 days	F. J. Laver (8-31)	Australia v England at Manchester	1909
39 years 14 days	**J. M. Anderson (5-62)**	**England v India at Lord's**	**2021**
39 years 6 days	R. J. Hadlee (5-53)	New Zealand v England at Birmingham	1990

* *Barnes took five or more 13 times after his 39th birthday, including twice in his final Test.*

FIVE STATS YOU MAY HAVE MISSED

BENEDICT BERMANGE

- At Nottingham, Ravindra Jadeja became the fifth Indian to complete the double of 2,000 runs and 200 wickets in Tests, after Kapil Dev, A. Kumble, Harbhajan Singh and R. Ashwin.

- At Nottingham and Lord's, India did not take a wicket with spin in successive Tests for only the second time; the first instances came against Pakistan, at Karachi and Faisalabad in 1989-90.

- Before Joe Root at Lord's, the only batsman known to have faced two hat-trick deliveries in an innings was Mohammad Ashraful, for Bangladesh against India at Dhaka in 2004-05. He too survived them – both bowled by Irfan Pathan.

- At Leeds, Root became the first captain to top-score in five successive Test innings:

5	J. E. Root (England)	64, 109, 180*, 33, 121	**2021**
4	A. Melville (South Africa)....	103, 189, 104*, 117........	1938-39 to 1947
4	R. B. Simpson (Australia).....	67, 71, 153, 115........	1964-65
4	S. P. Fleming (New Zealand)....	21, 32, 274*, 69*.........	2002-03 to 2003

- In India's second innings at Leeds, Cheteshwar Pujara was unbeaten on 91 at the end of the third day, but dismissed without addition next morning. He became the third player to suffer that fate six times in Tests, after Chris Cairns (New Zealand) and Jacques Kallis (South Africa).

between evenly matched sides. But this would be to confuse a James Bond car chase with a drunk driver: both are weaving alarmingly across the road, upsetting fruit stalls, sending pedestrians ducking for cover, but only one really knows what they're doing.

While England's all-format players grappled with the novelty and razzmatazz of The Hundred, most of their Test specialists whiled away precious weeks in the nets, with virtually no first-class cricket to occupy them. This absurdity was underscored when Moeen Ali dashed from Birmingham Phoenix to Lord's for his first home Test in two years, with only a couple of days to reacquaint himself with a red ball. As it turned out, this series would be his Test swansong, and a fittingly emblematic end it was too: a bittersweet reminder of how one of England's most talented all-round cricketers had been mismanaged, messed around and generally set up to fail.

Home advantage is the most powerful weapon in Test cricket, but England contrived to hand it to their opponents. Indeed it was arresting how neatly the roles from 2018 were reversed. Here, it was England who looked sketchy and sleepy, who arrived underprepared with no real idea of their best XI and no real coherent playing strategy, and who lost pretty much all the big moments.

In mitigation, the unavailability of their four fastest bowlers – Stokes, Jofra Archer, Olly Stone and (for three of the four Tests) Mark Wood – deprived them of cutting edge, and forced them to rely on a conveyor belt of 82mph seam. The nous and experience of Stuart Broad, who tore a calf in the build-up to the Second Test and played no further part, were missed. But India also had to contend with injuries, most notably to Ishant Sharma, Mohammed Shami, Mayank Agarwal, Shubman Gill and Washington Sundar. Unlike England, they had the depth to cope.

After Gill flew home with a shin problem, and Agarwal was sidelined with concussion, Rahul effortlessly stepped into the breach, hitting 84 at Trent Bridge and a brilliant 129 at Lord's. When Shami was ruled out of the Fourth Test, Umesh Yadav took his place and mopped up six wickets. Such was India's wealth of reserve talent that Ravichandran Ashwin, perhaps the world's best spinner, did not play at all, amid whispers of a dysfunctional relationship with Kohli. A composite XI of those India managed without – others included Prithvi Shaw, Hanuma Vihari, Suryakumar Yadav, Wriddhiman Saha and Akshar Patel – would probably have given England a run for their money.

Perhaps most crucially, they recognised when to raise their game. In their two wins, both in London, Rohit Sharma set things up with masterful batting in alien conditions, belying his unimpressive overseas Test record to make 83 out of an opening stand of 126 in the first innings at Lord's, then hauling India back into the game at The Oval with 127 in almost six hours. And in both Tests, Bumrah – who had already taken nine wickets at Trent Bridge – burst through on the last afternoon, removing Root in the first over after tea on the fifth day at Lord's, then all but settling matters at The Oval by bowling Ollie Pope and Jonny Bairstow. He was rarely less than a thrilling sight. He even scored a few runs – despite starting the series with a batting average of 2.26 – most importantly on the final morning at Lord's, where Root lost the plot.

FEWEST TESTS TO TAKE 100 WICKETS FOR INDIA

18	R. Ashwin	OB	2013-14	24	R. A. Jadeja	SLA	2016-17
20	E. A. S. Prasanna	OB	1969-70	**24**	**J. J. Bumrah**	**RFM**	**2021**
21	A. Kumble	LB	1995-96	25	Kapil Dev	RFM	1979-80
22	S. P. Gupte	LB	1958-59	25	Harbhajan Singh	OB	2001-02
22	B. S. Chandrasekhar	LB	1972-73	28	B. S. Bedi	SLA	1972-73
22	P. P. Ojha	SLA	2012-13	28	D. R. Doshi	SLA	1982-83
23	M. H. Mankad	SLA	1952-53	28	I. K. Pathan	LFM	2007-08

If India were powered by a cast of several, it felt as if England were powered by a cast of one. Earlier in Root's captaincy, the burdens of leadership and batsmanship seemed to pull him in opposite directions – one demanding selflessness, the other selfishness. But he began to recognise his limitations as a captain, and to realise that the best way to help his side was by scoring runs in industrial quantities. Here, he surpassed even his loftiest ambitions. Continuing his stunning form from earlier in the year in Sri Lanka and India, Root made three times as many runs as any of his team-mates, top-scored in the first five innings out of seven, and hit all three of England's centuries.

This was a testament to his talent and rediscovered powers of concentration, but also an indictment of those around him. And so England were forced to continue their batting auditions. Dom Sibley and Zak Crawley failed to see out the series; their replacements, Haseeb Hameed and Dawid Malan, offered flickers of improvement, with Hameed and Rory Burns threatening to resemble an opening partnership. Above all, though, you got the sense that, as soon as Root departed, England were likely to crumble.

Socially distanced: Ravi Shastri at Leeds, where he believes he contracted Covid-19.

Two days before the Fourth Test, at the St James' Court hotel in London, Indian coach Ravi Shastri held a launch for his new book, *Stargazing: The Players in My Life*. Many of the Indian squad were present, as well as the ECB chief executive, Tom Harrison. Masks were not worn. Four days later, Shastri tested positive for Covid, and went into isolation, along with three members of India's support staff (two tested positive). And two days before the Fifth Test at Old Trafford, assistant physiotherapist Yogesh Parmar – who had been in close contact with many of the players – was found to have the virus.

Nobody can say for sure where Shastri became infected. He was adamant his book launch was not to blame, arguing in a *Guardian* interview that he probably caught the bug in Leeds. But the effect on the tourists, who had been away from home for more than three months and were now facing the prospect of having their return delayed – or their participation in the IPL scuppered – was seismic. Shortly before the teams were due to take the field, it was announced that, despite a full set of negative Covid tests, India had chosen not to play. For a few hours, chaos reigned. Administrators held high-level negotiations. Allegations of bad faith and self-interest abounded. Had the Test been forfeited, or just abandoned? Would it be rescheduled? And what were we all meant to do for the next five days?

You could understand England's chagrin: a chance to square the series had been snatched from them. There were rumours that India's bubble had not exactly been unburstable. But wherever the blame lay, England were hardly in a position to lecture anyone on biosecurity. On October 12, a man called Daniel Jarvis appeared at Croydon magistrates' court to plead not guilty to a charge of aggravated trespass. During the Test series, Jarvis – a YouTube prankster going by the nickname of Jarvo69 – had infiltrated the security cordon and made his way on to the outfield, not once but three times. At Lord's, he appeared after lunch in Indian kit in an attempt to pass himself off as a fielder; at Headingley, he walked out in batting gear after the dismissal of Rohit Sharma; at The Oval, he ran on and barged into a startled Bairstow, before being grappled to the ground by security staff.

Even if the joke was wearing thin, it was a surreal note in what had been a surreal summer: a series beginning in a haze of haste and confusion ultimately receded in similar fashion. The result of England v India was to be decided almost a year after it started, maybe with radically different teams. It would, surely, be the longest and weirdest series of them all.

INDIA TOURING PARTY

*V. Kohli, M. A. Agarwal, R. Ashwin, Avesh Khan, J. J. Bumrah, A. R. Easwaran, R. A. Jadeja, Mohammed Shami, R. R. Pant, A. R. Patel, C. A. Pujara, A. M. Rahane, K. L. Rahul, W. P. Saha, I. Sharma, R. G. Sharma, P. P. Shaw, M. Siraj, S. N. Thakur, M. S. Washington Sundar, G. H. Vihari, S. A. Yadav, U. T. Yadav.

S. Gill, part of the squad for the World Test Championship final against New Zealand in June, went home injured before the England leg of the tour. Avesh Khan (like Easwaran, promoted from the reserves to the main party) and Washington Sundar were injured while playing for the County Select XI against the Indians. Shaw and S. A. Yadav arrived from a white-ball series in Sri Lanka to replace them. P. M. Krishna and A. R. Nagwaswalla were travelling reserves.

Coach: R. J. Shastri. *Batting coach*: V. Rathore. *Bowling coach*: B. Arun. *Fielding coach*: R. Sridhar. *Logistics manager*: R. Upadhyaya. *Administrative manager*: G. Dongre. *Trainers*: S. Desai, N. Webb. *Training assistants*: D. Garani, D. V. G. I. Raghavindraa, B. G. U. N. Seneviratne. *Physiotherapists*: N. Patel, Y. Parmar. *Masseurs*: A. Kanade, R. Kumar. *Media manager*: M. Parikh. *Content producer*: R. Arora. *Analyst*: H. P. Mohan.

TEST MATCH AVERAGES

ENGLAND – BATTING AND FIELDING

	T	I	NO	R	HS	100	50	Avge	Ct
J. E. Root	4	7	1	564	180*	3	1	94.00	7
†D. J. Malan	2	3	0	106	70	0	1	35.33	0
H. Hameed	3	5	0	140	68	0	2	28.00	0
J. M. Bairstow	4	7	0	184	57	0	1	26.28	9
†R. J. Burns	4	7	0	183	61	0	2	26.14	2
†S. M. Curran	3	5	1	74	32	0	0	18.50	1
†M. M. Ali	3	5	0	83	35	0	0	16.60	7
J. C. Buttler	3	5	0	72	25	0	0	14.40	18
C. Overton	2	3	0	43	32	0	0	14.33	3
D. P. Sibley	2	4	0	57	28	0	0	14.25	1
O. E. Robinson............	4	7	1	45	15	0	0	7.50	1
†J. M. Anderson............	4	7	3	4	2	0	0	1.00	1

Played in one Test: †S. C. J. Broad 4, 0 (2 ct); Z. Crawley 27, 6; D. W. Lawrence 0, 25; O. J. D. Pope 81, 2; C. R. Woakes 50, 18 (1 ct); M. A. Wood 5, 0*.

BOWLING

	Style	O	M	R	W	BB	5I	Avge
C. R. Woakes	RFM	47	14	138	7	4-55	0	19.71
C. Overton	RFM	62.3	16	168	8	3-14	0	21.00
O. E. Robinson	RFM	166.2	47	448	21	5-65	2	21.33
J. M. Anderson	RFM	163.3	51	370	15	5-62	1	24.66
M. A. Wood	RF	42.1	6	142	5	3-51	0	28.40
M. M. Ali	OB	86	3	299	6	2-84	0	49.83
S. M. Curran	LFM	74	10	238	3	2-27	0	79.33

Also bowled: S. C. J. Broad (RFM) 25–4–88–1; J. E. Root (OB) 18–2–40–1.

INDIA – BATTING AND FIELDING

	T	I	NO	R	HS	100	50	Avge	Ct
R. G. Sharma	4	8	1	368	127	1	2	52.57	3
K. L. Rahul	4	8	0	315	129	1	1	39.37	3
S. N. Thakur	2	3	0	117	60	0	2	39.00	0
C. A. Pujara	4	8	1	227	91	0	2	32.42	0
V. Kohli	4	7	0	218	55	0	2	31.14	6
†R. A. Jadeja	4	7	0	160	56	0	1	22.85	1
†R. R. Pant	4	7	0	146	50	0	1	20.85	14
Mohammed Shami	3	5	1	75	56*	0	1	18.75	1
J. J. Bumrah	4	7	2	87	34*	0	0	17.40	0
A. M. Rahane	4	7	0	109	61	0	1	15.57	1
I. Sharma	2	4	1	34	16	0	0	11.33	1
M. Siraj	4	6	4	14	7*	0	0	7.00	2

Played in one Test: U. T. Yadav 10, 25.

BOWLING

	Style	O	M	R	W	BB	5I	Avge
J. J. Bumrah	RFM	151	40	375	18	5-64	1	20.83
S. N. Thakur	RFM	49	7	154	7	2-22	0	22.00
U. T. Yadav	RF	37.2	4	136	6	3-60	0	22.66
Mohammed Shami	RFM	96.5	19	303	11	4-95	0	27.54
M. Siraj	RFM	126.5	22	430	14	4-32	0	30.71
I. Sharma	RFM	56	7	174	5	3-69	0	34.80
R. A. Jadeja	SLA	123	27	272	6	2-36	0	45.33

For the World Test Championship final, see page 823.

COUNTY SELECT XI v INDIANS

At Chester-le-Street, July 20–22. Drawn. Toss: Indians. First-class debut: J. E. K. Rew.
India were originally scheduled to play two four-day warm-up matches against India A at Northampton and Leicester, before evolving pandemic regulations forced a change of plan. Intra-squad warm-ups were arranged, but their management were keen for a first-class fixture, so the ECB

mustered a scratch side. With the exception of Hameed, it was filled with development players rather than Test hopefuls – though it was bolstered by the tourists' own Avesh Khan and Washington Sundar, after James Bracey had a Covid contact, and Zak Chappell was injured. But Avesh broke his left thumb trying to stop a return drive from Vihari, and Sundar had a finger broken batting against Mohammed Siraj, ruling both out of the tour. There was a failure for Rohit Sharma, named as captain while Virat Kohli rested a stiff back, but the rest of the top order got a start. Rahul batted three hours for a century, as did Jadeja for 75, and they put on 127 for the fifth wicket before the last five fell for 29, Miles taking four for six with the new ball, including his 300th first-class wicket. Replying to 311, the County Select XI received a lesson in English-style seam bowling, and only Hameed – who boosted his Test credentials by grinding out 112 – exceeded 33. On the third morning, the Indians – 91 in front – gave their batsmen time in the middle rather than trying to conjure a result. Jadeja added another half-century, and Sharma set a notional target of 284 shortly before tea; nobody objected when bad light brought an early end.

Close of play: first day, Indians 306-9 (Bumrah 3, Siraj 1); second day, County Select XI 220.

Indians

*R. G. Sharma c Carson b James	9			
M. A. Agarwal b James	28	– (1) c Washington Sundar b Carson	47	
C. A. Pujara st Rew b Carson	21	– (2) c sub (R. Ahmed) b Carson	38	
G. H. Vihari c Miles b Patterson-White	24	– (3) not out	43	
†K. L. Rahul retired out	101			
R. A. Jadeja c Libby b Miles	75	– (4) retired out	51	
S. N. Thakur b Miles	20	– (5) not out	6	
A. R. Patel c Rew b Miles	0			
U. T. Yadav c Libby b Patterson-White	12			
J. J. Bumrah b Miles	5			
M. Siraj not out	3			
B 6, lb 1, nb 6	13	Lb 1, w 5, nb 1	7	

1/33 (1) 2/41 (2) 3/67 (3) (93 overs) 311
4/107 (4) 5/234 (5) 6/282 (7)
7/282 (8) 8/290 (6) 9/302 (9) 10/311 (10)

1/87 (1) (3 wkts dec, 55 overs) 192
2/98 (2) 3/182 (4)

Miles 17.1–4–45–4; Avesh Khan 9.5–2–41–0; James 12–3–32–2; Patterson-White 27–2–80–2; Carson 18–1–71–1; Rhodes 7–1–25–0; Yates 2–0–10–0. *Second innings*—Miles 8–0–41–0; James 9–3–22–0; Rhodes 5–1–17–0; Carson 22–2–64–2; Patterson-White 11–0–47–0.

County Select XI

H. Hameed c Rahul b Thakur	112	– (2) not out	13	
J. D. Libby b Yadav	12	– (1) not out	17	
R. M. Yates c Rahul b Bumrah	1			
M. S. Washington Sundar c Sharma b Siraj	1			
*W. M. H. Rhodes b Yadav	11			
L. W. James c Thakur b Yadav	27			
†J. E. K. Rew c Sharma b Jadeja	2			
L. A. Patterson-White c Yadav b Patel	33			
J. J. Carson b Siraj	3			
C. N. Miles not out	1			
Avesh Khan absent hurt				
B 2, lb 8, nb 7	17	Nb 1	1	

1/20 (2) 2/24 (3) 3/29 (4) (82.3 overs) 220
4/56 (5) 5/131 (6) 6/159 (7)
7/198 (1) 8/208 (9) 9/220 (8)

(no wkt, 15.5 overs) 31

Yadav 15–7–22–3; Bumrah 15–6–29–1; Siraj 13–2–32–2; Thakur 14–6–31–1; Jadeja 15–3–55–1; Patel 10.3–3–41–1. *Second innings*—Bumrah 5–2–11–0; Thakur 5–2–11–0; Siraj 3–0–4–0; Yadav 2.5–1–5–0.

Umpires: Hassan Adnan and P. R. Pollard.

ENGLAND v INDIA

First LV= Insurance Test

JAMES COYNE

At Nottingham, August 4–8. Drawn. England 2pts (after 2pt penalty), India 2pts (after 2pt penalty). Toss: England.

Time was when England captains were besieged by all manner of problems peripheral to their on-field role. Barmaids, Tiger Moths, facial hair – everything seemed to weigh down the man who had to toss up, then go out and score the runs. There will always be an ambassadorial aspect to the job. But central contracts, and the army of ECB pen-pushers and tracksuits, were supposed to have lightened the load. It didn't appear that way for Root. It just looked as if old issues had been replaced by modern ones.

Whether grappling with the day-to-day grind of biosecurity; a schedule and selection still skewed towards white-ball cricket two years after World Cup success; the loss of the injured Jofra Archer and the recuperating Ben Stokes; uncertainty over the Ashes tour… Root's Test team seemed disproportionately affected. And then there was The Hundred,

Here's to you, Mr Robinson: Joe Root welcomes Ollie Robinson to the five-for club.

which had dominated the calendar and the conversation leading into this series. Root was himself the poster boy for Trent Rockets, as any spectator who made the walk across the river from Nottingham station could see.

Somehow, he managed to block all this out to produce one of his best innings. It was unclear whether his new status as a Hundred local added to the noise, but he was carried along by a cacophonous crowd through the nerviest moments of England's second innings, to a century which ranked alongside any of the game's great backs-to-the-wall performances. Mike Atherton, who had played one of his own, at Johannesburg, called it a "privilege" to be on commentary as India's fast bowlers, led by the electrifying Bumrah, threw everything at Root. (The privilege was not extended to Sky's other premier commentator: Nasser Hussain was busy at The Hundred.) His runs ensured England didn't lose – as they never had in 20 previous Tests where he had scored a century. But the coolness with which India knocked off the first 52 of their required 209 on the fourth evening for the loss of Rahul suggested that, had rain not washed out the last day, that link might easily have been severed.

Reporters who closely follow the England team had expressed concern for Root's well-being after hearing his voice crack on a pre-match Zoom call, when he said of Stokes: "I just want my friend to be OK." Tellingly, he had shifted his customary eve-of-game press conference to two days before the Test, to free up his mind in plenty of time. In the warmer afterglow of his century on the fourth day, he insisted he was coping – and that, far from suffering white-ball overload, he had been aided by the one-day series against Sri Lanka, which helped him stand taller at the crease, and restored pace through his wrists. His balance looked improved, his cover-driving and clips off his pads serene. One thing was certain: the disparity between him and his team-mates was unsustainable. Root's match haul of 173 made him the first in the world to pass 1,000 Test runs in the calendar year; next for England were Lawrence (354) and Sibley (345), and neither was long for this side.

FASTEST TO 1,000 RUNS IN A CALENDAR YEAR

May 3	M. Amarnath (I)	1983		Jul 27	D. G. Bradman (Aus)	1948
Jun 3	I. V. A. Richards (WI)	1976		Jul 27	A. D. Mathews (SL)	2014
Jul 1	R. Dravid (I)	2006		Jul 30	B. C. Lara (WI)	2004
Jul 5	D. L. Amiss (E)	1974		Aug 2	G. C. Smith (SA)	2008
Jul 18	K. C. Sangakkara (SL)	2014		**Aug 7**	**J. E. Root (E)**	**2021**

At the toss, Stokes struggled to recall the names of his five debutants – "Can someone help me out?" – yet that appeared to be his lone concern as England brushed aside Pakistan in 57 overs. Not since March 1985, and the plate final of the Rothmans Cup in Sharjah, also against Pakistan, had an England team boasted so few caps: 70 then, 124 now, of which Stokes had 98. Inevitably, his team became known as "Ben's Babes". Mahmood gave them a dream

Despite Burns's fifth-ball departure to Bumrah, the top order did actually grit their teeth on the first morning. After a fortnight of 100-ball whacking, there was much tittering as England took 15 minutes to score a run, and Sibley 25; the first boundary, by Crawley, took 34. But it was also a reflection of how India, who had spent a few weeks in the nets since the World Test Championship final, with just one warm-up match, hit their straps right away. Sibley's 18 was the lowest unbeaten score by an England opener in a complete pre-lunch session since Chris Smith ground out 12 at Karachi in 1983-84. But the real crime was that he gave it away so soon after, pushing a catch to the split field set by Kohli for one of England's crabbier players.

As for their decline from 138 for three to 183 all out – their lowest first-innings total in a home Test against India when batting first – anything more would have been an overachievement, since Bairstow, Buttler and Curran were all facing a red ball for the first time since the winter Tests in the subcontinent. The batting coach, Marcus Trescothick, agreed it was inadequate preparation. Buttler's slim pickings in the opening game of a series continued: an 18-ball duck, then bowled for 17 leaving a straight one from Thakur, India's useful fourth seamer.

Luckily for England, on a second day strafed to 33.4 overs by rain and gloom, the conditions were tough for any batsman, and Anderson, now 39, was in the fettle to exploit them. After Robinson persuaded Rohit to hook the last ball before lunch to fine leg, ending a skilful opening stand of 97, Pujara looked all at sea. He soon nicked a booming outswinger, then Kohli thrust out on fourth stump, and edged to Buttler. After 454 deliveries to him dating back to August 2014, including three dropped catches, Anderson

Scything and skying: Ravindra Jadeja follows through with more than a flourish.

had finally dismissed him in a Test again. The haywire Rahane almost ran himself out once, then did so.

India had lost four for 15, and their lead might have been negligible were it not for England's slip catching, so shoddy that they tumbled to tenth in the world over the previous three years in this key department. Drops by Sibley and Root were the costliest, and helped Rahul – on 52 and 78 – cast aside unpleasant memories of opening in England in 2018. He was no shrinking violet: on the third day, the umpires were keen to get on with it, but Rahul took the arrival of a small grey cloud overhead as his cue to walk off towards the pavilion. Relations between the sides did not improve.

Anderson did eventually have him caught behind on 84, overtaking Anil Kumble to become the third-highest Test wicket-taker, with 620. But his old ally Broad, on the sixth anniversary of his eight for 15 here against Australia, was struggling in the crosswinds; in search of a change of luck in the second innings, he dug out the previous summer's lockdown bandana. His travails were offset by a successful return from suspension for Robinson, who looked heir presumptive to the new ball – so long as he stayed out of bother. While no one could quibble with the control and movement which earned him a five-wicket haul in his second Test – a chance he feared he might never get – a shushing send-off after he cut short Jadeja's jaunty innings on 56 was a small sign, ahead of an Australia tour, that he might be too easy to wind up. With the Indian tail at times swinging themselves off their feet (Bumrah even hit his first Test six), England eventually conceded 95 on first innings.

Back in the rubble of their first-day collapse, Root had constructed a minor gem, his first fifty in 12 Test innings, passing Alastair Cook's England-record tally of 15,737 runs in all formats. Now his strategy was hanging by a thread: by requesting a strip with an

MOST RUNS FOR ENGLAND IN ALL FORMATS

		M	Tests	ODIs	T20Is	100	Avge
16,602	J. E. Root	298	9,600	6,109	893	39	48.97
15,737	A. N. Cook....	257	12,472	3,204	61	38	42.88
13,779	K. P. Pietersen .	275	8,181	4,422*	1,176	32	44.30
13,331	I. R. Bell......	287	7,727	5,416	188	26	40.27
13,190	G. A. Gooch ...	243	8,900	4,290	–	28	40.58

* Pietersen also scored 18 ODI runs for an ICC World XI.

As at January 16, 2022.

ample topping of grass – making the selection of a frontline spinner near-impossible – then choosing to make first use of it, he had gambled that conditions would ease by the time England batted again.

Sure enough, the heavy roller had flattened out the worst indentations, and the showery weather was quelling any reverse swing. But Root could not have foreseen that the new ball chosen by Kohli would barely swing at all. A rare chance to play straight threw Root's ailing partners a lifeline, even if none looked like clinging on for long. For England to reach 300, which now seemed the bare minimum, the captain would have to be around for most of it.

The way he throttled back and forth, as conditions, partners and the balance of power changed, was exemplary. And Bumrah was a constant menace, eventually adding five wickets to his first-innings four. Root was skittish as he neared 50, then 100 – including 12 nervy balls on 97, when Buttler had just gone, and the lead was not yet 150 – but otherwise he straddled the line between risk and reward to perfection.

Batting seemed to have become relatively easy on the fourth day, until around 2pm when the gloom descended and the lights came on. Wherever Root takes his place in the pantheon, Hutton or Gooch never had to contend with these Dukes balls zipping around off a floodlit surface. Suddenly Bumrah produced a leaping inswinger, which Sibley – after 132 balls with nary a flutter of the eyes at the off side – tried to leather through the covers, and Pant took a spectacular diving catch off the inside edge.

As that brought in the belligerent Bairstow, Root sensed the moment to hunker down. It was a masterful shifting through the gears, and you couldn't imagine anyone else in his side possessing such skill or temperament. That yawning gap, between one superb batsman and the mediocrity of others, was England's biggest worry.

Player of the Match: J. E. Root. *Attendance:* 61,165.

Close of play: first day, India 21-0 (Sharma 9, Rahul 9); second day, India 124-5 (Rahul 57, Pant 7); third day, England 25-0 (Burns 11, Sibley 9); fourth day, India 52-1 (Sharma 12, Pujara 12).

England

R. J. Burns lbw b Bumrah	0	– c Pant b Siraj	18
D. P. Sibley c Rahul b Mohammed Shami	18	– c Pant b Bumrah	28
Z. Crawley c Pant b Siraj	27	– c Pant b Bumrah	6
*J. E. Root lbw b Thakur	64	– c Pant b Bumrah	109
J. M. Bairstow lbw b Mohammed Shami	29	– c Jadeja b Siraj	30
D. W. Lawrence c Pant b Mohammed Shami	0	– lbw b Thakur	25
†J. C. Buttler c Pant b Bumrah	0	– b Thakur	17
S. M. Curran not out	27	– c Siraj b Bumrah	32
O. E. Robinson c Mohammed Shami b Thakur	0	– c Rahane b Mohammed Shami	15
S. C. J. Broad lbw b Bumrah	4	– b Bumrah	0
J. M. Anderson b Bumrah	1	– not out	0
B 1, lb 8, nb 4	13	B 5, lb 2, w 6, nb 10	23

1/0 (1) 2/42 (3) 3/66 (2) (65.4 overs) 183   1/37 (1) 2/46 (3) (85.5 overs) 303
4/138 (5) 5/138 (6) 6/145 (7)   3/135 (2) 4/177 (5)
7/155 (4) 8/155 (9) 9/160 (10) 10/183 (11)   5/211 (6) 6/237 (7) 7/274 (4)
  8/295 (8) 9/295 (10) 10/303 (9)

Bumrah 20.4–4–46–4; Mohammed Shami 17–2–28–3; Siraj 12–2–48–1; Thakur 13–3–41–2; Jadeja 3–0–11–0. *Second innings*—Bumrah 19–2–64–5; Siraj 25–3–84–2; Mohammed Shami 15.5–1–72–1; Thakur 13–1–37–2; Jadeja 13–3–39–0.

India

R. G. Sharma c Curran b Robinson	36	– (2) not out	12
K. L. Rahul c Buttler b Anderson	84	– (1) c Buttler b Broad	26
C. A. Pujara c Buttler b Anderson	4	– not out	12
*V. Kohli c Buttler b Anderson	0		
A. M. Rahane run out (Bairstow)	5		
†R. R. Pant c Bairstow b Robinson	25		
R. A. Jadeja c Broad b Robinson	56		
S. N. Thakur c Root b Anderson	0		
Mohammed Shami b Robinson	13		
J. J. Bumrah c Broad b Robinson	28		
M. Siraj not out	7		
B 6, lb 6, nb 8	20	Lb 1, nb 1	2

1/97 (1) 2/104 (3) 3/104 (4) (84.5 overs) 278   1/34 (1) (1 wkt, 14 overs) 52
4/112 (5) 5/145 (6) 6/205 (2)
7/205 (8) 8/232 (7) 9/245 (9) 10/278 (10)

Anderson 23–8–54–4; Broad 20–3–70–0; Robinson 26.5–6–85–5; Curran 15–2–57–0. *Second innings*—Anderson 5–1–12–0; Broad 5–1–18–1; Robinson 4–0–21–0.

Umpires: M. A. Gough and R. A. Kettleborough.   Third umpire: R. K. Illingworth.
Referee: B. C. Broad.

ENGLAND v INDIA

Second LV= Insurance Test

LAWRENCE BOOTH

At Lord's, August 12–16. India won by 151 runs. Toss: England. India 12pts.

Hell, wrote Sartre, is other people. But Virat Kohli had something more specific in mind. Addressing his team on the Lord's outfield shortly after lunch on the last day, he told them that – for England's batsmen – "hell" would be the next 60 overs. In fact, their torment proved less prolonged: when Mohammed Siraj bowled Anderson with the fifth ball of the 52nd, England, undone by the ferocity of the bowling, fielding and sledging, were all out for 120. A few hours earlier, India had been facing defeat; now they celebrated a stirring victory, their eighth in 65 Tests in England. It was arguably their most memorable, undoubtedly their most fractious.

The match had turned upside-down on the last morning, when Mohammed Shami and Bumrah took advantage of England's decision to spread the field and bowl short. Between them, the pair had failed to get off the mark in 40 Test innings out of 102, including first-innings ducks here; they possessed batting averages of 11 and three. With India eight down and just 182 ahead, two straight balls ought to have been enough to earn England a modest run-chase.

But they were distracted: apparently forgetting the score, they attempted to settle one. Late on the third evening, Bumrah had bowled a ten-ball over to Anderson, overstepping four times and peppering him with bouncers. Anderson was unimpressed, Bumrah

Flinch and miss: James Anderson gets a working-over at Lord's...

Mike Hewitt, Getty Images

…and makes his feelings known at the end of the third day.

unrepentant. The image of Root walking off after a majestic 180 not out was marred by a squabble behind him: Anderson v India, with Bumrah's arms outstretched as he argued his case. Things reportedly got uglier in the Long Room.

Fast-forward to the fifth morning, when Bumrah arrived to a volley of words from Buttler; soon, he suffered a blow to the head from Wood. Yet the tactics suited India: with five men on the boundary waiting for a swipe, England were spurning bowled and leg-before. And they suited Kohli, who heckled from the balcony, stoking grievance for the afternoon. Root grew frazzled, dropping Bumrah at slip off Ali on 22; Shami grew emboldened, bringing up his second Test half-century with a heaved six off Ali into the Grand Stand. Nine balls after lunch, with the stand worth 89 in 20 overs – an Indian ninth-wicket record in England – Kohli declared, setting 272 in 60. Only New Zealand, against Sri Lanka at Kandy in 1983-84, had won a Test after making a post-lunch declaration on the last day. And yet it was clear only one team could win from here.

The same had seemed true for much of the first day, when – after being put in under grey skies – India batted with skill and heart against a tweaked attack. Wood came in for Stuart Broad, who had expected to win his 150th cap but tore a calf after jumping a hurdle in training, and missed the rest of the summer; Ali replaced Dan Lawrence, adding balance in his first home Test since the 2019 Ashes; and Hameed returned after an absence of nearly five years, ousting Zak Crawley, who had averaged 11 since making 267 against Pakistan 12 months earlier. India, denied a crack at victory in the First Test by rain, made one change – Ishant Sharma, fit again, for the injured Shardul Thakur.

England had feared Anderson might miss out, too, after tightness in his thigh two days out. The suggestion irked him; predictably enough, he claimed the game's first wicket. The problem was that, by the time he bowled Rohit for a calmly authoritative 83, his best score outside India, the total was 126. Rahul had been the silent partner but, when he lifted Ali for a straight six – having moved to 22 in 107 boundaryless balls – it brought up the highest opening stand by a team inserted at Lord's, beating 114 between Alastair Cook and Andrew Strauss against South Africa in 2008. Anderson quickly added Pujara, poking to third slip, but Rahul took over, and Kohli bedded in, until Robinson had him caught in the cordon to end a stand of 117. By then, Rahul had completed his sixth Test hundred, and fifth abroad. The tourists closed on 276 for three – a triumph in the conditions.

But this was a game that refused to stand still. From the second ball next morning, Rahul mistimed Robinson to extra cover. From the seventh, Rahane fiddled Anderson to first slip. Pant capered to 37 before edging Wood, and Shami whacked Ali to midwicket. Jadeja resisted, but the last eight had fallen for 97, and Anderson finished with five for 62 – his seventh Test five-wicket haul at Lord's, and 31st in all. The gap between this and his first (also at Lord's, against Zimbabwe in 2003) was a Test-record 18 years 81 days, beating West Indies off-spinner Lance Gibbs. Trying to predict when he might call it a day was like trying to choose the lottery numbers.

England's openers put on a careful 23 by tea, after which Sibley immediately flicked Siraj to short midwicket, a shot that had cost him in Nottingham. Out walked Hameed, as Lord's held its breath for a player whose absence from the side had at times felt permanent.

ENGLAND OPENERS MAKING A DUCK IN THE SAME INNINGS

H. Sutcliffe and E. Paynter	1st inns v New Zealand at Christchurch. . .	1932-33
M. H. Denness and D. L. Amiss	2nd inns v Pakistan at Hyderabad	1972-73
D. W. Randall and G. Boycott	1st inns v Australia at Perth	1979-80
G. A. Gooch and R. T. Robinson	2nd inns v West Indies at Kingston	1985-86
M. E. Trescothick and A. J. Strauss . . .	2nd inns v Pakistan at Faisalabad.	2005-06
R. J. Burns and D. P. Sibley	**2nd inns v India at Lord's**	**2021**

He offered a nervous, crooked prod to his first ball – full, straight, 85mph – and was bowled. India's adrenalin was pumping. To Kohli's irritation, Siraj used up two reviews against Root, who nonchalantly moved past Graham Gooch's 8,900 and into second on England's Test list behind Cook.

Burns went shortly before stumps for 49, but next morning Root and Bairstow flourished in the best batting conditions of the match. With their stand worth 121, Bairstow – reaching 50 for the first time in 20 innings – flapped Siraj to slip, victim of an all-too-obvious short-ball trap. Root, though, was untouchable. He brought up his 22nd Test hundred, ticked off 9,000 Test runs, and remained above the fray as others came and went, including Curran first ball. As he had the previous afternoon, Root defused the hat-trick delivery. After Bumrah roughed him up, Shami bowled Anderson to end the day, and England had 391, a lead of 27. Only once at Lord's, against Australia in 1930, had they lost after making more in their first innings. And they had never lost when Root made a century.

Next day, that rule looked safe. Wood knocked over the openers, and Curran induced a fatal prod from Kohli not long before lunch, sprinting off deliriously towards square leg. At 56 for three, ahead by 29, India needed solidity. It came from two out-of-form veterans. Pujara focused on defence, scoring 12 from his first 113 balls, and earning mock applause when he reached 20, from 131. Rahane was a touch more adventurous, but the afternoon session brought 49 runs in 28 wicketless overs, as if both teams were steeling themselves for the final push.

Not until the stand was worth 100 in almost 50 overs did the game enter its next phase: Wood dug one in, and Pujara flinched to Root, the floating slip. His 45 had consumed 206 deliveries, and given India hope – only for Ali to remove Rahane and Jadeja in quick succession. When Robinson did for Pant and Ishant Sharma next morning, England were 15 minutes' sensible cricket away from chasing under 200 in two and a half sessions. Instead, they lost their heads, allowing Kohli to deliver his pep-talk with conviction rather than hope. Bumrah, he felt, had been treated with disrespect by England's fielders. It was time to return the favour.

From the start, India oozed venom, and the batsmen had no antidote. Burns spooned a leading edge to cover in the first over; Sibley edged behind in the second. For the first time in 531 home Tests, both England openers had made a duck in the same innings. Hameed was missed by Rohit in the slips on four, but lbw to Ishant on nine. Sensing the

Philip Brown, Popperfoto/Getty Images

Getting out of hand: Joe Root despairs as Jasprit Bumrah plays the innings of his life.

worst, England's fans lapped up more heartening news elsewhere, giving Andrew Strauss a standing ovation as he walked round the boundary: the Red for Ruth campaign, in honour of his wife, who had died of cancer in 2018, had raised over £1m. Back in the middle, India struck a blow either side of tea: Bairstow lbw on review to Ishant; Root, top-scoring for the fourth innings in a row, caught by Kohli at slip off Bumrah for 33. Kohli soon dropped Buttler, which for a while looked costly. Buttler and Ali survived nearly 16 overs, before Siraj did for Ali and Curran, who completed the first king pair in a Lord's Test. But Robinson got stuck in, too, earning the compliment of regular chit-chat from Kohli, who marched about like a maharajah.

Finally, with nine overs to go, India broke through. Thanks to a clever slower ball, Bumrah won an lbw shout on review against Robinson from round the wicket, and three deliveries later Siraj ended Buttler's two and a half hours' resistance. He then bowled

KING PAIRS FOR ENGLAND

W. Attewell	v Australia at Sydney	1891-92
E. G. Hayes	v South Africa at Cape Town	1905-06
J. M. Anderson	v India at Visakhapatnam	2016-17
S. M. Curran	**v India at Lord's**	**2021**

Anderson third ball – his eighth wicket of the match, and England's seventh duck. As Root reflected on a seventh game without a win, grimly taking the blame for his last-morning tactics, India were still bristling. "You go after one of us, all 11 will come right back," said Rahul. Once, his team would have been the bullied, not the bullies. But times change, and India – only a few hours after contemplating defeat – led 1–0.

Player of the Match: K. L. Rahul.   *Attendance:* 137,204.

Close of play: first day, India 276-3 (Rahul 127, Rahane 1); second day, England 119-3 (Root 48, Bairstow 6); third day, England 391; fourth day, India 181-6 (Pant 14, I. Sharma 4).

India

R. G. Sharma b Anderson	83	– (2) c Ali b Wood	21
K. L. Rahul c Sibley b Robinson	129	– (1) c Buttler b Wood	5
C. A. Pujara c Bairstow b Anderson	9	– c Root b Wood	45
*V. Kohli c Root b Robinson	42	– c Buttler b Curran	20
A. M. Rahane c Root b Anderson	1	– c Buttler b Ali	61
†R. R. Pant c Buttler b Wood	37	– c Buttler b Robinson	22
R. A. Jadeja c Anderson b Wood	40	– b Ali	3
Mohammed Shami c Burns b Ali	0	– (9) not out	56
I. Sharma lbw b Anderson	8	– (8) lbw b Robinson	16
J. J. Bumrah c Buttler b Anderson	0	– not out	34
M. Siraj not out	0		
B 8, lb 5, nb 2	15	B 2, lb 12, nb 1	15

1/126 (1) 2/150 (3) 3/267 (4) (126.1 overs) 364
4/278 (2) 5/282 (5) 6/331 (6)
7/336 (8) 8/362 (9) 9/364 (10) 10/364 (7)

1/18 (1) (8 wkts dec, 109.3 overs) 298
2/27 (2) 3/55 (4)
4/155 (3) 5/167 (5)
6/175 (7) 7/194 (6) 8/209 (8)

Anderson 29–7–62–5; Robinson 33–10–73–2; Curran 22–2–72–0; Wood 24.1–2–91–2; Ali 18–1–53–1. *Second innings*—Anderson 25.3–6–53–0; Robinson 17–6–45–2; Wood 18–4–51–3; Curran 18–3–42–1; Ali 26–1–84–2; Root 5–0–9–0.

England

R. J. Burns lbw b Mohammed Shami	49	– c Siraj b Bumrah	0
D. P. Sibley c Rahul b Siraj	11	– c Pant b Mohammed Shami	0
H. Hameed b Siraj	0	– lbw b I. Sharma	9
*J. E. Root not out	180	– c Kohli b Bumrah	33
J. M. Bairstow c Kohli b Siraj	57	– lbw b I. Sharma	2
†J. C. Buttler b I. Sharma	23	– c Pant b Siraj	25
M. M. Ali c Kohli b I. Sharma	27	– c Kohli b Siraj	13
S. M. Curran c R. G. Sharma b I. Sharma	0	– c Pant b Siraj	0
O. E. Robinson lbw b Siraj	6	– lbw b Bumrah	9
M. A. Wood run out (Jadeja/Pant)	5	– not out	0
J. M. Anderson b Mohammed Shami	0	– b Siraj	0
B 5, lb 6, w 5, nb 17	33	B 17, lb 7, w 1, nb 4	29

1/23 (2) 2/23 (3) 3/108 (1) (128 overs) 391
4/229 (5) 5/283 (6) 6/341 (7)
7/341 (8) 8/357 (9) 9/371 (10) 10/391 (11)

1/1 (1) 2/1 (2) (51.5 overs) 120
3/44 (3) 4/67 (5)
5/67 (4) 6/90 (7) 7/90 (8)
8/120 (9) 9/120 (6) 10/120 (11)

I. Sharma 24–4–69–3; Bumrah 26–6–79–0; Mohammed Shami 26–3–95–2; Siraj 30–7–94–4; Jadeja 22–1–43–0. *Second innings*—Bumrah 15–3–33–3; Mohammed Shami 10–5–13–1; Jadeja 6–3–5–0; Siraj 10.5–3–32–4; I. Sharma 10–3–13–2.

Umpires: M. A. Gough and R. K. Illingworth.   Third umpire: R. A. Kettleborough.
Referee: B. C. Broad.

> **"** Another tour would not take place until 1948-49, by which time Collins had been deselected: her chance of an overseas Test had vanished for ever. It haunted her for decades. 'The disappointment at not going was intense,' she wrote in 1985."
> Women's cricket during the war, page 60

ENGLAND v INDIA

Third LV= Insurance Test

KIT HARRIS

At Leeds, August 25–28. England won by an innings and 76 runs. Toss: India. England 12pts.

Gloom, monopolised for so long by the English, hung heavy over Headingley. The pendulum of public morale had swung. To many, it felt like the 1990s again: the top three struggling, the fastest bowlers crocked, the best spinner omitted, a wicketkeeping experiment failed, and an injury list longer than a parish register. This was not the team England's supporters had learned to believe in: this was the mismatched outfit the Barmy Army had been mustered to serve.

The selection carousel continued to turn. England omitted Dom Sibley, after 160 runs in eight innings, and recalled Malan. Dropped from the Test team in 2018, when the national selector, Ed Smith, said he "might be better suited to overseas conditions", Malan had played one red-ball innings in 12 months, though that was 199 here, for Yorkshire against Sussex in June. Mark Wood's shoulder, meanwhile, had not recovered after he jarred it in the field at Lord's. The like-for-like replacement might have been Saqib Mahmood, but Root preferred Craig Overton; his reference to Overton's "highest release point in our squad" smacked more of data than daring.

After eight successive wrong calls in England, Kohli said he was surprised to win the toss. India had not lost a Test here since 1967, though this was only their fourth match in that time. On their previous visit, in 2002, they had scored 628 on a light-coloured pitch and won by an innings. Kohli had concluded this strip might be similar. But like the clouds, it had a dark tinge; there was moisture overhead and underfoot. Shortly before the start, he suggested England was "the toughest country to bat in". Almost immediately, India proved him right.

The Barmy Army's trumpeter played "Jerusalem", but met only apprehensive silence from the stands. The anxiety lasted six minutes. Anderson's fifth ball found Rahul's edge and Buttler's gloves, and the home fans breathed a sigh of relief. In Anderson's third over, Pujara snicked a perfect leg-cutter, and they punched the air. In his sixth, Kohli got a little touch on a big drive, and they were out of their seats. It was his 50th consecutive international innings without a century, and the seventh time he had been dismissed by Anderson – whose opening spell was 8–5–6–3. Only Australian off-spinner Nathan Lyon had removed Kohli as often in Tests.

Curran and Ali were brought on, and Rohit off-drove his first boundary after 57 minutes. But when Robinson returned for a burst before lunch, and coaxed a feather from Rahane, India's morning had yielded 56 for four. After the break, Pant decided not to die wondering, preferring suicide with his questions answered: a wild cut, without the room for it, gave Buttler a fifth catch. Only one other keeper had caught the first five in a Test innings: Australia's Brad Haddin, against India at Brisbane in 2014-15, when his victims also included Pujara, Kohli and Rahane.

BATTED – AND BRUISED

India's lowest Test totals after choosing to bat:

75	v West Indies at Delhi	1987-88
76	v South Africa at Ahmedabad	2007-08
78	**v England at Leeds**	**2021**
96	v England at Lord's	1979
104†	v Australia at Mumbai	2004-05
106	v Pakistan at Lucknow	1952-53

† *India's lowest winning first-innings total.*

Now, even the second-string bowlers were irrepressible. Rohit had battled to 19 but, seeking a second boundary in nearly three hours, hoicked Overton to mid-on; next ball, Shami fished, and found third slip. Ishant averted the hat-trick. Moments later, Curran, too, was on a hat-trick, after pinning Jadeja and Bumrah. Four wickets had fallen on 67, in six deliveries. The crowd were stunned into near-silence. When Overton removed Siraj, India were all out for 78, their lowest total against England for 47 years.

England had lost only three Tests after bowling a team out for under 100 in the first innings; India had never won after failing to reach three figures. But England still had to bat. By the time Ishant's wayward first over had yielded nine – 11.5% of India's total – nerves were settling. Burns and Hameed weathered a spell of 8–5–8–0 from Bumrah either side of tea. In the evening, Burns – after a working-over from Shami – rediscovered his deftness against seam, the bat almost sympathetically recoiling after each clip or push, like a pulled punch. Then came spin, and he punched a pull for four from Jadeja's first ball. Hameed was assertive but not showy. A series of statement defensives was punctuated by bold back-foot drives for four off all four pacemen. India began to wilt. Someone on the Western Terrace threw a bouncy ball on to the outfield, near Siraj, which upset Kohli. But then, didn't everything? A rattled Siraj bounced Burns, who hooked him for six. Kohli steamed. Hameed's late cut brought up the 100 partnership, England's third for the first wicket in 56 Tests. Both batsmen reached chanceless fifties, and England reached the close 42 ahead – wicketless, almost disbelieving.

JUST A PERFECT DAY

Teams taking a first-innings lead, without losing a wicket, on the first day of a Test:

New Zealand (160-0) v Pakistan (104) at Hamilton	2000-01
England (157-0) v Australia (98) at Melbourne	2010-11
England (120-0) v India (78) at Leeds	**2021**

The second day also brought gloom, in the form of chill and cloud, and news of the death of Ted Dexter; England wore black armbands. Shami finally nipped one back through Burns, and the stand ended at 135 from 303 balls – England's highest and longest opening partnership since Cook and Hameed posted 180 at Rajkot in 2016-17. Hameed now appeared spellbound. On the first day, he had reached 60 off 130 balls; on the second, he added eight in 65, before Jadeja beat his lunge. Root arrived on his nirvanic plane, and it was India's turn to be transfixed: as though cursed to aid him, Bumrah gifted England five runs with two wild overthrows.

A hapless father among unruly boys, Kohli looked exasperated, which merely made his young charges more hyperactive. England were 182 for two at lunch. The Indians dined in silence, no doubt under the glare of that parental eye. Root reached his fifty, and Malan carved the second new ball for three fours, before bringing up his own half-century. The last time England's top four had all passed 50 was against New Zealand at Dunedin in 2012-13 (Cook, Compton, nightwatchman Finn and Trott). The lead was 220 when – just before tea – Siraj implored Kohli to review Malan's feint down the leg side. DRS showed a tickle, and he was gone for 70. His partnership of 139 with Root was only the second hundred stand between two Yorkshire batsmen in a Leeds Test (after Root and Bairstow's 124 against New Zealand in 2013).

When the players returned, the umpires discovered Pant had used sticking tape to bind the fourth and fifth fingers of his gloves, apparently in breach of Law 27.2. He was told to remove it, and no more was said. Root continued sublimely to 23rd Test hundred, his sixth of 2021, equalling England's record for a calendar year (alongside Denis Compton in 1947 and Michael Vaughan in 2002). He was also the fifth to score eight against India, after Sobers, Richards, Ponting and Steve Smith.

Gareth Copley, Getty Images

Jump cut: Haseeb Hameed evades a rasping shot by Cheteshwar Pujara.

At last, and too late, wickets began to fall. Bairstow edged Shami to slip, and Buttler clipped him to midwicket. Root's reverse sweep took him to 500 runs in the series (next came Rahul, with 244), and England were more than 300 ahead when he was castled by Bumrah. He left the stage to a rapturous ovation. Ali holed out with a devil-may-care hoick off Jadeja; Curran, dismissed by the last three balls he had faced, kept out the fourth, but eventually hooked Siraj to long leg.

The third day dawned colder still, and England's slide continued, from 350 for three to 432. But, for India, the collapse was a mirage of sunlit uplands: in reality, they had reached only base camp and, 354 behind, had Everest to climb. It was overcast and murky – the floodlights were on for most of the day – but they fought their way uphill. Rahul hung around for an hour and a half scoring eight, only to be brilliantly caught, left-handed, by Bairstow at second slip.

After lunch, a small plane circled the ground, pulling a banner which read "Sack the ECB & Save Test Cricket" – an incongruous message, given the excitement of the series, and the determination to stage it. India had their own Test to save, as England's patience faltered. Ali was given a funky field, with three in the deep, including cow corner, but Pujara milked him for singles. Curran banged it in from round the wicket, but Rohit's swatted pulls showed what he thought of *that*. Robinson, alone in his patience, hit Rohit in front. Anderson was dragged back into battle, but conceded 20 from two overs. Curran tried bouncing Kohli, too, with the effectiveness of a pea shooter. When the light became bad, Root bowled himself and Ali to hasten the new ball; Kohli donned a cap. India had batted 80 overs, and were 215 for two at the close.

England fans fretted on day four. Were these still the bad old times? India were only 139 behind. A target of 150 could be tough – hell, 100 might. But the new ball came immediately, and a tumultuous session saw them lose eight for 63, barely better than their first-innings collapse of eight for 57. Pujara was first to go, lbw on review, without adding to his overnight 91. Anderson was all over Kohli, but a catch behind was overruled by DRS – the noise was bat on pad – and he reached his first fifty of the series.

Instead, it was Robinson who drew Kohli's edge, before Rahane nibbled at Anderson's irresistible line and length – his first second-innings wicket in seven games. Pant, as if in self-parody, ran down the pitch to meet his first and second balls, then prodded his seventh to third slip. Ali ripped one through Shami's gate. Robinson celebrated his five-for twice

– an lbw against Shami was overturned, then Ishant got a nick behind – and Jadeja's duel with Overton went four, four, four, out. Siraj lasted two balls, and it was all done at 12.43pm. Robinson won the match award, and Root, who had overtaken Vaughan's England record of 26 Test wins as captain, said he had never seen anyone take to Test cricket as seamlessly.

England had shown all the determination and dominance that had typified the best of their cricket in the 21st century. Whether this was a return to form, or a momentary uptick in the decline, was a matter for Kennington.

Player of the Match: O. E. Robinson. *Attendance:* 66,296.

Close of play: first day, England 120-0 (Burns 52, Hameed 60); second day, England 423-8 (Overton 24, Robinson 0); third day, India 215-2 (Pujara 91, Kohli 45).

India

R. G. Sharma c Robinson b Overton	19	– lbw b Robinson	59
K. L. Rahul c Buttler b Anderson	0	– c Bairstow b Overton	8
C. A. Pujara c Buttler b Anderson	1	– lbw b Robinson	91
*V. Kohli c Buttler b Anderson	7	– c Root b Robinson	55
A. M. Rahane c Buttler b Robinson	18	– c Buttler b Anderson	10
†R. R. Pant c Buttler b Robinson	2	– c Overton b Robinson	1
R. A. Jadeja lbw b Curran	4	– c Buttler b Overton	30
Mohammed Shami c Burns b Overton	0	– b Ali	6
I. Sharma not out	8	– c Buttler b Robinson	2
J. J. Bumrah lbw b Curran	0	– not out	1
M. Siraj c Root b Overton	3	– c Bairstow b Overton	0
Lb 11, nb 5	16	B 4, lb 4, w 2, nb 5	15

1/1 (2) 2/4 (3) 3/21 (4)   (40.4 overs) 78   1/34 (2) 2/116 (3)   (99.3 overs) 278
4/56 (5) 5/58 (6) 6/67 (1)   3/215 (4) 4/237 (4)
7/67 (8) 8/67 (7) 9/67 (10) 10/78 (11)   5/239 (5) 6/239 (6) 7/254 (8)
                                      8/257 (9) 9/278 (7) 10/278 (11)

Anderson 8–5–6–3; Robinson 10–3–16–2; Curran 10–2–27–2; Ali 2–0–4–0; Overton 10.4–5–14–3. *Second innings*—Anderson 26–11–63–1; Robinson 26–6–65–5; Overton 18.3–6–47–3; Curran 9–1–40–0; Ali 14–1–40–1; Root 6–1–15–0.

England

R. J. Burns b Mohammed Shami	61	C. Overton lbw b Mohammed Shami 32
H. Hameed b Jadeja	68	O. E. Robinson b Bumrah 0
D. J. Malan c Pant b Siraj	70	J. M. Anderson not out 0
*J. E. Root b Bumrah	121	B 8, lb 4, w 1, nb 8 21
J. M. Bairstow c Kohli b Mohammed Shami	29	
†J. C. Buttler c I. Sharma		1/135 (1) 2/159 (2) (132.2 overs) 432
b Mohammed Shami	7	3/298 (3) 4/350 (5)
M. M. Ali c sub (A. R. Patel) b Jadeja	8	5/360 (6) 6/383 (4) 7/383 (7)
S. M. Curran c sub (M. A. Agarwal) b Siraj	15	8/418 (8) 9/431 (9) 10/432 (10)

I. Sharma 22–0–92–0; Bumrah 27.2–10–59–2; Mohammed Shami 28–8–95–4; Siraj 23–3–86–2; Jadeja 32–8–88–2.

Umpires: R. A. Kettleborough and A. G. Wharf.   Third umpire: R. K. Illingworth.
Referee: B. C. Broad.

" The ice cream queues routinely outstripped those for beer."
The women's Hundred, page 1200

ENGLAND v INDIA

Fourth LV= Insurance Test

HUGH CHEVALLIER

At The Oval, September 2–6. India won by 157 runs. Toss: England. India 12pts.

Was it Rohit Sharma who swung this match? The only centurion in a game that toyed with greatness, he was the linchpin of India's second-innings fightback. Without his imposing, effortless century, it might have been England, not India, 2–1 up with one (in theory) to play. Rohit was as unworried by a 99-run deficit as he was unflurried by the home attack, and he showed how the best players transcend format: labelled a white-ball specialist incapable of dominating in Tests outside the subcontinent, he emphatically proved otherwise. He wasn't always watertight – Burns twice offered a lifeline – but Rohit was nothing if not watchable. When he fell, at 236 for two, Kohli inherited a lead of 137. And some weary England bowlers.

Or should India thank the unstoried Shardul Thakur? He was injured at Lord's and unwanted at Leeds, but in only his fourth Test he contributed two fifties, one a game-shifting innings of pure chutzpah, the other an act of such maturity it belied a first-class average of 16. For a player of Thakur's instincts, blocking is rarely the answer at 127 for

FASTEST TEST FIFTIES BY BALLS IN ENGLAND

31	S. N. Thakur	India v England at The Oval	2021
32	I. T. Botham	England v New Zealand at The Oval	1986
33	C. A. Roach	West Indies v England at The Oval	1933
33	Kapil Dev	India v England at Manchester	1982
33	Harbhajan Singh	India v England at Nottingham	2002
33	S. C. J. Broad	England v West Indies at Manchester	2020
35	G. N. Yallop	Australia v England at Manchester	1981
35	Kapil Dev	India v England at Lord's	1982
35	D. A. Warner	Australia v England at Birmingham	2015

seven, so he was perhaps liberated by the hole in which India languished. "Beefy" reached his half-century in 31 balls, snatching the record for the fastest Test fifty in England from a more famous wearer of the nickname. The second, level-headed, contribution cemented Indian ascendancy, while his three wickets were Pope (top-scorer in England's first innings), Burns (half-century in the second) and Root (no explanation required).

Rohit and Thakur played crucial roles, yet it was the unorthodox menace of Jasprit Bumrah that really set a tiger among the Oval pigeons. Match figures of four for 94 don't roar so loudly, yet he ripped the game from England. He had already lopped off the openers on the first evening, and his new-found batting expertise chipped in useful runs. But on the last afternoon he was briefly irresistible. England had lunched on 131 for two, their hopes of reaching 368 still aflicker if they could up the tempo on a somnolent pitch.

Jadeja broke through first, bowling the diligent Hameed, perhaps unsettled by the need for speed. The ball had slumbered after a helter-skelter first day, but Bumrah now found reverse swing. And when he added 90mph pace, he was terrifying. The delivery that toppled Pope angled in on a fuller length, then nipped back a fraction to clatter into the stumps. Though a beauty, it was a warm-up. In his next over, an inswinging yorker zeroed in to the base of leg: too fast, too accurate, too good for Bairstow. Similar deliveries soon after would have spelled the end of a lesser player than Root. Bumrah's post-lunch spell boiled down to 6–3–6–2, not bad in anyone's book, and yet so much more.

Fetch that: Rohit Sharma brings up his hundred with a six off Moeen Ali.

Philip Brown, Popperfoto/Getty Images

India's victory – 50 years after their only other win at The Oval – was inked in even before a firm prod by Ali popped straight to short leg, reducing England to 147 for six. That wicket, the fourth to fall for six runs in six overs, was a second for the persevering Jadeja, whose ability to land the ball in the rough had become a mounting threat, especially for left-handers. And it helped quell incredulity from much of India that Ravichandran Ashwin was still not playing. The last rites were dragged beyond tea, mainly by Woakes, before an anticlimactic end: Anderson reviewed his dismissal for caught behind, causing the small army of stewards to lumber on, off and – verdict upheld – back on again.

Each team had two changes from Leeds. India brought in Yadav and Thakur for Mohammed Shami and Ishant Sharma, both suffering niggles, while England preferred Woakes, playing a first-class game for the first time in over a year, to Sam Curran. Jos Buttler – absent for the birth of daughter Margot – was replaced by Pope. Bairstow took the gloves.

Though the match ended in sultry, almost subcontinental, heat, it had begun beneath Kennington cloud heavy enough for the floodlights to be ablaze; a green strip gave Root extra encouragement to bowl, even if it committed England to batting last. Thirteen wickets on an eventful Thursday justified the choice: not since 1926 had more fallen on the opening day of an Oval Test which, unusually, was not scheduled to mark the end of the Test summer. The ground also wore a new face, having undergone significant redevelopment at the Pavilion End.

The first skirmishes went to India, with 28 flowing in seven overs. The next seven, all maidens, went to England, as the ball began to deviate. Woakes had Rohit caught behind in his first over, while Rahul was undone by late swing from Robinson: 28 for two. An unexpectedly expensive Anderson removed Pujara, and the experiment of Jadeja at No. 5 paid few dividends when he edged Woakes to make it 69 for four. He should have been Woakes's second slip victim in two overs, but Root, apparently expecting Burns to lunge for the ball, had given Kohli a life on 22. The groan/cheer – delete according to allegiance – from the first of five full houses was deafening. How much would the lapse cost?

The answer was 28, and England's rescuer was Robinson, who removed Kohli for the third time in six innings when he nicked behind. Shortly after tea, India were floundering at 127 for seven. Anyone switching on at this juncture might have thought they were watching a highlights package. In his record-breaking fifty, Thakur walloped six fours and three sixes, progress soon made to look almost pedestrian by the last five deliveries of the innings: thumped Thakur four; his dismissal (lbw on review); dropped-catch-turned-run-out to despatch Bumrah; Siraj single; acrobatic overhead catch by Bairstow to do for Yadav.

India's total of 191 wasn't so shoddy in the conditions, and there was time for their lot to get better. Iffy technique hastened the departure of England's openers, but the last victim of the day was the treasure India sought. All series, Root had sailed along in form sublime enough to move top of the Test rankings, but Yadav sank him with one that swung away, seamed in and pecked the off bail. A Rootless England anchored for the night at 53 for three.

Though not obvious at the time, this was when the Test was won and lost. England did well to recover from 62 for five, but batting at The Oval is easiest on the second day, and they squandered ideal conditions. They seemed content simply to gain a lead. The two returnees could take least blame: Pope, who began with a first-class average at his home ground of over 100, made a classy 81, his first Test fifty in 16 innings, while Woakes reprised Thakur, if at a gentler rate. Others were more reprehensible: Ali, vice-captain in Buttler's absence, threw away an innings of growing beauty. A ruthless England would have reached more than 290.

As they had the night before, India ended on a high. In 16 overs, they made 43 for none, even if Rohit should have been sent back on six, when Burns lost sight of the ball. The lack of a dependable second slip was another way in which England missed Ben Stokes. And this drop did prove expensive.

The third was a long day for England, who gained no help from sullen skies. Despite the lack of sun, the Indians made hay, none more than Rohit, whose sumptuous hundred was his first in overseas Tests. At 236 for one after 80 overs, Root eagerly took the new ball. Its first delivery, a Robinson long hop, deserved punishment. But Rohit's pull fetched up at long leg, and an innings of utmost languor ended with an utter clanger. If England sensed an opening after a better ball claimed Pujara the same over, however, they could not exploit it.

Gloom ended play early, with India 270 for three, though the only significant sideways movement of the day was yet to come. That evening, India coach Ravi Shastri's lateral flow test was positive, setting in train a course of events that culminated in the cancellation of the decisive Manchester game. The Covid news – three other coaching staff were now in quarantine – emerged on a sunny Sunday morning, when England did manage inroads. Woakes removed Jadeja and an out-of-sorts Rahane, before Kohli went for a sparkling 44: Ali found scant spin, but a tight line (and a smart slip catch by Overton) proved fatal. Kohli's sequence without a Test hundred now stretched to 21 innings, much the longest of his career, while Ali – in what turned out to be his last Test – overtook Jim Laker's total of 193 wickets.

PUNCHING ABOVE THEIR POSITION

Fifty in each innings of a Test from No. 8 or lower:

51 and 69	E. P. Nupen	South Africa v England at Durban	1927-28
117 and 57*	E. L. Dalton	South Africa v England at The Oval	1935
92 and 63	A. P. E. Knott	England v Australia at The Oval	1972
85 and 51	G. J. Whittall	Zimbabwe v South Africa at Bloemfontein	1999-2000
69 and 115	Harbhajan Singh	India v New Zealand at Ahmedabad	2010-11
51 and 50	P. M. Siddle	Australia v India at Delhi	2012-13
58 and 63*	Bhuvneshwar Kumar	India v England at Nottingham	2014
54* and 58*	W. P. Saha	India v New Zealand at Kolkata	2016-17
57 and 60	**S. N. Thakur**	**India v England at The Oval**	**2021**

Nupen batted at No. 9 in the first innings, Siddle and Bhuvneshwar Kumar at No. 9 in both.

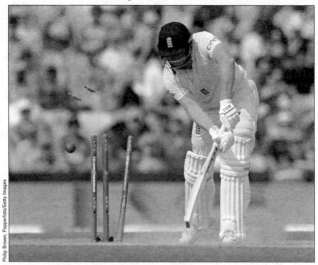

Yorkie yorked: Jonny Bairstow is poleaxed by Jasprit Bumrah's searing inswinger.

Even before the seventh-wicket pair frolicked on the flat pitch, India led by 213. With Pant happy to cede the role of aggressor to Thakur, they put on 100. And to add salt to the wound and runs to the target, Bumrah clomped 24 against an exhausted attack. Root had been reluctant to give long spells to Ali or Overton, which asked too much of the series-long workhorses, Robinson and Anderson. If Robinson's pace was visibly down, the Burnley Express was more a Burnley rail-replacement bus service.

But England persevered, and dismissed India for 466 soon after tea. The target was 368. Romantics among home supporters pointed to the Miracle of Headingley 2019. Realists, while doffing their caps to the openers – who reached the close at 77 – begged to differ. This is England, they said, and England do not achieve record run-chases twice in a generation, let alone twice in three seasons.

First to go was Burns, in the 41st over, the delivery after he had helped bring up England's second three-figure opening stand in two games. He fell for exactly 50, as someone did in all four innings, a curiosity unique in Test cricket. More significantly, Thakur had unearthed a smidgen of movement. England had no option but to increase the scoring-rate, prompting both an uncharacteristic swipe by Hameed – the chance barely registered on the difficulty scale, though Siraj at mid-on still botched it – and the second wicket. Whether Malan was too slow setting off, or Hameed too quick to take a risk, was arguable, but the run-out ended a hesitant knock by Malan, who had struggled against Jadeja.

England reached 141 for two, all results theoretically possible, before things fell apart. Kohli was unfazed by their healthy start, and adroitly manoeuvred his bowling resources around Jadeja at the Vauxhall End. That allowed him to apply intense pressure from the other. Charging in with the pavilion behind him, Bumrah delivered victory.

Player of the Match: R. G. Sharma.   *Attendance:* 111,217.

Close of play: first day, England 53-3 (Malan 26, Overton 1); second day, India 43-0 (Sharma 20, Rahul 22); third day, India 270-3 (Kohli 22, Jadeja 9); fourth day, England 77-0 (Burns 31, Hameed 43).

India

R. G. Sharma c Bairstow b Woakes	11	– c Woakes b Robinson	127
K. L. Rahul lbw b Robinson	17	– c Bairstow b Anderson	46
C. A. Pujara c Bairstow b Anderson	4	– c Ali b Robinson	61
*V. Kohli c Bairstow b Robinson	50	– c Overton b Ali	44
R. A. Jadeja c Root b Woakes	10	– lbw b Woakes	17
A. M. Rahane c Ali b Overton	14	– lbw b Woakes	0
†R. R. Pant c Ali b Woakes	9	– c and b Ali	50
S. N. Thakur lbw b Woakes	57	– c Overton b Root	60
U. T. Yadav c Bairstow b Robinson	10	– c Ali b Overton	25
J. J. Bumrah run out (Burns)	0	– c Ali b Woakes	24
M. Siraj not out	1	– not out	3
Lb 8	8	Lb 7, nb 2	9

1/28 (1) 2/28 (2) 3/39 (3)   (61.3 overs) 191   1/83 (2) 2/236 (1)   (148.2 overs) 466
4/69 (5) 5/105 (4) 6/117 (6)   3/237 (3) 4/296 (5)
7/127 (7) 8/190 (8) 9/190 (10) 10/191 (9)   5/296 (6) 6/312 (4) 7/412 (8)
                                                            8/414 (7) 9/450 (10) 10/466 (9)

Anderson 14–3–41–1; Robinson 17.3–9–38–3; Woakes 15–6–55–4; Overton 15–2–49–1. *Second innings*—Anderson 33–10–79–1; Robinson 32–7–105–2; Woakes 32–8–83–3; Overton 18.2–3–58–1; Ali 26–0–118–2; Root 7–1–16–1.

England

R. J. Burns b Bumrah	5	– c Pant b Thakur	50
H. Hameed c Pant b Bumrah	0	– b Jadeja	63
D. J. Malan c Sharma b Yadav	31	– run out (sub M. A. Agarwal/Pant)	5
*J. E. Root b Yadav	21	– b Thakur	36
C. Overton c Kohli b Yadav	1	– (9) b Yadav	10
O. J. D. Pope b Thakur	81	– (5) b Bumrah	2
†J. M. Bairstow lbw b Siraj	37	– (6) b Bumrah	0
M. M. Ali c Sharma b Jadeja	35	– (7) c sub (S. A. Yadav) b Jadeja	0
C. R. Woakes run out (Pant/Bumrah)	50	– (8) c Rahul b Yadav	18
O. E. Robinson b Jadeja	5	– not out	10
J. M. Anderson not out	1	– c Pant b Yadav	2
B 1, lb 14, nb 8	23	B 2, lb 5, nb 7	14

1/5 (1) 2/6 (2) 3/52 (4)   (84 overs) 290   1/100 (1) 2/120 (3)   (92.2 overs) 210
4/53 (5) 5/62 (3) 6/151 (7)   3/141 (2) 4/146 (5)
7/222 (8) 8/250 (6) 9/255 (10) 10/290 (9)   5/146 (6) 6/147 (7) 7/182 (4)
                                                        8/193 (8) 9/202 (9) 10/210 (11)

Yadav 19–2–76–3; Bumrah 21–6–67–2; Thakur 15–2–54–1; Siraj 12–4–42–1; Jadeja 17–1–36–2. *Second innings*—Yadav 18.2–2–60–3; Bumrah 22–9–27–2; Jadeja 30–11–50–2; Siraj 14–0–44–0; Thakur 8–1–22–2.

Umpires: R. K. Illingworth and A. G. Wharf.   Third umpire: M. A. Gough.
Referee: B. C. Broad.

> **"**
> At one in the morning just before the Lord's Test, he was enjoying a night at the Embassy Club in Bond Street when the message arrived. 'If the selectors had informed me a bit earlier,' he said, 'I should have gone to bed at a timely hour and knocked off a cigar or two.'"
> A history of selection, page 93

ENGLAND v INDIA

Fifth LV= Insurance Test

CHRIS STOCKS

At Manchester, September 10. Postponed.

The first indication that the Fifth Test was in doubt came when India failed to turn up for training on the eve of the game. The culprit was Covid. Head coach Ravi Shastri, bowling coach Bharat Arun and fielding coach R. Sridhar had all tested positive during the Fourth Test. Now, assistant physiotherapist Yogesh Parmar – who had been working closely with the team because senior physio Nitin Patel, a close contact of Shastri, had been self-isolating – joined them. That sent the entire touring party into isolation, as they awaited the results of a fresh round of PCR tests.

The fate of the match – and the series, with India 2–1 up – seemingly hung on their outcome. But murmurs were already surfacing that the players would be reluctant to take the field in any case: because of their proximity to Parmar, they feared some might have contracted the virus, but too recently to produce a positive result.

Indian nerves were exacerbated by the fact that the players' families had been travelling with them throughout a tour that began in early June. Anyone testing positive would be subject to a ten-day isolation period, and miss the restart of the Indian Premier League in the United Arab Emirates, scheduled to begin five days after the end of this series.

Still, when all tests came back negative just before 6pm, the ECB announced the match was on. Behind the match, a core group of senior players, led by Kohli, were adamant they wanted to call it off. Shortly before midnight, they delivered a letter, signed by the whole squad, stating as much to the BCCI. Stunned, the ECB were in discussions with their Indian counterparts into the early hours, trying to save a match worth up to £40m in broadcast and other revenues. Their attempts came to nothing.

At 8.45 next morning, an ECB statement confirmed the cancellation: "Due to fears of a further increase in the number of Covid cases inside the camp, India are regrettably unable to field a team." Briefly, the statement included the suggestion that India had "forfeited"

Nothing to see here: the Old Trafford scoreboard wrongly announces India's forfeiture.

THE TESTS THAT NEVER WERE

Test matches scheduled but not played:

Rain.	England v Australia at Manchester	1890
Rain.	England v Australia at Manchester	1938
Rain.	Australia v England at Melbourne	1970-71
Expulsion of Robin Jackman	West Indies v England at Georgetown.	1980-81
Assassination of Indira Gandhi	Pakistan v India at Karachi	1984-85
Terrorist bomb in Colombo	Sri Lanka v New Zealand at Kandy	1986-87
Terrorist bomb in Colombo	Sri Lanka v New Zealand at Colombo (SSC)	1986-87
Rain.	New Zealand v Pakistan at Dunedin	1988-89
Rain.	West Indies v England at Georgetown.	1989-90
Curfew and civil unrest.	Sri Lanka v Pakistan at Colombo (SSC)	1994-95
Poor visibility due to fog	Pakistan v Zimbabwe at Faisalabad	1998-99
Rain.	New Zealand v India at Dunedin	1998-99
Terrorist bomb in Karachi.	Pakistan v New Zealand at Karachi	2002
Terrorist shootings in Christchurch	New Zealand v Bangladesh at Christchurch	2018-19
Concerns over pandemic	Pakistan v Bangladesh at Karachi	2019-20
Player concerns over pandemic	**England v India at Manchester**	**2021**

The list excludes scheduled series cancelled in their entirety (e.g. during the Covid pandemic), and Tests postponed but eventually played.

---

the game, implying the series would be drawn 2–2; the verb was quickly removed, since it carried far-reaching implications, both for the result of the Test, and the ECB's hopes of insurance money.

The Indian board later released their own statement: it had been a "joint decision", and they would work with their English counterparts to reschedule the match. They added: "The BCCI has always maintained that the safety and well-being of the players is of paramount importance, and there will be no comprise [*sic*] on that aspect. The BCCI would like to thank the ECB for their co-operation and understanding in these trying times. We would like to apologise to the fans for not being able to complete an enthralling series."

Lancashire allowed a few hundred spectators into the ground, to avoid the risk of congestion on the streets outside. With several days' supply of alcohol in danger of going to waste, pints sold for £1. Some fans played cricket on the Old Trafford concourse. It was an eerie sight.

Aware that the ECB's insurance policy would not cover an abandonment caused by Covid, chief executive Tom Harrison said: "This is not a Covid cancellation. This is a match cancelled because of serious concerns over the mental health and well-being of one of the teams." Many were blaming the IPL, and indeed it had been reported before the tour that India wanted to move the Manchester Test to July, or cancel it altogether. That suspicion was now reinforced when their players flew out en masse the following day to the UAE, where they would undergo six days' quarantine. "Let me be super clear," said Harrison. "I don't think the IPL has anything to do with this."

The real losers were Lancashire and the estimated 85,000 fans who had planned to attend the first four days. "We're absolutely devastated for all the disruption caused to ticket holders and hospitality buyers," said Daniel Gidney, the club's chief executive. "They've looked forward to this for a long time. I'm incredibly sorry."

As well as alcohol, Lancashire had ordered five days' worth of food for fans, media, players and hospitality guests. Some was donated to local charities – the only good news to emerge from a grim day.

AUSTRALIA v ENGLAND IN 2021-22

Gideon Haigh

Test matches (5): Australia 4 (52pts), England 0 (–4pts).

English cricket teams have made some inglorious tours of Australia down the decades, but few have matched these Ashes for one-sidedness. The whitewash of 1920-21 was partly pardoned by the toll of war; those of 2006-07 and 2013-14 involved the expiry of some fine careers. The capitulation of Joe Root's Englishmen was ignominious and abject on every level. If it were possible for a team to lose in the nets, they would have done so. Australia were seldom extended, and never for long.

England held out for a draw in the Fourth Test at Sydney, where rain limited the available overs, and No. 11 James Anderson dead-batted the last in poor light precluding the use of faster bowlers. But the margins of defeat were definitive: nine wickets at the Gabba, 275 runs at Adelaide Oval, an innings and 14 runs at the Melbourne Cricket Ground, 146 runs at Bellerive Oval. England's average first-innings score barely exceeded 200; the batters totalled 17 noughts and one spirited hundred from Jonny Bairstow, as Australia brought an abrupt end to Root's record-breaking solo year. Not one player can claim to have enhanced his reputation. By early February, two men higher up the chain of accountability had gone: head coach Chris Silverwood, and managing director of men's cricket Ashley Giles. Chief executive Tom Harrison, who – like Giles – was present for the completion of the fiasco in Hobart, remained in place. Assistant coach Graham Thorpe was also sacked.

The tour's portents, it is true, had always been grim. England had struggled through another northern summer under the pall of Covid. Ben Stokes, having played one day of first-class cricket since sustaining a bad finger break at the outset of the IPL, was wrestling with his mental health. Although he declared his availability at the eleventh hour, long-term injuries to Jofra Archer and Olly Stone deprived England of two of their quickest bowlers, while stress fractures ruled out Sam Curran. Before the schedule of five Tests in six weeks was agreed, there were also months of high-stakes diplomacy about biosecurity protocols between the ECB and Cricket Australia, at a time when entry to Australia was heavily restricted – specifically, what level of restriction would satisfy state governments and public health authorities without antagonising visiting players and their families. Indeed, Western Australia's border controls were so strict that, after the series had begun, the final Test was moved from Perth to Hobart.

The delay in confirming the tour went down poorly in Australia, quick to detect any sense of English diffidence as the series loomed. "No one is forcing you to come," declared Australia's 2019 Ashes captain, Tim Paine, on October 1. "If you don't want to come, don't come. The Ashes are going ahead. The First Test is on December 8, whether Joe is here or not." The First Test did proceed on the specified date; it was Paine, on his 37th birthday, who was missing.

Off the middle, at the double: Travis Head top-scored with 357 runs, including two hundreds.

He spent it in seclusion, having stepped down on November 19 following revelations of sexually explicit messages to a Cricket Tasmania employee four years earlier. Fast bowler Pat Cummins was appointed a week later, with Steve Smith his deputy; Smith would briefly resume the captaincy when Cummins was ruled out of the Second Test by a Covid contact.

By the time Paine resigned, an England squad as near as possible to full strength (at least on paper) had converged on the Gold Coast in tranches – first Root, Stokes, Anderson, Stuart Broad and the balance of the Test specialists, followed by those involved in the T20 World Cup. The ECB puffed the party's readiness, participating in a six-episode BBC podcast series, "Project Ashes", about the tour's granular level of planning, preparation and war-gaming, whose measures included the despatch of a shadow squad, England Lions. The podcast's going-to-air coincided with the unravelling of these schemes, initially in the face of an old enemy: the weather. A scheduled three-day match between England and the Lions at Peter Burge Oval was abandoned after 29 overs, and a four-day game at Ian Healy Oval after 78, to be replaced by some listless middle practice. The Lions remained for a fixture against Australia A that coincided with the First Test, then flew home, causing one to question why they had come at all.

So scant had the opportunities been to prime Anderson and Broad that Silverwood deemed them unready for selection in Brisbane, leaving England's two most prolific wicket-takers to run drinks to an attack of Chris Woakes, Ollie Robinson and Mark Wood, who had never previously bowled in harness. It was as though England were treating the First Test as a warm-up for the Second. So began a succession of odd, opaque selections that puzzled players almost as much as pundits.

Root called correctly at the Gabba under overcast skies on a seam-friendly pitch but, without Anderson and Broad, lacked the confidence to bowl first. It's not as if the Ashes would have been all that different had Australia batted that morning, but at least Rory Burns's career would have been spared a wrong turning: with the first delivery of the series, he was bowled behind his legs by a full, fast, swinging ball from Mitchell Starc, and his tour never recovered.

With only 147 to defend, England's attack had little room to manoeuvre, and Jack Leach less. Poorly protected by Root, he was gored by the left-handers David Warner and Travis Head. Although Root and Dawid Malan finally wrested a session from Australia in the second innings, England surrendered their last eight wickets for 74 in a morning, to lose in Brisbane for the seventh time in their last nine visits. So much for Project Ashes. Mike Tyson proved more relevant: everyone has a plan until they're punched in the mouth.

It grew ever harder to follow Silverwood's thinking. When he finally chose Anderson and Broad in Adelaide, England left out the speedy Wood and the benighted Leach, leaving the team with a configuration they claimed to have forsworn: a kludge of right-arm seamers of roughly the same speed and trajectory. Broad was omitted again in Melbourne, on a surface that would

---

SITTING DUCKS

Most different players from one Test team making nought in a calendar year:

		0	Tests	
21	England	31	13	1994
21	England	54	16	1998
20	West Indies	36	8	1999
20	Sri Lanka	35	13	2017
20	**England**	**54**	**15**	**2021**

---

have suited him, and Leach recalled, in conditions that didn't. Silverwood kept faith with Haseeb Hameed, who appeared increasingly overwhelmed; he recalled Ollie Pope, who continued his year-long regression, and Robinson, despite his air of apathy and indolence. Was it a coincidence that England played their best cricket in Sydney, where Bairstow in the first innings and Zak Crawley in the second gave free rein to their attacking instincts, while their coach was in isolation, having tested positive for Covid?

The brief optimism that accompanied the reunion of Root and Stokes faded quickly. Root's form ebbed under the strain of being England's key wicket. His attempts to cleave to his natural game kept costing him outside off stump. Stokes appeared first underdone then overwrought, his back-and-across step defiant but defensive. He removed Warner in his first over of the series, only for the delivery to be judged a no-ball. His bowling was rarely effective and, at Sydney, injurious. By Hobart, he could not bowl at all.

Cummins, by contrast, looked confident in everything he did, right to the finish when, in an intelligent gesture, he banished champagne from the traditional Australian celebration out of sensitivity to the religious convictions

Victor, Victoria: Scott Boland won the Mullagh Medal in his native Melbourne.

of Usman Khawaja. The historic objection to fast-bowler captains was made to seem like the anathematising of split infinitives or the superstitious aversion to 13th floors. He did not miss a trick in the field, and his bowling remained superb, little flattered by 21 wickets at 18, for even his unsuccessful spells contributed to the cumulative pressure. He somehow did not take a wicket in the last hour of the second day at the MCG, but nobody who watched four English wickets fall amid vintage Australian celebration will forget it.

Cummins was also favoured by selectors (George Bailey, Tony Dodemaide and coach Justin Langer) who got almost everything right. They stuck with Starc, who alone among the frontline seamers bowled in all five Tests, took 19 wickets at 25, offered his captain variation in speed and angle to which England had no counter, and provided useful runs. They showed faith in Cameron Green, who came into the series with one Test half-century and zero Test wickets. After a tentative beginning, he buttressed the batting with 228 runs at 32; bouncing the ball as much as anyone on either side from his 6ft 6in, he claimed 13 wickets at 15; he was impassable in the gully. Just 22, he is a formidable cricketer in the making.

Australia had opted for Head rather than Khawaja at the Gabba, and he made a vivid, counterpunching 152 in 148 deliveries, which proved the series' highest. They drafted Jhye Richardson and Michael Neser at Adelaide, when Josh Hazlewood was injured and Cummins rendered ineligible by contact with a Covid case: Richardson took five for 42, and Neser looked the part.

And when those two pulled up sore, Australia recruited 32-year-old local boy Scott Boland for the Boxing Day Test on the basis of an outstanding MCG record. It proved fully justified. The second Indigenous man to play Test cricket, he won the Mullagh Medal – the individual award for the Melbourne Test, named after Indigenous cricket's original pioneer. But having been chosen as the horse for a particular course, Boland produced bowling in Sydney and Hobart that was similarly accurate, persistent and inventive. He would probably have been nowhere near calculations had his Victorian team-mate James Pattinson not retired from international cricket on the eve of the season. As it was, his 18 wickets cost less than ten each.

When Head returned a Covid positive after Melbourne, Khawaja seized his opportunity in Sydney with a brace of hundreds. Recalled for Hobart at the expense of Marcus Harris, Head made another bustling century, which secured him the Compton–Miller Medal for Player of the Series. After four years trying, he looked to have nailed down a spot.

It will be remembered as a bowler's series – no bad thing, in its way. The Australian summer was mild, thanks to La Niña; the home pitches were often spicy; the umpiring, provided by Australians, was quick on the finger. Had

BEST BOWLING AVERAGE IN AN ASHES SERIES

	W					W			
7.54	24	R. Peel (E).........	1888		**9.55**	**18**	**S. M. Boland (A)**	**2021-22**
7.76	17	J. Briggs (E).........	1886		9.60	46	J. C. Laker (E).......	1956
8.56	16	G. A. Lohmann (E) ...	1886-87		10.88	17	R. M. Ellison (E).....	1985
9.47	17	C. T. B. Turner (A) ...	1886-87		12.11	17	W. H. Lockwood (E)..	1902

Minimum: 15 wickets.

English fans known in advance that Warner would average 34, Steve Smith 30, and Marnus Labuschagne be restricted to a single hundred, they'd have been delighted. England's bowling figures read quite respectably, and in Wood they had the swiftest bowler on either side, not to mention the most cheerful.

Still, six of his 17 wickets came in his final innings, Anderson and Broad had a single genuinely effective Test each, neither Woakes nor Stokes had any impact, and Leach (six wickets at 53) was colossally outperformed by Nathan Lyon (16 at 23), despite Lyon not bowling at all in the abrupt Fifth Test. Most disappointing was Robinson, who has attributes of a fine Test bowler, but who frustrated management with his fitness. The propensity England exhibited for starting a spell with either a half-volley or a no-ball remained uncorrected for the whole series.

Neither team was served by outstanding wicketkeeping. Alex Carey, in his first series, a last-minute inclusion for Paine after being his long-term understudy, struggled to achieve a rapport with Warner at first slip, and passed 25 only twice; Jos Buttler showed flaws in technique and concentration, and was a stationary target at the crease while a broken finger at Sydney ended his tour. How to reconcile his T20I career strike-rate of 141 with his series strike-rate of 27? In the absence of answers, his Test career looked vulnerable.

One of the stranger features of the series was the teams' relations with their respective coaches. Langer's successes here, and earlier at the T20 World Cup, did not appear to have endeared him to senior players. The criticism had

FIVE STATS YOU MAY HAVE MISSED

BENEDICT BERMANGE

- The First Test, in Brisbane, was the first in which every player took at least one wicket or catch. Every England player featured in the scorecard for the Australians' first innings, the third such occurrence in Tests.

- Pat Cummins became the fourth Australian to make his first-class captaincy debut in a Test, after Dave Gregory (in the first Test match, 1876-77), Kim Hughes (against Pakistan in 1978-79) and Michael Clarke (against England in 2010-11).

- In England's first innings at Adelaide, James Anderson became the first player to be not out in 100 Test innings. He is well clear of Courtney Walsh (West Indies), in second place with 61.

- In terms of deliveries, it was the third-quickest Ashes defeat:

Balls	Winner		
3,991	Australia	....	2001
4,751	Australia	....	1921
5,115	**Australia**	....	**2021-22**
5,184	Australia	....	1950-51
5,380	Australia	....	2002-03

- Cameron Green scored 228 runs at 32 and took 13 wickets at 15. No Australian has scored more at a higher average and taken more wickets at a lower average in a Test series.

previously been that he wanted to do everything; now, the murmur was that he was erring the other way, leaning heavily on assistant Andrew McDonald. Cummins's seeming reluctance to recommend a renewal of Langer's contract, expiring in May, invited criticism from Australia's powerful lobby of ex-players, including Steve Waugh, Shane Warne and Ricky Ponting. But, in early February, Langer stepped down, having rejected CA's derisory offer of a new six-month contract.

England's players, by contrast, continued to laud Silverwood – at least in public – and Silverwood to laud himself: "I would love the chance to put some of this right. I think I can do that. I know I am a good coach. I would love to be given the opportunity, but there are certain things out of my hands at the moment." It was the voice of a soft-headed, self-championing mediocrity. But, in England's Test record since the start of 2021, of four wins and ten defeats, spoke for itself. His end was inevitable.

ENGLAND TOURING PARTY

*J. E. Root (Yorkshire), J. M. Anderson (Lancashire), J. M. Bairstow (Yorkshire), D. M. Bess (Yorkshire), S. W. Billings (Kent), S. C. J. Broad (Nottinghamshire), R. J. Burns (Surrey), J. C. Buttler (Lancashire), Z. Crawley (Kent), H. Hameed (Nottinghamshire), D. W. Lawrence (Essex), M. J. Leach (Somerset), D. J. Malan (Yorkshire), C. Overton (Somerset), O. J. D. Pope (Surrey), O. E. Robinson (Sussex), B. A. Stokes (Durham), C. R. Woakes (Warwickshire), M. A. Wood (Durham).

Stokes, taking a mental health break, was not in the original squad, but was added before departure. Buttler flew home with a broken finger after the Fourth Test, and was replaced by Billings, who had been playing in the BBL.

Head coach: C. E. W. Silverwood. *Assistant coaches:* P. D. Collingwood, G. P. Thorpe. *Batting consultant:* I. J. L. Trott. *Bowling coach:* J. Lewis. *Spin-bowling coach:* J. S. Patel. *Wicketkeeping consultant:* J. S. Foster. *Coaching consultant:* A. G. Botha. *Team manager:* A. W. Bentley. *Analyst:* R. Lewis. *Doctors:* A. Biswas, Moiz Moghal. *Physiotherapists:* C. A. de Weymarn, B. Langley. *Nutritionist:* E. Gardner. *Strength and conditioning:* P. C. F. Scott, D. Veness. *Psychologist:* J. Bickley. *Massage therapist:* M. Saxby. *Security managers:* W. Carr, C. Rhooms. *Head of team communications:* D. M. Reuben. *Digital:* G. Stobart. *Covid operations officer:* S. Elworthy.

TEST MATCH AVERAGES

AUSTRALIA – BATTING AND FIELDING

	T	I	NO	R	HS	100	50	Avge	Ct
†U. T. Khawaja	2	4	1	255	137	2	0	85.00	2
†T. M. Head	4	6	0	357	152	2	1	59.50	3
M. Labuschagne	5	9	1	335	103	1	2	41.87	5
†M. A. Starc	5	7	3	155	39*	0	0	38.75	1
†D. A. Warner	5	8	0	273	95	0	2	34.12	5
C. D. Green	5	8	1	228	74	0	2	32.57	4
S. P. D. Smith	5	8	0	244	93	0	2	30.50	11
†M. S. Harris	4	7	1	179	76	0	1	29.83	1
N. M. Lyon	5	5	2	76	31	0	0	25.33	4
†A. T. Carey	5	9	0	183	51	0	1	20.33	23
P. J. Cummins	4	5	0	72	24	0	0	14.40	2
S. M. Boland	3	3	1	24	10*	0	0	12.00	4

Played in one Test: †J. R. Hazlewood 0* (2 ct); M. G. Neser 35, 3; †J. A. Richardson 9, 8.

BOWLING

	Style	O	M	R	W	BB	5I	Avge
S. M. Boland	RFM	81.1	31	172	18	6-7	1	9.55
C. D. Green	RFM	80.4	22	205	13	3-21	0	15.76
P. J. Cummins	RF	126.4	31	379	21	5-38	1	18.04
N. M. Lyon	OB	163.1	47	377	16	4-91	0	23.56
J. A. Richardson	RFM	38.1	13	120	5	5-42	1	24.00
J. R. Hazlewood	RFM	27	10	74	3	2-42	0	24.66
M. A. Starc	LF	152.1	32	482	19	4-37	0	25.36

Also bowled: T. M. Head (OB) 1–1–0–0; M. Labuschagne (LB) 12–2–40–0; M. G. Neser (RFM) 24–5–61–2; S. P. D. Smith (LB) 5–2–10–1.

ENGLAND – BATTING AND FIELDING

	T	I	NO	R	HS	100	50	Avge	Ct
J. M. Bairstow	2	4	0	194	113	1	0	48.50	1
J. E. Root	5	10	0	322	89	0	3	32.20	6
Z. Crawley	3	6	0	166	77	0	1	27.66	8
†D. J. Malan	5	10	0	244	82	0	2	24.40	2
C. R. Woakes	3	6	0	146	44	0	0	24.33	0
†B. A. Stokes	5	10	0	236	66	0	2	23.60	3
J. C. Buttler	4	8	1	107	39	0	0	15.28	12
†S. C. J. Broad	3	6	3	42	15	0	0	14.00	2
†R. J. Burns	3	6	0	77	34	0	0	12.83	2
†M. J. Leach	3	6	2	51	26	0	0	12.75	0
O. J. D. Pope	3	6	0	67	35	0	0	11.16	4
M. A. Wood	4	8	0	86	39	0	0	10.75	1
H. Hameed	3	6	0	80	27	0	0	10.00	3
†J. M. Anderson	3	6	4	13	5*	0	0	6.50	0
O. E. Robinson	4	8	1	38	22	0	0	5.42	1

Played in one Test: S. W. Billings 29, 1 (5 ct).

BOWLING

	Style	O	M	R	W	BB	5I	Avge
J. M. Anderson	RFM	104	36	187	8	4-33	0	23.37
O. E. Robinson	RFM/OB	106.2	34	281	11	3-58	0	25.54
S. C. J. Broad	RFM	118.4	23	342	13	5-101	1	26.30
M. A. Wood	RF	121.1	15	453	17	6-37	1	26.64
J. E. Root	OB	57	4	234	5	2-27	0	46.80
M. J. Leach	SLA	73.5	3	321	6	4-84	0	53.50
C. R. Woakes	RFM	88.4	22	332	6	2-64	0	55.33
B. A. Stokes	RFM	63.3	6	286	4	3-113	0	71.50

Also bowled: D. J. Malan (LB) 11–0–61–2.

At Brisbane (Peter Burge Oval), November 23–25, 2021 (not first-class). **Drawn. ‡England XI 98-0** (29 overs) (H. Hameed 53*) **v England Lions.** *Rory Burns (39*) and Haseeb Hameed made it through the first morning, before thunderstorms arrived. Each side chose from 12 players.*

At Brisbane (Ian Healy Oval), November 30–December 3, 2021 (not first-class). **Drawn. England Lions 226-4** (78 overs) **v ‡England XI.** *The weather prevented play on the first two days; on the third, England's Test bowlers got some overs under their belts, though James Anderson, Stuart Broad and Jack Leach went wicketless. The final day was given up to practice in the middle. Each side chose from 13 players.*

AUSTRALIA v ENGLAND

First Test

Geoff Lemon

At Brisbane, December 8–11, 2021. Australia won by nine wickets. Australia 12pts, England –8pts (after 8pt penalty). Toss: England. Test debut: A. T. Carey.

There is nothing like a wicket from the first ball of the series. A four, a six, a wide to second slip – all can be made good as the over goes on. At the Gabba, the left-handed Burns received several Starc staples at once: a ball pitched up, swinging, angled down leg. He walked across his stumps, as ever, but perhaps a little more than usual, striving for decisiveness while racked by nerves. If he had time for a thought, it would have been annoyance at moving too far to glance to fine leg. But Starc swung it back and, instead of missing the stumps, it smashed into leg. Brisbane's stands were in uproar.

Ashes Tests here have a sense of inevitability. The preliminaries of any match report – two England wins in Brisbane from 19 previous attempts since the Second World War –

DISMISSED BY THE FIRST BALL OF A TEST SERIES

Batter	Bowler		
H. Sutcliffe	F. T. Badcock	England v New Zealand at Christchurch .	1932-33
T. S. Worthington . .	E. L. McCormick	England v Australia at Brisbane	1936-37
S. J. Cook†	Kapil Dev	South Africa v India at Durban	1992-93
Hannan Sarkar	P. T. Collins	Bangladesh v West Indies at Dhaka	2002-03
Hannan Sarkar	P. T. Collins	Bangladesh v West Indies at Gros Islet . .	2003-04
Wasim Jaffer	Mashrafe bin Mortaza .	India v Bangladesh at Chittagong	2007
T. G. McIntosh	Mohammad Amir	New Zealand v Pakistan at Dunedin	2009-10
K. L. Rahul	R. A. S. Lakmal	India v Sri Lanka at Kolkata	2017-18
D. Elgar	J. M. Anderson	South Africa v England at Centurion	2019-20
Abdul Malik† . . .	**B. Muzarabani**	**Afghanistan v Zimbabwe at Abu Dhabi** .	**2020-21**
R. J. Burns	**M. A. Starc**	**England v Australia at Brisbane**	**2021-22**

† *On Test debut.*

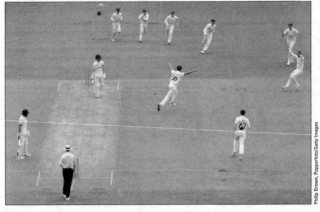

Off and running: Mitchell Starc bowls Rory Burns with the first ball of the series.

could be copied and pasted for each new tour, with only the length of the streak requiring an update. Australia's unbeaten run here against allcomers had ended in January 2021 – unusually, the final Test – when India recorded the first visiting win for 32 years, but that offered only a little encouragement to an England team without the Indians' depth of talent.

It was no surprise, then, that Australia's administration were determined to make sure the First Test returned to Brisbane, even among the Covid havoc. The surprise was that England acquiesced. When they landed in Australia, Queensland required every traveller to undergo two weeks of quarantine. Victoria and New South Wales did not, and Queensland's requirement expired shortly after this Test finished. Had the tourists arrived in Melbourne or Sydney, they could have played two weeks' worth of warm-up matches; had Brisbane's Test been a week later, they could have gone there directly. Instead, they spent that unnecessary fortnight's isolation in a resort hotel, trained only occasionally because of incessant rain, and managed barely a day of the intra-squad cricket that constituted their preparation. Some of Australia's T20 World Cup party had been in the same situation, but the rest had been playing Sheffield Shield cricket for two months.

Faced with a green pitch grown juicy under covers, Root won a toss that will be debated long into the future, and chose to bat, reasoning that – after a difficult start – there would be runs once the surface had settled. He was correct, the only problem being that by then Australia were batting. England's task of getting through the early conditions had failed, beginning with Burns.

Hazlewood was next to the party, hitting his trademark hard length to undo Malan with bounce, before going fuller to Root with a straight line and movement away. England's captain had scored 1,455 Test runs in the calendar year, but couldn't add another. Poking to first slip, he had his fourth duck in eight Ashes innings; Hazlewood had now removed him eight times in Tests, more than any other bowler. Then it was Cummins, the new captain, coming wide on the crease around the wicket to Stokes, who was squared up: Labuschagne swooped low at third slip, and England were in tatters at 29 for four.

Hameed and Pope improved that to 59 by lunch, but Cummins had Hameed edging to second slip in the first over after the break. Pope and, in particular, Buttler played their shots in an entertaining stand of 52, but Buttler feathered Starc, Pope hooked to long leg to give Green his first Test wicket, and Cummins picked off the lower order to become the first to

BRISBANE NOTES AND QUOTES

Queensland's draconian border restrictions, which required 14 days of quarantine – but were relaxed just after the Test concluded – dissuaded many media from attending. One of the those spared the hardship was Glenn McGrath – a New South Welshman now living further north – who kicked off the series on Channel Seven by claiming: "I'm not one for predictions." Moments later, he went for his traditional 5–0 to Australia. By the end of the Test, Ricky Ponting had joined him.

The border issues hung over the Test, and led to various failures of technology. There was a shortage of technicians, and Real Time Snicko was unavailable throughout. At one stage, DRS went down completely. And with England collapsing on the fourth day, footage on the world feed was lost because of a power outage: pictures went missing for almost 30 minutes. Back in London, BT Sport had to make do with punditry from Steve Harmison and Alastair Cook based on grainy footage via a phone on the boundary.

Shortly before the blackout – and after 11 months on 399 – Nathan Lyon had picked up his 400th Test wicket: Malan, caught at bat–pad. Earlier, Malan revealed the landmark should have arrived a day earlier. On the third afternoon, he was on 37 when a ball looped off his pad, via his glove, back to Lyon, who hardly appealed. "I think I might have got away with one," he told ABC Grandstand. "I gloved one straight to him, so that could've been his 400th wicket."

The eyes of the cricketing world were on Brisbane, and some were green. Despite gaining ICC Full Member status in 2017, Ireland have played just three Test matches, leading their captain, Andy Balbirnie, to tweet: "Test cricket looks fun. Anyone want a game?? Seriously".

Notes and Quotes compiled by Will Macpherson

collect a Test five-for on his first day as captain since Pakistan's Imran Khan at Edgbaston in 1982. How quickly the Tim Paine sexting scandal had faded. Australia had wrapped up the innings in 50.1 overs, at which point rain washed out the final session, when England might have fancied a bowl. To their chagrin, the second day began in bright sunshine.

There had been plenty of reaction to England's bowling selections, with Broad left out at a ground where his previous three visits had brought him 12 wickets at 24, and after the 2019 Ashes, in which he had been all over Warner and Harris. Leach's left-arm spin was preferred, despite the fact he had spent the English season on the bench. Woakes, meanwhile, bowled the first over, which he had not done in a Test since Mirpur in 2016-17. In the end it was irrelevant. Whoever bowled, a first innings of 147 would not have backed them up.

Fielding errors did not help, and they were manifold. The automated no-ball technology had failed, so on-field umpires were monitoring the crease for the first time in a Test since 2019, and missed four oversteps in a row from Stokes. The fourth bowled Warner, on 17, only for the transgression to be picked up on a replay (only wicket-taking deliveries were being checked). Warner was on 48 when Burns dropped a slip catch off Robinson, and on 60 when he stepped down the wicket after flicking to short leg, where Hameed missed a simple throw as the batsman lay stranded.

Labuschagne was more fluent, and with Warner laid into Leach in a stream of sixes and fours. When Labuschagne cut him to backward point for 74, to end a second-wicket stand of 156, it was completely against the run of play. Smith, England's Gabba tormentor in 2017-18, was hurried by Wood's pace, and edged behind. But England's problems in Australia have not always been caused by the best home players: they have allowed the lesser lights to make telling contributions, too.

In this case it was Head, who came in with Australia already 42 in front. Warner's scratchy start had become 94, before he chipped a Robinson slower ball to mid-off soon after tea, and Green was bowled leaving the next delivery. Yet in the company of Carey, Cummins and Starc, Head played with freedom, lashing through point, driving through cover, pulling from a decent length, clubbing spin down the ground. Even a beamer from the fiery Wood, which ricocheted via glove to chin, couldn't shake him. Leach ended the

Long leg, long levers: Josh Hazlewood catches Ollie Pope.

day with one for 95 from 11 overs, Head with 112, having become the first Australian to score an Ashes century in a session since Adam Gilchrist at Perth in 2006-07. He returned on the third morning to belt onwards to 152 from 148 balls, last to fall when making room to cut Wood; Australia's lead was 278.

Burns fell early again, this time to a Cummins leaper, while Hameed showed some poise in his 27. His wicket brought Malan and Root together before mid-afternoon drinks, and they produced England's few good hours of the match, staying the course until stumps, and taking the score to 220 for two; as each moved to within 20 of a century, the deficit shrank to 58. It was a glorious partnership, the left-handed Malan attacking Lyon's off-spin, Root playing sumptuous straight-drives off the quicks, and moving past Michael Vaughan's national record 1,481 Test runs in a calendar year, in 2002. For a night, England could dream of a comeback.

Like all dreams, it ended in the morning. When Malan fell bat–pad after a stand of 162 in 52 overs, Lyon had his long-awaited 400th Test wicket, having spent nearly two years in the 390s. Three overs later, Root tried to glide Green, and nicked behind for 89, his highest score in Australia. It was the beginning of the end: England went down quickly, as did – for half an hour – television coverage. The collapse was eight for 74, with all the bowlers bar Starc involved, in ideal batting conditions under sunny skies. Australia were

FASTEST ASHES HUNDREDS BY BALLS

57	A. C. Gilchrist (Australia) at Perth	2006-07
76	G. L. Jessop (England) at The Oval	1902
85	J. Darling (Australia) at Sydney	1897-98
85	**T. M. Head (Australia) at Brisbane**	**2021-22**
86	I. T. Botham (England) at Leeds	1981
86	I. T. Botham (England) at Manchester	1981
88	R. R. Lindwall (Australia) at Melbourne	1946-47
94	A. C. Gilchrist (Australia) at Sydney	2002-03
95	V. T. Trumper (Australia) at Manchester	1902
100	V. T. Trumper (Australia) at Sydney	1903-04

Details of balls faced are not known for many early innings.

ruthless, England inexplicable. On Test debut, wicketkeeper Carey held a record eight catches (Australia's Brian Taber, at Johannesburg in 1966-67, and England's Chris Read, against New Zealand at Edgbaston in 1999, both made eight dismissals in their first Test too, comprising seven catches and a stumping).

The debris left Australia a fourth-innings target of 20. Warner did not come out to bat, nursing bruised ribs courtesy of blows from Stokes and Wood, and Carey fell cheaply in his place, edging the impressive Robinson. But shortly after lunch on the fourth day, Australia had charged to a 1–0 lead. England's reward for a morale-sapping experience was to lose eight World Test Championship points, and each player's entire match fee, for being miles behind the over-rate. Another southern Ashes series had – from the very first ball – begun according to the playbook.

Player of the Match: T. M. Head.   *Attendance:* 98,779.

Close of play: first day, England 147; second day, Australia 343-7 (Head 112, Starc 10); third day, England 220-2 (Malan 80, Root 86).

England

R. J. Burns b Starc	0	– (2) c Carey b Cummins ... 13
H. Hameed c Smith b Cummins	25	– (1) c Carey b Starc ... 27
D. J. Malan c Carey b Hazlewood	6	– c Labuschagne b Lyon ... 82
*J. E. Root c Warner b Hazlewood	0	– c Carey b Green ... 89
B. A. Stokes c Labuschagne b Cummins	5	– c Green b Cummins ... 14
O. J. D. Pope c Hazlewood b Green	35	– c Smith b Lyon ... 4
†J. C. Buttler c Carey b Starc	39	– c Carey b Hazlewood ... 23
C. R. Woakes c Hazlewood b Cummins	21	– c Carey b Green ... 16
O. E. Robinson c Carey b Cummins	0	– c Head b Lyon ... 8
M. A. Wood c Harris b Cummins	8	– b Lyon ... 6
M. J. Leach not out	2	– not out ... 0
Lb 5, w 1	6	B 4, lb 5, w 6 ... 15

1/0 (1) 2/11 (3) 3/11 (4)   (50.1 overs) 147
4/29 (5) 5/60 (2) 6/112 (7)
7/118 (6) 8/122 (9) 9/144 (10) 10/147 (8)

1/23 (2) 2/61 (1)   (103 overs) 297
3/223 (3) 4/229 (4)
5/234 (6) 6/266 (5) 7/268 (7)
8/286 (9) 9/296 (10) 10/297 (8)

Starc 12–2–35–2; Hazlewood 13–4–42–2; Cummins 13.1–3–38–5; Lyon 9–2–21–0; Green 3–1–6–1. *Second innings*—Starc 20–3–77–1; Hazlewood 14–6–32–1; Cummins 20–6–51–2; Lyon 34–5–91–4; Green 12–3–23–2; Labuschagne 3–0–14–0.

Australia

D. A. Warner c Stokes b Robinson	94	
M. S. Harris c Malan b Robinson	3	– not out ... 9
M. Labuschagne c Wood b Leach	74	– not out ... 0
S. P. D. Smith c Buttler b Wood	12	
T. M. Head b Wood	152	
C. D. Green b Robinson	0	
†A. T. Carey c Pope b Woakes	12	– (1) c Buttler b Robinson ... 9
*P. J. Cummins c Hameed b Root	12	
M. A. Starc b Burns b Woakes	35	
N. M. Lyon c Robinson b Wood	15	
J. R. Hazlewood not out	0	
B 4, lb 6, w 2, nb 4	16	Nb 2 ... 2

1/10 (2) 2/166 (3) 3/189 (4)   (104.3 overs) 425
4/195 (1) 5/195 (6) 6/236 (7)
7/306 (8) 8/391 (9) 9/420 (10) 10/425 (5)

1/16 (1)   (1 wkt, 5.1 overs) 20

Woakes 25–8–76–2; Robinson 23–8–58–3; Wood 25.3–4–85–3; Stokes 12–0–65–0; Leach 13–0–102–1; Root 6–0–29–1. *Second innings*—Robinson 3–0–13–1; Woakes 2–0–3–0; Wood 0.1–0–4–0.

Umpires: P. R. Reiffel and R. J. Tucker.   Third umpire: P. Wilson.
Referee: D. C. Boon.

AUSTRALIA v ENGLAND

Second Test

DANIEL BRETTIG

At Adelaide, December 16–20, 2021 (day/night). Australia won by 275 runs. Australia 12pts. Toss: Australia. Test debut: M. G. Neser.

Adelaide, we were told, was England's best chance. The influence of the pink ball and the floodlights was made clear well before both sides landed in South Australia: Anderson and Broad, held back from a green seamer in Brisbane, would be unleashed for the Second Test. That thinking was drawn from the back half of the Adelaide Test in 2017-18, when Anderson swung the ball round corners in the second innings, and gave England a glimpse of a thrilling chase.

Now, as Australia shrugged off the loss of a second captain almost as comfortably as they had the resignation of Tim Paine, England went 2–0 down for the eighth time in nine visits. They did so in a manner so similar to the corresponding match four years earlier that it was as if a script were being followed. The genre? Misadventure.

DIFFERENT AUSTRALIAN CAPTAINS IN SUCCESSIVE TESTS

4	W. L. Murdoch, T. P. Horan, H. H. Massie and J. M. Blackham	1884-85
4	H. H. Massie, J. M. Blackham, T. P. Horan and H. J. H. Scott	1884-85 to 1886
3	W. Bardsley, H. L. Collins and J. Ryder	1926 to 1928-29
3	A. L. Hassett, I. W. G. Johnson and A. R. Morris	1953 to 1954-55
3	R. R. Lindwall, I. W. G. Johnson and I. D. Craig	1956-57 to 1957-58
3	**T. D. Paine, P. J. Cummins and S. P. D. Smith**	**2020-21 to 2021-22**

Whatever plans had crossed the minds of Root and Silverwood before this trip, they could not have envisaged the events that unfolded after the teams settled into their shared lodgings at the Crowne Plaza near Rundle Street, a short drive from the ground. Only one Test into his captaincy career, Cummins was ruled out on the morning of the game after a diner at the next table the night before had learned, mid-meal, that he was Covid-positive. Under the state's stringent health regulations, Cummins was deemed a close contact. Already without Hazlewood, who had strained his side at Brisbane, the Australians' pace attack looked vulnerable. In came Michael Neser, for a belated debut at the age of 31, and Jhye Richardson, for his first Test in nearly three years.

It all meant that, when Smith walked out for his first toss as captain since losing the job during the sandpaper saga more than three and a half years earlier, three different men had led Australia in three successive Tests for the first time in more than six decades. After the coin fell favourably for Australia under sunny afternoon skies, Anderson and Broad caused discomfort for the openers, with Broad mischievously asking Warner – whom he had dismissed seven times for 35 runs during the 2019 Ashes – whether he was still batting on off stump. It was Harris, though, who fell first, brilliantly caught down leg by Buttler off Broad for three. But it soon became clear England were repeating the mistakes of 2017-18, bowling too short to coax drives and edges. They were economical but unthreatening, reflected by a close-of-play 221 for two. Worse, Buttler had dropped Labuschagne twice – on 21, high down the leg side off Stokes, and minutes before stumps, on 95 off Anderson, a regulation chance to his right.

By then, Warner – who had overcome a slow start, as well as the sore ribcage suffered at Brisbane – had fallen in the nineties for the second innings in succession, spanking a Stokes long hop to cover. Pondering in that evening's press conference why the batsmen

Philip Brown, Popperfoto/Getty Images

Out of hand: Marnus Labuschagne is dropped by Jos Buttler on 21.

had been able to play and miss so often, Warner reasoned that Anderson, Broad, Woakes and Robinson were bowling a length that would have hit the stumps in England, but not in Australia. "I batted out of my crease, and Marnus did too, to be able to leave the ball on a good length," he said. "We backed ourselves that it would go over the stumps." English frustration had led to a bizarre plan B from Root: Stokes hurled down bouncer after bouncer as the lights enveloped the oval, creating the sort of atmosphere in which England ought to have attacked the outside edge.

Next day, Labuschagne reached his first Ashes hundred, from his 287th ball – the slowest in any Test for Australia since nightwatchman Jason Gillespie took 296 during his double-century against Bangladesh at Chittagong in April 2006. He was caught behind moments later off a Robinson no-ball, then trapped by the same bowler as he offered no shot.

But Australia, and especially Smith, made mainly untroubled progress in temperatures touching 37°C. Root did bowl Head for 18, but it wasn't until Stokes found some wobble on the second afternoon – producing a delivery of rare precision to beat Green and flick off stump – that England came closer to the ideal length. Anderson removed Smith for 93, but Australia were not dislodged until Carey had reached a maiden Test fifty, Starc and Neser posted pesky thirties, and Richardson smote a six into a rapturous members' enclosure.

England's openers emerged on the second evening to face a swinging, seaming new ball, and both departed – before a nearby lightning strike forced an early closure. Burns, beaten for pace, bounce and movement by Starc, did little wrong; Hameed, bunting straight to mid-on the full ball England had declined to bowl, did plenty, gifting Neser a wicket with his second delivery in Tests.

As at the Gabba, Root and Malan held the Australians up with a partnership of real verve. Root had broken three national captaincy records by completely another fifty – for the 37th time (beating Alastair Cook), the 11th in the Ashes (Peter May), and the seventh in Australia (Archie MacLaren). Lacking Cummins and Hazlewood, and with England 150 for two, Smith looked momentarily short of options. Into the breach stepped Green. After a couple of exploratory overs before the first interval, he added several kilometres of pace, and inches of bounce, to a questioning line around fifth stump. Root, always keen

ADELAIDE NOTES AND QUOTES

Stuart Broad – finally – became the tenth player to win 150 Test caps, and England marked the occasion by pulling together a video containing messages from family, friends and former team-mates. There were speeches from James Anderson and Joe Root, a bottle of vintage red, a signed Nottingham Forest shirt and a drawing of him walking off after his eight for 15 against Australia in 2015 at Trent Bridge. The artist was England's fielding coach, Carl Hopkinson.

The first day's play was overshadowed by the drama of Australian captain Pat Cummins being ruled out because he had been a close contact of a Covid case at the Little Hunter steak house. The contact turned out to be a grade cricketer from Sydney who knew Cummins's dinner companion, and came over to say hello – only to receive a message soon after informing him of his positive status. It could have been worse: Mitchell Starc and Nathan Lyon were both eating at the same restaurant, but were sitting outside.

Lyon had picked up his 400th Test wicket in Brisbane, though that was not enough to impress Kevin Pietersen, who took issue with England's approach on the third day at Adelaide. "Can SOMEONE please smack Lyon?!?!!" he tweeted. "FFS! Off-spinner with zero variations and bowling on world cricket's flattest road!!!!" Moments later, Lyon removed Chris Woakes and Ollie Robinson. "Wonder if Kev is watching," mused Ricky Ponting on commentary.

The game began with the ringing of the Bradshaw Bell, cast by the South Australia Cricket Association in honour of their former chief executive Keith Bradshaw, who had died a month earlier at the age of 58. A former secretary of MCC, he had introduced the custom of inviting a guest to ring the bell at Lord's five minutes before the start of each day of a Test. First to ring Adelaide's new bell were his partner, Helen Todd, and daughters Juliet and Eliza.

for bat on ball, succumbed to an outside edge, and swished his bat in unveiled anger. He proceeded to watch the innings disintegrate against Starc. Lyon, too, played his part, with an exceptional spell that pressured his quarry, and made a mess of Pope, who looked like an overawed Ian Bell in 2005. In all, England's last eight fell for 86, on a pitch still good for batting.

Australia, as four years earlier, waived the follow-on, despite a lead of 237, and once again stuttered through the third innings as England pitched fuller. Root, unaccountably doing pre-play throwdowns without a box, had taken a blow from the spin coach Jeetan Patel that required a trip to hospital, so Stokes assumed temporary command. Root returned after Robinson, who had bowled respectably throughout, resorted to off-breaks – another sign that England had been wrong to discard Leach. Soon, Root and Malan both took wickets with their part-timers, while Leach watched.

BRIGADIERS OF BLOCK

Lowest strike-rates (runs per 100 balls) in an innings lasting 200 balls or more:

%	R	B			
8.96	20	223	Hanif Mohammad	Pakistan v England at Lord's	1954
10.24	25	244	H. M. Amla	South Africa v India at Delhi	2015-16
11.76	40	340	H. L. Collins	Australia v England at Manchester	1921
12.34	29*	235	R. C. Russell	England v South Africa at Johannesburg	1995-96
12.56	**26**	**207**	**J. C. Buttler**	**England v Australia at Adelaide**	**2021-22**
13.71	38	277	T. E. Bailey	England v Australia at Leeds	1953
14.07	38	270	I. D. Craig	Australia v England at Manchester	1956
14.47	43	297	A. B. de Villiers	South Africa v India at Delhi	2015-16
14.58	35	240	C. J. Tavaré	England v India at Chennai	1981-82
14.73	42	285	B. Mitchell	South Africa v England at Cape Town	1938-39
15.00	33	220†	A. B. de Villiers	South Africa v Australia at Adelaide	2012-13

† *Also the most balls faced without hitting a boundary, where known.*

Striding edge: Jhye Richardson on his way to a five-for in his only Test of the series.

Set 468 in four and a bit sessions, England lost Hameed right away, touching a Richardson delivery that climbed, before Malan and Burns were each winkled out by sustained plans. Root, accompanied by Stokes, fought desperately to get to the close, and passed Cook's England-record 4,844 Test runs as captain. Starc, however, found the right line and length to hit him amidships once more and, after a prolonged delay, Root – still uncomfortable – stretched out to edge Starc's second ball of the night's final over. In every way, it was an excruciating passage for England, who closed on 82 for four.

Victory for Australia on day five looked more or less a matter of time, particularly after Pope fell in the third over to Starc, and Lyon won an lbw verdict on review 11 overs later against Stokes. That made it 105 for six. Had Carey not courteously allowed an edge from Buttler off the excellent Starc to pass between him and Warner at first slip, the game might have ended in a hurry. Instead, Buttler dug deep, and with Woakes held up the Australians for more than 31 overs.

The second new ball was always lurking, though, and Richardson used it superbly. His nip-backer to burst through Woakes was one of the deliveries of the series, while Buttler, after more than four and a quarter hours, stepped on his stumps trying to work Richardson for a single. Australia won with time to spare, Richardson finishing with five for 42.

Root, clearly angry, spoke of lessons not learned, while Silverwood compelled the batters to rewatch their dismissals in the dressing-room. "The disappointing thing is we made the same mistakes as last week," lamented Root. "We just can't afford to do that." To heighten the sense of internal disquiet, Anderson and Broad used their newspaper columns to duel with Root, Silverwood and the coaching staff over the matter of length. Australia, it must be said, bowled similarly, but with extra pace.

Smith, meanwhile, could barely believe his luck. As for Cummins, he watched most of the match from home in Sydney, having been spirited out of South Australia on a charter flight. However chaotic the circumstances, he was now fresh and ready for Boxing Day.

Player of the Match: M. Labuschagne. *Attendance:* 112,468.

Close of play: first day, Australia 221-2 (Labuschagne 95, Smith 18); second day, England 17-2 (Malan 1, Root 5); third day, Australia 45-1 (Harris 21, Neser 2); fourth day, England 82-4 (Stokes 3).

Australia

M. S. Harris c Buttler b Broad	3	– (2) c Buttler b Broad	23
D. A. Warner c Broad b Stokes	95	– (1) run out (Broad/Buttler)	13
M. Labuschagne lbw b Robinson	103	– (4) c Stokes b Malan	51
*S. P. D. Smith lbw b Anderson	93	– (5) c Buttler b Robinson	6
T. M. Head b Root	18	– (6) c Stokes b Robinson	51
C. D. Green b Stokes	2	– (7) not out	33
†A. T. Carey c Hameed b Anderson	51	– (8) b Root	6
M. A. Starc not out	39	– (9) c Pope b Root	19
M. G. Neser c Broad b Stokes	35	– (3) b Anderson	3
J. A. Richardson c Buttler b Woakes	9	– c Buttler b Malan	8
Lb 9, w 5, nb 11	25	B 3, lb 8, w 1, nb 5	17

1/4 (1) 2/176 (2)   (9 wkts dec, 150.4 overs) 473   1/41 (1)   (9 wkts dec, 61 overs) 230
3/241 (3) 4/291 (5)   2/48 (3) 3/48 (2)
5/294 (6) 6/385 (4)   4/55 (5) 5/144 (6) 6/173 (4)
7/390 (8) 8/448 (9) 9/473 (10)   7/180 (8) 8/216 (9) 9/230 (10)

N. M. Lyon did not bat.

Anderson 29–10–58–2; Broad 26–6–73–1; Woakes 23.4–6–103–1; Robinson 27–13–45–1; Stokes 25–2–113–3; Root 20–2–72–1. *Second innings*—Anderson 10–6–8–1; Broad 10–3–27–1; Robinson 15–2–54–2; Woakes 12–3–46–0; Root 6–1–27–2; Stokes 2–0–24–0; Malan 6–0–33–2.

England

H. Hameed c Starc b Neser	6	– (2) c Carey b Richardson	0
R. J. Burns c Smith b Starc	4	– (1) c Smith b Richardson	34
D. J. Malan c Smith b Starc	80	– lbw b Neser	20
*J. E. Root c Smith b Green	62	– c Carey b Starc	24
B. A. Stokes b Green	34	– lbw b Lyon	12
O. J. D. Pope c Labuschagne b Lyon	5	– c Smith b Starc	4
†J. C. Buttler c Warner b Starc	0	– hit wkt b Richardson	26
C. R. Woakes b Lyon	24	– b Richardson	44
O. E. Robinson lbw b Lyon	0	– c Smith b Lyon	8
S. C. J. Broad c Head b Starc	9	– not out	9
J. M. Anderson not out	5	– c Green b Richardson	2
Lb 6, nb 1	7	B 2, lb 3, nb 4	9

1/7 (2) 2/12 (1) 3/150 (4)   (84.1 overs) 236   1/4 (2) 2/48 (3)   (113.1 overs) 192
4/157 (3) 5/164 (6) 6/169 (7)   3/70 (1) 4/82 (4)
7/202 (8) 8/204 (9) 9/220 (5) 10/236 (10)   5/86 (6) 6/105 (5) 7/166 (8)
                                         8/178 (9) 9/182 (7) 10/192 (11)

Starc 16.1–6–37–4; Richardson 19–4–78–0; Neser 11–0–33–1; Lyon 28–11–58–3; Green 10–3–24–2. *Second innings*—Starc 27–10–43–2; Richardson 19.1–9–42–5; Lyon 39–16–55–2; Neser 13–5–28–1; Green 9–5–9–0; Labuschagne 4–2–10–0; Smith 1–1–0–0; Head 1–1–0–0.

Umpires: R. J. Tucker and P. Wilson.   Third umpire: P. R. Reiffel.
Referee: D. C. Boon.

AUSTRALIA v ENGLAND

Third Test

LAWRENCE BOOTH

At Melbourne, December 26–28, 2021. Australia won by an innings and 14 runs. Australia 12pts. Toss: Australia. Test debut: S. M. Boland.

Nearly a week later, long after Australia's fast bowlers had torn into England's top order on a gladiatorial evening at the MCG, Stokes still sounded awestruck. A withering 58-minute

Dan Peled, AFP/Getty Images

Down pat: back after a Covid scare, Cummins knocks over England's top three.

spell had reduced England to 22 for four, more or less settling the Test – and the Ashes. The ground was not quite half full, yet the mood was febrile, the noise deafening. For Crawley, Malan, Hameed and nightwatchman Leach, it was too much. Stokes, though – two not out at stumps – said the experience was "pretty special". In an era when Test cricket is struggling to keep the white-ball wolf from the door, this was sport at its most feral.

Softened up that night, England disintegrated next morning, as debutant seamer Scott Boland – a 32-year-old Melburnian of Aboriginal descent – picked up six for seven by hitting a length, finding movement, and catching the edge. Records tumbled almost as fast as wickets: England's total of 68 was their lowest in Australia since 1903-04, and their ninth Test defeat in 2021 (only Bangladesh, in 2003, had lost as many). Four ducks took their haul for the year to 54, equalling their own world record, set in 1998. And you had to go back to 1888 to find a lower Ashes total in an innings win than Australia's 267. There was no kind way of putting it: England had been pulverised.

It went without saying that Covid played a part. With Australia set to resume their first innings on the second morning, news emerged of positive cases in the England camp: six, it turned out, split evenly between coaching staff and family members. About to leave for the ground, the players got back off the team bus, and retreated inside their hotel for more swabs. The game eventually restarted half an hour late, at which point England bowled with a purpose rarely seen all tour. Had this not been the Ashes, they might have been on the first plane home.

As his side swung between illness and insult, Root's pre-match promise of a rousing response to Brisbane and Adelaide rang hollow. Four changes suggested revolution, but there was nothing new about Crawley (in for Burns), Bairstow (replacing Pope), Wood or Leach (ousting Woakes and Broad). Shuffling their pack, England hoped to turn up an ace. Instead, they batted like jokers.

After winning a good toss following a half-hour delay for rain on Boxing Day, Cummins – back from a Covid scare of his own – reduced them to 61 for three at lunch on a pitch dotted with tufts of green. Hameed edged behind for a duck, Crawley squirted to gully, and Malan – in the morning's final over – was caught at slip, to end a careful 14. While Root was there, clambering past South African Graeme Smith's 1,656 in 2008 on the list

MELBOURNE NOTES AND QUOTES

The build-up was dominated by the fallout of a story in *The Guardian*, which revealed that England had held a candid debrief immediately after Adelaide, in which their batting performances were eviscerated by the coaches, and senior players offered frank opinions.

That did not stop England getting funky with the techniques of Burns and Haseeb Hameed. Working with coaching consultant Ant Botha, they were spotted batting on one leg in the MCG nets – apparently to help them with their balance. Mike Atherton called it "a little strange". His *Times* colleague Steve James – another former Test opener – said it "beggared belief".

The criticism of England carried on after their innings defeat, when none of their players appeared on the outfield as Joe Root did post-match interviews. Their absence irritated Michael Vaughan, who was working for Fox Sports. "I didn't like the fact that the England players went straight down into the dressing-room," said Vaughan. "Of course, you're embarrassed. You've just performed poorly, you've just been bowled out for 68. Show face, get on the pitch, support your captain."

It was reported that head coach Chris Silverwood would be the first victim of a post-series clearout. One name thrown into the ring by the media was Ricky Ponting, who had spent the series eviscerating England – "the worst-performing team in Australia ever" – and Root's captaincy. Another candidate was Gary Kirsten, who had been overlooked for Silverwood in 2019. But he hurt his chances by making clear his interest while Silverwood – isolating because of Covid – was still in the job.

---

of annual Test tallies, England could conceive of 250. But soon after reaching a high-calibre half-century, he edged a low-calibre slash at Starc. Having pledged to "bang out a hundred", Root banged his bat: for the ninth time in 22 Test innings in Australia, he had fallen between 50 and 89.

It was the first of a quartet of suicidal strokes from England's middle-order seniors. Before tea, Stokes was caught at backward point attempting to ramp Green; after it, Bairstow tried to steer Starc over the cordon, and gloved to gully. In between, in the last over before the break, came the worst of the lot, arguably the worst of the tour. Buttler ran at Lyon, aiming down the ground. Instead, he presented a simple catch to deep square leg. Robinson played a few shots, but 185 was anaemic. Warner and Harris rammed home its inadequacy, raising Australia's 50 in 12.1 overs, before Warner was squared up by Anderson and caught low in the gully – momentary respite from the one-way traffic.

After the delayed start to the second morning, England briefly fought back. Lyon, the nightwatchman, nicked Robinson, before Labuschagne poked Wood's third ball to Root, whom he had just replaced at the top of the Test rankings. When Anderson bowled Smith off the edge, Australia were four down, still 75 behind. Either side of lunch, however, Root let them off the hook. Trying to ease Leach back in after his butchering at Brisbane, he set defensive fields, while a leg-side line allowed Harris and Head simple runs. After a fifth-wicket stand of 61, both fell before Australia had the lead, to slip catches by Root – Head off Robinson, Harris off Anderson, three short of equalling his Test-best 79. But the last four wickets added 87, opening up an 82-run advantage, and leaving England's top order with a tricky mini-session.

MOST TEST FIFTIES IN AUSTRALIA WITHOUT A HUNDRED

	I				*I*	
9	22	B. M. Laird (A)		6	31	A. C. Bannerman (A)
9	**27**	**J. E. Root (E)**		6	29	V. S. Ransford (A)
8	27	T. W. Hayward (E)		6	46	R. Benaud (A)
8	91	S. K. Warne (A)		6	24	P. N. Toohey (A)
8	20	N. Hussain (E)		6	25	A. J. Lamb (E)
7	49	M. G. Johnson (A)				

Flying fling: Haseeb Hameed tries to run out top-scorer Marcus Harris.

It quickly became traumatic. Starc had Crawley caught behind, dangling his bat, and next ball trapped Malan, back in his crease: out, said umpire Wilson; clipping leg bail, said DRS. Root emerged to a cacophony. The Ashes were on the line, and so was England's credibility, or what little remained. The hat-trick delivery, full and swinging, was almost perfect: to roars of disappointment, Root played and missed. But the crowd – fuelled by festive drinks – were in the mood for wickets. With his third ball, Boland had Hameed caught behind off a half-forward fiddle; with his fifth, he bowled Leach, who shouldered arms as if bearing in mind England's pre-match admission they had played too many shots during the first two Tests. Theatrically, Stokes delayed his entrance, hoping to run down the clock and eat up an over. When he appeared, it was to jeers. Next morning, he told team-mates it was the first time he had been "taken aback by an atmosphere". Somehow, he and Root reached the close, with England 51 behind.

ENGLAND'S LOWEST TOTALS IN AUSTRALIA

45	Sydney	1886-87	72†	Sydney‡	1894-95
61	Melbourne	1901-02	75	Melbourne	1894-95
61	Melbourne	1903-04	77	Sydney	1884-85
65†	Sydney‡	1894-95	79†	Brisbane	2002-03
68	**Melbourne**	**2021-22**	87	Melbourne	1958-59

† *One man absent.*   ‡ *In the same match.*

With their best batsman and resident miracle worker both at the crease, they went into the third day trying to convince themselves all was not lost. Reality kicked in as early as the fifth over, when Starc zipped one through Stokes's defence. Enter Boland, his figures already 1–0–1–2. He had Bairstow dropped by Green in the gully off his first ball, then leg-before to his fifth. When, in his next over, Root edged to slip, England were 61 for seven. Boland, Australia's oldest fast-bowling debutant since Geff Noblet in March 1950, was charging in like a 20-year-old. And, just like the collapse, his spell was rewriting records on the hoof. A return catch off Wood gave him a five-for in his first 19 balls, equalling the Test record set by Australia's Ernie Toshack against India at Brisbane in 1947-48, and matched by Stuart Broad against Australia at Trent Bridge in 2015. That

LOWEST TEST TOTALS TO WIN BY AN INNINGS

153†	Australia v South Africa (36 and 45) at Melbourne	1931-32
172	England v Australia (81 and 70) at Manchester	1888
199-8 dec	Australia v New Zealand (42 and 54) at Wellington	1945-46
218	West Indies v Pakistan (131 and 77†) at Lahore	1986-87
230	Pakistan v Sri Lanka (109 and 101†) at Kandy	1985-86
246	England v New Zealand (200 and 26) at Auckland.	1954-55
265	England v South Africa (115 and 117) at Cape Town.	1895-96
267-2 dec	England v New Zealand (67 and 129) at Leeds.	1958
267	**Australia v England (185 and 68) at Melbourne**	**2021-22**
269	England v New Zealand (47 and 74) at Lord's	1958

† *One man absent.*

became six in 21 when he removed Robinson – another victim of near flawless slip catching, another index of Australian superiority. Only Jermaine Lawson, with six for three for West Indies against Bangladesh at Dhaka in 2002, had taken a cheaper Test six-for. And it was all over when Green bowled Anderson, to complete a third-morning slump of six for 22 in 66 deliveries.

The Mullagh Medal was named after the Indigenous Australian all-rounder Unaarrimin ("Johnny Mullagh", as he became known) who starred on the Aboriginals' 1868 tour of England. In only its second year as the match award at the Melbourne Test – India's Ajinkya Rahane was the first recipient – it went to Boland, Australia's second male Test cricketer of Aboriginal descent, after Jason Gillespie. He wore the medal proudly, and a big smile: "I thought it was going to be really tough, a big step up." This sounded more of an insult to England than he presumably intended, though England invited their own mockery, too: head coach Chris Silverwood told BT Sport there were "positives" to derive from the debacle.

It meant Australia had retained the Ashes in a record 20 days and 50 minutes after the series began with Burns's Brisbane first-baller, and extended England's winless sequence in Australia to 13 Tests, another unwanted record. All that remained was to play for pride, though why that should appear out of nowhere was anyone's guess.

Player of the Match: S. M. Boland.   *Attendance:* 140,671.
Close of play: first day, Australia 61-1 (Harris 20, Lyon 0); second day, England 31-4 (Root 12, Stokes 2).

England

H. Hameed c Carey b Cummins.	0	– c Carey b Boland	7
Z. Crawley c Green b Cummins.	12	– c Carey b Starc	5
D. J. Malan c Warner b Cummins	14	– lbw b Starc	0
*J. E. Root c Carey b Starc.	50	– c Warner b Boland	28
B. A. Stokes c Lyon b Green	25	– (6) b Starc.	11
J. M. Bairstow c Green b Starc.	35	– (7) lbw b Boland	5
†J. C. Buttler c Boland b Lyon.	3	– (8) not out.	5
M. A. Wood lbw b Boland.	6	– (9) c and b Boland	0
O. E. Robinson c Boland b Lyon.	22	– (10) c Labuschagne b Boland.	0
M. J. Leach b Smith b Lyon.	13	– (5) b Boland	0
J. M. Anderson not out.	0	– b Green.	2
Lb 4, nb 1	5	Lb 5	5

1/4 (1) 2/13 (2) 3/61 (3)   (65.1 overs) 185
4/82 (4) 5/115 (5) 6/128 (7)
7/141 (8) 8/159 (6) 9/176 (10) 10/185 (9)

1/7 (1) 2/7 (3)   (27.4 overs) 68
3/22 (1) 4/22 (5)
5/46 (6) 6/60 (7) 7/61 (4)
8/65 (9) 9/65 (10) 10/68 (11)

Starc 15–3–54–2; Cummins 15–2–36–3; Boland 13–2–48–1; Green 8–4–7–1; Lyon 14.1–1–36–3.
Second innings—Starc 10–3–29–3; Cummins 10–4–19–0; Boland 4–1–7–6; Green 3.4–0–8–1.

Australia

M. S. Harris c Root b Anderson	76	*P. J. Cummins c Hameed b Anderson	21
D. A. Warner c Crawley b Anderson	38	M. A. Starc not out	24
N. M. Lyon c Buttler b Robinson	10	S. M. Boland c Crawley b Wood	6
M. Labuschagne c Root b Wood	1	B 2, lb 4, w 1, nb 5	12
S. P. D. Smith b Anderson	16		
T. M. Head c Root b Robinson	27	1/57 (2) 2/76 (3) 3/84 (4) (87.5 overs)	267
C. D. Green lbw b Leach	17	4/110 (5) 5/171 (6) 6/180 (1)	
†A. T. Carey c Buttler b Stokes	19	7/207 (7) 8/219 (8) 9/253 (9) 10/267 (11)	

Anderson 23–10–33–4; Robinson 19.2–4–64–2; Wood 19.5–2–71–2; Stokes 10.4–1–47–1; Leach 15–0–46–1.

Umpires: P. R. Reiffel and P. Wilson.   Third umpire: R. J. Tucker.
Referee: D. C. Boon.

AUSTRALIA v ENGLAND

Fourth Test

DEAN WILSON

At Sydney, January 5–9, 2022. Drawn. Australia 4pts, England 4pts. Toss: Australia.

Few grounds have tugged at the heartstrings quite like Sydney, with its mix of historic pavilions and tasteful redevelopment. It has witnessed many magic moments, with this century's including Steve Waugh's Ashes hundred off the final ball of the day in 2002-03, and Michael Clarke's record-breaking 329 not out against India nine years later. Then there was this game, which offered gems throughout – and a dramatic finale.

For those lucky enough to be there, the sight of the elegant Usman Khawaja, recalled after an absence of two and a half years, celebrating twin centuries in front of wife Rachel

Cameron Spencer, Getty Images

An Australian dream: Usman Khawaja en route to the first of his two hundreds.

and daughter Aisha, was a special treat. His journey from Pakistan, via grade and state cricket, to Australia's Test side in 2010-11 had not, back then, been something he was keen to talk about. He wanted to be known as just another Australian wearing the Baggy Green, not necessarily the first Muslim.

This time he was 35, more mature, and returning as a respected senior pro. It helped that the global conversation on race and diversity had reached Australia. Much had been made at Melbourne of the debut of Boland, and his Indigenous heritage. Now Khawaja was ready to embrace his background. "People talk about the American dream," he said after the first of his hundreds. "I am living the Australian dream. My parents came here from Pakistan to give us a better life, and I am representing Australia in our national sport. The love I got out there, I will never forget."

His chance had come about because Travis Head was in isolation after catching Covid. He was not alone. Match referee David Boon had also been laid low (he was replaced by Steve Bernard), while four of England's backroom team – Chris Silverwood plus three of

---

TWIN HUNDREDS IN AN ASHES TEST

W. Bardsley (A)	136 and 130 at The Oval	1909
H. Sutcliffe (E)	176 and 127 at Melbourne	1924-25
W. R. Hammond (E)	119* and 177 at Adelaide	1928-29
D. C. S. Compton (E)	147 and 103* at Adelaide†	1946-47
A. R. Morris (A)	122 and 124* at Adelaide†	1946-47
S. R. Waugh (A)	108 and 116 at Manchester	1997
M. L. Hayden (A)	197 and 103 at Brisbane	2002-03
S. P. D. Smith (A)	144 and 142 at Birmingham . . .	2019
U. T. Khawaja (A)	**137 and 101* at Sydney**	**2021-22**

† *The same match.*

---

his assistants, Jon Lewis, Jeetan Patel and Darren Veness – were still isolating in Melbourne. It left them with a skeleton staff: Graham Thorpe, wicketkeeping consultant James Foster and coaching consultant Ant Botha. To help out, Thorpe asked his former Surrey and England colleague Adam Hollioake if he might head south from his home on the Gold Coast. Hollioake was happy to help, and made the seven-hour drive – only to be ruled out after a close contact tested positive.

After all that, Australia won the toss and, ignoring the weather that would restrict the first day to 46.5 overs, chose to bat. It took England until the 21st to strike, as Broad – omitted, to his chagrin, at Melbourne on a pitch that appeared well suited to him – removed Warner for the 13th time in Tests, caught at second slip by Crawley. Harris, buoyed by a half-century at the MCG, dropped anchor to score 38 in more than three hours, before he was prised out by Anderson, who now had a Test wicket in each of the 20 years in which he had played Test cricket, beating 19 by Garry Sobers and Muttiah Muralitharan. Shortly after Labuschagne fell – once more to Wood's pace – Australia closed on 126 for three.

Next day, Smith and Khawaja took their partnership to 115, batting with patience and serenity – so much so that England soon resorted to intimidatory bowling to try to shift the game. Not for the first time, the task fell to Stokes, who caused discomfort for both batsmen. Five balls into his fourth over, however, he pulled up with a side injury – a low-grade tear, it emerged, that stopped him bowling again in the series. England's injury problems were not over: two hours later, Buttler's left index finger took an awkward blow behind the stumps; scans revealed a break, though not before he had continued until the end of the innings, and held another catch.

A bowler light, England had to wait until the second new ball for their next breakthroughs: Broad had Smith caught behind for 67 – his tenth score of 50-plus in his

Philip Brown, PopperFoto/Getty Images

Jonny B. Good: broken finger and all, Bairstow hits out en route to a counter-punching century.

13th Test innings on his home ground – and quickly added Green. In between, Khawaja brought up a half-century from 134 balls, then upped the tempo. His second fifty came from 67, and he marked his ninth Test century with a knee-pumping celebration inspired by basketball's LeBron James. He went on to 137, giving his team a grip on the game they never relinquished, and was finally out, to Broad, who became the seventh visiting seamer aged 35 or more to take a Test five-for in Australia (the sixth had been Anderson, four years earlier at Adelaide).

The declaration, at 416 for eight, left England's openers five overs to survive, which they managed. Any optimism was scotched by the dismissal of Hameed next morning, soon followed by 70 balls which produced no runs and three wickets, including Root, carving Boland high to second slip for a duck: 22 without loss had become 36 for four. The paralysis ended when Stokes, visibly hampered by his injury, thick-edged Boland for a single. Slowly, the momentum changed, and with Bairstow he added 128, only England's third century partnership of the series. Stokes finally fell leg-before to Lyon for 66, and next ball – from Cummins – Bairstow was hit on the end of his right thumb.

But adrenaline is a powerful drug and, after Buttler departed for a tame duck, Bairstow continued in pugnacious style, reaching his seventh Test hundred – a characteristic riposte to those who had questioned him. They included a group of fans who had abused him about his weight as he walked off at tea, and were soon ejected, missing some rich entertainment: Bairstow went after Lyon, and Wood – up at No. 8 – struck 39 from 41 balls, including a trio of pulled sixes off Cummins.

As well as Bairstow played, England were all out inside ten overs on the fourth morning for 294; Boland finished with a cheap four-for, before Australia set about turning a lead of 122 into an impossible target. First, though, an early burst of activity reduced them to 86 for four, with Ollie Pope taking three catches as Buttler's replacement behind the stumps, and later adding a fourth, to equal the record in a Test innings for a substitute fielder, held by Pakistan's Younis Khan and India's Wriddhiman Saha (on the same ground, a year earlier). Smith was fourth out, to Leach, but not before scoring his 3,000th Ashes run, in his 54th innings – the second-fastest, behind Don Bradman (38).

SYDNEY NOTES AND QUOTES

With England's coaching staff depleted by Covid, the dropped duo of Ollie Pope and Rory Burns fed nicks to the slips in practice, and threw to batters in the nets. "You almost go back to club cricket," said Ben Stokes.

The Covid outbreak – and Sydney's overwhelmed health system – meant England were being tested so regularly they were going in for the next round before receiving results for the last. Their team photo was taken with the players socially distanced.

Another to go down with the virus was Glenn McGrath, ruled out of the Pink Test which raises money for breast cancer care in honour of his late wife, Jane. But that, and smaller crowds than usual, did not prevent his foundation raising a record-breaking figure of more than \$A5m.

After Jimmy Anderson secured a draw by blocking out a maiden, he spoke about the experience on the BBC podcast "Tailenders". "Five balls from Steve Smith, he landed them really well, but the sixth – I don't think Steve would begrudge me using the word 'pie'. When I shook his hand I said: 'What was that?' He said: 'The pressure got to me.'"

Khawaja tapped into his first-innings form, and this time found an ally in Green. They added 179, as Khawaja became the ninth to score two hundreds in an Ashes Test, and the third to score two at the SCG, after Doug Walters against West Indies in 1968-69, and Ricky Ponting against South Africa in 2005-06. The declaration, which denied Leach the chance of a hat-trick, was perhaps a little late, leaving a fanciful target of 388 and a potential 109 overs for England to survive. The odds were stacked against them, but 11 wicketless overs that evening was a solid start.

On the final day, Australia made consistent inroads, but never sparked an all-out collapse. England were three down at lunch, including Crawley for a glittering 77; and, after rain had lopped off seven crucial overs, they were four down at tea, taken with 35

ROCK BOTTOM AT THE TOP

Lowest average by an England opener in a Test series:

10.00	H. Hameed	v Australia	2021-22
10.50	P. F. Warner	v South Africa	1905-06
12.12	G. A. Gooch	v Australia	1981
12.77	A. Lyth	v Australia	2015
13.75	M. A. Atherton	v Australia	1998-99

Minimum: seven innings.

Gooch's figures exclude 42 runs from No. 4 in the Fourth Test.

to go. Everyone fought hard: all the top seven, plus Leach and Broad, would spend at least 39 minutes at the crease, with Stokes lasting almost three hours in making his second sixty of the game.

But he fiddled Lyon to slip, then Cummins – armed with the second new ball – won lbw shouts against Buttler and Wood within three deliveries. When Boland had Bairstow, on 41, taken at silly point via bat and pad, Australia had more than ten overs to prise out the final two wickets. Leach, though, was resolute, as if reliving his part in the miracle of Headingley 2019, and Broad a willing accomplice.

As men gathered round the bat, and the light faded, Australia had to rely on spin for the last four overs. And with the final ball of the second, Leach edged Smith to slip, sparking huge celebrations. Out walked Anderson, whose first task was to watch Broad negotiate a maiden from Lyon. His second was to deny Smith, which he did with ease, averting the possibility of England's third 5–0 whitewash in five visits. "The minute I got out there," he said later, "Stuart Broad was telling me what to do: 'Get a big stride in, smother the ball, don't let the bounce beat your bat.' I was like: 'It's all right mate, I've played before, it's fine.'" And so it was. Just.

Player of the Match: U. T. Khawaja. *Attendance:* 110,285.

Close of play: first day, Australia 126-3 (Smith 6, Khawaja 4); second day, England 13-0 (Hameed 2, Crawley 2); third day, England 258-7 (Bairstow 103, Leach 4); fourth day, England 30-0 (Crawley 22, Hameed 8).

Australia

D. A. Warner c Crawley b Broad	30	– (2) c sub (†O. J. D. Pope) b Wood	3
M. S. Harris c Root b Anderson	38	– (1) c sub (†O. J. D. Pope) b Leach	27
M. Labuschagne c Buttler b Wood	28	– c sub (†O. J. D. Pope) b Wood	29
S. P. D. Smith c Buttler b Broad	67	– b Leach	23
U. T. Khawaja b Broad	137	– not out	101
C. D. Green c Crawley b Broad	5	– c Root b Leach	74
†A. T. Carey c Bairstow b Root	13	– c sub (†O. J. D. Pope) b Leach	0
*P. J. Cummins c Buttler b Broad	24		
M. A. Starc not out	34		
N. M. Lyon not out	16		
Lb 8, w 12, nb 4	24	Lb 3, w 5	8

1/51 (1) 2/111 (2)   (8 wkts dec, 134 overs) 416   1/12 (2)   (6 wkts dec, 68.5 overs) 265
3/117 (3) 4/232 (4)   2/52 (1) 3/68 (3)
5/242 (6) 6/285 (7) 7/331 (8) 8/398 (5)   4/86 (4) 5/265 (6) 6/265 (7)

S. M. Boland did not bat.

Anderson 30–9–54–1; Broad 29–5–101–5; Stokes 13.5–3–37–0; Wood 26.1–6–76–1; Leach 24–2–89–0; Malan 3–0–15–0; Root 8–0–36–1. *Second innings*—Anderson 12–1–34–0; Broad 11–3–31–0; Wood 15–0–65–2; Leach 21.5–1–84–4; Root 7–0–35–0; Malan 2–0–13–0.

England

H. Hameed c Starc	6	– (2) c Carey b Boland	9
Z. Crawley b Boland	18	– (1) lbw b Green	77
D. J. Malan c Khawaja b Green	3	– b Lyon	4
*J. E. Root c Smith b Boland	0	– c Carey b Boland	24
B. A. Stokes lbw b Lyon	66	– c Smith b Lyon	60
J. M. Bairstow c Carey b Boland	113	– c Labuschagne b Boland	41
†J. C. Buttler c Khawaja b Cummins	0	– lbw b Cummins	11
M. A. Wood c Lyon b Cummins	39	– lbw b Cummins	0
M. J. Leach c Cummins b Lyon	10	– c Warner b Smith	26
S. C. J. Broad c Carey b Boland	15	– not out	8
J. M. Anderson not out	4	– not out	0
B 9, lb 6, w 3, nb 2	20	Lb 7, nb 3	10

1/22 (1) 2/36 (2) 3/36 (4)   (79.1 overs) 294   1/46 (2)   (9 wkts, 102 overs) 270
4/36 (3) 5/164 (5) 6/173 (7)   2/74 (3) 3/96 (1)
7/245 (8) 8/266 (9) 9/289 (6) 10/294 (10)   4/156 (4) 5/193 (5) 6/218 (7)
                                       7/218 (8) 8/237 (6) 9/270 (9)

Cummins 20–6–68–2; Starc 16–2–56–1; Boland 14.1–6–36–4; Green 9–4–24–1; Lyon 17–0–88–2; Labuschagne 3–0–7–0. *Second innings*—Starc 18–2–68–0; Cummins 22–5–80–2; Boland 24–11–30–3; Lyon 22–10–28–2; Green 10–1–38–1; Labuschagne 2–0–9–0; Smith 4–1–10–1.

Umpires: P. R. Reiffel and R. J. Tucker.   Third umpire: P. Wilson.
Referee: S. R. Bernard.

AUSTRALIA v ENGLAND

Fifth Test

SIMON WILDE

At Hobart, January 14–16, 2022 (day/night). Australia won by 146 runs. Australia 12pts. Toss: England. Test debut: S. W. Billings.

England's hopes of building on their gritty showing in Sydney, and exploiting the switch to a second pink-ball match of the series, speedily came to nothing. Bellerive Oval was the beneficiary of Perth's removal from the schedule because of Western Australia's strict Covid protocols, and became the first new Ashes venue in Australia since the WACA in 1970-71. In order to keep the hours in line with prime-time television audiences in the eastern states, and the slots the game would have occupied had it proceeded in Western Australia, the Test was a day/nighter starting at 3pm, bringing the floodlights into full effect for the third session. When the cricket continued until 10.30 on the second evening to make up overs lost to rain on the first, it was thought to be the latest England had played Test cricket.

The game did not go that late again. On the third evening, the English batsmen discarded wickets so readily they seemed as frightened of the dark as they were of Cummins and Starc. After reaching 68 – the highest opening stand of the series – in pursuit of 271, England shed all ten wickets for 56 in 22.4 overs, a capitulation that betrayed broken minds and methods. Fittingly, the end came when Cummins cleaned up Robinson, who was standing somewhere between the stumps and the dressing-room. In all, England's two innings lasted 86.3 overs, 38 balls fewer than at Melbourne.

It was an eventful and dramatic game, but another unsatisfactory advert for floodlit Test cricket. The crowds totalled 25,801 across three days – the smallest attendance for an Ashes Test since 22,617 watched the final match of the Packer-affected series of 1978-79

Worth the wait: England's 30-year-old debutant, Sam Billings, catches Marnus Labuschagne – his first Test victim.

Robert Cianflone, Getty Images

MOST TEST WICKETS AGAINST AUSTRALIA

		T	*BB*	*Avge*
148	I. T. Botham (England)...........	36	6-78	27.65
135	C. A. Walsh (West Indies)	38	6-54	28.68
131	**S. C. J. Broad (England)**.........	**35**	**8-15**	**29.05**
130	R. J. Hadlee (New Zealand)	23	9-52	20.56
128	C. E. L. Ambrose (West Indies)	27	7-25	21.23
128	R. G. D. Willis (England).........	35	8-43	26.14
112	**J. M. Anderson (England)**	**35**	**6-47**	**33.76**
111	A. Kumble (India)................	20	8-141	30.32
109	W. Rhodes (England)	41	8-68	24.00
106	S. F. Barnes (England)............	20	7-60	21.58

at the SCG. And, on another sporting pitch, the floodlights further assisted the bowlers: of the 34 wickets on the second and third days, 16 fell in the two late sessions.

England had made five changes: Pope, debutant Billings and Woakes came in for the injured trio of Bairstow, Buttler (who had already returned home) and Anderson, who had a hamstring niggle; Hameed was dropped for Burns, and Leach for Robinson, as it was reasoned (correctly) that conditions would not assist spin and, with Stokes unfit to bowl, England needed four seamers. Australia kept faith with Lyon's off-breaks, though they went unused. Once the seriousness of Buttler's finger injury in Sydney had become clear, Billings received an emergency call, having been about to leave the country following a Big Bash stint, and was asked to join the team in Sydney. That was a ten-hour drive from Carrara, where he had played his last match, to avoid any possible Covid contacts as he transferred into England's bubble. He batted enterprisingly for 29 in the first innings, took five catches behind the stumps in the second, and was praised for his energy and enthusiasm.

Root had chosen to bowl on an emerald green pitch, and could scarcely have hoped for a better start than three wickets (all caught in the slips) inside ten overs, including both Warner and Smith for ducks, for the first time in 244 international innings together.

SIX WICKETS IN A TEST INNINGS AT HOBART

6-31	S. K. Warne	Australia v New Zealand	1993-94
6-37	**M. A. Wood**	**England v Australia**............	**2021-22**
6-40	D. A. J. Bracewell	New Zealand v Australia.........	2011-12
6-46	Saqlain Mushtaq	Pakistan v Australia.............	1999-2000
6-66	R. J. Ratnayake	Sri Lanka v Australia	1989-90
6-77	K. J. Abbott	South Africa v Australia	2016-17
6-89	J. R. Hazlewood............	Australia v South Africa	2016-17

Robinson accounted for both, but two overs into the second session, he hobbled from the field with a back spasm; at stumps, bowling coach Jon Lewis bluntly assessed his lack of fitness. Between the wickets of Warner and Smith, Broad's precision earned him the scalp of Khawaja, but things could have been even better had Crawley, who would take four catches in the innings, not put down Labuschagne off Robinson before he had scored.

The nature of Australia's counter-attack, led by Labuschagne and the irrepressible Head, replacing Harris after returning from his Covid-enforced absence, showed their confidence. The pitch was difficult and, had they simply looked to survive, they would have surely perished. But they thrashed the bowling off its line and length in a stand of 71 from 74 balls, with Wood, whose first three overs cost 31, and Woakes bearing the brunt. Labuschagne hit nine fours in his 44 before falling – literally – to Broad, bowled behind his legs as his tumbled over his feet, and landed face first on the pitch.

Robert Cianflone, Getty Images

Tasmanian devilry: Mark Wood powers towards career-best figures.

With England down to three seamers for most of the afternoon, Head found another willing ally in Green: they put on 121 in 26 overs as Wood continued to leak runs, obliging Root to give himself ten overs (the game's only spin). Head ducked into a bouncer from Wood and was struck on the hand by Woakes, but still raced to a second sparkling century of the series, off 112 balls. England regained some control when Head and Green fell either side of the second interval but, when the umpires ended play early at 9.05 for rain so light no one would have known the reason had the fourth official not put up his umbrella, Australia were already a useful 241 for six.

England had their moments next day, but were always chasing the game. Wood's pace was too much for Starc and Cummins, but Lyon took on his short ball, hooking three sixes in a breezy 31 that hoisted Australia above 300 – the outer limits of what England could hope to match. When Broad bowled Lyon to finish the innings, he had 128 Test wickets against Australia, level with Bob Willis on England's list, and behind only Ian Botham. Later in the day, after the batsmen did not last even 50 overs, he would take sole ownership of second place.

They were fortunate to last that long. Burns should have been out in Starc's opening over, but a feathered catch to the keeper went undetected by the umpire and unchallenged by the fielders. No matter: in the next over, he responded slowly to Crawley's perilous call for a single, then failed to dive for his ground and was beaten by Labuschagne's throw; it was Burns's eighth duck in his last 22 Test innings. Crawley was smartly caught at short leg by Head for 18, before a partnership of 49 between Malan and Root restored a little order, although – with Malan on 13 – Australia again did not to pursue an appeal for caught behind which would have been upheld.

Again, though, it was immaterial: Cummins removed Malan and Root in successive overs, with Root's lbw the first time all series he had not been caught in the cordon. An off-balance Stokes cut Starc lazily to point, before Pope was caught behind off Boland, inexplicably pushing at one on sixth stump. If Warner hadn't dropped Woakes first ball, England would have been 110 for seven. Woakes was missed again, on five, also off Boland, but rode his luck to put on 42 with Billings, and top-score with 36.

Even so, Australia's lead of 115 felt almost insurmountable, though England's bowlers exploited favourable conditions in the 80 minutes before stumps. Warner was well taken by

HOBART NOTES AND QUOTES

On the morning of his first Test innings, Sam Billings received a message from Australia's captain, Pat Cummins – once a team-mate at Penrith CC, a western suburb of Sydney. It featured a scorecard from a game in 2013 in which Billings made a five-ball duck, and Cummins an unbeaten century.

Jane Howlett, Tasmania's minister for sport, described the Test as the biggest sporting event the island had seen. But one local not there to lap it up was former Australia captain Tim Paine, who had lost his job because of a sexting scandal, and had disappeared to Queensland for a family holiday.

The eruption of a volcano in the islands of Tonga in the South Pacific, more than 2,500 miles north-east, meant Tasmanians awoke on the third and final day to a tsunami warning. Bellerive Oval, however, stands on a relatively protected part of the River Derwent, and spectators staying across the water in Hobart's centre were not put off catching the free ferry laid on by the authorities from Constitution Dock.

Among the first England players to leave Tasmania was Dawid Malan, who had learned on the second evening that his wife, Claire, had given birth six weeks early to their first child, Summer Skye, by emergency C-section.

An early-hours drinking session after the Test, involving Joe Root, James Anderson, assistant coach Graham Thorpe, plus Australians Nathan Lyon, Travis Head and Alex Carey, was quietly broken up by police. They had been called to the Crowne Plaza, where both teams were staying, because Thorpe had been smoking a cigar inside the hotel. Footage soon spread across social media. He had filmed the moment the players dispersed, though it was unclear how it reached the public domain.

Pope at backward point to condemn him to a second Ashes pair, and a 14th dismissal by Broad; Labuschagne fell to Woakes, and a terrific short ball from Wood took Khawaja's glove.

The early exchanges next day belonged to Wood, whose unsettling pace and tireless energy earned him four more wickets, three in a six-over opening burst that included Head and Smith, who was caught hooking. He took his haul of Test wickets past Frank Tyson (76) and Harold Larwood (78), by reputation the two England bowlers whose pace he most closely matched. Had Woakes not overstepped when he bowled Carey on 19, Australia would have been 91 for seven, 206 in front. But Carey survived to make a valuable 49 and, realistically, take the game beyond England. Soon after the first interval, Wood left the field holding aloft the ball for career-best figures of six for 37, the best for England in Australia since Matthew Hoggard's seven for 109 at Adelaide in 2006-07.

Crawley and Burns, whose untied shoulder-length hair suggested he was determined to play freely, struck several crisp fours against a ball that was not swinging, while also enjoying considerable luck: one lbw appeal by Starc against Burns, unchallenged, showed three reds. Australia grew anxious, and wasted a review, but need not have worried. On the stroke of the second break, Green's bounce induced Burns into playing on and, after the restart, the floodgates opened.

Green struck Malan on the head, then bowled him with a fuller ball, before having Crawley caught behind – his third wicket in 20 deliveries. Stokes aimlessly swung Starc to deep square leg and, when Root was bowled by a grubber from Boland, he had to laugh at his misfortune. England could not get off the field fast enough. Billings chipped to mid-on, and Pope, completing an awful return, was bowled behind his legs. Woakes edged a hack, Wood pulled on to his own stumps, and Robinson stepped away. It would have taken longer to shoot fish in a barrel.

Player of the Match: T. M. Head.   *Attendance:* 25,801.

Compton–Miller Medal: T. M. Head.

Close of play: first day, Australia 241-6 (Carey 10, Starc 0); second day, Australia 37-3 (Smith 17, Boland 3).

Australia

D. A. Warner c Crawley b Robinson	0	– c Pope b Broad	0
U. T. Khawaja c Root b Broad	6	– c Billings b Wood	11
M. Labuschagne b Broad	44	– c Billings b Woakes	5
S. P. D. Smith c Crawley b Robinson	0	– c Malan b Wood	27
T. M. Head c Robinson b Woakes	101	– (6) c Billings b Wood	8
C. D. Green c Crawley b Wood	74	– (7) lbw b Broad	23
†A. T. Carey b Woakes	24	– (8) c Billings b Broad	49
M. A. Starc c Burns b Wood	3	– (9) c Pope b Wood	1
*P. J. Cummins c Crawley b Wood	2	– (10) b Wood	13
N. M. Lyon b Broad	31	– (11) not out	4
S. M. Boland not out	10	– (5) c Billings b Wood	8
B 3, lb 3, w 2	8	B 1, lb 3, w 1, nb 1	6

1/3 (1) 2/7 (2) 3/12 (4)   (75.4 overs) 303
4/83 (3) 5/204 (5) 6/236 (6)
7/246 (8) 8/252 (9) 9/280 (7) 10/303 (10)

1/0 (1) 2/5 (3)   (56.3 overs) 155
3/33 (2) 4/47 (5)
5/59 (6) 6/63 (4) 7/112 (7)
8/121 (9) 9/151 (8) 10/155 (10)

Broad 24.4–4–59–3; Robinson 8–3–24–2; Wood 18–1–115–3; Woakes 15–2–64–2; Root 10–1–35–0. *Second innings*—Broad 18–2–51–3; Woakes 11–3–40–1; Robinson 11–4–23–0; Wood 16.3–2–37–6.

England

R. J. Burns run out (Labuschagne)	0	– b Green	26
Z. Crawley c Head b Cummins	18	– c Carey b Green	36
D. J. Malan c Carey b Cummins	25	– b Green	10
*J. E. Root lbw b Cummins	34	– b Boland	11
B. A. Stokes c Lyon b Starc	4	– c Lyon b Starc	5
O. J. D. Pope c Carey b Boland	14	– b Cummins	5
†S. W. Billings c Boland b Green	29	– c Cummins b Boland	1
C. R. Woakes c Carey b Starc	36	– c Carey b Boland	5
M. A. Wood b Cummins	16	– b Cummins	11
S. C. J. Broad b Starc	0	– (11) not out	1
O. E. Robinson not out	0	– (10) b Cummins	0
B 4, lb 8	12	Lb 13	13

1/2 (1) 2/29 (2) 3/78 (3)   (47.4 overs) 188
4/81 (4) 5/85 (5) 6/110 (6)
7/152 (7) 8/182 (8) 9/182 (10) 10/188 (9)

1/68 (1) 2/82 (3)   (38.5 overs) 124
3/83 (2) 4/92 (5)
5/101 (4) 6/107 (7) 7/107 (6)
8/115 (8) 9/123 (9) 10/124 (10)

Starc 10–1–53–3; Cummins 13.4–2–45–4; Boland 14–6–33–1; Green 10–0–45–1. *Second innings*—Starc 8–0–30–1; Cummins 12.5–3–42–3; Boland 12.5–5–18–3; Green 6–1–21–3.

Umpires: R. J. Tucker and P. Wilson.   Third umpire: P. R. Reiffel.
Referee: D. C. Boon.

PART FOUR

English Domestic Cricket

FIRST-CLASS AVERAGES IN 2021

BATTING AND FIELDING

(Qualification: 10 innings)

		M	I	NO	R	HS	100	50	Avge	Ct/St
1	O. J. D. Pope (Surrey & England)	12	19	3	1,028	274	3	1	64.25	7
2	D. G. Bedingham (Durham)	13	20	3	1,029	257	3	3	60.52	11
3	H. M. Amla (Surrey)	13	20	3	994	215*	3	2	58.47	2
4	C. B. Cooke (Glam)	14	21	7	816	205*	4	1	58.28	40/1
5	J. D. Libby (Worcs & County Select XI)	15	25	5	1,104	180*	4	4	55.20	8
6	†M. S. Harris (Leics)	8	13	1	655	185	3	1	54.58	7
7	J. E. Root (Yorks & England)	11	19	1	952	180*	4	2	52.88	12
8	B. C. Brown (Sussex)	12	21	2	976	157	4	2	51.36	27/3
9	E. G. Barnard (Worcs)	13	18	3	746	128	2	3	49.73	12
10	K. S. Carlson (Glam)	14	23	4	928	170*	3	5	48.84	3
11	J. J. Bohannon (Lancs)	15	20	2	878	170	2	5	48.77	7
12	L. Gregory (Somerset)	9	10	2	389	107	1	3	48.62	7
13	†K. K. Jennings (Lancs)	10	13	1	577	132	2	3	48.08	8
14	†T. J. Haines (Sussex)	13	25	0	1,176	156	5	6	47.04	2
15	D. W. Lawrence (Essex & England)	13	18	2	746	152*	1	5	46.62	8
16	J. A. Leaning (Kent)	13	21	5	745	127*	1	6	46.56	11
17	†G. S. Ballance (Yorks)	10	14	1	594	101*	1	4	45.69	3
18	L. J. Hill (Leics)	14	22	1	944	145	3	5	44.95	3
19	R. G. Sharma (Indians)	6	11	1	441	127	1	2	44.10	6
20	B. T. Foakes (Surrey)	8	10	2	350	133	1	2	43.75	16/2
21	J. L. Smith (Surrey)	12	17	2	656	138	3	1	43.73	15/1
22	M. J. J. Critchley (Derbys)	14	26	3	1,000	109	1	8	43.47	8
23	D. I. Stevens (Kent)	12	18	3	650	190	3	2	43.33	4
24	H. J. Swindells (Leics)	13	19	3	693	171*	2	3	43.31	27/1
25	†R. J. Burns (Surrey & England)	15	25	1	1,038	132	2	10	43.25	8
26	H. R. Hosein (Derbys)	8	14	5	371	83*	0	4	41.22	11
27	J. M. Vince (Hants)	13	20	0	816	231	1	4	40.80	16
28	S. D. Robson (Middx)	14	27	1	1,047	253	3	2	40.26	16
29	†B. T. Slater (Notts)	14	24	3	837	114*	2	5	39.85	8
30	T. B. Abell (Somerset)	12	20	2	711	132*	1	4	39.50	11
31	†R. M. Yates (Warwicks & County Select XI)	15	25	2	907	132*	5	3	39.43	21
32	H. Hameed (Notts, Cty Select XI & England)	15	26	2	944	114*	3	6	39.33	11
33	†L. Wood (Lancs)	10	13	2	431	119	1	1	39.18	3
34	†A. G. H. Orr (Sussex)	7	14	0	548	119	1	3	39.14	1
35	†A. Z. Lees (Durham)	11	17	1	625	129	1	5	39.06	6
36	†A. Lyth (Yorks)	14	22	1	819	153	3	3	39.00	25
37	†L. W. P. Wells (Lancs)	13	18	2	613	103	1	3	38.31	18
38	H. C. Brook (Yorks)	14	22	1	797	118	2	5	37.95	17
39	P. J. Malan (Warwicks)	6	10	1	339	141	1	1	37.66	0
40	†M. D. Stoneman (Surrey & Middx)	14	22	0	827	174	4	3	37.59	2
41	T. Westley (Essex)	13	18	1	631	213	3	1	37.11	5
42	†B. M. Duckett (Notts)	13	21	2	705	177*	1	4	37.10	15
43	†R. S. Vasconcelos (Northants)	14	24	1	845	185*	2	2	36.73	32/1
44	S. R. Hain (Warwicks)	15	26	2	881	118	1	7	36.70	21
45	†M. A. H. Hammond (Glos)	9	17	2	547	94	0	4	36.46	11
46	†P. I. Walter (Essex)	13	16	1	544	96	0	4	36.26	5
47	O. G. Robinson (Kent)	13	21	1	725	120	2	3	36.25	38/1
48	J. M. Clarke (Notts)	13	22	1	760	109	1	7	36.19	8
49	A. M. Rossington (Northants)	11	16	1	537	94	0	4	35.80	24/2
50	A. L. Davies (Lancs)	14	21	2	670	84	0	6	35.26	18/4
51	J. A. Haynes (Worcs)	9	14	0	491	97	0	4	35.07	8
52	R. I. Keogh (Northants)	14	24	2	766	126	2	4	34.81	1

		M	I	NO	R	HS	100	50	Avge	Ct/St
53	R. G. White (*Middx*)	14	26	4	765	120	2	4	34.77	19
54	C. N. Ackermann (*Leics*)	10	15	1	485	126*	1	3	34.64	20
55	D. L. Lloyd (*Glam*)	14	25	1	828	121	1	4	34.50	7
56	D. J. Vilas (*Lancs*)	15	18	1	584	189	1	2	34.35	20
57	W. L. Madsen (*Derbys*)	11	20	0	675	111	1	4	33.75	20
58	I. G. Holland (*Hants*)	14	24	1	766	146*	2	4	33.30	8
59	†B. A. Godleman (*Derbys*)	10	18	2	530	100*	1	3	33.12	5
60	†J. R. Bracey (*Glos & England*)	13	24	2	723	118	1	6	32.86	39
61	S. T. Evans (*Leics*)	11	18	0	591	138	3	1	32.83	3
62	D. P. Sibley (*Warwicks & England*)	14	24	3	687	80	0	6	32.71	4
63	L. W. James (*Notts & County Select XI*)	13	19	1	585	91	0	5	32.50	1
64	E. Barnes (*Leics*)	10	12	4	259	83*	0	2	32.37	4
65	†A. N. Cook (*Essex*)	14	19	0	611	165	2	2	32.15	16
66	D. A. Douthwaite (*Glam*)	13	16	1	482	96	0	4	32.13	3
67	†N. R. T. Gubbins (*Middx & Hants*)	14	26	2	769	137*	2	5	32.04	7
68	†L. A. Patterson-White (*Notts & Cty Select XI*)	15	21	3	571	101	1	3	31.72	4
69	†S. M. Davies (*Somerset*)	13	22	2	634	87	0	5	31.70	37/1
70	A. G. Salter (*Glam*)	10	11	4	221	90	0	1	31.57	2
71	†L. A. Procter (*Northants*)	13	21	2	597	93	0	5	31.42	2
72	G. K. Berg (*Northants*)	9	10	3	216	69*	0	1	30.85	3
73	†N. L. J. Browne (*Essex*)	14	19	2	524	102	1	4	30.82	6
74	†W. M. H. Rhodes (*Warwicks & Cty Select XI*)	16	28	2	800	156	1	5	30.76	13
75	E. J. H. Eckersley (*Durham*)	13	18	1	520	113*	1	3	30.58	28/1
76	†T. J. Moores (*Notts*)	12	19	3	486	97	0	3	30.37	52/2
77	A. K. Dal (*Derbys*)	8	13	2	333	106	1	1	30.27	6
78	S. S. Eskinazi (*Middx*)	9	17	2	453	102	1	2	30.20	4
	I. A. Cockbain (*Glos*)	6	11	1	302	117	1	2	30.20	1
80	S. J. Mullaney (*Notts*)	14	22	0	657	117	1	3	29.86	6
81	D. K. Ibrahim (*Sussex*)	6	11	0	328	94	0	3	29.81	3
82	M. J. Lamb (*Warwicks*)	14	24	5	565	67	0	3	29.73	5
83	S. A. Northeast (*Hants, Yorks & Notts*)	12	18	2	474	118	1	3	29.62	4
84	M. G. K. Burgess (*Warwicks*)	15	22	0	651	101	1	3	29.59	44/5
85	†R. A. Jadeja (*Indians*)	6	11	0	317	75	0	3	28.81	1
86	†M. H. Azad (*Leics*)	12	20	2	518	152	2	1	28.77	4
87	C. A. Pujara (*Indians*)	6	12	1	309	91	0	2	28.09	0
88	M. A. Jones (*Durham*)	8	13	1	337	81	0	2	28.08	2
89	D. J. Lamb (*Lancs*)	11	14	1	365	125	1	1	28.07	5
90	Z. Crawley (*Kent & England*)	15	27	2	691	90	0	6	27.64	12
91	†W. T. Root (*Glam*)	11	18	2	442	110*	1	1	27.62	4
92	J. M. Cox (*Kent*)	13	23	2	579	90	0	4	27.57	10
93	B. W. M. Mike (*Leics*)	13	19	1	495	74	0	4	27.50	2
	S. J. Croft (*Lancs*)	11	14	2	330	103*	1	1	27.50	8
95	J. T. A. Burnham (*Durham*)	10	15	2	357	102*	1	1	27.46	3
96	†S. A. Zaib (*Northants*)	13	22	1	576	135	1	3	27.42	4
97	A. J. A. Wheater (*Essex*)	14	16	0	434	87	0	2	27.12	23/4
98	†K. H. D. Barker (*Hants*)	10	15	1	379	84	0	3	27.07	1
99	J. Leach (*Worcs*)	13	19	5	377	84	0	1	26.92	2
100	K. C. Brathwaite (*Glos*)	6	11	0	295	60	0	1	26.81	6
101	†J. A. Simpson (*Middx*)	13	22	2	535	95*	0	3	26.75	50/3
102	†C. D. J. Dent (*Glos*)	12	23	2	560	91*	0	5	26.66	5
	L. D. McManus (*Hants*)	11	14	2	320	91	0	2	26.66	28/1
104	J. H. Davey (*Somerset*)	12	16	7	238	75*	0	1	26.44	2
105	S. R. Harmer (*Essex*)	14	16	4	317	82*	0	1	26.41	14
106	D. J. Bell-Drummond (*Kent*)	10	17	1	419	114	1	2	26.18	2
107	R. N. ten Doeschate (*Essex*)	10	12	0	314	56	0	3	26.16	9
108	T. C. Lace (*Glos*)	14	26	4	573	118	1	3	26.04	9
109	D. R. Briggs (*Warwicks*)	13	20	4	413	66*	0	3	25.81	4
110	B. D. Guest (*Derbys*)	12	20	1	489	116	1	1	25.73	26/3
111	B. A. Raine (*Durham*)	13	15	3	308	74	0	2	25.66	3
112	†T. P. Alsop (*Hants*)	14	24	2	564	149	2	0	25.63	14

		M	I	NO	R	HS	100	50	Avge	Ct/St
113	A. D. Thomason (*Sussex*)	9	17	2	379	78*	0	3	25.26	16
114	B. L. D'Oliveira (*Worcs*)	14	21	2	480	71	0	3	25.26	4
115	†M. J. Leach (*Somerset*)	10	15	4	276	49	0	0	25.09	2
116	†R. S. Patel (*Surrey*)	6	10	0	250	62	0	2	25.00	3
117	L. A. Dawson (*Hants*)	12	20	2	449	152*	1	1	24.94	17
118	G. A. Bartlett (*Somerset*)	11	16	1	373	100	1	2	24.86	2
119	†S. van Zyl (*Sussex*)	9	17	0	422	113	1	3	24.82	4
120	M. E. Milnes (*Kent*)	8	14	4	244	78	0	1	24.40	7
121	J. A. Tattersall (*Yorks, Glos & Surrey*)	8	13	2	267	86*	0	2	24.27	23
122	O. E. Robinson (*Sussex & England*)	11	16	2	337	67	0	2	24.07	4
123	G. C. H. Hill (*Yorks*)	7	11	0	263	71	0	1	23.90	1
124	†S. G. Borthwick (*Durham*)	13	20	0	474	100	1	3	23.70	14
125	†E. N. Gay (*Northants*)	9	17	0	391	101	1	1	23.00	5
126	†E. J. Byrom (*Somerset & Glam*)	7	10	1	206	78	0	1	22.88	2
127	J. C. Hildreth (*Somerset*)	13	20	0	456	107	1	1	22.80	14
128	T. T. Bresnan (*Warwicks*)	11	16	2	315	68*	0	1	22.50	18
129	†G. H. S. Garton (*Sussex*)	7	11	0	247	97	0	1	22.45	4
130	†T. G. R. Clark (*Sussex*)	7	13	2	240	54*	0	1	21.81	6
131	O. B. Cox (*Worcs*)	14	21	2	413	60*	0	2	21.73	42/2
132	C. Overton (*Somerset & England*)	10	14	1	280	74	0	2	21.53	12
133	D. K. H. Mitchell (*Worcs*)	14	23	1	470	113	1	3	21.36	13
	O. J. Carter (*Sussex*)	6	12	1	235	51	0	1	21.36	14
135	F. S. Organ (*Hants*)	6	10	0	213	67	0	1	21.30	6
136	M. de Lange (*Somerset*)	10	14	0	297	75	0	2	21.21	4
	L. P. Goldsworthy (*Somerset*)	10	15	1	297	48	0	0	21.21	1
138	T. A. I. Taylor (*Northants*)	11	17	2	316	50	0	1	21.06	6
139	D. M. Bess (*Yorks*)	14	20	1	399	56	0	2	21.00	4
	M. W. Parkinson (*Lancs*)	12	12	9	63	21*	0	0	21.00	1
141	R. F. Higgins (*Glos*)	13	19	1	376	73	0	1	20.88	3
142	F. J. Hudson-Prentice (*Derbys & Sussex*)	12	20	3	354	67	0	1	20.82	5
143	T. E. Bailey (*Lancs*)	13	16	6	330	63	0	2	20.62	1
144	†J. A. Thompson (*Yorks*)	13	20	0	411	57	0	1	20.55	4
145	M. H. Wessels (*Worcs*)	7	10	0	202	60	0	2	20.20	3
146	T. Köhler-Cadmore (*Yorks*)	11	18	0	353	89	0	1	19.61	21
147	†T. A. Lammonby (*Somerset*)	13	22	2	392	100	1	2	19.60	7
148	J. J. Carson (*Sussex & County Select XI*)	15	24	4	388	87	0	3	19.40	4
149	R. Clarke (*Surrey*)	11	13	3	192	65	0	1	19.20	13
150	T. Banton (*Somerset*)	8	14	1	245	51*	0	1	18.84	5
151	†J. L. du Plooy (*Derbys*)	13	24	1	428	98	0	2	18.60	5
152	G. H. Roderick (*Worcs*)	7	11	2	167	42*	0	0	18.55	1
153	J. J. Weatherley (*Hants*)	13	22	0	406	78	0	1	18.45	21
	†J. M. Cooke (*Glam*)	8	13	2	203	68	0	1	18.45	7
155	M. D. Taylor (*Glos*)	9	12	3	166	56	0	1	18.44	0
156	C. J. C. Wright (*Leics*)	12	16	2	257	87	0	1	18.35	2
157	†T. M. Head (*Sussex*)	6	11	1	183	49*	0	0	18.30	3
158	M. K. Andersson (*Middx*)	13	24	0	439	88	0	2	18.29	6
159	B. T. J. Wheal (*Hants*)	13	16	6	181	46*	0	0	18.10	2
160	R. P. Jones (*Lancs*)	9	11	0	199	58	0	1	18.09	11
161	†M. D. E. Holden (*Middx*)	10	19	1	325	52	0	1	18.05	6
162	T. van der Gugten (*Glam*)	11	13	2	194	85*	0	1	17.63	5
163	J. L. Denly (*Kent*)	9	14	0	246	63	0	1	17.57	1
164	P. S. P. Handscomb (*Middx*)	7	13	0	227	70	0	1	17.46	3
165	S. C. Kerrigan (*Northants*)	11	19	6	224	45*	0	0	17.23	3
166	T. C. Fell (*Worcs*)	12	19	0	324	69	0	2	17.05	9
167	K. J. Abbott (*Hants*)	11	12	3	148	58	0	1	16.44	1
168	H. G. Duke (*Yorks*)	9	13	1	197	54	0	2	16.41	31
169	J. Clarke (*Surrey*)	12	14	1	208	61*	0	2	16.00	2
	D. Paterson (*Notts*)	12	15	11	64	22	0	0	16.00	4
171	B. A. Hutton (*Notts*)	8	11	0	174	51	0	1	15.81	8
172	C. F. Parkinson (*Leics*)	13	18	2	253	41	0	0	15.81	2

		M	I	NO	R	HS	100	50	Avge	Ct/St
173	D. Y. Pennington (*Worcs*)	10	14	4	156	56	0	1	15.60	1
174	T. S. Roland-Jones (*Middx*)	6	11	2	138	46*	0	0	15.33	0
175	†B. J. Curran (*Northants*)	7	10	0	148	36	0	0	14.80	6
176	C. O. Thurston (*Northants*)	6	10	0	142	48	0	0	14.20	3
177	M. G. Hogan (*Glam*)	13	14	6	113	54	0	1	14.12	2
178	†D. M. W. Rawlins (*Sussex*)	10	17	0	233	58	0	1	13.70	3
179	†L. M. Reece (*Derbys*)	9	17	0	231	63	0	1	13.58	3
180	†M. L. Cummins (*Kent*)	8	10	2	108	28*	0	0	13.50	1
181	C. Rushworth (*Durham*)	13	13	6	91	31	0	0	13.00	3
182	S. A. Patterson (*Yorks*)	13	17	2	191	47*	0	0	12.73	3
183	C. N. Miles (*Warwicks & County Select XI*)	13	18	4	177	30*	0	0	12.64	5
184	B. W. Aitchison (*Derbys*)	13	20	4	200	50	0	1	12.50	12
185	J. A. Porter (*Essex*)	12	13	7	73	30	0	0	12.16	1
186	N. J. Selman (*Glam*)	5	10	0	121	69	0	1	12.10	3
187	L. J. Fletcher (*Notts*)	13	17	5	140	51	0	1	11.66	1
188	J. J. Bumrah (*Indians*)	6	10	2	92	34*	0	0	11.50	1
189	S. J. Cook (*Essex*)	13	13	2	126	37	0	0	11.45	1
190	D. A. Payne (*Glos*)	10	12	3	102	34	0	0	11.33	6
191	B. O. Coad (*Yorks*)	10	13	5	84	33*	0	0	10.50	0
192	S. Mahmood (*Lancs*)	8	11	4	73	20	0	0	10.42	2
193	D. Olivier (*Yorks*)	7	11	5	61	21	0	0	10.16	1
194	T. A. Wood (*Derbys*)	7	13	0	129	31	0	0	9.92	6
195	G. S. Virdi (*Surrey*)	11	12	6	59	47	0	0	9.83	1
196	†O. J. Hannon-Dalby (*Warwicks*)	8	11	6	48	26	0	0	9.60	2
197	L. C. Norwell (*Warwicks*)	13	18	5	120	30*	0	0	9.23	1
198	S. Conners (*Derbys*)	10	16	3	114	39	0	0	8.76	1
199	†S. C. J. Broad (*Notts & England*)	8	12	0	102	41	0	0	8.50	2
200	E. R. Bamber (*Middx*)	12	22	4	151	25	0	0	8.38	2
201	D. J. Worrall (*Glos*)	8	12	3	75	24	0	0	8.33	0
202	J. A. Brooks (*Somerset*)	6	10	4	47	15	0	0	7.83	0
203	†T. J. Murtagh (*Middx*)	12	20	7	88	31	0	0	6.76	3
204	†J. M. Anderson (*Lancs & England*)	10	12	7	29	8*	0	0	5.80	3
205	H. T. Crocombe (*Sussex*)	9	17	2	83	46*	0	0	5.53	0
206	B. W. Sanderson (*Northants*)	13	17	3	72	20	0	0	5.14	2
207	Mohammad Abbas (*Hants*)	10	14	7	28	6	0	0	4.00	2
208	S. F. Hunt (*Sussex*)	6	10	4	12	7	0	0	2.00	1

BOWLING

(Qualification: 10 wickets)

		Style	O	M	R	W	BB	5I	Avge
1	Zafar Gohar (*Glos*)	SLA	117.3	32	287	20	6-43	3	14.35
2	S. J. Cook (*Essex*)	RFM	382.2	128	837	58	5-20	3	14.43
3	L. J. Fletcher (*Notts*)	RFM	420.5	135	984	66	7-37	4	14.90
4	R. Ashwin (*Indians & Surrey*)	OB	83	23	171	11	6-27	1	15.54
5	Mohammad Abbas (*Hants*)	RFM	309.5	113	651	41	6-11	3	15.87
6	T. G. Southee (*New Zealand*)	RFM	83.1	19	192	12	6-43	1	16.00
7	C. Overton (*Somerset & England*)	RFM	333	109	818	50	5-25	4	16.36
8	S. Snater (*Essex*)	RM	168.5	42	511	31	7-98	2	16.48
9	M. G. Neser (*Glam*)	RFM	127	29	386	23	5-39	1	16.78
10	J. D. M. Evison (*Notts*)	RM	82.1	23	249	14	5-21	1	17.78
11	L. C. Norwell (*Warwicks*)	RFM	435.3	125	1,073	59	6-49	3	18.18
12	O. E. Robinson (*Sussex & England*)	RFM/OB	415.2	107	1,096	61	9-78	4	17.96
13	D. Paterson (*Notts*)	RFM	352.5	98	971	54	5-90	1	17.98
14	C. R. Woakes (*England & Warwicks*)	RFM	119.3	37	343	19	4-55	0	18.05
15	C. Rushworth (*Durham*)	RFM	435.3	125	1,073	59	6-49	3	18.18
16	{ T. S. Roland-Jones (*Middx*)	RFM	167.4	38	460	25	5-36	1	18.40
	{ K. A. Jamieson (*New Zealand & Surrey*)	RFM	93	39	184	10	5-31	1	18.40

	Style	O	M	R	W	BB	5I	Avge
18 K. H. D. Barker (*Hants*)	LFM	310	88	755	41	7-46	3	18.41
19 D. I. Stevens (*Kent*)	RM	284	93	725	39	5-53	2	18.58
20 T. J. Murtagh (*Middx*)	RFM	402.4	113	1,079	58	5-64	1	18.60
21 T. A. Boult (*New Zealand*)	LFM	75.2	14	205	11	4-85	0	18.63
22 T. E. Bailey (*Lancs*)	RFM	368	111	955	51	7-37	1	18.72
23 M. D. Fisher (*Yorks*)	RFM	121	29	393	20	5-41	1	19.65
24 W. M. H. Rhodes (*Warwicks & Cty Slct XI*)	RFM	190	53	523	26	5-23	1	20.11
25 M. W. Parkinson (*Lancs*)	LB	352.5	90	818	40	7-126	1	20.45
26 K. A. J. Roach (*Surrey*)	RFM	134	28	452	22	8-40	2	20.54
27 J. A. Thompson (*Yorks*)	RFM	329.5	91	949	46	5-52	1	20.63
28 N. N. Gilchrist (*Kent*)	RFM	160.1	26	620	30	5-38	1	20.66
29 E. R. Bamber (*Middx*)	RFM	407	111	1,084	52	5-41	1	20.84
30 S. C. J. Broad (*Notts & England*)	RFM	241.1	53	630	30	4-37	0	21.00
31 C. N. Miles (*Warwicks & Cty Select XI*)	RFM	327.4	68	988	47	5-28	3	21.02
32 D. A. Payne (*Glos*)	LFM	258.2	59	719	34	6-56	2	21.14
33 B. A. Carse (*Durham*)	RF	203.2	26	724	34	5-49	2	21.29
34 M. E. Milnes (*Kent*)	RFM	205.3	42	687	32	6-53	2	21.46
35 K. J. Abbott (*Hants*)	RFM	329.3	87	996	46	6-44	3	21.65
36 D. R. Briggs (*Warwicks*)	SLA	309	82	722	33	4-36	0	21.87
37 B. O. Coad (*Yorks*)	RFM	287.1	79	766	35	4-48	0	21.88
38 S. T. Finn (*Middx*)	RFM	68.2	4	266	12	5-77	1	22.16
39 J. H. Davey (*Somerset*)	RFM	292.2	84	781	35	5-30	2	22.31
40 R. F. Higgins (*Glos*)	RFM	443	118	1,143	51	5-46	2	22.41
41 B. A. Raine (*Durham*)	RFM	406.1	128	968	43	5-9	2	22.51
42 G. Stewart (*Kent*)	RFM	120	31	384	17	5-23	1	22.58
43 J. M. Anderson (*Lancs & England*)	RFM	287	90	659	29	7-19	2	22.72
44 C. J. C. Wright (*Leics*)	RFM	351	74	1,116	49	7-53	4	22.77
45 M. R. Quinn (*Kent*)	RFM	149.3	34	413	18	4-54	0	22.94
46 D. J. Worrall (*Glos*)	RFM	249.5	80	621	27	5-54	2	23.00
47 P. Coughlin (*Durham*)	RFM	88.4	22	279	12	5-64	1	23.25
48 S. R. Harmer (*Essex*)	OB	558.4	182	1,233	53	9-80	3	23.26
49 B. W. Aitchison (*Derbys*)	RFM	275.4	50	792	34	6-28	1	23.29
50 B. A. Hutton (*Notts*)	RFM	254	75	679	29	5-62	2	23.41
51 J. A. Atkins (*Sussex*)	RFM	137.4	14	469	20	5-51	2	23.45
52 W. D. Parnell (*Northants*)	LFM	114.4	26	427	18	5-64	2	23.72
53 S. Mahmood (*Lancs*)	RFM	233.1	52	669	28	5-47	1	23.89
54 D. J. Willey (*Yorks*)	LFM	148.3	30	479	20	5-61	1	23.95
55 P. M. Siddle (*Essex*)	RFM	176.2	37	488	20	6-38	1	24.40
56 T. J. Price (*Glos*)	RM	128	37	368	15	4-72	0	24.53
57 J. A. Porter (*Essex*)	RFM	299.4	73	842	34	4-31	0	24.76
58 G. K. Berg (*Northants*)	RFM	199.4	48	600	24	5-18	1	25.00
59 M. A. R. Cohen (*Derbys*)	LFM	99.5	19	280	11	5-43	1	25.45
60 S. A. Patterson (*Yorks*)	RFM	364	111	815	32	4-26	0	25.46
61 M. S. Crane (*Hants*)	LB	195.5	39	587	23	5-41	1	25.52
62 J. C. Tongue (*Worcs*)	RFM	115.5	18	358	14	5-39	1	25.57
63 M. G. Hogan (*Glam*)	RFM	332.5	78	874	34	5-28	1	25.70
64 B. T. J. Wheal (*Hants*)	RFM	298.5	62	882	34	4-59	0	25.94
65 S. C. Kerrigan (*Northants*)	SLA	298.5	57	766	29	5-39	2	26.41
66 D. L. Lloyd (*Glam*)	RM	170.3	24	558	21	4-11	0	26.57
67 M. J. Potts (*Durham*)	RFM	204.3	51	613	23	4-32	0	26.65
68 J. J. Bumrah (*Indians*)	RFM	207.4	59	507	19	5-64	1	26.68
69 B. W. Sanderson (*Northants*)	RFM	435.2	117	1,155	43	5-28	3	26.86
70 T. A. I. Taylor (*Northants*)	RFM	263.2	63	783	29	5-41	1	27.00
71 L. A. Procter (*Northants*)	RM	115.5	29	352	13	5-42	1	27.07
72 Mohammed Shami (*Indians*)	RFM	133.4	30	410	15	4-76	0	27.33
73 M. E. T. Salisbury (*Durham*)	RFM	142.4	38	440	16	4-74	0	27.50
74 M. A. Wood (*Durham & England*)	RF	181	36	580	21	3-28	0	27.61
75 W. S. Davis (*Leics*)	RFM	157.4	32	416	15	5-66	1	27.73
76 J. A. R. Harris (*Glam & Middx*)	RFM	110.2	6	389	14	3-50	0	27.78
77 L. B. K. Hollman (*Middx*)	LB	105.4	16	363	13	5-65	2	27.92

		Style	O	M	R	W	BB	5I	Avge
78	N. Wagner (*New Zealand*)	LFM	101	24	280	10	3-18	0	28.00
79	J. Clark (*Surrey*)	RFM	276	36	904	32	6-21	2	28.25
80	S. Conners (*Derbys*)	RFM	225.5	44	750	26	5-83	1	28.84
81	F. J. Hudson-Prentice (*Derbys & Sussex*)	RFM	240.2	52	752	26	5-68	1	28.92
82	D. T. Moriarty (*Surrey*)	SLA	181.4	31	521	18	6-60	1	28.94
83	C. F. Parkinson (*Leics*)	SLA	479.4	122	1,432	50	5-45	3	29.04
84	O. J. Hannon-Dalby (*Warwicks*)	RFM	258.5	73	698	24	5-76	1	29.08
85	M. Siraj (*Indians*)	RFM	142.5	24	466	16	4-32	0	29.12
86	R. J. W. Topley (*Surrey*)	LFM	199.3	46	616	21	5-66	1	29.33
87	L. W. James (*Notts & County Select XI*)	RFM	160	33	478	16	4-51	0	29.87
88	J. Leach (*Worcs*)	RFM	428	108	1,141	38	5-68	1	30.02
89	M. D. Taylor (*Glos*)	LM	266.1	67	818	27	5-40	1	30.29
90	T. van der Gugten (*Glam*)	RFM	274.3	54	823	27	4-34	0	30.48
91	L. Gregory (*Somerset*)	RFM	209.3	60	645	21	5-68	1	30.71
92	O. P. Stone (*Warwicks & England*)	RF	149.3	25	492	16	4-89	0	30.75
93	D. Y. Pennington (*Worcs*)	RFM	282.4	57	898	29	5-32	1	30.96
94	M. J. Leach (*Somerset*)	SLA	241	77	562	18	6-43	1	31.22
95	M. K. Andersson (*Middx*)	RFM	250.1	41	916	29	4-27	0	31.58
96	D. M. Bess (*Yorks*)	OB	405.4	122	912	28	7-43	2	32.57
97	C. A. J. Morris (*Worcs*)	RFM	189.3	45	621	19	6-52	1	32.68
98	L. A. Patterson-White (*Notts & Cty Slct XI*)	SLA	323	72	876	26	5-41	1	33.69
99	D. Olivier (*Yorks*)	RFM	175.1	26	610	18	4-61	0	33.88
100	D. J. Lamb (*Lancs*)	RFM	280.5	67	780	23	4-60	0	33.91
101	J. O. Baker (*Worcs*)	SLA	144.2	30	408	12	3-49	0	34.00
102	M. de Lange (*Somerset*)	RF	231.5	49	685	20	4-55	0	34.25
103	G. S. Virdi (*Surrey*)	OB	299.4	48	961	28	6-171	1	34.32
104	L. A. Dawson (*Hants*)	SLA	257	55	624	18	5-45	1	34.66
105	T. T. Bresnan (*Warwicks*)	RFM	175	59	453	13	3-35	0	34.84
106	H. W. Podmore (*Kent*)	RFM	114.3	16	419	12	4-77	0	34.91
107	G. P. Balderson (*Lancs*)	RFM	152.5	29	427	12	3-21	0	35.58
108	R. Clarke (*Surrey*)	RFM	197.5	45	582	16	3-34	0	36.37
109	L. Wood (*Lancs*)	LFM	205	32	660	18	3-31	0	36.66
110	J. J. Carson (*Sussex & County Select XI*)	OB	489.4	68	1,471	40	5-85	1	36.77
111	S. F. Hunt (*Sussex*)	LFM	127.5	18	487	13	3-47	0	37.46
112	H. T. Crocombe (*Sussex*)	RFM	211	29	756	20	4-92	0	37.80
113	S. G. Borthwick (*Durham*)	LB	130.5	22	455	12	4-32	0	37.91
114	A. S. Joseph (*Worcs*)	RFM	158	21	574	15	2-22	0	38.26
115	M. J. J. Critchley (*Derbys*)	LB	343.3	42	1,230	32	5-67	1	38.43
116	B. C. Cullen (*Middx*)	RFM	109.2	19	393	10	3-30	0	39.30
117	E. Barnes (*Leics*)	RFM	204.2	30	724	18	4-61	0	40.22
118	J. A. Brooks (*Somerset*)	RFM	142	28	499	12	4-77	0	41.58
119	E. G. Barnard (*Worcs*)	RFM	368.1	83	1,052	25	4-43	0	42.08
120	T. B. Abell (*Somerset*)	RM	168.3	44	558	13	3-63	0	42.92
121	G. H. S. Garton (*Sussex*)	LFM	134.5	11	559	13	4-69	0	43.00
122	B. W. M. Mike (*Leics*)	RFM	256	40	1,002	23	4-34	0	43.56
123	N. L. Buck (*Northants*)	RFM	107.4	11	436	10	3-65	0	43.60
124	A. G. Salter (*Glam*)	OB	218.5	41	687	15	4-18	0	45.80
125	D. A. Douthwaite (*Glam*)	RFM	181.1	18	781	17	2-16	0	45.94
126	L. M. Reece (*Derbys*)	LFM	183.3	46	555	12	2-25	0	46.25
127	B. L. D'Oliveira (*Worcs*)	LB	253.4	29	808	15	3-95	0	53.86

BOWLING STYLES

LB	Leg-breaks (6)		**RF**	Right-arm fast (4)
LFM	Left-arm fast medium (12)		**RFM**	Right-arm fast medium (82)
LM	Left-arm medium (1)		**RM**	Right-arm medium (7)
OB	Off-breaks (7)		**SLA**	Slow left-arm (9)

Note: The total comes to 128 because O. E. Robinson has two styles of bowling.

INDIVIDUAL SCORES OF 100 AND OVER

There were **157** three-figure innings in 134 first-class matches in 2021, which was 107 more than in the shortened 2020 season of 54 matches, but 48 fewer than in 2019, when 149 matches were played. Nine were double-hundreds, compared with five in 2020 and 11 in 2019. The list includes 146 in the County Championship (compared with 164 in 2019) plus two in the Bob Willis Trophy.

R. M. Yates (5)
120* Warwicks v Essex, Birmingham
104 Warwicks v Worcs, Birmingham
102 Warwicks v Durham, Birmingham
132* Warwicks v Somerset, Birmingham
113 Warwicks v Lancs, Lord's

B. C. Brown (4)
127 Sussex v Yorks, Leeds
100* Sussex v Glam, Hove
133* Sussex v Leics, Leicester
157 Sussex v Derbys, Hove

C. B. Cooke (4)
102* Glam v Yorks, Leeds
136 Glam v Northants, Northampton
133* Glam v Northants, Cardiff
205 Glam v Surrey, The Oval

J. D. Libby (4)
180* Worcs v Essex, Chelmsford
117 Worcs v Notts, Worcester
126 Worcs v Durham, Worcester
125* Worcs v Sussex, Worcester

J. E. Root (4)
101 Yorks v Kent, Canterbury
109 England v India, Nottingham
180* England v India, Lord's
121 England v India, Leeds

H. M. Amla (3)
215* Surrey v Hants, The Oval
173 Surrey v Glos, The Oval
163 Surrey v Glam, The Oval

D. G. Bedingham (3)
180* Durham v Notts, Nottingham
257 Durham v Derbys, Chester-le-Street
121 Durham v Worcs, Worcester

K. S. Carlson (3)
127* } Glam v Sussex, Cardiff
132 }
170* Glam v Northants, Cardiff

S. T. Evans (3)
138 Leics v Surrey, The Oval
102 Leics v Glos, Bristol
112 Leics v Surrey, Leicester

T. J. Haines (3)
155 Sussex v Lancs, Manchester
103 Sussex v Northants, Hove
156 Sussex v Middx, Hove

H. Hameed (3)
111 }
114* } Notts v Worcs, Worcester
112 Cty Slct XI v Indians, Chester-le-Street

M. S. Harris (3)
101 Leics v Surrey, Leicester
185 Leics v Middx, Leicester
148 Leics v Glos, Leicester

L. J. Hill (3)
121 Leics v Glos, Bristol
113 Leics v Derbys, Derby
145 Leics v Sussex, Leicester

A. Lyth (3)
115* Yorks v Glam, Leeds
116 Yorks v Kent, Canterbury
153 Yorks v Notts, Nottingham

O. J. D. Pope (3)
245 Surrey v Leics, The Oval
131 Surrey v Hants, The Oval
274 Surrey v Glam, The Oval

S. D. Robson (3)
165 Middx v Somerset, Lord's
154 Middx v Leics, Northwood
253 Middx v Sussex, Hove

J. L. Smith (3)
123 Surrey v Leics, The Oval
123 Surrey v Northants, Northampton
138 Surrey v Glam, The Oval

D. I. Stevens (3)
116* Kent v Northants, Northampton
190 Kent v Glam, Canterbury
107* Kent v Leics, Leicester

M. D. Stoneman (3)
119 Surrey v Leics, Leicester
174 Middx v Sussex, Hove
109 Middx v Kent, Canterbury

T. Westley (3)
213   Essex v Worcs, Chelmsford
113   Essex v Worcs, Worcester
106   Essex v Derbys, Chelmsford

T. P. Alsop (2)
119   Hants v Leics, Leicester
149   Hants v Glos, Southampton

M. H. Azad (2)
144*   Leics v Surrey, The Oval
152   Leics v Sussex, Leicester

E. G. Barnard (2)
128   Worcs v Essex, Chelmsford
112*   Worcs v Warwicks, Worcester

J. J. Bohannon (2)
127*   Lancs v Yorks, Manchester
170   Lancs v Warwicks, Manchester

H. C. Brook (2)
113   Yorks v Northants, Northampton
118   Yorks v Somerset, Scarborough

R. J. Burns (2)
104*   Surrey v Middx, The Oval
132   England v New Zealand, Lord's

A. N. Cook (2)
115   Essex v Worcs, Worcester
165   Essex v Surrey, The Oval

N. R. T. Gubbins (2)
124   Middx v Surrey, The Oval
137*   Hants v Glos, Cheltenham

I. G. Holland (2)
146*   Hants v Middx, Southampton
114   Hants v Glos, Southampton

K. K. Jennings (2)
114   Lancs v Yorks, Manchester
132   Lancs v Yorks, Leeds

R. I. Keogh (2)
124   Northants v Kent, Northampton
126   Northants v Glam, Northampton

K. L. Rahul (2)
101   Indians v Cty Slct XI, Chester-le-Street
129   India v England, Lord's

O. G. Robinson (2)
120   Kent v Northants, Canterbury
112   Kent v Middx, Canterbury

B. T. Slater (2)
114*   Notts v Worcs, Worcester
107   Notts v Derbys, Derby

H. J. Swindells (2)
103   Leics v Surrey, Leicester
171*   Leics v Somerset, Taunton

R. S. Vasconcelos (2)
154   Northants v Kent, Northampton
185*   Northants v Glam, Northampton

R. G. White (2)
120   Middx v Derbys, Lord's
110*   Middx v Sussex, Hove

W. A. Young (2)
124   Durham v Warwicks, Chester-le-Street
103   Durham v Worcs, Chester-le-Street

The following each played one three-figure innings:

T. B. Abell, 132*, Somerset v Glos, Bristol; C. N. Ackermann, 126*, Leics v Middx, Leicester.

G. S. Ballance, 101*, Yorks v Hants, Southampton; G. A. Bartlett, 100, Somerset v Hants, Taunton; D. J. Bell-Drummond, 114, Kent v Lancs, Canterbury; C. G. Benjamin, 127, Warwicks v Lancs, Manchester; S. G. Borthwick, 100, Durham v Essex, Chelmsford; J. R. Bracey, 118, Glos v Somerset, Taunton; N. L. J. Browne, 102, Essex v Glam, Cardiff; M. G. K. Burgess, 101, Warwicks v Worcs, Birmingham; J. T. A. Burnham, 102*, Durham v Worcs, Chester-le-Street.

J. M. Clarke, 109, Notts v Yorks, Nottingham; I. A. Cockbain, 117, Glos v Leics, Bristol; D. P. Conway, 200, New Zealand v England, Lord's; S. J. Croft, 103*, Lancs v Northants, Manchester.

A. K. Dal, 106, Derbys v Leics, Derby; L. A. Dawson, 152*, Hants v Leics, Leicester; C. de Grandhomme, 174*, Hants v Surrey, Southampton; B. M. Duckett, 177*, Notts v Worcs, Nottingham.

E. J. H. Eckersley, 113*, Durham v Notts, Nottingham; S. S. Eskinazi, 102, Middx v Glos, Cheltenham.

H. Z. Finch, 115, Kent v Sussex, Canterbury; B. T. Foakes, 133, Surrey v Glos, Bristol.

E. N. Gay, 101, Northants v Kent, Canterbury; B. A. Godleman, 100*, Derbys v Leics, Derby; L. Gregory, 107, Somerset v Hants, Taunton; B. D. Guest, 116, Derbys v Leics, Derby.

S. R. Hain, 118, Warwicks v Lancs, Manchester; J. C. Hildreth, 107, Somerset v Surrey, The Oval.

T. C. Lace, 118, Glos v Hants, Cheltenham; D. J. Lamb, 125, Lancs v Kent, Canterbury; T. A. Lammonby, 100, Somerset v Lancs, Taunton; D. W. Lawrence, 152*, Essex v Derbys, Chelmsford; J. A. Leaning, 127*, Kent v Sussex, Hove; A. Z. Lees, 129, Durham v Warwicks, Chester-le-Street; D. L. Lloyd, 121, Glam v Surrey, The Oval.

W. L. Madsen, 111, Derbys v Sussex, Hove; D. J. Malan, 199, Yorks v Sussex, Leeds; P. J. Malan, 141, Warwicks v Worcs, Worcester; D. K. H. Mitchell, 113, Worcs v Warwicks, Worcester; S. J. Mullaney, 117, Notts v Essex, Nottingham.

S. A. Northeast, 118, Hants v Middx, Southampton.

A. G. H. Orr, 119, Sussex v Kent, Canterbury.

L. A. Patterson-White, 101, Notts v Somerset, Taunton.

W. M. H. Rhodes, 156, Warwicks v Lancs, Lord's; W. T. Root, 110*, Glam v Yorks, Leeds.

R. G. Sharma, 127, India v England, The Oval.

G. L. van Buuren, 110*, Glos v Surrey, Bristol; S. van Zyl, 113, Sussex v Glam, Cardiff; D. J. Vilas, 189, Lancs v Sussex, Manchester; J. M. Vince, 231, Hants v Leics, Leicester.

L. W. P. Wells, 103, Lancs v Somerset, Taunton; L. Wood, 119, Lancs v Kent, Canterbury.

S. A. Zaib, 135, Northants v Sussex, Northampton.

FASTEST HUNDREDS BY BALLS...

67	D. I. Stevens	Kent v Leicestershire, Leicester.
81	J. M. Vince	Hampshire v Leicestershire, Leicester.
85	G. S. Ballance	Yorkshire v Hampshire, Southampton.
92	D. I. Stevens	Kent v Glamorgan, Canterbury.
94	G. L. van Buuren	Gloucestershire v Surrey, Bristol.
99	T. A. Lammonby	Somerset v Lancashire, Taunton.

...AND THE SLOWEST

288	H. Hameed	Nottinghamshire v Worcestershire, Worcester (*2nd inns*).
283	A. Z. Lees	Durham v Warwickshire, Chester-le-Street.
273	S. S. Eskinazi	Middlesex v Gloucestershire, Cheltenham.
268	H. Hameed	Nottinghamshire v Worcestershire, Worcester (*1st inns*).
268	B. T. Slater	Nottinghamshire v Worcestershire, Worcester.
267	R. J. Burns	England v New Zealand, Lord's.
261	J. D. Libby	Worcestershire v Essex, Chelmsford.
260	J. J. Bohannon	Lancashire v Yorkshire, Manchester.

TEN WICKETS IN A MATCH

There were **13** instances of bowlers taking ten or more wickets in a first-class match in 2021, seven more than in 2020 but ten fewer than in 2019. All were in the County Championship.

S. R. Harmer (2)
10-136 Essex v Durham, Chelmsford
12-202 Essex v Derbys, Chelmsford

The following each took ten wickets in a match on one occasion:

K. J. Abbott, 11-85, Hants v Middx, Lord's.

S. J. Cook, 10-41, Essex v Northants, Chelmsford.

L. J. Fletcher, 10-57, Notts v Worcs, Nottingham.

L. B. K. Hollman, 10-155, Middx v Sussex, Hove.

C. F. Parkinson, 10-108, Leics v Glos, Leicester; W. D. Parnell, 10-143, Northants v Yorks, Leeds; D. A. Payne, 11-87, Glos v Middx, Lord's.

K. A. J. Roach, 10-80, Surrey v Hants, The Oval; O. E. Robinson, 13-128, Sussex v Glam, Cardiff.

B. W. Sanderson, 10-99, Northants v Sussex, Northampton.

Zafar Gohar, 11-101, Glos v Durham, Bristol.

LV= COUNTY CHAMPIONSHIP IN 2021

NEVILLE SCOTT

Division One 1 *Warwickshire* 2 *Lancashire*
Division Two 1 *Essex* *Division Three* 1 *Kent*

Robert Graves, the author of *I, Claudius*, also wrote a memoir of the Great War called *Goodbye To All That*. Cricket's own Graves – Colin, who chaired the ECB from 2015 to 2020 – could perhaps have offered a more prophetic work: *Goodbye to the Championship*. Not that Graves, who arranged a financial bonus for those who delivered The Hundred yet favoured a Championship third division of part-timers playing three-day matches, was alone in devaluing the competition. Two predecessors, Lord MacLaurin and Giles Clarke, were also drawn from retail, and presided over a ruling body notably unsullied by cricketers; one proposed a return to amateurs, the other a T20 financial deal with a Texan chancer soon to be jailed for fraud. The Championship has long been sidelined.

COUNTY CHAMPIONSHIP DIVISION TABLES

Division One

		M	W	L	D	Bonus pts Bat	Bowl	Pen	Group pts	Final pts
1	Warwickshire.....	5	3	1	1	8	13	0	21	77
2	Lancashire	5	2.5	1	1.5	10	11.5	0	16.5	73.5
3	Nottinghamshire ..	5	3	2	0	10	15	0	5	73
4	Hampshire	5	2	1.5	1.5	2.5	15	0	8.5	61.5
5	Yorkshire	5	1	2.5	1.5	4	12.5	0	4.5	44.5
6	Somerset	5	0.5	4	0.5	6.5	14	1	18.5	31.5

Division Two

		M	W	L	D	Bonus pts Bat	Bowl	Pen	Group pts	Final pts	Avge
1	Essex	5	4	0	1	9	15	0	19	96	19.2
2	Gloucestershire ...	5	3.5	1.5	0	5.5	14.5	0	12	76	15.2
3	Durham	4	1	2	1	8	12	0	4	44	11
4	Northamptonshire .	5	1.5	2	1.5	5.5	12.5	0	16	54	10.8
5	Surrey	4	0.5	1.5	2	8	8	0	13	40	10
6	Glamorgan.......	5	0	3.5	1.5	12.5	10	0	11.5	34.5	6.9

Division Three

		M	W	L	D	Bonus pts Bat	Bowl	Pen	Group pts	Final pts
1	Kent.............	5	4	0	1	7	15	0	11	94
2	Middlesex	5	3.5	1.5	0	9.5	15	0.5	13	80
3	Worcestershire ...	5	2.5	2	0.5	8.5	15	0	18.5	67.5
4	Leicestershire.....	5	1.5	2.5	1	9.5	13	0	11.5	54.5
5	Derbyshire	5	1	2.5	1.5	11	12.5	0	9.5	51.5
6	Sussex	5	0	4	1	13	9	0	12	30

Win = 16pts; draw = 8pts. Penalties were for slow over-rates.

Group points were carried forward from the earlier stage; each team retained half their points from their two fixtures against the other qualifier from their group.

Division Two teams were ranked on average points per match after Durham v Surrey was cancelled because of a Covid outbreak.

But it faced a near existential crisis, in the light of Azeem Rafiq's revelations about racism, part of a wider issue of England cricket's lack of inclusivity – so glaringly unacknowledged by the game's stewards for 30 years. Even ignoring official overseas players, more than 11% of last year's Championship appearances were made by men whose upbringing was in South Africa, Zimbabwe, Australia or New Zealand. They were more than twice as likely to play county cricket as men of a minority ethnic background raised in Britain. And too many counties still relied on the privately educated. The "optics" (a buzzword the ECB's marketing gurus relish) are appalling: only the privileged need apply. Sponsors and sports editors, reluctant to back the game, will be even more resistant if this is the image the Championship projects. England's core problem for decades has been the lack of a critical mass of recreational players at the base; it hardly helps that such passionate home resources as remain are criminally untapped.

At least the 2022 campaign will avoid the predictable flaws of the 2021 conference-style Championship. In October, the ECB asked the counties to retain the format, but could not persuade enough to endorse it. Ian Watmore, who had succeeded Graves barely a year earlier, resigned, recognising that he had lost their confidence. So this season will at last implement the plan for a ten-team first division plus a second tier of eight, scheduled for 2020 before the pandemic overturned all plans. Justly, the divisions will be based on the final placings in 2019, rather than last summer's standings, a decision which penalised only Nottinghamshire and Durham, reprieving Surrey and Kent. Yorkshire were threatened with demotion in the wake of their racism crisis, but spared after wholesale changes of personnel.

The two divisions could have been reintroduced last year, with points per match to decide the tables in case of Covid-related cancellations (a fallback used anyway in 2021). Instead, the format involved three groups of six, each side playing ten games. The group tables then filtered the counties into three divisions, with the winner of the top division becoming county champions.

Effectively, it meant the best sides might spend eight matches eliminating also-rans before playing their true rivals once, and the title essentially came down to a dozen games in September. The best six teams were engaged in a frantic scramble on deliberately poor pitches as late-season victory became all. In the final three rounds, five of the nine games saw wickets fall at an average cost of under 20. They had tense, exciting finishes, yet were no kind of substitute for sustained quality between the best talents across a summer. The humbler divisions became immaterial.

Virtue prevailed. **Warwickshire**, the only side whose seven home games all reached the fourth day, claimed the title. In the group phase, they had scored just 1.3 more runs per wicket lost than per wicket taken, but repeatedly showed they knew how to win; **Lancashire**, eventual runners-up, sailed through their group phase (their advantage on the runs-per-wicket reckoning was 15), yet fell short in September's scramble.

Somerset, who headed their group despite carrying an eight-point pitch penalty from 2019, lost key bowlers for the division games, and soon became passengers. **Yorkshire** won half their group fixtures, but started the divisional stage with a huge handicap: they had fared poorly in both Roses matches, and teams took forward half the points gained in their two meetings with fellow qualifiers from their group, which meant they had 4.5 to Lancashire's 16.5. Meanwhile, Warwickshire had finished behind **Nottinghamshire** in their group but, thanks to beating them twice, entered Division One 16 points ahead of them.

One innings in mid-April proved crucial come September. At Trent Bridge, Warwickshire needed 333 to win against an attack led by Stuart Broad, and found themselves 184 for six, with Dom Sibley unavailable after breaking his finger. In a spirited win, they got home, helping to build that advantage of carried-over points which settled the title. Two games later, at Derby, Nottinghamshire broke their sorry run of 30 first-class matches without victory; they were to finish the season with seven wins.

As the last two days of the Championship began, four sides were still in it. Yet Warwickshire needed not only to beat Somerset but ideally to add seven

PRELIMINARY GROUP TABLES

Group One

		M	W	L	D	Bonus pts Bat	Bowl	Pen	Pts
1	Nottinghamshire.......	10	4	2	4	26	29	0	151
2	Warwickshire..........	10	4	1	5	17	25	1	145
3	Durham	10	3	2	5	17	30	3	132
4	Essex	10	3	2	5	15	26	0	129
5	Worcestershire........	10	1	3	6	24	21	0	109
6	Derbyshire	10	0	5	5	10	23	1	72

Group Two

		M	W	L	D	Bonus pts Bat	Bowl	Pen	Pts
1	Somerset.............	10	4	1	5	26	26	8	148
2	Hampshire	10	4	2	4	23	26	0	145
3	Gloucestershire	10	5	3	2	14	21	0	131
4	Surrey	10	2	2	6	19	24	0	123
5	Leicestershire.........	10	2	4	4	22	25	0	111
6	Middlesex............	10	2	7	1	15	30	1	84

Group Three

		M	W	L	D	Bonus pts Bat	Bowl	Pen	Pts
1	Lancashire	10	4	1	5	22	24	0	150
2	Yorkshire	10	5	1	4	14	23	0	149
3	Glamorgan	10	2	2	6	18	29	0	127
4	Northamptonshire	10	3	3	4	22	21	0	123
5	Kent	10	0	3	7	15	26	0	97
6	Sussex	10	1	5	4	18	28	0	94

Win = 16pts; draw = 8pts.

Somerset had 8pts deducted for a poor pitch in 2019; other penalties were for slow over-rates.

The top two teams in each group advanced to Division One, the middle two to Division Two, and the bottom two to Division Three. Each county carried forward half the points from their two fixtures against the other qualifier from their group.

bonus points as insurance against Hampshire beating Lancashire. Thanks to Danny Briggs, they grasped a fourth batting point, with their final pair together and three balls to spare. But, on a placid Edgbaston surface, Somerset then allowed them only two bowling points, and finished 22 ahead on first innings, with just four sessions to come.

In April, **Hampshire's** hopes had rested on overseas imports Mohammad Abbas and Kyle Abbott, potentially the competition's most lethal new-ball pair, but they played only the first seven games together, and were never in harness in the final stages. Even so, Hampshire would take the title if they could win in Liverpool on a dubious pitch almost the September norm. Suggestions at lunch that there could be a tie seemed less fanciful when, in mounting panic, Lancashire's ninth wicket fell two runs short of victory. If they tied and Warwickshire drew, Nottinghamshire – well on their way to beating Yorkshire – would seize the crown.

Half an hour from the close, however, Brummie cheering greeted the news that Lancashire had scraped home. All would now rest on the final day at Edgbaston: Warwickshire's title if they won, Lancashire's if not. A win seemed unlikely by the time the home side declared, after the game had produced 1,050 runs for 23 wickets in 300 overs, and set 273 from 79. But, defying the pitch, they proved unstoppable; Somerset succumbed 55 minutes after tea. In his first season at the club, Mark Robinson followed his mentor Peter Moores by becoming the second coach to claim Championship titles with two counties. A week later, he added the Bob Willis Trophy after his team thrashed Lancashire at Lord's.

"We believe if you play good cricket on these kinds of surfaces, keep games alive and go deep, you can still force results," he said. "But you need the weather. Teams are trying to fast-track wins, and pitches have gone down in my five years away from county cricket, with a lot of medium-pacers dominating. The ECB really must look at that." Chastened by England's Ashes debacle, the ECB did at least rejig fixtures: in 2022, there would be 40 four-day games in June and July, up from 17 in 2021. Even so, two-thirds of the tournament would be played either before May 22 or after September 5, with August remaining a no-go area for first-class cricket.

Back in April, snow in Leeds had forced Yorkshire and Glamorgan to abandon play on the third day of the season, and sleet glinting on shaven heads was a common sight in the spring. With a tournament run-rate of 51 per 100 balls, the slowest since 2000, all seamers prospered, none more than Nottinghamshire's Luke Fletcher, a richly popular star of the summer. But notions that the format gave everyone a chance of glory were fatuous. Of the 48 group games between sides who would have been placed in different divisions on the 2019 placings, second-tier teams won six and lost 21. There *is* a way of restoring a measure of equality to the Championship, but it would entail the ECB devising rules to grant serious financial redress to the lowly clubs whose best talents are lured away.

Essex, who had collected the 2019 Championship and the Bob Willis Trophy in 2020, confirmed how hard it is to win three long-form titles on the bounce. It has not been achieved since Yorkshire in 1968, despite ten sides claiming back-to-back trophies in the meantime. Essex had to settle for winning Division Two; they were oddly lacklustre from the off, and ended with acrimony over an alleged drinking culture, something of a storm in a beer glass. Behind them were **Gloucestershire**, who in July had fallen perhaps a dozen overs short of the draw that would have taken them, not opponents Hampshire, into Division One.

Durham became a force again, and were livid when Surrey pleaded unable to fulfil a fixture due to Covid, the one match cancelled in the tournament. Depleted by injury and England calls, **Surrey** enjoyed their finest hour when Hashim Amla helped grind out 122 for eight in 104.5 overs to deny Hampshire; Keith Barker's first 101 balls cost two singles. **Northamptonshire** were on the wrong side of two remarkable results, losing to Yorkshire by one run – the first such defeat in the Championship since 1995 – and then to Essex, who celebrated the autumn equinox by winning in 579 balls. Discounting single-innings games or forfeitures, it was the shortest victory since Surrey beat Worcestershire in 529 to claim the 1954 title. **Glamorgan**, the side most reliant on players raised abroad, finished bottom of Division Two but had the cash to sign Sam Northeast, the roving Old Harrovian, who should become the first British specialist batter to represent five counties.

Like Nottinghamshire, fellow East Midlanders Derbyshire and Leicestershire had endured lengthy runs without a Championship win in the past decade. Neither promised the resurgence found at Trent Bridge – they were shuffled into Division Three – but **Leicestershire** won three home matches, two by an innings, while **Derbyshire** dumped the wooden spoon on **Sussex** by winning their final game (their sole success). Of others in the basement, **Worcestershire** never got going, but injury-hit **Kent** were belatedly more like the team of recent summers, romping through their four games and superbly sealing victory in the last, just when **Middlesex** seemed to have found their best XI.

MILLENNIAL MEN

Bowlers who have reached 1,000 first-class wickets in the 21st century:

	Matches taken	Date of 1,000th	Complete career figures		
			M	W	Avge
Wasim Akram	244	May 4, 2001	257	1,042	21.64
P. C. R. Tufnell	297	July 29, 2001	316	1,057	29.35
D. E. Malcolm	290	May 31, 2002	304	1,054	30.33
Mushtaq Ahmed*.....	233	April 19, 2004	309	1,407	25.67
M. Muralitharan......	173	May 6, 2004	232	1,374	19.64
M. P. Bicknell	273	May 28, 2004	292	1,061	25.06
S. K. Warne	232	March 13, 2005	301	1,319	26.11
A. R. Caddick........	227	August 10, 2005	275	1,180	26.59
A. Kumble	213	July 2, 2006	244	1,136	25.83
R. D. B. Croft........	349	September 12, 2007	407	1,175	35.08
Danish Kaneria.......	201	December 14, 2011	206	1,023	26.18
H. M. R. K. B. Herath .	253	March 17, 2017	270	1,080	25.15
D. S. Hettiarachchi....	234	May 23, 2019	234	1,001	23.51
J. M. Anderson......	262	July 5, 2021	270	1,026	24.69

* *Mushtaq Ahmed's 1,000th victim was Martin Bicknell, who matched the feat 39 days later.*

Only Anderson has 1,000 in the 21st century (Danish Kaneria managed 989 after January 1, 2000).

Kent's Darren Stevens, three weeks shy of his 45th birthday, became the oldest to make a Championship hundred for 35 years; six weeks later, he hammered 190 from 149 balls and put on 166 for the ninth wicket with Miguel Cummins, who contributed one. His 96% share was the highest for any first-class century partnership. Stevens also survived a spell of seven for 19 from Lancashire's James Anderson, whose fifth scalp made him the first to record 1,000 wickets entirely in the 21st century. Down in the Hove kindergarten, by contrast, Danial Ibrahim became the youngest to reach a Championship fifty, at 16 years 299 days; he was one of 14 responsible for over half Sussex's appearances who, before 2021, had played only 20 Championship or Bob Willis Trophy games between them.

Unlike Surrey, Kent hurriedly gathered a scratch team when Covid forced their regulars into isolation on the eve of a game with Sussex; even then, Nathan Gilchrist had to isolate after day one. In their next match – 47 days later, at the end of the white-ball-only zone – they had ten changes from the earlier starting XI. There had been two instances of nine in the Championship, the more recent when Gloucestershire began the 1919 season with only two who had appeared in their previous game, in September 1914. Covid thus managed what the Great War could not. Happily, none of Gloucester's missing had fallen in battle.

In August, Worcestershire and Brett D'Oliveira met a Sussex side fielding debutant Archie Lenham. For the first time, opposing teams in a Championship match both included cricketers whose fathers and grandfathers had also played for their respective counties. The Lenhams spanned 66 seasons – a lifetime's watching for some devotees, most of whom relish these small delights of a competition whose integrity and lineage they cherish. Who at the ECB might credit such innocent folly?

Pre-season betting (best available prices): 6-1 Essex; 7-1 Somerset and Yorkshire; 9-1 Nottinghamshire; 10-1 Kent and Lancashire; 12-1 Hampshire, Middlesex and Surrey; 16-1 Sussex, WARWICKSHIRE and Worcestershire; 28-1 Gloucestershire; 36-1 Derbyshire and Northamptonshire; 66-1 Durham, Glamorgan and Leicestershire.

Prize money

Division One
£530,000 for winners: WARWICKSHIRE.
£260,000 for runners-up: LANCASHIRE.
£120,000 for third: NOTTINGHAMSHIRE.
£75,000 for fourth: HAMPSHIRE.
£67,000 for fifth: YORKSHIRE.
£60,000 for sixth: SOMERSET.

Division Two
£53,000 for winners: ESSEX.
£46,000 for runners-up: GLOUCESTERSHIRE.
£40,000 for third: DURHAM.
£33,000 for fourth: NORTHAMPTONSHIRE.
£27,000 for fifth: SURREY.
£20,000 for sixth: GLAMORGAN.

Division Three
£13,000 for winners: KENT.
£7,000 for runners-up: MIDDLESEX.

Leaders: *Group One* – from April 11 Durham, Essex and Nottinghamshire; April 18 Essex and Warwickshire; April 25 Warwickshire; May 9 Nottinghamshire; May 16 Essex; May 23 Nottinghamshire; May 29 Essex; June 5 Warwickshire; July 6 Nottinghamshire.
Group Two – from April 11 Hampshire; May 2 Gloucestershire; June 6 Somerset.
Group Three – from April 11 Lancashire; April 18 Sussex; April 25 Lancashire; May 16 Yorkshire; May 23 Lancashire; July 6 Yorkshire; July 14 Lancashire.

Bottom place: *Group One* – from April 11 Derbyshire; April 18 Durham and Nottinghamshire; April 25 Nottinghamshire; May 2 Derbyshire.
Group Two – from April 11 Leicestershire; April 18 Middlesex; April 25 Leicestershire; May 30 Middlesex.
Group Three – from April 11 Yorkshire; April 18 Glamorgan and Northamptonshire; April 25 Kent; June 6 Sussex.

Leaders: *Division One* – from July 14 Warwickshire; September 8 Nottinghamshire; September 14 Hampshire; September 24 Warwickshire. Warwickshire became champions on September 24.
Division Two – from July 14 Essex.
Division Three – from July 14 Worcestershire; September 9 Middlesex; September 24 Kent.

Bottom place: *Division One* – from July 14 Yorkshire; September 8 Somerset.
Division Two – from July 14 Durham; September 8 Glamorgan.
Division Three – from July 14 Derbyshire; September 8 Sussex.

Scoring of Points in the 2021 County Championship

(*a*) For a win, 16 points plus any points scored in the first innings.
(*b*) In a tie, each side score eight points, plus any points scored in the first innings.
(*c*) In a drawn match, each side score eight points, plus any points scored in the first innings.
(*d*) First-innings points (awarded only for performances in the first 110 overs of each first innings and retained whatever the result of the match):
 (i) A maximum of five batting points to be available: 200 to 249 runs – 1 point; 250 to 299 runs – 2 points; 300 to 349 runs – 3 points; 350 to 399 runs – 4 points; 400 runs or over – 5 points. Penalty runs awarded within the first 110 overs of each first innings count towards the award of bonus points.
 (ii) A maximum of three bowling points to be available: 3 to 5 wickets taken – 1 point; 6 to 8 wickets taken – 2 points; 9 to 10 wickets taken – 3 points.
(*e*) If a match is abandoned without a ball being bowled, each side score eight points.
(*f*) If a match is abandoned due to a pitch rated unfit, the visiting team shall be awarded 16 points plus bonus points already achieved, or 20 points, whichever is the greater. The home team shall be awarded 0 points and any bonus points rescinded. The visiting team shall be credited with a win and the home team a loss for tie-breaker purposes. This does not preclude further action being taken against the home team through the disciplinary process.
(*g*) The teams that finish first and second in each of the three groups shall progress to Division One; the teams that finish third and fourth shall progress to Division Two; and the teams that finish fifth and sixth shall progress to Division Three. Should any sides in a group be equal on points, the following tie-breakers will be applied in the order stated: most wins, fewest losses, team achieving most points in head-to-head contests, most wickets taken, most runs scored.
(*h*) Should any group match be cancelled, all group positions shall be determined on average points per completed match. The tie-breaker shall be net runs per wicket, defined as runs per wicket scored by a team minus runs per wicket scored against that team.
(*i*) Each team shall carry forward half the aggregate number of points scored in the two matches against the team that goes through to the division from the same group. For tie-break purposes, each team shall also carry forward half the number of wins and losses from the two matches against the other team, as well as half the wickets taken and runs scored. If only one result can be carried forward, the teams will carry forward all the points from that match, plus the result, wickets and runs for tie-break purposes. If both matches between the teams were cancelled, each team shall carry forward the average number of points carried forward by the other four teams in their new division.
(*j*) In the divisional stage, each team shall play one match against each of the four teams that have come from other groups.
(*k*) If any divisional match is cancelled, divisional positions shall be determined on average points per completed match. The tie-breaker shall be net runs per wicket, as above, in all divisional matches including those carried forward from the group stage.
(*l*) The minimum over-rate to be achieved by counties will be 16 overs per hour. Overs will be calculated at the end of the match, and penalties applied on a match-by-match basis. For each over (ignoring fractions) that a side have bowled short of the target number, one point will be deducted from their group total.

Under ECB playing conditions, two extras were awarded for every no-ball bowled, whether scored off or not, and one for every wide. With no-balls, any runs off the bat were credited to the batter, and leg-byes and byes were counted as such, in addition to the initial two extras; runs scored off wides, including byes, were counted as wides, in addition to the initial one-run extra. Any penalties off no-balls or wides were counted as penalty runs, in addition to the initial extras.

CONSTITUTION OF COUNTY CHAMPIONSHIP

At least four possible dates have been given for the start of county cricket in England. The first, patchy, references began in 1825. The earliest mention in any cricket publication is 1864. For many years, the County Championship was considered to have started in 1873, when regulations governing qualification first applied; indeed, a special commemorative stamp was issued by the Post Office in 1973. However, the Championship was not formally organised until 1890, and before then champions were proclaimed by the press; sometimes publications differed in their views, and no definitive list of champions can start before that date. Eight teams contested the 1890 competition – Gloucestershire, Kent, Lancashire, Middlesex, Nottinghamshire, Surrey, Sussex and Yorkshire. Somerset joined the following year, and in 1895 the Championship began to acquire something of its modern shape, when Derbyshire, Essex, Hampshire, Leicestershire and Warwickshire were added. At that point, MCC officially recognised the competition's existence. Worcestershire, Northamptonshire and Glamorgan were admitted in 1899, 1905 and 1921 respectively, and are regarded as first-class from these dates. An invitation in 1921 to Buckinghamshire to enter the Championship was declined, owing to the lack of necessary playing facilities, and an application by Devon in 1948 was unsuccessful. Durham were admitted in 1992, and granted first-class status prior to their pre-season tour of Zimbabwe.

In 2000, the Championship was split for the first time into two divisions, on the basis of counties' standings in the 1999 competition. From 2000 onwards, the bottom three teams in Division One were relegated at the end of the season, and the top three teams in Division Two promoted. From 2006, this was changed to two teams relegated and two promoted. In 2016, two were relegated and one promoted, to create divisions of eight and ten teams. In 2019, one was relegated and three promoted, to change the balance to ten teams in Division One and eight in Division Two.

There was no County Championship in 2020, however, because of the Covid-19 pandemic; it was replaced by an alternative competition, the Bob Willis Trophy. In 2021, the Championship was played in two phases: three conference groups, followed by three divisions based on the group results. The winners of Division One were champions, but also played the runners-up for the Bob Willis Trophy. The Championship reverted to two divisions of ten and eight in 2022, as determined by the placings in 2019.

COUNTY CHAMPIONS

The title of champion county is unreliable before 1890. In 1963, *Wisden* formally accepted the list of champions "most generally selected" by contemporaries, as researched by Rowland Bowen (see *Wisden 1959*, page 91). This appears to be the most accurate available list but has no official status. The county champions from 1864 to 1889 were, according to Bowen: 1864 Surrey; 1865 Nottinghamshire; 1866 Middlesex; 1867 Yorkshire; 1868 Nottinghamshire; 1869 Nottinghamshire and Yorkshire; 1870 Yorkshire; 1871 Nottinghamshire; 1872 Nottinghamshire; 1873 Gloucestershire and Nottinghamshire; 1874 Gloucestershire; 1875 Nottinghamshire; 1876 Gloucestershire; 1877 Gloucestershire; 1878 undecided; 1879 Lancashire and Nottinghamshire; 1880 Nottinghamshire; 1881 Lancashire; 1882 Lancashire and Nottinghamshire; 1883 Nottinghamshire; 1884 Nottinghamshire; 1885 Nottinghamshire; 1886 Nottinghamshire; 1887 Surrey; 1888 Surrey; 1889 Lancashire, Nottinghamshire and Surrey.

1890	Surrey	1896	Yorkshire	1902	Yorkshire
1891	Surrey	1897	Lancashire	1903	Middlesex
1892	Surrey	1898	Yorkshire	1904	Lancashire
1893	Yorkshire	1899	Surrey	1905	Yorkshire
1894	Surrey	1900	Yorkshire	1906	Kent
1895	Surrey	1901	Yorkshire	1907	Nottinghamshire

1908	Yorkshire	1952	Surrey	1987	Nottinghamshire
1909	Kent	1953	Surrey	1988	Worcestershire
1910	Kent	1954	Surrey	1989	Worcestershire
1911	Warwickshire	1955	Surrey	1990	Middlesex
1912	Yorkshire	1956	Surrey	1991	Essex
1913	Kent	1957	Surrey	1992	Essex
1914	Surrey	1958	Surrey	1993	Middlesex
1919	Yorkshire	1959	Yorkshire	1994	Warwickshire
1920	Middlesex	1960	Yorkshire	1995	Warwickshire
1921	Middlesex	1961	Hampshire	1996	Leicestershire
1922	Yorkshire	1962	Yorkshire	1997	Glamorgan
1923	Yorkshire	1963	Yorkshire	1998	Leicestershire
1924	Yorkshire	1964	Worcestershire	1999	Surrey
1925	Yorkshire	1965	Worcestershire	2000	Surrey
1926	Lancashire	1966	Yorkshire	2001	Yorkshire
1927	Lancashire	1967	Yorkshire	2002	Surrey
1928	Lancashire	1968	Yorkshire	2003	Sussex
1929	Nottinghamshire	1969	Glamorgan	2004	Warwickshire
1930	Lancashire	1970	Kent	2005	Nottinghamshire
1931	Yorkshire	1971	Surrey	2006	Sussex
1932	Yorkshire	1972	Warwickshire	2007	Sussex
1933	Yorkshire	1973	Hampshire	2008	Durham
1934	Lancashire	1974	Worcestershire	2009	Durham
1935	Yorkshire	1975	Leicestershire	2010	Nottinghamshire
1936	Derbyshire	1976	Middlesex	2011	Lancashire
1937	Yorkshire	1977 {	Middlesex	2012	Warwickshire
1938	Yorkshire		Kent	2013	Durham
1939	Yorkshire	1978	Kent	2014	Yorkshire
1946	Yorkshire	1979	Essex	2015	Yorkshire
1947	Middlesex	1980	Middlesex	2016	Middlesex
1948	Glamorgan	1981	Nottinghamshire	2017	Essex
1949 {	Middlesex	1982	Middlesex	2018	Surrey
	Yorkshire	1983	Essex	2019	Essex
1950 {	Lancashire	1984	Essex	2021	Warwickshire
	Surrey	1985	Middlesex		
1951	Warwickshire	1986	Essex		

Notes: Since the Championship was constituted in 1890, it has been won outright as follows: Yorkshire 32 times, Surrey 19, Middlesex 11, Essex, Lancashire and Warwickshire 8, Kent and Nottinghamshire 6, Worcestershire 5, Durham, Glamorgan, Leicestershire and Sussex 3, Hampshire 2, Derbyshire 1.

The title has been shared three times since 1890, involving Middlesex twice, Kent, Lancashire, Surrey and Yorkshire.

There was no County Championship in 2020 because of the Covid-19 pandemic. An alternative competition, the Bob Willis Trophy, was won by Essex. In 2021, the same trophy was awarded to Warwickshire as winners of a one-off match between the Championship winners and runners-up.

Wooden spoons: Since the major expansion of the Championship from nine teams to 14 in 1895, the counties have finished outright bottom as follows: Derbyshire 16, Leicestershire 14, Somerset 12, Glamorgan and Northamptonshire 11, Gloucestershire and Sussex 9, Nottinghamshire 8, Worcestershire 6, Durham and Hampshire 5, Warwickshire 3, Essex and Kent 2, Yorkshire 1. Lancashire, Middlesex and Surrey have never finished bottom. Leicestershire have also shared bottom place twice, once with Hampshire and once with Somerset.

From 1977 to 1983 the Championship was sponsored by Schweppes, from 1984 to 1998 by Britannic Assurance, from 1999 to 2000 by PPP healthcare, in 2001 by Cricinfo, from 2002 to 2005 by Frizzell, from 2006 to 2015 by Liverpool Victoria (LV), from 2016 to 2019 by Specsavers, and from 2021 by LV again.

COUNTY CHAMPIONSHIP – FINAL POSITIONS, 1890–2021

	Derbyshire	Durham	Essex	Glamorgan	Gloucestershire	Hampshire	Kent	Lancashire	Leicestershire	Middlesex	Northamptonshire	Nottinghamshire	Somerset	Surrey	Sussex	Warwickshire	Worcestershire	Yorkshire
1890	–	–	–	–	6	–	3	2	–	7	–	5	–	1	8	–	–	3
1891	–	–	–	–	9	–	5	2	–	3	–	4	5	1	7	–	–	8
1892	–	–	–	–	7	–	7	4	–	5	–	2	3	1	9	–	–	6
1893	–	–	–	–	9	–	4	2	–	3	–	6	8	5	7	–	–	1
1894	–	–	–	–	9	–	4	4	–	3	–	7	6	1	8	–	–	2
1895	5	–	9	–	4	10	14	2	12	6	–	12	8	1	11	6	–	3
1896	7	–	5	–	10	8	9	2	13	3	–	6	11	4	14	12	–	1
1897	14	–	3	–	5	9	12	1	13	8	–	10	11	2	6	7	–	4
1898	9	–	5	–	3	12	7	6	13	2	–	8	13	4	9	9	–	1
1899	15	–	6	–	9	10	8	4	13	2	–	10	13	1	5	7	12	3
1900	13	–	10	–	7	15	3	2	14	7	–	5	11	7	3	6	12	1
1901	15	–	10	–	14	7	7	3	12	2	–	9	12	6	4	5	11	1
1902	10	–	13	–	14	15	7	5	11	12	–	3	7	4	2	6	9	1
1903	12	–	8	–	13	14	8	4	14	1	–	5	10	11	2	7	6	3
1904	10	–	14	–	9	15	3	1	7	4	–	5	12	11	6	7	13	2
1905	14	–	12	–	8	16	6	2	5	11	13	10	15	4	3	7	8	1
1906	16	–	7	–	9	8	1	4	15	11	11	5	11	3	10	6	14	2
1907	16	–	7	–	10	12	8	6	11	5	15	1	14	4	13	9	2	2
1908	14	–	11	–	10	9	2	7	13	4	15	8	16	3	5	12	6	1
1909	15	–	14	–	16	8	1	2	13	6	7	10	11	5	4	12	8	3
1910	15	–	11	–	12	6	1	4	10	3	9	5	16	2	7	14	13	8
1911	14	–	6	–	12	11	2	4	15	3	10	8	16	5	13	1	9	7
1912	12	–	15	–	11	6	3	4	13	5	2	8	14	7	10	9	16	1
1913	13	–	15	–	9	10	1	8	14	6	4	5	16	3	7	11	12	2
1914	12	–	8	–	16	5	3	11	13	2	9	10	15	1	6	7	14	4
1919	9	–	14	–	8	7	2	5	9	13	12	3	5	4	11	15	–	1
1920	16	–	9	–	8	11	5	2	13	1	14	7	10	3	6	12	15	4
1921	12	–	15	17	7	6	4	5	11	1	13	8	10	2	9	16	14	3
1922	11	–	8	16	13	6	4	5	14	7	15	2	10	3	9	12	17	1
1923	10	–	13	16	11	7	5	3	14	8	17	2	9	4	6	12	15	1
1924	17	–	15	13	6	12	5	4	11	2	16	6	8	3	10	9	14	1
1925	14	–	7	17	10	9	5	3	12	6	11	4	15	2	13	8	16	1
1926	11	–	9	8	15	7	3	1	16	6	16	4	14	5	10	12	17	2
1927	5	–	8	15	12	13	4	1	7	9	16	2	14	6	10	11	17	3
1928	10	–	16	15	5	12	2	1	9	8	13	3	14	6	7	11	17	4
1929	7	–	12	17	4	11	8	2	9	6	13	1	15	10	4	14	16	2
1930	9	–	6	11	2	13	5	1	12	16	17	4	13	8	7	15	10	3
1931	7	–	10	15	2	12	3	6	16	11	17	5	13	8	4	9	14	1
1932	10	–	14	15	13	8	3	6	12	10	16	4	7	5	2	9	17	1
1933	6	–	4	16	10	14	5	3	17	12	13	8	11	9	2	7	15	1
1934	3	–	8	13	7	14	5	1	12	10	17	9	15	11	2	4	16	5
1935	2	–	9	13	15	16	10	4	6	3	17	5	14	11	7	8	12	1
1936	1	–	9	16	4	10	8	11	15	2	17	5	7	6	14	13	12	3
1937	3	–	6	7	4	14	12	9	16	2	17	10	13	8	5	11	15	1
1938	5	–	6	16	10	14	9	4	15	2	17	12	7	3	8	13	11	1
1939	9	–	4	13	3	15	5	6	17	2	16	12	14	8	10	11	7	1
1946	15	–	8	6	5	10	6	3	11	2	16	13	4	11	17	14	8	1
1947	5	–	11	9	2	16	4	3	14	1	17	11	11	6	9	15	7	7
1948	6	–	13	1	8	9	15	5	11	3	17	14	12	2	16	7	10	4
1949	15	–	9	8	7	16	13	11	17	1	6	11	9	5	13	4	3	1
1950	5	–	17	11	7	12	9	1	16	14	10	15	7	1	13	4	6	3

	Derbyshire	Durham	Essex	Glamorgan	Gloucestershire	Hampshire	Kent	Lancashire	Leicestershire	Middlesex	Northamptonshire	Nottinghamshire	Somerset	Surrey	Sussex	Warwickshire	Worcestershire	Yorkshire
1951	11	–	8	5	12	9	16	3	15	7	13	17	14	6	10	1	4	2
1952	4	–	10	7	9	12	15	3	6	5	8	16	17	1	13	10	14	2
1953	6	–	12	10	6	14	16	3	3	5	11	8	17	1	2	9	15	12
1954	3	–	15	4	13	14	11	10	16	7	7	5	17	1	9	6	11	2
1955	8	–	14	16	12	3	13	9	6	5	7	11	17	1	4	9	15	2
1956	12	–	11	13	3	6	16	2	17	5	4	8	15	1	9	14	9	7
1957	4	–	5	9	12	13	14	6	17	7	2	15	8	1	9	11	16	3
1958	5	–	6	15	14	2	8	7	12	10	4	17	3	1	13	16	9	11
1959	7	–	9	6	2	8	13	5	16	10	11	17	12	3	15	4	14	1
1960	5	–	6	11	8	12	10	2	17	3	9	16	14	7	4	15	13	1
1961	7	–	6	14	5	1	11	13	9	3	16	17	10	15	8	12	4	2
1962	7	–	9	14	4	10	11	16	17	13	8	15	6	5	12	3	2	1
1963	17	–	12	2	8	10	13	15	16	6	7	9	3	11	4	14	5	1
1964	12	–	10	11	17	12	7	14	16	6	3	15	8	4	9	2	1	5
1965	9	–	15	3	10	12	5	13	14	6	2	17	7	8	16	11	1	4
1966	9	–	16	14	15	11	4	12	8	12	5	17	3	7	10	6	2	1
1967	6	–	15	14	17	12	2	11	2	7	9	15	8	4	13	10	5	1
1968	8	–	14	3	16	5	2	6	9	10	13	4	12	15	17	11	7	1
1969	16	–	6	1	2	5	10	15	14	11	9	8	17	3	7	4	12	13
1970	7	–	12	2	17	10	1	3	15	16	14	11	13	5	9	7	6	4
1971	17	–	10	16	8	9	4	3	5	6	14	12	7	1	11	2	15	13
1972	17	–	5	13	3	9	2	15	6	8	4	14	11	12	16	1	7	10
1973	16	–	8	11	5	1	4	12	9	13	3	17	10	2	15	7	6	14
1974	17	–	12	16	14	2	10	8	4	6	3	15	5	7	13	9	1	11
1975	15	–	7	9	16	3	5	4	1	11	8	13	12	6	17	14	10	2
1976	15	–	6	17	3	12	14	16	4	1	2	13	7	9	10	5	11	8
1977	7	–	6	14	3	11	1	16	5	1	9	17	4	14	8	10	13	12
1978	14	–	2	13	10	8	1	12	6	3	17	7	5	16	9	11	15	4
1979	16	–	1	17	10	12	5	13	6	14	11	9	8	3	4	15	2	7
1980	9	–	8	13	7	17	16	15	10	1	12	3	5	2	4	14	11	6
1981	12	–	5	14	13	7	9	16	8	4	15	1	3	6	2	17	11	10
1982	11	–	7	16	15	3	13	12	2	1	9	4	6	5	8	17	14	10
1983	9	–	1	15	12	3	7	4	2	6	14	10	8	11	5	16	17	13
1984	12	–	1	13	17	15	5	16	4	3	11	2	7	8	6	9	10	14
1985	13	–	4	12	3	2	9	14	16	1	10	8	17	6	7	15	5	11
1986	11	–	1	17	2	6	8	15	7	12	9	4	16	3	14	12	5	10
1987	6	–	12	13	10	5	14	2	3	16	7	1	11	4	17	15	9	8
1988	14	–	3	10	15	2	17	5	7	12	9	11	4	16	6	1	13	8
1989	6	–	2	17	9	6	15	4	13	3	5	11	14	12	10	8	1	16
1990	12	–	2	8	13	3	16	6	7	1	11	13	15	9	17	5	4	10
1991	3	–	1	12	13	9	6	8	16	15	10	4	17	5	11	2	6	14
1992	5	18	1	14	10	15	2	12	8	11	3	4	9	13	7	6	17	16
1993	15	18	11	3	17	13	8	13	9	1	4	7	5	6	10	16	2	12
1994	17	16	6	18	12	13	9	10	2	4	5	3	11	7	8	1	15	13
1995	14	17	5	16	6	13	18	4	7	2	3	11	9	12	15	1	10	8
1996	2	18	5	10	13	14	4	15	1	9	16	17	11	3	12	8	7	6
1997	16	17	8	1	7	14	2	11	10	4	15	13	12	8	18	4	3	3
1998	10	14	18	12	4	6	11	2	1	17	15	16	9	5	7	8	13	3
1999	9	8	12	14	18	7	5	2	3	16	13	17	4	1	11	10	15	6
2000	9	8	2	3	4	7	6	2	4	8	1	7	5	1	9	6	5	3
2001	9	8	9	8	4	2	3	6	5	5	7	7	2	4	1	3	6	1
2002	6	9	1	5	8	7	3	4	5	2	7	3	8	1	6	2	4	9
2003	9	6	7	5	3	8	4	2	9	6	2	8	7	3	1	5	1	4

	Derbyshire	Durham	Essex	Glamorgan	Gloucestershire	Hampshire	Kent	Lancashire	Leicestershire	Middlesex	Northamptonshire	Nottinghamshire	Somerset	Surrey	Sussex	Warwickshire	Worcestershire	Yorkshire
2004	8	9	5	3	6	2	2	8	6	4	9	1	4	3	5	1	7	3
2005	9	2	5	9	8	2	5	1	7	6	4	1	8	7	3	4	6	3
2006	5	7	3	8	7	3	5	2	4	9	6	8	9	1	1	4	2	6
2007	6	2	4	9	7	5	7	8	3	3	5	2	1	4	1	8	9	6
2008	6	1	5	8	9	3	8	5	7	3	4	2	4	9	6	1	2	7
2009	6	1	2	5	4	6	1	4	9	8	3	2	3	7	8	5	9	7
2010	9	5	9	3	5	7	8	4	4	8	6	1	2	7	1	6	2	3
2011	5	3	7	6	4	9	8	1	9	1	3	6	4	2	5	2	7	8
2012	1	6	5	6	9	4	3	8	7	3	8	5	2	7	4	1	9	2
2013	8	1	3	8	6	4	7	1	9	5	2	7	6	9	3	4	5	2
2014	4	5	3	8	7	1	6	8	9	7	9	4	6	5	3	2	2	1
2015	8	4	3	4	6	7	7	2	9	2	5	3	6	1	8	5	9	1
2016	9	4	1	8	6	8	2	7	7	1	5	9	2	5	4	6	3	3
2017	8	9	1	7	6	5	5	2	10	7	3	2	6	3	4	8	1	4
2018	7	8	3	10	5	5	2	7	4	9	6	2	1	3	1	8	4	4
2019	7	5	1	3	3	4	1	10	8	2	8	2		6	6	7	9	5
2021	5	3	1	6	2	4	1	2	4	2	4	3	6	5	6	1	3	5

2020   The County Championship was replaced by the Bob Willis Trophy, and won by Essex.

For the 2000–2021 Championships, Division One placings are in bold, Division Two in italic, Division Three in roman.

MATCH RESULTS, 1864–2021

County	Years of Play	Played	Won	Lost	Drawn	Tied	% Won
Derbyshire	1871–87; 1895–2021	2,606	636	965	1,004	1	24.40
Durham	1992–2021	469	128	192	149	0	27.29
Essex	1895–2021	2,571	767	734	1,064	6	29.83
Glamorgan	1921–2021	2,096	458	728	910	0	21.85
Gloucestershire	1870–2021	2,849	838	1,041	968	2	29.41
Hampshire	1864–85; 1895–2021	2,679	709	894	1,072	4	26.46
Kent	1864–2021	2,964	1,060	883	1,016	5	35.76
Lancashire	1865–2021	3,042	1,122	632	1,284	4	36.88
Leicestershire	1895–2021	2,536	563	931	1,041	1	22.20
Middlesex	1864–2021	2,746	997	705	1,039	5	36.30
Northamptonshire	1905–2021	2,303	581	785	934	3	25.22
Nottinghamshire	1864–2021	2,876	869	793	1,213	1	30.21
Somerset	1882–85; 1891–2021	2,579	636	985	954	4	24.66
Surrey	1864–2021	3,120	1,210	699	1,207	4	38.78
Sussex	1864–2021	3,015	860	1,028	1,121	6	28.52
Warwickshire	1895–2021	2,552	716	725	1,109	2	28.05
Worcestershire	1899–2021	2,488	643	871	972	2	25.84
Yorkshire	1864–2021	3,144	1,358	560	1,224	2	43.19
Cambridgeshire	1864–69; 1871	19	8	8	3	0	42.10
		23,327	14,159	14,159	9,142	26	

Matches abandoned without a ball bowled are excluded. Figures include the Bob Willis Trophy.

Counties participated in the years shown, except that there were no matches in 1915–1918 and 1940–1945; Hampshire did not play inter-county matches in 1868–1869, 1871–1874 and 1879; Worcestershire did not take part in the Championship in 1919.

COUNTY CHAMPIONSHIP STATISTICS FOR 2021

County		For			Runs scored		Against	
	Runs	Wickets	Avge	per 100 balls	Runs	Wickets	Avge
Derbyshire (5)........	5,477	234	23.40	50.68	5,862	178	32.93
Durham (3).........	5,466	169	32.34	51.81	5,316	222	23.94
Essex (1)...........	4,950	164	30.18	50.18	4,532	210	21.58
Glamorgan (6).......	5,864	186	31.52	55.17	6,152	172	35.76
Gloucestershire (2)....	5,833	215	27.13	49.76	6,026	217	27.76
Hampshire (4)........	5,726	203	28.20	49.48	5,694	237	24.02
Kent (1)............	5,831	204	28.58	54.11	5,471	190	28.79
Lancashire (2).......	5,836	181	32.24	51.83	5,615	218	25.75
Leicestershire (4)	6,491	199	32.61	52.43	6,710	189	35.50
Middlesex (2)........	6,125	250	24.50	50.20	6,200	237	26.16
Northamptonshire (4)..	5,769	214	26.95	52.40	5,836	187	31.20
Nottinghamshire (3)...	6,342	205	30.93	52.82	5,528	244	22.65
Somerset (6)........	5,707	207	27.57	55.63	5,439	178	30.55
Surrey (5)...........	5,547	159	34.88	50.82	5,704	165	34.56
Sussex (6)..........	6,631	242	27.40	51.69	6,979	177	39.42
Warwickshire (1)	6,563	224	29.29	48.48	5,689	233	24.41
Worcestershire (3)	5,797	201	28.84	50.16	6,963	188	37.03
Yorkshire (5)........	5,504	205	26.84	49.94	5,743	220	26.10
	105,459	3,662	28.79	51.47	105,459	3,662	28.79

2021 Championship positions are shown in brackets; Division One in bold, Division Two in italic, Division Three in roman.

ECB PITCHES TABLE OF MERIT IN 2021

	First-class	One-day		First-class	One-day
Derbyshire	5.57	5.42	Northamptonshire	5.13	5.67
Durham	4.43	5.71	Nottinghamshire	5.00	5.43
Essex	4.86	5.69	Somerset	5.57	5.88
Glamorgan	4.00	5.08	Surrey	5.25	5.57
Gloucestershire	5.13	5.25	Sussex	5.29	5.33
Hampshire	4.43	5.54	Warwickshire........	5.50	5.84
Kent	5.14	5.54	Worcestershire.......	5.00	5.27
Lancashire	5.43	5.39	Yorkshire...........	5.13	5.54
Leicestershire........	5.14	5.60			
Middlesex/MCC	4.70	5.55			

Each umpire in a match marks the pitch on the following scale: 6 – Very good; 5 – Good; 4 – Above average; 3 – Below average; 2 – Poor; 1 – Unfit.

The tables, provided by the ECB, cover major matches, including Tests, Under-19 internationals and women's internationals, played on all grounds under the county's jurisdiction. Middlesex pitches at Lord's are the responsibility of MCC. The "First-class" column includes women's and Under-19 Tests.

Derbyshire and Somerset had the highest marks for first-class cricket, while Somerset had the best for one-day cricket; excluding outgrounds, the highest marks were 5.67 for Old Trafford (first-class) and 5.90 for Canterbury (one-day). The ECB point out that the tables of merit are not a direct assessment of the groundsmen's ability. Marks may be affected by many factors, including weather, soil conditions and the resources available.

COUNTY CAPS AWARDED IN 2021

Durham*	W. A. Young.
Essex	P. M. Siddle.
Glamorgan	K. S. Carlson, M. G. Neser, W. T. Root.
Gloucestershire*	K. C. Brathwaite, D. C. Goodman, G. D. Phillips, O. J. Price, J. A. Tattersall, J. D. Warner, B. J. J. Wells, Zafar Gohar.
Hampshire	T. P. Alsop, K. H. D. Barker, M. S. Crane, I. G. Holland, L. D. McManus, J. J. Weatherley, B. T. J. Wheal.
Kent	J. A. Leaning, M. E. Milnes.
Lancashire	J. J. Bohannon, S. Mahmood.
Leicestershire	L. J. Hill, C. J. C. Wright.
Northamptonshire	R. S. Vasconcelos, G. G. White.
Nottinghamshire	J. M. Clarke, B. A. Hutton, T. J. Moores, D. Paterson, B. T. Slater.
Somerset	J. H. Davey, M. T. C. Waller.
Surrey	H. M. Amla.
Sussex	T. J. Haines.
Warwickshire	T. T. Bresnan, D. R. Briggs, M. G. K. Burgess.
Worcestershire*	J. O. Baker, A. S. Joseph, G. H. Roderick, I. S. Sodhi.
Yorkshire	H. C. Brook.

* Durham and Gloucestershire now award caps to all first-class players; Worcestershire have replaced caps with colours awarded to all Championship players (or, in 2020, the Bob Willis Trophy).

  No caps were awarded by Derbyshire or Middlesex.

COUNTY TESTIMONIALS AWARDED FOR 2022

Glamorgan	*M. G. Hogan.	Middlesex	*E. J. G. Morgan.

*   Testimonial originally awarded for 2020, but extended because of the Covid-19 crisis.

No other county had confirmed a testimonial for 2022 when Wisden *went to press.*

Streets ahead: Will Rhodes drives towards a hundred.

BOB WILLIS TROPHY IN 2021

Paul Edwards

LANCASHIRE v WARWICKSHIRE

At Lord's, September 28–October 1. Warwickshire won by an innings and 199 runs. Toss: Warwickshire. First-class debut: M. S. Johal.

A game scheduled for five days stretched barely an hour into the fourth morning, and rarely looked like a contest between the best county teams in the land. No disrespect to either side should be inferred. Warwickshire had won the Championship a week earlier, and no amount of champagne could dull their intent to secure another trophy; that it was named after one of their most famous sons only sharpened their resolve. Lancashire, by contrast, had headed the table for one night, while they celebrated a breathtaking victory over Hampshire, before their title dreams were shattered. By the time they arrived at Lord's, they were running on empty: the last thing they needed was to be put in at 10.30 on a pitch with early life. A collapse to 12 for six in nine overs was reminiscent of some one-day finals on this ground, and offered an effective counter to the idea that one late-season match should decide the Championship. This is not to detract from Warwickshire's seamers: Norwell began the carnage with his 50th wicket of the season, Miles collected five, and 19-year-old Manraj Johal three on first-class debut. Only four Lancashire players managed more than a single – well over half their 78 came from Wood at No. 8 – and by the end of the opening day Warwickshire had established a 42-run lead without losing a wicket. It was already difficult to imagine them failing to win. Next morning, Yates made his fifth century of the season (he and Norwell were selected for their first Lions tour a fortnight later), and by tea Rhodes had crowned the most memorable week of his career with his first hundred for over a year. Parkinson held Lancashire's attack together, but a deficit of 440 meant their chief objective was recovering a little self-respect. Balderson compiled their only half-century of the match, but Davies ran himself out in his last innings before joining Warwickshire, and Briggs bowled effectively on a receptive pitch. A smattering of spectators saw the champions complete Lancashire's fourth-heaviest defeat early on October 1 – the first first-class cricket played in England in October since 1864, when Cambridgeshire & Yorkshire beat Kent & Nottinghamshire at Newmarket. "We wanted to send out a statement, why we are champions, and I've think we've done that today," said Rhodes. "Doing it for Bob, with that Warwickshire connection, is fantastic."

Close of play: first day, Warwickshire 120-0 (Yates 69, Sibley 49); second day, Warwickshire 464-7 (Rhodes 151, Miles 12); third day, Lancashire 171-6 (Jones 0, Wood 13).

Lancashire

G. P. Balderson c Bresnan b Norwell	1	– b Norwell	65
†A. L. Davies c and b Miles	7	– run out (Miles)	11
L. W. P. Wells b Miles	0	– c Burgess b Bresnan	41
J. J. Bohannon c Sibley b Johal	17	– c Hain b Norwell	8
*D. J. Vilas lbw b Miles	0	– c Hain b Miles	25
S. J. Croft lbw b Miles	0	– c Bresnan b Briggs	3
R. P. Jones c Burgess b Norwell	1	– lbw b Briggs	18
L. Wood not out	46	– b Johal	28
T. E. Bailey lbw b Johal	0	– c Burgess b Norwell	24
J. M. Blatherwick c Hain b Johal	0	– st Burgess b Briggs	11
M. W. Parkinson c Burgess b Miles	4	– not out	0
Nb 2	2	Lb 2, w 1, nb 4	7

1/8 (1) 2/8 (2) 3/9 (3)   (27.5 overs) 78   1/23 (2) 2/94 (3)   (68.2 overs) 241
4/9 (5) 5/11 (6) 6/12 (7)   3/120 (4) 4/143 (1)
7/47 (4) 8/57 (9) 9/57 (10) 10/78 (11)   5/158 (6) 6/158 (5) 7/195 (8)
                                     8/212 (7) 9/233 (10) 10/241 (9)

Norwell 6–2–9–2; Miles 9.5–1–28–5; Johal 8–3–29–3; Bresnan 4–2–12–0. *Second innings*—Norwell 14.2–2–60–3; Miles 15–1–67–1; Bresnan 8–0–24–1; Briggs 19–1–58–3; Johal 10–2–30–1; Yates 2–2–0–0.

Warwickshire

R. M. Yates c Wells b Parkinson	113	L. C. Norwell b Blatherwick	2
D. P. Sibley lbw b Bailey	57	M. S. Johal b Parkinson	19
*W. M. H. Rhodes b Blatherwick	156		
S. R. Hain b Blatherwick	55	B 4, lb 20, w 2, nb 10	36
M. J. Lamb b Wells	0		
†M. G. K. Burgess st Davies b Parkinson	44	1/133 (2) 2/243 (1) (147.3 overs)	518
T. T. Bresnan c Wells b Parkinson	4	3/340 (4) 4/341 (5)	
D. R. Briggs c Davies b Wells	2	5/425 (6) 6/439 (7) 7/442 (8)	
C. N. Miles not out	30	8/469 (9) 9/487 (10) 10/518 (11)	

Bailey 28–3–112–1; Blatherwick 26–6–80–3; Balderson 24–1–83–0; Wood 16–2–64–0; Parkinson 31.3–3–78–4; Wells 22–3–77–2.

Umpires: M. Burns and D. J. Millns.   Third umpire: A. G. Wharf.
Referee: D. A. Cosker.

The Bob Willis Trophy, named after the late England and Warwickshire bowler, was created in 2020 for the short first-class county competition devised after the Covid pandemic derailed the County Championship. The trophy was retained in 2021 for a one-off match between the Championship winners and runners-up, with a £50,000 prize.

DERBYSHIRE

Can Arthur ride to the rescue?

MARK EKLID

Dismay is such a regular visitor to the County Ground that it stores its favourite pint pot behind the members' bar. Yet even those Derbyshire followers scarred by the longest memories struggled to recall a season so draining. It ended with the head of cricket, Dave Houghton, leaving – almost with an air of relief – after his third spell at the county, where he was always more comfortable coaching than managing.

But the club pulled off a coup when they unveiled his replacement in November. Mickey Arthur had coached his native South Africa, plus Australia, Pakistan and, most recently, Sri Lanka. If he was prepared to commit himself to the long-term project of rebuilding Derbyshire, perhaps there was hope.

Sympathy is limited when an underperforming club blame ill fortune. Still, for a county such as Derbyshire to break the cycle, almost all their plans have to pay off: the margins between success and failure are tighter. And little went to plan in 2021.

Overseas signings can make a crucial difference, and Derbyshire pinned their hopes on two Australians. Tall fast bowler Billy Stanlake was recruited for all formats – an ambition bordering on the fanciful for a player dogged by injury and with little first-class experience. Quarantine regulations delayed his debut until the fifth Championship match, against Essex; he took two wickets in 17 overs, then returned home with a stress fracture of the back. Explosive one-day batsman Ben McDermott, on a white-ball contract deferred from the Covid-hit 2020 season, was drafted into the Championship side on Stanlake's departure. But he played only twice, scoring 49 in four innings, before being called up by Australia – just as the Vitality Blast began – to prepare for their tours of the West Indies and Bangladesh.

Two previous hirings, West Indian Ravi Rampaul and New Zealander Logan van Beek, signed short-term deals to cover for the Australians, in the Royal London Cup and the Blast respectively, but their returns were modest. Neither tournament lifted many Derbyshire spirits, though an extraordinary innings from Tom Wood, who scored the county's fastest one-day century in a rain-shortened game against Nottinghamshire, brought them a memorable victory – the only one in the Royal London Cup. They struggled to find 11 fit players; for one game, Daryn Smit, the head of talent pathway, had to be coaxed out of retirement to keep wicket. They won four Blast matches and tied another, but lacked the edge McDermott and Stanlake might have provided.

In the Championship, overcaution cost Derbyshire victory in their second match, at home to Worcestershire, and they did not earn another opportunity until they won at Hove in the final round, beating the only county to end below them. Those two games provided their largest totals of the season (390 and

Jacques Feeney, Getty Images

Ben Aitchison

465), but they batted woefully the rest of the time, especially in the first innings: there were just ten batting points and one century from ten matches in the Championship's group stage. They ended that first phase with nine totals under 200 in 12 attempts, in which even their highest score – 270 – failed to avert an innings defeat.

It did not help that their senior batsmen struggled. Wayne Madsen, who missed three months with a ruptured hamstring, and captain Billy Godleman, so out of touch he took a four-week midsummer break, ended the season in better shape, but still below their usual standards. Derbyshire could not afford either to fail again. Leus du Plooy barely got going, with eight ducks in 24 Championship innings; neither did Luis Reece, who had borne a heavy burden with bat and ball in previous years, and was expected to miss much of 2022 recovering from shoulder and knee surgery. His extended absence will be sorely felt – though the first signing from Arthur's extensive contacts book was Pakistan opener Shan Masood, followed by Sri Lanka seamer Suranga Lakmal.

Wicketkeeper Harvey Hosein, one of the few to score runs in the early weeks, suffered two concussions and announced his retirement, aged 25, in October, while left-arm seamer Michael Cohen was ruled out by a lower back problem in July. Dustin Melton, the Zimbabwe-born pace bowler registered as an overseas player while completing his qualification, appeared in just five Championship matches because of a heel injury; the loss of Alex Hughes's medium-pace in white-ball cricket, through a side strain, was another setback.

Brooke Guest, in his first full season with the county, was a more than adequate deputy for Hosein, with gloves and bat. Ben Aitchison and Sam Conners were the pick of a young seam attack, collecting 60 Championship wickets between them. Fynn Hudson-Prentice was another key member, before the lure of a return to Sussex proved too strong, though his departure allowed Anuj Dal greater scope to push his claims as an all-rounder.

The brightest light amid the gloom was Matt Critchley. Appropriately, he struck the final ball of the season for the two runs needed to clinch victory over Sussex, and complete 1,000 in the Championship for the first time – one of only five in the country to reach the landmark. Recognition of his ability spread as his leg-spin grew more effective; unfortunately, that resulted in a move to Essex when his contract expired. His loss was a grave blow to the team Arthur inherited.

DERBYSHIRE RESULTS

County Championship matches – Played 14: Won 1, Lost 7, Drawn 6.
Vitality T20 Blast matches – Played 12: Won 4, Lost 7, Tied 1. Cancelled 2.
Royal London Cup matches – Played 8: Won 1, Lost 6, No result 1.

LV= County Championship, 6th in Group 1, 5th in Division 3;
Vitality T20 Blast, 8th in North Group; Royal London Cup, 9th in Group 2.

COUNTY CHAMPIONSHIP AVERAGES, BATTING AND FIELDING

Cap		Birthplace	M	I	NO	R	HS	100	Avge	Ct/St
2019	M. J. J. Critchley....	Preston	14	26	3	1,000	109	1	43.47	8
	H. R. Hosein.......	Chesterfield‡....	8	14	5	371	83*	0	41.22	11
2011	W. L. Madsen	Durban, SA	11	20	0	675	111	1	33.75	20
2015	†B. A. Godleman....	Islington	10	18	2	530	100*	1	33.12	5
	A. K. Dal	Newcastle-u-Tyne	8	13	2	333	106	1	30.27	6
	B. D. Guest......	Manchester	12	20	1	489	116	1	25.73	26/3
	†J. L. du Plooy††....	Pretoria, SA......	13	24	1	428	98	0	18.60	5
	F. J. Hudson-Prentice	Haywards Heath ..	9	15	2	209	31*	0	16.07	2
	H. R. C. Came	Basingstoke	3	5	0	68	45	0	13.60	1
2019	†L. M. Reece......	Taunton	9	17	0	231	63	0	13.58	3
	B. W. Aitchison	Southport	13	20	4	200	50	0	12.50	12
	B. R. McDermott¶..	Caboolture, Aus..	2	4	0	49	25	0	12.25	1
	A. T. Thomson	Macclesfield....	4	6	0	65	18	0	10.83	1
2017	A. L. Hughes	Wordsley	5	9	1	84	25	0	10.50	1
	T. A. Wood	Derby‡........	7	13	0	129	31	0	9.92	6
	S. Conners	Nottingham	10	16	3	114	39	0	8.76	1
	D. R. Melton¶.....	Harare, Zimbabwe	5	8	3	39	15	0	7.80	2
	†M. A. R. Cohen††...	Cape Town, SA ..	5	8	1	41	11	0	5.85	1
	G. L. S. Scrimshaw	Burton-on-Trent ..	3	5	3	5	5*	0	2.50	1

Also batted: M. H. McKiernan (*Billinge*) (1 match) 23 (1 ct); E. H. T. Moulton (*Preston*) (2 matches) 6*, 3; B. Stanlake¶ (*Hervey Bay, Australia*) (1 match) 0, 8.

‡ *Born in Derbyshire.*   ¶ *Official overseas player.*   †† *Other non-England-qualified.*

BOWLING

	Style	O	M	R	W	BB	5I	Avge
B. W. Aitchison	RFM	275.4	50	792	34	6-28	1	23.29
F. J. Hudson-Prentice.............	RFM	182	47	548	23	5-68	1	23.82
M. A. R. Cohen	LFM	99.5	19	280	11	5-43	1	25.45
S. Conners	RFM	225.5	44	750	26	5-83	1	28.84
M. J. J. Critchley.................	LB	343.3	42	1,230	32	5-67	1	38.43
L. M. Reece.....................	LFM	183.3	46	555	12	2-25	0	46.25

Also bowled: A. K. Dal (RFM) 110–18–298–9; J. L. du Plooy (SLA) 8–1–21–0; A. L. Hughes (RM) 31–8–83–1; M. H. McKiernan (LB) 4–0–16–0; W. L. Madsen (OB) 43.5–8–130–4; D. R. Melton (RFM) 93–15–390–9; E. H. T. Moulton (RFM) 40–8–159–3; G. L. S. Scrimshaw (RFM) 35–6–154–3; B. Stanlake (RFM) 17–2–91–2; A. T. Thomson (OB) 53.2–6–186–7.

LEADING VITALITY BLAST AVERAGES (100 runs/15 overs)

Batting	Runs	HS	Avge	SR	Ct/St		Bowling	W	BB	Avge	ER
L. M. Reece.....	351	59	29.25	171.21	7		M. J. J. Critchley..	12	4-48	25.91	6.76
B. D. Guest	137	34*	22.83	134.31	10/1		G. L. S. Scrimshaw	14	3-23	16.85	7.61
F. J. Hudson-Prentice	134	41	13.40	131.37	4		A. T. Thomson ..	4	3-23	34.75	8.17
J. L. du Plooy ...	395	92	39.50	131.22	8		C. McKerr.......	5	2-23	38.20	9.09
T. A. Wood	142	63*	47.33	125.66	3		L. M. Reece......	5	2-24	27.40	9.13
H. R. C. Came ...	207	56	18.81	119.65	5		F. J. Hudson-Prentice	16	3-36	20.31	9.55
M. J. J. Critchley .	252	80*	28.00	117.75	9		L. V. van Beek...	16	3-22	22.56	9.80

LEADING ROYAL LONDON CUP AVERAGES (100 runs/4 wickets)

Batting	Runs	HS	Avge	SR	Ct/St
F. J. Hudson-Prentice	261	93	65.25	118.09	2
B. A. Godleman .	128	116	64.00	92.08	0
T. A. Wood	191	109	31.83	115.06	0
B. D. Guest	170	74	28.33	77.98	4/1
H. R. C. Came ...	141	57	23.50	85.45	0
M. H. McKiernan	113	38	22.60	129.88	4

Bowling	W	BB	Avge	ER
G. L. S. Scrimshaw	3	2-41	28.66	8.60
T. A. Wood	3	1-13	31.00	5.47
A. T. Thomson .	5	2-37	35.20	6.28
F. J. Hudson-Prentice	6	3-37	37.83	6.10
M. H. McKiernan	3	1-26	66.66	6.89
R. Rampaul	3	1-15	86.00	6.00

FIRST-CLASS COUNTY RECORDS

Highest score for	274	G. A. Davidson v Lancashire at Manchester......	1896
Highest score against	343*	P. A. Perrin (Essex) at Chesterfield.............	1904
Leading run-scorer	23,854	K. J. Barnett (avge 41.12).....................	1979–98
Best bowling for	10-40	W. Bestwick v Glamorgan at Cardiff	1921
Best bowling against	10-45	R. L. Johnson (Middlesex) at Derby	1994
Leading wicket-taker	1,670	H. L. Jackson (avge 17.11)	1947–63
Highest total for	801-8 dec	v Somerset at Taunton.......................	2007
Highest total against	677-7 dec	by Yorkshire at Leeds.......................	2013
Lowest total for	16	v Nottinghamshire at Nottingham	1879
Lowest total against	23	by Hampshire at Burton-upon-Trent	1958

LIST A COUNTY RECORDS

Highest score for	173*	M. J. Di Venuto v Derbys County Board at Derby .	2000
Highest score against	158	R. K. Rao (Sussex) at Derby	1997
Leading run-scorer	12,358	K. J. Barnett (avge 36.67)....................	1979–98
Best bowling for	8-21	M. A. Holding v Sussex at Hove...............	1988
Best bowling against	8-66	S. R. G. Francis (Somerset) at Derby	2004
Leading wicket-taker	246	A. E. Warner (avge 27.13)	1985–95
Highest total for	366-4	v Combined Universities at Oxford............	1991
Highest total against	369-6	by New Zealanders at Derby..................	1999
Lowest total for	60	v Kent at Canterbury........................	2008
Lowest total against	42	by Glamorgan at Swansea....................	1979

TWENTY20 COUNTY RECORDS

Highest score for	111	W. J. Durston v Nottinghamshire at Nottingham ..	2010
Highest score against	158*	B. B. McCullum (Warwickshire) at Birmingham ..	2015
Leading run-scorer	3,010	W. L. Madsen (avge 30.71, SR 134.31)	2010–21
Best bowling for	5-27	T. Lungley v Leicestershire at Leicester	2009
Best bowling against	5-14	P. D. Collingwood (Durham) at Chester-le-Street .	2008
Leading wicket-taker	55	M. J. J. Critchley (avge 26.21, ER 7.55)	2016–21
Highest total for	⎰ 222-5	v Yorkshire at Leeds........................	2010
	⎱ 222-5	v Nottinghamshire at Nottingham	2017
Highest total against	249-8	by Hampshire at Derby......................	2017
Lowest total for	72	v Leicestershire at Derby....................	2013
Lowest total against	84	by West Indians at Derby	2007

ADDRESS

The Incora County Ground, Nottingham Road, Derby DE21 6DA; 01332 388 101; info@ derbyshireccc.com; www.derbyshireccc.com. Twitter: @DerbyshireCCC.

OFFICIALS

Captain B. A. Godleman	**President** J. G. Wright
Head of cricket 2021 D. L. Houghton	**Chair** R. I. Morgan
2022 J. M. Arthur	**Chief executive** R. Duckett
Head of talent pathway D. Smit	**Head groundsman** N. Godrich
	Scorer J. M. Brown

GROUP ONE

At Birmingham, April 8–11. DERBYSHIRE drew with WARWICKSHIRE.

DERBYSHIRE v WORCESTERSHIRE

At Derby, April 15–18. Drawn. Derbyshire 15pts, Worcestershire 14pts. Toss: Worcestershire. County debut: A. S. Joseph.

Derbyshire's first home fixture since September 2019 – the County Ground had served as an international biosecure bubble in 2020 – nearly produced a win: Worcestershire were eight down with 14 overs to go, and play ended with seven fielders round the bat. Though Derbyshire had started the final day 353 ahead, they batted on for ten overs to raise the target to 398 in 84. The caution seemed irrelevant when Worcestershire slid to 83 for six, before Cox and Barnard survived 32 overs. Critchley struck twice, but Cox remained immovable. Even so, this was Critchley's match – the first Derbyshire player to score four fifties in the first two Championship games of a season, and the second to combine a century, half-century and five wickets in an innings, after fellow leg-spinner Garnet Lee against Leicestershire in 1928. Critchley might have added a second hundred, but was bowled for 84, undone by low bounce. His fifth wicket had been the West Indian fast bowler Alzarri Joseph, last out for a forceful 46 on Championship debut, just after securing Worcestershire's third batting point with a six.

Close of play: first day, Derbyshire 360-8 (Hosein 65, Aitchison 3); second day, Worcestershire 243-7 (Barnard 11, Joseph 10); third day, Derbyshire 268-5 (Hosein 33, Hudson-Prentice 10).

Derbyshire

L. M. Reece lbw b Leach	3	– c Cox b Joseph	17
*B. A. Godleman c Cox b Leach	50	– retired hurt	5
J. L. du Plooy b D'Oliveira	98	– b Barnard	28
W. L. Madsen c Mitchell b Pennington	1	– lbw b Mitchell	66
M. J. J. Critchley lbw b Barnard	109	– b Mitchell	84
†H. R. Hosein not out	83	– not out	55
A. K. Dal lbw b Barnard	0	– b D'Oliveira	7
F. J. Hudson-Prentice c Cox b Joseph	6	– not out	31
M. A. R. Cohen lbw b Joseph	0		
B. W. Aitchison c Cox b Barnard	11		
S. Conners b Barnard	0		
B 21, lb 6, nb 2	29	B 5, lb 12, nb 2	19

1/4 (1) 2/141 (2) 3/146 (4)   (111.2 overs) 390   1/58 (1)   (5 wkts dec, 80 overs) 312
4/217 (3) 5/338 (5) 6/338 (7)   2/78 (3) 3/207 (4)
7/355 (8) 8/355 (9) 9/384 (10)   4/238 (5) 5/249 (7)
10/390 (11)   110 overs: 384-9

In the second innings Godleman retired hurt at 5-0.

Leach 21–3–69–2; Pennington 19–2–69–1; Joseph 24–3–108–2; Barnard 25.2–4–67–4; D'Oliveira 19–3–41–1; Mitchell 3–0–9–0. *Second innings*—Leach 18–1–58–0; Pennington 7–1–43–0; D'Oliveira 24–0–104–1; Barnard 8–1–21–1; Joseph 8–1–35–1; Mitchell 15–1–34–2.

Worcestershire

D. K. H. Mitchell b Hudson-Prentice	9	– c Godleman b Critchley	8
J. D. Libby lbw b Conners	0	– b Hudson-Prentice	21
T. C. Fell lbw b Conners	69	– c Aitchison b Hudson-Prentice	13
G. H. Roderick c and b Critchley	12	– lbw b Aitchison	22
B. L. D'Oliveira c Madsen b Critchley	27	– c Hudson-Prentice b Aitchison	3
M. H. Wessels b Critchley	60	– lbw b Aitchison	2
†O. B. Cox b Reece	24	– not out	60
E. G. Barnard c Madsen b Critchley	23	– lbw b Critchley	35
A. S. Joseph b Critchley	46	– lbw b Critchley	4
*J. Leach c Critchley b Hudson-Prentice	7	– not out	9
D. Y. Pennington not out	0		
B 7, lb 13, nb 8	28	B 4, lb 4, nb 8	16

1/1 (2) 2/22 (1) 3/63 (4) (102 overs) 305 1/25 (1) (8 wkts, 83.5 overs) 193
4/121 (3) 5/135 (5) 6/217 (6) 2/33 (2) 3/54 (3)
7/231 (7) 8/282 (8) 9/299 (10) 10/305 (9) 4/64 (5) 5/72 (6)
6/83 (4) 7/168 (8) 8/176 (9)

Conners 18–2–54–2; Reece 16–4–41–1; Hudson-Prentice 25–5–50–2; Critchley 25–5–67–5; Aitchison 9–3–20–0; Cohen 13–2–50–0; Madsen 6–4–3–0. *Second innings*—Conners 11–5–24–0; Reece 8–1–19–0; Hudson-Prentice 14–4–38–2; Critchley 32.5–13–76–3; Aitchison 12–5–18–3; Cohen 6–3–10–0.

Umpires: P. K. Baldwin and R. T. Robinson.   Referee: W. R. Smith.

At Chester-le-Street, April 22–25. DERBYSHIRE drew with DURHAM.

DERBYSHIRE v NOTTINGHAMSHIRE

At Derby, April 29–May 1. Nottinghamshire won by 310 runs. Nottinghamshire 21pts, Derbyshire 3pts. Toss: Derbyshire.

Nottinghamshire achieved their first first-class victory in 31 games and 1,043 days, a sequence stretching back to June 2018, when they beat Essex at Chelmsford. They did it with five sessions to spare, after claiming all ten Derbyshire wickets on the third morning: Broad extracted two in the first over. Notionally pursuing 470, the hosts folded for 159, and suffered their biggest Championship defeat by runs since 1904, also against Nottinghamshire. It might have been their heaviest in all first-class cricket but for Aitchison's belligerent maiden run-a-ball fifty. On the opening day, Slater, with his second successive century, and Clarke had done much to decide the balance of the contest when they exploited poor bowling in a third-wicket stand of 163. That was followed by 16 falling for 148 in the second half of the day. Fletcher's five for 28 helped Nottinghamshire to a lead of 151, but they opted to bat again, before Hameed and Duckett made their advantage unassailable. Hudson-Prentice took four wickets in each innings, beating his previous best return of three.

Close of play: first day, Derbyshire 86-8 (Guest 6, Aitchison 0); second day, Derbyshire 23-0 (Reece 13, Wood 9).

Nottinghamshire

B. T. Slater lbw b Critchley	107	– b Reece	24
H. Hameed c du Plooy b Reece	0	– b Critchley	94
B. M. Duckett c Madsen b Hudson-Prentice	14	– c du Plooy b Hudson-Prentice	87
J. M. Clarke c Hosein b Aitchison	66	– c Wood b Hudson-Prentice	53
L. W. James lbw b Hudson-Prentice	1	– c Wood b Scrimshaw	7
*S. J. Mullaney lbw b Hudson-Prentice	2	– c Hosein b Scrimshaw	10
†T. J. Moores c Scrimshaw b Reece	26	– c Madsen b Hudson-Prentice	27
L. A. Patterson-White b Aitchison	23	– c Wood b Madsen	3
S. C. J. Broad c Wood b Hudson-Prentice	3	– b Hudson-Prentice	3
L. J. Fletcher c Madsen b Aitchison	0	– c Guest b Madsen	0
D. Paterson not out	0	– not out	0
B 4, lb 2, nb 8	14	B 2, lb 4, nb 4	10

1/2 (2) 2/31 (3) 3/194 (4)   (68.4 overs) 256   1/29 (1) 2/186 (3)   (70.4 overs) 318
4/195 (5) 5/197 (6) 6/205 (1)   3/239 (2) 4/259 (5)
7/242 (7) 8/254 (8) 9/254 (10) 10/256 (9)   5/275 (6) 6/308 (4) 7/315 (7)
                                       8/315 (8) 9/315 (10) 10/318 (9)

Conners 11–0–53–0; Reece 18.5–5–89–2; Hudson-Prentice 16.4–5–36–4; Aitchison 10–2–27–3; Critchley 6–0–20–1; Scrimshaw 7–1–25–0. *Second innings*—Conners 7–1–42–0; Reece 11.5–1–42–1; Hudson-Prentice 12.4–1–40–4; Critchley 17.1–0–104–1; Aitchison 5–1–25–0; Scrimshaw 11–2–40–2; Madsen 6–0–19–2.

Derbyshire

L. M. Reece c Moores b Broad	11	– c Clarke b Broad	15
T. A. Wood run out (Fletcher)	10	– b Fletcher	31
J. L. du Plooy lbw b Paterson	11	– lbw b Broad	0
*W. L. Madsen lbw b Broad	0	– c Moores b Paterson	21
M. J. J. Critchley c Moores b Paterson	33	– b Paterson	1
†H. R. Hosein lbw b Fletcher	2	– c Moores b Paterson	0
G. L. S. Scrimshaw c Moores b Fletcher	0	– (11) not out	5
B. D. Guest b Fletcher	10	– (7) c Moores b Fletcher	10
F. J. Hudson-Prentice b Fletcher	0	– (8) c Hameed b Broad	13
B. W. Aitchison c Hameed b Fletcher	0	– (9) b Patterson-White	50
S. Conners not out	12	– (10) c Paterson b Broad	4
B 5, lb 11	16	B 5, lb 2, nb 2	9

1/20 (1) 2/35 (2) 3/37 (4)   (34.5 overs) 105   1/26 (1) 2/26 (3)   (41.5 overs) 159
4/55 (3) 5/80 (6) 6/80 (5)   3/53 (4) 4/57 (5)
7/82 (7) 8/82 (9) 9/86 (10) 10/105 (8)   5/63 (6) 6/77 (2) 7/84 (7)
                                      8/123 (8) 9/153 (10) 10/159 (9)

Broad 13–3–33–2; Fletcher 14.5–6–28–5; Paterson 7–2–28–2. *Second innings*—Broad 13–2–37–4; Fletcher 11–3–32–2; Paterson 9–5–30–3; James 4–0–14–0; Mullaney 1–0–4–0; Patterson-White 3.5–0–35–1.

Umpires: R. T. Robinson and B. V. Taylor. Referee: S. J. Davis.

At Chelmsford, May 13–16. DERBYSHIRE lost to ESSEX by an innings and 15 runs.

DERBYSHIRE v DURHAM

At Derby, May 20–23. Drawn. Derbyshire 13pts, Durham 12pts. Toss: Durham.

Spectators returned to the County Ground, with a small crowd braving rain, wind and bad light, which ruined the contest: only 17 overs were possible in the first two days. A week after he became Durham's leading first-class wicket-taker, Rushworth's six for 49 took him past 500 in the Championship (excluding 16 in the 2020 Bob Willis Trophy). The only chance of a result was for

Derbyshire to impose the follow-on. That looked possible when Durham were 57 for five with nearly two sessions left, but Eckersley's 82 steered them to safety. Aitchison claimed a career-best six for 28 – the best figures for Derbyshire against Durham, beating Graeme Welch's six for 30 at Chester-le-Street in 2001 – and Critchley collected his 100th first-class victim. Guest kept wicket for Derbyshire after Hosein was concussed, hit on the back of the helmet by Carse on the third day; Dal took Hosein's place in the team.

Close of play: first day, Derbyshire 48-0 (Guest 23, Godleman 24); second day, no play; third day, Durham 20-2 (Bancroft 9, Borthwick 2).

Derbyshire

B. D. Guest lbw b Rushworth	30	A. K. Dal lbw b Rushworth	13
*B. A. Godleman c Bancroft b Rushworth	41	S. Conners c Lees b Rushworth	0
J. L. du Plooy c Poynter b Wood	0	D. R. Melton not out	3
W. L. Madsen lbw b Carse	42		
M. J. J. Critchley c Carse b Rushworth	49	B 1, lb 17, w 1, nb 4	23
†H. R. Hosein retired hurt	0		—
F. J. Hudson-Prentice b Rushworth	26	1/71 (1) 2/72 (3) 3/72 (2) (87.4 overs) 258
A. L. Hughes b Wood	7	4/171 (5) 5/181 (4) 6/195 (8)
B. W. Aitchison c Poynter b Carse	24	7/235 (9) 8/245 (7) 9/245 (11) 10/258 (10)

Hosein retired hurt at 176-4. Dal replaced Hosein, as a concussion substitute.

Rushworth 19.4–6–49–6; Wood 23–6–84–2; Raine 22–10–36–0; Carse 16–5–51–2; Borthwick 7–0–20–0.

Durham

C. T. Bancroft lbw b Critchley	39	B. A. Carse c Aitchison b Critchley	25
A. Z. Lees c †Guest b Aitchison	1	M. A. Wood c Conners b Aitchison	1
B. A. Raine c Hudson-Prentice b Aitchison	0	C. Rushworth not out	4
*S. G. Borthwick c †Guest b Aitchison	14	B 6, lb 18, nb 2	26
D. G. Bedingham c Dal b Aitchison	0		—
J. T. A. Burnham c †Guest b Conners	6	1/13 (2) 2/17 (3) 3/43 (4) (67.4 overs) 208
E. J. H. Eckersley lbw b Aitchison	82	4/43 (5) 5/57 (6) 6/117 (1)
†S. W. Poynter c du Plooy b Critchley	10	7/165 (8) 8/187 (7) 9/197 (10) 10/208 (9)

Conners 8–2–16–1; Melton 14–4–45–0; Aitchison 16–5–28–6; Hudson-Prentice 6–4–3–0; Critchley 13.4–0–54–3; Hughes 8–3–27–0; du Plooy 2–0–11–0.

Umpires: P. J. Hartley and R. T. Robinson.   Referee: D. A. Cosker.

At Worcester, May 27–30. DERBYSHIRE lost to WORCESTERSHIRE by an innings and 23 runs.

DERBYSHIRE v WARWICKSHIRE

At Derby, June 3–5. Warwickshire won by 191 runs. Warwickshire 20pts (after 1pt penalty), Derbyshire 2pts (after 1pt penalty). Toss: Derbyshire.

Conditions that suited swing bowling tested the batsmen – 18 wickets fell on the second day – and Warwickshire stood up to the challenge better. Hain and Burgess made telling contributions after Godleman put them in and Conners removed their first four wickets. A total of 274 looked modest. From 54 for one, however, Derbyshire lost nine for 67 to Miles and Norwell. Warwickshire declined to enforce the follow-on but, with Cohen taking his first five-wicket haul for Derbyshire, batted poorly second time round. A target of 309, with more than five sessions to play, was not impossible, only for the home batting to crumble again, bowled out before tea on the third afternoon. Both teams lost a point for a slow over-rate, but Warwickshire moved back to the top of Group One with their fourth straight victory. Derbyshire remained bottom, without a win.

Close of play: first day, Warwickshire 272-9 (Miles 15, Hannon-Dalby 0); second day, Warwickshire 132-7 (Briggs 6, Miles 0).

Warwickshire

*W. M. H. Rhodes c Godleman b Conners	8	– b Conners	3
R. M. Yates c Madsen b Conners	37	– b Reece	5
P. J. Malan b Conners	0	– c Guest b Cohen	0
S. R. Hain c Madsen b Reece	77	– lbw b Cohen	46
M. J. Lamb c Reece b Conners	7	– c Cohen b Aitchison	34
†M. G. K. Burgess c Guest b Cohen	71	– c Aitchison b Cohen	28
T. T. Bresnan c Madsen b Hughes	17	– c Madsen b Conners	7
D. R. Briggs c Guest b Aitchison	20	– c Guest b Cohen	12
C. N. Miles c Madsen b Cohen	17	– not out	12
L. C. Norwell c and b Reece	1	– c Conners	5
O. J. Hannon-Dalby not out	0	– c Aitchison b Cohen	0
Lb 15, nb 4	19	Lb 3	3

1/14 (1) 2/16 (3) 3/93 (2) (99.3 overs) 274
4/105 (5) 5/179 (4) 6/222 (7)
7/252 (6) 8/262 (8) 9/269 (10) 10/274 (9)

1/4 (1) 2/5 (3) (58 overs) 155
3/18 (2) 4/85 (5)
5/107 (4) 6/126 (7) 7/128 (6)
8/145 (8) 9/154 (10) 10/155 (11)

Conners 18–4–46–4; Cohen 17.3–3–44–2; Reece 14–3–25–2; Aitchison 13–2–56–1; Hughes 7–2–9–1; Dal 12–1–38–0; Critchley 18–1–41–0. *Second innings*—Conners 16–4–41–3; Cohen 16–2–43–5; Reece 7–2–25–1; Aitchison 11–2–32–1; Critchley 5–1–9–0; Hughes 3–1–2–0.

Derbyshire

L. M. Reece lbw b Hannon-Dalby	3	– c Burgess b Hannon-Dalby	0
*B. A. Godleman c Burgess b Miles	32	– c Bresnan b Hannon-Dalby	3
†B. D. Guest c Burgess b Norwell	23	– c Burgess b Miles	17
W. L. Madsen lbw b Miles	15	– c and b Rhodes	29
B. R. McDermott c Yates b Miles	2	– c Yates b Hannon-Dalby	21
M. J. J. Critchley c Burgess b Miles	5	– lbw b Hannon-Dalby	0
A. L. Hughes c Burgess b Norwell	4	– lbw b Rhodes	5
A. K. Dal c Bresnan b Norwell	0	– c Yates b Norwell	22
M. A. R. Cohen c Burgess b Miles	11	– st Burgess b Briggs	4
B. W. Aitchison c Bresnan b Norwell	0	– c Hannon-Dalby b Briggs	0
S. Conners not out	5	– not out	4
B 17, lb 4	21	B 8, lb 4	12

1/8 (1) 2/54 (2) 3/76 (4) (39.4 overs) 121
4/82 (5) 5/92 (6) 6/96 (3)
7/98 (8) 8/101 (7) 9/101 (10) 10/121 (9)

1/3 (2) 2/8 (1) (39.5 overs) 117
3/36 (3) 4/77 (4)
5/80 (6) 6/85 (5) 7/85 (7)
8/105 (9) 9/113 (8) 10/117 (10)

Hannon-Dalby 9–2–33–1; Norwell 13–3–24–4; Miles 11.4–5–30–5; Rhodes 3–1–3–0; Bresnan 3–2–10–0. *Second innings*—Hannon-Dalby 12–5–24–4; Norwell 11–2–43–1; Miles 11–3–25–1; Rhodes 4–1–11–2; Briggs 1.5–0–2–2.

Umpires: N. J. Llong and B. V. Taylor.   Referee: S. G. Hinks.

At Nottingham, July 4–6. DERBYSHIRE lost to NOTTINGHAMSHIRE by an innings and 36 runs.

DERBYSHIRE v ESSEX

At Derby, July 11–12. Drawn. Derbyshire 9pts, Essex 11pts. Toss: Derbyshire. Championship debut: J. D. S. Neesham.

The match was called off on the second morning after a Derbyshire player tested positive for Covid-19. The rest of the team were deemed close contacts, and all went into self-isolation. It was a tame end to Essex's faint hopes of retaining their Championship and Bob Willis Trophy titles. The ECB confirmed the result as a draw, though even a maximum-points win would not have earned

Essex a top-two finish in their group (and qualification for the first division). They had started well on an absorbing first day. Taking advantage of Critchley's decision to bat in overcast conditions – the floodlights were already on – they bagged full bowling points inside two sessions; 146 was Derbyshire's sixth consecutive total under 150. But, long before Essex could claim a batting point, the game reached its abrupt conclusion.

Close of play: first day, Essex 86-3 (Browne 28, Neesham 10).

Derbyshire

L. M. Reece lbw b Snater	16		F. J. Hudson-Prentice lbw b Neesham	11
T. A. Wood b S. J. Cook	2		M. A. R. Cohen not out	9
B. D. Guest b Porter	13		B. W. Aitchison c Harmer b Neesham	0
J. L. du Plooy lbw b Snater	43		Lb 6, w 3, nb 2	11
*M. J. J. Critchley lbw b S. J. Cook	9			
H. R. C. Came c Wheater b Harmer	7		1/8 (2) 2/25 (1) 3/31 (3)	(57.1 overs) 146
†H. R. Hosein c Wheater b Porter	12		4/59 (5) 5/78 (6) 6/97 (7)	
A. T. Thomson b Snater	13		7/119 (4) 8/128 (8) 9/141 (9) 10/146 (11)	

Porter 14–4–31–2; S. J. Cook 16–4–36–2; Snater 14–0–45–3; Neesham 4.1–0–15–2; Harmer 9–3–13–1.

Essex

N. L. J. Browne not out	28
A. N. Cook b Reece	30
*T. Westley c Hosein b Hudson-Prentice	1
M. S. Pepper c Guest b Hudson-Prentice	12
J. D. S. Neesham not out	10
Lb 4, w 1	5

1/37 (2) 2/45 (3)   (3 wkts, 38 overs)   86
3/63 (4)

R. N. ten Doeschate, †A. J. A. Wheater, S. R. Harmer, S. Snater, S. J. Cook and J. A. Porter did not bat.

Cohen 12–2–28–0; Hudson-Prentice 10–2–24–2; Aitchison 5–1–18–0; Reece 7–3–11–1; Critchley 4–3–1–0.

Umpires: N. A. Mallender and J. D. Middlebrook.   Referee: P. M. Such.

DIVISION THREE

At Lord's, August 30–September 2. DERBYSHIRE lost to MIDDLESEX by 112 runs.

DERBYSHIRE v LEICESTERSHIRE

At Derby, September 5–8. Drawn. Derbyshire 11pts, Leicestershire 13pts. Toss: Leicestershire. County debut: E. H. T. Moulton.

Derbyshire stared embarrassment in the face on the third morning: 56 for five in reply to Leicestershire's 528. Then Guest and Dal hit maiden hundreds while adding 227 – a county sixth-wicket record, beating 212 by Garnet Lee and Stan Worthington against Essex at Chesterfield in 1932. Even so, a total of 340 condemned them to follow on, 188 behind. But Godleman's unbeaten century, supported by Critchley, secured a draw. In the first five months of the season, Derbyshire had managed one first-class hundred; here, three different batsmen reached the landmark, the first time the county had achieved this since 2008 at Northampton. Leicestershire had also enjoyed batting in hot weather. Hill scored his second Championship century of the season after acting-captain Parkinson won the toss (Colin Ackermann was serving a one-match ban, after the team's seventh disciplinary offence in 12 months). Wright, whose dissent had triggered Ackermann's suspension, followed a career-best 87 as nightwatchman with his 500th first-class wicket, the start of Derbyshire's top-order collapse.

Close of play: first day, Leicestershire 282-3 (Hill 86, Wright 13); second day, Derbyshire 41-3 (Godleman 12, Critchley 9); third day, Derbyshire 313-8 (Conners 9, Aitchison 3).

Leicestershire

M. H. Azad c Madsen b Aitchison	25		*C. F. Parkinson c Aitchison b Critchley	1
S. T. Evans c Guest b Moulton	88		W. S. Davis not out	1
G. H. Rhodes b Critchley	54			
L. J. Hill c Guest b Aitchison	113		B 8, lb 12, nb 4	24
C. J. C. Wright st Guest b Thomson	87			
L. P. J. Kimber c Guest b Aitchison	0		1/52 (1) 2/127 (3)	(169.2 overs) 528
†H. J. Swindells c Critchley b Thomson	76		3/266 (2) 4/348 (4) 5/348 (6)	
B. W. M. Mike c and b Critchley	37		6/416 (5) 7/489 (8) 8/519 (7)	
E. Barnes c Aitchison b Thomson	22		9/523 (10) 10/528 (9)	110 overs: 322-3

Conners 24–6–68–0; Aitchison 28–6–71–3; Moulton 24–4–85–1; Critchley 45–5–144–3; Dal 21–4–56–0; Thomson 27.2–4–84–3.

Derbyshire

T. A. Wood c Swindells b Wright	13	– c Swindells b Wright	0
*B. A. Godleman c Swindells b Wright	14	– not out	100
J. L. du Plooy c Swindells b Davis	4	– c Swindells b Wright	10
W. L. Madsen c Swindells b Davis	2	– c Azad b Wright	21
M. J. J. Critchley b Mike	17	– not out	59
†B. D. Guest c Swindells b Parkinson	116		
A. K. Dal c Kimber b Mike	106		
A. T. Thomson lbw b Parkinson	10		
S. Conners c Kimber b Mike	9		
B. W. Aitchison lbw b Barnes	16		
E. H. T. Moulton not out	6		
B 5, lb 8, nb 14	27	B 4, lb 1, nb 8	13

1/18 (1) 2/23 (3) 3/31 (4)   (130.5 overs) 340   1/0 (1)   (3 wkts, 62.3 overs) 203
4/45 (2) 5/56 (5) 6/283 (7)   2/18 (3) 3/64 (4)
7/298 (8) 8/303 (6) 9/314 (9)
10/340 (10)   110 overs: 298-7

Wright 26–9–55–2; Davis 21–4–62–2; Mike 21–3–88–3; Barnes 22.5–5–56–1; Parkinson 29–16–34–2; Rhodes 8–1–17–0; Kimber 3–1–15–0. *Second innings*—Wright 9–0–36–3; Davis 8–0–17–0; Barnes 5–0–15–0; Mike 9–0–39–0; Parkinson 19.3–5–49–0; Rhodes 12–1–42–0.

Umpires: R. J. Bailey and I. N. Ramage.   Referee: T. J. Boon.

DERBYSHIRE v KENT

At Derby, September 12–15. Kent won by 130 runs. Kent 21pts, Derbyshire 3pts. Toss: Derbyshire.
    Kent rested key players ahead of the Blast finals the following weekend, lost a full day to rain, and still comfortably completed a third successive victory, just after tea on the last. Godleman had put them in after winning a favourable toss, but Derbyshire performed poorly in the first two sessions: Kent reached 237 for three, thanks to half-centuries from Crawley, who was dropped twice, Bell-Drummond and Leaning, before Conners and Aitchison mopped up the lower order. Stewart tightened Kent's hold with five cheap wickets, and Derbyshire were again grateful to Conners for a career-best 39 at No. 9, though he paid for it with an ankle injury which prevented him bowling in the second innings. The third-day washout sharpened Kent's sense of urgency: they ran up 64 in nine overs before declaring. But Derbyshire proved incapable of seeing out 85 overs. Only Dal's dogged unbeaten 58 and a flurry from Aitchison took them into the final session, as Gilchrist finished with seven wickets in the match.
    Close of play: first day, Derbyshire 1-1 (Godleman 0); second day, Kent 147-1 (Cox 58, Bell-Drummond 17); third day, no play.

Kent

Z. Crawley c Guest b Melton	53	– c Godleman b Dal	68
J. M. Cox b Aitchison	10	– c Guest b Critchley	81
D. J. Bell-Drummond c Madsen b Dal	69	– not out	51
J. A. Leaning not out	82	– not out	4
*S. W. Billings c and b Dal	36		
†O. G. Robinson st Guest b Critchley	1		
G. Stewart c Guest b Conners	16		
H. W. Podmore c Madsen b Aitchison	2		
N. N. Gilchrist c Aitchison b Conners	10		
J. E. G. Logan lbw b Aitchison	0		
J. Singh c Guest b Aitchison	0		
B 4, lb 1, w 1	6	B 4, w 3	7

1/16 (2) 2/119 (1) 3/142 (3) (91.5 overs) 285
4/237 (5) 5/242 (6) 6/266 (7)
7/269 (8) 8/284 (9) 9/285 (10) 10/285 (11)

1/114 (1) (2 wkts dec, 50 overs) 211
2/200 (2)

Conners 19–3–67–2; Aitchison 20.5–1–83–4; Melton 14–4–55–1; Dal 18–6–29–2; Critchley 15–2–38–1; du Plooy 5–1–8–0. *Second innings*—Aitchison 13–0–45–0; Dal 13–1–48–1; Melton 14–1–64–0; Critchley 9–0–48–1; du Plooy 1–0–2–0.

Derbyshire

H. R. C. Came b Stewart	1	– c Robinson b Stewart	11
*B. A. Godleman c Leaning b Gilchrist	31	– c Singh b Gilchrist	27
J. L. du Plooy c Leaning b Stewart	0	– lbw b Stewart	0
W. L. Madsen c Leaning b Gilchrist	14	– lbw b Podmore	13
M. J. J. Critchley c Robinson b Stewart	27	– c Crawley b Gilchrist	13
T. A. Wood b Stewart	0	– b Singh	14
†B. D. Guest lbw b Podmore	5	– c Robinson b Gilchrist	12
A. K. Dal c Leaning b Stewart	7	– not out	58
S. Conners c Bell-Drummond b Podmore	39	– (11) b Gilchrist	7
B. W. Aitchison c Bell-Drummond b Gilchrist	13	– (9) c Gilchrist b Singh	36
D. R. Melton not out	4	– (10) lbw b Podmore	1
Lb 3, nb 12	15	Lb 1, w 1, nb 16	18

1/1 (1) 2/1 (3) 3/29 (4) (43.3 overs) 156
4/71 (5) 5/73 (6) 6/80 (7)
7/93 (8) 8/134 (2) 9/148 (9) 10/156 (10)

1/27 (1) 2/27 (3) (58.5 overs) 210
3/55 (4) 4/55 (2)
5/85 (6) 6/89 (5) 7/102 (7)
8/172 (9) 9/175 (10) 10/210 (11)

Podmore 16–4–51–2; Stewart 13–7–23–5; Gilchrist 8.3–1–64–3; Singh 6–1–15–0. *Second innings*—Podmore 14–0–48–2; Stewart 9–1–45–2; Gilchrist 10.5–1–30–4; Singh 10–1–42–2; Logan 9–1–26–0; Leaning 5–1–16–0; Bell-Drummond 1–0–2–0.

Umpires: N. G. B. Cook and T. Lungley. Referee: T. J. Boon.

At Hove, September 21–23. DERBYSHIRE beat SUSSEX by nine wickets. *Derbyshire complete their only first-class win in the battle to avoid the wooden spoon.*

DURHAM

Two steps forward, one knock back

SIMON SINCLAIR

"If you asked us at the start of the year, we might have had a few doubts, but now we're realising that the club are back on track," said Durham's new captain, Scott Borthwick, summing up the optimism at Chester-le-Street after a promising 2021. They reached their first final in five years, and finished third in the second of three County Championship divisions – putting them in the top half of the 18 first-class counties. But, in October, the ECB announced that, after the Covid-dictated interlude of the past two seasons, the Championship would revert to two divisions in 2022 – and teams would be placed according to their performances in 2019. That year, Durham had finished fifth in Division Two, so there they remained.

It was a disappointing setback. Their run to the Royal London Cup final, along with an innings victory over eventual county champions Warwickshire, had shown the team were recovering from the sanctions that had derailed them after the 2016 season, imposed as part of an ECB financial bailout. There was still work ahead. In the one-day final, some players seemed overwhelmed by the occasion, and they lost to Glamorgan. The challenge for high performance coach James Franklin and director of cricket Marcus North was to build on the fightback, and reclaim a place in the county game's elite.

Talent from the North-East and further afield drove their progress, but one class act had seen Durham through it all. In May, Chris Rushworth succeeded his former new-ball partner Graham Onions as the county's leading first-class wicket-taker. Onions had surpassed the previous record-holder, Simon Brown, just before his departure in 2017, and Rushworth overtook his 527 during a resounding victory over Worcestershire. Unfortunately, it was the week before Covid restrictions were relaxed to allow spectators, so there was no crowd to cheer him on, though his father, Joe, embraced him on the boundary. Rushworth turned 35 in July, but showed no signs of slowing down, and passed 50 Championship wickets for the sixth time in his career. The records he sets may never be broken.

South African batsman David Bedingham had displayed flashes of his talent in the truncated 2020 summer, but this time fulfilled his promise in a marvellous season. He looked almost nonchalant at the crease, and in April the runs flowed with such ease that there was talk of 1,000 by the end of May. (A temporary falling-off, and the hiatus in the first-class programme, kept him waiting until September.) The highlight was a sumptuous 257 against Derbyshire, the county's second-best score after Martin Love's 273 in 2003. Bedingham did claim a record by adding an unbeaten 53 in the second innings, becoming the first Durham player to accumulate 300 in a single game. He also excelled in white-ball formats, drawing attention from a

David Bedingham

Will Matthews, MI News & Sport/Alamy

number of other counties. Given the exodus of talent after the ECB sanctions, it was a sign of Durham's improving fortunes that he remained loyal, signing a three-year extension to his contract that would keep him at Riverside until 2025.

Further evidence that the club could attract and retain quality had come when Borthwick returned, after four seasons with Surrey, to take up the captaincy of the first-class and 50-over sides. His red-ball form was up and down, but he was named the Most Valuable Player of the Royal London Cup, combining 260 runs with ten wickets. Borthwick's captaincy skills improved in leaps and bounds.

Australian Cameron Bancroft returned to lead the side in the Blast, where Durham finished seventh in their group. But he was less successful than New Zealand opener Will Young, who played in the early Championship rounds and contributed centuries to wins over Warwickshire and Worcestershire. Fellow opener Alex Lees scored 625 in the Championship and 562 in the Royal London Cup.

Durham have a proud tradition of fast bowlers: Stephen Harmison, Liam Plunkett, Mark Wood and Onions all rolled off their production line and into England shirts. Born in South Africa but England-qualified since 2019, Brydon Carse joined them: he made his international debut in July, after a Covid outbreak forced a reshuffle in the ranks for the one-day series with Pakistan. He helped England pull off a 3–0 win, taking five wickets in the last game, and was also knocking at the door of the Test team after claiming 34 at 21 in the Championship. Another Durham bowler who could enter the international arena is Matthew Potts, whose 16 wickets in the Blast earned him a contract with Northern Superchargers in The Hundred. He improved with the red ball, collecting eight wickets at Worcester and Northampton, where he also scored a career-best 81.

Cameron Steel moved to Surrey, initially on loan, and wicketkeeper Stuart Poynter left – after losing the gloves to Ned Eckersley – as did batter Jack Burnham. Former Gloucestershire off-spinner George Drissell signed in November, while Dutch seamer Paul van Meekeren, who played in the white-ball competitions, travelled the other way. In February, Durham signed Keegan Petersen, who had starred in South Africa's home Test win against India. He planned to be available for seven Championship fixtures, before his side's Test series against England in August.

Off the pitch, Durham continued to develop plans for a hotel within the Riverside ground, emulating Old Trafford and the Rose Bowl. This was first mooted before their fall from grace, but the club hoped their economic strategy had learned from those mistakes, and could build a sound structure that would allow Durham to compete in the upper echelons of the county game.

DURHAM RESULTS

County Championship matches – Played 13: Won 4, Lost 3, Drawn 6. Cancelled 1.
Vitality T20 Blast matches – Played 14: Won 5, Lost 8, No result 1.
Royal London Cup matches – Played 10: Won 7, Lost 2, No result 1.

LV= County Championship, 3rd in Group 1, 3rd in Division 2;
Vitality T20 Blast, 7th in North Group; Royal London Cup, finalists.

COUNTY CHAMPIONSHIP AVERAGES, BATTING AND FIELDING

Cap		Birthplace	M	I	NO	R	HS	100	Avge	Ct/St
2017	†L. Trevaskis	*Carlisle*	3	4	2	135	77*	0	67.50	2
2020	D. G. Bedingham††	*George, SA*	13	20	3	1,029	257	3	60.52	11
2021	W. A. Young¶	*New Plymouth, NZ*	4	7	0	278	124	2	39.71	1
2018	†A. Z. Lees	*Halifax*	11	17	1	625	129	1	39.06	6
2019	E. J. H. Eckersley	*Oxford*	13	18	1	520	113*	1	30.58	28/1
2017	M. J. Potts	*Sunderland‡*	7	9	2	206	81	0	29.42	3
2018	M. A. Jones††	*Ormskirk*	8	13	1	337	81	0	28.08	2
2015	G. Clark	*Whitehaven*	3	4	1	83	42	0	27.66	0
2015	J. T. A. Burnham	*Durham‡*	10	15	2	357	102*	1	27.46	3
2020	S. R. Dickson	*Johannesburg, SA*	3	4	1	79	46	0	26.33	0
2019	C. T. Bancroft¶	*Attadale, Australia*	5	8	1	183	46*	0	26.14	4
2011	†B. A. Raine	*Sunderland‡*	13	15	3	308	74	0	25.66	3
2009	†S. G. Borthwick	*Sunderland‡*	13	20	0	474	100	1	23.70	14
2016	B. A. Carse	*Port Elizabeth, SA*	8	9	2	161	40*	0	23.00	2
2012	P. Coughlin	*Sunderland‡*	4	5	0	89	48	0	17.80	3
2018	M. E. T. Salisbury	*Chelmsford*	4	5	0	75	41	0	15.00	0
2016	S. W. Poynter††	*Hammersmith*	6	8	2	85	52*	0	14.16	22
2010	C. Rushworth	*Sunderland‡*	13	13	6	91	31	0	13.00	3

Also batted: †B. A. Stokes§ (*Christchurch, NZ*) (cap 2010) (1 match) did not bat (1 ct); M. A. Wood§ (*Ashington*) (cap 2011) (3 matches) 17, 12, 1.

‡ *Born in Durham.* § *ECB contract.* ¶ *Official overseas player.* †† *Other non-England-qualified.*

Durham now award caps on first-class debut for the county.

BOWLING

	Style	O	M	R	W	BB	5I	Avge
C. Rushworth	RFM	435.3	125	1,073	59	6-49	3	18.18
B. A. Carse	RF	203.2	26	724	34	5-49	2	21.29
B. A. Raine	RFM	406.1	128	968	43	5-9	2	22.51
P. Coughlin	RFM	88.4	22	279	12	5-64	1	23.25
M. A. Wood	RF	79	19	233	10	3-28	0	23.30
M. J. Potts	RFM	204.3	51	613	23	4-32	0	26.65
M. E. T. Salisbury	RFM	142.4	38	440	16	4-74	0	27.50
S. G. Borthwick	LB	130.5	22	455	12	4-32	0	37.91

Also bowled: E. J. H. Eckersley (OB) 4–1–7–0; B. A. Stokes (RFM) 17–1–55–3; L. Trevaskis (SLA) 81.4–27–176–9.

LEADING VITALITY BLAST AVERAGES (100 runs/15 overs)

Batting	Runs	HS	Avge	SR	Ct
D. G. Bedingham	298	65	22.92	152.82	1
B. A. Carse	150	51	37.50	148.51	4
G. Clark	272	40	20.92	147.02	2
E. J. H. Eckersley	146	50*	24.33	130.35	5
S. R. Dickson	318	53	35.33	128.22	5
C. T. Bancroft	283	76*	25.72	119.91	6
B. A. Stokes	103	35	17.16	117.04	4
B. A. Raine	116	32	11.60	112.62	3

Bowling	W	BB	Avge	ER
L. Trevaskis	7	1-19	42.42	7.61
S. G. Borthwick	7	2-30	42.71	7.86
B. A. Raine	10	3-19	32.60	8.50
B. A. Carse	6	3-30	43.50	8.55
B. A. Stokes	8	4-27	21.12	8.89
M. J. Potts	16	3-27	26.50	9.15

LEADING ROYAL LONDON CUP AVERAGES (100 runs/4 wickets)

Batting	Runs	HS	Avge	SR	Ct/St	Bowling	W	BB	Avge	ER
G. Clark	646	141*	80.75	98.92	4	C. Rushworth	17	4-37	19.29	4.57
A. Z. Lees	562	126*	70.25	86.99	4	P. A. van Meekeren	14	3-33	22.14	5.53
S. R. Dickson	293	103*	58.60	113.12	2	L. Doneathy	8	4-36	37.50	6.61
S. G. Borthwick	260	76	43.33	79.02	10	J. O. I. Campbell	6	3-58	37.66	6.45
D. G. Bedingham	292	67	41.71	140.38	3	S. G. Borthwick	10	2-44	42.30	5.21
L. Doneathy	152	69*	38.00	116.03	5	L. Trevaskis	7	3-38	57.28	5.27
C. T. Bancroft	189	60*	31.50	105.00	9/1					

FIRST-CLASS COUNTY RECORDS

Highest score for	273	M. L. Love v Hampshire at Chester-le-Street.	2003
Highest score against	501*	B. C. Lara (Warwickshire) at Birmingham	1994
Leading run-scorer	12,030	P. D. Collingwood (avge 33.98).	1996–2018
Best bowling for	10-47	O. D. Gibson v Hampshire at Chester-le-Street	2007
Best bowling against	9-34	J. A. R. Harris (Middlesex) at Lord's.	2015
Leading wicket-taker	**564**	C. Rushworth (avge 22.22).	**2010–21**
Highest total for	648-5 dec	v Nottinghamshire at Chester-le-Street	2009
Highest total against	810-4 dec	by Warwickshire at Birmingham	1994
Lowest total for	61	v Leicestershire at Leicester.	2018
Lowest total against	18	by Durham MCCU at Chester-le-Street	2012

LIST A COUNTY RECORDS

Highest score for	164	B. A. Stokes v Nottinghamshire at Chester-le-St.	2014
Highest score against	174	J. M. Bairstow (Yorkshire) at Leeds.	2017
Leading run-scorer	6,007	P. D. Collingwood (avge 33.00).	1995–2018
Best bowling for	7-32	S. P. Davis v Lancashire at Chester-le-Street.	1983
Best bowling against	6-22	A. Dale (Glamorgan) at Colwyn Bay	1993
Leading wicket-taker	298	N. Killeen (avge 23.96)	1995–2010
Highest total for	**405-4**	**v Kent at Beckenham**	**2021**
Highest total against	361-7	by Essex at Chelmsford	1996
Lowest total for	72	v Warwickshire at Birmingham	2002
Lowest total against	63	by Hertfordshire at Darlington	1964

TWENTY20 COUNTY RECORDS

Highest score for	108*	P. D. Collingwood v Worcestershire at Worcester.	2017
Highest score against	127	T. Köhler-Cadmore (Worcs) at Worcester	2016
Leading run-scorer	3,206	P. Mustard (avge 25.04, SR 121.99)	2003–16
Best bowling for	5-6	P. D. Collingwood v Northants at Chester-le-St.	2011
Best bowling against	5-11	J. W. Shutt (Yorkshire) at Chester-le-Street	2019
Leading wicket-taker	93	G. R. Breese (avge 21.56, ER 6.76)	2004–14
Highest total for	225-2	v Leicestershire at Chester-le-Street	2010
Highest total against	225-6	by Worcestershire at Worcester	2016
Lowest total for	78	v Lancashire at Chester-le-Street	2018
Lowest total against	47	by Northamptonshire at Chester-le-Street	2011

ADDRESS

Emirates Riverside, Chester-le-Street, County Durham DH3 3QR; 0191 387 1717; reception@durhamcricket.co.uk; www.durhamcricket.co.uk. Twitter: @DurhamCricket.

OFFICIALS

Captain S. G. Borthwick
Director of cricket M. J. North
High performance coach J. E. C. Franklin
Academy director J. B. Windows

Chair Lord Botham
Chief executive T. J. Bostock
Head groundsman V. Demain
Scorer W. R. Dobson

GROUP ONE

At Nottingham, April 8–11. DURHAM drew with NOTTINGHAMSHIRE. *David Bedingham and Ned Eckersley add 254*, a Durham fifth-wicket record.*

At Chelmsford, April 15–18. DURHAM lost to ESSEX by 44 runs.

DURHAM v DERBYSHIRE

At Chester-le-Street, April 22–25. Drawn. Durham 14pts, Derbyshire 11pts. Toss: Durham. First-class debut: G. L. S. Scrimshaw.

Bedingham celebrated his 27th birthday with a century, converted a maiden double into Durham's second-highest score next day, and added an unbeaten fifty on the third, to finish with the highest individual match aggregate for the county. In the first three games of the season, he had accumulated 565 at 141. But neither Bedingham nor Rushworth, whose six-wicket assault on Derbyshire set up a 208-run first-innings lead, could secure Durham's first win of the season. Arriving in the third over, after Conners struck with successive balls, Bedingham shared three century partnerships – with Lees, Burnham and Eckersley – on his way to an outstanding 257. He fell 16 short of Martin Love's county record, against Hampshire in 2003, and his match total of 310 beat Michael Di Venuto's 293 against Sussex in 2009. Second time round, Borthwick declared late on the third evening, leaving Derbyshire to chase 384, or bat out the final day. Raine led the charge, but Madsen and Critchley shared a defiant stand of 138 to usher in the draw.

Close of play: first day, Durham 307-4 (Bedingham 170, Eckersley 18); second day, Derbyshire 148-5 (Madsen 76, Hosein 5); third day, Derbyshire 10-0 (Reece 8, Wood 2).

Durham

A. Z. Lees b Conners	39	– not out		78
W. A. Young c Madsen b Conners	1	– b Hudson-Prentice		21
*S. G. Borthwick lbw b Conners	0	– lbw b Critchley		15
D. G. Bedingham c Hosein b Conners	257	– not out		53
J. T. A. Burnham c Hosein b Critchley	75			
E. J. H. Eckersley lbw b Aitchison	34			
†S. W. Poynter c Guest b Scrimshaw	2			
P. Coughlin c Hosein b Hudson-Prentice	10			
B. A. Raine c Wood b Critchley	21			
M. E. T. Salisbury c Hosein b Conners	14			
C. Rushworth not out	11			
B 3, lb 7, w 1	11	B 6, lb 2		8

1/7 (2) 2/7 (3) 3/108 (1)   (147.4 overs) 475   1/36 (2)   (2 wkts dec, 44.5 overs) 175
4/242 (5) 5/351 (6) 6/368 (7)   2/83 (3)
7/398 (8) 8/429 (9) 9/458 (4)
10/475 (10)   110 overs: 343-4

Conners 24.4–4–83–5; Reece 24–9–59–0; Aitchison 18–3–50–1; Hudson-Prentice 20.4–6–59–1; Critchley 36–1–135–2; Scrimshaw 12–3–54–1; Madsen 12.2–3–25–0. *Second innings*—Conners 6–0–18–0; Reece 6–2–11–0; Aitchison 3–1–6–0; Hudson-Prentice 8–1–27–1; Madsen 9–1–37–0; Critchley 12.5–0–68–1.

Derbyshire

L. M. Reece c Poynter b Rushworth	15	– lbw b Borthwick	32
T. A. Wood b Rushworth	3	– b Raine	25
J. L. du Plooy lbw b Rushworth	0	– lbw b Raine	29
*W. L. Madsen c Burnham b Coughlin	76	– c Poynter b Raine	74
M. J. J. Critchley b Rushworth	40	– lbw b Coughlin	69
B. W. Aitchison b Raine	2		
†H. R. Hosein c Bedingham b Salisbury	63	– (6) not out	34
B. D. Guest c Poynter b Rushworth	37	– (7) not out	15
F. J. Hudson-Prentice b Salisbury	12		
S. Conners c Lees b Rushworth	0		
G. L. S. Scrimshaw not out	0		
B 6, lb 13	19	Lb 2	2

1/15 (2) 2/15 (3) 3/26 (1)   (83.1 overs) 267   1/41 (2)   (5 wkts, 97 overs) 280
4/132 (5) 5/137 (6) 6/148 (4)   2/75 (1) 3/93 (3)
7/231 (8) 8/266 (9) 9/267 (10) 10/267 (7)   4/231 (5) 5/233 (4)

Rushworth 22–6–58–6; Salisbury 16.1–4–64–2; Raine 23–6–56–1; Coughlin 17–4–49–1; Borthwick 5–0–21–0. *Second innings*—Rushworth 21–4–51–0; Salisbury 15–6–39–0; Raine 24–7–58–3; Coughlin 20–4–76–1; Borthwick 16–5–54–1; Eckersley 1–1–0–0.

Umpires: R. A. Kettleborough and N. A. Mallender.   Referee: W. M. Noon.

DURHAM v WARWICKSHIRE

At Chester-le-Street, April 29–May 1. Durham won by an innings and 127 runs. Durham 21pts, Warwickshire 1pt. Toss: Durham.
    Durham logged their first first-class win since September 2019, against group leaders Warwickshire, who had just beaten defending champions Essex. Rain delayed the start by an hour – then Raine (and Wood, making his first red-ball appearance for Durham since 2018) had Warwickshire in ruins at 30 for eight half an hour after lunch, though Miles and Norwell helped them reach 87. Raine finished with five for nine from 13 overs. By the close, openers Lees and Young had given Durham a one-run lead, and they went on to prove there were no demons in the pitch: a stand of 208 was a first-wicket record for this fixture. Though Bedingham failed, Carse and Wood pushed the lead past 300, before tormenting Warwickshire with their pace. Carse claimed five as the visitors were skittled again, subsiding inside three days. It was their heaviest defeat by Durham – who moved second in the group, a point behind Warwickshire.
    Close of play: first day, Durham 88-0 (Lees 41, Young 45); second day, Durham 287-4 (Lees 126, Eckersley 7).

Warwickshire

*W. M. H. Rhodes lbw b Raine	10	– c Bedingham b Wood	3
R. M. Yates b Wood	1	– c Borthwick b Rushworth	34
G. H. Vihari lbw b Raine	8	– lbw b Rushworth	0
S. R. Hain b Raine	1	– c Bedingham b Carse	21
M. J. Lamb b Wood	2	– b Carse	19
†M. G. K. Burgess b Raine	3	– c Poynter b Raine	27
T. T. Bresnan b Raine	1	– not out	39
D. R. Briggs c Rushworth b Wood	4	– c Lees b Carse	7
C. N. Miles c Borthwick b Carse	22	– b Carse	0
L. C. Norwell c Poynter b Carse	25	– b Carse	0
O. J. Hannon-Dalby not out	3	– c Borthwick b Rushworth	8
B 4, lb 3	7	B 4, lb 9, nb 6	19

1/6 (2) 2/18 (3) 3/19 (1)   (42.5 overs) 87   1/7 (1) 2/8 (3)   (67.3 overs) 177
4/22 (5) 5/22 (4) 6/25 (6)   3/58 (2) 4/82 (4)
7/30 (8) 8/30 (7) 9/82 (9) 10/87 (10)   5/93 (5) 6/127 (6) 7/141 (8)
                                                      8/149 (9) 9/149 (10) 10/177 (11)

Rushworth 10–2–28–0; Wood 12–2–28–3; Raine 13–8–9–5; Carse 7.5–3–15–2. *Second innings*—Rushworth 17.3–5–36–3; Wood 15–5–27–1; Raine 14–6–31–1; Carse 14–1–49–5; Borthwick 7–1–21–0.

Durham

A. Z. Lees c Bresnan b Norwell	129	B. A. Raine c and b Briggs	14
W. A. Young lbw b Norwell	124	M. A. Wood b Briggs	17
*S. G. Borthwick lbw b Miles	21	B 2, lb 10	12
D. G. Bedingham b Norwell	2		
J. T. A. Burnham lbw b Briggs	1	1/208 (2) (9 wkts dec, 145 overs)	391
E. J. H. Eckersley lbw b Hannon-Dalby	26	2/256 (3) 3/266 (4) 4/269 (5)	
†S. W. Poynter c Rhodes b Briggs	5	5/307 (1) 6/314 (7) 7/320 (6)	
B. A. Carse not out	40	8/341 (9) 9/391 (10) 110 overs: 272-4	

C. Rushworth did not bat.

Hannon-Dalby 36–11–69–1; Norwell 31–8–58–3; Miles 20–2–81–1; Bresnan 13–4–26–0; Rhodes 11–3–34–0; Briggs 31–6–93–4; Yates 3–0–18–0.

Umpires: M. A. Gough and R. J. Warren.   Referee: W. R. Smith.

DURHAM v WORCESTERSHIRE

At Chester-le-Street, May 13–16. Durham won by 258 runs. Durham 20pts, Worcestershire 4pts. Toss: Worcestershire.

Rushworth became Durham's leading first-class wicket-taker on his way to match figures of nine for 108, which secured a second successive win. He was kept waiting by rain on the final morning, and when play did start could not break Worcestershire's opening partnership. But in his next spell he found Haynes's edge; Bedingham held the catch at first slip to give Rushworth his 528th wicket for Durham, passing Graham Onions's 527. Covid restrictions meant the stands were empty but, after accepting his team-mates' congratulations, he was able to salute his father, watching from the health club car park, and go across to hug him at the end of the over. Then it was back to business: along with Wood and Carse, he worked through the line-up, before Borthwick completed victory. On the first day, Durham were inserted in overcast conditions, but Lees advanced to 99 before being caught behind just before tea. Next day, Rushworth took centre-stage, claiming a five-wicket haul – his 28th – to pull level with Onions, and bowl out Worcestershire, 33 behind. Young (in his last match before joining New Zealand) and Burnham scored second-innings centuries, while Eckersley blasted six sixes in a 57-ball 86, allowing Durham to declare for the third match running, and set a target of 423.

Close of play: first day, Worcestershire 6-0 (Mitchell 1, Libby 5); second day, Durham 79-1 (Young 37, Borthwick 24); third day, Worcestershire 60-0 (Mitchell 45, Libby 14).

Durham

A. Z. Lees c Cox b Leach	99	– b Morris	12
W. A. Young lbw b Leach	5	– lbw b Tongue	103
*S. G. Borthwick c Fell b Morris	4	– c Cox b Leach	27
D. G. Bedingham c Wessels b Morris	24	– c Cox b Tongue	33
J. T. A. Burnham lbw b Tongue	23	– not out	102
E. J. H. Eckersley b Tongue	0	– c D'Oliveira b Morris	86
†S. W. Poynter c Wessels b Barnard	1	– not out	7
B. A. Carse not out	38		
B. A. Raine b Tongue	8		
M. A. Wood b Tongue	12		
C. Rushworth b Tongue	2		
B 12, lb 14, w 2, nb 2	30	B 10, w 2, nb 2, p 5	19

1/23 (2) 2/36 (3) 3/86 (4)   (82.2 overs) 246   1/28 (1)   (5 wkts dec, 110.5 overs) 389
4/127 (5) 5/131 (6) 6/136 (7)   2/82 (3) 3/151 (4)
7/183 (1) 8/198 (9) 9/242 (10) 10/246 (11)   4/232 (2) 5/378 (6)

Leach 18–5–54–2; Barnard 19–8–45–1; Morris 17–4–61–2; Tongue 19.2–3–39–5; D'Oliveira 9–2–21–0. *Second innings*—Leach 23–4–52–1; Tongue 21–3–59–2; Barnard 22–8–56–0; Morris 23.5–5–114–2; Mitchell 7–3–20–0; D'Oliveira 14–0–73–0.

Worcestershire

D. K. H. Mitchell lbw b Rushworth	5	– c Burnham b Wood	62
J. D. Libby c Poynter b Raine	24	– lbw b Wood	36
T. C. Fell b Carse	44	– lbw b Carse	1
J. A. Haynes lbw b Rushworth	8	– c Bedingham b Rushworth	24
B. L. D'Oliveira lbw b Raine	10	– c Poynter b Wood	7
M. H. Wessels b Rushworth	13	– lbw b Rushworth	0
†O. B. Cox c Poynter b Wood	2	– lbw b Rushworth	11
E. G. Barnard lbw b Rushworth	2	– c Poynter b Carse	1
*J. Leach not out	42	– lbw b Rushworth	5
J. C. Tongue b Carse	17	– not out	12
C. A. J. Morris b Rushworth	21	– c Poynter b Borthwick	0
B 12, lb 9, nb 4	25	Lb 5	5

1/22 (1) 2/36 (2) 3/60 (4)   (69.4 overs) 213   1/79 (1) 2/89 (3)   (60.2 overs) 164
4/88 (5) 5/106 (3) 6/116 (6)   3/119 (4) 4/134 (5)
7/120 (8) 8/126 (7) 9/158 (10) 10/213 (11)   5/135 (6) 6/135 (2) 7/136 (8)
                                                            8/148 (9) 9/157 (7) 10/164 (11)

Rushworth 18.4–5–56–5; Wood 15–3–47–1; Raine 17–6–27–2; Carse 17–2–47–2; Borthwick 2–0–15–0. *Second innings*—Rushworth 20–6–52–4; Wood 14–3–47–3; Raine 10–3–16–0; Carse 9–0–34–2; Borthwick 7.2–1–10–1.

Umpires: M. A. Gough and S. J. O'Shaughnessy.   Referee: P. Whiticase.

At Derby, May 20–23. DURHAM drew with DERBYSHIRE.

DURHAM v ESSEX

At Chester-le-Street, May 27–29. Essex won by 195 runs. Essex 19pts, Durham 3pts. Toss: Durham.
    For the second time in 2021, Durham came out swinging at Essex, only for the champions to teach them a lesson. Riverside's first crowd since September 2019 saw the visitors bowled out for 182 – more than half of which came from Pepper, called up because Dan Lawrence had joined the Test squad. He batted three and a half hours, almost converting a maiden fifty into a century, before Rushworth and Raine removed the last five in 17 balls. But Durham were 58 for six by the close, and

---

MOST LBWs IN A FIRST-CLASS MATCH

20	West Indies v Pakistan at Providence	2010-11
20	Guyana v Jamaica at Providence	2019-20
19	Patiala v Delhi at Patiala	1953-54
19	Uttar Pradesh v Railways at Lucknow	2017-18
19	**Durham v Essex at Chester-le-Street**	**2021**

*There have been 11 instances of 18, six in the UK, including **Glamorgan v Sussex at Cardiff** in 2021.*

---

next day Porter, Sam Cook and Siddle finished them off for 99. The cascade of wickets continued as Essex slid to 53 for five, just 136 ahead. But ten Doeschate and Wheater restored their advantage in a clinical stand of 125, and Durham eventually faced a daunting chase of 385. They displayed more application second time round, but the Essex seamers' brilliance won the game in three days. There were 19 lbws in all, more than any previous UK fixture, and one short of the world record.
    Close of play: first day, Durham 58-6 (Eckersley 9); second day, Essex 263-8 (Harmer 30, S. J. Cook 11).

Essex

N. L. J. Browne b Potts	23	– lbw b Raine	6
A. N. Cook lbw b Rushworth	2	– b Rushworth	7
*T. Westley lbw b Raine	0	– lbw b Raine	1
M. S. Pepper lbw b Rushworth	92	– c Eckersley b Carse	16
P. I. Walter b Raine	28	– c Eckersley b Raine	22
R. N. ten Doeschate lbw b Borthwick	8	– lbw b Carse	55
†A. J. A. Wheater c Eckersley b Rushworth	8	– run out (Potts)	81
S. R. Harmer lbw b Raine	1	– not out	47
P. M. Siddle b Raine	1	– c Eckersley b Carse	5
S. J. Cook lbw b Rushworth	0	– lbw b Raine	22
J. A. Porter not out	0	– b Raine	0
B 5, lb 8, nb 6	19	B 21, lb 12, nb 6	39

1/25 (2) 2/33 (1) 3/40 (3) (62.2 overs) 182
4/104 (5) 5/139 (6) 6/179 (4)
7/180 (8) 8/182 (7) 9/182 (10) 10/182 (9)

1/13 (1) 2/15 (2) (89.5 overs) 301
3/15 (3) 4/53 (5)
5/53 (4) 6/178 (6) 7/231 (7)
8/242 (9) 9/285 (10) 10/301 (11)

Rushworth 16–7–32–4; Potts 17–4–45–1; Raine 14.2–2–45–4; Carse 11–1–30–0; Borthwick 4–1–17–1. *Second innings*—Rushworth 26–4–58–1; Potts 20–2–54–0; Raine 23.5–5–64–5; Carse 15–1–69–3; Borthwick 5–0–23–0.

Durham

C. T. Bancroft lbw b Siddle	20	– b Porter	4
A. Z. Lees lbw b Porter	0	– c Browne b ten Doeschate	48
*S. G. Borthwick lbw b S. J. Cook	8	– lbw b S. J. Cook	29
M. A. Jones lbw b S. J. Cook	4	– lbw b S. J. Cook	35
D. G. Bedingham b S. J. Cook	10	– b Porter	32
J. T. A. Burnham lbw b Siddle	2	– b Siddle	5
†E. J. H. Eckersley lbw b S. J. Cook	16	– b Siddle	6
B. A. Carse b Siddle	10	– b Porter	7
B. A. Raine not out	12	– c Wheater b Siddle	2
M. J. Potts c Wheater b Porter	8	– b Porter	11
C. Rushworth b Porter	0	– not out	5
B 4, lb 1, nb 4	9	Lb 5	5

1/1 (2) 2/33 (3) 3/33 (1) (47.4 overs) 99
4/37 (4) 5/40 (6) 6/58 (5)
7/79 (7) 8/79 (8) 9/99 (10) 10/99 (11)

1/8 (1) 2/47 (3) (87 overs) 189
3/104 (2) 4/137 (4)
5/151 (6) 6/161 (7) 7/170 (8)
8/171 (9) 9/173 (9) 10/189 (10)

Porter 12.4–5–27–3; S. J. Cook 21–11–38–4; Siddle 14.5–5–29–3. *Second innings*—Porter 19–9–31–4; S. J. Cook 19–7–39–2; Siddle 23–6–47–3; Harmer 23–9–57–0; ten Doeschate 3–0–10–1.

Umpires: J. D. Middlebrook and D. J. Millns.   Referee: T. J. Boon.

At Worcester, June 3–5. DURHAM beat WORCESTERSHIRE by ten wickets.

At Birmingham, July 4–7. DURHAM drew with WARWICKSHIRE.

DURHAM v NOTTINGHAMSHIRE

At Chester-le-Street, July 11–14. Drawn. Nottinghamshire 14pts, Durham 10pts (after 1pt penalty). Toss: Durham.

Nottinghamshire arrived confident of securing their place in Division One, while Durham – 15 points behind them and nine behind Warwickshire – still harboured their own hopes, and shortened the boundaries to the minimum allowed in an attempt to force victory. It was the visitors who capitalised, however, putting 328 on the board thanks to half-centuries from Slater and Patterson-White. Rain wiped out the second day, but Nottinghamshire were sure of their berth once Broad and Evison surged through the home batting (with Clarke becoming their fourth keeper in three Championship games). Evison claimed a maiden five-wicket haul and, by restricting Durham to 165, increased his side's advantage to an unbridgable 19 points. The final day was a damp squib, and a draw agreed an hour before the close; by then, Warwickshire had also drawn, ensuring Durham would be in Division Two. They did possess the group stage's leading run-scorer, Bedingham, with 945; among the wicket-takers, Rushworth's 46 put him second only to Nottinghamshire's Fletcher, who had 47.

Close of play: first day, Nottinghamshire 312-9 (Patterson-White 66, Fletcher 8); second day, no play; third day, Nottinghamshire 125-5 (Evison 4, Mullaney 0).

Nottinghamshire

B. T. Slater b Raine	60	– c Eckersley b Potts	19
H. Hameed b Rushworth	12	– b Borthwick	58
B. G. Compton c Borthwick b Rushworth	16	– c Jones b Salisbury	20
†J. M. Clarke b Salisbury	48	– c Bancroft b Potts	16
L. W. James b Raine	16	– b Salisbury	0
*S. J. Mullaney c Eckersley b Raine	39	– (7) b Potts	21
L. A. Patterson-White b Rushworth	73	– (8) c Raine b Borthwick	19
J. D. M. Evison lbw b Rushworth	8	– (6) c Raine b Salisbury	13
B. A. Hutton lbw b Potts	8	– b Salisbury	22
S. C. J. Broad c Potts b Salisbury	9	– c and b Borthwick	9
L. J. Fletcher not out	17	– not out	8
B 8, lb 2, nb 12	22	B 4, lb 2, nb 6	12

1/15 (2) 2/59 (3) 3/130 (1) (100.2 overs) 328
4/153 (4) 5/171 (5) 6/228 (6)
7/255 (8) 8/276 (9) 9/301 (10) 10/328 (7)

1/44 (2) 2/85 (3) (64.3 overs) 217
3/110 (4) 4/115 (5)
5/121 (6) 6/150 (7) 7/161 (6)
8/196 (9) 9/201 (8) 10/217 (10)

Rushworth 26.2–7–75–4; Potts 24–5–84–1; Salisbury 21–4–67–2; Raine 25–9–63–3; Borthwick 4–0–29–0. *Second innings*—Rushworth 15–2–54–0; Potts 18–4–55–3; Raine 13–6–28–0; Salisbury 13–3–42–3; Borthwick 5.3–1–32–4.

Durham

C. T. Bancroft lbw b Broad	0	– lbw b Broad	22
M. A. Jones lbw b Broad	5	– b Patterson-White	46
*S. G. Borthwick c Hutton b Evison	38	– c Clarke b James	25
D. G. Bedingham lbw b Evison	30	– b Mullaney	36
S. R. Dickson c Clarke b Evison	0	– not out	28
J. T. A. Burnham b Fletcher	23	– not out	5
†E. J. H. Eckersley lbw b Evison	0		
B. A. Raine c James b Evison	12		
M. J. Potts not out	27		
M. E. T. Salisbury c Hutton b Patterson-White	4		
C. Rushworth c Slater b Broad	5		
B 13, lb 2, nb 6	21	B 20, lb 4, nb 2	26

1/0 (1) 2/13 (2) 3/77 (4) (54.1 overs) 165
4/85 (5) 5/86 (3) 6/86 (7)
7/116 (8) 8/138 (6) 9/150 (10) 10/165 (11)

1/55 (1) (4 wkts, 55 overs) 188
2/112 (3) 3/136 (2)
4/174 (4)

Broad 12.1–2–36–3; Fletcher 13–5–34–1; James 16–6–14–0; Hutton 13–3–36–0; Evison 8–2–21–5; Patterson-White 2–1–9–1. *Second innings*—Broad 7–1–22–1; Fletcher 6–1–8–0; Hutton 6–0–30–0; Evison 4–1–9–0; Patterson-White 17–3–53–1; James 4–1–18–1; Mullaney 9–2–16–1; Slater 2–0–8–0.

Umpires: R. J. Bailey and N. Pratt. Referee: J. J. Whitaker.

DIVISION TWO

DURHAM v SURREY

At Chester-le-Street, August 30. Cancelled.

Two days before the scheduled start, Surrey announced that a player had tested positive for Covid. As "a significant number" of their squad were close contacts, and required to self-isolate, it was decided the fixture could not go ahead. In accordance with the tournament regulations, the ECB announced that rankings in Division Two would be determined by average points per completed match.

DURHAM v GLAMORGAN

At Chester-le-Street, September 5–8. Durham won by an innings and 42 runs. Durham 24pts, Glamorgan 2pts. Toss: Durham. County debut: E. J. Byrom.

Three weeks after losing the Royal London Cup final to Glamorgan, Durham dominated this encounter so thoroughly that they leapt from the bottom of the division to joint-second. On the opening day, they skittled the visitors for 97 – the lowest total in this fixture – with Coughlin, on his return after a thigh injury, collecting four wickets in 23 balls. Durham were in the lead by tea, and marched on to 503, their highest total of 2021, with seven scores of 46 or more, but no hundreds: Jones's 81 was the lowest top-score in a Championship innings of 500-plus. Glamorgan resumed needing 406 to make them bat again. Douthwaite and Salter mustered 163 for the seventh wicket, but only delayed defeat until the fourth morning. Rushworth became the second bowler to reach 50 first-class wickets in the season; Coughlin completed victory with the 100th of his career, as five more gave him nine for 75 in the match.

Close of play: first day, Durham 223-3 (Bedingham 44, Dickson 4); second day, Glamorgan 71-2 (Rutherford 32, Byrom 17); third day, Glamorgan 333-7 (Salter 82, van der Gugten 7).

Glamorgan

H. D. Rutherford c Coughlin b Rushworth	43	– c Lees b Rushworth	71
D. L. Lloyd lbw b Rushworth	4	– c Trevaskis b Potts	6
N. J. Selman c Coughlin b Raine	15	– c Eckersley b Coughlin	4
E. J. Byrom c Eckersley b Rushworth	3	– b Coughlin	17
K. S. Carlson lbw b Coughlin	17	– b Raine	14
*†C. B. Cooke lbw b Coughlin	3	– c Eckersley b Coughlin	5
D. A. Douthwaite b Coughlin	0	– c Potts b Trevaskis	96
A. G. Salter c Eckersley b Raine	2	– c Eckersley b Coughlin	90
T. van der Gugten b Raine	0	– not out	26
L. J. Carey c Rushworth b Coughlin	6	– b Rushworth	0
M. G. Hogan not out	1	– c Eckersley b Coughlin	4
Lb 3	3	B 15, lb 12, nb 4	31

1/9 (2) 2/63 (1) 3/63 (3)   (32 overs) 97
4/73 (4) 5/79 (6) 6/79 (7)
7/86 (8) 8/86 (9) 9/90 (5) 10/97 (10)

1/20 (2) 2/38 (3)   (130 overs) 364
3/99 (4) 4/128 (1)
5/128 (5) 6/151 (6) 7/314 (7)
8/358 (8) 9/359 (10) 10/364 (11)

Rushworth 10–4–26–3; Potts 9–2–32–0; Raine 8–3–25–3; Coughlin 5–1–11–4. *Second innings—* Rushworth 30–9–86–2; Potts 27–6–85–1; Coughlin 23–7–64–5; Raine 25–9–62–1; Trevaskis 15–3–25–1; Borthwick 10–4–15–0.

Durham

A. Z. Lees lbw b Hogan	55	L. Trevaskis not out	55
M. A. Jones c Cooke b van der Gugten	81	M. J. Potts not out	26
*S. G. Borthwick c Lloyd b van der Gugten	29	B 4, lb 4, w 1, nb 4	13
D. G. Bedingham b Hogan	47		
S. R. Dickson b Hogan	46	1/119 (1)　(8 wkts dec, 131.1 overs)	503
†E. J. H. Eckersley c Selman b Carey	57	2/172 (3) 3/203 (2)	
P. Coughlin c Selman b van der Gugten	20	4/234 (4) 5/315 (5) 6/335 (6)	
B. A. Raine c Byrom b Salter	74	7/361 (7) 8/459 (8)　110 overs: 401-7	

C. Rushworth did not bat.

Hogan 28–5–80–3; Carey 20–1–75–1; van der Gugten 27–5–82–3; Douthwaite 16–0–95–0; Lloyd 18.1–2–62–0; Salter 22–1–101–1.

Umpires: I. D. Blackwell and N. Pratt.　Referee: S. G. Hinks.

At Northampton, September 12–15. DURHAM drew with NORTHAMPTONSHIRE.

At Bristol, September 21–22. DURHAM lost to GLOUCESTERSHIRE by seven wickets.

ESSEX

All that glitters…

P A U L   H I S C O C K

Essex had a frustrating summer, despite winning their sixth trophy in six years. They had lifted the County Championship in 2019, but missed out on the chance to defend the title when they failed to navigate the conference system. Consigned to Division Two for the business end of the season, they won three of their four matches by an innings, and might have beaten Surrey, too, but for a third-day washout. Essex thus collected the second-tier trophy, but the players were not particularly delighted. "We didn't feel great taking a photo next to the Division Two champions board," said Dan Lawrence, captain in the final match. "It isn't something we will celebrate. We're a club who want to be winning Division One."

Only two red-ball games were lost – away to Warwickshire and Nottinghamshire, who both qualified for the first division – but six were drawn, including the last group game, at Derby, which was called off on the second day after a Covid outbreak.

Sam Cook was Essex's bowler of the summer. He allied consistency to an extra yard of pace and, moving the ball in the air and off the pitch, mopped up 58 wickets – five more than Simon Harmer, who continued to torment opposing batsmen with his off-breaks, and returned a career-best nine for 80 against Derbyshire, at Chelmsford in May. There was general relief when he signed a new four-year deal in December. The following month, he was named in South Africa's Test squad, more than six years after his last cap.

Dutch international Shane Snater grew in stature after taking over as third seamer when Peter Siddle returned to Australia in June, citing personal reasons. Snater collected 31 wickets, and provided important support for the reliable new-ball pair of Cook and Jamie Porter.

In nine of their 14 Championship matches, Essex had just one visit to the crease. The classy Lawrence led the way with 640 runs between international commitments, and staked a claim for a regular England place. Alastair Cook, long retired from Test duty, occasionally shone, not least during a wonderful 165 at The Oval. He carries on, and a reasonable summer should see him reach 10,000 first-class runs for Essex. In all, there were seven centuries; regular skipper Tom Westley scored three, but otherwise did little. The improving Paul Walter made several important middle-order contributions, although he fell tantalisingly short of a maiden century when dismissed for 96 against Gloucestershire in September. Adam Wheater was consistent behind the stumps, and chipped in with valuable runs.

In white-ball cricket, Essex reached the semi-final of the Royal London Cup before losing to the eventual winners, Glamorgan. Harmer took 18 wickets, and hit three late sixes to secure a dramatic tie at Old Trafford, and qualification

Justin Setterfield, Getty Images

Sam Cook

from the group stage. There was a return to bowling form for 41-year-old Ryan ten Doeschate, who claimed 15 at less than 20 with his medium-pacers. In September, the popular ten Doeschate, captain for the 2017 and 2019 Championship wins, announced his retirement from county cricket after 19 seasons at Chelmsford, and joined Kent as batting coach.

Alastair Cook made 415 runs at 51 in the Royal London – only the Durham pair of Graham Clark and Alex Lees scored more – while Westley had 413 at 52. Essex gleaned most satisfaction, however, from the emergence of Josh Rymell and Feroze Khushi, who both struck precocious maiden centuries. Rymell, just 20, hit a superb 121 in the quarter-final to set up a total that proved far beyond Yorkshire, while Khushi, two years older, made 109 in the group game against Durham at Riverside.

The batting was less impressive in the T20 Blast, and Essex finished seventh in their group, with only five victories. The bowling was better: Harmer and Aron Nijjar were a strong spin combination, while Sam Cook's 20 wickets helped earn him a wild-card call-up for Trent Rockets in The Hundred.

Varun Chopra, who had two spells with Essex, retired after failing to make a first-team appearance for them in 2021, while seamer Matt Quinn joined Kent, after finding his opportunities limited by youngsters Ben Allison and Jack Plom. The batting was strengthened by the acquisition of the hard-hitting Matt Critchley, who also bowls leg-spin, from Derbyshire.

Off the field, discontent rumbled on all season. Ronnie Irani, a former club captain, stepped down as cricket committee chairman in August, ostensibly to concentrate on his business interests (he also left the board in October). His constant presence around the dressing-room had not been popular with the first team or the coaching staff, especially after he alleged there was a drinking culture within the squad – which they vehemently denied.

Former Essex batsman John Stephenson returned to Chelmsford as chief executive in October, after 17 years with MCC at Lord's. He was almost immediately faced with a crisis when John Faragher, the chairman, resigned following allegations he had used racist language at a board meeting four years previously, which he too denied. The board subsequently announced an inquiry into why the original incident – and others of alleged racism levelled by former players Jahid Ahmed, Maurice Chambers and Zoheb Sharif – was not properly investigated at the time. Katharine Newton QC was appointed to lead the independent probe. "There is no place for discrimination of any kind at Essex," said Stephenson. "This is a proud club with a zero-tolerance policy towards racism." But in February, the ECB charged them with bringing the game into disrepute, leaving the case in the hands of the Cricket Discipline Commission.

ESSEX RESULTS

County Championship matches – Played 14: Won 6, Lost 2, Drawn 6.
Vitality T20 Blast matches – Played 14: Won 5, Lost 8, No result 1.
Royal London Cup matches – Played 10: Won 6, Lost 3, Tied 1.

LV= County Championship, 4th in Group 1, winners of Division 2;
Vitality T20 Blast, 7th in South Group; Royal London Cup, semi-finalists.

COUNTY CHAMPIONSHIP AVERAGES, BATTING AND FIELDING

Cap		Birthplace	M	I	NO	R	HS	100	Avge	Ct/St
2017	D. W. Lawrence	Leytonstone‡	10	13	1	640	152*	1	53.33	8
2013	T. Westley	Cambridge	13	18	1	631	213	3	37.11	5
	†P. I. Walter	Basildon‡	13	16	1	544	96	0	36.26	5
2005	†A. N. Cook	Gloucester	14	19	0	611	165	2	32.15	16
2015	†N. L. J. Browne	Leytonstone‡	14	19	2	524	102	1	30.82	6
	M. S. Pepper	Harlow‡	6	7	0	204	92	0	29.14	3
2020	A. J. A. Wheater	Leytonstone‡	14	16	0	434	87	0	27.12	23/4
2018	S. R. Harmer¶	Pretoria, SA	14	16	4	317	82*	0	26.41	14
2006	R. N. ten Doeschate††	Port Elizabeth, SA . .	10	12	0	314	56	0	26.16	9
	S. Snater††	Harare, Zimbabwe . .	9	8	2	99	48	0	16.50	1
2015	J. A. Porter	Leytonstone‡	12	13	7	73	30	0	12.16	1
2020	S. J. Cook	Chelmsford‡	13	13	2	126	37	0	11.45	1
2021	P. M. Siddle¶	Traralgon, Australia .	9	2	2	70	20	0	10.00	1

Also batted: B. M. J. Allison (*Colchester‡*) (2 matches) 13, 4, 52 (1 ct); †J. D. S. Neesham¶ (*Auckland, NZ*) (1 match) 10*; †A. S. S. Nijjar (*Goodmayes‡*) (1 match) 2; J. S. Rymell (*Ipswich*) (3 matches) 0, 14, 9 (2 ct).

‡ *Born in Essex.*   ¶ *Official overseas player.*   †† *Other non-England-qualified.*

BOWLING

	Style	O	M	R	W	BB	5I	Avge
S. J. Cook	RFM	382.2	128	837	58	5-20	3	14.43
S. Snater	RM	168.5	42	511	31	7-98	2	16.48
S. R. Harmer	OB	558.4	182	1,233	53	9-80	5	23.26
P. M. Siddle	RFM	176.2	37	488	20	6-38	1	24.40
J. A. Porter	RFM	299.4	73	842	34	4-31	0	24.76

Also bowled: B. M. J. Allison (RFM) 36–7–94–1; A. N. Cook (OB) 1–0–5–0; D. W. Lawrence (OB) 49.1–7–155–5; J. D. S. Neesham (RFM) 4.1–0–15–2; A. S. S. Nijjar (SLA) 13–5–21–0; R. N. ten Doeschate (RM) 9–0–35–1; P. I. Walter (LM) 34–4–120–2; T. Westley (OB) 10–1–12–0.

LEADING VITALITY BLAST AVERAGES (100 runs/15 overs)

Batting	Runs	HS	Avge	SR	Ct/St	Bowling	W	BB	Avge	ER
D. W. Lawrence	252	60	42.00	145.66	4	A. S. S. Nijjar . . .	13	2-19	26.69	6.87
J. D. S. Neesham	189	53	17.18	135.00	7	S. R. Harmer . . .	19	4-24	18.31	7.40
A. J. A. Wheater	209	49	20.90	133.12	7/5	S. J. Cook	20	4-15	18.25	7.82
M. S. Pepper . . .	260	55*	26.00	131.31	7	J. D. S. Neesham .	5	2-11	47.60	8.50
S. R. Harmer . . .	109	31	18.16	129.76	6	J. A. Porter.	2	1-19	80.00	10.00
T. Westley.	198	53	28.28	124.52	0	J. H. Plom	9	3-31	29.11	10.91
W. E. L. Buttleman	158	56*	19.75	119.69	2/1					
P. I. Walter	120	45	13.33	115.38	5					

LEADING ROYAL LONDON CUP AVERAGES (100 runs/4 wickets)

Batting	Runs	HS	Avge	SR	Ct/St
A. N. Cook	455	110	56.87	87.66	5
J. S. Rymell. . . .	331	121	55.16	71.95	4
T. Westley.	415	87*	51.87	85.56	4
F. I. N. Khushi .	234	109	46.80	86.98	2
A. S. S. Nijjar . .	115	32*	38.33	127.77	3
S. R. Harmer . . .	134	32*	33.50	112.60	8
P. I. Walter	157	50	31.40	98.74	3
A. J. A. Wheater	211	77	30.14	119.88	10/2
R. N. ten Doeschate	113	45	14.12	79.02	4

Bowling	W	BB	Avge	ER
S. R. Harmer	18	3-42	19.55	3.62
R. N. ten Doeschate	15	4-34	19.60	4.95
S. Snater	13	4-48	21.69	5.35
T. Westley	8	3-33	25.50	4.43
A. S. S. Nijjar	12	2-26	37.58	5.17
J. H. Plom	6	3-34	40.50	6.62
B. M. J. Allison . .	7	2-33	50.14	6.13

FIRST-CLASS COUNTY RECORDS

Highest score for	343*	P. A. Perrin v Derbyshire at Chesterfield		1904
Highest score against	332	W. H. Ashdown (Kent) at Brentwood		1934
Leading run-scorer	30,701	G. A. Gooch (avge 51.77)		1973–97
Best bowling for	10-32	H. Pickett v Leicestershire at Leyton		1895
Best bowling against	10-40	E. G. Dennett (Gloucestershire) at Bristol		1906
Leading wicket-taker	1,610	T. P. B. Smith (avge 26.68)		1929–51
Highest total for	761-6 dec	v Leicestershire at Chelmsford		1990
Highest total against	803-4 dec	by Kent at Brentwood		1934
Lowest total for	20	v Lancashire at Chelmsford		2013
Lowest total against	14	by Surrey at Chelmsford		1983

LIST A COUNTY RECORDS

Highest score for	201*	R. S. Bopara v Leicestershire at Leicester		2008
Highest score against	158*	M. W. Goodwin (Sussex) at Chelmsford		2006
Leading run-scorer	16,536	G. A. Gooch (avge 40.93)		1973–97
Best bowling for	8-26	K. D. Boyce v Lancashire at Manchester		1971
Best bowling against	7-29	D. A. Payne (Gloucestershire) at Chelmsford		2010
Leading wicket-taker	616	J. K. Lever (avge 19.04)		1968–89
Highest total for	391-5	v Surrey at The Oval		2008
Highest total against	373-5	v Nottinghamshire at Chelmsford		2017
Lowest total for	57	v Lancashire at Lord's		1996
Lowest total against	41	by Middlesex at Westcliff-on-Sea		1972
	41	by Shropshire at Wellington		1974

TWENTY20 COUNTY RECORDS

Highest score for	152*	G. R. Napier v Sussex at Chelmsford.		2008
Highest score against	153*	L. J. Wright (Sussex) at Chelmsford		2014
Leading run-scorer	3,471	**R. N. ten Doeschate (avge 27.76, SR 135.79)**		**2003–21**
Best bowling for	6-16	T. G. Southee v Glamorgan at Chelmsford		2011
Best bowling against	5-11	Mushtaq Ahmed (Sussex) at Hove.		2005
	5-11	T. G. Helm (Middlesex) at Lord's		2017
Leading wicket-taker	126	R. S. Bopara (avge 25.66, ER 7.57)		2003–19
Highest total for	242-3	v Sussex at Chelmsford		2008
Highest total against	**236-3**	**by Kent at Canterbury.**		**2021**
Lowest total for	74	v Middlesex at Chelmsford		2013
Lowest total against	82	by Gloucestershire at Chelmsford		2011

ADDRESS

The Cloud County Ground, New Writtle Street, Chelmsford CM2 0PG; 01245 252420; questions@essexcricket.org.uk; www.essexcricket.org.uk. Twitter: @EssexCricket.

OFFICIALS

Captain T. Westley
(Twenty20) S. R. Harmer
Head coach A. McGrath
Academy director B. Hyam

President D. L. Acfield
**Chief executive
and interim chair** J. P. Stephenson
Head groundsman S. G. Kerrison
Scorer A. E. Choat

GROUP ONE

ESSEX v WORCESTERSHIRE

At Chelmsford, April 8–11. Drawn. Essex 13pts, Worcestershire 12pts. Toss: Essex. County debut: G. H. Roderick.

The pitch proved benign, despite the early April start, and two marathon innings ensured the draw which ended Essex's run of 11 home wins in red-ball cricket. First Westley timed the ball well, especially on his favoured leg side, collecting 32 fours in a nine-hour 213. It was his second double-century (after 254, also against Worcestershire, in 2016), and more than he had managed in the entire Bob Willis Trophy season in 2020. He shared several useful stands, the biggest 157 for the sixth wicket with Wheater. Sam Cook reduced Worcestershire to 32 for three on the second evening, then added a fourth next morning, all without cost in 12 balls. But Libby proved unshiftable. He batted for 11 hours 21 minutes, the longest Championship innings since Jason Gallian (312) lasted two minutes longer for Lancashire against Derbyshire at Old Trafford in 1996; he became the first Worcestershire player to carry his bat since Daryl Mitchell in 2015, and spent the entire match on the field. Barnard survived almost five and a half hours, and scored a maiden century, helping Libby put on 244, a seventh-wicket record for this fixture. They were not separated until lunch was looming on the fourth day; before Pennington's maiden fifty rubber-stamped the draw.

Close of play: first day, Essex 207-3 (Westley 84, Walter 26); second day, Worcestershire 43-3 (Libby 21, D'Oliveira 6); third day, Worcestershire 350-6 (Libby 141, Barnard 116).

Essex

N. L. J. Browne c Libby b Barnard	26	– not out	7
A. N. Cook lbw b Morris	15	– b Leach	12
*T. Westley c Barnard b D'Oliveira	213	– not out	8
D. W. Lawrence lbw b Barnard	46		
P. I. Walter c Mitchell b Barnard	38		
R. N. ten Doeschate lbw b D'Oliveira	30		
†A. J. A. Wheater c Barnard b D'Oliveira	87		
S. R. Harmer lbw b Morris	1		
B. M. J. Allison c Libby b Morris	13		
S. J. Cook not out	2		
B 4, lb 6, w 1, nb 8	19	Lb 1	1

1/30 (2) 2/57 (1) (9 wkts dec, 157.4 overs) 490   1/17 (2) (1 wkt, 10 overs) 28
3/130 (4) 4/254 (5)
5/304 (6) 6/461 (3) 7/465 (8)
8/487 (9) 9/490 (7)   110 overs: 305-5

J. A. Porter did not bat.

Leach 29–5–90–0; Pennington 27–3–91–0; Morris 27–5–95–3; Barnard 27–6–67–3; D'Oliveira 36.4–6–95–3; Mitchell 4–0–20–0; Libby 7–0–22–0. *Second innings*—Leach 4–1–14–1; Pennington 4–1–9–0; Barnard 1–1–0–0; Morris 1–0–4–0.

Worcestershire

D. K. H. Mitchell b S. J. Cook	16	D. Y. Pennington st Wheater b Harmer	56
J. D. Libby not out	180	C. A. J. Morris lbw b Harmer	6
T. C. Fell c Harmer b S. J. Cook	0		
G. H. Roderick c Westley b S. J. Cook	0	B 2, lb 15, nb 4	21
B. L. D'Oliveira lbw b S. J. Cook	6		
M. H. Wessels lbw b Porter	54	1/32 (1) 2/32 (3) 3/32 (4) (177.3 overs) 475
†O. B. Cox lbw b Harmer	7	4/43 (5) 5/132 (6) 6/145 (7)
E. G. Barnard b Lawrence	128	7/389 (8) 8/390 (9) 9/465 (10)
*J. Leach c Wheater b Allison	1	10/475 (11) 110 overs: 316-6

Porter 31–4–99–1; S. J. Cook 37–10–100–4; Harmer 61.3–20–126–3; Lawrence 10–1–30–1; Allison 25–6–67–1; Walter 9–1–31–0; Westley 4–0–5–0.

Umpires: N. A. Mallender and D. J. Millns.   Referee: A. J. Swann.

ESSEX v DURHAM

At Chelmsford, April 15–18. Essex won by 44 runs. Essex 19pts, Durham 5pts. Toss: Essex. County debut: W. A. Young.

Essex returned to winning ways, but only after they were skittled for 96 – their lowest against Durham – as the ball nibbled around on the first day, which featured 18 wickets in all. The only batting highlight was a superb century from Borthwick, with 15 crisp fours; next day, Poynter and Salisbury stretched their ninth-wicket stand to 94 and Durham's lead to 163. Essex were just one in front when ten Doeschate was fifth out on the second evening, but Walter and Allison scored maiden Championship fifties, and Sam Cook dug in for two hours, equalling his career-best, before becoming a fifth victim for the lively Carse. Durham eventually needed 168, but lost the openers for ducks, the New Zealander Will Young going first ball. Borthwick and Burnham fought to the third-day close, but Harmer – who had warmed up with five first-innings wickets – removed them both in four balls next morning. That prised open the door: Durham had been 83 for three, but slumped to 123 all out, Harmer finishing with his 22nd five-wicket haul for Essex, and his sixth ten-for.

Close of play: first day, Durham 148-8 (Poynter 3, Salisbury 3); second day, Essex 208-6 (Walter 49, Harmer 6); third day, Durham 60-3 (Borthwick 9, Burnham 31).

Essex

N. L. J. Browne b Rushworth	0	– b Rushworth	4
A. N. Cook lbw b Rushworth	6	– c Burnham b Salisbury	12
*T. Westley c Poynter b Salisbury	4	– c Bedingham b Carse	38
D. W. Lawrence b Salisbury	32	– c Young b Carse	76
P. I. Walter b Carse	7	– c Poynter b Carse	77
R. N. ten Doeschate c Eckersley b Carse	4	– c and b Borthwick	16
†A. J. A. Wheater b Raine	18	– c Poynter b Borthwick	6
S. R. Harmer c Bedingham b Raine	0	– lbw b Raine	6
B. M. J. Allison c Poynter b Rushworth	4	– lbw b Carse	52
S. J. Cook c Bedingham b Carse	15	– c Poynter b Carse	37
J. A. Porter not out	1	– not out	3
Lb 1, nb 4	5	Lb 3	3

1/0 (1) 2/7 (3) 3/15 (2)   (41.3 overs) 96
4/32 (5) 5/36 (6) 6/74 (7)
7/74 (4) 8/76 (8) 9/82 (9) 10/96 (10)

1/6 (1) 2/19 (2)   (122.2 overs) 330
3/122 (3) 4/139 (4)
5/164 (6) 6/180 (7) 7/208 (8)
8/266 (5) 9/319 (9) 10/330 (10)

Rushworth 11–8–13–3; Salisbury 11–4–25–2; Raine 12–5–20–2; Carse 7.3–1–37–3. *Second innings*—Rushworth 24–5–55–1; Salisbury 27–7–67–1; Raine 25–7–67–1; Carse 27.2–3–82–5; Borthwick 17–1–52–2; Eckersley 2–0–4–0.

Durham

A. Z. Lees c Wheater b S. J. Cook	5	– lbw b Porter	0
W. A. Young c Lawrence b Harmer	24	– b S. J. Cook	0
*S. G. Borthwick b Lawrence	100	– c Westley b Harmer	24
D. G. Bedingham c Westley b Harmer	0	– c Allison b S. J. Cook	18
J. T. A. Burnham b S. J. Cook	1	– c Westley b Harmer	43
E. J. H. Eckersley c A. N. Cook b Harmer	4	– c Lawrence b Harmer	13
†S. W. Poynter not out	52	– lbw b S. J. Cook	1
B. A. Carse b Lawrence	0	– (9) lbw b Harmer	15
B. A. Raine c A. N. Cook b Harmer	1	– (8) lbw b Harmer	3
M. E. T. Salisbury c ten Doeschate b Harmer	41	– b Porter	2
C. Rushworth c A. N. Cook b S. J. Cook	15	– not out	2
B 8, lb 8	16	Lb 2	2

1/11 (1) 2/98 (2) 3/104 (4)   (82.3 overs) 259
4/114 (5) 5/141 (6) 6/143 (3)
7/143 (8) 8/144 (9) 9/238 (10) 10/259 (11)

1/0 (2) 2/0 (1)   (56.4 overs) 123
3/20 (4) 4/83 (5)
5/87 (3) 6/88 (7) 7/91 (8)
8/108 (6) 9/121 (9) 10/123 (10)

Porter 15–2–59–0; S. J. Cook 20.3–6–57–3; Allison 6–0–20–0; Harmer 34–12–79–5; Lawrence 7–1–28–2. *Second innings*—Porter 13.4–5–33–2; S. J. Cook 13–6–17–3; Harmer 24–8–57–5; Allison 5–1–7–0; Lawrence 1–0–7–0.

Umpires: P. J. Hartley and B. V. Taylor.   Referee: W. M. Noon.

At Birmingham, April 22–25. ESSEX lost to WARWICKSHIRE by seven wickets. *Essex's first defeat in 22 matches.*

At Worcester, April 29–May 2. ESSEX drew with WORCESTERSHIRE.

At Nottingham, May 6–9. ESSEX lost to NOTTINGHAMSHIRE by an innings and 30 runs. *Shane Snater takes a career-best seven for 98.*

ESSEX v DERBYSHIRE

At Chelmsford, May 13–16. Essex won by an innings and 15 runs. Essex 24pts, Derbyshire 1pt. Toss: Derbyshire. County debut: B. Stanlake.

Essex emphatically atoned for an innings defeat at Trent Bridge, and went top of the group. After an opening-day washout, the tall Australian fast bowler Billy Stanlake endured a horror start to his Derbyshire career, sending down six no-balls – and aborting his run-up five times – as his first four overs cost 25. He eventually located his radar, and removed both openers in quick succession after lunch (Browne's dismissal for 59 reduced his average against Derbyshire to 213). But that brought together Westley and Lawrence, who each cruised to a century during a stand of 221. Lawrence finished unbeaten on 152, from 133 balls, with six sixes (three in succession off Critchley, to bring up maximum batting points) and 16 fours. Derbyshire were three down by the end of the second day, and fared little better on the third, with only Brooke Guest escaping the twenties, as Harmer ran riot for career-best figures of nine for 80. He found the going harder in the follow-on, but still finished with 12. Derbyshire batted better, with Guest again catching the eye – he completed the maiden fifty that just eluded him in the first innings – though wickets fell regularly. Ten Doeschate took six catches in the match, all at short leg, to equal the Essex record by a fielder. Four days later, it was announced that Stanlake had a stress fracture of the back, and was flying home.

Close of play: first day, no play; second day, Derbyshire 35-3 (Guest 14, Hughes 5); third day, Derbyshire 97-1 (Godleman 39, Guest 56).

Essex

N. L. J. Browne c Madsen b Stanlake		59
A. N. Cook c Godleman b Stanlake		58
*T. Westley c du Plooy b Critchley		106
D. W. Lawrence not out		152
P. I. Walter not out		12
Lb 5, w 2, nb 18		25

1/137 (1)   (3 wkts dec, 76 overs) 412
2/138 (2) 3/359 (3)

R. N. ten Doeschate, †A. J. A. Wheater, S. R. Harmer, S. Snater, S. J. Cook and J. A. Porter did not bat.

Stanlake 17–2–91–2; Reece 13–0–47–0; Melton 13–2–53–0; Hudson-Prentice 12–1–75–0; Critchley 12–0–87–1; Hughes 6–0–33–0; Madsen 3–0–21–0.

Derbyshire

L. M. Reece lbw b Harmer	2	– b Porter	0
*B. A. Godleman c ten Doeschate b Lawrence	9	– lbw b Porter	45
B. D. Guest c ten Doeschate b Harmer	49	– lbw b S. J. Cook	65
J. L. du Plooy c Lawrence b Harmer	2	– c A. N. Cook b Snater	39
A. L. Hughes st Wheater b Harmer	22	– (9) c Walter b S. J. Cook	8
W. L. Madsen c Lawrence b Harmer	23	– (5) c ten Doeschate b Harmer	36
M. J. J. Critchley c and b Harmer	4	– (6) c A. N. Cook b Porter	25
†H. R. Hosein c ten Doeschate b Harmer	9	– (7) c ten Doeschate b Harmer	5
F. J. Hudson-Prentice not out	3	– (8) c ten Doeschate b Harmer	8
B. Stanlake b Harmer	0	– c Westley b S. J. Cook	8
D. R. Melton c and b Harmer	15	– not out	2
B 1, lb 7	8	B 6, lb 4	10

1/10 (1) 2/16 (2) 3/27 (4)   (56.5 overs) 146
4/71 (5) 5/103 (6) 6/109 (7)
7/127 (8) 8/128 (3) 9/128 (10) 10/146 (11)

1/14 (2) 2/111 (2)   (92.4 overs) 251
3/118 (3) 4/193 (5)
5/193 (4) 6/218 (1) 7/226 (8)
8/234 (6) 9/248 (10) 10/251 (9)

Harmer 25.5–9–80–9; Lawrence 11–2–20–1; S. J. Cook 7–2–8–0; Porter 8–1–18–0; Snater 5–2–12–0. *Second innings*—Porter 19–5–41–3; S. J. Cook 16.4–5–45–3; Harmer 45–9–122–3; Snater 10–2–27–1; Lawrence 2–1–6–0.

Umpires: I. D. Blackwell and Hassan Adnan.   Referee: J. J. Whitaker.

ESSEX v WARWICKSHIRE

At Chelmsford, May 20–23. Drawn. Essex 12pts, Warwickshire 11pts. Toss: Warwickshire.

The loss of more than 200 overs condemned this match to a draw. There was time for Sibley to have a useful workout in his first game since breaking a finger a month earlier: he made a typically doughty 43 before Bresnan added an equally disciplined half-century. After negotiating some testing deliveries from Siddle, who finished with his best figures for Essex on a pitch that helped the seamers, both fell to Sam Cook – Bresnan was tenth out as the last three wickets went down at the same score. Siddle had been presented with his county cap (and his 2019 Championship medal) at lunch on the first day. Alastair Cook replied in kind, also surviving over two and a half hours, before ten Doeschate and Harmer gave Essex a handy lead. The weather permitted less than 23 overs on the final day.

Close of play: first day, Warwickshire 159-7 (Bresnan 47, Briggs 1); second day, Essex 16-1 (A. N. Cook 11, Westley 1); third day, Warwickshire 0-0 (Briggs 0, Rhodes 0).

Warwickshire

*W. M. H. Rhodes c Browne b Siddle	10	– (2) not out	22
D. P. Sibley c Harmer b S. J. Cook	43	– (3) not out	2
R. M. Yates b Siddle	0		
P. J. Malan c Westley b Porter	7		
S. R. Hain lbw b Siddle	10		
†M. G. K. Burgess b Siddle	35		
T. T. Bresnan c A. N. Cook b S. J. Cook	50		
O. P. Stone c Harmer b S. J. Cook	4		
D. R. Briggs c Walter b Siddle	5	– (1) c Lawrence b S. J. Cook	37
L. C. Norwell b Siddle	0		
O. J. Hannon-Dalby not out	0		
Lb 2	2	B 1, lb 4	5

1/22 (1) 2/24 (3) 3/37 (4)   (69.2 overs) 166
4/56 (5) 5/76 (2) 6/132 (6)
7/141 (8) 8/166 (9) 9/166 (10) 10/166 (7)

1/63 (1)   (1 wkt, 23.5 overs) 66

Porter 16–5–40–1; S. J. Cook 18.2–3–48–3; Siddle 21–5–38–6; Harmer 12–3–30–0; Walter 2–0–8–0. *Second innings*—S. J. Cook 8.5–5–7–1; Porter 4–0–19–0; Siddle 5–1–24–0; Harmer 6–3–11–0.

Essex

N. L. J. Browne c Burgess b Norwell	4	P. M. Siddle c Hain b Bresnan	2
A. N. Cook c Yates b Rhodes	57	S. J. Cook b Briggs	5
*T. Westley c Burgess b Hannon-Dalby	8	J. A. Porter c Burgess b Stone	5
D. W. Lawrence b Norwell	14	Lb 4	4
P. I. Walter lbw b Rhodes	22		
R. N. ten Doeschate c Burgess b Norwell	56	1/9 (1) 2/29 (3) 3/77 (4) (82.3 overs)	217
†A. J. A. Wheater c and b Rhodes	0	4/100 (2) 5/121 (5) 6/125 (7)	
S. R. Harmer not out	40	7/169 (6) 8/180 (9) 9/203 (10) 10/217 (11)	

Stone 19.3–3–62–1; Norwell 18–1–48–3; Hannon-Dalby 19–3–65–1; Rhodes 11–4–21–3; Bresnan 10–3–8–1; Briggs 5–0–9–1.

Umpires: B. J. Debenham and I. J. Gould. Referee: P. Whitticase.

At Chester-le-Street, May 27–29. ESSEX beat DURHAM by 195 runs.

ESSEX v NOTTINGHAMSHIRE

At Chelmsford, June 3–6. Drawn. Essex 11pts, Nottinghamshire 13pts. Toss: Nottinghamshire.

Once again, the weather played spoilsport: the second day was washed out, and only 37.3 overs were possible on the fourth. Nottinghamshire had rebuilt solidly on the first, following a shaky start, which included Clarke retiring after being hit on the arm by Sam Cook. He returned to top-score with a confident 67, while James and Mullaney – who was dropped twice before reaching double figures – also contributed half-centuries. Harmer, wicketless in the previous two matches, now claimed four, which took him to 250 in the Championship; Walter was taken out of the attack after sending down two beamers. Essex's batsmen also hit early problems, sliding to 15 for three, but Westley continued his good home form with a workmanlike 71, and six others reached double figures as the deficit was whittled down to 83. Hutton, who bowled tightly throughout, rounded things off to finish with five wickets. There was little prospect of a result by the fourth morning, but time for Siddle to take a wicket in what turned out to be his last match for Essex before returning to Australia for personal reasons.

Close of play: first day, Nottinghamshire 248-6 (Clarke 57, Patterson-White 17); second day, no play; third day, Essex 180-7 (Harmer 15, Snater 17).

Nottinghamshire

B. T. Slater lbw b Snater	25	– (2) not out	19
B. G. Compton c A. N. Cook b Siddle	11	– (1) c A. N. Cook b Siddle	8
B. M. Duckett lbw b Siddle	2	– b Snater	16
J. M. Clarke c Snater b Harmer	67	– not out	1
L. W. James c A. N. Cook b Siddle	54		
*S. J. Mullaney c A. N. Cook b Snater	55		
†T. J. Moores b S. J. Cook	12		
L. A. Patterson-White b Harmer	31		
B. A. Hutton lbw b Harmer	10		
L. J. Fletcher c Walter b Harmer	0		
D. Paterson not out	11		
B 6, lb 1, nb 8	15		

1/24 (2) 2/26 (3) 3/48 (1)	(118.1 overs) 293	1/11 (1)	(2 wkts, 27.2 overs) 44
4/171 (5) 5/176 (6) 6/190 (7)		2/35 (3)	
7/261 (4) 8/272 (8) 9/272 (10)			
10/293 (9)	110 overs: 268-7		

In the first innings Clarke, when 11, retired hurt at 54-3 and resumed at 176-5.

S. J. Cook 30–11–64–1; Siddle 25–6–87–3; Snater 24–11–45–2; Harmer 33.1–11–71–4; Walter 4–1–14–0; ten Doeschate 2–0–5–0. *Second innings*—S. J. Cook 5–1–10–0; Siddle 6.2–2–10–1; Harmer 11–5–11–0; Snater 5–2–13–1.

Essex

N. L. J. Browne c Moores b Hutton	6	S. Snater lbw b Hutton	24
A. N. Cook c Moores b Hutton	5	P. M. Siddle not out	11
*T. Westley b Patterson-White	71	S. J. Cook b Hutton	6
M. S. Pepper c Moores b Fletcher	7	B 9, lb 7, nb 6	22
P. I. Walter b Patterson-White	21		
R. N. ten Doeschate c Clarke b Hutton	14	1/11 (1) 2/14 (2) 3/15 (4) (89.1 overs) 210	
†A. J. A. Wheater c Compton b James	10	4/70 (5) 5/108 (6) 6/143 (3)	
S. R. Harmer lbw b Fletcher	20	7/143 (7) 8/193 (9) 9/195 (8) 10/210 (11)	

Fletcher 21–9–32–2; Hutton 26.1–9–65–5; Paterson 17–4–34–0; Patterson-White 16–4–37–2; James 9–2–26–1.

Umpires: I. D. Blackwell and N. A. Mallender.   Referee: A. J. Swann.

At Derby, July 11–12. ESSEX drew with DERBYSHIRE. *The match is called off before the second day when a Derbyshire player tests positive for Covid-19. Essex fail to qualify for Division One.*

DIVISION TWO

At Cardiff, August 30–September 1. ESSEX beat GLAMORGAN by an innings and 74 runs.

ESSEX v GLOUCESTERSHIRE

At Chelmsford, September 5–7. Essex won by an innings and three runs. Essex 21pts, Gloucestershire 3pts. Toss: Essex.

This match was all but decided on the first morning, when Gloucestershire were put in – and shot out for 76. Porter, in his 100th first-class game, and Sam Cook reduced them to 32 for six, then Harmer mopped up, ending the innings with his 300th wicket since joining Essex in 2017. The home side also struggled, dipping to 32 for four before Walter took charge. He spent 20 balls on nought, batted responsibly for 270 minutes, and was unlucky to miss a maiden century, thanks to a juggled chance at third slip by Lace (who went on to collect a pair). Fifteen wickets went down on the first day but, with the pitch flattening out, Essex's last seven all reached double figures, and they eventually led by 200. Gloucestershire put up sterner resistance second time round, with Charlesworth and Bracey both surviving nearly two and a half hours, but Harmer and Cook instigated a collapse of six for 11. The ninth-wicket pair resisted stoutly on the third morning, before Harmer had Zafar Gohar caught at slip. When Higgins was run out, Gloucestershire were just short of making Essex bat again.

Close of play: first day, Essex 150-5 (Walter 71, Wheater 30); second day, Gloucestershire 132-5 (Dent 9).

Gloucestershire

B. G. Charlesworth lbw b Porter	12	– lbw b Harmer	49
M. A. H. Hammond lbw b Porter	5	– lbw b Snater	17
†J. R. Bracey c Wheater b S. J. Cook	3	– c Harmer b S. J. Cook	50
*C. D. J. Dent c Harmer b Porter	8	– b Harmer	11
T. C. Lace b S. J. Cook	0	– (7) c Harmer b S. J. Cook	0
G. L. van Buuren b S. J. Cook	4	– (8) lbw b S. J. Cook	0
R. F. Higgins c Pepper b Harmer	25	– (9) run out (Snater)	38
O. J. Price c Browne b Porter	3	– (6) run out (Rymell)	1
Zafar Gohar c Rymell b Harmer	12	– (10) c A. N. Cook b Harmer	24
T. J. Price not out	1	– (5) c Browne b Harmer	1
D. A. Payne b Harmer	0	– not out	0
Lb 2, w 1	3	Lb 6	6

1/13 (2) 2/20 (1) 3/28 (3)	(28 overs)	76
4/28 (5) 5/28 (4) 6/32 (6)		
7/47 (8) 8/73 (9) 9/76 (7) 10/76 (11)		

1/35 (2) 2/93 (1)	(90.1 overs)	197
3/123 (3) 4/124 (5)		
5/132 (6) 6/134 (7) 7/134 (8)		
8/134 (4) 9/188 (10) 10/197 (9)		

Porter 10–3–32–4; S. J. Cook 10–2–27–3; Snater 5–2–13–0; Harmer 3–1–2–3. *Second innings—* Porter 16–4–39–0; S. J. Cook 20.1–7–31–3; Harmer 40–12–78–4; Snater 12–2–40–1; Westley 2–0–3–0.

Essex

N. L. J. Browne c Bracey b Payne	7	S. Snater c Hammond b Zafar Gohar	10
A. N. Cook lbw b Higgins	15	S. J. Cook not out	22
*T. Westley lbw b T. J. Price	2	J. A. Porter c Payne b Zafar Gohar	17
M. S. Pepper c Bracey b Payne	8	Lb 4, nb 2	6
P. I. Walter c Lace b Payne	96		
J. S. Rymell c Hammond b Zafar Gohar	14	1/10 (1) 2/22 (2) 3/28 (3) (102.4 overs) 276	
†A. J. A. Wheater c O. J. Price b T. J. Price	34	4/32 (4) 5/75 (6) 6/154 (7)	
S. R. Harmer c Lace b Higgins	45	7/225 (5) 8/227 (8) 9/244 (9) 10/276 (11)	

Payne 22–4–71–3; Higgins 23–7–60–2; T. J. Price 22–7–62–2; Zafar Gohar 32.4–11–77–3; O. J. Price 3–1–2–0.

Umpires: N. L. Bainton and T. Lungley.   Referee: W. R. Smith.

At The Oval, September 12–15. ESSEX drew with SURREY.

ESSEX v NORTHAMPTONSHIRE

At Chelmsford, September 21–22. Essex won by an innings and 44 runs. Essex 19pts, Northamptonshire 3pts. Toss: Northamptonshire.

Essex romped to the second division title with their third innings victory out of four. They were helped by an abject performance from Northamptonshire, who slumped to their lowest total since 1946 (when they made 39 against Gloucestershire at Peterborough), and prolonged the match only half an hour into the second day. No fewer than 25 wickets tumbled on the first, on a pitch that helped the bowlers, but not excessively; there was an end-of-term feeling about much of the play. For Essex, the second-tier trophy was no major cause for celebration, after the successes of recent years. "We didn't feel great taking a photo next to the Division Two board," said Lawrence, who

KEEPING IT BRIEF

The shortest completed County Championship matches scheduled for four days (by overs):

96.3	**Essex (170) beat Northamptonshire (81 and 45) at Chelmsford**	**2021**
109.5	Kent (167) beat Northamptonshire (69 and 86) at Canterbury	1999
120.1	Somerset (169 and 30-0) beat Kent (139 and 59) at Canterbury	2019
127	Essex (191 and 151-0 dec) beat Leicestershire (52-2 dec and 176) at Colchester	2007
130.1	Sussex (300) beat Somerset (76 and 108) at Horsham	2013

The Championship first included four-day games in 1988. Games with forfeited innings are not counted. The shortest Championship match was Middlesex (86) v Somerset (35 and 44) at Lord's in 1899, which lasted 70 five-ball overs.

captained for the first time, while Tom Westley awaited the birth of his first child. The only man to reach double figures in the visitors' shambolic 86-minute second innings was Procter, who was last out for 24 to give Sam Cook – impeccable in line and length – match figures of ten for 41, including Kerrigan for a pair. The rot set in early. After Rossington decided to bat, he was one of seven to fall lbw in the first innings, as Cook and Porter bowled consistently. Essex took the lead within 15 overs, but wickets continued to tumble: only Lawrence and Wheater passed 30, though a modest total turned out to be more than enough. For Northamptonshire's outgoing head coach, David Ripley, it was a miserable end to a ten-year reign.

Close of play: first day, Northamptonshire 23-5 (Procter 14).

Northamptonshire

†R. S. Vasconcelos lbw b Porter	2	– lbw b S. J. Cook		1
E. N. Gay lbw b Porter	38	– c Wheater b Porter		1
L. A. Procter b Porter	4	– c Wheater b S. J. Cook		24
R. I. Keogh lbw b S. J. Cook	6	– c A. N. Cook b S. J. Cook		2
S. A. Zaib lbw b Snater	4	– (7) c Browne b Snater		0
*A. M. Rossington lbw b S. J. Cook	14	– (8) b Snater		4
J. J. Cobb lbw b S. J. Cook	1	– (9) c Pepper b Snater		0
T. A. I. Taylor c Wheater b S. J. Cook	0	– (10) c Lawrence b Snater		8
J. J. G. Sales c A. N. Cook b Porter	12	– (6) b S. J. Cook		0
S. C. Kerrigan lbw b S. J. Cook	0	– (5) c Wheater b S. J. Cook		0
C. J. White not out	0	– not out		0
		Lb 5		5

1/2 (1) 2/14 (3) 3/25 (4)   (34.5 overs)   81   1/1 (1) 2/3 (2)   (18.2 overs)   45
4/36 (5) 5/59 (2) 6/60 (7)   3/21 (4) 4/23 (5)
7/60 (8) 8/81 (6) 9/81 (10) 10/81 (9)   5/23 (6) 6/24 (7) 7/30 (8)
                                                               8/30 (9) 9/41 (10) 10/45 (3)

Porter 11.5–3–31–4; S. J. Cook 12–5–21–5; Harmer 5–1–9–0; Snater 6–1–20–1. *Second innings—*
Porter 4–0–11–1; S. J. Cook 8.2–4–20–5; Harmer 3–2–2–0; Snater 3–0–7–4.

Essex

N. L. J. Browne c sub (G. K. Berg) b White	20	S. Snater c Vasconcelos b White		4
A. N. Cook c Cobb b Taylor	18	S. J. Cook c Vasconcelos b White		4
J. S. Rymell b Procter	9	J. A. Porter not out		0
*D. W. Lawrence c sub (G. K. Berg) b Procter	33	Lb 3, w 1		4
M. S. Pepper c Zaib b Taylor	13			
P. I. Walter b Taylor	26	1/39 (1) 2/39 (2) 3/70 (3) (43.2 overs) 170		
†A. J. A. Wheater b Taylor	34	4/83 (4) 5/120 (5) 6/121 (6)		
S. R. Harmer c Sales b White	5	7/136 (8) 8/148 (9) 9/160 (10) 10/170 (7)		

Taylor 13.2–1–67–4; White 14–4–40–4; Procter 6–3–22–2; Kerrigan 5–1–11–0; Sales
2–0–19–0; Keogh 3–0–8–0.

Umpires: N. A. Mallender and M. J. Saggers.   Referee: P. M. Such.

GLAMORGAN

Silverware at last

EDWARD BEVAN

Glamorgan are not accustomed to winning trophies – their last had been in 2004 – so there was satisfaction when they lifted the Royal London Cup. They defeated Essex in the semi, when Joe Cooke followed a five-wicket haul with an unbeaten 66, then Durham in the final – despite losing five first-team players to The Hundred. With the one-day captain David Lloyd among those seconded to the new competition, the squad were led by Kiran Carlson. He visibly enjoyed the experience, and contributed to success in the final with a brilliant 82 from 59 balls. A Thursday at Trent Bridge might have lacked the atmosphere of a Saturday at Lord's, but over 7,000 still turned out for an entertaining contest.

However, Glamorgan made little impact in the other competitions. One hundred years after they joined the County Championship, they finished bottom of the second division – effectively 12th overall. They won only two matches, and lost three of the last four, two by an innings and the other by ten wickets.

Head coach Matthew Maynard had been optimistic before the season: "This is an opportunity to play and challenge the leading teams in the country." But Glamorgan's performances were so poor during the final month that he said the team had "an obligation to the supporters to turn things around". They did draw the last game, at The Oval, but it took place on a lifeless pitch on which 1,394 runs were scored for the loss of ten wickets.

The season had started promisingly, with Glamorgan well placed on the third day in Yorkshire, only for a snowstorm at lunch to prevent any play until the following morning. Wins against Kent and Lancashire raised hopes of further success in the second half – but, with the intrusion of The Hundred, and the other players getting very little cricket during the Championship's six-week break, form suffered.

Glamorgan were abysmal in the T20 Blast: nine defeats and three victories meant they propped up the South Group. The last game reflected their limitations, as Hampshire romped to 187 in 13 overs. Maynard pointed to the absence of Marnus Labuschagne and Nick Selman (later released) for several games because of Covid, but Colin Ingram's loss of form did not help. He managed only 174 runs from 12 innings, and that included a 75. The South African-born Ingram had often been the club's top scorer in previous seasons. He still has a year left on his overseas contract, but he has now moved full-time to Wales.

Carlson, Lloyd and wicketkeeper Chris Cooke were the leading batsmen in Championship cricket. Carlson hit 928 runs, including three hundreds, two in the same game against Sussex. Cooke averaged 58, and struck a career-best unbeaten 205 in the Oval run-fest. Lloyd, promoted to open at the start of the season, responded well to his new role, but there is still a need for an

Dan Mullan, Getty Images

Kiran Carlson

established opening pair. Cooke, who had led in red-ball cricket for three years, left the post at the end of the summer, and was succeeded by Lloyd.

Hamish Rutherford, the former New Zealand Test opener, replaced Labuschagne as an overseas player. He featured in the Royal London and the last four Championship matches, contributing useful innings without reaching three figures. Eddie Byrom joined on loan from Somerset for the final three games, and agreed a two-year contract. Sam Northeast, formerly of Kent and Hampshire, was also recruited in an effort to strengthen the batting. But there were rumblings about the lack of Welsh-born players coming through the Academy; only Carlson and Lloyd featured regularly in senior cricket.

Labuschagne and fellow Australian Michael Neser were scheduled to return as the overseas players in 2022, but much will again depend on the pandemic and their international commitments. Neser appeared in only five matches, but proved a potent new-ball partner for Michael Hogan, who again spearheaded the attack. He turns 41 in May, and has hinted this could be his final season. Many hope he stays longer: the club can ill afford to lose such a loyal and dedicated performer. James Harris has returned after eight years with Middlesex, and will bolster the attack. Off-spinner Andrew Salter had his moments – mostly in white-ball games – but Glamorgan have lacked a frontline slow bowler since the days of Robert Croft and Dean Cosker.

The club are in a stable financial position, benefiting from hosting Welsh Fire's Hundred games, but there may be no more first-class cricket at St Helen's in Swansea. The famous seaside ground where Garry Sobers struck Malcolm Nash for six sixes in an over, and the Australians were defeated in 1964 and 1968, is owned by the local council, though there has been little or no recent investment. The facilities are, according to Glamorgan's chief executive Hugh Morris, "in a very poor state indeed" – sad news for those who have enjoyed watching cricket there.

In the wake of the ECB's plan to tackle racism, chairman Gareth Williams set out Glamorgan's strategy to improve diversity on and off the field. In 2020, two Pakistan-born players who had appeared for the Second XI accused the club of racism, but this was resolved after talks with Morris; one of the players is now a consultant coach with the county. "I am happy to report we have not had a single complaint," said Williams, "and are constantly in touch and working together with those from Black, Asian and minority ethnic backgrounds."

GLAMORGAN RESULTS

County Championship matches – Played 14: Won 2, Lost 5, Drawn 7.
Vitality T20 Blast matches – Played 14: Won 3, Lost 9, No result 2.
Royal London Cup matches – Played 10: Won 6, Lost 2, No result 2.

LV= County Championship, 3rd in Group 3, 6th in Division 2;
Vitality T20 Blast, 9th in South Group; Royal London Cup, winners.

COUNTY CHAMPIONSHIP AVERAGES, BATTING AND FIELDING

Cap		Birthplace	M	I	NO	R	HS	100	Avge	Ct/St
2016	C. B. Cooke	Johannesburg, SA ..	14	21	7	816	205*	4	58.28	40/1
2021	K. S. Carlson	Cardiff‡..........	14	23	4	928	170*	3	48.84	3
	†H. D. Rutherford¶..	Dunedin, NZ	4	7	0	260	71	0	37.14	0
	C. Z. Taylor	Newport‡	6	8	2	215	84	0	35.83	2
2019	D. L. Lloyd	St Asaph‡	14	25	1	828	121	1	34.50	7
2019	M. Labuschagne¶....	Klerksdorp, SA ...	6	9	2	228	77	0	32.57	1
	D. A. Douthwaite....	Kingston-u-Thames	13	16	1	482	96	0	32.13	3
	A. G. Salter	Haverfordwest‡....	10	11	4	221	90	0	31.57	3
	†E. J. Byrom.......	Harare, Zimbabwe ..	3	5	0	151	78	0	30.20	1
2021	†W. T. Root	Sheffield	11	18	2	442	110*	1	27.62	4
	†J. M. Cooke.......	Hemel Hempstead ..	8	13	2	203	68	0	18.45	7
2018	T. van der Gugten†† .	Sydney, Australia ..	11	13	2	194	85*	0	17.63	5
	L. J. Carey	Carmarthen‡......	3	5	0	78	29	0	15.60	0
2013	M. G. Hogan††	Newcastle, Australia	13	14	6	113	54	0	14.12	2
	N. J. Selman	Brisbane, Australia..	5	10	0	121	69	0	12.10	3
	†W. J. Weighell	Middlesbrough	4	5	0	52	21	0	10.40	2
	A. Balbirnie¶	Dublin, Ireland	3	6	0	57	29	0	9.50	3

Also batted: J. A. R. Harris (*Morriston‡*) (cap 2010) 2 (matches) 17, 18* (1 ct); †C. A. Ingram¶ (*Port Elizabeth, SA*) (1 match) 7, 27; J. P. McIlroy (*Hereford*) (2 matches) 0; M. G. Neser¶ (*Pretoria, SA*) (cap 2021) (5 matches) 17, 24, 17* (3 ct); S. J. Reingold (*Cape Town, SA*) 9, 4 (1 ct); R. A. J. Smith (*Glasgow*) (1 match) 8, 4.

‡ *Born in Wales.* ¶ *Official overseas player.* †† *Other non-England-qualified.*

BOWLING

	Style	O	M	R	W	BB	5I	Avge
M. G. Neser	RFM	127	29	386	23	5-39	1	16.78
M. G. Hogan	RFM	332.5	78	874	34	5-28	1	25.70
D. L. Lloyd..................	RM	170.3	24	558	21	4-11	0	26.57
T. van der Gugten............	RFM	274.3	54	823	27	4-34	0	30.48
A. G. Salter	OB	218.5	41	687	15	4-18	0	45.80
D. A. Douthwaite.............	RFM	181.1	18	781	17	2-16	0	45.94

Also bowled: A. Balbirnie (OB) 3–0–17–0; E. J. Byrom (LB) 16–0–64–2; L. J. Carey (RFM) 54–9–179–4; K. S. Carlson (OB) 14.3–4–43–1; C. B. Cooke (RM) 3–0–19–0; J. M. Cooke (RFM) 11–0–51–0; J. A. R. Harris (RFM) 44.5–3–159–4; M. Labuschagne (LB) 32.2–3–127–2; J. P. McIlroy (LFM) 38–10–131–1; S. J. Reingold (OB) 6–1–15–3; W. T. Root (OB) 13–0–64–0; H. D. Rutherford (SLA) 8–1–26–1; R. A. J. Smith (RM) 22–3–84–1; C. Z. Taylor (OB) 146.2–16–484–5; W. J. Weighell (RM) 80.1–9–359–7.

LEADING VITALITY BLAST AVERAGES (100 runs/15 overs)

Batting	Runs	HS	Avge	SR	Ct/St
D. A. Douthwaite ..	203	53	20.30	**153.78**	2
D. L. Lloyd......	302	52	25.16	**147.31**	2
M. Labuschagne ..	390	93*	55.71	**140.79**	5
K. S. Carlson...	141	32	12.81	**127.02**	3
N. J. Selman	130	65	21.66	**126.21**	5
C. A. Ingram ...	174	75	15.81	**104.19**	4
C. B. Cooke ...	122	26	13.55	**103.38**	9/1

Bowling	W	BB	Avge	ER
R. I. Walker.....	8	3-15	16.00	**7.11**
R. A. J. Smith ...	4	2-13	34.50	**7.26**
P. Sisodiya......	7	2-22	36.57	**8.25**
D. A. Douthwaite	15	3-28	19.60	**8.48**
M. Labuschagne .	9	2-22	21.44	**8.77**
A. G. Salter	7	2-31	34.71	**9.34**
T. van der Gugten	7	3-16	41.71	**9.62**
W. J. Weighell ...	3	1-22	65.00	**11.47**

LEADING ROYAL LONDON CUP AVERAGES (100 runs/4 wickets)

Batting	Runs	HS	Avge	SR	Ct/St
N. J. Selman ...	421	140	52.62	73.60	9
T. N. Cullen ...	175	58*	35.00	79.18	18/1
J. M. Cooke	174	66*	34.80	119.17	4
H. D. Rutherford	308	86	34.22	93.61	1
K. S. Carlson...	232	82	29.00	98.72	5
W. T. Root	191	67	23.87	77.01	2
S. J. Reingold ..	187	40	20.77	59.74	8

Bowling	W	BB	Avge	ER
M. G. Hogan	16	4-33	12.56	2.99
J. M. Cooke.....	20	5-61	14.30	4.55
A. G. Salter	9	3-37	18.22	3.72
W. J. Weighell...	8	3-7	21.12	5.60
L. J. Carey	12	2-24	29.33	5.55
S. J. Reingold ...	5	1-16	32.60	6.03

FIRST-CLASS COUNTY RECORDS

Highest score for	309*	S. P. James v Sussex at Colwyn Bay............	2000
Highest score against	322*	M. B. Loye (Northamptonshire) at Northampton ...	1998
Leading run-scorer	34,056	A. Jones (avge 33.03)	1957–83
Best bowling for	10-51	J. Mercer v Worcestershire at Worcester.........	1936
Best bowling against	10-18	G. Geary (Leicestershire) at Pontypridd	1929
Leading wicket-taker	2,174	D. J. Shepherd (avge 20.95).................	1950–72
Highest total for	718-3 dec	v Sussex at Colwyn Bay	2000
Highest total against	750	by Northamptonshire at Cardiff................	2019
Lowest total for	22	v Lancashire at Liverpool	1924
Lowest total against	33	by Leicestershire at Ebbw Vale	1965

LIST A COUNTY RECORDS

Highest score for	169*	J. A. Rudolph v Sussex at Hove...............	2014
Highest score against	268	A. D. Brown (Surrey) at The Oval.............	2002
Leading run-scorer	12,278	M. P. Maynard (avge 37.66)	1985–2005
Best bowling for	7-16	S. D. Thomas v Surrey at Swansea	1998
Best bowling against	7-30	M. P. Bicknell (Surrey) at The Oval	1999
Leading wicket-taker	356	R. D. B. Croft (avge 31.96)	1989–2012
Highest total for	429	v Surrey at The Oval	2002
Highest total against	438-5	by Surrey at The Oval	2002
Lowest total for	42	v Derbyshire at Swansea	1979
Lowest total against	{ 59	by Combined Universities at Cambridge........	1983
	{ 59	by Sussex at Hove	1996

TWENTY20 COUNTY RECORDS

Highest score for	116*	I. J. Thomas v Somerset at Taunton.............	2004
Highest score against	117	M. J. Prior (Sussex) at Hove	2010
Leading run-scorer	2,205	C. A. Ingram (avge 34.45, SR 152.91)	2015–21
Best bowling for	5-14	G. G. Wagg v Worcestershire at Worcester.......	2013
Best bowling against	6-5	A. V. Suppiah (Somerset) at Cardiff	2011
Leading wicket-taker	100	D. A. Cosker (avge 30.32, ER 7.79)	2003–16
Highest total for	240-3	v Surrey at The Oval	2015
Highest total against	239-5	by Sussex at Hove	2010
Lowest total for	44	v Surrey at The Oval	2019
Lowest total against	81	by Gloucestershire at Bristol	2011

ADDRESS

Sophia Gardens, Cardiff CF11 9XR; 029 2040 9380; info@glamorgancricket.co.uk; www.glamorgan cricket.com. Twitter: @GlamCricket.

OFFICIALS

Captain 2021 C. B. Cooke
2022 D. L. Lloyd
(50-over) K. S. Carlson
Director of cricket M. A. Wallace
Head coach M. P. Maynard
Head of talent development R. V. Almond

President G. Elias
Chair G. Williams
Chief executive H. Morris
Head groundsman R. Saxton
Scorer/archivist A. K. Hignell

GROUP THREE

At Leeds, April 8–11. GLAMORGAN drew with YORKSHIRE.

GLAMORGAN v SUSSEX

At Cardiff, April 15–18. Sussex won by eight wickets. Sussex 24pts, Glamorgan 4pts. Toss: Sussex. County debut: W. J. Weighell. Championship debut: H. T. Crocombe.

Glamorgan paid for a disappointing first-innings batting performance, as a young Sussex side collected maximum points with shadows lengthening on the final day. Put in, Glamorgan were soon 23 for three and, though Lloyd and Carlson repaired the damage, the Irish off-spinner Carson lopped off the tail. Carlson had a lucky escape at 91, when Garton at slip dropped a chance off Tim Clark's first delivery in first-class cricket (in his seventh match). Sussex were riding high at 212 for

BOWLERS WITH SIX LBWs IN A FIRST-CLASS INNINGS

M. C. Ilott	Essex v Northamptonshire at Luton	1995
W. P. U. J. C. Vaas . .	Western Province v Southern Province at Colombo (RPS)	2004-05
Tabish Khan	Karachi Whites v Khan Research Laboratories at Karachi (NBP)	2011-12
O. E. Robinson	**Sussex v Glamorgan at Cardiff**	**2021**
C. J. C. Wright	**Leicestershire v Gloucestershire at Bristol**	**2021**

one in reply, then lost four in a hurry. But van Zyl completed a confident century, before Garton, with a career-best, and Robinson piled on 134 in 27 overs to take the advantage close to 200. Robinson soon weighed in with the ball as well, and Glamorgan looked sunk at 150 for five, before Carlson's second century gave them strong hopes of a draw. Taylor, who batted for five hours, put on 117 with him, and Douthwaite helped extend the lead past 150 – only for Robinson to snap up the last four in ten balls. He finished with nine for 78 – his best figures, and the best of the 2021 season – and 13 in the match. Sussex glimpsed victory again, and Thomason led the charge with his second fifty of the game. There were 18 lbws in all, equalling the Championship record (subsequently broken in Durham's match against Essex at Chester-le-Street).

Close of play: first day, Sussex 99-0 (Thomason 52, Haines 43); second day, Sussex 481-9 (Robinson 67, Crocombe 0); third day, Glamorgan 258-5 (Carlson 129, Taylor 33).

Glamorgan

N. J. Selman lbw b Robinson	0	– lbw b Robinson	11
D. L. Lloyd c Garton b Crocombe	84	– lbw b Robinson	19
A. Balbirnie lbw b Robinson	4	– lbw b Robinson	29
W. T. Root lbw b Crocombe	1	– lbw b Crocombe	8
K. S. Carlson not out	127	– c Thomason b Robinson	132
*†C. B. Cooke lbw b Robinson	13	– c Brown b Robinson	12
C. Z. Taylor c van Zyl b Robinson	3	– c van Zyl b Robinson	84
D. A. Douthwaite c Clark b Meaker	36	– lbw b Robinson	26
T. van der Gugten c Brown b Carson	5	– (10) lbw b Robinson	0
W. J. Weighell lbw b Carson	0	– (9) lbw b Robinson	0
M. G. Hogan st Brown b Carson	0	– not out	0
B 4, lb 6, nb 2	12	B 5, lb 14, w 1, nb 8	28

1/0 (1) 2/22 (3) 3/23 (4)	(75 overs) 285	1/29 (2) 2/30 (1)	(127.1 overs) 349
4/133 (5) 5/169 (6) 6/179 (7)		3/46 (4) 4/95 (3)	
7/266 (8) 8/277 (9) 9/285 (10) 10/285 (11)		5/150 (6) 6/267 (5) 7/346 (8)	
		8/346 (9) 9/348 (10) 10/349 (7)	

Robinson 18–3–50–4; Crocombe 15–3–44–2; Garton 12–0–72–0; van Zyl 4–1–12–0; Meaker 16–2–62–1; Carson 7–2–14–3; Clark 3–0–21–0. *Second innings*—Robinson 30.1–10–78–9; Crocombe 20–3–85–1; Meaker 16–1–57–0; Carson 32–8–62–0; Garton 7–0–19–0; Rawlins 20–4–29–0; Clark 2–2–0–0.

Sussex

A. D. Thomason c and b Hogan	67	– not out		78
T. J. Haines lbw b Hogan	87	– c Balbirnie b Hogan		6
S. van Zyl c Cooke b van der Gugten	113	– c Cooke b Lloyd		12
T. G. R. Clark c Weighell b Douthwaite	19	– not out		54
*†B. C. Brown c Cooke b Douthwaite	0			
D. M. W. Rawlins lbw b Taylor	2			
G. H. S. Garton lbw b Hogan	97			
O. E. Robinson lbw b Hogan	67			
S. C. Meaker lbw b Lloyd	6			
J. J. Carson lbw b Lloyd	0			
H. T. Crocombe not out	0			
B 4, lb 9, nb 10	23	Lb 2, nb 2		4

1/115 (1) 2/212 (2) 3/254 (4)   (123.3 overs) 481   1/15 (2)   (2 wkts, 40.1 overs) 154
4/254 (5) 5/261 (6) 6/330 (3)   2/42 (3)
7/464 (7) 8/478 (9) 9/478 (10)
10/481 (8)   110 overs: 454-6

Van der Gugten 20–3–79–1; Hogan 23.3–4–46–4; Weighell 15–0–96–0; Douthwaite 18–2–72–2; Lloyd 15–2–57–2; Taylor 29–2–97–1; Root 3–0–21–0. *Second innings*—Hogan 9–1–24–1; van der Gugten 10–1–42–0; Lloyd 5–0–22–1; Douthwaite 4–0–13–0; Taylor 8–1–24–0; Weighell 4.1–0–27–0.

Umpires: B. J. Debenham and A. G. Wharf.   Referee: P. Whitticase.

At Northampton, April 22–25. GLAMORGAN lost to NORTHAMPTONSHIRE by seven wickets.

GLAMORGAN v KENT

At Cardiff, April 29–30. Glamorgan won by ten wickets. Glamorgan 19pts, Kent 3pts. Toss: Glamorgan. Championship debut: J. M. Cooke.

A low-scoring match hurtled to a conclusion at 5.45 on the second day, with the oldest men on either side making significant contributions. For Kent, Stevens marked turning 45 with a five-for; he was the oldest to take a Championship wicket on his birthday since 46-year-old Jim Sims, for Middlesex against Northamptonshire in May 1949. But on a well-grassed pitch, he was trumped by Glamorgan's Australian seamer Hogan, nearly 40, whose own five-wicket haul demolished Kent for 74 in their second innings. They had done little better in the first, shot out for 138 – after being 88 for one – with four wickets apiece for van der Gugten and Lloyd, whose modest seamers produced his best figures. Glamorgan polished off a small target quickly, Lloyd collecting all the runs. Labuschagne had fallen down the pavilion steps shortly before his first game of the season, having recently arrived from Australia. A scan of his hand revealed no break, but he was soon trapped lbw by Stevens – a moment that went viral.

Close of play: first day, Glamorgan 109-2 (Lloyd 54, Root 34).

Kent

*D. J. Bell-Drummond b van der Gugten	31	– c C. B. Cooke b Hogan	13
J. M. Cox c C. B. Cooke b Lloyd	30	– lbw b Hogan	6
Z. Crawley c C. B. Cooke b van der Gugten	33	– b Hogan	1
J. L. Denly lbw b Lloyd	0	– lbw b Lloyd	10
J. A. Leaning c C. B. Cooke b Hogan	2	– lbw b Hogan	8
H. G. Kuhn lbw b Hogan	8	– (8) lbw b van der Gugten	14
†O. G. Robinson c Lloyd b van der Gugten	17	– (6) c C. B. Cooke b Hogan	8
D. I. Stevens b Lloyd	5	– (7) b Lloyd	0
M. E. Milnes lbw b van der Gugten	1	– lbw b Harris	12
F. J. Klaassen lbw b Lloyd	5	– not out	0
M. L. Cummins not out	1	– b Harris	0
Lb 4, w 1	5	Nb 2	2

1/54 (1) 2/88 (2) 3/88 (4)   (45.3 overs) 138
4/93 (5) 5/107 (6) 6/120 (3)
7/131 (8) 8/131 (7) 9/136 (10) 10/138 (9)

1/18 (2) 2/19 (1)   (26.5 overs) 74
3/30 (3) 4/30 (4)
5/41 (6) 6/46 (5) 7/54 (7)
8/72 (8) 9/74 (9) 10/74 (11)

Carey 11–3–33–0; Hogan 11–0–33–2; van der Gugten 11.3–1–41–4; Harris 5–1–16–0; Lloyd 7–2–11–4. *Second innings*—Carey 5–1–15–0; Hogan 10–3–28–5; Lloyd 6–0–21–2; van der Gugten 3–0–5–1; Harris 2.5–0–5–2.

Glamorgan

J. M. Cooke c Kuhn b Stevens	0	– not out	0
D. L. Lloyd lbw b Stevens	62	– not out	19
M. Labuschagne lbw b Stevens	11		
W. T. Root lbw b Milnes	37		
K. S. Carlson c Crawley b Stevens	15		
*†C. B. Cooke b Milnes	0		
C. Z. Taylor lbw b Milnes	7		
J. A. R. Harris not out	18		
T. van der Gugten c Robinson b Stevens	10		
L. J. Carey b Cummins	14		
M. G. Hogan c Milnes b Klaassen	1		
B 2, lb 16, nb 4	22		

1/1 (1) 2/33 (3) 3/120 (2)   (61.5 overs) 197
4/124 (4) 5/124 (6) 6/140 (5)
7/148 (7) 8/159 (9) 9/188 (10) 10/197 (11)

(no wkt, 2.2 overs) 19

Milnes 20–3–46–3; Stevens 23–9–53–5; Klaassen 9.5–0–49–1; Cummins 9–2–31–1. *Second innings*—Cummins 1.2–1–6–0; Klaassen 1–0–13–0.

Umpires: N. L. Bainton and I. D. Blackwell.   Referee: P. M. Such.

At Manchester, May 6–9. GLAMORGAN drew with LANCASHIRE.

GLAMORGAN v YORKSHIRE

At Cardiff, May 13–16. Drawn. Glamorgan 11pts, Yorkshire 12pts. Toss: Yorkshire. First-class debut: H. G. Duke.

Billy Root, who was capped during the match, had scored a century against Yorkshire in April, but now brother Joe fell one short of a family double, chopping on against Douthwaite's medium-pace. Even so, his innings rescued Yorkshire from 36 for four, and later 111 for eight; a ninth-wicket stand of 118 with Patterson helped establish a healthy lead. After the first day was washed out, Glamorgan had endured familiar problems, crashing from 69 for two to 82 for seven. Going in again, they lost Labuschagne for a duck – his first four Championship innings of the season had produced 33 runs – and had only just cleared the deficit by the third-day close. But the weather had the last word, allowing 13 overs on the final day, and leaving Carlson stranded in sight of another hundred. The game was broadcast by Sky Sports, who had airtime to fill following the mid-tournament postponement of the IPL because of the Covid outbreak.

Close of play: first day, no play; second day, Yorkshire 69-4 (Root 34, Bess 16); third day, Glamorgan 108-3 (Lloyd 40, Carlson 44).

Glamorgan

J. M. Cooke lbw b Thompson	5	– c Duke b Coad	6
D. L. Lloyd b Patterson	31	– lbw b Coad	40
M. Labuschagne lbw b Coad	10	– b Thompson	0
W. T. Root c and b Brook	23	– lbw b Brook	13
K. S. Carlson c Köhler-Cadmore b Patterson	4	– not out	88
*†C. B. Cooke lbw b Brook	3	– not out	8
D. A. Douthwaite lbw b Brook	0		
M. G. Neser c Lyth b Thompson	24		
A. G. Salter not out	24		
T. van der Gugten c Köhler-Cadmore b Patterson	9		
M. G. Hogan c Root b Willey	7		
B 8, lb 1	9	B 4, lb 5	9

1/11 (1) 2/34 (3) 3/69 (2) (53.5 overs) 149 1/16 (1) (4 wkts, 40 overs) 164
4/73 (5) 5/73 (4) 6/73 (7) 2/17 (3) 3/43 (4)
7/82 (6) 8/117 (8) 9/128 (10) 10/149 (11) 4/117 (2)

Coad 12–2–40–1; Thompson 13–4–33–2; Willey 7.5–0–25–1; Patterson 13–3–27–3; Brook 8–2–15–3. *Second innings*—Coad 9–3–16–2; Thompson 13–2–44–1; Patterson 7–0–36–0; Brook 4–0–14–1; Willey 7–0–45–0.

Yorkshire

A. Lyth c Carlson b Neser	0	D. J. Willey c J. M. Cooke b Douthwaite	3
T. Köhler-Cadmore b Hogan	1	*S. A. Patterson not out	47
G. S. Ballance c J. M. Cooke b Neser	7	B. O. Coad c Neser b Salter	0
J. E. Root b Douthwaite	99	B 18, lb 10, nb 2	30
H. C. Brook lbw b Neser	11		
D. M. Bess c Lloyd b Neser	20	1/0 (1) 2/6 (2) 3/10 (3) (75.3 overs) 230
†H. G. Duke c J. M. Cooke b Neser	0	4/36 (5) 5/78 (6) 6/78 (7)
J. A. Thompson lbw b Hogan	12	7/91 (8) 8/111 (9) 9/229 (4) 10/230 (11)

Neser 15–5–39–5; Hogan 16–5–42–2; van der Gugten 18–3–37–0; Lloyd 8–2–28–0; Douthwaite 8–1–22–2; Labuschagne 3–0–13–0; Salter 7.3–1–21–1.

Umpires: N. J. Llong and M. J. Saggers.   Referee: S. Cummings.

At Canterbury, May 20–23. GLAMORGAN drew with KENT.

GLAMORGAN v LANCASHIRE

At Cardiff, June 3–5. Glamorgan won by six wickets. Glamorgan 19pts, Lancashire 3pts. Toss: Glamorgan.

Glamorgan beat Lancashire at home for the first time since 1996, when the teams' current coaches, Matthew Maynard and Glen Chapple, were both playing (Maynard came out on top then too, hitting 214). A seaming pitch meant another low-scoring encounter, including 19 wickets on the first day, when members were allowed back after 623 days, as part of a Welsh government Covid test event.

Glamorgan were indebted to their Australian imports: the nippy Neser took seven wickets in the match, four lbw, while Labuschagne top-scored in both innings after scraping together only 44 runs in his previous six. Hogan, another Australian (though England-qualified), chipped in with two wickets, including his 400th in first-class cricket for Glamorgan. In testing conditions, a target of 188 – the highest total of the match – might have proved tricky: Glamorgan had lost nine for 76 in their first innings; Lancashire nine for 92 in their second. But Lloyd and Joe Cooke started positively with a stand of 72, and Labuschagne kept the scoreboard ticking over, reaching his half-century in 54 balls with just four fours, as Lancashire suffered their first defeat of the season, little more than an hour into the third morning.

Close of play: first day, Glamorgan 150-9 (Neser 17, Hogan 0); second day, Glamorgan 137-3 (Labuschagne 32, Carlson 14).

Lancashire

K. K. Jennings b Hogan	3	– lbw b Weighell	12
A. L. Davies c Salter b Weighell	21	– lbw b Neser	47
L. W. P. Wells lbw b Weighell	10	– b Douthwaite	26
J. J. Bohannon c B. C. Cooke b Neser	14	– b Neser	7
L. S. Livingstone c C. B. Cooke b Lloyd	17	– c Neser b Douthwaite	14
*†D. J. Vilas lbw b Hogan	12	– lbw b Neser	12
L. Wood lbw b Neser	28	– run out (Labuschagne)	0
D. J. Lamb lbw b Neser	12	– c C. B. Cooke b Lloyd	19
T. E. Bailey b Douthwaite	31	– c C. B. Cooke b Neser	0
S. Mahmood b Douthwaite	4	– b Lloyd	12
M. W. Parkinson not out	6	– not out	6
Lb 4, w 1, nb 10	15	B 1, lb 8	9

1/5 (1) 2/32 (3) 3/37 (2) (56.1 overs) 173
4/66 (4) 5/86 (6) 6/86 (5)
7/122 (7) 8/143 (8) 9/164 (10) 10/173 (9)

1/38 (1) 2/72 (3) (51.1 overs) 164
3/88 (2) 4/109 (4)
5/113 (5) 6/113 (7) 7/124 (6)
8/124 (9) 9/153 (8) 10/164 (10)

Neser 15-3–46–3; Hogan 11–1–30–2; Weighell 12–2–46–2; Douthwaite 7.1–1–16–2; Lloyd 8–1–24–1; Salter 3–0–7–0. *Second innings*—Neser 13–1–53–4; Hogan 12–1–19–0; Weighell 8–2–23–1; Lloyd 12.1–3–28–2; Douthwaite 6–0–32–2.

Glamorgan

J. M. Cooke b Bailey	14	– c Livingstone b Parkinson	38
D. L. Lloyd b Mahmood	21	– c Jennings b Bailey	41
M. Labuschagne lbw b Lamb	44	– not out	63
W. T. Root lbw b Bailey	0	– lbw b Mahmood	3
K. S. Carlson lbw b Bailey	12	– c Vilas b Wood	16
*†C. B. Cooke c Bohannon b Lamb	0	– not out	17
D. A. Douthwaite c Wood b Mahmood	18		
M. G. Neser not out	17		
W. J. Weighell c Vilas b Wood	13		
A. G. Salter lbw b Mahmood	0		
M. G. Hogan run out (Bailey/Vilas)	0		
B 4, lb 3, nb 4	11	B 1, lb 7, nb 2	10

1/38 (2) 2/74 (1) 3/74 (4) (39.2 overs) 150
4/92 (5) 5/97 (6) 6/102 (3)
7/127 (7) 8/144 (9) 9/145 (10) 10/150 (11)

1/72 (1) (4 wkts, 58.1 overs) 188
2/95 (2) 3/102 (4)
4/146 (5)

Bailey 11–3–40–3; Mahmood 11.2–1–34–3; Wood 9–0–42–1; Lamb 8–1–27–2. *Second innings*—Bailey 20.1–0–61–1; Mahmood 10–1–29–0; Lamb 10–1–35–1; Parkinson 6–0–22–1; Livingstone 1–0–5–0; Wells 1–0–1–0.

Umpires: P. K. Baldwin and A. G. Wharf. Referee: T. J. Boon.

At Hove, July 4–7. GLAMORGAN drew with SUSSEX.

GLAMORGAN v NORTHAMPTONSHIRE

At Cardiff, July 11–14. Drawn. Glamorgan 16pts, Northamptonshire 10pts. Toss: Northamptonshire. Championship debuts: H. O. M. Gouldstone, C. J. White.

Northamptonshire faced a struggle as soon as Glamorgan declared before play on the final day. Needing 247 to avoid an innings defeat, they lost Vasconcelos second ball, and were without both Berg (who injured his ankle warming up before the second day) and Procter, who had returned home after a second family bereavement in a week. Keogh was allowed to retire at 3pm, just after reaching 50, to watch his grandmother's funeral on his laptop. Despite all this, they survived: Keogh returned to finish undefeated on 71, while the 20-year-old debutant wicketkeeper Harry Gouldstone – son of former county batsman Mark – resisted for more than four hours. The internet came in useful again: his mother, holidaying in Portugal, delightedly followed his dogged display. Earlier, Salter polished off Northamptonshire's first innings with a career-best four for 18, then Glamorgan piled up a huge lead. As the sun finally shone after two rain-affected days, Labuschagne – fresh from scoring 276 for the Second XI, also against Northamptonshire – purred to 77, before shouldering arms to a straight one from Procter. Carlson and Chris Cooke took over, sharing an unbroken partnership of 307, a county fifth-wicket record, surpassing the 264 of Maurice Robinson and Stan Montgomery against Hampshire at Bournemouth in 1949. But Northamptonshire clung on.

Close of play: first day, Northamptonshire 128-4 (Thurston 36, Zaib 18); second day, Glamorgan 52-2 (Labuschagne 17, Root 6); third day, Glamorgan 462-4 (Carlson 170, C. B. Cooke 133).

Northamptonshire

*R. S. Vasconcelos c Carlson b van der Gugten	25	– c C. B. Cooke b Neser	0
E. N. Gay c C. B. Cooke b van der Gugten	22	– c C. B. Cooke b Neser	19
C. O. Thurston c Root b Hogan	48	– c C. B. Cooke b Neser	29
R. I. Keogh c Root b van der Gugten	12	– not out	71
L. A. Procter lbw b Neser	3		
S. A. Zaib c Labuschagne b Salter	50	– (5) run out (Labuschagne/ C. B. Cooke)	19
†H. O. M. Gouldstone not out	17	– (6) not out	67
S. C. Kerrigan c van der Gugten b Salter	0	– (7) c C. B. Cooke b Hogan	36
B. W. Sanderson lbw b Salter	5		
C. J. White c van der Gugten b Salter	10		
G. K. Berg absent hurt			
Lb 21, nb 2	23	Lb 2, w 5, nb 2	9

1/40 (2) 2/55 (1) 3/87 (4)   (77.3 overs) 215   1/0 (1)   (5 wkts, 92.4 overs) 250
4/94 (5) 5/181 (3) 6/181 (6)   2/39 (2) 3/52 (3)
7/191 (8) 8/197 (9) 9/215 (10)   4/97 (5) 5/226 (7)

In the second innings Keogh, when 50, retired not out at 140-4 and resumed at 226-5.

Neser 18–2–51–1; Hogan 16–7–29–1; van der Gugten 19–2–46–3; Douthwaite 9–1–36–0; Lloyd 5–1–14–0; Salter 10.3–4–18–4. *Second innings*—Neser 20–5–52–3; Hogan 13.4–3–46–1; van der Gugten 12–2–33–0; Salter 21–4–40–0; Labuschagne 16–3–47–0; Root 2–0–9–0; Douthwaite 5–1–12–0; Lloyd 3–1–9–0.

Glamorgan

J. M. Cooke c Vasconcelos b Sanderson	16
D. L. Lloyd c Vasconcelos b Procter	13
M. Labuschagne b Procter	77
W. T. Root b Procter	45
K. S. Carlson not out	170
*†C. B. Cooke not out	133
B 2, lb 5, w 1	8

1/28 (1)   (4 wkts dec, 113 overs) 462
2/32 (2) 3/154 (3)
4/155 (4)   110 overs: 443-4

D. A. Douthwaite, M. G. Neser, A. G. Salter, T. van der Gugten and M. G. Hogan did not bat.

Sanderson 25–5–85–1; White 26–0–122–0; Procter 20–2–77–3; Kerrigan 29–2–106–0; Keogh 9–0–32–0; Zaib 2–0–19–0; Gay 2–0–14–0.

Umpires: G. D. Lloyd and T. Lungley.   Referee: S. G. Hinks.

DIVISION TWO

GLAMORGAN v ESSEX

At Cardiff, August 30–September 1. Essex won by an innings and 74 runs. Essex 22pts, Glamorgan 3pts. Toss: Glamorgan. First-class debut: J. S. Rymell. Championship debut: S. J. Reingold.

Glamorgan subsided to defeat early on the third day, though the damage had been done on the first, after Cooke surprisingly opted to bat on a green-tinged pitch. Six wickets went down in the opening session, and it was 86 for eight before Douthwaite, who hit eight fours, put on 46 with Carey; medium-pacer Snater finished with six. Essex lost Alastair Cook for a third-ball duck, but Browne – who survived a straightforward chance to Lloyd at second slip off Hogan when eight – ensured a big lead with his first century for over two years. Pepper contributed a breezy 63 and, although the 20-year-old debutant Josh Rymell was lbw first ball, Snater made 48 to swell the advantage to 186 by tea on the second day. Glamorgan were quickly in trouble again: both openers departed for ducks, and they nosedived to 29 for six before Cooke ensured the match would reach a third day. Next morning, Sam Cook polished off the last three wickets – including Carey for an 17-ball 29 – to finish with five. Carlson had been awarded his county cap on the first day, but suffered a rare double failure.

Close of play: first day, Essex 92-2 (Browne 50, Lawrence 29); second day, Glamorgan 71-6 (Cooke 39, Salter 11).

Glamorgan

H. D. Rutherford c Pepper b Harmer	31	– lbw b Porter	0
D. L. Lloyd c Harmer b S. J. Cook	0	– lbw b S. J. Cook	0
S. J. Reingold c Harmer b Snater	9	– run out (Snater)	4
W. T. Root lbw b Snater	0	– lbw b Porter	4
K. S. Carlson c A. N. Cook b Snater	13	– b S. J. Cook	8
*†C. B. Cooke b Snater	0	– not out	47
D. A. Douthwaite c Porter b Snater	39	– lbw b Snater	1
A. G. Salter c Lawrence b Harmer	7	– b Porter	11
T. van der Gugten b Harmer	3	– c Wheater b S. J. Cook	4
L. J. Carey c Harmer b Snater	29	– c Rymell b S. J. Cook	29
M. G. Hogan not out	1	– b S. J. Cook	0
Lb 2	2	B 4	4

1/8 (2) 2/39 (3) 3/39 (4)	(44.5 overs) 134	1/0 (1) 2/2 (2)	(33.5 overs) 112
4/55 (5) 5/55 (6) 6/57 (1)		3/8 (3) 4/16 (4)	
7/69 (8) 8/86 (9) 9/132 (7) 10/134 (10)		5/20 (5) 6/29 (7) 7/73 (8)	
		8/78 (9) 9/112 (10) 10/112 (11)	

Porter 11–2–36–0; S. J. Cook 7–3–11–1; Snater 11.5–5–39–6; Harmer 15–6–46–3. *Second innings*—Porter 8–1–35–3; S. J. Cook 10.5–1–37–5; Snater 6–1–17–1; Harmer 7–0–17–0; Westley 2–0–2–0.

Essex

N. L. J. Browne c Douthwaite b Reingold	102	S. J. Cook lbw b Carey	0
A. N. Cook c Cooke b Carey	0	J. A. Porter not out	0
*T. Westley c Cooke b van der Gugten	8		
D. W. Lawrence c van der Gugten b Salter	34	B 5, lb 16, nb 6	27
M. S. Pepper c and b Reingold	63		
J. S. Rymell lbw b Douthwaite	0	1/8 (2) 2/41 (3)	(101.2 overs) 320
†A. J. A. Wheater b Carey	36	3/100 (4) 4/208 (1)	
S. R. Harmer c Cooke b Reingold	2	5/215 (6) 6/217 (5) 7/233 (8)	
S. Snater c van der Gugten b Salter	48	8/312 (7) 9/320 (10) 10/320 (9)	

P. I. Walter replaced Lawrence, who left to join England's Test squad.

Hogan 17–8–37–0; Carey 18–4–56–3; van der Gugten 18–2–57–1; Salter 23.2–6–51–2; Lloyd 6–1–15–0; Douthwaite 13–1–68–1; Reingold 6–1–15–3.

Umpires: B. J. Debenham and R. T. Robinson.   Referee: S. G. Hinks.

At Chester-le-Street, September 5–8. GLAMORGAN lost to DURHAM by an innings and 42 runs.

GLAMORGAN v GLOUCESTERSHIRE

At Cardiff, September 12–15. Gloucestershire won by ten wickets. Gloucestershire 22pts, Glamorgan 5pts. Toss: Gloucestershire. First-class debut: B. J. J. Wells.

Another insipid performance saw Glamorgan droop to a third successive heavy defeat, as Gloucestershire wrapped up their seventh win of the season before lunch on the final day. Initially, it seemed as if Dent had erred in fielding first, as Glamorgan's openers Rutherford and Lloyd put on 136. But the bowlers made inroads – Tom Price took three wickets in 13 balls – before a patient innings from Byrom, who lasted 277 minutes in his first home appearance for his new county, earned a third batting point. A good diving catch from Cooke sent back Hammond – Hogan's 400th Championship wicket – but Dent made a solid 75 before becoming Salter's 100th first-class victim. With van Buuren contributing 65, honours were roughly even by lunch on the third day: Gloucestershire were seven in front but eight down. Then Price swung the match with a maiden fifty, adding 69 with Payne and 40 with Warner. Now 110 adrift, Glamorgan collapsed in familiar fashion: they were 57 for six by the close, and next morning the Pakistan slow left-armer Zafar Gohar mopped up.

Close of play: first day, Glamorgan 264-6 (Byrom 60, Salter 26); second day, Gloucestershire 224-4 (van Buuren 65, Wells 23); third day, Glamorgan 57-6 (Douthwaite 4, Salter 0).

Glamorgan

H. D. Rutherford b Warner	62	– c Hammond b Zafar Gohar	17
D. L. Lloyd c sub (O. J. Price) b Higgins	73	– c Hammond b Payne	17
N. J. Selman c Wells b Payne	1	– c sub (O. J. Price) b Zafar Gohar	0
E. J. Byrom b Payne	78	– b Higgins	8
K. S. Carlson c sub (O. J. Price) b T. J. Price	17	– c sub (O. J. Price) b Zafar Gohar	0
*†C. B. Cooke b T. J. Price	6	– c Dent b van Buuren	6
D. A. Douthwaite lbw b T. J. Price	0	– b Higgins	14
A. G. Salter b Payne	26	– lbw b Zafar Gohar	19
R. A. J. Smith c Lace b Higgins	8	– b Zafar Gohar	4
T. van der Gugten c Wells b Higgins	14	– c van Buuren b Zafar Gohar	14
M. G. Hogan not out	0	– not out	9
B 9, lb 7, nb 8	24	B 4, lb 6, nb 6	16
	309		**124**

1/136 (2) 2/137 (3) 3/149 (1)   (107.3 overs) 309
4/179 (5) 5/191 (6) 6/191 (7)
7/264 (8) 8/279 (9) 9/307 (4) 10/309 (10)

1/39 (2) 2/39 (1)   (42 overs) 124
3/42 (3) 4/46 (5)
5/48 (4) 6/57 (6) 7/84 (8)
8/94 (9) 9/102 (7) 10/124 (10)

Payne 26–8–61–3; Higgins 27.1–2–90–3; Warner 16–5–40–1; T. J. Price 18–7–44–3; Zafar Gohar 17–2–47–0; Charlesworth 1.2–0–9–0; van Buuren 2–0–2–0. *Second innings*—Payne 9–2–37–1; Higgins 11–1–29–2; Zafar Gohar 18–7–43–6; van Buuren 4–2–5–1.

Gloucestershire

*C. D. J. Dent b Salter	75	– (2) not out. ... 11
M. A. H. Hammond c Cooke b Hogan	34	– (1) not out. ... 4
T. C. Lace c Cooke b Lloyd	12	
G. L. van Buuren lbw b Lloyd	65	
R. F. Higgins lbw b Salter	0	
†B. J. J. Wells c Lloyd b van der Gugten	40	
B. G. Charlesworth b Smith	44	
Zafar Gohar c Cooke b Hogan	5	
T. J. Price lbw b Hogan	71	
D. A. Payne c Cooke b Douthwaite	34	
J. D. Warner not out	10	
B 4, lb 18, w 1, nb 6	29	

1/63 (2) 2/90 (3) 3/184 (1)   (140.4 overs) 419   (no wkt, 1.3 overs) 15
4/184 (5) 5/224 (4) 6/268 (6)
7/279 (8) 8/310 (7) 9/379 (10)
10/419 (9)   110 overs: 327-8

Hogan 27.4–6–49–3; Smith 22–3–84–1; van der Gugten 25–3–76–1; Salter 42–14–93–2; Lloyd 13–2–53–2; Douthwaite 11–0–42–1. *Second innings*—Salter 1–0–9–0; Carlson 0.3–0–6–0.

Umpires: I. D. Blackwell and N. Pratt.   Referee: S. G. Hinks.

At The Oval, September 21–24. GLAMORGAN drew with SURREY. *Chris Cooke makes an undefeated 205 in Glamorgan's 672 for six, their third-highest total; Surrey respond with 722 for four.*

GLOUCESTERSHIRE

Winning isn't everything

Alex Winter

What a year it almost was. Gloucestershire played themselves into contention in all three competitions – yet came away with nothing. In the Championship, no county could match their eight victories, which made 2021 their most successful season since 1998; in the Royal London, they made the knockouts; and in the Blast, they fell just short.

Their Championship start was near perfect: four wins and a draw from five was their best since the days of the Graces, and there were some notable scalps. The highlight, naturally, was beating Somerset at Taunton for the first time since 1993; victory by eight wickets restored pride after the humiliation of 2020, when they were dismissed for 76 and 70.

The success was in part down to James Bracey, whose 478 runs in those five matches earned a Test debut against New Zealand. But it went badly, prompting some to write off his international career after eight runs in three innings. He managed just 236 in the last five Championship matches, though England took him on the Lions tour of Australia, where he made a century. David Payne was also called up, after Covid forced England into selecting a second-string ODI squad against Pakistan. It meant he missed a vital game at Cheltenham (and he didn't play for England either).

Defeat by Hampshire ended Gloucestershire's tilt at a maiden Championship, when a draw would have taken them into Division One; another ten overs at the crease might have been enough. Their batting in that game – indeed all season – let them down. Of the specialists, only Bracey, Miles Hammond and Ian Cockbain averaged over 30, and no county earned fewer batting points than Gloucestershire's 18. West Indies Test captain Kraigg Brathwaite played six matches, hitting only one fifty.

In September, Australian international Marcus Harris was signed on a two-year deal to play all formats. It was hailed as a statement of intent by chief executive Will Brown, as the club laid out their strategy for winning a first Championship by 2025. In October, Steve Snell, the county's former wicketkeeper, was recruited to the new post of performance director, overseeing talent development. In November, Gloucestershire appointed former South Africa batsman Dale Benkenstein head coach, with Ian Harvey continuing as assistant. They will also have a new club captain after Chris Dent stood down. His four summers in charge brought Championship promotion in 2019 – which finally takes effect in 2022.

The new set-up inherits a skilful attack, if one without much pace (though the arrival of Pakistan's Naseem Shah should help). Ryan Higgins claimed 51 wickets, his most productive summer, while the excellent Payne took 34 at 21. Australian international Dan Worrall worked hard for 27, but in July announced

Philip Brown, Getty Images

David Payne

he would take advantage of a UK passport and join Surrey as a local player – to the exasperation of many.

Gloucestershire's other overseas signings proved match-winners. New Zealander Glenn Phillips was a batting star of the T20 Blast, while Pakistan left-arm spinner Zafar Gohar bowled his side to Championship victories at Cardiff and Bristol, leaving them second in Division Two. Zafar returns for 2022; Dutch seamer Paul van Meekeren will also be available.

Phillips hit 500 runs in the Blast (behind only Leicestershire's Josh Inglis), including 36 sixes – a tournament record – yet Gloucestershire still couldn't reach the quarters. The batting was hindered by Cockbain sustaining an ankle injury that kept him out of four matches.

As in the Championship, the Blast campaign ended in a showdown in the last group fixture, this time at Somerset. Gloucestershire seemed in control, before conceding a scarcely believable 101 in six overs. Their chase never got going and – despite sitting in the top four almost all tournament – they crashed out. They would already have secured a place in the quarters had they beaten Surrey at Cheltenham two days earlier, but they lost that heavily too.

At least there was a festival at Cheltenham after a Covid-enforced absence in 2020. Even so, the College Ground had to welcome reduced numbers when the lifting of restrictions was pushed back to late July. But since it was not classified as a stadium, crowds of a similar size to Bristol were admitted. The scene was a throwback to former times: no temporary stands, but seats arranged nine or ten deep around the Chapel End boundary.

In August, Gloucestershire did squeeze through to the knockout stage of the Royal London Cup, but were again roundly beaten by Surrey. The tournament had included an encouraging performance from 20-year-old Ben Charlesworth, whose unbeaten 99 brought victory over Hampshire. In an otherwise modest year for Tom Lace, another attractive young batter, he hit his maiden Gloucestershire century in the Championship defeat by Hampshire.

There was mixed news for young siblings. Tom and Ollie Price did well late in the summer – and both agreed two-year deals. But the Hankinses, George and Harry, were released. Meanwhile, Ben Wells, a 21-year-old wicketkeeper-batsman, was signed from the Somerset Academy, and given a first-class debut at Cardiff. Seamer Ajeet Dale, also 21, arrived from Hampshire.

An otherwise positive summer featured two unwelcome incidents. The county were criticised for staging the women's Test between England and India on a wicket previously used for a T20 match, though the ECB was blamed for the late scheduling. More seriously, former fast bowler and club legend Syd Lawrence revealed in a Sky Sports documentary that he had suffered racial abuse from a team-mate. Gloucestershire offered an unreserved apology.

GLOUCESTERSHIRE RESULTS

County Championship matches – Played 14: Won 8, Lost 4, Drawn 2.
Vitality T20 Blast matches – Played 14: Won 6, Lost 6, No result 2.
Royal London Cup matches – Played 8: Won 4, Lost 4. Cancelled 1.

LV= County Championship, 3rd in Group 2, 2nd in Division 2;
Vitality T20 Blast, 6th in South Group; Royal London Cup, quarter-finalists.

COUNTY CHAMPIONSHIP AVERAGES, BATTING AND FIELDING

Cap		Birthplace	M	I	NO	R	HS	100	Avge	Ct
2021	J. A. Tattersall.........	Harrogate	2	4	1	162	86*	0	54.00	2
2016	G. L. van Buuren¶....	Pretoria, SA.....	6	9	2	354	110*	1	50.57	3
2016	†J. R. Bracey.........	Bristol	11	21	2	715	118	1	37.63	33
2013	†M. A. H. Hammond...	Cheltenham‡......	9	17	2	547	94	0	36.46	11
2020	T. J. Price.........	Oxford.........	6	9	4	177	71	0	35.40	1
2011	I. A. Cockbain......	Liverpool.........	6	11	1	302	117	1	30.20	1
2021	K. C. Brathwaite¶....	St Michael, Barbados	6	11	0	295	60	0	26.81	6
2010	†C. D. J. Dent........	Bristol.........	12	23	2	560	91*	0	26.66	5
2010	J. M. R. Taylor......	Banbury.........	3	5	0	133	40	0	26.60	1
2016	J. Shaw.........	Wakefield.........	4	6	2	105	41*	0	26.25	1
2020	T. C. Lace.........	Hammersmith......	14	26	4	573	118	1	26.04	9
2018	†B. G. Charlesworth...	Oxford.........	3	5	0	112	49	0	22.40	0
2018	R. F. Higgins.........	Harare, Zimbabwe	13	19	1	376	73	0	20.88	3
2013	G. T. Hankins......	Bath.........	5	7	1	120	37	0	20.00	6
2013	M. D. Taylor.........	Banbury.........	9	12	3	166	56	0	18.44	0
2021	G. D. Phillips¶......	East London, SA ...	3	6	0	109	47	0	18.16	5
2021	O. J. Price.........	Oxford.........	4	7	0	110	33	0	15.71	4
2020	G. F. B. Scott.........	Hemel Hempstead ...	5	7	0	100	31	0	14.28	3
2021	†Zafar Gohar¶.......	Lahore, Pakistan	4	6	0	78	30	0	13.00	0
2011	D. A. Payne.........	Poole.........	10	12	3	102	34	0	11.33	6
2013	T. M. J. Smith......	Eastbourne.........	5	8	1	76	47	0	10.85	2
2021	D. C. Goodman......	Ashford, Kent	4	5	3	20	9*	0	10.00	0
2018	D. J. Worrall¶.......	Melbourne, Australia ..	8	12	3	75	24	0	8.33	4

Also batted: J. D. Warner (*Wakefield*) (cap 2021) (2 matches) 10, 10* (1 ct); B. J. J. Wells (*Bath*)
(cap 2021) (1 match) 40 (2 ct).

‡ *Born in Gloucestershire.* ¶ *Official overseas player.*

Gloucestershire award caps on first-class debut.

BOWLING

	Style	O	M	R	W	BB	5I	Avge
Zafar Gohar	SLA	117.3	32	287	20	6-43	3	14.35
D. A. Payne	LFM	258.2	59	719	34	6-56	2	21.14
R. F. Higgins	RFM	443	118	1,143	51	5-46	2	22.41
D. J. Worrall.........	RFM	249.5	80	621	27	5-54	2	23.00
T. J. Price.........	RM	128	37	368	15	4-72	0	24.53
M. D. Taylor.........	LM	266.1	67	818	27	5-40	1	30.29

Also bowled: K. C. Brathwaite (OB) 4–0–16–0; B. G. Charlesworth (RM) 7.2–0–37–0; C. D. J.
Dent (SLA) 0–18–0; D. C. Goodman (RM) 104–25–252–5; M. A. H. Hammond (RM)
19–2–85–3; G. D. Phillips (OB) 40–3–159–4; O. J. Price (OB) 33–5–100–0; G. F. B. Scott (RM)
51–13–149–2; J. Shaw (RFM) 86–10–333–9; T. M. J. Smith (SLA) 104–8–303–4; G. L. van
Buuren (SLA) 48.4–11–119–7; J. D. Warner (RFM) 37.3–7–118–4.

LEADING VITALITY BLAST AVERAGES (100 runs/15 overs)

Batting	Runs	HS	Avge	SR	Ct/St	**Bowling**	W	BB	Avge	ER
G. D. Phillips ...	500	94*	55.55	**163.39**	7/1	T. M. J. Smith....	10	2-17	29.40	**7.17**
C. D. J. Dent ...	241	42	26.77	**150.62**	4	B. A. C. Howell ..	15	4-15	23.40	**8.10**
R. F. Higgins ...	113	43	37.66	**143.03**	2	J. Shaw	13	3-32	21.38	**8.17**
B. A. C. Howell..	246	53*	24.60	**142.19**	2	D. A. Payne	12	3-30	26.50	**8.83**
I. A. Cockbain ..	244	72	40.66	**135.55**	1	D. J. Worrall	3	2-33	91.66	**8.87**
M. A. H. Hammond..	222	44	18.50	**130.58**	6	R. F. Higgins	11	3-18	24.09	**9.75**
J. M. R. Taylor .	227	38	22.70	**119.47**	6					

LEADING ROYAL LONDON CUP AVERAGES (100 runs/4 wickets)

Batting	Runs	HS	Avge	SR	Ct/St
G. F. B. Scott...	238	66*	59.50	84.39	3
B. G. Charlesworth	260	99*	52.00	82.27	1
J. M. R. Taylor .	257	67*	51.40	93.11	3
G. L. van Buuren	202	51*	33.66	83.12	2
J. R. Bracey	161	90	32.20	90.96	8/1
C. D. J. Dent ...	190	112*	31.66	96.93	3

Bowling	W	BB	Avge	ER
G. L. van Buuren .	11	3-32	28.09	4.61
D. J. Worrall.....	7	4-58	32.85	5.49
M. D. Taylor....	7	2-22	33.00	4.62
T. M. J. Smith....	9	3-28	33.88	4.26
J. Shaw.........	8	4-36	35.25	5.64
J. D. Warner ...	6	3-42	41.00	5.34

FIRST-CLASS COUNTY RECORDS

Highest score for	341	C. M. Spearman v Middlesex at Gloucester	2004
Highest score against	319	C. J. L. Rogers (Northamptonshire) at Northampton	2006
Leading run-scorer	33,664	W. R. Hammond (avge 57.05).................	1920–51
Best bowling for	10-40	E. G. Dennett v Essex at Bristol	1906
Best bowling against	{ 10-66	A. A. Mailey (Australians) at Cheltenham	1921
	{ 10-66	K. Smales (Nottinghamshire) at Stroud............	1956
Leading wicket-taker	3,170	C. W. L. Parker (avge 19.43).................	1903–35
Highest total for	695-9 dec	v Middlesex at Gloucester..................	2004
Highest total against	774-7 dec	by Australians at Bristol	1948
Lowest total for	17	v Australians at Cheltenham	1896
Lowest total against	12	by Northamptonshire at Gloucester................	1907

LIST A COUNTY RECORDS

Highest score for	177	A. J. Wright v Scotland at Bristol	1997
Highest score against	190	J. M. Vince (Hampshire) at Southampton	2019
Leading run-scorer	7,825	M. W. Alleyne (avge 26.89)	1986–2005
Best bowling for	7-29	D. A. Payne v Essex at Chelmsford...........	2010
Best bowling against	6-16	Shoaib Akhtar (Worcestershire) at Worcester....	2005
Leading wicket-taker	393	M. W. Alleyne (avge 29.88)	1986–2005
Highest total for	401-7	v Buckinghamshire at Wing	2003
Highest total against	496-4	by Surrey at The Oval	2007
Lowest total for	49	v Middlesex at Bristol	1978
Lowest total against	48	by Middlesex at Lydney	1973

TWENTY20 COUNTY RECORDS

Highest score for	126*	M. Klinger v Essex at Bristol...................	2015
Highest score against	116*	C. L. White (Somerset) at Taunton	2006
Leading run-scorer	**3,308**	**I. A. Cockbain** (avge 33.41, SR 131.47)	**2011–21**
Best bowling for	5-16	T. M. J. Smith v Warwickshire at Birmingham	2020
Best bowling against	5-16	R. E. Watkins (Glamorgan) at Cardiff	2009
Leading wicket-taker	**131**	**B. A. C. Howell** (avge 19.44, ER 7.20)	**2012–21**
Highest total for	254-3	v Middlesex at Uxbridge	2011
Highest total against	250-3	by Somerset at Taunton	2006
Lowest total for	68	v Hampshire at Bristol	2010
Lowest total against	97	by Surrey at The Oval	2010

ADDRESS

The Bristol County Ground, Nevil Road, Bristol BS7 9EJ; 0117 910 8000; reception@glosccc.co.uk; www.gloscricket.co.uk. Twitter: @Gloscricket.

OFFICIALS

Captain 2021 C. D. J. Dent
Head coach 2021 I. J. Harvey
2022 D. M. Benkenstein
Performance director S. D. Snell
Head of talent pathway T. H. C. Hancock

President R. A. Gibbons
Chair D. Jones
Chief executive W. G. Brown
Head groundsman S. P. Williams
Scorer A. J. Bull

GROUP TWO

GLOUCESTERSHIRE v SURREY

At Bristol, April 8–11. **Gloucestershire won by eight wickets.** Gloucestershire 22pts, Surrey 4pts. Toss: Gloucestershire. Championship debut: A. A. P. Atkinson.

A disciplined Gloucestershire performance gave Ian Harvey victory in his first game as interim head coach. Surrey were under par with the bat in the first innings – Burns and Pope continued to struggle after poor winters with England – then terrible with the ball, conceding an opening stand of 139 from 28 overs as Gloucestershire raced into the ascendancy. Topley took his first five-wicket haul in senior cricket since 2014 (also against Gloucestershire, though for Essex); the hosts still earned a three-figure lead. Surrey were five down and only 81 ahead by tea on the third day but, with the attack a bowler light after Shaw picked up a groin injury, Foakes battled back with his 11th first-class hundred, and fourth against these opponents. The progress was wasted in a collapse of five for 15, and Gloucestershire were set 228 in 63 overs. Van Buuren's 94-ball hundred helped them gallop to their first win over Surrey for ten years.

Close of play: first day, Surrey 220-9 (Topley 6, Virdi 4); second day, Gloucestershire 311-8 (J. M. R. Taylor 26, M. D. Taylor 13); third day, Surrey 232-5 (Foakes 81, Clark 23).

Surrey

*R. J. Burns c Hankins b Payne	4	– c Payne b Scott	74
M. D. Stoneman lbw b Higgins	8	– lbw b Higgins	16
H. M. Amla lbw b Shaw	56	– c Bracey b M. D. Taylor	0
O. J. D. Pope c Scott b Shaw	22	– c Bracey b M. D. Taylor	0
†B. T. Foakes lbw b Higgins	26	– c Bracey b M. D. Taylor	133
J. L. Smith b Shaw	20	– b Payne	27
J. Clark c Bracey b Higgins	8	– b M. D. Taylor	52
J. Overton b Payne	40	– lbw b Higgins	1
A. A. P. Atkinson b Shaw	8	– lbw b Higgins	0
R. J. W. Topley c Bracey b Payne	6	– not out	1
G. S. Virdi not out	4	– run out (Lace)	1
B 9, lb 9	18	B 9, lb 7, nb 12	28
	—		—
(70.3 overs)	220	(104 overs)	333

1/8 (1) 2/12 (2) 3/48 (4) 4/109 (3) 5/136 (5) 6/144 (7) 7/169 (6) 8/185 (9) 9/207 (8) 10/220 (10)

1/41 (2) 2/46 (3) 3/48 (4) 4/145 (1) 5/187 (6) 6/318 (7) 7/327 (8) 8/327 (9) 9/331 (5) 10/333 (11)

Payne 17.3–4–49–3; Higgins 19–10–35–3; Shaw 16–2–48–4; M. D. Taylor 12.3–3–44–0; Scott 6–1–26–0. *Second innings*—Payne 22–3–75–1; Higgins 26–8–62–3; M. D. Taylor 29–6–94–4; Shaw 1–0–3–0; van Buuren 13–3–28–0); Scott 13–2–55–1.

Gloucestershire

†J. R. Bracey lbw b Virdi	54	– c Clark b Virdi	14
*C. D. J. Dent b Topley	78	– not out	91
T. C. Lace lbw b Virdi	65	– c Pope b Topley	0
G. L. van Buuren c Foakes b Topley	0	– not out	110
G. T. Hankins lbw b Topley	22		
R. F. Higgins lbw b Atkinson	16		
J. M. R. Taylor b Topley	27		
G. F. B. Scott c Overton b Atkinson	4		
D. A. Payne c Stoneman b Topley	0		
M. D. Taylor not out	17		
J. Shaw c Foakes b Atkinson	3		
B 1, lb 19, nb 20	40	B 1, w 1, nb 12	14
	—		—
(94 overs)	326	(2 wkts, 37.1 overs)	229

1/139 (1) 2/147 (2) 3/157 (4) 4/209 (5) 5/234 (6) 6/262 (3) 7/281 (8) 8/282 (9) 9/313 (7) 10/326 (11)

1/35 (1) 2/36 (3)

Topley 24–7–66–5; Atkinson 23–3–78–3; Overton 17–6–50–0; Clark 20–3–69–0; Virdi 10–0–43–2. *Second innings*—Topley 11–1–60–1; Atkinson 2–0–21–0; Virdi 11–4–54–1; Overton 7.1–1–44–0; Clark 6–0–49–0.

Umpires: I. D. Blackwell and R. White. Referee: T. J. Boon.

At Taunton, April 15–18. GLOUCESTERSHIRE beat SOMERSET by eight wickets. *Gloucestershire's first Championship victory at Taunton since 1993.*

At Southampton, April 22–25. GLOUCESTERSHIRE drew with HAMPSHIRE. *Gloucestershire's last pair survive 17.3 overs.*

GLOUCESTERSHIRE v LEICESTERSHIRE

At Bristol, April 29–May 2. Gloucestershire won by four wickets. Gloucestershire 19pts, Leicestershire 6pts. Toss: Gloucestershire.

Gloucestershire achieved the second-highest successful Championship chase in their history. They were 52 for three when Bracey fell after lunch, with Leicestershire sniffing their first victory of the season. But Lace and Cockbain steadied the innings, while Klein dropped out of the attack with an injured hamstring. After tea, needing 216 from 37, Gloucestershire accelerated, with Cockbain striking four sixes in his first Championship hundred since 2014. Though Parkinson claimed three

GLOUCESTERSHIRE'S HIGHEST WINNING FOURTH-INNINGS TOTALS

392-4	v Yorkshire (*set 389*) at Bristol	1948
353-8	v Loughborough UCCE (*351*) at Bristol	2008
348-6	**v Leicestershire (*348*) at Bristol**	**2021**
346-6	v Sussex (*346*) at Cheltenham	1992
333-6	v Warwickshire (*329*) at Birmingham	1987
333-8	v Hampshire (*331*) at Southampton	1998
329-4	v Glamorgan (*328*) at Bristol	1988
323-3	v Leicestershire (*323*) at Leicester	2006
320-5	v Worcestershire (*315*) at Worcester	2016
317-7	v Worcestershire (*317*) at Cheltenham	1937

late wickets, they won with 22 balls in hand. Earlier, Evans had scored his second century in two games, and Hill his second in seven seasons. Wright tightened the visitors' grip when he brought about a Gloucestershire collapse of five for 22, en route to a career-best seven for 53; his six lbws in the innings equalled the first-class record, already matched by Sussex's Ollie Robinson at Cardiff a fortnight before. The lower order engineered a recovery, but Leicestershire led by 146. Bad light and rain cost their batsmen 22 overs on the third day, however, and left them scrambling to get the equation right on the fourth. They set 348 in 82, but it was not enough.

Close of play: first day, Leicestershire 264-4 (Hill 77, Swindells 3); second day, Gloucestershire 176-6 (Hankins 29, Smith 19); third day, Leicestershire 125-3 (Patel 24, Hill 22).

Leicestershire

M. H. Azad lbw b Worrall	0	– (2) c Bracey b Higgins 24
S. T. Evans c Lace b Worrall	102	– (1) c Hankins b Higgins 22
M. S. Harris c Bracey b Worrall	62	– b Shaw 23
R. K. Patel b Worrall	2	– c Bracey b Worrall 44
L. J. Hill b Higgins	121	– b Higgins 38
†H. J. Swindells lbw b Higgins	5	– not out 28
B. W. M. Mike c †Lace b Shaw	54	– b Higgins 2
*C. F. Parkinson lbw b Smith	19	– run out (Cockbain) 3
C. J. C. Wright b Worrall	22	– c and b Higgins 3
D. Klein b Shaw	0	
H. A. Evans not out	4	– (10) run out (Dent) 0
B 10, lb 11, w 5, nb 4	30	B 6, lb 4, nb 4 14

1/0 (1) 2/127 (3) 3/129 (4)   (144.1 overs) 421
4/249 (2) 5/268 (6) 6/360 (5)
7/393 (8) 8/405 (7) 9/405 (10)
10/421 (9)   110 overs: 326-5

1/38 (1)   (9 wkts dec, 49.4 overs) 201
2/77 (3) 3/77 (2)
4/156 (4) 5/178 (5) 6/180 (7)
7/186 (8) 8/201 (9) 9/201 (10)

Worrall 34.1–9–79–5; Higgins 31–7–65–2; Goodman 24–5–72–0; Shaw 23–3–87–2; Smith 32–4–97–1. *Second innings*—Worrall 16–5–67–1; Higgins 16.4–2–62–5; Goodman 9–0–29–0; Shaw 8–0–33–1.

Gloucestershire

K. C. Brathwaite lbw b Wright	9	– c Patel b H. A. Evans 16
*C. D. J. Dent c Swindells b Wright	53	– c Swindells b Mike 9
†J. R. Bracey lbw b Parkinson	27	– b Mike 20
T. C. Lace c Harris b Klein	4	– c Patel b Parkinson 97
I. A. Cockbain lbw b Wright	0	– c Harris b Parkinson 117
R. F. Higgins lbw b Wright	5	– c Wright b Parkinson 33
G. T. Hankins lbw b Wright	37	– not out 7
T. M. J. Smith lbw b Wright	47	– not out 10
D. J. Worrall b Parkinson	11	
J. Shaw not out	41	
D. C. Goodman lbw b Wright	0	
B 12, lb 7, nb 22	41	B 15, lb 8, nb 16 39

1/28 (1) 2/99 (3) 3/99 (2)   (78.2 overs) 275
4/99 (5) 5/103 (4) 6/121 (6)
7/194 (7) 8/215 (9) 9/273 (8) 10/275 (11)

1/23 (1)   (6 wkts, 78.2 overs) 348
2/37 (2) 3/52 (3)
4/276 (4) 5/327 (5) 6/327 (6)

Wright 24.2–8–53–7; H. A. Evans 17–2–58–0; Klein 8.5–1–40–1; Mike 14–3–56–0; Parkinson 14.1–3–49–2. *Second innings*—Wright 18–3–80–0; H. A. Evans 15–3–73–1; Mike 16.2–2–65–2; Parkinson 26–1–93–3; Hill 3–0–14–0.

Umpires: R. K. Illingworth and N. J. Llong.   Referee: P. Whitticase.

At Lord's, May 6–8. GLOUCESTERSHIRE beat MIDDLESEX by seven wickets.

GLOUCESTERSHIRE v SOMERSET

At Bristol, May 20–23. Drawn. Gloucestershire 10pts, Somerset 13pts. Toss: Gloucestershire.

The return of spectators should have made this meeting of the group's top two sides – arguably the most meaningful West Country derby since 1998, when Somerset scuppered Gloucestershire's title bid – an occasion to savour. The weather dictated otherwise, halting play after 20.2 overs on the first morning, preventing a restart until the third day, and restricting the fourth to 32 balls. Even so, day three did some justice to the billing. Unbeaten Gloucestershire were on the cusp of rolling Somerset over, and preserving local bragging rights. But Abell, with his – and Somerset's – first century of the summer, transformed the mood. His eighth-wicket stand of 116 with Gregory helped bring three batting points, and denied Gloucestershire a third bowling point. The skies cleared enough next day to allow Overton and Davey to reduce Gloucestershire to 27 for six, and restore a little pride after defeat at Taunton.

Close of play: first day, Somerset 45-1 (Byrom 22, Abell 19); second day, no play; third day, Gloucestershire 16-2 (Brathwaite 13, Smith 0).

Somerset

E. J. Byrom c Brathwaite b Payne	38	L. Gregory b Taylor	57
T. A. Lammonby run out (Cockbain)	3	J. H. Davey not out	0
*T. B. Abell not out	132	B 6, lb 25, nb 2	33
J. C. Hildreth b Payne	15		
G. A. Bartlett lbw b Worrall	5	1/4 (2) (8 wkts dec, 101.3 overs)	300
L. P. Goldsworthy c Bracey b Worrall	2	2/85 (1) 3/127 (4)	
†S. M. Davies c Dent b Worrall	0	4/135 (5) 5/143 (6)	
C. Overton c Bracey b Higgins	15	6/143 (7) 7/176 (8) 8/292 (9)	

M. J. Leach did not bat.

Payne 23–6–58–2; Higgins 26–10–51–1; Taylor 26–5–95–1; Worrall 20.3–4–52–3; Smith 6–0–13–0.

Gloucestershire

K. C. Brathwaite c Abell b Davey	15	M. A. H. Hammond not out	0
*C. D. J. Dent c Goldsworthy b Overton	0		
†J. R. Bracey c Davies b Davey	1	Nb 2	2
T. M. J. Smith lbw b Overton	3		
T. C. Lace c Davies b Overton	0	1/5 (2) 2/14 (3) (6 wkts, 14.2 overs)	27
I. A. Cockbain b Overton	1	3/21 (4) 4/21 (5)	
R. F. Higgins not out	5	5/21 (1) 6/27 (6)	

M. D. Taylor, D. A. Payne and D. J. Worrall did not bat.

Overton 7.2–3–16–4; Davey 7–3–11–2.

Umpires: P. K. Baldwin and S. J. O'Shaughnessy.   Referee: P. M. Such.

At The Oval, May 27–30. GLOUCESTERSHIRE lost to SURREY by an innings and 47 runs.

At Leicester, June 3–5. GLOUCESTERSHIRE lost to LEICESTERSHIRE by an innings and 93 runs.

GLOUCESTERSHIRE v MIDDLESEX

At Cheltenham, July 5–8. Gloucestershire won by 164 runs. Gloucestershire 20pts, Middlesex 3pts. Toss: Middlesex. First-class debuts: O. J. Price; J. M. de Caires. Championship debuts: T. J. Price; D. J. Mitchell.

The sense that life was returning to normal was enhanced when the gates of Cheltenham College were opened to cricket, having stayed shut throughout 2020, and Gloucestershire achieved an important win. They should have made more from 153 for two, with Hammond hitting 75, but still took a match-winning lead as Middlesex suffered their worst collapse of the season – and there had been a few – losing eight for 25 in barely ten overs. Bracey then hit his first fifty since his ill-fated England call-up, and the lead was made unassailable by the 20-year-old Ollie Price, and his brother Tom, 18 months his senior. Eskinazi scored his first Championship century since 2017, as Middlesex – set an implausible 420 – recovered from eight for two to reach 201 for three, knuckling down for 100 overs. But the work was undone as the last six fell for 14. Matt Taylor took four in ten, and finished with career-best match figures of nine for 59. Payne and Simpson were added to England's replacement white-ball squad, and substituted on the second morning; Bracey took over as Gloucestershire captain. Josh de Caires, son of former England captain Mike Atherton, endured a difficult first-class debut.

Close of play: first day, Gloucestershire 248; second day, Gloucestershire 198-6 (O. J. Price 2, T. J. Price 0); third day, Middlesex 97-3 (Eskinazi 48, Mitchell 21).

Gloucestershire

M. A. H. Hammond c Eskinazi b Bamber	75	– c †White b Cullen	46
G. F. B. Scott b Murtagh	5	– lbw b Bamber	0
†J. R. Bracey c Simpson b Cullen	38	– c Eskinazi b Mitchell	88
T. C. Lace c Simpson b Bamber	31	– b Andersson	7
G. D. Phillips c Handscomb b Cullen	13	– c Robson b Andersson	9
J. M. R. Taylor lbw b Mitchell	5	– c †White b Mitchell	40
O. J. Price b Bamber	31	– c †White b Murtagh	33
T. J. Price c Simpson b Murtagh	13	– not out	35
M. D. Taylor not out	14	– b Mitchell	0
*D. A. Payne c Simpson b Mitchell	2		
D. J. Worrall c Simpson b Cullen	5	– (10) c †White b Mitchell	0
D. C. Goodman (did not bat)		– (11) c Bamber b Murtagh	7
B 10, lb 4, nb 2	16	Lb 7	7

1/7 (2) 2/87 (3) 3/153 (1)   (94.1 overs) 248   1/8 (2) 2/82 (1)   (72.2 overs) 272
4/166 (4) 5/176 (5) 6/187 (6)   3/106 (4) 4/132 (5)
7/223 (8) 8/227 (7) 9/239 (10) 10/248 (11)   5/189 (6) 6/198 (3) 7/262 (7)
                                                       8/263 (9) 9/263 (10) 10/272 (11)

Goodman replaced Payne, who left to join England's one-day squad.

Murtagh 22–8–40–2; Bamber 22–7–39–3; Andersson 9–1–43–0; Cullen 19.1–7–57–3; Mitchell 9–2–32–2; Sowter 13–4–23–0. *Second innings*—Murtagh 14.2–2–49–2; Bamber 16–4–51–1; Cullen 14–1–57–1; Mitchell 10–0–42–4; de Caires 3–0–7–0; Andersson 8–0–26–2; Sowter 7–0–33–0.

Middlesex

S. D. Robson b Worrall	37	– (2) lbw b M. D. Taylor	0
J. M. de Caires lbw b M. D. Taylor	5	– (1) c Phillips b Worrall	4
S. S. Eskinazi c Bracey b Goodman	6	– c O. J. Price b Worrall	102
*P. S. P. Handscomb c Bracey b M. D. Taylor	21	– lbw b Worrall	14
D. J. Mitchell lbw b Worrall	0	– lbw b M. D. Taylor	73
R. G. White c Hammond b M. D. Taylor	5	– c J. M. R. Taylor b Worrall	32
M. K. Andersson c Phillips b T. J. Price	5	– c Bracey b M. D. Taylor	0
N. A. Sowter c Phillips b M. D. Taylor	0	– c Hammond b M. D. Taylor	0
B. C. Cullen lbw b T. J. Price	5	– c Bracey b M. D. Taylor	0
E. R. Bamber lbw b T. J. Price	0	– c Lace b Worrall	3
T. J. Murtagh not out	1	– not out	0
B 1, nb 10, p 5	16	B 7, lb 8, nb 12	27

1/8 (2) 2/34 (3) 3/76 (1)   (36 overs) 101   1/4 (1) 2/8 (2)   (127.3 overs) 255
4/76 (5) 5/88 (4) 6/93 (7)   3/56 (4) 4/201 (3)
7/93 (6) 8/100 (8) 9/100 (9) 10/101 (10)   5/241 (5) 6/241 (7) 7/241 (8)
                                                       8/241 (9) 9/250 (10) 10/255 (6)

White replaced †J. A. Simpson, who left to join England's one-day squad.

Worrall 11–2–26–2; M. D. Taylor 9–3–19–4; T. J. Price 8–2–29–3; Goodman 7–1–16–1; O. J. Price 1–0–5–0. *Second innings*—Worrall 27.3–14–54–5; M. D. Taylor 29–13–40–5; T. J. Price 24–8–47–0; Goodman 14–4–26–0; Scott 9–5–11–0; O. J. Price 17–4–34–0; Phillips 5–1–15–0; Hammond 2–0–13–0.

Umpires: G. D. Lloyd and M. Newell.   Referee: W. R. Smith.

GLOUCESTERSHIRE v HAMPSHIRE

At Cheltenham, July 11–14. Hampshire won by seven wickets. Hampshire 22pts, Gloucestershire 2pts. Toss: Gloucestershire.

Needing at least a draw to seal a place in Division One, Gloucestershire won the toss, and their openers survived the first hour. But that was as good as it got: seven of their top eight made a start, but none passed Phillips's 47. Weatherley and Holland put that into perspective by opening with 174, before Gubbins made his first century for his new county, having just left Middlesex. Hampshire's total was boosted by 81 extras, the most conceded by Gloucestershire. That included 48 byes, equalling the Championship record, by Kent at Northampton in 1955. Gloucestershire had to survive the final day – which they had achieved in the reverse fixture – and Lace's maiden century for them raised hopes. But he shouldered arms to a straight delivery, providing a fifth first-class wicket in six seasons for Weatherley's off-spin, before Ollie Price was caught at leg slip via short leg's back. Had Gloucestershire batted another ten overs, they would probably have saved the game, but Hampshire leapfrogged them in the table, ending their dreams of a maiden title.

Close of play: first day, Gloucestershire 214-6 (J. M. R. Taylor 34, O. J. Price 18); second day, Hampshire 270-5 (Gubbins 31, McManus 14); third day, Gloucestershire 107-3 (Lace 25, Phillips 16).

Gloucestershire

M. A. H. Hammond c McManus b de Grandhomme	31	– b Crane	15
G. F. B. Scott lbw b de Grandhomme	31	– c Holland b Crane	29
*†J. R. Bracey b Wheal	0	– b Abbott	8
T. C. Lace lbw b Abbott	19	– lbw b Weatherley	118
G. D. Phillips c de Grandhomme b Wheal	47	– lbw b de Grandhomme	16
R. F. Higgins b Crane	25	– c de Grandhomme b Barker	26
J. M. R. Taylor c Gubbins b Abbott	34	– b Abbott	27
O. J. Price c McManus b de Grandhomme	18	– c Prest b Crane	23
T. J. Price not out	6	– not out	18
M. D. Taylor lbw b de Grandhomme	0	– lbw b Wheal	0
D. J. Worrall c Alsop b Crane	9	– c Crane b Wheal	0
B 1, lb 4, nb 4	9	B 12, lb 10, nb 8	30

1/61 (2) 2/66 (3) 3/72 (1)   (73.4 overs) 229   1/47 (1) 2/54 (2)   (126.1 overs) 310
4/104 (4) 5/139 (6) 6/173 (5)   3/68 (3) 4/107 (5)
7/214 (7) 8/214 (8) 9/214 (10) 10/229 (11)   5/202 (6) 6/258 (7) 7/270 (4)
                                          8/309 (8) 9/310 (10) 10/310 (11)

Barker 12–0–42–0; Abbott 18–4–48–2; Wheal 12–1–43–2; de Grandhomme 18–9–31–4; Crane 12.4–0–55–2; Prest 1–0–5–0. *Second innings*—Barker 17–6–37–1; Abbott 25–6–84–2; Wheal 25.1–10–59–2; Crane 39–17–55–3; de Grandhomme 11–4–31–0; Weatherley 9–2–22–1.

Hampshire

J. J. Weatherley c Phillips b Higgins	78	– c Bracey b Worrall	0
I. G. Holland c Bracey b Phillips	74	– lbw b Worrall	19
T. P. Alsop c Phillips b Higgins	15	– lbw b Worrall	9
N. R. T. Gubbins not out	137	– not out	13
T. J. Prest c O. J. Price b Worrall	18		
C. de Grandhomme c O. J. Price b Higgins	0	– (5) not out	12
†L. D. McManus c Higgins b Scott	39		
K. H. D. Barker c sub (D. C. Goodman) b Phillips	31		
M. S. Crane not out	13		
B 48, lb 11, w 2, nb 20	81	Lb 3	3

1/174 (2) 2/186 (1)   (7 wkts dec, 143 overs) 486   1/0 (1)   (3 wkts, 10.3 overs) 56
3/195 (3) 4/229 (5)   2/20 (3) 3/37 (2)
5/232 (6) 6/361 (7) 7/458 (8)   110 overs: 326-5

*K. J. Abbott and B. T. J. Wheal did not bat.

Worrall 30–10–60–1; Higgins 35–11–92–3; M. D. Taylor 27–5–76–0; T. J. Price 15–4–58–0; O. J. Price 9–0–52–0; Phillips 14–1–67–2; Scott 13–5–22–1. *Second innings*—Worrall 5.3–1–21–3; Higgins 4–0–25–0; M. D. Taylor 1–0–7–0.

Umpires: P. R. Pollard and R. A. White.   Referee: D. A. Cosker.

DIVISION TWO

GLOUCESTERSHIRE v NORTHAMPTONSHIRE

At Bristol, August 30–September 2. Gloucestershire won by six wickets. Gloucestershire 19pts, Northamptonshire 6pts. Toss: Gloucestershire. County debut: Zafar Gohar.

At 153 for nine, in reply to 327, Gloucestershire looked out of it. But Taylor and Warner battled for nearly 27 overs to spark a remarkable turnaround. Saving the follow-on was crucial, since it condemned Northamptonshire to batting in the trickiest conditions of the game: under gloomy skies and blazing floodlights, every ball was a challenge. In the first innings, the home attack had squandered a useful toss, and Rossington made a summer's-best 94, but they were now more ruthless, with Higgins claiming five for 46, his own best of the season. Kerrigan scrapped and slugged on the final morning to push the target above 250, which seemed daunting, only for the sun to smile on Gloucestershire's chase. Hammond survived a sharp slip chance early on, and led the assault in yet another season's best. Van Buuren, whose first-innings fifty had averted disaster, helped finish the job with another, which he reached from 43 balls.

Close of play: first day, Northamptonshire 232-5 (Rossington 66, Gouldstone 32); second day, Gloucestershire 90-6 (van Buuren 19, Zafar Gohar 3); third day, Northamptonshire 92-7 (Taylor 5, Kerrigan 0).

Northamptonshire

R. S. Vasconcelos c Hammond b Price	37	– b Taylor	26
E. N. Gay lbw b Taylor	44	– b Price	0
L. A. Procter c and b Price	2	– lbw b Higgins	9
R. I. Keogh b Taylor	18	– lbw b Price	4
S. A. Zaib c Hammond b Warner	8	– c Bracey b Warner	14
*†A. M. Rossington b Price	94	– b Higgins	18
H. O. M. Gouldstone b Higgins	43	– b Higgins	7
T. A. I. Taylor c Bracey b Warner	24	– lbw b Higgins	8
S. C. Kerrigan c Warner b Higgins	7	– b Higgins	27
B. W. Sanderson lbw b Price	2	– c Bracey b Price	1
C. J. White not out	15	– not out	1
B 4, lb 9, nb 20	33	B 4, lb 3, w 1, nb 6	14

1/67 (1) 2/73 (3) 3/102 (2)   (98.3 overs) 327   1/4 (2) 2/21 (3)   (38.1 overs) 129
4/115 (4) 5/147 (5) 6/271 (7)   3/26 (4) 4/57 (1)
7/275 (6) 8/290 (9) 9/293 (10) 10/327 (8)   5/61 (5) 6/85 (7) 7/92 (6)
         8/97 (8) 9/100 (10) 10/129 (9)

Higgins 25–10–41–2; Taylor 18–3–90–2; Price 20–5–72–4; Warner 16.3–2–54–2; Charlesworth 6–0–28–0; Zafar Gohar 11–3–19–0; van Buuren 2–0–10–0. *Second innings*—Higgins 14.1–4–46–5; Price 13–2–39–3; Taylor 6–2–13–1; Warner 5–0–24–1.

Gloucestershire

B. G. Charlesworth c Taylor b Sanderson	0	– b Procter	7
M. A. H. Hammond c Gay b Sanderson	10	– b Taylor	94
†J. R. Bracey c Gay b Sanderson	7	– c Rossington b Taylor	4
*C. D. J. Dent b Procter	21	– c Rossington b Kerrigan	26
T. C. Lace c Vasconcelos b Procter	12	– not out	67
G. L. van Buuren lbw b Kerrigan	56	– not out	53
R. F. Higgins c Rossington b Procter	8		
Zafar Gohar lbw b Procter	7		
T. J. Price b Kerrigan	16		
M. D. Taylor not out	24		
J. D. Warner c Vasconcelos b Procter	10		
B 4, lb 6, nb 10	20	Lb 3, w 5, nb 8	16

1/0 (1) 2/20 (3) 3/21 (2)   (90.5 overs) 191   1/23 (1)   (4 wkts, 80.4 overs) 267
4/53 (5) 5/56 (4) 6/83 (7)   2/40 (3) 3/111 (4)
7/101 (8) 8/146 (9) 9/153 (6) 10/191 (11)   4/168 (2)

Sanderson 21–7–39–3; White 19–3–44–0; Taylor 19–10–42–0; Procter 18.5–5–42–5; Kerrigan 13–5–14–2. *Second innings*—Sanderson 18–5–50–0; White 11–1–45–0; Procter 14–4–30–1; Taylor 13–1–41–2; Kerrigan 18–2–80–1; Keogh 6.4–0–18–0.

Umpires: S. J. O'Shaughnessy and I. N. Ramage.   Referee: P. M. Such.

At Chelmsford, September 5–7. GLOUCESTERSHIRE lost to ESSEX by an innings and three runs.

At Cardiff, September 12–15. GLOUCESTERSHIRE beat GLAMORGAN by ten wickets.

GLOUCESTERSHIRE v DURHAM

At Bristol, September 21–22. Gloucestershire won by seven wickets. Gloucestershire 20pts, Durham 3pts. Toss: Durham.

A summer of steady Championship cricket for Durham ended with a mighty crash: spun out twice, they succumbed inside two days to only their third defeat. Raine railed against a used wicket after the visitors fell apart on the first day to slow left-armers Zafar Gohar and van Buuren. But it was simply the familiar frustration of a county cricketer ill-equipped to play the turning ball. Gloucestershire, who fared little better while Durham's own left-arm spinner, Trevaskis, was taking a maiden five-for, were boosted by Zafar: his five boundaries brought an unexpected batting point and a handy lead. Raine was the only Durham player to get to grips with the task second time around, and did at least prevent an innings defeat. Zafar ended with 11 for 101, taking his figures from his last three innings to 17 for 144; his final wicket, Trevaskis, came via a ricochet to wicketkeeper Bracey off the helmet of Lace at short leg. Play on the first morning was interrupted after five deliveries when an air ambulance attending a nearby address landed on the outfield.

Close of play: first day, Gloucestershire 146-6 (Scott 10).

Durham

A. Z. Lees c Hammond b Zafar Gohar	40	– lbw b Zafar Gohar 9
M. A. Jones lbw b Payne	6	– run out (Bracey)................. 17
*S. G. Borthwick c Hammond b Payne	0	– lbw b Zafar Gohar 4
D. G. Bedingham c Hammond b Zafar Gohar	19	– lbw b Zafar Gohar 8
†E. J. H. Eckersley c Dent b van Buuren	20	– c Bracey b Higgins.............. 7
G. Clark b van Buuren	16	– b Zafar Gohar 17
P. Coughlin c Payne b Zafar Gohar	9	– c van Buuren b Zafar Gohar..... 2
B. A. Raine c Payne b Zafar Gohar	16	– not out 38
L. Trevaskis c Scott b Zafar Gohar	11	– c Bracey b Zafar Gohar 3
M. J. Potts c and b van Buuren	4	– lbw b van Buuren 14
C. Rushworth not out	0	– b van Buuren 0
B 1, lb 9	10	B 4, nb 8 12

1/25 (2) 2/25 (3) 3/72 (4)   (45.5 overs) 140   1/22 (1) 2/30 (2)   (52.4 overs) 131
4/77 (1) 5/109 (5) 6/118 (6)   3/30 (3) 4/39 (5)
7/124 (7) 8/125 (9) 9/140 (10) 10/140 (8)   5/49 (4) 6/59 (7) 7/71 (6)
                                                     8/87 (9) 9/125 (10) 10/131 (11)

Payne 8–2–13–2; Higgins 7–3–22–0; Zafar Gohar 15.5–2–50–5; T. J. Price 8–2–17–0; van Buuren 7–0–28–3. *Second innings*—Payne 11–3–23–0; Higgins 12–1–40–1; Zafar Gohar 23–7–51–6; van Buuren 3.4–0–6–2; O. J. Price 3–0–7–0.

Gloucestershire

C. D. J. Dent c Borthwick b Rushworth	0	– lbw b Rushworth	22
M. A. H. Hammond c Potts b Trevaskis	8	– c Eckersley b Rushworth	11
*†J. R. Bracey lbw b Raine	27	– not out	11
T. C. Lace lbw b Trevaskis	17	– (5) not out	1
G. L. van Buuren b Raine	62		
G. F. B. Scott lbw b Raine	21		
R. F. Higgins b Trevaskis	10		
O. J. Price c Bedingham b Trevaskis	1		
T. J. Price lbw b Trevaskis	16		
Zafar Gohar c Rushworth b Coughlin	30	– (4) c Lees b Trevaskis	0
D. A. Payne not out	14		
B 7, lb 5	12	B 4, lb 1, nb 4	9

1/0 (1) 2/30 (2) 3/42 (3)   (74.4 overs) 218   1/37 (2)   (3 wkts, 9.1 overs) 54
4/93 (4) 5/127 (5) 6/146 (7)   2/42 (1) 3/45 (4)
7/148 (8) 8/174 (9) 9/174 (6) 10/218 (10)

Rushworth 12–6–17–1; Potts 2–0–13–0; Trevaskis 33–12–78–5; Raine 16–6–39–3; Coughlin 6.4–3–26–1; Borthwick 5–1–33–0. *Second innings*—Rushworth 5–0–26–2; Trevaskis 4.1–0–23–1.

Umpires: B. J. Debenham and G. D. Lloyd.   Referee: D. E. Malcolm.

HAMPSHIRE

But no cigar

Pat Symes

Going into the last fortnight of the season, Hampshire had a chance of lifting both major trophies, and came within one ball of winning the County Championship for the first time in 48 years. But a brittle top order let them down at key moments – and they ended with little to show for a lopsided summer.

This was never truer than in the T20 Blast. After nine of their 14 group matches, Hampshire looked dead and buried, with more points from washouts than from a solitary victory. However, the arrival of powerful New Zealand all-rounder Colin de Grandhomme restored self-belief, and six victories sped them past the quarters and on to finals day. Their semi, against Somerset, was another nailbiter, and just a few more runs – they managed 150 – would probably have taken them through.

In the Championship, Hampshire had been slightly more consistent, and deserved their place in Division One, which they began in fourth. That is where they finished, after the tense denouement at Aigburth. Hampshire were defending a target of 196 on a turning wicket, leg-spinner Mason Crane was bowling beautifully and, with Lancashire nine down, one ball would have sufficed. Last man Matt Parkinson survived two from Crane, and the winning runs came next over.

A rousing start – there were big wins over Leicestershire and Middlesex – augured well but, at home to Gloucestershire, Hampshire could not prise apart the last pair. In other years, such frustration might have proved decisive come the end of September, but in 2021 counties carried forward only points gained against their fellow qualifiers. So although the next game, at The Oval, brought defeat by an innings and 289 – the club's heaviest in 110 years – it too had no lasting effect, since Hampshire ended up in a different division from Surrey (and Gloucestershire).

Hampshire's success, particularly in the Championship, came thanks to a quality attack, as incisive as any. The seam trio of Kyle Abbott, Mohammad Abbas and Keith Barker shared 128 wickets, all at a bargain rate. Abbas and Barker both took 41 at well under 20, and Abbott 46 at under 22. Abbott has proved to be one of Hampshire's best imports, and his 11 for 85 against Middlesex at Lord's showed he could win matches on his own. Perhaps crucially, he missed the last three fixtures with a foot injury.

Pakistan Test bowler Abbas brought a wealth of international experience, and at Southampton he ran through Middlesex, taking five wickets in 13 balls, including a hat-trick en route to match figures of nine for 39. Barker, oddly discarded by Warwickshire in 2018, added left-arm variety, and had a superb summer; he was named the Red Ball Bowler of the Year and the Players' Player of the Year. There was also sterling support from the much-improved

Brad Wheal, who took 34 Championship wickets, plus 17 in the Blast. Spinners Crane and Liam Dawson each made vital contributions. In December, Graeme Welch was appointed bowling coach.

Brad Wheal

The batting was another story. James Vince, the captain, hit 816 runs at 40, including a majestic 231 at Leicester, and he grew in stature after his first international century; he also led Southern Brave to The Hundred title. But opener Ian Holland faded after a bright start, while Joe Weatherley, strong in the Blast, was poor in the Championship. Lewis McManus marred a decent summer behind the stumps by being docked three disciplinary points for claiming a stumping against Leicestershire when the ball was in his other glove. It did not help that Aneurin Donald missed a second season with a knee injury. Sussex wicketkeeper Ben Brown was recruited in January to add spine.

Promising pace bowler Scott Currie took 19 cheap wickets in the Blast, while Crane grabbed 16 to help engineer the turnaround. The highlight of Hampshire's campaign came when they beat holders Nottinghamshire in the quarter-finals: having made just 125, they won by two runs. But in the semi, the Somerset tail crashed 50 off 18 to win by two wickets. Hampshire later bolstered their white-ball strength by signing the big-hitting Ross Whiteley from Worcestershire.

Royal London Cup hopes were hindered by losing six players to The Hundred and, though other counties lost more, Hampshire were not serious challengers. Nick Gubbins, newly arrived from Middlesex as a mid-season replacement for the unhappy Sam Northeast – who went first to Yorkshire, then Nottinghamshire and finally Glamorgan – hit 318 runs, including an unbeaten 131 against Sussex, Hampshire's only century. Young South African seamer John Turner looked a useful discovery, but Hampshire won only three games. Another encouraging prospect was 18-year-old batter Tom Prest. He played two Championship and 14 white-ball games, and in May sat his geography A-level at school in Dorset before rushing to Southampton for a Second XI Championship match against Sussex; he hit a triple-hundred, and Hampshire later won the tournament. Prest and Currie both signed contracts.

The Rose Bowl, farmland on the edge of the Downs until 1997, was the centre of global attention in June, when it hosted the ICC World Test Championship final between India and New Zealand. Covid had precipitated a move from Lord's, yet this was a huge vote of confidence for the venue, which has rapidly become a major centre of international cricket.

HAMPSHIRE RESULTS

County Championship matches – Played 14: Won 6, Lost 3, Drawn 5.
Vitality T20 Blast matches – Played 16: Won 7, Lost 6, No result 3.
Royal London Cup matches – Played 8: Won 3, Lost 4, No result 1.

LV= County Championship, 2nd in Group 2, 4th in Division 1;
Vitality T20 Blast, semi-finalists; Royal London Cup, 6th in Group 1.

COUNTY CHAMPIONSHIP AVERAGES, BATTING AND FIELDING

Cap		Birthplace	M	I	NO	R	HS	100	Avge	Ct/St
2013	J. M. Vince	Cuckfield	13	20	0	816	231	1	40.80	13
2021	I. G. Holland	Stevens Point, USA	14	24	1	766	146*	2	33.30	8
2019	S. A. Northeast	Ashford, Kent	8	13	2	358	118	1	32.54	0
	†N. R. T. Gubbins	Richmond	6	11	2	255	137*	1	28.33	6
2021	†K. H. D. Barker	Manchester	10	15	1	379	84	0	27.07	1
2021	L. D. McManus	Poole	11	14	2	320	91	0	26.66	28/1
2021	†T. P. Alsop	High Wycombe	14	24	2	564	149	2	25.63	14
2013	L. A. Dawson	Swindon	12	20	2	449	152*	1	24.94	17
	F. S. Organ	Sydney, Australia	6	10	0	213	67	0	21.30	6
2021	J. J. Weatherley	Winchester‡	13	22	0	406	78	0	18.45	21
2021	B. T. J. Wheal††	Durban, SA	13	16	6	181	46*	0	18.10	2
2017	K. J. Abbott¶	Empangeni, SA	11	12	3	148	58	0	16.44	1
2021	M. S. Crane	Shoreham-by-Sea	6	7	1	92	28	0	15.33	2
	J. K. Fuller	Cape Town, SA	2	4	0	34	21	0	8.50	0
	Mohammad Abbas¶	Sialkot, Pakistan	10	14	7	28	6	0	4.00	2

Also batted: S. W. Currie (*Poole*) (1 match) 4, 1 (1 ct); C. de Grandhomme¶ (*Harare, Zimbabwe*) (2 matches) 174*, 0, 12* (2 ct); T. J. Prest (*Wimborne*) (2 matches) 18 (1 ct); C. T. Steel (*Greenbrae, USA*) (1 match) 15, 14.

‡ *Born in Hampshire.* ¶ *Official overseas player.* †† *Other non-England-qualified.*

BOWLING

	Style	O	M	R	W	BB	5I	Avge
Mohammad Abbas	RFM	309.5	113	651	41	6-11	3	15.87
K. H. D. Barker	LFM	310	88	755	41	7-46	3	18.41
K. J. Abbott	RFM	329.3	87	996	46	6-44	3	21.65
M. S. Crane	LB	195.5	39	587	23	5-41	1	25.52
B. T. J. Wheal	RFM	298.5	62	882	34	4-59	0	25.94
L. A. Dawson	SLA	257	55	624	18	5-45	1	34.66

Also bowled: S. W. Currie (RFM) 27.5–2–109–4; C. de Grandhomme (RFM) 37–20–68–6; J. K. Fuller (RFM) 17–4–37–3; I. G. Holland (RFM) 147.1–35–433–6; F. S. Organ (OB) 73–20–205–8; T. J. Prest (OB) 1–0–5–0; J. M. Vince (RM) 13–1–85–1; J. J. Weatherley (OB) 9–2–22–1.

LEADING VITALITY BLAST AVERAGES (100 runs/15 overs)

Batting	Runs	HS	Avge	SR	Ct/St		**Bowling**	W	BB	Avge	ER
C. de Grandhomme	150	46	21.42	**153.06**	3		L. A. Dawson	10	3-24	24.90	**7.11**
J. J. Weatherley	410	71	37.27	**141.86**	2		M. S. Crane	16	3-23	23.87	**7.79**
L. D. McManus	199	60*	19.90	**140.14**	12/6		B. T. J. Wheal	17	3-39	20.82	**7.86**
D. J. M. Short	316	69	26.33	**138.59**	5		S. W. Currie	19	4-24	12.84	**7.87**
J. K. Fuller	194	38	19.40	**135.66**	9		C. P. Wood	3	2-26	25.00	**7.92**
J. M. Vince	373	102	31.08	**135.63**	11		D. J. M. Short	6	2-25	38.00	**8.76**
T. J. Prest	135	59*	22.50	**115.38**	4						

LEADING ROYAL LONDON CUP AVERAGES (100 runs/4 wickets)

Batting	Runs	HS	Avge	SR	Ct
N. R. T. Gubbins .	318	131*	53.00	99.06	1
T. P. Alsop.....	238	68	39.66	78.54	2
L. D. McManus ..	133	50	33.25	96.37	3
J. K. Fuller.....	125	54	25.00	113.63	2
F. S. Organ	120	79	24.00	71.85	3
J. J. Weatherley .	155	54	22.14	67.09	5
T. J. Prest......	108	41	15.42	71.52	1

Bowling	W	BB	Avge	ER
N. R. T. Gubbins .	4	4-38	20.25	5.40
S. W. Currie	6	3-58	22.00	7.13
I. G. Holland.....	8	4-12	23.75	4.41
J. A. Turner	7	3-44	27.85	5.41
K. J. Abbott	7	5-43	37.28	5.03
J. K. Fuller	4	1-25	47.00	5.87

FIRST-CLASS COUNTY RECORDS

Highest score for	316	R. H. Moore v Warwickshire at Bournemouth	1937
Highest score against	303*	G. A. Hick (Worcestershire) at Southampton	1997
Leading run-scorer	48,892	C. P. Mead (avge 48.84)	1905–36
Best bowling for	9-25	R. M. H. Cottam v Lancashire at Manchester	1965
Best bowling against	10-46	W. Hickton (Lancashire) at Manchester	1870
Leading wicket-taker	2,669	D. Shackleton (avge 18.23)	1948–69
Highest total for	714-5 dec	v Nottinghamshire at Southampton	2005
Highest total against	742	by Surrey at The Oval	1909
Lowest total for	15	v Warwickshire at Birmingham.................	1922
Lowest total against	23	by Yorkshire at Middlesbrough.................	1965

LIST A COUNTY RECORDS

Highest score for	190	J. M. Vince v Gloucestershire at Southampton ...	2019
Highest score against	203	A. D. Brown (Surrey) at Guildford	1997
Leading run-scorer	12,034	R. A. Smith (avge 42.97)......................	1983–2003
Best bowling for	7-30	P. J. Sainsbury v Norfolk at Southampton.......	1965
Best bowling against	7-22	J. R. Thomson (Middlesex) at Lord's	1981
Leading wicket-taker	411	C. A. Connor (avge 25.07).....................	1984–98
Highest total for	371-4	v Glamorgan at Southampton	1975
Highest total against	360-7	by Somerset at Southampton	2018
Lowest total for	43	v Essex at Basingstoke........................	1972
Lowest total against	⎰ 61	by Somerset at Bath..........................	1973
	⎱ 61	by Derbyshire at Portsmouth	1990

TWENTY20 COUNTY RECORDS

Highest score for	124*	M. J. Lumb v Essex v Southampton	2009
Highest score against	116*	L. J. Wright (Sussex) at Southampton	2014
Leading run-scorer	**4,303**	**J. M. Vince (avge 31.87, SR 134.68)**	**2010–21**
Best bowling for	6-19	Shaheen Shah Afridi v Middlesex at Southampton ..	2020
Best bowling against	6-28	J. K. Fuller (Middlesex) at Southampton..........	2019
Leading wicket-taker	**150**	**C. P. Wood (avge 26.64, ER 8.25)**.............	**2010–21**
Highest total for	249-8	v Derbyshire at Derby	2017
Highest total against	220-4	by Somerset at Taunton	2010
Lowest total for	85	v Sussex at Southampton	2008
Lowest total against	67	by Sussex at Hove	2004

ADDRESS

The Ageas Bowl, Botley Road, West End, Southampton SO30 3XH; 023 8047 2002; enquiries@ageasbowl.com; www.ageasbowl.com. Twitter: @hantscricket.

OFFICIALS

Captain J. M. Vince
Director of cricket G. W. White
First-team manager A. V. Birrell
Head of player development C. R. M. Freeston

President N. E. J. Pocock
Chair R. G. Bransgrove
Chief executive D. Mann
Head groundsman S. Lee
Scorer A. C. Mills

GROUP TWO

At Leicester, April 8–11. HAMPSHIRE beat LEICESTERSHIRE by an innings and 105 runs. *James Vince hits 231.*

HAMPSHIRE v MIDDLESEX

At Southampton, April 15–18. Hampshire won by 249 runs. Hampshire 22pts, Middlesex 3pts. Toss: Hampshire.

Mohammad Abbas marked his home debut with an outstanding spell of five wickets in 13 balls, including a hat-trick. As Middlesex set about replying to 319, he dismissed Holden and Gubbins with the last two balls of his first over, then stand-in captain Eskinazi with the first of his next. Within 16 overs, they were 31 for six – all to Abbas – and were soon shot out for 79; they never recovered. On a pitch favouring the seamers, Holland top-scored in both Hampshire totals, starting with a composed 64 on the first day, when Finn took four wickets in his first red-ball game since September 2019. By the end of the second day, Hampshire were 444 ahead, and only two down; Eskinazi admitted "tears were almost shed" in the Middlesex dressing-room. Holland went on to a career-best unbeaten 146, sharing a third-wicket stand of 257 with Northeast. Middlesex's pursuit of 531 was in vain, though half-centuries from Gubbins and White provided small compensation. Abbas added three wickets to finish with match figures of nine for 39 from 31 overs.

Close of play: first day, Hampshire 281-8 (Abbott 35, Wheal 11); second day, Hampshire 204-2 (Holland 90, Northeast 99); third day, Middlesex 208-4 (White 73, Andersson 25).

Hampshire

J. J. Weatherley st Simpson b Bamber	16	– c Andersson b Roland-Jones	1
I. G. Holland c Robson b Roland-Jones	64	– not out	146
T. P. Alsop c Sowter b Finn	19	– c Simpson b Bamber	0
S. A. Northeast c Simpson b Andersson	63	– b Finn	118
*J. M. Vince c Eskinazi b Andersson	9	– lbw b Finn	0
L. A. Dawson c Andersson b Finn	22	– not out	9
†L. D. McManus b Sowter	4		
K. J. Abbott b Finn	58		
M. S. Crane c Robson b Bamber	18		
B. T. J. Wheal not out	21		
Mohammad Abbas c Simpson b Finn	4		
Lb 12, w 1, nb 8	21	B 6, lb 5, w 1, nb 4	16

1/26 (1) 2/77 (3) 3/128 (2)   (110.2 overs) 319   1/1 (1)   (4 wkts dec, 67 overs) 290
4/143 (5) 5/191 (6) 6/196 (7)   2/2 (3) 3/259 (4)
7/221 (4) 8/252 (9) 9/313 (8)   4/273 (5)
10/319 (11)   110 overs: 319-9

Bamber 27–8–79–2; Roland-Jones 29–8–54–1; Finn 25.2–1–96–4; Andersson 19–3–53–2; Sowter 10–1–25–1. *Second innings*—Bamber 11–1–52–1; Roland-Jones 8–5–7–1; Andersson 8–1–41–0; Sowter 25–2–114–0; Finn 11–0–47–2; Robson 4–0–18–0.

Middlesex

S. D. Robson c Weatherley b Mohammad Abbas	18	– (2) b Mohammad Abbas	19
M. D. E. Holden c Weatherley b Mohammad Abbas	2	– (1) lbw b Abbott	10
N. R. T. Gubbins lbw b Mohammad Abbas	0	– c Dawson b Holland	67
*S. S. Eskinazi c McManus b Mohammad Abbas	3	– c Weatherley b Mohammad Abbas	1
R. G. White lbw b Mohammad Abbas	0	– lbw b Holland	73
M. K. Andersson lbw b Mohammad Abbas	0	– c McManus b Holland	26
†J. A. Simpson c Dawson b Wheal	16	– c Weatherley b Mohammad Abbas	21
T. S. Roland-Jones b Abbott	5	– lbw b Abbott	5
N. A. Sowter not out	24	– lbw b Abbott	9
S. T. Finn c McManus b Wheal	3	– not out	13
E. R. Bamber c McManus b Wheal	0	– c McManus b Dawson	24
Lb 8	8	B 13	13

1/2 (2) 2/2 (3) 3/8 (4)   (34.4 overs) 79
4/14 (5) 5/14 (6) 6/31 (1)
7/36 (8) 8/75 (7) 9/79 (10) 10/79 (11)

1/30 (2) 2/32 (1)   (99 overs) 281
3/33 (4) 4/155 (3)
5/208 (5) 6/219 (6) 7/235 (8)
8/235 (7) 9/245 (9) 10/281 (11)

Abbott 11–3–36–1; Mohammad Abbas 11–6–11–6; Holland 6–3–4–0; Crane 3–0–11–0; Wheal 3.4–0–9–3. *Second innings*—Abbott 19–3–64–3; Mohammad Abbas 20–10–28–3; Dawson 17–5–44–1; Wheal 16–3–40–0; Crane 18–1–73–0; Holland 9–4–19–3.

Umpires: N. J. Llong and T. Lungley. Referee: J. J. Whitaker.

HAMPSHIRE v GLOUCESTERSHIRE

At Southampton, April 22–25. Drawn. Hampshire 12pts, Gloucestershire 11pts. Toss: Hampshire.
Hampshire were denied a third successive substantial victory by a plucky last-wicket stand between Shaw and Dominic Goodman, an Exeter University student in only his second first-class match. The hosts had dominated from the start, as Holland and Alsop – who added 228 for the second wicket – each scored their second century of the summer. Gloucestershire needed 321 just to avoid the follow-on but, despite half-centuries from Brathwaite, Bracey and Higgins, they fell short by one run, with Mohammad Abbas taking four, including his 500th first-class wicket, and Dawson and Crane spinning out six. Put in again, they were soon back in trouble, as Wheal and Abbott took turns at breaking through the middle order. Defeat seemed certain when Shaw and Goodman came together, with the lead just 11. But amid mounting tension, and surrounded by a ring of close fielders, the final pair proved stoic heroes, holding out for 17.3 overs to ensure Gloucestershire's unlikely salvation.
Close of play: first day, Hampshire 292-3 (Alsop 127, Crane 0); second day, Gloucestershire 114-2 (Bracey 46, Lace 0); third day, Gloucestershire 14-0 (Brathwaite 10, Dent 2).

Hampshire

J. J. Weatherley lbw b Goodman	8	B. T. J. Wheal not out	15
I. G. Holland lbw b Worrall	114	Mohammad Abbas b Higgins	5
T. P. Alsop c Bracey b Higgins	149		
S. A. Northeast c Bracey b Taylor	24	B 6, lb 14, nb 10	30
M. S. Crane c Bracey b Higgins	4		
*J. M. Vince c Bracey b Worrall	52	1/19 (1) 2/247 (2) (144.1 overs) 470
L. A. Dawson b Higgins	65	3/291 (4) 4/302 (5) 5/332 (3)
†L. D. McManus c Dent b Worrall	0	6/403 (6) 7/403 (8) 8/419 (9)
K. J. Abbott lbw b Worrall	4	9/452 (7) 10/470 (11) 110 overs: 322-4

Worrall 31–11–75–4; Higgins 32.1–9–78–4; Taylor 27–6–102–1; Goodman 25–8–54–1; Shaw 22–2–107–0; Brathwaite 4–0–16–0; Dent 3–0–18–0.

Gloucestershire

K. C. Brathwaite c McManus b Dawson	60	– c Abbott b Dawson	21
*C. D. J. Dent lbw b Mohammad Abbas	6	– c Dawson b Wheal	10
†J. R. Bracey b Mohammad Abbas	65	– c Holland b Dawson	9
T. C. Lace c McManus b Mohammad Abbas	20	– c Weatherley b Wheal	38
I. A. Cockbain b Mohammad Abbas	24	– lbw b Abbott	36
R. F. Higgins b Crane	73	– b Abbott	29
G. T. Hankins lbw b Crane	31	– c Vince b Wheal	8
M. D. Taylor c Vince b Dawson	11	– lbw b Crane	4
D. J. Worrall b Crane	5	– b Wheal	0
J. Shaw b Dawson	12	– not out	23
D. C. Goodman not out	2	– not out	9
B 8, lb 1, nb 2	11	B 7, lb 1, nb 2	10

1/18 (2) 2/106 (1) 3/151 (4)   (132.1 overs) 320   1/33 (2)   (9 wkts, 97 overs) 197
4/158 (3) 5/207 (5) 6/283 (7)   2/33 (1) 3/50 (3)
7/288 (6) 8/298 (9) 9/313 (10)   4/103 (4) 5/133 (5) 6/154 (6)
10/320 (8)   110 overs: 273-5   7/161 (7) 8/161 (9) 9/161 (8)

Abbott 20–4–50–0; Mohammad Abbas 19–5–41–4; Dawson 41.1–12–80–3; Holland 13–3–45–0;
Crane 27–4–70–3; Wheal 12–4–25–0. *Second innings*—Mohammad Abbas 18–8–31–0; Abbott
19–8–27–2; Wheal 21–6–59–4; Dawson 20–7–27–2; Crane 19–5–45–1.

Umpires: B. J. Debenham and D. J. Millns.   Referee: S. Cummings.

At The Oval, April 29–May 1. HAMPSHIRE lost to SURREY by an innings and 289 runs.
Hampshire's heaviest defeat since 1911.

HAMPSHIRE v SOMERSET

At Southampton, May 6–9. Somerset won by ten wickets. Somerset 22pts, Hampshire 3pts. Toss:
Somerset.

Overton and Davey took seven wickets each as Hampshire slid to their second resounding defeat
in nine days. The toss, won by Somerset, proved crucial. Gregory took four for 26 in seamer-friendly
conditions as Hampshire were bowled out for under 100 in successive first innings, a fate they had
not met since 1965. Though Somerset lost five wickets by the close of the first day, they were more
resolute on the second, building a lead of 257, with Overton's 74 from No. 9 the game's highest
score. Hampshire relied upon fortune and fortitude in their second innings. Rain ruled out all but 57
balls on the third day; on the fourth, Weatherley reached 44 from 209, and Organ used up 108
making seven. Barker counter-punched with an unbeaten 52 from No. 10, but Overton and Davey
proved irresistible, sharing all ten wickets, before Byrom took one ball to knock off a target of two.

Close of play: first day, Somerset 142-5 (Abell 52, Leach 3); second day, Hampshire 92-3
(Weatherley 31, Northeast 1); third day, Hampshire 110-4 (Weatherley 34, Vince 5).

Hampshire

J. J. Weatherley c Davies b Abell	20	– c Davies b Davey	44
I. G. Holland c Overton b Gregory	4	– lbw b Overton	19
T. P. Alsop lbw b Davey	5	– c Davey b Overton	32
S. A. Northeast run out (Bartlett)	4	– (5) c Bartlett b Overton	9
*J. M. Vince b Overton	6	– (6) c Davies b Overton	42
L. A. Dawson c Gregory b Overton	0	– (7) lbw b Davey	0
†L. D. McManus b Gregory	13	– (8) c Hildreth b Davey	19
F. S. Organ c Davies b Gregory	11	– (9) c Overton b Davey	7
K. H. D. Barker c Davies b Gregory	10	– (10) not out	52
K. J. Abbott c Davies b Overton	3	– (4) lbw b Overton	0
Mohammad Abbas not out	0	– lbw b Davey	0
B 1, lb 2	3	B 8, lb 9, w 5, nb 12	34

1/7 (2) 2/26 (3) 3/36 (4)   (40.3 overs) 79
4/36 (1) 5/37 (6) 6/42 (5)
7/65 (8) 8/68 (8) 9/75 (10) 10/79 (9)

1/31 (2) 2/87 (3)   (131 overs) 258
3/89 (4) 4/103 (5)
5/130 (1) 6/134 (7) 7/177 (6)
8/186 (8) 9/250 (9) 10/258 (11)

Gregory 13.3–6–26–4; Overton 11–5–16–2; Davey 11–2–32–2; Abell 5–3–2–1. *Second innings*—Gregory 28–9–77–0; Overton 40–17–66–5; Davey 24–10–30–5; Abell 17–6–34–0; Leach 22–9–34–0.

Somerset

E. J. Byrom c Holland b Mohammad Abbas	11	– not out	2
T. A. Lammonby lbw b Barker	0	– not out	0
*T. B. Abell b Abbott	64		
J. C. Hildreth lbw b Abbott	14		
G. A. Bartlett c Dawson b Abbott	27		
L. P. Goldsworthy b Holland	24		
M. J. Leach c Dawson b Barker	34		
†S. M. Davies b Mohammad Abbas	33		
C. Overton b Barker	74		
L. Gregory not out	33		
J. H. Davey c Vince b Barker	7		
B 7, lb 4, nb 4	15		

1/11 (2) 2/11 (1) 3/36 (4)   (99 overs) 336   (no wkt, 0.1 overs) 2
4/90 (5) 5/137 (6) 6/189 (3)
7/193 (7) 8/268 (8) 9/328 (9) 10/336 (11)

Barker 24–5–67–4; Mohammad Abbas 31–8–86–2; Abbott 26–5–88–3; Holland 11–1–59–1; Dawson 7–1–25–0. *Second innings*—Holland 0.1–0–2–0.

Umpires: G. D. Lloyd and A. G. Wharf.   Referee: D. A. Cosker.

At Lord's, May 13–15. HAMPSHIRE beat MIDDLESEX by seven wickets. *Kyle Abbott takes 11 wickets.*

HAMPSHIRE v LEICESTERSHIRE

At Southampton, May 19–22. Drawn. Hampshire 12pts, Leicestershire 11pts. Toss: Leicestershire.
    Rain, which severely disrupted all four days, denied Hampshire the possibility of inflicting a second heavy defeat on Leicestershire. In ideal pace-bowling conditions, the visitors had restricted them to 233, with the raw Barnes and the experienced Wright claiming four wickets apiece. Holland proved the only batsman on either side to master the conditions for any time, and even he was dropped on nine en route to 82; no one else passed 32. Leicestershire had no answer to Abbott and Mohammad Abbas, who took nine for 66 between them; at 54 for nine, they needed 30 to avoid the

follow-on. Thanks to Barnes and Alex Evans, they succeeded – just. Vince tried to keep the match alive by forfeiting Hampshire's second innings, in the hope that a target of 150 in 22 overs might be tempting. It was not: after Abbott struck early, Azad and Harris played out time. The weather permitted only 124 overs in all. This was the first match at the Rose Bowl open to spectators since September 2019 – and they included the New Zealand tourists watching from their hotel balconies as they quarantined before their test series against England.

Close of play: first day, Hampshire 53-1 (Holland 24, Alsop 15); second day, Hampshire 223-7 (Barker 15, Abbott 5); third day, Leicestershire 28-5 (Patel 13, Swindells 2).

Hampshire

J. J. Weatherley c Ackermann b Wright	...	11
I. G. Holland lbw b Barnes	....	82
T. P. Alsop c Ackermann b H. A. Evans	..	25
S. A. Northeast b Wright	....	2
*J. M. Vince lbw b Barnes	....	32
L. A. Dawson lbw b Barnes	....	19
†J. C. McManus lbw b H. A. Evans	......	15
K. H. D. Barker c Patel b Wright	....	24

K. J. Abbott lbw b Wright	....	5
B. T. J. Wheal c Azad b Barnes	....	1
Mohammad Abbas not out	....	0
Lb 7, nb 10	....	17

1/20 (1) 2/102 (3) 3/105 (4) (71 overs) 233
4/141 (2) 5/172 (5) 6/191 (6)
7/218 (7) 8/232 (8) 9/233 (9) 10/233 (10)

Wright 24–4–71–4; H. A. Evans 16–2–50–2; Griffiths 9–2–34–0; Barnes 19–4–61–4; Ackermann 3–0–10–0.

Hampshire forfeited their second innings.

Leicestershire

M. H. Azad lbw b Abbott	....	0	– not out	....	3
S. T. Evans lbw b Mohammad Abbas	....	5	– lbw b Abbott	....	8
M. S. Harris b Mohammad Abbas	....	2	– not out	....	7
*C. N. Ackermann b Abbott	....	2		
L. J. Hill c McManus b Abbott	....	3		
R. K. Patel c McManus b Abbott	....	27		
†H. J. Swindells c Dawson b Abbott	....	8		
C. J. C. Wright c Dawson b Mohammad Abbas	...	3		
G. T. Griffiths b Abbott	....	1		
E. Barnes not out	....	17		
H. A. Evans c McManus b Wheal	....	10		
B 2, lb 2, nb 2	....	6	B 4, lb 4	....	8

1/5 (1) 2/5 (2) 3/8 (3)   (35.5 overs) 84   1/13 (2)   (1 wkt, 17 overs) 26
4/10 (4) 5/17 (5) 6/35 (7)
7/40 (8) 8/47 (9) 9/54 (6) 10/84 (11)

Mohammad Abbas 16–6–19–3; Abbott 14–2–47–6; Wheal 3.5–2–4–1; Barker 2–0–10–0. *Second innings*—Abbott 6–3–6–1; Mohammad Abbas 8–4–8–0; Barker 3–1–4–0.

Umpires: N. J. Llong and M. J. Saggers.   Referee: T. J. Boon.

At Taunton, June 3–6. HAMPSHIRE drew with SOMERSET.

HAMPSHIRE v SURREY

At Southampton, July 4–7. Drawn. Hampshire 15pts, Surrey 11pts. Toss: Surrey. First-class debuts: T. J. Prest; B. B. A. Geddes. County debut: N. R. T. Gubbins. Championship debuts: C. de Grandhomme; K. A. Jamieson.

An epic last-day rearguard led by Amla, who made an unbeaten 37 in six and a half hours, saved Surrey from seemingly inevitable defeat. Following on 416 behind after being bundled out for 72 – their lowest total against Hampshire since 1986 – they had closed the third day at six for two. When nightwatchman Virdi fell next morning, it was nine for three. But Amla knuckled down to face

278 balls – though he was dropped with Surrey still 17 overs from safety – and received support from Patel, who helped him see out 29 overs, and Smith. Further assistance came from 19-year-old Ben Geddes, drafted in mid-match for his first-class debut after Jacks was called up to England's replacement one-day squad (Hampshire's 18-year-old Tom Prest replaced Vince for the same reason). In all, the final day yielded 116 runs in 96.2 overs, with 57 maidens; Barker alone bowled 14 of them, and ended up with three for nine from 22, as Surrey closed on 122 for eight. Earlier, de Grandhomme, fresh from New Zealand's World Test Championship success at this ground, returned – now as a Hampshire player – to record a career-best unbeaten 174. In a remarkable second-day revival, he turned 221 for seven into 488, putting on 127 for the eighth wicket with Organ, and 114 for the last with Wheal. His compatriot Jamieson, Player of the Match in that WTC final, bowled just six overs in his first Championship game for Surrey before he suffered a glute injury, ending his short stint at the club.

Close of play: first day, Hampshire 229-7 (de Grandhomme 48, Organ 3); second day, Surrey 42-4 (Amla 24, Jacks 1); third day, Surrey 6-2 (Virdi 1).

Hampshire

J. J. Weatherley c Burns b Clark	13		K. J. Abbott c Smith b Overton	7
I. G. Holland b Clark	58		B. T. J. Wheal lbw b Virdi	45
T. P. Alsop c Smith b Clark	29			
N. R. T. Gubbins c Smith b Overton	17		B 6, lb 16, nb 16	38
*J. M. Vince lbw b Clarke	16			
C. de Grandhomme not out	174		1/21 (1) 2/79 (3) (134.5 overs)	488
†L. D. McManus c Smith b Clark	24		3/104 (4) 4/135 (5) 5/155 (2)	
K. H. D. Barker c Patel b Clarke	0		6/216 (7) 7/221 (8) 8/348 (9)	
F. S. Organ c Overton b Jacks	67		9/374 (10) 10/488 (11) 110 overs: 381-9	

T. J. Prest replaced Vince, who left to join England's one-day squad.

Jamieson 6–3–10–0; Clark 33–4–110–4; Clarke 29–3–114–2; Overton 25–2–81–2; Virdi 14.5–0–51–1; Patel 15–4–50–0; Jacks 11–0–45–1; Burns 1–0–5–0.

Surrey

*R. J. Burns c Weatherley b Barker	1		– c Gubbins b Wheal	0
M. D. Stoneman c Weatherley b Abbott	0		– lbw b Barker	1
H. M. Amla b Barker	29		– (4) not out	37
R. S. Patel b Barker	11		– (5) b Abbott	16
†J. L. Smith b Barker	0		– (6) c Holland b Organ	14
W. G. Jacks retired not out	1			
B. B. A. Geddes lbw b Abbott	4		– b de Grandhomme	15
J. Clark b Wheal	7		– lbw b Barker	4
J. Overton lbw b Abbott	4		– b Organ	11
R. Clarke b Wheal	0		– not out	2
K. A. Jamieson not out	0			
G. S. Virdi run out (Abbott)	0		– (3) c Organ b Barker	3
B 6, lb 1, nb 8	15		B 4, lb 15	19

1/0 (2) 2/8 (1) 3/34 (4)   (31.4 overs) 72   1/5 (2)   (8 wkts, 104.5 overs) 122
4/34 (5) 5/51 (7) 6/51 (3)   2/6 (1) 3/9 (3) 4/30 (5)
7/66 (8) 8/66 (9) 9/66 (10) 10/72 (12)   5/60 (6) 6/87 (7) 7/97 (8) 8/116 (9)

In the first innings Jacks retired not out at 42-4 to join England's one-day squad. Geddes replaced him.

Barker 14–6–24–4; Abbott 12.4–4–31–3; Wheal 5–1–10–2. *Second innings*—Barker 22–17–9–3; Abbott 23.5–16–19–1; Wheal 22–9–26–1; Organ 25–14–35–2; de Grandhomme 8–7–6–1; Holland 4–0–8–0.

Umpires: I. J. Gould and C. M. Watts.   Referee: S. G. Hinks.

At Cheltenham, July 11–14. HAMPSHIRE beat GLOUCESTERSHIRE by seven wickets. *Hampshire overtake Gloucestershire to qualify for Division One.*

DIVISION ONE

HAMPSHIRE v YORKSHIRE

At Southampton, August 30–September 2. Drawn. Hampshire 11pts, Yorkshire 12pts. Toss: Hampshire.

Abbott and Wheal – Hampshire's last pair, and both nursing injuries – got off the treatment table to deny Yorkshire in a tense conclusion. They came together with 46 balls remaining, and clung on, despite ten close fielders. Hampshire had been set a nominal 393 in 115 overs, and survival was the limit of their ambitions. The pitch, lively for the first half of the match, had flattened out, and Yorkshire worked hard for wickets: nightwatchman Crane faced 197 deliveries in more than four hours, while Vince curbed his attacking instinct to make 42 from 151. When he fell lbw to Thompson, it was 177 for nine – and so it stayed. Run-scoring had been tricky on the first two days, when Yorkshire carved out a lead of 80. Outstanding in both innings, Thompson finished with match figures of seven for 53. The third day also belonged to Yorkshire, thanks to half-centuries from Hill and Köhler-Cadmore, and an unbeaten 85-ball hundred from Ballance, who crashed seven leg-side sixes, including five off Dawson; it was his fifth century in his last seven innings at the Rose Bowl, which was also the scene, in 2014, of one of his four Test hundreds. Needing eight wickets on the final day, Yorkshire ended up with cause to regret delaying their declaration.

Close of play: first day, Yorkshire 197-6 (Bess 45, Thompson 15); second day, Yorkshire 34-1 (Hill 10, Köhler-Cadmore 16); third day, Hampshire 26-2 (Weatherley 16, Crane 0).

Yorkshire

A. Lyth lbw b Abbott	6	– c McManus b Wheal	7
G. C. H. Hill lbw b Abbott	31	– c McManus b Holland	55
T. Köhler-Cadmore c McManus b Abbott	20	– c Dawson b Crane	89
G. S. Ballance c Weatherley b Dawson	42	– not out	101
H. C. Brook b Wheal	13	– c Gubbins b Vince	12
D. M. Bess b Barker	54	– (7) c McManus b Barker	0
†H. G. Duke c Weatherley b Wheal	12	– (8) not out	1
J. A. Thompson b Wheal	15	– (6) c Vince b Barker	33
M. D. Fisher lbw b Crane	17		
*S. A. Patterson not out	9		
B. O. Coad lbw b Crane	0		
B 4, lb 16, nb 4	24	B 4, lb 5, w 3, nb 2	14

1/13 (1) 2/60 (2) 3/84 (3)   (106.1 overs) 243   1/7 (1)   (6 wkts dec, 87 overs) 312
4/114 (5) 5/138 (4) 6/159 (7)   2/128 (2) 3/206 (3)
7/197 (8) 8/215 (6) 9/239 (9) 10/243 (11)   4/231 (5) 5/295 (6) 6/296 (7)

Barker 26–6–52–1; Abbott 20–6–47–3; Wheal 24–8–47–3; Holland 15–9–21–0; Dawson 16–2–38–1; Crane 5.1–0–18–2. *Second innings*—Barker 18–5–39–2; Wheal 4–1–16–1; Holland 12–4–21–0; Dawson 35–7–104–0; Crane 12–1–68–1; Vince 6–0–55–1.

Hampshire

J. J. Weatherley c Duke b Fisher	1	– lbw b Thompson	43
I. G. Holland lbw b Coad	0	– c Brook b Coad	3
T. P. Alsop b Bess	12	– c Ballance b Bess	7
N. R. T. Gubbins c Brook b Coad	15	– (5) c and b Fisher	6
*J. M. Vince c Hill b Fisher	49	– (6) lbw b Thompson	42
L. A. Dawson lbw b Thompson	11	– (7) lbw b Fisher	0
†L. D. McManus c Duke b Bess	7	– (8) b Thompson	8
K. H. D. Barker c Köhler-Cadmore b Thompson	2	– (9) c Duke b Thompson	4
M. S. Crane c Lyth b Thompson	4	– (4) c Lyth b Fisher	28
K. J. Abbott not out	21	– not out	9
B. T. J. Wheal c Duke b Coad	12	– not out	0
B 15, lb 8, nb 6	29	B 8, lb 13, nb 6	27

1/1 (2) 2/1 (1) 3/16 (4)   (62.3 overs) 163   1/9 (2)   (9 wkts, 115 overs) 177
4/86 (5) 5/93 (3) 6/109 (6)   2/26 (3) 3/74 (1)
7/113 (8) 8/121 (7) 9/123 (9) 10/163 (11)   4/86 (5) 5/120 (4) 6/124 (7)
                                       7/138 (8) 8/159 (9) 9/177 (6)

Coad 12.3–4–29–3; Fisher 10–4–28–2; Patterson 9–4–14–0; Thompson 12–3–35–3; Bess 19–4–34–2. *Second innings*—Coad 16–9–16–1; Fisher 21–8–42–3; Thompson 17–11–18–4; Bess 33–21–43–1; Lyth 7–6–2–0; Patterson 17–10–27–0; Hill 4–1–8–0.

Umpires: N. J. Llong and J. D. Middlebrook.   Referee: P. Whitticase.

At Birmingham, September 5–8. HAMPSHIRE beat WARWICKSHIRE by 60 runs. *Hampshire recover after being dismissed for 89 in their first innings.*

HAMPSHIRE v NOTTINGHAMSHIRE

At Southampton, September 12–14. Hampshire won by 122 runs. Hampshire 20pts, Nottinghamshire 3pts. Toss: Hampshire.

For two days, pace bowlers collected wickets on a green pitch giving them every encouragement. Against Hutton and Paterson, Hampshire plodded to 226, a total that would have been fewer but for five dropped catches (four off the luckless Evison). Nottinghamshire fared worse, conceding a deficit of 71 after Barker, in his 13th season, claimed seven in an innings for the first time. The second day, which brought 16 wickets, closed with Hampshire seven down, 204 ahead. Next morning, they took their lead to 249 but, with the pitch now taking spin – slow left-armer Patterson-White claimed a career-best five for 41 – Nottinghamshire's predicament was precarious. In fact, they made a decent start, reaching 64 for one, before Dawson and Organ turned the match. The two spinners took the last eight wickets, and Dawson's five for 45 were his best figures for nine years. The defeat dented Nottinghamshire's Championship hopes: Hampshire replaced them at the top with one game to go. Beaten captain Mullaney described the pitch as "unacceptable for first-class cricket". Sam Northeast, still employed by Hampshire but on loan at Trent Bridge, was left out at the last minute after the cancellation of the Manchester Test allowed Hameed to play.

Close of play: first day, Nottinghamshire 29-1 (Slater 18, Duckett 9); second day, Hampshire 133-7 (Barker 11, Wheal 1).

Hampshire

J. J. Weatherley c Duckett b Hutton	11	– c Moores b Fletcher	7
I. G. Holland lbw b Fletcher	3	– c sub (C. G. Harrison) b Paterson	16
†T. P. Alsop b Paterson	16	– c Hameed b Paterson	0
N. R. T. Gubbins b Evison	54	– lbw b Paterson	2
*J. M. Vince c Hameed b Hutton	30	– b Fletcher	52
L. A. Dawson c Duckett b Paterson	31	– lbw b Patterson-White	29
K. H. D. Barker c Patterson-White b Paterson	19	– (8) c Paterson b Patterson-White	29
J. K. Fuller b Hutton	13	– (10) c Mullaney b Patterson-White	21
F. S. Organ b Fletcher	36	– (7) lbw b Patterson-White	11
B. T. J. Wheal b Mullaney	0	– (9) st Moores b Patterson-White	3
Mohammad Abbas not out	2	– not out	0
B 7, lb 4	11	B 4, lb 4	8

1/15 (1) 2/15 (2) 3/45 (3)   (82.2 overs) 226   1/26 (2) 2/26 (3)   (65.4 overs) 178
4/87 (5) 5/131 (4) 6/154 (6)   3/28 (1) 4/28 (4)
7/183 (8) 8/188 (7) 9/193 (10) 10/226 (9)   5/110 (6) 6/116 (5) 7/126 (7)
8/146 (9) 9/169 (8) 10/178 (10)

Fletcher 15.2–8–32–2; Hutton 18–7–40–3; Evison 14–4–52–1; Paterson 19–7–52–3; Patterson-White 7–0–19–0; Mullaney 9–3–20–1. *Second innings*—Fletcher 23–6–39–2; Hutton 9–2–31–0; Paterson 9–4–17–3; Mullaney 6–0–24–0; Evison 3–0–18–0; Patterson-White 15.4–4–41–5.

Nottinghamshire

B. T. Slater c Weatherley b Barker	55	– c Gubbins b Dawson	25
H. Hameed c Alsop b Barker	2	– c Organ b Mohammad Abbas	8
B. M. Duckett c Alsop b Barker	9	– lbw b Mohammad Abbas	33
J. M. Clarke c Wheal b Barker	0	– c Weatherley b Dawson	9
*S. J. Mullaney lbw b Barker	2	– c Weatherley b Dawson	3
†T. J. Moores lbw b Barker	4	– b Organ	8
L. A. Patterson-White b Wheal	53	– c and b Organ	4
J. D. M. Evison c Alsop b Barker	1	– c Gubbins b Dawson	22
B. A. Hutton c Organ b Fuller	16	– b Organ	3
L. J. Fletcher not out	3	– lbw b Dawson	4
D. Paterson c Gubbins b Wheal	6	– not out	4
Lb 2, nb 2	4	B 1, lb 3	4
	—		—
	155		127

1/11 (2) 2/29 (3) 3/29 (4)   (52.1 overs) 155   1/20 (2) 2/64 (3)   (54.3 overs) 127
4/31 (5) 5/39 (6) 6/109 (1)   3/72 (1) 4/80 (5)
7/115 (8) 8/145 (7) 9/145 (9) 10/155 (11)   5/81 (4) 6/86 (7) 7/97 (6)
     8/105 (9) 9/118 (10) 10/127 (8)

Barker 20–5–46–7; Mohammad Abbas 16–4–43–0; Wheal 6.1–0–24–2; Holland 2–0–16–0; Fuller 4–0–15–1; Dawson 3–0–8–0; Organ 1–0–1–0. *Second innings*—Barker 13–4–28–0; Mohammad Abbas 13–5–28–2; Dawson 17.3–4–45–5; Organ 11–2–22–3.

Umpires: M. Burns and M. J. Saggers.   Referee: W. M. Noon.

At Liverpool, September 21–23. HAMPSHIRE lost to LANCASHIRE by one wicket. *Hampshire are unable to take the tenth wicket that would have brought them the Championship.*

KENT

Blast furnace

FRED ATKINS

Kent emerged from lockdown's long, dark night of the soul, faced up to the twin threats of Covid and The Hundred, and emerged with a first trophy in 14 years. They packed more drama into a single season than they had into some decades.

Head coach Matt Walker said before the season that Kent had assembled "the best squad we've had for a very, very long time". Yet there was open revolt among some fans after a disastrous start to the Championship. A draw at Northampton was followed by three wallopings – by Yorkshire, Lancashire and Glamorgan, though even in defeat Kent began to show fight. They ended the run, managing six consecutive draws, one of which, against Glamorgan at Canterbury, was memorable for an innings for the ages from Darren Stevens, who hit a staggering 190 in gale-force winds. For once, his annual contract question was resolved early, with a one-year extension agreed in June; he responded by ending the Championship campaign third in the list of Kent run-scorers – behind Jack Leaning and wicketkeeper Ollie Robinson – and top of the wicket-takers. Not bad for a 45-year-old.

However, it was the decision to recall him to the T20 side after a three-season absence that perhaps turned a promising white-ball team into champions. The Blast revitalised the club. With fans allowed back in increasing numbers, the St Lawrence became a cacophonous furnace, and the Spitfires kept finding ways to win, whatever the circumstances: after a rout of Surrey at The Oval, a positive Covid test for an unnamed player sent the entire squad into isolation. With just a day before the start of the Canterbury Festival, Kent considered cancelling the Championship fixture with Sussex, but Walker, director of cricket Paul Downton and chief executive Simon Storey were determined to keep the show on the road – and scrambled 11 second-teamers or free agents. Playing against his former club (and wearing his old Sussex helmet, with the crest obscured), Harry Finch seized his chance, scoring a match-saving century on the final day. Scottish internationals Calum MacLeod, Safyaan Sharif and George Munsey were then recruited for an emphatic Blast win over Middlesex at Lord's, guaranteeing a home quarter-final. But more trouble lay in store.

The Royal London campaign was an almost unmitigated flop. In the opening match, at Beckenham, Kent asked Durham to bat, and dropped three catches. Those reprieved added another 225 runs, and Kent, chasing 406, lost by a country mile. Their only win came at Radlett against Middlesex – their favourite opponents in 2021.

Fans were almost universally hostile to The Hundred, which arguably hit Kent harder than any other county: ten of their drafted players – Zak Crawley, Daniel Bell-Drummond, Joe Denly, Sam Billings, Alex Blake, Jordan Cox, Adam Milne, Qais Ahmad, Matt Milnes and Fred Klaassen – returned to play

Darren Stevens

the quarter-final against Warwickshire. That team had a notable absentee: Stevens was less than thrilled when he was told he had been omitted. "You get us to finals day," he responded, "and I'll win you the comp." In the most raucous atmosphere seen at Canterbury for years, Kent throttled Warwickshire. Billings, the captain, was ecstatic, but there were signs that online criticism had rattled him. "People think I don't care," he said. "I think they're delusional."

In reality, he was one of a core of Kent-born players desperate to make their own history, rather than be reminded of the achievements of others by the monuments to county legends dotted around the ground. In the build-up, he spoke of how he had watched the 2007 final as a teenager at his old club, Hartley. Crawley had been nine years old, watching on TV with his parents in Sevenoaks, when Stevens, then 31, hit the winning boundary.

Milne's unavailability meant a recall for Stevens, who was heavily involved in both games, though the show was ultimately stolen by the 20-year-old Cox. At Edgbaston, journalists were asked if they might mention the work done by the Professional Cricketers' Trust in combatting poor mental health. Cox endured a first-baller in the semi-final against Sussex, and left the field to quacking over the PA system. Such ridicule probably wasn't what the PCT were envisaging. But, against Somerset in the final, Cox was unstoppable.

Until he smote a high-class 58 not out from 28 balls, Kent seemed to be heading for no more than 140; a total of 167 made them slight favourites. Cox then caught Will Smeed in the deep, a split second before Bell-Drummond careered into him and the foam boundary. The umpires wrongly ruled that Cox had – through a deliberate act by Bell-Drummond – had become part of the boundary, and awarded a six. The error spurred MCC into a lengthy clarification.

Cox, who really did catch Smeed later that over, then produced a moment of breathtaking athleticism. His staggering leap beyond the boundary prevented a certain six by Gregory – and he had the presence of mind to pat the ball into the hands of the waiting Milnes.

Kent carried the euphoria of Edgbaston into their final Championship fixture – against Middlesex. Though they were contesting no more than the Division Three title, they showed true steel. Asked to make 373, they rose to the challenge, and an electrifying innings from Tawanda Muyeye steered them to an exhilarating two-wicket win. Canterbury begins 2022 a happier place than it has been for years.

KENT RESULTS

County Championship matches – Played 14: Won 4, Lost 3, Drawn 7.
Vitality T20 Blast matches – Played 17: Won 12, Lost 4, No result 1.
Royal London Cup matches – Played 8: Won 1, Lost 5, No result 2.

LV= County Championship, 5th in Group 3, winners of Division 3;
Vitality T20 Blast, winners; Royal London Cup, 9th in Group 1.

COUNTY CHAMPIONSHIP AVERAGES, BATTING AND FIELDING

Cap		Birthplace	M	I	NO	R	HS	100	Avge	Ct/St
2021	J. A. Leaning	Bristol	13	21	5	745	127*	1	46.56	11
2005	D. I. Stevens	Leicester	12	18	3	650	190	0	43.33	4
	O. G. Robinson	Sidcup‡	13	21	1	725	120	2	36.25	38/1
	T. S. Muyeye††	Harare, Zimbabwe .	4	6	2	142	89	0	35.50	0
2019	Z. Crawley§	Bromley‡	12	21	2	637	90	0	33.52	9
2015	S. W. Billings	Pembury‡	4	5	0	149	72	0	29.80	6
	J. M. Cox	Margate‡	13	23	2	579	90	0	27.57	10
2015	D. J. Bell-Drummond	Lewisham‡	10	17	1	419	114	1	26.18	2
2021	M. E. Milnes	Nottingham	8	14	4	244	78	0	24.40	2
2019	H. W. Podmore	Hammersmith	5	6	1	107	37	0	21.40	0
	M. K. O'Riordan	Pembury‡	7	7	0	140	47	0	20.00	4
	G. Stewart††	Kalgoorlie, Australia	6	9	2	134	40	0	19.14	0
2008	J. L. Denly	Canterbury‡	9	14	0	246	63	0	17.57	1
	M. R. Quinn††	Auckland, NZ	6	5	3	32	13*	0	16.00	0
2018	H. G. Kuhn¶	Piet Retief, SA	4	8	0	108	32	0	13.50	4
	†M. L. Cummins¶	St Michael, Barbados	8	10	2	108	28*	0	13.50	1
	†J. E. G. Logan	Wakefield	4	6	1	51	21	0	10.20	0
	N. N. Gilchrist	Harare, Zimbabwe .	9	8	1	52	13	0	7.42	2
	F. J. Klaassen	Haywards Heath...	2	4	1	8	5	0	2.66	0

Also batted: H. Z. Finch (*Hastings*) (1 match) 24, 115; J. A. Gordon (*Coffs Harbour, Australia*) (1 match) 8, 0; Hamidullah Qadri (*Kandahar, Afghanistan*) (1 match) 30*, 4; H. F. Houillon (*Greenwich‡*) (1 match) 0, 9 (3 ct); D. J. Lincoln (*Frimley*) (1 match) 0, 41 (1 ct); J. Singh (*Denmark Hill*) (2 matches) 2, 0 (1 ct); B. J. Wightman (*Warwick*) (1 match) 0, 0*.

‡ *Born in Kent.*   § *ECB contract.*   ¶ *Official overseas player.*   †† *Other non-England-qualified.*

BOWLING

	Style	O	M	R	W	BB	5I	Avge
D. I. Stevens	RM	284	93	725	39	5-53	2	18.58
N. N. Gilchrist	RFM	160.1	26	620	30	5-38	1	20.66
M. E. Milnes	RFM	205.3	42	687	32	6-53	2	21.46
G. Stewart	RFM	120	31	384	17	5-23	1	22.58
M. R. Quinn	RFM	149.3	34	413	18	4-54	0	22.94
H. W. Podmore	RFM	114.3	16	419	12	4-77	0	34.91

Also bowled: D. J. Bell-Drummond (RM) 19-3-70-3; J. M. Cox (RM) 1-0-3-0; M. L. Cummins (RF) 162.2-19-622-6; J. L. Denly (LB) 89.2-12-274-4; Hamidullah Qadri (OB) 17-2-44-1; F. J. Klaassen (LFM) 42.5-3-172-3; J. A. Leaning (OB) 103.5-12-356-6; J. E. G. Logan (SLA) 47.1-11-119-8; M. K. O'Riordan (OB) 50-9-145-2; J. Singh (RFM) 40-5-140-7; B. J. Wightman (RM) 12-4-23-0.

LEADING VITALITY BLAST AVERAGES (100 runs/15 overs)

Batting	Runs	HS	Avge	SR	Ct/St	Bowling	W	BB	Avge	ER
D. J. Bell-Drummond	492	88	37.84	155.69	6	Qais Ahmad	10	2-13	28.60	6.65
Z. Crawley	380	69	31.66	150.79	4	J. L. Denly	11	3-31	21.72	7.31
D. I. Stevens	153	47*	21.85	142.99	0	A. F. Milne	7	4-38	16.57	7.73
J. M. Cox	367	64	52.42	142.24	13/2	M. E. Milnes	22	5-22	15.40	8.00
O. G. Robinson	103	48	34.33	139.18	3	F. J. Klaassen	19	4-17	19.63	8.64
J. A. Leaning	321	81*	29.18	131.02	12	D. I. Stevens	11	3-32	26.18	9.00
J. L. Denly	213	44	15.21	118.33	8	G. Stewart	9	3-33	27.55	9.78
S. W. Billings	116	56	23.20	114.85	3/2					

LEADING ROYAL LONDON CUP AVERAGES (100 runs/3 wickets)

Batting	Runs	HS	Avge	SR	Ct
Hamidullah Qadri	103	42*	103.00	85.83	1
H. G. Munsey ...	302	108	60.40	95.87	1
M. K. O'Riordan .	119	60	39.66	85.61	2
H. Z. Finch......	152	84	25.33	77.55	2
T. S. Muyeye....	140	30	23.33	99.29	1
O. G. Robinson ..	155	75	22.14	74.51	4

Bowling	W	BB	Avge	ER
N. N. Gilchrist	8	5-45	22.62	7.09
Hamidullah Qadri..	4	3-47	38.00	6.33
M. R. Quinn	6	2-28	41.00	7.02
M. E. Milnes.......	3	1-29	51.00	6.37
J. E. G. Logan.....	3	2-45	69.00	6.27
G. Stewart........	3	1-26	70.00	6.02

FIRST-CLASS COUNTY RECORDS

Highest score for	332	W. H. Ashdown v Essex at Brentwood	1934
Highest score against	344	W. G. Grace (MCC) at Canterbury	1876
Leading run-scorer	47,868	F. E. Woolley (avge 41.77)	1906–38
Best bowling for	10-30	C. Blythe v Northamptonshire at Northampton	1907
Best bowling against	10-48	C. H. G. Bland (Sussex) at Tonbridge	1899
Leading wicket-taker	3,340	A. P. Freeman (avge 17.64)...................	1914–36
Highest total for	803-4 dec	v Essex at Brentwood	1934
Highest total against	676	by Australians at Canterbury	1921
Lowest total for	18	v Sussex at Gravesend	1867
Lowest total against	16	by Warwickshire at Tonbridge.................	1913

LIST A COUNTY RECORDS

Highest score for	150*	J. L. Denly v Glamorgan at Canterbury........	2018
Highest score against	167*	P. Johnson (Nottinghamshire) at Nottingham	1993
Leading run-scorer	7,814	M. R. Benson (avge 31.89)	1980–95
Best bowling for	8-31	D. L. Underwood v Scotland at Edinburgh	1987
Best bowling against	6-5	A. G. Wharf (Glamorgan) at Cardiff	2004
Leading wicket-taker	530	D. L. Underwood (avge 18.93)	1963–87
Highest total for	{ 384-6	v Berkshire at Finchampstead	1994
	{ 384-8	v Surrey at Beckenham	2018
Highest total against	405-4	**by Durham at Beckenham**	**2021**
Lowest total for	60	v Somerset at Taunton	1979
Lowest total against	60	by Derbyshire at Canterbury	2008

TWENTY20 COUNTY RECORDS

Highest score for	127	J. L. Denly v Essex at Chelmsford.............	2017
Highest score against	151*	C. H. Gayle (Somerset) at Taunton	2015
Leading run-scorer	**3,723**	**J. L. Denly (avge 28.41, SR 126.84)**	**2004–21**
Best bowling for	5-11	A. F. Milne v Somerset at Canterbury	2017
Best bowling against	5-17	G. M. Smith (Essex) at Chelmsford............	2012
Leading wicket-taker	119	J. C. Tredwell (avge 28.46, ER 7.32)...........	2003–17
Highest total for	**236-3**	**v Essex at Canterbury**	**2021**
Highest total against	250-6	by Surrey at Canterbury	2018
Lowest total for	72	v Hampshire at Southampton	2011
Lowest total against	**80**	**by Middlesex at Lord's**	**2021**

ADDRESS

The Spitfire Ground, St Lawrence, Old Dover Road, Canterbury CT1 3NZ; 01227 456886; feedback@kentcricket.co.uk; www.kentcricket.co.uk. Twitter: @KentCricket.

OFFICIALS

Captain S. W. Billings
Director of cricket P. R. Downton
Head coach M. J. Walker
Head of talent pathway M. M. Patel

President Y. N. Neame
Chair S. R. C. Philip
Chief executive S. G. B. Storey
Head groundsman A. Llong
Scorers L. A. R. Hart

GROUP THREE

At Northampton, April 8–11. KENT drew with NORTHAMPTONSHIRE. *Darren Stevens, aged 44, becomes the oldest to score a Championship hundred since 1986.*

KENT v YORKSHIRE

At Canterbury, April 15–18. Yorkshire won by 200 runs. Yorkshire 23pts, Kent 5pts. Toss: Yorkshire.
The elegance and determination of Lyth proved the difference in a lop-sided encounter. Exasperated at falling three short of a century in the first innings – when consistent scoring down the card took Yorkshire to 379 – he emitted a roar of delight that echoed round a deserted ground on reaching three figures in the second. Root's praise for Lyth's fluency was so effusive it led to questions about an international recall, questions Root dealt with as deftly as he had Kent's attack: he too made a second-innings hundred, helping set a target of 445. Kent froze, in more than one sense. The ground and office staff tried to prevent hypothermia by wearing ugly bobble hats, while the top order batted like rabbits mesmerised by headlights. Twice they stumbled to 86 for five. The exceptions were Stevens and, more surprisingly, Milnes, whose resolve as nightwatchman lasted over four and a half hours and took the game into the final session. When he was finally removed, by Willey, he was so dejected he was unable to lift his bat to acknowledge his team-mates' applause.

Close of play: first day, Yorkshire 358-8 (Willey 25, Patterson 34); second day, Yorkshire 6-0 (Lyth 6, Köhler-Cadmore 0); third day, Kent 33-2 (Bell-Drummond 24, Milnes 0).

Yorkshire

A. Lyth c Robinson b Milnes	97	– c Cox b Milnes	116
T. Köhler-Cadmore c Robinson b Stevens	14	– c Cox b Stewart	3
T. W. Loten c Robinson b Podmore	27	– lbw b Milnes	21
J. E. Root c Robinson b Milnes	11	– b Denly	101
H. C. Brook lbw b Cummins	54	– not out	66
†J. A. Tattersall c Stevens b Leaning	11		
D. M. Bess lbw b Stevens	36		
J. A. Thompson c Robinson b Stevens	34	– (6) b Denly	6
D. J. Willey not out	37		
*S. A. Patterson c sub (F. J. Klaassen) b Milnes	38		
D. Olivier b Stevens	5		
B 5, lb 8, nb 2	15	B 4, lb 5, nb 8	17

1/28 (2) 2/124 (3) 3/143 (4)   (105.2 overs) 379   1/24 (2)   (5 wkts dec, 75.2 overs) 330
4/150 (1) 5/219 (5) 6/240 (6)   2/99 (4) 3/218 (1)
7/292 (7) 8/299 (8) 9/362 (10) 10/379 (11)   4/314 (4) 5/330 (6)

Podmore 10–1–53–1; Stevens 19.2–3–60–4; Milnes 21–3–76–3; Cummins 18–1–92–1; Stewart 17–5–50–0; Denly 14–6–27–0; Leaning 6–3–8–1. *Second innings*—Milnes 18–1–68–2; Stewart 10–1–32–1; Stevens 9–1–41–0; Cummins 14–0–48–0; Denly 13.2–2–0–61–2; Leaning 11–0–71–0.

Kent

*D. J. Bell-Drummond lbw b Willey	13	– b Willey	24
J. M. Cox lbw b Patterson	38	– b Willey	0
Z. Crawley b Olivier	1	– c Lyth b Thompson	4
J. L. Denly lbw b Patterson	17	– (5) c Tattersall b Thompson	30
J. A. Leaning c Tattersall b Patterson	0	– (6) c Köhler-Cadmore b Thompson	0
†O. G. Robinson c Tattersall b Thompson	44	– c Tattersall b Olivier	28
D. I. Stevens lbw b Brook	52	– (8) c Root b Willey	47
G. Stewart c Tattersall b Olivier	40	– (9) not out	8
M. E. Milnes not out	26	– (4) lbw b Willey	78
M. L. Cummins c Köhler-Cadmore b Olivier	13	– lbw b Willey	12
H. W. Podmore absent hurt		– absent hurt	
B 7, lb 14	21	B 8, lb 5	13

1/18 (1) 2/25 (3) 3/59 (4)   (87.1 overs) 265   1/13 (2) 2/33 (3)   (88.4 overs) 244
4/59 (5) 5/86 (2) 6/156 (6)   3/34 (1) 4/86 (5) 5/86 (6)
7/205 (7) 8/247 (8) 9/265 (10)   6/148 (7) 7/223 (4) 8/224 (8) 9/244 (10)

Willey 14–1–47–1; Olivier 18.1–1–55–3; Patterson 18–3–43–3; Thompson 16–2–52–1; Bess 9–1–32–0; Brook 12–4–15–1. *Second innings*—Willey 16.4–3–61–5; Olivier 18–2–57–1; Thompson 12–6–24–3; Patterson 14–5–23–0; Bess 23–10–57–0; Brook 2–0–6–0; Root 3–1–3–0.

Umpires: I. J. Gould and M. J. Saggers. Referee: T. J. Boon.

KENT v LANCASHIRE

At Canterbury, April 22–25. Lancashire won by an innings and five runs. Lancashire 22pts, Kent 2pts. Toss: Kent. County debut: L. W. P. Wells.

Lancashire gained their first innings victory over Kent for 68 years thanks in part to the leg-spin of the indefatigable Parkinson. He claimed match figures of nine for 164 from a mammoth 62 overs, including a career-best seven for 126 when Kent followed on, 356 behind. Bell-Drummond had reckoned it a bowl-first wicket, and his logic looked sound as Lancashire faltered to 190 for six on the first evening. But it looked rickety next day after Wood and Lamb, Nos 8 and 9, had made near-chanceless hundreds in a spirit-crushing stand of 187, a Lancashire record for the eighth wicket. Both hit personal-bests. Kent's half-hearted reply – Crawley alone made more than 21, while Bailey and Wood shared seven wickets – was short enough for Vilas to reinsert them. Bell-Drummond and Cox fared better: an opening stand of 176 was larger and longer than their entire first innings. And at 234 for one on the fourth morning, a Lancashire win seemed improbable. "I don't think many teams in the country would have won from there," said Parkinson.

Close of play: first day, Lancashire 260-7 (Wood 28, Lamb 12); second day, Kent 85-4 (Crawley 60, Kuhn 1); third day, Kent 209-1 (Bell-Drummond 108, Crawley 13).

Lancashire

K. K. Jennings c Leaning b Stevens	16	T. E. Bailey c Crawley b Leaning		47
†A. L. Davies c Robinson b Milnes	1	M. W. Parkinson not out		1
L. W. P. Wells c Robinson b Cummins	45			
J. J. Bohannon lbw b Cummins	87	B 8, lb 14, w 1, nb 4		27
S. J. Croft lbw b Stevens	2			
*D. J. Vilas lbw b Klaassen	53	1/5 (2) 2/30 (1) 3/80 (3)	(167.2 overs)	525
R. P. Jones st Robinson b Leaning	2	4/85 (5) 5/187 (6) 6/190 (7)		
L. Wood c Robinson b Milnes	119	7/248 (4) 8/435 (8) 9/516 (9)		
D. J. Lamb b Klaassen	125	10/525 (10)	110 overs: 300-7	

Milnes 32–7–90–2; Stevens 26–13–44–2; Klaassen 32–3–110–2; Cummins 33–5–100–2; Denly 13–0–58–0; Leaning 31.2–5–101–2.

Kent

*D. J. Bell-Drummond c Davies b Wood	3	– b Bohannon	114
J. M. Cox c Wells b Bailey	0	– c Jones b Parkinson	80
Z. Crawley c Davies b Bailey	60	– lbw b Parkinson	36
J. L. Denly c Wells b Wood	4	– b Lamb	31
J. A. Leaning c sub (J. M. Blatherwick) b Wood	12	– c and b Parkinson	0
H. G. Kuhn c Jones b Parkinson	21	– lbw b Lamb	32
†O. G. Robinson b Bailey	21	– not out	28
D. I. Stevens lbw b Parkinson	1	– c Jones b Parkinson	0
M. E. Milnes not out	17	– lbw b Parkinson	14
F. J. Klaassen c Jennings b Bailey	0	– c Croft b Parkinson	3
M. L. Cummins c Vilas b Bohannon	19	– c Jennings b Parkinson	0
Lb 5, nb 6	11	Lb 3, nb 10	13

1/3 (2) 2/9 (1) 3/23 (4) (50.3 overs) 169   1/176 (2) 2/234 (1) (138 overs) 351
4/76 (5) 5/85 (3) 6/123 (6)   3/238 (3) 4/238 (5)
7/127 (8) 8/133 (7) 9/133 (10) 10/169 (11)   5/305 (6) 6/310 (4) 7/311 (8)
                                     8/327 (9) 9/349 (10) 10/351 (11)

Bailey 15–4–46–4; Wood 13–1–38–3; Lamb 10–0–31–0; Parkinson 10–0–38–2; Bohannon 2.3–0–11–1. *Second innings*—Bailey 26–5–81–0; Wood 22–3–53–0; Lamb 27–8–57–2; Parkinson 52–8–126–7; Bohannon 8–0–27–1; Jones 1–0–2–0; Wells 1–0–1–0; Croft 1–0–1–0.

Umpires: N. J. Llong and B. V. Taylor. Referee: A. J. Swann.

At Cardiff, April 29–30. KENT lost to GLAMORGAN by ten wickets. *Darren Stevens takes his 30th five-for, but Kent are dismissed for 74 in their second innings.*

At Leeds, May 6–9. KENT drew with YORKSHIRE.

At Hove, May 13–16. KENT drew with SUSSEX.

KENT v GLAMORGAN

At Canterbury, May 20–23. Drawn. Kent 12pts, Glamorgan 11pts. Toss: Glamorgan.
An innings of astonishing brilliance lit up this otherwise drab, weather-beaten affair. Put in, Kent had plummeted to 128 for eight when Stevens, whose last six innings had all been in single figures, decided to harness the gales that were buffeting the ground and take a calculated risk. Reasoning that anything airborne would swirl awkwardly, he aimed for the sightscreens; two of his 15 sixes cleared them altogether. His striking was as extraordinary as it was brutal, with exactly 150 coming in boundaries. To say he dominated a stand of 166 – a ninth-wicket record in this fixture – was a gross understatement. Cummins, though, did his bit, stoically keeping out 55 balls before Stevens lofted to

---

I COULDN'T HAVE DONE IT WITHOUT YOU

Highest percentage of first-class century stands by one player:

96.38	166 (9th)	D. I. Stevens (160)/M. L. Cummins (1)	Kent v Glam at Canterbury	2021
95.32	107 (10th)	H. J. Enthoven (102)/W. F. F. Price (3) .	Middx v Sussex at Lord's. . . .	1930
95.00	100 (10th)	G. Stewart (95)/I. A. A. Thomas (1) . . .	Kent v Middx at Canterbury .	2018
94.96	139 (10th)	K. P. Pietersen (132)/M. P. Dunn (5). . .	Surrey v Leics at The Oval. . .	2015
94.39	107 (8th)	B. L. D'Oliveira (101)/B. M. Brain (4) .	Worcs v Notts at Worcester . .	1966
93.42	152 (10th)	E. B. Alletson (142)/W. Riley (10)	Notts v Sussex at Hove	1911
92.12	127 (9th)	Imran Khan (117)/N. Gifford (10).	Worcs v Northants at N'hampton	1976
91.45	117 (10th)	V. Subramanya (107)/B. S. Chandrasekhar (10).	Mysore v Madras at Madras. .	1966-67
91.00	100* (10th)	D. Tallon (91)/G. Noblet (9)	D. G. Bradman's XI v A. L. Hassett's XI at Melbourne	1948-49
91.00	100 (2nd)	B. J. Booth (91)/S. Jayasinghe (91)	Leics v Northants at N'hampton	1964

Figures in brackets are runs scored during the partnership, which may not be the complete innings. Where the scores do not constitute the whole partnership, the balance comes from extras.

---

long-on for 190 from 149. Even so, his hunch about catching had proved astute: he was dropped three times, including by Labuschagne, whom he later trapped lbw (just as he had when Glamorgan ran away with the match at Cardiff three weeks earlier). For the first time all season, Kent looked well placed. But just 38 balls were possible on Saturday and, though the sides tried to contrive a finish next day, rain ended play at lunchtime. Back at the start, members had been welcomed to the St Lawrence for the first time in 602 days, though any euphoria dissipated rather more quickly than the pools on the outfield. Of the 950 who turned up, all but about 200 had gone by the time play began shortly before 4.30. Kent reached the close at 70 for two, then fell apart as seamers van der Gugten and Neser took four wickets each. Some fans feared a repeat of the Cardiff humiliation, but instead came one of the more arresting performances by a 45-year-old at Canterbury.
Close of play: first day, Kent 70-2 (Cox 26, Leaning 1); second day, Glamorgan 55-2 (J. M. Cooke 10, Root 21); third day, Glamorgan 64-3 (Root 26, Carlson 0).

Kent

†O. G. Robinson c Lloyd b van der Gugten.......	43	– c C. B. Cooke b Neser............	14
J. M. Cox b Neser....................	27	– not out.......................	27
Z. Crawley c Lloyd b van der Gugten...........	0	– not out.......................	18
J. A. Leaning lbw b Neser...................	2		
*S. W. Billings lbw b van der Gugten...........	11		
D. J. Bell-Drummond lbw b Neser..............	0		
D. I. Stevens c Carlson b Labuschagne..........	190		
M. K. O'Riordan c C. B. Cooke b van der Gugten .	0		
N. N. Gilchrist lbw b Neser..................	12		
M. L. Cummins b Labuschagne...............	7		
M. R. Quinn not out......................	7		
B 1, lb 6, w 1.........................	8	Lb 1....................	1

1/60 (1) 2/62 (3) 3/73 (4) (76.2 overs) 307 1/28 (1) (1 wkt dec, 10 overs) 60
4/78 (2) 5/80 (6) 6/84 (5)
7/92 (8) 8/128 (9) 9/294 (7) 10/307 (10)

Neser 20–5–67–4; Hogan 15–2–67–0; Douthwaite 11–3–44–0; van der Gugten 19–11–34–4; Salter 2–0–32–0; Lloyd 5–0–29–0; Labuschagne 4.2–0–27–2. *Second innings*—Neser 4–0–28–1; van der Gugten 4–1–18–0; Hogan 1–0–2–0; Douthwaite 1–0–11–0.

Glamorgan

J. M. Cooke b Quinn....................	10	– not out.......................	6
D. L. Lloyd lbw b Quinn..................	4	– b Quinn.......................	17
M. Labuschagne lbw b Stevens..............	11	– not out.......................	0
W. T. Root not out......................	26		
K. S. Carlson not out....................	0		
Lb 5, nb 8.........................	13		

1/5 (2) 2/16 (3) 3/60 (1) (3 wkts dec, 26 overs) 64 1/23 (2) (1 wkt, 7 overs) 23

*†C. B. Cooke, D. A. Douthwaite, M. G. Neser, A. G. Salter, T. van der Gugten and M. G. Hogan did not bat.

Quinn 10–4–10–2; Stevens 8–4–18–1; Cummins 5–0–25–0; Gilchrist 3–0–6–0. *Second innings*—Quinn 4–2–14–1; Stevens 3–1–9–0.

Umpires: R. K. Illingworth and J. D. Middlebrook.   Referee: S. J. Davis.

KENT v NORTHAMPTONSHIRE

At Canterbury, June 3–6. Drawn. Kent 14pts, Northamptonshire 13pts. Toss: Northamptonshire.
    Northamptonshire dominated the first day after opting to bat. Gay passed his previous best of 77 with a six, but grew jittery as he approached three figures – and later thanked Procter for helping him to the landmark. They closed on 362 for five but, after the second day was washed out, could add only 30 more on the third; 392 was far fewer than had seemed likely at 314 for two. There were five catches for Robinson, including his 100th in first-class matches, and five wickets for Stevens. Robinson swapped his pads, and sped to a run-a-ball 120, greatly outscoring Cox in an opening stand of 161. Bell-Drummond made a bold declaration 62 behind, which appeared to wrongfoot Northamptonshire. Whenever they edged towards safety, Kent took a wicket – including one for Cummins, who ended a disappointing spell at the club with some fire and brimstone. But the wise head of Rossington guided them past tea, and a draw was agreed at 4.50. Robinson had also been in the news before the game. It is a quirk of the circuit that there are two Kent-born cricketers called Ollie Robinson (who also share a birthday). But the laughter stopped when Kent's Robinson was dragged into the row engulfing his Sussex namesake, whose Test debut had been marred by the disclosure of offensive tweets. It was sad, if predictable, that social media would confuse the two,

but surprising – and alarming – when local news group Kent Online illustrated an article with the wrong Robinson. They offered a "sincere apology" and agreed to pay compensation.

Close of play: first day, Northamptonshire 362-5 (Zaib 17, Taylor 19); second day, no play; third day, Kent 330-5 (Muyeye 3, Stevens 3).

Northamptonshire

R. S. Vasconcelos c Robinson b Quinn	66	– c Robinson b Stevens	9
E. N. Gay c Robinson b Leaning	101	– lbw b Stevens	8
L. A. Procter lbw b Quinn	81	– (7) run out (Bell-Drummond)	17
R. I. Keogh c Cox b Stevens	38	– c Robinson b Cummins	12
S. A. Zaib c Robinson b Stevens	21	– c Robinson b Gilchrist	6
*†A. M. Rossington b Stevens	4	– not out	59
T. A. I. Taylor lbw b Stevens	25	– (8) c Cox b Gilchrist	12
G. K. Berg c Leaning b Quinn	10	– (3) c Cox b Gilchrist	21
N. L. Buck c Robinson b Quinn	4	– lbw b Denly	6
S. C. Kerrigan not out	2	– not out	7
B. W. Sanderson c Robinson b Stevens	4		
B 8, lb 12, nb 16	36	B 8, lb 5, nb 14	27

1/135 (1) 2/235 (2) 3/314 (3)   (104.4 overs) 392
4/314 (4) 5/318 (6) 6/366 (5)
7/373 (7) 8/386 (9) 9/387 (8) 10/392 (11)

1/10 (2)   (8 wkts dec, 69 overs) 184
2/25 (1) 3/50 (4)
4/60 (3) 5/73 (5)
6/124 (7) 7/138 (8) 8/150 (9)

Quinn 26–5–86–4; Stevens 26.4–7–73–5; Cummins 13–0–54–0; Gilchrist 13–2–70–0; O'Riordan 6–0–27–0; Leaning 13–0–34–1; Denly 4–0–11–0; Bell-Drummond 3–0–17–0. *Second innings—* Quinn 13–2–26–0; Stevens 15–5–42–2; Gilchrist 15–0–57–3; Cummins 14–4–32–1; Denly 7–2–6–1; Leaning 2–1–1–0; Bell-Drummond 2–1–4–0; Cox 1–0–3–0.

Kent

†O. G. Robinson lbw b Buck	120	D. I. Stevens not out	3
J. M. Cox lbw b Kerrigan	90	Lb 4, nb 4	8
J. L. Denly c Zaib b Keogh	63		
J. A. Leaning c Rossington b Zaib	24	1/161 (1) (5 wkts dec, 69 overs) 330
*D. J. Bell-Drummond lbw b Kerrigan	19	2/277 (2) 3/281 (3)
T. S. Muyeye not out	3	4/318 (5) 5/326 (4)

M. K. O'Riordan, N. N. Gilchrist, M. L. Cummins and M. R. Quinn did not bat.

Sanderson 15–3–54–0; Berg 11–2–55–0; Taylor 13–6–33–0; Buck 13–0–69–1; Kerrigan 14–1–80–2; Keogh 2–0–28–1; Zaib 1–0–7–1.

Umpires: I. J. Gould and I. N. Ramage.   Referee: P. Whiticase.

KENT v SUSSEX

At Canterbury, July 11–14. Drawn. Kent 11pts, Sussex 11 pts. Toss: Kent. First-class debuts: J. A. Gordon, H. F. Houillon, D. J. Lincoln, J. Singh, B. J. Wightman; H. D. Ward. County debut: H. Z. Finch. Championship debut: J. M. Coles.

At 7pm, just 16 hours before the start of Canterbury Week, an unidentified member of the Kent T20 squad who had just beaten Surrey at The Oval tested positive for Covid, forcing 14 players into isolation. Determined that the festival should go ahead, staff worked through the night to scramble a team of second-string cricketers and red-ball specialists, captained by Kuhn. They faced a similarly inexperienced Sussex side – for the first time in Championship history, half the players in the game were 20 or younger – but the contest, delayed an hour to lessen the administrative headache, proved compelling. Eighteen-year-old seamer Jas Singh ripped out Sussex's top order on a surface offering little to the bowlers, before Atkins, aged 19, reduced Kent to 69 for six in reply to 181; Podmore and Hamidullah Qadri kept Kent's deficit to 16. The Sussex openers then put on 209: Orr recorded a maiden century, while Haines fell for 94. By now, Bailey Wightman had replaced Gilchrist, also forced into quarantine. Kent were set 349 on the final morning, and for a while the chase looked on: Finch, who had been playing for Hastings Priory when called to Canterbury, anchored the innings against his old county (and covered his helmet's Sussex logo with duct tape). But the wickets of Dan Lincoln and Finch took the wind from Kent sails and, when Hunt removed Qadri, Sussex needed – but could not manage – three wickets in five overs.

Close of play: first day, Kent 69-5 (Finch 24, Podmore 3); second day, Kent 122-7 (Hamidullah Qadri 12, Wightman 0); third day, Sussex 277-3 (Head 29, Carter 15).

Sussex

A. G. H. Orr c O'Riordan b Singh	21	– c Lincoln b Singh	119
T. J. Haines c Kuhn b Singh	25	– lbw b Quinn	94
H. D. Ward lbw b Gilchrist	4	– c Kuhn b Quinn	6
T. M. Head c Kuhn b Singh	12	– not out	49
†O. J. Carter c Houillon b Singh	32	– c O'Riordan b Quinn	18
J. M. Coles lbw b Hamidullah Qadri	36	– not out	23
D. K. Ibrahim c Houillon b Gilchrist	6		
*O. E. Robinson c Houillon b Podmore	21		
J. J. Carson not out	13		
S. F. Hunt lbw b Podmore	0		
J. A. Atkins b Podmore	0		
B 6, lb 5	11	B 11, lb 3, w 1, nb 8	23

1/50 (1) 2/51 (2) 3/61 (3) (57.5 overs) 181 1/209 (1) (4 wkts dec, 99 overs) 332
4/81 (4) 5/132 (5) 6/143 (7) 2/230 (3) 3/259 (2)
7/143 (6) 8/173 (8) 9/173 (10) 10/181 (11) 4/285 (5)

Podmore 12.5–2–49–3; Quinn 15.5–5–26–0; Gilchrist 12–3–24–2; Singh 11–2–51–4; Hamidullah Qadri 7–1–20–1. *Second innings*—Podmore 27–3–96–0; Quinn 24–2–118–3; Singh 13–1–32–1; Hamidullah Qadri 10–1–24–0; Wightman 12–4–23–0; O'Riordan 13–3–25–0.

Kent

J. A. Gordon lbw b Robinson	8	– c Carter b Robinson	0
M. K. O'Riordan lbw b Atkins	18	– run out (Haines)	47
H. Z. Finch lbw b Atkins	24	– c Carter b Hunt	115
*H. G. Kuhn b Atkins	8	– b Carson	4
D. J. Lincoln b Atkins	0	– c Robinson b Carson	41
†H. F. Houillon lbw b Robinson	0	– c Ibrahim b Carson	9
H. W. Podmore c Carter b Hunt	37	– not out	36
Hamidullah Qadri not out	30	– lbw b Hunt	4
B. J. Wightman b Atkins	0	– not out	0
M. R. Quinn c Carter b Robinson	11		
J. Singh lbw b Hunt	2		
B 13, lb 3, w 1, nb 10	27	B 2, lb 1, nb 16	19

1/20 (1) 2/48 (2) 3/56 (4) (51.5 overs) 165 1/0 (1) (7 wkts, 85.4 overs) 275
4/56 (5) 5/57 (6) 6/69 (3) 2/120 (2) 3/128 (4)
7/119 (7) 8/123 (9) 9/162 (10) 10/165 (11) 4/214 (5) 5/224 (6) 6/257 (3) 7/265 (8)

Wightman replaced N. N. Gilchrist, as a Covid substitute.

Robinson 18–4–54–3; Hunt 11.5–3–24–2; Atkins 14–1–51–5; Carson 5–1–16–0; Ibrahim 3–1–4–0. *Second innings*—Robinson 18–6–66–1; Hunt 17.5–5–48–2; Carson 32.4–7–87–3; Atkins 5–0–24–0; Coles 11–0–41–0; Haines 2–0–6–0.

Umpires: Hassan Adnan and B. V. Taylor. Referee: S. Cummings.

DIVISION THREE

At Leicester, August 30–September 1. KENT beat LEICESTERSHIRE by 132 runs. *After three defeats and seven draws, Kent win their first Championship match of the season.*

KENT v WORCESTERSHIRE

At Canterbury, September 5–7. Kent won by an innings and 56 runs. Kent 23pts, Worcestershire 3pts. Toss: Kent.

A thin layer of mist persuaded Crawley – Kent's fifth captain of the season – to bowl, and in a trice Worcestershire were floundering at 18 for four. All had gone to Milnes, who had no idea that – at lunch, and in front of his family – he would be presented with his cap. There was a brief rally from the middle order, but Gilchrist snatched a career-best five for 38, including the last four in 16 balls, to dismiss Worcestershire for 133. Kent then wobbled to 22 for three, before Leaning and Robinson brought stability in a stand of 75. By stumps, they were already 51 ahead, with six wickets in hand. With bright-and-breezy contributions from Stevens and Billings (replacing O'Riordan after England released him), Kent enjoyed a 260-run lead. And by the time the second day ended, a demoralised Worcestershire were six down for 91. Asked if the day could have gone any better, Leaning – dismissed for a high-class 97 – said "I'd have liked three more runs." Leach hit a gutsy unbeaten 49 next morning, but could not prevent Kent coasting to their first innings victory over Worcestershire since 1968.

Close of play: first day, Kent 184-4 (Leaning 52, Stevens 56); second day, Worcestershire 91-6 (Barnard 10, Cox 2).

Worcestershire

D. K. H. Mitchell c Cox b Milnes	4	– b Stevens	14
J. D. Libby b Milnes	2	– lbw b Stewart	23
T. C. Fell c Robinson b Milnes	3	– lbw b Gilchrist	11
J. A. Haynes b Gilchrist	8	– lbw b Stevens	26
B. L. D'Oliveira lbw b Milnes	1	– c Robinson b Gilchrist	0
E. G. Barnard c Robinson b Stevens	25	– lbw b Stewart	44
†O. B. Cox not out	41	– (8) lbw b Milnes	2
*J. Leach b Gilchrist	38	– (9) not out	49
J. O. Baker b Gilchrist	0	– (10) b Stevens	1
D. Y. Pennington lbw b Gilchrist	3	– (11) c Crawley b Gilchrist	13
A. W. Finch b Gilchrist	2	– (7) c Robinson b Stewart	1
Lb 2, nb 4	6	B 5, lb 11, nb 4	20

1/4 (1) 2/9 (2) 3/16 (3)   (39.4 overs) 133
4/18 (5) 5/32 (4) 6/54 (6)
7/119 (8) 8/119 (9) 9/123 (10) 10/133 (11)

1/19 (1) 2/51 (2)   (60.5 overs) 204
3/55 (3) 4/55 (5)
5/87 (4) 6/88 (7) 7/101 (8)
8/157 (6) 9/168 (10) 10/204 (11)

Milnes 12–3–35–4; Stevens 10–4–19–1; Gilchrist 11.4–2–38–5; Stewart 6–0–39–0. *Second innings*—Milnes 11–2–51–1; Stevens 19–7–49–3; Stewart 16–4–51–3; Gilchrist 13.5–3–36–3; Logan 1–0–1–0.

Kent

*Z. Crawley c Cox b Pennington	5	N. N. Gilchrist c Cox b Finch	8
J. M. Cox c Baker b Pennington	1	J. E. G. Logan b Baker	12
J. L. Denly lbw b Leach	9		
J. A. Leaning c Barnard b Pennington	97	B 1, lb 8, w 1, nb 12	22
†O. G. Robinson c Cox b Pennington	50		
D. I. Stevens c Barnard b Finch	66	1/5 (1) 2/10 (2) 3/22 (3) (114.2 overs) 393
S. W. Billings c Pennington b Baker	72	4/97 (5) 5/200 (6) 6/306 (4)
G. Stewart st Cox b Baker	24	7/322 (7) 8/348 (8) 9/371 (10)
M. E. Milnes not out	27	10/393 (11) 110 overs: 372-9

Billings replaced M. K. O'Riordan after being released from the England squad.

Leach 26–10–53–1; Pennington 24–2–80–4; Barnard 22–3–73–0; Finch 15–0–83–2; Baker 22.2–3–76–3; D'Oliveira 3–0–17–0; Mitchell 2–0–2–0.

Umpires: Hassan Adnan and P. R. Pollard.   Referee: P. M. Such.

At Derby, September 12–15. KENT beat DERBYSHIRE by 130 runs.

KENT v MIDDLESEX

At Canterbury, September 21–24. Kent won by two wickets. Kent 19pts, Middlesex 3pts. Toss: Kent.

The title-decider – admittedly for Division Three – proved a classic. After two modest first-innings totals, leaders Middlesex (who had plummeted from 121 for two to 147 all out) had a nine-run advantage over second-placed Kent, but then Stoneman's brisk century threatened to bat the hosts out of contention. Milnes was again a handful, and his five wickets – plus a career-best three for Bell-Drummond – just kept Middlesex within bounds. Even so, a steep target of 373 became steeper

---

KENT'S HIGHEST SUCCESSFUL RUN-CHASES

429-5	v Worcestershire at Canterbury .	2004	382-5 v Lancashire at Dover 1939
418-8	v Lancashire at Canterbury	2013	**375-8 v Middlesex at Canterbury . . 2021**
416-6	v Surrey at Blackheath.	1934	360-4 v Lancashire at Liverpool 2002
411-8	v Gloucestershire at Cheltenham	2013	356-3 v Middlesex at Lord's 2006
403-7	v Leicestershire at Leicester . . .	2001	354-6 v Australians at Canterbury . . . 1975

Kent's only higher fourth-innings total is 447-9 (set 485) to draw v Hampshire at Canterbury in 2005.

---

still after Kent lurched to 103 for four, only for a fluctuating match to shift their way in a combative stand of 172 between the fluent and the flamboyant. Robinson glided past three figures, but fell to the last ball of the third evening, leaving the dashing Muyeye to fight on next day, when another 98 were needed. A maiden fifty already under his belt, he seemed bound for a century, but was run out by a direct hit from Roland-Jones on 89. Stevens followed, which asked the last three to find 63. O'Riordan and Stewart took Kent to the brink, and Milnes edged Roland-Jones for four to settle it.

Close of play: first day, Kent 82-4 (Robinson 11, Milnes 0); second day, Middlesex 298-6 (Simpson 21, Hollman 29); third day, Kent 275-5 (Muyeye 76).

Middlesex

S. D. Robson c Robinson b Gilchrist	13	– (2) c Robinson b Stevens 19
M. D. Stoneman b Stevens.	59	– (1) b Bell-Drummond. 109
S. S. Eskinazi lbw b Stevens	15	– lbw b Bell-Drummond. 31
R. G. White not out	29	– c Cox b Milnes 38
M. D. E. Holden lbw b Stevens	0	– b Milnes 8
M. K. Andersson b Stewart	0	– c Robinson b Bell-Drummond 15
†J. A. Simpson c Robinson b Stevens	6	– b Milnes 46
L. B. K. Hollman lbw b O'Riordan	0	– c Gilchrist b O'Riordan 29
T. S. Roland-Jones c Stevens b Milnes	9	– c Leaning b Milnes. 6
E. R. Bamber c Leaning b Gilchrist	0	– b Milnes 25
*T. J. Murtagh b Milnes.	0	– not out 5
B 4, lb 10, nb 2	16	B 25, lb 5, nb 2 32

1/21 (1) 2/58 (3) 3/121 (2)	(60.5 overs)	147	1/47 (2) 2/115 (3) (86.4 overs) 363
4/121 (5) 5/122 (6) 6/129 (7)			3/199 (4) 4/223 (5)
7/130 (8) 8/143 (9) 9/144 (10) 10/147 (11)			5/243 (1) 6/248 (6) 7/304 (8)
			8/319 (9) 9/336 (7) 10/363 (10)

Milnes 14.5–5–31–2; Stevens 15–8–21–4; Gilchrist 15–6–34–2; Stewart 11–3–33–1; O'Riordan 5–1–14–1. *Second innings*—Milnes 19.4–3–87–5; Stewart 10–3–29–0; Gilchrist 18–3–93–0; Stevens 5–1–18–1; Bell-Drummond 13–2–47–3; O'Riordan 16–3–44–1; Leaning 5–0–15–0.

Kent

*Z. Crawley c Simpson b Bamber	20	– lbw b Roland-Jones	47
J. M. Cox b Murtagh	2	– c White b Murtagh	1
D. J. Bell-Drummond lbw b Murtagh	20	– c Eskinazi b Bamber	15
J. A. Leaning b Andersson	27	– lbw b Andersson	7
†O. G. Robinson b Bamber	14	– c Simpson b Murtagh	112
M. E. Milnes c Hollman b Andersson	16	– (10) not out	9
T. S. Muyeye c Simpson b Andersson	30	– (6) run out (Roland-Jones)	89
D. I. Stevens b Bamber	4	– (7) c Robson b Roland-Jones	14
M. K. O'Riordan b Roland-Jones	0	– (8) c Robson b Andersson	26
G. Stewart lbw b Roland-Jones	0	– (9) not out	37
N. N. Gilchrist not out	0		
B 2, lb 1, nb 2	5	Lb 16, nb 2	18

1/7 (2) 2/31 (1) 3/57 (3)   (54.4 overs) 138   1/9 (2)   (8 wkts, 105.2 overs) 375
4/82 (4) 5/90 (5) 6/112 (6)   2/48 (3) 3/69 (4)
7/122 (8) 8/130 (9) 9/130 (10) 10/138 (7)   4/103 (1) 5/275 (5)
                                           6/295 (6) 7/310 (7) 8/358 (8)

Murtagh 15–5–35–2; Bamber 19–6–36–3; Andersson 12.4–3–44–3; Roland-Jones 8–2–20–2. *Second innings*—Murtagh 25–11–45–2; Bamber 23–4–78–1; Roland-Jones 22.2–5–69–2; Andersson 17–0–86–2; Hollman 15–0–75–0; Robson 3–0–6–0.

Umpires: M. Burns and B. V. Taylor.   Referee: J. J. Whitaker.

LANCASHIRE

Agony at Aigburth

PAUL EDWARDS

After Lancashire lost at Trent Bridge on September 8, two journalists were discussing the prospects for the rest of the Championship season. One sought to look on life's brighter side: "If Lancashire win their last two matches…" But his grumpy chum was having none of it: "…they might just about come second."

As things turned out, Dane Vilas's talented young team did win their last two matches in Division One, and did finish runners-up, to Warwickshire. But events did not take the anticlimactic course the gloomy hack had envisaged – at least, not until the final hours of the competition. Lancashire had trounced Somerset by ten wickets, then claimed an absurdly tense one-wicket victory over Hampshire at Liverpool, to supplant them at the top of the table with a day to go. Officials invited supporters and the media to watch the last day of Warwickshire's game on a huge screen at Old Trafford, hoping Somerset would hold on for a draw, and make Lancashire champions for the first time since 2011. Yet, by the time around 20 folk had turned up, it was clear where the trophy was going. The bleak vastness of The Point suited the mood; some looked out on a stadium being prepared for the pop concert that had forced Lancashire to play at an outground in late September, and pondered whether, had they been at headquarters, they might have gained the four batting points that would have swung the title their way.

It was a grim end to a Championship season that had promised much; annihilation by Warwickshire the following week, in a one-off match at Lord's for the Bob Willis Trophy, gave the knife an extra twist. By then, Lancashire probably found it hard to look back with satisfaction on a campaign in which they had won six of their 14 four-day games, and come close to reaching the semi-finals of both white-ball competitions. Yet they had played some fine cricket and would have been worthy champions. Significantly, they are nowhere near their peak, and can harbour realistic hopes of challenging again in 2022. There were no retirements, though some junior players were released, and the signing of Phil Salt from Sussex should compensate for Alex Davies's departure to Warwickshire.

The best bowler was Tom Bailey, who took 51 wickets in 13 first-class matches and rarely gave opposing batsmen any peace. Saqib Mahmood offered strong support in eight games before injury curtailed his season. Two of James Anderson's four appearances were rain-ruined affairs in which he never took the field; when unleashed on Glamorgan and Kent, he helped himself to 11 in 46 overs, including a career-best seven for 19, and his 1,000th first-class wicket. Luke Wood and Danny Lamb performed capably. The leading spinner was Matt Parkinson, although it would be a sad comment on English cricket if slow left-armer Tom Hartley were to become a white-ball specialist. Parkinson could both contain batsmen and interrogate their defensive techniques. His 40 first-class wickets at a shade over 20 did him justice – and some went viral.

Lancashire lost two Championship matches, at Cardiff and Trent Bridge, which exposed their occasional batting frailties. Josh Bohannon, however, remained exempt from serious criticism. His 878 first-class runs included masterful centuries against Yorkshire and Warwickshire; he and Keaton Jennings were the only two to average over 40 in all first-class matches. So it was invaluable that many of their

Gareth Copley, Getty Images

Matt Parkinson

team-mates had all-round skills: Wood and Lamb made centuries to set up victory at Canterbury, while Bailey's 330 first-class runs included two fifties and several other useful innings; Luke Wells, who plainly enjoyed his first season after moving from Sussex, added 18 catches, mostly at slip, and three vital wickets at Taunton to his 613 runs. The team found ways to win in a manner reminiscent of their Championship triumph ten seasons earlier. The only difference was that Warwickshire, runners-up then, claimed the pennant.

Lancashire also looked capable of winning a white-ball trophy, but their limited-overs cricket never quite matched their Championship form. Although they qualified for the T20 Blast knockout with four wins in their last five group games, their batting was too often dependent on Jennings or Finn Allen of New Zealand. Both were missing – through injury and international call-up – for the quarter-final in August, along with Parkinson, who had Covid. Somerset won easily.

Prospects seemed brighter in the Royal London Cup: the depth of the squad enabled Lancashire to choose competitive teams, despite losing regulars to The Hundred. Led by Bailey in Vilas's absence, they won three of their first four games. A place in the knockouts looked certain, before Essex's Simon Harmer hit Steven Croft for three successive sixes in the last over to clinch a tie, ensuring his side's qualification at Lancashire's expense.

In June, it was announced that Paul Allott would be stepping down as director of cricket after four years; at the end of the season, Mark Chilton, a former captain and more recently assistant coach, was named as his successor.

There was embarrassment when it was revealed that, like England's Ollie Robinson, five players had posted racist and misogynist tweets, though some were a decade earlier, as teenagers. The club carried out an investigation but did not publish the results; it was understood the players were given anti-discrimination training. But in February the ECB imposed a one-match ban (plus a further four suspended) and a fine of £1,500 on Davies, by now on Warwickshire's books.

LANCASHIRE RESULTS

County Championship and Bob Willis Trophy matches – Played 15: Won 6, Lost 3, Drawn 6.
Vitality T20 Blast matches – Played 15: Won 7, Lost 6, Tied 1, No result 1.
Royal London Cup matches – Played 8: Won 3, Lost 2, Tied 1, No result 2.

LV= County Championship, 1st in Group 3, 2nd in Division 1; Bob Willis Trophy, runners-up;
Vitality T20 Blast, quarter-finalists; Royal London Cup, 4th in Group 1.

COUNTY CHAMPIONSHIP AND BOB WILLIS TROPHY AVERAGES
BATTING AND FIELDING

Cap		Birthplace	M	I	NO	R	HS	100	Avge	Ct/St
2021	J. J. Bohannon	*Bolton*‡	15	20	2	878	170	2	48.77	7
2018	†K. K. Jennings	*Johannesburg, SA* ...	10	13	1	577	132	2	48.08	8
	†L. Wood	*Sheffield*	10	13	2	431	119	1	39.18	3
	†L. W. P. Wells	*Eastbourne*	13	18	2	613	103	1	38.31	18
2017	A. L. Davies	*Darwen*‡	14	21	2	670	84	0	35.26	18/4
2018	D. J. Vilas¶	*Johannesburg, SA* ..	15	18	1	584	189	1	34.35	20
	D. J. Lamb	*Preston*‡	11	14	1	365	125	1	28.07	5
2010	S. J. Croft	*Blackpool*‡	11	14	2	330	103*	0	27.50	8
	†G. P. Balderson	*Manchester*‡	6	9	1	211	77	0	26.37	0
2019	M. W. Parkinson ...	*Bolton*‡	12	12	9	63	21*	0	21.00	1
2018	T. E. Bailey	*Preston*‡	13	16	0	330	63	0	20.62	1
	†T. W. Hartley	*Ormskirk*‡	3	4	1	61	25	0	20.33	2
	R. P. Jones	*Warrington*	9	11	0	199	58	0	18.09	11
2017	L. S. Livingstone	*Barrow-in-Furness* ..	6	7	0	77	25	0	11.00	5
2021	S. Mahmood	*Birmingham*	8	11	4	73	20	0	10.42	2
	J. M. Blatherwick ...	*Nottingham*	4	5	0	17	11	0	3.40	1

Also batted: †J. M. Anderson§ (*Burnley*‡) (cap 2003) (4 matches) 5*, 8* (1 ct); G. I. D. Lavelle (*Ormskirk*‡) (2 matches) 4, 32, 0 (5 ct).

‡ *Born in Lancashire.* § *ECB contract.* ¶ *Official overseas player.*

BOWLING

	Style	O	M	R	W	BB	5I	Avge
J. M. Anderson	RFM	46	19	83	11	7-19	1	7.54
T. E. Bailey	RFM	368	111	955	51	7-37	1	18.72
M. W. Parkinson	LB	352.5	90	818	40	7-126	1	20.45
S. Mahmood	RFM	233.1	52	669	28	5-47	1	23.89
D. J. Lamb	RFM	280.5	67	780	23	4-60	0	33.91
G. P. Balderson	RFM	152.5	29	427	12	3-21	0	35.58
L. Wood	LFM	205	32	660	18	3-31	0	36.66

Also bowled: J. M. Blatherwick (RFM) 66.1–14–236–9; J. J. Bohannon (RFM) 31.1–5–94–3; S. J. Croft (RFM/OB) 22–3–77–0; T. W. Hartley (SLA) 83–32–143–4; R. P. Jones (LB) 3–0–7–1; L. S. Livingstone (LB) 91–17–248–4; D. J. Vilas (OB) 1–0–6–0; L. W. P. Wells (LB) 68–13–186–9.

LEADING VITALITY BLAST AVERAGES (100 runs/15 overs)

Batting	Runs	HS	Avge	SR	Ct/St		Bowling	W	BB	Avge	ER
F. H. Allen	399	73*	33.25	159.60	4		T. W. Hartley ..	12	4-16	28.16	6.62
L. S. Livingstone	279	94*	55.80	147.61	2		S. J. Croft	5	1-7	29.80	7.09
A. L. Davies....	260	83*	20.00	128.71	6		L. W. P. Wells ..	3	1-15	39.33	7.37
R. P. Jones	161	61*	53.66	127.77	2		L. S. Livingstone	3	1-22	58.00	7.56
K. K. Jennings ..	298	88	42.57	126.80	4		L. Wood	13	4-20	28.07	8.29
J. C. Buttler ...	127	55	25.40	123.30	1/1		M. W. Parkinson	13	3-23	23.30	8.41
D. J. Vilas	221	42	20.09	122.77	4/1		D. J. Lamb	11	3-23	30.27	8.53
S. J. Croft	240	41	34.28	120.00	9						

LEADING ROYAL LONDON CUP AVERAGES (100 runs/4 wickets)

Batting	Runs	HS	Avge	SR	Ct/St
D. J. Lamb	147	86*	49.00	133.63	5
S. J. Croft	183	93	45.75	73.79	6
K. K. Jennings	133	47	44.33	57.57	0
R. P. Jones	220	72	44.00	67.48	1
L. W. P. Wells	158	66*	31.60	77.07	3
J. J. Bohannon	163	52	27.16	69.65	1
G. I. D. Lavelle	100	52	25.00	96.15	6/1

Bowling	W	BB	Avge	ER
T. E. Bailey	10	3-23	20.70	3.69
J. P. Morley	9	2-22	24.88	4.00
G. P. Balderson	5	3-25	27.20	5.03
D. J. Lamb	10	5-30	29.80	5.65
L. W. P. Wells	4	2-33	33.00	5.28
L. J. Hurt	8	3-55	33.50	5.95

FIRST-CLASS COUNTY RECORDS

Highest score for	424	A. C. MacLaren v Somerset at Taunton	1895
Highest score against	315*	T. W. Hayward (Surrey) at The Oval	1898
Leading run-scorer	34,222	E. Tyldesley (avge 45.20)	1909–36
Best bowling for	10-46	W. Hickton v Hampshire at Manchester	1870
Best bowling against	10-40	G. O. B. Allen (Middlesex) at Lord's	1929
Leading wicket-taker	1,816	J. B. Statham (avge 15.12).	1950–68
Highest total for	863	v Surrey at The Oval	1990
Highest total against	707-9 dec	by Surrey at The Oval	1990
Lowest total for	25	v Derbyshire at Manchester	1871
Lowest total against	20	by Essex at Chelmsford	2013

LIST A COUNTY RECORDS

Highest score for	166	D. J. Vilas v Nottinghamshire at Nottingham	2019
Highest score against	186*	C. G. Greenidge (West Indians) at Liverpool	1984
Leading run-scorer	11,969	N. H. Fairbrother (avge 41.84).	1982–2002
Best bowling for	6-10	C. E. H. Croft v Scotland at Manchester	1982
Best bowling against	8-26	K. D. Boyce (Essex) at Manchester.	1971
Leading wicket-taker	480	J. Simmons (avge 25.75)	1969–89
Highest total for	406-9	v Nottinghamshire at Nottingham	2019
Highest total against	417-7	by Nottinghamshire at Nottingham	2019
Lowest total for	59	v Worcestershire at Worcester	1963
Lowest total against	52	by Minor Counties at Lakenham	1998

TWENTY20 COUNTY RECORDS

Highest score for	108	K. K. Jennings v Durham at Chester-le-Street	2020
Highest score against	108*	I. J. Harvey (Yorkshire) at Leeds	2004
Leading run-scorer	**3,920**	**S. J. Croft (avge 29.47, SR 123.38)**	**2006–21**
Best bowling for	5-13	S. D. Parry v Worcestershire at Manchester	2016
Best bowling against	6-19	T. T. Bresnan (Yorkshire) at Leeds	2017
Leading wicket-taker	118	S. D. Parry (avge 24.88, ER 7.14)	2009–20
Highest total for	231-4	v Yorkshire at Manchester	2015
Highest total against	211-5	by Derbyshire at Derby	2017
Lowest total for	83	v Durham at Manchester	2020
Lowest total against	53	by Worcestershire at Manchester	2016

ADDRESS

Emirates Old Trafford, Talbot Road, Manchester M16 0PX; 0161 282 4000; enquiries@lancashirecricket.co.uk; www.lancashirecricket.co.uk. Twitter: @lancscricket.

OFFICIALS

Captain D. J. Vilas
Director of cricket 2021 P. J. W. Allott
2022 M. J. Chilton
Head coach G. Chapple
Head of talent pathway C. T. Benbow

President Sir Howard Bernstein
Chair A. E. Anson
Chief executive D. Gidney
Head groundsman M. Merchant
Scorers C. Rimmer and G. L. Morgan

GROUP THREE

LANCASHIRE v SUSSEX

At Manchester, April 8–11. Drawn. Lancashire 16pts, Sussex 14pts. Toss: Sussex. First-class debut: S. F. Hunt. Championship debuts: T. W. Hartley; J. J. Carson.

This match was moved to Old Trafford after an infestation of leatherjackets damaged the Hove outfield. The crane fly larvae might have found Manchester less hospitable: snow briefly covered the ground before play was called off on the final afternoon. The first two days included a substantial century from each side. Haines was dropped three times, twice in single figures, and hit on the hand, but batted almost six hours for a career-best 155 that rescued Sussex from 40 for four. Next day, Vilas responded in kind after arriving at 41 for three. He and Jones took heavy toll of the off-spinner Carson's early overs, though he recovered well and would dismiss both. Sean Hunt, a 19-year-old left-arm seamer, claimed three economical wickets on debut, but Vilas steered Lancashire to maximum bonus points and what might have been a match-winning lead. After an intense fourth morning, when Mahmood struck twice in five deliveries, Sussex were about to pull level when the snow intervened. They celebrated the draw with a snowball fight on the outfield.

Close of play: first day, Sussex 291-9 (Meaker 27, Hunt 1); second day, Lancashire 339-5 (Vilas 158, Wood 27); third day, Sussex 38-0 (Thomason 23, Haines 14).

Sussex

A. D. Thomason b Mahmood	3	– not out	46
T. J. Haines c Davies b Bailey	155	– c Hartley b Mahmood	26
S. van Zyl lbw b Bailey	0	– lbw b Mahmood	4
T. G. R. Clark c Lamb b Wood	0	– not out	14
*†B. C. Brown c Croft b Bailey	4		
D. M. W. Rawlins lbw b Wood	18		
G. H. S. Garton c Jennings b Lamb	10		
O. E. Robinson c Davies b Mahmood	59		
S. C. Meaker not out	30		
J. J. Carson lbw b Lamb	4		
S. F. Hunt lbw b Bailey	7		
B 2, lb 7, nb 2	11	B 4, lb 5, nb 4	13

1/3 (1) 2/6 (3) 3/14 (4)   (100.4 overs) 301   1/72 (1)   (2 wkts, 56.3 overs) 103
4/40 (5) 5/106 (6) 6/127 (7)   2/80 (3)
7/253 (8) 8/277 (2) 9/290 (10) 10/301 (11)

Bailey 22.4–6–48–4; Mahmood 20–5–61–2; Wood 17–2–59–2; Lamb 16–3–55–2; Hartley 17–1–48–0; Bohannon 6–1–16–0; Croft 2–0–5–0. *Second innings—*Bailey 11.3–2–19–0; Mahmood 13–5–19–2; Hartley 17–9–21–0; Lamb 10–3–24–0; Wood 5–1–11–0.

Lancashire

K. K. Jennings c Thomason b Robinson	4	T. W. Hartley run out (van Zyl)	4
†A. L. Davies lbw b Hunt	61	S. Mahmood not out	0
J. J. Bohannon c Brown b Robinson	10		
S. J. Croft c Brown b Garton	3	B 4, lb 9, nb 8	21
*D. J. Vilas c Thomason b Carson	189		
R. P. Jones c Clark b Carson	58	1/8 (1) 2/30 (3) (109.4 overs) 407
L. Wood lbw b Hunt	32	3/41 (4) 4/132 (2)
D. J. Lamb lbw b Hunt	1	5/257 (6) 6/350 (7) 7/354 (8)
T. E. Bailey run out (Garton)	24	8/394 (9) 9/404 (10) 10/407 (5)

Robinson 23–4–69–2; Hunt 21–4–47–3; Garton 20–3–78–1; Meaker 12–1–56–0; Carson 24.4–3–106–2; Rawlins 9–0–38–0.

Umpires: N. L. Bainton and M. J. Saggers. Referee: P. Whitticase.

LANCASHIRE v NORTHAMPTONSHIRE

At Manchester, April 15–18. Lancashire won by 206 runs. Lancashire 21pts, Northamptonshire 3pts.
Toss: Lancashire.

Lancashire achieved victory in the final hour of a game in which much of the resistance came from two old boys, Kerrigan and Procter. Kerrigan marked his return by bowling 34 overs of left-arm spin for four wickets, exhibiting the sort of control some had thought now beyond him, while Taylor also finished with four, despite injuring his finger. Lancashire's seamers were well supported by Parkinson, in his first first-class match since September 2019, as they reduced Northamptonshire to 87 for eight. Rossington and Kerrigan almost doubled that, before Parkinson bowled Rossington with a ripper pitching well outside leg, then turning to clip off stump; the similarity to Shane Warne's dismissal of Mike Gatting in the 1993 Test here sent social media into a frenzy. Croft's unbeaten century raised Lancashire's lead to 424, and Northamptonshire's chances of surviving nearly four sessions looked negligible at 96 for six. But Procter batted over six hours and was last out, one of a few crucial umpiring decisions that went against his side. Parkinson's match figures were six for 88 from 52.3 overs.

Close of play: first day, Lancashire 264-8 (Hartley 10, Mahmood 15); second day, Lancashire 60-0 (Jennings 23, Davies 36); third day, Northamptonshire 59-3 (Vasconcelos 22, Procter 15).

Lancashire

K. K. Jennings c Vasconcelos b Taylor	13	– lbw b Sanderson	27
†A. L. Davies run out (Taylor)	57	– c Vasconcelos b Taylor	36
J. J. Bohannon lbw b Kerrigan	68	– b Keogh	22
S. J. Croft c Rossington b Taylor	26	– not out	103
*D. J. Vilas lbw b Kerrigan	26	– run out (Taylor)	24
R. P. Jones st Rossington b Kerrigan	13	– run out (Gay)	8
L. Wood b Sanderson	23	– c sub (G. K. Berg) b Buck	17
T. E. Bailey lbw b Taylor	9	– c Procter b Buck	34
T. W. Hartley c Curran b Kerrigan	25	– not out	8
S. Mahmood c Buck b Taylor	20		
M. W. Parkinson not out	21		
Lb 4	4	B 6, lb 10, w 1	17

1/39 (1) 2/97 (2) 3/143 (4)   (115.2 overs) 305   1/64 (1)   (7 wkts dec, 81 overs) 296
4/171 (3) 5/205 (6) 6/212 (5)   2/64 (2) 3/123 (3)
7/236 (8) 8/242 (7) 9/269 (10)   4/163 (5) 5/172 (6) 6/204 (7) 7/266 (8)
10/305 (9)   110 overs: 292-9

Sanderson 28–6–59–1; Taylor 26.2–8–91–4; Buck 14–1–51–0; Procter 11.2–2–33–0; Kerrigan 34–8–60–4; Keogh 2–0–7–0. *Second innings*—Sanderson 13.3–3–40–1; Taylor 17–2–38–1; Kerrigan 3–0–19–0; Buck 18–3–70–2; Procter 5–1–20–0; Keogh 25–3–93–1.

Northamptonshire

B. J. Curran c Hartley b Mahmood	9	– c Jones b Mahmood	14
R. S. Vasconcelos c Bailey b Wood	15	– b Parkinson	35
E. N. Gay c Jennings b Mahmood	7	– c Croft b Mahmood	0
R. I. Keogh lbw b Bailey	29	– c Croft b Bailey	4
L. A. Procter c Bohannon b Parkinson	6	– c Croft b Parkinson	93
S. A. Zaib c Croft b Parkinson	4	– (7) lbw b Parkinson	4
*†A. M. Rossington b Parkinson	49	– (6) c Jennings b Wood	8
T. A. I. Taylor b Bailey	3	– st Davies b Jones	13
N. L. Buck lbw b Bailey	0	– c Davies b Wood	20
S. C. Kerrigan not out	45	– b Wood	0
B. W. Sanderson run out (Croft)	0	– not out	5
Lb 6, nb 4	10	B 8, lb 5, nb 4, p 5	22

1/13 (1) 2/23 (3) 3/45 (2)   (62 overs) 177   1/19 (1) 2/19 (3)   (105.3 overs) 218
4/68 (5) 5/73 (6) 6/73 (4)   3/26 (4) 4/76 (2)
7/87 (8) 8/87 (9) 9/169 (7) 10/177 (11)   5/87 (6) 6/96 (7) 7/152 (8)
                                 8/196 (9) 9/196 (10) 10/218 (5)

Bailey 10–2–32–3; Mahmood 16–4–38–2; Wood 14–1–42–1; Parkinson 20–3–49–3; Hartley 2–0–10–0. *Second innings*—Bailey 17–5–39–1; Mahmood 19–4–53–2; Parkinson 32.3–16–39–3; Wood 13–4–31–3; Hartley 17–7–22–0; Croft 6–2–12–0; Jones 1–0–4–1.

Umpires: M. Burns and R. A. Kettleborough.   Referee: P. M. Such.

At Canterbury, April 22–25. LANCASHIRE beat KENT by an innings and five runs. *Luke Wood and Danny Lamb add a county record 187 for the eighth wicket.*

At Hove, April 29–May 2. LANCASHIRE beat SUSSEX by five wickets.

LANCASHIRE v GLAMORGAN

At Manchester, May 6–9. Drawn. Lancashire 14pts, Glamorgan 14pts. Toss: Glamorgan. County debut: M. G. Neser.

A rain-wrecked match featured one notable duel when Anderson, who had missed almost all the 2019 Ashes through injury, dismissed Labuschagne, who had made his name in that series, for 12 just after lunch on the first day. Some portrayed it as an early blow ahead of England's winter tour of Australia, but Glamorgan still accumulated a respectable 344 thanks to half-centuries from Lloyd, Taylor and Douthwaite. Any possibility of a result vanished with a third-day washout, but the cricket retained its intensity. Australian all-rounder Michael Neser bowled thriftily on his debut for Glamorgan: at one point, he had figures of 9–8–1–1. But Jennings's third consecutive fifty and Bohannon's third in six innings helped Lancashire towards three batting bonus points, even if it took the last-wicket pair, Parkinson and Anderson, to achieve that goal late on the final evening.

Close of play: first day, Glamorgan 117-3 (Root 11, Carlson 0); second day, Lancashire 22-0 (Jennings 8, Davies 14); third day, no play.

Glamorgan

J. M. Cooke b Mahmood	15	A. G. Salter not out	7
D. L. Lloyd c Vilas b Wood	78	T. van der Gugten c Wood b Mahmood	23
M. Labuschagne c Vilas b Anderson	12		
W. T. Root lbw b Anderson	11	B 1, lb 2, nb 8	11
K. S. Carlson c Anderson b Wood	18		
*†C. B. Cooke c Livingstone b Bohannon	33	1/35 (1) 2/82 (3)	(109.5 overs) 344
C. Z. Taylor lbw b Mahmood	58	3/117 (2) 4/121 (4)	
D. A. Douthwaite lbw b Anderson	61	5/153 (5) 6/190 (6) 7/271 (8)	
M. G. Neser c Jennings b Parkinson	17	8/314 (9) 9/314 (7) 10/344 (11)	

Anderson 24–10–40–3; Mahmood 18.1–3–66–3; Wood 23–1–91–2; Lamb 17–3–70–0; Parkinson 17–5–46–1; Bohannon 4.4–0–15–1; Livingstone 6–1–13–0.

Lancashire

K. K. Jennings c Taylor b Salter	64	S. Mahmood c and b Neser	9
A. L. Davies c C. B. Cooke b Neser	15	M. W. Parkinson not out	16
L. W. P. Wells c Douthwaite b Salter	30	J. M. Anderson not out	5
J. J. Bohannon c Salter b Taylor	53	B 6, lb 2, w 1	9
L. S. Livingstone c J. M. Cooke			
b van der Gugten	25	1/24 (2)	(9 wkts dec, 94.3 overs) 301
*†D. J. Vilas c J. M. Cooke b Douthwaite	25	2/86 (3) 3/132 (1)	
L. Wood c C. B. Cooke b Douthwaite	28	4/183 (5) 5/208 (4) 6/230 (6)	
D. J. Lamb b Lloyd	22	7/265 (9) 8/278 (9) 9/286 (8)	

Neser 22–8–50–2; Lloyd 6.3–2–12–1; van der Gugten 19–2–51–1; Douthwaite 14–2–56–2; Taylor 11–1–35–1; Salter 13–2–49–2; Labuschagne 9–0–40–0.

Umpires: N. G. B. Cook and M. A. Gough.   Referee: S. Cummings.

At Northampton, May 20–23. LANCASHIRE drew with NORTHAMPTONSHIRE.

LANCASHIRE v YORKSHIRE

At Manchester, May 27–30. Lancashire won by an innings and 79 runs. Lancashire 22pts, Yorkshire 1pt. Toss: Yorkshire. Championship debut: G. C. H. Hill.

Lancashire's first crowd in 20 months saw an astonishing start. Electing to bat in the sunshine, Yorkshire crashed to 40 for seven before lunch. It needed Harry Duke, in his second match, to restore some sanity with the tail. When Lancashire declared with a lead of 350 on the third afternoon, Yorkshire's first defeat of the season seemed inevitable. But a valiant fight ended with only 40 balls left, when Parkinson had Bess caught at slip. It was Lancashire's first Roses victory since 2011, and only their second by an innings at Old Trafford since 1913; it took their lead over second-placed Yorkshire in Group Three to 24 points. Earlier, their 509 equalled their third-highest Roses total. Jennings scored his first first-class century since the Galle Test of November 2018, and Bohannon the second of his career: he brought up 300 with a six that hit the scorers' window. But Lyth and Köhler-Cadmore resisted for nearly two and a half hours when Yorkshire resumed, and it took Mahmood's maiden five-wicket haul to decide the match. In successive overs on the final morning, he bowled Fraine and Patterson; when he returned, with ten overs remaining, he had Thompson and Coad caught behind. An epic encounter attracted 615,000 livestream views.

Close of play: first day, Lancashire 95-1 (Jennings 22, Wells 11); second day, Lancashire 350-6 (Bohannon 47, Lamb 4); third day, Yorkshire 85-2 (Fraine 6, Patterson 2).

Yorkshire

A. Lyth c Lamb b Bailey	4	– c Wells b Parkinson ... 39
T. Köhler-Cadmore lbw b Lamb	10	– lbw b Mahmood ... 32
W. A. R. Fraine c Vilas b Mahmood	0	– b Mahmood ... 6
H. C. Brook run out (Davies)	0	– (5) lbw b Parkinson ... 52
G. C. H. Hill c Livingstone b Bailey	2	– (6) b Bailey ... 18
D. M. Bess c Lamb b Wood	3	– (7) c Livingstone b Parkinson ... 46
†H. G. Duke c Vilas b Bailey	52	– (8) b Wood ... 29
J. A. Thompson c Jennings b Wood	10	– (9) c Vilas b Mahmood ... 14
*S. A. Patterson c Parkinson	27	– (4) b Mahmood ... 8
B. O. Coad not out	32	– c Vilas b Mahmood ... 0
D. Olivier c Wells b Lamb	10	– not out ... 0
B 1, nb 8	9	B 14, lb 3, nb 10 ... 27
	159	**271**

1/4 (1) 2/9 (3) 3/9 (4)   (64.1 overs) 159
4/11 (5) 5/21 (6) 6/21 (2)
7/40 (8) 8/117 (9) 9/121 (7) 10/159 (11)

1/72 (1) 2/82 (2)   (136.2 overs) 271
3/87 (3) 4/92 (4)
5/151 (6) 6/180 (5) 7/238 (8)
8/271 (9) 9/271 (10) 10/271 (7)

Bailey 14–11–6–3; Mahmood 15–2–49–1; Lamb 11.1–3–26–2; Wood 11–2–51–2; Parkinson 13–3–26–1. *Second innings*—Bailey 19–11–30–1; Mahmood 26–9–47–5; Parkinson 41.2–17–61–3; Livingstone 22–5–58–0; Lamb 14–6–23–0; Wood 13.5–35–1; Wells 1–1–0–0.

Lancashire

K. K. Jennings c Köhler-Cadmore b Coad	114	T. E. Bailey b Hill ... 12
A. L. Davies c Duke b Olivier	52	S. Mahmood run out (Hill) ... 0
L. W. P. Wells c Köhler-Cadmore b Thompson	60	B 11, lb 10, nb 14 ... 35
J. J. Bohannon not out	127	
L. S. Livingstone c Olivier b Thompson	6	1/71 (2) (9 wkts dec, 173.4 overs) 509
*†D. J. Vilas c Köhler-Cadmore b Coad	35	2/246 (1) 3/246 (3)
L. Wood c Duke b Thompson	7	4/252 (5) 5/309 (6)
D. J. Lamb c Patterson b Bess	61	6/340 (7) 7/490 (8)
		8/506 (9) 9/509 (10)

M. W. Parkinson did not bat.

110 overs: 324-5

Coad 26–12–65–2; Thompson 25–5–86–3; Patterson 27–11–46–0; Olivier 24–4–95–1; Bess 43.4–10–120–1; Brook 17–4–37–0; Hill 11–2–39–1.

Umpires: S. J. O'Shaughnessy and A. G. Wharf.   Referee: S. Cummings.

At Cardiff, June 3–5. LANCASHIRE lost to GLAMORGAN by six wickets. *Lancashire become the last county to lose their unbeaten record in 2021.*

LANCASHIRE v KENT

At Manchester, July 4–7. Drawn. Lancashire 13pts, Kent 11pts. Toss: Kent.

A masterclass of swing bowling from Anderson on the second afternoon carried him past 1,000 first-class wickets to a career-best seven for 19, and overshadowed the rest of the game: a draw confirmed Lancashire's qualification for Division One. Rain had wiped out the first four sessions, so Denly's decision to bat, in cloudy conditions on a pitch that had been covered, was baffling. In a single ten-over spell from the end bearing his name, Anderson opened with three wicket-maidens,

---

BOWLERS WHOSE CAREER-BEST INCLUDED THEIR 1,000TH WICKET

8-18	A. V. Bedser..............	Surrey v Nottinghamshire at The Oval............	1952
8-45	A. Jepson	Nottinghamshire v Leicestershire at Nottingham	1958
7-19	D. Wilson...............	Yorkshire v MCC at Scarborough	1969
7-19	**J. M. Anderson**	**Lancashire v Kent at Manchester**	**2021**

Wilson later took eight for 36 for MCC v Ceylon in 1969-70.

Research: Andrew Samson

---

and reached four figures with two more: when Kuhn edged behind to provide the landmark, his analysis was 7–5–3–5. "I thought at first they were going a bit over the top for a five-wicket celebration," he said; he had known he was in the 990s, but not the precise number. Another two swiftly followed – all seven caught in the cordon – to beat his seven for 42 against West Indies at Lord's in 2017, when he claimed his 500th Test wicket. The only man to take him on was Stevens, who hit three fours in his last three overs. Though only one third of his wickets were for Lancashire, Anderson said it was "really special" to do it on the ground where he took his first, Ian Ward of Surrey, in 2002, and paid tribute to his mentor Glen Chapple, who had retired with 985. Kent were all out in just over two hours, but had Lancashire five down by the close. Wood made 63 not out on a rain-shortened third day, and Vilas declared, 185 ahead, before play restarted on the final afternoon. Hartley, who like Muyeye had entered the game after Parkinson and Crawley were called up for England's replacement one-day squad, claimed a career-best four, putting Kent in danger at 134 for eight. But Yorkshire exiles Leaning and Logan survived the last 19 overs.

Close of play: first day, no play; second day, Lancashire 108-5 (Croft 8, Jones 7); third day, Lancashire 259-9 (Wood 63, Anderson 8).

Kent

Z. Crawley c Jones b Anderson	0				
J. M. Cox c Wells b Anderson	1	– c Wells b Anderson	11		
*L. J. Denly lbw b Lamb	12	– c Davies b Lamb	17		
†O. G. Robinson c Vilas b Anderson	0	– (1) c Vilas b Wood	2		
J. A. Leaning c Jones b Anderson	2	– (4) not out	53		
H. G. Kuhn c Vilas b Anderson	0	– (5) c Wells b Hartley	21		
D. I. Stevens c Davies b Lamb	19	– lbw b Wells	17		
M. E. Milnes c Vilas b Anderson	1	– c Vilas b Hartley	2		
H. W. Podmore c Vilas b Anderson	3	– b Hartley.....................	0		
J. E. G. Logan c Vilas b Lamb	11	– not out	3		
M. R. Quinn not out	13				
T. S. Muyeye (did not bat)		– (6) lbw b Hartley	7		
B 4, lb 4, nb 4.......................	12	B 3, lb 7, nb 6	16		
	74		149		

1/0 (1) 2/1 (2) 3/5 (4)	(26.2 overs)	74
4/17 (5) 5/19 (6) 6/19 (3)		
7/24 (8) 8/34 (9) 9/51 (7) 10/74 (10)		

1/13 (1)	(8 wkts, 74 overs)	149
2/31 (2) 3/40 (3)		
4/71 (5) 5/103 (6)		
6/129 (7) 7/134 (8) 8/134 (9)		

Muyeye replaced Crawley, who left to join England's one-day squad.

Anderson 10–5–19–7; Wood 10–2–31–0; Lamb 6.2–3–16–3. *Second innings*—Anderson 12–4–24–1; Wood 14–4–34–1; Hartley 30–15–42–4; Lamb 8–1–31–1; Wells 10–5–8–1.

Lancashire

K. K. Jennings c Crawley b Quinn	14	T. W. Hartley c Cox b Quinn	24
A. L. Davies c Cox b Quinn	47	J. M. Anderson not out	8
L. W. P. Wells c Denly b Milnes	3		
J. J. Bohannon b Logan	14	B 2, lb 4, nb 10	16
*†D. J. Vilas c Crawley b Stevens	8		
S. J. Croft b Stevens	13	1/64 (2) 2/67 (1) (9 wkts dec, 91 overs) 259
R. P. Jones c Stevens b Logan	47	3/67 (3) 4/89 (5)
L. Wood not out	63	5/93 (4) 6/117 (6)
D. J. Lamb c Stevens b Logan	2	7/186 (7) 8/190 (9) 9/248 (10)

Hartley replaced M. W. Parkinson, who left to join England's one-day squad.

Podmore 13–3–45–0; Stevens 20–5–49–2; Milnes 10–1–40–1; Quinn 15–2–37–3; Logan 19–4–45–3; Denly 6–1–12–0; Leaning 8–0–25–0.

Umpires: S. J. O'Shaughnessy and R. A. White.   Referee: D. A. Cosker.

At Leeds, July 11–14. LANCASHIRE drew with YORKSHIRE. *Keaton Jennings scores his second Roses hundred of the season as Lancashire finish top of Group Three.*

DIVISION ONE

LANCASHIRE v WARWICKSHIRE

At Manchester, August 30–September 2. Drawn. Lancashire 12pts, Warwickshire 12pts. Toss: Warwickshire. County debut: C. K. Holder. Championship debuts: G. I. D. Lavelle; C. G. Benjamin.
  Warwickshire began the Championship's second stage as Division One leaders, carrying forward 21 points from their group, to third-placed Lancashire's 16.5. They adopted a cautious approach. Despite a 237-run partnership between Chris Benjamin and Hain on the opening day, much of the innings was tedious: with only 58 runs in 32 overs next morning, they failed to collect a third batting point. Benjamin, who had scored fifties on T20 and List A debut, went one better in his first Championship match, with a century, while Hain made his first hundred in over two years. In reply, Bohannon recorded his second of the season, sharing three-figure stands with Wells and Vilas, who reached 50 for the first time since April, but Norwell's accuracy earned Warwickshire a 30-run lead. On the final day, they ensured they could not lose: Sibley, recently dropped by England, scored 57 in three and a half hours, and was praised by coach Mark Robinson for his selflessness. He was one of four victims for Parkinson, who bowled 45 overs unchanged, including 40 on the final day.
  Close of play: first day, Warwickshire 259-3 (Hain 113, Rhodes 5); second day, Lancashire 100-1 (Wells 35, Bohannon 59); third day, Warwickshire 52-1 (Sibley 17, Benjamin 28).

Warwickshire

R. M. Yates c Jones b Bailey	4	– b Mahmood	1
D. P. Sibley lbw b Bailey	3	– b Parkinson	57
C. G. Benjamin c Vilas b Mahmood	127	– lbw b Parkinson	42
S. R. Hain lbw b Bailey	118	– c sub (R. J. Gleeson) b Livingstone	48
*W. M. H. Rhodes b Mahmood	10	– c Wells b Parkinson	7
M. J. Lamb b Parkinson	36	– not out	36
†M. G. K. Burgess c Wells b Parkinson	26	– c Bohannon b Parkinson	22
D. R. Briggs c Wells b Parkinson	11	– not out	11
C. N. Miles lbw b Mahmood	11		
L. C. Norwell not out	1		
C. K. Holder lbw b Mahmood	6		
B 1, lb 7, w 6, nb 4	18	B 5, lb 8, nb 2	15

1/4 (1) 2/7 (2) 3/244 (3)   (139.1 overs) 371   1/5 (1)   (6 wkts dec, 100 overs) 239
4/268 (4) 5/272 (5) 6/322 (7)   2/68 (3) 3/129 (2)
7/340 (8) 8/359 (6) 9/363 (9)   4/169 (4) 5/173 (6) 6/211 (7)
10/371 (11)
                   110 overs: 298-5

Bailey 23–9–53–3; Mahmood 28.1–7–77–4; Lamb 17–4–54–0; Balderson 21–6–47–0; Parkinson 41.1–10–96–3; Livingstone 4.5–0–21–0; Wells 3–0–14–0; Jones 1–0–1–0. *Second innings—* Bailey 5–3–8–0; Mahmood 10.3–3–28–1; Parkinson 45–16–94–4; Lamb 10–4–27–0; Livingstone 22–5–54–1; Balderson 7–4–9–0; Vilas 1–0–6–0.

Lancashire

G. P. Balderson lbw b Norwell	0	S. Mahmood not out		5
L. W. P. Wells b Norwell	45	M. W. Parkinson lbw b Norwell		3
J. J. Bohannon st Burgess b Briggs	170			
*D. J. Vilas c Yates b Norwell	67	B 7, lb 7, w 3, nb 2		19
R. P. Jones lbw b Norwell	0			—
L. S. Livingstone b Norwell	12	1/6 (1) 2/115 (2)	(118.3 overs)	341
†G. I. D. Lavelle lbw b Miles	4	3/244 (4) 4/244 (5) 5/272 (6)		
D. J. Lamb b Briggs	8	6/286 (7) 7/305 (8) 8/321 (9)		
T. E. Bailey c Burgess b Briggs	8	9/338 (3) 10/341 (11)	110 overs: 321-8	

Norwell 20.3–8–57–6; Holder 21–4–69–0; Briggs 38–10–78–3; Miles 20–2–72–1; Rhodes 13–3–27–0; Yates 3–0–18–0; Lamb 3–0–6–0.

Umpires: I. D. Blackwell and R. J. Warren.   Referee: T. J. Boon.

At Nottingham, September 5–8. LANCASHIRE lost to NOTTINGHAMSHIRE by 102 runs.

At Taunton, September 12–14. LANCASHIRE beat SOMERSET by ten wickets.

LANCASHIRE v HAMPSHIRE

At Liverpool, September 21–23. Lancashire won by one wicket. Lancashire 19pts, Hampshire 3pts. Toss: Lancashire.

Lancashire were nine down when Vilas swept Dawson to square leg, to snatch victory in a heart-stopping match – and leapfrog to the top of Division One. Had Vilas fallen, Hampshire would have been champions; had the game been tied, Nottinghamshire would have had a chance. As it was, Lancashire would win the Championship if Warwickshire failed to beat Somerset down at Edgbaston. For the moment, at least, players and supporters celebrated, their joy tinged with relief. Displaced to Aigburth by a pop concert at Old Trafford, the home side were proceeding smoothly in pursuit of 196 on the third afternoon. On a turning pitch, Vilas finally brought on his leg-spinner, Crane, in the 36th over – a delay which cost them dearly. He removed Bohannon with his third ball, and trapped Croft after tea. But Vilas steered Lancashire to 177 for five. Then Crane's superb bowling claimed three in 23 deliveries – and he also ran out Bailey. Last man Parkinson blocked two balls before Vilas's match-winning boundary. The third evening's climax followed two days of seesawing fortunes. Hampshire had battled hard to reach 143, and their seamers reduced Lancashire to 47 for seven, only for Croft, Wood and Bailey to deploy the long handle. Leading by two runs, the visitors were in trouble again at 24 for four, but a partnership of 80 between Vince and Dawson put criticism of the pitch in perspective. Bailey finished with a career-best seven for 37, and 50 first-class wickets in the season, to set up the final drama – and Hampshire's agony. "Jesus, it can be a cruel game," said Crane. Not that he knew it, but he was speaking for both sides: next day, Warwickshire saw off Somerset, pipping Lancashire to the title.

Close of play: first day, Lancashire 25-3 (Bohannon 11, Blatherwick 4); second day, Hampshire 158-7 (Wheal 0, Organ 0).

Hampshire

J. J. Weatherley c Davies b Balderson	18	– (3) b Bailey	33
I. G. Holland c Vilas b Bailey	1	– (1) c Bohannon b Bailey	0
†T. P. Alsop c Lamb b Balderson	24	– (4) c Davies b Bailey	2
N. R. T. Gubbins c Davies b Balderson	0	– (5) b Balderson	6
*J. M. Vince c Davies b Balderson	4	– (6) lbw b Parkinson	69
L. A. Dawson run out (Bailey)	10	– (7) b Bailey	41
K. H. D. Barker c Davies b Wood	9	– (10) c Davies b Bailey	4
F. S. Organ c Bohannon b Parkinson	8	– (9) lbw b Bailey	8
M. S. Crane c Wood b Parkinson	25	– (2) b Bailey	0
B. T. J. Wheal lbw b Parkinson	5	– (8) not out	13
Mohammad Abbas not out	0	– c Davies b Balderson	6
B 8, lb 5	13	Lb 8, w 1, nb 2	11

1/1 (2) 2/43 (3) 3/43 (4)   (73.2 overs) 143
4/48 (1) 5/71 (6) 6/71 (5)
7/91 (7) 8/120 (8) 9/132 (10) 10/143 (9)

1/0 (1) 2/1 (2)   (74.2 overs) 193
3/15 (4) 4/24 (5)
5/78 (3) 6/158 (6) 7/158 (7)
8/176 (9) 9/186 (10) 10/193 (11)

Bailey 16–6–24–2; Lamb 10–1–21–0; Wood 10–3–21–1; Balderson 14–3–21–3; Blatherwick 12–5–34–0; Parkinson 11.2–5–9–3. *Second innings*—Bailey 24.9–9–37–7; Blatherwick 7–1–27–0; Balderson 21.2–4–49–2; Lamb 4–0–21–0; Wood 5–0–22–0; Parkinson 10–3–18–1; Wells 3–0–11–0.

Lancashire

G. P. Balderson c Alsop b Mohammad Abbas	5	– b Dawson	12
†A. L. Davies b Mohammad Abbas	4	– c Crane b Barker	44
L. W. P. Wells lbw b Barker	0	– c Vince b Wheal	39
J. J. Bohannon c Weatherley b Barker	13	– c Vince b Crane	18
J. M. Blatherwick c Holland b Mohammad Abbas	4	– (10) c Weatherley b Crane	1
*D. J. Vilas c Dawson b Barker	7	– (5) not out	47
S. J. Croft c Dawson b Mohammad Abbas	40	– (6) lbw b Crane	20
D. J. Lamb c Weatherley b Barker	0	– (7) c Weatherley b Crane	5
L. Wood c Alsop b Wheal	37	– (8) c Weatherley b Crane	3
T. E. Bailey c Holland b Mohammad Abbas	23	– (9) run out (Crane)	0
M. W. Parkinson not out	4	– not out	0
Lb 4	4	B 5, lb 4	9

1/6 (2) 2/9 (3) 3/15 (1)   (54 overs) 141
4/27 (4) 5/27 (5) 6/47 (6)
7/47 (8) 8/93 (9) 9/131 (7) 10/141 (10)

1/55 (1)   (9 wkts, 66.2 overs) 198
2/57 (2) 3/112 (4)
4/118 (3) 5/151 (6) 6/177 (7)
7/187 (8) 8/193 (9) 9/194 (10)

Barker 21–6–51–4; Mohammad Abbas 22–5–48–5; Wheal 10.3–3–36–1; Dawson 1–0–2–0. *Second innings*—Barker 13–1–47–1; Mohammad Abbas 16–3–40–0; Dawson 14.2–5–35–1; Wheal 7–1–26–1; Crane 16–3–41–5.

Umpires: P. J. Hartley and A. G. Wharf.   Referee: S. Cummings.

At Lord's, September 28–October 1. LANCASHIRE lost to WARWICKSHIRE by an innings and 199 runs. *In the Bob Willis Trophy match between the champions and runners-up, Lancashire suffer their fourth-heaviest innings defeat, and their worst since 1950. See page 463.*

LEICESTERSHIRE

Healthy progress, ill discipline

RICHARD RAE

Progress was modest, but few would dispute that Leicestershire were moving in the right direction. Whether that momentum would make them trophy contenders in 2022 remained to be seen: at the summer's end, head coach Paul Nixon said he felt his squad were two years from that goal. But given the miseries of recent years, most supporters would surely settle for that. The post-season appointment of Claude Henderson as the club's first director of cricket – with Nixon retaining control of the first team – certainly suggested ambition.

In the group stage of the Championship, there were home wins against Middlesex and Gloucestershire, and solid draws with Surrey (twice), Hampshire and Somerset. Had a dominant performance at Bristol been converted into victory, Leicestershire would have qualified for Division Two instead of Surrey. While the defeats tended to be heavy, it was a respectable effort in a high-quality group. In Division Three, triumph against Sussex kept the team upbeat, and ensured fourth place.

There was obvious improvement in the batting: 14 centuries compared with six in 2019 – three each by Lewis Hill, Sam Evans and Marcus Harris, two by Hassan Azad and Harry Swindells, and one by Colin Ackermann. Hill, who had ceded the keeper's gloves to Swindells in 2020, was initially unsure of his place, but the change focused his mind, and he scored 944 runs at nearly 45.

Swindells was equally successful. His match-saving unbeaten 171 at Taunton typified his determination; he was consistent enough to stay at No. 6, and his wicketkeeping steadily got better. Openers Evans and Azad made their centuries only on good pitches and, since neither reached 600 runs, questions remained. Harris, conversely, was a model of accumulation, happy to bat time, and it was disappointing when he declined to return in 2022, preferring a two-year deal with Gloucestershire. He will be replaced as overseas player by South African Wiaan Mulder. The club captain, Ackermann, made an unbeaten century in the win over Middlesex, but struggled to convert starts.

Pre-season concerns over whether the attack could routinely dismiss opponents twice proved justified: they did so only five times out of 14. The efforts of seamer Chris Wright and left-arm spinner Callum Parkinson were gallant, but masked a lack of depth. Wright mixed lively outswing with nip-backers to collect 49 wickets, and at the age of 36 registered career-bests with bat and ball. He claimed his 500th first-class victim, and was awarded his county cap in September, as was Hill. Parkinson, 11 years Wright's junior, took 50, including career-best match figures of ten for 108 against Gloucestershire. Already the club's primary limited-overs weapon, he proved just as effective in the Championship, confidently giving the ball air and occasionally finding sharp turn.

The pace-bowling group will remain a work in progress. Dieter Klein was released, after six years at the club, but Roman Walker made his loan from Glamorgan permanent, Tom Scriven was an off-season signing from Hampshire, and left-arm seamer Beuran Hendricks was hired from South Africa.

Alex Pantling, Getty Images

Lewis Hill

One more win in the Vitality Blast and the Royal London Cup could have sent Leicestershire to the knockout stages in both. They had come within a delivery of reaching the Blast finals day in 2020, so having the 2021 tournament's leading run-scorer (Josh Inglis, with 531) and wicket-taker (Naveen-ul-Haq, with 26) might have tipped the balance – but losing the first five games left too much to do. Naveen returns for the Blast, with fellow Afghan Rahmanullah Gurbaz.

Similarly, relinquishing only Ackermann and Parkinson to The Hundred raised hopes for the Royal London, with Hill as acting-captain. But failure to beat Warwickshire when apparently cruising to victory cost Leicestershire a place in the knockouts, even though they won their final three games. Still, new talent was unearthed: the promising 16-year-old leg-spinner Rehan Ahmed and the powerful striker Louis Kimber signed their first contracts.

Leicestershire were involved in several on-field controversies. The first, on April 10, saw Azad given out stumped after Hampshire wicketkeeper Lewis McManus knocked off the bails with his left glove while holding the ball, some distance away, in his right. Video of the incident circulated rapidly and, though Hampshire captain James Vince said Azad would have been recalled "if we'd realised what happened", there was no apology.

Not that Leicestershire could occupy the moral high ground during the Blast, when they received five separate disciplinary sanctions between June 13 and July 1. This brought the 12-month total to six, and a seventh later triggered a one-match suspension for Ackermann as captain. Additionally, in the Blast match against Northamptonshire on June 29, the live stream showed Ben Mike twisting his spikes on the pitch. The ECB's Cricket Discipline Commission handed Mike a two-match ban. Leicestershire had to remain clean until August 2, 2022, or face a deduction of 12 points in the Championship, or two in the Blast or Cup.

Restrictions on attendance continued to affect income: CEO Sean Jarvis said they were around £250,000 down. The club announced Mehmooda Duke, the first woman to chair a first-class county, would step down in March 2022 after three years, but she quit in November, saying "cricket has been torn apart" by racism, and calling for "fresh leadership at national level". There was also a farewell to the man who literally pulled the strings at Grace Road: Dave Goodacre, who operated the scorebox for nearly two decades.

LEICESTERSHIRE RESULTS

County Championship matches – Played 14: Won 3, Lost 6, Drawn 5.
Vitality T20 Blast matches – Played 14: Won 6, Lost 8.
Royal London Cup matches – Played 8: Won 4, Lost 3, No result 1.

LV= County Championship, 5th in Group 2, 4th in Division 3;
Vitality T20 Blast, 6th in North Group; Royal London Cup, 4th in Group 2.

COUNTY CHAMPIONSHIP AVERAGES, BATTING AND FIELDING

Cap		Birthplace	M	I	NO	R	HS	100	Avge	Ct/St
	†M. S. Harris¶	Perth, Australia	8	13	1	655	185	3	54.58	7
	G. H. Rhodes	Birmingham	3	4	0	208	90	0	52.00	2
2021	L. J. Hill	Leicester‡	14	22	1	944	145	3	44.95	3
	H. J. Swindells	Leicester‡	13	19	3	693	171*	2	43.31	27/1
2019	C. N. Ackermann††	George, SA	10	15	1	485	126*	1	34.64	20
	S. T. Evans	Leicester‡	11	18	0	591	138	1	32.83	3
	E. Barnes	York	10	12	4	259	83*	0	32.37	4
	L. P. J. Kimber	Scunthorpe	4	6	1	151	71	0	30.20	6
	†M. H. Azad	Quetta, Pakistan	12	20	2	518	152	2	28.77	4
	B. W. M. Mike	Nottingham	13	19	1	495	74	0	27.50	2
	†H. E. Dearden	Bury	3	6	0	126	62	0	21.00	1
	R. K. Patel	Chigwell	5	7	0	143	44	0	20.42	4
2021	C. J. C. Wright	Chipping Norton	12	16	2	257	87	0	18.35	2
	C. F. Parkinson	Bolton	13	18	2	253	41	0	15.81	2
	G. T. Griffiths	Ormskirk	5	6	3	44	16	0	14.66	0
	W. S. Davis	Stafford	6	7	3	54	42	0	13.50	3
	A. Sakande	Chester	3	4	2	23	9	0	11.50	2
	†H. A. Evans	Bedford	4	6	2	29	12	0	7.25	0
	D. Klein††	Lichtenburg, SA	3	4	0	12	12	0	3.00	0

Also batted: †S. D. Bates (*Leicester‡*) (1 match) 0, 6 (2 ct, 1 st); J. P. Inglis¶ (*Leeds*) (2 matches) 27, 49, 52 (4 ct).

‡ *Born in Leicestershire.* ¶ *Official overseas player.* †† *Other non-England-qualified.*

BOWLING

	Style	O	M	R	W	BB	5I	Avge
C. J. C. Wright	RFM	351	74	1,116	49	7-53	4	22.77
W. S. Davis	RFM	157.4	32	416	15	5-66	1	27.73
C. F. Parkinson	SLA	479.4	122	1,452	50	5-45	3	29.04
E. Barnes	RFM	204.2	30	724	18	4-61	0	40.22
B. W. M. Mike	RFM	256	40	1,002	23	4-34	0	43.56

Also bowled: C. N. Ackermann (OB) 96–22–324–9; H. E. Dearden (OB) 0.5–0–8–0; H. A. Evans (RFM) 79–8–297–4; G. T. Griffiths (RFM) 92–8–388–7; L. J. Hill (RM) 4–0–22–0; L. P. J. Kimber (OB) 3–1–15–0; D. Klein (LFM) 53.5–5–254–4; G. H. Rhodes (OB) 32–2–97–0; A. Sakande (RFM) 89.2–14–309–7.

LEADING VITALITY BLAST AVERAGES (100 runs/15 overs)

Batting	Runs	HS	Avge	SR	Ct/St		Bowling	W	BB	Avge	ER
J. P. Inglis	531	118*	48.27	**175.82**	6/2		S. Steel	5	2-17	33.40	**6.59**
A. M. Lilley	351	99*	27.00	**148.72**	13		C. F. Parkinson	18	4-35	23.38	**7.51**
B. W. M. Mike	130	31	21.66	**147.72**	7		A. M. Lilley	6	3-26	34.16	**8.20**
C. N. Ackermann	263	46	23.90	**139.89**	7		C. N. Ackermann	12	3-35	33.25	**8.34**
L. P. J. Kimber	102	53	17.00	**137.83**	6		Naveen-ul-Haq	26	3-26	17.57	**8.67**
L. J. Hill	191	59	19.10	**129.05**	6		G. T. Griffiths	14	4-24	29.00	**10.50**
R. K. Patel	175	35	15.90	**127.73**	7						
S. Steel	304	54*	27.63	**108.96**	0						

LEADING ROYAL LONDON CUP AVERAGES (100 runs/4 wickets)

Batting	Runs	HS	Avge	SR	Ct/St		Bowling		W	BB	Avge	ER
M. S. Harris	232	127	58.00	86.56	1		B. W. M. Mike ...		9	3-34	25.66	6.63
L. J. Hill	322	108	46.00	94.42	3		W. S. Davis......		6	2-40	30.50	6.31
R. K. Patel	319	118	45.57	95.50	5		G. H. Rhodes		7	3-44	35.28	4.94
H. J. Swindells ..	179	75	35.80	82.11	8/2		E. Barnes........		9	2-34	38.44	5.78
L. P. J. Kimber..	197	85	32.83	104.78	1		D. Klein........		4	2-62	46.00	6.13
A. M. Lilley	162	46	27.00	137.28	4		A. M. Lilley		4	3-49	46.25	5.44
							G. T. Griffiths		4	2-34	49.25	5.96
							R. Ahmed		5	2-25	63.60	5.74

FIRST-CLASS COUNTY RECORDS

Highest score for	309*	H. D. Ackerman v Glamorgan at Cardiff..........	2006
Highest score against	355*	K. P. Pietersen (Surrey) at The Oval	2015
Leading run-scorer	30,143	L. G. Berry (avge 30.32)	1924–51
Best bowling for	10-18	G. Geary v Glamorgan at Pontypridd	1929
Best bowling against	10-32	H. Pickett (Essex) at Leyton	1895
Leading wicket-taker	2,131	W. E. Astill (avge 23.18)................	1906–39
Highest total for	701-4 dec	v Worcestershire at Worcester............	1906
Highest total against	761-6 dec	by Essex at Chelmsford	1990
Lowest total for	25	v Kent at Leicester	1912
Lowest total against	{ 24	by Glamorgan at Leicester..............	1971
	{ 24	by Oxford University at Oxford..............	1985

LIST A COUNTY RECORDS

Highest score for	201	V. J. Wells v Berkshire at Leicester..............	1996
Highest score against	201*	R. S. Bopara (Essex) at Leicester...............	2008
Leading run-scorer	8,216	N. E. Briers (avge 27.66)..................	1975–95
Best bowling for	6-16	C. M. Willoughby v Somerset at Leicester	2005
Best bowling against	6-21	S. M. Pollock (Warwickshire) at Birmingham......	1996
Leading wicket-taker	308	K. Higgs (avge 18.80)	1972–82
Highest total for	406-5	v Berkshire at Leicester	1996
Highest total against	458-4	by India A at Leicester.................	2018
Lowest total for	36	v Sussex at Leicester	1973
Lowest total against	{ 62	by Northamptonshire at Leicester	1974
	{ 62	by Middlesex at Leicester	1998

TWENTY20 COUNTY RECORDS

Highest score for	**118***	**J. P. Inglis v Worcestershire at Leicester**.......	**2021**
Highest score against	103*	A. N. Petersen (Lancashire) at Leicester.........	2016
Leading run-scorer	1,579	M. J. Cosgrove (avge 27.22, SR 132.24)..........	2005–19
Best bowling for	7-18	C. N. Ackermann v Warwickshire at Leicester	2019
Best bowling against	5-17	T. E. Bailey (Lancashire) at Leicester...........	2020
Leading wicket-taker	70	**C. F. Parkinson** (avge 23.98, ER 7.56)	2017–21
Highest total for	229-5	v Warwickshire at Birmingham	2018
Highest total against	255-2	by Yorkshire at Leicester	2019
Lowest total for	90	v Nottinghamshire at Nottingham	2014
Lowest total against	72	by Derbyshire at Derby	2013

ADDRESS

Uptonsteel County Ground, Grace Road, Leicester LE2 8EB; 0116 283 2128; enquiries@ leicestershireccc.co.uk; www.leicestershireccc.co.uk. Twitter: @leicsccc.

OFFICIALS

Captain C. N. Ackermann
Director of cricket C. W. Henderson
Head coach P. A. Nixon
President J. Birkenshaw

Chair 2021 M. Duke
2022 (interim) J. Duckworth
Chief executive S. M. Jarvis
Head groundsman A. B. Ward
Scorer P. J. Rogers

GROUP TWO

LEICESTERSHIRE v HAMPSHIRE

At Leicester, April 8–11. Hampshire won by an innings and 105 runs. Hampshire 24pts, Leicestershire 2pts. Toss: Hampshire. County debut: Mohammad Abbas.

Hampshire completed a near flawless innings victory half an hour into the final morning – but Vince, who had set up their 612 for five, found himself answering questions about a controversial dismissal the previous afternoon. Azad was given out stumped after wicketkeeper McManus knocked off the bails with his left hand while he raised the ball in his right, appealing for a catch. Leicestershire issued a statement expressing their disappointment, and McManus was later given a three-point penalty for misconduct. Vince said he would have recalled Azad had he understood what happened, and that McManus had whipped the bails off instinctively: "He's pretty down about how it looks." Earlier, the headlines dwelt on Vince's 231 from 220 deliveries, which equalled Jimmy Adams's county record against Leicestershire. Adding 224 with Alsop and 194 with Dawson, whose unbeaten 152 needed just 139 balls, he helped Hampshire beat the record total for this fixture, their 548 for six at Southampton in 1927. A balanced attack then made the most of a pitch offering unexpected pace for early April. Crane's leg-spin claimed six of the 14 home wickets that fell on the third day, while Abbott's seamers collected five in all.

Close of play: first day, Hampshire 431-4 (Vince 168, Dawson 51); second day, Leicestershire 151-4 (Ackermann 36, Swindells 39); third day, Leicestershire 279-8 (Wright 25, Griffiths 8).

Hampshire

J. J. Weatherley c Swindells b Griffiths....	41	†L. D. McManus not out..............	17
I. G. Holland c Swindells b Wright.......	11	B 5, lb 14, w 1, nb 2	22
T. P. Alsop c Mike b H. A. Evans.........	119		
S. A. Northeast lbw b Wright	19	1/37 (2)	(5 wkts dec, 120 overs) 612
*J. M. Vince c Swindells b Parkinson......	231	2/75 (1) 3/127 (4)	
L. A. Dawson not out	152	4/351 (3) 5/545 (5)	110 overs: 513-4

K. J. Abbott, M. S. Crane, B. T. J. Wheal and Mohammad Abbas did not bat.

Wright 26–5–111–2; H. A. Evans 26–1–98–1; Griffiths 18–2–92–1; Mike 15–1–82–0; Parkinson 26–3–155–1; Ackermann 9–0–55–0.

Leicestershire

S. T. Evans lbw b Abbott................	3	– b Abbott........................	8
M. H. Azad c Dawson b Abbott............	27	– st McManus b Dawson............	18
H. E. Dearden c McManus b Wheal	42	– lbw b Crane	62
*C. N. Ackermann run out (Vince).........	37	– c Weatherley b Mohammad Abbas ..	5
L. J. Hill c Dawson b Mohammad Abbas	3	– c Vince b Wheal.................	65
†H. J. Swindells c Dawson b Crane	59	– lbw b Crane	34
B. W. M. Mike c McManus b Abbott.......	4	– c McManus b Crane..............	3
C. F. Parkinson c Dawson b Crane	6	– lbw b Wheal....................	31
C. J. C. Wright b Crane	0	– not out	41
G. T. Griffiths not out..................	8	– lbw b Abbott	16
H. A. Evans c Holland b Wheal	12	– b Mohammad Abbas	2
Lb 1	1	B 8, lb 6, nb 6............	20

1/15 (1) 2/49 (2) 3/81 (3)	(76.5 overs) 202	1/12 (1) 2/59 (2)	(95.5 overs) 305
4/84 (5) 5/152 (4) 6/163 (7)		3/94 (4) 4/104 (3)	
7/177 (8) 8/182 (6) 9/187 (9) 10/202 (11)		5/182 (6) 6/194 (7) 7/240 (5)	
		8/265 (8) 9/292 (10) 10/305 (11)	

Mohammad Abbas 15–7–27–1; Abbott 14–5–27–3; Holland 10–3–35–0; Wheal 10.5–3–39–2; Dawson 12–4–24–0; Crane 15–2–49–3. *Second innings:* Abbott 17–4–53–2; Mohammad Abbas 15.5–9–41–2; Wheal 12–0–57–2; Dawson 19–5–30–1; Holland 3–1–8–0; Crane 29–6–102–3.

Umpires: M. A. Gough and B. V. Taylor. Referee: S. Cummings.

At The Oval, April 15–18. LEICESTERSHIRE drew with SURREY.

LEICESTERSHIRE v SOMERSET

At Leicester, April 22–24. Somerset won by nine wickets. Somerset 22pts, Leicestershire 4pts. Toss: Leicestershire. County debut: M. S. Harris.

Outstanding fast bowling from Overton, who had match figures of 35.4–19–64–8, enabled Somerset to win in three days, even if the margin exaggerated their control. His accuracy and pace, plus the flight and guile of Leach, were the difference, though Leicestershire could point to the rejection of a run-out appeal against Abell, on 15 – replays showed him short of his ground – as well as their own fielding errors: Abell was also dropped on his way to 88, the game's highest score. Both sides reckoned 300 was par, but Leicestershire began with 233. Next day, their captain Ackermann was struck on the forehead at slip after a ball from Parkinson deflected off Swindells, and replaced by concussion substitute Rishi Patel. But the middle order converted an 85-run deficit into a lead of 77, with five wickets in hand, before a double strike from Overton. Lammonby, whose first five innings of the season had produced 13 runs, coasted home with 70 not out.

Close of play: first day, Somerset 53-3 (Abell 13, Leach 10); second day, Leicestershire 48-3 (Patel 27, Hill 7).

Leicestershire

M. H. Azad c Davies b Abell	36	– c Davies b Davey		0
M. S. Harris b Gregory	19	– c Lammonby b Overton		7
H. E. Dearden lbw b Gregory	7	– c Abell b Overton		1
*C. N. Ackermann lbw b de Lange	4			
L. J. Hill c Banton b Overton	68	– c Gregory b Leach		47
†H. J. Swindells c Hildreth b Overton	1	– c Davies b Overton		49
B. W. M. Mike lbw b Leach	26	– c Lammonby b de Lange		37
C. F. Parkinson not out	27	– lbw b Overton		4
C. J. C. Wright b Lammonby	4	– c Davies b Leach		6
D. Klein b Leach	12	– c de Lange b Leach		0
G. T. Griffiths c Davies b Overton	12	– not out		3
R. K. Patel (did not bat)		– (4) c Hildreth b Overton		27
B 8, lb 1, nb 8	17	B 2, lb 6, nb 10		18

1/40 (2) 2/56 (3) 3/68 (4)	(82.4 overs)	233
4/68 (1) 5/74 (6) 6/133 (7)		
7/180 (5) 8/185 (9) 9/213 (10) 10/233 (11)		

1/1 (1) 2/2 (3)	(70.4 overs)	199
3/21 (2) 4/48 (4)		
5/126 (5) 6/162 (6) 7/168 (8)		
8/187 (9) 9/187 (10) 10/199 (7)		

Patel replaced Ackermann, as a concussion substitute.

Overton 17.4–9–39–3; Davey 12–2–36–0; Gregory 13–3–39–2; de Lange 14–3–41–1; Abell 9–4–26–1; Lammonby 10–2–20–1; Leach 7–1–23–2. *Second innings*—Overton 18–10–25–5; Davey 10–1–39–1; Gregory 11–3–41–0; Leach 20–8–43–3; de Lange 10.4–2–40–1; Lammonby 1–0–3–0.

Somerset

T. Banton lbw b Klein	15	– b Wright		8
T. A. Lammonby lbw b Wright	8	– not out		70
*T. B. Abell c Harris b Mike	88	– not out		35
J. C. Hildreth c Ackermann b Klein	5			
M. J. Leach b Mike	26			
G. A. Bartlett c Dearden b Mike	48			
†S. M. Davies c Harris b Griffiths	59			
C. Overton c Patel b Parkinson	24			
L. Gregory lbw b Parkinson	0			
J. H. Davey not out	11			
M. de Lange b Wright	0			
B 14, lb 5, w 1, nb 14	34	B 1, lb 1, w 1, nb 2		5

1/25 (2) 2/25 (1) 3/39 (4)	(80.2 overs)	318
4/102 (5) 5/214 (3) 6/219 (6)		
7/289 (8) 8/297 (9) 9/317 (7) 10/318 (11)		

1/10 (1)	(1 wkt, 26.5 overs)	118

Wright 18.2–6–57–2; Klein 17–1–74–2; Mike 14–2–50–3; Griffiths 14–1–42–1; Parkinson 17–2–76–2. *Second innings*—Wright 5–2–16–1; Klein 4–1–18–0; Mike 3–1–10–0; Parkinson 8–1–29–0; Hill 1–0–8–0; Griffiths 5–0–27–0; Dearden 0.5–0–8–0.

Umpires: R. J. Bailey and R. T. Robinson.	Referee: J. J. Whitaker.

At Bristol, April 29–May 2. LEICESTERSHIRE lost to GLOUCESTERSHIRE by four wickets.

LEICESTERSHIRE v SURREY

At Leicester, May 6–9. Drawn. Leicestershire 15pts, Surrey 13pts. Toss: Leicestershire. County debut: E. Barnes.

The loss of the third day to heavy rain, and half the fourth to an unfit outfield, spoiled a potentially exciting game on a good pitch taking spin. Three centuries helped Leicestershire build an imposing first-innings 496. Australia's Harris scored his first county hundred; an over later, Sam Evans reached his third in his last three matches; and Swindells – like Evans, a Leicester-born product of the club Academy – recorded the first of his career, after last man Alex Evans averted a hat-trick from Virdi. On the second afternoon, Burns passed 10,000 first-class runs during an unbroken opening partnership of 146 with Stoneman, but it was a day and a half before Surrey could resume, with 48 overs remaining. Stoneman completed a pleasing hundred, and Wright followed a seven-for at Bristol with five as Surrey's last eight fell for 69.

Close of play: first day, Leicestershire 306-6 (Swindells 25, Mike 0); second day, Surrey 146-0 (Burns 74, Stoneman 59); third day, no play.

Leicestershire

S. T. Evans c Smith b Virdi	112	C. J. C. Wright lbw b Virdi		0
M. H. Azad c Foakes b Topley	5	H. A. Evans not out		1
M. S. Harris lbw b Virdi	101			
*C. N. Ackermann lbw b Topley	33	B 4, lb 11, nb 8		23
L. J. Hill c Foakes b Clarke	18			
†H. J. Swindells st Foakes b Virdi	103	1/13 (2) 2/208 (3)	(141.2 overs)	496
E. Barnes b Virdi	5	3/243 (1) 4/277 (4) 5/304 (5)		
B. W. M. Mike c Clark b Overton	74	6/305 (7) 7/433 (8) 8/485 (9)		
C. F. Parkinson c Smith b Virdi	25	9/485 (10) 10/496 (6)	110 overs: 380-6	

Topley 29–6–110–2; Overton 21–2–65–1; Clarke 22–8–45–1; Clark 23–1–85–0; Virdi 44.2–3–171–6; Burns 2–0–5–0.

Surrey

*R. J. Burns c Parkinson b Wright	75	R. J. W. Topley c Hill b Parkinson		10
M. D. Stoneman c Ackermann b Wright	119	G. S. Virdi not out		0
H. M. Amla c Ackermann b Mike	15			
O. J. D. Pope b Wright	33	B 8, lb 6, w 1, nb 10		25
†B. T. Foakes b Parkinson	0			
J. L. Smith b Wright	0	1/164 (1) 2/201 (3)	(87.5 overs)	324
J. Clark b Wright	16	3/255 (4) 4/256 (5)		
J. Overton c Barnes b Parkinson	15	5/257 (6) 6/275 (7) 7/292 (2)		
R. Clarke b Barnes	16	8/298 (8) 9/320 (10) 10/324 (9)		

Wright 24–7–60–5; H. A. Evans 5–0–18–0; Parkinson 28–5–107–3; Ackermann 8–0–27–0; Barnes 9.5–0–49–1; Mike 13–1–49–1.

Umpires: I. J. Gould and R. K. Illingworth.	Referee: P. Whitticase.

At Southampton, May 19–22. LEICESTERSHIRE drew with HAMPSHIRE.

LEICESTERSHIRE v MIDDLESEX

At Leicester, May 27–30. Leicestershire won by five wickets. Leicestershire 19pts, Middlesex 5pts. Toss: Middlesex.

Leicestershire secured their first win in 11 first-class matches as Middlesex again failed to capitalise on a strong position – this time 243 ahead on the third morning with nine wickets standing. A calm unbeaten 95 from Simpson had been the spine of a solid first innings, before Bamber, Helm and Andersson, whose four for 27 was a county-best, ran through the home batting. But Wright picked up his third five-for in four games to keep Leicestershire interested. Although a target of 378 looked formidable, Harris scored a superb 185 and put on 243 with Ackermann, a third-wicket record between these sides. A slight wobble once Harris was dismissed might have been worse had Ackermann not been dropped at third man with 38 required, shortly after reaching his first first-class century for three years. It was Leicestershire's third-highest successful run-chase in the Championship; they had managed 394 to beat Derbyshire in 1947, and 382 against Northamptonshire in 1980. All three came at Grace Road, where this victory completed a happy return for home spectators. For Middlesex, who replaced them at the bottom of the group, this was a sixth defeat in eight.

Close of play: first day, Middlesex 260-7 (Simpson 73, Helm 16); second day, Middlesex 57-1 (Eskinazi 31, Gubbins 20); third day, Leicestershire 75-1 (Evans 26, Harris 41).

Middlesex

S. D. Robson lbw b Parkinson	23	– (2) lbw b Wright	6
S. S. Eskinazi c Ackermann b Davis	38	– (1) b Wright	46
N. R. T. Gubbins lbw b Davis	21	– b Mike	38
*P. S. P. Handscomb lbw b Barnes	26	– c Swindells b Mike	36
R. G. White c Ackermann b Parkinson	16	– b Davis	10
†J. A. Simpson not out	95	– c Evans b Wright	17
M. K. Andersson lbw b Parkinson	0	– lbw b Wright	4
L. B. K. Hollman b Barnes	32	– c Ackermann b Wright	26
T. G. Helm c Swindells b Mike	17	– b Wright	1
E. R. Bamber c Swindells b Mike	4	– lbw b Parkinson	8
T. N. Walallawita b Wright	6	– not out	1
B 5, lb 4, nb 8	17	B 10, lb 6, w 1, nb 8	25

1/52 (1) 2/76 (3) 3/91 (2)   (111 overs) 295   1/11 (2) 2/84 (1)   (82.1 overs) 218
4/118 (4) 5/132 (5) 6/132 (7)   3/102 (3) 4/119 (5)
7/222 (8) 8/262 (9) 9/286 (10)   5/163 (6) 6/174 (7) 7/174 (4)
10/295 (11)   8/179 (9) 9/216 (10) 10/218 (8)
110 overs: 288-9

Wright 19-2-69-1; Barnes 17-3-48-2; Davis 25-6-68-2; Parkinson 29-10-76-3; Ackermann 14-8-17-0; Mike 7-5-8-2. *Second innings*—Wright 23.1-6-48-6; Davis 13-4-30-1; Mike 13-1-42-2; Parkinson 14-2-40-1; Ackermann 4-3-7-0; Barnes 15-2-35-0.

Leicestershire

M. H. Azad c Eskinazi b Bamber	0	– c Walallawita b Bamber	1
S. T. Evans c Simpson b Andersson	15	– c Simpson b Helm	26
M. S. Harris lbw b Helm	3	– c Simpson b Walallawita	185
*C. N. Ackermann c Robson b Helm	8	– not out	126
L. J. Hill b Andersson	39	– lbw b Walallawita	2
†H. J. Swindells lbw b Andersson	1	– b Bamber	12
B. W. M. Mike lbw b Andersson	0	– not out	9
C. F. Parkinson lbw b Bamber	41		
C. J. C. Wright lbw b Bamber	23		
E. Barnes b Hollman	6		
W. S. Davis not out	0		
		B 6, lb 11	17

1/2 (1) 2/9 (3) 3/17 (4)   (55.1 overs) 136   1/2 (1)   (5 wkts, 123.1 overs) 378
4/40 (5) 5/42 (6) 6/42 (7)   2/83 (2) 3/326 (3)
7/86 (5) 8/125 (8) 9/136 (9) 10/136 (10)   4/332 (5) 5/355 (6)

Bamber 16-6-36-3; Helm 16-1-49-2; Andersson 11-3-27-4; Walallawita 8-2-22-0; Hollman 4.1-2-2-1. *Second innings*—Bamber 26-5-75-2; Helm 32-7-74-1; Andersson 19-2-54-0; Walallawita 24-1-84-2; Hollman 21.1-2-72-0; Gubbins 1-0-2-0.

Umpires: M. Newell and R. T. Robinson.   Referee: S. J. Davis.

LEICESTERSHIRE v GLOUCESTERSHIRE

At Leicester, June 3–5. **Leicestershire** won by an innings and 93 runs. Leicestershire 23pts, Gloucestershire 2pts. Toss: Leicestershire. County debut: G. D. Phillips.

Leicestershire recorded consecutive Championship victories for the first time since 2018, and their first back-to-back home wins in the same season since 2006. Gloucestershire, unbeaten in their first six matches, suffered their second innings defeat in a week, and lost top spot in Group Two. Asked for a pitch assisting the spinners, groundsman Andy Ward obliged. Leicestershire claimed first use and, thanks to Harris's third century in four games, as well as fifties from Ackermann and Hill, piled up 451. Perhaps still smarting from losing to Surrey, Gloucestershire seemed almost resigned once Ackermann, coming on in the 14th over, spun his first delivery sharply to hit the top of Dent's off stump. Only Hammond survived long, before he was bowled attempting a reverse sweep. When they followed on, 293 behind, Parkinson and Wright reduced them to 31 for five. Cockbain and Tattersall, on loan from Yorkshire, compiled a century stand, but the end came inside three days. Parkinson, relishing the turn, took five in each innings for a career-best ten for 108.

Close of play: first day, Leicestershire 357-5 (Swindells 25, Mike 2); second day, Gloucestershire 5-1 (Hammond 0).

Leicestershire

S. T. Evans c Lace b Phillips	27	E. Barnes b Shaw		10
M. H. Azad c Smith b Payne	4	W. S. Davis b Shaw		0
M. S. Harris lbw b Phillips	148			
*C. N. Ackermann b Hammond	57	B 25, lb 21, nb 8		54
L. J. Hill b Worrall	56			
†H. J. Swindells c Cockbain b Smith	36	1/10 (2) 2/64 (1)	(132 overs)	451
B. W. M. Mike lbw b Worrall	24	3/224 (4) 4/299 (3) 5/337 (5)		
C. F. Parkinson not out	24	6/379 (6) 7/405 (7) 8/436 (9)		
C. J. C. Wright c Shaw b Hammond	11	9/451 (10) 10/451 (11)	110 overs: 383-6	

Worrall 23–8–57–2; Payne 19–4–46–1; Shaw 16–3–55–2; Higgins 25–5–73–0; Phillips 21–1–77–2; Smith 19–0–60–1; Hammond 9–1–37–2.

Gloucestershire

M. A. H. Hammond b Parkinson	67	– c Azad b Wright	8
*C. D. J. Dent b Ackermann	12	– c Ackermann b Parkinson	5
G. D. Phillips c Harris b Parkinson	16	– lbw b Parkinson	8
T. C. Lace c Swindells b Ackermann	1	– c Swindells b Wright	4
I. A. Cockbain c Davis b Parkinson	4	– c Ackermann b Parkinson	59
R. F. Higgins b Parkinson	0	– c Hill b Parkinson	0
†J. A. Tattersall c Evans b Wright	18	– c Ackermann b Parkinson	51
T. M. J. Smith c Ackermann	1	– lbw b Ackermann	5
D. A. Payne not out	11	– b Ackermann	4
J. Shaw lbw b Parkinson	7	– b Ackermann	19
D. J. Worrall lbw b Wright	0	– not out	17
B 4, lb 5, nb 10	19	B 1, lb 9, nb 10	20

1/48 (2) 2/81 (3) 3/95 (4)	(50.3 overs) 158	1/5 (2) 2/17 (1)	(70 overs) 200
4/114 (5) 5/114 (6) 6/123 (1)		3/23 (4) 4/29 (3)	
7/128 (8) 8/144 (7) 9/153 (10) 10/158 (11)		5/31 (6) 6/150 (7) 7/155 (5)	
		8/160 (9) 9/165 (8) 10/200 (10)	

Wright 11.3–2–32–2; Davis 5–1–17–0; Parkinson 18–6–45–5; Ackermann 16–3–55–3. *Second innings*—Parkinson 32–12–63–5; Ackermann 13–5–44–3; Wright 13–4–36–2; Mike 7–0–27–0; Barnes 5–0–20–0.

Umpires: N. G. B. Cook and R. J. Warren. Referee: W. M. Noon.

At Taunton, July 4–7. LEICESTERSHIRE drew with SOMERSET.

At Northwood, July 11–14. LEICESTERSHIRE lost to MIDDLESEX by 121 runs.

DIVISION THREE

LEICESTERSHIRE v KENT

At Leicester, August 30–September 1. Kent won by 132 runs. Kent 20pts, Leicestershire 3pts. Toss: Kent. Championship debut: L. P. J. Kimber.

A game described as "bizarre" by players on both sides saw Kent recover from 116 for seven on the opening day to record their first victory of the season. On a pitch that helped the spinners from the start, Parkinson took four wickets, before fellow left-armer Logan – having added 68 for Kent's tenth with Leaning – claimed three as Leicestershire were skittled. Kent led by 123, extending it to 265 by the time Stevens arrived. At the end of day two, he had 55 – and last man Logan for company – but next morning raced to an unbeaten 107 in a further 28 balls; in all, he faced just 70. Of the 120 Kent added after the fall of the fifth wicket, Stevens made all but 13; of the tenth-wicket stand of 62, Logan made four. Parkinson's five-for seemed forgotten. Leicestershire had little chance of reaching a target of 386, and none at all after Milnes reduced them to 20 for six by lunch; his eventual six for 53 was his best return. But Mike hit a 52-ball 70, Barnes an unbeaten 70, and Davis a career-best 42, as the last four wickets thrashed 233 in 39 overs. Leicestershire eventually fell short by 133; Kent's two last-wicket stands had totalled 130. For only the third time in first-class cricket, there were three tenth-wicket partnerships of 50 or more.

Close of play: first day, Leicestershire 66-5 (Kimber 13, Mike 14); second day, Kent 210-9 (Stevens 55, Logan 4).

Kent

Z. Crawley b Parkinson	50	– b Parkinson	26
J. M. Cox c Ackermann b Wright	0	– c Ackermann b Parkinson	38
J. L. Denly c Ackermann b Parkinson	29	– lbw b Mike	20
J. A. Leaning not out	75	– c Ackermann b Parkinson	34
*†S. W. Billings b Parkinson	11	– c Swindells b Barnes	19
O. G. Robinson c Hill b Parkinson	7	– b Barnes	5
D. I. Stevens c Kimber b Wright	0	– not out	107
G. Stewart lbw b Wright	3	– b Barnes	1
M. E. Milnes b Barnes	22	– lbw b Parkinson	5
N. N. Gilchrist run out (Evans/Swindells)	0	– b Parkinson	0
J. E. G. Logan run out (Hill/Swindells)	21	– b Ackermann	4
Lb 6, nb 8	14	B 1, lb 2	3

1/3 (2) 2/79 (1) 3/80 (3)   (70 overs) 232
4/96 (5) 5/106 (6) 6/106 (7)
7/116 (8) 8/158 (9) 9/164 (10) 10/232 (11)

1/49 (1) 2/84 (3)   (61 overs) 262
3/84 (2) 4/128 (5)
5/142 (6) 6/166 (4) 7/167 (8)
8/190 (9) 9/200 (10) 10/262 (11)

Wright 17–2–59–3; Davis 9–2–31–0; Barnes 11–1–44–1; Parkinson 28–9–68–4; Mike 3–0–22–0; Ackermann 2–0–2–0. *Second innings*—Wright 10–1–44–0; Davis 6–1–15–0; Parkinson 23–9–75–5; Mike 7–0–51–1; Ackermann 6–2–17–1; Barnes 9–1–57–3.

Leicestershire

M. H. Azad c Billings b Stevens	18	– lbw b Stevens 0
S. T. Evans c Leaning b Milnes	10	– lbw b Milnes 1
*C. N. Ackermann c Billings b Stewart	2	– c Crawley b Milnes 2
L. J. Hill b Stewart	0	– c Billings b Milnes 5
L. P. J. Kimber lbw b Milnes	13	– b Milnes 4
†H. J. Swindells lbw b Logan	4	– b Milnes 0
B. W. M. Mike lbw b Milnes	17	– c Leaning b Logan 70
C. F. Parkinson lbw b Logan	2	– c Billings b Logan 17
E. Barnes not out	22	– not out 70
C. J. C. Wright c Crawley b Logan	7	– c Billings b Milnes 22
W. S. Davis c Leaning b Stewart	0	– c Billings b Gilchrist 42
B 6, lb 5, w 1, nb 2	14	B 11, lb 5, nb 4 20

1/26 (2) 2/31 (3) 3/33 (4)   (44.1 overs) 109   1/3 (2) 2/3 (1)   (51.2 overs) 253
4/33 (1) 5/47 (6) 6/70 (5)   3/5 (3) 4/17 (5)
7/73 (7) 8/100 (8) 9/101 (11) 10/109 (10)   5/17 (6) 6/20 (4) 7/97 (8)
                                                  8/128 (7) 9/161 (10) 10/253 (11)

In the first innings Barnes, when 14, retired hurt at 93-7 and resumed at 101-9.

Milnes 11–5–24–3; Stevens 13–5–34–1; Stewart 9–3–20–3; Logan 8.1–4–8–3; Denly 3–0–12–0. *Second innings*—Milnes 12–5–53–6; Stevens 9–3–24–1; Gilchrist 7.2–1–43–1; Stewart 2–0–21–0; Logan 10–2–39–2; Denly 9–1–36–0; Leaning 2–0–21–0.

Umpires: I. J. Gould and C. M. Watts. Referee: A. J. Swann.

At Derby, September 5–8. LEICESTERSHIRE drew with DERBYSHIRE.

LEICESTERSHIRE v SUSSEX

At Leicester, September 12–15. Leicestershire won by an innings and five runs. Leicestershire 24pts, Sussex 5pts. Toss: Sussex. First-class debut: T. I. Hinley.

Sussex, with an eye on the upcoming Vitality Blast finals day, named an inexperienced side for this game, including five teenagers and two 20-year-olds. As they neared the close of the first day on 291 for two, their plan seemed to be working. Brown made a fine century, though Hudson-Prentice was ruled out of the rest of the match after being hit on the hand by Sakande, and two late wickets meant they were effectively 310 for five. Next morning, Wright finished with six for 94, despite a hamstring injury, as Sussex slipped to 359. The collapse proved costly, as Leicestershire racked up 492 for four, with Azad and Hill both recording career-bests in a third-wicket stand of 248, and Kimber a maiden Championship fifty. A washed-out third day prompted quick runs on the fourth, which left the visitors an apparently manageable 48 overs to survive. With Wright now unable to bowl, Sussex reached 117 for three, 16 runs short of parity and 14 overs from safety. But they capitulated in 11, falling just short of making Leicestershire bat again as Mike and Parkinson – captain because Ackermann was missing for personal reasons – took four apiece.

Close of play: first day, Sussex 310-4 (Brown 111, Hinley 6); second day, Leicestershire 291-2 (Azad 122, Hill 109); third day, no play.

Sussex

A. G. H. Orr c Barnes b Wright	40	– c Swindells b Parkinson	34
*T. J. Haines c Rhodes b Mike	71	– lbw b Barnes	31
B. C. Brown not out	133	– c Sakande b Mike	12
F. J. Hudson-Prentice retired hurt	7	– absent hurt	
†O. J. Carter b Sakande	40	– (4) c Evans b Mike	9
D. M. W. Rawlins c Swindells b Wright	4	– (5) c Swindells b Mike	21
T. I. Hinley c Barnes b Wright	19	– (6) b Parkinson	1
J. J. Carson c Swindells b Wright	0	– (7) lbw b Parkinson	2
H. T. Crocombe b Wright	7	– (8) lbw b Mike	0
S. F. Hunt b Wright	0	– (9) not out	1
J. P. Sarro c Sakande b Barnes	0	– (10) c Swindells b Parkinson	1
B 10, lb 8, nb 20	38	B 5, lb 5, nb 6	16

1/106 (1) 2/170 (2) 3/291 (5)   (107.4 overs) 359   1/57 (1) 2/77 (3)   (45.2 overs) 128
4/302 (6) 5/334 (7) 6/334 (8)   3/83 (2) 4/117 (5) 5/120 (6)
7/352 (9) 8/352 (10) 9/359 (11)   6/122 (4) 7/122 (8) 8/122 (7) 9/128 (10)

In the first innings Hudson-Prentice retired hurt at 185-2.

Wright 29–3–94–6; Sakande 22–3–77–1; Mike 16–2–55–1; Barnes 17.4–2–62–1; Parkinson 16–3–38–0; Rhodes 7–0–15–0. *Second innings*—Sakande 8–0–48–0; Mike 14–4–34–4; Barnes 9–3–18–1; Parkinson 14.2–6–18–4.

Leicestershire

M. H. Azad c sub (A. M. Foreman) b Crocombe	152	†H. J. Swindells not out	69
S. T. Evans c Rawlins b Hunt	0	B 9, lb 1, nb 20	30
G. H. Rhodes b Haines	37	1/5 (2) (4 wkts dec, 102 overs) 492
L. J. Hill c sub (A. M. Foreman) b Crocombe	145	2/108 (3) 3/356 (4)
L. P. J. Kimber not out	59	4/362 (1)

B. W. M. Mike, *C. F. Parkinson, E. Barnes, C. J. C. Wright and A. Sakande did not bat.

Hunt 21–0–127–1; Crocombe 21–3–70–2; Carson 23–0–90–0; Sarro 9–0–64–0; Haines 9–2–21–1; Rawlins 13–0–75–0; Hinley 6–0–35–0.

Umpires: M. Newell and R. T. Robinson.   Referee: J. J. Whitaker.

At Worcester, September 21–23. LEICESTERSHIRE lost to WORCESTERSHIRE by ten wickets.

MIDDLESEX

All change at Lawless Lord's

Kevin Hand

The season began with a whiff of optimism, especially as the Australian batsman Peter Handscomb was due to take up his post as captain – a year late, thanks to Covid. Coach Stuart Law and managing director of cricket Angus Fraser were bullish. But the bubble soon burst.

After news broke of a pension shortfall for players and staff, dating back more than a decade, Middlesex lost seven of their first nine Championship matches, sentencing them to the third tier at the sharp end of the season – bitter stuff for a team which had won the title in 2016. The story was similarly dire in white-ball cricket: eighth in both their Vitality Blast and Royal London groups. Change was inevitable – and it started from the top.

First, chief executive Richard Goatley, who joined as finance director in 2005, stepped down because of ill health. Then Fraser was moved sideways into a new role, bringing young players through from club cricket to the county side. Improving this pathway had been one of the main tasks he set himself when originally appointed.

Fraser's departure from day-to-day involvement with the first team left Law in sole charge. The idea was to make accountability more apparent – which he found out the hard way when, despite a late run of success in the lowest tier of the Championship, he paid with his own job, even though there was a year left on his four-year contract. His assistant, Nic Pothas, departed too. Law was perhaps unlucky that he had arrived at a time of rebuilding, with the side in the second division of the Championship. He had improved the one-day performances – at least until last year – but red-ball results ultimately counted against him. Andrew Cornish, the new chief executive, said the decisions were not "taken lightly."

In January, it was announced that Richard Johnson, the former Middlesex seamer who had left the coaching staff on Law's arrival in 2019, would return after a spell at Surrey, and become first-team coach. He will be working alongside Alan Coleman, who was promoted from Second XI coach to head of men's performance, and club coach Rory Coutts.

There should certainly be enough young talent to work with. In 2020 and 2021, some 11 players aged 25 or under had featured in the first team, as "Fraser's Fledglings" started to make a mark. Robbie White hit 765 runs in the Championship, and centuries in the wins over Derbyshire and Sussex. Blake Cullen and Joe Cracknell were fast-tracked to The Hundred, while leg-spinner Luke Hollman took ten wickets at Hove, a match-winning performance on a true pitch.

A more experienced recruit also made his presence felt. The 34-year-old former Test opener Mark Stoneman joined from Surrey on a three-year deal in

August. Shrugging off a pair on debut against Derbyshire at Lord's, he crashed 174 in the run-fest at Hove, sharing a county-record opening partnership of 376 with Sam Robson, who made 253. Robson showed signs of a return to the form that brought him seven Test caps in 2014, and was one of only five in the country to make 1,000 in the Championship.

Robbie White

Stoneman replaced Nick Gubbins, who moved to Hampshire in an effort to reignite his own international ambitions. Gubbins had been Middlesex's Player of the Year in the Championship-winning season of 2016, but underwhelming since. He did make 124 against Surrey in his penultimate match – then hit another century in his second game for his new side. There were dressing-room grumbles about the pitches at Lord's not helping the batsmen, which contributed to Gubbins's decision.

The bowling may also look unfamiliar in 2022. Steven Finn, who spent the winter showcasing his talents as a commentator during the Ashes, has joined Sussex. He played only two Championship matches in 2021, but had been part of the furniture at Lord's since 2005, when he made his debut as a gangly 16-year-old. Finn took 394 first-class wickets for Middlesex at 28 – and 125 in 36 Tests for England.

James Harris returned to Glamorgan after nine seasons, but there will be one reassuringly recognisable face in the attack: Tim Murtagh took 58 wickets at 18 in the summer he turned 40 and, after eventually signing a new contract, was appointed club captain. It is a largely ceremonial role, although he will fill in on the field if Australia come calling for Handscomb, whose first season in charge was tough: a debut duck was followed by a run of low scores. A maiden fifty seemed likely to bring victory at The Oval, before it rained.

Murtagh's new-ball partner is expected to be the exciting Pakistan Test left-armer Shaheen Shah Afridi. Middlesex's batsmen will be relieved to have him on their side: playing against them for Hampshire in the Blast in 2020, he took four wickets with the last four balls of the match at the Rose Bowl, finishing with six for 19, all bowled. They will be backed up by the enthusiastic Ethan Bamber, who took 52 Championship wickets, while all-rounder Martin Andersson allied 29 to 439 runs.

In January, club chairman Mike O'Farrell was forced to apologise after telling the DCMS select committee that Middlesex's attempts to recruit a wider range of players had been hampered because the local black community preferred football, and young Asians were too busy studying. He said he was "devastated" by what he called a misunderstanding. Soon after, Middlesex became the first county to sign the Muslim Athlete charter, in an attempt to build "greater understanding of the needs and requirements of its Muslim players and followers."

MIDDLESEX RESULTS

County Championship matches – Played 14: Won 5, Lost 8, Drawn 1.
Vitality Blast matches – Played 14: Won 4, Lost 9, No result 1.
Royal London Cup matches – Played 7: Won 2, Lost 4, No result 1. Cancelled 1.

LV= County Championship, 6th in Group 2, 2nd in Division 3;
Vitality T20 Blast, 8th in South Group; Royal London Cup, 8th in Group 1.

COUNTY CHAMPIONSHIP AVERAGES, BATTING AND FIELDING

Cap		Birthplace	M	I	NO	R	HS	100	Avge	Ct/St
	†M. D. Stoneman	Newcastle-u-Tyne .	4	7	0	354	174	2	50.57	0
2013	S. D. Robson.......	Paddington, Aus ..	14	27	1	1,047	253	3	40.26	16
	R. G. White........	Ealing‡	14	26	4	765	120	2	34.77	19
2016	†N. R. T. Gubbins....	Richmond........	8	15	0	514	124	1	34.26	1
	D. J. Mitchell¶	Hamilton, NZ....	2	4	0	134	73	0	33.50	0
2018	S. S. Eskinazi.....	Johannesburg, SA .	9	17	2	453	102	1	30.20	8
2011	†J. A. Simpson......	Bury...........	13	22	2	535	95*	0	26.75	50/3
	†L. B. K. Hollman ...	Islington‡........	6	9	1	176	46	0	22.00	3
	M. K. Andersson....	Reading........	13	24	0	439	88	0	18.29	6
	†M. D. E. Holden	Cambridge.......	10	19	1	325	52	0	18.05	6
	†T. N. Walallawita ...	Colombo, SL	4	6	3	54	20*	0	18.00	2
	P. S. P. Handscomb¶	Box Hill, Australia	7	13	0	227	70	0	17.46	3
2012	T. S. Roland-Jones ..	Ashford‡........	6	11	2	138	46*	0	15.33	0
	B. C. Cullen	Isleworth‡......	4	5	0	55	27	0	11.00	0
	N. A. Sowter	Penrith, Australia .	3	6	1	46	24*	0	9.20	3
2015	J. A. R. Harris.....	Morriston.......	3	6	0	55	26	0	9.16	1
	†J. L. B. Davies	Reading........	2	4	0	35	24	0	8.75	1
	E. R. Bamber	Westminster‡.....	12	22	4	151	25	0	8.38	2
2019	T. G. Helm........	Stoke Mandeville..	4	8	2	49	17	0	8.16	1
	J. M. de Caires	Paddington‡......	2	4	0	28	17	0	7.00	1
2008	†T. J. Murtagh	Lambeth........	12	20	7	88	31	0	6.76	3
2009	S. T. Finn	Watford........	2	4	1	17	13*	0	5.66	0

Also batted: J. B. Cracknell (*Enfield‡*) (1 match) 13, 7 (2 ct).

‡ *Born in Middlesex.*   ¶ *Official overseas player.*   †† *Other non-England-qualified.*

BOWLING

	Style	O	M	R	W	BB	5I	Avge
T. S. Roland-Jones...............	RFM	167.4	38	460	25	5-36	1	18.40
T. J. Murtagh	RFM	402.4	113	1,079	58	5-64	1	18.60
E. R. Bamber	RFM	407	111	1,084	52	5-41	1	20.84
S. T. Finn	RFM	68.2	4	266	12	5-77	1	22.16
J. A. R. Harris.................	RFM	65.3	3	230	10	3-50	0	23.00
L. B. K. Hollman	LB	105.4	16	363	13	5-65	2	27.92
M. K. Andersson	RFM	250.1	41	916	29	4-27	0	31.58
B. C. Cullen	RFM	109.2	19	393	10	3-30	0	39.30

Also bowled: J. M. de Caires (RM) 3–0–7–0; N. R. T. Gubbins (LB) 1–0–2–0; T. G. Helm (RFM) 131.1–21–413–8; M. D. E. Holden (OB) 1–0–8–0; D. J. Mitchell (RM) 44–8–142–9; S. D. Robson (LB/RM) 17–0–72–2; N. A. Sowter (LB) 68–7–237–2; T. N. Walallawita (SLA) 102.2–20–326–3.

LEADING VITALITY BLAST AVERAGES (100 runs/15 overs)

Batting	Runs	HS	Avge	SR	Ct/St
P. R. Stirling	130	58	26.00	152.94	1
D. J. Mitchell	209	58	26.12	144.13	4
C. J. Green	107	26*	35.66	140.78	3
S. S. Eskinazi ...	399	102*	44.33	140.49	6
J. B. Cracknell ...	281	77	25.54	137.07	6
E. J. G. Morgan	133	38	26.60	129.12	4
J. A. Simpson ...	143	62	14.30	126.54	7/5
L. B. K. Hollman	130	51	16.25	123.80	9
M. D. E. Holden	120	50*	20.00	110.09	9

Bowling	W	BB	Avge	ER
Mujeeb Zadran ..	10	2-18	16.60	6.91
N. A. Sowter	15	3-13	20.00	7.50
T. G. Helm......	5	2-30	43.00	8.26
L. B. K. Hollman	5	2-10	21.77	8.52
B. C. Cullen.....	20	4-32	16.35	8.79
S. T. Finn.......	19	4-19	21.78	8.96
C. J. Green......	10	5-32	23.10	9.24

LEADING ROYAL LONDON CUP AVERAGES (100 runs/4 wickets)

Batting	Runs	HS	Avge	SR	Ct/St	Bowling	W	BB	Avge	ER
M. K. Andersson	133	44*	133.00	147.77	3	L. B. K. Hollman	8	4-56	24.50	5.29
S. S. Eskinazi	201	130	50.25	104.14	2	E. R. Bamber	10	3-41	29.70	6.02
S. D. Robson	169	76	42.25	99.41	3	J. A. R. Harris	7	2-45	42.85	6.00
M. D. E. Holden	201	94	40.20	87.39	2	T. N. Walallawita	4	2-54	71.75	5.21
J. L. B. Davies	164	70	32.80	106.49	1					
R. G. White	140	55	28.00	67.30	4/1					
P. S. P. Handscomb	130	75	21.66	94.20	3					

FIRST-CLASS COUNTY RECORDS

Highest score for	331*	J. D. B. Robertson v Worcestershire at Worcester	1949
Highest score against	341	C. M. Spearman (Gloucestershire) at Gloucester	2004
Leading run-scorer	40,302	E. H. Hendren (avge 48.81)	1907–37
Best bowling for	10-40	G. O. B. Allen v Lancashire at Lord's	1929
Best bowling against	9-38	R. C. Robertson-Glasgow (Somerset) at Lord's	1924
Leading wicket-taker	2,361	F. J. Titmus (avge 21.27)	1949–82
Highest total for	**676-5 dec**	v Sussex at Hove	**2021**
Highest total against	850-7 dec	by Somerset at Taunton	2007
Lowest total for	20	v MCC at Lord's	1864
Lowest total against	31	by Gloucestershire at Bristol	1924
	31	by Glamorgan at Cardiff	1997

LIST A COUNTY RECORDS

Highest score for	166	M. D. E. Holden v Kent at Canterbury	2019
Highest score against	166	L. J. Wright (Sussex) at Lord's	2019
Leading run-scorer	12,029	M. W. Gatting (avge 34.96)	1975–98
Best bowling for	7-12	W. W. Daniel v Minor Counties East at Ipswich	1978
Best bowling against	6-27	J. C. Tredwell (Kent) at Southgate	2009
Leading wicket-taker	491	J. E. Emburey (avge 24.68)	1975–95
Highest total for	380-5	v Kent at Canterbury	2019
Highest total against	368-2	by Nottinghamshire at Lord's	2014
Lowest total for	23	v Yorkshire at Leeds	1974
Lowest total against	41	by Northamptonshire at Northampton	1972

TWENTY20 COUNTY RECORDS

Highest score for	129	D. T. Christian v Kent at Canterbury	2014
Highest score against	123	I. A. Cockbain (Gloucestershire) at Bristol	2018
Leading run-scorer	3,318	D. J. Malan (avge 32.85, SR 128.00)	2006–19
Best bowling for	6-28	J. K. Fuller v Hampshire at Southampton	2018
Best bowling against	6-19	Shaheen Shah Afridi (Hampshire) at Southampton	2020
Leading wicket-taker	116	**S. T. Finn (avge 22.25, ER 8.25)**	**2008–21**
Highest total for	227-4	v Somerset at Taunton	2019
Highest total against	254-3	by Gloucestershire at Uxbridge	2011
Lowest total for	**80**	**v Kent at Lord's**	**2021**
Lowest total against	74	by Essex at Chelmsford	2013

ADDRESS

Lord's Cricket Ground, London NW8 8QN; 020 7289 1300; enquiries@middlesexccc.com; www.middlesexccc.com. Twitter: @Middlesex_CCC.

OFFICIALS

Captain P. S. P. Handscomb
(Twenty20) E. J. G. Morgan
Director of cricket 2021 A. R. C. Fraser
Head of men's performance cricket 2022 A. Coleman
Head coach 2021 S. G. Law
Club coach 2022 R. I. Coutts
First team coach R. L. Johnson

President M. W. W. Selvey
Chair M. I. O'Farrell
Chief executive A. J. Cornish
Head groundsman K. McDermott
Scorer D. K. Shelley

GROUP TWO

MIDDLESEX v SOMERSET

At Lord's, April 8–11. Somerset won by four wickets. Somerset 19pts, Middlesex 6pts. Toss: Somerset. County debut: M. de Lange. Championship debut: T. A. Lammonby.

When Somerset were 89 for nine in reply to 313, it seemed Middlesex were cruising to victory in their first red-ball game at Lord's for over 18 months. Even after de Lange and Leach added 83 for the last wicket to save the follow-on, things looked rosy for the home side. But they collapsed from 113 for three to 143 all out on the third morning, and Somerset hunted down a target of 285. Abell led the way with an impressive 84 and, after a wobble to 187 for six, Bartlett and Gregory, who had begun the game with a five-for, did the rest in a composed 19-over stand; soon after, the rain returned. Back on the first day, Robson – initially wearing three sweaters to combat the chill, and dropped three times before reaching 50 – hit 165, the first century of the season; he was seventh out at 263, having passed 10,000 career runs. Then Middlesex's new-ball pair, Murtagh and Bamber (17 years his junior), hooped it around, sharing seven cheap wickets. On a pitch tailor-made for seam, slow left-armer Leach had match figures of 33.4–9–61–4.

Close of play: first day, Middlesex 293-8 (Roland-Jones 19, Bamber 2); second day, Middlesex 87-2 (Gubbins 37, Eskinazi 28); third day, Somerset 112-3 (Abell 62, Bartlett 2).

Middlesex

S. D. Robson c Abell b Gregory	165	– (2) c Davies b Overton	13
M. D. E. Holden c Banton b Overton	4	– (1) c Davies b Overton	1
N. R. T. Gubbins lbw b Davey	21	– c Gregory b Overton	37
*S. S. Eskinazi lbw b Gregory	22	– c Overton b Davey	53
R. G. White c Gregory b Leach	17	– c Gregory b Leach	2
M. K. Andersson c Davies b Davey	8	– lbw b Leach	12
†J. A. Simpson c Davies b Gregory	11	– lbw b Davey	1
T. S. Roland-Jones lbw b Overton	26	– lbw b Davey	0
T. G. Helm c Hildreth b Gregory	9	– c Davies b Gregory	5
E. R. Bamber b Gregory	9	– lbw b Leach	1
T. J. Murtagh not out	4	– not out	6
B 1, lb 6, nb 10	17	B 8, lb 4	12

1/17 (2) 2/62 (3) 3/142 (4)   (102.4 overs) 313
4/197 (5) 5/218 (6) 6/254 (7)
7/263 (1) 8/281 (9) 9/309 (10) 10/313 (8)

1/1 (1) 2/14 (2)   (51.4 overs) 143
3/88 (3) 4/113 (5)
5/127 (4) 6/131 (7) 7/131 (8)
8/131 (6) 9/137 (9) 10/143 (10)

Overton 21.4–6–66–2; Davey 18–3–62–2; de Lange 14–3–41–0; Gregory 20–4–68–5; Leach 22–6–43–1; Abell 7–1–26–0. *Second innings—*Gregory 12–3–47–1; Overton 13–4–26–3; de Lange 4–0–24–0; Davey 11–3–16–3; Leach 11.4–3–18–3.

Somerset

T. Banton b Bamber	6	– lbw b Roland-Jones	37
T. A. Lammonby c Simpson b Murtagh	5	– c Eskinazi b Bamber	0
*T. B. Abell c Robson b Murtagh	4	– c Simpson b Bamber	84
J. C. Hildreth lbw b Bamber	20	– lbw b Roland-Jones	11
G. A. Bartlett c Simpson b Bamber	0	– not out	76
†S. M. Davies lbw b Roland-Jones	23	– lbw b Bamber	0
C. Overton b Roland-Jones	14	– c Simpson b Murtagh	5
L. Gregory b Murtagh	10	– not out	62
J. H. Davey b Murtagh	4		
M. de Lange b Andersson	51		
M. J. Leach not out	28		
Lb 3, nb 4	7	Lb 6, nb 4	10

1/7 (2) 2/15 (3) 3/15 (1)   (48.5 overs) 172
4/17 (5) 5/40 (4) 6/72 (7)
7/83 (8) 8/87 (6) 9/89 (9) 10/172 (10)

1/0 (2)   (6 wkts, 77.2 overs) 285
2/79 (1) 3/101 (4)
4/163 (5) 5/175 (6) 6/187 (7)

Murtagh 14–3–46–4; Bamber 13–7–24–3; Helm 9–0–36–0; Roland-Jones 9–2–31–2; Robson 2–0–15–0; Andersson 1.5–0–17–1. *Second innings*—Murtagh 21–3–71–1; Bamber 20.2–2–77–3; Roland-Jones 21–2–75–2; Helm 12–1–42–0; Andersson 3–0–14–0.

Umpires: R. A. Kettleborough and C. M. Watts.   Referee: D. A. Cosker.

At Southampton, April 15–18. MIDDLESEX lost to HAMPSHIRE by 249 runs. *Middlesex are all out for 79 in their first innings.*

MIDDLESEX v SURREY

At Lord's, April 22–24. Middlesex won by ten wickets. Middlesex 21pts, Surrey 3pts. Toss: Middlesex. First-class debut: L. B. K. Hollman. County debut: P. S. P. Handscomb.

Middlesex avoided a third successive defeat with a dominant display, inspired by their seamers, who shared 18 wickets (there was a run-out, and the other went to the debutant leg-spinner, Luke Hollman). Surrey had been shot out on the first day for 154, with Amla picking up the first half of a four-ball pair. Middlesex were ahead on the second morning, even though Handscomb, their new captain – who had replaced stand-in skipper Stevie Eskinazi in the side after quarantining on arrival from Australia – was out for a third-ball duck. Surrey shelled five chances, which allowed Middlesex to recover from 16 for three, all to Topley in nine deliveries. Robson, who batted for five and a half hours for the second home game in a row, put on 133 with White, and later Roland-Jones thumped seven boundaries. He then took four wickets as Surrey struggled again, despite Burns's 54, and Middlesex's openers completed the job before lunch on the third day. Roland-Jones finished with match figures of seven for 70, but a few days later picked up a knee injury which would keep him out for almost four months.

Close of play: first day, Middlesex 114-3 (Robson 46, White 52); second day, Surrey 105-3 (Burns 54, Foakes 16).

Surrey

*R. J. Burns c Robson b Murtagh	8	– c Simpson b Bamber	54
M. D. Stoneman c Simpson b Roland-Jones	44	– lbw b Bamber	2
H. M. Amla lbw b Murtagh	0	– lbw b Roland-Jones	0
O. J. D. Pope c Robson b Roland-Jones	22	– c Simpson b Andersson	32
†B. T. Foakes c Simpson b Roland-Jones	11	– c Robson b Murtagh	17
J. L. Smith b Murtagh	19	– lbw b Bamber	11
J. Clark c Gubbins b Murtagh	0	– b Roland-Jones	4
R. Clarke run out (Gubbins)	28	– lbw b Murtagh	3
R. J. W. Topley b Bamber	10	– b Roland-Jones	4
K. A. J. Roach b Hollman	8	– not out	0
G. S. Virdi not out	0	– c Simpson b Roland-Jones	0
B 1, lb 2, w 1	4	Lb 3	3

1/22 (1) 2/22 (3) 3/51 (4)   (55.4 overs) 154   1/16 (2) 2/20 (3)   (52 overs) 130
4/72 (5) 5/107 (6) 6/107 (2)   3/79 (4) 4/105 (1)
7/107 (7) 8/124 (9) 9/153 (10) 10/154 (8)   5/113 (5) 6/117 (6) 7/124 (7)
                                                          8/130 (9) 9/130 (9) 10/130 (11)

Murtagh 15–8–28–4; Bamber 14–2–51–1; Roland-Jones 14.4–4–41–3; Andersson 10.4–2–27–0; Hollman 2–1–4–1. *Second innings*—Murtagh 19–9–30–2; Bamber 11–2–30–3; Roland-Jones 12–4–29–4; Andersson 5–1–22–1; Hollman 5–0–16–0.

Middlesex

S. D. Robson lbw b Topley	95	– (2) not out	7
M. D. E. Holden c Burns b Topley	3	– (1) not out	11
N. R. T. Gubbins b Topley	4		
*P. S. P. Handscomb b Topley	0		
R. G. White b Clark	72		
†J. A. Simpson c Foakes b Clark	3		
M. K. Andersson b Clarke	13		
T. S. Roland-Jones not out	46		
L. B. K. Hollman c Virdi b Clark	2		
E. R. Bamber c Clarke b Roach	13		
T. J. Murtagh c Amla b Clarke	0		
B 14, lb 3	17		

1/8 (2) 2/16 (3) 3/16 (4)　　　(100.5 overs) 268　　　(no wkt, 2.3 overs) 18
4/149 (5) 5/161 (6) 6/189 (7)
7/215 (1) 8/228 (9) 9/261 (10) 10/268 (11)

Roach 25–7–53–1; Topley 26–7–56–4; Clark 21–4–58–3; Clarke 20.5–2–76–2; Virdi 8–3–8–0. *Second innings*—Roach 1.3–0–13–0; Topley 1–0–5–0.

Umpires: N. L. Bainton and M. A. Gough.　　Referee: P. Whitticase.

At Taunton, April 29–May 2. MIDDLESEX lost to SOMERSET by four wickets.

MIDDLESEX v GLOUCESTERSHIRE

At Lord's, May 6–8. Gloucestershire won by seven wickets. Gloucestershire 21pts, Middlesex 4pts. Toss: Gloucestershire. Championship debut: T. N. Walallawitta.

Middlesex had already lost twice to Somerset, and their West Country woes continued with a crushing three-day defeat by Gloucestershire, who remained top of the group. Again, poor batting on a sporting pitch was to blame. White stood alone on the first day, reaching the seventies (though not three figures) for the fourth match running, but a collective second-innings failure, in which only Gubbins and Simpson passed 15, made the result a formality. Gloucestershire knocked off the 90 they needed, with the former Middlesex player Lace rubbing salt into the wound. Bracey, dropped twice, had top-scored in their first innings with 75, while Cockbain and Higgins – another Middlesex old boy – ensured a small but significant lead. Left-arm seamer Payne finished with a career-best 11 for 87. The match was televised by Sky Sports, using the cameras in place for online streaming, after the cancellation of the IPL a few days earlier.

Close of play: first day, Gloucestershire 19-1 (Brathwaite 5, Taylor 2); second day, Middlesex 26-3 (Gubbins 7, Bamber 0).

Middlesex

S. D. Robson lbw b Higgins	12	– (2) lbw b Higgins	8
M. D. E. Holden lbw b Taylor	16	– (1) c and b Payne	7
N. R. T. Gubbins c Hankins b Payne	18	– lbw b Payne	52
*P. S. P. Handscomb b Payne	10	– c Bracey b Taylor	4
R. G. White not out	76	– (6) b Payne	1
†J. A. Simpson lbw b Smith	17	– (7) c and b Payne	40
M. K. Andersson lbw b Taylor	20	– (8) c Brathwaite b Payne	15
J. A. R. Harris b Payne	8	– (9) lbw b Payne	0
E. R. Bamber c Bracey b Higgins	3	– (5) c Bracey b Higgins	0
T. N. Walallawita c Smith b Payne	4	– not out	11
T. J. Murtagh b Payne	0	– c Bracey b Worrall	6
B 12, lb 14	26	B 5, lb 3	8

1/23 (1) 2/48 (2) 3/61 (4)   (80.5 overs) 210
4/78 (3) 5/117 (6) 6/159 (7)
7/184 (8) 8/195 (9) 9/210 (10) 10/210 (11)

1/12 (2) 2/16 (1)   (51.1 overs) 152
3/23 (4) 4/45 (5)
5/46 (6) 6/109 (3) 7/134 (7)
8/134 (9) 9/135 (8) 10/152 (11)

Payne 18.5–6–31–5; Higgins 23–7–49–2; Worrall 17–4–47–0; Taylor 16.5–5–36–2; Smith 6–0–21–1. *Second innings*—Payne 17–5–56–6; Higgins 16–2–54–2; Worrall 9.1–4–15–1; Taylor 9–4–19–1.

Gloucestershire

K. C. Brathwaite c Robson b Harris	33	– lbw b Harris	21
*C. D. J. Dent run out (Walallawita)	10	– b Bamber	25
M. D. Taylor c Simpson b Andersson	13		
†J. R. Bracey c Harris b Andersson	75	– (3) c Murtagh b Bamber	13
T. C. Lace lbw b Murtagh	2	– (4) not out	31
I. A. Cockbain b Harris	51	– (5) not out	1
R. F. Higgins lbw b Murtagh	49		
G. T. Hankins c Robson b Andersson	11		
T. M. J. Smith c Simpson b Bamber	7		
D. A. Payne c Handscomb b Bamber	10		
D. J. Worrall not out	3		
B 2, lb 3, nb 4	9	Lb 2	2

1/13 (2) 2/43 (3) 3/89 (1)   (87.2 overs) 273
4/100 (5) 5/191 (6) 6/205 (4)
7/235 (8) 8/260 (7) 9/264 (9) 10/273 (10)

1/34 (2)   (3 wkts, 26.2 overs) 93
2/50 (3) 3/87 (1)

Murtagh 22–6–57–2; Bamber 22.2–8–34–2; Harris 15–1–49–2; Andersson 15–3–64–3; Walallawita 12–1–58–0; Robson 1–0–6–0. *Second innings*—Murtagh 6–1–17–0; Bamber 9–3–29–2; Andersson 6–2–12–0; Harris 4–0–28–1; Walallawita 1.2–0–5–0.

Umpires: P. R. Pollard and B. V. Taylor.   Referee: P. M. Such.

MIDDLESEX v HAMPSHIRE

At Lord's, May 13–15. Hampshire won by seven wickets. Hampshire 20pts, Middlesex 3pts. Toss: Hampshire. Championship debuts: B. C. Cullen, J. L. B. Davies.

A fifth defeat out of six piled the pressure on Middlesex's coaching staff, with supporters becoming ever more vocal after another dire batting display on another seam-friendly surface. Hampshire had bowled them out for 79 in Southampton a month earlier, and now Middlesex again collapsed, despite a nuggety 51 from Gubbins in the first innings. Hampshire were also up against it, at 73 for six late on the second day (only 36 overs had been possible on the first), but 62 from Vince and a county-best 84 from Barker, which contained four forthright sixes, put them in front. Hampshire's cosmopolitan new-ball pair took over. Mohammad Abbas had picked up nine wickets in the victory at the Rose Bowl, and now Abbott went two better: as Middlesex's second innings sank without trace, they collected eight for 65 between them. Hampshire were relieved to reach their target in the last over of the third day, despite some brief rain breaks, as more bad weather was forecast for the fourth.

Close of play: first day, Middlesex 90-4 (Gubbins 21, Simpson 20); second day, Hampshire 131-7 (Barker 23, Abbott 0).

Middlesex

S. D. Robson c Dawson b Abbott	20	– (2) lbw b Mohammad Abbas	5
J. L. B. Davies c Dawson b Wheal	24	– (1) c McManus b Abbott	8
N. R. T. Gubbins b Mohammad Abbas	51	– c McManus b Abbott	2
*P. S. P. Handscomb b Abbott	0	– lbw b Abbott	24
R. G. White b Abbott	3	– c and b Mohammad Abbas	5
†J. A. Simpson lbw b Abbott	20	– b Wheal	9
M. K. Andersson lbw b Mohammad Abbas	5	– lbw b Barker	9
J. A. R. Harris b Mohammad Abbas	0	– lbw b Abbott	16
B. C. Cullen c Vince b Abbott	27	– lbw b Mohammad Abbas	11
E. R. Bamber lbw b Abbott	7	– lbw b Abbott	4
T. J. Murtagh not out	12	– not out	0
B 1, lb 2	3	B 4, lb 4	8

1/33 (1) 2/47 (2) 3/52 (4)   (68.1 overs) 172   1/13 (2) 2/17 (1)   (29.5 overs) 101
4/56 (5) 5/91 (6) 6/100 (7)   3/26 (3) 4/41 (5)
7/100 (8) 8/153 (3) 9/159 (9) 10/172 (10)   5/49 (4) 6/67 (7) 7/67 (6)
                                         8/95 (8) 9/97 (9) 10/101 (10)

Barker 15–4–38–0; Mohammad Abbas 21–7–46–3; Wheal 13–3–39–1; Abbott 18.1–6–44–6; Dawson 1–0–2–0. *Second innings*—Mohammad Abbas 10–4–24–3; Abbott 9.5–2–41–5; Wheal 5–0–10–1; Barker 5–1–18–1.

Hampshire

J. J. Weatherley c Andersson b Bamber	3	– lbw b Bamber	7
I. G. Holland b Bamber	0	– lbw b Murtagh	22
T. P. Alsop lbw b Murtagh	6	– (4) not out	9
S. A. Northeast lbw b Harris	11	– (5) not out	18
*J. M. Vince b Cullen	62		
L. A. Dawson c White b Murtagh	13	– (3) lbw b Murtagh	7
†L. D. McManus lbw b Bamber	1		
K. H. D. Barker c Handscomb b Harris	84		
K. J. Abbott b Cullen	6		
B. T. J. Wheal b Simpson b Murtagh	6		
Mohammad Abbas not out	0		
Lb 8, w 2, nb 6	16	Lb 3	3

1/2 (2) 2/9 (1) 3/9 (3)   (73 overs) 208   1/24 (1)   (3 wkts, 15.3 overs) 66
4/37 (4) 5/67 (6) 6/73 (7)   2/33 (3) 3/40 (2)
7/127 (5) 8/143 (9) 9/177 (10) 10/208 (8)

Murtagh 16–5–48–3; Bamber 20–5–55–3; Harris 13–1–53–2; Cullen 14–5–32–2; Andersson 10–3–12–0. *Second innings*—Bamber 8–4–17–1; Cullen 4–0–17–0; Murtagh 3.3–0–29–2.

Umpires: N. L. Bainton and N. A. Mallender. Referee: W. M. Noon.

At The Oval, May 20–23. MIDDLESEX drew with SURREY.

At Leicester, May 27–30. MIDDLESEX lost to LEICESTERSHIRE by five wickets.

At Cheltenham, July 5–8. MIDDLESEX lost to GLOUCESTERSHIRE by 164 runs.

MIDDLESEX v LEICESTERSHIRE

At Northwood, July 11–14. Middlesex won by 121 runs. Middlesex 21pts (after 1pt penalty), Leicestershire 4pts. Toss: Middlesex. First-class debut: J. B. Cracknell. County debut: A. Sakande.

Middlesex's victory still left them 27 points adrift of Leicestershire at the bottom of the group, although they did at least foil the visitors' attempt at a second big turnaround. At Grace Road in May, Leicestershire had chased down 378 after trailing by 159; here they were set 293 after a first-innings deficit of 96. Four wickets for Murtagh – leading Middlesex for the first time, as Handscomb had tested positive for Covid – prevented a repeat. A serene innings from Robson, who batted seven hours for his first century since the opening day of the season, had underpinned Middlesex. He put on 73 for the first wicket with de Caires, who survived a bang on the helmet from Mike, before dragging him into his stumps. The lower order was dismantled by Davis, who had gone wicketless on the first day but, moving the ball around, snapped up the last five on the second. Middlesex's seamers then restricted Leicestershire to 228, the main resistance coming from Ackermann and Inglis. Davis was a thorn again as Middlesex tottered to 17 for four, with Ackermann taking three sharp slip catches, but the recalled Eskinazi – who had torn a groin muscle in the first innings – emerged with a runner, and survived for 224 minutes to stretch the lead. With 89 overs to see out, Leicestershire reached 153 for five in the 57th, but the rest tumbled for 18.

Close of play: first day, Middlesex 280-3 (Robson 138, Cracknell 11); second day, Leicestershire 174-5 (Ackermann 65, Mike 1); third day, Middlesex 176-7 (Eskinazi 53, Sowter 10).

Middlesex

S. D. Robson c Inglis b Davis	154	– c Ackermann b Davis	4
J. M. de Caires b Mike	17	– c Ackermann b Sakande	2
S. S. Eskinazi retired hurt	23	– (7) not out	66
M. D. E. Holden c Inglis b Barnes	28	– (3) c Inglis b Davis	0
D. J. Mitchell c Swindells b Sakande	38	– lbw b Mike	23
J. B. Cracknell lbw b Sakande	13	– (4) c Ackermann b Davis	7
†R. G. White c Inglis b Davis	5	– (6) c Barnes b Parkinson	34
J. A. R. Harris lbw b Davis	5	– lbw b Barnes	26
N. A. Sowter b Davis	3	– c Harris b Parkinson	10
E. R. Bamber not out	8	– c Mike b Parkinson	6
*T. J. Murtagh c Parkinson b Davis	4	– c Davis b Parkinson	0
B 7, lb 9, nb 10	26	B 4, lb 6, nb 8	18

1/73 (2) 2/171 (4) 3/266 (5)	(108.4 overs)	324	1/6 (1) 2/6 (2)	(77.4 overs)	196
4/282 (6) 5/295 (7) 6/304 (1)			3/6 (3) 4/17 (4)		
7/311 (8) 8/312 (9) 9/324 (11)			5/55 (5) 6/82 (6) 7/159 (8)		
			8/176 (9) 9/196 (10) 10/196 (11)		

In the first innings Eskinazi retired hurt at 126-1.

Davis 27.4–4–66–5; Sakande 22–4–80–2; Barnes 16–2–49–1; Parkinson 23–6–62–0; Mike 20–7–51–1. *Second innings*—Davis 14–6–21–3; Sakande 16–6–38–1; Barnes 14–2–43–1; Mike 13–3–49–1; Parkinson 20.4–10–35–4.

Leicestershire

S. T. Evans c Sowter b Murtagh	4	– b Murtagh	0
L. J. Hill lbw b Murtagh	9	– c de Caires b Harris	17
M. S. Harris c White b Harris	31	– b Sowter	46
*C. N. Ackermann b Bamber	82	– c White b Murtagh	16
†J. P. Inglis b Bamber	49	– c White b Murtagh	52
H. J. Swindells c Sowter b Murtagh	6	– c Cracknell b Bamber	11
B. W. M. Mike c White b Mitchell	10	– c White b Mitchell	7
C. F. Parkinson c White b Mitchell	1	– b Murtagh	0
E. Barnes c White b Harris	4	– lbw b Harris	6
A. Sakande not out	8	– b Harris	9
W. S. Davis c Cracknell b Bamber	11	– not out	0
Lb 5, nb 8	13	B 1, lb 5, w 1	7

1/4 (1) 2/29 (2) 3/52 (3) (86 overs) 228
4/149 (5) 5/170 (6) 6/195 (7)
7/197 (8) 8/206 (9) 9/216 (4) 10/228 (11)

1/0 (1) 2/64 (2) (61 overs) 171
3/72 (3) 4/100 (4)
5/129 (6) 6/153 (5) 7/153 (8)
8/161 (9) 9/163 (7) 10/171 (10)

Murtagh 20–5–49–3; Bamber 26–7–54–3; Harris 20–1–50–2; Mitchell 15–3–43–2; Sowter 5–0–27–0. *Second innings*—Murtagh 15.3–5–36–4; Bamber 14–5–39–1; Harris 13.3–0–50–3; Mitchell 10–3–25–1; Sowter 8–0–15–1.

Umpires: B. J. Debenham and M. Newell. Referee: A. J. Swann.

DIVISION THREE

MIDDLESEX v DERBYSHIRE

At Lord's, August 30–September 2. Middlesex won by 112 runs. Middlesex 21pts, Derbyshire 4pts. Toss: Middlesex. County debut: M. D. Stoneman.

In his first match since a knee injury in April, Roland-Jones took three wickets in ten balls to derail Derbyshire's pursuit of 334. He might have nabbed Critchley as well, only for three fielders to converge on a top edge without any of them calling for it. The first of his victims had been Godleman, formerly of Middlesex, whose 70 put his side on track after a sticky start: 46 balls before a run was scored. Roland-Jones finished it off with two more wickets, but was well supported by Murtagh (who claimed seven in the match) and Bamber, parsimonious in the second innings after a career-best five for 41 in the first. Earlier, White had given Middlesex the upper hand with his maiden first-class century, before du Plooy missed three figures for Derbyshire. Determined batting down the order – Murtagh made 31 from No. 11 in a last-wicket stand of 58 – enabled Middlesex to set a testing target, although Mark Stoneman completed a four-ball pair on his first appearance since leaving Surrey.

Close of play: first day, Middlesex 218-5 (White 101, Simpson 29); second day, Derbyshire 201-9 (Conners 2, Aitchison 4); third day, Derbyshire 42-1 (Godleman 21, Wood 18).

Middlesex

S. D. Robson lbw b Conners	9	– (2) b Thomson	52
M. D. Stoneman lbw b Conners	0	– (1) b Conners	0
S. S. Eskinazi lbw b Reece	5	– c Dal b Conners	23
R. G. White c Critchley b Conners	120	– c Guest b Aitchison	0
M. D. E. Holden lbw b Reece	13	– c Aitchison b Thomson	44
M. K. Andersson c Critchley b Thomson	53	– lbw b Dal	42
†J. A. Simpson c Aitchison b Dal	36	– c Guest b Dal	12
T. S. Roland-Jones c and b Dal	6	– not out	33
E. R. Bamber c Wood b Critchley	7	– c Guest b Critchley	1
T. N. Walallawita not out	20	– b Thomson	12
*T. J. Murtagh c Critchley b Aitchison	5	– c Dal b Aitchison	31
B 1, lb 5, nb 2	8	Lb 6	6

1/5 (2) 2/10 (1) 3/14 (3) (88.2 overs) 282
4/52 (5) 5/157 (6) 6/236 (7)
7/244 (8) 8/256 (9) 9/263 (4) 10/282 (11)

1/0 (1) 2/40 (2) (64.3 overs) 256
3/45 (4) 4/98 (2)
5/141 (5) 6/177 (7) 7/178 (6)
8/179 (9) 9/198 (10) 10/256 (11)

Conners 18–2–65–3; Reece 21–4–84–2; Aitchison 19.2–6–37–1; Dal 17–3–52–2; Thomson 5–1–13–1; Critchley 8–2–25–1. *Second innings*—Conners 10–2–53–2; Reece 5–0–31–0; Aitchison 12.3–1–37–2; Thomson 17–1–71–3; Dal 8–2–22–2; Critchley 12–1–36–1.

Derbyshire

L. M. Reece c White b Murtagh	24	– c Simpson b Murtagh	0
*B. A. Godleman c White b Bamber	0	– c Andersson b Roland-Jones	70
T. A. Wood b Bamber	1	– lbw b Murtagh	18
J. L. du Plooy c Simpson b Murtagh	90	– b Murtagh	13
M. J. J. Critchley lbw b Murtagh	5	– c Robson b Andersson	58
A. L. Hughes c Holden b Murtagh	5	– c Robson b Roland-Jones	1
†B. D. Guest c Simpson b Andersson	5	– b Roland-Jones	0
A. K. Dal b Bamber	48	– run out (Andersson)	19
A. T. Thomson c Simpson b Bamber	16	– b Roland-Jones	18
S. Conners c Andersson b Bamber	6	– c Holden b Roland-Jones	2
B. W. Aitchison not out	4	– not out	12
Lb 1	1	B 6, lb 4	10
	—		—
	205		221

1/4 (2) 2/14 (3) 3/48 (1)   (61.5 overs) 205   1/0 (1) 2/42 (3)   (81.2 overs) 221
4/54 (5) 5/60 (6) 6/76 (7)   3/60 (4) 4/140 (2)
7/167 (4) 8/195 (8) 9/196 (9) 10/205 (10)   5/147 (6) 6/147 (7) 7/185 (8)
                                           8/185 (5) 9/198 (10) 10/221 (9)

Murtagh 17–1–60–4; Bamber 15.5–5–41–5; Andersson 10–3–39–1; Roland-Jones 14–0–51–0; Walallawita 5–1–13–0. *Second innings*—Murtagh 18–6–48–3; Bamber 21–10–35–0; Andersson 15–4–48–1; Roland-Jones 16.2–5–36–5; Walallawita 10–2–36–0; Holden 1–0–8–0.

Umpires: P. J. Hartley and Hassan Adnan.   Referee: S. J. Davis.

At Hove, September 6–9. MIDDLESEX beat SUSSEX by an innings and 54 runs. *Sam Robson and Mark Stoneman share a county-record opening stand of 376.*

MIDDLESEX v WORCESTERSHIRE

At Lord's, September 12–15. Middlesex won by 101 runs. Middlesex 19pts, Worcestershire 3pts. Toss: Worcestershire.

A fourth consecutive win kept Middlesex top of Division Three, and suggested a corner might have been turned after a wretched run in all formats. It was their best Championship sequence in a season since eight in 1995. In a low-scoring game, they owed much to Holden, who made 52 (his only first-class half-century of a subdued season) and 46. Worcestershire were no pushovers, with their captain Leach to the fore, and claimed a narrow lead after 18 wickets went down on the first day. They were helped by No. 10 Josh Baker's entertaining unbeaten 61, which featured ten fours and a six; he had managed only 18 runs in four previous first-class innings. Trailing by 27, Middlesex were under pressure in the third innings again, and lost Stoneman for his third duck in four Lord's innings since his arrival (this one lasted 36 balls). But from an unpromising 39 for four, the middle order manoeuvred Middlesex into calmer waters, with Nos 5 to 8 all reaching 45, before Morris took the last three wickets in nine balls to finish with six. After the third day was washed out, Worcestershire needed 221 but, with the seamers in control on another helpful Lord's surface, they lasted less than 36 overs. Roderick remained unbeaten with 42 in 140 minutes.

Close of play: first day, Worcestershire 113-8 (Morris 15, Baker 11); second day, Middlesex 233-6 (Simpson 59, Hollman 40); third day, no play.

Middlesex

S. D. Robson b Leach	20	– (2) c Cox b Leach	22
M. D. Stoneman lbw b Leach	12	– (1) lbw b Morris	0
S. S. Eskinazi lbw b Morris	7	– c Roderick b Morris	8
R. G. White lbw b Barnard	1	– c Mitchell b Morris	4
M. D. E. Holden c Mitchell b Barnard	52	– c Mitchell b Pennington	46
M. K. Andersson c Mitchell b Leach	0	– lbw b Barnard	45
†J. A. Simpson b Pennington	12	– c Haynes b Leach	59
L. B. K. Hollman b Barnard	4	– c Cox b Morris	46
T. S. Roland-Jones b Barnard	1	– lbw b Morris	1
E. R. Bamber not out	10	– not out	7
*T. J. Murtagh c Libby b Pennington	6	– c D'Oliveira b Morris	0
B 4, lb 9, nb 6	19	B 5, lb 4	9

1/33 (2) 2/47 (3) 3/48 (4)   (51 overs) 144
4/73 (1) 5/81 (6) 6/108 (7)
7/123 (8) 8/126 (5) 9/127 (9) 10/144 (11)

1/21 (1) 2/31 (3)   (93.4 overs) 247
3/39 (4) 4/39 (2)
5/105 (6) 6/153 (5) 7/239 (7)
8/240 (9) 9/241 (8) 10/247 (11)

Leach 14–4–30–3; Pennington 13–4–29–2; Barnard 15–3–43–4; Morris 9–1–29–1. *Second innings*—Leach 24–12–35–2; Pennington 16–5–54–1; Barnard 14–2–45–1; Morris 22.4–8–52–6; Baker 12–1–44–0; D'Oliveira 5–1–8–0.

Worcestershire

D. K. H. Mitchell c Simpson b Murtagh	4	– c Robson b Murtagh	7
J. D. Libby lbw b Bamber	13	– c Simpson b Bamber	6
G. H. Roderick c Simpson b Roland-Jones	42	– not out	42
J. A. Haynes lbw b Murtagh	0	– b Roland-Jones	9
B. L. D'Oliveira c Murtagh b Bamber	3	– c Simpson b Roland-Jones	2
E. G. Barnard c Eskinazi b Murtagh	4	– c Simpson b Andersson	28
†O. B. Cox c Eskinazi b Bamber	0	– lbw b Andersson	4
*J. Leach lbw b Murtagh	21	– b Bamber	11
C. A. J. Morris b Murtagh	20	– (10) b Andersson	1
J. O. Baker not out	61	– (9) b Bamber	2
D. Y. Pennington lbw b Hollman	3	– c Simpson b Bamber	1
		B 1, lb 5	6

1/12 (1) 2/24 (2) 3/25 (4)   (43.4 overs) 171
4/28 (5) 5/37 (6) 6/44 (7)
7/81 (3) 8/101 (8) 9/130 (9) 10/171 (11)

1/12 (2) 2/20 (1)   (35.3 overs) 119
3/39 (4) 4/51 (5)
5/94 (6) 6/98 (7) 7/113 (8)
8/115 (9) 9/118 (10) 10/119 (11)

Murtagh 17–4–64–5; Bamber 13–1–52–3; Andersson 5–0–28–0; Roland-Jones 8–0–24–1; Hollman 0.4–0–3–1. *Second innings*—Murtagh 11–1–40–1; Bamber 11.3–3–28–4; Andersson 7–2–22–3; Roland-Jones 6–1–23–2.

Umpires: N. L. Bainton and R. A. White. Referee: A. J. Swann.

At Canterbury, September 21–24. MIDDLESEX lost to KENT by two wickets. *Kent chase down 373 to pip Middlesex to the divisional title.*

NORTHAMPTONSHIRE

A chapter ends for the talented Mr Ripley

Andrew Radd

Significant change was in the air even before the close of an underwhelming season for Northamptonshire, which began promisingly enough but ended in acute embarrassment. Being dismissed for 45, their lowest first-class total since 1946, and defeated in 96.3 overs by Essex at Chelmsford – the shortest completed Championship match scheduled for four days – was a miserable way for David Ripley to sign off as head coach after nine years.

He had announced his intention to step down in an emotional statement to the club's AGM a couple of weeks earlier. Former captain Alex Wakely, whose successful partnership with Ripley yielded the Twenty20 title in 2013 and 2016, retired from the professional game at the end of May, while another central figure in those triumphs – South African batsman Richard Levi – was released. Promoted from assistant coach to succeed Ripley (who will remain at the club in a development capacity), John Sadler admitted after the Chelmsford debacle that some of the players had "run out of steam".

Just two more runs could have made a big difference to Northamptonshire's season. Momentum from a successful long run-chase against Glamorgan in the third round of Championship fixtures continued into a memorable contest with Yorkshire at Headingley. On the threshold of winning there for the first time in 31 years, Northamptonshire lost by one run. There was plenty of fighting talk about being the better side, but the result seemed to sap the team's belief. More tangibly, despite home-and-away victories over Sussex, they needed to beat Yorkshire in the return at Wantage Road to sustain realistic hopes of a place in Division One. On a deliberately bowler-friendly pitch, Northamptonshire – a man short in the first innings because Luke Procter had suffered a family bereavement – lost another close game. Finishing fourth in Division Two was a disappointment, though it proved academic: the club's 2019 promotion finally takes effect in 2022.

Even more frustrating were the white-ball performances. Five defeats plus a no-result at the start of the Vitality Blast set the tone, and Ripley revealed later that the contrast with past T20 glories – packed houses replaced by grumbling spectators drifting away early – was a big factor in his decision. Hopes were high for the Royal London Cup, with Northamptonshire losing fewer players to The Hundred than most, but only Derbyshire finished below them. Since winning the Blast in 2016, they have reached the T20 knockouts just once, and not at all in the 50-over tournament. Reviving their fortunes in these competitions will be Sadler's most pressing task. In December, he was joined by Ben Smith, formerly of Leicestershire and Worcestershire, as batting coach.

Still only 23, Ricardo Vasconcelos underlined his immense value, and was the Players' Player of the Season. He didn't miss a single competitive match,

Andy Kearns, Getty Images

Ricardo Vasconcelos

scored most runs in every format, and deputised as captain and wicketkeeper. His workload was not ideal, and probably contributed to a falling-off in his Championship form, after a blistering start brought 397 runs, including two centuries, in his first five innings. Ben Curran had been earmarked as Vasconcelos's red-ball opening partner, but his lack of runs forced a reappraisal, and Emilio Gay seized his opportunity with a maiden first-class century, against Kent at Canterbury. Saif Zaib was another young batsman to prove his versatility, while the more experienced Rob Keogh (the only other ever-present) enjoyed an outstanding season, securing a new two-year deal. His undefeated 71 – interrupted by a family funeral which he attended online – to help save the match at Cardiff, and 99 in the exciting victory over Surrey, were among the innings of the season. The batting will be bolstered in 2022 by the signing of New Zealand international Will Young, who hopes to be available for most of the Championship and one-day games, while his compatriot, all-rounder Jimmy Neesham, joins for the Blast.

With the ball, Ben Sanderson proved as challenging as ever when conditions offered help. He and Gareth Berg (now 41) formed an incisive new-ball partnership, sharing 19 wickets in the home Championship victory over Sussex, before Berg suffered a freak ankle injury during a warm-up in July, and couldn't play again. Tom Taylor, in his first full season with Northamptonshire, was a hard-working addition; his bowling statistics did not reflect his worth. Simon Kerrigan's return to full-time county cricket was welcomed around the circuit, and his left-arm spin was rarely collared.

The progression of several youngsters from the club's talent pathway represented perhaps the most positive feature of the summer. James Sales, the 18-year-old son of former county captain David, pulled the winning boundary on first-class debut against Surrey, and followed up with a half-century at home to Durham; he soon earned a professional contract. Left-arm wrist-spinner Fred Heldreich, wicketkeeper-batsman Harry Gouldstone, and all-rounder Gus Miller all signed rookie terms for 2022.

At the end of the season, chairman Gavin Warren declared that, after five years of focusing on survival, the priority now was ensuring the club's relevance. He strengthened relationships with neighbouring National Counties – a task expected to form a key part of Ripley's new responsibilities.

Northamptonshire put out an anti-racism statement after former fast bowler Maurice Chambers alleged he had been abused by a team-mate during his time at the club in 2014 and 2015.

NORTHAMPTONSHIRE RESULTS

County Championship matches – Played 14: Won 4, Lost 5, Drawn 5.
Vitality T20 Blast matches – Played 13: Won 4, Lost 8, No result 1. Cancelled 1.
Royal London Cup matches – Played 8: Won 2, Lost 4, No result 2.

LV= County Championship, 4th in Group 3, 4th in Division 2;
Vitality Blast, 9th in North Group; Royal London Cup, 8th in Group 2.

COUNTY CHAMPIONSHIP AVERAGES, BATTING AND FIELDING

Cap		Birthplace	M	I	NO	R	HS	100	Avge	Ct/St
2021	†R. S. Vasconcelos†† .	Johannesburg, SA . .	14	24	1	845	185*	2	36.73	32/1
2019	A. M. Rossington	Edgware	11	16	1	537	94	0	35.80	24/2
2019	R. I. Keogh	Dunstable	14	24	2	766	126	2	34.81	1
2020	†L. A. Procter	Oldham	13	21	2	597	93	0	31.42	2
	G. K. Berg	Cape Town, SA	9	10	3	216	69*	0	30.85	3
	J. J. G. Sales	Northampton‡.	3	6	2	112	53	0	28.00	1
	†S. A. Zaib	High Wycombe	13	22	1	576	135	1	27.42	4
	H. O. M. Gouldstone . .	Kettering‡.	4	8	2	155	67*	0	25.83	0
	†E. N. Gay	Bedford	9	17	0	391	101	1	23.00	5
	T. A. I. Taylor	Stoke-on-Trent	11	17	2	316	50	0	21.06	6
	S. C. Kerrigan	Preston	11	19	6	224	45*	0	17.23	3
	†W. D. Parnell¶	Port Elizabeth, SA . .	6	7	0	107	54	0	15.28	0
	†B. J. Curran	Northampton‡.	7	10	0	148	36	0	14.80	6
	†C. J. White	Kendal.	4	7	5	29	15*	0	14.50	0
	C. O. Thurston	Cambridge	6	10	0	142	48	0	14.20	3
	N. L. Buck	Leicester	4	6	1	69	21*	0	13.80	1
2018	B. W. Sanderson	Sheffield	13	17	3	72	20	0	5.14	2

Also batted: J. J. Cobb (*Leicester*) (cap 2018) (1 match) 1, 0 (1 ct); A. G. Wakely (*Hammersmith*)
(cap 2012) (1 match) 4 (1 ct).

‡ *Born in Northamptonshire.* ¶ *Official overseas player.* †† *Other non-England-qualified.*

BOWLING

	Style	O	M	R	W	BB	5I	Avge
W. D. Parnell	LFM	114.4	26	427	18	5-64	2	23.72
G. K. Berg	RFM	199.4	48	600	24	5-18	1	25.00
S. C. Kerrigan	SLA	298.5	57	766	29	5-39	2	26.41
B. W. Sanderson	RFM	435.2	117	1,155	43	5-28	3	26.86
T. A. I. Taylor	RFM	263.2	63	783	29	5-41	1	27.00
L. A. Procter	RM	115.5	29	352	13	5-42	1	27.07
N. L. Buck	RFM	107.4	11	436	10	3-65	0	43.60

Also bowled: E. N. Gay (RM) 5–0–22–1; R. I. Keogh (OB) 126.4–15–462–5; J. J. G. Sales (RM)
40–9–154–3; C. J. White (RFM) 94–10–319–5; S. A. Zaib (SLA) 43.1–6–139–3.

LEADING VITALITY BLAST AVERAGES (100 runs/15 overs)

Batting	Runs	HS	Avge	SR	Ct/St	**Bowling**	W	BB	Avge	ER
J. J. Cobb	185	63	30.83	**165.17**	6	Mohammad Nabi .	9	2-23	24.00	**6.00**
A. M. Rossington .	136	59	17.00	**144.68**	3/2	F. J. Heldreich . . .	5	2-17	23.40	**6.50**
S. A. Zaib	134	36	19.14	**139.58**	3	G. G. White	15	4-26	23.66	**8.12**
R. I. Keogh	347	56	49.57	**125.72**	3	W. D. Parnell. . . .	8	2-28	43.25	**8.68**
Mohammad Nabi .	131	32	18.71	**118.01**	3	B. W. Sanderson .	6	3-21	40.16	**9.77**
R. S. Vasconcelos	364	78*	33.09	**117.79**	6/2	T. A. I. Taylor . . .	11	3-33	31.09	**9.96**
W. D. Parnell . .	129	25	14.33	**105.73**	5	B. D. Glover	4	1-21	43.25	**10.59**

LEADING ROYAL LONDON CUP AVERAGES (100 runs/4 wickets)

Batting	Runs	HS	Avge	SR	Ct/St	Bowling	W	BB	Avge	ER
T. A. I. Taylor ..	145	65*	72.50	93.54	2	B. W. Sanderson .	15	3-29	16.80	4.65
L. A. Procter ...	110	48	55.00	74.32	1	S. A. Zaib	5	3-37	18.40	4.18
E. N. Gay	189	84*	37.80	89.15	3	C. J. White	10	4-20	22.00	5.11
R. I. Keogh	160	52	32.00	103.22	3	T. A. I. Taylor....	9	3-24	26.44	5.80
R. S. Vasconcelos	218	88	31.14	83.84	8/1	S. C. Kerrigan ..	6	4-48	31.83	4.91
B. J. Curran	182	94	30.33	88.78	1					
S. A. Zaib	132	43	26.40	88.00	2					

FIRST-CLASS COUNTY RECORDS

Highest score for	331*	M. E. K. Hussey v Somerset at Taunton	2003
Highest score against	333	K. S. Duleepsinhji (Sussex) at Hove	1930
Leading run-scorer	28,980	D. Brookes (avge 36.13)	1934–59
Best bowling for	10-127	V. W. C. Jupp v Kent at Tunbridge Wells.........	1932
Best bowling against	10-30	C. Blythe (Kent) at Northampton	1907
Leading wicket-taker	1,102	E. W. Clark (avge 21.26).	1922–47
Highest total for	781-7 dec	v Nottinghamshire at Northampton	1995
Highest total against	701-7 dec	by Kent at Beckenham......................	2017
Lowest total for	12	v Gloucestershire at Gloucester...............	1907
Lowest total against	33	by Lancashire at Northampton.................	1977

LIST A COUNTY RECORDS

Highest score for	172*	W. Larkins v Warwickshire at Luton	1983
Highest score against	184	M. J. Lumb (Nottinghamshire) at Nottingham ...	2016
Leading run-scorer	11,010	R. J. Bailey (avge 39.46)	1983–99
Best bowling for	7-10	C. Pietersen v Denmark at Brøndby	2005
Best bowling against	7-35	D. E. Malcolm (Derbyshire) at Derby	1997
Leading wicket-taker	251	A. L. Penberthy (avge 30.45).	1989–2003
Highest total for	425	v Nottinghamshire at Nottingham	2016
Highest total against	445-8	by Nottinghamshire at Nottingham	2016
Lowest total for	41	v Middlesex at Northampton	1972
Lowest total against	56	by Leicestershire at Leicester.................	1964
	56	by Denmark at Brøndby.......................	2005

TWENTY20 COUNTY RECORDS

Highest score for	111*	L. Klusener v Worcestershire at Kidderminster.....	2007
Highest score against	161	A. Lyth (Yorkshire) at Leeds...................	2017
Leading run-scorer	2,597	A. G. Wakely (avge 26.23, SR 117.67)...........	2009–20
Best bowling for	6-21	A. J. Hall v Worcestershire at Northampton	2008
Best bowling against	5-6	P. D. Collingwood (Durham) at Chester-le-Street...	2011
Leading wicket-taker	77	**G. G. White** (avge 29.03, ER 8.23)	**2007–21**
Highest total for	231-5	v Warwickshire at Birmingham.................	2018
Highest total against	260-4	by Yorkshire at Leeds.......................	2017
Lowest total for	47	v Durham at Chester-le-Street	2011
Lowest total against	86	by Worcestershire at Worcester...............	2006

ADDRESS

County Ground, Abington Avenue, Northampton NN1 4PR; 01604 514455; info@nccc.co.uk; www.nccc.co.uk. Twitter: @NorthantsCCC.

OFFICIALS

Captain A. M. Rossington
    (ltd-overs) J. J. Cobb
Head coach 2021 D. Ripley
Assistant coach 2021/Head coach 2022
    J. L. Sadler
Academy director K. J. Innes

President Lord Naseby
Chair G. G. Warren
Chief executive R. Payne
Head groundsman C. Harvey
Scorer A. C. Kingston

GROUP THREE

NORTHAMPTONSHIRE v KENT

At Northampton, April 8–11. Drawn. Northamptonshire 15pts, Kent 14pts. Toss: Northamptonshire. County debut: M. L. Cummins.

Batsmen prospered in bitterly cold and cheerless conditions, with interruptions for bad light, rain, sleet and – on the second and fourth days – snow. Northamptonshire took three early wickets, before Leaning put on 89 with Cox and 98 with Robinson. Buck struck twice shortly before the close, but Kent were boosted on the second morning by Stevens's belligerent century. Three weeks before his 45th birthday, he drove powerfully, becoming the oldest to reach three figures in the Championship since Yorkshire's Geoffrey Boycott (45 years 272 days) and Leicestershire's Chris Balderstone (45 years 247 days), both in July 1986. A last-wicket stand of 63 between Stevens and Kent debutant Miguel Cummins was a record in this fixture. Vasconcelos then mastered the bowling with a dazzling display. In all, he hit 20 fours, including three in three balls from Cummins to move to 106. Keogh completed a more circumspect century, and – just – secured maximum batting points: he and Buck scrambled a bye off the last ball of the 110th over. When more snow fell on the final afternoon, no one complained. The game proved Wakely's last for Northamptonshire; less than seven weeks later, he announced his retirement, at the age of 32.

Close of play: first day, Kent 309-7 (Stevens 34, Milnes 5); second day, Northamptonshire 91-1 (Vasconcelos 54, Gay 1); third day, Northamptonshire 301-5 (Keogh 66, Rossington 9).

Kent

*D. J. Bell-Drummond lbw b Sanderson	9	– lbw b Sanderson	5
J. M. Cox c Gay b Buck	62	– not out	18
Z. Crawley c Rossington b Berg	14	– not out	19
J. L. Denly b Berg	1		
J. A. Leaning c Rossington b Gay	79		
†O. G. Robinson c Thurston b Buck	84		
D. I. Stevens not out	116		
G. Stewart b Buck	5		
M. E. Milnes c Wakely b Taylor	14		
H. W. Podmore st Rossington b Keogh	29		
M. L. Cummins b Taylor	24		
B 1, lb 17	18		

1/14 (1) 2/36 (3) 3/38 (4)   (128.5 overs) 455   1/7 (1)   (1 wkt, 13.1 overs) 42
4/127 (2) 5/225 (5) 6/296 (6)
7/304 (8) 8/328 (9) 9/392 (10)
10/455 (11)   110 overs: 374-8

Sanderson 28–4–113–1; Taylor 26.5–6–83–2; Buck 24–3–84–3; Berg 26–12–56–2; Keogh 21–0–93–1; Gay 3–0–8–1. *Second innings*—Taylor 7–0–32–0; Sanderson 6–3–6–1; Berg 0.1–0–4–0.

Northamptonshire

B. J. Curran b Cummins	24
R. S. Vasconcelos c Cox b Leaning	154
E. N. Gay c Robinson b Stevens	5
A. G. Wakely c Milnes b Stevens	4
C. O. Thurston b Podmore	22
R. I. Keogh c sub (M. K. O'Riordan) b Podmore	124
*A. M. Rossington b Stewart	35
T. A. I. Taylor c sub (F. J. Klaassen) b Stewart	6
N. L. Buck not out	21
G. K. Berg c Robinson b Podmore	0
B. W. Sanderson b Podmore	0
B 3, lb 10, nb 26	39

1/77 (1) 2/96 (3)   (123.4 overs) 434
3/106 (4) 4/135 (5) 5/277 (2)
6/362 (7) 7/394 (8) 8/428 (6)
9/434 (10) 10/434 (11)   110 overs: 400-7

Podmore 21.4–3–77–4; Stevens 19–1–59–2; Milnes 24–4–86–0; Cummins 19–0–90–1; Stewart 17–4–41–2; Leaning 13–1–43–1; Denly 10–0–25–0.

Umpires: R. J. Bailey and P. R. Pollard.   Referee: J. J. Whitaker.

At Manchester, April 15–18. NORTHAMPTONSHIRE lost to LANCASHIRE by 206 runs.

NORTHAMPTONSHIRE v GLAMORGAN

At Northampton, April 22–25. Northamptonshire won by seven wickets. Toss: Northamptonshire. Northamptonshire 22pts, Glamorgan 7pts. County debut: W. D. Parnell.

Second-best for much of the game, Northamptonshire brushed aside a last-day target of 355 in 79 overs, thanks mainly to Vasconcelos and Keogh, who added 239 in 46 to help them to the third-highest successful chase in their history. Put in, Glamorgan had recovered from 211 for six, a century from Cooke lifting them to 407. Northamptonshire then slipped to 76 for five, with Harris – back at

---

NORTHAMPTONSHIRE'S HIGHEST SUCCESSFUL RUN-CHASES

395-4	v Middlesex at Northampton ...	2010	330-5	v Hampshire at Southampton .	2003
384-8	v Worcestershire at Northampton	1961	330-7	v Derbyshire at Derby	2017
357-3	**v Glamorgan at Northampton .**	**2021**	324-8	v Derbyshire at Derby	1980
353-9	v Durham at Northampton	2002	322-9	v Kent at Maidstone.........	1997
334-3	v Essex at Wellingborough ...	1955	321-6	v Middlesex at Northampton .	1986
333-5	v Warwickshire at Birmingham ..	1982	321-9	v Sussex at Hastings	1986
332-3	v Somerset at Taunton	1990	316-7	v Surrey at The Oval	1994

Northamptonshire's highest fourth-innings total is 411 (set 416) at Gloucester in 2007. They also scored 390-9 (set 427) to draw at Derby in 2015.

---

his first club on a fortnight's loan from Middlesex – claiming his first wicket for Glamorgan since August 2014. But the last five added 288, to restrict the deficit to 43; one of three half-centuries came from Parnell, the South African whose Northamptonshire debut had been delayed after he was pinged by the NHS Covid-19 test-and-trace system. Cooke and Carlson were impressive again, and the visitors declared before lunch on the final day. But Vasconcelos cracked 25 fours (and a six) in a career-best 185 not out from 221 balls, and Keogh hit 19 in 126 from 140, as Glamorgan's attack grew ragged, and Northamptonshire won with 38 balls to spare.

Close of play: first day, Glamorgan 324-7 (Cooke 107, Harris 7); second day, Northamptonshire 251-7 (Parnell 25, Berg 15); third day, Glamorgan 205-4 (Carlson 25, Cooke 9).

Glamorgan

N. J. Selman b Berg	17	–	c †Vasconcelos b Berg...........	69
D. L. Lloyd c Thurston b Parnell	65	–	c †Vasconcelos b Buck	38
A. Balbirnie lbw b Berg	3	–	c sub (B. D. Glover) b Buck....	0
W. T. Root lbw b Parnell	13	–	c †Vasconcelos b Sanderson	56
K. S. Carlson b Zaib...................	54	–	c Sanderson b Buck	59
*†C. B. Cooke c Vasconcelos b Buck	136	–	not out	57
C. Z. Taylor b Zaib...................	0	–	not out	16
D. A. Douthwaite b Berg	44			
J. A. R. Harris c Rossington b Sanderson	17			
W. J. Weighell c Rossington b Parnell...........	18			
M. G. Hogan not out	25			
Lb 11, nb 4..........................	15		B 4, lb 10, nb 2.............	16

1/66 (1) 2/74 (3) 3/100 (2)   (113.1 overs) 407   1/54 (2)   (5 wkts dec, 82 overs) 311
4/105 (4) 5/211 (5) 6/211 (7)   2/54 (3) 3/154 (1)
7/303 (8) 8/349 (9) 9/375 (10)   4/169 (4) 5/280 (5)
10/407 (6)   110 overs: 375-8

Sanderson 26–5–93–1; Buck 23.4–2–97–1; Parnell 20–3–82–3; Berg 25–6–69–3; Keogh 6–1–23–0; Zaib 12.3–2–32–2. *Second innings*—Sanderson 20–3–80–1; Berg 19–2–60–1; Buck 15–2–65–3; Parnell 15–5–58–0; Zaib 13–2–34–0.

Northamptonshire

B. J. Curran c Cooke b Weighell	36	– lbw b Taylor	24
R. S. Vasconcelos c Root b Lloyd	8	– not out	185
C. O. Thurston run out (Weighell)	1	– c Balbirnie b Weighell	0
R. I. Keogh lbw b Harris	20	– c Cooke b Lloyd	126
L. A. Procter c Cooke b Douthwaite	10	– not out	13
S. A. Zaib c Harris b Lloyd	41		
*†A. M. Rossington lbw b Hogan	76		
W. D. Parnell b Weighell	54		
G. K. Berg not out	69		
N. L. Buck c Weighell b Harris	18		
B. W. Sanderson b Hogan	2		
B 9, lb 13, w 1, nb 6	29	B 7, lb 1, w 1	9

1/12 (2) 2/17 (3) 3/54 (4)   (105 overs) 364   1/81 (1)   (3 wkts, 72.4 overs) 357
4/76 (1) 5/76 (5) 6/202 (6)   2/82 (3) 3/321 (4)
7/213 (7) 8/321 (8) 9/355 (10) 10/364 (11)

Hogan 21–7–64–2; Lloyd 16–2–63–2; Harris 21–2–65–2; Weighell 21–4–56–2; Douthwaite 9–0–46–1; Taylor 17–2–48–0. *Second innings*—Hogan 13–3–66–0; Lloyd 10.4–0–47–1; Harris 16–0–73–0; Taylor 17–1–75–1; Weighell 9–0–50–1; Douthwaite 4–0–21–0; Balbirnie 3–0–17–0.

Umpires: P. J. Hartley and S. J. O'Shaughnessy.   Referee: T. J. Boon.

At Leeds, April 29–May 2. NORTHAMPTONSHIRE lost to YORKSHIRE by one run. *Northamptonshire's narrowest defeat, having twice lost by two runs.*

NORTHAMPTONSHIRE v SUSSEX

At Northampton, May 6–9. Northamptonshire won by an innings and 120 runs. Northamptonshire 24pts, Sussex 3pts. Toss: Northamptonshire. First-class debut: J. P. Sarro. County debut: T. M. Head.
    Sanderson and Berg shared 19 wickets as Northamptonshire made good the loss of the third day to rain. The result felt inevitable when Sussex crashed to 25 for seven on the first morning on a well-grassed pitch, before Robinson – dropped three times – ensured they reached three figures. He then removed Curran with the second ball of the reply, and 19-year-old Joe Sarro trapped Vasconcelos with his fifth delivery in first-class cricket, but the rest of the attack failed to sustain the pressure. Zaib completed his maiden century, and put on 198 in 47 overs for the sixth wicket with Rossington. Taylor and Berg ensured maximum batting points, and Northamptonshire glimpsed a two-day victory, before van Zyl and Brown dug in. After a blank Saturday, Berg (who finished with career-best match figures of nine for 90) and Sanderson all but settled the issue next morning, with Rawlins completing a pair. Taylor, though, claimed the final wicket. "He obviously hadn't read the script," said Sanderson, whose third career haul of ten was his second against Sussex.
    Close of play: first day, Northamptonshire 214-5 (Zaib 66, Rossington 27); second day, Sussex 154-4 (van Zyl 71, Brown 30); third day, no play.

Sussex

A. D. Thomason c Rossington b Sanderson	8	– c Curran b Sanderson	7
T. J. Haines c Vasconcelos b Sanderson	0	– c Taylor b Berg	18
S. van Zyl b Sanderson	3	– c Vasconcelos b Sanderson	72
T. M. Head c Vasconcelos b Berg	9	– c Rossington b Berg	8
T. G. R. Clark lbw b Sanderson	1	– b Sanderson	13
*†B. C. Brown lbw b Berg	0	– lbw b Berg	39
D. M. W. Rawlins c Vasconcelos b Berg	0	– c Rossington b Berg	0
O. E. Robinson not out	49	– lbw b Sanderson	23
S. C. Meaker c Rossington b Berg	23	– c Rossington b Sanderson	6
J. J. Carson b Berg	10	– b Taylor	10
J. P. Sarro c Berg b Sanderson	0	– not out	7
Lb 3	3	B 4, lb 6, nb 2	12

1/1 (2) 2/10 (1) 3/19 (3)   (42.2 overs) 106   1/24 (2) 2/34 (1)   (63.2 overs) 215
4/21 (4) 5/21 (6) 6/21 (5)   3/55 (4) 4/68 (5)
7/25 (7) 8/81 (9) 9/105 (10) 10/106 (11)   5/159 (3) 6/160 (7) 7/169 (6)
                                        8/194 (9) 9/205 (8) 10/215 (10)

Sanderson 15.2–4–28–5; Taylor 8–0–37–0; Berg 13–5–18–5; Parnell 6–1–20–0. *Second innings—* Sanderson 22–5–71–5; Berg 21–5–72–4; Taylor 8.2–3–22–1; Parnell 5–2–17–0; Keogh 4–0–9–0; Procter 3–0–14–0.

Northamptonshire

B. J. Curran lbw b Robinson	0	G. K. Berg c Sarro b Head	38
R. S. Vasconcelos lbw b Sarro	8	B. W. Sanderson not out	1
C. O. Thurston c van Zyl b Robinson	24		
R. I. Keogh c Thomason b Robinson	66	B 7, lb 8, nb 10	25
L. A. Procter b Robinson	13		
S. A. Zaib lbw b Rawlins	135	1/0 (1) 2/8 (2) (9 wkts dec, 102 overs) 441
*†A. M. Rossington c Head b Sarro	87	3/36 (3) 4/60 (5)
T. A. I. Taylor not out	44	5/148 (4) 6/346 (6)
W. D. Parnell c Brown b Robinson	0	7/354 (7) 8/357 (9) 9/420 (10)

Robinson 26–7–58–5; Sarro 14–1–71–2; Meaker 21–1–83–0; Clark 15–0–58–0; Carson 5–0–34–0; Haines 2–0–16–0; Rawlins 12–1–53–1; Thomason 3–0–30–0; Head 4–1–23–1.

Umpires: N. L. Bainton and P. K. Baldwin.   Referee: W. M. Noon.

NORTHAMPTONSHIRE v LANCASHIRE

At Northampton, May 20–23. Drawn. Northamptonshire 8pts, Lancashire 8pts. Toss: Northamptonshire.
Excitement about the return of spectators to Wantage Road for the first time since September 2019 was doused by the weather, which allowed only 34.3 overs. With the floodlights on, a crowd of just under 500 saw Lancashire openers Jennings and Davies make a brisk start, but play was halted by rain after 70 minutes, and did not resume until 2.30 on the third day, when Berg removed Jennings. A storm then left the outfield white with hailstones, and only 38 deliveries were possible on the fourth.
Close of play: first day, Lancashire 59-0 (Jennings 23, Davies 34); second day, no play; third day, Lancashire 75-1 (Davies 45, Wells 0).

Lancashire

K. K. Jennings c Rossington b Berg	27
A. L. Davies not out	51
L. W. P. Wells not out	7
B 1, lb 2	3

1/63 (1)   (1 wkt, 34.3 overs) 88

J. J. Bohannon, L. S. Livingstone, *†D. J. Vilas, S. J. Croft, L. Wood, T. E. Bailey, M. W. Parkinson and J. M. Anderson did not bat.

Sanderson 14.3–2–45–0; Berg 13–4–28–1; Taylor 4–1–5–0; Parnell 3–1–7–0.

Northamptonshire

B. J. Curran, R. S. Vasconcelos, L. A. Procter, R. I. Keogh, S. A. Zaib, *†A. M. Rossington, T. A. I. Taylor, W. D. Parnell, G. K. Berg, S. C. Kerrigan, B. W. Sanderson.

Umpires: R. J. Bailey and R. A. Kettleborough. Referee: J. J. Whitaker.

At Hove, May 27–30. NORTHAMPTONSHIRE beat SUSSEX by seven wickets.

At Canterbury, June 3–6. NORTHAMPTONSHIRE drew with KENT.

NORTHAMPTONSHIRE v YORKSHIRE

At Northampton, July 4–6. Yorkshire won by 53 runs. Yorkshire 19pts, Northamptonshire 3pts. Toss: Yorkshire. County debut: S. A. Northeast.

Victory inside three days ultimately secured Yorkshire a place in Division One, while Northamptonshire's quest for a first Championship title was put on hold for another year. One run had separated the sides at Headingley in May, and another close contest unfolded on a wearing pitch already used for three T20 Blast fixtures. After winning an important toss, which meant the home side would have to bat last, Yorkshire were held together by Hill, who opened for the first time and survived a slip chance off Parnell on 31; he went on to score exactly half their runs by the time he was seventh out. In reply to 158, Northamptonshire looked set for a useful lead at 88 for two, until Bess – flighting and drifting the ball cleverly in a stiff breeze – returned a career-best seven for 43. Kerrigan then blended modest turn with excellent control to keep them in contention, but Brook's skilful and diligent century, lasting four and a half hours, in effect decided the result. Set 206, Northamptonshire crumbled to 43 for five, before Procter – who had missed the first innings because of a family bereavement – Taylor and Kerrigan offered spirited but unavailing resistance.

Close of play: first day, Northamptonshire 61-2 (Vasconcelos 32, Berg 0); second day, Yorkshire 159-6 (Brook 76, Thompson 6).

Yorkshire

A. Lyth c Vasconcelos b Sanderson	0	– c Vasconcelos b Sanderson	5
G. C. H. Hill lbw b Keogh	71	– b Kerrigan	13
S. A. Northeast c Vasconcelos b Taylor	3	– st Vasconcelos b Kerrigan	1
G. S. Ballance c Thurston b Kerrigan	22	– lbw b Kerrigan	26
H. C. Brook c Sanderson b Kerrigan	7	– c Zaib b Kerrigan	113
D. M. Bess c Vasconcelos b Berg	10	– lbw b Parnell	10
†H. G. Duke lbw b Taylor	5	– b Kerrigan	13
J. A. Thompson lbw b Parnell	22	– c Vasconcelos b Sanderson	6
*S. A. Patterson c Zaib b Keogh	0	– c Gay b Sanderson	0
B. O. Coad b Parnell	0	– c and b Taylor	8
D. Olivier not out	3	– not out	0
B 5, lb 8, nb 2	15	B 8, lb 4	12
	158		**217**

1/4 (1) 2/21 (3) 3/65 (4) (64.3 overs) 158
4/91 (5) 5/112 (6) 6/126 (7)
7/142 (2) 8/142 (9) 9/153 (10) 10/158 (8)

1/22 (2) 2/24 (3) (83.2 overs) 217
3/24 (1) 4/64 (4)
5/105 (6) 6/140 (7) 7/167 (8)
8/189 (9) 9/207 (10) 10/217 (5)

Sanderson 12–6–24–1; Berg 10–0–37–1; Taylor 11–6–14–2; Parnell 11.3–4–26–2; Kerrigan 13–2–36–2; Keogh 7–4–8–2. *Second innings*—Sanderson 20–4–70–3; Berg 3–0–12–0; Kerrigan 30.2–12–39–5; Keogh 16–2–41–0; Taylor 9–1–25–1; Parnell 5–1–18–1.

Northamptonshire

*†R. S. Vasconcelos c Duke b Bess	55	– lbw b Patterson	10
E. N. Gay lbw b Bess	21	– c Northeast b Bess	8
S. C. Kerrigan c Ballance b Patterson	1	– (10) c Duke b Olivier	29
G. K. Berg c Patterson b Bess	8	– (8) c Northeast b Coad	0
C. O. Thurston c Duke b Bess	1	– (3) c Ballance b Patterson	1
R. I. Keogh c Lyth b Olivier	9	– (4) c Brook b Bess	6
S. A. Zaib lbw b Bess	11	– (6) c Lyth b Olivier	9
T. A. I. Taylor not out	42	– (7) lbw b Coad	40
W. D. Parnell lbw b Bess	0	– run out (Thompson)	3
B. W. Sanderson c Lyth b Bess	5	– (11) lbw b Olivier	0
L. A. Procter absent		– (5) not out	42
B 1, lb 9, nb 4	14	B 4	4

1/54 (2) 2/61 (3) 3/88 (4)	(61.4 overs) 170	1/17 (1) 2/19 (3)	(52 overs) 152
4/93 (5) 5/106 (1) 6/110 (6)		3/19 (2) 4/28 (4)	
7/146 (7) 8/150 (9) 9/170 (10)		5/43 (6) 6/97 (7) 7/97 (8)	
		8/103 (9) 9/152 (10) 10/152 (11)	

Coad 7–0–35–0; Thompson 7–1–18–0; Bess 24.4–11–43–7; Patterson 16–3–47–1; Olivier 7–1–17–1. *Second innings*—Coad 9–2–33–2; Patterson 11–2–22–2; Bess 24–9–59–2; Olivier 8–1–34–3.

Umpires: T. Lungley and B. V. Taylor.   Referee: P. M. Such.

At Cardiff, July 11–14. NORTHAMPTONSHIRE drew with GLAMORGAN.

DIVISION TWO

At Bristol, August 30–September 2. NORTHAMPTONSHIRE lost to GLOUCESTERSHIRE by six
   wickets.

NORTHAMPTONSHIRE v SURREY

At Northampton, September 5–8. Northamptonshire won by two wickets. Northamptonshire 19pts,
Surrey 5pts. Toss: Surrey. First-class debut: J. J. G. Sales.
   A quarter of a century after his father, David, scored a double-century on first-class debut,
18-year-old James Sales marked his own by pulling the winning boundary, as Northamptonshire
secured a first Championship victory over Surrey since 2004 – when Sales senior was captain. An
engrossing contest hung in the balance on the final afternoon, with Northamptonshire chasing 320.
They reached 271 for four, thanks to Gay, Keogh (who fell for 99) and Procter, only for Topley and
Clark, armed with the second new ball, to bowl Surrey back into contention. Taylor steadied nerves,
before Sales finished the job. Surrey's decision to bat on a pitch offering early help to the seamers
had looked set to backfire, until Smith, who survived a slip chance on ten, and Jacks added 145 for

the fifth wicket. But the last six fell for 46, as Taylor collected his first five-wicket haul for Northamptonshire, whose reply fell away after a promising start. Surrey appeared to have taken a decisive grip when Atkinson and Virdi each made a career-best during a last-wicket stand of 83. Instead, the hosts pulled off their highest chase against them, beating 316 for seven at The Oval in 1994. The two head coaches, Alec Stewart and David Ripley, each deputised as square-leg umpire on the second day after Russell Warren was taken ill. During the game, it was announced that Ripley would be stepping down from his role at the end of the season.

Close of play: first day, Northamptonshire 7-0 (Vasconcelos 4, Gay 2); second day, Surrey 102-4 (Amla 26, Jacks 20); third day, Northamptonshire 106-2 (Gay 44, Keogh 46).

Surrey

C. T. Steel lbw b Sanderson	0	– c Rossington b Procter	17
R. S. Patel c Rossington b Taylor	35	– b Procter	19
*H. M. Amla b Taylor	0	– (4) c Rossington b Kerrigan	26
L. J. Evans b Taylor	4	– (3) b Sales	11
†J. L. Smith b Sanderson	123	– lbw b Kerrigan	7
W. G. Jacks b Kerrigan	60	– b Kerrigan	50
J. Clark lbw b Sanderson	15	– c Gay b Sanderson	2
R. Clarke c Rossington b Taylor	0	– c Rossington b Taylor	5
A. A. P. Atkinson c Rossington b Sanderson	3	– not out	41
R. J. W. Topley c Vasconcelos b Taylor	0	– b Kerrigan	0
G. S. Virdi not out	0	– c Rossington b Taylor	47
B 4, nb 8	12	B 4, lb 5, nb 4	13

1/0 (1) 2/11 (3) 3/15 (4)   (90.3 overs) 252
4/61 (2) 5/206 (6) 6/231 (7)
7/232 (8) 8/237 (9) 9/250 (10) 10/252 (5)

1/38 (1) 2/45 (2)   (104.3 overs) 238
3/49 (3) 4/75 (5)
5/102 (4) 6/117 (7) 7/125 (8)
8/155 (6) 9/155 (10) 10/238 (11)

Sanderson 19.3–11–32–4; Taylor 19–6–41–5; Sales 10–2–39–0; Procter 7–2–25–0; Kerrigan 23–4–59–1; Keogh 4–0–24–0; Zaib 8–2–28–0. *Second innings*—Sanderson 24–8–42–1; Taylor 14.3–1–54–2; Sales 13–4–35–1; Procter 14–3–40–2; Kerrigan 29.2–8–36–4; Keogh 7–3–20–0; Zaib 2.4–0–2–0.

Northamptonshire

R. S. Vasconcelos c Patel b Clark	24	– c Smith b Clarke	11
E. N. Gay c Smith b Topley	24	– lbw b Clark	50
L. A. Procter c Jacks b Topley	12	– (5) c Smith b Topley	57
R. I. Keogh b Atkinson	5	– c Evans b Clark	99
S. A. Zaib b Clarke	37	– (7) c Smith b Topley	6
*†A. M. Rossington lbw b Clarke	15	– c Steel b Clark	32
H. O. M. Gouldstone b Clarke	8	– (3) lbw b Clark	3
T. A. I. Taylor b Virdi	12	– c Smith b Clark	25
J. J. G. Sales lbw b Atkinson	2	– not out	7
S. C. Kerrigan not out	6	– not out	0
B. W. Sanderson lbw b Steel	2		
Lb 11, w 1, nb 12	24	B 3, lb 11, w 2, nb 16	32

1/43 (1) 2/66 (2) 3/73 (3)   (58.5 overs) 171
4/73 (4) 5/95 (6) 6/105 (7)
7/125 (8) 8/138 (9) 9/168 (5) 10/171 (11)

1/24 (1)   (8 wkts, 99.1 overs) 322
2/37 (3) 3/122 (2)
4/205 (4) 5/271 (5)
6/271 (6) 7/287 (7) 8/318 (8)

Topley 14–4–33–2; Atkinson 14–3–48–2; Clarke 15–6–34–3; Clark 10–3–27–1; Virdi 4–2–9–1; Steel 1.5–0–9–1. *Second innings*—Topley 22–6–59–2; Atkinson 8–1–25–0; Clarke 15–4–36–1; Clark 26–3–76–5; Virdi 14–2–45–0; Steel 13.1–1–67–0; Jacks 1–1–0–0.

Umpires: M. Newell and R. J. Warren.   Referee: D. A. Cosker.
A. J. Stewart and D. Ripley deputised for Warren on the second afternoon; M. J. Saggers replaced him from the second evening.

NORTHAMPTONSHIRE v DURHAM

At Northampton, September 12–15. Drawn. Northamptonshire 10pts, Durham 13pts. Toss: Northamptonshire.

The loss of the third day to rain probably cost Durham their first Championship victory at Wantage Road since 1999. After two poor days, Northamptonshire had also pulled themselves together: Sales contributed a maiden first-class fifty, Kerrigan kept out 135 balls, and No. 11 White helped negotiate the final 35. On the opening day, Rushworth and Potts had taken full advantage of careless shot selection, dismissing Northamptonshire in two sessions. Durham's top order struggled too, although Bedingham had time to chalk up 1,000 first-class runs for the season, before he was run out by Keogh. But the visitors rallied, first through Borthwick, then a pair of 22-year-olds – Trevaskis and Potts – whose stand of 149 in 35 overs fell one short of the county's ninth-wicket record. Northamptonshire's efforts were summed up when Clark was dropped twice in the slips off two balls from White. With a lead of 217, Durham were still favourites, despite the weather. But from 129 for seven midway through the final afternoon, Northamptonshire dug deep – aided by an increasingly benign pitch. Potts's match figures of eight for 116 proved in vain.

Close of play: first day, Durham 108-4 (Borthwick 54, Clark 23); second day, Northamptonshire 10-0 (Vasconcelos 5, Gay 4); third day, no play.

Northamptonshire

R. S. Vasconcelos c Eckersley b Rushworth	4	– c Eckersley b Rushworth	24
E. N. Gay c Eckersley b Rushworth	17	– c Borthwick b Potts	26
L. A. Procter c Eckersley b Trevaskis	76	– lbw b Raine	44
R. I. Keogh c Coughlin b Rushworth	9	– lbw b Raine	16
S. A. Zaib c Eckersley b Raine	10	– c Eckersley b Potts	6
*†A. M. Rossington lbw b Potts	10	– c Bedingham b Potts	4
H. O. M. Gouldstone c Eckersley b Potts	8	– b Rushworth	2
J. J. G. Sales not out	38	– c Trevaskis b Potts	53
S. C. Kerrigan b Potts	1	– not out	28
B. W. Sanderson lbw b Potts	0	– lbw b Borthwick	17
C. J. White b Trevaskis	0	– not out	3
B 8, lb 2	10	B 5, lb 3	8

1/10 (1)　2/35 (2)　3/55 (4)	(55.3 overs)	183
4/74 (5)　5/91 (6)　6/107 (7)		
7/173 (3)　8/182 (9)　9/182 (10)　10/183 (11)		

1/46 (2)	(9 wkts, 97 overs)	231
2/62 (1)　3/86 (4)		
4/102 (5)　5/108 (6)　6/111 (7)		
7/129 (3)　8/197 (8)　9/221 (10)		

Rushworth 14–2–50–3; Raine 14–3–34–1; Potts 12–4–42–4; Coughlin 9–1–27–0; Trevaskis 6.3–2–20–2. *Second innings*—Rushworth 20–6–41–2; Potts 20–4–68–4; Trevaskis 23–10–30–0; Raine 15–5–32–2; Borthwick 11–4–26–1; Coughlin 8–2–26–0.

Durham

A. Z. Lees b Sanderson	0	M. J. Potts b Sanderson	81
M. A. Jones lbw b Sanderson	18	C. Rushworth c Kerrigan b Sales	5
*S. G. Borthwick b Kerrigan	73		
D. G. Bedingham run out (Keogh)	10	B 4, lb 5, w 1, nb 2	12
†E. J. H. Eckersley lbw b Sales	2		
G. Clark b Kerrigan	42		400
P. Coughlin c Vasconcelos b White	48		
B. A. Raine b Sanderson	32		
L. Trevaskis not out	77		

1/0 (1)　2/20 (2)　3/35 (4)	(130 overs)	400
4/49 (5)　5/142 (6)　6/163 (6)		
7/225 (7)　8/236 (8)　9/385 (6)		
10/400 (11)	110 overs: 281-8	

Sanderson 24–9–41–4; White 24–2–68–1; Sales 15–3–61–2; Procter 17–7–49–0; Kerrigan 34–3–112–2; Keogh 12–3–43–0; Zaib 4–0–17–0.

Umpires: B. J. Debenham and P. J. Hartley.　Referee: P. M. Such.

At Chelmsford, September 21–22. NORTHAMPTONSHIRE lost to ESSEX by an innings and 44 runs. *Northamptonshire are dismissed for 81 and 45 in the shortest Championship match in the four-day era.*

NOTTINGHAMSHIRE

Oh pants, it's Hants!

JON CULLEY

The bare facts of 2021 are that Nottinghamshire let two chances of silverware slip through their grasp. Defending their Vitality Blast title, they lost a home quarter-final they looked bound to win; and they were in pole position for their first County Championship in 11 years, only to suffer a heavy defeat in the penultimate round. In both instances, the banana skin was Hampshire.

Seven Championship victories, however, made this a year of progress. When it began, Nottinghamshire had not won a first-class match in 27 attempts since June 2018, and had finished bottom of Division One in 2019. The Bob Willis Trophy in 2020 provided glimpses of improvement, but no wins, and the dismal sequence continued in their first three games in April. Yet when the tide turned – after 1,043 days, on May 1 at Derby – it came rushing in.

Nottinghamshire finished top of their preliminary group, above eventual champions Warwickshire. After they beat Somerset and Lancashire easily in the opening rounds of Division One, the title was theirs to lose. But that changed with the defeat in Southampton. Despite victory over Yorkshire in the final round, they finished third, half a point behind runners-up Lancashire. Ultimately, two group losses against Warwickshire proved fatal; that meant they carried forward only five points into Division One, to Warwickshire's 21. And, despite amassing 219 points across 14 matches – more than any other county – they start 2022 in Division Two, thanks to an ECB decision that the Championship would revert to the placings decided before the pandemic, when Nottinghamshire were at their nadir.

Stalwart seamer Luke Fletcher was the primary architect of the three wins that started the recovery, taking 25 wickets at seven apiece, including a career-best six for 24 against Essex, immediately followed by seven for 37 against Worcestershire. His final return of 66 at 14 was his best in 13 first-class summers, and made him the country's leading wicket-taker; he was named Championship Player of the Year by the PCA and the Cricket Writers' Club.

Another seamer, South African Dane Paterson, who had been expected to join as a Kolpak in 2020 before the pandemic (and a serious chest injury) intervened, arrived as an overseas player. Despite having had no cricket for a year, he collected 54 wickets – the first time two Nottinghamshire bowlers had taken 50-plus in the same Championship season since Vasbert Drakes and Paul Franks in 1999. Paterson was contracted to return in 2022.

Brett Hutton, back after three seasons with Northamptonshire, claimed 29 in eight matches, and Stuart Broad gave good value with 23 in five. Liam Patterson-White, Lyndon James and Joey Evison – three young, home-produced all-rounders – shared 52 wickets and made useful batting contributions to

Harry Trump, Getty Images

Ben Slater

Division One wins: Patterson-White, a left-arm spinner, scored his first century, against Somerset, James a career-best 91 against Lancashire, and Evison, the youngest at 19, a maiden fifty against Yorkshire.

There remains room for improvement among the mainstream batters. Ben Slater, who has become a reliable opener, was the most productive, with 837 at nearly 40. But more was expected of Ben Duckett: a superb unbeaten 177 against Worcestershire apart, his other 20 innings yielded 528. Joe Clarke, meanwhile, converted only one of his eight fifties.

Haseeb Hameed continued his rehabilitation. On a placid surface at Worcester, he made twin hundreds for the second time in his career, batting for a combined 13 hours and 44 minutes. In addition to 679 for Nottinghamshire, he reached a century for a County Select XI against the Indians and two sixties in three Tests against India, after an England recall. That gave him 944 first-class runs, his highest aggregate since he topped 1,000 in his first full season with Lancashire in 2016.

The captain, Steven Mullaney, made 117 to help set up an innings victory over Essex, and guided his team out of their trough. For good measure, he took on the Blast captaincy when Dan Christian was called up by Australia: Nottinghamshire won the North Group comfortably, only to founder in a low-scoring quarter-final on a tired Trent Bridge track. They were 66 for one chasing 126, collapsed to 109 for nine, and lost by two runs.

Clarke's 136 against Northamptonshire was the 2021 Blast's highest score, and Alex Hales hit his fifth T20 hundred. Leg-spinner Calvin Harrison – taken on after a pre-season match in which he combined a century with three wickets for Oxford UCCE against Nottinghamshire – was a real find, with 20 wickets; his economy-rate of 6.78 was bettered only by veteran left-arm spinner Samit Patel, whose three for four against Worcestershire was the most frugal four-over spell in the 19 seasons of England's domestic T20 competition. Spin trio Harrison, Patel and Matt Carter took 54 between them, while Jake Ball, who missed most of the Championship through injury, had 18.

In his valedictory season, 40-year-old Peter Trego led an otherwise youthful side in the Royal London Cup; they won three of their six completed matches, but did not qualify. James and Patterson-White claimed five-wicket hauls in victories over Warwickshire and Northamptonshire, and Sol Budinger made a maiden half-century at York.

Despite reports of interest from Pakistan, head coach Peter Moores signed a three-year contract, keeping him at Trent Bridge until 2024. In addition to Trego's retirement, Tom Barber and Ben Compton were released. Back in May, left-arm swing bowler Harry Gurney – who hadn't played since 2019 – called it a day because of a shoulder injury.

NOTTINGHAMSHIRE RESULTS

County Championship matches – Played 14: Won 7, Lost 3, Drawn 4.
Vitality T20 Blast matches – Played 15: Won 9, Lost 3, Tied 3.
Royal London Cup matches – Played 8: Won 3, Lost 3, No result 2.

LV= County Championship, 1st in Group 1, 3rd in Division 1;
Vitality T20 Blast, quarter-finalists; Royal London Cup, 5th in Group 2.

COUNTY CHAMPIONSHIP AVERAGES, BATTING AND FIELDING

Cap		Birthplace	M	I	NO	R	HS	100	Avge	Ct/St
2021	†B. T. Slater	Chesterfield	14	24	3	837	114*	2	39.85	8
2020	H. Hameed	Bolton	11	19	1	679	114*	2	37.72	11
2019	†B. M. Duckett.	Farnborough, Kent .	13	21	2	705	177*	1	37.10	15
2021	J. M. Clarke	Shrewsbury	13	22	1	760	109	1	36.19	8
	L. W. James	Worksop‡	12	18	1	558	91	0	32.82	1
	†L. A. Patterson-White	Sunderland	14	20	3	538	101	1	31.64	4
2021	†T. J. Moores	Brighton	12	19	3	486	97	0	30.37	52/2
2013	S. J. Mullaney	Warrington	14	22	0	657	117	1	29.86	6
	J. D. M. Evison	Peterborough	4	6	0	121	58	0	20.16	0
2021	D. Paterson¶	Cape Town, SA . . .	12	15	11	64	22	0	16.00	4
2021	B. A. Hutton	Doncaster	8	11	0	174	51	0	15.81	8
	Z. J. Chappell	Grantham	3	5	1	61	22	0	15.25	0
2008	†S. C. J. Broad§	Nottingham‡	5	7	0	87	41	0	12.42	0
2014	L. J. Fletcher	Nottingham‡	13	17	5	140	51	0	11.66	1
	†B. G. Compton	Durban, SA	3	5	0	55	20	0	11.00	2

Also batted: J. T. Ball (*Mansfield‡*) (cap 2016) (1 match) 4; S. A. Northeast (*Ashford, Kent*)
(2 matches) 34, 65, 13 (2 ct); D. J. Schadendorf†† (*Harare, Zimbabwe*) (1 match) 24 (4 ct).

‡ Born in Nottinghamshire.   § ECB contract.   ¶ Official overseas player.   †† Other non-England-qualified.

BOWLING

	Style	O	M	R	W	BB	5I	Avge
L. J. Fletcher	RFM	420.5	135	984	66	7-37	4	14.90
S. C. J. Broad	RFM	150	34	368	23	4-37	0	16.00
J. D. M. Evison.	RM	82.1	23	249	14	5-21	1	17.78
D. Paterson	RFM	352.5	98	971	54	5-90	2	17.98
B. A. Hutton	RFM	254	75	679	29	5-62	2	23.41
L. W. James	RFM	139	27	424	14	4-51	0	30.28
L. A. Patterson-White	SLA	285	70	749	24	5-41	1	31.20

Also bowled: J. T. Ball (RFM) 17.3–7–43–2; Z. J. Chappell (RFM) 100–21–306–6; B. M. Duckett
(OB) 3–0–17–0; S. J. Mullaney (RM) 151.2–29–423–7; B. T. Slater (OB) 2–0–8–0.

LEADING VITALITY BLAST AVERAGES (100 runs/15 overs)

Batting	Runs	HS	Avge	SR	Ct/St
J. M. Clarke . . .	408	136	37.09	180.53	6
A. D. Hales	482	101*	43.81	178.51	7
B. M. Duckett . .	383	74*	34.81	158.26	9
S. J. Mullaney . .	169	43*	15.36	136.29	13
S. R. Patel	309	64*	30.90	131.48	7
P. D. Trego . . .	125	35	17.85	123.76	3
T. J. Moores . . .	145	48	13.18	112.40	5/6

Bowling	W	BB	Avge	ER
S. R. Patel	16	3-4	21.56	6.63
C. G. Harrison . . .	20	4-17	13.90	6.78
M. Carter	18	3-17	20.66	7.01
S. J. Mullaney . . .	11	3-33	24.90	7.82
L. J. Fletcher	13	3-31	28.61	9.07
J. T. Ball	18	4-11	15.44	9.37

LEADING ROYAL LONDON CUP AVERAGES (90 runs/4 wickets)

Batting	Runs	HS	Avge	SR	Ct/St
B. T. Slater	395	86	56.42	90.80	4
H. Hameed	107	103	53.50	109.18	2
M. Montgomery	200	35	40.00	85.10	2
D. Schadendorf .	95	44*	23.75	110.46	6/1
S. G. Budinger .	165	71	20.62	123.13	1
P. D. Trego	95	39	11.87	77.86	4

Bowling	W	BB	Avge	ER
L. W. James.....	5	5-48	9.60	5.33
L. A. Patterson-White	13	5-19	14.46	5.37
L. J. Fletcher	6	4-30	21.83	5.95
D. Paterson	8	3-25	26.37	6.80
B. A. Hutton	6	2-22	30.83	4.86
J. D. M. Evison ..	4	2-33	40.75	7.08

FIRST-CLASS COUNTY RECORDS

Highest score for	312*	W. W. Keeton v Middlesex at The Oval	1939
Highest score against	345	C. G. Macartney (Australians) at Nottingham	1921
Leading run-scorer	31,592	G. Gunn (avge 35.69)	1902–32
Best bowling for	10-66	K. Smales v Gloucestershire at Stroud.	1956
Best bowling against	10-10	H. Verity (Yorkshire) at Leeds	1932
Leading wicket-taker	1,653	T. G. Wass (avge 20.34)	1896–1920
Highest total for	791	v Essex at Chelmsford.	2007
Highest total against	781-7 dec	by Northamptonshire at Northampton	1995
Lowest total for	13	v Yorkshire at Nottingham.	1901
Lowest total against	16	by Derbyshire at Nottingham.................	1879
	16	by Surrey at The Oval	1880

LIST A COUNTY RECORDS

Highest score for	187*	A. D. Hales v Surrey at Lord's	2017
Highest score against	191	D. S. Lehmann (Yorkshire) at Scarborough.	2001
Leading run-scorer	11,237	R. T. Robinson (avge 35.33)	1978–99
Best bowling for	6-10	K. P. Evans v Northumberland at Jesmond	1994
Best bowling against	7-41	A. N. Jones (Sussex) at Nottingham	1986
Leading wicket-taker	291	C. E. B. Rice (avge 22.60).....................	1975–87
Highest total for	445-8	v Northamptonshire at Nottingham	2016
Highest total against	425	by Northamptonshire at Nottingham............	2016
Lowest total for	57	v Gloucestershire at Nottingham	2009
Lowest total against	43	by Northamptonshire at Northampton	1977

TWENTY20 COUNTY RECORDS

Highest score for	136	**J. M. Clarke v Northants at Northampton**	**2021**
Highest score against	111	W. J. Durston (Derbyshire) at Nottingham	2010
Leading run-scorer	3,985	A. D. Hales (avge 30.41, SR 150.77)	2009–15
Best bowling for	5-22	G. G. White v Lancashire at Nottingham..........	2013
Best bowling against	5-13	A. B. McDonald (Leicestershire) at Nottingham	2010
Leading wicket-taker	181	S. R. Patel (avge 26.30, ER 7.28)...............	2003–21
Highest total for	227-3	v Derbyshire at Nottingham...................	2017
Highest total against	229-5	**by Warwickshire at Nottingham.**	**2021**
Lowest total for	91	v Lancashire at Manchester	2006
Lowest total against	63	**by Warwickshire at Birmingham**	**2021**

ADDRESS

Trent Bridge, West Bridgford, Nottingham NG2 6AG; 0115 982 3000; questions@nottsccc.co.uk; www.trentbridge.co.uk. Twitter: @TrentBridge.

OFFICIALS

Captain S. J. Mullaney
    (Twenty20) D. T. Christian
    (List A) H. Hameed
Director of cricket M. Newell
Head coach P. Moores
Elite pathway manager M. Wood

President S. B. Hassan
Chair J. P. Moore
Chief executive L. J. Pursehouse
Head groundsman S. Birks
Scorers R. Marshall and A. Cusworth

GROUP ONE

NOTTINGHAMSHIRE v DURHAM

At Nottingham, April 8–11. Drawn. Nottinghamshire 13pts, Durham 13pts. Toss: Nottinghamshire. Championship debut: D. G. Bedingham.

Nottinghamshire's winless streak extended to 28 first-class matches, but they avoided defeat, despite Durham controlling most of the first three days. Borthwick gave his bowlers a full day to take ten wickets: they managed five. After Durham had made 330, Moores arrived at 66 for five, and batted patiently before being stranded on 96, ensuring Nottinghamshire trailed by only 63. But their bowling was seriously weakened; Ball had dropped out with a sore back on the second morning, and Hutton suffered a side strain on the third afternoon. Durham took full advantage: Bedingham scored fluently in a career-best 180, as he and Eckersley shared an unbroken stand of 254, a county fifth-wicket record. Still, Nottinghamshire survived the final day. In only his third first-class match since his debut in 2018, the 22-year-old all-rounder Lyndon James made a career-best unbeaten 79.

Close of play: first day, Durham 241-7 (Carse 21, Raine 20); second day, Nottinghamshire 165-7 (Moores 40, Hutton 12); third day, Durham 332-4 (Bedingham 180, Eckersley 113).

Durham

A. Z. Lees run out (Clarke)	58	– lbw b Fletcher	0
M. A. Jones c Hameed b Ball	0	– b Hutton	5
*S. G. Borthwick lbw b Ball	0	– c Duckett b Hutton	1
D. G. Bedingham c Moores b Fletcher	57	– not out	180
J. T. A. Burnham c Moores b Fletcher	42	– c Moores b Mullaney	18
E. J. H. Eckersley c Hutton b Mullaney	19	– not out	113
†S. W. Poynter c Moores b James	7		
B. A. Carse lbw b Hutton	25		
B. A. Raine not out	59		
M. E. T. Salisbury c Hutton b Fletcher	14		
C. Rushworth lbw b Mullaney	31		
B 4, lb 10, nb 4	18	B 8, lb 5, nb 2	15

1/5 (2) 2/5 (3) 3/93 (4) 4/144 (1) (121.2 overs) 330
5/180 (5) 6/196 (6) 7/196 (7)
8/250 (8) 9/271 (10) 10/330 (11)   110 overs: 282-9

1/0 (1)   (4 wkts dec, 76 overs) 332
2/5 (3) 3/22 (2)
4/78 (5)

Ball 17.3–7–43–2; Hutton 24–7–59–1; Fletcher 29.3–10–83–3; Mullaney 13.2–5–37–2; Patterson-White 21–4–57–0; James 16–4–37–1. *Second innings*—Fletcher 17–4–41–1; Hutton 10.5–3–33–2; James 12–0–57–0; Mullaney 23–2–89–1; Patterson-White 10.1–0–82–0; Duckett 3–0–17–0.

Nottinghamshire

B. T. Slater c Poynter b Salisbury	0	– lbw b Borthwick	73
H. Hameed b Salisbury	10	– b Rushworth	0
B. M. Duckett c Poynter b Carse	24	– lbw b Rushworth	12
J. M. Clarke c Poynter b Salisbury	0	– c Bedingham b Salisbury	38
L. W. James c Poynter b Carse	28	– not out	79
*S. J. Mullaney c Bedingham b Rushworth	11	– b Salisbury	69
†T. J. Moores not out	96	– not out	7
L. A. Patterson-White c Poynter b Rushworth	26		
B. A. Hutton lbw b Salisbury	51		
L. J. Fletcher lbw b Carse	0		
J. T. Ball c Carse	4		
B 4, lb 7, nb 6	17	B 8, lb 10, nb 2	20

1/1 (1) 2/26 (2) 3/26 (4)   (74.1 overs) 267
4/46 (3) 5/66 (6) 6/85 (5)
7/141 (8) 8/230 (9) 9/231 (10) 10/267 (11)

1/5 (2)   (5 wkts, 83.3 overs) 298
2/21 (3) 3/88 (4)
4/159 (1) 5/283 (6)

Rushworth 21–9–41–2; Salisbury 19–3–74–4; Raine 15–1–48–0; Carse 16.1–2–86–4; Borthwick 3–0–7–0. *Second innings*—Rushworth 17–4–36–2; Salisbury 20.3–7–62–2; Raine 20–5–61–0; Carse 13–0–69–0; Borthwick 13–0–52–1.

Umpires: B. J. Debenham and I. J. Gould.   Referee: P. M. Such.

NOTTINGHAMSHIRE v WARWICKSHIRE

At Nottingham, April 15–18. Warwickshire won by three wickets. Warwickshire 20pts, Nottinghamshire 5pts. Toss: Nottinghamshire. County debuts: D. Paterson; G. H. Vihari.

Victory continued to elude Nottinghamshire, despite a strong position on the final morning: Warwickshire were three down, still needing 248, and Sibley would bat only if necessary, having broken a finger fielding. But he was spared, as the experienced Bresnan saw his side home. Hain and Lamb had batted bravely in the face of hostile bowling by Broad, but the South African seamer Dane Paterson, on county debut, took three quick wickets after lunch, leaving Warwickshire 184 for six, before Bresnan and Stone added 113. Nottinghamshire had held the upper hand since the first afternoon, when Patterson-White's career-best 73 helped them recover from 119 for six. Broad then claimed three wickets, including India's Hanuma Vihari for a 23-ball duck, and Paterson mopped up to secure a lead of 72. Fifties from Hameed and Clarke extended that, though left-arm spinner Briggs checked Nottinghamshire's progress by striking three times in four balls. But when Patterson-White trapped Rhodes at the end of the third day, the odds seemed against Warwickshire's chase of 333.

Close of play: first day, Warwickshire 24-2 (Rhodes 18, Briggs 0); second day, Nottinghamshire 128-2 (Hameed 51, Clarke 50); third day, Warwickshire 85-3 (Hain 20).

Nottinghamshire

B. T. Slater c Hain b Stone	5	–	lbw b Stone	2
H. Hameed c Sibley b Rhodes	19	–	c Burgess b Rhodes	53
B. M. Duckett lbw b Bresnan	17	–	lbw b Rhodes	25
J. M. Clarke c Burgess b Stone	29	–	c Burgess b Stone	56
L. W. James run out (Rhodes)	11	–	lbw b Stone	31
*S. J. Mullaney c Vihari b Rhodes	31	–	c Yates b Briggs	42
†T. J. Moores b Rhodes	31	–	b Briggs	7
L. A. Patterson-White not out	73	–	b Briggs	0
S. C. J. Broad c Bresnan b Rhodes	21	–	c Hain b Hannon-Dalby	1
Z. J. Chappell c Hain b Bresnan	22	–	not out	17
D. Paterson c Lamb b Bresnan	0	–	c Hannon-Dalby b Briggs	22
B 1, lb 5, w 1, nb 2, p 5	14		Lb 2, nb 2	4

1/11 (1) 2/44 (2) 3/44 (3)   (88 overs) 273
4/63 (5) 5/105 (6) 6/119 (4)
7/182 (7) 8/210 (9) 9/273 (10) 10/273 (11)

1/3 (1) 2/55 (3)   (88.2 overs) 260
3/131 (2) 4/141 (4)
5/198 (5) 6/218 (6) 7/218 (8)
8/219 (7) 9/221 (9) 10/260 (11)

Hannon-Dalby 24–7–56–0; Stone 20–4–67–2; Bresnan 17–6–48–3; Rhodes 18–4–53–4; Briggs 8–1–27–0; Vihari 1–0–11–0. *Second innings*—Hannon-Dalby 19–7–53–1; Stone 21–3–66–3; Bresnan 10–2–37–0; Rhodes 14–5–31–2; Briggs 23.2–4–68–4; Yates 1–0–3–0.

Warwickshire

*W. M. H. Rhodes c Moores b Broad	22	– lbw b Patterson-White	44
R. M. Yates c Moores b Chappell	0	– lbw b Broad	2
G. H. Vihari c Hameed b Broad	0	– b James	8
D. R. Briggs lbw b Broad	36	– (9) not out	16
S. R. Hain lbw b Patterson-White	72	– (4) c Moores b Paterson	57
M. J. Lamb c Duckett b James	7	– (5) b Paterson	50
†M. G. K. Burgess lbw b Paterson	36	– (6) b Paterson	1
T. T. Bresnan c Hameed b Paterson	12	– (7) not out	68
O. P. Stone not out	0	– (8) c Moores b Broad	43
O. J. Hannon-Dalby lbw b Paterson	0		
D. P. Sibley absent hurt			
B 4, lb 2, nb 10	16	B 19, lb 14, w 5, nb 6	44

1/4 (2) 2/23 (3) 3/30 (1) (70.4 overs) 201   1/13 (2) (7 wkts, 121.5 overs) 333
4/113 (4) 5/138 (6) 6/176 (5)   2/34 (3) 3/85 (1)
7/200 (8) 8/201 (7) 9/201 (10)   4/174 (4) 5/181 (5) 6/184 (6) 7/297 (8)

Broad 19–5–50–3; Chappell 14–4–40–1; Paterson 15.4–1–61–3; Mullaney 8–3–9–0; Patterson-White 8–3–10–1; James 6–0–25–1. *Second innings*—Broad 30–8–54–2; Chappell 15–4–50–0; James 11–1–42–1; Paterson 29.5–6–77–3; Patterson-White 21–5–52–1; Mullaney 15–4–25–0.

Umpires: N. A. Mallender and S. J. O'Shaughnessy.   Referee: D. A. Cosker.

At Worcester, April 22–25. NOTTINGHAMSHIRE drew with WORCESTERSHIRE. *Haseeb Hameed scores twin centuries.*

At Derby, April 29–May 1. NOTTINGHAMSHIRE beat DERBYSHIRE by 310 runs. *Nottinghamshire claim their first first-class win since June 2018, following 18 defeats and 12 draws.*

NOTTINGHAMSHIRE v ESSEX

At Nottingham, May 6–9. Nottinghamshire won by an innings and 30 runs. Nottinghamshire 22pts, Essex 3pts. Toss: Nottinghamshire.

Confidence buoyed after their barren first-class run ended at Derby, Nottinghamshire went top of Group One when they sealed victory over defending champions Essex with two sessions in hand, despite losing the third day to rain. On a green pitch, Essex had been routed for 99 on the first. Fletcher, in the form of his life, enjoyed a spell of 7–3–11–5 after lunch, concluding in a triple-wicket maiden, to earn a career-best six for 24. Snater, Essex's Zimbabwe-born Netherlands seamer, responded with seven for 98 in his second Championship game. But, as conditions eased, a century from Mullaney and 51 from James, who displayed a calm temperament and sound technique, set up a lead of 224. James went on to extract Cook before the third-day washout. Resuming 95 behind, with seven wickets left, Essex should at least have made Nottinghamshire bat again. But Fletcher removed Browne, for his second half-century of the match, and James dismissed ten Doeschate and Wheater in a double-wicket maiden. The last six fell for 29 to a combination of poor shots and good bowling, with James's four for 51 another career-best.

Close of play: first day, Nottinghamshire 188-4 (James 42, Mullaney 63); second day, Essex 129-3 (Browne 60, Walter 14); third day, no play.

Essex

N. L. J. Browne c Slater b Fletcher	53	– c Moores b Fletcher	64
A. N. Cook c Moores b Broad	3	– lbw b James	35
*T. Westley b Fletcher	1	– c Moores b Broad	1
D. W. Lawrence lbw b James	14	– b Paterson	11
P. I. Walter lbw b Broad	0	– c Duckett b James	30
R. N. ten Doeschate lbw b Fletcher	6	– lbw b James	21
†A. J. A. Wheater c Moores b Fletcher	5	– b James	0
S. R. Harmer lbw b James	8	– lbw b Paterson	0
S. Snater c Moores b Fletcher	0	– not out	12
P. M. Siddle lbw b Fletcher	0	– c Duckett b Paterson	6
J. A. Porter not out	0	– c Moores b Fletcher	1
B 1, lb 8	9	Lb 7, nb 6	13

1/23 (2) 2/34 (3) 3/61 (4)   (41 overs) 99   1/63 (2) 2/68 (3)   (85.2 overs) 194
4/62 (5) 5/80 (6) 6/86 (7)   3/89 (4) 4/137 (1)
7/99 (1) 8/99 (9) 9/99 (10) 10/99 (8)   5/165 (6) 6/165 (7) 7/170 (8)
                                          8/174 (5) 9/185 (10) 10/194 (11)

Broad 9–0–31–2; Fletcher 16–7–24–6; Paterson 11–2–32–0; James 5–3–3–2. *Second innings—* Broad 18–5–46–1; Fletcher 21.2–10–42–2; Paterson 20–8–41–3; James 20–6–51–4; Paterson-White 6–2–7–0.

Nottinghamshire

B. T. Slater c Walter b Snater	14		S. C. J. Broad c Cook b Snater	41
H. Hameed c Harmer b Snater	49		L. J. Fletcher lbw b Snater	2
B. M. Duckett c Wheater b Porter	0		D. Paterson not out	1
J. M. Clarke c Wheater b Snater	15			
L. W. James c Harmer b Snater	51		B 5, lb 6	11
*S. J. Mullaney b Siddle	117			
†T. J. Moores c Wheater b Snater	0		1/31 (1) 2/34 (3) 3/77 (4) (86 overs)	323
L. A. Patterson-White c ten Doeschate			4/84 (2) 5/207 (5) 6/207 (7)	
b Harmer	22		7/253 (8) 8/319 (6) 9/322 (10) 10/323 (9)	

Porter 21–2–75–1; Siddle 22–4–72–1; Snater 26–6–98–7; Harmer 12–3–40–1; Walter 1–0–7–0; ten Doeschate 4–0–20–0.

Umpires: R. J. Bailey and S. J. O'Shaughnessy.   Referee: T. J. Boon.

NOTTINGHAMSHIRE v WORCESTERSHIRE

At Nottingham, May 20–23. Nottinghamshire won by an innings and 170 runs. Nottinghamshire 24pts, Worcestershire 1pt. Toss: Worcestershire.

After Nottinghamshire had waited 30 games for a win, three came along at once – though the first spectators inside Trent Bridge for 20 months had to endure two days of awful weather which allowed only 95 balls. Nottinghamshire eventually wrapped up another assertive innings victory, skittling Worcestershire for 80 on the final morning, then for 150 when they followed on. Duckett had scored a superb unbeaten 177, from 196 balls, adding 205 with James – a county fourth-wicket record against Worcestershire – and 142 in 20 overs with Mullaney, on the way to 400 for five and maximum batting points. Fletcher then improved his career-best for the second match running: his seven for 37 included three lbws in five deliveries, in another triple-wicket maiden, as Worcestershire folded. Three more in the second innings gave him ten in a match for the first time, in his 122nd first-class appearance, aged 32. Libby showed some fight against his former team-mates, before an excellent low catch at square leg by Paterson, who later removed four of the last five.

Close of play: first day, Nottinghamshire 51-3 (Duckett 11); second day, no play; third day, Worcestershire 53-6 (Cox 8, Tongue 7).

Nottinghamshire

B. T. Slater c Cox b Pennington	15	†T. J. Moores not out		1
H. Hameed c Cox b Joseph	24	B 4, lb 6, w 1, nb 6		17
B. M. Duckett not out	177			
J. M. Clarke c Cox b Pennington	0	1/38 (1)	(5 wkts dec, 84.3 overs)	400
L. W. James c D'Oliveira b Mitchell	78	2/50 (2) 3/51 (4)		
*S. J. Mullaney c Cox b Tongue	88	4/256 (5) 5/398 (6)		

L. A. Patterson-White, S. C. J. Broad, L. J. Fletcher and D. Paterson did not bat.

Leach 18–2–70–0; Tongue 11.3–0–75–1; Pennington 19–4–66–2; Joseph 18–0–80–1; Mitchell 14–0–77–1; D'Oliveira 4–0–22–0.

Worcestershire

D. K. H. Mitchell lbw b Fletcher	9	– c Moores b Fletcher		1
J. D. Libby c Slater b Fletcher	2	– c Paterson b Broad		64
T. C. Fell c Moores b Broad	10	– c Slater b Fletcher		13
J. A. Haynes lbw b Fletcher	14	– c and b Fletcher		0
B. L. D'Oliveira lbw b Fletcher	0	– c Mullaney b Paterson		31
M. H. Wessels lbw b Fletcher	0	– c Duckett b James		10
†O. B. Cox c Moores b Broad	19	– lbw b Paterson		0
J. C. Tongue c Moores b Fletcher	7	– (10) b Paterson		6
A. S. Joseph c Moores b Fletcher	4	– (8) c Moores b Broad		4
*J. Leach not out	7	– (9) lbw b Paterson		7
D. Y. Pennington c Duckett b Broad	4	– not out		1
B 1, lb 3	4	B 10, lb 2, w 1		13

1/6 (2) 2/21 (3) 3/21 (1) (32.5 overs) 80	1/7 (1) 2/63 (3) (57.4 overs) 150
4/21 (5) 5/21 (6) 6/46 (4)	3/63 (4) 4/103 (2)
7/54 (8) 8/60 (9) 9/74 (7) 10/80 (11)	5/124 (6) 6/129 (7) 7/136 (5)
	8/136 (8) 9/149 (10) 10/150 (9)

Broad 13.5–4–28–3; Fletcher 16–6–37–7; Paterson 3–0–11–0. *Second innings*—Broad 15–4–31–2; Fletcher 8–1–20–3; James 11–4–23–1; Paterson 18.4–6–49–4; Patterson-White 5–2–15–0.

Umpires: B. V. Taylor and A. G. Wharf.   Referee: W. M. Noon.

At Birmingham, May 27–30. NOTTINGHAMSHIRE lost to WARWICKSHIRE by 170 runs.

At Chelmsford, June 3–6. NOTTINGHAMSHIRE drew with ESSEX.

NOTTINGHAMSHIRE v DERBYSHIRE

At Nottingham, July 4–6. Nottinghamshire won by an innings and 36 runs. Nottinghamshire 22pts, Derbyshire 3pts. Toss: Nottinghamshire. First-class debut: D. J. Schadendorf.

Nottinghamshire clinched victory in three days, despite losing half the first to rain, and returned to the top of their group, well positioned to qualify for Division One. On a pitch initially so green it could barely be distinguished from its neighbours – though it held fewer terrors than first feared – Derbyshire progressed uneasily to 91 for five on the first day, before subsiding for 149 on the second; 36 of the 79 overs were maidens. Duckett, standing in as wicketkeeper while Tom Moores self-isolated, followed four catches with an unbeaten 69, which remained the match's highest score, but departed next morning to join England's emergency one-day squad. His replacement was Dane Schadendorf, a Zimbabwe Under-19 international, who batted nicely and kept efficiently: he too held four catches, dropped none and conceded no byes. Fletcher took five wickets for the fourth time in the season, as Derbyshire folded again. Their coach, Dave Houghton, could not explain their poor form, though he praised "bright spark" Hudson-Prentice, who had claimed a career-best five for 68. Within a week, he announced he would be returning to Sussex.

Close of play: first day, Derbyshire 91-5 (du Plooy 21, Hudson-Prentice 13); second day, Nottinghamshire 256-7 (Duckett 69, Hutton 14).

Derbyshire

L. M. Reece c Duckett b Fletcher	6	– lbw b Paterson	21
T. A. Wood lbw b Hutton	9	– c Compton b Fletcher	3
B. D. Guest c Duckett b James	7	– c †Schadendorf b Hutton	18
J. L. du Plooy c Duckett b Fletcher	30	– b Paterson	1
*M. J. J. Critchley c Hameed b Evison	23	– c †Schadendorf b Evison	36
†H. R. Hosein lbw b Fletcher	0	– lbw b Fletcher	28
F. J. Hudson-Prentice c Patterson-White b Paterson	30	– c †Schadendorf b Fletcher	9
A. T. Thomson lbw b Paterson	6	– c Hutton b Fletcher	2
M. A. R. Cohen c Duckett b Hutton	10	– lbw b Paterson	0
B. W. Aitchison c Slater b Evison	15	– not out	0
G. L. S. Scrimshaw not out	0	– c †Schadendorf b Fletcher	0
Lb 5, nb 8	13	Lb 2, nb 2	4

1/16 (1) 2/20 (2) 3/40 (3) (79.1 overs) 149   1/13 (2) 2/35 (3) (46.4 overs) 122
4/75 (5) 5/76 (6) 6/117 (7)   3/46 (4) 4/55 (1)
7/117 (4) 8/127 (9) 9/143 (9) 10/149 (10)   5/100 (5) 6/115 (7) 7/121 (8)
  8/122 (9) 9/122 (6) 10/122 (11)

Fletcher 24–10–36–3; Hutton 23–10–35–2; Paterson 15–9–24–2; James 8–2–25–1; Evison 9.1–5–24–2. *Second innings*—Fletcher 11.4–3–28–5; Hutton 12–4–26–1; Paterson 11–2–22–3; Evison 9–2–34–1; James 3–0–10–0.

Nottinghamshire

B. T. Slater c Reece b Hudson-Prentice	7	B. A. Hutton lbw b Hudson-Prentice	23
H. Hameed c Hosein b Hudson-Prentice	57	D. J. Schadendorf b Reece	24
B. G. Compton c Thomson b Hudson-Prentice	0	L. J. Fletcher c du Plooy b Aitchison	14
*S. J. Mullaney c Aitchison b Hudson-Prentice	42	D. Paterson not out	2
L. W. James c Critchley b Cohen	33	B 4, lb 3, nb 10	17
†B. M. Duckett retired not out	69	
L. A. Patterson-White c Aitchison b Cohen	0	1/25 (1) 2/25 (3) 3/103 (4) (88.4 overs) 307
J. D. M. Evison c Hosein b Aitchison	19	4/122 (2) 5/183 (5) 6/183 (7)

7/223 (8) 8/283 (9) 9/305 (11) 10/307 (10)

Duckett retired not out at 256-7. Schadendorf replaced Duckett, who left to join England's one-day squad.

Cohen 21–2–65–2; Hudson-Prentice 25–7–68–5; Reece 10.4–2–33–1; Aitchison 17–1–54–2; Scrimshaw 5–0–35–0; Critchley 6–0–27–0; Thomson 4–0–18–0.

Umpires: N. L. Bainton and N. Pratt.   Referee: T. J. Boon.

At Chester-le-Street, July 11–14. NOTTINGHAMSHIRE drew with DURHAM. *Nottinghamshire head Group One.*

DIVISION ONE

At Taunton, August 30–September 1. NOTTINGHAMSHIRE beat SOMERSET by an innings and 160 runs.

NOTTINGHAMSHIRE v LANCASHIRE

At Nottingham, September 5–8. Nottinghamshire won by 102 runs. Nottinghamshire 21pts, Lancashire 3pts. Toss: Lancashire.

Lancashire resistance took the match into its final hour, before Nottinghamshire's second successive win put them top of Division One. Mullaney's declaration, 443 ahead, had given his bowlers 135 overs to take ten wickets: they needed 124, though Fletcher's fifth legitimate delivery brought his 400th first-class victim, trapping Davies for a pair. On a benign pitch, Balderson batted more than five hours for a career-best 77, while Lamb and Bailey added 108, a county ninth-wicket record against Nottinghamshire, thwarting Patterson-White's attempts to spin them out. Then, after 30 overs' defiance, Patterson removed Bailey's middle stump. Mahmood, using a runner after a side strain on the opening day, survived 13 balls, before Hutton had him caught at short leg. Lamb and Bailey had shared eight wickets in Nottinghamshire's first innings, which fell away from 211 for three. But Hutton's five for 62 wrecked Lancashire's reply, earning a home lead of 104, before James and Moores built up a huge advantage for Nottinghamshire in a sixth-wicket partnership of 176. The only disappointment was that both holed out in sight of a century, which would have been James's first.

Close of play: first day, Lancashire 28-2 (Balderson 19, Lamb 1); second day, Nottinghamshire 127-5 (James 18, Moores 11); third day, Lancashire 115-1 (Wells 57, Balderson 45).

Nottinghamshire

B. T. Slater c Lavelle b Bailey	8	– b Balderson	16
B. M. Duckett c Mahmood b Lamb	59	– lbw b Lamb	44
S. A. Northeast c Lavelle b Bailey	65	– c Lavelle b Bailey	13
J. M. Clarke lbw b Lamb	54	– c Jones b Balderson	22
L. W. James c Bohannon b Bailey	21	– c Bohannon b Wells	91
*S. J. Mullaney c Wells b Balderson	4	– c Lavelle b Bailey	1
†T. J. Moores lbw b Wells	12	– c Croft b Wells	97
L. A. Patterson-White c Jones b Lamb	6	– not out	37
B. A. Hutton c Lavelle b Lamb	0	– c sub (J. M. Blatherwick) b Bailey	1
L. J. Fletcher c sub (L. J. Hurt) b Bailey	27	– not out	5
D. Paterson not out	2		
Lb 8, nb 6	14	B 4, lb 3, w 1, nb 4	12

1/22 (1) 2/97 (2) 3/164 (3)   (82.2 overs) 272   1/51 (1)   (8 wkts dec, 107 overs) 339
4/211 (5) 5/223 (4) 6/223 (6)   2/71 (2) 3/85 (3)
7/230 (8) 8/230 (9) 9/260 (7) 10/272 (10)   4/102 (6) 5/107 (6)
                                    6/283 (7) 7/314 (5) 8/315 (9)

Bailey 19.2–6–48–4; Mahmood 14.3–1–68–0; Lamb 23–5–60–4; Balderson 20.3–2–72–1; Wells 4–0–11–1; Croft 1–0–5–0. *Second innings*—Bailey 25–8–84–3; Lamb 24–7–62–1; Balderson 20–5–52–2; Bohannon 10–4–25–0; Wells 16–1–55–2; Croft 12–1–54–0.

Lancashire

G. P. Balderson c Patterson-White b Fletcher	19	– (3) c Paterson b Patterson-White	77
A. L. Davies c Moores b Hutton	0	– lbw b Fletcher	0
L. W. P. Wells c Slater b Hutton	8	– (1) c Moores b Paterson	59
D. J. Lamb c Moores b Hutton	2	– (9) not out	68
J. J. Bohannon c Duckett b Hutton	35	– (4) lbw b Paterson	8
*D. J. Vilas lbw b Hutton	15	– (5) lbw b Hutton	3
R. P. Jones c Northeast b Hutton	14	– (6) b Fletcher	33
S. J. Croft b Paterson	24	– (7) c Duckett b Paterson	6
†G. I. D. Lavelle c Moores b Fletcher	32	– (8) lbw b Fletcher	0
T. E. Bailey lbw b Paterson	0	– b Paterson	52
S. Mahmood not out	0	– c Slater b Hutton	5
Lb 2, nb 4	6	B 10, lb 6, nb 14	30

1/4 (2) 2/24 (3) 3/32 (1)   (52.3 overs) 168   1/5 (2) 2/122 (1)   (123.1 overs) 341
4/82 (5) 5/82 (6) 6/111 (7)   3/138 (4) 4/146 (5)
7/124 (6) 8/156 (8) 9/164 (10) 10/168 (9)   5/192 (3) 6/210 (6) 7/210 (7)
                                    8/210 (8) 9/318 (10) 10/341 (11)

Fletcher 14.3–3–47–2; Hutton 19–5–62–5; Paterson 16–7–39–3; Mullaney 3–1–18–0. *Second innings*—Fletcher 28–7–103–3; Hutton 25.1–6–86–2; Paterson 32–12–78–4; Patterson-White 32–17–39–1; Mullaney 6–1–19–0.

Umpires: N. G. B. Cook and P. J. Hartley.   Referee: A. J. Swann.

At Southampton, September 12–14. NOTTINGHAMSHIRE lost to HAMPSHIRE by 122 runs.

NOTTINGHAMSHIRE v YORKSHIRE

At Nottingham, September 21–24. Nottinghamshire won by five wickets. Nottinghamshire 21pts, Yorkshire 3pts. Toss: Yorkshire.

Nottinghamshire had begun the season without a first-class win since 2018, but ended it with seven – and could have claimed their first Championship title since 2010 had results elsewhere gone their way. As it was, their failure by four runs to collect a third batting point left them half a point short of finishing runners-up and qualifying for the Bob Willis Trophy match. Clarke reached his first first-class century for 12 months on a bowler-friendly pitch – Lyth dropped him twice in the slips before finally hanging on – and Evison scored a maiden fifty, while 20-year-old Duke held six catches, one short of the Yorkshire record. But 296 looked formidable when the visitors succumbed for 73, their worst against Nottinghamshire since 1906: Fletcher charged to 66 wickets in the season, more than anyone else, and Evison picked up four for 13. Yorkshire redeemed themselves following on, especially the out-of-form Lyth, who would have been omitted but for Ballance falling ill. He compiled 153, his highest Championship score since a double-century against Surrey in 2016. Still, Nottinghamshire chased down 174 with nearly two sessions to spare, completing their first Championship win over Yorkshire for a decade.

Close of play: first day, Nottinghamshire 292-9 (Evison 58, Paterson 0); second day, Yorkshire 169-3 (Lyth 74); third day, Nottinghamshire 42-1 (Slater 15, Duckett 23).

Nottinghamshire

B. T. Slater c Duke b Hill	18	– not out ... 79
H. Hameed c Duke b Fisher	23	– c Lyth b Coad ... 4
B. M. Duckett c Bess b Hill	7	– b Thompson ... 54
J. M. Clarke c Lyth b Coad	109	– c Köhler-Cadmore b Bess ... 10
*S. J. Mullaney c Duke b Coad	31	– b Coad ... 9
†T. J. Moores c Duke b Thompson	9	– c Fraine b Coad ... 7
L. A. Patterson-White c Duke b Coad	16	– not out ... 4
J. D. M. Evison lbw b Thompson	58	
B. A. Hutton c Duke b Revis	9	
L. J. Fletcher c Thompson b Revis	4	
D. Paterson not out	4	
B 2, lb 4, nb 2	8	B 4, lb 3 ... 7

1/45 (2) 2/47 (1) 3/70 (3)   (97.3 overs) 296   1/9 (2)   (5 wkts, 48 overs) 174
4/119 (5) 5/147 (6) 6/173 (7)   2/107 (3) 3/130 (4)
7/270 (4) 8/282 (9) 9/292 (10) 10/296 (8)   4/143 (5) 5/163 (6)

Coad 25–7–75–3; Fisher 18–3–69–1; Thompson 20.3–6–55–2; Hill 9–3–32–2; Revis 9–2–19–2; Bess 11–1–27–0; Brook 5–1–13–0. *Second innings*—Coad 17–0–58–3; Fisher 8–1–26–0; Thompson 8–0–42–1; Bess 12–2–35–1; Hill 3–1–6–0.

Yorkshire

A. Lyth lbw b Hutton	...	4 – c Moores b Evison	153
G. C. H. Hill c Hameed b Fletcher	...	5 – run out (sub C. G. Harrison)	34
T. Köhler-Cadmore b Fletcher	...	0 – lbw b Patterson-White	49
W. A. R. Fraine c Moores b Fletcher	...	12 – (5) lbw b Hutton	3
H. C. Brook c Moores b Evison	...	12 – (6) c Hutton b Paterson	42
J. A. Thompson lbw b Evison	...	16 – (7) c Duckett b Mullaney	31
M. L. Revis c Hutton b Evison	...	0 – (8) c Clarke b Paterson	34
D. M. Bess c Hutton b Evison	...	12 – (9) lbw b Hutton	8
†H. G. Duke b Paterson	...	0 – (10) lbw b Hutton	7
M. D. Fisher c Moores b Paterson	...	4 – (4) lbw b Paterson	0
*B. O. Coad not out	...	0 – not out	3
B 4, lb 2, nb 2	8	B 20, lb 12	32

1/5 (2) 2/5 (3) 3/21 (1) (29.2 overs) 73
4/21 (4) 5/45 (6) 6/45 (7)
7/60 (5) 8/63 (9) 9/73 (8) 10/73 (10)

1/65 (2) 2/168 (3) (142.2 overs) 396
3/169 (4) 4/182 (5)
5/261 (6) 6/335 (7) 7/347 (1)
8/356 (9) 9/368 (10) 10/396 (8)

Fletcher 8–3–31–3; Hutton 7–3–12–1; Paterson 7.2–1–11–2; Evison 7–3–13–4. *Second innings*—Fletcher 23–7–68–0; Hutton 34–8–101–3; Evison 28–6–78–1; Paterson 21.2–5–39–3; Mullaney 19–3–50–1; Patterson-White 17–6–28–1.

Umpires: R. J. Bailey and R. A. Kettleborough.   Referee: T. J. Boon.

SOMERSET

Top flight, crash landing

RICHARD LATHAM

It says a lot about expectations at Taunton that, despite overcoming an eight-point penalty to qualify for Division One in the second phase of the County Championship, and reaching the Vitality Blast final, Somerset endured an ultimately disappointing 2021. When it mattered most, their form deserted them: a combination of top-order frailty and a weakened attack, deprived of Craig Overton and Lewis Gregory through England duty and injury, resulted in a dramatic slump.

In the four-day game, Somerset soon made good the deficit incurred for producing a poor pitch in the Championship decider against Essex in 2019. The first five matches resulted in victories over Middlesex (twice), Leicestershire and Hampshire, as Overton enhanced his Test prospects with 32 wickets. The next five were drawn, but they had done enough – not only to top the group, but to enter Division One in second place. Hopes were high for the long-awaited maiden Championship title.

Who could have predicted, then, that all four divisional matches would bring thumping defeats? Two were by an innings, one by ten wickets, the other by 118 runs. Not for the first time, Somerset's players had to watch as their opponents – Warwickshire – were crowned champions after the final game.

It wasn't difficult to diagnose the problem. Of the regular top six, only skipper Tom Abell, with 711 runs at nearly 40, could hold his head high. The others shone only occasionally: James Hildreth moved third in Somerset's all-time first-class runs table when he overtook Peter Wight's aggregate of 16,965; George Bartlett scored a hundred against Hampshire; Tom Banton, Tom Lammonby and Lewis Goldsworthy were never dull. But none averaged 25. New Zealand's Devon Conway prospered in two games, and proved a popular member of the dressing-room, having previously played for Somerset Second XI as an unknown in 2010. He will surely be invited back when international commitments allow. Pakistan's Azhar Ali returned to shore up the batting for the last three matches, but scored only 177 runs in six innings.

Somerset simply could not make totals that put pressure on the opposition. Even in the early successes, the lower order often rescued them, and the bowlers rarely had many runs to play with. Overton, who ended with 42 wickets at 15, added half a yard of pace, while Josh Davey confirmed his emergence as a key member of the attack with 35 at 22. But Gregory was rarely at his best. Between England call-ups, The Hundred and back problems, he played only one of the last six games – as a specialist batsman.

South African fast bowler Marchant de Lange, beginning a two-year contract as an overseas player, took 20 wickets in ten appearances. Australians Peter Siddle and Matt Renshaw signed for 2022. Jack Leach, no longer helped by the surfaces at the County Ground, claimed just 18, six in one Surrey innings at The Oval, but he earned a place – along with Overton – in England's Ashes party. Steve Davies kept wicket consistently well and, at times, looked in prime form with the bat; a top score of 87 was a letdown.

The Vitality Blast was a mirror image of the Championship: Somerset won only one of their first five matches, then seven of the last nine. The difference was the availability of Conway, who entered the fray in the seventh game, and scored 45 or more in five of his eight innings, topping the averages

Josh Davey

with 309 at 61. Abell wasn't far behind (295 at 59), while headlines were grabbed by 19-year-old Will Smeed, whose 385 at 32 included 34 fours and 19 sixes, earning him selection for Birmingham Phoenix in The Hundred, where he also excelled. Lammonby and Banton showed flashes of brilliance – Banton smashed the only century, in a ten-wicket thrashing of eventual champions Kent. With the ball, de Lange led the way with 18 wickets, while Roelof van der Merwe underlined his value as an economical left-arm spinner and superb fielder.

On finals day, Somerset snatched a thrilling two-wicket win over Hampshire in the semi. It had seemed hopeless: when Abell was seventh out, they needed 48 from 20, but Ben Green and then Davey pulled it off with two balls remaining. In their fifth Blast final (a record), Somerset needed 168 to win, but plunged from 61 for two to 119 for nine – and now there was no escape. They were runners-up for the fourth time (also a record) since their 2005 title.

In the Royal London Cup, Somerset failed to make the knockout stage, winning just three of their eight games. But their performances, under new 50-over captain Green, offered cause for optimism. Even though nine players were lost to The Hundred, crowds of up to 5,000 flocked to watch the greenhorns: Kasey Aldridge and Ned Leonard bowled well, and made Championship debuts; Sonny Baker, James Rew and George Thomas were selected by England Under-19. Though not all the youngsters succeeded – Eddie Byrom moved to Glamorgan, and Sam Young was later released – their approach was exhilarating, and suggested the future of Somerset cricket was not only safe, but exciting.

In November, seamer Jack Brooks apologised for tweets in 2012 in which he referred to two other players as "negro". The club called the comments unacceptable, and said he would take part in "extensive training on equality, diversity and inclusion". Brooks also said sorry for calling Indian Cheteshwar Pujara "Steve" during their time at Yorkshire.

SOMERSET RESULTS

County Championship matches – Played 14: Won 4, Lost 5, Drawn 5.
Vitality T20 Blast matches – Played 17: Won 10, Lost 5, No result 2.
Royal London Cup matches – Played 8: Won 3, Lost 3, No result 2.

LV= County Championship, 1st in Group 2, 6th in Division 1;
Vitality T20 Blast, finalists; Royal London Cup, 7th in Group 2.

COUNTY CHAMPIONSHIP AVERAGES, BATTING AND FIELDING

Cap		Birthplace	M	I	NO	R	HS	100	Avge	Ct/St
2015	L. Gregory	Plymouth	9	10	2	389	107	1	48.62	7
2018	T. B. Abell	Taunton‡	12	20	2	711	132*	1	39.50	11
2017	†S. M. Davies	Bromsgrove	13	22	2	634	87	0	31.70	37/1
2018	R. E. van der Merwe††	Johannesburg, SA . .	6	8	0	241	88	0	30.12	4
2019	Azhar Ali¶	Lahore, Pakistan . . .	3	6	0	177	60	0	29.50	2
2021	J. H. Davey††	Aberdeen	12	16	7	238	75*	0	26.44	2
2017	†M. J. Leach§	Taunton‡	10	15	4	276	49	0	25.09	2
	G. A. Bartlett	Frimley	11	16	1	373	100	1	24.86	2
2016	C. Overton	Barnstaple	8	11	1	237	74	0	23.70	9
2007	J. C. Hildreth	Milton Keynes	13	20	0	456	107	1	22.80	14
	B. G. F. Green	Exeter	4	8	1	154	43	0	22.00	2
	M. de Lange¶	Tzaneen, SA	10	14	0	297	75	0	21.21	4
	L. P. Goldsworthy . . .	Truro	10	15	1	297	48	0	21.21	1
	†T. A. Lammonby	Exeter	13	22	2	392	100	1	19.60	7
	T. Banton	Chiltern	8	14	1	245	51*	0	18.84	5
	†E. J. Byrom††	Harare, Zimbabwe .	4	5	1	55	38	0	13.75	1
	J. A. Brooks	Oxford	6	10	4	47	15	0	7.83	0

Also batted: K. L. Aldridge (*Bristol*) (1 match) did not bat; †D. P. Conway¶ (*Johannesburg, SA*) (2 matches) 88, 21, 12 (3 ct); E. O. Leonard (*Hammersmith*) (1 match) 4*, 6 (1 ct).

‡ *Born in Somerset.* § *ECB contract.* ¶ *Official overseas player.* †† *Other non-England-qualified.*

BOWLING

	Style	O	M	R	W	BB	5I	Avge
C. Overton	RFM	270.3	93	650	42	5-25	4	15.47
J. H. Davey	RFM	292.2	84	781	35	5-30	2	22.31
L. Gregory	RFM	209.3	60	645	21	5-68	1	30.71
M. J. Leach	SLA	241	77	562	18	6-43	1	31.22
M. de Lange	RF	231.5	49	685	20	4-55	0	34.25
J. A. Brooks	RFM	142	28	499	12	4-77	0	41.58
T. B. Abell	RM	168.3	44	558	13	3-63	0	42.92

Also bowled: K. L. Aldridge (RM) 22–2–101–0; L. P. Goldsworthy (SLA) 24–8–45–0; B. G. F. Green (RFM) 40–11–93–1; T. A. Lammonby (LM) 77–13–287–4; E. O. Leonard (RM) 18–2–85–1; R. E. van der Merwe (SLA) 96.1–26–241–8.

LEADING VITALITY BLAST AVERAGES (100 runs/15 overs)

Batting	Runs	HS	Avge	SR	Ct/St	**Bowling**	W	BB	Avge	ER
T. Banton	243	107*	27.00	**176.08**	8/3	C. Overton	13	3-28	20.30	**7.13**
T. A. Lammonby .	219	90	27.37	**162.22**	3	R. E. van der Merwe	11	4-27	18.09	**7.19**
T. B. Abell	295	78*	59.00	**161.20**	4	L. P. Goldsworthy	9	3-14	25.11	**7.29**
B. G. F. Green . . .	129	43*	21.50	**135.78**	10	J. A. Brooks	8	2-33	28.00	**7.68**
W. C. F. Smeed . .	385	63*	32.08	**132.30**	8	B. G. F. Green . . .	4	2-34	44.00	**8.38**
J. C. Hildreth . . .	206	72*	25.75	**132.05**	1	M. de Lange	18	3-18	22.72	**8.52**
D. P. Conway . .	309	81*	61.80	**125.60**	5	M. T. C. Waller . .	5	2-26	48.20	**8.60**
L. P. Goldsworthy	172	48	17.20	**110.25**	3	J. H. Davey	13	4-34	19.46	**9.79**
						L. Gregory	12	5-24	18.83	**9.82**

LEADING ROYAL LONDON CUP AVERAGES (100 runs/4 wickets)

Batting	Runs	HS	Avge	SR	Ct
L. P. Goldsworthy	381	96	63.50	87.18	2
B. G. F. Green	110	87	55.00	123.59	1
J. C. Hildreth	306	110	51.00	103.72	2
S. M. Davies	269	94	38.42	103.46	10
G. A. Bartlett	159	108	31.80	98.75	2

Bowling	W	BB	Avge	ER
B. G. F. Green	8	3-64	22.37	5.18
J. H. Davey	8	4-57	24.62	5.62
S. Baker	10	3-46	33.00	6.03
K. L. Aldridge	6	3-39	34.83	6.96

FIRST-CLASS COUNTY RECORDS

Highest score for	342	J. L. Langer v Surrey at Guildford	2006
Highest score against	424	A. C. MacLaren (Lancashire) at Taunton	1895
Leading run-scorer	21,142	H. Gimblett (avge 36.96)	1935–54
Best bowling for	10-49	E. J. Tyler v Surrey at Taunton	1895
Best bowling against	10-35	A. Drake (Yorkshire) at Weston-super-Mare	1914
Leading wicket-taker	2,165	J. C. White (avge 18.03)	1909–37
Highest total for	850-7 dec	v Middlesex at Taunton	2007
Highest total against	811	by Surrey at The Oval	1899
Lowest total for	25	v Gloucestershire at Bristol	1947
Lowest total against	22	by Gloucestershire at Bristol	1920

LIST A COUNTY RECORDS

Highest score for	184	M. E. Trescothick v Gloucestershire at Taunton	2008
Highest score against	167*	A. J. Stewart (Surrey) at The Oval	1994
Leading run-scorer	7,374	M. E. Trescothick (avge 36.87)	1993–2014
Best bowling for	8-66	S. R. G. Francis v Derbyshire at Derby	2004
Best bowling against	7-39	A. Hodgson (Northamptonshire) at Northampton	1976
Leading wicket-taker	309	H. R. Moseley (avge 20.03)	1971–82
Highest total for	413-4	v Devon at Torquay	1990
Highest total against	429-9	by Nottinghamshire at Taunton	2017
Lowest total for	⎰ 58	v Essex at Chelmsford	1977
	⎱ 58	v Middlesex at Southgate	2000
Lowest total against	60	by Kent at Taunton	1979

TWENTY20 COUNTY RECORDS

Highest score for	151*	C. H. Gayle v Kent at Taunton	2015
Highest score against	122*	J. J. Roy (Surrey) at The Oval	2015
Leading run-scorer	**3,900**	**J. C. Hildreth (avge 24.52, SR 124.64)**	**2004–21**
Best bowling for	6-5	A. V. Suppiah v Glamorgan at Cardiff	2011
Best bowling against	5-11	A. F. Milne (Kent) at Taunton	2017
Leading wicket-taker	⎰ 137	A. C. Thomas (avge 20.17, ER 7.67)	2008–15
	⎱ **137**	**M. T. C. Waller (avge 24.69, ER 7.36)**	**2009–21**
Highest total for	250-3	v Gloucestershire at Taunton	2006
Highest total for	231-5	by Kent at Canterbury	2018
Lowest total for	82	v Kent at Taunton	2010
Lowest total against	73	by Warwickshire at Taunton	2013

ADDRESS

Cooper Associates County Ground, St James's Street, Taunton TA1 1JT; 01823 425301; enquiries@somersetcountycc.co.uk; www.somersetcountycc.co.uk. Twitter: @SomersetCCC.

OFFICIALS

Captain T. B. Abell
Director of cricket A. Hurry
Head coach J. I. D. Kerr
Academy director 2021 S. D. Snell
Head of talent pathway M. Drakeley

President B. C. Rose
Chair G. M. Baird
Chief executive G. M. Hollins
Head groundsman S. Hawkins
Scorer L. M. Rhodes

GROUP TWO

At Lord's, April 8–11. SOMERSET beat MIDDLESEX by four wickets. *Somerset overcome a first-innings deficit of 141.*

SOMERSET v GLOUCESTERSHIRE

At Taunton, April 15–18. Gloucestershire won by eight wickets. Gloucestershire 22pts, Somerset 6pts. Toss: Gloucestershire. First-class debut: D. C. Goodman. County debut: K. C. Brathwaite.

Victory over Middlesex had allowed Somerset to more than wipe out their eight-point penalty after they produced a pitch rated "poor" for the 2019 Championship decider, but now they were brought crashing to earth by their arch-rivals. Top-order problems resurfaced as they slipped to 110 for five in their first innings, and 88 for seven in the second, with Lammonby completing a pair. Their frailty was punished by a Gloucestershire team for whom Bracey scored 201 runs for once out in eight and a quarter hours of patient batting. His first-innings century had kept them in the game, and he added a crucial 71 for the eighth wicket with Taylor, who progressed to a maiden fifty, reducing the deficit to three. Overton bowled his heart out, and his battle with Bracey, especially on a feisty third evening, was Championship cricket of the highest calibre. Higgins claimed seven wickets for a disciplined Gloucestershire seam attack, featuring an impressive debut from Dom Goodman, a 20-year-old at Exeter University. Despite defiant batting from Davies, Overton and Hildreth, and genuine pace from de Lange, Gloucestershire needed only 153 to achieve their first Championship win at Taunton since 1993. For Somerset, it was a first home defeat in four years.

Close of play: first day, Gloucestershire 13-0 (Brathwaite 2, Dent 9); second day, Gloucestershire 301-8 (Taylor 53, Payne 9); third day, Gloucestershire 28-1 (Brathwaite 8, Bracey 10).

Somerset

T. Banton b Payne	29	– c Dent b Taylor	18
T. A. Lammonby c Hankins b Higgins	0	– c Bracey b Higgins	0
*T. B. Abell lbw b Taylor	26	– lbw b Higgins	6
J. C. Hildreth c Lace b Taylor	17	– lbw b Goodman	64
G. A. Bartlett lbw b Higgins	22	– c Bracey b Goodman	0
†S. M. Davies b Payne	87	– c Hankins b Payne	12
C. Overton c Hankins b Higgins	54	– b Higgins	2
L. Gregory c Scott b Payne	13	– c Higgins b Taylor	8
J. H. Davey c Brathwaite b Goodman	17	– c Brathwaite b Higgins	22
M. de Lange c Lace b Taylor	37	– lbw b van Buuren	0
M. J. Leach not out	0	– not out	4
Lb 8, nb 2	10	Lb 9, nb 4	13

1/4 (2) 2/42 (1) 3/69 (3) (94.1 overs) 312 1/2 (2) 2/18 (3) (65.5 overs) 149
4/80 (4) 5/110 (5) 6/226 (7) 3/36 (1) 4/37 (5)
7/255 (8) 8/264 (6) 9/312 (9) 10/312 (10) 5/68 (6) 6/71 (7) 7/88 (8)
8/142 (4) 9/143 (10) 10/149 (9)

Payne 21–4–72–3; Higgins 24–6–71–3; Taylor 17.1–2–67–3; Goodman 14–4–36–1; van Buuren 8–3–23–0; Scott 10–0–35–0. *Second innings*—Payne 16–3–48–1; Higgins 16.5–5–29–4; Taylor 13–4–27–2; Goodman 11–3–19–2; van Buuren 9–3–17–1.

Gloucestershire

K. C. Brathwaite lbw b Overton	18	– b de Lange	36
*C. D. J. Dent c Davies b de Lange	50	– b Overton	9
†J. R. Bracey c Hildreth b Gregory	118	– not out	83
T. C. Lace c Banton b Overton	7	– not out	20
G. L. van Buuren c Gregory b Overton	4		
R. F. Higgins c Hildreth b Davey	23		
G. T. Hankins lbw b de Lange	4		
G. F. B. Scott c Overton b Gregory	10		
M. D. Taylor lbw b de Lange	56		
D. A. Payne c and b de Lange	12		
D. C. Goodman not out	2		
Lb 3, nb 2	5	B 4, w 2, nb 2	8
	309	(2 wkts, 41.1 overs)	**156**

1/41 (1) 2/87 (2) 3/105 (4)   (110.1 overs) 309   1/10 (2)   (2 wkts, 41.1 overs) 156
4/119 (5) 5/160 (6) 6/177 (7)   2/89 (1)
7/203 (8) 8/274 (3) 9/304 (10)
10/309 (9)   110 overs: 309-9

Gregory 20–5–72–2; Overton 24–6–63–3; Davey 15–3–43–1; de Lange 21.1–3–63–4; Leach 29–10–64–0; Abell 1–0–1–0. *Second innings*—Gregory 10–1–30–0; Overton 14–2–52–1; Leach 11.1–2–57–0; de Lange 6–2–13–1.

Umpires: N. L. Bainton and R. K. Illingworth.   Referee: S. Cummings.

At Leicester, April 22–24. SOMERSET beat LEICESTERSHIRE by nine wickets.

SOMERSET v MIDDLESEX

At Taunton, April 29–May 2. Somerset won by four wickets. Somerset 21pts, Middlesex 7pts. Toss: Somerset. First-class debut: L. P. Goldsworthy.

For the second time in three weeks, Somerset overturned an apparently lost cause against Middlesex, this time with the help of aggressive bowling from Overton. From 44 without loss in their second innings, a lead of 133, the visitors lost ten for 73, as Overton claimed five for 34. But there was still work to do. Set 207, Somerset lost Banton first ball to the relentless Murtagh, and collapsed to 123 for six; then the 20-year-old Lewis Goldsworthy, on first-class debut, and Davies, nearly 15 years his senior, put on an unbroken 86. Gubbins and White appeared to have given Middlesex control on the first day, while on the second Hildreth overtook Bill Alley's haul of 16,644 first-class runs for Somerset, and moved up to fourth on their all-time list; only Harold Gimblett, Marcus Trescothick and Peter Wight lay ahead. But five wickets for Finn (and five catches by Simpson) earned Middlesex a lead of 89, which grew into three figures before Davey removed Robson to begin the fightback. On the third morning, Jack Brooks became county cricket's first Covid substitute, replacing Gregory, whose girlfriend had reported symptoms of the virus; Gregory himself had tested positive at the Pakistan Super League in March.

Close of play: first day, Middlesex 308-6 (White 70, Hollman 3); second day, Somerset 178-4 (Bartlett 43, Goldsworthy 34); third day, Somerset 104-4 (Abell 43).

Middlesex

S. D. Robson c Davies b Gregory	6	– (2) c Banton b Davey	18
M. D. E. Holden c Davies b Overton	49	– (1) c Davies b Overton	30
N. R. T. Gubbins b Overton b Gregory	75	– c Davies b Davey	3
*P. S. P. Handscomb			
run out (sub R. E. van der Merwe)	17	– c Davies b Abell	0
R. G. White c Hildreth b Davey	92	– lbw b Overton	10
†J. A. Simpson c Hildreth b Lammonby	33	– c Abell b Davey	7
M. K. Andersson lbw b Overton	38	– c and b Overton	8
L. B. K. Hollman b Overton	16	– not out	21
T. G. Helm not out	0	– lbw b Overton	13
S. T. Finn lbw b Davey	0	– lbw b Overton	1
T. J. Murtagh c Bartlett b Davey	8	– b Abell	0
B 4, lb 11, nb 8	23	B 1, lb 5	6

1/17 (1) 2/82 (2) 3/129 (4)   (110 overs) 357   1/44 (2) 2/48 (1)   (50 overs) 117
4/170 (3) 5/239 (6) 6/294 (7)   3/50 (4) 4/54 (3)
7/332 (8) 8/349 (5) 9/349 (10) 10/357 (11)   5/62 (6) 6/77 (7) 7/82 (5)
8/102 (9) 9/110 (10) 10/117 (11)

Overton 28–12–60–3; Gregory 26–6–87–2; Davey 14–5–33–3; Abell 23–7–66–0; Leach 7–0–28–0; Lammonby 12–1–68–1. *Second innings*—Overton 19–7–34–5; Brooks 8–1–35–0; Davey 16–5–28–3; Abell 7–3–14–2.

Somerset

T. Banton lbw b Murtagh	3	– b Murtagh	0
T. A. Lammonby c Simpson b Finn	13	– lbw b Murtagh	9
*T. B. Abell c Andersson b Finn	41	– lbw b Murtagh	49
J. C. Hildreth c Simpson b Murtagh	39	– c White b Andersson	43
G. A. Bartlett c Simpson b Helm	55	– (6) lbw b Murtagh	12
L. P. Goldsworthy c Simpson b Helm	39	– (7) not out	41
†S. M. Davies c Holden b Finn	2	– (8) not out	44
C. Overton not out	38		
J. H. Davey c Helm b Finn	8		
M. J. Leach c Holden b Finn	16	– (5) c Holden b Finn	5
J. A. Brooks c Simpson b Murtagh	1		
B 4, lb 2, nb 2, p 5	13	B 4, nb 2	6

1/16 (2) 2/16 (1) 3/86 (4)   (80.2 overs) 268   1/0 (1)   (6 wkts, 57.4 overs) 209
4/98 (3) 5/188 (6) 6/195 (5)   2/17 (2) 3/95 (4)
7/218 (7) 8/228 (9) 9/267 (10) 10/268 (11)   4/104 (3) 5/118 (3) 6/123 (6)

Brooks replaced L. Gregory, as a Covid substitute.

Murtagh 22.2–7–49–3; Helm 20–5–56–2; Finn 20–2–77–5; Andersson 11–3–54–0; Hollman 7–0–21–0. *Second innings*—Murtagh 21–4–53–4; Helm 12–1–52–0; Finn 12–1–46–1; Andersson 10–0–39–1; Hollman 2.4–0–15–0.

Umpires: M. Burns and I. J. Gould.   Referee: W. M. Noon.

At Southampton, May 6–9. SOMERSET beat HAMPSHIRE by ten wickets.

SOMERSET v SURREY

At Taunton, May 13–16. Drawn. Somerset 9pts, Surrey 9pts. Toss: Somerset.

Burns warmed up for the New Zealand Test series with a fourth successive half-century in a match ruined by the weather. After rain washed out the first day, he rode his luck once play began at two on the second, before settling in. He added 76 for the second wicket with Amla, who gifted Gregory his 300th first-class wicket by pulling a long hop to long leg. Burns fell five balls later, but only nine overs were possible on the third day, and none on the last. For Somerset, Steven Davies was undergoing a medical procedure, so Banton kept wicket for the first time in a first-class match – and caught Pope.

Close of play: first day, no play; second day, Surrey 191-4 (Foakes 13, Smith 18); third day, Surrey 206-4 (Foakes 16, Smith 27).

Surrey

*R. J. Burns b de Lange	55	J. L. Smith not out		27
M. D. Stoneman c van der Merwe b Gregory	18	B 8, lb 14, w 2, nb 4		28
H. M. Amla c Byrom b Gregory	29			—
O. J. D. Pope c Banton b Abell	33	1/43 (2) 2/119 (3)	(4 wkts, 68 overs)	206
†B. T. Foakes not out	16	3/119 (1) 4/168 (4)		

W. G. Jacks, J. Clark, J. Overton, R. Clarke and K. A. J. Roach did not bat.

Gregory 22–7–64–2; Davey 20–7–39–0; de Lange 15–2–48–1; Abell 11–4–33–1.

Somerset

E. J. Byrom, T. A. Lammonby, *T. B. Abell, J. C. Hildreth, G. A. Bartlett, L. P. Goldsworthy, †T. Banton, L. Gregory, R. E. van der Merwe, J. H. Davey, M. de Lange.

Umpires: N. G. B. Cook and R. J. Warren.   Referee: D. A. Cosker.

At Bristol, May 20–23. SOMERSET drew with GLOUCESTERSHIRE.

SOMERSET v HAMPSHIRE

At Taunton, June 3–6. Drawn. Somerset 15pts, Hampshire 14pts. Toss: Hampshire. County debut: C. T. Steel.

Somerset's habit of losing early wickets continued as they slumped to 43 for five after being put in, with Barker claiming four for seven in nine overs. But, in front of Taunton's first crowd of the summer, that was as good as it got for Hampshire. Gregory and van der Merwe, in his first innings of the season, put on 171 in 35 overs for the eighth wicket, before the last two added a further 76. Barker finished with six for 72, his best figures for Hampshire, and his best for nearly seven years. The visitors slipped to 148 for six when Northeast fell for 67, but McManus, dismissed for 91 in the first over of the third day, fashioned a recovery to 311, despite five wickets for Davey. Somerset then built soundly on a lead of 49. Davies, promoted to open, took his match aggregate to 129, while Abell contributed a technically superb 98, and Bartlett a sweetly timed century. Keen to stay in the group's top two, Abell took no chances over a final-day declaration after Banton's brisk half-century had established a lead of 458. Some felt he should have closed the innings the previous evening, but that was rendered academic by afternoon rain.

Close of play: first day, Somerset 360; second day, Hampshire 285-7 (McManus 91, Organ 21); third day, Somerset 323-6 (Bartlett 74).

Somerset

E. J. Byrom b Barker	0	– c McManus b Abbott	4
†S. M. Davies c McManus b Barker	47	– lbw b Organ	82
*T. B. Abell c Dawson b Barker	8	– b Organ	98
J. C. Hildreth c McManus b Barker	1	– c and b Organ	13
G. A. Bartlett lbw b Barker	0	– c Vince b Wheal	100
L. P. Goldsworthy c McManus b Wheal	7	– c Alsop b Holland	36
T. Banton b Barker	45	– (8) not out	51
L. Gregory b Abbott	107		
R. E. van der Merwe run out (Wheal)	88		
J. H. Davey not out	22	– (7) c McManus b Barker	6
M. de Lange c Organ b Wheal	17		
B 8, lb 4, nb 6	18	B 11, lb 1, w 5, nb 2	19

1/0 (1) 2/20 (3) 3/26 (4) (83.2 overs) 360 1/13 (1) (7 wkts dec, 103.1 overs) 409
4/26 (5) 5/43 (6) 6/108 (7)   2/152 (2) 3/182 (4)
7/113 (2) 8/284 (9) 9/338 (8) 10/360 (11)   4/203 (3) 5/311 (6) 6/323 (7) 7/409 (5)

Barker 24–5–72–6; Abbott 24–2–132–1; Wheal 17.2–1–66–2; Holland 12–1–58–0; Dawson 4–0–12–0; Organ 2–1–8–0. *Second innings*—Barker 24–6–79–1; Abbott 17–2–90–1; Wheal 20.1–2–67–1; Organ 29–3–115–3; Holland 13–1–46–1.

Hampshire

C. T. Steel c and b de Lange	15	– lbw b Gregory	14
I. G. Holland c van der Merwe b Davey	9	– b Gregory	9
T. P. Alsop c Abell b de Lange	4	– not out	23
S. A. Northeast c Davies b Abell	67	– not out	19
*J. M. Vince c sub (K. L. Aldridge) b Davey	29		
L. A. Dawson c Hildreth b Abell	3		
†L. D. McManus c Abell b Davey	91		
K. H. D. Barker c Gregory b Davey	33		
F. S. Organ lbw b Gregory	26		
K. J. Abbott not out	10		
B. T. J. Wheal lbw b Davey	9		
B 2, lb 3, nb 10	15	B 8, lb 5, nb 10	23

1/15 (2) 2/30 (3) 3/31 (1) (104.2 overs) 311 1/30 (1) (2 wkts, 33.3 overs) 88
4/97 (5) 5/110 (6) 6/148 (4)   2/39 (2)
7/235 (8) 8/286 (7) 9/292 (9) 10/311 (11)

Davey 25.2–5–78–5; Gregory 24–7–76–1; de Lange 22–7–46–2; Abell 22–8–55–2; van der Merwe 11–0–51–0. *Second innings*—Gregory 10–6–18–2; Davey 9–3–23–0; de Lange 5–0–13–0; van der Merwe 7–0–16–0; Abell 2.3–0–5–0.

Umpires: P. J. Hartley and S. J. O'Shaughnessy. Referee: S. J. Davis.

SOMERSET v LEICESTERSHIRE

At Taunton, July 4–7. Drawn. Somerset 15pts, Leicestershire 14pts. Toss: Leicestershire. First-class debut: K. L. Aldridge. Championship debuts: D. P. Conway; J. P. Inglis.

Somerset, leading the group, knew a high-scoring draw would almost guarantee qualification for Division One, and preserve hopes of a maiden title. Unsurprisingly, they produced a pitch which frustrated all the bowlers. Leicestershire elected to field and, despite an opening stand of 143 between Devon Conway – who made 88 in his first Championship appearance – and Davies, their call seemed to have paid off when Somerset subsided to 224 for seven. But van der Merwe hit 76 from No. 8, Davey a career-best unbeaten 75 from No. 9, and de Lange 75 off 63 from No. 10, including six sixes, as the last three wickets added 237, allowing a declaration. Overton was summoned to England's one-day squad at the close of the second day; Hildreth took over as captain, and debutant all-rounder Kasey Aldridge was drafted in. From 272 for seven, Swindells – who extended his second first-class century to 171 – and Barnes each hit a career-best in an unbroken eighth-wicket partnership of 203, surpassing the club record of 195 by James Taylor and Jigar Naik against Derbyshire in 2009. Leicestershire edged ahead before rain curtailed the game at lunch on the final day, but Somerset went to The Oval needing only a draw.

Close of play: first day, Somerset 242-7 (van der Merwe 18, Davey 4); second day, Leicestershire 95-3 (Ackermann 22, Inglis 15); third day, Leicestershire 390-7 (Swindells 119, Barnes 54).

Somerset

D. P. Conway b Parkinson	88		M. de Lange c Harris b Parkinson	75
†S. M. Davies b Davis	65		J. A. Brooks not out	0
L. P. Goldsworthy c Ackermann b Davis	3		B 15, w 5, nb 10	30
J. C. Hildreth c Swindells b Griffiths	23			
G. A. Bartlett lbw b Mike	10		1/143 (2) 3/171 (1) (9 wkts dec, 115 overs) 461
T. A. Lammonby c Ackermann b Griffiths	14		2/151 (3) 3/171 (1)	
*C. Overton c Swindells b Griffiths	5		4/182 (5) 5/206 (6)	
R. E. van der Merwe c Davis b Barnes	75		6/213 (4) 7/224 (7)	
J. H. Davey not out	75		8/326 (8) 9/446 (10) 110 overs: 433-8

K. L. Aldridge replaced Overton, who left to join England's one-day squad.

Davis 29–4–89–2; Barnes 19–4–96–1; Mike 20–4–70–1; Griffiths 20–1–93–3; Parkinson 27–4–98–2.

Leicestershire

L. J. Hill lbw b Overton	14		C. F. Parkinson c Conway b de Lange	12
R. K. Patel c Overton b Brooks	21		E. Barnes not out	83
M. S. Harris c Davies b Davey	21		B 5, lb 2, nb 12	19
*C. N. Ackermann b de Lange	67			
J. P. Inglis lbw b Brooks	27		1/36 (1) 2/44 (2) (7 wkts, 152 overs) 475
†H. J. Swindells not out	171		3/60 (3) 4/117 (5) 5/177 (4)	
B. W. M. Mike c Hildreth b de Lange	40		6/256 (7) 7/272 (8) 110 overs: 350-7

G. T. Griffiths and W. S. Davis did not bat.

Overton 12–3–33–1; Davey 14–3–34–1; Brooks 29–9–76–2; de Lange 30–4–110–3; Aldridge 22–2–101–0; van der Merwe 18–6–40–0; Lammonby 17–3–58–0; Goldsworthy 10–3–16–0.

Umpires: N. A. Mallender and J. D. Middlebrook.   Referee: J. J. Whitaker.

At The Oval, July 11–14. SOMERSET drew with SURREY. *Somerset are bowled out for 69 in their second innings, but head Group Two.*

DIVISION ONE

SOMERSET v NOTTINGHAMSHIRE

At Taunton, August 30–September 1. Nottinghamshire won by an innings and 160 runs. Nottinghamshire 23pts, Somerset 2pts. Toss: Somerset. County debut: S. A. Northeast.

Entering Division One in second place, Somerset slumped to their heaviest defeat for a decade, and their first by Nottinghamshire at Taunton since 1985. Despite a depleted seam attack – Craig Overton was with England, and Lewis Gregory had a back injury – Somerset had chosen to field, and stayed in contention on the first day, before losing the plot on the second. Patterson-White scored his first century in senior cricket, and helped pile on 240 for the last four wickets, as Somerset erred in line and length. Replying to 448, they were totally outplayed. After a feeble first innings of 107, they followed on early on the third day, when they lasted longer, thanks to late-order resistance. But Fletcher and Paterson brought their combined match haul to 14. Somerset captain Abell, in his first

Championship match since a hamstring injury in June, offered a candid assessment: "Not enough character or backbone".

Close of play: first day, Nottinghamshire 282-6 (Moores 26, Patterson-White 46); second day, Somerset 87-7 (Leach 6, Davey 0).

Nottinghamshire

B. T. Slater c Lammonby b Brooks	3	L. J. Fletcher c Lammonby b van der Merwe	51
B. M. Duckett c van der Merwe b Brooks	24	D. Paterson not out	3
S. A. Northeast lbw b Davey	34		
J. M. Clarke c Davies b Abell	59	B 5, lb 5, nb 14	24
L. W. James c Davies b Abell	30		
*S. J. Mullaney lbw b de Lange	42	1/7 (1) 2/44 (2) (142.1 overs) 448	
†T. J. Moores c Davies b Lammonby	46	3/97 (3) 4/140 (4) 5/194 (5)	
L. A. Patterson-White lbw b Leach	101	6/208 (6) 7/332 (7) 8/381 (8)	
B. A. Hutton c Davey b Abell	31	9/410 (9) 10/448 (10) 110 overs: 371-7	

Davey 30–10–96–1; Brooks 28–6–94–2; de Lange 26–5–78–1; Abell 25–5–84–3; Leach 25–7–57–1; Lammonby 5–1–23–1; van der Merwe 3.1–0–6–1.

Somerset

†S. M. Davies lbw b Fletcher	1	– c Moores b Fletcher	2
T. A. Lammonby c Moores b Fletcher	10	– c Clarke b Hutton	34
*T. B. Abell c Moores b Fletcher	35	– c Moores b Paterson	11
J. C. Hildreth lbw b Paterson	12	– b Fletcher	4
L. P. Goldsworthy c Moores b Fletcher	5	– b Paterson	11
T. Banton c Moores b Paterson	6	– lbw b Paterson	17
R. E. van der Merwe lbw b Hutton	2	– c Northeast b Paterson	0
M. J. Leach c Clarke b Hutton	10	– st Moores b Patterson-White	35
J. H. Davey c Moores b Paterson	6	– not out	20
M. de Lange b Hutton	6	– c Mullaney b Patterson-White	36
J. A. Brooks not out	4	– b Fletcher	4
Lb 2, nb 8	10	Lb 3, nb 4	7

1/2 (1) 2/51 (2) 3/52 (3)	(38.5 overs)	107
4/68 (5) 5/72 (4) 6/77 (7)		
7/87 (6) 8/97 (8) 9/101 (9) 10/107 (10)		

1/10 (1) 2/39 (3)	(66.3 overs)	181
3/44 (4) 4/59 (2)		
5/85 (6) 6/85 (7) 7/86 (5)		
8/132 (8) 9/170 (10) 10/181 (11)		

Fletcher 11–4–21–4; Hutton 16.5–5–42–3; Paterson 11–1–42–3. *Second innings*—Fletcher 14.3–5–29–3; Hutton 10–3–21–1; Paterson 16–6–46–4; Mullaney 7–1–28–0; Patterson-White 19–7–54–2.

Umpires: D. J. Millns and P. R. Pollard.   Referee: S. Cummings.

At Scarborough, September 5–6. SOMERSET lost to YORKSHIRE by an innings and 33 runs.

SOMERSET v LANCASHIRE

At Taunton, September 12–14. Lancashire won by ten wickets. Lancashire 23pts, Somerset 3pts. Toss: Somerset. First-class debut: E. O. Leonard.

Somerset avoided the ignominy of three successive innings defeats – but only just. They chose to bowl with a second-string attack – Jack Leach was awaiting the result of a Covid test, while Craig Overton and Josh Davey had joined Lewis Gregory on the injury list – but were erratic and profligate. Wells hit 20 fours in a powerful 103, and three others scored half-centuries, as Lancashire ran up 373. On the second afternoon, Blatherwick, in his first Championship bowl for Lancashire, took four for 28 as Somerset were skittled for 90. Following on, they threw caution to the wind: Lammonby struck 100 from 103 balls, his fourth first-class century, and Azhar Ali was approaching 50 as the total raced to 194 for one in 35 overs. But it was merely a pause in the decline. Wells suddenly took three for eight, and Abell bagged his second duck of the day; Somerset's flickering hopes of a first Championship trophy were extinguished next morning. Lancashire knocked off their target of 32 without fuss, and returned home with ambitions of clinching the title in Liverpool. Hildreth overtook Peter Wight's career aggregate of 16,965 to become the third-highest Somerset run-scorer, after Harold Gimblett and Marcus Trescothick.

Close of play: first day, Lancashire 364-8 (Bailey 54, Blatherwick 1); second day, Somerset 226-4 (Hildreth 22, Goldsworthy 5).

Lancashire

G. P. Balderson c Lammonby b Leonard	22	– not out		10
†A. L. Davies c Davies b Brooks	3	– not out		22
L. W. P. Wells c Hildreth b Abell	103			
J. J. Bohannon c Leonard b Abell	50			
*D. J. Vilas lbw b Brooks	36			
R. P. Jones c Hildreth b Abell	5			
S. J. Croft c Davies b de Lange	71			
D. J. Lamb lbw b Brooks	0			
T. E. Bailey b de Lange	63			
J. M. Blatherwick c Abell b Brooks	1			
M. W. Parkinson not out	0			
Lb 13, nb 6	19			

1/27 (1) 2/27 (2) 3/182 (3)   (99.3 overs) 373   (no wkt, 6 overs) 32
4/195 (4) 5/201 (6) 6/266 (5)
7/268 (8) 8/363 (7) 9/371 (10) 10/373 (9)

Brooks 22-3-77-4; Leonard 15-2-68-1; Abell 7-0-63-3; de Lange 20.3-5-75-2; Green 12-0-38-0; Lammonby 10-3-25-0; van der Merwe 13-5-14-0. *Second innings*—Brooks 3-0-15-0; Leonard 3-0-17-0.

Somerset

B. G. F. Green b Bailey	0	– st Davies b Parkinson		31
T. A. Lammonby lbw b Bailey	6	– lbw b Wells		100
Azhar Ali lbw b Bailey	39	– st Davies b Wells		50
*T. B. Abell c Davies b Balderson	0	– c Vilas b Wells		0
J. C. Hildreth c Wells b Balderson	2	– c Blatherwick b Bailey		26
L. P. Goldsworthy c Jones b Blatherwick	15	– lbw b Bailey		21
†S. M. Davies c Davies b Blatherwick	1	– not out		22
R. E. van der Merwe b Blatherwick	4	– c Wells b Balderson		23
M. de Lange b Lamb	0	– c Jones b Blatherwick		0
J. A. Brooks c Lamb b Blatherwick	1	– b Balderson		15
E. O. Leonard not out	4	– c Davies b Blatherwick		6
B 5, lb 11, nb 2	18	Lb 4, nb 16		20

1/0 (1) 2/31 (3) 3/32 (4)   (38.2 overs) 90   1/69 (1) 2/194 (2)   (72.1 overs) 314
4/38 (5) 5/65 (6) 6/67 (7)   3/194 (4) 4/199 (3)
7/71 (8) 8/76 (9) 9/81 (10) 10/90 (3)   5/233 (5) 6/248 (6) 7/279 (8)
                                              8/280 (9) 9/301 (10) 10/314 (11)

Bailey 9.2-4-9-3; Lamb 12-2-25-1; Balderson 7-3-12-2; Blatherwick 10.2-2-28-4. *Second innings*—Bailey 19-1-81-2; Balderson 18-1-82-2; Blatherwick 11.1-0-67-2; Parkinson 10-1-49-1; Lamb 7-2-23-0; Wells 7-3-8-3.

Umpires: G. D. Lloyd and S. J. O'Shaughnessy.   Referee: S. J. Davis.

At Birmingham, September 21–24. SOMERSET lost to WARWICKSHIRE by 118 runs.

SURREY

The in-and-out club

RICHARD SPILLER

What had been billed as Surrey's delayed 175th anniversary celebration became a prolonged leaving party. Despite determining that events planned for 2020 – but derailed by Covid – should not be lost altogether, the county witnessed the retirement of four senior players and the departure of another.

Just as significantly, chief executive Richard Gould moved to Bristol City FC after a highly profitable decade in charge at The Oval, during which membership rocketed to more than 14,000. He was replaced by the former South African Test player Steve Elworthy, tempted across the river from the ECB. And in January, head coach Vikram Solanki left to become director of cricket at the IPL's new Ahmedabad franchise. He was replaced on an interim basis by former club captain Gareth Batty, who had recently retired at the age of 43. Batty will be assisted by Jim Troughton and Azhar Mahmood, now that Richard Johnson has returned to Middlesex. Academy director Gareth Townsend, meanwhile, left after 27 years.

The upheaval began during an undistinguished season in which Surrey won two of their 13 Championship matches, and failed to make the T20 Blast knockouts, though they did reach the Royal London Cup semi-finals.

In all, 34 players took the field, including five captains: a revolving door might have been useful in the pavilion. International commitments, the IPL and The Hundred all took their toll, as did injury. The most serious was the torn hamstring suffered by wicketkeeper Ben Foakes, who was out for three months after slipping on the dressing-room floor, while overseas pacemen Sean Abbott and Kyle Jamieson both broke down mid-match.

Yet gloom was rarely in the air. When fans returned, they could sit in the £31m One Oval Square development, renamed the M. A. R. Galadari Stand. Surrey also purchased the old Ovalhouse Theatre, over the road from the ground, with a view to a hotel development. Perhaps the most remarkable achievement was reducing a projected loss of £4m to a more manageable £1.5m. It was estimated the first year of the Covid crisis had cost around £5m, so the sold-out India Test was a boon.

Since claiming the Championship in 2018, Surrey have won only five of their 33 four-day matches, and lost 13. They rarely threatened to qualify for the top division. Failure to beat the two sides that finished below them proved key: Surrey shared two high-scoring draws with Leicestershire and, after being routed at Lord's, needed a shower to avoid losing twice to Middlesex. After being condemned to the second division, a trip to Durham was cancelled when a Surrey player tested positive for Covid. They then lost at Northampton, batted out time after following on against Essex, and took part in a run-orgy against Glamorgan at The Oval. Losing the toss nine times did not help.

Surrey began the Vitality Blast with three comfortable wins, and looked capable of reprising their appearance in the final in 2020. But rain ruined the next two matches, after which they lost the Curran brothers and Jason Roy to England. The next nine games produced only three victories, and Hampshire squeezed past them into the quarter-finals. The absence of injured seamers Abbott and Reece Topley was a major blow. Little was expected in the Royal London Cup, yet a largely young and untested side relished their opportunities, before losing to Durham in the semi-final.

Charlie Crowhurst, Getty Images

Jamie Smith

Surrey's outstanding performer was Jamie Smith, who turned 21 in July. He top-scored overall with 1,268 runs, and filled in capably for Foakes. Despite captaining for much of the Royal London run, he rarely looked overburdened, and deserved his England Lions tour call-up.

The Championship batting was uneven, the totals veering from massive to paltry. Rory Burns could scarcely be blamed, with a century and seven fifties in nine appearances between Test calls, while Hashim Amla fell six short of 1,000 runs, and led epic rearguards against Hampshire and Essex. Ollie Pope was Bradmanesque at The Oval, where two of his three centuries became doubles, but 33 was his best elsewhere. Mark Stoneman continued his fitful form since his superb first season in 2017 and, when Middlesex offered a three-year contract, he was allowed to depart early.

West Indian paceman Kemar Roach added bite to the bowling early on, claiming 22 wickets in five matches. Topley made a mark, Jordan Clark improved, and Rikki Clarke was always tidy. But batting struggles meant Surrey could rarely field both their promising spinners, Amar Virdi and Dan Moriarty (a fixture in white-ball matches). Jamie Overton found form elusive before injury ended his season in July, while India's Ravichandran Ashwin took seven wickets in a one-off appearance, against Somerset.

In the Blast, Surrey relied too heavily on Will Jacks, who augmented 393 attractive runs with handy off-spin. Seamer Gus Atkinson's 15 wickets highlighted his potential. In the Royal London, the Singaporean strokemaker Tim David smashed two centuries which left spectators in peril. Ryan Patel threw off his shackles, while Smith and Stoneman weighed in strongly.

It wasn't all about exits. Surrey signed seamer Dan Worrall from Gloucestershire, while Chris Jordan returns after almost a decade at Sussex to captain the T20 side. All-rounder Cameron Steel arrived from Durham in July.

Still, the final moments were devoted to farewells. Stoneman and former England fast bowler Liam Plunkett – who achieved little in three years at The Oval – had already gone. Batty's off-spin was economical as ever, while seamer Jade Dernbach faded away after 18 years of hard toil. Rikki Clarke, who first played for Surrey aged 19 in 2001, fought nobly throughout and, if his talents were waning, he remained a valuable servant to the last ball.

SURREY RESULTS

County Championship matches – Played 13: Won 2, Lost 3, Drawn 8. Cancelled 1.
Vitality T20 Blast matches – Played 14: Won 6, Lost 5, No result 3.
Royal London Cup matches – Played 10: Won 5, Lost 3, No result 2.

LV= County Championship, 4th in Group 2, 5th in Division 2;
Vitality T20 Blast, 5th in South Group; Royal London Cup, semi-finalists.

COUNTY CHAMPIONSHIP AVERAGES, BATTING AND FIELDING

Cap		Birthplace	M	I	NO	R	HS	100	Avge	Ct/St
2018	O. J. D. Pope§	Chelsea	9	13	2	861	274	3	78.27	6
2021	H. M. Amla¶	Durban, SA	13	20	3	994	215*	3	58.47	2
2014	†R. J. Burns§	Epsom‡	9	14	1	617	104*	1	47.46	5
2016	B. T. Foakes	Colchester	8	10	2	350	133	1	43.75	16/2
	J. L. Smith	Epsom‡	12	17	2	656	138	3	43.73	15/1
	W. G. Jacks	Chertsey‡	6	5	1	146	60	0	36.50	4
2018	†M. D. Stoneman	Newcastle-u-Tyne	10	15	0	473	119	1	31.53	2
	†R. S. Patel	Sutton‡	6	10	0	250	62	0	25.00	3
	J. Overton	Barnstaple	8	9	1	154	50	0	19.25	6
2005	R. Clarke	Orsett	11	13	3	192	65	0	19.20	13
	A. A. P. Atkinson	Chelsea	2	4	1	52	41*	0	17.33	0
	J. Clark	Whitehaven	12	14	1	208	61*	0	16.00	2
	C. T. Steel	Greenbrae, USA	2	4	0	45	28	0	11.25	1
	G. S. Virdi	Chiswick	11	12	6	59	47	0	9.83	1
	R. J. W. Topley	Ipswich	9	9	2	31	10	0	4.42	5

Also batted: S. A. Abbott¶ (*Windsor, Australia*) (1 match) 40 (1 ct); R. Ashwin¶ (*Madras, India*) (1 match) 0, 0* (1 ct); †M. P. Dunn (*Egham‡*) (1 match) 23 (1 ct); L. J. Evans (*Lambeth‡*) (2 matches) 6, 4, 11 (2 ct); B. A. Geddes (*Epsom‡*) (1 match) 4, 15; K. A. Jamieson¶ (*Auckland, NZ*) (1 match) 0*; †D. T. Moriarty (*Reigate‡*) (4 matches) 4, 0, 8 (2 ct); K. A. J. Roach¶ (*Checker Hall, Barbados*) (5 matches) 8, 0*, 5; J. A. Tattersall (*Harrogate*) (1 match) 4 (5 ct); J. P. A. Taylor (*Stoke-on-Trent*) (1 match) 19.

‡ *Born in Surrey.*   § *ECB contract.*   ¶ *Official overseas player.*

BOWLING

	Style	O	M	R	W	BB	5I	Avge
K. A. J. Roach	RFM	134	28	452	22	8-40	2	20.54
J. Clark	RFM	276	36	904	32	6-21	2	28.25
D. T. Moriarty	SLA	181.4	31	521	18	6-60	1	28.94
R. J. W. Topley	LFM	199.3	46	616	21	5-66	1	29.33
G. S. Virdi	OB	299.4	48	961	28	6-171	1	34.32
R. Clarke	RFM	197.5	45	582	16	3-34	0	36.37

Also bowled: S. A. Abbott (RFM) 15–8–27–2; R. Ashwin (OB) 58–13–126–7; A. A. P. Atkinson (RFM) 47–7–172–5; R. J. Burns (RM) 7–1–22–0; M. P. Dunn (RFM) 36.2–2–145–0; W. G. Jacks (OB) 64–9–216–4; K. A. Jamieson (RFM) 6–3–10–0; J. Overton (RFM) 142.1–30–454–6; R. S. Patel (RM) 23.5–5–80–0; C. T. Steel (LB) 24.1–1–120–1; M. D. Stoneman (OB) 3–0–13–0; J. P. A. Taylor (RFM) 15.1–5–44–2.

LEADING VITALITY BLAST AVERAGES (100 runs/15 overs)

Batting	Runs	HS	Avge	SR	Ct		Bowling	W	BB	Avge	ER
W. G. Jacks	393	87	35.72	**170.12**	2		D. T. Moriarty	11	3-26	23.18	**6.71**
J. Overton	134	28	14.88	**167.50**	5		W. G. Jacks	4	2-7	35.25	**6.71**
J. J. Roy	139	64	34.75	**147.87**	3		G. J. Batty	8	2-21	31.37	**6.78**
O. J. D. Pope	168	60	42.00	**141.17**	2		J. Overton	4	2-14	34.00	**8.00**
L. J. Evans	298	65	24.83	**127.35**	2		A. A. P. Atkinson	15	4-36	14.86	**8.36**
J. L. Smith	297	60	33.00	**125.84**	4		J. Clark	5	1-20	52.60	**10.31**

LEADING ROYAL LONDON CUP AVERAGES (100 runs/4 wickets)

Batting	Runs	HS	Avge	SR	Ct/St	Bowling	W	BB	Avge	ER
T. H. David....	340	140*	68.00	150.44	6	C. McKerr......	18	4-64	21.44	6.00
J. L. Smith....	315	85	63.00	80.35	11/2	C. T. Steel.....	10	4-33	22.00	4.88
R. S. Patel.....	386	131	55.14	113.19	5	A. A. P. Atkinson	5	4-43	22.60	7.06
M. D. Stoneman	329	117	54.83	79.27	5	D. T. Moriarty...	15	4-30	23.80	4.36
R. Clarke......	165	82	33.00	89.67	4	T. H. David	4	2-32	25.00	4.00
						M. P. Dunn	11	2-44	37.54	6.11
						R. Clarke.......	4	1-16	70.50	4.58

FIRST-CLASS COUNTY RECORDS

Highest score for	357*	R. Abel v Somerset at The Oval	1899
Highest score against	366	N. H. Fairbrother (Lancashire) at The Oval......	1990
Leading run-scorer	43,554	J. B. Hobbs (avge 49.72)	1905–34
Best bowling for	10-43	T. Rushby v Somerset at Taunton	1921
Best bowling against	10-28	W. P. Howell (Australians) at The Oval	1899
Leading wicket-taker	1,775	T. Richardson (avge 17.87)	1892–1904
Highest total for	811	v Somerset at The Oval	1899
Highest total against	863	by Lancashire at The Oval	1990
Lowest total for	14	v Essex at Chelmsford	1983
Lowest total against	16	by MCC at Lord's	1872

LIST A COUNTY RECORDS

Highest score for	268	A. D. Brown v Glamorgan at The Oval........	2002
Highest score against	187*	A. D. Hales (Nottinghamshire) at Lord's.......	2017
Leading run-scorer	10,358	A. D. Brown (avge 32.16)	1990–2008
Best bowling for	7-30	M. P. Bicknell v Glamorgan at The Oval	1999
Best bowling against	7-15	A. L. Dixon (Kent) at The Oval..............	1967
Leading wicket-taker	409	M. P. Bicknell (avge 25.21).................	1986–2005
Highest total for	496-4	v Gloucestershire at The Oval	2007
Highest total against	429	by Glamorgan at The Oval	2002
Lowest total for	64	v Worcestershire at Worcester................	1978
Lowest total against	44	by Glamorgan at The Oval	1999

TWENTY20 COUNTY RECORDS

Highest score for	131*	A. J. Finch v Sussex at Hove	2018
Highest score against	129	C. S. Delport (Essex) at Chelmsford	2019
Leading run-scorer	3,322	J. J. Roy (avge 31.04, SR 148.30)	2008–21
Best bowling for	6-24	T. J. Murtagh v Middlesex at Lord's	2005
Best bowling against	5-16	S. T. Finn (Middlesex) at Lord's	2010
Leading wicket-taker {	114	G. J. Batty (avge 26.40, ER 7.11)	2010–21
{	114	J. W. Dernbach (avge 27.11, ER 8.41)	2005–21
Highest total for	250-6	v Kent at Canterbury	2018
Highest total against	240-3	by Glamorgan at The Oval.....................	2015
Lowest total for	88	v Kent at The Oval..........................	2012
Lowest total against	44	by Glamorgan at The Oval.....................	2019

ADDRESS

The Kia Oval, Kennington, London SE11 5SS; 0203 946 0100; enquiries@surreycricket.com;
www.kiaoval.com. Twitter: @surreycricket.

OFFICIALS

Captain R. J. Burns	**President** D. J. Pakeman
(Twenty20) C. J. Jordan	**Chair** R. W. Thompson
Director of cricket A. J. Stewart	**Chief executive 2021** R. A. Gould
Head coach 2021 V. S. Solanki	**2022** S. Elworthy
Interim head coach 2022 G. J. Batty	**Head groundsman** L. E. Fortis
Head of talent pathway C. G. Taylor	**Scorer** D. Beesley

GROUP TWO

At Bristol, April 8–11. SURREY lost to GLOUCESTERSHIRE by eight wickets.

SURREY v LEICESTERSHIRE

At The Oval, April 15–18. Drawn. Surrey 15pts, Leicestershire 13pts. Toss: Leicestershire. County debut: K. A. J. Roach.

Bat held sway over ball on a placid pitch. Sam Evans dominated a rain-shortened first day with a maiden Championship hundred, often working the ball square on the off side, though he was dropped by Burns at slip when 42, and might have been run out for 98. He and Hill fell in quick succession next morning, and Leicestershire's other batsmen wasted much of their good work. Surrey also risked missing out, until Foakes joined Pope, back to his best after a difficult tour of India, in a stand of 229. Then Smith, en route to his first Championship hundred, blitzed away during a partnership of 234, while Pope eased to the third double among his ten first-class centuries. He batted for seven hours, cuffing 30 fours, before falling for 245, just as he was threatening to emulate Kevin Pietersen's triple-century in Leicestershire's previous Championship match at The Oval, in 2015. Burns declared at 672 – Surrey's highest against Leicestershire – and left his bowlers more than a day to bowl the visitors out again. They rarely looked like doing so; the compact Azad batted through, finishing with a career-best. There were no spectators – but there was a lot of noise, from the construction of the new M. A. R. Galadari Stand.

Close of play: first day, Leicestershire 215-3 (Evans 100, Hill 20); second day, Surrey 253-3 (Pope 92, Foakes 68); third day, Leicestershire 21-0 (Azad 13, Evans 5).

Leicestershire

M. H. Azad c Dunn b Overton	55	– not out	144
S. T. Evans b Virdi	138	– c Smith b Clark	22
H. E. Dearden c Foakes b Clark	14	– lbw b Clark	0
*C. N. Ackermann lbw b Clark	15	– c Foakes b Virdi	29
L. J. Hill b Clark	70	– not out	69
†H. J. Swindells b Roach	20		
B. W. M. Mike c Burns b Virdi	20		
C. F. Parkinson c Overton b Roach	2		
C. J. C. Wright run out (Roach)	16		
D. Klein b Virdi	0		
G. T. Griffiths not out	4		
Lb 7, nb 14	21	B 4, lb 10, w 1, nb 16	31

1/130 (1) 2/147 (3) 3/176 (4)   (117.3 overs) 375   1/82 (2)   (3 wkts, 92 overs) 295
4/298 (2) 5/312 (5) 6/339 (6)   2/82 (3) 3/143 (4)
7/353 (8) 8/353 (7) 9/353 (10)
10/375 (9)   110 overs: 350-6

Roach 29–4–100–2; Dunn 22–1–86–0; Virdi 26.3–8–75–3; Overton 20–6–55–1; Clark 20–0–52–3. *Second innings*—Roach 16–4–59–0; Dunn 14–1–59–0; Virdi 33–9–73–1; Overton 11–3–28–0; Clark 11–3–37–2; Burns 4–1–12–0; Stoneman 3–0–13–0.

Surrey

*R. J. Burns lbw b Parkinson	36	M. P. Dunn b Mike	23
M. D. Stoneman c Swindells b Griffiths	24		
H. M. Amla lbw b Griffiths	22	B 6, lb 16, w 1, nb 12	35
O. J. D. Pope st Swindells b Ackermann	245		
†B. T. Foakes b Klein	87		
J. L. Smith b Ackermann	123		
J. Clark not out	61		
J. Overton run out (Griffiths)	16		

K. A. J. Roach and G. S. Virdi did not bat.

1/43 (2)   (8 wkts dec, 141.4 overs) 672
2/83 (3) 3/93 (1)
4/322 (5) 5/556 (4) 6/575 (6)
7/613 (8) 8/672 (9)   110 overs: 451-4

Klein 24–2–122–1; Wright 21–4–87–0; Griffiths 26–2–100–2; Mike 13.4–0–79–1; Parkinson 36–2–172–1; Ackermann 21–1–90–2.

Umpires: G. D. Lloyd and P. R. Pollard.   Referee: S. J. Davis.

At Lord's, April 22–24. SURREY lost to MIDDLESEX by ten wickets.

SURREY v HAMPSHIRE

At The Oval, April 29–May 1. Surrey won by an innings and 289 runs. Surrey 24pts, Hampshire 1pt. Toss: Surrey. Championship debut: S. W. Currie.

Sent in on an unusually green Oval pitch, group leaders Hampshire succumbed for 92 shortly after lunch, paving the way for their heaviest innings defeat for 110 years, and Surrey's largest victory for 15. The nagging Clark found late swing and seam, and reaped a career-best, helped by sharp catching, particularly from Foakes. Only Holland and McManus averted complete meltdown. Hampshire's seamers could find less assistance, and Amla – fresh from a pair at Lord's – regained his best form during a trio of century stands. That included 257 with Pope, who made 131 in under four hours, taking his first-class average at The Oval to 105 (and against Hampshire to 113). Amla batted for over eight, and amassed 215 before retiring ahead of the third day with a stiff neck. Until then, he had been bothered more by the local wildlife than the visiting bowlers: one cover-drive was stopped in the outfield by a pigeon, and he was bowled by Dawson as he stepped away, distracted by a passing bird (dead ball was called). Seamer Scott Currie improved his figures on his last day as a teenager, but Hampshire's batting misfired again. Roach had enjoyed little luck in his county stint thus far, but now cashed in: searing inswing brought him a career-best eight for 40, three to catches from Clarke, who held six in the match. McManus was again the best of his side's batsmen, compiling 51 in three hours.

Close of play: first day, Surrey 131-1 (Burns 61, Amla 59); second day, Surrey 513-3 (Amla 215, Smith 66).

Hampshire

J. J. Weatherley c Foakes b Roach	9	– lbw b Clarke	14
I. G. Holland lbw b Clarke	22	– lbw b Roach	18
T. P. Alsop c Foakes b Clarke	5	– c Clarke b Roach	6
S. A. Northeast c Clarke b Clark	4	– c Clarke b Roach	0
*J. M. Vince c Foakes b Clark	0	– c Foakes b Clarke	10
L. A. Dawson c Clarke b Clark	0	– lbw b Roach	33
†L. D. McManus not out	31	– c Foakes b Roach	51
S. W. Currie c Foakes b Roach	4	– lbw b Roach	1
K. J. Abbott c Foakes b Clark	4	– c Clarke b Roach	21
B. T. J. Wheal c Clarke b Clark	5	– lbw b Roach	0
Mohammad Abbas c Burns b Clark	0	– not out	4
Nb 8	8	B 4, lb 15, nb 2	21

1/20 (1) 2/37 (3) 3/44 (4)	(34.3 overs) 92	1/35 (1) 2/43 (2) (60.3 overs) 179
4/44 (5) 5/44 (2) 6/44 (6)		3/43 (4) 4/44 (3)
7/53 (8) 8/70 (9) 9/92 (10) 10/92 (11)		5/60 (5) 6/114 (6) 7/120 (8)
		8/166 (9) 9/166 (10) 10/179 (7)

Roach 10–3–40–2; Overton 3–1–9–0; Clarke 11–5–22–2; Clark 10.3–3–21–6. *Second innings*—Roach 18.3–7–40–8; Overton 17–5–52–0; Clarke 13–3–31–2; Clark 11–3–33–0; Virdi 1–0–4–0.

Surrey

*R. J. Burns b Dawson	80	R. Clarke c and b Currie	14
M. D. Stoneman c McManus b Abbott	7		
H. M. Amla retired hurt	215	B 6, lb 5, w 2, nb 2	15
O. J. D. Pope c Wheal b Currie	131		
J. L. Smith c Vince b Currie	78	(7 wkts dec, 142.5 overs)	560
†B. T. Foakes c McManus b Currie	7		
J. Clark b Wheal	0		
J. Overton not out	13		

1/31 (2) (7 wkts dec, 142.5 overs) 560
2/156 (1) 3/413 (4)
4/526 (6) 5/527 (7)
6/533 (5) 7/560 (9) 110 overs: 439-3

K. A. J. Roach and G. S. Virdi did not bat.

In the first innings Amla retired hurt at 513-3.

Abbott 15–2–62–1; Mohammad Abbas 19–5–69–0; Holland 26–3–63–0; Wheal 25–0–114–1; Currie 27.5–2–109–4; Dawson 23–1–102–1; Vince 7–1–30–0.

Umpires: P. K. Baldwin and R. A. Kettleborough.   Referee: T. J. Boon.

At Leicester, May 6–9. SURREY drew with LEICESTERSHIRE.

At Taunton, May 13–16. SURREY drew with SOMERSET.

SURREY v MIDDLESEX

At The Oval, May 20–23. Drawn. Surrey 11pts, Middlesex 11pts. Toss: Middlesex.

Spectators returned at last – 3,500 on the opening day – though blustering winds and rain interruptions punctuated an engrossing derby. Openers Burns and Stoneman rode their luck to reach 135, before Middlesex's younger seamers discovered a fuller length and a straighter line, and triggered a dramatic collapse of six for seven in 50 balls just before tea (and a downpour that ended play). Only 74 overs were possible on the first two days, but the match went into overdrive on the third, when Roach's fierce spell rocked Middlesex's top order, and Clark mopped up. The visitors were indebted to a counter-attack from Simpson, but still trailed by 30. Burns and Stoneman then added another 135, equalling the record for highest identical starts in a first-class match (set by Kepler Wessels and John Barclay for Sussex against Somerset at Hove in 1979). Burns reached three figures after five successive half-centuries, then set Middlesex 290 in what rain reduced to 62 overs. They relished the improved conditions, and had a sniff at 219 for two in the 50th. But after a shower stole five more overs, the well-set pair of Handscomb (whose previous eight Championship innings had produced 60 runs) and Gubbins fell to catches in the deep off Roach, who finished with another five wickets to round off his Surrey stint.

Close of play: first day, Surrey 146-6 (Amla 6, Clarke 4); second day, Surrey 185-8 (Topley 0, Roach 0); third day, Surrey 135-0 (Burns 61, Stoneman 74).

Surrey

*R. J. Burns lbw b Bamber	64	– not out	104
M. D. Stoneman c Simpson b Cullen	63	– c Simpson b Bamber	74
H. M. Amla b Helm	24	– c Davies b Murtagh	43
O. J. D. Pope lbw b Andersson	0	– not out	37
†B. T. Foakes c Simpson b Andersson	0		
J. L. Smith c White b Helm	0		
J. Clark lbw b Andersson	1		
R. Clarke c Simpson b Cullen	19		
R. J. W. Topley lbw b Cullen	0		
K. A. J. Roach c White b Helm	5		
G. S. Virdi not out	0		
B 4, lb 9, w 1	14	B 1	1

1/135 (2) 2/135 (1) 3/140 (4)   (77.1 overs) 190   1/135 (2)   (2 wkts dec, 56.1 overs) 259
4/140 (5) 5/141 (6) 6/142 (7)   2/206 (3)
7/185 (3) 8/185 (8) 9/190 (9) 10/190 (10)

Murtagh 19–8–37–0; Bamber 19–6–33–1; Helm 19.1–6–47–3; Andersson 7–1–30–3; Cullen 13–3–30–3. *Second innings*—Murtagh 17–2–73–1; Cullen 15.1–0–70–0; Bamber 9–0–39–1; Helm 11–0–57–0; Andersson 4–0–19–0.

Middlesex

S. D. Robson c Foakes b Roach	17	– (2) c Clarke b Topley	32
J. L. B. Davies c Foakes b Roach	1	– (1) c Pope b Roach	2
N. R. T. Gubbins lbw b Topley	1	– c Burns b Roach	124
*P. S. P. Handscomb b Roach	5	– c Pope b Roach	70
R. G. White lbw b Clark	9	– (8) not out	1
†J. A. Simpson c Pope b Clark	68	– (5) b Roach	4
M. K. Andersson c Clarke b Topley	26	– (6) b Roach	7
B. C. Cullen b Roach	12		
T. G. Helm c Amla b Clark	4	– (7) not out	0
E. R. Bamber not out	11		
T. J. Murtagh c Stoneman b Clark	0		
Lb 2, nb 4	6	W 2, nb 8	10

1/18 (2) 2/19 (1) 3/19 (3)   (46.3 overs) 160   1/18 (1)   (6 wkts, 56.3 overs) 250
4/27 (4) 5/60 (5) 6/98 (7)   2/47 (2) 3/219 (4)
7/140 (8) 8/147 (9) 9/152 (6) 10/160 (11)   4/227 (5) 5/243 (3) 6/247 (6)

Topley 11–3–33–2; Roach 15–1–61–4; Clarke 7–3–23–0; Clark 13.3–0–41–4. *Second innings*—Topley 12.3–2–44–1; Roach 19–2–86–5; Clarke 12–2–47–0; Clark 7–0–31–0; Virdi 6–0–42–0.

Umpires: I. D. Blackwell and G. D. Lloyd. Referee: S. Cummings.

SURREY v GLOUCESTERSHIRE

At The Oval, May 27–30. Surrey won by an innings and 47 runs. Surrey 22pts, Gloucestershire 2pts. Toss: Surrey. County debuts: S. A. Abbott; J. A. Tattersall. Championship debut: D. T. Moriarty.

Amla's carefully crafted 173, his second eight-hour vigil in three home games, set Surrey up to end Gloucestershire's unbeaten start. Dropped at slip by Hammond off Tom Smith when 76, the 39-year-old Amla was relentless, seemingly relishing his extra responsibility: in a side with six changes, he had replaced Burns – now in the England bubble – as captain. Payne and Higgins kept the scoring-rate within bounds, at least until No. 9 Clarke cracked 65, including four successive fours off Taylor. The pitch had been used against Middlesex the previous week, prompting Surrey to include two spinners, which paid dividends once Brathwaite was removed on the third morning; Hammond alone, last out after nearly four hours of neat footwork and resolute defence, survived for long. Virdi and Moriarty shared nine wickets as Gloucestershire slid to 158, a deficit of 315. It was slow left-armer Moriarty's fourth haul of five or more in successive innings, in just his third first-class game; only Brian Langford, for Somerset in 1953, had matched this start since the Second

World War. Following on, Gloucestershire were in danger of losing in three days when Australian seamer Sean Abbott struck twice; he soon tore a hamstring, ending his brief stay as an overseas player. But Virdi punched more holes in the batting, and only Jonny Tattersall (on loan from Yorkshire) delayed Surrey on the final morning.

Close of play: first day, Surrey 285-5 (Amla 103, Overton 50); second day, Gloucestershire 45-1 (Brathwaite 27, Hammond 4); third day, Gloucestershire 124-5 (Hammond 38, Tattersall 15).

Surrey

M. D. Stoneman lbw b Higgins	22	D. T. Moriarty b Higgins	4
R. S. Patel c Brathwaite b Payne	62	G. S. Virdi not out	4
*H. M. Amla b Hammond	173		
†J. L. Smith c Brathwaite b Payne	2	B 5, lb 16	21
L. J. Evans c Tattersall b Taylor	6		
W. G. Jacks b Higgins	24	1/50 (1) 2/105 (2) (158 overs) 473
J. Overton c Tattersall b Payne	50	3/123 (4) 4/133 (5) 5/181 (6)
S. A. Abbott lbw b Smith	40	6/285 (7) 7/346 (8) 8/428 (3)
R. Clarke b Higgins	65	9/468 (9) 10/473 (10) 110 overs: 321-6

Payne 28–5–79–3; Higgins 29–8–69–4; Worrall 25–8–68–0; Taylor 27–6–89–1; Smith 41–4–112–1; Hammond 8–1–35–1.

Gloucestershire

K. C. Brathwaite lbw b Virdi	38	– c and b Overton	28
*C. D. J. Dent c Moriarty b Virdi	14	– lbw b Abbott	14
M. A. H. Hammond c Overton b Moriarty	77	– c Smith b Moriarty	45
T. C. Lace c Clarke b Moriarty	0	– b Abbott	0
I. A. Cockbain c Abbott b Virdi	1	– b Virdi	6
R. F. Higgins b Moriarty	0	– st Smith b Virdi	11
†J. A. Tattersall c Overton b Moriarty	7	– not out	86
T. M. J. Smith c Jacks b Moriarty	2	– lbw b Overton	1
M. D. Taylor b Jacks	12	– c sub (N. M. J. Reifer) b Virdi	15
D. A. Payne b Moriarty	1	– c Evans b Virdi	14
D. J. Worrall not out	1	– b Moriarty	24
B 5	5	B 8, lb 14, nb 2	24

1/39 (2) 2/84 (1) 3/85 (4) (75.5 overs) 158   1/38 (1) 2/42 (2) (78.5 overs) 268
4/88 (5) 5/89 (6) 6/111 (7)   3/44 (4) 4/58 (5)
7/113 (8) 8/144 (9) 9/153 (10) 10/158 (3)   5/84 (6) 6/138 (3) 7/139 (8)
  8/181 (9) 9/212 (10) 10/268 (11)

Abbott 10–5–22–0; Clarke 3–1–4–0; Virdi 26–7–46–3; Moriarty 26.5–7–60–6; Overton 4–1–14–0; Jacks 6–4–7–1. *Second innings*—Moriarty 28.5–5–82–2; Virdi 26–2–96–4; Jacks 6–1–27–0; Overton 13–2–36–2; Abbott 5–3–5–2.

Umpires: I. J. Gould and B. V. Taylor.   Referee: J. J. Whitaker.

At Southampton, July 4–7. SURREY drew with HAMPSHIRE. *Hashim Amla makes 37 in 387 minutes.*

SURREY v SOMERSET

At The Oval, July 11–14. Drawn. Surrey 11pts, Somerset 14pts. Toss: Somerset. County debut: R. Ashwin.

Hildreth's studious century on a used pitch helped Somerset reach 429 on a truncated second day. After Jamie Overton limped off with a calf strain, Surrey leaned on a spin-heavy attack, led by the Indian Ravichandran Ashwin, who took the new ball in a one-off county appearance. Burns and

Stoneman began the reply with an opening stand of 98, before Leach took advantage of a brittle batting order, despite having just emerged from ten days' quarantine. He wheeled down 20 maidens, and was well supported by fellow slow left-armer van der Merwe. Somerset were assured of a top-two spot in the group as long as they avoided defeat, which explained Hildreth's decision – early on the fourth day, with his bowlers rested – not to enforce the follow-on. Ashwin had struggled for wickets in the first innings, then been dismissed first ball, but now gained sharp turn. Backed by the enthusiastic Moriarty and excellent close catching, he took six wickets to shoot Somerset out for 69, which left Surrey requiring 259 from 57 overs. Amla and Smith ensured they were not embarrassed, and for Somerset a draw ensured a place in Division One. Of the game's 34 wickets, 30 fell to spin.

Close of play: first day, Somerset 280-6 (van der Merwe 6, Green 4); second day, Surrey 24-0 (Burns 18, Stoneman 4); third day, Surrey 239-8 (Clarke 15).

Somerset

D. P. Conway b Clark	21	– b Moriarty	12
†S. M. Davies lbw b Virdi	42	– c Smith b Ashwin	7
T. A. Lammonby b Ashwin	42	– c Clarke b Ashwin	3
*J. C. Hildreth b Clark	107	– lbw b Ashwin	14
L. P. Goldsworthy c Smith b Clark	48	– lbw b Moriarty	1
G. A. Bartlett lbw b Clarke	2	– b Ashwin	12
R. E. van der Merwe c Patel b Virdi	41	– lbw b Ashwin	7
B. G. F. Green c Clarke b Virdi	43	– b Ashwin	3
M. J. Leach not out	28	– c sub (N. M. J. Reifer) b Moriarty	2
M. de Lange c Clarke b Moriarty	29	– b Moriarty	3
J. A. Brooks c Ashwin b Moriarty	9	– not out	1
B 10, lb 5, nb 2	17	B 4	4

1/31 (1) 2/76 (2) 3/113 (3)   (148.5 overs) 429   1/9 (1) 2/13 (3)   (29.1 overs) 69
4/257 (5) 5/260 (6) 6/276 (4)   3/31 (4) 4/32 (5)
7/337 (7) 8/370 (8) 9/415 (10)   5/39 (1) 6/55 (6) 7/58 (7)
10/429 (11)   110 overs: 303-6   8/65 (9) 9/67 (8) 10/69 (10)

Ashwin 43–9–99–1; Clark 27–5–75–3; Moriarty 30.5–5–109–2; Overton 4–1–20–0; Virdi 29–5–86–3; Patel 1–0–1–0; Clarke 14–4–24–1. *Second innings*—Ashwin 15–4–27–6; Virdi 7–2–18–0; Moriarty 7.1–1–20–4.

Surrey

*R. J. Burns c Leach b van der Merwe	50	– b van der Merwe	12
M. D. Stoneman c Davies b Leach	67	– c Green b Leach	8
H. M. Amla c and b Leach	16	– lbw b van der Merwe	28
R. S. Patel c Conway b Leach	22	– c and b van der Merwe	6
†J. L. Smith c Davies b Leach	21	– not out	46
R. Ashwin c Conway b Leach	0	– not out	0
J. Clark c Hildreth b van der Merwe	33		
R. Clarke not out	16		
J. Overton b van der Merwe	4		
D. T. Moriarty lbw b van der Merwe	0		
G. S. Virdi lbw b Leach	0		
B 6, lb 3, nb 2	11	B 4, lb 1, w 1	6

1/98 (1) 2/136 (2) 3/145 (3)   (114.1 overs) 240   1/25 (1)   (4 wkts, 41 overs) 106
4/178 (5) 5/178 (6) 6/191 (4)   2/25 (2) 3/40 (4)
7/233 (7) 8/239 (9) 9/239 (10)   4/106 (3)
10/240 (11)   110 overs: 239-9

Brooks 14–1–59–0; de Lange 18.5–5–38–0; Leach 35.1–20–43–6; Green 12–6–19–0; van der Merwe 27–11–54–4; Goldsworthy 8–2–18–0. *Second innings*—van der Merwe 17–4–60–3; Leach 11–4–23–1; Goldsworthy 6–3–11–0; Green 7–2–7–0.

Umpires: P. J. Hartley and R. J. Warren.   Referee: S. J. Davis.

DIVISION TWO

At Chester-le-Street, August 30. DURHAM v SURREY. Cancelled. *The match is called off after a Surrey player tests positive for Covid-19.*

At Northampton, September 5–8. SURREY lost to NORTHAMPTONSHIRE by two wickets.

SURREY v ESSEX

At The Oval, September 12–15. Drawn. Surrey 9pts, Essex 15pts. Toss: Essex. County debut: J. A. Tattersall. Championship debut: J. P. A. Taylor.

Alastair Cook underlined why he was still widely regarded as England's best opener, ensuring Essex made hay. He batted throughout the first day against a tidy but unthreatening attack, and glided to 165 next morning – his 69th first-class century, and fifth at The Oval. He had put on 120 with Westley, then a lively 145 in 41 overs with Lawrence. Jonny Tattersall, whistled up on loan from Yorkshire as Jamie Smith was injured, became only the second Surrey wicketkeeper (after Ben Foakes in 2015) to make five dismissals in the first innings of his debut, and assisted in another when

PLAYERS APPEARING FOR THREE COUNTIES IN A CHAMPIONSHIP SEASON

K. W. Hogg	Lancashire, Nottinghamshire and Worcestershire	2007
S. A. Northeast	**Hampshire, Nottinghamshire and Yorkshire**	**2021**
J. A. Tattersall	**Gloucestershire, Surrey and Yorkshire**	**2021**

Walter's edge rebounded from his arm to Pope at gully. Surrey's reply started disastrously, both Steel and Patel bagging ducks, and they were thankful for Amla's steadiness against an attack led by Porter. Still, defeat looked certain before the third day was washed out. On the fourth, Amla, who batted for more than seven hours in the match, ground his way to 84, while James Taylor hung on for nearly two. Surrey still had to follow on, but were never in much danger of defeat in a game whose end was signalled by a rare comic over from Cook.

Close of play: first day, Essex 299-3 (A. N. Cook 140, Porter 0); second day, Surrey 107-7 (Amla 58, Taylor 2); third day, no play.

Essex

N. L. J. Browne c Tattersall b Clark	13	S. Snater not out		0
A. N. Cook c Tattersall b Moriarty	165	S. J. Cook lbw b Taylor		0
*T. Westley c Tattersall b Clarke	47			
D. W. Lawrence lbw b Moriarty	78	B 4, lb 21, nb 4		29
J. A. Porter c Tattersall b Clarke	30			
P. I. Walter c Pope b Jacks	33	1/29 (1) 2/149 (3)	(143.1 overs)	439
†A. J. A. Wheater b Topley	39	3/294 (4) 4/348 (5) 5/379 (2)		
S. R. Harmer lbw b Topley	3	6/415 (6) 7/428 (8) 8/439 (7)		
A. S. S. Nijjar c Tattersall b Taylor	2	9/439 (9) 10/439 (11)	110 overs: 356-4	

Topley 24–7–58–2; Clark 25–2–85–1; Clarke 19–1–62–2; Taylor 15.1–5–44–2; Moriarty 35–5–85–2; Jacks 14–2–33–1; Steel 9–0–44–0; Patel 2–0–3–0.

Surrey

C. T. Steel c A. N. Cook b Porter.............	0	– b Snater.......................	28
R. S. Patel lbw b S. J. Cook...................	0	– c Lawrence b Harmer............	17
*H. M. Amla lbw b Harmer....................	84	– not out.......................	34
O. J. D. Pope c Wheater b Porter.............	5	– not out.......................	27
W. G. Jacks lbw b Snater....................	11		
R. Clarke st Wheater b Harmer..............	12		
J. Clark c Wheater b S. J. Cook..............	5		
†J. A. Tattersall c Browne b Harmer...........	4		
J. P. A. Taylor c Walter b Snater.............	19		
D. T. Moriarty c Wheater b Porter............	8		
R. J. W. Topley not out......................	0		
B 5, lb 6, nb 2.........................	13	B 2, lb 3, nb 2.............	7

1/0 (1) 2/0 (2) 3/19 (4) (86.3 overs) 161   1/28 (2) (2 wkts, 36 overs) 113
4/52 (5) 5/78 (6) 6/87 (7)   2/66 (1)
7/98 (8) 8/142 (9) 9/161 (3) 10/161 (10)

Porter 18.3–9–27–3; S. J. Cook 16–5–31–2; Harmer 31–14–49–3; Nijjar 13–5–21–0; Snater 8–1–22–2. *Second innings*—Porter 6–1–29–0; S. J. Cook 5–0–18–0; Harmer 15–5–37–1; Snater 9–2–19–1; A. N. Cook 1–0–5–0.

Umpires: P. K. Baldwin and B. V. Taylor.   Referee: W. R. Smith.

SURREY v GLAMORGAN

At The Oval, September 21–24. Drawn. Surrey 13pts, Glamorgan 13pts. Toss: Glamorgan.

Over four days of late-summer London sunshine, records and bowlers's hearts were broken – and batting averages restored. A plumb pitch offered amiable bounce and negligible seam movement, and never changed. Lloyd's highest score made sure the visitors did not waste batting first, then on the second day Chris Cooke cashed in for a maiden double-century, and the first by a Glamorgan wicketkeeper. When Surrey finally went in, after tea, Smith drove crisply on the way to his third Championship century of the summer. But the main course was a stand of 362 between Amla and Pope, a third-wicket record for the fixture, beating the 244 of Andy Sandham and Tom Barling at Cardiff Arms Park in 1936; both teams made their third-highest total. Pope – leading Surrey for the first time – went on to his fourth double-century, before falling for 274, one run short of restoring his first-class average at The Oval to 100; it stalled at a Bradmanesque 99.94. He batted for 376 minutes

HIGHEST FIRST-CLASS AVERAGE ON A SINGLE GROUND

	Runs	100		
165.28	1,157	6	A. J. Pienaar..........	Oudtshoorn
132.18	**1,454**	**5**	**R. A. Jadeja..........**	**Rajkot (Saurashtra CA)**
116.25	1,395	5	A. Jadeja.............	Faridabad (Nahar Singh Stadium)
106.30	2,445	12	A. V. Mankad........	Bombay (Wankhede Stadium)
105.42	1,476	4	G. A. Headley........	Kingston (Melbourne Park)
105.41	5,060	19	V. M. Merchant	Bombay (Brabourne Stadium)
104.41	1,253	7	G. S. Sobers	Georgetown
103.17	4,024	19	D. G. Bradman	Melbourne
103.07	**1,443**	**5**	**D. P. Conway........**	**Wellington**
99.94	**1,799**	**8**	**O. J. D. Pope ....**	**The Oval**

Qualification: 15 innings.   *As at January 16, 2022.*

RIVAL CAPTAINS SCORING DOUBLE-HUNDREDS

Barbados (C. L. Walcott 209) v Trinidad (J. B. Stollmeyer 208) at Bridgetown.........	1950-51
Guyana (C. L. Hooper 222) v Leeward Islands (S. C. Williams 252*) at Albion	2001-02
Pakistan (Younis Khan 313) v Sri Lanka (D. P. M. D. Jayawardene 240) at Karachi.....	2008-09
Baroda (D. Hooda 293*) v Punjab (Yuvraj Singh 260) at Delhi......................	2016-17
Surrey (O. J. D. Pope 274) v Glamorgan (C. B. Cooke 205*) at The Oval	**2021**

(Amla for 413) and hit 35 fours and a six from 345 balls, before becoming Rutherford's maiden first-class victim as Glamorgan gave everyone a bowl (Hogan kept wicket at the end). The overall match average of 139 runs per wicket had been exceeded only once in the Championship: Warwickshire and Worcestershire managed 146 at Edgbaston in 1978. It all made for an unusual end to the 20-year career of Rikki Clarke, who tweeted after Glamorgan's innings: "Didn't have 177 overs in the dirt planned for my last game."

Close of play: first day, Glamorgan 379-4 (Carlson 45, C. B. Cooke 44); second day, Surrey 45-0 (Smith 23, Patel 22); third day, Surrey 387-2 (Amla 87, Pope 95).

Glamorgan

H. D. Rutherford lbw b Virdi	36	C. Z. Taylor not out	38
D. L. Lloyd c Jacks b Virdi	121	B 2, lb 24, w 1, nb 4	31
J. M. Cooke c Pope b Moriarty	68		
E. J. Byrom st Foakes b Moriarty	45	1/86 (1) (6 wkts dec, 177 overs)	672
K. S. Carlson c Moriarty b Jacks	69	2/211 (3) 3/287 (4)	
*†C. B. Cooke not out	205	4/289 (2) 5/429 (5)	
D. A. Douthwaite c Jacks b Virdi	59	6/618 (7)	110 overs: 419-4

A. G. Salter, M. G. Hogan and J. P. McIlroy did not bat.

Topley 25–3–92–0; Clark 12–2–55–0; Clarke 17–3–64–0; Moriarty 53–8–165–2; Virdi 39–1–140–3; Jacks 26–1–104–1; Patel 5–1–26–0.

Surrey

J. L. Smith c C. B. Cooke b Byrom	138	
R. S. Patel c Lloyd b Byrom	62	
H. M. Amla c Hogan b Carlson	163	
*O. J. D. Pope b Rutherford	274	
†B. T. Foakes not out	53	
R. Clarke not out	12	
B 10, lb 7, w 1, nb 2	20	

1/140 (2)	(4 wkts dec, 196 overs)	722
2/247 (1) 3/609 (3)		
4/677 (4)	110 overs: 372-2	

W. G. Jacks, J. Clark, D. T. Moriarty, R. J. W. Topley and G. S. Virdi did not bat.

Hogan 19–7–46–0; McIlroy 23–4–93–0; Salter 43–5–180–0; Lloyd 7–1–14–0; Taylor 41–4–127–0; Byrom 16–0–64–2; Douthwaite 11–1–48–0; J. M. Cooke 11–0–51–0; Rutherford 8–1–26–1; Carlson 14–3–37–1; C. B. Cooke 3–0–19–0.

Umpires: I. D. Blackwell and N. J. Llong.   Referee: W. M. Noon.

SUSSEX

A wooden spoonful of sugar…

Bruce Talbot

The last time Sussex finished bottom of the Championship, in 2000, the players were booed on the committee-room balcony after losing to Gloucestershire in two days. Chris Adams, the captain, and coach Peter Moores nearly paid with their jobs – yet within three years they had led Sussex to the first of three titles in five summers.

In the final game of the 2021 season, Sussex lost by nine wickets to Derbyshire – their ninth defeat, confirming the wooden spoon. Yet as the players left the field, most members stood to applaud. They had seen only three home wins in all competitions, and the keyboard warriors had the club management in their sights. But the more reasoned view was that Sussex's long-term future looked good – even if there might be more pain to endure first.

There was certainly none of the militancy among members that had brought the overthrow of the committee in 1997 after a raft of senior players departed. Chief executive Rob Andrew and director of cricket Keith Greenfield admitted there were too many youngsters in the Championship team. They also acknowledged they needed to sign more multi-format cricketers: of those who lost to Derbyshire, only Delray Rawlins and Harrison Ward had played the Blast semi-final a few days earlier.

Bringing back all-rounder Fynn Hudson-Prentice from Derbyshire was a start. Sussex also recruited Steven Finn from Middlesex, to provide experience in all formats; Greenfield insisted that Finn, after two red-ball appearances in two seasons, still had a role in four-day cricket. Of the squad which finished third in Division Two in 2018, a dozen had gone by the end of 2021, including Stiaan van Zyl, who returned to South Africa. Aaron Thomason also moved on, while Stuart Meaker and Mitch Claydon retired.

In January, another departure was confirmed when Ben Brown announced he was joining Hampshire, after 22 seasons at Hove. For five, he had led Sussex capably, often in difficult circumstances, and his removal from the captaincy in July was a surprise. He also lost the wicketkeeping gloves to Oli Carter, a further blow to his pride. But his move up to No. 3 seemed a success: in the last three Championship games, he hit two centuries and an eighty.

He certainly bore no grudge towards replacement captain Tom Haines, who was happy to take his counsel. Towards the end of the season, as his young team tired mentally and physically, there was little the 22-year-old Haines could do to stem the tide, but it didn't affect his batting. He finished 2021 as the country's leading first-class run-scorer, with 1,176, including three hundreds.

What Sussex hadn't expected were such meagre Championship returns from their two most experienced batters. Australian Travis Head averaged 18, and

Naomi Baker, Getty Images

Tom Haines

failed to reach 50 in 11 innings, while van Zyl's form tailed off after a hundred in the solitary win, against Glamorgan in April. Head, who during the winter was Player of the Series in the Ashes, returns for 2022, when he will be red-ball captain; Haines continues to lead the one-day team.

All season, Sussex gave plenty of opportunity to their youngsters, almost all developed in the Academy or local private schools, with whom Sussex have strong links. At just over 20, the team beaten by Worcestershire in August had the youngest average age in Championship history, while ten of those who faced Middlesex at Hove were educated in the county (and all spent at least part of their education in the private sector).

Several made an impression: opening batsman Ali Orr, all-rounder Dan Ibrahim (at 16 the youngest ever to make a Championship fifty), seamers Henry Crocombe and Jamie Atkins, and leg-spinner Archie Lenham (the first to appear in the Blast who had not been born when Twenty20 started in 2003). Off-spinner Jack Carson, the only ever-present of the 26 to represent Sussex in the Championship, struggled with a knee injury in the second half of the season, but finished with 37 wickets from 450 overs, and spun the ball hard. "We have a five-year strategy and, if these lads can keep improving, we will have a very competitive team in all formats by then," said Greenfield. The hope is they won't be tempted by more money elsewhere.

Andrew insisted Sussex's *raison d'être* was to produce England cricketers, so there was justifiable pride that five played at international level in 2021, even if two moved on: Phil Salt departed for Lancashire, while Chris Jordan returned to Surrey. They left big holes in the T20 side, though Tymal Mills, recalled by England for the World Cup, and Ravi Bopara signed new contracts. Sussex were also confident Rashid Khan would return for the whole of the Blast, as the 2022 tournament is being played in one block. Prolific Pakistan batter Mohammad Rizwan also joins in April.

Rashid's cameo with the bat had settled a tight quarter-final against Yorkshire, after Sussex did well to get through the group stage: five no-results included a home game against Surrey, abandoned when one more ball would have brought victory. As on their last appearance at finals day in 2018, they badly missed Rashid, and a timid display in the semi against Kent ended in defeat. In their Royal London group, Sussex finished a disappointing seventh.

With the wage bill slashed, they were confident of a small profit in 2022, despite the pandemic. Much of the summer was played out to the sound of building work, as the development at the entrance to Hove took shape. The apartments should be ready by the end of 2022, guaranteeing future income. The success of Sussex's recruitment policy may determine the value of the new penthouses.

SUSSEX RESULTS

County Championship matches – Played 14: Won 1, Lost 9, Drawn 4.
Vitality T20 Blast matches – Played 16: Won 7, Lost 4, No result 5.
Royal London Cup matches – Played 8: Won 2, Lost 4, No result 2.

LV= County Championship, 6th in Group 3, 6th in Division 3;
Vitality T20 Blast, semi-finalists; Royal London Cup, 7th in Group 1.

COUNTY CHAMPIONSHIP AVERAGES, BATTING AND FIELDING

Cap		Birthplace	M	I	NO	R	HS	100	Avge	Ct/St
2014	B. C. Brown	Crawley‡	12	21	2	976	157	4	51.36	27/3
2021	†T. J. Haines	Crawley‡	13	24	0	1,016	156	3	47.04	2
	†A. G. H. Orr	Eastbourne‡	7	14	0	548	119	1	39.14	1
	F. J. Hudson-Prentice	Haywards Heath‡	3	5	1	145	67	0	36.25	3
2019	O. E. Robinson	Margate	6	8	1	250	67	0	35.71	2
	D. K. Ibrahim	Burnley	6	11	0	328	94	0	29.81	3
	A. D. Thomason	Birmingham	9	17	2	379	78*	0	25.26	16
2019	†S. van Zyl¶	Cape Town, SA	9	17	0	422	113	1	24.82	4
	J. M. Coles	Aylesbury	2	4	1	72	36	0	24.00	1
	†G. H. S. Garton	Brighton‡	7	11	0	247	97	0	22.45	4
	†T. G. R. Clark	Haywards Heath‡	7	13	2	240	54*	0	21.81	6
	O. J. Carter	Eastbourne‡	6	12	1	235	51	0	21.36	14
	J. J. Carson	Craigavon, Ireland	14	23	4	385	87	0	20.26	3
	†T. M. Head¶	Adelaide, Australia	6	11	1	183	49*	0	18.30	3
	S. C. Meaker	Pietermaritzburg, SA	6	9	1	113	30*	0	14.12	2
	†D. M. W. Rawlins	Bermuda	10	17	0	233	58	0	13.70	3
	H. T. Crocombe	Eastbourne‡	9	17	2	83	46*	0	5.53	0
	J. A. Atkins	Redhill	5	9	5	21	10*	0	5.25	0
	†H. D. Ward	Oxford	3	6	0	30	19	0	5.00	2
	J. P. Sarro	Eastbourne‡	3	6	3	8	7*	0	2.66	1
	S. F. Hunt	Guildford	6	10	4	12	7	0	2.00	0

Also batted: J. C. Archer§ (*Bridgetown, Barbados*) (cap 2017) (1 match) 2; W. A. T. Beer (*Crawley‡*) (1 match) 19, 23*; †M. E. Claydon (*Fairfield, Australia*) (1 match) 22*; †T. I. Hinley (*Frimley*) (1 match) 19, 1; A. D. Lenham (*Eastbourne‡*) (1 match) 20, 9.

‡ *Born in Sussex.*   § *ECB contract.*   ¶ *Official overseas player.*

BOWLING

	Style	O	M	R	W	BB	5I	Avge
O. E. Robinson	RFM/OB	207	49	547	33	9-78	2	16.57
J. A. Atkins	RFM	137.4	14	469	20	5-51	2	23.45
J. J. Carson	OB	449.4	65	1,336	37	5-85	1	36.10
S. F. Hunt	LFM	127.5	18	487	13	3-47	0	37.46
H. T. Crocombe	RFM	211	29	756	20	4-92	0	37.80
G. H. S. Garton	LFM	134.5	11	559	13	4-69	0	43.00

Also bowled: J. C. Archer (RF) 18-4-43-3; W. A. T. Beer (LB) 29-6-70-3; T. G. R. Clark (RM) 33-3-120-1; M. E. Claydon (RFM) 17-3-54-2; J. M. Coles (SLA) 22-0-92-0; T. J. Haines (RM) 41-4-114-1; T. M. Head (OB) 27.4-4-109-1; T. I. Hinley (SLW) 6-0-35-0; F. J. Hudson-Prentice (RFM) 58.2-5-204-3; D. K. Ibrahim (RM) 67.4-11-236-3; A. D. Lenham (LB) 13-0-71-1; S. C. Meaker (RFM) 135.4-11-525-9; D. M. W. Rawlins (SLA) 171-17-573-4; J. P. Sarro (RM) 43-3-220-4; A. D. Thomason (RFM) 3-0-30-0; S. van Zyl (RM) 11-2-22-1; H. D. Ward (OB) 1-0-2-0.

LEADING VITALITY BLAST AVERAGES (100 runs/15 overs)

Batting	Runs	HS	Avge	SR	Ct/St
D. M. W. Rawlins	155	50*	25.83	155.00	2
L. J. Wright	370	77	41.11	151.63	5
P. D. Salt	302	77*	33.55	147.31	7/2
R. S. Bopara	259	62*	32.37	122.16	3
T. M. Head	108	27	15.42	112.50	6

Bowling	W	BB	Avge	ER
R. S. Bopara	8	3-15	20.37	7.08
G. H. S. Garton	11	3-19	15.81	7.25
A. D. Lenham	11	4-26	17.63	7.46
W. A. T. Beer	9	2-20	31.11	7.77
D. Wiese	11	2-16	17.54	7.82
T. S. Mills	7	3-20	14.11	8.00
C. J. Jordan	8	3-30	26.37	8.11
O. E. Robinson	5	2-15	30.40	9.30

LEADING ROYAL LONDON CUP AVERAGES (100 runs/4 wickets)

Batting	Runs	HS	Avge	SR	Ct/St	Bowling	W	BB	Avge	ER
T. M. Head	291	56	58.20	111.92	3	J. M. Coles	8	3-27	27.12	4.45
B. C. Brown	252	105	50.40	95.81	4	W. A. T. Beer	8	2-30	29.25	4.68
T. J. Haines	252	123	36.00	83.72	3	D. Wiese	7	2-44	37.28	7.05
A. G. H. Orr	144	108	28.80	68.57	0	D. K. Ibrahim	5	2-54	39.40	5.62
D. Wiese	132	36	26.40	126.92	2	A. D. Lenham	8	4-59	40.12	6.05
O. J. Carter	151	59	25.16	95.56	7/2	J. P. Sarro	4	2-41	47.25	7.26

FIRST-CLASS COUNTY RECORDS

Highest score for	344*	M. W. Goodwin v Somerset at Taunton	2009
Highest score against	322	E. Paynter (Lancashire) at Hove	1937
Leading run-scorer	34,150	J. G. Langridge (avge 37.69)	1928–55
Best bowling for	10-48	C. H. G. Bland v Kent at Tonbridge	1899
Best bowling against	9-11	A. P. Freeman (Kent) at Hove	1922
Leading wicket-taker	2,211	M. W. Tate (avge 17.41)	1912–37
Highest total for	742-5 dec	v Somerset at Taunton	2009
Highest total against	726	by Nottinghamshire at Nottingham	1895
Lowest total for	{ 19	v Surrey at Godalming	1830
	{ 19	v Nottinghamshire at Hove	1873
Lowest total against	18	by Kent at Gravesend	1867

LIST A COUNTY RECORDS

Highest score for	171	D. Wiese v Hampshire at Southampton	2019
Highest score against	198*	G. A. Gooch at Hove	1982
Leading run-scorer	7,969	A. P. Wells (avge 31.62)	1981–96
Best bowling for	7-41	A. N. Jones v Nottinghamshire at Nottingham	1986
Best bowling against	8-21	M. A. Holding (Derbyshire) at Hove	1988
Leading wicket-taker	370	R. J. Kirtley (avge 22.35)	1995–2010
Highest total for	399-4	v Worcestershire at Horsham	2011
Highest total against	377-9	by Somerset at Hove	2003
Lowest total for	49	v Derbyshire at Chesterfield	1969
Lowest total against	36	by Leicestershire at Leicester	1973

TWENTY20 COUNTY RECORDS

Highest score for	153*	L. J. Wright v Essex at Chelmsford	2014
Highest score against	152*	G. R. Napier (Essex) at Chelmsford	2008
Leading run-scorer	4,887	L. J. Wright (avge 33.47, SR 149.22)	2004–21
Best bowling for	5-11	Mushtaq Ahmed v Essex at Hove	2005
Best bowling against	{ 5-14	A. D. Mascarenhas (Hampshire) at Hove	2004
	{ 5-14	K. J. Abbott (Middlesex) at Hove	2015
Leading wicket-taker	106	W. A. T. Beer (avge 27.04, ER 7.48)	2008–21
Highest total for	242-5	v Gloucestershire at Bristol	2016
Highest total against	242-3	by Essex at Chelmsford	2008
Lowest total for	67	v Hampshire at Hove	2004
Lowest total against	85	by Hampshire at Southampton	2008

ADDRESS

The 1st Central County Ground, Eaton Road, Hove BN3 3AN; 01273 827100; info@sussexcricket.co.uk; www.sussexcricket.co.uk. Twitter: @SussexCCC.

OFFICIALS

Captain 2021 B. C. Brown	**President** Sir Rod Aldridge
2022 T. M. Head	**Chair** R. C. Warren
(Twenty20) L. J. Wright	**Chief executive** C. R. Andrew
(List A) T. J. Haines	**Head groundsperson** B. J. Gibson
Director of cricket K. Greenfield	**Scorer** G. J. Irwin
Head coach I. D. K. Salisbury	
(Twenty20) R. J. Kirtley	
Academy director M. H. Yardy	

GROUP THREE

At Manchester, April 8–11. SUSSEX drew with LANCASHIRE. *This game was moved from Hove because of an infestation of leatherjackets.*

At Cardiff, April 15–18. SUSSEX beat GLAMORGAN by eight wickets. *Ollie Robinson takes 13 wickets, including nine in the second innings.*

SUSSEX v YORKSHIRE

At Hove, April 22–25. Yorkshire won by 48 runs. Yorkshire 19pts, Sussex 4pts. Toss: Yorkshire.

Spin accounted for 16 wickets on an unusually dry early-season pitch, with Bess's six for 53 hastening a Yorkshire victory after they were outplayed for the first four sessions. On a surface which turned from the start, a target of 235 proved beyond Sussex, who should have established a bigger first-innings advantage. After dismantling Yorkshire for 150 and gaining a lead three wickets down, they lost seven for 53, squandering the hard work of Haines, whose 86 was the mainstay of their 221. England coach Chris Silverwood had turned up on the opening day to watch Robinson, though he must have been as impressed by Garton's consistent swing and pace, and by Carson, whose off-spin lost little in comparison with Bess. Still only 20, Carson found turn and bounce, and bowled with control. Among his five second-innings wickets were Root and the patient Ballance who, in his first match for Yorkshire after illness and anxiety kept him out in 2020, batted three hours for an invaluable 74. Willey and Olivier then added a crucial 51 for the last wicket. That seemed to tilt the game the visitors' way; Bess confirmed it.

Close of play: first day, Sussex 118-3 (Haines 71, Clark 7); second day, Yorkshire 163-5 (Ballance 36, Patterson 4); third day, Sussex 136-6 (Brown 26).

Yorkshire

A. Lyth c Clark b Garton	42	– lbw b Robinson	66
T. Köhler-Cadmore b Garton	17	– st Brown b Carson	21
G. S. Ballance c Garton b Hunt	18	– lbw b Carson	74
J. E. Root lbw b Garton	5	– c Brown b Carson	5
H. C. Brook b Rawlins	14	– c Brown b Garton	12
†J. A. Tattersall c Brown b Hunt	7	– c Garton b Carson	8
D. M. Bess c Brown b Rawlins	17	– (8) lbw b Robinson	19
J. A. Thompson lbw b Carson	5	– (9) c Thomason b Robinson	13
D. J. Willey c and b Robinson	13	– (10) not out	28
*S. A. Patterson c Brown b Robinson	3	– (7) b Garton	12
D. Olivier not out	1	– lbw b Carson	21
B 2, lb 6	8	B 9, lb 7, nb 10	26

1/60 (1) 2/61 (2) 3/75 (4) (50.5 overs) 150
4/102 (3) 5/102 (5) 6/126 (7)
7/126 (6) 8/140 (8) 9/149 (10) 10/150 (9)

1/90 (2) 2/96 (1) (103.4 overs) 305
3/113 (4) 4/134 (5)
5/157 (6) 6/194 (7) 7/226 (3)
8/251 (9) 9/254 (8) 10/305 (11)

Robinson 7.5–1–17–2; Hunt 11–3–45–2; Crocombe 4–0–19–0; Garton 11–4–25–3; Carson 11–1–24–1; Rawlins 6–2–12–2. *Second innings*—Robinson 24–5–73–3; Crocombe 11–3–22–0; Carson 39.4–7–85–5; Garton 14–2–69–2; Rawlins 15–2–40–0.

Sussex

A. D. Thomason c Brook b Thompson	20	– b Bess	10
T. J. Haines b Bess	86	– c Tattersall b Thompson	37
S. van Zyl c Köhler-Cadmore b Olivier	16	– b Bess	24
H. T. Crocombe c Tattersall b Olivier	0	– (10) c Willey b Bess	4
T. G. R. Clark b Olivier	33	– (4) c Brook b Bess	6
*†B. C. Brown lbw b Patterson	37	– (5) b Thompson	46
D. M. W. Rawlins c Root b Olivier	2	– (6) c Köhler-Cadmore b Bess	0
G. H. S. Garton c Köhler-Cadmore b Patterson	14	– (7) c Tattersall b Bess	21
O. E. Robinson b Patterson	0	– (8) lbw b Patterson	6
J. J. Carson b Patterson	0	– (9) c Lyth b Root	18
S. F. Hunt not out	0	– not out	2
Lb 5, nb 8	13	B 6, lb 2, nb 4	12

1/60 (1) 2/104 (3) 3/104 (4)   (76.3 overs) 221
4/168 (5) 5/168 (2) 6/179 (7)
7/212 (6) 8/212 (9) 9/212 (10) 10/221 (8)

1/45 (1) 2/64 (2)   (69.5 overs) 186
3/81 (4) 4/86 (3)
5/86 (6) 6/136 (7) 7/145 (5)
8/180 (9) 9/180 (5) 10/186 (10)

Willey 9–0–35–0; Olivier 15–2–61–4; Patterson 12.3–3–26–4; Root 4–0–6–0; Bess 25–6–55–1; Thompson 11–3–33–1. *Second innings*—Olivier 4–0–23–0; Thompson 11–2–31–2; Willey 2–0–13–0; Bess 29.5–9–53–6; Patterson 12–3–32–1; Root 11–3–26–1.

Umpires: I. D. Blackwell and P. R. Pollard.   Referee: D. A. Cosker.

SUSSEX v LANCASHIRE

At Hove, April 29–May 2. Lancashire won by five wickets. Lancashire 20pts, Sussex 6pts. Toss: Sussex. First-class debut: J. A. Atkins.

Lancashire completed a third successive victory shortly after lunch on the final day, but were pushed hard by Sussex, who again failed to win key passages. The pitch was slow, but they should have made more first-innings runs, given that six of the top seven reached 30; van Zyl's 79 was full of attractive off-side shots. Davies and Jennings gave Lancashire a solid start, but five wickets tumbled for 15 as Carson, despite modest turn, caused problems. Armed with a lead of 98, Sussex seemed set to boss the match, only to crash to 52 for five. Bailey led a disciplined seam attack – though the spinners would claim the last four wickets – and despite resistance from Rawlins, Sussex were dismissed for 154, setting Lancashire 253. Davies rode his luck to hit a 59-ball 73, his boisterous approach unsettling Sussex, with only Carson able to restrain him. Jennings, who had made 60 runs in four innings before this game, was steadier and his aggregate of 151 for once proved the difference.

Close of play: first day, Sussex 318-7 (Garton 30, Carson 13); second day, Lancashire 193-6 (Bohannon 26, Lamb 18); third day, Lancashire 124-2 (Jennings 35, Mahmood 1).

Sussex

A. D. Thomason b Bailey	0	– c Wells b Lamb	9
T. J. Haines c Vilas b Mahmood	58	– lbw b Bailey	19
S. van Zyl c Wells b Livingstone	79	– c Livingstone b Bailey	5
T. G. R. Clark lbw b Bailey	30	– lbw b Bailey	4
*†B. C. Brown lbw b Lamb	46	– lbw b Lamb	3
D. M. W. Rawlins c Wells b Parkinson	42	– b Parkinson	45
G. H. S. Garton c Mahmood b Lamb	35	– lbw b Mahmood	19
S. C. Meaker lbw b Bailey	7	– c Croft b Livingstone	9
J. J. Carson b Lamb	13	– lbw b Parkinson	21
H. T. Crocombe run out (Lamb)	2	– lbw b Livingstone	2
J. A. Atkins not out	0	– not out	4
B 8, lb 3, w 1, nb 4	16	B 5, lb 5, nb 4	14

1/6 (1) 2/139 (2) 3/153 (3)   (102.2 overs) 328
4/197 (4) 5/259 (6) 6/275 (5)
7/292 (8) 8/323 (9) 9/328 (10) 10/328 (7)

1/28 (1) 2/28 (2)   (46.1 overs) 154
3/37 (3) 4/38 (4)
5/52 (5) 6/87 (7) 7/106 (8)
8/139 (9) 9/148 (6) 10/154 (10)

Bailey 23–8–69–3; Mahmood 22–5–73–1; Lamb 23.2–8–59–3; Parkinson 9–0–53–1; Livingstone 25–5–63–1. *Second innings*—Bailey 10–5–28–3; Mahmood 10–2–29–1; Lamb 13–2–39–2; Livingstone 10.1–1–34–2; Parkinson 3–0–14–2.

Lancashire

K. K. Jennings c van Zyl b Carson	60	– not out	91
A. L. Davies b Carson	34	– b Meaker	73
L. W. P. Wells c Brown b Meaker	28	– lbw b Carson	12
J. J. Bohannon lbw b Atkins	37	– (6) c Clark b Crocombe	46
S. J. Croft c Brown b Carson	3	– (7) not out	16
*†D. J. Vilas b Atkins	0		
L. S. Livingstone c Thomason b Carson	0	– (5) c Rawlins b Carson	3
D. J. Lamb lbw b Meaker	27		
T. E. Bailey b Crocombe	3		
S. Mahmood not out	11	– (4) st Brown b Carson	7
M. W. Parkinson c Brown b Meaker	2		
B 11, lb 9, w 3, nb 2	25	Lb 4, w 1, nb 2	7
	230	(5 wkts, 68.2 overs)	255

1/93 (2) 2/137 (1) 3/145 (3) (98.2 overs) 230
4/150 (5) 5/151 (6) 6/152 (7)
7/205 (4) 8/215 (9) 9/228 (8) 10/230 (11)

1/102 (2) (5 wkts, 68.2 overs) 255
2/123 (3) 3/147 (4)
4/153 (5) 5/224 (6)

Crocombe 16–1–40–1; Atkins 20–4–50–2; Garton 11–1–33–0; Meaker 13.2–4–22–3; Haines 3–0–3–0; Carson 29–6–51–4; Rawlins 6–0–11–0. *Second innings*—Crocombe 10–0–59–1; Atkins 11–1–41–0; Meaker 16.2–1–62–1; Garton 4–0–29–0; Carson 24–5–45–3; Rawlins 3–0–15–0.

Umpires: P. J. Hartley and N. A. Mallender.   Referee: J. J. Whitaker.

At Northampton, May 6–9. SUSSEX lost to NORTHAMPTONSHIRE by an innings and 120 runs.
Sussex's heaviest defeat by Northamptonshire.

SUSSEX v KENT

At Hove, May 13–16. Drawn. Sussex 13pts, Kent 11pts. Toss: Sussex. First-class debut: T. S. Muyeye.

This was Archer's only first-class game of the summer, and first in the Championship since September 2018. His fitness dominated the narrative. He took two wickets on the opening day in the first of three probing spells – helping dismiss Kent for a shoddy 145 – and talked optimistically of playing in the New Zealand Test series. Instead, he bowled just five overs on the second and, when Brown threw him the ball on a much-curtailed third, Archer said he wasn't fit; Brown didn't look happy, but later blamed a "miscommunication". Within a week, Archer was undergoing surgery on his problematic right elbow. That was not Brown's only frustration. Careless batting cost Sussex the chance to build a match-winning lead – a familiar criticism – before a surface on which 20 wickets had fallen in the first five sessions went to sleep. The last two days were affected by rain, but Kent declined to set a target. Leaning, their sole batting success in the first innings, as well as Crawley and Robinson, all opted for time at the crease after the county's chastening start to the season.

Close of play: first day, Sussex 51-2 (van Zyl 16, Head 0); second day, Kent 138-2 (Crawley 61, Leaning 18); third day, Kent 220-3 (Leaning 61, Robinson 11).

Kent

*D. J. Bell-Drummond c Garton b Archer	2	– c Clark b Robinson	27
J. M. Cox b Robinson	24	– lbw b Archer	12
Z. Crawley c Brown b Archer	7	– c Thomason b Carson	85
J. A. Leaning c Thomason b Robinson	63	– not out	127
†O. G. Robinson c Haines b Garton	4	– lbw b Clark	85
T. S. Muyeye lbw b Robinson	1	– not out	12
D. I. Stevens c Thomason b Garton	0		
M. K. O'Riordan c Thomason b Garton	9		
N. N. Gilchrist c and b Carson	13		
M. L. Cummins b Carson	4		
M. R. Quinn not out	0		
B 4, lb 7, w 5, nb 2	18	B 15, lb 17, w 1, nb 6	39

1/3 (1) 2/11 (3) 3/70 (2)   (54.3 overs) 145   1/22 (2)   (4 wkts dec, 111 overs) 387
4/85 (5) 5/86 (6) 6/91 (7)   2/59 (1) 3/189 (3)
7/112 (8) 8/140 (4) 9/142 (9) 10/145 (10)   4/361 (5)

Robinson 18–4–29–3; Archer 13–4–29–2; Garton 17–1–65–3; Clark 2–0–4–0; Carson 4.3–1–7–2. *Second innings*—Robinson 24–5–53–1; Archer 5–0–14–1; Garton 21–0–88–0; Rawlins 28–4–86–0; Clark 11–1–37–1; Carson 14–1–57–1; Haines 1–0–1–0; Head 7–1–19–0.

Sussex

A. D. Thomason c O'Riordan b Gilchrist	21	O. E. Robinson c Crawley b Quinn	25
T. J. Haines c Robinson b Stevens	14	J. C. Archer c Robinson b Quinn	2
S. van Zyl lbw b Gilchrist	52	J. J. Carson not out	4
T. M. Head b Stevens	20	B 11, lb 5, nb 8	24
T. G. R. Clark b Gilchrist	42		
*†B. C. Brown c Robinson b Stevens	34	1/24 (2) 2/51 (1) 3/103 (4) (76.3 overs) 256
D. M. W. Rawlins lbw b Quinn	6	4/123 (3) 5/184 (5) 6/202 (6)
G. H. S. Garton c Robinson b Quinn	12	7/212 (8) 8/241 (8) 9/245 (10) 10/256 (9)

Quinn 19.3–4–54–4; Stevens 22–6–64–3; Cummins 19–4–67–0; Gilchrist 14–1–51–3; O'Riordan 2–0–4–0.

Umpires: G. D. Lloyd and D. J. Millns.   Referee: S. J. Davis.

SUSSEX v NORTHAMPTONSHIRE

At Hove, May 27–30. Northamptonshire won by seven wickets. Northamptonshire 21pts, Sussex 3pts. Toss: Sussex.

A young Sussex side without their spearhead, Ollie Robinson, refused to buckle – though they never properly recovered from 67 for eight just after lunch on the first day. "Not much has changed, has it?" cried one of the 800 spectators, as crowds returned to Hove for the first time since September 2019. That Sanderson was their nemesis came as little surprise. His late away movement unsettled a phalanx of left-handers, and his six wickets took his tally against Sussex in the month to 16 at just 12. A merry ninth-wicket stand of 99 between Carson and Crocombe avoided ignominy, and the deficit seemed likely to be modest when Northamptonshire lost Zaib for 64 at 205 for nine. However, Berg and Sanderson took the lead to 81, before Kerrigan's attacking left-arm spin strengthened their advantage. Haines, though, became the first Sussex batsman to score a century at Hove for two years – and Brown was caught on the boundary aiming to become the second. But a target of 218 never looked too demanding: conditions improved, and Zaib sealed a Northamptonshire victory in a flurry of attacking shots an hour into the final day.

Close of play: first day, Northamptonshire 91-4 (Zaib 14, Kerrigan 3); second day, Sussex 142-4 (Haines 64, Brown 34); third day, Northamptonshire 131-2 (Procter 47, Keogh 24).

Sussex

A. D. Thomason lbw b Sanderson	4	– c Rossington b Sanderson	8
T. J. Haines c Vasconcelos b Berg	13	– c Taylor b Kerrigan	103
S. van Zyl c Vasconcelos b Sanderson	5	– c and b Kerrigan	17
T. M. Head c Berg b Sanderson	1	– c Vasconcelos b Kerrigan	0
T. G. R. Clark b Taylor	11	– c Curran b Berg	13
*†B. C. Brown c Rossington b Parnell	9	– c Procter b Kerrigan	95
D. M. W. Rawlins lbw b Parnell	2	– b Taylor	15
G. H. S. Garton lbw b Sanderson	12	– c Vasconcelos b Taylor	0
J. J. Carson c Taylor b Sanderson	52	– lbw b Kerrigan	35
H. T. Crocombe not out	46	– lbw b Taylor	0
J. A. Atkins c Curran b Berg	5	– not out	0
B 9, lb 4, nb 2	15	B 6, lb 3, w 1, nb 2	12

1/8 (1) 2/28 (2) 3/29 (4)   (59.3 overs) 175
4/30 (3) 5/51 (6) 6/55 (5)
7/57 (7) 8/67 (8) 9/166 (9) 10/175 (11)

1/10 (1) 2/77 (3)   (99.1 overs) 298
3/79 (4) 4/98 (5)
5/209 (2) 6/232 (7) 7/232 (8)
8/297 (9) 9/298 (10) 10/298 (6)

Sanderson 18–2–45–5; Berg 13.3–1–31–2; Parnell 10–2–27–2; Taylor 12–1–36–1; Kerrigan 6–0–23–0. *Second innings*—Sanderson 24–6–53–1; Berg 20–1–79–1; Taylor 13–1–43–3; Parnell 6–1–29–0; Kerrigan 34.1–5–70–5; Keogh 2–0–15–0.

Northamptonshire

B. J. Curran c Brown b Crocombe	7	– c Brown b Atkins	10
R. S. Vasconcelos c Brown b Garton	20	– run out (Haines)	38
L. A. Procter c Brown b Atkins	9	– c Thomason b Atkins	51
R. I. Keogh c Rawlins b Carson	24	– not out	60
S. A. Zaib c Brown b Atkins	64	– not out	47
S. C. Kerrigan b Garton	15		
*†A. M. Rossington c Clark b Garton	28		
T. A. I. Taylor run out (Head)	3		
W. D. Parnell c Head b Crocombe	1		
G. K. Berg not out	43		
B. W. Sanderson b Garton	20		
Lb 11, w 1, nb 10	22	B 9, lb 1, nb 2	12

1/11 (1) 2/42 (3) 3/53 (2)   (81.5 overs) 256
4/81 (4) 5/107 (6) 6/160 (7)
7/167 (8) 8/176 (9) 9/205 (5) 10/256 (11)

1/15 (1)   (3 wkts, 61.4 overs) 218
2/57 (2) 3/141 (3)

Crocombe 19–4–44–2; Atkins 21–4–49–2; Garton 14.5–0–69–4; Carson 18–2–60–1; Rawlins 9–0–23–0. *Second innings*—Crocombe 4–0–22–0; Atkins 16–1–39–2; Carson 13–2–46–0; Rawlins 20–2–71–0; Garton 3–0–12–0; Head 5.4–1–18–0.

Umpires: P. K. Baldwin and N. J. Llong.   Referee: W. M. Noon.

At Leeds, June 3–6. SUSSEX lost to YORKSHIRE by an innings and 30 runs.

SUSSEX v GLAMORGAN

At Hove, July 4–7. Drawn. Sussex 12pts, Glamorgan 12pts. Toss: Sussex. First-class debut: O. J. Carter.

With eight players self-isolating and three injured or with England, Sussex had a troubled build-up. Yet had it not been for rain, which badly disrupted the first and third days, they might have won. Nineteen-year-old Ollie Carter became their sixth first-class debutant of the summer, and shaped up well, though it was the left-handed opener Ali Orr – 20, and also from Eastbourne – who made the bigger impression, at least in the second innings. Both had fallen cheaply on the first day, as Sussex slipped to 34 for four before recovering to 226 thanks to an even more precocious talent: Ibrahim now had two first-class fifties before turning 17. Glamorgan trailed by 11, but soon reduced the hosts to 19 for three. Orr, exhibiting maturity in his shot selection, especially against the experienced new-ball pair of Hogan and van der Gugten, put on 43 with Carter, then 100 with Brown, who later went to his 20th first-class century with a six. He promptly declared, setting 275 in 51 overs, which he admitted was cautious. Although Carson plugged away, Glamorgan gained the draw that confirmed a place in Division Two.

Close of play: first day, Sussex 161-7 (Ibrahim 41); second day, Glamorgan 205-9 (Salter 6, Hogan 11); third day, Sussex 111-4 (Orr 54, Brown 25).

Sussex

A. G. H. Orr lbw b van der Gugten	4	–	lbw b Lloyd		80
A. D. Thomason c C. B. Cooke b van der Gugten	5	–	c C. B. Cooke b van der Gugten		1
S. van Zyl b Hogan	5	–	lbw b van der Gugten		0
T. M. Head lbw b van der Gugten	47	–	c J. M. Cooke b Hogan		5
O. J. Carter lbw b Weighell	3	–	c and b Salter		22
*†B. C. Brown c C. B. Cooke b Douthwaite	22	–	not out		100
D. K. Ibrahim st C. B. Cooke b Salter	58	–	lbw b van der Gugten		17
W. A. T. Beer c J. M. Cooke b Hogan	19	–	not out		23
J. J. Carson b Hogan	0				
S. C. Meaker c van der Gugten b Salter	23				
M. E. Claydon not out	22				
Lb 8, nb 10	18		B 8, lb 3, nb 4		15

1/6 (2) 2/13 (3) 3/23 (1)	(75.3 overs) 226	1/10 (2)	(6 wkts dec, 79 overs) 263
4/34 (5) 5/75 (6) 6/96 (4)		2/10 (3) 3/19 (4)	
7/161 (8) 8/163 (9) 9/194 (10) 10/226 (7)		4/62 (5) 5/162 (1) 6/198 (7)	

Hogan 22–4–46–3; van der Gugten 21–7–45–3; Weighell 8–1–36–1; Douthwaite 10–1–54–1; Lloyd 5–1–14–0; Salter 9.3–2–23–2. *Second innings*—Hogan 21–5–38–1; van der Gugten 23–4–94–3; Salter 21–2–63–1; Weighell 3–0–25–0; Douthwaite 4–0–19–0; Lloyd 7–0–13–1.

Glamorgan

J. M. Cooke lbw b Meaker	6	–	c Thomason b Beer		19
D. L. Lloyd b Meaker	38	–	c Thomason b Meaker		17
C. A. Ingram c Brown b Claydon	7	–	c Thomason b Carson		27
W. T. Root lbw b van Zyl	37	–	c Carter b Carson		12
K. S. Carlson c Thomason b Claydon	17	–	c Head b Carson		23
*†C. B. Cooke c Thomason b Carson	29				
D. A. Douthwaite c Carter b Beer	17	–	not out		14
W. J. Weighell b Beer	21				
A. G. Salter not out	16	–	(6) not out		19
T. van der Gugten c Meaker b Carson	1				
M. G. Hogan b Carson	11				
B 2, lb 7, nb 6	15		B 20, lb 1, nb 2		23

1/15 (1) 2/28 (3) 3/82 (2)	(64.5 overs) 215	1/20 (2)	(5 wkts, 50.2 overs) 154
4/111 (5) 5/117 (4) 6/157 (7)		2/63 (3) 3/79 (4)	
7/187 (6) 8/187 (8) 9/188 (10) 10/215 (11)		4/95 (1) 5/131 (5)	

Claydon 12–1–51–2; Meaker 13–0–58–2; Carson 16.5–2–39–3; Ibrahim 5–0–19–0; van Zyl 7–1–10–1; Beer 11–0–29–2. *Second innings*—Claydon 5–2–3–0; Meaker 5–1–22–1; Carson 20.2–5–61–3; Beer 18–6–41–1; Head 2–1–6–0.

Umpires: B. J. Debenham and R. J. Warren.   Referee: A. J. Swann.

At Canterbury, July 11–14. SUSSEX drew with KENT. *Sussex finish bottom of their group.*

DIVISION THREE

At Worcester, August 30–September 2. SUSSEX lost to WORCESTERSHIRE by six wickets.

SUSSEX v MIDDLESEX

At Hove, September 6–9. Middlesex won by an innings and 54 runs. Middlesex 24pts, Sussex 3pts. Toss: Middlesex.

An excellent pitch yielded runs, records, and a positive result. Middlesex's total – their highest, beating 642 for three against Hampshire at Southampton 98 years earlier – contained a faultless career-best 253 by Robson. With Stoneman, who had collected a pair in his only previous game since leaving Surrey, he put on 376, a Middlesex first-wicket record (four more than Mike Gatting and Justin Langer managed against Essex at Southgate in 1998). White's second century in two games rubbed Sussex noses in it. Haines and Brown, not keeping wicket in a Championship game

NO SAFETY IN NUMBERS

First-class teams twice making 300, and losing by an innings:

Victoria (315 & 322) lost to New South Wales (775) by inns and 138 at Sydney........	1881-82
Gentlemen (303 & 308) lost to Players (647) by inns and 36 at The Oval..............	1899
Victoria (332 & 311) lost to New South Wales (675) by inns and 32 at Sydney.........	1913-14
West Indies (357 & 319) lost to Australia (758-8 dec) by inns and 82 at Kingston......	1954-55
Karachi Blues (314 & 316) lost to Karachi Whites (762) by inns and 132 at Karachi.....	1956-57
Lahore City (302 & 320) lost to Karachi Blues (802-8 dec) by inns and 180 at Peshawar .	1994-95
Sussex (342 & 316) lost to Glamorgan (718-3 dec) by inns and 60 at Colwyn Bay	2000
Somerset (318 & 322) lost to Worcestershire (696-8 dec) by inns and 56 at Worcester ...	2005
Baluchistan (308 & 345) lost to NWFP (664-6 dec) by inns and 11 at Peshawar	2007-08
Sri Lanka (393 & 309) lost to India (726-9 dec) by inns and 24 at Mumbai	2009-10
Bangladesh A (346 & 326) lost to SA A (676-9 dec) by inns and four at Mirpur	2009-10
Kenya (304 & 325) lost to Namibia (630-7 dec) by inns and one at Windhoek	2012-13
Sussex (319 & 303) lost to Middlesex (676-5 dec) by inns and 54 at Hove..........	**2021**

for the first time since 2014, also found conditions to their liking, but the game pivoted Middlesex's way at 222 for one, when Brown became the first of five victims for Hollman. A wobble later turned into a full-blown collapse, with the last six wickets falling for 12. Haines, after making a career-best 156, led the resistance in the follow-on too, and was the first in the country to reach 1,000 runs. Middlesex, though, chipped away, and Hollman, who had managed just two wickets in his first three matches, claimed ten for 155; not since Yorkshire's Adil Rashid at Worcester in 2011 had a leg-spinner taken ten in an away Championship game.

Close of play: first day, Middlesex 400-2 (Robson 192, White 2); second day, Sussex 103-0 (Orr 17, Haines 73); third day, Sussex 88-3 (Haines 39, Garton 9).

Middlesex

S. D. Robson c Haines b Carson	253	†J. A. Simpson not out	2
M. D. Stoneman c Carter b Crocombe	174	B 7, lb 10, w 5, nb 22	44
S. S. Eskinazi c Carter b Hunt..........	4		
R. G. White not out....................	110	1/376 (2) (5 wkts dec, 161 overs)	676
M. D. E. Holden c Brown b Carson	1	2/397 (3) 3/494 (1)	
M. K. Andersson c Brown b Rawlins	88	4/499 (5) 5/673 (6) 110 overs: 468-2	

L. B. K. Hollman, B. C. Cullen, T. N. Walallawitta and *T. J. Murtagh did not bat.

Hunt 23–2–108–1; Hudson-Prentice 30–1–94–0; Crocombe 22–1–88–1; Ibrahim 7–0–51–0; Carson 46–4–183–2; Rawlins 27–2–110–1; Haines 6–0–25–0.

Sussex

A. G. H. Orr c Simpson b Cullen	18	– b Hollman	20
*T. J. Haines c Simpson b Murtagh	156	– c Walallawita b Hollman	87
B. C. Brown st Simpson b Hollman	80	– st Simpson b Hollman	10
G. H. S. Garton c White b Hollman	10	– (5) c Simpson b Hollman	17
D. K. Ibrahim c Hollman b Robson	4	– (6) c Murtagh b Hollman	15
F. J. Hudson-Prentice c Simpson b Murtagh	25	– (7) c Simpson b Walallawita	67
†O. J. Carter c Holden b Hollman	5	– (8) not out	31
D. M. W. Rawlins b Hollman	0	– (9) c Hollman b Murtagh	18
J. J. Carson c Simpson b Hollman	0	– (10) b Murtagh	6
H. T. Crocombe b Andersson	0	– (11) lbw b Andersson	4
S. F. Hunt not out	2	– (4) lbw b Robson	0
B 9, lb 5, nb 4	18	B 9, lb 9, nb 10	28

1/104 (1) 2/222 (3) 3/250 (4)   (95.4 overs) 319   1/58 (1) 2/74 (3)   (89.2 overs) 303
4/271 (5) 5/307 (6) 6/308 (2)   3/79 (4) 4/108 (5)
7/308 (8) 8/308 (9) 9/317 (7) 10/319 (10)   5/142 (6) 6/223 (2) 7/245 (7)
    8/278 (9) 9/290 (10) 10/303 (11)

Murtagh 16–5–28–2; Cullen 20–2–99–1; Andersson 13.4–3–47–1; Walallawita 24–11–58–0;
Hollman 20–5–65–5; Robson 2–0–8–1. *Second innings*—Murtagh 16–4–47–2; Cullen
10–1–31–0; Walallawita 18–2–50–1; Andersson 12.2–1–48–1; Hollman 28–6–90–5; Robson
5–0–19–1.

Umpires: N. J. Llong and C. M. Watts.   Referee: D. E. Malcolm.

At Leicester, September 12–15. SUSSEX lost to LEICESTERSHIRE by an innings and five runs.
Sussex's first innings defeat by Leicestershire since 1999.

SUSSEX v DERBYSHIRE

At Hove, September 21–23. Derbyshire won by nine wickets. Derbyshire 24pts, Sussex 5pts. Toss:
Derbyshire.

Derbyshire's only victory of the summer was Sussex's fourth consecutive defeat, and it consigned
them to the wooden spoon for the first time since 2000. The winning runs came from Critchley,
promoted so he could have a tilt at reaching four figures for the first-class season. He cut it fine: no
other Derbyshire player had ended on exactly 1,000. Although they had seen three home victories all
year (none in the Championship), it was a surprise that some Sussex members gave the team a
standing ovation; a few more may have wondered whether to renew their membership for more
"bloody development cricket". It had been a good toss to win, and Madsen's century set up a decent
Derbyshire total. In response, Sussex's youngsters played some weary shots. They were indebted to
Brown's fourth hundred of the year; a total of 300 was the highest for an innings containing six
ducks. When Godleman became the first Derbyshire captain to impose the follow-on since he did so
in 2016, Brown's third-ball duck scuttled hopes of a fightback, and an innings defeat was avoided
only by Rawlins chancing his arm with the tail.

Close of play: first day, Derbyshire 371-5 (Guest 30, Dal 5); second day, Sussex 255-6 (Brown
150, Carson 27).

Derbyshire

H. R. C. Came lbw b Crocombe	45	– (2) b Crocombe	4
*B. A. Godleman c Carter b Atkins	52		
J. L. du Plooy c Ibrahim b Crocombe	0	– not out	4
W. L. Madsen c Orr b Hunt	111		
M. J. J. Critchley b Atkins	85	– (1) not out	15
†B. D. Guest lbw b Atkins	30		
A. K. Dal not out	49		
M. H. McKiernan c Carter b Hunt	23		
B. W. Aitchison c Brown b Crocombe	2		
D. R. Melton c Ibrahim b Crocombe	8		
E. H. T. Moulton c Brown b Atkins	3		
B 12, lb 19, nb 26	57		

1/89 (1) 2/89 (3) 3/185 (2)   (118.4 overs) 465   1/9 (2)   (1 wkt, 3.4 overs) 23
4/308 (4) 5/353 (5) 6/374 (6)
7/428 (8) 8/439 (9) 9/453 (10)
10/465 (11)   110 overs: 428-6

Hunt 23–1–88–2; Crocombe 26–4–92–4; Atkins 24.4–1–117–4; Ibrahim 16–2–54–0; Haines 11–1–24–0; Carson 14–1–47–0; Rawlins 3–0–10–0; Ward 1–0–2–0. *Second innings*—Crocombe 2–0–8–1; Ibrahim 1.4–0–15–0.

Sussex

A. G. H. Orr c Guest b Aitchison	0	– c Guest b Moulton	21
*T. J. Haines c Guest b Melton	18	– run out (Aitchison/Guest)	26
B. C. Brown c McKiernan b Aitchison	157	– b Moulton	0
D. K. Ibrahim c Madsen b Aitchison	1	– (5) lbw b Melton	29
H. D. Ward lbw b Aitchison	0	– (4) b Critchley	19
†O. J. Carter c Came b Melton	51	– lbw b Melton	4
D. M. W. Rawlins c and b Melton	0	– st Guest b Madsen	58
J. J. Carson not out	64	– c Guest b Dal	16
H. T. Crocombe lbw b Critchley	0	– b Madsen	2
S. F. Hunt b Critchley	0	– c Aitchison b Dal	0
J. A. Atkins b Critchley	0	– not out	0
Lb 1, nb 8	9	B 4, lb 1, w 1, nb 6	12

1/0 (1) 2/36 (2) 3/44 (4)   (84.4 overs) 300   1/43 (1) 2/43 (3)   (50.3 overs) 187
4/46 (5) 5/188 (6) 6/188 (7)   3/51 (2) 4/92 (4)
7/275 (3) 8/276 (9) 9/300 (10) 10/300 (11)   5/105 (6) 6/116 (5) 7/168 (8)
                                  8/172 (9) 9/173 (10) 10/187 (7)

Aitchison 21–2–80–4; Melton 14–2–57–3; Dal 17–1–36–0; Moulton 11–2–50–0; Critchley 17.4–1–60–3; McKiernan 4–0–16–0. *Second innings*—Aitchison 12–3–22–0; Melton 8–1–40–2; Critchley 19–6–71–1; Moulton 5–2–24–2; Dal 4–0–17–2; Madsen 2.3–0–8–2.

Umpires: N. L. Bainton and P. K. Baldwin. Referee: S. G. Hinks.

WARWICKSHIRE

A match made in Hull

PAUL BOLTON

Warwickshire's eighth Championship, achieved through resilience and a strong team ethic, was also a personal triumph for their new head coach, Mark Robinson. Four years after he guided England to the women's World Cup, and more than a decade after he coached Sussex to back-to-back Championships, he transformed an underperforming side. Having spent 18 months freelancing after losing his England job, Robinson returned to the county circuit, older and certainly wiser. He inherited a squad with a blend of youth and experience – but soon identified a lack of confidence, after two indifferent seasons in four-day cricket. The players responded to his perceptive approach, not least captain Will Rhodes, with whom he established an effective working relationship – perhaps helped by their mutual support of Hull City FC (both grew up there).

Rhodes was disappointed with his own form, until his century helped secure victory in the Bob Willis Trophy, but he compensated with astute captaincy, selfless cameos and important wickets. It was fitting that his catch clinched the decisive victory over Somerset. That win, after tea on day four, typified Warwickshire's season. They repeatedly had to dig deep, with three of their four group-stage victories settled in the final session.

The pitches at Edgbaston made for compelling cricket, but Robinson occasionally wondered if they were too good. Rob Yates certainly enjoyed them, hitting his four Championship centuries at home. He combined his Warwickshire commitments with a degree at Birmingham University, and broke his away drought in the Bob Willis Trophy at Lord's, booking a place on England Lions' trip to Australia. The other four Championship hundreds were struck by Sam Hain – the only batsman, apart from Yates, to top 800 runs – Michael Burgess, Chris Benjamin (on Championship debut against Lancashire) and Pieter Malan. That hundred aside, Malan and fellow overseas player Hanuma Vihari together contributed just 298 runs in 15 innings. But Chris Woakes, in his first appearances in the Championship for three years, after he unexpectedly became available following the cancellation of the Fifth Test against India, and opted out of his IPL contract, took 12 wickets in the last two games.

The regular seam attack were led by two Gloucestershire exiles, Liam Norwell and Craig Miles, who shared 86 Championship wickets, and added 11 in the Bob Willis Trophy. Norwell topped 50 in a season for the third time in a career blighted by injury – his 13 red-ball appearances more than doubled his tally for the previous three summers combined. He rediscovered his nip, and received an England Lions call.

Oliver Hannon-Dalby's season was curtailed by a foot injury, and Olly Stone's by a stress fracture of the back. Tim Bresnan made some typically wholehearted contributions with bat and ball, either side of a mid-season calf problem, and was sharp in the slips, holding six catches in the second innings against Yorkshire, on his return to Headingley. Having helped him resurrect his career, bowling coach Graeme Welch left in December for the same role at Hampshire. In the new year, Bresnan announced his retirement.

Rob Yates

Danny Briggs enjoyed a new lease of life following his move from Sussex, taking 33 first-class wickets – his most in ten years. The senior spinner, he also made important runs down the order. After an eight-year absence, he was recalled by England – part of an emergency squad, picked because of the first-choice team's Covid isolation – though he did not play. He was awarded his county cap in September, as was Burgess, who was excellent behind the stumps; he will face competition in 2022 from Alex Davies, the talented wicketkeeper-batsman signed from Lancashire.

Warwickshire had mixed fortunes in white-ball cricket, reaching the quarter-finals of the Vitality Blast, and missing out on the knockout stages of the Royal London Cup. The absence of most of the frontline bowlers, through injury or involvement in The Hundred, meant 19 players were used in the 50-over competition. Four were brought in on three-week contracts: Jordan Bulpitt, Karl Carver, Ashish Chakrapani and Kiel van Vollenhoven. There were hints of promise from rookies Jacob Bethell, a Barbadian 17-year-old all-rounder at Rugby School, and seamer Manraj Johal, plus maiden centuries from Yates, Ed Pollock and Matt Lamb. Pollock played in 12 Blast matches, but was left out of the quarter-final defeat at Canterbury. At the end of the season, he moved to Worcestershire – where he had been in the Academy – in search of red-ball opportunities: despite scoring 1,568 runs in 71 limited-overs matches for Warwickshire, he never played a Championship game. Off-spinner Alex Thomson moved to Derbyshire in June.

The majority of Edgbaston's Blast matches were played on hybrid pitches, including one on which the ground's lowest-score record was broken twice in three days: first Yorkshire were shot out for 81 in a match that lasted 24.2 overs, then Warwickshire collapsed to 63 against Nottinghamshire. On both occasions, the pitch was blameless. The West Indian all-rounder Carlos Brathwaite topped the bowling table with 18 wickets, and scored 183 quickfire runs. He confirmed a return for the 2022 Blast, this time as captain.

WARWICKSHIRE RESULTS

County Championship and Bob Willis Trophy matches – Played 15: Won 7, Lost 2, Drawn 6.
Vitality T20 Blast matches – Played 15: Won 7, Lost 7, No result 1.
Royal London Cup matches – Played 8: Won 4, Lost 4.

LV= County Championship, 2nd in Group 1, winners of Division 1; Bob Willis Trophy, winners;
Vitality T20 Blast, quarter-finalists; Royal London Cup, 6th in Group 2.

COUNTY CHAMPIONSHIP AND BOB WILLIS TROPHY AVERAGES
BATTING AND FIELDING

Cap		Birthplace		M	I	NO	R	HS	100	Avge	Ct/St
	†R. M. Yates	Solihull‡		14	24	2	906	132*	5	41.18	21
	P. J. Malan¶	Nelspruit, SA		6	10	1	339	141	1	37.66	0
2019	D. P. Sibley§	Epsom		10	16	2	527	80	0	37.64	2
2018	S. R. Hain	Hong Kong		15	26	2	881	118	1	36.70	21
	C. G. Benjamin	Johannesburg, SA ..		3	6	0	198	127	1	33.00	1
2020	†W. M. H. Rhodes	Nottingham		15	27	2	789	156	1	31.56	13
	M. J. Lamb	Wolverhampton		14	24	5	565	67	0	29.73	5
2021	M. G. K. Burgess ..	Epsom		15	22	0	651	101	1	29.59	44/5
2021	D. R. Briggs	Newport, IoW		13	20	4	413	66*	0	25.81	4
2021	T. T. Bresnan	Pontefract		11	16	2	315	68*	0	22.50	18
	G. H. Vihari¶	Kakinada, India		3	6	0	100	52	0	16.66	3
2020	O. P. Stone	Norwich		4	5	1	63	43	0	15.75	0
	C. N. Miles	Swindon		12	17	3	176	30*	0	12.57	4
2019	†O. J. Hannon-Dalby ..	Halifax		8	11	6	48	26	0	9.60	2
	L. C. Norwell	Bournemouth.....		13	18	5	120	30*	0	9.23	1

Also batted: †J. G. Bethell (*Barbados*) (1 match) 15, 8 (1 ct); E. A. Brookes (*Solihull‡*) (1 match)
did not bat; C. K. Holder¶ (*Barbados*) (2 matches) 6, 0*, 0; M. S. Johal (*Birmingham‡*) (1 match)
19; J. B. Lintott (*Taunton*) (1 match) 15 (1 ct); R. N. Sidebottom†† (*Shepparton, Australia*)
(2 matches) 0, 1; C. R. Woakes§ (*Birmingham‡*) (2 matches) 9, 0, 10 (1 ct).

‡ *Born in Warwickshire.* § *ECB contract.* ¶ *Official overseas player.* †† *Other non-England-qualified.*

BOWLING

	Style	O	M	R	W	BB	5I	Avge
C. R. Woakes..................	RFM	72.3	23	205	12	3-26	0	17.08
L. C. Norwell.................	RFM	367	101	964	54	6-57	2	17.85
W. M. H. Rhodes.............	RFM	178	51	481	26	5-23	1	18.50
C. N. Miles..................	RFM	302.3	64	902	43	5-28	3	20.97
D. R. Briggs.................	SLA	309	82	722	33	4-36	0	21.87
O. J. Hannon-Dalby..........	RFM	258.5	73	698	24	5-76	1	29.08
O. P. Stone.................	RF	124.3	20	395	13	4-89	0	30.38
T. T. Bresnan...............	RFM	175	59	453	13	3-35	0	34.84

Also bowled: E. A. Brookes (RFM) 7–2–22–0; C. K. Holder (RFM) 45–9–177–2; M. S. Johal
(RFM) 18–5–59–4; M. J. Lamb (RFM) 21–2–50–2; J. B. Lintott (SLW) 39–2–103–0; R. N.
Sidebottom (RFM) 46–9–113–0; G. H. Vihari (OB) 1–0–11–0; R. M. Yates (OB) 49–9–108–3.

LEADING VITALITY BLAST AVERAGES (100 runs/15 overs)

Batting	Runs	HS	Avge	SR	Ct/St
C. R. Brathwaite	183	52*	22.87	**150.00**	4
E. J. Pollock....	245	62	22.27	**144.11**	4
S. R. Hain	398	83*	39.80	**139.16**	11
W. M. H. Rhodes	258	79	19.84	**134.37**	9
A. J. Hose	185	46*	18.50	**133.09**	7
T. T. Bresnan ..	109	34*	21.80	**122.47**	2
M. G. K. Burgess	107	41	11.88	**97.27**	4/6

Bowling	W	BB	Avge	ER
D. R. Briggs	15	3-35	24.33	**7.04**
J. B. Lintott.....	15	4-20	20.26	**7.06**
C. R. Brathwaite..	18	3-7	17.61	**8.16**
C. N. Miles.....	15	3-19	25.80	**8.23**
T. T. Bresnan ..	16	4-26	17.50	**8.88**
W. M. H. Rhodes .	14	4-34	11.71	**9.11**

LEADING ROYAL LONDON CUP AVERAGES (100 runs/4 wickets)

Batting	Runs	HS	Avge	SR	Ct/St	Bowling	W	BB	Avge	ER
M. J. Lamb	360	119*	60.00	96.77	2	W. M. H. Rhodes	8	3-40	18.12	5.57
D. R. Mousley .	166	61	41.50	109.21	2	G. A. Garrett	5	3-50	27.00	5.00
R. M. Yates ...	282	103	40.28	92.76	4	J. G. Bethell.....	11	4-36	27.36	5.28
M. G. K. Burgess	275	73	39.28	80.17	10/2	E. A. Brookes ...	7	3-15	29.57	6.75
E. J. Pollock ..	237	103*	33.85	92.57	2	M. S. Johal......	7	2-35	32.57	5.47
W. M. H. Rhodes	204	65	29.14	76.11	4	M. J. Lamb	4	4-35	37.75	5.39
J. G. Bethell ...	141	66	23.50	94.63	2	K. Carver.......	5	2-35	40.60	5.07
E. A. Brookes ..	107	63	21.40	86.29	8					

FIRST-CLASS COUNTY RECORDS

Highest score for	501*	B. C. Lara v Durham at Birmingham..............	1994
Highest score against	322	I. V. A. Richards (Somerset) at Taunton	1985
Leading run-scorer	35,146	D. L. Amiss (avge 41.64).......................	1960–87
Best bowling for	10-41	J. D. Bannister v Combined Services at Birmingham ..	1959
Best bowling against	10-36	H. Verity (Yorkshire) at Leeds	1931
Leading wicket-taker	2,201	W. E. Hollies (avge 20.45)	1932–57
Highest total for	810-4 dec	v Durham at Birmingham	1994
Highest total against	887	by Yorkshire at Birmingham	1896
Lowest total for	16	v Kent at Tonbridge...........................	1913
Lowest total against	15	by Hampshire at Birmingham	1922

LIST A COUNTY RECORDS

Highest score for	206	A. I. Kallicharran v Oxfordshire at Birmingham....	1984
Highest score against	172*	W. Larkins (Northamptonshire) at Luton	1983
Leading run-scorer	11,254	D. L. Amiss (avge 33.79).......................	1963–87
Best bowling for	7-32	R. G. D. Willis v Yorkshire at Birmingham	1981
Best bowling against	6-27	M. H. Yardy (Sussex) at Birmingham	2005
Leading wicket-taker	396	G. C. Small (avge 25.48).......................	1980–99
Highest total for	392-5	v Oxfordshire at Birmingham	1984
Highest total against	415-5	by Nottinghamshire at Nottingham	2016
Lowest total for	59	v Yorkshire at Leeds	2001
Lowest total against	56	by Yorkshire at Birmingham	1995

TWENTY20 COUNTY RECORDS

Highest score for	158*	B. B. McCullum v Derbyshire at Birmingham	2015
Highest score against	115	M. M. Ali (Worcestershire) at Birmingham........	2018
Leading run-scorer	**2,341**	**S. R. Hain (avge 37.75, SR 129.91)**.............	**2016–21**
Best bowling for	5-19	N. M. Carter v Worcestershire at Birmingham	2005
Best bowling against	7-18	C. N. Ackermann (Leicestershire) at Leicester	2019
Leading wicket-taker	141	J. S. Patel (avge 24.76, ER 6.99)................	2009–20
Highest total for	242-2	v Derbyshire at Birmingham	2015
Highest total against	231-5	by Northamptonshire at Birmingham	2018
Lowest total for	**63**	**v Nottinghamshire at Birmingham**.............	**2021**
Lowest total against	**81**	**by Yorkshire at Birmingham**	**2021**

ADDRESS

Edgbaston Stadium, Birmingham B5 7QU; 0121 369 1994/0330 551 1994; info@edgbaston.com; www.edgbaston.com. Twitter: @WarwickshireCCC.

OFFICIALS

Captain W. M. H. Rhodes
   (Twenty20) C. R. Braithwaite
Director of cricket P. Farbrace
First-team coach M. A. Robinson
High performance manager P. Greetham
President Earl of Aylesford

Chair M. McCafferty
Chief executive S. J. Cain
Head groundsman G. Barwell
Scorer M. D. Smith

GROUP ONE

WARWICKSHIRE v DERBYSHIRE

At Birmingham, April 8–11. Drawn. Warwickshire 12pts, Derbyshire 11pts. Toss: Warwickshire. County debut: D. R. Briggs. Championship debuts: B. W. Aitchison, M. A. R. Cohen.

A match played in Arctic conditions was ended by a fourth-afternoon snowstorm, with matters evenly balanced. In numbing cold on a seamer-friendly pitch, only Critchley and Lamb batted with any fluency. With Reece, Critchley had shored up Derbyshire's first innings after Norwell and Hannon-Dalby made the most of the conditions; Norwell's five wickets included two in his first over, as three of the top four made ducks. A home win appeared likely when Derbyshire's attacking instincts got them into more trouble on the third day, with Hannon-Dalby taking all the wickets as they declined to 71 for five, including du Plooy for a pair. Rain gave them the opportunity to regroup: on the final morning, in the best weather of the match, Critchley and the obdurate Hosein added 113 in 36 overs. The eventual target before the weather closed in was 213 in 41 – which might have tested Warwickshire had they batted as sketchily as in their first innings against an inexperienced attack, although Lamb did last three hours for 54.

Close of play: first day, Warwickshire 13-1 (Sibley 3, Yates 10); second day, Warwickshire 169-5 (Lamb 41, Bresnan 27); third day, Derbyshire 71-5 (Critchley 23, Hosein 0).

Derbyshire

L. M. Reece c Hain b Norwell	63	– (2) c Burgess b Hannon-Dalby	3
*B. A. Godleman c Burgess b Norwell	0	– (1) c Yates b Hannon-Dalby	20
A. K. Dal b Norwell	0	– lbw b Hannon-Dalby	4
J. L. du Plooy b Hannon-Dalby	0	– lbw b Hannon-Dalby	0
W. L. Madsen c Yates b Hannon-Dalby	15	– c Yates b Hannon-Dalby	20
M. J. J. Critchley c Bresnan b Norwell	64	– lbw b Norwell	83
†H. R. Hosein c Hain b Norwell	2	– not out	78
F. J. Hudson-Prentice c Briggs b Rhodes	14	– c Burgess b Rhodes	21
M. A. R. Cohen c Bresnan b Miles	4	– c Hain b Miles	3
B. W. Aitchison not out	11	– c Hain b Miles	3
S. Conners c Hain b Briggs	9	– c Burgess b Norwell	4
B 1, lb 6	7	Lb 1, nb 4	5

1/0 (2) 2/0 (3) 3/7 (4) (78.2 overs) 189
4/50 (5) 5/143 (1) 6/147 (7)
7/162 (6) 8/164 (8) 9/168 (9) 10/189 (11)

1/13 (2) 2/17 (3) (72.4 overs) 244
3/17 (4) 4/34 (1)
5/71 (5) 6/184 (6) 7/219 (8)
8/227 (9) 9/233 (10) 10/244 (11)

Hannon-Dalby 20–6–45–2; Norwell 18–7–32–5; Miles 16–4–44–1; Bresnan 12–6–33–0; Briggs 9.2–3–27–1; Rhodes 3–2–1–1. *Second innings*—Hannon-Dalby 20.1–1–76–5; Norwell 17.4–1–87–2; Bresnan 10–4–24–0; Miles 9–2–25–2; Rhodes 14–6–28–1; Briggs 2–1–3–0.

Warwickshire

*W. M. H. Rhodes lbw b Conners	0	– not out	5
D. P. Sibley c Hosein b Conners	29	– not out	0
R. M. Yates c Madsen b Hudson-Prentice	40		
S. R. Hain c Madsen b Aitchison	14		
M. J. Lamb c Madsen b Critchley	54		
†M. G. K. Burgess c Hosein b Aitchison	7		
T. T. Bresnan b Reece	35		
C. N. Miles c Dal b Cohen	14		
D. R. Briggs lbw b Cohen	11		
L. C. Norwell lbw b Critchley	4		
O. J. Hannon-Dalby not out	0		
B 1, lb 4, w 2, nb 6	13	Nb 2	2

1/0 (1) 2/50 (3) 3/77 (4) (75.2 overs) 221
4/106 (2) 5/114 (6) 6/182 (7)
7/206 (5) 8/212 (8) 9/221 (10) 10/221 (9)

(no wkt, 4.1 overs) 7

Conners 13–4–40–2; Reece 20–8–38–1; Hudson-Prentice 15–6–45–1; Aitchison 7–2–31–2; Cohen 14.2–5–40–2; Critchley 6–0–22–2. *Second innings*—Conners 2.1–0–7–0; Reece 2–2–0–0.

Umpires: R. K. Illingworth and A. G. Wharf.   Referee: W. R. Smith.

At Nottingham, April 15–18. WARWICKSHIRE beat NOTTINGHAMSHIRE by three wickets.

WARWICKSHIRE v ESSEX

At Birmingham, April 22–25. Warwickshire won by seven wickets. Warwickshire 21pts, Essex 5pts. Toss: Essex.

Warwickshire inflicted Essex's first defeat in 22 first-class matches, thanks to a stylish century from Yates. His calm temperament and crisp square-driving had previously prompted comparisons with Alastair Cook. Now, with Cook watching from slip, Yates guided a perfectly paced chase, completed with eight balls to spare. They had needed 256 in 82 overs, with Harmer expected to be the match-winner – but he could find only slow turn, and ended up with his most expensive wicketless analysis for Essex. Walter's awkward left-arm pace appeared a bigger threat, but he was used sparingly; Yates cashed in, having delayed an essay on the significance of gorilla chest-beating for his English Language degree at Birmingham University. Harmer had made a significant contribution, but with the bat: his four-hour unbeaten 82 in the second innings, after Lawrence's equally dogged 55, helped Essex rally from 36 for five. Warwickshire had also needed lower-order runs, which restricted their first-innings deficit to 11; Briggs marshalled the resistance as the last two wickets added 91. On the opening day, regular strikes for Hannon-Dalby and Stone kept Essex's total within bounds – four reached 46, but none exceeded Browne's 68.

Close of play: first day, Warwickshire 7-0 (Rhodes 7, Yates 0); second day, Warwickshire 243-8 (Briggs 32, Miles 22); third day, Essex 213-9 (Harmer 62, Porter 1).

Essex

N. L. J. Browne c Burgess b Stone	68	– lbw b Miles	8
A. N. Cook c Burgess b Miles	46	– c Yates b Hannon-Dalby	10
*T. Westley lbw b Miles	4	– c Rhodes b Miles	5
D. W. Lawrence c Lamb b Stone	5	– run out (Miles)	55
P. I. Walter c Vihari b Stone	66	– c Burgess b Hannon-Dalby	1
R. N. ten Doeschate c Hain b Hannon-Dalby	56	– lbw b Stone	7
†A. J. A. Wheater c Burgess b Stone	23	– c Vihari b Miles	30
S. R. Harmer lbw b Hannon-Dalby	0	– not out	82
P. M. Siddle b Hannon-Dalby	14	– c Burgess b Miles	20
S. J. Cook c Hain b Hannon-Dalby	6	– c Miles b Stone	7
J. A. Porter not out	5	– lbw b Briggs	11
Lb 2	2	B 5, lb 2, w 1	8

1/55 (2) 2/63 (3) 3/72 (4)   (89.5 overs) 295   1/16 (2) 2/23 (3)   (94 overs) 244
4/186 (1) 5/197 (5) 6/243 (7)   3/24 (1) 4/25 (5)
7/248 (8) 8/266 (9) 9/276 (10) 10/295 (6)   5/36 (6) 6/93 (7) 7/137 (4)
                                                     8/169 (9) 9/202 (10) 10/244 (11)

Hannon-Dalby 20.5–7–73–4; Stone 21–3–89–4; Rhodes 13–2–41–0; Miles 13–4–35–2; Bresnan 6–1–32–0; Briggs 14–3–19–0; Yates 2–0–4–0. *Second innings*—Stone 26.5–5–65–2; Miles 22–3–70–4; Hannon-Dalby 19–7–35–2; Bresnan 4–0–16–0; Briggs 20–5–45–1; Rhodes 3–0–6–0.

Warwickshire

*W. M. H. Rhodes b Siddle	26	– c Wheater b S. J. Cook 11
R. M. Yates b S. J. Cook	4	– not out 120
G. H. Vihari c Wheater b Porter	32	– c Wheater b Walter 52
S. R. Hain b Harmer	36	– c S. J. Cook b Walter 60
M. J. Lamb b Siddle	47	– not out 6
†M. G. K. Burgess st Wheater b Harmer	2	
T. T. Bresnan b Harmer	21	
O. P. Stone lbw b Siddle	16	
D. R. Briggs not out	66	
C. N. Miles lbw b Porter	25	
O. J. Hannon-Dalby lbw b Harmer	3	
Lb 4, nb 2	6	B 5, lb 2 7

1/16 (2) 2/34 (1) 3/83 (3) (111.1 overs) 284   1/11 (1) (3 wkts, 80.4 overs) 256
4/119 (4) 5/129 (6) 6/155 (7)   2/126 (3) 3/244 (4)
7/186 (8) 8/193 (5) 9/259 (10)
10/284 (11)   110 overs: 275-9

Porter 29–8–70–2; S. J. Cook 26–8–69–1; Siddle 18–1–52–3; Harmer 38.1–11–89–4. *Second innings*—Porter 12–0–59–0; S. J. Cook 14.4–3–36–1; Siddle 14–3–41–0; Harmer 32–9–88–0; Walter 5–0–18–2; Lawrence 3–0–7–0.

Umpires: M. Burns and A. G. Wharf.   Referee: S. J. Davis.

At Chester-le-Street, April 29–May 1. WARWICKSHIRE lost to DURHAM by an innings and 127 runs. *Warwickshire collapse to 30 for eight in their first innings.*

WARWICKSHIRE v WORCESTERSHIRE

At Birmingham, May 6–9. Drawn. Warwickshire 13pts, Worcestershire 14pts. Toss: Worcestershire. County debut: P. J. Malan.

The loss of the third day to rain meant a match that had been nicely balanced petered out into a draw. Yates made another fluent century, his second in two innings at Edgbaston, though he was assisted by wayward bowling in helpful conditions on the first morning. When Worcestershire's attack finally switched on their radar, Warwickshire laboured, until Burgess played with growing assurance, eventually reaching his first hundred since he moved from Sussex in 2019. Barnard deserved a five-for, but had two chances dropped at slip, including Burgess on 41. Libby continued his productive start to the summer, but was unsettled by the pace of Stone, who went round the wicket and had him taken at short leg after he had hit 13 fours in his 74. When Stone's effectiveness was restricted by a sore toe, Haynes prospered – but missed out on a maiden century when he was run out while backing up, as Norwell deflected a straight-drive from Barnard into the stumps.

Close of play: first day, Warwickshire 271-7 (Burgess 65, Briggs 4); second day, Worcestershire 198-4 (Haynes 52, Wessels 17); third day, no play.

Warwickshire

*W. M. H. Rhodes c Cox b Leach	10	– c Barnard b Joseph	25
R. M. Yates c Cox b D'Oliveira	104	– c Cox b Leach	5
P. J. Malan b Barnard	32	– c Wessels b Joseph	28
S. R. Hain b D'Oliveira	8	– not out	6
M. J. Lamb c Cox b Leach	11	– not out	5
†M. G. K. Burgess c Fell b Barnard	101		
T. T. Bresnan c Cox b Barnard	20		
O. P. Stone b Tongue	0		
D. R. Briggs lbw b Tongue	24		
L. C. Norwell b Joseph	7		
O. J. Hannon-Dalby not out	4		
B 4, lb 8, nb 10	22	B 1	1

1/20 (1) 2/97 (3) 3/133 (4)   (117.2 overs) 343   1/5 (2) 2/44 (3)   (3 wkts, 25 overs) 70
4/154 (5) 5/224 (2) 6/262 (7)   3/63 (1)
7/263 (8) 8/316 (9) 9/339 (10)
10/343 (6)   110 overs: 316-8

Leach 25.6–6–62–2; Tongue 26–3–82–2; Joseph 23–3–80–1; Barnard 21.2–6–76–3; D'Oliveira 22–3–31–2. *Second innings*—Leach 4–1–19–1; Barnard 5–1–13–0; Tongue 8–1–15–0; Joseph 6–0–22–2; Mitchell 1–1–0–0; Libby 1–1–0–0.

Worcestershire

D. K. H. Mitchell lbw b Norwell	12	A. S. Joseph c Yates b Briggs	17
J. D. Libby c Hain b Stone	74	*J. Leach not out	8
T. C. Fell c Burgess b Rhodes	20	B 5, lb 7, w 3	15
J. A. Haynes run out (Norwell)	87		
B. L. D'Oliveira c Burgess b Rhodes	15	1/38 (1) (8 wkts dec, 113 overs) 364
M. H. Wessels c Hain b Bresnan	17	2/84 (3) 3/125 (2)
†O. B. Cox lbw b Hannon-Dalby	23	4/161 (5) 5/198 (6) 6/228 (7)
E. G. Barnard not out	76	7/289 (4) 8/337 (9) 110 overs: 350-8

J. C. Tongue did not bat.

Stone 17–2–46–1; Norwell 28–7–85–1; Hannon-Dalby 28–6–87–1; Bresnan 9–2–34–1; Rhodes 12–2–39–2; Briggs 19–2–61–1.

Umpires: I. D. Blackwell and M. J. Saggers. Referee: S. J. Davis.

At Chelmsford, May 20–23. WARWICKSHIRE drew with ESSEX.

WARWICKSHIRE v NOTTINGHAMSHIRE

At Birmingham, May 27–30. Warwickshire won by 170 runs. Warwickshire 22pts, Nottinghamshire 5pts. Toss: Nottinghamshire.

Spectators returned to Edgbaston for the first time since a friendly in July 2020, and saw Warwickshire complete a quickfire double over Nottinghamshire. Briggs produced an excellent all-round display: he made valuable runs down the order, then bowled his left-arm spin with skill and accuracy to claim his best first-class figures since September 2016 (when he was playing for Sussex). Rhodes returned to form with two half-centuries; after he was dropped behind on six in the first innings, it needed a reflex catch at short leg to deny him his first hundred of the season. Paterson took three quick wickets with the second new ball on his way to his first county five-for, but Norwell and Hannon-Dalby clobbered 52 in a carefree last-ditch stand. Norwell then claimed four wickets, helping Warwickshire to a 44-run lead, but it took a seventh-wicket partnership of 103 between Burgess and Briggs to convert that advantage into a match-winning one. Nottinghamshire set off optimistically after a target of 309 in 74 overs, but by the time they abandoned the chase – once Hannon-Dalby had removed Clarke and Mullaney – they were struggling to save the game.

Close of play: first day, Warwickshire 250-6 (Lamb 43, Briggs 0); second day, Nottinghamshire 173-3 (Clarke 48, James 4); third day, Warwickshire 201-6 (Burgess 61, Briggs 16).

Warwickshire

*W. M. H. Rhodes c Hameed b Patterson-White	91	– b Chappell ... 63
R. M. Yates b James	8	– b Patterson-White ... 26
P. J. Malan lbw b Mullaney	17	– c Patterson-White b Chappell ... 6
S. R. Hain lbw b Paterson	61	– c Moores b Chappell ... 5
M. J. Lamb c sub (B. A. Hutton) b Paterson	67	– lbw b Fletcher ... 7
†M. G. K. Burgess lbw b Paterson	3	– c Mullaney b Patterson-White ... 80
T. T. Bresnan c Hameed b Paterson	0	– c Moores b Fletcher ... 0
D. R. Briggs c Moores b Paterson	7	– b Fletcher ... 50
C. N. Miles c Slater b Fletcher	2	– run out (Slater) ... 1
L. C. Norwell not out	30	– b Fletcher ... 0
O. J. Hannon-Dalby c Mullaney b Patterson-White	26	– not out ... 4
B 7, lb 4, nb 18	29	B 1, lb 9, nb 12 ... 22

1/32 (2) 2/78 (3) 3/163 (1)   (119.1 overs) 341   1/76 (2) 2/95 (3)   (85.1 overs) 264
4/238 (4) 5/244 (6) 6/248 (7)   3/113 (4) 4/116 (1)
7/262 (8) 8/277 (9) 9/289 (5)   5/134 (5) 6/134 (7) 7/237 (6)
10/341 (11)   110 overs: 303-9   8/250 (9) 9/259 (8) 10/264 (10)

Fletcher 30–9–67–1; Chappell 17–3–64–0; Paterson 28–4–90–5; James 12–2–36–1; Mullaney 12–3–21–1; Patterson-White 20.1–2–52–2. *Second innings*—Fletcher 14.1–3–38–4; Chappell 22–5–64–3; Paterson 14–2–72–0; Patterson-White 23–4–45–2; James 3–0–16–0; Mullaney 9–1–19–0.

Nottinghamshire

B. T. Slater c Burgess b Norwell	77	– c Burgess b Bresnan ... 27
H. Hameed b Norwell	39	– c Burgess b Norwell ... 2
B. M. Duckett b Norwell	4	– c Yates b Briggs ... 23
J. M. Clarke lbw b Bresnan	61	– st Burgess b Hannon-Dalby ... 20
L. W. James b Miles	4	– c Burgess b Briggs ... 19
*S. J. Mullaney b Briggs	28	– c Yates b Hannon-Dalby ... 8
†T. J. Moores c and b Rhodes	13	– b Rhodes ... 21
L. A. Patterson-White c Burgess b Briggs	36	– b Miles ... 11
Z. J. Chappell c Lamb b Norwell	12	– c Hain b Briggs ... 1
L. J. Fletcher c Burgess b Rhodes	2	– b Briggs ... 1
D. Paterson not out	8	– not out ... 1
B 4, lb 5, nb 4	13	B 2, lb 1, w 1 ... 4

1/72 (2) 2/78 (3) 3/156 (1)   (95.2 overs) 297   1/8 (2) 2/48 (3)   (65.3 overs) 138
4/177 (5) 5/203 (4) 6/227 (6)   3/52 (1) 4/79 (4)
7/237 (7) 8/270 (9) 9/277 (10) 10/297 (8)   5/89 (6) 6/123 (7) 7/129 (5)
                                        8/135 (9) 9/136 (8) 10/138 (10)

Hannon-Dalby 21–6–57–0; Norwell 20–7–64–4; Bresnan 16–7–28–1; Miles 14–1–62–1; Briggs 16.2–5–53–2; Rhodes 8–1–24–2. *Second innings*—Hannon-Dalby 11–5–25–2; Norwell 12–2–35–1; Briggs 24.3–14–36–4; Bresnan 4–0–21–1; Miles 7–1–12–1; Rhodes 5–3–6–1; Yates 2–2–0–0.

Umpires: G. D. Lloyd and R. J. Warren.   Referee: P. M. Such.

At Derby, June 3–5. WARWICKSHIRE beat DERBYSHIRE by 191 runs.

WARWICKSHIRE v DURHAM

At Birmingham, July 4–7. Drawn. Warwickshire 11pts, Durham 11pts (after 2pt penalty). Toss: Durham.

The loss of six sessions to rain – including the entire first day – reduced the match to a battle for bonus points, which Durham won, only to be brought back to parity by a deduction for a slow over-rate. Asked to bat, and with Potts testing them repeatedly in a game dominated by right-arm seam, Warwickshire had Yates to thank for their 237; his 102 was his third century of the season. But he was pinned by Raine, before the last six fell for 16. The next morning began with a swap of personnel, enforced by the selection of England's emergency one-day squad: Brookes for Briggs; Burnham and Clark for Stokes and Carse. But little was required of them until the fourth. There was time for Miles to complete his second five-for in two matches, but Bedingham was marooned on 92 when the weather closed in.

Close of play: first day, no play; second day, Durham 20-1 (Bancroft 7, Potts 1); third day, Durham 173-5 (Bedingham 37, Eckersley 18).

Warwickshire

R. M. Yates lbw b Raine 102	C. N. Miles c Eckersley b Raine	2
D. P. Sibley c Eckersley b Potts 0	L. C. Norwell not out	0
P. J. Malan c Eckersley b Carse 31	R. N. Sidebottom c Eckersley b Raine	0
S. R. Hain c Bancroft b Stokes 30	Lb 4, nb 10	14
*W. M. H. Rhodes c Jones b Rushworth 39	
M. J. Lamb c Raine b Stokes 8	1/12 (2) 2/70 (3) 3/142 (4) (95 overs) 237
†M. G. K. Burgess lbw b Rushworth 0	4/195 (1) 5/221 (5) 6/221 (6)
D. R. Briggs c and b Stokes 11	7/225 (7) 8/237 (8) 9/237 (9) 10/237 (11)

E. A. Brookes replaced Briggs, who left to join England's one-day squad.

Rushworth 21–8–35–2; Potts 19–10–37–1; Raine 22–9–51–3; Stokes 17–1–55–3; Carse 15–2–52–1; Eckersley 1–0–3–0.

Durham

C. T. Bancroft lbw b Miles 34	J. T. A. Burnham c Yates b Miles	2
M. A. Jones b Miles. 8	G. Clark not out	8
M. J. Potts b Miles. 35	B 4, lb 11, w 1, nb 6	22
*S. G. Borthwick b Rhodes. 20	
D. G. Bedingham not out 92	1/14 (2) 2/82 (3) (7 wkts, 90 overs) 253
S. R. Dickson lbw b Miles. 5	3/89 (1) 4/135 (4)
†E. J. H. Eckersley c Hain b Yates 27	5/140 (6) 6/213 (7) 7/220 (8)

B. A. Raine and C. Rushworth did not bat.

Burnham and Clark replaced B. A. Stokes and B. A. Carse, who left to join England's one-day squad.

Norwell 22–8–40–0; Miles 23–9–62–5; Sidebottom 18–3–51–0; Rhodes 17–5–54–1; Brookes 7–2–22–0; Yates 3–0–9–1.

Umpires: P. R. Pollard and I. N. Ramage.   Referee: S. Cummings.

At Worcester, July 11–14. WARWICKSHIRE drew with WORCESTERSHIRE.

DIVISION ONE

At Manchester, August 30–September 2. WARWICKSHIRE drew with LANCASHIRE.

WARWICKSHIRE v HAMPSHIRE

At Birmingham, September 5–8. Hampshire won by 60 runs. Hampshire 19pts, Warwickshire 3pts. Toss: Warwickshire.

Hampshire won handsomely thanks to a magnificent fightback. After the start had been delayed by an hour following a positive Covid test in their camp, they were dismissed for 89, having reached 44 for one; Rhodes destroyed the middle order to take five for 23. Warwickshire were equally feckless, crashing to 11 for four. Their eventual lead of 27 – on a day of 20 wickets – seemed hardly worthwhile; Mohammad Abbas and Barker finished with five apiece. Hampshire then struggled to 208 for eight second time round, before Barker and Wheal applied themselves for 42 overs, adding 93. Pursuing 296, Warwickshire dug in, helped when Abbas went off with an injured ankle. Early on the fourth morning, they had inched their way to 157 for two, with Yates going well. But he was trapped by Fuller for 77, and Abbas returned, foot securely strapped, to take two key wickets with the second new ball. The last five went for 23, as Hampshire moved third, above Warwickshire.

Close of play: first day, Hampshire 41-0 (Weatherley 17, Holland 18); second day, Hampshire 260-8 (Barker 49, Wheal 20); third day, Warwickshire 139-2 (Yates 70, Hain 5).

Hampshire

J. J. Weatherley lbw b Miles	4	– lbw b Norwell	24
I. G. Holland c Yates b Holder	28	– c Yates b Norwell	44
†T. P. Alsop c Burgess b Rhodes	15	– st Burgess b Briggs	33
N. R. T. Gubbins c Briggs b Rhodes	0	– c Rhodes b Briggs	5
*J. M. Vince c Norwell b Rhodes	21	– c Lamb b Miles	48
L. A. Dawson c Lamb b Rhodes	1	– lbw b Norwell	3
F. S. Organ c Yates b Rhodes	9	– lbw b Norwell	16
K. H. D. Barker c Rhodes b Norwell	3	– (9) c Benjamin b Holder	75
J. K. Fuller c Yates b Norwell	0	– (8) b Miles	0
B. T. J. Wheal not out	0	– not out	46
Mohammad Abbas c Hain b Miles	1	– c Yates b Briggs	6
Lb 2, nb 2	7	B 8, lb 8, w 6	22

1/6 (1) 2/44 (3) 3/44 (4)   (28.1 overs) 89
4/48 (2) 5/51 (6) 6/71 (7)
7/74 (8) 8/74 (9) 9/88 (5) 10/89 (11)

1/55 (1) 2/109 (2)   (133.4 overs) 322
3/116 (4) 4/137 (3)
5/156 (6) 6/173 (5) 7/173 (8)
8/208 (7) 9/301 (9) 10/322 (11)

Miles 6.1–0–25–2; Norwell 9–4–13–2; Holder 5–1–23–1; Rhodes 8–3–23–5. *Second innings—* Norwell 28–5–72–4; Miles 30–12–61–2; Holder 19–4–85–1; Rhodes 5–1–20–0; Briggs 49.4–20–66–3; Yates 2–0–2–0.

Warwickshire

R. M. Yates lbw b Barker	0	– lbw b Fuller	77
D. P. Sibley c Vince b Mohammad Abbas	6	– c Alsop b Dawson	47
C. G. Benjamin c Weatherley b Barker	5	– c Barker b Dawson	12
S. R. Hain c Alsop b Mohammad Abbas	41	– c Alsop b Mohammad Abbas	18
*W. M. H. Rhodes c Holland b Mohammad Abbas	0	– c Alsop b Mohammad Abbas	17
M. J. Lamb c Alsop b Barker	6	– not out	32
†M. G. K. Burgess c Weatherley b Mohammad Abbas	27	– c Alsop b Barker	11
D. R. Briggs c Mohammad Abbas b Barker	19	– lbw b Fuller	11
C. N. Miles c Weatherley b Barker	0	– c Vince b Dawson	0
L. C. Norwell c Vince b Mohammad Abbas	6	– run out (Dawson/Fuller)	0
C. K. Holder not out	0	– c Alsop b Wheal	0
B 1, lb 1, nb 4	6	B 5, lb 5	10

1/5 (1) 2/11 (3) 3/11 (2)   (46 overs) 116
4/11 (5) 5/26 (6) 6/87 (7)
7/104 (8) 8/105 (9) 9/112 (10) 10/116 (8)

1/99 (2) 2/119 (3)   (108.4 overs) 235
3/157 (1) 4/170 (4)
5/191 (5) 6/212 (7) 7/231 (8)
8/232 (9) 9/233 (10) 10/235 (11)

Mohammad Abbas 18–8–29–5; Barker 16–5–43–5; Holland 5–0–17–0; Wheal 5–0–21–0; Dawson 2–0–4–0. *Second innings*—Mohammad Abbas 21–9–32–2; Barker 21–5–49–1; Wheal 18.4–4–45–1; Fuller 13–4–22–2; Organ 5–0–24–0; Dawson 24–2–42–3; Holland 6–2–11–0.

Umpires: I. J. Gould and J. D. Middlebrook.   Referee: S. J. Davis.

At Leeds, September 12–15. WARWICKSHIRE beat YORKSHIRE by 106 runs.

WARWICKSHIRE v SOMERSET

At Birmingham, September 21–24. Warwickshire won by 118 runs. Warwickshire 22pts, Somerset 5pts (after 1pt penalty). Toss: Somerset.

Warwickshire clinched their eighth County Championship with a barnstorming performance on the fourth day. For the first three, they had been anxiously monitoring events at Liverpool, where rivals Lancashire were hosting leaders Hampshire, and they initially focused on bonus points, knowing they could drop no more than one to stay in charge of their own fate. After fighting fifties from Sibley, Rhodes and Hain, they reached 339 for nine from 109 overs. With every fielder on the boundary, Briggs hit Brooks's next three deliveries for four, four and six to secure a fourth batting point, and later raised a 30-ball half-century with his third six. Somerset, though, at last summoned the resilience that had eluded them in Division One. Four batsmen passed 50, and Leach's 49 in nearly three hours deprived Warwickshire of a third bowling point. But news that Lancashire had triumphed at Aigburth simplified matters: win the game, win the title. On the third evening, they tore into the Somerset bowling at five an over; the rate exceeded seven next morning, as Yates brought up his fourth century of the summer, all at Edgbaston. The declaration was tantalising: Somerset needed to survive 79 overs (or, less likely, score 273) to make Lancashire champions. But Warwickshire were irresistible. They did their job with 27 overs to spare, thanks to relentless pressure from Woakes, who had to ask the England management for dispensation to play. It had been four years since his last Championship appearance at Edgbaston, but the wait was worth it.

Close of play: first day, Warwickshire 283-4 (Hain 83, Burgess 16); second day, Somerset 239-5 (Davies 48, Gregory 15); third day, Warwickshire 179-1 (Yates 72, Rhodes 42).

Warwickshire

R. M. Yates c Abell b Davey	3	–	not out	132
D. P. Sibley c Davies b Brooks	56	–	c Green b Davey	50
*W. M. H. Rhodes c Davies b Lammonby	60	–	run out (Overton/Davies)	62
S. R. Hain b Brooks	83	–	lbw b Brooks	3
M. J. Lamb lbw b Brooks	44	–	not out	27
†M. G. K. Burgess c Davies b Overton	20			
C. R. Woakes c Lammonby b Overton	10			
T. T. Bresnan c and b Overton	1			
D. R. Briggs not out	53			
L. C. Norwell c Azhar Ali b Overton	5			
C. N. Miles c and b Overton	7			
B 13, lb 4, nb 8	25		Lb 10, w 6, nb 4	20

1/3 (1) 2/124 (3) 3/139 (2)   (112.5 overs) 367   1/119 (2)   (3 wkts dec, 51 overs) 294
4/261 (5) 5/287 (6) 6/293 (4)   2/226 (3) 3/231 (4)
7/297 (7) 8/304 (8) 9/322 (10)
10/367 (11)   110 overs: 359-9

Overton 30.5–8–88–5; Davey 19–9–54–1; Brooks 25–8–83–3; Leach 19–4–55–0; Abell 10–2–50–0; Lammonby 9–2–20–1. *Second innings*—Overton 14–1–66–0; Davey 9–1–55–1; Leach 5–0–34–0; Brooks 13–0–60–1; Lammonby 5–0–27–0; Abell 5–0–42–0.

Somerset

B. G. F. Green b Woakes	14	– c Burgess b Bresnan	18
T. A. Lammonby c and b Briggs	59	– c Bresnan b Briggs	11
Azhar Ali c Rhodes b Bresnan	60	– c Hain b Woakes	3
*T. B. Abell c Burgess b Norwell	14	– c Yates b Miles	0
L. P. Goldsworthy c Woakes b Briggs	13	– c Yates b Miles	31
†S. M. Davies c Burgess b Bresnan	52	– b Norwell	13
L. Gregory lbw b Woakes	68	– c Burgess b Miles	31
C. Overton lbw b Bresnan	2	– b Woakes	4
M. J. Leach c Rhodes b Briggs	49	– b Woakes	9
J. H. Davey c Bresnan b Woakes	16	– not out	15
J. A. Brooks not out	8	– c Rhodes b Norwell	4
B 6, lb 20, nb 8	34	Lb 13, nb 2	15

1/36 (1) 2/104 (2) 3/132 (4)   (136.3 overs) 389
4/167 (3) 5/187 (5) 6/247 (6)
7/271 (8) 8/325 (7) 9/381 (9)
10/389 (10)   110 overs: 334-8

1/31 (2) 2/35 (1)   (52 overs) 154
3/35 (3) 4/56 (4)
5/73 (5) 6/85 (6) 7/90 (8)
8/106 (9) 9/149 (7) 10/154 (11)

Woakes 30.3–6–100–3; Norwell 26–12–63–1; Bresnan 20–8–35–3; Miles 24–4–61–0; Briggs 27–6–77–3; Rhodes 6–2–21–0; Lamb 3–1–6–0. *Second innings*—Woakes 16–8–39–3; Norwell 13–5–40–2; Bresnan 13–5–36–1; Briggs 1–1–0–1; Miles 9–1–26–3.

Umpires: S. J. O'Shaughnessy and R. J. Warren.   Referee: D. A. Cosker.

At Lord's, September 28–October 1. WARWICKSHIRE beat LANCASHIRE by an innings and 199 runs. *Warwickshire add the Bob Willis Trophy to the Championship title. See page 463.*

WORCESTERSHIRE

Bowling seam's the problem

JOHN CURTIS

Worcestershire's latest difficulties were reflected by results: for the first time since 2016, they failed to challenge in the latter stages of any competition. They were unable to capitalise on positive starts in the Royal London Cup or Vitality Blast, finished second from bottom in their County Championship group, then third out of six in Division Three.

In September, Joe Leach – long a talisman with the red ball – stood down as club captain after five years. Shortly before, his predecessor, the long-serving opener Daryl Mitchell, announced his retirement. In 221 first-class games for Worcestershire across 17 seasons, he scored 13,518 runs; in total, he played 537 senior matches, all but seven for the county (he played once for MCC, and spent 2011-12 with Zimbabwe's Mountaineers). Earlier in the year, he had concluded his chairmanship of the Professional Cricketers' Association after consecutive two-year terms.

At the end of July, the club parted company with the experienced Riki Wessels; Ross Whiteley, having helped Southern Brave win The Hundred, headed to Hampshire after nine seasons at New Road. Confirming Wessels's departure, Paul Pridgeon, the former Worcestershire seamer who is now chairman of the steering committee, spoke of the need to "introduce more opportunities for our young batsmen".

The club had planned to harness the experience of Matthew Wade, who in November helped Australia lift the T20 World Cup. But when he was picked up in the IPL auction for the first time, in February 2022, Worcestershire instead turned to the former Pakistan captain Azhar Ali, who had proved a popular overseas player at Somerset. They were hoping he would be available for the whole season.

Opener Jake Libby was again Worcestershire's red-ball rock in the Championship, with four centuries; only Sussex's Tom Haines surpassed his 1,075 runs at 56. Since signing from Nottinghamshire ahead of the 2020 season, Libby has twice been the first-class competition's second-highest run-scorer. Club officials believe international recognition is around the corner, and had acknowledged his influence by appointing him vice-captain.

Ed Barnard's wish to bat in the top six was granted towards the end of the season, and his best-ever campaign realised 746 runs at just under 50, with two centuries. But he lacked support: Jack Haynes was the only other player to average over 27, and there was just one more hundred, from Mitchell, against Warwickshire. Gareth Roderick experienced a difficult first season after his move from Gloucestershire, managing a best of 42 not out from 11 innings. Ben Cox (who averaged 21) and Tom Fell (17) produced just four

James Chance, Getty Images

Ed Barnard

half-centuries in 40 innings between them. To help remedy the problem, Ed Pollock moved down from Edgbaston.

Head coach Alex Gidman was satisfied that Worcestershire had become harder to beat, but their attack laboured on lifeless pitches, and could not cash in when opportunities arose on seam-friendly surfaces at Derby and Nottingham. West Indies paceman Alzarri Joseph struggled to fire on all cylinders during his two-month stint. Dillon Pennington managed some impressive spells, including for Birmingham Phoenix in The Hundred, but blew hot and cold. Josh Tongue, still beset by injuries, took a five-wicket haul on the first day of the Championship match at Durham; Pat Brown, 18 months after representing England's T20 team in New Zealand, made no county appearances at all because of a back injury, though he played six times for the Phoenix.

The leg-breaks of Brett D'Oliveira, who will take over as club captain in 2022, backed up the seam attack, but the big plus was the emergence of 18-year-old slow left-armer Josh Baker. He finished his exams at Malvern College in June, took a hat-trick for the Second XI, and was fast-tracked into the senior team. He demonstrated unwavering control – remarkable in one so young – and never looked out of place; his inclusion in the England Under-19 squad during the winter was well merited. New Zealand leg-spinner Ish Sodhi, in his sole Championship appearance, took six for 89 against the eventual champions, Warwickshire.

In the Blast, D'Oliveira showed his all-round quality, finishing as the club's leading run-scorer and most economical bowler. Libby translated his Championship form into T20 success, and Charlie Morris finished his first full Blast campaign as leading wicket-taker. Pennington was a handful with the new ball, while Sodhi and Australian seamer Ben Dwarshuis had their moments, though Dwarshuis did not prove quite as reliable as hoped. Defeats in their last two group games cost Worcestershire a quarter-final place.

It was a similar scenario in the Royal London Cup, with victories in the first three games including a memorable 182-run triumph at Chelmsford, where Haynes scored his maiden senior century during a club-record opening stand of 243 with D'Oliveira. No win came in the remaining five matches, though the promise shown by Baker and Jacques Banton – brother of Somerset's Tom – provided consolation.

WORCESTERSHIRE RESULTS

County Championship matches – Played 14: Won 3, Lost 5, Drawn 6.
Vitality T20 Blast matches – Played 14: Won 6, Lost 6, Tied 1, No result 1.
Royal London Cup matches – Played 8: Won 3, Lost 4, No result 1.

LV= County Championship, 5th in Group 1, 3rd in Division 3;
Vitality T20 Blast, 5th in North Group; Royal London Cup, 5th in Group 1.

COUNTY CHAMPIONSHIP AVERAGES, BATTING AND FIELDING

Colours		Birthplace	M	I	NO	R	HS	100	Avge	Ct/St
2020	J. D. Libby	Plymouth	14	23	4	1,075	180*	4	56.57	6
2015	E. G. Barnard	Shrewsbury	13	18	3	746	128	2	49.73	12
2019	J. A. Haynes	Worcester‡	9	14	0	491	97	0	35.07	8
2012	J. Leach	Stafford	13	19	5	377	84	0	26.92	2
2012	B. L. D'Oliveira	Worcester‡	14	21	2	480	71	0	25.26	4
2009	O. B. Cox	Wordsley‡	14	21	2	413	60*	0	21.73	42/2
2005	D. K. H. Mitchell	Badsey‡	14	23	1	470	113	1	21.36	13
2019	M. H. Wessels	Maroochydore, Aus	7	10	0	202	60	0	20.20	3
2014	C. A. J. Morris	Hereford	6	8	2	116	50	0	19.33	0
2021	G. H. Roderick	Durban, SA	7	11	2	167	42*	0	18.55	1
2021	A. S. Joseph¶	Antigua	6	8	0	148	61	0	18.50	0
2013	T. C. Fell	Hillingdon	12	19	0	324	69	0	17.05	9
2021	J. O. Baker	Redditch‡	5	7	2	84	61*	0	16.80	4
2018	D. Y. Pennington	Shrewsbury	10	14	4	156	56	0	15.60	1
2017	J. C. Tongue	Redditch‡	4	6	1	66	17	0	13.20	0
2019	A. W. Finch	Wordsley‡	3	4	1	37	31	0	12.33	0

Also batted: I. S. Sodhi¶ (*Ludhiana, India*) (colours 2021) (1 match) 13; †R. A. Whiteley (*Sheffield*) (colours 2013) (2 matches) 22, 8, 4 (1 ct).

‡ *Born in Worcestershire.* ¶ *Official overseas player.*

Worcestershire award colours to all Championship players.

BOWLING

	Style	O	M	R	W	BB	5I	Avge
J. C. Tongue	RFM	115.5	18	358	14	5-39	1	25.57
J. Leach	RFM	428	108	1,141	38	5-68	1	30.02
D. Y. Pennington	RFM	282.4	57	898	29	5-32	1	30.96
C. A. J. Morris	RFM	189.3	45	621	19	6-52	1	32.68
J. O. Baker	SLA	144.2	30	408	12	3-49	0	34.00
A. S. Joseph	RFM	158	21	574	15	2-22	0	38.26
E. G. Barnard	RFM	368.1	83	1,052	25	4-43	0	42.08
B. L. D'Oliveira	LB	253.4	29	808	15	3-95	0	53.86

Also bowled: A. W. Finch (RM) 76–13–250–8; J. D. Libby (OB) 38.2–5–129–1; D. K. H. Mitchell (RM) 93.5–15–291–4; I. S. Sodhi (LB) 49.2–3–148–6; R. A. Whiteley (LM) 10–1–33–1.

LEADING VITALITY BLAST AVERAGES (100 runs/15 overs)

Batting		Runs	HS	Avge	SR	Ct/St
M. M. Ali		106	52	26.50	**145.20**	1
O. B. Cox		275	61*	30.55	**132.21**	5/3
M. H. Wessels		300	77	27.27	**132.15**	8
B. L. D'Oliveira		358	69	29.83	**130.18**	7
R. A. Whiteley		237	42	26.33	**127.41**	8
E. G. Barnard		106	43*	15.14	**120.45**	3
J. D. Libby		315	78*	31.50	**108.24**	2

Bowling		W	BB	Avge	ER
B. L. D'Oliveira		5	3-15	23.60	**5.90**
I. S. Sodhi		11	4-24	32.81	**7.68**
D. Y. Pennington		13	4-24	20.00	**8.38**
E. G. Barnard		4	1-11	49.25	**8.82**
B. J. Dwarshuis		15	4-31	27.93	**8.91**
C. A. J. Morris		17	3-21	23.41	**9.51**

LEADING ROYAL LONDON CUP AVERAGES (100 runs/4 wickets)

Batting	Runs	HS	Avge	SR	Ct
J. A. Haynes	362	153	51.71	94.27	3
B. L. D'Oliveira	267	123	44.50	103.08	2
J. Leach	169	88	42.25	109.03	4
J. D. Libby	239	76	34.14	84.45	0
T. C. Fell	172	58	24.57	83.90	2
E. G. Barnard	111	39*	18.50	75.00	3

Bowling	W	BB	Avge	ER
J. Banton	4	3-15	13.75	4.58
B. L. D'Oliveira	7	3-8	26.28	5.04
E. G. Barnard	9	2-25	29.44	5.63
A. W. Finch	6	2-54	37.00	6.00
J. O. Baker	7	2-53	39.00	6.02
J. Leach	6	3-28	40.83	5.56
C. A. J. Morris	4	1-31	66.50	6.18

FIRST-CLASS COUNTY RECORDS

Highest score for	405*	G. A. Hick v Somerset at Taunton	1988
Highest score against	331*	J. D. B. Robertson (Middlesex) at Worcester	1949
Leading run-scorer	34,490	D. Kenyon (avge 34.18)	1946–67
Best bowling for	9-23	C. F. Root v Lancashire at Worcester	1931
Best bowling against	10-51	J. Mercer (Glamorgan) at Worcester	1936
Leading wicket-taker	2,143	R. T. D. Perks (avge 23.73)	1930–55
Highest total for	701-6 dec	v Surrey at Worcester	2007
Highest total against	701-4 dec	by Leicestershire at Worcester	1906
Lowest total for	24	v Yorkshire at Huddersfield	1903
Lowest total against	30	by Hampshire at Worcester	1903

LIST A COUNTY RECORDS

Highest score for	192	C. J. Ferguson v Leicestershire at Worcester	2018
Highest score against	161*	S. R. Hain (Warwickshire) at Worcester	2019
Leading run-scorer	16,416	G. A. Hick (avge 44.60)	1985–2008
Best bowling for	7-19	N. V. Radford v Bedfordshire at Bedford	1991
Best bowling against	7-15	R. A. Hutton (Yorkshire) at Leeds	1969
Leading wicket-taker	370	S. R. Lampitt (avge 24.52)	1987–2002
Highest total for	404-3	v Devon at Worcester	1987
Highest total against	399-4	by Sussex at Horsham	2011
Lowest total for	58	v Ireland v Worcester	2009
Lowest total against	45	by Hampshire at Worcester	1988

TWENTY20 COUNTY RECORDS

Highest score for	127	T. Köhler-Cadmore v Durham at Worcester	2016
Highest score against	141*	C. L. White (Somerset) at Worcester	2006
Leading run-scorer	**2,695**	**M. M. Ali (avge 28.97, SR 141.61)**	2007–21
Best bowling for	5-24	A. Hepburn v Nottinghamshire at Worcester	2017
Best bowling against	6-21	A. J. Hall (Northamptonshire) at Northampton	2008
Leading wicket-taker	**101**	**D. K. H. Mitchell (avge 29.69, ER 7.68)**	2005–21
Highest total for	227-6	v Northamptonshire at Kidderminster	2007
Highest total against	233-6	by Yorkshire at Leeds	2017
Lowest total for	53	v Lancashire at Manchester	2016
Lowest total against	93	by Gloucestershire at Bristol	2008

ADDRESS

County Ground, New Road, Worcester WR2 4QQ; 01905 748474; info@wccc.co.uk; www.wccc.co.uk. Twitter: @WorcsCCC.

OFFICIALS

Captain 2021 J. Leach
2022 B. L. D'Oliveira
(Twenty20) M. M. Ali
First-team coach A. P. R. Gidman
Head of player development K. Sharp

Academy coach E. J. Wilson
President C. Crawford
Chair F. Hira
Head groundsman T. R. Packwood
Scorer S. M. Drinkwater

GROUP ONE

At Chelmsford, April 8–11. WORCESTERSHIRE drew with ESSEX. *Jake Libby plays the second-longest Championship innings recorded by minutes.*

At Derby, April 15–18. WORCESTERSHIRE drew with DERBYSHIRE.

WORCESTERSHIRE v NOTTINGHAMSHIRE

At Worcester, April 22–25. Drawn. Worcestershire 15pts, Nottinghamshire 12pts. Toss: Worcestershire.
Nottinghamshire opener Haseeb Hameed faced 635 balls in total, a Championship record. In all, he batted for 13 hours 44 minutes, believed to be the longest by anyone in a Championship match. He scored twin centuries for the second time in his career, having previously done so for Lancashire against Yorkshire at Manchester in 2016. On a slow, low pitch, Worcestershire's openers had put on 140, with Libby continuing his fine form. Then, after a slide to 216 for seven, the last three wickets doubled the total during 78 overs of defiance; a tenth-wicket stand of 81 between Leach and Morris, who contributed ten, ate up 141 minutes. Nottinghamshire also stumbled once the openers were parted, at 115; Morris claimed three wickets in 15 balls, and the last five were swept away for 15 runs,

MOST BALLS FACED IN A COUNTY CHAMPIONSHIP MATCH

635	H. Hameed (111 and 114*) ..	Nottinghamshire v Worcestershire at Worcester .	2021
625	J. Cox (216 and 129*)	Somerset v Hampshire at Southampton	1999
606	I. R. Bell (262* and 62*).....	Warwickshire v Sussex at Horsham	2004
602	J. E. R. Gallian (312 and 11) ..	Lancashire v Derbyshire at Manchester	1996

Balls faced went unrecorded in many early Championship matches.

starting with Moores for a lively 62. But Hameed, eighth out of 111, represented a solid wall and, when Slater rejoined him in the follow-on, after tea on the third day, they could not be parted. It was the fifth time a pair of Nottinghamshire openers had posted a century and a double-century stand in a first-class match; their unbroken 236 was a Nottinghamshire record for the first wicket against Worcestershire, beating 220 between George Gunn and "Dodger" Whysall at Trent Bridge in 1924.
Close of play: first day, Worcestershire 305-7 (Barnard 40, Joseph 46); second day, Nottinghamshire 99-0 (Slater 41, Hameed 51); third day, Nottinghamshire 87-0 (Slater 45, Hameed 37).

Worcestershire

D. K. H. Mitchell c Moores b Fletcher	59	
J. D. Libby c Moores b Fletcher	117	
T. C. Fell lbw b Chappell	1	
G. H. Roderick c Moores b Paterson	1	
B. L. D'Oliveira run out (Fletcher)	3	
M. H. Wessels b Patterson-White	13	
†O. B. Cox lbw b Patterson-White	0	
E. G. Barnard c Moores b Patterson-White .	58	
A. S. Joseph c Clarke b Chappell	61	

*J. Leach c Mullaney b Patterson-White.... 84
C. A. J. Morris not out 10

B 10, lb 13, nb 6 29

1/140 (1) 2/141 (3)   (145.1 overs)   436
3/156 (4) 4/169 (5) 5/210 (6)
6/216 (2) 7/216 (8) 8/330 (9)
9/355 (8) 10/436 (10)   110 overs: 352-8

Chappell 32–5–88–2; Paterson 22–4–76–1; Fletcher 30–5–64–2; Patterson-White 41.1–6–114–4; Mullaney 11–0–44–0; James 9–1–27–0.

Nottinghamshire

B. T. Slater c Mitchell b D'Oliveira	45	– not out	114
H. Hameed c Cox b Leach	111	– not out	114
B. M. Duckett c Barnard b Joseph	5		
J. M. Clarke b Morris	27		
L. W. James lbw b Morris	4		
*S. J. Mullaney b Morris	2		
†T. J. Moores c Leach b D'Oliveira	62		
L. A. Patterson-White lbw b Leach	0		
Z. J. Chappell run out (Mitchell)	9		
L. J. Fletcher not out	2		
D. Paterson b Joseph	0		
B 4, lb 3, nb 2	9	B 5, lb 2, w 1	8

1/115 (1) 2/130 (3) 3/164 (4) (104.4 overs) 276
4/168 (5) 5/172 (6) 6/261 (7)
7/261 (8) 8/266 (2) 9/276 (9) 10/276 (11)

(no wkt dec, 109 overs) 236

Leach 22–6–61–2; Morris 20–8–30–3; Joseph 18.4–4–33–2; Barnard 12–2–35–0; Mitchell 6–3–6–0; Libby 4–0–8–0; D'Oliveira 22–3–96–2. *Second innings*—Leach 14–4–30–0; Morris 15–5–27–0; Barnard 15–4–32–0; Joseph 11–4–18–0; D'Oliveira 22–1–62–0; Mitchell 21–4–39–0; Libby 11–3–21–0.

Umpires: R. K. Illingworth and R. J. Warren. Referee: P. M. Such.

WORCESTERSHIRE v ESSEX

At Worcester, April 29–May 2. Drawn. Worcestershire 11pts, Essex 12pts. Toss: Essex. Championship debut: S. Snater.

As in the previous week, an easy pitch squeezed the life out of the contest, though this time it was Worcestershire's turn to follow on, and escape with a comfortable draw. When Joseph trapped Browne after lunch on the first day, it was the first wicket their attack had taken at home in nine and a half hours. Alastair Cook's 25th first-class century for Essex, Westley's 23rd overall, plus a near miss for Lawrence, helped the visitors to their highest total in five years, since making 601 for five, also against Worcestershire. Occasional leg-spinner D'Oliveira bowled 46 overs as the seamers were spared apparently pointless exertions. In response to a mammoth 561, Mitchell and Libby began with another century stand; Fell and D'Oliveira followed suit, but Worcestershire could not save the follow-on. Only two sessions remained, however, and survival was easy. With the last eight (full) days at New Road yielding just 40 wickets at an average above 50, Sam Cook had match figures of 40–19–67–6.

Close of play: first day, Essex 266-2 (Westley 75, Lawrence 33); second day, Worcestershire 37-0 (Mitchell 17, Libby 15); third day, Worcestershire 302-5 (Wessels 24, Cox 23).

Essex

N. L. J. Browne lbw b Joseph	26	S. Snater b D'Oliveira	1
A. N. Cook b Joseph	115	P. M. Siddle not out	11
*T. Westley c Cox b Libby	113	B 4, lb 3, nb 12	19
D. W. Lawrence lbw b Pennington	90		
P. I. Walter c Fell b Mitchell	65	1/71 (1) (8 wkts dec, 174 overs) 561
R. N. ten Doeschate lbw b D'Oliveira	41	2/210 (2) 3/340 (3)
†A. J. A. Wheater b D'Oliveira	23	4/390 (4) 5/463 (5) 6/471 (6)
S. R. Harmer not out	57	7/510 (7) 8/524 (9) 110 overs: 300-2

S. J. Cook did not bat.

Morris 26–7–105–0; Pennington 28–7–65–1; Joseph 24–3–92–2; Barnard 30–12–59–0; D'Oliveira 46–6–147–3; Mitchell 11–2–41–1; Libby 9–1–45–1.

Worcestershire

D. K. H. Mitchell c ten Doeschate b Harmer	67	– b S. J. Cook	20
*J. D. Libby b Harmer	41	– not out	52
T. C. Fell c Wheater b S. J. Cook	53	– lbw b S. J. Cook	35
G. H. Roderick b Harmer	0	– not out	13
B. L. D'Oliveira c Wheater b Snater	67		
M. H. Wessels b S. J. Cook	33		
†O. B. Cox b S. J. Cook	37		
E. G. Barnard b Harmer	1		
A. S. Joseph lbw b S. J. Cook	0		
D. Y. Pennington b Lawrence	30		
C. A. J. Morris not out	8		
B 4, lb 11, nb 12	27	B 8, lb 1	9

1/111 (2) 2/132 (1) 3/132 (4)	(138.1 overs)	364	1/24 (1)	(2 wkts, 57 overs) 129
4/243 (5) 5/259 (6) 6/313 (6)			2/105 (3)	
7/326 (7) 8/326 (9) 9/326 (8)				
10/364 (10)	110 overs: 300-5			

S. J. Cook 29–12–60–4; Siddle 25–4–71–0; Harmer 49–18–85–4; Lawrence 11.1–2–38–1; Snater 17–4–77–1; Walter 7–2–18–0. *Second innings*—S. J. Cook 11–7–7–2; Harmer 24–8–34–0; Siddle 3–0–17–0; Snater 7–1–17–0; Walter 6–0–24–0; Lawrence 4–0–19–0; Westley 2–1–2–0.

Umpires: G. D. Lloyd and R. A. White.   Referee: S. Cummings.

At Birmingham, May 6–9. WORCESTERSHIRE drew with WARWICKSHIRE.

At Chester-le-Street, May 13–16. WORCESTERSHIRE lost to DURHAM by 258 runs.

At Nottingham, May 20–23. WORCESTERSHIRE lost to NOTTINGHAMSHIRE by an innings and 170 runs.

WORCESTERSHIRE v DERBYSHIRE

At Worcester, May 27–30. Worcestershire won by an innings and 23 runs. Worcestershire 23pts, Derbyshire 4pts. Toss: Worcestershire. County debut: B. R. McDermott.

With spectators returning to New Road, Pennington produced career-best bowling performances two days running as Worcestershire completed their only group win. His match figures of nine for 76 reflected a pitch with considerably more pace and bounce than the previous two here. After Mitchell had fallen to the first ball of the game, Haynes came close to a maiden hundred, and was distraught when he pulled a long hop from Critchley to deep midwicket. Barnard enhanced his reputation as a genuine all-rounder with a rapid 90 and, from 248 for six, shepherded the tail to 421. In Derbyshire's reply, Critchley, who had managed 193 runs and eight wickets when the teams met in April, made an unbeaten 81, but the home seamers ensured they failed to avoid the follow-on – by two runs. They offered still less resistance second time round, losing eight for 57 as Pennington claimed a maiden first-class five-for.

Close of play: first day, Worcestershire 336-7 (Barnard 48); second day, Derbyshire 91-3 (Madsen 31, McDermott 18); third day, Derbyshire 112-6 (Madsen 43, Hughes 3).

Worcestershire

D. K. H. Mitchell lbw b Conners	0	A. S. Joseph c Godleman b Melton	12
J. D. Libby run out (Critchley)	26	*J. Leach b Melton	5
T. C. Fell c Guest b Conners	12	D. Y. Pennington not out	24
J. A. Haynes c Melton b Critchley	97	Lb 11, w 2	13
R. A. Whiteley c Madsen b Melton	22		
B. L. D'Oliveira c Hughes b Hudson-		1/0 (1) 2/21 (3) (121.2 overs) 421	
Prentice	71	3/62 (2) 4/115 (5) 5/229 (4)	
†O. B. Cox c Guest b Aitchison	49	6/248 (6) 7/336 (7) 8/364 (9)	
E. G. Barnard c McDermott b Critchley	90	9/376 (10) 10/421 (8) 110 overs: 373-8	

Conners 20–5–73–2; Melton 16–1–76–3; Hudson-Prentice 27–5–83–1; Aitchison 23–3–52–1; Hughes 7–2–12–0; Critchley 23.2–1–97–2; Madsen 5–0–17–0.

Derbyshire

†B. D. Guest c Whiteley b Leach	20	– c Cox b Pennington	7
*B. A. Godleman c Fell b Pennington	10	– c Mitchell b Joseph	21
J. L. du Plooy lbw b Barnard	7	– c and b D'Oliveira	19
W. L. Madsen c Mitchell b Barnard	51	– c Cox b Leach	45
B. R. McDermott c Mitchell b Pennington	25	– lbw b Pennington	1
M. J. J. Critchley not out	81	– c Fell b Pennington	6
F. J. Hudson-Prentice c Haynes b Leach	25	– b D'Oliveira	0
A. L. Hughes c Cox b Pennington	25	– not out	7
B. W. Aitchison lbw b Joseph	1	– c Cox b Pennington	0
S. Conners b Joseph	4	– b Pennington	9
D. R. Melton c Fell b Pennington	5	– c Mitchell b Joseph	1
B 4, lb 2, nb 10	16	B 1, lb 4, w 5, nb 2	12

1/14 (2) 2/32 (1) 3/58 (3) (82.4 overs) 270
4/109 (5) 5/137 (4) 6/193 (7)
7/250 (8) 8/251 (9) 9/261 (10) 10/270 (11)

1/16 (1) 2/46 (2) (58.2 overs) 128
3/71 (3) 4/72 (5)
5/92 (6) 6/93 (7) 7/116 (4)
8/117 (9) 9/127 (10) 10/128 (11)

Leach 23–4–64–2; Pennington 19.4–4–44–4; Barnard 16–1–53–2; Joseph 18–2–78–2; Whiteley 3–0–11–0; Mitchell 3–0–14–0. *Second innings*—Leach 13–4–17–1; Pennington 14–4–32–5; Barnard 12–2–25–0; Joseph 7.2–1–28–2; D'Oliveira 12–3–21–2.

Umpires: R. J. Bailey and B. J. Debenham. Referee: D. A. Cosker.

WORCESTERSHIRE v DURHAM

At Worcester, June 3–5. Durham won by ten wickets. Durham 23pts, Worcestershire 3pts. Toss: Durham.

Libby and Bedingham each ticked off a third century of the summer, and ended the game as the Championship's two leading run-scorers, but Bedingham was the happier, as Durham beat Worcestershire for the second time in three weeks. The hosts never recovered from being bowled out cheaply, a consequence of poor shot selection and high-quality bowling from Carse and Potts, whose four for 32 was a career-best. Bedingham and Jones cemented Durham's strong response with a fifth-wicket stand of 171, before the second new ball sparked a collapse. Tongue finished with four, including Bedingham, but the difference was still 250. Worcestershire lost half their wickets for 121, but Libby again showed his quality, reaching his hundred after being dropped on 76, then caught off a no-ball on 95. He and the lower order chiselled out a lead of 86, with Potts collecting four more. But it was easy for Durham: Bancroft and the promoted Jones reached the target in the third day's final over.

Close of play: first day, Durham 140-4 (Jones 12, Bedingham 6); second day, Worcestershire 99-3 (Libby 51, Tongue 10).

Worcestershire

D. K. H. Mitchell lbw b Carse	6	– c Carse b Potts	2
J. D. Libby c Lees b Carse	13	– st Eckersley b Borthwick	126
T. C. Fell lbw b Potts	1	– lbw b Potts	21
G. H. Roderick lbw b Potts	0	– b Rushworth	0
R. A. Whiteley c Borthwick b Raine	8	– (6) c Bancroft b Raine	4
B. L. D'Oliveira not out	39	– (7) b Potts	46
†O. B. Cox c Eckersley b Potts	11	– (8) c Borthwick b Rushworth	26
E. G. Barnard c Eckersley b Carse	20	– (9) not out	34
*J. Leach c Borthwick b Carse	0	– (10) c Eckersley b Potts	19
J. C. Tongue lbw b Raine	9	– (5) lbw b Rushworth	15
D. Y. Pennington c Borthwick b Potts	0	– c Borthwick b Carse	5
B 12, lb 6, nb 6	24	B 15, lb 11, nb 12	38

1/19 (2) 2/20 (3) 3/20 (4)   (50.3 overs) 131
4/20 (5) 5/47 (5) 6/82 (7)
7/111 (8) 8/111 (9) 9/124 (10) 10/131 (11)

1/7 (1) 2/74 (3)   (102.5 overs) 336
3/81 (4) 4/115 (5)
5/121 (6) 6/227 (7) 7/269 (2)
8/282 (9) 9/328 (10) 10/336 (11)

Rushworth 12–2–30–0; Potts 12.3–4–32–4; Carse 13–4–25–4; Raine 13–3–26–2. *Second innings—* Rushworth 26.2–8–68–3; Potts 24–6–66–4; Carse 21.3–1–78–1; Raine 22–4–70–1; Borthwick 9–3–28–1.

Durham

C. T. Bancroft c Fell b Tongue	18	– not out	46
A. Z. Lees c Cox b Whiteley	52		
*S. G. Borthwick c Barnard b Tongue	42		
M. A. Jones c Cox b Leach	78	– (2) not out	34
M. J. Potts c Cox b Tongue	0		
D. G. Bedingham lbw b Tongue	121		
J. T. A. Burnham c Cox b Pennington	9		
†E. J. H. Eckersley c Cox b Leach	8		
B. A. Carse c Barnard b Pennington	1		
B. A. Raine c Libby b Barnard	16		
C. Rushworth not out	11		
B 11, lb 5, w 1, nb 8	25	B 4, lb 4, w 1	9

1/34 (1) 2/103 (3) 3/134 (3)   (109.3 overs) 381
4/134 (5) 5/305 (4) 6/328 (7)
7/341 (8) 8/342 (9) 9/367 (6) 10/381 (10)

(no wkt, 20.2 overs) 89

Leach 25–6–84–2; Pennington 23–5–79–2; Tongue 25–6–73–4; Barnard 25.3–6–84–1; Whiteley 7–1–22–1; D'Oliveira 4–0–23–0. *Second innings—* Leach 4–1–18–0; Pennington 5–1–19–0; Tongue 5–2–15–0; Barnard 6–1–19–0; Libby 0.2–0–10–0.

Umpires: N. L. Bainton and D. J. Millns. Referee: J. J. Whitaker.

WORCESTERSHIRE v WARWICKSHIRE

At Worcester, July 11–14. Drawn. Worcestershire 12pts, Warwickshire 14pts. Toss: Warwickshire. First-class debuts: J. O. Baker; J. B. Lintott. Championship debut: I. S. Sodhi.

Warwickshire sealed their place in Division One with a high-scoring draw, as Pieter Malan, their overseas player, finally demonstrated his quality. He had averaged only 15 in his eight Championship innings before this game, but managed runs in both innings before he returned home to South Africa. Worcestershire had selected three spinners and, on a worn pitch, all were in action before lunch on the first day. Slow left-armer Josh Baker made his debut only days after finishing his education at

Malvern College; he showed promise and control in dismissing Hain and Rhodes. New Zealand leg-spinner Sodhi, signed primarily for the Vitality Blast, finished with six for 89, but there was no great turn; Malan and Sibley confidently added 220 for the second wicket. Worcestershire's reply was underpinned by Mitchell's first century of the summer, and a second for Barnard, promoted to the top six. They declared with a lead of 52, but Yates and Malan ensured Warwickshire suffered no last-day alarms.

Close of play: first day, Warwickshire 245-4 (Rhodes 11, Lamb 0); second day, Worcestershire 152-2 (Mitchell 83, Haynes 42); third day, Worcestershire 415-8 (Barnard 98, Finch 29).

Warwickshire

R. M. Yates lbw b Leach	0	– c Cox b Baker	88
D. P. Sibley c Cox b Finch	80	– c Cox b Finch	41
P. J. Malan c Mitchell b Sodhi	141	– not out	77
S. R. Hain lbw b Baker	11	– not out	0
*W. M. H. Rhodes c Libby b Baker	60		
M. J. Lamb lbw b Sodhi	44		
†M. G. K. Burgess b Sodhi	4		
C. N. Miles c Cox b Sodhi	16		
J. B. Lintott c Fell b Sodhi	15		
L. C. Norwell not out	17		
R. N. Sidebottom lbw b Sodhi	1		
B 2, nb 4	6	B 2, lb 2, w 5	9

1/0 (1) 2/220 (3) 3/222 (2)   (120.2 overs) 395   1/76 (2)   (2 wkts dec, 59.5 overs) 215
4/245 (4) 5/338 (5) 6/343 (7)   2/215 (1)
7/344 (6) 8/368 (9) 9/393 (8)
10/395 (11)   110 overs: 359-7

Leach 17–6–46–1; Finch 23–4–75–1; Barnard 20–2–78–0; Baker 22–1–73–2; Sodhi 30.2–3–89–6; D'Oliveira 8–0–32–0. *Second innings*—Leach 6–2–16–0; Baker 17–3–67–1; Finch 6–0–14–1; Sodhi 19–0–59–0; Barnard 2–0–9–0; Libby 6–0–23–0; Mitchell 3.5–0–23–0.

Worcestershire

D. K. H. Mitchell lbw b Norwell	113	A. W. Finch c Burgess b Norwell	31
J. D. Libby lbw b Norwell	22	J. O. Baker not out	12
T. C. Fell lbw b Yates	2	B 15, lb 7, nb 2	24
J. A. Haynes c Miles b Lamb	65		
B. L. D'Oliveira c Burgess b Rhodes	18	1/68 (2) (9 wkts dec, 174 overs) 447	
E. G. Barnard not out	112	2/73 (3) 3/203 (4)	
†O. B. Cox c and b Rhodes	1	4/214 (1) 5/245 (5)	
*J. Leach c Burgess b Yates	34	6/247 (7) 7/294 (8)	
I. S. Sodhi c Lintott b Lamb	13	8/324 (9) 9/425 (10) 110 overs: 276-6	

Norwell 30–7–69–3; Miles 21–4–61–0; Lintott 39–2–103–0; Sidebottom 28–6–62–0; Yates 31–5–54–2; Lamb 15–1–38–2; Rhodes 10–3–38–2.

Umpires: N. G. B. Cook and C. M. Watts. Referee: T. J. Boon.

DIVISION THREE

WORCESTERSHIRE v SUSSEX

At Worcester, August 30–September 2. Worcestershire won by six wickets. Worcestershire 20pts, Sussex 5pts. Toss: Sussex. First-class debut: A. D. Lenham.

Sussex selected six teenagers – a Championship record, surpassing the five they had fielded at Canterbury in July – in a team whose average age was 20. The presence of 17-year-old Archie Lenham opposite Brett D'Oliveira meant that, for the first time in Championship history, three successive generations had played each other while representing the same teams: Les Lenham and Basil D'Oliveira, followed by Neil Lenham and Damian D'Oliveira. Sussex competed strongly, and held the upper hand more than once, but Worcestershire prevailed when Libby's fourth century of the season guided them to a target of 315 with four overs to spare. Sussex's first fightback had been led by Carson, who came in at 138 for seven – including a duck for Hudson-Prentice, back at Sussex after five years. Caught off a no-ball when two, he hit four sixes in a career-best 87, until he fell to Leach, who claimed his first five-wicket haul for two years. Replying to 264, Worcestershire reached 174 for four, but lost six for 39 as Sarro and Crocombe – both 19 – earned Sussex a 51-run lead. Leach had them three for three; Baker's later double-strike, including Orr for a second half-century in the match, made it 98 for five. Danial Ibrahim – 17 days younger than Lenham – had added 94 to his first-innings 48 when he became Leach's ninth victim, preventing him becoming the youngest Championship centurion. Worcestershire's pursuit began badly, but Libby was their rock, and overtook Durham's David Bedingham as the season's leading run-scorer. He shared stands of 105 with Haynes, and 86 with Cox, before D'Oliveira accelerated to the line with a 26-ball half-century.

Close of play: first day, Sussex 254-9 (Carson 81, Sarro 0); second day, Worcestershire 186-7 (Leach 9, Baker 0); third day, Sussex 199-6 (Ibrahim 56, Lenham 4).

Sussex

A. G. H. Orr hit wkt b Finch	52	– c and b Baker 57
*T. J. Haines lbw b Leach	20	– c Fell b Leach 0
H. D. Ward c Haynes b Finch	1	– lbw b Leach 0
J. M. Coles b Pennington	12	– lbw b Leach 1
†O. J. Carter b Leach	0	– c and b Baker 20
F. J. Hudson-Prentice c Cox b Leach	0	– st Cox b Baker 46
D. K. Ibrahim lbw b Leach	48	– c Cox b Leach 94
A. D. Lenham c Cox b Barnard	20	– c Cox b Finch 9
J. J. Carson b Leach	87	– c Baker b Finch 15
H. T. Crocombe lbw b D'Oliveira	9	– c Barnard b Pennington 6
J. P. Sarro not out	0	– not out 0
B 8, lb 3, nb 4	15	Lb 11, nb 4 15

1/29 (2) 2/46 (3) 3/66 (4)   (82.4 overs) 264
4/71 (5) 5/75 (6) 6/97 (1)
7/138 (8) 8/183 (7) 9/249 (10) 10/264 (9)

1/1 (2) 2/1 (3)   (84.5 overs) 263
3/3 (4) 4/87 (5)
5/98 (1) 6/185 (6) 7/208 (8)
8/234 (9) 9/253 (10) 10/263 (7)

Leach 22.4–6–68–5; Pennington 19–6–66–1; Barnard 13–4–34–1; Finch 15–6–32–2; Baker 12–2–42–0; D'Oliveira 1–0–11–1. *Second innings*—Leach 21.5–3–68–4; Pennington 15–2–52–1; Finch 13–3–46–2; Baker 19–4–49–3; Barnard 12–1–37–0.

Worcestershire

D. K. H. Mitchell c Carter b Ibrahim	16	– b Crocombe 19
J. D. Libby b Hudson-Prentice	28	– not out 125
T. C. Fell c Ward b Carson	11	– c Hudson-Prentice b Crocombe 4
J. A. Haynes b Ibrahim	47	– c and b Hudson-Prentice 62
B. L. D'Oliveira c Carter b Sarro	38	– (6) not out. 56
E. G. Barnard c Carson b Sarro	17	
†O. B. Cox c Carter b Crocombe	0	– (5) c Ward b Lenham 37
*J. Leach lbw b Crocombe	18	
J. O. Baker c Carter b Crocombe	5	
D. Y. Pennington c and b Hudson-Prentice	6	
A. W. Finch not out	3	
Lb 2, nb 22	24	B 6, lb 1, w 1, nb 4 12

1/44 (2) 2/63 (1) 3/71 (3)   (64 overs) 213
4/147 (4) 5/174 (6) 6/175 (7)
7/177 (5) 8/201 (8) 9/202 (9) 10/213 (10)

1/39 (1)   (4 wkts, 74.2 overs) 315
2/49 (3) 3/154 (4)
4/240 (5)

Hudson-Prentice 13–3–49–2; Sarro 13–1–53–2; Crocombe 16–5–44–3; Ibrahim 9–4–9–2; Carson 11–0–40–1; Lenham 1–0–11–0; Coles 1–0–5–0. *Second innings*—Hudson-Prentice 15.2–1–61–1; Sarro 7–1–32–0; Crocombe 9–1–39–2; Carson 16–0–58–0; Ibrahim 5–1–12–0; Lenham 12–0–60–1; Coles 10–0–46–0.

Umpires: N. L. Bainton and N. Pratt.   Referee: D. W. Headley.

At Canterbury, September 5–7. WORCESTERSHIRE lost to KENT by an innings and 56 runs.

At Lord's, September 12–15. WORCESTERSHIRE lost to MIDDLESEX by 101 runs.

WORCESTERSHIRE v LEICESTERSHIRE

At Worcester, September 21–23. Worcestershire won by ten wickets. Worcestershire 23pts, Leicestershire 3pts. Toss: Leicestershire. First-class debut: S. D. Bates.

Mitchell brought down the curtain on a 17-season career – from start to finish at Worcestershire – and received a guard of honour from the Leicestershire players for his final innings. Fittingly, he was at the crease when Libby hit the winning run. The visitors had given a debut to wicketkeeper Sam Bates, after Harry Swindells and opener Sam Evans were forced to self-isolate. Kimber confirmed his promise, top-scoring with 71 out of 222, but Worcestershire scored exactly 200 more, as seven of the top eight made at least 35. Libby passed 1,000 runs for the first time, and nightwatchman Morris made his first Championship half-century. They put on 125 for the second wicket; Barnard and Cox later added 116 for the seventh. Parkinson became only the fourth English spinner to take 50 wickets in a Championship season since 2012. Leach, who had announced he was standing down after five years as captain, helped reduce Leicestershire to 35 for four, but Rhodes staved off an innings defeat with a career-best 90. A target of 12 allowed Mitchell to bask in a heartfelt ovation.

Close of play: first day, Worcestershire 30-1 (Libby 16, Morris 6); second day, Worcestershire 378-6 (Barnard 44, Cox 52).

Leicestershire

M. H. Azad c Mitchell b Leach	2	– c Cox b Leach	4
R. K. Patel c Leach b Barnard	22	– b Leach	0
G. H. Rhodes c Haynes b Pennington	27	– c Cox b Pennington	90
L. J. Hill c Haynes b Barnard	40	– c Haynes b Leach	2
L. P. J. Kimber lbw b Leach	71	– c Barnard b Morris	4
B. W. M. Mike c Libby b Baker	3	– lbw b Barnard	58
†S. D. Bates c Haynes b Baker	0	– c Haynes b Barnard	6
E. Barnes b Morris	13	– b Baker	5
*C. F. Parkinson lbw b Pennington	17	– c Barnard b Pennington	21
C. J. C. Wright b Leach	2	– not out	10
A. Sakande not out	2	– c Barnard b Pennington	4
B 4, lb 9, nb 10	23	Lb 5, nb 2	7

1/6 (1) 2/47 (2) 3/87 (3) (82.3 overs) 222
4/112 (4) 5/133 (6) 6/133 (7)
7/160 (8) 8/218 (5) 9/220 (9) 10/222 (10)

1/3 (2) 2/16 (1) (81 overs) 211
3/28 (4) 4/35 (5)
5/123 (6) 6/131 (7) 7/146 (8)
8/192 (9) 9/207 (3) 10/211 (11)

Leach 17.3–5–38–3; Pennington 17–5–41–2; Morris 15–1–59–1; Barnard 13–3–40–2; Baker 20–7–31–2. *Second innings*—Leach 18–7–25–3; Pennington 13–1–59–3; Morris 13–1–45–1; Barnard 12–2–41–2; Baker 20–9–26–1; D'Oliveira 2–1–4–0; Mitchell 3–1–6–0.

Worcestershire

D. K. H. Mitchell c Kimber b Wright	8	– not out		9
J. D. Libby c Kimber b Wright	77	– not out		3
C. A. J. Morris b Parkinson	50			
G. H. Roderick c Kimber b Barnes	35			
J. A. Haynes st Bates b Parkinson	44			
B. L. D'Oliveira c Azad b Parkinson	37			
E. G. Barnard c Bates b Wright	48			
†O. B. Cox c Bates b Sakande	59			
*J. Leach c Wright b Sakande	12			
J. O. Baker c Rhodes b Sakande	3			
D. Y. Pennington not out	10			
B 9, lb 12, nb 18	39			

1/14 (1) 2/139 (3) 3/153 (2)   (119.2 overs) 422   (no wkt, 2.4 overs) 12
4/210 (4) 5/265 (6) 6/270 (5)
7/386 (7) 8/398 (8) 9/411 (9)
10/422 (10)   110 overs: 386-6

Wright 31–6–97–3; Sakande 21.2–1–66–3; Mike 17–1–75–0; Barnes 14–1–70–1; Parkinson 31–7–70–3; Rhodes 5–0–23–0. *Second innings*—Wright 1.4–0–11–0; Barnes 1–0–1–0.

Umpires: N. G. B. Cook and Hassan Adnan.   Referee: W. R. Smith.

YORKSHIRE

The world turned upside down

GRAHAM HARDCASTLE

Yorkshire's performances counted for nothing compared with events off the field, as reports of racism at the club became cricket's biggest story. The storm, centring on former player Azeem Rafiq, led the BBC news on November 16, when Rafiq, former chair Roger Hutton, his replacement Lord (Kamlesh) Patel of Bradford and ECB chief executive Tom Harrison sat in front of parliament's Digital, Culture, Media and Sport select committee. They had been summoned to answer questions after Yorkshire released only a summary of an independent report they had commissioned into Rafiq's complaints; it said there was insufficient evidence to prove institutional racism. Since then, it had emerged that the batter Gary Ballance called him "Paki".

Rafiq's allegations were published in August 2020, and the club finally released the redacted report in September 2021, but the scandal gathered pace in the autumn, and the ramifications were seismic. After Yorkshire stated they were taking no disciplinary action, all their major sponsors pulled out, and the ECB suspended Headingley from hosting international cricket. Hutton resigned, soon followed by chief executive Mark Arthur.

Patel became Yorkshire's new chair, and swiftly announced a six-figure settlement of Rafiq's employment tribunal case. "I have been appointed with a clear remit of righting the wrongs of the past, and making sure this club is an inclusive home for aspiring players of the future," he said.

Further change was on the way. In December, Patel sacked 16 members of staff, including the entire coaching team. Director of cricket Martyn Moxon and first-team coach Andrew Gale, both implicated by Rafiq, headed the departures. Former England bowler Darren Gough was installed as managing director of cricket to the end of the 2022 season. In January, he brought in his old England team-mates Steve Harmison and Ryan Sidebottom to help on an interim basis. A fortnight later, Ottis Gibson, the Barbadian who had been in charge of West Indies and South Africa, was appointed head coach. A threat that the ECB might relegate Yorkshire to Division Two of the Championship disappeared, and there was even talk that they had done enough for their international fixtures to be restored. Despite all that, there was dissent from the club's old guard.

Moxon and Gale had already been under pressure for cricketing reasons. Although Yorkshire were the only county to qualify for the Championship's Division One plus both limited-overs knockouts, they remained without a trophy since 2015. In the end, they finished fifth in Division One, and lost in the quarter-finals of the Royal London Cup and the Vitality Blast.

Their greatest quality and biggest weakness went hand in hand. They often dragged themselves back into matches after the batting had struggled. In nine

Harry Brook

of 13 Championship first innings, they failed to reach 250. Still, they conjured victories: they beat Sussex (away) and Northamptonshire (home and away) after conceding leads. The home win against Northamptonshire in May was by a single run, as Yorkshire defended 220. But four months later at Southampton, in the first round of Division One, Hampshire's last-wicket pair, Kyle Abbott and Brad Wheal, repelled 46 balls to secure the draw. Had Yorkshire won, they could well have mounted a title challenge.

There were seven captains across all competitions. Steve Patterson and David Willey, the permanent Championship and T20 skippers, were supplemented by Joe Root, Adam Lyth, Dom Bess, Ballance and Ben Coad, as injury and unavailability bit. Ten players, plus Gale, disappeared during The Hundred, which made qualification for the Royal London Cup knockouts the team's biggest achievement.

A number of youngsters shone. At Leicester in July, wicketkeeper Harry Duke became the county's second-youngest List A centurion, at 19 years 322 days. (The youngest was Sachin Tendulkar in 1992, aged 19 years 100 days.) In the same game, George Hill (aged 20) hit a career-best unbeaten 90, and his skilful seamers later claimed three in six balls to wreck a run-chase by Glamorgan, the eventual champions, on a turgid Cardiff pitch. Promoted to open in the Championship, Hill scored two fifties.

But the standout was 22-year-old Harry Brook. He made 797 Championship runs plus 486 in the Blast, and was named Young Player of the Year by the PCA and the Cricket Writers' Club. Two Championship hundreds doubled his career total. Brook was pipped as Yorkshire's leading run-scorer by Lyth, whose 819 included three hundreds – two in the first two matches.

Jordan Thompson led the bowling, with 46 wickets, and always seemed to make something happen. Dawid Malan was dismissed for the second 199 of his career in an innings win over Sussex, a classy performance which helped earn a Test recall. Bess, in his first season as a permanent Yorkshire player after appearing on loan in 2019, collected 40 wickets and 450 runs in all formats, including key hauls in Championship wins at Hove and Northampton. South African quick bowler Duanne Olivier (an overseas player since Kolpak status was abolished) battled a back injury, and took only 19 wickets in eight games across two competitions.

Pakistan seamer Haris Rauf signed in December, as part of a partnership with Lahore Qalandars: Brook joined the Qalandars for the Pakistan Super League in early 2022, and Patel talked about learning from their players' development programme to improve access to the sport. They later partnered with South Africa's Titans, too. It fitted in with his mission to "win back pride" for Yorkshire. "We aim to become a beacon to which the rest of the sport can aspire," he said.

YORKSHIRE RESULTS

County Championship matches – Played 14: Won 6, Lost 3, Drawn 5.
Vitality T20 Blast matches – Played 14: Won 7, Lost 6, No result 1. Cancelled 1.
Royal London Cup matches – Played 9: Won 4, Lost 3, No result 2.

LV= County Championship, 2nd in Group 3, 5th in Division 1;
Vitality T20 Blast, quarter-finalists; Royal London Cup, quarter-finalists.

COUNTY CHAMPIONSHIP AVERAGES, BATTING AND FIELDING

Cap		Birthplace	M	I	NO	R	HS	100	Avge	Ct
2012	†G. S. Ballance	Harare, Zimbabwe	10	14	1	594	101*	1	45.69	3
2016	†D. J. Willey	Northampton	6	8	4	165	41*	0	41.25	1
2010	†A. Lyth	Whitby‡	14	22	1	819	153	3	39.00	25
2021	H. C. Brook	Keighley‡	14	22	1	797	118	2	37.95	17
2012	J. E. Root§	Sheffield‡	5	8	0	291	101	1	36.37	4
	G. C. H. Hill	Keighley‡	7	11	0	263	71	0	23.90	1
	D. M. Bess§	Exeter	14	20	1	399	56	0	21.00	4
	†J. A. Thompson	Leeds‡	13	20	0	411	57	0	20.55	4
2019	T. Köhler-Cadmore	Chatham	11	18	0	353	89	0	19.61	21
	H. G. Duke	Wakefield‡	9	13	1	197	54	0	16.41	31
	J. A. Tattersall	Harrogate‡	5	8	1	101	26	0	14.42	16
	T. W. Loten	York‡	2	4	0	57	27	0	14.25	0
2012	S. A. Patterson	Beverley‡	13	17	2	191	47*	0	12.73	3
	M. D. Fisher	York‡	5	7	2	55	17	0	11.00	1
2018	B. O. Coad	Harrogate‡	10	13	5	84	33*	0	10.50	0
2020	D. Olivier¶	Groblersdal, SA	7	11	5	61	21	0	10.16	1
	W. A. R. Fraine	Huddersfield‡	3	6	0	35	12	0	5.83	1

Also batted: D. J. Leech (*Middlesbrough‡*) (1 match) did not bat; †D. J. Malan§ (*Roehampton*) (2 matches) 199, 9, 12 (2 ct); S. A. Northeast (*Ashford, Kent*) (2 matches) 3, 1 (2 ct); M. L. Revis (*Steeton‡*) (1 match) 0, 34.

‡ *Born in Yorkshire.* § *ECB contract.* ¶ *Official overseas player.*

BOWLING

	Style	O	M	R	W	BB	5I	Avge
M. D. Fisher	RFM	121	29	393	20	5-41	1	19.65
J. A. Thompson	RFM	329.5	91	949	46	5-52	1	20.63
B. O. Coad	RFM	287.1	79	766	35	4-48	0	21.88
D. J. Willey	LFM	148.3	30	479	20	5-61	1	23.95
S. A. Patterson	RFM	364	111	815	32	4-26	0	25.46
D. M. Bess	OB	405.4	122	912	28	7-43	2	32.57
D. Olivier	RFM	175.1	26	610	18	4-61	0	33.88

Also bowled: H. C. Brook (RM) 82.1–18–194–7; G. C. H. Hill (RFM) 48–12–128–7; D. J. Leech (RFM) 17–1–79–0; A. Lyth (OB) 13–8–6–0; M. L. Revis (RM) 9–2–19–2; J. E. Root (OB) 27–4–74–1.

LEADING VITALITY BLAST AVERAGES (90 runs/15 overs)

Batting	Runs	HS	Avge	SR	Ct
J. A. Thompson	215	74	26.87	185.34	7
J. M. Bairstow	295	112	73.75	175.59	2
H. C. Brook	486	91*	69.42	149.07	9
A. Lyth	232	52	17.84	145.91	12
G. S. Ballance	159	55	22.71	128.22	0
T. Köhler-Cadmore	168	55	42.00	126.31	3
J. E. Root	97	49	24.25	105.43	2

Bowling	W	BB	Avge	ER
D. M. Bess	11	3-17	18.27	6.70
L. H. Ferguson	14	4-24	19.21	7.27
A. U. Rashid	5	3-32	29.80	7.45
M. D. Fisher	12	2-15	26.75	8.75
D. J. Willey	7	3-44	23.00	8.94
M. J. Waite	9	2-17	29.33	9.26
J. A. Thompson	14	4-44	21.14	9.86

LEADING ROYAL LONDON CUP AVERAGES (100 runs/4 wickets)

Batting	Runs	HS	Avge	SR	Ct/St
M. J. Waite	159	44	39.75	116.05	0
G. C. H. Hill ..	222	90*	37.00	86.04	1
W. A. Luxton ..	165	68	33.00	86.38	1
W. A. R. Fraine .	227	69*	32.42	113.50	4
M. L. Revis....	186	58*	31.00	109.41	5
H. G. Duke	206	125	29.42	79.23	4/1
G. S. Ballance . .	180	54	25.71	77.58	9
J. A. Tattersall .	153	70	25.50	85.95	5

Bowling	W	BB	Avge	ER
J. R. Sullivan	5	4-11	15.80	5.64
G. C. H. Hill	10	3-47	24.90	5.29
M. J. Waite	12	5-59	26.66	6.27
M. W. Pillans....	8	4-26	31.37	7.38
B. O. Coad......	8	3-30	35.62	4.88
M. L. Revis	5	2-43	45.80	5.32

FIRST-CLASS COUNTY RECORDS

Highest score for	341	G. H. Hirst v Leicestershire at Leicester	1905
Highest score against	318*	W. G. Grace (Gloucestershire) at Cheltenham....	1876
Leading run-scorer	38,558	H. Sutcliffe (avge 50.20)	1919–45
Best bowling for	10-10	H. Verity v Nottinghamshire at Leeds	1932
Best bowling against	10-37	C. V. Grimmett (Australians) at Sheffield	1930
Leading wicket-taker	3,597	W. Rhodes (avge 16.02)	1898–1930
Highest total for	887	v Warwickshire at Birmingham.................	1896
Highest total against	681-7 dec	by Leicestershire at Bradford..................	1996
Lowest total for	23	v Hampshire at Middlesbrough	1965
Lowest total against	13	by Nottinghamshire at Nottingham	1901

LIST A COUNTY RECORDS

Highest score for	191	D. S. Lehmann v Nottinghamshire at Scarborough ..	2001
Highest score against	177	S. A. Newman (Surrey) at The Oval	2009
Leading run-scorer	8,699	G. Boycott (avge 40.08).................	1963–86
Best bowling for	7-15	R. A. Hutton v Worcestershire at Leeds	1969
Best bowling against	7-32	R. G. D. Willis (Warwickshire) at Birmingham	1981
Leading wicket-taker	308	C. M. Old (avge 18.96)	1967–82
Highest total for	411-6	v Devon at Exmouth	2004
Highest total against	375-4	by Surrey at Scarborough..................	1994
Lowest total for	54	v Essex at Leeds.................	2003
Lowest total against	23	by Middlesex at Leeds	1974

TWENTY20 COUNTY RECORDS

Highest score for	161	A. Lyth v Northamptonshire at Leeds	2017
Highest score against	111	D. L. Maddy (Leicestershire) at Leeds...........	2004
Leading run-scorer	**3,159**	**A. Lyth (avge 26.32, SR 144.70)**	**2008–21**
Best bowling for	6-19	T. T. Bresnan v Lancashire at Leeds	2017
Best bowling against	5-43	L. J. Fletcher (Nottinghamshire) at Nottingham	2020
Leading wicket-taker	118	T. T. Bresnan (avge 24.72, ER 8.09).............	2003–19
Highest total for	260-4	v Northamptonshire at Leeds	2017
Highest total against	231-4	by Lancashire at Manchester	2015
Lowest total for	**81**	**v Warwickshire at Birmingham**	**2021**
Lowest total against	90	by Glamorgan at Cardiff	2016

ADDRESS

Headingley, Leeds LS6 3DP; 0344 504 3099; cricket@yorkshireccc.com; www.yorkshireccc.com.
Twitter: @YorkshireCCC.

OFFICIALS

Captain S. A. Patterson
    (Twenty20) D. J. Willey
Director of cricket 2021 M. D. Moxon
Managing director of cricket 2022 D. Gough
First-team coach 2021 A. W. Gale
    2022 O. D. Gibson
2nd XI/Academy director 2021 I. M. Dews

President G. A. Cope
Chair 2021 C. N. R. Hutton
    2022 Lord Patel of Bradford
Chief executive 2021 M. A. Arthur
Head groundsman A. Fogarty
Scorer J. T. Potter

GROUP THREE

YORKSHIRE v GLAMORGAN

At Leeds, April 8–11. Drawn. Yorkshire 11pts, Glamorgan 14pts. Toss: Yorkshire. First-class debut: J. P. McIlroy. Championship debut: C. Z. Taylor.

Glamorgan and Billy Root had the better of this battle with Yorkshire and his elder brother Joe. But their hopes of a first victory in this fixture since 1999 were blocked by snow on the third day, which prevented any play after lunch. Next morning, Billy brought up a determined century, working two to leg off Joe's spin during an unbroken 212-run stand with Cooke, a fifth-wicket record between these sides. Cooke declared on reaching his own hundred, setting Yorkshire 379 in 76; they were 47 for three when Joe Root fell cheaply a second time, but Lyth's well-paced unbeaten 115 ensured a comfortable draw. Glamorgan bowled 25 overs of spin to offset a slow over-rate. Put in on the first day, they had recovered from 29 for three through Billy Root and Carlson, and then from 132 for seven thanks to half-centuries from Douthwaite, van der Gugten (a career-best) and Hogan. Yorkshire faltered in reply – Joe Root horribly miscued a full toss from off-spinner Taylor – and trailed by 137. Their problems grew when muscle strains ruled out Coad, who had taken seven wickets, and Fisher. But the snow enabled their survival.

Close of play: first day, Glamorgan 310-8 (van der Gugten 80, Hogan 40); second day, Glamorgan 68-4 (Root 25, Cooke 17); third day, Glamorgan 161-4 (Root 77, Cooke 57).

Glamorgan

N. J. Selman b Coad	4	– c Tattersall b Coad	0
D. L. Lloyd b Fisher	4	– c Brook b Coad	16
A. Balbirnie lbw b Patterson	16	– c Brook b Olivier	5
W. T. Root c Tattersall b Coad	43	– not out	110
K. S. Carlson c Lyth b Olivier	55	– c Tattersall b Coad	0
*†C. B. Cooke c Köhler-Cadmore b Patterson	1	– not out	102
C. Z. Taylor b Fisher	9		
D. A. Douthwaite b Coad	57		
T. van der Gugten not out	85		
M. G. Hogan c Patterson b Coad	54		
J. P. McIlroy lbw b Patterson	0		
Lb 2	2	Lb 8	8
	330		241

1/8 (1) 2/12 (2) 3/29 (3)   (101.4 overs) 330
4/111 (5) 5/112 (6) 6/128 (7)
7/132 (4) 8/254 (8) 9/326 (10) 10/330 (11)

1/0 (1)   (4 wkts dec, 78.4 overs) 241
2/17 (3) 3/29 (2)
4/29 (5)

Coad 26–5–94–4; Fisher 21–3–78–2; Patterson 23.4–8–51–3; Olivier 19–6–69–1; Bess 9–1–23–0; Root 3–0–13–0. *Second innings*—Coad 7–3–18–3; Olivier 14–4–33–1; Patterson 14–6–30–0; Bess 25.4–3–83–0; Root 5–0–20–0; Brook 13–1–49–0.

Yorkshire

A. Lyth lbw b Douthwaite	52	– not out	115
T. Köhler-Cadmore c Cooke b Hogan	11	– c Cooke b van der Gugten	4
T. W. Loten b Hogan	0	– lbw b Hogan	9
J. E. Root c Douthwaite b Taylor	16	– c Balbirnie b Douthwaite	13
H. C. Brook lbw b Lloyd	40	– c Root b Hogan	60
†J. A. Tattersall lbw b van der Gugten	15	– not out	15
D. M. Bess not out	38		
M. D. Fisher c Cooke b McIlroy	6		
*S. A. Patterson c Selman b Lloyd	3		
B. O. Coad c Taylor b Douthwaite	5		
D. Olivier c Cooke b Taylor	3		
Nb 4	4	Lb 5, nb 2	7
	193		223

1/19 (2) 2/31 (3) 3/79 (1)   (58.2 overs) 193
4/79 (4) 5/129 (6) 6/149 (5)
7/160 (8) 8/167 (9) 9/175 (10) 10/193 (11)

1/19 (2)   (4 wkts, 66 overs) 223
2/32 (3) 3/47 (4)
4/178 (5)

Hogan 13–4–50–2; van der Gugten 12–3–48–1; Root 2–0–6–0; McIlroy 9–4–12–1; Douthwaite 11–3–39–2; Taylor 4.2–1–16–2; Lloyd 7–1–22–2. *Second innings*—van der Gugten 13–4–35–1; Hogan 13–2–32–2; Douthwaite 9–1–35–1; McIlroy 6–2–26–0; Taylor 19–4–62–0; Root 6–0–28–0.

Umpires: P. K. Baldwin and R. J. Warren.   Referee: W. M. Noon.

At Canterbury, April 15–18. YORKSHIRE beat KENT by 200 runs.

At Hove, April 22–25. YORKSHIRE beat SUSSEX by 48 runs.

YORKSHIRE v NORTHAMPTONSHIRE

At Leeds, April 29–May 2. Yorkshire won by one run. Yorkshire 20pts, Northamptonshire 4pts. Toss: Northamptonshire.

Yorkshire's third one-run win in 3,684 first-class matches was secured by the man who completed the second – Patterson. Their first had come against Middlesex at Bradford in 1976, but their second, against Loughborough UCCE in 2007, ended with Patterson bowling the last two in the final over. This time, a 50-minute rain break at the fall of the ninth wicket, when Northamptonshire needed 14 for their first victory at Headingley in 31 seasons, heightened nerves during an early tea. On resuming, Parnell, who had claimed five in each innings with his left-arm seam, inched towards the target of 220. Then, with two required, Patterson nipped one away to find his edge; the keeper held on to clinch a third successive win. An absorbing contest was played in bowler-friendly conditions. Sanderson bowled Lyth with its first ball, and Yorkshire were 80 for five before Bess chivvied 56, the game's highest score. Northamptonshire in turn were 81 for five, but fifties from Zaib and Taylor earned a 28-run lead. The home side were just 121 ahead in the second innings when Willey arrived at No. 10; against his old county, he contributed a valuable 41, including three leg-side sixes off Berg, ran out Vasconcelos with a direct hit late on the third day, and collected six wickets in all. Parnell almost swung it – until Patterson celebrated another heist.

Close of play: first day, Northamptonshire 36-0 (Curran 14, Vasconcelos 21); second day, Yorkshire 43-3 (Ballance 8, Patterson 0); third day, Northamptonshire 94-4 (Procter 20, Zaib 1).

Yorkshire

A. Lyth b Sanderson	0	– c Taylor b Berg			27
T. Köhler-Cadmore b Berg	42	– c Vasconcelos b Sanderson			0
W. A. R. Fraine lbw b Berg	11	– lbw b Parnell			3
G. S. Ballance c Curran b Parnell	4	– c Curran b Parnell			16
H. C. Brook lbw b Parnell	0	– (6) c Keogh b Parnell			39
†J. A. Tattersall c Berg b Sanderson	26	– (7) c Vasconcelos b Taylor			18
D. M. Bess c Kerrigan b Berg	56	– (8) lbw b Sanderson			32
J. A. Thompson b Parnell	17	– (9) c Vasconcelos b Kerrigan			37
D. J. Willey c Vasconcelos b Parnell	12	– (10) not out			41
*S. A. Patterson c Vasconcelos b Parnell	9	– (5) lbw b Parnell			4
D. Olivier not out	0	– b Parnell			11
B 19, lb 9, w 1	29	B 12, lb 6, w 1			19

1/0 (1) 2/66 (3) 3/76 (4) (63.3 overs) 206   1/12 (2) 2/25 (3) (78.4 overs) 247
4/76 (5) 5/80 (2) 6/137 (6)   3/35 (1) 4/55 (4)
7/160 (8) 8/186 (9) 9/206 (7) 10/206 (10)   5/60 (5) 6/86 (7) 7/145 (8)
    8/149 (6) 9/214 (9) 10/247 (11)

Sanderson 21–8–48–2; Taylor 14.5–5–34–0; Parnell 15.3–4–64–5; Berg 13–6–32–3. *Second innings*—Sanderson 21–8–37–2; Taylor 15–4–45–1; Parnell 17.4–2–79–5; Berg 12–4–47–1; Kerrigan 13–4–21–1.

Northamptonshire

B. J. Curran c Brook b Patterson	15	– lbw b Thompson	9
*†R. S. Vasconcelos c Köhler-Cadmore b Patterson	47	– run out (Willey)	41
C. O. Thurston c Lyth b Thompson	13	– lbw b Thompson	0
R. I. Keogh c Köhler-Cadmore b Patterson	1	– c Köhler-Cadmore b Willey	5
L. A. Procter c Brook b Thompson	4	– c Tattersall b Willey	27
S. A. Zaib b Willey	55	– c Köhler-Cadmore b Olivier	25
T. A. I. Taylor b Bess	50	– lbw b Patterson	1
W. D. Parnell c Köhler-Cadmore b Willey	16	– c Tattersall b Patterson	33
G. K. Berg not out	11	– c Tattersall b Willey	16
S. C. Kerrigan c Lyth b Willey	8	– c Lyth b Olivier	12
B. W. Sanderson c Tattersall b Thompson	4	– not out	4
B 5, lb 5	10	B 24, lb 17, nb 4	45

1/47 (1) 2/76 (3) 3/76 (2)   (88.5 overs) 234
4/81 (4) 5/81 (5) 6/173 (6)
7/199 (7) 8/217 (8) 9/229 (10) 10/234 (11)

1/9 (1) 2/17 (3)   (73.5 overs) 218
3/38 (4) 4/74 (2)
5/115 (5) 6/136 (7) 7/146 (6)
8/178 (9) 9/206 (10) 10/218 (8)

Willey 18–5–43–3; Thompson 18.5–6–58–3; Patterson 18–9–35–3; Olivier 16–2–56–0; Brook 3–1–8–0; Bess 15–6–24–1. *Second innings*—Patterson 25.5–5–53–2; Thompson 14–2–51–2; Willey 18–4–39–3; Olivier 14–2–33–2; Bess 2–1–1–0.

Umpires: N. G. B. Cook and D. J. Millns.   Referee: D. A. Cosker.

YORKSHIRE v KENT

At Leeds, May 6–9. Drawn. Yorkshire 13pts, Kent 14pts. Toss: Yorkshire. County debut: M. R. Quinn. Championship debut: N. N. Gilchrist.

Rain washed out the third day, and a wet outfield prevented play before 2.45 on the fourth, ensuring a drab draw. Crawley had lit up the first with flashes of quality as he battled to 90 on a slow surface, supported by former Yorkshire player Leaning, who scored 47, following a pair when the sides met at Canterbury. Kent reached the close on 224 for seven, but a 60-run stand from O'Riordan and Cummins, who hit Patterson for two sixes, pushed them past 300 in the morning. By stumps, Ballance had 91 out of Yorkshire's 240 for five but, when he resumed after the four lost sessions, he was run out just short of his first century since July 2019, having missed the intervening season through illness and injury. Kent's 20-year-old seamer Gilchrist – like Ballance, Harare-born – took four wickets in his second first-class match.

Close of play: first day, Kent 224-7 (O'Riordan 4, Gilchrist 3); second day, Yorkshire 240-5 (Ballance 91, Bess 4); third day, no play.

Kent

*D. J. Bell-Drummond c Brook b Coad	4	M. L. Cummins not out	28
J. M. Cox c Lyth b Patterson	20	M. R. Quinn c and b Bess	1
Z. Crawley c Root b Patterson	90		
J. L. Denly c Lyth b Thompson	3	B 4, lb 8, nb 4	16
J. A. Leaning c Lyth b Brook	47		
†O. G. Robinson c Thompson b Coad	38	1/4 (1) 2/46 (2) (111.3 overs) 305
D. I. Stevens c Tattersall b Coad	9	3/65 (4) 4/144 (3) 5/206 (5)
M. K. O'Riordan b Olivier	40	6/216 (6) 7/217 (7) 8/244 (9)
N. N. Gilchrist b Thompson	9	9/304 (8) 10/305 (11) 110 overs: 300-8

Coad 22–4–53–3; Thompson 23–11–41–2; Patterson 21–7–58–2; Olivier 18–1–77–1; Bess 22.3–4–56–1; Brook 4–2–2–1; Root 1–0–6–0.

Yorkshire

A. Lyth c Cummins b Stevens	23	B. O. Coad not out	33
T. Köhler-Cadmore b Gilchrist	14	D. Olivier c O'Riordan b Leaning	7
G. S. Ballance run out (O'Riordan)	96		
J. E. Root c Robinson b Quinn	41	Lb 2, nb 10	12
H. C. Brook lbw b Gilchrist	59		
†J. A. Tattersall c Robinson b Denly	1	1/39 (1) 2/48 (2) (105.3 overs)	321
D. M. Bess b Stevens	15	3/131 (4) 4/233 (5)	
J. A. Thompson c Robinson b Gilchrist	18	5/236 (6) 6/246 (3) 7/256 (7)	
*S. A. Patterson c Robinson b Gilchrist	2	8/269 (9) 9/304 (8) 10/321 (11)	

Cummins 17–2–77–0; Stevens 22–10–48–2; Quinn 23–8–42–1; Gilchrist 18–3–74–4; O'Riordan 8–2–31–0; Leaning 7.3–1–21–1; Denly 10–2–26–1.

Umpires: P. J. Hartley and R. A. Kettleborough.   Referee: J. J. Whitaker.

At Cardiff, May 13–16. YORKSHIRE drew with GLAMORGAN.

At Manchester, May 27–30. YORKSHIRE lost to LANCASHIRE by an innings and 79 runs. *Yorkshire's first defeat at Old Trafford since July 2000.*

YORKSHIRE v SUSSEX

At Leeds, June 3–6. Yorkshire won by an innings and 30 runs. Yorkshire 23pts, Sussex 4pts. Toss: Yorkshire. First-class debuts: D. K. Ibrahim, A. G. H. Orr.

Dan Ibrahim became the youngest to score a Championship half-century, aged 16 years 299 days – beating Bilal Shafayat of Nottinghamshire by 61 days. His composed 55 helped an inexperienced Sussex reach 313, after Brown's pugnacious 127 fashioned a recovery from four. But Yorkshire still pulled off an innings win with 32 balls to spare, thrilling the home crowd on their return to

YOUNGEST PLAYERS WITH A FIRST-CLASS FIFTY IN THE UK

Years Days

15	116	Hasan Raza (56)	Pakistan A v Derbyshire at Derby	1997
16	54	W. W. F. Pullen (71)	Gloucestershire v Yorkshire at Cheltenham	1882
16	112	†B. A. Godleman (69*)	Middlesex v Cambridge UCCE at Cambridge	2005
16	182	†P. Willey (78)	Northamptonshire v Cambridge Univ at Cambridge	1966
16	258	Mushfiqur Rahim (63)	Bangladeshis v Sussex at Hove	2005
16	267	Majid Khan (51*)	Pakistan Eaglets v Kent at Dartford	1963
16	**299**	**†D. K. Ibrahim (55)**	**Sussex v Yorkshire at Leeds**	**2021**
16	315	†R. G. Williams (64)	Northamptonshire v Oxford University at Oxford	1974
16	360	†B. M. Shafayat (72)	Nottinghamshire v Middlesex at Nottingham	2001

† *On first-class debut.*

Pullen's innings predated the formal constitution of the County Championship in 1890. Ibrahim made another fifty aged 16 years 330 days, and Hasan Raza scored three further fifties on Pakistan A's tour. Mushfiqur Rahim became the youngest player to score a first-class hundred in the UK, aged 16 years 263 days, for Bangladeshis v Northamptonshire.

Headingley. This was also their first chance to see Malan since he joined in 2020. His classy 199, in his first appearance of the season, underpinned a total of 558 and a lead of 245, though he was bowled by off-spinner Carson one short of becoming the first to score successive double-centuries for Yorkshire, after his 219 against Derbyshire the previous August. Entering the final session, Sussex looked likely to survive, on 165 for four; debutant opener Ali Orr had made an excellent 67. But once Thomason was caught driving to slip for 52, they lost five for seven to Bess and Willey, slipping to 187 for nine. Brown and Atkins held out for 11 overs before Brown was bowled by fellow captain Patterson.

Close of play: first day, Sussex 267-5 (Brown 126, Ibrahim 37); second day, Yorkshire 272-2 (Malan 103, Ballance 74); third day, Sussex 38-0 (Orr 23, Haines 12).

Sussex

A. G. H. Orr c sub (D. Olivier) b Brook	15	– b Bess	67
T. J. Haines c Brook b Willey	2	– c Lyth b Bess	24
S. van Zyl c Duke b Thompson	15	– c Duke b Thompson	0
A. D. Thomason c Malan b Thompson	40	– c Lyth b Bess	52
T. M. Head c Duke b Thompson	14	– c Köhler-Cadmore b Coad	18
*†B. C. Brown c Duke b Coad	127	– b Patterson	22
D. K. Ibrahim c Brook b Coad	55	– c Lyth b Bess	0
J. J. Carson not out	10	– c Thompson b Willey	5
S. C. Meaker b Patterson	9	– c Brook b Willey	0
H. T. Crocombe lbw b Willey	1	– c Duke b Willey	0
J. A. Atkins run out (Willey)	2	– not out	10
B 11, lb 8, nb 4	23	B 4, lb 11, nb 2	17

1/8 (2) 2/25 (3) 3/38 (1) (115.3 overs) 313   1/60 (2) 2/61 (3) (113.4 overs) 215
4/68 (5) 5/175 (4) 6/269 (7) 7/296 (7)   3/125 (1) 4/164 (5)
8/310 (9) 9/311 (10) 10/313 (11) 110 overs: 308-7   5/180 (4) 6/180 (7) 7/187 (8)
   8/187 (9) 9/187 (10) 10/215 (6)

Coad 26–7–64–2; Willey 21–3–83–2; Thompson 24–8–53–3; Patterson 25.3–11–42–1; Brook 8–1–24–1; Bess 11–2–28–0. *Second innings*—Coad 20–11–43–1; Willey 19–10–26–3; Thompson 24–6–55–1; Bess 35–15–51–4; Patterson 9.4–1–21–1; Lyth 6–2–4–0.

Yorkshire

A. Lyth b Atkins	48	*S. A. Patterson c and b Carson	8
T. Köhler-Cadmore lbw b Ibrahim	25	B. O. Coad b Atkins	1
D. J. Malan b Carson	199		
G. S. Ballance c Brown b Carson	77	B 9, lb 11, w 3, nb 16	39
H. C. Brook b Atkins	49		
D. M. Bess c Brown b Meaker	8	1/83 (2) 2/95 (1) (145 overs) 558
†H. G. Duke lbw b Atkins	54	3/275 (4) 4/374 (5) 5/402 (6)
J. A. Thompson c Meaker b Atkins	42	6/459 (3) 7/535 (7) 8/542 (8)
D. J. Willey not out	8	9/555 (10) 10/558 (11) 110 overs: 419-5

Crocombe 16–1–80–0; Atkins 26–2–98–5; Meaker 23–0–103–1; Ibrahim 21–3–72–1; Carson 43–7–124–3; Haines 7–1–18–0; Head 9–0–43–0.

Umpires: R. J. Bailey and G. D. Lloyd. Referee: P. M. Such.

At Northampton, July 4–6. YORKSHIRE beat NORTHAMPTONSHIRE by 53 runs. *Yorkshire qualify for Division One.*

YORKSHIRE v LANCASHIRE

At Leeds, July 11–14. Drawn. Yorkshire 8pts, Lancashire 11pts. Toss: Yorkshire. County debut: J. M. Blatherwick. Championship debuts: D. J. Leech; G. P. Balderson.

Yorkshire's final group match was switched from Scarborough to Headingley because of Covid precautions, but only 119.2 overs were possible. The first day was played in full, the second washed out, and the third delayed until noon by a wet outfield. Then Dominic Leech collided with the concrete base of the Western Terrace while fielding, and dislocated his left knee. The umpires called an early tea – because of concerns about boggy run-ups, rather than a direct consequence of his injury – and the crowd jeered through two inspections in bright sunshine. But play never resumed: the final day was abandoned, and Yorkshire announced they would relay the outfield in the winter. As both sides had already for Division One, the fixture had extra significance because they would carry forward half their head-to-head points. Lancashire followed victory at Old Trafford by securing three batting points here, while Yorkshire failed to get any for bowling, so they entered the next phase with 16.5 and 4.5 respectively. On the opening day, Jennings and Davies had cast doubt on Patterson's decision to bowl under overcast skies by accumulating 163. Jennings's 20th first-class hundred made him the 14th Lancashire player to score two Roses centuries in a season; Bohannon, stranded on 74, might have become the 15th, and Wells was left three short of a maiden hundred for the club.

Close of play: first day, Lancashire 273-2 (Wells 35, Bohannon 7); second day, no play; third day, Lancashire 411-2 (Wells 97, Bohannon 74).

Lancashire

K. K. Jennings c and b Thompson		132
A. L. Davies lbw b Thompson		84
L. W. P. Wells not out		97
J. J. Bohannon not out		74
B 12, lb 11, w 1		24

1/163 (2)	(2 wkts, 119.2 overs)	411
2/256 (1)	110 overs: 342-2	

*†D. J. Vilas, S. J. Croft, R. P. Jones, G. P. Balderson, T. E. Bailey, J. M. Blatherwick and J. M. Anderson did not bat.

Coad 24–4–53–0; Leech 17–1–79–0; Thompson 20–5–76–2; Patterson 25–4–94–0; Brook 6–2–7–0; Bess 23.2–3–76–0; Hill 4–1–3–0.

Yorkshire

A. Lyth, G. C. H. Hill, S. A. Northeast, G. S. Ballance, H. C. Brook, D. M. Bess, †H. G. Duke, J. A. Thompson, *S. A. Patterson, B. O. Coad, D. J. Leech.

Umpires: I. J. Gould and N. J. Llong.   Referee: W. R. Smith.

DIVISION ONE

At Southampton, August 30–September 2. YORKSHIRE drew with HAMPSHIRE.

YORKSHIRE v SOMERSET

At Scarborough, September 5–6. Yorkshire won by an innings and 33 runs. Yorkshire 22pts, Somerset 3pts. Toss: Somerset.

When the Championship's final phase had begun in August, the points carried forward put Somerset second, and Yorkshire bottom, of Division One. But this two-day result meant they had swapped places within two rounds: Somerset suffered a second successive innings defeat, while Yorkshire raised hopes of a title challenge. Three players in their early twenties starred. Fisher exploited Scarborough's pace and bounce to dismiss the visitors early on the first afternoon, with a career-best five for 41. Next day, his opening burst of 6–5–2–4 left them a sorry 18 for five; eventual match figures of nine for 64 were another best. In between, Brook, just handed his county cap, elegantly steered Yorkshire into the lead by the first-day close, then advanced to his second century of the season in the morning. All-rounder Thompson's 57 helped extend the advantage to 174, and he added three wickets, winning the game when he bowled de Lange with one ball of the extra half-hour to go. Green's 32 – from No. 8 – was Somerset's highest score of the match.

Close of play: first day, Yorkshire 159-5 (Brook 79, Duke 4).

Somerset

*T. B. Abell c Duke b Fisher	2	– b Fisher	14
T. A. Lammonby c Brook b Willey	8	– c Brook b Willey	0
Azhar Ali b Thompson	24	– c Lyth b Fisher	1
J. C. Hildreth c Lyth b Hill	24	– lbw b Fisher	2
G. A. Bartlett c Duke b Hill	4	– lbw b Fisher	0
†S. M. Davies c Köhler-Cadmore b Fisher	15	– c Köhler-Cadmore b Hill	25
T. Banton c Duke b Thompson	0	– c Duke b Thompson	10
B. G. F. Green not out	13	– b Thompson	32
M. J. Leach c Lyth b Fisher	4	– c Lyth b Bess	26
J. H. Davey lbw b Fisher	4	– not out	5
M. de Lange b Fisher	22	– b Thompson	21
B 8, lb 6	14	B 4, lb 1	5

1/2 (1) 2/14 (2) 3/64 (4)   (42 overs) 134   1/2 (2) 2/7 (3)   (51.5 overs) 141
4/68 (5) 5/68 (3) 6/68 (7)   3/17 (4) 4/17 (5)
7/86 (6) 8/100 (9) 9/108 (10) 10/134 (11)   5/18 (1) 6/45 (7) 7/69 (6)
                                            8/111 (9) 9/115 (8) 10/141 (11)

Fisher 11–1–41–5; Willey 7–3–22–1; Patterson 6–2–9–0; Thompson 11–4–36–2; Hill 7–2–12–2. *Second innings*—Fisher 9–5–23–4; Willey 9–1–40–1; Patterson 12–5–18–0; Thompson 8.5–1–32–3; Hill 5–2–11–1; Bess 8–3–12–1.

Yorkshire

A. Lyth c Davies b de Lange	0	D. J. Willey c and b de Lange	23
G. C. H. Hill c Hildreth b Davey	29	M. D. Fisher not out	15
T. Köhler-Cadmore c Abell b Davey	1	*S. A. Patterson c Azhar Ali b de Lange	0
G. S. Ballance c Abell b Davey	32	B 8, lb 4, nb 2	14
H. C. Brook c Abell b Green	118		
D. M. Bess st Davies b Leach	10	1/1 (1) 2/51 (2) 3/51 (3) (103.3 overs) 308
†H. G. Duke b Davey	9	4/89 (4) 5/122 (6) 6/179 (7)
J. A. Thompson c Lammonby b de Lange	57	7/230 (5) 8/285 (8) 9/296 (9) 10/308 (11)

Köhler-Cadmore, when 1, retired hurt at 16-1 and resumed at 51-2.

Davey 28–9–72–4; de Lange 25.3–8–55–4; Abell 17–1–57–0; Lammonby 8–1–43–0; Green 9–3–29–1; Leach 16–3–40–1.

Umpires: R. T. Robinson and R. A. White.   Referee: J. J. Whitaker.

YORKSHIRE v WARWICKSHIRE

At Leeds, September 12–15. Warwickshire won by 106 runs. Warwickshire 19pts, Yorkshire 3pts. Toss: Yorkshire. First-class debut: J. G. Bethell.

Neither side passed 176 in a match dominated by swing and seam, but Warwickshire won decisively, jumping to second in Division One, while Yorkshire slid to fifth, ending their Championship bid. Eighteen wickets had fallen on the first day, and 15 on the second; after a third-day washout, Warwickshire snapped up the remaining seven before lunch. Yorkshire had also struck seven times before lunch, on the opening day, but a punchy 66 from Burgess helped the visitors reach 155. Then Woakes – like Malan, released by England after the Old Trafford Test was cancelled – claimed three wickets in his first Championship appearance for three years. Yorkshire closed on 95 for eight, and could add only 13 at the start of day two. Sibley made a dogged 45 and Burgess an aggressive 37 to build on Warwickshire's advantage, although Thompson collected a Championship-best five. A target of 224 grew more daunting when former local hero Bresnan brilliantly caught Malan one-handed off the last ball of the day – the third of six catches he took at first slip as Yorkshire crumbled for 117. Norwell bowled superbly in both innings, while Patterson picked up his 450th first-class wicket – debutant Jacob Bethell, the 2021 Wisden Schools Cricketer of the Year.

Close of play: first day, Yorkshire 95-8 (Ballance 51, Patterson 1); second day, Yorkshire 50-3 (Ballance 21); third day, no play.

Warwickshire

*W. M. H. Rhodes c Duke b Coad	13	– b Patterson	12
D. P. Sibley lbw b Fisher	11	– c Duke b Thompson	45
C. G. Benjamin b Patterson	9	– c Lyth b Thompson	3
S. R. Hain c Bess b Coad	0	– c Duke b Thompson	0
M. J. Lamb b Patterson	16	– b Patterson	0
†M. G. K. Burgess c Bess b Coad	66	– c Brook b Fisher	37
C. R. Woakes lbw b Patterson	9	– c Duke b Thompson	0
T. T. Bresnan lbw b Hill	4	– lbw b Coad	36
J. G. Bethell c Duke b Patterson	15	– b Fisher	8
C. N. Miles c Duke b Coad	0	– not out	17
L. C. Norwell not out	4	– c Malan b Thompson	13
B 4, lb 4	8	B 4, lb 1	5

1/24 (2) 2/24 (1) 3/24 (4)   (42.4 overs) 155   1/23 (1) 2/26 (3)   (61.4 overs) 176
4/48 (3) 5/55 (5) 6/71 (7)   3/26 (4) 4/27 (5)
7/103 (8) 8/133 (9) 9/134 (10) 10/155 (6)   5/97 (2) 6/97 (7) 7/108 (6)
                                                        8/130 (9) 9/163 (8) 10/176 (11)

Coad 11.4–0–48–4; Fisher 10–3–38–1; Patterson 14–3–34–4; Thompson 5–0–24–0; Hill 2–0–3–1. *Second innings*—Coad 17–6–26–1; Fisher 13–1–48–2; Patterson 12.5–3–27–2; Thompson 15.4–3–52–5; Hill 3–0–14–0; Brook 0.1–0–4–0.

Yorkshire

A. Lyth lbw b Norwell	1	– c Bresnan b Miles	14
G. C. H. Hill lbw b Woakes	4	– c Bresnan b Woakes	1
D. J. Malan c Bethell b Woakes	9	– c Bresnan b Norwell	12
G. S. Ballance b Miles	58	– c Hain b Woakes	21
H. C. Brook lbw b Woakes	15	– c Bresnan b Woakes	9
D. M. Bess b Norwell	1	– (7) lbw b Bresnan	4
†G. Duke lbw b Norwell	7	– (8) c and b Miles	8
J. A. Thompson c Rhodes b Miles	5	– (6) c Bresnan b Norwell	18
M. D. Fisher c Bresnan b Miles	0	– not out	13
*S. A. Patterson b Norwell	6	– c Bresnan b Miles	5
B. O. Coad not out	0	– c Rhodes b Norwell	2
Lb 2	2	Lb 8, nb 2	10

1/5 (2) 2/5 (1) 3/27 (4)   (42.5 overs) 108   1/1 (2) 2/18 (1)   (49.3 overs) 117
4/63 (5) 5/64 (6) 6/76 (7)   3/50 (3) 4/50 (4)
7/91 (8) 8/93 (9) 9/108 (10) 10/108 (4)   5/69 (5) 6/82 (7) 7/95 (8)
                                                      8/105 (6) 9/114 (10) 10/117 (11)

Woakes 12–3–40–3; Norwell 14–6–27–4; Bresnan 7–2–18–0; Miles 9.5–3–21–3. *Second innings*—Woakes 14–6–26–3; Norwell 15.3–4–38–3; Miles 11–2–34–3; Bresnan 9–5–11–1.

Umpires: N. J. Llong and N. A. Mallender. Referee: S. Cummings.

At Nottingham, September 21–24. YORKSHIRE lost to NOTTINGHAMSHIRE by five wickets.

VITALITY BLAST IN 2021

Nick Friend

1 Kent   2 Somerset   3= Hampshire, Sussex

As so often, another county season finished with Darren Stevens at its centre. Now aged 45, he claimed his third T20 title – his first since 2007 – as Kent came out on top after a frenetic finals day. The eerie tranquillity 12 months earlier of a campaign conducted behind closed doors was long gone, and Edgbaston's sense of carnival had returned.

For the first time in the competition's history, the last four came from the same group, with Kent joined by Somerset, Hampshire and Sussex. It might easily have been otherwise: the quarter-finals were chaotic, dramatic affairs. Sussex, who reached the knockout stages for a fourth successive season but again ended without silverware, were indebted to a spectacular cameo from Rashid Khan. He hit 27 from nine balls against Yorkshire – in a game played at Durham's Riverside because Headingley was preparing for an England–India Test. Kent ought not to have had enough runs against Warwickshire, whose season included the discovery of batter Chris Benjamin and left-arm wrist-spinner Jake Lintott, both stars of The Hundred. Lancashire were armed with Liam Livingstone – the white-ball whacker of the summer – but found themselves outhit when Somerset overhauled a target of 185 with time to spare. And in one of the all-time-great Blast matches, Hampshire defended 125 against reigning champions Nottinghamshire, who crumbled in front of the TV cameras.

After 2020's pared-down format had meant three groups of six for the first time since 2013 – a pandemic-induced decision – the Blast reverted to its two-pool system, with the South Group providing the four semi-finalists. Kent, the eventual champions, might have improved on nine group wins had a Covid outbreak not forced them to select an emergency XI for their last two. Even so, they beat Middlesex when their T20 debutant left-arm spinner Elliot Hooper snatched three wickets, and was named Player of the Match. Kent also drafted in Scottish internationals George Munsey, Calum MacLeod and Safyaan Sharif. All told, Sam Billings's men fielded 25 players, including Jordan Cox, who shone in the final with a counter-attacking half-century and an astonishing piece of boundary fielding to provide a catch for Matt Milnes, the tournament's second-leading wicket-taker, with 22.

He finished four behind Leicestershire's Afghan seamer, Naveen-ul-Haq, whose success was a strong nod to the county's recruitment policy. They also brought in Australian wicketkeeper-batter Josh Inglis, who made hundreds against Northamptonshire and Worcestershire, and hit 531 runs – more than anyone else – at a strike-rate of 175. But Paul Nixon's team, a decade on from the last of their three titles, failed to qualify from the North Group. Behind Inglis in the list of run-scorers was New Zealand's Glenn Phillips; on two successive days, he made 94 not out for Gloucestershire, though they

At his peak: Samit Patel was the most economical of any bowler to take 15 wickets; he also hit 309 runs at a healthy lick, and held seven catches.

couldn't replicate their 2020 run to the knockouts; his 36 sixes were 12 clear of the field.

The leading homegrown batters – by weight of runs – were Kent's Daniel Bell-Drummond and Yorkshire's Harry Brook. Meanwhile, Hampshire's Joe Weatherley enjoyed much his most profitable T20 season, but his 71 could not prevent a thrilling Somerset win in the semi-finals. For Sussex, the tournament marked the end of an era: in the semi-final defeat by Kent, Chris Jordan and Phil Salt made their last appearances. Salt headed for Lancashire, and Jordan rejoined Surrey – two more high-profile departures from Hove. But Sussex also brought in youth: Archie Lenham, the third generation of his family to represent them, became the second-youngest debutant in the competition's history, after Hamidullah Qadri, and the first born after the inaugural Twenty20 Cup to take part. Indeed, Stevens had claimed his first T20 crown in 2004, a fortnight after Lenham's birth: 17 years on, they were on opposite sides at Edgbaston. Experience won.

Stevens was not the only veteran to prosper. Samit Patel became just the sixth player (after Dwayne Bravo, Dan Christian, Andre Russell, Kieron Pollard and Shakib Al Hasan) to combine 5,000 runs and 250 wickets in T20 cricket. Patel might have added to his figures, had Nottinghamshire not imploded with finals day in sight. Their juggernaut victory in 2020 seemed to have put to bed any doubts over their big-game mettle, after letting slip a winning position in the 2019 semi-final. But Christian, who had inspired the previous year's triumph, was unexpectedly recalled by Australia, and missed the entire tournament. Not that Nottinghamshire appeared especially weakened until the quarter-final collapse against Hampshire, when they plummeted from

66 for one to 123 all out, three short of victory. Though dripping in frustration, they could look back with satisfaction at the signing of leg-spinner Calvin Harrison, briefly of Hampshire. He took 20 wickets in 15 games – more than any other slow bowler. Likewise, they claimed the most points in the group stage, despite ties against Worcestershire, Lancashire and Derbyshire.

For Derbyshire, things ended in anticlimax, with positive Covid cases causing the cancellation of their last games, against Northamptonshire and Yorkshire. Luckily, there was little riding on them in terms of qualification, but the North Group was determined on a points-per-game basis. Derbyshire's all-round season of misery was possibly tempered by a rare piece of silverware: James Farnsworth – dressed as Freddie the Falcon – became just the second person to retain the mascot race.

The 2021 Blast also had a small influence on The Hundred, its upstart young sibling. The wildcard draft allowed each franchise to pick a player – supposedly based on T20 performances – to add to their roster. Seamers Blake Cullen and Sam Cook were two such beneficiaries: they picked up 20 wickets apiece for Middlesex and Essex, neither of whom seriously challenged for a knockout place. The 2022 Blast will be played in a single block, with finals day on July 16 – back to midsummer for the first time since Middlesex won at Southampton in 2008. Perhaps that will reduce no-results. While only three occurred in the North Group, there were ten in the South, half of which blighted Sussex's season. The sun shone in neighbouring Kent – and even in Birmingham, after dark.

FINAL GROUP TABLES

	North Group	P	W	L	T	NR	Pts	Avge pts	NRR
1	NOTTINGHAMSHIRE	14	9	2	3	0	21	1.50	1.50
2	YORKSHIRE............	13	7	5	0	1	15	1.15	0.30
3	LANCASHIRE...........	14	7	5	1	1	16	1.14	0.20
4	WARWICKSHIRE........	14	7	6	0	1	15	1.07	0.00
5	Worcestershire	14	6	6	1	1	14	1.00	−0.62
6	Leicestershire	14	6	8	0	0	12	0.85	−0.01
7	Durham...............	14	5	8	0	1	11	0.78	−0.22
8	Derbyshire	12	4	7	1	0	9	0.75	−0.32
9	Northamptonshire.......	13	4	8	0	1	9	0.69	−0.87

Derbyshire's last two matches were cancelled because of a positive Covid test within their team; no points were awarded for these games. Rankings in the North Group were decided by average points per match.

	South Group	P	W	L	T	NR	Pts	NRR
1	KENT..................	14	9	4	0	1	19	0.65
2	SOMERSET.............	14	8	4	0	2	18	0.37
3	SUSSEX...............	14	6	3	0	5	17	0.47
4	HAMPSHIRE...........	14	6	5	0	3	15	0.38
5	Surrey	14	6	5	0	3	15	0.33
6	Gloucestershire........	14	6	6	0	2	14	0.20
7	Essex.................	14	5	8	0	1	11	−0.46
8	Middlesex	14	4	9	0	1	9	−0.38
9	Glamorgan	14	3	9	0	2	8	−1.37

Prize money

£270,000 for winners: KENT.
£120,000 for runners-up: SOMERSET.
£33,000 for losing semi-finalists: HAMPSHIRE and SUSSEX.
£7,500 for losing quarter-finalists: LANCASHIRE, NOTTINGHAMSHIRE, WARWICKSHIRE and YORKSHIRE.
Match-award winners received: £2,500 in the final, £1,000 in the semi-finals, £500 in the quarters, and £225 in group games. The Most Valuable Player (Samit Patel of Nottinghamshire) received £2,500.

VITALITY BLAST AVERAGES

BATTING (300 runs)

		M	I	NO	R	HS	100	50	Avge	SR	4	6
1	J. M. Clarke (*Notts*)	12	12	1	408	136	1	1	37.09	**180.53**	36	23
2	A. D. Hales (*Notts*)	15	15	4	482	101*	1	2	43.81	**178.51**	61	23
3	J. P. Inglis (*Leics*)	14	14	3	531	118*	2	1	48.27	**175.82**	63	24
4	†L. M. Reece (*Derbys*)	12	12	0	351	59	0	4	29.25	**171.21**	37	18
5	W. G. Jacks (*Surrey*)	12	1	393	87	0	3	35.72	**170.12**	50	17	
6	G. D. Phillips (*Glos*)	12	12	3	500	94*	0	3	55.55	**163.39**	30	36
7	F. H. Allen (*Lancs*)	13	13	1	399	73*	0	4	33.25	**159.60**	43	15
8	†B. M. Duckett (*Notts*)	13	12	1	383	74*	0	3	34.81	**158.26**	47	10
9	D. J. Bell-Drummond (*Kent*) .	14	14	1	492	88	0	6	37.84	**155.69**	38	20
10	L. J. Wright (*Sussex*)	11	10	1	370	77	0	4	41.11	**151.63**	46	10
11	Z. Crawley (*Kent*)	12	12	0	380	69	0	1	31.66	**150.79**	39	14
12	H. C. Brook (*Yorks*)	13	13	6	486	91*	0	2	69.42	**149.07**	41	20
13	A. M. Lilley (*Leics*)	14	14	1	351	99*	0	1	27.00	**148.72**	32	18
14	P. D. Salt (*Sussex*)	12	11	2	302	77*	0	3	33.55	**147.31**	31	12
	D. L. Lloyd (*Glam*)	12	12	0	302	52	0	2	25.16	**147.31**	31	15
16	J. M. Cox (*Kent*)	14	12	5	367	64	0	3	52.42	**142.24**	25	10
17	J. J. Weatherley (*Hants*) . . .	13	13	2	410	71	0	2	37.27	**141.86**	23	20
18	M. Labuschagne (*Glam*) . . .	8	8	1	390	93*	0	4	55.71	**140.79**	35	11
19	S. S. Eskinazi (*Middx*)	11	11	2	399	102*	1	3	44.33	**140.49**	51	5
20	S. R. Hain (*Warwicks*)	14	13	3	398	83*	0	4	39.80	**139.16**	27	11
21	†D. J. M. Short (*Hants*)	12	12	0	316	69	0	1	26.33	**138.59**	38	12
22	J. M. Vince (*Hants*)	12	12	0	373	102	1	1	31.08	**135.63**	50	6
23	W. C. F. Smeed (*Somerset*) . .	14	13	1	385	63*	0	3	32.08	**132.30**	34	19
24	M. H. Wessels (*Worcs*)	11	11	0	300	77	0	3	27.27	**132.15**	33	6
25	S. R. Patel (*Notts*)	15	13	3	309	64*	0	2	30.90	**131.48**	28	11
26	†J. L. du Plooy (*Derbys*) . . .	12	12	2	395	92	0	3	39.50	**131.22**	26	14
27	J. A. Leaning (*Kent*)	14	13	2	321	81*	0	3	29.18	**131.02**	20	13
28	B. L. D'Oliveira (*Worcs*) . .	13	13	1	358	69	0	3	29.83	**130.18**	37	8
29	S. R. Dickson (*Durham*) . . .	11	11	2	318	53	0	2	35.33	**128.22**	23	7
30	R. I. Keogh (*Northants*)	12	12	5	347	56	0	3	49.57	**125.72**	22	8
31	†D. P. Conway (*Somerset*) . .	8	8	3	309	81*	0	4	61.80	**125.60**	41	2
32	†R. S. Vasconcelos (*Nhants*) .	12	12	1	364	78*	0	2	33.09	**117.79**	44	4
33	S. Steel (*Leics*)	12	12	1	304	54*	0	2	27.63	**108.96**	22	7
34	J. D. Libby (*Worcs*)	13	13	3	315	78*	0	2	31.50	**108.24**	20	1

BOWLING (15 wickets)

		Style	Balls	Dots	R	W	BB	4i	Avge	SR	ER
1	S. R. Patel (*Notts*)	SLA	312	116	345	16	3-4	0	21.56	19.50	**6.63**
2	C. G. Harrison (*Notts*)	LB	246	74	278	20	4-17	2	13.90	12.30	**6.78**
3	M. Carter (*Notts*)	OB	318	103	372	18	3-17	0	20.66	17.66	**7.01**
4	D. R. Briggs (*Warwicks*) . . .	SLA	311	99	365	15	3-35	0	24.33	20.73	**7.04**
5	J. B. Lintott (*Warwicks*)	SLW	258	68	304	15	4-20	1	20.26	17.20	**7.06**
6	S. R. Harmer (*Essex*)	OB	282	89	348	19	4-24	2	18.31	14.84	**7.40**
7	N. A. Sowter (*Middx*)	LB	240	84	300	15	3-13	0	20.00	16.00	**7.50**
8	C. F. Parkinson (*Leics*)	SLA	336	116	421	18	4-35	1	23.38	18.66	**7.51**

		Style	Balls	Dots	R	W	BB	4i	Avge	SR	ER
9	M. S. Crane (*Hants*)	LB	294	102	382	16	3-23	0	23.87	18.37	**7.79**
10	S. J. Cook (*Essex*)	RFM	280	105	365	20	4-15	1	18.25	14.00	**7.82**
11	B. T. J. Wheal (*Hants*)	RFM	270	99	354	17	3-39	0	20.82	15.88	**7.86**
12	S. W. Currie (*Hants*)	RFM	186	65	244	19	4-24	2	12.84	9.78	**7.87**
13	T. S. Mills (*Sussex*)	LF	180	73	240	17	3-20	0	14.11	10.58	**8.00**
14	M. E. Milnes (*Kent*)	RFM	254	89	339	22	5-22	2	15.40	11.54	**8.00**
15	B. A. C. Howell (*Glos*)	RFM	260	68	351	15	4-15	1	23.40	17.33	**8.10**
16	G. G. White (*Northants*) . . .	SLA	262	74	355	15	4-26	1	23.66	17.46	**8.12**
17	C. R. Brathwaite (*Warwicks*) .	RFM	233	90	317	18	3-7	0	17.61	12.94	**8.16**
18	C. N. Miles (*Warwicks*) . . .	RFM	282	97	387	15	3-19	0	25.80	18.80	**8.23**
19	A. A. P. Atkinson (*Surrey*) . . .	RFM	160	46	223	15	4-36	2	14.86	10.66	**8.36**
20	D. A. Douthwaite (*Glam*) . .	RFM	208	77	294	15	3-28	0	19.60	13.86	**8.48**
21	M. de Lange (*Somerset*) . . .	RF	288	84	409	18	3-18	0	22.72	16.00	**8.52**
22	F. J. Klaassen (*Kent*)	LFM	259	87	373	19	4-17	2	19.63	13.63	**8.64**
23	Naveen-ul-Haq (*Leics*)	RFM	316	119	457	26	3-26	0	17.57	12.15	**8.67**
24	B. C. Cullen (*Middx*)	RFM	223	87	327	20	4-32	2	16.35	11.15	**8.79**
25	T. T. Bresnan (*Warwicks*) . . .	RFM	189	60	280	16	4-26	1	17.50	11.81	**8.88**
26	B. J. Dwarshuis (*Worcs*) . . .	LFM	282	106	419	15	4-31	1	27.93	18.80	**8.91**
27	S. T. Finn (*Middx*)	RFM	277	95	414	19	4-19	1	21.78	14.57	**8.96**
28	M. J. Potts (*Durham*)	RFM	278	93	424	16	3-27	0	26.50	17.37	**9.15**
29	J. T. Ball (*Notts*)	RFM	178	62	278	18	4-11	1	15.44	9.88	**9.37**
30	C. A. J. Morris (*Worcs*)	RFM	251	77	398	17	3-21	0	23.41	14.76	**9.51**
31	F. Hudson-Prentice (*Derbys*) .	RFM	204	72	325	16	3-36	0	20.31	12.75	**9.55**
32	L. V. van Beek (*Derbys*) . . .	RFM	221	84	361	16	3-22	0	22.56	13.81	**9.80**

LEADING WICKETKEEPERS

Dismissals	M		Dismissals	M	
18 (12ct, 6st)	13	L. D. McManus (*Hants*)	11 (10ct, 1st)	12	B. D. Guest (*Derbys*)
12 (7ct, 5st)	10	A. J. A. Wheater (*Essex*)	11 (5ct, 6st)	13	T. J. Moores (*Notts*)
12 (7ct, 5st)	12	J. A. Simpson (*Middx*)	10 (9ct, 1st)	11	C. B. Cooke (*Glam*)
11 (8ct, 3st)	10	T. Banton (*Somerset*)	10 (4ct, 6st)	14	M. G. K. Burgess (*Warwicks*)

J. M. Cox (Kent) made three catches and two stumpings in five matches as wicketkeeper, in addition to ten catches in nine when not keeping wicket.

LEADING FIELDERS

Ct	M		Ct	M	
13	14	A. M. Lilley (*Leics*)	12	14	J. A. Leaning (*Kent*)
13	15	S. J. Mullaney (*Notts*)	11	14	J. M. Vince (*Hants*)
12	10	A. J. Blake (*Kent*)	11	14	S. R. Hain (*Warwicks*)
12	13	A. Lyth (*Yorks*)			

NORTH GROUP

DERBYSHIRE

At Derby, June 13. **Warwickshire won by three wickets.** ‡Derbyshire **160-8** (20 overs) (F. J. Hudson-Prentice 41); **Warwickshire 161-7** (19 overs) (D. R. Mousley 56). *PoM: D. R. Mousley. Attendance: 516. Derbyshire were 84-5 before Fynn Hudson-Prentice's 22-ball 41 helped them finish on 160. Despite Dan Mousley's second T20 fifty, the contest was still in the balance when Warwickshire were 129-6, needing 32 off 19. But Carlos Brathwaite (16 off ten) and – in his first appearance of the season – Chris Woakes (13* off five) showed their international class.*

At Derby, June 15 (floodlit). **Lancashire won by seven wickets.** ‡Derbyshire **196-5** (20 overs) (H. R. C. Came 56, J. L. du Plooy 92; T. E. Bailey 3-34); **Lancashire 197-3** (18.2 overs) (L. S. Livingstone 45, A. L. Davies 83*, D. J. Vilas 40*). *PoM: A. L. Davies. Attendance: 558. No team had ever scored as many as 197 chasing at Derby, so the home side could feel confident after Harry*

Came, with his first fifty for Derbyshire, and Leus du Plooy, a career-best 92 in 56, shared a third-wicket century stand. Lancashire lost Finn Allen first ball, but coasted to victory thanks to Alex Davies (83* in 54), supported by Liam Livingstone and Dane Vilas.

At Derby, June 17 (floodlit). **Derbyshire won by five wickets.** ‡**Northamptonshire 141-8** (20 overs) (R. S. Vasconcelos 38, G. G. White 37); **Derbyshire 143-5** (18.2 overs) (J. L. du Plooy 48*, M. J. J. Critchley 41). *PoM:* J. L. du Plooy. *County debut:* Mohammad Nabi (Northamptonshire). *Attendance:* 660. Northamptonshire struggled to 51-5 in nine overs, and were then squeezed by seamer George Scrimshaw, who bowled straight through his stint for 24–15–31–1, before a flurry brought 41 in the last three. Du Plooy and Matt Critchley kept Derbyshire's pursuit of 142 straightforward: their fourth-wicket stand of 81 reduced the target to 14 off 23.

At Derby, June 22 (floodlit). **Leicestershire won by 42 runs. Leicestershire 174-8** (20 overs) (S. Steel 46, C. N. Ackermann 37, L. P. J. Kimber 53; F. J. Hudson-Prentice 3-36); ‡**Derbyshire 132** (18.4 overs) (H. R. C. Came 40). *PoM:* L. P. J. Kimber. *Attendance:* 747. A maiden T20 fifty from Louis Kimber revived Leicestershire from 80-5; they smashed 47 off their last three overs. In contrast, Derbyshire began strongly, with Came scoring 40 out of 60-0 from seven, but melted away: the next 11.4 brought 72-10. The following day, it was announced Critchley would replace Billy Godleman as captain for the rest of the tournament.

At Derby, June 25 (floodlit). **Tied. Nottinghamshire 137-9** (20 overs) (J. M. Clarke 36; M. H. McKiernan 3-9); ‡**Derbyshire 137-9** (20 overs) (L. M. Reece 51). *PoM:* M. J. J. Critchley. *Attendance:* 767. Derbyshire needed ten off 14 balls, with five wickets in hand, for their first T20 win over Nottinghamshire in six years. Then Calvin Harrison and Luke Fletcher grabbed four for one to turn the contest on its head. Critchley needed five off Harrison's final delivery: he drove to long-on, where he was dropped by Sol Budinger, and the ball dribbled over the boundary for Nottinghamshire's third tie of the season. Earlier, Matt Carter and Jake Ball put on a club-record 27* for their last wicket.

At Derby, July 2 (floodlit). **Worcestershire won by 14 runs.** ‡**Worcestershire 167-6** (20 overs) (B. L. D'Oliveira 43, O. B. Cox 30, R. A. Whiteley 37; J. W. Dernbach 3-23); **Derbyshire 153-8** (20 overs) (L. M. Reece 39, T. A. Wood 46; C. A. J. Morris 3-21). *PoM:* B. L. D'Oliveira. *County debut:* J. W. Dernbach (Derbyshire). *Attendance:* 750. Brett D'Oliveira and Ross Whiteley set up a challenging target, despite three wickets from Jade Dernbach – replacing his Surrey colleague Conor McKerr on loan to Derbyshire. The home side were marginally ahead on the powerplay, but their later batting lacked poise, and Tom Wood deserved better support. When Daryl Mitchell had du Plooy caught behind, he became the first to take 100 T20 wickets for Worcestershire.

At Derby, July 18. **Derbyshire v Yorkshire. Cancelled.** *A positive Covid test in the Derbyshire camp a week earlier, following their win at Durham, required the full first-team squad to self-isolate, forcing the cancellation of their last two Blast games, and a Championship match against Essex.*

Derbyshire away matches

June 9: lost to Lancashire by six wickets.
June 11: beat Leicestershire by 23 runs.
June 18: lost to Nottinghamshire by two runs.
June 20: lost to Yorkshire by 39 runs.

June 24: beat Warwickshire by five wickets.
July 9: beat Durham by six wickets.
July 16: cancelled v Northamptonshire.

DURHAM

At Chester-le-Street, June 11 (floodlit). **Durham won by 20 runs. Durham 181-8** (20 overs) (G. Clark 34, B. A. Carse 51; J. A. Thompson 4-44); ‡**Yorkshire 161-6** (20 overs) (J. M. Bairstow 67, H. C. Brook 41). *PoM:* B. A. Carse. *Attendance:* 3,892. Brydon Carse gave Durham a winning start with his maiden T20 fifty, against a strong Yorkshire. Coming in at 95-6, he lifted them to 181 with a brilliant 51 in 31 balls. There were solid efforts from Jonny Bairstow and Harry Brook, but Carse bowled Bairstow, then caught Brook off a skyer, and the visitors came up short.

At Chester-le-Street, June 15 (floodlit). **Nottinghamshire won by 13 runs.** ‡**Nottinghamshire 195-5** (20 overs) (A. D. Hales 96*, B. M. Duckett 52); **Durham 182-8** (20 overs) (D. G. Bedingham 65, G. Clark 39; M. Carter 3-43). *PoM:* A. D. Hales. *Attendance:* 2,866. Alex Hales blasted 96* from 54 balls and put on 126 for Nottinghamshire's third wicket with Ben Duckett, propelling them towards an imposing 195. Undaunted, David Bedingham and Graham Clark opened with 73 – before Durham lost three wickets in eight deliveries, two to Matt Carter's off-spin, and the chase wilted.

At Chester-le-Street, June 17 (floodlit). **Durham won by six wickets.** ‡**Lancashire 151-6** (20 overs) (L. S. Livingstone 65; M. J. Potts 3-34); **Durham 153-4** (17.4 overs) (D. G. Bedingham 58). *PoM:* D. G. Bedingham. *Attendance:* 2,541. *Bedingham and Clark shared another powerful opening stand, of 76 – and this time it led to a comfortable victory. Bedingham's 39-ball 58, with three sixes, gave the middle order plenty of time to whittle down the target. Earlier, Matty Potts had shackled Lancashire's potent line-up with three wickets, including Liam Livingstone for a forceful 65.*

At Chester-le-Street, June 20. **Durham won by 22 runs.** ‡**Durham 185-4** (20 overs) (C. T. Bancroft 76*, S. R. Dickson 30); **Warwickshire 163-8** (20 overs) (W. M. H. Rhodes 36, S. R. Hain 35; B. A. Carse 3-30). *PoM:* C. T. Bancroft. *County debut:* J. G. Bethell (Warwickshire). *Attendance:* 3,044. *Ben Stokes scored a rapid 29, took a wicket and held two catches in his first game for Durham in nearly three years – and his first for any side since breaking his finger at the IPL in April. But two colleagues took centre-stage. Cameron Bancroft hit 76*, his first T20 half-century for Durham, to steer them to a competitive 185. Then Carse claimed a career-best 3-30 to stymie Warwickshire's charge.*

At Chester-le-Street, June 23 (floodlit). **Northamptonshire won by nine wickets.** ‡**Durham 157-5** (20 overs) (S. R. Dickson 51*); **Northamptonshire 158-1** (17.5 overs) (R. S. Vasconcelos 78*, A. M. Rossington 59). *PoM:* A. M. Rossington. *County debut:* F. J. Heldreich (Northamptonshire). *Attendance:* 3,991. *A record Northamptonshire opening stand – 125 in 13.3 overs – brought their first T20 win of the summer. Ricardo Vasconcelos's 78* was his highest score in the format, while Rossington's aggressive 59 off 38 put Durham on the back foot. Bedingham had fallen to the second ball of the match, and it took Sean Dickson's maiden T20 fifty to set any sort of target.*

At Chester-le-Street, July 2 (floodlit). **Leicestershire won by eight wickets** (DLS). **Durham 115-4** (15.1 overs) (G. Clark 40, S. R. Dickson 35*); ‡**Leicestershire 88-2** (8.2 overs) (J. P. Inglis 35*, C. N. Ackermann 36*). *PoM:* C. N. Ackermann. *Attendance:* 3,142. *Afghan seamer Naveen-ul-Haq removed Stokes and Bancroft in his first over to reduce Durham to 25-3, though they fought back to 115-4 before rain curtailed the innings. Leicestershire's target was revised to 88 in nine overs; after an early wobble, Josh Inglis and Colin Ackermann put Durham to the sword.*

At Chester-le-Street, July 9 (floodlit). **Derbyshire won by six wickets. Durham 176-9** (20 overs) (B. A. Raine 32, S. R. Dickson 37, S. G. Borthwick 33; A. T. Thomson 3-23); ‡**Derbyshire 180-4** (20 overs) (T. A. Wood 32, J. L. du Plooy 47, M. J. J. Critchley 33*, B. D. Guest 34*). *PoM:* M. J. J. Critchley. *County debuts:* L. Doneathy, P. A. van Meekeren (Durham). *Attendance:* 3,268. *Derbyshire arrived bottom of the table, but inflicted a third successive defeat on Durham when Brooke Guest slammed Ben Raine to the rope off the final ball. Dickson and Scott Borthwick had guided Durham to a defendable 176, and the game looked to be in their hands when 18-year-old Luke Doneathy bowled Leus du Plooy, leaving the visitors to get 61 off six overs. But Guest and Matt Critchley kept their composure.*

Durham away matches

June 13: beat Leicestershire by two wickets.
June 18: no result v Yorkshire.
June 25: lost to Worcestershire by eight wickets.
June 26: beat Warwickshire by 34 runs.

June 30: lost to Northamptonshire by 30 runs.
July 16: lost to Lancashire by six runs.
July 18: lost to Nottinghamshire by 78 runs.

LANCASHIRE

At Manchester, June 9. **Lancashire won by six wickets.** ‡**Derbyshire 168-7** (20 overs) (L. M. Reece 59, J. L. du Plooy 34; M. W. Parkinson 3-28); **Lancashire 171-4** (19.3 overs) (L. S. Livingstone 94*, J. C. Buttler 30). *PoM:* L. S. Livingstone. *County debuts:* F. H. Allen (Lancashire); A. T. Thomson (Derbyshire). *Attendance:* 2,462. *Covid-19 regulations allowed a maximum of 4,000 fans to watch the return of the Blast, and a healthy crowd saw Liam Livingstone bat through a T20 innings for the first time, securing a comfortable victory with his tenth over. He also hit two sixes in his 58-ball 94*, and shared fifty partnerships with New Zealand opener Finn Allen, Jos Buttler and Dane Vilas. Former Lancashire player Luis Reece (59 in 32) had helped Derbyshire to 168, despite three wickets from Matt Parkinson.*

At Manchester, June 10 (floodlit). **Lancashire won by 16 runs.** ‡**Lancashire 172-8** (20 overs) (F. H. Allen 73*, G. T. Griffiths 4-24); **Leicestershire 156-5** (20 overs) (S. Steel 54*, J. P. Inglis 34, R. K. Patel 32). *PoM:* F. H. Allen. *County debuts:* J. P. Inglis, Naveen-ul-Haq, S. Steel (Leicestershire). *Attendance:* 2,480. *Two more openers batted throughout their innings. Allen reached his first fifty* *for Lancashire and ensured a defendable target, despite a career-best 4-24 from Gavin Griffiths, who removed Livingstone and Alex Davies in a double-wicket maiden. Scott Steel anchored Leicestershire's steady pursuit, but slow left-armer Tom Hartley's four overs cost just 18.*

At Manchester, June 20. **Tied.** ‡**Nottinghamshire 172** (20 overs) (A. D. Hales 33, B. M. Duckett 35, T. J. Moores 48; D. J. Lamb 3-23); **Lancashire 172-4** (20 overs) (K. K. Jennings 88, F. H. Allen 60). *PoM:* K. K. Jennings. *Attendance:* 3,630. *The match was tied when Steven Mullaney's throw from extra cover dismissed Keaton Jennings, trying to complete a second run. Lancashire had been on course while Allen and Jennings were putting on 118 for the first wicket, though Samit Patel conceded only 14 singles and a four in 24 deliveries. Once he dismissed Allen, the innings stuttered. They needed eight off two balls, from Luke Fletcher: Jennings swung the first over midwicket for six, before being run out. Ben Duckett and Tom Moores had earlier set up a competitive 172 for Nottinghamshire, despite Danny Lamb's T20-best 3-23.*

At Manchester, July 1. **Lancashire won by 34 runs.** ‡**Lancashire 159-6** (20 overs) (K. K. Jennings 34, R. P. Jones 49*); **Worcestershire 125** (18.3 overs) (O. B. Cox 36; S. Mahmood 4-25, T. W. Hartley 4-16). *PoM:* R. P. Jones. *Attendance:* 1,840. *Lancashire were an indifferent 85-4 before Rob Jones took control, batting shrewdly on a used pitch for 49*, his highest T20 score. Chasing 160, Worcestershire were bowled out for 125, with four wickets apiece for Saqib Mahmood and Hartley: Mahmood topped and tailed the innings, while Hartley's career-best four-for included Riki Wessels and Ross Whiteley with successive deliveries in the tenth.*

At Manchester, July 9 (floodlit). **Lancashire won by eight wickets.** ‡**Northamptonshire 142-8** (20 overs) (L. J. Hurt 3-22); **Lancashire 144-2** (15.4 overs) (F. H. Allen 66, K. K. Jennings 54*). *PoM:* F. H. Allen. *Attendance:* 3,549. *Northamptonshire chose to bat, but started and ended poorly: they lost the openers in the first two overs, and four for 13 in the last three. In between, Rob Keogh held the innings together, despite a leg injury. Allen and Jennings responded with 112 in 11.2 overs, and Lancashire coasted home.*

At Manchester, July 16 (floodlit). **Lancashire won by six runs.** ‡**Lancashire 199-5** (20 overs) (F. H. Allen 66, K. K. Jennings 43, A. L. Davies 56); **Durham 193-5** (20 overs) (D. G. Bedingham 50, G. Clark 37, S. R. Dickson 53). *PoM:* A. L. Davies. *Attendance:* 3,872. *Lancashire scored 75 in their powerplay, thanks to Allen, whose fifty in 21 balls was one slower than Buttler's county record. He and Jennings put on 101, their third century group stand, and Davies maintained the momentum. Even so, a target of 200 looked achievable: Durham's own powerplay brought 78-0, with David Bedingham (50 in 24) playing the Allen role. Sean Dickson's 53 and Brydon Carse's 18-ball 29* kept the game alive, but 15 off the last proved too much, ruling them out of the quarter-finals.*

At Manchester, July 17 (floodlit). **Lancashire won by four wickets.** ‡**Yorkshire 128-7** (20 overs) (J. E. Root 32, G. S. Ballance 31; L. Wood 4-20); **Lancashire 131-6** (19 overs) (L. W. P. Wells 30). *PoM:* L. Wood. *Attendance:* 4,432. *Victory ensured a quarter-final for Lancashire, who ended the group phase unbeaten at home. It began to go wrong for Yorkshire when Vilas took a superb one-handed diving catch off Luke Wood's first delivery to remove Adam Lyth; Wood finished with a career-best 4-20. Lancashire needed only 129 but, after Allen and Jennings hurtled to 37 in 2.3 overs, they too struggled on a tricky pitch against a varied attack. Luke Wells joined Steven Croft to add 54, taking them within 11 of victory. Yorkshire and their acting-captain, Joe Root, were praised for declining to run out Croft when he collapsed mid-pitch with cramp.*

Lancashire away matches

June 13: lost to Worcestershire by eight wickets.
June 15: beat Derbyshire by seven wickets.
June 17: lost to Durham by six wickets.
June 18: no result v Warwickshire.
June 25: lost to Northants by seven wickets.
June 26: lost to Nottinghamshire by seven runs.
July 2: lost to Yorkshire by nine runs.

LEICESTERSHIRE

At Leicester, June 11 (floodlit). **Derbyshire won by 23 runs. Derbyshire 209-6** (20 overs) (L. M. Reece 51, M. J. J. Critchley 80*, A. L. Hughes 38; Naveen-ul-Haq 3-26); ‡**Leicestershire 186** (19 overs) (R. K. Patel 35; L. V. van Beek 3-37). *PoM:* M. J. J. Critchley. *County debut:* H. R. C. Came (Derbyshire). *Attendance:* 703. *All-rounders Matt Critchley (80* off 45) and Luis Reece (51 off 29) each thumped four sixes in a Derbyshire fifth-wicket record stand of 85; Afghan seamer*

Naveen-ul-Haq claimed three wickets on his home debut. Netherlands pacer Logan van Beek then took 3-37, and Critchley 2-31 with his leg-breaks, as Leicestershire succumbed to scoreboard pressure. Eight reached double figures, but none exceeded Rishi Patel's 35 off 20.

At Leicester, June 13. **Durham won by two wickets. ‡Leicestershire 168-9** (20 overs) (S. Steel 53, A. M. Lilley 31; M. J. Potts 3-27, B. A. Raine 3-19); **Durham 170-8** (19 overs) (D. G. Bedingham 38, E. J. H. Eckersley 50*, L. Trevaskis 30*; A. M. Lilley 3-26). *PoM:* E. J. H. Eckersley. *County debut:* L. P. J. Kimber (Leicestershire). *Attendance:* 714. *Defending 168-9, Leicestershire threw away apparently certain victory after Durham collapsed to 108-8, still requiring 61 from 40 balls. Former Leicestershire player Ned Eckersley (50* off 36) and Liam Trevaskis (30* off 20) did it with an over to spare. A calamitous 19th was begun by Naveen with Durham needing 23. Then came a missed catch, two beamers (one ramped for four), Naveen's withdrawal from the attack and six off the free hit, bowled by Ben Mike. A stand of 62* was Durham's highest for the ninth wicket.*

At Leicester, June 16 (floodlit). **Warwickshire won by 35 runs. Warwickshire 190-7** (20 overs) (W. M. H. Rhodes 79, S. R. Hain 45; B. W. M. Mike 4-22); **‡Leicestershire 155** (20 overs) (S. Steel 46, R. K. Patel 30; D. R. Briggs 3-35, T. T. Bresnan 3-29). *PoM:* W. M. H. Rhodes. *Attendance:* 729. *Warwickshire's fourth successive away win was facile, as Leicestershire appeared to lose confidence against the group leaders. Will Rhodes, with a career-best 79 off 40, and Sam Hain put on 114 for the third wicket; Hain passed Ian Bell's haul of 2,152 to become Warwickshire's highest T20 run-scorer. Though Mike, who also returned a career-best (4-22), and Naveen kept the target to 191, three wickets in the powerplay dragged Leicestershire's chase off course.*

At Leicester, June 25 (floodlit). **Leicestershire won by 34 runs. ‡Leicestershire 207-3** (20 overs) (S. Steel 32, A. M. Lilley 99*, C. N. Ackermann 40); **Yorkshire 173** (19.5 overs) (G. S. Ballance 34, H. C. Brook 33; C. F. Parkinson 4-35). *PoM:* A. M. Lilley. *Attendance:* 788. *Arron Lilley's career-best 99* off 55 gave Leicestershire a third straight win – and a chance of reaching the knockout stage. He hit four sixes, added 90 for the third wicket with Colin Ackermann, and would have made a century but for a short run earlier in his innings. Yorkshire, missing six players to England or injury, found 208 beyond them, and Callum Parkinson collected 4-35 as they buckled.*

99 NOT OUT IN T20s IN THE UK

<table>
<tr><td>S. M. Davies . .</td><td>Surrey (203-2) beat Sussex by 18 runs at Whitgift School, Croydon . . . . . .</td><td>2011</td></tr>
<tr><td>J. M. Vince . . .</td><td>Hampshire (187-4) beat Kent by six wickets at Canterbury . . . .</td><td>2015</td></tr>
<tr><td>J. L. Denly . . .</td><td>Kent (160-5) lost to Gloucestershire by eight wickets at Canterbury . . . . . .</td><td>2018</td></tr>
<tr><td>A. Balbirnie . . .</td><td>Glamorgan (188-4) beat Gloucestershire by 17 runs at Cardiff . . . .</td><td>2020</td></tr>
<tr><td>**A. M. Lilley** . .</td><td>**Leicestershire (207-3) beat Yorkshire by 34 runs at Leicester** . . . .</td><td>**2021**</td></tr>
</table>

Davies, Balbirnie and Lilley are yet to hit a Twenty20 hundred.

At Leicester, June 29 (floodlit). **Northamptonshire won by five wickets. ‡Leicestershire 138** (19.5 overs) (S. Steel 44, H. J. Swindells 32); **Northamptonshire 141-5** (18.2 overs) (R. S. Vasconcelos 30, R. I. Keogh 34*). *PoM:* F. J. Heldreich. *Attendance:* 621. *Northamptonshire's five spinners combined for seven wickets in 15 overs – and 19-year-old slow left-armer Freddie Heldreich (2-17) stood out. Harry Swindells hit three consecutive sixes off the pace of Wayne Parnell, but 138 proved insufficient. Rob Keogh anchored the chase, completed with ten balls to spare.*

At Leicester, July 16 (floodlit). **Leicestershire won by two wickets. Nottinghamshire 173** (19.2 overs) (J. M. Clarke 57, B. M. Duckett 45; Naveen-ul-Haq 3-33, C. N. Ackermann 3-35); **‡Leicestershire 177-8** (19.4 overs) (J. P. Inglis 42, A. M. Lilley 42; S. J. Mullaney 3-33). *PoM:* A. M. Lilley. *Attendance:* 788. *Nottinghamshire, top of the table and guaranteed a home quarter-final, suffered their second defeat, after failing to build on Joe Clarke's explosive 57 off 27. They were 110-2 after ten, but managed only 63 more. Josh Inglis (42 off 19) raced away in pursuit of 174, and Lilley, who held four catches and took 1-20 in a full spell, joint-top-scored. Leicestershire stuttered after both fell, but crawled over the line.*

At Leicester, July 18 (floodlit). **Leicestershire won by seven wickets. ‡Worcestershire 169-6** (20 overs) (J. D. Libby 35, R. A. Whiteley 31, E. G. Barnard 43*); **‡Leicestershire 171-3** (17.5 overs) (J. P. Inglis 118*). *PoM:* J. P. Inglis. *Attendance:* 762. *Inglis, dropped by Daryl Mitchell at extra cover on 14, made his second century of the tournament – and a career-best – as Leicestershire breezed past a target of 170. His 118* off 61 included ten sixes, was the club's highest innings, and* *made him the top run-scorer of the group stage (531). His stand of 111* with Swindells (22*) was also a club record for the fourth wicket. In the Worcestershire innings, Naveen's 2-32 had given him the corresponding bowling achievement (26), and Parkinson overtook Claude Henderson's tally of 69 as Leicestershire's leading wicket-taker in T20s. The result shut Worcestershire out of the quarter-finals, and put Warwickshire through.*

Leicestershire away matches

June 10: lost to Lancashire by 16 runs.
June 15: lost to Yorkshire by 18 runs.
June 20: beat Northamptonshire by 34 runs.
June 22: beat Derbyshire by 42 runs.

June 27: lost to Worcestershire by seven wickets.
July 1: lost to Nottinghamshire by six wickets.
July 2: beat Durham by eight wickets.

NORTHAMPTONSHIRE

At Northampton, June 11 (floodlit). **Worcestershire won by 32 runs. Worcestershire 185-7** (20 overs) (B. L. D'Oliveira 43, M. M. Ali 52; B. W. Sanderson 3-21, T. A. I. Taylor 3-33); ‡**Northamptonshire 153-9** (20 overs) (S. A. Zaib 36). *PoM:* M. M. Ali. *Attendance:* 939. *Brett D'Oliveira and Moeen Ali, who hit four sixes in his 30-ball 52, put Worcestershire on top in a second-wicket stand worth 94 in nine overs. Northamptonshire hit back, with seamers Ben Sanderson and Tom Taylor taking three-fors, but the batting stumbled. Levi departed to the first ball of the innings, and Ali (24–8–21–2) completed an outstanding performance by dismissing Wayne Parnell and Rob Keogh in successive overs.*

At Northampton, June 13 (floodlit). **Nottinghamshire won by 14 runs.** ‡**Nottinghamshire 214-7** (20 overs) (J. M. Clarke 136); **Northamptonshire 200-7** (20 overs) (J. J. Cobb 62, R. I. Keogh 45; J. T. Ball 3-58). *PoM:* J. M. Clarke. *Attendance:* 925. *Joe Clarke made Northamptonshire pay dearly for dropping him at mid-off on 29, hitting 11 sixes and six fours in an exquisite 96-ball 136, a Nottinghamshire record. The next-highest scorer was Peter Trego, with 24. Northamptonshire were in the hunt while Josh Cobb and Keogh were adding 104 in ten overs, but Cobb injured his hamstring, and later required a runner, which hampered the chase – as did Matt Carter's tidy off-spin. While every other bowler in the match conceded at least 7.50 an over, his four cost 15.*

T20 CENTURIES FOR NOTTINGHAMSHIRE

136	J. M. Clarke . .	v Northamptonshire at Northampton	2021
113*	D. T. Christian . .	v Northamptonshire at Northampton	2018
110	M. H. Wessels .	v Derbyshire at Nottingham	2017
101*	**A. D. Hales . . .**	**v Lancashire at Nottingham.**	**2021**
101	A. D. Hales . . .	v Yorkshire at Nottingham	2017
100*	J. M. Clarke . . .	v Durham at Chester-le-Street	2020

At Northampton, June 15 (floodlit). **Warwickshire won by 55 runs.** ‡**Warwickshire 170-3** (20 overs) (P. J. Malan 63, S. R. Hain 69*); **Northamptonshire 115** (18.5 overs) (R. S. Vasconcelos 36; J. B. Lintott 4-20). *PoM:* J. B. Lintott. *Attendance:* 913. *Warwickshire made light of losing Ed Pollock to the game's first ball and, thanks to Pieter Malan and Sam Hain, who together crashed 90 off 51 deliveries, reached a challenging 170. On a pitch used for the third time in five days, Northamptonshire reached 65-2 in the ninth, before losing three wickets in five balls, two to Jake Lintott's left-arm wrist-spin; he finished with a career-best 4-20. A last-wicket stand of 33 gave the score some respectability, but not much.*

At Northampton, June 20. **Leicestershire won by 34 runs.** ‡**Leicestershire 200-2** (20 overs) (J. P. Inglis 103*, A. M. Lilley 44, C. N. Ackermann 31*); **Northamptonshire 166-7** (20 overs) (R. E. Levi 30, Mohammad Nabi 32, R. I. Keogh 45*; J. P. Inglis). *PoM:* J. P. Inglis. *Attendance:* 986. *Neither side had won so far, and a brilliant, chanceless 62-ball 103* from Josh Inglis ensured it was Leicestershire who broke their duck. His century featured four sixes and 13 fours, while Arron Lilley – who survived a stumping chance on 12 – cleared the boundary three times. After Lilley fell for 44, Colin Ackermann helped Inglis add 101* in nine overs. Northamptonshire never looked likely to reach a target of 201, despite the efforts of Mohammad Nabi and Keogh.*

At Northampton, June 25 (floodlit). **Northamptonshire won by seven wickets. ‡Lancashire 130-7** (20 overs) (S. J. Croft 35*); **Northamptonshire 131-3** (18.2 overs) (R. S. Vasconcelos 41). *PoM:* Mohammad Nabi. *Attendance:* 965. *Nabi, whose four overs cost just 18, set the tone for a disciplined Northamptonshire performance in the field: Ricardo Vasconcelos pulled off a tough catch at midwicket, and there was a superb direct hit from Tom Taylor at long leg. Steven Croft and Danny Lamb (20 from 12) had steadied Lancashire from 81-5, but their total was well below par. Vasconcelos batted steadily, before a stand of 54* between Keogh and Nabi brought Northamptonshire a second successive victory.*

At Northampton, June 30 (floodlit). **Northamptonshire won by 30 runs. Northamptonshire 173-5** (20 overs) (R. S. Vasconcelos 60, B. J. Curran 62); **‡Durham 143** (20 overs) (S. R. Dickson 40, M. J. Potts 40*; G. G. White 4-26). *PoM:* B. J. Curran. *County debut:* H. M. Crawshaw (Durham). *Attendance:* 966. *Watched over the internet by brothers Tom and Sam in the England squad hotel, Ben Curran zoomed to a 19-ball half-century. The last of four successive fours off Ben Stokes took him past 50 inside the powerplay, and he shared an opening stand of 101 with Vasconcelos. Durham exerted some control at the end of the Northamptonshire innings, only to crumble to 11-4 in reply; they never properly recovered. Left-arm spinner Graeme White claimed his 74th T20 wicket – passing David Willey's Northamptonshire record – when he dismissed Eckersley, and took two more.*

At Northampton, July 16 (floodlit). **Northamptonshire v Derbyshire. Cancelled.** *This match was called off because of a Covid outbreak in the Derbyshire squad.*

Northamptonshire away matches

June 17: lost to Derbyshire by five wickets.
June 18: no result v Worcestershire.
June 23: beat Durham by nine wickets.
June 26: lost to Yorkshire by 82 runs.

June 29: beat Leicestershire by five wickets.
July 9: lost to Lancashire by eight wickets.
July 18: lost to Warwickshire by 14 runs.

NOTTINGHAMSHIRE

At Nottingham, June 11 (floodlit). **Warwickshire won by 18 runs. Warwickshire 229-5** (20 overs) (A. J. Hose 32, E. J. Pollock 62, S. R. Hain 53*, C. R. Brathwaite 44); **‡Nottinghamshire 211-9** (20 overs) (B. M. Duckett 51, T. J. Moores 38). *PoM:* C. R. Brathwaite. *Attendance:* 3,915. *Ed Pollock (62 off 34 balls), Sam Hain (53* off 28) and Carlos Brathwaite (44 off 18) helped Warwickshire reach the highest total conceded by Nottinghamshire, and a Trent Bridge record. They plundered 95 off the last six overs, with Brathwaite thumping Peter Trego for four sixes and a four in the 19th. Ben Duckett's 27-ball 51 kept Nottinghamshire in it, but his team-mates could not match their opponents' late explosion.*

At Nottingham, June 18 (floodlit). **Nottinghamshire won by two runs. Nottinghamshire 152-6** (15 overs) (B. M. Duckett 38, S. R. Patel 64*; L. V. van Beek 3-22, G. L. S. Scrimshaw 3-36); **‡Derbyshire 150-6** (15 overs) (L. M. Reece 56, L. du Ploy 58*). *PoM:* S. R. Patel. *County debut:* S. G. Budinger (Nottinghamshire). *Attendance:* 3,592. *On a day so wet that six of the eight Blast games were abandoned, Nottinghamshire did well to stage a match of 15 overs a side. Samit Patel inspired their narrow win: his 32-ball 64* was the game's highest score, and his 2-14 made him the first English player to combine 250 T20 wickets with 5,000 runs. For Derbyshire, Luis Reece and Leus du Ploy hit fifties, but 20 off the final over was just too much.*

At Nottingham, June 22 (floodlit). **Nottinghamshire won by ten wickets. Worcestershire 86-8** (20 overs) (S. R. Patel 3-4; J. T. Ball 3-17); **‡Nottinghamshire 89-0** (6.2 overs) (A. D. Hales 60*). *PoM:* S. R. Patel. *Attendance:* 3,144. *It was another record-breaking day for Patel. An analysis of 3-4 was English T20 cricket's most economical four-over spell, and made him the second to take 100 T20 wickets at a single ground, after Shakib Al Hasan at Mirpur. Worcestershire limped to 86 in 20 overs, and Nottinghamshire won in 6.2 overs, with Alex Hales smashing 60* off 24. The 82 balls remaining were a domestic record for an unshortened match, surpassing 75, when Hampshire beat Gloucestershire at Bristol in 2010.*

At Nottingham, June 26. **Nottinghamshire won by seven wickets. Nottinghamshire 173-6** (20 overs) (A. D. Hales 101*); **‡Lancashire 166-7** (20 overs) (A. L. Davies 39, S. J. Croft 41, L. Wood 33*; M. Carter 3-17). *PoM:* A. D. Hales. *Attendance:* 4,242. *Hales's run-spree continued with 101* off 66, his fifth T20 century – and second for Nottinghamshire. Though his only meaningful support* *came from Steven Mullaney (25), they had a total they could defend. For Lancashire, Alex Davies hit five of his 15 balls for six, but became one of three victims for tall off-spinner Matt Carter, who like team-mate Calvin Harrison conceded less than a run a ball.*

At Nottingham, July 1. **Nottinghamshire won by six wickets. Leicestershire 154** (20 overs) (H. J. Swindells 36; L. J. Fletcher 3-31, C. G. Harrison 3-20); ‡**Nottinghamshire 156-4** (17.5 overs) (B. T. Slater 48, S. R. Patel 63*). *PoM:* S. R. Patel. *Attendance:* 4,051. *Nottinghamshire strengthened their position with a sixth win. Ben Slater, brought in for his first T20 match since 2018 because three players were ill or self-isolating, hit 48 in 31 balls to back up Patel's 63*; he was dropped once, and Patel twice. Earlier, Harrison's career-best 3-20 helped dismiss Leicestershire for 154.*

At Nottingham, July 9 (floodlit). **Nottinghamshire won by ten wickets.** ‡**Yorkshire 60-3** (7 overs); **Nottinghamshire 65-0** (3.4 overs) (A. D. Hales 31*). *PoM:* S. R. Patel. *Attendance:* 4,169. *A match limited to seven overs a side by rain produced Nottinghamshire's second ten-wicket win of the season, and secured a home quarter-final. They took 22 deliveries to overhaul Yorkshire's 60-3. Hales hit four of his last five balls for six – one from Matthew Fisher, four from Josh Poysden.*

At Nottingham, July 18 (floodlit). **Nottinghamshire won by 78 runs. Nottinghamshire 221-4** (20 overs) (A. D. Hales 35, B. M. Duckett 74*, S. R. Patel 34, S. J. Mullaney 43*); ‡**Durham 143** (16 overs) (M. J. Potts 30; C. G. Harrison 4-36). *PoM:* B. M. Duckett. *Attendance:* 3,950. *Nottinghamshire completed the group stage with nine wins after piling up 221-4: Duckett scored 74* from 41, and Mullaney 43* from 17. Durham's Brydon Carse needed stitches after a Hales drive struck him on the ear as he followed through; Luke Doneathy replaced him, as a concussion substitute, and was last out as Durham surrendered in 16 overs. Harrison's 4-36 gave him 18 wickets, level with Jake Ball (now with England) as Nottinghamshire's leading T20 bowlers.*

Nottinghamshire away matches

June 9: tied with Worcestershire.
June 13: beat Northamptonshire by 14 runs.
June 15: beat Durham by 13 runs.
June 20: tied with Lancashire.

June 25: tied with Derbyshire.
July 2: beat Warwickshire by 114 runs.
July 16: lost to Leicestershire by two wickets.

WARWICKSHIRE

At Birmingham, June 18 (floodlit). **Warwickshire v Lancashire. Abandoned.**

At Birmingham, June 24 (floodlit). **Derbyshire won by five wickets. Warwickshire 167-9** (20 overs) (E. J. Pollock 46, M. G. K. Burgess 41, T. T. Bresnan 34*; G. L. S. Scrimshaw 3-23); ‡**Derbyshire 170-5** (19.1 overs) (T. A. Wood 63*, J. L. du Plooy 57). *PoM:* J. L. du Plooy. *A post-match pitch invasion by several hundred students marred Derbyshire's first win at Edgbaston in ten years. Around a third of the 6,000 spectators had been lured from local universities by the prospect of cheap alcohol, and evidently took the event's title – "Invades Edgbaston" – too literally. Warwickshire's chief executive, Stuart Cain, described the incident as disgraceful, and promised a life ban for identifiable offenders. Tom Wood, with his second successive half-century (63* off 48), and Leus du Plooy (57 off 34) led Derbyshire's chase of 168 with a stand of 90 in ten overs.*

At Birmingham, June 26. **Durham won by 34 runs. Durham 164-8** (20 overs) (B. A. Stokes 35, C. T. Bancroft 60; C. R. Brathwaite 3-32); ‡**Warwickshire 130** (18.3 overs) (W. M. H. Rhodes 45, M. J. Lamb 39; B. A. Stokes 4-27). *PoM:* B. A. Stokes. *Warwickshire slipped to a second home defeat in 48 hours as Ben Stokes, continuing his recovery from a finger injury, starred for Durham. He clobbered 35 off 25 – though he was overshadowed by Cameron Bancroft's 60 off 45 – then took a well-judged running catch to dismiss Ed Pollock, before filleting Warwickshire's middle order with 4-27.*

At Birmingham, June 30 (floodlit). **Warwickshire won by ten wickets.** ‡**Yorkshire 81** (15.5 overs) (C. R. Brathwaite 3-7, C. N. Miles 3-19); **Warwickshire 86-0** (8.3 overs) (E. J. Pollock 33*, A. J. Hose 46*). *PoM:* C. R. Brathwaite. *Records tumbled in a match lasting 24.2 overs, after Yorkshire collapsed for their lowest total, the lowest against Warwickshire, and the lowest at Edgbaston – though that record would fall two days later. After Lyth had taken 15 from the first five balls, Yorkshire imploded in an array of cross-batted strokes. There were only eight boundaries in their 81; Pollock and Adam Hose hit 14 in Warwickshire's first ten-wicket win.*

At Birmingham, July 2 (floodlit). **Nottinghamshire won by 114 runs. Nottinghamshire 177-9** (20 overs) (B. M. Duckett 39, A. D. Hales 34, S. R. Patel 41; J. B. Lintott 3-28, W. M. H. Rhodes 3-40); ‡**Warwickshire 63** (13.4 overs) (J. T. Ball 4-11, C. G. Harrison 4-17). *PoM:* S. R. Patel. *Warwickshire's 63 was their lowest total, and the lowest against Nottinghamshire. The slow bowlers prospered: Jake Lintott in the Nottinghamshire innings, Calvin Harrison in the reply. Harrison registered career-best figures – as did Jake Ball – including a triple-wicket maiden, giving Nottinghamshire their first three-figure margin of victory, and Warwickshire their heaviest defeat. Carlos Brathwaite withdrew from Warwickshire's squad after a positive Covid test.*

LOWEST T20 TOTALS IN THE UK

44	Glamorgan v Surrey at The Oval	2019
47	Northamptonshire v Durham at Chester-le-Street	2011
53	Worcestershire v Lancashire at Manchester	2016
63	**Warwickshire v Nottinghamshire at Birmingham**	**2021**
67	Sussex v Hampshire at Hove	2004
68	Sussex v Surrey at Hove	2007
68	Gloucestershire v Hampshire at Bristol	2010

The lowest in a T20 international is 79 by Australia v England at Southampton in 2005.

At Birmingham, July 16 (floodlit). **Warwickshire won by 17 runs. ‡Warwickshire 169-5** (20 overs) (S. R. Hain 83*, C. R. Brathwaite 52*); **Worcestershire 152-6** (20 overs) (J. D. Libby 36). *PoM:* S. R. Hain. *County debut:* K. R. Mayers (Warwickshire). *A furious onslaught from Brathwaite and Sam Hain, scoring 53 in the last three overs, brought Warwickshire back from 63-5. Their stand of 106* in 11 overs was a county sixth-wicket record. Worcestershire captain Ed Barnard made 13 bowling changes, but gave Pennington – the pick of his attack – only two overs. Worcestershire were 74-2 in the 11th, but could not maintain the momentum.*

At Birmingham, July 18. **Warwickshire won by 14 runs. ‡Warwickshire 191-6** (20 overs) (A. J. Hose 37, W. M. H. Rhodes 32, C. G. Benjamin 60*); **Northamptonshire 177-8** (20 overs) (R. S. Vasconcelos 39, J. J. Cobb 35, R. I. Keogh 55*; W. M. H. Rhodes 3-41). *PoM:* C. G. Benjamin. *County debut:* C. G. Benjamin (Warwickshire). *South Africa-born Chris Benjamin, recruited from Durham University as wicketkeeping back-up, announced himself by smashing 60* off 34 on debut, and adding 84 with Will Rhodes. Northamptonshire needed 192, and Josh Cobb (35 off 18) and Rob Keogh (55* off 33) put on 65, but three spinners kept them in check. Having won, Warwickshire had to wait four hours to find out whether they would proceed to the quarter-finals. The news that Leicestershire had beaten Worcestershire confirmed they would.*

Warwickshire away matches

June 10: lost to Yorkshire by six wickets.
June 11: beat Nottinghamshire by 18 runs.
June 13: beat Derbyshire by three wickets.
June 15: beat Northamptonshire by 55 runs.

June 16: beat Leicestershire by 35 runs.
June 20: lost to Durham by 22 runs.
July 9: lost to Worcestershire by 49 runs.

WORCESTERSHIRE

At Worcester, June 9 (floodlit). **Tied. Worcestershire 152-6** (20 overs) (J. D. Libby 52*, R. A. Whiteley 42); ‡**Nottinghamshire 152-8** (20 overs) (J. M. Clarke 45, A. D. Hales 31, P. D. Trego 35). *PoM:* J. M. Clarke. *County debuts:* B. J. Dwarshuis, I. S. Sodhi (Worcestershire); C. G. Harrison (Nottinghamshire). *Attendance:* 745. *Jake Libby and Ross Whiteley added 78 off 57 for the fifth wicket, giving Worcestershire a defendable 152-6. Nottinghamshire were cruising when Joe Clarke and Alex Hales opened with 76 in 5.5 overs but, on a slow pitch, the spin of Moeen Ali and Ish Sodhi pegged them back. Still, only ten were needed from 12 – and five from the final over – but Peter Trego, attempting two from the last ball, was run out by Ed Barnard. Josh Tongue, who bowled the last, had conceded 26 in his previous two.*

At Worcester, June 13. **Worcestershire won by eight wickets.** ‡Lancashire 132-4 (20 overs) (J. C. Buttler 55); **Worcestershire 133-2** (17.2 overs) (M. H. Wessels 40, B. L. D'Oliveira 61*). *PoM:* B. L. D'Oliveira. *Attendance:* 784. *The slow pitch from the previous home game was used again, and turned out to be even slower. Jos Buttler hit 55 off 46, but Lancashire's 132-4 proved insufficient. Riki Wessels (40 off 27) and Brett D'Oliveira (61* off 45) effectively settled the outcome with an opening stand of 79 in nine overs.*

At Worcester, June 16 (floodlit). **Yorkshire won by 94 runs.** Yorkshire 216-6 (20 overs) (J. M. Bairstow 112, T. Köhler-Cadmore 53; B. J. Dwarshuis 4-31); ‡**Worcestershire 122** (16.3 overs) (M. H. Wessels 32, M. M. Ali 39, R. A. Whiteley 30; A. U. Rashid 3-32). *PoM:* J. M. Bairstow. *Attendance:* 830. *Having scored five off ten balls, Jonny Bairstow changed his bat and smashed 107 off the next 40 – including ten sixes – in a brutal display (the last 56, from 17, came after he suffered an ankle injury and was given a runner). His stand of 146 in 12 overs with Tom Köhler-Cadmore (53 off 33) was Yorkshire's third-wicket record. Only Ben Dwarshuis escaped the carnage, and Worcestershire never looked like challenging their target of 217.*

T20 CENTURIES FOR YORKSHIRE

161	A. Lyth	v Northamptonshire at Leeds		2017
118	D. J. Willey	v Worcestershire at Leeds		2017
112	**J. M. Bairstow**	**v Worcestershire at Worcester**		**2021**
109	I. J. Harvey	v Derbyshire at Leeds		2005
108*	I. J. Harvey	v Lancashire at Leeds		2004
102*	J. M. Bairstow	v Durham at Chester-le-Street		2014
101*	H. H. Gibbs	v Northamptonshire at Northampton		2010

At Worcester, June 18 (floodlit). **Worcestershire v Northamptonshire. Abandoned.**

At Worcester, June 25 (floodlit). **Worcestershire won by eight wickets.** ‡Durham 178-8 (20 overs) (D. G. Bedingham 44; C. A. J. Morris 3-37); **Worcestershire 181-2** (19.3 overs) (B. L. D'Oliveira 67, J. D. Libby 78*). *PoM:* J. D. Libby. *Attendance:* 1,218. *Libby and D'Oliveira each achieved career-bests during a second-wicket stand of 145 which earned Worcestershire their first win in five. A six and four from Ben Cox in Matty Potts's final over sealed a chase of 179. Durham had stumbled after David Bedingham's 44 off 26, with Dwarshuis again tidy, and Charlie Morris returning his best figures. Ben Stokes laboured to a run-a-ball 20, while his three overs cost 40, as he continued his comeback from injury.*

At Worcester, June 27. **Worcestershire won by seven wickets.** Leicestershire 156-7 (20 overs) (L. J. Hill 59); ‡**Worcestershire 157-3** (19.1 overs) (M. H. Wessels 46, B. L. D'Oliveira 69). *PoM:* B. L. D'Oliveira. *Attendance:* 1,284. *D'Oliveira improved his personal-best for the second time in 48 hours as Worcestershire again triumphed in the last over. His opening stand of 103 in 12.2 overs with Wessels was Worcestershire's highest for any wicket against Leicestershire. Earlier, Dillon Pennington had helped reduce Leicestershire to 59-5 in the 12th, but Lewis Hill's career-best 59 put a reasonable 156 on the board.*

At Worcester, July 9 (floodlit). **Worcestershire won by 49 runs.** ‡**Worcestershire 174-6** (20 overs) (M. H. Wessels 35, B. L. D'Oliveira 45, O. B. Cox 43; W. M. H. Rhodes 4-34); **Warwickshire 125** (18 overs) (E. J. Pollock 53; I. S. Sodhi 4-24, B. L. D'Oliveira 3-15). *PoM:* B. L. D'Oliveira. *Attendance:* 1,275. *A fine all-round performance from D'Oliveira sealed this local derby for Worcestershire. Wessels – in his final appearance for them – had contributed 35 to an opening stand with him of 70. Pursuing 175, Warwickshire were well placed at 81-2, but D'Oliveira picked up three wickets in nine balls, and Sodhi four in eight; the two leg-spinners had a combined 7-39 off eight overs.*

Worcestershire away matches

June 11: beat Northamptonshire by 32 runs.
June 22: lost to Nottinghamshire by ten wickets.
June 23: lost to Yorkshire by 12 runs.
July 1: lost to Lancashire by 34 runs.

July 2: beat Derbyshire by 14 runs.
July 16: lost to Warwickshire by 17 runs.
July 18: lost to Leicestershire by seven wickets.

YORKSHIRE

At Leeds, June 10 (floodlight). **Yorkshire won by six wickets. Warwickshire 144-8** (20 overs) (S. R. Hain 59; J. A. Thompson 3-23); ‡**Yorkshire 147-4** (18.3 overs) (J. M. Bairstow 34, T. Köhler-Cadmore 31*). PoM: J. A. Thompson. *County debuts:* L. H. Ferguson (Yorkshire); C. R. Brathwaite (Warwickshire). *Attendance:* 4,249. *Five of Yorkshire's top six chipped in to overhaul a target of 145 with ease. Jonny Bairstow got them going with three sixes in a breezy 34, before Will Fraine (19* off eight) finished things off. But the game's only fifty was Sam Hain's measured innings, which steered Warwickshire from 6-2 to respectability. Bustling seamer Jordan Thompson took two running return catches as he matched his T20-best 3-23.*

At Leeds, June 15 (floodlight). **Yorkshire won by 18 runs.** ‡**Yorkshire 240-4** (20 overs) (A. Lyth 51, J. M. Bairstow 82, D. J. Willey 44, H. C. Brook 48*); **Leicestershire 222-8** (20 overs) (J. P. Inglis 82, C. N. Ackermann 32, B. W. M. Mike 31; D. J. Willey 3-44). PoM: J. M. Bairstow. *Attendance:* 4,264. *An aggregate of 462 equalled the tournament record, and included 29 sixes. The top score on each side was 82, from Bairstow and Josh Inglis: Bairstow shared 113 for Yorkshire's first wicket with Adam Lyth, both reaching 50 in 28 balls, but Inglis (a Leeds-born Australian) got there in 20, steering Leicestershire to 146-3. Even after he was brilliantly caught by Thompson – one-handed at deep cover – lower-order runs reduced the target to 31 off two overs. But New Zealand pace bowler Lockie Ferguson (2-28) conceded only eight in the 19th, and captain David Willey four in the last.*

<hr>

MOST SIXES IN AN ENGLAND DOMESTIC T20 GAME

31	Essex (20) beat v Surrey (11) at Chelmsford	....	2019
31	Leicestershire (19) lost to Yorkshire (12) at Leicester	....	2019
29	Essex (15) lost to Glamorgan (14) at Chelmsford	....	2017
29	**Yorkshire (15) beat Leicestershire (14) at Leeds**	....	**2021**
27	Yorkshire (13) beat Worcestershire (14) at Leeds	....	2017
27	Middlesex (11) lost to Surrey (16) at The Oval	....	2018
26	Surrey (14) lost to Glamorgan (12) at The Oval	....	2015

There are no instances of a game containing 25 sixes, but seven of 24, including **Hampshire (12) beat Glamorgan (12) at Southampton in 2021.**

<hr>

At Leeds, June 18 (floodlight). **Yorkshire v Durham. Abandoned.**

At Leeds, June 20. **Yorkshire won by 39 runs. Yorkshire 174-6** (20 overs) (J. E. Root 49, H. C. Brook 48*; G. L. S. Scrimshaw 3-30); ‡**Derbyshire 135** (19 overs) (F. J. Hudson-Prentice 34; L. H. Ferguson 3-21, D. M. Bess 3-21). PoM: H. C. Brook. *Attendance:* 4,224. *Joe Root just missed his sixth fifty in seven Blast innings going back to 2018, but his first white-ball game leading Yorkshire – regular captain Willey was one of four team-mates absent with England's T20 squad – was a success. He added 57 in six overs with Harry Brook before being caught at mid-on off seamer George Scrimshaw, who claimed a career-best 3-30. But Ferguson and Dom Bess both returned 3-21 as Derbyshire fell well short.*

At Leeds, June 23 (floodlight). **Yorkshire won by 12 runs.** ‡**Yorkshire 191-5** (20 overs) (H. C. Brook 83*, J. A. Thompson 66*; D. Y. Pennington 4-24); **Worcestershire 179-5** (20 overs) (M. H. Wessels 77, O. B. Cox 61*). PoM: J. A. Thompson. *Attendance:* 4,258. *Yorkshire were reeling on 15-4 when Dillon Pennington struck three times in the third over and trapped Root in the fifth – both maidens. He also had Brook dropped on two in the seventh. But Brook and Thompson transformed the match with a fabulous stand of 141* in nine overs, a sixth-wicket record for all T20 cricket in England. Brook smashed six sixes in his 54-ball 83*; Thompson, even more brutal, five in 66* off 28. Riki Wessels and Ben Cox fought back, adding 68 as Worcestershire recovered from 50-3, but 23 off the last over was too much.*

At Leeds, June 26 (floodlight). **Yorkshire won by 82 runs.** ‡**Yorkshire 224-3** (20 overs) (M. D. Stoneman 50, J. A. Thompson 74, H. C. Brook 45*); **Northamptonshire 142** (19.3 overs) (R. I. Keogh 36; D. M. Bess 3-17). PoM: J. A. Thompson. *County debut:* M. D. Stoneman (Yorkshire). *Attendance:* 4,081. *With Root no longer available, Thompson was promoted to No. 3 – and responded with a blistering career-best 74, off 35 balls with seven sixes. He was supported by 50 from Mark Stoneman, on loan from Surrey, and 45* from Brook, who helped Gary Ballance take 27 off the last* *over as Yorkshire passed 200 for the third time in 12 days. Bess's 3-17, his best T20 return, reduced Northamptonshire to 78-4, before Rob Keogh provided a little resistance. A fancy-dress pitch invasion saw a parrot rugby-tackled by a pirate.*

At Leeds, July 2 (floodlit). **Yorkshire won by nine runs.** ‡**Yorkshire 180-4** (20 overs) (A. Lyth 52, H. C. Brook 91*); **Lancashire 171-8** (20 overs) (K. K. Jennings 37, R. P. Jones 61*, S. J. Croft 41; L. H. Ferguson 4-24). *PoM:* H. C. Brook. *Attendance:* 4,449. *A hat trick by Ferguson – Yorkshire's first in T20 cricket – to end the match secured their first T20 Roses win since 2017, and left them well placed to reach the knockouts. Lancashire started the final over needing 20, and had reduced that to ten off three before Ferguson removed Luke Wells, Luke Wood and Tom Hartley. Earlier, Brook's career-best 91* off 50 took his tournament average to 115. Rob Jones's maiden T20 fifty put Lancashire back in the game after they were 70-4, but he was stranded as Ferguson wrapped things up in style.*

Yorkshire away matches

June 11: lost to Durham by 20 runs.
June 16: beat Worcestershire by 94 runs.
June 25: lost to Leicestershire by 34 runs.
June 30: lost to Warwickshire by ten wickets.

July 9: lost to Nottinghamshire by ten wickets.
July 17: lost to Lancashire by four wickets.
July 18: cancelled v Derbyshire.

SOUTH GROUP

ESSEX

At Chelmsford, June 11 (floodlit). **Hampshire won by 13 runs. Hampshire 155-6** (20 overs) (J. J. Weatherley 42); ‡**Essex 142** (19.2 overs) (T. Westley 44). *PoM:* C. P. Wood. *Attendance:* 403. *Hampshire reached 52-1 after seven, but on a slow pitch found it difficult to accelerate. Joe Weatherley made a responsible 42, while Jamie Fuller's robust 26 contained both his team's sixes. The Essex reply began at a similar tempo and, at 80-3 in the tenth, they seemed on course. But Tom Westley was run out and, despite handy knocks by Paul Walter (29) and Jimmy Neesham (28), the innings dribbled away. Chris Wood (1-15) and Liam Dawson (1-17) kept a lid on the scoring.*

At Chelmsford, June 15 (floodlit). **Sussex won by seven wickets. Essex 128-8** (20 overs) (M. S. Pepper 38; G. H. S. Garton 3-31); ‡**Sussex 130-3** (14 overs) (L. J. Wright 75). *PoM:* L. J. Wright. *Attendance:* 476. *Victory by seven wickets (with six overs unused) confirmed the one-sidedness of this game. A frugal Sussex attack had taken wickets at regular intervals to deny Essex any momentum; George Garton led the way with 3-31, while Michael Pepper fought hardest, contributing a 25-ball 38. Sussex captain Luke Wright, back after splitting the webbing on his hand, hit a 44-ball 75, and shared fifty stands with Phil Salt and Travis Head. Sussex had three wins from three.*

At Chelmsford, June 18 (floodlit). **Essex v Gloucestershire. Abandoned.** *For the fifth season running, this fixture saw no play. Covid had scuppered the 2020 match (which vanished from the schedule once a revised competition shifted from two groups to three), while rain washed out four.*

At Chelmsford, June 25 (floodlit). **Kent won by 28 runs (DLS). Kent 167-9** (20 overs) (Z. Crawley 43, D. J. Bell-Drummond 50; S. R. Harmer 4-26); ‡**Essex 31-4** (5 overs). *PoM:* D. J. Bell-Drummond. *Attendance:* 704. *Put in, Kent set off at breakneck speed and, at 82-0 after the powerplay, were eyeing 200-plus. But spin slowed them, and after 12 overs they were 111-5. Dan Lawrence became the first Essex player to hold four outfield catches – three off Simon Harmer – and a target of 168 seemed gettable. Essex, though, made an abysmal start, and when lightning, followed by rain, drove the players from the field, they were well adrift.*

At Chelmsford, June 29 (floodlit). **Essex won by six wickets (DLS). Essex 151-4** (18.1 overs) (A. J. A. Wheater 49, M. S. Pepper 55*); ‡**Somerset 153** (20 overs) (D. P. Conway 53; J. H. Plom 3-31, S. R. Harmer 4-24). *PoM:* M. S. Pepper. *Attendance:* 548. *Although Devon Conway hit a resilient 53, Somerset lost their way after reaching a confident 107-2. The destroyer, once again, was Harmer, who took three wickets in the 14th; seamer Jack Plom claimed a career-best 3-31. A maiden T20 fifty from Pepper guided Essex – whose target was reduced to 148 in 19 overs – to their first home win of the tournament, and only their fourth since the start of 2018.*

At Chelmsford, July 1. **Essex won by eight wickets.** ‡**Glamorgan 104** (17 overs); **Essex 108-2** (12.2 overs) (A. J. A. Wheater 39, D. W. Lawrence 55*). *PoM:* D. W. Lawrence. *Attendance:* 606. *This was a drubbing: Covid precautions had robbed Glamorgan of key players such as Marnus Labuschagne, but a total of 104 was lamentable – even on a hybrid pitch used for a fifth time. Essex shared the wickets, with Sam Cook, Plom and Harmer taking two each. There was also one for Lawrence, who then made the most of two drops to hit the game's only half-century.*

At Chelmsford, July 18. **Middlesex won by nine runs.** ‡**Middlesex 169-5** (20 overs) (S. D. Robson 60, D. J. Mitchell 43); **Essex 160-9** (20 overs) (T. Westley 37; S. T. Finn 3-25). *PoM:* S. D. Robson. *County debut:* J. S. Rymell (Essex). *Attendance:* 605. *Neither side could reach the knockouts, but victory for Middlesex ensured they avoided the wooden spoon. In only his seventh T20 game in 14 seasons at Middlesex, Robson reached a maiden 50, and gained useful support from Daryl Mitchell. Essex looked in control at 93-2 in the 11th, before the departure of Westley derailed the chase. Steven Finn claimed three as Essex's T20 season ran out of steam.*

Essex away matches

June 9: beat Somerset by three wickets.
June 13: lost to Glamorgan by seven wickets.
June 20: lost to Kent by 67 runs.
June 21: beat Surrey by eight wickets.

June 24: beat Middlesex by two wickets.
July 9: lost to Sussex by six wickets.
July 16: lost to Hampshire by 18 runs.

GLAMORGAN

At Cardiff, June 10 (floodlit). **Gloucestershire won by four runs.** ‡**Gloucestershire 179-6** (20 overs) (G. D. Phillips 44, B. A. C. Howell 30; D. A. Douthwaite 3-28); **Glamorgan 175-9** (20 overs) (M. Labuschagne 93*; B. A. C. Howell 3-39). *PoM:* M. Labuschagne. *Attendance:* 545. *Marnus Labuschagne, playing his first T20 game for Glamorgan, almost brought them success with a 56-ball 93*, but few others did much in pursuit of 180. There was also fading light to contend with: one floodlight was out of order, which meant the other three could not be used (play began at 5.30 and the sun set three hours later, just as the match reached its climax). New Zealand's Glenn Phillips, also a county debutant, had made an immediate impression for Gloucestershire with 44 off 32, as their last five overs yielded 66. Benny Howell then supplemented his 15-ball 30 with three wickets, as Labuschagne played his lone hand. With 19 needed from the last over, he managed 14.*

At Cardiff, June 13. **Glamorgan won by seven wickets. Essex 153-6** (20 overs) (W. E. L. Buttleman 36); ‡**Glamorgan 156-3** (19 overs) (N. J. Selman 65, M. Labuschagne 59). *PoM:* N. J. Selman. *Attendance:* 564. *This time a Labuschagne half-century did bring a Glamorgan victory. After Will Buttleman and Michael Pepper (29) had given Essex a bright start, their team-mates struggled to 153-6 against an accurate attack. In reply, a partnership of 100 by Nick Selman and Labuschagne did the trick.*

At Cardiff, June 16 (floodlit). **Kent won by 40 runs.** ‡**Kent 144-7** (20 overs) (S. W. Billings 30, J. M. Cox 32*); **Glamorgan 104** (17.4 overs) (M. E. Milnes 5-22). *PoM:* M. E. Milnes. *Attendance:* 889. *Glamorgan's target of 145 appeared gettable, but the Kent seamers expertly exploited a pitch of variable bounce; Matt Milnes returned his best white-ball figures. Glamorgan were never in contention once they had lost three for seven mid-chase. Earlier, Sam Billings had helped stabilise the Kent innings, before Jordan Cox provided a late boost.*

At Cardiff, June 18 (floodlit). **Glamorgan won by 21 runs.** ‡**Glamorgan 150-9** (20 overs) (C. A. Ingram 75; B. C. Cullen 3-33, S. T. Finn 4-19); **Middlesex 129-9** (20 overs) (P. R. Stirling 46, E. J. G. Morgan 33; T. van der Gugten 3-16). *PoM:* C. A. Ingram. *Attendance:* 1,182. *Having scored 33 in four games, Colin Ingram was promoted to open, and scored exactly half Glamorgan's 150-9. Eight batsmen failed to reach double figures, and the next-best was 18 by No. 10 Timm van der Gugten. Middlesex appeared on course when Paul Stirling and Eoin Morgan shared 61 for the third wicket but, after both were out in successive overs, there was little else.*

At Cardiff, June 29 (floodlit). **Glamorgan won by one run. Glamorgan 153-6** (20 overs) (K. S. Carlson 32, D. L. Lloyd 41, W. T. Root 41*); ‡**Surrey 152-9** (20 overs) (O. J. D. Pope 60, K. A. Jamieson 31). *PoM:* W. T. Root. *County debut:* S. J. Pearce (Glamorgan). *Attendance:* 991. *Surrey needed 13 from the final over, bowled by van der Gugten. A Gareth Batty single gave the strike to Kyle Jamieson, who struck a six. But only four runs came from the next three balls, leaving two from the last: Jamieson played it back to the bowler, and was run out. Not long before, Ollie Pope* *appeared to be guiding Surrey to their target of 154, but Kiran Carlson's throw beat him, and the bowlers clawed their way back. Glamorgan had been indebted to Billy Root, who hit Gus Atkinson for four sixes in their final over.*

At Cardiff, July 2 (floodlit). **Sussex won by 33 runs. ‡Sussex 201-8** (20 overs) (P. D. Salt 63, L. J. Wright 77; R. I. Walker 3-44, D. A. Douthwaite 3-28); **Glamorgan 168** (18.4 overs) (D. L. Lloyd 51, D. A. Douthwaite 35; A. D. Lenham 4-26). *PoM:* A. D. Lenham. *Attendance:* 1,540. *Phil Salt (63 off 35) and Luke Wright (77 off 41) gave Sussex a rousing start of 144 off 12.2 overs. Though Dan Douthwaite dismissed both in three balls, the damage was done, and a target of 202 was never in Glamorgan's sights. Their only fight came from David Lloyd (51 off 29), as 16-year-old Archie Lenham took 4-26 with his leg-spin.*

YOUNGEST TO TAKE FOUR WICKETS IN A T20 IN THE UK

Yrs	Days			
16	**344**	**A. D. Lenham (4-26)** ..	Sussex v Glamorgan at Cardiff	**2021**
17	187	M. D. Fisher (5-22)	Yorkshire v Derbyshire at Leeds.............	2015
19	38	L. Gregory (4-15)	Somerset v Gloucestershire at Bristol...........	2011
19	41	J. A. R. Harris (4-23)...	Glamorgan v Northamptonshire at Cardiff	2009
19	75	S. M. Curran (4-13)....	Surrey v Gloucestershire at The Oval	2017
19	**93**	**B. C. Cullen (4-32)....**	Middlesex v Somerset at Taunton	**2021**
19	104	C. R. Woakes (4-21) ...	Warwickshire v Somerset at Taunton	2008
19	104	G. H. S. Garton (4-16)..	Sussex v Glamorgan at Hove	2016
19	111	L. Trevaskis (4-16)	Durham v Lancashire at Manchester............	2018
19	137	D. Y. Pennington (4-9) .	Worcestershire v Northamptonshire at Worcester ..	2018

At Cardiff, July 16 (floodlit). **Somerset won by 74 runs. ‡Somerset 181-5** (20 overs) (D. P. Conway 70*, T. A. Lammonby 34; R. I. Walker 3-15); **Glamorgan 107** (17.4 overs) (L. P. Goldsworthy 3-14, R. E. van der Merwe 3-20). *PoM:* D. P. Conway. *Attendance:* 917. *Glamorgan were soundly beaten. Somerset's foundation had been laid by Devon Conway (70 off 52), who put on 52 for the first wicket with Steven Davies, then 65 for the fifth with Tom Lammonby. Glamorgan then folded, as three left-arm spinners – Jack Leach (2-32), Lewis Goldsworthy and Roelof van der Merwe – shared eight wickets.*

Glamorgan away matches

June 14: lost to Surrey by five wickets.
June 19: no result v Somerset.
June 22: no result v Sussex.
June 24: lost to Gloucestershire by 34 runs.

June 27: lost to Middlesex by seven wickets.
July 1: lost to Essex by eight wickets.
July 18: lost to Hampshire by six wickets.

GLOUCESTERSHIRE

At Bristol, June 11 (floodlit). **Sussex won by five wickets. Gloucestershire 177-7** (20 overs) (G. D. Phillips 42; G. H. S. Garton 3-19); **‡Sussex 178-5** (17.2 overs) (P. D. Salt 77*, G. H. S. Garton 46; J. Shaw 3-32). *PoM:* P. D. Salt. *County debut:* A. D. Lenham (Sussex). *Attendance:* 2,848. *There were 19 sixes in all, most to the short Kennington Avenue boundary. After Sussex slipped to 52-4 in pursuit of 178, Phil Salt and George Garton blasted 92 in nine overs to help win the game with ease. At 16 years and 323 days, leg-spinner Archie Lenham – son of Neil and grandson of Les, both of Sussex – became the second-youngest in T20 county cricket, after Hamidullah Qadri of Derbyshire. Lenham took 1-34. For Gloucestershire, there had been six scores between 13 and 24, plus Glenn Phillips's brisk 42.*

At Bristol, June 20. **Gloucestershire v Hampshire.** Abandoned.

At Bristol, June 22 (floodlit). **Gloucestershire won by eight wickets. Kent 147-7** (20 overs) (Z. Crawley 43, J. M. Cox 36*); **‡Gloucestershire 149-2** (13.4 overs) (M. A. H. Hammond 33, C. D. J. Dent 37, I. A. Cockbain 30*, G. D. Phillips 41*). *PoM:* G. D. Phillips. *Attendance:* 1,256. *Zak Crawley was the only Kent batsman properly to get to grips with a sluggish surface, though there were useful late runs from Jordan Cox. Gloucestershire found few issues, and Phillips's three sixes brought them home in style.*

At Bristol, June 24 (floodlit). **Gloucestershire won by 34 runs. Gloucestershire 216-2** (20 overs) (M. A. H. Hammond 35, B. A. C. Howell 53*, G. D. Phillips 94*); ‡**Glamorgan 182-8** (20 overs) (D. L. Lloyd 44, M. Labuschagne 33, D. A. Douthwaite 35). *PoM:* G. D. Phillips. *Attendance:* 1,866. *Phillips's purple patch grew more vivid. He was on 25 from 18 balls when he put his foot to the floor: the next 23 yielded 69, as he hit the first of two scores of 94* on consecutive days. He and Benny Howell shared a club-record third-wicket stand of 130* in 64 balls, and propelled Gloucestershire to 216-2. For Glamorgan, Dan Douthwaite, who had conceded 23 off his last over, hit 35 off 17. Gloucestershire went top.*

At Bristol, July 1. **Somerset won by eight wickets. Gloucestershire 161-7** (20 overs) (M. A. H. Hammond 44, B. A. C. Howell 52; L. Gregory 5-24); ‡**Somerset 165-2** (19.2 overs) (D. P. Conway 81*, W. C. F. Smeed 36, L. P. Goldsworthy 39*). *PoM:* L. Gregory. *Attendance:* 3,088. *Gloucestershire didn't make the most of being 79-1 in the 11th. Instead, Lewis Gregory collected a white-ball-record 5-24, limiting Somerset's target to 162. Devon Conway, dropped in the first over, marshalled an unspectacular chase with his third T20 fifty in a row, putting on 78 with Will Smeed and 79 with a less fluent Lewis Goldsworthy.*

At Cheltenham, July 9 (floodlit). **Gloucestershire won by ten runs. Gloucestershire 171-8** (20 overs) (I. A. Cockbain 34, J. R. Bracey 33, R. F. Higgins 43); ‡**Middlesex 161-8** (20 overs) (M. D. E. Holden 50*; B. A. C. Howell 3-23). *PoM:* R. F. Higgins. *Attendance:* 2,850. *Until Ryan Higgins helped plunder 52 from the final four overs, Gloucestershire were meandering. They had lurched to 26-3, before a breezy 33 from James Bracey – his first score above 11 in seven T20 innings – engineered a partial recovery. Middlesex were never quite up with the rate; three cheap wickets for Howell slowed them further, and Max Holden's 50* came too late.*

At Cheltenham, July 16. **Surrey won by seven wickets. Gloucestershire 177-9** (20 overs) (B. A. C. Howell 30, G. D. Phillips 48; A. A. P. Atkinson 4-37); ‡**Surrey 178-3** (18.2 overs) (J. L. Smith 60, L. J. Evans 58). *PoM:* G. J. Batty. *Attendance:* 3,174. *A win for Gloucestershire would have taken them into the knockouts, and eliminated their opponents. But Surrey's victory meant both sides still had a chance of the quarters. On a sticky afternoon, Gloucestershire had enjoyed a good start – 69-1 in the eighth – but then struggled. Spinners Gareth Batty and Dan Moriarty had combined figures of 4-48, while seamer Gus Atkinson took 4-37. Jamie Smith and Laurie Evans made light work of the target, and Surrey gave their run-rate a useful boost.*

Gloucestershire away matches

June 10: beat Glamorgan by four runs.
June 13: lost to Kent by five runs.
June 17: beat Middlesex by two runs.
June 18: no result v Essex.

June 25: beat Sussex by 27 runs.
July 2: lost to Hampshire by ten runs.
July 18: lost to Somerset by 23 runs.

HAMPSHIRE

At Southampton, June 28 (floodlit). **Hampshire v Middlesex. Abandoned.** *After seven away fixtures while the Rose Bowl was staging international cricket, Hampshire returned home to a downpour.*

At Southampton, June 30 (floodlit). **Surrey won by 20 runs. Surrey 146-7** (20 overs) (J. L. Smith 59; S. W. Currie 3-21); ‡**Hampshire 126-8** (20 overs) (A. A. P. Atkinson 3-21). *PoM:* J. L. Smith. *Attendance:* 2,542. *Hampshire at last took the field for a home T20 game, but suffered a fifth defeat. Surrey openers Will Jacks and Jamie Smith put on 51 inside six overs, before the innings fell away against Scott Currie's pace; there was no boundary in the last five overs. Needing an apparently modest 147, Hampshire laboured to 34-1 in the powerplay. Jamie Overton (2-14) was most miserly, and top-scorer was 18-year-old Canford schoolboy Tom Prest, with 20. Surrey now led the group; Hampshire were bottom.*

At Southampton, July 2 (floodlit). **Hampshire won by ten runs. ‡Hampshire 176-6** (20 overs) (T. J. Prest 59*, J. J. Weatherley 30, J. K. Fuller 38); **Gloucestershire 166-5** (20 overs) (C. D. J. Dent 42, G. D. Phillips 57, J. M. R. Taylor 30). *PoM:* T. J. Prest. *Attendance:* 2,480. *On his third county appearance, Prest was instrumental in Hampshire's win, only their second in seven completed matches. Top-scoring for the second game running, he put on 73 for the sixth wicket with James Fuller, to ensure a useful total. Gloucestershire made a decent start and, at 115-2 after 14, with Chris Dent and Glenn Phillips having added 82, were well placed. However, intelligent bowling left them needing 20 from Chris Wood's final over, which proved too many.*

At Southampton, July 9 (floodlit). **Hampshire won by 75 runs.** ‡**Hampshire 175-6** (20 overs) (J. J. Weatherley 50, L. D. McManus 60*); **Somerset 100** (16 overs) (S. W. Currie 4-24). *PoM:* J. J. Weatherley. *County debut:* T. E. Albert (Hampshire). *Attendance:* 2,797. *Hampshire recovered from 22-3 thanks to fifties from Weatherley and Lewis McManus, whose 36-ball 60* was a career-best. A below-strength Somerset lost the prolific Devon Conway to the second ball of their reply, from Wood (captain in James Vince's absence), and couldn't settle. Currie picked up four wickets, and was supported by Brad Wheal (18–13–6–2).*

At Southampton, July 16. **Hampshire won by 18 runs.** ‡**Hampshire 171-8** (20 overs) (J. M. Vince 63, D. J. M. Short 30, C. de Grandhomme 32; S. J. Cook 3-34); **Essex 153** (19.2 overs) (T. Westley 39, D. W. Lawrence 60). *PoM:* J. M. Vince. *Attendance:* 3,240. *Buoyed by his first international century three days earlier, Vince guided a resurgent Hampshire to victory. After choosing to bat, he gave the innings its backbone, eventually falling for a 46-ball 63. Essex looked in control during a second-wicket stand of 80 in nine overs between Tom Westley and Dan Lawrence. But Mason Crane had Westley neatly stumped, and wickets kept falling, with all six bowlers managing at least one.*

At Southampton, July 16 (floodlit). **Hampshire won by six wickets.** ‡**Sussex 183-6** (20 overs) (L. J. Wright 54, R. S. Bopara 62); **Hampshire 184-4** (19.2 overs) (J. M. Vince 102, D. J. M. Short 35). *PoM:* J. M. Vince. *Attendance:* 3,240. *Vince's day got better as he powered Hampshire to their second win of a double-header – and collected his second match award. Sussex had coasted to a challenging total thanks to fifties from Luke Wright and Ravi Bopara; without four tight overs from Liam Dawson (2-15), they might have been out of sight. Vince, though, was in ebullient form, dominating an opening stand of 120 in 12 overs with D'Arcy Short. Two balls after reaching his second T20 hundred, he fell hit wicket, for the first time in 660 professional innings. It was the only success of an expensive evening for Ollie Robinson (1-40). Hampshire had no problem knocking off the 16 they still needed.*

At Southampton, July 18. **Hampshire won by six wickets. Glamorgan 184-4** (20 overs) (D. L. Lloyd 52, M. Labuschagne 78; B. T. J. Wheal 3-39); ‡**Hampshire 187-4** (13 overs) (J. M. Vince 39, D. J. M. Short 69, J. J. Weatherley 43*). *PoM:* D. J. M. Short. *Attendance:* 2,196. *Hampshire, in sixth, were the form team, yet their odds of progress were slim. They had to win handsomely enough to overtake Surrey's net run-rate, and hope Gloucestershire lost. It helped that Surrey were not playing, and that Vince won the toss: bowling first meant Hampshire would know the scale of the task. First, though, they had to contain Glamorgan, and in particular David Lloyd and Marnus Labuschagne, who between them smote ten sixes. If a target of 185 was tough, reaching it by the first ball of the 15th was tougher. But the hundred came up in seven overs and, though three wickets fell in 13 balls, the runs never dried up. Short battered 69 from 30, Joe Weatherley 43* from 13. Astonishingly, the hosts achieved their fifth successive win with seven overs unused. And when Gloucestershire did lose, Hampshire had made the knockouts.*

Hampshire away matches

June 9: lost to Kent by 38 runs.
June 11: beat Essex by 13 runs.
June 12: lost to Sussex by nine wickets.
June 15: lost to Middlesex by three wickets.

June 18: no result v Surrey.
June 20: no result v Gloucestershire.
June 25: lost to Somerset by seven runs.

KENT

At Canterbury, June 9 (floodlit). **Kent won by 38 runs. Kent 176-6** (20 overs) (J. L. Denly 44, D. J. Bell-Drummond 42, O. G. Robinson 48; M. S. Crane 3-23); ‡**Hampshire 138-9** (20 overs) (J. M. Vince 34, J. J. Weatherley 37; F. J. Klaassen 4-32). *PoM:* F. J. Klaassen. *County debuts:* J. E. G. Logan (Kent); D. J. M. Short (Hampshire). *Attendance:* 1,044. *Kent started so brutally – Joe Denly and Daniel Bell-Drummond made 86 in seven overs – that Hampshire seemed happy to opt for containment. James Vince and D'Arcy Short began the ascent on 177 almost as well, and collected 51 from the powerplay, before Darren Stevens, playing his first Twenty20 game for Kent since 2017, struck first ball; it was his 100th T20 wicket for the county. Fred Klaassen dismantled the middle order as Hampshire fell behind the rate.*

At Canterbury, June 11 (floodlit). **Kent won by 16 runs. Kent 178-8** (20 overs) (J. A. Leaning 64, J. M. Cox 64; C. J. Green 5-32); ‡**Middlesex 162-8** (20 overs) (L. B. K. Hollman 51, N. A. Sowter 31*; D. I. Stevens 3-32). *PoM:* J. A. Leaning. *Attendance:* 838. *A defiant partnership of 123 – a record for Kent's fifth wicket – between Jack Leaning and Jordan Cox rescued them from 47-4 after* *seven. Then, in an eventful last over, off-spinner Chris Green conceded eight runs and took four wickets, including a hat-trick that brought him an all-format career-best 5-32. Stevens responded with three wickets in a raucous atmosphere, reducing Middlesex to 98-6. Luke Hollman and Nathan Sowter showed fight, but could not mount a serious tilt at the target.*

At Canterbury, June 13 (floodlit). **Kent won by five runs.** ‡**Kent 183-5** (20 overs) (D. J. Bell-Drummond 51, J. A. Leaning 81*; D. A. Payne 3-30); **Gloucestershire 178-8** (20 overs) (C. D. J. Dent 40, G. D. Phillips 38, B. A. C. Howell 44). *PoM:* J. A. Leaning. *County debut:* Qais Ahmed (Kent). *Attendance:* 997. Kent slumped, revived, wobbled and – thanks to Klaassen – triumphed. With Benny Howell and Graeme van Buuren well set, Gloucestershire needed a gettable ten off the last over. But Klaassen bowled Howell and had Matt Taylor caught from the first two balls. Singles were scrambled off the third and fourth, before van Buuren fell attempting a second. Six off the last would bring a tie, but Josh Shaw could manage only one. Earlier, Leaning, who came in at 16-3, cracked a career-best 81* off 51.

At Canterbury, June 20. **Kent won by 67 runs. Kent 236-3** (20 overs) (Z. Crawley 69, D. J. Bell-Drummond 88, J. A. Leaning 42*); ‡**Essex 169** (19.2 overs) (A. J. A. Wheater 46, S. R. Harmer 31; J. A. Leaning 3-15). *PoM:* J. A. Leaning. *Attendance:* 1,164. Bell-Drummond thought the chances of a commanding score on a damp Canterbury wicket were zero, and would also have bowled. But once he and Zak Crawley realised the ease of the track, they changed plan. After an opening stand of 145 inside 12 overs, Leaning pummelled 42* from 17 to whizz Kent to 236. Essex, who had never conceded more, recovered from 83-6, yet never came near their target. All six Kent bowlers were in the wickets, with Leaning taking a format-best 3-15. For the third home game in succession, he picked up the match award.

HIGHEST T20 TOTALS BY KENT

236-3	v Essex at Canterbury	**2021**	217	v Gloucestershire at Gloucester	2010
231-7	v Surrey at The Oval	2015	210-4	v Hampshire at Beckenham	2018
231-5	v Somerset at Canterbury	2018	209-5	v Middlesex at Lord's	2020
227-7	v Somerset at Taunton	2015	208-4	v Middlesex at Canterbury	2014
221-2	v Essex at Chelmsford	2017	207-2	v Surrey at The Oval	2017

At Canterbury, June 28 (floodlit). **Somerset won by ten wickets.** Kent 168-8 (20 overs) (Z. Crawley 39, J. L. Denly 36; L. Gregory 4-27); ‡**Somerset 169-0** (15.4 overs) (T. Banton 107*, D. P. Conway 51*). *PoM:* T. Banton. *Attendance:* 1,070. *"It's probably the best I've played,"* said Tom Banton after his match-winning century, sounding as excited as if he had just finished a shift delivering parcels. The ground had been shrouded in fog for the Kent innings, though Bell-Drummond refused to blame the conditions, simply saying that *"we never really got going"* in a toothless bowling display. Banton reached his hundred from 47 balls, and hit seven sixes; Devon Conway was happy to stay in his shadow. Their stand of 169* was a Somerset record for the first wicket, and the highest unbroken T20 partnership on British soil.

At Canterbury, July 2 (floodlit). **Kent won by 11 runs.** ‡**Kent 191-4** (20 overs) (J. L. Denly 36, J. A. Leaning 50, J. M. Cox 61*); **Surrey 180-6** (20 overs) (W. G. Jacks 87, L. J. Evans 57; A. F. Milne 4-38). *PoM:* W. G. Jacks. *Attendance:* 1,319. The increasingly potent Leaning–Cox axis added 90 in nine overs, and ensured Surrey faced a daunting target. But so imperious was Will Jacks in the reply that Laurie Evans later admitted he thought victory was *"in the bag"*; Jacks eventually fell for a T20-best 87 from 54 balls. However, Qais Ahmad's stifling leg-spin meant 18 were needed off the last. Three balls yielded six, before Adam Milne took what he described as a *"horrendous"* hat-trick.

At Canterbury, July 18 (floodlit). **Sussex won by four wickets.** ‡**Kent 130-7** (20 overs) (H. Z. Finch 30, C. S. MacLeod 31; R. S. Bopara 3-15); **Sussex 134-6** (17.1 overs) (L. J. Wright 39, D. M. W. Rawlins 33; H. W. Podmore 3-35). *PoM:* R. S. Bopara. *Attendance:* 1,123. Kent were certain to head the group, and their severely weakened team – 15 were in quarantine – had less to play for than Sussex, for whom a win would guarantee progress. Scots internationals George Munsey, Safyaan Sharif and Calum MacLeod, whose 31 was the top score in a modest 130, had been drafted in by Kent, while Sussex included Jofra Archer, back briefly after an elbow injury. His 0-20 from three overs was outshone by Ravi Bopara. Sussex wobbled when Luke Wright and Bopara fell in the same over, but Crawley stumbled trying to catch Delray Rawlins, and Harry Podmore's three-wicket burst came too late.

Kent away matches

June 15: lost to Somerset by 47 runs.
June 16: beat Glamorgan by 40 runs.
June 22: lost to Gloucestershire by eight wickets.
June 25: beat Essex by 28 runs (DLS).

June 29: no result v Sussex.
July 9: beat Surrey by nine wickets.
July 16: beat Middlesex by 77 runs.

MIDDLESEX

At Lord's, June 10 (floodlit). **Surrey won by 54 runs. Surrey 223-7** (20 overs) (J. J. Roy 45, W. G. Jacks 70; N. A. Sowter 3-40); ‡**Middlesex 169-9** (20 overs) (S. S. Eskinazi 36, P. R. Stirling 58, E. J. G. Morgan 32; S. M. Curran 4-29). *PoM:* W. G. Jacks. *County debut:* C. J. Green (Middlesex). *Attendance:* 5,709. *Surrey made the highest T20 total at Lord's as Jacks pummelled his fifty from 15 deliveries. All told, 66 of his 24-ball 70 came in boundaries, and he made Jason Roy look pedestrian. A chastening evening for Middlesex saw Blake Cullen removed from the attack for two beamers, both uppercut for six by Tom Curran; it meant Surrey scored 18 from one legitimate ball of the 19th over, which was finished by Ethan Bamber and cost 28. Paul Stirling hit 58 from 28, but Sam Curran took advantage of Middlesex risk-taking to net four wickets.*

FASTEST T20 FIFTIES BY BALLS IN THE UK

13	M. E. Trescothick	.....	Somerset v Hampshire at Taunton	....	2010
14	G. L. Brophy	....	Yorkshire v Derbyshire at Derby	....	2006
15	**W. G. Jacks**		**Surrey v Middlesex at Lord's**	....	**2021**
16	A. D. Hales	....	Nottinghamshire v Derbyshire at Nottingham	....	2010
16	D. T. Christian	....	Nottinghamshire v Leicestershire at Nottingham	....	2016
16	L. Ronchi	....	Leicestershire v Durham at Leicester	....	2017
16	A. J. Finch	....	Surrey v Middlesex at The Oval	....	2018
17	M. J. Lumb	....	Nottinghamshire v Leicestershire at Nottingham	....	2016
17	M. H. Wessels	....	Nottinghamshire v Worcestershire at Nottingham	....	2016
17	B. M. Duckett	....	Northamptonshire v Nottinghamshire at Northampton	.....	2018
17	M. H. Wessels	....	Nottinghamshire v Worcestershire at Worcester	....	2018
17	**L. S. Livingstone**		**England v Pakistan at Nottingham**	....	**2021**

At Radlett, June 15. **Middlesex won by three wickets. Hampshire 215-6** (20 overs) (J. M. Vince 31, D. J. M. Short 48, J. J. Weatherley 41, L. D. McManus 47); ‡**Middlesex 217-7** (19.4 overs) (J. B. Cracknell 77, J. A. Simpson 62; M. S. Crane 3-35). *PoM:* J. B. Cracknell. *Attendance:* 671. *In retrospect, a series of surrendered starts – the top five all fell between 23 and 48 – cost Hampshire, though at the halfway point a total of 215 seemed plenty. It took a late onslaught from Chris Green, who had earlier conceded 55, to ensure Middlesex crossed the line – after Joe Cracknell and John Simpson had put on a club-record 122 for the fourth wicket in ten overs.*

At Radlett, June 17. **Gloucestershire won by two runs** (DLS). **Middlesex 179-5** (20 overs) (J. B. Cracknell 67, E. J. G. Morgan 38); ‡**Gloucestershire 157-5** (18 overs) (C. D. J. Dent 32, I. A. Cockbain 62*). *PoM:* I. A. Cockbain. *Attendance:* 494. *In a farcical finish in gathering gloom – both captains criticised a 5.30 start at a ground without floodlights – Middlesex began to walk off in the belief they had won on DLS. Poor visibility had forced Eoin Morgan to resort to spin once the umpires made it clear it was too dark for anything else; with Gloucestershire ahead on DLS, he obliged. But when Middlesex got their noses in front, Morgan switched to pace in the expectation it would prompt the end of the game. However, the umpires ruled the light had improved, and play could continue. Finn conceded 15 from the 18th, only for rain to fall. Had Ian Cockbain hit Finn for four, not six, off the last, the game would have been tied. Cracknell had earlier made another fifty.*

At Lord's, June 24 (floodlit). **Essex won by two wickets. Middlesex 183-2** (20 overs) (S. S. Eskinazi 102*); ‡**Essex 184-8** (20 overs) (D. W. Lawrence 59, M. S. Pepper 43, J. D. S. Neesham 30; D. J. Mitchell 3-24). *PoM:* D. W. Lawrence. *County debut:* D. J. Mitchell (Middlesex). *Attendance:* 6,221. *A maiden T20 century from Steve Eskinazi proved in vain, because runs from the other end came too* *slowly. He managed a strike-rate of 167, but neither Cracknell (29 off 23) nor Daryl Mitchell (29 off 24) could match his pace, despite Middlesex having wickets in hand. Essex seemed on the brink of a straightforward victory when, with Dan Lawrence on 57 and Jimmy Neesham on 28, they needed 16 from two overs. But both fell to Tom Helm, then three more to Mitchell. With four required off the last ball, a thick edge from Simon Harmer flew to the boundary.*

At Radlett, June 27. **Middlesex won by seven wickets.** ‡**Glamorgan 170-8** (20 overs) (D. A. Douthwaite 53, W. J. Weighell 51; D. J. Mitchell 3-37); **Middlesex 171-3** (17.4 overs) (S. S. Eskinazi 91*, D. J. Mitchell 32). *PoM:* S. S. Eskinazi. *Attendance: 407. Eskinazi enjoyed another day in the sun – had Middlesex needed more, he might have made successive hundreds – and this time steered his side to an easy win. So poor was Glamorgan's rejigged top order (Marnus Labuschagne and Nick Selman were both unavailable) that it looked as if Middlesex might be chasing under 100. But James Weighell joined Dan Douthwaite at 76-6, and they added 88 – a seventh-wicket record in all county cricket – at more than 11 an over. After three wickets with his medium-pace, Mitchell clonked 32 off 13 balls to hasten the end.*

At Lord's, July 1. **Middlesex won by 63 runs. Middlesex 166-7** (20 overs) (S. S. Eskinazi 59, M. D. E. Holden 38); ‡**Sussex 103-9** (20 overs) (N. A. Sowter 3-13, B. C. Cullen 3-21). *PoM:* S. S. Eskinazi. *County debut:* H. D. Ward (Sussex). *Attendance: 6,861. At 134-2 after 14, Middlesex were on course for many more than 166, but the wheels came off, partly against the death bowling of Tymal Mills (2-31). As was now customary, Eskinazi was the bedrock of the innings: four consecutive scores of 59 or more atoned for a total of 70 from his first five knocks. But if Middlesex had made a mess, it was nothing compared with Sussex. Travis Head top-scored with 23, while leg-spinner Nathan Sowter and seamer Cullen each took three wickets.*

At Lord's, July 16 (floodlit). **Kent won by 77 runs.** ‡**Kent 157-8** (20 overs) (H. G. Kuhn 42, H. Z. Finch 47; B. C. Cullen 4-33); **Middlesex 80** (16.3 overs) (E. O. Hooper 3-24). *PoM:* E. O. Hooper. *County debuts:* V. Chopra (Middlesex); E. O. Hooper, C. S. MacLeod, H. G. Munsey, S. M. Sharif (Kent). *Attendance: 7,652. In the dying moments of Middlesex's shambolic reply – their worst T20 total, and the lowest against Kent – there were ironic cheers for the 17 added by the last pair. That included a standing ovation when No. 11 Mujeeb Zadran struck the innings' only six, 13 overs after Cracknell had hit his only four. If Middlesex looked as though they had been forced to assemble a scratch team because of Covid, in reality Kent. Two years after a Championship game for Sussex, left-arm spinner Elliot Hooper took a three-for on T20 debut. Earlier, the 19-year-old Cullen had claimed four, including Harry Finch, another recruit from Sussex, for 47.*

No. 11 TOP-SCORES IN A T20 INNINGS

24*	M. F. Cleary	....	Leicestershire (97-9) v Durham at Leicester	 2004
16*	H. G. D. Nayanakantha	..	Ragama (89) v Army at Colombo (CCC)	 2006-07
15	R. Casimir	....	Dominica (77) v Barbados at Coolidge	 2007-08
17*	M. T. Chinouya	....	Centrals (121) v Easterns at Harare (Country Club)	... 2007-08
19*	G. J-P. Kruger	....	Lions (104-9) v Dolphins at Johannesburg	 2007-08
23*	H. D. N. de Silva	......	Panadura (59) v Chilaw Marians at Colombo (Colts)	.. 2011-12
20	P. Jaswal	....	Himachal Pradesh (76) v Punjab at Delhi	 2014-15
26*	A. A. S. Silva	....	Saracens (95) v Bloomfield at Colombo (Colts)	 2015-16
19*	Zahir Khan	....	Brisbane Heat (109) v Perth Scorchers at Carrara	 2019-20
13	**Mujeeb Zadran**	**.......**	**Middlesex (80) v Kent at Lord's**	**................** **2021**
20	**P. Vekaria**	**..........**	**Rwanda (115) v Malawi at Kigali**	**..............** **2021-22**

Casimir and Vekaria were joint-top scorers.

Middlesex away matches

June 11: lost to Kent by 16 runs.
June 18: lost to Glamorgan by 21 runs.
June 25: lost to Surrey by five wickets.
June 28: no result v Hampshire.

July 2: lost to Somerset by five runs.
July 9: lost to Gloucestershire by ten runs.
July 18: beat Essex by nine runs.

SOMERSET

At Taunton, June 9 (floodlit). **Essex won by three wickets. Somerset 185-7** (20 overs) (J. C. Hildreth 39, B. G. F. Green 43*; S. J. Cook 3-14); ‡**Essex 187-7** (18.5 overs) (P. I. Walter 45, J. D. S. Neesham 53; J. H. Davey 3-39, M. de Lange 3-35). *PoM:* J. D. S. Neesham. *County debut: J. D. S. Neesham (Essex). Attendance: 1,144. Handed the role of opener at the age of 36, James Hildreth responded with 39 off 18, as Somerset plundered 57 from the first three overs. But they were pegged back by seamer Sam Cook, before Essex's overseas recruit, New Zealander James Neesham, blitzed a 23-ball half-century to see them home with seven balls to spare.*

At Taunton, June 11 (floodlit). **Surrey won by seven wickets. Somerset 187-6** (20 overs) (J. C. Hildreth 31, T. B. Abell 69); ‡**Surrey 188-3** (16 overs) (J. J. Roy 30, L. J. Evans 65, S. M. Curran 72*). *PoM:* S. M. Curran. *Attendance: 1,149. Despite Tom Abell's stylish 69 off 44, Somerset's 187 was below par on a road of a pitch, on which Surrey raced to victory. Sam Curran's career-best 72* off 36 featured six sixes; Laurie Evans (65 off 34) also batted brilliantly in their stand of 104 in 8.5 overs, a Surrey record for the third wicket.*

At Taunton, June 15 (floodlit). **Somerset won by 47 runs. Somerset 204-7** (20 overs) (T. B. Abell 68, L. P. Goldsworthy 48; G. Stewart 3-33); ‡**Kent 157** (18 overs) (Z. Crawley 48, J. M. Cox 33; M. de Lange 3-18). *PoM:* T. B. Abell. *Attendance: 1,575. Abell's ability to score quickly with textbook shots, and the precocious talent of 20-year-old Lewis Goldsworthy, helped rescue Somerset with a fourth-wicket stand of 90 in 7.4 overs. Responding to an imposing 204, Kent struggled, not least during three rapid overs from Marchant de Lange; only Zak Crawley (48 off 23) fired.*

At Taunton, June 19 (floodlit). **Somerset v Glamorgan. Abandoned.**

At Taunton, June 25 (floodlit). **Somerset won by seven runs. Somerset 172-9** (20 overs) (T. Banton 77, W. C. F. Smeed 63*; S. W. Currie 4-31); ‡**Hampshire 165-8** (20 overs) (D. J. M. Short 37, C. de Grandhomme 66; L. Gregory 3-46). *PoM:* T. Banton. *County debuts: D. P. Conway (Somerset); C. de Grandhomme, T. J. Prest (Hampshire). Attendance: 1,953. Having scored 33 runs in five innings, Tom Banton finally rediscovered his touch, with 77 off 37 including eight fours and five sixes. Teenager Will Smeed (63* off 44), oozed class. Requiring 173, Hampshire fell to 16-2, before Colin de Grandhomme marked his county debut with 66 off 34, but de Lange's four overs for 13 proved decisive.*

At Taunton, July 2 (floodlit). **Somerset won by five runs** (DLS). **Somerset 152** (18.1 overs) (D. P. Conway 45, W. C. F. Smeed 33; B. C. Cullen 4-32); ‡**Middlesex 114-6** (16 overs) (N. A. Sowter 37*; C. Overton 3-28). *PoM:* B. C. Cullen. *Attendance: 1,889. Blake Cullen's hat-trick went unnoticed by team-mates, spectators – and Cullen himself. By sending back Goldsworthy with the last ball of the 14th over, then returning for the 18th to dismiss Ben Green and de Lange, he joined two New Zealanders – Adam Milne (Kent) and Lockie Ferguson (Yorkshire) – among the day's three hat-trick takers. Craig Overton, captaining Somerset for the first time, had made a golden duck, as his team were bowled out for 152. But he roared back with the ball, taking three as Middlesex also faltered, after a sprightly 37* off 24 by Nathan Sowter. When rain fell, they were five behind on DLS.*

TWENTY20 HAT-TRICKS FOR MIDDLESEX

D. P. Nannes	v Essex at Chelmsford	2008
T. S. Roland-Jones	v Glamorgan at Cardiff	2019
C. J. Green	**v Kent at Canterbury**	**2021**
B. C. Cullen	**v Somerset at Taunton**	**2021**

At Taunton, July 18 (floodlit). **Somerset won by 23 runs. Somerset 183-7** (20 overs) (W. C. F. Smeed 39, T. A. Lammonby 90); ‡**Gloucestershire 160-6** (20 overs) (I. A. Cockbain 72). *PoM:* T. A. Lammonby. *Attendance: 2,054. Somerset were boosted by an astonishing assault from Tom Lammonby. Arriving at 74-4 in the 13th (it was soon 89-5), he played one of the great T20 innings seen at Taunton, sailing to a 22-ball half-century – his first in the format – and eventually smashing*

90 off 36, with 11 fours and four sixes; he was run out off the final ball of the innings. Shellshocked Gloucestershire never recovered, despite Ian Cockbain's own fireworks (72 off 46); Overton and Jack Brooks conceded just 37 from their eight overs. The result ensured Somerset a home quarter-final, and knocked out their opponents.

Somerset away matches

June 18: no result v Sussex.
June 23: beat Surrey by seven wickets.
June 28: beat Kent by ten wickets.
June 29: lost to Essex by six wickets.

July 1: beat Gloucestershire by eight wickets.
July 9: lost to Hampshire by 75 runs.
July 16: beat Glamorgan by 74 runs.

SURREY

At The Oval, June 14 (floodlit). **Surrey won by five wickets. Glamorgan 166-8** (20 overs) (N. J. Selman 43, M. Labuschagne 74; D. T. Moriarty 3-26); ‡**Surrey 167-5** (18.2 overs) (J. J. Roy 64, L. J. Evans 39, J. L. Smith 35*). *PoM:* J. J. Roy. *Attendance:* 3,055. *Jason Roy's 64 off 36 all but decided the match, after Marnus Labuschagne's 74 from 51 provided the substance of Glamorgan's 166; left-arm spinner Dan Moriarty claimed three wickets. Roy's charge was augmented by Laurie Evans's punchy 39 and Jamie Smith's mature 35*, which overcame a slip from 88-1 to 101-4.*

At The Oval, June 17 (floodlit). **No result. Surrey 53-2** (5 overs) (W. G. Jacks 38*) v ‡**Sussex.** *Attendance:* 2,723. *Rain ended the match after five eventful overs. Roy was spectacularly caught off the second ball by Archie Lenham at fine leg, before Will Jacks took 26 from Tymal Mills's only over, the third, which cost 28 in all. Dropped off the first ball, he hit the next three for six.*

At The Oval, June 18 (floodlit). **Surrey v Hampshire. Abandoned.**

At The Oval, June 21 (floodlit). **Essex won by eight wickets. Surrey 118** (16.4 overs) (J. Clark 30; S. J. Cook 4-15); ‡**Essex 119-2** (15.3 overs) (W. E. L. Buttleman 56*, A. J. A. Wheater 30). *PoM:* S. J. Cook. *County debut:* B. B. A. Geddes (Surrey). *Attendance:* 1,526. *Surrey's first defeat began to look inevitable when they slipped to 39-4 in a game reduced to 17 overs a side. Debutant Ben Geddes made 28, but Sam Cook led the attack outstandingly to claim 4-15. With Essex needing only 119, openers Will Buttleman and Adam Wheater effectively settled victory by hitting 67 in eight overs.*

At The Oval, June 23 (floodlit). **Somerset won by seven wickets. Surrey 146-8** (20 overs) (W. G. Jacks 65; M. J. Leach 3-28); ‡**Somerset 149-3** (18.4 overs) (J. C. Hildreth 72*, W. C. F. Smeed 42). *PoM:* J. C. Hildreth. *Attendance:* 3,829. *James Hildreth marked his 200th T20 match by hitting the winning runs, having dominated a second-wicket stand of 103 off 63 with Will Smeed; Surrey's 146-8 looked thin. Jacks had enjoyed himself in the early stages, with six fours and three sixes, but Somerset's spinners took control. Max Waller's overs cost only 17, while Jack Leach, playing his first T20 game in ten seasons as a professional, took 3-28 and ran out Evans.*

LIFELONG LOYALISTS

Most T20 appearances for one team, without ever playing for another:

205	J. C. Hildreth (Somerset)	2004 to 2021
177	D. K. H. Mitchell (Worcestershire)	2005 to 2021
143	M. T. C. Waller (Somerset)	2009 to 2021
136	M. A. Wallace (Glamorgan)	2003 to 2016
133	A. G. Wakely (Northamptonshire)	2009 to 2020

At The Oval, June 25 (floodlit). **Surrey won by five wickets. Middlesex 174-7** (20 overs) (S. S. Eskinazi 64, D. J. Mitchell 58; A. A. P. Atkinson 4-36); ‡**Surrey 175-5** (19 overs) (W. G. Jacks 47, O. J. D. Pope 52*). *PoM:* O. J. D. Pope. *County debut:* K. A. Jamieson (Surrey). *Attendance:* 3,905. *A double-wicket maiden from Jacks set Middlesex back, but Steve Eskinazi and Daryl Mitchell added 106 in 12 overs. An attack including three leg-spinners – Nathan Sowter, Luke*

Hollman and Nick Gubbins, who shared all five wickets – troubled Surrey. They needed 57 from the last four overs, and got there in three: Ollie Pope held his nerve, and Jamie Overton (24* off ten) blasted three sixes.

At The Oval, July 9 (floodlit). **Kent won by nine wickets. Surrey 128-7** (20 overs) (J. Clark 37*); ‡**Kent 129-1** (15.3 overs) (J. L. Denly 31, D. J. Bell-Drummond 53*, O. G. Robinson 45*). PoM: D. J. Bell-Drummond. *County debut:* T. H. David (Surrey). *Attendance:* 4,373. *Kent outclassed Surrey, whose meagre total never posed any threat. Fast bowler Adam Milne's 2-13 set the tone, and Jordan Clark's 37* was the best Surrey could muster. Their underpowered attack were picked off easily: Daniel Bell-Drummond and Ollie Robinson made 65 in 7.1 overs as the Spitfires flew to their target.*

Surrey away matches

June 10: beat Middlesex by 54 runs.
June 11: beat Somerset by seven wickets.
June 27: no result v Sussex.
June 29: lost to Glamorgan by one run.

June 30: beat Hampshire by 20 runs.
July 2: lost to Kent by 11 runs.
July 16: beat Gloucestershire by seven wickets.

SUSSEX

At Hove, June 12 (floodlit). **Sussex won by nine wickets.** ‡**Hampshire 154-7** (20 overs) (J. M. Vince 36; A. D. Lenham 3-14); **Sussex 155-1** (16.2 overs) (P. D. Salt 72*, R. S. Bopara 56*). PoM: A. D. Lenham. *Attendance:* 2,209. *On his home debut, 16-year-old leg-spinner Archie Lenham had an unforgettable night, taking a wicket with his first ball and adding two more to claim the match award. Although eight Hampshire batters made double figures, only James Vince and James Fuller (26*) passed 18. Phil Salt and Ravi Bopara put on £118* from 74 balls for Sussex's second wicket, with Bopara making what was then his highest score for them.*

At Hove, June 18 (floodlit). **Sussex v Somerset. Abandoned.**

At Hove, June 22 (floodlit). **Sussex v Glamorgan. Abandoned.** *Sussex's third no-result in a row.*

At Hove, June 25 (floodlit). **Gloucestershire won by 27 runs. Gloucestershire 162-5** (20 overs) (G. D. Phillips 94*, J. M. R. Taylor 38; T. S. Mills 3-20); ‡**Sussex 135** (19.5 overs) (L. J. Wright 33, O. E. Robinson 31; R. F. Higgins 3-18, B. A. C. Howell 4-15). PoM: G. D. Phillips. *Attendance:* 2,380. *For the second game running, New Zealand international Glenn Phillips made 94* in a Gloucestershire win, and shared a club-record fifth-wicket stand with James Taylor. This time, he had to oversee a recovery from 35-4 at the end of the powerplay, and was a little more circumspect. He did not hit the first of his five sixes until his 26th ball; then he cut loose. Benny Howell's clever variations ensured his efforts were not wasted.*

At Hove, June 27. **No result. Surrey 175-7** (20 overs) (J. L. Smith 57, L. J. Evans 31; T. S. Mills 3-21); ‡**Sussex 43-1** (4.5 overs). *Attendance:* 2,353. *Once again, the weather turned against Sussex, this time at a crucial – not to say cruel – juncture. One more ball would have constituted a match (meaning that, at 24.5 overs, this was the longest possible T20 game to end in a no-result). But in poor light and with rain falling, Luke Wright was hit on the helmet from the fourth delivery of Kyle Jamieson's second over. The umpires allowed one more ball, then took the players from the field, with Sussex well ahead of the five-over DLS par score – even if they lost a wicket. Neither they nor the 2,500 crowd were happy: "The lads are gutted," said coach James Kirtley. "But they've shown incredible character in what might have been a provocative situation." Surrey had earlier built a decent total around Jamie Smith's maiden T20 fifty, while Tymal Mills took 3-21.*

At Hove, June 29 (floodlit). **Sussex v Kent. Abandoned.** *The fifth Sussex game (and fourth at home) not to reach a result.*

At Hove, July 9 (floodlit). **Sussex won by six wickets. Essex 146-9** (20 overs) (T. Westley 53, M. S. Pepper 38; C. J. Jordan 3-30); ‡**Sussex 148-4** (18.3 overs) (R. S. Bopara 62*, D. M. W. Rawlins 50*). PoM: R. S. Bopara. *Attendance:* 2,415. *Bopara, against the county where he spent 18 seasons,* *and Rawlins guided Sussex home after an uncertain start: 67-4 at halfway in reply to Essex's 146. Bopara was the steadier, improving his highest Sussex score to 62* from 46, with Rawlins, whose fourth six delivered victory, the more flamboyant. Essex had reached 121-3 thanks to Tom Westley's fifty, but his departure sparked a collapse of six for 22. Sussex went second in the group.*

Sussex away matches

June 11: beat Gloucestershire by five wickets.
June 15: beat Essex by seven wickets.
June 17: no result v Surrey.
July 1: lost to Middlesex by 63 runs.

July 2: beat Glamorgan by 33 runs.
July 16: lost to Hampshire by six wickets.
July 18: beat Kent by four wickets.

QUARTER-FINALS

At Chester-le-Street, August 24 (floodlit). **Sussex won by five wickets.** ‡Yorkshire 177-7 (20 overs) (T. Köhler-Cadmore 55, G. S. Ballance 55; T. S. Mills 3-39); **Sussex 178-5** (19.4 overs) (L. J. Wright 54; J. A. Thompson 3-28). PoM: Rashid Khan. *Attendance:* 1,500. *Afghan leg-spinner Rashid Khan won the match with the bat, taking Sussex to finals day for the first time since 2018. He came in at 135-4, with 43 required off 21 balls, and hit a whirlwind 27* from nine. That included sixes off Matthew Fisher and Jordan Thompson, and three successive fours in an expensive 19th over from David Willey, which left Sussex needing six off the last. Yorkshire had been 33-3 after electing to bat on a good pitch with short boundaries, but were revived by fifties from Tom Köhler-Cadmore and the more fluent Gary Ballance. Luke Wright's belligerent 54 gave Sussex a good start, but three wickets from Thompson seemed to have put Yorkshire on top – until Rashid arrived. The match was played at Durham's HQ as Yorkshire, who had earned a home quarter-final, were about to host a Test at Headingley.*

At Nottingham, August 25 (floodlit). **Hampshire won by two runs.** Hampshire 125-9 (20 overs) (T. J. Prest 44, J. K. Fuller 30; D. Paterson 3-22); ‡**Nottinghamshire 123** (19.4 overs) (J. M. Clarke 42; L. A. Dawson 3-24). PoM: L. A. Dawson. *Attendance:* 14,042. *Defending champions Nottinghamshire were favourites, having dominated the North Group, while Hampshire scraped through from the South on net run-rate. And for three-quarters of the match, the odds only shortened. Put in on a worn pitch, Hampshire made their lowest T20 total of the season. They were 40-5 after nine overs, and their best stand was 49 between Tom Prest and James Fuller. Chasing 126, Nottinghamshire cruised to 66-1, only to lose a calamitous seven for 30, with two each for Liam Dawson and Scott Currie. Even so, after Matt Carter hit three sixes, they effectively needed just two from the last over; if tied on runs and wickets, they would go through on a better score in the powerplay. Yet Carter was at the wrong end and, after failing to find a single from Brad Wheal's first three balls, last man Dane Paterson attacked the fourth and edged behind. A crowd of 14,042 was a record for a domestic midweek fixture at Trent Bridge.*

At Taunton, August 26 (floodlit). **Somerset won by seven wickets.** Lancashire 184-9 (20 overs) (J. J. Bohannon 35, D. J. Vilas 42, R. P. Jones 38*; R. E. van der Merwe 4-27, M. de Lange 3-41); ‡**Somerset 185-3** (18.1 overs) (W. C. F. Smeed 44, T. B. Abell 78*, T. A. Lammonby 47*). PoM: T. B. Abell. *Attendance:* 3,886. *An explosive start from Josh Bohannon (35 off 20) and Liam Livingstone (25 off 10) was built on by Dane Vilas, and propelled Lancashire past 100 within ten overs. But Roelof van der Merwe's wild celebration on dismissing Livingstone announced a key moment, and his left-arm spin claimed three more wickets in a below-par total of 184. Somerset were lagging behind, requiring 70 from 36, but Tom Abell (78* off 45) and Tom Lammonby (47* off 26) blitzed the winning runs with 11 balls to spare.*

At Canterbury, August 27 (floodlit). **Kent won by 21 runs.** Kent 162-7 (20 overs) (D. J. Bell-Drummond 53, S. W. Billings 56; T. T. Bresnan 4-26); ‡Warwickshire 141 (J. B. Lintott 41; M. E. Milnes 4-24). PoM: S. W. Billings. *Attendance:* 3,116. *A boisterous capacity crowd saw Kent reach their first finals day since 2009. Sam Billings feared it was going to be one of those nights, when his drive ricocheted off the non-striker's wicket to Jake Lintott, who uprooted two* *stumps to run out the dangerous Daniel Bell-Drummond. Billings later became one of four victims for Tim Bresnan, but by then he had steered Kent towards a decent 162. If Warwickshire were confident at the break, they were in trouble at 55-6 in the 11th, as Kent fielded out of their skins. Lower-order flailing, especially from Lintott, gave the visitors fleeting hope, but 25 off the last was beyond them. Matt Milnes took wickets with the final two deliveries.*

FINALS DAY REPORTS BY RICHARD GIBSON

SEMI-FINALS

HAMPSHIRE v SOMERSET

At Birmingham, September 18. Somerset won by two wickets. Toss: Somerset.

"We got a get-out-of-jail card," admitted Gregory, the Somerset captain. It was hard to disagree, after a spectacular tail-end heist extended Hampshire's run of semi-final defeats to five in nine T20 tournaments, and sent Somerset to a record fifth final. When Abell lofted Currie to deep midwicket immediately after reaching 50, Somerset – seven down – needed 48 from 20 balls. It looked for all the world as though Hampshire, having defended 125 in the quarters against Nottinghamshire, would make their first Edgbaston final after six defeats in the semis. But Green, who had made eight off ten, thrashed 27 from his next seven, only to hole out to long-on. With 12 needed off seven, in came Davey, buoyed by his four wickets; he hit his second ball, from Wheal, for a straight six, and his third for the match-winning four. Hampshire had begun poorly, losing three wickets in four overs, which would have been four in six had Somerset had sufficient fielders in the ring. Weatherley noticed, and knew he was safe to throw caution to the wind: a steepling top edge was held by Banton, running towards square leg – and Dawson clonked six from the resulting free hit. The savvy Weatherley held the innings together as wickets fell, though his 50-ball 71 could not quite bring enough runs.

Player of the Match: J. H. Davey.   *Attendance (for all three matches on finals day):* 24,789.

Hampshire

		B	4/6
1 *J. M. Vince *c 1 b 9*..........	2	7	0
2 T. E. Albert *c 1 b 10*	5	7	1
3 T. J. Prest *b 10*..............	0	1	0
4 J. J. Weatherley *c 4 b 11*	71	50	2/5
5 L. A. Dawson *b 8*............	18	19	0/1
6 †L. D. McManus *c 1 b 5*	4	7	0
7 J. K. Fuller *run out (3/1)*......	22	19	1/1
8 C. P. Wood *b 10*	18	6	1/2
9 S. W. Currie *b 10*............	0	2	0
10 M. S. Crane *not out*	3	3	0
11 B. T. J. Wheal *run out (6/11)*..	0	0	0
B 2, lb 2, w 1, nb 2	7		

6 overs: 45-3   (20 overs) **150**

1/8 2/8 3/26 4/65 5/80 6/111 7/133 8/133 9/149

Overton 18–11–15–1; Davey 24–11–34–4; van der Merwe 24–7–30–0; Goldsworthy 24–9–21–1; Green 6–2–4–1; de Lange 24–7–42–1.

Somerset

		B	4/6
1 †T. Banton *c 3 b 11*	6	11	0
2 W. C. F. Smeed *c 1 b 8*	15	16	3
3 R. E. van der Merwe *c 1 b 9* ...	2	3	0
4 T. B. Abell *c 7 b 9*	50	35	3/2
5 L. P. Goldsworthy *run out (7/6)*	3	5	0
6 T. A. Lammonby *lbw b 10*.....	0	1	0
7 *L. Gregory *b 5*	18	20	1
8 B. G. F. Green *c 3 b 8*	35	18	1/3
9 C. Overton *not out*	11	6	0/1
10 J. H. Davey *not out*	11	3	1/1
Lb 2.......................	2		

6 overs: 30-3   (19.4 overs) **153-8**

1/15 2/19 3/29 4/34 5/34 6/79 7/103 8/139

11 M. de Lange did not bat.

Wood 24–11–26–2; Wheal 22–7–40–1; Currie 24–7–30–2; Crane 24–7–27–1; Dawson 24–6–28–1.

Umpires: M. Burns and G. D. Lloyd.   Third umpire: N. L. Bainton.
Referee: W. M. Noon.

KENT v SUSSEX

At Birmingham, September 18. Kent won by 21 runs. Toss: Kent.

When Darren Stevens won his first Twenty20 title in 2004, Archie Lenham was a newborn baby. Now the oldest and youngest players to feature on finals day came face to face. Stevens, recalled in place of the injured Alex Blake, was happy in the spotlight. He built on Bell-Drummond's 51-ball 82 – the spine of the innings, and his sixth half-century of the competition – with a flurry of boundaries. As usual, Kent had chosen to bat, though it did not go wholly to plan: from three superb powerplay overs, Garton took two for 12, while three wickets in five balls later reduced them to 94 for five. There were also two tidy overs from Lenham; had Rashid Khan been available, Kent might have buckled. Instead, Stevens joined Bell-Drummond, put on a brisk 42 for the sixth wicket and, to the delight of the crowd, dabbed, scooped and drove his side towards 168. Klaassen's potency in the powerplay meant they barely missed Adam Milne, who had gone to the IPL: from the moment he had Salt caught behind in the second over, wickets fell regularly, including one for Stevens, who nipped out the dangerous Wiese. At 57 for five, Sussex hopes rested on Garton, whose savage hitting had been a feature of their season. His third six took him to 41 from 22, but next ball he sliced to short third man – and the end was in sight. Klaasen wrapped things up with a career-best four for 17.

Player of the Match: D. J. Bell-Drummond.

Kent

		B	4/6
1 Z. Crawley *b 7*	9	9	1
2 D. J. Bell-Drummond *c 3 b 8*	82	51	7/2
3 J. L. Denly *c 8 b 7*	3	8	0
4 *†S. W. Billings *b 3*	14	14	1
5 J. A. Leaning *b 10*	0	2	0
6 J. M. Cox *c 1 b 10*	0	1	0
7 D. I. Stevens *not out*	47	28	7
8 G. Stewart *c 1 b 10*	3	6	0
9 Qais Ahmad *run out (1)*	2	2	0
10 M. E. Milnes *not out*	0	0	0
B 1, lb 1, w 4, nb 2	8		

6 overs: 53-2   (20 overs)   **168-8**

1/24 2/51 3/93 4/94 5/94 6/136 7/160 8/163

11 F. J. Klaassen did not bat.

Garton 24–10–24–2; Wiese 6–1–15–0; Mills 24–9–33–3; Jordan 24–5–36–1; Lenham 12–1–13–0; Beer 18–4–24–0; Bopara 12–5–21–1.

Sussex

		B	4/6
1 †P. D. Salt *c 4 b 11*	9	6	2
2 *L. J. Wright *b 10*	10	9	2
3 R. S. Bopara *c 4 b 9*	22	20	2/1
4 D. M. W. Rawlins *c 5 b 11*	2	7	0
5 D. Wiese *b 7*	3	7	0
6 H. D. Ward *c 2 b 5*	21	18	2
7 G. H. S. Garton *c 8 b 10*	41	23	4/3
8 C. J. Jordan *c 2 b 11*	13	10	0/1
9 W. A. T. Beer *not out*	11	9	1
10 T. S. Mills *b 10*	6	4	1
11 A. D. Lenham *c 9 b 11*	1	2	0
Lb 5, w 3	8		

6 overs: 40-3   (19.1 overs)   **147**

1/15 2/31 3/39 4/43 5/57 6/89 7/119 8/136 9/146

Denly 12–6–16–0; Klaassen 19–11–17–4; Milnes 18–5–22–3; Stewart 12–6–15–0; Qais Ahmad 24–11–32–1; Stevens 12–2–22–1; Leaning 18–7–18–1.

Umpires: G. D. Lloyd and M. J. Saggers.   Third umpire: N. L. Bainton.
Referee: W. M. Noon.

FINAL

KENT v SOMERSET

At Birmingham, September 18. Kent won by 25 runs. Toss: Somerset.

This was one of the great I-told-you-so tales. When Stevens was omitted from the quarter-final against Warwickshire, he struck a bargain with Billings, his captain, and Matt Walker, the coach. "I was devastated, but one thing I did say was: 'You get us to finals day, and I'll win you the comp.'"

Ashley Allen, Getty Images

Flight control: Jordan Cox intercepts the ball as he leaps over the boundary, patting it back to Matt Milnes before touching the ground.

Stevens did not let his colleagues down: at 45, he became a Twenty20 champion for the third time – and was involved in the moment that effectively settled the contest.

It was Cox, however, almost 25 years younger, who was the chief protagonist. Somerset needed 74 from 39 when Stevens came on to bowl; Gregory middled a pull, which was heading over the ropes and into the Hollies Stand. But Cox soared high beyond the boundary, and slapped the ball back into the grasp of the gleeful Milnes. It was a relay catch of the utmost skill – Cox seemed to hang in the air for an eternity – and a full house rose as one.

None wore a wider smile than Stevens. After three years out of Kent's T20 team, he had played every group game bar two (when he had to self-isolate), and looked forward to many more: "I've got no interest in stopping. As long as I keep looking after my body, as long as the eyes stay good, I'll be all right." Now, a flicked six in an eight-ball cameo was followed by some steady bowling, as Kent decided pace off the ball was the route to success. Leg-spinners Denly and Qais Ahmed shared five wickets, including Smeed and Abell, the only Somerset batters to pass 16.

Earlier, slow left-armer van der Merwe helped limit Kent to 118 for five after 17 (and showed Billings how he should approach the Somerset response). But as in the semi-final, Kent unleashed a late assault, inspired this time by the ferocious Cox: he cracked another 38 from 11 balls, as 49 came from the last three overs. Putting a golden duck in the afternoon behind him, he ended with a crucial half-century, reached with a flat six pulled off his 26th delivery.

In a final as enthralling as any in the competition's history, there was no shortage of incident, including a protracted umpiring error. When Smeed was on 36, he slog-swept Denly to deep midwicket, where Cox completed the catch, despite Bell-Drummond clattering into him a fraction of a second later, and then the foam boundary marker too. After much consolation, the umpires signalled six. But Cox had stayed on the field, and MCC later confirmed Smeed should have been out. It mattered not: three balls later, another blow into the night sky by Smeed off Denly was swallowed – by Cox. By the time Somerset managed their next boundary, they had slipped to 100 for seven in the 16th, en route to a record fourth defeat in the final, and Stevens was about to keep his promise.

Player of the Match: J. M. Cox.   *Player of the Tournament:* S. R. Patel.

Kent

	B	4/6
1 Z. Crawley *c 5 b 3* 41	33	4
2 D. J. Bell-Drummond *c 2 b 7*... 18	15	1/1
3 J. L. Denly *c 4 b 7* 0	1	0
4 *†S. W. Billings *c 6 b 7*...... 2	5	0
5 J. A. Leaning *c 8 b 10* 27	29	2
6 J. M. Cox *not out* 58	28	3/3
7 D. I. Stevens *run out (9)*...... 12	8	0/1
8 G. Stewart *run out (10)* 2	2	0
9 Qais Ahmad *not out* 0	0	0
B 1, lb 2, w 2, nb 2 7		

6 overs: 46-2 (20 overs) 167-7

1/44 2/44 3/52 4/75 5/111 6/141 7/151

10 M. E. Milnes and 11 F. J. Klaassen did not bat.

Overton 24–6–37–0; Davey 24–4–41–1; van der Merwe 24–11–19–3; Goldsworthy 24–7–27–1; Green 12–2–17–0; de Lange 12–1–23–0.

Somerset

	B	4/6
1 †T. Banton *st 4 b 3* 0	2	0
2 W. C. F. Smeed *c 6 b 3* 43	32	2/2
3 L. P. Goldsworthy *c 2 b 11* 3	7	0
4 T. B. Abell *c 11 b 9* 26	20	3
5 T. A. Lammonby *lbw b 3* 9	11	0
6 *L. Gregory *c 10 b 7* 6	8	0
7 R. E. van der Merwe *c 3 b 9* ... 4	5	0
8 B. G. F. Green *c 2 b 8* 9	12	0
9 C. Overton *c 5 b 10* 13	8	1/1
10 J. H. Davey *not out* 16	9	0/1
11 M. de Lange *not out* 8	6	0/1
W 5 5		

6 overs: 47-2 (20 overs) 142-9

1/0 2/3 3/61 4/79 5/89 6/94 7/95 8/113 9/119

Denly 24–10–31–3; Klaassen 12–6–17–1; Stewart 18–5–28–1; Milnes 18–4–17–1; Qais Ahmad 24–9–19–2; Stevens 24–5–30–1.

Umpires: M. Burns and M. J. Saggers. Third umpire: N. L. Bainton.
Referee: W. M. Noon.

T20 BLAST FINALS

2003 SURREY beat Warwickshire by nine wickets at Nottingham.
2004 LEICESTERSHIRE beat Surrey by seven wickets at Birmingham.
2005 SOMERSET beat Lancashire by seven wickets at The Oval.
2006 LEICESTERSHIRE beat Nottinghamshire by four runs at Nottingham.
2007 KENT beat Gloucestershire by four wickets Birmingham.
2008 MIDDLESEX beat Kent by three runs at Southampton.
2009 SUSSEX beat Somerset by 63 runs at Birmingham.
2010 HAMPSHIRE beat Somerset by losing fewer wickets with the scores tied at Southampton.
2011 LEICESTERSHIRE beat Somerset by 18 runs at Birmingham.
2012 HAMPSHIRE beat Yorkshire by ten runs at Cardiff.
2013 NORTHAMPTONSHIRE beat Surrey by 102 runs (D/L) at Birmingham.
2014 WARWICKSHIRE beat Lancashire by four runs at Birmingham.
2015 LANCASHIRE beat Northamptonshire by 13 runs at Birmingham.
2016 NORTHAMPTONSHIRE beat Durham by four wickets at Birmingham.
2017 NOTTINGHAMSHIRE beat Warwickshire by 22 runs at Birmingham.
2018 WORCESTERSHIRE beat Sussex by five wickets at Birmingham.
2019 ESSEX beat Worcestershire by four wickets at Birmingham.
2020 NOTTINGHAMSHIRE beat Surrey by six wickets at Birmingham.
2021 KENT beat Somerset by 25 runs at Birmingham.

ROYAL LONDON CUP IN 2021

Kit Harris

1 Glamorgan   2 Durham   3= Essex, Surrey

There were fears that, for the second year running, the Royal London Cup wouldn't go ahead. Rebranded as a "development" competition for up-and-coming county players – presumably alongside down-and-going veterans – it was in danger of experiencing, at best, an identity crisis, and at worst, a terminal decline. The Hundred, scheduled alongside it, rostered 98 county-contracted players, and borrowed another nine as injuries, positive Covid tests and the notorious "ping" withered the counties' strength. The cancellation of Derbyshire's last two Vitality Blast games prompted press-box harbingers of doom to sound the death knell for the Cup. As late as seven days before the first games, ECB chief executive Tom Harrison was imploring the national press to believe that the tournament would be played for the first time since 2019, if in a desperate tenor: "I'm sincerely hoping it will be. Absolutely."

But go ahead it did and, everything reckoned, it flourished. The assumption that this competition would spell disaster for the poorer counties was quashed when Glamorgan claimed a List A title for only the fourth time, ending a 17-year trophy drought. Topping a tight group – a single win separated the first seven teams – they defeated Essex in an enthralling home semi-final, and met fellow minnows Durham in the decider. There were no ringers, no hired hands. They did it the old-fashioned way, using only 14 players in their campaign, nine of whom appeared in every match. On the eve of the final, they opted not to recall their Hundred contingent, but to stick with those who had got them there. "It wouldn't be fair on these guys not to give them the opportunity," said their coach, David Harrison. Despite being underdogs – they had won nothing since 2004, whereas Durham had lifted two one-day trophies, in 2007 and 2014 – Glamorgan boasted unity and consistency.

More than that, their semi-final win was sealed by an unbroken century stand between two undiscovered gems. Joe Cooke scored 66 and took five for 61. Scouted from Hertfordshire, he had not played a senior white-ball game before July; now, he appeared in every match, and finished as the tournament's highest wicket-taker, with 20 at 14. Meanwhile, Tom Cullen, their new white-ball wicketkeeper, chalked up 19 dismissals, six more than anyone else.

Fresh faces were the singular characteristic of the tournament. In its three previous seasons, there had been 66 List A debutants; this year, there were 100. In their opening games, Sussex fielded nine, and Warwickshire eight. Like Cooke and Cullen, dozens seized their opportunity. All six bowlers who claimed five-fors did so for the first time. Liam Patterson-White's figures of 10–3–19–5 against Northamptonshire were the best of the season; his team-mate, Lyndon James, took five in only his second game. While greenhorns filled their bowling boots, the evergreens were not to be outdone. Kyle Abbott, in his 109th match, registered his first five-wicket haul. Essex's 41-year-old

Golden Graham: Durham opener Graham Clark was the competition's top-scorer.

Ryan ten Doeschate took 15 at 20, and Glamorgan's 40-year-old Michael Hogan 16 at 12. His economy-rate was under three.

Batsmen had to contend with rain and unfamiliar venues, but there were 22 totals over 300, with only Glamorgan and Lancashire failing to reach the mark. Durham exceeded it three times, and their 405 for four against Kent – the year's highest total – included an opening stand of 242 between Graham Clark and Alex Lees. A week later, they put on 230 against Gloucestershire. The pair dominated the season's scoring: Clark became the eighth to score 600 one-day runs in an English domestic season since the reduction to a single tournament in 2010. His 646 included three hundreds and 101 boundaries, 43 more than the next best, Lees, who made two centuries in his 562.

Surrey likewise found breathtaking run-making form, not least through the signing of Tim David who, in 2018, had become the first Singapore international to join the global T20 circuit. His 340 runs came at the astonishing strike-rate of 150, and his stand-out innings – an unbeaten 140 from 70 balls against Warwickshire at The Oval – contained 11 sixes. His team-mate Ryan Patel put Nottinghamshire to the sword at Guildford, clouting ten sixes in his 131 off 70; Jamie Smith hit 54 off 19 in the same innings. Tom Wood, of Derbyshire, blitzed 109 from 59 at home, also against Nottinghamshire. In all, 37 centuries were scored by 31 batsmen; for 21, it was their first in the format. Essex's Feroze Khushi got one in his first match; Harry Duke, of Yorkshire, in his second.

The tournament prompted understandable grumbles. For the eighth season since 2006, there wasn't a complete set of quarter-finals: each group's second- and third-placed teams played off for a semi-final against the leaders. The final itself, the 89th in a major domestic List A competition, suffered the unprecedented twin humiliations of a move to midweek *and* away from Lord's. With apologies to Trent Bridge, a showpiece should never suffer such ignominy; the ECB later protested it was a one-off.

There is no doubt squads were stretched. Yorkshire bade adieu to 11 players at the start of The Hundred. Kent, Nottinghamshire and Surrey parted with nine; Lancashire, Somerset and Sussex lost eight. Of these, all except Yorkshire later surrendered a further player to The Hundred once their county campaign was under way, as did Middlesex, Northamptonshire and Warwickshire. Only two of these nine players (Nottinghamshire's Luke Fletcher and Somerset's Marchant de Lange) returned in time for the Cup's closing stages. Factoring in injuries and England selection, Surrey and Sussex had only 60% of their players available; six more counties could call on less than 70% of their staff. Several were forced to sign more players – in some cases, on one-month contracts – just to make it through. Kent used every player they could. Ultimately, though, of the 463 county-contracted cricketers, 54 were fit to play, but didn't.

While the ECB's restructuring took with one hand, it gave back with the other. In 2019, Royal London had voiced their "continued support" of all English one-day cricket, and now increased the prize fund – unchanged since their sponsorship began in 2014 – by 36%. Glamorgan took home £209,000, which was £55,000 more than Somerset two years earlier.

The talent drain had a counterbalance. The counties retained the services of 26 foreign players – The Hundred boasted only 21 – and scores of Academy graduates gaped down the pitch at the likes of Hashim Amla, Cameron Bancroft and Travis Head. Many even felled them.

There was good news for spectators, too, as the number of counties who took one-day cricket into their hinterlands doubled to eight. List A matches were seen, once again, at Sookholme (for the first time since 2018), Chesterfield, Guildford and Scarborough (no games since 2016); Sedbergh and York made their one-day bows. There may yet be a way back for festival cricket at Blackpool, Swansea and Horsham. Scarborough's Five Counties Cricket Week featured a home game for Durham, much to the chagrin of the locals, who chuntered about interlopers from up north.

Surrey and Yorkshire accompanied Glamorgan out of their group – defending champions Somerset were top at one stage, but lost their last three games. Yorkshire were swept aside by Essex in their play-off, but another stunning David century saw Surrey through against Gloucestershire, only for them to be Clark-and-Leesed when they met Durham. That group was looking close, too, until a Covid outbreak in the Gloucestershire squad forced them to pull out of their match against Middlesex at Radlett. The final positions were thus decided, as had become the norm, by each team's percentage of their potential points. Middlesex's president, Mike Selvey, gave voice to their scorn, saying his team should have been awarded the game. "Wait for the controversy at the top when the table is finalised," he tweeted. He then called for a one-point-each abandonment – but Gloucestershire would still have progressed, and Middlesex would have advanced only from eighth to seventh. There was no controversy, save for his suggestion that teams laid low by Covid should forfeit their matches, which failed to grasp the spirit of the age.

FINAL GROUP TABLES

	Group A	P	W	L	T	NR	Pts	Avge pts	NRR
1	DURHAM	8	6	1	0	1	13	1.63	0.92
2	ESSEX	8	5	2	1	0	11	1.38	0.24
3	GLOUCESTERSHIRE	7	4	3	0	0	8	1.14	0.09
4	Lancashire	8	3	2	1	2	9	1.13	0.01
5	Worcestershire	8	3	4	0	1	7	0.88	0.26
6	Hampshire	8	3	4	0	1	7	0.88	0.16
7	Sussex.	8	2	4	0	2	6	0.75	−0.69
8	Middlesex.	7	2	4	0	1	5	0.71	−0.29
9	Kent	8	1	5	0	2	4	0.50	−1.26

Middlesex v Gloucestershire was cancelled because of a Covid outbreak in the Gloucestershire squad; no points were awarded for the game. Rankings in Group A were decided by average points per match.

	Group B	P	W	L	T	NR	Pts	NRR
1	GLAMORGAN	8	4	2	0	2	10	0.82
2	SURREY	8	4	2	0	2	10	0.41
3	YORKSHIRE.	8	4	2	0	2	10	−0.02
4	Leicestershire	8	4	3	0	1	9	−0.43
5	Nottinghamshire.	8	3	3	0	2	8	0.69
6	Warwickshire.	8	3	3	0	2	8	−0.03
7	Somerset.	8	3	3	0	2	8	−0.41
8	Northamptonshire.	8	2	4	0	2	6	−0.41
9	Derbyshire	8	1	6	0	1	3	−0.56

Prize money

£209,000 for winners: GLAMORGAN.
£105,000 for runners-up: DURHAM.
£30,000 for losing semi-finalists: ESSEX and SURREY.

AVERAGES

BATTING (275 runs)

		M	I	NO	R	HS	100	50	Avge	SR	4	6
1	G. Clark (*Durham*)	9	9	1	646	141*	3	1	80.75	98.92	96	5
2	†A. Z. Lees (*Durham*)	9	9	1	562	126*	2	4	70.25	86.99	53	5
3	T. H. David (*Surrey*)	10	8	3	340	140*	2	1	68.00	150.44	27	20
4	L. P. Goldsworthy (*Somerset*)	8	7	1	381	96	0	4	63.50	87.18	31	6
5	J. L. Smith (*Surrey*)	10	7	2	315	85	0	3	63.00	80.35	27	11
6	†H. G. Munsey (*Kent*)	7	5	0	302	108	1	2	60.40	95.87	41	4
7	M. J. Lamb (*Warwicks*) . .	8	7	1	360	119*	1	2	60.00	76.75	33	3
8	S. R. Dickson (*Durham*). .	9	8	3	293	103*	1	1	58.60	113.12	23	9
9	†T. M. Head (*Sussex*)	7	7	2	291	56	0	3	58.20	111.92	25	8
10	†A. N. Cook (*Essex*).	10	10	2	455	110	1	3	56.87	87.66	57	0
11	†B. T. Slater (*Notts*)	8	8	1	395	86	0	4	56.42	90.80	51	2
12	J. S. Rymell (*Essex*)	7	6	0	331	121	1	1	55.16	71.95	31	3
13	†R. S. Patel (*Surrey*).	10	8	1	386	131	2	1	55.14	113.19	33	16
14	†M. D. Stoneman (*Surrey*) .	9	8	2	329	117	1	1	54.83	79.27	33	5
15	†N. R. T. Gubbins (*Hants*) .	7	7	1	318	131*	1	2	53.00	99.06	26	7
16	N. J. Selman (*Glam*)	10	9	1	421	140	1	2	52.62	73.60	34	1

		M	I	NO	R	HS	100	50	Avge	SR	4	6
17	T. Westley (*Essex*)	10	10	2	415	87*	0	4	51.87	85.56	53	0
18	J. A. Haynes (*Worcs*)	7	7	0	362	153	1	2	51.71	94.27	40	3
19	J. C. Hildreth (*Somerset*) .	8	7	1	306	110	1	2	51.00	103.72	28	8
20	L. J. Hill (*Leics*)	8	7	0	322	108	2	1	46.00	94.42	29	3
21	R. K. Patel (*Leics*)	8	8	1	319	118	1	1	45.57	95.50	38	4
22	D. G. Bedingham (*Durham*)	8	7	0	292	67	0	4	41.71	140.38	26	14
23	†R. M. Yates (*Warwicks*) . .	7	7	0	282	103	1	2	40.28	92.76	33	4
24	M. G. K. Burgess (*Warwicks*)	8	8	1	275	73	0	2	39.28	80.17	29	1
25	†H. D. Rutherford (*Glam*) .	10	9	0	308	86	0	4	34.22	93.61	36	7

BOWLING (10 wickets)

		Style	O	M	R	W	BB	4I	Avge	SR	ER
1	M. G. Hogan (*Glam*)	RFM	67.1	7	201	16	4-33	1	12.56	25.18	2.99
2	J. M. Cooke (*Glam*)	RFM	62.5	2	286	20	5-61	1	14.30	18.85	4.55
3	L. A. Patterson-White (*Notts*)	SLA	35	3	188	13	5-19	1	14.46	16.15	5.37
4	B. W. Sanderson (*Northants*)	RFM	54.1	7	252	15	3-29	0	16.80	21.66	4.65
5	C. Rushworth (*Durham*) . . .	RFM	71.4	6	328	17	4-37	1	19.29	25.29	4.57
6	S. R. Harmer (*Essex*)	OB	97	9	352	18	3-42	0	19.55	32.33	3.62
7	R. N. ten Doeschate (*Essex*)	RM	59.2	0	294	15	4-34	1	19.60	23.73	4.95
8	T. E. Bailey (*Lancs*)	RFM	56	6	207	10	3-23	0	20.70	33.60	3.69
9	C. McKerr (*Surrey*)	RFM	64.2	0	386	18	4-64	1	21.44	21.44	6.00
10	S. Snater (*Essex*)	RM	52.4	3	282	13	4-48	1	21.69	24.30	5.35
11	C. T. Steel (*Surrey*)	LB	45	1	220	10	4-33	2	22.00	27.00	4.88
	C. J. White (*Northants*)	RFM	43	3	220	10	4-20	1	22.00	25.80	5.11
13	P. A. van Meekeren (*Durham*)	RFM	56	2	310	14	3-33	0	22.14	24.00	5.53
14	D. T. Moriarty (*Surrey*)	SLA	81.5	7	357	15	4-30	1	23.80	32.73	4.36
15	G. C. H. Hill (*Yorks*)	RFM	47	2	249	10	3-47	0	24.90	28.20	5.29
16	M. J. Waite (*Yorks*)	RFM	51	4	320	12	5-59	1	26.66	25.50	6.27
17	J. G. Bethell (*Warwicks*) . . .	SLA	57	0	301	11	4-36	1	27.36	31.09	5.28
18	G. L. van Buuren (*Glos*) . . .	SLA	67	0	309	11	3-32	0	28.09	36.54	4.61
19	L. J. Carey (*Glam*)	RFM	63.2	2	352	12	2-24	0	29.33	31.66	5.55
20	E. R. Bamber (*Middx*)	RFM	49.2	0	297	10	3-41	0	29.70	29.60	6.02
21	D. J. Lamb (*Lancs*)	RFM	52.4	3	298	10	5-30	1	29.80	31.60	5.65
22	S. Baker (*Somerset*)	RFM	54.4	2	330	10	3-46	0	33.00	32.80	6.03
23	M. P. Dunn (*Surrey*)	RFM	67.3	2	413	11	2-44	0	37.54	36.81	6.11
24	A. S. S. Nijjar (*Essex*)	SLA	87.1	2	451	12	2-26	0	37.58	43.58	5.17
25	S. G. Borthwick (*Durham*) .	LB	81.1	0	423	10	2-44	0	42.30	48.70	5.21

LEADING WICKETKEEPERS

Dismissals	M			Dismissals	M	
19 (18ct, 1st)	10	T. N. Cullen (*Glam*)		10 (8ct, 2st)	6	H. J. Swindells (*Leics*)
13 (11ct, 2st)	10	J. L. Smith (*Surrey*)		10 (10ct)	8	S. M. Davies (*Somerset*)
12 (10ct, 2st)	8	M. G. K. Burgess (*Warwicks*)		10 (9ct, 1st)	9	C. T. Bancroft (*Durham*)
12 (10ct, 2st)	9	A. J. A. Wheater (*Essex*)				

LEADING FIELDERS

Ct	M			Ct	M	
10	9	S. G. Borthwick (*Durham*)		8	8	G. H. Rhodes (*Leics*)
9	9	G. S. Ballance (*Yorks*)		8	10	S. R. Harmer (*Essex*)
9	10	N. J. Selman (*Glam*)		8	10	S. J. Reingold (*Glam*)
8	8	E. A. Brookes (*Warwicks*)				

GROUP ONE

DURHAM

At Scarborough, July 29. **Gloucestershire won by four wickets. Durham 335-4** (50 overs) (G. Clark 140, A. Z. Lees 85, C. T. Bancroft 31, S. R. Dickson 46*; D. J. Worrall 4-58); **‡Gloucestershire 336-6** (49.4 overs) (B. G. Charlesworth 87, T. C. Lace 38, J. R. Bracey 90, J. M. R. Taylor 49*). *County debut:* J. D. Warner (Gloucestershire). *Attendance:* 841. Durham had planned to host a Royal London game at North Marine Road in July 2020, as part of Scarborough's Five Counties Cricket Week; the pandemic wiped it out, but they agreed to return a year later. It produced their only defeat of the group stage, after Jack Taylor fired Gloucestershire over the line: needing 16 off the last over, he hit Chris Rushworth for six, four and six. Graham Clark and Alex Lees had put Durham in a strong position with their second double-century opening stand in three innings, and the club's highest – 230 – for any wicket against these opponents. But Ben Charlesworth and James Bracey added 118 for Gloucestershire's third to give them a chance, which Taylor seized with a 28-ball 49*.

HIGHEST SUCCESSFUL ONE-DAY CHASES BY GLOUCESTERSHIRE

336-6 (49.4 overs)	v **Durham** at Scarborough	**2021**
335-6 (44.1 overs)	v Middlesex at Southgate	2005
306-6 (59.3 overs)	v Leicestershire at Leicester	1983
302-7 (39.5 overs)	v Middlesex at Cheltenham	2010
294-6 (48.2 overs)	v Somerset at Bristol	2008

At Gosforth, August 5. **Durham won by 87 runs. Durham 327-6** (50 overs) (A. Z. Lees 59, D. G. Bedingham 60, S. R. Dickson 103*, L. Doneathy 69*); **‡Lancashire 240** (44.3 overs) (J. J. Bohannon 52, R. P. Jones 65, G. I. D. Lavelle 38; L. Doneathy 4-36). *County debut:* T. R. Cornall (Lancashire). *Attendance:* 1,900. Durham returned to South Northumberland CC and inflicted a heavy defeat on Lancashire. Sean Dickson scored a maiden one-day century, in 75 balls, and added 156* – a county seventh-wicket record, and an all-wicket best against Lancashire – with 19-year-old Luke Doneathy, who followed 69* with 4-36 for his seamers, both career-bests. Only Josh Bohannon and Rob Jones made much headway in pursuit of 328.

At Chester-le-Street, August 8. **Durham won by two wickets** (DLS). **Essex 227-6** (45 overs) (F. I. N. Khushi 109, J. S. Rymell 40; J. O. I. Campbell 3-58); **‡Durham 233-8** (44.1 overs) (A. Z. Lees 126*). *County debut:* L. M. Benkenstein (Essex). *Attendance:* 2,304. Durham took a major stride towards the knockouts when Lees guided them to a last-over win. In a nervy run-chase, he kept his composure in a career-best 126*; none of his team-mates passed 24. Rain had interrupted Essex's innings, revising the target to 232 in 45; Feroze Khushi reached a run-a-ball century on List A debut, adding 101 with Josh Rymell. Leg-spinner Luc Benkenstein, son of Dale, who led Durham for three seasons, took 1-30 on his Essex debut.

At Chester-le-Street, August 12. **Durham won by nine wickets. Hampshire 225-9** (50 overs) (F. S. Organ 79, T. A. R. Scriven 42; C. Rushworth 4-37, P. A. van Meekeren 3-33); **‡Durham 228-1** (40.4 overs) (G. Clark 141*, S. G. Borthwick 71*). *County debut:* F. S. Middleton (Hampshire). *Attendance:* 1,710. Durham's fourth successive win ushered them smoothly into the semi-finals, after Clark and Scott Borthwick hammered Hampshire for 211*, the club's second-wicket record. Clark reached 140 for the third time in three weeks, raising his tournament average to 93. Earlier, Rushworth and Paul van Meekeren reduced Hampshire to 65-6 by the 16th over; Felix Organ and Tom Scriven helped them to 225, but Durham cantered home.

Durham away matches

July 22: beat Kent by 103 runs.
July 25: no result v Sussex.

July 27: beat Middlesex by two runs (DLS).
August 10: beat Worcestershire by 46 runs.

ESSEX

At Chelmsford, July 25. **Essex won by nine wickets. Middlesex 212** (45.4 overs) (M. D. E. Holden 36, R. G. White 47, J. L. B. Davies 70; S. Snater 3–45); ‡**Essex 213-1** (39 overs) (A. N. Cook 92*, T. Westley 87*). *Attendance: 979. The visitors' inexperience was clear: seven failed to reach double figures, though Jack Davies – one of five Middlesex players on List A debut – showed promise with a calm and responsible 70. Shane Snater snaffled three wickets. Alastair Cook put on 54 with Will Buttleman, then 159* with Tom Westley, as Essex cruised to victory with 11 overs to spare.*

At Chelmsford, July 29 (day/night). **Worcestershire won by 182 runs. Worcestershire 338-7** (50 overs) (J. A. Haynes 153, B. L. D'Oliveira 123); ‡**Essex 156** (31.3 overs) (A. N. Cook 42, A. J. A. Wheater 77; J. Leach 3–28, B. L. D'Oliveira 3–8). *Attendance: 1,274. A glittering stand between Jack Haynes and Brett D'Oliveira ensured a one-sided contest. Haynes recorded his maiden century in senior cricket, and D'Oliveira his first List A hundred, as they put on 243 in 36 overs – a record opening partnership for Worcestershire, and their highest for any wicket against Essex. D'Oliveira was finally dismissed for 123 off 116, and Haynes for 153 off 128. A total of 338-7 almost felt anticlimactic, though it was a record in the fixture, beating Essex's 287-3 at Chelmsford in 1997; Snater leaked 83. D'Oliveira then added a career-best 3-8 as Essex suffered their heaviest defeat. Adam Wheater's 77 stood out in an innings containing five ducks.*

ESSEX'S HEAVIEST ONE-DAY DEFEATS BY RUNS

182	v Worcestershire at Chelmsford	**2021**
179	v Australians at Chelmsford	2012
178	v Worcestershire at Chelmsford	1995
178	v Glamorgan at Cardiff	2001
177	v South Africans at Chelmsford	1998

At Chelmsford, August 1. **Essex won by nine wickets.** ‡**Kent 158** (47.5 overs) (H. G. Munsey 39); **Essex 159-1** (31.1 overs) (A. N. Cook 77*, T. Westley 69*). *Attendance: 1,251. Kent lost three wickets in an underwhelming powerplay that realised 31 and included a 17-ball duck for Harry Finch. Against a mean Essex attack, they never recovered: six bowlers took at least one wicket, and none cost more than five an over; Simon Harmer's off-breaks yielded an impeccable 2-21. Cook and Westley then enjoyed an untroubled second-wicket stand of 127*, as victory came with almost 19 overs in hand. Partly because of The Hundred, Kent were missing a team's worth of first-choice players, and remained without a Royal London win.*

At Chelmsford, August 10. **Essex won by 97 runs. Essex 321-8** (50 overs) (J. S. Rymell 78, F. I. N. Khushi 77, A. J. A. Wheater 53); ‡**Sussex 224** (43.2 overs) (T. M. Head 38, J. M. Coles 32, D. Wiese 36; J. H. Plom 3–52, R. N. ten Doeschate 4–34). *Attendance: 1,799. Essex qualified for the knockouts after Josh Rymell, with a first one-day half-century, and Feroze Khushi batted beautifully for seventies. Wheater (53 off 29) and Aron Nijjar (28* off 16) helped plunder 98 from the last ten overs. In reply, eight reached double figures for Sussex, but Travis Head's 38 proved the top score; Ryan ten Doeschate finished with his best one-day analysis for Essex since 2007.*

Essex away matches

July 22: beat Hampshire by three wickets.   August 8: lost to Durham by two wickets (DLS).
August 3: beat Gloucestershire by two wickets.   August 12: tied with Lancashire.

GLOUCESTERSHIRE

At Bristol, July 25. **Lancashire won by six wickets. Gloucestershire 171** (48 overs) (G. F. B. Scott 43, M. D. Taylor 51*; D. J. Lamb 5–30); ‡**Lancashire 177-4** (43.4 overs) (K. K. Jennings 47, L. W. P. Wells 31; J. Shaw 4–36). *County debut: B. J. J. Wells (Gloucestershire). Attendance: 1,303. Once Lancashire's Danny Lamb had ripped through the middle order – his three for two in 11 balls* *left Gloucestershire 63-5 – the game was as good as over. George Scott and Matt Taylor did put on 69, helping them to 171, but Lamb finished with 5-30, his best in all formats. Josh Shaw, with a one-day-best 4-36, averted a complete walkover.*

At Bristol, July 27. **Worcestershire won by 11 runs** (DLS). **Worcestershire 228-7** (40.3 overs) (J. A. Haynes 59, J. D. Libby 33, J. J. Dell 32); ‡**Gloucestershire 82-4** (11 overs) (G. L. van Buuren 38*). *Attendance: 963. Rain played havoc with this match, forcing four interruptions and ultimately setting Gloucestershire 94 in 11 overs. Graeme van Buuren manoeuvred them into a promising position but, with 26 needed from three, the runs dried up, and they managed 14. Worcestershire had relied on Jack Haynes for their runs, though there were several useful contributions, including 21* from 18-year-old Josh Baker, whose left-arm spin would keep Gloucestershire quiet at the death.*

At Bristol, August 3. **Essex won by two wickets. Gloucestershire 204** (49.1 overs) (J. M. R. Taylor 62, G. F. B. Scott 64; S. Snater 4-48); ‡**Essex 207-8** (50 overs) (T. Westley 71, J. S. Rymell 30, A. S. S. Nijjar 32*; G. L. van Buuren 3-32). *Attendance: 1,330. Another fighting stand from Scott and a Taylor (this time Matt's brother Jack) dug Gloucestershire out of a hole. They came together at 73-5 and added 99; both made sixties, and ensured there was at least something to defend. When Tom Westley was run out (by Matt Taylor) for a diligent 71, Essex were 153-8 in the 44th. From there, Gloucestershire should have won, but Aron Nijjar and Shane Snater picked up the pace: Snater, who had taken four wickets, cut the winning boundary from the last ball.*

At Bristol, August 6. **Gloucestershire won by seven wickets.** ‡**Hampshire 204-8** (37 overs) (T. P. Alsop 57, T. J. Prest 41; G. L. van Buuren 3-36); **Gloucestershire 205-3** (35.3 overs) (B. G. Charlesworth 99*, J. M. R. Taylor 67*). *Attendance: 1,120. After rain had reduced the game to 37 overs a side, Hampshire seemed in control at 90-0 in the 17th. Once Tom Prest fell for a bright 41, though, the innings fell away, and the only other player to reach 30 was fellow opener Tom Alsop. When Gloucestershire stumbled to 75-3, it was anyone's game. But the 20-year-old Ben Charlesworth, who narrowly missed a maiden century, and the more experienced Jack Taylor added 130*.*

Gloucestershire away matches

July 29: beat Durham by four wickets.
August 1: beat Sussex by three runs (DLS).

August 8: cancelled v Middlesex.
August 12: beat Kent by eight wickets.

HAMPSHIRE

At Southampton, July 22. **Essex won by three wickets. Hampshire 273** (49.1 overs) (N. R. T. Gubbins 62, J. J. Weatherley 54, L. D. McManus 50; S. Snater 3-62, S. R. Harmer 3-42); ‡**Essex 275-7** (44.3 overs) (T. Westley 69, M. S. Pepper 34, P. I. Walter 35, S. R. Harmer 32*; S. W. Currie 3-58). *County debut: J. A. Turner (Hampshire). Attendance: 2,215. South African-born pace bowler John Turner, aged 20, celebrated his Hampshire debut by claiming the wicket of Alastair Cook with his fifth delivery. That reduced Essex to 8-2 on a placid pitch, but the next seven all made at least 25, as Essex's strength in depth guided them home. There at the end were Simon Harmer and Aron Nijjar, whose spin had earlier claimed combined figures of 5-90.*

At Southampton, July 27. **Hampshire won by 98 runs.** ‡**Hampshire 328-7** (50 overs) (T. P. Alsop 68, T. J. Prest 34, N. R. T. Gubbins 131*, J. K. Fuller 54); **Sussex 230** (41.2 overs) (T. G. R. Clark 32, T. M. Head 52; N. R. T. Gubbins 4-38). *Attendance: 1,843. Nick Gubbins dominated this match from the moment he arrived at 81-1. If his unbeaten hundred was no great surprise – all told, he had hit 11 centuries for Middlesex – then his figures of 4-38 undoubtedly were. In 57 previous List A games, he had sent down two wicketless overs of leg-spin (both in the last match, against Essex). Now, fifth change, he bowled four middle-order batters, including Travis Head, to repel a young Sussex side's assault on 329. Earlier, Gubbins had cracked 131* from 119 balls, adding 116 for the sixth wicket with James Fuller.*

At Southampton, August 1. **Lancashire won by 51 runs** (DLS). **Hampshire 162** (43.1 overs) (N. R. T. Gubbins 31, L. D. McManus 45; T. E. Bailey 3-23, G. P. Balderson 3-25); ‡**Lancashire 115-2** (25.3 overs) (L. W. P. Wells 66*). *Attendance: 2,994. Seamers Tom Bailey and George Balderson – bowling for the first time in a one-day match – took advantage of some flimsy Hampshire batting to dismiss them with 41 balls unused. Luke Wells, with a career-best 66*, and Rob Jones then put together 71* for Lancashire's third wicket; when rain arrived in the 26th over, they were way ahead on DLS.*

At Southampton, August 4. **Hampshire won by six wickets.** ‡**Worcestershire 176** (39 overs) (B. L. D'Oliveira 40, J. Leach 34*; J. A. Turner 3-44, K. J. Abbott 5-43); **Hampshire 180-4** (39.5 overs) (T. P. Alsop 50, N. R. T. Gubbins 59, J. J. Weatherley 33). *Attendance: 2,401. Hampshire's South African opening pair, Turner and Kyle Abbott, took eight wickets between them after Worcestershire squandered winning the toss. It was the first time Abbott had claimed five List A wickets, in his 109th game. Tom Alsop and Gubbins both hit a fifty as Hampshire ran out easy winners.*

Hampshire away matches

July 30: no result v Middlesex.
August 6: lost to Gloucestershire by seven wickets.

August 8: beat Kent by six wickets (DLS).
August 12: lost to Durham by nine wickets.

KENT

At Beckenham, July 22. **Durham won by 103 runs. Durham 405-4** (50 overs) (G. Clark 141, A. Z. Lees 100, D. G. Bedingham 67, C. T. Bancroft 60*); ‡**Kent 302-8** (50 overs) (H. G. Munsey 96, H. Z. Finch 64, Hamidullah Qadri 42*; C. Rushworth 3-29). *Attendance: 918. Invited to bat at a ground known as a bowlers' graveyard, Durham sailed past their highest limited-overs score (and the highest against Kent). Hundreds from openers Graham Clark and Alex Lees – who put on 242 in 34 overs, an all-wicket club record in this fixture – were followed by rapid innings from David Bedingham (67 off 38) and Cameron Bancroft (60* off 37). Durham were helped by dropped catches, while Matt Quinn's 1-97 equalled Kent's most expensive one-day figures. The scorecard entry "c Borthwick b Rushworth" appeared three times at the start of the reply and, though George Munsey and Harry Finch put on 138, the rate was always beyond Kent.*

HIGHEST LIMITED-OVERS TOTALS FOR DURHAM

405-4	v Kent at Beckenham	**2021**
353-8	v Nottinghamshire at Chester-le-Street.	2014
349-7	v Leicestershire at Leicester	2015
342-5	v Northamptonshire at Chester-le-Street.	2019
340-6	v Leicestershire at Leicester	2016

At Beckenham, July 28. **No result. Lancashire 71-0** (14.5 overs) (J. J. Bohannon 39*) v ‡**Kent.** *Attendance: 871. Keaton Jennings and Josh Bohannon made untrammelled progress for Lancashire, before rain called a halt.*

At Beckenham, August 8. **Hampshire won by six wickets** (DLS). **Kent 105** (22.5 overs) (I. G. Holland 4-12); ‡**Hampshire 107-4** (18.2 overs) (T. P. Alsop 37, I. G. Holland 30*). *Attendance: 715. An atrocious performance by Kent meant they could not progress. In a match initially reduced to 27 overs a side, Ollie Robinson (27) and Tawanda Muyeye (24) began steadily; at 63-1 after 11, there were few signs of what lay ahead. But nine fell for 42, with Ian Holland grabbing a white-ball-best 4-12. The Hampshire reply – they were set 107 in 24 after more rain interrupted Kent's innings – began uncertainly, but Holland ushered in victory.*

At Beckenham, August 12. **Gloucestershire won by eight wickets. Kent 218-9** (50 overs) (O. G. Robinson 75, T. S. Muyeye 30, D. I. Stevens 40; G. L. van Buuren 3-34); ‡**Gloucestershire 219-2** (37.4 overs) (C. D. J. Dent 112*, G. L. van Buuren 51*). *Attendance: 1,122. When Lancashire failed to win at Old Trafford – they tied with Essex – this facile victory took Gloucestershire to the knockouts, in third place; Kent, meanwhile, were last. Robinson made his highest one-day score, and Darren Stevens produced an entertaining cameo, but once again Kent struggled for runs. In reply, Gloucestershire captain Chris Dent hit a run-a-ball century and added 106* with Graeme van Buuren, whose left-arm spin had taken 3-34.*

Kent away matches

July 25: lost to Worcs by three wickets.
July 30: no result v Sussex (DLS).

August 1: lost to Essex by nine wickets.
August 6: beat Middlesex by 21 runs.

LANCASHIRE

At Sedbergh, July 23. **Lancashire won by two wickets.** ‡Sussex 270-9 (50 overs) (T. J. Haines 38, T. M. Head 56, O. J. Carter 55, D. K. Ibrahim 46, W. A. T. Beer 40; L. J. Hurt 3-55); **Lancashire 274-8** (49 overs) (D. J. Vilas 31, R. P. Jones 35, D. J. Lamb 86*, T. E. Bailey 45; A. D. Lenham 4-59). *Attendance: 906. Nine Sussex players, including captain Tom Haines, were making List A debuts, but they pushed Lancashire all the way in a magnificent contest at Sedbergh School. That had seemed unlikely when they were 101-4. But Oli Carter's 55, and forties from Dan Ibrahim and Will Beer, piloted a recovery, before leg-spinner Archie Lenham, on his 17th birthday, reduced Lancashire to 115-7. Then Danny Lamb and Tom Bailey shared a superbly judged stand of 112, a county eighth-wicket record. Though Lenham claimed Bailey as his fourth victim, Lamb's 69-ball 86*, his maiden one-day half-century, settled matters.*

At Manchester, August 3. **Middlesex won by six runs.** ‡Middlesex 257 (49.3 overs) (S. S. Eskinazi 45, S. D. Robson 76, M. K. Andersson 42*; T. E. Bailey 3-33); **Lancashire 251** (49.2 overs) (K. K. Jennings 42*, R. P. Jones 72, S. J. Croft 41, D. J. Lamb 33; E. R. Bamber 3-49, L. B. K. Hollman 4-56). *Attendance: 1,615. Lancashire needed 14 off the last over, from Ethan Bamber, with one wicket left but Lamb in full flow: a no-ball, a boundary and a wide brought it down to seven off five, before Bamber bowled Lamb with the second legitimate delivery. Despite Sam Robson's fluent 76, Middlesex's total would have been inadequate without Martin Andersson, who added 67 for the last two wickets with Thilan Walallawita and Bamber. Lancashire's pursuit of 258 was going well until Keaton Jennings tore his calf, ending his season. Luke Hollman took four crucial wickets, including George Balderson and Rob Jones (for a career-best 72) in his eighth over.*

At Manchester, August 8. **Lancashire v Worcestershire. Abandoned.**

At Manchester, August 12. **Tied. Lancashire 250-6** (50 overs) (J. J. Bohannon 34, S. J. Croft 93, G. I. D. Lavelle 52); ‡Essex 250-8 (50 overs) (A. N. Cook 110, R. N. ten Doeschate 45). *Attendance: 1,836. Simon Harmer hit three successive sixes in the final over, then scrambled two off Steven Croft's last ball for a tie. That earned Essex a home quarter-final, and knocked Lancashire out. Earlier, Croft's 93 had underpinned their 250-6: he put on 106 with George Lavelle, whose maiden one-day fifty included three sixes, one landing on the pavilion balcony. Alastair Cook anchored Essex's chase with his 13th List A century but, when he and Adam Wheater fell to successive deliveries from Croft, and Aron Nijjar first ball to Wells, they needed 21 off the last over to tie. Harmer rose gloriously to the challenge.*

Lancashire away matches

July 25: beat Gloucestershire by six wickets. August 1: beat Hampshire by 51 runs (DLS).
July 28: no result v Kent. August 5: lost to Durham by 87 runs.

MIDDLESEX

At Radlett, July 27. **Durham won by two runs** (DLS). ‡Durham 288-8 (50 overs) (G. Clark 65, S. G. Borthwick 76, D. G. Bedingham 41, L. Doneathy 50); **Middlesex 225-9** (36 overs) (P. S. P. Handscomb 75, R. G. White 55; P. A. van Meekeren 3-47). *Attendance: 582. Durham captain Scott Borthwick played a crucial role to shut Middlesex out in a close finish. He top-scored with 76, supported by half-centuries from Graham Clark and Luke Doneathy, as Durham set 289. Peter Handscomb and Robbie White rebuilt after Middlesex lost three early wickets with a stand of 130, but when both fell in quick succession shortly before a rain-break at 32 overs, they had dropped behind on DLS. There was time for four more overs, from which they needed 55. A canny 34th, from Borthwick, cost just four, but Thilan Walallawita hit the last four balls of the 35th, bowled by Liam Trevaskis, for 18, to leave 16 required off the last. It proved chaotic: Paul van Meekeren took a wicket with each of the first two balls, then conceded two fours, two wides and a single. Tim Murtagh, though, couldn't score five from the last.*

At Radlett, July 30. **Middlesex v Hampshire. Abandoned.**

At Radlett, August 6. **Kent won by 21 runs. Kent 217-9** (35 overs) (J. A. Leaning 35, H. G. Munsey 59, M. K. O'Riordan 60, Hamidullah Qadri 35*; E. R. Bamber 3-41); ‡Middlesex 196 (32.3 overs) (M. D. E. Holden 32, J. M. de Caires 43, J. A. R. Harris 34; N. N. Gilchrist 5-45, Hamidullah Qadri 3-47). *County debut: T. L. Greatwood (Middlesex). Attendance: 607. Nathan Gilchrist's first one-*

day five-for kept Middlesex at bay in a match reduced to 35 overs a side. Kent recovered from 7-2 through half-centuries from George Munsey and Marcus O'Riordan, who added 69 for the seventh wicket with Hamidullah Qadri; seamer Toby Greatwood (2-30) bowled sharply on debut. Middlesex were rarely in it, falling to 88-6 as Gilchrist ripped out the middle order. Joshua de Caires and James Harris put on 57, but the asking-rate was excessive, and Gilchrist mopped up the tail.

At Radlett, August 8. **Middlesex v Gloucestershire. Cancelled.** *The day before the game, Gloucestershire announced a Covid outbreak in their squad, and the ECB confirmed the cancellation of the fixture. Neither team were awarded points, and Group One positions would be decided by average points per completed match. Andrew Cornish, Middlesex's chief executive, said it was "extremely disappointing to hear that our opponents tomorrow are only able to field one player not in isolation". His president, Mike Selvey, tweeted: "A team that doesn't put a side out? Bottom line is you forfeit, surely."*

Middlesex away matches

July 25: lost to Essex by nine wickets.
August 1: beat Worcestershire by 13 runs.

August 3: beat Lancashire by six runs.
August 12: lost to Sussex by three runs.

SUSSEX

At Hove, July 25. **Sussex v Durham. Abandoned.**

At Hove, July 30. **No result** (DLS). **Sussex 209-7** (29 overs) (T. G. R. Clark 44, T. M. Head 52, B. C. Brown 38, D. Wiese 31; N. N. Gilchrist 3-45); ‡**Kent 50-1** (5.4 overs). *Attendance:* 1,538. *For the sixth white-ball game out of nine, a Sussex home match fell foul of the weather. Ben Brown, making his first appearance since losing the captaincy, and Travis Head, with his third fifty in three Royal London games, gave Sussex hope in an innings reduced first to 31 overs, then 29. Ollie Robinson (23) and former Sussex Academy player Tawanda Muyeye (24*) put Kent on course, but the rain returned.*

At Hove, August 1. **Gloucestershire won by three runs** (DLS). **Gloucestershire 218-8** (42 overs) (B. G. Charlesworth 39, J. M. R. Taylor 52, G. F. B. Scott 38); ‡**Sussex 214** (40.5 overs) (B. C. Brown 63, O. J. Carter 59; J. D. Warner 3-42, T. M. J. Smith 3-28). *Attendance:* 1,326. *After Brown hit 63, the game's top-scorer, a ninth-wicket stand of 62 from 38 balls, including a career-best 59 from 19-year-old wicketkeeper Ollie Carter, put Sussex in sight of a notable victory. But he fell 15 short of a tweaked target of 218 from 42, before his junior partner, Archie Lenham, was run out by Tom Lace with four needed. Sussex were now winless from five games. The Gloucestershire innings relied on a brisk sixth-wicket stand of 71 between Jack Taylor and George Scott.*

At Hove, August 12. **Sussex won by three runs.** ‡**Sussex 333-4** (50 overs) (B. C. Brown 105, T. J. Haines 123, T. M. Head 46*, D. Wiese 33); **Middlesex 330-8** (50 overs) (M. D. E. Holden 94, V. Chopra 45, J. L. B. Davies 51, M. K. Andersson 44*). *Attendance:* 1,682. *Brown and Tom Haines, captains old and new, each made a maiden one-day hundred as Sussex piled up 333-4. They put on a county-record 219 for the second wicket, and 130 came off the last ten overs. Four scores of 40 or more kept Middlesex in it, and they were arguably favourites with eight needed off five, but Wiese – whose previous ball had gone for six – conceded only four singles. Defeat ended Middlesex's faint hopes, while Sussex had been unable to progress anyway.*

Sussex away matches

July 23: lost to Lancashire by two wickets.
July 27: lost to Hampshire by 98 runs.

August 6: beat Worcestershire by two wickets.
August 10: lost to Essex by 97 runs.

WORCESTERSHIRE

At Worcester, July 25. **Worcestershire won by three wickets. Kent 322-7** (50 overs) (H. G. Munsey 108, H. Z. Finch 84); ‡**Worcestershire 323-7** (49.1 overs) (J. A. Haynes 77, T. C. Fell 57, E. G. Barnard 39*, J. Leach 88). *County debut:* J. Banton (Worcestershire). *Attendance:* 1,445. *Worcestershire captain Joe Leach's 88 off 51 – including seven sixes – turned the match on its head after his team had been 184-6 in the 34th, still needing 139. His partnership of 134 in 15 with Ed Barnard was a club seventh-wicket record. Kent owed their 322-7 to George Munsey's maiden one-day century; his fourth-wicket stand of 184 with Harry Finch was their highest for any wicket against Worcestershire.*

At Worcester, August 1. **Middlesex won by 13 runs.** ‡**Middlesex 302-5** (41 overs) (M. D. E. Holden 39, S. S. Eskinazi 130, S. D. Robson 57, M. K. Andersson 38*); **Worcestershire 289-7** (41 overs) (B. L. D'Oliveira 74, T. C. Fell 58, J. D. Libby 58). *Attendance:* 2,008. *Back after a groin injury, Steve Eskinazi made a one-day-best 130 off 101 to set Middlesex up for victory in a rain-reduced game. Martin Andersson (38* off 11) helped ensure 46 came from the last 16. Brett D'Oliveira and Tom Fell gave Worcestershire hope with a second-wicket stand of 116, and Jake Libby fought hard, but Middlesex always had just enough control.*

At Worcester, August 6. **Sussex won by two wickets.** ‡**Worcestershire 233-9** (50 overs) (J. D. Libby 40, J. Banton 33; J. M. Coles 3-27, A. D. Lenham 3-53); **Sussex 234-8** (49.3 overs) (A. G. H. Orr 108, T. J. Haines 46, T. M. Head 38*; J. Banton 3-15). *Attendance:* 1,373. *Spinners James Coles and Archie Lenham, both 17, collected three wickets apiece, but Worcestershire recovered from 137-7 to reach 233-9. Sussex were cruising at 182-2, Ali Orr bringing up his first century with the fourth of five sixes. But four wickets fell for 15 – three to Jacques Banton, brother of Somerset's Tom – and seven were still needed as Josh Baker began the final over. He removed Lenham first ball, only for Travis Head – once of Worcestershire – to see Sussex home with a six.*

At Worcester, August 10. **Durham won by 46 runs.** ‡**Durham 289-9** (50 overs) (A. Z. Lees 93, D. G. Bedingham 66, E. J. H. Eckersley 36); **Worcestershire 243** (45.1 overs) (J. D. Libby 76, Extras 30; P. A. van Meekeren 3-45, L. Trevaskis 3-38). *Attendance:* 1,793. *On a pitch used for all four of New Road's matches, Durham reached the knockouts. Alex Lees provided their glue, before acceleration from David Bedingham (66 off 41, with six sixes) and Ned Eckersley (36 off 27, with two) lifted them to a score that proved beyond Worcestershire. Paul van Meekeren made early inroads, then Liam Trevaskis worked his way through the middle order; only Libby made a major contribution.*

Worcestershire away matches

July 27: beat Gloucestershire by 11 runs (DLS).
July 29: beat Essex by 182 runs.
August 4: lost to Hampshire by six wickets.
August 8: no result v Lancashire.

GROUP TWO

DERBYSHIRE

At Derby, July 27. **Warwickshire won by eight wickets** (DLS). **Derbyshire 200-9** (42 overs) (H. R. C. Came 45, F. J. Hudson-Prentice 51*; J. G. Bethell 3-32); ‡**Warwickshire 207-2** (37 overs) (E. J. Pollock 103*, R. M. Yates 60). *County debuts:* J. Bulpitt, K. Carver (Warwickshire). *Attendance:* 545. *Rain delayed the start, then interrupted Derbyshire's innings, and Warwickshire's eventual target was 205 from 42. Ed Pollard's 103* – his first List A century – saw them home with five to spare. Derbyshire openers Harry Came and Tom Wood (28) had put on 82 in 16, but they faltered once Jacob Bethell, a 17-year-old slow left-armer born in Barbados, made the breakthrough. Fynn Hudson-Prentice's 51* took them to 200. There was little doubt of the outcome once Pollock and Rob Yates opened with 121 in 24.*

At Derby, July 30. **Glamorgan v ‡Derbyshire. Abandoned.** *County debut:* M. D. Wagstaff (Derbyshire). *Rain relented long enough to allow the toss – Derbyshire decided to field – which made this an uneventful county debut for 17-year-old Mitchell Wagstaff.*

At Chesterfield, August 8. **Yorkshire won by eight wickets. Derbyshire 108-6** (10 overs) (F. J. Hudson-Prentice 38*; J. R. Sullivan 4-11); ‡**Yorkshire 109-2** (8.4 overs) (W. A. R. Fraine 69*). *Attendance:* 589. *Yorkshire won a rain-shortened ten-over thrash with eight balls in hand, after Will Fraine reached 50 on 19 – a List A record for his county – and finished with 69* off 32. Came and Wagstaff had begun with 40 for Derbyshire, but leg-spinner Josh Sullivan checked their progress with three wickets in four balls in the sixth over. Hudson-Prentice hit back with 38* in 17, which gave them a chance – until Fraine intervened.*

At Derby, August 12. **Surrey won by eight wickets.** ‡**Derbyshire 215** (46.2 overs) (M. D. Wagstaff 36, M. H. McKiernan 38; C. McKerr 3-43, D. T. Moriarty 3-44); **Surrey 219-2** (37 overs) (M. D. Stoneman 35, R. S. Patel 111*, T. H. David 52*). *Attendance:* 916. *Already condemned to bottom place in their group, Derbyshire were handicapped when Hudson-Prentice withdrew after testing* *positive for Covid. They failed to see out their 50 overs, whereas Surrey cruised into the quarter-finals. Ryan Patel took apart a modest target of 216, with 111* – his second one-day century, both in this tournament. He put on 92 for the first wicket with Mark Stoneman, and 95* for the third with Tim David (52* from 38).*

Derbyshire away matches

July 22: lost to Leicestershire by six wickets.
July 25: lost to Somerset by six wickets.

August 1: lost to Northamptonshire by eight wickets.
August 4: beat Nottinghamshire by 41 runs.

GLAMORGAN

At Cardiff, July 22. **Glamorgan won by two wickets.** ‡**Warwickshire 221** (49.2 overs) (C. G. Benjamin 50, M. G. K. Burgess 73; J. M. Cooke 3-35); **Glamorgan 225-8** (49.4 overs) (K. S. Carlson 60, W. T. Root 50; J. G. Bethell 4-36). *County debuts:* S. J. Reingold, H. D. Rutherford (Glamorgan); A. M. Chakrapani, M. S. Johal, K. T. van Vollenhoven (Warwickshire). *Attendance:* 732. Twelve players made List A debuts, and none did better than Warwickshire's 17-year-old Rugby schoolboy Jacob Bethell, who took 4-36 with his left-arm spin. But his efforts were in vain, like those of fellow newcomer Chris Benjamin, whose 50 as opener earned him a call-up for Birmingham Phoenix's Hundred squad at Edgbaston the following day. Glamorgan overhauled a target of 222 with two balls to spare, thanks to a 101-run stand between Kiran Carlson and Billy Root, and 30* for the ninth wicket between Roman Walker and Lukas Carey.*

At Cardiff, August 3. **Glamorgan won by five wickets.** ‡**Surrey 132** (44.1 overs) (R. Clarke 35; A. G. Salter 3-37); **Glamorgan 133-5** (26.5 overs) (H. D. Rutherford 58, S. J. Reingold 40). *Attendance:* 791. Michael Hogan dismissed Mark Stoneman with the first ball of the game, and Surrey continued to struggle against an accurate Glamorgan attack, with Andrew Salter recording career-best figures; Hogan's ten overs cost only 18. Needing just 133, Glamorgan lost Nick Selman early, but Hamish Rutherford and Steven Reingold put on 86. A few late wickets flattered Surrey.*

At Cardiff, August 8. **Glamorgan won by eight wickets.** **Nottinghamshire 73** (20.2 overs) (W. J. Weighell 3-7); ‡**Glamorgan 76-2** (16 overs) (N. J. Selman 37*). *County debut:* S. I. M. King (Nottinghamshire). *Attendance:* 683. In a game reduced to 23 overs a side, Glamorgan consolidated their position as group leaders by outclassing an inexperienced Nottinghamshire. Only Sam King, whose first appearance for the visitors was as a concussion substitute after Lyndon James was hit on the helmet by James Cooke, and 17-year-old Fateh Singh, another debutant, reached double figures, as Nottinghamshire subsided to their lowest one-day total against Glamorgan. Selman guided the hosts to their target without fuss.*

At Cardiff, August 12. **Yorkshire won by four runs. Yorkshire 230** (48.5 overs) (J. A. Tattersall 53, M. J. Waite 44; W. J. Weighell 3-55, J. M. Cooke 3-40); ‡**Glamorgan 226-8** (50 overs) (H. D. Rutherford 58, N. J. Selman 92; G. C. H. Hill 3-49). *Attendance:* 1,054. Yorkshire won, and matched Glamorgan's points tally – as did Surrey, at Derby – but the hosts topped the table on net run-rate, and advanced to a home semi-final, leaving the other two to contest the quarters. Yorkshire had come back strongly twice. From 132-7, they were rescued by a stand of 84 in 11 overs between Jonny Tattersall and Matthew Waite. Then, after Glamorgan reached 180-1, with Selman eyeing a hundred, seven tumbled for 43, including two in the last over from Waite: defending 11, he conceded five.*

Glamorgan away matches

July 25: beat Northamptonshire by 59 runs.
July 28: lost to Somerset by one run (DLS).

July 30: no result v Derbyshire.
August 5: no result v Leicestershire.

LEICESTERSHIRE

At Leicester, July 22. **Leicestershire won by six wickets.** ‡**Derbyshire 275-7** (50 overs) (B. A. Godleman 116, B. D. Guest 40, H. R. Hosein 38; A. M. Lilley 3-49); **Leicestershire 279-4** (46.3 overs) (N. R. Welch 32, R. K. Patel 70, M. S. Harris 75, L. J. Hill 51, G. H. Rhodes 39*). *County debuts:* C. R. Marshall, N. O. Priestley (Derbyshire). *Attendance:* 718. Derbyshire captain Billy Godleman, having scored his seventh one-day century after a month away from the game, felt

275 was defendable, even on a flat Grace Road pitch. Lewis Hill, leading Leicestershire for the first time, helped prove him wrong, adding a half-century to seventies from Rishi Patel and Marcus Harris as his side cruised home. Earlier, opener Nick Welch had slipped, hit his wicket and dislocated his knee; he was stretchered off, and missed the rest of the tournament. Meanwhile, Derbyshire wicketkeeper Harvey Hosein was struck on the head while batting, and replaced in the field by coach Ajmal Shahzad; Brooke Guest took the gloves.

At Leicester, July 25. **Yorkshire won by seven wickets.** ‡**Leicestershire 327-7** (50 overs) (M. S. Harris 127, L. J. Hill 108; M. J. Waite 5-59); **Yorkshire 329-3** (47.5 overs) (W. A. R. Fraine 45, H. G. Duke 125, G. S. Ballance 43, G. C. H. Hill 90*). *County debut:* R. Ahmed (Leicestershire). *Attendance:* 674. *Nineteen-year-old Harry Duke's first century in senior cricket led Yorkshire to their highest successful chase against Leicestershire, in their 1,000th List A match. He became the second-youngest to score a one-day hundred for the county, after Sachin Tendulkar in 1992. Leicestershire had posted an imposing 327-7, Harris scoring his maiden one-day century at the 48th attempt, and adding 212 for the third wicket with Hill, who scored his second; it was a club all-wicket record against Yorkshire. Matthew Waite claimed his first one-day five-for (six team-mates managed two for 263 between them). Then Duke and George Hill put on 172 for Yorkshire's third, as the home bowlers toiled in vain.*

At Leicester, August 5. **No result** (DLS). **Glamorgan 277-8** (50 overs) (N. J. Selman 140, S. J. Reingold 38, W. T. Root 67; G. H. Rhodes 3-44); ‡**Leicestershire 0-0** (1 over). *Attendance:* 482. *Nick Selman made a sparkling 140 off 144 balls, his first one-day century, before being run out in the final over of the Glamorgan innings. But rain meant it counted for nothing. Leicestershire off-spinner George Rhodes claimed a career-best 3-44 and held three catches.*

At Leicester, August 7. **Leicestershire won by one run** (DLS). **Leicestershire 253-9** (50 overs) (H. J. Swindells 75, A. M. Lilley 41, E. Barnes 33*; C. T. Steel 4-33); ‡**Surrey 225** (38.5 overs) (R. S. Patel 52, J. L. Smith 34, R. Clarke 82; B. W. M. Mike 3-34). *County debut:* C. T. Steel (Surrey). *Attendance:* 424. *Needing four from Ben Mike's final over, Surrey scored two and lost three wickets – including Rikki Clarke for 82 – as Leicestershire completed a sensational comeback. Their own moderate total had centred on a career-best 75 from opener Harry Swindells, and featured a crucial last-wicket stand of 36* between Ed Barnes and Will Davis. On List A debut, Cameron Steel conceded no boundaries in taking 4-33 from ten. Rain adjusted Surrey's target to 227 in 39 and, at 173-3 in the 29th, they were on track. But Rehan Ahmed, a 16-year-old leg-spinner, triggered a collapse of seven for 52.*

Leicestershire away matches

July 29: lost to Warwickshire by seven runs.   August 10: beat Somerset by four wickets.
August 1: lost to Nottinghamshire by seven wickets.   August 12: beat Northamptonshire by four runs (DLS).

NORTHAMPTONSHIRE

At Northampton, July 25. **Glamorgan won by 59 runs. Glamorgan 295-6** (50 overs) (H. D. Rutherford 86, N. J. Selman 33, C. Z. Taylor 36, T. N. Cullen 58*, J. M. Cooke 33*); ‡**Northamptonshire 236** (44.2 overs) (B. J. Curran 55, S. A. Zaib 41, T. A. I. Taylor 65*; M. G. Hogan 3-26, J. M. Cooke 3-32). *County debut:* A. W. Gorvin (Glamorgan). *Attendance:* 549. *The patience of Glamorgan's top order in gloomy, overcast conditions – exemplified by Hamish Rutherford's 86 off 97 balls – was followed by strong acceleration from Tom Cullen and Joe Cooke, who put on 68* from the last 32 balls. Cooke backed up his 33* off 18 with three wickets as Northamptonshire fell short, despite strong hitting from Tom Taylor. Michael Hogan also managed a cheap three-for.*

At Northampton, August 1. **Northamptonshire won by eight wickets. Derbyshire 177-9** (28 overs) (B. D. Guest 45, F. J. Hudson-Prentice 64; C. J. White 4-20, B. W. Sanderson 3-29); ‡**Northamptonshire 183-2** (27.3 overs) (R. S. Vasconcelos 50, E. N. Gay 84*, R. I. Keogh 33*). *Attendance:* 424. *In a match reduced to 28 overs a side, Derbyshire crashed to 8-4 inside two overs from Jack White – who finished with four – and Ben Sanderson. Brooke Guest and Fynn Hudson-Prentice (64 off 43) added 106 in 14 to keep them afloat, helping No. 9 Nils Priestley (25*) help them past 121-8 into 177-9. But Emilio Gay (84* off 73) and Ricardo Vasconcelos put Northamptonshire on course for a century stand, and Rob Keogh (33* off 16) ensured their first win of the competition, with three balls to spare. Mitchell Wagstaff, after not taking the field in his first match, had fallen to the first ball of the game.*

At Northampton, August 8. **Northamptonshire won by 81 runs** (DLS). **Northamptonshire 305-6** (46 overs) (R. S. Vasconcelos 88, B. J. Curran 94, R. I. Keogh 35); ‡**Somerset 223** (40.5 overs) (L. P. Goldsworthy 80, J. H. Davey 53; S. C. Kerrigan 4-48, L. A. Procter 3-40). *County debut: J. J. G. Sales (Northamptonshire). Attendance: 650. Somerset's decision to bowl backfired, as Vasconcelos and Ben Curran added 129 in 20 overs for the second wicket either side of a rain interruption which lopped four off both innings. Each faced 93 balls, with Curran's 94 a career-best. Chasing 306, Somerset were five down for 89, before Lewis Goldsworthy's powerful 80 off 61. But with 97 needed, he trod on his stumps against Sanderson, whose first five overs had cost just five; Simon Kerrigan mopped up his first one-day four-for, a decade after his debut. During the interval, Northamptonshire announced that the Pavilion End would be renamed the David Capel End, honouring the Test all-rounder, who died in 2020.*

At Northampton, August 12. **Leicestershire won by four runs** (DLS). ‡**Leicestershire 271** (50 overs) (R. K. Patel 41, A. M. Lilley 46, L. P. J. Kimber 63, R. Ahmed 40*; B. W. Sanderson 3-30, S. A. Zaib 3-37); **Northamptonshire 261-9** (48 overs) (E. N. Gay 42, L. A. Procter 48, R. I. Keogh 52, S. A. Zaib 43). *Attendance: 749. Yorkshire's narrow win over Glamorgan, achieved while this game was in progress, meant victory for Leicestershire was not enough to send them through. Rishi Patel and Arron Lilley had flourished briefly, but it took runs from Louis Kimber and Rehan Ahmed to give them a substantial total on a pitch helping spin. From 53-0 in ten overs, Northamptonshire – whose target had been reduced by rain to 266 from 48 – lost three for three in ten balls. Luke Procter, Keogh and Saif Zaib led a recovery, but 11 off the final over proved just beyond them.*

Northamptonshire away matches

July 28: no result v Yorkshire.
July 30: no result v Surrey.

August 6: lost to Warwickshire by 134 runs.
August 10: lost to Nottinghamshire by two wickets.

NOTTINGHAMSHIRE

At Sookholme, July 30. **No result. Nottinghamshire 92-2** (21 overs) (B. T. Slater 42*, M. Montgomery 31*) v ‡**Somerset**. *County debut: E. O. Leonard (Somerset). Attendance: 797. Rain limited the action to 78 minutes, with Ben Slater and Matthew Montgomery unable to expand their third-wicket stand of 69*.*

At Sookholme, August 1. **Nottinghamshire won by seven wickets. Leicestershire 144** (43.1 overs) (B. W. M. Mike 34, R. Ahmed 35*; L. J. Fletcher 4-30, D. Paterson 3-25); ‡**Nottinghamshire 145-3** (20.2 overs) (B. T. Slater 38, P. D. Trego 39). *Attendance: 1,079. The weather was kinder on Nottinghamshire's return to Welbeck CC, but the ball swung and seamed on an overcast morning. Luke Fletcher exploited conditions brilliantly, bowling his ten in a single spell; by the time Leicestershire saw the back of him, they were 54-6. Their only decent stand was 70 for the eighth wicket, between Ben Mike and 16-year-old Rehan Ahmed, who scored 35* in his third senior match. As the clouds gave way to sunshine, Nottinghamshire romped to their target.*

At Derby, August 4. **Derbyshire won by 41 runs. Derbyshire 258-6** (27 overs) (H. R. C. Came 57, T. A. Wood 109; L. A. Patterson-White 3-41); ‡**Nottinghamshire 217** (27 overs) (B. A. Hutton 46; F. J. Hudson-Prentice 3-37). *Attendance: 756. Officially a home game for Nottinghamshire, this match was staged at Derby because of the Trent Bridge Test, and the start delayed because part of the square was wet. But Derbyshire completed their only win of the tournament (and their first against Nottinghamshire in List A cricket since 2004) after setting a target in 27 overs that might have been testing in 50. Harry Came and Tom Wood scored maiden one-day half-centuries, and Wood converted his into Derbyshire's fastest one-day hundred, from 55 balls. For Nottinghamshire, only Brett Hutton (46 off 20) exceeded 30.*

At Grantham, August 10. **Nottinghamshire won by two wickets.** ‡**Northamptonshire 210** (49.5 overs) (E. N. Gay 40, L. A. Procter 44; L. A. Patterson-White 5-19); **Nottinghamshire 211-8** (49.4 overs) (B. T. Slater 53, B. G. Compton 71, M. Montgomery 31; T. A. I. Taylor 3-24).

Attendance: 1,258. Nottinghamshire kept their hopes of qualifying alive when Dane Paterson hit Ben Sanderson over his head for six, clinching victory with two balls to spare. Liam Patterson-White's 5-19, his best figures in any format, had helped dismiss Northamptonshire for 210. It did not seem a challenging target, and Ben Compton (grandson of Denis) took the hosts much of the way with his maiden fifty in senior cricket. But Tom Taylor's 3-24 – his best white-ball return – pegged them back, until Paterson wrapped it up. This was Nottinghamshire's second home game at Grantham, following a washout in 2019.

Nottinghamshire away matches

July 25: beat Warwickshire by 86 runs.
July 27: lost to Surrey by 33 runs (DLS).

August 6: no result v Yorkshire.
August 8: lost to Glamorgan by eight wickets.

SOMERSET

At Taunton, July 25 (day/night). **Somerset won by six wickets. Derbyshire 298** (49.3 overs) (B. D. Guest 74, F. J. Hudson-Prentice 93; S. Baker 3-46, B. G. F. Green 3-64); ‡**Somerset 299-4** (48 overs) (S. M. Davies 94, J. C. Hildreth 110, L. P. Goldsworthy 57*). *County debuts: S. Baker, S. J. Young (Somerset). Attendance: 3,300. Somerset began their title defence by giving one-day debuts to five players. But old hands Steve Davies, with 94 off 72, and James Hildreth, who battled cramp, required a runner and still brought up his eighth one-day hundred for the club, guided them towards a target of 299. They put on 120, then Hildreth and Lewis Goldsworthy shared 105. Fynn Hudson-Prentice and Brooke Guest had posted career-bests for Derbyshire, added 142 for the fourth wicket, but 18-year-old seamer Sonny Baker pegged them back.*

At Taunton, July 28. **Somerset won by one run** (DLS). **Somerset 180-7** (37 overs) (L. P. Goldsworthy 41, B. G. F. Green 87; M. G. Hogan 4-33); ‡**Glamorgan 179-9** (37 overs) (W. T. Root 37, T. N. Cullen 37; K. L. Aldridge 3-39). *County debut: G. S. Drissell (Somerset). Attendance: 1,555. Michael Hogan single-handedly reduced Somerset to 26-4, which soon became 49-5, but Ben Green, the new List A captain, rescued them with 87. Set a revised 181 in 37 overs, Glamorgan were kept in contention by 37s from Billy Root and Tom Cullen, and – with the last pair at the crease – needed six off the final delivery. Andy Gorvin smacked Goldsworthy back over his head, but the ball pitched just short of the boundary, handing Somerset their first one-run win for 20 years.*

At Taunton, August 1. **Somerset won by five wickets. Yorkshire 158-5** (20 overs) (M. L. Revis 58*, W. Luxton 31*); ‡**Somerset 159-5** (19.1 overs) (J. C. Hildreth 61*). *County debut: J. E. K. Rew (Somerset). Attendance: 4,000. Rain kept a (Covid) capacity crowd waiting for four and a half hours, before Yorkshire teenagers Matthew Revis, with a maiden one-day fifty, and Will Luxton shared a sixth-wicket stand of 69*. Getting on for twice their age, Hildreth responded with 61* off 34, as Somerset won a 20-over match with five balls to spare.*

At Taunton, August 10. **Leicestershire won by four wickets. Somerset 326-7** (50 overs) (S. M. Davies 61, G. A. Bartlett 108, G. W. Thomas 75; B. W. M. Mike 3-75); ‡**Leicestershire 327-6** (44.4 overs) (R. K. Patel 40, L. J. Hill 107, AM. Lilley 39, L. P. J. Kimber 85). *County debut: G. W. Thomas (Somerset). Attendance: 3,200. Leicestershire pulled off their highest successful chase, beating 324-4 in a 40-over game against the same opponents at Grace Road in 2013. They were inspired by a fifth-wicket stand of 158 in 18 between their captain, Lewis Hill, who made a run-a-ball century, and Louis Kimber, whose punishing 85 off 57 included five sixes; Marchant de Lange's eight overs disappeared for 80. A high Somerset total had looked unlikely at 104-5, before George Bartlett hit a maiden one-day century (his 108 off 89 contained eight sixes) and put on 182 in 26 overs with 17-year-old George Thomas, Somerset's best stand for any wicket against Leicestershire. But their knockout hopes faded as the visitors took control of the pursuit.*

Somerset away matches

July 30: no result v Nottinghamshire.
August 5: no result v Surrey.

August 8: lost to Northamptonshire by 81 runs (DLS).
August 12: lost to Warwickshire by three wickets.

SURREY

At Guildford, July 27. **Surrey won by 33 runs** (DLS). **Surrey 311-8** (30 overs) (M. D. Stoneman 43, R. S. Patel 131, J. L. Smith 54); ‡**Nottinghamshire 266-7** (30 overs) (B. T. Slater 69, S. G. Budinger 45, J. D. M. Evison 54, D. J. Schadendorf 44*; C. McKerr 3-41). *Attendance:* 2,452. *A run-glut at Woodbridge Road came after rain had interrupted Surrey's innings at 29-1 off eight. They smashed 282 off the remaining 22, including 23 sixes. Ryan Patel (131 off 70) struck ten, reaching his maiden one-day century off 59. Jamie Smith cracked a 16-ball fifty, the joint-fastest in England. Seamer Joey Evison's four overs leaked 55. After Nottinghamshire were set an adjusted 300 off 30, Ben Slater and Sol Budinger began with 71 off 5.5, but the pace slackened, and Matt Dunn produced a double-wicket maiden.*

FASTEST LIST A FIFTIES BY BALLS IN THE UK

16	G. D. Rose	Somerset v Glamorgan at Neath	1990
16	**J. L. Smith**	**Surrey v Nottinghamshire at Guildford**	**2021**
17	D. J. Hussey	Nottinghamshire v Derbyshire at Nottingham	2007
17	J. C. Buttler	Somerset v Glamorgan at Taunton	2010
19	D. R. Smith	Sussex v Yorkshire at Scarborough	2009
19	S. J. Walters	Glamorgan v Lancashire at Colwyn Bay	2011
19	**W. A. R. Fraine**	**Yorkshire v Derbyshire at Chesterfield**	**2021**
20	J. M. Kemp	Kent v Sussex at Tunbridge Wells	2006
20	P. D. Trego	Somerset v Glamorgan at Taunton	2011

At The Oval, July 30. **No result. Northamptonshire 31-1** (5.3 overs) v ‡**Surrey.** *County debut:* N. J. H. Kimber (Surrey). *Attendance:* 3,130.

At The Oval, August 5. **No result** (DLS). ‡**Somerset 220** (48.3 overs) (S. M. Davies 45, L. P. Goldsworthy 96; D. T. Moriarty 4-30); **Surrey 66-0** (8 overs) (B. B. A. Geddes 31*). *Attendance:* 3,593. *Surrey were denied almost certain victory when rain stopped play eight overs into their pursuit of a revised 147 in 25. Tournament regulations required ten overs to constitute a match and, though they were already ahead of the ten-over DLS par score, Somerset might yet have taken wickets to raise the bar. But for Lewis Goldsworthy's adventurous 96, the game would have been over long before its damp denouement. Dropped early off Dan Moriarty, who finished with a career-best 4-30, he was caught at deep midwicket seeking his century.*

At The Oval, August 10. **Surrey won by seven wickets.** ‡**Warwickshire 268-9** (50 overs) (E. J. Pollock 30, M. J. Lamb 31, C. N. Miles 31*, Extras 31; C. McKerr 4-64, C. T. Steel 4-39); **Surrey 269-3** (39.4 overs) (B. B. A. Geddes 32, R. S. Patel 36, T. H. David 140*, J. L. Smith 45*). *Attendance:* 3,609. *Every Warwickshire batsman reached double figures, but none passed 31, as Conor McKerr and Cameron Steel shared the first eight wickets. Arriving at 59-2 in the 22nd, Surrey's Singapore international Tim David battered 140* off 70, reaching his maiden one-day century off 55, the fastest for the club since Ali Brown's 50-ball hundred against Gloucestershire at The Oval in 2007. David added 154* in 19 overs with Smith – a Surrey all-wicket record in this fixture – to book a place in the quarter-finals.*

Surrey away matches

July 22: beat Yorkshire by five wickets.   August 7: lost to Leicestershire by one run (DLS).
August 3: lost to Glamorgan by five wickets.   August 12: beat Derbyshire by eight wickets.

WARWICKSHIRE

At Birmingham, July 25. **Nottinghamshire won by 86 runs. Nottinghamshire 323** (49.4 overs) (B. T. Slater 86, H. Hameed 103, M. Montgomery 35; W. M. H. Rhodes 3-40); ‡**Warwickshire 237** (44 overs) (R. M. Yates 103, W. M. H. Rhodes 39, M. J. Lamb 38; L. W. James 5-48, L. A. Patterson-White 3-46). *County debut:* M. Montgomery (Nottinghamshire). *Attendance:* 711. *Maiden List A centuries for Haseeb Hameed and Rob Yates were both followed by a batting collapse.*

Warwickshire's was the more spectacular: from 226-4 in the 42nd, they lost 6-11, the final three in an over from seamer Lyndon James, who had not bowled in his previous one-day game, two years earlier, but finished with five. Injuries and unavailability meant Warwickshire were without ten bowlers, while Nottinghamshire – whose last seven had fallen for 60 – included four format debutants.

At Birmingham, July 29. **Warwickshire won by seven runs. ‡Warwickshire 303-6** (50 overs) (R. M. Yates 72, M. J. Lamb 119*, E. A. Brookes 63); **Leicestershire 296-9** (50 overs) (H. J. Swindells 69, R. K. Patel 118; G. A. Garrett 3-50, W. M. H. Rhodes 3-49). *Attendance: 802. Matthew Lamb converted his first one-day fifty into a century, putting on 153 – a Warwickshire sixth-wicket record – with Ethan Brookes, who also registered a first fifty. They turned a precarious 121-5 into an impressive 303-6, but Rishi Patel countered with a century of his own, having added 159 in 25 overs for Leicestershire's first wicket with Harry Swindells. The initiative was squandered, though, by feckless batting against an inexperienced Warwickshire attack. Leicestershire required 83 from 15.2 overs with eight wickets in hand but, by the time 15 were needed from the last, the final pair were at the crease, and could muster only seven against Will Rhodes. "Every middle-order player has had a soft dismissal," said head coach Paul Nixon. "It was unprofessional. I'm devastated."*

At Birmingham, August 6. **Warwickshire won by 134 runs. Warwickshire 278-6** (46 overs) (W. M. H. Rhodes 65, M. G. K. Burgess 73, M. J. Lamb 65, D. R. Mousley 54); **‡Northamptonshire 144** (33.4 overs) (T. A. I. Taylor 57*; E. A. Brookes 3-15). *Attendance: 728. Michael Burgess, with a career-best 73, and Rhodes rescued Warwickshire from 11-2 with a partnership of 133. Lamb and Dan Mousley then added 114 for the fifth, and put the match beyond Northamptonshire. Tom Taylor's defiant 57* gave the reply a veneer of respectability, after Charlie Thurston top-edged a pull off Ethan Brookes into his chin, and retired hurt.*

At Birmingham, August 12. **Warwickshire won by three wickets. ‡Somerset 287-8** (50 overs) (S. M. Davies 46, L. P. Goldsworthy 79, J. C. Hildreth 72; M. J. Lamb 4-35); **Warwickshire 289-7** (49 overs) (E. J. Pollock 44, M. G. K. Burgess 38, M. J. Lamb 92, D. R. Mousley 37, J. G. Bethell 37; J. H. Davey 4-57). *Attendance: 728. Ben Green returned to lead Somerset after isolating because of Covid. But his team's quarter-final hopes were dashed by Lamb, who took his first one-day wickets, then hit another stylish half-century. Earlier, Lewis Goldsworthy and James Hildreth had put on a run-a-ball 118 for Somerset's third wicket.*

Warwickshire away matches

July 22: lost to Glamorgan by two wickets. August 3: lost to Yorkshire by 39 runs.
July 27: beat Derbyshire by eight wickets (DLS). August 10: lost to Surrey by seven wickets.

YORKSHIRE

At Scarborough, July 22. **Surrey won by five wickets. Yorkshire 165** (34.1 overs) (G. S. Ballance 39, M. L. Revis 43; A. A. P. Atkinson 4-43); **‡Surrey 168-5** (39.1 overs) (M. D. Stoneman 73*; M. W. Pillans 4-57). *County debut: N. M. J. Reifer (Surrey). Attendance: 2,727. Both teams fielded four List A debutants, but it was an easy win for Surrey. Gus Atkinson – one of the newcomers – collected 4-43 on a fast, bouncy pitch as Yorkshire were skittled for 165. Mark Stoneman, who had just played four T20 matches for Yorkshire on loan, supervised the chase with a measured 73*; his opening partner, Hashim Amla, passed 10,000 one-day runs before becoming the first of four wickets for fellow South African Mat Pillans, once of Surrey.*

At Scarborough, July 28. **No result. Yorkshire 222** (49.3 overs) (W. Luxton 68, M. W. Pillans 40; C. J. White 3-38, T. A. I. Taylor 3-64); **‡Northamptonshire 2-0** (0.5 overs). *County debut: W. Luxton (Yorkshire). Attendance: 2,169. Yorkshire's batters had another bad day, against List A debutant Jack White on a pacy surface: his eight-over opening spell brought him 3-28. When Tom Taylor added a couple, they had slumped to 69-6, and it took an eye-catching, leg-side-dominant 68 from 18-year-old Will Luxton, on county debut, to drag them past 200. His eighth-wicket stand of 93 with Pillans was a Yorkshire record. Rain limited Northamptonshire's reply to five balls.*

At York, August 3. **Yorkshire won by 39 runs. Yorkshire 320-7** (50 overs) (H. G. Duke 42, G. S. Ballance 54, G. C. H. Hill 64, J. A. Tattersall 70, M. J. Waite 42*); **‡Warwickshire 281** (47.2 overs) (W. M. H. Rhodes 37, M. G. K. Burgess 33, D. R. Mousley 61, J. G. Bethell 66; B. O. Coad 3-30, G. C. H. Hill 3-47). *Attendance: 2,925. George Garrett struck twice in the opening over of Clifton*

Park's first one-day match. But Yorkshire surged to 320-7, thanks to half-centuries from Gary Ballance, George Hill and Jonathan Tattersall, plus a blistering 16-ball 42* from Matthew Waite, who hit 30 off Ethan Brookes in the final over; a hamstring injury prevented Garrett bowling at the death. Waite went on to dismiss both Warwickshire openers. Maiden fifties from List A debutant Dan Mousley and Jacob Bethell revived the innings from 134-5, but their stand of 115 came too late.

At York, August 6. **No result. Nottinghamshire 185-5** (33 overs) (B. T. Slater 74, S. G. Budinger 71; M. W. Pillans 4-26) v ‡**Yorkshire.** *County debuts: J. R. Sullivan (Yorkshire); F. Singh (Nottinghamshire). Attendance: 1,724. Yorkshire finally won the toss, only for rain to intervene. Ben Slater and Sol Budinger, who struck four sixes, opened for Nottinghamshire with a forceful 146, but Pillans hit back with four wickets in 13 balls. After the weather closed in, a fire alarm forced the players to leave the pavilion for 15 minutes. Both sides stayed in the frame for the knockouts.*

Yorkshire away matches

July 25: beat Leicestershire by seven wickets.
August 1: lost to Somerset by five wickets.

August 8: beat Derbyshire by eight wickets.
August 12: beat Glamorgan by four runs.

QUARTER-FINALS

At Chelmsford, August 14. ‡**Essex won by 129 runs. Essex 317-5** (50 overs) (J. S. Rymell 121, T. Westley 33, P. I. Walter 33, A. J. A. Wheater 34, S. R. Harmer 31*; G. C. H. Hill 3-51); **Yorkshire 188** (38.4 overs) (W. A. R. Fraine 31, W. Luxton 34, M. L. Revis 42, M. J. Waite 31; J. H. Plom 3-34, T. Westley 3-33). *Attendance: 681. Josh Rymell, just 20, underlined his potential with a magnificent maiden hundred, full of cultured and powerful drives, to take Essex to an imposing total. Yorkshire reached 68-1 in reply, but too slowly – and it was soon 88-5 as Essex's spin trio of Simon Harmer, Aron Nijjar and Tom Westley took control. They finished with a combined 20–1–84–7, and seamer Jack Plom a career-best 3-34. Essex hurried into the last four with their biggest win over Yorkshire in 18 years.*

At The Oval, August 15. **Surrey won by five wickets. Gloucestershire 242-7** (50 overs) (G. L. van Buuren 37, G. F. B. Scott 66*, T. M. J. Smith 51*); ‡**Surrey 246-5** (42.4 overs) (T. H. David 102, J. L. Smith 69*). *Attendance: 1,508. A Gloucestershire-record eighth-wicket stand of 105* between George Scott and Tom Smith rescued them from 137-7 in the 33rd – not the first time they had depended on runs from their lower-middle order. Surrey spinners Dan Moriarty and Tim David had exerted a stranglehold, and together claimed 4-62. A target of 243 was not too onerous, though Surrey slipped to 92-3 in the 15th. David's uncomplicated style had been enjoying rich returns, and his second hundred in three matches – his sequence now read 140*, 52*, 102 – battered Gloucestershire into submission. There was useful support from the 21-year-old captain, Jamie Smith, and victory was emphatic.*

SEMI-FINALS

GLAMORGAN v ESSEX

At Cardiff, August 16. Glamorgan won by five wickets. Toss: Glamorgan.

A pair of career-best performances from Joe Cooke sent Glamorgan to their first one-day final for eight years, after Essex had set them a challenging target on a good surface. He began with five for 61, the best one-day figures at Cardiff since 2012, to limit the damage when the visitors reached 225 for three in the 40th. A mid-innings stutter by Glamorgan threatened to undo the top order's good work, but Cooke and Cullen forged an unbeaten partnership of 111. Cooke capped his 56-ball 66 by driving Harmer into the River Taff to seal victory with two overs to spare. Essex had made a good start, with an opening stand of 111 between Rymell and Cook, visibly annoyed to be stumped off a wide from Reingold's off-spin; Walter's aggressive 50 backed them up. Cooke's accurate medium-pace kept the lower order in check, while Hogan's ten overs cost just 21. Rutherford's 44-ball 67, his fourth half-century of the competition, gave Glamorgan early impetus. At 151 for one in the 24th, they were well on course, before four fell for 31, including Selman for a steady 59. Cooke, though, was not finished, giving Glamorgan supporters less than three days to arrange a midweek trip to Nottingham for the final.

Attendance: 1,061.

Essex

J. S. Rymell c Salter b Cooke	44	B. M. J. Allison c Carlson b Hogan		3
A. N. Cook st Cullen b Reingold	68	J. H. Plom not out		0
*T. Westley c Reingold b Cooke	31			
F. I. N. Khushi c Cullen b Salter	26	B 8, lb 6, w 8, nb 4		26
P. I. Walter c and b Carey	50			
R. N. ten Doeschate c Cullen b Weighell	2	1/111 (2) 2/146 (1)	(49.4 overs)	289
†A. J. A. Wheater c Reingold b Cooke	16	3/162 (3) 4/225 (4) 5/228 (6)		
S. R. Harmer c Reingold b Cooke	21	6/259 (7) 7/268 (5) 8/270 (9)		
A. S. S. Nijjar c Reingold b Cooke	2	9/281 (10) 10/289 (8)	10 overs: 46-0	

Hogan 10–1–21–1; Carey 8–0–53–1; Weighell 8–0–64–1; Cooke 9.4–0–61–5; Salter 10–0–39–1; Reingold 4–0–37–1.

Glamorgan

H. D. Rutherford c Walter b Harmer	67	J. M. Cooke not out		66
N. J. Selman c Wheater b Westley	59			
*K. S. Carlson c Rymell b Westley	36	Lb 7, w 4		11
W. T. Root c sub (L. M. Benkenstein)				
b ten Doeschate	3	1/95 (1) 2/151 (3)	(5 wkts, 48 overs)	293
S. J. Reingold b Nijjar	10	3/156 (4) 4/180 (5)		
†T. N. Cullen not out	41	5/182 (2)	10 overs: 78-0	

A. G. Salter, W. J. Weighell, L. J. Carey and M. G. Hogan did not bat.

Plom 7–0–47–0; Allison 4–0–46–0; Nijjar 10–0–52–1; Harmer 10–0–54–1; ten Doeschate 7–0–46–1; Westley 10–0–41–2.

Umpires: M. Burns and I. J. Gould.   Referee: P. M. Such.

DURHAM v SURREY

At Chester-le-Street, August 17. Durham won by five wickets. Toss: Durham.

Durham booked a place in their first Royal London Cup final since winning the inaugural tournament in 2014. An early burst from Rushworth – three in his first four overs, including Pope for a six-ball duck – had Surrey floundering, before their captain, Smith, joined former Durham player Stoneman to steady the ship. They added 155, with Stoneman – in his first innings back in the North-East since leaving in 2016 – run out in the last over. His century set a competitive target of 281, but Lees and Borthwick, who was dropped twice, provided a solid foundation in a second-wicket stand of 119, and Bedingham blasted 56 in 35 deliveries. By the time he holed out, Durham were on their way to Trent Bridge.

Attendance: 1,883.

Surrey

M. D. Stoneman run out (Clark/Bancroft)	117	C. McKerr not out		1
R. S. Patel c Bedingham b Rushworth	9	D. T. Moriarty not out		2
O. J. D. Pope b Rushworth	0	B 3, lb 8, w 7, nb 4		22
T. H. David c Bancroft b Rushworth	3			
*†J. L. Smith lbw b Borthwick	85	1/18 (2) 2/24 (3)	(8 wkts, 50 overs)	280
R. Clarke c Rushworth b Doneathy	12	3/40 (4) 4/195 (5)		
C. T. Steel lbw b Borthwick	1	5/216 (6) 6/223 (7)		
N. M. J. Reifer run out (Doneathy/Bancroft)	28	7/270 (1) 8/278 (8)	10 overs: 47-3	

M. P. Dunn did not bat.

Salisbury 7–0–52–0; Rushworth 10–1–49–3; Campbell 5–0–43–0; Trevaskis 10–0–34–0; Borthwick 10–0–44–2; Doneathy 8–0–47–1.

Durham

G. Clark c Reifer b Dunn	46	L. Trevaskis not out	4
A. Z. Lees lbw b David	75	Lb 1, w 3	4
*S. G. Borthwick c Pope b Dunn	71		
D. G. Bedingham c Reifer b Clarke	56	1/64 (1) 2/183 (2) (5 wkts, 47.3 overs)	281
†C. T. Bancroft not out	24	3/222 (3) 4/273 (4)	
S. R. Dickson b McKerr	1	5/276 (6) 10 overs: 47-0	

L. Doneathy, M. E. T. Salisbury, C. Rushworth and J. O. I. Campbell did not bat.

Dunn 7–0–49–2; Clarke 8.3–1–42–1; McKerr 9–0–50–1; David 10–0–45–1; Steel 6–0–49–0; Moriarty 7–0–45–0.

Umpires: P. J. Hartley and G. D. Lloyd.   Referee: J. J. Whitaker.

FINAL

DURHAM v GLAMORGAN

Elizabeth Ammon

At Nottingham, August 19. Glamorgan won by 58 runs. Toss: Durham.

Glamorgan's cabinet had been empty for 17 years. What's more, it hadn't contained a single knockout trophy, until they beat Durham on a sunny, late-summer Thursday in Nottingham. Yes, a Thursday; no, not at Lord's. To make way for the climax of The Hundred, the final of what was once the most prestigious day in the domestic calendar now had a midweek slot at Trent Bridge, just two days after the second semi-final.

Yet none of that mattered to Carlson and his team-mates, as they lifted the trophy in front of Glamorgan's supporters, small in number but loud in voice. To them, the location – like the scheduling – was irrelevant. For the 7,228 people who defied the ECB's best attempts to make it as a difficult as possible to attend, this was a thoroughly absorbing day. And it was Carlson who laid the foundations for victory with a career-best 82 from 59 balls; Salter provided support with a useful 33, and later added three cheap wickets with his off-spin.

After Durham had won the toss, Rushworth – still going strong at 35 – got them off to a good start, taking the prize wicket of Rutherford, caught at long leg in the fifth over. The removal of Reingold in the 12th brought Carlson to the crease – and began a third-wicket partnership with Selman of 106 in less than 16 overs, of which Carlson's share was 81. But Potts, back from his stint in The Hundred, took three for one in eight balls, including Root for a golden duck, and Glamorgan were grateful for a series of contributions from their lower order, turning 160 for five in the 30th into 296 for nine.

Durham's reply began solidly, with Clark producing the form that had helped him average 86 in the competition. But his solid 40 was ended by Salter, who had already bowled the equally prolific Lees with one that turned sharply. Weighell chipped in with the wicket of Borthwick and, when Salter disposed of Bedingham for a duck, Durham – whose powerful top order had made them pre-match favourites – had slumped to 74 for four in the 19th.

A dynamic 85-run partnership between Dickson and Bancroft dragged them back in contention, but Bancroft's departure for 55, holing out to deep midwicket, left them needing 138 from 16.5 overs. Dickson was left playing a lone hand, as he tried both to keep up with the rate and marshal the lower order. But no one else could pass ten, as Cooke and Carey picked up two each.

It was fitting that the winning moment came from 40-year-old Hogan, with a perfect back-of-a-length seamer to remove Rushworth first ball. It was his 16th wicket of the tournament, taken at an average of 12, and an economy-rate of under three. Grasping the trophy, he could barely conceal his joy. "We've been trying 17 seasons to get this," he said.

Player of the Match: A. G. Salter.   *Attendance:* 7,228.

Glamorgan

H. D. Rutherford c Lees b Rushworth	15	
N. J. Selman c Lees b Potts	36	
S. J. Reingold c Bancroft b Raine	14	
*K. S. Carlson c Bancroft b Potts	82	
W. T. Root lbw b Potts	0	
†T. N. Cullen c and b Doneathy	24	
J. M. Cooke c Potts b Borthwick	29	
A. G. Salter c Bancroft b Raine	33	
W. J. Weighell c Clark b Raine	15	

L. J. Carey not out 19
M. G. Hogan not out 12

B 2, lb 7, w 6, nb 2 17

1/20 (1) 2/51 (3)   (9 wkts, 50 overs) 296
3/157 (2) 4/157 (5)
5/160 (4) 6/203 (7) 7/240 (6)
8/250 (8) 9/263 (9)   10 overs: 44-1

Rushworth 10–2–37–1; Potts 10–2–55–3; Raine 10–0–58–3; Doneathy 2.5–0–32–1; Trevaskis 9–0–53–0; Borthwick 8.1–0–52–1.

Durham

G. Clark c Weighell b Salter	40	
A. Z. Lees b Salter	15	
*S. G. Borthwick c Reingold b Weighell	10	
†C. T. Bancroft c sub (A. W. Gorvin) b Reingold	55	
D. G. Bedingham c Weighell b Salter	0	
S. R. Dickson not out	84	
B. A. Raine c Hogan b Cooke	10	
L. Doneathy c Carlson b Carey	10	

M. J. Potts c Cullen b Carey 0
L. Trevaskis c Selman b Cooke 9
C. Rushworth c Cullen b Hogan 0
Lb 4, w 1 5

1/47 (2) 2/64 (1) 3/73 (3)   (45.1 overs) 238
4/74 (5) 5/159 (4) 6/198 (7)
7/226 (8) 8/227 (9) 9/238 (10)
10/238 (11)   10 overs: 45-0

Hogan 7.1–0–27–1; Carey 8–1–47–2; Salter 10–0–42–3; Weighell 8–0–43–1; Cooke 9–0–57–2; Reingold 3–0–18–1.

Umpires: N. A. Mallender and S. J. O'Shaughnessy.   Third umpire: M. Burns.
Referee: D. A. Cosker.

THE MEN'S HUNDRED IN 2021

GEORGE DOBELL

1 Southern Brave   2 Birmingham Phoenix   3 Trent Rockets

On a balmy night at Lord's, as Southern Brave's death bowlers were choking the life out of the Birmingham Phoenix run-chase in The Hundred's maiden final, and a full house looked on in appreciation, it was hard to fathom all the criticism. Wasn't this – a high-profile, high-quality, short-form competition played, in part at least, on free-to-air television – exactly what English cricket had been crying out for? What harm could there be in a freshly branded tournament which appealed to a young, more diverse audience?

There was, for sure, plenty to admire. The Phoenix, joyfully and astutely captained by Moeen Ali, generated a level of support that domestic T20 had struggled to achieve in Birmingham, and played attractive cricket, characterised by Liam Livingstone's devastating batting and Adam Milne's potent bowling. It took an outstanding Brave team, characterised by Jake Lintott's left-arm wrist-spin and Tymal Mills's left-arm pace, to deny them.

Many of the numbers were persuasive. According to the ECB, over 16m watched some of the tournament on TV, with over 9m having seen no other ECB-administered cricket in 2021. More than 510,000 tickets were issued, 59% to under-45s; over half had not previously bought a ticket for a game in England. But a cigarette, a fry-up and a gallon of wine can all be pleasurable, too. It was the collateral damage which fuelled The Hundred's critics.

The competition had endured a long and difficult pregnancy. It had taken years of cajoling – including financial inducement – to persuade the 18 first-class counties to back an eight-team event, only for the pandemic to delay the launch by 12 months. When it finally came to life, the circumstances were imperfect, as problems with international travel led to a plethora of withdrawals: some big names, typically those expecting to play in the IPL and T20 World Cup, were reluctant to spend more time in biobubbles. The ECB claimed the tournament would feature "the best v the best", which sounded hubristic.

The big sell was understandable, since the ECB had bet the farm – financially and reputationally – on The Hundred's success. The set-up costs had been vast. Leaked figures suggested annual expenditure of around £35m (against a UK broadcast deal of £36.5m a year), but this excluded various expenses, not least the £1.3m per annum paid to every county and MCC for each of the first five seasons (£123.5m in total) to allow the competition to proceed. That cast doubt on the ECB's claim that The Hundred would produce a financial windfall. Even before Covid, their reserves had fallen from £73m to roughly zero. The appointment of extra staff, many tasked with bringing the tournament to fruition, was certainly a factor.

It was also prioritised over existing formats, and given the prime summer weeks. The T20 Blast, for years the counties' cash cow, was played in a window 40% smaller than previous seasons, with fixtures squeezed into less

Requited glove: Finn Allen and Liam Livingstone of Birmingham Phoenix during their stand at Leeds.

attractive slots: Surrey, for example, hosted six games in 12 days; attendances suffered. The Championship, too, was hit, with eight rounds before the end of May, and four from August 30. The standard of pitches did nothing to quieten the debate about the competition's ability to prepare Test cricketers.

Then there was the impact on the Test side itself. Since most of England's stars had already been allowed to participate in the IPL, several faced India with little red-ball cricket behind them. Dawid Malan had played one first-class innings in the year before his Test recall, while Jonny Bairstow had gone five months without one before the First Test against India. Joe Root gently called for better surfaces and more prioritisation of Test cricket, but was anyone in authority listening?

Hardest hit was the 50-over Royal London Cup. With the best 100 or so white-ball players absent, and the biggest grounds often busy, it was reduced to a development competition, with many matches played on outgrounds. This brought opportunity for youngsters. But with teenagers proliferating, the gap between county and international cricket became a chasm. It seemed an odd way to build on England's 2019 World Cup success.

Yet few would dispute that something needed to be done. The sport's relevance in England and Wales had been declining for years. With many school playing fields sold, and almost all cricket behind a TV paywall, the game had become the preserve of the privately educated, or those exposed to it in an earlier generation. It desperately needed an influx of younger people in general, and women in particular.

The ECB were also keen to diversify their income, amid fears of Test cricket's diminishing appeal to broadcasters. They wanted a competition which, like the IPL or BBL, could command global interest, and said they had conducted research suggesting a new audience could be attracted by shorter games, less jargon, lower ticket prices, greater exposure across mainstream media, and a more welcoming attitude to women and children. Even The Hundred's harshest critics could see the reasoning.

But if quicker games were the aim, why introduce a tactical timeout? And if they wanted to attract young families, why start some games at 7pm? As for an audience beyond white males, was it wise to appoint a coach – Darren Lehmann at Northern Superchargers – who had once been punished for hurling racist abuse? Might not many of the same outcomes have been achieved by adapting existing formats, without any of the complications or controversies? After all, when the ECB secured their lucrative 2017 broadcast deal, worth £1.1bn, the new competition was intended to be a T20; the 100-ball idea came along later.

The Hundred, then, divided opinion long before a ball was bowled. A survey on its eve by the Cricket Supporters' Association found 63% of cricket lovers felt negatively towards it. Welsh Fire, meanwhile, promised to "prove the haters wrong". To county supporters who had legitimate concerns for the future, such language felt like a slap in the face. In a letter to *The Cricketer*, Don Root, grandfather of Joe, called the tournament "just about as welcome… as Covid". He spoke for many who wondered if it was an attempt to reduce the number of first-class counties by stealth.

But, as the ECB pointed out, The Hundred wasn't necessarily aimed at Root senior. It was aimed at the new audience – at least initially, until the board realised they also required the buy-in of existing supporters. Within a couple of games, some of the reservations had disappeared. Above all, The Hundred was still cricket. An open-minded observer could appreciate good batting and bowling, and sharp fielding. And while some of the innovations – for example, umpires waving a card to signal the end of each "set" (not "over") – felt contrived, others had merit. Bowling two consecutive sets from the same end helped the flow; penalising slow over-rates by adding a fielder to the inner ring for the final set discouraged dawdling.

Some adapted better than others. **London Spirit**, captained by Eoin Morgan and coached by Shane Warne, lost six of their seven completed matches. Australia's Glenn Maxwell pulled out relatively late, and three England players without red-ball contracts when signed by the Spirit (Mark Wood, Zak Crawley and Dan Lawrence) appeared only four times between them because of Test duty. But an experienced middle order containing Morgan, Ravi Bopara (whose top score was 17) and Joe Denly rarely came to life, and Mohammad Amir, their star overseas player, was underwhelming.

Welsh Fire fared little better despite winning their first two games – the only two in which Bairstow, who made a half-century in both, was available. They then lost five in a row, stumbling to the tournament's heaviest defeat, a 93-run drubbing by Birmingham. With Tom Banton struggling and Jake Ball injured, too much was required of Ben Duckett, the second-highest run-scorer in the competition. Only a ferocious 80 from 35 balls by New Zealand's Glenn Phillips against the Spirit spared them the wooden spoon.

Trent Rockets had their moments, and won their first three. Marchant de Lange claimed the competition's first five-for, and Rashid Khan justified his stellar reputation. But a lack of runs from Alex Hales, Malan and D'Arcy Short

THE HUNDRED ATTENDANCE FIGURES

	Biggest	Smallest	Average	Total
Birmingham Phoenix (Birmingham)	17,778	12,137	15,512	62,047
London Spirit (Lord's)	23,892	22,889	23,406	† 70,217
Manchester Originals (Manchester)	14,864	11,660	13,354	† 40,061
Northern Superchargers (Leeds)	12,538	10,324	11,495	45,981
Oval Invincibles (The Oval)	21,279	18,126	19,615	78,460
Southern Brave (Southampton)	11,778	9,204	10,786	43,143
Trent Rockets (Nottingham)	12,783	11,483	12,337	49,348
Welsh Fire (Cardiff)	9,261	3,021	5,670	22,680

† *Excluding one abandoned fixture. Group games only.*

proved costly, and they fell away, skittled for 96 in the eliminator by Southern Brave. **Oval Invincibles** and **Manchester Originals** – who, inevitably perhaps, lost two home games to rain – also failed to mount a sustained challenge. Only **Northern Superchargers** passed 200, in a match billed as a local derby against the Originals: John Simpson thrashed 71 from 28 balls, and Steven Finn, who bowled only 15, became the first to concede 50. Despite the sustained excellence of Adil Rashid, the competition's joint-highest wicket-taker on 12 (with Milne, de Lange and Rashid Khan), they never fully recovered from failing to win any of their first three matches, and frontline seamers David Willey and Brydon Carse were expensive. The loss of Adam Lyth and the impressive Harry Brook, who both tested positive for Covid, for the final couple of matches didn't help.

But such withdrawals presented opportunities. Chris Benjamin had been a professional cricketer for only a few weeks, and played just one T20 match when he was drafted into the Phoenix squad as a last-minute replacement for the injured Adam Hose. In the tournament's second game, he made a match-clinching 24 not out. Will Smeed, a 19-year-old from Somerset, also enjoyed an outstanding start to life at the Phoenix, hitting 146 from 79 balls in his first three innings. Tom David, a Singaporean who was nobody's idea of a star overseas player, produced some of the most exciting moments of the final, with a six-ball 15 and a bullet throw to run out Livingstone. Lintott, a part-time teacher from Taunton, ended up a trophy winner.

Birmingham Phoenix would have been worthy champions, having gone into the final after winning five in succession. Livingstone ended up with 348 runs, 116 clear of the field. His strike-rate of 178 and tally of 27 sixes were competition-bests. Such was his dominance, his dismissal in the final was the game's decisive moment. Their batting line-up also boasted Ali and New Zealand's Finn Allen, while the bowling, led by the speed of Milne and boosted by the wiles of Imran Tahir and Benny Howell, was scarcely less potent.

That the Phoenix were denied was largely due to the excellence of **Southern Brave's** bowling. Mills, full of pace and guile, was masterful at the death, and claimed four for 21 from 36 balls in the two knockout games. With George Garton offering left-arm swing early on, Lintott miserly and dangerous in the middle overs, and Chris Jordan adding experience at the end, they could make almost any chase a challenge. Southern Brave managed only one of the tournament's 13 highest totals, but their captain, James Vince, consistently helped them to competitive scores, while Alex Davies and Quinton de Kock chipped in. Losing their first two games left little margin for error, but they won their last seven, and underlined the coaching credentials of the calm Mahela Jayawardene.

Possibly because the women's games took place before the men's as double-headers, some pitches were tired, resulting in lower scores than expected. The addition of musical acts between innings was incongruous: because stages overlooked the pitch, the acts seemed to be performing to a bunch of cricketers doing their warm-ups. Some of the coverage was hard to stomach. The BBC, in particular, seemed so desperate to see The Hundred win favour that they lost sight of their trademark objectivity: poor fielding and empty seats were passed over. News that a few ECB executives stood to share a bonus of £2.1m did nothing to assuage the suspicion that it was those with a direct interest in the competition's success who cheered loudest.

But it was fun. And, despite the withdrawals, it stood up as a high-quality tournament. Whether The Hundred turns out to be monster or saviour, though, remains to be seen.

FINAL TABLE

	P	W	L	NR/A	Pts	NRR
BIRMINGHAM PHOENIX .	8	6	2	0	12	21.74
SOUTHERN BRAVE	8	5	2	1	11	0.68
TRENT ROCKETS........	8	5	3	0	10	0.69
Oval Invincibles	8	4	3	1	9	2.46
Northern Superchargers	8	3	4	1	7	10.19
Manchester Originals	8	2	4	2	6	−7.21
Welsh Fire...............	8	3	5	0	6	−16.53
London Spirit	8	1	6	1	3	−12.82

Net run-rate calculated per 100 balls rather than per five-ball over.

Prize money

£150,000 for winners: SOUTHERN BRAVE.
£75,000 for runners-up: BIRMINGHAM PHOENIX.
£50,000 for third place: TRENT ROCKETS.
£10,000 for Most Valuable Player: L. S. Livingstone (Birmingham Phoenix).
£5,000 for leading run-scorer: L. S. Livingstone (Birmingham Phoenix).
£5,000 for leading wicket-taker: A. F. Milne (Birmingham Phoenix).
£5,000 for leading fielder: Q. de Kock (Southern Brave).
£5,000 for Moment of the Hundred: Imran Tahir (Birmingham Phoenix) – hat-trick v Welsh Fire.

AVERAGES

BATTING (100 runs)

	M	I	NO	R	HS	50	Avge	SR	4	6
1 L. S. Livingstone (*Phoenix*)	9	9	3	348	92*	3	58.00	178.46	22	27
2 W. G. Jacks (*Invincibles*)	8	7	0	146	44	0	20.85	175.90	16	8
3 W. C. F. Smeed (*Phoenix*)	6	6	1	166	65*	1	33.20	172.91	13	10
4 †Q. de Kock (*Brave*)............	9	8	2	202	72*	2	33.66	172.64	21	8

		M	I	NO	R	HS	50	Avge	SR	4	6
5	J. M. Bairstow (*Fire*)	2	2	0	128	72	2	64.00	**170.66**	10	8
6	P. R. Stirling (*Brave*)	6	5	0	132	61	1	26.40	**167.08**	10	10
7	†J. A. Simpson (*Superchargers*)	7	6	2	152	71*	1	38.00	**165.21**	19	4
8	S. R. Patel (*Rockets*)	9	8	2	179	46*	0	29.83	**157.01**	12	11
9	†D. J. Willey (*Superchargers*)	7	7	1	132	81*	1	22.00	**155.29**	6	9
10	H. C. Brook (*Superchargers*)	5	5	1	189	62	1	47.25	**153.65**	17	7
11	A. M. Rossington (*Spirit*)	6	6	0	140	46	0	23.33	**152.17**	16	4
12	L. J. Evans (*Invincibles*)	8	7	4	123	67*	1	41.00	**151.85**	6	7
13	J. M. Clarke (*Originals*)	7	7	0	127	58	1	18.14	**151.19**	14	5
14	†M. A. H. Hammond (*Phoenix*)	9	7	3	114	44*	0	28.50	**150.00**	14	2
	T. Köhler-Cadmore (*Superchargers*)	4	4	0	111	71	1	27.75	**150.00**	10	5
	F. H. Allen (*Phoenix*)	8	8	0	165	43	0	20.62	**150.00**	18	5
17	J. J. Roy (*Invincibles*)	8	7	2	186	56*	2	37.20	**148.80**	17	9
18	†M. M. Ali (*Phoenix*)	7	7	0	225	59	1	32.14	**148.02**	13	15
19	G. D. Phillips (*Fire*)	8	8	2	214	80	2	35.66	**146.57**	14	12
20	†R. A. Whiteley (*Brave*)	10	7	3	133	44*	0	33.25	**144.56**	13	7
21	P. D. Salt (*Originals*)	7	7	0	122	30	0	17.42	**141.86**	18	1
22	†J. L. du Plooy (*Fire*)	6	6	0	147	43	0	24.50	**141.34**	6	7
23	†B. M. Duckett (*Fire*)	8	8	0	232	65	2	29.00	**137.27**	28	3
24	C. G. Benjamin (*Phoenix*)	9	7	4	112	37*	0	37.33	**136.58**	11	4
25	†C. Munro (*Originals*)	7	7	2	165	45	0	33.00	**136.36**	18	6
26	J. P. Inglis (*Spirit*)	8	7	0	173	72	2	24.71	**136.22**	18	5
27	†E. J. G. Morgan (*Spirit*)	8	7	1	151	41	0	25.16	**136.03**	6	9
28	A. L. Davies (*Brave*)	10	9	2	202	50	1	28.85	**132.89**	20	3
29	A. D. Hales (*Rockets*)	9	9	1	185	40*	0	23.12	**132.14**	20	6
30	S. W. Billings (*Invincibles*)	8	7	1	143	49	0	23.83	**131.19**	12	4
31	†C. A. Ingram (*Invincibles*)	8	7	1	120	81*	1	20.00	**130.43**	9	5
32	J. M. Vince (*Brave*)	10	9	1	229	60	2	28.62	**129.37**	26	6
33	L. Gregory (*Rockets*)	9	7	2	107	28*	0	21.40	**128.91**	10	4
34	†D. J. Malan (*Rockets*)	9	9	1	214	62*	3	26.75	**121.59**	26	4
35	†D. J. M. Short (*Rockets*)	9	9	3	156	69*	2	26.00	**120.93**	20	2
36	C. A. Lynn (*Superchargers*)	7	7	0	150	48	0	21.42	**118.11**	14	5

BOWLING (80 balls)

		Style	Balls	Dots	R	W	BB	4I	Avge	SR	ER
1	A. F. Milne (*Phoenix*)	RF	135	74	129	12	3-15	0	10.75	11.25	**95.55**
2	T. S. Mills (*Brave*)	LF	187	84	208	8	3-8	0	26.00	23.37	**111.22**
3	Mohammad Nabi (*Spirit*)	OB	95	34	107	6	2-19	0	17.83	15.83	**112.63**
4	M. W. Parkinson (*Originals*)	LB	109	42	127	9	4-9	1	14.11	12.11	**116.51**
5	B. A. C. Howell (*Phoenix*)	RFM	170	55	204	11	2-12	0	18.54	15.45	**120.00**
	M. S. Crane (*Spirit*)	LB	115	43	138	6	1-16	0	23.00	19.16	**120.00**
7	Mujeeb Zadran (*Superchargers*)	OB	130	48	157	6	2-6	0	26.16	21.66	**120.76**
8	S. P. Narine (*Invincibles*)	OB	130	48	158	7	3-11	0	22.57	18.57	**121.53**
9	Qais Ahmad (*Fire*)	LB	155	51	189	8	4-13	1	23.62	19.37	**121.93**
10	J. B. Lintott (*Brave*)	SLW	165	55	209	11	3-14	0	19.00	15.00	**126.66**
11	A. U. Rashid (*Superchargers*)	LB	135	57	173	12	3-13	0	14.41	11.25	**128.14**
12	T. W. Hartley (*Originals*)	SLA	100	41	130	7	3-27	0	18.57	14.28	**130.00**
13	S. R. Patel (*Rockets*)	SLA	134	46	176	8	3-20	0	22.00	16.75	**131.34**
14	M. de Lange (*Rockets*)	RF	119	49	157	12	5-20	1	13.08	9.91	**131.93**
15	Rashid Khan (*Rockets*)	LB	170	67	231	12	3-16	0	19.25	14.16	**135.88**
16	D. R. Briggs (*Brave*)	SLA	90	32	123	7	2-17	0	17.57	12.85	**136.66**
17	M. J. Potts (*Superchargers*)	RFM	80	34	110	3	1-23	0	36.66	26.66	**137.50**
18	L. H. Ferguson (*Originals*)	RF	80	24	111	4	2-37	0	27.75	20.00	**138.75**
19	Imran Tahir (*Phoenix*)	LB	174	47	245	10	5-25	1	24.50	17.40	**140.80**
20	S. Mahmood (*Invincibles*)	RFM	120	43	173	5	2-19	0	34.60	24.00	**144.16**

		Style	Balls	Dots	R	W	BB	4I	Avge	SR	ER
21	M. Carter (*Rockets*)	OB	130	47	188	9	3-17	0	20.88	14.44	**144.61**
22	T. Shamsi (*Invincibles*)	SLW	115	30	167	7	3-25	0	23.85	16.42	**145.21**
23	M. M. Ali (*Phoenix*)	OB	90	28	131	4	1-15	0	32.75	22.50	**145.55**
24	T. K. Curran (*Invincibles*) . . .	RFM	122	38	179	10	3-29	0	17.90	12.20	**146.72**
25	G. H. S. Garton (*Brave*)	LFM	155	68	230	10	3-18	0	23.00	15.50	**148.38**
26	J. D. S. Neesham (*Fire*)	RFM	80	26	121	7	3-5	0	17.28	11.42	**151.25**
27	C. J. Jordan (*Brave*)	RFM	180	48	280	9	2-15	0	31.11	20.00	**155.55**
28	R. J. W. Topley (*Invincibles*) .	LFM	109	41	172	4	1-14	0	43.00	27.25	**157.79**
29	D. J. Willey (*Superchargers*) .	LFM	99	38	160	5	2-9	0	32.00	19.80	**161.61**
30	M. J. J. Critchley (*Fire*)	LB	85	24	138	4	1-20	0	34.50	21.25	**162.35**
31	C. R. Brathwaite (*Originals*) . .	RFM	90	23	148	3	2-13	0	49.33	30.00	**164.44**
32	B. C. Cullen (*Spirit*)	RFM	120	49	204	10	3-37	0	20.40	12.00	**170.00**
33	D. A. Payne (*Fire*)	LFM	125	44	222	6	3-38	0	37.00	20.83	**177.60**
34	R. E. van der Merwe (*Spirit*) . .	SLA	100	23	178	5	2-35	0	35.60	20.00	**178.00**
35	P. R. Brown (*Phoenix*)	RFM	85	19	167	6	3-27	0	27.83	14.16	**196.47**
36	T. G. Helm (*Phoenix*)	RFM	82	21	168	5	2-37	0	33.60	16.40	**204.87**

Economy-rate calculated per 100 balls rather than per five-ball over.

LEADING WICKETKEEPERS

Dismissals	M			Dismissals	M	
12 (11ct, 1st)	9	Q. de Kock (*Brave*)		7 (5ct, 2st)	9	T. J. Moores (*Rockets*)
8 (6ct, 2st)	7	J. A. Simpson (*Superchargers*)		6 (4ct, 2st)	6	A. M. Rossington (*Spirit*)

LEADING FIELDERS

Ct	M			Ct	M	
7	10	A. L. Davies (*Brave*)		6	8	R. S. Bopara (*Spirit*)

At The Oval, July 22 (floodlit). **Oval Invincibles won by nine runs. Oval Invincibles** 145-8 (100 balls) (S. W. Billings 49; F. J. Klaassen 3-23); ‡**Manchester Originals** 136-7 (100 balls) (C. R. Brathwaite 37). *PoM:* S. W. Billings. *Attendance:* 18,126. *A captain's-knock 49 off 30 from Sam Billings, in his first innings since contracting Covid a fortnight earlier, helped Oval Invincibles complete a women's and men's double over Manchester Originals. Assisted by Tom Curran's 29* off 18, he turned a shaky 48-4 into a testing 145-8. The Originals' reply began scratchily. Phil Salt fell in Sam Curran's first set of five, and Jos Buttler had faced only ten balls out of 34 by the time he got a leading edge to cover off Sunil Narine. Nathan Sowter's leg-spin caused further damage but, from 69-5 off 60, Carlos Brathwaite and Calvin Harrison put on 53. They were never quite up with the rate, however, and the Currans closed the game out. "It's great to get a first win on the board, and follow the ladies' example," said Billings.*

At Birmingham, July 23 (floodlit). **Birmingham Phoenix won by three wickets. London Spirit** 144-6 (100 balls) (Z. Crawley 64); ‡**Birmingham Phoenix** 148-7 (97 balls) (M. M. Ali 40). *PoM:* Z. Crawley. *Attendance:* 12,137. *In the clash between Britain's two biggest cities, the smaller triumphed. Zak Crawley, who had glued London Spirit together after they were put in, survived until the penultimate delivery. He tucked in to Tom Helm at both ends of the innings, though Helm eventually dismissed him for a 40-ball 64. Most threatening of the Birmingham attack was Adam Milne: he had two catches dropped, and was alone in costing under a run a ball. In reply, the Phoenix lost regular wickets and, when Moeen Ali departed for a steady 40 to make it 98-5 after 71, they were wobbling. A dash of aggression from the unheralded Chris Benjamin (24* from 15) did the trick.*

At Nottingham, July 24. **Trent Rockets won by nine wickets.** ‡**Southern Brave 126-8** (100 balls) (R. A. Whiteley 39*; M. de Lange 5-20); **Trent Rockets 127-1** (82 balls) (D. J. M. Short 51*, D. J. Malan 62*). *PoM:* M. de Lange. *Attendance:* 12,783. *Trent Rockets began with a comfortable victory, D'Arcy Short and Dawid Malan knocking off a modest target after Alex Hales fell to the second delivery of the chase. Earlier, Marchant de Lange – a late signing – was the sixth bowler tried by the Rockets. He dismissed Delray Rawlins with his first ball, a 90mph tester on a good length, soon added Colin de Grandhomme, and finished with 20–10–20–5, the tournament's best figures. Spinners Joe Root (1-17) and Rashid Khan (0-28) also kept the brakes on as Southern Brave were limited to 126 – a comeback of sorts from 71-6 after 65.*

At Leeds, July 24 (floodlit). **Welsh Fire won by five runs. Welsh Fire 173-4** (100 balls) (J. M. Bairstow 56, B. M. Duckett 41, J. D. S. Neesham 30*); ‡**Northern Superchargers 168-7** (100 balls) (H. C. Brook 35; Qais Ahmad 4-13). *PoM:* Qais Ahmad. *Attendance:* 10,324. *Jonny Bairstow – leading the away team on his home ground – galloped to 56 in 36, steering Welsh Fire to 93 off 63 before he fell to Ben Stokes, acting-captain for Superchargers as Faf du Plessis had concussion. Jimmy Neesham smashed 30* from 11 to lift them to 173. Harry Brook's five sixes in a 31-ball 62 kept the Superchargers in it, despite Jake Ball dismissing Stokes for just five. After Brook was plumb lbw to 20-year-old Afghan leg-spinner Qais Ahmad (20–8–13–4), Matty Potts (20* off ten) reduced the target to 11 off five: Ball restricted them to singles.*

At Lord's, July 25. **Oval Invincibles v ‡London Spirit. Abandoned.** *Heavy rain turned the Lord's outfield into a lake, and led to the competition's first abandonment.*

At Manchester, July 25 (floodlit). **Manchester Originals won by six wickets.** ‡**Birmingham Phoenix 87** (84 balls) (M. W. Parkinson 4-9); **Manchester Originals 89-4** (73 balls) (J. C. Buttler 30). *PoM:* M. W. Parkinson. *Attendance:* 13,537. *Matt Parkinson exploited a used pitch to pull the rug from beneath the Phoenix, who became the first side – men's or women's – to be dismissed inside 100 balls. He removed his Lancashire team-mate Liam Livingstone with his first delivery, and picked up another three in his last four, to claim figures of 19–11–9–4. Fellow leg-spinner Harrison also took two, as the Phoenix careered from 80-5 to 87 all out. The Originals lost four in reply – three to spin – but Buttler hurried them towards victory, which came with 27 deliveries unused.*

At Nottingham, July 26 (floodlit). **Trent Rockets won by two wickets.** ‡**Northern Superchargers 132** (99 balls) (H. C. Brook 38, J. A. Simpson 42; Rashid Khan 3-31, M. de Lange 3-22); **Trent Rockets 134-8** (94 balls) (A. D. Hales 40*). *PoM:* Rashid Khan. *Attendance:* 11,483. *While fourth-wicket pair Brook and John Simpson were crunching 61 in 40, the Superchargers looked set for a big score – but they slipped from 107-4 to 109-8, three to successive balls from Rashid Khan and de Lange. The Rockets then stumbled too: 20-0 became 20-3, with Malan and Root out for ducks to their Yorkshire team-mate Adil Rashid, and they later looked sunk at 103-8 after 82. But one delivery after opener Hales had been irritated than a single was disallowed because of an intruder on the pitch, he was gifted a six when Stokes spilled a straightforward catch over the long-off boundary. Hales made the most of his let-off: with Matt Carter – a late inclusion after Steven Mullaney was forced to self-isolate – he completed victory by smashing David Willey over midwicket.*

At Cardiff, July 27 (floodlit). **Welsh Fire won by 18 runs. Welsh Fire 165-4** (100 balls) (T. Banton 34, J. M. Bairstow 72, B. M. Duckett 53); ‡**Southern Brave 147-7** (100 balls) (J. M. Vince 40; J. D. S. Neesham 3-5). *PoM:* J. M. Bairstow. *Attendance:* 3,021. *Bairstow led Welsh Fire to another win in his last match before joining England's Test squad. His 39-ball 72 was the highest yet by a man in The Hundred, and he added 116 in 63 with Ben Duckett, before Danny Briggs removed him and Neesham with consecutive deliveries. The Brave were 85-1 at the halfway mark, but Ball – wearing a black armband for his old bowling coach, Mike Hendrick, who had died that day – bowled Devon Conway. Then Neesham had James Vince mistiming to long-on, and held a catch at long-off. With 29 needed off 15, he returned to take two wickets, and ensure victory for the Fire.*

At Manchester, July 28 (floodlit). **Manchester Originals v Northern Superchargers. Abandoned.**

At Lord's, July 29 (floodlit). **Trent Rockets won by seven runs. Trent Rockets 123-4** (100 balls) (D. J. M. Short 69*); ‡**London Spirit 116-8** (100 balls) (S. R. Patel 3-20, M. Carter 3-17). *PoM:* D. J. M. Short. *Attendance:* 23,892. *When the Rockets were 99-4 with seven balls left, an adequate total seemed unlikely, but Short crashed 24, and ended with 69* from 47. On another reused strip, scoring was always tricky, especially against slow bowling, and the Spirit's chase never gained much rhythm. Six reached double figures, but only Roelof van der Merwe passed 18. The Rockets sent down 75 balls of spin for a combined return of 8-70; for 25 balls of seam, it was 0-43.*

At Southampton, July 30 (floodlit). **Southern Brave won by four wickets. Birmingham Phoenix 151-3** (100 balls) (L. S. Livingstone 68*, M. A. H. Hammond 44*); ‡**Southern Brave 152-6** (97 balls) (J. M. Vince 60, D. P. Conway 34; A. F. Milne 3-15). *PoM:* J. M. Vince. *Attendance:* 11,778. *A partnership of 104* between Livingstone (68* from 44) and Miles Hammond muscled the Phoenix past 150, after they lost Finn Allen and Ali (for a three-ball duck) to left-arm wrist-spinner Jake Lintott. But it wasn't quite enough: Vince belted 60 from 38, before Chris Jordan (17* from nine) took the Brave home, despite a tight performance from New Zealand seamer Milne (20–11–15–3).*

At Cardiff, July 31. **Manchester Originals won by seven wickets.** ‡**Welsh Fire 150-6** (100 balls) (B. M. Duckett 32, J. L. du Plooy 43, M. J. J. Critchley 30*); **Manchester Originals 153-3** (95 balls) (P. D. Salt 30, J. M. Clarke 58, C. Munro 33*). *PoM:* J. M. Clarke. *Attendance:* 5,286. *A punishing opening stand of 95 in 48 balls between Salt and Joe Clarke (58 off 31) turned the Originals' pursuit of 151 into a formality, and condemned the Fire to their first defeat. Their innings had centred on 43 off 22 from Leus du Plooy, who had recently completed ten days' isolation following the abandonment of the Championship match between Derbyshire and Essex at Chesterfield. Matt Critchley, also of Derbyshire, contributed 30* off 17.*

At Leeds, July 31 (floodlit). **Northern Superchargers won by six wickets.** ‡**Oval Invincibles 127-6** (100 balls) (J. J. Roy 52*, T. K. Curran 34; A. U. Rashid 3-13); **Northern Superchargers 128-4** (97 balls) (C. A. Lynn 48, H. C. Brook 47*). *PoM:* H. C. Brook. *Attendance:* 10,859. *Northern Superchargers secured their first win, after two defeats and a washout. Adil Rashid had Oval Invincibles on the run at 60-6 – they hit only four boundaries in their first 78 balls, including three sixes from Narine – until Tom Curran joined Jason Roy, who batted throughout the Invincibles' innings. They more than doubled the total. In reply, Chris Lynn managed only a run a ball, but helped Brook get the Superchargers to 97-2. Brook became the tournament's leading run-scorer, with 147, and Simpson (19*), who arrived in the closing stages, lifted Curran into the stands for the winning six.*

At Birmingham, August 1. **Birmingham Phoenix won by six wickets. Trent Rockets 144-6** (100 balls) (A. D. Hales 38, D. J. Malan 51, S. R. Patel 31); ‡**Birmingham Phoenix 145-4** (74 balls) (F. H. Allen 43, W. C. F. Smeed 36; Rashid Khan 3-26). *PoM:* W. C. F. Smeed. *Attendance:* 17,479. *After three wins out of three, the Rockets were brought down to earth by a resurgent Phoenix. Milne provided characteristic precision at the start – he removed the dangerous Short for a duck – and finished with 20–14–13–2. The cornerstone of the Rockets innings was Malan, yet on a decent strip his 51 from 41 felt underpowered. Hales (38 from 22) and Samit Patel (31 from 19) showed more urgency, even if neither could compare with 19-year-old Will Smeed, who lit up the Phoenix reply. His 36 occupied 13 balls, part of a ferocious opening stand of 60 in 22 with Allen (43 off 23), which allowed later consolidation, if needed. It wasn't: victory came with 26 unused.*

At Lord's, August 1 (floodlit). **Southern Brave won by four runs. Southern Brave 145-6** (100 balls) (A. L. Davies 50); ‡**London Spirit 141-7** (100 balls) (A. M. Rossington 45, J. P. Inglis 55). *PoM:* C. J. Jordan. *Attendance:* 23,436. *London Spirit, whose coach, Shane Warne, was in isolation after a positive Covid test, almost pulled off their first win. Adam Rossington (45 in 21) and Josh Inglis romped to 68-0 in 25 balls, the best powerplay of The Hundred; Inglis batted into the closing stages, but no one else reached double figures, and with 18 needed off 15 he was caught behind by a leaping Quinton de Kock. Tight bowling by Jordan and Tymal Mills clinched the tournament's narrowest win. Earlier, the Spirit had restricted Southern Brave to 145; despite Alex Davies's half-century.*

At The Oval, August 2 (floodlit). **Oval Invincibles won by six wickets. Welsh Fire 121-7** (100 balls) (B. M. Duckett 65; T. K. Curran 3-29); ‡**Oval Invincibles 124-4** (93 balls) (S. W. Billings 40*). *PoM:* S. W. Billings. *Attendance:* 21,279. *On a two-paced pitch, Welsh Fire mustered a modest total, despite Duckett repeatedly finding the leg-side boundary in his 52-ball 65. Josh Cobb was run out at the non-striker's end when Reece Topley got a touch on a Duckett drive: he slid his bat in safely, then inexplicably withdrew it. In pursuit of 122, Will Jacks hit 20 off nine, but a double strike from Neesham had Oval Invincibles faltering at 48-3. Billings and Laurie Evans hurried them home, though, with Evans lifting David Payne for four, six and six to finish it.*

At Lord's, August 3 (floodlit). **Northern Superchargers won by 63 runs.** ‡**Northern Superchargers 155-3** (100 balls) (D. J. Willey 81*); **London Spirit 92-9** (100 balls) (B. A. Raine 3-20). *PoM:* D. J. Willey. *Attendance:* 22,889. *Willey ran amok as London Spirit slumped to another defeat. First he thrashed 81* off 45, including six sixes – his highest score in any format for three years. Then he removed the Spirit openers in the opening ten balls of the chase, and sent down 15 of the innings' first 20. From 49-2, the hosts subsided to 92-9, having made neither head nor tail of Mujeeb Zadran, who took 2-6 from his 20.*

At Birmingham, August 4 (floodlit). **Birmingham Phoenix won by six wickets. Oval Invincibles 172-3** (100 balls) (J. J. Roy 38, C. A. Ingram 81*); ‡**Birmingham Phoenix 174-4** (94 balls) (W. C. F. Smeed 45, M. M. Ali 49, C. G. Benjamin 37*). *PoM:* C. G. Benjamin. *Attendance:* 14,653. *This was a run extravaganza: 346 was the tournament's highest aggregate. An Invincibles total of 172-3 might have borne out their name but, against a batting line-up now firing on all cylinders, it proved flimsy. Four of the Phoenix top five hit 23 or more at a rate of 160-plus, and they won easily. Smeed maintained his sharp form with 45 off 28, though the pace quickened further thanks to Ali (49 from 26) and Benjamin, who lashed 37* from 16. It had been a breezy affair earlier, too, with Colin Ingram scything 81* from 43.*

At Manchester, August 5 (floodlit). **No result. Manchester Originals 98-3** (71 balls) (C. Munro 41*) v ‡*Southern Brave. Attendance:* 11,660. *Rain cut the game to 90 balls a side, then 85, and returned to end it. The Originals' second no-result put them level with Birmingham Phoenix and Trent Rockets at the top of the table.*

At Cardiff, August 6 (floodlit). **Trent Rockets won by six wickets. Welsh Fire 139-8** (100 balls) (G. D. Phillips 50, J. L. du Plooy 30; Wahab Riaz 4-30); ‡**Trent Rockets 140-4** (90 balls) (S. R. Patel 46*). *PoM:* S. R. Patel. *Attendance:* 5,112. *Welsh Fire lost their third successive game, after a late-innings batting failure. A fourth-wicket stand of 72 off 46 between Glenn Phillips and du Plooy was followed by a collapse of four for 13, courtesy of Wahab Riaz's late-swinging yorkers. Trent Rockets' stop-start chase was teetering when Hales (26) holed out to Qais Ahmad. But Patel (46* off 20, with five sixes) and Lewis Gregory (22* off 17, having been bowled by a Payne no-ball on seven) blitzed 69* off 33 to take the Rockets clear at the top.*

At Southampton, August 7 (floodlit). **Southern Brave won by five wickets. ‡Northern Superchargers 128-6** (100 balls) (D. J. Vilas 35*); **Southern Brave 131-5** (95 balls) (Q. de Kock 72*). *PoM:* Q. de Kock. *Attendance:* 10,712. *De Kock, with 72* off 45, asserted his class to take Southern Brave home with five balls to spare; his team's next-best score was 20, from fellow opener Paul Stirling. Chasing a modest 129, the Brave had lost three in nine balls to the off-breaks of Lyth – who had been bowled by the game's first ball, from George Garton – and the leg-breaks of Adil Rashid. But while de Kock was there, the result was in little doubt. The Superchargers' innings had never got going, and expert death bowling from Jordan and Mills, who didn't concede a boundary from the last 13 balls, kept things under control.*

At The Oval, August 8 (floodlit). **Oval Invincibles won by nine runs. Oval Invincibles 125-6** (65 balls) (J. J. Roy 56*); ‡**Trent Rockets 116-8** (65 balls) (S. P. Narine 3-11). *PoM:* J. J. Roy. *Attendance:* 19,382. *Roy proved the difference in a rain-shortened match. He was dropped on 18 by Rashid Khan, and made the most of it by collaring the Rockets attack for 56 from 29; next-highest for the Invincibles was Extras, with 14. Short then fell for a duck, one of three wickets for Narine, and the Rockets – though never out of the game – were always behind the rate. They fought on, with Gregory hitting 28* off 12 from No. 7, but a beery crowd cheered a home win at 10.27pm. The Rockets clung on at the top; the Invincibles climbed to second.*

At Birmingham, August 9 (floodlit). **Birmingham Phoenix won by 93 runs. Birmingham Phoenix 184-5** (100 balls) (W. C. F. Smeed 65*, M. M. Ali 59; L. S. Livingstone 31; D. A. Payne 3-38); ‡**Welsh Fire 91** (74 balls) (I. A. Cockbain 32; Imran Tahir 5-25). *PoM:* Imran Tahir. *Attendance:* 17,778. *Imran Tahir completed The Hundred's biggest win with its first hat-trick, and was the second to take five wickets. Birmingham Phoenix's 184-5 was the highest total yet, and Welsh Fire's 91 the second-lowest, undercut only by the Phoenix's own 87 in Manchester, and outstripped here by a single partnership: Smeed (65* in 38 balls) and Ali (59 in 28) added 92, and hit nine sixes. Payne picked up three late home wickets, but was upstaged by Tahir, who had Qais Ahmed caught slogging, Matt Milnes lbw and Payne bowled. It was the Phoenix's fourth win, all at Edgbaston.*

At Manchester, August 10 (floodlit). **London Spirit won by six runs. ‡London Spirit 142-6** (100 balls) (A. M. Rossington 46; T. W. Hartley 3-27); **Manchester Originals 136-9** (100 balls) (C. N. Ackermann 53, C. R. Brathwaite 30; B. T. J. Wheal 4-17). *PoM:* B. T. J. Wheal. *Attendance:* 14,864. *London Spirit claimed their first win, after a meltdown by Manchester Originals. Having fought back from 21-3, they needed 17 from 12 balls with six wickets in hand, only to lose four for ten: Brad Wheal removed Colin Ackermann for 53, before Brathwaite (30 off 19) sliced Blake Cullen to deep cover. Three then fell in the final five, from Wheal, including Fred Klaassen, who trod on his stumps with six required for a last-ball tie. Earlier, Rossington led the way for Spirit with 46 off 29. But progress was tricky against the speed of Lockie Ferguson – he reached 94mph – and the turn of Parkinson, who also performed an outstanding leap to catch Rossington's reverse sweep.*

At Southampton, August 11 (floodlit). **Southern Brave won by eight wickets. Welsh Fire 144-5** (100 balls) (T. Banton 36, G. D. Phillips 30*, J. L. du Plooy 30); ‡**Southern Brave 147-2** (87 balls) (Q. de Kock 57*, J. M. Vince 53). *PoM:* Q. de Kock. *Attendance:* 11,449. *Once again, the Brave were grateful to Jordan and Mills, who went for just 25 from the last 20 balls of the Fire's innings, and de Kock, who got little of the strike but guided them home with 57* off 32. There was assistance from Briggs, opening the bowling with his left-arm spin and taking 2-17, and Vince (53 off 39), who put on 86 with de Kock. While the Brave went top, the Fire were now out of contention for the knockouts, having lost five in a row.*

At Leeds, August 12 (floodlit). **Northern Superchargers won by 69 runs. Northern Superchargers 200-5** (100 balls) (D. J. Vilas 36, J. A. Simpson 71*); ‡**Manchester Originals 131** (99 balls) (B. A. Raine 3-15). *PoM:* J. A. Simpson. *Attendance:* 12,538. *At 106-4 after 65, Northern Superchargers looked on course for a decent score, but a blistering innings transmuted decent to daunting, and brought up the competition's only total of 200. Simpson hit 11 fours and two sixes, and – in a fifth-wicket stand with Dane Vilas worth 90 – hit 71* from 28. Manchester fluffed four catches, as the bowlers suffered: Steve Finn's 15 deliveries went for 51, much the most expensive return of the tournament. (Ackermann's 20, though, cost just 17.) In reply, no one bettered Brathwaite's 21. Ben Raine picked up 3-15.*

At Nottingham, August 13 (floodlit). **Birmingham Phoenix won by 16 runs. Birmingham Phoenix 166-6** (100 balls) (L. S. Livingstone 50, M. A. H. Hammond 38*); ‡**Trent Rockets 150-9** (100 balls) (S. J. Mullaney 49; P. R. Brown 3-27). *PoM:* L. S. Livingstone. *Attendance:* 12,694. *Birmingham Phoenix shrugged off the loss of Ali, a late call-up for the Lord's Test. Livingstone, who deputised as captain, took them to three figures with 50 in 31, before he was caught going for a fourth six: Mullaney parried it as he crossed the boundary, then jumped back to complete the catch. Hammond's 20-ball 38* lifted the target to 167. Dillon Pennington, on tournament debut, bowled 15 of the first 20 deliveries in Trent Rockets' reply, dismissed Malan and Hales in a five-ball maiden, conceded just 11 and was not needed again, as Pat Brown collected three.*

At The Oval, August 14 (floodlit). **Oval Invincibles won by two wickets. ‡London Spirit 146-7** (100 balls) (J. L. Denly 35, E. J. G. Morgan 41; T. Shamsi 3-25); **Oval Invincibles 147-8** (95 balls) (W. G. Jacks 44, L. J. Evans 67*). *PoM:* L. J. Evans. *Attendance:* 19,673. *Evans's breathtaking 67* off 37 took Oval Invincibles to a narrow win, and second in the table. At 14-3, and 52-4, they were struggling, but Jacks (44 off 26) swept and pulled with panache, and – despite another flurry of wickets – Evans applied the coup de grace with a swashbuckling six over long-on. London Spirit had sprinted to 49 before Rossington (28 off 20) played on, then Eoin Morgan thumped five sixes in his 20-ball 41. But Tabraiz Shamsi removed Morgan and Ravi Bopara in two balls, the first of five to tumble in 17, and it needed van der Merwe (20* off 10) to provide late momentum.*

At Nottingham, August 15 (floodlit). **Trent Rockets won by seven wickets. ‡Manchester Originals 135-8** (100 balls) (C. Munro 45; Rashid Khan 3-16); **Trent Rockets 136-3** (95 balls) (D. J. Malan 52, S. R. Patel 35*). *PoM:* D. J. Malan. *Attendance:* 12,388. *Playing against a backdrop of a worsening political situation in Afghanistan, Rashid Khan inspired Trent Rockets to a victory that ensured a place in the knockouts. At 70-1 off 41, the Originals had been flying. But they stuttered, managing 65-7 off the last 59, as Rashid took 3-16 and held two catches. Malan then broke the back of the chase with 52 off 46, before Patel finished the job in a hurry.*

At Southampton, August 16 (floodlit). **Southern Brave won by six wickets. Oval Invincibles 134-7** (100 balls) (W. G. Jacks 39, A. J. Blake 44*; J. B. Lintott 3-14); ‡**Southern Brave 135-4** (95 balls) (A. L. Davies 40*, C. de Grandhomme 40*). *PoM:* A. L. Davies. *Attendance:* 9,204. *A fifth-wicket stand of 67* between Davies and de Grandhomme sped Southern Brave into the eliminator at the expense of the Invincibles, whose away form – three defeats and a no-result – was their undoing. Jacks had propelled them to 46-0 from 16 balls but, after his departure, the innings lost its way. Alex Blake shoved it back on course with a forthright 44*, though a total of 134 felt light. Left-arm wrist-spinner Lintott had figures of 20-6-14-3. The Brave began badly, lurching to 14-2, but rebuilt. At 68-4, the game seemed evenly poised – then came the match-winning partnership.*

At Leeds, August 17 (floodlit). **Birmingham Phoenix won by eight wickets. Northern Superchargers 143-8** (100 balls) (C. A. Lynn 34, T. Köhler-Cadmore 71; L. S. Livingstone 3-25); ‡**Birmingham Phoenix 147-2** (74 balls) (F. H. Allen 42, L. S. Livingstone 92*). *PoM:* L. S. Livingstone. *Attendance:* 12,260. *Birmingham Phoenix's sixth win, with 26 balls in hand, secured* *top place in the table, and direct entry to the final. That was by no means certain when the Superchargers openers ran up 95 in 54 – Köhler-Cadmore slammed 66464 off Brown – as if intent on reprising the 200 their side had scored five days earlier. But Livingstone found Lynn's edge, and quickly added Willey and Vilas. Next, Livingstone put on 106 in 51 with Allen. He reached a 20-ball fifty, the fastest in The Hundred, with his seventh six, while his tenth took him to 92* off 40 – matching Jemimah Rodrigues for the highest score in the format.*

At Cardiff, August 18 (floodlit). **Welsh Fire won by three wickets. London Spirit 163-5** (100 balls) (J. P. Inglis 72, J. B. Cracknell 35; R. F. Higgins 3-21); ‡**Welsh Fire 165-7** (98 balls) (G. D. Phillips 80; B. C. Cullen 3-37, B. T. J. Wheal 3-30). *PoM:* G. D. Phillips. *Attendance:* 9,261. *A show-stealing innings from Phillips made up for Welsh Fire's mediocre bowling and fielding. He hit five fours and seven sixes in a 36-ball 80, out of 111 while he was at the crease. A successful chase had seemed unlikely after London Spirit racked up 163-5, with Inglis blasting 72 off 45. Cobb's sprawling boundary catch of Rossington, and Ryan Higgins's 3-21, reined in the scoring, but Morgan (25 off 12) finished with a flourish. Welsh Fire were 2-2, then 20-3, before Phillips intervened. When he went, 51 were needed from 37, but Cobb's 28* off 15 clinched it. Welsh Fire sneaked into seventh place, consigning London Spirit to the wooden spoon.*

ELIMINATOR

SOUTHERN BRAVE v TRENT ROCKETS

At The Oval, August 20 (floodlit). Southern Brave won by seven wickets. Toss: Southern Brave.

Fortune favoured the Brave in a desperately one-sided match that secured them a place in the final against Birmingham Phoenix. Opting to field, their seam attack blew the Rockets apart: Garton's sharp bounce lopped off Malan, Hales and Short; Overton's cutters clipped the wings of Mullaney and Patel; Jordan's examination-by-variation was failed by Moores and Carter; Mills's pinpoint yorkers ensured there would be no late boost. The Rockets barely got off the launch pad: Patel top-scored with 20, and Mills took three for eight. Requiring just 97, the Brave batted in an atmosphere of anticlimax. De Lange bowled beautifully: he had taken five wickets in the corresponding group game, and now had a hand in all three. But, for the Brave, this was barely a bump in the road. The 32 balls they left unused were the most in any game of the tournament.

Player of the Match: G. H. S. Garton. *Attendance:* 21,458.

Trent Rockets

		B	4/6
1 D. J. Malan *c 2 b 8*	14	8	3
2 A. D. Hales *c 2 b 8*	3	6	0
3 D. J. M. Short *c 10 b 8*	6	6	1
4 S. J. Mullaney *b 9*	5	4	1
5 S. R. Patel *c 11 b 9*	20	21	1/1
6 *L. Gregory *c 1 b 10*	11	17	1
7 †T. J. Moores *c 9 b 7*	19	12	0/2
8 Rashid Khan *c 6 b 10*	2	9	0
9 M. Carter *c 2 b 7*	0	2	0
10 M. de Lange *c 2 b 10*	7	6	0/1
11 S. J. Cook *not out*	0	0	0
B 4, lb 1, w 4	9		

25 balls: 31-4 (91 balls) 96

1/15 2/18 3/24 4/31 5/62 6/82 7/87 8/88 9/96

Garton 20–10–18–3; Overton 20–10–25–2; Mills 16–10–8–3; Jordan 15–7–15–2; Lintott 20–11–25–0.

Southern Brave

		B	4/6
1 P. R. Stirling *c 10 b 9*	31	19	3/2
2 †Q. de Kock *c 11 b 10*	6	4	1
3 *J. M. Vince *not out*	45	27	6/2
4 A. L. Davies *c 7 b 10*	3	6	0
5 R. A. Whiteley *not out*	7	12	1
B 4, lb 1	5		

25 balls: 50-1 (68 balls) 97-3

1/22 2/69 3/83

6 T. H. David, 7 C. J. Jordan, 8 G. H. S. Garton, 9 C. Overton, 10 T. S. Mills and 11 J. B. Lintott did not bat.

Carter 10–4–17–1; Cook 18–6–26–0; de Lange 20–12–16–2; Rashid Khan 15–8–26–0; Patel 5–1–7–0.

Umpires: D. J. Millns and R. J. Warren. Third umpire: N. L. Bainton.
Referee: W. M. Noon.

FINAL

BIRMINGHAM PHOENIX v SOUTHERN BRAVE

Matt Roller

At Lord's, August 21 (floodlit). Southern Brave won by 32 runs. Toss: Birmingham Phoenix.

A fast, flat throw from the boundary was the defining moment of the first men's Hundred final. After hitting an unbeaten 40-ball 92 in Birmingham Phoenix's last group game, Livingstone had pulled his third and fourth deliveries for six, and clubbed 45 off 18 when he sliced Jordan to deep cover midway through their chase. Diving forward, Whiteley could only parry the ball on the half-volley, but Tim David, who had run back from inside the ring, picked it up and fired it to the keeper's end. His direct hit found Livingstone, who had dawdled over the first run, just short of his ground aiming for a second. Such was his importance, it felt as though it had sealed the title for Southern Brave.

David ran off in open-mouthed disbelief. A Singapore international with a couple of seasons in the Big Bash – though only one fifty in 23 innings – he had expected to spend the week holidaying in London between stints for Surrey and St Lucia Kings. But he was drafted in to the Brave squad when Colin de Grandhomme joined New Zealand. He had neither batted nor bowled in the eliminator, but here he hit two of his six balls for six, held a superb low catch to dismiss Bedingham at the start of the Phoenix reply, and now removed the ferocious Livingstone.

To get this far, the Brave had relied on a versatile attack, with Jordan and left-armers Mills, Garton and Lintott forming the core. But after they were put in – following a bizarre toss, which had to be repeated when the coin lodged on its side by the edge of the stage – they set up victory thanks to two of the Blast's more experienced batters. The first was Stirling, Middlesex's resident six-hitter during his Lord's career. He was quickly into his groove, despite Milne – the tournament's most dangerous bowler – dismissing the in-form de Kock for seven, and Tahir outfoxing Vince. Stirling, though, walloped six sixes, and his 36-ball 61 built an ideal platform for Whiteley (and, briefly, David) to swing hard at the death. If Milne was unhittable – he took two from eight from 20 – his team-mates were not. Whiteley crashed eight of his 19 balls for boundaries, mostly down the ground.

The Phoenix also lost two early wickets. The Brave's decision to pick Overton as a specialist new-ball bowler rather than Danny Briggs's left-arm spin soon paid off when he had his Somerset team-

Galloping George: Garton topped 90mph for Southern Brave in the final.

mate Smeed caught at point. Livingstone briefly looked as if he could overhaul the target on his own, clattering Lintott for 14 from three deliveries, only for David's throw to shatter stumps, and dreams. Ali, released by England between the Lord's and Headingley Tests, was unusually scratchy and, when he holed out to long-on for 36, the game was up.

Player of the Match: P. R. Stirling.   *Attendance:* 24,556.
Most Valuable Player of the Tournament: L. S. Livingstone.

Southern Brave

		B	4/6
1 †Q. de Kock *c 9 b 8*	7	7	0/1
2 P. R. Stirling *c 6 b 7*	61	36	2/6
3 *J. M. Vince *b 11*	4	8	0
4 A. L. Davies *c 11 b 8*	27	20	1/1
5 T. H. David *c 1 b 4*	15	6	0/2
6 R. A. Whiteley *not out*	44	19	4/4
7 C. J. Jordan *not out*	5	4	0
Lb 5	5		

25 balls: 25-1   (100 balls)   168-5

1/15 2/35 3/85 4/103 5/145

8 G. H. S. Garton, 9 C. Overton, 10 T. S. Mills and 11 J. B. Lintott did not bat.

Milne 20–14–8–2; Pennington 10–4–29–0; Imran Tahir 20–3–33–1; Howell 20–6–34–1; Brown 15.2–2–36–0; Livingstone 10–3–18–1; Ali 5–1–5–0.

Birmingham Phoenix

		B	4/6
1 D. G. Bedingham *c 5 b 8*	0	2	0
2 W. C. F. Smeed *c 4 b 9*	2	6	0
3 *M. M. Ali *c 9 b 11*	36	30	1/3
4 L. S. Livingstone *run out (5)*	46	19	4/4
5 M. A. H. Hammond *c 8 b 10*	3	4	0
6 †C. G. Benjamin *not out*	23	25	1/1
7 B. A. C. Howell *not out*	20	14	3
Lb 2, w 4	6		

25 balls: 28-2   (100 balls)   136-5

1/0 2/14 3/70 4/83 5/97

8 A. F. Milne, 9 D. Y. Pennington, 10 P. R. Brown and 11 Imran Tahir did not bat.

Garton 20–12–27–1; Overton 20–8–26–1; Mills 20–11–13–1; Lintott 20–6–30–1; Jordan 20–5–38–0.

Umpires: M. J. Saggers and A. G. Wharf.   Third umpire: N. J. Llong.
Referee: S. Cummings.

THE UNIVERSITIES IN 2021

The university cricket season was again severely impacted by Covid, as it had been in 2020. The British Universities and Colleges Sports board tried to arrange as many games as restrictions allowed. "The season was deemed to be an 'extraordinary' one, in which there would be no promotion or relegation, and the focus was on facilitating fixtures rather than competitive matches," said Neal Kington of BUCS. "The men's national league was split into two pools to reduce the teams' travel requirements."

Loughborough finished top in the north, a point ahead of Leeds/Bradford, with Durham and Cambridge further behind. Oxford led the way in the south, a point clear of Cardiff; Exeter and Bristol made up the group. But Cardiff came out on top in the Championship final against Oxford at Kibworth, as Glamorgan's Steven Reingold – who won the match with a six – finished 97 not out.

The senior teams were once again called University Centres of Cricketing Excellence, as MCC had ended their funding of the project after 15 years; the ECB provided some financial support instead. The UCCEs (and Exeter University) continued to provide early-season practice for county sides, but the games were no longer first-class, and all involved teams of more than 11 players. Taylor Cornall and Josh de Caires both reached centuries in a stand of 270 for Leeds/Bradford against Yorkshire at Headingley, while Oxford's Calvin Harrison made a hundred against Nottinghamshire. Durham seamer Mungo Russell took five for 24 as Worcestershire were bowled out for 150.

The Varsity Match, already stripped of first-class status, suffered a further blow when, a few days before it was due to start, the authorities at Oxford and Cambridge ruled out sporting contests in either city. Thanks to herculean behind-the-scenes efforts, the game was shifted to Teddington CC's ground at Bushy Park, near Hampton Court, where an entertaining three days ended with Cambridge just failing to reach a target of 58 in nine overs. They did win the 50-over fixture, still played at Lord's, but Oxford came out on top in the T20.

Oxford's George Hargrave made an undefeated 105 in the 50-over match, to follow 100 in the corresponding fixture in 2020, and 146 in the four-day game in 2019. He was only the fourth man to score three centuries in official Varsity Matches, after M. J. K. Smith for Oxford in 1954/55/56, and the Cambridge pair of Robin Boyd-Moss (1982/83) and Matthew Hughes, who made first-class hundreds in 2015 and 2016, and another in the one-day game in 2018. Boyd-Moss also scored 100 in a 50-over match in 1982, though that was not part of the official one-day series between the universities. Sian Kelly scored three centuries for Oxford's women against Cambridge between 2015 and 2016.

THE UNIVERSITY MATCHES IN 2021

At Cambridge, May 14. **Oxford University won by nine wickets.** ‡Cambridge University 101-7 (20 overs); **Oxford University 103-1** (11.5 overs) (T. R. W. Gnodde 64*, O. Z. Mohamed 32*). *Oxford eased to victory in the annual Varsity T20, which resumed after not being played in 2020. Cambridge had decided to bat, but were 7-2 after three overs, and never really recovered; their* *highest score was Jovan Dhariwal's 24. Oxford lost George Hargrave second ball, but had no further problems: Tom Gnodde, who hit five fours and four sixes, and Omar Mohamed hurried them home with a stand of 103*.*

At Lord's, May 23. **Cambridge University won by four wickets** (DLS). ‡**Oxford University 229-4** (29 overs) (G. T. Hargrave 105*, T. R. W. Gnodde 41); **Cambridge University 218-6** (28.3 overs) (N. P. Taylor 36, A. J. Moen 34, A. R. Amin 93*; O. J. Allsop 3-37). *PoM:* A. R. Amin. *Hargrave reprised his hundred in this match in 2020 to set up a challenging total; he and Gnodde put on 91 in nine overs for the fourth wicket. Several rain interruptions meant it became a 29-over game, and Cambridge's target was adjusted to 215. They made a solid start – 76-1 in the 12th – but seized up, and looked out of it at 124-5 in the 20th. Thanks to a remarkable blitz from Aaran Amin, though, they sprinted home with three deliveries to spare: he crashed eight sixes in his 50-ball 93*, including three in an over from Owen Marshall's off-breaks. In front of a smattering of spectators who constituted the first crowd in any match at Lord's for 20 months, Amin ended the game with his 12th boundary, a six off Will Barker, who finished with 3.3-0-47-0.*

At Teddington, July 7–9 (not first-class). **Drawn. Cambridge University 314** (134.1 overs) (N. P. Taylor 39, E. R. B. Hyde 31, J. S. Dhariwal 42, A. R. Amin 58, J. C. Vitali 38; C. E. Mingard 3-89, O. J. Marshall 3-61) **and 52-6** (9 overs) (J. Pyman 3-25); ‡**Oxford University 138** (51 overs) (G. T. Hargrave 43, O. J. Marshall 37; J. C. Vitali 3-51, J. W. Gammell 3-24) **and 233** (105.5 overs) (R. Wight 40, J. C. Searle 44, F. J. H. Foster 31, Extras 30; A. R. Amin 3-38). *The match was originally scheduled to be played in the Parks from July 5–8, but a decision by the university authorities not to permit inter-varsity contests in Oxford (or Cambridge) during the pandemic led to a late move to Teddington CC. It became a three-day match, which proved crucial in the end. When Oxford dipped to 123-7 in the follow-on – still 53 behind with more than half the third day to go – heavy defeat looked certain. But the tail dug in: No. 8 Robert Wight survived for 152 minutes, then captain Chris Searle (127 minutes) and Freddie Foster (97) put on 61 for the ninth wicket. Off-spinner Amin finished with figures of 36–17–38–3. Cambridge eventually needed 58 from nine but, with James Pyman taking a wicket in each of his first three overs, they fell just short, and Oxford escaped with a draw.*

MCC IN 2021

STEVEN LYNCH

The welcome return of spectators enlivened the season at Lord's. Some were allowed in for the one-day Varsity Match in May, and gradually all restrictions were eased. Two Tests were successfully staged: England drew with New Zealand, but later collapsed against India. Covid uncertainties meant the inaugural World Test Championship final – which featured the two visiting teams – moved to Southampton. But Lord's did host London Spirit's matches in the new men's and women's Hundred competitions.

The most obvious manifestations of the Lord's redevelopment were the new Compton and Edrich Stands at the Nursery End, while a popular innovation was the Father Time Wall, along an extensive stretch of the inner perimeter behind the Grand Stand. Members and other supporters could purchase (from £200 upwards) a plaque on the wall, which also featured depictions of major moments from the ground's history.

MCC's first overseas president, Kumar Sangakkara, completed his tenure, extended by a year after the blank 2020 season. His successor was the former England captain Clare Connor, the club's first female figurehead. Bruce Carnegie-Brown, the chairman of Lloyd's of London, succeeded Gerald Corbett as MCC chair.

There was sombre news off the field. Ted Dexter died in August, aged 86; a familiar face at Lord's for decades, he was England's most charismatic batsman of his time, and MCC's president in 2002-03. Among others who passed away were Keith Bradshaw, secretary and chief executive from 2006 until he returned to his native Australia in 2011. Late in the year came news of the death of 110-year-old Eileen Ash, who played Test cricket before the Second World War. Her portrait now hangs in the Pavilion.

The former England batsman John Stephenson left after 17 years as assistant secretary (cricket) to become Essex's CEO; he was replaced by the former Tasmania and Somerset batsman (and Australian Test selector) Jamie Cox. Lockdown losses inevitably meant scrutiny of staffing levels: Michael Capitelli, the membership manager, retired after 45 years' service, while maintenance manager Jon Hawke – whose brother, father and grandfather had all worked at Lord's – left after almost 40. Others accepted redundancy packages, including Pavilion-based PAs Deborah Moore (after more than 40 years) and Sara Hales (over 30). The *Daily Mail* discovered that the two men had been given honorary life membership, but the women had not.

After an unavoidable reduction in 2020, MCC's out-match programme returned in record style: 536 men's games made it the club's busiest season, although a few were cancelled because of Covid. In all, 230 matches were won, 61 drawn, one tied, 99 lost, and 145 abandoned or cancelled. MCC women's teams played 33, winning 16, drawing two and losing seven, with eight abandoned. In April, two women's teams had contested the first match at Lord's under the regulations for The Hundred.

THE NATIONAL COUNTIES IN 2021

Richard Logan

There was a new dawn – but also the end of an era – as National Counties cricket emerged from a year of Covid complications. For the first time, competitive matches were played under the auspices of the National Counties Cricket Association, which had succeeded the Minor Counties CA in 2019.

Covid's lingering impact meant the T20 competition was cancelled for the second year running. But the 50-over Trophy and three-day Championship took place with minimal disruption. In the Championship, the Eastern and Western Divisions were split into two leagues of five, based on finishing positions two years earlier, with promotion and relegation for 2022.

Berkshire won the one-day competition for the fifth time – their eighth trophy in five seasons – after crushing Cumbria in front of a large crowd at Wormsley. But hopes of a record fifth consecutive Championship title were ended by Oxfordshire, who routed them by 285 runs at Thame. It was Berkshire's first three-day defeat in seven years.

After the Trophy final, three Berkshire stalwarts announced their retirement. James Morris, an inspirational captain, had forged a strong partnership with coach Tom Lambert, which made their side arguably the most successful ever at this level. But a knee injury prevented Morris from playing in his farewell season, so his brother Richard deputised – before hanging up his boots too. Slow left-armer Chris Peploe, once of Middlesex, took more than 300 wickets in all formats in a Berkshire career that began in 2009. He will be missed – though not by opposing batsmen.

Having ended Berkshire's long unbeaten run, **Oxfordshire** went on to top the group, then beat Suffolk by 178 runs in a compelling Championship final at Tring Park, an impressive new venue. Oxfordshire's win – their first since 1989 – ensured the title stayed in the Western Division, and sent Gareth Andrew, the former Somerset, Worcestershire and Hampshire all-rounder, into retirement with a trophy. Andrew took 125 wickets – 89 in the Championship – and scored more than 900 runs across the three formats in three highly productive seasons as Oxfordshire's professional. But they were certainly not a one-man team. Their links with Sussex's Academy began to bear fruit, with James Coles and Harrison Ward both playing for Sussex's first team, as well as making valuable contributions for Oxfordshire.

Suffolk's appearance in their first Championship final since 2005 owed much to a remarkable unbroken last-wicket partnership between Adam Mansfield and Ben Claydon, who snatched victory over Staffordshire in their last group match, at Copdock. **Norfolk**, who had beaten Cambridgeshire earlier in the day, appeared to be heading for the final instead, when Suffolk lost their ninth wicket, still 89 short of a stiff target of 370. But Claydon, who had been unable to bat in the first innings because of a back injury, hobbled out to join Mansfield, and scored a maiden half-century in just his second match, to spirit Suffolk home with seven balls to spare.

Berkshire's 151-run victory over Cumbria had been the heaviest in a Trophy final since the competition started in 1983, and followed a much narrower win over the same opponents in the 2019 final. There was another difference: before the season, Cumberland had become **Cumbria**, a subtle but significant change which aligned them more closely with the county's cricket board, and abandoned an administrative name that disappeared in 1974. The result was an identity that was more relevant to clubs and players in Cumbria; the profile of the side changed too, with home-grown youngsters replacing the more senior players who, in the past, had been brought in from leagues beyond Cumbria's boundaries which had no obvious affinity with the county.

In a season when masks, hand-sanitiser and lateral-flow tests were a daily requirement, disruption was never far away. Norfolk's home Championship game against Suffolk at Horsford was called off on the second morning after one of the home players tested positive for Covid. The teams had changed at opposite ends of the Manor Park ground, and contact been kept to a minimum – but strict protocols meant it was enough to halt the game. **Shropshire**, meanwhile, had to move their Trophy match against Staffordshire to Oswestry, after a Covid outbreak led to the closure of the pavilion at Wem.

After **Cambridgeshire** were beaten in a bowl-out by Cumbria in the Trophy semi-final at Keswick, they also returned a positive test, putting their Championship match against Staffordshire the following week in jeopardy. Cambridgeshire fulfilled the fixture, but probably wished they hadn't: a much-changed team were shot out for 40 (the joint-lowest Championship total in 36 years) and 87. Staffordshire's victory by an innings and 275 runs was their biggest.

The pandemic also disrupted the showcase matches between the National Counties and their first-class counterparts, which had been cancelled completely in 2020. In the games that survived this time, the minnows generally acquitted themselves well, with **Wales NC** and **Cornwall** beating Glamorgan and Somerset. Steve Reingold and Sam Pearce, who featured in Wales's three-wicket win in Cardiff, later helped Glamorgan win the Royal London Cup. Cambridgeshire slow left-armer Harrison Craig enjoyed himself against Essex at Chelmsford, taking five for 14, including the wicket of Alastair Cook. Essex, who were 112 for six at one stage, won a rain-affected contest by 25 runs.

An NCCA representative side also made their competitive debut a successful one, winning the Dream11 European Championship, a T10 competition staged in Malaga in Spain over two weeks in September and October. The NCCA team, coached by Lambert and captained by Berkshire's Dan Lincoln, represented England against emerging European nations, and hammered Belgium by ten wickets in the final.

NATIONAL COUNTIES CHAMPIONSHIP IN 2021

Eastern Division One

		P	W	D	L	Bat	Bowl	Pts
1	Suffolk	4	3	1	0	9	14	75
2	Norfolk	4	3	1	0	5	16	73
3	Staffordshire	4	1	1	2	12	16	48
4	Lincolnshire	4	0	2	2	6	13	27
5	Cambridgeshire	4	0	1	3	4	13	21

Western Division One

		P	W	D	L	Bat	Bowl	Pts
1	Oxfordshire	4	3	0	1	10	15	73
2	Berkshire	4	2	1	1	8	15	59
3	Cheshire	4	1	1	2	8	15	47
4	Dorset	4	1	1	2	4	15	39
5	Wiltshire	4	0	2	2	2	14	24

Eastern Division Two

		P	W	D	L	Bat	Bowl	Pts
1	BEDFORDSHIRE	4	2	2	0	9	16	65
2	Buckinghamshire	4	2	1	1	5	16	57
3	Hertfordshire	3*	1	1	1	7	8	43
4	Cumbria	3*	1	0	2	3	12	27
5	Northumberland	4	1	3	0	2	16	34

* *Hertfordshire v Cumbria was abandoned without a ball bowled; both teams were awarded 8pts.*

Western Division Two

		P	W	D	L	Bat	Bowl	Pts
1	HEREFORDSHIRE	4	3	1	0	9	16	77
2	Shropshire	4	2	1	1	6	15	57
3	Cornwall	4	1	2	1	4	16	44
4	Wales National Counties	4	0	3	1	8	16	36
5	Devon	4	0	1	3	5	16	25

LEADING AVERAGES IN 2021

BATTING (250 runs)

		M	I	NO	R	HS	100	50	Avge	Ct/St
1	S. S. Arthurton (*Norfolk*)	3	5	1	291	158*	1	0	72.75	3
2	O. Ebsworth-Burland (*Oxfordshire*)	2	4	0	269	117	1	1	67.25	0
3	G. G. Wagg (*Shropshire*)	4	8	0	453	126	2	1	56.62	1
4	Z. A. Malik (*Staffordshire*)	4	7	0	383	102	1	2	54.71	1
5	E. D. Woods (*Berkshire*)	4	7	1	321	122*	1	1	53.50	1
6	N. A. Hammond (*Herefordshire*)	4	7	1	309	114	1	0	51.50	4
7	C. L. Herring (*Wales NC*)	4	6	0	309	110	1	3	51.50	9/1
8	M. W. Thompson (*Devon*)	4	8	2	305	90*	0	2	50.83	6
9	O. M. D. Kolk (*Wales NC*)	4	6	0	289	134	1	1	48.16	1
10	A. J. Mellor (*Staffordshire*)	4	7	0	315	140	2	0	45.00	11/2
11	A. J. Woodland (*Buckinghamshire*)	4	8	2	268	109	1	0	44.66	1
12	J. M. Kettleborough (*Bedfordshire*)	4	7	1	265	106	2	1	44.16	3
13	C. J. Haggett (*Devon*)	4	7	0	298	109	1	1	42.57	0
14	J. S. Kendall (*Lincolnshire*)	4	8	1	292	61	0	2	41.71	3
15	G. R. Thurstance (*Bedfordshire*)	4	7	0	273	86	0	3	39.00	3
16	B. J. Chapman-Lilley (*Herefordshire*)	4	8	1	270	125	1	1	38.57	6
17	T. M. Cosford (*Oxfordshire*)	4	8	0	300	96	0	2	37.50	3
18	M. J. Hill (*Staffordshire*)	4	7	0	254	88	0	2	36.28	1
19	A. G. Oxley (*Suffolk*)	4	7	0	250	121	1	1	35.71	5
20	G. G. Tait (*Oxfordshire*)	5	10	2	269	71	0	2	33.62	6
21	M. Campopiano (*Oxfordshire*)	5	10	0	294	90	0	2	29.40	7

BOWLING (15 wickets)

		Style	O	M	R	W	BB	5I	Avge
1	B. Fletcher (*Dorset*)	LFM	72.3	16	172	16	7-28	1	10.75
2	C. D. R. Parsons (*Buckinghamshire*) .	RFM	126	43	288	25	4-38	0	11.52
3	T. Brett (*Bedfordshire*)	SLA	158.2	47	352	30	6-52	3	11.73
4	B. E. I. Morgan (*Herefordshire*)	RFM	93	36	196	16	4-32	0	12.25
5	E. D. Woods (*Berkshire*)	OB	122.5	36	299	24	6-101	2	12.45
6	G. G. Wagg (*Shropshire*)	LM/SLA	114.3	26	300	22	6-53	2	13.63
7	G. M. Andrew (*Oxfordshire*)	RFM	188	57	361	25	5-39	1	14.44
8	J. W. Rudge (*Herefordshire*)	RFM	103.4	34	254	17	4-22	0	14.94
9	A. J. Hanby (*Norfolk*)	RM	102	26	293	18	6-32	1	16.27
10	K. A. Bull (*Wales NC*)	OB	119.4	20	304	18	5-59	2	16.88
11	M. B. Wareing (*Suffolk*)	LFM	89.3	17	274	16	5-25	2	17.12
12	M. Siddall (*Cumbria*)	SLA	123.3	31	313	17	6-82	2	18.41
13	B. W. Stolworthy (*Norfolk*)	RFM	119.2	29	300	15	4-38	0	20.00
14	D. J. Wainwright (*Cheshire*)	SLA	146.5	40	360	17	6-38	1	21.17
15	R. N. W. Pack (*Dorset*)	SLA	134.4	26	338	15	6-38	1	22.53
16	T. W. W. Rash (*Suffolk*)	RFM	130	31	347	15	5-29	1	23.13
17	M. T. Coles (*Bedfordshire*)	RFM	148	37	465	19	5-71	0	24.47
18	E. A. F. Whiteford (*Cornwall*)	OB	138.2	15	447	18	5-58	1	24.83
19	H. E. Craig (*Cambridgeshire*)	SLA	158	21	509	19	8-76	1	26.78
20	M. H. A. Footitt (*Lincolnshire*)	LFM	127	30	411	15	4-106	0	27.40

TROPHY FINAL

At Wormsley, September 2. **Berkshire won by 151 runs. Berkshire 260-8** (50 overs) (S. D. Perera 84, T. E. Albert 76; J. A. McGown 4-50); ‡**Cumbria 109** (34.1 overs) (M. H. Sempill 39; J. A. J. Rishton 4-16, L. E. Beaven 3-20). *A lively second-wicket stand of 132 between Savin Perera and 19-year-old Toby Albert set Berkshire up, although seamer James McGown's four wickets kept the target within bounds. But Cumbria never got close, with Andy Rishton helping reduce them to 31-6; he finished with figures of 10–2–16–4, including Cumbria's captain, Gary Pratt, for ten. Matt Sempill survived 60 balls for his 39, but of the rest only No. 10 McGown (26*) reached double figures as Berkshire completed a thumping victory.*

CHAMPIONSHIP FINAL

At Tring, September 5–8. **Oxfordshire won by 178 runs. Oxfordshire 248** (81.1 overs) (O. Ebsworth-Burland 33, T. M. Cosford 46, J. A. Cater 56; J. A. Beaumont 3-39) **and 311** (115.1 overs) (H. G. K. Smith 33, O. Ebsworth-Burland 38, M. Campopiano 31, J. A. Cater 35, G. M. Andrew 38, R. R. L. Shurmer 36; J. S. Gatting 3-57, J. A. Beaumont 5-59; ‡**Suffolk 213** (87.4 overs) (J. J. Cantrell 49, T. W. W. Rash 30, A. P. Mansfield 34; G. M. Andrew 3-56) **and 168** (86.4 overs) (J. Marston 61, B. D. Shepperson 32; O. D. Clarke 5-59). *The much-travelled all-rounder Gareth Andrew – 37, and in probably his final game for Oxfordshire – did much to settle the outcome. In a second innings in which six men made it into the thirties (but not beyond), he came in at 195-7, and helped stretch a lead of 230 to an imposing 346, helped by a ninth-wicket stand of 55 with Robbie Shurmer. Suffolk had 13 overs to negotiate on the third evening, but slumped to 13-3, with Andrew removing opener Darren Ironside for a duck. Joe Marston led the final-day resistance, but slow left-armer Jacob Clarke made regular inroads, and Oxfordshire completed their first Championship title at this level since 1989.*

SECOND ELEVEN CHAMPIONSHIP IN 2021

		P	W	L	D	A	Bonus points Bat	Bowl	Pts	Avge pts
1	Hampshire	9	7	1	1	0	16	27	163	18.11
2	Durham	9	5	1	2	1	17	22	143	15.88
3	Leicestershire	7	4	2	1	0	17	20	109	15.57
4	Middlesex	9	5	2	1	1	13	23	132	14.66
5	Yorkshire	11	3	1	6	1	29	26	159	14.45
6	Glamorgan	10	4	2	2	2	20	19	135	13.50
7	Nottinghamshire	11	4	4	3	0	28	29	145	13.18
8	Worcestershire	8	3	2	2	1	18	15	105	13.12
9	Essex	9	3	3	2	1	22	24	107	11.88
10	Lancashire	12	3	3	5	1	22	23	141	11.75
11	Gloucestershire	10	3	4	3	0	13	19	112	11.20
12	Northamptonshire	9	3	4	2	0	14	17	95	10.55
13	Somerset	9	3	5	1	0	10	25	91	10.11
14	Warwickshire	10	3	4	1	2	8	20	100	10.00
15	Surrey	7	1	3	3	0	13	17	70	10.00
16	Sussex	9	0	6	3	0	21	17	62	6.88
17	Kent	7	0	6	1	0	9	18	35	5.00
18	Derbyshire	10	1	5	2	2	12	19	41	4.10

Win = 16pts; draw = 8pts. A combined Kent and Sussex team played two games; both counties took the points gained in those fixtures.

Essex deducted 11pts for a slow over-rate. Derbyshire deducted 38pts for fielding an unregistered player in three matches.

LEADING AVERAGES IN 2021

BATTING (400 runs)

		M	I	NO	R	HS	100	50	Avge	Ct/St
1	S. S. Eskinazi (*Middx*)	4	7	2	449	244*	1	1	89.80	6
2	J. A. Haynes (*Worcs*)	5	8	1	566	177*	2	2	80.85	0
3	L. P. Goldsworthy (*Somerset*)	4	7	1	444	110	2	3	74.00	3
4	T. A. R. Scriven (*Hants*)	6	8	2	440	117	2	2	73.33	3
5	M. A. Jones (*Durham*)	5	8	2	436	200*	1	2	72.66	1
6	A. L. Hughes (*Derbys*)	6	9	2	489	231*	2	1	69.85	5
7	W. A. R. Fraine (*Yorks*)	6	8	0	497	186	2	1	62.12	8
8	A. P. Beard (*Essex*)	7	11	3	481	125*	1	4	60.12	1
9	E. N. Gay (*Northants*)	6	8	0	471	189	1	3	58.87	1
10	†A. G. H. Orr (*Sussex*)	7	13	2	590	109	2	3	53.63	3/2
11	G. I. D. Lavelle (*Lancs*)	8	12	2	517	174	2	1	51.70	6/2
12	J. D. M. Evison (*Notts*)	9	10	0	513	152	1	4	51.30	2
13	B. G. Compton (*Notts*)	10	14	2	613	204*	2	1	51.08	24
14	G. C. H. Hill (*Yorks*)	5	9	0	449	207	1	1	49.88	6
15	J. J. Dell (*Worcs*)	5	9	0	444	116	2	1	49.33	2
16	T. S. S. Mackintosh (*Durham*)	6	9	0	428	143	2	2	47.55	10/1
17	S. G. Budinger (*Notts*)	9	13	0	572	118	2	3	44.00	7
18	A. H. Miller (*Northants*)	9	11	1	402	83	0	3	40.20	1
19	T. R. Cornall (*Kent, Lancs, Worcs*)	8	13	1	473	112	2	1	39.41	9
20	B. D. Birkhead (*Yorks*)	10	16	3	467	101*	1	2	35.92	20/3
21	J. H. Wharton (*Yorks*)	10	16	0	560	88	0	6	35.00	6
22	M. Montgomery (*Notts*)	10	13	1	419	147	1	2	34.91	5
23	J. E. K. Rew (*Somerset*)	7	14	2	413	71*	0	2	34.41	24/1
24	J. Broad (*Derbys, Surrey*)	8	16	2	456	120	1	1	32.57	2
25	S. J. Young (*Somerset*)	9	17	1	512	203*	1	1	32.00	10

† *Two games for a combined Kent and Sussex team.*

BOWLING (18 wickets)

		Style	O	M	R	W	BB	5I	Avge
1	L. Trevaskis (*Durham*)	SLA	139.4	42	314	23	5-69	1	13.65
2	S. W. Currie (*Hants*)	RFM	110.1	28	334	22	4-19	0	15.18
3	J. D. M. Evison (*Notts*)	RM	193.4	52	559	35	7-25	2	15.97
4	J. P. Morley (*Lancs*)	SLA	218	58	502	28	7-59	2	17.92
5	A. S. S. Nijjar (*Essex*)	SLA	110	20	373	20	6-37	2	18.65
6	B. G. F. Green (*Somerset*)	RFM	126.5	34	370	18	4-52	0	20.55
7	J. W. Shutt (*Yorks*)	OB	214.5	51	571	29	5-94	1	19.68
8	J. O. I. Campbell (*Durham*)	LFM	185.4	48	529	26	5-20	1	20.34
9	B. G. F. Green (*Somerset*)	RFM	126.5	34	370	18	4-52	0	20.55
10	Z. J. Chappell (*Notts*)	RFM	142	42	372	18	4-32	0	20.66
11	M. S. Johal (*Warks*)	RFM	147.4	25	472	22	5-15	2	21.45
12	N. A. Sowter (*Middx*)	LB	168	26	494	22	4-69	0	22.45
13	A. S. Dale (*Glos, Hants*)	RFM	149.2	38	472	21	4-10	0	22.47
14	A. Sakande (*Leics*)	RFM	213	55	664	29	5-32	2	22.89
15	A. P. Beard (*Essex*)	RFM	164.1	34	549	23	4-77	0	23.86
16	M. E. T. Salisbury (*Durham*)	RFM	162.1	31	575	24	6-47	2	23.95
17	D. J. Leech (*Yorks*)	RM	177.5	42	582	24	5-28	1	24.25
18	T. L. Greatwood (*Middx*)	RFM	132.4	30	446	18	5-79	1	24.77
19	J. A. Turner (*Hants*)	RFM	168	36	549	22	3-10	0	24.95
20	T. H. S. Pettman (*Notts*)	RFM	297.2	65	840	32	5-30	3	26.25
21	E. O. Leonard (*Somerset*)	RM	242.3	49	831	30	5-76	1	27.70
22	G. S. Drissell (*Durham, Somerset, Worcs*)	OB	238	48	730	25	4-28	0	29.20
23	C. McKerr (*Surrey*)	RFM	180	47	526	18	5-35	1	29.22
24	T. E. Barber (*Notts*)	LFM	193.5	24	834	18	2-43	0	46.33

SECOND ELEVEN TWENTY20 FINAL

At Arundel, June 24. **Warwickshire won by 54 runs**. ‡**Warwickshire 149-5** (20 overs) (M. Montgomery 60); **Sussex 95** (16.2 overs) (G. A. Garrett 5-19). *South African Matthew Montgomery, who hit a 50-ball 66 in the semi-final against Middlesex, played a similar innings in the final, top-scoring with 60 from 43. Six Sussex batters fell for between 11 and 15, as George Garrett, a 21-year-old seamer from Hertfordshire, grabbed five.*

There was no Second Eleven Trophy in 2021.

LEAGUE CRICKET IN 2021

GEOFFREY DEAN

After a reduced 2020, all the ECB's premier leagues enjoyed a full season. But coronavirus still caused problems. Paul Bedford, the national manager for leagues and competitions, said they inconvenienced almost every club, every week: "Teams were taken out through isolation requirements, and clubs were often only able to field two XIs instead of three. Some were more severely affected, and there were instances of clubs having to shut down for a week." Bedford, who has been at the ECB for 14 years, described it as the hardest season he could recall for league administrators. "If it wasn't Covid issues, with government restrictions in the early stages of the season and local isolations later on, it was hosing down with rain," he said. "In the Surrey Championship, for example, on only two Saturdays out of 18 could you play without a delayed start or an interruption."

A third factor also took up time: the introduction of the ECB's new "safe hands management" system. "To be a flagship club, you needed to satisfy DBS [disclosure and barring service] security checks," Bedford explained. "The majority of sides in the top two divisions of premier leagues have done a tremendous job. It was about ensuring that cricket is safe for all juniors, and as attractive as we can make it. But clubs had a difficult time encouraging all their coaches to get their certification."

Frequent cancellations led several leagues to adopt an average-points system. The Birmingham League was one; their champions, Berkswell, had three matches cancelled by Covid. "We'd moved away from average points in the past, but it made for a sensible decision," said Bedford. "I hope the usual aggregate points system can return in 2022."

Castleford won the North Yorkshire League, also on average points, and were crowned overall champions of Yorkshire – contested by the winners of the county's four premier leagues. The final was held at Headingley in September: Castleford edged it by six runs over Woodlands, the Bradford League winners, who had lost the previous final, in 2019, to Sheriff Hutton Bridge. Castleford owed a lot to their opening pair, Chesney Hughes and Liam Hyde, whose stand of 103 laid the basis for a total of 241. Hughes had made a double-century on his previous appearance at Headingley, for Derbyshire against Yorkshire in 2013, and top-scored with 61 this time. He later delivered a good final over, with Woodlands needing 13, to clinch the trophy.

Although they lost in the play-off semis, Richmondshire won the North Yorkshire & South Durham League for the third year running. They claimed the title with a winning draw at runners-up Barnard Castle, thanks to a superb all-round performance from Sam Wood, who followed seven for 30 with an important 40.

"It was one of the best days I've had on a pitch," said Wood. "Barnard Castle are our biggest rivals, and they knocked us out of three cups this year – so to win it there was very special." Berkswell also claimed a hat-trick of titles, trouncing nearest challengers Leamington by eight wickets on the last day to go through the Birmingham League season unbeaten.

Nantwich secured their fifth Cheshire League title in 12 years after a brilliant 76-ball 104 from Luke Robinson helped see off second-placed Didsbury. "No one can bowl to him when he's in that mood," said Ray Doyle, Nantwich's captain. "On his day, he's as good as anyone in amateur cricket."

Heathcoat, whose 2019 Devon League title was the first in their 128-year history, secured another after slipping up only once. "We used 20 players, and all had moments of brilliance," said their skipper, Peter Randerson. In the Essex League, Chelmsford also romped to the title, as Jack Sterland led from the front with 1,010 runs, including 196 against Harold Wood, the highest of his five centuries. "This year felt like a proper competitive season again," he said.

In the South Wales Premier League, where no competitive cricket was played in 2020, St Fagans retained their title, but newly promoted Swansea enjoyed a wonderful season, finishing second and reaching three finals. They won two – the Welsh Cup and the South Wales T20 Cup – but lost to Newport in the T20 final. "If you'd have offered me three cup finals and second in the league at the start of the season, I'd have bitten your hand off," said Swansea's captain, Brad Wadlan, who led the way in the league with 736 runs.

Chris Aspin writes: The Lancashire League returned to the two-division structure introduced in 2019, but suspended in 2020. Coronavirus still disrupted several fixtures, and prevented some overseas players from reaching the UK; nine substitute pros turned out on the opening day, when newcomers Greenmount beat Accrington by seven runs. Rawtenstall's 59-year-old captain Keith Roscoe took his 1,800th wicket in the league, and later claimed six for 63 to become its most successful amateur bowler, overtaking Fred Duerr's 1,811 for Bacup and Ramsbottom between 1902 and 1929. Roscoe took his first wicket in 1979, for Bacup, and joined Rawtenstall ten years later.

The Championship and Second Division were both decided on the last afternoon: Burnley triumphed for the 17th time, finishing three points clear of Darwen, while Haslingden led Greenmount by eight in the second tier (both were promoted). Crompton, penalised 45 for breaching league rules, and Colne, who won only once, were relegated. In the 50-over Worsley Cup, Lowerhouse beat Clitheroe to take the trophy for the fourth time. Francois Haasbroek, the South African, atoned for a golden duck with six for 35, including a hat-trick.

It was a batsman's season: there were 19 centuries in the first division, 35 in the second. At the other extreme, seven Nelson batsmen failed to score when Accrington dismissed them for 35, which included 14 extras.

Thikshila de Silva, Great Harwood's Sri Lankan pro, made a league-record 219 not out against Bacup. He faced 126 balls, and hit 15 sixes; his side amassed 344 for six and won by 218 runs. Church piled up 400 for four at Rawtenstall, beating Accrington's 386 on the same ground ten years earlier; Indian professional Sagar Trivedi reached 50 off 15 balls, and 100 off 28 (a league record), as Church won by 174 runs.

Five scored 1,000, two in the top division – Ashar Zaidi, the Norden pro, headed the averages with 1,010 at 101, while James Price (Middleton) made 1,109 at 65. In the second tier, de Silva hit 1,113 at 69, Usman Tariq (Nelson) 1,110 at 55, with five centuries, and Chesney Hughes (Greenmount) 1,048 at 87. Josh Tolley of Norden led the amateurs with 865. Hughes (159 not out) and fellow opener Andy Kerr (127) put on 320 against East Lancashire, the highest partnership for any wicket since the Lancashire League was founded in 1892. Greenmount finished with 341 for two, then Callum Hunter took seven for 27 as East Lancs (who went through the season without employing a professional, a first for the league) were bundled out for 141. Greenmount also skittled Rawtenstall for 41, after making 326. A first-wicket stand of 191 by Josh Tolley (135) and Hashum Malik (104) helped Norden to a massive victory over Walsden – for whom, earlier in the season, openers Josh Gale and Jake Hooson had put on 142 against both Colne and Lowerhouse.

Haslingden enjoyed two ten-wicket wins, against Rawtenstall, after Hunsley picked up five for 30, and East Lancs, who were bowled out for 43, with Garry Sudworth taking five for five. Graham Knowles retired aged 48, having scored 13,902 runs for Haslingden, a total exceeded by only four others in league history. In all, he hit 15 centuries, including an unbeaten 183 at Rawtenstall in 1998, the highest in the league by an amateur. As a schoolboy in 1988, he had played alongside his father, Bryan, another local legend.

Five bowlers reached 50 wickets, four in the top division. Walsden's off-spinner Umesh Karunaratne picked up 62 at 12, Zaidi 53 at 12, Darwen's David Bowden – the top amateur – 52 at 11, and Daryn Smit (Ramsbottom) 50 at 14. De Silva took 56 at 17 for Great Harwood in Division Two, whose leading amateur was Accrington's Toby Bulcock, with 47 at 13.

In August, Accrington could field only ten against Bacup, and failed to raise a Second XI the same day. A fortnight earlier, they had recalled Len Dewhurst, who at 60 became the oldest to take a wicket for them, against East Lancs. After running into more personnel problems, Accrington called up 20-year-old Alice Clarke, the first woman to play at the league's highest level. She kept wicket, took a catch and conceded no byes, but Accrington suffered their eighth successive defeat. In the next game, she was joined by her father, Damian, who had last played for the club in 2012, and Accrington defeated Nelson. Leg-spinner Louis Russell, just 13, took three for 18 on his debut for Littleborough, against Rishton.

Darwen won the T20 competition for the first time, beating Clitheroe in a rerun of the previous year's final, with their Indian pro Atharwa Taide making 101. Earlier, Norden lost their first five wickets for six, and were all out for a record low of 25 – including nine extras – against Littleborough. Walsden beat Ramsbottom after Joe Gale struck five sixes and a four off the final over. For Greenmount, Hughes smashed 127 off 62, but Middleton still sailed home by nine wickets. And Rawtenstall's Sri Lankan pro, Saliya Saman Jeewantha, struck 76 off 23, with 11 sixes, against Greenmount.

Burnley reached the final of the Lancashire Cup, played at Old Trafford, but lost by seven wickets to Ormskirk from the Liverpool Competition.

ECB PREMIER LEAGUE TABLES IN 2021

An asterisk denotes one tie.

Birmingham & District

		P	W	L	Avge
1	**Berkswell**	20	13	0	**15.55**
2	Leamington	22	10	4	12.81
3	Knowle & Dorridge....	21	7	5	12.81
4	Kidderminster.......	22	8	8	12.72
5	Barnt Green	21	5	6	10.47
6	Shrewsbury	21	5	8	10.42
7	Shifnal.............	20	6	6	10.10
8	Moseley...........	21	6	7	9.95
9	Smethwick.........	22	7	8	9.81
10	Ombersley........	21	6	8	9.47
11	Walsall...........	20	4	6	8.75
12	W. Bromwich Dartmouth .	21	2	13	7.04

Cornwall

		P	W	L	Pts
1	**Penzance**...........	17	15	0	**322**
2	Truro.............	18	11	5	249
3	St Just	18	9	8	228
4	Redruth	18	9	6	222
5	St Austell..........	18	7	9	198
6	Camborne	17	7	8	197
7	Wadebridge	17	6	9	195
8	Werrington........	17	6	9	188
9	Callington	16	5	9	185
10	Grampound Road	18	2	14	93

Bradford

		P	W	L	Quot
1	**Woodlands**	22	17	3	**2.51**
2	Townville.........	22	17	3	1.48
3	New Farnley........	22	14	5	1.84
4	Hanging Heaton	22	12*	6	1.16
5	Pudsey St Lawrence ...	22	11	7	1.33
6	Farsley...........	22	10	8	1.06
7	Methley...........	22	10	9	0.94
8	Bradford & Bingley.....	22	7	12	0.74
9	Cleckheaton	22	5*	15	0.69
10	Batley...........	22	3	17	0.54
11	Morley...........	22	5	15	0.60
12	Wrenthorpe	22	5	14	0.57

*Wrenthorpe deducted 164pts and Methley
    28pts for fielding an ineligible player*

Derbyshire

		P	W	L	Pts
1	**Sandiacre Town**.......	22	18	3	**418**
2	Ockbrook & Borrowash ..	22	17	4	407
3	Ticknall............	22	17	5	396
4	Denby	22	12	7	333
5	Spondon	22	10	9	289
6	Langley Mill United	22	9	10	285
7	Alvaston & Boulton.....	22	10	11	278
8	Swarkestone.........	22	9	12	265
9	Marehay..........	22	7	13	233
10	Eckington..........	22	7	14	228
11	Chesterfield	22	6	14	219
12	Elvaston...........	22	0	20	86

Cheshire County League

		P	W	L	Pts
1	**Nantwich**...........	22	14	5	**402**
2	Didsbury	22	12	5	378
3	Chester Boughton Hall...	22	11	5	364
4	Oulton Park	22	8	5	297
5	Alderley Edge........	22	9	6	296
6	Widnes	22	7	8	279
7	Oxton	22	6	9	271
8	Hyde	22	7	9	269
9	Neston	22	6	7	255
10	Toft..............	22	5	10	231
11	Timperley	22	4	13	197
12	Cheadle	22	4	11	184

Devon

		P	W	L	Avge
1	**Heathcoat**	18	11	4	**17.83**
2	Sandford	18	8	4	14.38
3	Plymouth	18	7	5	13.66
4	Bovey Tracey	18	8	6	13.35
5	Sidmouth	18	5	6	11.63
6	Paignton	18	6	6	11.58
7	Cornwood	18	4	7	10.63
8	Hatherleigh	18	5	8	10.23
9	Exeter	18	4	9	10.00
10	Exmouth	18	4	10	8.60

East Anglian

		P	W	L	Pts
1	**Sawston & Babraham**	22	13	3	**406**
2	Swardeston	22	10	4	351
3	Mildenhall	22	10	4	342
4	Great Witchingham	22	10	6	334
5	Bury St Edmunds	22	10	7	317
6	Cambridge	22	8	6	314
7	Saffron Walden	22	7	11	299
8	Copdock & Old Ipswichian	22	6	7	261
9	Sudbury	22	4	9	231
10	Frinton-on-Sea	22	4	10	221
11	Horsford	22	3	9	196
12	Burwell & Exning	17	3	12	188

Essex League

		P	W	L	Pts
1	**Chelmsford**	18	**13**	**2**	**312**
2	Wanstead & Snaresbrook	18	10	5	277
3	Brentwood	18	11	3	275
4	Hornchurch	18	7	7	221
5	Belhus	18	7	8	218
6	Hadleigh & Thundersley	17	8	7	205
7	Colchester & East Essex	18	6	9	185
8	Chingford	18	5	6	169
9	Harold Wood	18	3	12	115
10	Billericay	18	1	13	92

Hertfordshire League

		P	W	L	Pts
1	**Harpenden**	18	9	4	**331**
2	Totteridge Millhillians	18	9	4	322
3	Radlett	18	8	7	309
4	Hertford	18	8	5	283
5	Welwyn Garden City	18	7	5	278
6	Hoddesdon	18	9*	6	277
7	North Mymms	18	7*	6	262
8	Potters Bar	18	6	6	259
9	West Herts	18	7*	10	238
10	Reed	18	2	15	136

Hoddesdon tied two games.

Home Counties

		P	W	L	Pts
1	**High Wycombe**	18	12*	1	**315**
2	Henley	18	11*	2	285
3	Banbury	18	8*	4	249
4	Aston Rowant	18	7	6	245
5	Datchet	18	7	7	232
6	Buckingham Town	18	6	6	207
7	Finchampstead	18	4	8	183
8	Oxford	18	4	10	182
9	Thame Town	18	5	9	177
10	Tring Park	18	3*	10	133

Finchampstead deducted 11pts for fielding an unregistered player.

Kent

		P	W	L	Pts
1	**Bexley**	18	14	4	**268**
2	Sandwich Town	18	12	3	257
3	Tunbridge Wells	18	11	5	234
4	Sevenoaks Vine	18	9	8	202
5	Bickley Park	18	8	8	195
6	Blackheath	18	7	10	179
7	Lordswood	18	6	8	176
8	Beckenham	18	7	10	174
9	Holmesdale	18	5	11	155
10	Bromley	18	2	14	97

Leicestershire & Rutland League

		P	W	L	Pts
1	**Kibworth**	22	**15**	**6**	**430**
2	Loughborough Town	22	14	7	415
3	Sileby Town	22	12	9	372
4	Langtons	22	12	9	368
5	Leicester Ivanhoe	22	11	10	367
6	Kegworth Town	22	10	11	359
7	Oakham	22	10	10	352
8	Newtown Linford	22	10	11	343
9	Rothley Park	22	9	12	324
10	Syston Town	22	9	10	312
11	Barrow Town	22	9	11	310
12	Cropston	22	3	18	209

Lincolnshire Cricket Board

		P	W	L	Pts
1	**Bourne**	18	14	2	**303**
2	Grantham	18	13	4	282
3	Bracebridge Heath	18	10	5	236
4	Sleaford	18	9	6	224
5	Lindum	18	8	8	206
6	Scunthorpe Town	18	8	6	203
7	Market Deeping	18	5	10	161
8	Boston	18	5	11	153
9	Louth	18	3	12	108
10	Woodhall Spa	18	2	13	105

Liverpool & District Competition

		P	W	L	Pts
1	**Northern**	22	**15**	**3**	**391**
2	Wallasey	22	13	4	356
3	Leigh	22	12	5	316
4	Ormskirk	22	10	7	285
5	Formby	22	9	6	268
6	Rainhill	22	8	8	251
7	Wigan	22	7	11	228
8	Orrell Red Triangle	22	7	8	227
9	New Brighton	22	7	12	225
10	Southport & Birkdale	22	5	11	200
11	Bootle	22	5	8	200
12	Sefton Park	22	1	16	116

Middlesex

		P	W	L	Pts
1	Crouch End	18	11	3	126
2	North Middlesex	18	10	3	123
	Teddington	18	11	4	123
4	Shepherds Bush	18	9	6	106
5	Twickenham	18	8	7	101
6	Richmond	18	8	7	93
7	Ealing	18	6	9	74
8	Hampstead	18	5	9	67
9	Brondesbury	18	4	10	54
10	Finchley	18	0	14	14

Northamptonshire League

		P	W	L	Pts
1	Peterborough Town	20	14	0	339
2	Finedon Dolben	20	14	3	325
3	Geddington	20	11	6	266
	Old Northamptonians	20	11	7	266
5	Oundle Town	20	9	6	265
6	Brigstock	20	9	5	254
7	Rushden & Higham Town	20	8	10	225
8	Desborough Town	20	5	10	168
9	Overstone Park	20	3	11	152
10	Brixworth	20	2	13	114
11	Horton House	20	1	16	97

North East

		P	W	L	Avge
1	South Northumberland	21	12	1	16.71
2	Burnmoor	22	12	4	16.40
3	Benwell Hill	21	11	2	15.04
4	Chester-le-Street	22	11	4	14.63
5	Hetton Lyons	22	7	9	11.31
6	Eppleton	22	7	9	11.18
7	Tynemouth	22	8	8	11.18
8	Felling	22	7	11	9.36
9	Whitburn	22	5	11	8.81
10	Burnopfield	22	5	10	8.50
11	Washington	22	4	12	7.90
12	Sacriston	20	4	12	7.20

North Staffs & South Cheshire League

		P	W	L	Pts
1	J & G Meakin	22	12	5	323
2	Longton	22	13	5	317
3	Porthill Park	22	10	6	312
4	Checkley	22	11	4	292
5	Bagnall Norton	22	9	8	253
6	Burslem	22	8	11	243
7	Cheadle	22	7	9	238
8	Moddershall & Oulton	22	6	11	234
	Stone	22	8	8	234
10	Leek	22	7	10	214
11	Whitmore	22	9	10	208
12	Ashcombe Park	22	3	16	156

Whitmore were deducted 20pts for fielding an ineligible player; Porthill Park were awarded 15pts for a Covid cancellation.

North Wales League

		P	W	L	Pts
1	St Asaph	22	17	3	242
2	Menai Bridge	22	16	3	235
3	Bangor	22	14	3	203
4	Northop	22	11	6	176
5	Mochdre	22	10	7	158
6	Pwllheli	22	10	9	151
7	Brymbo	22	8	9	134
	Gresford	22	7	10	134
9	Llandudno	22	6	14	111
10	Llay Welfare	22	4	13	92
11	Conwy	22	4	15	82
12	Denbigh	22	1	16	46

North Yorkshire & South Durham League

		P	W	L	Avge
1	Richmondshire	21	13	3	18.04
2	Barnard Castle	21	9	1	16.47
3	Billingham Synthonia	20	9	5	14.00
4	Hartlepool	22	9	7	13.54
5	Saltburn	21	8	5	13.33
6	Stokesley	21	8*	8	12.42
7	Marton	21	7	7	12.33
8	Thornaby	21	8	6	12.23
9	Middlesbrough	22	6*	10	10.90
10	Great Ayton	21	6	9	10.33
11	Normanby Hall	22	4	11	9.22
12	Marske	21	2	15	8.00

Northern

		P	W	L	Pts
1	Blackpool	22	13	2	238
2	Lancaster	22	12	5	212
	Netherfield	22	11	7	212
4	Longridge	22	11	4	208
5	Garstang	22	9	6	206
6	Kendal	22	9*	9	167
7	Leyland	22	6	6	154
8	Fulwood & Broughton	22	6	9	144
9	St Annes	22	4	10	134
10	Chorley	22	5	10	133
11	Morecambe	22	4	10	131
12	Fleetwood	22	5*	15	101

Nottinghamshire Cricket Board

		P	W	L	Pts
1	Kimberley Institute	22	14	5	128
2	Cavaliers & Carrington	22	16	4	126
3	Radcliffe-on-Trent	22	15	5	126
4	Cuckney	22	15	5	118
5	Papplewick & Linby	22	12	7	100
6	Clifton Village	22	9	10	82
7	Wollaton	22	9	11	76
8	Plumtree	22	9*	10	76
9	Hucknall	22	6	12	62
10	Attenborough	22	6*	14	46
11	Caythorpe	22	4	14	38
12	Mansfield Hosiery Mills	22	2	18	20

Final positions also determined by NRR.

South Wales Division One

		P	W	L	Pts
1	St Fagans	18	12	3	258
2	Swansea.............	18	10	5	235
3	Newport............	18	10	6	234
4	Neath...............	18	8	7	204
5	Bridgend Town	18	7	8	195
6	Port Talbot Town	18	8	6	192
7	Ammanford	18	6	8	171
8	Cardiff.............	18	5	12	160
9	Pontarddulais	18	5	10	149
10	Mumbles	18	4	10	138

Southern

		P	W	L	Avge
1	South Wilts	18	12	3	18.13
2	St Cross Symondians....	18	9	5	16.00
3	Bournemouth	18	9	6	14.20
4	Bashley (Rydal)......	18	7	6	14.00
5	Hants CCC Academy....	18	7	6	13.61
6	Havant..............	18	5	6	12.72
7	Hook & Newnham	18	5	7	12.00
8	Burridge	18	6	10	10.62
9	Lymington	18	5	11	10.50
10	Alton..............	18	4	9	9.92

Burridge deducted 10pts for fielding an
ineligible player.

Surrey Championship

		P	W	L	Pts
1	East Molesey	18	12	2	294
2	Sunbury............	18	10	4	244
3	Weybridge	18	9	4	236
4	Esher...............	18	6	6	189
5	Wimbledon	18	6	7	183
6	Reigate Priory	18	6	8	175
7	Normandy	18	5	9	156
8	Ashtead	18	4	7	148
9	Banstead	18	4	8	147
10	Cranleigh..........	18	4	11	113

Cranleigh deducted 10pts for fielding an
unregistered player.

Sussex League

		P	W	L	Pts
1	Preston Nomads	18	11	3	389
2	East Grinstead	18	10	4	357
3	Roffey.............	18	8	5	324
4	Three Bridges.......	18	7	5	309
5	Middleton-on-Sea	18	7	7	300
6	Eastbourne............	18	7	8	269
	Hastings & St Leonards ..	18	5	8	265
8	Brighton & Hove	18	5	9	253
9	Cuckfield	18	4	9	248
10	Haywards Heath	18	4	10	215

West of England

		P	W	L	Pts
1	Clevedon............	18	13	4	274
2	Potterne	18	11	5	270
3	Bath	18	10	4	241
4	Lansdown	18	10	5	240
5	Bedminster..........	18	8	7	208
6	Bridgwater..........	18	6*	9	197
7	Taunton Deane	18	7	8	178
8	Chippenham.........	18	4	11	178
9	Cheltenham	18	3	11	148
10	Downend	18	5*	11	146

Potterne (15), Bridgwater (15) and
Cheltenham (14) had points added after a
Covid concession.

Yorkshire North

		P	W	L	Avge
1	Castleford............	20	14	2	7.80
2	Yorkshire Academy.....	13	9*	3	7.00
3	Scarborough..........	21	11	6	6.57
4	Woodhouse Grange.....	21	10	9	5.90
5	Clifton Alliance	21	10	9	5.71
	Sheriff Hutton Bridge ..	21	10	10	5.71
7	Dunnington	22	9	11	5.00
8	York	22	7	11	4.63
9	Acomb..............	20	8*	11	4.55
10	Driffield Town	20	8	10	4.40
	Harrogate...........	20	6	10	4.40
12	Stamford Bridge	21	5	13	3.90

Driffield given a disciplinary penalty of 12pts.

Yorkshire South

		P	W	L	Pts
1	Appleby Frodingham ..	22	16	3	212
2	Sheffield Collegiate.....	22	13	5	180
3	Treeton	22	13	7	178
4	Wakefield Thornes	22	11	7	166
5	Barnsley Woolley Miners ..	22	12	7	164
6	Elsecar.............	22	9	8	144
7	Whitley Hall........	22	8	10	126
8	Tickhill............	22	8	10	120
9	Doncaster Town	22	7	13	118
10	Cawthorne	22	7	11	118
11	Hallam.............	22	5	12	98
12	Wickersley Old Village ..	22	2	18	38

Final positions also determined by NRR.

LANCASHIRE LEAGUE TABLES IN 2021

Division One

		P	W	L	Pts
1	Burnley	22	15	5	189
2	Darwen	22	15	6	186
3	Norden	22	14	6	174
4	Walsden	22	13	6	169
5	Clitheroe	22	12	7	163
6	Lowerhouse	22	12	6	154
7	Ramsbottom	22	10	11	134
8	Todmorden	22	8	12	117
9	Rochdale	22	7	12	110
10	Middleton	22	6	14	87
11	Crompton	22	5	15	40
12	Colne	22	1	18	36

Crompton deducted 45pts for a breach of League rules.

Division Two

		P	W	L	Pts
1	Haslingden	22	15	4	192
2	Greenmount	22	15	4	184
3	Littleborough	22	14	4	174
4	Church	22	12	6	169
5	Enfield	22	13	7	165
6	Bacup	22	9	9	120
7	Great Harwood	22	8	11	113
8	Accrington	22	6	13	105
9	Rawtenstall	22	6	11	102
10	East Lancashire	22	5	13	88
11	Rishton	22	3	14	71
12	Nelson	22	4	14	70

OTHER LEAGUE WINNERS IN 2021

Airedale & Wharfedale	Saltaire
Bolton	Horwich RMI
Cambs & Hunts	Histon
Cumbria	Furness
Greater Manchester	Prestwich
Huddersfield	Hoylandswaine
Norfolk Alliance	Downham Stow
North Essex	Coggeshall
Northumberland & Tyneside Senior	Consett
Pembrokeshire	Neyland
Quaid-e-Azam	Kashmir
Ribblesdale	Settle
Shropshire	Worfield
South Wales Association	Llanelli
Thames Valley	Beaconsfield
Two Counties	Witham
Warwickshire	Stratford-upon-Avon
Worcestershire	Stourbridge

ECB CLUB CUPS IN 2021

ROYAL LONDON CLUB CHAMPIONSHIP

Teams from Somerset are used to claiming the runner-up pennant. Bath, three times the losing finalists at Lord's, had never held the trophy, and no side from the county had reached the final of the Club Championship since they lost to Sandiacre Town, 18 years previously. Sandiacre had added another title, in 2014, but Bath must have wondered if their turn would ever come again.

It did. And anyone who witnessed their semi-final crushing of Brentwood would have been forgiven for feeling this was their year. In the event, the final was played at Wormsley, which might have helped break the spell, but they needed to beat Sandiacre Town, in a replay of the 2003 final, when Bath required 14 to win with four wickets in hand, but lost by one run.

Sandiacre were in imperious form, though they had relied heavily on Conor Marshall (four for 27 against Leamington in the quarter-final, and an unbeaten 75 against South Northumberland in the semi) and Luke Thomas (56 in the quarter, having scored 120 and 77 not out in the early rounds).

Bath had progressed with the help of three dashing blades: Ben Wells, who hit 139 off 86 balls against Bashley; Tim Rouse, whose 100 had seen off Bridgwater; and Bradley Porteous, who played the key innings in the quarter-final at Weybridge (75) and the semi (84). But, in the final, Wells was absent, Rouse failed, and Porteous was sawn off; it fell to Wells's brother Sam – still smarting from the news that Somerset were not renewing his contract – to play the winning hand.

The 2019 champions, Swardeston, had lost on the last ball of their second-round match against Cambridge. Luke O'Donnell (Three Bridges) was the top scorer (424 at 141), and Bath's Paul Muchall, formerly of Kent and Gloucestershire, took the most wickets (14 at 12). The highest score was Oliver Wilkin's 144 off 106 for Finchampstead versus Ealing; the best figures were Karanpal Singh's six for 25 for Welwyn Garden City against Peterborough Town. It was a credit to all the clubs that, despite the pandemic, they were able to complete a tournament which has now been won by 14 different teams in the last 14 seasons.

Semi-final   At Bath, August 29. **Bath won by 197 runs. Bath 254-8** (40 overs) (B. G. Porteous 84, A. A. Morrison 62); ‡**Brentwood 57** (23.3 overs) (P. B. Muchall 5-11, J. Arney 3-23).

Semi-final   At Gosforth, August 29. **Sandiacre Town won by six wickets. South Northumberland 183-8** (40 overs) (S. J. D. Bell 64, A. D. Cragg 58, D. M. Wheeldon 3-28, J. R. Jordison 3-31); ‡**Sandiacre Town 184-4** (38.4 overs) (S. McNeill 60, C. R. Marshall 75*).

FINAL

BATH v SANDIACRE TOWN

At Wormsley, September 12. Bath won by 81 runs. Toss: Bath.

Sam Young returned after two months of Somerset duty to lead Bath to their first national title, in their fourth final. He hit 78 off 81, with six fours and three sixes, after Sandiacre had nabbed two early wickets, including another former Somerset player, Tim Rouse. Bradley Porteous was Young's first partner, and they added 71; Paul Muchall then helped him put on 62. There was a stutter, but Jack Scrivens hit strongly, and Matthew Newbold paid a premium for his three wickets. Sandiacre, needing 221, lost the openers – including the dangerous Luke Thomas for six – to George Axtell, and James Arney made it 57 for four. Young effectively decided the match by running out Connor Marshall. Scott McNeill's lone hand, an unbeaten 75, added late runs, but when John Jordison – the sole survivor from the 2003 final between these teams – was eighth out at 133, Bath knew they had done it at last.

Player of the Match: S. Young.

Bath

B. G. Porteous lbw b Marshall	34		J. Arney run out (Anderson)		10
T. D. Rouse c Anderson b Wheeldon	1		M. Cadywould not out		6
A. A. Morrison b McFadyean	0				
S. Young b Newbold	78		Lb 6, w 20, nb 1		27
P. B. Muchall c Wheeldon b Newbold	21				—
*S. A. Mount c Needham b McIlroy	8		1/7 (2) 2/9 (3) 3/80 (1) (8 wkts, 40 overs)		220
†J. T. H. Scrivens not out	34		4/142 (5) 5/154 (6)		
K. Hopper c Thomas b Newbold	1		6/163 (4) 7/165 (8) 8/204 (9)		8 overs: 19-2

G. Axtell did not bat.

Wheeldon 8–2–28–1; McFadyean 7–0–33–1; Jordison 7–0–48–0; Marshall 8–0–21–1; Newbold 8–0–63–3; McIlroy 2–0–21–1.

Sandiacre Town

J. Chapman c Morrison b Axtell	4		R. McFadyean lbw b Rouse		2
L. Thomas c Scrivens b Axtell	6		M. R. S. Newbold b Porteous		1
S. B. McNeill not out	75				
C. McIlroy b Arney	8		B 1, lb 2, w 8, nb 2		13
J. Needham c Scrivens b Arney	0				—
C. R. Marshall run out (Young)	6		1/4 (1) 2/22 (2) 3/43 (4) (34 overs)		139
*†W. Anderson c Scrivens b Muchall	7		4/57 (5) 5/76 (6) 6/95 (7)		
D. M. Wheeldon b Rouse	12		7/124 (8) 8/133 (9) 9/136 (10)		
J. R. Jordison c Scrivens b Muchall	5		10/139 (11)		8 overs: 25-2

Axtell 5–0–19–2; Muchall 8–2–32–2; Arney 8–1–22–2; Porteous 3–0–19–1; Cadywould 2–0–8–0; Rouse 8–1–36–2.

Umpires: A. Oram and A. Seymour.

VITALITY CLUB T20

Having done the double in 2019, Swardeston were conspicuous by their absence in the later stages. They had fallen to eventual semi-finalists Brentwood, themselves destroyed by Tunbridge Wells, who went on to blindside Barnard Castle in the final. Three centuries were scored in the season, the fastest by Pershore opener Mike Green, who hit 115 off 44 balls – with ten fours and ten sixes – against Waltham. He was later stranded on 99 not out (from 61) against Quatt.

North final At Denby, August 15. **Barnard Castle won by nine wickets.** ‡**Alderley Edge 135-9** (20 overs) (F. Usher 3-21); **Barnard Castle 137-1** (12.5 overs) (S. Seth 83*).

South final At Basingstoke, August 15. **Tunbridge Wells won by nine wickets. Brentwood 140-8** (20 overs); **Tunbridge Wells 142-1** (16.4 overs) (V. Bhatia 58*, A. Williams 56*).

Final At Northampton, September 19. **Tunbridge Wells won by five wickets.** ‡**Barnard Castle 125-5** (20 overs) (K. Carver 55*); **Tunbridge Wells 128-5** (18.3 overs) (A. Williams 53*).

THE VONEUS VILLAGE CUP IN 2021

Benj Moorehead

Fifty years since it spluttered into life, the Village Cup rumbled on, no mean feat given that idling away a Sunday afternoon at cow corner is not as common as it was in the 1970s. There were 347 entrants in 2021, more than the competition had seen for a decade or more, and the Lord's final attracted around 1,500 spirited villagers. After three seasons without one, it had the backing of a headline sponsor – Voneus, who aim to provide broadband to hard-to-reach places, far-flung villages among them.

Calmore Sports, making their Village Cup debut, became the first New Forest side to win the trophy. They play at Loperwood Park in Hampshire, tucked inside the forest's eastern edge (or, if you're Boris Johnson, a ten-minute drive from Peppa Pig World). As Calmore forged their way to Lord's, the local community rallied to the cause. "When we played Rockhampton from the West Country in the quarter-final, we had to go down to the pub and ask if we could have a keg of cider, because they had drunk it all by two o'clock," said club captain Mark Lavelle. For the rain-hit semi against Stoke Green, members of nearby Paultons CC unearthed an emergency supply of sawdust and a Super Sopper. Lavelle estimated that Calmore raised £15,000 from those two home matches, both of which drew crowds of several hundred.

While he took 17 wickets at 11 with left-arm spin, Steve Wright's left-arm seam produced 22 maidens from 64 overs. Will Brewster, until recently Hampshire CCC's media manager, was recast as a star opener, and made fifties in the quarter- and semi-finals. There was a cameo by Yannick de Mezieres Lepervanche, a South African who studied at Solent University. Yet they were all trumped by Ben Johns, who began with two ducks and finished with three half-centuries – including an unbeaten 58 at Lord's, to go with an extraordinary catch in front of the Mound Stand. A stocky left-hander, Johns made his Calmore debut in 2013 aged 15, and has not missed a league game. "I think it's up to 130 in a row," he said. "I don't know how it's happened or where the years have gone, but I get to play with ten of my mates every single week."

Twice, Calmore nearly threw it away: against Cookham Dean (Berkshire), they lost seven for 45 chasing 121, and then seven for 28 during a tie against Goatacre (Wiltshire); Calmore went through after losing fewer wickets overall. In contrast, the Cheshire side Alvanley brushed aside four previous winners on their way to the final. Their strength was in the bowling, led by Jimmy Ecclestone, brother of England spinner Sophie, and Stephen Charles, who took a hat-trick against Neyland (Dyfed) in the semi-final. Simon Gee held the middle order together, and made six stumpings. No one scored a hundred or took a five-for, illustrating the collective consistency.

Back in April, Oxford Downs managed three centuries and a pair of five-fors in two matches. First, they despatched Horley by 247 runs, then The Baldons by 376 – the highest margin of victory in the Village Cup – with Tom Costley smashing 141 from 68 balls in a total of 420, before their opponents were rolled for 44. But Oxford Downs were knocked out by Langford in the next round on wickets lost, after a last-ball run-out left the scores tied.

Thomas Morgan produced the all-round performance of the summer: 90 not out and seven for 19 for Ynystawe, the 2001 champions, against Tondu in the Glamorgan and Gwent regional final. But for the second year running, Ynystawe were beaten in a bowl-out, losing 1–0 (11 attempts each) to Rockhampton.

FINAL

CALMORE SPORTS v ALVANLEY

At Lord's, September 19. Calmore Sports won by six wickets. Toss: Calmore Sports.

Ben Johns won this match with the bat, though it will be better remembered for his incredible catch. Put in, Alvanley had limped to 73 for two in the 24th over after a superb opening spell of 8–6–5–2 by Steve Wright, a left-arm seamer who conceded only a no-ball and a streaky boundary. Stephen Charles then whipped a delivery sweetly off his toes towards the Mound Stand – but Johns leapt, like a gibbon from down the road at London Zoo, and plucked it from the sky. Simon Gee hit 28, but the innings never caught fire before the players went off for rain, with Alvanley 150 for seven after 36. They did not reappear for three hours, when Calmore Sports were set a revised target of 112 from 20. Chris Charles, brother of Stephen, took wickets in his first two overs, the second with a lethal inducker, before a pair of sharp stumpings by Gee left Calmore needing 57 from 42 balls. But no one could not dislodge Johns, who batted patiently before clearing his front leg to pull Lee Ainsworth for the first six of the innings in the 16th over. It went for 18, and changed the game. Three more sixes followed, and Calmore cantered to victory with seven balls to spare.

Player of the Match: B. Johns.

Alvanley

*M. J. Rowlands b Wright.	18
A. L. Reid c West b Wright.	16
S. T. Charles c Johns b Perry.	13
†S. P. Gee c Perry b Lavelle	28
L. Ainsworth c West b Johnson.	26
A. Bennion c and b Lavelle.	15
C. Fletcher not out.	12
C. Wright run out (Wright)	0
C. I. Charles not out	5
Lb 3, w 13, nb 1.	17
	150

1/30 (2) 2/37 (1)   (7 wkts, 36 overs) 150
3/73 (3) 4/96 (4)
5/119 (6) 6/145 (5) 7/145 (8)   8 overs: 30-0

J. Ecclestone and B. Tumilty did not bat.

Wright 8–6–5–2; West 4–0–24–0; Lavelle 6–1–26–2; Perry 8–0–36–1; Carty 8–0–35–0; Manning 1–0–12–0; Johnson 1–0–9–1.

Calmore Sports

W. P. Brewster c Gee b C. I. Charles	0
B. D. Johns not out	58
S. C. Johnson b C. I. Charles.	1
M. J. Taylor st Gee b Tumilty	16
J. W. Manning st Gee b Tumilty	4
*M. I. Lavelle not out	15
B 1, lb 2, w 14, nb 1	18
	112

1/1 (1) 2/10 (3)   (4 wkts, 18.5 overs) 112
3/45 (4)
4/55 (5)   4 overs: 14-2

†M. O. Bailey, B. M. Perry, M. J. West, S. W. Wright and L. C. Carty did not bat.

C. I. Charles 3.5–0–17–2; Ecclestone 3–0–17–0; Ainsworth 3–0–30–0; S. T. Charles 4–0–15–0; Tumilty 4–0–16–2; Rowlands 1–0–14–0.

Umpires: T. J. Dorr and R. Ellis.

DISABILITY CRICKET IN 2021

Good news from Yorkshire, at last

STEVE MORGAN

"If you can't see it, you can't be it." So says Ian Martin, the ECB's head of disability cricket. And rarely was his mantra more relevant. The second summer of Covid posed continuing problems for cricketers everywhere, but arguably these were felt more keenly on the game's margins.

In another Groundhog Day year on the international scene, England's Physical Disability XI were the only one of four sides to play any kind of competitive fixture. But it was worth the wait: a strong Lord's Taverners XI, captained by Matthew Hoggard and featuring Sam Northeast, as well as former county stalwarts Steve Kirby and Steffan Jones, were beaten by five wickets at Tring. The PD XI needed 249 and, with the scores level, Matt Askin's boundary off the penultimate ball from Kirby was a moment to savour, after a chase set up by opener Angus Brown, with 91 from 95 balls, and Will Flynn's dashing 76 from 72. It would be another three months before the squad's first training retreat in two years, at Edgbaston in November.

The year had other highlights. A goal of establishing 100 disability "champion" clubs nationwide (a cornerstone of the ECB's Inspiring Generations five-year plan) was surpassed within weeks; 300 became the aim by the end of 2024. In April, a four-year partnership was announced worth £2m between the ECB and the Lord's Taverners, to extend playing opportunities through the charity's Super 1s programme. Community hubs will be set up for those aged 12 to 25 across all 39 English counties. Disabled youngsters should be able to play cricket in at least ten further regions this summer.

The lack of international cricket lent sharp focus to the Disability Premier League, a ground-breaking pan-disability competition successfully trialled in August and September at Neston CC (Cheshire), Valley End CC (Surrey) and Loughborough University. The DPL started with four teams, using a five-tier grading system for players, who are chosen by draft. In 2022, the teams will play a T20 round robin in August; the aim is to help bridge the gap between domestic and international cricket.

Surrey won the D40 National League: Jonny Gale's side were unbeaten in their six matches, and ended up six points clear of Middlesex. Lancashire and Surrey won the Division Two North and South titles. In Blind cricket, Metro won the National League Division One, while Sussex Sharks topped the second tier.

Yorkshire cricket endured a troubled season elsewhere, but the efforts of Alex Jervis – a mainstay of England's Learning Disability side – made him a shoo-in as the ECB Disability Cricketer of the Year; the award was presented at the Cricket Writers' Club lunch in October. Disappointed by the quality of Yorkshire's disability set-up, Jervis decided to do something

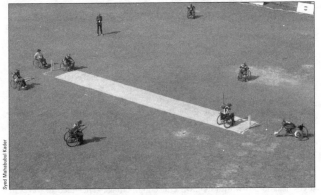

Syed Mahabubul Kader

Level playing field: Team Red take on Team Green in Dhaka, Bangladesh.

about it. He has so far helped raise more than £10,000, ensuring a return to competitive hard-ball cricket after seven years. A member of England's LD Ashes winners in 2019, he scouted and coached players himself, and organised profiles for the website.

On a more surreal note, Liam O'Brien of England's PD side turned his lockdown lay-off to good use: he became Europe's No. 1 player of the American football video game "Madden", winning several online events.

Covid permitting, England's Visually Impaired, Deaf and Learning Disability sides will head Down Under in June for Ashes series (it should be third time lucky for the VI players, after two postponements). Featuring a mix of 40- and 20-over games, this combined tour will be the biggest yet undertaken in the disabled game – a huge moment for all involved, and sure to increase its profile. As Martin says, "There's a lot of cricket – but there's no cricket like this."

SENIOR CRICKET IN 2021

ROAD SAFETY SERIES

The pandemic prompted the suspension of several international tournaments, but the 359-day hiatus in the Road Safety Series must have been the longest. A BCCI-approved T20 competition for retired international cricketers, it began in March 2020, and saw India crowned champions in March 2021. The five teams boasted an impressive roll call: Brett Lee (Australia), Virender Sehwag, Yuvraj Singh and Sachin Tendulkar (India), Sanath Jayasuriya and Muttiah Muralitharan (Sri Lanka), Jonty Rhodes (South Africa), Shivnarine Chanderpaul and Brian Lara (West Indies).

It wasn't plain sailing. Only four matches were possible before Covid forced a shutdown. That the tournament restarted said as much about the lure of the rupee as it did about the determination of its organiser, Ravi Gaikwad. The Australians, led by Lee – and whose "legends" included Pat Richards, a former rugby league pro with no known cricketing heritage – declined to travel to India for the resumption. Teams from England (led by Kevin Pietersen) and Bangladesh were hurriedly added, though neither made it to the semi-finals. Sri Lanka's Tillekeratne Dilshan scored most runs (271) and took most wickets (12), but his team lost to India in the final: Yuvraj and Yusuf Pathan smacked half-centuries, and Jayasuriya couldn't quite muster the aggression of old in the chase.

Semi-finals India beat West Indies; Sri Lanka beat South Africa.

Final At Raipur, March 21, 2021 (floodlit). **India won by 14 runs. India 181-4** (20 overs) (Yuvraj Singh 60, Y. K. Pathan 62*); ‡**Sri Lanka 167-7** (20 overs) (S. T. Jayasuriya 43).

COUNTY CHAMPIONSHIP

The ECB managed to stage a full veterans' County Championship programme. Essex won the Over-50 competition thanks to an astonishing run-glut from Giles Ecclestone: 775 at 155 with five centuries. In the Over-60s, Kent were champions, while Surrey's Donald Taylor hit an unbeaten 180 against Hampshire. Surrey took the Over-70 title; Gloucestershire's Keith Daniels scored 908 at 48, and Alan May's 33 wickets for Sussex included seven for 25 against Berkshire.

Over-50 County Championship
Semi-finals Lancashire beat Devon; Essex beat Hampshire.
Final At Kibworth, September 19. **Essex won by six wickets. Lancashire 183-7** (C. Turner 84); ‡**Essex 187-4** (36 overs) (G. W. Ecclestone 80).

Over-60 County Championship
Semi-finals Warwickshire beat Lancashire; Kent beat Essex.
Final At Great Tew, September 21. **Kent won by six wickets. Warwickshire 188-9** (M. I. N. Eames 61; R. Staple 5-41); ‡**Kent 191-4** (J. Butterworth 80).

Over-70 County Championship
Semi-finals Cheshire beat Wales; Surrey beat Essex.
Final At Kidderminster, September 2. **Surrey won by nine wickets.** ‡**Cheshire 182-5** (40 overs) (S. C. Yates 54); **Surrey 186-1** (35.1 overs) (A. Peters 96*).

ENGLAND UNDER-19 v WEST INDIES UNDER-19 IN 2021

Under-19 one-day internationals (6): England 4, West Indies 2

Two years after their last home appearance, England's youth squad arrived in metropolitan Kent to begin a six-match ODI series with their West Indian contemporaries; neither team had taken the field since the ICC Under-19 World Cup, 19 months earlier. The hosts won 4–2, a score which might easily have been reversed, but for their pair of thrilling one-wicket victories.

England named Jacob Bethell – Barbados-born, newly signed by Warwickshire via Rugby School and later named Wisden Schools Cricketer of the Year – and Hampshire's Tom Prest as joint-captains. When both were recalled by their counties mid-series (as was Archie Lenham of Sussex), James Rew skippered in the final game. No player on either side had previously appeared at this level, though several hinted they might climb higher. For England, a promising top five (George Thomas, George Bell, Rehan Ahmed, Bethell and Rew) all hit over 125 runs, including at least one half-century, at 39 or more. Glamorgan wicketkeeper Alex Horton made ten dismissals – the most for England in any bilateral youth series – and Sonny Baker, a swing bowler from Somerset, led the attack with ten wickets.

The West Indies team comprised four Trinidadians, three Barbadians, three Nevisians, two each from Guyana, Jamaica and St Lucia – including the captain, 17-year-old Ackeem Auguste – and one each from Grenada and St Maarten. Their coach was the former Barbados player Rohan Nurse, who counted Curtly Ambrose among his assistants. Unsurprisingly, the attack was strong: seamers Johann Layne and Andel Gordon were impressive throughout, as was leg-spinner Isai Thorne. The batting, however, repeatedly let them down. The exceptions were Teddy Bishop – the outstanding player of the series, on either side – who scored 271 at 54, and Matthew Nandu, who hit fifties in the last two games.

SQUADS

England   *J. G. Bethell (Warwickshire), *T. J. Prest (Hampshire), R. Ahmed (Leicestershire), T. H. Aspinwall (Lancashire), S. Baker (Somerset), N. A. Barnwell (Surrey), G. J. Bell (Lancashire), J. A. Boyden (Lancashire), J. M. Coles (Sussex), A. J. Horton (Glamorgan), D. K. Ibrahim (Sussex), A. D. Lenham (Sussex), W. A. Luxton (Yorkshire), H. W. Petrie (Hampshire), J. E. K. Rew (Somerset), J. J. G. Sales (Northamptonshire), F. Singh (Nottinghamshire), G. W. Thomas (Somerset). *Coach:* R. K. J. Dawson.

Bethell (for the first and second games) and Prest (for the next three) were named as joint-captains. Both were recalled by their counties before the sixth, when Rew took over. Sales was recalled by Northamptonshire before the series began.

West Indies   *A. W. J. Auguste, O. Amory, A. Amurdan, J. Beckford, T. J. Bishop, C. Bowen-Tuckett, M. Clarke, R. A. Clarke, G. Depeiza, N. Edward, A. Gordon, S. Hackett, J. Jagessar, J. Layne, A. Mahase, M. Nandu, I. Thorne, V. J. Singh. *Coach:* R. R. Nurse.

First Under-19 one-day international At Beckenham, September 4. **England won by 166 runs.** **England 289-9** (50 overs) (J. G. Bethell 69, J. E. K. Rew 59, A. J. Horton 53; I. Thorne 3-51); ‡**West Indies 123** (29.1 overs) (R. Ahmed 3-22, T. J. Prest 5-18). *An emphatic all-round performance gave England their largest victory by runs against a Test nation. Jacob Bethell and James Rew both passed 50 in their third-wicket stand of 87, but the West Indies seamers fought back to reduce the hosts from 149-2 to 204-7. Alex Horton's 48-ball 53 ensured the early work was not in vain. Needing 290, West Indies reached 90-2 in the 18th, then lost eight for 33. Rehan Ahmed and Tom Prest shared those eight as the visitors recorded their shortest completed innings against England; Prest's figures (6–2–18–5) were England's sixth-best.*

Second Under-19 one-day international At Beckenham, September 6. **England won by one wicket.** ‡**West Indies 180** (39.3 overs) (T. J. Bishop 97*; T. J. Prest 3-36, J. G. Bethell 3-29); **England 181-9** (38 overs) (J. E. K. Rew 53; I. Thorne 3-54). *A thriller went England's way thanks to a last-wicket stand of 19* between Fateh Singh and Nathan Barnwell. First, though, came Teddy Bishop's extraordinary knock for West Indies: arriving at first drop, when Matthew Nandu retired hurt – hit in the ribs by Sonny Baker – he scored 97* off 104. After Anderson Amurdan's 27, no one else bettered Isai Thorne, who made 11 out of a seventh-wicket stand of 54. Requiring 181, and with Rew past 50, England slipped up again: 143-4 became 162-9. But the last pair crept to the target, assisted by six wides, the last of which clinched the game. In all, West Indies conceded 26 in wides, with Thorne alone contributing ten.*

Third Under-19 one-day international At Beckenham, September 8. **West Indies won by two wickets.** ‡**England 239-9** (50 overs); **West Indies 241-8** (47 overs) (T. J. Bishop 133; N. A. Barnwell 3-30). *Bishop would not be denied twice, hitting the highest score by a West Indian No. 3, as his team took their turn to win a nailbiter. England had recovered from 120-6 to post a competitive 239-9, in which George Bell top-scored with 44. Arriving early again – it was 12-2 after Barnwell sent back Justin Jagessar and Amurdan – Bishop again stood head and shoulders above the rest: while he made 133 off 117, none of his team-mates passed 21. Only four West Indians had ever scored more, among them Nicholas Pooran and Chris Gayle. But when James Coles bowled him, they still needed 12, with three wickets in hand. Barnwell dismissed McKenny Clarke, but Johann Layne finished it with a six, sealing West Indies' narrowest win batting second.*

Fourth Under-19 one-day international At Canterbury (Polo Farm), September 10. **England won by nine wickets.** **West Indies 135** (40.5 overs) (S. Baker 3-37, T. H. Aspinwall 3-28); ‡**England 136-1** (17.5 overs) (G. W. Thomas 59*, J. G. Bethell 67). *An untroubled opening partnership of 117 between George Thomas and Bethell helped England to victory with more than 32 overs remaining; never had they won at home with more time to spare. West Indies had laboured to 135, with only Rivaldo Clarke (37) and Giovonte Depeiza (32) finding any fluency. It proved woefully inadequate as Thomas and Bethell compiled England's first century opening stand against West Indies.*

Fifth Under-19 one-day international At Canterbury (Polo Farm), September 14. **England won by one wicket** (DLS). **West Indies 166** (41 overs) (M. Nandu 51); ‡**England 170-9** (42 overs) (G. J. Bell 60*; A. Gordon 3-37, J. Layne 3-40). *Before 2021, England had achieved a one-wicket victory only once, against Australia in Dubai in 2013-14; now they did it for the second time in nine days. The heroes were Bell – who faced 115 balls for 60* – and last man Baker, who survived 17 minutes without scoring while his partner knocked off the 12 required. West Indies had fallen short again: the fit-again Nandu top-scored with 51, but a promising 101-2 became an unfulfilling 166. England, becalmed at 93-5 after 25, were pepped up by Coles's 27-ball 31, but lost four for 20 as they chased a revised target of 170 in 43. Bell just needed someone to hang on at the other end: enter Baker, as England secured the series with a game to spare.*

Sixth Under-19 one-day international At Canterbury (Polo Farm), September 17. **West Indies won by 17 runs.** ‡**West Indies 230** (50 overs) (M. Nandu 80; R. Ahmed 3-30); **England 213** (45 overs) (R. Ahmed 68*; V. J. Singh 4-51). *Vasant Singh, a leg-spinner, undid England in their chase of a moderate 231. West Indies had been in trouble at 107-5 after Ahmed took three quick wickets, before Nandu saved them with a backs-to-the-wall 80. Baker (4-41) was irresistible at the death but, for the first time in the series, West Indies batted out their overs – just. Thomas and Rew began the pursuit with a sprightly 52, then Singh chipped away, and all looked lost at 135-7. Ahmed took charge with an unbeaten half-century to bring up the 200 but, for once, England's tail could not cling on.*

YOUTH CRICKET IN 2021

Following the success of their All Stars programme, launched in 2017 for those aged five to eight, the ECB launched Dynamos, for the eight-to-11 age group – in the hope of reversing the decline of cricket among primary-school children. The Dynamos programme had initially been unveiled in February 2020; soon after, the UK was in lockdown.

It eventually got going in May 2021, with the aim of adding 35,000 children to the 65,000 signed up for All Stars. Every child was given a personalised cricket shirt, and the cost of an eight-week course was £40, significantly less than joining a private club's colts section. The challenge will come when those children want to make the transition to a club's age-group teams, when costs increase.

For county Under-18 boys, the Championship returned after being suspended in 2020, but Surrey were denied the chance to defend their 2019 title when the ECB decided not to bring the six regional winners together for national finals (nor do they plan to do so in 2022). The 24 teams, comprising the first-class counties plus six others, each played three games; no team won all three, but Middlesex accrued most points. The Cup, a 50-over competition, was also restricted to regions; Northamptonshire won all their matches. The Cup final will return this year, and a national T20 will be established.

Two Glamorgan colts topped the run-scoring across formats: Harry Friend of Newport (611) and Callum Nicholls of St Fagans (528). Gloucestershire's Max Shepherd, of Bourton Vale, took 31 wickets, including seven for 53 in the Championship against Wales. The highest Championship score was 151 not out by Ben Walken for Lancashire against Cheshire; Hampshire's Bertie Foreman had the best bowling performance, taking seven for 39 against Sussex. Somerset's Josh Thomas hit 157 from 115 balls against Devon in the Cup; his county team-mate Sonny Baker returned the best Cup figures – playing *for* Devon – with six for 24 against Gloucestershire.

Berkshire gained the most points in the regional girls' Under-18 Cup; Staffordshire won all six of their games in the Under-15 equivalent. National finals in both formats will make a comeback this year.

The county boys' Under-15 Cup barely got off the ground. Only Durham, Cumberland and Northumberland played more than once; Durham's Joseph Davis scored the only hundred. The ECB are replacing the competition with an Under-16 Cup in 2022 – which means the same cohort will have another opportunity.

The Under-14 Cup was also hampered, but that didn't stop Northamptonshire's Shaynan Patel hitting 455 runs, including an innings of 267 from 106 balls – with 24 fours and 24 sixes – in a 45-over game against Lincolnshire. His side racked up 478 for seven, and won by 373 runs.

Vitality again sponsored junior T20 competitions for clubs, though there were no national finals at Under-19, owing to the pressures of public exams. Knowle & Dorridge, from Warwickshire, won the boys' Under-15 final, and Surrey's Esher were Under-13 champions. Porthill Park, in Staffordshire, won the girls' national finals in both age groups.

THE 2021 ECB DAVID ENGLISH BUNBURY FESTIVAL

The cream of the UK's teenage cricketing talent converged, after a one-year hiatus, for the 34th Bunbury Festival. As ever, each of the four Bunbury regions pulled together an extended list of their best club and county Under-15 players, and whittled them down to a squad for the festival in August.

Even in the pre-festival intra-squad games, there were several outstanding performances as boys jostled for the selectors' eye. For the Midlands, Sam Seecharan and Arush Buchake scored hundreds, as did Yousuf Choudhary for London & East. Lucas Selby, going in at No. 10 in a North game, hit 71 not out from 43 balls, much of it from the bowling of Corey Flintoff, son of Andrew. South & West warmed up by beating Hampshire Under-16; London & East saw off Middlesex Under-15.

The festival's opening Sunday saw the T20 play-offs. London & East's 147 for six was overhauled by the Midlands, and the North's 103 for eight was easily surpassed by South & West, for whom Ben Salter had taken four for 15. On Monday, in the 50-over round robin, London & East scored 323 for six to beat the North, thanks to wicketkeeper Dylan Rawal's quickfire 73; the Midlands were guided to a testing target of 262 against South & West by fifties from Buchake, Seecharan and Jack Home. The following day, London & East saw 323 for six on the scoreboard again – only this time they conceded it, and lost, as the Midlands were powered by another Seecharan half-century, including five sixes; the North triumphed after Michael Vaughan's son Archie dismissed the South & West top three. After a rest day, South & West beat London & East in a rain-affected game; the Midlands made it a clean sweep when Tazeem Chaudry Ali's five for 34 helped bowl out the North for 160 and, despite parsimony from Vaughan, surpassed it with three wickets in hand.

On the final day, the Midlands had a chance to make it a double when they faced South & West in the T20 final. The weather again threatened, and the Midlands made slow progress to 118 for eight. Despite three wickets from Chaudry Ali, South & West eased home.

Across all the games, Fin Hill of South & West was top scorer (390), and the Midlands' Farhan Ahmed leading wicket-taker (24). Aged just 13, he took six for 60 against London & East and was Player of the Festival. "He is a fine ambassador for his school and county, and I am sure he will be for his country in the near future," said David English. He is as good a judge as anyone. Since he named John Crawley the best player of the first tournament in 1987, over 1,000 Bunbury cricketers have made first-class debuts – and 119 have gone on to represent England. "This is the first step on the golden pathway to winning an England cap," English told *Sky Sports*. "Seeing them test their skills against the best in the country is very important to me, because I could never play cricket like that – so the next best thing was to give someone else the opportunity."

SCHOOLS CRICKET IN 2021

REVIEW BY DOUGLAS HENDERSON

To borrow from another sport, schools cricket in 2021 was not so much a game of two halves as a country riven in two. While a dozen or so schools flourished – fitting in 20 games or more – a large number never got on the pitch. That explains why this section is thinner than usual: nearly 50 regular entries, many of them well-known cricketing centres, played so little it made no sense to record what passed for a season. Even those who did send in reports often had no one fulfilling the normal criteria of 150 runs or ten wickets. As always, though, the leading player in each category is given.

Back in the spring, I optimistically wrote at Schools Cricket Online:

> The 2021 season in theory could possibly be the best for years, indeed decades, as it promises a full term with no public exams, no revision mania, no reading weeks, no post-exam exeats and all the rest of the nonsense which has plagued schools and ruined the schools cricket season.

Little did I reckon with the advent of the dreaded Teacher-Assessed Grades, or TAGs. In effect, they became not just teachers of a full timetable, but exam boards too, setting, marking and scrupulously moderating exam-type papers. Meanwhile the boards, who did much less than in a normal year, still collected the usual £220m in fees: a scandal seemingly noticed only by Alice Thomson in *The Times*. It also meant pupils often had to sit more not-quite-exams than ever. Far from being a golden summer with time away from study, it was the opposite, as teachers and pupils suffered from appalling burnout.

There was another, allied problem. Even when heads were prepared to risk playing rival schools, they often had to cope with a block cancellation, sometimes at very short notice.

One positive was that the Covid pandemic helped foster a second, late-summer season. In September 2020, when close-contact sports such as rugby were out of the question, First XIs played as many as ten fixtures. These autumn-term matches are included in the school-by-school reports that follow, since they are the same academic year as the more familiar early-summer games. Even if a split season is unlikely to become established – rugby and football will doubtless force their way back – it proved such a success that some schools are determined to continue playing at least a few games. It helps that September weather is often blissful.

Several schools were forced, either by government diktat or local preference, to field teams entirely from a single year-group bubble. While this allowed a reasonable standard, the team fielded were not a true First XI. And even if a representative team were available, the weather was not always accommodating – unlike the beautiful lost spring and summer of 2020.

So it is something of a wonder that schools cricket happened at all and, in some cases, flourished. A welcome addition to this section are the results of matches played by several girls' teams. In recent years, the growth of the women's game, boosted by the success of the England team, has been phenomenal, and this can now be seen in these pages.

Of the six players to average over 100, just two did so from at least four completed innings. Jacob Bethell batted seven times (twice not out) in compiling 654 runs for Rugby, and averaged a phenomenal 130. He also scored a double-hundred against historic rivals Marlborough. There were three more doubles. Daniel Stock of Myerscough (Manchester) hit an unbeaten 212; meanwhile, Harry Gallian, whose Test-playing father, Jason, is cricket master

WISDEN SCHOOLS CRICKETERS OF THE YEAR

2007	Jonny Bairstow	St Peter's School, York
2008	James Taylor	Shrewsbury School
2009	Jos Buttler	King's College, Taunton
2010	Will Vanderspar	Eton College
2011	Daniel Bell-Drummond	Millfield School
2012	Tom Abell	Taunton School
2013	Tom Köhler-Cadmore	Malvern College
2014	Dylan Budge	Woodhouse Grove
2015	Ben Waring	Felsted School
2016	A. J. Woodland	St Edward's School, Oxford
2017	Teddie Casterton	RGS, High Wycombe
2018	Nathan Tilley	Reed's School
2019	Tawanda Muyeye	Eastbourne College
2020	No award	
2021	**Jacob Bethell**	**Rugby School**

at Felsted, made 225 on the same day as Wellingborough's James Sales, son of Northamptonshire's David, struck 215 not out. By a considerable margin, Gallian was the leading run-scorer, with 1,107: next, over 200 behind, was Alex Horton from St Edward's, Oxford.

With around half of schools playing no more than ten matches – many of them 20-over or 100-ball affairs – it was nigh impossible for bowlers to approach 40 wickets, the usual benchmark of a strong season. However, Eton and Epsom both managed over 20 fixtures, and their bowlers were correspondingly more successful: George Weldon of Eton collected 46, and Epsom's Harry Jackson 40. Meanwhile, Yousef Majid of Cranleigh took 42 from just nine matches, though as a left-arm spinner – not subject to as many ECB restrictions as fast bowlers – he sent down roughly as many overs. In a two-day match against Hurstpierpoint, he twice opened the bowling, taking eight for 15 in the first innings and 14 for 75 in the match; it's easy to see why his captain kept him on for the entire game.

Remarkably, the National Schools T20 competition did reach a conclusion, despite several rounds being unplayed with three weeks to go. And finals day survived a wretched Arundel forecast: not until the last 15 minutes did light rain start to fall, prompting the DLS target to be displayed on the scoreboard. In the end, although King's, Taunton, had by that metric been ahead in the closing stages, Malvern triumphed for the second successive time. It was hard

Jacob Bethell of Rugby School: Wisden Cricketer of the Year for 2021.

to say whom the damp conditions hampered more: the batsmen, slipping as they ran; or the bowlers, struggling to grip the ball. Sedbergh and Tonbridge were the beaten semi-finalists.

Before the denouement, the competition had produced some extraordinary performances: with 12 needed off two balls, Jamie Treasure of Warwick hit two sixes to clinch the game against King Edward's, Birmingham; Hampton's Pravin Kinharan took five for one, including a hat-trick; and when Myerscough and Sedbergh both made 207, they (erroneously) resorted to a super over, when the result should have been determined by wickets lost. Happily, Sedbergh, who would have won on the simpler tiebreak, prevailed in extra time, when ten played nine. Meanwhile, two Felsted teams – boys and girls – tied games on the same day, on adjacent pitches.

There was, however, a hidden casualty from one year of no cricket, and another of only sporadic play. According to Martin Speight, the former Sussex player now coaching at Sedbergh, players lost "cricketing intelligence". Even on finals day at Arundel, four of the best cricketing schools all showed signs of inexperience: many silly run-outs or near misses, and injudicious slogging when accumulation was needed.

The choice of Wisden Schools Cricketer was difficult. Yousef Majid at Cranleigh (Ollie Pope's *alma mater*) came close. Still a Year 12, he took those 14 wickets in the two-day game against MCC, and has already played for Sussex Seconds. Another in the frame, and also with a season still to play, was Felsted's Harry Gallian, the only cricketer to reach 1,000 runs.

But the winner is Jacob Bethell of Rugby School, England Under-19 and Warwickshire. His housemaster at Rugby, the former Warwickshire captain Michael Powell, would not be surprised to see the England team added to the list in the coming years. "He's the complete package for an all-rounder – a hugely talented top-order bat, a more than useful left-arm spinner and one of the most gifted fielders I've come across. And he's a hard worker who grabs every opportunity he can. There's something of the Vaughan or Trescothick about him. I can see him scoring more and more runs the higher in the game he reaches."

Bethell has cricket in his blood. His grandfather played alongside Garry Sobers for Barbados in the 1960s, and his father for Derbyshire Seconds in the early 1990s. Like them, Jacob was born in Barbados, and West Indies were starting to take a serious interest when he was as young as 11. He has, though, committed himself to England (and played Championship cricket for Warwickshire). Growing up in the Caribbean and facing his share of fast bowling also helped the left-handed Jacob become a prodigious hooker and puller. In 2021, his sumptuous double-hundred against Marlborough underlined his powers of concentration, and his ability to produce the goods when it matters. He is the 14th Wisden Schools Cricketer of the Year.

In February 2022, long after this section was completed, came the sad and unexpected news that Douglas Henderson, *Wisden's* schools correspondent, had died. He first compiled these pages for the 2006 edition, so this was his 17th review. His energy, enthusiasm and trenchant opinion suffused all he did, not least the research to determine each edition's Schools Cricketer of the Year. A full obituary will appear in *Wisden 2023*.

MCC Schools v ESCA

At Lord's, September 7. **MCC Schools won by two wickets**. ESCA 253 (44.3 overs) (K. Patel 32, K. Smith 72, S. J. Seecharan 75; T. F. Debenham 4-21); ‡MCC Schools 256-8 (48 overs) (C. Dickinson 35, J. W. Baird 82, A. Shetty 64*).

MCC Schools *J. W. Baird (*Millfield*), T. F. Debenham (*New Hall*), C. Dickinson (*Scarborough College*), H. G. R. Gallian (*Felsted*), T. Hinley (*Eastbourne College*), B. M. James (*Epsom College*), D. Khalid (*Haileybury*), Y. Majid (*Cranleigh*), N. Shaikh (*Repton*), A. Shetty (*Manchester GS*), S. Srikanthan (*Bishop Vesey's GS*).

ESCA *K. Smith (*King's School, Canterbury*), N. B. Cornwell (*Queen's School, Bushey*), R. Evitts (*John Taylor HS, Burton*), M. Killeen (*Park View Academy of Sport*), R. Lewis (*Shrewsbury*), B. McKinney (*Seaham HS*), K. Patel (*St Paul's*), H. L. Seagrave (*Haileybury*), S. J. Seecharan (*Tonbridge*), J. Stanley (*Thomas Telford*), J. Thomas (*King's College, Taunton*).

SCHOOLS AVERAGES

BEST BATTING AVERAGE (4 completed innings)

		I	NO	Runs	HS	100	Avge
1	J. G. Bethell (*Rugby School*)	7	2	654	202	3	130.80
2	L. Maher (*Wycliffe College*)	9	5	400	100*	1	100.00
3	J. J. du'Gay (*Blundell's School*)	13	7	576	82*	0	96.00
4	J. J. G. Sales (*Wellingborough School*)	5	1	361	215*	1	90.25
5	H. G. R. Gallian (*Felsted School*)	16	3	1,107	225	4	85.15
6	T. Hinley (*Eastbourne College*)	10	2	665	141	2	83.12
7	G. J. Taylor (*King's School, Rochester*)	9	4	382	103*	1	76.40
8	B. Walkden (*Myerscough College*)	10	3	531	150*	3	75.85
9	A. A. Blundell (*Solihull School*)	6	2	303	102*	2	75.75
10	S. James (*Brentwood School*)	9	4	377	102*	1	75.40
11	H. R. Friend (*Monmouth School*)	9	3	447	105*	3	74.50
12	B. Butterfield (*Reigate Grammar School*)	7	2	369	91*	0	73.80
13	A. J. Rosslee (*Millfield School*)	7	2	359	137*	1	71.80
14	H. T. Fermor (*King's School, Rochester*)	12	4	563	115	2	70.37
15	B. H. P. Kearin (*Chigwell School*)	8	2	405	95	0	67.50
16	J. Little (*Myerscough College*)	10	4	402	95*	0	67.00
17	J. E. Rew (*King's College, Taunton*)	9	3	394	100*	1	65.66
18	S. S. E. Gumbs (*Bradfield College*)	12	3	589	154*	3	65.44
19	D. Stock (*Myerscough College*)	12	4	510	212*	1	63.75
20	A. D. King (*Ratcliffe College*)	9	2	439	108	1	62.71
21	B. G. G. Garrett (*Epsom College*)	20	8	739	111*	2	61.58
22	H. Usman (*Chigwell School*)	8	2	369	105*	1	61.50
23	T. A. Harper (*Woodbridge School*)	5	0	307	90	0	61.40
24	A Buchake (*Uppingham School*)	9	2	428	107	1	61.14

V. Patel (Aldenham), S. A. Ford (RGS, Worcester), M. Pumfrey (St Edward's Girls), C. X. C. Mannix (Abingdon), I. B. K. Wakeford (Oundle Girls), T. R. J. Cosh (Bromsgrove), B. C. Wood (Giggleswick), A. Singh (Llandaff), H. W. H. Mountford (Denstone) and J. C. Bradley (Eastbourne) would have qualified for this table had they had sufficient completed innings.

MOST RUNS

		I	NO	Runs	HS	100	Avge
1	H. G. R. Gallian (*Felsted School*)	16	3	1,107	225	4	85.15
2	A. J. Horton (*St Edward's School, Oxford*)	21	4	906	128*	2	53.29
3	D. Khalid (*Haileybury*)	23	6	854	121	1	50.23
4	O. H. Cox (*Malvern College*)	22	3	837	94	0	44.05
5	T. R. Thanawalla (*Hampton School*)	17	2	816	134	2	54.40
6	R. J. Noble (*Stowe School*)	22	6	797	114	1	49.81
7	J. M. Connell (*Harrow School*)	17	2	787	119*	3	52.46
8	J. J. Fielding (*Shrewsbury School*)	21	3	779	123*	1	43.27
9	T. W. Boorman (*Malvern College*)	22	4	771	91	0	42.83
10	G. T. Freeman (*Eton College*)	22	3	766	103	1	40.31
11	B. G. G. Garrett (*Epsom College*)	20	8	739	111*	2	61.58
12	S. J. Meadows (*Worksop College*)	22	3	738	128*	2	38.84
13	J. G. Weir (*Eton College*)	22	4	715	128*	2	39.72
14	W. G. Meacock (*Haileybury*)	22	9	714	102*	1	54.92
15	B. Hildebrand (*Epsom College*)	20	2	696	132*	2	38.66
16	W. J. La Fontaine Jackson (*Winchester College*)	18	3	680	112*	1	45.33
17	T. Hinley (*Eastbourne College*)	10	2	665	141	2	83.12
18	S. M. Hadfield (*Tonbridge School*)	19	2	662	112*	1	38.94
19	J. T. P. Willis (*Hurstpierpoint College*)	22	3	657	101*	1	34.57
20	J. G. Bethell (*Rugby School*)	7	2	654	202	3	130.80
21	J. P. Cronie (*Stowe School*)	16	1	628	131	1	41.86
22	D. P. Ormond (*St George's College, Weybridge*)	14	2	627	159*	1	52.25
23	F. Clinton (*Charterhouse*)	14	0	626	80	0	44.71
24	E. B. Bruce (*Hampton School*)	14	0	601	79	0	42.92

BEST BOWLING AVERAGE (10 wickets)

		O	M	R	W	BB	Avge
1	K. B. Jivanji (*Ratcliffe College*)	13.3	0	49	11	5-15	4.45
2	D. J. Clarke (*Queen Elizabeth's Hospital, Bristol*)	25	1	86	16	4-17	5.37
3	I. F. Atherton (*Lancaster RGS*)	23	6	63	11	4-23	5.72
4	N. V. Gorantla (*The Perse School*)	25	1	87	12	4-22	7.25
5	H. W. Grayson (*Wellingborough School*)	19.2	0	93	12	5-11	7.75
6	N. Gough (*RGS, Newcastle*)	24	8	94	12	6-8	7.83
7	L. R. B. Hill (*RGS, Guildford*)	34.1	6	87	11	4-12	7.90
8	S. A. H. S. Eley (*KCS, Wimbledon*)	42.2	8	123	15	6-20	8.20
9	F. S. Landa (*Trent College*)	89.4	10	201	24	5-47	8.37
10	I. Ahmed (*John Lyon School*)	31.3	3	127	15	3-1	8.46
11	A. S. Vydianath (*King Edward's School, Birmingham*)	43.5	3	189	22	7-11	8.59
12	J. M. Coles (*Magdalen College School*)	70	18	175	20	6-29	8.75
	E. R. Payne-Cooke (*Haileybury Girls*)	26	2	105	12	4-16	8.75
14	M. M. Allen (*Haileybury Girls*)	25.3	4	99	11	3-9	9.00
15	A. S. Padki (*Haberdashers' Boys' School*)	112.2	27	255	28	5-34	9.10
16	S. G. Kirk (*Wellingborough School*)	29	4	101	11	3-10	9.18
17	Y. Patel (*John Lyon School*)	22	1	104	11	3-6	9.45
18	B. A. G. Higton (*Marlborough College*)	111.2	17	345	35	5-5	9.85
19	R. Kundaje (*Stamford School*)	109	14	300	30	7-45	10.00
	A. M. Vaughan (*Millfield School*)	31	3	120	12	2-7	10.00
21	R. K. Randev (*Merchant Taylors' School, Northwood*) .	20.4	5	102	10	6-12	10.20
22	J. A. Liddle (*King's School, Chester*)	44	6	184	18	3-6	10.22
23	S. G. L. Kanakala (*RGS, Newcastle*)	71	7	211	20	5-20	10.55
24	S. F. Hall (*Skinners' School*)	24.0	0	129	12	4-18	10.75
25	B. J. Schofield (*Lancaster RGS*)	64	17	183	17	5-15	10.76
26	L. Pearson-Taylor (*Millfield School*)	32	2	142	13	3-19	10.92

MOST WICKETS

		O	M	R	W	BB	Avge
1	G. P. le H. Weldon (*Eton College*)	165	32	473	46	5-27	10.28
2	Y. Majid (*Cranleigh School*)	154.3	45	332	42	8-15	7.90
3	H. D. Jackson (*Epsom College*)	137	10	539	40	5-25	13.47
4	H. L. Seagrave (*Haileybury*)	142.4	12	543	39	5-12	13.92
5	E. S. J. Hilditch (*Eton College*)	181	27	558	38	5-26	14.68
6	B. A. G. Higton (*Marlborough College*)	111.2	17	345	35	5-5	9.85
7	J. Nash (*Gresham's School*)	135.3	21	482	34	5-8	14.17
8	A. T. Drew (*Hurstpierpoint College*)	107.1	13	486	33	6-23	14.72
	A. C. Beagles (*Eton College*)	162.2	36	522	33	4-24	15.81
10	R. Kundaje (*Stamford School*)	109	14	300	30	7-45	10.00
	S. Brown (*St Edward's School, Oxford*)	122.4	11	450	30	4-24	15.00
	J. P. W. O'Connor (*Felsted School*)	97	7	431	29	4-11	14.86
	A. J. Gallimore (*Shrewsbury School*)	114	15	432	29	5-13	14.89
12	B. James (*Epsom College*)	127	11	464	29	5-24	16.00
	M. Ndlela (*Gresham's School*)	110	19	470	29	4-14	16.20
	L. D. Hart (*Gresham's School*)	131.3	17	610	29	5-27	21.03
	R. J. Noble (*Stowe School*)	108	5	615	29	6-45	21.20
18	A. S. Padki (*Haberdashers' Boys' School*)	112.2	27	255	28	5-34	9.10
	J. P. Cronie (*Stowe School*)	89.5	11	330	28	5-25	11.78
	B. N. Sheopuri (*Harrow School*)	122.1	16	459	28	7-52	16.39
	J. A. Blackburn (*Worksop College*)	122	5	513	28	4-36	18.32
	J. E. Dickenson (*Malvern College*)	96.1	2	513	28	3-16	18.32
23	B. Hildebrand (*Epsom College*)	95.1	2	448	27	5-30	16.59
	J. O. Baker (*Malvern College*)	99	12	390	27	3-16	14.44

OUTSTANDING SEASONS (minimum 6 matches)

	P	W	L	T	D	A	%W
Blundell's School	15	14	0	1	0	0	93.33
Solihull School	7	6	1	0	0	3	85.71
Bromsgrove School	6	5	1	0	0	12	83.33
Queen Elizabeth's Hospital, Bristol	6	5	0	1	0	8	83.33
Tonbridge School	22	18	2	0	2	0	81.82
Hampton School	16	13	3	0	0	1	81.25
Stowe School	21	17	2	0	2	0	80.95
John Lyon School	10	8	1	0	1	4	80.00
King's College, Taunton	15	12	3	0	0	6	80.00
Wellingborough School	9	7	2	0	0	3	77.78
Eton College	21	16	4	0	1	1	76.19
RGS Newcastle	8	6	2	0	0	0	75.00
RGS Guildford	11	8	3	0	0	1	72.73
St Edward's School, Oxford (Boys)	22	16	4	0	2	1	72.73
Malvern College	22	16	6	0	0	0	72.73
Llandaff Cathedral School	7	5	2	0	0	3	71.43
Marlborough College (Boys)	17	12	5	0	0	1	70.59
Simon Langton School for Boys	10	7	3	0	0	0	70.00

*Glasgow HS (100%), Oundle School (Girls) (100%) and St Edward's School, Oxford (Girls) (75%)
would have qualified for this table had they played sufficient matches.*

SCHOOLS A–Z

In the results line, A = abandoned without a ball bowled. An asterisk indicates captain. The qualification for the averages (which include Twenty20, but not overseas tour games) is 150 runs or ten wickets. Counties have been included for all schools. Since cricket does not follow the current complex system of administrative division, *Wisden* adheres to the county boundaries in existence before the dissolution of Middlesex in 1965. Schools affected by those and subsequent boundary changes – such as Eton College, which was removed from Buckinghamshire and handed to Berkshire – are listed under their former county.

Abingdon School *Berkshire*
P11 W7 L3 D1 A3

Master i/c J. M. Golding   **Coach** Dr C. J. Burnand

The long-awaited season began with an excellent victory over Berkhamsted, when Liam Hilditch hit an outstanding century. Momentum, though, was dissipated by the weather, even if there were memorable performances from Freddie Smith, who led the way with the bat, and Freddie Merrett, who took a fine hat-trick against MCC, and spearheaded the bowling.
Batting C. X. C. Mannix 241 at 120.50; *F. E. H. Smith 397 at 49.62; L. M. Hilditch 238 at 39.66.
Bowling R. J. J. King 12 at 10.17; F. J. K. Merrett 15 at 15.53.

Aldenham School *Hertfordshire*
P6 W3 L2 D1

Master i/c J. A. Coleman   **Coach** D. J. Goodchild

In a curtailed season, Aldenham played good cricket across limited-overs and declaration formats. The highlight was chasing 283 to beat the John Dewes Memorial XI, with captain Viren Patel scoring 120 not out.
Batting *V. Patel 190 at 190.00; J. Seimon 206 at 41.20.
Bowling The leading bowler was T. Francis, who took nine wickets at 17.67.

Alleyn's School *Surrey*
P10 W5 L4 D1 A1

Master i/c R. N. Ody   **Coach** P. D. Bone

It was wonderful to play ten matches, all after half-term. The first team shared the London Schools' cup final with Westminster. A committed band of Year 13s were brilliantly led by co-captains Josh Shattock and Abe Wood.
Batting *A. B. Wood 273 at 39.00; *J. J. Shattock 178 at 22.25; L. M. Stylianou 198 at 22.00.
Bowling E. P. Marshall 11 at 19.00; A. B. Wood 11 at 19.64.

Alex Davidson, ECB/Getty Images

Bedford's wicketkeeper Charlie Mumford averaged almost 50; Tom Prest, from Canford, played for Hampshire on T20 finals day.

Bedford School *Bedfordshire*
P12 W7 L5

Master i/c I. G. S. Steer   **Coach** T. Brett

Bedford had a steady season, and results improved once fifth-form boys were included. The highlight was an excellent win at Eton, while the outstanding player was keeper-batsman Charlie Mumford.

Batting C. S. Mumford 540 at 49.09; A. R. Chandrapu 161 at 32.20; A. W. Houghton 283 at 31.44; *H. J. Warren 169 at 18.77; R. S. Mehmi 173 at 15.72.

Bowling R. S. Mehmi 10 at 14.70; V. Somal 13 at 17.38; A. W. Houghton 16 at 18.94; D. J. Sheemar 13 at 21.67.

Berkhamsted School *Hertfordshire*
P15 W6 L6 D3 A5

Master i/c G. R. A. Campbell   **Coaches** D. J. Gibson and B. R. Mahoney

A young team improved over the summer to record some superb results. Captain Archie Palmer and Charlie Doe excelled with the bat, while spinners Sikandar Rizwan, Ben Oldham and Teddy Fleming led the bowling.

Batting C. A. J. Doe 426 at 35.50; *A. C. Palmer 356 at 29.66; B. J. S. Oldham 258 at 23.45; R. J. Treadwell 150 at 12.50.

Bowling B. J. S. Oldham 17 at 17.35; S. A. Rizwan 20 at 17.45; B. J. Miles 10 at 17.80; T. J. Fleming 17 at 19.82; C. O. Barrett 11 at 20.64.

Bishop's Stortford College *Hertfordshire*
P4 L4

Master i/c N. D. Hughes   **Coach** D. J. Clutterbuck

In what were a challenging couple of years, there were only four matches, but the team were superbly captained by William Cutlan-Smyth, who batted well, and was ably supported by Thomas Howes.

Batting The leading batter was T. D. Howes, who hit 88 runs at 22.00.

Bowling The leading bowler was T. D. Howes, who took six wickets at 24.17.

Bloxham School *Oxfordshire*
P14 W4 L9 D1 A5

Master i/c G. N. Webber   **Coach** R. S. Lovering

The school had a tough fixture list, but a young side did well. Highlights included an excellent draw against MCC, and convincing wins over South Oxford Amateurs, Bedford Modern and Old Bloxhamists. The outstanding cricketer was Ben England.

Batting J. B. England 290 at 36.25; J. Gurney 250 at 22.72; *G. King 182 at 16.54.

Bowling A. Maginnis 11 at 26.45; J. B. England 11 at 28.27.

Blundell's School *Devon*
P15 W14 T1

Master i/c L. J. Lewis

The first team had their best season for many years, and went unbeaten in 15 matches; a tie was the only (slight) hiccup. They were capably led by Joseph du'Gay, who averaged 96 with the bat.

Batting J. J. du'Gay 576 at 96.00; E. J. Carter 165 at 41.25; T. J. Hatton 265 at 37.85; S. J. Broomhead 262 at 32.75; T. C. A. Reynolds 279 at 27.90; H. D. S. Southgate 194 at 27.71; W. J. Bucknell 313 at 26.08.

Bowling T. D. Murphy 23 at 13.35; B. M. Coen 20 at 14.05; T. J. Hatton 23 at 14.57; T. P. Dos Santos 21 at 14.62; T. C. A. Reynolds 13 at 21.15.

Bradfield College (Boys) *Berkshire*
P21 W13 L5 D3 A3

Master i/c M. S. Hill
Coaches J. R. Wood and C. P. Ellison

Bradfield College (Girls) *Berkshire*
P9 W5 L3 D1 A2

Master i/c M. S. Hill
Coaches P. J. Clegg and C. C. Doherty

Captain Sheridon Gumbs's 154 not out against MCC was the champagne moment of a successful and enjoyable season. Most impressive was the way this group of players raised the profile of cricket at Bradfield: a real Covid bounceback. A young girls' team benefited from the encouraging leadership of Year 13 Fionnhuala Davies, who in turn was supported by Emma Seligman and Rosie Talbot. Outstanding performances came from Ava Lee and Poppy Tulloch, both in Year 10.

Batting (boys) *S. S. E. Gumbs 589 at 65.44; Z. B. Lion-Cachet 295 at 36.87; S. W. Negus 293 at 32.55; J. M. Sheldon 360 at 27.69; C. J. Keyes 261 at 18.64; L. R. Pincus 154 at 17.11; M. J. Layton 155 at 14.09.

Bowling (boys) J. H. Rank 17 at 16.41; M. W. A. McKenzie 26 at 20.04; O. R. Pincus 11 at 23.18; M. J. Layton 16 at 23.50; B. C. Armstrong 11 at 24.36.

Batting (girls) A. G. Lee 292 at 58.40; P. G. Tulloch 216 at 36.00.

Bowling (girls) The leading bowler was A. G. Lee, who took nine wickets at 9.78.

Brentwood School *Essex*
P11 W6 L4 T1 A2

Master i/c O. C. Prior
Coach J. C. Mickleburgh

After a disrupted beginning, the season included a tie against Felsted – Callum Balsom hit 64 – and a final-ball defeat by Ipswich, when Jack Levy made 54. James Abbott scored 82 in a ten-wicket victory against Bancroft's, while Surya James reached three figures against Old Brentwoods. The team took part in a small 100-ball festival, when James hit an unbeaten 81 on his last appearance.

Batting S. James 377 at 75.40; T. V. Don Balage 356 at 35.60; *J. S. Levy 249 at 31.12; C. Balsom 266 at 29.55.

Bowling J. D. Abbott 14 at 14.50.

Bromsgrove School *Worcestershire*
P6 W5 L1 A12

Master i/c D. J. Fallows
Coach K. Evenson

A frustrating season contained just six games, and only one was a 50-over contest. There were, though, strong performances by Freddie Fallows with the ball, and Tom Cosh with the bat. The Under-15s won the county final, against Malvern, thanks in part to Lucas Ingram; the Under-17s reached their national quarter-finals. Oliver Davidson has represented Scotland, and Fallows has a place at the Leicestershire CCC Academy.

Batting T. R. J. Cosh 166 at 83.00.

Bowling F. Fallows 12 at 8.67.

Bryanston School *Dorset*
P14 W6 L7 D1 A7

Master i/c S. D. Morris
Coaches R. J. Scott and C. G. D. Carmichael

The school played stylish cricket when the weather allowed, reaching the Dorset 100-ball final in May, and accumulating several convincing victories in June. The highlight was bowling out the Old Boys for 73 before lunch (following dramatic defeats in 2018 and 2019).

Batting F. S. Young 214 at 21.40; *J. N. Castleton 200 at 20.00; H. D. H. Hartley 195 at 19.50; T. B. Johnson 153 at 17.00.

Bowling F. S. Young 18 at 14.89; J. L. Hartley 10 at 20.10; S. A. I. Macdonald 10 at 22.40.

Caterham School *Surrey*
P8 W3 L4 D1 A4

Master i/c J. N. Batty

Caterham were well led by Ben Haynes, winning matches against Reigate, Alleyn's and Sevenoaks. All-rounder Nathan Barnwell was the outstanding player, and there were excellent contributions from Jonny Naylor and Freddie Knox.

Batting N. Barnwell 289 at 41.28; J. Naylor 179 at 35.80; *B. Haynes 190 at 27.14; F. Knox 162 at 23.14.

Bowling N. Barnwell 11 at 18.91.

Charterhouse *Surrey* P11 W5 L6 A6
Master i/c M. P. Bicknell
Rain and Covid made this a tough year. Ayush Patel and Freddie Clinton batted superbly, and were supported by Sam Thomas. Luke Griffiths, aged 15, led the attack well, while Jonty Postlewhite bowled off-spin with great skill.
Batting *A. A. Patel 547 at 45.58; F. Clinton 626 at 44.71; S. N. S. Thomas 330 at 27.50; J. W. Postlewhite 235 at 23.50; J. R. Kher 224 at 17.23.
Bowling J. A. Burns 14 at 15.57; A. A. Patel 16 at 15.63; J. W. Postlewhite 22 at 19.09; L. A. Griffiths 22 at 20.95; F. Clinton 15 at 26.20.

Cheltenham College *Gloucestershire* P12 W5 L6 D1 A2
Master i/c M. K. Coley **Coach** M. P. Briers
In a mixed season there were notable wins over Radley College, Free Foresters and MCC, when Will Taylor scored 110 not out. Will Blowers claimed 16 wickets with his off-spin, including 5-77 against Rugby.
Batting W. G. I. Taylor 343 at 38.11; O. I. Elliott 294 at 26.72; *Z. J. French 247 at 22.45; T. L. I. Nicholson 161 at 17.88.
Bowling E. L. M. Buttress 14 at 21.57; W. R. G. Blowers 16 at 25.06.

Chigwell School *Essex* P8 W4 L4 A6
Master i/c F. A. Griffith **Coach** Mohammad Akhtar
Ben Kearin showed great leadership skills and played several wonderful innings, though the only hundred came from Haaris Usman. There were fine bowling performances from Usman, Dominic Tunks, Aditya Singh and Ben Copsey; others chipped in. The highlight of the season was victory against MCC – a superb team performance.
Batting *B. H. P. Kearin 405 at 67.50; H. Usman 369 at 61.50; G. Nair 193 at 24.12.
Bowling D. Tunks 10 at 13.60; H. Usman 11 at 13.91.

Chislehurst & Sidcup Grammar School *Kent* P4 W1 L1 D2 A5
Master i/c R. A. Wallbridge **Coach** D. F. J. Hathrill
The school were admirably led by Seb Naylor, who topped the batting; Oli Smith's off-spin proved useful too. The weather and the pandemic reduced opportunities, though a rare, hard-fought draw with MCC was a reminder of the joy of school cricket.
Batting The leading batter was *S. R. G. Naylor, who hit 90 runs at 30.00.
Bowling The leading bowler was O. V. C. Smith, who took seven wickets at 12.14.

Christ's Hospital *Sussex* P7 W1 L6 A2
Master i/c D. H. Messenger **Coach** T. E. Jesty
A young squad struggled on their return to cricket after half-term. However, captain Louis Cooper batted well, while between them Max Hughes and Nick Kinnear claimed more than half the wickets.
Batting *G. L. Cooper 165 at 27.50.
Bowling M. Hughes 8 at 13.25.

Churcher's College *Hampshire* P8 W4 L4 A7
Master i/c R. Maier
Churcher's College were thrilled to be back on the field – and competing in the National T20 tournament for the first time was a highlight.
Batting J. D. Oliver 175 at 29.16.
Bowling The leading bowler was F. Brockwell, who took five wickets at 6.00.

Claysmore School *Dorset* P11 W4 L5 D2
Master i/c D. O. Conway
With the welcome reintroduction of fixtures, the boys were eager to go. Cricket week proved the most successful of recent years, and this group of players have great potential.
Batting W. Tripcony 248 at 31.00; J. G. Parsons 272 at 27.20.
Bowling E. A. L. Rimmer 10 at 13.50; *T. R. H. Berry 11 at 14.91.

Clifton College *Gloucestershire* P13 W9 L4 A9
Master i/c J. C. Bobby **Coach** J. R. A. Williams
One positive of the pandemic has been schools cricket in September, and it was great to have a full programme after losing all the 2020 season. The first team – ably led by Ollie Meadows – proved a talented squad and played excellent cricket. Only three have left, so there is optimism for 2022, which will again see games in September.

Batting B. I. Kellaway 347 at 57.83; *O. J. Meadows 423 at 47.00; J. P. Phillips 218 at 36.33; S. P. Sainsbury 322 at 32.20; W. Naish 210 at 30.00.
Bowling B. I. Kellaway 14 at 14.07; H. N. Saleem 10 at 16.20; W. Naish 12 at 18.58.

Colston's School *Gloucestershire*
P7 W2 L5

Master i/c L. M. Evans
Coach P. M. Muchall

After seemingly endless disruption, it was refreshing to see cricket again. Although results weren't always favourable, the future looks encouraging: most of the side should be available for 2022.
Batting D. G. M. Broome 262 at 43.66.
Bowling E. R. Dryell 12 at 15.08.

Cranleigh School *Surrey*
P9 W4 L2 D3 A7

Master i/c A. P. Forsdike
Coaches S. D. Welch and G. V. Pritchard

Having lost the early season to Covid, the first team packed matches into the second half of term. Slow left-armer Yousef Majid stood out, taking 42 wickets in nine games. Tom Lawes proved a capable captain.
Batting S. S. D. Shanmugavel 263 at 29.22; L. La Costa 261 at 29.00; *T. E. Lawes 213 at 21.30; W. S. B. Bovill 179 at 17.90.
Bowling Y. Majid 42 at 7.90; T. E. Lawes 10 at 13.90.

Dauntsey's School *Wiltshire*
P12 W6 L6 A4

Master i/c T. W. Butterworth

This was a positive summer for a side in transition, despite the challenging circumstances caused by the weather and pandemic. The team progressed, with satisfying performances later in the season including a good win against MCC.
Batting *R. Glover 261 at 29.00; T. Spencer 277 at 25.18; H. E. H. Barker 219 at 24.33; W. J. Hyde 159 at 14.15.
Bowling A. T. D. R. Richardson 15 at 16.00; C. J. Hodgson 13 at 16.69; W. J. Hyde 10 at 21.50; H. E. H. Barker 11 at 27.09.

Denstone College *Staffordshire*
P8 W2 L5 D1 A9

Master i/c S. M. Guy
Coach C. J. Prosser

This was a challenging season. Many fixtures were cancelled because of the weather or Covid but, when the opportunity arose, the team embraced the chance for a proper game of cricket with open arms, from Twenty20 to two days – and much in between.
Batting H. W. H. Mountford 186 at 62.00; W. C. Alsbury 171 at 34.20; W. J. Rhodes 152 at 25.33; *G. I. Park 165 at 23.57.
Bowling W. J. Rhodes 13 at 16.62; G. I. Park 10 at 20.10; R. B. Hughes 10 at 23.30.

Dr Challoner's Grammar School *Buckinghamshire*
P8 W5 L3 A2

Master i/c N. J. S. Buchanan

Dr Challoner's enjoyed a good season, and the side were intelligently led by Theo Weatherall. Runs and wickets came from all players, leading to several good victories. Hannah Davis and Eva Barrett became the first girls to represent the school at cricket, and performed with distinction.
Batting *T. G. Weatherall 234 at 46.80; J. P. Tollerfield 172 at 34.40; T. W. Whittington 165 at 23.57.
Bowling The leading bowler was D. Malhi, who took nine wickets at 11.67.

Dover College *Kent*
P10 W3 L6 T1 A3

Master i/c J. R. Payne
Coach E. O. Breeze

After such a long absence, it was wonderful to have cricket again, with senior pupils James Hide and Harvey Mashiter-Yates excelling in their final year. Most games were settled by fine margins, rarely in our favour. The squad contained many young pupils, who will have learned from the experience.
Batting *J. S. Hide 196 at 24.50.
Bowling H. Mashiter-Yates 11 at 20.00.

Downside School *Somerset*
P13 W2 L11 A4

Master i/c G. E. Setterfield

A young Downside first team benefited from a season of learning experiences. The squad fought hard in competitive fixtures against strong opposition, and were a credit to the school in both red-and pink-ball games; they seem well set for 2022.
Batting N. C. Viljoen 329 at 29.90; L. M. D. Matthews 151 at 25.16; *L. Hansom 151 at 15.10.
Bowling J. C. Last-Sutton 15 at 14.47; H. D. R. Clark 12 at 19.50.

Dulwich College *Surrey*
P15 W4 L9 D2 A3

Master i/c R. G. Coughtrie
Coach A. E. N. Riley

Mikyle Ossman captained the First XI admirably. Wet weather made for helpful seam conditions, and Toby Kemp and Magnus Broadley exploited them superbly. Exciting prospects suggest future seasons may bring success.

Batting *M. S. M. Ossman 252 at 21.00; J. D. Reisser-Weston 167 at 11.92.
Bowling T. W. Kemp 22 at 14.55; M. B. H. Broadley 16 at 19.06; M. S. M. Ossman 11 at 23.64.

Durham School *County Durham*
P4 W1 L3 A11

Master i/c M. B. Fishwick

Plenty of planning and much optimism for a full season sadly led to just four fixtures: Barnard Castle, RGS Newcastle, MCC and Durham U-17s. All were competitive games. The young talent should make further progress in 2022.

Batting D. M. Hogg 171 at 57.00.
Bowling The leading bowler was C. J. Brown, who took eight wickets at 17.13.

Eastbourne College *Sussex*
P13 W8 L4 D1 A5

Master i/c R. S. Ferley
Coach J. C. Tredwell

This proved a promising year in both 50- and 20-over cricket, with the boys showing a great attitude in an interrupted season. Tom Hinley batted magnificently, playing some great innings.

Batting *T. Hinley 665 at 83.12; J. C. Bradley 184 at 61.33; W. T. C. Chambers 204 at 34.00; *O. H. Streets 234 at 33.42; T. R. Lock 165 at 20.62.
Bowling A. Kent 10 at 5.10; E. Bawa 13 at 17.77; N. James 10 at 19.90; T. Hinley 13 at 26.08.

The Edinburgh Academy *Midlothian*
P10 W5 L4 D1 A4

Master i/c R. W. Sales
Coach A. D. W. Patterson

The Academy had a mixed summer, which started well before petering out. The young side kept at it during the short season, and will benefit from more fixtures (and a tour to Barbados). Notable performances included a draw against a strong MCC side and twice beating local rivals George Watson's and Stewart's Melville.

Batting B. D. Murray 232 at 46.40; W. S. A. Hood 167 at 20.87; W. Hodgson 182 at 20.22.
Bowling W. S. A. Hood 10 at 18.60; A. T. B. Stirling 10 at 19.60; R. L. Duff 10 at 22.60; C. A. S. Lamond 10 at 23.50.

Elizabeth College, Guernsey *Channel Islands*
P16 W11 L3 D2

Master i/c T. P. Eisenhuth
Coach L. B. Ferbrache

Ben Ferbrache proved a highly capable leader, consistently drawing the best from his team.

Batting C. R. W. Birch 377 at 47.12; P. W. Birch 273 at 34.12; M. K. Thomas 208 at 29.71; C. G. Clapham 188 at 26.85; M. J. M. Clayon 267 at 19.07.
Bowling O. F. Clapham 21 at 17.62; L. Steyn 16 at 18.19; B. E. Johnson 15 at 24.07.

Ellesmere College *Shropshire*
P6 W1 L5 A6

Master i/c G. Owen
Coach R. Jones

Cricket eventually resumed at half-term. The aim was to re-establish the game (and its wider culture) after so long an absence. A young squad, made up from four year-groups and just one Year 13, developed well; all the games proved to be competitive.

Batting The leading batter was O. R. W. Moore, who hit 140 runs at 23.33.
Bowling The leading bowler was W. G. Owen, who took seven wickets at 11.86.

Eltham College *Kent*
P10 W4 L6 A5

Master i/c J. L. Baldwin
Coach Yasir Arafat

Fixtures did not start until June because of the pandemic, but there was still time for good wins against Judd, Colfe's and Caterham. Joseph Bilsby captained excellently, contributing with bat and ball. Under-14 student Akhil Venugopalan made an impact, and looks one for the future.

Batting B. M. N. Mirchandani 301 at 50.16; C. L. Smith 153 at 30.60; R. Taraq 171 at 28.50; *J. P. J. Bilsby 164 at 27.33; R. Parikh 151 at 25.16.
Bowling B. J. Davis 10 at 17.40.

Emanuel School *Surrey*
P16 W3 L11 D2 A2

Master i/c C. M. Booth
Coach M. G. Stear

A season aimed at providing as much cricket as possible was a clear success: there were 16 games, with 20 students representing the First XI or Senior XI. Highlights included wins against London Oratory and Kingston Grammar, and it was a delight to welcome MCC back. In a difficult time for

Harry Gallian totted up 1,107 runs for Felsted, while Cranleigh's Yousef Majid claimed 42 wickets.

all players, wicketkeeper Luke Johnstone hit two half-centuries; captain Billy Hughes – a fine all-rounder – and Ben Winnick led the bowling with ten wickets, while Ethan Wirasinha took nine.
Batting L. D. Johnston 201 at 25.12.
Bowling B. T. Winnick 10 at 19.30; *B. Hughes 10 at 22.70.

Epsom College *Surrey*
P22 W15 L4 D3 A2
Master i/c D. C. Shirazi   **Coach** S. A. Whatling
Epsom had a busy and successful summer. They were superbly led by Brandon James, who combined almost 600 runs with 29 wickets. Ben Garrett was a strong performer at the top of the order, while Brendan Hildebrand proved a talented all-rounder. Many return for 2022.
Batting B. G. G. Garrett 739 at 61.58; *B. M. James 592 at 49.33; B. Hildebrand 696 at 38.66; W. Hodgson 384 at 34.90; T. Lynagh 270 at 20.76.
Bowling H. D. Jackson 40 at 13.48; K. Jain 18 at 14.11; B. M. James 29 at 16.00; B. Hildebrand 27 at 16.59; O. H. King 20 at 20.60.

Eton College *Buckinghamshire*
P21 W16 L4 D1 A1
Master i/c T. W. Roberts   **Coach** R. R. Montgomerie
Eton completed 21 matches, despite pandemic and weather. Unbeaten until half-term, they benefited from a potent seam attack led by George Weldon (46 wickets) and captain Angus Beagles (33). Off-spinner Edward Hilditch also took 38. Few sides made 200 against Eton, hastening victory in overs and declaration matches. Openers George Freeman and James Weir both hit more than 700 runs.
Batting G. T. Freeman 766 at 40.31; J. G. Weir 715 at 39.72; C. D. D. Whipple 495 at 29.11; M. R. L. Russell 467 at 27.47; M. J. J. Glyn 320 at 24.61; *A. C. Beagles 278 at 23.16; G. P. L. Weldon 177 at 22.12; O. C. A. Stone 155 at 9.68.
Bowling G. P. L. Weldon 46 at 10.28; E. S. J. Hilditch 38 at 14.68; A. C. Beagles 33 at 15.82; A. M. Varma 21 at 21.57; O. C. A. Stone 13 at 28.77; F. H. Catherwood 18 at 29.94.

Felsted School *Essex*
P16 W10 L5 T1 A1
Master i/c J. E. R. Gallian   **Coaches** C. S. Knightley, A. Mohindru and N. J. Lockhart
The First XI's excellent season brought many good victories, and they reached the last 16 of the National T20 Independent Schools tournament. The leading batsman was Harry Gallian, with 1,107 runs. Josh O'Connor was an astute captain, and also the leading wicket-taker, with 29.
Batting H. G. R. Gallian 1,107 at 85.15; W. G. B. Forsey 275 at 34.38; D. T. Karr 313 at 22.36; O. G. Dias 168 at 16.80; H. M. W. Wiseman 180 at 15.00; F. P. F. Latham 181 at 13.92.
Bowling *J. P. W. O'Connor 29 at 14.86; O. G. Dias 16 at 19.31; H. G. R. Gallian 14 at 20.93; A. M. L. Murphy 18 at 22.89; K. A. Morley-Jacob 15 at 29.13; H. Peddy 10 at 32.60.

Fettes College *Midlothian*

P7 W1 L5 D1 A2

Master i/c A. B. Russell   **Coach** J. Dickinson

Perhaps unsurprisingly, given the circumstances, this proved a difficult season. The few games that were played were all in short format, and – despite plenty of endeavour – the batters struggled to score quickly enough.

Batting M. C. F. Hughson 163 at 27.16.

Bowling The leading bowler was *O. J. Norton, who took six wickets at 14.00.

Forest School *Essex*

P19 W12 L7

Master i/c J. F. Perham   **Coach** J. Ormsby

Cricket is now a major sport for both boys (320) and girls (160). Our girls have developed their skills, and now compete weekly, making it through to the last 16 and eight of their national competitions. Forest now have 18 county representatives – a robust cricketing culture.

Batting A. S. Aiyar 416 at 34.66; J. G. Feather 474 at 31.60; P. G. Miller 162 at 23.14; T. J. Bentley 194 at 21.55; H. J. Sewell 291 at 19.40; S. F. Miller 189 at 17.18.

Bowling A. S. Rashid 15 at 11.80; T. J. Bentley 25 at 12.20; K. A. Arawawwala 21 at 13.19; J. J. Kathuria 16 at 15.06; P. G. Miller 17 at 15.76.

Framlingham College *Suffolk*

P15 W6 L9 A2

Master i/c C. D. Gange

Given the previous 18 months, the quality and volume of fixtures came as a delight. Huge credit goes to all squad members for their commitment in a challenging period. Year 11 all-rounder Jayden Borges, and batters Will White and Henry Bevan (both Year 13), made significant contributions.

Batting J. O. K. Borges 596 at 45.84; L. C. Francis-Smith 255 at 19.61; *H. T. J. Bevan 239 at 18.38; B. C. Farrant 240 at 17.14; F. J. H. Royall 163 at 16.30; W. H. White 184 at 12.26.

Bowling J. O. K. Borges 21 at 13.43; B. Sunderland 12 at 18.00; H. T. J. Bevan 19 at 18.32; W. H. White 24 at 20.63; J. C. W. Bishopp 11 at 25.00.

Giggleswick School *Yorkshire*

P1 L1 A2

Master i/c A. J. Galley   **Coach** A. S. Silva

With Covid and the weather curtailing the season, the school resorted largely to internal matches. The only external fixture to survive was against RGS Lancaster where, despite an aggressive 65 from Barney Wood, the first team were defeated by six wickets.

Batting The leading batter was B. C. Wood, who hit 65 runs at 65.00.

Bowling The leading bowler was M. Seddon, who took two wickets at 12.00.

The Glasgow Academy *Lanarkshire*

P2 W1 L1 A3

Master i/c V. Hariharan

After a blank 2020, there was a glimmer of hope in 2021. Five fixtures were arranged, but travel restrictions and isolation issues allowed only two T20 fixtures against local schools, High School of Glasgow and Kelvinside Academy. With high participation levels, there is plenty of hope for 2022.

Batting A. R. Harden 34 at 17.00.

Bowling B. G. Thomson 2 at 5.00.

The High School of Glasgow *Lanarkshire*

P3 W3

Master i/c S. C. Leggat   **Coach** K. J. A. Robertson

In a disrupted season, the school played only three games – but won them all. The young team benefited from excellent performances from Ibrahim Faisal and Chris Collins with the bat, and Akshat Gupta and Faisal with the ball.

Batting The leading batter was I. Faisal, who hit 141 runs at 47.00.

Bowling The leading bowler was A. Gupta, who took six wickets at 4.83.

Gordonstoun School *Morayshire*

P2 L2

Master i/c R. Denyer   **Coach** R. S. Glen

A frustrating summer saw few games and few senior participants. There were, though, positives in the number of junior students enjoying cricket, and the emphasis is now on rebuilding.

Batting The leading batter was H. G. Diggle, who hit 84 runs at 42.00.

Bowling The leading bowler was A. H. Goldring.

Danyaal Khalid was in prolific early-season form for Haileybury; Johnny Connell hit three hundreds for Harrow.

Gresham's School *Norfolk*   P25 W12 L10 T1 D2

Master i/c D. J. Atkinson   **Coach** C. Brown

The school had an outstanding 2021: the Under-16s won the Midland section of the National Cup, and the Under-15 boys reached the regional finals day. The first team's season was disrupted by Covid and the weather, but they still managed 25 games. Joe Nash led the attack, and the Ndlela – Sakhumuzi and Mgcinumuzi – brothers managed the batting.

Batting E. A. E. Hart 402 at 33.50; *S. Ndlela 499 at 33.26; C. G. Hood 392 at 32.66; A. Jones 416 at 27.73; M. Ndlela 482 at 26.77; *B. A. Wilcox 315 at 21.00; H. W. Nunn 277 at 19.78; L. D. Hart 188 at 11.75.

Bowling J. Nash 34 at 14.18; H. J. Adams 11 at 14.82; M. Ndlela 29 at 16.21; H. J. Seagon 12 at 17.58; L. D. Hart 29 at 21.03; S. Ndlela 23 at 25.17; F. O. Lowe 13 at 27.69.

The Haberdashers' Boys' School *Hertfordshire*   P13 W8 L2 D3 A5

Master i/c D. H. Kerry

An excellent season saw the school play competitive, high-standard cricket. The highlights were a six-wicket win against St Albans in a two-day game that went to the last over – Ashish Padki took 10-70 in the match – and a convincing 117-run victory over Merchant Taylors'.

Batting J. S. Madan 308 at 51.33; C. Mullapudi 321 at 35.66; J. E. J. Cobb 378 at 34.36; S. J. Singh 292 at 26.54; N. Shah 168 at 21.00; K. V. Patel 159 at 19.87.

Bowling A. S. Padki 28 at 9.11; *J. P. Granger 10 at 12.40; M. Muralitharan 13 at 14.46; Z. A. Kureshi 18 at 15.72; K. F. J. Dubignon 10 at 21.70; C. Mullapudi 11 at 22.91.

Haileybury (Boys) *Hertfordshire*   P22 W14 L6 D2 A13
Haileybury (Girls) *Hertfordshire*   P7 W2 L5 A9

Master i/c R. C. Kitzinger   **Coach** C. E. Igolen-Robinson

Fixtures began in September 2020, and the team were superbly captained by wicketkeeper-batsman Bill Meacock. Danyaal Khalid scored 440 runs in the first two weeks of May, while all-rounders Ben Spencer, Harry Seagrave, Leighton Gibbs and Dylan van der Westhuizen contributed heavily to a successful summer. The girls were well led by opening bowler Ella Payne-Cook, whose pace and bounce were complemented by Tilly Allen's swing. Hillary Hawthorne batted well, but – in a young side – often ran out of partners.

Batting (boys) *W. G. Meacock 714 at 54.92; D. Khalid 854 at 50.23; D. van der Westhuizen 526 at 23.90; B. T. Spencer 286 at 23.83; H. L. Seagrave 223 at 20.27; L. E. Gibbs 264 at 17.60; K. F. Forbes-Sobers 201 at 14.35.
Bowling (boys) H. L. Seagrave 39 at 13.92; B. T. Spencer 23 at 17.04; A. B. Wells 10 at 20.00; T. Wrigley 21 at 22.81; D. van der Westhuizen 11 at 32.36.
Batting (girls) The leading batter was H. J. Hawthorne, who hit 133 runs at 26.60.
Bowling (girls) E. R. Payne-Cooke 12 at 8.75; M. M. Allen 11 at 9.00.

Hampton School *Middlesex*

Master i/c A. M. Banerjee
P16 W13 L3 A1
Coach C. P. Harrison

Hampton enjoyed another excellent season, which included games in September 2020. An outstanding performance by Tanmay Thanawalla, who scored 816 runs, was backed up by Eddie Bruce's 601 and captain Matthew Avant-Smith's 520. Avant-Smith, Pravin Kiritharan and Kyle Shah led the attack.
Batting T. R. Thanawalla 816 at 54.40; E. B. Bruce 601 at 42.92; A. R. Bhat 501 at 35.78; *M. Avant-Smith 520 at 32.50; P. D. Kiritharan 350 at 31.81; M. H. Ford 301 at 27.36.
Bowling K. A. Seth 24 at 11.96; P. D. Kiritharan 26 at 12.62; T. J. Gallatley 10 at 14.10; A. H. Simonds-Gooding 10 at 17.20; A. V. Zotov 12 at 18.92; M. Avant-Smith 16 at 19.56.

Harrow School *Middlesex*

Master i/c J. Marsden
P17 W10 L5 D2 A4
Coach M. R. Ramprakash

A young Harrow side performed impressively in a challenging summer, with their two-day victory against Oxford University the highlight. They were captained brilliantly by Tej Sheopuri, while Johnny Connell hit three centuries. Brij Sheopuri, Jasper Gray and John Richardson took 70 wickets between them.
Batting J. M. Connell 787 at 52.46; V. R. Patel 449 at 40.81; M. P. Ferreira 317 at 39.62; G. L. Cutler 162 at 32.40; *T. N. Sheopuri 415 at 29.64; C. J. Ellis 280 at 17.50.
Bowling J. T. Nelson 16 at 14.75; B. N. Sheopuri 28 at 16.39; J. L. Gray 22 at 19.59; C. J. Ellis 14 at 23.07; J. Z. R. Richardson 20 at 24.30.

Hurstpierpoint College *Sussex*

Master i/c J. E. Anyon
P22 W14 L7 D1 A2
Coach M. P. Nash

The high point of a successful season for a young side was victory in the Langdale Trophy. Aidan Drew was the leading wicket-taker with 33, and Joe Willis the leading run-scorer with 657. Bertie Foreman and Henry Rogers were selected to represent the South-East at Under-17 and Under-15 respectively.
Batting *A. M. Foreman 415 at 34.58; J. T. P. Willis 657 at 34.57; O. W. Jago-Lewis 532 at 33.25; *F. C. Longley 173 at 24.71; A. T. Drew 232 at 21.09; *O. A. Haines 328 at 17.26.
Bowling C. M. S. Mullins 12 at 12.00; A. T. Drew 33 at 14.73; A. M. Foreman 24 at 20.83; P. M. W. Norton-Smith 11 at 23.18; J. S. Addison 25 at 25.76; O. A. Haines 11 at 35.00.

John Hampden Grammar School *Buckinghamshire*

Master i/c S. K. Parbery
P14 W5 L7 D2 A2

Most of the scheduled fixture list was played, including two festivals and the annual game against MCC. Will Midwinter had an excellent final season, and his 91 not out against RGS High Wycombe secured a memorable victory by two wickets. Year 10 all-rounder Lochie Christopherson and Year 12 opening batsman Will Shurrock also performed consistently.
Batting W. C. S. Midwinter 406 at 40.60; W. Z. Shurrock 243 at 30.38; B. A. Sidders 171 at 21.38.
Bowling C. S. Midwinter 10 at 13.40; L. T. Christopherson 20 at 13.55.

John Lyon School *Middlesex*

Master i/c A. S. Ling
P10 W8 L1 D1 A4
Coach S. H. Cloete

John Lyon had an outstanding summer, losing only once and winning the Under-19 Middlesex Cup for the seventh time, more than any other school. Of the many excellent performances, Kahil Jariwala's 95 v MCC was the most memorable.
Batting Y. Patel 231 at 46.20; K. N. Jariwala 267 at 38.14; A. Sundaram 264 at 37.71.
Bowling I. Ahmed 15 at 8.47; Y. Patel 11 at 9.45; S. Vaid 10 at 12.60; *A. Sutaria 16 at 13.19; R. Raval 10 at 17.30.

The Judd School *Kent*

Master i/c R. M. Richardson
P8 W3 L5 A7
Coach C. K. Dobson

In a difficult year marred by many cancellations, the school still managed eight games. Max Moen proved a capable captain, and was the leading run-scorer; Satvik Vyakarnam took most wickets. There were also promising performances from Ekansh Singh and Angus Hall (Year 10s).
Batting The leading batter was *M. P. Moen, who hit 138 runs at 34.50.
Bowling The leading bowler was S. Vyakarnam, who took seven wickets at 12.43.

Hampton's reliable batsman Tanmay Thanawalla scored 816 runs at 54.

Kimbolton School *Huntingdonshire*   P5 W3 L1 D1 A8
Master i/c M. S. Gilbert   **Coach** A. J. Tudor
A thrilling last-ball victory over a strong MCC XI was a highlight of a short season. Oliver Greenhow showed glimpses of his all-round talent, while the progress of fast bowler Henry Leigh-Smith and wicketkeeper-batsman Ben Rowbotham gives plenty of hope for 2022.
Batting B. Rowbotham 175 at 43.75; *O. J. Greenhow 181 at 36.20.
Bowling H. N. Leigh-Smith 11 at 14.45.

King Edward's School, Birmingham *Warwickshire*   P19 W12 L6 D1 A4
Master i/c L. M. Roll   **Coach** N. W. Round
Playing 19 matches was a triumph for the First XI, and they won a dozen. A coherent blend of four year groups, the team demonstrated the enjoyment of schools cricket.
Batting Y. Khalil 340 at 34.00; P. S. Gajula 338 at 33.80; S. R. Gunarathne 346 at 31.45; D. R. Gandhewar 439 at 27.43; *M. S. Dogra 371 at 23.18; V. V. Iyer 250 at 19.23.
Bowling A. S. Vydianath 22 at 8.59; D. R. Gandhewar 23 at 16.70; P. S. Gajula 17 at 21.00; M. F. Saeed 12 at 22.25; V. V. Iyer 15 at 24.40.

King Edward VI School, Southampton *Hampshire*   P10 W4 L5 D1 A4
Master i/c A. D. Penn
An excellent game against Winchester College ended in defeat, but the outstanding games were wins over Dauntsey's and MCC. Year 11s Kamran Dhariwal and Hamish Croft were the leading performers; Year 9 Charlie Aspinall made a match-winning fifty on debut.
Batting K. S. Dhariwal 305 at 33.88; H. W. M. Croft 152 at 25.33.
Bowling The leading bowler was N. A. M. Damley-Jones, who took seven wickets at 22.71.

King's College, Taunton *Somerset*   P15 W12 L3 A6
Master i/c R. J. Woodman   **Coach** P. D. Lewis
It was a season to be proud of, with many turning out for the first team. King's reached the final of the National T20 competition. In another enjoyable Woodard Cricket Festival, the school hosted Hurstpierpoint, Bloxham, Worksop and MCC.
Batting J. E. Rew 394 at 65.66; H. Smeed 390 at 39.00; G. W. Thomas 341 at 34.10; S. J. Crimp 157 at 31.40; W. J. Chesterman 275 at 30.55; L. G. Del-Bianco 151 at 30.20; T. Ingham-Hill 205 at 25.62.
Bowling C. Sharland 10 at 17.20; G. W. Thomas 11 at 17.82; H. Smeed 16 at 19.50; W. J. Chesterman 13 at 24.15.

King's College School, Wimbledon Surrey P16 W9 L6 D1 A2
Master i/c T. Gwynne

Despite playing the early season as an Under-18 year-group bubble, this was a successful season with several excellent victories. Captain Pranav Khera led from the front with nearly 600 runs, including two sublime centuries. Leg-spinner Kairan Sivapathasundram was the pick of the bowlers, and displayed impressive control. The most exciting moment came against MCC, when Seth Eley took six for 20 before lunch in a superb display of fast bowling; the game ended in a one-run defeat.

Batting *P. Khera 599 at 42.78; W. M. Barnett 305 at 23.46; Z. Irtiza-Ali 206 at 22.88; H. T. Nicholls 166 at 18.44.

Bowling S. A. H. S. Eley 15 at 8.20; K. Sivapathasundram 25 at 13.60; F. N. Johnson 10 at 16.90; J. Southorn 12 at 22.25.

The King's School, Canterbury Kent P10 L10 A2
Master i/c R. A. L. Singfield Coach M. A. Ealham

Remaining in year-group bubbles for the entire term made it a difficult summer. The Year 13s fought hard and were admirably led by Fred Sharp, the top run-scorer. Will Allen claimed 15 wickets.

Batting *F. H. A. Sharp 312 at 34.66; J. E. Anderson 201 at 25.12.

Bowling W. T. B. Allen 15 at 17.73.

The King's School, Chester Cheshire P14 W8 L6 A6
Master i/c S. Neal Coaches S. C. Wundke and S. R. Egerton

A talented young side enjoyed an encouraging season. Jake Liddle's reliability with bat and ball is shown in the averages, while Rishi Muthuvelu's spin took most wickets. Rohit Kaimal and Charles Williams played many useful innings.

Batting J. A. Liddle 419 at 38.09; R. A. Kaimal 318 at 28.90; C. E. Williams 228 at 25.33; R. Muthuvelu 191 at 19.10; *H. T. E. Goodfellow 155 at 11.92.

Bowling J. A. Liddle 18 at 10.22; R. Muthuvelu 20 at 14.25.

The King's School in Macclesfield Cheshire P5 W1 L4 A9
Master i/c P. J. Langley Coach A. J. Harris

King's enjoyed their return to competitive cricket. The team largely comprised Year 13s, though several lower-school pupils showed great promise for the future. This, plus new indoor facilities, makes for exciting times.

Batting J. W. Chong 150 at 30.00.

Bowling The leading bowler was *B. M. Kersh, who took eight wickets at 13.00.

King's School, Rochester Kent P12 W8 L4 A4
Master i/c C. H. Page Coach D. A. Saunders

Harrison Fermor (the first pupil to pass 500 runs since 2005) and George Taylor batted well. Pick of the bowlers were Tom Fox and James Watkins, while Pierce Sinden's six for two against Duke of York's was remarkable.

Batting G. J. Taylor 382 at 76.40; H. T. Fermor 563 at 70.37; *T. J. Fox 189 at 27.00.

Bowling T. J. Fox 12 at 15.75; J. P. R. Watkins 12 at 23.17; H. T. Fermor 10 at 28.50.

The King's School, Worcester Worcestershire P14 L14 A6
Master i/c S. D. Greenall Coach A. A. D. Gillgrass

It proved a tough season for an inexperienced team. They had their moments, but a lack of regular runs meant wins were elusive. Wicketkeeper Cameron Jones stood out with gloves and bat.

Batting A. C. Terry 167 at 23.85; *O. W. G. Preston 228 at 22.80; J. T. T. Richardson 195 at 21.66; C. Jones 228 at 19.00.

Bowling E. W. P. Thrush 14 at 20.79; G. R. F. Bartram 13 at 22.08.

Lancaster Royal Grammar School Lancashire P13 W7 L4 T1 D1 A7
Master i/c G. A. J. Mason Coach C. Wilkinson

Superb early-season form brought good wins against Bolton, Cheadle Hulme, Rossall and Giggleswick; batsman James McWilliam and wicketkeeper Will Beedon excelled. The highlight of a miserable later season – when the weather and Covid wreaked havoc – was an exciting tie with the Old Lancastrians.

Batting B. D. Rosbottom 258 at 36.85; J. P. McWilliam 285 at 31.66; A. T. Parkinson 205 at 25.62.

Bowling I. F. Atherton 11 at 5.73; *B. J. Schofield 17 at 10.76; J. A. Eccles 13 at 11.85; B. D. Rosbottom 13 at 12.85; F. W. Deeks 16 at 16.50.

Langley Park School for Boys *Kent* P18 W11 L7 A1
Master i/c J. M. A. Batten

A relatively green first team enjoyed success, claiming the school's first Kent Cup since 2013. There were excellent contributions across the squad, with Andrew Pomering and Harry Roberts starring with the bat, and William East and Alex Davison with the ball.

Batting H. C. Roberts 508 at 36.28; *A. G. Pomering 432 at 33.23; I. W. Loader 392 at 23.05; W. J. East 339 at 21.18; Z. J. Desouza 255 at 18.21.

Bowling M. O. Balmain 16 at 12.31; H. C. Roberts 12 at 13.75; W. J. East 22 at 16.77; A. W. Davison 20 at 17.40; N. Malhotra 18 at 19.44; A. G. Pomering 13 at 20.54; L. MacKenzie 12 at 25.08.

Leicester Grammar School *Leicestershire* P3 W1 L2 A2
Master i/c L. Potter

Covid delayed the season until after half-term. A good win against King's School, Grantham, was the best result. Rohan Kelkar left after a successful school career and two years as captain. Vivek Bulsara, Will Earland and Saurav Thakrar will also be missed.

Batting The leading batter was J. D. Modhvadia, who hit 76 runs at 25.33.

Bowling The leading bowler was R. A. Pateman, who took three wickets at 28.67.

The Leys School *Cambridgeshire* P14 W8 L5 D1 A1
Master i/c R. I. Kaufman **Coach** W. J. Earl

The Leys' first team had another excellent season, which included wins over Haileybury and Gresham's. The performance of the season was Issy Routledge taking five for 43 against MCC. The future looks bright for this young side.

Batting N. R. M. Thain 176 at 58.66; *S. R. M. Thain 314 at 44.85; R. C. B. Bramley 348 at 31.63; W. M. P. Routledge 280 at 23.33; J. R. H. Davies 158 at 17.55.

Bowling H. J. Gadsby 22 at 11.73; S. H. Aldous 15 at 12.60; S. R. M. Thain 16 at 17.19.

The Cathedral School, Llandaff *Glamorgan* P7 W5 L2 A3
Master i/c J. R. Murphy **Coach** D. L. Williams

Despite a month of rain in May, there was at last some cricket: fantastic innings by Avaneesh Shah and Aryan Singh saw both score over 150 runs. Ollie Sherwood led the attack, followed by Singh.

Batting A. Singh 188 at 62.66; A. P. Shah 172 at 57.33.

Bowling O. J. Sherwood 7 at 12.86.

Lord Wandsworth College *Hampshire* P12 W6 L6 A3
Master i/c E. H. Ikin

Despite the captain, Joe Wheeler, being injured for most of the season, impressive performances from a young team gave promise for the future. Gemma Lane and Finty Trussler both gained contracts with Southern Vipers, and led a strong girls' side to the college's first victory over MCC Women.

Batting S. L. Ruffell 264 at 33.00; A. J. Campbell 154 at 30.80; R. F. Wollen 170 at 21.25; A. H. Oscroft 165 at 18.33.

Bowling S. L. Ruffell 15 at 16.00; I. T. Low 10 at 19.00.

Loughborough Grammar School *Leicestershire* P5 W3 L1 D1 A12
Master i/c M. I. Gidley

With Covid scuppering cricket before half-term and the weather after, it was a short season. Two Year 11 players, batsman George Royle and bowler Sam Joy, were the leading performers.

Batting G. Royle 166 at 55.33.

Bowling S. Joy 10 at 11.50.

Magdalen College School *Oxfordshire* P11 W6 L3 D2 A6
Master i/c C. J. W. Boyle **Coach** A. A. Duncan

There was frustration, especially in the first half of term, but a great group of boys had a superb season. Anton Eisner captained brilliantly, and the squad worked tirelessly to improve their skills.

Batting J. M. Coles 333 at 47.57; *A. E. L. Eisner 262 at 29.11; W. J. Price 291 at 29.10.

Bowling J. M. Coles 20 at 8.75; A. Joshi 14 at 18.64; S. J. Down 10 at 23.10; A. E. L. Eisner 10 at 26.40.

Ben Higton had a superb all-round season for Marlborough; Sonny Baker, from King's, Taunton, has signed for Somerset.

Malvern College *Worcestershire*   P22 W16 L6
Master i/c M. A. Hardinges   **Coach** N. A. Brett

Between them, a total of 16 wins – against Eton, Harrow, Tonbridge, Repton and Stowe, among others – and a second successive triumph in the National T20 Cup made for a magnificent summer. Oliver Cox was the top run-scorer, while left-arm spinner Josh Baker signed for Worcestershire.

Batting O. H. Cox 837 at 44.05; T. W. Boorman 771 at 42.83; R. M. Edavalath 504 at 33.60; M. N. Holland 253 at 31.62; A. J. G. Catto 258 at 23.45; *J. E. Dickenson 291 at 19.40; J. O. Baker 252 at 18.00.

Bowling J. O. Baker 27 at 14.44; R. M. Edavalath 23 at 17.26; J. E. Dickenson 28 at 18.32; A. J. G. Catto 18 at 21.78; T. I. Burrowes 11 at 24.82.

The Manchester Grammar School *Lancashire*   P8 W6 L2 A3
Master i/c M. Watkinson

Despite Covid restrictions, there was a full season of first-team cricket. George Bell missed some school games playing for Lancashire Seconds, while Arav Shetty enjoyed an outstanding summer. The most notable victory came against Sedbergh, when Shetty hit a century and Lachlan Anson took five for 23.

Batting A. Shetty 449 at 74.83; G. Bell 185 at 37.00; R. Premrajh 193 at 27.57; A. Hasan 152 at 25.33.

Bowling The leading bowler was J. Clift, who took nine wickets at 14.66.

Marlborough College (Boys) *Wiltshire*   P17 W12 L5 A3
Master i/c M. P. L. Bush   **Coach** M. W. Alleyne

Marlborough College (Girls) *Wiltshire*   P8 W4 L3 T1 A2
Master i/c M. P. L. Bush   **Coaches** M. W. Alleyne and C. M. Edwards

In a summer beset by Covid restrictions, 22 boys featured in the first team. Despite the instability, it was great to be playing again. Captain Freddie Kottler set an excellent example, and Wiltshire all-rounder Ben Higton was outstanding. It was also an enjoyable return to action for the girls who, on a competitive circuit, fought out a memorable tie with Wellington. Rose Curtis and Ruby Lee's partnership of 128 helped secure victory in a tough contest against Rugby.

Batting (boys) *F. J. A. Kottler 358 at 39.77; B. A. G. Higton 326 at 36.22; W. J. Pembroke 348 at 34.80; D. S. Corbett 390 at 32.50; W. J. Hammersley 343 at 31.18; S. T. Martin-Jenkins 193 at 27.57; C. J. M. Brook 151 at 21.57.
Bowling (boys) B. A. G. Higton 35 at 9.86; S. M. Montgomery 20 at 14.50; S. T. Martin-Jenkins 25 at 16.04; A. A. G. Del Mar 21 at 17.29; H. G. W. Mayne 14 at 22.14.
Batting (girls) The leading batter was R. E. G. Lee, who hit 92 runs at 46.00.
Bowling (girls) The leading bowler was *C. J. Stafford, who took seven wickets at 12.43.

Merchant Taylors' School, Northwood *Hertfordshire* P18 W10 L7 D1 A1

Master i/c I. McGowan

Despite year-group bubbling and poor weather, the various school teams managed 160 games involving 140 pupils; there were excellent new block fixtures against Hampton, Haileybury and Dulwich. The school reached Middlesex Cup Finals at Under-12, Under-14 and Under-15 level, and have reinvigorated the Under-16s (Colts) with games against Cranleigh, Hurstpierpoint, RGS Guildford and Tonbridge.

Batting *R. K. Randev 266 at 38.00; A. S. Sawant 255 at 28.33; K. Patwal 182 at 26.00; A. S. Patel 322 at 24.76; G. Muralitharan 297 at 21.21; D. B. McLeish 169 at 21.12; D. B. Justus 158 at 15.80.
Bowling R. K. Randev 10 at 10.20; A. D. Whiteside 10 at 14.30; S. S. Shankar 13 at 17.77; S. Ganesh 23 at 17.91; A. C. Shah 11 at 18.27; D. B. Justus 19 at 19.37; A. Sheikh 13 at 23.08.

Millfield School *Somerset* P24 W16 L6 D2 A2

Master i/c M. Garaway   **Coaches** J. Moore, E. H. Harris and K. Peters

The Meyer's XI defeated several county Academies, the Under-15 boys reached the regional finals of the National Cup, while the Under-14 boys won the county cup and qualified for the Lord Taverners' Cup in 2022. Meanwhile, the Under-18 girls lost to eventual winners Bede's in the semi-final of the National T20 competition. Adam Rosslee and Jamie Baird were the outstanding batters, with leg-spinner Kamran Khanna the top wicket-taker. Luke Pearson-Taylor took two hat-tricks, and Callum Harvey one – to snatch the game from Wiltshire Under-18s.

Batting A. J. Rosslee 359 at 71.80; C. F. Harvey 355 at 44.37; D. C. Kelly 200 at 40.00; J. W. Baird 403 at 36.63; C. G. Melly 381 at 34.63; G. R. E. Gallmann-Findlay 233 at 33.28; E. Wade 334 at 30.36; *B. A. Beaumont 339 at 28.25; J. R. Eckland 282 at 21.69; J. J. Kelly 215 at 17.91.
Bowling A. M. Vaughan 12 at 10.00; L. Pearson-Taylor 13 at 10.92; K. K. Khanna 24 at 16.13; D. C. Kelly 18 at 18.11; C. F. Harvey 22 at 20.50; J. F. Hawksworth 21 at 23.38; B. Fitch 11 at 23.45; A. A. Rao 16 at 29.44.

Monkton Combe School *Somerset* P9 W2 L6 D1 A2

Masters i/c M. B. Abington and M. B. Hunt   **Coach** R. D. Staunton

A young, talented and enthusiastic fielding side played nine matches. Highlights were an unbeaten century against Downside by captain Ed Walker, and the emerging talent of Matty Garrod, who reads the game very well for such a young player.

Batting M. J. Garrod 242 at 34.57; *E. A. Walker 261 at 32.62.
Bowling H. T. Betts 13 at 14.23; M. J. Garrod 11 at 16.00.

Monmouth School *Monmouthshire* P12 W7 L5 A6

Master i/c A. J. Jones   **Coach** S. P. James

In a truncated season, Harry Friend hit three centuries, two against his Glamorgan Academy colleagues.

Batting *H. R. Friend 447 at 74.50; S. J. Wingwood 242 at 48.40; J. Harris 153 at 38.25; J. Middlecote 151 at 37.75; H. Caldicott 211 at 35.16.
Bowling S. J. Swingwood 21 at 15.29; H. R. Friend 11 at 15.91; T. Mayell 13 at 17.69; E. Sivak 12 at 29.58.

Myerscough College (Manchester) *Lancashire* P17 W11 L6 A1

Master i/c D. P. Atkinson   **Coach** B. J. Pelser

The college, who had an enjoyable season despite the inevitable pandemic restrictions, were delighted to reach the T20 North-West finals, and the last 16 of the Under-17s cup. The cricket played was excellent, with many individual records broken.

Batting *B. Walkden 531 at 75.85; J. Little 402 at 67.00; D. Stock 510 at 63.75; L. Young 263 at 52.60; M. Fisher 255 at 42.50; A. McLoughlin 181 at 36.20; Z. Perren 302 at 30.20.
Bowling I. Brooks 18 at 16.28; T. Phipps 16 at 17.31; J. Massey 16 at 19.38; D. Newton 15 at 21.93.

Oakham School *Rutland* P12 W5 L7
Master i/c N. C. Johnson
Understandable rustiness, a lack of incisive bowling, and having to play in a bubble of schools led to modest results. Year 12 Freddie Fairey led the batting with three centuries; eight of the squad should return in 2022.
Batting J. R. Begy 287 at 41.00; F. L. Fairey 415 at 37.72; B. R. Collinson 253 at 31.62; J. D. C. Johnson 314 at 31.40; *J. A. M. Tattersall 279 at 25.36; N. G. Shaw 185 at 23.12.
Bowling B. R. Collinson 12 at 15.83; J. A. M. Tattersall 14 at 26.14; J. D. C. Johnson 12 at 26.33.

The Oratory School *Oxfordshire* P16 W8 L6 D2 A5
Master i/c S.Tomlinson
The First XI were superbly captained by Toby Winterbottom, and they grew as a team during the season to record some fine results. With the next crop of juniors coming through, the school look forward to the future. The continuing progress of the girls' programme is another cause of optimism.
Batting K. M. Tappan 268 at 20.61; *T. T. Winterbottom 210 at 17.50; H. Thorby 205 at 17.08; D. Watts 151 at 16.77; C. Thomas 158 at 14.36; O. I. Simmons 162 at 13.50.
Bowling O. H. Winterbottom 14 at 11.43; T. T. Winterbottom 12 at 13.00; C. Thomas 16 at 15.00; O. I. Simmons 14 at 15.93; A. Mew 11 at 16.64.

Oundle School (Boys) *Northamptonshire* P12 W4 L7 D1 A6
Oundle School (Girls) *Northamptonshire* P4 W4 A6
Master i/c D. W. Foster   Coach M. J. Roberts
The boys had some tough matches during a mixed season. In his first season bowling off-spin, Will Park prospered with bat and ball. The girls performed brilliantly, winning all of their four official games. Imogen Wakeford struck a sublime 127 not out, while many others made important contributions.
Batting (boys) W. G. De Capell Brooke 347 at 28.91; *O. R. R. Thain 259 at 25.90; W. R. J. Park 208 at 20.80; E. R. P. Stanton 211 at 17.58; H. Boston 157 at 17.44.
Bowling (boys) W. R. J. Park 16 at 18.25; F. L. Fairey 10 at 19.90; J. O. C. Howard 14 at 20.21; H. Boston 13 at 28.54.
Batting (girls) I. B. K. Wakeford 190 at 95.00.
Bowling (girls) The leading bowler was G. C. Park, who took six wickets at 3.66.

The Perse School *Cambridgeshire* P11 W3 L7 D1 A5
Master i/c S. M. Park
In a frustrating year of school sport, it was a delight to play some cricket. Nikhil Gorantla and Henry Howarth had excellent seasons in their final year of schoolboy cricket.
Batting *N. V. Gorantla 327 at 46.71; H. J. S. Howarth 287 at 35.87.
Bowling N. V. Gorantla 12 at 7.25.

Pocklington School *Yorkshire* P10 W3 L6 D1
Master i/c D. Byas
Henry Kay (114 not out) and Harry Jones (100 not out) both hit fine centuries, and gained some powerful support from Harry Jackson. He made a lightning unbeaten 63 against Hymer's, reaching his fifty from just 15 deliveries.
Batting H. Kay 284 at 31.55; H. Jackson 252 at 25.20; J. Matthews 184 at 18.40.
Bowling H. Jackson 14 at 16.29; H. Kay 11 at 24.73.

Queen Elizabeth's Hospital, Bristol *Gloucestershire* P6 W5 T1 A8
Master i/c P. E. Joslin   Coach D. C. Forder
This was a frustrating summer for a strong squad of largely Year 13 cricketers, with Covid issues preventing them from playing eight games. When they did actually meet opponents, Fuzael Ahmed led an unbeaten side.
Batting The leading batter was *F. J. Ahmed, who hit 122 runs at 24.40.
Bowling D. J. Clarke 16 at 5.38.

Radley College *Oxfordshire* P19 W7 L11 D1 A2
Master i/c S. H. Dalrymple   Coach A. R. Wagner
The results may have been slightly disappointing, but what mattered was the joy of being back on the field. Zayn Hussain captained the side. The batting relied heavily on Ethan Berlusconi, while Hussain and Freddie Loveland shared the majority of the wickets.

Batting E. A. Berlusconi 580 at 44.61; B. G. Tucker 312 at 28.36; J. R. J. Hayes 362 at 25.85; R. M. Harrap 269 at 24.45; G. P. Acheson-Gray 225 at 15.00; J. S. Sharp 231 at 14.43.
Bowling F. J. Loveland 22 at 17.68; B. G. Tucker 12 at 19.42; *Z. Hussain 22 at 19.45; J. R. J. Hayes 12 at 23.83; M. C. L. Jardine-Brown 12 at 25.33; B. M. Wilson 13 at 31.85.

Ratcliffe College *Leicestershire*　　　　　　　　　　P10 W5 L4 D1 A5
Master i/c E. O. Woodcock
It was pleasing to get some semblance of a season after 2020. Aled King captained an inexperienced side admirably and scored prolifically. The bowling and fielding were strong, which helped compensate for too great a reliance on King for runs.
Batting *A. D. King 439 at 62.71.
Bowling K. B. Jivanji 11 at 4.45; A. D. King 16 at 12.81; J. E. Davies 11 at 14.45.

Reed's School *Surrey*　　　　　　　　　　　　　　　P11 W3 L8 A4
Master i/c M. R. Dunn
Alex Lewis led the team well in difficult circumstances and, despite the impediments of Covid and rain, his side made fantastic progress. Maxwell Dunn spearheaded the attack with pace and hostility, while Lewis batted fluently.
Batting C. Dasghose 181 at 45.25; *A. C. Lewis 321 at 29.18; K. Patel 185 at 26.42; M. M. Dunn 200 at 25.00; A. G. Spencer 191 at 23.87.
Bowling B. L. Way 10 at 19.00; A. C. Lewis 11 at 20.82; M. M. Dunn 17 at 25.29.

Reigate Grammar School *Surrey*　　　　　　　　　　P7 W2 L5 A5
Master i/c J. M. C. Leck　　　　　　　　　　　　　　**Coach** S. J. Woodward
In a season blighted by Covid restrictions and injuries, a very young first team worked hard. Performances improved significantly, and the experience should stand the squad in good stead.
Batting B. Butterflate 369 at 73.80.
Bowling The leading bowler was B. Butterfield, who took eight wickets at 24.00.

Repton School *Derbyshire*　　　　　　　　　　　　P13 W5 L6 D2 A5
Master i/c C. M. W. Read　　　　　　　　　　　　　**Coach** C. M. Simons
What with pandemic cancellations and dodging the rain, Repton had a mixed season. The school had a notable win against Shrewsbury, and a National T20 Cup run to the last 16 – not bad for a team containing three Under-15s. Disappointingly, though, there was neither century nor five-wicket haul.
Batting M. Y. Bin Naeem 211 at 35.16; O. Randall 222 at 31.71; N. Shaikh 308 at 28.00; A. Harrison 199 at 19.90; O. L. Reddy 198 at 19.80; *A. L. Haleem 217 at 18.08.
Bowling A. Harrison 15 at 18.33; N. Shaikh 10 at 29.50; W. R. Orpin 11 at 29.73.

Rossall School *Lancashire*　　　　　　　　　　　　P6 W2 L4 A6
Master i/c S. I. Roberts　　　　　　　　　　　　　　**Coach** J. E. Boyne
Half the games of a frustrating season were abandoned. Matthew Wood started well with 74 against MCC, and Will Robinson batted reliably. The highlight of the season came from captain Joey Warwick, who took five for two against Kirkham.
Batting W. H. Robinson 152 at 30.40.
Bowling *J. F. Warwick 10 at 11.80.

Royal Grammar School Guildford *Surrey*　　　　　　P11 W8 L3
Master i/c R. C. Black　　　　　　　　　　　　　　　**Coach** M. W. Barnes
An excellent season included winning the RGS Festival for the first time since 2015. Thomas Humphreys, who hit most runs and took most wickets, had a superb summer as captain.
Batting *T. M. Humphreys 423 at 42.30; R. G. Gupta 239 at 23.90; D. R. Patel 154 at 17.11.
Bowling L. R. B. Hill 11 at 7.91; H. M. C. Turrell 10 at 12.60; S. H. Stuart-Reckling 13 at 14.69; T. M. Humphreys 15 at 16.93.

Royal Grammar School High Wycombe *Bucks*　　　　P18 W3 L11 D4 A5
Master i/c A. H. Fletcher　　　　　　　　　　　**Coaches** O. R. W. Shaw and C. Parsons
Despite regular team changes allowing players to be tried for the first time in competitive situations, a young XI improved during the term, culminating in several outstanding individual and team performances at the RGS Festival.
Batting D. Yatigammana 242 at 22.00; *P. Mahesh 169 at 18.77.
Bowling M. Mahesh 13 at 12.77; J. Berry 10 at 24.20; A. Tiwari 10 at 24.90.

Royal Grammar School Newcastle *Northumberland* P8 W6 L2

Master i/c M. J. Smalley   **Coach** D. Shurben

Fixtures resumed in June and, despite isolations – most notably for captain Cal Fletcher – the side acquitted themselves brilliantly. The school relished hosting the RGS Festival. Nathan Gough, Sree Kanakala, Matt Nice and Bobby Green all had moments in the sun.

Batting R. Green 299 at 42.71; M. Nice 247 at 30.87; N. Gough 219 at 27.37.

Bowling N. Gough 12 at 7.83; S. G. L. Kanakala 20 at 10.55.

Royal Grammar School Worcester *Worcestershire* P11 W7 L4

Master i/c P. J. Newport   **Coach** P. J. Scott

Centuries by Sam Ford (in a nine-wicket victory over local rivals King's, Worcester) and Sebastian Scott were the first since 2018. The side enjoyed full participation in the RGS Festival, hosted by Newcastle in July.

Batting S. A. Ford 154 at 154.00; S. G. T. Scott 258 at 43.00; J. E. J. Rees 254 at 36.28; *B. R. Sutton 325 at 36.11.

Bowling W. Godwin 13 at 15.69; B. W. Whitton 10 at 17.10; B. J. Hallam 16 at 18.00.

Rugby School *Warwickshire* P12 W7 L4 D1 A3

Master i/c A. E. L. Thomson   **Coach** N. J. Tester

Rugby recorded their first victory over Marlborough in more than 25 years. Jacob Bethell led the team with the bat, scoring 654 runs in seven innings, including 202 in the Marlborough match. Freddie Fowler took 21 wickets at 19. Five Under-15 players made their debuts for the XI.

Batting *J. G. Bethell 654 at 130.80; A. J. Price 374 at 31.16; H. G. Butler 222 at 18.50; E. G. King 157 at 13.08.

Bowling O. H. Phillips 17 at 17.41; F. G. Fowler 21 at 19.81; J. Jacob 19 at 30.95.

St Albans School *Hertfordshire* P7 W2 L4 D1 A6

Master i/c M. C. Ilott

After Covid delayed the start of the season, there were several promising performances, especially from the captain, Steven Perrin. Seven of the first team have left, so there is an opportunity for younger players to shine as the rebuild begins.

Batting *S. T. Perrin 235 at 58.75.

Bowling J. Barwick 11 at 19.64; F. Reid 10 at 19.90.

St Benedict's School, Ealing *Middlesex* P16 W7 L8 D1 A3

Master i/c K. Newell

The team played positive cricket, but the bowling was not always penetrative. All-rounder Ethan Wetherell enjoyed a successful final season as captain.

Batting J. H. Braddock 434 at 33.38; *E. G. Wetherell 314 at 24.15; J. A. Barrett 257 at 19.76; H. J. Manners 181 at 18.10; B. Morris 159 at 17.66.

Bowling E. G. Wetherell 10 at 17.30.

St Edward's School, Oxford (Boys) *Oxfordshire* P22 W16 L4 D2 A1
St Edward's School, Oxford (Girls) *Oxfordshire* P4 W3 L1 A1

Master i/c R. G. Craze   **Coach** D. P. Simpkins

An experienced, talented team won the John Harvey Cup for the sixth time in nine years after defeating Marlborough, Radley and Winchester. There were further excellent victories against Harrow and Rugby, while the Under-17s reached the semi-finals of the *Cricket Paper* National Cup. The inaugural season for the girls' First XI was a great success, with the side playing on the main square for the first time. Superb victories against Haileybury, Marlborough and Rugby highlighted the talent of the team; with only one player leaving, the side promise to be as strong in 2022.

Batting (boys) A. J. Horton 906 at 53.29; S. Brown 552 at 46.00; *L. A. Charlesworth 254 at 28.22; J. E. Marsh 393 at 26.20; E. Hyman 235 at 26.11; K. Barman 317 at 22.64; A. T. Turner 168 at 21.00; D. Driscoll 155 at 19.37.

Bowling (boys) S. Brown 30 at 15.00; C. Z. F. Turner 22 at 18.45; G. McLeod 16 at 19.00; A. T. Turner 19 at 19.68; L. A. Charlesworth 14 at 20.86; J. E. Marsh 14 at 28.29.

Batting (girls) The leading batter was *M. Pumfrey, who hit 133 runs at 133.00.

Bowling (girls) The leading bowler was R. A. Freeland, who took six wickets at 9.83.

St George's College, Weybridge *Surrey*　　P18 W10 L7 D1 A3
Master i/c D. P. Keighley

The college were fortunate to get in plenty of games, and welcomed the return of cricket week. Daniel Ormond led from the front, scoring at a prolific rate, averaging over 50 and hitting 39 sixes. There were many great performances from the bowlers, with the attacking off-spinner Sam Burnley shining brightest.

Batting *D. P. Ormond 627 at 52.25; O. N. Pascall 164 at 41.00; F. G. Brennen 276 at 30.66; S. Burnley 257 at 28.55; J. A. Cake 254 at 25.40; L. J. Richards 218 at 19.81.
Bowling S. Burnley 24 at 19.67; G. T. C. Allom 19 at 19.68; E. O'Donovan 14 at 24.64; C. J. B. Tonkin 14 at 27.79; F. G. Brennen 10 at 32.60.

St Joseph's College *Surrey*　　P9 W6 L3 A3
Master i/c E. M. Tyler　　**Coach** M. D. Hunn

The 2021 season was a successful one, particularly the record number of teams competing on a weekend. Josh Bowyer broke the first-team record with an incredible 186 against Woodbridge School.

Batting *E. T. Lucking 278 at 39.71; J. W. Bowyer 395 at 39.50.
Bowling H. Hitchen 16 at 11.88; T. Marston 14 at 17.57.

St Lawrence College *Kent*　　P16 W10 L5 D1 A6
Master i/c S. M. Simmons　　**Coach** G. O. Jones

Five of the 16 matches were played in September 2020. The outstanding performers were captain Joe McCaffrey, Archie Ralph-Harding, George Kidd, Duncan Moore and Ollie Jordan-Smith. The highlight of the season was victory over Whitgift.

Batting G. C. T. Kidd 423 at 32.53; *J. R. P. McCaffrey 259 at 28.77; D. A. Moore 319 at 24.53; A. E. Ralph-Harding 232 at 19.33; T. R. Marshall 157 at 14.27.
Bowling J. R. P. McCaffrey 22 at 15.41; O. A. Jordan-Smith 18 at 16.28; W. E. A. Ansell 18 at 16.28; A. E. Ralph-Harding 13 at 16.54; K. Moore 12 at 18.92.

St Paul's School *Surrey*　　P9 W4 L4 D1 A5
Master i/c N. E. Briers

The school enjoyed impressive wins against the Old Paulines, St John's Leatherhead, Dulwich and Reed's – despite being restricted to a bubble of Year 13s, plus one high performer from Year 10. There were narrow defeats by full-strength sides from Hampton and RGS Guildford. Fifteen-year-old Krish Patel hit a brilliant century against a powerful Eton team, made a hundred for the Surrey Under-18 Academy XI against Whitgift, and was selected for Surrey Seconds.

Batting K. Patel 356 at 50.85; A. Sofat 271 at 30.11; A. A. P. Hillman 211 at 26.37; *F. W. J. Harrison 170 at 21.25; A. Malik 186 at 20.66.
Bowling A. Sofat 16 at 17.63; F. W. J. Harrison 17 at 18.06.

St Peter's School, York *Yorkshire*　　P10 W6 L3 D1
Master i/c G. J. Sharp

In a season curtailed by academic commitments and Covid restrictions, the XI were well led by Harvey Gration, who in turn was supported by senior players. A group of younger boys showed immense promise, particularly Hugo Nixon, Will Warren, William Bramley and Wills Bennison.

Batting *H. Gration 195 at 32.50; A. Wood 181 at 30.16; W. Bennison 155 at 22.14.
Bowling H. Gration 19 at 13.68; O. J. Tomalin 14 at 15.71; W. Bennison 15 at 16.00; E. Watson 15 at 16.67; F. H. Southgate 13 at 18.46.

Sedbergh School *Yorkshire*　　P10 W5 L5 A16
Master i/c M. P. Speight

Perhaps the most startling figure was the loss of 16 fixtures: rain was the cause before half-term, Covid after. The upshot was just one 50-over match, and the team never found their style of play. The best cricket came in the National T20, when a strong pace attack and the batting of captain Leo Johnson took them to the semis. The North-West T20 final, against Myerscough, was a classic: Sedbergh won on fewer wickets after both sides made 207.

Batting *L. S. Johnson 282 at 40.28; G. P. Barnes 185 at 26.42; T. Aspinwall 167 at 20.87.
Bowling J. A. Dickinson 12 at 18.33.

Sherborne School *Dorset*   P8 W2 L5 D1 A3
Master i/c A. D. Nurton   **Coach** M. G. Pardoe
All summer, Sherborne fought hard with the ball and in the field, but a lack of runs made winning a challenge. A youngish squad have the opportunity to improve in 2022, particularly in the new Dorset 100-ball competition.
Batting J. J. E. Meaker 175 at 25.00; M. G. Dowling 155 at 22.14.
Bowling C. W. M. Wills 7 at 28.29.

Shiplake College *Oxfordshire*   P17 W5 L10 D2
Master i/c P. M. McCraw   **Coach** C. J. Ellison
A young First XI made pleasing progress, illustrated by a number of victories after half-term. The side were led well by opening batsman and top scorer Jai Angell, who returns for 2022. Monty McLaren-Clarke and Oliver Stalder also prospered.
Batting J. Angell 473 at 29.56; O. C. G. Stalder 352 at 23.46; M. Griffiths 178 at 17.80; H. R. Kunzig 166 at 15.09.
Bowling M. G. McLaren-Clarke 15 at 24.00; J. Rogers 15 at 26.33; O. C. G. Stalder 13 at 31.46; H. F. C. Batchelor 13 at 31.92.

Shrewsbury School *Shropshire*   P21 W11 L10
Master i/c A. S. Barnard   **Coach** A. J. Shantry
Shrewsbury School capped 16 players, with five Under-15s and four Under-16s making their debuts. Results and teamwork improved as the side got to know one another. The season culminated at the Silk Trophy, where the squad showed their best form.
Batting J. J. Fielding 779 at 43.27; H. R. Cooke 443 at 26.05; J. E. Home 390 at 26.00; J. O. Parry 242 at 16.13; B. J. Lees 188 at 10.44.
Bowling A. J. Gallimore 29 at 14.90; A. Shukla 17 at 15.24; H. D. Walker 19 at 16.63; J. S. S. Proctor 16 at 19.44; H. R. Cooke 19 at 19.47; J. O. Parry 15 at 23.20; J. P. Pattenden 12 at 25.92.

Simon Langton School for Boys *Kent*   P10 W7 L3
Master i/c J. K. R. Whitnell
A tough draw in both national competitions meant first-round exits. But the team improved markedly, and fantastic contributions from captain and all-rounder Nathan Fox led to finishing as runners-up to Langley Park in the Kent Cup, and beating MCC for the first time. The T20 Kent Cup final was cancelled after the tragic death of Ed Glover, one of our first team.
Batting *N. M. Fox 454 at 50.44; B. J. B. Carpenter-Friend 288 at 48.00; H. A. Legg 221 at 44.20.
Bowling N. M. Fox 20 at 11.95; D. Gunathilake 10 at 25.60.

The Skinners' School *Kent*   P11 W6 L5 A4
Master i/c W. G. Burrows
In a season ruined by weather, a young First XI could be incredibly proud of their performance on a relatively strong school circuit. Ben Adams and Scott Hall led the way with the bat, while Dan Brice, in his first year in the side, made an impression with the ball.
Batting S. F. Hall 283 at 40.42; B. M. G. Adams 339 at 37.66.
Bowling S. F. Hall 12 at 10.75; D. T. Brice 16 at 14.56; J. M. H. Nicholson 12 at 17.58.

Solihull School *Warwickshire*   P7 W6 L1 A3
Master i/c D. L. Maddy   **Coach** D. Smith
After almost two years without cricket, the 2021 season proved a huge success throughout the school. The first team were intelligently captained by Alfie Blundell, and it is sad to see the group of senior players leave.
Batting *A. A. Blundell 303 at 75.75; J. P. Gordon 217 at 54.25; L. P. Horgan 170 at 34.00.
Bowling The leading bowler was S. Graham, who took eight wickets at 22.25.

Stamford School *Lincolnshire*   P10 W6 L4 A1
Master i/c D. W. Headley   **Coach** C. A. Esson
Senior players Charlie Agnew, Ewan Laughton, Ben Potter and Cormac Calnan all batted reliably, and were bolstered by the emerging Ben Saunders. The 6ft 7in left-arm seamer Josh Hull and magical leg-spinner Rohan Kundaje were outstanding in their first season.
Batting B. M. Saunders 263 at 37.57; S. G. Potter 228 at 28.50; C. O. Agnew 237 at 26.33; C. Calnan 236 at 26.22; *E. R. Laughton 250 at 25.00.
Bowling R. Kundaje 30 at 10.00; J. O. Hull 22 at 12.55.

For Stowe, Rhys Noble made 797 runs and took 29 wickets.

Stowe School *Buckinghamshire*

P21 W17 L2 D2

Master i/c J. A. Knott   **Coach** P. R. Arnold

The team reached the quarter-finals of the National T20 and won the Silk Trophy. Rhys Noble and James Cronie had fine all-round seasons, while Year 10 pupils Aadi Sharma and Wilf Pickard made an impact; Sharma was selected to represent the South & West at the Bunbury Festival.

Batting R. J. Noble 797 at 49.81; *J. P. Cronie 628 at 41.86; J. A. L. Mercer 419 at 32.23; A. Sharma 431 at 30.78; A. R. Short 267 at 22.25; G. H. S. Hooper 307 at 19.18.

Bowling J. P. Cronie 28 at 11.79; A. Sharma 23 at 15.65; W. J. Pickard 21 at 16.67; R. J. Noble 29 at 21.21; H. J. Julyan 12 at 22.67; R. G. Hesketh 24 at 23.04; J. A. L. Mercer 14 at 28.64.

Sutton Valence School *Kent*

P5 W3 L1 T1 A7

Master i/c V. J. Wells

Just five matches were possible – with many cancelled because of the weather or Covid – which was a disappointment for a good side. There was time, though, for Oliver Patel to score 107 not out, and for Year 11 bowlers Henry Martin and George Sturges to make an impact.

Batting O. C. S. Patel 151 at 37.75.

Bowling The leading bowler was G. J. C. Sturges, who took seven wickets at 13.86.

Taunton School *Somerset*

P13 W4 L8 D1 A8

Master i/c P. N. Sanderson   **Coach** M. E. Trescothick

A wet summer brought eight cancellations, but Taunton finished strongly after half-term with wins over Wellington, Millfield and King's, Taunton. The highest run-scorer was Jacob Hockey, while Ben Coston hit his maiden first-team hundred; spinner Alfie Macdonald took most wickets.

Batting J. L. Hockey 291 at 41.57; B. J. Coston 246 at 35.14; A. J. Small 196 at 24.50.

Bowling A. G. Macdonald 10 at 11.30.

Tiffin School *Surrey*

P13 W7 L5 D1 A2

Master i/c M. J. Williams   **Coach** K. Balasubramaniam

A diet of short-form cricket was mercifully relieved by a return to all-day matches towards the close of the season. A young side bursting with talent improved with every match to finish with a fine record under its excellent captain, Dru Shori.

Batting *D. Shori 408 at 37.09; R. Rafiq 225 at 28.12; S. Tamilarasan 195 at 19.50; D. Vasireddy 205 at 18.63.

Bowling P. Sivagnanasundaram 21 at 14.14; D. Shori 10 at 20.40; A. J. Cormack 12 at 23.42.

Tonbridge School *Kent*

P22 W18 L2 D2

Master i/c R. J. M. Stephen **Coaches** C. D. Morgan and I. Baldock

Tonbridge's First XI had an excellent summer. They were led by wicketkeeper Tom Geffen, while Sam Hadfield scored consistently and Joe Baldwin made an immense all-round contribution. Reaching the semi-finals of the National T20 at Arundel was a highlight, although they fell just short in their chase against Malvern.

Batting D. W. Beazleigh 268 at 44.66; S. J. Seecharan 208 at 41.60; J. W. B. Baldwin 440 at 40.00; S. M. Hadfield 662 at 38.94; H. C. Bevan-Thomas 483 at 32.20; F. Kirkland 259 at 28.77; S. J. S. Baldwin 312 at 26.00; *T. S. A. Geffen 415 at 21.84; O. F. M. Sykes 163 at 16.30.

Bowling S. J. S. Baldwin 24 at 14.13; J. W. B. Baldwin 26 at 19.85; S. M. Hadfield 21 at 19.86; H. C. Bevan-Thomas 18 at 24.61; T. J. Masding 17 at 25.35; A. A. Ramanathan 13 at 32.15.

Trent College *Derbyshire*

P16 W10 L6 A4

Master i/c S. A. J. Boswell **Coach** P. Johnson

This was a frustrating term for many reasons. It was, though, great to see students playing competitive cricket again. First-team captain Kieran Pell hit most runs, just ahead of Mitchell Wagstaff. The bowling was inconsistent, leading to poor performances in the National Cup competitions. However, Fateh Landa's five-wicket haul in a two-day game was a highlight.

Batting M. D. Wagstaff 423 at 38.45; K. J. Pell 456 at 32.57; F. S. Landa 230 at 20.90; L. H. W. Stentiford 223 at 18.58; M. Hill 167 at 15.18; S. Q. Haider 178 at 13.69.

Bowling F. S. Landa 24 at 8.38; M. D. Wagstaff 15 at 12.80; J. P. Glover 14 at 15.00; R. A. Mukherjee 11 at 15.45; Q. S. Haider 11 at 17.18.

University College School, Hampstead *Middlesex*

P6 W2 L4

Master i/c D. J. Brown **Coaches** A. P. van de Looy and A. R. Wilkes

The 2021 season was an odd one, since the school remained in year-group bubbles; matches started after half-term. The First XI fixtures were shared between two year groups over six matches.

Batting The leading batter was A. M. Fowler, who hit 99 runs at 19.80.

Bowling The leading bowler was O. J. Morgan-Wynne, who took six wickets at 13.33.

Uppingham School *Rutland*

P9 W2 L5 D2

Master i/c A. P. Siddall **Coach** T. R. Ward

A season of rebuilding largely involved Years 12 and 11, who showed promise. There was a victory over Oundle, and a T20 win against Oakham, as well as a narrow defeat by Rugby. The future of Uppingham cricket looks exciting.

Batting A. Buchake 428 at 61.14; *F. G. H. Read 224 at 37.33; A. W. B. Macdonald 174 at 24.85.

Bowling F. Dutton 12 at 23.83; F. D. A. Riddington 15 at 24.00; C. Sprott 11 at 27.00.

Warwick School *Warwickshire*

P8 W3 L4 D1 A7

Master i/c S. R. G. Francis **Coaches** C. Roberts and S. Thompson

The Year 13 XI took to the field all season, and depended on captain Ibrahim Afzal and Jamie Treasure for the bulk of the runs; Treasure won a T20 cup match with three sixes in the final over. Gabriel D'Souza, Peter Dobson and Adam Lane all signed off after four or more years in the firsts.

Batting J. A. Treasure 286 at 47.66; I. I. Afzal 283 at 35.37.

Bowling The leading bowler was G. M. D'Souza, who took eight wickets at 27.63.

Wellingborough School *Northamptonshire*

P9 W7 L2 A3

Master i/c G. E. Houghton **Coach** A. J. Doig

This was a truncated season owing to Covid and poor weather. The First XI won our own two-day T20 festival, and overall results were good. Captain James Sales appeared regularly for Northamptonshire Seconds, and made a sublime 215 not out in a 40-over game against Kimbolton.

Batting *J. J. G. Sales 361 at 90.25; B. A. Dunkley 254 at 31.75; B. D. Sales 195 at 27.85.

Bowling H. W. Grayson 12 at 7.75; S. G. Kirk 11 at 9.18; A. D. Dunkley 12 at 13.42.

Wellington College *Berkshire*

P14 W8 L5 D1 A1

Master i/c D. M. Pratt **Coach** P. R. Mann

The season began after lockdown and saw the first team reach the quarter-finals of the National T20 tournament, before local Covid guidance forced them to stop playing on June 16. Opening bowler Harry Petrie proved an astute captain.

Batting N. E. A. Harris 398 at 36.18; M. S. Bradbury 270 at 27.00; J. Crerar 184 at 18.40; J. A. D. Lewis 227 at 17.46.
Bowling *H. W. Petrie 15 at 12.60; S. F. Daniel 21 at 13.00; M. S. Bradbury 12 at 18.25; O. O. Henry 12 at 22.00.

Wells Cathedral School *Somerset* P14 W6 L6 D2 A2
Master i/c T. Webley   **Coach** J. R. Boot
It was a delight for the First XI to be playing cricket again on Cedars Field after a blank 2020. The boys played some brilliant cricket, and put on a fantastic display in Wells cricket week, which included a fine draw against a strong MCC side.
Batting B. Furlong 489 at 44.45; J. P. Denegri 335 at 25.76; W. H. Rowley 289 at 22.23; C. J. Tucker 202 at 20.20.
Bowling B. Furlong 24 at 16.17; L. Deans 12 at 22.83; W. H. Rowley 14 at 28.64.

Westminster School *Middlesex* P13 W7 L3 D3
Master i/c J. D. Kershen   **Coach** S. K. Ranasinghe
After no cricket the year before, 2021 brought a sixth London Schools' Under-19 Cup title, along with several other wins. Gaurav Kocher led the side ably, and proved a talented all-rounder, as did Will Whiu. The batting was led by Tarun Eapen, Ben Preston and wicketkeeper Ewan Hincks. The outstanding bowler was Mikaeel Toosy, while Ibrahim Ahmad provided fine support.
Batting T. M. Eapen 334 at 30.36; B. B. L. Preston 290 at 26.36; *G. Kocher 258 at 25.80; J. E. Hincks 200 at 22.22; W. J. M. Whiu 215 at 17.91.
Bowling M. Toosy 22 at 15.45; W. J. M. Whiu 13 at 16.00; M. I. Ahmad 10 at 32.10; G. Kocher 10 at 34.30.

Whitgift School *Surrey* P18 W8 L10 A3
Master i/c D. M. Ward   **Coach** N. M. Kendrick
The First XI were inexperienced, with only three having played for them before. George Roberts led the batting and Krish Anand the bowling, while the whole team contributed to excellent wins over Cranleigh and Hampton, and to a very narrow defeat by Harrow – all a great advert for school cricket.
Batting G. W. M. Roberts 506 at 42.16; T. C. Lloyd 271 at 27.10; V. L. Jani 264 at 24.00; T. Patel 192 at 24.00; B. E. C. Karpal 189 at 23.62; S. E. McDowall 208 at 20.80; *J. J. Baxter 251 at 17.92; A. S. Gill 279 at 17.43.
Bowling J. J. Baxter 17 at 18.12; K. Anand 26 at 18.27; S. Sivaranjan 18 at 18.39; M. N. Shroff 15 at 19.33; B. E. C. Karpal 17 at 24.94; T. Patel 10 at 53.50.

Wilson's School *Surrey* P17 W8 L9 A2
Master i/c A. P. Parkinson
A disappointing season brought more defeats than victories. On several occasions the team failed to capitalise on strong positions. The best performance came in the National T20 Tournament, when Whitgift were beaten by 16 runs.
Batting *A. Dutta 343 at 34.30; P. Madan 362 at 27.84; F. H. R. Michael 298 at 22.92.
Bowling N. Viamalanathan 12 at 15.08; D. A. Read 21 at 17.19; J. Ellis 12 at 20.42.

Winchester College *Hampshire* P19 W9 L7 D3 A1
Master i/c J. M. Burridge   **Coach** P. N. Gover
Batsmen Wilf La Fontaine Jackson and Caspar Byers, the captain, led a young side, particularly in T20s, where Byers was often dominant in the powerplay. Chris Batten and Zain Malik also made good impressions.
Batting W. J. La Fontaine Jackson 680 at 45.33; C. J. Batten 366 at 30.50; *C. A. S. Byers 429 at 28.60; H. W. T. Nicholls 268 at 17.86; Z. A. Malik 231 at 14.43; D. J. Hall 156 at 13.00.
Bowling S. Morgan 17 at 12.53; Z. A. Malik 26 at 15.38; S. C. Tall 12 at 17.75; P. A. L. Fisher 19 at 26.11; D. J. Hall 12 at 28.08; C. R. I. Whillock 16 at 37.31.

Woodbridge School *Suffolk* P5 L5
Master i/c I. J. Simpson,   **Coach** D. A. Brous
This was a short season because of several cancellations. Thomas Harper batted superbly, and suggested he will be an excellent captain in 2022.
Batting *T. A. Harper 307 at 61.40.
Bowling The leading bowler was T. A. Harper, who took eight wickets at 6.62.

Worksop College *Nottinghamshire*

P22 W7 L15 A2

Master i/c N. J. Longhurst   **Coach** I. C. Parkin

The team saved their best performances for the knockout competitions, reaching the last eight of the National T20 and last 16 of the Under-17 Cup. Sam Meadows struck two centuries, while captain James Blackburn showed great control with his left-arm spin.

Batting S. J. Meadows 738 at 38.84; J. Davies 267 at 20.53; L. J. Hogg 296 at 18.50; *J. A. Blackburn 197 at 16.41; I. B. Parkin 280 at 15.55; P. S. Pothula 215 at 15.35; J. W. Thompson 222 at 13.87; W. E. Booth 231 at 12.83; S. H. Ali 231 at 12.15.

Bowling J. A. Blackburn 28 at 18.32; B. L. Tomlinson 21 at 24.05; P. S. Pothula 17 at 25.76; I. B. Parkin 19 at 26.47; J. W. Thompson 16 at 33.12.

Worth School *Sussex*

P15 W6 L5 D4 A8

Master i/c R. Chaudhuri

A strange season left the first team unfulfilled. A strong side never got into a rhythm, though Anish Padalkar, Jacob McLoughlin, Mali Lewis and Oliver Havas all made regular contributions. It will be tough to fill their shoes, but the younger players look a talented bunch.

Batting A. Padalkar 219 at 43.80; J. P. McLoughlin 194 at 32.33; M. B. Lewis 150 at 25.00.

Bowling J. P. McLoughlin 14 at 16.00; O. D. Havas 13 at 20.23.

Wrekin College *Shropshire*

P11 W5 L4 D2 A6

Master i/c J. Shaw

All those who played in the first team did an outstanding job. Year 13 Luke Thornton led the side capably, and was well supported by Patrick Ward-Clayton. All-rounder Matthew Lamb had another superb season.

Batting M. J. Lamb 285 at 47.50; P. J. Ward-Clayton 172 at 34.40; *L. Thornton 234 at 33.42.

Bowling L. Thornton 16 at 14.44; M. J. Lamb 15 at 15.07.

Wycliffe College *Gloucestershire*

P9 W5 L4 A6

Master i/c M. J. Kimber   **Coach** B. W. Gannon

Liberty Maher led the batting and averaged exactly 100, while captain Oliver Wood bowled economically with little luck.

Batting L. Maher 400 at 100.00; H. W. Murray 271 at 54.20; O. Gabb 242 at 34.57.

Bowling The leading bowler was F. A. Christie, who took nine wickets at at 23.89.

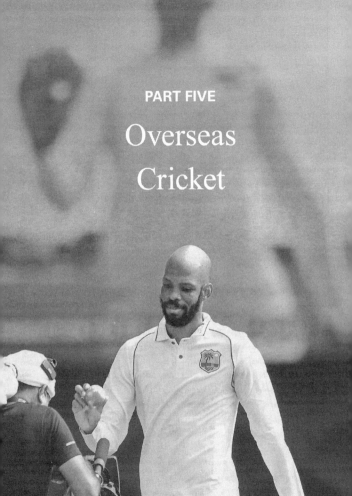

PART FIVE

Overseas
Cricket

INTERNATIONALS CANCELLED OR POSTPONED BY THE PANDEMIC

Jan	ICC under-19 Women's World Cup – postponed to December, then January 2023
	Australia Women v India Women – postponed to September (3 ODIs and 3 T20Is)
	Afghanistan v Zimbabwe – postponed to March (2 Tests and 3 T20Is)
	United Arab Emirates v Ireland – Second and Third ODIs cancelled
	Australia v New Zealand – postponed to January 2022 (3 ODIs and 1 T20I)
Feb	ICC Women's World Cup – postponed to March and April 2022
	ICC World Cup League Two (Nepal tri-series) – postponed to February 2022
	Zimbabwe Women v Pakistan Women – cancelled (3 T20Is)
Mar	South Africa v Australia – postponed (3 Tests)
	Zimbabwe v Ireland – postponed to April 2022 (3 ODIs and 1 3T20Is)
	ICC World Cup League Two (Oman tri-series) – postponed to September (6 ODIs)
May	ICC World Cup League Two (PNG tri-series) – postponed to November 2022
	Netherlands v England – postponed to June 2022 (3 ODIs)
	Asia Cup – postponed to 2023
Jun	Ireland v Pakistan – postponed indefinitely (2 T20Is)
Jul	Ireland v Zimbabwe – postponed to August (3 ODIs and 5 T20Is)
	ICC World Cup League Two (Scotland tri-series) – postponed to July 2022
	West Indies v Pakistan – First T20I cancelled
	Sri Lanka v Afghanistan – cancelled (3 ODIs and 3 T20Is)
Aug	ICC World Cup League Two (USA tri-series) – postponed indefinitely
	ICC World Cup Challenge League (Group A) – postponed to July 2022 (15 ODIs)
Sep	ICC World Cup Challenge League (Group B) – postponed to July 2022 (15 ODIs)
	England v India – Fifth Test postponed to July 2022
	Bangladesh v England – postponed to March 2023 (3 ODIs and 3 T20Is)
	ICC Women's T20 World Cup Pacific qualifier – cancelled
Oct	ICC Men's T20 World Cup Europe qualifier (group stages) – cancelled
	ICC Men's T20 World Cup Pacific qualifier – cancelled
Nov	ICC Women's World Cup qualifier – cancelled after 11 of 25 ODIs
	ICC World Cup League Two (Namibia tri-series) – cancelled after two of eight ODIs
	South Africa v Netherlands – Second and Third ODIs cancelled
	ICC Men's T20 World Cup Asia qualifier (Group B) – cancelled
Dec	Pakistan v West Indies – postponed to June 2022 (3 ODIs)
	USA v Ireland – cancelled (3 ODIs)

WORLD TEST CHAMPIONSHIP 2019–2021

As New Zealand and India contested the final of the inaugural World Test Championship in June, many were startled to discover that the league stage was still in progress. While the first day of the final at Southampton was washed out, West Indies and South Africa were beginning the Second Test, in St Lucia, of a series postponed from July 2020, but technically part of the tournament. Both were in the table's bottom half, so the result could not have affected the finalists, but South Africa's 2–0 victory was enough to squeeze past Pakistan to fifth place, which doubled their share of the prize money.

The finalists had been settled since the start of March, when India completed a 3–1 win over England; had they lost the last Test, Australia would have joined New Zealand, who had qualified in February, but victory ensured India headed the table. Two further series were played after that (and before West Indies hosted South Africa), both in the lower reaches of the table: Sri Lanka drew two Tests in the Caribbean, before beating Bangladesh 1–0 at home.

The Covid-19 pandemic had played havoc with the schedule in 2020, causing the ICC to change the rules mid-tournament: rather than have each of the top nine Test sides complete their scheduled six series, the rankings were determined by the percentage of possible points earned in series that were actually played.

Of the 27 series originally planned, 23 and a half took place. Four of the teams – India, England, Sri Lanka and West Indies – completed their six series. Bangladesh managed three and a half: their second match against Pakistan had been scheduled two months after the first, by which time all cricket had ground to a halt, also preventing tours by Australia and New Zealand. More controversially, Australia withdrew from a tour of South Africa in February 2021, so finished with just four series. They would, however, have qualified but for a four-point deduction because of a slow over-rate during their home series with India; without that penalty, they would have tied with New Zealand on 70%, and gone through on a better runs-per-wicket ratio.

CHAMPIONSHIP TABLE

		Series	Tests	W	L	D	Pen	Pts	Potential points	%
1	INDIA	6	17	12	4	1	0	520	720	72.22
2	NEW ZEALAND . . .	5	11	7	4	0	0	420	600	70.00
3	Australia.	4	14	8	4	2	4	332	480	69.16
4	England	6	21	11	7	3	0	442	720	61.38
5	South Africa.	5	13	5	8	0	6	264	600	44.00
6	Pakistan	5.5	12	4	5	3	0	286	660	43.33
7	Sri Lanka	6	12	2	6	4	0	200	720	27.77
8	West Indies	6	13	3	8	2	6	194	720	26.94
9	Bangladesh.	3.5	7	0	6	1	0	20	420	4.76

Penalties deducted for slow over-rates. Teams tied on percentage separated by runs-per-wicket ratio (runs scored per wicket lost, divided by runs conceded per wicket taken).

Shortly before the final, the ICC announced changes to the regulations for the next cycle of the World Test Championship, which began in August 2021 when England hosted India. Again, the aim was for every team to play six series, three home and three away, each consisting of at least two Tests. But the original system, whereby a maximum of 120 points were available per series – so that a win in a two-Test series earned 60 points, compared with 24 for a win in a five-Test series – had been perceived as confusing. In future, the ICC said each Test would be worth the same number of points, but they would use the percentage system, introduced as an emergency measure during the pandemic, to rank teams, dividing the points they gained by the total available.

Prize money

$1.6m for winners: NEW ZEALAND.
$800,000 for runners-up: INDIA.
$450,000 for third: AUSTRALIA.

$350,000 for fourth: ENGLAND.
$200,000 for fifth: SOUTH AFRICA.
$100,000 each for remaining four teams.

HOW THE POINTS WORKED

Up to 120 points were available for each series. How they were awarded for each match depended on the number of individual Tests played:

	Win	Draw	Tie
Five-Test series	24	8	12
Four-Test series	30	10	15
Three-Test series	40	13	20
Two-Test series	60	20	30

WORLD TEST CHAMPIONSHIP – THE FINAL

INDIA v NEW ZEALAND

Hugh Chevallier

At Southampton, June 18–23. New Zealand won by eight wickets. Toss: New Zealand.

A performance of breathtaking class from Kyle Jamieson decided this low-scoring, slow-burning classic. Indeed, such was the quality, intensity and brio of the whole contest that it almost floored its critics. The World Test Championship, they argued, was itself flawed if determined by a one-off game. They had a point: the essence of long-form cricket is the ebb and flow of momentum over a number of matches – and it felt wrong that the only fixture of the entire competition not to be part of a series was its climax. Kohli, the Indian captain, was clear: "I am not in absolute agreement with deciding the best Test side in the world over the course of one game." That may or may not have contained a hidden complaint, while the canny Ravi Shastri, may or may not have damned with faint praise when he said victory had gone to the better team "in the conditions."

Space in the international schedule, of course, was at a premium, so a complex matrix of 60 Tests boiled down to this solitary game, played in a three-quarters-empty stadium. The blank seats did not reflect a lack of interest, but adherence to pandemic regulations, which had also forced a move from Lord's. The standard of play would have graced any ground, yet for much of the game it looked as if it would count for naught, the crown shared. That would have been an uncomfortable outcome for all, including the ICC, but they had wisely built in a reserve day. It was not a six-day Test, they insisted: there was simply the facility to make up overs lost during the first five, which turned out to be a whopping 225, exactly half the scheduled 450.

On the face of it, there was no contest. India, a nation of 1.4 billion cricket obsessives, were up against a country whose five million prefer rugby. Yet there were at least five reasons why New Zealand were favourites when, after an opening-day washout, play started on the second morning.

First, preparation: they had just outclassed England in two Tests, while India made do with a low-level intra-squad warm-up containing more hyphens than meaning. Second, familiar conditions: the south coast in a damp June is more Christchurch than Chennai. Then, selection: India ignored the forecast and included two spinners – admittedly, each had at least one Test century – while their opponents opted for a full-out seam attack. If that gave India the semblance of balance, their pace trio would flag under the workload, while New Zealand's quintet stayed fresh. Fourth, a lack of ego. Finally, the toss: both bearded wonders were keen to field under scowling skies, but Williamson called correctly. Could the bowlers make the most of his fortune?

IT'S THE TAKING PART THAT MATTERS

Most wicketless overs in a Test by a player making a pair:

53–5–140–0	A. Mishra	India v South Africa at Nagpur	2009-10
43–11–134–0	Manjural Islam	Bangladesh v Zimbabwe at Harare	2000-01
41–15–107–0	R. J. Bright	Australia v Pakistan at Faisalabad	1982-83
41–5–112–0	C. A. Walsh	West Indies v New Zealand at Wellington	1999-2000
40–1–189–0	B. A. Mavuta	Zimbabwe v Bangladesh at Mirpur	2018-19
36.4–11–92–0	**J. J. Bumrah**	**India v New Zealand at Southampton**	**2021**
36–7–115–0	H. M. R. K. B. Herath	Sri Lanka v Pakistan at Galle	2000
35–6–106–0	A. Nehra	India v Australia at Melbourne	2003-04
35–7–74–0	**T. G. Southee**	**New Zealand v India at Mumbai**	**2021-22**
33–8–91–0	R. M. Hogg	Australia v India at Delhi	1979-80

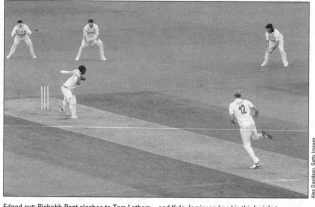

Alex Davidson, Getty Images

Edged out: Rishabh Pant slashes to Tom Latham – and Kyle Jamieson has his third wicket.

It seemed not. Runs didn't exactly gush – they never did – but the flow was steady. Under lights, Southee and Boult swung the ball, only for their width to diminish the threat. And when Jamieson was cracked to the fence in his first over, India were 41 for none, at four an over. Gill, with 19 off 24, and Rohit were enjoying themselves, but tighter lines and fuller lengths turned off the tap. The 6ft 8in Jamieson became a towering example of accuracy: of his 46 overs in the match, 22 were maidens, and he conceded four boundaries – all in the first innings. The pressure told. When Rohit drove without conviction at a ball that left him late, the edge was born mainly of frustration. At third slip, Southee made up for an insipid opening spell with a magnificent diving catch that snapped a useful stand of 62.

Gill, his progress reduced to a crawl, went for a 64-ball 28, undone by a sumptuous one–two–three in left-armer Wagner's first over. Two balls had swung back in, prompting Gill to assume the next – ostensibly identical – would too. But it held its own, and Watling, in his last Test before retirement, did the rest. At 63 for two, India needed glue, and who better to provide it than the adhesive Pujara? Trouble was, he had come unstuck in the last couple of years – 28 century-less innings at less than 30 – and these were unstinting bowlers in gnarly conditions. He did hit his 36th and 37th balls for four, but missed his 54th, a nip-backer from Boult, and was lbw for eight: 88 for three.

The rest of the day, ended before five by a third stoppage for bad light, also made unmissable viewing. This was Test cricket red in tooth and claw – a batting great and his high-class deputy scrapping for survival as vultures circled. That Kohli and Rahane reached the close at 146 for three was an achievement: in one over, a rejuvenated Southee beat both twice, and they struggled for a loose ball to punish.

India had painstakingly pieced together a potential advantage, but it took three overs next morning for New Zealand to puncture it. Kohli, who battled three and a quarter hours for 44, missed a sizzling Jamieson inducker, and lost a review into the bargain. The bowlers ratcheted the screws ever tighter: the day had contained four scoring shots in 54 deliveries when an unusually restrained Pant ran out of restraint. Latham clung on, despite a kitchen sink flying nearby. And when Rahane let his monumental concentration lapse, wafting a Wagnerian short ball to square leg, India were 182 for six. Ashwin swatted a few cheerful runs, but the end came in haste: Jamieson, head and shoulders the best of a bellicose bunch, claimed five for 31.

TESTS IN ENGLAND WITH PLAY ON A SIXTH DAY

England (405 and 251) lost to Australia (695) by an innings and 39 runs at The Oval 1930
Don Bradman hits 232, while England leg-spinner Ian Peebles takes 6-204.

England (284 and 356) lost to Australia (399 and 242-5) by five wickets at The Oval 1972
Ian and Greg Chappell add 201 for the third wicket; Dennis Lillee has match figures of 10-181.

Australia (532-9 dec and 40-2) drew with England (191 and 538) at The Oval 1975
The longest first-class match in England at 32 hours 17 mins; Bob Woolmer scores 149 from 390 balls.

India (217 and 170) lost to New Zealand (249 and 140-2) by eight wickets at Southampton 2021
India's first Test at a neutral ground; there was no play on the scheduled first or fourth days.

How good was India's 217? Could their bowlers match the New Zealanders' venom? Ishant and Bumrah found more seam movement than swing, yet allowed Latham and Conway to leave with impunity. The disciplined Mohammed Shami did make them play, discomfiting both with pace and bounce, but the breakthrough came an hour or so after tea when Latham misread Ashwin's spin and popped the ball to short extra. Grind forward another hour, and Conway, the game's first half-centurion, had cause to regret a Pieteresnesque flamingo shot that fetched up with mid-on. Moments later, bad light chased the players from the field at 101 for two; the late wicket was reward for Indian perseverance, yet the balance had tilted south.

The less written about Monday, notionally the fourth day, the better. Suffice to say there was more spray (plenty) than play (none). After rain pilfered yet another hour on Tuesday morning, even incurable optimists wondered if either side could engineer a result, the more so once Williamson had taken 51 balls in adding two to his overnight 12. Though some called his approach ponderous, even irresponsible, it was in reality a testament to the precision of the bowling. Yet as maiden begat maiden, they also begat wickets. Shami, dangerous as ever, and Ishant grabbed four to leave New Zealand 162 for six, shifting more weight on to the captain's shoulders.

India, who had made 20 more at the fall of the sixth wicket, failed to cement their position: on a pitch with little for the spinners, their overworked seamers were tiring. Jamieson cracked a handy 21 and, when Williamson – at last nibbling one he might have left – went for 49 from 177 balls, New Zealand noses were in front. Southee confirmed the superiority of their tail with a brisk 30. A lead of 32 was solid gold but, with four sessions left, time was running out for them to cash it in.

Invigorated by his batting, Southee was irresistible. Before the fifth day was out, he had both openers lbw, with Rohit's wicket a minor classic. The swing sequence of away–away–away–away–in out-Wagnered Gill's first-innings in–in–away. At stumps, India had ticked off New Zealand's lead and made it their own; all that was needed now was the sixth-day sun to shine. And, *mirabile dictu*, it did.

The path to an Indian victory was narrow, convoluted and led through territory marked "Here be dragons". New Zealand's route, though easier to discern, was not without risk. And looming over the drama was an hourglass: 98 overs, and counting. Kohli was key. He had stoutly come in the night before – no nightwatchman for him – and been clonked on the helmet by Southee. Now he faced the biggest and fiercest of the Antipodean dragons, emanating menace, breathing fire. Our era knows few doughtier knights, but Sir Virat was no match for this foe, his armour scant protection. Leaden of foot, he nicked a Jamieson thunderbolt – and the champion was slain.

In his next over, Jamieson despatched Pujara, gobbled up in the slips by Taylor. That left India 72 for four, just 40 to the good, and the match slithering from their grasp. Pant, though, picked up the gauntlet and, lance in hand, rode his luck after Southee, in a rare false move by the New Zealand cordon, gave him a life. He shrugged off the loss of Rahane and, at 142 for five not long after lunch, India supporters were growing vocal, their team scraping runs to push for victory. It mightn't need many.

Nathan Stirk, ICC/Getty Images

Bromance: Virat Kohli and Kane Williamson – rivals at Southampton, friends around the world.

Nor would it be. Pant's buccaneering innings ended in a staggering catch by Nicholls, back-pedalling at breakneck speed from gully; as predicted, the tail added little. All three innings had borne the hallmarks (and scars) of aggressive bowling of the highest calibre – the fielding wasn't bad, either – and a Test that had crawled into life on a soggy Saturday, but seemed moribund after a monsoonal Monday, was now whistling towards a vibrant conclusion on a wondrous Wednesday.

New Zealand's target was 139 in 53 overs: not mission impossible, yet trickier than it sounded, with the ball singing from the hand rather than pinging from the bat. And although Ishant and Shami beat the openers umpteen times, it was Ashwin who prised them apart. He lured Latham down the pitch, and deceived him all ends up – Pant removed the bails. Four overs later, Ashwin set hearts thumping by trapping Conway. As the hourglass emptied, New Zealand contended with world-class spin as well as seam. So far, the match had tiptoed along at less than two and a half an over. Now the required rate touched three.

But at the crease were Williamson and Taylor, New Zealand's highest Test run-scorers, and two of their calmest heads. The equation had always favoured them, and inexorably they pulled away. Kohli could not reconcile the opposing imperatives of wicket-taking and run-saving and, when at 84 for two Taylor was dropped at first slip off the ill-fated Bumrah, few doubted Pujara had also dropped the mace. The steadfast Williamson became only the second in the match to make a fifty, as boundaries, once rare as hen's teeth, grew commonplace in the evening sun, removing time – then India – from the reckoning. In the ultimate hour of the ultimate day of "The Ultimate Test" (© ICC), there was another grassed catch but, more importantly, the clipped four from Taylor that atoned for a different final, played at Lord's two years earlier. Then, New Zealand had been the unluckiest team in cricket. Now, they topped the world.

Player of the Match: K. A. Jamieson. *Attendance:* 12,622.

Close of play: first day, no play; second day, India 146-3 (Kohli 44, Rahane 29); third day, New Zealand 101-2 (Williamson 12, Taylor 0); fourth day, no play; fifth day, India 64-2 (Pujara 12, Kohli 8).

India

R. G. Sharma c Southee b Jamieson	34	– lbw b Southee	30
S. Gill c Watling b Wagner	28	– lbw b Southee	8
C. A. Pujara lbw b Boult	8	– c Taylor b Jamieson	15
*V. Kohli lbw b Jamieson	44	– c Watling b Jamieson	13
A. M. Rahane c Latham b Wagner	49	– c Watling b Boult	15
†R. R. Pant c Latham b Jamieson	4	– c Nicholls b Boult	41
R. A. Jadeja c Watling b Boult	15	– c Watling b Wagner	16
R. Ashwin c Latham b Southee	22	– c Taylor b Boult	7
I. Sharma c Taylor b Jamieson	4	– (10) not out	1
J. J. Bumrah lbw b Jamieson	0	– (11) c Latham b Southee	0
Mohammed Shami not out	4	– (9) c Latham b Southee	13
Lb 3, nb 2	5	B 1, lb 8, w 1, nb 1	11

1/62 (1) 2/63 (2) 3/88 (3)   (92.1 overs) 217
4/149 (4) 5/156 (6) 6/182 (5)
7/205 (8) 8/213 (9) 9/213 (10) 10/217 (7)

1/24 (2) 2/51 (1)   (73 overs) 170
3/71 (4) 4/72 (3)
5/109 (5) 6/142 (7) 7/156 (6)
8/156 (8) 9/170 (9) 10/170 (11)

Southee 22–6–64–1; Boult 21.1–4–47–2; Jamieson 22–12–31–5; de Grandhomme 12–6–32–0; Wagner 15–5–40–2. *Second innings*—Southee 19–4–48–4; Boult 15–2–39–3; Jamieson 24–10–30–2; Wagner 15–2–44–1.

New Zealand

T. W. M. Latham c Kohli b Ashwin	30	– st Pant b Ashwin	9
D. P. Conway c Mohammed Shami b I. Sharma	54	– lbw b Ashwin	19
*K. S. Williamson c Kohli b I. Sharma	49	– not out	52
L. R. P. L. Taylor c Gill b Mohammed Shami	11	– not out	47
H. M. Nicholls c R. G. Sharma b I. Sharma	7		
†B-J. Watling b Mohammed Shami	1		
C. de Grandhomme lbw b Mohammed Shami	13		
K. A. Jamieson c Bumrah b Mohammed Shami	21		
T. G. Southee b Jadeja	30		
N. Wagner c Rahane b Ashwin	0		
T. A. Boult not out	7		
B 4, lb 16, nb 6	26	Lb 11, nb 2	13

1/70 (1) 2/101 (2) 3/117 (4)   (99.2 overs) 249
4/134 (5) 5/135 (6) 6/162 (7)
7/192 (8) 8/221 (3) 9/234 (10) 10/249 (9)

1/33 (1)   (2 wkts, 45.5 overs) 140
2/44 (2)

I. Sharma 25–9–48–3; Bumrah 26–9–57–0; Mohammed Shami 26–8–76–4; Ashwin 15–5–28–2; Jadeja 7.2–2–20–1. *Second innings*—I. Sharma 6.2–2–21–0; Mohammed Shami 10.5–3–31–0; Bumrah 10.4–2–35–0; Ashwin 10–5–17–2; Jadeja 8–1–25–0.

Umpires: M. A. Gough and R. K. Illingworth.   Third umpire: R. A. Kettleborough.
Referee: B. C. Broad.

WORLD TEST CHAMPIONSHIP 2021–2023

The second World Test Championship began in August 2021, when England met India, who had lost the inaugural final to New Zealand seven weeks earlier. As before, the championship was contested by the top nine teams in the Test rankings, each playing six of the other sides. By January 2022, eight of the 27 scheduled series had taken place, most consisting of just two Tests.

Under the new system, whereby each Test was worth the same number of points, but teams were ranked on the percentage of points they might have achieved, Sri Lanka were on top, thanks to a 100% record from their two Tests against West Indies. Australia were next, on 86%, the fruits of their 4–0 victory in the Ashes – the only Test cricket they had played over the previous 12 months. England, meanwhile, were propping up the table with 9%. Even if they had not lost half the 20 points they had earned across their series with India and Australia to penalties for slow over-rates, 18% would have kept them firmly at the bottom, below Bangladesh and West Indies.

The previous finalists were floating mid-table. India, the only side to have played three series, had led England (before the final Test was postponed) and beaten New Zealand, but lost 2–1 to South Africa, which left them with 49% of their potential points after an over-rate penalty. Meanwhile, New Zealand were on 33% after losing one Test in India and another – more unexpectedly – at home to Bangladesh. South Africa's victory over India put them in the top half of the table with 66%, while Pakistan were in third place on 75% after drawing a series in the West Indies and winning one in Bangladesh. But there was much to play for ahead of the final in March 2023.

CHAMPIONSHIP TABLE

		Series	Tests	W	L	D	Pen	Pts	Potential points	%
1	Sri Lanka	1	2	2	0	0	0	24	24	100.00
2	Australia	1	5	4	0	1	0	52	60	86.66
3	Pakistan.	2	4	3	1	0	0	36	48	75.00
4	South Africa	1	3	2	1	0	0	24	36	66.66
5	India	3*	9	4	3	2	3	53	108	49.07
6	New Zealand....	2	4	1	2	1	0	16	48	33.33
7	Bangladesh	2	4	1	3	0	0	12	48	25.00
8	West Indies	2	4	1	3	0	0	12	48	25.00
9	England.	2*	9	1	6	2	10	10	108	9.25

Win = 12pts; draw = 4pts; tie = 6pts. Penalties are deducted for slow over-rates.

* *England v India to be completed in July 2022.*

To January 16, 2022.

WORLD CUP SUPER LEAGUE 2020–2022

The table for the World Cup Super League, a qualifying tournament for the men's World Cup in 2023, looked rather different from the World Test Championship at the end of 2021: England were on top, rather than languishing at the bottom.

This was partly because the table was ordered by total points achieved, rather than a percentage of those possible: unlike the World Test Championship, the league was designed on the premise that each team would play the same number of matches – 24, three each against eight of the other 12 sides. No one had played more than England's 15 ODIs by the end of the year, and no one had won as many as nine matches. But on percentages, they were behind New Zealand and Afghanistan, who had whitewashed their only opponents (Bangladesh and Ireland, respectively), plus Bangladesh and Australia, who had won two-thirds of their matches. Zimbabwe were bottom by any measure, with two wins in nine games.

The league is contested by the ICC's 12 Full Members plus the Netherlands, who won the World Cricket League Championship in December 2017. India, the hosts of the 2023 World Cup, and the other top seven will qualify automatically, while the bottom five will join teams from lower leagues in a further qualifying tournament.

SUPER LEAGUE TABLE

		M	W	L	NR	Pen	Pts	NRR	%
1	England	15	9	5	1	0	95	0.83	63.33
2	Bangladesh	12	8	4	0	0	80	0.32	66.66
3	Australia	9	6	3	0	0	60	0.63	66.66
4	Ireland	15	4	9	2	0	50	−0.47	33.33
5	India	9	5	4	0	1	49	−0.07	54.44
6	Sri Lanka	15	4	10	1	3	42	−0.30	28.00
7	Pakistan	9	4	5	0	0	40	−0.23	44.44
8	West Indies	9	4	5	0	0	40	−0.97	44.44
9	South Africa	10*	3	5	2	1	39	−0.02	39.00
10	New Zealand	3	3	0	0	0	30	2.35	100.00
11	Afghanistan	3	3	0	0	0	30	0.52	100.00
12	Netherlands	4*	2	1	1	0	25	−0.04	62.50
13	Zimbabwe	9	2	6	1	0	25	−0.78	27.77

Win = 10pts, no result = 5pts. Penalties are deducted for slow over-rates.

* South Africa's last two matches against the Netherlands were postponed because of Covid issues in November 2021.

To December 31, 2021.

THE MEN'S T20 WORLD CUP IN 2021-22

LAWRENCE BOOTH

1 Australia   2 New Zealand   3= England, Pakistan

As Aaron Finch, captain of the new T20 world champions, got up to leave the tournament's last press conference, he was asked whether he had chosen heads or tails a few hours earlier. "Heads," he said. A good call, then? Finch smiled. "Yeah, a good call."

On one level, Australia's triumph had all the ingredients of a decent story, not least since they had scratched their last remaining limited-overs itch. Going into the final, five different teams had lifted the trophy in its six editions since 2007 (West Indies had won twice). But neither the Australians – nor New Zealand, their opponents – were among them. Now they had a full cabinet: men's and women's 50- and 20-over World Cups, plus men's Champions Trophy. As Finch rhapsodised about dressing-room harmony, his team-mates could be heard celebrating raucously next door. It might have been no coincidence that the anthem pulsating through the wall was "Freed From Desire".

On another level, though, he embodied Napoleon's dictum about preferring lucky generals to good ones. Finch had endured a quiet tournament as an opening batsman: a best of 44 in seven innings, and four single-figure scores, including two ducks. But he had won six tosses, bowling – and emerging victorious – each time. On the other occasion, his team were thrashed by England – only one side that night looked potential champions, and it wasn't Australia.

In fairness, he did not shy away from his good fortune in a tournament too dependent on the flip of a coin. Of the 33 games in the Super 12 and knockout stages, the toss-winning captain bowled on 26 occasions, and won 19. (Four of the seven defeats were suffered by Afghanistan, Bangladesh, Namibia and Scotland.) Only the Afghans, confident in leg-spinner Rashid Khan's ability to defend most totals, routinely chose to bat. Otherwise, the toss-losing captain could often be seen turning to expectant colleagues on the outfield and playing an imaginary forward defensive – as New Zealand's Kane Williamson did, with a rueful smile, half an hour before the final.

It had not always been thus. On the morning of the apparently seminal Australia–England clash, T20 international cricket had achieved perfect equilibrium: of 1,320 matches (excluding ties, no-results and abandonments), 660 had been won setting a target, 660 chasing. But evening dew in the United Arab Emirates made bowling second a hazard: the ball grew slippery, and substitutes ran on and off with fresh towels draped over their forearms, like lackeys at a five-star spa. To compound the imbalance, batting became more straightforward, since the ball skidded on: low first-innings scores on slow pitches were easy meat. Playing in the afternoon *was* possible: 13 of the Super 12 games started at two. But with temperatures touching the mid-thirties, it wasn't much fun walking from taxi to press box, let alone fielding for 20 overs. Neither did afternoon starts suit India, who would have hosted this World Cup

Spun gold: Adam Zampa took 13 wickets for Australia.

but for Covid, and whose huge, lucrative TV audience – an hour and a half ahead of the Gulf – needed their cricket fix before bedtime.

And so the World Cup soldiered on, and captains did their best to tiptoe around the subject. To refer to the influence of the toss was to risk making excuses; to ignore it altogether sounded delusional. The trophy in the bag, Finch could afford cheerful honesty: "I tried to play the toss factor down throughout the tournament, because I thought we'd have to bat first at some point, but it did play a big part, to be honest. You saw the dew out there: the slower balls were not holding in the wicket. I don't know how I did it. Maybe it was just fate."

None of this, though, could detract from the spirit of an **Australia** side who had recently suffered 4–1 defeats in the West Indies and Bangladesh, and were no one's favourites. Embodying their renaissance was David Warner, who had just been ditched at the IPL by Sunrisers Hyderabad. Had Kusal Perera, Sri Lanka's wicketkeeper, not dropped the clanger of the tournament on the sixth day of the Super 12s, things might have panned out differently. Warner, 18 at the time, went on to make 65 off 42 balls, and grew in stature: 89 not out off 56 against West Indies, 49 off 30 in the semi-final against Pakistan (when he failed to review a non-existent edge), then 53 off 38 in the final. After Warner was named Player of the Tournament, Finch said he had predicted as much a month earlier to Australian head coach Justin Langer. Not fate, perhaps, but a decent prophecy.

As vital was the leg-spin of Adam Zampa, who was usually economical, even by the standards of the middle overs, and took a cheap five-for against Bangladesh. Josh Hazlewood provided Test-match rigour with the new ball, despite not having played a T20 international from March 2016 until September 2020. He saved his best for last, inducing stasis in New Zealand's top order. Then there was Mitchell Marsh, trying his luck at No. 3 – a position he had not filled until July. Omitted against England, he battered a half-century against West Indies, then an unbeaten 77 off 50 in the final. Two years earlier, during an Ashes Test at The Oval, he had half-jokingly claimed: "Most of Australia hates me." Maybe the match award in a World Cup final changed a few minds.

Australia's turning point, though, had come in the semi against Pakistan, when Marcus Stoinis and Matthew Wade joined forces at 96 for five in the 13th over in pursuit of 177. The equation was pared down to 50 off four. Soon after, Hasan Ali dropped Wade at deep midwicket off Shaheen Shah Afridi. Wade hit the next three balls for six, sealing victory with an over to spare, and stunning a crowd made up almost entirely of green and white; only India, whose UAE diaspora accounts for over a third of the population of ten million, filled the venues more reliably.

A similar story had unfolded in the first semi-final the night before, down the coast in Abu Dhabi, where **New Zealand** needed 57 off four against England – only for Jimmy Neesham, the forgotten man of the 2019 World Cup final super over at Lord's, to get stuck into Chris Jordan. Like Australia, the New Zealanders won by five wickets with six balls to spare. While they had laid one ghost to rest, another lay in wait. Their record in tournament play against the Australians was atrocious, and in the final they batted – initially at least – as if determined to repeat history. A ten-over score of 57 for one reflected their anxiety and left them too much to do, despite Williamson's puckish 85.

Afterwards, Williamson – battling to be heard over Australian jubilation – bridled uncharacteristically when it was suggested his side had again fallen at the last. "Don't forget the World Test Championship," he said. So close to a treble of trophies across the formats, New Zealand remained without a limited-overs World Cup.

Unlike the finalists, Pakistan and England got their timing wrong. For **Pakistan**, the Super 12s had been a joyous procession, starting with a ten-wicket demolition of India, their first victory against them at any World Cup. Along the way, fans could enjoy the skilful opening partnership of Mohammad Rizwan and Babar Azam, who managed seven half-centuries between them, the exclamation-mark sixes of Asif Ali, and the theatrical energy of Afridi's new-ball bursts. As ever, they were more watchable than anyone.

But if there was a criticism of the openers, it was their strike-rates: Rizwan 127, Babar 126 – decent, but not destructive. And in the semi-final, Babar's 39 off 34 balls played into Australian hands, when the side batting first really needed to make 20 above par to counteract the effects of the dew. The only unbeaten team going into the semis, Pakistan mislaid their verve when it mattered.

While Babar was able to name an unchanged side throughout, **England** suffered key injuries at cruel moments. Eoin Morgan's team had hoped to become the first to simultaneously hold both World Cups. And things were looking good, especially after a masterful hundred from Jos Buttler, on a sticky Sharjah surface against Sri Lanka, helped make them the first to win a Super 12 floodlit game after being put in, and set up a fourth victory from four.

But Tymal Mills, their late-overs specialist, limped out of that match – and the World Cup – with a thigh injury. And when he was followed by Jason Roy, who tore a calf muscle in the defeat by South Africa, England had lost two

In his stride: Pakistan's Babar Azam topped the run-scoring table.

crucial figures. It didn't help that the build-up to the semi-final was spent answering questions about the racism scandal engulfing Yorkshire back home. Then, after losing the toss to New Zealand, they watched the out-of-form Jonny Bairstow, Roy's replacement as opener, scratch his way to 13 off 17 deliveries. Later, Chris Woakes, so potent with the new ball, took his analysis in death overs to 57 off three, including seven sixes. Ultimately, England – already without Jofra Archer and Ben Stokes – tried to force square pegs into round holes, with predictable consequences.

That said, they had plenty of success. Buttler was arguably the tournament's most cherished wicket, and brutalised Australia. Moeen Ali and his off-breaks opened the attack in four games out of six, though he didn't bowl at all against Australia or New Zealand – a reflection of the obsession with match-ups. And Liam Livingstone almost won the semi-final with his protean spin. But Morgan the batsman looked a fading force, and Dawid Malan – No. 1 in the rankings at the start, though Babar overtook him by the end – never got going.

The greatest disappointments were the favourites, **India**. They might have been able to write off their defeat by Pakistan as an aberration had they not then flopped against New Zealand. Since it was assumed the New Zealanders (who had also lost to Pakistan) would beat Scotland, Namibia and Afghanistan, that game felt like a quarter-final, only nine days into the Super 12s. Group Two deteriorated into a series of hammerings, redeemed only by the faint possibility of a rousing conclusion: could Afghanistan upset New Zealand, and so assist India? In keeping with the competition's overall lack of tension, they never came close.

For Virat Kohli, stepping down as T20 captain at the end, it was an unusually anonymous few weeks. After a slow fifty against Pakistan that summed up his team's lethargy, he batted only twice more, promoting bigger hitters ahead of him in search of a pick-me-up for India's net run-rate. Thrashings of the group's three weakest sides were in vain. The staging of the postponed second half of the IPL in the UAE had been regarded as a boon for India's players: if nothing else, went the argument, they would be acclimatised. But they also looked tired. It felt like heresy to say it but, since the IPL's inception in 2008, India had not won the T20 World Cup.

If **South Africa** had paid more heed to their net run-rate, they – not Australia – might have reached the last four. After an opening defeat by the Australians, they won their next four, becoming the first to beat England, thanks to a dominant stand between Rassie van der Dussen and Aiden Markram, and a last-over hat-trick from Kagiso Rabada. But they paid the price for dithering in pursuit of 85 to beat Bangladesh: apparently aiming for victory in 15 overs, they seemed content to have won in 13.3. Two days later, Australia bowled the Bangladeshis out for 73, and obliterated the target in 6.2. The difference was a place in the semi-finals.

South Africa, though, might have been distracted. Before the game against Australia, their players assumed a variety of anti-racism poses. It looked messy and incoherent: when the photo went viral, Cricket South Africa sprang into action. Hours before their second match, against West Indies, CSA sought to convey unity via a three-line whip: everyone had to take a knee, and everyone obliged – except Quinton de Kock, who refused to say why, and pulled out of the game. South Africa won, but few performances all competition were more impressive than the post-match press conference by their captain, Temba Bavuma, who managed to express disappointment in a team-mate without explicitly condemning him.

De Kock soon said sorry, and was straight back in the side, though his inconsistency was not unique. Many sides took a knee for their first game (Pakistan placed hands on hearts), but not thereafter; England, who hadn't taken a knee since the summer of 2020, did so only because their "moment of unity" T-shirts fell foul of ICC kit regulations. Not for the first time, cricket was making the simple seem difficult.

Elsewhere, highlights were scarce. **Sri Lanka** uncovered new batting gems in Charith Asalanka and Pathum Nissanka, while the leg-breaks and googlies of Wanindu Hasaranga de Silva, who collected a hat-trick against South Africa, took him top of the rankings. Much was made of the fact that **West Indies** had won two of the previous three editions, but their most recent triumph had been five and a half years earlier, and the first nearly a decade back. Their players were old – only two were under 26 – and it showed. Lendl Simmons and Chris Gayle both averaged nine; Dwayne Bravo and Andre Russell six. Talk of an era's end felt a couple of years too late.

Afghanistan were hit by the mid-tournament retirement of former captain Asghar Afghan, but could never be discounted while Rashid and Mujeeb Zadran were twirling in unison. Mujeeb, however, was limited by injury to three matches, and the batting flopped in the must-win encounter with New Zealand. **Bangladesh's** delicate touch game might have suited their big-turning pitches at home, but was badly exposed; among their batsmen, the highest strike-rate was captain Mahmudullah's modest 120.

Taking a stand (well, sort of): South Africa's players adopt various expressions of anti-racism.

It was left to **Scotland** and **Namibia** to provide the fairytales. The Scots pulled off the biggest surprise when they beat Bangladesh in the First Round, and in left-arm spinner Mark Watt had one of the most consistent bowlers. Opener George Munsey connected with some meaty reverse sweeps, but only Richie Berrington passed 50 (twice), and their Super 12 defeat by Namibia –

THE BIG SIX

Players appearing in all seven T20 World Cups:

	M	R	HS	Avge	W	BB	Avge
D. J. Bravo (West Indies).....	34	530	66*	21.20	27	4-38	28.96
C. H. Gayle (West Indies)....	33	965	117	34.46	10	2-17	26.50
Mahmudullah (Bangladesh)...	30	363	50	18.15	8	2-13	34.62
Mushfiqur Rahim (Bangladesh)	33	402	57*	17.47	–	–	–
Shakib Al Hasan (Bangladesh)	31	698	84	26.84	41	4-9	17.29
R. G. Sharma (India)........	33	847	79*	38.50	0	–	–

inspired by the giant, blond, left-arm quick Ruben Trumpelmann – was a blow. **Ireland**, too, had suffered at Namibia's hands in the first round, though not before all-rounder Curtis Campher had taken four wickets in four balls against the **Netherlands**. For joint-hosts **Oman** and the engaging but outclassed **Papua New Guinea**, there was little to celebrate.

As for Australia, perhaps their dressing-room gusto in the hours after their triumph made sense. Thanks to Covid's reconfiguration of the schedule, they had less than a year to enjoy being world champions, before a title defence on home turf. "Come on, Finchy!" urged a voice from next door, mid-press conference. Cricket's insane fixture list leaves little room to breathe, let alone eat, drink or be merry. For Australia, there really was no time like the present.

NATIONAL SQUADS

* Captain. † Did not play.

Afghanistan *Mohammad Nabi, Asghar Afghan, †Fareed Ahmad, Gulbadeen Naib, Hamid Hassan, †Hashmatullah Shahidi, Hazratullah Zazai, Karim Janat, Mohammad Shahzad, Mujeeb Zadran, Najibullah Zadran, Naveen-ul-Haq, Rahmanullah Gurbaz, Rashid Khan, Sharafuddin Ashraf, †Usman Ghani. *Coach:* L. Klusener.

Asghar Afghan announced his retirement; and was replaced by Sharafuddin Ashraf.

Australia *A. J. Finch, A. C. Agar, P. J. Cummins, J. R. Hazlewood, †J. P. Inglis, M. R. Marsh, G. J. Maxwell, †K. W. Richardson, S. P. D. Smith, M. A. Starc, M. P. Stoinis, †M. J. Swepson, M. S. Wade, D. A. Warner, A. Zampa. *Coach:* J. L. Langer.

Bangladesh *Mahmudullah, Afif Hossain, Liton Das, Mehedi Hasan snr, Mohammad Naim, Mohammad Saifuddin, Mushfiqur Rahim, Mustafizur Rahman, Nasum Ahmed, Nurul Hasan, †Rubel Hossain, Shakib Al Hasan, Shamim Hossain, Shoriful Islam, Soumya Sarkar, Taskin Ahmed. *Coach:* R. C. Domingo.

Mohammad Saifuddin was ruled out with a back injury and replaced by Rubel Hossain. Shakib Al Hasan withdrew with a hamstring strain and was not replaced.

England *E. J. G. Morgan, M. M. Ali, J. M. Bairstow, S. W. Billings, J. C. Buttler, †T. K. Curran, C. J. Jordan, L. S. Livingstone, D. J. Malan, T. S. Mills, A. U. Rashid, J. J. Roy, †R. J. W. Topley, †J. M. Vince, †D. J. Willey, C. R. Woakes, M. A. Wood. *Coach:* C. E. W. Silverwood.

S. M. Curran was originally named, but omitted before the tournament due to a back injury, and replaced by T. K. Curran. Mills suffered a thigh strain and was replaced by Topley. Roy was ruled out with a calf injury, and replaced by Vince.

India *V. Kohli, R. Ashwin, Bhuvneshwar Kumar, J. J. Bumrah, R. D. Chahar, V. V. Chakravarthy, R. A. Jadeja, I. P. Kishan, Mohammed Shami, H. H. Pandya, R. R. Pant, K. L. Rahul, R. G. Sharma, S. N. Thakur, S. A. Yadav. *Coach:* R. J. Shastri.

A. R. Patel was originally named, but the ICC allowed India to replace him with Thakur, having extended the deadline for nomination of final squads by five days.

Ireland *A. Balbirnie, M. R. Adair, C. Campher, G. J. Delany, †G. H. Dockrell, J. B. Little, †A. R. McBrine, K. J. O'Brien, N. A. Rock, S. Singh, P. R. Stirling, H. T. Tector, †L. J. Tucker, B. C. White, C. A. Young. *Coach:* G. X. Ford.

Namibia *M. G. Erasmus, S. J. Baard, K. J. Birkenstock, †M. D. du Preez, J. N. Frylinck, Z. E. Green, J. N. Loftie-Eaton, B. M. Scholtz, B. Shikongo, J. J. Smit, R. C. Trumpelmann, M. van Lingen, D. Wiese, C. G. Williams, H. N. Ya France. *Coach:* P. de Bruyn.

Netherlands *P. M. Seelaar, C. N. Ackermann, †P. R. P. Boissevain, B. N. Cooper, B. F. W. de Leede, S. A. Edwards, B. D. Glover, F. J. Klaassen, S. J. Myburgh, M. P. O'Dowd, R. N. ten Doeschate, L. V. van Beek, T. van der Gugten, R. E. van der Merwe, P. A. van Meekeren. *Coach:* R. J. Campbell.

New Zealand *K. S. Williamson, †T. D. Astle, T. A. Boult, †M. S. Chapman, D. P. Conway, †L. H. Ferguson, M. J. Guptill, †K. A. Jamieson, A. F. Milne, D. J. Mitchell, J. D. S. Neesham, G. D. Phillips, M. J. Santner, T. L. Seifert, I. S. Sodhi, T. G. Southee. *Coach:* G. R. Stead.

Ferguson withdrew with a calf tear, and was replaced by Milne.

Oman *Zeeshan Maqsood, Aqib Ilyas, Ayaan Khan, Bilal Khan, †N. Dhamba, Fayyaz Butt, S. Goud, Jatinder Singh, Kaleemullah, Khawar Ali, Mohammad Nadeem, Naseem Khushi, K. H. Prajapati, †Sufyan Mehmood, Suraj Kumar. *Coach:* L. R. D. Mendis.

Prajapati was a late replacement for Khurram Nawaz.

Pakistan *Babar Azam, Asif Ali, Fakhar Zaman, †Haider Ali, Haris Rauf, Hasan Ali, Imad Wasim, Mohammad Hafeez, †Mohammad Nawaz, Mohammad Rizwan, †Mohammad Wasim, †Sarfraz Ahmed, Shadab Khan, Shaheen Shah Afridi, Shoaib Malik. *Coach:* Saqlain Mushtaq.

Sohaib Maqsood was originally named, but was omitted before the tournament with a back injury, and replaced by Shoaib Malik.

Papua New Guinea *A. Vala, C. J. A. Amini, S. K. Atai, S. Bau, K. Doriga, H. Hiri, †J. Kila, K. V. Morea, N. Pokana, D. A. Ravu, L. Siaka, C. A. Soper, †G. Toka, T. P. Ura, N. Vanua. *Coach:* C. S. Sandri.

Scotland *K. J. Coetzer, R. D. Berrington, D. E. Budge, M. H. Cross, J. H. Davey, A. C. Evans, C. N. Greaves, †M. A. Jones, M. A. Leask, C. S. MacLeod, H. G. Munsey, S. M. Sharif, H. Tahir, C. D. Wallace, M. R. J. Watt, B. T. J. Wheal. *Coach:* S. Burger.

  Davey suffered a groin injury, and was replaced by Jones.

South Africa *T. Bavuma, Q. de. Kock, †B. C. Fortuin, R. R. Hendricks, H. Klaasen, K. A. Maharaj, A. K. Markram, D. A. Miller, †P. W. A. Mulder, †L. T. Ngidi, A. A. Nortje, D. Pretorius, K. Rabada, T. Shamsi, H. E. van der Dussen. *Coach:* M. V. Boucher.

Sri Lanka *M. D. Shanaka, K. I. C. Asalanka, P. V. D. Chameera, L. D. Chandimal, †A. Dananjaya, †D. M. de Silva, P. W. H. de Silva, K. B. U. Fernando, W. I. A. Fernando, C. Karunaratne, C. B. R. L. S. Kumara, P. Nissanka, M. D. K. J. Perera, P. B. B. Rajapaksa, M. M. Theekshana. *Coach:* J. M. Arthur.

West Indies *K. A. Pollard, †F. A. Allen, D. J. Bravo, R. L. Chase, †A. D. S. Fletcher, C. H. Gayle, S. O. Hetymer, J. O. Holder, E. Lewis, O. C. McCoy, N. Pooran, R. Rampaul, A. D. Russell, L. M. P. Simmons, †O. R. Thomas, H. R. Walsh. *Coach:* P. V. Simmons.

  Allen was ruled out with an ankle injury, and replaced by Hosein. McCoy was withdrawn with a leg injury, and replaced by Holder.

Attendance figures, provided by the ICC, have been rounded to the nearest 50.

FIRST ROUND TABLES

Group A
	P	W	L	Pts	NRR
SRI LANKA	3	3	0	6	3.75
NAMIBIA	3	2	1	4	−0.52
Ireland	3	1	2	2	−0.85
Netherlands	3	0	3	0	−2.46

Group B
	P	W	L	Pts	NRR
SCOTLAND	3	3	0	6	0.77
BANGLADESH	3	2	1	4	1.73
Oman	3	1	2	2	−0.02
Papua New Guinea	3	0	3	0	−2.65

SUPER 12 TABLES

Group One
	P	W	L	Pts	NRR
ENGLAND	5	4	1	8	2.64
AUSTRALIA	5	4	1	8	1.21
South Africa	5	4	1	8	0.73
Sri Lanka	5	2	3	4	−0.26
West Indies	5	1	4	2	−1.64
Bangladesh	5	0	5	0	−2.38

Group Two
	P	W	L	Pts	NRR
PAKISTAN	5	5	0	10	1.58
NEW ZEALAND	5	4	1	8	1.16
India	5	3	2	6	1.74
Afghanistan	5	2	3	4	1.05
Namibia	5	1	4	2	−1.89
Scotland	5	0	5	0	−3.54

DATA ANALYSIS AT THE MEN'S T20 WORLD CUP

To keep up, catch up with the match-ups

MATT ROLLER

Against West Indies and Bangladesh, Moeen Ali took four for 35 from seven overs. In England's third game, against Australia, he did not bowl, yet it barely raised an eyebrow. Everyone knew the reason was the major tactical theme of the World Cup: it's the match-ups, stupid.

The terminology is nascent, but the concept is captaincy stripped back to first principles: which bowler is best used when, and against whom? Such decisions have been made for centuries – Douglas Jardine's recognition that Australia's batting matched up poorly against hostile fast bowling defined the 1932-33 Ashes – but this tournament saw greater analysis and scrutiny than ever. Each batter's strike-rate against right- and left-arm pace (and in- and away-spin) was a staple of the ICC's broadcast, and bowlers' head-to-head records against batters flashed up continually.

Perhaps the simplest match-up is the general rule that, in T20, batters fare better against balls turning into them than turning away. In Ali's case, that meant regular use against left-handers, but shielding from the right-handed Aaron Finch – a notorious bully of off-spin – when he batted through to the 19th over.

England were more focused on match-ups than any other team. Nathan Leamon, their analyst, ran in-game simulations on his laptop in the dugout to determine who should bowl next, and to which field; he conveyed his findings via laminated cards on clipboards. In the semi-final against New Zealand, Liam Livingstone abandoned his usual ploy of exclusively bowling off-breaks to left-handers when he confronted Devon Conway; instead, armed with the knowledge that Conway is strong hitting against the spin, he resorted to leg-breaks. In the same game, Kane Williamson gave the usually influential Mitchell Santner just one over, after England sent in Ali, the world's fastest scorer against left-arm finger-spin, at No. 4.

In general, match-ups worked, even if some sides became obsessed. Against Sri Lanka, Mahmudullah persisted with off-spin against left-handers Charith Asalanka and Bhanuka Rajapaksa; two overs from him and Afif Hossain cost 31 and, by the time his main bowlers returned, Bangladesh had effectively lost. Increased attention to detail also denied Associate nations an advantage they had once held: Scotland's George Munsey must have hoped his unorthodox style would take opponents by surprise, but most stationed men for his trademark reverse sweep the moment he walked in.

Australia, the eventual champions, made only one change, for the England game, bringing in Ashton Agar for Mitchell Marsh in order to target England's right-handed openers. Agar took one for 15 (and made 20), but a lack of batting depth had rendered Australia shotless. Finch warned against getting "seduced into looking purely at match-ups… you probably go away from your own strengths". Marsh returned next game.

Finch's side were reckoned to have less of a focus on data, but the partnership of David Warner (left-handed, short, strong against spin) and Marsh (right-handed, tall, strong against pace) that won them the final was an example of how to blunt the impact of match-ups: pairing batters with complementary skills makes life tricky for the opposition. However, Australia's success was a reminder that, in a volatile format, tactical nous must be underpinned by talent.

STATISTICS

Leading run-scorers

	M	I	NO	R	HS	50	Avge	SR	4	6
Babar Azam (P)	6	6	1	303	70	4	60.60	126.25	28	5
†D. A. Warner (A)	7	7	1	289	89*	3	48.16	146.70	32	10
Mohammad Rizwan (P)	6	6	2	281	79*	3	70.25	127.72	23	12
J. C. Buttler (E)	6	6	3	269	101*	2	89.66	151.12	22	13
†K. I. C. Asalanka (SL)	6	6	1	231	80*	2	46.20	147.13	23	9
D. Wiese (Nam)	8	8	3	227	66*	1	45.40	127.52	13	11
P. Nissanka (SL)	8	8	0	221	72	3	27.62	117.55	19	5
K. S. Williamson (NZ)	7	7	2	216	85	1	43.20	115.50	20	5
D. J. Mitchell (NZ)	7	7	1	208	72*	1	34.66	140.54	15	10
M. J. Guptill (NZ)	7	7	0	208	93	1	29.71	120.93	21	8
K. L. Rahul (I)	5	5	1	194	69	3	48.50	152.75	19	7
M. R. Marsh (A)	6	5	2	185	77*	2	61.66	146.82	17	8
R. D. Berrington (Scot)	8	8	2	177	70	2	29.50	128.26	12	8
H. E. van der Dussen (SA)	5	5	2	177	94*	1	59.00	116.44	10	6

The only century was J. C. Buttler's 101 for England v Sri Lanka at Sharjah.*

Best strike-rates

	SR	Runs		SR	Runs
Shoaib Malik (P)	181.81	100	P. W. H. de Silva (SL)	148.75	119
†J. D. S. Neesham (NZ)	175.51	86	Jatinder Singh (Oman)	148.68	113
Mohammad Hafeez (P)	163.46	85	†K. I. C. Asalanka (SL)	147.13	231
M. A. Leask (Scot)	154.76	130	M. R. Marsh (A)	146.82	185
K. L. Rahul (I)	152.75	194	†D. A. Warner (A)	146.70	289
R. G. Sharma (I)	151.30	174	A. K. Markram (SA)	145.94	162
J. C. Buttler (E)	151.12	269	†P. B. B. Rajapaksa (SL)	143.51	155

Minimum: 75 runs.

Leading wicket-takers

	Style	Balls	Dots	R	W	BB	4I	Ave	SR	ER
P. W. H. de Silva (SL)	LB	180	80	156	16	3-9	0	9.75	11.25	5.20
A. Zampa (A)	LB	162	68	157	13	5-19	1	12.07	12.46	5.81
T. A. Boult (NZ)	LFM	166	85	173	13	3-17	0	13.30	12.76	6.25
Shakib Al Hasan (B)	SLA	132	59	123	11	4-9	1	11.18	12.00	5.59
J. R. Hazlewood (A)	RFM	144	74	175	11	4-39	1	15.90	13.09	7.29
A. A. Nortje (SA)	RF	116	65	104	9	3-8	0	11.55	12.88	5.37
Shadab Khan (P)	LB	138	65	138	9	4-26	1	15.33	15.33	6.00
A. U. Rashid (E)	LB	134	55	146	9	4-2	1	16.22	14.88	6.53
D. Pretorius (SA)	RFM	88	33	101	9	3-17	0	11.22	9.77	6.88
J. H. Davey (Scot)	RFM	105	36	123	9	4-18	1	13.66	11.66	7.02
J. N. Frylinck (Nam)	LFM	135	48	168	9	3-21	0	18.66	15.00	7.46
I. S. Sodhi (NZ)	LB	144	46	194	9	2-17	0	21.55	16.00	8.08
M. A. Starc (A)	LF	162	68	248	9	2-21	0	27.55	18.00	9.18

Most economical bowlers

	ER	Balls		ER	Balls
Bilal Khan (Oman)	4.45	66	M. M. Theekshana (SL)	5.48	150
J. B. Little (Ire)	4.91	72	M. M. Ali (E)	5.50	84
J. J. Bumrah (I)	5.08	112	Shakib Al Hasan (B)	5.59	132
Hamid Hassan (Afg)	5.18	66	Imad Wasim (P)	5.70	120
P. W. H. de Silva (SL)	5.20	180	L. S. Livingstone (E)	5.73	90
R. Ashwin (I)	5.25	72	Shoriful Islam (B)	5.75	73
A. A. Nortje (SA)	5.37	116	A. Zampa (A)	5.81	162
Mujeeb Zadran (Afg)	5.41	72	R. A. Jadeja (I)	5.94	102

Minimum: 60 balls.

Leading wicketkeepers

	Dismissals	M		Dismissals	M
M. S. Wade (A)	9 (9ct)	7	D. P. Conway (NZ)	4 (4ct)	5
M. H. Cross (Scot)	8 (6ct, 2st)	8	Mohammad Shahzad (Afg)	4 (4ct)	5
Nurul Hasan (B)	5 (5ct)	5	Mohammad Rizwan (P)	4 (4ct)	6
J. C. Buttler (E)	5 (4ct, 1st)	6	M. D. K. J. Perera (SL)	4 (3ct, 1st)	8
Z. E. Green (Nam)	5 (5ct)	8			

D. P. Conway played one match when not keeping wicket, but made no catches.

Leading fielders

	Ct	M		Ct	M
C. S. MacLeod (Scot)	8	7	Jatinder Singh (Oman)	5	3
S. P. D. Smith (A)	8	7	J. J. Roy (E)	5	5
Mohammad Naim (B)	6	7	Fakhar Zaman (P)	5	6
H. G. Munsey (Scot)	6	8			

FIRST ROUND

Reports by Paul Radley

GROUP A

At Abu Dhabi, October 18, 2021. **Ireland won by seven wickets.** ‡**Netherlands 106** (20 overs) (M. P. O'Dowd 51; M. R. Adair 3-9, C. Campher 4-26); **Ireland 107-3** (15.1 overs) (P. R. Stirling 30*, G. J. Delany 44). *PoM:* C. Campher. *Curtis Campher became the third player – after Afghanistan's Rashid Khan and Sri Lanka's Lasith Malinga – to take four wickets in four balls in a T20 international as Ireland outplayed the Netherlands. After conceding 12 in his first over, he apologised to his captain, Andy Balbirnie, but Campher returned for the tenth of the innings, and had Colin Ackermann caught down the leg side with a delivery initially ruled a wide, only for DRS to reveal a glove. He then trapped Ryan ten Doeschate and Scott Edwards with successive balls – thus taking Ireland's first senior international hat-trick – before Roelof van der Merwe dragged on, to make it 51-6. When opener Max O'Dowd fell to Mark Adair for 51, it was 88-7, before the Dutch lost their last three off the final three balls of the innings: two to Adair, one to a run-out. Five golden ducks were a record for a T20 international. Needing just 107, Ireland were anchored by Paul Stirling, and boosted by Gareth Delany's 29-ball 44. Fittingly, the winning run – with nearly five overs to spare – was scored by Campher. It was Ireland's first victory over the Dutch at a T20 World Cup following defeats in 2014 and 2016. "One freak over changed the whole game," said the Netherlands captain, Pieter Seelaar.*

Campher fire: Ireland's Curtis Campher took four wickets in four balls against the Netherlands.

At Abu Dhabi, October 18, 2021 (floodlit). **Sri Lanka won by seven wickets. Namibia 96** (19.3 overs) (M. M. Theekshana 3-25); ‡**Sri Lanka 100-3** (13.3 overs) (W. I. A. Fernando 30*, P. B. B. Rajapaksa 42*). *PoM:* M. M. Theekshana. *Namibia, the lowest-ranked side in the competition, were playing their first World Cup game since 2003, when they took part in the 50-over version. It was no surprise they showed signs of stage fright, reacting with coy self-consciousness every time they saw themselves on the big screens. They struggled to cope with Sri Lanka's bowlers, too, and Zane Green twice had to be treated after the pacy Dushmantha Chameera hit him on the helmet. Maheesh Theekshana, a 21-year-old off-spinner, removed both Green and opening partner Stephan Baard, and returned to bowl Jan Frylinck with a carrom ball – part of a Namibian collapse from 68-2 to 96. Pulses were racing on both sides as Sri Lanka slipped to 26-3, but Avishka Fernando and Bhanuka Rajapaksa (42* off 27 balls) added 74* in 8.2 overs to settle the matter.*

At Abu Dhabi, October 20, 2021. **Namibia won by six wickets. Netherlands 164-4** (20 overs) (M. P. O'Dowd 70, C. N. Ackermann 35); ‡**Namibia 166-4** (19 overs) (M. G. Erasmus 32, D. Wiese 66*). *PoM:* D. Wiese. *With England and New Zealand playing a televised warm-up game on the neighbouring Tolerance Oval, this match was a sideshow for many – but not for Namibia, who won their first game at any World Cup. The Dutch had posted a healthy 164-4, thanks to O'Dowd's second half-century; Ackermann backed him up, and Edwards (21* off 11) provided a late boost. But Namibia set aside their inexperience, and chased confidently after lurching to 52-3 in the ninth. Captain Gerhard Erasmus shared a fourth-wicket stand of 93 with David Wiese, the former South Africa all-rounder now playing for the country of his father's birth; his first international half-century (66* off 40) sealed an unexpected win with an over in hand. No team had reached a higher target at Abu Dhabi. "It feels awesome, to be honest," said Wiese.*

At Abu Dhabi, October 20, 2021 (floodlit). **Sri Lanka won by 70 runs. Sri Lanka 171-7** (20 overs) (P. Nissanka 61, P. W. H. de Silva 71; J. B. Little 4-23); †**Ireland 101** (18.3 overs) (A. Balbirnie 41; M. M. Theekshana 3-17). *PoM:* P. W. H. de Silva. *After overseeing Mumbai Indians' IPL campaign, Mahela Jayawardene opted to remain in the UAE for a stint as Sri Lanka's batting consultant, and pulled off a tactical masterstroke to change the course of the game. After Josh Little had reduced Sri Lanka to 8-3 in the second over, en route to a career-best 4-23, Jayawardene suggested Wanindu Hasaranga de Silva be promoted to No. 5. He counter-punched with 71 off 47, taking the game out of Ireland's grasp in a stand of 123 with Pathum Nissanka; both scored their first T20I half-centuries. A target of 172 was well beyond the Irish, who lost their last seven for 16 as Theekshana updated his career-best. The result dumped the Netherlands out, and sent Sri Lanka through to the Super 12.*

At Sharjah, October 22, 2021. **Namibia won by eight wickets. ‡Ireland 125-8** (20 overs) (P. R. Stirling 38; J. N. Frylinck 3-21); **Namibia 126-2** (18.3 overs) (M. G. Erasmus 53*). *PoM:* D. Wiese. *Namibia sent Ireland home and progressed to the Super 12. On a relaid pitch that had been lifeless during the IPL, Ireland chose to bat and made a sprightly start as Stirling and Kevin O'Brien put on 62. But once they went, the innings folded: Balbirnie did his best, making 21, but only three boundaries were hit after the powerplay, and nobody outside the top three reached double figures. For Namibia, Craig Williams and Green built a platform, from which Erasmus – with his sixth T20I half-century – and Wiese launched a charge to victory. Adair strained his side and limped off after bowling ten balls. Wiese (2-22 and 28* off 14) received the match award, but handed it to Erasmus, his captain. "This is his moment," he said.*

At Sharjah, October 22, 2021 (floodlit). **Sri Lanka won by eight wickets. Netherlands 44** (10 overs) (C. B. R. L. S. Kumara 3-7, P. W. H. de Silva 3-9); **‡Sri Lanka 45-2** (7.1 overs) (M. D. K. J. Perera 33*). *PoM:* C. B. R. L. S. Kumara. *Already out of the competition, the Netherlands played for pride, but found none, thanks to a rampant Sri Lanka, who bundled them out for 44 in a match lasting 103 balls. The Netherlands were put in, and quietly reached 19-1. But nine fell for 25 as Lahiru Kumara, who bowled fast for a career-best, and Hasaranga de Silva filled their boots. Only once had they scored fewer: 39 against the same opposition at Chittagong in the 2014 World T20, still the tournament's lowest. Nissanka registered the match's fifth duck, but Sri Lanka strolled to victory in 43 deliveries.*

GROUP B

At Al Amerat, October 17, 2021. **Oman won by ten wickets. Papua New Guinea 129-9** (20 overs) (A. Vala 56, C. J. A. Amini 37; Zeeshan Maqsood 4-20); **‡Oman 131-0** (13.4 overs) (Aqib Ilyas 50*, Jatinder Singh 73*). *PoM:* Zeeshan Maqsood. *T20I debuts:* Ayaan Khan, K. H. Prajapati (Oman). *Oman's home World Cup debut could not have gone better. The pictures beamed to the world from their charming ground in a suburb of Muscat, at the foot of the Hajar Mountains, were stunning. In the stands, Omani nationals wore dishdashas and carried home-made placards written in Arabic. Oman started perfectly, with new-ball bowlers Bilal Khan and Kaleemullah removing the openers without a run on the board. PNG captain Assad Vala and Charles Amini rallied with a stand of 81 in ten overs. But the innings turned on the smart run-out of Amini by Mohammad Nadeem. Oman's own captain Zeeshan Maqsood took 4-20 with his left-arm spin, including three in an over, as PNG collapsed to 118-9. Oman then steamrollered the chase, thanks to two home-grown openers. Jatinder Singh, the son of a carpenter for the Royal Oman Police who has lived in Muscat since 1975, made a T20I-best 73*; Aqib Ilyas, resident in Oman since he was six months old, belted 50*.*

At Al Amerat, October 17, 2021 (floodlit). **Scotland won by six runs. Scotland 140-9** (20 overs) (C. N. Greaves 45; Mehedi Hasan snr 3-19); **‡Bangladesh 134-7** (20 overs) (Mushfiqur Rahim 38; B. T. J. Wheal 3-24). *PoM:* C. N. Greaves. *A former driver for Amazon helped deliver one of Scotland's most memorable wins, and just their second in a World Cup, after beating Hong Kong at Nagpur in 2016. Aged 31, but appearing in only his second senior international, Chris Greaves played a key all-round role. First, his 28-ball 45 – including a remarkable reverse-swept six – helped the Scots rally from 53-6 to 140-9. Then, with Bangladesh appearing to have a grip on the chase at 65-2 after 11, and Shakib Al Hasan and Mushfiqur Rahim at the crease, Greaves's leg-spin removed both to swing the game in Scotland's favour. Hampshire seamer Brad Wheal dismissed Nurul Hasan and Mahmudullah in the 19th, and 24 off the last proved beyond the crestfallen Bangladeshis. "He was delivering parcels for Amazon not too long ago, and now is getting Player of the Match against Bangladesh," said Scotland's captain, Kyle Coetzer.*

At Al Amerat, October 19, 2021. **Scotland won by 17 runs. ‡Scotland 165-9** (20 overs) (M. H. Cross 45, R. D. Berrington 70; K. V. Morea 4-31, C. A. Soper 3-24); **Papua New Guinea 148** (19.3 overs) (N. Vanua 47; J. H. Davey 4-18). *PoM:* R. D. Berrington. *Richie Berrington starred with the bat as Scotland consolidated their opening-day success over Bangladesh by beating the weakest side in the group. This time, they were not quite as inspired, but they did not need to be against a rusty PNG. After left-arm seamer Kabua Morea took their first wicket at a World Cup, deceiving Coetzer with a slower ball, Berrington made 70 in a potent 49-ball innings. A third-wicket stand of 92 with Matt Cross (45 off 36) formed the bulk of their 165-9, though the innings tailed off badly from 151-3; Morea finished with 4-31. PNG then fell to 35-5 in the powerplay and, though Norman Vanua hit 47, Josh Davey saw a relieved Scotland to the win with a career-best 4-18.*

At Al Amerat, October 19, 2021 (floodlit). **Bangladesh won by 26 runs. ‡Bangladesh 153** (20 overs) (Mohammad Naim 64, Shakib Al Hasan 42; Bilal Khan 3-18, Fayyaz Butt 3-30); **Oman 127-9** (20 overs) (Jatinder Singh 40; Mustafizur Rahman 4-36, Shakib Al Hasan 3-28). PoM: Shakib Al Hasan. *The knowledge that defeat would send Bangladesh home seemed to fray their nerves rather than sharpen their focus. After choosing to bat, they were cautious in the powerplay, reaching 29-2, and were grateful for a sloppy fielding display by Oman. Mohammad Naim, brought in to open after the defeat by Scotland, was parried over the rope for six by Jatinder at deep backward point, then spilled in the next over by Kashyap Prajapati, who had earlier put down Liton Das. Naim made the most of his lives on his T20 World Cup debut, top-scoring with 64 from 50 balls and putting on 80 in nine overs with Shakib, before the last eight tumbled for 52; left-arm seamer Bilal picked up 3-18. But Shakib followed his 42 with 3-28, as Bangladesh squeezed the life out of Oman's chase. The pace of Mustafizur Rahman topped and tailed the innings. Despite lax Bangladesh catching, only Jatinder passed 21.*

At Al Amerat, October 21, 2021. **Bangladesh won by 84 runs. ‡Bangladesh 181-7** (20 overs) (Shakib Al Hasan 46, Mahmudullah 50); **Papua New Guinea 97** (19.3 overs) (K. Doriga 46*; Shakib Al Hasan 4-9). PoM: Shakib Al Hasan. *Bangladesh overpowered PNG, and improved their net run-rate sufficiently to confirm their place in the Super 12. Though their powerplay was sedate (45-1), Shakib upped the tempo with three sixes before falling to a stunning boundary catch from Amini who, before the game, had identified him as the player he was most looking forward to meeting. Mahmudullah (50 off 28) cut loose with three sixes of his own, and 58 came from the last four; Mohammad Saifuddin hit Chad Soper's final three deliveries for six, six and four. Needing 182, PNG disintegrated to 29-7 as Shakib took 4-9, including Amini for one; the first boundary came in the tenth over. Kiplin Doriga made a career-best 46* off 34, but PNG were all out short of three figures – and a country mile from the target.*

At Al Amerat, October 21, 2021 (floodlit). **Scotland won by eight wickets. ‡Oman 122** (20 overs) (Aqib Ilyas 37, Zeeshan Maqsood 34; J. H. Davey 3-25); **Scotland 123-2** (17 overs) (K. J. Coetzer 41, R. D. Berrington 31*). PoM: J. H. Davey. *The final match at Al Amerat was almost a winner-takes-all contest: because of the vagaries of net run-rate, Scotland could lose by one run and still beat Oman to the Super 12. Such niceties were rendered academic by the Scots' thumping win. Off the second ball of the innings, Jatinder ran himself out; three batsmen passed 20, but Davey was penetrative at the death. A target of 123 was child's play, and Coetzer – making light of a hand injury which had taken him off the field – oversaw a dominant chase, top-scoring with 41 to send Scotland through as group leaders, ahead of Bangladesh.*

SUPER 12 – GROUP 1

AUSTRALIA v SOUTH AFRICA

At Abu Dhabi, October 23, 2021. Australia won by five wickets. Toss: Australia.

As so often in their World Cup battles with South Africa, Australia emerged victorious, this time after Stoinis struck two fours in the final over. It was, though, a win set up by the pacemen, led by a rejuvenated Hazlewood. Fresh from winning the IPL in the UAE with Chennai Super Kings, he used his knowledge of conditions to spear the ball in just short of a length. After Bavuma played back to a straight one from Maxwell in the second over, Hazlewood transformed the powerplay into the first morning of a Test match, and snared van der Dussen with a good-length delivery. But he was fortunate to dismiss de Kock: the ball ballooned off the shoulder of the bat, over his head, and on to the stumps. South Africa could manage only 29 for three in six overs, and it remained an uphill battle – not least when they slipped from 80 for four to 83 for seven, following two wickets for Zampa and the run-out of Maharaj, who slipped as he attempted to regain his ground after trying to burgle an overthrow. Markram fought valiantly to give his bowlers something to defend which after a fiery start from Nortje and Rabada they nearly did.

The pressure was maintained by spinners Shamsi, the world's No. 1 T20 bowler, and Maharaj, while Markram pulled off a stunning diving catch at wide long-on to dismiss Smith. But Stoinis and Wade kept Australia ahead of the rate, and victory came with two balls remaining.   ZAAHIER ADAMS

Player of the Match: J. R. Hazlewood.   Attendance: 1,950.

South Africa

			B	4/6
1 *T. Bavuma *b* 5		12	7	2
2 †Q. de Kock *b* 11		7	12	1
3 H. E. van der Dussen *c* 7 *b* 11 ..		2	3	0
4 A. K. Markram *c* 5 *b* 9		40	36	3/1
5 H. Klaasen *c* 4 *b* 8		13	13	2
6 D. A. Miller *lbw b* 10		16	18	0
7 D. Pretorius *c* 7 *b* 10		1	2	0
8 K. A. Maharaj *run out (5/7)*		0	2	0
9 K. Rabada *not out*		19	23	1/1
10 A. A. Nortje *c* 2 *b* 9		2	3	0
11 T. Shamsi *not out*		0	1	0
B 2, lb 3, w 1		6		

6 overs: 29-3   (20 overs) 118-9

1/13 2/16 3/23 4/46 5/80 6/82 7/83 8/98 9/115

Starc   24–11–32–2;   Maxwell   24–7–24–1;
Hazlewood   24–15–19–2;   Cummins   24–14–17–1; Zampa 24–10–21–2.

Australia

			B	4/6
1 D. A. Warner *c* 5 *b* 9		14	15	3
2 *A. J. Finch *c* 9 *b* 10		0	5	0
3 M. R. Marsh *c* 3 *b* 8		11	17	1
4 S. P. D. Smith *c* 4 *b* 10		35	34	3
5 G. J. Maxwell *b* 11		18	21	1
6 M. P. Stoinis *not out*		24	16	3
7 †M. S. Wade *not out*		15	10	2
Lb 1, w 3		4		

6 overs: 28-2   (19.4 overs) 121-5

1/4 2/20 3/38 4/80 5/81

8 P. J. Cummins, 9 M. A. Starc, 10 A. Zampa and 11 J. R. Hazlewood did not bat.

Rabada   24–14–28–1;   Nortje   24–14–21–2;
Maharaj 24–6–23–1; Shamsi 24–9–22–1; Pretorius 22–4–26–0.

Umpires: M. A. Gough and N. N. Menon.   Third umpire: L. Rusere.
Referee: J. Srinath.

ENGLAND v WEST INDIES

At Dubai, October 23, 2021 (floodlit). England won by six wickets. Toss: England.

This was both sides' first T20 World Cup game since Carlos Brathwaite collared Ben Stokes in the 2016 final at Kolkata, prompting the captains to weigh up the past: Pollard suggested that match – and those four sixes – would be on English minds; Morgan denied any scars. Yet the phoney war could hardly have proved more irrelevant, as West Indies succumbed for 55, their second-lowest total (behind 45 against England at Basseterre in 2018-19), and Rashid took four for two, England's best figures (beating Jordan's four for six, in the same match). Just as central was Ali, who opened the bowling with his off-breaks, held a wonderful running catch over his shoulder to dismiss Lewis, then fiddled out Simmons and Hetmyer; two for 17 was his most economical four-over spell. When Mills, in his first England game since February 2017, out-thought Gayle, West Indies closed the powerplay on 31 for four. The rest of the innings was a mishmash of miscues, though Rashid – brought on for the right-handers – slid a beauty through Russell's defences. Only the Netherlands (twice, both against Sri Lanka, once on the eve of this game) had been dismissed for fewer at a T20 World Cup. England carelessly lost four wickets in their chase, including two to athletic return catches by left-arm spinner Hosein, but completed victory – their first in this competition against West Indies in six attempts – with 11.4 overs to spare. The match was done in 136 balls, the shortest of England's 744 non-rain-affected white-ball games. "As good as it gets," said Morgan. "Unacceptable," said Pollard. No one mentioned Kolkata.   LAWRENCE BOOTH

Player of the Match: M. M. Ali.   Attendance: 7,300.

West Indies

		B	4/6
1 L. M. P. Simmons *c 5 b 4*	3	7	0
2 E. Lewis *c 4 b 8*	6	5	0/1
3 C. H. Gayle *c 7 b 11*..........	13	13	3
4 S. O. Hetmyer *c 6 b 4*........	9	9	2
5 D. J. Bravo *c 3 b 9*	5	5	1
6 †N. Pooran *c 2 b 11*	1	9	0
7 *K. A. Pollard *c 3 b 10*	6	14	0
8 A. D. Russell *b 10*	0	2	0
9 A. J. Hosein *not out*	6	13	0
10 O. C. McCoy *c 1 b 10*	0	1	0
11 R. Rampaul *b 10*	3	8	0
W 3	3		

6 overs: 31-4   (14.2 overs)   **55**

1/8 2/9 3/27 4/31 5/37 6/42 7/44 8/49 9/49

Ali 24–18–17–2; Woakes 12–6–12–1; Mills 24–14–17–2; Jordan 12–9–7–1; Rashid 14–12–2–4.

England

		B	4/6
1 J. J. Roy *c 3 b 11*	11	10	0/1
2 †J. C. Buttler *not out*	24	22	3
3 J. M. Bairstow *c and b 9*	9	6	2
4 M. M. Ali *run out (2/10)*	3	4	0
5 L. S. Livingstone *c and b 9* ...	1	2	0
6 *E. J. G. Morgan *not out*	7	7	1
Nb 1....................	1		

6 overs: 39-3   (8.2 overs)   **56-4**

1/21 2/30 3/36 4/39

7 D. J. Malan, 8 C. R. Woakes, 9 C. J. Jordan, 10 A. U. Rashid and 11 T. S. Mills did not bat.

Hosein 24–9–24–2; Rampaul 12–7–14–1; McCoy 12–5–12–0; Pollard 2–0–6–0.

Umpires: Aleem Dar and M. Erasmus.   Third umpire: C. M. Brown.
Referee: D. C. Boon.

BANGLADESH v SRI LANKA

At Sharjah, October 24, 2021. Sri Lanka won by five wickets. Toss: Sri Lanka.

Sri Lanka fought back against fellow qualifiers Bangladesh, thanks to a superb unbeaten 80 off 49 balls from Asalanka, in only his fifth T20 international. First he added 69 for the second wicket with Nissanka, after Perera had been bowled by Nasum Ahmed from the fourth ball of the chase. Then, after Sri Lanka lost three for eight, with Shakib Al Hasan

MOST WICKETS AT T20 WORLD CUPS

41 **Shakib Al Hasan (Bangladesh)**	36 Saeed Ajmal (Pakistan)
39 Shahid Afridi (Pakistan)	35 Umar Gul (Pakistan)
38 S. L. Malinga (Sri Lanka)	35 B. A. W. Mendis (Sri Lanka)

striking twice, Asalanka and Rajapaksa thrashed 86 off 52 as Bangladesh grew sloppy in the field. The decisive over was the 16th: with Sri Lanka still needing 46, Mohammad Saifuddin disappeared for 22, of which 21 were scored by Rajapaksa. After Asalanka completed victory, Bangladesh captain Mahmudullah was criticised for holding back his two best bowlers – Shakib and left-arm quick Mustafizur Rahman – until it was too late. The game was ill-tempered: when Kumara removed Liton Das in the sixth over, the pair exchanged words, and needed to be separated by team-mates and the umpires; both lost a chunk of their match fee. After Mohammad Naim departed for 62, Mushfiqur Rahim smashed an unbeaten 57 off 37 against an attack missing injured mystery spinner Maheesh Theekshana, and including five seamers. Until Asalanka's intervention, Bangladesh's efforts looked enough. REX CLEMENTINE

Player of the Match: K. I. C. Asalanka.   *Attendance*: 4,800.

Bangladesh

	B	4/6
1 Mohammad Naim *c and b* 9....	62	52 6
2 Liton Das *c* 7 *b* 11	16	16 2
3 Shakib Al Hasan *b* 8	10	7 2
4 Mushfiqur Rahim *not out*	57	37 5/2
5 Afif Hossain *run out (11)*	7	6 1
6 *Mahmudullah *not out*	10	5 2
B 2, lb 3, w 1, nb 3	9	

6 overs: 41-1   (20 overs)   171-4

1/40 2/56 3/129 4/150

7 †Nurul Hasan, 8 Mehedi Hasan snr, 9 Mohammad Saifuddin, 10 Nasum Ahmed and 11 Mustafizur Rahman did not bat.

Karunaratne 18–8–12–1; K. B. U. Fernando 18–6–27–1; Chameera 24–4–41–0; Kumara 24–10–29–1; Asalanka 6–1–14–0; de Silva 18–1–29–0; Shanaka 12–3–14–0.

Sri Lanka

	B	4/6
1 †M. D. K. J. Perera *b* 10.......	1	3 0
2 P. Nissanka *b* 3...............	24	21 1/1
3 K. I. C. Asalanka *not out*	80	49 5/5
4 W. I. A. Fernando *b* 3	0	3 0
5 P. W. H. de Silva *c* 1 *b* 9	6	5 1
6 P. B. B. Rajapaksa *b* 10.......	53	31 3/3
7 *M. D. Shanaka *not out*	1	1 0
W 7	7	

6 overs: 54-1   (18.5 overs)   172-5

1/2 2/71 3/71 4/79 5/165

8 C. Karunaratne, 9 K. B. U. Fernando, 10 P. V. D. Chameera and 11 C. B. R. L. S. Kumara did not bat.

Nasum Ahmed 17–4–29–2; Mehedi Hasan snr 24–8–30–0; Mohammad Saifuddin 18–5–38–1; Shakib Al Hasan 18–8–17–2; Mustafizur Rahman 18–6–22–0; Mahmudullah 12–2–21–0; Afif Hossain 6–0–15–0.

Umpires: A. T. Holdstock and J. S. Wilson.   Third umpire: M. A. Gough.
Referee: J. Srinath.

SOUTH AFRICA v WEST INDIES

At Dubai, October 26, 2021. South Africa won by eight wickets. Toss: South Africa.

An important win for South Africa was overshadowed by the absence of one man. Not long before the start, wicketkeeper and opener Quinton de Kock pulled out for what his captain, Bavuma, described at the toss as "personal reasons". Those reasons were not hard to divine. That morning, Cricket South Africa had instructed their players to take a knee

---

LOWEST STRIKE-RATE IN A T20 WORLD CUP INNINGS

40.00	14 (35 balls)	Alok Kapali........	Bangladesh v South Africa at Cape Town.	2007-08
45.16	14 (31)	R. M. Haq.........	Scotland v Pakistan at Durban..........	2007-08
45.71	**16 (35)**	**L. M. P. Simmons ..**	**West Indies v South Africa at Dubai** ...	**2021-22**
50.00	17 (34)	G. C. Wilson.......	Ireland v West Indies at Providence	2010
54.54	18 (33)	D. O. Obuya	Kenya v Sri Lanka at Johannesburg......	2007-08
54.83	**17 (31)**	**H. G. Munsey**	**Scotland v Pakistan at Sharjah**.......	**2021-22**

Minimum: 30 balls.

---

before every match. It was, they said, "imperative for the team to be seen taking a united and consistent stand against racism, especially given SA's history". De Kock, who had declined to do so before a Test in the Caribbean four months earlier, decided on the way to the ground to opt out. Afterwards, an eloquent Bavuma said he had been "surprised and taken aback", but added: "Quinton is an adult. You have to respect his decision, whether you agree with it or not." South Africa had successfully put the controversy to one side, though not before Klaasen, now wearing the gloves, dropped an early chance. But they were helped by mystifying passivity from Simmons, who managed only 16 singles in 35 balls. Lewis, his opening partner, did his best to compensate, clonking six sixes, but Nortje's speed and guile were too good for West Indies, and 143 was modest. Bavuma's day got worse before it got better, when he was run out in the first over of the chase by Russell from mid-on. But Hendricks – de Kock's replacement as opener – pummelled 39, before Markram thrashed a 25-ball fifty in an unbroken stand of 83 with the steadier van der Dussen. LAWRENCE BOOTH

Player of the Match: A. A. Nortje. *Attendance:* 1,550.

West Indies

		B	4/6
1 L. M. P. Simmons *b 9*	16	35	0
2 E. Lewis *c 9 b 8*	56	35	3/6
3 †N. Pooran *c 6 b 8*	12	7	2
4 C. H. Gayle *c 5 b 7*	12	12	0/1
5 *K. A. Pollard *c 3 b 7*	26	20	2/1
6 A. D. Russell *b 10*	5	4	1
7 S. O. Hetmyer *run out (6/5)*	1	2	0
8 D. J. Bravo *not out*	8	5	1
9 H. R. Walsh *c 2 b 7*	0	1	0
10 A. J. Hosein *not out*	0	0	0
Lb 2, w 4, nb 1	7		

6 overs: 43-0 (20 overs) 143-8

1/73 2/87 3/89 4/121 5/132 6/133 7/137 8/137

11 R. Rampaul did not bat.

Markram 18–11–22–0; Rabada 24–11–27–1; Nortje 24–14–14–1; Maharaj 24–11–24–2; Shamsi 18–4–37–0; Pretorius 12–5–17–3.

South Africa

		B	4/6
1 *T. Bavuma *run out (6)*	2	3	0
2 R. R. Hendricks *c 7 b 10*	39	30	4/1
3 H. E. van der Dussen *not out*	43	51	3
4 A. K. Markram *not out*	51	26	2/4
Lb 1, w 8	9		

6 overs: 42-1 (18.2 overs) 144-2

1/4 2/61

5 †H. Klaasen, 6 D. A. Miller, 7 D. Pretorius, 8 K. A. Maharaj, 9 K. Rabada, 10 A. A. Nortje and T. Shamsi did not bat.

Hosein 24–9–27–1; Rampaul 18–6–22–0; Russell 20–3–36–0; Walsh 18–3–26–0; Bravo 24–11–23–0; Pollard 6–2–9–0.

Umpires: Aleem Dar and P. R. Reiffel. Third umpire: C. M. Brown.
Referee: D. C. Boon.

BANGLADESH v ENGLAND

At Abu Dhabi, October 27, 2021. England won by eight wickets. Toss: Bangladesh.

The first T20 game between the sides proved a non-event. In burning heat, England were in control of their only afternoon game of the competition for all but one over: the first, bowled by Ali, which cost ten. But he stayed on for a second, and got rid of openers Liton Das and Mohammad Naim in successive balls, courtesy of simple catches to deep backward square and mid-on. Like the unerring Woakes, who removed Shakib Al Hasan thanks to a smart grab by Rashid at short fine leg, and ended up conceding only 12 from his four overs, Ali bowled through the powerplay. From 27 for three, the innings did not improve; on a decent pitch, scarcely a shot was played in anger. Livingstone trapped Mushfiqur Rahim on review after he missed a reverse sweep, then had Mahmudullah skewing to backward point. In between, Afif Hossain was run out, having briefly imagined Mills's misfield invited a second. It took until the 19th over for Bangladesh to clear the fence – Nasum Ahmed did so twice off Rashid – but Mills docked the tail for his best figures in T20 internationals, and England needed just 125. Roy cut the first ball of the chase, from Shakib, for a four, then straight-drove Mustafizur Rahman for another. When Buttler was caught at long-off in the fifth, England had 39. Roy, swashbuckling his way to a 33-ball half-century, and Malan, back at No. 3 after his demotion against West Indies, confirmed their ascendancy in a stand of 73. A bloodless victory came with nearly six overs to spare. LAWRENCE BOOTH

Player of the Match: J. J. Roy.   *Attendance:* 2,800.

Bangladesh

		B	4/6
1 Liton Das *c 6 b 5*	9	8	2
2 Mohammad Naim *c 8 b 5*.....	5	7	0
3 Shakib Al Hasan *c 10 b 8*.....	4	7	0
4 Mushfiqur Rahim *lbw b 6* ...	29	30	3
5 *Mahmudullah *c 8 b 6*.......	19	24	1
6 Afif Hossain *run out (11/2)*	5	6	1
7 †Nurul Hasan *c 2 b 11*........	16	18	0
8 Mehedi Hasan snr *c 8 b 11*....	11	10	2
9 Nasum Ahmed *not out*	19	9	1/2
10 Mustafizur Rahman *b 11*	0	1	0
B 1, lb 1, w 5...............	7		

6 overs: 27-3   (20 overs) 124-9

1/14 2/14 3/26 4/63 5/73 6/83 7/98 8/124 9/124

11 Shoriful Islam did not bat.

Ali 18–9–18–2; Woakes 24–14–12–1; Rashid 24–8–35–0; Jordan 12–4–15–0; Mills 24–9–27–3; Livingstone 18–8–15–2.

England

		B	4/6
1 J. J. Roy *c 9 b 11*	61	38	5/3
2 †J. C. Buttler *c 2 b 9*	18	18	1/1
3 D. J. Malan *not out*.........	28	25	3
4 J. M. Bairstow *not out*	8	4	1
Lb 6, w 5.................	11		

6 overs: 50-1   (14.1 overs) 126-2

1/39 2/112

5 M. M. Ali, 6 L. S. Livingstone, 7 *E. J. G. Morgan, 8 C. R. Woakes, 9 C. J. Jordan, 10 A. U. Rashid and 11 T. S. Mills did not bat.

Shakib Al Hasan 18–5–24–0; Mustafizur Rahman 18–8–23–0; Shoriful Islam 19–6–26–1; Nasum Ahmed 18–5–26–1; Mehedi Hasan snr 12–1–21–0.

Umpires: N. N. Menon and L. Rusere.   Third umpire: R. J. Tucker.
Referee: J. Srinath.

AUSTRALIA v SRI LANKA

At Dubai, October 28, 2021 (floodlit). Australia won by seven wickets. Toss: Australia.

Australia's second win coincided with a return to form for Warner, who a month earlier had been dropped by Sunrisers Hyderabad at the IPL. Now, in pursuit of a modest 155, he survived a regulation leg-side catch to wicketkeeper Perera on 18 after gloving a pull off Chameera, and went on to a decisive 65 off 42 balls, with ten fours. "Everyone was talking about my form," he said, "which was not a thing I was worried about." The Australians had managed their chase cleverly, taking few risks against spinners Theekshana and Hasaranga de Silva, whose combined eight overs cost 49, but attacking the rest: nine overs of seam brought one for 106, as Warner and Finch began with a stand of 70 inside seven. Smith and Stoinis finished the job. Sri Lanka had also started well: 78 for one inside ten. But that became 94 for five against Starc, who thrillingly yorked Perera, and the unhittable

Zampa. Figures of two for 12 were his most economical four-over spell in T20 internationals; his next two cheapest had also come against Sri Lanka. Rajapaksa ensured they crossed 150, but it was not enough. REX CLEMENTINE

Player of the Match: A. Zampa. *Attendance:* 3,450.

Sri Lanka

			B	4/6
1 P. Nissanka	c 1 b 8	7	9	1
2 †M. D. K. J. Perera	b 9	35	25	4/1
3 K. I. C. Asalanka	c 4 b 10	35	27	4/1
4 W. I. A. Fernando	c 4 b 10	4	7	0
5 P. B. B. Rajapaksa	not out	33	26	4/1
6 P. W. H. de Silva	c 7 b 9	4	2	1
7 *M. D. Shanaka	c 7 b 8	12	19	1
8 C. Karunaratne	not out	9	6	1
	Lb 4, w 10, nb 1	15		

6 overs: 53-1   (20 overs) 154-6

1/15 2/78 3/86 4/90 5/94 6/134

9 P. V. D. Chameera, 10 M. M. Theekshana and 11 C. B. R. L. S. Kumara did not bat.

Starc 24–11–27–2; Hazlewood 24–12–26–0; Cummins 24–10–34–2; Maxwell 6–3–16–0; Stoinis 18–3–35–0; Zampa 24–12–12–2.

Australia

			B	4/6
1 D. A. Warner	c 5 b 7	65	42	10
2 *A. J. Finch	b 6	37	23	5/2
3 G. J. Maxwell	c 4 b 6	5	6	1
4 S. P. D. Smith	not out	28	26	1
5 M. P. Stoinis	not out	16	7	2/1
	W 2, nb 2	4		

6 overs: 63-0   (17 overs) 155-3

1/70 2/80 3/130

6 M. R. Marsh, 7 †M. S. Wade, 8 P. J. Cummins, 9 M. A. Starc, 10 A. Zampa and 11 J. R. Hazlewood did not bat.

Karunaratne 12–4–19–0; Theekshana 24–10–27–0; Chameera 18–4–33–0; Kumara 18–1–48–0; de Silva 24–10–22–2; Shanaka 6–2–6–1.

Umpires: Aleem Dar and R. K. Illingworth. Third umpire: M. Erasmus.
Referee: J. J. Crowe.

BANGLADESH v WEST INDIES

At Sharjah, October 29, 2021. West Indies won by three runs. Toss: Bangladesh. Twenty20 international debut: R. L. Chase.

The final margin was the closest of the competition, and both teams – desperate to avoid the third Super 12 defeat that would seal their exit – were left to reflect on an error-strewn game. Perhaps the difference was Holder, an injury replacement for fast bowler Obed McCoy: he struck two late sixes, took one for 22 from four overs, and used all his height to catch Liton Das, Bangladesh's top scorer, at long-on in the penultimate over. It had begun with Mahmudullah hitting Bravo's slower ball for six, but Bravo – who had gone for only three in the 17th – conceded just three from his next five deliveries. Bangladesh, whose noses had been in front for much of the chase, now needed 13 off the last but, despite fielding lapses, could not find the boundary, and Russell closed out the game with three balls in the blockhole. Each team suffered setbacks: Shakib Al Hasan sustained an early hamstring injury in the field, which hampered him for the rest of the game and put him out of the tournament, while Pollard retired ill mid-innings, and did not field – though he returned to hit a crucial final-ball six. Bangladesh began well, with two powerplay wickets, including Gayle, on an unsuccessful return to opening. But they gave early let-offs to Chase and Pooran, who struck four sixes in seven balls from the spinners. West Indies, meanwhile, missed three run-out chances – but stayed afloat. SIMON WILDE

Player of the Match: N. Pooran. *Attendance:* 9,400.

West Indies

		B	4/6
1 C. H. Gayle *b 8*	4	10	0
2 E. Lewis *c 5 b 10*	6	9	1
3 R. L. Chase *b 11*	39	46	2
4 S. O. Hetmyer *c 4 b 8*	9	7	1
5 *K. A. Pollard *not out*	14	18	0/1
6 A. D. Russell *run out (9)*	0	0	0
7 †N. Pooran *c 1 b 11*	40	22	1/4
8 D. J. Bravo *c 4 b 10*	1	3	0
9 J. O. Holder *not out*	15	5	0/2
B 1, lb 6, w 7	14		

6 overs: 29-2   (20 overs) 142-7

1/12 2/18 3/32 4/62 5/119 6/119 7/123

10 A. J. Hosein and 11 R. Rampaul did not bat.

Pollard, when 8, retired ill at 62-3 and resumed at 123-7.

Mehedi Hasan snr 24–9–27–2; Taskin Ahmed 24–13–17–0; Mustafizur Rahman 24–8–43–2; Shoriful Islam 24–11–20–2; Shakib Al Hasan 24–8–28–0.

Bangladesh

		B	4/6
1 Mohammad Naim *b 9*	17	19	2
2 Shakib Al Hasan *c 9 b 6*	9	12	1
3 †Liton Das *c 9 b 8*	44	43	4
4 Soumya Sarkar *c 1 b 10*	17	13	2
5 Mushfiqur Rahim *b 11*	8	7	1
6 *Mahmudullah *not out*	31	24	2/1
7 Afif Hossain *not out*	2	2	0
B 2, lb 1, w 8	11		

6 overs: 29-2   (20 overs) 139-5

1/21 2/29 3/60 4/90 5/130

8 Mehedi Hasan snr, 9 Taskin Ahmed, 10 Mustafizur Rahman and 11 Shoriful Islam did not bat.

Rampaul 24–8–25–1; Holder 24–11–22–1; Russell 24–9–29–1; Hosein 24–6–24–1; Bravo 24–8–36–1.

Umpires: A. T. Holdstock and R. J. Tucker.   Third umpire: P. R. Reiffel.
Referee: R. S. Madugalle.

SOUTH AFRICA v SRI LANKA

At Sharjah, October 30, 2021. South Africa won by four wickets. Toss: South Africa.

All eyes were on de Kock, who had apologised to the South African public and his team-mates for pulling out of the match against West Indies, and pledged to take a knee. He was true to his word, and attention quickly turned to an enthralling contest. After being put in, Sri Lanka were dismissed for 142, with opener Nissanka making an impressive 58-ball 72, but only Asalanka of the rest passing 11; as the last nine tumbled for 81, Shamsi and Pretorius each took three for 17. South Africa, though, made heavy weather of the

T20 WORLD CUP HAT-TRICKS

B. Lee	Australia v Bangladesh at Cape Town	2007-08
C. Campher	**Ireland v Netherlands at Abu Dhabi**	**2021-22**
P. W. H. de Silva	**Sri Lanka v South Africa at Sharjah**	**2021-22**
K. Rabada	**South Africa v England at Sharjah**	**2021-22**

chase. Hendricks, leg-before, and de Kock, skying a pull, fell in three balls to Chameera, before van der Dussen was run out by Shanaka. Bavuma supplied solidity with a run-a-ball 46 but, when he became the second victim of a Hasaranga de Silva hat-trick – his second in international cricket – that began in the 15th over and ended in the 18th, South Africa appeared to have botched it. The events of the previous few days, though, seemed to have fostered resilience. With 22 required off nine deliveries, Rabada clubbed Chameera over wide long-off, before Miller swung Kumara over midwicket for successive sixes in the 20th. Radaba sealed victory with a ball to go, when a thick outside edge flew to the boundary, sparking emotional scenes in the South African changing-room. "We had a job to do, and we had to dig deep," said Bavuma, who rewarded Miller – seemingly twice his size – with a touching bear hug.   ZAAHIER ADAMS

Player of the Match: T. Shamsi.   *Attendance:* 2,450.

Sri Lanka

		B	4/6
1 P. Nissanka *c 10 b 7*	72	58	6/3
2 †M. D. K. J. Perera *b 10*	7	10	1
3 K. I. C. Asalanka *run out (8/1)*	21	14	2/1
4 P. B. B. Rajapaksa *c and b 11*	0	3	0
5 W. I. A. Fernando *c and b 11*	3	5	0
6 P. W. H. de Silva *c 5 b 11*	4	5	0
7 *M. D. Shanaka *c 8 b 7*	11	12	2
8 C. Karunaratne *c 3 b 7*	5	5	0
9 P. V. D. Chameera *b 10*	3	4	0
10 M. M. Theekshana *not out*	7	3	1
11 C. B. R. L. S. Kumara *run out (1/10)*	0	1	0
Lb 7, w 2	9		

6 overs: 39-1   (20 overs) 142

1/20 2/61 3/62 4/77 5/91 6/110 7/131 8/131 9/142

Markram 12–4–8–0; Rabada 18–6–32–0; Nortje 24–11–27–2; Maharaj 24–5–34–0; Shamsi 24–13–17–3; Pretorius 18–9–17–3.

South Africa

		B	4/6
1 †Q. de Kock *c and b 9*	12	10	2
2 R. R. Hendricks *lbw b 9*	11	12	1
3 H. E. van der Dussen *run out (7)*	16	11	0
4 *T. Bavuma *c 1 b 6*	46	46	1/1
5 A. K. Markram *b 6*	19	20	2
6 D. A. Miller *not out*	23	13	0/2
7 D. Pretorius *c 4 b 6*	0	1	0
8 K. Rabada *not out*	13	7	1/1
Lb 3, w 2, nb 1	6		

6 overs: 40-2   (19.5 overs) 146-6

1/25 2/26 3/49 4/96 5/112 6/112

9 K. A. Maharaj, 10 A. A. Nortje and 11 T. Shamsi did not bat.

Chameera 24–12–27–2; Theekshana 24–1–31–0; Kumara 23–6–35–0; Karunaratne 18–5–23–0; de Silva 24–10–20–3; Shanaka 6–1–7–0.

Umpires: J. S. Wilson and P. Wilson.   Third umpire: Ahsan Raza.
Referee: J. J. Crowe.

AUSTRALIA v ENGLAND

At Dubai, October 30, 2021 (floodlit). England won by eight wickets. Toss: England.

After the hype, the rout. From the moment Warner edged the game's eighth ball, from Woakes to Buttler, England dominated this encounter between the group's last unbeaten sides. Woakes then stuck out a hand to intercept Smith's toe-ended pull off Jordan, before trapping Maxwell. When Rashid hurried a googly into Stoinis's pads, a repeat of his dismissal in the 50-over World Cup semi-final at Edgbaston in 2019, Australia were 21 for four, and reeling. Ali's off-breaks went unused as Morgan kept him away from Finch, but Livingstone stepped up to remove Wade during a tight four-over spell. After 16, Australia had inched to 75 for five. Five sixes from the lower order (three off the expensive Mills, two off Woakes) helped add 50, but wickets fell too: Jordan finished with three, and Australia's 125 was their lowest T20 total against England since their first meeting, in 2005, when they made 79 at the Rose Bowl. Roy and Buttler flew out of the blocks and, by the time Roy, reverse-sweeping, was leg-before on review to Zampa, they had 66 in just 6.2 overs. Buttler had already hit three sixes, two in succession off Starc, and brought up a 25-ball fifty with his fourth, a monstrous straight blow off Zampa. Malan came and went quietly, but Buttler added another six, and Bairstow thrashed two, as victory arrived with 50 balls to spare – 19 more than Australia's previous-quickest T20 defeat batting first. An ashen-faced Finch admitted: "It's why they've been the best in the world for a while." Morgan, though, was still drooling over Buttler: "When he comes off like that, it's very difficult to stop him."   LAWRENCE BOOTH

Player of the Match: C. J. Jordan.   *Attendance:* 8,800.

Australia

		B	4/6
1 D. A. Warner c 2 b 8	1	2	0
2 *A. J. Finch c 4 b 9	44	49	4
3 S. P. D. Smith c 8 b 9	1	5	0
4 G. J. Maxwell lbw b 8	6	9	0
5 M. P. Stoinis lbw b 10	0	4	0
6 †M. S. Wade c 1 b 6	18	18	2
7 A. C. Agar c 6 b 11	20	20	0/2
8 P. J. Cummins b 9	12	3	0/2
9 M. A. Starc c 2 b 11	13	6	1/1
10 A. Zampa run out (2/11)	1	4	0
11 J. R. Hazlewood not out	0	0	0
Lb 6, w 3	9		

6 overs: 21-3   (20 overs) 125

1/7 2/8 3/15 4/21 5/51 6/98 7/110 8/110 9/119

Rashid 24–12–19–1; Woakes 24–15–23–2; Jordan 24–12–17–3; Livingstone 24–10–15–1; Mills 24–8–45–2.

England

		B	4/6
1 J. J. Roy lbw b 10	22	20	1/1
2 †J. C. Buttler not out	71	32	5/5
3 D. J. Malan c 6 b 7	8	8	1
4 J. M. Bairstow not out	16	11	0/2
B 5, w 3, nb 1	9		

6 overs: 66-0   (11.4 overs) 126-2

1/66 2/97

5 M. M. Ali, 6 L. S. Livingstone, 7 *E. J. G. Morgan, 8 C. R. Woakes, 9 C. J. Jordan, 10 A. U. Rashid and 11 T. S. Mills did not bat.

Starc 18–6–37–0; Hazlewood 12–3–18–0; Cummins 6–3–14–0; Agar 16–7–15–1; Zampa 18–5–37–1.

Umpires: M. Erasmus and N. N. Menon.   Third umpire: H. D. P. K. Dharmasena.
Referee: R. S. Madugalle.

ENGLAND v SRI LANKA

At Sharjah, November 1, 2021 (floodlit). England won by 26 runs. Toss: Sri Lanka.

The question had gnawed away: how would England fare batting first? For Morgan, the answer eventually proved reassuring. Thanks to Buttler, who became their first player to make a century in all three formats, and smart fielding at the crux of Sri Lanka's chase, they became the first side in the Super 12 to win a floodlit match after being put in. Yet after ten overs they had run aground on a low Sharjah pitch against Sri Lanka's spinners, Hasaranga de Silva and Theekshana: 47 for three, with Morgan floundering. Buttler bided his time: he completed England's slowest World Cup half-century (45 balls) while becoming their second player – after Morgan – to pass 2,000 T20I runs, then opened up

MOST T20 INTERNATIONAL WINS AS CAPTAIN

43†	E. J. G. Morgan (England)	42	Asghar Afghan (Afghanistan)
42‡	M. S. Dhoni (India)	32†	V. Kohli (India)

† Including two super overs.   ‡ Including one bowl-out.

to supervise the addition of 116 from the last ten. Morgan finally accelerated, making 40 in a stand of 112 in 13 overs, before de Silva befuddled him. Buttler had 87 when the last over began, and took eight off Chameera's first three deliveries, including a two as Nissanka fumbled a tough catch at deep square. The next two were dots, before Chameera served up a leg-stump full toss: six into the stands, and a 67-ball hundred, England's fourth in T20s, after Alex Hales, Malan and Livingstone. Work remained,

Serving up a storm: Jos Buttler smashes an unbeaten 101 against Sri Lanka.

even after Rashid helped reduce Sri Lanka to 76 for five. Heavy dew meant England were furiously drying the ball after every delivery, while Mills walked off with a thigh strain that ended his World Cup. To add to the tension, de Silva and Shanaka were up with the rate. With 35 needed off 20, de Silva launched Livingstone high towards deep extra. Roy hared round from long-off and held the ball inches from the rope, before relaying it to substitute fielder Sam Billings. Soon after, Buttler hurled down the stumps as Shanaka considered a chancy single. In all, the last five tumbled for eight, handing England a win that looked easier on paper than in the flesh, and taking them within touching distance of the last four.   LAWRENCE BOOTH

Player of the Match: J. C. Buttler.   *Attendance:* 2,650.

England

		B	4/6
1 J. J. Roy *b* 7	9	6	1
2 †J. C. Buttler *not out*	101	67	6/6
3 D. J. Malan *b* 9	6	8	1
4 J. M. Bairstow *lbw b* 7	0	1	0
5 *E. J. G. Morgan *b* 7	40	36	1/3
6 M. M. Ali *not out*	1	2	0
Lb 1, w 5	6		

6 overs: 36-3   (20 overs)   163-4

1/13 2/34 3/35 4/147

7 L. S. Livingstone, 8 C. R. Woakes, 9 C. J. Jordan, 10 A. U. Rashid and 11 T. S. Mills did not bat.

12th man: S. W. Billings.

Chameera 24–8–43–1; de Silva 24–11–21–3; Kumara 24–9–44–0; Theekshana 24–13–13–0; Karunaratne 12–4–17–0; Shanaka 12–2–24–0.

Sri Lanka

		B	4/6
1 P. Nissanka *run out (5/2)*	1	1	0
2 †M. D. K. J. Perera *c 5 b 10*	7	9	0
3 K. I. C. Asalanka *c 6 b 10*	21	16	3/1
4 W. I. A. Fernando *lbw b 9*	13	14	1
5 P. B. B. Rajapaksa *c 1 b 8*	26	18	2/2
6 *M. D. Shanaka *run out (2)*	26	25	2/1
7 P. W. H. de Silva *c 12 b 7*	34	21	3/1
8 C. Karunaratne *c 1 b 6*	0	2	0
9 P. V. D. Chameera *c 3 b 9*	4	4	1
10 M. M. Theekshana *c 9 b 6*	2	2	0
11 C. B. R. L. S. Kumara *not out*	1	2	0
Lb 1, w 1	2		

6 overs: 40-3   (19 overs)   137

1/1 2/24 3/34 4/57 5/76 6/129 7/130 8/134 9/134

Ali 18–10–15–2; Woakes 15–6–25–1; Rashid 24–12–19–2; Jordan 24–11–24–2; Livingstone 24–6–34–1; Mills 9–2–19–0.

Umpires: A. T. Holdstock and R. J. Tucker.   Third umpire: J. S. Wilson.
Referee: D. C. Boon.

BANGLADESH v SOUTH AFRICA

At Abu Dhabi, November 2, 2021. South Africa won by six wickets. Toss: South Africa.

A straightforward win for South Africa, their third in succession, was not as valuable as it first seemed. Chasing just 85, after Rabada and Nortje had each taken a career-best three-for to blow Bangladesh away on an unfamiliarly hard, seaming Abu Dhabi surface, they used up 13.3 overs knocking off the runs, with van der Dussen making a leisurely 22 in 27, and Bavuma an unbeaten 31 in 28. In a group where net run-rate was looming as a tie-breaker, the caution felt misplaced. Still, the game had looked like a possible banana skin against Bangladesh opponents stocked with South African expertise: Russell Domingo and Ottis Gibson were their head coach and bowling coach, having filled the same roles with South Africa, while former Test batsman Ashwell Prince was their batting coach; in charge of fielding was Ryan Cook, yet another South African. It made no difference to a supine batting performance. Four Bangladeshis made ducks (three fell first ball), and only opener Liton Das and No. 8 Mehedi Hasan passed 11. Taskin Ahmed exploited the surface to take a couple of early wickets, but the result was never uncertain, despite South Africa's lack of urgency. Defeat meant Bangladesh – as well as Sri Lanka – were out.   ZAAHIER ADAMS

Player of the Match: K. Rabada.   *Attendance:* 4,950.

Bangladesh

		B	4/6
1 Mohammad Naim *c 2 b 8*		9	11 1
2 †Liton Das *lbw b 11*		24	36 1
3 Soumya Sarkar *lbw b 8*		0	1 0
4 Mushfiqur Rahim *c 2 b 8*		0	3 0
5 *Mahmudullah *c 4 b 10*		3	9 0
6 Afif Hossain *b 7*		0	1 0
7 Shamim Hossain *c 9 b 11*		11	20 0
8 Mehedi Hasan snr *c and b 10*		27	25 2/1
9 Taskin Ahmed *run out (5)*		3	5 0
10 Nasum Ahmed *hit wkt b 10*		0	1 0
11 Shoriful Islam *not out*		0	0 0
Lb 1, w 4, nb 2		7	

6 overs: 28-3   (18.2 overs)   84

1/22 2/22 3/24 4/34 5/34 6/45 7/64 8/77 9/84

Maharaj 24–9–23–0; Rabada 24–14–20–3; Nortje 20–15–8–3; Pretorius 18–8–11–1; Shamsi 24–13–21–2.

South Africa

		B	4/6
1 †Q. de Kock *b 8*		16	15 3
2 R. R. Hendricks *lbw b 9*		4	5 1
3 H. E. van der Dussen *c 11 b 10*		22	27 2
4 A. K. Markram *c 1 b 9*		0	4 0
5 *T. Bavuma *not out*		31	28 3/1
6 D. A. Miller *not out*		5	2 1
B 4, lb 1, w 3		8	

6 overs: 33-3   (13.3 overs)   86-4

1/6 2/28 3/33 4/80

7 D. Pretorius, 8 K. Rabada, 9 K. A. Maharaj, 10 A. A. Nortje and 11 T. Shamsi did not bat.

Taskin Ahmed 24–17–18–2; Shoriful Islam 24–17–15–0; Mehedi Hasan snr 15–5–19–1; Nasum Ahmed 12–5–22–1; Soumya Sarkar 6–2–7–0.

Umpires: R. K. Illingworth and P. R. Reiffel.   Third umpire: C. M. Brown.
Referee: J. J. Crowe.

AUSTRALIA v BANGLADESH

At Dubai, November 4, 2021. Australia won by eight wickets. Toss: Bangladesh.

Starc set the tone for an embarrassing mismatch by yorking Liton Das with the third ball of Bangladesh's last game of the tournament. They were ten for three after three overs, their top order badly missing the injured Shakib Al Hasan, and dismissed in double figures for the second time in three days; in his 118th international appearance, Zampa ran through the lower order for his maiden five-wicket haul. He would have claimed a first hat-trick too, had Wade not dropped Taskin Ahmed. It barely mattered: Australia had never bowled a side out so cheaply in T20s. To overtake South Africa on net run-rate, they had to

T20 FIVE-WICKET HAULS FOR AUSTRALIA

6-30	**A. C. Agar v New Zealand at Wellington**	**2020-21**
5-19	**A. Zampa v Bangladesh at Dubai**	**2021-22**
5-24	A. C. Agar v South Africa at Johannesburg	2019-20
5-27	J. P. Faulkner v Pakistan at Mohali.	2015-16

complete their chase within 50 balls: thanks to Finch's bottom-handed bludgeoning, they did it in 38. Marsh, restored to the side at No. 3 – Ashton Agar was left out as Australia adjusted their balance – pulled the winning six off Taskin to give them victory with 82 balls to spare. Soon after, the inquest into Bangladesh's miserable campaign began, with Mahmudullah saying his future as captain was out of his hands.   MATT ROLLER

Player of the Match: A. Zampa.   *Attendance:* 1,600.

Bangladesh

		B	4/6
1 Mohammad Naim *c 8 b 11*.	17	16	3
2 †Liton Das *b 9*	0	1	0
3 Soumya Sarkar *b 11*	5	8	1
4 Mushfiqur Rahim *lbw b 4*	1	2	0
5 *Mahmudullah *c 7 b 9*	16	18	2
6 Afif Hossain *c 2 b 10*	0	4	0
7 Shamim Hossain *c 7 b 10*.	19	18	1/1
8 Mehedi Hasan snr *lbw b 10*	0	1	0
9 Taskin Ahmed *not out*	6	11	0
10 Mustafizur Rahman *c 5 b 10* . . .	4	9	0
11 Shoriful Islam *c 2 b 10*.	0	2	0
Lb 1, w 4	5		
6 overs: 33-4 (15 overs)	73		

1/1 2/6 3/10 4/32 5/33 6/62 7/62 8/65 9/73

Starc 24–15–21–2; Hazlewood 12–10–8–2; Maxwell 12–7–6–1; Cummins 18–9–18–0; Zampa 24–14–19–5.

Australia

		B	4/6
1 D. A. Warner *b 11*	18	14	3
2 *A. J. Finch *b 9*	40	20	2/4
3 M. R. Marsh *not out*	16	5	2/1
4 G. J. Maxwell *not out*	0	0	0
Lb 1, w 2, nb 1	4		
6 overs: 67-2 (6.2 overs)	78-2		

1/58 2/67

5 S. P. D. Smith, 6 M. P. Stoinis, 7 †M. S. Wade, 8 P. J. Cummins, 9 M. A. Starc, 10 A. Zampa and 11 J. R. Hazlewood did not bat.

Taskin Ahmed 20–8–36–1; Mustafizur Rahman 12–3–32–0; Shoriful Islam 6–1–9–1.

Umpires: H. D. P. K. Dharmasena and N. N. Menon.   Third umpire: J. S. Wilson.
Referee: J. J. Crowe.

SRI LANKA v WEST INDIES

At Abu Dhabi, November 4, 2021 (floodlit). Sri Lanka won by 20 runs. Toss: West Indies.
   Before 2021, Asalanka and Nissanka had been little known even among Sri Lankan fans, but they further enhanced their reputations with a skilful 91-run stand in ten overs, as reigning champions West Indies were dumped out of the tournament. By the end of the game, Asalanka was the competition's leading run-scorer, with Nissanka a close second; Hasaranga de Silva, meanwhile, was the leading wicket-taker, after his two for 19 took his haul to 16 – a T20 World Cup record – at just nine apiece. West Indies' bowling, by contrast, lacked penetration and pace, and conceded 189. Many felt they had been over-reliant on players past their prime, and the onus fell on two of the younger generation.

Pooran's 46 kept them in the game after Binura Fernando had removed the openers in his first over, while Hetmyer's unbeaten 81 off 54 averted meltdown. When the 14th over began, West Indies required 83 – possible, given Hetmyer and Pollard had just come together, with Bravo and Holder to follow. But de Silva bowled Pollard first ball, then Bravo, both with a googly, and Hetmyer's late blows could not prevent a sorry end for a side who had won two of the previous three T20 World Cups.   REX CLEMENTINE

Player of the Match: K. I. C. Asalanka.   *Attendance:* 2,300.

Sri Lanka

		B	4/6
1 P. Nissanka *c 5 b 9*	51	41	5
2 †M. D. K. J. Perera *c and b 6*	29	21	2/1
3 K. I. C. Asalanka *c 5 b 6*	68	41	8/1
4 *M. D. Shanaka *not out*	25	14	2/1
5 C. Karunaratne *not out*	3	3	0
Lb 4, w 9	13		
6 overs: 48-1 (20 overs) 189-3			

1/42 2/133 3/179

6 W. I. A. Fernando, 7 P. B. B. Rajapaksa, 8 P. W. H. de Silva, 9 K. B. U. Fernando, 10 P. V. D. Chameera and 11 M. M. Theekshana did not bat.

12th man: D. M. de Silva.

Chase 2.4–6–0; Holder 2.4–7–37–0; Rampaul 2.4–8–37–0; Russell 2.4–8–33–2; Hosein 1.2–0–22–0; Bravo 2.4–4–42–1; Pollard 6–0–8–0.

West Indies

		B	4/6
1 C. H. Gayle *c 8 b 9*	1	5	0
2 E. Lewis *b 9*	8	6	2
3 †N. Pooran *c 12 b 10*	46	34	6/1
4 R. L. Chase *c 7 b 5*	9	8	2
5 S. O. Hetmyer *not out*	81	54	8/4
6 A. D. Russell *c and b 5*	2	4	0
7 *K. A. Pollard *b 8*	0	1	0
8 J. O. Holder *c 5 b 4*	8	5	0/1
9 D. J. Bravo *b 8*	2	3	0
10 A. J. Hosein *not out*	1	1	0
B 1, lb 2, w 7, nb 1	11		
6 overs: 52-3 (20 overs) 169-8			

1/1 2/10 3/47 4/77 5/94 6/107 7/117 8/131

11 R. Rampaul did not bat.

Theekshana 2.4–13–21–0; K. B. U. Fernando 1.2–6–24–2; Chameera 2.4–9–41–1; Karunaratne 2.4–11–43–2; Shanaka 1.2–3–18–1; de Silva 2.4–10–19–2.

Umpires: Aleem Dar and L. Rusere.   Third umpire: P. Wilson.
Referee: D. C. Boon.

AUSTRALIA v WEST INDIES

At Abu Dhabi, November 6, 2021. Australia won by eight wickets. Toss: Australia.

A few hours after Australia's bullish win, their place in the semi-finals – on net run-rate – was confirmed by South Africa's failure to beat England by the required amount. West Indies, meanwhile, dropped out of the top eight in the ICC rankings, which meant they would have to play in the First Round of the 2022 World Cup in Australia to qualify for the Super 12s. It was a sad farewell to international cricket for the 38-year-old Bravo, who made only ten and didn't manage a wicket; he later said the 42-year-old Gayle, who hit two sixes before he was bowled by Cummins, had only "halfway-retired". West Indies had raced to 30 from 13 balls, then lost three for five in eight – including two to Hazlewood, who finished with four for 39 after his first over cost 20. A 31-ball 44 from Pollard helped them to 157, before Hosein bowled Finch for nine. But Warner played some ferocious cuts and pulls on his way to a 29-ball half-century, and Marsh was elegant through the covers. By the time he drove Gayle to mid-off to depart for 53 off 32, he and Warner had put on 124, Australia's highest second-wicket stand; Gayle celebrated by playfully jumping on Marsh's back.   VINODE MAMCHAN

Player of the Match: D. A. Warner.   *Attendance:* 1,700.

West Indies

		B	4/6
1 C. H. Gayle *b* 8	15	9	0/2
2 E. Lewis *c 5 b* 10	29	26	5
3 †N. Pooran *c 3 b* 11	4	4	1
4 R. L. Chase *b* 11	0	2	0
5 S. O. Hetmyer *c 7 b* 11	27	28	2
6 *K. A. Pollard *c 4 b* 9	44	31	4/1
7 D. J. Bravo *c 1 b* 11	10	12	0/1
8 A. D. Russell *not out*	18	7	1/2
9 J. O. Holder *not out*	1	1	0
Lb 6, w 3	9		

6 overs: 50-3   (20 overs) 157-7

1/30 2/35 3/35 4/70 5/91 6/126 7/143

10 H. R. Walsh and 11 A. J. Hosein did not bat.

Starc 24–10–33–1; Hazlewood 24–8–39–4; Cummins 24–10–37–1; Maxwell 6–3–6–0; Marsh 18–7–16–0; Zampa 24–11–20–1.

Australia

		B	4/6
1 D. A. Warner *not out*	89	56	9/4
2 *A. J. Finch *b* 11	9	11	1
3 M. R. Marsh *c 9 b* 11	53	32	5/2
4 G. J. Maxwell *not out*	0	0	0
Lb 3, w 6, nb 1	10		

6 overs: 53-1   (16.2 overs) 161-2

1/33 2/157

5 S. P. D. Smith, 6 M. P. Stoinis, 7 †M. S. Wade, 8 P. J. Cummins, 9 M. A. Starc, 10 A. Zampa and 11 J. R. Hazlewood did not bat.

Hosein 24–9–29–1; Chase 8–3–17–0; Holder 12–4–26–0; Bravo 24–8–36–0; Walsh 12–3–18–0; Russell 12–1–25–0; Gayle 6–3–7–1.

Umpires: R. K. Illingworth and L. Rusere.   Third umpire: Aleem Dar.
Referee: J. Srinath.

ENGLAND v SOUTH AFRICA

At Sharjah, November 6, 2021 (floodlit). South Africa won by ten runs. Toss: England.
England's first defeat of the competition was made more painful by injury to Roy, who pulled up with a calf strain 38 runs into their pursuit of 190, and was ruled out of the tournament two days later. But while the result did not hamper their progress to the semi-finals, South Africa were squeezed out on net run-rate by Australia: needing to limit England to fewer than 132 to qualify, they had to settle for a narrow victory. Rabada's first three overs had cost 45, including three successive sixes from Livingstone in the 16th; the first, out of the ground over midwicket, measured 112 metres, the World Cup's biggest hit.

Hightailing it: Anrich Nortje hits 90mph as South Africa inflict England's first defeat.

Alex Davidson, Getty Images

Now, defending 14 off the last, Rabada began with a hat-trick, as Woakes, Morgan and Jordan were all caught on the slog. But it was immaterial. South Africa had begun slowly after being put in, with Hendricks, bowled sweeping by Ali, making two off eight. Rashid removed de Kock, caught at long-on, but Markram joined van der Dussen in a potent unbroken third-wicket stand of 103 in 8.4 overs, including eight sixes. Between them, Wood – in his first game of the tournament after injury to Tymal Mills – and Woakes were hit for seven. Van der Dussen's 94 off 60 was a career-best. England needed 87 to avoid being knocked out, and 106 to top the group. Buttler and Ali, promoted to No. 3, provided early impetus, but Shamsi's left-arm wrist-spin slowed them, and Rabada supplied the finishing touches. England wore black armbands in memory of Kent's Alan Igglesden, the former Test seamer who had died five days earlier.   LAWRENCE BOOTH

Player of the Match: H. E. van der Dussen.   *Attendance:* 4,500.

South Africa

		B	4/6
1 R. R. Hendricks *b 3*	2	8	0
2 †Q. de Kock *c 1 b 10*	34	27	4
3 H. E. van der Dussen *not out*	94	60	5/6
4 A. K. Markram *not out*	52	25	2/4
B 1, lb 3, w 3	7		

6 overs: 40-1   (20 overs) 189-2

1/15 2/86

5 *T. Bavuma, 6 D. A. Miller, 7 D. Pretorius, 8 K. Rabada, 9 K. A. Maharaj, 10 A. A. Nortje and 11 T. Shamsi did not bat.

Ali 24–8–27–1; Woakes 24–8–43–0; Rashid 24–4–32–1; Jordan 24–6–36–0; Wood 24–4–47–0.

England

		B	4/6
1 J. J. Roy *retired hurt*	20	15	4
2 †J. C. Buttler *c 5 b 10*	26	15	3/1
3 M. M. Ali *c 6 b 11*	37	27	3/2
4 J. M. Bairstow *lbw b 11*	1	3	0
5 D. J. Malan *c 8 b 7*	33	26	3/1
6 L. S. Livingstone *c 6 b 7*	28	17	1/3
7 *E. J. G. Morgan *c 9 b 8*	17	12	3
8 C. R. Woakes *c 10 b 8*	7	5	1
9 C. J. Jordan *c 6 b 8*	0	1	0
10 A. U. Rashid *not out*	2	2	0
11 M. A. Wood *not out*	1	1	0
Lb 2, w 3, nb 2	7		

6 overs: 59-1   (20 overs) 179-8

1/58 2/59 3/110 4/145 5/165 6/176 7/176 8/176

Roy retired hurt at 38-0.

Maharaj 18–8–23–0; Nortje 24–11–34–1; Rabada 24–6–48–3; Shamsi 24–13–24–2; Markram 12–4–18–0; Pretorius 18–7–30–2.

Umpires: C. M. Brown and J. S. Wilson.   Third umpire: P. Wilson.
Referee: D. C. Boon.

SUPER 12 – GROUP 2

INDIA v PAKISTAN

At Dubai, October 24, 2021 (floodlit). Pakistan won by ten wickets. Toss: Pakistan.

Indian World Cup wins over Pakistan had become so routine that, in advance, the pundits barely bothered to clear their throats. But Babar Azam chose to field after winning an important toss – the dew would be a problem for India's bowlers, not Pakistan's – and Shaheen Shah Afridi served up an electrifying opening burst, swinging a yorker on to Sharma's pads, then a good-length ball through Rahul's gate. When Yadav touched one from Hasan Ali that left him a fraction, India had lost three for 31 inside the powerplay. But Kohli accumulated with quiet panache, and Pant hit successive one-handed sixes off Hasan – slog-sweep followed by straight-drive. Pakistan, though, never quite lost control, despite a careless conclusion to Afridi's spell: two balls after foxing Kohli with a slow bouncer, he produced a wide full toss, which was steered for four by Pandya, and called a no-ball on height; the free hit led to five byes, as Afridi's wild run-out attempt hurtled past long-on.

Star of Pakistan: Mohammad Rizwan clips to leg in the ten-wicket defeat of India.

If 151 for seven seemed to give both sides a chance, Pakistan's openers saw it differently. Mohammad Rizwan drove Bhuvneshwar Kumar's second ball for four, and pulled his third for six; Babar repeated the dose off Jadeja. After ten overs, Pakistan had 71. Both batsmen mowed Chakravarthy into the leg-side stands, and Indian fans – sensing the worst – began to drift away. When Babar scampered the winning runs, Pakistan had their first victory in any World Cup over India, at the 13th attempt, and their first by ten wickets in all T20 games. As Pakistan's supporters disappeared joyously into the Dubai night, Kohli was both generous and subdued: "They outplayed us today." LAWRENCE BOOTH

Player of the Match: Shaheen Shah Afridi. *Attendance:* 16,550.

India

		B	4/6
1 K. L. Rahul *b 10*	3	8	0
2 R. G. Sharma *lbw b 10*	0	1	0
3 *V. Kohli *c 1 b 10*	57	49	5/1
4 S. A. Yadav *c 1 b 9*	11	8	1/1
5 †R. R. Pant *c and b 7*	39	30	2/2
6 R. A. Jadeja *c 12 b 9*	13	13	1
7 H. H. Pandya *c 2 b 11*	11	8	2
8 Bhuvneshwar Kumar *not out*	5	4	0
9 Mohammed Shami *not out*	0	0	0
B 6, lb 1, w 4, nb 1	12		

6 overs: 36-3   (20 overs) 151-7

1/1 2/6 3/31 4/84 5/125 6/133 7/146

10 J. J. Bumrah and 11 V. V. Chakravarthy did not bat.

Shaheen Shah Afridi 24–13–31–3; Imad Wasim 12–5–10–0; Hasan Ali 24–8–44–2; Shadab Khan 24–9–22–1; Mohammad Hafeez 12–3–12–0; Haris Rauf 24–8–25–1.

Pakistan

		B	4/6
1 †Mohammad Rizwan *not out*	79	55	6/3
2 *Babar Azam *not out*	68	52	6/2
Lb 1, w 4	5		

6 overs: 43-0   (17.5 overs) 152-0

3 Fakhar Zaman, 4 Mohammad Hafeez, 5 Shoaib Malik, 6 Asif Ali, 7 Shadab Khan, 8 Imad Wasim, 9 Hasan Ali, 10 Shaheen Shah Afridi and 11 Haris Rauf did not bat.

12th man: Mohammad Nawaz.

Bhuvneshwar Kumar 18–7–25–0; Mohammed Shami 23–5–43–0; Bumrah 18–7–22–0; Chakravarthy 24–6–33–0; Jadeja 24–8–28–0.

Umpires: M. Erasmus and C. B. Gaffaney. Third umpire: R. K. Illingworth.
Referee: D. C. Boon.

AFGHANISTAN v SCOTLAND

At Sharjah, October 25, 2021 (floodlit). Afghanistan won by 130 runs. Toss: Afghanistan.

In their first game since the fall of their country to the Taliban, Afghanistan's players cried during the national anthem. But from the moment their openers plundered 18 off the second over, from Leask, they gave their small but vociferous contingent in the crowd a performance to relish. As so often during their rise, victory was authored by spin bowling: Mujeeb Zadran and Rashid Khan combined to take nine for 29, as Scotland – from 28

MOST CONSECUTIVE T20 WINS IN ONE COUNTRY

17	**Afghanistan in the UAE**	. . . .	**2015-16 to 2021-22**
16	**Pakistan in the UAE**	. . . .	**2016-17 to 2021-22**
10	Australia in Australia.	. . . .	2005-06 to 2009-10
10	Afghanistan in India	. . . .	2015-16 to 2018-19
9†	**England in the UAE**	. . . .	**2011-12 to 2021-22**

† *Includes one super over.*

---

without loss – collapsed to 60, their lowest T20 total (behind 81 against South Africa at The Oval in 2009). With his array of variations from the front of the hand, Mujeeb ran through the top order; Rashid was yet to bowl, but it was already 37 for five. When he trapped Leask, Nos 3–6 had, uniquely in T20 internationals, all made a duck. That was one of five lbws, equalling the T20 record set three days earlier by the Netherlands' batters against Sri Lanka. Mujeeb was the first to take five in his maiden T20 World Cup game. Earlier, Hazratullah Zazai and Mohammad Shahzad helped Afghanistan to 55 for one in the powerplay, before Najibullah Zadran hit a brutal 59. The carnage only emphasised the excellence of Mark Watt, Scotland's left-arm spinner, who varied his angle and pace, and dismissed Hazratullah with a 67mph yorker. TIM WIGMORE

Player of the Match: Mujeeb Zadran. *Attendance:* 1,150.

Afghanistan

		B	4/6
1 Hazratullah Zazai b 8.	44	30	3/3
2 †Mohammad Shahzad c 7 b 10 .	22	15	2/1
3 Rahmanullah Gurbaz c 2 b 9 . . .	46	37	1/4
4 Najibullah Zadran c 11 b 10 . .	59	34	5/3
5 *Mohammad Nabi not out.	11	4	2
Lb 3, w 5.	8		

6 overs: 55-1   (20 overs)   190-4

1/54 2/82 3/169 4/190

6 Asghar Afghan, 7 Gulbadeen Naib, 8 Karim Janat, 9 Rashid Khan, 10 Naveen-ul-Haq and 11 Mujeeb Zadran did not bat.

Wheal 24–8–42–0; Leask 6–1–18–0; Sharif 24–10–33–2; Davey 24–3–41–1; Watt 24–15–23–1; Greaves 18–6–30–0.

Scotland

		B	4/6
1 H. G. Munsey b 11	25	18	2/2
2 *K. J. Coetzer b 11	10	7	2
3 C. S. MacLeod lbw b 11	0	1	0
4 R. D. Berrington lbw b 11	0	3	0
5 †M. H. Cross c 2 b 10	0	1	0
6 M. A. Leask lbw b 9	0	5	0
7 C. N. Greaves lbw b 9	12	12	1
8 M. R. J. Watt b 11	1	3	0
9 J. H. Davey lbw b 9.	4	7	0
10 S. M. Sharif not out	3	4	0
11 B. T. J. Wheal b 9	0	1	0
Lb 2, w 3.	5		

6 overs: 37-5   (10.2 overs)   60

1/28 2/28 3/28 4/30 5/36 6/38 7/45 8/53 9/60

Mohammad Nabi 6–3–11–0; Mujeeb Zadran 24–17–20–5; Naveen-ul-Haq 12–8–12–1; Rashid Khan 14–8–9–4; Karim Janat 6–2–6–0.

Umpires: H. D. P. K. Dharmasena and P. Wilson.   Third umpire: R. A. Kettleborough.
Referee: J. J. Crowe.

NEW ZEALAND v PAKISTAN

At Sharjah, October 26, 2021 (floodlit). Pakistan won by five wickets. Toss: Pakistan.

Just over a month earlier, New Zealand had abandoned their tour of Pakistan minutes before the start of a one-day international in Rawalpindi because of a security alert. Now, Pakistan's fans wanted revenge. The atmosphere at Sharjah matched the mood back home: their UAE expats were loud, and taunted the New Zealanders with chants of "security, security". Buoyed by their support – and their ten-wicket win over India – Pakistan's bowlers were in top form again. After Babar Azam won the toss, Shaheen Shah Afridi began with a maiden to Guptill, before the pace of Haris Rauf brought him a career-best four for 22. In between, Mitchell and Conway top-scored with 27 each, while Williamson made a laborious 26-ball 25 before he was run out by Hasan Ali off his own bowling. New Zealand failed to hit a boundary between the last ball of the 13th over and the last of the 17th, and were restricted to 134 for eight. But their own bowlers struck at regular intervals, with Southee's early dismissal of Babar his 100th in the format; only Sri Lanka's Lasith Malinga and Bangladesh's Shakib Al Hasan had beaten him to it (though Afghanistan's Rashid Khan would join them three days later). Sodhi won a pair of lbw shouts, while an outstanding full-length dive by Conway at long-off did for Mohammad Hafeez. When Boult trapped Imad Wasim, Pakistan needed 48 off 31. Asif Ali made it look easy, hitting Southee for successive sixes, then clouting Boult for a third. With Shoaib Malik adding one in between, off Santner, Pakistan raced to a cathartic victory. SHAHID HASHMI

Player of the Match: Haris Rauf. *Attendance:* 10,000.

New Zealand

			B	4/6
1 M. J. Guptill *b 11*		17	20	3
2 D. J. Mitchell *c 3 b 6*		27	20	1/2
3 *K. S. Williamson *run out (9)*		25	26	2/1
4 J. D. S. Neesham *c 3 b 4*		1	2	0
5 D. P. Conway *c 2 b 11*		27	24	3
6 G. D. Phillips *c 9 b 11*		13	15	1
7 †T. L. Seifert *c 4 b 10*		8	8	1
8 M. J. Santner *b 11*		6	5	1
9 I. S. Sodhi *not out*		2	2	0
B 1, lb 5, nb 2		8		

6 overs: 42-1 (20 overs) 134-8

1/36 2/54 3/56 4/90 5/116 6/116 7/125 8/134

10 T. G. Southee and 11 T. A. Boult did not bat.

Shaheen Shah Afridi 24–13–21–1; Imad Wasim 24–11–24–1; Hasan Ali 18–4–26–0; Haris Rauf 24–10–22–4; Shadab Khan 18–10–19–0; Mohammad Hafeez 12–5–16–1.

Pakistan

			B	4/6
1 †Mohammad Rizwan *lbw b 9*		33	34	5
2 *Babar Azam *b 10*		9	11	1
3 Fakhar Zaman *lbw b 9*		11	17	0/1
4 Mohammad Hafeez *c 5 b 8*		11	6	0/1
5 Shoaib Malik *not out*		26	20	2/1
6 Imad Wasim *lbw b 11*		11	12	1
7 Asif Ali *not out*		27	12	1/3
Lb 2, w 5		7		

6 overs: 30-1 (18.4 overs) 135-5

1/28 2/47 3/63 4/69 5/87

8 Shadab Khan, 9 Hasan Ali, 10 Shaheen Shah Afridi and 11 Haris Rauf did not bat.

Santner 24–7–33–1; Southee 24–14–25–1; Boult 22–12–29–1; Neesham 18–7–18–0; Sodhi 24–10–28–2.

Umpires: M. A. Gough and R. A. Kettleborough. Third umpire: P. Wilson.
Referee: R. S. Madugalle.

NAMIBIA v SCOTLAND

At Abu Dhabi, October 27, 2021 (floodlit). Namibia won by four wickets. Toss: Namibia.

The first meeting of two Associate nations in the main stages of a T20 World Cup went the way of Namibia, after their First Round wins over the Netherlands and Ireland. It was seldom in doubt after left-armer Trumpelmann collected an unprecedented three wickets in the opening over of a T20 international: Munsey was bowled first ball, MacLeod caught behind, and Berrington trapped by an inswinger. Scotland were already without their captain, Kyle Coetzer, because of a finger injury. Now, six balls in, they were without hope: two for three, with both runs from wides. Arriving soon after, at 18 for four, Leask showed power and selectivity to thrash 44 from 27 balls, but his dismissal, bowled by Smit as he sized up a short leg-side boundary, prevented a final flourish; Frylinck's accurate medium-pace earned two for ten. Even so, 109 for eight on a slow Abu Dhabi pitch was a recovery of sorts, and Scotland's spin trio – Greaves, Watt and Leask – hauled them back into the game. For the fifth consecutive match, left-armer Watt conceded under a run a ball; when he fired one down leg to have Williams stumped, Namibia were 67 for four in the 13th. But Scotland's chances of a Super 12 victory – and $40,000 – were thwarted by Smit and Wiese. TIM WIGMORE

Player of the Match: R. C. Trumpelmann. *Attendance:* 2,800.

Scotland

		B	4/6
1 H. G. Munsey *b 10*	0	1	0
2 †M. H. Cross *b 7*	19	33	1
3 C. S. MacLeod *c 3 b 10*	0	2	0
4 *R. D. Berrington *lbw b 10*	0	1	0
5 C. D. Wallace *lbw b 5*	4	13	0
6 M. A. Leask *b 6*	44	27	4/2
7 C. N. Greaves *run out (5)*	25	32	2
8 M. R. J. Watt *c 4 b 7*	3	6	0
9 J. H. Davey *not out*	5	5	0
Lb 5, w 4	9		

6 overs: 22-4   (20 overs) 109-8

1/0 2/2 3/2 4/18 5/57 6/93 7/99 8/109

10 S. M. Sharif and 11 B. T. J. Wheal did not bat.

Trumpelmann 24–17–17–3; Frylinck 24–14–10–2; Smit 24–11–20–1; Wiese 24–11–22–1; Scholtz 12–2–16–0; van Lingen 6–2–12–0; Ya France 6–3–7–0.

Namibia

		B	4/6
1 C. G. Williams *st 2 b 8*	23	29	0/1
2 M. van Lingen *c 4 b 10*	18	24	2
3 †Z. E. Green *c 1 b 7*	9	13	1
4 *M. G. Erasmus *b 6*	4	6	0
5 D. Wiese *c 8 b 6*	16	14	0/1
6 J. J. Smit *not out*	32	23	2/2
7 J. N. Frylinck *c 3 b 11*	2	4	0
8 H. N. Ya France *not out*	0	2	0
Lb 9, w 2	11		

6 overs: 29-1   (19.1 overs) 115-6

1/28 2/50 3/61 4/67 5/102 6/109

9 J. N. Loftie-Eaton, 10 R. C. Trumpelmann and 11 B. M. Scholtz did not bat.

Wheal 24–14–14–1; Davey 12–5–15–0; Sharif 19–8–21–1; Greaves 24–13–22–1; Watt 24–12–22–1; Leask 12–6–12–2.

Umpires: A. T. Holdstock and R. J. Tucker.   Third umpire: N. N. Menon.

Referee: J. Srinath.

AFGHANISTAN v PAKISTAN

At Dubai, October 29, 2021 (floodlit). Pakistan won by five wickets. Toss: Afghanistan.

Pakistan achieved a memorable win, their third in a row, with Asif Ali again to the fore. After spiriting them to victory over New Zealand with three sixes, he now smashed four, all in the 19th over off the hapless Karim Janat. Set 148, Pakistan had been on course at 122 for three with 19 deliveries to go, and Rashid Khan – who had conjured up a mesmeric display of leg-breaks and googlies – preparing to send down his last. He made it count: on 51, Babar Azam missed a heave, and was bowled. After Naveen-ul-Haq conceded only two in an immaculate 18th over, and had Shoaib Malik caught behind, Pakistan still needed 24. Asif, much-criticised in recent times, rose spectacularly to the challenge, hitting Karim's first ball over long-off, his third over midwicket, his fifth over long-off, and his sixth over extra cover; only a pair of perfect yorkers escaped punishment. Afghan fans in a large crowd were stunned. Outside the stadium, meanwhile, police had been called after thousands of ticketless supporters tried to force their way in; they were eventually dispersed, though the ICC promised an investigation. Earlier, Afghanistan had opted to bat, contrary to the tournament's prevailing wisdom. Three of their top five began with a six, but wickets were thrown away too, and from 76 for six they were thankful for an unbroken stand of 71 at ten an over from captain Mohammad Nabi and Gulbadeen Naib, one of his predecessors. Pakistan's biggest challenge in the chase was always going to be Rashid and Mujeeb Zadran, who picked up three for 40 between them; the wicket of Mohammad Hafeez made Rashid the fastest of the four bowlers to claim 100 in T20 internationals, in his 53rd match. Afghanistan had started to dream of a crucial win, until Asif provided a robust wake-up call.   SHAHID HASHMI

Player of the Match: Asif Ali.   *Attendance:* 15,000.

Afghanistan

		B	4/6
1 Hazratullah Zazai c 11 b 8	0	5	0
2 †Mohammad Shahzad c 2 b 10 .	8	9	1
3 Rahmanullah Gurbaz c 2 b 9 . . .	10	7	0/1
4 Asghar Afghan c and b 11	10	7	1/1
5 Karim Janat c 3 b 8	15	17	1/1
6 Najibullah Zadran c 1 b 7	22	21	3/1
7 *Mohammad Nabi not out	35	32	5
8 Gulbadeen Naib not out	35	25	4/1
Lb 3, w 6, nb 3	12		

6 overs: 49-4   (20 overs) 147-6

1/7 2/13 3/33 4/39 5/64 6/76

9 Rashid Khan, 10 Naveen-ul-Haq and 11 Mujeeb Zadran did not bat.

Shaheen Shah Afridi 24–12–22–1; Imad Wasim 24–14–25–2; Haris Rauf 24–9–37–1; Hasan Ali 24–12–38–1; Shadab Khan 24–15–22–1.

Pakistan

		B	4/6
1 †Mohammad Rizwan c 10 b 11	8	10	1
2 *Babar Azam b 9.	51	47	4
3 Fakhar Zaman lbw b 7	30	25	2/1
4 Mohammad Hafeez c 8 b 9	10	10	1
5 Shoaib Malik c 2 b 10	19	15	1/1
6 Asif Ali not out	25	7	0/4
7 Shadab Khan not out	0	1	0
Lb 2, w 2, nb 1	5		

6 overs: 38-1   (19 overs) 148-5

1/12 2/75 3/97 4/122 5/124

8 Imad Wasim, 9 Hasan Ali, 10 Shaheen Shah Afridi and 11 Haris Rauf did not bat.

Mujeeb Zadran 24–12–14–1; Mohammad Nabi 24–7–36–1;   Naveen-ul-Haq   18–6–22–1; Karim Janat 24–4–48–0; Rashid Khan 24–9–26–2.

Umpires: C. M. Brown and J. S. Wilson.   Third umpire: L. Rusere.
Referee: D. C. Boon.

AFGHANISTAN v NAMIBIA

At Abu Dhabi, October 31, 2021. Afghanistan won by 62 runs. Toss: Afghanistan.

Afghanistan gave their former captain Asghar Afghan a rousing send-off, after he announced on Facebook the day before that this would be his last match for his country. "I want more and more youngsters to get the opportunity to play for Afghanistan," he wrote. After contributing 31 off 23 balls to his side's 160 for five – a total boosted by a busy opening stand of 53 between Hazratullah Zazai and Mohammad Shahzad, who became the first for his country to pass 2,000 T20 runs, and a late flurry from Mohammad Nabi – Asghar walked off through an emotional guard of honour. Afghanistan would have managed more but for leg-spinner Nicol Loftie-Eaton, who got the ball to fizz off the pitch and claimed two for 21. But Namibia lost three in the powerplay and, when Hamid Hassan

– in his first T20 international for five and a half years – nailed Erasmus with an inswinging yorker, then had Smit caught behind for a duck, they were 56 for six after 11. He finished with three for nine, while Naveen-ul-Haq, who had grown up idolising him, also bagged three. Namibia failed to reach three figures, and Afghanistan remained second in the group, with half an eye on the semi-finals. DEIVARAYAN MUTHU

Player of the Match: Naveen-ul-Haq. *Attendance:* 600.

Afghanistan

			B	4/6
1 Hazratullah Zazai *c 2 b 7*		33	27	4/2
2 †Mohammad Shahzad *c 11 b 10*		45	33	3/2
3 Rahmanullah Gurbaz *lbw b 3*		4	8	0
4 Asghar Afghan *c 2 b 10*		31	23	3/1
5 Najibullah Zadran *lbw b 3*		7	11	1
6 *Mohammad Nabi *not out*		32	17	5/1
7 Gulbadeen Naib *not out*		1	1	0
Lb 1, w 6		7		

6 overs: 50-0   (20 overs) 160-5

1/53 2/68 3/89 4/113 5/148

8 Karim Janat, 9 Rashid Khan, 10 Naveen-ul-Haq and 11 Hamid Hassan did not bat.

12th man: Usman Ghani.

Trumpelmann 24–14–34–2; Smit 18–7–22–1; Wiese 24–9–33–0; Frylinck 18–6–34–0; Loftie-Eaton 24–11–21–2; Scholtz 6–1–8–0; Erasmus 6–2–7–0.

Namibia

			B	4/6
1 C. G. Williams *c 12 b 10*		1	3	0
2 M. van Lingen *c 11 b 10*		11	8	0/1
3 J. N. Loftie-Eaton *b 7*		14	16	0/1
4 *M. G. Erasmus *b 11*		12	14	1
5 †Z. E. Green *b 9*		1	7	0
6 D. Wiese *b 11*		26	30	2
7 J. J. Smit *c 2 b 11*		0	3	0
8 J. N. Frylinck *c 6 b 10*		6	14	0
9 H. N. Ya France *c and b 7*		3	5	0
10 R. C. Trumpelmann *not out*		12	9	2
11 B. M. Scholtz *not out*		6	11	0
Lb 2, w 4		6		

6 overs: 29-3   (20 overs) 98-9

1/2 2/16 3/29 4/36 5/56 6/56 7/69 8/77 9/80

Naveen-ul-Haq 24–10–26–3; Mohammad Nabi 12–6–17–0; Hamid Hassan 24–16–9–3; Gulbadeen Naib 24–12–19–2; Karim Janat 12–5–11–0; Rashid Khan 24–15–14–1.

Umpires: Ahsan Raza and C. B. Gaffaney.   Third umpire: P. R. Reiffel.
Referee: J. Srinath.

INDIA v NEW ZEALAND

At Dubai, October 31, 2021 (floodlit). New Zealand won by eight wickets. Toss: New Zealand.

Kohli sounded perplexed after a second insipid performance left India relying on results elsewhere to reach the last four, and New Zealand in charge of their own fate. "Quite bizarre," he said. His side had managed only eight fours and two sixes, then took their competition haul of wickets to just two. Against disciplined bowling, and mainly faultless fielding – though Milne dropped Sharma at fine leg first ball – India were curiously tentative, except when they were picking out men on the boundary. If a ten-over score of 48 for three wasn't bad enough, Kohli slog-swept the first delivery after mid-innings drinks to long-on. His 17-ball nine, and Pant's 19-ball 12, summed up the stodge. When Pandya upper-cut Boult in the 17th over, it was their first boundary in 71 – two short of their record drought in a T20 innings, against Australia at Melbourne in 2007-08. Between them, spinners Santner and Sodhi conceded just 32 in eight overs, while Boult finished with three for 20. Only a couple of blows from Jadeja – far too little, far too late – dragged the total to 110. The New Zealand chase was an amble. Guptill fell early to Bumrah's slower ball, but Mitchell – a novice opener – took toll of Jadeja en route to a format-best 49. Williamson barely broke sweat as New Zealand got home with 33 deliveries to spare, and Indian fans left the Dubai International Cricket Stadium early for a second Sunday in succession. LAWRENCE BOOTH

Player of the Match: I. S. Sodhi. *Attendance:* 14,250.

India

		B	4/6
1 K. L. Rahul c 2 b 9		18	16	3
2 I. P. Kishan c 2 b 11		4	8	1
3 R. G. Sharma c 1 b 10		14	14	1/1
4 *V. Kohli c 11 b 10		9	17	0
5 †R. R. Pant b 8		12	19	0
6 H. H. Pandya c 1 b 11		23	24	1
7 R. A. Jadeja not out		26	19	2/1
8 S. N. Thakur c 1 b 11		0	3	0
9 Mohammed Shami not out		0	0	0
Lb 2, w 2		4		

6 overs: 35-2   (20 overs)   110-7

1/11 2/35 3/40 4/48 5/70 6/94 7/94

10 J. J. Bumrah and 11 V. V. Chakravarthy did not bat.

Boult 24–13–20–3; Southee 24–11–26–1; Santner 24–11–15–0; Milne 24–10–30–1; Sodhi 24–9–17–2.

New Zealand

		B	4/6
1 M. J. Guptill c 8 b 10		20	17	3
2 D. J. Mitchell c 1 b 10		49	35	4/3
3 *K. S. Williamson not out		33	31	3
4 †D. P. Conway not out		2	4	0
Lb 1, w 6		7		

6 overs: 44-1   (14.3 overs)   111-2

1/24 2/96

5 G. D. Phillips, 6 J. D. S. Neesham, 7 M. J. Santner, 8 A. F. Milne, 9 T. G. Southee, 10 I. S. Sodhi and 11 T. A. Boult did not bat.

Chakravarthy 24–9–23–0; Bumrah 24–15–19–2; Jadeja 12–4–23–0; Mohammed Shami 6–1–11–0; Thakur 9–3–17–0; Pandya 12–2–17–0.

Umpires: M. Erasmus and R. A. Kettleborough.   Third umpire: A. T. Holdstock.
Referee: R. S. Madugalle.

NAMIBIA v PAKISTAN

At Abu Dhabi, November 2, 2021 (floodlit). Pakistan won by 45 runs. Toss: Pakistan.

Pakistan made it four out of four, after brilliant seventies by Mohammad Rizwan and Babar Azam, and a tight performance from their bowlers. Opting to bat on a greenish pitch – the first time in the tournament they had not chased – they had made a careful start. Namibia's left-arm quick Trumpelmann, who had dismantled Scotland's top order six days earlier, began with a maiden, and his second over cost two; the first powerplay yielded just 29, Pakistan's lowest six-over total with no wicket down. But from 59 off ten, with Rizwan a sedate 16 off 25, they produced fireworks. Rizwan and Babar became the first pair to share five three-figure stands in T20 internationals, before Rizwan and Mohammad Hafeez, with a 16-ball 32, extended the damage in the last ten overs to 130; Rizwan smashed the last, from Smit, for four fours and a six. Namibia batted valiantly, but Pakistan's varied attack kept them under control. Williams made a fighting 40, and Wiese – a regular in the PSL – 43 not out in 31, but Namibia were not in the hunt.   SHAHID HASHMI

Player of the Match: Mohammad Rizwan.   *Attendance:* 4,950.

Pakistan

			B	4/6
1 †Mohammad Rizwan *not out*...		79	50	8/4
2 *Babar Azam *c 9 b 5*........		70	49	7
3 Fakhar Zaman *c 8 b 9*.......		5	5	0
4 Mohammad Hafeez *not out*		32	16	5
Lb 3....................		3		

6 overs: 29-0   (20 overs)   189-2

1/113 2/122

5 Shoaib Malik, 6 Asif Ali, 7 Shadab Khan, 8 Imad Wasim, 9 Hasan Ali, 10 Shaheen Shah Afridi and 11 Haris Rauf did not bat.

Trumpelmann   24–11–36–0;   Wiese 24–10–30–1; Smit 24–5–50–0; Frylinck 24–5–31–1; Shikongo 12–1–19–0; Loftie-Eaton 12–2–20–0.

Namibia

			B	4/6
1 S. J. Baard *run out (11/1)*......		29	29	1/1
2 M. van Lingen *b 9*...........		4	2	1
3 C. G. Williams *c 9 b 7*.......		40	37	5/1
4 *M. G. Erasmus *c 7 b 8*.....		15	10	1/1
5 D. Wiese *not out*...........		43	31	3/2
6 J. J. Smit *c 3 b 11*..........		2	5	0
7 J. N. Loftie-Eaton *not out*		7	7	0
Lb 2, w 1, nb 1		4		

6 overs: 34-1   (20 overs)   144-5

1/8 2/55 3/83 4/93 5/110

8 †Z. E. Green, 9 J. N. Frylinck, 10 R. C. Trumpelmann and 11 B. Shikongo did not bat.

Shaheen Shah Afridi 24–11–36–0; Hasan Ali 24–12–22–1; Imad Wasim 18–11–13–1; Haris Rauf 24–14–25–1; Shadab Khan 24–6–35–1; Mohammad Hafeez 6–2–11–0.

Umpires: C. M. Brown and C. B. Gaffaney.   Third umpire: P. R. Reiffel.
Referee: J. J. Crowe.

NEW ZEALAND v SCOTLAND

At Dubai, November 3, 2021. New Zealand won by 16 runs. Toss: Scotland.

After a week to dwell on their opening two defeats in the Super 12s, Scotland received early cheer. In the fifth over, Sharif snared Mitchell, then saw his plan for Williamson bear fruit: a wide gully closed off his release shot – he steered his first delivery there along the ground – and he was strangled down leg for a fourth-ball duck. When Watt continued his memorable tournament by removing Conway, reverse-sweeping, with his first ball, New Zealand were 52 for three in the seventh. But Guptill defied two foes. First, Scotland's disciplined attack, especially early on in a partnership with Phillips eventually worth 105 in 12 overs. Second, the heat. Guptill often looked too exhausted to run more than a single, though it mattered little: his 93 included six fours and seven sixes, making him the first to clear the rope 150 times in T20 internationals. He also became the second, after Virat Kohli, to top 3,000 runs. Watt got through four superb overs for just 13, but a target of 173, even on a good batting track, felt beyond Scotland. Not that they were overawed: Cross hit Milne for five consecutive fours, Munsey struck Sodhi for successive sixes, and they reached 66 for one in the eighth. But, after a wide, Munsey perished attempting a third six, hitting a full toss to long-on. And Scotland's steady middle-order accumulation meant that, despite Leask's late flourish, New Zealand were merely challenged rather than threatened.   TIM WIGMORE

Player of the Match: M. J. Guptill.   *Attendance:* 650.

New Zealand

		B	4/6
1 M. J. Guptill *c 5 b 11*	93	56	6/7
2 D. J. Mitchell *lbw b 9*	13	11	1
3 *K. S. Williamson *c 3 b 9*	0	4	0
4 †D. P. Conway *c 3 b 8*	1	3	0
5 G. D. Phillips *c 7 b 11*	33	37	0/1
6 J. D. S. Neesham *not out*	10	6	1
7 M. J. Santner *not out*	2	3	0
Lb 5, w 15	20		

6 overs: 52-2   (20 overs) 172-5

1/35 2/35 3/52 4/157 5/157

8 A. F. Milne, 9 T. G. Southee, 10 I. S. Sodhi and 11 T. A. Boult did not bat.

Wheal 24–8–40–2; Sharif 24–13–28–2; Evans 24–6–48–0; Watt 24–12–13–1; Greaves 18–6–26–0; Leask 6–1–12–0.

Scotland

		B	4/6
1 H. G. Munsey *c 9 b 10*	22	18	1/2
2 *K. J. Coetzer *c 9 b 11*	17	11	4
3 †M. H. Cross *b 9*	27	29	5
4 R. D. Berrington *c 4 b 10*	20	17	1/1
5 C. S. MacLeod *b 11*	12	15	0
6 M. A. Leask *not out*	42	20	3/3
7 C. N. Greaves *not out*	8	10	0
Lb 2, w 6	8		

6 overs: 48-1   (20 overs) 156-5

1/21 2/66 3/76 4/102 5/106

8 M. R. J. Watt, 9 S. M. Sharif, 10 A. C. Evans and 11 B. T. J. Wheal did not bat.

Boult 24–12–29–2; Southee 24–13–24–1; Milne 24–10–36–0; Santner 24–8–23–0; Sodhi 24–7–42–2.

Umpires: Ahsan Raza and M. Erasmus.   Third umpire: N. N. Menon.
Referee: J. Srinath.

AFGHANISTAN v INDIA

At Abu Dhabi, November 3, 2021 (floodlit). India won by 66 runs. Toss: Afghanistan.

After crashing and burning against Pakistan and New Zealand, India finally came out to play. Only a big win, plus other results going their way, would give them any chance of reaching the last four on net run-rate. Kohli lost the toss for the 13th time in 14 internationals, and India were put in – but Rohit Sharma and Rahul overcame this inconvenience in style. Rohit cleared the long straight boundaries with timing and panache, before Rahul deployed his pick-up shots. Afghanistan's bowlers could neither beat the bat nor force error, as the total reached 140 – India's highest all-wicket stand at a T20 World Cup – before Rohit drove Karim Janat to extra cover. Seven runs later,

Rahul too was gone, but even this worked in India's favour on an evening when they didn't put a foot wrong. Kohli held himself back, promoting Pant and Pandya, and 210 was by a margin of 20 the tournament's highest score. Having gone strokeless against New Zealand, they had managed 19 fours and ten sixes. Naveen-ul-Haq's four overs cost an eye-watering 59, while even Rashid Khan went for 36. Afghanistan swung for the fences, as they had to, but managed only 144 for seven. Ashwin, playing for the injured Varun Chakravarthy, took two for 14 in his first white-ball international for over four years.   ANAND VASU

Player of the Match: R. G. Sharma.   *Attendance:* 4,250.

India

		B	4/6
1 K. L. Rahul *b 4*	69	48	6/2
2 R. G. Sharma *c 6 b 7*	74	47	8/3
3 †R. R. Pant *not out*	27	13	1/3
4 H. H. Pandya *not out*	35	13	4/2
B 2, lb 1, w 1, nb 1	5		

6 overs: 53-0   **(20 overs) 210-2**

1/140 2/147

5 *V. Kohli, 6 S. A. Yadav, 7 R. A. Jadeja, 8 R. Ashwin, 9 S. N. Thakur, 10 Mohammed Shami and 11 J. J. Bumrah did not bat.

Mohammad Nabi 6–2–7–0; Sharafuddin Ashraf 12–1–25–0; Naveen-ul-Haq 24–4–59–0; Hamid Hassan 24–10–34–0; Gulbadeen Naib 24–5–39–1; Rashid Khan 24–4–36–0; Karim Janat 6–2–7–1.

Afghanistan

		B	4/6
1 Hazratullah Zazai *c 9 b 11*	13	15	1/1
2 †Mohammad Shahzad *c 8 b 10*	0	4	0
3 Rahmanullah Gurbaz *c 4 b 7*	19	10	1/2
4 Gulbadeen Naib *lbw b 8*	18	20	3
5 Najibullah Zadran *b 8*	11	13	0/1
6 *Mohammad Nabi *c 7 b 10*	35	32	2/1
7 Karim Janat *not out*	42	22	3/2
8 Rashid Khan *c 4 b 10*	0	1	0
9 Sharafuddin Ashraf *not out*	2	3	0
W 4	4		

6 overs: 47-2   **(20 overs) 144-7**

1/13 2/13 3/48 4/59 5/69 6/126 7/127

10 Naveen-ul-Haq and 11 Hamid Hassan did not bat.

Mohammed Shami 24–13–32–3; Bumrah 24–13–25–1; Pandya 12–3–23–0; Jadeja 18–8–19–1; Ashwin 24–12–14–2; Thakur 18–2–31–0.

Umpires: R. A. Kettleborough and P. R. Reiffel.   Third umpire: Aleem Dar.
Referee: D. C. Boon.

NAMIBIA v NEW ZEALAND

At Sharjah, November 5, 2021. New Zealand won by 52 runs. Toss: Namibia.

An unbroken partnership of 76 between Phillips and Neesham set New Zealand up for their third win. Victory against Afghanistan in two days' time would guarantee the semi-finals. On a slow pitch with alarmingly low bounce – the game's 12th ball shot through like a grubber – the New Zealanders had been tied down, crawling along at a run a ball for 16 overs. Scholtz, Namibia's left-arm spinner, was particularly effective, while Erasmus, their captain, defied a broken right ring finger to get through four tight overs of off-spin.

But Phillips and Neesham added a competition-high 67 in the final four, cleverly targeting a 57-metre square boundary, and running Namibia ragged. The seamers veered between too full and too short on a surface that rewarded good lengths, and a target of 164 proved far beyond the Namibians, despite an attractive cameo from Baard. Sodhi had a brief scare after Wiese smashed a leg-break straight at him, through his hands and into his head, but he was cleared by concussion tests.   MATT ROLLER

Player of the Match: J. D. S. Neesham.   *Attendance:* 1,650.

New Zealand

			B	4/6
1 M. J. Guptill *c 9 b 5*			18	18	1/1
2 D. J. Mitchell *c 2 b 11*			19	15	2
3 *K. S. Williamson *b 3*			28	25	2/1
4 †D. P. Conway *run out (3/10)*			17	18	1
5 G. D. Phillips *not out*			39	21	1/3
6 J. D. S. Neesham *not out*			35	23	1/2
Lb 1, w 6			7

6 overs: 43-1   (20 overs) 163-4

1/30 2/43 3/81 4/87

7 M. J. Santner, 8 A. F. Milne, 9 T. G. Southee, 10 I. S. Sodhi and 11 T. A. Boult did not bat.

Scholtz 18–8–15–1; Trumpelmann 18–8–25–0; Wiese 24–5–40–1; Smit 12–3–27–0; Loftie-Eaton 12–1–24–0; Erasmus 24–11–22–1; Birkenstock 12–3–9–0.

Namibia

			B	4/6
1 S. J. Baard *b 7*			21	22	2
2 M. van Lingen *b 6*			25	25	2/1
3 *M. G. Erasmus *c 4 b 10*			3	4	0
4 †Z. E. Green *c 11 b 9*			23	27	1/1
5 D. Wiese *lbw b 9*			16	17	1/1
6 J. J. Smit *not out*			9	17	1
7 J. N. Loftie-Eaton *c 1 b 11*			0	2	0
8 C. G. Williams *c 5 b 11*			0	2	0
9 R. C. Trumpelmann *not out*			6	4	1
Lb 3, w 5			8

6 overs: 36-0   (20 overs) 111-7

1/47 2/51 3/55 4/86 5/102 6/103 7/105

10 K. J. Birkenstock and 11 B. M. Scholtz did not bat.

Southee 24–15–15–2; Boult 24–12–20–2; Milne 24–14–25–0; Santner 24–12–20–1; Neesham 6–1–6–1; Sodhi 18–9–22–1.

Umpires: P. R. Reiffel and P. Wilson.   Third umpire: Ahsan Raza.
Referee: R. S. Madugalle.

INDIA v SCOTLAND

At Dubai, November 5, 2021 (floodlit). India won by eight wickets. Toss: India.

India took a battering ram to Scotland as they clung on to their semi-final hopes. Their only obstacle was Munsey, who played a perfect pick-up off Bumrah, then went after Chakravarthy and Ashwin. Having scored 24 out of 27, he hit Mohammed Shami's slower ball to mid-on, and from then it was all India. Jadeja, completing a three-pronged spin attack, targeted the stumps to collect a career-best three for 15, Shami yorked MacLeod and Evans in three balls, and Scotland were all out for 85. Two wickets for Bumrah made him India's leading T20 wicket-taker, with 64, one more than leg-spinner Yuzvendra Chahal. India needed to boost their net run-rate in case it became relevant, and the urgency proved liberating. Rohit Sharma thrashed 30 off 16, while the innovative Rahul raced to 50 off 18, the fastest half-century of the tournament. Kohli, who had not batted against Afghanistan, faced only two balls as India reached the target in 39. Their powerplay score of 82 for two – the best of the competition – was a national record, as was victory with 81 balls to spare, beating 59 against the UAE at Mirpur in 2015-16. But they still needed Afghanistan to surprise New Zealand.　　ANAND VASU

　　Player of the Match: R. A. Jadeja.　　*Attendance:* 8,050.

Scotland

		B	4/6
1 H. G. Munsey *c 6 b 9*	24	19	4/1
2 *K. J. Coetzer *b 10*	1	7	0
3 †M. H. Cross *lbw b 7*	2	9	0
4 R. D. Berrington *b 7*	0	5	0
5 C. S. MacLeod *b 9*	16	28	0
6 M. A. Leask *lbw b 7*	21	12	2/1
7 C. N. Greaves *c 6 b 8*	1	7	0
8 M. R. J. Watt *b 10*	14	13	2
9 S. M. Sharif *run out (12)*	0	1	0
10 A. C. Evans *b 9*	0	1	0
11 B. T. J. Wheal *not out*	2	4	0
Lb 1, w 3	4		

6 overs: 27-2　　(17.4 overs)　　85

1/13 2/27 3/28 4/29 5/58 6/63 7/81 8/81 9/81

Bumrah　22–17–10–2;　Chakravarthy 18–10–15–0;　Ashwin　24–11–29–1; Mohammed　Shami　18–11–15–3;　Jadeja 24–12–15–3.

India

		B	4/6
1 K. L. Rahul *c 5 b 8*	50	19	6/3
2 R. G. Sharma *lbw b 11*	30	16	5/1
3 *V. Kohli *not out*	2	2	0
4 S. A. Yadav *not out*	6	2	0/1
W 1	1		

6 overs: 82-2　　(6.3 overs)　　89-2

1/70 2/82

5 †R. R. Pant, 6 H. H. Pandya, 7 R. A. Jadeja, 8 R. Ashwin, 9 Mohammed Shami, 10 J. J. Bumrah and 11 V. V. Chakravarthy did not bat.

12th man: I. P. Kishan.

Watt　12–3–20–1;　Wheal　12–2–32–1;　Evans 6–1–16–0;　Sharif　6–3–14–0;　Greaves 3–1–7–0.

　　Umpires: M. Erasmus and R. J. Tucker.　　Third umpire: J. S. Wilson.
　　　　　　　　Referee: J. J. Crowe.

AFGHANISTAN v NEW ZEALAND

At Abu Dhabi, November 7, 2021. New Zealand won by eight wickets. Toss: Afghanistan.
　　This was a quarter-final of sorts. Victory for New Zealand would guarantee them a place in the last four; victory for Afghanistan, though not out of contention, would favour India, who would be likely to qualify in second on net run-rate. But it turned into a stroll for the New Zealanders, who sealed their fourth successive World Cup semi-final – T20 or 50-over – with a characteristic cocktail of disciplined bowling, shrewd batting and outstanding fielding. Two brilliant catches – by Conway to dismiss Mohammad Shahzad, then by Neesham to account for Najibullah Zadran, who had held the innings together with 73 off 48 – helped restrict Afghanistan to 124. With their batsmen more comfortable against spin than speed, Williamson had hit them with pace: Boult (who finished with three for 17),

Southee and Milne all took a wicket during a powerplay yielding only 23 for three. Despite Najibullah's clean striking, especially off Santner, the innings lacked fluency. For the only time in the tournament, Neesham bowled four overs (for 24), with spinners Santner and Sodhi delivering four (for 40) between them. In the final over, a series of wide yorkers from Neesham to Rashid Khan produced just two runs. The chase suited New Zealand ideally. Guptill took them to 45 for one in the powerplay. Rashid bowled Guptill, before Williamson and Conway began circumspectly on a surface not conducive to timing, but a series of sweeps from Conway sealed an easy win. For TV executives, however, it was an unwelcome result: India were out before the semi-finals. TIM WIGMORE

Player of the Match: T. A. Boult. *Attendance:* 1,050.

Afghanistan

		B	4/6
1 Hazratullah Zazai *c 7 b 11*		2	4 0
2 †Mohammad Shahzad *c 4 b 8* . .		4	11 1
3 Rahmanullah Gurbaz *lbw b 9* . . .		6	9 1
4 Gulbadeen Naib *b 10*		15	18 1
5 Najibullah Zadran *c 6 b 11*		73	48 6/3
6 *Mohammad Nabi *c and b 9* . . .		14	20 0
7 Karim Janat *c 10 b 11*		2	2 0
8 Rashid Khan *c 3 b 6*		3	7 0
9 Mujeeb Zadran *not out*		0	1 0
B 1, lb 1, w 3		5	

6 overs: 23-3   (20 overs) 124-8

1/8 2/12 3/19 4/56 5/115 6/119 7/121 8/124

10 Naveen-ul-Haq and 11 Hamid Hassan did not bat.

Southee 24–15–24–2; Boult 24–14–17–3; Milne 24–12–17–1; Neesham 24–9–24–1; Santner 12–1–27–0; Sodhi 12–3–13–1.

New Zealand

		B	4/6
1 M. J. Guptill *b 8*		28	23 4
2 D. J. Mitchell *c 2 b 9*		17	12 3
3 *K. S. Williamson *not out*		40	42 3
4 †D. P. Conway *not out*		36	32 4
Lb 2, w 2		4	

6 overs: 45-1   (18.1 overs) 125-2

1/26 2/57

5 G. D. Phillips, 6 J. D. S. Neesham, 7 M. J. Santner, 8 A. F. Milne, 9 T. G. Southee, 10 I. S. Sodhi and 11 T. A. Boult did not bat.

Mohammad Nabi 24–10–26–0; Mujeeb Zadran 24–9–31–1; Naveen-ul-Haq 12–3–16–0; Hamid Hassan 18–10–14–0; Rashid Khan 24–5–27–1; Gulbadeen Naib 7–1–9–0.

Umpires: H. D. P. K. Dharmasena and L. Rusere. Third umpire: R. K. Illingworth.
Referee: J. Srinath.

PAKISTAN v SCOTLAND

At Sharjah, November 7, 2021 (floodlit). Pakistan won by 72 runs. Toss: Pakistan.

Pakistan remained the World Cup's only unbeaten side after another comprehensive win, with another unchanged team. As against Namibia, they were slow initially, Mohammad Rizwan caught behind for 15 off left-arm spinner Hamza Tahir, in his first World Cup match. Rizwan had still gone past Chris Gayle's record for most T20 runs in a calendar year (1,665 in 2015). Fakhar Zaman fell cheaply too, but Babar Azam and the explosive Shoaib Malik helped rack up a formidable 189 for four. Babar's fourth half-century equalled the record for a single T20 World Cup (by Australia's Matthew Hayden, now the Pakistan batting coach, in 2007, and Virat Kohli in 2014). And it broke another record: Kohli's 18 scores of 50-plus in all T20s in a calendar year, in 2016. Shoaib, meanwhile, launched six sixes in an 18-ball half-century, the joint-fastest in this World Cup, and Pakistan's fastest in any T20 international. In total, 129 came off last ten overs;

the 20th, bowled by Greaves, went for 26, and was the tournament's most costly. Scotland faced a hopeless task, though Berrington provided solace with a 34-ball fifty. Pakistan, who had now won their last 16 T20s in the UAE dating back five years, prepared for a semi-final against Australia in Dubai.   SHAHID HASHMI

Player of the Match: Shoaib Malik.   *Attendance:* 4,000.

Pakistan

		B	*4/6*
1 †Mohammad Rizwan *c 3 b 11*	15	19	0/1
2 *Babar Azam *c 1 b 7*	66	47	5/3
3 Fakhar Zaman *c 6 b 7*	8	13	0
4 Mohammad Hafeez lbw *b 9*	31	19	4/1
5 Shoaib Malik *not out*	54	18	1/6
6 Asif Ali *not out*	5	4	0
Lb 3, w 7	10		

6 overs: 35-0   (20 overs)   189-4

1/35 2/59 3/112 4/142

7 Shadab Khan, 8 Imad Wasim, 9 Hasan Ali, 10 Shaheen Shah Afridi and 11 Haris Rauf did not bat.

Tahir 24–10–24–1; Wheal 12–2–20–0; Sharif 24–8–41–1; Watt 24–8–41–0; Berrington 12–2–17–0; Greaves 24–8–43–2.

Scotland

		B	*4/6*
1 H. G. Munsey *c 11 b 7*	17	31	2
2 *K. J. Coetzer *b 9*	9	16	1
3 †M. H. Cross *run out (8)*	5	8	0
4 R. D. Berrington *not out*	54	37	4/1
5 D. E. Budge *b 7*	0	2	0
6 M. A. Leask *b 10*	14	14	2
7 C. N. Greaves *b 11*	4	12	0
8 M. R. J. Watt *not out*	2	3	0
B 1, lb 1, w 7, nb 3	12		

6 overs: 24-1   (20 overs)   117-6

1/23 2/36 3/41 4/41 5/87 6/114

9 S. M. Sharif, 10 B. T. J. Wheal and 11 H. Tahir did not bat.

Shaheen Shah Afridi 24–14–24–1; Imad Wasim 24–12–17–0; Haris Rauf 24–7–27–1; Hasan Ali 24–11–33–1; Shadab Khan 24–14–14–2.

Umpires: R. J. Tucker and P. Wilson.   Third umpire: A. T. Holdstock.
Referee: D. C. Boon.

INDIA v NAMIBIA

At Dubai, November 8, 2021 (floodlit). India won by nine wickets. Toss: India.

India's semi-final hopes had ended the previous afternoon, when New Zealand beat Afghanistan, but finishing touches remained. After his 50th match in charge, Kohli was stepping down as T20 captain, while head coach Ravi Shastri, his closest ally, was moving on after a four-year stint, an "emotional but very proud man". When India chose to bowl, the expectation was the game would follow a similar script to the one against Scotland. But Namibia refused to crumble: there was no major partnership, perhaps, and no defining performances, just doughty contributions all round. The innings, though, was stop–start, thanks in part to Jadeja, who rushed through his overs, attacked the stumps, and picked up his second match award, with figures of three for 16. At the other end, Ashwin tossed the ball up, and used his variations to collect three for 20. Wiese's 26 ensured Namibia got to 132 – unlikely to discomfit India on an excellent surface. Rohit Sharma, who followed Kohli and New Zealand's Martin Guptill past 3,000 runs in the format, and Rahul waded into the bowling, putting on 86 for the first wicket and ensuring the game was done in quick time. Kohli did not even bat, instead promoting Yadav in an attempt, he said, to give him a memory to take home.   ANAND VASU

Player of the Match: R. A. Jadeja.   *Attendance:* 9,050.

Namibia

		B	4/6
1 S. J. Baard *lbw b 7*	21	21	1/1
2 M. van Lingen *c 10 b 11*	14	15	2
3 C. G. Williams *st 5 b 7*	0	4	0
4 *M. G. Erasmus *c 5 b 8*	12	20	1
5 J. N. Loftie-Eaton *c 2 b 8*	5	5	0
6 D. Wiese *c 2 b 11*	26	25	2
7 J. J. Smit *c 2 b 7*	9	9	1
8 †Z. E. Green *b 8*	0	1	0
9 J. N. Frylinck *not out*	15	15	0
10 R. C. Trumpelmann *not out*	13	6	1/1
Lb 8, w 8, nb 1	17		

6 overs: 34-2   (20 overs)   **132-8**

1/33 2/34 3/39 4/47 5/72 6/93 7/94 8/117

11 B. M. Scholtz did not bat.

Mohammed Shami 24–9–39–0; Bumrah 24–14–19–2; Ashwin 24–13–20–3; Jadeja 24–13–16–3; Chahar 24–9–30–0.

India

		B	4/6
1 K. L. Rahul *not out*	54	36	4/2
2 R. G. Sharma *c 8 b 9*	56	37	7/2
3 S. A. Yadav *not out*	25	19	4
Lb 1	1		

6 overs: 54-0   (15.2 overs)   **136-1**

1/86

4 *V. Kohli, 5 †R. R. Pant, 6 H. H. Pandya, 7 R. A. Jadeja, 8 R. Ashwin, 9 R. D. Chahar, 10 Mohammed Shami and 11 J. J. Bumrah did not bat.

Trumpelmann 18–6–26–0; Wiese 12–7–18–0; Scholtz 6–3–11–0; Smit 12–2–17–0; Frylinck 12–1–19–1; Loftie-Eaton 24–7–31–0; van Lingen 8–2–13–0.

Umpires: C. M. Brown and R. K. Illingworth.   Third umpire: M. Erasmus.
Referee: J. J. Crowe.

SEMI-FINALS

ENGLAND v NEW ZEALAND

At Abu Dhabi, November 10, 2021 (floodlit). New Zealand won by five wickets. Toss: New Zealand.

A little over two years earlier, Jimmy Neesham had posted a tweet after New Zealand's super-over defeat by England in the 50-over World Cup final. "Kids, don't take up sport," he wrote. "Take up baking or something. Die at 60 really fat and happy." He had ignored his own advice – and now played a redemptive cameo on a dramatic night at the Sheikh Zayed Stadium. New Zealand, chasing 167, had just lost Conway and Phillips to the irrepressible Livingstone, and were slowing at precisely the wrong moment.

They needed 57, more than any team had required – and made – off the last four overs to win a T20 international. Neesham targeted Jordan, swatting him over midwicket for six – as he had against Jofra Archer in that super over – before whacking him through long-on for four. From the over's fourth legitimate delivery (Jordan, feeling the heat, had already bowled two wides), Neesham was brilliantly caught at long-on. Except he wasn't: just as Boult had trodden on the boundary at a crucial moment of England's chase at Lord's, Bairstow was unable to relay the ball to Livingstone before knee brushed foam: six more, in an over eventually costing 23. Neesham and Mitchell, who had calmly glued the chase together, then traded sixes in the 18th, bowled by Rashid. And though Neesham was caught by Morgan in the covers off its last delivery, his 27 off 11 had turned the tide. When Mitchell spanked Woakes for two sixes moments later, England were done, their plans for a third successive World Cup final now lost in the desert sand. "We're devastated," said Morgan; Williamson, preferring native understatement, was "chuffed".

England's own innings had never quite got going after they lost an important toss. The out-of-form Bairstow was no replacement for the injured Jason Roy, making 13 off 17, while Buttler's demise for 29 – missing a reverse sweep off Sodhi – seemed pivotal. But Malan made his best score of the tournament, and Ali his third half-century in T20 internationals. Boult went wicketless for the first time in the competition, and New Zealand's high fielding standards slipped. They had chased successfully against England

On the gas: Daryl Mitchell drives New Zealand to the final.

Gareth Copley, ICC/Getty Images

only once in seven T20 games and, when Woakes fiddled out Guptill and Williamson in another immaculate opening burst, it was 13 for two. Conway resuscitated the innings with a skilful 46, only to break his right hand punching his bat after he was stumped off Livingstone – self-inflicted, perhaps, but a cruel way to miss a World Cup final. Thanks to Neesham and Mitchell, New Zealand were soon there.   LAWRENCE BOOTH

Player of the Match: D. J. Mitchell.   *Attendance:* 6,400.

England

		B	4/6
1 †J. C. Buttler *lbw b 10*	29	24	4
2 J. M. Bairstow *c 3 b 8*	13	17	2
3 D. J. Malan *c 4 b 9*	41	30	4/1
4 M. M. Ali *not out*	51	37	3/2
5 L. S. Livingstone *c 7 b 6*	17	10	1/1
6 *E. J. G. Morgan *not out*	4	2	0
Lb 2, w 9	11		

6 overs: 40-1   (20 overs) **166-4**

1/37 2/53 3/116 4/156

7 S. W. Billings, 8 C. R. Woakes, 9 C. J. Jordan, 10 A. U. Rashid and 11 M. A. Wood did not bat.

Southee 24–11–24–1; Boult 24–8–40–0; Milne 24–7–31–1; Sodhi 24–6–32–1; Santner 6–2–8–0; Neesham 12–3–18–1; Phillips 6–1–11–0.

New Zealand

		B	4/6
1 M. J. Guptill *c 4 b 8*	4	3	1
2 D. J. Mitchell *not out*	72	47	4/4
3 *K. S. Williamson *c 10 b 8*	5	11	0
4 †D. P. Conway *st 1 b 5*	46	38	5/1
5 G. D. Phillips *c 7 b 5*	2	4	0
6 J. D. S. Neesham *c 6 b 10*	27	11	1/3
7 M. J. Santner *not out*	1	1	0
B 1, lb 4, w 4, nb 1	10		

6 overs: 36-2   (19 overs) **167-5**

1/4 2/13 3/95 4/107 5/147

8 A. F. Milne, 9 T. G. Southee, 10 I. S. Sodhi and 11 T. A. Boult did not bat.

Woakes 24–11–36–2; Jordan 18–9–31–0; Rashid 24–7–39–1; Wood 24–5–34–0; Livingstone 24–12–22–2.

Umpires: H. D. P. K. Dharmasena and M. Erasmus.   Third umpire: N. N. Menon.
Referee: D. C. Boon.

AUSTRALIA v PAKISTAN

At Dubai, November 11, 2021 (floodlit). Australia won by five wickets. Toss: Australia.

In Dubai, a chaser's paradise, Australia pulled off the most dramatic heist seen in, well, 24 hours, to book their place in an improbable final. Like New Zealand, Australia were on their last legs, requiring 12 an over with only the bowlers to come. Like New Zealand, a flurry of sixes took them home with five wickets and an entire over to spare. Like New Zealand, their heroes – Stoinis and Wade – were largely unheralded, not outright stars.

Pakistan had chosen the 11 players who had provided their five group wins. If that seems a mundane observation, it isn't: since their win over Scotland, Mohammad Rizwan had spent two nights in intensive care with a chest infection. Not that it was evident, as he and Babar Azam continued their profitable opening partnership after Finch chose the obvious option on winning the toss. They put on 71, laying the platform for Pakistan's 176, the highest first-innings total in Dubai all tournament. Babar was initially slick, but became stuck before falling on the stroke of drinks to the excellent Zampa. Rizwan found the boundary often, but played out too many dots, and was hit on the grille by Starc; he responded with a toothy grin. The openers bowed out as the tournament's leading run-scorers, while Rizwan became the first to 1,000 T20 international runs in a calendar year. As Pakistan's usual finishers crumbled around him, it took four sixes from Fakhar Zaman – who had also started slowly – to provide what felt a par score. He hung deep in his crease to hit hard down the ground, at one stage nearly decapitating umpire Gaffaney with a fizzing drive.

With a partisan crowd buzzing, everything seemed to be with Pakistan, especially when Shaheen Shah Afridi produced a stunning opening over. It cost one run, and saw Finch pinned lbw first ball, just as he had been in the 2019 World Cup semi-final against England. Warner and Marsh rebuilt, but Shadab Khan's introduction changed the game. Marsh was caught in the deep in his first over, Smith in similar fashion in his second. In his third, Warner was caught behind – he didn't review it, but replays revealed no edge. Finally, to complete the best men's T20 World Cup semi-final figures, Maxwell holed out switch-hitting. The crowd believed Shadab had handed Pakistan victory. Perhaps only Stoinis disagreed. With Australia needing 81 from 46 balls, he responded to Maxwell's dismissal by hitting the next ball for six, and continued to pick up boundaries. That allowed Wade to settle, but he was soon taking down Hasan Ali. Australia needed 20 from ten when Hasan shelled a simple chance in the deep off Wade. He scrambled two, then launched Afridi's next three balls for six, two of them fancy scoops. The apparent crisis enveloping Australia after their defeat by England seemed ancient history. WILL MACPHERSON

Player of the Match: M. S. Wade.   *Attendance:* 15,050.

Pakistan

		B	4/6
1 †Mohammad Rizwan *c 4 b 9* ...	67	52	3/4
2 *Babar Azam *c 1 b 10*	39	34	5
3 Fakhar Zaman *not out*	55	32	3/4
4 Asif Ali *c 4 b 8*..............	0	1	0
5 Shoaib Malik *b 9*	1	2	0
6 Mohammad Hafeez *not out*	1	1	0
B 5, lb 1, w 5, nb 2	13		

6 overs: 47-0   (20 overs) 176-4

1/71 2/143 3/158 4/162

7 Shadab Khan, 8 Imad Wasim, 9 Hasan Ali, 10 Shaheen Shah Afridi and 11 Haris Rauf did not bat.

Starc 2–4–10–38–2; Hazlewood 2–4–8–49–0; Maxwell 1–8–5–20–0; Cummins 2–4–9–30–1; Zampa 2–4–9–22–1; Marsh 6–1–11–0.

Australia

		B	4/6
1 D. A. Warner *c 1 b 7*........	49	30	3/3
2 *A. J. Finch *lbw b 10*.......	0	1	0
3 M. R. Marsh *c 4 b 7*........	28	22	3/1
4 S. P. D. Smith *c 3 b 7*	5	6	1
5 G. J. Maxwell *c 11 b 7*	7	10	0
6 M. P. Stoinis *not out*	40	31	2/2
7 †M. S. Wade *not out*	41	17	2/4
Lb 2, w 2, nb 3	7		

6 overs: 52-1   (19 overs) 177-5

1/1 2/52 3/77 4/89 5/96

8 P. J. Cummins, 9 M. A. Starc, 10 A. Zampa and 11 J. R. Hazlewood did not bat.

Shaheen Shah Afridi 2–4–12–35–1; Imad Wasim 1–8–6–25–0; Haris Rauf 1–8–6–32–0; Hasan Ali 2–4–3–44–0; Shadab Khan 2–4–11–26–4; Mohammad Hafeez 6–2–13–0.

Umpires: C. B. Gaffaney and R. A. Kettleborough.   Third umpire: J. S. Wilson.
Referee: J. J. Crowe.

FINAL

AUSTRALIA v NEW ZEALAND

Tim Wigmore

At Dubai, November 14, 2021 (floodlit). Australia won by eight wickets. Toss: Australia.

Seldom have Australia gone into a world event as unheralded as they did here. And yet, when Maxwell reverse-swept Southee for four, just after 9.20 in Dubai, their inaugural men's T20 World Cup trophy was sealed in imperious fashion. Australia's victory was, perhaps, best seen as a triumph of talent over planning: get the strongest players in the team, and worry about their roles later. Even a run of five bilateral series defeats before the tournament had not undermined head coach Justin Langer's belief that, with the talent of this XI, their qualities would overcome a lack of familiarity.

In the final, three men vindicated such thinking. Hazlewood had played just three matches in all T20 cricket between 2015 and 2019, yet his immaculate length – too short to play off the front foot, too full to comfortably rock back – yielded just 11 from three powerplay overs. He returned with leg-cutters and knuckle balls to dismiss Phillips and Williamson, for 85, and claim three for 16.

With Australia chasing 173, talent again won out. Warner, who had been sacked as captain and dropped by Sunrisers Hyderabad in the IPL, started slowly, but ruthlessly targeted New Zealand's spinners to make 53; he was named Player of the Tournament. Marsh, often ridiculed by fans at home and abroad, had started batting at No. 3 for Australia only in July, when a plethora of players missed a tour of the West Indies, and had been dropped ahead of the defeat by England a fortnight earlier. Emboldened by the selection of seven specialist batters, he flicked his first ball, from Milne, for six and struck his next two for four. He picked the right day for his highest T20 international score.

A place in the T20 World Cup final, after reaching the last two ODI finals and winning the World Test Championship, led many to hail New Zealand as the game's best all-format team. Yet such logic ran into the cold reality of Australia's hold over their trans-Tasman

Put that in your pipe: Mitchell Marsh silences the doubters with a match-winning innings.

Aamir Qureshi, AFP/Getty Images

rivals. This was their 17th consecutive victory in a limited-overs knockout match, a sequence stretching back to 1981.

Besides Finch winning the toss for the sixth time out of seven, the simplest explanation was that one team played T20 for their entire innings, and one for only half. New Zealand had started reasonably but, when Mitchell fell to Hazlewood in the fourth over, they appeared too concerned with avoiding more damage. New Zealand damaged themselves in an even graver way – they mustered two runs from each of the last two overs of the powerplay, normally among the highest-scoring. After ten, they were 57 for one; at the same stage, Australia would be one down as well, but for 82.

Williamson played what became the finest T20 innings of his life as he accelerated from a stodgy start – 21 off 21 balls when he was spilled by Hazlewood at fine leg off Starc. With a sequence of brilliant drives, he hit 64 from his last 27, including 39 in 12 from Starc, the latest to suffer when attempting to bowl yorkers; his analysis of none for 60 was the most expensive in a World Cup final. But even with 172 for four – the highest score in a final, though not for long – the suspicion was that New Zealand should have scored another 20 on an excellent pitch. Guptill, notionally their top-order aggressor, lacked timing and intent in a 35-ball 28; the in-form Neesham faced just seven, and launched Cummins for a straight six.

Given Australia's batting depth, New Zealand needed early wickets. They managed one, from the excellent Boult, but their spinners – not helped by the dew – wilted, yielding 63 from a combined six overs, as Williamson held his seamers back. By the time Boult returned for his third over and immediately bowled Warner, the fate of the match had apparently been sealed. While New Zealand's wait to lift a limited-overs World Cup continued, Australia had a first T20 trophy to go with five ODI titles.

Player of the Match: M. R. Marsh.   *Attendance:* 13,450.

Player of the Tournament: D. A. Warner.

New Zealand

			B	4/6
1 M. J. Guptill *c 6 b* 10			28	35 3
2 D. J. Mitchell *c 7 b* 11			11	8 0/1
3 *K. S. Williamson *c 5 b* 11			85	48 10/3
4 G. D. Phillips *c 4 b* 11			18	17 1/1
5 J. D. S. Neesham *not out*			13	7 0/1
6 †T. L. Seifert *not out*			8	6 1
B 1, lb 3, w 4, nb 1			9	

6 overs: 32-1   (20 overs) 172-4

1/28 2/76 3/144 4/148

7 M. J. Santner, 8 A. F. Milne, 9 T. G. Southee, 10 I. S. Sodhi and 11 T. A. Boult did not bat.

Starc 24–5–60–0; Hazlewood 24–18–16–3; Maxwell 18–5–28–0; Cummins 24–7–27–0; Zampa 24–7–26–1; Marsh 6–1–11–0.

Australia

			B	4/6
1 D. A. Warner *b* 11			53	38 4/3
2 *A. J. Finch *c 2 b* 11			5	7 1
3 M. R. Marsh *not out*			77	50 6/4
4 G. J. Maxwell *not out*			28	18 4/1
Lb 4, w 6			10	

6 overs: 43-1   (18.5 overs) 173-2

1/15 2/107

5 S. P. D. Smith, 6 M. P. Stoinis, 7 †M. S. Wade, 8 P. J. Cummins, 9 M. A. Starc, 10 A. Zampa and 11 J. R. Hazlewood did not bat.

Boult 24–14–18–2; Southee 23–6–43–0; Milne 24–12–30–0; Sodhi 18–3–40–0; Santner 18–4–23–0; Neesham 6–1–15–0.

Umpires: M. Erasmus and R. A. Kettleborough.   Third umpire: N. N. Menon.

Referee: R. S. Madugalle.

MEN'S T20 WORLD CUP FINALS

2007-08	INDIA beat Pakistan by five runs at Johannesburg	I. K. Pathan
2009	PAKISTAN beat Sri Lanka by eight wickets at Lord's	Shahid Afridi
2010	ENGLAND beat Australia by seven wickets at Bridgetown	C. Kieswetter
2012-13	WEST INDIES beat Sri Lanka by 36 runs at Colombo (RPS)	M. N. Samuels
2013-14	SRI LANKA beat India by six wickets at Mirpur	K. C. Sangakkara
2015-16	WEST INDIES beat England by four wickets at Kolkata	M. N. Samuels
2021-22	AUSTRALIA beat New Zealand by eight wickets at Dubai	M. R. Marsh

MRF TYRES ICC TEAM RANKINGS

TEST RANKINGS (As at January 16, 2022)

		Matches	Points	Rating
1	Australia	23	2,736	119
2	New Zealand	28	3,264	117
3	India	32	3,717	116
4	England	41	4,151	101
5	South Africa	23	2,271	99
6	Pakistan	30	2,787	93
7	Sri Lanka	30	2,485	83
8	West Indies	33	2,480	75
9	Bangladesh	22	1,157	53
10	Zimbabwe	11	342	31

Afghanistan had a rating of 30 and Ireland 0, but neither had played sufficient Tests to achieve a ranking.

ONE-DAY RANKINGS (As at December 31, 2021)

		Matches	Points	Rating
1	New Zealand	17	2,054	121
2	England	32	3,793	119
3	Australia	28	3,244	116
4	India	32	3,624	113
5	South Africa	25	2,459	98
6	Pakistan	27	2,524	93
7	Bangladesh	30	2,740	91
8	West Indies	30	2,523	84
9	Sri Lanka	32	2,657	83
10	Afghanistan	17	1,054	62
11	Netherlands	7	336	48
12	Ireland	25	1,145	46

Remaining rankings 13 Scotland (45), 14 Zimbabwe (38), 15 Oman (35), 16 Nepal (30), 17 United Arab Emirates (21), 18 Namibia (21), 19 USA (17), 20 Papua New Guinea (0).

TWENTY20 RANKINGS (As at December 31, 2021)

		Matches	Points	Rating
1	England	34	9,354	275
2	India	36	9,627	267
3	Pakistan	46	12,225	266
4	New Zealand	38	9,707	255
5	South Africa	35	8,858	253
6	Australia	40	9,927	248
7	Afghanistan	17	3,951	232
8	Sri Lanka	30	6,950	232
9	Bangladesh	37	8,529	231
10	West Indies	37	8,519	230
11	Zimbabwe	30	5,751	192
12	Nepal	19	3,556	187
13	Scotland	24	4,447	185
14	United Arab Emirates	15	2,750	183
15	Ireland	34	6,227	183
16	Namibia	25	4,435	177
17	Oman	13	2,260	174
18	Netherlands	23	3,922	171
19	Papua New Guinea	19	3,166	167

Remaining rankings 20 Singapore (140), 21 Qatar (128), 22 Canada (124), 23 Jersey (123), 24 Hong Kong (121), 25 Uganda (105), 26 Italy (104), 27 Kuwait (103), 28 USA (103), 29 Saudi Arabia (100), 30 Kenya (99), 31 Bermuda (88), 32 Malaysia (86), 33 Germany (86), 34 Bahrain (84), 35 Tanzania (82), 36 Denmark (77), 37 Botswana (76), 38 Guernsey (72), 39 Spain (70), 40 Romania (68), 41 Norway (67), 42 Nigeria (65), 43 Austria (58), 44 Belgium (56), 45 Sweden (54), 46 Philippines (48), 47 France (48), 48 Mexico (45), 49 Cayman Islands (44), 50 Vanuatu (44), 51 Portugal (43), 52 Ghana (42), 53 Isle of Man (41), 54 Luxembourg (38), 55 Argentina (38), 56 Bahamas (37), 57 Malawi (37), 58 Peru (36), 59 Fiji (35), 60 Finland (35), 61 Sierra Leone (33), 62 Hungary (33), 63 Samoa (32), 64= Costa Rica (32), Japan (32), 66 Belize (31), 67 Malta (31), 68 Panama (26), 69 Thailand (25), 70 Cyprus (21), 72 Czechia (21), 72 South Korea (20), 73 Greece (19), 74 Mozambique (16), 75 Rwanda (15), 76 Bhutan (12), 77 Bulgaria (11), 78 St Helena (9), 79 Seychelles (9), 80 Brazil (8), 81 Maldives (5), 82 Gibraltar (4), 83 Chile (4), 84 Myanmar (0), 85= eSwatini (0), Lesotho (0), China (0), Estonia (0), Serbia (0), Indonesia (0), Turkey (0).

The ratings are based on all Test series, one-day and Twenty20 internationals since May 1, 2018.

MRF TYRES ICC PLAYER RANKINGS

Introduced in 1987, the rankings have been backed by various sponsors, but were taken over by the ICC in January 2005. They rank cricketers on a scale up to 1,000 on their performances in Tests. The rankings take into account playing conditions, the quality of the opposition and the result of the matches. In August 1998, a similar set of rankings for one-day internationals was launched, and Twenty20 rankings were added in October 2011.

The leading players in the Test rankings on January 16, 2022, were:

	Batters	Points		Bowlers	Points
1	M. Labuschagne (A)	935	1	P. J. Cummins (A)	898
2	J. E. Root (E)	872	2	R. Ashwin (I)	839
3	K. S. Williamson (NZ)	862	3	K. Rabada (SA)	828
4	S. P. D. Smith (A)	845	4	K. A. Jamieson (NZ)	825
5	T. M. Head (A)	773	5	Shaheen Shah Afridi (P)	822
6	R. G. Sharma (I)	773	6	T. G. Southee (NZ)	795
7	V. Kohli (I)	767	7	J. M. Anderson (E)	788
8	F. D. M. Karunaratne (SL)	754	8	J. R. Hazlewood (A)	786
9	Babar Azam (P)	750	9	N. Wagner (NZ)	775
10	T. W. M. Latham (NZ)	728	10	J. J. Bumrah (I)	763

The leading players in the one-day international rankings on December 31, 2021, were:

	Batters	Points		Bowlers	Points
1	Babar Azam (P)	873	1	T. A. Boult (NZ)	737
2	V. Kohli (I)	844	2	J. R. Hazlewood (A)	709
3	R. G. Sharma (I)	813	3	Mujeeb Zadran (Afg)	708
4	L. R. P. L. Taylor (NZ)	801	4	C. R. Woakes (E)	700
5	A. J. Finch (A)	779	5	Mehedi Hasan (B)	692
6	J. M. Bairstow (E)	775	6	M. J. Henry (NZ)	691
7	D. A. Warner (A)	762	7	J. J. Bumrah (I)	679
8	S. D. Hope (WI)	758	8	M. A. Starc (A)	652
9	K. S. Williamson (NZ)	754	9	Shakib Al Hasan (B)	650
10	Q. de Kock (SA)	743	10	K. Rabada (SA)	643

The leading players in the Twenty20 international rankings on December 31, 2021, were:

	Batters	Points		Bowlers	Points
1	D. J. Malan (E)	805	1	P. W. H. de Silva (SL)	797
2	Babar Azam (P)	805	2	T. Shamsi (SA)	784
3	Mohammad Rizwan (P)	798	3	A. Zampa (A)	725
4	A. K. Markram (SA)	796	4	A. U. Rashid (E)	719
5	K. L. Rahul (I)	729	5	Rashid Khan (Afg)	710
6	A. J. Finch (A)	709	6	J. R. Hazlewood (A)	705
7	D. P. Conway (NZ)	703	7	Mujeeb Zadran (Afg)	679
8	J. C. Buttler (E)	674	8	A. A. Nortje (SA)	655
9	H. E. van der Dussen (SA)	669	9	Shadab Khan (P)	634
10	M. J. Guptill (NZ)	658	10	T. G. Southee (NZ)	633

INTERNATIONAL RESULTS IN 2021

TEST MATCHES

	Tests	W	L	D	% won	% lost	% drawn
Pakistan	9	7	2	0	**77.77**	22.22	0.00
Australia	5	3	1	1	**60.00**	20.00	20.00
India	14	8	3	3	**57.14**	21.42	21.42
New Zealand.......	6	3	1	2	**50.00**	16.66	33.33
South Africa	6	3	3	0	**50.00**	50.00	0.00
Afghanistan........	2	1	1	0	**50.00**	50.00	0.00
Sri Lanka	9	3	3	3	**33.00**	33.00	33.00
West Indies	10	3	5	2	**30.00**	50.00	20.00
England..........	15	4	9	2	**26.66**	60.00	13.33
Zimbabwe........	5	1	4	0	**20.00**	80.00	0.00
Bangladesh	7	1	5	1	**14.28**	71.42	14.28
Totals	44	37	37	7	**84.09**	84.09	15.90

Ireland played no Tests in 2021.

ONE-DAY INTERNATIONALS (Full Members only)

	ODIs	W	L	NR	% won	% lost
Afghanistan	3	3	0	0	**100.00**	0.00
New Zealand	3	3	0	0	**100.00**	0.00
England..........	9	6	2	1	**75.00**	25.00
Bangladesh	12	8	4	0	**66.66**	33.33
India	6	4	2	0	**66.66**	33.33
Australia	3	2	1	0	**66.66**	33.33
West Indies	9	4	5	0	**44.44**	55.55
South Africa	9	3	5	1	**37.50**	62.50
Pakistan	6	2	4	0	**33.33**	66.66
Sri Lanka	15	4	10	1	**28.57**	71.42
Ireland.	9	2	5	2	**28.57**	71.42
Zimbabwe.........	6	1	4	1	**20.00**	80.00
Totals	45	42	42	3		

The following teams also played official ODIs in 2021, some against Full Members (not included above): Scotland (P6 W4 L1 NR1); Oman (P10 W6 L3 NR1); Nepal (P6 W4 L2); Netherlands (P6 W3 L2 NR1); USA (P6 W3 L3); Namibia (P2 W1 L1); UAE (P2 W1 L1); PNG (P8 L8).

TWENTY20 INTERNATIONALS (Full Members only)

	T20Is	W	L	NR	% won	% lost
Pakistan	27	18	6	3	**75.00**	25.00
South Africa	23	15	8	0	**65.21**	34.78
England..........	17	11	6	0	**64.70**	35.29
India	14	8	6	0	**57.14**	42.85
New Zealand	21	11	10	0	**52.38**	47.61
Afghanistan	6	3	3	0	**50.00**	50.00
Australia..........	22	10	12	0	**45.45**	54.55
West Indies	25	9	13	3	**40.90**	59.09
Bangladesh	24	9	15	0	**37.50**	62.50
Sri Lanka	18	6	12	0	**33.33**	66.66
Ireland.	9	3	6	0	**33.33**	66.66
Zimbabwe.........	14	4	10	0	**28.57**	71.42
Totals	110	107	107	3		

All white-ball matches between Full Members only. The % won/lost excludes no-results. With the extension of Twenty20 international status to all Associate Members of the ICC, a further 59 teams also played official T20Is in 2021.

TEST AVERAGES IN CALENDAR YEAR 2021

BATTING (325 runs)

		T	I	NO	R	HS	100	50	Avge	SR	Ct/St
1	†F. D. M. Karunaratne (SL) ..	7	13	0	902	244	4	3	69.38	55.74	2
2	K. S. Williamson (NZ)	4	7	1	395	238	1	1	65.83	46.03	0
3	M. Labuschagne (A)	5	9	1	526	108	2	4	65.75	49.06	4
4	†D. P. Conway (NZ)	3	6	0	379	200	1	2	63.16	50.00	0
5	J. E. Root (E)	15	29	1	1,708	228	6	4	61.00	56.85	21
6	D. M. de Silva (SL)	6	10	1	530	166	2	2	58.88	55.03	12
7	†Fawad Alam (P)	9	13	3	571	140	3	2	57.10	49.69	7
8	†Tamim Iqbal (B)	4	8	1	383	92	0	4	54.71	77.84	1
9	S. P. D. Smith (A)	5	8	0	430	131	1	3	53.75	52.05	13
10	†H. D. R. L. Thirimanne (SL)	7	13	0	659	140	2	4	50.69	43.41	14
11	Abid Ali (P)	9	15	1	695	215*	2	2	49.64	48.87	5
12	Liton Das (B)	7	12	0	594	114	1	5	49.50	57.50	17/3
13	R. G. Sharma (I)	11	21	2	906	161	2	4	47.68	48.19	14
14	K. L. Rahul (I)	5	10	0	461	129	2	1	46.10	43.12	3
15	Mohammad Rizwan (P)	9	13	3	455	115*	1	2	45.50	50.16	26/1
16	†D. Elgar (SA)	6	11	1	442	127	1	3	44.20	54.77	7
17	M. A. Agarwal (I)	4	8	0	353	150	1	2	44.12	48.55	2
18	P. Nissanka (SL)	6	10	0	427	103	1	4	42.70	43.30	3
19	Azhar Ali (P)	9	15	2	549	126	1	3	42.23	44.34	3
20	†D. P. D. N. Dickwella (SL)..	7	12	1	463	96	0	3	42.09	63.86	21
21	†Mominul Haque (B)	7	13	1	503	127	2	1	41.91	47.85	0
22	N. E. Bonner (WI)	9	16	2	577	113*	1	4	41.21	35.55	9
23	Mushfiqur Rahim (B)	7	12	1	443	91	0	3	40.27	45.90	3
24	†R. R. Pant (I)	12	21	2	748	101	1	5	39.36	67.44	33/6
25	†Q. de Kock (SA)	6	10	1	348	141*	1	1	38.66	68.77	26
26	†Fahim Ashraf (P)	8	11	1	384	78*	0	3	38.40	49.80	4
27	H. E. van der Dussen (SA) . .	6	10	1	335	75*	0	3	37.22	41.66	7
28	A. D. Mathews (SL)	6	11	1	357	110	1	2	35.70	46.78	1
29	†K. R. Mayers (WI)	10	20	2	636	210*	1	2	35.33	61.98	5
30	Babar Azam (P)	8	13	1	416	77	0	4	34.66	48.48	5
31	A. K. Markram (SA)	6	11	1	346	108	1	2	34.60	44.70	9
32	K. C. Brathwaite (WI)	10	20	0	675	126	1	4	33.75	37.79	6
33	†Nazmul Hossain (B)	7	14	1	398	163	2	0	30.61	52.85	8
34	S. Gill (I)	9	17	1	478	91	0	4	29.87	54.19	5
35	V. Kohli (I)	11	19	0	536	72	0	4	28.21	44.07	14
36	C. A. Pujara (I)	14	26	1	702	91	0	6	28.08	34.17	8
37	†R. J. Burns (E)	10	19	0	530	132	1	3	27.89	41.34	7
38	B. O. P. Fernando (SL)	7	13	1	333	91	0	3	27.75	43.30	8
39	D. W. Lawrence (E)	8	15	2	354	81*	0	3	27.23	49.03	1
40	J. O. Holder (WI)	8	16	2	362	71*	0	2	25.85	55.26	13
41	R. Ashwin (I)	9	15	1	355	106	1	0	25.35	50.85	2
42	J. C. Buttler (E)	9	16	2	353	55	0	1	25.21	42.78	41/1
43	J. M. Bairstow (E)	9	17	1	391	57	0	1	24.43	48.45	11
44	J. Blackwood (WI)	10	20	0	488	68	0	2	24.40	45.99	9
45	J. Da Silva (WI)	10	19	3	385	92	0	2	24.06	34.04	36/2
46	O. J. D. Pope (E)	9	18	1	368	81	0	1	21.64	48.04	8
47	A. M. Rahane (I)	13	23	0	479	67	0	2	20.82	43.03	14
48	D. P. Sibley (E)	10	20	2	356	87	0	3	19.77	30.29	5

BOWLING (12 wickets)

		Style	O	M	R	W	BB	5I	Avge	SR	ER
1	A. R. Patel (I)	SLA	201.5	50	427	36	6-38	5	11.86	33.63	2.11
2	Hasan Ali (P)	RFM	212.3	49	659	41	5-27	5	16.07	31.09	3.10
3	R. Ashwin (I)	OB	387.1	82	899	54	6-61	3	16.64	43.01	2.32
4	L. T. Ngidi (SA) . . .	RFM	122.5	28	370	22	6-71	2	16.81	33.50	3.01

		Style	O	M	R	W	BB	5I	Avge	SR	ER
5	Shaheen Shah Afridi (P)	LFM	292.5	78	802	47	6-51	3	17.06	37.38	2.73
6	K. A. Jamieson (NZ)	RFM	188.2	67	473	27	6-48	3	17.51	41.85	2.51
7	P. A. K. P. Jayawickrama (SL)	SLW	132.5	36	328	18	6-92	2	18.22	44.27	2.46
8	P. J. Cummins (A)	RF	156.5	46	394	21	5-38	1	18.76	44.80	2.51
9	K. Rabada (SA)	RF	172	43	437	23	5-34	1	19.00	44.86	2.54
10	Sajid Khan (P)	OB	121.4	26	355	18	8-42	1	19.72	40.55	2.91
11	T. A. Boult (NZ)	LFM	114.5	23	330	16	4-85	0	20.62	43.06	2.87
12	A. Y. Patel (NZ)	SLA	143	33	434	21	10-119	3	20.66	40.85	3.03
13	A. A. Nortje (SA)	RF	157	34	519	25	6-56	2	20.76	37.68	3.30
14	O. E. Robinson (E)	RFM/OB	295.4	85	783	37	5-65	2	21.16	47.94	2.64
15	J. N. T. Seales (WI)	RM	100.4	23	341	16	5-21	1	21.31	37.75	3.38
16	R. T. M. Wanigamuni (SL)	OB	192.2	30	560	26	6-70	2	21.53	44.38	2.91
17	J. M. Anderson (E)	RFM	399.5	141	848	39	6-40	2	21.74	61.51	2.12
18	J. R. Hazlewood (A)	RFM	120.4	43	287	13	5-57	1	22.07	55.69	2.37
19	B. Muzarabani (Z)	RFM	156.1	35	425	19	4-48	0	22.36	49.31	2.72
20	Mohammed Shami (I)	RFM	166.4	38	517	23	5-44	1	22.47	43.47	3.10
21	J. O. Holder (WI)	RFM	227.4	57	503	22	5-27	1	22.86	62.09	2.20
22	S. N. Thakur (I)	RFM	108	16	371	16	4-61	0	23.18	40.50	3.43
22	T. G. Southee (NZ)	RFM	210.5	50	516	22	6-43	2	23.45	57.50	2.44
24	K. A. J. Roach (WI)	RFM	233.4	52	645	27	4-52	0	23.88	51.92	2.76
25	K. R. Mayers (WI)	RM	134	42	327	13	3-24	0	25.15	61.84	2.44
26	K. A. Maharaj (SA)	SLA	185.4	38	480	19	5-36	1	25.26	58.63	2.58
27	R. A. S. Lakmal (SL)	RFM	181	62	445	17	5-47	1	26.17	63.88	2.45
28	J. J. Bumrah (I)	RFM	308.4	78	796	30	5-64	1	26.53	61.73	2.57
29	D. M. Bess (E)	OB	136.1	16	452	17	5-30	1	26.58	48.05	3.31
30	L. Embuldeniya (SL)	SLA	316.1	78	871	32	7-137	3	27.21	59.28	2.75
31	Nauman Ali (P)	SLA	216.3	58	529	19	5-35	2	27.84	68.36	2.44
32	R. A. Jadeja (I)	SLA	217.2	53	476	16	4-40	0	29.75	81.50	2.19
33	M. Siraj (I)	RFM	292.5	63	929	31	5-73	1	29.96	56.67	3.17
34	J. A. Warrican (WI)	SLA	191.5	32	572	19	4-50	0	30.10	60.57	2.98
35	Taskin Ahmed (B)	RFM	116.2	27	393	13	4-82	0	30.23	53.69	3.37
36	Taijul Islam (B)	SLA	345.3	78	915	30	7-116	2	30.50	69.10	2.64
37	J. E. Root (E)	OB/LB	139.3	18	427	14	5-8	1	30.50	59.78	3.06
38	I. Sharma (I)	RFM	168.2	39	458	14	3-48	0	32.71	72.14	2.72
39	M. A. Starc (A)	LF	180.1	43	565	17	4-37	0	33.23	63.58	3.13
40	M. J. Leach (E)	SLA	299.5	40	1,020	30	5-122	1	34.00	59.96	3.40
41	M. A. Wood (E)	RF	202.3	33	661	19	3-51	0	34.78	63.94	3.26
42	M. V. T. Fernando (SL)	LFM	150.2	23	502	14	5-101	1	35.85	64.42	3.33
43	N. M. Lyon (A)	OB	260.1	78	612	17	4-91	0	36.00	91.82	2.35
44	Mehedi Hasan (B)	OB	332.1	66	918	25	5-82	1	36.72	79.72	2.76
45	M. M. Ali (E)	OB	147	13	525	14	4-98	0	37.50	63.00	3.57
46	R. R. S. Cornwall (WI)	OB	290.4	47	826	21	5-74	1	39.33	83.04	2.84
47	S. C. J. Broad (E)	RFM	179.1	48	474	12	4-48	0	39.50	89.58	2.64

MOST DISMISSALS BY A WICKETKEEPER

Dis		T			Dis		T		
42	(41ct, 1st)	9	J. C. Buttler (E)		27	(26ct, 1st)	9	Mohammad Rizwan (P)	
39	(33ct, 6st)	12	R. R. Pant (I)		26	(26ct)	6	Q. de Kock (SA)	
38	(36ct, 2st)	10	J. Da Silva (WI)		21	(21ct)	7	D. P. D. N. Dickwella (SL)	

MOST CATCHES IN THE FIELD

Ct	T			Ct	T		
21	15	J. E. Root (E)		14	11	V. Kohli (I)	
16	6	Imran Butt (P)		14	11	R. G. Sharma (I)	
14	7	H. D. R. L. Thirimanne (SL)		14	13	A. M. Rahane (I)	

ONE-DAY INTERNATIONAL AVERAGES
IN CALENDAR YEAR 2021

BATTING (225 runs)

		M	I	NO	R	HS	100	50	Avge	SR	4	6
1	J. S. Malhotra (USA)	6	6	3	261	173*	1	0	87.00	104.40	6	21
2	J. N. Malan (SA)	8	7	1	509	177*	2	2	84.83	92.04	49	11
3	†H. G. Munsey (Scot)	6	6	3	230	79*	0	1	76.66	81.85	14	9
4	†D. P. Conway (NZ)	3	3	0	225	126	1	1	75.00	88.23	26	0
5	Babar Azam (P)	6	6	0	405	158	2	1	67.50	108.00	48	7
6	S. D. Hope (WI)	5	5	0	310	110	1	2	62.00	79.28	27	3
7	†Fakhar Zaman (P)	6	6	0	365	193	2	0	60.83	91.93	35	13
8	M. D. Patel (USA)	6	6	2	238	100	1	1	59.50	79.06	14	4
9	†S. Dhawan (I)	6	6	1	297	98	0	3	59.40	91.95	36	3
10	J. M. Bairstow (E)	6	5	0	291	124	1	1	58.20	121.75	26	16
11	Mushfiqur Rahim (B)	9	9	2	407	125	1	2	58.14	76.64	25	3
12	H. E. van der Dussen (SA)	8	7	1	342	123*	1	2	57.00	95.53	28	6
13	P. R. Stirling (Ire)	14	14	1	705	131*	3	2	54.23	79.66	71	17
14	Mahmudullah (B)	12	11	3	399	76*	0	4	49.87	81.59	20	13
15	†E. Lewis (WI)	6	6	1	237	103	1	2	47.40	77.19	19	9
16	S. Singh (Ire)	13	9	3	280	100*	1	1	46.66	86.95	25	2
17	†M. D. Gunathilleke (SL)	6	6	0	271	96	0	2	45.16	92.49	35	4
18	†M. D. K. J. Perera (SL)	6	6	0	246	120	1	1	41.00	88.80	22	1
19	†K. I. C. Asalanka (SL)	8	8	0	326	77	0	3	40.75	85.78	23	4
20	†Shakib Al Hasan (B)	9	9	2	277	96*	0	2	39.57	70.30	22	1
21	W. I. A. Fernando (SL)	8	8	0	310	118	1	2	38.75	84.23	25	5
22	{ C. Campher (Ire)	7	6	0	232	56	0	2	38.66	80.83	17	2
	†Tamim Iqbal (B)	12	12	0	464	112	1	4	38.66	77.33	48	7
24	H. T. Tector (Ire)	14	14	2	454	79	0	4	37.83	75.66	32	9
25	†W. T. S. Porterfield (Ire)	6	6	0	226	75	0	3	37.66	65.88	26	1
26	†Zeeshan Maqsood (Oman)	10	9	1	270	58	0	2	33.75	69.05	18	8
27	A. Balbirnie (Ire)	14	14	1	421	102	1	3	32.38	71.96	43	3
28	D. M. de Silva (SL)	11	11	1	304	91	0	2	30.40	72.38	28	0
29	Jatinder Singh (Oman)	10	9	0	263	107	1	1	29.22	106.04	28	11
30	P. W. H. de Silva (SL)	14	14	1	356	80*	0	3	27.38	94.68	24	13
31	†Ayaan Khan (Oman)	10	9	0	241	83	0	1	26.77	61.47	16	4
32	Liton Das (B)	11	11	0	256	102	1	0	23.27	71.91	27	0
33	L. J. Tucker (Ire)	14	10	0	229	83	0	1	22.90	70.24	12	5
34	M. D. Shanaka (SL)	12	12	1	247	48*	0	0	22.45	70.77	13	5

BOWLING (9 wickets)

		Style	O	M	R	W	BB	4I	Avge	SR	ER
1	S. Lamichhane (Nepal)	LB	41.5	5	133	18	6-11	3	7.38	13.94	3.17
2	M. A. Starc (A)	LF	27.1	2	117	11	5-48	1	10.63	14.81	4.30
3	K. V. Morea (PNG)	LM	39	2	144	11	5-28	1	13.09	21.27	3.69
4	A. C. Evans (Scot)	RFM	34.4	2	145	11	5-43	1	13.18	18.90	4.18
5	S. Mahmood (E)	RFM	28	3	123	9	4-42	1	13.66	18.66	4.39
6	D. J. Willey (E)	LFM	27	2	144	9	4-64	1	16.00	18.00	5.33
7	S. N. Netralvalkar (USA)	LFM	50.1	5	198	12	4-29	1	16.50	25.08	3.94
8	Ayaan Khan (Oman)	SLA	59.2	7	210	12	4-36	1	17.50	29.66	3.53
9	Shakib Al Hasan (B)	SLA	81	5	298	17	5-30	2	17.52	28.58	3.67
10	C. A. Soper (PNG)	RFM	58	8	230	13	3-45	0	17.69	26.76	3.96
11	N. P. Kenjige (USA)	SLA	45.2	1	179	10	3-22	0	17.90	27.20	3.94
12	Khawar Ali (Oman)	LB	44.1	2	216	11	5-15	1	19.63	24.09	4.89
13	Mehedi Hasan (B)	OB	84	6	297	15	4-25	2	19.80	33.60	3.53
14	J. B. Little (Ire)	LFM	73	3	342	17	4-39	1	20.11	25.76	4.68
15	S. Singh (Ire)	OB	104.1	15	383	19	5-10	2	20.15	32.89	3.67
16	Zeeshan Maqsood (Oman)	SLA	79.4	5	339	16	4-28	1	21.18	29.87	4.25
17	Mustafizur Rahman (B)	LFM	76.5	4	388	18	3-16	0	21.55	25.61	5.04

		Style	O	M	R	W	BB	4I	Avge	SR	ER
18	A. J. Hosein (WI)	SLA	81.2	3	323	14	3-26	0	23.07	34.85	3.97
19	Bilal Khan (Oman)	LFM	71	3	357	15	4-47	1	23.80	28.40	5.02
20	K. A. Maharaj (SA)	SLA	68	3	290	12	3-38	0	24.16	34.00	4.26
21	B. Muzarabani (Z)	RFM	52.5	8	218	9	4-29	1	24.22	35.22	4.12
22	Haris Rauf (P)	RFM	51	1	318	13	4-65	1	24.46	23.53	6.23
23	A. R. McBrine (Ire)	OB	104	10	403	16	5-29	1	25.18	39.00	3.87
24	T. Shamsi (SA)	SLW	72.4	1	369	14	5-49	1	26.35	31.14	5.07
25	Bhuvneshwar Kumar (I)	RFM	48	0	252	9	3-42	0	28.00	32.00	5.25
26	A. S. Joseph (WI)	RFM	79.1	4	342	12	3-39	0	28.50	39.58	4.32
27	P. V. D. Chameera (SL)	RF	106.2	4	586	20	5-16	1	29.30	31.90	5.51
28	Mohammad Saifuddin (B)	RM	48.2	0	307	10	3-51	0	30.70	29.00	6.35
29	C. A. Young (Ire)	RFM	91.2	6	462	13	4-18	1	35.53	42.15	5.05
30	K. Rabada (SA)	RF	61.2	5	323	9	2-16	0	35.88	40.88	5.26
31	A. L. Phehlukwayo (SA)	RFM	62	1	403	11	3-56	0	36.63	33.81	6.50
32	Taskin Ahmed (B)	RFM	83.2	3	417	10	4-46	1	41.70	50.00	5.00
33	P. W. H. de Silva (SL)	LB	121	7	552	12	3-37	0	46.00	60.50	4.56

MOST DISMISSALS BY A WICKETKEEPER

Dis		M		Dis		M	
15	(15ct)	13	L. J. Tucker (Ire)	10	(8ct, 2st)	8	K. Doriga (PNG)
13	(12ct, 1st)	6	R. W. Chakabva (Z)	10	(8ct, 2st)	9	Mushfiqur Rahim (B)
11	(11ct)	6	M. H. Cross (Scot)				

Tucker played one further one-day international when not keeping wicket, taking two catches.

MOST CATCHES IN THE FIELD

Ct	M			Ct	M		
9	6	K. Bhurtel (Nepal)		7	11	Mehedi Hasan (B)	
7	8	Liton Das (B)		7	12	Tamim Iqbal (B)	
7	11	D. M. de Silva (SL)					

Liton Das played three further one-day internationals as wicketkeeper, taking three catches.

TWENTY20 INTERNATIONAL AVERAGES IN CALENDAR YEAR 2021

BATTING (350 runs)

		M	I	NO	R	HS	100	50	Avge	SR	4	6
1	†E. Lewis (WI)	18	18	1	489	79	0	4	28.76	155.73	42	37
2	R. G. Sharma (I)	11	11	0	424	74	0	5	38.54	150.88	39	23
3	†D. A. Miller (SA)	17	15	7	377	85*	0	2	47.12	149.60	23	18
4	A. K. Markram (SA)	18	16	3	570	70	0	4	43.84	148.82	44	27
5	J. J. Roy (E)	15	15	1	426	64	0	2	30.42	146.89	48	17
6	M. J. Guptill (NZ)	18	18	0	678	97	0	5	37.66	145.49	53	41
7	J. C. Buttler (E)	14	14	5	589	101*	1	4	65.44	143.30	49	26
8	†V. P. Thamotharam (Malta)	18	18	2	419	104*	1	1	26.18	140.13	34	20
9	Riazat Ali Shah (Uganda)	21	16	3	350	59	0	1	26.92	140.00	25	18
10	†D. P. Conway (NZ)	14	13	4	428	99*	0	2	47.55	135.01	45	9
11	Mohammad Rizwan (P)	29	26	8	1,326	104*	1	12	73.66	134.89	119	42
12	†Q. de Kock (SA)	14	14	2	524	72	0	5	43.66	131.32	54	12
13	†N. Pooran (WI)	25	21	2	484	64	0	2	25.47	130.45	31	32
14	M. R. Marsh (A)	21	20	3	627	77*	0	6	36.88	129.81	59	23
15	Babar Azam (P)	29	26	1	939	122	1	9	37.56	127.58	99	17
16	†Fakhar Zaman (P)	24	20	3	415	60	0	3	24.41	127.30	33	18
17	R. R. Hendricks (SA)	15	15	1	413	69	0	3	29.50	126.29	44	9
18	R. D. Berrington (Scot)	13	13	4	447	82*	0	4	49.66	125.91	31	18

		M	I	NO	R	HS	100	50	Avge	SR	4	6
19	P. R. Stirling (Ire)	16	16	2	482	115*	1	1	34.42	125.52	51	18
20	A. J. Finch (A)	17	17	1	459	79*	0	3	28.68	125.06	45	16
21	L. Bruce (Gibraltar) . . .	9	9	1	356	73	0	5	44.50	124.91	27	3
22	H. E. van der Dussen (SA)	16	14	4	391	94*	0	3	39.10	123.73	24	14
23	C. G. Williams (Namibia) .	14	14	0	378	81	0	4	27.00	117.02	40	11
24	†Afif Hossain (B)	27	25	4	390	49*	0	0	18.57	116.41	27	17
25	†D. J. Malan (E)	17	16	2	384	76	0	2	27.42	116.01	35	11
26	S. Ssesazi (Uganda)	16	16	2	483	63	0	4	34.50	112.06	52	15
27	R. B. Patel (Uganda) . . .	19	16	5	357	68*	0	1	32.45	111.56	35	5
28	H. Lakov (Bulgaria)	12	12	4	404	80	0	5	50.50	108.89	33	5
29	Saud Islam (Uganda) . .	20	19	2	452	75	0	3	26.58	106.10	43	9
30	Mahmudullah (B)	26	26	5	496	52	0	2	23.61	105.30	35	12
31	†Mohammad Naim (B) . . .	26	26	1	575	64	0	3	23.00	100.34	48	12
32	B. Arora (Malta)	17	17	4	406	66*	0	2	31.23	91.85	42	8
33	J. O. Adedeji (Nigeria) .	18	18	2	403	68	0	2	25.18	91.79	34	12

BOWLING (20 wickets)

		Style	O	D	R	W	BB	4I	Avge	SR	ER
1	D. M. Nakrani (Uganda) . .	LM	444	248	374	35	6-7	2	10.68	12.68	5.05
2	S. Conteh (Sierra Leone) .	RM	192	107	167	20	5-17	2	8.35	9.60	5.21
3	P. W. H. de Silva (SL) . . .	LB	462	203	419	36	4-9	1	11.63	12.83	5.44
4	T. Shamsi (SA)	SLW	504	221	481	36	4-25	2	13.36	14.00	5.72
5	Bilal Muhammad (Malta) .	LFM	404	216	403	24	4-10	1	16.79	16.83	5.98
6	Shakib Al Hasan (B)	SLA	418	178	422	25	4-9	2	16.88	16.72	6.05
7	P. Aho (Nigeria)	RFM	317	183	337	20	6-5	1	16.85	15.85	6.37
8	Mehedi Hasan snr (B) . . .	OB	489	211	529	23	3-19	0	23.00	21.26	6.49
9	Nasum Ahmed (B)	SLA	341	151	377	22	4-10	2	17.13	15.50	6.63
10	Shadab Khan (P)	LB	354	155	392	20	4-26	1	19.60	17.70	6.64
11	J. N. Frylinck (Namibia) .	LFM	267	111	306	23	6-24	1	13.30	11.60	6.87
12	J. R. Hazlewood (A)	RFM	328	163	376	23	4-39	1	16.34	14.26	6.87
13	Mustafizur Rahman (B) . .	LFM	417	188	487	28	4-12	2	17.39	14.89	7.00
14	A. U. Rashid (E)	LB	350	131	409	23	4-2	1	17.78	15.21	7.01
15	T. A. Boult (NZ)	LFM	352	167	415	23	3-17	0	18.04	15.30	7.07
16	A. Zampa (A)	LB	459	188	546	26	5-19	1	21.00	17.65	7.13
17	Washeem Abbas (Malta) .	RFM	381	166	459	29	5-37	2	15.82	13.13	7.22
18	P. V. D. Chameera (SL) . .	RF	415	184	502	22	4-17	1	22.81	18.86	7.25
19	T. G. Southee (NZ)	RFM	389	185	471	24	3-15	0	19.62	16.20	7.26
20	Shoriful Islam (B)	LFM	330	138	406	22	3-33	0	18.45	15.00	7.38
21	M. R. Adair (Ire)	RFM	292	124	363	24	4-23	1	15.12	12.16	7.45
22	Shaheen Shah Afridi (P) . .	LFM	457	218	599	23	3-26	0	26.04	19.86	7.86
23	L. M. Jongwe (Z)	RFM	304	109	400	26	4-18	1	15.38	11.69	7.89
24	Hasan Ali (P)	RFM	358	148	482	25	4-18	1	19.28	14.32	8.07
25	I. S. Sodhi (NZ)	LB	336	111	457	27	4-28	2	16.92	12.44	8.16
26	Haris Rauf (P)	RFM	459	150	637	25	4-22	1	25.48	18.36	8.32

MOST DISMISSALS BY A WICKETKEEPER

Dis		M			Dis		M	
23	(15ct, 8st)	13	I. A. Karim (Kenya)		17	(14ct, 3st)	21	Nurul Hasan (B)
22	(20ct, 2st)	27	Mohammad Rizwan (P)		14	(9ct, 5st)	7	S. Nadigotla (Romania)
21	(20ct, 1st)	22	M. S. Wade (A)		14	(10ct, 4st)	23	N. Pooran (WI)

Mohammad Rizwan and Pooran each played two further matches when not keeping wicket; Rizwan took two catches, and Pooran none.

MOST CATCHES IN THE FIELD

Ct	M			Ct	M	
17	29	Babar Azam (P)		14	18	M. J. Guptill (NZ)
15	18	A. K. Markram (SA)		13	26	Mohammad Naim (B)
15	24	Fakhar Zaman (P)				

AFGHANISTAN CRICKET IN 2021

Chaos in Kabul

MOHAMMAD IBRAHIM MOMAND

Given the passion and effort that went into Afghanistan's elevation to full international status in 2017, it has been a pity to witness the administrative and leadership woes that have beset their cricket since. It is hard to escape the conclusion that the opportunity has largely been missed.

After the poor showing at the 2019 World Cup, the Afghanistan Cricket Board turned on itself. Chairman Azizullah Fazli and chief executive Asadullah Khan were fired, only for the new chairman, Farhan Yusefzai, to fall out with the new chief executive, Lutfullah Stanikzai, and sack him after a year for "unsatisfactory performance and misbehaviour". His replacements came and went: Jaar Abdulrahimzai lasted four months, and Rahmatullah Qureishi five. Hamid Shinwari had just been appointed when Kabul fell to the Taliban in August.

They entered the ACB offices and immediately dismissed Farhan and Hamid, accusing them of abusing their authority. They reinstalled Azizullah but, while he was with the national team at the T20 World Cup, claimed they

AFGHANISTAN IN 2021

	Played	Won	Lost	Drawn/No result
Tests	2	1	1	–
One-day internationals	3	3	–	–
Twenty20 internationals	8	5	3	–

JANUARY	3 ODIs (in the UAE) v Ireland	(page 889)
FEBRUARY		
MARCH	2 Tests and 3 T20Is (in the UAE) v Zimbabwe	(page 891)
APRIL		
MAY		
JUNE		
JULY		
AUGUST		
SEPTEMBER		
OCTOBER	} T20 World Cup in the UAE	(page 830)
NOVEMBER		
DECEMBER		

Aamir Qureshi, Getty Images

Watching the watchers: A Taliban fighter monitors a trial match at Kabul in September, ahead of the T20 World Cup, between Peace Defenders and Peace Heroes.

had intended his appointment to be temporary, and replaced him with former all-rounder Mirwais Ashraf – whom they called "acting-chairman". Their choice of chief executive was Naseeb Khan: the seventh to hold the post in less than three years.

It means that, since Afghanistan's first Test, in June 2018, they have had more chief executives than they have played Tests: the clear challenge for Mirwais and Naseeb is to play more. But the role of the Taliban may prove counterproductive. It was widely reported that, under the new regime, women would not be allowed to play cricket, which prompted Australia to cancel a visit by Afghanistan's men for a standalone Test in late November. Mirwais and Naseeb claimed they were exploring ways to facilitate the women's game without violating strict Islamic law, and the ICC have formed a working group to support them.

Afghanistan's national team had begun 2021 with a clean sweep over Ireland in three one-dayers in the United Arab Emirates. Rahmanullah Gurbaz, a 19-year-old wicketkeeper on debut, hit 127 in the first game; Rahmat Shah struck his fifth ODI century in the second.

The only other senior bilateral event was a dual-format contest with Zimbabwe in the UAE, where honours were even in the two-match Test series. Seamers dominated the first game, when Afghanistan were bundled out for 131 and 135 to lose by ten wickets, but the second was remarkable for a partnership of 307 between Hashmatullah Shahidi – who hit the country's first Test double-century – and captain Asghar Afghan. Rashid Khan's 11 wickets ensured victory. Afghanistan whitewashed Zimbabwe in the T20s.

There was a hiatus of six months before the T20 World Cup in the UAE: the players were rusty, and it showed. Afghanistan had qualified directly for the Super 12 stage and, though they trounced their Associate opponents, Scotland and Namibia, they were easily beaten by Pakistan, India and New Zealand.

It had always been thought this might be Asghar's last global event, but his mid-tournament retirement came as a shock. He was considered a strong and wise leader, widely respected in Afghanistan, and had been expected – at the very least – to see the tournament through. The reality, perhaps, was that he'd had enough of the heat. On social media, there had been accusations of nepotism in selection, though these were unfair. It was Asghar who gave opportunities to the likes of Rashid Khan and Mujeeb Zadran, who promoted over 90% of Afghanistan's Under-19 class of 2018 to full senior honours, and who became the rock while adminstrators came and went. But there is only so much a man can take.

Despite the best intentions and manifold promises, the ACB postponed the Afghanistan Premier League once again. The franchise tournament, launched in 2018-19 and won by Balkh Legends, was postponed from 2019-20 because of financial problems, then in 2020-21 because of the pandemic. It seemed unlikely – even if foreign players were willing to appear – that a window could be found.

Youthful promise is, as ever, the hallmark of cricket in Afghanistan. Qais Ahmad is already in demand around the world's franchise tournaments. The likes of left-arm fast bowler Fazalhaq Farooqi, strong right-armer Mohammad Saleem Safi, left-arm wrist-spinner Noor Ahmad Lakanwal, Under-19 captain Suliman Safi Khan and his speedy team-mate Bilal Sami are being watched with excitement. Suliman and Bilal were key components of Afghanistan's progress to the semi-finals of the 2022 Under-19 World Cup, repeating their run from four years earlier.

In November, shortly after his appointment, Mirwais gave a frank appraisal of the year: "We beat Ireland and Zimbabwe, then there was little cricket, and the performance of the national team in the T20 World Cup was not good." He sounded positive regarding future relations with the Taliban government, however: "They helped us financially, getting us over 10m Afghanis [about £75,000] despite the banking crisis, and they arranged charter flights so we could get to the World Cup. We have been given their full support to fix things, make administrative reforms, and recruit coaching staff." Some remained sceptical: head coach Lance Klusener and bowling coach Shaun Tait resigned soon after.

The Ghazi Amanullah Khan one-day tournament in October 2020 was covered in Wisden 2021 *(page 622), and the Ahmad Shah Abdali first-class tournament and Ghazi Amanullah Khan one-day tournament in late 2021 will be covered under the 2021-22 season in* Wisden 2023.

AFGHANISTAN v IRELAND IN THE UAE IN 2020-21

Paul Radley

One-day internationals (3): Afghanistan 3 (30pts), Ireland 0 (0pts)

Labelling this series "Afghanistan v Ireland" felt like a misnomer: for several months, Ireland's matches had really been "Allcomers v Paul Stirling". His previous international innings before arriving in the Gulf had been a match-winning century against England in Southampton in August 2020. He had added another hundred against the UAE immediately before this series, and now two more against Afghanistan at Abu Dhabi's Sheikh Zayed Stadium – where he had made his first-class debut as a 17-year-old in March 2008 – to make it four ODI centuries in six innings. But Stirling, whose 285 runs at 95 accounted for 37% of Ireland's output, could not do it on his own, and Afghanistan swept the series 3–0.

Unlike Ireland, the Afghans had contributions from everyone: new players, long-serving seniors, Twenty20 superstars. In the first game, Rahmanullah Gurbaz, just 19, clouted nine sixes and made a hundred on debut. Rahmat Shah showed why he is regarded as their most technically sound batsman with a century in the second. And Rashid Khan applied the *coup de grâce* with four wickets in the third.

Rashid, Mohammad Nabi and Mujeeb Zadran were able to take part only after the sides agreed – at two weeks' notice – to push back the series by three days. They were returning from the Australian Big Bash, and needed the extra time to quarantine. Ireland's captain Andy Balbirnie was happy with the change, since the initial programme had his team playing seven ODIs in 16 days, including the UAE series. But the Irish could not derail an Afghan side whose progress was in contrast to their own struggles since both were granted Test status in 2017.

It was a dispiriting week for local Irish sports fans. The cricket team were whitewashed, while a couple of miles away golfer Rory McIlroy's challenge at the Abu Dhabi HSBC Championship fell short, and Conor McGregor was knocked out in UFC Fight Island. To add to the gloom, the former Ireland player, manager and selector Roy Torrens died on the eve of the second match. Stirling called it "crushing news".

IRELAND TOURING PARTY

*A. Balbirnie, M. R. Adair, C. Campher, G. J. Delany, S. C. Getkate, J. B. Little, A. R. McBrine, B. J. McCarthy, J. A. McCollum, K. J. O'Brien, C. Olphert, N. A. Rock, S. Singh, P. R. Stirling, H. T. Tector, L. J. Tucker, C. A. Young. *Coach:* G. X. Ford.

First one-day international At Abu Dhabi, January 21, 2021. **Afghanistan won by 16 runs.** ‡**Afghanistan 287-9** (50 overs) (Rahmanullah Gurbaz 127, Javed Ahmadi 38, Rashid Khan 55; A. R. McBrine 5-29); **Ireland 271-9** (50 overs) (P. R. Stirling 39, C. Campher 39, L. J. Tucker 83; Naveen-ul-Haq 3-68). *Afghanistan 10pts. PoM:* Rahmanullah Gurbaz. *ODI debuts:* Azmatullah Omarzai, Rahmanullah Gurbaz (Afghanistan). *Afghanistan were itching to get going after not playing for ten months. After fog delayed the start, Rahmanullah Gurbaz, a 19-year-old wicketkeeper in his* *maiden ODI, lit up their return. His first scoring shot, off his ninth ball, was a pulled six, and he scarcely looked back, hitting eight more (and eight fours) on the way to a run-a-ball 127. Off-spinner Andy McBrine, who had never taken more than three wickets in an ODI, pegged Afghanistan back with five in 31 deliveries, but No. 9 Rashid Khan flogged 55 from 30, with five sixes. Ireland were reasonably placed at 174-4 in the 37th, with wicketkeeper Lorcan Tucker going well – but when he was ninth out for a career-best 83, the game was up.*

Second one-day international   At Abu Dhabi, January 24, 2021. **Afghanistan won by seven wickets.** ‡**Ireland 259-9** (50 overs) (P. R. Stirling 128, C. Campher 47; Naveen-ul-Haq 4-42, Mujeeb Zadran 3-46); **Afghanistan 260-3** (45.2 overs) (Rahmanullah Gurbaz 31, Rahmat Shah 103*, Hashmatullah Shahidi 82). *Afghanistan 10pts. PoM: Rahmat Shah. After the sides had observed a minute's silence to mark the death of former Ireland player Roy Torrens, Paul Stirling paid tribute to his friend with the bat. He slammed 128, putting on 84 for the third wicket with Harry Tector (24) and 106 for the fourth with Curtis Campher, but regular strikes by seamer Naveen-ul-Haq and spinner Mujeeb Zadran kept the total within bounds. Afghanistan were 48-2 before Rahmat Shah, who made his fifth ODI century, and Hashmatullah Shahidi added 184 in 33 overs – a national record for the third wicket, beating the same pair's 144 against Bangladesh at Mirpur in 2016-17.*

Third one-day international   At Abu Dhabi, January 26, 2021. **Afghanistan won by 36 runs. Afghanistan 266-9** (50 overs) (Asghar Afghan 41, Mohammad Nabi 32, Gulbadeen Naib 36, Rashid Khan 48; C. A. Young 3-61, S. Singh 3-37); ‡**Ireland 230** (47.1 overs) (P. R. Stirling 118; Rashid Khan 4-29). *Afghanistan 10pts. PoM: Rashid Khan. PoS: P. R. Stirling. The young Irish team had handled Rashid Khan well in the first two matches, but now his four wickets – which took his overall ODI haul against Ireland to 55 at 17 – settled the outcome. He was helped when Mujeeb bowled Stirling for 118, including six sixes; it was his 12th ODI century. Ireland were chasing as many as 267 only because Rashid had top-scored with a 40-ball 48 after coming in at 163-7. Fog had delayed the start by an hour and a quarter.*

AFGHANISTAN v ZIMBABWE IN THE UAE IN 2020-21

PAUL RADLEY

Test matches (2): Afghanistan 1, Zimbabwe 1
Twenty20 internationals (3): Afghanistan 3, Zimbabwe 0

Both sides had gone over a year without a Test, so it was no surprise Afghanistan and Zimbabwe took time to get back into the groove. The First Test ended in two days – as much a symptom of Afghanistan's lack of red-ball cricket as the uncharacteristically generous covering of grass on the Abu Dhabi pitch. Zimbabwe won handsomely, but struggled on a more typical track in the Second, and went down to a heavy defeat themselves.

The pandemic played its part. Coronavirus had caused a blanket ban on sport in Zimbabwe from the New Year, and ahead of their trip to the United Arab Emirates, they had played only two intra-squad games as preparation, in a bio-bubble in Harare. Even the venue for this series was affected. It was initially scheduled for neighbouring Oman, with Al Amerat's scenic Academy ground set to become the latest boutique Test venue. But Oman's borders were closed as Covid cases spiked: instead of the jagged peaks of the Al-Hajar Mountains, the backdrop was provided by the futuristic main stand of Abu Dhabi's Sheikh Zayed Stadium.

This was the first time Afghanistan had been involved in a series worthy of the term: four previous Tests had all been one-offs, against different opponents. If having two matches proved anything, it was that they are quick learners. In the First Test, they were bowled out cheaply twice. But in the Second, they showed substance. Hashmatullah Shahidi batted for ten minutes shy of ten hours for his country's first double-century, while Rashid Khan (who missed the opening match with a finger injury) sent down 596 deliveries, and claimed 11 wickets. As temperatures soared, sandstorms blew in, and Zimbabwe's batsmen knuckled down, the Afghans refused to wilt.

Missing out on a rare series win was harsh on Zimbabwe's captain, Sean Williams, who made 264 runs and was the one consistently excellent performer on either side. Afghanistan knew his importance: when he came out to bat in the Second Test, their talkative wicketkeeper Afsar Zazai trumpeted: "Oh yes, boys. Come on. The real match starts now." Williams smiled, said "Thank you", and got to work. After a match-winning hundred in the First Test, his career-best 151 not out in the Second took Zimbabwe to within an hour of saving the game, and winning the series. It lifted his average in four Tests as captain to 96, against 27 in the ranks.

Williams had to cope without six first-choice players through illness or injury. Tendai Chatara, Craig Ervine, Kyle Jarvis, P. J. Moor, Brendan Taylor and white-ball captain Chamu Chibhabha were particularly missed in the Twenty20 games, in which Afghanistan (themselves without Mujeeb Zadran and Gulbadeen Naib, because of visa issues) won a series that resembled Groundhog Day: the margins of victory were 48, 45 and 47 runs.

ZIMBABWE TOURING PARTY

*S. C. Williams (T/20), R. P. Burl (T/20), R. W. Chakabva (T/20), Faraz Akram (20), T. S. Kamunhukamwe (20), K. T. Kasuza (T/20), W. N. Madhevere (T/20), W. P. Masakadza (T/20), P. S. Masvaure (T/20), B. A. Mavuta (T/20), T. K. Musakanda (T/20), R. Mutumbami (T/20), B. Muzarabani (T/20), R. Ngarava (T/20), V. M. Nyauchi (T/20), M. Shumba (20), Sikandar Raza (T/20), D. T. Tiripano (T/20). *Coach:* L. S. Rajput.

AFGHANISTAN v ZIMBABWE

First Test

At Abu Dhabi, March 2–3, 2021. Zimbabwe won by ten wickets. Toss: Afghanistan. Test debuts: Abdul Malik, Abdul Wasi, Munir Ahmad; W. N. Madhevere.

When Afghanistan started out in Test cricket in June 2018, they were razed by India in Bangalore, bowled out twice in two sessions. It was brutal stuff, but at least they could say they had been playing one of the world's best sides. When something similar happened here, that excuse would not do. Afghanistan lasted 47 overs in the first innings, and 45.3 in the second. They were certainly inexperienced – this was only their fifth Test, and their talismanic leg-spinner Rashid Khan was absent with a finger injury – but Zimbabwe had been almost as light on Test cricket over the same period, and their main destroyer was Blessing Muzarabani, a lanky seamer winning only his second cap.

Muzarabani did have the benefit of two seasons of county cricket with Northamptonshire to hone his craft. Conditions in the desert were a world away from Wantage Road, though there was some grass on the pitch, which is rare in the UAE. Muzarabani enjoyed it, and his burst after Afghanistan had chosen to bat proved decisive. He bowled the debutant opener Abdul Malik with the first delivery of the match, and he and new-ball partner Victor Nyauchi had seven wickets between them by the time Afghanistan subsided for 131 on the first afternoon.

Zimbabwe's top order, lacking regulars Craig Ervine and Brendan Taylor, both ill, had flaws of their own. But they had enough nous, in the form of Williams and Sikandar Raza, to chisel out a match-winning lead. After Wesley Madhevere became the match's second debutant to collect a first-ball duck – given lbw by Ahmed Shah Pakteen, the first Afghan

---

OUT TO THE FIRST BALL OF THE MATCH ON TEST DEBUT

S. J. Cook	South Africa v India at Durban	1992-93
L. V. Garrick.	West Indies v South Africa at Kingston.	2000-01
Abdul Malik	**Afghanistan v Zimbabwe at Abu Dhabi**.	**2020-21**

---

to stand in a Test – Raza came in at 38 for four to face a hat-trick ball from slow left-armer Hamza Hotak. Raza cut it for four, and Zimbabwe scarcely looked back. Although he was guilty of giving his wicket away, Raza's alliance of 71 with his captain began to shift the balance. Williams pressed on to an assured century, the second in his first three matches in charge, and his seventh-wicket stand of 75 with Chakabva swelled the lead.

A total of 250 left Zimbabwe 119 in front. For much of Afghanistan's faltering second attempt, that looked likely to be enough for a rare innings win. Nyauchi picked up three more wickets, while Tiripano also took three as Afghanistan managed just 135. Zimbabwe had to bat again, but needed only 20 balls to complete a thumping victory.

It was the second Test in a week to finish in two days, following England's collapse against India. Conditions here did not provoke such heated debate as in Ahmedabad, even if Williams did describe the pitch as like a carpet at one end and a dustbowl at the other.

Player of the Match: S. C. Williams.
Close of play: first day, Zimbabwe 133-5 (Williams 54, Burl 8).

Afghanistan

Abdul Malik b Muzarabani	0	– (2) c Chakabva b Nyauchi	0
Ibrahim Zadran c Musakanda b Nyauchi	31	– (1) c Chakabva b Tiripano	76
Rahmat Shah c Chakabva b Muzarabani	6	– (4) lbw b Nyauchi	0
Munir Ahmad c Sikandar Raza b Nyauchi	12	– (3) lbw b Muzarabani	1
Hashmatullah Shahidi b Nyauchi	5	– c Madhevere b Nyauchi	4
†Afsar Zazai c Chakabva b Tiripano	37	– lbw b Williams	0
*Asghar Afghan c Chakabva b Muzarabani	13	– b Muzarabani	14
Abdul Wasi c Kasuza b Sikandar Raza	3	– b Burl	9
Hamza Hotak not out	16	– not out	21
Yamin Ahmadzai c Tiripano b Williams	1	– c Williams b Tiripano	0
Zahir Khan c Williams b Muzarabani	0	– c Nyauchi b Tiripano	0
B 4, w 1, nb 2	7	B 4, lb 1, w 5	10

1/0 (1) 2/8 (3) 3/37 (4) (47 overs) 131
4/52 (2) 5/69 (5) 6/91 (7)
7/109 (6) 8/122 (8) 9/123 (10) 10/131 (11)

1/5 (2) 2/6 (3) (45.3 overs) 135
3/15 (4) 4/21 (5)
5/21 (6) 6/47 (7) 7/81 (8)
8/129 (1) 9/129 (10) 10/135 (11)

Muzarabani 12–3–48–4; Nyauchi 10–1–34–3; Tiripano 12–5–24–1; Burl 7–1–9–0; Williams 3–2–4–1; Sikandar Raza 3–0–8–1. *Second innings*—Muzarabani 8–4–14–2; Nyauchi 7–1–30–3; Williams 6–0–28–1; Tiripano 9.3–2–23–3; Burl 7–0–13–1; Sikandar Raza 4–0–16–0; Madhevere 4–1–6–0.

Zimbabwe

P. S. Masvaure lbw b Hamza Hotak	15	– not out	5
K. T. Kasuza b Yamin Ahmadzai	0	– not out	11
T. K. Musakanda b Hamza Hotak	7		
*S. C. Williams c Hashmatullah Shahidi b Hamza Hotak	105		
W. N. Madhevere lbw b Hamza Hotak	0		
Sikandar Raza c Abdul Malik b Hamza Hotak	43		
R. P. Burl lbw b Ibrahim Zadran	8		
†R. W. Chakabva c Abdul Malik b Zahir Khan	44		
D. T. Tiripano c Ibrahim Zadran b Zahir Khan	4		
B. Muzarabani not out	12		
V. M. Nyauchi b Hamza Hotak	0		
B 2, lb 8, w 1, nb 1	12	Lb 1	1

1/5 (2) 2/22 (3) 3/38 (1) 4/38 (5) (72 overs) 250
5/109 (6) 6/137 (7) 7/212 (8) 8/224 (9)
9/250 (4) 10/250 (11)

(no wkt, 3.2 overs) 17

Yamin Ahmadzai 17.1–2–48–1; Hamza Hotak 25.3–3–75–6; Zahir Khan 19–0–81–2; Abdul Wasi 8.5–3–23–0; Ibrahim Zadran 2–0–13–1. *Second innings*—Hamza Hotak 2–0–11–0; Yamin Ahmadzai 1.2–0–5–0.

Umpires: Ahmed Shah Pakteen and Aleem Dar.   Third umpire: Ahmed Shah Durrani.
Referee: R. S. Madugalle.

AFGHANISTAN v ZIMBABWE

Second Test

At Abu Dhabi, March 10–14, 2021. Afghanistan won by six wickets. Toss: Afghanistan. Test debuts: Sayed Shirzad, Shahidullah.

When sports stars achieve a milestone and point to the name on the back of their shirt, it does not always stem from look-at-me egomania. Many use it as a reminder of the family they are representing. After reaching his maiden Test century, Asghar Afghan was cheating a little: he had changed his last name in 2018 from Stanikzai, his tribe, to honour his country instead. And he had already patted the new crest – in use for the first time – on his chest.

Under that ACB logo is the number one, signifying that Asghar was the first player listed when Afghanistan started in Test cricket. He was also the only one left from the pioneering group of refugees who made up their first national team. Stung by the limp defeat the previous week, he was central to the turnaround that ended in a comfortable win, despite a twitchy run-chase on the final afternoon.

Asghar reached his century, amid a whirl of shots that would not have looked out of place on the streets where he learned the game. They came against Nyauchi's burst with the second new ball late on the first day, and Hashmatullah Shahidi followed him to three

---

DISMISSED FOR A DUCK IN FIRST THREE TEST INNINGS

T. A. Ward.......	South Africa v Australia and England in England	1912
R. A. L. Massie ...	Australia v England in England	1972
B. P. Bracewell ...	New Zealand v England in England	1978
M. G. Hughes	Australia v India and England in Australia........	1985-86 to 1986-87
M. S. Atapattu	Sri Lanka v India in India and Australia in Sri Lanka ..	1990-91 to 1992-93
S. L. Malinga....	Sri Lanka v Australia in Australia.................	2004
M. R. Gillespie ...	New Zealand v South Africa in SA and England in NZ.	2007-08
Kamrul Islam.....	Bangladesh v England in Bangladesh..............	2016-17
W. N. Madhevere	**Zimbabwe v Afghanistan in the UAE**	**2020-21**

Ward (who was part of two hat-tricks) and Madhevere both faced only five balls.

---

figures next morning. They put on 307 for the fourth wicket, dwarfing Afghanistan's previous best Test partnership – 139 by Ihsanullah Janat and Rahmat Shah against Ireland at Dehradun in March 2019. Asghar eventually departed for 164, but allowed Hashmatullah, who in all faced 443 balls in 590 minutes, to carry on to his country's maiden double before calling a halt at 545 for four. It was, by more than 200, their highest Test total.

One of the five changes Afghanistan had made from the First Test was the inclusion of Rashid Khan. The finger he had broken playing for Lahore Qalandars in the PSL got a severe workout: he delivered 99.2 overs across Zimbabwe's back-to-back innings, and finished with 11 for 275. It was the biggest workload for any bowler in a Test since Muttiah Muralitharan sent down 113.5 – and took 16 wickets – for Sri Lanka against England at The Oval in 1998.

It was to Zimbabwe's credit that Rashid was made to work hard. Mohan Singh, the groundsman, had shaved off the greenery, which blunted the seamers, but the slow bowlers had to earn their wickets too. And earn was the right word: it was pointed out that Rashid had pocketed around £400,000 for bowling 64 overs in 16 matches in the IPL late in 2020; his match fee here, for four balls short of 100 overs, was thought to be about £1,000.

Zimbabwe started promisingly, reaching 133 for one, before Masvaure fell for a patient 65. Sayed Shirzad, a bustling seamer making his debut, then dismissed Williams (top-edging a pull) and Madhevere (for a second golden duck) with successive balls. As in the First Test, Sikandar Raza entered on a hat-trick, and survived: he top-scored with 85, before becoming Rashid's fourth victim as Zimbabwe capsized for 287. Asghar asked them to follow on, 258 behind. They wobbled at 102 for four – the hapless Madhevere collected his third duck in three innings – and soon after Rashid claimed three wickets in eight balls.

He finished with a national-record seven in the second innings, as No. 9 Tiripano proved the most stubborn. He batted with remarkable determination to see out 258 balls, and put on 187 with Williams, a Zimbabwean eighth-wicket record (they had only six higher stands in all). Tiripano was finally trapped five short of a maiden Test century. At the other end, Williams proved unmovable, but ran out of partners just as an unlikely draw seemed possible. He finished with a career-best undefeated 151, after seven and three-quarter hours. Afghanistan knocked off the target of 108 with relative ease. "We missed out on the series by 60 minutes," said Williams.

Player of the Match: Hashmatullah Shahidi. *Player of the Series:* S. C. Williams.

Close of play: first day, Afghanistan 307-3 (Hashmatullah Shahidi 86, Asghar Afghan 106); second day, Zimbabwe 50-0 (Masvaure 29, Kasuza 14); third day, Zimbabwe 24-0 (Masvaure 3, Kasuza 20); fourth day, Zimbabwe 266-7 (Williams 106, Tiripano 63).

Afghanistan

Ibrahim Zadran c Sikandar Raza b Burl	72	– (2) c Musakanda b Burl	29
Javed Ahmadi c Williams b Nyauchi	4	– (1) b Muzarabani	4
Rahmat Shah run out (Musakanda/Chakabva)	23	– b Burl	58
Hashmatullah Shahidi not out	200	– (6) not out	6
*Asghar Afghan lbw b Sikandar Raza	164		
Nasir Ahmadzai not out	55	– (5) not out	4
Shahidullah (did not bat)		– (4) c Kasuza b Muzarabani	0
B 16, lb 1, w 5, nb 5	27	B 4, w 1, nb 2	7

1/6 (2) 2/56 (3)	(4 wkts dec, 160.4 overs) 545	1/8 (1) (4 wkts, 26.1 overs) 108
3/121 (1) 4/428 (5)		2/89 (2) 3/91 (4)
		4/101 (3)

†Afsar Zazai, Rashid Khan, Hamza Hotak and Sayed Shirzad did not bat.

Muzarabani 26–5–62–0; Nyauchi 24–4–102–1; Tiripano 20.4–1–83–0; Sikandar Raza 31–4–79–1; Williams 30–4–97–0; Burl 20–1–69–1; Madhevere 9–0–36–0. *Second innings*—Muzarabani 9.1–1–25–2; Nyauchi 6–1–28–0; Williams 3–0–18–0; Tiripano 4–0–17–0; Burl 4–1–16–2.

Zimbabwe

P. S. Masvaure b Hamza Hotak	65	– c and b Javed Ahmadi	15
K. T. Kasuza c Afsar Zazai b Rashid Khan	41	– c Rahmat Shah b Rashid Khan	30
T. K. Musakanda lbw b Rashid Khan	41	– lbw b Rashid Khan	15
*S. C. Williams c Hamza Hotak b Sayed Shirzad	8	– not out	151
W. N. Madhevere c Afsar Zazai b Sayed Shirzad	0	– c Afsar Zazai b Sayed Shirzad	0
Sikandar Raza c Rahmat Shah b Rashid Khan	85	– c Nasir Ahmadzai b Rashid Khan	22
R. P. Burl b Hamza Hotak	0	– lbw b Rashid Khan	0
†R. W. Chakabva c Ibrahim Zadran b Rashid Khan	33	– lbw b Rashid Khan	0
D. T. Tiripano c Nasir Ahmadzai b Hamza Hotak	3	– lbw b Rashid Khan	95
B. Muzarabani run out (Rahmat Shah/Rashid Khan)	0	– c Afsar Zazai b Hamza Hotak	17
V. M. Nyauchi not out	0	– lbw b Rashid Khan	0
B 2, lb 6, w 2, nb 1	11	B 12, lb 7, w 1	20

1/91 (2) 2/133 (1) 3/145 (3)	(91.3 overs) 287	1/44 (1) 2/46 (2) (148.5 overs) 365
4/145 (5) 5/186 (3) 6/189 (7)		3/101 (3) 4/102 (5)
7/242 (8) 8/251 (9) 9/287 (10) 10/287 (6)		5/140 (6) 6/140 (7) 7/142 (8)
		8/329 (9) 9/362 (10) 10/365 (11)

Sayed Shirzad 15–3–48–2; Hamza Hotak 32–6–73–3; Rashid Khan 36.3–3–138–4; Javed Ahmadi 8–1–20–0. *Second innings*—Sayed Shirzad 27–7–49–1; Rashid Khan 62.5–17–137–7; Hamza Hotak 34–7–104–1; Javed Ahmadi 16–5–40–1; Shahidullah 5–1–6–0; Asghar Afghan 1–0–1–0; Rahmat Shah 3–0–9–0.

Umpires: Ahmed Shah Pakteen and Aleem Dar. Third umpire: Ahmed Shah Durrani.
Referee: R. S. Madugalle.

First Twenty20 international At Abu Dhabi, March 17, 2021. **Afghanistan won by 48 runs. Afghanistan 198-5** (20 overs) (Rahmanullah Gurbaz 87, Asghar Afghan 55); ‡**Zimbabwe 150-7** (20 overs) (T. S. Kamunhukamwe 44; Rashid Khan 3-28). *PoM*: Rahmanullah Gurbaz. *Afghanistan unearthed another gem in wicketkeeper-batsman Rahmanullah Gurbaz. Only 19, he had made a century on ODI debut at this ground against Ireland in January; since then, he had played in the*

Abu Dhabi T10, and domestic 50-over cricket in Sharjah. He thus hit the ground running: a vicious 45-ball 87 included seven sixes against a weak attack, although he survived a simple chance to midwicket on 41, shelled by the unfortunate Wesley Madhevere, who had just collected three successive ducks in the Tests (and would make two and seven in this series). It set Afghanistan on course for a hefty total, as Sean Williams rued his decision to bowl. Zimbabwe got nowhere close in reply, with Rashid Khan taking three wickets.

Second Twenty20 international   At Abu Dhabi, March 19, 2021. **Afghanistan won by 45 runs.** ‡**Afghanistan** 193-5 (20 overs) (Usman Ghani 49, Karim Janat 53, Mohammad Nabi 40); **Zimbabwe** 148 (17.1 overs) (R. P. Burl 40; Rashid Khan 3-30). *PoM: Mohammad Nabi. Two all-rounders swung the match Afghanistan's way: Mohammad Nabi pummelled 40 from 15 deliveries, then took two wickets; Karim Janat, younger brother of Asghar Afhan, top-scored with a 38-ball 53, then wrapped up Zimbabwe's reply when he yorked Blessing Muzarabani. Rashid nabbed another three wickets, including Ryan Burl, who made 40 from No. 7.*

Third Twenty20 international   At Abu Dhabi, March 20, 2021. **Afghanistan won by 47 runs.** ‡**Afghanistan** 183-7 (20 overs) (Usman Ghani 39, Najibullah Zadran 72*); **Zimbabwe** 136-5 (20 overs) (T. K. Musakanda 30, Sikandar Raza 41*, R. P. Burl 39*). *PoM: Najibullah Zadran. PoS: Karim Janat. T20I debut: Fazal Haque (Afghanistan). A straightforward win, set up by Najibullah Zadran's 35-ball 72*, gave Asghar Afghan his 42nd in just 52 T20 internationals in charge, putting him above M. S. Dhoni as the most successful captain in the format. "It is good news for Afghanistan," he said. "We are new to cricket, so to have the No. 1 T20 captain is very big news for our people." His brother, Karim, won the series award for 100 runs and five wickets.*

AUSTRALIAN CRICKET IN 2021

Langer no longer

DANIEL BRETTIG

Power struggles defined Australian cricket in what its custodians had hoped would become a post-Covid world in 2021. Australia failed to play a single Test overseas for more than two years, creating a vacuum filled by questions about the way the men's team, in particular, were progressing.

Most concerning for their international standing was the last-moment cancellation of a tour of South Africa, ostensibly because Cricket Australia were unable to obtain fast-tracked vaccinations for their players. The global response was cynical: Australia's administrators had, it was felt, been eroding their credibility for years, with tours called off on flimsy premises.

Head coach Justin Langer, and his ally and team manager Gavin Dovey, were at the centre of rumours of player dissatisfaction, exacerbated by

AUSTRALIA IN 2021

	Played	Won	Lost	Drawn/No result
Tests	5	3	1	1
One-day internationals	3	2	1	–
Twenty20 internationals	22	10	12	–

DECEMBER — JANUARY	4 Tests, 3 ODIs and 3 T20Is (h) v India	(see *Wisden 2021*, page 630)
FEBRUARY — MARCH	5 T20Is (a) v New Zealand	(page 958)
APRIL		
MAY		
JUNE		
JULY	3 ODIs and 5 T20Is (a) v West Indies	(page 1046)
AUGUST	5 T20Is (a) v Bangladesh	(page 917)
SEPTEMBER		
OCTOBER — NOVEMBER	T20 World Cup in the UAE	(page 830)
DECEMBER — JANUARY	5 Tests (h) v England	(page 407)

For a review of Australian domestic cricket from the 2020-21 season, see page 902.

If the hat doesn't fit: Australia bid farewell to Justin Langer, their head coach.

Robert Cianflone, Getty Images

biobubbles, Test and T20 defeats at home by India, and for understrength Australian T20 teams in New Zealand, the West Indies and Bangladesh (one-day series wins against India and West Indies did little to ease concerns).

A meeting was convened – excluding Langer – between the three men's captains, plus CA chief executive Nick Hockley and chair Earl Eddings. A change of approach was agreed: the captains would be given more agency. Eddings was subsequently replaced as chair by Richard Freudenstein, and Dovey removed from team performance responsibilities; Michael Di Venuto and Jeff Vaughan were brought in as assistant coaches, while George Bailey took over from Trevor Hohns as chief selector.

The model seemed to be the highly successful women's side, in which coach Matthew Mott and selection chair Shawn Fegler had helped the captain, Meg Lanning, establish a set-up in which everyone knew what was expected of them. A multi-format series victory over India kept momentum going ahead of the 2021-22 Ashes, which they won easily, and the World Cup.

Bailey did not accompany the men to the UAE for the T20 World Cup, but his team ethos of "owning your own space" did – so too a clear on-field plan. Deep pace-bowling resources would be allied with the canny spin of Adam Zampa; Marcus Stoinis and Matthew Wade would act as middle-order "fixers". Despite a nervy opening win against South Africa and a thumping by England, Australia had enough breathing space to ease into the semis.

Facing an undefeated Pakistan, Aaron Finch's men had the fortune to be chasing, with a joyous stand of 81 off 41 balls between Stoinis and Wade seeing them to the final against New Zealand. It proved anticlimactic, fitting the pattern of Australian dominance in trans-Tasman tournament finals, but was still a memorable triumph, not least because Australia had been unfancied when the tournament began. The new approach had been vindicated. "Everything has really been player-driven," said seamer Josh Hazlewood.

Uncertainty had haunted the men's Ashes for much of the year, as CA and the ECB negotiated the finer points of quarantine and preparation, including the accommodation of English players' families. But it was the Queensland weather that had the greatest initial impact, England's pre-series practice being reduced to almost zero, even as Australia's players enjoyed Sheffield Shield games elsewhere in the country.

There was a major left turn a couple of weeks before the series, when Test captain Tim Paine resigned after the revelation that he had sent lewd texts to a former Cricket Tasmania staffer four years previously. His reputation as the country's best wicketkeeper was enhanced by Alex Carey's struggles as his replacement, but in captaincy terms it was hard to see the elevation of Pat Cummins as anything other than a net gain. He certainly got the best out of his fellow pacemen. From the moment they were granted first use of a Gabba greentop, and Rory Burns succumbed to the first ball of the series, it was a pageant of Australian fast-bowling supremacy, backed up by Nathan Lyon.

No batter dominated. David Warner, Marnus Labuschagne and Steve Smith made runs when it mattered. Travis Head's two counter-attacking hundreds won the series award. Usman Khawaja made a pair of cathartic centuries on his recall at Sydney, and was an articulate spokesperson for diversity: "Cricket's a very white sport, and has been for a long time in Australia, so unless things start changing from the top, it's very hard to funnel that down."

In Cameron Green, the Australians unearthed an all-rounder of the rarest calibre. And the fast-bowling mine kept turning up gems: even when injury restricted Hazlewood to a solitary Test, and Cummins was kept away from Adelaide by Covid protocols, Jhye Richardson stepped in with a five-for, and Scott Boland – handed a debut at Melbourne – stepped up with 18 wickets at under ten. Not only a Victorian, but a descendent of the Indigenous Gulidjan people, he became an instant hero, and a target for several counties.

Cummins led calmly on and off the field, a sense of serenity befitting his articulate, well-read and humble presence. Australia would probably have won 5–0 had they taken the last wicket at Sydney; English hand-wringing was a familiar response, though it should be balanced with Joe Root's team having fulfilled the tour in the first place. Under the continual threat of Covid, their visit was not to be taken for granted, but with gratitude.

Despite the successes, Langer's hold on power continued to slip away. In early February, CA belatedly and publicly had conversations that might have taken place after the Boxing Day Test. Langer's many friends and former team-mates went on the attack, somewhat overstating the role of the coach in the team process. What was undeniable was that Cummins, in sharply articulating the arguments for change, showed an authority never exhibited by Paine. Such leadership was needed for the challenges that lay ahead: a raft of postponed overseas trips beckoned, not least tours of Pakistan, Sri Lanka and India. There, the Australians' mettle would truly be tested.

ENGLAND LIONS IN AUSTRALIA IN 2021-22

A-Team Test (1): Australia A 1, England Lions 0

Two winters earlier, in Melbourne, England's second-string side had beaten their Australian counterparts for the first time, their heroes including five with Test experience, and four who would win a cap. This tour party was different. Of the 15 who travelled, six had not appeared at this level. Josh Bohannon and Rob Yates had forced their way in by weight of county runs, while Surrey's Jamie Smith was back-up wicketkeeper. Harry Brook replaced Dominic Sibley, who withdrew to work on his game. Warwickshire seamer Liam Norwell's call-up rewarded his role in their Championship win; and Sam Cook was squeezed in shortly before departure.

Just three of the squad had played Tests: James Bracey, Mason Crane and wicketkeeper Ben Foakes. Brydon Carse (who flew home early with a knee injury), Saqib Mahmood and Matt Parkinson had played limited-overs cricket for England, but this tour comprised only red-ball games: two practice matches with the Ashes squad, then an A-Team Test.

But awful weather allowed only 29 overs in the first, before the second was limited to a day. Before the Australia A game, just four of the Lions had batted (Tom Abell, Bracey, Foakes and captain Alex Lees); only Norwell had taken a wicket. And it was no surprise when Bess, omitted from England's team for the First Test, edged out Parkinson, who bowled only three overs on the tour, and Crane, who bowled none.

A dire batting performance scotched the Lions' chances of repeating their victory of 2019-20. Though Norwell took five to dismiss Australia A for 213, the visitors capitulated for 103 as Michael Neser bowled himself into the Second Ashes Test at Adelaide. Extraordinary hitting from Mitchell Marsh helped set a target of 460, before a battling century from Bracey proved in vain.

ENGLAND LIONS TOURING PARTY

*A. Z. Lees (Durham), T. B. Abell (Somerset), J. J. Bohannon (Lancashire), J. R. Bracey (Gloucestershire), H. C. Brook (Yorkshire), B. A. Carse (Durham), S. J. Cook (Essex), M. S. Crane (Hampshire), M. D. Fisher (Yorkshire), B. T. Foakes (Surrey), S. Mahmood (Lancashire), L. C. Norwell (Warwickshire), M. W. Parkinson (Lancashire), J. L. Smith (Surrey), R. M. Yates (Warwickshire). *Coach:* M. M. Patel.

D. P. Sibley chose to train in England, and was replaced by Brook; Cook was added to the squad before departure. Carse flew home with a knee injury.

For the warm-up matches between England Lions and the England XI, see page 415.

AUSTRALIA A v ENGLAND LIONS

At Brisbane (Ian Healy Oval), December 9–12, 2021. Australia A won by 112 runs. Toss: Australia A.

The match barely had a billing, since it was played at the same time as the First Test, a few miles away. Eyes were on the performances of Khawaja, beaten to the No. 5 Ashes berth by Travis Head, and Marsh, the match-winner in the previous month's T20 World Cup final. Both teams had jittery starts: no one reached 40 in either first innings. Australia A had lost five wickets to the accurate Norwell and four to the erratic Bess; Khawaja feathered Fisher. By the end of the first day, England

Lions were 13 for three; next day, Neser's pace and bounce skittled them for 103. The pitch eased, and Street's watchfulness took Australia A to the close, one down, 268 ahead. He reached his fifth first-class century on the third morning, having added 87 with Hunt, 88 with Renshaw and 94 with Maddinson, whose fifty came off 39 balls. Marsh eclipsed them all with seven sixes – four in a row off Yates – in a 27-ball unbeaten 60. The Lions were set 460, and on the last day, they found their fight, as Bracey ground out 113 from 295 balls, supported by gusty knocks from Bohannon and Foakes. But it came to naught.

Close of play: first day, England Lions 13-3 (Bracey 5, Fisher 0); second day, Australia A 158-1 (Street 76, Renshaw 34); third day, England Lions 136-3 (Bracey 57, Bohannon 29).

Australia A

B. E. Street c Lees b Bess	26	– not out	119
H. J. Hunt c Yates b Norwell	33	– c Foakes b Fisher	40
M. T. Renshaw c Mahmood b Norwell	38	– c Lees b Bess	43
*N. J. Maddinson c Abell b Bess	0	– c Yates b Bess	71
U. T. Khawaja c Foakes b Fisher	11	– c Foakes b Yates	5
M. R. Marsh c Bohannon b Bess	33	– not out	60
†J. P. Inglis c and b Norwell	6		
M. G. Neser c Foakes b Norwell	17		
M. T. Steketee c Bohannon b Bess	39		
M. J. Swepson c Foakes b Norwell	4		
S. M. Boland not out	0		
B 1, lb 2, w 1, nb 2	6	B 5, lb 2, w 1, nb 3	11

1/48 (1) 2/76 (1) 3/76 (4)   (70.5 overs) 213   1/87 (2)   (4 wkts dec, 87 overs) 349
4/99 (5) 5/126 (3) 6/148 (7)   2/175 (3) 3/269 (4)
7/157 (6) 8/195 (8) 9/213 (9) 10/213 (10)   4/278 (5)

Mahmood 15–4–37–0; Fisher 16–4–35–1; Norwell 16.5–2–58–5; Bess 23.5–5–80–4. *Second innings*—Mahmood 15.5–5–35–0; Fisher 13–3–49–1; Norwell 13–3–35–0; Bess 37–3–157–2; Yates 7–0–62–1; Brook 2–0–4–0.

England Lions

*A. Z. Lees c Inglis b Boland	2	– (2) b Boland	1
R. M. Yates c Renshaw b Neser	1	– (1) c Renshaw b Neser	41
J. R. Bracey c Khawaja b Marsh	5	– c Inglis b Steketee	113
T. B. Abell c Inglis b Steketee	5	– c Khawaja b Steketee	0
M. D. Fisher c Khawaja b Swepson	9	– (9) lbw b Renshaw	0
J. J. Bohannon c Khawaja b Marsh	22	– (5) c Renshaw b Neser	51
H. C. Brook c Steketee b Neser	17	– (6) c Hunt b Swepson	1
†B. T. Foakes c Renshaw b Neser	12	– (7) b Renshaw	73
D. M. Bess b Neser	15	– (8) b Maddinson	25
L. C. Norwell b Swepson	8	– c Hunt b Swepson	25
S. Mahmood not out	0	– not out	0
Lb 5, nb 2	7	Lb 6, w 1, nb 10	17

1/3 (1) 2/3 (2) 3/13 (4)   (43.3 overs) 103   1/2 (2) 2/68 (1)   (128.2 overs) 347
4/19 (3) 5/50 (6) 6/60 (5)   3/77 (4) 4/172 (5)
7/80 (7) 8/80 (8) 9/103 (10) 10/103 (9)   5/174 (6) 6/285 (3) 7/319 (7)
                                                       8/319 (9) 9/347 (8) 10/347 (10)

Neser 15.3–5–29–5; Boland 8–2–16–1; Steketee 7–1–12–1; Swepson 9–2–26–2; Marsh 4–0–15–1. *Second innings*—Neser 14–5–36–2; Boland 21–4–64–1; Marsh 9–2–29–0; Steketee 17–2–52–2; Swepson 46.2–10–124–2; Renshaw 14–7–26–2; Maddinson 3–1–4–1; Street 4–3–6–0.

Umpires: S. A. J. Craig and D. M. Koch. Referee: K. C. Wessels.

DOMESTIC CRICKET IN AUSTRALIA IN 2020-21

Peter English

At the start of another disrupted season, Australia's much-envied first-class domestic tournament was reduced to park cricket. All six teams began the Sheffield Shield in an Adelaide hub, playing on the suburban Park 25 (which had never staged a senior men's game before), Karen Rolton Oval (one previous first-class match) and Glenelg Oval. Most fixtures returned to the main stadiums when the tournament resumed in February, but travel restrictions prompted by Covid cut the Shield from ten rounds to eight, and the Marsh One-Day Cup from seven to five. Even so, the season ended in mid-April, a fortnight later than the previous record; for the first time, the Shield overlapped with matches in the English County Championship.

In the end, **Queensland** coped best, despite late summer rain washing out six days of play in Brisbane. They finished less than two points ahead of defending champions New South Wales, but won the final by an innings, with five sessions to spare. Because international commitments had been curtailed, both sides had Test players available, and more than 10,000 spectators made the most of free admission across the four days; with the boutique Allan Border Field overflowing, some had to be turned away.

Marnus Labuschagne, whose innings of 192 dominated the final, finished the tournament with 821 runs at 82, the third-highest aggregate after Western Australia's Cameron Green (922) and South Australia's Travis Head (893). Queensland also had the third-best wicket-taker, leg-spinner Mitchell Swepson, who might have headed the list had he not been restricted to five matches because of a stress fracture in his neck.

New South Wales experienced a topsy-turvy summer. In November, they were dismissed for 64 by Tasmania, but fought back to win; in March, Tasmania bowled them out for 32 – their lowest first-class total – and this time there was no way back. A few days before losing the Shield final to Queensland, they secured the Marsh Cup, beating Western Australia in the one-day final thanks to a century from Jack Edwards and four wickets from Sean Abbott; Sydney Sixers retained their Big Bash League title. Nathan Lyon took 42 Shield wickets, more than anyone else. His ten for 78 against Victoria, the best match return of his domestic career, took him to 600 first-class victims. Abbott combined 21 wickets with 570 runs.

Green sparkled for **Western Australia**, and made his Test debut against India. He scored 197 against New South Wales and 251 against Queensland, and also finished in the top five in the one-day competition. He was one of five Western Australians to register three Shield centuries, along with Cameron Bancroft, Shaun Marsh, wicketkeeper-batsman Josh Inglis and Sam Whiteman. While Green's bowling was less effective, after a back stress fracture the previous season, he picked up an Australian central contract.

Tasmania finished fourth in both competitions, despite the rout of New South Wales for 32, when Jackson Bird followed up a career-best 54 with seven for 18, his best figures; he finished the season with 35, second to Lyon. Alex Doolan, who played four Tests in 2014, retired as Tasmania's eighth-highest run-scorer in the Shield, with 5,978.

For **Victoria**, Will Pucovski and Marcus Harris put on 486 against South Australia, an all-wicket Shield record, beating 464 by Steve and Mark Waugh. Both reached double-hundreds, and Pucovski scored another against Western Australia, on the way to a Test debut, but concussion and shoulder surgery limited him to two Shield matches. Harris collected 695, while Scott Boland claimed 30 wickets, and Jon Holland 27.

The season was no walk in the park for **South Australia**, who failed to win a match in either competition, and finished bottom of the Shield for the ninth time in 12 seasons. Two stalwarts retired: Chadd Sayers and Callum Ferguson. Though they played one Test apiece, Sayers's 279 wickets for South Australia made him their third-highest wicket-taker in the Shield, while Ferguson was their fourth-highest run-scorer, with 8,318.

FIRST-CLASS AVERAGES IN 2020-21

BATTING (400 runs)

		M	I	NO	R	HS	100	Avge	Ct/St
1	W. J. Pucovski (*Victoria/Aus A/Aus*) ...	4	7	3	591	255*	2	118.20	3
2	J. P. Inglis (*Western Australia*)	8	12	4	585	153*	3	73.12	23/2
3	M. C. Henriques (*New South Wales*)	6	11	2	633	167	3	70.33	5
4	M. Labuschagne (*Queensland/Aus*)	12	18	0	1,247	192	5	69.27	10
5	C. D. Green (*West Australia/Aus A/Aus*)	14	22	3	1,283	251	4	67.52	9
6	B. R. McDermott (*Tasmania/Australia A*) .	5	9	2	462	107*	1	66.00	4
7	†M. T. Renshaw (*Queensland*)	8	10	2	500	168*	1	62.50	4
8	†U. T. Khawaja (*Queensland*)	8	10	2	473	131	2	59.12	11
9	†T. M. Head (*South Aus/Aus A/Aus*)	10	19	2	975	223	3	57.35	9
10	S. A. Abbott (*New South Wales/Aus A*) .	9	13	3	570	102*	1	57.00	7
11	†S. E. Marsh (*Western Australia*)	8	14	1	734	135	3	56.46	12
12	†M. S. Harris (*Victoria/Aus A/Australia*) .	11	19	3	829	239	2	51.81	6
13	C. T. Bancroft (*Western Australia*)	8	14	0	678	126	3	48.42	9
14	P. S. P. Handscomb (*Victoria*)	8	13	2	511	124*	1	46.45	14
15	A. M. Rahane (*Indians*)	6	12	2	455	117*	2	45.50	7
16	H. J. Hunt (*South Australia*)	7	14	0	628	127	2	44.85	5
17	J. J. Peirson (*Queensland*)	8	9	0	402	109	1	44.66	26
18	†J. R. Doran (*Tasmania*)	8	14	0	615	123	2	43.92	9
19	T. D. Paine (*Tasmania/Aus A/Australia*) .	12	20	5	602	111*	1	40.13	53/1
20	†S. M. Whiteman (*Western Australia*) ...	8	14	0	555	118	1	39.64	4
21	†M. S. Wade (*Tasmania/Australia*)	8	16	1	576	90	0	38.40	8
22	†H. J. Nielsen (*South Australia*)	7	14	0	503	114	1	35.92	7
23	B. J. Webster (*Tasmania*)	8	14	1	404	135*	1	31.07	12
24	†N. J. Maddinson (*Victoria/Australia A*) .	10	16	1	429	77	0	28.60	4

BOWLING (15 wickets)

		Style	O	M	R	W	BB	5I	Avge
1	J. D. Wildermuth (*Queensld/Aus A*) ...	RFM	161	45	467	22	4-21	0	21.22
2	J. M. Bird (*Tasmania/Australia A*) ...	RFM	318.1	92	810	36	7-18	1	22.50
3	P. J. Cummins (*Australia/NSW*)	RF	202.1	57	533	23	4-21	0	23.17
4	S. M. Boland (*Victoria*)	RFM	265.1	65	720	30	6-61	0	24.00
5	J. R. Hazlewood (*Australia/NSW*)	RFM	233.4	71	554	23	5-8	2	24.08
6	M. G. Neser (*Queensland/Aus A*)	RFM	233.1	67	534	22	5-27	2	24.27
7	H. N. A. Conway (*NSW/Aus A*)	RFM	178.4	51	505	19	6-39	1	26.57
8	B. J. Doggett (*Queensland*)	RFM	198.2	36	590	22	4-79	0	26.81
9	M. J. Swepson (*Queensland/Aus A*)..	LB	320	72	912	34	5-55	3	26.82
10	T. A. Copeland (*New South Wales*) ...	RFM	259.4	90	554	20	5-17	1	27.70
11	J. L. Pattinson (*Australia A/Victoria*) .	RFM	163	35	448	16	4-60	0	28.00
12	P. M. Siddle (*Tasmania*).............	RFM	212	70	507	18	3-17	0	28.16
13	S. A. Abbott (*NSW/Aus A*)...........	RFM	228.4	58	682	24	6-89	1	28.41
14	J. M. Holland (*Victoria*)	SLA	296.2	71	779	27	5-82	1	28.85
15	N. M. Lyon (*NSW/Australia*).........	OB	599.3	136	1,587	51	6-21	3	31.11
16	X. C. Bartlett (*Queensland*)	RFM	197.5	57	595	19	4-58	0	31.31
17	M. Siraj (*Indians*)	RFM	187.2	41	566	18	5-73	1	31.44
18	N. T. Ellis (*Tasmania*)	RFM	165.1	24	578	17	4-76	0	34.00
19	M. L. Kelly (*Western Australia*)	RFM	264.5	63	685	20	4-43	0	34.25
20	M. T. Steketee (*Queensland/Aus A*)..	RFM	254.1	57	733	21	5-37	1	34.90
21	M. J. Perry (*Victoria*)	RFM	166.1	36	536	15	3-25	0	35.73
22	W. J. Sutherland (*Victoria/Aus A*)	RFM	236	57	686	19	4-81	0	36.10
23	C. J. Gannon (*Western Australia*).....	RFM	315.5	80	950	24	3-65	0	39.58
24	B. J. Webster (*Tasmania*)............	OB	188.4	24	673	17	4-50	0	39.58
25	M. A. Starc (*NSW/Australia*).	LF	352.5	76	1,205	27	4-53	0	44.62

SHEFFIELD SHIELD IN 2020-21

	P	W	L	D	A	Bat	Bowl	Pts
						Bonus pts		
QUEENSLAND	8	3	1	3	1	5.87	5.3	33.17
NEW SOUTH WALES	8	3	2	3	0	4.51	6.0	31.51
Western Australia	8	2	1	5	0	7.37	4.0	28.37
Tasmania.	8	2	3	3	0	5.71	7.4	28.11
Victoria	8	1	1	6	0	4.16	5.6	21.76
South Australia	8	0	3	4	1	4.72	3.1	12.82

Outright win = 6pts; draw = 1pt; abandoned = 1pt. Bonus points awarded for the first 100 overs of each team's first innings: 0.01 batting points for every run over the first 200; 0.1 bowling points for each wicket taken.

FINAL

QUEENSLAND v NEW SOUTH WALES

At Brisbane (Allan Border Field), April 15–18, 2021. Queensland won by an innings and 33 runs. Toss: New South Wales.

Labuschagne's patient dedication played the central role in securing Queensland's ninth Shield title, all since 1994-95. His third century of the season against New South Wales was the first to result in victory – Queensland had lost by one wicket in November, and drawn in Wollongong earlier in April. In a match where no one else reached 50, his 192 neutered an attack including four Test bowlers. The New South Wales batting lacked the same depth, thanks to IPL call-ups, and had been dismissed soon after tea on the opening day. Seamers Neser and Wildermuth – whose international experience consisted of a couple of games apiece, nearly three years earlier – collected nine wickets between them. Then Labuschagne batted for nine and a half hours, five more than the whole New South Wales line-up had managed. Queensland's eventual lead was 246. They had the visitors five down again by the end of the third day, and three wickets for Swepson's leg-spin on the fourth morning meant it was all over by lunch. Because of the elongated Australian season, this final took place on the same dates as the second round of the County Championship. The last three league games, played on April 3–6, were the first instance of any Shield fixtures beginning in April.

Player of the Match: M. Labuschagne.

Close of play: first day, Queensland 58-1 (Street 14, Labuschagne 23); second day, Queensland 286-3 (Labuschagne 160, Renshaw 29); third day, New South Wales 140-5 (Abbott 20, Holt 10).

New South Wales

D. P. Hughes c Peirson b Wildermuth	19	– c Khawaja b Bartlett	40
M. R. Gilkes b Neser	6	– c Burns b Doggett	37
*K. R. Patterson c Peirson b Doggett	43	– c Renshaw b Doggett	13
J. J. Sangha c and b Neser	20	– lbw b Bartlett	14
J. R. Edwards c Peirson b Neser	0	– lbw b Bartlett	4
S. A. Abbott c Burns b Wildermuth	23	– c Burns b Neser	22
†B. J. H. Holt c Street b Wildermuth	6	– lbw b Swepson	29
M. A. Starc c Doggett b Wildermuth	4	– not out	27
T. A. Copeland not out	16	– c Peirson b Swepson	9
N. M. Lyon c Burns b Neser	1	– c Khawaja b Swepson	10
J. R. Hazlewood c Labuschagne b Neser	0	– c Peirson b Doggett	3
Lb 3, w 1, nb 1	5	B 2, lb 3	5

1/9 (2) 2/47 (1) 3/76 (4) (62.2 overs) 143   1/64 (1) 2/85 (3) (82.1 overs) 213
4/82 (5) 5/96 (3) 6/115 (7)   3/96 (2) 4/110 (4)
7/123 (8) 8/123 (6) 9/143 (10) 10/143 (11)   5/121 (5) 6/142 (6) 7/176 (7)
    8/190 (9) 9/206 (10) 10/213 (11)

Neser 13.2–6–27–5; Wildermuth 16–5–21–4; Bartlett 12–4–24–0; Doggett 15.3–3–38–1; Swepson 6–0–30–0. *Second innings*—Neser 22–6–41–1; Wildermuth 6–1–20–0; Swepson 24–1–68–3; Bartlett 16–7–42–3; Doggett 14.1–3–37–3.

Queensland

J. A. Burns c Holt b Hazlewood	20	M. J. Swepson c and b Abbott	8
B. E. Street c Copeland b Lyon	46	B. J. Doggett not out	1
M. Labuschagne c Copeland b Abbott	192		
*U. T. Khawaja c Holt b Starc	23	B 4, lb 3, nb 2	9
M. T. Renshaw b Copeland	34		
†J. J. Peirson c Copeland b Lyon	36	1/26 (1) 2/153 (2)	(149.3 overs) 389
J. D. Wildermuth c Holt b Abbott	15	3/213 (4) 4/299 (5)	
M. G. Neser c Gilkes b Lyon	0	5/351 (6) 6/370 (7) 7/371 (8)	
X. C. Bartlett lbw b Abbott	5	8/375 (3) 9/386 (9) 10/389 (10)	

Starc 22–8–52–1; Hazlewood 25–9–42–1; Copeland 26–8–73–1; Lyon 41–5–116–3; Abbott 28.3–4–71–4; Sangha 2–0–15–0; Edwards 5–1–13–0.

Umpires: S. J. Nogajski and P. Wilson.   Third umpire: D. M. Koch.
Referee: R. L. Parry.

SHEFFIELD SHIELD WINNERS

1892-93	Victoria	1936-37	Victoria	1982-83	New South Wales*
1893-94	South Australia	1937-38	New South Wales	1983-84	Western Australia
1894-95	Victoria	1938-39	South Australia	1984-85	New South Wales
1895-96	New South Wales	1939-40	New South Wales	1985-86	New South Wales
1896-97	New South Wales	1940–46	*No competition*	1986-87	Western Australia
1897-98	Victoria	1946-47	Victoria	1987-88	Western Australia
1898-99	Victoria	1947-48	Western Australia	1988-89	Western Australia
1899-1900	New South Wales	1948-49	New South Wales	1989-90	New South Wales
1900-01	Victoria	1949-50	New South Wales	1990-91	Victoria
1901-02	New South Wales	1950-51	Victoria	1991-92	Western Australia
1902-03	New South Wales	1951-52	New South Wales	1992-93	New South Wales
1903-04	New South Wales	1952-53	South Australia	1993-94	New South Wales
1904-05	New South Wales	1953-54	New South Wales	1994-95	Queensland
1905-06	New South Wales	1954-55	New South Wales	1995-96	South Australia
1906-07	New South Wales	1955-56	New South Wales	1996-97	Queensland*
1907-08	Victoria	1956-57	New South Wales	1997-98	Western Australia
1908-09	New South Wales	1957-58	New South Wales	1998-99	Western Australia*
1909-10	South Australia	1958-59	New South Wales	1999-2000	Queensland
1910-11	New South Wales	1959-60	New South Wales	2000-01	Queensland
1911-12	New South Wales	1960-61	New South Wales	2001-02	Queensland
1912-13	South Australia	1961-62	New South Wales	2002-03	New South Wales*
1913-14	New South Wales	1962-63	Victoria	2003-04	Victoria
1914-15	Victoria	1963-64	South Australia	2004-05	New South Wales*
1915–19	*No competition*	1964-65	New South Wales	2005-06	Queensland
1919-20	New South Wales	1965-66	New South Wales	2006-07	Tasmania
1920-21	New South Wales	1966-67	Victoria	2007-08	New South Wales
1921-22	Victoria	1967-68	Western Australia	2008-09	Victoria
1922-23	New South Wales	1968-69	South Australia	2009-10	Victoria
1923-24	Victoria	1969-70	Victoria	2010-11	Tasmania
1924-25	Victoria	1970-71	South Australia	2011-12	Queensland
1925-26	New South Wales	1971-72	Western Australia	2012-13	Tasmania
1926-27	South Australia	1972-73	Western Australia	2013-14	New South Wales
1927-28	Victoria	1973-74	Victoria	2014-15	Victoria
1928-29	New South Wales	1974-75	Western Australia	2015-16	Victoria*
1929-30	Victoria	1975-76	South Australia	2016-17	Victoria
1930-31	Victoria	1976-77	Western Australia	2017-18	Queensland
1931-32	New South Wales	1977-78	Western Australia	2018-19	Victoria
1932-33	New South Wales	1978-79	Victoria	2019-20	New South Wales†
1933-34	Victoria	1979-80	Victoria	2020-21	Queensland
1934-35	Victoria	1980-81	Western Australia		
1935-36	South Australia	1981-82	South Australia		

New South Wales have won the title 47 times, Victoria 32, Western Australia 15, South Australia 13, Queensland 9, Tasmania 3.

The tournament was the Pura Milk Cup in 1999-2000, and the Pura Cup from 2000-01 to 2007-08.

* *Second in table but won final. Finals were introduced in 1982-83.*

† *There was no final in 2019-20.*

MARSH ONE-DAY CUP IN 2020-21

50-over league plus final

	P	W	L	A	Bonus	Pts	NRR
NEW SOUTH WALES ..	5	4	0	1	2	19	1.50
WESTERN AUSTRALIA	5	3	1	1	4	17	1.31
Queensland.	5	3	1	1	2	15	1.02
Tasmania	5	2	3	0	2	10	0.02
Victoria	5	1	3	1	0	5	−1.22
South Australia.	5	0	5	0	0	0	−2.25

Win = 4pts; 1 bonus point awarded for achieving victory with a run-rate 1.25 times that of the opposition, and 2 bonus points for victory with a run-rate twice that of the opposition. Teams tied on points were ordered by net run-rate.

Final   At Sydney (Bankstown Oval), April 11, 2021. **New South Wales won by 102 runs.** ‡New **South Wales 251-8** (50 overs) (J. R. Edwards 108); **Western Australia 149** (40.3 overs). *Both sides lost their third wicket at 50, but Jack Edwards – a week short of his 21st birthday – joined opener Daniel Hughes (58) to add 118 for New South Wales. Recalled because their international batting stars had left for the IPL, he reached his second List A century to help them pass 250. Western Australia failed to recover from their early setbacks, as Sean Abbott (4-23) and Nathan Lyon (3-38) worked their way through the innings, before Mitchell Starc finished it off with nearly ten overs in hand.*

The KFC T20 Big Bash League has its own section (page 1115).

BANGLADESH CRICKET IN 2021

Spin over substance

UTPAL SHUVRO

By the end of the year, a disappointment lingered: the T20 World Cup. But perhaps Bangladesh's poor performance there was not a surprise: only once had they won a game beyond the preliminary stage, against West Indies in 2007. So why the gloom? The answer lay in their form before the tournament, when they won three consecutive T20 series – first in Zimbabwe, then at home against Australia and New Zealand. Admittedly, the visiting teams were understrength, but Bangladesh had beaten neither before, so hopes were high, especially as they dismissed Australia for 62 – their lowest total – en route to a 4–1 win, and New Zealand for 60 and 93.

The slow, low pitch at Mirpur proved a false friend. A vicious turner, it made batting so hazardous that Shakib Al Hasan remarked: "Careers will end if any batter plays 10–15 matches on these wickets." Despite the results, then, this was far from ideal preparation for the World Cup in the Gulf.

BANGLADESH IN 2021

	Played	Won	Lost	Drawn/No result
Tests	7	1	5	1
One-day internationals	12	8	4	–
Twenty20 internationals	27	11	16	–

For a review of Bangladesh domestic cricket from the 2020-21 season, see page 927.

The preliminary round, in Oman, began disastrously. Bangladesh never recovered from the shock of losing to Scotland in their opening game and, though wins over Oman and Papua New Guinea took them to the Super 12 stage, they lost all five of their matches; they finished, dispiritingly, with all-out totals of 84 against South Africa and 73 against Australia. There was hue and cry back home. The Bangladesh Cricket Board formed a fact-finding committee (of two), from which there was silence. It seemed more like a public relations move from a board given to intransigence: in October, Nazmul Hasan had been elected unopposed for a third term as president.

Though Bangladesh lost 16 of the record 27 T20s they played in the calendar year, they performed markedly better in ODIs, winning three series out of four. They beat West Indies and Sri Lanka at home, and Zimbabwe away, but were swept aside in New Zealand in both white-ball formats.

Bangladesh's Test report card made for unpleasant reading, although they did begin 2022 with a stunning victory over New Zealand, the World Test Champions, at Mount Maunganui. But they lost two Tests at home against a second-string West Indies team: an unbeaten fourth-innings double-century from Kyle Mayers guided the visitors to a historic win at Chittagong, then the tourists humiliatingly out-spun Bangladesh at Mirpur. After a high-scoring draw against Sri Lanka at Pallekele, Bangladesh lost the series when they ran into left-arm spinner Praveen Jayawickrama, who took 11 wickets on debut.

Their sole Test win came in Zimbabwe in July, but even that was overshadowed by the sudden retirement of Mahmudullah. Omitted from the squad, and without a red-ball contract, he was clearly not in the Test plans of coach Russell Domingo, who had reportedly told him to focus on the shorter forms. But with Tamim Iqbal and Mushfiqur Rahim injured, Mahmudullah received a late call-up, and – after a 17-month absence from Test cricket – scored a career-best 150 not out at Harare. Upon leaving the field, he informed his team-mates of his retirement. This was leaked to the press, and Nazmul accused Mahmudullah of being unprofessional, but his comrades gave him a guard of honour next day. No formal announcement was made until November, and Mahmudullah continued as T20 captain in the meantime.

Shakib's return, after he had served a one-year ban for failing to report a match-fixing approach, was a welcome boost. Though he was unavailable for a number of series – reasons varied from paternity leave to IPL commitments – his impact was immediate. On his comeback, an ODI against West Indies, he had figures of 7.2–2–8–4 and won the match award; he was later named Player of the Series. He then earned himself another ban, this time for three matches, after a display of petulance in a Dhaka Premier League T20 game in June. First he kicked the stumps after an lbw appeal was turned down; an over later, he ripped all three out of the ground. But he was instrumental in the T20 triumph over Australia, and stood out among the rubble of Bangladesh's World Cup. He became the highest wicket-taker in the tournament's history, and all T20 internationals. When Pakistan visited in December, he became the sixth (and fastest) player to score 4,000 runs and take 200 wickets in Tests, reaching the milestone in his 59th game. It was a rare highlight: Pakistan won all three T20s, and both Tests.

BANGLADESH v WEST INDIES IN 2020-21

MOHAMMAD ISAM

One-day internationals (3): Bangladesh 3 (30pts), West Indies 0 (0pts)
Test matches (2): Bangladesh 0 (0pts), West Indies 2 (120pts)

West Indies' hopes were not high as they embarked on this tour without a dozen regulars, who declined to travel. Bangladesh had been troublesome opponents at home in recent years, and their canny spinners were expected to outwit inexperienced adversaries. The home side did sweep the one-day series, in which the West Indians failed to reach 180 – and were on top in the First Test before a stunning turnaround, spearheaded by the debutant Kyle Mayers, whose unbeaten 210 had been bettered only once in the fourth innings of a successful Test run-chase, by Gordon Greenidge, a fellow Bajan. West Indies came out on top in a close-fought Second Test as well, to complete one of their finest performances of recent years. Leaving aside a one-off match against Afghanistan late in 2019, it was their first series win in Asia since beating Bangladesh 2–0 in November 2012.

Kraigg Brathwaite, the quiet understudy of Jason Holder, maintained this was not a second-string team. Mayers and Nkrumah Bonner, previously on the fringes, became heroes, while Rahkeem Cornwall proved a match-winner under pressure, and wicketkeeper Joshua Da Silva carved out important runs. Holder had been one of the 12 who turned down the trip – understandable given the number of tours West Indies had during the pandemic, and when there were lucrative franchise tournaments. The missing players were assured their absence would not be held against them, but by the end several might have been looking anxiously over their shoulder. Not long after, Brathwaite replaced Holder as full-time Test captain.

Bangladesh were shocked by their feeble performance in the Tests. It was their first international series since the pandemic, but they had crushed a much stronger West Indian side at home in 2018-19, and breezed through the

HIGHEST SCORE IN A SUCCESSFUL TEST RUN-CHASE

214*	C. G. Greenidge	West Indies (344-1) v England at Lord's	1984
210*	**K. R. Mayers**	**West Indies (395-7) v Bangladesh at Chittagong**	**2020-21**
182	A. R. Morris	Australia (404-3) v England at Leeds	1948
173*	D. G. Bradman	Australia (404-3) v England at Leeds	1948
173*	M. A. Butcher	England (315-4) v Australia at Leeds	2001
171*	Younis Khan	Pakistan (382-3) v Sri Lanka at Pallekele	2015
168	S. M. Nurse	West Indies (348-5) v New Zealand at Auckland	1968-69
160	J. Darling	Australia (276-4) v England at Sydney	1897-98
154*	G. C. Smith	South Africa (283-5) v England at Birmingham	2008
153*	B. C. Lara	West Indies (311-9) v Australia at Bridgetown	1998-99
153*	M. D. K. J. Perera	Sri Lanka (304-9) v South Africa at Durban	2018-19
151*	R. N. Harvey	Australia (336-5) v South Africa at Durban	1949-50

Morris and Bradman achieved the feat in the same innings.

one-dayers. They were not helped by a thigh injury to Shakib Al Hasan, which kept him on the sidelines after the second day of the First Test, but their three other spinners all underperformed on the fifth as Mayers took charge. Mominul Haque also came in for criticism for his reactive captaincy, and was outshone by Brathwaite, who extracted the best from veteran seamer Shannon Gabriel, and spinners Cornwall and Jomel Warrican.

The tour had started poorly for West Indies. In the 50-over games, they were forced to field nine debutants, of whom only Akeal Hosein, a left-arm spinner from Trinidad who had done well in the CPL, showed much gumption. The task of leading this callow bunch fell to Jason Mohammed, who had not played an international since July 2018. For Bangladesh, the focus was on Shakib, who did well on his return following a year's ban for failing to report a corrupt approach.

WEST INDIES TOURING PARTY

*K. C. Brathwaite (T), S. W. Ambris (50), J. Blackwood (T), N. E. Bonner (T/50), J. D. Campbell (T), R. R. S. Cornwall (T), J. Da Silva (T/50), S. T. Gabriel (T), J. N. Hamilton (50), K. J. Harding (50), K. A. R. Hodge (50), C. K. Holder (50), A. J. Hosein (50), A. S. Joseph (T/50), A. M. McCarthy (50), K. R. Mayers (T/50), S. A. R. Moseley (50), K. Y. Ottley (50), V. Permaul (T), R. Powell (50), R. A. Reifer (T/50), K. A. J. Roach (T), H. R. Walsh (50), J. A. Warrican (T). *Coach:* P. V. Simmons.

Mohammed captained in the ODIs, in which Walsh took no part after testing positive for Covid soon after arrival in Dhaka. R. Shepherd was originally selected, but returned a positive test prior to departure, and was replaced by Harding.

First one-day international   At Mirpur, January 20, 2021. **Bangladesh won by six wickets. West Indies 122** (32.2 overs) (K. R. Mayers 40; Hasan Mahmud 3-28, Shakib Al Hasan 4-8); ‡**Bangladesh 125-4** (33.5 overs) (Tamim Iqbal 44; A. J. Hosein 3-26). *Bangladesh 10pts. PoM:* Shakib Al Hasan. *ODI debuts:* Hasan Mahmud (Bangladesh); N. E. Bonner, J. Da Silva, C. K. Holder, A. J. Hosein, A. M. McCarthy, K. R. Mayers (West Indies). *Shakib Al Hasan marked his international comeback after a 12-month ban with Bangladesh's cheapest four-wicket haul in ODIs, against opponents fielding six debutants. Bowling slightly slower than before his break, he took control with a miserly spell, and finished with 7.2–2–8–4. Among the game's seven newcomers, a couple stood out on a sluggish pitch: Bangladesh seamer Hasan Mahmud finished with three wickets, as did Akeal Hosein, the Trinidadian left-arm spinner. Bangladesh's batsmen looked rusty in their first international for ten months, but had little difficulty knocking off a small target.*

Second one-day international   At Mirpur, January 22, 2021. **Bangladesh won by seven wickets. ‡West Indies 148** (43.4 overs) (R. Powell 41; Mehedi Hasan 4-25); **Bangladesh 149-3** (33.2 overs) (Tamim Iqbal 50, Shakib Al Hasan 43*). *Bangladesh 10pts. PoM:* Mehedi Hasan. *ODI debut:* K. Y. Ottley (West Indies). *This game followed a similar pattern, with Mustafizur Rahman taking early wickets, and the spinners making the ball grip on a rough pitch. For West Indies, only No. 8 Rovman Powell showed the technique required to survive, with 41 from 66 balls; no one else lasted an hour. Tamim Iqbal replied with a steady 50, and Liton Das and Nazmul Hossain, presented with an opportunity for cheap runs, fell softly, before Shakib ensured a series win for the Bangladeshis.*

Third one-day international   At Chittagong, January 25, 2021. **Bangladesh won by 120 runs. Bangladesh 297-6** (50 overs) (Tamim Iqbal 64, Shakib Al Hasan 51, Mushfiqur Rahim 64, Mahmudullah 64*); ‡**West Indies 177** (44.2 overs) (N. E. Bonner 31, R. Powell 47; Mohammad Saifuddin 3-51). *Bangladesh 10pts. PoM:* Mushfiqur Rahim. *PoS:* Shakib Al Hasan. *ODI debuts:* J. N. Hamilton, K. J. Harding (West Indies). *Bangladesh were indebted to their senior batsmen as they took their winning ODI streak over West Indies to eight: Tamim and Shakib rebuilt from 38-2 with a stand of 93, before Mushfiqur Rahim and Mahmudullah put on 72 for the fifth wicket.*

West Indies were then skittled for the third match running, with Powell – now up to No. 6 – top-scoring again. Mohammad Saifuddin claimed three wickets after replacing Rubel Hossain, as Bangladesh kickstarted their World Cup qualification campaign with a 3–0 whitewash.

BANGLADESH v WEST INDIES

First Test

At Chittagong, February 3–7, 2021. West Indies won by three wickets. West Indies 60pts. Toss: Bangladesh. Test debuts: N. E. Bonner, K. R. Mayers, S. A. R. Moseley.

At 59 for three, chasing a distant 395, West Indies looked dead in the water. Shakib Al Hasan had been ruled out of the series after straining his thigh on the second day, but Bangladesh's other spinners shared eight wickets in the first innings, and Mehedi Hasan's off-breaks had already claimed three more. Surely it was only a matter of time before another home win was chalked up – but two doughty debutants had other ideas. Kyle Mayers, a 28-year-old left-hander from Barbados, had been caught up in Hurricane Maria in September 2017: he was attending a training camp in Dominica, where the roof of his apartment was ripped off. But now he and Nkrumah Bonner, a 32-year-old Jamaican, weathered a Bangladeshi spin-storm with great composure.

The pair survived an hour until the fourth-day close, then gradually opened up next day. At first there were few thoughts of a win. Only one experienced batsman remained – Blackwood, the hero of West Indies' unlikely victory in Southampton several months previously – but for more than two sessions he was not required. Bonner and Mayers stayed until lunch, rarely chancing their arm, but pouncing on anything short from Mehedi and fellow off-spinner Nayeem Hasan. Slow left-armer Taijul Islam kept it tight, but could not break through. Mayers was driving well, while Bonner soaked up the pressure, occasionally leaning back to cut.

Mayers eventually reached three figures off 178 balls and, with no wickets going down before tea, West Indies looked good for a draw. With 129 more wanted, victory seemed optimistic – especially when Bonner was trapped by Taijul, after a partnership of 216 in 73 overs. Blackwood did not last long, aiming a rash shot at Nayeem, but wicketkeeper Da Silva – a veteran of one Test – dug in, while Mayers broke loose. With the spinners bowling erratically, he carved five sixes (he finished with seven, plus 20 fours), and became only the seventh – and second West Indian, after Lawrence Rowe – to make a double-century in his first Test. Da Silva fell with victory in sight after a stand of 100, of which his share was 20, and after Roach bagged a duck it was left to Mayers to seal a famous win with 15 balls to spare. "We never gave up," he said. "The captain and coach said you need to keep fighting on a pitch like this. It's a great feeling to be playing Test cricket."

HIGHEST PARTNERSHIPS BY TWO TEST DEBUTANTS

249 for 1st	Khalid Ibadulla/Abdul Kadir	P v A at Karachi	1964-65
216 for 4th	**N. E. Bonner/K. R. Mayers**	**WI v B at Chittagong**	**2020-21**
165 for 6th†	D. L. Houghton/A. Flower	Z v I at Harare	1992-93
161 for 1st	Tamim Iqbal/Junaid Siddique	B v NZ at Dunedin (University)	2007-08
142 for 3rd	G. A. Headley/F. I. de Caires	WI v E at Bridgetown	1929-30
134 for 2nd	Mohammad Hafeez/Yasir Hameed	P v B at Karachi	2003
124 for 4th	F. I. de Caires/J. E. D. Sealy	WI v E at Bridgetown	1929-30
121 for 5th	R. T. Ponting/S. G. Law	A v SL at Perth	1995-96
120 for 10th	R. A. Duff/W. W. Armstrong	A v E at Melbourne	1901-02
115 for 9th	R. E. Foster/A. E. Relf	E v A at Sydney	1903-04
114 for 7th†	K. J. O'Brien/S. R. Thompson	Ire v P at Malahide	2018

† *Country's inaugural Test match.*

Until this astonishing denouement, Bangladesh had largely bossed their first Test in almost a year. They batted circumspectly on the opening day, before Mehedi broke free on the second, completing a maiden century as the total rose to an imposing 430. In reply, Brathwaite made a solid 76, but the rest of the upper order struggled, before Blackwood and Da Silva put on 99. The problems were hardly surprising: West Indies had debutants at Nos 3, 4 and 5, the first such instance outside any country's inaugural Test since India at Lord's in 1946. The tail could make little of the spinners, and the last five tumbled for six; Mehedi added four wickets to his hundred.

Cornwall shared the new ball, and removed Tamim Iqbal and Nazmul Hossain in his first over, but 115 from Mominul Haque – his ninth Test century, and seventh at Chittagong, to go with two at Mirpur – took his side well ahead. Soon after he was out, Mominul declared with a lead of 394. Thanks to a couple of nerveless debutants, it wasn't enough, as West Indies ticked off the fifth-highest successful chase in Test history.

Player of the Match: K. R. Mayers.

Close of play: first day, Bangladesh 242-5 (Shakib Al Hasan 39, Liton Das 34); second day, West Indies 75-2 (Brathwaite 49, Bonner 17); third day, Bangladesh 47-3 (Mominul Haque 31, Mushfiqur Rahim 10); fourth day, West Indies 110-3 (Bonner 15, Mayers 37).

Bangladesh

Shadman Islam lbw b Warrican	59	– c Da Silva b Gabriel	5
Tamim Iqbal b Roach	9	– lbw b Cornwall	0
Nazmul Hossain run out (Roach/Da Silva/Mayers)	25	– c Blackwood b Cornwall	0
*Mominul Haque c Campbell b Warrican	26	– c Roach b Gabriel	115
Mushfiqur Rahim c Cornwall b Warrican	38	– lbw b Cornwall	18
Shakib Al Hasan c Brathwaite b Cornwall	68		
†Liton Das b Warrican	38	– (6) c Mayers b Warrican	69
Mehedi Hasan c sub (K. A. R. Hodge) b Cornwall	103	– (7) b Warrican	7
Taijul Islam c Da Silva b Gabriel	18	– (8) b Warrican	3
Nayeem Hasan b Bonner	24	– (9) not out	1
Mustafizur Rahman not out	3		
B 2, lb 7, w 5, nb 5	19	W 1, nb 4	5

1/23 (2) 2/66 (3) 3/119 (4)   (150.2 overs) 430   1/1 (2)   (8 wkts dec, 67.5 overs) 223
4/134 (1) 5/193 (5) 6/248 (7)   2/1 (3) 3/3 (1)
7/315 (6) 8/359 (9) 9/416 (10) 10/430 (8)   4/73 (5) 5/206 (6)
                                       6/214 (4) 7/222 (8) 8/223 (7)

Roach 20–5–60–1; Gabriel 26–4–69–1; Cornwall 42.2–5–114–2; Mayers 7–2–16–0; Warrican 48–8–133–4; Bonner 4–0–13–0. *Second innings*—Roach 7–1–17–0; Cornwall 27–2–81–3; Gabriel 12–0–37–2; Warrican 17.5–0–57–3; Bonner 2–0–13–0; Brathwaite 1–0–7–0; Mayers 1–0–11–0.

West Indies

*K. C. Brathwaite b Nayeem Hasan	76	– c sub (Yasir Ali) b Mehedi Hasan	20
J. D. Campbell lbw b Mustafizur Rahman	3	– lbw b Mehedi Hasan	23
S. A. R. Moseley lbw b Mustafizur Rahman	2	– lbw b Mehedi Hasan	12
N. E. Bonner c Nazmul Hossain b Taijul Islam	17	– lbw b Taijul Islam	86
K. R. Mayers lbw b Mehedi Hasan	40	– not out	210
J. Blackwood c Liton Das b Mehedi Hasan	68	– b Nayeem Hasan	9
†J. Da Silva c Liton Das b Nayeem Hasan	42	– b Taijul Islam	20
R. R. S. Cornwall b Mehedi Hasan	2	– (9) not out	0
K. A. J. Roach c sub (Mithun Ali) b Mehedi Hasan	0	– (8) c sub (Saif Hasan) b Mehedi Hasan	0
J. A. Warrican b Taijul Islam	4		
S. T. Gabriel not out	0		
Lb 1, nb 4	5	B 11, lb 4	15

1/11 (2) 2/24 (3) 3/75 (4)   (96.1 overs) 259   1/39 (2)   (7 wkts, 127.3 overs) 395
4/130 (1) 5/154 (5) 6/253 (7)   2/48 (1) 3/59 (3)
7/253 (6) 8/253 (9) 9/259 (8) 10/259 (10)   4/275 (4) 5/292 (6) 6/392 (7) 7/394 (8)

Mustafizur Rahman 15–4–46–2; Shakib Al Hasan 6–1–16–0; Mehedi Hasan 26–9–58–4; Taijul Islam 33.1–11–84–2; Nayeem Hasan 16–1–54–2. *Second innings*—Mustafizur Rahman 13–1–71–0; Taijul Islam 45–18–91–2; Mehedi Hasan 35–3–113–4; Nayeem Hasan 34.3–4–105–1.

Umpires: R. K. Illingworth and Sharfuddoula. Third umpire: Gazi Sohel.
Referee: Neeyamur Rashid.

BANGLADESH v WEST INDIES

Second Test

At Mirpur, February 11–14, 2021. West Indies won by 17 runs. West Indies 60pts. Toss: West Indies.

Mominul Haque admitted his side were shaken by events in Chittagong – and now they were rattled and finally rolled by the West Indian spinners. What had been expected to be a cakewalk for Bangladesh had turned into a 2–0 victory for the visitors, one of their most remarkable series wins of recent years. The lack of a Plan B from Mominul was a cause for concern, although a bigger issue was the bowling of his spinners.

Brathwaite was relieved to win the toss and bat, usually the best route to success at the Shere Bangla Stadium. He showed the way himself by battling almost three hours for 47, before falling to Soumya Sarkar, who had been drafted in to the 18-man squad to replace the injured Shakib Al Hasan. Bangladesh also included Abu Jayed instead of Mustafizur Rahman, who had encountered problems running on the danger area in the First Test.

Then came another notable performance from Bonner. His technique was unusual – rocking back and punching the ball square on either side – though the spinners could not take advantage. He had 74 by the end of the first day, but missed out on a century next morning. This time there was no collapse: Joseph hit out, galloping to 82 with five sixes and eight fours, while Da Silva made a resolute 92. They added 118 for the seventh wicket, and West Indies finished with 409, with Jayed's seamers bringing him four.

Gabriel, a more rapid proposition, blasted out Soumya and Nazmul Hossain in three balls, before Cornwall took over. His innocent-looking off-spin, delivered from a great height, helped reduce Bangladesh to 155 for six on the third morning. Liton Das and Mehedi Hasan steadied things with a stand of 126, before four wickets for 15 – two as Cornwall completed a five-for – sentenced them to a deficit of 113.

The momentum soon swung back Bangladesh's way, as their spinners finally made a mark. Taijul Islam and Nayeem Hasan shared seven as West Indies were bundled out for 117, and once again only Bonner survived for long. He scrapped more than three hours for 38, with Da Silva's 20 the next-highest contribution. Mayers, the hero of the First Test, failed to reach double figures in either innings. Mehedi struck only once, but the wicket of Shayne Moseley was his 100th in Tests.

Bangladesh needed 231 to share the series, and made a confident start: the openers put on 59 in 12 overs, before Soumya fell to part-time off-spinner Brathwaite's first ball. He thin-edged a cut, which was well caught by the plunging Cornwall at slip, and was given out on review after Richard Illingworth turned down the appeal. Brathwaite struck again soon after to remove Tamim Iqbal for a 46-ball 50, and nerves started to bother the Bangladesh batsmen. In all, nine reached double figures but, after Tamim's departure, no one hung around for long, until Mehedi threatened to win the match by himself.

He had put on 25 for the last wicket with the scoreless Jayed, when he pushed at Warrican and was taken low down by Cornwall – his third slip catch of an innings in which he bowled almost unchanged, to go with nine wickets in the match. The West Indian players went wild. Many jumped on Cornwall – or tried to – while the rest ran around the empty ground. "People wrote us off," said Brathwaite. "But we kept it simple, enjoyed it, and we proved them wrong."

Player of the Match: R. R. S. Cornwall.   *Player of the Series:* N. E. Bonner.

Close of play: first day, West Indies 223-5 (Bonner 74, Da Silva 22); second day, Bangladesh 105-4 (Mushfiqur Rahim 27, Mithun Ali 6); third day, West Indies 41-3 (Bonner 8, Warrican 2).

West Indies

*K. C. Brathwaite c Nazmul Hossain b Soumya Sarkar.	47	– c Liton Das b Nayeem Hasan	6
J. D. Campbell lbw b Taijul Islam	36	– b Taijul Islam	18
S. A. R. Moseley b Abu Jayed	7	– c Mithun Ali b Mehedi Hasan	7
N. E. Bonner c Mithun Ali b Mehedi Hasan	90	– b Nayeem Hasan	38
K. R. Mayers c Soumya Sarkar b Abu Jayed	5	– (6) lbw b Abu Jayed	6
J. Blackwood c and b Taijul Islam	28	– (7) st Liton Das b Taijul Islam	9
†J. Da Silva b Taijul Islam	92	– (8) c Soumya Sarkar b Taijul Islam	20
A. S. Joseph c Liton Das b Abu Jayed	82	– (9) c Nazmul Hossain b Taijul Islam	9
R. R. S. Cornwall not out	4	– (10) c Mushfiqur Rahim b Nayeem Hasan	1
J. A. Warrican c Liton Das b Abu Jayed	2	– (5) lbw b Abu Jayed	2
S. T. Gabriel c Mushfiqur Rahim b Taijul Islam	8	– not out	1
B 4, lb 2, nb 2	8	B 8, lb 4, nb 2	14

1/66 (2) 2/87 (3) 3/104 (1) (142.2 overs) 409 1/11 (1) 2/20 (3) (52.5 overs) 117
4/116 (5) 5/178 (6) 6/266 (4) 3/39 (2) 4/50 (5)
7/384 (7) 8/396 (8) 9/398 (10) 10/409 (11) 5/62 (6) 6/73 (7) 7/104 (8)
8/114 (9) 9/116 (4) 10/117 (10)

Abu Jayed 28–6–98–4; Mehedi Hasan 33–9–75–1; Nayeem Hasan 24–3–74–0; Taijul Islam 46.2–8–108–4; Soumya Sarkar 11–1–48–1. *Second innings*—Taijul Islam 21–4–36–4; Nayeem Hasan 15.5–5–34–3; Mehedi Hasan 6–1–15–1; Abu Jayed 10–4–32–2.

Bangladesh

Tamim Iqbal c Moseley b Joseph	44	– c Moseley b Brathwaite	50
Soumya Sarkar c Mayers b Gabriel	0	– c Cornwall b Brathwaite	13
Nazmul Hossain c Bonner b Gabriel	4	– c Moseley b Cornwall	11
*Mominul Haque c Da Silva b Cornwall	21	– c Cornwall b Warrican	26
Mushfiqur Rahim c Mayers b Cornwall	54	– c Da Silva b Warrican	14
Mithun Ali c Brathwaite b Cornwall	15	– c Bonner b Cornwall	10
†Liton Das c Blackwood b Cornwall	71	– c Da Silva b Cornwall	22
Mehedi Hasan c Brathwaite b Gabriel	57	– c Cornwall b Warrican	31
Nayeem Hasan c Blackwood b Cornwall	0	– (10) lbw b Brathwaite	14
Taijul Islam not out	13	– (9) lbw b Cornwall	8
Abu Jayed c Bonner b Joseph	1	– not out	0
B 5, w 1, nb 10	16	B 8, lb 4, nb 2	14

1/1 (2) 2/11 (3) 3/69 (4) (96.5 overs) 296 1/59 (2) 2/70 (1) (61.3 overs) 213
4/71 (1) 5/142 (6) 6/155 (5) 3/78 (3) 4/101 (5)
7/281 (7) 8/281 (9) 9/283 (8) 10/296 (11) 5/115 (6) 6/147 (4) 7/153 (7)
8/163 (9) 9/188 (10) 10/213 (8)

Gabriel 21–3–70–3; Cornwall 32–8–74–5; Joseph 17.5–3–60–2; Mayers 8–2–15–0; Warrican 13–2–48–0; Bonner 3–0–17–0; Brathwaite 2–0–7–0. *Second innings*—Cornwall 30–5–105–4; Joseph 2–0–16–0; Gabriel 2–0–8–0; Warrican 16.3–4–47–3; Brathwaite 11–1–25–3.

Umpires: R. K. Illingworth and Sharfuddoula.   Third umpire: Gazi Sohel.
Referee: Neeyamur Rashid.

BANGLADESH v SRI LANKA IN 2021

Mohammad Isam

One-day internationals (3): Bangladesh 2 (20pts), Sri Lanka 1 (10pts)

Less than a month after these two teams finished a Test series in Pallekele, which Sri Lanka won 1–0, they reconvened in Dhaka for three matches in the World Cup Super League. The games took place in the shadow of Covid, which had spiralled in Bangladesh, leading to a national lockdown a few weeks before the tour started. It meant all three were played in the National Stadium at Mirpur, with the players in a bubble in Dhaka's Pan-Pacific hotel, which had already successfully housed the West Indians (in January) and all the teams for two domestic tournaments. The Sri Lankans' quarantine period was disrupted by three suspected positive tests – although only Shiran Fernando, a seamer on his first senior tour, turned out to have Covid.

In the circumstances, it was a great effort to get the matches done and dusted. Bangladesh, who had lost nine of their previous ten internationals, won the first two comfortably, before Sri Lanka turned the tables in the third, thanks to a superb 120 from Kusal Perera, followed by five cheap wickets for the pacy Dushmantha Chameera. Perera captained the visitors, with Kusal Mendis as his deputy – both had been out of favour for more than a year – after Dimuth Karunaratne was omitted, along with fellow senior players Dinesh Chandimal, Suranga Lakmal and Angelo Mathews. It was a sign that Mickey Arthur, the coach, wanted more emphasis on fitness and fielding.

The absences meant Bangladesh had a distinct edge in experience, and they made it count. Tamim Iqbal captained shrewdly, Mushfiqur Rahim made 84 and 125 in the two victories, and there were telling spells from Mehedi Hasan, Mustafizur Rahman and Shakib Al Hasan. Sri Lanka bowled and fielded brightly, but batted well only in the last game.

SRI LANKA TOURING PARTY

*M. D. K. J. Perera, K. N. A. Bandara, P. V. D. Chameera, A. Dananjaya, D. M. de Silva, P. W. H. de Silva, D. P. D. N. Dickwella, A. M. Fernando, K. B. U. Fernando, S. A. Fernando, M. D. Gunathilleke, C. Karunaratne, B. K. G. Mendis, P. Nissanka, P. A. D. L. R. Sandakan, M. D. Shanaka, I. Udana, R. T. M. Wanigamuni. *Coach:* J. M. Arthur.

First one-day international At Mirpur, May 23, 2021 (day/night). **Bangladesh won by 33 runs.** ‡**Bangladesh 257-6** (50 overs) (Tamim Iqbal 52, Mushfiqur Rahim 84, Mahmudullah 54; D. M. de Silva 3-45); **Sri Lanka 224** (48.1 overs) (M. D. K. J. Perera 30, P. W. H. de Silva 74; Mehedi Hasan 4-30, Mustafizur Rahman 3-34). *Bangladesh 10pts. PoM:* Mushfiqur Rahim. *Bangladesh ended a ten-match winless streak with a crisp all-round performance. Skipper Tamim Iqbal showed the way with a watchful 52, then from 99-4 Mushfiqur Rahim and Mahmudullah put on 109. A total of 257-6 was not enough to spare the batsmen a broadside from the outspoken Bangladesh board president Nazmul Hossain during the innings break – but the bowlers ensured a happy ending. Sri Lanka dipped to 149-7 in the 35th, with Mehedi Hasan taking four wickets, before a rollicking 60-ball 74 from Wanindu Hasaranga de Silva, which included five sixes, narrowed the margin.*

Second one-day international   At Mirpur, May 25, 2021 (day/night). **Bangladesh won by 103 runs** (DLS). ‡**Bangladesh 246** (48.1 overs) (Mushfiqur Rahim 125, Mahmudullah 41; P. V. D. Chameera 3-44, P. A. D. L. R. Sandakan 3-54); **Sri Lanka 141-9** (40 overs) (Mehedi Hasan 3-28, Mustafizur Rahman 3-16). *Bangladesh 10pts. PoM: Mushfiqur Rahim. ODI debut: Shoriful Islam (Bangladesh). A series-clinching victory was set up by Mushfiqur's eighth ODI century, although his only stand of note was 87 for the fifth wicket with Mahmudullah. Late on, Mohammad Saifuddin was clattered on the head by Dushmantha Chameera; he was run out off the same ball, and felt groggy for the rest of the day. He was replaced by Taskin Ahmed, who became the first concussion substitute in an ODI. Three showers meant Sri Lanka's target was eventually revised to 245 in 40 overs, but they never got close, after another solid bowling performance from the home side. Eight Sri Lankans made double figures, but the highest score was Dhanushka Gunathilleke's 24. Mehedi took three more wickets, and moved second in the ICC bowling rankings.*

Third one-day international   At Mirpur, May 28, 2021 (day/night). **Sri Lanka won by 97 runs.** ‡**Sri Lanka 286-6** (50 overs) (M. D. Gunathilleke 39, M. D. K. J. Perera 120, D. M. de Silva 55*; Taskin Ahmed 4-46); **Bangladesh 189** (42.3 overs) (Mosaddek Hossain 51, Mahmudullah 53; P. V. D. Chameera 5-16). *Sri Lanka 10pts. PoM: P. V. D. Chameera. PoS: Mushfiqur Rahim. ODI debuts: K. B. U. Fernando, C. Karunaratne, R. T. M. Wanigamuni (Sri Lanka). Sri Lanka finally got their act together, thanks to their captain, Kusal Perera, who hit his sixth ODI century (and third against Bangladesh). He put on 82 for the first wicket with Gunathilleke, 69 for the third with Kusal Mendis (22), and 65 for the fourth with Dhananjaya de Silva, to set up the highest total of the series. Bangladesh quickly slipped to 28-3, but fifties from Mosaddek Hossain and the consistent Mahmudullah gave them a chance, before the last five wickets disappeared for 31. Chameera, who struck in his first over in each game, finished with a career-best 5-16. His figures had been bettered in Sri Lanka–Bangladesh ODIs only by his compatriot Chaminda Vaas, with 6-25 at Pietermaritzburg during the 2003 World Cup.*

BANGLADESH v AUSTRALIA IN 2021

Mohammad Isam

Twenty20 internationals (5): Bangladesh 4, Australia 1

Australia's preparations for the Twenty20 World Cup, already dented by a 4–1 defeat in the West Indies, took a further knock in Bangladesh, where the home side delivered an identical scoreline, their first series victory over these opponents in any format. The pitches were slow and turned a little, but this was not the typical subcontinental trial by spin: Bangladesh's left-arm seamers Mustafizur Rahman and Shoriful Islam split 14 wickets. Of the slow men, Nasum Ahmed took eight and Shakib Al Hasan seven, including his 100th in T20 internationals.

There had been long odds against the Australians turning up at all: they had called off series in Bangladesh before, and now had to contend with another wave of the pandemic. But the home board bent over backwards to accommodate their demands, including playing all the games in Mirpur, when the plan had been to share them with Chittagong, and spare the pitches in the Shere Bangla National Stadium. It helped that Cricket Australia were under different management: Nick Hockley, their new CEO, was not keen for his reign to start with another embarrassing withdrawal.

From their plane, the tourists were driven straight to a hotel in Dhaka, which closed its doors to others throughout their stay. CA insisted the Bangladeshis also underwent ten days' quarantine, which deprived them of middle-order batsmen Mushfiqur Rahim, whose parents had gone down with Covid, and Liton Das, whose father-in-law caught it too.

Already without the seven senior players who missed the tour of the West Indies – Pat Cummins, Glenn Maxwell, Jhye and Kane Richardson, Marcus Stoinis and David Warner opted out for personal reasons, while Steve Smith was resting an elbow injury – Australia had also lost their captain, Aaron Finch, after he injured his knee in the Caribbean.

Although Alex Carey had deputised in the 50-over matches there, Matthew Wade took the reins for this series. "These are certainly the toughest conditions to play T20 cricket in," he said afterwards. "There's no excuses. We had enough cricket in the West Indies to come and play good cricket – we just didn't. Credit to Bangladesh. We really had to scrounge, but their batsmen found a way, even though our spinners were exceptional."

In one respect, Wade was right: Ashton Agar and Mitch Swepson went for less than a run a ball, and Adam Zampa little more. But Australia's spinners did not take as many wickets as their home counterparts. Seamer Josh Hazlewood claimed eight, while Mitchell Marsh led the way for the batsmen with 156 runs. There were a couple of notable individual performances: the match Australia won was swung their way when Dan Christian clouted Shakib for five sixes in an over, while Tasmania seamer Nathan Ellis – a net bowler when the tour started – was called into the main squad, and marked his international debut with a hat-trick.

There were signs that all was not well within the Australian camp. Justin Langer's performance as coach had been under the spotlight even before these defeats, and he and Gavin Dovey, the tour manager, criticised the team's social-media man for posting a video on the board's official website of Bangladesh's celebrations after they clinched the series. "There was a difference of opinion," admitted Dovey. "In hindsight, it was one of those instances which should have taken place in private." At least viewers at home were spared the drubbing: failure to agree a broadcast deal meant this was the first men's series not screened in Australia since a tour of Pakistan in 1994-95.

AUSTRALIA TOURING PARTY

*M. S. Wade, A. C. Agar, W. A. Agar, J. P. Behrendorff, A. R. Carey, D. T. Christian, N. T. Ellis, J. R. Hazlewood, M. C. Henriques, B. R. McDermott, M. R. Marsh, R. P. Meredith, J. R. Philippe, M. A. Starc, M. J. Swepson, A. J. Turner, A. J. Tye, A. Zampa. Coach: J. L. Langer.

A. J. Finch was originally named as captain, but injured his knee during the tour of the West Indies; he was not replaced in the squad. Ellis and T. Sangha accompanied the tour as net bowlers; Ellis was elevated to the full squad when Meredith strained his side.

First Twenty20 international At Mirpur, August 3 (floodlit). **Bangladesh won by 23 runs. Bangladesh 131-7** (20 overs) (Mohammad Naim 30, Shakib Al Hasan 36; J. R. Hazlewood 3-24); ‡**Australia 108** (20 overs) (M. R. Marsh 45; Nasum Ahmed 4-19). PoM: Nasum Ahmed. *The unheralded slow left-armer Nasum Ahmed was the home hero, his four wickets tripling his haul from four previous T20Is. They included Mitchell Marsh, the only Australian to pass 14. They never threatened Bangladesh's 131-7, which had looked modest, but turned out to be the highest of the series. Mitchell Starc and Josh Hazlewood shared five wickets, but tight displays from Ashton Agar and Adam Zampa foreshadowed what was to come. Bangladesh began with three spinners: Alex Carey fell to the first ball of the reply, from Mehedi Hasan, and Australia were soon 11-3, before left-arm seamers Mustafizur Rahman (2-16) and Shoriful Islam (2-19) mopped up.*

Second Twenty20 international At Mirpur, August 4 (floodlit). **Bangladesh won by five wickets.** ‡**Australia 121-7** (20 overs) (M. R. Marsh 45, M. C. Henriques 30; Mustafizur Rahman 3-23); **Bangladesh 123-5** (18.4 overs) (Afif Hossain 37*). PoM: Afif Hossain. *Australia looked set to square the series when Bangladesh dipped to 67-5 in the 12th over, chasing 122. But the underrated pair of Afif Hossain, who hit five fours and a six, and wicketkeeper Nurul Hasan (22*), shared a stand of 56*, putting their side 2–0 up without further alarm. Afif collected the match award, but it might have gone to Shakib Al Hasan, who followed a tight spell (1-22) with 26 from 17 balls. Earlier, Mustafizur and Shoriful (2-27) had continued to prove awkward, taking 5-50 between them.*

Third Twenty20 international At Mirpur, August 6 (floodlit). **Bangladesh won by ten runs.** ‡**Bangladesh 127-9** (20 overs) (Mahmudullah 52; N. T. Ellis 3-34); **Australia 117-4** (20 overs) (B. R. McDermott 35, M. R. Marsh 51). PoM: Mahmudullah. T20I debut: N. T. Ellis (Australia). *Bangladesh clawed their way back from 3–2 after 13 balls to clinch their first series win over Australia in any format. First Mahmudullah, the captain, made a run-a-ball 52 to ensure a competitive total on another grudging surface, then his bowlers delivered the goods again. Australia were sitting pretty at 71-1 in the 14th, but Shakib bowled Ben McDermott, and Shoriful removed Moises Henriques. It boiled down to 34 from four overs, but Marsh was another victim for Shoriful, and Australia fell short once more. Earlier, Tasmania seamer Nathan Ellis, a late addition to the playing squad, marked his international debut with a hat-trick from the last three balls of Bangladesh's innings.*

HAT-TRICK ON INTERNATIONAL DEBUT

M. J. C. Allom.	England v New Zealand at Christchurch (Test)	1929-30
P. J. Petherick	New Zealand v Pakistan at Lahore (Test)	1976-77
P. W. H. de Silva.	Sri Lanka v Zimbabwe at Galle (ODI)	2017
D. S. M. Kumara	Sri Lanka v Bangladesh at Mirpur (ODI)	2017-18
N. T. Ellis	**Australia v Bangladesh at Mirpur (T20I)**	**2021**

D. W. Fleming took a hat-trick on his Test debut, for Australia v Pakistan at Rawalpindi in 1994-95, but had already appeared in ODIs; Taijul Islam (Bangladesh v Zimbabwe at Mirpur in 2014-15) and K. Rabada (South Africa v Bangladesh at Mirpur in 2015) both did so on ODI debut, having previously played in other formats.

Fourth Twenty20 international   At Mirpur, August 7 (floodlit). **Australia won by three wickets.** ‡**Bangladesh 104-9** (20 overs) (A. J. Tye 3-18, M. J. Swepson 3-12); **Australia 105-7** (19 overs) (D. T. Christian 39). *PoM:* M. J. Swepson. *A consolation win for Australia was effectively sealed in one over, the fourth of the chase, when Dan Christian clouted five sixes off Shakib (666066). He soon fell for 39, but had thrust Australia ahead of the rate, which gave them the breathing space to overcome a later wobble to 65-6. Ashton Agar took them close with a run-a-ball 27. Earlier, three wickets apiece for leg-spinner Mitch Swepson (including Mahmudullah and Nurul with successive balls) and Andrew Tye had condemned Bangladesh to the lowest total of the series – so far.*

Fifth Twenty20 international   At Mirpur, August 9 (floodlit). **Bangladesh won by 60 runs.** ‡**Bangladesh 122-8** (20 overs); **Australia 62** (13.4 overs) (Mohammad Saifuddin 3-12, Shakib Al Hasan 4-9). *PoM:* Shakib Al Hasan. *PoS:* Shakib Al Hasan. *At 38-2 in the eighth over, Australia looked on course to threaten a target of 123. But the innings melted like ice cream in the sun: the last eight dribbled away for 24 in just 39 balls, as the visitors plunged to their lowest T20 score, and*

AUSTRALIA'S LOWEST TOTALS IN T20 INTERNATIONALS

62	**(13.4 overs)**	**v Bangladesh at Mirpur**		**2021**
79	(14.3 overs)	v England at Southampton		2005
86	(16.2 overs)	v India at Mirpur		2013-14
89	(19.3 overs)	v Pakistan at Dubai		2012-13
89	(16.5 overs)	v Pakistan at Abu Dhabi		2018-19
108	(19.5 overs)	v Pakistan at Dubai		2008-09
108	**(20 overs)**	**v Bangladesh at Mirpur**		**2021**
117	(19.1 overs)	v Pakistan at Dubai		2018-19

---

shortest all-out innings. Mohammad Saifuddin claimed three wickets with his gentle seamers, while Shakib made up for his mauling in the previous match with 4-9, including his 100th in the format (Ashton Turner). Only Sri Lanka's Lasith Malinga, who finished on 107, had reached this landmark in T20 internationals.

BANGLADESH v NEW ZEALAND IN 2021-22

MOHAMMAD ISAM

Twenty20 internationals (5): Bangladesh 3, New Zealand 2

New Zealand's tour of Bangladesh, with five T20 games squeezed into ten days in Mirpur, was in stark contrast to Australia's trip that preceded it. Goodwill abounded: the visitors shook hands with their hosts (the Australians would not, on account of Covid), and the Bangladesh Cricket Board changed the start times to suit viewers in New Zealand (they had not for the Australians). At each toss, New Zealand captain Tom Latham – Kane Williamson was given the tour off, as were many of his first-team colleagues – greeted his opposite number, Mahmudullah, in Bengali; he later thanked the BCB for taking care of Finn Allen when he tested positive.

New Zealand also wished to avoid repeating Australia's on-field mistakes, and – to an extent – they succeeded. After being dismissed for 60 in the first game, they steadily improved, and were one hit away from winning the second, but they lost 3–2, their first T20 series defeat by Bangladesh. Latham top-scored with 159 runs, including a pair of unbeaten half-centuries, and left-arm spinner Ajaz Patel took ten economical wickets. The local stars were Mahmudullah (120 runs while being dismissed just twice), slow left-armer Nasum Ahmed and left-arm quick Mustafizur Rahman (eight cheap wickets each).

Critics, however, said the series was meaningless: New Zealand sent none of their T20 World Cup players – even head coach Gary Stead was rested – and the spin-friendly pitches on which Bangladesh prospered would not be reprised in the UAE. Bangladesh cast such reservations aside, saying their priority was to win, and their batsmen would be able to adjust in time for the World Cup.

NEW ZEALAND TOURING PARTY

*T. W. M. Latham, F. H. Allen, H. K. Bennett, T. A. Blundell, D. A. J. Bracewell, C. de Grandhomme, J. A. Duffy, S. C. Kuggeleijn, C. E. McConchie, R. Ravindra, B. V. Sears, B. M. Tickner, W. A. Young. *Coach:* G. Pocknall.

When Allen tested positive for Covid on the tour's second day, M. J. Henry was flown out as cover.

First T20 international At Mirpur, September 1, 2021. **Bangladesh won by seven wickets.** ‡**New Zealand 60** (16.5 overs) (Mustafizur Rahman 3-13); **Bangladesh 62-3** (15 overs). *PoM:* Shakib Al Hasan. *T20I debuts:* C. E. McConchie, R. Ravindra (New Zealand). *New Zealand were bowled out for their joint-lowest total, matching 60 against Sri Lanka at Chittagong in the 2014 World T20. Debutant opener Rachin Ravindra – named after Rahul Dravid and Sachin Tendulkar – made a golden duck, chipping one back to Mehedi Hasan, and within four overs New Zealand were 9-4. Tom Latham and Henry Nicholls both made 18; the last six fell for 17. Bangladesh were soon 7-2, but were rescued by Shakib Al Hasan, whose 25 was the match's top score. He said the pitch was worse than any in the previous month's series, when Australia had been dismissed for 62.*

Second T20 international At Mirpur, September 3, 2021. **Bangladesh won by four runs.** ‡**Bangladesh 141-6** (20 overs) (Mohammad Naim 39, Liton Das 33, Mahmudullah 37*; R. Ravindra 3-22); **New Zealand 137-5** (20 overs) (T. W. M. Latham 65*). *PoM:* Mahmudullah. *T20I debut:* B. V. Sears (New Zealand). *New Zealand needed six off the last ball, bowled by Mustafizur Rahman, but Latham – who had been in since the third over – managed only a single. Bangladesh had begun* *solidly: Mohammad Naim and Liton Das opened with 59 inside ten overs, before Ravindra's left-arm spin claimed 3-22, his best figures in all T20 cricket. Mahmudullah's late flurry raised the total to 141. Latham batted beautifully for 65* off 49, but his team fell behind the rate – Mehedi's four overs cost just 12, and brought the wickets of Tom Blundell and Nicholls – and New Zealand needed 20 from the last over. A no-balled beamer from Mustafizur kept the chase alive, but he prevailed in the end.*

Third T20 international   At Mirpur, September 5, 2021. **New Zealand won by 52 runs. ‡New Zealand 128-5** (20 overs) (H. M. Nicholls 36*, T. A. Blundell 30*); **Bangladesh 76** (19.4 overs) (A. Y. Patel 4-16, C. E. McConchie 3-15). *PoM:* A. Y. Patel. *New Zealand's continued improvement finally earned them a victory, when Bangladesh collapsed in pursuit of 129. Nicholls and Blundell had come together at 62-5, and put on 66*. Then the slow-bowling trio of Ajaz Patel, off-spinner Cole McConchie and Ravindra combined to take 8-44 from 12 overs, and drown Bangladesh, who were all at sea on an unpredictable surface. Mushfiqur Rahim top-scored with 20* as New Zealand dismissed Bangladesh for 76 for the second time in 2021, after Auckland in April.*

Fourth T20 international   At Mirpur, September 8, 2021. **Bangladesh won by six wickets. ‡New Zealand 93** (19.3 overs) (W. A. Young 46; Nasum Ahmed 4-10, Mustafizur Rahman 4-12); **Bangladesh 96-4** (19.1 overs) (Mahmudullah 43*). *PoM:* Nasum Ahmed. *Needing victory to stay in the series, New Zealand could muster only 93, having been 51-2. Slow left-armer Nasum Ahmed had been advised by captain Mahmudullah and spin coach Rangana Herath to counter Finn Allen's switch-hitting by bowling slowly. Instead, he pushed it through, and claimed a career-best 4-10. Mustafizur then stepped in, finishing with 4-12. Bangladesh took their time chasing, with Mahmudullah deciding on accumulation after the loss of three for single figures. Just five balls remained at the end, though this belied the one-sided nature of the match.*

Fifth T20 international   At Mirpur, September 10, 2021. **New Zealand won by 27 runs. ‡New Zealand 161-5** (20 overs) (F. H. Allen 41, T. W. M. Latham 50*); **Bangladesh 134-8** (20 overs) (Afif Hossain 49*). *PoM:* T. W. M. Latham. *Latham's second unbeaten half-century of the series helped New Zealand to 161-5, the highest score at Mirpur in the home summer, and brought a consolation win. Batting first, they had got off to a flier as Allen and Ravindra hit 58 inside six overs. In all, New Zealand managed six sixes, having struck four in the previous four games. Bangladesh paid for their caution at the start of their pursuit, and were 46-4 in the ninth. Though Afif Hossain and Mahmudullah added 63, the chase fizzled out once Mahmudullah went for 23.*

BANGLADESH v PAKISTAN IN 2021-22

Mohammad Isam

Twenty20 internationals (3): Bangladesh 0, Pakistan 3
Test matches (2): Bangladesh 0 (0pts), Pakistan 2 (24pts)

Spectators were admitted to Bangladeshi grounds for the first time since the pandemic began, but the national team failed to greet them with a return to form. They always seemed two steps behind Pakistan: the T20 games were as good as over each time Bangladesh's top order caved in, while Pakistan fought harder to win both Tests.

These were both teams' first outings after the T20 World Cup. Pakistan had just eight days between their semi-final defeat by Australia and the first game at Mirpur. Bangladesh, having already lost Shakib Al Hasan to a hamstring injury, controversially omitted Mushfiqur Rahim. Chief selector Minhazul Abedin insisted he was being rested; Mushfiqur said he had been dropped, and was summoned for a showdown with his board. Bangladesh were brushed aside in all three games.

On the morning of the First Test in Chittagong, a 6.2 magnitude earthquake struck neighbouring Myanmar; it was strong enough to shake the teams' hotel, and the players cowered in the corridor. A chemical factory next to the Sher-e-Bangla Stadium burned down, sending acrid smoke across the ground throughout the first day. Bangladesh's top order also collapsed, but were rescued by Mushfiqur and Liton Das, who scored his maiden Test hundred. Taijul Islam's seven wickets earned the hosts a lead, but Shaheen Shah Afridi's five-for kept Pakistan's target manageable, and Abid Ali helped chase it down.

The Second Test looked like being claimed by the rain, which forced Pakistan's first innings into the fourth afternoon. They declared on reaching 300, more in hope than with confidence, leaving themselves 116 overs to bowl Bangladesh out twice. Thanks to off-spinner Sajid Khan's 12 wickets, they pulled off a remarkable win in gathering gloom.

PAKISTAN TOURING PARTY

*Babar Azam (T/20), Asif Ali (20), Bilal Asif (T), Abdullah Shafiq (T), Abid Ali (T), Fahim Ashraf (T), Fakhar Zaman (20), Fawad Alam (T), Haider Ali (20), Haris Rauf (20), Hasan Ali (T/20), Iftikhar Ahmed (20), Imad Wasim (20), Imam-ul-Haq (T), Kamran Ghulam (20), Khushdil Shah (20), Mohammad Abbas (T), Mohammad Nawaz (T/20), Mohammad Rizwan (T/20), Mohammad Wasim (20), Naseem Shah (T), Nauman Ali (T), Sajid Khan (T), Saud Shakil (T), Shadab Khan (20), Shaheen Shah Afridi (T/20), Shahnawaz Dhani (20), Shoaib Malik (20), Sarfraz Ahmed (T/20), Usman Qadir (20), Zahid Mahmood (T). *Coach:* Saqlain Mushtaq.

Shoaib Malik returned home after the second T20 to be with his ill mother.

First Twenty20 international At Mirpur, November 19, 2021. ‡**Bangladesh 127-7** (20 overs) (Afif Hossain 36, Mehedi Hasan 30*; Hasan Ali 3-22). **Pakistan 132-6** (19.2 overs) (Fakhar Zaman 34, Khushdil Shah 34). *PoM:* Hasan Ali. *T20I debut:* Saif Hasan (Bangladesh). *Bangladesh started badly, and struggled to recover from 40-4, but a late burst from Mehedi Hasan got them into three* *figures. On a slow pitch, Pakistan needed nearly all their overs to reach their target of 128. Having slid to 24-4, they were rescued by a watchful stand of 56 between Fakhar Zaman and Khushdil Shah, before Shadab Khan and Mohammad Nawaz added 36* from 15.*

Second Twenty20 international   At Mirpur, November 20, 2021. ‡**Bangladesh 108-7** (20 overs) (Nazmul Hossain 40); **Pakistan 109-2** (18.1 overs) (Mohammad Rizwan 39, Fakhar Zaman 57*). *PoM:* Fakhar Zaman. *Having been rested for the first game, Shaheen Shah Afridi (2-15) gave Pakistan extra edge with the new ball: Nazmul Hossain's fluent 40 proved the lone hand in a mediocre display. Still not trusting the pitch, Pakistan chased without haste. Bangladesh dropped two sitters as a second-wicket stand of 85 between Mohammad Rizwan and Fakhar took the visitors most of the way home.*

Third Twenty20 international   At Mirpur, November 22, 2021. ‡**Bangladesh 124-7** (20 overs) (Mohammad Naim 47); **Pakistan 127-5** (20 overs) (Mohammad Rizwan 40, Haider Ali 45; Mahmudullah 3-10). *PoM:* Haider Ali. *PoS:* Mohammad Rizwan. *T20I debuts:* Shohidul Islam (Bangladesh); Shahnawaz Dhani (Pakistan). *Bangladesh lost again, but finally put up a contest, pushing Pakistan to the last ball. Rejigging their top order, Bangladesh initially had more momentum, but Mohammad Wasim (2-15) and Iftikhar Ahmed (0-13) pegged them back. Pakistan took their time in the pursuit, and kept wickets in hand: at 117-2, they needed eight from the final over, bowled by captain Mahmudullah after Taskin Ahmed suffered a hand injury. Sarfraz Ahmed missed the first ball, and was out to the second; Haider Ali left to the third. Iftikhar hit his first for six, then was caught going for the winning blow. With two needed from the last, Mahmudullah tried to surprise Mohammad Nawaz with an early release; the batsman pulled away, and was bowled. Mahmudullah asked if he had been ready and, when Nawaz said he hadn't, offered to bowl again. This time, Nawaz smashed a four.*

BANGLADESH v PAKISTAN

First Test

At Chittagong, November 26–30, 2021. Pakistan won by eight wickets. Pakistan 12pts. Toss: Bangladesh. Test debuts: Yasir Ali; Abdullah Shafiq.

Pakistan's margin of victory belies how hard-fought this contest was. In the first three days, Bangladesh twice hit back from desperate positions, but Pakistan held their nerve through decisive contributions from their opening batsmen and bowlers. Abid Ali and debutant Abdullah Shafiq shared hundred partnerships in both innings; Hasan Ali took five wickets in the first, and Shaheen Shah Afridi in the second.

Bangladesh had chosen to bat, and crashed to 49 for four in little over an hour. They were saved by Mushfiqur Rahim and Liton Das, whose fifth-wicket stand of 206 took them into the second day. Liton reached his maiden century, in his 26th Test, more than six years after his debut. His dismissal began a second slide of four for 49, but an enterprising unbeaten 38 from Mehedi Hasan helped raise a decent total of 330.

By the close, however, Abid and Abdullah had put on 145; Abdullah batted nearly four hours for his watchful 52, vindicating the selection of a youngster who had made only three first-class appearances before this tour. He was out, lbw to Taijul Islam, to the fifth delivery of day three, and Azhar Ali fell in identical fashion next ball. Taijul staged Bangladesh's second comeback, taking seven for 116; despite Abid's fourth Test century, they earned a first-innings lead of 44.

Pakistan now struck crucial blows: Afridi and Hasan removed the top five, including Nazmul Hossain and Mominul Haque for ducks. On the fourth morning, newcomer Yasir Ali had helped Bangladesh recover to 90 for five, when he was struck on the helmet by Afridi, and failed a concussion check. Nurul Hasan, Yasir's substitute, kept Liton company while he passed 50 again, but the last four fell for four runs.

This left Pakistan a target of 202, on a pitch which remained true. Abid and Abdullah reached the end of the day unseparated, with 109 on the board. By the time they were parted at 151 – Abdullah having made an attractive 73 – the result was no longer in doubt.

Abid missed out on twin centuries by nine runs, and a small crowd politely applauded Azhar's winning boundary.

Player of the Match: Abid Ali.

Close of play: first day, Bangladesh 253-4 (Mushfiqur Rahim 82, Liton Das 113); second day, Pakistan 145-0 (Abid Ali 93, Abdullah Shafiq 52); third day, Bangladesh 39-4 (Mushfiqur Rahim 12, Yasir Ali 8); fourth day, Pakistan 109-0 (Abid Ali 56, Abdullah Shafiq 53).

Bangladesh

Shadman Islam lbw b Hasan Ali	14	– lbw b Shaheen Shah Afridi	1
Saif Hasan c Abid Ali b Shaheen Shah Afridi	14	– c and b Shaheen Shah Afridi	18
Nazmul Hossain c Sajid Khan b Fahim Ashraf	14	– c Abdullah Shafiq	
		b Shaheen Shah Afridi	0
*Mominul Haque c Mohammad Rizwan b Sajid Khan	6	– c Azhar Ali b Hasan Ali	0
Mushfiqur Rahim c Mohammad Rizwan			
b Fahim Ashraf	91	– b Hasan Ali	16
†Liton Das lbw b Hasan Ali	114	– (7) lbw b Shaheen Shah Afridi	59
Yasir Ali b Hasan Ali	4	– (6) retired hurt	36
Mehedi Hasan not out	38	– lbw b Sajid Khan	11
Taijul Islam c Abdullah Shafiq		– (10) st Mohammad Rizwan	
b Shaheen Shah Afridi	11	b Sajid Khan	0
Abu Jayed c Abdullah Shafiq b Hasan Ali	8	– (11) c Mohammad Rizwan	
		b Shaheen Shah Afridi	0
Ebadat Hossain b Hasan Ali	0	– (12) not out	0
Nurul Hasan (did not bat)		– (9) c Fahim Ashraf b Sajid Khan	15
Lb 14, w 1, nb 1	16	B 1	1

1/19 (1) 2/33 (2) 3/47 (4)   (114.4 overs) 330   1/14 (1) 2/14 (3)   (56.2 overs) 157
4/49 (3) 5/255 (6) 6/267 (7)   3/15 (4) 4/25 (2)
7/276 (5) 8/304 (9) 9/330 (10) 10/330 (11)   5/43 (5) 6/115 (8) 7/153 (9)
                                                            8/157 (7) 9/157 (11) 10/157 (10)

In the second innings Yasir Ali retired hurt at 90-5. Nurul Hasan replaced him, as a concussion substitute.

Shaheen Shah Afridi 27–8–70–2; Hasan Ali 20.4–5–51–5; Fahim Ashraf 14–2–54–2; Sajid Khan 27–5–79–1; Nauman Ali 26–6–62–0. *Second innings*—Shaheen Shah Afridi 15–8–32–5; Hasan Ali 11–0–52–2; Fahim Ashraf 8–3–16–0; Nauman Ali 9–3–23–0; Sajid Khan 13.2–1–33–3.

Pakistan

Abid Ali lbw b Taijul Islam	133	– lbw b Taijul Islam	91
Abdullah Shafiq lbw b Taijul Islam	52	– lbw b Mehedi Hasan	73
Azhar Ali lbw b Taijul Islam	0	– not out	24
*Babar Azam b Mehedi Hasan	10	– not out	13
Fawad Alam c Liton Das b Taijul Islam	8		
†Mohammad Rizwan lbw b Ebadat Hossain	5		
Fahim Ashraf c Liton Das b Taijul Islam	38		
Hasan Ali st Liton Das b Taijul Islam	12		
Sajid Khan b Ebadat Hossain	5		
Nauman Ali lbw b Taijul Islam	8		
Shaheen Shah Afridi not out	13		
B 1, lb 1	2	B 2	2

1/146 (2) 2/146 (3) 3/169 (4)   (115.4 overs) 286   1/151 (2)   (2 wkts, 58.3 overs) 203
4/182 (5) 5/207 (6) 6/217 (1)   2/171 (1)
7/229 (8) 8/240 (9) 9/257 (10) 10/286 (7)

Abu Jayed 12–0–41–0; Ebadat Hossain 26–7–47–2; Taijul Islam 44.4–9–116–7; Mehedi Hasan 30–7–68–1; Mominul Haque 3–0–12–0. *Second innings*—Taijul Islam 28–4–89–1; Ebadat Hossain 8–2–30–0; Mehedi Hasan 18.3–4–59–1; Abu Jayed 4–0–23–0.

Umpires: M. A. Gough and Sharfuddoula.   Third umpire: Gazi Sohel.
Referee: Neeyamur Rashid.

BANGLADESH v PAKISTAN

Second Test

At Mirpur, December 4–8, 2021. Pakistan won by an innings and eight runs. Pakistan 12pts. Toss: Pakistan. Test debut: Mahmudul Hasan.

Sajid Khan came to Dhaka with six wickets from three Tests, and had to wait until the fourth day to bowl his off-breaks. Rain had dragged Pakistan's first innings beyond lunch, and Bangladesh started batting with only 116 overs left in the game. But Sajid's wait was rewarded. He claimed eight for 42, the fourth-best figures in Pakistan's history, and followed up with four for 86 to complete a remarkable victory.

Bangladesh were stunned. They had, at the toss, considered themselves reinforced. Shakib Al Hasan's hamstring had recovered in time for him to replace the concussed Yasir Ali, seamer Khaled Ahmed came in for Abu Jayed, and opener Mahmudul Hasan made

---

BEST TEST BOWLING FOR PAKISTAN

9-56	Abdul Qadir (LB)	v England at Lahore.	1987-88
9-86	Sarfraz Nawaz (RFM)	v Australia at Melbourne.	1978-79
8-41	Yasir Shah (LB).	v New Zealand at Dubai	2018-19
8-42	**Sajid Khan (OB). . . . .**	**v Bangladesh at Mirpur**	**2021-22**
8-58	Imran Khan (RFM)	v Sri Lanka at Lahore	1981-82
8-60	Imran Khan (RFM)	v India at Karachi.	1982-83
8-69	Sikander Bakht (RFM).	v India at Delhi	1979-80
8-164	Saqlain Mushtaq (OB).	v England at Lahore.	2000-01

---

his debut in place of Saif Hasan. After three days, they felt safe. As they took the field on the fourth morning, Pakistan were 188 for two in their first innings; rain had surely killed off the match.

But Pakistan declared as soon as they reached 300, catching Bangladesh off guard. They capitulated in 32 overs, equalling their lowest total at home (against West Indies at Dhaka in 2002-03) and missing the follow-on mark by 14. Nazmul Hossain and Shakib accounted for 63 of their 87. Sajid took seven of the first eight wickets; the other was a run-out.

The fifth day became a battle for survival and, before Sajid could even get his fingers twitching, Bangladesh were 25 for four against the new ball. Mushfiqur Rahim and Liton Das ate up time, adding 73 either side of lunch, only for Liton to pull a long hop from Sajid to square leg. Despite the danger, Shakib looked in sublime touch, off-driving Hasan for three successive fours. Though he lost Mushfiqur, run out when his bat bounced up before he had grounded it behind the line, Shakib became the sixth player – and fastest, in 59 Tests – to achieve the double of 4,000 runs and 200 wickets, after Garfield Sobers, Ian Botham, Kapil Dev, Daniel Vettori and Jacques Kallis.

When the last hour began, Bangladesh were 198 for six; Shakib and Mehedi Hasan had lasted 137 balls with few hazards. Babar Azam, with five first-class wickets to his name, decided to bowl only his second over in Tests (the first had come at the end of the previous day). His second delivery pinned Mehedi lbw. Next over, Sajid castled Shakib, completing his ten-wicket haul; Khaled soon became his 11th. Taijul Islam and Ebadat Hossain clung on but, with the light fading and Pakistan forbidden from bowling their quicks, Sajid had Taijul plumb in front, completing match figures of 12 for 128. With five overs remaining, Pakistan had completed a remarkable heist.

Player of the Match: Sajid Khan.   *Player of the Series:* Abid Ali.

Close of play: first day, Pakistan 161-2 (Azhar Ali 36, Babar Azam 60); second day, Pakistan 188-2 (Azhar Ali 52, Babar Azam 71); third day, no play; fourth day, Bangladesh 76-7 (Shakib Al Hasan 23, Taijul Islam 0).

Pakistan

Abid Ali b Taijul Islam		39
Abdullah Shafiq b Taijul Islam		25
Azhar Ali c Liton Das b Ebadat Hossain		56
*Babar Azam lbw b Khaled Ahmed		76
Fawad Alam not out		50
†Mohammad Rizwan not out		53
Lb 1		1

1/59 (2)   (4 wkts dec, 98.3 overs) 300
2/70 (1) 3/193 (3)
4/197 (4)

Fahim Ashraf, Hasan Ali, Sajid Khan, Nauman Ali and Shaheen Shah Afridi did not bat.

Ebadat Hossain 23–3–88–1; Khaled Ahmed 17.3–5–49–1; Shakib Al Hasan 19–7–52–0; Taijul Islam 25–6–73–2; Mehedi Hasan 14–2–37–0.

Bangladesh

Shadman Islam c Hasan Ali b Sajid Khan	3	– lbw b Shaheen Shah Afridi		2
Mahmudul Hasan c Babar Azam b Sajid Khan	0	– b Hasan Ali		6
Nazmul Hossain lbw b Sajid Khan	30	– c Fawad Alam b Shaheen Shah Afridi		6
*Mominul Haque run out (Hasan Ali)	1	– lbw b Hasan Ali		7
Mushfiqur Rahim c Fawad Alam b Sajid Khan	5	– run out (Abdullah Shafiq/		
		Mohammad Rizwan).		48
†Liton Das c and b Sajid Khan	6	– c Fawad Alam b Sajid Khan		45
Shakib Al Hasan c Azhar Ali b Sajid Khan	33	– b Sajid Khan		63
Mehedi Hasan b Sajid Khan	0	– lbw b Babar Azam		14
Taijul Islam lbw b Sajid Khan	0	– lbw b Sajid Khan		5
Khaled Ahmed b Shaheen Shah Afridi	0	– c Mohammad Rizwan b Sajid Khan		0
Ebadat Hossain not out	0	– not out		0
B 5, lb 3, nb 1	9	B 8, lb 1		9

1/1 (2) 2/20 (1) 3/22 (4)   (32 overs) 87   1/12 (2) 2/12 (1)   (84.4 overs) 205
4/31 (5) 5/46 (6) 6/65 (3)   3/19 (4) 4/25 (3)
7/71 (8) 8/76 (9) 9/77 (10) 10/87 (7)   5/98 (6) 6/147 (5) 7/198 (8)
                                                        8/200 (7) 9/204 (10) 10/205 (9)

Shaheen Shah Afridi 4–3–3–1; Nauman Ali 12–2–33–0; Sajid Khan 15–4–42–8; Babar Azam 1–0–1–0. *Second innings*—Shaheen Shah Afridi 15–5–31–2; Hasan Ali 11–3–37–2; Nauman Ali 20–5–41–0; Fahim Ashraf 4–4–0–0; Sajid Khan 32.4–8–86–4; Babar Azam 2–1–1–1.

Umpires: M. A. Gough and Sharfuddoula.   Third umpire: Gazi Sohel.
Referee: Neeyamur Rashid.

DOMESTIC CRICKET IN BANGLADESH IN 2020-21

UTPAL SHUVRO

First-class cricket almost disappeared from Bangladesh in the pandemic's shadow. After three tour matches in February 2021 – two Tests against West Indies and a three-day game in which Emerging Players beat Ireland Wolves – the National Cricket League began in late March, only to be postponed after two rounds. As Covid cases surged, the Bangladesh Cricket Board initially decided to stage all four third-round matches in two venues: seaside town Cox's Bazar, and Bangladesh Krira Shikkha Protisthan, a sports institute north-west of Dhaka. But Cox's Bazar became a hotspot for the coronavirus, so the government imposed restrictions on movement in the area. Sylhet had already struggled to put out a team in the second round after six players, including captain Alok Kapali, tested positive, and there were also cases in Rangpur's squad. The tournament never resumed; the NCL started afresh in October, its 23rd edition. No winner was declared for the 22nd, and the zonal first-class Bangladesh Cricket League did not take place at all in 2020-21 (nor was there a T20 Bangladesh Premier League).

In the second NCL round in March, left-arm spinner Sanjamul Islam recorded the most economical haul of ten or more wickets in Bangladeshi first-class cricket: his ten for 33 for Rajshahi against Barisal beat Ruyel Miah's 13 for 65 the previous season, for Sylhet against Chittagong.

Before the NCL, the board had introduced two new tournaments, to give players match practice. The 50-over BCB President's Cup, in October 2020, was a hurriedly organised intra-squad competition; Bangladesh's tour of Sri Lanka had just been postponed for the second time, so extra players were added to the preliminary squad to form three teams, named after their captains – Mahmudullah, Tamim Iqbal and Nazmul Hossain. Although they were effectively practice games, and lacked List A status, the tournament was competitive, as players embraced the chance to take the field for the first time in seven months. Prize money of 3.675m taka (over £30,000) also helped: Mahmudullah's XI collected nearly half that for winning the final against Nazmul's XI.

The Bangabandhu T20 league, in November and December, was contested by five divisional teams. Mahmudullah was the victorious captain again, contributing 70 in 48 balls to **Khulna's** victory over Chattogram in the final. Chattogram had headed the table, thanks to the tournament's leading run-scorer (Liton Das, with 393) and wicket-taker (Mustafizur Rahman, with 22).

The Dhaka Premier League – usually the country's only List A competition – had been called off after only two days in March 2020, but was staged in June 2021 as a T20 tournament. **Abahani** were champions, and the main talking point was a shocking incident in the early rounds, when international all-rounder Shakib Al Hasan, playing for Mohammedan, had an lbw appeal against Mushfiqur Rahim, the Abahani captain – and his national team-mate – turned down. He kicked the stumps, shouted at the umpire, then ripped out the stumps and hurled them at the pitch. Shakib was banned for three matches and fined 500,000 taka (about £4,300), but was playing for Bangladesh in Zimbabwe a few weeks later.

FIRST-CLASS AVERAGES IN 2020-21

BATTING (150 runs)

		M	I	NO	R	HS	100	Avge	Ct/St
1	Zahiduzzaman (*Dhaka Metropolis*)	2	4	2	207	71	0	103.50	2
2	†K. R. Mayers (*West Indies*)	2	4	1	261	210*	1	87.00	3
3	†Zakir Hasan (*Sylhet*)	2	4	0	343	159	2	85.75	0
4	Nasir Hossain (*Rangpur*)	2	4	1	245	115	1	81.66	1
5	Tushar Imran (*Khulna*)	2	4	1	218	116	1	72.66	0

		M	I	NO	R	HS	100	Avge	Ct/St
6	N. E. Bonner (*West Indies*)	2	4	0	231	90	0	57.75	3
7	Shahadat Hossain (*Emerging/Chittagong*)	3	5	1	228	108	1	57.00	1
8	Saif Hasan (*Emerging/Dhaka*)	3	5	0	284	127	1	56.80	1
9	Shuvagata Hom (*Dhaka*)	2	4	1	163	114	1	54.33	4
10	Liton Das (*Bangladesh*)	2	4	0	200	71	0	50.00	5/1
11	Mehedi Hasan (*Bangladesh*)	2	4	0	198	103	1	49.50	0
12	Yasir Ali (*Emerging/Chittagong*)	3	5	0	247	92	0	49.40	6
13	†Pinak Ghosh (*Chittagong*)	2	4	0	178	159	1	44.50	0
14	J. Da Silva (*West Indies*)	2	4	0	174	92	0	43.50	5
15	Asadullah Galib (*Sylhet*)	2	4	0	162	82	0	40.50	2
16	Mahmudul Hasan (*Emerging/Chittagong*)	3	5	0	198	78	0	39.60	4
17	†Mominul Haque (*Bangladesh/Chittagong*)	4	8	0	231	115	1	28.87	0

BOWLING (7 wickets, average 35.00)

		Style	O	M	R	W	BB	5I	Avge
1	Sanjamul Islam (*Rajshahi*)	SLA	23	10	33	10	6-15	1	3.30
2	Farhad Reza (*Rajshahi*)	RFM	43.2	12	81	7	4-44	0	11.57
3	Tanvir Islam (*Emerging/Barisal*)	SLA	92.2	24	238	17	8-51	2	14.00
4	Mukidul Islam (*Rangpur*)	RM	50.2	7	183	13	6-64	2	14.07
5	Abu Haider (*Dhaka Metropolis*)	LFM	48.3	16	106	7	3-34	0	15.14
6	Rahatul Ferdous (*Sylhet*)	SLA	42.1	6	122	8	7-75	1	15.25
7	Mehedi Hasan Rana (*Chittagong*)	LFM	69.3	15	170	10	4-35	0	17.00
8	Sohag Gazi (*Barisal*)	OB	43.2	6	142	8	6-65	1	17.75
9	Taijul Islam (*Bangladesh/Rajshahi*)	SLA	206.5	59	492	25	4-23	0	19.68
10	Hasan Murad (*Chittagong*)	SLA	75.2	15	185	9	5-72	1	20.55
11	Masum Khan (*Khulna*)	RFM	62.1	12	197	9	4-34	0	21.88
12	Abdul Halim (*Khulna*)	RM	70	15	207	8	4-62	0	25.87
13	Nazmul Islam (*Dhaka*)	SLA	132.1	23	337	13	6-64	1	25.92
14	Mehedi Hasan (*Bangladesh*)	OB	100	22	261	10	4-58	0	26.10
15	Shuvagata Hom (*Dhaka*)	OB	65	9	185	7	4-86	0	26.42
16	R. R. S. Cornwall (*West Indies*)	OB	131.2	20	374	14	5-74	1	26.71
17	J. A. Warrican (*West Indies*)	SLA	95.2	14	285	10	4-133	0	28.50
18	Abu Jayed (*Bangladesh/Sylhet*)	RFM	96	21	310	9	4-98	0	34.44

BANGABANDHU NATIONAL CRICKET LEAGUE IN 2020-21

Tier One

	P	W	L	D	Pts
Dhaka	2	1	0	1	13.71
Khulna	2	1	1	0	12.03
Rangpur	2	1	1	0	11.64
Sylhet	2	0	1	1	5.72

Tier Two

	P	W	L	D	Pts
Chittagong	2	1	0	1	13.31
Dhaka Metropolis	2	1	0	1	12.18
Rajshahi	2	1	1	0	11.00
Barisal	2	0	2	0	2.50

Outright win = 8pts; draw = 2pts. Bonus points awarded for the first 100 overs of each team's first innings, when each team have had the chance to face 100 overs or been bowled out: 0.01 batting points for every run over the first 250; 0.5 bowling points for the fifth, seventh and ninth wicket taken.

The final four rounds were cancelled because of the Covid-19 pandemic; no winner was declared, and there was no promotion or relegation.

NATIONAL CRICKET LEAGUE WINNERS

†1999-2000	Chittagong	2006-07	Dhaka	2014-15	Rangpur
2000-01	Biman Bangladesh Airlines	2007-08	Khulna	2015-16	Khulna
		2008-09	Rajshahi	2016-17	Khulna
2001-02	Dhaka	2009-10	Rajshahi	2017-18	Khulna
2002-03	Khulna	2010-11	Rajshahi	2018-19	Rajshahi
2003-04	Dhaka	2011-12	Rajshahi	2019-20	Khulna
2004-05	Dhaka	2012-13	Khulna	2020-21	*No winner*
2005-06	Rajshahi	2013-14	Dhaka		

† *The National Cricket League was not first-class in 1999-2000.*

Khulna have won the title 7 times, Rajshahi 6, Dhaka 5, Biman Bangladesh Airlines, Chittagong and Rangpur 1.

BANGABANDHU T20 CUP IN 2020-21

	P	W	L	Pts	NRR
Chattogram	8	7	1	14	1.15
Khulna.	8	4	4	8	0.01
Dhaka	8	4	4	8	−0.32
Barisal	8	3	5	6	−0.36
Rajshahi.	8	2	6	4	−0.45

3rd v 4th   Dhaka beat Barisal by nine runs.

1st v 2nd   Khulna beat Chattogram by 47 runs.

Final play-off   Chattogram beat Dhaka by seven wickets.

Final At Mirpur, December 18, 2020 (floodlit). **Khulna won by five runs. Khulna 155-7** (20 overs); ‡**Chattogram 150-6** (20 overs). *Mahmudullah led Khulna to victory after storming to a T20-best 70* in 48 balls, out of 112 added while he was at the crease; none of his team-mates passed 25. Saikat Ali tried to play the same role in Chattogram's reply, smashing four sixes in a maiden fifty. They needed 16 off the last over, bowled by Shahidul Islam, who had just returned from Narayanganj, where his father had died five days earlier; he restricted them to ten and claimed two wickets, including Saikat.*

DHAKA PREMIER LEAGUE IN 2020-21

50-over league plus Super League and Relegation League

Preliminary League	P	W	L	Pts		Super League	P	W	L	Pts
PRIME BANK	11	9	2	18		Abahani	16	12	4	24
PRIME DOLESHWAR. . .	11	7†	2	16		Prime Bank	16	11	5	22
ABAHANI	11	8	3	16		Prime Doleshwar	16	9‡	4	21
GAZI GROUP.	11	7	4	14		Gazi Group.	16	9*	6	19
MOHAMMEDAN	11	6*	4	13		Sheikh Jamal Dhanmondi .	16	9*	6	19
SH. JAM. DHANMONDI	11	6*	4	13		Mohammedan	16	7*	8	15
Brothers Union	11	4‡	4	11						
Shinepukur	11	4*	6	9						
Khelaghar Samaj Kalyan . .	11	4	7	8		**Relegation League**				
Legends of Rupganj	11	3*	7	7		Legends of Rupganj	13	5*	7	11
Old DOHS	11	2†	7	6		Old DOHS	13	3†	8	8
Partex	11	0*	10	1		Partex	13	0*	12	1

* *Plus one no-result.*   † *Plus two no-results.*   ‡ *Plus three no-results.*

The top six teams advanced to the Super League, carrying forward all their results from the Preliminary League, then playing the other five qualifiers again. Teams tied on points were separated on head-to-head results.

There was no Bangladesh Premier League in 2020-21.

INDIAN CRICKET IN 2021

Pride before the fall

SHARDA UGRA

For any side, winning 22 matches out of 36, reaching an ICC final and touching No. 1 in the Test rankings would constitute a good year. India ended 2021 having enjoyed their best-ever 12 months, and Ravi Shastri, their outgoing coach, lavished them with praise and hyperbole: they were, he suggested, one of the greatest teams of all time.

The only two chokes came in the final of the World Test Championship, unhelpfully scheduled in England in June, and at the T20 World Cup in the United Arab Emirates in November. Otherwise, India's engine was working at full throttle, and the overseas Test results were phantasmagorical. In January, they became the first team to beat Australia at Brisbane in over 32 years. By September, they were leading England in the Pataudi Trophy, to be completed

INDIA IN 2021

	Played	Won	Lost	Drawn/No result
Tests	14	8	3	3
One-day internationals	6	4	2	–
Twenty20 internationals	16	10	6	–

DECEMBER / JANUARY	4 Tests, 3 ODIs and 3 T20Is (a) v Australia	(see *Wisden 2021*, page 630)
FEBRUARY / MARCH	4 Tests, 3 ODIs and 5 T20Is (h) v England	(page 308)
APRIL		
MAY		
JUNE	World Test Championship final (in England) v New Zealand	(page 823)
JULY	3 ODIs and 3 T20Is (a) v Sri Lanka	(page 1015)
AUGUST / SEPTEMBER	4 Tests (a) v England	(page 377)
OCTOBER	T20 World Cup in the UAE	(page 830)
NOVEMBER	2 Tests and 3 T20Is (h) v New Zealand	(page 934)
DECEMBER / JANUARY	3 Tests and 3 ODIs (a) v South Africa	(page 992)

For a review of Indian domestic cricket from the 2020-21 season, see page 942.

Visionhaus, Getty Images

All over bar the shouting: Virat Kohli was replaced as captain in all three formats.

at Birmingham in 2022. In December, they were only the third visiting side in 26 years to win at Centurion. This was history-making as habit.

It seems unthinkable, then, that India's Test team were beset by uncertainty as 2022 dawned. South Africa came from behind to win the Freedom Series, the middle order were on life support, the bowling attack could no longer perform miracles, and the captain had vacated his post. This unnerving transformation took not weeks, but days.

Most expected India to complete their first Test series win in South Africa but, after Centurion, their lights were punched out. The teetering giant, if left unsupported, eventually falls. At the epicentre was the man who, disproportionately but inevitably, had been the centre of their cricketing universe for half a dozen years. Virat Kohli, captain, leader, legend, with his own superhero character on television (we were told, or rather sold), was not just *part* of the zeitgeist: he *was* the zeitgeist. And the rapid unravelling of his cult, in the last quarter of 2021, brought down the entire temple.

Within four months over the autumn, Kohli went from being the all-powerful, all-format captain to just another middle-order batsman entangled in a mid-career crisis. It had been 26 months, and 54 matches, since his last international century – and this from a player who, not long ago, had been in serious pursuit of Sachin Tendulkar's hundred hundreds. During that time, his Test average was 28, way off his career mark of over 50. In trying to balance his form with the captaincy, Kohli overreached a reasonable ambition – to return to voluminous run-making – by miscalculating his influence.

His decision to break the news of his resignation as national (and Royal Challengers Bangalore) T20 captain to his 180m followers on Instagram, a month before the World Cup, triggered events he could not have anticipated. He found himself at loggerheads with BCCI president Sourav Ganguly, over whether there had been conversations about splitting the white-ball captaincy. The board's subsequent decision to replace Kohli as ODI leader with Rohit Sharma was communicated via a single sentence at the bottom of a press release announcing the tour party for South Africa.

India's most successful Test captain continued his odyssey only as far as Cape Town. As defeat loomed, Kohli shouted into the stump microphone, accusing the television company of rigging DRS pictures in South Africa's favour. His tantrum gave the green light to K. L. Rahul and Ravichandran Ashwin to bawl similarly infantile comments down the wire. Two days later, with the series gone, Kohli quit the job he said he treasured most.

Until then, he had been strengthened by continual upheaval at the BCCI. From January 2017 to October 2019, the board were run by a government-appointed committee, and their head and chief executive quickly fell into fan-like adoration of their captain. They were bystanders when Anil Kumble was brusquely replaced as coach in favour of Shastri, Kohli's preferred candidate. Victories, at home and abroad, gave the Kohli–Shastri axis further muscle. Ganguly's was a lone voice in pointing out the dearth of ICC silverware.

Still, throughout 2021, India were cruising. Returning triumphantly from Australia, they beat England at home in all three formats, before travelling to the UK for the northern summer. Their bench strength was lauded, as they simultaneously sent a white-ball squad to Sri Lanka under Shikhar Dhawan (which won the ODIs but lost the T20s).

The World Test Championship final was decided by which set of batsmen better held their nerve against high-quality seam bowling. New Zealand prevailed, and India learned the hard way not to apply their standard template of five specialist bowlers, including two spinners, in all conditions. They put the lesson into practice by twice overturning Tests in London with fast and skilful bowling. At Lord's, they changed from Houdinis into hunters, after a tail-end partnership put England's target out of reach before they were steamrollered by the quicks. At The Oval, India conceded a 99-run lead, but Rohit Sharma's sublime century gave England a struggle in the fourth innings, and again the pacemen rolled them over.

Then came Manchester, where positive Covid tests in the Indian camp led not to the abandonment of the final Test (it was postponed until the following summer) but of good sense and manners. The BCCI had previously asked for the Test to be rescheduled, to create a six-week break before the resumption of the IPL. The ECB, with tickets already sold, declined. The positive results were India's escape route, on chartered flights, into their IPL bubbles.

Perhaps unexpectedly, the IPL did not translate into Indian success at the World Cup, which followed shortly afterwards at the same venues. India lost a World Cup match to Pakistan for the first time, then succumbed to New Zealand. Victories over Bangladesh, Afghanistan and Scotland were, by then, insufficient to take them to the semi-finals.

There was just enough time to welcome New Zealand to India for a vengeful shoeing in Tests and T20s, before the plane left for South Africa. Until then, India were flying. But they returned to earth with a thump: fifth place in the 2021–23 World Test Championship table, and the post-Kohli era arriving sooner, and more gloomily, than expected.

INDIA v NEW ZEALAND IN 2021-22

ANAND VASU

Twenty20 internationals (3): India 3, New Zealand 0
Test matches (2): India 1 (16pts), New Zealand 0 (4pts)

A meeting of the two top-ranked Test teams should have been the toast of the cricket world. Sadly, it was nothing of the sort. New Zealand flew to India straight after the T20 World Cup, and crammed in three more T20s before two Tests, the minimum qualification for the ICC's World Test Championship.

In June, the same sides contested the final of the first edition of the WTC, when New Zealand came out on top in Southampton. But priorities seemed to have changed. Several Indian players skipped this series, as a tour of South Africa was looming: Virat Kohli missed the T20s and the First Test, while Jasprit Bumrah, Rishabh Pant and Rohit Sharma were also given a breather. New Zealand rested Trent Boult, reasoning that the pitches would not be to his liking, while Devon Conway was absent after breaking a finger in the T20 World Cup semi-final. Kane Williamson sat out the T20s, then was ruled out of the Second Test with a recurrence of an elbow injury.

India atoned for recent defeats by New Zealand by winning all three T20s with something to spare. They also won the Test series, though the most striking performance came from New Zealand's slow left-armer Ajaz Patel, who took all ten wickets for 119 in the first innings in Mumbai, the city of his birth 33 years previously, and which his family had left for Auckland when he was 16. It put him alongside Jim Laker and Anil Kumble in the Test pantheon, if not quite in terms of impact: Laker, who finished with 19 at Old Trafford in 1956, was leading a rout, and Kumble also hastened his side to victory, at Delhi in 1998-99. At the Wankhede, Ajaz plugged away from one end, while none of his colleagues looked like taking a wicket at the other. In a nice touch by the broadcasters, he was interviewed by India's off-spinner Ravichandran Ashwin, who finished the match with eight wickets, and presented Ajaz with a shirt signed by the Indian team. "I was trying to be on the money every ball, because as soon as I miss, you guys would be on top," Ajaz told him. "So it has been a bit of a mind game. It was about trusting what you are doing is the right thing."

Overall, though, it seemed as if New Zealand's hectic schedule had caught up with them. Always a proud side, they scrapped hard to draw the First Test at Kanpur but, with Williamson joining Conway on the injured list, they never looked like saving the Second.

ALL TEN WICKETS IN A TEST INNINGS

51.2–23–53–10	J. C. Laker	England v Australia at Manchester	1956
26.3–9–74–10	A. Kumble	India v Pakistan at Delhi	1998-99
47.5–12–119–10	**A. Y. Patel**	**New Zealand v India at Mumbai**	**2021-22**

One-man band: Ajaz Patel celebrates again en route to all ten.

For India, the Tests again suggested a need for fresh blood in the middle order. Over the previous two years, Cheteshwar Pujara had averaged 27, Ajinkya Rahane 24, and even Kohli only 26. But, just as Sachin Tendulkar was undroppable, so is Kohli, and as long as he continued to underperform – he had still not scored an international century since November 2019 – it was difficult to leave out those around him. Meanwhile, the bench flexed their muscles: Shreyas Iyer began his career with 105 and 65 in the First Test, and Mayank Agarwal grabbed his chance with 150 and 62 in the Second.

Indian pitches continued to be confounding. They sometimes turn from the start, which in the past they rarely had; but even when they do not, teams seem to have trouble posting tall first-innings scores. India kicked off the Tests with 345 and 325, both below par, although New Zealand's collapse for 62 – the lowest in any Test in India – meant the hosts waltzed home in the Second Test, despite Patel's heroics.

NEW ZEALAND TOURING PARTY

*K. S. Williamson (T), T. D. Astle (20), T. A. Blundell (T), T. A. Boult (20), M. S. Chapman (20), L. H. Ferguson (20), M. J. Guptill (20), K. A. Jamieson (T), T. W. M. Latham (T), A. F. Milne (20), D. J. Mitchell (T/20), J. D. S. Neesham (20), H. M. Nicholls (T), A. Y. Patel (T), G. D. Phillips (T/20), R. Ravindra (T/20), M. J. Santner (T/20), T. L. Seifert (20), I. S. Sodhi (20), W. E. R. Somerville (T), T. G. Southee (T/20), L. R. P. L. Taylor (T), N. Wagner (T), W. A. Young (T). *Coach:* G. R. Stead.

Southee captained in the T20 series. T. A. Boult and C. de Grandhomme asked to miss the Test leg, citing bubble fatigue. D. P. Conway was originally selected for both squads, but injured his hand at the T20 World Cup; Ravindra was added for the T20s, and Mitchell for the Tests.

First Twenty20 international At Jaipur, November 17, 2021 (floodlit). **India won by five wickets. New Zealand 164-6** (20 overs) (M. J. Guptill 70, M. S. Chapman 63); ‡**India 166-5** (19.4 overs) (R. G. Sharma 48, S. A. Yadav 62). *PoM:* S. A. Yadav. *T20I debut:* V. R. Iyer (India). *Revenge was in the air after India had been dumped out of the T20 World Cup following defeats by Pakistan and New Zealand. Only three days after losing the final in Dubai, New Zealand were sent in at the Sawai Mansingh Stadium. Martin Guptill got plenty in his arc, clattering 70 off 42 balls; after Daryl Mitchell's golden duck, he and Mark Chapman put on 109 for the second wicket. Rohit Sharma – captaining while Virat Kohli sat out this series and the First Test – set up the chase with a 36-ball 48, then Suryakumar Yadav hit 62 from 40, with three sixes. When he was out in the 17th over, India wanted just 21 from 20, but tight bowling meant they still needed ten off the last, Mitchell's first. The debutant left-hander Venkatesh Iyer hit a four, but was then dismissed, before two wides gave Rishabh Pant the breathing space to finish things off.*

Second Twenty20 international At Ranchi, November 19, 2021 (floodlit). **India won by seven wickets. New Zealand 153-6** (20 overs) (M. J. Guptill 31, D. J. Mitchell 31, G. D. Phillips 34); ‡**India 155-3** (17.2 overs) (K. L. Rahul 65, R. G. Sharma 55; T. G. Southee 3-16). *PoM:* H. V. Patel. *T20I debut:* H. V. Patel (India). *Put in again, New Zealand began brightly, with Guptill cracking 14 off six balls. But Ravichandran Ashwin and Harshal Patel – a seamer making his international debut a few days before his 31st birthday, after leading the IPL wicket-takers – pulled things back. India's chase was helped a little by the dew, which hampered New Zealand's bowlers. Rohit smacked five sixes and, although two more wickets fell after an opening partnership with K. L. Rahul of 117, India strolled home.*

Third Twenty20 international At Kolkata, November 21, 2021 (floodlit). **India won by 73 runs.** ‡**India 184-7** (20 overs) (R. G. Sharma 56; M. J. Santner 3-27); **New Zealand 111** (17.2 overs) (M. J. Guptill 51; A. R. Patel 3-9). *PoM:* A. R. Patel. *PoS:* R. G. Sharma. *India swept the series with a comprehensive victory. Rohit won the toss again, but this time chose to bat, to give his team a different test. The restored Ishan Kishan helped him put on 69 in the powerplay, before becoming the first of three wickets in 11 balls for slow left-armer Mitchell Santner. When Rohit gave a return catch to leg-spinner Ish Sodhi, it was 103-4 in the 12th – but the unrelated Iyers, Shreyas (25 from 20) and Venkatesh (20 from 15), helped raise the total to 184. It proved more than enough. Guptill did well again, with 51 from 36, but no one else passed 17. Akshar Patel took three wickets in ten balls, including Chapman and Glenn Phillips for ducks, and finished with 3-9 from three overs, while Harshal (2-26) showed that his slower balls and cutters, so effective in the IPL, worked at international level too.*

INDIA v NEW ZEALAND

First Test

At Kanpur, November 25–29, 2021. Drawn. India 4pts, New Zealand 4pts. Toss: India. Test debuts: S. S. Iyer; R. Ravindra.

Over the years, the Green Park pitch had either been an underprepared turner – barely watered beforehand, and typically producing a three-day finish – or a slow, low surface leading to a turgid draw. This track was expected to help the spinners, but it proved benign. There was no turn on offer, not enough pace for the fast bowlers, and too little bounce to interest the close catchers.

India went in without six regulars. Virat Kohli missed this Test, and Jasprit Bumrah, Rishabh Pant, Mohammed Shami and Rohit Sharma the entire series; late on, K. L. Rahul

MOST FIVE-FORS IN FIRST FOUR TESTS

	Wkts		Debut
6	39	C. T. B. Turner (Australia)	1886-87
5	33	R. M. Hogg (Australia)	1978-79
5	**33**	**A. R. Patel (India)**	**2020-21**
5	31	T. Richardson (England)	1893
4	32	F. R. Spofforth (Australia)	1876-77
4	32	N. G. B. Cook (England)	1983
4	30	V. D. Philander (South Africa)	2011-12
4	26	S. F. Barnes (England)	1901-02

N. D. Hirwani (India) took 36 wickets in his first four Tests, with three five-fors.

was ruled out with a thigh strain. New Zealand, meanwhile, were without Trent Boult, who was rested, and Devon Conway, who had broken his hand punching his bat after being dismissed in the T20 World Cup semi-final. When the stand-in captain Rahane won the toss, all eyes were on an unfamiliar top order. Gill made a pretty half-century, but could not go on. Pujara, desperate for runs, poked at one from Southee that straightened, and feathered to the keeper, Blundell, who had replaced the retired B-J. Watling. And Rahane himself showed signs of touch before he chopped Jamieson into his stumps.

The hazard lights were on at 145 for four, but India were rescued by Shreyas Iyer, making his Test debut at 26 after more than 50 white-ball internationals. He began cautiously, but took control, driving fluently, unsettling New Zealand's three spinners, and looking comfortable against the quicks. He became the 16th Indian to score a century on Test debut and, with help from Jadeja and Ashwin, guided them to 345. On a pitch that offered little, the experienced Southee was the best of the bowlers, finishing with five for 69.

New Zealand's openers were soon into their stride, leaving the Indians to wonder where a wicket might come from. Latham and Young were assured against the spinners, looking more like specialists plucked from the Ranji Trophy than spooked tourists. Young was the aggressor early on, but Latham's decisive footwork was especially impressive. They were finally separated after more than four hours, having put on 151, New Zealand's second-highest opening stand in India, after 231 by Mark Richardson and Lou Vincent at Mohali in 2003-04. Young made 89, his highest score in his fifth Test, and Latham also missed out on a century, after 401 minutes and 282 balls. Both were victims of the uncapped Srikar Bharat, keeping wicket as Saha had a stiff neck.

The rest of the innings was a procession. The key wicket of Williamson went to Yadav, while slow left-armer Akshar Patel – attacking the stumps – picked up his fifth five-wicket bag in seven Test innings. New Zealand subsided for 296, a deficit of 49. The ever-inventive Ashwin, who took three wickets and went for less than two an over, twice darted across to the leg side immediately after bowling; he avoided the danger area, but umpire Nitin Menon was unhappy, as Ashwin was obscuring his view (and possibly impeding the non-striker); he pointed out that he might be prevented from judging an lbw appeal.

India soon dipped to 51 for five, only 100 in front. But Iyer rode to the rescue again, adding 65 to his first-innings hundred, while Saha – now recovered – made a painstaking 61 from 126 balls. He and Akshar put on 67 for the eighth wicket, before Rahane declared, setting New Zealand 284 in 98 overs.

STUMPED BY A SUBSTITUTE IN A TEST

Batsman	Sub keeper		
S. J. Snooke	N. C. Tufnell	South Africa v England at Durban	1909-10
Pervez Sajjad	B. E. Congdon	New Zealand v Pakistan at Lahore	1964-65
T. W. M. Latham	**K. S. Bharat**	**New Zealand v India at Kanpur**	**2021-22**

Few visiting teams have survived a full final day in India, but Kanpur's cool winter ensured the pitch did not break up. New Zealand were immediately into rearguard mode. Latham made 52 in 218 minutes, while Somerville – nightwatchman after Young had gone cheaply the previous evening – consumed more than two hours for 36. Ashwin eventually removed Latham, to pass Harbhajan Singh (417 wickets) on India's Test list; only Anil Kumble (619) and Kapil Dev (434) lay ahead. Jadeja made two important strikes, trapping Taylor and Williamson, but the resistance continued. Blundell lasted 44 minutes for two, and Jamieson half an hour for five; Rachin Ravindra, the Wellington-born debutant of Indian origin, faced 91 balls in 91 minutes as the spinners scooted through their overs, and remained undefeated.

When Jadeja won his fourth lbw decision of the innings, the last pair came together with 8.4 overs left. But the ball was not turning sharply, nor bouncing spitefully. Ajaz Patel negotiated 29 deliveries, as he and Ravindra made sure New Zealand achieved a tenth successive Test without defeat, a national record – by the barest of margins.

Player of the Match: S. S. Iyer.

Close of play: first day, India 258-4 (Iyer 75, Jadeja 50); second day, New Zealand 129-0 (Latham 50, Young 75); third day, India 14-1 (Agarwal 4, Pujara 9); fourth day, New Zealand 4-1 (Latham 2, Somerville 0).

India

M. A. Agarwal c Blundell b Jamieson	13	–	c Latham b Southee	17
S. Gill b Jamieson	52	–	b Jamieson	1
C. A. Pujara c Blundell b Southee	26	–	c Blundell b Jamieson	22
*A. M. Rahane b Jamieson	35	–	lbw b Patel	4
S. S. Iyer c Young b Southee	105	–	c Blundell b Southee	65
R. A. Jadeja b Southee	50	–	lbw b Southee	0
†W. P. Saha c Blundell b Southee	1	–	(8) not out	61
R. Ashwin b Patel	38	–	(7) b Jamieson	32
A. R. Patel c Blundell b Southee	3	–	not out	28
U. T. Yadav not out	10			
I. Sharma lbw b Patel	0			
B 5, lb 2, w 1, nb 4	12		B 3, lb 1	4

1/21 (1) 2/82 (2) 3/106 (3) (111.1 overs) 345
4/145 (4) 5/266 (6) 6/288 (7)
7/305 (5) 8/313 (9) 9/339 (8) 10/345 (11)

1/2 (2) (7 wkts dec, 81 overs) 234
2/32 (3) 3/41 (4)
4/51 (1) 5/51 (6) 6/103 (7) 7/167 (5)

Southee 27.4–6–69–5; Jamieson 23.2–6–91–3; Patel 29.1–7–90–2; Somerville 24–2–60–0; Ravindra 7–1–28–0. *Second innings*—Southee 22–2–75–3; Jamieson 17–6–40–3; Patel 17–3–60–1; Ravindra 9–3–17–0; Somerville 16–2–38–0.

New Zealand

T. W. M. Latham st sub (†K. Srikar Bharat) b Patel	95	–	b Ashwin	52
W. A. Young c sub (†K. Srikar Bharat) b Ashwin	89	–	lbw b Ashwin	2
*K. S. Williamson lbw b Yadav	18	–	(4) lbw b Jadeja	24
L. R. P. L. Taylor c sub (†K. Srikar Bharat) b Patel	11	–	(5) lbw b Jadeja	2
H. M. Nicholls lbw b Patel	2	–	(6) lbw b Patel	1
†T. A. Blundell b Patel	13	–	(7) b Ashwin	2
R. Ravindra b Jadeja	13	–	(8) not out	18
K. A. Jamieson c Patel b Ashwin	23	–	(9) lbw b Jadeja	5
T. G. Southee b Patel	5	–	(10) lbw b Jadeja	4
W. E. R. Somerville b Ashwin	6	–	(3) c Gill b Yadav	36
A. Y. Patel not out	5	–	not out	2
B 6, lb 4, w 1, nb 5	16		B 12, lb 1, nb 4	17

1/151 (2) 2/197 (3) 3/214 (4) (142.3 overs) 296
4/218 (5) 5/227 (1) 6/241 (7)
7/258 (6) 8/270 (9) 9/284 (8) 10/296 (10)

1/3 (2) 2/79 (3) (9 wkts, 98 overs) 165
3/118 (1) 4/125 (5)
5/126 (6) 6/128 (4)
7/138 (7) 8/147 (9) 9/155 (10)

Sharma 15–5–35–0; Yadav 18–3–50–1; Ashwin 42.3–10–82–3; Jadeja 33–10–57–1; Patel 34–6–62–5. *Second innings*—Ashwin 30–12–35–3; Patel 21–12–23–1; Yadav 12–2–34–1; Sharma 7–1–20–0; Jadeja 28–10–40–4.

Umpires: N. N. Menon and V. K. Sharma.   Third umpire: A. K. Chaudhary.
Referee: J. Srinath.

INDIA v NEW ZEALAND

Second Test

At Mumbai, December 3–6, 2021. India won by 372 runs. India 12pts. Toss: India.

It soon became clear the Wankhede pitch would suit India perfectly – a red-soil surface that would turn and bounce. Unlike at Kanpur, the edges would carry, and the straight ball could be lethal. And so India romped to a huge victory – though not before one of New Zealand's own spinners, the Mumbai-born Ajaz Patel, had become the third player in Test history to take ten wickets in an innings.

India were without Ravindra Jadeja, who injured his right forearm in the First Test, Ishant Sharma (dislocated finger) and Ajinkya Rahane (hamstring). It meant Rahane, capped 79 times but his place in doubt, was yet to play a Test at his home ground. For New Zealand, Kane Williamson had a recurrence of his elbow trouble (Mitchell replaced

---

BEST TEST BOWLING FIGURES IN CITY OF BIRTH

10-119	A. Y. Patel	New Zealand v India at Mumbai.	**2021-22**
9-51	M. Muralitharan	Sri Lanka v Zimbabwe at Kandy	2001-02
9-56	Abdul Qadir	Pakistan v England at Lahore	1987-88
9-95	J. M. Noreiga	West Indies v India at Port-of-Spain.	1970-71
8-15	S. C. J. Broad	England v Australia at Nottingham	2015
8-46	M. Muralitharan	Sri Lanka v West Indies at Kandy	2005
8-58	Imran Khan	Pakistan v Sri Lanka at Lahore	1981-82
8-60	R. L. Chase	West Indies v England at Bridgetown	2018-19
8-69	H. J. Tayfield	South Africa v England at Durban	1956-57
8-109	P. A. Strang.	Zimbabwe v New Zealand at Bulawayo.	2000-01
8-164	Saqlain Mushtaq	Pakistan v England at Lahore	2000-01

Noreiga was born about ten miles outside Port-of-Spain, and Chase around six from Bridgetown.

---

him), and left-arm quick Neil Wagner missed out again, which seemed odd. The absence of both captains from the previous match made this the only two-Test series, after South Africa v England in 1888-89, to feature four different men in charge.

Back after his break, Kohli won the toss, and no wicket went down for nearly two hours as Agarwal and Gill put on 80 – though they were helped by off-key performances from Southee and Jamieson, neither able to recapture their Kanpur spark.

From there, however, it was the Ajaz Patel show. Pressed into service by stand-in skipper Latham, he quickly settled into an excellent line and length with his slow left-armers. Gill edged to slip, then Pujara – who likes to run down the track to the spinners – yorked himself and was bowled for a duck. Four deliveries later, Kohli played outside the line, only for the ball to kiss the inside edge and, almost simultaneously, hit the pad. Given out by the on-field umpire Anil Chaudhary, Kohli was quick to review. Third umpire Virender Sharma watched several replays, but eventually determined there was not enough evidence to overturn the decision. "This is simply not out," pronounced the watching Shane Warne. Kohli had to go, stalking off with a word in Chaudhary's direction: 80 for none had become 80 for three.

It was left to Agarwal to anchor the innings. Using his crease to counter the spinners, and aiming straight against the quicker bowlers, he made 150 in seven hours 12 minutes, with 17 fours and four sixes. Support came from Akshar Patel, who went on to a maiden Test fifty, and helped India to 325. But the real story came from the other Patel: Ajaz sent down 47.5 overs, quietly and patiently, and took all ten. Unlike Jim Laker at Old Trafford in 1956, or Anil Kumble at Delhi in 1998-99, he did not hurtle to immortality, but got there bit by bit, mainly because none of his team-mates looked like buying a wicket.

A fast bowler turned spinner who had previously claimed only 29 Test victims, Patel finished with figures of 47.5–12–119–10, relegating Richard Hadlee's nine for 56 at Brisbane in 1985-86 to second place among New Zealand's best analyses. His success

---

BEST INNINGS FIGURES IN A TEST DEFEAT...

10-119	**A. Y. Patel**	New Zealand v India at Mumbai	**2021-22**
9-83	Kapil Dev	India v West Indies at Ahmedabad	1983-84
9-95	J. M. Noreiga	West Indies v India at Port-of-Spain	1970-71
9-102	S. P. Gupte	India v West Indies at Kanpur	1958-59
9-129	K. A. Maharaj	South Africa v Sri Lanka at Colombo (SSC) . .	2018

...AND BEST MATCH FIGURES IN VAIN

14-225	**A. Y. Patel**	New Zealand v India at Mumbai	**2021-22**
13-132	J. Srinath	India v Pakistan at Calcutta	1998-99
13-163	S. F. Barnes	England v Australia at Melbourne	1901-02
13-217	M. G. Hughes	Australia v West Indies at Perth	1988-89
13-244	T. Richardson	England v Australia at Manchester	1896

---

suggested their batsmen might be up against it once India's spinners got to work, and so it proved: they subsided for 62, their sixth-smallest Test innings, and the lowest on Indian soil, undercutting the home side's 75 against West Indies at Delhi in 1987-88.

In fact, the seam of Siraj had started the rot, with three wickets in seven balls, before the guile and class of Ashwin brought four for eight in eight overs. Only Latham and Jamieson scraped into double figures. The match was over as a contest, but Kohli batted again, despite a lead of 263, in an attempt to cajole his middle order into a semblance of form. Agarwal restated his case for a permanent place with 62; Pujara and Gill, who swapped places, each made 47, Kohli 36 in nearly two hours, and Akshar Patel biffed four late sixes as the lead disappeared over the horizon. Kohli eventually called a halt 539 ahead. Ajaz Patel claimed four more victims, and Ravindra three with his own left-arm tweakers, meaning all the wickets in the match went to bowlers of Indian origin – something that had not happened since the India–Pakistan encounters of the 1950s and '60s, when all Pakistan's players were from pre-Partition India.

New Zealand batted a little better second time round, with Mitchell and Nicholls at least averting a three-day defeat, but it was all over an hour into the fourth day, with Ashwin and fellow off-spinner Jayant Yadav, in his first Test for nearly five years, taking four wickets apiece. Ashwin finished with match figures of eight for 42, and 14 in the series. It was New Zealand's biggest defeat by runs, beating 358 by South Africa at Johannesburg in 2007-08. But the last word, if not the match award, went to Ajaz Patel. "The stars have aligned for me to have an occasion like that here in Mumbai, the place I was born," he said. "These kind of things don't really sink in until later. It is a special moment."

Player of the Match: M. A. Agarwal. *Player of the Series:* R. Ashwin.
Close of play: first day, India 221-4 (Agarwal 120, Saha 25); second day, India 69-0 (Agarwal 38, Pujara 29); third day, New Zealand 140-5 (Nicholls 36, Ravindra 2).

India

M. A. Agarwal c Blundell b Patel	150	– c Young b Patel	62
S. Gill c Taylor b Patel	44	– (3) c Latham b Ravindra	47
C. A. Pujara b Patel	0	– (2) c Taylor b Patel	47
*V. Kohli lbw b Patel	0	– b Ravindra	36
S. S. Iyer c Blundell b Patel	18	– b Ravindra	14
†W. P. Saha lbw b Patel	27	– c Jamieson b Ravindra	13
R. Ashwin b Patel	0		
A. R. Patel lbw b Patel	52	– (7) not out	41
J. Yadav c Ravindra b Patel	12	– (8) c and b Patel	6
U. T. Yadav not out	0		
M. Siraj c Ravindra b Patel	4		
B 13, lb 5	18	B 6, lb 3, nb 1	10

1/80 (2) 2/80 (3) 3/80 (4)   (109.5 overs) 325   1/107 (1)   (7 wkts dec, 70 overs) 276
4/160 (5) 5/224 (6) 6/224 (7)   2/115 (2) 3/197 (3)
7/291 (1) 8/316 (8) 9/321 (9) 10/325 (11)   4/211 (5) 5/217 (4) 6/238 (6) 7/276 (8)

Southee 22–6–43–0; Jamieson 12–3–36–0; Patel 47.5–12–119–10; Somerville 19–0–80–0;
Ravindra 4–0–20–0; Mitchell 5–3–9–0. *Second innings*—Southee 13–2–31–0; Patel 26–3–106–4;
Jamieson 8–2–15–0; Somerville 10–0–59–0; Ravindra 13–2–56–3.

New Zealand

*T. W. M. Latham c Iyer b Siraj	10	– lbw b Ashwin	6
W. A. Young c Kohli b Siraj	4	– c sub (S. A. Yadav) b Ashwin	20
D. J. Mitchell lbw b Patel	8	– c J. Yadav b Patel	60
L. R. P. L. Taylor b Siraj	1	– c Pujara b Ashwin	6
H. M. Nicholls b Ashwin	7	– st Saha b Ashwin	44
†T. A. Blundell c Pujara b Ashwin	8	– run out (sub K. Srikar Bharat/Saha)	0
R. Ravindra c Kohli b J. Yadav	4	– c Pujara b J. Yadav	18
K. A. Jamieson c Iyer b Patel	17	– lbw b J. Yadav	0
T. G. Southee c sub (S. A. Yadav) b Ashwin	0	– b J. Yadav	0
W. E. R. Somerville c Siraj b Ashwin	0	– c Agarwal b J. Yadav	1
A. Y. Patel not out	0	– not out	0
Lb 1, nb 2	3	B 9, lb 1, nb 2	12

1/10 (2) 2/15 (1) 3/17 (4)   (28.1 overs) 62   1/13 (1) 2/45 (2)   (56.3 overs) 167
4/27 (3) 5/31 (5) 6/38 (7)   3/55 (4) 4/128 (3)
7/53 (6) 8/53 (9) 9/62 (10) 10/62 (8)   5/129 (6) 6/162 (7) 7/165 (8)
                                                                                       8/165 (9) 9/167 (10) 10/167 (5)

U. T. Yadav 5–2–7–0; Siraj 4–0–19–3; Patel 9.1–3–14–2; Ashwin 8–2–8–4; J. Yadav 2–0–13–1.
Second innings—Siraj 5–2–13–0; Ashwin 22.3–9–34–4; Patel 10–2–42–1; J. Yadav 14–4–49–4;
U. T. Yadav 5–1–19–0.

Umpires: A. K. Chaudhary and N. N. Menon.   Third umpire: V. K. Sharma.
Referee: J. Srinath.

DOMESTIC CRICKET IN INDIA IN 2020-21

R. Mohan

For the first time since it began in 1934-35, the Ranji Trophy did not take place. Even the Second World War had not stopped India's first-class championship – but Covid did. At first it was postponed, as the pandemic not only delayed the 2020 IPL for six months, but moved it to the UAE, where it finally wound up in November. With the relaxing of national lockdowns, the BCCI were emboldened to stage the T20 Syed Mushtaq Ali Trophy in January, and followed up with the 50-over Vijay Hazare Trophy in February and March, along with the women's one-day tournament, before the next IPL started in April.

At the end of January, the board confirmed that the Ranji Trophy would not return until 2021-22. When the fixture list was released in July, it seemed as if the Duleep Trophy (the zonal first-class competition, which once functioned as a Test trial but had declined in recent years) might have gone for good. And it was not yet clear whether the Irani Cup (Ranji champions versus Rest of India) or the 50-over Deodhar Trophy (between India A, B and C) would reappear.

Mumbai, now regarded as the home of Indian white-ball cricket thanks to its successful IPL franchise, won their fourth Vijay Hazare title – and second in three seasons – in a high-scoring final against Uttar Pradesh. They chased down 313 with 51 balls to spare; there was an unbeaten century on each side, from UP's Madhav Kaushik and Mumbai's Aditya Tare. Dropped from the national team after an unhappy tour of Australia, Mumbai's 21-year-old opener Prithvi Shaw piled up 827 runs, a tournament record, including a double-century, three other hundreds, and a 39-ball 73 in the final. Another opener, Devdutt Padikkal – eight months younger than Shaw – matched his four centuries, in an aggregate of 737 for semi-finalists Karnataka.

Tamil Nadu are also a white-ball powerhouse, with their own T20 premier league, but their triumph in the Syed Mushtaq Ali Trophy was their first since 2006-07. Former Test wicketkeeper Dinesh Karthik was captain then and now – a tribute to his longevity and skilful marshalling of resources, with eight players unavailable for various reasons. Karthik had also led Tamil Nadu to the final the previous season, when they were runners-up to Karnataka, but this time they crushed Baroda on a square-turner in Ahmedabad.

In a reflection of India's political landscape, Wasim Jaffer, who had retired from first-class cricket in 2020 as record-holder for most runs in the Ranji Trophy, found himself under attack as coach of Uttarakhand: he was accused, unfairly, of communalism – favouring fellow Muslims – in his team selection. The players stood by him, but he resigned, citing interference by officials.

VIJAY HAZARE TROPHY IN 2020-21

Six 50-over leagues plus knockout

Qualifier Delhi beat Uttarakhand by four wickets.

Quarter-finals Gujarat beat Andhra by 117 runs; Karnataka beat Kerala by 80 runs; Mumbai beat Saurashtra by nine wickets; Uttar Pradesh beat Delhi by 46 runs.

Semi-finals Mumbai beat Karnataka by 72 runs; Uttar Pradesh beat Gujarat by five wickets.

Final At Delhi, March 14, 2021. **Mumbai won by six wickets. ‡Uttar Pradesh 312-4** (50 overs) (M. Kaushik 158*); **Mumbai 315-4** (41.3 overs) (A. P. Tare 118*). *The match was shaped by two maiden one-day hundreds. Madhav Kaushik batted throughout Uttar Pradesh's innings to set a target of 313. But Prithvi Shaw blasted 73 out of 89 in the first nine overs of Mumbai's reply, before Aditya Tare took up the baton, striking 18 fours as he rushed to 118* in 107 balls, claiming the trophy with more than eight overs in hand.*

SYED MUSHTAQ ALI TROPHY IN 2020-21

Six 20-over leagues plus knockout

Quarter-finals Punjab beat Karnataka by nine wickets; Tamil Nadu beat Himachal Pradesh by five wickets; Baroda beat Haryana by eight wickets; Rajasthan beat Bihar by 16 runs.

Semi-finals Baroda beat Punjab by 25 runs; Tamil Nadu beat Rajasthan by seven wickets.

Final At Ahmedabad, January 31, 2021 (floodlit). **Tamil Nadu won by seven wickets. Baroda 120-9** (20 overs); ‡**Tamil Nadu 123-3** (18 overs). *Dinesh Karthik put Baroda in on a turning pitch, and used four spinners before resorting to seam. Slow left-armer Manimaran Siddharth (4-20) ran through the line-up in his first match of the season, reducing Baroda to 36-6. Only Vishnu Solanki (49) stood firm, adding 58 with Atit Sheth (29), but Tamil Nadu eased past a target of 121.*

The Vivo Indian Premier League has its own section (page 1120).

RANJI TROPHY WINNERS

1934-35	Bombay	1963-64	Bombay	1992-93	Punjab
1935-36	Bombay	1964-65	Bombay	1993-94	Bombay
1936-37	Nawanagar	1965-66	Bombay	1994-95	Bombay
1937-38	Hyderabad	1966-67	Bombay	1995-96	Karnataka
1938-39	Bengal	1967-68	Bombay	1996-97	Mumbai
1939-40	Maharashtra	1968-69	Bombay	1997-98	Karnataka
1940-41	Maharashtra	1969-70	Bombay	1998-99	Karnataka
1941-42	Bombay	1970-71	Bombay	1999-2000	Mumbai
1942-43	Baroda	1971-72	Bombay	2000-01	Baroda
1943-44	Western India	1972-73	Bombay	2001-02	Railways
1944-45	Bombay	1973-74	Karnataka	2002-03	Mumbai
1945-46	Holkar	1974-75	Bombay	2003-04	Mumbai
1946-47	Baroda	1975-76	Bombay	2004-05	Railways
1947-48	Holkar	1976-77	Bombay	2005-06	Uttar Pradesh
1948-49	Bombay	1977-78	Karnataka	2006-07	Mumbai
1949-50	Baroda	1978-79	Delhi	2007-08	Delhi
1950-51	Holkar	1979-80	Delhi	2008-09	Mumbai
1951-52	Bombay	1980-81	Bombay	2009-10	Mumbai
1952-53	Holkar	1981-82	Delhi	2010-11	Rajasthan
1953-54	Bombay	1982-83	Karnataka	2011-12	Rajasthan
1954-55	Madras	1983-84	Bombay	2012-13	Mumbai
1955-56	Bombay	1984-85	Bombay	2013-14	Karnataka
1956-57	Bombay	1985-86	Delhi	2014-15	Karnataka
1957-58	Baroda	1986-87	Hyderabad	2015-16	Mumbai
1958-59	Bombay	1987-88	Tamil Nadu	2016-17	Gujarat
1959-60	Bombay	1988-89	Delhi	2017-18	Vidarbha
1960-61	Bombay	1989-90	Bengal	2018-19	Vidarbha
1961-62	Bombay	1990-91	Haryana	2019-20	Saurashtra
1962-63	Bombay	1991-92	Delhi	2020-21	*No competition*

Bombay/Mumbai have won the Ranji Trophy 41 times, Karnataka 8, Delhi 7, Baroda 5, Holkar 4, Bengal, Hyderabad, Madras/Tamil Nadu, Maharashtra, Railways, Rajasthan and Vidarbha 2, Gujarat, Haryana, Nawanagar, Punjab, Saurashtra, Uttar Pradesh and Western India 1.

IRISH CRICKET IN 2021

Not being put to the Test

IAN CALLENDER

Ireland ended 2021 casting around for a new head coach, and with two players isolating in Florida, unable to travel with the rest of the squad to the West Indies. It was a fair reflection of the state of Irish cricket, on and off the field. An external investigation was ordered into a T20 World Cup campaign which saw Ireland knocked out in the first round – but a wider review, including assessing the input (or lack of it) from board officials, might also have been worthwhile.

The year started with a one-day defeat by the UAE, and ended even more ignominiously, with a 1–1 draw in T20s against the USA. In all, Ireland won only ten of their 30 matches. The highlights were shared series against South Africa and Zimbabwe – but other lowlights included defeats by Afghanistan and the Netherlands.

Andrew Balbirnie, the captain, was not a happy man. Before the series in America, he hit out at poor facilities at home, and a lack of fixtures for the

IRELAND IN 2021

	Played	Won	Lost	Drawn/No result
Tests	–	–	–	–
One-day internationals	14	4	8	2
Twenty20 internationals	16	6	10	–

JANUARY	2 ODIs (a) v UAE	(page 1086)
	3 ODIs (in the UAE) v Afghanistan	(page 889)
FEBRUARY		
MARCH		
APRIL		
MAY		
JUNE	3 ODIs (a) v Netherlands	(page 1089)
JULY	3 ODIs and 3 T20Is (h) v South Africa	(page 947)
AUGUST SEPTEMBER	3 ODIs and 5 T20Is (h) v Zimbabwe	(page 950)
OCTOBER	3 T20Is (a) v UAE	(page 1091)
	T20 World Cup in the UAE	(page 830)
NOVEMBER		
DECEMBER	2 T20Is (a) v USA	(page 1093)

For a review of Irish domestic cricket from the 2021 season, see page 953.

Bowed, but unbeaten: Harry Tector is floored by Anrich Nortje, but Ireland shock South Africa at Malahide.

Ireland Wolves (the national A-Team). And he bemoaned the absence of Test matches: since the carnival atmosphere of their first, against Pakistan at Malahide in 2018, Ireland have managed only two more, none since the visit to Lord's in 2019. Frustrated, Balbirnie was reduced to a plaintive tweet during the Ashes: "Test cricket looks like fun. Anyone want a game?? Seriously."

Early exit from the T20 World Cup meant head coach Graham Ford stood down six months before the end of his four-year contract. He was popular with the players, but results were indifferent: Ireland had also failed to qualify for the 50-over World Cup in 2019, ending a run of eight global tournaments. His replacement was unveiled early in 2022: Heinrich Malan, another South African, who moved to New Zealand in 2013 to coach Central Districts, then Auckland Aces. He was New Zealand's assistant coach in England in 2021, but this will be his first lead role. Malan was due to begin a three-year contract in March, after Ireland's bid to reach the next T20 World Cup, in Australia later in 2022. They were condemned to another qualifying event after failing to make it out of their group in the UAE in 2021.

In the preliminary stage of the World Cup, Ireland had beaten the Netherlands, thanks to Curtis Campher's four wickets in four balls, and – after a predictable defeat by Sri Lanka – needed only to beat Namibia to progress. But six wickets tumbled for 31 in the last six overs, and Namibia passed a below-par total of 125 in the 19th. Kevin O'Brien scored 25 in his 380th – and possibly final – innings in all matches for Ireland, 250 in official internationals; he was left out of the squad that travelled to the USA in December.

That Namibian defeat, though, was not the low point of the year. In the first match in Florida, all looked hunky-dory as the USA struggled to 67 for four in

12 overs – but they hammered 121 off the last eight, and Ireland fell well short. It was the Americans' first victory over a Test-playing nation. Total embarrassment was avoided when Ireland clung on to win the second match by nine runs. It was their 16th T20 international of the year, but only the sixth victory. Three had come in the five-match series against Zimbabwe at home in August and September, but even then some batting deficiencies were shown up, as Ireland failed to chase 118 in the first game, and 125 in the last.

There were occasional bright spots. Paul Stirling was the dominant batsman once again. He clobbered a maiden T20I century, against Zimbabwe, and finished the year with 1,187 international runs, 518 more than any of his team-mates. And he was the leading scorer in the world in ODIs, with 705 (South Africa's Janneman Malan came next, with 509), including three centuries, all in defeat.

Balbirnie reached three figures only once, but his 102 came in the best team performance of the year, a maiden ODI victory over South Africa at Malahide, against an attack led by the fearsome pace pair of Kagiso Rabada and Anrich Nortje. Balbirnie had also made 65 in the first game, which was abandoned. In the third, Simi Singh hit a maiden century – the first in ODIs by a No. 8 – although South Africa squared the series.

There were new caps for the 21-year-old Neil Rock, who ended the year as the first-choice wicketkeeper in T20s, and William McClintock, a 24-year-old from Donemana, who slotted in as a middle-order power-hitter alongside the recalled Shane Getkate. Former captain Gary Wilson announced his retirement after 292 matches for Ireland in all formats over 15 years. He ended 2021 as interim assistant coach to Northamptonshire's David Ripley, who took temporary charge for the trip to the Americas.

Ireland's women, after 625 days without an international, had a busy and successful year. They won 12 of 17 matches, comfortably surpassing their previous best of eight from 22, in 2014. Gaby Lewis, who turned 21 in March 2022, was nominated for the ICC T20 Player of the Year award after making 325 runs, including a maiden century, against Germany. The team did not qualify for the 2022 World Cup but – now ranked tenth – will take part in the expanded World Cricket League, guaranteeing 27 ODIs over three years.

IRELAND v SOUTH AFRICA IN 2021

IAN CALLENDER

One-day internationals (3): Ireland 1 (15pts), South Africa 1 (15pts)
Twenty20 internationals (3): Ireland 0, South Africa 3

Temba Bavuma's squad flew straight to Dublin from a tour of the West Indies and, though they were spared quarantine, their whistle-stop schedule provided a potential excuse for their sluggish start to the ODI Super League: at the seventh attempt, Ireland achieved their first victory over South Africa. Thereafter, it was uphill for the home side, as the South Africans bounced back to share the points – the first game had been ruined by the weather – and then romped to a clean sweep in the T20 series.

South Africa's bowlers took only two wickets in the first 38 overs of the opening ODI, which rain curtailed 14 balls later; they fared little better in the second, as Ireland's captain, Andrew Balbirnie, scored 102 out of 290 for five. South Africa built a promising platform, but lost their last eight for 88, and Ireland won their fourth successive completed home match, having defeated Zimbabwe 3–0 in July 2019. The tourists had originally planned to rest Quinton de Kock, but felt obliged to select him for the final contest, when he scored his 15th century, in a 70-run victory.

In the T20s, it was the hosts' turn to be underprepared. While South Africa had just won a hard-fought five-match series in Grenada, Ireland were playing their first T20 in 16 months; that gap, combined with the visitors' superior bowling, resulted in three one-sided games. Each followed the same pattern: South Africa batted first, then Ireland lost early wickets, and never recovered. They were at least eight down on reaching 100 in every game and, among their batsmen, only Balbirnie totalled 50.

A fortnight before the South Africans arrived, Kevin O'Brien had announced his retirement from ODIs, after four runs in four games, to concentrate on the shorter form. But runs still proved elusive: he scored two from eight balls across the three T20s. South Africa's spinners were always on top, and their 15 wickets meant their batting did not necessarily have to fire, though David Miller was Player of the Series, scoring 36, 75 (both unbeaten) and 28.

For once, Ireland lacked a significant contribution from Paul Stirling, who reached double figures in five of the six matches, but never passed 27; he had scored only one half-century in 20 white-ball innings at Malahide. There were two recalls: George Dockrell, the left-arm spinner who had forged a new career with Leinster as a batsman, and former captain William Porterfield, who scored 63 in the first ODI, but injured a finger and did not play again.

SOUTH AFRICA TOURING PARTY

*T. Bavuma (50/20), Q. de Kock (50/20), B. C. Fortuin (50/20), B. E. Hendricks (50/20), R. R. Hendricks (50/20), H. Klaasen (50/20), G. F. Linde (50/20), K. A. Maharaj (50/20), J. N. Malan (50/20), A. K. Markram (50/20), D. A. Miller (50/20), P. W. A. Mulder (20), L. T. Ngidi (50/20), A. A. Nortje

(50/20), A. L. Phehlukwayo (50/20), D. Pretorius (50/20), K. Rabada (50/20), T. Shamsi (50/20), H. E. van der Dussen (50/20), K. Verreyne (50/20), L. B. Williams (50/20). *Coach:* M. V. Boucher.

S. S. B. Magala was originally selected, but sustained an ankle injury; B. E. Hendricks replaced him.

First one-day international   At Malahide, July 11, 2021. **No result. Ireland 195-4** (40.2 overs) (W. T. S. Porterfield 63, A. Balbirnie 65) **v ‡South Africa.** Ireland 5pts, South Africa 5pts. *The game was spoiled, but the Ireland batsmen proved they could be competitive, and South Africa's bowlers took time to adjust to the conditions. William Porterfield, restored to the Ireland line-up after being dropped in the Netherlands, showed class in making 63, his highest score since May 2019. A second-wicket partnership of 87 with Andrew Balbirnie was ended by Tabraiz Shamsi, before rain fell with Ireland 145-2 off 35; when play resumed, Kagiso Rabada dismissed Balbirnie and Harry Tector in the same over, just before the final interruption.*

Second one-day international   At Malahide, July 13, 2021. **Ireland won by 43 runs. Ireland 290-5** (50 overs) (A. Balbirnie 102, A. R. McBrine 30, H. T. Tector 79, G. H. Dockrell 45); **‡South Africa 247** (48.3 overs) (J. N. Malan 84, H. E. van der Dussen 49). Ireland 10pts. *PoM:* A. Balbirnie. *Temba Bavuma acknowledged his team had been outplayed by Ireland, who achieved their first ODI victory over South Africa. The tourists conceded 103 in the last ten overs, which Bavuma called criminal. They also missed four catches, including Tector first ball; he went on to make 79 from 68, and hit four sixes in a stand of 90 from 46 – the highest of Ireland's four fifty partnerships – with George Dockrell, who thrashed 45 from 23. Balbirnie was another beneficiary: dropped on 74, he went on to his seventh ODI hundred, and his sixth in a victory. Janneman Malan and Rassie van der Dussen added 108 for South Africa's third wicket but, with 132 needed from 17.4 overs, they stumbled. Dockrell, after 50 wicketless overs, got Malan for 84, before Andy McBrine trapped van der Dussen. In all, South Africa lost their last eight in 16 overs. Rabada was run out when Keshav Maharaj hit a high full toss to Curtis Campher at deep midwicket. Expecting a call of no-ball, he threw to the keeper, Lorcan Tucker, with Rabada – believing his partner to be out – lingering mid-pitch. When a TV replay confirmed the no-ball, the umpires ruled that the run-out stood, since the ball was not dead. Some observers raised Law 31.7 ("batsman leaving the wicket under a misapprehension"), but the South Africans had greater concerns.*

Third one-day international   At Malahide, July 16, 2021. **South Africa won by 70 runs. ‡South Africa 346-4** (50 overs) (J. N. Malan 177*, Q. de Kock 120, H. E. van der Dussen 30); **Ireland 276** (47.1 overs) (C. Campher 54, S. Singh 100*; A. L. Phehlukwayo 3-56, T. Shamsi 3-46). South Africa 10pts. *PoM:* J. N. Malan. *PoS:* J. N. Malan. *ODI debut:* L. B. Williams (South Africa). *South Africa brought in Quinton de Kock, but he was outshone by Malan, who hit 177*, his country's fourth-highest innings, including 16 fours and six sixes in 169 chanceless balls. De Kock's 120 from 91, with 11 fours and five sixes, was his 16th ODI hundred, while the partnership of 225 was South*

HIGHEST ODI SCORE BY NOs 8 TO 11

100*	S. Singh	Ireland v South Africa at Malahide	2021
95*	C. R. Woakes	England v Sri Lanka at Nottingham	2016
95*	**S. M. Curran**	**England v India at Pune**	**2020-21**
92*	A. D. Russell	West Indies v India at North Sound	2011
92	N. M. Coulter-Nile	Australia v West Indies at Nottingham	2019
86*	R. Rampaul	West Indies v India at Visakhapatnam	2011-12

Russell was batting at No. 9, Rampaul at No. 10, and the highest score by a No. 11 is 58 by Mohammad Amir for Pakistan v England at Nottingham in 2016.

Africa's fifth double-century opening stand, and the third involving de Kock. The hosts' faltering response included a wicket from Lizaad Williams's first ball in ODIs – the third South African to achieve the feat, after Martin van Jaarsveld and Monde Zondeki, both in 2002. From 92-6, Simi Singh fought back with a 91-ball 100, his first international century, and added 104 with Campher, an Ireland seventh-wicket record. Singh's last 32 runs came in 19 deliveries during a tenth-wicket stand of 47 with Craig Young; after 4,305 ODIs, it was the first time a player had scored a century batting in the bottom four.*

First Twenty20 international   At Malahide, July 19, 2021. **South Africa won by 33 runs. South Africa 165-7** (20 overs) (A. K. Markram 39; M. R. Adair 3-39); ‡**Ireland 132-9** (20 overs) (H. T. Tector 36, B. J. McCarthy 30*; T. Shamsi 4-27). *PoM:* T. Shamsi. *The first T20 between these teams was a one-sided affair. South Africa's innings was steady rather than spectacular, with a highest partnership of 36, between Miller and top-scorer Aidan Markram. Rabada hit four successive fours in the final over, from Mark Adair. Opening the bowling for South Africa, left-arm spinner George Linde saw his first ball of the tour slog-swept for six by Paul Stirling – then bowled him round his legs with his second. Shamsi spun a magic spell to take four wickets, including three in 11 balls. As in the final ODI, Ireland needed a last-wicket stand to restore some respectability in defeat. Set 166, they slumped to 88-9, before Barry McCarthy made 30* – his highest score in international cricket. His partnership of 44* with Josh Little was a tenth-wicket record for Ireland.*

Second Twenty20 international   At Belfast, July 22, 2021. **South Africa won by 42 runs.** ‡**South Africa 159-7** (20 overs) (D. A. Miller 75*, P. W. A. Mulder 36); **Ireland 117** (19.3 overs) (B. C. Fortuin 3-16, T. Shamsi 3-14). *PoM:* D. A. Miller. *South Africa clinched the series with another emphatic victory, but Ireland didn't help themselves with a poor fielding performance after a strong start. Stirling dismissed Bavuma and Malan – both slashing to short third man – with the game's second and fourth balls, and the visitors were 58-5 at halfway. The critical error came when Miller was dropped at the wicket on 19. He doubled the score with Wiaan Mulder, raised his half-century in the penultimate over, and hit four sixes in the last, from Little, to finish with 75* from 44. Needing 160, Ireland followed a familiar path, falling to a barrage of spin: Bjorn Fortuin, Shamsi and Markram had combined figures of 7-47. When Fortuin, playing his first game of the tour, took two wickets in the 15th over, Ireland were 93-8, and out of contention.*

Third Twenty20 international   At Belfast, July 24, 2021. **South Africa won by 49 runs.** ‡**South Africa 189-2** (20 overs) (T. Bavuma 72, R. R. Hendricks 69, D. A. Miller 36*); **Ireland 140-9** (20 overs). *PoM:* T. Bavuma. *PoS:* D. A. Miller. *T20I debut:* B. C. White (Ireland). *This game was played at the end of Northern Ireland's hottest week on record – the temperature routinely exceeded 30°C – and South Africa, despite making five changes, turned up the heat still further. Bavuma and Reeza Hendricks, dropped on 30 at long-on by debutant Ben White, each brought up a half-century in the 14th over, and put on 127. Bavuma's fifty was his first in this format. Miller added 36* from 17 in a daunting total of 189-2. Ireland replied with their highest score of the series – and met their heaviest defeat. Stirling and Balbirnie added 33 for the second wicket, as did McCarthy and Young for the ninth, but that was as good as it got. The gulf in class was illustrated by the innings' second halves: South Africa hit 126 for two from their last ten overs, Ireland 65 for six.*

IRELAND v ZIMBABWE IN 2021

Ian Callender

Twenty20 internationals (5): Ireland 3, Zimbabwe 2
One-day internationals (3): Ireland 1 (15pts), Zimbabwe 1 (15pts)

When Ireland won the T20 series, in which three consecutive victories – their first such run at home since their first game in 2008 – were bookended by two collapses, coach Graham Ford admitted he was alarmed by their inconsistency. His words were accurate and prophetic, as his team then blew hot and cold in the ODIs. It is a problem Ireland coaches have been trying to solve for years.

Still, there were promising signs ahead of the T20 World Cup. Kevin O'Brien, after six runs in seven international innings in 2021, returned to form with a total of 140 in the T20s, bettered only by Paul Stirling's 234, including his first century. Mark Adair took ten wickets at 5.70, despite missing the first two games with back spasms. In the ODIs, a resurgent William Porterfield and Harry Tector each scored two half-centuries, and off-spinner Andy McBrine conceded less than three an over.

Zimbabwe, owing to their suspension from ICC events, did not have the chance to qualify for the World Cup but, on this showing, would have struggled. Craig Ervine, who played two seasons for Northern Knights and several more as club professional at Lisburn, was given the captaincy, and dominated the batting in both formats, totalling 281. Blessing Muzarabani, the fastest bowler on either side, took six wickets at 16 in the ODIs, but lacked support. Brendan Taylor, meanwhile, announced his retirement from international cricket before the final ODI, recalling a 17-year career of "extreme highs and extreme lows", in which he made 9,938 runs in all formats for Zimbabwe; only the Flower brothers Andy (11,580) and Grant (10,028) had scored more.

ZIMBABWE TOURING PARTY

*C. R. Ervine, R. P. Burl, R. W. Chakabva, T. L. Chatara, L. M. Jongwe, T. S. Kamunhukamwe, W. N. Madhevere, T. R. Marumani, W. P. Masakadza, T. K. Musakanda, B. Muzarabani, D. N. Myers, R. Ngarava, M. Shumba, Sikandar Raza, B. R. M. Taylor, D. T. Tiripano, S. C. Williams. *Coach:* L. S. Rajput.

First Twenty20 international   At Clontarf, August 27. **Zimbabwe won by three runs. Zimbabwe 117-7** (20 overs) (R. W. Chakabva 47); ‡**Ireland 114-9** (20 overs) (R. P. Burl 3-22). PoM: R. Chakabva. T20I debuts: C. Campher, N. A. Rock (Ireland). *Ireland's losing run extended to four as Zimbabwe defended 117 at Clontarf, staging its first international since the square was relaid in 2019. The pitch was not to blame for the low totals, though: Zimbabwe struggled for touch and, after Regis Chakabva (47 off 28) departed in the 13th, they hit only one more four. Paul Stirling was dismissed before opening partner Kevin O'Brien for the first time in nine matches but, from 65-2 in the 11th, Ireland should have won easily. Ryan Burl dismissed George Dockrell and O'Brien with successive balls in a career-best 3-22, however, and in the last nine overs only Simi Singh scored more than singles. The last of his four boundaries came in the 18th; Ireland needed six from the 20th, but Richard Ngarava conceded just two. Only once had Zimbabwe successfully defended a lower total: 105 against West Indies (79-7) at Port-of-Spain in 2009-10.*

Second Twenty20 international   At Clontarf, August 29. **Ireland won by seven wickets.** ‡Zimbabwe 152-5 (20 overs) (M. Shumba 46*, R. P. Burl 37*; S. C. Getkate 3-20); **Ireland 153-3** (18.3 overs) (P. R. Stirling 37, K. J. O'Brien 60, G. H. Dockrell 33*). *PoM:* K. J. O'Brien. *O'Brien passed 50 for the first time in international cricket since October 2019 – a drought of 30 innings – as Ireland levelled the series with a much-improved batting display. Zimbabwe looked rusty, falling to 64-5 as Shane Getkate returned a career-best 3-20, before Milton Shumba and Burl turned the innings round with a stand of 88* off 59. The last four overs brought 49, and set Ireland a competitive 153. Stirling and O'Brien began the chase with 59 off 37; O'Brien, on 20 when Shumba dropped a return catch, cashed in for 60. Dockrell settled matters with three consecutive fours off Ngarava.*

Third Twenty20 international   At Bready, September 1. **Ireland won by 40 runs. Ireland 178-2** (20 overs) (P. R. Stirling 115*, A. Balbirnie 31); ‡Zimbabwe 138 (18.2 overs) (C. R. Ervine 33; M. R. Adair 3-11). *PoM:* P. R. Stirling. *T20I debut:* W. T. McClintock (Ireland). *With Ireland labouring at 33-1 after the powerplay, Stirling (then 24* off 26) sent a message back to the dressing-room that this was a "tough wicket". He scored 91 off his next 49, reached his century off 70, and hit eight fours and eight sixes in 115*. It was only the second century for Ireland in 104 T20 matches, after O'Brien's 124 against Hong Kong in Oman in 2019. The only disappointment for the crowd was that local hero William McClintock did not get to bat on his debut. Though Zimbabwe – whose highest successful chase was 172 – stayed ahead of their opponents' total for the first 18 overs, they were nine down by then, and two balls later Ireland had bowled out a Full Member for the first time, at the 37th attempt.*

Fourth Twenty20 international   At Bready, September 2. **Ireland won by 64 runs. Ireland 174-4** (20 overs) (P. R. Stirling 39, K. J. O'Brien 47, A. Balbirnie 36); ‡Zimbabwe 110-9 (20 overs) (M. R. Adair 4-23). *PoM:* M. R. Adair. *Another dominant win sealed the series for Ireland with a game in hand. They again passed 170, but this time it was a team effort: all six batsmen made double figures. Stirling and O'Brien put on 89 for the first wicket in ten overs (shared by six bowlers, in one-over spells), before both fell to Wellington Masakadza, whose 2-22 was Zimbabwe's highlight. The biggest cheer of the day, though, was for McClintock, who got off the mark from his first ball in international cricket. Requiring 175, Zimbabwe's batsmen were immediately under pressure as Mark Adair took three wickets in his first ten balls; when he held top-scorer Craig Ervine at long-on in the 14th, it was 74-7. He later obtained Blessing Muzarabani to return 4-23, his best figures. A last-wicket stand of 24* between Luke Jongwe and Ngarava was the highest of the innings.*

Fifth Twenty20 international   At Bready, September 4. **Zimbabwe won by five runs.** ‡Zimbabwe 124-4 (C. R. Ervine 67*; M. R. Adair 3-23); Ireland 119 (20 overs) (L. M. Jongwe 3-29, D. T. Tiripano 3-31). *PoM:* C. R. Ervine. *PoS:* P. R. Stirling. *Ervine's 67* – over half Zimbabwe's runs, and more than twice anyone else's score – was the high point of a tense match. He arrived in the second over, to face Adair's hat-trick ball, which went for two wides; though he saw the innings through, 124 was an unlikely winning total (he later admitted Zimbabwe felt they were 25–30 runs short). Even at 30-4, Ireland were in the game; Neil Rock, given a chance at No. 5, top-scored with 22 but, with 34 needed from 38, he holed out to deep square leg. With the final pair together, Craig Young hit Jongwe for six, and nine were needed from the last over – but Ngarava closed out the match again, restricting Josh Little to three. Andrew Balbirnie, the Ireland captain, called their performance "a bit of a blip".*

First one-day international   At Stormont, September 8. **Zimbabwe won by 38 runs. Zimbabwe 266-7** (50 overs) (B. R. M. Taylor 49, C. R. Ervine 64, S. C. Williams 33, Sikandar Raza 59*); ‡Ireland 228 (48.4 overs) (W. T. S. Porterfield 75, P. R. Stirling 32, H. T. Tector 50; B. Muzarabani 4-29). *Zimbabwe 10pts. PoM:* Sikandar Raza. *Zimbabwe had won only one of their six Super League games – defeating Pakistan in a super over in Rawalpindi – and doubled their points with an impressive all-round effort. The last 11 overs of each innings were in marked contrast: Zimbabwe scored 103-3 with 12 boundaries as Sikandar Raza went into overdrive; Ireland lost six for 39, of which 34 were singles. Zimbabwe ransacked the pacemen, who were hit for 192 in 27 overs; spinners Singh and Andy McBrine conceded 48 in 20. Against the new ball, Ireland went 24 deliveries without a run off the bat, but William Porterfield (75) added 64 with Stirling and 71 with Harry Tector. His dismissal, to a mistimed pull, began the collapse, in which Muzarabani took four wickets in 20 balls.*

Second one-day international   At Stormont, September 10. **No result. Ireland 282-8** (50 overs) (W. T. S. Porterfield 67, P. R. Stirling 33, A. Balbirnie 40, H. T. Tector 55, L. J. Tucker 32; R. Ngarava 3-52) v ‡Zimbabwe. *Ireland 5pts, Zimbabwe 5pts. ODI debut:* M. Shumba (Zimbabwe). *This was Ireland's second no-result of the summer – after the first ODI against South Africa at Malahide – and one which grieved them. No team had scored more than 242 (Pakistan, in 2011) in* *a successful chase at Stormont, so Ireland had every reason to back their total of 282. Porterfield put on 82 for the first wicket with Stirling, and 69 for the second with Balbirnie. When Porterfield was out in the 37th, the hosts were 153-3, but they had learned the lesson of two days prior; now they added 129 from the last 13. The 50th, bowled by Jongwe, went W1W6W14, including two run-outs, one off a wide. A cloudburst inundated the field during the interval.*

Third one-day international At Stormont, September 13. **Ireland won by seven wickets** (DLS). **Zimbabwe 131** (34 overs) (C. R. Ervine 57; J. B. Little 3-33, A. R. McBrine 3-26); ‡**Ireland 118-3** (22.2 overs) (P. R. Stirling 43, A. Balbirnie 34). *Ireland 10pts. PoM:* A. R. McBrine. *PoS:* W. T. S. Porterfield. *Brendan Taylor's final international game began with disappointment, was damp throughout, and ended in defeat. Wearing a shirt numbered 284 – his total appearances – he opened the batting and was first out, for seven, in a match reduced to 42 overs after morning rain. The blustery conditions were ideal for bowling: Little swung it around for 3-33, and McBrine let the wind help his drift to claim 3-26. More bad weather interrupted the Zimbabwe innings and, when they were all out for 131 from 34 overs, Ireland were given a DLS target of 126 from 35, which became 118 from 32 after another rain break. Out of the murk shone Stirling, whose untroubled 43 helped bring victory with nearly ten overs to spare. In levelling the series, Ireland moved fourth in the Super League – well among the qualification places – whereas Zimbabwe remained 12th, ahead of only the Netherlands.*

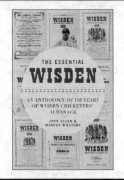

DOMESTIC CRICKET IN IRELAND IN 2021

Ian Callender

The Ireland selectors shuffled the pack in an attempt to stimulate more competitive domestic cricket. Since the interprovincial tournaments in all three formats were set up in 2013, Leinster had won 19 out of 23. So Cricket Ireland drew up a list of 48 players, and handed each of the four provincial teams a core squad of 12. Three internationals were transferred from Leinster to Munster, who had previously appeared only in the Twenty20 competition but now stepped up to contest the List A version as well. As in 2020, there were no first-class matches; with no Tests scheduled, the authorities chose to focus on white-ball cricket.

But some things never change: for the eighth successive season, **Leinster Lightning** were the 50-over champions. Still, the appointment of newly retired Ireland international Gary Wilson as head coach for **North West Warriors** sparked an improvement in their fortunes. They finished second to Leinster in the one-day cup, and won the T20 trophy for the first time since 2014 – with Leinster pushed down to third by **Northern Knights**.

The 50-over competition was effectively settled when Leinster and North West met for the second time, at Eglinton in May. North West set a target of 232, which Leinster passed with seven balls to spare: Ireland captain Andrew Balbirnie made 85 not out and George Dockrell 67, his third successive half-century in the competition. He had earlier hit a maiden hundred, against Northern, and was the leading run-scorer with 364 at 121, while Balbirnie averaged 109. Leinster's Barry McCarthy was the leading bowler with 17 at 12, including six for 39 against Munster, a tournament record.

The new selection policy did make **Munster Reds** more competitive, though they won only four of 12 completed matches across both formats. Murray Commins – son of South African Test player John – scored 352 one-day runs for Munster, and qualified for Ireland by residency in January 2022; Josh Manley, a South African-born Irish-passport holder, was second only to McCarthy, with 13 wickets.

In the T20 tournament, Munster relied heavily on Matt Ford (son of Graham, who stood down as Ireland head coach in November) and P. J. Moor, the Zimbabwean wicketkeeper. They were the only two to reach 200 runs for any side, with Moor's match-winning 58-ball 95 not out against Leinster the outstanding innings. Available to play for Ireland in late 2022, he could put pressure on current wicketkeepers Lorcan Tucker and Neil Rock. As in the longer format, the T20 decider took place between North West and Leinster, though on neutral ground, at Comber. Leinster fielded an entirely home-grown side, but missed internationals Balbirnie, McCarthy and Simi Singh; North West swept past a target of 114 inside 14 overs. Their leading scorer was William Porterfield (who no longer plays T20 internationals) with 190, and their best bowler Craig Young, with 12 wickets – though he finished second to Northern leg-spinner Ben White (17), who made his international debut against South Africa in July.

INTERPROVINCIAL CUP IN 2021

50-over league

	P	W	L	NR/A	Bonus	Pts	NRR
Leinster.........	6	4	1	1	2	20	0.66
North West......	6	3	2	1	1	15	0.32
Northern........	6	1	3	2	0	8	−0.56
Munster.........	6	1	3	2	0	8	−0.67

INTERPROVINCIAL TROPHY IN 2021

20-over league

	P	W	L	A	Bonus	Pts	NRR
North West	9	5	3	1	3	25	0.63
Northern	9	4	3	2	1	21	−0.53
Leinster.	9	3	4	2	2	18	0.20
Munster.	9	3	5	1	1	15	−0.41

Other domestic honours
Irish T20 Cup **Brigade**. Leinster League **Merrion**. Leinster Cup **Merrion**. Munster League **Cork County**. Munster T20 **Cork Harlequins**. Northern League **Waringstown**. Northern Cup **CIYMS**. Northern T20 **Carrickfergus**. North West League **Bready**. North West Cup **Brigade**. North West T20 **Brigade**.

INTERPROVINCIAL CHAMPIONS

2013	Leinster	2016	Leinster	2019	Leinster
2014	Leinster	2017	Leinster	2020	*No competition*
2015	Leinster	2018	North West	2021	*No competition*

The Interprovincial Championship was not first-class until 2017.

Leinster have won the title 6 times, North West 1.

NEW ZEALAND CRICKET IN 2021

Of mace and men

ANDREW ALDERSON

Fans in New Zealand have seldom experienced such euphoria: at 5.35am on June 24, Ross Taylor whipped Mohammed Shami off his pads to the square-leg boundary at Southampton, to secure an eight-wicket victory over India, and the inaugural World Test Championship mace. Back home, the team achieved instant immortality. The women's World Cup and men's Champions Trophy in 2000 had both resonated, but victory at the Rose Bowl came in what is touted as the ultimate form of the game.

Workplaces offered anecdotal evidence of the passion and support on show. Grey-partitioned cubicles became pop-up confessional booths to disclose nocturnal activities across the six nights of the final. The goodwill fostered by Kane Williamson's team was difficult to calculate, but selling cricket to the

NEW ZEALAND IN 2021

	Played	Won	Lost	Drawn/No result
Tests	6	3	1	2
One-day internationals	3	3	–	–
Twenty20 internationals	23	13	10	–

DECEMBER — JANUARY	2 Tests and 3 T20Is (h) v Pakistan	(see *Wisden 2021*, page 714)
FEBRUARY — MARCH	5 T20Is (h) v Australia	(page 958)
MARCH — APRIL	3 ODIs and 3 T20Is (h) v Bangladesh	(page 920)
MAY		
JUNE	2 Tests (a) v England	(page 342)
	World Test Championship final (in England) v India	(page 823)
JULY		
AUGUST		
SEPTEMBER	5 T20Is (a) v Bangladesh	(page 920)
OCTOBER — NOVEMBER	T20 World Cup in the UAE	(page 830)
NOVEMBER — DECEMBER	2 Tests and 3 T20Is (a) v India	(page 934)

For a review of New Zealand domestic cricket from the 2020-21 season, see page 963.

next generation should be a doddle. Even Sir Richard Hadlee declared this side "the best in our history". The defence rests, your honour.

Fortunately the triumph came before the Delta strain caused a Covid lockdown in August. The mace quarantined back in New Zealand with B-J. Watling, who retired after the game, and it was paraded from Tim Southee's Northland family farm to Invercargill in the south. Watling finished his 75-Test career with 265 wicketkeeping dismissals, the most by a New Zealander. He could also weld himself to the crease, often in a crisis, finishing with eight centuries and an average of 37. Watling shared in record sixth-wicket partnerships against five of the nine nations he played.

Other individual and team highlights masked what was sometimes a melancholic year in the grasp of Covid. Notably, in December, slow left-armer Ajaz Patel became the third bowler to take ten wickets in a Test innings, against India in Mumbai, the city of his birth. After Rachin Ravindra clasped a steepler at mid-on to complete the set, *The New Zealand Herald* ran the headline "One for the Ajaz". Patel's match figures of 14 for 225 were the best of any visiting player in India, and he was only the second New Zealander to take a first-class ten-for, after Canterbury's Albert Moss, on debut against Wellington in December 1889. But Patel was back on the field later in the day, after New Zealand were shredded for 62, the lowest Test total in India. A subsequent 372-run defeat thwarted hopes of a first series win in 12 attempts there, and ended a national-record run of ten matches without defeat.

Kyle Jamieson, though, continued his stellar start with the ball. He reached 50 wickets in his ninth Test – only seven had got there more quickly – including seven for 61 in the WTC final, where he was Player of the Match. Not long before that, Devon Conway had become the first man to score a double-century on Test debut in England, with a round 200 at Lord's. His overall contribution was underlined by averages of more than 50 in each format by the end of the year. Southee, who turned 33, married consistency to adaptability with 20 wickets at 20 in four Tests, and 24 at 19 in T20s.

Apart from that winning boundary in the WTC final, Taylor had a quiet year by his standards, the only other innings of note an important 80 at Edgbaston to help swing the Second Test New Zealand's way, and set up a first series win in England since 1999. Aged 37, he announced his retirement early in 2022, and bowed out by taking the final wicket as Bangladesh – after a stunning victory at Mount Maunganui – were crushed in Christchurch. He finished with 7,683 runs in Tests, 8,581 in ODIs, and 1,909 in T20s, and was the first to play 100 international matches in all three formats. His 290 at Perth in 2015-16 remains the highest Test score by a visiting batsman in Australia.

In the unfamiliar role of opener in Abu Dhabi in November, Daryl Mitchell guided New Zealand to their first T20 World Cup final with 72 in 47 balls, as they chased down England's 166; a devastating late burst from Jimmy Neesham proved equally crucial, as the task of scoring 57 from the last four overs was ticked off with six balls to spare. In the final, though, a side lacking Conway – he had broken a finger slapping his bat after getting out in the semi – went down to Australia, despite Williamson's 48-ball 85.

Security issues and the pandemic, however, cast a pall over the year. Any vaccine-driven respite to the airport/hotel/ground lifestyle of the modern

Philip Brown, Popperfoto/Getty Images

Nearly men no more: New Zealand celebrate the World Test Championship in Southampton.

professional was minimal. Travel bubbles remained in place, and player welfare clashed with commercial imperatives. Trent Boult was a good example: a man with a young family, he opted out of the Tests in India to return home after playing in the rejigged IPL, the T20 World Cup and the T20 series in India. Before that, a second-string side, none of whom went to the subsequent World Cup, had been sent to Bangladesh, and lost a T20 series 3–2.

The year was further compromised by the cancellation of New Zealand's first tour of Pakistan in 18 years, after government advice of a "specific, credible threat", according to NZC's chief executive David White. The Pakistan board were outraged, but New Zealand's prime minister, Jacinda Ardern, backed the move. She reported a couple of "pretty brief" conversations with her Pakistan counterpart, the World Cup-winning captain Imran Khan, who wanted to "come to an understanding how the decision had been made".

The women's team struggled home and away against England and Australia, the respective 50- and 20-over world champions. New Zealand won two of eight T20s and two of 11 ODIs; captain Sophie Devine and all-rounder Amelia Kerr both stepped away temporarily to nurture their mental health.

In August, came the news that former Test all-rounder Chris Cairns had undergone emergency surgery in Sydney at the age of 51 to combat a life-threatening heart condition. He subsequently suffered a stroke, resulting in paralysis, but embarked on rehabilitation in the hope of walking again. Then, in February, he was diagnosed with bowel cancer.

For fans at home, Spark Sport – the new rights-holding broadcaster – screened popular highlights packages. In another key development, NZC embraced the power of social media: the number of YouTube subscribers for domestic matches rocketed from fewer than 40,000 in 2019-20 to over a million in 2020-21. A further bouquet was reserved for the board's financial wizardry in turning a budgeted $NZ3.5m loss into a net surplus of $160,000 – a minor miracle considering the uncertainty of lockdowns, isolation requirements, travel restrictions and crowd limitations.

NEW ZEALAND v AUSTRALIA IN 2020-21

Mark Geenty

Twenty20 internationals (5): New Zealand 3, Australia 2

In a snapshot of modern cricketing times, and Australia's enviable depth, their selectors announced two separate tour squads in late January, totalling 37 players: one for three Tests in South Africa, the other for five Twenty20s in New Zealand. Only Aaron Finch's T20 side boarded their plane, however, after Cricket Australia abandoned the South African tour amid Covid concerns, alleging "an unacceptable level of health and safety risk to our players, support staff and the community".

Despite the cancellation, they despatched an unchanged squad across the Tasman Sea, for a series postponed a year earlier as the pandemic took hold. The likes of David Warner, Steve Smith, Pat Cummins and Mitchell Starc – as well as head coach Justin Langer – stayed at home, while Langer's assistant, Andrew McDonald, took charge of a party including three uncapped players: top-order batsman Josh Philippe, leg-spinner Tanveer Sangha and fast bowler Riley Meredith.

The New Zealand government's coronavirus alert levels and border controls ensured this was no ordinary next-door visit. Australia underwent 14 days of managed isolation at a Christchurch hotel and training venue, which ended on the eve of the first match, and caught a charter flight out of Wellington immediately after the last.

After sell-outs at Christchurch and Dunedin, a local outbreak forced Auckland to lock down, and the last two games were moved away from Eden Park and Mount Maunganui. That meant three in a row on the drop-in pitch at Wellington's Sky Stadium. Two were played behind closed doors, which cost New Zealand Cricket an estimated $NZ1.4m.

It was an entertaining, seesawing series: New Zealand moved into a 2–0 lead, before Australia fought back to make the last a decider, which was won by the hosts. Much interest centred on Finch and New Zealand's Martin Guptill. Both had suffered a slump in form, which extended into the opening game, but they recovered to finish as the leading run-scorers. Guptill collected two match awards and 218 runs, at a strike-rate of 159; Finch scored 197 at 134, including an unbeaten 79 in the fourth game.

Spin was also significant: New Zealand leg-spinner Ish Sodhi was Player of the Series for 13 wickets at 12, ahead of Australia's left-armer Ashton Agar, who mopped up in the third match with six for 30. Adam Zampa's presence denied Sangha a debut, but Meredith made an instant impression with his 150kph pace, and twice trapped New Zealand's captain Kane Williamson.

AUSTRALIAN TOURING PARTY

*A. J. Finch, A. C. Agar, J. P. Behrendorff, B. R. McDermott, M. R. Marsh, G. J. Maxwell, R. P. Meredith, J. R. Philippe, J. A. Richardson, K. W. Richardson, D. R. Sams, T. Sangha, D. J. M. Short, M. P. Stoinis, A. J. Turner, A. J. Tye, M. S. Wade, A. Zampa. *Coach*: A. B. McDonald.

First Twenty20 international   At Christchurch, February 22, 2021 (floodlit). **New Zealand won by 53 runs. New Zealand 184-5** (20 overs) (D. P. Conway 99*, G. D. Phillips 30); ‡**Australia 131** (17.3 overs) (M. R. Marsh 45; I. S. Sodhi 4-28). *PoM:* D. P. Conway. *T20I debut:* J. R. Philippe (Australia). *Hagley Oval's first floodlit international was also illuminated by Devon Conway, the South African-born batter playing his fifth innings for New Zealand. With a mixture of finesse, strokeplay and power, he steered them from 19-3 to 184-5. A crowd of 9,093 were on their feet as he faced Kane Richardson for the final delivery: a six and four had just carried him to 98 off 58 balls, but he missed a maiden international hundred when he hit a full toss to deep point for a single. Australia were never in the chase: Tim Southee and Trent Boult found sharp swing to destroy the top order. When Glenn Maxwell edged Southee, they were 19-4, and had no Conway to rescue them; Ish Sodhi picked up his best international return.*

Second Twenty20 international   At Dunedin (University Oval), February 25, 2021. **New Zealand won by four runs. New Zealand 219-7** (20 overs) (M. J. Guptill 97, K. S. Williamson 53, J. D. S. Neesham 45*; K. W. Richardson 3-43); ‡**Australia 215-8** (20 overs) (J. R. Philippe 45, M. P. Stoinis 78, D. R. Sams 41; M. J. Santner 4-31). *PoM:* M. J. Guptill. *After 11 T20I innings without a fifty, Martin Guptill boomed Jhye Richardson's first delivery over long-off, and was away. He was back to his old self in a spectacular 50-ball 97, including eight sixes, which overshadowed an effortless 53 off 35 from Kane Williamson. By the time Jimmy Neesham whipped six more sixes, including a reverse lap over third man, New Zealand had clouted 18, and amassed 219-7. But on the small University Oval no total is completely safe, especially against the power of Marcus Stoinis. When he arrived at 87-3, Australia needed 133 off 59, and they nearly got there: he and Daniel Sams blasted 92 off 36, and were 15 short of victory when Neesham was called up to bowl his only over. He removed Sams, then Stoinis – for 78 off 37 – with low full tosses, to put New Zealand 2–0 up.*

Third Twenty20 international   At Wellington (Sky Stadium), March 3, 2021 (floodlit). **Australia won by 64 runs. Australia 208-4** (20 overs) (A. J. Finch 69, J. R. Philippe 43, G. J. Maxwell 70); ‡**New Zealand 144** (17.1 overs) (M. J. Guptill 43, D. P. Conway 38; A. C. Agar 6-30). *PoM:* A. C. Agar. *T20I debut:* R. P. Meredith (Australia). *The key moment came in the first over, when Chris Gaffaney turned down Southee's theatrical lbw appeal against Aaron Finch; DRS had it clipping leg stump. The reprieve launched Finch's revival after a poor run in the BBL: he soon raised his half-century with a switch hit for six, en route to 69 off 44. Maxwell targeted the short boundaries, and one of the five sixes in his 31-ball 70 punched a hole in a plastic seat – empty, since there were no spectators. Chasing 209, New Zealand were rocked when debutant Riley Meredith trapped Williamson shuffling across, before Ashton Agar spun out Glenn Phillips, Conway and Neesham in five balls. He became the fourth to snare six in a T20 international.*

Fourth Twenty20 international   At Wellington (Sky Stadium), March 5, 2021 (floodlit). **Australia won by 50 runs. ‡Australia 156-6** (20 overs) (A. J. Finch 79*; I. S. Sodhi 3-32); **New Zealand 106** (18.5 overs) (K. A. Jamieson 30; K. W. Richardson 3-19). *PoM:* A. J. Finch. *With the latest Covid restrictions prompting New Zealand Cricket to stage six men's and women's T20Is at Wellington in five days, the drop-in pitch was bound to play tricks at some stage. Spinners' eyes lit up from the third over, when Mitchell Santner found dramatic turn and bounce, and New Zealand were sensing a series-clinching victory when Australia entered the 20th on 130-6, with Finch a relatively pedestrian 53 off 49. But he smote four sixes off Kyle Jamieson to lift Australia to 156 – probably par in these conditions. Needing under eight an over, but mistrusting the pitch, the New Zealanders went into their shells, and were later criticised by coach Gary Stead. Agar (24–17–11–2) set the tone, and fellow spinners Maxwell and Adam Zampa picked up two apiece. Only Jamieson's 30 off 18 helped them stagger past 100, as Australia levelled the series.*

Fifth Twenty20 international   At Wellington (Sky Stadium), March 7, 2021. **New Zealand won by seven wickets. ‡Australia 142-8** (20 overs) (A. J. Finch 36, M. S. Wade 44; I. S. Sodhi 3-24); **New Zealand 143-3** (15.3 overs) (D. P. Conway 36, M. J. Guptill 71, G. D. Phillips 34*). *PoM:* M. J. Guptill. *PoS:* I. S. Sodhi. *The shootout was scheduled at high noon, to allow the Australians to fly home later in the day. The turnstiles at the Cake Tin were finally unlocked, and a small crowd of 7,548 saw Guptill clinch the series with 71 off 46 balls; for the third time in his career, he struck a six on to the stadium roof at deep midwicket. He put on 106 for the 12th over with Conway, promoted to open in place of Tim Seifert, and hit Zampa's leg-spin for 64066 in the ninth. Though Guptill fell in sight of victory, Phillips finished the job with 27 deliveries to spare by clubbing two more sixes off Zampa. Earlier, New Zealand had bowled and fielded superbly. Sodhi picked up three, Boult and Santner were outstanding, and Phillips and Mark Chapman bowled some part-time spin on the ageing pitch. Only Matthew Wade reached 40 in Australia's sub-par 142.*

NEW ZEALAND v BANGLADESH IN 2020-21

Andrew Alderson

One-day internationals (3): New Zealand 3, Bangladesh 0
Twenty20 internationals (3): New Zealand 3, Bangladesh 0

This series was submerged beneath a number of higher-profile sporting events. Emirates Team New Zealand – a sailing syndicate with a patriotic magnetism – retained the America's Cup on Auckland's Waitemata Harbour; Super Rugby rumbled on; and the NZ Warriors took part in Australia's rugby league competition. And yet Bangladesh's visit should have caught the public eye: it was the only 50-over outing of the southern summer for New Zealand's World Cup runners-up, although injuries had deprived them of Kane Williamson (elbow), Ross Taylor (hamstring) and strike bowler Lockie Ferguson (back).

The snag was that Bangladesh's reputation preceded them: they had lost all 26 of their previous internationals in New Zealand (ignoring a World Cup victory over Scotland), and that sorry run was extended to 32, even after the home side rested their IPL players from the T20 series. It allowed new talent to emerge: Wellington opener Finn Allen came in after 512 runs at a strike-rate of 194 in the Super Smash, Will Young stepped up after years of service for Central Districts, and Wellington's Devon Conway took over the wicketkeeping gloves for the T20s, showcasing another skill in his seamless transition to the international ranks. He had earlier hit his maiden ODI hundred, as did Daryl Mitchell. Weaknesses were few, and New Zealand completed their sixth and seventh series wins of an unprecedented home season.

Bangladesh fielded a familiar-looking side, but could make little impression on a New Zealand juggernaut hardened by close encounters. The influence of former New Zealand captain Daniel Vettori, in a mentoring role with the visiting spinners, was negligible. The Bangladeshis endured 14 days of isolation in Christchurch with restricted training opportunities, but Tamim Iqbal, who captained in the 50-over matches before missing the T20s, praised their quarantine treatment. He also reiterated his respect for New Zealanders in general after the way they had embraced his side on their previous visit, in March 2019, when they missed being caught up in the Christchurch terror attack by a matter of minutes.

BANGLADESH TOURING PARTY

*Tamim Iqbal (50), Afif Hossain (50/20), Al-Amin Hossain (50/20), Hasan Mahmud (50/20), Liton Das (50/20), Mahmudullah (50/20), Mehedi Hasan jnr (50/20), Mehedi Hasan snr (50/20), Mithun Ali (50/20), Mohammad Naim (50/20), Mohammad Saifuddin (50/20), Mosaddek Hossain (50/20), Mushfiqur Rahim (50), Mustafizur Rahman (50/20), Nasum Ahmed (50/20), Nazmul Hossain (50/20), Rubel Hossain (50/20), Shoriful Islam (50/20), Soumya Sarkar (50/20), Taskin Ahmed (50/20). *Coach:* R. C. Domingo.

Tamim Iqbal was unavailable for the T20 series for personal reasons; Mahmudullah captained instead. Mushfiqur Rahim missed the T20s after a finger injury in the third ODI.

First one-day international   At Dunedin (University Oval), March 20, 2021. **New Zealand won by eight wickets. Bangladesh 131** (41.5 overs) (T. A. Boult 4-27); ‡**New Zealand 132-2** (21.2 overs) (M. J. Guptill 38, H. M. Nicholls 49*). *New Zealand 10pts. PoM:* T. A. Boult. *ODI debuts:* D. P. Conway, D. J. Mitchell, W. A. Young (New Zealand); Mehedi Hasan snr (Bangladesh). *The first scoring shot was an upper-cut six by Tamim Iqbal, but after that Bangladesh disappointed a student-stacked University Oval crowd by capsizing for 131 – including only eight fours and two more sixes, which New Zealand's openers exceeded by themselves. Fortunately for the spectators, the home side offered a stream of fielding highlights: Martin Guptill, Mitchell Santner and Henry Nicholls all snapped up sharp catches, while Jimmy Neesham's fingertips turned Mahmudullah's straight-drive into the run-out of Mithun Ali. Trent Boult's four wickets bookended the innings, and he was well supported. Guptill kept the crowd entertained, pinging three fours and four sixes in a 19-ball 38, which allowed his opening partner Nicholls to steer the chase with 49* from 53. The modest target was overhauled with 28.4 overs to spare, a result welcomed by publicans and restaurateurs as the crowd swept up Union Street East earlier than expected.*

Second one-day international   At Christchurch, March 23, 2021 (day/night). **New Zealand won by five wickets. Bangladesh 271-6** (50 overs) (Tamim Iqbal 78, Soumya Sarkar 32, Mushfiqur Rahim 34, Mithun Ali 73*); ‡**New Zealand 275-5** (48.2 overs) (D. P. Conway 72, T. W. M. Latham 110*, J. D. S. Neesham 30). *New Zealand 10pts. PoM:* T. W. M. Latham. *Bangladesh fared much better, posting a competitive target, but stand-in captain Tom Latham's 110* – his fifth ODI century – led New Zealand home. The key was his fourth-wicket partnership of 113 with Devon Conway, after they were wobbling at 53-3. Conway was eventually run out with 106 still needed from 99 balls, but Latham was helped by Neesham and Daryl Mitchell (12* from six), and some butterfingered fielding. Earlier, Tamim has knuckled down for 78 from 108, and the innings was spiced up by Mithun's inventive 57-ball 73*. New Zealand's win was laced with petulance: Kyle Jamieson was fined 15% of his match fee for dissent after TV umpire Wayne Knights disallowed a return catch off Tamim. The Laws say a player must have complete control over the ball, but Jamieson had grazed it along the ground. Next over, Neesham threw at the stumps in his follow-through and hit Tamim on the arm; his quick apology failed to convince the batsman, who remonstrated with the umpire while being treated by the physio.*

Third one-day international   At Wellington (Basin Reserve), March 26, 2021. **New Zealand won by 164 runs.** ‡**New Zealand 318-6** (50 overs) (D. P. Conway 126, D. J. Mitchell 100*, Rubel Hossain 3-70); **Bangladesh 154** (42.4 overs) (Mahmudullah 76*; M. J. Henry 4-27, J. D. S. Neesham 5-27). *New Zealand 10pts. PoM:* D. P. Conway. *PoS:* D. P. Conway. *A fifth-wicket partnership of 159 in 24 overs between Conway and Mitchell, who both made maiden ODI centuries, set up a total Bangladesh never threatened. Conway's still head enhanced his reputation as a poster boy for NZ's domestic nursery; he finished with 126 from 110 balls, while Mitchell's blend of hand speed and brute strength brought him 100* from 92. He scampered the two required for his hundred from the final delivery, but was lucky to get there, as Mushfiqur Rahim fumbled the return. The pressure of the chase then brought a lolly scramble for wickets: Neesham benefited with career-best ODI figures, after Matt Henry scalped the top three. The fielding highlight came from Boult, who dived one-handed near the third-man boundary to catch Liton Das, leaving Bangladesh 26-3. Mahmudullah dug in for 76* from 73 balls, with four defiant sixes, but New Zealand swept the series 3–0.*

First Twenty20 international   At Hamilton, March 28, 2021. **New Zealand won by 66 runs.** ‡**New Zealand 210-3** (20 overs) (M. J. Guptill 35, D. P. Conway 92*, W. A. Young 53); **Bangladesh 144-8** (20 overs) (Afif Hossain 45, Mohammad Saifuddin 34*; I. S. Sodhi 4-28). *PoM:* D. P. Conway. *T20I debuts:* F. H. Allen, W. A. Young (New Zealand); Nasum Ahmed, Shoriful Islam (Bangladesh). *Conway's dominance continued with 92* from 52 balls. He had a stroke of luck in the 15th over, slog-sweeping the debutant slow left-armer Nasum Ahmed to deep backward square, where Shoriful Islam's catch was ruled a six as no daylight could be discerned between boot and rope; it contributed to a sorrowful debut for Shoriful, whose four overs of left-arm seam had disappeared for 50. Will Young, in his first T20 international, gave the leg side preferential treatment in his 30-ball 53, but fellow debutant Finn Allen was bowled by the first ball of his international career, from Nasum. Bangladesh struggled after the introduction of leg-spinner Ish Sodhi for the sixth over: he dismantled the middle order with four wickets in eight balls, and equalled his format-best figures. At 59-6 after eight, the visitors were sunk.*

Second Twenty20 international   At Napier, March 30, 2021 (floodlit). **New Zealand won by 28 runs** (DLS). **New Zealand 173-5** (17.5 overs) (G. D. Phillips 58*, D. J. Mitchell 34*); ‡**Bangladesh 142-7** (16 overs) (Mohammad Naim 38, Soumya Sarkar 51). PoM: G. D. Phillips. *On a ground where the sun has stopped play and the super-sopper tractor been known to churn up the field, there was another threat to Napier's credibility – a blind DLS chase. After a shower, Bangladesh thought they needed 148 from 16 overs. But, at 12-0 after nine balls, match referee Jeff Crowe called a halt for five minutes, then said the target was 171 (originally announced as 170, to add further confusion). At 94-1 after ten, Bangladesh were in with a shout: Soumya Sarkar crashed 51 from 27, as the bowlers – including Adam Milne, in his first international since November 2018 – struggled to grip the ball. But the rate kept going up, before three wickets in five deliveries left Bangladesh reeling at 126-6, with only 11 left. Earlier, Allen had got off the mark in international cricket with a reverse-swept boundary, before Glenn Phillips used the depth of the crease in his 31-ball 58*. Crowe apologised to the tourists after the match, but skipper Mahmudullah was philosophical: "There was some confusion, and the DLS kept changing, but that can happen." Neesham, however, was embarrassed: "How is it possible to start a run-chase without knowing what you're chasing? Crazy stuff."*

Third Twenty20 international   At Auckland, April 1, 2021 (floodlit). **New Zealand won by 65 runs. New Zealand 141-4** (10 overs) (M. J. Guptill 44, F. H. Allen 71); ‡**Bangladesh 76** (9.3 overs) (T. G. Southee 3-15, T. D. Astle 4-13). *PoM*: F. H. Allen. *PoS*: G. D. Phillips. *If Allen had not smashed 71 from 29 balls, peppering the arc from long-off to square leg, the Eden Park groundstaff would have been contenders for the match award: helped by an improved drainage system, they remedied the soggy surface within minutes after heavy rain. A few dogged patrons remained for what became a ten-over contest, and were treated to fireworks from Guptill and Allen, who hit 85 from the first 34 balls; Bangladesh dropped four catches. Slogging was inevitable in pursuit of 142, and Bangladesh were skittled for 76. Leg-spinner Todd Astle, in his first T20I for more than 18 months, collected 4-13 from his two overs; his googly was bamboozling, and he varied his pace. Wicketkeeper Conway also caught the eye with a sharp stumping of Afif Hossain. New Zealand took their record against Bangladesh in 32 matches at home to 32–0 – seven T20Is, 16 ODIs and nine Tests.*

DOMESTIC CRICKET IN NEW ZEALAND IN 2020-21

Mark Geenty

The last time Peter Fulton was involved with Canterbury, in 2016-17, they won the four-day Plunket Shield and the 50-over Ford Trophy in his final season as a player. On his return as head coach in July 2020, after a short stint working with New Zealand's international batsmen, they repeated the double, and were tantalisingly close to an unprecedented treble, only for Wellington to snatch victory in the Super Smash final.

Canterbury secured their 20th Plunket Shield by a 40-point margin from Northern Districts, over eight rounds. Led by all-rounder Cole McConchie, they set off with back-to-back wins over defending champions Wellington, and their lively crop of seamers had given them a telling advantage by early November. Will Williams, a qualified flight instructor, sent stumps, bails and fielders in the cordon tumbling with his high, front-on action. He was the Shield's leading wicket-taker, with 31 at 17, including 12 in the victories over Wellington. Fraser Sheat and Ed Nuttall were also in the top eight, international Matt Henry made his presence felt in three matches, and all-rounder Daryl Mitchell proved the buy of the season. After eight years with Northern Districts, he was lured south, and in five games combined 17 wickets at 17 with 288 runs at 48.

Northern Districts got plenty of runs out of Joe Carter, whose 590 at 53 made him the tournament's top scorer, and former Test opener Jeet Raval (547), but missed Colin de Grandhomme, nursing an ankle injury, and had no one in the top 11 wicket-takers. **Otago** were a close third, with Hamish Rutherford (588) and Nick Kelly (579) just behind Carter. Left-arm wrist-spinner Michael Rippon was the Shield's leading slow bowler with 22, and also scored 497 runs. Seamer Michael Rae, who finished two wickets behind Williams, collected a hat-trick against Central Districts – remarkably, all three caught by Dale Phillips at short leg.

It was the season's third hat-trick, after two for **Auckland**: Kyle Jamieson's devastating swing snared one in their second match, also against Central Districts, followed in March by left-arm spinner Louis Delport as Northern Districts chased quick runs. In a hefty 232-run partnership against Wellington, Will and Robbie O'Donnell became the first brothers to score centuries in the same Auckland innings since Nessie and Cyril Snedden against Hawke's Bay in 1920-21 – and Will got another in the second innings. Like Otago and Auckland, **Central Districts** won twice, but **Wellington** never got going, and ended without a win. Bowling firepower was the issue, though there were 560 runs from captain Michael Bracewell (including three centuries against Auckland) and 456 from Devon Conway in his five appearances.

The Ford Trophy, coinciding with tours by West Indies and Pakistan, provided the sternest examination of depth: Tests and New Zealand A matches stretched the country's pool of 116 male professionals. Again, Canterbury and Northern Districts rose to the top in a quirky format, each pair of teams playing twice in three days at the same venue to save travel and accommodation costs post-Covid.

Canterbury's seven wins gave them a short cut to the final – 20 wickets meant Williams led the one-day wicket-takers, too – and Northern Districts overwhelmed third-placed Wellington in the play-off, where Henry Cooper's unbeaten 146 led them to 351, despite rain cutting the game to 42 overs a side. But Canterbury won the final at a canter. They benefited from a glut of T20 internationals in March, usually reserved for Test cricket, which enabled them to put out a daunting line-up, including Test batter Henry Nicholls, who scored 127 not out, while Ken McClure supplied the fireworks. He scored 480 at 68 in all, second only to Auckland's Will O'Donnell, who made 537 at 53.

At the season's end, the South African Rob Walter was appointed Central Districts' head coach after five years with Otago; their assistant coach, former Zimbabwe batsman Dion Ebrahim, took Walter's old job.

FIRST-CLASS AVERAGES IN 2020-21

BATTING (350 runs)

		M	I	NO	R	HS	100	Avge	Ct/St
1	K. S. Williamson (*New Zealand*)	3	4	0	639	251	3	159.75	1
2	W. T. O'Donnell (*Auckland*)	4	7	2	375	137*	2	75.00	3
3	†H. M. Nicholls (*Canterbury/New Zealand*)	7	9	0	634	174	2	70.44	7
4	C. D. Fletcher (*Canterbury/NZ A*)	10	14	5	586	157	2	65.11	33/3
5	R. R. O'Donnell (*Auckland*)	7	11	2	546	142	3	60.66	3
6	†L. J. Carter (*Canterbury*)	7	8	1	403	169	1	57.57	3
7	D. J. Mitchell (*Canterbury/New Zealand*)	8	9	1	441	103	2	55.12	14
8	†D. P. Conway (*Wellington*)	5	9	0	456	157	1	50.66	4
9	W. A. Young (*Central Dist/NZ A/NZ*)	7	10	2	393	133	2	49.12	4
10	†T. W. M. Latham (*Canterbury/NZ*)	9	12	0	568	106	1	47.33	16
11	†M. S. Chapman (*Auckland/NZ A*)	6	10	1	424	95	0	47.11	4
12	†J. A. Raval (*Northern Districts*)	8	13	1	547	161*	1	45.58	10
13	N. F. Kelly (*Otago*)	8	15	2	579	94	0	44.53	5
14	J. F. Carter (*Northern Districts/NZ A*)	11	17	2	657	146*	1	43.80	11
15	G. D. Phillips (*Auckland/New Zealand A*)	8	13	0	548	136	1	42.15	8
16	D. N. Phillips (*Otago*)	6	11	1	419	149	1	41.90	13
17	†M. G. Bracewell (*Wellington/NZ A*)	10	18	0	725	142	4	40.27	9
18	†H. D. Rutherford (*Otago*)	8	15	0	588	111	1	39.20	4
19	D. Cleaver (*Central Districts/NZ A*)	9	14	1	505	99	0	38.84	24
20	M. J. G. Rippon (*Otago/New Zealand A*)	9	16	3	504	106	1	38.76	6
21	†R. Ravindra (*Wellington/New Zealand A*)	9	15	1	536	144*	2	38.28	6
22	C. E. McConchie (*Canterbury/NZ A*)	10	13	2	420	124*	1	38.18	4
23	K. J. McClure (*Canterbury/NZ A*)	10	15	2	433	165	1	33.30	12
24	T. A. Blundell (*Wellington/New Zealand*)	12	19	1	558	113	3	31.00	10
25	G. R. Hay (*Central Districts*)	7	13	0	395	93	0	30.38	5
26	B-J. Watling (*Northern Districts/NZ*)	10	16	2	400	77	0	28.57	29
27	H. R. Cooper (*Northern Districts/NZ A*)	10	16	0	426	85	0	26.62	7

BOWLING (15 wickets)

		Style	O	M	R	W	BB	5I	Avge
1	K. A. Jamieson (*Auckland/NZ*)	RFM	230.1	77	548	47	6-48	6	11.65
2	W. S. A. Williams (*Canterbury*)	RM	275.5	99	528	31	5-26	2	17.03
3	S. B. Davey (*Canterbury*)	RM	113.1	34	279	15	5-19	1	18.60
4	S. H. A. Rance (*Central Districts*)	RM	112.1	18	339	18	5-64	1	18.83
5	D. J. Mitchell (*Canterbury/NZ*)	RM	135.4	34	341	18	5-44	1	18.94
6	J. A. Duffy (*Otago/New Zealand A*)	RFM	211	58	564	28	4-47	0	20.14
7	T. G. Southee (*Northern Districts/NZ*)	RFM	247.4	64	669	32	5-32	2	20.90
8	F. W. Sheat (*Canterbury*)	RM	203.3	57	565	27	5-25	2	20.92
9	M. J. Henry (*Canterbury/NZ A/NZ*)	RFM	203.5	58	477	21	6-53	1	22.71
10	D. A. J. Bracewell (*Central Dist/NZ A*)	RFM	210	44	569	24	6-42	1	23.70
11	N. G. Smith (*Otago/New Zealand A*)	RFM	160	49	393	16	3-29	0	24.56
12	N. Wagner (*Northern Districts/NZ*)	LFM	278	60	767	30	4-58	0	25.56
13	E. J. Nuttall (*Canterbury/NZ A*)	LFM	196.4	33	710	27	5-54	1	26.29
14	R. L. Toole (*Central Districts*)	LM	216.2	56	591	22	4-38	0	26.86
15	B. M. Tickner (*Central Districts/NZ A*)	RFM	234.2	43	759	28	5-80	1	27.10
16	S. C. Kuggeleijn (*Northern Dist/NZ A*)	RFM	204.2	32	643	22	7-45	1	29.22
17	I. G. McPeake (*Wellington*)	RFM	199.1	61	534	18	4-53	0	29.66
18	I. S. Sodhi (*Northern Districts/NZ A*)	LB	205.4	34	610	19	4-89	0	32.10
19	R. Ravindra (*Wellington/NZ A*)	SLA	154.2	26	549	16	6-89	1	34.31
20	M. J. G. Rippon (*Otago/NZ A*)	SLW	219	26	819	23	6-66	1	35.60
21	M. D. Rae (*Otago/New Zealand A*)	RFM	308	45	1,216	34	5-62	1	35.76
22	W. E. R. Somerville (*Auckland*)	OB	230	72	599	16	4-61	0	37.43
23	J. G. Walker (*Northern Districts*)	OB	229.4	62	573	15	3-48	0	38.20

PLUNKET SHIELD IN 2020-21

	P	W	L	D	Bonus pts Bat	Bonus pts Bowl	Pts	Net avge runs per wkt
Canterbury	8	5	0	3	19	30	109	14.45
Northern Districts	8	3	2	3	11	22	69	–2.14
Otago	8	2	4	2	13	26	63	–7.68
Auckland	8	2	0	5*	12	21	61	6.76
Central Districts	8	2	4	1*	7	21	56	–2.25
Wellington	8	0	4	4	12	25	37	–8.05

* *Plus one abandoned.*

Outright win = 12pts; abandoned = 4pts. Bonus points were awarded as follows for the first 110 overs of each team's first innings: one batting point for the first 200 runs, then for 250, 300 and 350; one bowling point for the third wicket taken, then for the fifth, seventh and ninth.

PLUNKET SHIELD WINNERS

1921-22	Auckland	1958-59	Auckland	1991-92	Central Districts / Northern Districts
1922-23	Canterbury	1959-60	Canterbury	1992-93	Northern Districts
1923-24	Wellington	1960-61	Wellington	1993-94	Canterbury
1924-25	Otago	1961-62	Wellington	1994-95	Auckland
1925-26	Wellington	1962-63	Northern Districts	1995-96	Auckland
1926-27	Auckland	1963-64	Auckland	1996-97	Canterbury
1927-28	Wellington	1964-65	Canterbury	1997-98	Canterbury
1928-29	Auckland	1965-66	Wellington	1998-99	Central Districts
1929-30	Wellington	1966-67	Central Districts	1999-2000	Northern Districts
1930-31	Canterbury	1967-68	Central Districts	2000-01	Wellington
1931-32	Wellington	1968-69	Auckland	2001-02	Auckland
1932-33	Otago	1969-70	Otago	2002-03	Auckland
1933-34	Auckland	1970-71	Central Districts	2003-04	Wellington
1934-35	Canterbury	1971-72	Otago	2004-05	Auckland
1935-36	Wellington	1972-73	Wellington	2005-06	Central Districts
1936-37	Auckland	1973-74	Wellington	2006-07	Northern Districts
1937-38	Auckland	1974-75	Otago	2007-08	Canterbury
1938-39	Auckland	1975-76	Canterbury	2008-09	Auckland
1939-40	Auckland	1976-77	Otago	2009-10	Northern Districts
1940–45	*No competition*	1977-78	Auckland	2010-11	Canterbury
1945-46	Canterbury	1978-79	Otago	2011-12	Northern Districts
1946-47	Auckland	1979-80	Northern Districts	2012-13	Central Districts
1947-48	Otago	1980-81	Auckland	2013-14	Canterbury
1948-49	Canterbury	1981-82	Wellington	2014-15	Canterbury
1949-50	Wellington	1982-83	Wellington	2015-16	Auckland
1950-51	Otago	1983-84	Canterbury	2016-17	Canterbury
1951-52	Canterbury	1984-85	Wellington	2017-18	Central Districts
1952-53	Otago	1985-86	Otago	2018-19	Central Districts
1953-54	Central Districts	1986-87	Central Districts	2019-20	Wellington
1954-55	Wellington	1987-88	Otago	2020-21	Canterbury
1955-56	Canterbury	1988-89	Auckland		
1956-57	Wellington	1989-90	Wellington		
1957-58	Otago	1990-91	Auckland		

Auckland have won the title outright 23 times, Wellington 21, Canterbury 20, Otago 13, Central Districts 10, Northern Districts 7. Central Districts and Northern Districts also shared the title once.

The tournament was known as the Shell Trophy from 1975-76 to 2000-01, and the State Championship from 2001-02 to 2008-09.

THE FORD TROPHY IN 2020-21

50-over league plus knockout

	P	W	L	A	Bonus	Pts	NRR
CANTERBURY	10	7	3	0	3	31	1.14
NORTHERN DISTRICTS	10	6	4	0	2	26	-0.09
WELLINGTON	10	5	4	1	0	22	-0.16
Otago	10	5	5	0	0	20	-0.61
Auckland	10	4	6	0	2	18	-0.23
Central Districts	10	2	7	1	2	12	-0.04

2nd v 3rd   At Hamilton, March 2, 2021 (day/night). **Northern Districts won by 138 runs** (DLS). **Northern Districts 351-8** (42 overs) (H. R. Cooper 146*); ‡**Wellington 145-7** (26.1 overs). *Henry Cooper set up a huge victory by scoring 146* in 94 balls – a maiden List A century – with seven sixes. He put on 136 in 14 overs with Joe Carter and, despite Colin de Grandhomme falling first ball, and bad weather trimming eight overs off their innings, Northern Districts reached 351, their second-highest one-day total. Tom Blundell responded with 80*, but Wellington looked beaten well before the rain returned.*

Final   At Christchurch, March 6, 2021 (day/night). **Canterbury won by eight wickets. ‡Northern Districts 289-7** (50 overs); **Canterbury 292-2** (45 overs) (H. M. Nicholls 127*). *Katene Clarke (with a career-best 82) and Carter (70) built a solid platform for Northern Districts in a second-wicket stand of 125, and de Grandhomme rounded off the innings with 57 off 37 balls. But Henry Nicholls anchored Canterbury's reply with 127* in 144, adding 113 with Chad Bowes (42) and 150 with the diminutive Ken McClure, who cracked 92 in 74 and hoisted four sixes over the vast Hagley Oval boundaries. Canterbury grabbed their first trophy of the season with five overs in hand.*

The Dream 11 Super Smash has its own section (page 1136).

PAKISTAN CRICKET IN 2021

Ramiz ruffles feathers

OSMAN SAMIUDDIN

On the surface, this looked like a messy year for Pakistan. Their national team visited eight countries. They didn't finish with the same coaches they started with (in fact, they didn't have a coach at all). A new board chairman made waves. Their most comprehensive home season in over a decade was severely hit by the withdrawal of New Zealand and England, bringing uncertainty to Pakistan's aim of welcoming back all international cricket. The Pakistan Super League was halted by Covid halfway through, and relocated to the UAE months later, with no spectators. A long-brewing tension between the PCB and the franchises over the financial model of the PSL threatened to cause fundamental schisms.

On the field, though, it seemed far from messy. No team among the ICC's Full Members had a better win/loss ratio across all formats than Pakistan: they

PAKISTAN IN 2021

	Played	Won	Lost	Drawn/No result
Tests	9	7	2	–
One-day internationals	6	2	4	–
Twenty20 internationals	29	20	6	3

DECEMBER	2 Tests and 3 T20Is (a) v New Zealand	(see *Wisden 2021*, page 714)
JANUARY	2 Tests and 3 T20Is (h) v South Africa	(page 970)
FEBRUARY		
MARCH		
APRIL	3 ODIs and 4 T20Is (a) v South Africa	(page 987)
MAY	2 Tests and 3 T20Is (a) v Zimbabwe	(page 1060)
JUNE		
JULY	3 ODIs and 3 T20Is (a) v England	(page 366)
AUGUST	2 Tests and 4 T20Is (a) v West Indies	(page 1049)
SEPTEMBER		
OCTOBER	T20 World Cup in the UAE	(page 830)
NOVEMBER	2 Tests and 3 T20Is (a) v Bangladesh	(page 922)
DECEMBER	3 T20Is (h) v West Indies	(page 978)

For a review of Pakistan domestic cricket from the 2020-21 season, see page 980.

Munir uz Zaman, AFP/Getty Images

The Mirpur miracle: Sajid Khan's 12 wickets magic a win over Bangladesh.

won 29 and lost 12. No team won more games, and – especially noteworthy, given the context of travel in the pandemic – no team played more often away from home.

The national team had begun 2021 in New Zealand, before hosting – then visiting – South Africa. From there, they travelled to Zimbabwe, the UK, the West Indies (Guyana and Jamaica), the T20 World Cup in the UAE, and Bangladesh. In all, Pakistan's men played 32 consecutive matches abroad, before West Indies arrived in Karachi in December. It felt as if Pakistan had done more than any other team to keep cricket going – hence the anger when New Zealand and England pulled out.

Everywhere Pakistan went, they played entertaining cricket. There was a taut one-wicket Test defeat in Jamaica, a rain-hit Test victory conjured out of two days' play in Mirpur, and fightback wins after being 27 for four against South Africa, and two for three against West Indies.

The highlight was their run to the semi-final of the T20 World Cup in November. That success was all the more surprising since they had ended up playing only one of their scheduled T20s in the lead-up: the weather washed out three games in the Caribbean, and the seven home fixtures against New Zealand and England were cancelled. The highlight of the highlight was a ten-wicket win over India in Dubai, a moment that not only kickstarted Pakistan's charge but provided a cathartic balm to a team accustomed to being bossed about by their neighbours at global competitions.

The key development was the emergence of a robust all-format core, led by the captain Babar Azam and built on Mohammad Rizwan (as much an on-field leader as Babar), Shaheen Shah Afridi and Hasan Ali. Rizwan had a record-breaking year as a T20 opener; Afridi and Hasan were the world's top two wicket-takers in all formats. Arrayed around them were format specialists such as Fawad Alam, Fahim Ashraf – at last, a genuine all-rounder – Shadab Khan and Haris Rauf. This had the makings of a great side.

Whether greatness is realised depends not just on the players, but the board that employ them. Once again, it was clear that the PCB's fortunes lay in the hands of the prevailing political power. After three years of relative stability, prime minister Imran Khan decided to shake things up. In came Ramiz Raja as chairman, for no reason other than Imran's wish for an ex-cricketer; he replaced Ehsan Mani, the non-cricketer Imran had appointed in 2018.

Ramiz brought the energy of a Tasmanian devil. Such was his intensity, Misbah-ul-Haq and Waqar Younis left their coaching positions even before he was in place, having learned the new boss was not a fan. Ramiz met Karachi businessmen to secure investment, no doubt leaning on his MBA from Punjab University. One investor reportedly offered him a "blank cheque" if Pakistan beat India at the T20 World Cup, though it had yet to materialise.

Acting as a quasi-manager, Ramiz called several meetings with the national team, had a say in selections and suggested coaching appointments. He planned to import drop-in pitches so Pakistan could better compete in Australia. He wanted bigger names at the PSL, and played hard ball with the franchises, telling them to agree a new financial model – or else. He even promised a pay increase for domestic cricketers. And this was all just in the first few weeks; there was no surprise when the chief executive, Wasim Khan, soon figured out there might be little left for him to do, and resigned.

What Ramiz could not control were the abrupt withdrawals of New Zealand and England. New Zealand's came on the morning of what would have been their first game in Pakistan for 18 years, the tourists having received what they said was a credible security threat. They refused to share details with either the PCB, or Imran's government. England's reasons for pulling out, shortly afterwards, seemed even more spurious.

Ramiz channelled the national anger, publicly reminding everyone of the debt world cricket owed Pakistan, as well as the intrinsic inequities of the game. Privately, he secured arrangements with both teams to tour in 2022-23, for more games than originally planned. Thanks to Ramiz's trailblazing, there could be entertaining times ahead.

PAKISTAN v SOUTH AFRICA IN 2020-21

DANYAL RASOOL

Test matches (2): Pakistan 2 (120pts), South Africa 0 (0pts)
Twenty20 internationals (3): Pakistan 2, South Africa 1

South Africa continued the return of international cricket to Pakistan; it was their first tour there for over 13 years. Following the spotlight on security for matches against Sri Lanka and Bangladesh, it was arguably the first time for a decade or more that the focus was on the play: at last, a top-tier nation had agreed to visit. Pakistan were undaunted, winning both Tests – a welcome boost after losing heavily in New Zealand – and pinching the T20 series at the death.

Pakistan have long considered themselves better players of fast bowling than the other subcontinental teams, but the threat posed by South Africa's potent pace trio – Kagiso Rabada, Anrich Nortje and Lungi Ngidi – led to the usually bouncy surfaces being toned down. Even so, Pakistani pitches are often resistant to attempts to turn them into lifeless dustbowls, and the wickets were shared around.

The series was in the balance until the final afternoon: South Africa, chasing 370, were 241 for three, after Aiden Markram past his century and Temba Bavuma set. But Markram and Quinton de Kock fell to Hasan Ali's first two legitimate deliveries with the second new ball, and the impressive Shaheen Shah Afridi helped wrap things up. De Kock had a miserable time in the Tests, making 46 runs in four attempts, and afterwards took a break from the game – and the captaincy.

The main difference between the sides was the depth of Pakistan's batting. In the First Test, they recovered from 27 for four thanks to a century from Fawad Alam at No. 6, from where Mohammad Rizwan also reached three figures in the Second.

Mark Boucher, South Africa's coach, was predictably disappointed after his side's fourth series defeat out of five (they had now lost ten of their last 13 Tests). "The way we played in big moments really cost us," he said. "Our match awareness – when to tighten the screws – was lacking. We created opportunities. We just didn't take them."

The T20s felt anticlimactic, particularly as several of South Africa's key players were being rested for a home series against Australia that never happened. Despite that, the visitors put together three spirited performances, and were unlucky not to come away with the spoils. Rizwan, who continued his surprising rise to 20-over stardom, catapulted Pakistan to victory in the end, with the home side holding their nerve better at key moments, as they had in the Tests. But the South Africans, who were captained by Heinrich Klaasen, were encouraged by pushing Pakistan all the way. It wasn't long before the teams locked horns again in white-ball cricket: a few weeks later, it was Pakistan's turn to tour South Africa.

SOUTH AFRICA TOURING PARTY

*Q. de Kock (T), T. Bavuma (T), N. Burger (20), O. A. Cele (20), C. J. Dala (20), D. M. Dupavillon (T), F. du Plessis (T), D. Elgar (T), S. J. Erwee (T), B. C. Fortuin (20), B. E. Hendricks (T), R. R. Hendricks (20), M. Jansen (T), H. Klaasen (20), G. F. Linde (T/20), K. A. Maharaj (T), J. N. Malan (20), A. K. Markram (T), D. A. Miller (20), P. W. A. Mulder (T), L. T. Ngidi (T), A. A. Nortje (T), K. D. Petersen (T), A. L. Phehlukwayo (20), D. Pretorius (T/20), K. Rabada (T), R. D. Rickelton (20), T. Shamsi (T/20), L. L. Sipamla (T/20), J. T. Smuts (20), G. J. Snyman (20), G. A. Stuurman (20), P. J. van Biljon (20), H. E. van der Dussen (T), K. Verreynne (T). *Coach:* M. V. Boucher.

Klaasen captained in the T20s. O. E. G. Baartman was originally named in the Test squad, but withdrew for medical reasons and was replaced by Jansen.

PAKISTAN v SOUTH AFRICA

First Test

At Karachi, January 26–29, 2021. Pakistan won by seven wickets. Pakistan 60pts. Toss: South Africa. Test debuts: Imran Butt, Nauman Ali.

The National Stadium was traditionally a Pakistani fortress, at least until England won in the dark in 2000-01 – and they had lost only once more in a total of 42 Tests there, on South Africa's previous visit in 2007-08. Dry, dusty winters with little rainfall mean the Karachi groundsman has no trouble preparing tracks favouring the slower bowlers, the area in which this South African side looked markedly inferior to their opponents. They seemed to believe the pre-match chatter about the pitch being a raging Bunsen, and prepared to field all three spinners, only for unorthodox left-armer Tabraiz Shamsi to suffer a back spasm shortly before the start.

His absence was a blow, but South Africa began brightly after winning the toss. They refused to let Pakistan's attack bog them down, marching along at more than four an over for much of the first session. But once the sun reached its zenith and the moisture drained from the surface, things began to fall apart. Aside from the early wicket that Shaheen Shah Afridi always seems to capture, Pakistan did little to earn their breakthroughs: several batsmen obligingly hit the self-destruct button, including van der Dussen, who was run out after a suicidal attempt at a single. Elgar's 58 was easily the highest contribution to a disappointing total of 220.

The home side had feared de Kock, but he was not in the right frame of mind for a long battle against spin. He batted as if high-risk shots against the debutant slow left-armer Nauman Ali were a substitute for a solid defensive technique, and it was little surprise to see him hole out at midwicket to a relatively harmless delivery. Bavuma and Linde

---

FEWEST BALLS TO REACH 200 TEST WICKETS

		M	*Avge*		
7,725	Waqar Younis (P)	38	20.61	v New Zealand at Christchurch	1995-96
7,848	D. W. Steyn (SA)	39	23.13	v West Indies at Port-of-Spain	2010
8,154	**K. Rabada (SA)**	**44**	**22.87**	**v Pakistan at Karachi**	**2020-21**
9,234	M. D. Marshall (WI)	42	21.64	v England at Port-of-Spain	1985-86
9,487	A. A. Donald (SA)	42	22.69	v Sri Lanka at Centurion	1997-98
9,672	I. T. Botham (E)	41	21.29	v Australia at The Oval	1981
9,860	V. D. Philander (SA)	54	21.83	v Australia at Johannesburg	2017-18
9,875	F. S. Trueman (E)	47	22.06	v Pakistan at Lord's	1962
9,896	**Mohammed Shami (I)**	**55**	**27.10**	**v South Africa at Centurion**	**2021-22**
10,136	J. Garner (WI)	44	20.33	v Australia at Brisbane	1984-85
10,194	D. Gough (E)	50	27.06	v Pakistan at Lord's	2001

Figures are at the time of the 200th wicket.

battened down the hatches, putting on 43 for the sixth wicket. But that partnership also ended with a careless run-out, before Yasir Shah picked up a couple of tailenders as the innings folded.

A ferocious spell of fast bowling in the first-day twilight demonstrated why Pakistan had aimed to prepare the slowest pitch that soil science would allow. Rabada and Nortje ripped through the top order, reducing them to 27 for four shortly before the close. But in what would become a familiar sight, the middle and lower order dug in. Fawad Alam, controversially omitted from the Test team for a decade despite prolific domestic form, scored a gritty, redemptive hundred in his home ground, while contributions right down to Yasir's unbeaten 38 from No. 11 resulted in a match-defining lead of 158. The innings illustrated the difference in quality between the sides' spinners: Linde and Maharaj were unable to trouble the batsmen as Nauman and Yasir had. Rabada did take three wickets, including his 200th – Hasan Ali – in his 44th Test.

South Africa were much more resolute in their second innings. A doughty stand of 127 between Markram, whose fifty occupied 158 balls, and van der Dussen took them into the lead for the loss of just one wicket, before a seismic shift. Van der Dussen popped Yasir to silly mid-off, the first of three late wickets on the third evening, culminating in Markram after more than five hours. The collapse extended to five for 17 next morning, when Hasan – playing his first Test in two years after a back injury threatened his career – bowled nightwatchman Maharaj with the day's first delivery, and de Kock was well held at short leg by Abid Ali off Yasir. But Bavuma accumulated 40, and Linde survived more than an hour before falling to a good catch by Imran Butt, another debutant, at leg slip. Pakistan still needed only 88 – not enough for South Africa's potent pacemen to defend, although Nortje removed both openers in his third over.

Pakistan's final-day hero had been the 34-year-old Nauman, who marked his belated debut with five for 35; he and Yasir both took seven in the match. Born in Khipro, a remote part of Sind, Nauman played no serious cricket until he was 14; none of his seven brothers progressed beyond the tape-ball version. His uncle, Rizwan Ahmed, played a solitary one-day international against Zimbabwe in February 2008. Nauman's match analysis of 42.3–12–73–7 was one for the family scrapbook.

Player of the Match: Fawad Alam.

Close of play: first day, Pakistan 33-4 (Azhar Ali 5, Fawad Alam 5); second day, Pakistan 308-8 (Hasan Ali 11, Nauman Ali 6); third day, South Africa 187-4 (Maharaj 2, de Kock 0).

South Africa

D. Elgar c Babar Azam b Nauman Ali	58	– (2) c Mohammad Rizwan b Yasir Shah	29
A. K. Markram c Imran Butt b Shaheen Shah Afridi	13	– (1) c Abid Ali b Nauman Ali	74
H. E. van der Dussen run out (Babar Azam/ Mohammad Rizwan)	17	– c Abid Ali b Yasir Shah	64
F. du Plessis c Mohammad Rizwan b Yasir Shah	23	– lbw b Yasir Shah	10
*†Q. de Kock c Imran Butt b Nauman Ali	15	– (6) c Abid Ali b Yasir Shah	2
T. Bavuma run out (Hasan Ali/Mohammad Rizwan)	17	– (7) lbw b Nauman Ali	40
G. F. Linde c sub (Mohammad Nawaz) b Hasan Ali	35	– (8) c Imran Butt b Nauman Ali	11
K. A. Maharaj b Yasir Shah	0	– (5) b Hasan Ali	2
K. Rabada not out	21	– b Nauman Ali	1
A. A. Nortje b Yasir Shah	0	– c Fawad Alam b Nauman Ali	0
L. T. Ngidi lbw b Shaheen Shah Afridi	8	– not out	3
B 5, lb 1, nb 7	13	Lb 1, w 1, nb 7	9

1/30 (2) 2/63 (3) 3/108 (4)   (69.2 overs) 220   1/48 (2) 2/175 (3)   (100.3 overs) 245
4/133 (5) 5/136 (1) 6/179 (6)   3/185 (4) 4/185 (1)
7/179 (8) 8/194 (7) 9/195 (10) 10/220 (11)   5/187 (5) 6/192 (6) 7/234 (8)
    8/238 (9) 9/240 (10) 10/245 (7)

Shaheen Shah Afridi 11.2–0–49–2; Hasan Ali 14–5–61–1; Fahim Ashraf 5–0–12–0; Nauman Ali 17–4–38–2; Yasir Shah 22–6–54–3. *Second innings*—Shaheen Shah Afridi 17–1–61–0; Hasan Ali 16–1–61–1; Nauman Ali 25.3–8–35–5; Yasir Shah 33–7–79–4; Fahim Ashraf 9–6–8–0.

Pakistan

Imran Butt c sub (K. D. Petersen) b Rabada	9	– c de Kock b Nortje	12
Abid Ali b Rabada	4	– b Nortje	10
Azhar Ali c de Kock b Maharaj	51	– not out	31
*Babar Azam lbw b Maharaj	7	– lbw b Maharaj	30
Shaheen Shah Afridi b Nortje	0		
Fawad Alam c Bavuma b Ngidi	109	– (5) not out	4
†Mohammad Rizwan c du Plessis b Ngidi	33		
Fahim Ashraf b Nortje	64		
Hasan Ali b Rabada	21		
Nauman Ali lbw b Maharaj	24		
Yasir Shah not out	38		
B 1, lb 7, nb 10	18	B 1, lb 2	3

1/5 (2) 2/15 (1) 3/26 (4) (119.2 overs) 378   1/22 (2) (3 wkts, 22.5 overs) 90
4/27 (5) 5/121 (3) 6/176 (7)   2/23 (1) 3/86 (4)
7/278 (6) 8/295 (8) 9/323 (9) 10/378 (10)

Rabada 27–7–70–3; Nortje 27–4–105–2; Ngidi 17–1–57–2; Maharaj 32.2–4–90–3; Linde 13–4–38–0; Markram 3–0–10–0. *Second innings*—Rabada 8–2–21–0; Nortje 7–1–24–2; Maharaj 1.5–0–12–1; Ngidi 3–0–17–0; Linde 3–0–13–0.

Umpires: Ahsan Raza and Aleem Dar.   Third umpire: Asif Yaqoob.
Referee: Mohammad Javed.

PAKISTAN v SOUTH AFRICA

Second Test

At Rawalpindi, February 4–8, 2021. Pakistan won by 95 runs. Pakistan 60pts. Toss: Pakistan.
Rawalpindi's cool, wet climate makes creating a dry, spin-bowling paradise a challenge. Pakistan's head coach Misbah-ul-Haq still hoped for such a pitch, to neutralise the South African fast bowlers, but there was an element of the unknown when his side decided to bat. Concerns about Pakistan's opening pair soon returned: in the first hour, they dipped to 22 for three. But the new captain, Babar Azam, after a rare failure in his first Test in charge, made a patient half-century, putting on 123 with Fawad Alam to set them back on track on a rain-affected opening day.

Nortje enjoyed himself next morning, his short stuff proving particularly menacing. Babar, who had survived three hours the previous day, fell second ball, Mohammad Rizwan went cheaply, and Fawad was run out. Fahim Ashraf stalled South Africa with an excellent unbeaten 78, but the tail could offer little against a bowler who often clocked 95mph. Nortje finished with five for 56, while Maharaj whirred through 45 overs and claimed three for 90.

BEST MATCH FIGURES IN PAKISTAN–SOUTH AFRICA TESTS

11-60	D. W. Steyn (6-8, 5-52)	v Pakistan at Johannesburg	2012-13
11-96	D. Olivier (6-37, 5-59)	v Pakistan at Centurion	2018-19
10-108	P. S. de Villiers (6-81, 4-27)	v Pakistan at Johannesburg	1994-95
10-114	**Hasan Ali (5-54, 5-60)**	**v South Africa at Rawalpindi**	**2020-21**
10-133	Waqar Younis (6-78, 4-55)	v South Africa at Port Elizabeth	1997-98
10-147	Saeed Ajmal (6-96, 4-51)	v South Africa at Cape Town	2012-13

Aamir Qureshi, AFP/Getty Images

Turning point: Rassie van der Dussen fails to hold a tight chance, and Mohammad Rizwan fights on.

Pakistan's 272 looked better when Elgar and van der Dussen departed to successive balls from the nippy, accurate Hasan Ali. The other bowlers made regular inroads, and South Africa subsided for 201, a significant deficit of 71. De Kock again attacked the spinners in carefree fashion, smashing five boundaries off his first eight balls on the second evening – but he fell to Shaheen Shah Afridi early next morning. Bavuma tried to shepherd the tail, but Hasan (and two run-outs) ensured there was not much resistance at the other end.

Suddenly, on a bizarre third evening, the pitch seemed to change character. Dust flew up as the ball ragged square, and slow left-armers Linde – who took a career-best five-for – and Maharaj reduced Pakistan to 76 for five. But South Africa's inability to dislodge the lower order cost them again. Fahim, once described by Pakistan's former head coach Mickey Arthur as "not an all-rounder, just a bowler", helped Rizwan put on 52. South Africa did not help themselves with poor fielding: from successive balls, Elgar put down a regulation slip catch before Fahim had scored, then van der Dussen at silly point could not quite latch on to a more difficult chance off Rizwan, who had four at the time. He kicked on to his first Test century, helped later by Yasir Shah and Nauman Ali, to set an unlikely target of 370 in a day and a half.

Now the inscrutable surface changed again, and gave little help to the spinners. The South Africans grafted to 127 for one by the end of the fourth day, and Markram continued to a century on the fifth. But Hasan put Pakistan in charge with a quick double strike, despatching van der Dussen and du Plessis, before Bavuma dropped anchor again.

At 241 for three, with 129 more needed, there was a lot riding on the second new ball. And it did the trick. Hasan quickly removed Markram for 108, and ended de Kock's miserable trip next ball. The lower order offered scant resistance: in all, the last seven wickets tumbled for 33. Hasan finished with a maiden Test haul of ten – and Pakistan's best match figures against South Africa – while Afridi mopped up the tail. Pakistan may have taken the scenic route, but they completed a satisfying 2–0 series win in entertaining style. Babar was only the fifth Pakistani to win his first Test series as captain.

Player of the Match: Hasan Ali.   *Player of the Series:* Mohammad Rizwan.

Close of play: first day, Pakistan 145-3 (Babar Azam 77, Fawad Alam 42); second day, South Africa 106-4 (Bavuma 15, de Kock 24); third day, Pakistan 129-6 (Mohammad Rizwan 28, Hasan Ali 0); fourth day, South Africa 127-1 (Markram 59, van der Dussen 48).

Pakistan

Imran Butt c de Kock b Maharaj	15	– lbw b Rabada ... 0
Abid Ali c Markram b Nortje	6	– c de Kock b Maharaj ... 13
Azhar Ali lbw b Maharaj	0	– lbw b Linde ... 33
*Babar Azam c du Plessis b Nortje	77	– lbw b Markram ... 8
Fawad Alam run out (Bavuma)	45	– c Markram b Linde ... 12
†Mohammad Rizwan c Rabada b Nortje	18	– not out ... 115
Fahim Ashraf not out	78	– c Nortje b Linde ... 29
Hasan Ali c Elgar b Maharaj	8	– lbw b Maharaj ... 5
Yasir Shah c and b Mulder	8	– c de Kock b Linde ... 23
Nauman Ali c Markram b Nortje	8	– c Elgar b Rabada ... 45
Shaheen Shah Afridi c Elgar b Nortje	0	– b Linde ... 4
B 2, lb 2, nb 5	9	B 9, nb 2 ... 11
	—	—
	272	298

1/21 (1) 2/21 (3) 3/22 (2) (114.3 overs) 272
4/145 (4) 5/149 (5) 6/190 (6)
7/221 (8) 8/251 (9) 9/272 (10) 10/272 (11)

1/0 (1) 2/28 (2) (102 overs) 298
3/45 (4) 4/63 (3)
5/76 (5) 6/128 (7) 7/143 (8)
8/196 (9) 9/293 (10) 10/298 (11)

Rabada 21–2–72–0; Nortje 24.3–8–56–5; Maharaj 45–11–90–3; Linde 5.5–2–4–0; Elgar 1.1–0–6–0; Mulder 17–7–40–1. *Second innings*—Rabada 14–3–34–2; Nortje 17–7–57–0; Maharaj 38–4–118–3; Mulder 7–1–16–0; Linde 26–9–64–5.

South Africa

D. Elgar c Mohammad Rizwan b Hasan Ali	15	– (2) c Mohammad Rizwan b Shaheen Shah Afridi . 17
A. K. Markram c Shaheen Shah Afridi b Nauman Ali	32	– (1) c Imran Butt b Hasan Ali ... 108
H. E. van der Dussen b Hasan Ali	0	– b Hasan Ali ... 48
F. du Plessis c Mohammad Rizwan b Fahim Ashraf	17	– lbw b Hasan Ali ... 5
T. Bavuma not out	44	– c Mohammad Rizwan b Shaheen Shah Afridi . 61
*†Q. de Kock b Shaheen Shah Afridi	29	– c Imran Butt b Hasan Ali ... 0
P. W. A. Mulder run out (Shaheen Shah Afridi/ Mohammad Rizwan)	33	– b Yasir Shah ... 20
G. F. Linde b Hasan Ali	21	– c Fahim Ashraf b Hasan Ali ... 4
K. A. Maharaj b Hasan Ali	1	– c Imran Butt b Shaheen Shah Afridi ... 0
K. Rabada run out (Abid Ali)	0	– b Shaheen Shah Afridi ... 0
A. A. Nortje b Hasan Ali	0	– not out ... 2
Nb 9	9	Lb 2, nb 7 ... 9
	—	—
	201	274

1/26 (1) 2/26 (3) 3/55 (4) (65.4 overs) 201
4/81 (2) 5/114 (6) 6/164 (7)
7/186 (8) 8/192 (9) 9/201 (10) 10/201 (11)

1/33 (2) 2/127 (3) (91.4 overs) 274
3/135 (4) 4/241 (1)
5/241 (6) 6/253 (5) 7/258 (8)
8/268 (9) 9/268 (10) 10/274 (7)

Shaheen Shah Afridi 13–2–37–1; Hasan Ali 15.4–2–54–5; Fahim Ashraf 8–2–20–1; Nauman Ali 17–8–36–1; Yasir Shah 12–2–54–0. *Second innings*—Shaheen Shah Afridi 21–6–51–4; Hasan Ali 16–2–60–5; Nauman Ali 20–6–63–0; Yasir Shah 23.4–5–56–1; Fahim Ashraf 10–2–37–0; Fawad Alam 1–0–5–0.

Umpires: Ahsan Raza and Aleem Dar. Third umpire: Asif Yaqoob.
Referee: Mohammad Javed.

First Twenty20 international At Lahore, February 11, 2021 (floodlit). **Pakistan won by three runs. Pakistan 169-6** (20 overs) (Mohammad Rizwan 104*); ‡**South Africa 166-6** (20 overs) (J. N. Malan 44, R. R. Hendricks 54). *PoM:* Mohammad Rizwan. *T20I debut:* G. J. Snyman (South Africa). *South Africa removed Babar Azam without scoring, prevented anyone other than Mohammad Rizwan from passing 21, and restricted Pakistan to 45 in the powerplay. It sounds like the perfect T20 script – yet they lost. The inclusion of Rizwan – derided for his stodginess – had been contentious, but he smashed 104* from 64 balls, with seven sixes, to become Pakistan's second T20 centurion, after Ahmed Shehzad against Bangladesh in 2013-14. He was responsible for over 60% of his side's runs,* *dragging them to 169, just about par for a flat surface at the Gaddafi Stadium. Janneman Malan looked set to make short work of the target with a 29-ball 44, but once Pakistan's spinners got going the chase fell apart. Leg-spinner Usman Qadir removed Malan and the debutant Jacques Snyman; both Qadir and slow left-armer Mohammad Nawaz conceded only 21 from their four overs as the asking-rate mounted. Some sloppiness in the field gave South Africa a sniff, and they needed six from the last ball – but Bjorn Fortuin could conjure only two off Fahim Ashraf.*

Second Twenty20 international   At Lahore, February 13, 2021 (floodlit). **South Africa won by six wickets.** Pakistan 144-7 (20 overs) (Mohammad Rizwan 51, Fahim Ashraf 30*; D. Pretorius 5-17); ‡South Africa 145-4 (16.2 overs) (R. R. Hendricks 42, P. J. van Biljon 42). *PoM:* D. Pretorius. *T20I debut:* G. A. Stuurman (South Africa). *Rizwan made another half-century, but this time South*

FIVE WICKETS IN T20s FOR SOUTH AFRICA

5-17	**D. Pretorius**	**v Pakistan at Lahore**	**2020-21**
5-19	R. McLaren	v West Indies at North Sound	2009-10
5-23	D. Wiese	v West Indies at Durban	2014-15
5-23	Imran Tahir	v Zimbabwe at East London	2018-19
5-24	Imran Tahir	v New Zealand at Auckland .	2016-17

Africa were not to be denied. Instead, seamer Dwaine Pretorius scripted a thumping win: his 5-17 was South Africa's best in the format. A 77-run stand between Reeza Hendricks and Pite van Biljon offset two early strikes from Shaheen Shah Afridi (18–12–18–2). David Miller and skipper Heinrich Klaasen then set up a decider with time to spare, putting on 40* in 23 balls.

Third Twenty20 international   At Lahore, February 14, 2021 (floodlit). **Pakistan won by four wickets.** South Africa 164-8 (20 overs) (D. A. Miller 85*; Zahid Mahmood 3-40); ‡Pakistan 169-6 (18.4 overs) (Mohammad Rizwan 42, Babar Azam 44; T. Shamsi 4-25). *PoM:* Mohammad Nawaz. *PoS:* Mohammad Rizwan. *T20I debut:* Zahid Mahmood (Pakistan). *Pakistan seemed to have wrapped the series up after a sensational first hour. But once Miller's dazzling power-hitting blew the match wide open, it was a surprise to see South Africa fall at the last. They had been reeling at 65-7 in the 11th, before Miller blasted seven sixes and five fours in his 45-ball 85* out of 118 added during his stay. Pakistan's openers started steadily, putting on 51 in the powerplay, but Rizwan and No. 3 Babar both fell when well set, leaving the game in the balance. With three overs to go, 28 were needed – but an erratic 19th from Andile Phehlukwayo, which included a wide, a no-ball and four legal deliveries, presented the match to the home side: Hasan Ali (20* from seven) smote two sixes and a four to bring a rapid end.*

PAKISTAN v NEW ZEALAND IN 2021-22

Danyal Rasool

In September 2021, the primary threat to professional cricket seemed to be Covid, not security. But on the morning of the first one-day international at Rawalpindi, it became clear something had gone badly wrong. Many journalists had been at the ground for several hours before the scheduled start, to contend with the complex security arrangements put in place for New Zealand's first tour of Pakistan in 18 years, comprising three ODIs and five T20s. But there was no sign of the players.

Then, shortly after 2pm, the Pakistan Cricket Board said New Zealand had "unilaterally" scrapped the tour because of a "specific and credible" security threat made known to their government – though not shared with Pakistan's administrators or security agencies. The tourists would fly home next day.

PCB chief executive Wasim Khan lashed out, saying the players' hotel had been "protected like a fortress", and insisting entry checkpoints at the ground ensured "complete safety". New Zealand's own security expert, he said, had given the plans a "clean bill of health". Adding that the cost to Pakistan cricket would run into millions of dollars, Wasim called the decision "gut-wrenching". Three days later, England pulled out of a short visit scheduled for October, citing "increasing concerns about travelling to the region", and bubble fatigue. Pakistan were thus denied their entire on-field preparation for the T20 World Cup.

It put a knot in local stomachs. Had the hopeful, peaceful years since the attack on Sri Lanka's team bus in Lahore in March 2009 been the exception? Had normal service been resumed? PCB chairman Ramiz Raja said these were "just stupid excuses to wriggle out of Pakistan. Sometimes it's security, sometimes the players are scared, sometimes they're mentally tired." He accused New Zealand, Australia and England of being part of a bloc "creating a cricket family which they do not want us to join".

The New Zealanders' withdrawal stirred memories of their aborted visit in 2002, following an explosion close to their hotel hours before the Karachi Test. But their return for a one-day series at the end of 2003 had passed without incident, and the Pakistanis had hosted several tours since the 2009 attack. Several of New Zealand's players, meanwhile, had appeared in the Pakistan Super League. Now, though, the hard work felt wasted.

NEW ZEALAND TOURING PARTY

*T. W. M. Latham (50/20), F. H. Allen (50/20), T. D. Astle (20), H. K. Bennett (50), D. A. J. Bracewell (50), M. S. Chapman (20), C. de Grandhomme (50/20), J. A. Duffy (50), M. J. Guptill (20), M. J. Henry (50/20), S. C. Kuggeleijn (50), C. E. McConchie (50), D. J. Mitchell (50/20), H. M. Nicholls (50), A. Y. Patel (50/20), R. Ravindra (50), B. V. Sears (20), I. S. Sodhi (20), B. M. Tickner (50/20), W. A. Young (50/20). *Coach:* G. D. Pocknall.

T. A. Blundell was chosen for both formats, but injured his thigh and was replaced by Mitchell.

PAKISTAN v WEST INDIES IN 2021-22

Shahid Hashmi

Twenty20 internationals (3): Pakistan 3, West Indies 0

Pakistan badly needed this series to take place. After New Zealand and England had withdrawn from their tours, threatening to precipitate another suspension of international cricket in the country, the PCB were understandably anxious. Their chairman, Ramiz Raja, ruled out a return to neutral venues such as the UAE and, mercifully, found West Indies eager to visit for three T20s and three one-day internationals.

Some of the tourists' box-office players were less keen. Shimron Hetmyer, Evin Lewis, Andre Russell – who in 2016 admitted he was scared of going to Pakistan – and Lendl Simmons demurred for "personal reasons". Jason Holder was rested, Fabian Allen and Obed McCoy were injured, and captain Kieron Pollard had not recovered from a hamstring strain sustained at the T20 World Cup. Nicholas Pooran led a young team who were nearly a Second XI. And things would soon get worse.

The minute the tourists landed, another old foe reared its head. Roston Chase, Sheldon Cottrell and Kyle Mayers were found to have Covid, and ruled out of the T20s. Pakistan enjoyed a clean sweep but, on the eve of the third game, three more West Indians tested positive. It took hours of persuasion to get them to complete the series, but playing the one-dayers was out of the question. Those games were put off until June 2022, giving Cricket West Indies another opportunity to persuade their big guns to travel.

WEST INDIES TOURING PARTY

*N. Pooran (50/20), D. M. Bravo (50/20), S. S. J. Brooks (50/20), R. L. Chase (50/20), S. S. Cottrell (20), D. C. Drakes (20), J. P. Greaves (50), A. J. Hosein (50/20), S. D. Hope (50/20), A. S. Joseph (50), B. A. King (20), K. R. Mayers (20), G. Motie (50), A. Phillip (50/20), R. Powell (20), R. A. Reifer (50), R. Shepherd (50/20), O. F. Smith (50/20), D. C. Thomas (50/20), O. R. Thomas (20), H. R. Walsh (50/20). *Coach:* P. V. Simmons.

K. A. Pollard was originally named as captain, but a hamstring injury ruled him out of the tour, and he was replaced by Thomas and Powell.

First Twenty20 international   At Karachi, December 13, 2021 (floodlit). **Pakistan won by 63 runs. Pakistan 200-6** (20 overs) (Mohammad Rizwan 78, Haider Ali 68, Mohammad Nawaz 30*); ‡**West Indies 137** (19 overs) (S. D. Hope 31; Mohammad Wasim 4-40, Shadab Khan 3-17). *PoM:* Haider Ali. *T20I debuts:* S. S. J. Brooks, D. C. Drakes (West Indies). *Babar Azam was caught behind off Akeal Hosein for a second-ball duck, but Pakistan piled up 200 thanks to fellow opener Mohammad Rizwan's brilliant 78. He added 105 for the third wicket with Haider Ali, whose 39-ball 68 included four sixes; Mohammad Nawaz then smote 30* off ten. West Indies, depleted by three Covid cases, had no answer to the hostile pace of Mohammad Wasim and wrist-spin of Shadab Khan, who between them took 7-57.*

Second Twenty20 international   At Karachi, December 14, 2021 (floodlit). **Pakistan won by nine runs. ‡Pakistan 172-8** (20 overs) (Mohammad Rizwan 38*, Haider Ali 31, Iftikhar Ahmed 32); **West Indies 163** (20 overs) (B. A. King 67, R. Shepherd 35*; Shaheen Shah Afridi 3-26). *PoM:* Shadab Khan. *The young West Indians, energised by opener Brandon King's first international half-century, fought to the last, but lost narrowly. Pakistan had managed 172, despite a second failure by Babar and* *a top score of just 38*, by Rizwan; Shadab (28* off 12) hit three late sixes. While King (67 off 43, with three sixes) was in, West Indies had a chance but, when he was fifth out at 118, they faltered. Romario Shepherd scored rapidly, but not rapidly enough: 23 from the last over proved out of reach.*

Third Twenty20 international   At Karachi, December 16, 2021 (floodlit). **Pakistan won by seven wickets. ‡West Indies 207-3** (20 overs) (B. A. King 43, S. S. J. Brooks 49, N. Pooran 64, D. M. Bravo 34*); **Pakistan 208-3** (18.5 overs) (Mohammad Rizwan 87, Babar Azam 79). *PoM:* Mohammad Rizwan. *PoS:* Mohammad Rizwan. *T20I debut:* G. Motie (West Indies). *Three more Covid cases in the West Indies camp nearly put paid to the match but, with just 12 fit players left in their T20I squad, and despite understandable concerns, they took the field (Devon Thomas was omitted). Perhaps surprisingly, they reached 207, their highest total against Pakistan. King hit 43 of*

HIGHEST T20 PARTNERSHIPS FOR PAKISTAN

197	Mohammad Rizwan/Babar Azam	....	v South Africa at Centurion ..	2020-21
158	Mohammad Rizwan/Babar Azam	....	v West Indies at Karachi.....	2021-22
152*	Mohammad Rizwan/Babar Azam	....	v India at Dubai	2021-22
150	Mohammad Rizwan/Babar Azam	....	v England at Nottingham	2021
143*	Ahmed Shehzad/Mohammad Hafeez........		v Zimbabwe at Harare	2013-14
142	Kamran Akmal/Salman Butt		v Bangladesh at Gros Islet	2010
142	Mukhtar Ahmed/Ahmed Shehzad		v Zimbabwe at Lahore........	2015

All were for the first wicket, except the Shehzad/Hafeez partnership, which was for the second.

---

the first 66, and Nicholas Pooran added 93 with Darren Bravo. It still wasn't enough, as Babar and Rizwan opened with their fifth hundred partnership of the year, one more than all Pakistan's other opening pairs had ever achieved, and their sixth overall, a T20I record. By the time they were parted, the chase had become a saunter.

First one-day international   At Karachi, December 18, 2021 (day/night). **Pakistan v West Indies. Postponed.**

Second one-day international   At Karachi, December 20, 2021 (day/night). **Pakistan v West Indies. Postponed.**

Third one-day international   At Karachi, December 22, 2021 (day/night). **Pakistan v West Indies. Postponed.**

DOMESTIC CRICKET IN PAKISTAN IN 2020-21

Danyal Rasool

The Quaid-e-Azam Trophy went to the final day, the final hour, the final moments – the most spectacular finish to a domestic first-class season since a hat-trick from Toby Roland-Jones at Lord's sealed the 2016 County Championship for Middlesex. At Karachi in January 2021, the first tie in a first-class final anywhere in the world meant **Khyber Pakhtunkhwa** and defending champions **Central Punjab** shared the title.

That Central Punjab took the game so deep after losing eight for 249 in pursuit of 356 was thanks to the heroism of their captain Hasan Ali: batting at No. 8, he was stranded on a magnificent 61-ball 106 when Khyber Pakhtunkhwa's off-spinner Sajid Khan dismissed last man Waqas Maqsood. It was Sajid's 67th wicket of the tournament, putting him six ahead of anyone else.

The Quaid-e-Azam was still looking to find its feet in its second season under a radically revamped format, with the number of teams reduced from 16 to six. This time, there were merely tweaks to the points system, including greater reward for dismissing the opposition within 100 overs for under 300, but the absence of substantial changes was notable in itself: at times, change has been the competition's only constant. It must have encouraged the Pakistan Cricket Board that, thanks to a more even distribution of talent, the quality of cricket looked superior to what had sometimes been served up by the previous bloated structure.

Though Central Punjab started as strong favourites to retain their title, they only just scraped through to the final: their first five league games brought three defeats and two draws, but once Hasan took charge they won four of the last five. Khyber Pakhtunkhwa lost their first game, but were not beaten again. It was a record-breaking year for their No. 4, Kamran Ghulam: his 1,249 runs at 62 broke the tournament record of 1,217, set by Saadat Ali back in 1983-84. It was especially impressive in a season less conducive to run-scoring than 2019-20; no one else reached 1,000, and there were just 47 centuries and two double-hundreds, down from 77 and eight a year earlier.

The shift away from domination by pace bowlers continued. For the second year running, the top three wicket-takers were spinners, with Sajid followed by slow left-armer Nauman Ali (61) and leg-spinner Zahid Mahmood (52). The most prolific fast bowler was Hasan, whose persistent back injuries had threatened to derail his career. His 43 Quaid-e-Azam wickets at 20 earned an international recall, which he marked by collecting four five-wicket hauls in four Tests, against South Africa and Zimbabwe.

The National T20 Cup, staged in the autumn of 2020, expanded from five league rounds to ten, with all six sides playing each other twice, before the top four advanced to the knockout. Although spectators were not allowed because of the Covid-19 pandemic, all games were televised, and there was a notable uptick in interest – seemingly from selectors as well as fans. Several players were rewarded with call-ups to the national side, including Central Punjab's Abdullah Shafiq, who scored a hundred on T20 debut, and Khushdil Shah, who smashed a 35-ball century in his breakout season. Khushdil's team, Southern Punjab, lost their first four matches before catching fire, sneaking into the semis on net run-rate when they raced past a target of 162 in 10.4 overs against Baluchistan in the last group game. They went on to the final, but there Mohammad Rizwan led Khyber Pakhtunkhwa to their first title of the season, after 67 from opener Fakhar Zaman made him the competition's leading run-scorer, with 420.

The Quaid-e-Azam Trophy was swiftly followed by the Pakistan One-Day Cup and produced the same finalists. This time, however, there was no close finish: Khyber Pakhtunkhwa romped home by seven wickets, with a century from Sahibzada Farhan steering them to victory over Central Punjab – and leaving them with at least one hand on each of the season's three domestic titles.

FIRST-CLASS AVERAGES IN 2020-21

BATTING (450 runs)

		M	I	NO	R	HS	100	Avge	Ct/St
1	Kamran Ghulam (*Khyber Pakhtunkhwa*) .	11	20	0	1,249	166	5	62.45	10
2	†Ayaz Tasawwar (*Baluchistan*).........	7	12	3	555	138*	1	61.66	10
3	Agha Salman (*Southern Punjab*)	10	19	3	941	169	2	58.81	8
4	†Fawad Alam (*Sindh/Pakistan*)	5	9	1	466	115	2	58.25	6
5	†Saud Shakil (*Sindh*).................	10	19	2	970	174	3	57.05	3
6	Asad Shafiq (*Sindh*).................	10	19	5	748	141	2	53.42	8
7	Hammad Azam (*Northern*)	10	18	2	846	145	2	52.87	5
8	Akbar-ur-Rehman (*Baluchistan*)......	8	14	0	727	164	2	51.92	6
9	†Mohammad Nawaz (*Northern*)	8	16	1	744	121	1	49.60	0
10	Saad Nasim (*Central Punjab*)	8	14	1	635	136*	1	48.84	12
11	Usman Salahuddin (*Central Punjab*) ..	11	21	2	924	219*	4	48.63	9
12	Adil Amin (*Khyber Pakhtunkhwa*)	10	19	1	864	172	1	48.00	4
13	†Zain Abbas (*Central Punjab*)	7	14	0	643	118	1	45.92	5
14	†Sharjeel Khan (*Sindh*)	8	15	0	656	133	2	43.73	4
15	†Umar Amin (*Northern*)	10	18	2	648	123	2	40.50	10
16	†Imran Farhat (*Baluchistan*)	8	14	1	517	116	1	39.76	3
17	†Israrullah (*Khyber Pakhtunkhwa*)	11	20	1	732	127	1	38.52	17
18	Khalid Usman (*Khyber Pakhtunkhwa*) ...	11	18	4	519	113*	1	37.07	6
19	Saif Badar (*Southern Punjab*)	8	16	1	542	81	0	36.13	4
20	†Imran Rafiq (*Southern Punjab*)	9	18	1	594	130	1	34.94	7
21	Mohammad Saad (*Central Punjab*).....	11	21	2	661	83	0	34.78	7
22	†Ali Zaryab (*Central Punjab*)	10	19	1	590	117	1	32.77	5
23	Nasir Nawaz (*Northern*)	7	14	0	450	68	0	32.14	3
24	†Umar Siddiq (*Southern Punjab*)	10	19	0	600	94	0	31.57	24/3
25	Rehan Afridi (*Khyber Pakhtunkhwa*)	11	19	1	561	127	1	31.16	26/9
26	Faizan Riaz (*Northern*)	9	18	2	495	146	1	30.93	14

BOWLING (15 wickets)

		Style	O	M	R	W	BB	5I	Avge
1	Hasan Ali (*Central Punjab/Pakistan*)	RFM	322.4	61	1,099	55	5-32	4	19.98
2	Irfanullah Shah (*Khyber Pakhtunkhwa*)	RFM	150.5	34	465	23	5-33	1	20.21
3	Waqas Maqsood (*Central Punjab*)...	LFM	301.2	78	893	41	6-25	1	21.78
4	Nauman Ali (*Northern/Pakistan*)	SLA	529.2	117	1,585	69	7-53	7	22.97
5	Aamer Yamin (*Southern Punjab*)....	RM	124	21	429	18	6-47	1	23.83
6	Sajid Khan (*Khyber Pakhtunkhwa*) ..	OB	512	78	1,681	67	6-71	5	25.08
7	Yasir Shah (*Baluchistan/Pakistan*)	LB	182.1	34	609	24	5-115	1	25.37
8	Jalat Khan (*Baluchistan*)	SLA	242	40	750	29	6-116	3	25.86
9	Zahid Mahmood (*Southern Punjab*) .	LB	340.2	34	1,401	52	6-57	3	26.94
10	Khurram Shehzad (*Baluchistan*)	RFM	129.5	17	502	18	5-27	1	27.88
11	Ahmed Safi (*Central Punjab*).......	SLA	263.3	37	993	34	5-106	1	29.20
12	Zia-ul-Haq (*Southern Punjab*)	LFM	143.2	19	504	17	7-35	1	29.64
13	Taj Wali (*Baluchistan*)	LFM	271.1	55	827	27	5-57	1	30.62
14	Tabish Khan (*Sindh*)...............	RFM	295.4	60	929	30	5-44	1	30.96
15	Khalid Usman (*Khyber Pakhtunkhwa*)	SLA	340.4	54	1,085	35	4-50	0	31.00
16	Kashif Bhatti (*Baluchistan*)	SLA	344.5	54	1,117	36	5-75	2	31.02
17	Shahnawaz Dahani (*Sindh*)........	RFM	224.5	39	811	26	4-79	0	31.19
18	Bilawal Iqbal (*Central Punjab*)	RFM	247.4	69	775	22	3-27	0	35.22
19	Arshad Iqbal (*Khyber Pakhtunkhwa*) .	RFM	163	26	546	15	3-42	0	36.40
20	Mohammad Nawaz (*Northern*)	SLA	229	42	823	22	5-69	2	37.40
21	Waqas Ahmed (*Northern*)	RF	233.2	35	870	19	4-78	0	45.78
22	Abrar Ahmed (*Sindh*)..............	OB	224.5	33	787	16	4-40	0	49.18
23	Mohammad Asghar (*Sindh*)	SLA	220.5	27	748	15	5-101	1	49.86

Overseas Cricket – Pakistan

QUAID-E-AZAM TROPHY IN 2020-21

	P	W	L	D	Bonus pts Bat	Bonus pts Bowl	Pts
KHYBER PAKHTUNKHWA....	10	5*	1	4	24	36	161
CENTRAL PUNJAB..........	10	4	3	3	18	40	137
Southern Punjab	10	4*	4	2	23	31	129
Baluchistan..................	10	3*	4	3	24	40	128
Northern	10	3	3	4	24	31	123
Sindh........................	10	1	5	4	18	33	87

* *One win by an innings.*

Outright win = 16pts; draw = 5pts. A further point was awarded for winning by an innings. Bonus points were awarded as follows for the first 100 overs of each team's first innings: one batting point for the first 200 runs, and then for 250, 300, 350 and 400; one bowling point for the third wicket taken, and then for the sixth and eighth; in addition, one bowling point for dismissing the opposition inside 100 overs for 251 to 300, two for 201 to 250 and three for 200 or less.

Final   At Karachi (National), January 1–5, 2021. **Tied. Central Punjab and Khyber Pakhtunkhwa shared the trophy. ‡Khyber Pakhtunkwa 300 and 312** (Kamran Ghulam 108); **Central Punjab 257-9 dec and 355** (Hasan Ali 106*). Central Punjab returned for their second successive final, but had to share the title with Khyber Pakhtunkhwa when the match was tied. After claiming 4-62, Hasan Ali declared 43 behind in the hope of setting up an outright result, but Central Punjab looked down and out at 202-7 in pursuit of 356. Then Hasan took charge, scoring a maiden century and supervising the addition of 153. With one run required, Kamran Ghulam ensured the tie with a catch at mid-on off Sajid Khan (4-86). Earlier, Kamran had followed his first-innings 76 with his fifth hundred of the season, which took him past Saadat Ali's record of 1,217 runs in a Quaid-e-Azam tournament, and helped set a target that was very nearly enough.

QUAID-E-AZAM TROPHY WINNERS

The competition has been contested sometimes by regional teams, sometimes by departments, sometimes by a mixture of the two, and now by six regional associations. Karachi teams have won the Quaid-e-Azam Trophy 20 times, PIA 7, National Bank 5, Lahore teams, Sui Northern Gas and United Bank 4, Habib Bank 3, Bahawalpur, Peshawar, Punjab, Railways and Sialkot 2, ADBP, Central Punjab, Faisalabad, Rawalpindi and WAPDA 1. Central Punjab and Khyber Pakhtunkhwa have also shared the title.

PAKISTAN ONE-DAY CUP IN 2020-21

50-over league plus knockout

Semi-finals   Central Punjab beat Sindh by 127 runs; Khyber Pakhtunkhwa tied with Northern but won a super over.

Final   At Karachi (State Bank), January 31, 2021. **Khyber Pakhtunkhwa won by seven wickets.** **Central Punjab 239** (47 overs) (Asif Afridi 5-39); ‡**Khyber Pakhtunkhwa 245-3** (36.1 overs) (Sahibzada Farhan 103*). *A few weeks after these teams shared the first-class title, Khyber Pakhtunkhwa made sure the one-day trophy was all theirs. Left-arm spinner Asif Afridi tied down Central Punjab with five wickets, before opener Sahibzada Farhan's run-a-ball century led them to victory with nearly 14 overs to spare.*

NATIONAL T20 CUP IN 2020-21

20-over league plus knockout

Semi-finals   Southern Punjab beat Northern by seven wickets; Khyber Pakhtunkhwa beat Sindh by eight wickets.

Final   At Rawalpindi, October 18, 2020 (floodlit). **Khyber Pakhtunkhwa won by ten runs.** **Khyber Pakhtunkhwa 206-4** (20 overs); ‡**Southern Punjab 196-8** (20 overs). *Khyber Pakhtunkhwa won their first title of the season after Fakhar Zaman (67) and Shoaib Malik (56* in 22) helped them pass 200. Shaheen Shah Afridi and Wahab Riaz claimed identical analyses of 3-36 as they topped and tailed Southern Punjab's innings, despite the efforts of Hussain Talat (63) and Mohammad Imran (38*), who hit three sixes in the final over.*

The HBL Pakistan Super League has its own section (page 1140).

SOUTH AFRICAN CRICKET IN 2021

De Kock's shocks

COLIN BRYDEN

Had India's 2021-22 tour been thwarted by the spread of the Omicron variant, the South African summer would have been denied its most joyous moment, when a largely inexperienced team came from behind to clinch the Test series. They won the last two matches by playing with the dogged determination of their captain, Dean Elgar, who made 96 not out in a successful chase at Johannesburg. The batting of Keegan Petersen, in only his second series, was a revelation, and the South African fast bowlers outshone their more heralded rivals, despite the absence of Anrich Nortje. His hip injury opened the door for the tall left-armer Marco Jansen, adding an exciting dimension to an attack led by Kagiso Rabada, who was back to his best form.

SOUTH AFRICA IN 2021

	Played	Won	Lost	Drawn/No result
Tests	6	3	3	–
One-day internationals	10	3	5	2
Twenty20 internationals	23	15	8	–

DECEMBER	2 Tests (h) v Sri Lanka	(see *Wisden 2021*, page 751)
JANUARY		
	2 Tests and 3 T20Is (a) v Pakistan	(page 970)
FEBRUARY		
MARCH		
APRIL	3 ODIs and 4 T20Is (h) v Pakistan	(page 987)
MAY		
JUNE	2 Tests and 5 T20Is (a) v West Indies	(page 1049)
JULY	3 ODIs and 3 T20Is (a) v Ireland	(page 947)
AUGUST		
SEPTEMBER	3 ODIs and 3 T20Is (a) v Sri Lanka	(page 1018)
OCTOBER	T20 World Cup in the UAE	(page 830)
NOVEMBER	1 ODI (h) v Netherlands	(page 991)
DECEMBER	3 Tests and 3 ODIs (h) v India	(page 992)
JANUARY		

For a review of South African domestic cricket from the 2020-21 season, see page 1002.

Matthew Lewis, ICC/Getty Images

Brought to kneel: Quinton de Kock finally follows CSA's instructions at the T20 World Cup.

The series had begun inauspiciously, as South Africa lost at Centurion. Later that evening came a statement from Quinton de Kock, the team's wicketkeeper and most talented batsman, announcing his immediate retirement from Tests. He had just turned 29. Already due to miss the last two games because of paternity leave, he had realised a need to spend more time with his family; despite signs of discontent, even disillusionment, earlier in the year, the news still came as a surprise.

The experiment of making de Kock captain in all formats had been aborted in March, when Elgar was named Test captain, with Temba Bavuma leading the white-ball teams. De Kock had never looked entirely comfortable in the role, and was more discomfited than most by the restrictions of biobubbles.

He was at the centre of controversy during the T20 World Cup in October, when he opted out of the match against West Indies rather than obey an edict from Cricket South Africa – issued on the morning of the game – for all the players to take the knee in solidarity with racial equality. After an online meeting with CSA officials, de Kock – himself part of a mixed-race family – apologised, and agreed to kneel in future. He made the point, though, that he had been "shocked" by the timing and directness of the instruction: "I felt like my rights were taken away."

It was a typical frustration of a year in which, until the India visit, the optimism at the end of 2020 was not fully realised. The interim CSA board, charged with paving the way for a new, majority-independent body, endured months of bickering and what looked at times like obstructionism from the members' council, consisting of the presidents of provincial unions. A new board were finally installed in June, and Lawson Naidoo – a respected lawyer who heads an organisation dedicated to upholding the South African constitution – was elected chairman. A 58-year-old lifelong follower of cricket, he still played the game socially. One of the new board members was Andrew Hudson, formerly a Test opener and chairman of selectors.

Much needed to be done to reverse years of decay and financial mismanagement, but progress was slow. One urgent task, to appoint a permanent chief executive, had not been completed by the end of the year.

In the meantime, hearings into allegations of racism in cricket were conducted by an ombudsman, Dumisa Ntsebeza. It became evident that there were occasions, particularly in the years immediately following unity in 1991, when the integration of black players into a white-dominated system lacked sensitivity. Ashwell Prince spoke of the pain of being labelled a "quota player", an unfair tag for a man with a batting average of 41 in 66 Tests. Ntsebeza recommended the appointment of a full-time ombudsman, and called for improved grievance and mediation procedures.

Several players, including former Test wicketkeeper Thami Tsolekile, alleged that racism played a role in their suspension on match-fixing charges, but Ntsebeza rejected such claims. However, director of cricket Graeme Smith and national team coach Mark Boucher were both implicated in allegations of racist behaviour, and CSA began a formal investigation.

Against this backdrop, it was not entirely surprising that results were chequered. At the beginning of the year, South Africa were beaten by Pakistan in four successive series: Tests and T20s away, one-dayers and T20s at home. There were signs of improvement in the West Indies, but a disappointing drawn one-day series in Ireland followed, before South Africa swept the T20s.

There was a similar pattern in Sri Lanka in September: South Africa lost the ODIs, but won their third T20 series in a row, before a creditable performance in the T20 World Cup. Having lost a close opener to Australia, they won their remaining four, and were denied a place in the semi-finals on net run-rate.

The Netherlands were invited to South Africa for a one-day series, but the first game was rained off, and the tour then fell victim to the spread of Omicron. At times, it seemed likely India's visit would go the same way. Somehow, it went ahead – and it was enthralling. Both sides' batsmen had to dig in against top-quality seam bowling on lively pitches. Elgar considered himself an "old-school" captain, who demanded absolute commitment from his men. Even after the Centurion defeat, he had their loyalty, and a 2–1 win was among South Africa's most satisfying.

SOUTH AFRICA v PAKISTAN IN 2020-21

NEIL MANTHORP

One-day internationals (3): South Africa 1, Pakistan 2
Twenty20 internationals (4): South Africa 1, Pakistan 3

Pakistan became only the second team, after Australia, to win more than one bilateral ODI series in South Africa. They did so thanks to record-breaking batting feats from Fakhar Zaman and Babar Azam, and clinical bowling when it mattered. They then won a T20 series in South Africa for the first time (excluding a one-off game in 2012-13). The fact that Cricket South Africa allowed five players to take up their IPL contracts after just two of the seven matches attracted opprobrium, but summed up their reliance on Indian money.

Temba Bavuma's appointment as limited-overs captain – the first black player to lead South Africa – was an important landmark, though he was not appointed because of the colour of his skin. A successful and ambitious skipper of Gauteng Lions, he had never disguised his desire to lead his country. While he was yet to establish himself as a regular in either white-ball format, it was hoped the captaincy would allow him to play with the freedom which comes with a guaranteed place. He made one, 92 and 20 in the 50-over matches, but a hamstring injury in the third ruled him out of the T20 series. Wicketkeeper Heinrich Klaasen, who had led the T20 side for three games at Lahore in February, stepped in. With Rassie van der Dussen missing the last two 20-over games because of a thigh strain, South Africa were at times without seven first-choice players. Having opted not to use former captain Faf du Plessis for either series, they were unusually short of experience.

Pakistan coach Misbah-ul-Haq said on arrival that victory would be "a great achievement" for his team, but that was based on history rather than form – of which the hosts had shown little. By the time Pakistan left, South Africa had won only two series out of 13 across all formats, and Misbah's opposite number, Mark Boucher, was under increasing pressure. He said he accepted "a massive amount of responsibility" for the results.

Babar Azam praised Fakhar for an "outstanding tour" which brought him 193 (off 155 balls) and 101 in the ODIs, and a match-winning 60 (off 34) in the third T20. But he was quick to recognise the role played by his bowlers, with Haris Rauf, Shaheen Shah Afridi and Hasan Ali all doing their bit.

PAKISTAN TOURING PARTY

*Babar Azam (50/20), Abdullah Shafiq (50), Arshad Iqbal (20), Asif Ali (50/20), Danish Aziz (50/20), Fahim Ashraf (50/20), Fakhar Zaman (50/20), Haider Ali (50/20), Haris Rauf (50/20), Hasan Ali (50/20), Imam-ul-Haq (50), Mohammad Hafeez (20), Mohammad Hasnain (50/20), Mohammad Nawaz (50/20), Mohammad Rizwan (50/20), Mohammad Wasim (50/20), Sarfaraz Ahmed (50/20), Shadab Khan (50), Shaheen Shah Afridi (50/20), Sharjeel Khan (20), Usman Qadir (50/20), Zahid Mahmood (20). *Coach:* Misbah-ul-Haq.

Saud Shakil withdrew from the tour with a leg injury, and was replaced by Asif Ali. Shadab Khan was ruled out of the T20 series with a toe injury.

First one-day international At Centurion, April 2, 2021. **Pakistan won by three wickets. South Africa 273-6** (50 overs) (H. E. van der Dussen 123*, D. A. Miller 50); ‡**Pakistan 274-7** (50 overs) (Imam-ul-Haq 70, Babar Azam 103, Mohammad Rizwan 40, Shadab Khan 33; A. A. Nortje 4-51). *Pakistan 10pts. PoM: Babar Azam. ODI debut: Danish Aziz (Pakistan). A glorious century from Babar Azam, who put on 177 with Imam-ul-Haq, set up a Pakistan victory which should have been sealed long before the last over, never mind the last ball. Chasing 274, the tourists reached 186-1 in the 32nd. But Anrich Nortje launched a bouncer barrage, and was rewarded with four for six in 18 deliveries, starting with Babar, who edged behind the ball after completing his 13th ODI hundred in only his 76th innings. Mohammad Rizwan's steadying innings ended with a pull, and Shadab Khan slashed Andile Phehlukwayo to deep cover. With 12 needed off eight balls, Lungi Ngidi bowled Shadab with a full toss, but it was called a no-ball on height; the free hit was smashed through extra cover. Even so, a single was still needed off the final delivery: Phehlukwayo's attempted yorker would have been a wide had Fahim Ashraf not slapped it past point. Earlier, South Africa were rescued from 55-4 by Rassie van der Dussen's maiden ODI century – after reaching 50 seven times in his first 16 innings (and averaging 70). He added a patient 116 with David Miller, then 64 with Phehlukwayo. But their total looked below par on a faultless surface.*

Second one-day international At Johannesburg, April 4, 2021. **South Africa won by 17 runs. South Africa 341-6** (50 overs) (Q. de Kock 80, A. K. Markram 39, T. Bavuma 92, H. E. van der Dussen 60, D. A. Miller 50*; Haris Rauf 3-54); ‡**Pakistan 324-9** (50 overs) (Fakhar Zaman 193, Babar Azam 31; A. A. Nortje 3-63). *South Africa 10pts. PoM: Fakhar Zaman. Fakhar Zaman hit one of the greatest one-day centuries in a losing cause, a bewildering 193 out of 324-9; Pakistan's next best was Babar's 31. It was the highest innings in an ODI chase, and the highest ODI score at the Wanderers, beating Herschelle Gibbs's 175 for South Africa against Australia in 2005-06. From an unpromising 205-7 in the 38th, Fakhar seemed able to hit every ball exactly where he wanted.*

HIGHEST ODI SCORES IN DEFEAT

194*	C. K. Coventry	Zimbabwe v Bangladesh at Bulawayo		2009
193	**Fakhar Zaman**	**Pakistan v South Africa at Johannesburg**		**2020-21**
181*	M. L. Hayden	Australia v New Zealand at Hamilton		2006-07
176*	E. Lewis	West Indies v England at The Oval		2017
175	S. R. Tendulkar	India v Australia at Hyderabad		2009-10
173	D. A. Warner	Australia v South Africa at Cape Town		2016-17
171*	R. G. Sharma	India v Australia at Perth		2015-16
167*	R. A. Smith	England v Australia at Birmingham		1993
164	R. T. Ponting	Australia v South Africa at Johannesburg		2005-06
162	C. H. Gayle	West Indies v England at St George's		2018-19
160*	T. M. Dilshan	Sri Lanka v India at Hobart		2011-12
160	T. M. Dilshan	Sri Lanka v India at Rajkot		2008-09

Five sixes came in six off Tabraiz Shamsi, as he singlehandedly reduced the equation to 38 off two overs. But his innings ended in controversy. Heading back for a second, he was deceived when Quinton de Kock, South Africa's wicketkeeper, pointed towards the bowler's end, to indicate that was where Aiden Markram's boundary throw was heading. Running to the striker's end, Fakhar slowed, and looked behind him. In fact, the ball came to his end, and a direct hit ran him out. The umpires took no action, and Fakhar diplomatically blamed himself. Temba Bavuma had played a crucial role in South Africa's huge total, adding 114 with de Kock, and 101 with van der Dussen; Miller then thrashed a 27-ball 50* to leave Pakistan facing a mountain they nearly scaled.

Third one-day international At Centurion, April 7, 2021. **Pakistan won by 28 runs. Pakistan 320-7** (50 overs) (Imam-ul-Haq 57, Fakhar Zaman 101, Babar Azam 94, Hasan Ali 32*; K. A. Maharaj 3-45); ‡**South Africa 292** (49.3 overs) (J. N. Malan 70, K. Verreynne 62, A. L. Phehlukwayo 54; Shaheen Shah Afridi 3-58, Mohammad Nawaz 3-34). *Pakistan 10pts. PoM: Babar Azam. PoS: Fakhar Zaman. ODI debut: Usman Qadir (Pakistan). Another century from Fakhar set up victory for Pakistan, and took him to 302 runs in six days – the highest aggregate compiled by South Africa in a three-match series. Babar's prolific form continued too, with 94 from 82 balls, after Imam-ul-Haq's measured 57 in an opening stand of 112. South Africa's spinners, led by Keshav Maharaj, thwarted Pakistan's progress, before Hasan Ali lofted slow left-armer Jon-Jon Smuts for four sixes* *in the 49th over, and Babar helped wallop Phehlukwayo for 18 in the last, falling in search of the six that would have brought him a hundred. Despite Janneman Malan's energetic 70, South Africa stumbled to 140-5 against the probing left-arm spin of Mohammad Nawaz and the turn of leg-spinner Usman Qadir, son of Abdul, in his first ODI. Kyle Verreynne underlined his promise with a mature fifty and a century stand with Phehlukwayo. But he heaved a slower ball from Haris Rauf to deep square leg, Phehlukwayo top-edged a slog off Hasan, and the chase petered out.*

First Twenty20 international   At Johannesburg, April 10, 2021. **Pakistan won by four wickets.** ‡**South Africa 188-6** (20 overs) (A. K. Markram 51, H. Klaasen 50, P. J. van Biljon 34); **Pakistan 189-6** (19.5 overs) (Mohammad Rizwan 74*, Fahim Ashraf 30; B. E. Hendricks 3-32). *PoM:* Mohammad Rizwan. *T20I debuts:* W. J. Lubbe, S. S. B. Magala, L. B. Williams (South Africa). *South African inexperience allowed Pakistan to steal a match they rarely looked like winning. The tourists needed 38 from three overs, but left-armer Beuran Hendricks – who had just removed Haider Ali and Nawaz in two balls – served up three full tosses, which Rizwan despatched for 14. It came down to 11 off the last over, bowled by Lizaad Williams, one of three South African debutants. Ashraf was dropped off the first ball and bowled by the second, before Rizwan and Hasan Ali scrambled the winning runs off the penultimate delivery. It was Pakistan's highest successful T20 chase, beating 187 (chasing 184) against Australia at Harare in 2018. Earlier, Malan had given South Africa the perfect start by targeting Shaheen Shah Afridi, while Markram and captain Heinrich Klaasen took heavy toll of an out-of-sorts attack, with only left-arm spinner Nawaz controlling the rate. But South Africa slowed disastrously: from the start of the 17th over to the end of the 19th, they managed just 15 runs (and lost three wickets) – a shortfall that not even Sisanda Magala's last-ball six off Afridi could make good.*

Second Twenty20 international   At Johannesburg, April 12, 2021. **South Africa won by six wickets.** ‡**Pakistan 140-9** (20 overs) (Babar Azam 50, Mohammad Hafeez 32; G. F. Linde 3-23, L. B. Williams 3-35); **South Africa 141-4** (14 overs) (A. K. Markram 54, H. Klaasen 36*). *PoM:* G. F. Linde. *South Africa galloped to a mediocre target, thanks to another half-century from Markram, and a stand of 49* in 3.4 overs between Klaasen (36* in 21 balls) and George Linde (20* in ten). Linde had already contributed three wickets with his left-arm spin (and held three catches), having struck with the game's first ball: charging down the pitch, Rizwan skyed to mid-on, ending a streak of ten consecutive scores of 40 or more in all T20s for his country and Multan Sultans. Babar made a run-a-ball 50, but Pakistan also struggled against South Africa's other slow bowler. Shamsi conceded 22 in his four overs. It wasn't plain sailing for the home side, as Magala inherited Dale Steyn's national record for the longest T20 over. He did well to concede only 18, after beginning with three no-balls and a wide; two more wides followed. Magala recovered to take 1-14 from his final three overs, and help suffocate the Pakistanis.*

Third Twenty20 international   At Centurion, April 14, 2021. **Pakistan won by nine wickets.** **South Africa 203-5** (20 overs) (J. N. Malan 55, A. K. Markram 63, H. E. van der Dussen 34*); ‡**Pakistan 205-1** (18 overs) (Mohammad Rizwan 73*, Babar Azam 122). *PoM:* Babar Azam.

HIGHEST PARTNERSHIPS IN T20 INTERNATIONALS

236 for 1st	Hazratullah Zazai/Usman Ghani	Afghanistan v Ireland at Dehradun	2018-19
223 for 1st	A. J. Finch/D. J. M. Short	Australia v Zimbabwe at Harare	2018
200 for 1st	H. G. Munsey/K. J. Coetzer	Scotland v Netherlands at Malahide	2019
197 for 1st	**Mohammad Rizwan/Babar Azam**	**Pakistan v SA at Centurion**	**2020-21**
184 for 3rd	D. P. Conway/G. D. Phillips	NZ v West Indies at Mount Maunganui	2020-21
182 for 3rd	D. J. Malan/E. J. G. Morgan	England v New Zealand at Napier	2019-20
171* for 1st	M. J. Guptill/K. S. Williamson	NZ v Pakistan at Hamilton	2015-16
170 for 1st	G. C. Smith/L. E. Bosman	SA v England at Centurion	2009-10
167* for 2nd	J. C. Buttler/D. J. Malan	England v SA at Cape Town	2020-21
166 for 2nd	D. P. M. D. Jayawardene/K. C. Sangakkara	Sri Lanka v West Indies at Bridgetown	2009-10

A sparkling 49-ball hundred from Babar condemned South Africa to a thrashing. He eventually fell for 122 from 59, Pakistan's highest T20 score, beating Ahmed Shehzad's 111 against Bangladesh in the 2013-14 World T20 at Mirpur. An opening stand of 197 with Rizwan, whose 47-ball 73 looked pedestrian by comparison, also broke records: an all-wicket best for Pakistan, and the highest by any T20 team in a chase, surpassing 194 between Aaron Finch and Jason Roy for Surrey against*

Middlesex at The Oval in 2018. Set 204, Pakistan also improved their highest successful T20 chase for the second time in five days. Their bowlers had been savaged too, as South Africa reached 140-1 with seven overs to go, following a third straight fifty for Markram (63 from 31) and a first in the format for Malan. But Pakistan fought back to keep the target within bounds.

Fourth Twenty20 international   At Centurion, April 16, 2021. **Pakistan won by three wickets. South Africa 144** (19.3 overs) (J. N. Malan 33, H. E. van der Dussen 52; Hasan Ali 3-40, Fahim Ashraf 3-17); ‡**Pakistan 149-7** (19.5 overs) (Fakhar Zaman 60). *PoM:* Fahim Ashraf. *PoS:* Babar Azam. *T20I debut:* P. W. A. Mulder (South Africa). *Pakistan developed wheel-wobble of extraordinary proportions in pursuit of a straightforward 145 in perfect conditions. Having reached 92-1 inside ten overs, they lost six for 37 in nine to a string of unnecessarily belligerent shots. Fakhar, who had eased to 60 off 33, miscued a drive off Williams, before Babar slashed to third man in the same over. Haider Ali was caught at deep square leg, the usually calm Mohammad Hafeez messed up a slog-sweep, and Asif Ali toe-ended a return catch. When Ashraf's ambitious back-foot drive found mid-on, Pakistan still needed 16 from nine balls. But Magala overstepped twice, and Nawaz restored order with a pair of sixes, the second – off Williams – sealing a series win with a ball to spare. Earlier, South Africa collapsed from a promising 109-2 in the 13th to 144, with Ashraf expertly throttling the innings. Only van der Dussen (52 from 36) wriggled free.*

SOUTH AFRICA v NETHERLANDS IN 2021-22

Firdose Moonda

One-day internationals (1): South Africa 0 (5pts), Netherlands 0 (5pts)

The Super League added context to an otherwise under-the-radar contest: having dropped points in Ireland and Sri Lanka, South Africa needed to sweep the three-match series to stay on track for automatic qualification for the 2023 World Cup. They were denied, but by a greater opponent than the Netherlands.

Anticipating a busy summer, the South Africans had chosen to rest six regulars, which made room for Wayne Parnell, the first of the recent Kolpaks to return to the national team. Khaya Zondo was recalled, while Zubayr Hamza and Sisanda Magala were given one-day debuts.

Ryan ten Doeschate had retired, but still travelled with the Netherlands as a mentor. Several of the squad had played domestic cricket in South Africa: useful expertise for them – and great targets for the first spectators permitted at matches since the start of the pandemic. But the crowd did not get to see much. The first match went ahead just as the Omicron variant was taking hold. Ryan Campbell, the Dutch coach, said his players were worried, but under "unbelievable pressure" to take the field. After rain curtailed the game, the remaining fixtures were postponed as the players' concerns held sway. They could not get a flight home until two days after the series was scheduled to finish.

NETHERLANDS TOURING PARTY

P. M. Seelaar, C. N. Ackermann, M. N. Ahmed, B. F. W. de Leede, S. A. Edwards, C. Floyd, B. D. Glover, B. H. G. Gorlee, V. J. Kingma, F. J. Klaassen, S. J. Myburgh, M. P. O'Dowd, S. Snater, T. van der Gugten, R. E. van der Merwe, M. S. Zulfiqar. Coach: R. J. Campbell.

First one-day international At Centurion, November 26, 2021. **No result. South Africa 277-8** (50 overs) (M. Z. Hamza 56, K. Verreynne 95, A. L. Phehlukwayo 48); ‡**Netherlands 11-0** (2 overs). *South Africa 5pts, Netherlands 5pts. ODI debuts: M. Z. Hamza, S. S. B. Magala (South Africa); C. N. Ackermann (Netherlands). Despite having never successfully chased against a team ranked in the top eight, the Netherlands chose to field in their first match against South Africa since 2013-14. Kyle Verreynne – dropped on 19 – laid a foundation with 95, before Andile Phehlukwayo and Keshav Maharaj added 68 for the eighth wicket. Even so, it was the first time South Africa had failed to reach 300 in an ODI against the Netherlands. An afternoon storm ended the chase after two overs.*

Second one-day international At Centurion, November 28, 2021. **South Africa v Netherlands. Cancelled.**

Third one-day international At Centurion, December 1, 2021. **South Africa v Netherlands. Cancelled.**

SOUTH AFRICA v INDIA IN 2021-22

Neil Manthorp

Test matches (3): South Africa 2 (24pts), India 1 (11pts)
One-day internationals (3): South Africa 3, India 0

This tour was delayed by a week while the effects of the Omicron variant were assessed, but the BCCI's decision to go ahead was received with extreme gratitude by Cricket South Africa, who feared financial ruin had the trip been cancelled. And CSA were further delighted by an exciting, low-scoring Test series, which the home side came from behind to win 2–1. It was the first time a series of three or more Tests had been won by a team that never reached 250.

Virat Kohli had made no secret of his desire to become the first Indian captain to win a Test series in South Africa. It started well enough, with a 113-run victory, but he was forced to sit out the Second Test because of a back spasm and, after his side slipped to a pair of seven-wicket defeats, he gave up the captaincy. He had already handed over the T20 leadership, after which the board stripped him of the ODI job too.

Neither side were at full strength. India were missing Rohit Sharma, their prolific opener (and new one-day captain), as well as the influential all-rounder Ravindra Jadeja. Both were injured, as was South Africa's fastest and most potent bowler, Anrich Nortje. The hosts also had to deal with the sudden retirement of Quinton de Kock – their wicketkeeper and best batsman – who caused a seismic shock by calling a halt to his Test career after the defeat at Centurion. Two weeks after his 29th birthday, de Kock said he wanted to spend more time with his family; his first child was born during the Second Test, for which he had already been granted paternity leave.

Another under immense pressure was South Africa's head coach, Mark Boucher. Between the Test and one-day series, CSA announced their intention to charge him with gross misconduct for "racist and/or subliminally racist behaviour" as a player 20 years earlier, and for his recent handling of the team, especially their initial inability to display a united stance in their support for the anti-racism movement. The seven-page rap sheet was leaked to the media between the second and third one-dayers, which rattled the players and made the subsequent series win all the more impressive. Boucher replied with a single paragraph, expressing his intention to defend himself against all the allegations.

India started as most had predicted – the only previous visitors to win an uncontrived Test at Centurion had been Australia. But then, unexpectedly, India lost the remaining five matches of the tour. If their Test batting was disappointing, South Africa's seamers were superb. Kagiso Rabada was fortunate his 41 no-balls were not more costly, but he led the attack well, and delivered 20 wickets at 19 apiece. Lungi Ngidi was just as lethal, with 15 at 15. But it was Marco Jansen's 19 wickets at 16 in his debut series which took everyone by surprise. A 6ft 9in left-arm seamer aged 21, he was thought to be in the Covid-enlarged squad purely as back-up, and his selection for the First Test caught many on the hop. After that, it was the batsmen who were hopping: apart from a nervous first spell, Jansen looked entirely comfortable, bowling with pace and, thanks to his lanky frame, conjuring bounce from awkward angles. He can bat, too, and could be a banker for South Africa for years to come. His arrival overshadowed the return of Duanne Olivier, his Kolpak days behind him.

Another discovery was Keegan Petersen who, at 28, was less of an overnight sensation. Solid and compact in defence, with a sweet cover-drive and simple, effective punches off the back foot, he made 62, 72 and 82 in the final two Tests, and finished as the series' leading scorer. Dean Elgar, the Test captain, who supervised a tricky chase to make it 1–1 at Johannesburg, and one-day skipper Temba Bavuma also got their heads down.

Equally unexpected was the decisive factor in South Africa's one-day success: spin. Not only did they play it with more skill than India, they bowled it better as well. Slow left-armer Keshav Maharaj dismissed Kohli twice, and went for a tick above 4.5 an over; Tabraiz Shamsi took four wickets in his two games, and even part-time off-spinner Aiden Markram sent down 17 overs at an economy-rate of just five. Meanwhile, India's vaunted spinners struggled. Ravichandran Ashwin took one for 121 in his two outings, while leggie Yuzvendra Chahal nursed figures of two for 147 in 29 overs.

INDIA TOURING PARTY

*V. Kohli (T/50), M. A. Agarwal (T), R. Ashwin (T/50), Bhuvneshwar Kumar (50), J. J. Bumrah (T/50), Y. S. Chahal (50), D. L. Chahar (50), S. Dhawan (50), R. S. Gaikwad (50), S. S. Iyer (T/50), V. R. Iyer (50), I. P. Kishan (50), P. M. Krishna (50), Mohammed Shami (T), P. K. Panchal (T), R. R. Pant (T/50), C. A. Pujara (T), A. M. Rahane (T), K. L. Rahul (T/50), W. P. Saha (T), N. Saini (50), I. Sharma (T), M. Siraj (T/50), S. N. Thakur (T/50), G. H. Vihari (T), J. Yadav (T/50), S. A. Yadav (50), U. T. Yadav (T). *Coach:* R. Dravid.

R. G. Sharma was originally named in both squads, and as captain for the ODIs, but withdrew because of a hamstring injury; Panchal replaced him for the Tests, while Rahul led in the ODIs. M. S. Washington Sundar was originally part of the 50-over squad, but was replaced by J. Yadav after testing positive for Covid. Chahar, Saini, A. R. Nagwaswalla and Saurabh Kumar accompanied the Test team as reserves; Saini joined the full 50-over squad when Siraj was injured.

TEST MATCH AVERAGES

SOUTH AFRICA – BATTING AND FIELDING

	T	I	NO	R	HS	100	50	Avge	Ct
T. Bavuma	3	6	3	221	52	0	2	73.66	3
†D. Elgar	3	6	1	235	96*	0	2	47.00	4
K. D. Petersen	3	6	0	276	82	0	3	46.00	8
H. E. van der Dussen	3	6	1	117	41*	0	0	23.40	4
K. A. Maharaj	3	4	0	66	25	0	0	16.50	2
M. Jansen	3	4	0	60	21	0	0	15.00	2
A. K. Markram	3	6	0	76	31	0	0	12.66	4
†K. Rabada	3	4	0	40	25	0	0	10.00	2
L. T. Ngidi	3	4	1	3	3	0	0	1.00	1

Played in two Tests: D. Olivier 1*, 10*; K. Verreynne 21, 0 (14 ct). Played in one Test: †Q. de Kock 34, 21 (7 ct); P. W. A. Mulder 12, 1 (4 ct).

BOWLING

	Style	O	M	R	W	BB	5I	Avge
L. T. Ngidi	RFM	83.4	25	225	15	6-71	1	15.00
M. Jansen	LF	103.3	29	313	19	4-31	0	16.47
K. Rabada	RF	119.1	23	381	20	4-42	0	19.05
D. Olivier	RFM	57	8	195	5	3-64	0	39.00

Also bowled: K. A. Maharaj (SLA) 32–5–119–1; P. W. A. Mulder (RFM) 29–8–74–0.

INDIA – BATTING AND FIELDING

	T	I	NO	R	HS	100	50	Avge	Ct
V. Kohli	2	4	0	161	79	0	1	40.25	2
K. L. Rahul	3	6	0	226	123	1	1	37.66	1
†R. R. Pant	3	6	1	186	100*	1	0	37.20	13
A. M. Rahane	3	6	0	136	58	0	1	22.66	2
M. A. Agarwal	3	6	0	135	60	0	1	22.50	1
C. A. Pujara	3	6	0	124	53	0	1	20.66	4
R. Ashwin	3	6	0	89	46	0	0	14.83	2
J. J. Bumrah	3	6	2	44	14*	0	0	11.00	1
S. N. Thakur	3	6	0	59	28	0	0	9.83	0
Mohammed Shami	3	6	0	25	9	0	0	4.16	1
M. Siraj	2	4	1	5	4*	0	0	1.66	1

Played in one Test: G. H. Vihari 20, 40*; U. T. Yadav 4*, 0.

BOWLING

	Style	O	M	R	W	BB	5I	Avge
S. N. Thakur	RFM	72.5	11	229	12	7-61	1	19.08
Mohammed Shami	RFM	102	23	294	14	5-44	1	21.00
J. J. Bumrah	RFM	104.5	26	281	12	5-42	1	23.41
M. Siraj	RFM	49	10	153	3	2-47	0	51.00
R. Ashwin	OB	64.1	11	182	3	2-18	0	60.66

Also bowled: U. T. Yadav (RF) 25–3–100–2.

SOUTH AFRICA v INDIA

First Test

At Centurion, December 26–30, 2021. India won by 113 runs. India 11pts (after 1pt penalty). Toss: India. Test debut: M. Jansen.

A Test match cannot be won on the first day, at least not by a batsman, but Rahul went a long way towards ensuring Indian supremacy with an exceptionally disciplined century in difficult conditions. His partnership of 117 with Karnataka team-mate Mayank Agarwal was only India's third century opening stand in eight tours of South Africa, and it laid the platform for their first victory at Centurion, where South Africa had won 21 of the previous 26 Tests.

Punching up – or down? Marco Jansen, the tallest current Test cricketer, and Temba Bavuma, the shortest.

Kohli's decision to bat under threatening grey skies was bold and, though the pitch lacked pace on the first day, there was plenty of movement to encourage the home fast-bowling trio. But they couldn't exploit it, aiming too short and failing to build pressure. As well as Rahul and Agarwal batted, it was the shots they didn't play which contributed as much to their success. On the rare occasions the seamers found the right lines and lengths, they were unable to tempt the batsmen to flirt.

The second day was lost to rain, but the third morning offered spectacular evidence both of how poorly South Africa had bowled, and how responsible the previous batting had been: the last seven wickets tumbled for 49, with Ngidi and Rabada reaping the benefits of attacking the stumps. India's four seamers then did the same, immediately and relentlessly: on a pitch starting to misbehave, South Africa were soon 32 for four. Bavuma – belligerent in attack, solid in defence – was helped by de Kock in a stand of 72 which held the tourists up, but no one looked comfortable. Mohammed Shami's control was outstanding and, had it not been for a couple of beefy contributions from Jansen and Rabada, the deficit of 130 would have been greater – but it still looked match-defining.

In such difficult batting conditions, every contribution was valuable, and seven of India's top eight now reached double figures, by varying methods. Rahul and Pujara survived 74 and 64 balls apiece, while Rahane and Pant chanced their arm. Rabada and Jansen both claimed four wickets with some probing deliveries, but that was par for the course on a pitch offering lateral movement and unpredictable bounce. Seven wickets fell to catches in the cordon.

Not even the most optimistic local supporter fancied South Africa to chase 305, especially after they lost four wickets before the end of the fourth day – including nightwatchman Maharaj, bowled by Bumrah from the final ball of the evening. If any hope remained, it was in the low-slung shape of Elgar, still there at stumps with a stubborn 52.

He should have gone on 63, when Shami dropped a sitter off his own bowling, but it was not expensive: Bumrah trapped him for 77 and the game was up. Bavuma remained stoically unbeaten, but de Kock's chop-on was symbolic of his team's tame surrender and his own frame of mind. Shortly after India's victory, he announced his retirement from Test cricket, a fortnight after turning 29.

Shami completed match figures of eight for 107, but Rahul's opening-day century was recognised by both captains – and the match award – as the greatest difference between the teams. The only cloud on India's horizon was a point penalty for a slow over-rate.

Player of the Match: K. L. Rahul.

Close of play: first day, India 272-3 (Rahul 122, Rahane 40); second day, no play; third day, India 16-1 (Rahul 5, Thakur 4); fourth day, South Africa 94-4 (Elgar 52).

India

K. L. Rahul c de Kock b Rabada	123	– c Elgar b Ngidi	23
M. A. Agarwal lbw b Ngidi	60	– c de Kock b Jansen	4
C. A. Pujara c Petersen b Ngidi	0	– (4) c de Kock b Ngidi	16
*V. Kohli c Mulder b Ngidi	35	– (5) c de Kock b Jansen	18
A. M. Rahane c de Kock b Ngidi	48	– (6) c van der Dussen b Jansen	20
†R. R. Pant c van der Dussen b Ngidi	8	– (7) c Ngidi b Rabada	34
R. Ashwin c Maharaj b Rabada	4	– (8) c Petersen b Rabada	14
S. N. Thakur c de Kock b Rabada	4	– (3) c Mulder b Rabada	10
Mohammed Shami c de Kock b Ngidi	8	– b Mulder b Rabada	1
J. J. Bumrah c Mulder b Jansen	14	– not out	7
M. Siraj not out	4	– b Jansen	0
B 4, lb 4, nb 11	19	B 17, lb 4, nb 6	27

1/117 (2) 2/117 (3) 3/199 (4) (105.3 overs) 327
4/278 (1) 5/291 (5) 6/296 (7)
7/296 (6) 8/304 (8) 9/308 (9) 10/327 (10)

1/12 (2) 2/34 (3) (50.3 overs) 174
3/54 (1) 4/79 (5)
5/109 (4) 6/111 (6) 7/146 (8)
8/166 (7) 9/169 (9) 10/174 (11)

Rabada 26–5–72–3; Ngidi 24–5–71–6; Jansen 18.3–4–69–1; Mulder 19–4–49–0; Maharaj 18–2–58–0. *Second innings*—Rabada 17–4–42–4; Ngidi 10–2–31–2; Jansen 13.3–4–55–4; Mulder 10–4–25–0.

South Africa

*D. Elgar c Pant b Bumrah	1	– (2) lbw b Bumrah	77
A. K. Markram b Mohammed Shami	13	– (1) b Mohammed Shami	1
K. D. Petersen b Mohammed Shami	15	– c Pant b Siraj	17
H. E. van der Dussen c Rahane b Siraj	3	– b Bumrah	11
T. Bavuma c Pant b Mohammed Shami	52	– (6) not out	35
†Q. de Kock b Thakur	34	– (7) b Siraj	21
P. W. A. Mulder c Pant b Mohammed Shami	12	– (8) c Pant b Mohammed Shami	1
M. Jansen lbw b Thakur	19	– (9) c Pant b Mohammed Shami	13
K. Rabada c Pant b Mohammed Shami	25	– (10) c Mohammed Shami b Ashwin	8
K. A. Maharaj c Rahane b Bumrah	12	– (5) b Bumrah	8
L. T. Ngidi not out	0	– c Pujara b Ashwin	0
Lb 4, nb 7	11	Lb 2, nb 5	7

1/2 (1) 2/25 (3) 3/30 (2) (62.3 overs) 197
4/32 (4) 5/104 (6) 6/133 (7)
7/144 (5) 8/181 (8) 9/193 (9) 10/197 (10)

1/1 (1) 2/34 (3) (68 overs) 191
3/74 (4) 4/94 (5)
5/130 (2) 6/161 (7) 7/164 (8)
8/190 (6) 9/191 (10) 10/191 (11)

Bumrah 7.2–2–16–2; Siraj 15.1–3–45–1; Mohammed Shami 16–5–44–5; Thakur 11–1–51–2; Ashwin 13–2–37–0. *Second innings*—Bumrah 19–4–50–3; Mohammed Shami 17–3–63–3; Siraj 18–5–47–2; Thakur 5–0–11–0; Ashwin 9–2–18–2.

Umpires: M. Erasmus and A. T. Holdstock.   Third umpire: A. Paleker.
Referee: A. J. Pycroft.

SOUTH AFRICA v INDIA

Second Test

At Johannesburg, January 3–6, 2022. South Africa won by seven wickets. South Africa 12pts. Toss: India.

Elgar played the lead role in one of South Africa's best Test run-chases with an unbeaten 96, spanning 188 balls in over five hours, on another pitch that offered lateral movement and inconsistent bounce. South Africa had never successfully chased down as many as 240 at the Wanderers, their previous-best being 220 against New Zealand in May 2006 (Australia made 310 for eight in 2011-12). India badly missed Kohli, who was ruled out with a sore back shortly before the game; Rahul took charge for the first time in a Test.

Elgar was beaten as often as anybody, and struck repeatedly on the body; he needed three lots of treatment, but never flinched, and completed the job he was unable to finish a week earlier.

The match had been turned on its head by Rabada, who claimed three wickets in 22 balls just as India were on the point of grabbing control on the third morning. The long-serving pair of Pujara and Rahane had both reached brave half-centuries during a partnership of 111 against some profligate bowling from Ngidi and Jansen; Rahane even cut Jansen for six over point. The first hour had produced 66 runs and, though India's lead was a modest 128, it seemed that could mushroom: the attack were uninspired, the batsmen set. Elgar gave a dressing-down during the drinks break, after which Rabada almost immediately had Rahane caught at slip with a searing leg-cutter, then pinned Pujara with a nip-backer. His second ball to Pant reared up and struck gloves in front of helmet; Pant charged down to the third and swung wildly, edging to Kyle Verreynne, the new keeper. It was a horrid response, in conditions where physical discomfort and pain were a prerequisite for success. "When KG's got his tail up, there's no better bowler," enthused Elgar.

Kohli's stand-in, Vihari, showed he had the stomach for the fight, and remained until the end, watching Thakur hit a breezy 28, but Rabada's spell had given South Africa a chance. Most believed it to be a long shot, but the doubters had not reckoned with Elgar's resolve.

India's first-innings 202 could have been worse: when Rahul's uncharacteristic hook was taken on the square-leg boundary, they were 116 for five, but Ashwin made a counter-punching 46 from No. 7. Jansen's later spells, marrying pace to steepling bounce, asked stern questions of the lower order's temperament and technique.

South Africa looked on course for a big lead when they reached 88 for one but, well as Petersen played for a maiden half-century in his fourth Test, wickets were always likely to fall in clusters. With Siraj nursing a thigh strain, Thakur stepped up with a virtuoso display of wobble-seam bowling, ideal for the surface. His career-best seven for 61 was hard-earned – and restricted the deficit to 27. Thakur's haul included the two top-scorers, Petersen caught at second slip and Bavuma glancing down leg.

The series' first moment of controversy and niggle had come with the dismissal of van der Dussen, when replays showed Pant catching an outside edge apparently on the half-volley. The evidence was inconclusive, so the decision was not overturned, but it came just 17 deliveries after he had claimed a catch off the same batter which had clearly bounced (and, for good measure, missed the bat). During lunch, South Africa's coach Mark Boucher spent ten minutes in the referee's room, asking whether van der Dussen could be recalled, as the wicket had fallen to the last delivery before the break. The officials indicated that he could – if India withdrew the appeal, which they did not.

South Africa started the fourth day on 118 for two, needing another 122. A tense finish was on the cards – but never happened. The pitch had flattened out, and the Indian attack looked listless: the only casualty as the hosts levelled the series was van der Dussen, uncontroversially caught at slip.

Player of the Match: D. Elgar.

Close of play: first day, South Africa 35-1 (Elgar 11, Petersen 14); second day, India 85-2 (Pujara 35, Rahane 11); third day, South Africa 118-2 (Elgar 46, van der Dussen 11).

India

*K. L. Rahul c Rabada b Jansen	50	– c Markram b Jansen	8
M. A. Agarwal c Verreynne b Jansen	26	– lbw b Olivier	23
C. A. Pujara c Bavuma b Olivier	3	– lbw b Rabada	53
A. M. Rahane c Petersen b Olivier	0	– c Verreynne b Rabada	58
G. H. Vihari c van der Dussen b Rabada	20	– not out	40
†R. R. Pant c Verreynne b Jansen	17	– c Verreynne b Rabada	0
R. Ashwin c Petersen b Jansen	46	– c Verreynne b Ngidi	16
S. N. Thakur c Petersen b Olivier	0	– c Maharaj b Jansen	28
Mohammed Shami c and b Rabada	9	– c Verreynne b Jansen	0
J. J. Bumrah not out	14	– c Jansen b Ngidi	7
M. Siraj c Verreynne b Rabada	1	– b Ngidi	0
B 8, lb 3, nb 5	16	B 16, lb 4, w 5, nb 8	33

1/36 (2) 2/49 (3) 3/49 (4)   (63.1 overs) 202
4/91 (5) 5/116 (1) 6/156 (6)
7/157 (8) 8/185 (9) 9/187 (7) 10/202 (11)

1/24 (1) 2/44 (2)   (60.1 overs) 266
3/155 (4) 4/163 (3)
5/167 (6) 6/184 (5) 7/225 (8)
8/228 (9) 9/245 (10) 10/266 (11)

Rabada 17.1–2–64–3; Olivier 17–1–64–3; Ngidi 11–4–26–0; Jansen 17–5–31–4; Maharaj 1–0–6–0. *Second innings*—Rabada 20–3–77–3; Olivier 12–1–51–1; Ngidi 10.1–2–43–3; Jansen 17–4–67–3; Maharaj 1–0–8–0.

South Africa

*D. Elgar c Pant b Thakur	28	– (2) not out	96
A. K. Markram lbw b Mohammed Shami	7	– (1) lbw b Thakur	31
K. D. Petersen c Agarwal b Thakur	62	– lbw b Ashwin	28
H. E. van der Dussen c Pant b Mohammed Shami	1	– c Pujara b Mohammed Shami	40
T. Bavuma c Pant b Thakur	51	– not out	23
†K. Verreynne lbw b Thakur	21		
M. Jansen c Ashwin b Thakur	21		
K. Rabada c Siraj b Mohammed Shami	0		
K. A. Maharaj b Bumrah	21		
D. Olivier not out	1		
L. T. Ngidi b Pant b Thakur	0		
B 4, lb 4, w 5, nb 3	16	B 1, lb 7, w 16, nb 1	25

1/14 (2) 2/88 (1) 3/101 (3)   (79.4 overs) 229
4/102 (4) 5/162 (6) 6/177 (5)
7/179 (8) 8/217 (9) 9/228 (7) 10/229 (11)

1/47 (1)   (3 wkts, 67.4 overs) 243
2/93 (3) 3/175 (4)

Bumrah 21–5–49–1; Mohammed Shami 21–5–52–2; Siraj 9.5–2–24–0; Thakur 17.5–3–61–7; Ashwin 10–1–35–0. *Second innings*—Bumrah 17–2–70–0; Mohammed Shami 17–3–55–1; Thakur 16–2–47–1; Siraj 6–0–37–0; Ashwin 11.4–2–26–1.

Umpires: M. Erasmus and A. Paleker. Third umpire: A. T. Holdstock.
Referee: A. J. Pycroft.

SOUTH AFRICA v INDIA

Third Test

At Cape Town, January 11–14, 2022. South Africa won by seven wickets. South Africa 12pts. Toss: India.

South Africa became only the third team to successfully chase more than 200 in consecutive Tests, and echoed the previous game by losing just three wickets in the process. Elgar's side had come from behind to clinch the series, and an increasingly petulant Kohli resigned as captain soon afterwards.

Desperate to add a series win in South Africa to his CV, alongside victory in Australia and a 2–1 lead in the incomplete series in England, he undertook unusually long periods of grim, shotless defence, and unleashed a series of outbursts on the third evening when, the game slipping away, he yelled accusations of bias into the stump microphone. But his most important error might have come before a ball was bowled, when he chose to bat on a thickly grassed pitch under grey skies. In 34 Tests at Newlands since South Africa's international return in 1992, batting first had resulted in just 11 victories, and 17 defeats.

Kohli was fastidious in defence in the first innings, facing 201 deliveries for his 79, but only Pujara (who helped him add 62 for the third wicket) and Pant (51 for the fifth) hung around for long. Eight men were caught between keeper and gully. Kohli left repeatedly, testament more to his skill than to poor bowling – but the South Africans were content to see him going nowhere at times. Eventually, with the No. 10 for company, he chased a wide one.

Not for the first time in the series, India relied on their seamers to keep them in the game: Bumrah produced an inspired spell, finishing with five for 42, including top-scorer Petersen, caught at slip for 72. He followed Kohli's example, although he rotated the strike more often during his four-hour stay. But he was also denied meaningful partnerships by his team-mates' inferior techniques against the seaming ball.

India's 13-run lead was worth only bragging rights, but early on the third day they were 58 for four, with Rabada and Jansen both striking twice. Markram and Elgar held good catches in the cordon, but Petersen's one-hander at leg slip to remove Pujara was outstanding. Kohli took obdurate defence to another level, this time grinding out 29 from 143 balls. For once, all eyes were on the other batsman: Pant seemed to be playing on a different surface. In the 48th over, he effortlessly hoisted Maharaj for consecutive sixes and, even after Kohli was finally out in the next over, he showed no signs of changing tack. Soon he slashed Olivier through the covers for two more boundaries. With the match precariously balanced, it felt as if Pant was changing the narrative again.

Any wag by India's tail might have made the difference, but the last four wickets managed only 36, of which Pant made 22, turning down another dozen to keep the strike, but still completed his fourth Test century, and third abroad, after The Oval (2018) and Sydney (2018-19). Jansen was too quick and hostile for the lower order, but only after Ngidi's second spell of 7–1–12–3 had exposed them, with Kohli, Ashwin and Thakur caught close in. All 20 Indian wickets fell to catches, a unique occurrence in a Test; in total, South Africa held on to 55, easily a record for a three-match series, beating 48 by New Zealand at home to Pakistan in 2009-10.

South Africa's quest for 212 started badly, when Markram edged Mohammed Shami to slip, but Elgar and Petersen were making solid if slow progress until Elgar was pinned by Ashwin on 22. A grimace was followed by a reluctant review, based more on hope than expectation. DRS showed the ball just clearing leg stump – and umpire Marais Erasmus was heard muttering "That's impossible." Kohli took the cue, though there was nothing mumbled about his rant down the stump mike at the host broadcaster: "Focus on your team while they shine the ball. Not just the opposition." Team-mates joined in, including Rahul, who said: "The whole country is playing against 11 guys." Ashwin added: "Surely you can find better ways to win, SuperSport!" The outbursts overlooked the fact that DRS is run by the independent Hawk-Eye set-up, and has nothing to do with the local production company. The chuntering continued for a while, and made for uneasy listening. Referee Andy Pycroft warned the Indians that a repeat might attract a fine, but no sanctions were applied. It was an unedifying episode.

Crucially for the match, and the series, 41 runs came in the nine overs following the collective meltdown, whereas only 19 had come from the previous nine. "It played nicely into our hands that, for a period of time, they forgot about the game," said Elgar. "I'm extremely happy it happened that way."

With Petersen punishing some errant bowling, South Africa finished the day needing another 111, and cruised home on the fourth morning. Petersen was the only casualty after an excellent 82, which earned him both the match and series awards. "It's not been easy," he admitted. "Challenging wickets, changing conditions. We've had to tough it out against a high-quality bowling attack. I enjoyed every moment."

Player of the Match: K. D. Petersen. *Player of the Series:* K. D. Petersen.

Close of play: first day, South Africa 17-1 (Markram 8, Maharaj 6); second day, India 57-2 (Pujara 9, Kohli 14); third day, South Africa 101-2 (Petersen 48).

India

K. L. Rahul c Verreynne b Olivier	12	– c Markram b Jansen		10
M. A. Agarwal c Markram b Rabada	15	– c Elgar b Rabada		7
C. A. Pujara c Verreynne b Jansen	43	– c Petersen b Jansen		9
*V. Kohli c Verreynne b Rabada	79	– c Markram b Ngidi		29
A. M. Rahane c Verreynne b Rabada	9	– c Elgar b Rabada		1
†R. R. Pant c Petersen b Jansen	27	– not out		100
R. Ashwin c Verreynne b Jansen	2	– c Jansen b Ngidi		7
S. N. Thakur c Petersen b Maharaj	12	– c Verreynne b Ngidi		5
J. J. Bumrah c Elgar b Rabada	0	– (11) c Bavuma b Jansen		2
U. T. Yadav not out	4	– (9) c Verreynne b Rabada		0
Mohammed Shami c Bavuma b Ngidi	7	– (10) c van der Dussen b Jansen		0
B 5, lb 1, nb 7	13	B 8, lb 9, w 2, nb 9		28

1/31 (1) 2/33 (2) 3/95 (3)   (77.3 overs) 223
4/116 (5) 5/167 (6) 6/175 (7)
7/205 (8) 8/210 (9) 9/211 (4) 10/223 (11)

1/20 (2) 2/24 (1)   (67.3 overs) 198
3/57 (3) 4/58 (5)
5/152 (4) 6/162 (7) 7/170 (8)
8/180 (9) 9/189 (10) 10/198 (11)

Rabada 22–4–73–4; Olivier 18–5–42–1; Jansen 18–6–55–3; Ngidi 14.3–7–33–1; Maharaj 5–2–14–1. *Second innings*—Rabada 17–5–53–3; Olivier 10–1–38–0; Jansen 19.3–6–36–4; Ngidi 14–5–21–3; Maharaj 7–1–33–0.

South Africa

*D. Elgar c Pujara b Bumrah	3	– (2) c Pant b Bumrah		30
A. K. Markram b Bumrah	8	– (1) c Rahul b Mohammed Shami		16
K. A. Maharaj b Yadav	25			
K. D. Petersen c Pujara b Bumrah	72	– (3) b Thakur		82
H. E. van der Dussen c Kohli b Yadav	21	– (4) not out		41
T. Bavuma c Kohli b Mohammed Shami	28	– (5) not out		32
†K. Verreynne c Pant b Mohammed Shami	0			
M. Jansen b Bumrah	7			
K. Rabada c Bumrah b Thakur	15			
D. Olivier not out	10			
L. T. Ngidi c Ashwin b Bumrah	3			
B 4, lb 4, w 1, nb 4, p 5	18	Lb 8, nb 3		11

1/10 (1) 2/17 (2) 3/45 (3)   (76.3 overs) 210
4/112 (5) 5/159 (6) 6/159 (7)
7/176 (8) 8/179 (4) 9/200 (9) 10/210 (11)

1/23 (1)   (3 wkts, 63.3 overs) 212
2/101 (2) 3/155 (3)

Bumrah 23.3–8–42–5; Yadav 16–3–64–2; Mohammed Shami 16–4–39–2; Thakur 12–2–37–1; Ashwin 9–3–15–0. *Second innings*—Bumrah 17–5–54–1; Mohammed Shami 15–3–41–1; Yadav 9–0–36–0; Thakur 11–3–22–1; Ashwin 11.3–1–51–0.

Umpires: M. Erasmus and A. T. Holdstock. Third umpire: A. Paleker.
Referee: A. J. Pycroft.

First one-day international At Paarl, January 19, 2022. **South Africa won by 31 runs.** ‡South Africa 296-4 (50 overs) (T. Bavuma 110, H. E. van der Dussen 129*); India 265-8 (50 overs) (S. Dhawan 79, V. Kohli 51, S. N. Thakur 50*). *PoM:* H. E. van der Dussen. *ODI debuts:* M. Jansen (South Africa); V. R. Iyer (India). *A fourth-wicket stand of 204 hustled South Africa to a total perhaps 30 above par. Rassie van der Dussen, often a slow starter, galloped from the off, and later* *applauded the anchor role played by Temba Bavuma, who finished with 110 from 143. He rotated the strike well, particularly against the spinners, while van der Dussen (129* from 96, with four sixes) punished the out-of-sorts Bhuvneshwar Kumar and Shardul Thakur. India were 138-1 at halfway, but Shikhar Dhawan was bowled aiming a cut at a Keshav Maharaj delivery that turned sharply into him, then Virat Kohli's sweep against Tabraiz Shamsi lobbed off the toe-end to midwicket. Rishabh Pant fell to a dazzling leg-side stumping by Quinton de Kock off seamer Andile Phehlukwayo, and Thakur's aggressive maiden ODI half-century only reduced the margin of defeat. These matches were not part of the Super League.*

Second one-day international   At Paarl, January 21, 2022. **South Africa won by seven wickets. ‡India 287-6** (50 overs) (K. L. Rahul 55, R. R. Pant 85, S. N. Thakur 40*); **South Africa 288-3** (48.1 overs) (J. N. Malan 91, Q. de Kock 78, T. Bavuma 35, A. K. Markram 37*, H. E. van der Dussen 37*). PoM: Q. de Kock. *The pitch used for the previous game was heavily watered and rolled in surface with more pace. De Kock took advantage with a bold and beautiful 66-ball 78, which put his side so far ahead in the chase that only cruise control was required to clinch the series. De Kock flicked, cut, drove and pulled at will – Bhuvneshwar and Ravichandran Ashwin suffered most – before a surprise full toss from Thakur hit him in front. He had put on 132 in 22 overs with Janneman Malan, who looked on course for a century until a Jasprit Bumrah off-cutter bounced steeply and ricocheted off his elbow on to the stumps. Earlier, K. L. Rahul's sluggish 55 from 79 balls did India few favours, though Pant was a cut above his team-mates. He belted 33 off Shamsi's first three overs but, just as he looked set to haul the target skywards, he hoisted him to long-on, and departed for 85.*

Third one-day international   At Cape Town, January 23, 2022. **South Africa won by four runs. South Africa 287** (49.5 overs) (Q. de Kock 124, H. E. van der Dussen 52, D. A. Miller 39; P. M. Krishna 3-59); **‡India 283** (49.2 overs) (S. Dhawan 61, V. Kohli 65, S. A. Yadav 39, D. L. Chahar 54; L. T. Ngidi 3-58, A. L. Phehlukwayo 3-40). PoM: Q. de Kock. PoS: Q. de Kock. *De Kock's commanding century should have made the game safe, but South Africa allowed India to recover from a seemingly hopeless position. They needed ten from the last three overs, with three wickets in hand – and lost. De Kock's ball-striking had been as hot as the weather, and by the time he hooked Bumrah to deep square leg for 124 in the 36th over, he had 229 runs in the series. After a stand of 144, van der Dussen departed the same way seven balls later, and hopes of a total around 320 disappeared too. India reached 116-1 before Dhawan top-edged a Phehlukwayo bouncer, then Pant suicidally charged down and sliced his first ball straight to deep cover. Non-striker Kohli turned his back in disgust; he carried on the hard work, but again fell to Maharaj, whose quicker ball looped off a leading edge. The match looked all over at 223-7, but Deepak Chahar slapped a few tired deliveries to the boundary, and reached 50 in 31 balls. Suddenly India were favourites again, only for Chahar to heave a Ngidi bouncer to midwicket. The last pair needed five from five balls, but Yuzvendra Chahal spliced Dwayne Pretorius to midwicket, and South Africa took the series 3–0.*

DOMESTIC CRICKET IN SOUTH AFRICA IN 2020-21

Colin Bryden

South Africa's franchise era came to an end in another season disrupted by Covid-19. Almost 17 years after six franchise teams contested a Pro20 tournament in April 2004, it wound up with the final of the Four-Day Franchise Series. The match was a curio in itself: the final had been phased out after 2005-06, but was reinstated as the competition had been split into two pools to save money.

It ended in an innings victory for the Durban-based **Dolphins** over the **Titans**, despite losing most of the first two days (of five) to rain or bad light. The Titans had been the most successful franchise, winning the four-day and one-day titles five times apiece (plus one shared in each competition), and the T20 tournament six times. But they could not bow out with another triumph. By contrast, this was the Dolphins' best season. Though they had shared the first two four-day franchise titles, they had never been sole winners, and had only two outright limited-overs trophies; in 2020-21, they reached the finals in all three formats. In addition to their four-day glory, they shared the Momentum One-Day Cup with Gauteng's **Lions**, who went on to beat them in the Betway T20 Challenge – one of only two defeats for the Dolphins across the three competitions (they had lost to the **Knights** in their second first-class fixture).

The Dolphins won four of their seven qualifying matches. Kingsmead was friendly to spin, and three of their slow bowlers appeared among the tournament's eight leading wicket-takers. Top was Keshav Maharaj, with 34; fellow left-armer Senuran Muthusamy had 28, and off-spinner Prenelan Subrayen 19. In the final, when Maharaj was on national duty, Subrayen and Muthusamy took 19 wickets between them. South Africa had also called up seven Titans players, including Aiden Markram, the competition's top scorer with 945 runs at 94, but this was not enough to explain their abject first-innings collapse for 53.

The four-day series should have finished a month earlier, but domestic cricket halted in mid-December after a Dolphins player tested positive for Covid in an earlier match with Titans, pushing the last two rounds and the final into March. The one-day cup was condensed into four weeks in the new year, in a biosecure environment in Potchefstroom, and the T20 competition, originally scheduled for March after being cancelled in 2019-20, was rushed through in ten days, in another bubble, in Durban.

Pool A of the one-day tournament was badly hit by rain: the Dolphins won the first two matches, and the remaining four were washed out. The weather was kinder when Pool B was staged the following week, with the Lions winning three. But rain returned to ruin the final. Play could not begin until the reserve day, and ended before enough overs had been bowled to constitute a match. In the T20 Challenge, the Dolphins won all five league games before their batting failed in the final against a Lions attack led by seamers Kagiso Rabada and Sisanda Magala.

The semi-professional provincial schedule was torn up because of the pandemic; the teams eventually managed two three-day matches and three one-day games each, with no trophies at stake. All national student, schools and age-group tournaments were cancelled.

In 2021-22, the six franchise teams disappeared, with 15 provincial teams stepping back into the limelight (rather than 12, as in an earlier rejected proposal). They were in two divisions, with Boland, Central Gauteng Lions, Eastern Province, Free State, KwaZulu-Natal Coastal, North West, Northerns and Western Province in the top tier, and Border, Easterns, KwaZulu-Natal Inland, Limpopo, Mpumalanga, Northern Cape and South Western Districts in the second. The main motivation for the change was financial: to reduce the number of teams overall, while an eight-strong premier division offered opportunities for more players at the highest domestic level. In a bonus, with Brexit forcing the end of Kolpak contracts in England, several players returned home to sign for provincial sides.

FIRST-CLASS AVERAGES IN 2020-21

BATTING (250 runs, average 25.00)

		M	I	NO	R	HS	100	Avge	Ct/St
1	K. Verreynne (*Cape Cobras*)	5	8	3	680	216*	2	97.14	18/1
2	A. K. Markram (*Titans/South Africa*). . .	9	15	3	1,054	204*	5	87.83	12
3	R. van Tonder (*Knights*)	7	13	1	721	200	2	60.08	6
4	P. J. Malan (*Cape Cobras*)	7	12	0	638	264	2	53.16	7
5	†R. D. Rickelton (*Lions*)	7	13	0	627	194	1	48.23	11
6	W. B. Marshall (*Lions/C Gauteng*) . . .	5	8	0	385	145	1	48.12	5
7	F. Behardien (*Knights*)	6	11	2	433	142	1	48.11	9
8	†D. Elgar (*Titans/South Africa*)	10	17	1	764	127	2	47.75	5
	R. S. Second (*Warriors*)	7	13	1	573	171	2	47.75	12
10	†S. J. Erwee (*Dolphins*)	8	13	1	569	199	2	47.41	7
11	†G. F. Linde (*Cape Cobras*)	5	8	1	322	107	1	46.00	3
12	K. D. Petersen (*Dolphins*)	8	13	2	484	173	1	44.00	9
13	†M. J. Ackerman (*Dolphins/KZN Coastal*) . .	9	13	1	520	122	1	43.33	8
14	†D. A. Hendricks (*Lions*)	7	13	0	562	130	2	43.23	1
15	R. R. Hendricks (*Lions*)	4	7	0	289	96	0	41.28	3
16	K. A. Maharaj (*Dolphins/South Africa*) . .	7	8	1	279	89	0	39.85	5
17	K. Zondo (*Dolphins*)	7	11	2	345	111	2	38.33	5
18	P. W. A. Mulder (*Lions/South Africa*) . . .	8	13	2	393	100*	1	35.72	5
19	M. Y. Vallie (*Warriors*)	6	11	0	380	85	0	34.54	2
20	M. P. Breetzke (*Warriors*)	5	10	1	303	77*	0	33.66	6
21	†N. Brand (*Titans*).	6	10	1	283	115	2	31.44	2
22	†S. Muthusamy (*Dolphins*)	7	11	1	310	79	0	31.00	1
23	†T. de Zorzi (*Cape Cobras*)	7	12	1	330	68	0	30.00	4
24	†E. M. Moore (*Warriors*)	6	11	0	316	155	1	28.72	2
25	†M. C. Kleinveldt (*Knights*)	7	13	1	333	77	0	27.75	0
26	S. Qeshile (*Warriors*)	6	11	1	260	97	0	26.00	20/1
27	H. E. van der Dussen (*Lions/S Africa*) . . .	7	11	1	259	107*	1	25.90	5
28	T. B. de Bruyn (*Titans*).	7	11	0	281	127	1	25.54	9

BOWLING (10 wickets, average 30.00)

		Style	O	M	R	W	BB	5I	Avge
1	P. Fojela (*Border*)	RFM	62.3	17	153	13	6-45	1	11.76
2	S. T. Ndwandwa (*SW Districts*)	SLA	70.2	18	166	12	7-38	1	13.83
3	S. Muthusamy (*Dolphins*)	SLA	156	40	407	28	6-79	1	14.53
4	D. Potgieter (*Lions*)	RFM	58.1	14	171	11	4-41	0	15.54
5	P. Subrayen (*Dolphins*)	OB	171.1	40	359	19	6-24	1	18.89
6	L. L. Sipamla (*Lions/South Africa*) . . .	RFM	114.5	17	423	22	5-37	1	19.22
7	C. P. Savage (*Cape Cobras*)	RF	83.4	25	251	12	5-77	1	20.91
8	G. F. Linde (*Cape Cobras*)	SLA	174.2	43	482	23	7-29	2	20.95
9	R. de Swardt (*Dolphins*)	RFM	109	35	235	11	4-41	0	21.36
10	N. Brand (*Titans*)	SLA	90	17	223	10	4-37	0	22.30
11	M. Pretorius (*Knights*)	RF	192	40	554	24	4-40	0	23.08
12	K. A. Maharaj (*Dolphins/South Africa*) .	SLA	287.5	55	790	34	7-48	4	23.23
13	D. M. Dupavillon (*Dolphins*)	RF	111.5	29	362	15	7-38	1	24.13
14	T. L. Moreki (*Cape Cobras*)	RFM	123.2	27	370	15	4-54	0	24.66
15	T. Shamsi (*Titans*)	SLW	129.5	16	420	17	8-32	1	24.70
16	B. E. Hendricks (*Lions*)	LFM	135.5	25	451	18	7-29	1	25.05
17	L. B. Williams (*Titans*)	RF	207.3	41	679	27	4-51	0	25.14
18	S. von Berg (*Knights*)	LB	256.3	44	745	29	5-93	1	25.68
19	A. A. Nortje (*South Africa/Warriors*) . .	RF	93.4	15	342	13	6-56	1	26.30
20	M. Jansen (*Warriors*)	LF	192	49	609	23	4-66	0	26.47
21	S. S. B. Magala (*Lions*)	RFM	105.2	12	468	16	6-60	1	29.25
22	J. T. Smuts (*Warriors*)	SLA	105	23	294	10	3-39	0	29.40
23	B. D. Walters (*Warriors*)	RFM	114.5	25	384	13	5-61	1	29.53

FOUR-DAY FRANCHISE SERIES IN 2020-21

Pool A	*P*	*W*	*L*	*D*	*Bonus pts* *Bat*	*Bowl*	*Pts*
DOLPHINS . . .	7	4	1	2*	24.08	26	126.08
Knights.	7	3	3	1	25.70	25	104.70
Lions	7	2	3	2	24.22	22	81.22†

Pool B	*P*	*W*	*L*	*D*	*Bonus pts* *Bat*	*Bowl*	*Pts*
TITANS.	7	2	1	4*	22.88	20	98.88
Cape Cobras. . .	7	1	2	4	24.58	22	86.58
Warriors.	7	2	4	1	14.68	24	76.68

Outright win = 16pts; draw = 6pts. Bonus points awarded for the first 100 overs of each team's first innings: one batting point for the first 150 runs and 0.02 of a point for every subsequent run; one bowling point for the third wicket taken and for every subsequent two.

* *One match halted because of a Covid-19 case.*

† *9pts deducted for slow over-rates in three separate matches.*

Final At Durban, March 25–29, 2021. **Dolphins won by an innings and 76 runs. Dolphins 295** (S. J. Erwee 100); **Titans 53** (P. Subrayen 6-24) **and 166** (S. Muthusamy 6-79). *Rain allowed only ten overs on the first day and none on the second; not until the fourth morning of five did the Dolphins complete their first innings, which depended heavily on a 135-run partnership between Sarel Erwee and Marques Ackerman (74). The Titans then folded for 53 against the spinners, the lowest total in their 17 seasons; it was also the lowest in a major domestic first-class final in any country, beating 61 by Tamil Nadu v Bombay in the 1972-73 Ranji Trophy and, closer to home, by Northern Transvaal v Transvaal in the 1984-85 Currie Cup. Off-spinner Prenelan Subrayen bowled throughout the innings for a career-best 22–7–24–6; when the Titans followed on, he made that 10-80, while slow left-armer Senuran Muthusamy finished with 9-91 (one man was run out).*

CHAMPIONS

1889-90	Transvaal
1890-91	Kimberley
1892-93	Western Province
1893-94	Western Province
1894-95	Transvaal
1896-97	Western Province
1897-98	Western Province
1902-03	Transvaal
1903-04	Transvaal
1904-05	Transvaal
1906-07	Transvaal
1908-09	Western Province
1910-11	Natal
1912-13	Natal
1920-21	Western Province
1921-22	{ Transvaal
	Natal
	Western Province
1923-24	Transvaal
1925-26	Transvaal
1926-27	Transvaal
1929-30	Transvaal
1931-32	Western Province
1933-34	Natal
1934-35	Transvaal
1936-37	Natal
1937-38	{ Natal
	Transvaal
1946-47	Natal
1947-48	Natal
1950-51	Transvaal
1951-52	Natal
1952-53	Western Province
1954-55	Natal
1955-56	Western Province
1958-59	Transvaal
1959-60	Natal
1960-61	Natal
1962-63	Natal
1963-64	Natal
1965-66	{ Natal
	Transvaal
1966-67	Natal
1967-68	Natal
1968-69	Transvaal
1969-70	{ Transvaal
	Western Province
1970-71	Transvaal
1971-72	Transvaal
1972-73	Transvaal
1973-74	Natal
1974-75	Western Province
1975-76	Natal
1976-77	Natal
1977-78	Western Province
1978-79	Transvaal
1979-80	Transvaal
1980-81	Natal
1981-82	Western Province
1982-83	Transvaal
1983-84	Transvaal
1984-85	Transvaal
1985-86	Western Province
1986-87	Transvaal
1987-88	Transvaal
1988-89	Eastern Province
1989-90	{ Eastern Province
	Western Province
1990-91	Western Province
1991-92	Eastern Province
1992-93	Orange Free State
1993-94	Orange Free State

1994-95	Natal	2004-05	Dolphins	2012-13	Cape Cobras
1995-96	Western Province		Eagles	2013-14	Cape Cobras
1996-97	Natal	2005-06	Dolphins	2014-15	Lions
1997-98	Free State		Titans	2015-16	Titans
1998-99	Western Province	2006-07	Titans	2016-17	Knights
1999-2000	Gauteng	2007-08	Eagles	2017-18	Titans
2000-01	Western Province	2008-09	Titans	2018-19	Lions
2001-02	KwaZulu-Natal	2009-10	Cape Cobras	2019-20	Lions
2002-03	Easterns	2010-11	Cape Cobras	2020-21	Dolphins
2003-04	Western Province	2011-12	Titans		

Transvaal/Gauteng have won the title outright 25 times, Natal/KwaZulu-Natal 21, Western Province 18, Titans 5, Cape Cobras 4, Lions and Orange Free State/Free State 3, Eagles/Knights and Eastern Province 2, Dolphins, Easterns and Kimberley 1. The title has been shared seven times as follows: Transvaal 4, Natal and Western Province 3, Dolphins 2, Eagles, Eastern Province and Titans 1.

The tournament was the Currie Cup from 1889-90 to 1989-90, the Castle Cup from 1990-91 to 1995-96, the SuperSport Series from 1996-97 to 2011-12, and the Sunfoil Series from 2012-13 to 2017-18. There was no sponsor from 2018-19 to 2020-21.

From 1971-72 to 1990-91, the non-white South African Cricket Board of Control (later the South African Cricket Board) organised their own three-day tournaments. These are now recognised as first-class (see *Wisden 2006*, pages 79–80). A list of winners appears in *Wisden 2007*, page 1346.

CSA PROVINCIAL THREE-DAY PROGRAMME IN 2020-21

Pool A KwaZulu-Natal Coastal W2; South Western Districts W1 L1; Boland L1 D1; Border L1 D1.
Pool B KwaZulu-Natal Inland W1 D1; Easterns W1 L1; Free State W1 L1; Limpopo L1 D1.
Pool C Eastern Province W1 D1; Central Gauteng D2; North West D2; Mpumalanga L1 D1.
Pool D Northerns W1 D1; Northern Cape D2; Western Province D2; South Africa U19 L1 D1.

These matches replaced the CSA Provincial Three-Day Cup, because of Covid-19; no trophy was awarded. Matches involving Limpopo, Mpumalanga and South Africa Under-19 did not have first-class status.

MOMENTUM ONE-DAY CUP IN 2019-20

50-over league plus knockout

Pool A	P	W	L	A	BP	Pts	Pool B	P	W	L	A	BP	Pts
DOLPHINS ..	4	2	0	2	1	13	LIONS	4	3	1	0	2	14
KNIGHTS ...	4	0	1	3	0	6	COBRAS	4	2	2	0	2	10
Titans	4	0	1	3	0	5*	Warriors	4	1	3	0	1	5

* *One point deducted for slow over-rate.*

Semi-finals Dolphins beat Cobras by three wickets; Lions v Knights was abandoned, but Lions advanced to the final on a better qualifying record.

Final At Potchefstroom, February 4–5, 2021. **No result; Lions and Dolphins shared the trophy. Lions** 225-7 (45 overs); ‡**Dolphins** 37-2 (10.2 overs). *There was no play on the day originally allotted; next day, the match was reduced to 45 overs a side, but it was not possible to complete the 20 overs of the Dolphins' innings necessary to constitute a game. It was the fourth time in nine seasons that the one-day final had been rained off. In the play that did take place, Dominic Hendricks and Nicky van den Bergh added 116 for the Lions' fourth wicket, but Eathan Bosch's 4-41 kept the total down.*

BETWAY T20 CHALLENGE IN 2020-21

20-over league plus knockout

	P	W	L	Bonus	Pts	NRR
DOLPHINS	5	5	0	1	21	0.81
LIONS	5	4	1	0	16	0.07
WARRIORS	5	2	3	1	9	0.23
Titans	5	2	3	0	8	−0.29
Cape Cobras	5	1	4	0	4	−0.14
Knights	5	1	4	0	4	−0.69

2nd v 3rd   Lions beat Warriors by seven wickets.

Final   At Durban, February 28, 2021. **Lions won by four wickets.** ‡Dolphins 107-7 (20 overs); **Lions 108-6** (19 overs). *After winning all five league games, the Dolphins were restricted to their lowest total of the tournament. Left-arm spinner Bjorn Fortuin dismissed Sarel Erwee in the opening over, and they were 14-3 by the fifth; Kagiso Rabada picked up 3-12 as the Dolphins limped into three figures. Lions opener Reeza Hendricks's run-a-ball 39 was the highest score of the match, and confirmed him as the tournament's leading run-scorer, with 257; Wiaan Mulder and Fortuin saw them over the line.*

CSA PROVINCIAL 50-OVER PROGRAMME IN 2020-21

Pool A KwaZulu-Natal Coastal W3; Boland W1 L2; Border W1 L2; SW Districts W1 L2.
Pool B Easterns W2 A1; Free State W2 A1; Limpopo W1 L2; KwaZulu-Natal Inland L3.
Pool C Central Gauteng W3; North West W2 L1; Eastern Province W1 L2; Mpumalanga L3.
Pool D Northern Cape W2 L1; Northerns W2 L1; South Africa U19 W2 L1; Western Province L3.

These matches replaced the CSA Provincial 50-Over Challenge, because of Covid-19; no trophy was awarded. Matches involving Limpopo, Mpumalanga and South Africa Under-19 did not have List A status.

SRI LANKAN CRICKET IN 2021

Points don't mean prizes

SA'ADI THAWFEEQ

Not for the first time, Sri Lanka's on-field exploits were undermined by the antics of the board. A controversial performance-based pay contract was proposed, three players were suspended for biobubble breaches, and Mickey Arthur was released as national team coach.

Disputes over the new contract began as soon as it was drawn up, shortly before the tour of England in June. It was the work of a four-man technical and advisory committee appointed by sports minister Namal Rajapaksa. All were cricket legends: Aravinda de Silva, Roshan Mahanama, Muttiah Muralitharan and Kumar Sangakkara. They had already succeeded in getting Tom Moody, one of Arthur's predecessors, appointed as director of cricket for a three-year term. He helped devise the new contracts, in which players would be given points for various elements of performance, and paid accordingly.

SRI LANKA IN 2021

	Played	Won	Lost	Drawn/No result
Tests	9	3	3	3
One-day internationals	15	4	10	1
Twenty20 internationals	20	8	12	–

DECEMBER }	2 Tests (a) v South Africa	(see *Wisden 2021*, page 751)
JANUARY	2 Tests (h) v England	(page 295)
FEBRUARY		
MARCH }	2 Tests, 3 ODIs and 3 T20Is (a) v West Indies	(page 1032)
APRIL	2 Tests (h) v Bangladesh	(page 1010)
MAY	3 ODIs (a) v Bangladesh	(page 915)
JUNE	3 ODIs and 3 T20Is (a) v England	(page 357)
JULY	3 ODIs and 3 T20Is (h) v India	(page 1015)
AUGUST		
SEPTEMBER	3 ODIs and 3 T20Is (h) v South Africa	(page 1018)
OCTOBER }	T20 World Cup in the UAE	(page 830)
NOVEMBER	2 Tests (h) v West Indies	(page 1020)
DECEMBER		

For a review of Sri Lankan domestic cricket from the 2020-21 season, see page 1027.

Honouring the pioneer: former captains Arjuna Ranatunga (foreground) and Aravinda de Silva (behind him) carry the coffin of Bandula Warnapura, Sri Lanka's first Test captain.

The committee reportedly gave 50% weighting to on-field performance since 2019, then 20% to fitness, and 10% each to leadership, professionalism and potential. The bone of contention was a lack of transparency. Several senior players had significant pay cuts, placing them below the level of more junior team-mates, but complained they were not told how many points they had scored for the various criteria. The number of centrally contracted players was also reduced, from 32 to 24.

Moody defended the plan: "This was not pulled out of thin air. It was done after thorough research, looking at other countries and how they contract their players. We put together what we thought was the best, most effective and fair system." Negotiations continued throughout the year; most players signed tour-by-tour contracts, though Angelo Mathews stood his ground and was left out for "personal reasons". The deadlock ended when Sri Lanka Cricket assured the players that "certain deficiencies" would be rectified when their contracts come up for renewal in 2022.

Things had been bad enough even before the contracts were proposed. Sri Lanka had lost two Tests in South Africa, then two at home to England. The chairman of selectors, Ashantha de Mel, resigned, and was replaced by Pramodya Wickremasinghe, who led a six-member selection committee appointed by Rajapaksa.

An all-format visit to the West Indies, crammed into March, brought T20 and one-day defeats, and two drawn Tests – all in Antigua. Sri Lanka finally tasted Test victory in Pallekele, where debutant Praveen Jayawickrama's 11 wickets clinched a two-match series against Bangladesh. A return leg of three ODIs, at Mirpur, was lost.

The tour of England produced five white-ball defeats and a washout, and was made worse by the suspensions of Niroshan Dickwella, Dhanushka

Gunathilleke and Kusal Mendis for leaving the team's Covid-secure hotel for a cigarette. They each received a one-year ban, a £35,000 fine, mandatory counselling from a doctor – and an undertaking from former Sri Lanka captain Arjuna Ranatunga that he would "slap them two or three times".

India sent a second-string team to Colombo in July, while their Test side were in England. They still beat Sri Lanka in the ODI series, but the hosts prevailed in the T20s. South Africa visited in September: Sri Lanka won the one-day rubber, but were whitewashed in the T20s.

That seemed far from ideal preparation for the T20 World Cup, but Sri Lanka started well enough, advancing through the first round with victories against Namibia, Ireland and the Netherlands, whom they bowled out for 44. The Super 12 stage began with a convincing triumph over Bangladesh, but defeats by Australia, South Africa and England followed. A consolation win against West Indies, the defending champions, could not mask the problems.

Arthur's two-year contract as head coach was not renewed, and he was snapped up by Derbyshire – his first role on the county circuit. His swansong was a two-Test series against West Indies in Galle, with both games won by huge margins. Despite the challenges of Covid, he left the national team in better shape than when he took over.

Shammi Silva had been re-elected in May for another two-year term as SLC president, and most office-holders were returned uncontested. A faction led by former Test captain Bandula Warnapura had initially challenged the incumbents, before withdrawing en masse, citing the "lack of a level playing field" in the electoral process. Five months after the elections, Warnapura died, aged 68, from diabetes.

Early in 2021, the courts had received a petition, whose signatories included Muralitharan and former international batsman Sidath Wettimuny, seeking an overhaul of SLC's "flawed" constitution. The case made little headway because of Covid restrictions, but was due to be heard this year.

SRI LANKA v BANGLADESH IN 2020-21

Sa'adi Thawfeeq

Test matches (2): Sri Lanka 1 (80pts), Bangladesh 0 (20pts)

This tour, postponed twice when the two boards could not agree details and dates during the pandemic, finally creaked underway in April 2021. It included only two Tests (three were originally planned), and took place in empty stadiums. After a high-scoring draw, Sri Lanka won the second match comfortably to complete their first series win at home since beating South Africa in July 2018. It was a personal triumph for the captain, Dimuth Karunaratne, who followed 244 in the First Test with 118 and 66 in the Second.

The pitch for the opening game had been expected to help the seamers, but turned out better for the batsmen – only 17 wickets went down for 1,289 runs, and the match referee, Ranjan Madugalle, rated the track as below average. For the second game, Sri Lanka shaved the surface to promote turn; they included two spinners, who came into their own as the match wore on. One of the new faces was 22-year-old slow left-armer Praveen Jayawickrama, who had just ten first-class matches under his belt, and was playing only because Lasith Embuldeniya, Duvindu Tillekeratne and Prabath Jayasuriya had all failed fitness tests. He seized his chance with both hands, claiming 11 wickets as Bangladesh succumbed for 251 and 227. Karunaratne said Jayawickrama had done the simple things well, and compared him to a recently retired local legend: "He pitches the ball in the right spot. That's something we saw from Rangana Herath."

Bangladesh were without Shakib Al Hasan and Mustafizur Rahman, both at the IPL. Mominul Haque, the captain, claimed their absence gave others an opportunity, but Shakib's all-round skills were particularly missed in the Second Test. Mominul made a mark in the opening match with a hundred – his 11th in Tests, but first outside Bangladesh. Nazmul Hossain extended his maiden century to 163, batting for nearly nine hours, but the experienced opener Tamim Iqbal missed out, falling in the nineties in both Tests.

BANGLADESH TOURING PARTY

*Mominul Haque, Abu Jayed, Ebadat Hossain, Liton Das, Mehedi Hasan snr, Mithun Ali, Mushfiqur Rahim, Nazmul Hossain, Saif Hasan, Shadman Islam, Shoriful Islam, Taijul Islam, Tamim Iqbal, Taskin Ahmed, Yasir Ali. *Coach:* R. C. Domingo.

Khaled Ahmed, Mukidul Islam, Nayeem Hasan, Nurul Hasan, Shohidul Islam and Shuvagata Hom also travelled, but were not included in the 15-man squad named before the First Test.

SRI LANKA v BANGLADESH

First Test

At Pallekele, April 21–25, 2021. Drawn. Sri Lanka 20pts, Bangladesh 20pts. Toss: Bangladesh.

The hosts had hoped to upset Bangladesh with a pitch that helped the seamers and nullified the spinners, but it remained flat throughout, and only 17 wickets fell. Sri Lanka did not complete their first innings, in which skipper Karunaratne made 244 and Dhananjaya de Silva 166, until lunch on the fifth day.

The track had a tinge of green at the toss, but it did not fool Bangladesh's captain, Mominul Haque, who had no hesitation in batting. Saif Hasan departed for a duck in the second over, but that was just about the end of the good news for Sri Lanka, whose bowlers varied their lengths too much. Left-handers Tamim Iqbal and Nazmul Hossain – badly dropped by Dickwella off Dhananjaya when 28 – put on 144, before Tamim dabbed at one from Vishwa Fernando that bounced more than he expected, and guided it straight to slip. He departed for 90, but Nazmul ploughed on, now with Mominul. By the close, Bangladesh had steamed to 302 for two, with a relieved Nazmul banking a maiden Test century after a run of failures. "Tamim *bhai* batted very well," he said. "He was scoring quickly, which allowed me to take a bit of time."

Mominul followed suit on a rain-reduced second day, with his 11th hundred in Tests, but first away from home (seven had come at Chittagong). The stand grew to 242, a third-wicket record for Bangladesh, beating 236 by Mominul and Mushfiqur Rahim against Sri Lanka at Chittagong in 2017-18. Nazmul finally pushed a return catch to Kumara after seven minutes short of nine hours, but Mushfiqur and Liton Das (selected to keep wicket as Mushfiqur had a finger injury) added contrasting half-centuries, before Mominul finally called a halt an hour into the third morning. Bowling was no fun on this pitch, although Lakmal was economical and Fernando persevered for his four wickets. Kumara, though, tweaked a hamstring and played no further part in the series; he had also limped out of his previous Test, against South Africa at Centurion in December. Spinners Dhananjaya and Wanindu Hasaranga de Silva had combined figures of one for 241, but even they were rarely collared: the scoring-rate was little more than three an over. "The plan was to cut down the runs and fence them in," said Fernando.

Bangladesh's spin-heavy attack had an even harder time. The Sri Lankan openers shared a century stand before Thirimanne was trapped by Mehedi Hasan, but Karunaratne kept going… and going. He had 85 by the end of the third day, and 234 at stumps on the fourth. It was his 11th Test century, and his first double. There was the odd close call, and when 82 he was given out lbw to Taijul Islam, but survived on review. Bangladesh failed to take a wicket in 86 overs on the fourth day, as Karunaratne and Dhananjaya batted relentlessly on. Dhananjaya finally fell in the fifth over of the final morning, after a partnership of 345, Sri Lanka's highest for any wicket against Bangladesh. After 656 minutes at the crease, Karunaratne spooned an attempted pull to midwicket, having hit 26 fours. His side had just nosed into the lead, but he did not declare until lunch, by which time their advantage was 107.

Bangladesh had a scare when Saif fell for one, taking his tally in five Test innings to 25, and Nazmul was bowled for a duck; Lakmal claimed both in nine balls. But Tamim hit out, clattering ten fours and three sixes, while Mominul dug in to ensure no more alarms, and rain eventually brought an early end. It was the first drawn Test in Sri Lanka since July 2014, after 28 positive results. "Maybe it was a little bit naive of me in terms of strategy – this was my first Test in Pallekele," said Sri Lanka's coach, Mickey Arthur. "We wanted to beat Bangladesh with a bit of pace and bounce, but it's just been extremely flat."

Player of the Match: F. D. M. Karunaratne.

Close of play: first day, Bangladesh 302-2 (Nazmul Hossain 126, Mominul Haque 64); second day, Bangladesh 474-4 (Mushfiqur Rahim 43, Liton Das 25); third day, Sri Lanka 229-3 (Karunaratne 85, D. M. de Silva 26); fourth day, Sri Lanka 512-3 (Karunaratne 234, D. M. de Silva 154).

Bangladesh

Tamim Iqbal c Thirimanne b M. V. T. Fernando	90	– not out	74
Saif Hasan lbw b M. V. T. Fernando	0	– c Dickwella b Lakmal	1
Nazmul Hossain c and b Kumara	163	– b Lakmal	0
*Mominul Haque c Thirimanne b D. M. de Silva	127	– not out	23
Mushfiqur Rahim not out	68		
†Liton Das c B. O. P. Fernando b M. V. T. Fernando	50		
Mehedi Hasan c Dickwella b Lakmal	3		
Taijul Islam c Dickwella b M. V. T. Fernando	2		
Taskin Ahmed not out	6		
B 9, lb 6, w 11, nb 6	32	Nb 2	2

1/8 (2) 2/152 (1)   (7 wkts dec, 173 overs) 541   1/21 (2)   (2 wkts, 33 overs) 100
3/394 (3) 4/424 (4)   2/27 (3)
5/511 (6) 6/515 (7) 7/524 (8)

Abu Jayed and Ebadat Hossain did not bat.

Lakmal 36–14–81–1; M. V. T. Fernando 35–9–96–4; Kumara 28–4–88–1; Mathews 7–1–14–0; D. M. de Silva 30–1–130–1; P. W. H. de Silva 36–2–111–0; Karunaratne 1–0–6–0. *Second innings*—Lakmal 8–2–21–2; M. V. T. Fernando 5–2–18–0; D. M. de Silva 11–1–46–0; P. W. H. de Silva 9–0–15–0.

Sri Lanka

*F. D. M. Karunaratne c Nazmul Hossain b Taskin Ahmed	244	P. W. H. de Silva b Taijul Islam	43
H. D. R. L. Thirimanne lbw b Mehedi Hasan	58	R. A. S. Lakmal not out	22
B. O. P. Fernando c Liton Das b Taskin Ahmed	20	M. V. T. Fernando not out	0
A. D. Mathews b Taijul Islam	25	B 4, lb 10, w 10, nb 3	27
D. M. de Silva b Taskin Ahmed	166		
P. Nissanka c Liton Das b Ebadat Hossain	12	1/114 (2) (8 wkts dec, 179 overs) 648	
†D. P. D. N. Dickwella run out (Mehedi Hasan/Liton Das)	31	2/157 (3) 3/190 (4)	
		4/535 (5) 5/544 (1)	
		6/553 (6) 7/585 (7) 8/647 (8)	

C. B. R. L. S. Kumara did not bat.

Abu Jayed 19–2–76–0; Taskin Ahmed 30–6–112–3; Ebadat Hossain 21–1–99–1; Mehedi Hasan 58–6–161–1; Taijul Islam 45–9–163–2; Mominul Haque 4–0–18–0; Saif Hasan 2–0–5–0.

Umpires: H. D. P. K. Dharmasena and R. S. A. Palliyaguruge.   Third umpire: R. R. Wimalasiri.
Referee: R. S. Madugalle.

SRI LANKA v BANGLADESH

Second Test

At Pallekele, April 29–May 3, 2021. Sri Lanka won by 209 runs. Sri Lanka 60pts. Toss: Sri Lanka. Test debuts: P. A. K. P. Jayawickrama; Shoriful Islam.

After the previous bore draw, the groundstaff shaved more grass off the pitch, ensuring there would be some turn later on. And although Sri Lanka's spinners were less experienced, they came out on top, helped by winning the toss and running up another huge total. The 22-year-old slow left-armer Praveen Jayawickrama took 11 wickets on his debut, and formed an impressive partnership with his Moors club-mate Ramesh Mendis Wanigamuni, whose off-breaks claimed six.

Karunaratne and Thirimanne had given their side the upper hand on the first day, both making centuries and putting on 209, to become Sri Lanka's first opening pair to share three successive hundred partnerships. Dropped by Nazmul Hossain at slip off Taskin Ahmed when 28, Karunaratne glided to his 12th Test hundred, and passed 5,000 runs.

It was a surprise when he was caught behind shortly after tea, a maiden Test wicket for 19-year-old Shoriful Islam, a tall left-arm seamer. Thirimanne went on to 140, before falling on the second morning. Oshada Fernando lasted more than five hours for 81 then, after a mini-collapse, Dickwella and Wanigamuni added 111 for the seventh wicket, before Karunaratne called a halt early on the third day. Taskin finished with four wickets, and might have had more: Nazmul shelled another regulation chance at slip off Wanigamuni towards the end.

Bangladesh made a solid start, with Tamim Iqbal dominating a first-wicket stand of 98, before Saif Hasan presented Jayawickrama with his first Test wicket. Nazmul collected his second successive duck, then Tamim again fell in sight of three figures, misreading Jayawickrama's arm-ball. There was a minor recovery as Mominul Haque and Mushfiqur Rahim put on 63, but both fell in the forties, and the tail did not hang around. The last seven wickets contributed only 37, and Jayawickrama was celebrating figures of six for 92, the best by a Sri Lankan on debut, undercutting Upul Chandana's six for 179 against Pakistan in the Asian Test Championship final at Dhaka in March 1999.

Karunaratne waived the follow-on despite a lead of 242, and added 66 – taking his haul for the series to 428 – as Sri Lanka set about establishing an unassailable advantage. Another slow left-armer, Taijul Islam, profited as the batsmen sought quick runs, and finished with five for 72, his best figures away from home. The eventual declaration,

---

BEST MATCH FIGURES ON TEST DEBUT

16-136	N. D. Hirwani	India v West Indies at Madras	1987-88
16-137	R. A. L. Massie	Australia v England at Lord's	1972
12-102	F. Martin	England v Australia at The Oval	1890
12-358	J. J. Krejza	Australia v India at Nagpur	2008-09
11-82	C. V. Grimmett	Australia v England at Sydney	1924-25
11-96	C. S. Marriott	England v West Indies at The Oval	1933
11-112	A. E. Hall	South Africa v England at Cape Town	1922-23
11-130	Mohammad Zahid	Pakistan v New Zealand at Rawalpindi	1996-97
11-145	A. V. Bedser	England v India at Lord's	1946
11-178	**P. A. K. P. Jayawickrama**	**Sri Lanka v Bangladesh at Pallekele**	**2020-21**
11-196	S. F. Burke	South Africa v New Zealand at Cape Town	1961-62
11-204	A. L. Valentine	West Indies v England at Manchester	1950

Marriott was appearing in his only Test; Burke, Krejza and Martin played just one more.

---

halfway through the fourth day, left a notional target of 437. Apart from a few desultory overs from Lakmal, the spinners bowled non-stop. Wanigamuni was first to strike, removing Tamim for a quickfire 24, and he later added the seasoned pair of Mominul and Mushfiqur. Poor light ended play an hour early with Bangladesh teetering at 177 for five, and praying for more bad weather on the final day.

But it dawned fine, and the match – as well as the series – was done and dusted before lunch. With the batsmen uncertain whether to play forward or back, Jayawickrama winkled out three more to finish with 11 for 178, another debut best for Sri Lanka, this time beating Akila Dananjaya's eight for 44 against Bangladesh at Mirpur in 2017-18. "He does the simple things well," said Karunaratne. "He makes the batsman play, and gives the ball a chance to do something. He played like a bowler who had more than his ten first-class matches."

Player of the Match: P. A. K. P. Jayawickrama. *Player of the Series:* F. D. M. Karunaratne.

Close of play: first day, Sri Lanka 291-1 (Thirimanne 131, B. O. P. Fernando 40); second day, Sri Lanka 469-6 (Dickwella 64, Wanigamuni 22); third day, Sri Lanka 17-2 (Karunaratne 13, Mathews 1); fourth day, Bangladesh 177-5 (Liton Das 14, Mehedi Hasan 4).

Sri Lanka

*F. D. M. Karunaratne c Liton Das b Shoriful Islam.	118 – (2) c sub (Yasir Ali) b Saif Hasan ... 66
H. D. R. L. Thirimanne c Liton Das b Taskin Ahmed	140 – (1) c Nazmul Hossain b Mehedi Hasan 2
B. O. P. Fernando c Liton Das b Mehedi Hasan ...	81 – st Liton Das b Taijul Islam........ 1
A. D. Mathews c Liton Das b Taskin Ahmed	5 – c sub (Yasir Ali) b Taijul Islam 12
D. M. de Silva c Nazmul Hossain b Taijul Islam..	2 – c Nazmul Hossain b Mehedi Hasan .. 41
P. Nissanka b Taskin Ahmed	30 – c Shoriful Islam b Taijul Islam....... 24
†D. P. D. N. Dickwella not out	77 – c Taijul Islam b Taskin Ahmed 24
R. T. M. Wanigamuni c Mushfiqur Rahim	
b Taskin Ahmed.	33 – c Tamim Iqbal b Taijul Islam....... 8
R. A. S. Lakmal (did not bat)	– b Taijul Islam............... 12
P. A. K. P. Jayawickrama (did not bat)	– not out 3
B 3, lb 2, w 1, nb 1.................	7 Nb 1 1

1/209 (1) 2/313 (2)   (7 wkts dec, 159.2 overs) 493   1/14 (1)   (9 wkts dec, 42.2 overs) 194
3/319 (4) 4/328 (5)   2/15 (3) 3/39 (4)
5/382 (6) 6/382 (3) 7/493 (8)   4/112 (2) 5/124 (5) 6/162 (6)
                                                             7/178 (7) 8/180 (8) 9/194 (9)

M. V. T. Fernando did not bat.

Abu Jayed 22–4–69–0; Taskin Ahmed 34.2–7–127–4; Mehedi Hasan 36–7–118–1; Shoriful Islam 29–6–91–1; Taijul Islam 38–7–83–1. *Second innings*—Mehedi Hasan 14–3–66–2; Shoriful Islam 1–0–8–0; Taijul Islam 19.2–2–72–5; Taskin Ahmed 4–0–26–1; Saif Hasan 4–0–22–1.

Bangladesh

Tamim Iqbal c Thirimanne b Jayawickrama	92 – c Dickwella b Wanigamuni 24
Saif Hasan c de Silva b Jayawickrama...........	25 – c Lakmal b Jayawickrama 34
Nazmul Hossain c Thirimanne b Wanigamuni	0 – b Jayawickrama 26
*Mominul Haque lbw b Wanigamuni	49 – b Wanigamuni 32
Mushfiqur Rahim lbw b Jayawickrama	40 – c de Silva b Wanigamuni 40
†Liton Das c Thirimanne b Jayawickrama.........	8 – lbw b Jayawickrama............. 17
Mehedi Hasan lbw b Jayawickrama.............	16 – c Nissanka b Jayawickrama 39
Taijul Islam hit wkt b Lakmal	9 – c Dickwella b de Silva 2
Taskin Ahmed lbw b Jayawickrama	0 – c Karunaratne b Wanigamuni 7
Shoriful Islam b Lakmal....................	0 – not out 0
Abu Jayed not out	0 – lbw b Jayawickrama 0
B 2, lb 9, nb 1........................	12 B 3, lb 2, nb 1............. 6

1/98 (2) 2/99 (3) 3/151 (1)   (83 overs) 251   1/31 (1) 2/73 (2)   (71 overs) 227
4/214 (5) 5/224 (4) 6/224 (6)   3/104 (3) 4/134 (4)
7/241 (7) 8/243 (9) 9/246 (10) 10/251 (8)   5/171 (5) 6/183 (6) 7/206 (9)
                                                          8/227 (8) 9/227 (7) 10/227 (11)

Lakmal 10–0–30–2; M. V. T. Fernando 7–1–19–0; Mathews 2–0–7–0; Wanigamuni 31–7–86–2; Jayawickrama 32–7–92–6; de Silva 1–0–6–0. *Second innings*—Lakmal 4–2–14–0; Wanigamuni 28–2–103–4; Jayawickrama 32–10–86–5; de Silva 7–1–19–1.

Umpires: H. D. P. K. Dharmasena and R. S. A. Palliyaguruge.   Third umpire: R. R. Wimalasiri.
Referee: R. S. Madugalle.

SRI LANKA v INDIA IN 2021

Fidel Fernando

One-day internationals (3): Sri Lanka 1 (9pts), India 2 (20pts)
Twenty20 internationals (3): Sri Lanka 2, India 1

In the run-up to this white-ball tour in July 2021, India had a problem. They had just contested the World Test Championship final in Southampton and, because their players would have had to undergo 14 days of quarantine in Colombo, plus another stint on their return, it was decided the main party should remain in the UK ahead of the Tests against England.

And so the BCCI sent a shadow squad to Sri Lanka – although that still meant an array of IPL stars. Shikhar Dhawan captained, with Bhuvneshwar Kumar his deputy, and the team also included Yuzvendra Chahal, Ishan Kishan, Hardik Pandya, Prithvi Shaw and Kuldeep Yadav, along with a cast of promising youngsters. There were advantages to this arrangement: the Indian board could keep their big guns fresh for the series they deemed important (which did not seem to extend far beyond England and Australia); the host board still received good TV revenue, as the vast Indian audience tuned in anyway; and the reserve players (both Dhawan and coach Rahul Dravid bridled at being termed "second-string") gained international experience. It was possible this sort of thing would be seen more often, depending how long international cricket had to exist in biosecure bubbles. During this trip, for example, India's players had to isolate for 45 days in all, for the sake of six days' cricket.

The changes made for a more competitive match-up: India's first-choice team would probably have made short work of the inexperienced Sri Lankans. After discussions between their head coach Mickey Arthur, director of cricket Tom Moody, and the technical committee headed by Aravinda de Silva, a number of senior players had been dropped from the white-ball plans. Lasith Malinga, Angelo Mathews and Tissara Perera were all left out; Perera reacted by announcing his retirement, and Malinga soon followed, while Mathews made himself unavailable for several months as he weighed up his options. Partly as a result, India's reserves took the 50-over series.

However, their bench strength was tested in the Twenty20 matches. After the first game, which India won comfortably, Krunal Pandya tested positive for Covid, and eight other players – deemed close contacts – had to self-isolate. The Indians might have abandoned the tour, but to their credit stayed on, and completed the series with a lopsided XI that included tailender Bhuvneshwar at No. 6; among several format debutants was the 30-year-old Kerala seamer Sandeep Warrier, who had started the tour as a net bowler. Sri Lanka won the last two games to shade the series, but India were not disgraced. "The balance of our team meant we were a couple of batsmen short, which was always challenging," said Dravid. "But the great positive for me was the way the guys fought."

INDIA TOURING PARTY

*S. Dhawan (50/20), Arshdeep Singh (20), Bhuvneshwar Kumar (50/20), Y. S. Chahal (50/20), D. L. Chahar (50/20), R. D. Chahar (50/20), V. V. Chakravarthy (50/20), R. D. Gaikwad (50/20), K. Gowtham (50/20), I. P. Kishan (50/20), D. B. Padikkal (50/20), M. K. Pandey (50/20), H. H. Pandya (50/20), K. H. Pandya (50/20), N. Rana (50/20), N. Saini (50/20), R. Sai Kishore (20), C. Sakariya (50/20), S. V. Samson (50/20), S. Sandeep Warrier (20), P. P. Shaw (50/20), Simarjeet Singh (20), K. Yadav (50/20), S. A. Yadav (50/20). Coach: R. Dravid.

Arshdeep Singh, Sai Kishore, I. C. Porel, Sandeep Warrier and Simarjeet Singh were originally named as net bowlers, but elevated to the T20 squad after K. H. Pandya tested positive for Covid, and eight close contacts (Chahal, D. L. Chahar, Gowtham, Kishan, Pandey, H. H. Pandya, Shaw and S. A. Yadav) were placed in isolation.

First one-day international At Colombo (RPS), July 18, 2021 (day/night). **India won by seven wickets.** ‡Sri Lanka 262-9 (50 overs) (W. I. A. Fernando 32, K. I. C. Asalanka 38, M. D. Shanaka 39, C. Karunaratne 43*); **India 263-3** (36.4 overs) (P. P. Shaw 43, S. Dhawan 86*, I. P. Kishan 59, S. A. Yadav 31*). *India 10pts. PoM:* P. P. Shaw. *ODI debuts:* P. B. B. Rajapaksa (Sri Lanka); I. P. Kishan, S. A. Yadav (India). *With No. 8 Chamika Karunaratne top-scoring, the Sri Lankans thought they had fought to a competitive score, despite not managing a fifty partnership – but India hunted down the target in ferocious style. Prithvi Shaw smoked the home pacemen through the covers in the powerplay and, when he departed for 43 off 24 balls, with nine fours, Shikhar Dhawan supervised the rest of the chase. He put on 85 in 12 overs with Ishan Kishan (59 from 42), then 72 with Manish Pandey and 48* with Suryakumar Yadav, who slapped 31* from 20.*

Second one-day international At Colombo (RPS), July 20, 2021 (day/night). **India won by three wickets.** ‡Sri Lanka 275-9 (50 overs) (W. I. A. Fernando 50, M. B. Ranasinghe 36, D. M. de Silva 32, K. I. C. Asalanka 65, C. Karunaratne 44*; Bhuvneshwar Kumar 3-54, Y. S. Chahal 3-50); **India 277-7** (49.1 overs) (M. K. Pandey 37, S. A. Yadav 53, K. H. Pandya 35, D. L. Chahar 69*; P. W. H. de Silva 3-37). *India 10pts, Sri Lanka –1pt. PoM:* D. L. Chahar. *Sri Lanka again thought they had got the job done when they reduced India to 116-5 after 18 overs in reply to another serviceable total, boosted by Charitha Asalanka's even-paced 65, and a second late burst from Karunaratne. But India had started quickly, which gave the later batsmen room for manoeuvre. Yadav made a bright 53, then from 193-7 Deepak Chahar – whose previous 17 internationals had produced 19 runs – spanked 69*, dominating an eighth-wicket stand of 84* with Bhuvneshwar Kumar (19*). Chahar targeted the left-arm wrist-spin of Lakshan Sandakan, who followed a first-ball duck with 1-71. Sri Lanka lost a point for a tardy over-rate.*

Third one-day international At Colombo (RPS), July 23, 2021 (day/night). **Sri Lanka won by three wickets (DLS).** ‡India 225 (43.1 overs) (P. P. Shaw 49, S. V. Samson 46, S. A. Yadav 40; A. Dananjaya 3-44, P. A. K. P. Jayawickrama 3-59); **Sri Lanka 227-7** (39 overs) (W. I. A. Fernando 76, P. B. B. Rajapaksa 65, Extras 30; R. D. Chahar 3-54). *Sri Lanka 10pts. PoM:* W. I. A. Fernando. *PoS:* S. A. Yadav. *ODI debuts:* R. D. Chahar, K. Gowtham, N. Rana, C. Sakariya, S. V. Samson (India). *With the series won, India shook up their side, awarding five new caps and changing most of their attack. Newcomer Sanju Samson was one of three to reach the forties, but spinners Akila Dananjaya and Praveen Jayawickrama shared six wickets as India declined from 157-3 to 195-8 in a rain-interrupted innings. Sri Lanka's target was revised to 227 in 47 overs, and they were sustained by a second-wicket stand of 109 between Avishka Fernando and Bhanuka Rajapaksa, who hit a maiden ODI fifty and a dozen fours in all. India's spinners caused problems too, but Sri Lanka eased home with eight overs remaining.*

First Twenty20 international At Colombo (RPS), July 25, 2021 (floodlit). **India won by 38 runs. India 164-5** (20 overs) (S. Dhawan 46, S. A. Yadav 50); ‡Sri Lanka 126 (18.3 overs) (K. I. C. Asalanka 44; Bhuvneshwar Kumar 4-22). *PoM:* Bhuvneshwar Kumar. *T20I debuts:* K. I. C. Asalanka, C. Karunaratne (Sri Lanka); V. V. Chakravarthy, P. P. Shaw (India). *Sri Lanka never threatened India's total. Despite losing Shaw to the first ball of the match, from Dushmantha Chameera, India made 51-1 in the powerplay, before Yadav's 34-ball 50 pushed them to 164. Sri Lanka were 111-4 in the 16th, but lost Asalanka and Wanindu Hasaranga de Silva without addition; Bhuvneshwar mopped up with three wickets in four balls.*

Second Twenty20 international At Colombo (RPS), July 27–28, 2021 (floodlit). **Sri Lanka won by four wickets. India 132-5** (20 overs) (S. Dhawan 40); ‡**Sri Lanka 133-6** (19.4 overs) (M. B. Ranasinghe 36, D. M. de Silva 40*). *PoM:* D. M. de Silva. *T20I debuts:* R. T. M. Wanigamuni (Sri Lanka); R. D. Gaikwad, D. B. Padikkal, N. Rana, C. Sakariya (India). *In a match delayed for a day after Krunal Pandya's positive Covid test, which also forced eight team-mates into isolation, a reshaped and bowler-heavy Indian XI battled to 132-5. Chameera was the most impressive home bowler, with 1-23, while Dananjaya dismissed top-scorer Dhawan and Samson on the way to 2-29. Sri Lanka made a slow start – 39-2 after seven – but, with late showers making the ball difficult to grip, a brisk 40* from Dhananjaya de Silva ensured a last-over victory.*

Third Twenty20 international At Colombo (RPS), July 29, 2021 (floodlit). **Sri Lanka won by seven wickets.** ‡**India 81-8** (20 overs) (P. W. H. de Silva 4-9); **Sri Lanka 82-3** (14.3 overs) (R. D. Chahar 3-15). *PoM:* P. W. H. de Silva. *PoS:* P. W. H. de Silva. *T20I debut:* S. Sandeep Warrier (India). *An injury to Navdeep Saini meant India had to include Sandeep Warrier, who had started the tour as one of five net bowlers. He sent down three decent overs for 23 – but in a lost cause, as India had managed only 81-8, the second-lowest score by a Test nation in a full 20 overs, after West Indies' 79-7 (chasing 106) against Zimbabwe at Port-of-Spain in 2009-10. The game was up at 36-5 after nine, with only bowlers to come. Hasaranga de Silva celebrated turning 24 with 4-9; only South African leg-spinner Imran Tahir (4-21 against the Netherlands in March 2014) had previously taken four in a T20 international on his birthday. Dhananjaya de Silva, with 23* from 20, made sure there were no slip-ups, as Sri Lanka claimed their first T20 series win over India in eight attempts.*

SRI LANKA v SOUTH AFRICA IN 2021-22

SA'ADI THAWFEEQ

One-day internationals (3): Sri Lanka 2 (20pts), South Africa 1 (10pts)
Twenty20 internationals (3): Sri Lanka 0, South Africa 3

South Africa relied on two strategies for this dual-format tour. First, their batsmen devoted themselves to perfecting the art of sweeping – orthodox and reverse – to counter Sri Lanka's spin threat. Second, they brought their own army of slow bowlers, to try to turn the local pitches to their advantage. They needed time to adjust but, once they had done so, seemed unbeatable. Having lost their captain, Temba Bavuma, to a freak thumb injury in the first match, and after conceding valuable Super League points in the one-dayers, South Africa's resolve and tenacity were impressive, and they won all three T20 games.

A batsman almost always stepped up: Aiden Markram with 96, and Janneman Malan with 121, in the ODIs; Quinton de Kock and Reeza Hendricks in the T20s. Keshav Maharaj took on the captain's role with confidence, and led the impressive attack, which included left-arm wrist-spinner Tabraiz Shamsi and slow-left armers George Linde (in the one-dayers) and Bjorn Fortuin (in the T20s). With support from Markram's off-breaks, South Africa's spinners took 35 of their 47 wickets across both series.

With the 2023 World Cup in mind, Sri Lanka had adopted a policy of developing their next generation and, to an extent, it paid off. Left-handed batsman Charith Asalanka and hard-hitting opener Aviskha Fernando set up success in the first ODI; mystery spinner Mahesh Theekshana bowled them to victory in the third, to clinch the series. But these efforts were nullified by South Africa's spin threat in the T20s, where Sri Lanka's preparation of turning tracks backfired. They used nine bowlers in the one-day games, and took only six wickets in the T20 series. At the end of the tour, captain Dasun Shanaka lamented the plan: "Had we prepared good pitches, we could have performed much better."

SOUTH AFRICA TOURING PARTY

*T. Bavuma (50), Q. de Kock (20), B. C. Fortuin (20), B. E. Hendricks (50/20), R. R. Hendricks (50/20), H. Klaasen (50/20), G. F. Linde (50/20), S. S. B. Magala (20), J. N. Malan (50), K. A. Maharaj (50/20), A. K. Markram (50/20), D. A. Miller (20), P. W. A. Mulder (20), L. T. Ngidi (20), A. A. Nortje (50/20), D. Pretorius (50/20), K. Rabada (20), T. Shamsi (50/20), L. Sipamla (50), H. E. van der Dussen (50/20), K. Verreynne (50), L. B. Williams (50/20). *Coach:* M. V. Boucher.

C. J. Dala was originally selected, but remained in South Africa after a positive Covid test, and was replaced by Sipamla. Bavuma broke his thumb in the first ODI; Maharaj took over as captain.

First one-day international At Colombo (RPS), September 2 (day/night). **Sri Lanka won by 14 runs.** ‡**Sri Lanka 300-9** (50 overs) (W. I. A. Fernando 118, D. M. de Silva 44, K. I. C. Asalanka 72); **South Africa 286-6** (50 overs) (A. K. Markram 96, T. Bavuma 38*, H. E. van der Dussen 59, H. Klaasen 36). *Sri Lanka 10pts. PoM:* W. I. A. Fernando. *Aviskha Fernando's 118, his third ODI century, came off 115 balls, and he shared half-century stands with Minod Ranasinghe (27), Dhananjaya de Silva and Charith Asalanka, who hit a career-best 72. Needing 301, South Africa were on course at 155-1 when Bavuma, trying to evade a return from the outfield, was hit on the* *thumb, ending a partnership of 97 with Aiden Markram, and his tour; it later emerged he had suffered a fracture. The momentum faltered and, though Markram reached his highest score in this format, the Sri Lankan bowlers choked the chase.*

Second one-day international At Colombo (RPS), September 4 (day/night). **South Africa won by 67 runs** (DLS). ‡**South Africa 283-6** (47 overs) (J. N. Malan 121, R. R. Hendricks 51, H. Klaasen 43); **Sri Lanka 197** (36.4 overs) (K. I. C. Asalanka 77, M. D. Shanaka 30, C. Karunaratne 36; T. Shamsi 5-49). *South Africa 10pts. PoM: J. N. Malan. ODI debut: G. F. Linde (South Africa). South Africa bounced back with a fine all-round performance to level the series. A delayed start reduced the game to 47 overs a side, and South Africa's 283-6 was built around Janneman Malan's third ODI century, supported by cameos from Reeza Hendricks and Heinrich Klaasen, whose 43 came off 27. Sri Lanka fell to 19-3, before Asalanka made 77, his second career-best in three days. Another shower adjusted the target to 265 from 41. Tabraiz Shamsi cleaned up with his first ODI five-for.*

Third one-day international At Colombo (RPS), September 7 (day/night). **Sri Lanka won by 78 runs.** ‡**Sri Lanka 203-9** (50 overs) (D. M. de Silva 31, K. I. C. Asalanka 47; K. A. Maharaj 3-38); **South Africa 125** (30 overs) (M. M. Theekshana 4-37). *Sri Lanka 10pts. PoM: P. V. D. Chameera. PoS: K. I. C. Asalanka. ODI debut: M. M. Theekshana (Sri Lanka). Sri Lanka claimed the series on a tricky pitch which turned from the start. It was an ideal stage for carrom-ball bowler Mahesh Theekshana, who bamboozled the South Africans with 4-37, including a wicket with his first ball in international cricket, as Malan edged to slip. He was the fourth Sri Lankan to achieve the feat, after Charitha Buddhika, Kaushal Lokuarachchi and Thilan Thushara. Sri Lanka had cautiously accumulated 203-9; Asalanka spent 71 balls over his 47, as South Africa sent down 40 overs of spin. But it was paceman Dushmantha Chameera who put South Africa on the back foot with two early wickets, and from 19-3 they never recovered: Klaasen top-scored with 22 as Theekshana ran through his repertoire.*

First Twenty20 international At Colombo (RPS), September 10 (floodlit). **South Africa won by 28 runs.** ‡**South Africa 163-5** (20 overs) (Q. de Kock 36, R. R. Hendricks 38, A. K. Markram 48); **Sri Lanka 135-6** (20 overs) (L. D. Chandimal 66*). *PoM: A. K. Markram. T20I debuts: M. M. Theekshana (Sri Lanka); K. A. Maharaj (South Africa). Keshav Maharaj, captaining South Africa on his T20I debut, led them to victory with crafty bowling in defence of a handy total. After Quinton de Kock and Reeza Hendricks opened with 73, Markram kept up the pace with a jaunty 48. Sri Lanka's batsmen didn't get going, with the exception of Dinesh Chandimal (66* off 54) and a late blast from Chamika Karunaratne (22* off 14). Bhanuka Rajapaksa made his third consecutive golden duck, after two in the ODI series, as Maharaj trapped him with his first ball in T20Is – the third South African to do so, after Alfonso Thomas and Rory Kleinveldt.*

Second Twenty20 international At Colombo (RPS), September 12 (floodlit). **South Africa won by nine wickets.** ‡**Sri Lanka 103** (18.1 overs) (M. D. K. J. Perera 30; A. K. Markram 3-21, T. Shamsi 3-20); **South Africa 105-1** (14.1 overs) (Q. de Kock 58*). *PoM: T. Shamsi. T20I debut: P. A. K. P. Jayawickrama (Sri Lanka). South Africa won the series thanks to a woeful Sri Lankan batting display. After Anrich Nortje dismissed Chandimal, they lost their remaining nine wickets to spin; the last four fell for three runs. Markram took three wickets for the first time in a T20I, as Sri Lanka equalled their lowest score against these opponents. With de Kock leading the way, South Africa knocked off the runs with nearly six overs to spare, interrupted only by a brief stoppage for rain.*

Third Twenty20 international At Colombo (RPS), September 14 (floodlit). **South Africa won by ten wickets.** ‡**Sri Lanka 120-8** (20 overs) (M. D. K. J. Perera 39); **South Africa 121-0** (14.4 overs) (R. R. Hendricks 56*, Q. de Kock 59*). *PoM: Q. de Kock. PoS: Q. de Kock. Sri Lanka capitulated again, posting a disappointing 120-8. But for Kusal Perera – returning to the side after he had injured a shoulder, and then been laid low by Covid – and another late charge from No. 9 Karunaratne (24*), they would have failed to reach 100. South Africa's chase was a breeze: de Kock and Hendricks each scored an unbeaten half-century, and their partnership of 121* was a team record for any wicket against Sri Lanka.*

SRI LANKA v WEST INDIES IN 2021-22

Sa'adi Thawfeeq

Test matches (2): Sri Lanka 2 (24pts), West Indies 0 (0pts)

West Indies arrived in Sri Lanka hoping to end the year with a series win in a spinners' paradise, having begun it with a 2–0 victory in another – Bangladesh. But things did not go to plan: they lost both Tests by large margins, and Sri Lanka maintained their tight grip on the Sobers–Tissera Trophy. That the home spinners accounted for 39 of West Indies' 40 wickets told a story.

On Galle's turning pitches, Sri Lanka's batting was held together by three players. Captain Dimuth Karunaratne, who hit 270 runs at 69, was in prime form, despite six months' absence from international cricket; his 147 and 83 in the First Test laid the foundation for victory. Dhananjaya de Silva's unbeaten 155 helped win the Second, after Sri Lanka had conceded a first-innings lead of 49. Pathum Nissanka, meanwhile, continued his bright start to Test cricket with three half-centuries.

Among the bowlers, Ramesh Mendis Wanigamuni confirmed his early promise with 18 wickets at 15, and his off-spin proved the ideal foil to slow left-armer Lasith Embuldeniya, who took 13 at 18. Their success was backed up by another slow left-armer, Praveen Jayawickrama, with seven at 21. In all, Sri Lanka's spinners sent down 298 overs, to their seamers' 27.

West Indies' own left-arm spinners, Jomel Warrican and Veerasammy Permaul, each registered career-best figures, and Roston Chase claimed a five-for with his off-breaks, but 84 overs of seam bowling brought the visitors three wickets. Kraigg Brathwaite, the captain, blamed his batsmen's failure to post challenging totals: West Indies managed three half-centuries between them, and a highest total of just 253, with only Nkrumah Bonner standing tall.

For the first time since the start of the pandemic, spectators were admitted at Galle, though not to capacity. At the end of the series, Mickey Arthur completed his two-year contract as Sri Lanka coach, and it was announced he would take the reins at Derbyshire.

WEST INDIES TOURING PARTY

*K. C. Brathwaite, J. Blackwood, N. E. Bonner, R. L. Chase, R. R. S. Cornwall, J. Da Silva, S. T. Gabriel, J. O. Holder, S. D. Hope, K. R. Mayers, V. Permaul, K. A. J. Roach, J. N. T. Seales, J. L. Solozano, J. A. Warrican. *Coach:* P. V. Simmons.

SRI LANKA v WEST INDIES

First Test

At Galle, November 21–25, 2021. Sri Lanka won by 187 runs. Sri Lanka 12pts. Toss: Sri Lanka. Test debut: J. L. Solozano.

By lunch on the first day, West Indies were already unhappy. They had dropped Karunaratne on 14, burned two of their three reviews, and lost debutant Jeremy Solozano, who was stretchered off after being struck on the helmet at short leg by a Karunaratne pull. Hope came on as a concussion substitute, and Solozano took no further part in the series.

Despite not having had any competitive cricket since April, Karunaratne showed few signs of rustiness, and put on 139 with Nissanka, his new partner. It was Sri Lanka's highest opening stand against West Indies, beating 130 between Michael Vandort and Malinda Warnapura in Guyana in 2007-08; Karunaratne's eventual 147 was his 13th Test hundred, and his fourth in 2021 alone (only England captain Joe Root had more). After Chase removed Fernando and Mathews in quick succession, Karunaratne found another ally in de Silva. Their fourth-wicket stand of 111 ended in strange fashion on the second morning, when de Silva defended a ball from Gabriel, only to see it bounce towards the stumps. He attempted to swat it away with his bat, missed, and tried again – but instead whacked his own wicket. Chandimal, returning to the role of specialist keeper while Niroshan Dickwella served a ban for a biobubble breach in England in June, contributed an enterprising 45, before Warrican and Chase, with his fourth Test five-for, wrapped up the innings.

A steady start from Brathwaite and Blackwood – promoted to makeshift opener – proved a false dawn for West Indies. Spin soon wove its web: after painstakingly reaching 46 from 20 overs, they lost six for 54 in the next 20, including nightwatchman Warrican, and Chase with two overs of the second day to go. But, needing 187 to save the follow-on, West Indies were helped by rain – which restricted the third day to 38 overs – and their lower order. Mayers and Holder extended their seventh-wicket stand to 63, before the careful Da Silva and more aggressive Cornwall added 49 for the ninth, obliging Sri Lanka to bat again.

The hosts still led by 156 and, with one eye on the weather, set off in search of quick runs. Karunaratne made a princely 83 – his sixth successive score of 50-plus – though he would have been out for 34 had West Indies reviewed an lbw shout from Cornwall. Mathews, overcoming a lean patch since a century against England at Galle in January, hit a rollicking unbeaten 69. Sri Lanka declared at tea on the penultimate afternoon, setting West Indies 348 in four sessions, and prompting optimistic references to their astounding chase of 395 to defeat Bangladesh at Chittagong in January.

Within 12 overs, however, the game was lost, as Mendis Wanigamuni and Embuldeniya reduced West Indies to 18 for six, at which point Wanigamuni had four for seven. Bonner and Da Silva took it to the final day, adding 100 in 45 overs, but Bonner was left stranded on 68, from 220 balls, as Embuldeniya completed a five-wicket haul and an emphatic win for Sri Lanka.

Player of the Match: F. D. M. Karunaratne.

Close of play: first day, Sri Lanka 267-3 (Karunaratne 132, de Silva 56); second day, West Indies 113-6 (Mayers 22, Holder 1); third day, West Indies 224-9 (Da Silva 11); fourth day, West Indies 52-6 (Bonner 18, Da Silva 15).

Sri Lanka

P. Nissanka c Cornwall b Gabriel	56	– c Hope b Cornwall	3
*F. D. M. Karunaratne st Da Silva b Chase	147	– c Blackwood b Cornwall	83
B. O. P. Fernando c Bonner b Chase	3	– lbw b Warrican	14
A. D. Mathews c Holder b Chase	3	– not out	69
D. M. de Silva hit wkt b Gabriel	61	– c and b Warrican	1
†L. D. Chandimal c Cornwall b Chase	45	– not out	10
R. T. M. Wanigamuni c Da Silva b Warrican	13		
R. A. S. Lakmal lbw b Warrican	11		
P. V. D. Chameera c Brathwaite b Warrican	3		
L. Embuldeniya c Blackwood b Chase	17		
P. A. K. P. Jayawickrama not out	8		
B 5, lb 6, nb 8	19	B 8, lb 2, nb 1	11

1/139 (1) 2/164 (3) 3/170 (4) (133.5 overs) 386   1/4 (1) (4 wkts dec, 40.5 overs) 191
4/281 (5) 5/296 (2) 6/331 (7)   2/39 (5) 3/162 (2)
7/355 (6) 8/361 (6) 9/361 (9) 10/386 (10)   4/163 (5)

Gabriel 19–2–69–2; Holder 19–9–24–0; Cornwall 27–3–91–0; Mayers 3–0–9–0; Warrican 32–5–87–3; Chase 28.5–3–83–5; Blackwood 1–0–6–0; Brathwaite 4–0–6–0. *Second innings*—Cornwall 15.5–0–60–2; Holder 5–0–19–0; Chase 6–1–28–0; Warrican 9–1–42–2; Gabriel 4–0–23–0; Brathwaite 1–0–9–0.

West Indies

Batsman	First innings		Second innings	
*K. C. Brathwaite c Nissanka b Wanigamuni	41	–	lbw b Wanigamuni	0
J. Blackwood lbw b Embuldeniya	20	–	c Mathews b Embuldeniya	9
N. E. Bonner c de Silva b Jayawickrama	1	–	not out	68
S. D. Hope c Fernando b Wanigamuni	10	–	b Wanigamuni	3
R. L. Chase c Fernando b Wanigamuni	4	–	b Embuldeniya	1
J. A. Warrican c Chandimal b Jayawickrama	1	–	(10) c Fernando b Embuldeniya	1
K. R. Mayers c Karunaratne b de Silva	45	–	(6) lbw b Wanigamuni	2
J. O. Holder c Chameera b Jayawickrama	36	–	(7) b Wanigamuni	0
†J. Da Silva not out	15	–	(8) c de Silva b Embuldeniya	54
R. R. S. Cornwall c Wanigamuni b Lakmal	39	–	(9) c Lakmal b Jayawickrama	13
S. T. Gabriel lbw b Jayawickrama	2	–	c de Silva b Embuldeniya	0
B 8, lb 5, w 3, nb 2	18		Lb 5, w 2, nb 2	9
	230			**160**

1/46 (2) 2/51 (3) 3/80 (1)   (85.5 overs)   230   1/3 (1) 2/11 (2)   (79 overs)   160
4/83 (4) 5/86 (6) 6/100 (5)   3/14 (4) 4/15 (5)
7/163 (7) 8/175 (8) 9/224 (10) 10/230 (11)   5/18 (6) 6/18 (7) 7/118 (8)
     8/149 (9) 9/156 (10) 10/160 (11)

Hope replaced J. L. Solozano, as a concussion substitute.

Lakmal 6–1–10–1; Chameera 8–0–14–0; Embuldeniya 32–11–67–1; Jayawickrama 19.5–6–40–4; Wanigamuni 17–1–75–3; de Silva 3–0–11–1. *Second innings*—Embuldeniya 29–12–46–5; Wanigamuni 31–5–64–4; Jayawickrama 14–6–28–1; de Silva 1–0–5–0; Chameera 4–0–12–0.

Umpires: H. D. P. K. Dharmasena and R. S. A. Palliyaguruge.   Third umpire: R. R. Wimalasiri.
Referee: R. S. Madugalle.

SRI LANKA v WEST INDIES

Second Test

At Galle, November 29–December 3, 2021. Sri Lanka won by 164 runs. Sri Lanka 12pts. Toss: Sri Lanka. Test debut: K. I. C. Asalanka.

Emboldened by the performance of their trio of spinners in the First Test, Sri Lanka left out fast bowler Dushmantha Chameera in favour of an extra batsman, handing Charith Asalanka his debut. Their only seamer was Lakmal, but even he proved one too many, as their three slow bowlers shared all 20 wickets in another rout. West Indies, who retained Hope while Solozano continued his recovery, stuck with two pacemen, though they brought in Roach for Shannon Gabriel. They omitted off-spinner Rahkeem Cornwall and recalled slow left-armer Veerasammy Permaul for his first Test since 2015.

Rain delayed the start until after tea on the first day and, predictably, Karunaratne batted again on winning the toss. By the close, Sri Lanka had a promising 113 for one, Karunaratne having prodded a return catch to Chase – the key wicket, according to West Indies captain Brathwaite. His words seemed apt next day, when Permaul's five for 35 – his first five-for – and fellow left-arm spinner Warrican's career-best four for 50 worked through the Sri Lankan order. Only opener Nissanka kept his head, with a diligent 73, as all ten fell for 98.

West Indies were 69 for one at tea, at which point the rain returned. But across the first 50 overs of the third day, they made serene progress, advancing to 166 for two thanks to a cautious 72 from Brathwaite. Embuldeniya ended his four and a half hours' resistance,

HIGHEST NINTH-WICKET PARTNERSHIPS FOR SRI LANKA

124	D. M. de Silva/L. Embuldeniya............	v West Indies at Galle.....	2021-22
118	T. T. Samaraweera/B. A. W. Mendis	v India at Colombo (PSO)...	2010
105	K. M. D. N. Kulasekara/W. P. U. J. C. Vaas.....	v England at Lord's........	2006
101†	S. T. Jayasuriya/C. R. D. Fernando	v Pakistan at Faisalabad	2004-05

† *Fernando contributed one run.*

however, before the new ball changed everything. Seven wickets fell for 73, as Wanigamuni took six for 70, his first five-wicket haul in Tests. Only a ninth-wicket stand of 38 between Mayers and Permaul set up a West Indies lead of 49.

Sri Lanka had not cleared the arrears when Karunaratne and Fernando were both run out and, when Asalanka fell on the fourth morning, they were just 24 ahead. Once again, though, Nissanka compiled a timely and mature half-century, restoring the balance through a stand of 78 with de Silva. West Indies chipped away, and things were still more or less even when the eighth wicket – the injured Mathews, who had a thigh strain – fell at 221, with Sri Lanka 172 ahead. But now the match swung firmly in their favour as de Silva, mixing careful defence with ambitious striking, put on 124 with Embuldeniya.

De Silva raised his eighth Test century – against seven different opponents – and enabled a declaration early on the fifth day, setting West Indies 297 in a minimum of 85 overs. Understandably, they aimed for survival; unsurprisingly, they failed. Their rearguard had started well enough, losing only the openers in the first 43 overs. Then Hope was the first of three victims in an over for Wanigamuni: he pulled a short one to square leg, Chase clipped to bat–pad first ball, and Mayers snicked a big turner. Embuldeniya and Wanigamuni shared all ten wickets, giving Wanigamuni match figures of 11 for 136. Sri Lanka's victory was a fine send-off for the coach, Mickey Arthur, who had reached the end of his two-year contract.

Player of the Match: D. M. de Silva. *Player of the Series:* R. T. M. Wanigamuni.

Close of play: first day, Sri Lanka 113-1 (Nissanka 61, Fernando 2); second day, West Indies 69-1 (Brathwaite 22, Bonner 1); third day, Sri Lanka 46-2 (Nissanka 21, Asalanka 4); fourth day, Sri Lanka 328-8 (de Silva 153, Embuldeniya 25).

Sri Lanka

P. Nissanka lbw b Permaul.....................	73	– (2) lbw b Chase	66
*F. D. M. Karunaratne c and b Chase	42	– (1) run out (Mayers).............	6
B. O. P. Fernando c Da Silva b Warrican	18	– run out (Blackwood/Da Silva)......	14
A. D. Mathews b Warrican	29	– (9) c Blackwood b Permaul	1
D. M. de Silva c Da Silva b Permaul...........	2	– not out	155
K. I. C. Asalanka c Bonner b Permaul	10	– (4) c Bonner b Permaul	19
†L. D. Chandimal lbw b Warrican...............	2	– (6) c and b Chase	2
R. T. M. Wanigamuni c Hope b Warrican.........	5	– (7) c Roach b Brathwaite	25
R. A. S. Lakmal c Warrican b Permaul	12	– (8) lbw b Permaul...............	7
L. Embuldeniya b Permaul....................	1	– b Holder	39
P. A. K. P. Jayawickrama not out	0		
Lb 7, nb 3...........................	10	B 4, lb 4, w 1, nb 2.........	11

1/106 (2) 2/139 (3) 3/152 (1)   (61.3 overs) 204   1/7 (1)   (9 wkts dec, 121.4 overs) 345
4/154 (5) 5/169 (6) 6/169 (7)   2/39 (3) 3/73 (4)
7/178 (8) 8/187 (10) 9/200 (9) 10/204 (4)   4/151 (2) 5/157 (6) 6/208 (7)
                                              7/219 (8) 8/221 (9) 9/345 (10)

In the first innings Mathews, when 12, retired hurt at 162-4 and resumed at 187-8.

Roach 6–2–12–0; Holder 8–2–23–0; Mayers 2–0–13–0; Permaul 13–3–35–5; Chase 14–0–64–1; Warrican 18.3–5–50–4. *Second innings*—Permaul 40–4–106–3; Chase 27–2–82–2; Warrican 29–5–76–0; Roach 8–0–27–0; Holder 9.4–1–26–1; Brathwaite 5–0–11–1; Bonner 3–1–9–0.

West Indies

*K. C. Brathwaite b Embuldeniya	72	– lbw b Wanigamuni	6
J. Blackwood lbw b Jayawickrama	44	– c de Silva b Embuldeniya	36
N. E. Bonner lbw b Wanigamuni	35	– b Embuldeniya	44
S. D. Hope lbw b Wanigamuni	22	– c Lakmal b Wanigamuni	16
R. L. Chase c Asalanka b Wanigamuni	10	– c Fernando b Wanigamuni	0
K. R. Mayers not out	36	– c de Silva b Wanigamuni	0
J. O. Holder lbw b Wanigamuni	4	– c de Silva b Embuldeniya	3
†J. Da Silva b Wanigamuni	0	– not out	4
K. A. J. Roach c de Silva b Jayawickrama	8	– lbw b Embuldeniya	13
V. Permaul b Embuldeniya	15	– lbw b Wanigamuni	1
J. A. Warrican c sub (C. Karunaratne) b Wanigamuni	1	– c de Silva b Embuldeniya	3
Nb 6	6	B 4, lb 2	6

1/62 (2) 2/137 (3) 3/166 (1)   (104.2 overs) 253   1/15 (1) 2/65 (2)   (56.1 overs) 132
4/180 (5) 5/191 (4) 6/197 (7)   3/92 (4) 4/92 (5)
7/197 (8) 8/208 (9) 9/246 (10) 10/253 (11)   5/92 (6) 6/103 (7) 7/108 (3)
                                         8/128 (9) 9/129 (10) 10/132 (11)

Lakmal 9–3–22–0; Embuldeniya 35–13–94–2; Jayawickrama 25–4–59–2; de Silva 1–0–8–0. *Second innings*—Embuldeniya 20.1–6–35–5; Wanigamuni 25–6–66–5; Jayawickrama 10–3–23–0; Asalanka 1–0–2–0.

Umpires: H. D. P. K. Dharmasena and R. S. A. Palliyaguruge.   Third umpire: L. E. Hannibal.
Referee: R. S. Madugalle.

SRI LANKA UNDER-19 v ENGLAND UNDER-19 IN 2021-22

Under-19 one-day internationals (5): Sri Lanka 3, England 2

In between lockdowns, red lists and quarantines, England managed to send a youth squad to Sri Lanka for a five-match one-day series, in preparation for the Under-19 World Cup in the West Indies in January 2022. They retained most of their summer squad, omitting only the injured Harry Petrie and Archie Lenham; despite a back problem, Sonny Baker made the trip, in order to work on his recovery outdoors with bowling coach Stuart Barnes. Three were called up for the first time: batsman Harry Crawshaw, seamer Ben Cliff and slow left-armer Josh Baker. Sri Lanka named a squad of 14 but, having sealed the series with a match to spare, brought in four debutants.

England edged the opener, but the next three were a harrowing trial by spin. The damage was done by two slow-left armers – captain Dunith Wellalage (who finished with nine wickets at seven) and Wanuja Sahan (seven at 11) – and leg-spinner Raveen de Silva (seven at 14). Will Luxton was the only England batsman to stay afloat, scoring 150 runs at 50, including one of their two half-centuries; wicketkeeper James Rew made the other. On raging turners, Tom Prest and Rehan Ahmed formed a useful spin pairing, but Sri Lanka were up to the challenge, and three batsmen shone: Pawan Pathiraja (195 at 49, including 113 in the second match), Wellalage (139 at 46) and Ranuda Somarathne (129 at 32).

There was also plenty of attention for Sri Lanka's unusual pace-bowling tyro, 18-year-old Matheesha Pathirana, whose slingy action and impressive speed had brought him to the attention of Chennai Super Kings – and the label "the next Malinga". His deployment was erratic: in his four games, he was the seventh, fourth, sixth and ninth to bowl. His bowling was just as erratic: he sent down 16 wides.

ENGLAND TOURING PARTY

*J. G. Bethell (Warwickshire), *T. J. Prest (Hampshire), R. Ahmed (Leicestershire), T. H. Aspinwall (Lancashire), J. O. Baker (Worcestershire), S. Baker (Somerset), N. A. Barnwell (Surrey), G. J. Bell (Lancashire), J. A. Boyden (Lancashire), B. M. Cliff (Yorkshire), J. M. Coles (Sussex), H. M. Crawshaw (Durham), A. J. Horton (Glamorgan), D. K. Ibrahim (Sussex), W. A. Luxton (Yorkshire), J. E. K. Rew (Somerset), J. J. G. Sales (Northamptonshire), F. Singh (Nottinghamshire), G. W. Thomas (Somerset). *Coach:* R. K. J. Dawson.

Bethell (for the first and second games) and Prest (third, fourth and fifth) were named as joint-captains. S. Baker was a non-playing squad member.

First Under-19 one-day international At Colombo (SSC), November 30, 2021. **England won by 25 runs. England 242** (49.3 overs) (D. N. Wellalage 5-30); **‡Sri Lanka 217** (47.3 overs) (R. Somarathne 57, D. N. Wellalage 68; J. A. Boyden 3-27). *A dominant performance from Sri Lanka captain Dulith Wellalage was ruined by a collapse that cost victory. England were 66-1 when he came on to bowl his slow left-armers; he took 5-30, keeping the target to a gettable 243. Sri Lanka stuttered from 51-0 to 69-4, but Ranuda Somarathne added 102 with Wellalage for the sixth wicket. After the skipper departed, 27 were needed from 24 with four wickets in hand – but they fell for one, including three in an over from left-arm seamer Josh Boyden.*

Second Under-19 one-day international   At Colombo (SSC), December 3, 2021. **Sri Lanka won by 148 runs.** ‡**Sri Lanka 251-4** (50 overs) (P. Pathiraja 113, R. Somarathne 58*). **England 103** (31.4 overs) (J. E. K. Rew 50; W. Sahan 5-21). *Pawan Pathiraja, a left-hander from Kandy, hit an imperious century, putting on 68 with Shevon Daniel, 105 with Somarathne and 60* with Wellalage. Facing a daunting target of 252, the tourists disintegrated against slow left-armer Wanuja Sahan, whose 5-21 were Sri Lanka's best figures against England. Only James Rew had any answer, accumulating a competent half-century.*

Third Under-19 one-day international   At Colombo (SSC), December 5, 2021. **Sri Lanka won by two wickets.** ‡**England 114** (34.3 overs) (D. N. Wellalage 3-13); **Sri Lanka 115-8** (44 overs). *England faced another slow-bowling examination, but almost defended 114. Left-arm seamer Yasiru Rodrigo dismissed Jacob Bethell with the first ball of the match, then George Bell in the third over, before England lost eight wickets to spin. Off-spinner Tom Prest opened England's bowling with a spell of one for four from seven overs, and his final figures of 10–5–13–1 included a ball that went for five wides. Sri Lanka inched to the target as wickets fell and, from 96-8, Rodrigo and Matheesha Pathirana painstakingly accrued the 19 needed.*

Fourth Under-19 one-day international   At Colombo (SSC), December 8, 2021. **Sri Lanka won by 126 runs.** ‡**Sri Lanka 243-7** (50 overs) (P. Pathiraja 60, K. H. R. A. de Silva 59; B. M. Cliff 3-43); **England 117** (33.3 overs) (K. H. R. A. de Silva 3-6). *Sri Lanka sealed the series with a thumping victory, similar to their win in the second game. Pathiraja top-scored again, adding 111 for the fourth wicket with Raveen de Silva. Prest was economical but wicketless; seamer Ben Cliff bowled with heart. England were 83-2 in the 21st but, when top-scorer George Thomas was run out for 40, Sri Lanka's six spinners ran riot. The last eight fell for 34, as all but Pathiraja and wicketkeeper Anjala Bandara had a bowl.*

Fifth Under-19 one-day international   At Colombo (SSC), December 10, 2021. **England won by 48 runs. England 214-8** (50 overs) (W. A. Luxton 84*; W. V. V. Ranpul 4-45); ‡**Sri Lanka 166** (35.1 overs) (S. Rajapaksa 66; T. J. Prest 6-41). *England claimed a consolation win, thanks to two outstanding performances. Will Luxton's 84* – he retired with heat exhaustion in the 45th over – was their top score of the series (and only their second half-century). Then, despite 66 from Sadisha Rajapaksa, Prest swept Sri Lanka aside with 6-41, England's second-best figures in Youth ODIs, after Justin Bishop's 7-41 against West Indies at Chelmsford in 2001.*

DOMESTIC CRICKET IN SRI LANKA IN 2020-21

Sa'adi Thawfeeq

In August 2020, Sri Lanka Cricket completed the top tier of the 2019-20 first-class Premier League, after a five-month suspension because of the pandemic, but no first-class domestic cricket was played in 2020-21. The board found time only for the limited-overs tournaments, conducted in biobubbles under strict Covid protocols.

The two major trophies were won by the traditional powers of the domestic circuit, Nondescripts and Sinhalese. Despite missing nine regulars – five on the sick list, four on national duty – a young **Nondescripts** team pulled off a resounding 145-run win over Ragama in the final of the 50-over competition. Both teams had won seven matches out of seven, but this was a one-sided game: Under-19 international Kamil Mishara struck his third century of the tournament, before Ragama's batting folded with nearly 20 overs to spare.

Earlier in the competition, Tissara Perera, once the national white-ball captain, became the first Sri Lankan to hit six sixes in an over, against Bloomfield's occasional leg-spinner Dilhan Cooray. Entering with 20 balls of the Army's innings to go, he raced to fifty in 13 – one short of the world record, set by Kaushalya Weeraratne in the same competition in 2005-06. A couple of days earlier, there had been a delay at the Arons CC ground, where Nondescripts arrived to play Kalutara Town: one boundary was found to be only 45 metres away, so the groundstaff had to cut back shrubs to increase the distance to 52. The match was reduced to 49 overs a side, and the interval shortened, but Nondescripts bowled out Kalutara in 28.

The SLC T20 tournament was won by **Sinhalese**, led by Charith Asalanka – who made his international debut a few months later, and could be a future Sri Lanka captain. In the final, against the Army, he was outshone by an unbeaten 71 from wicketkeeper Krishan Sanjula Arachchige, who then held three catches as the Army were dismissed for 117. Sinhalese had also appeared in the final of the Under-23 limited-overs tournament – delayed until February by the pandemic, after the group rounds were completed in October – but succumbed by 59 runs to Lankan, who carried off their first major trophy.

MAJOR CLUBS LIMITED-OVERS TOURNAMENT IN 2020-21

Four 50-over mini-leagues plus knockout

Quarter-finals Army beat Sinhalese by 17 runs; Badureliya beat Moors by seven wickets; Nondescripts beat Navy by 167 runs; Ragama beat Tamil Union by six wickets.

Semi-finals Nondescripts beat Badureliya by 18 runs; Ragama beat Army by eight wickets.

Final At Colombo (SSC), April 11, 2021. **Nondescripts won by 145 runs.** ‡Nondescripts 286-7 (50 overs) (R. V. P. K. Mishara 113); *Ragama 141* (30.3 overs). *Nondescripts won their seventh 50-over title – second only to Sinhalese – after Kamil Mishara added 137 with Kaveen Bandara, and 98 with captain Angelo Perera. Ragama could not get even halfway to a target of 287, as seamers Lahiru Kumara (3-30) and Chamika Karunaratne (4-37) ran through them.*

SRI LANKA CRICKET TWENTY20 TOURNAMENT IN 2020-21

Four 20-over mini-leagues plus knockout

Quarter-finals Army beat Negombo by six runs; Colombo beat Ragama by 57 runs; Kurunegala Youth beat Nondescripts by 63 runs; Sinhalese beat Colts by six wickets.

Semi-finals Army beat Kurunegala Youth by nine wickets; Sinhalese beat Colombo by 32 runs.

Final At Colombo (SSC), March 20, 2021. **Sinhalese won by 29 runs.** ‡**Sinhalese 146-5** (20 overs); **Army 117** (19.2 overs). *Krishan Sanjula Arachchige's career-best 71* led Sinhalese to 146-5, which proved more than enough to defeat the Army. Wickets fell steadily in the chase to a combination of seam and spin, with only Ashan Randika (44) and Himasha Liyanage (32) reaching double figures.*

The Lanka Premier League has its own section (page 1144).

FIRST-CLASS CHAMPIONS

1988-89	{ Nondescripts { Sinhalese	1998-99	Bloomfield	2010-11	Bloomfield
1989-90	Sinhalese	1999-2000	Colts	2011-12	Colts
1990-91	Sinhalese	2000-01	Nondescripts	2012-13	Sinhalese
1991-92	Colts	2001-02	Colts	2013-14	Nondescripts
1992-93	Sinhalese	2002-03	Moors	2014-15	Ports Authority
1993-94	Nondescripts	2003-04	Bloomfield	2015-16	Tamil Union
1994-95	{ Bloomfield { Sinhalese	2004-05	Colts	2016-17	Sinhalese
		2005-06	Sinhalese	2017-18	Chilaw Marians
1995-96	Colombo	2006-07	Colombo	2018-19	Colombo
1996-97	Bloomfield	2007-08	Sinhalese	2019-20	Colombo
1997-98	Sinhalese	2008-09	Colts	2020-21	*No competition*
		2009-10	Chilaw Marians		

Sinhalese have won the title outright 8 times, Colts 6, Bloomfield and Colombo 4, Nondescripts 3, Chilaw Marians 2, Moors, Ports Authority and Tamil Union 1. Sinhalese have shared it twice, Bloomfield and Nondescripts once each.

The tournament was known as the Lakspray Trophy from 1988-89 to 1989-90, the P. Saravanamuttu Trophy from 1990-91 to 1997-98, and the Premier League from 1998-99.

WEST INDIAN CRICKET IN 2021

Big hits, small returns

VANEISA BAKSH

West Indies went into the T20 World Cup as title defenders, but were eliminated without putting up much of a fight, summing up a tough 2021 for the men's team. Sixteen victories in 44 games across the formats was a poor showing; many of the 23 defeats were drubbings. By December, they were eighth in the Test and one-day rankings, and ninth in T20s.

Things had seemed so promising in January. Though numerous regulars declined to tour Bangladesh, and a makeshift team under Jason Mohammed had been swept aside in the one-dayers, West Indies redeemed themselves in the two Tests. Kraigg Brathwaite was named captain, laid foundations with the bat and proved a prudent choice as stand-in for Jason Holder, who had opted out of the tour. The star was Kyle Mayers who, in a superb run-chase at Chittagong, became the sixth to score a double-century on Test debut.

Kieron Pollard, who had excused himself from the trip, returned to lead West Indies' white-ball teams when Sri Lanka visited in March. Spirits

WEST INDIES IN 2021

	Played	Won	Lost	Drawn/No result
Tests	10	3	5	2
One-day internationals	9	4	5	–
Twenty20 internationals	25	9	13	3

JANUARY	2 Tests and 3 ODIs (a) v Bangladesh	(page 909)
FEBRUARY		
MARCH	⎫ 2 Tests, 3 ODIs and 3 T20Is (h) v Sri Lanka	(page 1032)
APRIL	⎭	
MAY		
JUNE	⎫ 2 Tests and 5 T20Is (h) v South Africa	(page 1039)
JULY	3 ODIs and 5 T20Is (h) v Australia	(page 1046)
AUGUST	⎭ 2 Tests and 4 T20Is (h) v Pakistan	(page 1049)
SEPTEMBER		
OCTOBER	⎫ T20 World Cup in the UAE	(page 830)
NOVEMBER	⎭ 2 Tests (a) v Sri Lanka	(page 1020)
DECEMBER	3 T20Is (a) v Pakistan	(page 978)

For a review of West Indian domestic cricket from the 2020-21 season, see page 1056.

Spent force: Chris Gayle is blown out by Pat Cummins at the T20 World Cup.

remained high as the visitors were vanquished in both formats. Brathwaite again led for the Tests and, though both were drawn, West Indies had enjoyed their first four-match unbeaten run since 2012-13.

It proved a false dawn. Progress was hijacked by off-field events: mainly Covid and its mutations, but also dodgy selection decisions. By June, when South Africa arrived, it was obvious Brathwaite had become the No. 1 choice as Test skipper. The South Africans dominated, winning both Tests by large margins and claiming the T20 series. When Australia came in July, Nicholas Pooran was given a shot as T20 captain, and West Indies won 4–1, but Pollard was back in charge for the ODI series, which was lost.

There hardly seemed time for a breather, as Pakistan were the fourth visitors to the Caribbean, starting their T20 series two days after the last Australia game. But three of the games were washed out, and Pakistan won the other. The First Test produced a thrilling one-wicket win for West Indies – a low-scoring game which twisted and turned until last pair Kemar Roach and Jayden Seales crept over the line. Pakistan roared back to square the series.

By now, two major issues had become the focus of attention. The first was the team's attitude to batting. It seemed every format merited the same approach: power hitting, the long-time hallmark of West Indian cricket, though apparently unsupported by thought or technique. The bowling had improved considerably, but injudicious batting had rendered the team lopsided. The second concern was the whim of the selectors, who compounded the first by regularly opting for muscularity over finesse.

It all came to a head as the T20 World Cup loomed. The selection of Chris Gayle appeared to be based on his record-breaking career, rather than form or fitness. The press and public were indignant: while Gayle had apparently been given an automatic pass, Holder was merely a reserve. Sunil Narine was also omitted, despite his economy-rate of 4.4 in the Caribbean Premier League.

West Indies' insipid showing was an indictment of the flawed thinking. The vaunted power-players swiped mightily at shadows, a display of recklessness that wasted some valiant bowling. Twice champions, West Indies were all out for 55 against England, and their sole win came against Bangladesh. One meme, depicting a trio of roughnecks lurking in an alley, wielding huge rocks, said: "Fans, waiting for West Indies to reach home."

Neither was Gayle impressive off the field, laying into Curtly Ambrose for commenting on his lack of runs. When Dwayne Bravo diplomatically announced his international retirement, Gayle bragged that he was ready for more, and suggested Cricket West Indies lay on a farewell T20 for him in Jamaica, against Ireland in January 2022. It provoked an already seething public, especially when the board said they would consider the idea. Administrators once defined by their antagonistic stance toward the players now seemed more willing to kowtow to their big names.

West Indies lost two Tests in Sri Lanka, then were decimated in Pakistan – first in three T20s (with Pooran captaining) by a home team on top form, then by Covid, which prompted the cancellation of the one-dayers.

In December, it was announced that the contracts of head selector Roger Harper and his assistant Miles Bascombe would not be renewed, and an interim panel would be convened by Phil Simmons. On New Year's Eve, the squads for the Ireland white-ball series were named: the captaincy was back with Pollard, Holder was recalled, and Gayle was out. In his absence, West Indies lost the 50-over series, before the T20s were cancelled because of another Covid situation.

The women's team sailed a steady course in terms of team politics, but the pandemic kept capsizing fixtures, and the role of captain changed as often as it did among the men. In June, Stafanie Taylor led West Indies to T20 and ODI series victories against Pakistan. Then South Africa visited: the T20s series was drawn, but West Indies – initially led by Anisa Mohammed, then Deandra Dottin – went down heavily in the one-dayers. A visit to Pakistan ahead of the World Cup qualifier was successful, but the qualifier in Zimbabwe was rocked by Covid. After its curtailment, the team (and coach Courtney Walsh) were stranded for 11 days in Oman, while CWI attempted to arrange flights. There was a consolation: West Indies were one of the lucky teams to qualify for the World Cup on ranking.

After a sterling stint as a player, broadcaster and author, Michael Holding announced his retirement from media work in September, aged 67. His late flowering as an activist, bringing to wider consciousness the struggles of black cricketers, served as a poignant reminder of the power of the mind.

WEST INDIES v SRI LANKA IN 2020-21

Colin James

Twenty20 internationals (3): West Indies 2, Sri Lanka 1
One-day internationals (3): West Indies 3 (30pts), Sri Lanka 0 (–2pts)
Test matches (2): West Indies 0 (40pts), Sri Lanka 0 (40pts)

This series – the first international cricket in the Caribbean since January 2020 – came close to cancellation in early February when Sri Lanka head coach Mickey Arthur and senior batsman Lahiru Thirimanne tested positive for Covid-19. The original plan had been to start with the Tests and move on to the limited-overs matches, but the white-ball games were shunted forward. Both Arthur and Thirimanne flew with the Sri Lankan squad, though not Lahiru Kumara, who tested positive just before departure.

In another blow for the tourists, Chaminda Vaas, recently reappointed for a fourth stretch as fast-bowling coach, resigned at the eleventh hour. Sri Lanka Cricket accused him of holding the game "at ransom", and were scathing about his motives, which they said were "based on personal monetary gain". There was more. Visa issues prevented the Twenty20 captain, Dasun Shanaka, from joining his colleagues, and the leadership passed to Angelo Mathews. He played the 20-over games, but on the morning of the second one-day international announced he was leaving the tour for personal reasons.

All eight matches were staged in Antigua, where both teams could stay in biosecure conditions. The three Twenty20 internationals were held at the Coolidge Ground, while the ODIs and two Tests were played at the Sir Vivian Richards Stadium at North Sound. Spectators were barred.

There was also uncertainty about the home Test captain. Jason Holder had led his side with distinction in England the previous July but, unsure about Covid, had been one of ten players to opt out of the recent trip to Bangladesh. There, replacement captain Kraigg Brathwaite guided an understrength team to a 2–0 victory. It made selection for this series a tricky business, and divided opinion among the region's luminaries. Clive Lloyd and Andy Roberts publicly lobbied for change; Viv Richards also gave Brathwaite a ringing endorsement. But Curtly Ambrose and Ian Bishop reasoned that one swallow did not make a summer. The selectors, however, chose to reward Brathwaite.

Jimmy Adams, CWI's director of cricket, paid tribute to Holder's five-year stint as Test captain. The highest-ranked all-rounder in the Test game, he was retained for the Sri Lanka matches, but of the other Bangladesh absentees only Darren Bravo made the red-ball squad, though not the team. Roston Chase, vice-captain in England and New Zealand in 2020, was unlucky to miss out, as was Shamarh Brooks.

West Indies prevailed in both white-ball formats, though Mathews's side did win a T20, their only victory of the tour. A couple of familiar faces reappeared in the 20-over games: Chris Gayle, now 41, returned after 18 months out of the West Indies team, while Fidel Edwards, two years younger, came back for the first time since November 2012. Neither made an especially compelling case for age, and both were outshone by Kieron Pollard, who hit six sixes in an over off Akila Dananjaya in the first T20. In the ODIs, there were centuries for Shai Hope and Evin Lewis as West Indies chased successfully on all three occasions.

The hosts had slightly the better of the drawn Tests, but largely placid pitches at North Sound made it difficult to dismiss the obdurate Sri Lankans twice. For them, there were strong performances from opening batsman Thirimanne, who hit 240 runs at 60, and opening bowler Suranga Lakmal, who took 11 wickets at 21.

SRI LANKA TOURING PARTY

*F. D. M. Karunaratne (T/50/20), K. N. A. Bandara (50/20), P. V. D. Chameera (T/50/20), L. D. Chandimal (T/50/20), A. Dananjaya (20), D. M. de Silva (T), P. W. H. de Silva (T/50/20), D. P. D. N. Dickwella (T/20), L. Embuldeniya (T), A. M. Fernando (T/50/20), A. N. P. R. Fernando (50/20), B. O. P. Fernando (T/50/20), M. V. T. Fernando (T), M. D. Gunathilleke (50/20), R. A. S. Lakmal (T/50/20), L. M. D. Madushanka (20), A. D. Mathews (T/50/20), P. H. K. D. Mendis (T/50/20), P. Nissanka (T/50/20), N. L. T. C. Perera (50/20), P. A. D. L. R. Sandakan (50/20), M. D. Shanaka (T/50), A. R. S. Silva (T), H. D. R. L. Thirimanne (T), R. T. M. Wanigamuni (T/20). *Coach:* J. M. Arthur.

C. B. R. L. S. Kumara, originally named in the white-ball squads, tested positive for Covid before the party left for the Caribbean, and was replaced by Lakmal (who was retained for the Tests). Mathews, who led the team in the T20I series after Shanaka arrived late because of visa issues, withdrew from the squad for personal reasons after the first ODI.

First Twenty20 international At Coolidge, Antigua, March 3, 2021 (floodlit). **West Indies won by four wickets. Sri Lanka 131-9** (20 overs) (D. P. D. N. Dickwella 33, P. Nissanka 39); ‡**West Indies 134-6** (13.1 overs) (K. A. Pollard 38; A. Dananjaya 3-62, P. W. H. de Silva 3-12). *PoM:* K. A. Pollard. *T20I debuts:* K. Sinclair (West Indies); K. N. A. Bandara, P. Nissanka (Sri Lanka). *This astonishing match included both a hat-trick and six sixes in an over – both involving the diminutive off-spinner Akila Dananjaya. In his second over (the fourth of the innings), with West Indies 52-0, he had Evin Lewis caught at long-off for a ten-ball 28, trapped the returning Chris Gayle for a golden duck, and induced an edge from Nicholas Pooran for another first-baller.*

SIX SIXES IN AN OVER

Batsman	Bowler		
G. S. Sobers.	M. A. Nash	Nottinghamshire v Glamorgan at Swansea (FC)	1968
R. J. Shastri	T. Raj	Bombay v Baroda at Bombay (FC)	1984-85
H. H. Gibbs	D. L. S. van Bunge	South Africa v Netherlands at Basseterre (ODI)	2006-07
Yuvraj Singh	S. C. J. Broad . . .	India v England at Durban (T20I)	2007-08
R. A. Whiteley . . .	K. Carver.	Worcestershire v Yorkshire at Leeds (T20)	2017
Hazratullah Zazai .	Abdullah Mazari .	Kabul Zwanan v Balkh Legends at Sharjah (T20)	2018-19
L. J. Carter.	A. P. Devcich . . .	Northern Dist v Canterbury at Christchurch (T20)	2019-20
K. A. Pollard . . .	**A. Dananjaya** . . .	**West Indies v Sri Lanka at Coolidge (T20I)** . .	**2020-21**
N. L. T. C. Perera	P. D. M. A. Cooray	Army v Bloomfield at Panagoda (List A)	2020-21
J. S. Malhotra . . .	G. Toka	USA v Papua New Guinea at Al Amerat (ODI)	2021-22

Dananjaya then ran into Kieron Pollard, wholly unfazed by what had gone before: his next six balls sailed over the boundary between midwicket and wide long-off. By the end of the powerplay, the hosts were a T20I-record 98-4, heading for victory. Fellow spinner Wanindu Hasaranga de Silva removed Pollard (for 38 from 11 deliveries) and Fabian Allen in two balls, and the urgency went out of the game. Dananjaya ended with 3-62 – the most expensive three-wicket return in all Twenty20 cricket – and an intriguing ball-by-ball analysis: 000116 | 4WWW14 | 666666 | 610101. Earlier, Sri Lanka had lost their way from a steady 71-1 in the tenth. Fidel Edwards claimed 1-29 in his first game for West Indies since 2012.

Second Twenty20 international   At Coolidge, Antigua, March 5, 2021 (floodlit). **Sri Lanka won by 43 runs.** ‡**Sri Lanka 160-6** (20 overs) (M. D. Gunathilleke 56, P. Nissanka 37); **West Indies 117** (18.4 overs) (P. W. H. de Silva 3-17, P. A. D. L. R. Sandakan 3-10). *PoM:* P. W. H. de Silva. *Openers Dhanushka Gunathilleke (56 off 42) and Pathum Nissanka (37 off 23) laid the foundation for a daunting score by hammering 95 off 62 balls, but again Sri Lanka went off the boil. They pottered for more than eight overs without a boundary, and needed a brisk 19* from Wanindu Hasaranga de Silva to scrape 160. As it turned out, though, they had plenty to halt an eight-game losing streak. As before, Dananjaya took the new ball and removed Lewis, but there the similarity ceased: his four overs cost 13 (and his first three just six). Lendl Simmons and Gayle fostered some West Indian optimism by taking the score to 45-1, but Hasaranga de Silva dismissed both in the seventh, and the middle order fell away to 66-6. Pollard, at No. 7, could contribute only 13 off 15 (with just one six this time), and the top score was a seven-ball 23 from Obed McCoy at No.10. Wrist-spinners Hasaranga de Silva and (left-armer) Lakshan Sandakan did the damage.*

Third Twenty20 international   At Coolidge, Antigua, March 7, 2021 (floodlit). **West Indies won by three wickets.** ‡**Sri Lanka 131-4** (20 overs) (L. D. Chandimal 54*, K. N. A. Bandara 44*); **West Indies 134-7** (19 overs) (P. A. D. L. R. Sandakan 3-29). *PoM:* F. A. Allen. *The deciding game was the closest. With 18 balls left, West Indies were 105-7, needing 27. Allen, who had come in to face a hat-trick ball from Sandakan, then belted three sixes off the penultimate over – bowled by Dananjaya – to secure the series. A target of 132 would not usually have caused problems but, on a grudging strip, runs did not come easily. Sri Lanka had been kept in check by Allen's left-arm spin (1-13) and were in trouble at 46-4 in the tenth. But a stand of 85* between Dinesh Chandimal and Ashen Bandara repaired the damage, if at an unspectacular rate. Five of West Indies' top six made starts, but wickets fell regularly until Allen saw them home. Sandakan claimed another three wickets, while Dananjaya leaked 53.*

First one-day international   At North Sound, Antigua, March 10, 2021. **West Indies won by eight wickets.** ‡**Sri Lanka 232** (49 overs) (M. D. Gunathilleke 55, F. D. M. Karunaratne 52, K. N. A. Bandara 50); **West Indies 236-2** (47 overs) (E. Lewis 65, S. D. Hope 110, D. M. Bravo 37*). *West Indies 10pts. PoM:* S. D. Hope. *ODI debuts:* K. N. A. Bandara, P. Nissanka (Sri Lanka). *West Indies romped to victory thanks to a stylish century from Shai Hope on his return to international cricket after being dropped for the Test tour of New Zealand, and opting out of the trip to Bangladesh. It was his tenth ODI hundred, in his 74th innings. On a true pitch, he put on 143 for the first wicket with Lewis, and 72 for the second with Darren Bravo. The Sri Lankans, who also enjoyed a century opening stand, had seemed bound for more than 232, but lost wickets carelessly – and one controversially. Gunathilleke became the eighth player in over 4,000 one-day internationals to be dismissed obstructing the field, when he knocked the ball backwards with his boot, out of the reach of Pollard, the bowler, after thinking better of a single. The on-field officials referred the decision to the third umpire, Joel Wilson, who detected intention on the batsman's part; others were less sure. Ashen Bandara bolstered the middle order with 50 on debut, but Sri Lanka failed to bat out their overs – a steep decline after a healthy start.*

Second one-day international   At North Sound, Antigua, March 12, 2021. **West Indies won by five wickets.** ‡**Sri Lanka 273-8** (50 overs) (M. D. Gunathilleke 96, L. D. Chandimal 71, P. W. H. de Silva 47; J. N. Mohammed 3-47); ‡**West Indies 274-5** (49.4 overs) (E. Lewis 103, S. D. Hope 84, N. Pooran 35*). *West Indies 10pts. PoM:* E. Lewis. *West Indies won the game, and series, with two balls to spare – a tighter finish than seemed likely after Lewis and Hope had put on 192 for the first wicket on another bone-hard pitch. Lewis reached his century from 116 balls (at least 20 more than any of his three previous hundreds), while Hope took up where he left off in the last game, making a steady 84 from 108. The pair departed in successive overs, and the wobble grew more concerning when Bravo and Pollard fell cheaply to leave the hosts needing 41 from 25 balls. Pooran, however, remained steadfast. Gunathilleke top-scored for Sri Lanka for the third game in a row, and oversaw a recovery from 50-3 during a 100-run stand with Chandimal; Hasaranga de Silva gave the innings a late flourish with 47 from 31; off-spinner Jason Mohammed, bowling a full ten overs for the first time in ODIs, took a career-best 3-47.*

Third one-day international   At North Sound, Antigua, March 14, 2021. **West Indies won by five wickets. Sri Lanka 274-6** (50 overs) (M. D. Gunathilleke 36, F. D. M. Karunaratne 31, K. N. A. Bandara 55*, P. W. H. de Silva 80*; A. J. Hosein 3-33); ‡**West Indies 276-5** (48.3 overs) (S. D. Hope 64, D. M. Bravo 102, K. A. Pollard 53*). *West Indies 10pts, Sri Lanka –2pts. PoM:* D. M. Bravo. *PoS:* S. D. Hope. *ODI debut:* A. Phillip (West Indies). *Another game, another West Indies success after winning the toss and fielding. The last time they had won consecutive ODIs against Sri*

Lanka was 2008. On this occasion, their centurion was Darren Bravo, whose previous international hundred had come in October 2016, and who had not reached 40 in 24 innings. He and the indefatigable Hope added 109 for the third wicket, before Hope was dismissed for 64, his lowest score of the series. It was his sixth score of 50-plus in a row (all against Sri Lanka); only Pakistan's Javed Miandad had managed a longer run. Pollard then cantered his side past their target. Gunathilleke had got Sri Lanka's innings off to another crisp start. Two of his younger team-mates also confirmed their credentials: Bandara hit a second fifty in his third ODI, while Hasaranga de Silva clubbed a career-best 80* of 60 balls. Left-arm spinner Akeal Hosein claimed 3-33, but Trinidadian seamer Anderson Phillip went wicketless on debut. Sri Lanka were deducted two points for a slow over-rate.

WEST INDIES v SRI LANKA

First Test

At North Sound, Antigua, March 21–25. Drawn. West Indies 20pts, Sri Lanka 20pts. Toss: West Indies. Test debut: P. Nissanka.

A pair of responsible second-innings centuries, one from Sri Lanka's Pathum Nissanka and the other from West Indies' Nkrumah Bonner, dug each side out of a hole. Both players belied their inexperience: the 22-year-old Nissanka was on debut, while Bonner, though ten years older, was in his third Test. Ultimately, however, the bowlers could not find enough in an unhelpful pitch, and the game ended in stalemate.

Brathwaite, retained as captain after Holder preferred not to tour Bangladesh, chose to bowl on a pitch with grass and moisture. It was the right decision: helped by Brathwaite's brilliant run-out of Oshada Fernando, West Indies reduced their opponents to 92 for five. Sri Lanka rallied but, once Dickwella was smartly held by Cornwall at slip to make it 150 for six, a terminal slide was on. While Roach was consistently hostile, Holder proved the chief destroyer: his five for 27 was his eighth – and cheapest – five-for. Among the victims was the stubborn left-hander Thirimanne, who dragged on a seemingly harmless ball after resisting for nearly five hours.

A total of 169 was poor but, despite three of the top four passing 30, West Indies were shakily placed at 133 for five on the second day. The lead was just two when Cornwall, at No. 9, galumphed to the crease. He is reputed to weigh 22 stone, and he put plenty behind the two sixes and nine fours that punctuated a feisty maiden Test fifty. With Da Silva he added 90, an eighth-wicket record (for a week) between these sides. The diligent and reliable Lakmal, added to the tour party only after Lahiru Kumara tested positive for Covid-19, took a career-best five for 47 in his 63rd Test.

A lead of 102 looked useful, the more so after Karunaratne again fell cheaply. But Thirimanne proved as resolute as before, and now found support from Oshada: they pushed Sri Lankan noses ahead during a stand of 162, ended when Oshada edged Mayers, a maiden Test wicket for his medium-pace. Chandimal went in identical fashion soon after and, when Roach castled Thirimanne, the momentum had tilted back towards West Indies: Sri Lanka were effectively 87 for four.

But Nissanka bolstered the innings in two important partnerships: 70 with de Silva and 179 with Dickwella (a sixth-wicket record in this fixture), as Sri Lanka raised their sights from preventing defeat to engineering victory. Initially a study in defence – he did not score from his first 20 balls – Nissanka remained as patient as he was determined. From his 240th, he became the first Sri Lankan to hit a century on debut since Thilan Samaraweera in 2001; a dozen balls later, he holed out to deep backward square in an effort to up the rate. His partner, Dickwella, had led a charmed life – at one stage the ball rolled back on to the stumps but did not dislodge the bails – until, one shot from a maiden century, he dragged on against Roach. It was the 17th time he had been unable to convert a fifty into a hundred – a Test record, one clear of Indian opener Chetan Chauhan.

The dogged Sri Lankan innings came to an end in its 150th over, leaving West Indies a target of 375 in a little under four sessions. The previous month, they had hauled in a target of 395 in Chittagong, so it was improbable rather than impossible. On such a slow pitch, though, Brathwaite considered the risks of strokeplay too severe, and opted for survival. Campbell departed on the fourth evening, but the other West Indians all hung around as the pitch refused to misbehave. All the same, Bonner's achievement should not be underplayed: like Nissanka, he produced an innings of self-denial. Bonner took three balls longer to reach his hundred, by which time the draw was safe.

Player of the Match: N. E. Bonner.

Close of play: first day, West Indies 13-0 (Brathwaite 3, Campbell 7); second day, West Indies 268-8 (Cornwall 60, Roach 4); third day, Sri Lanka 255-4 (de Silva 46, Nissanka 21); fourth day, West Indies 34-1 (Brathwaite 8, Bonner 15).

Sri Lanka

*F. D. M. Karunaratne c Campbell b Cornwall	12	– (2) c Campbell b Roach	3
H. D. R. L. Thirimanne b Holder	70	– (1) b Roach	76
B. O. P. Fernando run out (Brathwaite)	4	– c Da Silva b Mayers	91
L. D. Chandimal c Da Silva b Holder	4	– c Da Silva b Mayers	4
D. M. de Silva b Roach	13	– b Joseph	50
P. Nissanka c Holder b Roach	9	– c Roach b Cornwall	103
†D. P. D. N. Dickwella b Cornwall b Holder	32	– b Roach	96
R. A. S. Lakmal c Brathwaite b Holder	3	– run out (Blackwood/Da Silva)	8
P. V. D. Chameera b Roach	2	– c Mayers b Cornwall	6
L. Embuldeniya lbw b Holder	3	– c Holder b Cornwall	10
M. V. T. Fernando not out	1	– not out	0
B 4, lb 6, w 5, nb 1	16	B 13, lb 5, nb 11	29

1/17 (1) 2/29 (3) 3/54 (4) (69.4 overs) 169   1/8 (2) 2/170 (3) (149.5 overs) 476
4/76 (5) 5/92 (6) 6/150 (7)   3/178 (4) 4/189 (1)
7/160 (2) 8/163 (8) 9/164 (9) 10/169 (10)   5/259 (6) 6/438 (6) 7/460 (7)
   8/462 (8) 9/476 (10) 10/476 (9)

Roach 16–2–47–3; Gabriel 9–2–22–0; Cornwall 14–6–25–1; Joseph 11–2–32–0; Holder 17.4–6–27–5; Mayers 2–0–6–0. *Second innings*—Roach 27–3–74–3; Gabriel 18–2–67–0; Holder 22–4–40–0; Joseph 21–2–83–1; Cornwall 42.5–4–137–3; Brathwaite 9–1–30–0; Mayers 9–2–24–2; Blackwood 1–0–3–0.

West Indies

*K. C. Brathwaite c de Silva b Lakmal	3	– b Embuldeniya	23
J. D. Campbell c Dickwella b Chameera	42	– c Dickwella b M. V. T. Fernando	11
N. E. Bonner lbw b Embuldeniya	31	– not out	113
K. R. Mayers c de Silva b Lakmal	45	– c Thirimanne b Embuldeniya	52
J. Blackwood b Lakmal	2	– b M. V. T. Fernando	4
J. O. Holder b Lakmal	19	– not out	18
†J. Da Silva c Dickwella b Chameera	46		
A. S. Joseph c Chandimal b Lakmal	0		
R. R. S. Cornwall b M. V. T. Fernando	61		
K. A. J. Roach not out	5		
S. T. Gabriel lbw b M. V. T. Fernando	0		
B 1, lb 6, w 1, nb 9	17	B 4, lb 8, nb 3	15

1/13 (1) 2/69 (3) 3/95 (2) (103 overs) 271   1/12 (2) (4 wkts, 100 overs) 236
4/120 (5) 5/133 (4) 6/169 (6)   2/78 (1)
7/171 (8) 8/261 (7) 9/271 (9) 10/271 (11)   3/183 (4) 4/204 (5)

Lakmal 25–9–47–5; M. V. T. Fernando 17–6–52–2; Chameera 22–1–71–2; Embuldeniya 28–6–64–1; de Silva 11–2–30–0. *Second innings*—Lakmal 25–10–33–0; M. V. T. Fernando 19–0–73–2; Embuldeniya 28–9–62–2; Chameera 18–3–44–0; de Silva 10–5–12–0.

Umpires: G. O. Brathwaite and J. S. Wilson. Third umpire: N. Duguid.
Referee: R. B. Richardson.

WEST INDIES v SRI LANKA

Second Test

At North Sound, Antigua, March 29–April 2. Drawn. West Indies 20pts, Sri Lanka 20pts. Toss: Sri Lanka.

Brathwaite compiled a patient century in the first innings and came within 15 of another in the second, but once again an unyielding pitch and obdurate opposition ensured a draw. Set 377 in around seven hours, Sri Lanka showed immense resolve, and finished on 193 for two when the players shook hands.

The concentration shown by Brathwaite was such that, across the first four days, he faced 507 balls and batted over 13 and a half hours. He had endured 37 Test innings without a century, and this – his ninth – took him past 4,000 runs. His first-innings defiance helped West Indies recover, first from an unsteady 120 for four, then from an uncertain 222 for seven, when he was joined by Cornwall. They added 103, raising the eighth-wicket record between these sides for the second time in a week. Cornwall's contribution was 73 from 92 balls, his captain's 26 from 96.

> The pitch, sound in nature as well as name, had the last word.

Lakmal proved the most potent of the Sri Lankan bowlers, as he had in the previous game, even if he was gifted a wicket or two. One of his victims was Bonner, brought crashing down to earth after edging an attempted cut into the stumps. Brathwaite, who also dragged on a cut, was last out for 126. Chameera claimed three, while Dickwella held five catches. A total of 354 was probably more than Karunaratne had envisaged when he chose to bowl.

Matters didn't immediately improve for the Sri Lankan captain: his disappointing tour continued when Bonner pulled off a stupendous one-handed diving catch in the slips. In better nick was Thirimanne, who hit a third successive fifty before he too dragged on. At 77 for three, Sri Lanka had got into a muddle, and required a series of scores from the middle order to get them out. First came a stand of 75, halted when Chandimal hooked Gabriel to deep square leg. A few overs later, Dhananjaya de Silva and new partner Nissanka were culpable too. Between them, they declined to review the lbw that did for Dhananjaya: replays showed the ball missing leg.

Nissanka made amends with a useful half-century and, when Roach ended the innings in a hurry on the fourth morning – almost 50 overs had been lost to the weather on the third – Sri Lanka trailed by 96. If West Indies were well placed – the more so after Embuldeniya hurt his leg sliding in the outfield, and was stretchered off – they threatened to squander their advantage through excess of caution. None of the top three seemed in the mood to hasten a declaration, and the run-rate did not take off until Brathwaite was fourth out, for 85. Mayers had picked up the tempo a little, though the real impetus came in an unbroken fifth-wicket stand between Holder and Da Silva, which added 53 at more than seven. Despite that, West Indies had time for just nine overs on the fourth evening, and could not break through.

Nor did they break through next morning, when they were hampered by a late start and a brief downpour. None of the seven previous opening stands of these two Tests had passed 18, but now Thirimanne and Karunaratne reached three figures. Eventually, Joseph found the edge of Thirimanne's bat, and he fell for 39, his lowest score of the series. There was some redemption for Karunaratne, who made a patient 75, and another second-innings half-century for Oshada Fernando. But the pitch, sound in nature as well as name, had the last word, and the game was called off early.

Player of the Match: K. C. Brathwaite.   *Player of the Series:* R. A. S. Lakmal.

Close of play: first day, West Indies 287-7 (Brathwaite 99, Cornwall 43); second day, Sri Lanka 136-3 (Chandimal 34, de Silva 23); third day, Sri Lanka 250-8 (Nissanka 49, Embuldeniya 0); fourth day, Sri Lanka 29-0 (Thirimanne 17, Karunaratne 11).

West Indies

*K. C. Brathwaite b Chameera	126	– b Chameera ... 85
J. D. Campbell c Dickwella b Lakmal	5	– c Dickwella b Lakmal ... 10
N. E. Bonner b Lakmal	0	
K. R. Mayers c Dickwella b M. V. T. Fernando	49	– lbw b Lakmal ... 55
J. Blackwood c Dickwella b Lakmal	18	– (3) c Dickwella b Chameera ... 18
J. O. Holder c Thirimanne b de Silva	30	– (5) not out ... 71
†J. Da Silva c Dickwella b Chameera	1	– (6) not out ... 20
A. S. Joseph lbw b Embuldeniya	29	
R. R. S. Cornwall c M. V. T. Fernando b Lakmal	73	
K. A. J. Roach c Dickwella b Chameera	9	
S. T. Gabriel not out	1	
Lb 6, nb 7	13	B 2, lb 12, w 1, nb 6 ... 21

1/11 (2) 2/15 (3) 3/86 (4)   (111.1 overs) 354   1/14 (2)   (4 wkts dec, 72.4 overs) 280
4/120 (5) 5/171 (6) 6/185 (7)   2/58 (3) 3/140 (4)
7/222 (8) 8/325 (9) 9/351 (10) 10/354 (1)   4/227 (1)

Lakmal 28–11–94–4; M. V. T. Fernando 27–4–71–1; Embuldeniya 25–5–88–1; Chameera 21.1–4–69–3; de Silva 10–3–26–1. *Second innings*—Lakmal 14–3–62–2; M. V. T. Fernando 12.4–1–49–0; de Silva 28–3–81–0; Chameera 18–0–74–2.

Sri Lanka

*F. D. M. Karunaratne c Bonner b Joseph	1	– (2) lbw b Mayers ... 75
H. D. R. L. Thirimanne b Roach	55	– (1) c Cornwall b Joseph ... 39
B. O. P. Fernando lbw b Mayers	18	– not out ... 66
L. D. Chandimal c sub (H. R. Walsh) b Gabriel	44	– not out ... 10
D. M. de Silva lbw b Blackwood	39	
P. Nissanka c sub (H. R. Walsh) b Roach	51	
†D. P. D. N. Dickwella c Da Silva b Holder	20	
R. A. S. Lakmal c Brathwaite b Joseph	6	
P. V. D. Chameera c Da Silva b Holder	2	
L. Embuldeniya not out	5	
M. V. T. Fernando c Da Silva b Roach	0	
B 4, lb 5, w 1, nb 7	17	Lb 1, w 1, nb 1 ... 3

1/18 (1) 2/64 (3) 3/77 (2)   (107 overs) 258   1/101 (1)   (2 wkts, 79 overs) 193
4/152 (4) 5/177 (5) 6/203 (7)   2/146 (2)
7/214 (8) 8/231 (9) 9/258 (6) 10/258 (11)

Roach 18–5–58–3; Gabriel 16–3–37–1; Joseph 22–4–64–2; Holder 21–3–39–2; Mayers 11–7–10–1; Cornwall 15–5–25–0; Blackwood 4–0–16–1. *Second innings*—Roach 12–2–33–0; Holder 10–3–24–0; Cornwall 26.4–8–53–0; Gabriel 5.2–2–20–0; Joseph 10–2–33–1; Blackwood 6–1–17–0; Brathwaite 3–0–7–0; Mayers 6–4–5–1.

Umpires: G. O. Brathwaite and J. S. Wilson.   Third umpire: N. Duguid.
Referee: R. B. Richardson.

WEST INDIES v SOUTH AFRICA IN 2021

Craig Cozier

Test matches (2): West Indies 0 (–6pts), South Africa 2 (120pts)
Twenty20 internationals (5): West Indies 2, South Africa 3

A tour imperilled by chaos at Cricket South Africa, then by an untimely Covid spike that necessitated logistical gymnastics from the West Indian board, ended in double success for the visitors: a comprehensive Test sweep followed by Twenty20 victory in a series that went to the wire.

The Tests were South Africa's first in the Caribbean for 11 years, and their first visit of any kind since they were part of a one-day tri-series in 2016. The matches were originally slated for Trinidad, but thanks to coronavirus they were shifted late on to St Lucia and Grenada. To the relief of Cricket West Indies, everything passed off without a hitch. One oddity was that the games were part of the 2019–21 World Test Championship, even though the second started on the same day as the WTC final between India and New Zealand in Southampton. Thanks to an over-rate penalty, West Indies actually lost points.

South Africa had slipped to seventh in the rankings after losing ten of their previous 13 Tests, but dominated both matches, even though West Indies had climbed above them following impressive victories in Bangladesh in February, and a home draw against Sri Lanka. The South Aficans' hostile pacemen – Kagiso Rabada, Anrich Nortje and Lungi Ngidi – found two lively pitches in St Lucia to their liking, and shared 27 wickets. They were helped by slick catching in the cordon, which ensured Dean Elgar made a successful start as permanent Test captain. And when West Indies belatedly showed brief signs of a rearguard, slow left-armer Keshav Maharaj produced a hat-trick, only South Africa's second in a Test.

Elgar's appointment liberated Quinton de Kock, who had looked burdened by his role as all-format skipper-cum-keeper. He batted beautifully throughout, starting with an unbeaten 141 in the First Test. Then came an equally confident 96 to set the tone in the Second; he added 255 at a strike-rate of 141 in the T20s. "He was the X factor," said South Africa's delighted coach, Mark Boucher. "The outfield was very slow during his 141: that could have been 200. And the 96 was worth 120–130."

West Indies were simply not good enough with the bat in the Tests. Kraigg Brathwaite, the captain, was unable to build on a promising series against Sri Lanka, and totals of 97, 162, 149 and 165 – with just two half-centuries – showed up the imperfect techniques which coach Phil Simmons admitted needed work. Brathwaite was blunt: "We didn't bat well. Full stop." The bowling was a different story. Kemar Roach led the attack in favourable conditions, while 19-year-old Jayden Seales showed promise in his maiden series. But they couldn't make up for the batting deficiencies.

The T20s were harder fought, but West Indies (with Jason Holder the only survivor from the Test defeats) were undone by quality spin and the red-hot form of de Kock. Left-arm wrist-spinner Tabraiz Shamsi went for just four an over, and took seven wickets, as South Africa won their first T20 series under Boucher after five defeats. Temba Bavuma, having recovered from hamstring and finger injuries that kept him out of the Tests, basked in a 3–2 victory on his first assignment as 20-over captain.

The first innings of each match was in the 160s, but West Indies hit 53 sixes to South Africa's 23, and scored 62% of their runs in boundaries. However, their high-risk approach also frittered away winning positions. "We had three opportunities to try to chase down 160-odd, and we couldn't get over the line," said captain Kieron Pollard, as he eyed the upcoming defence of the T20 World Cup his side won early in 2016. "The most disappointing thing is that we keep making the same mistakes, and that's the definition of insanity."

SOUTH AFRICA TOURING PARTY

*D. Elgar (T), T. Bavuma (T/20), Q. de Kock (T/20), S. J. Erwee (T), B. C. Fortuin (20), B. E. Hendricks (T/20), R. R. Hendricks (20), M. Jansen (T), H. Klaasen (20), G. F. Linde (T/20), S. S. B. Magala (20), K. A. Maharaj (T), J. N. Malan (20), A. K. Markram (T/20), D. A. Miller (20), P. W. A. Mulder (T/20), L. T. Ngidi (T/20), A. A. Nortje (T/20), K. D. Petersen (T), A. L. Phehlukwayo (20), K. Rabada (T/20), T. Shamsi (T/20), P. Subrayen (T), H. E. van der Dussen (T/20), K. Verreynne (T/20), L. B. Williams (T/20). *Coach:* M. V. Boucher.

Bavuma captained in the T20 matches. D. Pretorius was originally named for the T20s, but tested positive for Covid-19 shortly before the series, and was replaced by Mulder; B. E. Hendricks was added to the squad.

WEST INDIES v SOUTH AFRICA

First Test

At Gros Islet, St Lucia, June 10–12, 2021. South Africa won by an innings and 63 runs. South Africa 60pts. Toss: West Indies. Test debuts: J. N. T. Seales; K. D. Petersen, K. Verreynne.

Brathwaite's bold decision to bat on a lively, grass-tinged pitch backfired when South Africa's pacemen exposed faulty techniques. A first-day rout for 97 – West Indies' lowest against these opponents – was a hole from which they could not escape, especially after de Kock's sublime unbeaten 141. More excellent bowling from the seamers enabled South Africa to clinch victory on the stroke of lunch on the third day, emphatically ending a run of nine away defeats since their win at Trent Bridge in July 2017.

West Indies had started in upbeat mood, after winning two and drawing two of their four Tests in 2021. And they began promisingly: the openers had almost negotiated a tricky first hour when Hope – recalled after almost a year – had his off stump disturbed by Nortje. The next ball rattled Bonner's helmet, a blow that ultimately removed him from the match with concussion. Nortje's demolition of the top order continued: an over later, his nip-backer castled the strokeless Brathwaite.

Bonner eventually gave de Kock catching practice off Rabada, before Nortje removed Mayers and Blackwood to ill-judged forcing strokes either side of lunch. Ngidi, economical but wicketless in the first session, now snared the last five, all to outside edges, as West Indies' collapse extended to eight for 52.

On a pitch that offered pace, bounce and seam movement throughout, the slips remained busy when South Africa started their reply. Elgar went for a duck in the first over, thanks to Blackwood's superb diving effort off Roach, before Markram's half-century stabilised the innings. But batting remained a challenge. The 19-year-old Trinidadian debutant fast bowler Jayden Seales had proudly received his maroon cap from Curtly Ambrose, and kept his team in the contest by striking three times before the close of a first day of 14 wickets. Seales broke through with his sixth ball, which Keegan Petersen (another debutant) deflected to second slip. Later Markram, after an important 60, and Kyle Verreynne – the third new cap, boasting a first-class average of 56 – were both caught behind.

When van der Dussen fell early on the second day, West Indies had a glimmer: South Africa were 65 ahead, with a longish tail to follow. But de Kock provided backbone, crafting a masterpiece in his maiden first-class innings in the Caribbean, and turning his sixth Test century into a career-best. Hard graft brought him fifty from 98 balls, exactly the "boring" cricket Elgar, his new captain, had called for. Mark Boucher, the coach, preferred "disciplined".

A flurry of wickets after a stand of 53 with Mulder left South Africa 233 for eight, but de Kock now took charge. He carted two leg-side sixes and a four in an over from Seales with the new ball, and the third of his seven sixes – swung disdainfully to leg off Mayers – took him to three figures. He celebrated with a three-fingered salute to a military friend whose

---

FEWEST FIRST-CLASS GAMES BEFORE WEST INDIES TEST DEBUT

1	C. C. Passailaigue	v England at Kingston	1929-30
1	G. Gladstone Morais	v England at Kingston	1929-30
1	C. C. Griffith	v England at Port-of-Spain	1959-60
1	F. H. Edwards	v Sri Lanka at Kingston	2002-03
1	**J. N. T. Seales**	**v South Africa at Gros Islet**	**2021**
2	M. G. Grell	v England at Port-of-Spain	1929-30
2	E. E. Achong	v England at Port-of-Spain	1929-30
2	R. L. Fuller	v England at Kingston	1934-35
2	G. S. Sobers	v England at Kingston	1953-54
2	D. T. Dewdney	v Australia at Bridgetown	1954-55
2	C. K. Singh	v England at Port-of-Spain	1959-60
2	L. A. King	v India at Kingston	1961-62

---

finger had been shot off in Afghanistan, and pointed to a bat sticker plugging the Rockwood rhino conservancy in South Africa's Northern Cape. Two miscued pulls off Holder were the only let-offs: when de Kock had 83, Mayers missed a difficult catch at deep square, while a no-ball provided a reprieve at 118, when Mayers held an easier chance.

Resuming 225 behind, West Indies lost Brathwaite and Kieran Powell (Bonner's concussion substitute, in his first Test innings since December 2018) to Rabada. Nortje removed Hope and Mayers, and only Chase survived for long, eating up 202 minutes. Rabada returned to dismantle the lower order, and complete his first Test five-for in 33 innings since March 2018, sending Da Silva's off stump flying. West Indies' 200th Test defeat came when Seales edged yet another catch to the cordon. Rabada, Nortje and Ngidi had combined figures of 18 for 189.

Before the first ball, the West Indians had continued their practice of taking a knee to highlight racial and social injustice, a gesture that started in England in 2020. The South Africans offered respectful support: some took a knee, others raised a fist. De Kock did neither, and later said: "I'll keep my reasons to myself." By the end of the match, the spotlight had shifted to his exploits on the field.

Player of the Match: Q. de Kock.

Close of play: first day, South Africa 128-4 (van der Dussen 34, de Kock 4); second day, West Indies 82-4 (Chase 21, Blackwood 10).

West Indies

*K. C. Brathwaite b Nortje	15	– lbw b Rabada	7
S. D. Hope b Nortje	15	– (3) c Mulder b Nortje	12
N. E. Bonner c de Kock b Rabada	10		
R. L. Chase c Markram b Ngidi	8	– b Maharaj	62
K. R. Mayers c van der Dussen b Nortje	1	– c Mulder b Nortje	12
J. Blackwood c Petersen b Nortje	1	– c van der Dussen b Rabada	13
J. O. Holder c Markram b Ngidi	20	– b Maharaj	4
†J. Da Silva c Mulder b Ngidi	0	– b Rabada	9
R. R. S. Cornwall c Markram b Ngidi	13	– c van der Dussen b Rabada	0
K. A. J. Roach c de Kock b Ngidi	1	– not out	13
J. N. T. Seales not out	0	– c Mulder b Nortje	3
K. O. A. Powell (did not bat)		– (2) lbw b Rabada	14
Lb 4, w 6, nb 3	13	B 8, lb 2, w 1, nb 2	13
1/24 (2) 2/31 (1) 3/45 (3) 4/46 (5) 5/56 (6) 6/56 (4) 7/56 (8) 8/74 (9) 9/80 (10) 10/97 (7) (40.5 overs)	97	1/12 (1) 2/25 (2) 3/37 (3) 4/51 (5) 5/97 (6) 6/125 (7) 7/140 (4) 8/141 (9) 9/146 (8) 10/162 (11) (64 overs)	162

Powell replaced Bonner, as a concussion substitute.

Rabada 10–2–24–1; Ngidi 13.5–7–19–5; Nortje 11–3–35–4; Maharaj 4–3–6–0; Mulder 2–0–9–0. *Second innings*—Rabada 20–9–34–5; Ngidi 13–3–31–0; Nortje 14–5–46–3; Mulder 6–1–18–0; Maharaj 11–5–23–2.

South Africa

*D. Elgar c Blackwood b Roach	0
A. K. Markram c Da Silva b Seales	60
K. D. Petersen c Holder b Seales	19
H. E. van der Dussen c Hope b Holder	46
K. Verreynne c Da Silva b Seales	6
†Q. de Kock not out	141
P. W. A. Mulder c Da Silva b Holder	25
K. A. Maharaj c Powell b Cornwall	0
K. Rabada c Holder b Roach	4
A. A. Nortje c Hope b Holder	7
L. T. Ngidi c Da Silva b Holder	0
B 4, lb 1, w 3, nb 6	14
1/0 (1) 2/34 (3) 3/113 (2) 4/119 (5) 5/162 (4) 6/215 (7) 7/222 (8) 8/233 (9) 9/312 (10) 10/322 (11) (96.5 overs)	322

Roach 20–3–64–2; Holder 20.5–4–75–4; Seales 21–6–75–3; Mayers 8–2–28–0; Cornwall 18–1–61–1; Chase 9–5–14–0.

Umpires: G. O. Brathwaite and J. S. Wilson. Third umpire: L. S. Reifer.
Referee: R. B. Richardson.

WEST INDIES v SOUTH AFRICA

Second Test

At Gros Islet, St Lucia, June 18–21, 2021. South Africa won by 158 runs. South Africa 60pts, West Indies –6pts (after 6pt penalty). Toss: West Indies.

South Africa were pushed harder across the four days, but their bowling quality again proved too much for punch-drunk West Indies batting, before a historic hat-trick from Maharaj set up another dominant victory. It was South Africa's first overseas series win since New Zealand in 2016-17.

Brathwaite and Phil Simmons, West Indies' captain and coach, had vigorously defended their decision to bat in the First Test. Now they chose to bowl, on a less grassy pitch, and with overcast conditions ripe for exploitation. Gabriel, back after a hamstring injury, struck with his third ball, which Markram slapped to point, before Seales claimed Petersen again, to a catch at second slip, and Roach found exaggerated seam movement to castle a disbelieving van der Dussen as he shouldered arms. South Africa were reeling at 37 for three, but after lunch Verreynne helped Elgar add 87 before gloving Gabriel down the leg side. Elgar eventually fell for a gritty 77, compiled in almost six hours, but de Kock again made batting look simple. On the second day, he glided to 96, before nicking one from Mayers which rebounded from the keeper's gloves to Hope in the gully. The tail was soon lopped off; a total below 300 gave West Indies a chink of light.

But the gains made by the bowlers were lost by the batsmen. It took just one delivery for the rot to set in, as Brathwaite gloved Rabada's loosener down leg. In the fourth over, Ngidi claimed Powell, who had replaced the still-infirm Bonner, then Nortje made it 30 for three when Chase nudged to short square leg. Hope and Blackwood added 43 for the fifth wicket, but it was fleeting resistance. South Africa's fourth seamer, Mulder, ploughed through the lower order and, with the last four wickets tumbling for six in 21 balls, the innings folded for 149 – exactly half South Africa's total.

The home attack were again left to pick up the pieces, and they mounted a good fightback on the third day, despite a limping Gabriel being limited to six overs. Roach dislodged both openers cheaply, Holder delighted in de Kock's dismissal for a duck, and Mayers advanced his all-round credentials with three cheap wickets from each-way swing. South Africa were 73 for seven, a lead of 222, halfway through the day. But van der Dussen contributed a forthright unbeaten 75, swelling the target to 324. He added 70 with Rabada, whose career-best 40 – plus five wickets – clinched the match award.

West Indies' openers survived six overs until the close, and memories were kindled overnight of the successful quest for 395 to defeat Bangladesh in February. But reality soon returned: Rabada ended Brathwaite's miserable series (28 runs in four attempts), and quickly snuffed out Hope. Although Powell and Mayers added 64 – West Indies' sole half-century stand of the series – the pursuit never looked likely. Mayers's debut double-hundred had inspired that Chittagong chase, but this surface did not suit his attacking instincts. He eventually top-edged Rabada, and Elgar hauled in a tough skyer running back from slip.

Powell swung Maharaj straight to deep square, and next ball Holder's prod ended up in the hands of short leg. Frenzied celebrations followed when Mulder plucked a one-handed stunner at leg slip off Da Silva: Maharaj had a hat-trick, only the second for South Africa in Tests after the controversial bent-armed seamer Geoff Griffin against England at Lord's in 1960. With Chase nursing a leg injury, Maharaj sealed victory half an hour before tea with his fifth wicket.

Only a few dozen fully vaccinated spectators turned up each day – despite a maximum of 400 allowed – and a handful waving South African flags stayed to watch Elgar lift the sponsors' cup. The Sir Vivian Richards Trophy had accidentally been left behind in Cricket South Africa's offices in Johannesburg, but it did little to sour the mood.

Player of the Match: K. Rabada.   *Player of the Series:* Q. de Kock.

Close of play: first day, South Africa 218-5 (de Kock 59, Mulder 2); second day, West Indies 149; third day, West Indies 15-0 (Brathwaite 5, Powell 9).

South Africa

*D. Elgar b Mayers	77	– (2) c Holder b Roach	10	
A. K. Markram c Chase b Gabriel	0	– (1) c Holder b Roach	4	
K. D. Petersen c Holder b Seales	7	– b Mayers	18	
H. E. van der Dussen b Roach	4	– not out	75	
K. Verreynne c Da Silva b Gabriel	27	– c Da Silva b Mayers	6	
†Q. de Kock c Hope b Mayers	96	– c Da Silva b Holder	0	
P. W. A. Mulder c Da Silva b Roach	8	– c Hope b Mayers	0	
K. A. Maharaj c Da Silva b Holder	12	– c Holder b Seales	6	
K. Rabada not out	21	– c sub (D. M. Bravo) b Roach	40	
A. A. Nortje c Seales b Mayers	1	– c Da Silva b Roach	3	
L. T. Ngidi c sub (D. M. Bravo) b Roach	1	– st Da Silva b Brathwaite	6	
B 9, lb 20, w 12, nb 3	44	B 1, lb 1, w 4	6	

1/1 (2) 2/26 (3) 3/37 (4) (112.4 overs) 298 1/4 (1) 2/33 (2) (53 overs) 174
4/124 (5) 5/203 (1) 6/239 (7) 3/44 (3) 4/52 (5)
7/275 (8) 8/275 (6) 9/281 (10) 10/298 (11) 5/53 (6) 6/54 (7) 7/73 (8)
8/143 (9) 9/152 (10) 10/174 (11)

Roach 21.4–6–45–3; Gabriel 16–4–65–2; Seales 19–4–44–1; Holder 21–5–47–1; Chase 15–4–26–0; Mayers 15–6–28–3; Brathwaite 5–0–14–0. *Second innings*—Roach 13–1–52–4; Gabriel 6–0–28–0; Seales 11–3–34–1; Mayers 9–2–24–3; Holder 11–2–24–1; Brathwaite 3–0–10–1.

West Indies

*K. C. Brathwaite c de Kock b Rabada	0 – c Elgar b Rabada	6
K. O. A. Powell lbw b Ngidi	5 – c Nortje b Maharaj	51
S. D. Hope b Ngidi	43 – c Markram b Rabada	2
R. L. Chase c Verreynne b Nortje	4 – absent hurt	
K. R. Mayers c Markram b Maharaj	12 – (4) c Elgar b Rabada	34
J. Blackwood c Elgar b Maharaj	49 – (5) c de Kock b Ngidi	25
J. O. Holder c Petersen b Rabada	0 – (6) c Petersen b Maharaj	0
†J. Da Silva c de Kock b Mulder	7 – (7) c Mulder b Maharaj	0
K. A. J. Roach c de Kock b Mulder	1 – (8) c Ngidi b Maharaj	27
J. N. T. Seales c Verreynne b Mulder	0 – (9) c Nortje b Maharaj	7
S. T. Gabriel not out	0 – (10) not out	2
B 6, lb 3, w 5, nb 4	18	B 4, lb 3, w 2, nb 2	11

1/0 (1) 2/8 (2) 3/30 (4)   (54 overs) 149   1/16 (1) 2/26 (3)   (58.3 overs) 165
4/54 (5) 5/97 (3) 6/115 (7)   3/90 (4) 4/107 (2)
7/143 (8) 8/145 (9) 9/145 (10) 10/149 (6)   5/107 (6) 6/107 (7)
                                               7/147 (5) 8/158 (8) 9/165 (9)

Rabada 13–6–24–2; Ngidi 7–0–27–2; Nortje 12–0–41–1; Maharaj 18–2–47–2; Mulder 4–3–1–3. *Second innings*—Rabada 16–3–44–3; Ngidi 10–2–29–1; Maharaj 17.3–7–36–5; Nortje 11–3–35–0; Mulder 4–0–14–0.

Umpires: G. O. Brathwaite and J. S. Wilson.   Third umpire: L. S. Reifer.
Referee: R. B. Richardson.

First Twenty20 international   At St George's, Grenada, June 26, 2021. **West Indies won by eight wickets. South Africa 160-6** (20 overs) (Q. de Kock 37, H. E. van der Dussen 56*); ‡**West Indies 161-2** (15 overs) (A. D. S. Fletcher 30, E. Lewis 71, C. H. Gayle 52*). PoM: E. Lewis. *West Indies may have been overwhelmed in the Tests, but their white-ball specialists ensured a comfortable victory in the shortest format. The move to Grenada brought a changing of the guard: only Jason Holder played for the hosts in both series. After a disciplined bowling display restricted South Africa to 160, a six-fest was ignited by Evin Lewis, who smote seven in his 35-ball 71; Kagiso Rabada's first over cost 15, and Lungi Ngidi's 20. Chris Gayle and Andre Russell each cleared the ropes three more times as West Indies coasted home; they had only once scored more to win a T20 in the Caribbean (194-1 against India at Kingston in 2017). Earlier, Russell's dismissal of Quinton de Kock slowed South Africa after they had gambolled to 53-1 in the powerplay, and left-arm spinner Fabian Allen (2-18) kept it tight.*

Second Twenty20 international   At St George's, Grenada, June 27, 2021. **South Africa won by 16 runs. South Africa 166-7** (20 overs) (R. R. Hendricks 42, T. Bavuma 46; O. C. McCoy 3-25); ‡**West Indies 150-9** (20 overs) (A. D. S. Fletcher 35, F. A. Allen 34; K. Rabada 3-37). PoM: G. F. Linde. *South Africa squared the series thanks to spinners George Linde (24–14–19–2) and Tabraiz Shamsi (24–11–16–1), who kept the West Indian hitters in check; Nicholas Pooran, Kieron Pollard and Russell all fell cheaply to catches in the deep. There was no comeback from 105-7 in the 17th, despite a defiant 12-ball 34 from Allen, which included five sixes. South Africa had shot out of the blocks, openers Reeza Hendricks and de Kock (26) putting on 73 in 6.5 overs. But both fell to the Guyanese off-spinner Kevin Sinclair (2-23), before left-arm seamer Obed McCoy claimed three.*

Third Twenty20 international   At St George's, Grenada, June 29, 2021. **South Africa won by one run. South Africa 167-8** (20 overs) (Q. de Kock 72, H. E. van der Dussen 32; O. C. McCoy 4-22, D. J. Bravo 3-25); ‡**West Indies 166-7** (20 overs). PoM: T. Shamsi. *The closest match of the tour hinged on the final two overs. First Anrich Nortje conceded only four in the 19th, then Rabada successfully defended 15; Allen's last-ball six made the margin appear tighter than it was. It crowned a disciplined performance by the South African attack, especially Shamsi (24–11–13–2), the top-ranked bowler in the format. West Indies had looked on course at 96-3 by halfway, but wickets came* *at regular intervals; the top score was Lewis's 27, although Russell clouted successive sixes off Nortje before perishing for 25 in search of another. Earlier, de Kock had continued his purple patch with 72 from 51, countering career-best figures from McCoy and a typically canny performance from Dwayne Bravo.*

Fourth Twenty20 international   At St George's, Grenada, July 1, 2021. **West Indies won by 21 runs. West Indies 167-6** (20 overs) (L. M. P. Simmons 47, K. A. Pollard 51*); ‡**South Africa 146-9** (20 overs) (Q. de Kock 60; D. J. Bravo 4-19). *PoM:* K. A. Pollard. *In a seesaw series, it was West Indies' turn to follow a middling batting display with a stifling bowling performance, to set up a decider. Temba Bavuma's decision to give the first over to occasional off-spinner Aiden Markram did not work – Lendl Simmons blitzed 20 – but the middle order misfired again, before Pollard punched 51* from 25 balls, with five sixes; 66 came from the last four overs. Pollard then entrusted the new ball to Fidel Edwards (aged 39) and Gayle (41), who had Hendricks stumped from his first delivery in T20Is for over five years; he celebrated with a slightly stiff cartwheel, in imitation of his team-mate Sinclair, 20 years his junior. Inevitably, de Kock provided the sternest resistance but, when Bravo winkled him out in the 18th over, the game was up. Bravo, in his 78th T20I, finished with his best figures.*

Fifth Twenty20 international   At St George's, Grenada, July 3, 2021. **South Africa won by 25 runs.** ‡**South Africa 168-4** (20 overs) (Q. de Kock 60, A. K. Markram 70); **West Indies 143-9** (20 overs) (E. Lewis 52, S. O. Hetmyer 33; L. T. Ngidi 3-32). *PoM:* A. K. Markram. *PoS:* T. Shamsi. *T20I debut:* A. J. Hosein (West Indies). *South Africa pinched the series at the last, with much of the credit going to de Kock, who rounded off a superb tour with 60 from 42, and Shamsi, whose 24–16–11–1 took his series haul to 7-80 from 20 overs. After Bavuma fell in the first, de Kock and Markram (70 from 48) piled on 128; only 32 came from the last five after they were separated, but South Africa had plenty. Lewis teed off for 52 from 34, but Shimron Hetmyer was the only other batsman to get going. Wiaan Mulder, in for the injured Nortje, sealed the deal in the 15th, when Pollard (after straining a hamstring sprinting a single) and Russell clubbed successive wide full tosses straight to fielders.*

WEST INDIES v AUSTRALIA IN 2021

CRAIG COZIER

Twenty20 internationals (5): West Indies 4, Australia 1
One-day internationals (3): Australia 2 (20pts), West Indies 1 (10pts)

It was bound to be a challenging tour for Australia, with several of their white-ball superstars unavailable. But after being overpowered 4–1 in the T20s, and despite a Covid-19 scare in Barbados, they ended on a high with a hard-fought 2–1 success in the ODI series.

The players were based in biosecure hubs in St Lucia and Barbados, so when West Indies manager Rawl Lewis apparently tested positive in Bridgetown, hours before the second ODI, the tour hung in the balance. The result of the Covid test was later confirmed as an administrative error by local health officials, and hastily arranged meetings between the two boards calmed nerves. The match itself was played two days after the toss.

Australia's depleted squad provided further evidence of the waning importance of national duty: Cricket Australia allowed Pat Cummins, Glenn Maxwell, Kane and Jhye Richardson, Daniel Sams, Marcus Stoinis and David Warner to rest. The absence of Steve Smith (elbow injury) and Marnus Labuschagne (contracted to Glamorgan) further weakened their resources. What might have been viewed as a lost opportunity to fine-tune plans ahead of the T20 World Cup was portrayed by national selector Trevor Hohns as a chance for fringe players. Only Mitchell Marsh seized it, finishing the T20s as Australia's leading run-scorer (227) and wicket-taker (eight). In the fourth match, his career-bests with bat and ball brought about their sole win.

West Indies were also far from full strength. Nicholas Pooran deputised as captain for Kieron Pollard, who had strained a hamstring against South Africa. Obed McCoy (shin splints) and Fidel Edwards (triceps) were limited to two games, and Jason Holder was rested. The recalled Hayden Walsh grabbed his chance, earning 12 wickets with his controlled leg-spin.

While Pollard returned for the ODIs, Australia lost their captain: Aaron Finch jarred his right knee in the final T20, and flew home for surgery. Alex Carey took over and, leaning heavily on his experienced new-ball pair of Mitchell Starc and Josh Hazlewood, maintained his team's 26-year unbeaten record in ODI series against West Indies.

Pollard called the Kensington Oval's sluggish pitches "unacceptable for international cricket" and "absolutely ridiculous". But there were no such complaints from Starc, whose 11 wickets made him an obvious Player of the Series, nor Hazlewood, who had a remarkable economy-rate of 2.07. And the teams were in harmony on more significant matters: before the start of every match, the Australians took a knee in solidarity with West Indies.

AUSTRALIA TOURING PARTY

A. J. Finch, A. C. Agar, W. A. Agar, J. P. Behrendorff, A. T. Carey, D. T. Christian, J. R. Hazlewood, M. C. Henriques, B. R. McDermott, M. R. Marsh, R. P. Meredith, J. R. Phillipe, M. A. Starc, M. J. Swepson, A. J. Turner, A. J. Tye, M. S. Wade, A. Zampa. Coach: J. L. Langer.

Carey captained in the ODIs after Finch sustained a knee injury and flew home. N. T. Ellis and T. Sangha were travelling reserves.

First Twenty20 international   At Gros Islet, St Lucia, July 9, 2021 (floodlit). **West Indies won by 18 runs. West Indies 145-6** (20 overs) (A. D. Russell 51, J. R. Hazlewood 3-12); **‡Australia 127** (16 overs) (M. S. Wade 33, M. R. Marsh 51; O. C. McCoy 4-26, H. R. Walsh 3-23). *PoM:* O. C. McCoy. *Though Australia bossed the game for long periods, West Indies found decisive late-overs heroes in both innings. Andre Russell's 51 off 26 – surprisingly, his maiden T20I half-century, in his 47th innings – breathed life into a score of 76-4 off 14, after Josh Hazlewood conceded three in his three powerplay overs. Russell's fifth – and final – six soared 103 metres over midwicket. Australia's pursuit of 146 was powered by a cameo from Matthew Wade (33 off 14) and a first fifty for Mitchell Marsh (51 off 31). But from 108-4 in the 11th, they lost six for 19 as left-arm seamer Obed McCoy's clever variations sparked panic.*

Second Twenty20 international   At Gros Islet, St Lucia, July 10, 2021 (floodlit). **West Indies won by 56 runs. West Indies 196-4** (20 overs) (L. M. P. Simmons 30, S. O. Hetmyer 61, D. J. Bravo 47*); **Australia ‡140** (19.2 overs) (M. R. Marsh 54; H. R. Walsh 3-29). *PoM:* S. O. Hetmyer. *A record fourth-wicket stand of 103 off 61 between Shimron Hetmyer (a career-best 61 off 36) and Dwayne Bravo (47* off 34) provided the foundation for West Indies. Another Russell assault (24* off eight) put the finishing touches to a formidable total. Australia's chase soon hit the skids: Wade fell second ball, and Fidel Edwards's dipping slower delivery tricked Aaron Finch. Marsh's second successive half-century stabilised the middle order but, once he swatted Hayden Walsh to long-off, Australia suffered another collapse – seven for 39 this time – and went down with a whimper.*

Third Twenty20 international   At Gros Islet, St Lucia, July 12, 2021 (floodlit). **West Indies won by six wickets. ‡Australia 141-6** (20 overs) (A. J. Finch 30, M. C. Henriques 33); **West Indies 142-4** (14.5 overs) (C. H. Gayle 67, N. Pooran 32*; R. P. Meredith 3-48). *PoM:* C. H. Gayle. *Chris Gayle sealed the series for West Indies, ending a lengthy slump in form with a thunderous 67 off 38 that made light work of Australia's modest 141-6. Slamming seven sixes in his first T20I half-century for five years, he became the first to reach 14,000 runs in all 20-over cricket. He credited a pep talk from his injured captain, Kieron Pollard, for motivating him: "Just respect the Universe Boss, and let him play cricket and have some fun." Australia's innings had been stifled by the spin of Walsh and Fabian Allen, who dismissed the in-form Marsh for nine, and caught a reflex parry by Bravo to remove Finch.*

Fourth Twenty20 international   At Gros Islet, St Lucia, July 14, 2021 (floodlit). **Australia won by four runs. ‡Australia 189-6** (20 overs) (A. J. Finch 53, M. R. Marsh 75; H. R. Walsh 3-27); **West Indies 185-6** (20 overs) (L. M. Simmons 72, E. Lewis 31; M. R. Marsh 3-24). *PoM:* M. R. Marsh. *A career-best all-round show from Marsh, and a deadly final over from Mitchell Starc, delivered a nail-biting victory for Australia. Marsh, whose 44-ball 75 was his third half-century of the series, added 114 for the second wicket with Finch, forming the cornerstone of a challenging 189-6. Evin Lewis and Lendl Simmons (72 off 48) launched West Indies' chase emphatically, but the middle order stagnated against Marsh. Russell and Allen fought back and, when Riley Meredith conceded 25 – including four sixes – off the 19th, they needed 11 from the last. But Starc nailed his yorkers, and Russell refused singles off the first five balls in vain hope of clearing the fence – which he did, too late, from the sixth.*

Fifth Twenty20 international   At Gros Islet, St Lucia, July 16, 2021 (floodlit). **West Indies won by 16 runs. ‡West Indies 199-8** (20 overs) (E. Lewis 79, N. Pooran 31; A. J. Tye 3-37); **Australia 183-9** (20 overs) (A. J. Finch 34, M. R. Marsh 30; S. S. Cottrell 3-28, A. D. Russell 3-43). *PoM:* E. Lewis. *PoS:* H. R. Walsh. *A six-hitting onslaught by Lewis (79 off 34) ended the largely one-sided series with an exclamation mark. He cleared the boundary nine times, and passed 100 T20I sixes in his 42nd innings – the fastest to the mark. There were cameos from Gayle, who slammed Adam Zampa's first over for 20, and Nicholas Pooran, who took 25 from Mitchell Swepson's third. Andrew Tye helped limit the damage, and the last six overs produced only 37. Finch and Marsh threatened to make it a contest, as Australia raced past 90 in the tenth, but Allen's 15-metre sprint and dive at long-on got rid of Finch. No other batsman passed his 34 as a difficult chase fizzled out.*

First one-day international At Bridgetown, Barbados, July 20, 2021 (floodlit). **Australia won by 133 runs** (DLS). ‡**Australia 252-9** (49 overs) (J. R. Philippe 39, A. T. Carey 67, A. J. Turner 49; H. R. Walsh 5-39) **v West Indies 123** (26.2 overs) (K. A. Pollard 56; M. A. Starc 5-48, J. R. Hazlewood 3-11). *Australia 10pts. PoM: M. A. Starc. ODI debuts: W. A. Agar, B. R. McDermott, J. R. Philippe (Australia). Alex Carey made a successful debut as Australian captain, top-scoring with 67, before a fiery new-ball blitz from Starc and Hazlewood inspired a comprehensive triumph. Openers Josh Philippe and Ben McDermott – two of three Australian debutants – anchored the innings with 51, but Akeal Hosein and Alzarri Joseph brought the hosts back, sharing four wickets. Carey shifted the tide again, sharing 104 with Ashton Turner, before the last five went for 29, all to Walsh in a maiden five-wicket haul. Three brief rain delays left West Indies needing 257 in 49, but they never came close. Starc held a return catch to despatch Lewis first ball, then sent Jason Mohammed's off-stump cartwheeling: 4-2 became 27-6. Pollard's counter-attacking half-century provided some respite, before Starc returned to wrap things up with his eighth five-for.*

Second one-day international At Bridgetown, Barbados, July 22 and 24, 2021 (floodlit). **West Indies won by four wickets.** ‡**Australia 187** (47.1 overs) (M. S. Wade 36, A. Zampa 36, W. A. Agar 41; A. S. Joseph 3-39, A. J. Hosein 3-30); **West Indies 191-6** (38 overs) (S. D. Hope 38, N. Pooran 59*; J. O. Holder 52; M. A. Starc 3-26). *West Indies 10pts. PoM: N. Pooran. ODI debut: R. P. Meredith (Australia). The toss was held on July 22, but the match postponed because of a positive Covid case among the West Indian backroom staff; after subsequent tests proved negative, the match began two days later. The toss stood, but Australia were allowed to replace Hazlewood with Wes Agar. They were quickly reduced to 45-6, but Wade and the lower order – Agar's 41 was his best in List A cricket – avoided capitulation. When Hosein bowled a no-ball in the 17th over, Pollard was fielding at short leg; unable to change positions for the free hit, he decided instead to avert the risk of injury, and left the field for one delivery, which Starc drove harmlessly to long-on. Defending a handy target of 188, Starc then dismissed Lewis and Darren Bravo in two balls and, when Zampa's googly got Pollard, West Indies were 72-5. But Pooran – dropped by Moises Henriques on 26, with 65 still required – added 93 with Jason Holder, and saw his team home.*

Third one-day international At Bridgetown, Barbados, July 26, 2021 (floodlit). **Australia won by six wickets.** ‡**West Indies 152** (45.1 overs) (E. Lewis 55; M. A. Starc 3-43); **Australia 153-4** (30.3 overs) (A. T. Carey 35, M. S. Wade 51*). *Australia 10pts. PoM: A. C. Agar. PoS: M. A. Starc. Australia's attack again exposed West Indian top-order frailties, and this time there was no fightback. Lewis was struck on the helmet by Hazlewood and retired hurt at 14-0; he returned at 71-5 and batted through for 55* – but nobody else passed 18. West Indies' 152 hardly seemed enough, but Australia also failed to cope with a surface so difficult that Pollard bowled a few exploratory overs of off-spin. Wade, though, drew on his experience to control a stand of 54* with Ashton Agar, and steer a winning course.*

WEST INDIES v PAKISTAN IN 2021

CRAIG COZIER

Twenty20 internationals (4): West Indies 0, Pakistan 1
Test matches (2): West Indies 1 (12pts), Pakistan 1 (12pts)

West Indies' busy year continued with a visit from Pakistan, who won the disrupted T20 series and shared the spoils in the two Tests. At first glance, that seemed a satisfactory haul, but the visitors were left to reflect on their tour with a tinge of regret, after losing the First Test by one wicket.

The white-ball leg had been marred by foul weather – no surprise in the heart of the Caribbean's rainy season. Pakistan won the only game that reached a conclusion, but the series was hardly ideal preparation for the T20 World Cup. Five matches had been planned, but a Covid scare during the Australians' recent visit to the Caribbean meant the first was cancelled, before rain spoiled three of the others.

The Tests, part of the new 2021–23 World Championship cycle, were spared the worst of the weather, and followed a similar pattern to Pakistan's previous tours: close, competitive, compelling. On their last visit, four years earlier, then-skipper Misbah-ul-Haq bade farewell to international cricket with a memorable last-gasp victory in Dominica to secure a 2–1 series win. Misbah returned as head coach, and his charges showed great spirit to fight back from defeat in the First Test to win the Second. Dropped catches in the tense final stages of that opening match had cost them, as West Indies held on for their third one-wicket victory – the 15th in all Tests.

Both games were played at Sabina Park in Jamaica, where the seamers relished sporting pitches and were helped by a high standard of catching in the cordon. Fragile batting resulted in low-scoring contests – but the team that batted marginally better emerged victorious in both. A steely 97 by captain Kraigg Brathwaite and an aggressive second-innings 55 by Jermaine Blackwood were the cornerstones of West Indies' victory in a dramatic opener. Fawad Alam's unbeaten 124 then provided a winning platform – alongside Babar Azam's 75 – in the second match.

Left-armer Shaheen Shah Afridi was a constant menace, making good use of his height, pace, bounce and swing, with new ball and old, and claiming the series award for 18 wickets at 11. For West Indies, Jayden Seales might not yet possess all Afridi's gifts but, in only his second series, and not yet 20, he led the home attack with 11 wickets, including a maiden five-for. Kemar Roach and Jason Holder also did well with the ball, while their batting was crucial in the First Test.

The tour marked the end of Misbah's spell as coach. He missed the final day of the series after a positive Covid test, which forced him to extend his stay in Jamaica to fulfil a ten-day quarantine period. The tough grind of bubble life and its challenges were among the factors he cited in his resignation after two years in the job. Bowling coach Waqar Younis – another with a year left on his contract – also stepped down, giving the Pakistan board's new chairman Ramiz Raja a clean slate when he took over shortly afterwards.

PAKISTAN TOURING PARTY

*Babar Azam (T/20), Abdullah Shafiq (T), Abid Ali (T), Arshad Iqbal (20), Azam Khan (20), Azhar Ali (T), Fahim Ashraf (T), Fakhar Zaman (20), Fawad Alam (T), Haris Rauf (20), Hasan Ali (T/20), Imad Wasim (20), Imran Butt (T), Mohammad Abbas (T), Mohammad Hafeez (20), Mohammad Hasnain (20), Mohammad Nawaz (T/20), Mohammad Rizwan (T/20), Mohammad Wasim (20), Naseem Shah (T), Nauman Ali (T), Sajid Khan (T), Sarfraz Ahmed (T/20), Saud Shakil (T), Shadab Khan (20), Shaheen Shah Afridi (T/20), Shahnawaz Dahani (T), Sharjeel Khan (20), Sohaib Maqsood (20), Usman Qadir (20), Yasir Shah (T), Zahid Mahmood (T). *Coach:* Misbah-ul-Haq.

Haris Rauf and Mohammad Nawaz were originally included in the Test squad, but released after the T20s. Haider Ali was named in the T20 squad, but withdrawn after breaching Covid protocols during the Pakistan Super League, and replaced by Sohaib Maqsood.

First Twenty20 international At Bridgetown, Barbados, July 27, 2021. **West Indies v Pakistan. Cancelled.** *This match was called off after the preceding Australian series was extended following a positive Covid test.*

Second Twenty20 international At Bridgetown, Barbados, July 28, 2021. **No result. West Indies 85-5** (9 overs) v ‡**Pakistan.** *T20I debut: Mohammad Wasim (Pakistan). Rain started as the national anthems were played, forcing a reduction to nine overs a side – but showers lurked, and only one innings was completed. There was time for Mohammad Wasim, a 19-year-old debutant fast bowler, to fell Lendl Simmons with a bouncer; he retired hurt with concussion, and played no further part in the series. Wasim later captured his first international wicket, when Chris Gayle holed out at long-on. Kieron Pollard slammed 22* from nine balls, including a towering six from Shaheen Shah Afridi's final delivery which cleared the Greenidge & Haynes Stand.*

Third Twenty20 international At Providence, Guyana, July 31, 2021. **Pakistan won by seven runs. Pakistan 157-8** (20 overs) (Mohammad Rizwan 46, Babar Azam 51; J. O. Holder 4-26); ‡**West Indies 150-4** (20 overs) (E. Lewis 35*, N. Pooran 62*). *PoM: Mohammad Hafeez. Pakistan completed what turned out to be a series-clinching victory when Pollard fell in the final over. That left West Indies needing 18 from four balls, but Afridi produced two dots. Pakistan's challenging total was set up by their top order, who propelled them to 134-2 after 16, Babar Azam top-scoring with 51 from 40 balls, before a rash of late wickets. When West Indies batted, the canny Mohammad Hafeez scooted through his four overs for six runs (and the wicket of Andre Fletcher). Evin Lewis made 35 before retiring with a side strain, and Nicholas Pooran clattered six sixes in a 33-ball 62*. But Pollard found timing elusive, and West Indies came up just short.*

Fourth Twenty20 international At Providence, Guyana, August 1, 2021. **No result. ‡West Indies 15-0** (1.2 overs) v Pakistan. *This game consisted of seven minutes, eight deliveries, and two huge sixes from Fletcher – one off Hafeez, the parsimonious hero of the previous day.*

Fifth Twenty20 international At Providence, Guyana, August 3, 2021. **No result. West Indies 30-0** (3 overs) v ‡**Pakistan.** *Ashen skies and incessant rain halted proceedings after West Indies had made a bright start, with Fletcher thumping two more sixes off Hafeez. There was never much prospect of a resumption, and Babar was eventually presented with the series trophy in a tent behind the players' dugouts. No Player of the Series was named.*

> **"** My toddler threw a toy car at the telly the other day. I know he shouldn't have done it, but he's got a good arm."
> People, page 180

WEST INDIES v PAKISTAN

First Test

At Kingston, Jamaica, August 12–15, 2021. West Indies won by one wicket. West Indies 12pts. Toss: West Indies.

A pulsating contest, which ebbed and flowed across four days, was settled in intoxicating fashion by Roach's cover-driven two, in an unwavering last-wicket stand of 17 with the youthful Seales. Roach had bowled outstandingly on Sabina Park's seam-friendly surface, while Seales had taken eight wickets; overall, there were 13 catches for the keepers and seven in the slips, while spin failed to strike once. Pakistan had their opportunities, but dropped catches in the final stages cost them dear; it seemed harsh that the excellence of Shaheen Shah Afridi – who took four wickets in each innings – went unrewarded in the end.

Roach and Seales had done the early damage after Pakistan were sent in. Seales, taking the new ball in the absence of the unfit Shannon Gabriel, probed away as Pakistan dipped to 101 for five, before a restorative stand of 85 between left-handers Fawad Alam and Fahim Ashraf. They were separated by Chase's throw from square leg, which heralded one of the match's many collapses: the last five wickets tumbled for 31, the final three without addition.

Pakistan were buoyed by Mohammad Abbas's double strike on the first evening, ripping out Powell and Bonner with successive balls in the third over. Next day, West Indies' efforts mirrored their opponents': from 100 for five, an important stand regained the initiative, as Brathwaite and Holder – captains new and old – put on 96. The broad-batted Brathwaite drove imperiously, and a tenth Test hundred was there for the taking when he was run out by Hasan Ali's direct hit from fine leg as he tried to pinch a second. It was a rare error of judgment during six hours in the middle. Da Silva, with 21 in an hour and a half, ensured an advantage of 36.

The balance of power continued to fluctuate. Another dicey start by Pakistan, including ducks for Imran Butt and Fawad, saw them decline to 65 for four. Babar Azam's elegant half-century – and useful stands with Mohammad Rizwan and Fahim – shifted things their way again, but the fourth morning belonged emphatically to West Indies. Mayers produced a corker to square up Babar, who nicked to slip, while Seales polished off the innings with a maiden five-for, completed when Roach at fine leg calmly held on to a swirling skyer from Hasan Ali. This time Pakistan's last five wickets had mustered 35. Brathwaite described Seales as "a star in the making."

A target of 168 was not straightforward, as imperfect West Indian batting techniques faced Pakistan's quality pace attack. Afridi proved too much at first, reducing the hosts to 16 for three, including the important scalp of Brathwaite. Blackwood counter-punched in typical fashion, shifting the tide in a stand of 68 with Chase. But the

Randy Brooks, AFP/Getty Images

Five star: teenager Jayden Seales makes a mark.

YOUNGEST TO TAKE A TEST FIVE-FOR FOR WEST INDIES

Yrs	Days			
19	**338**	**J. N. T. Seales (5-55)**	**v Pakistan at Kingston**	**2021**
20	41	A. L. Valentine (8-104†)	v England at Manchester	1950
20	313	D. J. Bravo (6-55)	v England at Manchester	2004
20	331	J. J. C. Lawson (6-3)	v Bangladesh at Dhaka	2002-03
21	18	K. A. J. Roach (6-48)	v Bangladesh at St George's	2009
21	56	S. Ramadhin (6-86)	v England at Lord's	1950
21	93	W. W. Hall (6-50)	v India at Kanpur	1958-59
21	136	R. A. Harper (6-57)	v England at Manchester	1984
21	141	F. H. Edwards (5-36†)	v Sri Lanka at Kingston	2003
21	166	I. R. Bishop (6-87)	v India at Bridgetown	1988-89

† *On debut. Only the first instance is shown for each player.*

pendulum swung once more, thanks to a sensational slip catch from Butt to remove Blackwood. Mayers completed a pair and, when Holder lost his off stump to Hasan, tea was taken at 114 for seven, with West Indies still 54 short.

But Pakistan's fielding standards slipped, and West Indies took heavy toll. Abbas at long leg could not cling on to a tough top edge from Da Silva, then wicketkeeper Mohammad Rizwan fumbled a thick inside edge from Roach. Afridi finally claimed Da Silva, his fourth wicket – and, at 142 for eight, Pakistan remained favourites. For the first time, West Indies were in danger of losing a Test after being set fewer than 200 (they had previously won 55 and drawn six).

Afridi should have celebrated a fifth wicket, but Hasan's miss at deep square leg breathed fresh life into Roach, on 16, as well as the smattering of groundstaff, who had become increasingly vocal. Hasan looked to have made amends with his third wicket, when Rizwan sprinted to haul in Warrican's top edge. Their last pair at the crease, West Indies needed 17. As the tension ratcheted up, another Roach edge flew just beyond Rizwan's despairing dive, and away for four. Three balls later, his assured push through the covers off Hasan sealed a gripping contest. West Indies had won only twice by one wicket, against Australia at Bridgetown in 1998-99 (after a Brian Lara masterclass) and Pakistan in Antigua the following season. "A remarkable Test," said a relieved Brathwaite.

Player of the Match: J. N. T. Seales.

Close of play: first day, West Indies 2-2 (Brathwaite 1, Chase 0); second day, West Indies 251-8 (Da Silva 20, Warrican 1); third day, Pakistan 160-5 (Babar Azam 54, Fahim Ashraf 12).

Pakistan

Imran Butt b Roach	11	– lbw b Roach	0
Abid Ali c Da Silva b Seales	9	– c Holder b Seales	34
Azhar Ali c Holder b Seales	17	– b Roach	23
*Babar Azam c Da Silva b Roach	30	– c Holder b Mayers	55
Fawad Alam b Holder	56	– c Da Silva b Seales	0
†Mohammad Rizwan c Chase b Holder	23	– c Da Silva b Holder	30
Fahim Ashraf run out (Chase)	44	– c Da Silva b Roach	20
Yasir Shah c Da Silva b Mayers	0	– c Da Silva b Seales	4
Hasan Ali c Mayers b Seales	14	– c Roach b Seales	28
Shaheen Shah Afridi not out	0	– lbw b Seales	0
Mohammad Abbas c Da Silva b Holder	0	– not out	1
B 4, lb 5, nb 4	13	B 4, lb 2, nb 2	8

1/21 (1) 2/21 (2) 3/68 (3)   (70.3 overs) 217   1/1 (1) 2/56 (3)   (83.4 overs) 203
4/68 (4) 5/101 (6) 6/186 (7)   3/65 (2) 4/65 (5)
7/190 (8) 8/217 (9) 9/217 (5) 10/217 (11)   5/121 (6) 6/168 (7) 7/170 (4)
                                                          8/180 (8) 9/192 (10) 10/203 (9)

Roach 16–4–47–2; Seales 16–3–70–3; Mayers 14–5–28–1; Holder 15.3–3–26–3; Chase 8–1–33–0; Warrican 1–0–4–0. *Second innings*—Roach 19–8–30–3; Seales 15.4–3–55–5; Mayers 15–5–33–1; Holder 18–6–36–1; Warrican 7–2–28–0; Chase 6–2–12–0; Brathwaite 3–1–3–0.

West Indies

*K. C. Brathwaite run out (Hasan Ali)	97	– c Mohammad Rizwan b Shaheen Shah Afridi .	2
K. O. A. Powell c Imran Butt b Mohammad Abbas	0	– lbw b Shaheen Shah Afridi	4
N. E. Bonner lbw b Mohammad Abbas	0	– b Shaheen Shah Afridi	5
R. L. Chase c Mohammad Rizwan b Hasan Ali	21	– c Imran Butt b Fahim Ashraf	22
J. Blackwood c Mohammad Abbas b Shaheen Shah Afridi .	22	– c Imran Butt b Hasan Ali	55
K. R. Mayers lbw b Shaheen Shah Afridi	0	– c Imran Butt b Fahim Ashraf	0
J. O. Holder c Mohammad Rizwan b Fahim Ashraf	58	– b Hasan Ali	16
†J. Da Silva lbw b Shaheen Shah Afridi	21	– c Mohammad Rizwan b Shaheen Shah Afridi .	13
K. A. J. Roach lbw b Mohammad Abbas	13	– not out	30
J. A. Warrican b Shaheen Shah Afridi	1	– c Mohammad Rizwan b Hasan Ali . .	6
J. N. T. Seales not out	0	– not out	2
B 3, lb 11, nb 6	20	B 2, lb 10, nb 1	13

1/1 (2) 2/1 (3) 3/51 (4) (89.4 overs) 253
4/100 (5) 5/100 (6) 6/196 (7)
7/221 (1) 8/249 (9) 9/252 (10) 10/253 (8)

1/4 (2) (9 wkts, 56.5 overs) 168
2/15 (1) 3/16 (3)
4/84 (4) 5/92 (6) 6/111 (5)
7/114 (7) 8/142 (8) 9/151 (10)

Mohammad Abbas 22–9–43–3; Shaheen Shah Afridi 21.4–6–59–4; Yasir Shah 13–1–46–0; Fahim Ashraf 14–6–37–1; Hasan Ali 19–4–54–1. *Second innings*—Mohammad Abbas 12–5–27–0; Shaheen Shah Afridi 17–4–50–4; Hasan Ali 16.5–5–37–3; Fahim Ashraf 8–1–29–2; Yasir Shah 3–0–13–0.

Umpires: G. O. Brathwaite and J. S. Wilson. Third umpire: L. S. Reifer.
Referee: R. B. Richardson.

WEST INDIES v PAKISTAN

Second Test

At Kingston, Jamaica, August 20–24, 2021. Pakistan won by 109 runs. Pakistan 12pts. Toss: West Indies.

Pakistan shrugged off a terrible start, and the handicap of losing four sessions to bad weather, to seal a series-levelling win an hour after tea on the final day. They were indebted to a fifth Test century from Fawad Alam, and a career-best haul of ten for 94 from Shaheen Shah Afridi, two left-handers at opposite ends of their careers. Babar Azam was influential too. First, his silky 75 helped redeem Pakistan after they were put in again and lost three quick wickets. Then, three days later, his bold declaration – setting West Indies 329 in around 130 overs – showed confidence in his potent attack.

Babar's early rescue mission had come in association with Fawad, who continued to make up for lost time after a decade in the international wilderness. They joined forces after Roach and Seales had disposed of the openers and Azhar Ali, to make it two for three inside 15 minutes. But Babar's classical driving, on both sides of the wicket, complemented the fidgety Fawad, who peppered the off side behind square. In a seesaw series, they shifted the momentum in a fourth-wicket stand of 158 in four and a half hours.

The energy-sapping August heat eventually brought West Indies respite, when Fawad was reluctantly forced to retire hurt with severe leg cramps on 76. Babar, in sight of three figures, was a third victim for the impeccable Roach soon afterwards – but Pakistan still ended the first day in control, at 212 for four.

Rain erased the second, though inadequate covers did not help. And when the third was halted after eight balls because Holder's run-up was impeded by a boggy patch created by the previous day's leaks, a draw loomed. Play finally restarted after lunch, however, and Seales struck with the second new ball, breaking a 50-run partnership (spread across three days) between Mohammad Rizwan and Fahim Ashraf. Then Holder removed Rizwan and Nauman Ali with consecutive deliveries. But Fawad – now fully rehydrated – dug in with the tail, powering on to three figures. He celebrated in increasingly familiar fashion, mimicking a heroic horseback scene from the popular Turkish drama series *Ertugrul Ghazi*. This was his fourth century in ten Tests since his recall in England in 2020.

Babar declared nine down, before Afridi's new-ball swing prised out the openers. By stumps, West Indies were tottering at 39 for three. Next morning, Bonner and Blackwood battled in a stand of 60 but, once they were separated, the innings subsided swiftly: in all, six wickets crashed for 45. Successive balls from Mohammad Abbas accounted for Bonner and Mayers (for a third duck in a row), while Fawad's diving gully catch off Afridi sent back Blackwood. Afridi scythed through the lower order to claim six for 51; Holder's aggressive 26 was not enough to turn the tide.

Bolstered by a lead of 152, Pakistan's openers – who had struggled until now – piled on 70 in less than ten overs on the fourth afternoon. The innings raced along, and Babar, who eventually picked up long-on, was happy to offer the carrot of a chase.

West Indies closed at 49 for one, with Powell's careless run-out the only blemish, but next day Pakistan's probing seam continued to breach leaden-footed defence. Hasan Ali trapped Bonner, before another sensational slip catch from Imran Butt accounted for Chase. Nauman Ali's slow left-armers then claimed the key wickets of Blackwood and Brathwaite either side of lunch.

Mayers and Holder put on 46, before Afridi ended their aggressive resistance to make it 159 for seven, but a shower brought an early tea, to jangle Pakistan's nerves. The bad weather, though, didn't stick around long. Holder drove Nauman to extra cover, and Afridi dazzled again with the second new ball, removing Roach and Da Silva in three deliveries to complete a deserved victory.

Player of the Match: Shaheen Shah Afridi.   *Player of the Series:* Shaheen Shah Afridi.
Close of play: first day, Pakistan 212-4 (Mohammad Rizwan 22, Fahim Ashraf 23); second day, no play; third day, West Indies 39-3 (Bonner 18, Joseph 0); fourth day, West Indies 49-1 (Brathwaite 17, Joseph 8).

Pakistan

Abid Ali c Blackwood b Roach	1	– (2) c sub (S. D. Hope) b Joseph	29
Imran Butt c Da Silva b Seales	1	– (1) c Bonner b Mayers	37
Azhar Ali c Da Silva b Roach	0	– c Blackwood b Brathwaite	22
*Babar Azam c Holder b Roach	75	– c Bonner b Joseph	33
Fawad Alam not out	124		
†Mohammad Rizwan lbw b Holder	31	– (7) not out	10
Fahim Ashraf lbw b Seales	26	– (6) lbw b Holder	9
Nauman Ali c Da Silva b Holder	0		
Hasan Ali run out (Bonner/Da Silva)	9	– (5) c Da Silva b Holder	17
Shaheen Shah Afridi c Powell b Seales	19		
Mohammad Abbas not out	0		
B 1, lb 9, nb 6	16	B 5, lb 6, w 7, nb 1	19

1/2 (1) 2/2 (3) 3/2 (2)   (9 wkts dec, 110 overs) 302   1/70 (2)   (6 wkts dec, 27.2 overs) 176
4/168 (4) 5/218 (7) 6/231 (6)   2/90 (1) 3/107 (3)
7/231 (8) 8/267 (9) 9/302 (10)   4/145 (5) 5/160 (6) 6/176 (4)

In the first innings Fawad Alam, when 76, retired hurt at 160-3 and resumed at 218-5.

Roach 27–9–68–3; Seales 15–4–31–3; Joseph 18–1–75–0; Holder 23–9–46–2; Mayers 17–5–34–0; Chase 8–0–32–0; Bonner 1–0–6–0; Brathwaite 1–1–0–0. *Second innings*—Roach 3–1–11–0; Seales 3–0–32–0; Holder 6–0–27–2; Joseph 4.2–0–24–2; Mayers 7–0–43–1; Brathwaite 4–0–28–1.

West Indies

*K. C. Brathwaite b Shaheen Shah Afridi	4	– c Fawad Alam b Nauman Ali	39
K. O. A. Powell lbw b Shaheen Shah Afridi	5	– run out (Shaheen Shah Afridi)	23
N. E. Bonner c Mohammad Rizwan b Mohammad Abbas	37	– (4) lbw b Hasan Ali	2
R. L. Chase b Fahim Ashraf	10	– (5) c Imran Butt b Hasan Ali	0
A. S. Joseph c Babar Azam b Shaheen Shah Afridi	4	– (3) c Mohammad Rizwan b Shaheen Shah Afridi	17
J. Blackwood c Fawad Alam b Shaheen Shah Afridi	33	– c Mohammad Rizwan b Nauman Ali	25
K. R. Mayers c Mohammad Rizwan b Mohammad Abbas	0	– c Mohammad Rizwan b Shaheen Shah Afridi	32
J. O. Holder c Mohammad Rizwan b Shaheen Shah Afridi	26	– c Fawad Alam b Nauman Ali	47
†J. Da Silva lbw b Mohammad Abbas	6	– c Fahim Ashraf b Shaheen Shah Afridi	15
K. A. J. Roach c Babar Azam b Shaheen Shah Afridi	8	– lbw b Shaheen Shah Afridi	7
J. N. T. Seales not out	0	– not out	0
Lb 10, w 1, nb 6	17	B 4, lb 2, w 1, nb 5	12

1/8 (2) 2/9 (1) 3/34 (4)   (51.3 overs) 150
4/45 (5) 5/105 (3) 6/105 (7)
7/109 (6) 8/116 (9) 9/143 (8) 10/150 (10)

1/34 (2) 2/65 (3)   (83.2 overs) 219
3/69 (4) 4/73 (5)
5/101 (6) 6/113 (1) 7/159 (7)
8/199 (8) 9/212 (10) 10/219 (9)

Mohammad Abbas 18–6–44–3; Shaheen Shah Afridi 17.3–7–51–6; Hasan Ali 8–1–30–0; Fahim Ashraf 7–4–14–1; Nauman Ali 1–0–1–0. *Second innings*—Mohammad Abbas 14–3–42–0; Shaheen Shah Afridi 17.2–5–43–4; Hasan Ali 14–6–37–2; Fahim Ashraf 13–5–36–0; Nauman Ali 22–7–52–3; Fawad Alam 3–1–3–0.

Umpires: G. O. Brathwaite and J. S. Wilson.   Third umpire: N. Duguid.
Referee: R. B. Richardson.

DOMESTIC CRICKET IN THE WEST INDIES IN 2020-21

Haydn Gill

The pandemic severely impacted the West Indies domestic season. As the Caribbean grappled with increased Covid cases across the region, Cricket West Indies were in a quandary; ultimately, they decided to forgo the first-class tournament for the first time since 1967-68, and scale down the limited-overs competition. The possibility of staging the four-day tournament later in 2021 was eventually abandoned, with the more profitable Caribbean Premier League given priority.

The Super50, staged in February, was cut from ten teams to six, with a single round robin rather than two zonal groups playing two rounds each. Financial constraints meant there was no room for the last two champions – Combined Campuses & Colleges and West Indies Emerging Players – or for the USA and Canada. There were only 19 matches, down from 43 the previous season; and, to restrict the risk of infection from the movement of players and officials, the tournament was staged in one country, Antigua, and two venues, the Sir Vivian Richards Stadium at North Sound and the Coolidge Cricket Ground.

Even so, the shortened Super50 was largely welcomed. One bonus was the availability of most West Indies players, often on international duty during domestic events. **Trinidad & Tobago**, fielding a host of big names, made the most of it, winning all their seven matches. Though it was the first time they had reached the final for five years, they extended their record number of one-day titles to 12 (plus one shared).

Trinidad successfully chased targets in their five league matches and the semi-final against Jamaica. In the final, however, Guyana put them in. They responded by smashing 362 for five, the highest total of the season, then dismissing Guyana for 210. The mammoth score was set up by 146 from opener Lendl Simmons, his second century in his fourth innings of the competition. He was one of three Trinidadian batsmen who headed the run-charts: the list was topped by Jason Mohammed, who scored 327 at 81 in seven innings, followed by left-hander Evin Lewis (318 at 45) and Simmons (316 at 79). The team also provided two of the top four wicket-takers: Ravi Rampaul grabbed 14, while fellow pacer Anderson Phillip claimed 11, and made his international debut a fortnight later in a one-day series with Sri Lanka. Seasoned leg-spinner Imran Khan, like Rampaul aged 36, and slow left-armer Akeal Hosein contributed to Trinidad's success with eight apiece.

Two little-known bowlers also took the opportunity to enhance their credentials: Guyanese left-arm spinner Gudakesh Motie was the leading wicket-taker with 17, and Quinton Boatswain, a fast bowler from Montserrat, matched Rampaul by collecting 14 for Leeward Islands.

CG INSURANCE SUPER50 CUP IN 2020-21

50-over league plus knockout

	P	W	L	Pts	NRR
TRINIDAD & TOBAGO.....	5	5	0	20	1.07
GUYANA.................	5	4	1	16	1.07
WINDWARD ISLANDS	5	2	3	8	–0.71
JAMAICA	5	2	3	8	–0.78
Barbados................	5	1	4	4	0.23
Leeward Islands	5	1	4	4	–0.73

Semi-finals Trinidad & Tobago beat Jamaica by six wickets; Guyana beat Windward Islands by 95 runs.

Fifth-place play-off Leeward Islands beat Barbados by seven wickets.

Final At Coolidge, February 27, 2021 (day/night). **Trinidad & Tobago won by 152 runs. Trinidad & Tobago 362-5** (50 overs) (L. M. P. Simmons 146); ‡**Guyana 210** (43.5 overs). *Lendl Simmons and Evin Lewis (57) dashed to 121 inside 20 overs, and Simmons added another 100 with Darren Bravo as Trinidad & Tobago advanced to their second-highest 50-over total (after 409-6 v Northern Windwards in 2001-02). Ravi Rampaul reduced Guyana to 55-6 in ten overs, and finished with 4-52, though Raymon Reifer gave the innings some respectability; he was stranded on 97* when Jayden Seales (3-40) sealed Trinidad's victory.*

REGIONAL CHAMPIONS

1965-66	Barbados	1984-85	Trinidad & Tobago	2003-04	Barbados
1966-67	Barbados	1985-86	Barbados	2004-05	Jamaica
1967-68	*No competition*	1986-87	Guyana	2005-06	Trinidad & Tobago
1968-69	Jamaica	1987-88	Jamaica	2006-07	Barbados
1969-70	Trinidad	1988-89	Jamaica	2007-08	Jamaica
1970-71	Trinidad	1989-90	Leeward Islands	2008-09	Jamaica
1971-72	Barbados	1990-91	Barbados	2009-10	Jamaica
1972-73	Guyana	1991-92	Jamaica	2010-11	Jamaica
1973-74	Barbados	1992-93	Guyana	2011-12	Jamaica
1974-75	Guyana	1993-94	Leeward Islands	2012-13	Barbados
1975-76	{ Trinidad / Barbados	1994-95	Barbados	2013-14	Barbados
		1995-96	Leeward Islands	2014-15	Guyana
1976-77	Barbados	1996-97	Barbados	2015-16	Guyana
1977-78	Barbados	1997-98	{ Leeward Islands / Guyana	2016-17	Guyana
1978-79	Barbados			2017-18	Guyana
1979-80	Barbados	1998-99	Barbados	2018-19	Guyana
1980-81	Combined Islands	1999-2000	Jamaica	2019-20	Barbados
1981-82	Barbados	2000-01	Barbados	2020-21	*No competition*
1982-83	Guyana	2001-02	Jamaica		
1983-84	Barbados	2002-03	Barbados		

Barbados have won the title outright 22 times, Jamaica 12, Guyana 10, Trinidad/Trinidad & Tobago 4, Leeward Islands 3, Combined Islands 1. Barbados, Guyana, Leeward Islands and Trinidad have also shared the title.

The tournament was known as the Shell Shield from 1965-66 to 1986-87, the Red Stripe Cup from 1987-88 to 1996-97, the President's Cup in 1997-98, the Busta Cup from 1998-99 to 2001-02, the Carib Beer Cup from 2002-03 to 2007-08, the Headley–Weekes Trophy from 2008-09 to 2012-13, the President's Trophy in 2013-14, the WICB Professional Cricket League from 2014-15 (though it was sponsored by Digicel in 2016-17), and the West Indies Championship from 2018-19.

The Caribbean Premier League has its own section (page 1147).

ZIMBABWE CRICKET IN 2021

No country for old mistakes

LIAM BRICKHILL

Zimbabwean cricket endured one of its most difficult year yet. From the gut-punch revelations of Heath Streak's malfeasance, to Brendan Taylor's retirement and subsequent downfall, the disappointment at the cancellation of the women's T20 World Cup qualifiers, and Sikandar Raza's career-threatening battle with a bone marrow infection, there was little respite.

Then there were the biobubbles, the lockdowns, and the myriad struggles of daily life in Zimbabwe. Attempts at normality were thwarted by the appearance of new coronavirus variants, and everything was cloaked in the feverish weathers of a changing climate. And yet, in this land of Balancing Rocks and Msasa forests that wash wine-red over the countryside each spring, the rain still falls and cricket is still played.

Indeed, the year started with a flourish. Test captain Sean Williams led his side to a ten-wicket win over Afghanistan with a cut-and-thrust hundred on an unusually green Abu Dhabi strip. In what was their only complete Test

ZIMBABWE IN 2021

	Played	Won	Lost	Drawn/No result
Tests	5	1	4	–
One-day internationals	6	1	4	1
Twenty20 internationals	17	6	11	–

JANUARY		
FEBRUARY		
MARCH	2 Tests and 3 T20Is (in the UAE) v Afghanistan	(page 891)
APRIL	} 2 Tests and 3 T20Is (h) v Pakistan	(page 1060)
MAY		
JUNE		
JULY	1 Test, 3 ODIs and 3 T20Is (h) v Bangladesh	(page 1066)
AUGUST	3 ODIs and 5 T20Is (a) v Ireland	(page 950)
SEPTEMBER	} 3 T20Is (a) v Scotland	(page 1090)
OCTOBER		
NOVEMBER		
DECEMBER		

For a review of Zimbabwean domestic cricket from the 2020-21 season, see page 1071.

performance of the year, the fast bowlers also prospered. But Afghanistan scorched Zimbabwe in the second match, Pakistan immolated them twice by an innings, and Bangladesh made it four defeats in a row. There was, as ever, evidence of potential and grit, but the Test players remained frustrated by an inability to bring everything together when it mattered: they won moments, occasionally sessions, but rarely games.

The men's white-ball teams could stand a little taller, despite chastening series defeats by Bangladesh in ODIs, and Afghanistan and Ireland in T20s. But Zimbabwe reached 1–1 in T20 series against Pakistan and Bangladesh, before losing both deciders. The honours were shared in a one-day series in Ireland, and the year ended with a T20 series triumph over Scotland in the rimy twilight of the British summer.

That European jaunt provided the stage for Taylor's international swansong. While his exit took everyone by surprise, there had been signs he was getting ready to say goodbye. Usually the sturdy mettle in the middle, his batting took on an urgent, freeform quality, as though seeking to express the full bloom of his repertoire, no matter the format or situation. At the time, it seemed almost irresponsible; in hindsight, it made sense. In January 2022, pre-empting an ICC statement, he admitted consorting with match-fixers, and a drug habit. He was banned from cricket for three and a half years.

Taylor was not the first pillar to fall, nor even the tallest. The previous April, news had broken of an eight-year ban for Streak – a Zimbabwean cricket legend – following breaches of the ICC's anti-corruption code. His crude unveiling left sadness that a reputation could be thrown away for such perfidy.

Though much is taken, much abides. There are other cricketers here, and good ones. Mary-Anne Musonda, captain of the women's side, is a brilliant leader and a scene-stealing batter who has what it takes to succeed in the modern game. Her run-a-ball hundred to secure victory over Ireland in Zimbabwe's first women's ODI was the highlight of the year. Zimbabwe will need more of the same as they continue to strive towards a dream deferred: an appearance at a global women's tournament.

Blessing Muzarabani has rattled stumps, pinged helmets, and won friends wherever he has gone. Craig Ervine is ageing like a fine Mukuyu Merlot, Williams evergreen in the middle order, and Raza back at the top of his game, capping the year with a career-best 226 in the Logan Cup. New and talented game-changers have been found, such as Wesley Madhevere, Ryan Burl, Richard Ngarava and Luke Jongwe.

And they all have something to look forward to: in November, it was announced that Zimbabwe would co-host the 2027 World Cup, alongside South Africa and Namibia. Before then, they have T20 World Cup qualifiers, at home, in 2022. Despite a flawed and imbalanced global system, there is opportunity yet for the Zimbabwean cricketer.

ZIMBABWE v PAKISTAN IN 2020-21

Liam Brickhill

Twenty20 internationals (3): Zimbabwe 1, Pakistan 2
Test matches (2): Zimbabwe 0, Pakistan 2

More than seven years on from their previous Test series in Zimbabwe, Pakistan began the second leg of their trip in high spirits after winning both white-ball series in South Africa. They left Zimbabwe in much the same mood, having overcome what resistance the hosts offered in the T20 series, and flattened them in the two Tests.

Their opponents, of course, were expected to put up even less of a fight than their southern neighbours, and Pakistan's coach Misbah-ul-Haq called Zimbabwe a side with "nothing to lose". But it would not be true to suggest they had nothing to play for. They were still reeling from the news, which broke a week before the first T20, that their former captain and coach Heath Streak had been banned for eight years because of corruption, and were desperate to change the headlines. They nearly did so, pushing Pakistan hard in the 20-over games, despite the absence of several key players.

Brendan Taylor missed the first T20 through illness, while Sean Williams – Zimbabwe's regular captain – was ruled out of the Tests by a hand injury. Craig Ervine played only in the first T20, when he strained a calf muscle, and opening batsman Prince Masvaure missed the Second Test with a fractured thumb. Sikandar Raza, meanwhile, the talismanic all-rounder whose mere presence had for years bolstered Zimbabwe's self-belief, had been struck down with a bone-marrow infection in his right arm on the squad's return from the UAE. There were fears the problem might be cancerous, but mercifully they proved groundless.

This lengthy injury list gutted the middle order, and it was the batting that repeatedly let them down: Regis Chakabva alone passed 50 in the Tests. Of the replacements and newcomers, only all-rounder Luke Jongwe, recalled after a five-year absence from international cricket, acquitted himself well; his four wickets set up Zimbabwe's unlikely win in the second T20.

Pakistan had no such problems. In every match bar that defeat, at least one member of their top order made a decisive contribution, exemplified by Mohammad Rizwan's excellence in the T20 series, which brought him 186 runs from 139 balls for once out, and Abid Ali's unbeaten 215 in the Second Test. The bowlers shared the spoils and outclassed their opponents, none more so than Hasan Ali, finally resembling the exciting cricketer who had burst on to the international scene in 2016. He produced a match-turning spell in the T20 decider, and ran rampant across the two Tests, taking 14 wickets at just under nine apiece. Shaheen Shah Afridi was not far behind, with ten at 16. Babar Azam had a quiet tour by his standards, with one fifty in five innings, but took his tally as captain of a new-look Test team to four wins out of four.

PAKISTAN TOURING PARTY

*Babar Azam (T/20), Abdullah Shafiq (T), Abid Ali (T), Agha Salman (T), Arshad Iqbal (20), Asif Ali (20), Azhar Ali (T), Danish Aziz (20), Fahim Ashraf (T/20), Fakhar Zaman (20), Fawad Alam (T), Haider Ali (20), Haris Rauf (T/20), Hasan Ali (T/20), Imran Butt (T), Mohammad Hafeez (20), Mohammad Hasnain (20), Mohammad Nawaz (T/20), Mohammad Rizwan (T/20), Mohammad Wasim (20), Nauman Ali (T), Sajid Khan (T), Sarfraz Ahmed (T/20), Saud Shakil (T), Shaheen Shah Afridi (T/20), Shahnawaz Dani (20), Sharjeel Khan (20), Tabish Khan (T), Usman Qadir (20), Zahid Mahmood (T). *Coach:* Misbah-ul-Haq.

All-rounder Shadab Khan was originally selected for the T20 series, but pulled out after injuring a toe in South Africa. Leg-spinner Zahid Mahmood was chosen in his place, only to opt out because he was anxious about travelling by himself; he joined the tour for the Test series, when he was able to fly from Pakistan with his Test colleagues.

First Twenty20 international At Harare, April 21, 2021. **Pakistan won by 11 runs. Pakistan 149-7** (20 overs) (Mohammad Rizwan 82*); ‡**Zimbabwe 138-7** (20 overs) (C. R. Ervine 34, L. M. Jongwe 30*; Usman Qadir 3-29). *PoM:* Mohammad Rizwan. *T20I debuts:* T. R. Marumani (Zimbabwe); Danish Aziz (Pakistan). *Mohammad Rizwan proved the difference, contributing 82* to a Pakistan total of 149-7, in which the next highest score was 15 from debutant Danish Aziz. Dropped on 13 at mid-on by Tinashe Kamunhukamwe – part of a sloppy Zimbabwean fielding effort – Rizwan chaperoned the middle order, then led the charge at the death, plundering 20 from the final over, bowled by Richard Ngarava. Zimbabwe were well placed at 77-2 in the 11th, before losing four for 18 in 18 deliveries to spin. Mohammad Hafeez bowled four overs in a T20I for the first time since 2013-14 (and claimed his first wicket for two and a half years), while Usman Qadir's leg-breaks collected three. Luke Jongwe fought back, but 20 off the final over proved too many against Haris Rauf's nerveless changes of pace and pinpoint yorkers.*

Second Twenty20 international At Harare, April 23, 2021. **Zimbabwe won by 19 runs. Zimbabwe 118-9** (20 overs) (T. S. Kamunhukamwe 34); ‡**Pakistan 99** (19.5 overs) (Babar Azam 41; L. M. Jongwe 4-18). *PoM:* L. M. Jongwe. *T20I debut:* Arshad Iqbal (Pakistan). *Zimbabwe staged a remarkable turnaround to register their first T20 victory over Pakistan, at the 16th attempt. The tourists had seemed in charge after six bowlers claimed at least one wicket on a sluggish surface, limiting the total to 118-9; opener Kamunhukamwe alone passed 18. Pakistan's chase began slowly, but they were in contention at 78-3 in the 16th – only to lose seven for 21. Ninety-nine was their lowest T20 total since 2015-16, and the first time Zimbabwe had bowled them out in the format. Employing a mixture of cutters and slower balls, Jongwe collected the best T20I figures by a Zimbabwean – three wickets in the last over – beating Wellington Masakadza's 4-28 against Scotland at Nagpur in 2015-16; he celebrated his wickets by removing a shoe and using it to make an imaginary phone call. This was Zimbabwe's first T20 win at home since 2016, and ended a nine-match losing streak. Babar Azam described his side's performance as "very painful".*

Third Twenty20 international At Harare, April 25, 2021. **Pakistan won by 24 runs.** ‡**Pakistan 165-3** (20 overs) (Mohammad Rizwan 91*, Babar Azam 52; L. M. Jongwe 3-37); **Zimbabwe 141-7** (20 overs) (W. N. Madhevere 59, T. R. Marumani 35; Hasan Ali 4-18). *PoM:* Hasan Ali. *PoS:* Mohammad Rizwan. *A finely balanced decider did not swing Pakistan's way until the closing moments. With Zimbabwe 102-1 in the 14th, needing 64 more, an electric finish loomed. But Mohammad Hasnain bowled Tadiwanashe Marumani, before Hasan Ali removed Wessly Madhevere following an exuberant half-century, and asphyxiated Zimbabwe's charge to finish with a T20I-best 4-18. Opting for first use of a fresh pitch, Pakistan had lost Sharjeel Khan in the powerplay, before Rizwan put on 126 with Babar, who became the fastest to 2,000 T20I runs: this was his 52nd innings, beating Virat Kohli's 56. But it was Rizwan who shone, favouring the leg side as he blunted Zimbabwe's attack with a 60-ball 91*. It was his seventh score of 50-plus in his last 11 T20I innings (and his fifth unbeaten), after no half-century in his first 17.*

ZIMBABWE v PAKISTAN

First Test

At Harare, April 29–May 1, 2021. Pakistan won by an innings and 116 runs. Toss: Zimbabwe. Test debuts: R. Kaia, R. Ngarava, M. Shumba; Sajid Khan.

If Zimbabwe largely kept pace with Pakistan during the Twenty20s, a gulf was immediately apparent in the Test format. Pakistan's fast bowlers dismantled their opponents on the first day, before their batsmen ambled to a healthy lead. The hosts then wilted against Hasan Ali's intensity in their second innings, and the match was over inside three days. The most significant Zimbabwean achievement came from Langton Rusere, the first black African to stand in a Test. The DRS was absent but, unlike his compatriots, he put in a near-flawless performance.

Zimbabwe, who were missing several key players through illness or injury, won the toss, but that was where their luck ended. They lost both openers within 40 minutes, and continued to struggle, with Hasan and Shaheen Shah Afridi taking four wickets each. Debutant Roy Kaia top-scored with 48, but his team-mates found ways to get themselves in, then out. Zimbabwe were dismissed by tea.

Imran Butt and Abid Ali settled in, compiling their first century stand as opening partners. Next morning, Abid was dismissed via a juggled slip catch from Taylor, ending a stand of 115 in 44 overs, and the glacial pace briefly surged when Tiripano nipped out Azhar Ali and Babar Azam with consecutive deliveries. It was Babar's first golden duck in Test cricket, but by then Pakistan were in the lead. Zimbabwe's woes mounted when Masvaure at short leg endured a fierce blow to his left hand just below the thumb; scans revealed a fracture, and he played no further part in the series.

After more than five and a half hours, Butt fell in sight of a maiden hundred, feathering a loose drive in his first moment of real indiscretion, but his departure brought little relief for the bowlers, as Fawad Alam and Mohammad Rizwan put on 107. The second new ball brought Rizwan's demise, when he chopped an indipper from Muzarabani on to his stumps for 45, but Fawad cruised to 50 and beyond. He had converted each of his three previous Test half-centuries into a hundred, and there was a sense of inevitability about his fourth. Zimbabwe chipped away at the other end, but Fawad ticked on steadily, and some typically bellicose hitting from Hasan pushed the game forward. By the time Fawad was last out for 140 an hour into the third day, a fourth wicket for the persevering Muzarabani, the lead had swelled to 250.

A fired-up Hasan then got to work on Zimbabwe, who crumbled. The end might have come even sooner had Pakistan held all their chances, but that couldn't prevent another collapse: 134 all out, this time, in 46 overs, with Hasan picking up a career-best five for 36. It was Pakistan's first Test win away from home (and outside the UAE) since Lord's 2018.

Player of the Match: Hasan Ali.

Close of play: first day, Pakistan 103-0 (Imran Butt 43, Abid Ali 56); second day, Pakistan 374-6 (Fawad Alam 108, Hasan Ali 21).

Zimbabwe

P. S. Masvaure c Imran Butt b Shaheen Shah Afridi	11	– absent hurt	
K. T. Kasuza b Hasan Ali	0	– (1) lbw b Hasan Ali	28
T. K. Musakanda b Nauman Ali	14	– (2) run out (Sajid Khan/ Mohammad Rizwan)	43
*B. R. M. Taylor c Fahim Ashraf b Hasan Ali	5	– c Hasan Ali b Nauman Ali	29
M. Shumba run out (Imran Butt/Sajid Khan)	27	– (3) c Mohammad Rizwan b Nauman Ali	4
R. Kaia lbw b Hasan Ali	48	– (5) lbw b Fahim Ashraf	0
†R. W. Chakabva c Imran Butt b Hasan Ali	19	– (6) not out	14
D. T. Tiripano not out	28	– (7) b Hasan Ali	2
T. S. Chisoro b Shaheen Shah Afridi	9	– (8) c Imran Butt b Hasan Ali	0
B. Muzarabani b Shaheen Shah Afridi	14	– (9) b Hasan Ali	2
R. Ngarava b Shaheen Shah Afridi	1	– (10) b Hasan Ali	5
		B 2, lb 5	7

1/0 (2)　2/18 (1)　3/30 (3)　　　　(59.1 overs)　176　　1/48 (1)　2/68 (3)　　　　(46.2 overs)　134
4/30 (4)　5/89 (5)　6/124 (6)　　　　　　　　　　　　　　3/92 (2)　4/95 (5)
7/127 (7)　8/141 (9)　9/164 (10)　10/176 (11)　　　　　5/117 (4)　6/124 (7)
　　　　　　　　　　　　　　　　　　　　　　　　　　　7/124 (8)　8/128 (9)　9/134 (10)

Shaheen Shah Afridi 15.1–5–43–4; Hasan Ali 15–2–53–4; Nauman Ali 11–2–29–1; Fahim Ashraf 7–3–14–0; Sajid Khan 11–1–37–0. *Second innings*—Shaheen Shah Afridi 11–1–35–0; Hasan Ali 12.2–2–36–5; Fahim Ashraf 10–2–22–1; Nauman Ali 9–1–27–2; Sajid Khan 4–0–7–0.

Pakistan

Imran Butt c Chakabva b Ngarava	91	Sajid Khan c Chakabva b Ngarava		7
Abid Ali c Taylor b Chisoro	60	Shaheen Shah Afridi not out		4
Azhar Ali c Musakanda b Tiripano	36			
*Babar Azam c Kaia b Tiripano	0	B 1, lb 3, w 1, nb 8		13
Fawad Alam c Chakabva b Muzarabani	140			
†Mohammad Rizwan b Muzarabani	45	1/115 (2) 2/176 (3)	(133 overs)	426
Fahim Ashraf c Chisoro b Tiripano	0	3/182 (4) 4/226 (1)		
Hasan Ali c Chakabva b Muzarabani	30	5/333 (6) 6/334 (7) 7/395 (8)		
Nauman Ali c Musakanda b Muzarabani	0	8/395 (9) 9/412 (10) 10/426 (5)		

Muzarabani 31–8–73–4; Ngarava 29–4–104–2; Chisoro 34–7–89–1; Tiripano 23–6–89–3; Shumba 9–3–29–0; Kaia 7–0–38–0.

Umpires: M. Erasmus and L. Rusere.   Third umpire: I. Chabi.
Referee: A. J. Pycroft.

ZIMBABWE v PAKISTAN

Second Test

At Harare, May 7–10, 2021. Pakistan won by an innings and 147 runs. Toss: Pakistan. Test debuts: L. M. Jongwe; Tabish Khan.

Zimbabwe dragged this Test into the fourth day, but their domination by Pakistan's insatiable batsmen and varied bowling attack was even more complete than it had been the previous week. Victory by an innings and 147 supplanted the First Test as Pakistan's second-largest outside Asia, behind an innings-and-166-run win over New Zealand at Dunedin in 1972-73.

Statistical highlights abounded, starting with a 236-run stand between Abid Ali and Azhar Ali after Pakistan had opted to bat. It was their second-highest partnership for any wicket against Zimbabwe, behind 313 (for the eighth) between Wasim Akram and Saqlain Mushtaq at Sheikhupura in 1996-97, and a Test record for the second wicket at Harare. The feat was the greater given the vim shown by Zimbabwe's opening pair of Muzarabani and Ngarava, who quickly accounted for Imran. Both found an extra yard and significant lift with the new ball.

Support was lacking, however, and the pressure built up by Zimbabwe in the morning drained away in the afternoon, as first Azhar, then Abid, eased to hundreds. Muzarabani hit back with the second new ball, dismissing Azhar, Babar Azam and Fawad Alam in successive overs. And when Pakistan reached 341 for seven shortly before lunch on the second day, Zimbabwe were not out of it. Instead, Nauman Ali joined Abid in a 169-run eighth-wicket stand – another ground record – and left Zimbabwe deflated. While Abid reached a double-century in cruise control, Nauman shifted through the gears, accelerating dramatically after passing 50. It took a sharp piece of work from Chakabva to get rid of him, three short of what would have been a maiden first-class hundred; it was the first stumping off a wide in Test history.

Pakistan's 510 for eight reflected a decent pitch, which made Zimbabwe's reply all the limper. Seamer Tabish Khan, at 36 Pakistan's oldest Test debutant in 66 years, celebrated with a wicket in his first over (after 598 at first-class level), and Zimbabwe lost three more before stumps. The procession continued on the third morning, as Hasan Ali's waspish pace and curve produced another career-best: five for 27 was his fourth five-for in his last five Test innings, which had now yielded 24 wickets at under ten.

A mammoth 378 behind, Zimbabwe followed on after lunch, and a punch-drunk middle order went down swinging. Chakabva repeatedly lifted Pakistan's spinners over the leg side on his way to 80, while Taylor unfurled an array of strokes that would not have been out of place in T20. He had hit ten fours from 30 deliveries when he was given out for 49, strangled down leg off Shaheen Shah Afridi. Taylor disagreed with Marais Erasmus's decision, and his show of dissent drew a reprimand from match referee Andy Pycroft.

Nauman collected a five-for as Zimbabwe quickly folded, and Afridi rattled through the tail with a succession of zippy yorkers amid lengthening shadows. Luke Jongwe, on Test debut, and No. 11 Muzarabani forced the match into the fourth morning, when the

---

THREE FROM ONE TEAM TAKING FIVE-FORS IN THE SAME TEST

G. Giffen (5-76), S. T. Callaway (5-37); A. E. Trott (8-43)	A v E at Adelaide . . .	1894-95
S. F. Barnes (5-56), C. Blythe (5-63); W. Rhodes (5-83)	E v A at Manchester .	1909
D. K. Lillee (5-15), M. H. N. Walker (5-48); J. R. Thomson (5-38)	E v A at Birmingham	1975
D. R. Doshi (5-39), Kapil Dev (5-70), Madan Lal (5-23)	I v E at Bombay	1981-82
P. R. Reiffel (6-71); T. B. A. May (5-89), S. K. Warne (5-82) . . .	A v E at Birmingham	1993
Hasan Ali (5-27); Shaheen Shah Afridi (5-52), Nauman Ali (5-86)	**P v Z at Harare**	**2020-21**

---

formalities were completed in five overs. But there was time for more stats: Afridi's fifth wicket made this the first time three Pakistan bowlers had taken five-wicket hauls in the same Test. It was also only the second time – after George Hirst and Colin Blythe for England against Australia at Birmingham in 1909 – that two left-armers had removed five in the same innings.

Player of the Match: Abid Ali. *Player of the Series:* Hasan Ali.
Close of play: first day, Pakistan 268-4 (Abid Ali 118, Sajid Khan 1); second day, Zimbabwe 52-4 (Chakabva 28, Chisoro 1); third day, Zimbabwe 220-9 (Jongwe 31, Muzarabani 0).

Pakistan

Imran Butt c Tiripano b Ngarava.	2	Nauman Ali st Chakabva b Chisoro	97
Abid Ali not out.	215		
Azhar Ali c Shumba b Muzarabani	126	B 7, lb 8, w 5, nb 2	22
*Babar Azam c Kasuza b Muzarabani.	2		
Fawad Alam b Muzarabani	5	1/12 (1) (8 wkts dec, 147.1 overs)	510
Sajid Khan c Chakabva b Tiripano	20	2/248 (3) 3/252 (4)	
†Mohammad Rizwan c Ngarava b Chisoro .	21	4/264 (5) 5/303 (6)	
Hasan Ali c Chakabva b Jongwe.	0	6/340 (7) 7/341 (8) 8/510 (9)	

Tabish Khan and Shaheen Shah Afridi did not bat.

Muzarabani 29–6–82–3; Ngarava 24–5–58–1; Jongwe 17–1–68–1; Tiripano 22–5–83–1; Chisoro 40.1–7–131–2; Shumba 11–1–73–0.

Zimbabwe

Batsman	1st innings		2nd innings	
K. T. Kasuza	b Hasan Ali	4	b Nauman Ali	22
T. K. Musakanda	lbw b Tabish Khan	0	c Mohammad Rizwan b Shaheen Shah Afridi	8
†R. W. Chakabva	c Abid Ali b Hasan Ali	33	c Babar Azam b Nauman Ali	80
*B. R. M. Taylor	c Mohammad Rizwan b Shaheen Shah Afridi	9	c Mohammad Rizwan b Shaheen Shah Afridi	49
M. Shumba	lbw b Sajid Khan	2	c Imran Butt b Nauman Ali	16
T. S. Chisoro	c Imran Butt b Hasan Ali	1	(9) b Shaheen Shah Afridi	8
L. M. Jongwe	b Hasan Ali	19	(6) c Mohammad Rizwan b Shaheen Shah Afridi	37
D. T. Tiripano	c sub (Saud Shakil) b Sajid Khan	23	(7) lbw b Nauman Ali	0
R. Kaia	c Azhar Ali b Hasan Ali	11	(8) c Sajid Khan b Nauman Ali	0
R. Ngarava	not out	15	b Shaheen Shah Afridi	0
B. Muzarabani	run out (Imran Butt/Mohammad Rizwan)	7	not out	4
Extras	B 4, lb 3, w 1	8	B 1, lb 5, nb 1	7

1/0 (2) 2/23 (1) 3/40 (4)   (60.4 overs) 132
4/47 (5) 5/53 (6) 6/68 (3)
7/77 (7) 8/108 (8) 9/110 (9) 10/132 (11)

1/13 (2) 2/63 (1)   (68 overs) 231
3/142 (4) 4/170 (3)
5/188 (5) 6/196 (7) 7/196 (8)
8/205 (9) 9/205 (10) 10/231 (6)

Shaheen Shah Afridi 14–4–34–1; Tabish Khan 15–8–22–1; Hasan Ali 13–4–27–5; Nauman Ali 6–3–3–0; Sajid Khan 12.4–6–39–2. *Second innings*—Shaheen Shah Afridi 20–5–52–5; Tabish Khan 11–3–46–0; Hasan Ali 10–7–9–0; Sajid Khan 6–1–32–0; Nauman Ali 21–3–86–5.

Umpires: M. Erasmus and L. Rusere.   Third umpire: I. Chabi.
Referee: A. J. Pycroft.

ZIMBABWE v BANGLADESH IN 2021

Liam Brickhill

Test match (1): Zimbabwe 0, Bangladesh 1
One-day internationals (3): Zimbabwe 0 (0pts), Bangladesh 3 (30pts)
Twenty20 internationals (3): Zimbabwe 1, Bangladesh 2

These two teams, once evenly matched, now had different orbits: Zimbabwe were not part of the World Test Championship, nor would they appear at the Twenty20 World Cup. The one-day internationals had Super League points at stake, but the gulf was clear even there: Bangladesh were near the top of the table, Zimbabwe at the bottom. The results reflected it.

Zimbabwe were also hindered by the absence of key personnel. Sean Williams, the Test captain, and Craig Ervine were forced to isolate after family members tested positive for Covid. Sikandar Raza returned during the white-ball games after a lengthy lay-off caused by a bone-marrow infection in his right arm, but was not yet back to his best. And Kyle Jarvis had announced his retirement from all cricket in June, after a year battling injury and illness. This meant the hosts had to field several inexperienced players. Despite the results, there was enough mettle shown by the likes of Dion Myers, Wesley Madhevere, Takudzwanashe Kaitano, Ryan Burl and Blessing Muzarabani to suggest that Zimbabwe's next generation possess talent.

Yet Bangladesh won all three series, and were the better team throughout. Zimbabwe bossed moments – sometimes whole sessions – but were often sloppy: they sent down 19 no-balls during the Test, and conceded more extras than their opponents in five of the six white-ball matches. Bangladesh did the basics better, and held their nerve when it mattered.

This was all the more impressive given the problems thrown their way. Tamim Iqbal arrived trying to manage a recurring knee injury and, though he played in the first warm-up, he missed the Test. Mushfiqur Rahim was nursing a hairline fracture to his left index finger which stopped him from keeping wicket in that game; he then flew home before the ODIs to deal with a family emergency. Left-arm seamer Mustafizur Rahman bowled just five deliveries in the limited-overs warm-up before straining his ankle, and played in only two white-ball games.

Bangladesh were never able to play their first-choice XI – but their bench strength meant it mattered little. Mahmudullah, a late addition to the Test squad, responded with a career-best 150 not out before surprising everyone by announcing his Test retirement mid-match.

Several other tourists advanced from the fringes, but one old campaigner was never far from the centre of Bangladesh's success. Shakib Al Hasan was injured for the home series against West Indies earlier in the year, before opting out of a Test series in Sri Lanka to take part in the IPL. But he took five wickets in the Test, won the second ODI virtually off his own bat, and commanded respect every time he bowled.

BANGLADESH TOURING PARTY

Mominul Haque (T), Abu Jayed (T), Afif Hossain (50/20), Aminul Islam (20), Ebadat Hossain (T), Liton Das (T/50/20), Mahmudullah (T/50), Mehedi Hasan snr (T/50), Mehedi Hasan jnr (20), Mithun Ali (50), Mohammad Naim (50/20), Mohammad Saifuddin (50/20), Mosaddek Hossain (50), Mushfiqur Rahim (T/20), Mustafizur Rahman (50/20), Nasum Ahmed (T), Nazmul Hossain (T), Nayeem Hasan (T), Nurul Hasan (T/50/20), Rubel Hossain (50), Saif Hasan (T), Shadman Islam (T), Shakib Al Hasan (T/50/20), Shamim Hossain (20), Shoriful Islam (T/50/20), Soumya Sarkar (20), Taijul Islam (T/50), Tamim Iqbal (T/50/20), Taskin Ahmed (T/50/20), Yasir Ali (T). Coach: R. C. Domingo.

Tamim Iqbal captained in the 50-over matches, and Mahmudullah in the T20s. Mahmudullah was a late addition to the Test party after injuries to others. Mushfiqur Rahim returned home after the Test, for personal reasons.

ZIMBABWE v BANGLADESH

Only Test

At Harare, July 7–11, 2021. Bangladesh won by 220 runs. Toss: Bangladesh. Test debuts: T. Kaitano, D. N. Myers.

For Bangladesh, Shadman Islam scored a maiden Test hundred, Nazmul Hossain cantered to his second, Taskin Ahmed made a career-best 75, and Mehedi Hasan picked up nine wickets. For Zimbabwe, Brendan Taylor played two explosive knocks, and debutant Takudzwanashe Kaitano two adhesive innings. But they were all overshadowed by Mahmudullah.

A late inclusion in Bangladesh's squad, and almost 18 months after his previous Test, he entered on the first afternoon at 132 for six. In his 50th match, he compiled a career-best 150 in nearly seven hours, breaking several national records – then surprised everyone by retiring from Test cricket. The news leaked out on the third day, and was confirmed when his team lined up for a guard of honour on the fifth. If this really was the end for the 35-year-old Mahmudullah, he signed off in style. First, he and Liton Das put on 138 for the seventh wicket, before Liton departed for 95, having increased his career-best by one. Then, after Mehedi fell first ball, Mahmudullah was joined by Taskin in a match-defining stand of 191 – a Bangladesh record for the ninth wicket, beating the 184 he added with Abul Hasan against West Indies at Khulna in 2012-13.

The Zimbabweans let several chances slip, and frustration spilled over into aggression on the second morning, when both Muzarabani and Taskin attracted the attention of match referee Andy Pycroft for an incident that escalated quickly from jovial to jowl-to-jowl. After evading a bouncer, Taskin performed a cheeky jig at the crease; Muzarabani responded with a verbal barrage, following through until his face was pressed into the batsman's grille. "I told him to do something with the ball rather than abusing me," shrugged Taskin; the pair were later fined 15% of their match fee.

Whatever fire the Zimbabweans had in their bellies was quickly extinguished: Mahmudullah moved up a gear as he neared his hundred, and Taskin joined in merrily. By the time the partnership was finally broken just before tea on the second day, four runs short of the overall Test record for the ninth wicket. In all, the last four wickets had added 336 – even though two made ducks.

At first, Zimbabwe made a decent fist of the riposte. The new opening pair of Shumba and Kaitano added 61, before Taylor (standing in as captain for the quarantined Sean Williams) launched an audacious salvo. But after he fell for a two-hour 81, no one could give much support to Kaitano, who extended his maiden Test innings to 87 in over seven and a half hours. Apart from Chakabva's 31 not out, the longest stay was Maruma's 34-minute duck. Mehedi and Shakib Al Hasan shared nine wickets, several courtesy of ambitious sweeps. Nearly 200 ahead, Bangladesh were batting again on the third evening, and soon in complete control: Shadman and Nazmul piled on an unbroken 196 before the declaration. Nazmul, who zoomed along at a run a ball, hit six sixes, as Zimbabwe's plans disintegrated.

Asked to bat four sessions to save the game – 477 was an impossible target – Zimbabwe's top order, Taylor aside, aimed for survival. Kaitano presented a dead bat, contributing two to a second-wicket stand of 95. His first run came with the total on 72, easily a Test record for an opener (against Bangladesh at Chittagong in 2004-05, another Zimbabwean debutant, Barney Rogers, opened his account with the score on 39). Taylor, meanwhile, attacked with even more gusto than in the first innings, reaching his fifty off 34 deliveries, equalling the Zimbabwean record set by Andy Blignaut against Pakistan at Harare in 2002-03. But, after hurtling to 92 with 16 fours, he chipped his 73rd ball back to Mehedi. "I felt I left so many runs out there," he said.

Kaitano finally fell, late on the third evening, after making seven in 146 minutes; on one, he had survived a sitter to Ebadat Hossain at fine leg off Mehedi. Next day, Tiripano's gritty rearguard merely delayed the inevitable as the middle order folded again, with Maruma and Kaia both collecting pairs; Kaia's misery was compounded when he was reported for a suspect action after 23 wicketless overs of off-spin. Before Mehedi brought the curtain down, there was just enough time for Muzarabani to answer Taskin's dance-off challenge, showcasing a few of his own moves to accompany some lusty blows.

Player of the Match: Mahmudullah.

Close of play: first day, Bangladesh 294-8 (Mahmudullah 54, Taskin Ahmed 13); second day, Zimbabwe 114-1 (Kaitano 33, Taylor 37); third day, Bangladesh 45-0 (Shadman Islam 22, Saif Hasan 20); fourth day, Zimbabwe 140-3 (Myers 18, Tiripano 7).

Bangladesh

Saif Hasan b Muzarabani	0	– (2) c Myers b Ngarava	43
Shadman Islam c Taylor b Ngarava	23	– (1) not out	115
Nazmul Hossain c Myers b Muzarabani	2	– not out	117
*Mominul Haque c Myers b Nyauchi	70		
Mushfiqur Rahim lbw b Muzarabani	11		
Shakib Al Hasan c Chakabva b Nyauchi	3		
†Liton Das c Nyauchi b Tiripano	95		
Mahmudullah not out	150		
Mehedi Hasan lbw b Tiripano	0		
Taskin Ahmed b Shumba	75		
Ebadat Hossain lbw b Muzarabani	0		
B 10, lb 11, w 2, nb 16	39	B 1, w 5, nb 3	9

1/4 (1) 2/8 (3) 3/68 (2) (126 overs) 468   1/88 (2)   (1 wkt dec, 67.4 overs) 284
4/106 (5) 5/109 (6) 6/132 (4)
7/270 (7) 8/270 (9) 9/461 (10) 10/468 (11)

Muzarabani 29-4-94-4; Ngarava 23-5-83-1; Tiripano 23-5-58-2; Nyauchi 17-1-92-2; Myers 3-1-13-0; Shumba 21-4-64-1; Kaia 10-0-43-0. *Second innings*—Muzarabani 12-4-27-0; Ngarava 9-0-36-1; Tiripano 11-2-33-0; Nyauchi 10-1-36-0; Shumba 12.4-0-67-0; Kaia 13-2-84-0.

Zimbabwe

M. Shumba lbw b Shakib Al Hasan	41	– c sub (Yasir Ali) b Taskin Ahmed	11
T. Kaitano c Liton Das b Mehedi Hasan	87	– lbw b Shakib Al Hasan	7
*B. R. M. Taylor c sub (Yasir Ali) b Mehedi Hasan	81	– c and b Mehedi Hasan	92
D. N. Myers c Mehedi Hasan b Shakib Al Hasan	27	– c Shadman Islam b Mehedi Hasan	26
T. H. Maruma lbw b Shakib Al Hasan	0	– (6) lbw b Mehedi Hasan	0
R. Kaia c Liton Das b Taskin Ahmed	0	– (7) lbw b Taskin Ahmed	0
†R. W. Chakabva not out	31	– (8) b Taskin Ahmed	1
D. T. Tiripano lbw b Mehedi Hasan	2	– (5) c Liton Das b Ebadat Hossain	52
V. M. Nyauchi b Mehedi Hasan	0	– c Shakib Al Hasan b Taskin Ahmed	10
B. Muzarabani b Mehedi Hasan	2	– not out	30
R. Ngarava c Nazmul Hossain b Shakib Al Hasan	0	– b Mehedi Hasan	10
B 3, lb 2	5	B 5, lb 11, nb 1	17

1/61 (1) 2/176 (3) 3/225 (4)   (111.5 overs) 276   1/15 (1) 2/110 (3)   (94.4 overs) 256
4/228 (5) 5/229 (6) 6/261 (2)   3/132 (2) 4/159 (4)
7/263 (8) 8/263 (9) 9/269 (10) 10/276 (11)   5/159 (6) 6/160 (7) 7/164 (8)
                                                      8/198 (9) 9/239 (5) 10/256 (11)

Taskin Ahmed 24–10–46–1; Ebadat Hossain 21–8–58–0; Shakib Al Hasan 34.5–10–82–4; Mehedi Hasan 31–5–82–5; Mominul Haque 1–0–3–0. *Second innings*—Shakib Al Hasan 25–9–44–1; Mehedi Hasan 30.4–10–66–4; Taskin Ahmed 24–4–82–4; Ebadat Hossain 11–2–39–1; Mahmudullah 4–0–9–0.

Umpires: M. Erasmus and L. Rusere.   Third umpire: I. Chabi.
Referee: A. J. Pycroft.

First one-day international   At Harare, July 16, 2021. **Bangladesh won by 155 runs. Bangladesh 276-9** (50 overs) (Liton Das 102, Mahmudullah 33, Afif Hossain 45; L. M. Jongwe 3-51); ‡**Zimbabwe 121** (28.5 overs) (R. W. Chakabva 54; Shakib Al Hasan 5-30). *PoM:* Liton Das. *ODI debuts:* T. R. Marumani, D. N. Myers (Zimbabwe). *Put in, Bangladesh lost their captain Tamim Iqbal without a run on the board, and were wobbling at 74-4 before Liton Das's fourth ODI century – and third against Zimbabwe – lifted them towards a formidable total on a sluggish pitch. Three wickets fell in successive balls in the 49th over, bowled by Luke Jongwe, the third to a run-out. Zimbabwe made a similar start, slipping to 78-4 – but there was no comeback, as Shakib Al Hasan got to work. The wicket of Brendan Taylor (in his 200th match) took Shakib past Mashrafe bin Mortaza's 269 as Bangladesh's leading ODI wicket-taker, and he added four to finish with his fifth five-for against Zimbabwe. Regis Chakabva biffed two sixes in a 51-ball 54, but the rest offered little resistance.*

Second one-day international   At Harare, July 18, 2021. **Bangladesh won by three wickets.** ‡**Zimbabwe 240-9** (50 overs) (B. R. M. Taylor 46, D. N. Myers 34, W. N. Madhevere 56, Sikandar Raza 30; Shoriful Islam 4-46); **Bangladesh 242-7** (49.1 overs) (Shakib Al Hasan 96*). *Bangladesh 10pts. PoM:* Shakib Al Hasan. *On a two-paced pitch, Shakib showed remarkable composure to shepherd a tricky chase. He made 96*, but the next-best was 28* from Mohammad Saifuddin, who joined him at 173-7 in the 39th, with 68 more needed. Zimbabwe built pressure – there were only three boundaries in the last 20 overs – but missed crucial chances, including a run-out when Saifuddin was at the wrong end. They might have been defending a stiffer target had Taylor not been given out – hit wicket off Shoriful Islam – by TV umpire Langton Rusere, even though he had finished his shot when he absent-mindedly swung his bat into his stumps. Taylor had looked in ominous touch and, though Wesley Madhevere made an enterprising fifty, Zimbabwe never quite regained their momentum.*

Third one-day international   At Harare, July 20, 2021. **Bangladesh won by five wickets. Zimbabwe 298** (49.3 overs) (R. W. Chakabva 84, D. N. Myers 34, Sikandar Raza 57, R. P. Burl 59; Mohammad Saifuddin 3-87, Mustafizur Rahman 3-57); ‡**Bangladesh 302-5** (48 overs) (Liton Das 32, Tamim Iqbal 112, Shakib Al Hasan 30, Mithun Ali 30, Nurul Hasan 45*). *Bangladesh 10pts. PoM:* Tamim Iqbal. *PoS:* Shakib Al Hasan. *A career-best 84 from Chakabva, plus punchy fifties from Sikandar Raza and Ryan Burl, gave Zimbabwe a good chance of a consolation victory, and some important points. But Tamim's calculated assault turned a challenging chase into a simple one. He reached the fastest of his 14 one-day hundreds, from his 87th ball, before Nurul Hasan, in his first ODI since December 2016, sealed the 50-over whitewash with a rapid 45*. By then, Zimbabwe had lost the plot, conceding 27 extras and missing several opportunities.*

First Twenty20 international   At Harare, July 22, 2021. **Bangladesh won by eight wickets.** ‡**Zimbabwe 152** (19 overs) (R. W. Chakabva 43, D. N. Myers 35; Mustafizur Rahman 3-31); **Bangladesh 153-2** (18.5 overs) (Mohammad Naim 46*, Soumya Sarkar 50). *PoM:* Soumya Sarkar. *T20I debut:* D. N. Myers (Zimbabwe). *Bangladesh's pacemen shared eight wickets, before Mohammad Naim and Soumya Sarkar set up victory with their first century opening stand in T20 internationals. Zimbabwe had actually outscored them in the powerplay, and looked good at 91-2 at halfway. But they slumped alarmingly, losing eight for 61, and were bowled out with an over to spare. Naim and Sarkar were initially circumspect, particularly against Blessing Muzarabani, whose first three overs yielded just eight, but Zimbabwe again let things slip in the field. The partnership was eventually broken by Chakabva, who parried a return behind his back into the stumps to run out Sarkar, but it was a rare moment of slickness.*

Second Twenty20 international   At Harare, July 23, 2021. **Zimbabwe won by 23 runs.** ‡**Zimbabwe 166-6** (20 overs) (W. N. Madhevere 73, R. P. Burl 34*; Shoriful Islam 3-33); **Bangladesh 143** (19.5 overs) (L. M. Jongwe 3-31, W. P. Masakadza 3-20). *PoM:* W. N. Madhevere. *T20I debut:* Shamim Hossain (Bangladesh). *Zimbabwe finally won a match, tightening up in all areas, while Bangladesh's fielders had an off day. Madhevere cracked a career-best 73, with three straight sixes, before Burl took over, targeting deep midwicket as 54 came from the last five overs.*

Muzarabani was held back until the third over, but struck twice in his first four balls; this time, his team-mates offered more support, conceding fewer extras and taking their opportunities. Slow left-armer Wellington Masakadza had a busy time: after taking three wickets in his first ten balls, he held three catches in the outfield, the last to level the series.

Third Twenty20 international   At Harare, July 25, 2021. **Bangladesh won by five wickets.** ‡**Zimbabwe 193-5** (20 overs) (W. N. Madhevere 54, R. W. Chakabva 48, R. P. Burl 31*); **Bangladesh 194-5** (19.2 overs) (Soumya Sarkar 68, Mahmudullah 34, Shamim Hossain 31*). *PoM:* Soumya Sarkar. *PoS:* Soumya Sarkar. *The decider was played on the same pitch as the high-scoring third ODI, and proved similarly profitable for batsmen. Madhevere swatted five sixes in one Taskin Ahmed over on his way to another fifty as Zimbabwe's openers put on 63 in six overs. Chakabva dealt in sixes, smashing six before falling in search of another, thanks to a relayed boundary catch which Naim, running at full tilt from fine leg, parried back to Shamim Hossain. Burl helped navigate a minor wobble to finish with a flourish, but Sarkar's all-round effort proved the difference: his 2-19 reined Zimbabwe in when they looked set for 200-plus, then a quickfire 68 underpinned the chase. Bangladesh still needed 61 from 39 when he fell, but 20-year-old Shamim, in only his second international, hit six fours from 15 deliveries as they clinched the series with four balls to spare.*

DOMESTIC CRICKET IN ZIMBABWE IN 2020-21

JOHN WARD

The Zimbabwe domestic season was again curtailed by the Covid-19 pandemic, but this time the three provincial competitions were all completed; the previous year, the T20 tournament was cancelled, and the other two left unfinished.

The four-day Logan Cup had first-time winners – **Rocks** (formerly Southern Rocks), the Masvingo-based side disbanded after 2013-14. They were resuscitated after Rangers, the young team drawn from the Alistair Campbell high performance programme, fell victim to the pandemic and dropped out after a single season. Southern Rocks had generally been a weak side, so, in addition to restoring players who had been reassigned to other provinces, Zimbabwe Cricket gave them some promising youngsters to ensure they were competitive.

Perhaps ZC overcompensated: Rocks won all their four matches. The brothers Roy and Innocent Kaia, who returned from Mountaineers, were the tournament's top run-scorers with 374 and 368 respectively, both averaging over 60; the most successful bowler was Tendai Chisoro, who came back from Rhinos to claim 18 wickets at 17. Sadly, the residents of Masvingo never saw their reborn team in action: the competition was staged in Harare without spectators, and the players were isolated throughout.

Plans for each team to play the others twice, in all three formats, were ruined by a second wave of the virus; Zimbabwe was locked down from New Year until mid-March and, when the restrictions were finally lifted, there was time to complete only a single round-robin in each competition.

Four centuries were scored in the ten Logan Cup matches, the highest 164 by Regis Chakabva for Eagles against Tuskers. The most exciting match was between Rhinos and Mountaineers. Set 371, Rhinos squeezed home when last man Tafara Chingwara scored the winning run. It was one of three defeats for **Mountaineers**, the powerhouse of the last few seasons; badly weakened by retirements and the transfer of several top players, they gleaned their only points from a draw with Tuskers.

Mountaineers also finished bottom of the Pro50 tournament, won by **Rhinos**, who beat Rocks in the final – their first trophy in any format in their 12 seasons. Opener Takudzwa Kaitano scored 122 in the final, which made him the tournament's top run-scorer with 247 at 49; he was backed up by fast bowler Carl Mumba, who totalled 158 in four innings without being dismissed, at a strike-rate of 147. John Nyumbu headed the wicket-takers with 11 for Tuskers at just under 12, five coming in the third-place play-off against Eagles.

In between, the Domestic Twenty20 competition was staged over a week in April. **Tuskers** and **Eagles** won three games apiece, and the final went to Tuskers, for whom Craig Ervine scored 250 in all, including 120 not out against Mountaineers. But the discovery of the tournament was 19-year-old Tadiwanashe Marumani of Rocks, whose 228 runs at 57 led to his international debut, against Pakistan, a few days later. Donald Tiripano took 11 wickets for Mountaineers, but could lift them only to fourth.

The season had begun in October with a month-long National Premier League, designed by ZC to strengthen club cricket. It was a 45-over competition for nine teams (four from Harare, two from Bulawayo and one each from Mutare, Kwekwe and Masvingo), which produced some good cricket and introduced some promising young players to a higher standard. Takashinga tied on points with Midwest, but had won their head-to-head fixture, and were declared winners. Roy Kaia shone here, too, with 241 runs, 20 wickets and seven catches for Takashinga, while Midwest's Tarisai Musakanda scored 307 at 38, including 142 against Gladiators. Nick Welch, who had made his first-class debut for Eagles in 2013-14 aged 16, and is now at Leicestershire, scored 184 in three matches for Harare Kings, including a superb 132 not out. Gladiators' left-arm spinner Malcom Chikuwa collected 23 wickets at eight.

FIRST-CLASS AVERAGES IN 2020-21

BATTING (125 runs in 4 innings, average 20.00)

		M	I	NO	R	HS	100	Avge	Ct/St
1	I. Kaia (*Rocks*)	4	6	0	368	99	0	61.33	4
2	T. H. Maruma (*Mountaineers*)	3	5	1	222	143	1	55.50	2
3	R. W. Chakabva (*Eagles/Zimbabwe*)	5	8	1	371	164	1	53.00	14/1
4	C. Kunje (*Rhinos*)	4	7	1	277	79	0	46.16	0
5	W. T. Mashinge (*Rocks*)	4	6	1	228	73	0	45.60	1
6	R. Nyathi (*Rhinos*)	4	6	0	263	84	0	43.83	1
7	R. Kaia (*Rocks/Zimbabwe*)	6	10	0	433	133	1	43.30	2
8	T. Kaitano (*Rhinos*)	4	7	0	302	86	0	43.14	3
9	S. W. Masakadza (*Mountaineers*)	3	6	0	249	89	0	41.50	2
10	P. J. Moor (*Tuskers*)	4	7	0	274	85	0	39.14	5
11	A. Odendaal (*Rocks*)	3	4	0	147	80	0	36.75	0
12	†C. R. Ervine (*Tuskers*)	4	7	0	246	97	0	35.14	4
13	B. R. M. Taylor (*Rhinos/Zimbabwe*)	3	6	0	208	86	0	34.66	4
14	T. T. Munyonga (*Mountaineers*)	4	7	0	240	79	0	34.28	6
15	J. Gumbie (*Mountaineers*)	4	8	0	265	62	0	33.12	4
16	L. M. Jongwe (*Tuskers/Zimbabwe*)	5	9	1	242	53	0	30.25	1
17	†P. S. Masvaure (*Rhinos/Zimbabwe*)	4	6	1	150	64	0	30.00	1
18	D. N. Myers (*Mountaineers*)	4	8	0	225	116	1	28.12	3
19	†B. S. Mudzinganyama (*Rocks*)	4	6	1	135	43	0	27.00	1
20	B. N. Evans (*Eagles*)	4	5	0	131	43	0	26.20	2
21	K. O. Maunze (*Eagles*)	4	6	0	149	51	0	24.83	1
22	†M. Shumba (*Tuskers/Zimbabwe*)	5	9	0	202	79	0	22.44	1
23	G. Chirimuuta (*Mountaineers*)	3	6	0	133	89	0	22.16	0
24	K. T. Kasuza (*Mountaineers/Zimbabwe*)	3	6	0	125	70	0	20.83	1

BOWLING (8 wickets, average 35.00)

		Style	O	M	R	W	BB	5I	Avge
1	Hasan Ali (*Pakistan*)	RFM	50.2	15	125	14	5-27	2	8.92
2	S. Snater (*Rocks*)	RM	27	5	94	8	5-45	1	11.75
3	L. T. Chivanga (*Eagles*)	RFM	56	14	147	10	4-47	0	14.70
4	Shaheen Shah Afridi (*Pakistan*)	LFM	60.1	15	164	10	5-52	1	16.40
5	Faraz Akram (*Eagles*)	RM	48.4	14	148	9	4-30	0	16.44
6	B. N. Evans (*Eagles*)	RFM	73.1	22	194	11	5-25	1	17.63
7	W. P. Masakadza (*Mountaineers*)	SLA	82.2	34	180	10	3-42	0	18.00
8	Nauman Ali (*Pakistan*)	SLA	47	9	145	8	5-86	1	18.12
9	R. Kaia (*Rocks/Zimbabwe*)	RM	69.1	10	224	12	6-34	2	18.66
10	T. Mutsamba (*Rocks*)	RFM	68	22	180	9	4-33	0	20.00
11	T. Chingwara (*Rhinos*)	RFM	72.5	13	266	13	4-26	0	20.46
12	B. Muzarabani (*Rocks/Zimbabwe*)	RFM	82.3	19	232	11	4-45	0	21.09
13	A. Odendaal (*Rocks*)	LFM	61.3	14	212	10	3-33	0	21.20
14	T. Mufudza (*Eagles*)	OB	66	17	178	8	3-37	0	22.25
15	J. C. Nyumbu (*Tuskers*)	OB	134	31	368	16	4-45	0	23.00
16	V. M. Nyauchi (*Mountaineers*)	RFM	70.3	18	216	9	3-28	0	24.00
17	T. S. Chisoro (*Rocks/Zimbabwe*)	SLA/LFM	207.3	52	540	21	4-37	0	25.71
18	B. A. Mavuta (*Rhinos*)	LB	96.4	13	374	14	4-14	0	26.71
19	A. Ndlovu (*Tuskers*)	SLA	90	18	274	10	5-60	1	27.40
20	T. T. Munyonga (*Mountaineers*)	OB	67.3	5	244	8	4-35	0	30.50
21	L. M. Jongwe (*Tuskers/Zimbabwe*)	RFM	76.2	11	278	9	3-69	0	30.88
22	C. T. Mumba (*Rhinos*)	RFM	87.4	24	278	9	5-77	1	30.88
23	C. Chitumba (*Mountaineers*)	RFM	79	19	249	8	4-66	0	31.12
24	D. N. Myers (*Mountaineers*)	RFM	53.5	8	251	8	2-61	0	31.37
25	R. Ngarava (*Eagles/Zimbabwe*)	LFM	91	18	285	9	4-46	0	31.66

LOGAN CUP IN 2020-21

	P	W	L	D	Pts
Rocks	4	4	0	0	40
Eagles	4	2	1	1	25
Rhinos	4	1	1	2	20
Tuskers	4	0	2	2	10
Mountaineers	4	0	3	1	5

Win = 10pts; draw = 5pts.

LOGAN CUP WINNERS

1993-94	Mashonaland U24	2007-08	Northerns
1994-95	Mashonaland	2008-09	Easterns
1995-96	Matabeleland	2009-10	Mashonaland Eagles
1996-97	Mashonaland	2010-11	Matabeleland Tuskers
1997-98	Mashonaland	2011-12	Matabeleland Tuskers
1998-99	Matabeleland	2012-13	Matabeleland Tuskers
1999-2000	Mashonaland	2013-14	Mountaineers
2000-01	Mashonaland	2014-15	Matabeleland Tuskers
2001-02	Mashonaland	2015-16	Mashonaland Eagles
2002-03	Mashonaland	2016-17	Manicaland Mountaineers
2003-04	Mashonaland	2017-18	Manicaland Mountaineers
2004-05	Mashonaland	2018-19	Mountaineers
2005-06	*No competition*	2019-20	*No winner*
2006-07	Easterns	2020-21	Rocks

Mashonaland/Northerns/Mashonaland Eagles have won the title 12 times, Easterns/Mountaineers/
Manicaland Mountaineers and Matabeleland/Matabeleland Tuskers 6, Mashonaland Under-24 and
Rocks 1.

PRO50 CHAMPIONSHIP IN 2020-21

50-over league

	P	W	L	Pts	NRR
ROCKS	4	3	1	30	1.48
RHINOS	4	3	1	30	1.28
Tuskers	4	3	1	30	−0.09
Eagles	4	1	3	10	−1.26
Mountaineers	4	0	4	0	−1.39

Third-place play-off At Harare (Old Hararians), April 28, 2021. **Tuskers won by 85 runs.**
Tuskers 221 (49 overs) (D. Jakiel 5-21); ‡**Eagles 136** (36.1 overs) (J. C. Nyumbu 5-21). *Brian
Chari smashed eight sixes in a run-a-ball 92, and added 114 with Clive Madande (46), before
Tuskers' last seven fell for 23, five to seamer Daniel Jakiel. But Eagles suffered a similar collapse –
seven for 27 – as off-spinner John Nyumbu matched Jakiel's return.*

Final At Harare (Takashinga), April 28, 2021. **Rhinos won by 47 runs. Rhinos 297-8** (50 overs)
(T. Kaitano 122); ‡**Rocks 250** (49 overs). *Rhinos claimed their first trophy in any tournament after
opener Takudzwanashe Kaitano batted through 46 overs for a maiden century, and No. 8 Carl
Mumba hit three sixes in a 14-ball 28*. Leg-spinner Brandon Mavuta picked up three wickets and a
run-out as Rocks were dismissed with an over to spare.*

DOMESTIC TWENTY20 CHAMPIONSHIP IN 2020-21

20-over league

	P	W	L	Pts	NRR
TUSKERS	4	3	1	30	1.50
EAGLES	4	3	1	30	0.48
Rocks	4	2	2	20	0.33
Mountaineers	4	2	2	20	−0.39
Rhinos	4	0	4	0	−1.98

Third-place play-off   At Harare (Old Hararians), April 16, 2021. **Rocks won by two wickets.**
‡**Mountaineers 160-5** (20 overs); **Rocks 161-8** (18.4 overs). *Late collapses had capsized Rocks'*
previous two run-chases, and this time they slipped from 129-2 to 159-8, before the tail ensured that
the work of Tadiwanashe Marumani (51) and Richmond Mutumbami (41) was not wasted.

Final   At Harare (Takashinga), April 16, 2021. **Tuskers won by 69 runs. Tuskers 179-6** (20 overs);
‡**Eagles 110** (15 overs) (A. Ndlovu 5-20). *Tuskers crushed Eagles with five overs to spare after*
Ainsley Ndlovu struck twice in his first 11 balls, then returned to wrap up the innings with three in
eight. Earlier, Craig Ervine (65 in 47) and Sean Williams (50 in 29) put on 86 in nine overs, before
Milton Shumba's 30 in 18 raised the target to a daunting 180.

A-TEAM TOURS IN 2021

BANGLADESH EMERGING PLAYERS v IRELAND WOLVES IN 2020-21

A-Team Test match (1): Bangladesh EP 1, Ireland Wolves 0
A-Team one-day internationals (5): Bangladesh EP 4, Ireland Wolves 0
A-Team Twenty20 internationals (2): Bangladesh EP 1, Ireland Wolves 0

Ireland tested out their bench strength with a visit to Bangladesh early in 2021. Harry Tector's side failed to record a win, but came close in three of the 50-over matches. Their batting proved equal to the task in the white-ball games, but the bowlers struggled against precocious opponents, notably Mahmudul Hasan, Shamim Hossain and Towhid Hridoy, who had all been part of the team that won the Under-19 World Cup in February 2020. The trip was nearly derailed by a Covid scare, when a positive result for Ruhan Pretorius – a late call-up – was announced during the first one-day game, which was immediately abandoned. It proved a false positive, and Pretorius cracked 90 in the next match.

Touring party *H. T. Tector, M. R. Adair, C. Campher, P. K. D. Chase, G. J. Delany, S. T. Doheny, J. J. Garth, S. C. Getkate, G. I. Hume, J. L. Lawlor, J. B. Little, J. A. McCollum, R. Pretorius, N. A. Rock, L. J. Tucker, B. C. White. *Coach:* G. X. Ford.

G. H. Dockrell was originally named as captain for the Test, but opted out of the tour at a late stage, and was replaced by Pretorius.

Test match At Chittagong, February 26–28, 2021. **Bangladesh Emerging Players won by an innings and 23 runs. ‡Ireland Wolves 151** (67 overs) (C. Campher 39; Tanvir Islam 5-55) **and 139** (74.3 overs) (H. T. Tector 55; Tanvir Islam 8-51); **Bangladesh Emerging Players 313** (90.4 overs) (Saif Hasan 49, Tanzid Hasan 41, Mahmudul Hasan 42, Yasir Ali 92, Towhid Hridoy 36; M. R. Adair 3-22, G. I. Hume 3-56). *PoM:* Tanvir Islam. *First-class debuts:* Akbar Ali, Mahmudul Hasan, Shahadat Hosain (Bangladesh Emerging Players); C. Campher (Ireland Wolves). *Slow left-armer Tanvir Islam took his maiden first-class five-for in the first innings, and dismantled Ireland Wolves with eight in the second.*

First one-day international At Chittagong, March 5, 2021. **No result. Bangladesh Emerging Players 122-4** (30 overs) (Saif Hasan 31, Towhid Hridoy 44*) v **‡Ireland Wolves.** *The match was stopped when it was announced that Ireland's Ruhan Pretorius had tested positive for Covid. It was later shown to be a false positive, and he and the other players were cleared to continue the series.*

Second one-day international At Chittagong, March 7, 2021. **Bangladesh Emerging Players won by four wickets. Ireland Wolves 263-7** (50 overs) (J. A. McCollum 41, R. Pretorius 90, S. T. Doheny 37, H. T. Tector 31); **‡Bangladesh Emerging Players 264-6** (49.4 overs) (Saif Hasan 36, Mahmudul Hasan 66, Yasir Ali 31, Towhid Hridoy 31, Shamim Hossain 53*). *PoM:* Shamim Hossain. *Spared isolation, Pretorius top-scored with 90, as Ireland Wolves posted a competitive score. When Towhid Hridoy fell in the 45th over of the reply, making it 214-5, the tourists smelled victory – but Shamim Hossain hit 53* from 39 to take his side over the line in the final over.*

Third one-day international At Chittagong, March 9, 2021 (day/night). **Bangladesh Emerging Players won by six wickets. Ireland Wolves 260-7** (50 overs) (J. A. McCollum 40*, H. T. Tector 36, C. Campher 43, L. J. Tucker 82*; Mukidul Islam 3-53); **‡Bangladesh Emerging Players 264-4** (45.3 overs) (Saif Hasan 120, Towhid Hridoy 43*, Shamim Hossain 44*). *PoM:* Saif Hasan. *Wicketkeeper Lorcan Tucker's 52-ball 82*, which followed some handy contributions from the top order, hauled Ireland Wolves to another serviceable total, but opener Saif Hasan made light of the target. He scored 120 of the first 195 runs, hitting five sixes and 11 fours, before Towhid and Shamim finished things off with 69* in six overs.*

Fourth one-day international At Mirpur, March 12, 2021. **Bangladesh Emerging Players won by eight wickets. Ireland Wolves 182** (46.2 overs) (M. R. Adair 40, R. Pretorius 35; Sumon Khan 4-31); **‡Bangladesh Emerging Players 186-2** (41.3 overs) (Mahmudul Hasan 80*, Towhid Hridoy 88*). *PoM:* Sumon Khan. *The Bangladeshis clinched the series with another regulation victory. Ireland Wolves recovered from 112-7 thanks to a stand of 57 between Pretorius and Graham Hume (29*), but the total never looked enough. Although the home side lurched to 10-2, Mahmudul Hasan and Towhid calmly put on 176*.*

Fifth one-day international   At Mirpur, March 14, 2021. **Bangladesh Emerging Players won by five runs. Bangladesh Emerging Players 260** (49.4 overs) (Anisul Islam 41, Mahmudul Hasan 123, Mahidul Islam 33; M. R. Adair 3-27); ‡**Ireland Wolves 255-9** (50 overs) (S. T. Doheny 81, M. R. Adair 45, N. A. Rock 35; Saif Hasan 3-31). *PoM:* Mahmudul Hasan. *Another tenacious performance almost brought an Irish win: Stephen Doheny anchored the chase, but three wickets for Saif Hasan's off-breaks put the brakes on, and the later batsmen could not quite seal a consolation victory. Earlier, Mahmudul had dominated the Bangladesh innings with 123 from 135 balls.*

First Twenty20 international   At Mirpur, March 16, 2021. **Bangladesh Emerging Players won by 30 runs. Bangladesh Emerging Players 184-7** (20 overs) (Saif Hasan 48, Towhid Hridoy 58); ‡**Ireland Wolves 154** (18.1 overs) (L. J. Tucker 38; Sumon Khan 4-28). *PoM:* Sumon Khan. *Bangladesh galloped to 184 thanks to Towhid, with a 35-ball 58, and Shamim, who clouted four sixes in his 28 from 11. The Wolves lost Gareth Delany for a duck in the first over, and were never really on terms. Seamer Sumon Khan took the last three wickets in seven balls.*

Second Twenty20 international   At Mirpur, March 18, 2021. **Bangladesh Emerging Players v Ireland Wolves. Cancelled.** *The match was called off when the tourists were advised to fly home early, with new Covid restrictions set to be introduced for those arriving in Ireland.*

IRELAND WOLVES v NETHERLANDS A IN 2021

A-Team one-day internationals (3): Ireland Wolves 2, Netherlands A 1

The Dutch A-Team, captained by wicketkeeper Scott Edwards, made a brief trip in May, playing three 50-over matches behind closed doors at Oak Hill CC in Co. Wicklow, about 30 miles south of Dublin. Ireland Wolves won the first, boosted by a remarkable unbroken tenth-wicket partnership of 89 between Shane Getkate and Peter Chase. The other matches were low-scoring affairs, after both captains defied conventional wisdom and batted first on winning the toss: Ireland Wolves were bowled out for 94 in the second game, and Netherlands A for 105 in the third.

Touring party   *S. A. Edwards, P. R. P. Boissevain, B. N. Cooper, B. F. W. de Leede, A. Dutt, V. J. Kingma, R. Klein, Musa Ahmed, S. J. Myburgh, A. J. Staal, L. V. van Beek, P. A. van Meekeren, Vikramjit Singh, T. P. Visée. Coach:* R. J. Campbell.

First one-day international   At Oak Hill, May 11, 2021. **Ireland Wolves won by 94 runs. Ireland Wolves 276-9** (50 overs) (H. T. Tector 69, G. H. Dockrell 34, S. C. Getkate 74*; P. R. P. Boissevain 3-46); ‡**Netherlands A 182** (45.5 overs) (T. P. Visée 42, L. V. van Beek 59*). *At 187-9 in the 42nd over, Ireland Wolves looked set for a modest total – but Shane Getkate blasted eight sixes from 40 balls, and put on 89* for the last wicket with Peter Chase (28* from 30), to raise a scarcely believable 276. Both Dutch openers went for nought, and Bas de Leede's golden duck made it 4-3; embarrassment loomed at 40-6, but Logan van Beek shared stands of 48 with Tobias Visée for the seventh wicket, and 56 with Vivian Kingma (26) for the last.*

HIGHEST TENTH-WICKET STANDS IN LIST A MATCHES

128	A. Ashish Reddy/M. Ravi Kiran .	Hyderabad v Kerala at Secunderabad	2014-15
109	**R. Punia/Umar Nazir**	**Jammu & Kashmir v Andhra at Mumbai** .	**2021-22**
106*	I. V. A. Richards/M. A. Holding .	West Indies v England at Manchester.	1984
103	Mohammad Amir/Saeed Ajmal .	Pakistan v New Zealand at Abu Dhabi	2009-10
102*	T. A. Bula/F. de Wet	North West v Free State at Potchefstroom . . .	2005-06
102	S. R. Hain/M. W. Parkinson . . .	England Lions v West Indies A at Coolidge . .	2017-18
99*	R. Rampaul/K. A. J. Roach	West Indies v India at Visakhapatnam	2011-12
89*	**S. C. Getkate/P. K. D. Chase** . .	**Ireland Wolves v Netherlands A at Oak Hill**	**2021**
85	F. A. Allen/J. Royal	Jamaica v Leeward Islands at North Sound	2020-21
84	G. Khera/D. S. Hettiarachchi. . . .	Police v Galle at Colombo (Police).	2018-19

Second one-day international   At Oak Hill, May 12, 2021. **Netherlands A won by five wickets.** ‡**Ireland Wolves 94** (23.5 overs) (S. C. Getkate 32, C. A. Young 30; V. J. Kingma 3-5); **Netherlands A 98-5** (16.3 overs) (S. A. Edwards 36*, T. P. Visée 33). *Rain forced a reduction to 40 overs a side. With Ireland Wolves' top three all failing to score, they collapsed to 55-8 in the 17th, before Getkate and Craig Young guided them close to three figures; Kingma finished with 5–3–5–3. The total was nowhere near enough, though there was time for Chase to inflict another duck on de Leede.*

Third one-day international   At Oak Hill, May 13, 2021. **Ireland Wolves won by five wickets.** ‡**Netherlands A 105** (28.5 overs) (G. J. McCarter 6-32, B. C. White 3-16); **Ireland Wolves 110-5** (20.4 overs) (H. T. Tector 57*). *Even though Ireland had struggled after opting to bat the previous day, the Dutch captain Scott Edwards also chose to take first strike. Again it proved disastrous: Netherlands A were sunk at 46-5 in the ninth, with four wickets for Graeme McCarter, who finished with 6-32. De Leede finally got off the mark, then fell lbw for one. Ireland Wolves wobbled to 29-3 in the 11th, but skipper Harry Tector clinched the series with 4446 off Paul van Meekeren.*

ZIMBABWE A v SOUTH AFRICA A IN 2021

A-Team one-day internationals (4): Zimbabwe A 1, South Africa 3
A-Team Test matches (2): Zimbabwe A 0, South Africa A 1

South Africa A hopped across the border, and outclassed their Zimbabwean hosts. They won three of the four 50-over games with ease, tripping up only in a rain-affected encounter, then dominated the first four-day game, in which captain Zubayr Hamza made an undefeated 222. There were also centuries for the consistent Ryan Rickelton and Sinethemba Qeshile, who shared the wicketkeeping duties. Zimbabwe A, for whom Tadiwanashe Marumani and Dion Myers showed promise, hit back on the first day of the next match, bowling the South Africans out for 282, but changing Covid regulations meant no further play was possible.

Touring party *M. Z. Hamza (FC/50), O. A. Cele (FC), C. J. Dala (50), T. B. de Bruyn (FC/50), T. de Zorzi (FC/50), D. M. Dupavillon (FC/50), A. D. Galiem (FC), D. A. Hendricks (FC), R. R. Hendricks (50), W. J. Lubbe (FC/50), S. S. B. Magala (50), J. N. Malan (50), E. M. Moore (FC), S. Muthusamy (FC), T. I. Ntuli (FC), A. L. Phehlukwayo (50), D. Pretorius (50), M. Pretorius (FC), S. Qeshile (FC/50), R. D. Rickelton (FC/50), L. L. Sipamla (FC/50), G. A. Stuurman (FC/50), R. van Tonder (FC). *Coach:* M. Maketa.

First one-day international   At Harare, May 29, 2021. **South Africa A won by six wickets. Zimbabwe A 319-9** (50 overs) (C. J. Chibhabha 37, T. R. Marumani 82, D. N. Myers 96, M. Shumba 30; L. L. Sipamla 3-40, D. Pretorius 3-39); ‡**South Africa A 320-4** (42.5 overs) (J. N. Malan 82, R. R. Hendricks 52, M. Z. Hamza 49, T. B. de Bruyn 113*; T. Mufudza 4-87). *Zimbabwe A's total, boosted by sizeable contributions from opener Tadiwanashe Marumani and Dion Myers (run out for 96) seemed to have set up a challenging total. But the experienced South Africans cruised past it: Janneman Malan and Reeza Hendricks put on 115 for the second wicket, then their captain, Zubayr Hamza, sat back as Theunis de Bruyn cracked six sixes and seven fours in his 113* from 64 balls. Tapiwa Mufudza, a 30-year-old off-spinner, took all four wickets to fall – but they cost him 87.*

Second one-day international   At Harare, May 31, 2021. **South Africa A won by 184 runs. South Africa A 365-6** (50 overs) (J. N. Malan 53, R. D. Rickelton 169, R. R. Hendricks 51, M. Z. Hamza 37*); ‡**Zimbabwe A 181** (35.3 overs) (T. R. Marumani 48, D. N. Myers 70; S. Muthusamy 4-37). *A virtuoso performance from wicketkeeper Ryan Rickelton blasted South Africa A out of sight: he hit 169 from 150 balls, sharing partnerships of 120 with Malan and 137 with Hendricks. Zimbabwe A lost Chamu Chibhabha first ball, and again the only sustained resistance came from Marumani and Myers, who put on 75.*

Third one-day international   At Harare, June 2, 2021. **Zimbabwe A won by 22 runs** (DLS). ‡**South Africa A 226-9** (50 overs) (T. de Zorzi 60, W. J. Lubbe 31, C. J. Dala 45; D. N. Myers 3-18); **Zimbabwe A 170-4** (37 overs) (C. J. Chibhabha 85*, M. Shumba 50*). *Zimbabwe A had the better of the match from the start, reducing the visitors to 74-6, before Tony de Zorzi and the tail muscled the total past 200. Zimbabwe A were 46-4, before Chibhabha and Milton Shumba put on 124*. When rain ended play, they were comfortably ahead of the DLS requirement of 149.*

Fourth one-day international   At Harare, June 4, 2021. **South Africa A won by 116 runs. South Africa A 281-6** (50 overs) (R. D. Rickelton 40, R. R. Hendricks 89, T. de Zorzi 55, T. B. de Bruyn 40*; L. M. Jongwe 3-47); ‡**Zimbabwe A 165** (38.2 overs) (M. Shumba 35, L. M. Jongwe 30; S. Muthusamy 4-36). *South Africa A took the series 3–1 with a disciplined all-round performance. Consistent batting, led by Hendricks, lifted them to 281, then the bowlers kept the pressure on: only one went for more than 4.6 an over. Slow left-armer Senuran Muthusamy took four wickets as Zimbabwe A came up well short.*

First Test   At Harare, June 7–10, 2021. **South Africa A won by an innings and 166 runs.** ‡**Zimbabwe A 344** (105.4 overs) (M. Shumba 74, D. N. Myers 69, R. Kaia 32, R. Mutumbami 51; D. M. Dupavillon 5-69, L. L. Sipamla 3-76) **and 93** (45.3 overs) (T. H. Maruma 33; G. A. Stuurman 3-18, D. M. Dupavillon 3-28); **South Africa A 603-4 dec** (135 overs) (E. M. Moore 93, R. D. Rickelton 109, M. Z. Hamza 222*, S. Qeshile 124*, Extras 34; R. Kaia 3-98). *Batsmen enjoyed themselves at first on a flat pitch, though fast bowler Daryn Dupavillon stuck to his task to take five wickets as Zimbabwe A reached 344. A second-wicket stand of 179 between Eddie Moore and Rickelton put South Africa A in charge, then skipper Hamza whisked them out of sight with his second double-century. He shared a fifth-wicket stand of 338* with wicketkeeper Sinethemba Qeshile, who hit his own maiden hundred (his previous-highest was 99). Trailing by 259, Zimbabwe A lost two wickets to Dupavillon on the third evening, and disintegrated next morning, not helped by having to use concussion substitutes for their first-innings top-scorers Shumba and Myers, who were both hit on the head while batting.*

Second Test   At Harare, June 13–16, 2021. **Drawn. South Africa A 282** (88.5 overs) (E. M. Moore 44, R. D. Rickelton 92, T. de Zorzi 59; W. N. Madhevere 5-49) v ‡**Zimbabwe A.** *This match was called off after the first day, when the Zimbabwe government announced new regulations because of rising Covid numbers. Rickelton had followed his century in the previous match with 92, but a maiden five-for for Wesley Madhevere – whose off-breaks had captured only six previous first-class wickets – pegged the South Africans back.*

SRI LANKA A v PAKISTAN SHAHEENS IN 2021-22

A-Team Test matches (2): Sri Lanka A 0, Pakistan Shaheens 0
A-Team one-day internationals (3): Sri Lanka A 0, Pakistan Shaheens 1

Pakistan Shaheens, captained by Saud Shakil and coached by 1992 World Cup winner Ijaz Ahmed, had much the better of their trip to Sri Lanka late in 2021. Bad weather probably cost them victory in the opening four-day game, and impinged on the second, although Sri Lanka batted much better in their second innings after being rolled for 67 in the first. They looked to have unveiled a gem in 20-year-old opener Kamil Mishara, who made 98 in both matches. But their batting proved fragile again in the first 50-over game, the only one to escape the weather, as they were bundled out for 102. The visitors, by contrast, had three different century-makers, plus a potent attack spearheaded by Naseem Shah, still only 18 but already with a Test hat-trick to his name.

Touring party *Saud Shakil (FC/50), Abbas Afridi (50), Abdullah Shafiq (FC/50), Abrar Ahmed (FC/50), Agha Salman (FC/50), Ahmed Safi (FC), Akif Javed (50), Arshad Iqbal (FC/50), Irfanullah Shah (FC/50), Kamran Ghulam (FC/50), Khurram Shehzad (FC/50), Mohammad Haris (FC/50), Mohammad Taha (FC/50), Naseem Shah (FC/50), Omair Bin Yousuf (FC/50), Qasim Akram (FC/50), Salman Khan (FC), Usman Salahuddin (FC), Zahid Mahmood (FC/50). *Coach:* Ijaz Ahmed.

Haider Ali was originally named as vice-captain, but was a late inclusion in the full Pakistan squad for the T20 World Cup. He was replaced by Mohammad Taha.

First Test   At Pallekele, October 28–31, 2021. **Drawn. Sri Lanka A 141** (46 overs) (M. V. T. Fernando 30*; Naseem Shah 5-53, Khurram Shehzad 3-25) **and 144-2** (30.3 overs) (R. V. P. K. Mishara 98); ‡**Pakistan Shaheens 324-2 dec** (115 overs) (Saud Shakil 118*, Omair Bin Yousuf 93, Kamran Ghulam 58*). *First-class debut:* Mohammad Haris (Pakistan Shaheens). *Sri Lanka A had rain to thank for escaping with a draw. Only 22 overs were possible on the first day – during which they slumped to 61-6 – followed by 47 on the second and 39 on the third, as Pakistan Shaheens looked to build their advantage. The tourists' captain, Saud Shakil, eventually put on 206 with Omair Bin Yousuf, but there was not enough time to force a result, and the match was called off after Sri Lanka A's 20-year-old opener Kamil Mishara just missed out on a maiden century.*

Second Test At Pallekele, November 4–7, 2021. **Drawn. ‡Pakistan Shaheens 394** (106 overs) (Abdullah Shafiq 117, Kamran Ghulam 45, Agha Salman 103, Naseem Shah 31; C. D. Gunasekara 6-83); **Sri Lanka A 67** (22.2 overs) (Naseem Shah 4-28, Khurram Shehzad 3-10) **and 317-6** (86.4 overs) (R. V. P. K. Mishara 98, W. S. R. Samarawickrama 151*). *Pakistan Shaheens looked on course for a crushing victory when they bowled Sri Lanka A out for 67 after centuries from Abdullah Shafiq and Agha Salman had underpinned a total of 394. Only 30 overs were possible on the third day, and Sri Lanka A saw out the fourth with something to spare. Mishara was out for 98 for the second match in a row, but home captain Sadeera Samarawickrama made up for a golden duck in the first innings with 151*, which included 26 fours and a six. The Shaheens' wicketkeeper Mohammad Haris took six catches in the first innings.*

First one-day international At Dambulla, November 11, 2021. **Pakistan Shaheens won by six wickets. Sri Lanka A 102** (32.2 overs) (P. H. K. D. Mendis 34; Khurram Shehzad 3-19, Abbas Afridi 4-30); **‡Pakistan Shaheens 103-4** (21.2 overs) (Omair Bin Yousuf 38). *The home side's batting problems continued: both openers departed for ducks, and soon it was 19-4. Abbas Afridi, a 20-year-old seamer, took four wickets. The only hiccup during the Shaheens' chase came when off-spinner Ashian Daniel – also 20 – struck twice in three balls to make it 76-4.*

Second one-day international At Dambulla, November 13, 2021. **No result. Pakistan Shaheens 0-0** (1 over) **v ‡Sri Lanka A.**

Third one-day international At Dambulla, November 15, 2021. **No result. Pakistan Shaheens 167-4** (32 overs) (Omair Bin Yousuf 59, Saud Shakil 59*) **v ‡Sri Lanka A.**

SOUTH AFRICA A v INDIA A

A-Team Test matches (3): South Africa A 0, India A 0

A month before their senior sides locked horns in a Test series, the A-Teams of South Africa and India played three four-day games. All were drawn, with quick scoring difficult on slowish pitches at Bloemfontein's Maungaung Oval. Of the tourists, captain Priyank Panchal and Hanuma Vihari would return for the Tests (Vihari played at Johannesburg when Virat Kohli was injured), while Deepak Chahar and Ishan Kishan took part in the ODIs that followed. The giant left-arm paceman Marco Jansen caught the eye for the home side with six wickets and a fighting 70 not out; he made his full Test debut shortly afterwards.

Touring party *P. K. Panchal, R. N. B. Apparajith, D. L. Chahar, R. D. Chahar, A. R. Easwaran, K. Gowtham, S. N. Khan, I. P. Kishan, A. R. Nagwaswalla, D. B. Padikkal, I. C. Porel, N. Saini, Saurabh Kumar, P. P. Shaw, Umran Malik, G. H. Vihari, U. D. Yadav. *Coach: S. H. Kotak. Kishan and D. L. Chahar were late additions to the squad.

First Test At Bloemfontein, November 23–26, 2021. **Drawn. South Africa A 509-7 dec** (135.3 overs) (P. J. Malan 163, T. de Zorzi 117, J. F. Smith 52, S. Qeshile 82*, G. F. Linde 51); **‡India A 308-4** (93.1 overs) (P. P. Shaw 48, P. K. Panchal 96, A. R. Easwaran 103). *PoM: P. J. Malan. First-class debut: Umran Malik (India A). Rain washed out the final day, but the match already seemed destined for a draw. Centuries from captain Pieter Malan and Tony de Zorzi, who came together at 14-2 and added 217, were followed by middle-order application to take South Africa A's total past 500. India A also hunkered down: after a 45-ball cameo from Prithvi Shaw, skipper Priyank Panchal put on 142 with Abhimanyu Easwaran.*

Second Test At Bloemfontein, November 30–December 3, 2021. **Drawn. ‡South Africa A 297** (105.5 overs) (S. J. Erwee 38, R. van Tonder 34, M. Z. Hamza 31, S. Qeshile 32, G. F. Linde 44, M. Jansen 70*; N. Saini 3-67, I. C. Porel 3-49) **and 212** (58.5 overs) (S. J. Erwee 41, P. J. Malan 31, R. van Tonder 33; I. C. Porel 3-33); **India A 276** (74.5 overs) (P. P. Shaw 42, G. H. Vihari 54, I. P. Kishan 49, S. N. Khan 71*; G. A. Stuurman 4-48, M. Jansen 3-44) **and 155-3** (41.3 overs) (A. R. Easwaran 55, G. H. Vihari 72*; G. A. Stuurman 3-51). *PoM: G. H. Vihari. A rain-shortened third day harmed chances of a positive result, as India A's eventual target of 234 proved out of reach. The highlight of South Africa A's first innings was 70* from No. 8 Marco Jansen, the 6ft 9in left-arm seamer who would soon make his full Test debut. Hanuma Vihari then applied himself for four hours for 54, before Sarfaraz Khan's more forthright 71. India A looked favourites when the home side dipped to 123-6 – only 144 ahead – but Jansen and Glenton Stuurman extended the lead. Stuurman then took three wickets, giving him seven in the match, but Vihari spent another three hours at the crease.*

Third Test   At Bloemfontein, December 6–9, 2021. **Drawn.** ‡**South Africa A 268** (94.5 overs) (S. J. Erwee 75, T. de Zorzi 58, K. Zondo 56; D. L. Chahar 4-45, N. Saini 3-51) **and 311-3 dec** (86 overs) (S. J. Erwee 97, M. Z. Hamza 125*, T. de Zorzi 33); **India A 276** (90.1 overs) (G. H. Vihari 63, I. P. Kishan 91; M. Jansen 3-48, L. L. Sipamla 5-99) **and 90-3** (17 overs) (P. P. Shaw 38). *PoM:* L. L. Sipamla. *Both sides found it hard to push the scoring along, averaging around three an over in their respective first innings. India A pinched a narrow lead, thanks to adhesive innings from Vihari (63 from 170 balls) and Ishan Kishan (91 from 153) in the face of probing spells from Jansen and Lutho Sipamla. When South Africa A batted again, Sarel Erwee and Zubayr Hamza also took their time, sharing a second-wicket stand of 178 in 54 overs; Hamza's eventual 125* lasted four minutes short of six hours, while Erwee batted for 628 minutes in the match for his 172 runs. The players shook hands after 17 overs of India A's second innings.*

For Australia A v England Lions, see page 900.

THE LEADING ASSOCIATE NATIONS IN 2021

For the first 11 months, 2021 could hardly have gone better for Namibian cricket: the national team held their own at the T20 World Cup in the UAE, and the ICC announced that Namibia, along with South Africa and Zimbabwe, would co-host the 2027 World Cup. Preparation for the trip to the Gulf had gone well, with successful home series against Uganda, an Emerging South Africa team, a Zimbabwean invitation side and the South African Titans. There were warm-up victories over the UAE, Scotland and Papua New Guinea (twice) and, though they did lose to Oman and Scotland, they were clearly ready for their T20 World Cup debut.

After their opening game brought heavy defeat by Sri Lanka, **Namibia** – the lowest-ranked of the 16 teams – handsomely beat the Netherlands and Ireland to book a place in the Super 12 stage. Next came victory against Scotland, when Ruben Trumpelmann provided one of the tournament's highlights: three wickets in an electrifying first over. Afghanistan ended the run, and there were defeats by three other Test nations, but by getting this far Namibia automatically qualified for the 2022 T20 World Cup. Players such as Trumpelmann, David Wiese (sixth-highest run-scorer, with 227 at 45), captain Gerhard Erasmus (who overcame a broken finger to hit 151 at 21), medium-pacer Jan Frylinck and spinner Bernard Scholtz all enhanced their reputations.

But in late November, the emergence of Covid's Omicron variant in neighbouring South Africa ruined a three-team instalment of World Cup League Two in Windhoek. Oman and Namibia met twice, with each winning once, before the fixtures were cancelled; the UAE never took the field.

On the local scene, Windhoek High School Old Boys reasserted their dominance of club cricket when they won the 50-over Premier League title for the second year in a row. In the final, they overcame Wanderers by nine wickets, with Craig Williams scoring 68 and Wimpie Viljoen an unbeaten 63.

Nepal found new stars, and a new controversy. Coached by Dav Whatmore (who had guided Sri Lanka to World Cup glory in 1996), they adopted a fearless approach – winning hearts and matches. In April, Nepal beat the Netherlands and Malaysia in a home T20 tournament. The elegant batter Kushal Bhurtel, who made his debut in the tri-series, became the first to score half-centuries in his first three T20 internationals; he then made it four in five.

In September, Nepal went to Oman, where they won two ODIs against PNG, before playing four League Two matches, against Oman and the USA, winning and losing to both. Whatmore resigned during the trip, ending a successful year-long stint; pressures caused by the pandemic were a factor. Against PNG, Nepal's globe-trotting spinner Sandeep Lamichhane claimed four for 35, followed by a national-record six for 11, while Rohit Paudel made 86 and 62 not out. Pubudu Dassanayake, the Sri Lankan-Canadian who had coached Nepal from 2011 to 2015, was reappointed in December.

When he arrived, Nepali cricket was in the throes of a serious dispute. National captain Gyanendra Malla, vice-captain Dipendra Singh Airee and two other players had spoken publicly of their dissatisfaction with the handling of central contracts, and were sacked by the Cricket Association of Nepal, who

Mountain Man: Sandeep Lamichhane took 31 international wickets in 2021, at nine each.

made Lamichhane captain. However, at least half a dozen other players supported Malla, and they boycotted a training camp in late December. Dassanayake will need to sort out the situation if the team are going to cope with a busy schedule in 2022.

The Netherlands had not played since November 2019, and a rusty T20 squad travelled, 18 months later, to Nepal for a triangular tournament also involving Malaysia. They beat both other teams once, and tied their second game against Malaysia, before being flattened by the hosts in the final. In May, they shared a two-match one-day series against Scotland in Rotterdam, then moved on to Utrecht for three 50-over encounters with Ireland as part of the World Cup Super League. Despite being understrength, the Netherlands prevailed 2–1. These games were the first to be broadcast live on Dutch TV.

Then in October came the T20 World Cup, when the county players would bolster the team. But any optimism didn't last long: the Netherlands crashed to three defeats, the most humiliating at the hands of Sri Lanka, who dismissed them for 44 (their second-lowest total, behind the 39 they made, also against Sri Lanka, in this tournament in 2013-14). Ryan ten Doeschate retired from all cricket on the morning of the rout. His international debut had been in 2006, and his final ODI average of 67 was at the end of 2021 the highest by any player, male or female. The Netherlands were due to play three ODIs – part of the World Cup Super League – against South Africa in Centurion towards the end of the year. The first was ruined by rain, the last two by Omicron.

For the top tier (*Topklasse*) only, there was a full domestic programme. Punjab of Rotterdam became national champions for the first time, while neighbours VOC won the T20 Cup. Kampong of Utrecht and Salland of Deventer were promoted from the league below. Of the 12 teams in the *Topklasse*, six have grass wickets, the highest number yet.

In the autumn, Clayton Floyd became the first century-maker in the inaugural ten-over European Cricket Championship, held on the Costa del Sol. He made 115 from 25 balls for the Dutch team against Romania, and was named the MVP. Meanwhile, at La Manga, Frédérique Overdijk snatched seven for three against France, the best T20 international figures by anyone, male or female. Her colleague Sterre Kalis earned a full-time contract with Northern Diamonds.

Oman took advantage of an opportunity brought about by the pandemic. The T20 World Cup was forced to relocate from India to the UAE, and Oman – who were taking part – offered to provide a venue. Pankaj Khimji, chair of Oman Cricket, invited ICC officials to look at the facilities, and they were so impressed they gave the Al Amerat stadium – in the mountains above Muscat – six first round matches. Oman opened the tournament by hosting PNG, whom they bested by ten wickets. Although they then underperformed against Bangladesh and Scotland, the Muscat venue attracted large, exuberant crowds, which was not always the case at the tournament's other venues in the UAE. (Afghanistan are considering using the ground for Tests.)

Oman's preparations had not been ideal: from October 2020 to September 2021, they had not taken the field and, when matches did restart, they were in the 50-over format of League Two. They enjoyed a run of four home wins – against Nepal, USA (twice) and PNG – before losing to Scotland; the chance for instant revenge disappeared in a rainstorm. Oman entertained Sri Lanka in a couple of 20-over practice games before the World Cup. In late November, they flew to Namibia for the resumption of League Two, but Omicron intervened after two matches against the hosts. However, they ended 2021 comfortably top of the table.

Papua New Guinea's international campaign in 2021 was compressed into 46 days across September and October, and did not go well. The appointment in March of Australian-born Italian cricketer Carl Sandri as coach barely made a difference, and PNG's losing streak in ODIs, stalled by almost two years without a fixture, reached 16. In 2019, they had taken comfort from an excellent T20 run, but now lost all five games, including three at the World Cup. Their maiden appearance at the tournament was perhaps most eye-catching for their dazzling shirts. A 17-run defeat by Scotland was as good as it got.

There was no cricket for the women's side, who were forced to withdraw from the 50-over World Cup Qualifier after several tested positive for Covid shortly before departure for Zimbabwe. Their regional T20 World Cup Qualifier was cancelled, with PNG progressing by virtue of their ranking. The pandemic also put paid to the regional qualifier for the Under-19 World Cup, though PNG's recent record was good enough for them to reach the tournament, held in the Caribbean early in 2022.

It was perhaps indicative of the year that the planned finale to the domestic season – a match between the best players from Hanuabada and the best from the rest of the country – was postponed because of flooding at Amini Park.

For three months from September, the **UAE** became the centre of world cricket. First, the interrupted IPL was played to its conclusion across Abu Dhabi, Dubai and Sharjah. With one day's gap, the same venues then hosted the T20 World Cup. Once that was done, it was on to the Abu Dhabi T10.

Throughout, the leading players of the host nation were the ghosts at the feast. Amid the fog of a corruption scandal from two years earlier, the UAE had failed to qualify for a World Cup scheduled for Australia in 2020. The fact it was switched to the Emirates made their omission galling – more so when the UAE outplayed Ireland in Dubai, a series organised to give the Irish practice for the World Cup. At the start of the year, they had beaten them in the first one-day international of a Covid-afflicted series that ended 1–1.

To cap it all, UAE players even missed out on a pay day at the Abu Dhabi T10 League – their own domestic franchise competition. The event clashed with a rearranged tour of Namibia for a League Two tri-series, also involving Oman. And that too was scuppered on the day of the UAE's first match, when the onset of the Omicron variant prompted a hasty retreat.

If the year starts with the number two, then it must be another year in which **USA** makes more headlines off the field than on. The failure to hold constitutionally mandated elections – a recurring theme of the USACA era – blighted USA Cricket in only their fourth year of existence. So much for the lofty promises of 2018, when they claimed they would not repeat the sins of their predecessor (which had prompted their expulsion by the ICC).

In March, two board members sued half their fellow directors, plus CEO Iain Higgins, over alleged constitutional violations that contributed to the failure to hold elections on time. The suit, initially dismissed on procedural grounds, was refiled, and the legal wrangling continued into 2022. Whether for this or for other reasons, Higgins resigned in November, after a little more than two years in the role. There may be light at the end of the tunnel: days after Higgins's departure, the USA were awarded co-hosting rights – along with Cricket West Indies – for the 2024 men's T20 World Cup.

After almost 18 months without internationals, the USA made a splash in their second match back. In Oman in September, Jaskaran Singh Malhotra cracked 16 sixes against Papua New Guinea, including six in an over. He finished unbeaten on 173, the first ODI hundred for the USA. The second, by Monank Patel, came four days later against Nepal, though in a losing cause.

Both the USA women and men produced dominant performances to win their T20 World Cup regional qualifiers. And Christmas came three days early when the men beat Ireland by 26 runs in Florida, their first T20 win over a Full Member. They triumphed despite losing key players Steven Taylor, Aaron Jones and Karima Gore to Covid. That victory underscored their promise on the field. If only they can get things right off it.

Reporting by Helge Schutz, Ujjwal Acharya, Dave Hardy, Paul Bird, Andrew Nixon, Paul Radley and Peter Della Penna.

CRICKET IN SCOTLAND IN 2021

Knocking on the door

WILLIAM DICK

Following the famine of the previous year, 2021 was a comparative feast for Scottish cricket. After winning a T20 international against Zimbabwe in Edinburgh, history was made when the national team made it past the group stage of a global tournament for the first time, reaching the Super 12s at the T20 World Cup in October. Though they then lost five out of five, their earlier performances – particularly a victory over Bangladesh – raised the profile of the sport at home, and of Scottish cricket more widely.

Tony Brian, the chair of Cricket Scotland, was optimistic about the chances of Test status: "Beating Bangladesh, who were then ranked sixth, is a fairly major upset, and the sort of thing that gets you on people's radars." Already a director at the ICC, Brian has some lobbying to do. Of the 30 criteria that must be met, Scotland fail to meet only one: to have beaten four Full Members, ranked in the top ten, in an ODI or T20 in the last eight years, ICC tournaments excluded. Under this criterion, Scotland have beaten only England (in 2018), but have requested a rule change, to reflect the increase in Full Members to 12, which would add victories over Ireland (2019) and Zimbabwe (2021). "That's a discussion to take place with the ICC," says Brian. "I think people will listen." The ICC were due to review Scotland's application in the summer of 2023.

They remained in contention for a place in the 2023 World Cup, thanks to a pair of 50-over victories against Papua New Guinea and one against Oman in a qualifying tournament in September. Played in Muscat, the round robin nearly brought a second win against the hosts, only for Cyclone Shaheen to blow in, recalling a washout against the United Arab Emirates two years earlier, when rare rain came to Sharjah.

Though the seniors were successful, the Under-19s suffered a major disappointment by failing to reach their World Cup in January 2022. Having beaten Ireland in the group stage of the qualifying tournament, they lost to them in the final.

Scotland's women continued their steady progress towards the 2023 T20 World Cup, topping their group in Europe to reach the global qualifying tournament. The Bryce sisters, Kathryn and Sarah, along with Abtaha Maqsood, featured in the inaugural edition of The Hundred.

In the domestic season, Heriot's won a memorable Eastern Premier League and Scottish Cup double, while Clydesdale prevailed in a final-day decider against Ferguslie to take the Western Premier League title; there was no play-off to determine the national champions. Carlton completed a treble of sorts, winning the men's and women's T20 cups, plus the women's Premier League. The Regional Pro50 – contested by representative teams from the east, west and Highlands, plus an Academy side – was won by Western Warriors. An inaugural Women's Super Series featured two teams – coached by Peter Ross and Daniel Sutton – in a ten-match T20 series, which they drew.

Domestic honours
Eastern Premier League **Heriot's**. Western Premier League **Clydesdale**. Scottish Cup **Heriot's**. Men's Twenty20 Cup **Carlton**. Regional Pro50 **Western Warriors**. Women's Premier League **Carlton**. Women's Twenty20 Cup **Carlton**. Women's Super Series **Ross XI** and **Sutton XI** (shared).

UNITED ARAB EMIRATES v IRELAND IN 2020-21

One-day internationals (2): UAE 1, Ireland 1

Five months had elapsed since Ireland's last international. If that offered plenty of time to savour an exhilarating victory over World Cup winners England in Southampton, it offered nothing in terms of development. By the time their team were eventually reunited, they were desperate to resume. The main focus of the trip to Abu Dhabi was a three-match Super League series against Afghanistan, but first they had four matches against the hosts. On the eve of the series, Kevin O'Brien said the target was nothing less than a 4–0 win.

For reasons many and varied, it did not work as planned. First, the UAE proved unexpectedly obstinate: Ireland had won all six previous one-day encounters and, when they had last met, in March 2018, the margin of victory was 226 runs, the biggest in their history. Yet the UAE began with a comfortable win in the opening match, thanks to hundreds from C. P. Rizwan and Mohammad Usman. And in the days that followed, it looked as though there might be no chance for revenge.

On the morning of the first match, the UAE had announced that two players had tested positive for Covid-19; the game went ahead but, after more cases emerged in the next few days, the remaining matches were suspended. The local authorities were using the track-and-trace technology that had helped facilitate the return of international cricket in the UK in 2020, and allowed a successful IPL to be staged in the UAE a few months earlier. The upshot was the home players had to isolate in their hotel rooms for eight days, throwing the tour into doubt. The second and third games were cancelled, and the last delayed until four days after the series had originally been due to finish.

It meant that Ireland, who had avoided the disease, were again kicking their heels. In order to fill the time, they organised a practice game against Afghanistan in the nine-day break between the two ODIs. They lost, but it seemed to galvanise them. As unsatisfactory as the series was, Ireland were at least able to halve it, thanks to a straightforward win inspired by Simi Singh, who contributed two career-bests: a maiden fifty and figures of five for ten constituted a good day's work. PAUL RADLEY

First one-day international   At Abu Dhabi, January 8, 2021. **United Arab Emirates won by six wickets. ‡Ireland 269-5** (50 overs) (P. R. Stirling 131*, A. Balbirnie 53); **United Arab Emirates 270-4** (49 overs) (C. P. Rizwan 109, Mohammad Usman 102*). *PoM:* C. P. Rizwan. *ODI debuts:* A. Sharafu, Kashif Daud (UAE). *As an electrical engineer for a construction company, C. P. Rizwan had worked throughout the UAE's lockdown in 2020. When time permitted, his wife, Fathima, would give him throwdowns in the front room of their flat in Sharjah. It seemed to do the trick. The UAE celebrated their return to competitive cricket for the first time in nearly 11 months with only their second ODI victory over an ICC Full Member, having beaten Zimbabwe in March 2018. Rizwan, who reached his maiden century from his 131st ball, gained invaluable support from fellow centurion Mohammad Usman. They came together at 51-3, and added 184 – a UAE record for any wicket – to put the pursuit of 270 beyond doubt. Usman hit the winning run from his 107th delivery, having reached his first ODI century with a four from his 106th ball. Ireland had relied on Paul Stirling, whose 131* was his tenth, and second in a row, after walloping 142 against England the previous August.*

Second one-day international   At Abu Dhabi, January 12, 2021. **Cancelled.**

Third one-day international   At Abu Dhabi, January 14, 2021. **Cancelled.**

Fourth one-day international   At Abu Dhabi, January 18, 2021. **Ireland won by 112 runs. Ireland 228-6** (50 overs) (H. T. Tector 33, L. J. Tucker 42, C. Campher 56, S. Singh 54*; Zahoor Khan 3-35); **‡United Arab Emirates 116** (36 overs) (S. Singh 5-10). *PoM:* S. Singh. *PoS:* C. Campher. *After a few false starts because of the Covid-19 outbreak in the UAE camp, it was announced – with less than a day's warning – that the sides would meet for a second and final time. Put in, Ireland lurched to 10-3, with the experienced trio of Kevin O'Brien, Stirling and Andy Balbirnie gone by the fifth over. The clatter of wickets slowed, before Curtis Campher, striking his third half-century in his fourth ODI innings, and Simi Singh (his first in 20) put on 91 to help lift the tourists to 228. Singh had barely started: his off-spin then claimed the UAE's top five to derail their chase, and he ended with 10–4–10–5.*

NAMIBIA v UGANDA IN 2020-21

Twenty20 internationals (3): Namibia 3, Uganda 0

Captained by wicketkeeper Arnold Otwani, Uganda gained valuable experience during a short tour of Namibia in April. There were three T20 internationals: Namibia won them all, though the Ugandans had a sniff in the second match. They reduced Namibia to 34 for four, but made a poor start themselves and were behind on DLS when it rained. The trip concluded with two 50-over matches (not official ODIs, as Uganda do not have that status); Namibia won both. Ronak Patel scored 105 in the first game, to help Uganda recover from nine for four, while Stephen Baard hammered 145 for Namibia in the second.

First Twenty20 international At Windhoek, April 3, 2021. **Namibia won by seven wickets.** ‡**Uganda 134-5** (20 overs) (R. B. Patel 35*); **Namibia 135-3** (14.5 overs) (M. G. Erasmus 62*). *PoM:* M. G. Erasmus. *T20I debuts:* M. D. du Preez, J. N. Loftie-Eaton (Namibia); C. Kyewuta, R. B. Patel (Uganda). *Namibia were 12-2 in the chase, but their captain, Gerhard Erasmus, stopped the rot with 62* from 36 balls.*

Second Twenty20 international At Windhoek, April 5, 2021. **Namibia won by 20 runs** (DLS). ‡**Namibia 134-6** (20 overs) (J. J. Smit 40, M. D. du Preez 33*; Riazat Ali Shah 3-23); **Uganda 65-5** (12.4 overs) (K. Waiswa 33). *PoM:* J. J. Smit. *T20I debuts:* Saud Islam, J. Sebanja (Uganda). *After two wickets in four balls from seamer Riazat Ali Shah, Namibia dipped to 34-4. They scrambled another 100, then Uganda also began badly (16-4). Ronak Patel (19*) shored things up, but Kenneth Waiswa fell to the last ball before rain set in, leaving Uganda's DLS target 86.*

Third Twenty20 international At Windhoek, April 5, 2021. **Namibia won by 65 runs.** ‡**Namibia 189-3** (20 overs) (C. G. Williams 81, J. P. Kotze 37, J. J. Smit 35*); **Uganda 124** (20 overs) (Riazat Ali Shah 33; T. Lungameni 3-30, J. N. Frylinck 3-21). *PoM:* C. G. Williams. *Craig Williams's 81 from 49 balls was his highest score in T20Is, and lifted Namibia to a total that proved more than enough.*

NEPAL TWENTY20 TRI-SERIES IN 2021

1 Nepal   2 Netherlands   3 Malaysia

Nepal shrugged off the late withdrawal of their long-serving former captain Paras Khadka, who had suffered a shoulder injury; he would retire a few months later. The 24-year-old opener Khushal Bhurtel started his international career with 62, 61 not out and 62, and added 77 in the final, in which Nepal steamrollered the Netherlands, who were handicapped by the absence of their English county players. The third team were Malaysia, who almost upset the Dutch in a rain-affected tie.

At Kirtipur, April 17, 2021. **Nepal won by nine wickets. Netherlands 136-4** (20 overs) (S. A. Edwards 30, B. F. W. de Leede 41); ‡**Nepal 141-1** (15 overs) (K. Bhurtel 62, Aasif Sheikh 54*). *PoM:* K. Bhurtel. *T20I debuts:* S. Alam, K. Bhurtel, Aasif Sheikh (Nepal); A. Dutt, J. L. de Mey (Netherlands). *Debutant Khushal Bhurtel and his opening partner, Aasif Sheikh, settled the match with a stand of 116 in 12.4 overs.*

At Kirtipur, April 18, 2021. **Netherlands won by 15 runs.** ‡**Netherlands 191-2** (20 overs) (M. P. O'Dowd 133*, S. A. Edwards 31); **Malaysia 176-8** (20 overs) (Virandeep Singh 87). *PoM:* M. P. O'Dowd. *New Zealand-born Max O'Dowd extended the Netherlands' first T20I century to the fifth-highest score in the format; the previous-best by an Associate batsman was George Munsey's 127* for Scotland v Netherlands at Malahide in September 2019. In all, O'Dowd hit 15 fours and six sixes from 73 balls. Malaysia slipped to 20-3 in the fourth over of the chase, but Virandeep Singh kept them interested.*

At Kirtipur, April 19, 2021. **Nepal won by nine wickets. Malaysia 109** (16.5 overs) (K. C. Karan 3-17); ‡**Nepal 113-1** (12.1 overs) (K. Bhurtel 61*, Aasif Sheikh 42). *PoM:* K. C. Karan. *Bhurtel slammed five sixes (and three fours) in a 26-ball half-century, and shared another century opening stand with Sheikh (102 this time).*

At Kirtipur, April 20, 2021. **Netherlands won by three wickets.** ‡Nepal 206-6 (20 overs) (K. Bhurtel 62, D. S. Airee 60); **Netherlands 209-7** (19.3 overs) (B. N. Cooper 55, B. F. W. de Leede 81*, P. M. Seelaar 31; S. Lamichhane 4-48). PoM: B. F. W. de Leede. *Bhurtel made his third half-century in three matches, before Dipendra Airee biffed 60 from 30, with five sixes. Ben Cooper and Bas de Leede both reached 50 in 32 balls, with de Leede – whose previous-highest in the format was 41 – going on to 81* from 42, with five sixes and seven fours, as the Netherlands chased down their lofty target.*

At Kirtipur, April 21, 2021. **Tied** (DLS). **Netherlands 107-4** (13 overs) (B. N. Cooper 54*, P. M. Seelaar 37); ‡**Malaysia 91-4** (10 overs) (Syed Aziz 30). PoM: B. N. Cooper. *The Netherlands almost slipped up in a rain-affected match. First they declined to 22-3 in the fourth, before being rescued by Cooper (54 off 32) and captain Pieter Seelaar. Malaysia's target was revised to 92 in ten, and they looked on course at 57-0 in the seventh, only to be pegged back. They needed two from the last two balls, but Vivian Kingma trapped Aminuddin Ramly, then Sharvin Muniandy could only scamper a bye to tie.*

At Kirtipur, April 22, 2021. **Nepal won by 69 runs.** Nepal 217-7 (20 overs) (Aasif Sheikh 42, G. Malla 41, D. S. Airee 33, K. C. Karan 45); ‡**Malaysia 148** (19.1 overs) (Ahmed Faiz 31, Aminuddin Ramly 41; S. Kami 3-20, S. Lamichhane 3-42, K. S. Airee 3-16). PoM: S. Kami. *T20I debut: K. S. Airee (Nepal). Malaysia were never in the hunt after another solid batting performance from Nepal, which included 19 sixes (and nine fours). K. C. Karan hit seven in a 13-ball 45; seamer Dhivendran Mogan's four overs cost 63.*

NEPAL 6pts, NETHERLANDS 5pts, Malaysia 1pt.

Final At Kirtipur, April 24, 2021. **Nepal won by 142 runs.** Nepal 238-3 (20 overs) (K. Bhurtel 77, G. Malla 33, K. Malla 50*, D. S. Airee 48*); ‡**Netherlands 96** (17.2 overs) (K. C. Karan 3-11). PoM: K. C. Karan. *The final was disappointingly one-sided: the Netherlands crumbled after Nepal hurtled to the highest score of the tournament. At 17 years 50 days, Kushal Malla was the youngest to score a half-century in a T20 international, though he lost the record to Gibraltar's Louis Bruce (16) in August; his 50* came from 24 balls, and included five of his side's 15 sixes. Leg-spinner Sandeep Lamichhane finished the tournament with 13 wickets, six more than Karan; team-mate Bhurtel topped the run-scorers with 278 in his maiden series.*

NETHERLANDS v SCOTLAND IN 2021

One-day internationals (2): Netherlands 1, Scotland 1

Scotland's brief tour of the Netherlands in May gave both teams an opportunity to play outside their World Cup qualification tournaments. Together with the absence of spectators, this lent proceedings an informal air. In an unusually wet spring, the first game was reduced to 33 overs, and the second brought forward a day to avoid a likely washout. Despite sitting a tier higher than Scotland in the ICC pyramid, the Netherlands were far from clear favourites. With much of their side playing county cricket, their batting looked fragile, but their seam attack had depth. Scotland were nearly at full strength, and their more experienced middle order helped them square the series.   Bertus de Jong

First one-day international At Rotterdam, May 19. **Netherlands won by 14 runs.** ‡**Netherlands 163-8** (33 overs) (M. P. O'Dowd 82); **Scotland 149-3** (33 overs) (V. J. Kingma 3-21). *ODI debuts: L. V. van Beek, A. Dutt (Netherlands). Morning rain threatened an abandonment, but allowed a 33-over contest. Opener Max O'Dowd held the Netherlands together with 82, supported by Logan van Beek (24) at No. 8; they added 42, the highest partnership. Needing 164, Scotland slumped to 31-3 against Vivian Kingma (who finished with a career-best 3-21) and Paul van Meekeren (2-28). Richie Berrington (41) and George Munsey (27) were both dropped while adding 69, but the recovery faltered when the quicks returned: 100-3 became 121-7, which left too much for the tail.*

Second one-day international At Rotterdam, May 20. **Scotland won by six wickets.** ‡**Netherlands 171** (48.4 overs) (S. A. Edwards 56; A. C. Evans 5-43); **Scotland 172-4** (42.1 overs) (H. G. Munsey 79*). *ODI debut: P. R. P. Boissevain (Netherlands). A bad forecast and good sense brought the second match forward a day. The Dutch chose to bat again, on a sluggish pitch. The seamers had the best of it: Ali Evans's 5-43 was his maiden ODI five-for, and the Netherlands were dismissed for 171. Wicketkeeper Scott Edwards top-scored with 56, his first half-century in senior cricket. Kingma* *and van Meekeren continued to prove a handful, reducing Scotland to 34-3, and debutant legspinner Phillipe Boissevain got Berrington. But that was the last fortune the hosts enjoyed, as George Munsey (79*) and Dylan Budge (40*) calmly accumulated 106* for the fifth wicket.*

NETHERLANDS v IRELAND IN 2021

One-day internationals (3): Netherlands 2 (20pts), Ireland 1 (10pts)

Since the teams last met in an ODI, in 2013, their paths had diverged markedly: Ireland had become a Test nation, while the Netherlands lost their ODI status and had to claw their way back up the pile. But they regained their status in 2018, and were the only non-Test team in the Super League. It was a disappointment they were denied their core middle order by county cricket; Ireland, meanwhile, were without the injured Curtis Campher and Gareth Delaney. Following a miserably wet May, Utrecht could offer only slow and uneven pitches for its first ODIs. It did not make for an ideal introduction for viewers of the first cricket broadcast live on Dutch television, despite a lastball thriller in the first game. BERTUS DE JONG

First one-day international At Utrecht, June 2. **Netherlands won by one run. ‡Netherlands 195** (50 overs) (T. van der Gugten 49; C. A. Young 3-34, J. B. Little 3-32); **Ireland 194-9** (50 overs) (P. R. Stirling 69, S. Singh 45; P. M. Seelaar 3-27). *Netherlands 10pts. PoM:* T. van der Gugten. The Netherlands held off Ireland's late challenge as a back-and-forth tussle went to the final ball. The Dutch were soon in trouble, when Josh Little's three quick wickets reduced them to 53-5. Bas de Leede and Saqib Zulfiqar added 49, but both went at 102, and it needed an eighth-wicket stand of 72 between Logan van Beek and Timm van der Gugten – who top-scored with 49 – to nurse the total to 195. Ireland were 11-3, before Paul Stirling, followed by Simi Singh, fought back. Little required three to win from the last delivery, bowled by van Beek, but his scoop brought only a single.

Second one-day international At Utrecht, June 4. **Ireland won by eight wickets. ‡Netherlands 157** (49.2 overs) (M. P. O'Dowd 36; C. A. Young 4-18, J. B. Little 4-39); **Ireland 158-2** (43 overs) (P. R. Stirling 52, A. Balbirnie 63*, H. T. Tector 30*). *Ireland 10pts. PoM:* J. B. Little. Ireland levelled the series after Craig Young and Little – with a career-best 4-39 – shared eight wickets. Stephan Myburgh and Max O'Dowd had begun with 44, but Little had Myburgh chopping on, and Ben Cooper caught behind fending at a lifter next ball. The hosts sank to 116-8, before van Beek and Brandon Glover put on 30. Even so, 158 was a paltry target and, if the pitch seemed a little flatter in the second innings, so did the bowling. William Porterfield was yorked by van Beek in the second over, but Ireland had plenty of time to accumulate. Stirling and captain Andrew Balbirnie shared 82, then Harry Tector added 67* with his skipper to see it through.

Third one-day international At Utrecht, June 7. **Netherlands won by four wickets. ‡Ireland 163** (49.2 overs) (H. T. Tector 58, G. H. Dockrell 40; F. J. Klaassen 3-23, L. V. van Beek 3-29); **Netherlands 166-6** (45.5 overs) (S. J. Myburgh 74, M. P. O'Dowd 36; S. Singh 3-29). *Netherlands 10pts. PoM:* S. J. Myburgh. *ODI debut:* Musa Ahmed (Netherlands). The Netherlands claimed the series after an Irish collapse gave them a chasable target of 164. Fred Klaassen had ended Kevin O'Brien's final ODI innings for a four-ball duck. Tector and George Dockrell came together at 28-3 and added 89, but Dockrell's dismissal triggered a slide of seven for 46 as the Dutch seamers ran amok. Myburgh clipped the first ball of the Netherlands reply – bowled by Barry McCarthy – for six, and went on to the highest score of the series. After an opening stand of 66 with O'Dowd, he was eventually fourth out, six short of victory, but Ireland's late wickets were in vain.

PAPUA NEW GUINEA v USA IN OMAN IN 2021

One-day internationals (2): Papua New Guinea 0, USA 2

Papua New Guinea, captained by Asad Vala, warmed up for their World Cup League Two matches in Oman with two ODIs against both the USA and Nepal. They lost all four – and things did not improve, as they then lost all four League Two matches as well. In the second game against the USA, the shell-shocked Papuans had to watch Jaskaran Singh Malhotra blast 173 not out, including 16 sixes – six in the final over of the innings.

First one-day international   At Al Amerat, September 6, 2021. **USA won by seven wickets.** ‡**Papua New Guinea 158** (44.2 overs) (A. Vala 61, S. Bau 31; N. P. Kenjige 3-22, N. K. Patel 4-30); **USA 159-3** (28.2 overs) (S. R. Taylor 82, M. D. Patel 34*). *PoM:* S. R. Taylor. *ODI debuts:* S. J. Modani, G. Singh (USA). *PNG's captain Asad Vala held his side's innings together with 61, but the USA completed a routine victory, opener Steve Taylor hitting seven sixes in his 55-ball 82.*

Second one-day international   At Al Amerat, September 9, 2021. **USA won by 134 runs. USA 271-9** (50 overs) (J. S. Malhotra 173*); ‡**Papua New Guinea 137** (37.1 overs) (L. Siaka 30, N. Vanua 30; A. A. Paradkar 4-26). *PoM:* J. S. Malhotra. *ODI debut:* A. A. Paradkar (USA). *Jaskaran Singh Malhotra, whose previous-highest in ODIs was 18, hit 16 sixes – six in the last over of the innings, from seamer Gaudi Toka – as he extended the USA's first century in ODIs to a towering 173*, the highest by a No. 5 in the format, beating a record held by A. B. de Villiers. Only Scotland's Calum MacLeod, with 175 against Canada in 2013-14, had made a bigger score for a current Associate nation, although Paul Stirling hit 177 against Canada in 2010, before Ireland were granted Test status. Only Eoin Morgan, with 17 sixes in his 148 for England v Afghanistan in the 2019 World Cup, had hit more in an innings (there have been three other cases of 16, by de Villiers, Chris Gayle and Rohit Sharma). PNG barely made it halfway to their distant target, with the 20-year-old left-arm seamer Abhishek Paradkar taking four wickets on debut.*

NEPAL v PAPUA NEW GUINEA IN OMAN IN 2021

One-day internationals (2): Papua New Guinea 0, Nepal 2

Papua New Guinea's main problem was flaky batting – their highest total across the four matches against the USA and Nepal was just 158. They found Nepal's leg-spinner Sandeep Lamichhane almost impossible to read: he had overall figures of ten for 46.

First one-day international   At Al Amerat, September 7, 2021. **Nepal won by two wickets.** ‡**Papua New Guinea 134** (33 overs) (L. Siaka 30; S. Lamichhane 4-35); **Nepal 135-8** (39.3 overs) (Aasif Sheikh 30, R. K. Paudel 41; G. Toka 3-18). *PoM:* S. Lamichhane. *ODI debuts:* K. Bhurtel, Aasif Sheikh, B. Sob (Nepal). *Nepal were making a hash of a regulation chase when they dipped to 82-7 in the 28th, after Gaudi Toka took two in two – but Rohit Kumar Paudel and Sompal Kami (22*) put on 52 to take the scores level. Nepal seamer Bikram Sob had earlier taken the wicket of Tony Ura with his first ball in international cricket.*

Second one-day international   At Al Amerat, September 10, 2021 (day/night). **Nepal won by 151 runs.** ‡**Nepal 233** (49.3 overs) (G. Malla 45, R. K. Paudel 86, K. C. Karan 42; C. A. Soper 3-45); **Papua New Guinea 82** (19.1 overs) (S. Lamichhane 6-11). *PoM:* S. Lamichhane. *ODI debut:* K. V. Morea (PNG). *After restricting Nepal to 233, in which the highlight was Paudel's careful 86, PNG looked for a morale-boosting victory. But they were soon 11-2, then folded to Sandeep Lamichhane's leg-breaks and googlies. When he started his spell, PNG had 39-2; ten overs later, they were all out for 82, with Lamichhane improving his ODI-best figures to 6-11.*

SCOTLAND v ZIMBABWE IN 2021

Twenty20 internationals (3): Scotland 1, Zimbabwe 2

Scotland played their first T20 matches at home since 2018, and their victory over Zimbabwe was their third T20 triumph over a Test nation, after Bangladesh in Ireland. Though Scotland hit their highest home total in the decider, Zimbabwe clinched the series with a clinical chase.

First Twenty20 international   At Edinburgh, September 15. **Scotland won by seven runs.** ‡**Scotland 141-6** (20 overs) (R. D. Berrington 82*); **Zimbabwe 134-9** (20 overs) (M. Shumba 45*; S. M. Sharif 4-24). *PoM:* R. D. Berrington. *Richie Berrington's 82* off 61 enabled them to recover from 30-4, and set a target of 142. Zimbabwe rallied after losing Wesley Madhevere to the first ball of the innings, but fell short, despite a heroic 45* off 30 from Milton Shumba. Safyaan Sharif (4-24) equalled his career-best figures.*

Second Twenty20 international At Edinburgh, September 17. **Zimbabwe won by ten runs.** ‡**Zimbabwe 136-5** (20 overs) (C. R. Ervine 30, S. C. Williams 60*); **Scotland 126** (19.4 overs) (R. D. Berrington 42, M. H. Cross 42). *PoM:* R. Ngarava. *T20I* debut: I. Kaia (Zimbabwe). It was Zimbabwe's turn to defend a moderate score by a narrow margin; they had Craig Ervine and Stuart Williams's fourth-wicket stand of 71 to thank for their recovery from 20-3. Tendai Chatara (2-28) and Richard Ngarava (2-13) then had Scotland on the rack at 16-4, before Berrington and Matthew Cross rallied with 75. They needed 27 from 18 with five wickets in hand, but canny bowling from slow left-armer Wellington Masakadza shut the door on the chase.

Third Twenty20 international At Edinburgh, September 19. **Zimbabwe won by six wickets.** ‡**Scotland 177-4** (20 overs) (H. G. Munsey 54, R. D. Berrington 44, C. S. MacLeod 39*); **Zimbabwe 180-4** (19.1 overs) (W. N. Madhevere 43, M. Shumba 66*). *PoM:* M. Shumba. Scotland hit their highest home T20 total, but a riotous innings from Shumba took Zimbabwe to victory. George Munsey had got the hosts off to an explosive start with 54 off 30; his opening partner Kyle Coetzer made six and, when Oliver Hairs was out for eight, Scotland were 72-2. Berrington and MacLeod added 70. Needing 178, Zimbabwe were 63-3 in the tenth, before Shumba cut loose: his 29-ball 66* included two fours and six sixes, and formed the bulk of a fourth-wicket stand of 99 off 52 with Medhevere.

UNITED ARAB EMIRATES v NAMIBIA IN 2021-22

Twenty20 internationals (1): United Arab Emirates 0, Namibia 1

This final tune-up before the T20 World Cup was a mishmash of seven games called the Summer T20 Bash: a one-off between the United Arab Emirates and Namibia (their first meeting), a three-match rubber between the UAE and Ireland, and a tri-series featuring Namibia, Scotland and Papua New Guinea.

In the first of these, Sussex all-rounder David Wiese made his debut for Namibia – the country of his father's birth – after playing the last of his 26 internationals for South Africa in 2016. Now a veteran of seven T20 tournaments around the world, his presence galvanised his adoptive team. His new team-mate Jan Frylinck, also born in South Africa, became the second seamer, after Deepak Chahar, to take six wickets in a T20 international (two more six-fors would follow, for Nigeria and Uganda, by the end of the month). PAUL RADLEY

At Dubai (ICC Academy), October 5, 2021. **Namibia won by 17 runs.** Namibia **159-8** (20 overs) (S. J. Baard 39, C. G. Williams 57; Zahoor Khan 4-29); ‡**United Arab Emirates 142-9** (20 overs) (Waseem Muhammad 39; J. N. Frylinck 6-24). *PoM:* J. N. Frylinck. *T20I debuts:* Kashif Daud, Waseem Muhammad (UAE); R. C. Trumpelmann (Namibia). Jan Frylinck, a South Africa-born leftarm seamer, became the fifth bowler to take a six-wicket haul in T20Is, grabbing victory for Namibia in their first match against the UAE, who had not played since February (they were also missing their coach, Robin Singh, who was with Mumbai Indians in the IPL). David Wiese had a quiet debut for Namibia, who owed their 159-8 to Craig Williams's 57 off 37. Zahoor Khan, who had been working with Chennai Super Kings as a net bowler, took three wickets in six balls to finish with 4-29, a career-best. Wiese dismissed Chirag Suri in the fifth over of the UAE reply, and then it was the Frylinck show.

UNITED ARAB EMIRATES v IRELAND IN 2021-22

Twenty20 internationals (3): United Arab Emirates 2, Ireland 1

Ireland expected to beat the UAE handsomely, but the second game exposed their over-reliance on openers Paul Stirling and Kevin O'Brien, and their series ended in defeat, insult and injury. A savage hundred by Waseem Muhammad, familiar to few outside the UAE, dented Irish egos, while their captain, Andy Balbirnie, was helped from the field after injuring his left foot trying to sweep. The UAE regarded their comeback as further proof that they should be playing in what they regarded as their home World Cup. They had missed out on qualification because of a corruption scandal which saw six of their players banned for a total of 41 years. PAUL RADLEY

At Dubai (ICC Academy), October 7, 2021. **Ireland won by seven wickets. ‡United Arab Emirates 123-7** (20 overs) (Mohammad Usman 35; C. Campher 3-19); **Ireland 124-3** (18.5 overs) (P. R. Stirling 53, K. J. O'Brien 46; Basil Hameed 3-20). PoM: C. Campher. T20I debut: S. M. Sharma (UAE). *Even allowing for the UAE's rustiness – and the slowness of the pitch – their performance was supine. They laboured against the medium-pace of Josh Little and Curtis Campher: only Mohammad Usman passed 20. The UAE did not reach 100 until the 19th over, while Ireland lost their first wicket at 90 in the 13th. When Paul Stirling went for 53, he was the first of three victims for leg-spinner Basil Hameed, who had not bowled in any of his five previous T20Is. But no one else managed a wicket, and Kevin O'Brien made 46 as the chase became a cakewalk.*

At Dubai (ICC Academy), October 8, 2021. **United Arab Emirates won by 54 runs. United Arab Emirates 163-4** (20 overs) (C. Suri 51, Mohammad Usman 32, Basil Hameed 39*); **‡Ireland 109** (18.4 overs) (Akif Raja 3-22, K. P. Meiyappan 4-25). PoM: K. P. Meiyappan. T20I debuts: Akif Raja, K. P. Meiyappan (UAE). *After the previous day's defeat, the UAE showed they were up for the fight, with their two debutants sharing seven wickets. Seamer Akif Raja dismissed Ireland's experienced top three – Stirling, O'Brien and Andrew Balbirnie – in the powerplay, before legspinner Karthik Meiyappan picked up 4-25. Earlier, Suri had made 51, though the innings lacked impetus: when he departed at 109-3, there were only five overs remaining. But Hameed (39* off 20) and Kashif Daud, a Sharjah-based coach who had made his international debut, aged 34, against the Irish in January, and was piqued by seamer Mark Adair's sledging, smashed 47* off the last 21 balls to reach a total that proved beyond their opponents.*

At Dubai (ICC Academy), October 10, 2021. **United Arab Emirates won by seven wickets. Ireland 134-5** (20 overs) (P. R. Stirling 40, K. J. O'Brien 54; Rohan Mustafa 3-23); **‡United Arab Emirates 139-3** (16.1 overs) (Waseem Muhammad 107*). PoM: Waseem Muhammad. *Within UAE domestic cricket, Waseem Muhammad was already a star. A 12-ball fifty, against high-quality bowling in February's T10 League, had established his reputation; now he announced himself at international level with a breathtaking hundred. Ireland had appeared set for an imposing total when Stirling and O'Brien put on 85 inside 12 overs, but Rohan Mustafa dismissed both en route to 3-23, Balbirnie suffered a toe injury, and the eventual target of 135 was far from intimidating. Even so, the chase was astonishing. Waseem hit 80 of his 107 in boundaries, taking 36 balls to pass 50, and another 24 to reach three figures, matching Shaiman Anwar's UAE record 60-ball century, against Papua New Guinea in 2016-17. He made 77% of the total, and sealed the win with a straight six out of the ground, interrupting a football match.*

UNITED ARAB EMIRATES TWENTY20 TRI-SERIES IN 2021-22

1 Namibia   2 Scotland   3 Papua New Guinea

In the round-robin, Namibia extended their winning streak to six, Richie Berrington scored 102 in two innings for Scotland, and Papua New Guinea lost both their matches.

At Dubai (ICC Academy), October 8, 2021. **Scotland won by eight wickets. ‡Papua New Guinea 154-5** (20 overs) (A. Vala 55, S. Bau 38*); **Scotland 156-2** (17.5 overs) (H. G. Munsey 50, R. D. Berrington 41*). PoM: H. G. Munsey. T20I debuts: K. V. Morea (PNG), C. N. Greaves (Scotland). *In the first game of the tri-series, 11 days before these teams met again in the T20 World Cup, Scotland recorded a straightforward victory, clinching a clinical chase with 13 balls to spare. Asad Vala had led Papua New Guinea from the front with 55, and was supported by Sese Bau's sprightly 38*, but their scoring was pegged back by a tidy spell of 1-17 from leg-spinner Chris Greaves, an uncontracted amateur on leave from his job as an Amazon delivery driver. Scotland rarely looked troubled as they cruised towards a target of 155. George Munsey hit 50 off 33, and a stand of 72* off 52 between Richie Berrington and Calum MacLeod (27*) settled matters.*

At Dubai (ICC Academy), October 9, 2021. **Namibia won by five wickets. Scotland 137-8** (20 overs) (R. D. Berrington 61); **‡Namibia 138-5** (17.4 overs) (S. J. Baard 39, C. G. Williams 50). PoM: C. G. Williams. *These teams' only previous meeting, in 2019, had also come at this ground. Then, Namibia had won batting first; now, they won chasing. Scotland's 137-8 was insipid: Ruben Trumpelmann dismissed Kyle Coetzer and Matthew Cross early, Frylinck (2-24) was economical again, and only Berrington showed much pluck, with a 46-ball 61. Namibia lost Zane Green for a* *golden duck to Josh Davey, but Stephan Baard and Williams (50 off 37) shared a second-wicket partnership of 93 off 58. Though the stand was broken at halfway, and Namibia wobbled, 38 from ten overs was too few for Scotland to defend.*

At Dubai (ICC Academy), October 10, 2021. **Namibia won by 14 runs. Namibia 174-6** (20 overs) (C. G. Williams 57, J. J. Smit 48); ‡**Papua New Guinea 160-6** (20 overs) (T. P. Ura 69). *PoM:* J. J. Smit. *T20I debut:* M. van Lingen (Namibia). *Namibia concluded the round-robin by defeating Papua New Guinea – their sixth consecutive win. Williams scored his third half-century in a row and, supported by J. J. Smit's 48 off 34, helped post the highest total of the series – though Wiese failed again. Despite losing Vala for one, PNG started well: Tony Ura (69 off 43) and Charles Amini (25) brought the score to 71-1 in the ninth, but the innings stuttered against Smit (2-24) and Frylinck. Simon Atai (28 off 25) injected late momentum, but there was too much to do.*

USA v IRELAND IN 2021-22

Twenty20 internationals (2): USA 1, Ireland 1

Ireland's brief visit to Florida late in 2021 started with embarrassment, and ended with a scramble for the airport. In the first T20, the United States bounced back from 16 for four to reach 188, then kept Ireland down to 162, sealing their first victory over a Test-playing country in any official international (their previous T20 wins had come against Argentina, Bahamas, Belize, Bermuda and Panama, plus two against the Cayman Islands). Ireland squared the series with a nervy victory in the second match, before Covid-19 intervened. First, one of the umpiring team tested positive, forcing the cancellation of the first ODI when the other officials were pinged as close contacts; then "multiple" players returned positives as well, leading to the remaining two games being called off. The Irish team flew out of Miami on December 31 for a white-ball series in the West Indies, which will be reported in *Wisden 2023*.

First Twenty20 international At Lauderhill, December 22, 2021. **USA won by 26 runs.** ‡**USA 188-6** (20 overs) (S. J. Modani 50, G. Singh 65, M. O. Kain 39*; B. J. McCarthy 4-30); **Ireland 162-6** (20 overs) (P. R. Stirling 31, L. J. Tucker 57*). *PoM:* G. Singh. *T20I debuts:* R. R. Behara, M. O. Kain, S. J. Modani, R. M. Scott, Yasir Mohammad (USA). *A fifth-wicket stand of 110 between Sushant Modani and the former Guyana batsman Gajanand Singh helped the USA recover from 12-4, then 39* in 15 balls from Marty Kain swelled the total to 188. It proved enough for a historic victory, the USA's first over a Full Member nation: Ireland could muster only 162, despite a fighting half-century from Lorcan Tucker. "We just weren't good enough today and we deserved to lose," said their captain, Andy Balbirnie.*

Second Twenty20 international At Lauderhill, December 23, 2021 (floodlit). **Ireland won by nine runs. Ireland 150** (18.5 overs) (L. J. Tucker 84; S. N. Netravalkar 3-33); ‡**USA 141-7** (20 overs) (C. Campher 4-25). *PoM:* L. J. Tucker. *T20I debut:* V. M. Maghela (USA). *Another excellent innings from Tucker, who made 84 from 56 balls, spared Ireland's blushes: the next-highest was Curtis Campher's 17, as they reached a modest 150. In the field, Ireland were also indebted to Campher, who ran out opener Ryan Scott, then took four wickets to disrupt the USA's victory charge. They needed 17 from Mark Adair's final over, but managed only seven, as the relieved Irish squared the series.*

First one-day international At Lauderhill, December 26, 2021. **USA v Ireland. Cancelled.** *This match was called off when one of the umpiring team tested positive for Covid-19, forcing the other officials to isolate.*

Second one-day international At Lauderhill, December 28, 2021. **USA v Ireland. Cancelled.** *More positive tests, this time from the players on both sides, forced the cancellation of this match and the next.*

Third one-day international At Lauderhill, December 30, 2021. **USA v Ireland. Cancelled.**

MEN'S WORLD CUP QUALIFIERS IN 2021

The ICC's restructured competition to provide a clearer route to World Cup qualification began in August 2019, and is due to run to February 2023.

The Super League (see page 829) comprises the 12 Full members, plus the Netherlands (the leading Associate). The top seven plus India, the hosts, advance to the 2023 World Cup. The bottom five proceed to the Qualifier.

League Two (whose matches have ODI status) is scheduled to finish by February 2023, and comprises seven more leading Associates, ranked 14th to 20th; the top three proceed to the Qualifier, but the bottom four reach the Qualifier play-off.

The Challenge League (which does not have ODI status) is scheduled to finish by July 2022, and comprises the 12 Associates ranked 21st to 32nd; the top two reach the Qualifier play-off.

Of the six teams in the Qualifier play-off, the top two proceed to the Qualifier. Of the ten teams in the Qualifier, the top two advance to the 2023 World Cup.

LEAGUE TWO IN 2021

As in 2020, when no action was possible after February, several matches fell foul of the pandemic. Three rounds were rescheduled – in Oman in September and October, and Namibia in November – but the last six games were called off after the Omicron variant emerged in southern Africa. By the end of the year, Oman were top, with Scotland well placed. Six of the seven teams remained in contention for the Qualifier.

WORLD CUP LEAGUE TWO, 2019–23

	P	W	L	NR	Pts	NRR
Oman	20	14	5	1	29	0.25
Scotland	12	7	3	2	16	0.21
United States of America	16	7	9	0	14	−0.22
Namibia	9	5	4	0	10	0.06
Nepal	8	4	4	0	8	0.46
United Arab Emirates	7	3	3	1	7	−0.00
Papua New Guinea	12	0	12	0	0	−0.67

As at December 31, 2021.

At Al Amerat, Oman, September 13, 2021. **Nepal won by five wickets. ‡United States of America** 230-9 (50 overs) (M. D. Patel 100); **Nepal 231-5** (49 overs) (K. Bhurtel 84, R. K. Paudel 62*, B. Bhandari 37). PoM: K. Bhurtel. ODI debut: S. Krishnamurthi (USA). *Wicketkeeper Monank Patel scored the USA's second ODI hundred, four days after his team-mate Jaskaran Singh Malhotra made the first. But measured knocks from opener Khushal Bhurtel (who had earlier pouched three good catches) and 19-year-old Rohit Kumar Paudel gave Nepal victory in the first completed match in this competition since they bowled the USA out for 35 in Kirtipur in February 2020.*

At Al Amerat, September 14, 2021 (day/night). **Oman won by five wickets. ‡Nepal 196** (47.4 overs) (Aasif Sheikh 90; Bilal Khan 4-47); **Oman 200-5** (31.1 overs) (Jatinder Singh 107, Mohammad Nadeem 38*). PoM: Jatinder Singh. ODI debuts: Ayaan Khan, N. Dhamba, Shoaib Khan (Oman). *Jatinder Singh, who faced only 62 balls and hit 12 fours and six sixes, scored his maiden international century as Oman sauntered past Nepal's modest total, in which Aasif Sheikh alone passed 21 in the face of a lively spell from left-arm seamer Bilal Khan. Mohammad Nadeem ended the match with a six off Bikram Sob.*

At Al Amerat, September 16, 2021 (day/night). **Oman won by four wickets. United States of America 178** (44.4 overs) (K. I. Gore 44, E. H. Hutchinson 49*); ‡**Oman 179-6** (49.4 overs) (Zeeshan Maqsood 31, Mohammad Nadeem 32, Suraj Kumar 35; S. N. Netravalkar 3-39). *PoM:* Mohammad Nadeem. *ODI debut:* D. O. D. Rikhi (USA). *A ninth-wicket stand of 66 between Karima Gore (born in the Bronx) and Elmore Hutchinson helped the USA recover from 96-8. Oman were 20-2 after 15 balls, but then found scoring difficult. Steve Taylor whisked through ten overs, taking 1-24 with his medium-pacers, but Oman eventually crept home in the last over.*

At Al Amerat, September 17, 2021 (day/night). **United States of America won by six wickets. Nepal 174** (48 overs) (K. Bhurtel 36, G. Malla 55; K. Phillip 3-43, S. N. Netravalkar 4-29); ‡**United States of America 175-4** (29.3 overs) (S. R. Taylor 92, M. D. Patel 38*, J. S. Malhotra 36*). *PoM:* S. R. Taylor. *ODI debuts:* G. K. Jha (Nepal); K. Phillip (USA). *Two wickets in two balls from seamer K. C. Karan (2-23) briefly threatened to derail the USA's chase but, from 119-4, Patel and Malhotra calmly added 56* in the next ten overs.*

At Al Amerat, September 19, 2021 (day/night). **Nepal won by seven wickets. Oman 121** (37.1 overs) (Zeeshan Maqsood 41; K. C. Karan 4-25, S. Lamichhane 4-18); ‡**Nepal 122-3** (18.2 overs) (Aasif Sheikh 40, G. Malla 52*). *PoM:* K. C. Karan. *ODI debut:* Sufyan Mehmood (Oman). *Only Zeeshan Maqsood made more than 13, as leg-spinner Sandeep Lamichhane gutted the middle order with three wickets in six balls to reduce Oman to 43-6. Sheikh and captain Gyanendra Malla then made sure of a quick finish with a stand of 95 in 12 overs, to give Dav Whatmore – the Australian who coached Sri Lanka to the World Cup title in 1996 – a winning send-off in his last match in charge of Nepal.*

At Al Amerat, September 20, 2021 (day/night). **Oman won by 72 runs. Oman 274-7** (50 overs) (Jatinder Singh 42, Ayaan Khan 41, Zeeshan Maqsood 53, Naseem Khushi 35*; N. P. Kenjige 3-49); ‡**United States of America 202** (39.5 overs) (M. D. Patel 56, G. Singh 48; Khawar Ali 3-49, Ayaan Khan 4-36). *PoM:* Ayaan Khan. *ODI debut:* P. D. Macchi (Oman). *A consistent Oman batting display – eight men reached double figures, and the other made nine – raised a total that proved beyond the Americans, with spinners Khawar Ali (leg-breaks) and Ayaan Khan (slow left-arm) sharing seven wickets.*

* * *

At Al Amerat, September 25, 2021. **Scotland won by six wickets. Papua New Guinea 197** (47.4 overs) (C. A. Soper 46*, D. A. Ravu 32; G. T. Main 3-33, H. Tahir 3-36); ‡**Scotland 198-4** (43 overs) (M. H. Cross 70, C. S. MacLeod 45). *PoM:* M. H. Cross. *A stand of 66 between Chad Soper and Damien Ravu rescued PNG from 125-8, but Matt Cross made sure there were no Scottish slip-ups with a 75-ball 70. George Munsey (27*) ended the match with a six off Norman Vanua.*

At Al Amerat, September 26, 2021. **Oman won by 110 runs. Oman 250-7** (50 overs) (Aaqib Ilyas 34, Ayaan Khan 44, Suraj Kumar 62*); ‡**Papua New Guinea 140** (42.2 overs) (J. Kila 36; Zeeshan Maqsood 4-28, Ayaan Khan 3-12). *PoM:* Zeeshan Maqsood. *ODI debut:* K. H. Prajapati (Oman). *PNG's batting again proved fragile, with Oman's captain, Zeeshan Maqsood, delivering an accurate spell of left-arm spin.*

At Al Amerat, September 28, 2021. **Scotland won by 18 runs.** ‡**Scotland 273-6** (50 overs) (K. J. Coetzer 60, R. D. Berrington 97, D. E. Budge 32*); **Oman 255-9** (50 overs) (Jatinder Singh 64, Aaqib Ilyas 33, S. Goud 54*; C. B. Sole 3-79). *PoM:* R. D. Berrington. *Richie Berrington hit five sixes and five fours, passing 2,000 runs in ODIs, before being run out from the penultimate ball of Scotland's innings. Oman looked out of it at 155-7 in the 38th, but Sandeep Goud, helped by wicketkeeper Naseem Khushi (27) and Kaleemullah (20), hauled them close.*

At Al Amerat, September 29, 2021 (day/night). **Scotland won by four wickets.** ‡**Papua New Guinea 226-8** (50 overs) (A. Vala 30, N. Vanua 57, C. A. Soper 39*; A. C. Evans 3-42, M. A. Leask 3-19); **Scotland 228-6** (48.5 overs) (K. J. Coetzer 81, M. A. Leask 51*). *PoM:* M. A. Leask. *Another PNG recovery – from 97-6 this time – put the Scots under pressure, especially when Cross fell for a duck. Skipper Kyle Coetzer made a sedate 81, but from 167-6 after 42 Scotland needed a brisk half-century from Michael Leask, who had earlier taken three wickets with his off-breaks.*

At Al Amerat, October 1, 2021 (day/night). **Oman won by three wickets. Papua New Guinea 150** (43.2 overs) (A. Vala 62; Khawar Ali 5-15); ‡**Oman 151-7** (35.5 overs) (Aaqib Ilyas 56; K. V. Morea 5-28). *PoM:* Khawar Ali. *Leg-spinner Khawar Ali achieved his first five-for in ODIs, as did PNG's left-arm seamer Kabua Morea, who had never taken more than two in an innings. It left the Barramundis with an unenviable record to this point of the tournament: played 12, lost 12.*

At Al Amerat, October 2, 2021 (day/night). **No result.** ‡Scotland 100-3 (23.2 overs) (H. G. Munsey 58*) **v Oman.** *Heavy rain from Cyclone Shaheen ended the match – and Scotland's hopes of four wins in a week.*

* * *

At Windhoek, Namibia, November 26, 2021. **Namibia won by 40 runs. Namibia 228** (50 overs) (M. van Lingen 51, C. G. Williams 37, J. J. Smit 56; Zeeshan Maqsood 3-30); ‡Oman 188 (46.5 overs) (Zeeshan Maqsood 58, S. Goud 50; J. J. Smit 5-26). *PoM:* J. J. Smit. *ODI debuts:* M. D. du Preez, R. C. Trumpelmann, M. van Lingen (Namibia). *Half-centuries from the debutant Michael van Lingen and Johannes Smit (captaining in the absence of Gerhard Erasmus, who broke a finger during the T20 World Cup) pushed Namibia to 228. Oman looked sunk at 70-5, before Zeeshan and Goud put on 106 – but seamers Smit and Ruben Trumpelmann removed the last five for 12 to seal a home win.*

At Windhoek, November 27, 2021. **Oman won by nine runs.** ‡Oman 291-9 (50 overs) (K. H. Prajapati 52, Aaqib Ilyas 43, Ayaan Khan 83; R. C. Trumpelmann 5-76); **Namibia 282-9** (50 overs) (Z. E. Green 47, C. G. Williams 38, J. J. Smit 94; Zeeshan Maqsood 3-45). *PoM:* Ayaan Khan. *ODI debut:* J. N. Loftie-Eaton (Namibia). *Oman turned the tables, with Ayaan following a maiden half-century with a tight spell (9–1–38–1). Smit, who had never passed 56 in ODIs, made 94, but Namibia's hopes ended when he fell to the first ball of the 49th over.*

At Windhoek, November 29, 2021. **Oman v United Arab Emirates. Abandoned.** *The rapid spread of the Omicron Covid variant caused this match – and the remaining five in this round – to be called off.*

At Windhoek, November 30, 2021. **Namibia v United Arab Emirates. Cancelled.**

At Windhoek, December 2, 2021. **Oman v United Arab Emirates. Cancelled.**

At Windhoek, December 4, 2021. **Namibia v Oman. Cancelled.**

At Windhoek, December 5, 2021. **Namibia v United Arab Emirates. Cancelled.**

At Windhoek, December 6, 2021. **Oman v United Arab Emirates. Cancelled.**

CHALLENGE LEAGUE IN 2021

By the end of 2021, Canada and Singapore led the way in Group A, both with four wins from five games. In Group B, Uganda were in pole position, having won all five matches, and Hong Kong were a little way off in second.

MEN'S T20 WORLD CUP QUALIFIERS IN 2021

JAMES COYNE

It's hardly the most pressing of global issues, but spare a thought for the 33 men's national teams knocked out of qualification for the 2022 T20 World Cup without even playing their scheduled matches. The ICC attempted to make up for time lost to Covid, but the comprehensive qualification pathway contained some bumps in the road.

Europe's regional groups, involving 24 teams, were twice rearranged, then cancelled. As in all such cases, the highest-placed teams in the ICC rankings progressed. For the regional finals in Spain, Italy brought several recent professionals, born in South Africa with Italian heritage: Jade Dernbach, Grant Stewart and player/coach Gareth Berg. They failed to progress to the global stage, though, pipped to second place by Germany on net run-rate, despite beating them by one run in their last game. **Germany** advanced as runners-up to **Jersey**. Denmark's campaign was hamstrung by a dispute which prompted six players to withdraw on the eve of departure. Chasing Jersey's 94, they were all out for 89.

Andy Moles, who had coached Hong Kong, Kenya, Scotland and Afghanistan, was signed as head coach by the Bahamas – returning to international cricket after eight years – ahead of the Americas competition.

MOST ECONOMICAL FOUR-OVER SPELLS IN T20

24–24–0–2	A. K. Karnewar	**Manipur v Vidarbha at Mangalagiri**	**2021-22**
24–24–0–2	Saad Bin Zafar	**Canada v Panama at Coolidge**	**2021-22**
24–23–1–2	Mohammad Irfan	St Kitts & Nevis v Barbados at Bridgetown .	2018
24–23–2–2	C. H. Morris	Cape Cobras v Lions at Johannesburg.	2014-15
24–22–2–4	U. W. M. B. C. A. Welegedara .	Sinhalese v Tamil Union at Colombo (CCC)	2014-15
24–22–2–2	V. R. Iyer	**Bihar v Madhya Pradesh at Delhi (Palam)**	**2021-22**

As expected, the **USA** and **Canada** ran away with it, but Panama played some remarkable matches. They posted 111 for nine against Argentina, after their last pair put on an unbeaten 62. In reply to Canada's 245 for one, they were dismissed for 37, with Saad Bin Zafar taking two for none in four overs.

Africa's regional groups made full use of the Gahanga International Stadium in Kigali, Rwanda, and scheduled 27 matches in just over a month. The rest were held at the nearby Integrated Polytechnic Regional College. Its competitive pitch played into the hands of Uganda's Dinesh Nakrani, who took six for seven against Lesotho (bowled out for 26), and five for eight against the Seychelles. Mozambique's Francisco Couana became the first to combine a century with five wickets in a T20I, against Cameroon. The Cameroonians, meanwhile, lost an extraordinary match to Tanzania: requiring 241, they were 54 for one, before being bowled out for 62. James Moses played for Botswana aged 56. Uganda and Tanzania came through the groups, and both beat Kenya at the regional finals; **Uganda** advanced in first place.

With governments in the Far East persevering with stricter Covid measures than elsewhere, the Asia and Pacific regional qualifiers were worst hit. The eight-team Pacific competition was completely shelved – the **Philippines** progressed on ranking alone – as was one of Asia's regional groups, sending **Hong Kong** straight through. The other group did go ahead, with **Bahrain** advancing to the Global Qualifiers.

REGIONAL QUALIFIERS

Africa (in Rwanda, October–November 2021) **Group A** UGANDA 12pts, Ghana 10, Malawi 8, Rwanda 6, Seychelles 4, eSwatini 2, Lesotho 0. **Group B** TANZANIA 8pts, Botswana 6, Sierra Leone 4, Mozambique 2, Cameroon 0. **Final** UGANDA 10pts, Kenya 8, Tanzania 6, Nigeria 0. *Kenya and Nigeria had a bye to the final as the two highest-ranked teams. Cameroon, eSwatini, Lesotho, Seychelles and Tanzania played their first T20 internationals.* **Qualified** Uganda.

Americas (in Antigua, November 2021) USA 12pts, CANADA 10, Bermuda 8, Argentina 4, Bahamas 4, Panama 2, Belize 2. *Bahamas played their first T20 international.* **Qualified** USA and Canada.

Asia (in Qatar and Malaysia, October–November 2021) **Group A** BAHRAIN 6pts, Qatar 6, Kuwait 4, Saudi Arabia 4, Maldives 0. *Bahrain qualified on head-to-head result.* **Group B** Bhutan, China, HONG KONG, Malaysia, Myanmar and Thailand. *Group B was cancelled due to the pandemic; the highest-ranked team qualified.* **Qualified** Bahrain and Hong Kong.

Europe (in Spain, October 2021) **Group A** Bulgaria, Cyprus, France, Israel, ITALY, Malta, Norway, Spain. **Group B** Finland, GERMANY, Gibraltar, Greece, Guernsey, Hungary, Luxembourg, Sweden. **Group C** Austria, Belgium, Czechia, DENMARK, Isle of Man, Portugal, Romania, Serbia. **Final** JERSEY 12pts, GERMANY 6, Italy 6, Denmark 0. *All groups were cancelled due to the pandemic; the highest-ranked teams progressed to the final. Jersey had a bye to the final as the highest-ranked team.* **Qualified** Jersey and Germany.

Pacific (in Japan, October 2021) Cook Islands, Fiji, Indonesia, Japan, PHILIPPINES, Samoa, South Korea, Vanuatu. *Cancelled due to the pandemic; the highest-ranked team qualified.* **Qualified** Philippines.

GLOBAL QUALIFIERS

The eight regional qualifiers progressed to the Global Qualifiers in February and July 2022, with the four lowest-placed teams from the T20 World Cup 2021 (Ireland, the Netherlands, Oman and Papua New Guinea), and the next four highest-ranked teams (Nepal, UAE, Singapore and Zimbabwe). Four teams from the Global Qualifiers will reach the T20 World Cup in 2022.

OTHER MEN'S TWENTY20 INTERNATIONALS IN 2021

Austria meet their Waterloo

Tailenders are often unpredictable, but in the helter-skelter world of Associate cricket, strange things can happen. Belgium had fallen to 14 for eight in the second match of their 2–1 series win over Austria at Waterloo in July. Then No. 8 Saber Zakhil struck 100 not out from 47 balls, the first T20I century by a batter below the top six, and added an unbroken 132 for the ninth wicket with Saqlain Ali, a world record for any of the last four wickets; his team won on DLS.

They had already made waves a fortnight earlier, in Malta. Leading a five-match series 2–1, they were 74 for nine – only for opener Sherul Mehta and No. 11 Khalid Ahmadi to add 54. Malta were all out four short, whereupon the umpires belatedly awarded them five penalty runs: during the innings break, a Belgian player had apparently threatened to kill one of the them (invoking Law 42.5). Belgium won the decider.

For the Maltese, it was one extraordinary event after another. In the Continental Cup in Romania (won by the hosts), they had an unbeaten 55 taken off them by Luxembourg's Tony Whiteman, at 52 years 101 days the oldest player to score a T20I half-century; they then lost the third-place play-off to Hungary, who had not played a T20I before the tournament. Malta's home quadrangular series saw them defeat Switzerland – also making their full international debut – in the final. They then drew a two-match series with Gibraltar after an abandonment and an unusual tie on DLS (Malta 145, Gibraltar 52 for two).

Cyprus hosted Estonia for both teams' international bows: Cyprus won 2–0 before both were bested by the Isle of Man in a tri-series. Other triangular tournaments were won by Austria (in Czechia), and by Portugal and Germany at home. France played their first T20I, at the German event. Bulgaria hosted a quadrangular for Balkan teams, won by Romania.

Sweden played their first T20I, and won their second, in a 2–1 defeat by Denmark, before drawing 2–2 with Finland. Spain's 2–1 win over Germany suggested the Germans had been lucky to advance, on ranking alone, in the T20 World Cup qualifying.

Few teams can have made such an enigmatic first appearance on the international stage as Rwanda, who began a five-match series against Ghana with a thrilling one-wicket victory. At 2–1 up, Rwanda must have felt confident: chasing 167, they were 30 for one after five overs when rain came, but rather than wait for it to stop, they conceded the match, left the ground – and were thrashed in the fifth. Sierra Leone also won their debut game, but suffered a 5–1 defeat by Nigeria, themselves the whipping-boys in a tri-series in Uganda, where they managed a solitary, narrow win over Kenya as the hosts took the tournament.

CRICKET ROUND THE WORLD IN 2021

COMPILED BY JAMES COYNE AND TIMOTHY ABRAHAM

DREAM11 EUROPEAN CHAMPIONSHIP 2021

For most of the pandemic years of 2020 and 2021, the European Cricket Network delivered a non-stop roadshow of domestic club tournaments across 19 countries. The beast – in the form of TV and streaming agreements, sponsorship deals and online betting – needs constant feeding.

The logic of ECN founder Daniel Weston was that all the successful football, handball and volleyball leagues of Europe are based on historic clubs rooted in towns and cities – though he may have also twigged it would be easier to exert influence over spit-and-sawdust grassroots set-ups than national boards, the ICC or other private tycoons.

But the appeal of a European Championship played by national teams was easy to see. And, unlike the European Cricket Series club tournaments squirreled away in a subscription streaming package, BT Sport in the UK and Fox Sports in Australia bought up the TV rights.

Come September 2021, Covid restrictions had relented sufficiently for 15 national teams to fly to the Costa del Sol, inland from Malaga. Ireland, Scotland and Denmark refused the ECN's invitation, while the Netherlands, who were warming up for the T20 World Cup in the Gulf, sent a second-string side. With the county season still in full swing, England were represented by a team drawn from the National (formerly Minor) Counties, but with some first-class experience in their ranks. There was amusement when the England XI lost to Belgium and Italy, but those defeats were offset by 17 wins, and they landed the title. Harrison Ward and Dan Lincoln walloped 595 and 594 runs each at strike-rates of 264 and 225 – and with a class of strokeplay befitting their Sussex and Kent helmets.

The games, following the ECN's favoured T10 format, were played on a matting wicket, which allowed 98 fixtures in 26 days – as many as five a day on the same ground. The small dimensions of the Cartama Oval meant Twenty20-scale scores in just 60 balls, and brought regular cries of "*Seis carreras mas!*" and "Maximooo!" from the exuberant commentators.

Even they were beginning to sound jaded by the final, when Belgium's Sherry Butt hit four sixes in a row off England's Welsh leg-spinner, Sam Pearce (the tournament's leading wicket-taker), and Ward heaved the first three balls of the reply over the ropes too. The Netherlands had reached 200 (of which 172 came in boundaries) against whipping boys Romania, though the Dutch did lose to Portugal – another nation luring South Africans with heritage in the old country, such as the punchy left-hander Sharn Gomes, who struck 56.

The stratospheric boundary count left fielding captains with nothing to lose. Whether a joke, stunt or protest at the imbalance between bat and ball, Finland captain Jonathan Scamans posted eight slips and a leg gully for the first delivery of England's innings… and Luke Webb almost edged it. When the clip, evoking a West Indies field from the late 1970s, emerged on social media, the clicks came flooding in – which pretty much seems the point of all ECN activity. Italy's Baljit Singh – slayer of England – did actually hold a slip catch, against Germany.

Gideon Haigh once asked whether cricket made money in order to exist, or existed in order to make money – and there is little doubt of the main aim of Weston's company. The hope must be that it cuts through to enough European youngsters looking for an alternative to football. At the cavalcade on the Costa del Sol, the English and the Dutch aside, there were a mere handful of genuinely homegrown cricketers. The jury is out.   JAMES COYNE

ISRAEL

A cricket club opening their underground shelter to civilians fleeing rocket attacks might sound shocking elsewhere, but less so in the Holy Land. When the conflict between Israel and the occupied Palestinian territories ignited again in May 2021, missiles were fired into Israel, prompting retaliatory airstrikes on the Gaza Strip. In Beersheba, the largest city in Israel's southern Negev, Indian researchers at Ben-Gurion University were seeking sanctuary from the bombardment. Some knew Beersheba CC from their weekend cricket and headed for the clubhouse's underground refuge. There was a certain irony: it was in Beersheba that the Israel Cricket Association first pioneered cricket-based integration projects between Jewish and Bedouin children in 2009. Most of the 300-odd cricketers in Israel are of Indian-Jewish descent, and clustered in the towns of the Negev. Israel's appearances at international tournaments have sometimes been met with protests from civilians, even opposing teams, and they no longer fly in tracksuits or blazers bearing the ICA emblem incorporating the Star of David. But they were denied even that experience by Covid, which put paid to their T20 World Cup qualifier. The establishment of diplomatic relations between Israel and the UAE in 2020 does at least mean Israeli cricket officials can now fly to ICC meetings. When the ICC first moved to Dubai in the mid-2000s, the ICA's then-chairman Stanley Perlman (and long-time *Wisden* contributor) had to fly in on his South African passport.   JAMES COYNE

MALTA

It's fitting that Malta has hosted tournaments in the European Cricket Series – the venture aimed at gaming and fantasy-league platforms in the subcontinent – given the country's transformation into a gambling mecca. Around 15% of Malta's income is derived from the online gaming industry, and the country has become a hub for offshore British and European gambling companies. But the entry of a team in the ECS, representing Gozo, the second island of the Maltese archipelago, was chastening: they were bundled out for six by eventual champions Super Kings, losing a T10 match by an astronomical 194 runs. There were eight Gozitan ducks, six golden. Since then, they have prospered, with two league wins in 2021, and there is excitement about a permanent

JOHN LENNON AND CRICKET

Wicket to ride

Timothy Abraham

Wander through the colourful Plaza de las Flores in Almería and you may stumble across a bronze statue of John Lennon strumming a guitar. It was during a six-week stay in the Andalusian city in 1966 that Lennon part-composed "Strawberry Fields Forever" and began wearing his Windsor glasses. Almería was also where he briefly rekindled an interest in a sport he had not played since his youth.

Despite the appeal of Liverpool or Everton, it seems cricket rather than football stirred something in Lennon while growing up at his aunt Mimi Smith's house in Woolton. Lennon's half-sister, Julia Baird, says he was a "fast bowler and terrifying batsman". She adds: "We played with a proper willow bat and a leather ball. It was uber-competitive. There were plenty of injuries."

Whatever passion Lennon had for the game appeared to peter out during his rebellious teenage years at Quarry Bank High School – save for running a book on the outcomes of school matches with lifelong friend Pete Shotton. Quarry Bank did play Paul McCartney's Liverpool Institute High School for Boys. But while McCartney also dabbled, the pair seemingly never crossed paths on the pitch. By his own admission, McCartney was not much of a player, and "happy when they stuck me in the outfield, where the ball hardly ever reached me, and I could just dawdle about". Lennon had a bat of his own, though, which was in a glass case at a wine bar on Penny Lane, until it closed a few years ago.

In his early twenties, Lennon was still living in Mimi's semi, when she welcomed Frank Duckworth (later of the Duckworth/Lewis/Stern method) as a lodger for three months in 1962. Duckworth was studying for a PhD in metallurgy at the University of Liverpool, while Lennon was playing gigs at the Cavern Club, but there were no discussions about the County Championship. "I exchanged words with him only once," Duckworth remembered. "I said, 'Hello John', and he replied 'Um'. I heard him playing a few chords in his bedroom occasionally."

Four years later, with Beatlemania gripping the globe, the Fab Four took a holiday after an arduous worldwide tour. McCartney went to Africa, George Harrison to India, while Ringo Starr caught up with family. Lennon, though, spent part of the break filming his only non-musical acting role, as the fresh-faced, wise-cracking Private Gripweed in the black comedy *How I Won the War*, based on a Patrick Ryan novel. Though the arid landscape of Almería is better known as the location for Sergio Leone's spaghetti westerns starring Clint Eastwood, Spain now passed as North Africa, with Michael Crawford in the lead role. Every day, Lennon was driven to the desert backdrop for filming in his black Rolls-Royce, where he kept his stash of drugs.

One of the early sequences depicts a game of cricket in England, in which Lennon quips to Crawford: "May I rub your ball, sir? It gives me great pleasure." The action then switches to the Western Desert campaign, and a mission for Lennon, the bumbling Crawford and the rest of their regiment to schlep a roller and other equipment across the desert to create an "advanced area cricket pitch". Lennon features in a farcical scene, fielding at mid-on, while Roy Kinnear bats and the visiting officers sneer – "what rotten bowling!" – despite the death toll racked up in establishing the pitch.

Austrian photographer Zdenko Hirschler took stills of several impromptu games during breaks in filming, with Lennon an eager participant (see page 50). Dressed in green military fatigues, he looks a little uncomfortable at the crease, but his grip is orthodox and he appears a predominantly front-foot player. Crawford recalled that "John became quite a good bowler" in Almería. "The only time he had a little trouble was when I was batting. He couldn't tell which were the wickets and which were my legs." Even the American director Richard Lester joined in: "John bowled with such force he hit my leg and nearly broke it in two!"

In the film, Lennon's character dies after being shot. Lennon, who initially refused to do the scene, told Lester he was haunted by visions of violent death. *How I Won the War* was released in 1967, and poorly received, though it did gain a cult following – and was praised for its anti-war message.

That was the end of Lennon's relationship with cricket, though not Almería's. Nestled among the Cabrera mountains, just up the coast, is the Desert Springs Resort, where cricket has gained a foothold since 2008. English counties and schools have used the facilities for pre-season training, as did the England team for camps before the 2015 Ashes and 2017 Champions Trophy.

In 2021, it received ICC accreditation to hold one-day internationals, the only ground in mainland Europe (the Netherlands apart) to achieve such status. "With the warm temperatures here during the English winter, this is an all-year-round cricket venue," says Nick Gaywood, the former Devon left-arm spinner overseeing cricket operations. "We have held ICC Associate tournaments, and there's no reason why it couldn't be used to stage high-profile ODI and T20 matches for Full Members in future."

cricket facility on Gozo. Maltese cricket has heritage: W. G. Grace opened the batting for Lord Sheffield's XI at Valletta's Naval Ground en route to Australia in 1891-92; Wally Hammond also played there as a boy, when his father, William, was stationed with the Royal Garrison Artillery. The Floriana Parade Ground, which hosted even earlier cricket, is now a car park, its patrons unaware that the block of sandstone at one end, measuring nine metres by three, was once an immovable sightscreen. Following Malta's independence in 1964, the United Services Ground was renamed the Marsa Sports Club. In the era of low-cost flights, Malta has become a favourite year-round destination for touring teams taking advantage of the climate and Marsa's excellent facilities. A tapeball league involving 16 teams and over 100 players has opened cricket up to many newcomers. At the same time, the Malta Schools Cricket Project was launched, resulting in another 11 qualified ICC Level 2 coaches and 40 Maltese PE teachers (16 women) trained to instruct cricket. Participation exploded, with 14 sides now competing in the T20 Malta Cricket League, and a steady growth in international fixtures. In summer 2021, Malta pushed Belgium (25 places above them in the T20 rankings) in a 3–2 home defeat. And in Portugal, Malta's Bikram Arora (66 not out) and Varun Thamotharam (104 not out) added 166 against Gibraltar, breaking the T20I fourth-wicket record of 161 by Australia's David Warner and Glenn Maxwell at Johannesburg in 2015-16.   CHARLES FELLOWS-SMITH

SPAIN

In May 2021, the people of Barcelona were presented with 822 potential projects for inclusion in the city's participatory budget, and the €1.3m (£1.1m) proposal to "renovate the sports field Julià de Capmany for the playing of cricket and minority sports" finished second in Sants-Montjuïc, the 1992 Olympics district. "There are a lot of South Asians living in Sants-Montjuïc, but it was still a surprise to receive the number of votes we did," said Damien McMullen, the Australian president of Barcelona International CC. His club are one of 25 in the Federació Catalana de Criquet, with perhaps 20 more existing outside official auspices, and there are around 700 cricketers in Catalonia. Cricket was played on the Julià de Capmany municipal field in hilly Montjuïc from 2012 to 2020, but it fell into disrepair and, after arsonists set light to the changing-rooms, the council knocked down the buildings and closed the gates. Pop-up street cricket, familiar across Europe, has forced the local authorities to start engaging with cricket organisations. "I think the deciding factor in the vote was the sheer number of kids from a South Asian background whacking balls around on the streets and constantly getting moved along by locals or the police," chuckles McMullen. "Catalans have come to realise there's a need for a place for these kids to play and practise nearby." The *federació* were astute enough to enlist local cultural centres to their cause, and front their PR campaign with the girls of Cricket Jove Barcelona, some clad in headscarves, to ram home the idea of cricket as a tool of inclusion in increasingly multicultural Spain. As such, junior and women's cricket will be given pride of place on the revamped ground, though artists' impressions

View of the terraces: cricket at Zuoz.

incorporate American Football goalposts too. Hifsa Butt, a 20-year-old of Pakistani heritage, said: "We want to play proper cricket, with 11 players, with a hard ball – not a tennis ball, like we use indoors. So now we need a proper cricket pitch with real, not synthetic, grass." In bone-dry Catalonia, that will bring its own problem. "You usually have about two overs before the shine is completely ripped off the ball, and if there's a chance for a diving catch you think twice," says McMullen. "You don't come across many grassy wickets or outfields in Catalonia."   JAMES COYNE

SWITZERLAND

Headquarters of United Nations agencies, the Red Cross and myriad other international bodies, Switzerland is returning from ten years as a cricketing pariah. Their absence was a shame, given the majesty of the ground used by the pupils of Lyceum Alpinum Zuoz, in the Engadin Valley of the eastern Swiss Alps. Zuoz hosted the 1997 European Nations Cup final – a game chosen as one of *Wisden's* 100 matches of the 20th century, mainly because France's No. 11 had staggered a crucial leg-bye before collapsing with a fractured skull inflicted by Germany's opening bowler. But the Swiss Cricket Association, an ICC member since 1985, were expelled from the global cricket family in 2012 because of the emergence of a rival national governing body, the Schweizer-ischer Cricket Verband. Instead of giving up, the SCA re-formed as Cricket Switzerland in 2014, and set their sights on the long climb back to acceptance.

Four years later, they gained the approval of the Swiss Olympic Association – opening important doors which had been shut by the rift. When Alex Mackay took over as chief executive in 2014, there were 14 clubs. There are now 33, with two more hoping to join. In the 2021 season, there were 200 children playing cricket every weekend in Zurich; local clubs lack the manpower to take on more. International tournaments and domestic leagues did not stop during Switzerland's isolation, and the lake at St Moritz hosted the famous Cricket on Ice tournament. The national team contain two sets of brothers: Asad and Osama Mahmood, and Arjun and Ashwin Vinod. As Cricket Switzerland are now in the ICC stable, costs such as flights and hotels will be covered, allowing money to be directed to the grassroots. A five-year contract with live-streaming network CricHQ and an agreement with digital marketeers Key & Eagle should help attract sponsors. An overture to Roger Federer, whose interest in the sport was encouraged by his South African mother, Lynette, might give Swiss cricket a further injection of publicity. All the while, Mackay will be making the teas, agreeing to umpire at the last minute, and putting out boundary markers on a Saturday morning. CHARLIE INGLEFIELD

TAJIKISTAN

When Tajikistan became the ICC's 106th member in 2021, it marked quite an achievement for Central Asia's poorest country, where wrestling and horseback sports take centre stage. Deemed too bourgeois for the Soviet Union, cricket was turfed out of the region in 1917. It made a surprising return to Tajikistan in the 1960s, when some shepherds began playing cricket on their *jailoo* (summer pastures); the best guess is they picked it up from visiting Indians or Pakistanis. The game was spread by these unconventional wandering sides, until Abdurasul Saraev – son of one of the shepherds – founded the Tajikistan Cricket Federation in 2009. His successor, Najibullo Ruzi, has put in place the infrastructure to achieve ICC Associate Membership, and secured government funding to raise cricket's profile. There are now six men's teams, who contest T20 tournaments at a football stadium in Dushanbe, the capital. The Laws have been translated into Tajik, and cricket is taught (with a soft ball) in 30 schools. There is plenty of natural talent among the 4,000 regular cricketers: boys and girls in Tajikistan grow up playing *chilikdangal*, a street game in which players hit a small stick with a longer one. Players get to bat only if they run the hitter out, so most Tajiks are crack fielders. The team in the town of Kulob play in the foothills of the Wakhan Corridor, a mountain pass at an altitude of 16,000ft that forms the border with Afghanistan. It is largely thanks to receiving equipment and support from the Afghan side of the mountains that cricket has been able to develop. A key figure at the TCF is Asadullah Khan, a former Afghanistan batsman who introduced women's cricket from scratch a decade ago, claiming they would soon be among the best teams in Asia. Although they are not yet at that level, Asadullah still organises two Tajik women's sides, who host touring groups

CRICKET ON HMS QUEEN ELIZABETH

The day the crocodiles were in church

Daz Hoare

It has been an honour and a privilege to organise cricket for the nation's flagship aircraft carrier. Not that it's easy. As front and centre of Operation Fortis – part of the UK's strategic defence- and foreign-policy tilt towards the Indo–Pacific region – HMS *Queen Elizabeth* habitually carries up to 1,600 personnel and 24 fighter jets, and can travel 500 miles a day.

The security considerations surrounding a £3.2bn ship mean we cannot disclose our location too far in advance. But just ahead of a port visit, I email every local club, and am like a kid on Christmas Eve waiting for the replies. My method is the friendly request, far removed from the 19th century Royal Navy captains challenging locals to prove their manliness on the field. We have players from all over the Commonwealth in our team, and most ranks from able rate to commander.

Following intense fast-jet trials off the US eastern seaboard in late 2019, *Queen Elizabeth* docked in Mayport, Florida, and the crew prepared for the ship's maiden cricket fixture, on the banks of the St Mary's River, which marks the Georgia–Florida border. As we arrived, the home side, Camden County CC, were cutting overgrown grass with machetes. When a couple of balls disappeared into the surrounding woodland, they laughed: "Don't worry, they're either asleep in there, or in church." We eventually realised "they" were crocodiles, alligators and snakes. Despite an unbeaten 57 from our captain, Sqn Ldr Paul Elliot, *Big Lizzie's* first game brought narrow defeat, but memorable home cooking and friends for life, not least Camden's 61-year-old wicketkeeper, Patrick Bishop.

As the world grappled with Covid-19, *Queen Elizabeth* mainly stayed in British waters, and prepared for the role of fleet flagship of the Royal Navy. In May 2021, we embarked on a 28-week deployment to the Far East and back. As we sailed through the Mediterranean, the crew of passing ships cast quizzical glances at the games of cricket on our upper deck: we had acquired our own pop-up net and mat for training (a few net balls were lost overboard). In Sicily, we conducted a session on the jetty, and even the local *carabinieri* helped out with fielding.

Then came a reply to sate our competitive juices: a T20 game against British Forces Cyprus at Happy Valley CC. (This is within British Overseas Territory, and local cricketers must submit their details in advance to gain access.) If you approach from the top of the valley, a lush ground – dug into the rugged hillside, with the Mediterranean a short plunge down a dirt track – heaves into view. It is paradise for the cricketer but, with an intense sun and no wind, the basin became an oven, making boundaries preferable to scampered twos. When we bowled, it helped that "Bungy" Williams was hit for six: our tatty old ball was lost, and the replacement swung far more obligingly. A 62-run win was followed by a swim and a beer.

As we sailed through the Suez Canal, a reply came from the small North Pacific island of Guam (see *Wisden 2020*), home of a US naval base. Guam CC had been unable to take the field in over two years. We were playing about as far from the Greenwich meridian as possible: 11,700 nautical miles. The bowling was always from one end to avoid the glare of the setting sun.

We turned west for home, entertaining the prospect of a match in Oman while it was hosting the T20 World Cup. Sadly, we had to be content with training on the jetty at Al Duqm. We had one last chance to pull on our whites in the winter sun of Mallorca, before returning to our families for Christmas. Cricket is everywhere, and I hope to be telling these stories to the grandchildren.

Daz Hoare is the outgoing chief petty officer of physical training on HMS Queen Elizabeth.

– a girls' school from India were recent visitors – on the concrete *maidon* in the picturesque town of Vahdat. Coaches from neighbouring countries are being invited to run courses at a fledgling academy, with Shahid Afridi and Mohammad Nabi lined up in 2022. A dedicated cricket ground is under construction in Dushanbe, where the men's national team will be able to play their first T20 internationals. With life in Afghanistan uncertain since the Taliban's return, the TCF have even invited the Afghanistan Cricket Board to share the ground, so Afghan teams have a home closer to Kabul than their usual haunts in India and the UAE.   JONATHAN CAMPION

TOKELAU

The victorious cricketers of "America" begin a celebratory jig, before grabbing buckets and joyously smearing the crestfallen "England" players in turquoise paint. Both teams sit down with the crowd for fish stew and coconut milk, as the Stars and Stripes, and Cross of St George, flutter in the warm breeze at St Peter's field. Every January, *Egelani* v *Amelika* (England v America) is one of the most colourful and fiercely contested highlights of the Tokelauan sporting calendar. The overarm bowling actions and strokeplay are familiar, but the bats and Laws have been adapted: *kilikiti*, Tokelau's national sport, is almost cricket – but not quite. Popular across Polynesia, it was introduced by Christian missionaries during the 1800s. Each year, 12–15 large-scale *kilikiti* matches are played across Tokelau, usually around Christmas and Easter, but sometimes on Mother's or Father's Day, and at weddings. Tokelau, with a population just under 1,500, is a remote New Zealand dependency in the Pacific, and *kilikiti* is played on its three atolls (Atafu, Nukunonu and Fakaofo). Nukunonu's big game divides the atoll into players from the north (*Egelani*) and south (*Amelika*) – names adopted shortly after the Second World War – for a seven-round tournament. "We used to play cricket every day for weeks at a time," remembers Ioane Tumua, an elder of team *Amelika*. "But we didn't have work back then, and lived off the land, so it was a simpler time." The field in Nukunonu was constructed in the 1960s by filling a saltwater lagoon with baskets of coral gravel – some argue the pitches are better than the drop-in wickets used in Australia. While *kilikiti* is played in good spirits, the terminology is distinctly Tokelauan, and reflects its origin as a substitute for war. It isn't a game, but a *taua* (battle); a batter isn't out, but *mate* (dead). Almost the entire atoll is involved, with multiple generations taking the field at the same time. This year's tournament, won by *Amelika*, was broadcast live on Facebook, so that overseas Tokelauans could feel part of the action. Some Tokelauans take an interest in New Zealand's fortunes on TV, but so far standard cricket has yet to catch on, according to Elena Pasilio, who reports on *kilikiti* for Nukunonu's *Te Uluga Talafau* newspaper. Cricket (as most know it) has been played at a decent level by players of Tokelauan descent, and notably by Fa'amele Pedro-Epati, who played *kilikiti* as a youngster. She represents New Zealand at indoor cricket, and plays at good club level in Auckland for Waitakere.   ADAM HOPKINS

UKRAINE

As he went around the classroom asking pupils to nominate their favourite colours for the umpteenth time, Kobus Olivier could see he was losing the attention of his English language students. Then the idea came to him: could cricket energise these young Ukrainians? The sport had been his life – growing up in Johannesburg, coaching in the townships with Bob Woolmer and pro-ing in England, before briefly serving as chief executive of Cricket Kenya. Olivier was running his own cricket academy in Dubai until he experienced a blissful summer in Kiev, and emigrated on a whim. Having landed a job as an English teacher in one of Kiev's exclusive private schools – he can speak barely a word of Ukrainian or Russian – he found cricket was a hit. "After all those years under the Soviet system, where everything was a little predictable, young people are clamouring for something new," said Olivier. "In terms of a foothold in schools, we're already ahead of the Netherlands." He dug into his extensive contacts book to secure a crateful of kit from Neal Radford at the Lord's Taverners, plus seven Kwik Cricket sets from Shyam Bhatia, the Dubai steel magnate who owns a cricket museum in Jumeirah. In 2021, Bhatia was named patron of the Ukraine Cricket Federation at a dinner thrown in his honour, and a cricket exchange programme set up between Kiev and Dubai. Olivier has met Ukraine's deputy minister of sports, hoping to persuade the government to add cricket to the national curriculum, and help it spread beyond a cluster of exclusive international schools. And cricket's USP? His answer won't please everyone. "I'm selling it as a British sport. I talk about the heritage of the game, and how it compares to Wimbledon. Ukraine is trying desperately to improve its English proficiency. There are more than 300 after-school English classes in Kiev, so what I say is that you learn English in my cricket classes, and you learn a new skill too." The challenge will be to knit his grassroots project together with the existing cricket scene in Ukraine, which is dominated by South Asian immigrants, mostly drawn by the reputation of the medical universities. In the north-eastern city of Kharkiv, a few hundred miles from the ongoing stand-off between Ukrainian and pro-Russia separatist troops in Donbas, Hardeep Singh, president of the UCF, runs an accommodation business which houses as many as 5,000 South Asian medical students. He is building Ukraine's first proper cricket ground. Until now, local cricketers have played their tapeball and hardball leagues virtually in isolation. When he arrived, Olivier was the only qualified coach in Ukraine, and the UCF cannot access ICC courses while they are not a member. But discussions have opened with the ICC over Associate status, which could be forthcoming as early as 2023. JAMES COYNE

VENEZUELA

The message inscribed on a cricket bat at the Uribana Penitentiary Centre in Barquisimeto reads: "*Defensa de los derechos humano*" (in defence of human rights). It was once used at club matches in Maracaibo and Caracas, but is now a brutal weapon. Prison officers use it to beat inmates, many incarcerated for criticising Venezuela's socialist president, Nicolás Maduro. How the bat ended up in the jail is unclear, though perhaps it was left behind by a cricketer fleeing a country in turmoil: since 2014, more than 5.9m have escaped Venezuela's political chaos, socio-economic instability and humanitarian crisis. Caracas Sports Club are nestled in El Peñón, away from the city and with views of the El Ávila mountain range – and cricket is hanging by a thread. Heavy-duty machinery cut into the hillside to create a striking ground in 1951, and a hooked six might rebound off a rockface. But few have been hit of late. CSC's cricket-playing members have dwindled and, even with guests, there are barely enough to scrape together a team – let alone two – for a twice-monthly knockabout. "It's a far cry from the glory days when we'd have ex-Test players from the West Indies squaring off against each other every weekend," sighs Robin Jones, a silver-haired Barbadian who recently, and reluctantly, left Venezuela. "We still played a fair bit until 2005, when it became too dangerous for many visitors." Most Venezuelan migrants have headed to other parts of Spanish-speaking Latin America, but 24,000 made the seven-mile trip across the Gulf of Paria to Trinidad. Since baseball is more popular than football in Venezuela, it is no surprise that a few have taken to cricket, joining in scratch games on the beach and elsewhere. Any attempts to watch Trinbago Knight Riders in the CPL, however, have been thwarted because of the difficulty of acquiring tickets without an ID card. The grass still gets cut once a week at CSC, and the artificial pitch plays pretty well, if one day Venezuela is stable enough for cricket to return.   TIMOTHY ABRAHAM

PART SIX

Overseas
Franchise
Cricket

OVERSEAS FRANCHISE CRICKET IN 2020-21

Freddie Wilde

Last year, the primary challenge facing the Twenty20 circuit was simply ensuring leagues were played during the global lockdown. As the world learned to live with Covid, the focus shifted to getting cricketers on the field, while navigating quarantines, isolations and biobubbles. This further complicated an already transient landscape: withdrawals and postponements abounded but, with large broadcast contracts to be fulfilled, the show had to go on.

But not everywhere. The second season of the Afghanistan Premier League had been delayed a year, to 2020-21, on account of funding problems, but was postponed again as the pandemic took hold. The coup by the Taliban suggested any staging was unlikely in the near future. Covid, though, was the main cause of cancellations: the Mzansi Super League, scheduled for November 2020, and the Bangladesh Premier League, for March 2021, were both cancelled. The debut of the Euro Slam, hosted by Ireland, Scotland and the Netherlands, and originally slated for the summer of 2019, was deferred yet again, to 2022.

It was touch-and-go for the **Indian Premier League**, which was suspended midway through, and completed in the UAE. The IPL had planned a mega-auction ahead of the 2021 edition, to give franchises the chance to rebuild from scratch, but this was put back a year, which should have hurt the ageing Chennai Super Kings. Rather than use the regular auction to attempt an ambitious overhaul, they retained the bulk of their squad and made small tweaks with huge consequences: they won their fourth IPL title and, given the circumstances, their most impressive.

Chennai's signing of Moeen Ali, deployed in an attacking role at No. 3, the rise of Ruturaj Gaikwad (the tournament's leading run-scorer, with 635) and the establishment of batting depth (Dwayne Bravo was at No. 9) allowed them to adopt a super-aggressive approach. This was a departure from the combination of strong bowling and stable batting that had underpinned their first three titles. The last five IPLs have been won by either Chennai or Mumbai Indians, who had been looking to complete a hat-trick of victories, but finished fifth. The 2022 mega-auction and the addition of two new franchises, in Ahmedabad and Lucknow, mean these two giants will have to grow again.

The **Big Bash League** introduced a number of new rules, with varying degrees of success. The powerplay was split in two: a mandatory block of four overs at the start, and a two-over Power Surge, activated by the batting team. It added intrigue, and prompted tactical debate. However, the Bash Boost – a bonus point for the higher team score after ten overs – produced mixed results, and the X Factor option, to deploy a substitute player, was rarely used.

As in the IPL, the historically strong teams continued to dominate: the well-rounded Sydney Sixers beat Perth Scorchers in the final, despite the Scorchers having re-energised their squad, CSK-style, by concentrating on batting depth. The Sixers' experienced line-up was complemented by Josh Philippe, the league's best young batting talent.

The **Caribbean Premier League** was deservedly won by one of the season's break-out teams: St Kitts and Nevis Patriots, who turned their 2020 wooden spoon to gold. They had arguably the most impressive draft in T20 history: Evin Lewis made 426 runs, with a strike-rate of 163, and was well supported by youngsters Sherfane Rutherford and Dominic Drakes – the hero of a thrilling final against St Lucia Kings.

The Kings' head coach, Andy Flower, was a common feature among successful teams. He led Delhi Bulls to the **T10 League** final in the UAE, Trent Rockets to the men's Hundred eliminator, and Multan Sultans to their first **Pakistan Super League**, another competition that suffered a Covid hiatus. Multan's captain, Mohammad Rizwan, decided to remodel himself as an opening batsman. It proved an inspired decision: he broke the record for the most T20 runs in a calendar year, with 2,036.

Rashid Khan continued to stand out as the world's best T20 bowler, and did so against the backdrop of political turmoil at home. In the inaugural **Lanka Premier League**, he had competition from local spinner Wanindu Hasaranga de Silva, who was adjudged the Most Valuable Player, having taken Jaffna Stallions to the title with his array of googlies and middle-order hitting. The LPL was one of the feel-good stories of the year, showcasing the domestic talent that promises a brighter future for Sri Lanka's ailing national team.

In the **Super Smash**, Wellington Firebirds romped to the title after winning nine of their ten group games. They boasted the tournament's two highest run-scorers in Finn Allen (512 runs, strike-rate 194) and Devon Conway (455 runs, strike-rate 136).

Meanwhile, a tactic emerged: to attack the post-powerplay overs with specialist spin-hitters. England's Liam Livingstone combined brutal power (he struck 86 sixes in the year) with off- and leg-spin bowling, depending on the match-up. Singapore-born Australian Tim David punished slow-bowling attacks in the BBL, CPL and PSL with low hands and a front-foot bias. To counter this new threat, bowling teams turned to enforcers – bowlers who send it down fast and short – such as Lockie Ferguson, Tymal Mills and Anrich Nortje. These methods are likely to shape the game in the coming years, unsettling the traditional pace–spin–pace deployment inherited from ODI cricket, and pushing T20's claim as the most strategic format.

ROLL OF HONOUR

Afghanistan	Afghanistan Premier League	*Not held*
Australia	Big Bash League	Sydney Sixers
Bangladesh	Bangladesh Premier League	*Not held*
India	Indian Premier League	Chennai Super Kings
Ireland	Euro Slam	*Launch postponed to 2022*
Pakistan	Pakistan Super League	Multan Sultans
New Zealand	Super Smash	Wellington Firebirds
South Africa	Mzansi Super League	*Not held*
Sri Lanka	Lanka Premier League	Jaffna Stallions
West Indies	Caribbean Premier League	St Kitts and Nevis Patriots
United Arab Emirates	T10 League	Northern Warriors

THE LEADING TWENTY20 CRICKETER IN 2021

Mohammad Rizwan

Alan Gardner

Twenty20 batting is supposed to be a volatile, high-variance occupation: boom-boom or bust. Occasionally, a player produces a purple patch to rise above the hurly-burly. But no one has had a year of such sustained run-scoring as Pakistan's Mohammed Rizwan. Never mind seeing it well: he was batting as if blessed with foresight. And in a sense he was. After starring in Pakistan's ten-wicket demolition of India at the T20 World Cup, his clarity of purpose was summed up by a viral video from the ICC that spliced his pre-game routine of visualisation alongside the boundaries he struck during his 55-ball 79.

Rizwan had begun the year uncertain of his place, either for his country or in the Pakistan Super League. "My T20 career looked finished to me," he said. Before October 2020, he had opened only eight times in T20; a little over a year later, he was one half of Pakistan's most-successful opening partnership ever, as well as the captain who had led his new team, Multan Sultans, to their first PSL title.

The bare numbers had a formidable heft. Rizwan peeled off 1,326 T20I runs at 73 – breaking the calendar record, set by Ireland's Paul Stirling in 2019, by almost 600. In all T20 cricket, he made 2,036 at 56. No one – not Chris Gayle, not Virat Kohli, not Rizwan's opening partner, Babar Azam, who last year scored 1,779 himself – had ever got near 2,000.

He had debuted for Pakistan in April 2015, but struggled to hold down a spot in any format. In February 2021, a few days after his maiden Test hundred, he raised three figures for the first time in T20s, an unbeaten 104 from 64 balls against South Africa in Lahore.

That was the numerical high point, though it was downhill from there only in the sense that Rizwan was nigh-on unstoppable. He made 30 or more in two-thirds of his 45 T20 innings, and was dismissed in single figures just six times. From stand-in opener, promoted as an experiment in Babar's absence in New Zealand in 2020-21, Rizwan became a standard-bearer for consistency in the face of T20's slings and arrows.

His efforts were not quite enough to take Pakistan all the way at the T20 World Cup, though his 67 off 52 in the semi-final against Australia almost helped them overcome the disadvantage of batting first. It emerged he had spent the previous two nights in hospital with a severe chest infection. "I want to do what nobody else is doing, because if somebody's done it, then that's just ordinary," he said. There was nothing ordinary about Rizwan's rise.

THE LEADING TWENTY20 CRICKETER IN THE WORLD

2018	Rashid Khan (Afghanistan)		2021	Kieron Pollard (West Indies)
2019	Rashid Khan (Afghanistan)		**2022**	**Mohammad Rizwan (Pakistan)**
2020	Andre Russell (West Indies)			

KFC TWENTY20 BIG BASH LEAGUE IN 2020-21

Daniel Cherny

1 Sydney Sixers   2 Perth Scorchers

The shifting Covid situation in 2020 hampered most Australian industries, but particularly professional sport, and perhaps no competition more than the BBL. As outbreaks flared up all over the place, there were considerable implications for travel between the main cities, throwing into confusion a tournament normally spanning six states and two territories.

The fixture list changed more often than a contentious piece of legislation, and some players struggled with the protocols restricting contact with the outside world. Brisbane Heat's captain, Chris Lynn, and English batsman Dan Lawrence were fined for a social outing involving a photo with a fan and a proscribed taxi trip (after testing negative for the virus, they were allowed to play the next game, but had to prepare separately). Melbourne Renegades' Will Sutherland was fined for a game of golf and a meal with friends. Sutherland's should-have-been team-mate Imran Tahir opted out altogether; after weeks in bio-bubbles at the IPL and PSL, he declined to put himself through further quarantine.

Given the challenges, it was remarkable that at least one match was played in each of the six states, though the biggest number – 13 – took place in the Australian Capital Territory. That was one of two initial hubs, along with Tasmania, before games spread to Queensland and South Australia, then Western Australia and Victoria. But there were forced changes up to the end, when a flash lockdown meant Perth Scorchers had to switch a home knockout game to Canberra. And because of ongoing issues in New South Wales, only one fixture was played in Sydney: the final. There, **Sydney Sixers** claimed a second successive title, equalling the record of three set by the Scorchers, their defeated opponents. Two of their batters – James Vince and Josh Philippe – passed 500 runs. It was an 11th domestic trophy for their coach, Greg Shipperd, who had also won nine across three formats with Victoria. But there was an unfortunate postscript a few months later, when the Sixers' popular general manager Jodie Hawkins departed in a Cricket NSW restructure.

The tournament introduced three key innovations: the Power Surge, effectively a floating two-over powerplay (with the initial powerplay cut to four); the Bash Boost, a bonus point for whichever side had the higher total after ten overs; and the X-Factor, an opportunity to introduce a full substitute after ten overs of the first innings. The X-Factor did not catch on. The Bash Boost created some interesting moments, but was criticised for rewarding mediocrity: teams who lost early wickets while chasing put their foot down in the hope of collecting a point from a heavy defeat.

Indeed, in the last league match, the drama was sapped out of a potentially thrilling finish. To qualify as one of the five teams in the knockouts, **Melbourne Stars** needed a win plus the Boost point, but knew they were out as soon as the Sixers overtook their halfway score inside eight overs. It was only the second time they had missed the final stages. **Perth Scorchers** and **Brisbane Heat** made slow starts, but surged home to qualify. Second-placed Perth were fired up by England's Liam Livingstone and New Zealand's Colin Munro, while Jhye Richardson took 29 wickets, five more than anyone else; the Heat relied heavily on Lynn's spasmodic brilliance. **Sydney Thunder** defied the impositions in New South Wales to qualify in third place. They were fuelled by Alex Hales, the tournament's leading run-scorer with 543, including a record 30 sixes and a century which helped them reach 232 against the Sixers – the highest total in ten BBL seasons. **Adelaide Strikers** had an up-and-down campaign, but squeezed into the final five at the expense of the Stars and **Hobart Hurricanes**, who blew a strong first half – much of it in Tasmania – to flop at the back end. They lost on the last day of the league stage to the otherwise lamentable **Melbourne Renegades**, who claimed back-to-back wooden spoons as Aaron Finch endured a lean spell.

That last day of the league, January 26, was shrouded in controversy after Cricket Australia decided against marketing it as Australia Day, which commemorates the arrival of the First Fleet of white settlers in 1788. It prompted an angry reaction from the prime minister, Scott Morrison – and a forthright riposte from the Sixers' Indigenous all-rounder, Dan Christian, who called on him to follow CA's example.

BIG BASH LEAGUE AVERAGES IN 2020-21

BATTING (250 runs, strike-rate 125.00)

		M	I	NO	R	HS	100	50	Avge	SR	4	6
1	D. T. Christian (*Sydney S*)..	16	14	6	272	61*	0	2	34.00	182.55	21	18
2	A. D. Hales (*Sydney T*)	15	15	1	543	110	1	3	38.78	161.60	54	30
3	B. C. J. Cutting (*Sydney T*)..	15	13	6	280	34*	0	0	40.00	157.30	26	16
4	C. A. Lynn (*Brisbane H*)...	13	13	0	458	69	0	5	35.23	154.72	39	26
5	T. H. David (*Hobart H*)....	14	14	5	279	58	0	1	31.00	153.29	19	14
6	J. R. Philippe (*Sydney S*)...	16	16	0	508	95	0	3	31.75	149.41	55	14
7	M. R. Marsh (*Perth S*).....	15	14	6	315	57*	0	3	39.37	147.88	27	13
8	J. C. Silk (*Sydney S*)	16	14	4	382	78	0	1	38.20	144.69	41	5
9	J. M. Vince (*Sydney S*)	16	16	2	537	98*	0	4	38.35	143.58	59	11
10	G. J. Maxwell (*Melb S*)...	14	13	1	379	71*	0	3	31.58	143.56	32	17
11	S. W. Billings (*Sydney T*)..	11	10	1	260	83	0	2	28.88	142.85	21	9
12	M. P. Stoinis (*Melbourne S*)..	13	13	1	396	97*	0	3	33.00	142.44	40	17
13	†J. B. Weatherald (*Adel S*)..	15	15	3	433	80*	0	3	36.08	141.04	37	22
14	J. P. Inglis (*Perth S*)	17	16	4	413	72*	0	3	34.41	140.00	40	9
15	B. R. McDermott (*Hob H*) ..	12	12	1	402	96	0	3	36.54	139.58	28	21
16	L. S. Livingstone (*Perth S*).	14	14	0	426	77	0	3	30.42	133.96	26	28
17	†D. P. Hughes (*Sydney S*) ...	16	16	3	331	96	0	2	25.46	131.34	24	11
18	J. J. Roy (*Perth S*)	12	12	1	355	74*	0	2	32.27	130.51	43	7
19	P. D. Salt (*Adelaide S*).....	15	15	0	310	59	0	2	20.66	130.25	29	9
20	†C. Munro (*Perth S*)	16	15	1	443	82	0	4	31.64	128.03	32	19
21	†U. T. Khawaja (*Sydney T*)..	15	15	1	338	49	0	0	24.14	127.54	45	3
22	M. A. Bryant (*Brisbane H*)..	14	14	0	302	40	0	0	21.57	127.42	34	8
23	†C. A. Ingram (*Hobart H*)...	10	10	0	258	55	0	1	25.80	127.09	25	9
24	†S. E. Marsh (*Melbourne R*)..	12	12	0	312	87	0	3	26.00	126.82	23	10
25	N. C. R. Larkin (*Melb S*)...	11	10	3	276	70	0	2	39.42	126.60	32	5
26	J. J. Peirson (*Brisbane H*) ..	17	16	9	324	69*	0	1	46.28	126.56	22	7

BOWLING (12 wickets)

		Style	Balls	Dots	R	W	BB	4I	Avge	SR	ER
1	Mujeeb Zadran (*Bris H*) .	OB	180	77	188	14	5-15	1	13.42	12.85	**6.26**
2	Rashid Khan (*Adelaide S*)	LB	234	93	268	16	3-18	0	16.75	14.62	**6.87**
3	S. N. J. O'Keefe (*Sydney S*)	SLA	294	100	340	15	3-15	0	22.66	19.60	**6.93**
4	J. P. Behrendorff (*Perth S*)	LFM	318	156	373	16	2-17	0	23.31	19.87	**7.03**
5	A. Zampa (*Melbourne S*)	LB	271	97	332	19	5-17	1	17.47	14.26	**7.35**
6	J. D. Wildermuth (*Bris H*)	RFM	252	101	312	13	3-23	0	24.00	19.38	**7.42**
7	P. M. Siddle (*Adelaide S*)	RFM	260	106	323	19	5-16	1	17.00	13.68	**7.45**
8	J. A. Richardson (*Perth S*)	RFM	369	168	474	29	4-24	2	16.34	12.72	**7.70**
9	Fawad Ahmed (*Perth S*) .	LB	339	107	436	15	3-25	0	29.06	22.60	**7.71**
10	R. P. Meredith (*Hobart H*)	RFM	302	123	394	16	3-21	0	24.62	18.87	**7.82**
11	S. M. Boland (*Hobart H*)	RFM	326	140	432	17	4-41	1	25.41	19.17	**7.95**
12	A. J. Tye (*Perth S*)	RFM	325	127	433	21	4-20	1	20.61	15.47	**7.99**
13	K. W. Richardson (*Melb R*)	RFM	243	100	324	15	3-22	0	21.60	16.20	**8.00**
14	X. C. Bartlett (*Brisbane H*)	RFM	246	96	328	12	3-24	0	27.33	20.50	**8.00**
15	C. R. Brathwaite (*Sydney S*)	RFM	288	100	385	16	4-18	1	24.06	18.00	**8.02**
16	T. Sangha (*Sydney T*) . . .	LB	285	98	384	21	4-14	1	18.28	13.57	**8.08**
17	P. Hatzoglou (*Melb R*) . .	LB	282	103	389	17	3-43	0	22.88	16.58	**8.27**
18	N. T. Ellis (*Hobart H*) . . .	RFM	322	110	446	20	4-34	1	22.30	16.10	**8.31**
19	B. Stanlake (*Melbourne S*)	RFM	233	101	324	13	3-25	0	24.92	17.92	**8.34**
20	W. A. Agar (*Adelaide S*) .	RFM	328	140	457	22	4-27	1	20.77	14.90	**8.35**
21	C. J. Green (*Sydney T*) . .	OB	234	73	336	13	4-34	1	25.84	18.00	**8.61**
22	D. T. Christian (*Sydney S*)	RFM	270	76	398	15	3-36	0	26.53	18.00	**8.84**
23	B. J. Dwarshuis (*Sydney S*)	LFM	273	110	403	24	4-13	1	16.79	11.37	**8.85**
24	L. C. Hatcher (*Melbourne S*)	RFM	208	70	308	13	3-28	0	23.69	16.00	**8.88**
25	M. T. Steketee (*Brisbane H*)	RFM	338	129	522	24	4-33	1	21.75	14.08	**9.26**
26	N. J. McAndrew (*Sydney T*)	RFM	264	96	429	15	3-41	0	28.60	17.60	**9.75**

KFC TWENTY20 BIG BASH LEAGUE IN 2020-21

	P	W	L	NR	Boost	Pts	NRR
SYDNEY SIXERS	14	9	5	0	9	36	0.25
PERTH SCORCHERS . .	14	8	5	1	6.5	32	0.85
SYDNEY THUNDER . .	14	8	6	0	7	31	0.94
BRISBANE HEAT	14	7	7	0	8	29	−0.28
ADELAIDE STRIKERS .	14	7	7	0	7	28	0.10
Hobart Hurricanes	14	7	7	0	7	28	−0.18
Melbourne Stars.	14	5	8	1	7.5	24	0.14
Melbourne Renegades . . .	14	4	10	0	4	16	−1.72

Win = 3pts; no result = 1.5pts. Bash Boost point (for team with more runs after ten overs of each innings) = 1pt, or 0.5pts each in a no-result.

4th v 5th At Brisbane, January 29, 2021 (floodlit). **Brisbane Heat won by six wickets.** ‡**Adelaide Strikers 130-7** (20 overs) (J. B. Weatherald 32; M. Labuschagne 3-13); **Brisbane Heat 131-4** (18.5 overs) (J. L. Denly 41, J. J. Peirson 47*). PoM: J. J. Peirson. *The Strikers chose to bat, but became badly bogged down by the leg-spin of Marnus Labuschagne and Mitchell Swepson (2-23). Labuschagne then fell cheaply as the Heat stumbled to 23-3, before Joe Denly and Jimmy Peirson dug them out of the hole.*

1st v 2nd At Canberra, January 30, 2021 (floodlit). **Sydney Sixers won by nine wickets.** ‡**Perth Scorchers 167-6** (20 overs) (C. Munro 30, J. P. Inglis 69*, A. J. Turner 33); **Sydney Sixers 168-1** (17 overs) (J. R. Philippe 45, J. M. Vince 98*). PoM: J. M. Vince. *The Sixers quickly removed Perth's dangerous English openers, Jason Roy and Liam Livingstone; then, despite a 41-ball 69* from Josh Inglis, easily overhauled them on a benign Manuka Oval pitch. James Vince and Josh Philippe opened with 92 in 8.5 overs, and Vince was 98* from 53 with one run required; a bouncer from Andrew Tye was called wide, denying him a sublime century. "I hope he didn't mean it," said Vince.*

3rd v winners of first play-off At Canberra, January 31, 2021 (floodlit). **Brisbane Heat won by seven wickets. Sydney Thunder 158-8** (20 overs) (S. W. Billings 34, B. C. J. Cutting 34*); ‡**Brisbane Heat 162-3** (19.1 overs) (M. Labuschagne 32, S. D. Heazlett 74*, J. J. Peirson 43*). *PoM:* S. D. Heazlett. *Plenty of Thunder batsmen got starts, but none could pass 34, though Ben Cutting ensured they took 48 off the last four overs. Chasing 159, the Heat started badly again – 14-2 – but Sam Heazlett smacked 74* in 49 balls to eliminate the Thunder and enter the final play-off. He put on 92* in 7.1 overs with Peirson, who scored a handy 43* in 24.*

Losers of second play-off v winners of third play-off At Canberra, February 4, 2021 (floodlit). **Perth Scorchers won by 49 runs** (DLS). **Perth Scorchers 189-1** (18.1 overs) (C. T. Bancroft 58*, L. S. Livingstone 77, M. R. Marsh 49*); ‡**Brisbane Heat 150-9** (18 overs) (J. A. Burns 38; A. M. Hardie 3-46). *PoM:* L. S. Livingstone. *The Scorchers ended Brisbane's run of four wins after Livingstone snatched the game from their hands. He smashed 77 in 39 balls, with six sixes, out of a stand of 114 with his new opening partner, Cameron Bancroft, who was promoted because of Roy's ankle injury, and went on to add 75* with Mitchell Marsh. Later, the resurgent Jason Behrendorff removed Denly and Chris Lynn with successive deliveries (though he was the Heat's leading run-scorer, Lynn never got going in the knockouts). That helped ensure the final would be played by the tournament's two best – and historically most successful – sides.*

FINAL

SYDNEY SIXERS v PERTH SCORCHERS

At Sydney, February 6, 2021 (floodlit). Sydney Sixers won by 27 runs. Toss: Perth Scorchers.

After two months on the road, the Sixers arrived home at the SCG, and claimed back-to-back titles. It was their fourth meeting of the season with the Scorchers, and their third win. As in their previous encounter, a week earlier, Vince was denied a hundred, though less controversially – this time he was caught at backward point off Fawad Ahmed. But he had been the thorn in Perth's side again, nullifying the attack led by Behrendorff and Richardson as he raced to 95 out of 140; none of his team-mates passed 20. The Scorchers needed 189, and Bancroft and Livingstone made a promising start, with 45 in 4.5 overs, before Bird removed both. Christian, who had joined the Sixers after a lean summer with the Renegades in 2019-20, took two wickets in the final over, proving his Midas touch was back, and completing a comfortable victory.

Player of the Match: J. M. Vince. *Player of the Tournament:* J. R. Philippe (Sydney Sixers).

Sydney Sixers

		B	4/6
1 †J. R. Philippe *run out (9/7)*...	9	8	0/1
2 J. M. Vince *c 5 b 11*.........	95	60	10/3
3 D. P. Hughes *c 3 b 8*	13	10	0/1
4 *M. C. Henriques *c 7 b 9*.....	18	11	2
5 J. C. Silk *not out*..........	17	11	2
6 D. T. Christian *c 3 b 9*	20	14	1/1
7 C. R. Brathwaite *c 10 b 8*.....	10	6	2
Lb 4, w 2	6		

4 overs: 31-1 (20 overs) 188-6

1/28 2/66 3/114 4/140 5/177 6/188

8 S. A. Abbott, 9 B. J. Dwarshuis, 10 S. N. J. O'Keefe and 11 J. M. Bird did not bat.

Behrendorff 24–8–36–0; Richardson 24–7–45–2; Tye 24–11–29–2; Fawad Ahmed 18–5–16–1; Hardie 18–5–37–0; Livingstone 12–4–21–0.

Perth Scorchers

		B	4/6
1 C. T. Bancroft *c 2 b 11*........	30	19	4/1
2 L. S. Livingstone *c 5 b 11*	45	35	3/2
3 C. Munro *c 4 b 8*	2	4	0
4 †J. P. Inglis *c 4 b 9*.........	22	20	2
5 M. R. Marsh *c 2 b 9*	11	10	1
6 *A. J. Turner *c 11 b 8*	11	9	1
7 A. M. Hardie *c 10 b 9*	26	13	1/2
8 J. A. Richardson *not out*......	7	7	0
9 A. J. Tye *c 4 b 6*............	0	3	0
10 J. P. Behrendorff *c 8 b 6*......	0	1	0
11 Fawad Ahmed *not out*	0	0	0
Lb 2, w 4, nb 1	7		

4 overs: 43-0 (20 overs) 161-9

1/45 2/56 3/95 4/116 5/117 6/142 7/157 8/159 9/160

Bird 18–8–14–2; Dwarshuis 24–9–37–3; Abbott 18–3–33–2; Christian 24–10–25–2; O'Keefe 24–8–26–0; Brathwaite 12–2–24–0.

Umpires: S. J. Nogajski and P. Wilson. Third umpire: G. A. Abood.
Referee: R. W. Stratford.

BIG BASH FINALS

2011-12	SYDNEY SIXERS beat Perth Scorchers by seven wickets at Perth.	
2012-13	BRISBANE HEAT beat Perth Scorchers by 34 runs at Perth.	
2013-14	PERTH SCORCHERS beat Hobart Hurricanes by 39 runs at Perth.	
2014-15	PERTH SCORCHERS beat Sydney Sixers by four wickets at Canberra.	
2015-16	SYDNEY THUNDER beat Melbourne Stars by three wickets at Melbourne.	
2016-17	PERTH SCORCHERS beat Sydney Sixers by nine wickets at Perth.	
2017-18	ADELAIDE STRIKERS beat Hobart Hurricanes by 25 runs at Adelaide.	
2018-19	MELBOURNE RENEGADES beat Melbourne Stars by 13 runs at Melbourne (Dock).	
2019-20	SYDNEY SIXERS beat Melbourne Stars by 19 runs at Sydney.	
2020-21	SYDNEY SIXERS beat Perth Scorchers by 27 runs at Sydney.	

BIG BASH LEAGUE RECORDS

Highest score	147*	M. P. Stoinis .	Melbourne S v Sydney S at Melbourne	2019-20
	130*	M. S. Wade . .	Hobart H v Adelaide S at Adelaide	2019-20
	122*	D. J. M. Short.	Hobart H v Brisbane H at Brisbane. . . .	2017-18
Fastest 50 – balls	12	C. H. Gayle . .	Melbourne R v Adelaide S at Melbourne	2015-16
Fastest 100 – balls	39	C. J. Simmons	Perth S v Adelaide S at Perth	2013-14
Most sixes – innings	11	C. H. Gayle . .	Sydney T v Adelaide S at Sydney.	2011-12
	11	C. J. Simmons	Perth S v Sydney S at Sydney	2013-14
	11	C. A. Lynn. .	Brisbane H v Perth S at Perth	2016-17
	11	C. A. Lynn. .	Brisbane H v Sydney S at Sydney.	2019-20
Most runs – season	705	M. P. Stoinis (avge 54.23, SR 136.62) for Melbourne S		2019-20
Most sixes – season	30	**A. D. Hales for Sydney T**		**2020-21**
Most runs – career	2,790	**C. A. Lynn** (avge 37.20, SR 150.97)		**2011-12 to 2020-21**
	2,431	**A. J. Finch** (avge 34.23, SR 134.60)		**2011-12 to 2020-21**
	2,205	**G. J. Maxwell** (avge 32.42, SR 149.08) . . .		**2011-12 to 2020-21**
Most 100s – career	2	A. T. Carey (2016-17 to 2020-21), A. J. Finch (2011-12 to 2020-21), U. T. Khawaja (2011-12 to 2020-21), D. J. M. Short (2016-17 to 2020-21), C. J. Simmons (2013-14 to 2015-16), L. J. Wright (2011-12 to 2017-18)		
Best SR – career†	152.11	**A. D. Hales** (1,474 runs, avge 33.50)		**2012-13 to 2020-21**
Most sixes – career	172	**C. A. Lynn**		**2011-12 to 2020-21**
Best bowling	6-7	S. L. Malinga. .	Melbourne S v Perth S at Perth	2012-13
	6-11	I. S. Sodhi	Adelaide S v Sydney T at Sydney . . .	2016-17
	5-14	D. T. Christian. .	Hobart H v Adelaide S at Hobart	2016-17
Most econ four overs	3-3	M. G. Johnson .	Perth S v Melbourne S at Perth	2016-17
Most expensive analysis	0-61	B. J. Dwarshuis	Sydney S v Melbourne S at Melbourne	2019-20
Most wickets – season	30	D. R. Sams (avge 15.36, ER 7.83) for Sydney T		2019-20
Most wickets – career	111	**B. Laughlin** (avge 24.26, ER 8.08)		**2011-12 to 2020-21**
	106	**S. A. Abbott** (avge 21.04, ER 8.52)		**2011-12 to 2020-21**
	98	**K. W. Richardson** (avge 22.90, ER 7.82). . .		**2011-12 to 2020-21**
Best ER – career‡	5.40	S. L. Malinga (300 balls, avge 15.00).		2012-13 to 2013-14
Highest total	232-5	**Sydney T v Sydney S at Adelaide**.		**2020-21**
	223-8	Hobart H v Melbourne R at Melbourne (Dock)		2016-17
	222-4	Melbourne R v Hobart H at Melbourne (Dock)		2016-17
Lowest total	57	Melbourne R v Melbourne S at Melbourne (Dock)		2014-15
Highest successful chase	223-8	Hobart H v Melbourne R at Melbourne (Dock)		2016-17
Highest match aggregate	445-12	Melbourne R v Hobart H at Melbourne (Dock)		2016-17

† *Career strike-rate: minimum 500 runs.*   ‡ *Career economy-rate: minimum 300 balls.*

VIVO INDIAN PREMIER LEAGUE IN 2021

Anand Vasu

1 Chennai Super Kings   2 Kolkata Knight Riders

In 2020, the pandemic had delayed the tournament for six months and forced a move to the United Arab Emirates. This time, to enable it to be held safely in India, logistics experts had advised using as few venues as possible, and proposed three, all in Maharashtra: the Wankhede Stadium in Mumbai, the DY Patil Stadium in Navi Mumbai, and the MCA Stadium in Gahunje, on the outskirts of Pune. This would allow teams to travel entirely by road, reducing the risk of breaching the biosecure bubble. To even up the playing field, it was proposed that no team would play at their traditional home ground.

When the BCCI unveiled their schedule for the 2021 IPL, it provoked incredulity. They had rejected the experts' proposals, and wanted the tournament's climax – the four knockout games – to be played at the new stadium in Ahmedabad, which had just been renamed after prime minister Narendra Modi. Once that was cleared, it was impossible to deny other state associations. So the format adopted was a "cluster-caravan": the eight teams would spend a couple of weeks in Chennai and Mumbai, then move to Ahmedabad and Delhi for a fortnight, then to Bangalore and Kolkata, and finally back to Ahmedabad.

They got halfway through the fixture list – 29 out of 60 matches – before it collapsed. The cricket had kept going as the latest Covid wave in India reached horrific levels and, when the BCCI finally called a halt, it was not in response to the mass deaths but because the virus had penetrated the bubble. Half a dozen individuals, including players, across four franchises tested positive, and the entire Delhi Capitals team were isolated as a precaution.

The tournament halted in early May, and did not resume until September, when it returned to the UAE, shoehorned in ahead of the T20 World Cup – also displaced to the UAE from India. By October, a sense of order was restored, with M. S. Dhoni lifting the trophy, as the most consistent team, **Chennai Super Kings**, bounced back from a dire 2020. But the miracle was that the IPL was completed at all.

When the suspension came, Virat Kohli's **Royal Challengers Bangalore** had been enjoying an unusually bright run. Glenn Maxwell, now with his fourth team, had at last found his home, helping them to third place, with five wins from seven matches – behind Chennai, on net run-rate, and leaders **Delhi Capitals**, who had six wins from eight.

The top three would remain the same when the league stage concluded, five months later. But there were significant changes elsewhere. The long break affected defending champions **Mumbai Indians** – notorious slow starters – more than anyone else, as they effectively had two mini-campaigns to run. They had hauled themselves into fourth place before the tournament ground to a halt, but could not regain their momentum, and missed the play-offs.

Kolkata Knight Riders moved in the other direction: they had lost five of their seven games in India, and were next to bottom, but in the UAE Eoin Morgan showed exceptional captaincy. Despite his own poor form, he more than justified his place, shepherding his side's strong comeback: the Knight Riders eventually fought their way to the final, beating Bangalore (with two balls to spare) and Delhi (with one) in the play-offs. Delhi Capitals had been the team to beat for the best part of the tournament, but Kolkata chased down 136 thanks to an opening stand of 96 from Shubman Gill and Venkatesh Iyer – the left-hand batter who was perhaps the find of the IPL year – despite a collapse of six for seven in the closing overs.

They joined Chennai in the final in Dubai, a thousand miles from Ahmedabad and 138 days later than planned. But there was a sense of inevitability about the game: if the Super Kings make it to the back end, they usually seal the deal. Sure enough, openers Faf du Plessis and Ruturaj Gaikwad rustled up a quick 61, and du Plessis batted through the innings for 86 out of an imposing 192 for three. For the Knight Riders, Gill and Iyer made an even better start, raising 91, but the middle order folded.

Chennai had based their campaign on the starts provided by du Plessis and Gaikwad, who ended up in a shoot-out for the Orange Cap awarded to the leading run-scorer: Gaikwad finished with 635 at an average of 45 and a strike-rate of 136, with du Plessis two behind. **Punjab Kings** (formerly Kings XI Punjab) also relied heavily on their openers, K. L. Rahul and Mayank Agarwal, but this did not work out so well: they finished sixth.

Sunrisers Hyderabad never got going, with a single win in India and only two in the UAE. They were in such disarray that they sacked David Warner as captain, then dropped him altogether. Almost as ineffective were **Rajasthan Royals**. Apart from the occasional rush from Sanju Samson, who had acquired a reputation for striking once and doing not much more, the Royals had little to write home about, though their plans were scuppered when two of their England stars – Jofra Archer and Ben Stokes – were injured, and a third, Jos Buttler, did not return in September.

For Bangalore, the brightest light was Harshal Patel, whose 32 wickets equalled Dwayne Bravo's eight-year record for an IPL season. Nine came in victories over Mumbai Indians: he dismissed three in four balls in Chennai, then followed up with a hat-trick in Dubai.

Saikat Das, Sportzpics/IPL

Unstoppable: Bangalore's Harshal Patel tears in against Mumbai Indians at Dubai, scene of his hat-trick.

In 2022, the IPL was set to expand to ten teams, with the addition of two new franchises representing Ahmedabad and Lucknow. India's women were still awaiting their own league, however; in 2021, there was no attempt to stage the minimalist Women's T20 Challenge which had run alongside the men's play-offs in the previous three seasons.

INDIAN PREMIER LEAGUE AVERAGES IN 2021

BATTING (200 runs)

		M	I	NO	R	HS	100	50	Avge	SR	4	6
1	†S. O. Hetmyer (*Delhi C*)..	14	13	6	242	53*	0	1	34.57	**168.05**	19	12
2	P. P. Shaw (*Delhi C*).....	15	15	0	479	82	0	4	31.93	**159.13**	56	18
3	J. C. Buttler (*Rajasthan R*)	7	7	0	254	124	1	0	36.28	**153.01**	27	13
4	A. T. Rayudu (*Chen SK*) .	16	13	4	257	72*	0	2	28.55	**151.17**	16	17
5	K. A. Pollard (*Mumbai I*) .	14	13	5	245	87*	0	1	30.62	**148.48**	16	16
6	A. B. de Villiers (*RC Bang*)	15	14	4	313	76*	0	2	31.30	**148.34**	23	16
7	†Y. B. Jaiswal (*Rajasthan R*)	10	10	0	249	50	0	1	24.90	**148.21**	32	10
8	†R. A. Jadeja (*Chennai SK*)	16	12	9	227	62*	0	1	75.66	**145.51**	19	9
9	G. J. Maxwell (*RC Bang*) .	15	14	2	513	78	0	6	42.75	**144.10**	48	21
10	S. A. Yadav (*Mumbai I*) ..	14	14	0	317	82	0	2	22.64	**143.43**	40	10
11	J. M. Bairstow (*S Hyd'bad*)	7	7	1	248	63*	0	2	41.33	**141.71**	20	15
12	M. A. Agarwal (*Punjab K*)	12	12	1	441	99*	0	4	40.09	**140.44**	42	18
13	R. A. Tripathi (*Kol KR*) ..	17	16	2	397	74*	0	2	28.35	**140.28**	41	11
14	K. L. Rahul (*Punjab K*) ..	13	13	3	626	98*	0	6	62.60	**138.80**	48	30
15	F. du Plessis (*Chennai SK*)	16	16	2	633	95*	0	6	45.21	**138.20**	60	23
16	†M. M. Ali (*Chennai SK*)..	15	15	1	357	58	0	1	25.50	**137.30**	31	19
17	S. V. Samson (*Raj R*)	14	14	2	484	119	1	2	40.33	**136.72**	45	17
18	R. D. Gaikwad (*Chen SK*)	16	16	2	635	101*	1	4	45.35	**136.26**	64	23
19	†I. P. Kishan (*Mumbai I*) ..	10	10	1	241	84	0	2	26.77	**133.88**	21	10
20	K. D. Karthik (*Kol KR*)...	17	15	5	223	40	0	0	22.30	**131.17**	22	7
21	†R. R. Pant (*Delhi C*)	16	16	4	419	58*	0	3	34.91	**128.52**	42	10
22	†V. R. Iyer (*Kolkata KR*) .	5	5	0	370	67	0	4	41.11	**128.47**	37	14
23	R. G. Sharma (*Mumbai I*).	13	13	0	381	63	0	1	29.30	**127.42**	33	14
24	†D. B. Padikkal (*RC Bang*)	14	14	1	411	101*	1	1	31.61	**125.30**	44	14
25	†S. Dhawan (*Delhi C*)	16	16	1	587	92	0	3	39.13	**124.62**	63	16
26	M. K. Pandey (*S Hyd'bad*)	8	8	2	292	69*	0	3	48.66	**123.72**	21	10
27	†N. Rana (*Kolkata KR*)....	17	16	3	383	80	0	2	29.46	**121.97**	34	17
28	V. Kohli (*RC Bangalore*) ..	15	15	1	405	72*	0	3	28.92	**119.46**	43	9
29	†S. R. Dube (*Rajasthan R*) .	9	9	1	230	64*	0	1	28.75	**119.17**	18	10
30	S. Gill (*Kolkata KR*)......	17	17	0	478	57	0	3	28.11	**118.90**	50	12
31	†Q. de Kock (*Mumbai I*)...	11	11	1	297	70*	0	2	29.70	**116.01**	29	7
32	K. S. Williamson (*S Hyd*) .	10	10	4	266	66*	0	2	44.33	**113.19**	29	2

BOWLING (10 wickets)

		Style	Balls	Dots	R	W	BB	4I	Avge	SR	ER
1	A. A. Nortje (*Delhi C*) ..	RF	182	84	187	12	2-12	0	15.58	15.16	**6.16**
2	R. Bishnoi (*Punjab K*) ..	LB	216	87	230	12	3-24	0	19.16	18.00	**6.38**
3	S. P. Narine (*Kolkata KR*)	OB	336	131	361	16	4-21	1	22.56	21.00	**6.44**
4	V. V. Chakravarthy (*KKR*)	LB	408	149	448	18	3-13	0	24.88	22.66	**6.58**
5	A. R. Patel (*Delhi C*)...	SLA	276	99	306	15	3-21	0	20.40	18.40	**6.65**
6	Rashid Khan (*S Hyd'bad*)	LB	336	130	375	18	3-36	0	20.83	18.66	**6.69**
7	M. Siraj (*RC Bangalore*)	RFM	312	147	353	11	3-27	0	32.09	28.36	**6.78**
8	Y. S. Chahal (*RC Bang*) .	LB	318	127	374	18	3-11	0	20.77	17.66	**7.05**
9	R. A. Jadeja (*Chennai SK*)	SLA	294	104	346	13	3-13	0	26.61	22.61	**7.06**
10	S. P. Mavi (*Kolkata KR*).	RFM	193	91	233	11	4-21	1	21.18	17.54	**7.24**

		Style	Balls	Dots	R	W	BB	4I	Avge	SR	ER
11	Aavesh Khan (*Delhi C*) .	RM	366	156	450	24	3-13	0	18.75	15.25	**7.37**
12	R. D. Chahar (*Mumbai I*)	LB	258	93	318	13	4-27	1	24.46	19.84	**7.39**
13	J. J. Bumrah (*Mumbai I*).	RFM	330	142	410	21	3-36	0	19.52	15.71	**7.45**
14	L. H. Ferguson (*Kol KR*)	RF	180	76	224	13	3-18	0	17.23	13.84	**7.46**
15	Mohammed Shami (*Pun K*)	RFM	316	145	395	19	3-21	0	20.78	16.63	**7.50**
16	J. O. Holder (*S Hyderabad*)	RFM	191	75	247	16	4-52	1	15.43	11.93	**7.75**
17	D. J. Bravo (*Chennai SK*)	RFM	202	73	263	14	3-24	0	18.78	14.42	**7.81**
18	T. A. Boult (*Mumbai I*). .	LFM	308	138	406	13	3-28	0	31.23	23.69	**7.90**
19	H. V. Patel (*RC Bangalore*)	RFM	338	122	459	32	5-27	2	14.34	10.56	**8.14**
20	K. Rabada (*Delhi C*)	RF	336	135	456	15	3-36	0	30.40	22.40	**8.14**
21	C. Sakariya (*Rajasthan R*)	LFM	312	113	426	14	3-31	0	30.42	22.28	**8.19**
22	Arshdeep Singh (*Pun K*) .	RFM	248	88	342	18	5-32	1	19.00	13.77	**8.27**
23	D. L. Chahar (*Chen SK*) .	RFM	324	132	451	14	4-13	2	32.21	23.14	**8.35**
24	J. R. Hazlewood (*Ch SK*)	RFM	210	87	293	11	3-24	0	26.63	19.09	**8.37**
25	Mustafizur Rahman (*Raj R*)	LFM	311	113	436	14	3-20	0	31.14	22.21	**8.41**
26	S. N. Thakur (*Chen SK*) .	RFM	359	137	527	21	3-28	0	25.09	17.09	**8.80**
27	P. M. Krishna (*Kol KR*) .	RFM	231	102	351	12	3-30	0	29.25	19.25	**9.11**
28	C. H. Morris (*Rajasthan R*) .	RFM	246	91	376	15	4-23	1	25.06	16.40	**9.17**
29	A. D. Russell (*Kolkata KR*).	RFM	114	39	188	11	5-15	1	17.09	10.36	**9.89**

INDIAN PREMIER LEAGUE IN 2021

	P	W	L	Pts	NRR
DELHI CAPITALS	14	10	4	20	0.48
CHENNAI SUPER KINGS	14	9	5	18	0.45
ROYAL CHALLENGERS BANGALORE . . .	14	9	5	18	−0.14
KOLKATA KNIGHT RIDERS	14	7	7	14	0.58
Mumbai Indians	14	7	7	14	0.11
Punjab Kings.	14	6	8	12	−0.00
Rajasthan Royals.	14	5	9	10	−0.99
Sunrisers Hyderabad	14	3	11	6	−0.54

At Chennai, April 9, 2021 (floodlit). **Royal Challengers Bangalore won by two wickets. Mumbai Indians 159-9** (20 overs) (C. A. Lynn 49, S. A. Yadav 31; H. V. Patel 5-27); ‡**Royal Challengers Bangalore 160-8** (20 overs) (V. Kohli 33, G. J. Maxwell 39, A. B. de Villiers 48). *PoM:* H. V. Patel. *A last-ball victory for RCB meant reigning champions Mumbai Indians still hadn't won their opening fixture since 2012. They would have been defending more than 160, but an astonishing final over from seamer Harshal Patel yielded four wickets and just one run; having never taken more than three in 96 previous T20 matches, he finished with 5-27. Bangalore were coasting at 98-2 in the 13th, but lost four – including Virat Kohli and Glenn Maxwell – for 24 in 25 balls. It needed the cool head of A. B. de Villiers (48 off 27) to get them close, though his late run-out ensured a tight finish.*

At Mumbai, April 10, 2021 (floodlit). **Delhi Capitals won by seven wickets. Chennai Super Kings 188-7** (20 overs) (M. M. Ali 36, S. K. Raina 54, S. M. Curran 34); ‡**Delhi Capitals 190-3** (18.4 overs) (P. P. Shaw 72, S. Dhawan 85). *PoM:* S. Dhawan. *Chennai Super Kings did their best to recover from 7-2 in the third over: Moeen Ali and Suresh Raina steered them out of trouble, before Sam Curran (34 off 15) sped them towards a decent total. He was especially brutal on his brother Tom, who conceded 23 from the 19th. On a flat Wankhede pitch, though, it was too few. Prithvi Shaw and Shikhar Dhawan opened with 138, which took the pressure off the middle order.*

At Chennai, April 11, 2021 (floodlit). **Kolkata Knight Riders won by ten runs. Kolkata Knight Riders 187-6** (20 overs) (N. Rana 80, R. A. Tripathi 53); ‡**Sunrisers Hyderabad 177-5** (20 overs) (M. K. Pandey 61*, J. M. Bairstow 55). *PoM:* N. Rana. *Nitish Rana anchored the Knight Riders' innings with a 56-ball 80, while Rahul Tripathi slapped 53 from 29; the Afghan spinners Mohammad Nabi and Rashid Khan had 4-56 in their eight overs. The Sunrisers quickly lost openers David Warner and Wriddhiman Saha and, although Manish Pandey and Jonny Bairstow dragged them back with 92 in 11 overs, the bowlers kept control. The 40-year-old Harbhajan Singh made his debut for KKR after 160 matches for Mumbai Indians and Chennai Super Kings.*

At Mumbai, April 12, 2021 (floodlit). **Punjab Kings won by four runs. Punjab Kings 221-6** (20 overs) (K. L. Rahul 91, C. H. Gayle 40, D. Hooda 64; C. Sakariya 3-31); ‡**Rajasthan Royals 217-7** (20 overs) (S. V. Samson 119; Arshdeep Singh 3-35). PoM: S. V. Samson. *Rajasthan's new captain, Sanju Samson, made the most of two lives to strike the tournament's first hundred – as he had in 2017 and 2019. His seventh six brought their target down to five off two balls, but he turned down a single, before Deepak Hooda caught him at deep cover to seal Punjab's victory. Earlier, Hooda had smashed 64 off 28, including five sixes in seven balls, and added 105 in eight overs with K. L. Rahul, who fell in the 20th to Chetan Sakariya, a left-arm swing bowler from Gujarat on IPL debut. But the biggest talking point was a delivery from Rajasthan leg-spinner Riyan Parag Das to Chris Gayle: his arm was nearly perpendicular to his shoulder, and some felt he was bowling underarm, contrary to Law 21.1.2; an MCC tweet described it as "borderline". In the same over, Gayle sliced an off-break to Ben Stokes at long-on. Stokes – whom Gayle had just hit for his 350th IPL six – broke his finger taking the catch, and was out for ten weeks.*

At Chennai, April 13, 2021 (floodlit). **Mumbai Indians won by ten runs. Mumbai Indians 152** (20 overs) (R. G. Sharma 43, S. A. Yadav 56; A. D. Russell 5-15); ‡**Kolkata Knight Riders 142-7** (20 overs) (N. Rana 57, S. Gill 33; R. D. Chahar 4-27). PoM: R. D. Chahar. *It was a game of two collapses. Mumbai scored 81-1 in their first ten overs, with Suryakumar Yadav to the fore, followed by 71-9 in their second. Mixing up his pace and angles, Andre Russell snaffled five wickets in two overs. Then Kolkata had a go: 72-0 in the ninth, but 70-7 off their final 68 deliveries, as excessive aggression gave way to excessive caution against Mumbai's spinners: Rahul Chahar's leg-breaks brought 4-27, while left-armer Krunal Pandya had figures of 24–13–13–1. It was Kolkata's 12th defeat in their last 13 matches against Mumbai.*

At Chennai, April 14, 2021 (floodlit). **Royal Challengers Bangalore won by six runs. Royal Challengers Bangalore 149-8** (20 overs) (V. Kohli 33, G. J. Maxwell 59; J. O. Holder 3-30); ‡**Sunrisers Hyderabad 143-9** (20 overs) (D. A. Warner 54, M. K. Pandey 38; Shahbaz Ahmed 3-7). PoM: G. J. Maxwell. *The match turned on the 17th over of the reply, bowled by Shahbaz Ahmed, a brisk left-arm spinner in only his fourth IPL game. It began with Hyderabad sitting pretty at 115-2 but, six balls and three mis-hits later, they were 116-5. Bangalore held on to log a second win. Their innings had not gone to plan, either – from 91-2, they lurched to 109-6 against Rashid Khan. Maxwell saved them: 43 IPL games after his last half-century, he pinged 59 from 41.*

At Mumbai, April 15, 2021 (floodlit). **Rajasthan Royals won by three wickets. Delhi Capitals 147-8** (20 overs) (R. R. Pant 51; J. D. Unadkat 3-15); ‡**Rajasthan Royals 150-7** (19.4 overs) (D. A. Miller 62, C. H. Morris 36*; Aavesh Khan 3-32). PoM: J. D. Unadkat. *Delhi limped to 36-3 in the powerplay, with left-arm seamer Jaydev Unadkat dismissing Shaw, Dhawan and Ajinkya Rahane, before Rishabh Pant cracked 51 from 32 balls. Mustafizur Rahman kept things quiet, but a target of 148 looked more imposing after Rajasthan endured an even worse powerplay – 26-3. They were 90-6 after 15 overs, at which point there had been no sixes in the game (Delhi's had been the first IPL innings at the Wankhede without one). But David Miller biffed two, before departing for 62 from 43, then his fellow South African Chris Morris hacked 36* from 18, putting on 46* with Unadkat (11*) as Rajasthan surged home.*

At Mumbai, April 16, 2021 (floodlit). **Chennai Super Kings won by six wickets. Punjab Kings 106-8** (20 overs) (M. Shahrukh Khan 47; D. L. Chahar 4-13); ‡**Chennai Super Kings 107-4** (15.4 overs) (F. du Plessis 36*, M. M. Ali 46). PoM: D. L. Chahar. *The clash of Kings was effectively settled in the first seven overs: by then, Punjab were 26-5, their heavyweight batters all gone, and Deepak Chahar had 4-13. Though Shahrukh Khan dragged them into three figures with a career-best 47, Chennai needed only 107. Faf du Plessis and the fluent Ali coasted to 90-1, and three wickets were just a hiccup before Sam Curran hit the winning four with 26 balls to spare.*

At Chennai, April 17, 2021 (floodlit). **Mumbai Indians won by 13 runs. ‡Mumbai Indians 150-5** (20 overs) (Q. de Kock 40, R. G. Sharma 32, K. A. Pollard 35*); **Sunrisers Hyderabad 137** (19.4 overs) (D. A. Warner 36, J. M. Bairstow 43; T. A. Boult 3-28, R. D. Chahar 3-19). PoM: K. A. Pollard. *Victory, at last, for a team who chose to bat. Mumbai's 150 looked middling, but scoring had become tougher as the innings progressed: other than openers Quinton de Kock and Rohit Sharma, only Kieron Pollard (35* off 22) passed 12, and he was dropped by Vijay Shankar on 18. Warner and Bairstow, Hyderabad's prolific openers, raced out of the traps, before Bairstow (43 off 22) trod on his stumps trying to ramp Krunal Pandya. From 67-0 in seven overs, they lost all ten for 70, as Trent Boult and Rahul Chahar picked up three-fors.*

At Chennai, April 18, 2021 (floodlit). **Royal Challengers Bangalore won by 38 runs.** ‡Royal Challengers Bangalore 204-4 (20 overs) (G. J. Maxwell 78, A. B. de Villiers 76*); Kolkata Knight Riders 166-8 (20 overs) (A. D. Russell 31; K. A. Jamieson 3-41). PoM: A. B. de Villiers. *Maxwell carried on where he left off against Hyderabad, and Bangalore made it three from three. This fifty came at a faster lick – he hit 78 from 49 balls, and tucked in to the mystery spin of Varun Chakravarthy, whose two early wickets had included Kohli. Maxwell, though, was outshone: de Villiers walloped 43 of the 56 that gushed from the last three overs, and finished with 76* from 34. Kolkata got off to a decent start – 57-1 in the sixth – but no one managed more than Russell's 31, as he tried to make amends for leaking 38 from his two overs.*

At Mumbai, April 18, 2021 (floodlit). **Delhi Capitals won by six wickets. Punjab Kings 195-4** (20 overs) (K. L. Rahul 61, M. A. Agarwal 69); ‡Delhi Capitals 198-4 (18.2 overs) (P. P. Shaw 32, S. Dhawan 92). PoM: S. Dhawan. *Punjab's total was a slight disappointment after Rahul and Mayank Agarwal kicked off with 122 in 12.4 overs. An eventful second over – left-arm seamer Lukman Meriwala's first in the IPL – included a dropped catch, a misfield, a no-ball, three fours and a six. Dhawan shot out of the blocks in reply, putting on 59 with Shaw and 48 with Steve Smith (nine). He eventually perished for 92 from 49, with 15 boundaries, but Marcus Stoinis and Lalit Yadav, in only his second IPL game, eased Delhi over the line.*

At Mumbai, April 19, 2021 (floodlit). **Chennai Super Kings won by 45 runs. Chennai Super Kings 188-9** (20 overs) (F. du Plessis 33; C. Sakariya 3-36); ‡Rajasthan Royals 143-9 (20 overs) (J. C. Buttler 49; M. M. Ali 3-7). PoM: M. M. Ali. *Chennai's 188-9 was the highest IPL total in which no one reached 40 (previously 184-8 by Mumbai Indians v Rising Pune Supergiant in April 2017); their top score, 33, came from du Plessis, who was out one short of 6,000 T20 runs. Jos Buttler led Rajasthan's reply but, once he was bowled by a Ravindra Jadeja delivery that pitched leg then hit middle and off, the Royals collapsed from 87-2 to 95-7, with Ali claiming three in five balls en route to his best IPL return.*

At Chennai, April 20, 2021 (floodlit). **Delhi Capitals won by six wickets.** ‡Mumbai Indians 137-9 (20 overs) (R. G. Sharma 44; A. Mishra 4-24); Delhi Capitals 138-4 (19.1 overs) (S. Dhawan 45, S. P. D. Smith 33). PoM: A. Mishra. *Amit Mishra's leg-breaks proved decisive on a sluggish Chepauk surface. After Mumbai had rushed to 67-1 in the seventh, he collected 4-24; from their final 13.1 overs, they managed just 70-8. Delhi took their time – Dhawan scored 45 off 42, and Smith 33 off 29 – but were in no danger of falling short.*

At Chennai, April 21, 2021 (floodlit). **Sunrisers Hyderabad won by nine wickets.** ‡Punjab Kings 120 (19.4 overs) (K. K. Ahmed 3-21); Sunrisers Hyderabad 121-1 (18.4 overs) (D. A. Warner 37, J. M. Bairstow 63*). PoM: J. M. Bairstow. *On a pitch that turned from the start, slow left-armer Abhishek Sharma and Rashid Khan never let Punjab settle, enjoying a combined return of 48–21–41–3. Rashid was tricky to read, for batter and keeper: Bairstow missed a chance to stump Moises Henriques, though the error was not costly. By then, Nicholas Pooran had collected a third duck in four innings – run out without facing – while left-arm seamer Khaleel Ahmed picked up three wickets. Warner, whose direct hit despatched Pooran, fell for a run-a-ball 37, but Bairstow and Kane Williamson guided the Sunrisers to their first victory; Punjab had now lost three in a row.*

At Mumbai, April 21, 2021 (floodlit). **Chennai Super Kings won by 18 runs. Chennai Super Kings 220-3** (20 overs) (R. D. Gaikwad 64, F. du Plessis 95*); ‡Kolkata Knight Riders 202 (19.1 overs) (K. D. Karthik 40, A. D. Russell 54, P. J. Cummins 66*; D. L. Chahar 4-29, L. T. Ngidi 3-28). PoM: F. du Plessis. *CSK openers Ruturaj Gaikwad (64 from 42) and du Plessis (95* from 60) began with a stand of 115, and the other batsmen kept the pressure on; Jadeja hit the only ball he faced for six. With Deepak Chahar taking four quick wickets, KKR looked out of it at 31-5 – but Russell flogged 54 from 22, then Pat Cummins (whose four overs had disappeared for 58) crashed a T20-best 66* from 34; both hit six sixes. Amazingly, the target was in sight – but the last three all fell for ducks (two to run-outs), and the Super Kings could breathe again.*

At Mumbai, April 22, 2021 (floodlit). **Royal Challengers Bangalore won by ten wickets. Rajasthan Royals 177-9** (20 overs) (S. R. Dube 46, R. Tewatia 40; M. Siraj 3-27, H. V. Patel 3-47); ‡Royal Challengers Bangalore 181-0 (16.3 overs) (V. Kohli 72*, D. B. Padikkal 101*). PoM: D. B. Padikkal. *Bangalore strolled to a fourth straight victory, and their fourth ten-wicket win in all IPL games, a record. Mohammed Siraj had set the tone, reducing Rajasthan to 18-3, though resistance from Shivam Dube and Rahul Tewatia helped lift the target to 178. Then Devdutt Padikkal raced to a 51-ball century, including six sixes; at 20 years 289 days, he was the third-youngest (after Manish Pandey and Rishabh Pant) to record an IPL hundred. Kohli's 72* from 47 made him the first to 6,000 IPL runs.*

At Chennai, April 23, 2021 (floodlit). **Punjab Kings won by nine wickets. Mumbai Indians 131-6** (20 overs) (R. G. Sharma 63, S. A. Yadav 33); ‡**Punjab Kings 132-1** (17.4 overs) (K. L. Rahul 60*, C. H. Gayle 43*). PoM: K. L. Rahul. *This was a stroll in the Chepauk for Punjab, as Rahul (60* off 52) marshalled the pursuit of a modest 132, putting on 53 with Agarwal, then an increasingly fluent 79* with Gayle (43* off 35). Mumbai had struggled for their timing on a pitch that thwarted strokeplay: even Rohit Sharma needed 52 balls for his 63.*

At Mumbai, April 24, 2021 (floodlit). **Rajasthan Royals won by six wickets. Kolkata Knight Riders 133-9** (20 overs) (R. A. Tripathi 36; C. H. Morris 4-23); ‡**Rajasthan Royals 134-4** (18.5 overs) (S. V. Samson 42*). PoM: C. H. Morris. *Kolkata never hit their stride. They were a hesitant 25-1 at the end of the powerplay, then 61-4 in the 11th after Eoin Morgan was run out without facing. Things didn't improve, and Morris grabbed the last four to finish with his best IPL figures in his 75th game. Chakravarthy claimed a couple of wickets when Rajasthan replied, but Samson calmly steered them home.*

At Mumbai, April 25, 2021 (floodlit). **Chennai Super Kings won by 69 runs.** ‡**Chennai Super Kings 191-4** (20 overs) (R. D. Gaikwad 33, F. du Plessis 50, R. A. Jadeja 62*; H. V. Patel 3-51); **Royal Challengers Bangalore 122-9** (20 overs) (D. B. Padikkal 34; R. A. Jadeja 3-13). PoM: R. A. Jadeja. *After another du Plessis half-century, Jadeja – dropped on nought – smashed 62* off 28, with five sixes, to lift CSK to 191. Harshal Patel began the last over with figures of 3-14, but 37 came from it as Jadeja tucked in for 6666264 (the third delivery was a no-ball). It equalled the IPL's most expensive over: Prasanth Parameswaran of Kochi Tuskers also conceded 36 plus a no-ball to RCB's Chris Gayle at Bangalore in 2011. The final total proved more than enough. Sam Curran had Kohli caught behind for eight; later, Jadeja bowled Maxwell and de Villiers in three balls, and finished with 3-13. Shardul Thakur (1-11) was even more parsimonious, as RCB lost their unbeaten record.*

At Chennai, April 25, 2021 (floodlit). **Delhi Capitals won the super over, after a tie.** ‡**Delhi Capitals 159-4** (20 overs) (P. P. Shaw 53, R. R. Pant 37, S. P. D. Smith 34*); **Sunrisers Hyderabad 159-7** (20 overs) (J. M. Bairstow 38, K. S. Williamson 66*; Aavesh Khan 3-34). PoM: P. P. Shaw. *Asked if he was tired of super overs, Williamson said he was tired of losing them; this was his third such defeat with the Sunrisers, on top of three for New Zealand. His 66* had tied the main match, and he was back at the crease for the showdown. Both super overs were bowled by spinners. Akshar Patel, in his first game post-Covid, conceded seven, after the umpires called one short as David Warner returned for a second; that left Rashid Khan to defend eight, and Delhi won with a leg-bye. Ravichandran Ashwin, who had taken one wicket in four outings for the Capitals, announced he was taking a break to support his family as India's Covid crisis mounted.*

At Ahmedabad, April 26, 2021 (floodlit). **Kolkata Knight Riders won by five wickets. Punjab Kings 123-9** (20 overs) (M. A. Agarwal 31, C. J. Jordan 30; P. M. Krishna 3-30); ‡**Kolkata Knight Riders 126-5** (16.4 overs) (R. A. Tripathi 41, E. J. G. Morgan 47*). PoM: E. J. G. Morgan. *Morgan helped Kolkata off the bottom of the table, taking his side to their second win out of six with a calm 47* off 40 after they had slipped to 17-3. His stand of 66 with Tripathi (41 off 32) proved decisive. Punjab had found scoring tricky in the tournament's first game at Ahmedabad's rechristened Narendra Modi Stadium: not until Chris Jordan's 30 off 18 at No. 8 did anyone score at better than a run a ball.*

At Ahmedabad, April 27, 2021 (floodlit). **Royal Challengers Bangalore won by one run. Royal Challengers Bangalore 171-5** (20 overs) (R. M. Patidar 31, A. B. de Villiers 75*); ‡**Delhi Capitals 170-4** (20 overs) (R. R. Pant 58*, S. O. Hetmyer 53*). PoM: A. B. de Villiers. *This was the fourth time Delhi had been involved in a game decided by one run – and the third time in a row they had lost. Shimron Hetmyer could not keep the strike in the last over, when they needed 14. He had been middling everything, carting Kyle Jamieson for three sixes in the 18th, but not Mohammed Siraj's second ball of the 20th – a yorker that yielded just a single. Pant flashed two fours at the end, but it wasn't quite enough. Hetmyer, 53* from 25, was distraught. The architect of Bangalore's innings had been de Villiers, whose 75* came from 42, including 22 off the last, bowled by Stoinis (who contributed a wide). De Villiers became the sixth to rack up 5,000 IPL runs, after Raina, Kohli, Rohit Sharma, Warner and Dhawan; his strike-rate of 150 was much the fastest.*

At Delhi, April 28, 2021 (floodlit). **Chennai Super Kings won by seven wickets.** ‡**Sunrisers Hyderabad 171-3** (20 overs) (D. A. Warner 57, M. K. Pandey 61); **Chennai Super Kings 173-3** (18.3 overs) (R. D. Gaikwad 75, F. du Plessis 56; Rashid Khan 3-36). PoM: R. D. Gaikwad. *Warner became the fourth to reach 10,000 runs in all T20 cricket, but his 57 used up 55 balls – the slowest* *of his 54 IPL scores of 50-plus. Pandey hit 61 from 46, while Williamson swiped 26* from ten. But the total never looked enough, especially once Gaikwad and du Plessis led off with 129 in 13 overs. Three wickets for Rashid Khan slowed the charge, but CSK completed their fifth successive win with something to spare.*

At Delhi, April 29, 2021 (floodlit). **Mumbai Indians won by seven wickets. Rajasthan Royals 171-4** (20 overs) (J. C. Buttler 41, Y. B. Jaiswal 32, S. V. Samson 42, S. R. Dube 35); ‡**Mumbai Indians 172-3** (18.3 overs) (Q. de Kock 70*, K. H. Pandya 39). PoM: Q. de Kock. *The second match at Delhi produced figures almost identical to the first. Steady scoring by Rajasthan's top four got them to 171, though Jasprit Bumrah bowled two overs for just eight runs (plus a leg-bye) at the death. De Kock bounced back after a couple of cheap dismissals – both in defeat – to bat through Mumbai's innings for 70* off 50, securing victory with seven wickets and nine balls in hand.*

At Ahmedabad, April 29, 2021 (floodlit). **Delhi Capitals won by seven wickets. Kolkata Knight Riders 154-6** (20 overs) (S. Gill 43, A. D. Russell 45*); ‡**Delhi Capitals 156-3** (16.3 overs) (P. P. Shaw 82, S. Dhawan 46; P. J. Cummins 3-24). PoM: P. P. Shaw. *Shaw became the first to take six fours off the opening over of a T20 game, to set Delhi up for a win that took them joint-top with Chennai and Bangalore. With Kolkata defending 155 after Russell's late flurry (45* off 27), Shivam Mahi began with a wide, before Shaw pummelled the next six to the boundary, en route to an 18-ball half-century (and, eventually, a 41-ball 82). By the time Dhawan fell for a more sedate 46, he and Shaw had put on 132 inside 14 overs, and the game was up.*

At Ahmedabad, April 30, 2021 (floodlit). **Punjab Kings won by 34 runs. Punjab Kings 179-5** (20 overs) (K. L. Rahul 91*, C. H. Gayle 46); ‡**Royal Challengers Bangalore 145-8** (20 overs) (V. Kohli 35, R. M. Patidar 31, H. V. Patel 31; H. Brar 3-19). PoM: H. Brar. *Harpreet Brar, a little-known left-arm spinner from Uttar Pradesh playing his fourth IPL game, snatched victory for Punjab by dismissing Kohli and Maxwell (bowled by successive deliveries) and de Villiers (caught at extra cover) at no cost in seven balls. They were his first IPL wickets. At 62-1 from ten, Bangalore were vaguely on course; at 69-4 in the 13th, they were shipping water fast. Earlier, Rahul dominated the Kings' innings, pummelling 91*. He and Gayle added 80, before Punjab lurched from 99-1 to 118-5. Harpreet, though, joined Rahul and scored 25* from 17.*

At Delhi, May 1, 2021 (floodlit). **Mumbai Indians won by four wickets. Chennai Super Kings 218-4** (20 overs) (F. du Plessis 50, M. M. Ali 58, A. T. Rayudu 72*); ‡**Mumbai Indians 219-6** (20 overs) (Q. de Kock 38, R. G. Sharma 35, K. H. Pandya 32, K. A. Pollard 87*; S. M. Curran 3-34). PoM: K. A. Pollard. *The battle of the IPL's most successful teams was wrenched the way of five-times champions Mumbai by Pollard, who hammered 87* from 34, with eight sixes (three in four balls from Jadeja). Lungi Ngidi's four overs cost 62, while Thakur had 1-56. Three-times champions Chennai had looked set for a sixth successive victory while Ambati Rayudu was clattering seven sixes in 72* from 27, to build on a stand of 108 between du Plessis and Ali, who cleared the ropes nine times between them. Mumbai had only 81-3 at halfway, but Pollard had just arrived: 138 came from the second ten overs. Three late wickets from Sam Curran threatened to deny him but, with 16 required from the last, from Ngidi, Pollard completed victory with 044062. He turned down a single from the fourth delivery, and finished the job by blocking a yorker wide of long-on.*

At Delhi, May 2, 2021 (floodlit). **Rajasthan Royals won by 55 runs. Rajasthan Royals 220-3** (20 overs) (J. C. Buttler 124, S. V. Samson 48); ‡**Sunrisers Hyderabad 165-8** (20 overs) (M. K. Pandey 31, J. M. Bairstow 30; Mustafizur Rahman 3-20, C. H. Morris 3-29). PoM: J. C. Buttler. *After five defeats in six games, the Sunrisers installed Williamson as captain instead of Warner, who also lost his place, but it did not change their luck. Buttler plundered 124 in 64 balls – his maiden T20 hundred in his 260th innings – and added 150 in 13.4 with Samson, helping to set 221. Hyderabad's new opening pair, Pandey and Bairstow, put on 57 in six overs, but after them only Williamson reached 20, as Mustafizur collected three cheap wickets.*

At Ahmedabad, May 2, 2021 (floodlit). **Delhi Capitals won by seven wickets. Punjab Kings 166-6** (20 overs) (M. A. Agarwal 99*; K. Rabada 3-36); ‡**Delhi Capitals 167-3** (17.4 overs) (P. P. Shaw 39, S. Dhawan 69*). PoM: M. A. Agarwal. *Delhi's openers again took control of a chase, lifting their side top of the table with a sixth win in eight. Shaw fell for 39 off 22 balls after the powerplay had produced 63, but Dhawan (69* off 47) stayed until the end, backed by Hetmyer's four-ball 16*. Punjab's innings had been dominated by first-time captain Agarwal (K. L. Rahul had appendicitis). His 99* from 58 was well clear of the next-best contribution: a run-a-ball 26 from the world's top-ranked T20I batsman Dawid Malan, making his IPL debut. It was to be his only game. The following day, Kolkata's match against Bangalore was postponed, after two of their players tested positive for Covid, while the Delhi team, who had played the Knight Riders a few days earlier, were asked to isolate in their hotel; on May 4, the tournament was suspended.*

* * *

At Dubai, September 19, 2021 (floodlit). **Chennai Super Kings won by 20 runs. ‡Chennai Super Kings 156-6** (20 overs) (R. D. Gaikwad 88*); **Mumbai Indians 136-8** (20 overs) (S. S. Tiwary 50*; D. J. Bravo 3-25). PoM: R. D. Gaikwad. *After a hiatus of 139 days, the tournament resumed in the UAE, and Chennai quickly reasserted their dominance, pulling level with Delhi at the top. Gaikwad's 88* off 58 was the catalyst for their turnaround from 7-3 (plus Rayudu retired hurt with a bruised elbow, courtesy of Adam Milne). When Dhoni went cheaply it was 24-4, but Gaikwad added 81 with Jadeja, then 39 off 16 with Dwayne Bravo, to post a challenging 156-6. Mumbai struggled to get Deepak Chahar's seamers away, and faltered to 94-6 before Saurabh Tiwary found some impetus with 50*. Bravo's death variations ensured nothing came of it.*

At Abu Dhabi, September 20, 2021 (floodlit). **Kolkata Knight Riders won by nine wickets. ‡Royal Challengers Bangalore 92** (19 overs) (V. V. Chakravarthy 3-13, A. D. Russell 3-9); **Kolkata Knight Riders 94-1** (10 overs) (S. Gill 48, V. R. Iyer 41*). PoM: V. V. Chakravarthy. *Kolkata (seventh beforehand) trounced Bangalore (third) with a superb display that belied the table. Kohli's indifferent form – one fifty in seven innings – continued when he fell for five; at 41-1 in the sixth, though, there were few signs of what was to come. Tight bowling and loose batting led to nine wickets cascading for 51, including de Villiers for a golden duck. Chakravarthy's spin deceived the middle order, while Russell bowled an impeccable line. Kolkata knocked off the small target in ten overs, with left-hander Venkatesh Iyer 41* on IPL debut.*

At Dubai, September 21, 2021 (floodlit). **Rajasthan Royals won by two runs. Rajasthan Royals 185** (20 overs) (E. Lewis 36, Y. B. Jaiswal 49, M. K. Lomror 43; Mohammed Shami 3-21, Arshdeep Singh 5-32); **‡Punjab Kings 183-4** (20 overs) (K. L. Rahul 49, M. A. Agarwal 67, N. Pooran 32). PoM: K. Tyagi. *Punjab had the match in the bag at 178-2, with two established batters needing eight off two overs. But Rajasthan staged an astonishing coup: Mustafizur confined them to four singles, then Kartik Tyagi conceded just one, and had two caught behind. Put in by Punjab (who omitted Gayle on his 42nd birthday), Evin Lewis and Yashasvi Jaiswal raced to 54 in the sixth over before left-armer Arshdeep Singh broke through, en route to a career-best 5-32. Mahipal Lomror smote four sixes in a 17-ball 43, but the Royals' last six fell for 19. When Rahul (dropped three times) and Agarwal opened with 120 inside 12 overs, victory seemed a foregone conclusion.*

At Dubai, September 22, 2021 (floodlit). **Delhi Capitals won by eight wickets. ‡Sunrisers Hyderabad 134-9** (20 overs) (K. Rabada 3-37); **Delhi Capitals 139-2** (17.5 overs) (S. Dhawan 42, S. S. Iyer 47*, R. R. Pant 35*). PoM: A. A. Nortje. *This game went ahead despite Sunrisers left-arm seamer T. Natarajan testing positive for Covid, which forced six members of the Hyderabad entourage – including team-mate Vijay Shankar – into isolation. Their fortunes did not pick up on the field, as they slumped to their seventh defeat in eight. Delhi's South African fast bowlers, Anrich Nortje (2-12) and Kagiso Rabada, took five wickets between them, and no Hyderabad batsman passed Abdul Samad's 28. The Capitals then soared back to the top, thanks to Shreyas Iyer and Pant (35* off 21).*

At Abu Dhabi, September 23, 2021 (floodlit). **Kolkata Knight Riders won by seven wickets. Mumbai Indians 155-6** (20 overs) (R. G. Sharma 33, Q. de Kock 55); **‡Kolkata Knight Riders 159-3** (15.1 overs) (V. R. Iyer 53, R. A. Tripathi 74*; J. J. Bumrah 3-43). PoM: S. P. Narine. *Tripathi's blistering 74* off 42 rocketed Kolkata to victory. His second-wicket stand of 88 off 52 with Venkatesh Iyer (53 off 30) sealed the game, after Iyer and Gill had put on 40 in three overs. The match had started well for Mumbai, as Rohit Sharma and de Kock opened with 78, but Sunil Narine (1-20) choked them with canny change-ups, and Ferguson's pace ruled out a revival. Bumrah took all three wickets in Kolkata's chase – Morgan's wretched form continued, and he was fined £24,000 for his team's slow over-rate – but no bowler was spared as Iyer and Tripathi cut loose.*

At Sharjah, September 24, 2021 (floodlit). **Chennai Super Kings won by six wickets. Royal Challengers Bangalore 156-6** (20 overs) (V. Kohli 53, D. B. Padikkal 70; D. J. Bravo 3-24); **‡Chennai Super Kings 157-4** (18.1 overs) (R. D. Gaikwad 38, F. du Plessis 31, A. T. Rayudu 32). PoM: D. J. Bravo. *A seemingly rejuvenated Bangalore sailed to 111-0 in 13 overs, with Kohli and Padikkal passing 50. Yet it might have been more, and the middle order's attempts to accelerate against the slower-ball variations of Bravo and Thakur (2-29) shifted the momentum towards Chennai, whose mastery of the last seven overs limited the scoring to 45-6. Their openers Gaikwad and du Plessis then accumulated calmly – putting on 71 by the ninth – and the Bangalore attack couldn't apply pressure. Victory put CSK level with Delhi again.*

At Abu Dhabi, September 25, 2021. **Delhi Capitals won by 33 runs. Delhi Capitals 154-6** (20 overs) (S. S. Iyer 43); ‡**Rajasthan Royals 121-6** (20 overs) (S. V. Samson 70*). PoM: S. S. Iyer. *As in Delhi's previous win, Iyer and Nortje played key roles. Iyer led their batting with 43 – despite only three boundaries – before Hetmyer hit 28 off 16, and the lower order lifted them past 150. During the interval, Iyer told Nortje it was difficult to hit straight, which helped him work out the length to bowl: he dismissed Jaiswal with his first delivery, finished with 2-18, and conceded just one four. Samson compiled 70*, but only one other Royals batter reached double figures – and Samson was fined for a slow over-rate for the second match running.*

At Sharjah, September 25, 2021 (floodlit). **Punjab Kings won by five runs. Punjab Kings 125-7** (20 overs) (J. O. Holder 3-19); ‡**Sunrisers Hyderabad 120-7** (20 overs) (W. P. Saha 31, J. O. Holder 47*; R. Bishnoi 3-24). PoM: J. O. Holder. *Jason Holder's late heroics could not spare Hyderabad from another defeat. He hit five sixes in a 29-ball 47* (his team-mates managed two fours between them), but was unable to add a sixth, off IPL debutant Nathan Ellis's final ball, to force a super over. He had been left with too much to do: 20 in the powerplay was the lowest in the Sunrisers' history. Mohammed Shami had struck two early blows, removing Warner and Williamson, while Ravi Bishnoi's googlies outwitted the middle order. Earlier, Holder had taken three cheap wickets as Punjab themselves struggled on a slow Sharjah surface.*

At Abu Dhabi, September 26, 2021. **Chennai Super Kings won by two wickets. ‡Kolkata Knight Riders 171-6** (20 overs) (R. A. Tripathi 45, N. Rana 37*); **Chennai Super Kings 172-8** (20 overs) (R. D. Gaikwad 40, F. du Plessis 43, M. M. Ali 32; S. P. Narine 3-41). PoM: R. A. Jadeja. *Deepak Chahar slog-swept the match's last ball – his first – for a single to clinch a thriller for Chennai. The match was unremarkable until the endgame: Tripathi continued his good form for Kolkata, top-scoring with 45, and Dinesh Karthik blasted a late 26 off 11; Sam Curran's spell cost 56. Chennai were cruising towards their target of 172; then, needing 34 from 21 with seven wickets in hand, they lost Ali, Suresh Raina and Dhoni in six balls. Soon the equation was 24 from ten, but Jadeja hit 6644 off Prasidh Krishna to leave four needed from the final over. Narine nipped out Curran and Jadeja, leaving Chahar with one ball to become a hero.*

At Dubai, September 26, 2021 (floodlit). **Royal Challengers Bangalore won by 54 runs. Royal Challengers Bangalore 165-6** (20 overs) (V. Kohli 51, K. Srikar Bharat 32, G. J. Maxwell 56; J. J. Bumrah 3-36); ‡**Mumbai Indians 111** (18.1 overs) (R. Sharma 43; H. V. Patel 4-17, Y. S. Chahal 3-11). PoM: G. J. Maxwell. *This time, Bangalore really were rejuvenated: they crushed Mumbai, whose pursuit of 166 had started swimmingly. At 69-1 after eight, they looked in control, but no one other than the openers – Rohit (43 off 28) and de Kock (24 off 23) – could manage double figures or a run a ball. Yuzvendra Chahal's leg-breaks caused problems, though it was the seam of Harshal which tore Mumbai apart: three succumbed to the first three balls of the 17th, all to slower deliveries. Earlier, Kohli had become the fifth player – and first Indian – to reach 10,000 T20 runs, after Gayle, Pollard (the second victim in Harshal's hat-trick), Shoaib Malik and Warner.*

At Dubai, September 27, 2021 (floodlit). **Sunrisers Hyderabad won by seven wickets. ‡Rajasthan Royals 164-5** (20 overs) (Y. B. Jaiswal 36, S. V. Samson 82); **Sunrisers Hyderabad 167-3** (18.3 overs) (J. J. Roy 60, K. S. Williamson 51*). PoM: J. J. Roy. *The Sunrisers completed only their second win – with ex-captain Warner left to watch from the hotel (coach Trevor Bayliss said he wanted young players to experience the set-up at the ground). Replacing him, Jason Roy made his debut for the Sunrisers, and added 57 for each of the first two wickets, with Saha (18) and Williamson, who completed victory – and his fifty – with successive fours off Mustafizur. Earlier, another half-century from Samson meant he briefly overtook Dhawan as the tournament's leading run-scorer; he added 56 with Jaiswal and 84 with Lomror.*

At Sharjah, September 28, 2021. **Kolkata Knight Riders won by three wickets. Delhi Capitals 127-9** (20 overs) (S. P. D. Smith 39, R. R. Pant 39); ‡**Kolkata Knight Riders 130-7** (18.2 overs) (S. Gill 30, N. Rana 36*; Aavesh Khan 3-13). PoM: S. P. Narine. *Tempers frayed when Delhi pinched a second run from the last ball of their penultimate over – the result of a ricochet off Pant, after Tripathi shied at the stumps. To Kolkata's annoyance, Ashwin called Pant through for an overthrow; when Ashwin was dismissed by the first delivery of the next over, he exchanged words with the bowler, Southee, and Morgan, Kolkata's captain. The spat spilled over into the press conferences, with Pant claiming the second run "was in the spirit of the game", and on to Twitter, where Ashwin said he hadn't seen the ball deflect off his partner, but would have run even if he had; he also chastised Southee and Morgan for taking the "moral high ground". Kolkata had the last laugh, winning by three wickets thanks to Nitish Rana's 36* off 27, but not before Ashwin had removed Morgan for a duck, celebrating the wicket with relish. Earlier, Delhi had lost seven for 50 after reaching 77-2 in the 13th.*

At Abu Dhabi, September 28, 2021 (floodlit). **Mumbai Indians won by six wickets. Punjab Kings 135-6** (20 overs) (A. K. Markram 42); ‡**Mumbai Indians 137-4** (19 overs) (S. S. Tiwary 45, H. H. Pandya 40*). PoM: K. A. Pollard. *Pollard bowled six balls, faced seven, and was named Player of the Match, with 2-8 and 15*, as Mumbai chased down 136. A fifth-wicket stand of 61 between Aiden Markram and Hooda had rescued Punjab after a collapse from 36-0 to 48-4, with Pollard reaching 300 T20 wickets when he dismissed Gayle and Rahul. Mumbai also laboured on a slow surface, and needed 40 from 23 soon after Pollard joined Hardik Pandya. But Pandya – missed on seven – came to life. With five wanted from seven, he lofted Shami to long-on, where Hooda dropped the ball over the rope.*

At Dubai, September 29, 2021 (floodlit). **Royal Challengers Bangalore won by seven wickets. Rajasthan Royals 149-9** (20 overs) (E. Lewis 58, Y. B. Jaiswal 31; H. V. Patel 3-34); ‡**Royal Challengers Bangalore 153-3** (17.1 overs) (K. Srikar Bharat 44, G. J. Maxwell 50*). PoM: Y. S. Chahal. *Another one-sided game involving Bangalore saw a helter-skelter Rajasthan collapse from a healthy position. After Lewis had shared an opening stand of 77 with Jaiswal, then guided the Royals to 100-1 after 11 overs, it all went wrong. George Garton broke through by taking pace off the ball and finding Lewis's edge, Harshal picked up a three-for, and spinners Chahal and Shahbaz shared 4-28 from six overs. Rajasthan's last nine produced 49 runs and eight wickets. Bangalore could chase brisk innings from Srikar Bharat (44 from 35) and Maxwell (50* from 30) for improving their net run-rate.*

At Sharjah, September 30, 2021 (floodlit). **Chennai Super Kings won by six wickets. Sunrisers Hyderabad 134-7** (20 overs) (W. P. Saha 44; J. R. Hazlewood 3-24); ‡**Chennai Super Kings 139-4** (19.4 overs) (R. D. Gaikwad 45, F. du Plessis 41; J. O. Holder 3-27). PoM: J. R. Hazlewood. *Chennai's ninth win meant they were the first to reach the knockouts, while the Sunrisers' ninth defeat ended their faint hopes. Though Williamson fell cheaply, to Bravo, Saha scored 44 out of 74 before he was fourth out, but there were no boundaries for eight overs mid-innings, and it took the lower order to get them to 134, with three cheap wickets for Josh Hazlewood. Gaikwad and du Plessis opened with 75 in ten overs and, after Holder dismissed both, Dhoni completed the job with a six into the stands.*

At Dubai, October 1, 2021 (floodlit). **Punjab Kings won by five wickets. Kolkata Knight Riders 165-7** (20 overs) (V. R. Iyer 67, R. A. Tripathi 34, N. Rana 31; Arshdeep Singh 3-32); ‡**Punjab Kings 168-5** (19.3 overs) (K. L. Rahul 67, M. A. Agarwal 40). PoM: K. L. Rahul. *The Kings stayed in the race for the play-offs, though the only immediate beneficiary of their last-over win were Delhi Capitals, now guaranteed a knockout spot. Venkatesh Iyer and Tripathi had added 72 off 55 for the Knight Riders' second wicket; Rana maintained the momentum, but Morgan made only two, his fourth consecutive single-figure score. Rahul and Agarwal then opened Punjab's reply with 70 off 53 but, with 11 needed from ten, Tripathi insisted he had caught Rahul at deep midwicket; after several replays, the third umpire concluded the ball had been grassed. Iyer did get Rahul in the 20th, and the Kings wanted four from four when Tripathi dropped another skyer – off Shahrukh Khan – over the boundary.*

At Sharjah, October 2, 2021. **Delhi Capitals won by four wickets. Mumbai Indians 129-8** (20 overs) (S. A. Yadav 33; Aavesh Khan 3-15, A. R. Patel 3-21); ‡**Delhi Capitals 132-6** (19.1 overs) (S. S. Iyer 33*). PoM: A. R. Patel. *A disciplined seventh-wicket stand of 39* off 36 – the highest of the game – between Iyer and Ashwin secured victory for Delhi after they slid to 93-6 in pursuit of 130. Mumbai had managed as many as 129 only because of the profligacy of Rabada and Rabada, who conceded 74 from their eight overs; the rest combined to take 7-55 from 12, with seamer Aavesh Khan and spinner Akshar Patel collecting three each. Mumbai's attack were more consistent – five bowlers took a wicket – but there was little scoreboard pressure, and Delhi kept their heads.*

At Dubai, October 2, 2021 (floodlit). **Rajasthan Royals won by seven wickets. Chennai Super Kings 189-4** (20 overs) (R. D. Gaikwad 101*, R. A. Jadeja 32*; R. Tewatia 3-39); ‡**Rajasthan Royals 190-3** (17.3 overs) (Y. B. Jaiswal 50, S. R. Dubey 64*). PoM: R. D. Gaikwad. *This was not a night to be a bowler. With hindsight, Chennai – who were sure of progressing – may have eased off a little, but while they were batting they seemed to be progressing nicely. The in-form Gaikwad dominated the innings, reaching 50 from his 43rd delivery, and smashing the last ball, his 60th, for six to raise a maiden T20 century. Of the Royals' bowlers, Mustafizur (0-51) suffered most, though Chennai's opening pair, Sam Curran and Hazlewood, both proved costlier, leaking 109 from eight wicketless overs. None of the Rajasthan batters missed out and, despite a demanding target, victory came with 15 balls unused.*

At Sharjah, October 3, 2021. **Royal Challengers Bangalore won by six runs. ‡Royal Challengers Bangalore 164-7** (20 overs) (D. B. Padikkal 40, G. J. Maxwell 57; Mohammed Shami 3-49, M. C. Henriques 3-12); **Punjab Kings 158-6** (20 overs) (K. L. Rahul 39, M. A. Agarwal 57; Y. S. Chahal 3-29). *PoM:* G. J. Maxwell. *Bangalore became the third side to reach the knockouts. Henriques had chopped short their opening stand of 68, dismissing Kohli (25), Christian (first ball) and Padikkal in seven deliveries. (On 35, Padikkal had survived a DRS review, despite the ball apparently brushing his gloves.) Maxwell and de Villiers rebuilt, adding 73, and when Maxwell became the first of Shami's three victims in the final over he had made 57 from 33. Punjab started convincingly: openers Rahul and Agarwal piled on 91 by the 11th. But once the partnership was broken, Chahal also struck three times in seven balls, and the lower order could not keep up.*

At Dubai, October 3, 2021 (floodlit). **Kolkata Knight Riders won by six wickets. ‡Sunrisers Hyderabad 115-8** (20 overs); **Kolkata Knight Riders 119-4** (19.4 overs) (S. Gill 57). *PoM:* S. Gill. *Gill shone on a testing pitch that defeated almost everyone else, hitting ten fours in a 51-ball 57 – his first half-century of the tournament. At 44-2 off ten overs, Kolkata were taking the long route to a target of 116, keeping debutant Umran Malik – who cranked it up to 93mph – and Rashid Khan's deft variations at bay. But Gill upped the tempo, and kept his side on course for the play-offs. Hyderabad had struggled against spin; Williamson's 26 was their best score, before he was run out by Shakib Al Hasan in his follow-through.*

At Dubai, October 4, 2021 (floodlit). **Delhi Capitals won by three wickets. Chennai Super Kings 136-5** (20 overs) (A. T. Rayudu 55*); **‡Delhi Capitals 139-7** (19.4 overs) (S. Dhawan 39). *PoM:* A. R. Patel. *Delhi held their nerve to regain pole position from Chennai. Batting first on a greenish pitch, the Super Kings – leaders on net run-rate – had been choked by Akshar Patel (2-18), with only Rayudu (55* off 43) escaping the stranglehold. Chennai lost just five wickets in tottering to 136; Delhi were six down before reaching three figures – Shardul Thakur (2-13) posed the main threat – but had time in hand. Hetymer (28* off 18, after being dropped on 12 by substitute Krishnappa Gowtham) hit out, while Akshar clung on, scoring five of the 36 they added. With two needed from four, he succumbed to Bravo, but Rabada glanced his first ball to the boundary.*

At Sharjah, October 5, 2021 (floodlit). **Mumbai Indians won by eight wickets. Rajasthan Royals 90-9** (20 overs) (N. M. Coulter-Nile 4-14, J. D. S. Neesham 3-12); **‡Mumbai Indians 94-2** (8.2 overs) (I. P. Kishan 50*). *PoM:* N. M. Coulter-Nile. *After their emphatic win against CSK, the Royals were hurled back to earth, scraping together just 90-9, the second-lowest IPL total by a team batting 20 overs (behind Kolkata's 84-8 v Bangalore in October 2020). A slow, low surface discouraged strokeplay, but the Mumbai seamers had fun: Nathan Coulter-Nile ran in hard to collect 4-14, while Jimmy Neesham took pace off and claimed 3-12 – both IPL-bests. With Bumrah contributing 2-14, the trio had combined figures of 9-40 from 12 overs. Thanks to a murderous 50* from 25 by Ishan Kishan, it took Mumbai just 50 balls to flatten – and eliminate – Rajasthan.*

At Abu Dhabi, October 6, 2021 (floodlit). **Sunrisers Hyderabad won by four runs. Sunrisers Hyderabad 141-7** (20 overs) (J. J. Roy 44, K. S. Williamson 31; H. V. Patel 3-33); **‡Royal Challengers Bangalore 137-6** (20 overs) (D. B. Padikkal 41, G. J. Maxwell 40). *PoM:* K. S. Williamson. *Already qualified, Bangalore were now targeting a top-two finish – but they came a cropper against bottom-placed Hyderabad. All went to plan as Kohli put the Sunrisers in and restricted them to 141 – half from one stand, between Roy and Williamson. Then Bhuvneshwar Kumar trapped Kohli in the chase's first over, and Padikkal's 41 used up 52 balls. Maxwell (40 from 25) kept them on course, until Williamson ran him out, with 50 required off 35. When Holder conceded five off the 19th over, RCB needed 13 off the last, from Bhuvneshwar: de Villiers hit the fourth ball for six, but managed only a single off the last two deliveries – both full tosses.*

At Dubai, October 7, 2021. **Punjab Kings won by six wickets. Chennai Super Kings 134-6** (20 overs) (F. du Plessis 76); **‡Punjab Kings 139-4** (13 overs) (K. L. Rahul 98*; S. N. Thakur 3-28). *PoM:* K. L. Rahul. *A masterly 42-ball 98* from Rahul gave Punjab a minute chance of progressing, if Rajasthan thrashed Kolkata that evening. Chennai had relied on du Plessis's 76 off 55, which featured the only two sixes of the innings, both – with two fours, and his dismissal by Shami – in its last eight balls. A total of 134 was a fair recovery from 61-5 after 12. But Rahul quickly put that into perspective, hitting 15 boundaries, which matched Chennai's combined total; the last of his eight sixes sealed the game, with seven overs to go. Despite three defeats in a row, Chennai were by now sure of second place.*

At Sharjah, October 7, 2021 (floodlit). **Kolkata Knight Riders won by 86 runs. Kolkata Knight Riders 171-4** (20 overs) (S. Gill 56, V. R. Iyer 38); ‡**Rajasthan Royals 85** (16.1 overs) (R. Tewatia 44; S. P. Mavi 4-21, L. H. Ferguson 3-18). *PoM:* S. P. Mavi. *Kolkata romped to victory, after Rajasthan failed to reach 100 for the second time in three days. Gill and Iyer opened with 79 to launch the Knight Riders towards 171. The Royals were soon 1-2, and never recovered. In the confusion, Shivam Dube walked out instead of Anuj Rawat, their intended No. 4, and the umpires refused to allow the error to be corrected, as he had already crossed the boundary. Rawat did not have long to wait. Rajasthan's 85 was their third-worst total, while Kolkata had only once won by more than 86 runs: in the very first IPL match, in 2008, they beat Bangalore by 140. Sitting fourth, they were all but certain of making the cut.*

At Abu Dhabi, October 8, 2021 (floodlit). **Mumbai Indians won by 42 runs.** ‡**Mumbai Indians 235-9** (20 overs) (I. P. Kishan 84, S. A. Yadav 82; J. O. Holder 4-52); **Sunrisers Hyderabad 193-8** (20 overs) (J. J. Roy 34, A. Sharma 33, M. K. Pandey 69*). *PoM:* I. P. Kishan. *Defending champions Mumbai amassed 235-9 – their highest IPL total – yet still crashed out. Reaching the play-offs had been almost impossible, since they needed to win by at least 170 to sneak past Kolkata on run-rate. They gave it their best, though, zooming to 83-1 in six overs and not letting up; Suryakumar Yadav walloped 82 from 40, while Kishan's brutal 84 came from 32. There were four expensive wickets for Holder and five catches for Mohammad Nabi (equalling the T20 record for an outfielder). The Sunrisers, though rooted to the foot of the table, stamped out Mumbai's hopes by the end of the powerplay, when they were 70-1; Manish Pandey hit 69 off 41, but a target of 236 was never attainable.*

FASTEST IPL FIFTIES

14	K. L. Rahul	Kings XI Punjab v Delhi Daredevils at Mohali	2017-18
15	Y. K. Pathan	Kolkata KR v Sunrisers Hyderabad at Kolkata	2013-14
15	S. P. Narine	Kolkata KR v RC Bangalore at Bangalore	2016-17
16	S. K. Raina	Chennai SK v Kings XI Punjab at Mumbai	2013-14
16	**I. P. Kishan**	**Mumbai Indians v Sunrisers Hyderabad at Abu Dhabi**	**2021**

Kishan is also one of eight players to have hit a 17-ball fifty in the IPL.

At Dubai, October 8, 2021 (floodlit). **Royal Challengers Bangalore won by seven wickets. Delhi Capitals 164-5** (20 overs) (P. P. Shaw 48, S. Dhawan 43); ‡**Royal Challengers Bangalore 166-3** (20 overs) (K. Srikar Bharat 78*, G. J. Maxwell 51*). *PoM:* K. Srikar Bharat. *The league stage ended with two simultaneous matches, an IPL first, but this one had little significance, with the teams already locked into first and third in the table. Leaders Delhi looked likely to chalk up an 11th win: Shaw and Dhawan put on 88 in ten overs, Hetmyer (29) topped them up to 164, and Bangalore were 6-2 when Nortje removed Padikkal and Kohli. At the halfway mark, they were only 61-3, with de Villiers just gone and 104 required. But Srikar Bharat and Maxwell chipped away until the target was 19 off two overs – only for Nortje to restrict them to four singles in the 19th. Aavesh Khan conceded nine in five balls: six off one to win. Then he bowled a leg-side wide, and Bharat smacked the next, a full toss, over long-on, reaching victory and a T20-best 78*.*

Play-offs

1st v 2nd   At Dubai, October 10, 2021 (floodlit). **Chennai Super Kings won by four wickets. Delhi Capitals 172-5** (20 overs) (P. P. Shaw 60, R. R. Pant 51*, S. O. Hetmyer 37); ‡**Chennai Super Kings 173-6** (19.4 overs) (R. D. Gaikwad 70, R. V. Uthappa 63; T. K. Curran 3-29). *PoM:* R. D. Gaikwad. *Gaikwad powered Chennai in an exciting chase, which Dhoni sealed with two balls to spare, sending the Super Kings straight to the final. Shaw had got Delhi off to a flyer with 60 off 34; then Pant (51* off 35, including a brace of one-handed sixes) and Hetmyer (37 off 24) added 83. But Gaikwad (70 off 50) and Robin Uthappa (63 off 44) upstaged them, putting on 110 in 12.5 for Chennai's second. Tom Curran was the catalyst for the fall of three for six in eight balls, and removed Ali at the start of the final over, from which 13 were needed. Dhoni hit three consecutive fours – interrupted by a wide – to complete the job like the fabled finisher of old.*

3rd v 4th At Sharjah, October 11, 2021 (floodlit). **Kolkata Knight Riders won by four wickets.** ‡**Royal Challengers Bangalore 138-7** (20 overs) (V. Kohli 39; S. P. Narine 4-21); **Kolkata Knight Riders 139-6** (19.4 overs). PoM: S. P. Narine. *Narine ended Bangalore's tournament. His 4-21 included Kohli, de Villiers and Maxwell, before he hit Dan Christian for three consecutive sixes (either side of a wide) in the chase. Kohli's 39 proved the game's top score, and Bangalore were scratchy, failing to clear the rope in their 138-7; Kolkata hit five sixes to stay well ahead of the rate. Kohli buckled under the pressure: after a petulant response to an lbw decision (which he overturned on review) he earned a dressing-down from umpire Virender Sharma; when Kolkata needed seven from the final over, he had left only Christian or Maxwell to bowl it. A first-ball four from Shakib rendered his choice (Christian) academic. Kohli had already announced he was giving up the captaincy; under his leadership, Bangalore had won 66 games and lost 70, with their best finish runners-up in 2016.*

Final play-off At Sharjah, October 13 (floodlit). **Kolkata Knight Riders won by three wickets. Delhi Capitals 135-5** (20 overs) (S. Dhawan 36, S. S. Iyer 30*); ‡**Kolkata Knight Riders 136-7** (19.5 overs) (S. Gill 46, V. R. Iyer 55). PoM: V. R. Iyer. *Delhi's tournament ended in a third successive defeat, although Kolkata – requiring 13 from 25 with nine wickets in hand – almost self-destructed. Delhi bowled well, but the only plausible explanation was panic. Barely a run was scored as wicket followed wicket – the last four all scoreless – to leave the Knight Riders needing six from two. Tripathi eventually found the middle of his bat, and tonked Ashwin, whose over had already claimed two ducks, back over his head. All five Kolkata bowlers had earlier kept a lid on the scoring and, when Iyer followed up their parsimony by hitting the game's only fifty in pursuit of a modest 136, the Delhi goose was surely cooked. It did not give up without a fight.*

FINAL

CHENNAI SUPER KINGS v KOLKATA KNIGHT RIDERS

At Dubai, October 15, 2021 (floodlit). Chennai Super Kings won by 27 runs. Toss: Kolkata Knight Riders.
    Kolkata arrived on a roll. Since the tournament had resumed in the UAE, they had won seven matches, more than any other side, including four in a row to reach the final. But the one team they had not been able to beat were Chennai. For the third time after they walked out together, Morgan won the toss; for the third time, Dhoni ended triumphant. After the Super Kings were put in, du Plessis batted throughout the innings for 86; he was dismissed by the final ball, aiming for the

Out on their own: Chennai openers Faf du Plessis and Ruturaj Gaikwad, leading scorers in the IPL.

boundary which would have made him the leading run-scorer in this tournament, but finished two behind his opening partner, Gaikwad. He had put on 61 with Gaikwad, 63 with Uthappa and 68 with Ali. The 56 given away by Ferguson matched the runs he had conceded across eight overs in the two play-offs. Still, the Knight Riders were up with the rate when Gill and Iyer opened with 91 – until Thakur struck twice in three deliveries, starting a collapse of eight for 34 in six overs. Kolkata hung on to the end, but 31 off six balls was well beyond them.

Player of the Match: F. du Plessis.

Player of the Tournament: H. V. Patel (Royal Challengers Bangalore).

Chennai Super Kings

	B	4/6
1 R. D. Gaikwad *c 10 b 4*	32	27 3/1
2 F. du Plessis *c 2 b 10*	86	59 7/3
3 R. V. Uthappa *lbw b 4*	31	15 0/3
4 M. M. Ali *not out*	37	20 2/3
B 1, lb 1, w 3, nb 1	6	

6 overs: 50-0   (20 overs) 192-3

1/61 2/124 3/192

5 A. T. Rayudu, 6 *†M. S. Dhoni, 7 R. A. Jadeja, 8 D. J. Bravo, 9 S. N. Thakur, 10 D. L. Chahar and 11 J. R. Hazlewood did not bat.

Shakib Al Hasan 18–6–33–0; Mavi 24–8–32–1; Ferguson 24–4–56–0; Chakravarthy 24–5–38–0; Narine 24–6–26–2; Iyer 6–2–5–0.

Kolkata Knight Riders

	B	4/6
1 S. Gill *lbw b 10*	51	43 6
2 V. R. Iyer *c 7 b 9*	50	32 5/3
3 N. Rana *c 2 b 9*	0	1 0
4 S. P. Narine *c 7 b 11*	2	2 0
5 *E. J. G. Morgan *c 10 b 11*	4	8 0
6 †K. D. Karthik *c 5 b 7*	9	7 0/1
7 Shakib Al Hasan *lbw b 7*	0	1 0
8 R. A. Tripathi *c 4 b 9*	2	3 0
9 L. H. Ferguson *not out*	18	11 1/1
10 S. P. Mavi *c 10 b 8*	20	13 1/2
11 V. V. Chakravarthy *not out*	0	0 0
W 8, nb 1	9	

6 overs: 55-0   (20 overs) 165-9

1/91 2/93 3/97 4/108 5/119 6/120 7/123 8/125 9/164

Chahar 24–10–32–1; Hazlewood 24–10–29–2; Thakur 24–11–38–3; Bravo 24–9–29–1; Jadeja 24–9–37–2.

Umpires: R. K. Illingworth and N. N. Menon.   Third umpire: S. Ravi.
Referee: J. Srinath.

INDIAN PREMIER LEAGUE FINALS

2007-08 RAJASTHAN ROYALS beat Chennai Super Kings by three wickets at Mumbai.
2008-09 DECCAN CHARGERS beat Royal Challengers Bangalore by six runs at Johannesburg.
2009-10 CHENNAI SUPER KINGS beat Mumbai Indians by 22 runs at Mumbai.
2010-11 CHENNAI SUPER KINGS beat Royal Challengers Bangalore by 58 runs at Chennai.
2011-12 KOLKATA KNIGHT RIDERS beat Chennai Super Kings by five wickets at Chennai.
2012-13 MUMBAI INDIANS beat Chennai Super Kings by 23 runs at Kolkata.
2013-14 KOLKATA KNIGHT RIDERS beat Kings XI Punjab by three wickets at Bangalore.
2014-15 MUMBAI INDIANS beat Chennai Super Kings by 41 runs at Kolkata.
2015-16 SUNRISERS HYDERABAD beat Royal Challengers Bangalore by eight runs at Bangalore.
2016-17 MUMBAI INDIANS beat Rising Pune Supergiant by one run at Hyderabad.
2017-18 CHENNAI SUPER KINGS beat Sunrisers Hyderabad by eight wickets at Mumbai.
2018-19 MUMBAI INDIANS beat Chennai Super Kings by one run at Hyderabad.
2020 MUMBAI INDIANS beat Delhi Capitals by five wickets at Dubai.
2021 CHENNAI SUPER KINGS beat Kolkata Knight Riders by 27 runs at Dubai.

INDIAN PREMIER LEAGUE RECORDS

Highest score	175*	C. H. Gayle	RC Bangalore v Pune Warriors at Bangalore	2012-13
	158*	B. B. McCullum	Kolkata KR v RC Bangalore at Bangalore	2007-08
	133*	A. B. de Villiers	RC Bangalore v Mumbai Indians at Mumbai	2014-15
Fastest 50 – balls	14	K. L. Rahul	KXI Punjab v Delhi Daredevils at Mohali	2017-18
Fastest 100 – balls	30	C. H. Gayle	RC Bangalore v Pune Warriors at Bangalore	2012-13
Most sixes – innings	17	C. H. Gayle	RC Bangalore v Pune Warriors at Bangalore	2012-13

Most runs – season	973	V. Kohli (avge 81.08, SR 152.03) for RC Bangalore....	2015-16
Most sixes – season	59	C. H. Gayle for RC Bangalore	2011-12
Most runs – career	**6,283**	**V. Kohli (avge 37.39, SR 129.94)**	**2007-08 to 2021**
	5,784	S. Dhawan (avge 34.84, SR 126.64)	2007-08 to 2021
	5,611	R. G. Sharma (avge 31.17, SR 130.39).......	2007-08 to 2021
Most 100s – career	6	C. H. Gayle............................	2008-09 to 2021
Best SR – career†	178.57	A. D. Russell (1,700 runs, avge 29.31)	2011-12 to 2021
Most sixes – career	357	C. H. Gayle............................	2008-09 to 2021
Best bowling	6-12	A. S. Joseph . Mumbai Indians v S Hyderabad at Hyderabad	2018-19
	6-14	Sohail Tanvir . Rajasthan Royals v Chennai SK at Jaipur	2007-08
	6-19	A. Zampa ... Rising Pune S v S Hyderabad at Visakhapatnam...................	2015-16
Most econ four overs	0-6	F. H. Edwards Deccan C v Kolkata KR at Cape Town ..	2008-09
	1-6	A. Nehra .... Delhi D v KXI Punjab at Bloemfontein ..	2008-09
	1-6	Y. S. Chahal . RC Bangalore v Chennai SK at Chennai ..	2018-19
Most expensive analysis	0-70	B. Thampi... S Hyderabad v RCB at Bangalore	2017-18
Most wickets – season	32	D. J. Bravo (avge 15.53, ER 7.95) for Chennai SK	2012-13
	32	**H. V. Patel (avge 14.34, ER 8.14) for RC Bangalore ..**	**2021**
Most wickets – career	170	S. L. Malinga (avge 19.79, ER 7.14)	2008-09 to 2018-19
	167	D. J. Bravo (avge 24.31, ER 8.36)	2007-08 to 2021
	166	A. Mishra (avge 23.95, ER 7.35)	2007-08 to 2021
Best ER – career‡	6.33	Rashid Khan (1,812 balls, avge 20.55)	2016-17 to 2021
Highest total	263-5	RC Bangalore v Pune Warriors at Bangalore.........	2012-13
	248-3	RC Bangalore v Gujarat Lions at Bangalore	2015-16
Lowest total	49	RC Bangalore v Kolkata KR at Kolkata	2016-17
Highest successful chase	226-6	Rajasthan R v Kings XI Punjab at Sharjah............	2020
Highest match aggregate	469-10	Chennai SK v Rajasthan Royals at Chennai	2009-10

†   *Career strike-rate: minimum 500 runs.*   ‡   *Career economy-rate: minimum 300 balls.*

DREAM11 SUPER SMASH IN 2020-21

Mark Geenty

1 Wellington Firebirds   2 Canterbury Kings

Finn Allen's move south to Wellington had not exactly set the cricket world ablaze. In the Plunket Shield, he collected a pair on debut for his new team, at No. 6, and totalled 40 from his next four innings. A promising young batsman who had scored a century against the England tourists the previous summer, he needed sparking up.

Then, on Christmas Eve, the first day of the Super Smash, he was picked as a pinch-hitter for Wellington Firebirds. It was only his third T20 match, four years after the first. He was a revelation, blasting 53 off 23 balls to beat his old Auckland team-mates, and never looked back. Allen hit six half-centuries and 512 runs – only two men had beaten that in a single Super Smash – at an average of 56 and strike-rate of 193. He fearlessly charged the fast bowlers, including the daunting figure of Kyle Jamieson. His ball-striking was unmatched, the sound off the bat like a rifle shot; he cleared the rope 25 times, the highlight a monster switch-hit off Mitchell Santner, New Zealand's premier white-ball spinner, playing for Northern Knights. But Allen's lucky bat, held together with tape, broke in the final, against Canterbury Kings, after hitting three fours in the run-chase. He fell next over, leaving Devon Conway to step up with an unbeaten 63-ball 93, which his captain, Michael Bracewell, labelled the best Conway innings he had seen. It secured back-to-back titles for **Wellington Firebirds**.

Conway's 455 (strike-rate 135) made him the tournament's second-highest run-scorer, not long after he became eligible for New Zealand and made his long-awaited international debut. With new-ball pair Hamish Bennett and Logan van Beek both snaring 13 wickets, and all-rounder Jimmy Neesham 12, the Firebirds won ten out of 11.

Central Stags and **Canterbury Kings** contested a cliffhanger of a preliminary final, after winning six matches each. Stags batsman Will Young hit a whirlwind 101 off 47, with ten sixes, but all-rounder Daryl Mitchell helped the Kings reach a target of 181. Mitchell was fourth on the run-list with 374, behind George Worker's 424 for the Stags, and added ten wickets with his medium-pacers. These teams also supplied the leading wicket-takers: Central's Blair Tickner, with 17, and Canterbury's Matt Henry, with 14.

Outside the three play-off teams, **Northern Knights** won five and lost five, while **Auckland Aces** and **Otago Volts**, both qualifiers the previous season, managed only two victories apiece.

There were no overseas players, because of border restrictions caused by the pandemic, but a gap in New Zealand's international fixture list allowed some big-name cameos: Kane Williamson appeared twice for the Knights, and twice guided them home in run-chases. Ross Taylor played six matches for the Stags, and hit 65 off 36 balls against the Kings at Napier, in an ultimately unsuccessful bid to win back his place in the national T20 side.

That match was notable not only for Taylor's pyrotechnics, but for the Napier city council's solution to the problem of the setting sun dazzling batters, which had held up a one-day international against India for 40 minutes two years earlier. They unveiled a giant shade sail, 12 metres square, above the Chapman Stand; hoisted by a crane, it could be moved to match the sun's course, and they hoped it would protect McLean Park's international status.

DREAM 11 SUPER SMASH AVERAGES IN 2020-21

BATTING (150 runs, strike-rate 100.00)

		M	I	NO	R	HS	100	50	Avge	SR	4	6
1	F. H. Allen (*Wellington F*)	11	11	2	512	92*	0	6	56.88	**193.93**	56	25
2	D. A. J. Bracewell (*Cent S*)	11	11	6	223	55*	0	2	44.60	**181.30**	17	13
3	W. A. Young (*Central S*) .	7	7	0	297	101	1	2	42.42	**174.70**	14	21
4	†A. P. Devcich (*Northern K*)	10	9	2	286	102	1	1	40.85	**169.23**	20	20
5	G. D. Phillips (*Auckland A*)	9	9	0	156	68	0	1	17.33	**162.50**	11	13
6	†M. S. Chapman (*Auck A*) .	5	5	0	219	73	0	2	43.80	**162.22**	22	10
7	J. A. Clarkson (*Central S*)	11	11	1	280	78	0	1	28.00	**159.09**	19	14
8	C. D. Fletcher (*Cant K*) . .	12	9	3	189	72	0	1	31.50	**157.50**	15	9
9	R. R. O'Donnell (*Auck A*)	10	10	3	254	61	0	1	36.28	**156.79**	19	11
10	C. J. Bowes (*Canterbury K*)	12	12	1	271	72	0	1	24.63	**152.24**	32	10
11	†H. D. Rutherford (*Otago V*)	10	10	0	166	49	0	0	16.60	**146.90**	22	6
12	B. J. Horne (*Auckland A*) .	10	10	3	163	63	0	1	23.28	**145.53**	8	9
13	A. K. Kitchen (*Otago V*) .	10	10	1	229	57*	0	1	25.44	**142.23**	15	14
14	K. J. McClure (*Cant K*) . .	12	12	1	187	40	0	0	17.00	**140.60**	22	7
15	T. A. Blundell (*Well F*). . . .	8	8	1	187	62*	0	1	26.71	**139.55**	20	5
16	†G. H. Worker (*Central S*) .	11	11	0	424	106	1	2	38.54	**138.56**	40	16
17	N. T. Broom (*Otago V*). . .	10	10	0	292	57	0	1	29.20	**137.08**	30	8
18	†D. P. Conway (*Well F*)	10	10	3	455	93*	0	5	65.00	**135.82**	52	9
19	†S. M. Solia (*Auckland A*) . .	10	10	0	266	75	0	2	26.60	**135.02**	29	5
20	D. J. Mitchell (*Cant K*). . .	10	10	0	374	88	0	3	37.40	**135.01**	26	10
21	W. T. O'Donnell (*Auck A*)	8	7	1	212	50*	0	1	35.33	**124.70**	15	8
22	C. E. McConchie (*Cant K*)	12	11	3	298	56*	0	1	37.25	**120.16**	23	5
23	†M. G. Bracewell (*Well F*) . .	11	8	3	155	47*	0	0	31.00	**116.54**	11	3
24	†N. F. Kelly (*Otago V*). . . .	10	9	0	195	75	0	1	21.66	**116.07**	22	6
25	T. L. Seifert (*Northern K*)	10	10	0	281	74	0	2	28.10	**115.63**	26	10
26	D. Cleaver (*Central S*) . . .	11	11	0	177	33	0	0	16.09	**107.92**	21	3

BOWLING (6 wickets, economy-rate 10.00)

		Style	Balls	Dots	R	W	BB	4I	Avge	SR	ER
1	J. R. Lennox (*Central S*)	SLA	90	41	82	6	3-20	0	13.66	15.00	**5.46**
2	J. G. Walker (*Northern K*)	OB	150	53	167	9	2-14	0	18.55	16.66	**6.68**
3	B. V. Sears (*Wellington F*)	RFM	132	59	151	9	4-21	1	16.77	14.66	**6.86**
4	T. D. Astle (*Canterbury K*)	LB	252	76	294	9	2-12	0	32.66	28.00	**7.00**
5	M. J. G. Rippon (*Otago V*)	SLW	222	68	268	10	2-19	0	26.80	22.20	**7.24**
6	P. F. Younghusband (*Well F*)	LB	204	61	253	9	2-25	0	28.11	22.66	**7.44**
7	H. K. Bennett (*Well F*)	RFM	254	108	328	13	2-13	0	25.23	19.53	**7.74**
8	L. V. van Beek (*Well F*) . .	RFM	252	89	327	13	3-28	0	25.15	19.38	**7.78**
9	T. G. Southee (*Northern K*)	RFM	90	35	118	8	3-41	0	14.75	11.25	**7.86**
10	J. D. S. Neesham (*Well F*)	RFM	160	56	210	12	3-11	0	17.50	13.33	**7.87**
11	R. Ravindra (*Wellington F*)	SLA	138	28	186	6	2-22	0	31.00	23.00	**8.08**
12	A. Y. Patel (*Central S*) . . .	SLA	248	92	335	7	3-34	0	47.85	35.42	**8.10**
13	R. M. ter Braak (*Auckland A*)	LFM	125	49	170	11	3-26	0	15.45	11.36	**8.16**
14	M. J. Henry (*Cant K*) . . .	RFM	250	89	345	14	3-25	0	24.64	17.85	**8.28**
15	B. M. Tickner (*Central S*)	RFM	252	111	349	17	3-23	0	20.52	14.82	**8.30**

		Style	Balls	Dots	R	W	BB	4I	Avge	SR	ER
16	E. J. Nuttall (*Cant K*) . . .	LFM	192	74	272	11	3-18	0	24.72	17.45	**8.50**
17	D. A. J. Bracewell (*Cent S*) .	RFM	233	83	341	10	3-38	0	34.10	23.30	**8.78**
18	M. G. Bracewell (*Well F*) .	OB	90	19	133	8	4-28	1	16.62	11.25	**8.86**
19	D. J. Mitchell (*Cant K*) . .	RM	178	49	266	10	2-21	0	26.60	17.80	**8.96**
20	M. J. McClenaghan (*Ot V*) .	LFM	232	78	352	12	3-36	0	29.33	19.33	**9.10**
21	J. A. Clarkson (*Central S*)	RM	106	37	161	6	2-30	0	26.83	17.66	**9.11**
22	J. F. A. Field (*Central S*)	RFM	198	64	307	10	2-26	0	30.70	19.80	**9.30**
23	S. C. Kuggeleijn (*North K*) .	RFM	192	76	304	12	2-26	0	25.33	16.00	**9.50**
24	W. E. R. Somerville (*Auck A*)	OB	186	58	298	12	3-18	0	24.83	15.50	**9.61**
25	W. S. A. Williams (*Cant K*)	RM	162	36	263	8	2-18	0	32.87	20.25	**9.74**
26	M. B. Bacon (*Otago V*) .	RM	107	38	175	9	3-18	0	19.44	11.88	**9.81**

DREAM11 SUPER SMASH IN 2020-21

	P	W	L		Pts	NRR
WELLINGTON FIREBIRDS . . .	10	9	1		36	1.52
CENTRAL STAGS	10	6	4		24	0.59
CANTERBURY KINGS	10	6	4		24	0.08
Northern Knights	10	5	5		20	−0.44
Auckland Aces	10	2	8		8	−0.38
Otago Volts	10	2	8		8	−1.45

2nd v 3rd At Auckland (Eden Park Outer Oval), February 11, 2021. **Canterbury Kings won by four wickets.** ‡**Central Stags 180-7** (20 overs) (W. A. Young 101); **Canterbury Kings 181-6** (19.5 overs) (D. J. Mitchell 88, C. D. Fletcher 72). *Will Young batted for all but 11 deliveries of the Central Stags innings; he hit ten sixes, a tournament record, and was run out off the final ball for 101 in 47. That looked enough to get the Stags into the final when Canterbury Kings were 38-4, but Daryl Mitchell and Cam Fletcher added 132, a T20 fifth-wicket record in New Zealand, in 13.3 overs, and the Kings scraped home with a ball to spare.*

Final At Wellington (Basin Reserve), February 13, 2021. **Wellington Firebirds won by five wickets. Canterbury Kings 175-8** (20 overs) (C. J. Bowes 37, D. J. Mitchell 35, C. E. McConchie 44; L. V. van Beek 3-28); ‡**Wellington Firebirds 178-5** (19.4 overs) (D. P. Conway 93*). *The Firebirds retained the title in front of a crowd of 5,545. Mitchell steered the Kings to 106-2 in the 12th over, but their scoring-rate dipped slightly, despite 29 in 15 from Henry Shipley, leaving a target of 176. Though Finn Allen departed for 16, Devon Conway unleashed his power game, manipulating the field and pacing his innings to perfection: he completed victory with his 12th boundary to finish with 93* in 63.*

SUPER SMASH FINALS

2005-06	CANTERBURY WIZARDS beat Auckland Aces by six wickets at Auckland.
2006-07	AUCKLAND ACES beat Otago Volts by 60 runs at Auckland.
2007-08	CENTRAL STAGS beat Northern Knights by five wickets at New Plymouth.
2008-09	OTAGO VOLTS headed the table; the final against Canterbury Wizards at Dunedin was washed out.
2009-10	CENTRAL STAGS beat Auckland Aces by 78 runs at New Plymouth.
2010-11	AUCKLAND ACES beat Central Stags by four runs at Auckland.
2011-12	AUCKLAND ACES beat Canterbury Wizards by 44 runs at Auckland.
2012-13	OTAGO VOLTS beat Wellington Firebirds by four wickets at Dunedin.
2013-14	NORTHERN KNIGHTS beat Otago Volts by five wickets at Hamilton.
2014-15	WELLINGTON FIREBIRDS beat Auckland Aces by six wickets at Hamilton.
2015-16	AUCKLAND ACES beat Otago Volts by 20 runs at New Plymouth.
2016-17	WELLINGTON FIREBIRDS beat Central Stags by 14 runs at New Plymouth.
2017-18	KNIGHTS beat Central Stags by nine wickets at Hamilton.
2018-19	CENTRAL STAGS beat Knights by 67 runs at Hamilton.
2019-20	WELLINGTON FIREBIRDS beat Auckland Aces by 22 runs at Wellington.
2020-21	WELLINGTON FIREBIRDS beat Canterbury Kings by five wickets at Wellington.

SUPER SMASH RECORDS

Highest score	120*	M. J. Guptill. . . .	Auckland A v Canterbury W at Rangiora	2011-12
	116*	G. D. Phillips. . .	Auckland A v Central S at Auckland .	2016-17
	116	D. P. M. D.		
		Jayawardene . .	Central S v Otago V at New Plymouth	2016-17
Fastest 50 – balls	14	K. Noema-Barnett	Central S v Otago V at Invercargill. . .	2010-11
Fastest 100 – balls	40	T. L. Seifert	Knights v Auckland A at Mt Maunganui	2017-18
Most sixes – innings	10	**W. A. Young** . . .	**Central S v Canterbury K at Auckland**	**2020-21**
Most runs – season	584	J. D. Ryder (avge 58.40, SR 174.32) for Wellington F. .		2012-13
Most sixes – season	39	J. D. Ryder for Wellington F.		2012-13
Most runs – career	**2,838**	**N. T. Broom (avge 28.09, SR 123.12)**.		**2005-06 to 2020-21**
	2,798	**G. H. Worker (avge 28.26, SR 127.18)** . . .		**2008-09 to 2020-21**
	2,336	R. J. Nicol (avge 30.33, SR 121.09).		2005-06 to 2017-18
Most 100s – career	2	D. P. Conway (2017-18 to 2020-21), B. B. McCullum (2005-06 to 2011-12), **G. D. Phillips (2016-17 to 2020-21)**		
Best SR – career*	188.68	F. H. Allen (517 runs, avge 51.70).		2016-17 to 2020-21
Most sixes – career	107	C. de Grandhomme		2006-07 to 2020-21
Best bowling	6-7	K. A. Jamieson .	Canterbury K v Auckland A at Auckland	2018-19
	6-23	T. S. Nethula . .	Knights v Central S at Napier.	2018-19
	6-28	I. G. Butler . . .	Otago V v Auckland A at Dunedin. . . .	2009-10
	6-28	B. Laughlin . . .	Northern K v Wellington F at Wellington	2013-14
Most econ four overs	6-7	K. A. Jamieson .	Canterbury K v Auckland A at Auckland	2018-19
Most expensive analysis	0-70	A. W. Mathieson	Central S v Auckland A at Auckland . .	2015-16
Most wickets – season	22	K. A. Jamieson (avge 12.77, ER 7.33) for Canterbury K		2018-19
Most wickets – career	125	A. M. Ellis (avge 22.35, ER 8.32)		2006-07 to 2019-20
	109	R. M. Hira (avge 22.48, ER 7.24).		2006-07 to 2019-20
	92	L. J. Woodcock (avge 23.46, ER 7.65).		2005-06 to 2018-19
Best ER – career†	6.45	D. L. Vettori (682 balls, avge 22.24)		2005-06 to 2014-15
Highest total	249-3	Otago V v Central S at New Plymouth.		2016-17
	248-4	Central S v Otago V at New Plymouth.		2016-17
Lowest total	72	Wellington F v Northern Knights at Hamilton		2015-16
Highest successful chase	222-3	Canterbury K v Knights at Christchurch.		2019-20
Highest match aggregate	497-7	Central S v Otago V at New Plymouth.		2016-17

* *Career strike-rate: minimum 500 runs.* † *Career economy-rate: minimum 300 balls.*

THE HBL PAKISTAN SUPER LEAGUE IN 2020-21

Mazher Arshad

1 Multan Sultans   2 Peshawar Zalmi

For the second year running, the coronavirus pandemic cut the Pakistan Super League in two. The sixth PSL tournament started in Karachi in February – with crowds allowed at 20% of ground capacity – and was supposed to be completed in Lahore in March, but a Covid outbreak forced a postponement halfway through the group stages.

Things started to go wrong on March 1, when Islamabad United's Australian leg-spinner Fawad Ahmed tested positive for Covid-19 before a match against Quetta Gladiators. It was postponed for a day, but went ahead despite two more positive tests (Islamabad's Lewis Gregory, Quetta's Tom Banton); so did a double-header on March 3. Though the Pakistan Cricket Board offered vaccines to players and officials, trust in the biosecure bubble was fading. Another Australian, Dan Christian, decided to leave Karachi Kings (whose fielding coach had also tested positive). As the infection continued to spread, the PCB called a halt.

A new window to resume the tournament was found, in June, but a third Covid wave in Pakistan compelled the board to shift it to Abu Dhabi. That brought further challenges: travel restrictions complicated the logistics of getting visas for Pakistan and Indian nationals, who formed most of the television crew, as well as flying them in. The league finally resumed on June 9. By then, the six teams had been forced to call up new players, as many of those who had appeared in Karachi, including a dozen from England, were no longer available.

Multan Sultans, the eventual winners, enjoyed a big turnaround in Abu Dhabi, where they won four games out of five to finish second in the table, after a single win in Karachi. They were led by a dynamic captain, Mohammad Rizwan, the competition's second-most prolific batsman with 500 runs, who had joined them only in January, after failing to win a regular place in the Karachi side. Sohaib Maqsood, the Player of the Tournament for his 428 runs at a strike-rate of 156, was central to Multan's campaign, as was 22-year-old Shahnawaz Dahani, the leading wicket-taker with 20; he was named Bowler of the Tournament and Best Emerging Cricketer.

Multan were first-time finalists, whereas their opponents, **Peshawar Zalmi**, got there for the fourth time in five seasons – and were runners-up for the third. Coach Daren Sammy's strategy of loading the squad with power-hitters paid off, and Afghan batter Hazratullah Zazai, one of the second-half replacements, led the late charge with 212 runs and a strike-rate of 185. The captain, left-arm seamer Wahab Riaz, took 18 wickets.

Islamabad United, bottom in the previous tournament, were transformed. They became the first team to win eight group matches – and scored a PSL record 247 – only to lose their play-offs to Multan and Peshawar.

Defending champions **Karachi Kings** were one of four teams tied on ten points in the league stage, and squeezed into the play-offs on net run-rate, but could go no further, though they had the leading run-scorer in Babar Azam (554). **Lahore Qalandars**, who had won three of their four games in Karachi, nosedived in Abu Dhabi, failing to reach the play-offs for the fifth time in six seasons, despite a formidable attack: Rashid Khan, Shaheen Shah Afridi, Haris Rauf and James Faulkner claimed 50 wickets between them.

The wooden spoon went to **Quetta Gladiators**, who conceded 9.36 per over, the worst economy-rate; they won only twice. Losing overseas players such as Dale Steyn, Chris Gayle and Banton, who all left after the Karachi leg, did not help. Faf du Plessis, who did come to Abu Dhabi, went home early after suffering concussion and memory loss during a fielding collision.

PAKISTAN SUPER LEAGUE AVERAGES IN 2020-21

BATTING (150 runs)

		M	I	NO	R	HS	100	50	Avge	SR	4	6
1	†Hazratullah Zazai (*Pesh Z*) ..	5	5	0	212	77	0	3	42.40	185.96	24	14
2	Mohammad Nabi (*Kar K*)	5	5	2	174	67	0	2	58.00	179.38	16	11
3	†C. Munro (*Islamabad U*) .	7	7	2	285	90*	0	2	57.00	169.64	37	11
4	Asif Ali (*Islamabad U*) ..	12	10	2	224	75	0	1	28.00	167.16	15	18
5	T. H. David (*Lahore Q*) ..	6	6	2	180	64*	0	1	45.00	166.66	11	12
6	†R. R. Rossouw (*Multan S*)	12	12	3	177	50	0	1	19.66	158.03	20	7
7	Sohaib Maqsood (*Multan S*)	12	12	3	428	65*	0	5	47.55	156.77	39	22
8	†S. E. Rutherford (*Pesh Z*)	13	12	4	276	56	0	1	34.50	153.33	16	21
9	†U. T. Khawaja (*Islamabad U*)	7	7	2	246	105*	1	1	49.20	152.79	31	5
10	Shoaib Malik (*Peshawar Z*)	13	13	3	354	73	0	2	35.40	149.36	29	17
11	†Sharjeel Khan (*Karachi K*)	11	11	0	338	105	1	1	30.72	148.24	31	23
12	†Shan Masood (*Multan S*) .	7	7	0	209	73	0	2	29.85	142.17	25	7
13	Mohammad Hafeez (*Lah Q*)	10	10	2	271	73*	0	2	33.87	138.26	22	14
14	Sarfraz Ahmed (*Quetta G*)	10	10	3	321	81	0	3	45.85	137.76	35	7
15	†Khushdil Shah (*Multan S*)	11	9	5	165	44*	0	0	41.25	137.50	7	10
16	Haider Ali (*Peshawar Z*) .	9	9	1	166	50	0	1	20.75	137.18	16	8
17	J. M. Vince (*Multan S*) ..	5	5	0	174	84	0	1	34.80	135.93	20	5
18	†Azam Khan (*Quetta G*)...	10	10	0	174	47	0	0	17.40	133.84	18	7
19	Babar Azam (*Karachi K*) .	11	11	3	554	90*	0	7	69.25	132.53	56	12
20	Kamran Akmal (*Pesh Z*) ..	13	13	0	283	59	0	2	21.76	129.22	39	7
21	†B. R. Dunk (*Lahore Q*)...	10	9	1	163	57*	0	1	20.37	128.34	13	7
22	Mohammad Rizwan (*Mul S*)	12	12	1	500	82*	0	4	45.45	127.87	56	10
23	Iftikhar Ahmed (*Isbad U*)	12	9	3	221	71*	0	1	36.83	123.46	16	9
24	Usman Khan (*Quetta G*)..	6	6	0	150	81	0	1	25.00	121.95	16	5
25	†Fakhar Zaman (*Lahore Q*)	10	10	1	287	83	0	2	31.88	121.09	26	11
26	†Hussain Talat (*Islamabad U*)	11	8	1	156	42	0	0	22.28	103.31	13	1

BOWLING (7 wickets)

		Style	Balls	Dots	R	W	BB	4I	Avge	SR	ER
1	Rashid Khan (*Lahore Q*) .	LB	192	90	175	11	5-20	1	15.90	17.45	**5.46**
2	J. P. Faulkner (*Lahore Q*)	LFM	144	71	156	13	3-19	0	12.00	11.07	**6.50**
3	Hasan Ali (*Islamabad U*) .	RFM	239	118	269	13	2-14	0	20.69	18.38	**6.75**
4	Mohammad Irfan (*Pesh Z*)	LFM	240	112	271	10	3-27	0	27.10	24.00	**6.77**
5	Fahim Ashraf (*Isbad U*) ..	RFM	168	71	190	9	3-11	0	21.11	18.66	**6.78**
6	Imran Tahir (*Multan S*) ..	LB	150	49	170	13	3-7	0	13.07	11.53	**6.80**
7	Imran Khan (*Multan S*) ..	RFM	150	63	179	12	3-24	0	14.91	12.50	**7.16**
8	Khurram Shehzad (*Qu G*)	RFM	96	41	116	7	3-14	0	16.57	13.71	**7.25**
9	Shaheen Shah Afridi (*La Q*) .	LFM	240	113	292	16	3-14	0	18.25	15.00	**7.30**

		Style	Balls	Dots	R	W	BB	4I	Avge	SR	ER
10	B. Muzarabani (*Multan S*) .	RFM	112	57	144	10	3-31	0	14.40	11.20	**7.71**
11	Imad Wasim (*Karachi K*).	SLA	186	75	241	7	2-2	0	34.42	26.57	**7.77**
12	S. Mahmood (*Peshawar Z*)	RFM	109	43	145	12	3-12	0	12.08	9.08	**7.98**
13	Mohammad Imran (*Pesh Z*)	LFM	249	85	340	9	2-47	0	37.77	27.66	**8.19**
14	Shadab Khan (*Isbad U*) . .	LB	234	98	325	9	2-14	0	36.11	26.00	**8.33**
15	Mohammad Wasim (*Is U*) .	RFM	240	85	336	12	4-31	1	28.00	20.00	**8.40**
16	Shahnawaz Dahani (*Mul S*) .	RFM	242	106	340	20	4-5	2	17.00	12.10	**8.42**
17	Mohammad Hasnain (*QG*) .	RF	197	85	292	9	2-18	0	32.44	21.88	**8.89**
18	Arshad Iqbal (*Karachi K*)	RFM	174	56	260	8	3-16	0	32.50	21.75	**8.96**
19	Wahab Riaz (*Peshawar Z*) .	LF	282	120	422	18	4-17	1	23.44	15.66	**8.97**
20	Waqas Maqsood (*Kar K*)	LFM	123	35	192	7	2-21	0	27.42	17.57	**9.36**
21	Haris Rauf (*Lahore Q*) . . .	RFM	212	84	342	10	3-38	0	34.20	21.20	**9.67**
22	Mohammad Ilyas (*Kar K*)	RFM	107	43	173	8	3-39	0	21.62	13.37	**9.67**
23	Umaid Asif (*Peshawar Z*)	RFM	189	59	306	8	2-17	0	38.25	23.62	**9.71**

PAKISTAN SUPER LEAGUE IN 2020-21

	P	W	L	Pts	NRR
ISLAMABAD UNITED	10	8	2	16	0.85
MULTAN SULTANS	10	5	5	10	1.05
PESHAWAR ZALMI	10	5	5	10	0.58
KARACHI KINGS	10	5	5	10	−0.11
Lahore Qalandars	10	5	5	10	−0.58
Quetta Gladiators	10	2	8	4	−1.78

1st v 2nd At Abu Dhabi, June 21, 2021 (floodlit). **Multan Sultans won by 31 runs. ‡Multan Sultans 180-5** (20 overs) (Sohaib Maqsood 59, J. Charles 41, Khushdil Shah 42*); **Islamabad United 149** (19 overs) (U. T. Khawaja 70; Sohail Tanvir 3-17, B. Muzarabani 3-31). *PoM:* Sohail Tanvir. *Multan's victory over table-toppers Islamabad earned them their first PSL final. Both sides lost two top-order batters for ducks, but Sohaib Maqsood, backed up by forceful innings from Johnson Charles and Khushdil Shah, ensured an imposing total for Multan, whereas Islamabad's Usman Khawaja (70 in 40) found little support.*

3rd v 4th At Abu Dhabi, June 21, 2021 (floodlit). **Peshawar Zalmi won by five wickets. Karachi Kings 175-7** (20 overs) (Babar Azam 53, N. L. T. C. Perera 37); ‡**Peshawar Zalmi 176-5** (19.5 overs) (Hazratullah Zazai 77, Shoaib Malik 30). *PoM:* Hazratullah Zazai. *Peshawar knocked out the reigning champions thanks to another tour de force from Hazratullah Zazai. On debut a week earlier – also against Karachi – he had equalled the PSL record with a 17-ball fifty; this time he took 23, and finished with 77 from 38, all but seven coming in boundaries. Babar Azam's seventh fifty of this tournament proved in vain.*

Final play-off At Abu Dhabi, June 22, 2021 (floodlit). **Peshawar Zalmi won by eight wickets. Islamabad United 174-9** (20 overs) (C. Munro 44, Hasan Ali 45); ‡**Peshawar Zalmi 177-2** (16.5 overs) (Hazratullah Zazai 66, J. W. Wells 55*, Shoaib Malik 32*). *PoM:* Hazratullah Zazai. *Islamabad were 110-8 before Hasan Ali's 16-ball 45 set a more challenging target. But Hazratullah continued to run riot, with 66 in 44. He added 126 with Jon Wells – a 32-year-old Tasmanian on PSL debut – before Shoaib Malik clinched a place in the final with three fours off Hasan Ali. Peshawar fielded a couple of overs with ten men when the umpires were initially sceptical about an injury to Mohammad Irfan.*

Final At Abu Dhabi, June 24, 2021 (floodlit). **Multan Sultans won by 47 runs. Multan Sultans 206-4** (20 overs) (Shan Masood 37, Mohammad Rizwan 30, Sohaib Maqsood 65*, R. R. Rossouw 50); ‡**Peshawar Zalmi 159-9** (20 overs) (Kamran Akmal 36, Shoaib Malik 48; Imran Tahir 3-33). *PoM:* Sohaib Maqsood. *PoT:* Sohaib Maqsood. *Peshawar suffered a double blow earlier in the day when batter Haider Ali and seamer Umaid Asif were suspended for meeting people outside the team's biosecure bubble. Haider was replaced in Pakistan's squad to tour England by Maqsood, who proceeded to guide Multan to their first PSL title. His fifth half-century – 65* in 35 balls – and 50 in 21 from Rilee Rossouw, with whom he added 98 in 7.2 overs, helped them mount the third-highest total of this tournament. Blessing Muzarabani removed Hazratullah cheaply in the reply, and Imran Tahir struck three times in four balls to crush Peshawar's hopes.*

PAKISTAN SUPER LEAGUE FINALS

2015-16   ISLAMABAD UNITED beat Quetta Gladiators by six wickets at Dubai.
2016-17   PESHAWAR ZALMI beat Quetta Gladiators by 58 runs at Lahore.
2017-18   ISLAMABAD UNITED beat Peshawar Zalmi by three wickets at Dubai.
2018-19   QUETTA GLADIATORS beat Peshawar Zalmi by eight wickets at Karachi.
2019-20   KARACHI KINGS beat Lahore Qalandars by five wickets at Lahore.
2020-21   MULTAN SULTANS beat Peshawar Zalmi by 47 runs at Abu Dhabi.

PAKISTAN SUPER LEAGUE RECORDS

Highest score	127*	C. A. Ingram	Karachi K v Quetta G at Sharjah ...	2018-19
	117*	C. S. Delport	Islamabad U v Lahore Q at Karachi	2018-19
	117	Sharjeel Khan ...	Islamabad U v Peshawar Z at Dubai	2015-16
Fastest 50 – balls	17	Kamran Akmal ..	Peshawar Z v Karachi K at Lahore .	2017-18
	17	Asif Ali	Islamabad U v Lahore Q at Karachi	2018-19
	17	**Hazratullah Zazai**	**Peshawar Z v Karachi K at Abu Dhabi**	**2020-21**
Fastest 100 – balls	43	R. R. Rossouw...	Multan S v Quetta G at Multan	2019-20
Most sixes – innings	12	B. R. Dunk	Lahore Q v Karachi K at Lahore ...	2019-20
Most runs – season	**554**	**Babar Azam (avge 69.25, SR 132.53) for Karachi K .**		**2020-21**
Most sixes – season	28	Kamran Akmal for Peshawar Z....................		2017-18
Most runs – career	**2,070**	**Babar Azam (avge 43.12, SR 121.55) ....**		**2015-16 to 2020-21**
	1,820	Kamran Akmal (avge 27.57, SR 136.84)..		2015-16 to 2020-21
	1,481	Shoaib Malik (avge 32.19, SR 128.11)....		2015-16 to 2020-21
Most 100s – career	3	Kamran Akmal		2015-16 to 2019-20
Best SR – career†	166.24	K. A. Pollard (650 runs, avge 32.50)		2016-17 to 2018-19
Most sixes – career	84	**Kamran Akmal**		**2015-16 to 2020-21**
Best bowling	6-16	R. S. Bopara	Karachi K v Lahore Q at Sharjah .	2015-16
	6-19	Fahim Ashraf	Islamabad U v Lahore Q at Karachi	2018-19
	6-24	Umar Gul	Multan S v Quetta G at Dubai ...	2017-18
Most econ four overs	2-4	Mohammad Nawaz	Quetta G v Lahore Q at Dubai ...	2017-18
Most expensive analysis	**0-65**	**Zafar Gohar.....**	**Islamabad U v Pesh Z at Abu Dhabi**	**2020-21**
Most wickets – season	25	Hasan Ali (avge 13.64, ER 6.77) for Peshawar Z......		2018-19
Most wickets – career	**94**	**Wahab Riaz (avge 19.61, ER 7.38) ......**		**2015-16 to 2020-21**
	72	Hasan Ali (avge 20.88, ER 7.33)		2015-16 to 2020-21
Best ER – career‡	6.22	S. P. Narine (396 balls, avge 20.55).......		2016-17 to 2017-18
Highest total	**247-2**	**Islamabad U v Peshawar Z at Abu Dhabi**		**2020-21**
	238-3	Islamabad U v Lahore Q at Karachi		2018-19
	232-6	**Peshawar Z v Islamabad U at Abu Dhabi**		**2020-21**
Lowest total	59	Lahore Q v Peshawar Z at Dubai		2016-17
Highest successful chase	204-4	Lahore Q v Multan S at Sharjah		2018-19
Highest match aggregate	**479-8**	**Islamabad U v Peshawar Z at Abu Dhabi**		**2020-21**

† *Career strike-rate: minimum 500 runs.*   ‡ *Career economy-rate: minimum 300 balls.*

MY11CIRCLE LANKA PREMIER LEAGUE IN 2020-21

Sa'adi Thawfeeq

1 Jaffna Stallions   2 Galle Gladiators

Sri Lanka had long looked enviously at high-profile T20 competitions in other Test nations – and some saw the lack of such a tournament as a factor in the gradual decline of the national side. World T20 runners-up in 2009 and 2012, champions in 2014, Sri Lanka had failed to gain automatic entry to the Super 12 stage of the 2021 T20 World Cup; instead they found themselves in the qualifying groups, competing with the likes of Oman, Scotland and Namibia.

If the idea of the Lanka Premier League was straightforward, its creation had been anything but. The LPL was expected to start in 2018, but administrative headaches caused numerous delays – even before coronavirus struck. That it got off the ground in November was quite an achievement. Once again, though, there was rescheduling. The August start was shunted to November 7, then twice more, before finally settling on November 26. Despite all that, the tournament turned out to be a huge success.

Although the LPL could not match the IPL in terms of star names, there were many positives. The matches were exciting, competitive and – most importantly – actually happening, while tournaments around the world had been cancelled. And the LPL unearthed several capable young cricketers who might have been lost in the backwaters of Sri Lankan cricket. Among them were Dhananjaya Lakshan, a seam-bowling all-rounder named the Emerging Player of the Tournament; Nuwan Thushara, who has a slingy action reminiscent of Lasith Malinga; Jaffna's teenage leg-spinner Vijayakanth Viyaskanth, and off-spinner Sahan Arachchi.

Dasun Shanaka, captain of the oddly spelled Dambulla Viiking, voiced a widespread sentiment when he said the LPL was "vital to our cricket future. We are getting a look at cricketers we otherwise wouldn't. We were judging players from their international performances, but we were putting inexperienced players into international cricket. Once they play a tournament like this, they know what to expect."

Because of Covid, Hambantota's Mahinda Rajapaksa Stadium hosted all 23 matches, which might have led to tired pitches – but didn't. The three-week competition could hardly have enjoyed a more thrilling start, with Colombo Kings defeating Kandy Tuskers in a super over after both made 219.

The eventual winners were **Jaffna Stallions**, led by all-rounder Tissara Perera, though they had finished only third in the league stage (whose purpose was to reduce five teams to four for the knockouts). **Galle Gladiators** won just two of their eight games, yet scraped through in fourth; in a tense semi-final, they overcame **Colombo Kings**, who had topped the table with six victories. In the other semi, Jaffna had a more comfortable victory over **Dambulla Viiking**. The team to miss out, on net run-rate, were **Kandy Tuskers**.

The Gladiators would have been left far behind without opener Dhanushka Gunathilleke, the tournament's leading scorer by a country mile. He went off the boil in the knockouts (scoring 13 and one), but in the first eight games he averaged 77, never made fewer than 30, and contributed 37% of his side's runs. Next-heaviest scorer was Colombo's Laurie Evans – imported from Sussex – with 289; he hit the only century of the competition, against Jaffna.

One player stood head and shoulders above the others in the bowling, too. Jaffna leg-spinner Wanindu Hasaranga de Silva claimed 17 wickets – Lakshan was next with 13 – and had a phenomenal economy-rate of 5.18. No one else to send down at least three overs cost less than 6.44. Overseas names fared well, with Afghan wrist-spinner Qais Ahmad as notable for his parsimony (6.50) as his 12 wickets. With Pakistanis unable to play in the IPL, several – including Mohammad Amir, Shoaib Malik and Shahid Afridi – turned out here. West Indian Andre Russell combined eight cheap wickets with 169 runs at almost two a ball. In the five-over thrash against the Gladiators, he spanked 65 from 19 as the Kings rocketed to 96.

The success of the inaugural LPL prompted Sri Lanka Cricket to expand the competition for its second season. For 2021, a team representing Trincomalee, on the island's east coast, were due to join in.

LANKA PREMIER LEAGUE AVERAGES IN 2020-21

BATTING (140 runs)

		M	I	NO	R	HS	100	50	Avge	SR	4	6
1	N. L. T. C. Perera (*Jaffna S*) .	10	8	2	261	97*	0	2	43.50	223.07	22	19
2	A. D. Russell (*Colombo K*) ..	8	7	1	169	65*	0	1	28.16	194.25	20	10
3	Azam Khan (*Galle G*)	10	9	2	215	55	0	1	30.71	186.95	19	16
4	L. J. Evans (*Colombo K*)	8	8	3	289	108*	1	2	57.80	170.00	24	18
5	P. B. B. Rajapaksa (*Galle G*)	10	8	1	180	40	0	0	25.71	163.63	19	11
6	M. D. Shanaka (*Dambulla V*)	9	9	2	278	73	0	2	39.71	161.62	24	14
7	Rahmanullah Gurbaz (*Kandy T*)	8	8	0	169	53	0	1	21.12	157.94	19	11
8	D. P. D. N. Dickwella (*Dam V*)	9	9	1	270	65	0	2	33.75	148.35	32	8
9	M. D. Gunathilleke (*Galle G*)	10	10	2	476	94*	0	4	59.50	144.68	67	8
10	A. K. Perera (*Dambulla V*) ..	7	7	2	227	74*	0	1	45.40	141.87	20	8
11	D. A. S. Gunaratne (*Kandy T*)	8	8	4	168	52*	0	1	42.00	141.17	19	2
12	B. K. G. Mendis (*Kandy T*) ..	8	8	1	263	68	0	2	37.57	139.89	18	17
13	S. R. Patel (*Dambulla V*)....	9	9	0	189	58	0	1	21.00	136.95	16	8
14	W. I. A. Fernando (*Jaffna S*) .	9	8	1	275	92*	0	2	39.28	134.80	17	20
15	M. D. K. J. Perera (*Kandy T*)	8	8	0	209	87	0	1	26.12	132.27	24	4
16	B. R. M. Taylor (*Kandy T*) ..	6	6	1	144	51*	0	1	28.80	129.72	17	5
17	L. D. Chandimal (*Colombo K*)	9	8	2	246	80	0	2	41.00	129.47	35	6
18	Shoaib Malik (*Jaffna S*).....	10	9	1	203	59	0	1	25.37	120.83	15	3
19	D. J. Bell-Drummond (*Col K*)	7	6	0	151	70	0	1	25.16	117.96	13	6
20	W. U. Tharanga (*Dambulla V*)	8	8	0	196	77	0	1	24.50	108.28	26	3

BOWLING (5 wickets)

		Style	Balls	Dots	R	W	BB	4I	Avge	SR	ER
1	P. W. H. de Silva (*Jaffna S*) ...	LB	222	109	192	17	3-15	0	11.29	13.05	5.18
2	Qais Ahmad (*Colombo K*)	LB	180	76	195	12	3-24	0	16.25	15.00	6.50
3	A. D. Mathews (*Colombo K*) ...	RM	103	56	117	5	1-9	0	23.40	20.60	6.81
4	R. T. M. Wanigamuni (*Dam V*) ..	OB	102	37	120	6	2-28	0	20.00	17.00	7.05
5	R. A. S. Lakmal (*Jaffna S*)	RFM	114	53	139	8	2-27	0	17.37	14.25	7.31

		Style	Balls	Dots	R	W	BB	4I	Avge	SR	ER
6	Usman Shinwari (*Jaffna S*) …	LFM	126	67	158	9	3-16	0	17.55	14.00	**7.52**
7	D. A. S. Gunaratne (*Kandy T*) . .	RFM	156	51	196	9	2-20	0	21.77	17.33	**7.53**
8	N. L. T. C. Perera (*Jaffna S*) …	RFM	103	31	131	5	2-9	0	26.20	20.60	**7.63**
9	P. M. Pushpakumara (*Dam V*) . .	SLA	108	34	139	8	2-19	0	17.37	13.50	**7.72**
10	Mohammad Amir (*Galle G*)…	LFM	228	106	294	11	5-26	1	26.72	20.72	**7.73**
11	S. R. Patel (*Dambulla V*) …	SLA	160	58	209	7	2-26	0	29.85	22.85	**7.83**
12	C. A. K. Rajitha (*Dambulla V*) . .	RFM	108	46	145	6	2-16	0	24.16	18.00	**8.05**
13	S. M. A. Priyanjan (*Colombo K*) .	OB	96	33	130	5	2-4	0	26.00	19.20	**8.12**
14	I. Udana (*Colombo K*) ……	LFM	167	64	240	5	3-25	0	48.00	33.40	**8.62**
15	P. A. D. Lakshan (*Galle G*) …	RFM	156	57	225	13	3-36	0	17.30	12.00	**8.65**
16	A. N. P. R. Fernando (*Kandy T*) . .	RFM	159	60	233	8	3-36	0	29.12	19.87	**8.79**
17	A. D. Russell (*Colombo K*) …	RFM	78	32	116	8	3-18	0	14.50	9.75	**8.92**
18	P. V. D. Chameera (*Colombo K*) .	RF	167	62	256	8	2-27	0	32.00	20.87	**9.19**
19	P. A. D. L. R. Sandakan (*Galle G*)	SLW	174	47	272	12	3-32	0	22.66	14.50	**9.37**
20	D. Olivier (*Jaffna S*)………	RFM	157	59	266	10	4-44	1	26.60	15.70	**10.16**
21	Naveen-ul-Haq (*Kandy T*) ….	RFM	108	33	183	8	3-44	0	22.87	13.50	**10.16**
22	Anwar Ali (*Dambulla V*) …..	RFM	123	38	226	9	3-37	0	25.11	13.66	**11.02**

LANKA PREMIER LEAGUE IN 2020-21

	P	W	L	NR	Pts	NRR
COLOMBO KINGS …………	8	6	2	0	12	0.44
DAMBULLA VIIKING……….	8	5	2	1	11	−0.19
JAFFNA STALLIONS ……….	8	4	3	1	9	0.78
GALLE GLADIATORS ………	8	2	6	0	4	−0.20
Kandy Tuskers ………………	8	2	6	0	4	−0.77

1st v 4th   At Hambantota, December 13, 2020 (floodlit). **Galle Gladiators won by two wickets. Colombo Kings 150-9** (20 overs) (D. J. Bell-Drummond 70; P. A. D. L. R. Sandakan 3-32); ‡**Galle Gladiators 151-8** (19.5 overs) (P. B. B. Rajapaksa 33, P. A. D. Lakshan 31*). *PoM:* P. A. D. Lakshan. *Fourth beat first in a game awash with errors. Galle needed 17 from ten balls when Colombo's Qais Ahmad dropped a straightforward catch. He recovered quickly, but fluffed the ensuing run-out chance. With the equation reading 15 from six, Qais dropped another. Dhananjaya Lakshan, twice the beneficiary, slammed 11 off the first four balls, before Lakshan Sandakan hit his first for four. Earlier, Daniel Bell-Drummond had been given at least three lives en route to 70.*

2nd v 3rd   At Hambantota, December 14, 2020 (floodlit). **Jaffna Stallions won by 37 runs. Jaffna Stallions 165-9** (20 overs) (W. I. A. Fernando 39, J. Charles 76); ‡**Dambulla Viiking 128** (19.1 overs) (W. U. Tharanga 33; P. W. H. de Silva 3-15). *PoM:* J. Charles. *Once again, a shelled catch proved costly: Jaffna opener Johnson Charles had not scored when he top-edged to Kasun Rajitha at fine leg. His eventual 76 from 56 proved the mainstay of the innings, which tailed off badly – there were four run-outs in 25 balls – from a promising 108-1 after 12. In the event, they had plenty. Wanindu Hasaranga de Silva bamboozled everyone with googlies, and Dambulla never came close.*

Final   At Hambantota, December 16, 2020 (floodlit). **Jaffna Stallions won by 53 runs.** ‡**Jaffna Stallions 188-6** (20 overs) (Shoaib Malik 46, D. M. de Silva 33, N. L. T. C. Perera 39*; P. A. D. Lakshan 3-36); **Galle Gladiators 135-9** (20 overs) (P. B. B. Rajapaksa 40, Azam Khan 36). *PoM:* Shoaib Malik. *PoT:* P. W. H. de Silva (Jaffna Stallions). *The Stallions galloped to victory. Their top six all reached double figures, with Charles (26 from 15) again starting at a lick. Shoaib Malik and Dhananjaya de Silva then rebuilt from a shaky 70-3, adding 69 in seven overs and setting the stage for Tissara Perera, who clouted 39 off 14. All five bowlers cost at least nine an over. After ten balls, Galle were 7-3, with Dhanushka Gunathilleke, the tournament's leading scorer, run out after a mid-pitch collision with the bowler. Despite feisty innings from the captain, Bhanuka Rajapaksa, and keeper Azam Khan (both faced just 17 balls), Galle never got back in the game.*

THE HERO CARIBBEAN PREMIER LEAGUE IN 2021

Peter Miller

1 St Kitts & Nevis Patriots   2 St Lucia Kings

As the pandemic continued, the Caribbean Premier League was played entirely at Warner Park in St Kitts. Unlike 2020, spectators were allowed – up to half the ground's capacity – though they had to be fully vaccinated. With 33 matches on one square, there were concerns about how the pitches would play as the tournament progressed, but they proved unfounded: the cricket was excellent, and the finale thrilling.

The home team, **St Kitts & Nevis Patriots**, completed their rise from the bottom of the table in 2020 to first-time winners, securing a dramatic victory against St Lucia Kings with a scrabbled single off the last ball of the final. They were marshalled by captain Dwayne Bravo and their Australian coach Simon Helmot, and boosted by the return of Chris Gayle, after an absence of two seasons. But their most impressive player was Evin Lewis, who amassed 426 runs, including a record 38 sixes and his first CPL hundred.

The runners-up remained the same, though St Lucia Zouks had become **St Lucia Kings** after the franchise was bought by the consortium owning the IPL's Punjab Kings. Player of the Tournament Roston Chase outscored even Lewis, with 446, and took ten wickets. Faf du Plessis combined impressive leadership and batting form, including a T20-best 120 not out, but missed the knockouts with a groin injury. Singapore international Tim David was becoming one of the most useful players around, making 282 runs at a strike-rate of 146, while 22-year-old Jeavor Royal claimed 12 wickets with his left-arm spin.

The reigning champions, **Trinbago Knight Riders**, headed the league table again, but lost to St Lucia in the semi-finals. In 2020, they had shone in every department, winning all 12 games, but this time they leaned heavily on the bowlers. They managed only three fifties, of which the captain, Kieron Pollard, scored two. Ravi Rampaul, who returned to the CPL after a three-season hiatus, was the competition's leading wicket-taker, with 19, and spinners Sunil Narine and Akeal Hosein its most economical bowlers.

Guyana Amazon Warriors completed the semi-final line-up, but were knocked out by the Patriots. Their stars were Romario Shepherd and Odean Smith, who earned 18 victims apiece with their pace, and were vital contributors with the bat. Captain Nicholas Pooran finished with 263 runs, and Chandrapaul Hemraj made a hundred that suggested a player coming of age. The usually reliable Shoaib Malik, however, scored just 67 in ten innings.

Jamaica Tallawahs could be brutal – they piled up 255 for five against St Lucia in their opening match – but were inconsistent. They were bowled out four times in ten innings, once for 92 by Trinbago. Andre Russell had made a 14-ball fifty against St Lucia, but never reached those heights again. Opener

Kennar Lewis was a bright spot, and South African pace bowler Migael Pretorius collected 16 wickets at his first CPL, but they rarely clicked as a team.

Barbados Royals (another name-change, after the owners of Rajasthan Royals took a majority stake in the former Tridents) also missed the play-offs, for the second year running since they were champions in 2019. A talented squad fell foul of bad luck and bad form. Close calls went mostly against them – St Kitts & Nevis snatched a win when Sheldon Cottrell hit the last ball for six – and they were looking to rebuild in 2022.

CARIBBEAN PREMIER LEAGUE AVERAGES IN 2021

BATTING (150 runs)

		M	I	NO	R	HS	100	50	Avge	SR	4	6
1	A. D. Russell (*Jamaica T*)	10	10	3	160	50*	0	1	22.85	**175.82**	11	16
2	K. Lewis (*Jamaica T*)	10	10	0	262	89	0	2	26.20	**164.77**	20	20
3	†N. Pooran (*Guyana AW*)..	11	10	2	263	75*	0	1	32.87	**163.35**	12	25
4	*E. Lewis (*St K&N P*)	11	11	2	426	102*	1	3	47.33	**163.21**	25	38
5	K. A. Pollard (*Trinbago KR*)	11	10	3	261	58*	0	2	37.28	**158.18**	15	21
6	T. H. David (*St Lucia K*)	12	11	3	282	56	0	1	35.25	**146.11**	19	19
7	R. L. Chase (*St Lucia K*) .	12	12	3	446	85	0	4	49.55	**144.33**	35	24
8	F. du Plessis (*St Lucia K*) .	9	9	1	277	120*	1	1	34.62	**143.52**	22	12
9	†M. Deyal (*St Lucia K*). . . .	9	8	0	159	78	0	1	19.87	**135.89**	13	9
10	*C. Hemraj (*Guyana AW*) .	11	11	1	254	105*	1	0	25.40	**133.68**	20	16
11	†C. H. Gayle (*St K&N P*) . .	9	9	0	165	42	0	0	18.33	**128.90**	17	10
12	G. D. Phillips (*Barbados R*)	10	10	2	254	80*	0	2	31.75	**128.28**	16	16
13	†S. E. Rutherford (*St K&N P*)	11	10	3	262	58*	0	3	37.42	**127.18**	11	18
14	†Azam Khan (*Barbados R*)	8	8	0	178	50	0	1	22.25	**124.47**	11	12
15	B. A. King (*Guyana AW*) .	11	11	1	189	77	0	1	18.90	**123.52**	18	8
16	†K. R. Mayers (*Barbados R*)	8	8	1	160	81*	0	1	22.85	**123.07**	14	9
17	J. Charles (*Barbados R*) . .	10	10	0	216	40	0	0	21.60	**122.72**	21	12
18	†S. O. Hetmyer (*Guyana AW*)	11	10	1	218	54	0	2	24.22	**121.78**	15	9
19	A. D. S. Fletcher (*St Lucia K*)	12	12	1	229	81*	0	1	20.81	**120.52**	15	13
20	S. S. J. Brooks (*Jamaica T*)	9	8	1	214	47*	0	1	30.57	**118.88**	21	4
21	T. L. Seifert (*Trinbago KR*)	11	10	2	177	40*	0	1	22.12	**112.73**	17	8
22	L. M. P. Simmons (*Trin KR*)	11	11	0	193	70	0	1	17.54	**111.56**	19	8
23	R. Powell (*Jamaica T*) . . .	10	10	0	168	38	0	0	16.80	**106.32**	6	13
24	Mohammad Hafeez (*Guy AW*)	8	7	1	179	70	0	1	29.83	**102.28**	20	3
25	†C. Munro (*Trinbago KR*) .	11	11	2	267	47	0	0	29.66	**101.13**	20	10
26	D. C. Thomas (*St K&N P*)	9	9	1	196	55*	0	1	24.50	**95.60**	24	2

BOWLING (8 wickets)

		Style	Balls	Dots	R	W	BB	4I	Avge	SR	ER
1	S. P. Narine (*Trinbago KR*)	OB	240	143	175	12	2-9	0	14.58	20.00	**4.37**
2	A. J. Hosein (*Trinbago KR*)	SLA	252	143	207	13	2-12	0	15.92	19.38	**4.92**
3	Imad Wasim (*Jamaica T*)	SLA	138	70	137	9	3-15	0	15.22	15.33	**5.95**
4	Mohammad Amir (*Barb R*)	LFM	146	74	149	11	3-21	0	13.54	13.27	**6.12**
5	Imran Tahir (*Guyana AW*)	LB	252	118	269	13	3-34	0	20.69	19.38	**6.40**
6	Fawad Ahmed (*St K&N P*)	LB	204	92	222	11	2-14	0	20.18	18.54	**6.52**
7	G. Motie (*Guyana AW*) . .	SLA	114	52	124	8	3-25	0	15.50	14.25	**6.52**
8	R. L. Chase (*St Lucia K*) .	OB	228	108	263	10	2-33	0	26.30	22.80	**6.92**
9	J. Royal (*St Lucia K*)	SLA	162	87	196	12	3-19	0	16.33	13.50	**7.25**
10	O. F. Smith (*Guyana AW*)	RFM	213	100	268	18	3-20	0	14.88	11.83	**7.54**

		Style	Balls	Dots	R	W	BB	4I	Avge	SR	ER
11	A. S. Joseph (*St Lucia K*)	RFM	214	117	274	9	3-27	0	30.44	23.77	**7.68**
12	R. Shepherd (*Guyana AW*)	RFM	198	100	254	18	3-15	0	14.11	11.00	**7.69**
13	F. A. Allen (*St K&N P*) . .	SLA	204	77	263	9	2-30	0	29.22	22.66	**7.73**
14	P. A. van Meekeren (*St KNP*)	RFM	174	81	230	8	2-23	0	28.75	21.75	**7.93**
15	R. Rampaul (*Trinbago KR*)	RFM	232	107	308	19	4-29	1	16.21	12.21	**7.96**
16	J. L. Jaggesar (*St K&N P*)	OB	138	56	187	9	3-32	0	20.77	15.33	**8.13**
17	K. O. K. Williams (*St L K*)	RFM	143	58	200	11	4-24	1	18.18	13.00	**8.39**
18	Wahab Riaz (*St Lucia K*)	LF	222	99	313	11	2-16	0	28.45	20.18	**8.45**
19	D. C. Drakes (*St K&N P*)	LFM	232	96	331	16	3-26	0	20.68	14.50	**8.56**
20	Naveen-ul-Haq (*Guy AW*)	RFM	181	75	262	8	2-8	0	32.75	22.62	**8.68**
21	N. R. J. Young (*Barb B*) .	RM	94	36	140	8	3-24	0	17.50	11.75	**8.93**
22	D. Wiese (*St Lucia K*) . . .	RFM	96	35	146	11	5-25	2	13.27	8.72	**9.12**
23	Ali Khan (*Trinbago KR*) .	RFM	78	36	121	8	4-6	1	15.12	9.75	**9.30**
24	D. J. Bravo (*St K&N P*) . .	RFM	122	31	193	8	4-26	1	24.12	15.25	**9.49**
25	A. D. Russell (*Jamaica T*)	RFM	187	65	297	11	2-34	0	27.00	17.00	**9.52**
26	M. Pretorius (*Jamaica T*)	RFM	222	86	353	16	4-32	2	22.06	13.87	**9.54**
27	I. Udana (*Trinbago KR*) .	LFM	156	59	252	11	5-21	1	22.90	14.18	**9.69**

CARIBBEAN PREMIER LEAGUE IN 2021

	P	W	L	Pts	NRR
TRINBAGO KNIGHT RIDERS . . .	10	6	4	12	0.70
GUYANA AMAZON WARRIORS .	10	6	4	12	0.10
ST KITTS & NEVIS PATRIOTS .	10	6	4	12	−0.32
ST LUCIA KINGS	10	5	5	10	−0.15
Jamaica Tallawahs	10	4	6	8	0.12
Barbados Royals	10	3	7	6	−0.52

1st v 4th   At Basseterre, St Kitts, September 14, 2021. **St Lucia Kings won by 21 runs. ‡St Lucia Kings 205-4** (20 overs) (M. Deyal 78, R. L. Chase 36, D. Wiese 34*, T. H. David 38*); **Trinbago Knight Riders 184** (19.3 overs) (S. P. Narine 30; D. Wiese 5-39). PoM: D. Wiese. *St Lucia Kings reached their second successive final, after passing 200 against Trinbago, the defending champions. Mark Deyal slammed six sixes in a 44-ball 78 – his maiden T20 half-century – and put on 73 in 40 with acting-captain Andre Fletcher, whose share was three. A late assault from David Wiese and Tim David added 75* off 34. Wiese then ran through the Knight Riders, starting with his 200th T20 wicket and finishing with his second five-for in four days.*

2nd v 3rd   At Basseterre, St Kitts, September 14, 2021. **St Kitts & Nevis Patriots won by seven wickets. ‡Guyana Amazon Warriors 178-9** (20 overs) (S. O. Hetmyer 45*); **‡St Kitts & Nevis Patriots 181-3** (17.5 overs) (C. H. Gayle 42, E. Lewis 77*, D. J. Bravo 34). PoM: E. Lewis. *A dazzling 77* in 39 balls from Evin Lewis rushed the Patriots into the final. Three days earlier, he had smashed 11 sixes in an unbeaten century against Trinbago; this time, he hit eight, and shared stands of 76 in seven overs with Chris Gayle, then 88 in eight with Dwayne Bravo. Bravo's decision to bowl first had paid off when Guyana fell away from 88-2 at the halfway mark: six perished in the next seven overs, though four late sixes from Shimron Hetmyer raised the target to 179.*

Final   At Basseterre, St Kitts, September 15, 2021. **St Kitts & Nevis Patriots won by three wickets. ‡St Lucia Kings 159-7** (20 overs) (R. R. S. Cornwall 43, R. L. Chase 43, K. M. A. Paul 39); **St Kitts & Nevis Patriots 160-7** (20 overs) (J. Da Silva 37, D. C. Drakes 48*). PoM: D. C. Drakes. PoT: R. L. Chase. *St Kitts & Nevis Patriots clinched their first title off the last ball. Needing 21 from two overs, they scored 12 in the 19th, bowled by Wahab Riaz, but lost two wickets. Kesrick Williams then restricted them to four off four deliveries, before Dominic Drakes (48* off 24) drove him to the boundary, then hit the winning single. St Lucia Kings had chosen to bat, but were bogged down by spin: slow left-armer Fabian Allen conceded only 17 in four overs, and Roston Chase's 43 ate up 40 balls. It took Keemo Paul's 39 from 21, including three consecutive sixes off Drakes, to get them to 159. Chase bowled Gayle for a duck, then dived to catch Lewis for six, but the Patriots' middle order fought back to set up victory.*

CPL FINALS

2013   JAMAICA TALLAWAHS beat Guyana Amazon Warriors by seven wickets at Port-of-Spain.
2014   BARBADOS TRIDENTS beat Guyana Amazon Warriors by eight runs (D/L) at Basseterre.
2015   TRINIDAD & TOBAGO RED STEEL beat Barbados Tridents by 20 runs at Port-of-Spain.
2016   JAMAICA TALLAWAHS beat Guyana Amazon Warriors by nine wickets at Basseterre.
2017   TRINBAGO KNIGHT RIDERS beat St Kitts & Nevis Patriots by three wickets at Tarouba.
2018   TRINBAGO KNIGHT RIDERS beat Guyana Amazon Warriors by eight wickets at Tarouba.
2019   BARBADOS TRIDENTS beat Guyana Amazon Warriors by 27 runs at Tarouba.
2020   TRINBAGO KNIGHT RIDERS beat St Lucia Zouks by eight wickets at Tarouba.
2021   ST KITTS & NEVIS PATRIOTS beat St Lucia Kings by three wickets at Basseterre.

CPL RECORDS

Highest score	132*	B. A. King	Guyana AW v Barbados T at Providence	2019
	121*	A. D. Russell	Jamaica T v Trinbago KR at Port-of-Spain	2018
	120*	**F. du Plessis**	**St Lucia K v St Kitts & Nevis P at Basseterre**	**2021**
Fastest 50 – balls	**14**	**A. D. Russell**	**Jamaica T v St Lucia K at Basseterre**	**2021**
Fastest 100 – balls	40	A. D. Russell	Jamaica T v Trinbago KR at Port-of-Spain	2018
Most sixes – innings	13	A. D. Russell	Jamaica T v Trinbago KR at Port-of-Spain	2018
Most runs – season	567	C. Munro (avge 51.54, SR 140.34) for Trinbago KR		2018
Most sixes – season	**38**	**E. Lewis for St Kitts & Nevis P**		**2021**
Most runs – career	2,629	**L. M. P. Simmons (avge 31.67, SR 119.71)**		**2013 to 2021**
	2,519	**C. H. Gayle (avge 36.50, SR 133.13)**		**2013 to 2021**
	2,310	**A. D. S. Fletcher (avge 28.51, SR 118.52)**		**2013 to 2021**
Most 100s – career	4	C. H. Gayle		2013 to 2021
	4	D. R. Smith		2013 to 2019
Best SR – career†	173.37	**A. D. Russell (1,491 runs, avge 31.06)**		**2013 to 2021**
Most sixes – career	172	C. H. Gayle		2013 to 2021
Best bowling	6-6	Shakib Al Hasan	Barbados T v T&T RS at Bridgetown	2013
	5-3	Sohail Tanvir	Guyana AW v Barbados T at Bridgetown	2017
	5-15	Mohammad Nabi	St Lucia Z v St K&N P at Port-of-Spain	2020
Most econ four overs	2-1	Mohammad Irfan	Barbados T v St K&N P at Bridgetown	2018
Most expensive analysis	0-68	J. D. S. Neesham	Trinbago KR v St K&N P at Basseterre	2019
Most wickets – season	28	D. J. Bravo (avge 11.71, ER 7.34) for T&T RS		2015
Most wickets – career	114	**D. J. Bravo (avge 22.11, ER 8.64)**		**2013 to 2021**
	96	R. R. Emrit (avge 22.75, ER 7.64)		2013 to 2020
	90	**S. P. Narine (avge 20.07, ER 5.32)**		**2013 to 2021**
Best ER – career‡	5.32	**S. P. Narine (2,035 balls, avge 20.07)**		**2013 to 2021**
Highest total	267-2	Trinbago KR v Jamaica T at Kingston		2019
	255-5	**Jamaica T v St Lucia K at Basseterre**		**2021**
Lowest total	52	T&T RS v Barbados T at Bridgetown		2013
Highest successful chase	242-6	St Kitts & Nevis P v Jamaica T at Basseterre		2019
Highest match aggregate	493-7	Jamaica T v Trinbago KR at Kingston		2019

† *Career strike-rate: minimum 500 runs.*   ‡ *Career economy-rate: minimum 300 balls.*

T10 LEAGUE IN 2020-21

PAUL RADLEY

1 Northern Warriors   2 Delhi Bulls

The UAE is no stranger to franchise leagues, having hosted the IPL and PSL when they were forced out of their home countries. But it is unclear how much benefit Emirates cricket has derived from these guests. Though the large expatriate workforce from the subcontinent have lapped up the chance to see the stars of India and Pakistan on their doorstep, opportunities for domestic cricketers at those events have been nil. Even the UAE's own T10 competition has felt more like an imported product, with just one place per team reserved for home-based players. And that has felt like a push at times: the token local has often batted down the order and barely bowled.

But the ten-over league's fourth season changed that. UAE players showed they could be trusted, and spurred each other to greater heights. It started in the opening match, when wicketkeeper Abdul Shakoor blazed 73 in 28 balls to lead defending champions **Maratha Arabians** to victory against **Northern Warriors**, the eventual tournament winners. Shakoor, born and raised in Sharjah, had played nine internationals for the UAE, the last in March 2019; at best, he would be their fourth-choice keeper. The captions for the broadcast of the first match listed him as Abdul Shakoor Bangash, who had not played competitive cricket for nearly three years.

Other UAE internationals showed they could excel among more celebrated company too. Chirag Suri made runs for **Bangla Tigers**. Rohan Mustafa, vice-captain of **Team Abu Dhabi** (as deputy to Luke Wright), bowled thrifty off-spin in the powerplay; slow left-armer Sultan Ahmed (**Qalandars**) and seamer Zahoor Khan (**Deccan Gladiators**) were also parsimonious.

But the Warriors' Muhammad Waseem – born in Pakistan, based in the UAE – provided the high-water mark, matching the feat of the competition's most luminous star. Chris Gayle had been paid $95,000 to play for Team Abu Dhabi, but the returns on that investment were modest until he lashed a 12-ball half-century against the Arabians, on his way to 84 not out off 22. That equalled the T10's fastest fifty, by Afghanistan's Mohammad Shahzad in 2018-19. Two hours later, Waseem had a three-way share in the record, storming to an unbeaten 56 in 13 as the Warriors knocked off 98 to beat **Pune Devils** in 4.3 overs.

Waseem, whose tournament fee was $5,000, finished with 212 runs, the fourth-highest total, behind Qalandars' Sohail Akhtar (248), Warriors captain Nicholas Pooran (241), and Evin Lewis of **Delhi Bulls** (216). Pooran and Lewis had strike-rates above 240, but Waseem outshone both in the final: his 27 was the top score, before he was dismissed in sight of victory by his best friend Shiraz Ahmed. The Warriors became the first team to win the T10 twice, after brushing aside the Bulls – first-time finalists, though their captain, Dwayne Bravo, and coach, Andy Flower, had triumphed with the Arabians in 2019-20.

T10 LEAGUE IN 2020-21

	P	W	L	Pts	NRR
DELHI BULLS	6	5	1	10	3.38
NORTHERN WARRIORS	6	5	1	10	2.38
QALANDARS	6	5	1	10	1.53
TEAM ABU DHABI	6	3	3	6	1.14
Bangla Tigers	6	2	4	4	−0.49
Deccan Gladiators...........	6	2	4	4	−0.59
Maratha Arabians	6	1	5	2	−3.65
Pune Devils................	6	1	5	2	−3.83

Play-offs   **1st v 2nd** Delhi Bulls beat Northern Warriors by five wickets; **3rd v 4th** Team Abu Dhabi beat Qalandars by six wickets; **Final eliminator** Northern Warriors beat Team Abu Dhabi by seven wickets; **Third-place play-off** Team Abu Dhabi beat Qalandars by 21 runs.

Final   At Abu Dhabi, February 6, 2021 (floodlit). **Northern Warriors won by eight wickets. Delhi Bulls 81-9** (10 overs) (M. M. Theekshana 3-14); ‡**Northern Warriors 85-2** (8.2 overs). *Warriors captain Nicholas Pooran was lucky to be fit to lift the trophy: in a ferocious over from fellow West Indian Fidel Edwards, he was hit once in the grille and twice on the forearm, then trapped lbw. But his bowlers had already set up victory. Sri Lankan off-spinner Maheesh Theekshana and UAE seamer Junaid Siddique wrecked the Bulls' top order as they subsided to 81-9, the second-lowest first innings in the 2020-21 competition. Muhammad Waseem led the chase with 27, and the Warriors won with ten balls to spare.*

PART SEVEN

Women's Cricket

WOMEN'S CRICKET IN 2021

Thai-breaker

MELINDA FARRELL

The pandemic continued to have a disproportionate effect on international women's cricket, as many governing bodies prioritised the more lucrative men's game, while the need for biosecure bubbles and quarantine made touring difficult. Among the major nations, Sri Lanka fared worst, playing just twice all year – a warm-up and a match against the Netherlands in the World Cup Qualifier in Zimbabwe, before the tournament was curtailed by Covid.

Thailand were even more unlucky, their misfortune exposing a significant flaw in the ICC's plans. The Thais had made enormous strides to qualify for the T20 World Cup in Australia in 2019, where their cheery approach made them the tournament's feel-good story. The positive news continued with one-day series against Zimbabwe and a South Africa Emerging side, in which Thailand won three of their nine matches. At the World Cup Qualifier, they beats hosts Zimbabwe, Bangladesh and the USA, and were leading their group and on track to secure qualification – only for Covid to intervene. The ICC were forced to abandon the event, and decided that the rankings would determine the final qualifiers for the tournament proper, which was due to start in New Zealand in March 2022. Only Full Member nations appear on the official rankings, so there is no other route for countries such as Thailand to qualify, a situation that must be addressed in the next World Cup cycle.

At the other end of the scale, it was encouraging to see three multi-format series played in the space of eight months. Both England and Australia won home series against India, before Australia comfortably won the Ashes early in 2022.

The BBCI's willingness to engage meant the welcome return of India to Test cricket, for their first matches in almost seven years. Both games – against England at Bristol in June, and Australia at Carrara in September – were hard-fought, and a great advertisement for the longer format. When Australia's solitary Test with England (at Canberra in January 2022) was also drawn, in nerve-shredding fashion, many called for women's Tests, traditionally played over four days, to be extended to five. The players's voices were among the loudest and, if the multi-format concept remains popular, pressure will grow to schedule more.

In England, the women's Hundred made its highly anticipated arrival, a year late because of Covid. It proved a great success, building on the higher visibility of women's domestic cricket that started with the Kia Super League T20 competition, and quickly established itself as another attractive option for international players. It was the most upbeat story of the English summer.

Sadly, the BCCI have not shown the same support for the introduction of a women's IPL, an omission that has allowed other domestic tournaments to establish themselves, and nurture both home-grown and international talent. Several Indian players, including Harmanpreet Kaur and Jemimah Rodrigues, stayed in Australia after the internationals, and flourished in the Women's Big Bash League, which continued to attract big viewing figures.

Other organisations are closely watching the success of the various franchise tournaments, both in terms of broadcast audiences and crowd numbers. The new chair of the Pakistan Cricket Board, Ramiz Raja, said he wanted his country to be the first in Asia to form a women's T20 league – a move that would increase the onus on the BCCI to fast-track a women's IPL.

At the end of the year, news emerged of the first privately funded women's tournament, to be held in Dubai over a fortnight in May 2022. The FairBreak Invitational should feature six teams, with major players from Full Member countries alongside others from emerging nations such as Thailand, Vanuatu and Japan. The competition is being organised in conjunction with Cricket Hong Kong and, if it proves commercially viable, will be a significant step in the women's game, giving more opportunities for players from outside the leading nations.

But while there are encouraging prospects for a growing number of tournaments, Australia remain far ahead on the road to full professional status for both international and domestic players, and the results can clearly be seen on the field. During the white-ball tour of New Zealand, Meg Lanning's side set a record for consecutive one-day international wins, surpassing the 21 of their men's side, under Ricky Ponting, early in 2003. The winning streak was extended to 26 before it was broken by India later in the year.

The ECB are optimistic The Hundred will have a similar effect on professional standards to the boost Australia have enjoyed since the inception of the WBBL – but that has already been up and running for six years, so the Australians have a sizeable head start.

But when teams such as Sri Lanka play no international cricket for more than a year, and Thailand's door to a major ICC tournament is slammed shut on a technicality, the biggest danger to the growth of women's cricket remains the fact that only a few national boards have the financial means and the appetite to make the women's game a priority.

MRF TYRES ICC WOMEN'S RANKINGS

In 2015, the ICC introduced a table of women's rankings, which combined results from Tests, one-day internationals and Twenty20 internationals. In 2018, after Twenty20 international status was extended to all Associate women's teams, this was replaced by separate rankings for one-day and Twenty20 cricket.

ONE-DAY INTERNATIONAL TEAM RANKINGS

(As at December 31, 2021)

		Matches	Points	Rating
1	Australia............	17	2,746	162
2	South Africa.........	19	2,307	121
3	England	18	2,148	119
4	India...............	17	1,899	112
5	West Indies	20	1,778	89
6	New Zealand	19	1,668	88
7	Pakistan	20	1,339	67
8	Sri Lanka	5	233	47
9	Zimbabwe	8	0	0

Bangladesh had a rating of 95 and Ireland 48, but neither had played sufficient matches in the qualifying period (since October 2018) for a ranking.

TWENTY20 INTERNATIONAL TEAM RANKINGS

(As at December 31, 2021)

		Matches	Points	Rating
1	Australia............	20	5,824	291
2	England	25	7,157	286
3	India...............	23	6,081	264
4	New Zealand	17	4,487	264
5	South Africa.........	20	5,030	252
6	West Indies	19	4,691	247
7	Pakistan	18	4,027	224
8	Sri Lanka	8	1,600	200
9	Bangladesh..........	11	2,094	190
10	Thailand............	17	2,851	168
11	Zimbabwe	17	2,730	161
12	Ireland	20	3,209	160

Remaining rankings 13 Scotland (152), 14 PNG (130), 15 Nepal (128), 16 UAE (128), 17 Samoa (125), 18 Tanzania (112), 19 Uganda (104), 20 Netherlands (93), 21 Namibia (87), 22 Indonesia (85), 23 Kenya (84), 24 Hong Kong (78), 25 Germany (70), 26 China (67), 27 USA (62), 28 Brazil (58), 29 Vanuatu (54), 30 Japan (52), 31 Rwanda (49), 32 Malaysia (47), 33 Belize (45), 34 Myanmar (42), 35 Jersey (40), 36 Canada (35), 37 Nigeria (30), 38 France (26), 39 Oman (26), 40 Botswana (23), 41 Austria (23), 42 Bhutan (22), 43 Sierra Leone (21), 44 Kuwait (19), 45 South Korea (18), 46 Malawi (18), 47 Mexico (14), 48 Costa Rica (9), 49 Mozambique (3), 50 Qatar (3), 51= Argentina (0), Fiji (0), Mali (0), Norway (0).

> **"** There was no rest for the wicket: next ball, he played down the wrong line, and was bowled, for a gruesome pair."
> India v England, page 328

ICC WOMEN'S PLAYER RANKINGS

In October 2008, the ICC launched a set of rankings for women cricketers, on the same principles as those for men, based on one-day international performances. Twenty20 rankings were added in September 2012. There are no Test rankings.

The leading players in the women's one-day international rankings on December 31, 2021, were:

	Batters	Points			Bowlers	Points
1	L. Lee (SA)	761		1	J. L. Jonassen (A)	760
2	A. J. Healy (A)	750		2	J. N. Goswami (I)	727
3	M. D. Raj (I)	738		3	M. Schutt (A)	717
4	T. T. Beaumont (E)	728		4	M. Kapp (SA)	715
5	A. E. Satterthwaite (NZ)	717		5	S. Ecclestone (E)	701
6	S. S. Mandhana (I)	710		6	S. Ismail (SA)	688
7	M. M. Lanning (A)	699		7	K. H. Brunt (E)	666
8	B. L. Mooney (A)	690		8	A. Khaka (SA)	643
9	S. R. Taylor (WI)	676		9	A. Shrubsole (E)	598
10	H. C. Knight (E)	674		10	K. L. Cross (E)	589

The leading players in the women's Twenty20 international rankings on December 31, 2021, were:

	Batters	Points			Bowlers	Points
1	B. L. Mooney (A)	754		1	S. Ecclestone (E)	771
2	S. Verma (I)	726		2	S. Glenn (E)	744
3	S. S. Mandhana (I)	709		3	S. Ismail (SA)	718
4	M. M. Lanning (A)	698		4	M. Schutt (A)	699
5	S. F. M. Devine (NZ)	692		5	D. B. Sharma (I)	685
6	A. J. Healy (A)	673		6	J. L. Jonassen (A)	684
7	S. W. Bates (NZ)	649		7	K. H. Brunt (E)	681
8	L. Lee (SA)	629		8	Anam Amin (P)	668
9	S. R. Taylor (WI)	618		9	S. G. Molineux (A)	650
10	K. E. Bryce (Scot)	613		10	Diana Baig (P)	641
					G. L. Wareham (A)	641

WOMEN'S ONE-DAY INTERNATIONAL AVERAGES IN CALENDAR YEAR 2021

BATTING (200 runs)

		M	I	NO	R	HS	100	50	Avge	SR	4	6
1	L. Lee (SA)	11	11	4	632	132*	1	5	90.28	79.00	81	5
2	S. R. Taylor (WI)	8	7	3	347	105*	2	0	86.75	77.28	35	2
3	G. H. Lewis (Ire.)	5	5	1	299	96*	0	3	74.75	75.12	33	2
4	P. G. Raut (I)	6	6	2	295	104*	1	2	73.75	68.92	35	0
5	⎰ T. T. Beaumont (E.)	11	11	3	503	102	1	4	62.87	77.02	60	1
	⎱ M. D. Raj (I)	11	10	2	503	79*	0	6	62.87	66.71	48	3
7	†B. L. Mooney (A)	6	5	1	243	125*	1	1	60.75	92.04	23	0
8	†R. L. Haynes (A)	5	5	1	207	93*	0	2	51.75	81.81	20	0
9	Aliya Riaz (P)	11	11	3	382	81	0	2	47.75	70.87	25	9
10	Nida Dar (P)	10	10	2	363	87	0	2	45.37	66.48	28	3
11	M. du Preez (SA)	12	8	1	315	65*	0	3	45.00	70.31	26	2
12	A. J. Healy (A)	6	6	0	267	77	0	2	44.50	94.01	32	4
13	H. C. Knight (E)	11	11	1	423	101	1	2	42.30	80.11	44	1
14	†L. Paul (Ire.)	5	5	0	208	95	0	2	41.60	66.66	19	0
15	†A. E. Satterthwaite (NZ)	11	11	2	366	119*	1	2	40.66	71.06	36	2
16	L. Wolvaardt (SA)	12	12	1	440	80	0	5	40.00	70.62	56	0
17	D. J. S. Dottin (WI)	14	13	1	460	132	1	2	38.33	75.28	55	6
18	N. R. Sciver (E)	10	10	2	291	74*	0	2	36.37	88.71	34	2
19	†S. S. Mandhana (I)	11	11	1	352	86	0	2	35.20	86.69	49	3
20	H. K. Matthews (WI)	14	14	1	380	100*	1	1	29.23	64.40	46	0
21	A. E. Jones (E)	11	9	1	230	60	0	1	28.75	81.27	28	2
22	†B. M. Halliday (NZ)	11	10	0	279	60	0	2	27.90	74.20	28	3
23	Omaima Sohail (P)	12	12	0	330	62	0	2	27.50	66.00	34	0
24	R. S. Williams (WI)	9	9	1	219	78*	0	1	27.37	48.77	16	0
25	L. Winfield-Hill (E)	9	9	0	245	43	0	0	27.22	69.80	29	2
26	†L. Goodall (SA)	13	11	3	212	59*	0	1	26.50	54.35	14	0
27	†Muneeba Ali (P)	12	12	0	301	58	0	1	25.08	60.80	41	0

BOWLING (9 wickets)

		Style	O	M	R	W	BB	4I	Avge	SR	ER
1	Nahida Akter (B)	SLA	35	10	78	13	5-21	1	6.00	16.15	2.22
2	L. M. Kasperek (NZ)	OB	46	2	207	14	6-46	1	14.78	19.71	4.50
3	A. Khaka (SA)	RFM	77.4	12	238	14	4-40	1	17.00	33.28	3.06
4	A. Mohammed (WI)	OB	99.4	3	360	20	4-27	1	18.00	29.90	3.61
5	Anam Amin (P)	SLA	83.4	7	272	15	5-35	1	18.13	33.46	3.25
6	K. L. Cross (E)	RFM	71.3	2	314	17	5-34	1	18.47	25.23	4.39
7	C. E. Dean (E)	OB	41.2	1	192	10	4-36	1	19.20	24.80	4.64
8	S. E. Luus (SA)	LB	43	1	199	9	3-35	0	22.11	28.66	4.62
9	H. K. Matthews (WI)	OB	121	14	404	18	4-26	1	22.44	40.33	3.33
10	J. N. Goswami (I)	RFM	92	6	347	15	4-42	1	23.13	36.80	3.77
11	S. Ismail (SA)	RF	102	5	420	18	3-22	0	23.33	34.00	4.11
12	L. M. Tahuhu (NZ)	RFM	55	1	285	12	5-37	1	23.75	27.50	5.18
13	K. H. Brunt (E)	RFM	62.2	7	239	10	4-22	1	23.90	37.40	3.83
14	Fatima Sana (P)	RFM	88.4	6	498	20	5-39	2	24.90	26.60	5.61
15	S. Ecclestone (E)	SLA	107	10	407	16	3-33	0	25.43	40.12	3.80
16	Nashra Sandhu (P)	SLA	96.4	7	396	15	4-49	1	26.40	38.66	4.09
17	Diana Baig (P)	RFM	90.5	5	375	14	4-30	1	26.78	38.92	4.12
18	N. R. Sciver (E)	RFM	69.4	3	271	10	3-26	0	27.10	41.80	3.88
19	S. C. Selman (WI)	RFM	85.3	6	310	11	2-34	0	28.18	46.63	3.62
20	⎰ M. Kapp (SA)	RFM	89	10	321	11	3-24	0	29.18	48.54	3.60
	⎱ H. M. Rowe (NZ)	RM	61	2	321	11	4-47	1	29.18	33.27	5.26
22	S. F. M. Devine (NZ)	RM	57	2	297	9	2-26	0	33.00	38.00	5.21

WOMEN'S TWENTY20 INTERNATIONAL AVERAGES IN CALENDAR YEAR 2021

BATTING (150 runs, strike-rate 90.00)

		M	I	NO	R	HS	100	50	Avge	SR	4	6
1	L. Wolvaardt (SA)	8	8	5	161	53*	0	1	53.66	**161.00**	14	6
2	A. E. Jones (E)	9	8	2	151	43	0	0	25.16	**142.45**	18	3
3	F. O. Kibasu (Tanzania) . .	7	7	2	280	127*	1	1	56.00	**138.61**	40	0
4	S. Verma (I)	9	9	0	200	60	0	1	22.22	**134.22**	23	12
5	D. N. Wyatt (E)	9	9	1	252	89*	0	1	31.50	**133.33**	32	3
6	†S. S. Mandhana (I)	9	9	1	255	70	0	2	31.87	**131.44**	37	4
7	G. H. Lewis (Ire).	10	10	2	325	105*	1	1	40.62	**128.45**	43	4
8	L. Lee (SA).	8	8	0	232	75	0	2	29.00	**119.58**	35	2
9	N. R. Sciver (E)	9	9	1	153	55	0	1	19.12	**118.60**	18	2
10	†B. L. Mooney (A)	6	5	1	160	61*	0	2	40.00	**115.94**	20	0
11	†A. E. Satterthwaite (NZ) . .	9	8	0	189	49	0	0	23.62	**113.85**	26	1
12	S. A. Wittmann (Namibia)	12	11	2	245	93*	0	2	27.22	**112.90**	26	6
13	T. T. Beaumont (E).	9	9	0	303	97	0	3	33.66	**108.60**	37	2
14	K. Green (Namibia)	12	11	4	184	54*	0	1	26.28	**108.23**	25	2
15	G. Ishimwe (Rwanda). . . .	11	11	2	205	114*	1	0	22.77	**107.32**	23	0
16	T. Brits (SA).	5	5	3	153	66	0	2	76.50	**104.79**	15	1
17	M. T. Hill (Hong Kong) . .	5	5	1	161	55	0	1	40.25	**103.20**	14	0
18	M. I. Pascal (Tanzania). . .	6	6	2	171	54	0	1	42.75	**103.01**	19	0
19	A. Zepeda (Austria)	8	8	1	361	101	1	2	51.57	**102.55**	50	0
20	†T. Satish (UAE)	5	5	1	165	64*	0	1	41.25	**102.48**	13	0
21	†S. G. Mtae (Tanzania). . . .	7	7	0	161	52	0	1	23.00	**101.25**	21	0
22	S. R. Magar (Nepal)	7	7	2	221	82*	0	1	44.20	**98.22**	24	0
23	Q. A. Abel (Kenya)	6	6	2	165	47*	0	0	41.25	**97.05**	17	0
24	L. K. Delany (Ire)	11	10	1	190	61	0	1	21.11	**94.05**	21	1
25	M. Mupachikwa (Z)	8	8	2	227	42	0	0	37.83	**93.03**	27	0
26	R. Stokell (Ire)	11	11	1	195	48	0	0	19.50	**92.41**	23	2
27	Y. Khan (Namibia).	12	12	3	208	78*	0	1	23.11	**90.82**	20	2

BOWLING (11 wickets)

		Style	B	D	R	W	BB	4I	Avge	SR	ER
1	P. Z. Kamunya (Tanzania) .	RM	156	111	68	12	3-6	0	5.66	13.00	**2.61**
2	L. Cardoso (Brazil)	RFM	85	43	50	11	3-8	0	4.54	7.72	**3.52**
3	V. H. Hamunyela (Namibia).	OB	240	156	142	18	4-8	2	7.88	13.33	**3.55**
4	W. N. Mwatile (Namibia) .	RM	252	175	152	15	5-6	1	10.13	16.80	**3.61**
5	K. Green (Namibia).	RM	227	149	139	13	2-2	0	10.69	17.46	**3.67**
6	S. B. Wetoto (Kenya)	OB	130	76	82	17	6-16	2	4.82	7.64	**3.78**
7	S. F. Jerome (Tanzania) . .	RFM	153	89	97	14	3-7	0	6.92	10.92	**3.80**
8	E. Mbofana (Z)	RM	114	78	73	13	6-11	1	5.61	8.76	**3.84**
9	S. N. Shihepo (Namibia). .	RM	150	104	97	11	2-4	0	8.81	13.63	**3.88**
10	H. T. Ishimwe (Rwanda). .	RM	204	116	144	15	3-2	0	9.60	13.60	**4.23**
11	M. Vumiliya (Rwanda) . . .	LB	186	111	141	13	4-0	1	10.84	14.30	**4.54**
12	F. C. J. Overdijk (Neth). . .	RM	117	69	91	11	7-3	1	8.27	10.63	**4.66**
	L. Paul (Ire).	LM	180	92	140	12	4-16	1	11.66	15.00	**4.66**
14	L. N. M. Phiri (Z)	OB	147	89	115	16	5-6	2	7.18	9.18	**4.69**
15	L. Tshuma (Z)	RM	150	85	120	14	4-11	1	8.57	10.71	**4.80**
16	J. Efosa (Nigeria)	RM	187	100	176	11	2-15	0	16.00	17.00	**5.64**
17	S. Ecclestone (E).	SLA	197	98	189	11	3-35	0	17.18	17.90	**5.75**
18	S. Ismail (SA)	RF	132	64	143	11	5-12	1	13.00	12.00	**6.50**
19	S. Glenn (E).	LB	166	65	186	11	2-11	0	16.90	15.09	**6.72**

Details of dots are incomplete for Cardoso.

WOMEN'S INTERNATIONAL SERIES IN 2021

SOUTH AFRICA v PAKISTAN IN 2020-21

One-day internationals (3): South Africa 3, Pakistan 0
Twenty20 internationals (3): South Africa 2, Pakistan 1

When South Africa and Pakistan met in January 2021, neither had played since the Twenty20 World Cup, almost a year earlier. They returned in very different circumstances, with all six internationals staged behind closed doors at Kingsmead because of the Covid-19 crisis. Both teams had stand-in captains: Sune Luus stepped up to lead the home side, as Dane van Niekerk had a bad back, while Javeria Khan resumed the role for Pakistan after Bismah Maroof withdrew for family reasons.

South Africa won all but one of the matches, though the contests were often close, especially the opening game, which went to the final ball. Four players passed 100 runs in the one-day series – Aliya Riaz and Nida Dar for Pakistan, Laura Wolvaardt and Marizanne Kapp for South Africa – while Tazmin Brits scored 118 for once out in her two T20 innings. The pacy Shabnim Ismail took seven wickets in each series, and Kapp also bowled some key spells; Diana Baig took nine ODI wickets for Pakistan, though none in the T20s.

First one-day international   At Durban, January 20, 2021. **South Africa won by three runs. South Africa 200-9** (50 overs) (L. Wolvaardt 40, M. Kapp 47; Diana Baig 3-46); ‡**Pakistan 197-8** (50 overs) (Omaima Sohail 37, Nida Dar 59*; S. Ismail 3-42). *PoM:* S. Ismail. *ODI debut:* N. Mlaba (South Africa). *It looked like a straightforward home win when Pakistan were 78-5 in the 28th over, before Nida Dar and Aliya Riaz put on 51. Then, after Shabnim Ismail hit the stumps with successive deliveries, Diana Baig joined Dar to make a career-best 35* in a stand of 60* (a ninth-wicket record for Pakistan), aided by sloppy fielding. They needed 13 off the final over, and four off the last ball, but Nadine de Klerk held her nerve. Earlier, seamer Baig and off-spinner Dar (2-35) had helped restrict South Africa to four an over; they might not have reached 200 without Ismail's late run-a-ball 20.*

Second one-day international   At Durban, January 23, 2021. **South Africa won by 13 runs. South Africa 252-7** (50 overs) (L. Lee 47, S. E. Luus 32, M. Kapp 68*); ‡**Pakistan 239-8** (50 overs) (Omaima Sohail 41, Nida Dar 51, Aliya Riaz 81; M. Kapp 3-44, A. Khaka 4-40). *PoM:* M. Kapp. *This was proclaimed the Black ODI: the South Africans wore black, symbolising the fight against gender-based violence. The game produced another tight finish. Pakistan were 222-6 after 47 overs, whereas South Africa had been 207-6. But while Marizanne Kapp (68* in 45 balls) had led an assault which plundered 45 off their last three, Pakistan's chase petered out when Riaz fell for a career-best 81 – the tour's highest score. Kapp followed her half-century by removing the openers in her first two overs. She and Ayabonga Khaka, who took four for the first time, reduced Pakistan to 73-5, before Dar and Riaz added 111 (a record for Pakistan's sixth wicket) to revive chances of victory.*

Third one-day international   At Durban, January 26, 2021. **South Africa won by 32 runs. South Africa 201** (50 overs) (L. Lee 49, L. Wolvaardt 58, T. Chetty 34; Diana Baig 4-30); ‡**Pakistan 169** (48 overs) (Javeria Khan 33; S. Ismail 3-22, A. Khaka 3-29, S. E. Luus 3-35). *PoM:* S. Ismail. *PoS:* S. Ismail. *ODI debut:* T. Brits (South Africa). *Pakistan put South Africa in again, but it did not prove third time lucky. Lizelle Lee and Laura Wolvaardt opened confidently, and the hosts were 124-1 before two strikes from Baig in the 28th over triggered a collapse of four for eight. Trisha Chetty propelled them towards 200, before becoming the final victim in Baig's career-best 4-30. Pakistan must have fancied the target, but once more slipped to 73-5 – this time against Ismail and Sune Luus, who collected her 100th ODI wicket when she held a return catch off her opposite number, Javeria Khan. Khaka completed the whitewash with two overs to spare.*

First Twenty20 international   At Durban, January 29, 2021. **South Africa won by eight wickets.**
‡Pakistan 124-8 (20 overs) (Ayesha Naseem 31; M. Kapp 3-24); **South Africa 125-2** (19 overs)
(T. Brits 52*). *PoM:* T. Brits. *Riaz, leading Pakistan for the first time as Javeria had injured her
finger, chose to bat – but the top order still struggled, losing their fifth wicket in the seventies for the
fourth successive match. Ismail became the fourth woman to take 100 T20I wickets (among men,
only Lasith Malinga had done it). The tourists' recovery came from Ayesha Naseem and Dar, aged
16 and 34 respectively. South African opener Tazmin Brits guided her side to victory with an
unbeaten half-century; Kapp followed up three wickets by helping her add 69 in ten overs.*

Second Twenty20 international   At Durban, January 31, 2021. **South Africa won by 18 runs.**
South Africa 133-5 (20 overs) (T. Brits 66); ‡Pakistan 115-7 (20 overs) (Aliya Riaz 39, Ayesha
Naseem 33; S. Ismail 5-12). *PoM:* S. Ismail. *Ismail secured the series with her best return in all T20
cricket: she ended the powerplay with 18–11–9–3, and Pakistan in ruins at 20-4, before returning in
the game's final over to add Naseem and Riaz, who had put on 65, a sixth-wicket record for their
side. Brits had been in for all but five balls of South Africa's innings, reaching another fifty, though
none of her colleagues passed 15.*

Third Twenty20 international   At Durban, February 3, 2021. **Pakistan won by eight runs** (DLS).
Pakistan 127-6 (20 overs) (Javeria Khan 56*; N. P. Shangase 3-20); ‡South Africa 68-4 (12.3 overs).
PoM: Javeria Khan. *PoS:* T. Brits. *Javeria returned to lead Pakistan to their only victory of the tour
– despite Luus finally winning the toss. It owed much to Javeria's 56* in 50 balls, and her sixth-
wicket stand of 61 with Kainat Imtiaz in the last seven overs of their innings. South Africa limped to
45-4 as slow left-armer Anam Amin collected two wickets, including Kapp for a single, and were
behind on DLS when rain ended play.*

ZIMBABWE v PAKISTAN IN 2020-21

At the end of their tour of South Africa, Pakistan moved on to Zimbabwe, but
their three Twenty20 internationals had to be called off. They played the first
of three 50-over games on February 9, and won by 178 runs; these were not
official internationals, as the ICC did not restore ODI status for Zimbabwe
until April. Then Emirates Airlines announced that, because of the developing
Covid-19 situation, its flights to and from Zimbabwe (and South Africa, ruling
out the possibility of diverting the journey) would be suspended from February
13. The two boards agreed that the Pakistan squad should return home at once,
and they left Zimbabwe on February 12, the date scheduled for the second
one-day match. The remaining fixtures, including three official T20 internationals, were cancelled, though both sides said they hoped to reschedule. It was
another blow for Zimbabwe: financial issues and coronavirus meant the
women's team had not played an official international since May 2019.

NEW ZEALAND v ENGLAND IN 2020-21

One-day internationals (3): New Zealand 1, England 2
Twenty20 internationals (3): New Zealand 0, England 3

Concerns over the new UK variant of Covid-19 meant England's touring party
had to quarantine for ten days on arrival in New Zealand ahead of their first
ODI series since the end of 2019. The wait was worth it. With a year to go
before New Zealand hosted the postponed 50-over World Cup – whose final
should have taken place on the last day of this tour – England secured four
victories in both formats. Tammy Beaumont shone, scoring four half-centuries in her
six innings and 231 runs for once out in the ODIs, taking her top of the
rankings for the first time. Captain Heather Knight also flourished, before

hamstring trouble ruled her out of the final T20. Nat Sciver, vice-captain on the trip because Anya Shrubsole was at home nursing a knee injury, stepped in, completing a memorable tour: in the ODIs, she had averaged 48 with the bat, and 16 with the ball. For New Zealand, it was a sobering fortnight, though Amy Satterthwaite made a century in the third 50-over match – the only game the hosts won. The three T20 games formed double-headers with the men's T20 series between New Zealand and Australia, with all played in Wellington; originally, the second game had been scheduled for Auckland, and the third for Tauranga, but both were moved because of the Covid situation.

ENGLAND TOURING PARTY

*H. C. Knight, T. T. Beaumont, K. H. Brunt, K. L. Cross, F. R. Davies, S. I. R. Dunkley, S. Ecclestone, G. A. Elwiss, N. E. Farrant, S. Glenn, A. E. Jones, N. R. Sciver, M. K. Villiers, F. C. Wilson, L. Winfield-Hill, D. N. Wyatt. *Coach:* L. M. Keightley.
    I. E. C. M. Wong travelled with the party as a reserve.

First one-day international   At Christchurch, February 23, 2021 (day/night). **England won by eight wickets.** ‡**New Zealand 178** (45.1 overs) (H. N. K. Jensen 53, B. M. Halliday 50); **England 181-2** (33.4 overs) (T. T. Beaumont 71, H. C. Knight 67*). *PoM:* H. C. Knight. *ODI debuts:* B. M. Halliday, F. C. Jonas (New Zealand). *England's first ODI since December 2019 ended in a simple win, after Tammy Beaumont (71 off 86 balls) and captain Heather Knight (67* off 69) put on 94 for the second wicket. It was New Zealand's tenth ODI defeat in a row, a national record. Seven different bowlers took a wicket as they were dismissed for 178, despite maiden fifties for Hayley Jensen and debutant Brooke Halliday. But the best figures (2-31) were claimed by left-arm seamer Tash Farrant, in her second ODI, more than seven years after her first. Sophie Ecclestone's 2-36 included her 100th international wicket.*

Second one-day international   At Dunedin (University), February 26, 2021. **England won by seven wickets.** ‡**New Zealand 192** (49.5 overs) (B. M. Halliday 60; N. R. Sciver 3-26); **England 194-3** (37.4 overs) (T. T. Beaumont 72*, N. R. Sciver 63, A. E. Jones 46*). *PoM:* N. R. Sciver. *Another seventy from Beaumont ushered England to a series victory with more than 12 overs to spare. Set 193, they lost two early wickets, before she put on 103 with Nat Sciver (63 off 61), then 79* with Amy Jones (46* off 45). Earlier, Sciver had taken the new ball for the first time in an ODI since April 2018, and with fiancée Katherine Brunt reduced New Zealand to 27-4. That was soon 76-6, before Halliday and the lower order gave their bowlers something to defend. It was still nowhere near enough.*

Third one-day international   At Dunedin (University), February 28, 2021. **New Zealand won by seven wickets.** ‡**England 220** (47.5 overs) (T. T. Beaumont 88*, H. C. Knight 60; A. C. Kerr 4-42); **New Zealand 223-3** (46.4 overs) (A. E. Satterthwaite 119*, A. C. Kerr 72*). *PoM:* A. E. Satterthwaite. *New Zealand ended a losing streak of 11 thanks to a stand of 172* between Amy Satterthwaite, who made her seventh ODI hundred, and Amelia Kerr, who had already struck four times with her leg-breaks. It was the hosts' highest stand for the fourth wicket. At 51-3, they appeared to be heading for a whitewash, but Satterthwaite became the third New Zealander to pass 4,000 ODI runs, then inched ahead of Debbie Hockley's 4,066; only Suzie Bates (4,548) had more. The tourists had been on course for a big total at 140-2 in the 29th, after Beaumont and Knight added 109, as wickets fell regularly. Beaumont became the first woman to carry her bat for England in an ODI. No one else passed 15, and Kerr picked up the last three for one run in seven balls. The game was played behind closed doors after New Zealand was placed in a temporary Covid-19 lockdown.*

CARRYING BAT THROUGH WOMEN'S ODI INNINGS

		Total		
D. L. Thomas	70*	113	International XI v India at Napier	1981-82
D. A. Hockley	78*	158	New Zealand v Australia at Auckland	1996-97
P. Rau	67*	117	India v New Zealand at Lincoln	2000-01
C. N. I. M. Joyce	43*	107	Ireland v South Africa at Stellenbosch	2007-08
T. T. Beaumont	**88***	**220**	**England v New Zealand at Dunedin**	**2020-21**

First Twenty20 international At Wellington (Sky Stadium), March 3, 2021. **England won by seven wickets. New Zealand 96** (19.4 overs) (K. J. Martin 36); ‡**England 99-3** (16 overs) (D. N. Wyatt 33). *PoM:* S. Glenn. *T20I debut:* B. M. Halliday (New Zealand). *England breezed to victory, with Sciver to the fore. After removing Sophie Devine and Satterthwaite, New Zealand's two most dangerous batters, in her first two overs, she supervised the closing stages of a small run-chase with 26*. From 59-0 in the ninth, England had lost three for eight, including Knight, run out for a duck – but eased home with four overs to spare. Earlier, spinners Ecclestone and Sarah Glenn took 4-29 between them as New Zealand slumped to 96.*

Second Twenty20 international At Wellington (Sky Stadium), March 5, 2021. **England won by six wickets. New Zealand 123-9** (20 overs) (A. E. Satterthwaite 49; F. R. Davies 4-23); ‡**England 124-4** (17.2 overs) (T. T. Beaumont 63, H. C. Knight 39). *PoM:* F. R. Davies. *Beaumont scored her fourth half-century of the tour as England added the T20 series to their one-day victory. New Zealand had reached a promising 84-2 in the 12th, but fell away: the last 51 balls of their innings yielded 39 for seven. Kerr and Martin were stumped by Jones in the same over from Glenn, while seamer Freya Davies took 4-23, her best figures in international cricket.*

Third Twenty20 international At Wellington (Sky Stadium), March 7, 2021 (floodlit). **England won by 32 runs. England 128-9** (20 overs) (F. C. Wilson 31*; S. F. M. Devine 3-30); ‡**New Zealand 96** (18 overs) (M. K. Villiers 3-10). *PoM:* K. H. Brunt. *PoS:* T. T. Beaumont. *Brunt trapped both New Zealand openers for ducks in the first over of the chase as England easily defended a modest total, winning their 11th successive T20 match since defeat by South Africa in the World Cup in February 2020. Mady Villiers contributed a career-best 3-10 with her off-breaks, while Ecclestone (2-19) was as thrifty as usual. For the second time in five days, the home side were all out for 96. England had themselves slipped from 70-3 in the 12th, and were grateful for Fran Wilson's combative 31*. They were led for the first time by Sciver, after Knight injured a hamstring. It was England's 16th win in 17 completed T20 games against New Zealand going back to 2011.*

INDIA v SOUTH AFRICA IN 2020-21

One-day internationals (5): India 1, South Africa 4
Twenty20 internationals (3): India 1, South Africa 2

South Africa dominated their two white-ball series, with eight games squeezed into 17 days at Lucknow's Ekana Stadium. Two players stood out. Opener Lizelle Lee slammed 288 runs at 144 in the one-day games, then added a match-winning 70 in the second T20. And opening bowler Shabnim Ismail followed seven ODI wickets with four in the T20s. If a 4–1 win in the one-dayers was decisive, then victory in the 20-over matches – after a pair of 3–1 defeats by India in 2017-18 and 2019-20 – was almost as sweet for the South Africans. Their six wins all came batting second. For India, playing their first cricket since the final of the T20 World Cup, 364 days earlier, Punam Raut (263 runs at 87) and Mithali Raj (210 at 70, including her 10,000th international run) shone in the 50-over games, while slow left-armer Rajeshwari Gayakwad was unhittable in both formats. In the ODIs, she went at just 3.56 an over; in the T20s, at 4.75.

First one-day international At Lucknow, March 7, 2021. **South Africa won by eight wickets. India 177-9** (50 overs) (M. D. Raj 50, H. Kaur 40; S. Ismail 3-28); ‡**South Africa 178-2** (40.1 overs) (L. Lee 83*, L. Wolvaardt 80). *PoM:* S. Ismail. *ODI debut:* M. C. Patel (India). *South Africa's seventh win in a row equalled their ODI best, and was built on a partnership of 169 between Lizelle Lee and Laura Wolvaardt – the highest for the first wicket by any team against India, and an all-wicket record against them by South Africa. The hosts' batting had been rusty in their first ODI since November 2019. Mithali Raj helped them to 154-4 in the 38th, but her dismissal for 50 – one of three cheap wickets for Shabnim Ismail – slowed them down: the last 74 balls of the innings yielded five for 23. South Africa made light work of the chase.*

Second one-day international   At Lucknow, March 9, 2021. **India won by nine wickets. South Africa 157** (41 overs) (S. E. Luus 36, L. Goodall 49; J. N. Goswami 4-42, R. S. Gayakwad 3-37); ‡**India 160-1** (28.4 overs) (S. S. Mandhana 80*, P. G. Raut 62*). PoM: J. N. Goswami. *India turned the tables in style, coasting to victory with more than 21 overs in hand. Set a modest 158, they lost Jemimah Rodrigues early, before Smriti Mandhana (80* off 64, with ten fours and three sixes) and Punam Raut put on 138*, India's highest stand for any wicket against South Africa. The tourists had reached 80-2 in the 21st, but folded for 157, with four wickets for seamer Jhulan Goswami and three for slow left-armer Rajeshwari Gayakwad.*

Third one-day international   At Lucknow, March 12, 2021. **South Africa won by six runs** (DLS). **India 248-5** (50 overs) (P. G. Raut 77, M. D. Raj 36, H. Kaur 36, D. B. Sharma 36*); ‡**South Africa 223-4** (46.3 overs) (L. Lee 132*, M. du Preez 37). PoM: L. Lee. *A tour de force from Lee re-established South Africa's lead, in a game shortened by rain. Her career-best 132* from 131 balls – the first century by a South African against India – ensured they stayed ahead of the rate, despite the loss of Mignon du Preez and Marizanne Kapp in successive overs to make it 178-6. Earlier, Raj became the second player, after England's Charlotte Edwards, to bring up 10,000 international runs, and fell next ball. Raut top-scored with 77 in a solid total.*

Fourth one-day international   At Lucknow, March 14, 2021. **South Africa won by seven wickets. India 266-4** (50 overs) (P. S. Punia 32, P. G. Raut 104*, M. D. Raj 45, H. Kaur 54); ‡**South Africa 269-3** (48.4 overs) (L. Lee 69, L. Wolvaardt 53, L. Goodall 59*, M. du Preez 61). PoM: M. du Preez. *ODI debut: R. P. Yadav (India). South Africa claimed the series thanks to half-centuries from each of their top four. Chasing 267, Lee and Wolvaardt began with 116 in 23 overs, before Lara Goodall and du Preez hammered 103 for the third wicket inside 16. It was their highest successful chase, beating 265-5 against England at Centurion in 2015-16 – though they were helped by the absence from India's attack of Goswami, who had a hand injury, and Shikha Pandey, controversially rested from the series. Raut's century had been the centrepiece of India's total, which was boosted by Harmanpreet Kaur's 35-ball 54, her first ODI half-century since February 2018. Raj ticked off another milestone: the first woman to pass 7,000 ODI runs. Lee, meanwhile, rose seven places in the rankings, briefly claiming top spot from England's Tammy Beaumont.*

Fifth one-day international   At Lucknow, March 17, 2021. **South Africa won by five wickets. India 188** (49.3 overs) (H. Kaur 30*, M. D. Raj 79*; N. de Klerk 3-35); ‡**South Africa 189-5** (48.2 overs) (M. du Preez 57, A. E. Bosch 58, M. Kapp 36*; R. S. Gayakwad 3-13). PoM: A. E. Bosch. PoS: L. Lee. *ODI debut: C. Prathyusha (India). For the fifth game in a row, victory went to the chasing team, as South Africa completed a 4–1 win following careful fifties from du Preez and Anneke Bosch, her first in internationals. Chasing 189, they had been 27-3, and there was still work to do at 131-5. A punchy 36* from Kapp (who had earlier taken 1-25 from ten overs) sealed the win, despite the miserly Gayakwad (10–4–13–3). India had reached 124-3 before Harmanpreet retired with a hip injury; soon, they were all out for 188, leaving Raj stranded.*

First Twenty20 international   At Lucknow, March 20, 2021 (floodlit). **South Africa won by eight wickets. India 130-6** (20 overs) (H. Deol 52, J. I. Rodrigues 30; S. Ismail 3-14); ‡**South Africa 133-2** (19.1 overs) (A. E. Bosch 66*, S. E. Luus 43). PoM: A. E. Bosch. T20I debut: S. Dil Bahadur (India). *Three days after her maiden ODI fifty, Bosch managed her first in T20Is, as she and captain Sune Luus helped South Africa knock off a slim target. Earlier, Bosch had struck twice in an over as India lost four for 14 in their last three, and had to settle for 130-6, despite Harleen Deol's first international half-century. Ismail typified a strong South African performance in the field with figures of 24–16–14–3; India, by contrast, were sloppy.*

Second Twenty20 international   At Lucknow, March 21, 2021 (floodlit). **South Africa won by six wickets. India 158-4** (20 overs) (S. Verma 47, H. Deol 31, R. M. Ghosh 44*); ‡**South Africa 159-4** (20 overs) (L. Lee 70, L. Wolvaardt 53*). PoM: L. Wolvaardt. *Lee, the star of the ODIs, bludgeoned South Africa towards another series win with 70 in 45 balls, before Wolvaardt supplied the finishing touches with 53* off 39 – her fifth not-out in six T20 innings since dropping into the middle order. With six wickets left to chase 159, South Africa were grateful for a high no-ball from Arundhati Reddy, which Wolvaardt pulled for two. She added two from the free hit, then the winning single off the last delivery. Once more, India rued shoddy fielding, with Richa Ghosh putting down Lee on 30 and 60. Ghosh had cracked 44* off 26, to build on the work of her fellow 17-year-old Shafali Verma (47 off 31). But India's 158-4 wasn't quite enough.*

Third Twenty20 international   At Lucknow, March 23, 2021 (floodlit). **India won by nine wickets. South Africa 112-7** (20 overs) (R. S. Gayakwad 3-9); ‡**India 114-1** (11 overs) (S. Verma 60, S. S. Mandhana 48*). PoM: R. S. Gayakwad. PoS: S. Verma. T20I debut: A. Soni (India). *India* rattled to a consolation win with nine overs to spare, thanks to an opening stand of 96 in 8.3 between Verma, newly crowned the world's top-ranked T20 batter (for the second time), and Mandhana, captain in this series because of Harmanpreet's injury. Verma's 60 included 58 in boundaries (seven fours and five sixes). South Africa's innings had never got going: Luus top-scored with 28, and Gayakwad managed 3-9 in her four overs.

NEW ZEALAND v AUSTRALIA IN 2020-21

Twenty20 internationals (3): New Zealand 1, Australia 1
One-day internationals (3): New Zealand 0, Australia 3

Meg Lanning and her side had expected to visit New Zealand in early 2021 for the World Cup. They had probably pencilled in March 7 as the date they would lift the trophy, 364 days after winning the T20 version. But with the tournament postponed a year because of Covid-19, they settled for a world record, extending their run of one-day victories to 24 as they surged past the men's best, 21 by Ricky Ponting's Australians in 2003. The men achieved their feat in 134 days, while the women's stretched across three years. Four of their players – Ashleigh Gardner, Rachael Haynes, Alyssa Healy and Beth Mooney – had appeared in all 24, while five others appeared in at least 21 (none of the men managed more than 20). Healy scored 155 ODI runs at 51, while the Player of the Series was seamer Megan Schutt, who took seven wickets at 13. For New Zealand, off-spinner Leigh Kasperek collected nine for 70 in two matches, but none of her team-mates took more than two wickets. Amy Satterthwaite resumed the captaincy when Sophie Devine dropped out after one T20 game suffering from fatigue. The only blip in Australia's triumphal progress had come in the T20 matches, played as double-headers with the men's series against Bangladesh. New Zealand won the second, and the third was washed out, making this the first time since the 2017-18 Ashes that Australia had not won a series or tournament.

First Twenty20 international   At Hamilton, March 28, 2021 (floodlit). **Australia won by six wickets. New Zealand 130-6** (20 overs) (A. E. Satterthwaite 40; J. L. Jonassen 3-26); ‡**Australia 133-4** (18 overs) (A. K. Gardner 73*). *PoM:* A. K. Gardner. *Ellyse Perry returned for her first international since tearing her hamstring in the T20 World Cup, more than a year before; she did not bowl, but completed victory by striking Frankie Mackay for two fours. Mackay and Jess Kerr had rattled Australia early on – 14-3 in the fourth, with Beth Mooney out first ball – but Ash Gardner steered them towards victory with 73* in 48. Only Amy Satterthwaite had passed 20 for New Zealand, whose innings declined from 93-2 when she was caught by Perry.*

Second Twenty20 international   At Napier, March 30, 2021. **New Zealand won by four wickets. Australia 129-4** (20 overs) (B. L. Mooney 61*); ‡**New Zealand 131-6** (20 overs) (F. L. Mackay 46, A. C. Kerr 36). *PoM:* F. L. Mackay. *T20I debut: D. R. Brown (Australia). New Zealand captain Sophie Devine was rested because of exhaustion, but Mackay stepped up to open, despite a calf injury. She followed 2-20 with 46 in 39 balls, before becoming 18-year-old seamer Darcie Brown's first international victim. Amelia Kerr took New Zealand into three figures, but when she was bowled by Megan Schutt they needed 29 off 18. They scraped over the line when – with three required – Maddy Green bottom-edged the final ball for four. Australia had never found their fluency, though Mooney batted through the innings for 61*.*

Third Twenty20 international   At Auckland, April 1, 2021. **No result. Australia 14-1** (2.5 overs) v ‡**New Zealand.** *PoS:* J. M. Kerr. *Rain cut the match to 13 overs a side, then caused a washout after 17 deliveries, so the series was tied 1–1. It was the first time since November 2017 that Australia had failed to win a series. Though Perry never took the field, this was her 123rd T20I, beating New Zealander Suzie Bates's record.*

First one-day international   At Mount Maunganui, April 4, 2021. **Australia won by six wickets. New Zealand 212** (48.5 overs) (L. R. Down 90, A. E. Satterthwaite 32, A. C. Kerr 33; M. Schutt 4-32, N. J. Carey 3-34); ‡**Australia 215-4** (38.3 overs) (A. J. Healy 65, E. A. Perry 56*, A. K. Gardner 53*). *PoM*: M. Schutt. *Australia clocked up their 22nd successive ODI victory, beating the record of 21 they had shared with the Australian men's team of 2003. It was also Meg Lanning's 50th win in 58 ODIs as captain. With Devine absent and Mackay injured, Lauren Down opened – and sailed past 15, her previous best for New Zealand, to make 90. But once Amelia Kerr was given out, a doubtful stumping off Schutt, Down was one of eight wickets to tumble for 53. Alyssa Healy had scored only 14 in the T20Is, but bounced back with 65 in 68 balls. Perry reached 50 for the 30th time in ODIs, adding 78 with Healy and 79* with Gardner, as they coasted to the record.*

Second one-day international   At Mount Maunganui, April 7, 2021 (day/night). **Australia won by 71 runs. Australia 271-7** (50 overs) (R. L. Haynes 87, A. J. Healy 44, M. M. Lanning 49; L. M. Kasperek 6-46); ‡**New Zealand 200** (45 overs) (A. C. Kerr 47, B. M. Halliday 32; J. L. Jonassen 3-29). *PoM*: R. L. Haynes. *Australia retained the Rose Bowl, securing their 18th consecutive bilateral ODI series victory since 2014 – despite a remarkable performance from off-spinner Leigh Kasperek, the first woman to take six Australian wickets in an ODI. She put a brake on the later stages after Rachael Haynes had shared stands of 82 with Healy and 98 with Lanning. Down followed her 90 three days earlier with a duck; she and Satterthwaite were dismissed in the first nine balls of New Zealand's chase. Amelia Kerr fought back, but once again the lower order collapsed: the last five went for 26. Slow left-armer Jess Jonassen picked up three wickets and a run-out.*

Third one-day international   At Mount Maunganui, April 10, 2021 (day/night). **Australia won by 21 runs. Australia 149-7** (25 overs) (A. J. Healy 46; L. M. Kasperek 3-24); ‡**New Zealand 128-9** (25 overs). *PoM*: M. Schutt. *ODI debut*: D. R. Brown (Australia). *Not even the weather could prevent Australia extending their record run to 24 ODI wins, nine against New Zealand, including the last six. This also equalled their own record for successive unbeaten ODIs – they had won 23 and tied one between January 1978 and February 1985. Rain shortened the match to 25 overs a side, before Healy and Mooney (promoted to open) put on 73 in ten overs. Then Kasperek caught Mooney off Lea Tahuhu, and in the next over removed Healy, Gardner and Haynes – a triple-wicket maiden. Australia still managed to set a target of 150, and the New Zealanders struggled against the spinners; their highest score, 21*, came from Tahuhu at No. 9.*

ENGLAND v INDIA IN 2021

Kalika Mehta

Test match (1): England 0, India 0
One-day internationals (3): England 2, India 1
Twenty20 internationals (3): England 2, India 1
Overall points: England 10, India 6

It was a joyous occasion when England and India walked out for the opening match of the summer to cheers around the Bristol County Ground, after Covid-19 had forced England to play their home games behind closed doors in 2020. In further cause for celebration, they were wearing whites, a rare sight in modern women's cricket, though there was a distinct difference between the home side's cream kit and the visitors' brilliant white.

India had not worn theirs for nearly seven years – their previous Test was against South Africa in November 2014 – whereas the multi-format Ashes had given England a Test every two years. This was the first series (apart from the Ashes) to adopt the multi-format framework, with four points available for the Test, and two for each of the six white-ball games. England claimed overall victory, but not until the last: had India won the third Twenty20, at Chelmsford, the series would have been drawn.

Young driver: Shafali Verma is given licence to attack at Bristol.

In the Test, India fielded five debutants to England's one, and of their other six only captain Mithali Raj and seamer Jhulan Goswami had played more than two Tests. But Raj and Goswami, ever-present in India's ten previous Tests in the 21st century, were outshone by two of the newcomers, whose vim and vigour secured an unexpected draw. There had been questions over whether 17-year-old batting sensation Shafali Verma – the youngest Indian woman to make her Test debut since Rajani Venugopal, then 15, in 1984-85 – could translate her white-ball skills into the four-day game. Meanwhile, Sneh Rana was being given a second chance, more than five years after her last international. Verma played two dazzling innings, while Rana followed up four wickets by batting more than three hours to save the game. It ended with India eight down but 179 ahead after following on; a fifth day would almost certainly have yielded a result.

The ebbs and flows of the match showed the talent on both sides. England handed a cap to Sophia Dunkley – the first black woman to play Test cricket for them – and she stepped up to score an unbeaten 74. Captain Heather Knight, like Verma, just missed out on a century, while left-arm spinner Sophie Ecclestone collected four wickets in each innings. But the teams headed into the white-ball games on two points apiece, before England completed 2–1 wins in both the one-day and T20 series.

With the 50-over World Cup in New Zealand due to begin in March 2022 (a year late, because of the Covid crisis), the two sides – finalists in 2017 – were working out their likely line-ups, though both were due to tour Australia before the tournament. In the second ODI, at Taunton, Kate Cross repaid coach Lisa Keightley's faith by claiming only her second five-wicket haul, while Dunkley showed she could handle pressure and steady the middle order. Danni

Wyatt, now 30, was left out of the ODIs, but seized the chance to remind Keightley of her quality in the final T20, steering England to a series win with an unbeaten 89.

One of the biggest talking points in the 50-over matches was Raj's scoring-rate. Though she struck a half-century in all three, the first two came in losing causes, with India failing to set sufficiently challenging targets. Raj finished with 206 runs for twice out, returned to the top of the ODI rankings, and overtook Charlotte Edwards as the leading run-scorer across all women's internationals. She remained India's best one-day batter, but the game has evolved: she ate up valuable balls, and her strike rotation was slack.

In the field, too, there was more energy and bounce when Harmanpreet Kaur took charge – as she did in the second ODI, after Raj was injured batting, and in the T20s, when Raj did not play. Heading into the World Cup, India needed to inject some urgency to supplement her stability, if they were to repeat or improve on their performance as runners-up in 2017.

INDIAN TOURING PARTY

*M. D. Raj (T/50), S. D. Bahadur (20), T. Bhatia (T/50), E. K. Bisht (T/50/20), H. Deol (20), R. M. Ghosh (20), J. N. Goswami (T/50), H. Kaur (T/50/20), S. S. Mandhana (T/50/20), S. S. Pandey (T/50/20), P. S. Punia (T/50), S. Rana (T/50/20), P. G. Raut (T/50), A. Reddy (T/50/20), J. I. Rodrigues (T/50/20), I. T. Roy (T/50/20), D. B. Sharma (T/50/20), P. Vastrakar (T/50/20), S. Verma (T/50/20), P. Yadav (T/50/20), R. P. Yadav (T/50/20). *Coach:* R. R. Powar.

Kaur captained in the T20 series.

ENGLAND v INDIA

LV= Insurance Test Match

At Bristol, June 16–19. Drawn. England 2pts, India 2pts. Toss: England. Test debuts: S. I. R. Dunkley; T. Bhatia, S. Rana, D. B. Sharma, P. Vastrakar, S. Verma.

In the last Test between these sides, in 2014, India had pulled off a shock victory at Wormsley. Seven years on, England were hopeful of revenge on the final afternoon, when the tourists were seven down following on, and only 34 ahead. But Rana, at No. 8, held out for three and a quarter hours to ensure the points were shared.

There had been much talk about the fact that the teams would be playing on a pitch already used in a men's T20 game – home captain Knight said it was "not ideal". But when she decided to bat, on a slightly worn but perfectly decent strip, England made hay. Beaumont reached a fine half-century, before Verma's one-handed low catch at silly mid-on gave Rana her first Test wicket. Knight batted fluently, despite a slow over-rate, adding 90 for the third wicket with Sciver, but fell five short of her second Test century – one of four wickets in ten overs from Sharma and Rana in the evening session as England slipped from 230 for two to 251 for six. That became 270 for seven early next morning.

Dunkley, who had already created history as the first black woman to play Test cricket for England, remained composed, completing a maiden fifty. Alongside her, Shrubsole stood firm: they added 70 in ten overs before the declaration, just after lunch, on 396 for nine. Dunkley was 74 not out, the highest score on Test debut for England for 35 years.

India enjoyed a blistering start. Verma, at 17 the youngest of their five debutants, displayed scintillating timing as she reached her own maiden Test fifty in 83 balls, with 38 in boundaries. She and Mandhana piled on 167, before Verma, trying to bring up what would have been the first century on Test debut for an Indian, looked to smash Cross into the stratosphere, but ended up slicing to mid-off, and departed to a standing ovation. Her dismissal triggered a collapse: all ten fell for 64 as India subsided for 231, and followed on 165 behind. Slow left-armer Ecclestone took a Test-best four for 88, including Raj second ball. Only Sharma held out, for 29 in an hour and a half. That earned her promotion from No. 7 to No. 3 in the second innings, when Mandhana edged Brunt to slip on the stroke of lunch. Rain meant just 20 overs were bowled on the third afternoon, but that was

HIGHEST SCORE ON TEST DEBUT FOR ENGLAND...

117†	L. Cooke	v India at Collingham	1986
113	E. Bakewell	v Australia at Adelaide (Thebarton)	1968-69
74*	**S. I. R. Dunkley**	**v India at Bristol**	**2021**
72	M. E. Maclagan	v Australia at Brisbane (Exhibition)	1934-35
65	M. C. Godliman	v India at Taunton	2002

† *Cooke also scored 72 in her first innings.*

...AND INDIA

96†	**S. Verma**	**v England at Bristol**	**2021**
80*	**S. Rana**	**v England at Bristol**	**2021**
75	C. Aheer	v New Zealand at Nelson	1994-95
74	S. Rangaswamy	v West Indies at Bangalore	1976-77
71	S. Agarwal	v Australia at Ahmedabad	1983-84

† *Verma also scored 63 in her second innings.*

Twelve women have scored a century on Test debut; the record is 204 by M. A. J. Goszko for Australia v England at Shenley in 2001.

time enough for Verma to reach an even more sparkling half-century, from 63 balls, with ten fours. She succumbed to Ecclestone on the final morning, just after becoming the first woman to hit three sixes in a Test career, let alone a match. But Sharma pushed on to 54 before another rush of wickets – five for 28.

The tourists looked to be toppling until Rana became the first Indian (woman or man) to take four in an innings and score a half-century on Test debut. She and wicketkeeper Bhatia shared an unbroken stand of 104, which gradually quenched England's hopes, and led to criticism of their decision to pick only one frontline slow bowler. Knight later made the case for a fifth day – though, as the balance shifted, it might have been India who benefited.

Player of the Match: S. Verma.

Close of play: first day, England 269-6 (Dunkley 12, Brunt 7); second day, India 187-5 (Kaur 4, Sharma 0); third day, India 83-1 (Verma 55, Sharma 18).

England

L. Winfield-Hill c Bhatia b Vastrakar	35		S. Ecclestone c Pandey b Sharma	17	
T. T. Beaumont c Verma b Rana	66		A. Shrubsole b Rana	47	
*H. C. Knight lbw b Sharma	95		B 2, lb 1, w 1, nb 2	6	
N. R. Sciver lbw b Sharma	42				
†A. E. Jones lbw b Rana	1		1/69 (1)	(9 wkts dec, 121.2 overs)	396
S. I. R. Dunkley not out	74		2/140 (2) 3/230 (4)		
G. A. Elwiss c Sharma b Rana	5		4/236 (5) 5/244 (3) 6/251 (7)		
K. H. Brunt lbw b Goswami	8		7/270 (8) 8/326 (9) 9/396 (10)		

K. L. Cross did not bat.

Goswami 21–3–58–1; Pandey 15–3–61–0; Vastrakar 14–3–53–1; Rana 39.2–4–131–4; Sharma 27–5–65–3; Kaur 5–0–25–0.

India

S. S. Mandhana c Brunt b Sciver	78	– c Sciver b Brunt 8
S. Verma c Shrubsole b Cross	96	– c Brunt b Ecclestone 63
P. G. Raut lbw b Knight	2	– (4) c Ecclestone b Sciver 39
S. S. Pandey c and b Knight	0	– (9) c Jones b Sciver 18
*M. D. Raj c Beaumont b Ecclestone	2	– b Ecclestone 4
H. Kaur lbw b Ecclestone	4	– c Jones b Ecclestone 8
D. B. Sharma not out	29	– (3) b Ecclestone 54
†T. Bhatia lbw b Ecclestone	0	– (10) not out 44
S. Rana c Jones b Ecclestone	2	– (8) not out 80
P. Vastrakar b Brunt	12	– (7) b Knight 12
J. N. Goswami b Shrubsole	1	
B 4, lb 1	5	B 6, lb 6, w 1, nb 1 14

1/167 (2) 2/179 (1) 3/179 (4)   (81.2 overs) 231   1/29 (1)   (8 wkts, 121 overs) 344
4/183 (5) 5/183 (3) 6/187 (6)   2/99 (2) 3/171 (3)
7/187 (8) 8/197 (9) 9/230 (10) 10/231 (11)   4/175 (5) 5/175 (4)
                                            6/189 (7) 7/199 (6) 8/240 (9)

Brunt 11–2–42–1; Shrubsole 10.2–2–18–1; Sciver 10–3–22–1; Cross 12–4–40–1; Ecclestone 26–5–88–4; Knight 11–8–7–2; Dunkley 1–0–9–0. *Second innings*—Brunt 21–5–49–1; Shrubsole 13–2–52–0; Ecclestone 38–10–118–4; Cross 15–6–43–0; Knight 15–2–41–1; Sciver 16–9–21–2; Elwiss 3–1–8–0.

Umpires: S. Redfern and C. M. Watts.   Third umpire: I. J. Gould.
Referee: D. T. Jukes.

First one-day international   At Bristol, June 27. **England won by eight wickets. India 201-8** (50 overs) (P. G. Raut 32, M. D. Raj 72, D. B. Sharma 30; S. Ecclestone 3-40); ‡**England 202-2** (34.5 overs) (T. T. Beaumont 87*, N. R. Sciver 74*). *England 2pts. PoM*: T. T. Beaumont. *ODI debut*: S. I. R. Dunkley (England); S. Verma (India). *Shafali Verma could not sustain her Test form in her first ODI, though she hit three fours in her 15 before she skewed Katherine Brunt to mid-on. India took 15.4 overs to bring up their 50; though Mithali Raj top-scored with 72, she used up 108 balls, with Punam Raut and Deepti Sharma equally slow as they dawdled to 201. The evergreen Jhulan Goswami had Lauren Winfield-Hill (picked ahead of Danni Wyatt for the ODIs) caught behind in the fifth over, and Heather Knight struggled to 18 off 30. But Tammy Beaumont and Nat Sciver scored at a run a ball; their stand of 119* saw England win with 15 overs to spare.*

Second one-day international   At Taunton, June 30 (day/night). **England won by five wickets. India 221** (50 overs) (S. Verma 44, M. D. Raj 59; S. Ecclestone 3-33, K. L. Cross 5-34); ‡**England 225-5** (47.3 overs) (L. Winfield-Hill 42, S. I. R. Dunkley 73*, K. H. Brunt 33*). *England 2pts. PoM*: K. L. Cross. *Kate Cross dismantled India's batting with her first five-for in more than six years. After Verma and Smriti Mandhana opened with a stand of 56, she bowled Mandhana via the inside edge, had Jemimah Rodrigues caught at mid-on and held a return catch off Harmanpreet Kaur; Sharma was caught in the deep and Sneh Rana at mid-off. Verma was in decent touch again, but Sophie Ecclestone had her stumped off a slower ball. Raj's languid 59 off 92 helped India to 221, still below par. But after Goswami bowled Beaumont for ten, Poonam Yadav and Rana had England in trouble at 133-5. Sophia Dunkley steadied the ship, balancing attack and defence in an assured 73*, and adding 92* with Brunt.*

Third one-day international   At Worcester, July 3. **India won by four wickets. England 219** (47 overs) (L. Winfield-Hill 36, H. C. Knight 46, N. R. Sciver 49; D. B. Sharma 3-47); ‡**India 220-6** (46.3 overs) (S. S. Mandhana 49, M. D. Raj 75*). *PoS*: S. Ecclestone. *Raj's last game of the tour was her best, from her first correct call at the toss to the four that clinched her 84th ODI win as captain, beating Belinda Clark's record with Australia. On the way, she became the leading run-scorer in all women's internationals, overtaking Charlotte Edwards's 10,273. After rain shortened the match to 47 overs, Shikha Pandey trapped Beaumont for a four-ball duck; though several home batters contributed, India's slow bowlers, led by Sharma, kept things tight until the final over, when Cross hit Sharma for a four and a six that sailed over long-off. Cross went on to dismiss Verma for 19, toe-ending to cover, and when Sarah Glenn had Mandhana plumb, one shy of her fifty, the onus was on Raj. Exploiting some wayward bowling, she shared 50-run partnerships with Kaur and Rana, and finished on 75* as India narrowed the points gap in the series to 6–4.*

MOST RUNS IN WOMEN'S INTERNATIONALS

	Avge		*Tests*	*ODIs*	*T20Is*	
10,337	47.20	M. D. Raj (India)	669	7,304	2,364	1999 to 2021
10,273	37.49	C. M. Edwards (England)	1,676	5,992	2,605	1996 to 2015-16
8,052	41.08	S. R. Taylor (West Indies) . . .	–	4,931	3,121	2008 to 2021
7,849	36.17	S. W. Bates (New Zealand) . . .	–	4,548	3,301	2005-06 to 2020-21
7,024	43.35	M. M. Lanning (Australia) . . .	185	3,925	2,914	2010-11 to 2020-21

First Twenty20 international   At Northampton, July 9 (floodlit). **England won by 18 runs** (DLS). **England 177-7** (20 overs) (D. N. Wyatt 31, N. R. Sciver 55, A. E. Jones 43; S. S. Pandey 3-22); ‡**India 54-3** (8.4 overs). *England 2pts. PoM:* N. R. Sciver. *Victory ensured England could not lose the series, though the highlight was Harleen Deol's acrobatic fielding to dismiss Amy Jones. After taking a sensational overhead catch, and with her momentum carrying her over the boundary, she flicked the ball into the air, before diving back to collect it. But by then England were 166-5 in the 19th over: Jones had put on 78 in seven with Sciver, who hit her tenth T20I half-century. Wyatt, recalled for the T20 games, had struck 31 before being caught behind off Radha Yadav – who extended her record sequence of at least one wicket in a T20I innings to 27. Needing 178, India started disastrously when Brunt bowled Verma for a second-ball duck. Mandhana smacked six glorious fours, then slapped Sciver to deep backward square on 29, and Glenn removed Kaur for a single as rain began to fall; India were well behind a DLS target of 73.*

Second Twenty20 international   At Hove, July 11. **India won by eight runs. India 148-4** (20 overs) (S. Verma 48, H. Kaur 31); ‡**England 140-8** (20 overs) (T. T. Beaumont 59, H. C. Knight 30). *India 2pts. PoM:* D. B. Sharma. *Their backs against the wall, India fought their way to a narrow win, once again reducing the deficit in the series to two points. They got off to a flyer in an opening stand of 70 in nine overs, before Mandhana (20) was dismissed by Freya Davies, and Verma (a six and eight fours in a dazzling 48 off 38) holed out to Mady Villiers's first delivery. Kaur and Sharma (24*) helped them scrap to 148-4. Though Wyatt and Sciver – run out chancing a non-existent single – departed in England's first three overs, Beaumont and Knight put on 75. Beaumont reached a fluid 39-ball fifty, but was lbw mistiming a sweep off Sharma; Jones hit the next delivery back down the ground, and a fortuitous deflection off Sharma's right leg ran out Knight. Panic set in, with Dunkley and Villiers needlessly run out, and India kept the series alive.*

Third Twenty20 international   At Chelmsford, July 14 (floodlit). **England won by eight wickets.** ‡**India 153-6** (20 overs) (S. S. Mandhana 70, H. Kaur 36; S. Ecclestone 3-35); **England 154-2** (18.4 overs) (D. N. Wyatt 89*, N. R. Sciver 42). *England 2pts. PoS:* N. R. Sciver. *Wyatt's clinical 89* in 56 balls – her tenth T20I half-century – strengthened her bid to reclaim her ODI place before the World Cup. Mandhana's 70 off 51 had set up India's 153-6; if they could defend it, the series would be drawn. Beaumont was lbw to Sharma for 11, but Wyatt and Sciver, batting with confidence and flair, added 112 in 13 overs. Then Rana bowled Sciver to give India a glimmer of hope, which grew as Poonam Yadav conceded just three singles in the 18th. England required 13 off 12 deliveries, but Wyatt did it in four. She ran two off Sharma's first ball, lifted a six over deep square leg, swept behind square for four, then took a single to win the match, the T20 leg of the tour and the overall series.*

WEST INDIES v PAKISTAN IN 2021

Twenty20 internationals (3): West Indies 3, Pakistan 0
One-day internationals (5): West Indies 3, Pakistan 2

West Indies welcomed Courtney Walsh with some emphatic victories in their first series since his appointment as coach in October 2020. They won six of the eight games, sweeping the T20 series, then going 3–0 up in the one-dayers, before Pakistan won the last two. Kyshona Knight shone, scoring 219 runs over the eight matches, though the two outstanding innings came from captain Stafanie Taylor and opener Hayley Matthews, who both struck ODI hundreds. Off-spinner Anisa Mohammed also starred for West Indies, taking 15 wickets, matching Pakistani seamer Fatima Sana. The tourists' leading scorer was Omaima Sohail, with 191 runs, even though she played only in the one-day series.

First Twenty20 international   At North Sound, Antigua, June 30, 2021. **West Indies won by ten runs. West Indies 136-6** (20 overs) (H. K. Matthews 32, D. J. S. Dottin 31); ‡**Pakistan 126-6** (20 overs) (Ayesha Naseem 45*; S. S. Connell 3-21). *PoM:* S. S. Connell. *West Indies reached 136, thanks chiefly to openers Hayley Matthews, the third West Indian woman (after Stafanie Taylor and Deandra Dottin) to pass 1,000 T20I runs, and Dottin herself; the Knight twins, Kyshona and Kycia, were the next-highest scorers with 23 and 15. Meanwhile, when Nida Dar – whose four overs cost just 15 – removed Dottin, she became the fifth woman, and the first Pakistani of either gender, to 100 wickets in the format. Shamilia Connell's devastating opening spell reduced the visitors to 23-3, and it was soon 57-6. Despite a national-record seventh-wicket stand of 69* between Ayesha Naseem (45* from 33 balls) and Fatima Sana (24* from 21), who both finished with T20I bests, Pakistan couldn't make up the lost ground.*

Second Twenty20 international   At Coolidge, Antigua, July 2, 2021. **West Indies won by seven runs (DLS). ‡West Indies 125-6** (20 overs) (Kycia A. Knight 30*); **Pakistan 103-6** (18 overs). *PoM:* Kycia A. Knight. *A dramatic match took a worrying turn when two West Indians, Chinelle Henry and Chedean Nation, collapsed in separate incidents during the Pakistan reply. They were taken to hospital, and said to be "conscious and stable". The game continued, but Pakistan's hopes of levelling the series were scuppered by five run-outs, one short of the record for a T20I innings, by Singapore against Myanmar in 2019. They were seven behind DLS par when rain stopped play with two overs to go. West Indies had endured their own problems with the bat, slumping to 69-4, before Nation (28) and Kycia Knight gave them something to bowl at; 18 in wides by Pakistan's bowlers helped.*

Third Twenty20 international   At North Sound, Antigua, July 4, 2021. **West Indies won by six wickets. ‡Pakistan 102** (19.4 overs) (S. R. Taylor 4-17, A. Mohammed 3-24); **West Indies 106-4** (19.1 overs) (S. R. Taylor 43*). *PoM:* S. R. Taylor. *PoS:* S. S. Connell. *An all-round tour de force from Taylor led her team to a whitewash. Her off-breaks snapped up the last four Pakistani wickets, including a final-over hat-trick – only the second by a West Indian woman in a T20I, after fellow off-spinner Anisa Mohammed against South Africa at Tarouba in 2018. With Mohammed now chipping in too, West Indies needed just 103. At 17-3, they were in trouble. But Taylor judged the chase perfectly, adding 41 with Nation (20) – fit again after her scare two days earlier – and 48* with Kycia Knight (24*), to clinch an emphatic series win.*

First one-day international   At Coolidge, Antigua, July 7, 2021. **West Indies won by five wickets. Pakistan 205-9** (50 overs) (Muneeba Ali 36, Ayesha Zafar 46, Nida Dar 55; S. R. Taylor 3-29); ‡**West Indies 209-5** (47.5 overs) (S. R. Taylor 105*). *PoM:* S. R. Taylor. *ODI debut:* C. Isaac (West Indies). *Taylor dominated the opening game of the five-match series, reaching her first international century for nearly eight years to guide West Indies home with 13 balls to spare. The next-highest score was Nation's 23. Earlier, Taylor had taken three for 29 as she and Mohammed whittled away at Pakistan's middle order, after an opening stand of 70. Dar's 55 dragged the total towards 200, but Taylor made light work of the task, ending a run of 20 unconverted ODI half-centuries. "I've been dreaming of this day," she said.*

Second one-day international   At Coolidge, Antigua, July 9, 2021. **West Indies won by eight wickets. ‡Pakistan 120** (42.4 overs) (Muneeba Ali 37; A. Mohammed 4-27); **West Indies 121-2** (31.1 overs) (H. K. Matthews 49, Kyshona A. Knight 39*). *PoM:* H. K. Matthews. *Pakistan collapsed from 60-2 to 120, as Mohammed led a powerful performance from the West Indian spinners, taking 4-27. In all, the slow bowlers managed 8-89 from 32.4 overs. Then their openers, Matthews – whose off-breaks had picked up 2-17 – and Kyshona Knight, made sure the outcome was never in doubt with a partnership of 65. Both West Indies wickets fell to run-outs.*

Third one-day international   At North Sound, Antigua, July 12, 2021. **West Indies won by eight wickets. Pakistan 182** (49 overs) (Omaima Sohail 62; C. A. Henry 3-37, A. Mohammed 3-25); ‡**West Indies 183-2** (40.1 overs) (H. K. Matthews 100*, B. Cooper 45). *PoM:* H. K. Matthews. *ODI debut:* Ayesha Naseem (Pakistan). *A round 100* from Matthews, her second ODI century, gave West Indies an unassailable 3–0 lead. Earlier, she had taken 2-30 as Pakistan slipped from 143-3 to 182 in 15 chaotic overs – a collapse that included the stumping of Omaima Sohail for a career-best 62. There were also three wickets each for Mohammed and Henry. Matthews then put on 56 with Kyshona Knight, and a decisive 106 with Britney Cooper. Victory came with nearly ten overs to spare.*

Fourth one-day international At North Sound, Antigua, July 15, 2021. **Pakistan won by four wickets. West Indies 210** (49.4 overs) (Kyshona A. Knight 88, S. R. Taylor 49; Fatima Sana 4-30, Nashra Sandhu 4-49); ‡**Pakistan 211-6** (48.3 overs) (Sidra Ameen 41, Omaima Sohail 61). *PoM:* Fatima Sana. *ODI debut:* R. S. Williams (West Indies). *This time it was West Indies' turn to make a mess of batting first, as they lost eight for 39 after Kyshona Knight's 88 (a maiden international half-century) and Taylor's 49 had guided them to 171-2 with more than ten overs to go. Their stand of 142 was a third-wicket record for West Indies but, after that, only Rashada Williams (14), the debutant wicketkeeper, reached double figures. Seamer Sana (who produced a career-best) and slow left-armer Nashra Sandhu each picked up four. Another sixty from Sohail held the innings together, before Dar finished the job, taking Pakistan to their third-highest successful chase.*

Fifth one-day international At Coolidge, Antigua, July 18, 2021. **Pakistan won by 22 runs** (DLS). **Pakistan 190-8** (34 overs) (Muneeba Ali 39, Omaima Sohail 34); ‡**West Indies 171** (34 overs) (D. J. S. Dottin 37, B. Cooper 40; Fatima Sana 5-39). *PoM:* Fatima Sana. *PoS:* H. K. Matthews. *Rain disrupted the final match, but West Indies were still set a challenging target of 194 from 34 overs. Sohail was again in the runs – 34 took her series total to 191, more than anyone else on either side – before 28* from 19 balls by Sana made Pakistan's total competitive. Sana then set about West Indies' batting, with a maiden five-wicket haul. The last seven fell for 51 in ten overs as Pakistan pulled off a second successive consolation victory.*

WEST INDIES v SOUTH AFRICA

ALEX BRINTON

Twenty20 internationals (3): West Indies 1, South Africa 1
One-day internationals (5): West Indies 1, South Africa 4

South Africa's late-summer visit to the West Indies was mostly a success: though a bad batting performance cost them the T20 series, they triumphed emphatically in the one-dayers. Lizelle Lee led the run-scoring with 362 at 72 across both series, passing 1,000 in T20Is and 3,000 in ODIs, while Laura Wolvaardt totalled 232; no other batter managed even half as many. Economical bowling restricted West Indies in all the matches: in the one-day games, ten of South Africa's 11 bowlers conceded under four an over.

West Indies failed to build on the momentum gained by beating Pakistan in July. Head coach Courtney Walsh could hardly have been filled with hope by his attack: Hayley Matthews and Qiana Joseph were the top wicket-takers, with six, but managed less than one per innings. Rashada Williams continued to improve, playing three one-day matches and scoring 157 at 78, including her first international half-century. Such positives were scant: Deandra Dottin scored West Indies' only other 50; Lee had managed four on her own.

First T20 international At North Sound, Antigua, August 31. **No result.** ‡**South Africa 135-3** (20 overs) (L. Lee 30, M. Kapp 36, L. Wolvaardt 35*); **West Indies 21-1** (2.5 overs). *T20I debut:* Q. Joseph (West Indies). *The weather put a dampener on what might have been a good finish. South Africa made a moderate 135, Lizelle Lee and Marizanne Kapp keeping the score ticking, while Laura Wolvaardt (35* off 21) hit out; Qiana Joseph, a debutant left-arm quick, was economical (0-22). Deandra Dottin retired hurt with a leg injury after the third ball of West Indies' reply (she recovered for the next game), but the innings had barely begun when the rain came.*

Second T20 international At North Sound, Antigua, September 2. **South Africa won by 50 runs. South Africa 165-3** (20 overs) (L. Lee 75, L. Wolvaardt 33*); ‡**West Indies 115-8** (20 overs) (M. Kapp 3-31). *PoM:* L. Lee. *Wolvaardt (33* off nine) struck the last four deliveries of the South Africa innings for six to propel her side to 165, after Lee had built a platform with a 52-ball 75. Joseph was quick and tidy, claiming Dane van Niekerk as her first international wicket, but lacked support. West Indies were stifled by the seamers – Ayabonga Khaka conceded only eight – and never threatened. They found the boundary just 11 times, to South Africa's 23.*

Third T20 international At North Sound, Antigua, September 4. **West Indies won by five wickets. ‡South Africa 80-9** (20 overs) (K. Ramharack 3-8); **West Indies 81-5** (11.5 overs) (D. J. S. Dottin 31). PoM: K. Ramharack. *West Indies humiliated South Africa, restricting them to 80, then surpassing that with 8.1 overs to spare. The visitors were 12-4 in the third, their imposing top four all gone; Tazmin Brits and Sune Luus could only work the ball around in an attempt to limit the damage. Hayley Matthews conceded just nine, and off-spinner Karishma Ramharack ran through the lower order, taking a career-best 3-8. Though Matthews fell early, a second-wicket partnership of 53 between Dottin and Kyshona Knight extinguished South Africa's slender hopes. Four then fell for 16, but Chedean Nation hit the winning runs to square the series.*

First one-day international At Coolidge, Antigua, September 7. ‡**West Indies 153** (46.4 overs) (D. J. S. Dottin 38, Kycia A. Knight 39); **South Africa 157-2** (39.3 overs) (L. Lee 91*, L. Wolvaardt 36). PoM: L. Lee. *Lee seamlessly transferred formats, adding 91* to the 114 she had totalled in the T20 series as South Africa easily overhauled a modest target. West Indies were kept in check by the accuracy of Khaka (7.4–3–17–2) and van Niekerk (10–1–23–2); only Britney Cooper (who retired hurt on 23), Dottin and Kycia Knight reached double figures as the last eight fell for 83. In South Africa's pursuit of 154, Lee and Wolvaardt opened with 88, and Lee stayed to the end. "We need to go back to the drawing board, and come up with ways to score 200, which I know we have the ability to do," said Dottin.*

Second one-day international At Coolidge, Antigua, September 10. ‡**West Indies 120** (44.2 overs) (M. Kapp 3-24); **South Africa 121-1** (25.4 overs) (L. Wolvaardt 71*). PoM: L. Wolvaardt. *West Indies chose to bat again, but never recovered after slumping to 18-3, with Matthews, Kyshona Knight and Dottin all falling to Kapp. At 86-5, Shabika Gajnabi's stumping off the miserly van Niekerk (10–5–14–2) triggered another collapse. South Africa's pursuit was straightforward: Lara Goodall (25*) batted for the first time on tour, adding 86* for the second wicket with Wolvaardt (71*).*

Third one-day international At Coolidge, Antigua, September 13. **West Indies 157** (48.4 overs) (R. S. Williams 37, D. J. S. Dottin 71; S. Ismail 3-31); ‡**South Africa 158-2** (36.4 overs) (L. Lee 78*, L. Wolvaardt 53). PoM: S. Ismail. *Once more, West Indies were bundled out cheaply, and beaten in an easy chase. Dottin dominated their innings with 71, adding 77 for the second wicket with Rashada Williams (37), but the others scored 29 between them; there were 20 extras. Khaka (2-22) was economical again; Shabnim Ismail (3-31) took her first wickets of the tour, and ran out Ramharack first ball. Lee and Wolvaardt opened the reply with a stand of 122 – South Africa's highest for any wicket against West Indies. By the time they were parted by Joseph, the lone wicket-taker, the visitors had all but clinched the match, and the series.*

Fourth one-day international At North Sound, Antigua, September 16. **South Africa 185-6** (50 overs) (T. Brits 30, M. du Preez 65*); ‡**West Indies 150-9** (50 overs) (R. S. Williams 42; D. van Niekerk 3-23). PoM: D. van Niekerk. *ODI debut: C. S. Fraser (West Indies). West Indies won the toss, and this time chased. It nearly worked – they had South Africa 122-6 in the 36th, with Wolvaardt and van Niekerk out (Lee was rested). Then Mignon du Preez grasped her opportunity: her watchful 65*, plus wicketkeeper Sanalo Jafta's 28* off 46 – comprising 18 singles and five twos – inflated the total to 185-6. West Indies had successfully chased as many only three times, though that included July's win against Pakistan, so they had reason to hope, especially while Williams (42) was there. Nobody could stay with her, though, and when van Niekerk ran her out, the innings crumbled. Nos. 7 to 10 all scored eight (Aaliyah Alleyne was not out) as West Indies lost their sixth ODI in a row.*

Fifth one-day international At North Sound, Antigua, September 19. **West Indies won on a super over, following a tie.** ‡**West Indies 192-5** (50 overs) (R. S. Williams 78*, H. K. Matthews 48; N. de Klerk 3-33); **South Africa 192-7** (50 overs) (L. Lee 61, T. Brits 48, M. du Preez 46; S. S. Grimmond 4-33). PoM: S. S. Grimmond. *The first super over in a women's one-day international earned West Indies a consolation win: with the scores level, Nation hit Maria Klaas's final ball for four. Earlier, Williams continued her form with 78*, adding 97 for the fourth wicket with Matthews. Though Nadine de Klerk plugged away for a career-best 3-33, a total of 192-5 was competitive. Lee and Brits put on 111 for the first wicket, but South Africa lost three for three, then slid to 143-6 against Joseph and off-spinner Sheneta Grimmond. Six were needed off Dottin's final over, and one from the last ball – but du Preez was run out by Shakera Selman to force the tie-breaker. South Africa batted first: Dottin limited Lee and van Niekerk to six, then van Niekerk was run out from the first ball of West Indies' super over, bowled by Klaas. Nation scampered two from the second, but one short was called. It went to the wire again, before Nation on-drove a full toss to the boundary. West Indies were jubilant – and Lee furious: "You can't just have six balls. That's not going to define what's happened in an ODI."*

ENGLAND v NEW ZEALAND IN 2021

Raf Nicholson

Twenty20 internationals (3): England 2, New Zealand 1
One-day internationals (5): England 4, New Zealand 1

After a drubbing by England at home in February and March, New Zealand were a much improved side on the return visit, even though they lost both series again. Two of the eight matches were decided only in the final over, while a 4–1 scoreline in the one-day games belied their closeness. Disappointingly, the record crowds from the women's Hundred failed to transfer to the internationals – the biggest was 2,800 at Hove. And the one time the series made headlines came off the field, ahead of the third ODI in Leicester, when there was a security threat against the tourists after New Zealand Cricket pulled their men's team out of a trip to Pakistan. It was quickly deemed "not credible" by the ECB and NZC.

New Zealand welcomed back Suzie Bates, playing her first matches since shoulder surgery, as well as captain Sophie Devine, who had taken a two-month mental-health break earlier in the year; Devine hit a match-winning fifty in the second T20, at Hove. The workload of Lea Tahuhu, returning after three operations on her foot to remove a pre-cancerous mole, was carefully managed. She sat out the T20s and one ODI but, when she did play, looked her dangerous best, despite having lost some pace, and took five wickets in the one-day win at Leicester.

A recurring theme was the England batters' exhaustion after the longest season they had known: series against India and New Zealand flanked The Hundred, where most had played eight or nine games. Coach Lisa Keightley admitted that they had struggled with mental fatigue after living with strict Covid protocols for months on end. There were batting collapses in the first three ODIs, though Heather Knight and Tammy Beaumont bounced back with hundreds in the last two. Katherine Brunt was rested in four matches, Nat Sciver in one, and Knight missed the first two T20s as she battled a hamstring injury.

England introduced three players: Maia Bouchier, Charlie Dean and Emma Lamb, who was added to the squad after Bouchier and Dean were forced to wait on test results following possible contact with a Covid case. Off-spinner Dean boosted her claim for World Cup selection with ten wickets, equalling New Zealand seamer Hannah Rowe as the most successful bowler in the ODIs.

NEW ZEALAND TOURING PARTY

*S. F. M. Devine, S. W. Bates, L. R. Down, C. L. Green, M. L. Green, B. M. Halliday, H. N. K. Jensen, L. M. Kasperek, J. M. Kerr, J. T. McFadyen, K. J. Martin, T. M. M. Newton, M. M. Penfold, H. M. Rowe, A. E. Satterthwaite, L. M. Tahuhu. *Coach:* R. M. Carter.

R. A. Mair was originally selected, but withdrew because of a shin injury and was replaced by Penfold.

Dan Mullan, Getty Images

Dean of Worcester: in her second one-day international, off-spinner Charlie Dean takes four wickets.

First Twenty20 international   At Chelmsford, September 1 (floodlit). **England won by 46 runs. England 184-4** (20 overs) (T. T. Beaumont 97, A. E. Jones 31); ‡**New Zealand 138** (18.5 overs) (A. E. Satterthwaite 43). *PoM:* T. T. Beaumont. *T20I debut:* E. L. Lamb (England). *Heather Knight had pulled out the day before with a hamstring injury, but her side were unfazed, while New Zealand looked rusty after nearly five months without a match. Tammy Beaumont and Amy Jones smashed the 12th and 13th overs for 18 each. Beaumont – dropped twice – hit her fourth international fifty of the summer, but was caught off the penultimate delivery trying to reach a 65-ball century by ramping Hayley Jensen. England's 184-4 was their highest T20 total against New Zealand, who promptly sank to 4-2 – Sophie Devine lbw to Tash Farrant, playing her first international since March, and Suzie Bates bowled by Katherine Brunt's cross-seamer. Wickets continued to fall as New Zealand slogged away, and only Amy Satterthwaite reached 20. England's win was so resounding that debutant Emma Lamb did not face a delivery (she was the non-striker as Sophia Dunkley hit the final ball of the innings for four) or bowl.*

Second Twenty20 international   At Hove, September 4 (floodlit). **New Zealand won by four wickets. England 127-7** (20 overs) (D. N. Wyatt 35); ‡**New Zealand 128-6** (18.2 overs) (S. F. M. Devine 50). *PoM:* S. F. M. Devine. *T20I debut:* M. E. Bouchier (England). *Devine celebrated her 100th T20 international with a match-winning performance. After putting England in again, she reduced them to 25-3 by dismissing Nat Sciver and Jones, who holed out off consecutive deliveries; when Dunkley was caught and bowled by Leigh Kasperek, it was 61-4. A nervous Maia Bouchier ran erratically between the wickets, but her 25 was the highest score by an England player on T20 debut since the inaugural international, also at Hove, in 2004. Devine went after an under-par target of 128 with gusto, hitting four sixes over the leg side on her way to a 39-ball fifty. Mady Villiers, who had already demonstrated why she might be the world's best fielder by running out Bates with a direct hit from mid-on, finally saw Devine off with a diving catch at deep midwicket. But New Zealand won with ten balls to spare, helped by 19 in wides.*

Third Twenty20 international   At Taunton, September 9 (floodlit). **England won by four wickets. New Zealand 144-4** (20 overs) (S. W. Bates 34, S. F. M. Devine 35); ‡**England 145-6** (19.5 overs) (D. N. Wyatt 35, H. C. Knight 42, A. E. Jones 32; L. M. Kasperek 3-25). *PoM:* H. C. Knight. *PoS:* S. F. M. Devine. *England clinched the series with one ball to go when Dunkley slammed a full toss* *from Satterthwaite over midwicket. Knight, back for the decider, was steering her team towards victory when she was caught at mid-off with eight needed from seven, and Bouchier was bowled in the final over. But Dunkley held her nerve. Earlier, Bates – who became the first woman to play 250 internationals for New Zealand – got her side off to a flyer after Farrant put down a tricky return catch, and Devine also struck quick runs. Satterthwaite and Devine fell in quick succession, but New Zealand plundered 50 from the last four overs – Brooke Halliday clubbed Sophie Ecclestone for 15 in the 19th. A total of 144 looked solid, given a boggy outfield. Sciver and Wyatt both fell in the seventh to Kasperek, who later added Jones to stunt England's chase and finish as the series' leading wicket-taker, with six.*

First one-day international   At Bristol, September 16 (day/night). **England won by 30 runs. England 241** (49.3 overs) (T. T. Beaumont 44, H. C. Knight 89, K. H. Brunt 43; J. M. Kerr 3-42); ‡**New Zealand 211** (46.3 overs) (A. E. Satterthwaite 79*, S. F. M. Devine 34). PoM: H. C. Knight. ODI debut: C. E. Dean (England). *England reached 109-1, after Beaumont was dropped at first slip on five, but then lost four for 31. In her first game of the series, Lea Tahuhu rattled the stumps of Sciver and Jones, but Brunt added 88 with Knight, and the recovery led to a respectable 241. New Zealand's start was bafflingly slow: 17 in the first ten overs, as Brunt began with four maidens. It was 31-3 after Knight caught Bates and Green at slip and, though Satterthwaite made her 30th ODI score of 50-plus, wickets continued to fall. Charlie Dean claimed her first for England when she clipped Jess Kerr's off stump. Despite late flurries from Tahuhu and Kasperek, England won when Kasperek was run out by Lauren Winfield-Hill's throw from mid-on.*

Second one-day international   At Worcester, September 19. **England won by 13 runs** (DLS). **England 197** (43.3 overs) (L. Winfield-Hill 39, D. N. Wyatt 63*; H. M. Rowe 3-41, L. M. Kasperek 3-31); ‡**New Zealand 169** (39 overs) (K. L. Cross 3-43, C. E. Dean 4-36). PoM: D. N. Wyatt. *England again retrieved a difficult situation, with a little assistance from the weather. An inspired spell of 5–1–10–2 from Hannah Rowe, who removed Knight and Sciver with awayswingers, had helped reduce them to 85-5; Jones and Dunkley had played tired shots. The run-out of Winfield-Hill – a miscommunication with Wyatt left both at the non-striker's end – triggered another collapse, to 146-9. But Wyatt and Farrant added 51, a tenth-wicket record for England; Wyatt thumped Rowe for two sixes in her first ODI half-century on home soil. New Zealand were 111-4 after 23 overs, ten ahead on DLS, when rain halted play for an hour, revising the target to 183 in 42. Shortly afterwards, Sciver bowled Devine through the gate, and Dean collected 4-20 in a six-over spell that put paid to New Zealand's hopes.*

Third one-day international   At Leicester, September 21 (day/night). **New Zealand won by three wickets. England 178** (48.3 overs) (K. H. Brunt 49*; L. M. Tahuhu 5-37); ‡**New Zealand 181-7** (45.5 overs) (M. L. Green 70*, A. E. Satterthwaite 33; K. H. Brunt 4-22). PoM: M. L. Green. ODI debut: M. M. Penfold (New Zealand). *New Zealand defied a bomb threat to chalk up a win. Put in for the third time running, England's batters continued to struggle. Tahuhu's first international five-for in a ten-year career had them floundering at 78-7; disciplined line and length made up for her reduced speed after surgery. The other two fell to debutant seamer Molly Penfold, with Lauren Down's amazing diving catch at backward point removing Wyatt. Brunt gave herself something to bowl at, rampaging to 49* and adding 53 with Kate Cross, whose 29 was an international-best. Brunt then extracted both openers for single figures. But Maddy Green shouldered responsibility in her first half-century for New Zealand in over three years, putting on 72 with Satterthwaite and 52 with Halliday. A wobble – three for 12 – left them on 158-7, before Tahuhu completed victory with four overs to go when she lofted Farrant for six.*

Fourth one-day international   At Derby, September 23 (day/night). **England won by three wickets. New Zealand 244-8** (50 overs) (A. E. Satterthwaite 54, S. F. M. Devine 41, K. J. Martin 65*; C. E. Dean 3-52); ‡**England 245-7** (49.3 overs) (L. Winfield-Hill 33, H. C. Knight 101, A. E. Jones 40; H. M. Rowe 4-47). PoM: H. C. Knight. *England wrapped up the series in bizarre fashion: with the scores level, Katey Martin stumped Ecclestone, but the ball was called wide, which took precedence and completed their highest successful one-day chase. It owed much to Knight's first ODI hundred for four years, which kept England on track, despite Rowe's career-best 4-47. She and Jones added 100, before Jones toed Rowe to mid-off, and Dunkley fell for a duck. But Knight found another ally in Wyatt, who smashed a six in Rowe's last over on her way to a run-a-ball 27. Both fell to Devine in the 49th, leaving six to get off the final over; Anya Shrubsole hit Kasperek's first delivery down the ground for four before the unexpected twist. Knight had finally won the toss, and New Zealand were 33-3 when Bates ran herself out and Shrubsole bagged two early wickets in her first match of the series after spraining her ankle. Dropped catches paved the way for half-centuries from Satterthwaite and Martin, before hefty striking from Halliday (28) challenged England to score 245.*

Fifth one-day international   At Canterbury, September 26. **England won by 203 runs. England 347-5** (50 overs) (L. Winfield-Hill 43, T. T. Beaumont 102, N. R. Sciver 39, A. E. Jones 60, S. I. R. Dunkley 33*, D. N. Wyatt 43*); ‡**New Zealand 144** (35.2 overs) (K. L. Cross 3-44, H. C. Knight 3-24). *PoM:* T. T. Beaumont. *PoS:* H. C. Knight. *England finished in style, racking up 347-5 – their sixth-highest one-day total – and a mammoth 203-run win. Apart from Knight, who followed her century with a duck, all the batters pitched in, but the highlight was Beaumont's eighth ODI hundred, in front of a raucous home crowd; a few hours earlier, she had been among more than 30 women retrospectively awarded county caps by Kent. New Zealand missed several catches, including four off Winfield-Hill. Bates finally caught Beaumont at mid-on, but Dunkley and Wyatt added 79 in the last 6.2 overs; Wyatt's 20-ball 43* included four sixes. New Zealand were never up with an asking-rate of nearly seven. Shrubsole, finding lavish swing, had Bates caught skying to point; Ecclestone bowled Down, swiping wildly, before holding a return catch off Green; and Cross, bowling eight overs off the reel, dismissed Satterthwaite and Devine with successive deliveries. At 66-5, the match was as good as over. Knight confirmed the result with three late wickets.*

AUSTRALIA v INDIA IN 2021-22

GEOFF LEMON

One-day internationals (3): Australia 2, India 1
Test match (1): Australia 0, India 0
Twenty20 internationals (3): Australia 2, India 0
Overall points: Australia 11, India 5

Women's Test cricket witnessed the beginnings of a revival in 2021, when India toured England and Australia in the space of three months. BCCI president Sourav Ganguly and secretary Jay Shah seemed to have made the decision all but unilaterally, announcing Tests for both tours before the home boards had done so. It ended a stretch in which no women's Tests had been played, other than the Ashes, since 2014.

As with India's tour of England, and the Ashes, the Australian matches formed a multi-format series, with two points per win in the white-ball games, and four points for the one-off Test. The series opened the southern hemisphere season, and was relocated, at late notice, to three venues in Queensland because of interstate travel restrictions during the pandemic.

The result, 11–5 to Australia, did not reflect the contest. The Test ended with India in a dominant position, but rain spoiled their chances of pressing for a win, further underlining the need for women's Tests to be played over five days. India also lost a winning position to the weather in one of the T20s, having fumbled a victory in the final over of the second one-dayer. That handed Australia their 26th consecutive win in the format, extending the record for either gender that dated back to 2017. India ended the streak in the next match, another close finish – evidence of a young side growing in confidence against the best.

First one-day international   At Mackay, September 21, 2021. **Australia won by nine wickets. India 225-8** (50 overs) (Y. H. Bhatia 35, M. D. Raj 63, R. M. Ghosh 32*; D. R. Brown 4-33); ‡**Australia 227-1** (41 overs) (R. L. Haynes 93*, A. J. Healy 77, M. M. Lanning 53*). *Australia 2pts. PoM:* D. R. Brown. *ODI debuts:* H. J. Darlington (Australia); Y. H. Bhatia, R. M. Ghosh, Meghna Singh (India). *Australia dominated the opening match in the style that, in April, had seen them set a record for the most successive ODI wins. As so often since her India debut in 1999, captain Mithali*

Raj had to play a cautious role, accumulating 63 while 18-year-old seamer Darcie Brown blew away the top order. A sprightly 32* from wicketkeeper Richa Ghosh, a year younger, helped India to 225. Her opposite number, Alyssa Healy, pulled savagely, sharing an opening stand of 126 with Rachael Haynes, who then added 101 with Meg Lanning; all three made a half-century, with Haynes on 93* as Australia romped home.

Second one-day international   At Mackay, September 24, 2021 (day/night). **Australia won by five wickets. India 274-7** (50 overs) (S. S. Mandhana 86, R. M. Ghosh 44; T. M. McGrath 3-45); ‡**Australia 275-5** (50 overs) (B. L. Mooney 125*, T. M. McGrath 74, N. J. Carey 39*). *Australia 2pts. PoM:* B. L. Mooney. *ODI debut:* S. Verma (India). *Indian hearts were broken as Australia won after a video replay. With three needed from the last ball, bowled by Jhulan Goswami, Nicola Carey was caught at square leg off a full toss – only for India's jubilation to turn to horror when the third umpire ruled it a no-ball on height. From the next delivery, a free hit, Carey clipped two to midwicket, securing both the series and Australia's highest successful chase in a record winning streak now extended to 26. Earlier, India were powered by Smriti Mandhana, who hit Brown for three successive boundaries en route to 86. After Mandhana tired, Ghosh made 44 and Goswami's late striking (28*) boosted the total to 274. She then sent back Healy for a three-ball duck, before Australia slipped to 52-4. They looked done for, but Beth Mooney struck a career-best 125*, adding 126 with Tahlia McGrath and 97* with Carey. Australia began the last over needing 13. Thanks to an overthrow, a misfield, a no-ball full toss, a bye, a leg-bye and a scrambled two, that became three off one delivery – leading to the final drama.*

Third one-day international   At Mackay, September 26, 2021. **India won by two wickets.** ‡**Australia 264-9** (50 overs) (A. J. Healy 35, B. L. Mooney 52, A. K. Gardner 67, T. M. McGrath 47; J. N. Goswami 3-37, P. Vastrakar 3-46); **India 266-8** (49.3 overs) (S. Verma 50, Y. H. Bhatia 64, D. B. Sharma 31, S. Rana 30; A. J. Sutherland 3-30). *India 2pts. PoM:* J. N. Goswami. *ODI debut:* S. Campbell (Australia). *Goswami shook off her disappointment from two days earlier to produce a commanding new-ball display, and begin Australia's slide to their first ODI defeat in four years. They had chosen to bat, and Goswami soon despatched Haynes and Lanning; Mooney and Ashleigh Gardner turned things round with a partnership of 98, before seamer Pooja Vastrakar applied the brakes with a career-best 3-46. With India needing 265, Shafali Verma and Yastika Bhatia, who put on 101, each made a half-century, but the required rate was climbing. Then it was Carey's turn to reprieve a batter with a wicket off a no-ball – and Sneh Rana made her pay, striking three boundaries in the 47th. Fittingly, it fell to Goswami to make the winning hit.*

AUSTRALIA v INDIA

Test Match

At Carrara, September 30–October 3 (day/night). Drawn. Australia 2pts, India 2pts. Toss: Australia. Test debuts: D. R. Brown, S. Campbell, A. J. Sutherland, G. L. Wareham; Y. H. Bhatia, Meghna Singh.

The action moved to the Gold Coast for a day/night Test played with a pink ball on a drop-in pitch. Lanning put India in, hoping her tall fast bowlers, Darcie Brown and Stella Campbell – two of four Australian debutants – would find early movement; they didn't. Nerves might have played a part, as they repeatedly strayed short and wide. Mandhana, with her upright stance, seemed taller than she was, and had so much time to pull and cut. She found the boundary gracefully and repeatedly, batting throughout a rain-affected first day. Next morning, after she was caught off a Perry no-ball on 80, she went on to 127, the second century for India against Australia, after Sandhya Agarwal at Mumbai back in 1983-84.

The Indians eventually resorted to recklessness in the hope of ushering the game towards a result. Mandhana drove wildly to mid-off, and Raut walked after being given not out for a catch at the wicket. No batter fell to pace until well after the second new ball was taken, when Perry – improving with each spell – dismissed Yastika Bhatia, fourth out at 261. Rain intervened again, scotching nearly half the 200 overs scheduled for the first two days.

India finally called it quits after dinner on the third afternoon, having taken 145 overs to reach 377. The declaration allowed them to bowl just as the floodlights came in in the deepening dusk: Goswami dismissed openers Mooney and Healy, Meghna Singh

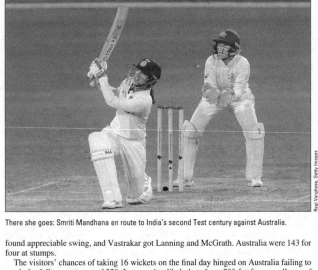

Regi Varghese, Getty Images

There she goes: Smriti Mandhana en route to India's second Test century against Australia.

found appreciable swing, and Vastrakar got Lanning and McGrath. Australia were 143 for four at stumps.

The visitors' chances of taking 16 wickets on the final day hinged on Australia failing to reach the follow-on target of 228. It seemed unlikely but, from 208 for four, a collapse of four for 15 meant they were five short of almost certain safety. But Perry was still there and, with an unbeaten 68, saw her team out of danger. Australia declared, 136 behind, in the vain hope of being set a target, but India, unable to score quickly enough, were not tempted. After Verma made a half-century, India eventually set Australia a notional 272 from 32 overs. Handshakes were offered before the final hour began. The overs lost – despite an extension to playing time, 83 were washed away – might have made all the difference.

Player of the Match: S. S. Mandhana.

Close of play: first day, India 132-1 (Mandhana 80, Raut 16); second day, India 276-5 (Sharma 12, T. Bhatia 0); third day, Australia 143-4 (Perry 27, Gardner 13).

India

S. S. Mandhana c McGrath b Gardner	127	– (2) c Gardner b Molineux	31
S. Verma c McGrath b Molineux	31	– (1) lbw b Wareham	52
P. G. Raut c Healy b Molineux	36	– (4) not out	41
*M. D. Raj run out (Sutherland)	30		
Y. H. Bhatia c Mooney b Perry	19	– (3) b Gardner	3
D. B. Sharma lbw b Campbell	66	– (5) not out	3
†T. Bhatia c Healy b Campbell	22		
P. Vastrakar c Mooney b Perry	13		
J. N. Goswami not out	7		
Meghna Singh not out	2		
B 3, lb 6, w 13, nb 2	24	B 5	5

1/93 (2) 2/195 (1) (8 wkts dec, 145 overs) 377 1/70 (2) (3 wkts dec, 37 overs) 135
3/217 (3) 4/261 (5) 2/74 (3) 3/122 (1)
5/274 (4) 6/319 (7) 7/359 (8) 8/369 (6)

R. S. Gayakwad did not bat.

Perry 27–4–76–2; Brown 10–0–49–0; Campbell 14–2–47–2; McGrath 16–3–40–0; Molineux 23–8–45–2; Gardner 30–11–52–1; Sutherland 17–6–31–0; Wareham 8–2–28–0. *Second innings*—Perry 5–1–14–0; Brown 4–0–15–0; Campbell 4–1–19–0; McGrath 2–0–6–0; Sutherland 2–0–10–0; Molineux 7–0–23–1; Gardner 10–1–31–1; Wareham 3–0–12–1.

Australia

†A. J. Healy c T. Bhatia b Goswami	29	– b Goswami	6
B. L. Mooney b Goswami	4	– c Gayakwad b Vastrakar	11
*M. M. Lanning lbw b Vastrakar	38	– not out	17
E. A. Perry not out	68	– not out	1
T. M. McGrath c Mandhana b Vastrakar	28		
A. K. Gardner c Raj b Sharma	51		
A. J. Sutherland c T. Bhatia b Meghna Singh	3		
S. G. Molineux lbw b Meghna Singh	2		
G. L. Wareham c T. Bhatia b Vastrakar	2		
D. R. Brown lbw b Sharma	8		
S. Campbell not out	0		
Lb 6, w 1, nb 1	8	Lb 1	1

1/14 (2) 2/63 (1)   (9 wkts dec, 96.4 overs) 241   1/8 (1) 2/28 (2) (2 wkts, 15 overs) 36
3/80 (3) 4/119 (5) 5/208 (6)
6/216 (7) 7/220 (8) 8/223 (9) 9/240 (10)

Goswami 22–7–33–2; Meghna Singh 19–2–54–2; Vastrakar 21.4–6–49–3; Gayakwad 18–1–63–0; Sharma 16–6–36–2. *Second innings*—Goswami 6–2–8–1; Meghna Singh 2–0–12–0; Vastrakar 5–1–13–1; Gayakwad 2–1–2–0.

Umpires: P. J. Gillespie and C. A. Polosak.   Third umpire: B. N. J. Oxenford.
Referee: R. W. Stratford.

First Twenty20 international   At Carrara, October 7, 2021 (floodlit). **No result. India 131-4** (15.2 overs) (J. I. Rodrigues 49*) **v ‡Australia.** *Australia 1pt, India 1pt. T20I debuts: H. J. Darlington, T. M. McGrath (Australia); Y. H. Bhatia, Renuka Singh (India). With India trailing 6–4 on points, but well set, rain again denied them a shot at victory. Harmanpreet Kaur, having recovered from a thumb injury, had returned to lead them, and was one of five batters to play a cameo as Jemimah Rodrigues extemporised for 49*. India were on track to improve their best score against Australia (177) when the weather stepped in.*

Second Twenty20 international   At Carrara, October 9, 2021 (floodlit). **Australia won by four wickets. India 118-9** (20 overs) (P. Vastrakar 37*); **‡Australia 119-6** (19.1 overs) (B. L. Mooney 34, T. M. McGrath 42*, R. S. Gayakwad 3-21). *Australia 2pts. PoM: T. M. McGrath. Australia remorselessly took advantage of India's run of bad fortune to claim an unbeatable points lead in the series. Pace did the damage, with Tayla Vlaeminck having both Indian openers caught within three overs. The visitors never recovered, despite Harmanpreet's rapid 28, and only a late attack from Vastrakar took the total to 118. India nearly defended it. Shikha Pandey's ball to dismiss Healy went viral on social media: angling away, it swung back from far outside off, seamed in further on pitching, and hit the top of middle. Rajeshwari Gayakwad then led the spinners in tightening the screws until Australia were 94-6, needing 25 from 20 balls. But McGrath, battering boundaries, came to the rescue again.*

Third Twenty20 international   At Carrara, October 10, 2021 (floodlit). **Australia won by 14 runs. Australia 149-5** (20 overs) (B. L. Mooney 61, T. M. McGrath 44*); **‡India 135-6** (20 overs) (S. S. Mandhana 52). *Australia 2pts. PoM: T. M. McGrath. With the series decided, the final match lacked urgency, though India still scrapped to get rid of Australia's top order cheaply – all except Mooney, who teamed up with the hard-hitting McGrath to set a target of 150. Mandhana scored 52, but took 49 balls, putting pressure on her partners, who succumbed to Australia's all-rounders. When she departed, India needed 58 from 31, and the game was up. The eventual margin of 14 runs flattered them: needing 36 from Carey's final over, Ghosh smacked a couple of sixes and a four. It wasn't enough but, as throughout the series, India had fought hard.*

ZIMBABWE v IRELAND IN 2021-22

One-day internationals (4): Zimbabwe 1, Ireland 3

Zimbabwe became the 17th country to field a women's one-day international team, and the first since Bangladesh in November 2011. They won their debut match, the fifth to achieve the feat, after England, Australia (both in 1973), South Africa (1997) and Bangladesh. Ireland had lost the last two of those games, and now made it three-times-unlucky against newcomers, but stormed back to win the remaining three matches. The series was bookended by two memorable centuries. Zimbabwe's Mary-Anne Musonda became the first captain to score a century on ODI debut. Also making her bow that day was 15-year-old Amy Hunter, a Belfast schoolgirl whose first three innings of two, one and four offered no clue as to what was to follow. In the final game, on her 16th birthday, she became the youngest cricketer – of either gender, in any format – to score a hundred in a senior international match.

First one-day international At Harare, October 5, 2021. **Zimbabwe won by four wickets. Ireland** 253-8 (50 overs) (L. K. Delany 88, S. M. Kavanagh 31); ‡**Zimbabwe** 254-6 (43.5 overs) (M. A. Musonda 103*, Extras 38). *PoM:* M. A. Musonda. *ODI debuts:* C. T. Dhururu, P. Marange, E. Mbofana, M. A. Musonda, P. Mujaji, M. Mupachikwa, A. R. Ndiraya, J. N. Nkomo, L. N. M. Phiri, N. Sibanda, L. Tshuma (Zimbabwe); G. Dempsey, A. Hunter, O. Prendergast, C. Raack (Ireland). *In Zimbabwe's first ODI, Mary-Anne Musonda, their captain, oversaw a tricky chase with a wise and well-paced 103*. Her bowlers had stuck at it after she won the toss, even as Laura Delany hit an 81-ball 88: seamer Loreen Tshuma conceded only 32 in her ten overs. Zimbabwe's target was 254 and, from 25-2, Musonda calmly took control, adding 57 with Ashley Ndiraya, 60 with Pellagia Mujaji and 57 with Josephine Nkomo. The chase had become a stroll by the time she reached her century from 110 balls.*

Second one-day international At Harare, October 7, 2021. **Ireland won by 80 runs. Ireland** 286-7 (50 overs) (L. Paul 96, G. H. Lewis 65, L. K. Delany 35, S. M. Kavanagh 34); ‡**Zimbabwe** 206-9 (50 overs) (J. N. Nkomo 70*; C. Murray 3-56). *PoM:* L. Paul. *ODI debut:* J. Maguire (Ireland). *Put in again, Ireland raised their game with an opening stand of 135 between Leah Paul and Gaby Lewis. Lewis's sprightly 65 was overshadowed by Paul's dominant 95, the highest score by an Ireland opener for 21 years (until Lewis surpassed her two days later). After Paul was caught behind, Delany and Shauna Kavanagh maintained the momentum, helping inflate the total to 286. Only once had Ireland scored more in an ODI: 309-2 against the Netherlands at Miskin, Wales, in 2005. Zimbabwe slid to 121-8, whereupon Nkomo – their most economical bowler – put on 69 with Nomvelo Sibanda. Her 70* ensured Zimbabwe salvaged some pride.*

Third one-day international At Harare, October 9, 2021. **Ireland won by eight wickets.** ‡**Zimbabwe** 178 (47 overs) (C. Raack 3-34); **Ireland** 179-2 (39 overs) (L. Paul 63, G. H. Lewis 96*). *PoM:* G. H. Lewis. *ODI debuts:* T. S. Granger, N. Gwanzura, A. T. Mazvishaya (Zimbabwe). *This time, Zimbabwe chose to bat, and had progressed to 76-2 in the 21st when Delany took the crucial wicket of Musonda; no one else passed 26. Celeste Raack's leg-breaks broke the middle order, and 178 was barely sufficient on a good surface. Paul and Lewis put that total into perspective with another century stand: their 145 was Ireland's second-highest opening partnership, after 181 between Anne Linehan and Mary-Pat Moore against Denmark in 1995. With the scores level, Lewis needed to clear the ropes for her maiden ODI hundred, but could manage only a single.*

Fourth one-day international At Harare, October 11, 2021. **Ireland won by 85 runs. Ireland** 312-3 (50 overs) (G. H. Lewis 78, A. Hunter 121*, L. K. Delany 68); ‡**Zimbabwe** 227-8 (50 overs) (A. R. Ndiraya 38, J. N. Nkomo 66, M. A. Musonda 36). *PoM:* A. Hunter. *PoS:* G. H. Lewis. *Amy Hunter, on her 16th birthday, became the youngest centurion, male or female, in international cricket. Batting at No. 3, she made 121* to carry Ireland to 312-3, their highest total. She added 104 with the in-form Lewis – whose third successive half-century took her to 263 runs in the series, both*

SIXTEEN-YEAR-OLD INTERNATIONAL CENTURIONS

16 years 0 days	A. Hunter......	**Ireland v Zimbabwe (ODI) at Harare**	**2021-22**
16 years 205 days	M. D. Raj	India v Ireland (ODI) at Milton Keynes........	1999
16 years 233 days	P. Alako	Uganda v Mali at (T20I) at Kigali	2019

Irish records – and 143 with Delany (68 off 53). "It's a bit surreal right now," said Hunter. "When I came to my hundred, I didn't know what to do – take my helmet off or keep it on – but it was unbelievable." Zimbabwe responded well: Nkomo scored her second fifty, and added 96 with Ndiraya; with pluck and resolve, the hosts batted through their overs again.

PAKISTAN v WEST INDIES IN 2020-21

Alex Brinton

One-day internationals (3): Pakistan 0, West Indies 3

When West Indies last visited Pakistan, in 2018-19, they played at Karachi's Southend Club; this time, they were upgraded to the National Stadium. Both teams were keen to use the series as a warm-up for the World Cup qualifiers in Zimbabwe a fortnight later, but Pakistan's preparations were disrupted when six players were forced to isolate, including Diana Baig and captain Javeria Khan, who sat out the first match; senior bowler Nida Dar also missed the series, following the death of her father. Pakistan had the leading wicket-taker in Anam Amin, who claimed nine at 11, but the West Indies' batting form – led by Deandra Dottin and Hayley Matthews, who combined for 302 runs – helped them to a clean sweep.

First one-day international   At Karachi, November 8, 2021. **West Indies won by 45 runs. West Indies 253-9** (50 overs) (D. J. S. Dottin 132, H. K. Matthews 57; Anam Amin 5-35); ‡**Pakistan 208-9** (50 overs) (Iram Javed 40, Aliya Riaz 46, H. K. Matthews 3-31). *PoM:* D. J. S. Dottin. *Deandra Dottin starred with a career-best 132, the fourth-highest innings for West Indies, and shared a third-wicket stand of 119 with Hayley Matthews; both were dismissed by slow left-armer Anam Amin, who took a career-best 5-35. Pakistan's chase of 254 never got going: Iram Javed and Aliya Riaz put on 57 for the fourth wicket, but were the only batters to reach 40, as Matthews claimed three.*

Second one-day international   At Karachi, November 11, 2021. **West Indies won by 37 runs. West Indies 153** (45.4 overs) (D. J. S. Dottin 34); ‡**Pakistan 116** (39.2 overs) (S. S. Connell 3-18, H. K. Matthews 4-26). *PoM:* H. K. Matthews. *Pakistan needed 43 from 14 overs with five wickets in hand, but capitulated to give West Indies the series. The tourists had been restricted to 153 by tight bowling from Anam and Nashra Sandhu, who both went for under three an over. Pakistan were sitting pretty at 111-5 after 36, but Matthews's dismissal of Fatima Sana triggered an astonishing collapse of five for five.*

Third one-day international   At Karachi, November 14, 2021. **West Indies won by six wickets. Pakistan 225-7** (50 overs) (Muneeba Ali 58, Aliya Riaz 44*); ‡**West Indies 226-4** (44 overs) (S. R. Taylor 102*, H. K. Matthews 49, C. N. Nation 51*). *PoM:* S. R. Taylor. *West Indies captain Stafanie Taylor lit up the final match with a spectacular unbeaten century, and guided her team to a 3–0 victory. Pakistan batted first this time, and opener Muneeba Ali made their only half-century of the series; all the top six chipped in to a competitive total of 225. Their hopes were raised when West Indies fell to 15-3, but Taylor serenely added 83 with Matthews and 128* with Chedean Nation, their fifth-wicket record.*

ZIMBABWE v BANGLADESH IN 2021-22

One-day internationals (3): Bangladesh 3, Zimbabwe 0

Little more than a month after their ODI debut, Zimbabwe were given a pasting by Bangladesh. Batting first in every match, they were all out three times while totalling 241; Bangladesh lost only six wickets in all. Their slow-left armer Nahida Akter filled her boots with 11 wickets at five; she was one of six to average under ten. For the hosts, Modester Mupachikwa hinted at batting ability, scoring 48 runs, and opening bowler Esther Mbofana showed accuracy, taking three wickets.

First one-day international   At Bulawayo, November 10, 2021. **Bangladesh won by eight wickets. Zimbabwe 48** (23.2 overs) (Jahanara Alam 3-18, Salma Khatun 3-6, Nahida Akter 3-2); ‡**Bangladesh 49-2** (10.4 overs). *PoM:* Jahanara Alam. *ODI debuts:* C. Chatonzwa, F. Chipare (Zimbabwe). *Zimbabwe were shot out for the lowest total in their nascent ODI history, as off-spinner Salma Khatun and left-arm spinner Nahida Akter combined for figures of 13.2–7–8–6. Only Precious Marange (17) reached double figures. Bangladesh sauntered to a paltry target.*

Second one-day international   At Bulawayo, November 13, 2021. **Bangladesh won by nine wickets. ‡Zimbabwe 121** (46.4 overs) (M. Mupachikwa 33, N. Gwanzura 35*; Nahida Akter 3-30); **Bangladesh 125-1** (Murshida Khatun 51*, Farzana Haque 53*) (24.3 overs). *PoM:* Farzana Haque. *ODI debut:* S. M. Mayers (Zimbabwe). *Zimbabwe made a better fist of things, though Salma and Nahida again posed problems, sharing five wickets. Nyasha Gwanzura applied herself, lasting 80 balls for 35*. A second-wicket stand of 115* between Murshida Khatun and Farzana Haque took Bangladesh home before the halfway point.*

Third one-day international   At Bulawayo, November 15, 2021. **Bangladesh won by seven wickets. ‡Zimbabwe 72** (27.2 overs) (S. M. Mayers 39; Nahida Akter 5-21); **Bangladesh 74-3** (18.2 overs) (Murshida Khatun 39*). *PoM:* Nahida Akter. *ODI debut:* Fariha Trisna (Bangladesh). *Once again, Zimbabwe had no answer to Nahida, who opened the bowling, claimed a career-best 5-21, and ran out Modester Mupachikwa. Opener Sharne Mayers top-scored with 39, and was ninth out. Bangladesh tried to get past 72 quickly, and lost three wickets on the way, but Zimbabwe soon fell to their sixth successive defeat.*

WOMEN'S WORLD CUP QUALIFIER IN 2021–22

This tournament was postponed twice, switched continents and folded halfway through because of a Covid outbreak, provoking an outcry from followers of women's cricket.

Originally scheduled for Sri Lanka in July 2020, it was initially delayed a year because of the pandemic, and later moved to Zimbabwe in November 2021. One of the ten teams, Papua New Guinea, pulled out a fortnight before the start when several players tested positive for Covid. The remaining sides played in two groups, to be followed by a Super Six: the top three would qualify for the World Cup in March 2022, and the next two would enter the Women's Championship in 2022–25, which was expanding from eight teams to ten.

On the penultimate day of the group rounds, Sri Lanka's match with West Indies was cancelled after positive tests in their camp. The other games went ahead but, by the time they finished, the ICC had called the tournament off. Apart from the cases affecting players, the spread of the Omicron variant had led to restrictions on travel from African countries, including Zimbabwe, and there were concerns the teams might be unable to get home.

The ICC determined the qualifiers through the official ODI rankings, which meant Bangladesh, Pakistan and West Indies would go to the World Cup, while Ireland and Sri Lanka joined the Women's Championship.

But there was general indignation at the injustice to Thailand, who had built on their encouraging performance at the Twenty20 World Cup in 2019-20 by beating Full Members Zimbabwe and Bangladesh, as well as the USA, and lost only to Pakistan. Because Thailand are not Full Members (a criterion based on men's cricket) they did not have ODI status or a ranking; this tournament was supposed to provide a route to both, and they seemed well on course before events off the field snatched away the chance until the next World Cup qualifying cycle. (The ICC also withdrew ODI status – originally promised to all the fixtures – from those involving the three Associate teams.)

Bangladesh pulled off a narrow win over Pakistan on the opening day, chasing down 202 thanks to an unbeaten fifty from Rumana Ahmed, only to succumb four days later to Thailand, whose seamer Nattaya Boochatham claimed five for 26. The other results were more predictable, with Associate sides the Netherlands and USA losing all their matches.

Group A	P	W	L	Pts	NRR	Group B	P	W	L	Pts	NRR
West Indies....	1	1	0	2	0.94	Thailand	4	3	1	6	0.48
Sri Lanka	1	1	0	2	0.77	Bangladesh	3	2	1	4	1.84
Ireland	2	1	1	2	−0.14	Pakistan.......	3	2	1	4	1.09
Netherlands ...	2	0	2	0	−0.67	Zimbabwe.....	3	1	2	2	−0.43
						USA	3	0	3	0	−3.61

Table shows all games played. Sri Lanka v West Indies was cancelled because of positive Covid tests, and the remaining group round and the Super Six were abandoned when the ICC called off the tournament.

WOMEN'S T20 WORLD CUP QUALIFIERS IN 2021

James Coyne

Most of the regional qualifiers were completed before the Omicron variant began to close borders once again. The European regional qualifier was moved from Scotland to La Manga in Spain, but the pitches were poor because staff had been furloughed. Turkey would have been the sixth European participants had their sports ministry been able to secure visas for Spain. Instead, it was France who assumed the role of plucky ingénues. Against the newcomers, Frédérique Overdijk of the Netherlands took seven for three, a T20 record for women or men. But France had an encouraging finale, when 23-year-old leg-spinner Marie Violleau, from Nantes – only a year of cricket and a few months of slow bowling under her belt – dismissed the accomplished Bryce sisters of **Scotland**, who won the competition.

The Americas qualifier was shifted from the USA to Mexico for ease of travel. For the first time in a decade, Argentina and Brazil had the chance to qualify for a women's World Cup. But on a spongy surface at the Reforma Athletic Club, Argentina were bundled out for 12 by their rivals. Brazil then stole second spot from Canada, in an incredible finish. Canada, chasing 49, needed three from the last over, bowled by 16-year-old seamer Laura Cardoso. After a dot ball, five wickets fell in consecutive deliveries: two run-outs bookended a hat-trick. The **USA** triumphed, as expected, boosted by Southern Vipers' Tara Norris, who had invoked her Philadelphian birthplace, and whose left-arm swing went at less than two an over. The USA's solitary defeat came after an unfathomable let-off for Canada's outstanding batter Divya Saxena. She skyed one, then ran towards the ball, distracting the converging fielders. Surprisingly, the umpires rejected an appeal for obstructing the field, and Saxena went on to play the decisive innings. If there was any unease, it wasn't evident in the post-tournament presentation, where Brazil captain Roberta Moretti Avery led all four teams in a chorus of *Alegria, alegria* ("joy" in Portuguese and Spanish), before her team-mates Erika Reinehr and Evelyn de Sousa put on a capoeira display.

To nobody's surprise, **Zimbabwe** advanced from the Africa region, and the **United Arab Emirates** pipped Hong Kong to the qualifying spot in the Asia competition. The sole victim of the pandemic was the Pacific qualifier, which was cancelled as the Omicron variant took hold; **Papua New Guinea** progressed as the team with the highest ranking.

REGIONAL QUALIFIERS

Africa (in Botswana, September 2021) **Group A** ZIMBABWE 10pts, TANZANIA 8, Rwanda 6, Botswana 4, Mozambique 2, eSwatini 0. **Group B** NAMIBIA 8pts, UGANDA 6, Nigeria 4, Sierra Leone 2, Cameroon 0. **Semi-finals** Zimbabwe beat Uganda; Namibia beat Tanzania. **Final** Zimbabwe beat Namibia. *Cameroon and eSwatini played their first T20 internationals.* **Qualified** Zimbabwe.

Americas (in Mexico, October 2021)   USA 10pts, Brazil 8, Canada 6, Argentina 0. **Qualified** USA.

Asia (in the UAE, November 2021)   UAE 10pts, Hong Kong 8, Nepal 6, Malaysia 4, Bhutan 2, Kuwait 0. **Qualified** UAE.

Europe (in Spain, August 2021)   SCOTLAND 8pts, Ireland 6, Netherlands 4, Germany 2, France 0. **Qualified** Scotland.

Pacific (in Samoa, September 2021)   Cook Islands, Fiji, Indonesia, Japan, Philippines, PAPUA NEW GUINEA, Samoa, Vanuatu. *Cancelled due to the pandemic; the highest-ranked team qualified.* **Qualified** Papua New Guinea.

GLOBAL QUALIFIER

The five regional qualifiers progressed to the Global Qualifier in July 2022, with the two lowest-placed teams from the T20 World Cup 2020 (Bangladesh and Thailand), and the next highest-ranked team (Ireland). Two teams from the Global Qualifier will reach the T20 World Cup in 2022.

THE INDOMITABLE LIONESS

Mankads can be beautiful too

MAEVA DOUMA

Taking the first wicket of the match on my Cameroon debut was incredible. But I could not have predicted how much more incredible the day would get. It was the women's T20 World Cup Africa regional qualifier in Botswana, in September, and Uganda had reached 153 for one. I noticed that their batters were backing up early, and the Mankad had worked for me before. Surely international players would be more careful, I thought. But I saw my chance, and took it with the third ball of the 16th over; two balls later, it worked again. It got even more extraordinary in the 20th over, when it worked twice more. I'd expected the non-strikers to get wise to the tactic, but they just kept leaving the crease. It had never happened more than once in an international match – that made getting four myself even more amazing.

I know it's a controversial mode of dismissal, but I don't see any problem. The Ugandans were disappointed to be out, but we all play by the same Laws, and they had to go. The batter is out of the crease and trying to get an advantage, and it is only right that the bowler has the chance to counter that. As a bowler, your priority is to get the batter on strike out. Against Sierra Leone, I took the first wicket by clean bowling their opener, as I had done against Uganda, and this is what really gives me pleasure. But if you see that the non-striker can be eliminated, then it is a beautiful opportunity to run her out.

I have spoken to many journalists since the match, and they were excited about what I did, rather than looking at the negative side. My team-mates supported me. I am sure opponents who have heard about our match against Uganda will now be more careful when I am bowling. That was certainly the case in our other three matches in Gaborone. I am still only 16, and very proud to have put Cameroon cricket in the public eye; I hope this will increase interest in cricket here. We love playing the game, and it means so much to represent our country. People might not like me Mankading, but I think it is a good tactic. I'm not going to stop.

Maeva Douma was speaking to John Wright.

OTHER WOMEN'S TWENTY20 INTERNATIONALS IN 2021

Zapped by Zepeda

It takes a hard heart not to have a soft spot for Thailand. Led by the irrepressible Naruemol Chaiwai, they continued to surprise and delight in equal measure. In August, they nearly beat Zimbabwe in the first meeting between the teams, then triumphed in the next two. In the opener, Zimbabwe were 72 for two but lost six for eight, before sneaking home by one wicket. Natthakan Chantham's unbeaten 88 set up a big total in the second game, as did Chanida Sutthiruang's whirlwind 46 not out in the third.

Having defeated Sri Lanka in 2018 and Ireland in 2019, Thailand have now beaten three Full Members, plus six of the eight leading Associates. Their record would be still better had the ICC not changed their mind about giving the women's World Cup qualifier – at which Thailand beat Bangladesh – full international status. Chaiwai's team ended 2021 ranked tenth in T20s.

In May, Ireland defeated Scotland 3–1 after losing the first game; in a low-scoring series, no batter reached 50, and Scotland never topped triple figures as Leah Paul took nine wickets at four. In July, Ireland beat the Netherlands 2–1 in a better series for the batters: Laura Delany made her only half-century of the year, as did Miranda Veringmeier and Babette de Leede (niece of former men's captain Tim) for the opposition. Gaby Lewis hit 325 runs at 40 in the calendar year.

But she was outscored by Andrea-Mae Zepeda, whose 361 at 51 led Austria to wins over Italy (3–2) and Belgium (3–0), both of whom played their first full women's internationals. Italy won their debut game, and successfully defended 99 (by one run) in their fifth. Belgium were zapped by Zepeda, who made 101, 65 and 84 not out, avenging Belgium's defeat of their men two months earlier; she was named ICC Women's Associate Cricketer of the Year.

In their 5–0 whitewash by Germany, France's batters reached 20 only three times in 37 innings; the team could muster no more than 85. Nepal thrice brushed Qatar aside, bowling them out for 27 in the first game. Sweden's first women's international was a success: they dismissed Norway for 52, and escaped to victory with two wickets in hand.

In the seventh edition of Rwanda's Kwibuka Cup, bat dominated ball to an almost ludicrous degree: Kenya's Sara Wetoto claimed 17 wickets at four, Victoria Hamunyela of Namibia took 15 at four, and Rwanda rolled Botswana for 29. There were just two half-centuries in the 14 games, both for Namibia: Sune Wittmann made 93 not out off 60 balls against Botswana, and Yasmeen Khan an unbeaten 78 to defeat Nigeria in the semi. Unbeaten all the way to the final, Namibia capitulated for 69 to Wetoto (six for 16), and Kenya grabbed the title.

REBEL WOMEN'S BIG BASH LEAGUE IN 2020-21

Daniel Cherny

1 Sydney Thunder   2 Melbourne Stars

Like so much of 2020, the sixth Women's Big Bash League was reshaped by Covid-19. In July, Cricket Australia had announced a relatively conventional schedule, with carnival weekends and matches staged in six states. But it soon became clear this was not feasible, especially once Victoria re-entered a hard lockdown. In September, CA bit the bullet, relocating the entire tournament to Sydney, where it would be held across five venues, with all eight teams based in a village in Sydney Olympic Park, and limited crowds.

Pulling all this off was no mean feat, given the still semi-professional nature of the competition. Many found hub life trying; one senior insider vowed never to do it again. And the early stages were marred by rain: eight of the first 13 fixtures produced no result.

Melbourne Stars shared the points in each of their first three games. But apart from the weather, not much could stop them during the round robin stage. Now coached by Trent Woodhill, the Stars – traditional stragglers – welcomed captain Meg Lanning and England all-rounder Nat Sciver back from Perth, and were catapulted up the table to reach the semi-finals for the first time. Lanning scored 493 runs, Sciver combined 252 runs and 19 wickets, and leg-spinner Alana King took 16 at 16. In the semi, they sailed past **Perth Scorchers**, who had recruited Australia opener Beth Mooney, the league's leading run-scorer with 551, and New Zealand's Sophie Devine, named Player of the Tournament again for her 460 runs and six wickets.

Though she led the Stars into their first final, Lanning's wait for a WBBL title continued when they succumbed to **Sydney Thunder** – inaugural winners in 2015-16 but empty-handed since. Thunder too had made useful acquisitions: England captain Heather Knight, who plundered 446 runs at 40, and, still more valuable, seamer Sammy-Jo Johnson, the tournament's leading wicket-taker with 22 at 14. They halted what looked like a match-winning run-chase by defending champions **Brisbane Heat** in the semi-final. Despite the loss of Johnson and Mooney, the Heat had finished second in the table, thanks to the spin of Jess Jonassen and Amelia Kerr.

The biggest disappointment was **Sydney Sixers** missing the knockouts for a second successive season, though this time it was down to net run-rate. The previous year they had been hit by an injury to Ellyse Perry; now they had no such excuse, with Perry and the hard-hitting Alyssa Healy among the top six scorers. Perry played the anchor role, but at times she weighed her side down: her 390 runs came at a strike-rate of just 96.

Adelaide Strikers also dropped out of the finals, with South Africa's Laura Wolvaardt replacing Devine but unable to emulate her consistency with the bat. **Hobart Hurricanes** floundered without Knight, finishing at the foot of the table. Just ahead were **Melbourne Renegades**; Amy Satterthwaite, back after maternity leave, struggled to find her best, while they badly missed Jess Duffin, who had given birth in June. In a curio of the hub-based league, New Zealander Rosemary Mair, one of a pool of replacement players, appeared for both Melbourne sides, after training with Perth Scorchers.

WOMEN'S BIG BASH LEAGUE AVERAGES IN 2020-21

BATTING (200 runs)

		M	I	NO	R	HS	100	50	Avge	SR	4	6
1	A. J. Healy (*Sydney S*) . . .	13	12	0	402	111	1	2	33.50	**161.44**	56	15
2	M. M. Lanning (*Melbourne S*)	15	14	2	493	77	0	6	41.08	127.72	66	10
3	S. F. M. Devine (*Perth S*) . .	12	12	3	460	103	1	3	51.11	126.37	42	18
4	H. C. Knight (*Sydney T*) . .	16	15	4	446	83	0	4	40.54	124.92	49	8
5	N. R. Sciver (*Melbourne S*)	14	13	6	252	47*	0	0	36.00	122.92	28	3
6	M. du Preez (*Melbourne S*)	15	13	1	380	61	0	4	31.66	122.58	46	6
7	L. Lee (*Melbourne R*)	13	12	0	261	79	0	1	21.75	121.96	28	10
8	E. J. Villani (*Melbourne S*)	15	14	1	360	56	0	2	27.69	120.80	51	7
9	†G. P. Redmayne (*Brisbane H*)	14	14	3	357	65	0	3	32.45	118.60	42	6
10	R. H. Priest (*Hobart H*) . .	13	13	3	354	92*	0	2	35.40	118.00	53	7
11	†B. L. Mooney (*Perth S*) . . .	14	14	4	551	75*	0	4	55.10	117.73	54	5
12	S. R. Taylor (*Adelaide S*) .	10	10	0	226	60	0	1	22.60	113.00	21	4
13	C. A. Webb (*Melbourne R*)	13	12	4	246	54*	0	1	30.75	112.32	17	6
14	†J. L. Jonassen (*Brisbane H*)	14	13	1	231	35	0	0	19.25	111.05	28	2
15	K. M. Mack (*Adelaide S*) .	14	12	0	251	58	0	2	20.91	109.60	27	1
16	†R. L. Haynes (*Sydney T*) . .	16	15	6	337	61*	0	2	37.44	109.41	35	6
17	L. Wolvaardt (*Adelaide S*)	14	14	1	347	68	0	2	26.69	104.83	28	8
18	E. A. Perry (*Sydney S*) . . .	13	12	4	390	72*	0	3	48.75	96.53	43	2
19	G. M. Harris (*Brisbane H*)	14	14	3	246	81*	0	2	22.36	95.71	25	7
20	†S. G. Molineux (*Melbourne R*)	12	11	0	221	52	0	1	20.09	93.24	29	0
21	R. C. Trenaman (*Sydney T*)	16	15	0	253	38	0	0	16.86	91.66	33	3
22	T. T. Beaumont (*Sydney S*)	16	15	0	209	30	0	0	13.93	90.47	24	2
23	T. M. McGrath (*Adelaide S*)	14	14	0	227	52	0	1	16.21	82.24	24	0
24	†A. E. Satterthwaite (*Melb R*)	13	12	2	204	48*	0	0	20.40	78.16	19	0

BOWLING (10 wickets, economy-rate 7.50)

		Style	Balls	Dots	R	W	BB	4I	Avge	SR	ER
1	A. C. Kerr (*Brisbane H*) .	LB	302	268	17	4-20	1	15.76	17.76	**5.32**
2	D. R. Brown (*Adelaide S*)	RFM	240	131	221	10	3-13	0	22.10	24.00	5.52
3	S. Ismail (*Sydney T*)	RF	306	163	284	14	3-10	0	20.28	21.85	5.56
4	S. L. Bates (*Sydney T*) . . .	RM	305	136	302	18	3-9	0	16.77	16.94	5.94
5	G. M. Harris (*Brisbane H*)	OB	138	60	137	13	4-16	1	10.53	10.61	5.95
6	A. M. King (*Melbourne S*)	LB	256	112	256	16	3-16	0	16.00	16.00	6.00
7	H. K. Matthews (*Hobart H*)	OB	192	82	193	12	3-15	0	16.08	16.00	6.03
8	M. Schutt (*Adelaide S*) . . .	RFM	293	164	295	11	3-7	0	26.81	26.63	6.04
9	T. C. J. Peschel (*Perth S*) . .	RM	276	147	282	13	2-5	0	21.69	21.23	6.13
10	M. Kapp (*Sydney S*)	RFM	246	136	252	13	3-14	0	19.38	18.92	6.14
11	H. J. Darlington (*Sydney T*)	RM	252	100	260	19	3-19	0	13.68	13.26	6.19
12	S. Glenn (*Perth S*)	LB	308	126	321	17	4-18	2	18.88	18.11	6.25
13	S. J. Coyte (*Adelaide S*) . .	RM	266	127	289	18	3-10	0	16.05	14.77	6.51
14	J. L. Jonassen (*Brisbane H*) .	SLA	264	116	287	17	4-28	1	16.88	15.52	6.52
15	S. J. Johnson (*Sydney T*) . .	RM	295	125	326	22	4-26	1	14.81	13.40	6.63
16	H. C. Knight (*Sydney T*) .	OB	138	37	153	10	3-4	0	15.30	13.80	6.65
17	S. Day (*Melbourne S*) . . .	SLA	208	71	231	11	3-16	0	21.00	18.90	6.66
18	N. R. Sciver (*Melbourne S*)	RM	270	113	302	19	4-29	1	15.89	14.21	6.71

		Style	Balls	Dots	R	W	BB	4I	Avge	SR	ER
19	N. M. Hancock (*Brisbane H*)	RM	223	110	252	11	2-16	0	22.90	20.27	**6.78**
20	H. L. Graham (*Perth S*) ..	RM	261	94	300	12	3-22	0	25.00	21.75	**6.89**
21	N. J. Carey (*Hobart H*) ...	RM	240	96	277	11	3-14	0	25.18	21.81	**6.92**
22	T. M. McGrath (*Adelaide S*)	RM	259	104	301	10	2-16	0	30.10	25.90	**6.97**
23	S. G. Molineux (*Melb R*) .	SLA	227	104	265	11	3-20	0	24.09	20.63	**7.00**
24	C. M. Leeson (*Melbourne R*)	RM	221	78	258	11	3-14	0	23.45	20.09	**7.00**
25	N. E. Bolton (*Perth S*) ...	RM	218	86	256	10	3-25	0	25.60	21.80	**7.04**
26	D. van Niekerk (*Sydney S*)	LB	247	78	300	10	2-24	0	30.00	24.70	**7.28**

WOMEN'S BIG BASH LEAGUE IN 2020-21

	P	W	L	NR/A	Pts	NRR
MELBOURNE STARS	14	8	3	3	19	0.96
BRISBANE HEAT..........	14	8	4	2	18	0.54
SYDNEY THUNDER	14	7	5	2	16	0.34
PERTH SCORCHERS........	14	6	6	2	14	0.35
Sydney Sixers	14	6	6	2	14	−0.08
Adelaide Strikers	14	6	7	1	13	0.13
Melbourne Renegades	14	4	8	2	10	−1.00
Hobart Hurricanes	14	3	9	2	8	−1.14

Semi-final   At North Sydney, November 25, 2020 (floodlit). **Melbourne Stars won by seven wickets. Perth Scorchers 125-8** (20 overs) (N. E. Bolton 32; A. M. King 3-16); ‡**Melbourne Stars 127-3** (16.2 overs) (N. R. Sciver 47*, A. J. Sutherland 30*). *PoM*: A. M. King. *Neither Sophie Devine nor Beth Mooney was able to break free from the Stars' grasp – there was only one boundary in the first 12 overs – and leg-spinner Alana King wreaked havoc from the moment she trapped Devine with her first delivery. A pearler from Heather Graham took out Meg Lanning's off stump, but Nat Sciver steered the Stars to a comfortable win, and their first WBBL final.*

Semi-final   At North Sydney, November 26, 2020 (floodlit). **Sydney Thunder won by 12 runs. Sydney Thunder 143-6** (20 overs) (R. L. Haynes 48*); ‡**Brisbane Heat 131** (18.3 overs) (L. M. Kimmince 37; H. J. Darlington 3-19). *PoM*: H. J. Darlington. *Brisbane Heat were eyeing a crack at a third successive title at 118-4, needing 26 from 30 balls. But there were two run-outs in the 16th over, before Hannah Darlington hit the stumps with consecutive deliveries in the 18th, and Sammy-Jo Johnson wrapped up victory with a low return catch. Rachael Haynes had steadied the Thunder's innings with 48*, though Amelia Kerr (1-19) and Nadine de Klerk (2-11) kept down the scoring-rate.*

FINAL

SYDNEY THUNDER v MELBOURNE STARS

At North Sydney, November 28, 2020 (floodlit). Sydney Thunder won by seven wickets. Toss: Melbourne Stars.

Melbourne Stars failed when it mattered most, scrabbling their way to 86 for nine, the lowest total in a WBBL final. It was the eighth time Meg Lanning had won the toss in this tournament: seven times she had chosen to field, but now – after six wins and a no-result – she decided to bat, and the Stars fell into a black hole. Shabnim Ismail made the most of the conditions, bowling her four overs off the reel, and removing Elyse Villani and Lanning cheaply. The tone was set as Ismail conceded only 12, and Sammy-Jo Johnson 11. A target of 87 posed little challenge, and the experienced pair of Heather Knight and Rachael Haynes guided the Thunder to their second title, with 38 balls in hand.

Player of the Match: S. Ismail.   *Player of the Tournament*: S. F. M. Devine (Perth Scorchers).

Melbourne Stars

		B	4/6
1 E. J. Villani c 5 b 10.	1	11	0
2 *M. M. Lanning c 7 b 10	13	15	1/1
3 M. du Preez lbw b 4	4	10	0
4 N. R. Sciver c 5 b 11	11	11	1
5 A. J. Sutherland c 5 b 9	20	20	1/1
6 A. M. King c 6 b 3	0	2	0
7 K. H. Brunt not out	22	27	0
8 E. A. Osborne c 5 b 4	6	11	0
9 T. Flintoff b 8	1	6	0
10 †N. M. Faltum run out (7/8) . .	3	7	0
Lb 3, w 2	5		

6 overs: 20-2　　　(20 overs)　　86-9

1/3 2/20 3/20 4/36 5/37 6/53 7/66 8/73 9/86

11 S. Day did not bat.

Ismail 24–16–12–2; Johnson 24–16–11–2; Bates 24–12–18–1; Darlington 24–12–15–1; Smith 12–6–18–1; Knight 12–4–9–1.

Sydney Thunder

		B	4/6
1 T. T. Beaumont lbw b 7	16	15	1/1
2 R. C. Trenaman c 1 b 9	23	26	5
3 H. C. Knight not out	26	19	2/1
4 S. J. Johnson b 6	1	5	0
5 *R. L. Haynes not out	21	17	2/1

6 overs: 30-1　　　(13.4 overs)　　87-3

1/24 2/44 3/54

6 P. E. S. Litchfield, 7 †T. B. Wilson, 8 H. J. Darlington, 9 L. G. Smith, 10 S. Ismail and 11 S. L. Bates did not bat.

Sciver 24–15–17–0; Brunt 24–11–24–1; King 22–11–30–1; Flintoff 6–3–6–1; Osborne 6–4–10–0.

Umpires: C. A. Polosak and E. Sheridan. Third umpire: A. K. Wilds.
Referee: S. R. Bernard.

WOMEN'S BIG BASH LEAGUE FINALS

2015-16　SYDNEY THUNDER beat Sydney Sixers by three wickets at Melbourne.
2016-17　SYDNEY SIXERS beat Perth Scorchers by seven runs at Perth.
2017-18　SYDNEY SIXERS beat Perth Scorchers by nine wickets at Adelaide.
2018-19　BRISBANE HEAT beat Sydney Sixers by three wickets at Sydney (Drummoyne Oval).
2019-20　BRISBANE HEAT beat Adelaide Strikers by six wickets at Brisbane (Allan Border Field).
2020-21　SYDNEY THUNDER beat Melbourne Stars by seven wickets at Sydney (North Sydney Oval).

WOMEN'S BIG BASH LEAGUE RECORDS

Highest score	114	A. K. Gardner	Sydney S v Melbourne S at North Sydney	2017-18
	112*	A. J. Healy. . .	Sydney S v Adel S at Sydney (Hurstville)	2018-19
	111	**A. J. Healy .**	**Sydney S v Melbourne S at North Sydney**	**2020-21**
	106*	A. J. Healy. . .	Sydney S v Melbourne Stars at Perth . .	2019-20
	106	A. J. Healy. . .	Sydney S v Adel S at Sydney (Hurstville)	2017-18
Fastest 50 – balls	22	A. K. Gardner	Sydney S v Melbourne S at North Sydney	2017-18
	22	L. Lee	Melbourne S v Sydney S at North Sydney	2017-18
Fastest 100 – balls	42	G. M. Harris .	Brisbane H v Melbourne S at Brisbane .	2018-19
Most sixes – innings	10	A. K. Gardner	Sydney S v Melbourne S at North Sydney	2017-18
Most runs – season	777	E. A. Perry (avge 86.33, SR 121.21) for Sydney S		2018-19
Most sixes – season	29	S. F. M. Devine for Adelaide S		2019-20
Most runs – career	3,127	**B. L. Mooney (avge 46.67, SR 121.72). . . .**		**2015-16 to 2020-21**
	3,002	E. A. Perry (avge 52.66, SR 104.27).		2015-16 to 2020-21
Most 100s – career	**4**	A. J. Healy		2015-16 to 2020-21
Best SR – career†	144.81	L. M. Kimmince (643 runs, avge 16.92) . .		2015-16 to 2020-21
Most sixes – career	106	S. F. M. Devine		2015-16 to 2020-21

Best bowling	5-15	M. R. Strano	Melb R v Melb S at Melbourne . .	2015-16
	5-17	A. E. Satterthwaite	Hobart H v Sydney T at Hobart . .	2016-17
	5-19	H. K. Matthews . .	Hobart H v Brisbane H at Hobart . .	2016-17
Most econ four overs	**3-7**	**M. Schutt. . . . . . .**	**Adel S v Syd S at Sydney (Drum).**	**2020-21**
	1-7	N. R. Sciver	Melb S v Melb R at Melbourne . .	2015-16
	1-7	K. M. Beams.	Melbourne S v Bris H at Mackay . .	2017-18
	0-7	L. M. M. Tahuhu .	Melbourne R v Sydney S at Geelong	2018-19
Most expensive analysis	2-54	S. G. Molineux . . .	Melbourne R v Bris H at Geelong .	2018-19
Most wickets – season	28	S. E. Aley (avge 11.75, ER 5.68) for Sydney S		2016-17
Most wickets – career	**104**	**M. R. Strano (avge 18.74, ER 6.52) . . . . . .**		**2015-16 to 2020-21**
	92	J. L. Jonassen (avge 21.22, ER 6.19)		2015-16 to 2020-21
	90	M. Kapp (avge 17.92, ER 5.31)		2015-16 to 2020-21
Best ER – career‡	5.16	J. L. Hunter (552 balls, avge 16.37)		2015-16 to 2017-18
Highest total	242-4	Sydney S v Melbourne S at North Sydney		2017-18
	206-1	Sydney S v Adelaide S at Sydney (Hurstville)		2018-19
	200-6	Sydney T v Melbourne R at North Sydney		2017-18
Lowest total	66	Hobart H v Sydney S at Brisbane		2016-17
	66	Brisbane H v Melbourne R at Melbourne (Dock)		2017-18
Highest successful chase	185-4	Melbourne R v Brisbane H at Brisbane (AB)		2019-20
Highest match aggregate	398-11	Sydney S v Melbourne S at North Sydney		2017-18

† *Career strike-rate: minimum 500 runs.*   ‡ *Career economy-rate: minimum 300 balls.*

WOMEN'S OVERSEAS DOMESTIC CRICKET IN 2020-21

AUSTRALIA

WOMEN'S NATIONAL CRICKET LEAGUE IN 2020-21

50-over league plus final

	P	W	L	T	A	Bonus	Adj	Pts	NRR
VICTORIA	8	6	2	0	0	3	–0.5	26.5	0.35
QUEENSLAND	8	4	3	0	1	4	0	21	1.15
Tasmania	8	4	3	1	0	1	0	19	–0.01
New South Wales	8	3	3	1	1	3	0	18	0.35
South Australia	8	4	4	0	0	2	0	18	0.15
Australian Capital Territory .	8	3	5	0	0	1	0	13	–0.64
Western Australia	8	2	6	0	0	2	–0.5	9.5	–1.00

Final   At St Kilda, March 27, 2021. **Queensland won by 112 runs. Queensland 317-8** (50 overs) (G. P. Redmayne 134*, M. C. Hinkley 53; K. J. Garth 3-45); ‡**Victoria 205** (42.4 overs) (C. G. Sippel 3-44, L. Mills 3-36, G. M. Harris 4-35). *Queensland won their first title, after New South Wales failed to reach the final for the first time in the WNCL's 25 seasons. Victoria had dominated the league, but lost more players to Australia's tour of New Zealand than their opponents – who had to pass a Covid test overnight when the rules for arrivals from Brisbane suddenly changed. Captain Georgia Redmayne batted throughout Queensland's innings for a career-best 134* and put on 111 with Mikayla Hinkley; she followed up with two catches and two stumpings as table-leaders Victoria were bowled out with seven overs to spare. Opener Elyse Villani was dismissed for 18, but her 611 runs equalled the third-highest total in a WNCL season, and made her Player of the Tournament.*

The Women's Big Bash League has its own section (page 1189).

INDIA

WOMEN'S SENIOR ONE-DAY TROPHY IN 2020-21

Six 50-over mini-leagues plus knockout

Elite A: JHARKHAND 16pts, ODISHA 16, Hyderabad 12, Gujarat 8, Chhattisgarh 4, Tripura 4.
Elite B: RAILWAYS 20pts, BENGAL 16, Haryana 12, Saurashtra 4, Assam 4, Uttarakhand 4.
Elite C: ANDHRA 20pts, Goa 12, Uttar Pradesh 12, Maharashtra 8, Rajasthan 4, Chandigarh 4.
Elite D: MADHYA PRADESH 16pts, Baroda 16, Kerala 12, Mumbai 12, Punjab 4, Nagaland 0. Madhya Pradesh advanced on head-to-head result.
Elite E: VIDARBHA 16pts, KARNATAKA 16, Delhi 12, Tamil Nadu 8, Himachal Pradesh 8, Meghalaya 0.
Plate: MIZORAM 20pts, Puducherry 20, Jammu & Kashmir 16, Bihar 12, Manipur 8, Sikkim 8, Arunachal Pradesh 0. Mizoram advanced on head-to-head result.

Play-off (third-best runner-up v Plate winner)   Odisha beat Mizoram by six wickets.
Quarter-finals   Jharkhand beat Karnataka by 20 runs, Railways beat Odisha by 68 runs, Andhra beat Vidarbha by 49 runs, Bengal beat Madhya Pradesh by 28 runs.
Semi-finals   Jharkhand beat Andhra by 27 runs, Railways beat Bengal by six wickets.

Final   At Rajkot, April 4, 2021. **Railways won by seven wickets.** ‡**Jharkhand 167** (50 overs) (S. Rana 3-33); **Railways 169-3** (37 overs) (S. Meghana 53, P. G. Raut 59). *Railways clinched their 12th title in the competition's 15th season (there was no winner in 2019-20, when the pandemic struck before the knockout stage). After Sabbhineni Meghana and Punam Raut shared a second-wicket stand of 107, they raced home with 13 overs in hand, as Sneh Rana hammered 34* in 22 balls. Earlier, Meghna Singh reduced Jharkhand to 30-3; Indrani Roy, the tournament's leading scorer, took her aggregate to 456 before she was stumped for 49, one of three victims for Rana.*

IRELAND

ARACHAS SUPER 50 CUP IN 2021

	P	W	L	NR/A	Pts	NRR
Scorchers	7	4	1	2	10	1.06
Typhoons	7	1	4	2	4	–1.06

ARACHAS SUPER 20 CUP IN 2021

	P	W	L	NR	Pts	NRR
Scorchers	6	4	1	1	9	0.56
Typhoons	6	1	4	1	3	–0.56

From 2015 to 2019, three teams played a combined 50-over/Twenty20 tournament, the Women's Super 3s. This was cut back to a 50-over competition for two sides in 2020, because of the pandemic, and in 2021 they contested two separate trophies. The Scorchers won both, with their captain, Gaby Lewis, scoring 405 runs in ten matches across the two formats, and off-spinner Eimear Richardson claiming 11 wickets in her four T20 games.

NEW ZEALAND

DREAM11 WOMEN'S SUPER SMASH IN 2020-21

20-over league plus knockout

	P	W	L	NR	Pts	NRR
CANTERBURY MAGICIANS . .	10	7	2	1	30	0.78
AUCKLAND HEARTS.	10	7	2	1	30	0.27
WELLINGTON BLAZE.	10	7	3	0	28	2.19
Northern Spirit	10	3	7	0	12	–0.86
Otago Sparks	10	3	7	0	12	–1.31
Central Hinds	10	2	8	0	8	–1.16

Play-off At Auckland, February 11, 2021. **Wellington Blaze won by 35 runs.** ‡**Wellington Blaze 150-6** (20 overs) (A. C. Kerr 54*); **Auckland Hearts 115-7** (20 overs). *Melie Kerr followed up her 44-ball 54* with 2-16, after Sophie Devine bowled Auckland opener Anna Peterson with the first delivery of the chase.*

Final At Wellington, February 13, 2021. **Canterbury Magicians won by four wickets. Wellington Blaze 125-8** (20 overs) (A. E. Satterthwaite 3-13); ‡**Canterbury Magicians 126-6** (19.4 overs) (A. C. Kerr 3-19). *Once Devine fell for 49, Wellington collapsed from 100-1 in the last six overs, with New Zealand captain Amy Satterthwaite claiming three wickets in eight balls – only for Canterbury to stagger to 60-6. Jess Kerr dismissed Satterthwaite for a duck, and her sister Melie claimed a hat-trick, all bowled by googlies. But Kate Ebrahim (45*) and Lea Tahuhu (38* off 20, including three sixes) steered them home in the final over. This was Canterbury's fifth Super Smash title, one behind Wellington.*

HALLYBURTON JOHNSTONE SHIELD IN 2020-21

50-over league plus final

	P	W	L	Bonus	Pts	NRR
CANTERBURY	10	7	3	5	33	0.96
AUCKLAND	10	7	3	5	33	–0.11
Central Districts	10	7	3	4	32	0.87
Northern Districts	10	5	5	4	24	0.16
Wellington.	10	4	6	3	19	–0.16
Otago.	10	0	10	0	0	–1.97

Final At Auckland, March 21, 2021. **Canterbury won by eight wickets.** ‡**Auckland 185** (47.5 overs) (K. T. Perkins 52; A. E. Satterthwaite 4-27); **Canterbury 188-2** (37.4 overs) (F. L. Mackay 94*, A. E. Satterthwaite 73). *Satterthwaite dominated Canterbury's charge to their second trophy of the season: she took four wickets to wrap up Auckland's innings, before sharing a second-wicket stand of 166 with captain Frankie Mackay. It was their 38th outright title in the original women's competition, going back to the 1940s, when matches were staged over two or three days, and their third double; Satterthwaite and Mackay had featured in all three, going back to 2007-08.*

PAKISTAN

PCB TRIANGULAR T20 WOMEN'S TOURNAMENT IN 2020-21

	P	W	L	NR/A	Pts	NRR
CHALLENGERS	4	2	0	2	6	0.28
DYNAMITES	4	2	1	1	5	0.17
Blasters	4	0	3	1	1	−0.39

Final At Rawalpindi, December 1, 2020. **Challengers won by seven runs. Challengers 133-7** (20 overs) (Subhana Tariq 3-37); ‡**Dynamites 126-6** (20 overs). *The Challengers claimed a narrow win, though none of their players bettered Kainat Hafeez's 31 in 27 balls or Syeda Aroob Shah's 2-21. For the Dynamites, leg-spinner Subhana Tariq claimed her only three wickets of the tournament, while opener Nahida Khan's 39, with two sixes, made her the leading run-scorer, with 154 from four matches.*

SOUTH AFRICA

CSA WOMEN'S PROVINCIAL PROGRAMME IN 2020-21

The 50-over Provincial League was cancelled because of the pandemic. Instead, the 16 teams played in four pools, with play-offs to settle promotion and relegation issues for 2021-22. The Provincial T20 competition was also cancelled.

WOMEN'S T20 SUPER LEAGUE IN 2020-21

	P	W	L	Pts	NRR
Coronations	3	2	1	4	1.05
Thistles	3	2	1	4	−0.20
Starlights	3	1	2	2	−0.16
Duchesses	3	1	2	2	−0.68

Thistles headed the table going into the final round, but collapsed for 44 in reply to Coronations' 103-9, enabling Coronations – whose line-up included internationals Laura Wolvaardt, Nadine de Klerk and Ayabonga Khaka – to win the league by virtue of that head-to-head result.

SRI LANKA

WOMEN'S DIVISION ONE IN 2020-21

50-over league

	P	W	L	Bonus	Pts	NRR
Navy	7	7	0	5	33	1.89
Air Force A	7	6	1	5	29	1.27
Army A	7	5	2	5	25	1.14
Chilaw Marians	7	4	3	2	18	−0.47
Seenigama	7	2	5	2	10	−0.57
Air Force B	7	2	5	1	9	−1.04
Colts	7	1	6	1	5	−1.16
Army B	7	1	6	0	4	−0.97

The Navy and Army A met in the final round, in a match that would decide the title. Chasing 139, the Navy recovered from 62-6 to scrape home by two wickets, thanks to 43 from Shashikala Siriwardene, preserving their 100% record. Slow left-arm Inoka Ranaweera's 4-27 in Army A's innings ensured she was the tournament's leading wicket-taker, with 25. Meanwhile, Air Force A finished runners-up after bowling out Army B for 92.

ZIMBABWE

FIFTY50 CHALLENGE IN 2020-21

	P	W	L	Pts	NRR
MOUNTAINEERS	6	4	2	40	0.33
RHINOS	6	4	2	40	0.31
Eagles	6	3	3	30	0.57
Tuskers	6	1	5	10	−1.37

Final   At Harare (Takashinga), December 6, 2020. **Mountaineers won by 62 runs** (DLS). **Rhinos 210** (46.2 overs) (J. N. Nkomo 85; F. Chipare 5-29); ‡**Mountaineers 198-4** (37.2 overs) (C. S. Mugeri-Tiripano 85). *Zimbabwe Cricket staged two new women's tournaments in tandem, with teams playing T20 and 50-over matches on successive days. Mountaineers won the inaugural Fifty50 Challenge. When rain ended play, they were well ahead of par, thanks to an opening stand of 126 in 25 overs from Chipo Mugeri-Tiripano and Loryn Phiri (43). Rhinos had relied heavily on Josephine Nkomo, the Player of the Tournament with 294 runs in all, but once she was out they collapsed from 182-3 to 210; Francesca Chipare cleaned up with 5-27.*

WOMEN'S T20 CUP IN 2020-21

	P	W	L	NR	Pts	NRR
EAGLES	6	4	1	1	9	0.71
TUSKERS	6	3	3	0	6	−0.47
Mountaineers	6	2	3	1	5	−0.04
Rhinos	6	2	4	0	4	−0.10

Final   At Harare (Takashinga), December 5, 2020. **Eagles won by eight wickets**. ‡**Tuskers 78-6** (20 overs); **Eagles 81-2** (14.1 overs). *Modester Mupachikwa led Eagles to the title, scoring 47* in 42 balls to complete the chase with 35 balls to spare. Seamer Precious Marange had taken 2-6 from her four overs as Tuskers struggled to 78.*

THE WOMEN'S HUNDRED IN 2021

Isabelle Westbury

1 Oval Invincibles   2 Southern Brave   3 Birmingham Phoenix

Revolution is rarely neat and tidy. Proponents of the women's game had, and still have, many reservations about The Hundred; they were not held only by stalwart supporters of the men's county sides. And yet its first edition was hailed as a triumph for women's cricket.

There were caveats. The Hundred's success was in part down to the contrast with what came before. The wider impact on the women's game, its grassroots, and club cricket, will take time to manifest. Heather Knight, the England captain who also led **London Spirit**, had already spoken about English cricket's failure to capitalise on the 2017 World Cup triumph. This time, she hoped, it would be different.

The Hundred was the first major tournament to include a women's competition alongside the men's from the off. (In Australia, the women's BBL kicked off four years after the men's; the IPL had yet to announce a women's league.) It pierced the public consciousness in the UK, something men's cricket had managed only rarely since the 2005 Ashes. A women's fixture was chosen for the opening game, a day before the men's equivalent, and the gamble paid off. It was a high-scoring match, with a family-friendly atmosphere, won by **Oval Invincibles** – the eventual champions – against **Manchester Originals**. And it was broadcast live on BBC Two. The double-headers for the remaining 33 fixtures also worked: high-profile television and radio personalities hired primarily for the men's games covered the women's too, and match reports included both.

It was not initially intended for women's fixtures to be staged as the first half of double-headers at the eight Test venues. But Covid intervened, and the ECB were keen to simplify logistics. They also marketed the tournaments as one, and ensured equal provision of training facilities, accommodation, transport and much else.

While the final was one-sided – thanks to a bowling masterclass from the Invincibles, and a batting calamity for the runaway table leaders **Southern Brave** – the standard was mostly high. In the absence of Australia's top players – withdrawn because of quarantine concerns ahead of their home series against India – other nationalities provided much of the entertainment. Dane van Niekerk, the South African captain, was named the Most Valuable Player after leading the Invincibles to the title and scoring 259 runs, more than anyone else. Just behind was **Northern Superchargers'** opener Jemimah Rodrigues, who revived her India prospects with three half-centuries, including 92 not out – the highest score of The Hundred, matched by the highest men's score – and caught the public imagination with her innovative strokeplay.

The calibre of Australia's second-tier players, drafted in as late replacements, demonstrated what a successful domestic competition might do for the

Too quick: Dane van Niekerk runs out Fi Morris in the final, and Oval Invincibles are one wicket from victory over Southern Brave.

English game. **Birmingham Phoenix's** Eve Jones, uncapped despite years of service to the domestic game, finished with 233 runs (fourth overall, and behind only one English player, the Brave's Sophia Dunkley). Among the bowlers, Tash Farrant (another Invincible) was the leading wicket-taker, with 18, and Kirsty Gordon's 15 for the Phoenix put her joint-second with Australian Sammy-Jo Johnson. Both Farrant and Gordon had lost England contracts, but forced their way back into the conversation. Invincibles opener Alice Capsey, who turned 17 during the tournament, hit the headlines with a rapid fifty on her Lord's debut, and later added the most economical 20-ball analysis – two for nine – with her off-spin. While **Trent Rockets** brought up the rear of the chasing pack, and **Welsh Fire** propped up the table, their better moments did not come solely from their internationals. A greater spread of success stories was an improvement on the Kia Super League, which ran from 2016 to 2019.

The women's Hundred contrasted with the men's, where crowds – critics quickly observed – continued to be largely composed of young men out for a good time, not a long time. But the earlier start of the women's matches, and their more approachable feel, helped create a carnival atmosphere for families; the fact that the tournament took place during the school holidays was also a boon. So-called fan experiences – food, music and games to accompany the on-field action – might be a distraction for the seasoned spectator, but formed part of the allure for the uninitiated. The ice-cream queues routinely outstripped those for beer. The gender of the players racing around in their brightly coloured shirts mattered little: this was new and thrilling, and young fans could make it their own.

Another significant difference from the men's game was that the best-known English cricketers are not primarily identified with their counties, where there has been no lasting legacy for women. That meant the storm of debate around the death of county cricket – *men's* county cricket – hardly brushed the women's game.

There were still unknowns. The absence of a marquee domestic T20 competition involving international players, after the KSL was sacrificed on the Hundred's altar, was part of the collateral damage, which may have ramifications at international level. And while a lot of money was spent on marketing and broadcasting, embarrassingly little reached the players. Though it was trumpeted that the prize money was the same in both tournaments, equal pay remained a long way off, with even the highest-paid women behind the lowest-paid men. But the women's arm is an integral part of the Hundred's commercial package, not an add-on – and it proved just as much a success as the men's equivalent. The pay issue had to be addressed, quickly.

There should also be a sharp eye on the evolution of the men's Hundred. For both arms to thrive, the tournament needs to retain its one-club, two-teams feel. Much was made of what the women's game might learn from the men's, but this flowed both ways, on and off the field. There was a close relationship between the teams at each club (in part dictated by Covid precautions), and a new interest in the women's game from men, including players, who had not been bothered before.

The Hundred was not made for women. It is not a beacon of gender equality. But the departure from the gendered structures of county cricket means the gap is closing faster than ever.

THE WOMEN'S HUNDRED IN 2021

	P	W	L	A	Pts	NRR
SOUTHERN BRAVE	8	7	1	0	14	21.12
OVAL INVINCIBLES	8	4	3	1	9	0.30
BIRMINGHAM PHOENIX	8	4	4	0	8	3.71
London Spirit	8	4	4	0	8	0.91
Manchester Originals	8	3	4	1	7	0.31
Northern Superchargers	8	3	4	1	7	−0.81
Trent Rockets	8	3	4	1	7	−5.86
Welsh Fire	8	2	6	0	4	−20.34

Net run-rate calculated per 100 balls rather than per five-ball over.

Prize money

£150,000 for winners: OVAL INVINCIBLES.
£75,000 for runners-up: SOUTHERN BRAVE.
£50,000 for third place: BIRMINGHAM PHOENIX.
£10,000 for Most Valuable Player: D. van Niekerk (Oval Invincibles).
£5,000 for leading run-scorer: D. van Niekerk (Oval Invincibles) 259.
£5,000 for leading wicket-taker: N. E. Farrant (Oval Invincibles) 18.
£5,000 for leading fielder: K. L. George (Welsh Fire).
£5,000 for Moment of The Hundred: D. van Niekerk (Oval Invincibles) – winning four in opening match v Manchester Originals.

THE WOMEN'S HUNDRED AVERAGES IN 2021

BATTING (100 runs)

		M	I	NO	R	HS	50	Avge	SR	4	6
1	D. R. Gibson (*Spirit*)	8	8	5	108	34*	0	36.00	**180.00**	16	2
2	A. E. Jones (*Phoenix*)	9	8	1	176	42*	0	25.14	**155.75**	25	2
3	J. I. Rodrigues (*Superchargers*)	7	7	1	249	92*	3	41.50	**150.90**	41	1
4	S. Verma (*Phoenix*)	8	8	1	171	76*	1	24.42	**142.50**	24	2
5	S. I. R. Dunkley (*Brave*)	9	9	3	244	58*	2	40.66	**141.86**	30	3
6	N. R. Sciver (*Rockets*)	8	7	0	220	54	1	31.42	**136.64**	32	2
7	R. H. Priest (*Rockets*)	8	7	0	138	76	1	19.71	**136.63**	20	5
8	†S. S. Mandhana (*Brave*)	7	7	1	167	78	2	27.83	**133.60**	17	6
9	H. L. Graham (*Rockets*)	8	7	2	125	44*	0	25.00	**132.97**	13	2
10	H. C. Knight (*Spirit*)	8	8	1	214	40	0	30.57	**130.48**	30	1
11	D. N. Wyatt (*Brave*)	9	9	1	208	69*	1	26.00	**129.19**	25	6
12	A. R. Capsey (*Invincibles*)	10	8	1	150	59	1	21.42	**126.05**	23	0
13	E. L. Lamb (*Originals*)	7	7	0	135	46	0	19.28	**125.00**	19	2
14	L. Lee (*Originals*)	7	7	2	215	68	1	43.00	**124.27**	31	3
15	M. Kapp (*Invincibles*)	5	5	1	150	38	0	37.50	**122.95**	17	4
16	E. A. Burns (*Phoenix*)	9	8	1	156	45	0	22.28	**121.87**	23	0
17	H. K. Matthews (*Fire*)	8	8	1	221	71*	1	31.57	**119.45**	30	3
18	L. Winfield-Hill (*Superchargers*)	7	7	0	118	64	1	16.85	**119.19**	14	2
19	†E. Jones (*Phoenix*)	9	9	1	233	64	2	29.12	**118.27**	34	3
20	D. J. S. Dottin (*Spirit*)	8	8	1	146	50*	1	20.85	**117.74**	21	3
21	L. Wolvaardt (*Superchargers*)	7	7	2	181	75*	1	36.20	**116.77**	24	1
22	B. F. Smith (*Fire*)	8	8	0	137	38	0	17.12	**115.12**	16	4
23	S. J. Johnson (*Rockets*)	8	7	0	120	33	0	17.14	**114.28**	10	7
24	H. Kaur (*Originals*)	3	3	1	104	49*	0	52.00	**109.47**	10	0
25	†G. P. Redmayne (*Fire*)	8	8	2	187	38*	0	31.16	**107.47**	21	0
26	D. van Niekerk (*Invincibles*)	10	9	3	259	67*	2	43.16	**105.71**	32	2
27	G. L. Adams (*Invincibles*)	10	9	1	133	42	0	16.62	**105.55**	18	1
28	T. T. Beaumont (*Spirit*)	6	6	0	139	42	0	23.16	**102.96**	11	1
29	A. N. Davidson-Richards (*Super*)	7	7	3	110	42	0	27.50	**102.80**	9	1
30	M. du Preez (*Originals*)	7	7	3	118	31	0	29.50	**101.72**	11	2
31	S. R. Taylor (*Brave*)	9	9	5	182	45*	0	45.50	**101.67**	15	1
32	K. M. Mack (*Phoenix*)	9	8	0	100	31	0	12.50	**101.01**	9	0
33	F. C. Wilson (*Invincibles*)	10	9	0	108	25	0	12.00	**92.30**	14	0
34	K. H. Brunt (*Rockets*)	8	7	1	120	43*	0	20.00	**89.55**	12	0

BOWLING (100 balls)

		Style	Balls	Dots	R	W	BB	4I	Avge	SR	ER
1	D. B. Sharma (*Spirit*)	OB	155	69	136	10	2-10	0	13.60	15.50	**87.74**
2	A. R. Capsey (*Invincibles*)	OB	135	61	122	10	2-9	0	12.20	13.50	**90.37**
3	S. Ismail (*Invincibles*)	RFM	115	69	105	3	1-14	0	35.00	38.33	**91.30**
4	A. Wellington (*Brave*)	LB	175	78	161	14	4-12	2	11.50	12.50	**92.00**
5	L. C. N. Smith (*Superchargers*)	SLA	132	60	122	9	3-14	0	13.55	14.66	**92.42**
6	A. Shrubsole (*Brave*)	RFM	155	79	146	9	4-13	1	16.22	17.22	**94.19**
7	S. Ecclestone (*Originals*)	SLA	140	70	141	5	2-11	0	28.20	28.00	**100.71**
8	N. E. Farrant (*Invincibles*)	LFM	179	82	185	18	4-10	1	10.27	9.94	**103.35**
9	D. van Niekerk (*Invincibles*)	LB	150	50	165	8	3-30	0	20.62	18.75	**110.00**
10	E. A. Burns (*Phoenix*)	OB	135	50	154	7	2-15	0	22.00	19.28	**114.07**
11	K. H. Brunt (*Rockets*)	RFM	127	62	145	5	2-19	0	29.00	25.40	**114.17**
12	S. J. Johnson (*Rockets*)	RFM	134	52	154	15	4-15	1	10.26	8.93	**114.92**
13	K. A. Levick (*Superchargers*)	LB	130	50	150	7	2-16	0	21.42	18.57	**115.38**
14	F. R. Davies (*Spirit*)	RFM	127	60	147	5	1-19	0	29.40	25.40	**115.74**
15	L. K. Bell (*Brave*)	RFM	165	75	191	12	3-22	0	15.91	13.75	**115.75**
16	C. E. Dean (*Spirit*)	OB	142	57	168	6	2-22	0	28.00	23.66	**118.30**
17	F. M. K. Morris (*Brave*)	OB	130	42	155	4	2-17	0	38.75	32.50	**119.23**

		Style	Balls	Dots	R	W	BB	4I	Avge	SR	ER
18	K. L. Cross (*Originals*)	RFM	136	62	169	12	3-19	0	14.08	11.33	124.26
19	K. L. Gordon (*Phoenix*).	SLA	170	62	212	15	3-14	0	14.13	11.33	124.70
20	H. K. Matthews (*Fire*)	OB	149	47	186	11	3-23	0	16.90	13.54	124.83
21	A. M. Maqsood (*Phoenix*)	LB	150	39	191	4	2-14	0	47.75	37.50	127.33
22	E. L. Arlott (*Phoenix*)	RFM	117	51	150	6	2-30	0	25.00	19.50	128.20
23	E. A. Russell (*Superchargers*) . .	RM	105	38	135	2	1-24	0	67.50	52.50	128.57
24	S. R. Taylor (*Brave*)	OB	115	39	148	3	1-15	0	49.33	38.33	128.69
25	M. K. Villiers (*Invincibles*) . . .	OB	125	47	163	6	2-19	0	27.16	20.83	130.40
26	A. Hartley (*Originals*)	SLA	135	42	179	8	3-29	0	22.37	16.87	132.59
27	G. A. Elwiss (*Phoenix*)	RFM	136	41	183	4	2-27	0	45.75	34.00	134.55
28	P. M. Cleary (*Fire*)	RM	130	63	175	6	2-21	0	29.16	21.66	134.61
29	I. E. C. M. Wong (*Phoenix*). . .	RFM	137	53	192	6	2-23	0	32.00	22.83	140.14
30	G. M. Hennessy (*Fire*)	RFM	110	37	155	2	2-24	0	77.50	55.00	140.90
31	S. Glenn (*Rockets*)	LB	125	39	178	5	1-17	0	35.60	25.00	142.40
32	B. F. Smith (*Fire*)	OB	134	49	193	4	1-16	0	48.25	33.50	144.02
33	A. N. Davidson-Richards (*Super*)	RFM	111	35	164	7	2-17	0	23.42	15.85	147.74

Economy-rate calculated per 100 balls rather than per five-ball over.

LEADING WICKETKEEPERS

Dismissals	M	
11 (8ct, 3st)	10	S. J. Bryce (*Invincibles*)
10 (2ct, 8st)	9	C. E. Rudd (*Brave*)
7 (4ct, 3st)	7	E. Threlkeld (*Originals*)

Dismissals	M	
7 (1ct, 6st)	9	A. E. Jones (*Phoenix*)
6 (1ct, 5st)	8	R. H. Priest (*Rockets*)

LEADING FIELDERS

Ct	M	
6	8	D. R. Gibson (*Spirit*)
6	9	M. E. Bouchier (*Brave*)

Ct	M	
6	10	A. R. Capsey (*Invincibles*)
6	10	G. J. Gibbs (*Invincibles*)

At The Oval, July 21 (floodlit). **Oval Invincibles won by five wickets. ‡Manchester Originals 135-6** (100 balls) (L. Lee 42; N. E. Farrant 3-25); **Oval Invincibles 139-5** (98 balls) (D. van Niekerk 56*, M. Kapp 38; K. L. Cross 3-28). PoM: D. van Niekerk. *Attendance:* 7,395. *The Hundred got off to a triumphant start as a surprisingly partisan crowd roared Oval Invincibles to a tense victory with two balls to spare. At 36-4 after 32, with three wickets for Manchester Originals captain Kate Cross, the Invincibles were hardly living up to their name. But Dane van Niekerk and Marizanne Kapp, the married couple from South Africa, responded with a stand of 73 in 50 balls, before Mady Villiers nervelessly helped van Niekerk over the line. Earlier, Kapp – who bowled the first ten balls of the tournament, from the Pavilion End – had taken two wickets, and Tash Farrant three, as the Originals made 135. Lizelle Lee's 42 was the largest contribution, Harmanpreet Kaur's 16-ball 29 the most languid. By the end, the outcome seemed incidental. "We were making history tonight, and the result was almost irrelevant," said Cross. Van Niekerk agreed: "The atmosphere was electric." This was a standalone game: the men's competition started the next day.*

At Birmingham, July 23. **London Spirit won by three wickets. Birmingham Phoenix 128-6** (100 balls) (E. Jones 47, A. E. Jones 33); **‡London Spirit 132-7** (96 balls) (N. D. Dattani 34). PoM: E. Jones. *Attendance:* 12,137. *Set 129, the Spirit were given a flying start by Naomi Dattani, but the fizz went out of their chase, and they careered from 81-2 to 124-7. They reached their target, however, thanks to No. 9 Danielle Gibson hitting her first two balls to the rope. Earlier, the Phoenix had also meandered, with the rest of the team unable to keep up with the Joneses: Eve and Amy (33 from 17) added 64 for the fourth wicket, but no one else passed 13. From 101-4 with 23 left, they should have made more than 128.*

At Nottingham, July 24. **Southern Brave won by 23 runs. Southern Brave 133-5** (100 balls) (S. R. Taylor 45*, A. Shrubsole 40*); **‡Trent Rockets 110-7** (100 balls) (N. R. Sciver 44; A. Shrubsole 4-13). PoM: S. R. Taylor. *Attendance:* 12,783. *A fine all-round performance by Southern Brave's captain Anya Shrubsole ensured they got off to a winning start. Entering at 57-5, she smacked 40**

Order of the Phoenix: Evelyn Jones, wicketkeeper Amy Jones and Abtaha Maqsood celebrate a wicket, as Birmingham Phoenix defend a total of 113 against Manchester Originals.

from 30 balls, and put on 76* with Stafanie Taylor (who later bowled tightly for 1-26). Then she had figures of 20–13–13–4, including wickets with three of the game's last four balls. Trent Rockets had looked in touch only while Nat Sciver was hitting 44 from 29, with eight fours. Southern Brave leg-spinner Amanda-Jade Wellington's 20–11–10–0 included a (five-ball) maiden.

At Leeds, July 24. **Northern Superchargers won by six wickets. Welsh Fire 130-8** (100 balls) (H. K. Matthews 30; L. C. N. Smith 3-14); ‡**Northern Superchargers 131-4** (85 balls) (J. I. Rodrigues 92*). *PoM:* J. I. Rodrigues. *Attendance: 10,324. Northern Superchargers were 19-4 after 18 balls, but Jemimah Rodrigues hit a sparkling 92* in 43, which would remain The Hundred's highest score (later equalled by Liam Livingstone). After a poor run for India, it was a return to form. She shared the first century partnership of the women's tournament with Alice Davidson-Richards, who contributed 23 as they coasted home. Welsh Fire openers Bryony Smith (19 in 11) and Hayley Matthews (30 in 20) had begun brightly but, after a couple of strikes from leg-spinner Katie Levick, the middle order lost momentum against Linsey Smith's slow left-armers.*

At Lord's, July 25. **Oval Invincibles won by 15 runs. Oval Invincibles 132-7** (100 balls) (A. R. Capsey 59); ‡**London Spirit 117-7** (100 balls) (H. C. Knight 40, D. R. Gibson 30*; D. van Niekerk 3-30). *PoM:* A. R. Capsey. *Attendance: 12,378. Sixteen-year-old Alice Capsey lit up Lord's on a grey afternoon with a brilliant 41-ball 59 studded with ten fours, to set the Invincibles up for victory in the tournament's first London derby. Capsey, awaiting her GCSE results, was the youngest to make fifty in a competitive game at Lord's, beating John Murray of Middlesex in 1952. "It's so historic," she said. "Even walking through the Long Room to go to the pitch brings its own excitement." Among her team-mates, only van Niekerk (29) passed 12. London Spirit never came close. Van Niekerk's leg-breaks brought three wickets, including England captain Heather Knight, who top-scored with 40, and late blows from Gibson (30* off 13) only narrowed the margin of defeat. The ECB later said they would reconsider their ticketing policy after more than 13,000 spectators were offered a full refund because the subsequent men's game was rained off. Had the men's game taken place, and the women's been abandoned, there would have been no refund.*

At Manchester, July 25. **Birmingham Phoenix won by 20 runs. ‡Birmingham Phoenix 113-9** (100 balls) (A. E. Jones 31; E. L. Lamb 3-16); **Manchester Originals 93-8** (100 balls) (H. Kaur 49*; K. L. Gordon 3-14). *PoM:* K. L. Gordon. *Attendance: 13,537. On a used pitch taking spin from the start, the Phoenix defended a modest 113. Their innings relied on another brisk thirty from Amy Jones, and an inventive 20 from Gwenan Davies, but the dangerous Shafali Verma never got going.*

The Manchester slowers sent down 65 balls, and together took 5-58; Emma Lamb, whose off-breaks claimed 3-16, became the first to bowl successive sets from different ends. The Phoenix also opened with spin, and left-armer Kirstie Gordon had a hand in the first three wickets, including a diving catch at extra cover. She and leg-spinner Abtaha Maqsood shared 5-28. Even Harmanpreet struggled for timing, and the rate ran away from the Originals, who proved the only team (male or female) to bat 100 balls for under 100.

At Nottingham, July 26. **Northern Superchargers won by 27 runs.** ‡**Northern Superchargers 149-7** (100 balls) (L. Winfield-Hill 33, J. I. Rodrigues 60, L. M. Kimmince 31; S. J. Johnson 4-15); **Trent Rockets 122-7** (100 balls) (N. R. Sciver 33, K. H. Brunt 43*). *PoM:* J. I. Rodrigues. *Attendance:* 11,483. *Led by Rodrigues, who stroked 60 from 41 balls with ten fours, and Laura Kimmince's blitz of 31 from 13, the Superchargers completed a second comfortable victory. Although Australian seamer Sammy-Jo Johnson ended with 20–9–15–4, a target of 150 always looked beyond the Rockets, especially once Sciver fell for 33. Katherine Brunt clouted 43* but, with spinners Linsey Smith (20–9–12–1) and Levick (20–10–20–2) clamping down, the closing stages were a formality.*

At Cardiff, July 27. **Southern Brave won by eight wickets. Welsh Fire 110-7** (100 balls) (H. K. Matthews 33); ‡**Southern Brave 112-2** (84 balls) (S. S. Mandhana 61*). *PoM:* S. S. Mandhana. *Attendance:* 3,021. *Matthews made another forceful start – she hit half Welsh Fire's 12 fours – after Shrubsole chose to bowl. But once 20-year-old seamer Lauren Bell (2-19) dismissed her and Sarah Taylor in two balls, they were 52-4 from 49. Georgia Hennessy (23*) nudged them into three figures. A key moment in Southern Brave's chase came when Nicole Harvey had Smriti Mandhana (then 26) badly dropped at deep midwicket. She did have Sophia Dunkley (16) caught at cover next ball, but Mandhana surged on to 61* in 39, sealing victory with her third six.*

At Manchester, July 28. **Manchester Originals v Northern Superchargers. Abandoned.** *This was the first of the women's matches to be affected by rain; the men's fixture was also washed out.*

At Lord's, July 29. **Trent Rockets won by 18 runs.** ‡**Trent Rockets 151-4** (100 balls) (R. H. Priest 76, N. R. Sciver 32); **London Spirit 133-7** (100 balls) (H. C. Knight 31). *PoM:* R. H. Priest. *Attendance:* 23,892. *Rachel Priest came good after two failures, cracking an imperious 42-ball 76, all but 12 in boundaries; she and the steadier Johnson put on 101 for the first wicket. With Sciver contributing a brutal 32, the Rockets became the first women's side to make 150. The Spirit used seven bowlers, but not Deandra Dottin, at the request of Cricket West Indies. Halfway through their reply, the Spirit were an encouraging 70-2, but Dottin was run out off the 51st for 29, and the zip went out of the innings. Pick of the bowlers was off-spinner Lucy Higham (2-12).*

At Southampton, July 30. **Southern Brave won by eight wickets. Birmingham Phoenix 140-4** (100 balls) (E. Jones 33, A. E. Jones 42*, K. M. Mack 31); ‡**Southern Brave 141-2** (82 balls) (D. N. Wyatt 69*, S. I. R. Dunkley 41). *PoM:* D. N. Wyatt. *Attendance:* 11,778. *Danni Wyatt thrashed 69* from 40, with four sixes and five fours, to make light of a testing target of 141 and give Southern Brave three wins out of three. She put on 60 for the second wicket with Dunkley, who hit seven fours but was unluckily run out when Maqsood dropped a return chance from Wyatt, which cannoned into the stumps. The Phoenix had earlier made a solid start, but Wellington (20–8–16–2) removed Verma and Eve Jones, before a stand of 72 from 43 between Amy Jones and Katie Mack.*

At Cardiff, July 31. **Welsh Fire won by nine wickets. Manchester Originals 120-6** (100 balls) (S. Ecclestone 31*); ‡**Welsh Fire 124-1** (88 balls) (H. K. Matthews 71*, G. P. Redmayne 38*). *PoM:* H. K. Matthews. *Attendance:* 5,286. *A second-wicket stand of 101* in 71 balls between Matthews (71* off 50) and Georgia Redmayne (38*) lifted Welsh Fire to their first victory, and kept their opponents winless. Lee had hit the first two balls of Manchester Originals' innings for four, only to be run out off the third; the next boundary did not come until the 37th delivery, by which time they had crept to 31-2. Sophie Ecclestone's late cameo (31* off 15) gave the Originals a semblance of a target to defend, and her left-arm spin proved hard to hit: 20–8–14–0. But the Fire could not be put out.*

At Leeds, July 31. **Northern Superchargers won by four runs. Northern Superchargers 109-8** (100 balls) (A. N. Davidson-Richards 42); ‡**Oval Invincibles 105-4** (100 balls). *PoM:* A. N. Davidson-Richards. *Attendance:* 10,859. *A low-scoring game produced the competition's closest result, though it was enough to put Northern Superchargers top of the table with their third win. Their hero was Davidson-Richards, who rescued them from 78-6 with a 30-ball 42, in a match where* *no one else reached 30. She then restricted Oval Invincibles to five off the last five deliveries of their innings, dismissing Sarah Bryce (29) and denying van Niekerk (27*) the strike. Earlier, the Invincibles' 16-year-old opening bat Capsey bowled for the first time, in her third game, and her off-breaks earned the tournament's most economical figures: 20–11–9–2.*

At Birmingham, August 1. **Trent Rockets won by 11 runs.** ‡**Trent Rockets 145-5** (100 balls) (H. L. Graham 44*); **Birmingham Phoenix 134-9** (100 balls) (S. J. Johnson 3-28). *PoM:* H. L. Graham. *Attendance:* 17,479. *The Rockets enjoyed another healthy opening stand between Johnson (29) and Priest (18), this time worth 46. Sciver, dropped on nine, kept the innings ticking, before Heather Graham gave it a hefty late boost. She whipped 44* from 21, as 63 came off the last 32. Issy Wong was removed from the attack for bowling two full tosses above waist height. In the Phoenix reply, Verma briefly looked a threat until a Brunt slower ball breached her defences. Johnson took three as wickets fell regularly, and the result was clear before Wong walloped 27 from 11.*

At Lord's, August 1. **Southern Brave won by seven wickets. London Spirit 93** (96 balls) (T. T. Beaumont 34; A. Wellington 4-14); ‡**Southern Brave 97-3** (92 balls). *PoM:* A. Wellington. *Attendance:* 23,436. *London Spirit became the first team bowled out in the women's tournament. Almost two-thirds of their 93 came either from Tammy Beaumont, who took 45 balls to compile 34, or Extras (27, including 25 in wides). Wellington began with a run-out, and added four wickets, among them Knight and Beaumont; her 14 dot balls included a maiden set. Southern Brave's 25-ball powerplay brought only 24-1 – six fewer than the Spirit's – as Deepti Sharma tied them in knots. Even so, Stafanie Taylor (29*) and Maia Bouchier (15*) completed the Brave's fourth straight victory. A crowd of 15,189 was believed to be the biggest for a women's domestic match in England; 15,000 were reported to have watched a Roses match in 1949, at Roundhay Park in Leeds. The record would be beaten within three weeks.*

At The Oval, August 2. **Welsh Fire won by 12 runs. Welsh Fire 112-6** (100 balls) (G. P. Redmayne 30); ‡**Oval Invincibles 100-9** (100 balls) (H. K. Matthews 3-23). *PoM:* S. J. Taylor. *Attendance:* 21,279. *A sluggish pitch made hitting difficult: Welsh Fire found the boundary only eight times to Oval Invincibles' ten. Matthews and Redmayne put on 47 in 31 balls, but the boost came from Sarah Taylor (29 off 24). Missed at long-on when 12, she danced down the pitch to drive, and improvised reverse hits over short third man. Hennessy was run out by a superb direct hit from wicketkeeper Bryce. Her opposite number, Taylor, put on an exemplary display in the defence of 112-6, which included running out Georgia Adams behind her back, as Welsh Fire's inspirational fielding kept their opponents at bay. Katie George stood out with a diving catch at deep midwicket off van Niekerk, followed by a brilliant reflex grab, at the third attempt, to dismiss Villiers – and the Invincibles proved not to be.*

At Lord's, August 3. **London Spirit won by seven wickets.** ‡**Northern Superchargers 126-5** (100 balls) (J. I. Rodrigues 57); **London Spirit 129-3** (98 balls) (T. T. Beaumont 42, D. J. S. Dottin 50*). *PoM:* D. J. S. Dottin. *Attendance:* 22,889. *Dottin's 34-ball 50* ensured the Superchargers slipped to their first defeat, though she inadvertently breached regulations on head protection by dispensing with her helmet when the Spirit required six off four: she hit the next two to the boundary. The result was tough on Rodrigues, whose 57 off 44 was her third half-century in four innings, and Linsey Smith, whose 2-15 included England captain Knight.*

At Birmingham, August 4. **Oval Invincibles won by eight wickets.** ‡**Birmingham Phoenix 129-9** (100 balls) (E. A. Burns 45; N. E. Farrant 3-23); **Oval Invincibles 133-2** (97 balls) (G. L. Adams 42, D. van Niekerk 67*). *PoM:* N. E. Farrant. *Attendance:* 14,653. *The scale of the Invincibles' victory was better expressed by wickets in hand (eight) than balls remaining (three). Needing 130, they timed their response to perfection, and reached 90 before losing Adams for 42, though she had twice been given a life in the field. Van Niekerk, however, kept going, finishing with 67* from 51. She had also helped rein the Phoenix in: the most economical bowler on either side, she sent down 20 balls of leg-spin for a return of 2-16. Farrant claimed three of the top seven. Without Erin Burns, the hosts would have struggled to make three figures.*

At Manchester, August 5. **Manchester Originals won by 17 runs** (DLS). **Southern Brave 123-7** (100 balls) (H. E. Jones 3-17, A. Hartley 3-29); ‡**Manchester Originals 97-1** (70 balls) (L. Lee 43*, E. L. Lamb 32). *PoM:* L. Lee. *Attendance:* 11,660. *The fifth round brought Manchester Originals' first win, and Southern Brave's first defeat. Hannah Jones, making her tournament debut, dismissed* *both Brave openers – Mandhana and Wyatt – and later bowled Shrubsole, matching fellow slow left-armer Alex Hartley's haul of three, as the visitors slid from 113-3 to 118-7. Lee and Lamb led the Originals' response, opening with 52 in 38 balls; Lee had advanced her own score to 43* when rain ended play, with Manchester comfortably ahead on DLS.*

At Cardiff, August 6. **Trent Rockets won by four wickets. Welsh Fire 102** (100 balls) (S. J. Johnson 3-24, H. L. Graham 3-14); **‡Trent Rockets 103-6** (92 balls) (N. R. Sciver 54). *PoM:* N. R. Sciver. *Attendance:* 5,112. *Trent Rockets made it three in a row after Welsh Fire collapsed. Openers Bryony Smith (27 off 16) and Matthews (28) put on 34, which improved to 75-2 with 39 balls remaining. Graham began the slide by having Matthews caught slicing to short third man; Sciver dived full length to catch Sophie Luff, and Priest pulled off three smart stumpings, as the last eight fell for 27. Requiring 103, the Rockets stumbled to 16-2, but Sciver (54 in 40) added 66 with Brunt to put the result beyond doubt.*

At Southampton, August 7. **Southern Brave won by seven wickets** (DLS). **Northern Superchargers 76-3** (73 balls); **‡Southern Brave 89-3** (62 balls) (S. I. R. Dunkley 50*, M. E. Bouchier 33*). *PoM:* S. I. R. Dunkley. *Attendance:* 10,712. *Dunkley's sparkling 50* off 28 took the Brave three points clear at the top after they made light work of a rain-affected chase. At 26-3 in pursuit of a revised 89 off 75, with two wickets for off-spinner Kalea Moore, they were struggling, but Bouchier (33* off 19) joined Dunkley in a stand of 63*. The Superchargers' innings had been curtailed after 73 deliveries; no one managed better than a run a ball.*

At The Oval, August 8. **Oval Invincibles v ‡Trent Rockets. Abandoned.** *Rain began after the Rockets decided to bat.*

At Birmingham, August 9. **Birmingham Phoenix won by ten wickets. Welsh Fire 127-9** (100 balls) (B. F. Smith 38); **‡Birmingham Phoenix 131-0** (76 balls) (S. Verma 76*, E. Jones 52*). *PoM:* S. Verma. *Attendance:* 17,778. *Verma, whose previous five innings for Birmingham Phoenix had totalled 71, came good at last, smashing a 22-ball fifty, the fastest of the tournament. She finished with 76* from 42 in an opening stand of 131* with Eve Jones (52* in 35). That brought two records: the highest partnership in The Hundred, by women or men, and the only ten-wicket win. For Welsh Fire, Bryony Smith alone passed 19, before she succumbed to the first of three run-outs.*

At Manchester, August 10. **London Spirit won by five wickets. ‡Manchester Originals 127-5** (100 balls) (E. L. Lamb 39, M. du Preez 31, S. Ecclestone 32*); **London Spirit 131-5** (98 balls) (H. C. Knight 35, D. B. Sharma 34*; A. Hartley 3-32). *PoM:* D. B. Sharma. *Attendance:* 14,864. *Lamb had scored 23 of the Originals' 30-0 when her opening partner, Lee, was lbw to Sharma for a seven-ball duck. Sharma conceded only ten, and had the dangerous Mignon du Preez brilliantly held in the deep by Gibson. Ecclestone's 32* included an imperious four and six down the ground, to help post a competitive 127-5. Cross and Hartley, close friends and co-presenters of the No Balls podcast, shared all the wickets as London Spirit slipped to 87-5, despite Knight's 35. They wanted 41 from 30, and Sharma took them home with 34*.*

At Southampton, August 11. **Southern Brave won by 39 runs. Southern Brave 166-3** (100 balls) (D. N. Wyatt 53, S. S. Mandhana 78); **‡Welsh Fire 127-4** (100 balls) (B. F. Smith 33, G. P. Redmayne 35*, S. N. Luff 30). *PoM:* S. S. Mandhana. *Attendance:* 11,449. *Southern Brave reached the final after a dominant opening stand of 107 off 69 between Wyatt (53 off 34) and Mandhana (78 off 52, after being caught off a Piepa Cleary no-ball on five). Their eventual total of 166-3 was comfortably the tournament's highest. Facing elimination, and devoid of confidence, Welsh Fire were never on terms. The Brave's opening pair of Shrubsole and Bell had combined figures of 30–11–33–0, Stafanie Taylor took 1-15 off 15, and no one made more than Redmayne's 35*.*

At Leeds, August 12. **Manchester Originals won by eight wickets. Northern Superchargers 126-5** (100 balls) (L. Wolvaardt 75*; K. L. Cross 3-19); **‡Manchester Originals 127-2** (86 balls) (L. Lee 68). *PoM:* K. L. Cross. *Attendance:* 12,538. *This match was dominated by a Mancunian bowler and two South African batters. Cross, the Mancunian, removed her fellow captain Lauren Winfield-Hill in her first set, then two more of the Superchargers' top order in her second, which – in the new parlance – she extended to a double-wicket maiden tenner. With Eleanor Threlkeld stumping the tournament's top scorer Rodrigues for seven, the Superchargers were drowning at 16-4. Laura Wolvaardt, though, revived them with a majestic 75* from 51 balls, even if 126 felt light – as Lee, her fellow South African, quickly proved. When she fell for a 40-ball 68, the score was 102-2, and victory assured.*

At Nottingham, August 13. **Birmingham Phoenix won by three wickets. Trent Rockets 125-7** (100 balls) (A. J. Freeborn 30; K. L. Gordon 3-26); ‡**Birmingham Phoenix 129-7** (94 balls) (E. A. Burns 38; S. J. Johnson 3-22). *PoM:* E. A. Burns. *Attendance:* 12,694. *Birmingham Phoenix were struggling at 71-6 chasing 126, but Burns stood her ground, and added 48 with Emily Arlott. With seven required, though, Burns holed out to become Johnson's third victim; Arlott would have been a fourth had a return catch not gone down, but she hit the next two deliveries for four. Earlier, Gordon had claimed three middle-order wickets, and Mack effected two run-outs, but a stand of 54 between Graham (26) and Abigail Freeborn gave Trent Rockets something to bowl at.*

At The Oval, August 14. **Oval Invincibles won by eight wickets. London Spirit 103-9** (100 balls) (T. T. Beaumont 42, H. C. Knight 34); ‡**Oval Invincibles 107-2** (87 balls) (G. L. Adams 37*). *PoM:* G. L. Adams. *Attendance:* 19,673. *Oval Invincibles' stunning fightback in the field put the mockers on London Spirit, triggering a collapse of eight for 23, and paving the way for a straightforward chase. Things had started well for the visitors, Beaumont and Knight sharing 11 fours in a second-wicket stand of 76 off 55. Beaumont's innings of lofted drives and hard sweeps was ended by Jo Gardner's bulletlike direct hit and, under pressure, no one else could find the rope. Between them, Capsey, Kapp and Shabnim Ismail sent down 60 balls for just 42. Though their total was weak, the Spirit were willing, and their hopes strengthened when van Niekerk was soon caught behind. Sharma conceded only 11, but Adams guided the Invincibles home.*

At Nottingham, August 15. **Manchester Originals won by nine wickets. Trent Rockets 122-6** (100 balls) (S. J. Johnson 33); ‡**Manchester Originals 124-1** (L. Lee 47*, E. L. Lamb 46). *PoM:* L. Lee. *Attendance:* 12,388. *The Originals were already out, but now dragged the Rockets down with them, thanks to a punishing opening stand of 96 in 67 balls between Lee and Lamb (46 off 31). The Rockets had been given a quick start by Johnson, who hit four sixes in her 20-ball 33, but made little headway against Ecclestone, whose 2-11 included 14 dots. A total of 122 felt at least 20 light, and the Rockets compounded a careless batting display by donating 16 in wides.*

At Southampton, August 16. **Southern Brave won by 30 runs. Southern Brave 115-3** (100 balls) (S. I. R. Dunkley 58*); ‡**Oval Invincibles 85** (94 balls) (D. van Niekerk 31; L. K. Bell 3-22, A. Wellington 4-12). *PoM:* S. I. R. Dunkley. *Attendance:* 9,204. *Southern Brave, already in the final, roundly beat the Invincibles, who had already booked their place in the eliminator thanks to Trent Rockets' defeat the previous day. On a slow pitch, scoring was never easy, though Dunkley – reprieved on two and 30 – enjoyed Villiers's off-breaks, which she hit for 25 from ten balls. More circumspect against others, she finished on 58* from 39. Then came a tour de force from Wellington. She came on after the powerplay, and immediately broke through. Almost unreadable in her flight, she took another in her third set to spark panic – and two more in her last, as the Brave hurtled from 64-2 to 85 all out, including an eight-ball sequence of five for one. If the Brave looked invincible, the Invincibles looked timorous.*

At Leeds, August 17. **Birmingham Phoenix won by 14 runs. Birmingham Phoenix 147-4** (100 balls) (E. Jones 64); ‡**Northern Superchargers 133-6** (100 balls) (L. Winfield-Hill 64, L. Wolvaardt 32). *PoM:* E. Jones. *Attendance:* 12,260. *Both sides were fighting for a place in the knockout: Birmingham Phoenix were almost there after a third successive win and Northern Superchargers' fourth successive defeat. Verma hit the first two balls of the match for four, then was caught low at short midwicket off the third. But Amy Jones kept up the momentum with 24 off 11, and the innings was anchored by opener Eve Jones, who struck 64 off 47, with three sixes. The Superchargers were on course as Winfield-Hill raced to 64 off 38 but, once she fell to a diving catch at third man, they tumbled from 97-1 to 119-5, with only one boundary in 31 deliveries. Barring a miracle for London Spirit the following day, the Phoenix would meet the Invincibles in the play-off.*

At Cardiff, August 18. **London Spirit won by seven wickets. Welsh Fire 95-9** (100 balls) (G. P. Redmayne 35); ‡**London Spirit 96-3** (58 balls) (H. C. Knight 34*, D. R. Gibson 34*). *PoM:* D. R. Gibson. *Attendance:* 9,261. *Welsh Fire, already nailed to the bottom of the table, completed an unhappy tournament. There was a glimpse of promise at 45-1, Bryony Smith having struck three early fours, and Redmayne reaching 35, but it was snuffed out by a collapse of eight for 46 in 60 balls. London Spirit's six-woman attack was a model of economy: nobody went for more than 1.10 runs per ball. Needing to reach their target of 96 from just 41 to progress to the eliminator, the Spirit had a go. Knight and Gibson, who had identical scores of 34* off 19 with seven fours, added 60 in 33, but at the crucial point they were still 33 short. Their victory was thus both a formality and a disappointment: they were pipped by Birmingham Phoenix – their equal on points and wins – by 2.8 runs per 100 balls.*

ELIMINATOR

OVAL INVINCIBLES v BIRMINGHAM PHOENIX

At The Oval, August 20. Oval Invincibles won by 20 runs. Toss: Birmingham Phoenix.

Kapp took charge of a low-scoring knockout with a doughty all-round contribution that propelled the Invincibles into the final. Opting to bowl on a slow pitch, the Phoenix despatched Adams and van Niekerk early. Kapp decided that batting the overs was the smart move, and provided glue; while Wilson and Capsey supplied pep. But it took the Invincibles 91 balls to reach 100, and four wickets fell in a late clatter. A target of 115 was eminently gettable, even after Kapp swiftly sent back Mack and Eve Jones; an untroubled stand of 52 between Amy Jones and Burns took the Phoenix to 66 for two. But Kapp returned to get rid of Burns, courtesy of a Farrant screamer at mid-off – and it proved the turning point, as eight fell for 28 in 45 balls. Farrant mopped up with four for ten, and Kapp held the winning catch to usher her team to Lord's.

Player of the Match: N. E. Farrant.   *Attendance:* 21,458.

Oval Invincibles

		B	4/6
1 G. L. Adams c 3 b 7	4	4	1
2 *D. van Niekerk c 6 b 9	2	7	0
3 F. C. Wilson c and b 10	21	17	4
4 M. Kapp c 9 b 4	37	37	4/1
5 A. R. Capsey run out (1/10)	26	20	3
6 M. K. Villiers c 1 b 10	4	7	0
7 J. L. Gardner run out (5/8)	2	2	0
8 G. J. Gibbs not out	6	12	6
9 †S. J. Bryce not out	0	0	0
Lb 1, w 5	6		

25 balls: 23-2   (100 balls) 114-7

1/5 2/15 3/36 4/90 5/100 6/100 7/106

10 N. E. Farrant and 11 S. Ismail did not bat.

Wong 15–8–27–1; Arlott 15–10–11–1; Gordon 20–8–22–2; Maqsood 15–7–18–0; Elwiss 20–5–22–0; Burns 15–5–13–1.

Birmingham Phoenix

		B	4/6
1 K. M. Mack c 9 b 4	0	3	0
2 E. Jones c 9 b 4	0	1	0
3 *†A. E. Jones c 2 b 10	35	25	6
4 E. A. Burns c 10 b 4	23	22	4
5 G. M. Davies c 9 b 10	12	16	2
6 M. Kelly c and b 2	4	7	0
7 I. E. C. M. Wong b 11	1	3	0
8 G. A. Elwiss c and b 5	2	3	0
9 E. L. Arlott c 11 b 10	2	7	0
10 K. L. Gordon c 4 b 10	5	6	0
11 A. M. Maqsood not out	1	1	0
B 3, lb 2, w 4	9		

25 balls: 30-2   (94 balls) 94

1/0 2/14 3/66 4/66 5/81 6/84 7/85 8/87 9/93

Kapp 15–7–21–3; Ismail 20–13–15–1; Farrant 19–13–10–4; van Niekerk 20–4–25–1; Capsey 20–9–18–1.

Umpires: R. J. Bailey and A. C. Harris.   Third umpire: N. L. Bainton.
Referee: T. J. Boon.

FINAL

OVAL INVINCIBLES v SOUTHERN BRAVE

Raf Nicholson

At Lord's, August 21. Oval Invincibles won by 48 runs. Toss: Southern Brave.

A tournament that had drawn huge crowds culminated with a record 17,116 spectators witnessing the first domestic women's final at Lord's – and an upset, with favourites Southern Brave skittled for 73. Shrubsole had opted to bowl; her experience and the youth of Lauren Bell had made a formidable new-ball pairing in the league games, and Bell's first set of five was a maiden, while Shrubsole soon had Adams caught at deep midwicket. Van Niekerk and Wilson put on 56, but it was slow going, with the Invincibles just 21 after the 25-ball powerplay. Wilson's 25 was her highest score of the tournament, but she was put down on one and 17, the ball slippery from persistent showers. The pair fell within six deliveries: Wilson was caught sweeping to deep midwicket, while van Niekerk hit a slower one from Bell to mid-off. But Kapp and Capsey, who drove sumptuously down the ground, helped the Invincibles add 51 from the last 30 balls. A total of 121 still looked under par – until Kapp (who had missed half the tournament with a thigh injury) shocked the Brave with an opening set of ten unplayable awayswingers. Wyatt edged behind, Dunkley nicked to slip, and Ireland's Gaby Lewis (playing only her second game, after Smriti Mandhana's return to India) was caught at short fine leg attempting to pull. All three went without scoring. Once Bouchier was run out by Wilson's direct hit from backward point and Ismail bounced out Wellington, the Brave were 11 for five, and the Invincibles had the title in the bag. Capsey claimed two scalps, giving her ten in her breakthrough tournament, before Kapp yorked Bell to wrap up a comprehensive win.

Player of the Match: M. Kapp.   *Attendance:* 17,116.
Most Valuable Player of the Tournament: D. van Niekerk.

Oval Invincibles

		B	4/6
1 G. L. Adams *c 1 b 7*	4	6	1
2 *D. van Niekerk *c 2 b 11*	26	29	3
3 F. C. Wilson *c 1 b 6*	25	29	3
4 M. Kapp *c 6 b 8*	26	14	4
5 A. R. Capsey *b 11*	18	12	3
6 M. K. Villiers *c 5 b 7*	13	7	2
7 J. L. Gardner *not out*	2	3	0
B 1, lb 1, w 5	7		

25 balls: 21-1   (100 balls) 121-6

1/5 2/61 3/64 4/98 5/114 6/121

8 G. J. Gibbs, 9 †S. J. Bryce, 10 N. E. Farrant and 11 S. Ismail did not bat.

Shrubsole 20–11–16–2; Bell 20–12–24–2; Wellington 20–5–24–1; Morris 20–7–30–1; Taylor 15–3–18–0; Norris 5–2–7–0.

Southern Brave

		B	4/6
1 D. N. Wyatt *c 9 b 4*	0	4	0
2 G. H. Lewis *c 5 b 4*	0	2	0
3 S. I. R. Dunkley *c 2 b 4*	0	2	0
4 S. R. Taylor *st 9 b 2*	18	22	2
5 M. E. Bouchier *run out (3)*	7	9	1
6 A. Wellington *c 5 b 11*	0	3	0
7 *A. Shrubsole *c 4 b 5*	1	3	0
8 F. M. K. Morris *run out (8/2)*	23	26	4
9 T. G. Norris *b 5*	11	14	1
10 †C. E. Rudd *not out*	7	6	0
11 L. K. Bell *b 4*	4	7	1
Lb 1, w 1	2		

25 balls: 11-3   (98 balls) 73

1/1 2/1 3/2 4/11 5/11 6/14 7/29 8/62 9/63

Kapp 18–13–9–4; Ismail 20–15–14–1; Farrant 20–10–12–0; Capsey 20–11–21–2; van Niekerk 20–9–16–1.

Umpires: S. J. O'Shaughnessy and S. Redfern.   Third umpire: N. J. Llong.
Referee: S. J. Davis.

RACHAEL HEYHOE FLINT TROPHY IN 2021

Syd Egan

1 Southern Vipers   2 Northern Diamonds   3 Central Sparks

The Rachael Heyhoe Flint Trophy, introduced for the Covid summer of 2020, returned for a second edition. Despite some changes in its structure, it came to the same conclusion when **Southern Vipers** beat **Northern Diamonds** in the final.

This time, the North and South groups were replaced by a single league for the eight teams, with the top side going straight to the final, and the next two entering a play-off. Four rounds were played in May and June before The Hundred, with most of the England players available for the first three, though they missed the matches in September.

The Vipers, defending champions, got off to a solid start, with Danni Wyatt scoring half-centuries in wins against **Lightning** and **South East Stars**. But **Central Sparks** made the headlines: England wicketkeeper-batter Amy Jones hit a run-a-ball 114 to beat the Diamonds at Headingley, then two days later, smashed 163 not out, the highest score of the tournament's two seasons, against **Western Storm** at Edgbaston. It wasn't chanceless – Jones was dropped four times – but it was majestic cricket from England's most elegant strokemaker, with the biggest of six sixes deposited far into the Hollies Stand.

That set the scene for an early-season showdown between the big batting guns of the Sparks and the Vipers at Hove – only for Emily Arlott, a little-heralded Worcestershire seamer, to steal the day for the Sparks. She ripped out the Vipers' heart in a remarkable quadruple-wicket maiden, culminating in a hat-trick, which left them reeling on 17 for five; she finished with five for 29 as they limped to 104 all out chasing 225, their first defeat of the regional era.

The Vipers got back on track with an eight-wicket win against Western Storm in the round before The Hundred. Off-spinner Charlie Dean took three for 27 on her ascent from unknown amateur to England ODI player in less than four months. Meanwhile, in Worcester, the Sparks were losing to **Thunder** by two wickets, despite an unbeaten century from skipper Eve Jones – on a used pitch condemned even by the victorious captain, Alex Hartley.

At the other end of the country, the Diamonds were climbing the ladder after their initial loss to the Sparks. A successful defence of 151 against Lightning was followed by a nine-wicket rout at Fenner's, where they bowled out Sunrisers for 53, with England veterans Katherine Brunt and Jenny Gunn claiming three wickets apiece. Back at Headingley, former England keeper-batter Sarah Taylor made a quiet debut for the Diamonds as they chased the Stars' 250 for six, thanks to half-centuries from Netherlands international Sterre Kalis, Gunn and Beth Langston. They finished the first stage of the tournament level with the Sparks on 13 points, one behind the Vipers.

When hostilities resumed in September, **Sunrisers** quickly dropped out of contention; for the second season running, they failed to record a win.

Improbably, the closest they came was against the table-topping Vipers, who ran up 309 for nine at Chelmsford, their highest total of the tournament, thanks to a century from Georgia Elwiss. In reply, Cordelia Griffith put on 75 with opening partner Grace Scrivens and 112 with Lissy Macleod. Griffith was finally trapped on 91 by a beauty from Lauren Bell. That brought in Fran Wilson, who scored an unbeaten 65 off 51; she needed six off the last ball, bowled by Elwiss, but managed four.

That result, plus victories for the Sparks and the Diamonds, meant those three had already qualified before the last round, but there was all to play for in terms of advancing directly to the final. When the Sparks failed to chase down 321 against Lightning, who were boosted by a 207-run stand from their Scottish internationals, the Bryce sisters Sarah (90) and Kathryn (162), the match between the Vipers and the Diamonds effectively turned into another play-off. The Diamonds started slowly, but a late surge driven by Bess Heath's 51-ball 71 set the Vipers 257, which they knocked with an over to spare. The Diamonds took the slower road to the final, beating the Sparks in the official play-off at Scarborough.

RACHAEL HEYHOE FLINT TROPHY AVERAGES IN 2021

BATTING (200 runs)

		M	I	NO	R	HS	100	50	Avge	SR	4	6
1	A. E. Jones (*Sparks*)	3	3	1	282	163*	2	0	141.00	115.57	30	9
2	B. A. M. Heath (*Diamonds*)	5	5	3	212	78*	0	2	106.00	111.57	25	2
3	H. C. Knight (*Storm*)	3	3	0	223	91	0	3	74.33	97.80	30	1
4	S. N. Luff (*Storm*)	7	7	1	417	157*	1	3	69.50	79.73	47	1
5	D. N. Wyatt (*Vipers*)	4	4	1	206	64*	0	3	68.66	80.46	25	0
6	G. A. Elwiss (*Vipers*)	7	7	2	265	112*	1	1	53.00	93.30	29	1
7	K. E. Bryce (*Lightning*)	7	7	0	353	162	1	2	50.42	80.96	39	3
8	E. L. Lamb (*Thunder*)	6	5	0	237	121	1	0	47.40	87.45	30	2
9	†E. Jones (*Sparks*)	8	8	1	299	100*	1	2	42.71	62.16	42	2
10	B. F. Smith (*Stars*)	6	6	0	252	84	0	2	42.00	67.44	31	0
11	S. L. Kalis (*Diamonds*)	9	8	1	290	76	0	2	41.42	66.66	30	1
12	C. L. Griffith (*Sunrisers*)	7	7	0	273	91	0	2	39.00	82.22	34	2
13	G. E. B. Boyce (*Thunder*)	7	7	0	232	91	0	2	33.14	67.44	31	0
14	†A. Campbell (*Diamonds*)	8	7	0	223	76	0	2	31.85	87.10	26	5
15	A. J. Macleod (*Sunrisers*)	7	7	0	214	79	0	1	30.57	74.30	28	0
16	G. L. Adams (*Vipers*)	8	8	0	233	77	0	3	29.12	64.90	24	0
17	S. J. Bryce (*Lightning*)	7	7	0	202	90	0	1	28.85	73.45	27	2

BOWLING (10 wickets)

		Style	O	M	R	W	BB	4I	Avge	SR	ER
1	C. E. Dean (*Vipers*)	OB	39.5	4	138	10	3-27	0	13.80	23.90	3.46
2	G. L. Adams (*Vipers*)	OB	37.5	2	173	12	4-35	1	14.41	18.91	4.57
3	K. L. Gordon (*Lightning*)	SLA	70	5	247	16	4-23	2	15.43	26.25	3.52
4	K. A. Levick (*Diamonds*)	LB	59.1	5	190	12	4-34	1	15.83	29.58	3.21
5	H. E. Jones (*Thunder*)	SLA	50	3	239	14	5-33	1	17.07	21.42	4.78
6	C. M. Taylor (*Vipers*)	OB	72	5	236	13	4-21	1	18.15	33.23	3.27

		Style	O	M	R	W	BB	4I	Avge	SR	ER
7	B. F. Smith (*Stars*)	OB	52.2	0	232	12	3-46	0	19.33	26.16	4.43
8	B. A. Langston (*Diamonds*)	RM	73.5	10	269	13	2-12	0	20.69	34.07	3.64
9	K. S. Castle (*Sunrisers*)	RM	47.4	3	211	10	3-40	0	21.10	28.60	4.42
10	I. E. C. M. Wong (*Sparks*)	RFM	63.5	7	299	14	5-49	1	21.35	27.35	4.68
11	E. L. Arlott (*Sparks*)	RFM	55	5	261	11	5-29	1	23.72	30.00	4.74
12	L. C. N. Smith (*Diamonds*)	SLA	73	10	286	12	5-34	1	23.83	36.50	3.91
13	R. A. Fackrell (*Sparks*)	OB	47	0	265	11	4-31	1	24.09	25.63	5.63
14	K. E. Bryce (*Lightning*)	RM	62.5	8	246	10	4-16	1	24.60	37.70	3.91
15	A. Hartley (*Thunder*)	SLA	68.5	8	295	10	2-17	0	29.50	41.30	4.28
16	T. G. Norris (*Vipers*)	LM	68.5	4	331	11	4-14	1	30.09	37.54	4.80

RACHAEL HEYHOE FLINT TROPHY IN 2021

50-over league plus knockout

	P	W	L	Bonus	Pts	NRR
SOUTHERN VIPERS	7	6	1	3	27	0.41
NORTHERN DIAMONDS	7	5	2	3	23	1.18
CENTRAL SPARKS	7	5	2	2	22	0.82
Lightning	7	3	4	1	13	0.27
South East Stars	7	3	4	1	13	−0.22
Western Storm	7	3	4	1	13	−0.46
Thunder	7	3	4	1	13	−0.62
Sunrisers	7	0	7	0	0	−1.59

Win = 4pts; 1 bonus pt awarded for achieving victory with a run-rate 1.25 times that of the opposition.

Play-off   At Scarborough, September 22. **Northern Diamonds won by six wickets.** †**Central Sparks 175-7** (50 overs) (G. M. Davies 42, R. A. Fackrell 42*); **Northern Diamonds 176-4** (32.5 overs) (S. L. Kalis 41*, A. Campbell 76). *Northern Diamonds trotted into their second final of the season – with 17 overs in hand. A strong bowling performance, with two wickets each for Beth Langston, Rachel Slater and Linsey Smith, restricted Central Sparks to 101-7 before Ria Fackrell and Emily Arlott (29*) shared a stand of 74* to set a target of 176. The Diamonds stuttered as Arlott struck twice in the ninth over, but Ami Campbell plundered a 78-ball 76 out of the 116 she added with Sterre Kalis. When she was out, they were on the brink of a comfortable win.*

FINAL

NORTHERN DIAMONDS v SOUTHERN VIPERS

At Northampton, September 25. Southern Vipers won by three wickets. Toss: Northern Diamonds.
   Roared on by a posse of hardcore fans, who defied a national petrol crisis to travel to Northampton, Southern Vipers pulled off a remarkable victory to retain the Trophy, turning the match into a repeat of the previous year's final, with Northern Diamonds runners-up again. Batting first, the Diamonds made a plodding start, reaching 81 for four at halfway. But Ami Campbell's 60 dragged them to 183, despite Georgia Adams claiming four for 35 with her part-time off-spin. Then Beth Langston bowled both Vipers openers for ducks in a masterful new-ball spell; by the time Jenny Gunn grabbed two in two, to leave the reigning champions 109 for seven, it seemed all over. But Emily Windsor and Tara Norris dug in, and ground out a gutsy stand of 78 which completed an unlikely win with two balls to spare.
   Player of the Match: E. L. Windsor.

Northern Diamonds

*H. J. Armitage b Scholfield	16
L. C. N. Smith c Lewis b Adams	31
S. L. Kalis lbw b Adams	18
L. Dobson b Taylor	0
A. Campbell c Windsor b Elwiss	60
†B. A. M. Heath lbw b Norris	25
J. L. Gunn c Lewis b Adams	2
B. A. Langston lbw b Adams	0
P. C. Graham b Taylor	0
K. A. Levick c Rudd b Norris	8
R. Slater not out	6
B 1, lb 4, w 11, nb 1	17

1/35 (1) 2/72 (2) 3/73 (4)   (49.2 overs) 183
4/73 (3) 5/112 (6) 6/115 (7)
7/115 (8) 8/116 (9) 9/144 (10)
10/183 (5)   10 overs: 34-0

Bell 10–0–46–0; Norris 10–1–36–2; Elwiss 6.2–0–25–1; Scholfield 3–1–10–1; Taylor 10–0–26–2; Adams 10–1–35–4.

Southern Vipers

*G. L. Adams b Langston	0
E. M. McCaughan b Langston	0
M. E. Bouchier st Heath b Levick	33
G. A. Elwiss c Heath b Graham	14
G. H. Lewis b Gunn	24
E. L. Windsor not out	47
P. J. Scholfield c Armitage b Gunn	9
†C. E. Rudd lbw b Gunn	0
T. G. Norris not out	40
Lb 4, w 16	20

1/0 (1) 2/6 (2)   (7 wkts, 49.4 overs) 187
3/47 (4) 4/62 (3)
5/93 (5) 6/109 (7)
7/109 (8)   10 overs: 41-2

L. K. Bell and C. M. Taylor did not bat.

Langston 9.4–0–40–2; Slater 4–0–14–0; Graham 6–1–38–1; Gunn 10–0–31–3; Levick 10–2–20–1; Smith 10–2–40–0.

Umpires: J. Naeem and N. Pratt.   Referee: J. J. Whitaker.

CHARLOTTE EDWARDS CUP IN 2021

Syd Egan

1 South East Stars   2 Northern Diamonds   3 Southern Vipers

The Kia Super League had been superseded by The Hundred as England's premier short-form competition for women, and the county T20 Cup reduced to a regional development tournament. But the ECB felt it important that the leading cricketers should continue to play T20 at domestic level: hence the Charlotte Edwards Cup – named after England's all-time leading run-scorer – for the eight regional teams already contesting the 50-over Rachael Heyhoe Flint Trophy. To counter criticism that, in 2020, a two-group system had prevented the second-best side (Western Storm, runners-up in the South Group) qualifying for the RHF final, it was set up so that three teams advanced to the knockouts: the two group-winners plus one of the runners-up.

In Group A, **Southern Vipers** – finalists in three of the four KSL seasons, and coached by Edwards – made the early running, with three big wins in July. Off-spinner Charlie Dean took a rare T20 five-for, against **Central Sparks**, and Maia Bouchier hit 53 not out in 43 balls against **South East Stars**; both made England debuts later in the summer. But when the competition resumed in August, after a break for The Hundred, the Vipers slithered to successive defeats. Eve Jones, the tournament's leading run-scorer with 276, and Marie Kelly shared an opening stand of 137 for the Sparks, and Kelly reached her maiden professional hundred with the winning four. Then the Stars beat them at home after 17-year-old Alice Capsey struck 61, dismissed both Vipers openers with the new ball, and finished with two for nine.

Meanwhile, Group B began with a series of low-scoring affairs, before **Thunder** bucked the trend by smashing the season's highest total – 186 for one – against the **Sunrisers** at Old Trafford: Emma Lamb was undefeated on 111, then claimed three for 16 as the Sunrisers subsided for 115. When the teams met again after The Hundred, they tied on 124, with 63 from the Sunrisers' Cordelia Griffith, daughter of former Derbyshire all-rounder Frank. But the Sunrisers, who never won after their opening game, and **Lightning**, who never won at all, ended up bottom of their groups.

The other six all entered the last group round with a chance of reaching finals day. The Stars, who were leading Group A, sealed direct qualification for the final in their second win over the Sparks. With Capsey rested after a nasty fall in the Vipers game, it was another teenager, Cambridge first-year veterinary student Emma Jones, who took up the cudgels, smacking 46 off 27 balls out of 165 for six. Meanwhile, in Group B, **Northern Diamonds** made sure of reaching the play-off with a bonus-point win over Thunder; that extra point meant they were level with **Western Storm**, who missed out again, with a lower net run-rate.

The Vipers claimed the third qualifying spot – thanks to three bonus points from July, which put them ahead of the Storm as the best of the runners-up.

Weakened by international call-ups, they lost the play-off to the Diamonds, who joined the Stars in the final, where Capsey stole the headlines again with a match-winning innings.

CHARLOTTE EDWARDS CUP AVERAGES IN 2021

BATTING (100 runs)

		M	I	NO	R	HS	100	50	Avge	SR	4	6
1	E. L. Lamb (*Thunder*)	4	4	1	218	111*	1	1	72.66	152.44	24	3
2	B. F. Smith (*Stars*)	7	7	0	162	42	0	0	23.14	148.62	28	2
3	A. R. Capsey (*Stars*)	6	6	1	203	61	0	1	40.60	130.96	24	3
4	M. Kelly (*Sparks*)	6	6	1	170	100*	1	0	34.00	127.81	27	1
5	G. L. Adams (*Stars*)	7	7	1	215	88*	0	2	35.83	119.44	35	0
6	C. L. Griffith (*Sunrisers*)	4	4	0	129	63	0	1	32.25	117.27	14	4
7	H. J. Armitage (*Diamonds*) . . .	8	8	2	141	59*	0	1	23.50	109.30	15	2
8	†E. Jones (*Sparks*)	6	6	1	276	76	0	3	55.20	108.66	31	6
9	S. N. Luff (*Storm*)	6	5	1	127	60*	0	1	31.75	105.83	12	1
10	B. A. M. Heath (*Diamonds*) . .	5	5	1	103	58*	0	1	25.75	105.10	16	0
11	P. A. Franklin (*Stars*)	6	6	1	112	30	0	0	22.40	103.70	14	1
12	A. J. Freeborn (*Lightning*)	6	6	0	161	61	0	1	26.83	99.38	18	2
13	M. E. Bouchier (*Vipers*)	4	4	2	104	53*	0	1	52.00	98.11	13	0
14	G. A. Elwiss (*Vipers*)	7	7	1	109	45	0	0	18.16	96.46	10	1
15	G. M. Hennessy (*Storm*)	6	6	2	120	62	0	1	30.00	83.33	12	0
16	E. Threlkeld (*Thunder*)	6	6	1	102	28	0	0	20.40	80.31	9	0
17	L. Dobson (*Diamonds*)	8	8	1	111	44*	0	0	15.85	79.28	13	3

BOWLING (7 wickets)

		Style	Balls	Dots	R	W	BB	4I	Avge	SR	ER
1	G. K. Davis (*Sparks*)	OB	72	38	55	8	4-12	1	6.87	9.00	4.58
2	N. Harvey (*Storm*)	LB	144	64	113	12	3-13	0	9.41	12.00	4.70
3	L. C. N. Smith (*Diamonds*)	SLA	192	92	156	10	2-12	0	15.60	19.20	4.87
4	A. L. MacDonald (*Diamonds*)	RM	156	71	127	9	4-17	1	14.11	17.33	4.88
5	E. L. Lamb (*Thunder*) . . .	OB	78	37	66	9	4-13	1	7.33	8.66	5.07
6	K. A. Levick (*Diamonds*) .	LB	180	84	153	10	2-19	0	15.30	18.00	5.10
7	B. F. Smith (*Stars*)	OB	155	74	138	14	4-15	1	9.85	11.07	5.34
8	D. R. Gibson (*Storm*)	RM	114	55	107	7	2-9	0	15.28	16.28	5.63
9	C. M. Taylor (*Vipers*)	OB	168	69	159	9	3-12	0	17.66	18.66	5.67
10	J. L. Gunn (*Diamonds*) . . .	RFM	171	81	165	13	4-15	2	12.69	13.15	5.78
11	A. R. Capsey (*Stars*)	OB	108	48	105	7	3-13	0	15.00	15.42	5.83
12	C. E. Dean (*Vipers*)	OB	89	51	91	7	5-19	1	13.00	12.71	6.13
13	T. G. Norris (*Vipers*)	LM	155	65	173	13	4-14	1	13.30	11.92	6.69
14	G. A. Elwiss (*Vipers*)	RFM	162	63	182	10	3-16	0	18.20	16.20	6.74
15	F. M. K. Morris (*Storm*) . .	OB	120	60	136	7	2-21	0	19.42	17.14	6.80

CHARLOTTE EDWARDS CUP IN 2021

20-over league plus knockout

Group A							
	P	W	L	T	Bonus	Pts	NRR
SOUTH EAST STARS	6	5	1	0	1	21	1.05
SOUTHERN VIPERS	6	4	2	0	3	19	0.87
Central Sparks	6	3	3	0	0	12	−0.66
Lightning	6	0	6	0	0	0	−1.13

Group B

	P	W	L	T	Bonus	Pts	NRR
NORTHERN DIAMONDS...	6	4	2	0	1	17	0.65
Western Storm............	6	4	2	0	1	17	0.18
Thunder.................	6	2	3	1	1	11	0.02
Sunrisers...............	6	1	4	1	0	6	−0.87

Win = 4pts; 1 bonus pt awarded for achieving victory with a run-rate 1.25 times that of the opposition.

Play-off At Southampton, September 5. **Northern Diamonds won by 18 runs.** ‡Northern **Diamonds 135-6** (20 overs) (L. Winfield-Hill 65); **Southern Vipers 117** (20 overs) (E. L. Windsor 32; J. L. Gunn 4-26). PoM: L. Winfield-Hill. *Lauren Winfield-Hill kept the Diamonds on course after their openers fell cheaply, with 65 off 49 balls, and Jenny Gunn provided a rousing finish with two sixes in their final over. She went on to claim four wickets, dismissing Vipers captain Georgia Adams in her first spell, and wrapping up the innings in her second.*

FINAL

NORTHERN DIAMONDS v SOUTH EAST STARS

At Southampton, September 5. South East Stars won by five wickets. Toss: Northern Diamonds.

Alice Capsey guided the Stars to the title, in front of a crowd of 1,200. The chase had got off to a rollicking start, with captain Bryony Smith and Aylish Cranstone plundering 71 off eight overs, before Cranstone stepped on her own stumps after a pull. Enter Capsey, who audaciously ramped her first ball for four. While another three wickets tumbled at the other end, she played with a calm confidence belying her 17 years, and added 51 with Alice Davidson-Richards, before completing victory with two overs in hand. Following the Diamonds' successful defence of 135 earlier in the day, Hollie Armitage had elected to bat again – and found herself at the crease in the powerplay, after Winfield-Hill went for a third-ball duck. She anchored the innings with an unbeaten 59, sharing a half-century partnership with Gunn to lift the target to 139.

Player of the Match: A. R. Capsey.

Northern Diamonds

		B	4/6
1 L. Dobson *c 9 b 6*.............	11	12	2
2 †B. A. M. Heath *run out (9)*...	22	22	3
3 L. Winfield-Hill *lbw b 4*......	0	3	0
4 *H. J. Armitage *not out*......	59	48	4
5 S. L. Kalis *c and b 1*.........	18	19	1
6 J. L. Gunn *not out*	22	16	2
Lb 1, w 5	6		

6 overs: 30-2　　　(20 overs) **138-4**

1/18 2/22 3/45 4/88

7 L. C. N. Smith, 8 A. L. MacDonald, 9 R. H. M. Hopkins, 10 R. Slater and 11 K. A. Levick did not bat.

Capsey 24–5–30–0; Moore 24–10–20–0; Davidson-Richards 24–4–28–1; Gibbs 12–5–13–1; Smith 24–10–22–1; Gregory 12–2–24–0.

South East Stars

		B	4/6
1 *B. F. Smith *b 7*..............	37	25	7
2 A. Cranstone *hit wkt b 8*......	35	27	4/1
3 A. R. Capsey *not out*	40	26	4/1
4 G. J. Gibbs *c 3 b 11*.........	3	6	0
5 P. A. Franklin *c 6 b 11*.......	0	2	0
6 A. N. Davidson-Richards *c 4 b 8*	18	20	0
7 K. E. White *not out*	1	2	0
W 5	5		

6 overs: 50-0　　　(18 overs) **139-5**

1/71 2/81 3/84 4/85 5/136

8 †K. M. Chathli, 9 E. W. S. Jones, 10 K. Moore and 11 D. L. Gregory did not bat.

Smith 24–11–29–1; Slater 6–1–14–0; Gunn 18–4–24–0; Levick 24–13–19–2; MacDonald 24–7–32–2; Armitage 12–4–21–0.

Umpires: S. M. Bartlett and S. Redfern.　　Referee: P. Whitticase.

OTHER ENGLAND DOMESTIC CRICKET IN 2021

The first ECB-organised county cricket for women since 2019 took place over four weekends in April and May. The Vitality Women's County T20 featured 36 teams in six regional groups; the North Group included Scotland A, the North East Warriors (a combined Durham–Northumberland team) and a North Representative XI drawn from across the region, while Wales played in the West Midlands Group.

Although it wound up on May 16, there was no finals day for the leading sides. Kent appeared the strongest, winning all six games they played (two were called off), despite missing not only their England stars but even some regional players in the run-up to the Rachael Heyhoe Flint Trophy. The ECB withdrew their centrally contracted players because the competition, classified as recreational cricket, had less strict Covid protocols than the RHF tournament, and they were anxious that the professionals should not be forced into quarantine by positive contacts. It reinforced county cricket's status at the bottom of the women's hierarchy.

Emma Lamb scored 233 at a strike-rate of 168 in four games for Lancashire, while the leading wicket-taker was Hampshire leg-spinner Finty Trussler, who collected 16 either side of her 18th birthday.

Kent did win the London Championship, first organised by the south-east counties in 2020, and now expanded to include Sussex. This was the only 50-over county competition following the demise of the County Championship after 2019. Kent won three matches before succumbing to title-holders Surrey in their last game.

The Under-18 County Cup (40 overs) was played in eight regional groups, and the Under-15 equivalent in nine; as in the senior county competition, there were no national finals.

The Vitality Club T20 Cup resumed after a year off; 2019's losing semi-finalists, Bridgwater and Sessay, reached the final, with **Bridgwater** claiming the trophy. In the Plate, **Thriplow** won their first national final on the same day that another Thriplow side handed out a 146-run thrashing in the East Anglian Premier League, which they went on to win in September.

VITALITY WOMEN'S COUNTY TWENTY20 IN 2021

East Group Hertfordshire 23pts, Buckinghamshire 18, Suffolk 18, Cambridgeshire 18, Huntingdonshire 3, Norfolk 2.

East Midlands Group Nottinghamshire 23, Lincolnshire 16, Shropshire 12, Derbyshire 11, Leicestershire 10, Northamptonshire 6.

North Group Lancashire 20, Scotland 18, North Representative XI 16, Yorkshire 14, North East Warriors 6, Cumbria 2.

South East Group Kent 26, Surrey 17, Hampshire 14, Sussex 14, Middlesex 13, Essex 2.

South West Group Gloucestershire 20, Devon 18, Dorset 14, Cornwall 12, Oxfordshire 12, Wiltshire 0.

West Midlands Group Somerset 22, Warwickshire 20, Worcestershire 12, Wales 8, Staffordshire 6, Berkshire 4.

LONDON CHAMPIONSHIP IN 2021

50-over league

Kent 52pts, Surrey 40, Middlesex 39, Sussex 23, Essex 9.

LONDON CUP IN 2021

At Radlett, June 21. **Middlesex won by eight wickets. Surrey 124-7** (20 overs) (H. V. Jones 42; K. L. Coppack 3-27); ‡**Middlesex 127-2** (18.2 overs) (N. D. Dattani 50). *Surrey were on the skids once Kate Coppack inflicted two ducks in her first two overs, and were 35-4 by the seventh. Hannah Jones (42 in 40) helped raise the target to 125, but Naomi Dattani's fifty ensured Middlesex's sixth title out of seven.*

VITALITY WOMEN'S CLUB T20 FINALS IN 2021

Cup final   At Kibworth, August 1. **Bridgwater won by 17 runs.** ‡**Bridgwater 110-9** (20 overs) (E. Geach 36); **Sessay 93-6** (20 overs) (O. Watson 33*). *Sessay had bowled out 2019 champions Bishop's Stortford for 68 in their semi-final, but Bridgwater took the cup, despite declining from 81-2; there were four run-outs, and at the finish four fell for one run in nine balls. They made sure of victory, however, when Georgia Tulip and Tilly Bond reduced Sessay to 41-5.*

Plate final   At Kibworth, August 1. **Thriplow won by nine wickets. Mildenhall 96-8** (20 overs); ‡**Thriplow 97-1** (17.3 overs) (I. Routledge 58*). *In an East Anglian face-off, Isabella Routledge swept Thriplow to victory with 58* from 48 balls. For Mildenhall, only Jasmine Westley reached 20, and once she was run out wickets fell steadily.*

THE UNIVERSITY MATCHES IN 2021

At Cambridge, May 14. **Oxford University won by 25 runs.** ‡**Oxford University 146-4** (20 overs) (V. M. Picker 34, A. Travers 81, Extras 30; A. P. Bebb 3-25); **Cambridge University 121-7** (20 overs) (E. W. S. Jones 63). *Vanessa Picker and Alex Travers (81 in 54 balls, and 12 fours) opened with 123 in 17 overs, before Alice Bebb picked up three wickets and caught Travers. Only Emma Jones (63 in 51) passed 19 in Cambridge's run-chase, where five batters were bowled and the other two run out.*

At Wormsley, June 28. **Oxford University won by 88 runs.** ‡**Oxford University 235-8** (50 overs) (A. Travers 75, M. Ross 34, Extras 45; A. P. Bebb 3-42); **Cambridge University 147** (43.1 overs) (E. W. S. Jones 33, Extras 32; S. Florides 3-22). *Oxford completed their eighth Varsity win across the two formats since losing the T20 fixture in June 2017. As in May, there was a half-century from Travers, three wickets for Bebb, and Jones provided Cambridge's only resistance. This time, four of Oxford's top five fell for single figures, before Maddy Ross and Shona McNab (a run-a-ball 25) gave Travers some support. Sophie Florides wrapped up victory with nearly seven overs in hand. There were 77 extras in all, including 65 from wides.*

PART EIGHT

Records and Registers

FIRST-CLASS FEATURES OF 2021

This section covers the calendar year. Some of the features listed occurred in series and seasons reported in *Wisden 2021* and some in series and seasons that will be reported in *Wisden 2023*; these items are indicated by [W21] or [W23].

Double-Hundreds (39)

	Mins	Balls	4	6		
311	561	343	40	4	Mohammad Huraira .	Northern v Baluchistan at Karachi.[W23]
303*	585	385	36	3	Ahsan Ali	Sindh v Central Punjab at Lahore.[W23]
274	371	345	35	1	‡O. J. D. Pope	Surrey v Glamorgan at The Oval.
264	670	507	26	4	P. J. Malan.	Cape Cobras v Knights at Cape Town.
257	540	410	33	0	D. G. Bedingham . . .	Durham v Derbyshire at Chester-le-Street.
253	561	337	34	3	Rizwan Hussain.	Central Punjab v S Punjab at Karachi.[W23]
253	462	356	30	1	S. D. Robson	Middlesex v Sussex at Hove.
251	445	343	29	5	C. D. Green.	Western Australia v Queensland at Brisbane.
245	420	272	30	0	‡O. J. D. Pope	Surrey v Leicestershire at The Oval.
244	656	437	26	0	F. D. M. Karunaratne	Sri Lanka v Bangladesh (1st Test) at Pallekele.
238	573	364	28	0	K. S. Williamson . . .	NZ v Pakistan (2nd Test) at Christchurch.[W21]
234*	370	245	25	9	N. F. Kelly.	Otago v Central Districts at Dunedin.[W23]
231	324	220	36	2	J. M. Vince	Hampshire v Leicestershire at Leicester.
228	476	321	18	1	‡J. E. Root.	England v Sri Lanka (1st Test) at Galle.
226	412	299	22	3	Sikandar Raza	Southern Rocks v Mountaineers at Harare.[W23]
223	347	245	31	1	T. M. Head	South Australia v Western Australia at Perth.
222*	344	240	28	3	M. Z. Hamza	South Africa A v Zimbabwe A at Harare.
221	452	274	23	4	Tayyab Tahir	Southern Punjab v Baluchistan at Multan.[W23]
220	440	364	21	3	Abdul Malik	Amo v Speen Ghar at Kandahar.[W23]
218	536	377	19	2	‡J. E. Root.	England v India (1st Test) at Chennai.
217	603	387	16	4	Towhid Hridoy	South Zone v North Zone at Chittagong.[W23]
216*	494	327	23	5	K. Verreynne.	Cape Cobras v Warriors at Cape Town.
215*	637	407	29	0	Abid Ali.	Pakistan v Zimbabwe (2nd Test) at Harare.
215*	491	367	22	0	H. M. Amla	Surrey v Hampshire at The Oval.
213	504	346	20	0	Faizan Riaz	Northern v Central Punjab at Lahore.[W23]
213	538	408	32	0	T. Westley	Essex v Worcestershire at Chelmsford.
211	489	333	26	0	Munir Ahmad	Boost v Speen Ghar at Kandahar.[W23]
210*	415	310	20	7	K. R. Mayers.	WI v Bangladesh (1st Test) at Chittagong.
206	294	221	27	4	Haider Ali	Northern v Central Punjab at Karachi.[W23]
205*	355	299	18	1	C. B. Cooke	Glamorgan v Surrey at The Oval.
204*	501	342	27	1	A. K. Markram	Titans v Knights at Centurion.
203*	584	388	24	2	Abdul Bangalzai	Baluchistan v Central Punjab at Lahore.[W23]
203*	407	309	20	3	Mohammad Saad. . . .	Central Punjab v Baluchistan at Lahore.[W23]
203*	456	299	26	2	K. Zondo	KZN Coastal v W Province at Cape Town.[W23]
202*	599	390	16	4	Imam-ul-Haq.	Baluchistan v Khyber Pakh at Lahore.[W23]
200*	590	443	21	1	Hashmatullah Shahidi	Afghanistan v Zim (2nd Test) at Abu Dhabi.
200*	496	319	20	0	J. N. Malan	Boland v Free State at Bloemfontein.[W23]
200	578	347	22	1	D. P. Conway	New Zealand v England (1st Test) at Lord's.
200	550	379	23	4	H. R. Cooper	Northern Districts v Otago at Alexandra.[W23]

‡   *O. J. D. Pope and J. E. Root each scored two double-hundreds.*

Hundred on First-Class Debut

133		B. L. Wiggins	Central Districts v Canterbury at Christchurch.

Hundred in Each Innings of a Match

M. G. Bracewell	105	119	Wellington v Auckland at Auckland.
K. S. Carlson.	127*	132	Glamorgan v Sussex at Cardiff.
H. Hameed	111	114*	Nottinghamshire v Worcestershire at Worcester.
W. T. O'Donnell	117	137*	Auckland v Wellington at Auckland.

Carrying Bat through Completed Innings

T. J. Dean.............	144*	Victoria (271) v New South Wales at Sydney.[W23]
D. P. Hughes	89*	New South Wales (247) v Victoria at Melbourne.[W23]
J. D. Libby............	180*	Worcestershire (475) v Essex at Chelmsford.

Most Sixes in an Innings

15	D. I. Stevens (190)	Kent v Glamorgan at Canterbury.
10	Sohag Gazi (113)	Barisal v Rajshahi at Cox's Bazar.[W23]
9	N. F. Kelly (234*)	Otago v Central Districts at Dunedin.[W23]

Longest Innings

Mins

681	J. D. Libby (180*)	Worcestershire v Essex at Chelmsford.
670	P. J. Malan (264)	Cape Cobras v Knights at Cape Town.
656	F. D. M. Karunaratne (244) ...	Sri Lanka v Bangladesh (1st Test) at Pallekele.
637	Abid Ali (215*)	Pakistan v Zimbabwe (2nd Test) at Harare.
603	Towhid Hridoy (217)	South Zone v North Zone at Chittagong.[W23]

Unusual Dismissals

Hit the Ball Twice

Ikram Alikhil (11)	Speen Ghar v Amo at Kandahar.[W23]

First-Wicket Partnership of 100 in Each Innings

115	236*	B. T. Slater/H. Hameed, Nottinghamshire v Worcestershire at Worcester.
135	135	R. J. Burns/M. D. Stoneman, Surrey v Middlesex at The Oval.
109	125	T. G. Mokoena/N. Brand, Northerns v KwaZulu-Natal Coastal at Centurion.[W23]
118	179*	Riaz Hussan/Sediqullah Atal, Band-e-Amir v Mis Ainak at Kandahar.[W23]
197	100	T. Ward/C. P. Jewell, Tasmania v Western Australia at Hobart.[W23]
146	151	Abid Ali/Abdullah Shafiq, Pakistan v Bangladesh (1st Test) at Chittagong.

Highest Wicket Partnerships

First Wicket

376	S. D. Robson/M. D. Stoneman, Middlesex v Sussex at Hove.
365	Mohammad Huraira/Sarmad Bhatti, Northern v Baluchistan at Karachi.[W23]
327	Mizanur Rahman/Mithun Ali, Central Zone v North Zone at Chittagong.[W23]
251	H. D. Rutherford/M. Renwick, Otago v Central Districts at Dunedin.[W23]

Second Wicket

304	Ahsan Ali/Ammad Alam, Sindh v Central Punjab at Lahore.[W23]
261	M. S. Harris/P. S. P. Handscomb, Victoria v New South Wales at Sydney.[W23]

Third Wicket

362	H. M. Amla/O. J. D. Pope, Surrey v Glamorgan at The Oval.
258	Amite Hasan/Towhid Hridoy, South Zone v North Zone at Chittagong.[W23]
257	I. G. Holland/S. A. Northeast, Hampshire v Middlesex at Southampton.
257	H. M. Amla/O. J. D. Pope, Surrey v Hampshire at The Oval.

Fourth Wicket

369	K. S. Williamson/H. M. Nicholls, New Zealand v Pakistan (2nd Test) at Christchurch.[W21]
345	F. D. M. Karunaratne/D. M. de Silva, Sri Lanka v Bangladesh (1st Test) at Pallekele.
308	Umar Amin/Faizan Riaz, Northern v Southern Punjab at Karachi.[W23]
307	Hashmatullah Shahidi/Asghar Afghan, Afghanistan v Zimbabwe (2nd Test) at Abu Dhabi.

Fifth Wicket

338* M. Z. Hamza/S. Qeshile, South Africa A v Zimbabwe A at Harare.
307* K. S. Carlson/C. B. Cooke, Glamorgan v Northamptonshire at Cardiff.
254* D. G. Bedingham/E. J. H. Eckersley, Durham v Nottinghamshire at Nottingham.

Sixth Wicket

305 L. J. Carter/C. D. Fletcher, Canterbury v Otago at Christchurch.
256 N. F. Kelly/M. W. Chu, Otago v Central Districts at Dunedin.[W23]
227 B. D. Guest/A. K. Dal, Derbyshire v Leicestershire at Derby.

Seventh Wicket

244 J. D. Libby/E. G. Barnard, Worcestershire v Essex at Chelmsford.
204 R. Mutumbami/R. Kaia, Southern Rocks v Tuskers at Harare.[W23]

Eighth Wicket

263 Abdul Wasi/Jamshid Khan, Amo v Band-e-Amir at Kandahar.[W23]
260 J. N. Malan/F. D. Adams, Boland v Free State at Bloemfontein.[W23]
212 Fazle Mahmud/Islamul Ahsan, Barisal v Rajshahi at Sylhet.[W23]
203* H. J. Swindells/E. Barnes, Leicestershire v Somerset at Taunton.
199* J. Pillay/A. Gqamane, Northerns v Western Province at Cape Town.[W23]

Ninth Wicket

191 Mahmudullah/Taskin Ahmed, Bangladesh v Zimbabwe (Only Test) at Harare.
166 D. I. Stevens/M. L. Cummins, Kent v Glamorgan at Canterbury.

Tenth Wicket

119 T. P. Kaber/S. H. Jamison, Border v KwaZulu-Natal Inland at East London.[W23]
114 C. de Grandhomme/B. T. J. Wheal, Hampshire v Surrey at Southampton.

Monopolising Runs Scored in a Partnership

160 out of 166 (96.38%) D. I. Stevens (160)/M. L. Cummins (1) (Ex 5) Kent v Glamorgan at Canterbury.

Monopolising Runs Scored while at the Wicket

190 out of 214 (88.78%) D. I. Stevens. Kent v Glamorgan at Canterbury.

Most Wickets in an Innings

10-36 S. A. Whitehead . . . South Western Districts v Easterns at Oudtshoorn.[W23]
10-119 A. Y. Patel . . . . New Zealand v India (2nd Test) at Mumbai.
9-78 O. E. Robinson . . . . Sussex v Glamorgan at Cardiff.
9-80 S. R. Harmer . . . . . Essex v Derbyshire at Chelmsford.
8-40 K. A. J. Roach . . . . Surrey v Hampshire at The Oval.
8-42 Sajid Khan . . . . Pakistan v Bangladesh (2nd Test) at Mirpur.
8-51 Tanvir Islam . . . . . . Bangladesh Emerging Players v Ireland Wolves at Chittagong.
8-98 Sanjamul Islam . . . . North Zone v East Zone at Rajshahi.[W23]

Most Wickets in a Match

15-100 S. A. Whitehead . . . South Western Districts v Easterns at Oudtshoorn.[W23]
14-225 A. Y. Patel . . . . New Zealand v India (2nd Test) at Mumbai.
13-128 O. E. Robinson . . . . Sussex v Glamorgan at Cardiff.
13-174 K. A. Maharaj . . . . . Dolphins v Lions at Johannesburg.
12-113 Nasum Ahmed . . . . Sylhet v Dhaka at Sylhet.[W23]
12-128 Sajid Khan . . . . Pakistan v Bangladesh (2nd Test) at Mirpur.
12-131 Mukidul Islam . . . . Rangpur v Khulna at Rangpur.
12-136 Zohaib Ahmadzai . . Amo v Band-e-Amir at Kandahar.[W23]
12-196 Nauman Ali . . . . . . Northern v Southern Punjab at Karachi.[W23]
12-202 S. R. Harmer . . . . . . Essex v Derbyshire at Chelmsford.

Hat-Tricks (6)

L. J. Delport	Auckland v Northern Districts at Whangarei.
K. A. Maharaj.	South Africa v West Indies (2nd Test) at Gros Islet.
Mohammad Abbas	Hampshire v Middlesex at Southampton.
Mohammad Ashraful	Barisal v Chittagong at Chittagong.[W23]
M. D. Rae	Otago v Central Districts at Dunedin.
Sharifullah	Dhaka Metropolis v Rajshahi at Cox's Bazar.[W23]

Match Double (100 runs and 10 wickets)

K. A. Maharaj.	12, 89; 6-126, 7-48	Dolphins v Lions at Johannesburg.
S. A. Whitehead	66, 45; 5-64, 10-36	South Western Districts v Easterns at Oudtshoorn.[W23]

Most Wicketkeeping Dismissals in an Innings

6 (5ct, 1st)	P. D. Bocock	Northern Districts v Otago at Dunedin.
6 (6ct)	H. G. Duke	Yorkshire v Nottinghamshire at Nottingham.
6 (6ct)	Mohammad Haris	Pakistan Shaheens v Sri Lanka A at Pallekele.
6 (6ct)	P. M. Nevill	New South Wales v Victoria at Sydney.
6 (6ct)	J. R. Philippe	Western Australia v South Australia at Perth.[W23]
6 (5ct, 1st)	Pritom Kumar	Rajshahi v Chittagong at Rajshahi.

Most Wicketkeeping Dismissals in a Match

9 (9ct)	Junaid Ali	Central Punjab v Southern Punjab at Karachi.[W23]
9 (8ct, 1st)	C. R. McLachlan	Wellington v Canterbury at Wellington.[W23]
9 (8ct, 1st)	Mohammad Haris	Pakistan Shaheens v Sri Lanka A at Pallekele.

Most Catches in an Innings in the Field

6	T. T. Bresnan	Warwickshire v Yorkshire at Leeds.
5	H. D. R. L. Thirimanne	Sri Lanka v England (2nd Test) at Galle.

Most Catches in a Match in the Field

7	T. T. Bresnan	Warwickshire v Yorkshire at Leeds.
6	M. M. Ali	England v India (4th Test) at The Oval.
6	R. Clarke	Surrey v Hampshire at The Oval.
6	S. P. D. Smith.	Australia v England (2nd Test) at Adelaide.
6	R. N. ten Doeschate	Essex v Derbyshire at Chelmsford.

No Byes Conceded in Total of 500 or More

J. J. Peirson	Queensland v Tasmania (500-6 dec) at Adelaide.[W23]
S. Qeshile	Warriors v Cape Cobras (513-6 dec) at Cape Town.
U. T. Yadav.	India A v South Africa A (509-7 dec) at Bloemfontein.

Highest Innings Totals

864-9 dec	Boost v Speen Ghar at Kandahar.[W23]
722-4 dec	Surrey v Glamorgan at The Oval.
676-5 dec	Middlesex v Sussex at Hove.
672-8 dec	Surrey v Leicestershire at The Oval.
672-6 dec	Glamorgan v Surrey at The Oval.
659-6 dec	New Zealand v Pakistan (2nd Test) at Christchurch.[W21]
648-8 dec	Sri Lanka v Bangladesh (1st Test) at Pallekele.
647-7 dec	Northerns v Western Province at Cape Town.[W23]
642-6 dec	Otago v Central Districts at Dunedin.[W23]
621-4 dec	Northern v Baluchistan at Karachi.[W23]
616-5 dec	Sindh v Central Punjab at Lahore.[W23]
612-5 dec	Hampshire v Leicestershire at Leicester.

Lowest Innings Totals

16†	Border v KwaZulu-Natal Coastal at Paarl.
32†	New South Wales v Tasmania at Hobart.
45	Northamptonshire v Essex at Chelmsford.
53	Titans v Dolphins at Durban.
54	Eastern Province v Gauteng at Port Elizabeth.[W23]
60	Barisal v Rajshahi at Savar.
62	New Zealand v India (2nd Test) at Mumbai.
65	Easterns v South Western Districts at Oudtshoorn.[W23]
67	Sylhet v Dhaka at Sylhet.[W23]
67	Sri Lanka A v Pakistan Shaheens at Pallekele.
68	England v Australia (3rd Test) at Melbourne.
69	Somerset v Surrey at The Oval.

† *One man absent.*

Matches Dominated by Batting (1,200 runs at 80 runs per wicket)

1,394 for 10 (139.40)	Glamorgan (672-6 dec) v Surrey (722-4 dec) at The Oval.
1,354 for 16 (84.62)	Boost (864-9 dec) v Speen Ghar (490-7) at Kandahar.[W23]

Most Individual Hundreds in an Innings

4	Northerns (647-7 dec) v Western Province at Cape Town.[W23]
4	Boost (864-9 dec) v Speen Ghar at Kandahar.[W23]

Most Individual Fifties in an Innings

7	Boost (864-9 dec) v Speen Ghar at Kandahar.[W23]
6	South Australia (482-8 dec) v New South Wales at Adelaide.
6	Khyber Pakhtunkhwa (557) v Baluchistan at Lahore.[W23]
6	Speen Ghar (490-7) v Boost at Kandahar.[W23]

Tied Match

Khyber Pakhtunkhwa (300 and 312) v Central Punjab (257-9 dec and 355) at Karachi.

Eleven Bowlers in an Innings

Glamorgan v Surrey (722-4 dec) at The Oval.

Most Extras in an Innings

b	lb	w	nb		
83	63	7	1	12	Boost (864-9 dec) v Speen Ghar at Kandahar.[W23]
81	48	11	2	20	Hampshire (486-7 dec) v Gloucestershire at Cheltenham.
64	27	8	17	12	New Zealand (659-6 dec) v Pakistan (2nd Test) at Christchurch.
57	12	19	0	26	Derbyshire (465) v Sussex at Hove.
54	25	21	0	8	Leicestershire (451) v Gloucestershire at Leicester.
54	33	9	5	7	Amo (447) v Band-e-Amir at Kandahar.[W23]
53	27	7	2	17	Baluchistan (571-7 dec) v Southern Punjab at Multan.[W23]
50	35	11	2	2	Speen Ghar (389) v Mis Ainak at Kandahar.[W23]

Career Aggregate Milestones

15,000 runs	D. Elgar.
10,000 runs	R. J. Burns, V. Kohli, S. D. Robson, J. M. Vince, D. A. Warner, B-J. Watling.
1,000 wickets	J. M. Anderson.
500 wickets	Enamul Haque, J. A. R. Harris, K. A. Maharaj, Mohammad Abbas, D. Olivier, Sohail Khan, C. J. C. Wright.
500 dismissals	T. D. Paine.

LIST A FEATURES OF 2021

Highest Individual Scores

230	T. M. Head	South Australia v Queensland at Adelaide.[W23]
227*	P. P. Shaw	Mumbai v Puducherry at Jaipur.
198	V. R. Iyer	Madhya Pradesh v Punjab at Indore.
193	Fakhar Zaman	Pakistan v South Africa at Johannesburg.
192	R. Samarth	Karnataka v Kerala at Delhi.
185*	P. P. Shaw	Mumbai v Saurashtra at Delhi.

Hundred on List A Debut

101	C. J. Briggs	South Australia (237) v Western Australia at Adelaide.
109	F. I. N. Khushi	Essex v Durham at Chester-le-Street.

Carrying Bat through Completed Innings

A. T. Carey	128*	Victoria (271) v New South Wales at Sydney.[W23]

Most Sixes in an Innings

16	J. S. Malhotra (173*)	USA v Papua New Guinea at Al Amerat.
11	F. H. Allen (128)	Wellington v Otago at Wellington.
11	T. H. David (140*)	Surrey v Warwickshire at The Oval.
11	I. P. Kishan (173)	Jharkhand v Madhya Pradesh at Indore.

Most Runs off One Over

36 (666666)	N. L. T. C. Perera off P. D. M. A. Cooray	Army v Bloomfield at Panagoda.
36 (666666)	J. S. Malhotra off G. Toka	USA v Papua New Guinea at Al Amerat.

Unusual Dismissals

Obstructing the Field

M. D. Gunathilleke (55)..........	Sri Lanka v West Indies at North Sound.
S. B. Harper (7)	Victoria v South Australia at Melbourne.
S. Qeshile (9)	Warriors v Lions at Potchefstroom.
Saud Shakil (12).................	Sindh v Baluchistan at Karachi.

Highest Wicket Partnerships

First Wicket
285* R. Samarth/D. B. Padikkal, Karnataka v Railways at Bangalore.
264 T. D. Agarwal/N. T. Tilak Varma, Hyderabad v Goa at Surat.

Second Wicket
244 J. B. Weatherald/T. M. Head, South Australia v Queensland at Adelaide.[W23]
239 D. L. S. Croospulle/P. H. K. D. Mendis, Chilaw Marians v Panadura at Katunayake.
226 H. J. Nielsen/T. M. Head, South Australia v Western Australia at Perth.
225 E. D. Kerkar/S. S. Kauthankar, Goa v Hyderabad at Surat.

Third Wicket
255 D. Shorey/N. Rana, Delhi v Puducherry at Jaipur.

Fourth Wicket
210 Mohammad Ikhlaq/Saad Nasim, Central Punjab v Khyber Pakhtunkhwa at Karachi.
205 P. S. P. Handscomb/J. A. Merlo, Victoria v South Australia at Melbourne.

Fifth Wicket
214 Y. Nahar/A. N. Kazi, Maharashtra v Mumbai at Jaipur.
213 M. L. Udawatte/Mohammed Shamaaz, Moors v Sinhalese at Colombo (SSC).
212 A. K. Perera/P. C. de Silva, Nondescripts v Tamil Union at Colombo (NCC).
202 K. D. Karthik/R. N. B. Indrajith, Tamil Nadu v Himachal Pradesh at Jaipur.[W23]

Sixth Wicket
227 Adil Amin/Mohammad Haris, Khyber Pakhtunkhwa v Baluchistan at Karachi.

Seventh Wicket
174* V. Vinod/S. Joseph, Kerala v Maharashtra at Rajkot.[W23]
156* S. R. Dickson/L. Doneathy, Durham v Lancashire at Gosforth.

Tenth Wicket
109 R. Punia/Umar Nazir, Jammu & Kashmir v Andhra at Mumbai.[W23]

Most Wickets in an Innings

7-31	S. Sharma............	Uttar Pradesh v Bihar at Alur.
7-46	U. A. Morais	Burgher v Bloomfield at Colombo (Bloomfield).

Hat-Tricks (4)

V. Arora	Himachal Pradesh v Maharashtra at Jaipur.
A. M. McCarthy	Jamaica v Barbados at Coolidge.
A. Rajpoot	Uttar Pradesh v Haryana at Mohali.[W23]
G. S. Sandhu............	Queensland v South Australia at Adelaide.[W23]

Most Wicketkeeping Dismissals in an Innings

7 (7ct)	I. P. Kishan	Jharkhand v Madhya Pradesh at Indore.
6 (4ct, 2st)	H. J. Patel	Gujarat v Jammu & Kashmir at Mumbai.[W23]

Highest Innings Totals

457-4	(50 overs)	Mumbai v Puducherry at Jaipur.
427-8	(50 overs)	Wellington v Otago at Wellington.
422-9	(50 overs)	Jharkhand v Madhya Pradesh at Indore.
405-4	(50 overs)	Durham v Kent at Beckenham.
402-3	(50 overs)	Madhya Pradesh v Punjab at Indore.

Lowest Innings Totals

30	(19.3 overs)	Ace Capital v Nondescripts at Colombo (NCC).
48	(14 overs)	Nagaland v Tripura at Jaipur.[W23]

Largest Victories

324 runs	Jharkhand 422-9 (50 overs) v Madhya Pradesh 98 (18.4 overs) at Indore.
267 runs	Karnataka 354-3 (50 overs) v Bihar 87 (27.2 overs) at Bangalore.

There were six wins by ten wickets.

Tied Matches

Lancashire 250-6 (50 overs) v Essex 250-8 (50 overs) at Manchester.
Boost 294-8 (50 overs) v Mis Ainak 294-5 (50 overs) at Kandahar.[W23]
Nondescripts 195 (43.1 overs) v Negombo 195 (42.3 overs) at Katunayake.[W23]
Punjab 288-8 (50 overs) v Goa 288-7 (50 overs) at Ranchi.[W23]

TWENTY20 FEATURES OF 2021

Highest Individual Scores

146*	P. Bisht	Meghalaya v Mizoram at Chennai.
140*	B. R. M. Taylor.	Rhinos v Eagles at Harare.
137*	M. Azharuddeen	Kerala v Mumbai at Mumbai.
136	J. M. Clarke.	Nottinghamshire v Northamptonshire at Northampton.
133*	M. P. O'Dowd.	Netherlands v Malaysia at Kirtipur.
127	B. R. McDermott. . . .	Hobart Hurricanes v Melbourne Renegades at Melbourne.[W23]

Most Sixes in an Innings

17	P. Bisht (146*)	Meghalaya v Mizoram at Chennai.
11	M. Azharuddeen (137*).	Kerala v Mumbai at Mumbai.
11	J. M. Clarke (136)	Nottinghamshire v Northamptonshire at Northampton.
11	E. Lewis (102*)	St Kitts & Nevis Patriots v Trinbago KR at Basseterre.

Most Runs off One Over

37 (666*6264)	R. A. Jadeja off H. V. Patel . . .	Chennai Super Kings v RC Bangalore at Mumbai.
36 (666666)	K. A. Pollard off A. Dananjaya	West Indies v Sri Lanka at Coolidge.

* *Jadeja's third six was off a no-ball.*

Unusual Dismissals

Obstructing the Field

Nurul Hasan (42).	Sheikh Jamal Dhanmondi v Prime Doleshwar at Mirpur.
Yeasin Arafat (2).	Mohammedan v Gazi Group Cricketers at Mirpur.

Highest Wicket Partnership

First Wicket
181* V. Kohli/D. B. Padikkal, Royal Challengers Bangalore v Rajasthan Royals at Mumbai.

Most Wickets in an Innings

6-5	P. Aho	Nigeria v Sierra Leone at Lagos.
6-7	D. M. Nakrani	Uganda v Lesotho at Kigali City.
6-18	H. Fennell	Argentina v Panama at North Sound.
6-19	A. R. Nagwaswalla	Gujarat v Maharashtra at Vadodara.
6-23	R. Dhawan.............	Himachal Pradesh v Jammu & Kashmir at Vadodara.[W23]
6-24	J. N. Frylinck..........	Namibia v United Arab Emirates at Dubai.
6-25	J. D. F. Vandersay.......	Colombo Stars v Kandy Warriors at Colombo (RPS).[W23]
6-30	A. C. Agar.............	Australia v New Zealand at Wellington.

Four Wickets in Four Balls

C. Campher............ Ireland v Netherlands at Abu Dhabi.

Four Wickets in Five Balls

D. A. Blignaut.......... Germany v Italy at Almeria.

There were 17 further hat-tricks in addition to Campher and Blignaut.

Outstanding Innings Analyses

4–4–0–2	A. K. Karnewar	Vidarbha v Manipur at Mangalagiri.[W23]
4–4–0–2	Saad Bin Zafar.........	Canada v Panama at Coolidge.

Most Catches in an Innings in the Field

5 Mohammad Nabi....... Sunrisers Hyderabad v Mumbai Indians at Abu Dhabi.

Highest Innings Totals

255-5	(20 overs)	Jamaica Tallawahs v St Lucia Kings at Basseterre.
247-2	(20 overs)	Islamabad United v Peshawar Zalmi at Abu Dhabi.
245-1	(20 overs)	Canada v Panama at Coolidge.

Lowest Innings Totals

26	(12.4 overs)	Lesotho v Uganda at Kigali City.
37	(17.2 overs)	Panama v Canada at Coolidge.
38	(10.1 overs)	Cameroon v Mozambique at Kigali.

Largest Victories

208 runs   Canada 245-1 (20 overs) v Panama 37 (17.2 overs) at Coolidge.

There were 25 wins by ten wickets.

There were six ties, excluding nine settled by a super over.

RECORDS

Compiled by Philip Bailey

This section covers
- first-class records to December 31, 2021 (page 1237).
- List A one-day records to December 31, 2021 (page 1265).
- List A Twenty20 records to December 31, 2021 (page 1269).
- All-format career records to December 31, 2021 (page 1272).
- Test records to January 16, 2022, the end of the Australia v England series (page 1273).
- Test records series by series (page 1308).
- one-day international records to December 31, 2021 (page 1354).
- Twenty20 international records to December 31, 2021 (page 1366).
- miscellaneous other records to December 31, 2021 (page 1373).
- women's Test records, one-day international and Twenty20 international records to December 31, 2021 (page 1377).

The sequence
- Test series records begin with those involving England, arranged in the order their opponents entered Test cricket (Australia, South Africa, West Indies, New Zealand, India, Pakistan, Sri Lanka, Zimbabwe, Bangladesh, Ireland, Afghanistan). Next come all remaining series involving Australia, then South Africa – and so on until Ireland v Afghanistan records appear on page 1350.

Notes
- Unless otherwise stated, all records apply only to first-class cricket. This is considered to have started in 1772, when Hambledon played All England.
- mid-year seasons taking place outside England are given simply as 2020, 2021, etc.
- (E), (A), (SA), (WI), (NZ), (I), (P), (SL), (Z), (B), (Ire), (Afg) indicates the nationality of a player or the country in which a record was made.
- in career records, dates in italic indicate seasons embracing two different years (i.e. non-English seasons). In these cases, only the first year is given, e.g. *2020* for 2020-21.

See also
- up-to-date records on www.wisdenrecords.com.
- Features of 2021 (page 1221).

CONTENTS

FIRST-CLASS RECORDS

BATTING RECORDS

LIST A ONE-DAY RECORDS

LIST A TWENTY20 RECORDS

ALL-FORMAT CAREER RECORDS

MEN'S TEST RECORDS

BATTING RECORDS

BOWLING RECORDS

ALL-ROUND RECORDS

WICKETKEEPING RECORDS

FIELDING RECORDS

TEAM RECORDS

PLAYERS

UMPIRES

TEST SERIES

MEN'S ONE-DAY INTERNATIONAL RECORDS

MEN'S TWENTY20 INTERNATIONAL RECORDS

MISCELLANEOUS RECORDS

WOMEN'S INTERNATIONAL RECORDS

NOTES ON RECORDS

All change, and all ten

STEVEN LYNCH

As explained on page 118, the main change to our Records section this year is the alignment with the Association of Cricket Statisticians and Historians' list of first-class matches, which has meant occasional amendments to old-established figures. But modern-day feats meant changes in other areas too. In Mumbai, New Zealand's Ajaz Patel became only the third bowler to take all ten wickets in a Test innings (and the first to do so in the city of his birth), while in Oudtshoorn in South Africa, Sean Whitehead of South Western Districts – another slow left-armer – took ten for 36 against Easterns (he managed 15 in the match and, batting at No. 8, scored 66 and 45).

Jimmy Anderson claimed his 1,000th first-class wicket, from the end that bears his name at Old Trafford. He was the 216th to get there but, given the general reduction in long-form matches, it's possible he will be the last: next on the list, with 889, is 40-year-old Tim Murtagh. For current batsmen, only Alastair Cook has as many as 20,000 first-class runs (a country mile behind Jack Hobbs's revised tally of 61,760). Joe Root should become the 14th to reach 10,000 in Tests during 2022.

Exotic locations catch the eye; among countries who played their first official T20 internationals in 2021 were Estonia and eSwatini. Peter Aho of Nigeria took six for five – the best figures in T20 internationals – against Sierra Leone at the University of Lagos. The equivalent women's record also changed hands: Frédérique Overdijk of the Netherlands claimed seven for three (six bowled, one lbw) as France were filleted for 33 at La Manga.

And keep an eye on India's Ranji Trophy. It resumed in 2022 after almost two Covid-affected years and, in one of the early games, Bihar's Sakibul Gani hit 341, the first triple-century by a first-class debutant. Next year's section is taking shape already.

ROLL OF DISHONOUR

The following players have either been banned after being found guilty of breaching anti-corruption codes, or have admitted to some form of on-field corruption:

Amir Hayat (UAE), Amit Singh (I), Ashfaq Ahmed (UAE), Ata-ur-Rehman (P), M. Azharuddin (I), A. Bali (I), G. H. Bodi (SA), A. Chandila (I), A. A. Chavan (I), P. Cleary (A), W. J. Cronje (SA), Danish Kaneria (P), L. H. D. Dilhara (SL), Ghulam Shabbir (UAE), H. H. Gibbs (SA), C. L. Hall (A), Haseeb Amjad (HK), Irfan Ahmed (HK), Irfan Ansari (UAE), A. Jadeja (I), S. T. Jayasuriya (SL), H. N. K. Jensen (NZ), Khalid Latif (P), J. Logan (A), K. S. Lokuarachchi (SL), P. Matshikwe (SA), N. E. Mbhalati (SA), M. D. Mishra (I), Mohammad Amir (P), Mohammad Ashraful (B), Mohammad Asif (P), Mohammad Irfan (P), Mohammad Naveed (UAE), Mohammad Nawaz (P), Nadeem Ahmed (HK), Nasir Jamshed (P), Naved Arif (P), M. O. Odumbe (Ken), A. N. Petersen (SA), M. Prabhakar (I), Qadeer Ahmed (UAE), Salim Malik (P), Salman Butt (P), M. N. Samuels (WI), Shafiqullah Shinwari (Afg), H. N. Shah (I), Shaiman Anwar (UAE), Shakib Al Hasan (B), Shariful Haque (B), Sharjeel Khan (P), Ajay Sharma (I), S. Sreesanth (I), S. J. Srivastava (I), H. H. Streak (Z), T. P. Sudhindra (I), J. Symes (SA), B. R. M. Taylor (Z), S. K. Trivedi (I), T. L. Tsolekile (SA), L. L. Tsotsobe (SA), Umar Akmal (P), L. Vincent (NZ), M. S. Westfield (E), H. S. Williams (SA), A. R. Yadav (I), Yousuf Mahmood (Oman), D. N. T. Zoysa (SL).

FIRST-CLASS RECORDS

This section covers first-class cricket to December 31, 2021. Bold type denotes performances in the calendar year 2021 or, in career figures, players who appeared in first-class cricket in that year.

BATTING RECORDS

HIGHEST INDIVIDUAL INNINGS

In all first-class cricket, there have been **232** individual scores of 300 or more. The highest are:

501*	B. C. Lara	Warwickshire v Durham at Birmingham	1994
499	Hanif Mohammad	Karachi v Bahawalpur at Karachi	1958-59
452*	D. G. Bradman	NSW v Queensland at Sydney	1929-30
443*	B. B. Nimbalkar	Maharashtra v Kathiawar at Poona	1948-49
437	W. H. Ponsford	Victoria v Queensland at Melbourne	1927-28
429	W. H. Ponsford	Victoria v Tasmania at Melbourne	1922-23
428	Aftab Baloch	Sind v Baluchistan at Karachi	1973-74
424	A. C. MacLaren	Lancashire v Somerset at Taunton	1895
405*	G. A. Hick	Worcestershire v Somerset at Taunton	1988
400*	B. C. Lara	West Indies v England at St John's	2003-04
394	Naved Latif	Sargodha v Gujranwala at Gujranwala	2000-01
390	S. C. Cook	Lions v Warriors at East London	2009-10
385	B. Sutcliffe	Otago v Canterbury at Christchurch	1952-53
383	C. W. Gregory	NSW v Queensland at Brisbane	1906-07
380	M. L. Hayden	Australia v Zimbabwe at Perth	2003-04
377	S. V. Manjrekar	Bombay v Hyderabad at Bombay	1990-91
375	B. C. Lara	West Indies v England at St John's	1993-94
374	D. P. M. D. Jayawardene	Sri Lanka v South Africa at Colombo (SSC)	2006
369	D. G. Bradman	South Australia v Tasmania at Adelaide	1935-36
366	N. H. Fairbrother	Lancashire v Surrey at The Oval	1990
366	M. V. Sridhar	Hyderabad v Andhra at Secunderabad	1993-94
365*	C. Hill	South Australia v NSW at Adelaide	1900-01
365*	G. S. Sobers	West Indies v Pakistan at Kingston	1957-58
364	L. Hutton	England v Australia at The Oval	1938
359*	V. M. Merchant	Bombay v Maharashtra at Bombay	1943-44
359*	S. B. Gohel	Gujarat v Orissa at Jaipur	2016-17
359	R. B. Simpson	NSW v Queensland at Brisbane	1963-64
357*	R. Abel	Surrey v Somerset at The Oval	1899
357	D. G. Bradman	South Australia v Victoria at Melbourne	1935-36
356	B. A. Richards	South Australia v Western Australia at Perth	1970-71
355*	G. R. Marsh	Western Australia v South Australia at Perth	1989-90
355*	K. P. Pietersen	Surrey v Leicestershire at The Oval	2015
355	B. Sutcliffe	Otago v Auckland at Dunedin	1949-50
354*	L. D. Chandimal	Army v Saracens at Katunayake	2020
353	V. V. S. Laxman	Hyderabad v Karnataka at Bangalore	1999-2000
352	W. H. Ponsford	Victoria v NSW at Melbourne	1926-27
352	C. A. Pujara	Saurashtra v Karnataka at Rajkot	2012-13
351*	S. M. Gugale	Maharashtra v Delhi at Mumbai	2016-17
351	K. D. K. Vithanage	Tamil Union v Air Force at Katunayake	2014-15
350	Rashid Israr	Habib Bank v National Bank at Lahore	1976-77

A fuller list can be found in Wisdens *up to 2011.*

DOUBLE-HUNDRED ON DEBUT

227	T. Marsden	Sheffield & Leicester v Nottingham at Sheffield	1826
207	N. F. Callaway†	New South Wales v Queensland at Sydney	1914-15
		In his only first-class innings. He was killed in action in France in 1917.	
240	W. F. E. Marx	Transvaal v Griqualand West at Johannesburg	1920-21
200*	A. Maynard	Trinidad v MCC at Port-of-Spain	1934-35
232*	S. J. E. Loxton	Victoria v Queensland at Melbourne	1946-47

215*	G. H. G. Doggart	Cambridge University v Lancashire at Cambridge . . .	1948
202	J. Hallebone	Victoria v Tasmania at Melbourne	1951-52
230	G. R. Viswanath	Mysore v Andhra at Vijayawada.	1967-68
260	A. A. Muzumdar	Bombay v Haryana at Faridabad.	1993-94
209*	A. Pandey	Madhya Pradesh v Uttar Pradesh at Bhilai	1995-96
210*	D. J. Sales	Northamptonshire v Worcestershire at Kidderminster	1996
200*	M. J. Powell	Glamorgan v Oxford University at Oxford	1997
201*	M. C. Juneja	Gujarat v Tamil Nadu at Ahmedabad	2011-12
213	Jiwanjot Singh	Punjab v Hyderabad at Mohali	2012-13
202	A. Gupta	Punjab v Himachal Pradesh at Dharamsala	2017-18
256*	Bahir Shah	Speen Ghar v Amo at Ghazi Amanullah Town	2017-18
203	B. D. Schmulian	C. Districts v N. Districts at Mount Maunganui	2017-18
228	M. Raghav	Manipur v Nagaland at Dimapur	2018-19
267*	A. R. Rohera	Madhya Pradesh v Hyderabad at Indore	2018-19
200*	Hanif Kunrai	Kunar v Kandahar at Asadabad.	2018-19
233*	Arslan Khan	Chandigarh v Arunachal Pradesh at Chandigarh.	2019-20

TWO SEPARATE HUNDREDS ON DEBUT

148	and 111	A. R. Morris	New South Wales v Queensland at Sydney	1940-41
152	and 102*	N. J. Contractor	Gujarat v Baroda at Baroda	1952-53
132*	and 110	Aamer Malik	Lahore A v Railways at Lahore	1979-80
130	and 100*	Noor Ali	Afghanistan v Zimbabwe XI at Mutare	2009
158	and 103*	K. H. T. Indika	Police v Seeduwa Raddoluwa at Colombo (Police)	2010-11
126	and 112	V. S. Awate	Maharashtra v Vidarbha at Nagpur.	2012-13
154*	and 109*	T. J. Dean	Victoria v Queensland at Melbourne	2015-16
102	and 142	Haji Murad	Amo v Speen Ghar at Ghazi Amanullah Town . .	2017-18

TWO DOUBLE-HUNDREDS IN A MATCH

| A. E. Fagg . . . . | 244 | 202* | Kent v Essex at Colchester. . . . . | 1938 |
| A. K. Perera . . . . | 201 | 231 | Nondescripts v Sinhalese at Colombo (PSO). | 2018-19 |

TRIPLE-HUNDRED AND HUNDRED IN A MATCH

| G. A. Gooch. . . . . | 333 | 123 | England v India at Lord's. . . . . | 1990 |
| K. C. Sangakkara . . . . . | 319 | 105 | Sri Lanka v Bangladesh at Chittagong . . . . . . | 2013-14 |

DOUBLE-HUNDRED AND HUNDRED IN A MATCH

In addition to Fagg, Perera, Gooch and Sangakkara, there have been **65** further instances of a batter scoring a double-hundred and a hundred in the same first-class match. The most recent are:

N. V. Ojha.	219*	101*	India A v Australia A at Brisbane	2014
S. D. Robson	231	106	Middlesex v Warwickshire at Lord's	2016
G. S. Ballance	108	203*	Yorkshire v Hampshire at Southampton	2017
B. O. P. Fernando	109	234	Chilaw Marians v Colts at Colombo (NCC) . .	2018-19
D. P. Sibley	215*	109	Warwickshire v Nottinghamshire at Nottingham	2019
R. Dalal	178	205*	Arunachal Pradesh v Mizoram at Puducherry	2019-20

Zaheer Abbas achieved the feat four times, for Gloucestershire between 1976 and 1981, and was not out in all eight innings. M. R. Hallam did it twice for Leicestershire, in 1959 and 1961; N. R. Taylor twice for Kent, in 1990 and 1991; G. A. Gooch for England in 1990 (see above) and Essex in 1994; M. W. Goodwin twice for Sussex, in 2001 and 2007; and C. J. L. Rogers for Northamptonshire in 2006 and for Derbyshire in 2010.

TWO SEPARATE HUNDREDS IN A MATCH MOST TIMES

R. T. Ponting	8	J. B. Hobbs	6	M. L. Hayden	5
Zaheer Abbas	8	G. M. Turner	6	G. A. Hick	5
W. R. Hammond	7	C. B. Fry.	5	C. J. L. Rogers	5
M. R. Ramprakash	7	G. A. Gooch	5	

W. Lambert scored 107 and 157 for Sussex v Epsom at Lord's in 1817, a feat not repeated until W. G. Grace's 130 and 102* for South of the Thames v North of the Thames at Canterbury in 1868.

FIVE HUNDREDS OR MORE IN SUCCESSION

D. G. Bradman (1938-39)	6	B. C. Lara (1993-94–1994)	5
C. B. Fry (1901)	6	P. A. Patel (2007–2007-08)	5
M. J. Procter (1970-71)	6	K. C. Sangakkara (2017)	5
M. E. K. Hussey (2003)	5	E. D. Weekes (1955-56)	5

Bradman also scored four hundreds in succession twice, in 1931-32 and 1948–1948-49; W. R. Hammond did it in 1936-37 and 1945–1946, and H. Sutcliffe in 1931 and 1939.

T. W. Hayward (Surrey v Nottinghamshire and Leicestershire), D. W. Hookes (South Australia v Queensland and New South Wales) and V. Sibanda (Zimbabwe XI v Kenya and Mid West v Southern Rocks) are the only players to score two hundreds in each of two successive matches. Hayward scored his in six days, June 4–9, 1906.

The most fifties in consecutive innings is ten – by E. Tyldesley in 1926, by D. G. Bradman in the 1947-48 and 1948 seasons and by R. S. Kaluwitharana in 1994-95.

MOST HUNDREDS IN A SEASON

D. C. S. Compton (1947)	18	T. W. Hayward (1906)	13
J. B. Hobbs (1925)	16	E. H. Hendren (1923)	13
W. R. Hammond (1938)	15	E. H. Hendren (1927)	13
H. Sutcliffe (1932)	14	E. H. Hendren (1928)	13
G. Boycott (1971)	13	C. P. Mead (1928)	13
D. G. Bradman (1938)	13	H. Sutcliffe (1928)	13
C. B. Fry (1901)	13	H. Sutcliffe (1931)	13
W. R. Hammond (1933)	13		
W. R. Hammond (1937)	13		

Since 1969 (excluding G. Boycott – above)

G. A. Gooch (1990)	12	M. R. Ramprakash (1995)	10
S. J. Cook (1991)	11	M. R. Ramprakash (2007)	10
Zaheer Abbas (1976)	11	G. M. Turner (1970)	10
G. A. Hick (1988)	10	Zaheer Abbas (1981)	10
H. Morris (1990)	10		

The most outside England is nine by V. Sibanda in Zimbabwe (2009-10), followed by eight by D. G. Bradman in Australia (1947-48), D. C. S. Compton (1948-49), R. N. Harvey and A. R. Morris (both 1949-50) all three in South Africa, M. D. Crowe in New Zealand (1986-87), Asif Mujtaba in Pakistan (1995-96), V. V. S. Laxman in India (1999-2000), M. G. Bevan in Australia (2004-05) and Zia-ul-Haq in Afghanistan (2017-18).

The most double-hundreds in a season is six by D. G. Bradman (1930), five by K. S. Ranjitsinhji (1900) and E. D. Weekes (1950), and four by Arun Lal (1986-87), C. B. Fry (1901), W. R. Hammond (1933 and 1934), E. H. Hendren (1929-30), V. M. Merchant (1944-45), C. A. Pujara (2012-13) and G. M. Turner (1971-72).

MOST DOUBLE-HUNDREDS IN A CAREER

D. G. Bradman	37	G. A. Gooch	13	J. L. Langer	12
W. R. Hammond	36	W. G. Grace	13	R. B. Simpson	12
E. H. Hendren	22	B. C. Lara	13	Younis Khan	12
M. R. Ramprakash	17	C. P. Mead	13	J. W. Hearne	11
H. Sutcliffe	17	W. H. Ponsford	13	L. Hutton	11
C. B. Fry	16	**C. A. Pujara**	**13**	D. S. Lehmann	11
G. A. Hick	16	K. C. Sangakkara	13	V. M. Merchant	11
J. B. Hobbs	16	J. T. Tyldesley	13	C. J. L. Rogers	11
C. G. Greenidge	14	P. Holmes	12	A. Sandham	11
K. S. Ranjitsinhji	14	Javed Miandad	12	G. Boycott	10

R. Dravid 10
M. W. Gatting 10
S. M. Gavaskar 10
J. Hardstaff jnr. 10
V. S. Hazare 10

B. J. Hodge 10
D. P. M. D. Jayawardene 10
I. V. A. Richards 10
A. Shrewsbury 10
R. T. Simpson 10

G. M. Turner 10
Zaheer Abbas 10

MOST HUNDREDS IN A CAREER

(100 or more)

		Total	100th 100				
		Total	Inns	Season	Inns	400+	300+	200+
1	J. B. Hobbs	199	1,325	1923	819	0	1	16
2	E. H. Hendren	170	1,300	1928-29	740	0	1	22
3	W. R. Hammond	167	1,005	1935	680	0	4	36
4	C. P. Mead	153	1,340	1927	892	0	0	13
5	G. Boycott	151	1,014	1977	645	0	0	10
	H. Sutcliffe	151	1,098	1932	702	0	1	17
7	F. E. Woolley	145	1,530	1929	1,029	0	1	9
8	G. A. Hick	136	871	1998	574	1	3	16
9	L. Hutton	129	814	1951	619	0	1	11
10	G. A. Gooch	128	990	1992-93	820	0	1	13
11	W. G. Grace	124	1,478	1895	1,103	0	3	13
12	D. C. S. Compton	123	839	1952	552	0	1	9
13	T. W. Graveney	122	1,223	1964	940	0	0	7
14	D. G. Bradman	117	338	1947-48	295	1	6	37
15	I. V. A. Richards	114	796	1988-89	658	0	1	10
	M. R. Ramprakash	114	764	2008	676	0	1	17
17	Zaheer Abbas	108	768	1982-83	658	0	0	10
18	A. Sandham	107	1,000	1935	871	0	1	11
	M. C. Cowdrey	107	1,130	1973	1,035	0	1	3
20	T. W. Hayward	104	1,138	1913	1,076	0	1	8
21	G. M. Turner	103	792	1982	779	0	1	10
	J. H. Edrich	103	979	1977	945	0	1	4
23	L. E. G. Ames	102	951	1950	916	0	0	9
	E. Tyldesley	102	961	1934	919	0	0	7
	D. L. Amiss	102	1,139	1986	1,081	0	0	3

In the above table, 200+, 300+ and 400+ include all scores above those figures.
Zaheer Abbas and G. Boycott scored their 100th hundreds in Test matches.

Current Players

The following who played in 2021 have scored 40 or more hundreds.

A. N. Cook 69
H. M. Amla 55
C. A. Pujara 50
J. C. Hildreth 47

D. Elgar 44
S. P. D. Smith 43
F. D. M. Karunaratne 42
Azhar Ali 41

G. S. Ballance 41
Fawad Alam 41

MOST RUNS IN A SEASON

	Season	M	I	NO	R	HS	100	Avge
D. C. S. Compton	1947	30	50	8	3,816	246	18	90.85
W. J. Edrich	1947	30	52	8	3,539	267*	12	80.43
T. W. Hayward	1906	36	61	8	3,518	219	13	66.37
L. Hutton	1949	33	56	6	3,429	269*	12	68.58
F. E. Woolley	1928	36	59	4	3,352	198	12	60.94
H. Sutcliffe	1932	35	52	7	3,336	313	14	74.13
W. R. Hammond	1933	34	54	5	3,323	264	13	67.81
E. H. Hendren	1928	35	54	7	3,311	209*	13	70.44
R. Abel	1901	38	68	8	3,309	247	7	55.15

3,000 in a season has been surpassed on 19 other occasions (a full list can be found in Wisden 1999 *and earlier editions). W. R. Hammond, E. H. Hendren and H. Sutcliffe are the only players to achieve the feat three times. K. S. Ranjitsinhji was the first to reach 3,000 in a season, with 3,159 in 1899. M. J. K. Smith (3,245 in 1959) and W. E. Alley (3,019 in 1961) are the only players except those listed above to have reached 3,000 since the Second World War.*

W. G. Grace scored 2,739 runs in 25 matches in 1871 – the first to reach 2,000 in a season. He made ten hundreds, including two double-hundreds, and averaged 78.25.

The highest aggregate in a season since the reduction of County Championship matches in 1969 was 2,755 by S. J. Cook (24 matches, 42 innings) in 1991, and the last to achieve 2,000 in England was M. R. Ramprakash (2,026 in 2007); C. A. Pujara scored 2,064 in India in 2016-17.

2,000 RUNS IN A SEASON MOST TIMES

J. B. Hobbs............ 17	F. E. Woolley......... 13	C. P. Mead........... 11
E. H. Hendren......... 15	W. R. Hammond 12	T. W. Hayward........ 10
H. Sutcliffe............ 15	J. G. Langridge........ 11	

Since the reduction of County Championship matches in 1969, G. A. Gooch is the only batter to have reached 2,000 in a season five times.

1,000 RUNS IN A SEASON MOST TIMES

Includes overseas tours and seasons

W. G. Grace............ 28	A. Jones.............. 23	G. Gunn.............. 20
F. E. Woolley 28	T. W. Graveney........ 22	T. W. Hayward........ 20
M. C. Cowdrey 27	W. R. Hammond 22	G. A. Hick 20
C. P. Mead........... 27	D. Denton 21	James Langridge 20
G. Boycott 26	J. H. Edrich 21	J. M. Parks........... 20
J. B. Hobbs 26	G. A. Gooch 21	M. R. Ramprakash...... 20
E. H. Hendren 25	W. Rhodes 21	A. Sandham........... 20
D. L. Amiss........... 24	D. B. Close 20	M. J. K. Smith 20
W. G. Quaife 24	K. W. R. Fletcher 20	C. Washbrook 20
H. Sutcliffe 24	M. W. Gatting 20	

F. E. Woolley reached 1,000 runs in 28 consecutive seasons (1907–1938), C. P. Mead in 27 (1906–1936).

Outside England, 1,000 runs in a season has been reached most times by D. G. Bradman (in 12 seasons in Australia).

Three batters have scored 1,000 runs in a season in each of four different countries: G. S. Sobers in West Indies, England, India and Australia; M. C. Cowdrey and G. Boycott in England, South Africa, West Indies and Australia.

HIGHEST AGGREGATES OUTSIDE ENGLAND

	Season	M	I	NO	R	HS	100	Avge
In Australia								
D. G. Bradman	1928-29	13	24	6	1,690	340*	7	93.88
In South Africa								
J. R. Reid................	1961-62	17	30	2	1,915	203	7	68.39
In West Indies								
E. H. Hendren	1929-30	11	18	5	1,765	254*	6	135.76
In New Zealand								
M. D. Crowe.............	1986-87	11	21	3	1,676	175*	8	93.11
In India								
C. A. Pujara.............	2016-17	17	29	4	2,064	256*	7	82.56
In Pakistan								
Saadat Ali	1983-84	14	27	1	1,649	208	4	63.42

	Season	M	I	NO	R	HS	100	Avge
In Sri Lanka								
R. P. Arnold	1995-96	16	24	3	1,475	217*	5	70.23
In Zimbabwe								
V. Sibanda.	2009-10	14	26	4	1,612	215	9	73.27
In Bangladesh								
Tushar Imran.	2016-17	12	16	2	1,249	220	5	89.21
In Afghanistan								
Zia-ul-Haq.	2017-18	17	31	4	1,616	148	8	59.85

The highest aggregate for a season in Ireland is 491 by W. T. S. Porterfield in 2018.

Excluding Pujara in India (above), the following aggregates of over 2,000 runs have been recorded in more than one country:

	Season	M	I	NO	R	HS	100	Avge
M. Amarnath (I/P/WI)	1982-83	21	34	6	2,234	207	9	79.78
J. R. Reid (A/SA/NZ)	1961-62	22	40	2	2,188	203	7	57.57
S. M. Gavaskar (P/I)	1978-79	21	30	6	2,121	205	10	88.37
R. B. Simpson (I/P/A/WI)...	1964-65	20	34	4	2,063	201	8	68.76
M. H. Richardson (Z/SA/NZ)	2000-01	21	34	3	2,030	306	4	65.48

The only other player to hit ten hundreds in an overseas season was V. V. S. Laxman in India and Australia in 1999-2000.

LEADING BATTERS IN AN ENGLISH SEASON

(Qualification: 8 completed innings)

Season	Leading scorer	Runs	Avge	Top of averages	Runs	Avge
1946	D. C. S. Compton	2,403	61.61	W. R. Hammond.	1,783	84.90
1947	D. C. S. Compton	3,816	90.85	D. C. S. Compton	3,816	90.85
1948	L. Hutton	2,654	64.73	D. G. Bradman	2,428	89.92
1949	L. Hutton	3,429	68.58	J. Hardstaff	2,251	72.61
1950	R. T. Simpson	2,576	62.82	E. D. Weekes	2,310	79.65
1951	J. D. Robertson	2,917	56.09	P. B. H. May	2,339	68.79
1952	L. Hutton	2,567	61.11	D. S. Sheppard	2,262	64.62
1953	W. J. Edrich.	2,557	47.35	R. N. Harvey.	2,040	65.80
1954	D. Kenyon	2,636	51.68	D. C. S. Compton	1,524	58.61
1955	D. J. Insole.	2,427	42.57	D. J. McGlew	1,871	58.46
1956	T. W. Graveney.	2,397	49.93	K. Mackay	1,103	52.52
1957	T. W. Graveney.	2,361	49.18	P. B. H. May	2,347	61.76
1958	P. B. H. May	2,231	63.74	P. B. H. May	2,231	63.74
1959	M. J. K. Smith	3,245	57.94	V. L. Manjrekar	755	68.63
1960	M. J. K. Smith	2,551	56.95	R. Subba Row	1,503	55.66
1961	W. E. Alley	3,019	56.96	W. M. Lawry.	2,019	61.18
1962	J. H. Edrich	2,482	51.70	R. T. Simpson	867	54.18
1963	J. B. Bolus	2,190	41.32	G. S. Sobers	1,333	47.60
1964	T. W. Graveney.	2,385	54.20	K. F. Barrington	1,872	62.40
1965	J. H. Edrich	2,319	62.67	M. C. Cowdrey	2,093	63.42
1966	A. R. Lewis	2,198	41.47	G. S. Sobers	1,349	61.31
1967	C. A. Milton	2,089	46.42	K. F. Barrington	2,059	68.63
1968	B. A. Richards.	2,395	47.90	G. Boycott.	1,487	64.65
1969	J. H. Edrich	2,238	69.93	J. H. Edrich	2,238	69.93
1970	G. M. Turner	2,379	61.00	G. S. Sobers	1,742	75.73
1971	G. Boycott.	2,503	100.12	G. Boycott.	2,503	100.12
1972	Majid Khan	2,074	61.00	G. Boycott.	1,230	72.35
1973	G. M. Turner	2,416	67.11	G. M. Turner	2,416	67.11
1974	R. T. Virgin	1,936	56.94	C. H. Lloyd.	1,458	63.39
1975	G. Boycott.	1,915	73.65	R. B. Kanhai	1,073	82.53
1976	Zaheer Abbas	2,554	75.11	Zaheer Abbas	2,554	75.11
1977	I. V. A. Richards	2,161	65.48	G. Boycott.	1,701	68.04

Season	Leading scorer	Runs	Avge	Top of averages	Runs	Avge
1978	D. L. Amiss	2,030	53.42	C. E. B. Rice	1,871	66.82
1979	K. C. Wessels	1,800	52.94	G. Boycott.	1,538	102.53
1980	P. N. Kirsten	1,895	63.16	A. J. Lamb	1,797	66.55
1981	Zaheer Abbas	2,306	88.69	Zaheer Abbas	2,306	88.69
1982	A. I. Kallicharran.	2,120	66.25	G. M. Turner.	1,171	90.07
1983	K. S. McEwan	2,176	64.00	I. V. A. Richards.	1,204	75.25
1984	G. A. Gooch	2,559	67.34	C. G. Greenidge	1,069	82.23
1985	G. A. Gooch	2,208	71.22	I. V. A. Richards.	1,836	76.50
1986	C. G. Greenidge.	2,035	67.83	C. G. Greenidge	2,035	67.83
1987	G. A. Hick	1,879	52.19	M. D. Crowe	1,627	67.79
1988	G. A. Hick	2,713	77.51	R. A. Harper	622	77.75
1989	S. J. Cook	2,241	60.56	D. M. Jones.	1,510	88.82
1990	G. A. Gooch	2,746	101.70	G. A. Gooch	2,746	101.70
1991	S. J. Cook	2,755	81.02	C. L. Hooper	1,501	93.81
1992	{ P. D. Bowler . . . . { M. A. Roseberry	2,044 2,044	65.93 56.77	Salim Malik	1,184	78.93
1993	G. A. Gooch	2,023	63.21	D. C. Boon	1,437	75.63
1994	B. C. Lara	2,066	89.82	J. D. Carr.	1,543	90.76
1995	M. R. Ramprakash. . .	2,258	77.86	M. R. Ramprakash . . .	2,258	77.86
1996	G. A. Gooch	1,944	67.03	S. C. Ganguly	762	95.25
1997	S. P. James.	1,775	68.26	G. A. Hick	1,524	69.27
1998	J. P. Crawley	1,851	74.04	J. P. Crawley	1,851	74.04
1999	S. G. Law	1,833	73.32	S. G. Law	1,833	73.32
2000	D. S. Lehmann.	1,477	67.13	M. G. Bevan	1,124	74.93
2001	M. E. K. Hussey	2,055	79.03	D. R. Martyn.	942	104.66
2002	I. J. Ward.	1,759	62.82	R. Dravid	773	96.62
2003	S. G. Law	1,820	91.00	S. G. Law	1,820	91.00
2004	R. W. T. Key	1,896	79.00	R. W. T. Key	1,896	79.00
2005	O. A. Shah.	1,728	66.46	M. E. K. Hussey	1,074	76.71
2006	M. R. Ramprakash. . .	2,278	103.54	M. R. Ramprakash . . .	2,278	103.54
2007	M. R. Ramprakash. . .	2,026	101.30	M. R. Ramprakash . . .	2,026	101.30
2008	S. C. Moore	1,451	55.80	T. Frost	1,003	83.58
2009	M. E. Trescothick	1,817	75.70	M. R. Ramprakash . . .	1,350	90.00
2010	M. R. Ramprakash. . .	1,595	61.34	J. C. Hildreth.	1,440	65.45
2011	M. E. Trescothick	1,673	79.66	I. R. Bell.	1,091	90.91
2012	N. R. D. Compton . . .	1,494	99.60	N. R. D. Compton . . .	1,494	99.60
2013	C. J. L. Rogers.	1,536	51.20	S. M. Katich	1,097	73.13
2014	A. Lyth	1,619	70.39	J. E. Root	1,052	75.14
2015	J. C. Hildreth	1,758	56.70	J. M. Bairstow.	1,226	72.11
2016	K. K. Jennings.	1,602	64.08	S. A. Northeast	1,402	82.47
2017	K. C. Sangakkara. . . .	1,491	106.50	K. C. Sangakkara	1,491	106.50
2018	R. J. Burns.	1,402	60.95	O. J. D. Pope.	1,098	61.00
2019	D. P. Sibley	1,575	68.47	O. J. D. Pope	812	101.50
2020	A. N. Cook	563	56.30	Z. Crawley	522	65.25
2021	**T. J. Haines**	**1,176**	**47.04**	**O. J. D. Pope**	**1,028**	**64.25**

The highest average recorded in an English season was 115.66 (2,429 runs, 26 innings) by D. G. Bradman in 1938.

In 1953, W. A. Johnston averaged 102.00 from 17 innings, 16 not out.

MOST RUNS

Dates in italics denote the first half of an overseas season; i.e. *1945* denotes the 1945-46 season.

		Career	M	I	NO	R	HS	100	Avge
1	J. B. Hobbs	1905–1934	834	1,325	107	61,760	316*	199	50.70
2	F. E. Woolley. . . .	1906–1938	978	1,530	84	58,959	305*	145	40.77
3	E. H. Hendren . . .	1907–1938	833	1,300	166	57,611	301*	170	50.80
4	C. P. Mead.	1905–1936	814	1,340	185	55,061	280*	153	47.67
5	W. G. Grace.	1865–1908	870	1,478	104	54,211	344	124	39.45

		Career	M	I	NO	R	HS	100	Avge
6	H. Sutcliffe......	1919–1945	754	1,098	124	50,670	313	151	52.02
7	W. R. Hammond .	1920–1951	634	1,005	104	50,551	336*	167	56.10
8	G. Boycott......	1962–1986	609	1,014	162	48,426	261*	151	56.83
9	T. W. Graveney ..	1948–*1971*	732	1,223	159	47,793	258	122	44.91
10	G. A. Gooch.....	1973–2000	581	990	75	44,846	333	128	49.01
11	T. W. Hayward ...	1893–1914	712	1,138	96	43,547	315*	104	41.79
12	D. L. Amiss	1960–1987	658	1,139	126	43,423	262*	102	42.86
13	M. C. Cowdrey ..	1950–1976	692	1,130	134	42,719	307	107	42.89
14	A. Sandham.....	1911–*1937*	643	1,000	79	41,284	325	107	44.82
15	G. A. Hick	*1983*–2008	526	871	84	41,112	405*	136	52.23
16	L. Hutton.......	1934–1960	513	814	91	40,140	364	129	55.51
17	W. Rhodes......	1898–1930	1,110	1,534	237	39,969	267*	58	30.81
18	M. J. K. Smith ...	1951–1975	637	1,091	139	39,832	204	69	41.84
19	J. H. Edrich	1956–1978	564	979	104	39,790	310*	103	45.47
20	R. E. S. Wyatt ...	1923–1957	739	1,141	157	39,405	232	85	40.04
21	D. C. S. Compton	1936–1964	515	839	88	38,942	300	123	51.85
22	E. Tyldesley.....	1909–1936	648	961	106	38,874	256*	102	45.46
23	J. T. Tyldesley ...	1895–1923	608	994	62	37,897	295*	86	40.66
24	K. W. R. Fletcher	1962–1988	730	1,167	170	37,665	228*	63	37.77
25	C. G. Greenidge..	1970–1992.	523	889	75	37,354	273*	92	45.88
26	J. W. Hearne.....	1909–1936	647	1,025	116	37,252	285*	96	40.98
27	L. E. G.Ames....	1926–1951	593	951	95	37,250	295	102	43.51
28	D. Kenyon	1946–1967	643	1,159	59	37,002	259	74	33.63
29	W. J. Edrich.....	1934–1958	571	964	92	36,965	310*	86	42.39
30	J. M. Parks......	1949–1976	739	1,227	172	36,673	205*	51	34.76
31	M. W. Gatting ...	1975–1998	551	861	123	36,549	258	94	49.52
32	D. Denton	1894–1920	742	1,161	70	36,440	221	69	33.40
33	G. H. Hirst......	1891–1929	826	1,217	152	36,356	341	60	34.13
34	I. V. A. Richards .	*1971*–1993	507	796	63	36,212	322	114	49.40
35	A. Jones........	1957–1983	645	1,168	72	36,049	204*	56	32.89
36	W. G. Quaife	1894–1928	719	1,203	185	36,012	255*	72	35.37
37	R. E. Marshall ...	*1945*–1972	602	1,053	59	35,725	228*	68	35.94
38	M. R. Ramprakash	1987–2012	461	764	93	35,659	301*	114	53.14
39	G. Gunn........	1902–1932	643	1,061	82	35,208	220	62	35.96

Some works of reference provide career figures which differ from those in this list, owing to the exclusion or inclusion of matches recognised or not recognised as first-class by Wisden, which now accepts the Association of Cricket Statisticians' list of first-class matches.

Current Players with 20,000 Runs

	Career	M	I	NO	R	HS	100	Avge
A. N. Cook........	2003–2021	324	568	42	24,841	294	69	47.22

HIGHEST CAREER AVERAGE

(Qualification: 10,000 runs)

Avge		Career	M	I	NO	R	HS	100
95.14	D. G. Bradman...	*1927*–1948	234	338	43	28,067	452*	117
71.64	V. M. Merchant ..	1929–1951	150	234	46	13,470	359*	45
67.46	A. K. Sharma ...	*1984*–2000	129	166	16	10,120	259*	38
65.18	W. H. Ponsford ..	1920–1934	162	235	23	13,819	437	47
64.99	W. M. Woodfull ..	1921–1934	174	245	39	13,388	284	49
58.38	V. S. Hazare ...	1934–1966	238	367	46	18,740	316*	60
58.24	A. L. Hassett	1932–1953	216	322	32	16,890	232	59
57.84	S. R. Tendulkar ..	1988–2013	310	490	51	25,396	248*	81
57.83	D. S. Lehmann...	1987–2007	284	479	33	25,795	339	82

Avge		*Career*	*M*	*I*	*NO*	*R*	*HS*	*100*
57.32	M. G. Bevan.	*1989–2006*	237	400	66	19,147	216	68
57.22	A. F. Kippax	*1918–1935*	175	256	33	12,762	315*	43
56.83	G. Boycott	*1962–1986*	609	1,014	162	48,426	261*	151
56.59	**S. P. D. Smith . . .**	***2007–2021***	**139**	**242**	**27**	**12,167**	**239**	**43**
56.55	C. L. Walcott	*1941–1963*	146	238	29	11,820	314*	40
56.40	**Fawad Alam . . . .**	***2003–2021***	**187**	**292**	**48**	**13,762**	**296***	**41**
56.37	K. S. Ranjitsinhji .	*1893–1920*	307	500	62	24,692	285*	72
56.22	R. B. Simpson . . .	*1952–1977*	257	436	62	21,029	359	60
56.10	W. R. Hammond .	*1920–1951*	634	1,005	104	50,551	336*	167
56.02	M. D. Crowe	*1979–1995*	247	412	62	19,608	299	71
55.90	R. T. Ponting . . .	*1992–2013*	289	494	62	24,150	257	82
55.51	L. Hutton	*1934–1960*	513	814	91	40,140	364	129
55.34	E. D. Weekes	*1944–1964*	152	241	24	12,010	304*	36
55.33	R. Dravid	*1990–2011*	298	497	67	23,794	270	68
55.11	S. V. Manjrekar . .	*1984–1997*	147	217	31	10,252	377	31

G. A. Headley scored 9,921 runs, average 69.86, between 1927-28 and 1954; V. G. Kambli scored 9,965 runs, average 59.67, between 1989-90 and 2004-05.

FASTEST FIFTIES

Minutes

11	C. I. J. Smith (66)	Middlesex v Gloucestershire at Bristol	1938
13	Khalid Mahmood (56)	Gujranwala v Sargodha at Gujranwala.	2000-01
14	S. J. Pegler (50)	South Africans v Tasmania at Launceston.	1910-11
14	F. T. Mann (53)	Middlesex v Nottinghamshire at Lord's.	1921
14	H. B. Cameron (56)	Transvaal v Orange Free State at Johannesburg.	1934-35
14	C. I. J. Smith (52)	Middlesex v Kent at Maidstone	1935

The number of balls taken to achieve fifties was rarely recorded until recently. C. I. J. Smith's two fifties (above) may have taken only 12 balls each. Khalid Mahmood reached his fifty in 15 balls.

Fifties scored in contrived circumstances and with the bowlers' compliance are excluded from the above list, including the fastest of them all, in 8 minutes (13 balls) by C. C. Inman, Leicestershire v Nottinghamshire at Nottingham, 1965, and 10 minutes by G. Chapple, Lancashire v Glamorgan at Manchester, 1993.

FASTEST HUNDREDS

Minutes

35	P. G. H. Fender (113*)	Surrey v Northamptonshire at Northampton	1920
40	G. L. Jessop (101)	Gloucestershire v Yorkshire at Harrogate	1897
40	Ahsan-ul-Haq (100*)	Muslims v Sikhs at Lahore.	1923-24
42	G. L. Jessop (191)	Gentlemen of South v Players of South at Hastings .	1907
43	A. H. Hornby (106)	Lancashire v Somerset at Manchester	1905
43	D. W. Hookes (107)	South Australia v Victoria at Adelaide.	1982-83
44	R. N. S. Hobbs (100)	Essex v Australians at Chelmsford.	1975

The fastest recorded authentic hundred in terms of balls received was scored off 34 balls by D. W. Hookes (above). Research of the scorebook has shown that P. G. H. Fender scored his hundred from between 40 and 46 balls. He contributed 113 to an unfinished sixth-wicket partnership of 171 in 42 minutes with H. A. Peach.

E. B. Alletson (Nottinghamshire) scored 189 out of 227 runs in 90 minutes against Sussex at Hove in 1911. It has been estimated that his last 139 runs took 37 minutes.

Hundreds scored in contrived circumstances and with the bowlers' compliance are excluded, including the fastest of them all, in 21 minutes (27 balls) by G. Chapple, Lancashire v Glamorgan at Manchester, 1993, 24 minutes (27 balls) by M. L. Pettini, Essex v Leicestershire at Leicester, 2006, and 26 minutes (36 balls) by T. M. Moody, Warwickshire v Glamorgan at Swansea, 1990.

FASTEST DOUBLE-HUNDREDS

Minutes

103	Shafiqullah Shinwari (200*)	Kabul v Boost at Asadabad	2017-18
113	R. J. Shastri (200*)	Bombay v Baroda at Bombay	1984-85
120	G. L. Jessop (286)	Gloucestershire v Sussex at Hove	1903
120	C. H. Lloyd (201*)	West Indians v Glamorgan at Swansea	1976
130	G. L. Jessop (234)	Gloucestershire v Somerset at Bristol	1905
131	V. T. Trumper (293)	Australians v Canterbury at Christchurch	1913-14

Shafiqullah faced 89 balls, which was also a record.

FASTEST TRIPLE-HUNDREDS

Minutes

181	D. C. S. Compton (300)	MCC v North Eastern Transvaal at Benoni	1948-49
205	F. E. Woolley (305*)	MCC v Tasmania at Hobart	1911-12
205	C. G. Macartney (345)	Australians v Nottinghamshire at Nottingham	1921
213	D. G. Bradman (369)	South Australia v Tasmania at Adelaide	1935-36

The fastest known triple-hundred in terms of balls received was scored off 191 balls by M. Marais for Border v Eastern Province at East London in 2017-18.

MOST RUNS IN A DAY BY ONE BATTER

390*	B. C. Lara (501*)	Warwickshire v Durham at Birmingham	1994
345	C. G. Macartney (345)	Australians v Nottinghamshire at Nottingham	1921
334*	W. H. Ponsford (352)	Victoria v New South Wales at Melbourne	1926-27
333	K. S. Duleepsinhji (333)	Sussex v Northamptonshire at Hove	1930
331*	J. D. Robertson (331*)	Middlesex v Worcestershire at Worcester	1949
325*	B. A. Richards (356)	South Australia v Western Australia at Perth	1970-71

*There have been another **14** instances of a batter scoring 300 in a day, most recently 319 by R. R. Rossouw, Eagles v Titans at Centurion in 2009-10 (see Wisden 2003, page 278, for full list).*

LONGEST INNINGS

Hrs	Mins			
16	55	R. Nayyar (271)	Himachal Pradesh v Jammu & Kashmir at Chamba	1999-2000
16	10	Hanif Mohammad (337)	Pakistan v West Indies at Bridgetown	1957-58
		Hanif believed he batted 16 hours 39 minutes.		
16	4	S. B. Gohel (359*)	Gujarat v Orissa at Jaipur	2016-17
15	7	V. A. Saxena (257)	Rajasthan v Tamil Nadu at Chennai	2011-12
14	38	G. Kirsten (275)	South Africa v England at Durban	1999-2000
14	32	K. K. Nair (328)	Karnataka v Tamil Nadu at Mumbai	2014-15
13	58	S. C. Cook (390)	Lions v Warriors at East London	2009-10
13	56	A. N. Cook (263)	England v Pakistan at Abu Dhabi	2015-16
13	43	T. Kohli (300*)	Punjab v Jharkhand at Jamshedpur	2012-13
13	41	S. S. Shukla (178*)	Uttar Pradesh v Tamil Nadu at Nagpur	2008-09
13	32	A. Chopra (301*)	Rajasthan v Maharashtra at Nasik	2010-11

1,000 RUNS IN MAY

	Runs	Avge
W. G. Grace, May 9 to May 30, 1895 (22 days)	1,016	112.88
Grace was 46 years old.		
W. R. Hammond, May 7 to May 31, 1927 (25 days)	1,042	74.42
Hammond scored his 1,000th run on May 28, thus equalling		
Grace's record of 22 days.		
C. Hallows, May 5 to May 31, 1928 (27 days)	1,000	125.00

1,000 RUNS IN APRIL AND MAY

		Runs	Avge
T. W. Hayward, April 16 to May 31, 1900		1,074	97.63
D. G. Bradman, April 30 to May 31, 1930		1,001	143.00
On April 30 Bradman was 75 not out.			
D. G. Bradman, April 30 to May 31, 1938		1,056	150.85
Bradman scored 258 on April 30, and his 1,000th run on May 27.			
W. J. Edrich, April 30 to May 31, 1938		1,010	84.16
Edrich was 21 not out on April 30. All his runs were scored at Lord's.			
G. M. Turner, April 24 to May 31, 1973		1,018	78.30
G. A. Hick, April 17 to May 29, 1988		1,019	101.90
Hick scored a record 410 runs in April, and his 1,000th run on May 28.			

MOST RUNS SCORED OFF AN OVER

(All instances refer to six-ball overs)

36	G. S. Sobers	off M. A. Nash, Nottinghamshire v Glam at Swansea (six sixes)....	1968
36	R. J. Shastri	off Tilak Raj, Bombay v Baroda at Bombay (six sixes)............	1984-85
34	E. B. Alletson	off E. H. Killick, Notts v Sussex at Hove (46604446 inc 2 nb)	1911
34	F. C. Hayes	off M. A. Nash, Lancashire v Glamorgan at Swansea (646666)	1977
34†	A. Flintoff	off A. J. Tudor, Lancs v Surrey at Manchester (64444660 inc 2 nb) .	1998
34	C. M. Spearman	off S. J. P. Moreton, Gloucestershire v Oxford UCCE at Oxford (666646) *Moreton's first over in first-class cricket.*	2005
32	C. C. Smart	off G. Hill, Glamorgan v Hampshire at Cardiff (664664)	1935
32	I. R. Redpath	off N. Rosendorff, Australians v OFS at Bloemfontein (666644) ...	1969-70
32	P. W. G. Parker	off A. I. Kallicharran, Sussex v Warwicks at Birmingham (466664).	1982
32	I. T. Botham	off I. R. Snook, England XI v C Dists at Palmerston North (466466)	1983-84
32	Khalid Mahmood	off Naved Latif, Gujranwala v Sargodha at Gujranwala (666662)...	2000-01

† *Altogether 38 runs were scored off this over, the two no-balls counting for two extra runs each under ECB regulations.*

The following instances have been excluded because of the bowlers' compliance: 34 – M. P. Maynard off S. A. Marsh, Glamorgan v Kent at Swansea, 1992; 34 – G. Chapple off P. A. Cottey, Lancashire v Glamorgan at Manchester, 1993; 34 – F. B. Touzel off F. J. J. Viljoen, Western Province B v Griqualand West at Kimberley, 1993-94. Chapple scored a further 32 off Cottey's next over.

There were 35 runs off an over received by A. T. Reinholds off H. T. Davis, Auckland v Wellington at Auckland 1995-96, but this included 16 extras and only 19 off the bat.

In a match against KwaZulu-Natal at Stellenbosch in 2006-07, W. E. September (Boland) conceded 34 in an over: 27 to M. Bekker, six to K. Smit, plus one no-ball.

In a match against Canterbury at Christchurch in 1989-90, R. H. Vance (Wellington) deliberately conceded 77 runs in an over of full tosses which contained 17 no-balls and, owing to the umpire's understandable miscalculation, only five legitimate deliveries.

The greatest number of runs scored off an eight-ball over is 34 (40446664) by R. M. Edwards off M. C. Carew, Governor-General's XI v West Indians at Auckland, 1968-69.

MOST SIXES IN AN INNINGS

23	C. Munro (281)	Auckland v Central Districts at Napier.............	2014-15
22	Shafiqullah Shinwari (200*)	Kabul v Boost at Asadabad......................	2017-18
19	P. B. B. Rajapaksa (268)	Burgher v Ports Authority at Colombo (Moors)......	2018-19
19	Najeeb Tarakai (200)	Speen Ghar v Mis Ainak at Asadabad	2018-19
17	B. O. P. Fernando (234)	Chilaw Marians v Colts at Colombo (NCC).........	2018-19
16	A. Symonds (254*)	Gloucestershire v Glamorgan at Abergavenny	1995
16	G. R. Napier (196)	Essex v Surrey at Croydon	2011
16	J. D. Ryder (175)	New Zealanders v Australia A at Brisbane..........	2011-12
16	Mukhtar Ali (168)	Rajshahi v Chittagong at Savar...................	2013-14

*There have been **seven** further instances of 15 sixes in an innings.*

MOST SIXES IN A MATCH

24	Shafiqullah Shinwari (22, 200*)	Kabul v Boost at Asadabad	2017-18
23	C. Munro (281)	Auckland v Central Districts at Napier	2014-15
21	R. R. Pant (117, 131)	Delhi v Jharkhand at Thumba	2016-17
20	A. Symonds (254*, 76)	Gloucestershire v Glam at Abergavenny	1995
19	B. O. P. Fernando (109, 234)	Chilaw Marians v Colts at Colombo (NCC)	2018-19
19	P. B. B. Rajapaksa (268)	Burgher v Ports Authority at Colombo (Moors) .	2018-19
19	Najeeb Tarakai (200)	Speen Ghar v Mis Ainak at Asadabad	2018-19

MOST SIXES IN A SEASON

80	I. T. Botham	1985		51	A. W. Wellard	1933
66	A. W. Wellard	1935		49	I. V. A. Richards	1985
65	Najeeb Tarakai	2017-18		48	A. W. Carr	1925
57	A. W. Wellard	1936		48	J. H. Edrich	1965
57	A. W. Wellard	1938		48	A. Symonds	1995

MOST BOUNDARIES IN AN INNINGS

	4/6			
72	62/10	B. C. Lara (501*)	Warwickshire v Durham at Birmingham . . .	1994
68	68/–	P. A. Perrin (343*)	Essex v Derbyshire at Chesterfield	1904
65	64/1	A. C. MacLaren (424)	Lancashire v Somerset at Taunton	1895
64	64/–	Hanif Mohammad (499)	Karachi v Bahawalpur at Karachi	1958-59
57	52/5	J. H. Edrich (310*)	England v New Zealand at Leeds	1965
57	52/5	Naved Latif (394)	Sargodha v Gujranwala at Gujranwala	2000-01
56	54/2	K. M. Jadhav (327)	Maharashtra v Uttar Pradesh at Pune	2012-13
55	55/–	C. W. Gregory (383)	NSW v Queensland at Brisbane	1906-07
55	53/2	G. R. Marsh (355*)	W. Australia v S. Australia at Perth	1989-90
55	51/3†	S. V. Manjrekar (377)	Bombay v Hyderabad at Bombay	1990-91
55	52/3	D. S. Lehmann (339)	Yorkshire v Durham at Leeds	2006
55	54/1	D. K. H. Mitchell (298)	Worcestershire v Somerset at Taunton	2009
55	54/1	S. C. Cook (390)	Lions v Warriors at East London	2009-10
55	47/8	R. R. Rossouw (319)	Eagles v Titans at Centurion	2009-10

† *Plus one five.*

PARTNERSHIPS OVER 500

624	for 3rd	K. C. Sangakkara (287)/D. P. M. D. Jayawardene (374), Sri Lanka v South Africa at Colombo (SSC)	2006
594*	for 3rd	S. M. Gugale (351*)/A. R. Bawne (258*), Maharashtra v Delhi at Mumbai .	2016-17
580	for 2nd	Rafatullah Mohmand (302*)/Aamer Sajjad (289), WAPDA v Sui Southern Gas at Sheikhupura	2009-10
577	for 4th	V. S. Hazare (288)/Gul Mahomed (319), Baroda v Holkar at Baroda	1946-47
576	for 2nd	S. T. Jayasuriya (340)/R. S. Mahanama (225), Sri Lanka v India at Colombo (RPS)	1997-98
574*	for 4th	F. M. M. Worrell (255*)/C. L. Walcott (314*), Barbados v Trinidad at Port-of-Spain	1945-46
561	for 1st	Waheed Mirza (324)/Mansoor Akhtar (224*), Karachi Whites v Quetta at Karachi	1976-77
555	for 1st	P. Holmes (224*)/H. Sutcliffe (313), Yorkshire v Essex at Leyton	1932
554	for 1st	J. T. Brown (300)/J. Tunnicliffe (243), Yorks v Derbys at Chesterfield . . .	1898
539	for 3rd	S. D. Jogiyani (282)/R. A. Jadeja (303*), Saurashtra v Gujarat at Surat . . .	2012-13
523	for 3rd	M. A. Carberry (300*)/N. D. McKenzie (237), Hants v Yorks at Southampton	2011
520*	for 5th	C. A. Pujara (302*)/R. A. Jadeja (232*), Saurashtra v Orissa at Rajkot . . .	2008-09
503	for 1st	R. G. L. Carters (209)/A. J. Finch (288*), Cricket Australia XI v New Zealanders at Sydney	2015-16
502*	for 4th	F. M. M. Worrell (308*)/J. D. C. Goddard (218*), Barbados v Trinidad at Bridgetown	1943-44
501	for 3rd	A. N. Petersen (286)/A. G. Prince (261), Lancs v Glam at Colwyn Bay . . .	2015

HIGHEST PARTNERSHIPS FOR EACH WICKET

First Wicket

561	Waheed Mirza/Mansoor Akhtar, Karachi Whites v Quetta at Karachi........	1976-77
555	P. Holmes/H. Sutcliffe, Yorkshire v Essex at Leyton........................	1932
554	J. T. Brown/J. Tunnicliffe, Yorkshire v Derbyshire at Chesterfield	1898
503	R. G. L. Carters/A. J. Finch, Cricket Australia XI v New Zealanders at Sydney .	2015-16
490	E. H. Bowley/J. G. Langridge, Sussex v Middlesex at Hove	1933

Second Wicket

580	Rafatullah Mohmand/Aamer Sajjad, WAPDA v Sui S. Gas at Sheikhupura....	2009-10
576	S. T. Jayasuriya/R. S. Mahanama, Sri Lanka v India at Colombo (RPS).......	1997-98
480	D. Elgar/R. R. Rossouw, Eagles v Titans at Centurion.....................	2009-10
475	Zahir Alam/L. S. Rajput, Assam v Tripura at Gauhati	1991-92
465*	J. A. Jameson/R. B. Kanhai, Warwickshire v Gloucestershire at Birmingham...	1974

Third Wicket

624	K. C. Sangakkara/D. P. M. D. Jayawardene, Sri Lanka v SA at Colombo (SSC)	2006
594*	S. M. Gugale/A. R. Bawne, Maharashtra v Delhi at Mumbai	2016-17
539	S. D. Jogiyani/R. A. Jadeja, Saurashtra v Gujarat at Surat	2012-13
523	M. A. Carberry/N. D. McKenzie, Hampshire v Yorkshire at Southampton.....	2011
501	A. N. Petersen/A. G. Prince, Lancashire v Glamorgan at Colwyn Bay	2015

Fourth Wicket

577	V. S. Hazare/Gul Mahomed, Baroda v Holkar at Baroda....................	1946-47
574*	C. L. Walcott/F. M. M. Worrell, Barbados v Trinidad at Port-of-Spain.......	1945-46
502*	F. M. M. Worrell/J. D. C. Goddard, Barbados v Trinidad at Bridgetown	1943-44
470	A. I. Kallicharran/G. W. Humpage, Warwickshire v Lancashire at Southport...	1982
462*	D. W. Hookes/W. B. Phillips, South Australia v Tasmania at Adelaide	1986-87

Fifth Wicket

520*	C. A. Pujara/R. A. Jadeja, Saurashtra v Orissa at Rajkot	2008-09
494	Marshall Ayub/Mehrab Hossain, Central Zone v East Zone at Bogra	2012-13
479	Misbah-ul-Haq/Usman Arshad, Sui N. Gas v Lahore Shalimar at Lahore	2009-10
464*	M. E. Waugh/S. R. Waugh, New South Wales v Western Australia at Perth....	1990-91
440*	D. B. Ravi Teja/R. Sanjay Yadav, Meghalaya v Mizoram at Kolkata	2019-20

Sixth Wicket

487*	G. A. Headley/C. C. Passailaigue, Jamaica v Lord Tennyson's XI at Kingston..	1931-32
428	W. W. Armstrong/M. A. Noble, Australians v Sussex at Hove	1902
417	W. P. Saha/L. R. Shukla, Bengal v Assam at Kolkata	2010-11
411	R. M. Poore/E. G. Wynyard, Hampshire v Somerset at Taunton	1899
399	B. A. Stokes/J. M. Bairstow, England v South Africa at Cape Town	2015-16

Seventh Wicket

460	Bhupinder Singh jnr/P. Dharmani, Punjab v Delhi at Delhi.................	1994-95
399	A. N. Khare/A. J. Mandal, Chhattisgarh v Uttarakhand at Naya Raipur	2019-20
371	M. R. Marsh/S. M. Whiteman, Australia A v India A at Brisbane	2014
366*	J. M. Bairstow/T. T. Bresnan, Yorkshire v Durham at Chester-le-Street	2015
347	D. St E. Atkinson/C. C. Depeiaza, West Indies v Australia at Bridgetown	1954-55
347	Farhad Reza/Sanjamul Islam, Rajshahi v Chittagong at Savar...............	2013-14

Eighth Wicket

433	A. Sims and V. T. Trumper, A. Sims' Aust. XI v Canterbury at Christchurch...	1913-14
392	A. Mishra/J. Yadav, Haryana v Karnataka at Hubli	2012-13
332	I. J. L. Trott/S. C. J. Broad, England v Pakistan at Lord's	2010
313	Wasim Akram/Saqlain Mushtaq, Pakistan v Zimbabwe at Sheikhupura	1996-97
292	R. Peel/Lord Hawke, Yorkshire v Warwickshire at Birmingham	1896

Ninth Wicket

283	A. Warren/J. Chapman, Derbyshire v Warwickshire at Blackwell	1910
268	J. B. Commins/N. Boje, South Africa A v Mashonaland at Harare	1994-95
261	W. L. Madsen/T. Poynton, Derbyshire v Northamptonshire at Northampton	2012
251	J. W. H. T. Douglas/S. N. Hare, Essex v Derbyshire at Leyton	1921
249*†	A. S. Srivastava/K. Seth, Madhya Pradesh v Vidarbha at Indore	2000-01

† *276 unbeaten runs were scored for this wicket in two separate partnerships; after Srivastava retired hurt, Seth and N. D. Hirwani added 27.*

Tenth Wicket

307	A. F. Kippax/J. E. H. Hooker, New South Wales v Victoria at Melbourne	1928-29
249	C. T. Sarwate/S. N. Banerjee, Indians v Surrey at The Oval	1946
239	Aqeel Arshad/Ali Raza, Lahore Whites v Hyderabad at Lahore	2004-05
235	F. E. Woolley/A. Fielder, Kent v Worcestershire at Stourbridge	1909
233	Ajay Sharma/Maninder Singh, Delhi v Bombay at Bombay	1991-92

There have been only 13 last-wicket stands of 200 or more.

UNUSUAL DISMISSALS

Handled the Ball

There have been **63** instances in first-class cricket. The most recent are:

W. S. A. Williams	Canterbury v Otago at Dunedin	2012-13
E. Lewis	Trinidad & Tobago v Leeward Islands at Port-of-Spain	2013-14
C. A. Pujara	Derbyshire v Leicestershire at Derby	2014
I. Khan	Dolphins v Lions at Johannesburg	2014-15
K. Lesporis	Windward Islands v Barbados at Bridgetown	2015-16
S. R. Dickson	Kent v Leicestershire at Leicester	2016
M. Z. Hamza	Cape Cobras v Knights at Bloemfontein	2016-17

Under the 2017 revision of the Laws, Handled the Ball was subsumed under Obstructing the Field.

Obstructing the Field

There have been **32** instances in first-class cricket. T. Straw of Worcestershire was given out for obstruction v Warwickshire in both 1899 and 1901. The most recent are:

W. E. Bell	Northern Cape v Border at Kimberley	2015-16
Jahid Ali	Pakistan A v Zimbabwe A at Bulawayo	2016-17
Ghamai Zadran	Mis Ainak v Boost at Ghazi Amanullah Town	2017-18
Rashid Zadran	Mis Ainak v Band-e-Amir at Kabul	2017-18
Zia-ur-Rehman	Mis Ainak v Amo at Khost	2017-18
R. P. Burl	Rising Stars v Harare Metropolitan Eagles at Harare	2017-18
K. Cotani	North West v Free State at Bloemfontein	2018-19
T. A. Blundell	Wellington v Otago at Wellington	2020-21

Hit the Ball Twice

There have been **22** instances in first-class cricket. The last occurrence in England involved J. H. King of Leicestershire v Surrey at The Oval in 1906. The most recent are:

Aziz Malik	Lahore Division v Faisalabad at Sialkot.	1984-85
Javed Mohammad	Multan v Karachi Whites at Sahiwal	1986-87
Shahid Pervez	Jammu & Kashmir v Punjab at Srinagar	1986-87
Ali Naqvi	PNSC v National Bank at Faisalabad	1998-99
A. George	Tamil Nadu v Maharashtra at Pune	1998-99
Maqsood Raza	Lahore Division v PNSC at Sheikhupura	1999-2000
D. Mahajan	Jammu & Kashmir v Bihar at Jammu	2005-06
Ikram Alikhil	**Speen Ghar v Amo at Kandahar.**	**2021-22**

Timed Out

There have been **six** instances in first-class cricket:

A. Jordaan	Eastern Province v Transvaal at Port Elizabeth (SACB match).	1987-88
H. Yadav	Tripura v Orissa at Cuttack.	1997-98
V. C. Drakes	Border v Free State at East London	2002-03
A. J. Harris	Nottinghamshire v Durham UCCE at Nottingham.	2003
R. A. Austin	Combined Campuses & Colleges v Windward Is at Arnos Vale	2013-14
C. Kunje	Bulawayo Met Tuskers v Manica Mountaineers at Bulawayo.	2017-18

BOWLING RECORDS

TEN WICKETS IN AN INNINGS

In the history of first-class cricket, there have been **84** instances of a bowler taking all ten wickets in an innings, plus a further three instances of ten wickets in 12-a-side matches. Occurrences since the Second World War:

	O	M	R		
*W. E. Hollies (Warwickshire).	20.4	4	49	v Notts at Birmingham	1946
J. M. Sims (East).	18.4	2	90	v West at Kingston	1948
T. E. Bailey (Essex).	39.4	9	90	v Lancashire at Clacton.	1949
J. K. Graveney (Glos.)	18.4	2	66	v Derbyshire at Chesterfield	1949
R. Berry (Lancashire).	36.2	9	102	v Worcestershire at Blackpool	1953
S. P. Gupte (President's XI)	24.2	7	78	v Combined XI at Bombay	1954-55
J. C. Laker (Surrey).	46	18	88	v Australians at The Oval	1956
J. C. Laker (England).	51.2	23	53	v Australia at Manchester	1956
G. A. R. Lock (Surrey).	29.1	18	54	v Kent at Blackheath.	1956
K. Smales (Nottinghamshire).	41.3	20	66	v Gloucestershire at Stroud.	1956
P. M. Chatterjee (Bengal).	19	11	20	v Assam at Jorhat.	1956-57
J. D. Bannister (Warwickshire).	23.3	11	41	v Comb. Services at Birmingham†	1959
A. J. G. Pearson (Cambridge U.)	30.3	8	78	v Leics at Loughborough	1961
N. I. Thomson (Sussex).	34.2	19	49	v Warwickshire at Worthing.	1964
P. J. Allan (Queensland).	15.6	3	61	v Victoria at Melbourne	1965-66
I. J. Brayshaw (W. Australia).	17.6	4	44	v Victoria at Perth.	1967-68
Shahid Mahmood (Karachi Whites).	25	5	58	v Khairpur at Karachi	1969-70
E. E. Hemmings (International XI)	49.3	14	175	v West Indies XI at Kingston	1982-83
P. Sunderam (Rajasthan).	22	5	78	v Vidarbha at Jodhpur.	1985-86
S. T. Jefferies (W. Province).	22.5	7	59	v Orange Free State at Cape Town	1987-88
Imran Adil (Bahawalpur).	22.5	3	92	v Faisalabad at Faisalabad	1989-90
G. P. Wickremasinghe (Sinhalese).	19.2	5	41	v Kalutara PCC at Colombo (SSC)	1991-92
R. L. Johnson (Middlesex).	18.5	6	45	v Derbyshire at Derby.	1994
Naeem Akhtar (Rawalpindi B).	21.3	10	28	v Peshawar at Peshawar	1995-96
A. Kumble (India).	26.3	9	74	v Pakistan at Delhi	1998-99
D. S. Mohanty (East Zone).	19	5	46	v South Zone at Agartala	2000-01
O. D. Gibson (Durham).	17.3	1	47	v Hampshire at Chester-le-Street	2007
M. W. Olivier (Warriors).	26.3	4	65	v Eagles at Bloemfontein	2007-08

	O	M	R		
Zulfiqar Babar (Multan)	39.4	3	143	v Islamabad at Multan.	2009-10
P. M. Pushpakumara (Colombo) .	18.4	5	37	v Saracens at Moratuwa	2018-19
S. A. Whitehead (SW Districts) .	**12.1**	**4**	**36**	**v Easterns at Oudtshoorn.**	**2021-22**
A. Y. Patel (New Zealand)	**47.5**	**12**	**119**	**v India at Mumbai**	**2021-22**

* *W. E. Hollies bowled seven and had three lbw. The only other instance of a bowler achieving the feat without the direct assistance of a fielder came in 1850 when J. Wisden bowled all ten, for North v South at Lord's.*

† *Mitchells & Butlers Ground.*

OUTSTANDING BOWLING ANALYSES

	O	M	R	W		
H. Verity (Yorkshire)	19.4	16	10	10	v Nottinghamshire at Leeds . . .	1932
G. Elliott (Victoria).	19	17	2	9	v Tasmania at Launceston.	1857-58
Ahad Khan (Railways)	6.3	4	7	9	v Dera Ismail Khan at Lahore . .	1964-65
J. C. Laker (England)	14	12	2	8	v The Rest at Bradford	1950
D. Shackleton (Hampshire)	11.1	7	4	8	v Somerset at Weston-s-Mare . .	1955
E. Peate (Yorkshire)	16	11	5	8	v Surrey at Holbeck.	1883
K. M. Dabengwa (Westerns) . . .	4.4	3	1	7	v Northerns at Harare	2006-07
F. R. Spofforth (Australians) . . .	8.3	6	3	7	v England XI at Birmingham . .	1884
W. A. Henderson (NE Transvaal) .	9.3	7	4	7	v OFS at Bloemfontein	1937-38
Rajinder Goel (Haryana).	7	4	4	7	v Jammu & K at Chandigarh. . . .	1977-78
N. W. Bracken (NSW)	7	5	4	7	v South Australia at Sydney . . .	2004-05
V. I. Smith (South Africans) . . .	4.5	3	1	6	v Derbyshire at Derby	1947
S. Costick (Victoria)	21.1	20	1	6	v Tasmania at Melbourne	1868-69
Israr Ali (Bahawalpur)	11	10	1	6	v Dacca U. at Bahawalpur.	1957-58
A. D. Pougher (MCC).	3	3	0	5	v Australians at Lord's	1896
G. R. Cox (Sussex)	6	6	0	5	v Somerset at Weston-s-Mare . .	1921
R. K. Tyldesley (Lancashire) . . .	5	5	0	5	v Leicestershire at Manchester .	1924
P. T. Mills (Gloucestershire). . . .	6.4	6	0	5	v Somerset at Bristol	1928

MOST WICKETS IN A MATCH

19-90	J. C. Laker	England v Australia at Manchester	1956
17-48†	C. Blythe	Kent v Northamptonshire at Northampton.	1907
17-50	C. T. B. Turner	Australians v England XI at Hastings	1888
17-54	W. P. Howell	Australians v Western Province at Cape Town	1902-03
17-56	C. W. L. Parker	Gloucestershire v Essex at Gloucester	1925
17-67	A. P. Freeman	Kent v Sussex at Hove	1922
17-86	K. J. Abbott	Hampshire v Somerset at Southampton	2019
17-89	W. G. Grace	Gloucestershire v Nottinghamshire at Cheltenham . . .	1877
17-89	F. C. L. Matthews	Nottinghamshire v Northants at Nottingham	1923
17-91	H. Dean	Lancashire v Yorkshire at Liverpool	1913
17-91†	H. Verity	Yorkshire v Essex at Leyton	1933
17-92	A. P. Freeman	Kent v Warwickshire at Folkestone	1932
17-103	W. Mycroft	Derbyshire v Hampshire at Southampton	1876
17-106	G. R. Cox	Sussex v Warwickshire at Horsham	1926
17-106†	T. W. J. Goddard	Gloucestershire v Kent at Bristol	1939
17-119	W. Mead	Essex v Hampshire at Southampton	1895
17-137	W. Brearley	Lancashire v Somerset at Manchester	1905
17-137	J. M. Davison	Canada v USA at Fort Lauderdale	2004
17-159	S. F. Barnes	England v South Africa at Johannesburg	1913-14
17-201	G. Giffen	South Australia v Victoria at Adelaide	1885-86
17-212	J. C. Clay	Glamorgan v Worcestershire at Swansea.	1937

† *Achieved in a single day.*

H. Arkwright took 18-96 for MCC v Gentlemen of Kent in a 12-a-side match at Canterbury in 1861. There have been **60** *instances of a bowler taking 16 wickets in an 11-a-side match, the most recent being 16-110 by P. M. Pushpakumara for Colombo v Saracens at Moratuwa, 2018-19.*

FOUR WICKETS WITH CONSECUTIVE BALLS

There have been **44** instances in first-class cricket. R. J. Crisp achieved the feat twice, for Western Province in 1931-32 and 1933-34. A. E. Trott took four in four balls and another hat-trick in the same innings for Middlesex v Somerset in 1907, his benefit match. Occurrences since 2007:

Tabish Khan	Karachi Whites v ZTBL at Karachi................................	2009-10
Kamran Hussain	Habib Bank v Lahore Shalimar at Lahore....................	2009-10
N. Wagner	Otago v Wellington at Queenstown.............................	2010-11
Khalid Usman	Abbottabad v Karachi Blues at Karachi......................	2011-12
Mahmudullah	Central Zone v North Zone at Savar	2013-14
A. C. Thomas	Somerset v Sussex at Taunton.....................................	2014
Taj Wali	Peshawar v Port Qasim Authority at Peshawar.............	2015-16
N. G. R. P. Jayasuriya	Colts v Badureliya at Maggona.............................	2015-16
K. R. Smuts	Eastern Province v Boland at Paarl	2015-16

In their match with England at The Oval in 1863, Surrey lost four wickets in the course of a four-ball over from G. Bennett.

Sussex lost five wickets in the course of the final (six-ball) over of their match with Surrey at Eastbourne in 1972. P. I. Pocock, who had taken three wickets in his previous over, captured four more, taking in all seven wickets with 11 balls, a feat unique in first-class matches. (The eighth wicket fell to a run-out.)

In 1996, K. D. James took four in four balls for Hampshire against Indians at Southampton and scored a century, a feat later emulated by Mahmudullah and Smuts.

HAT-TRICKS

Double Hat-Trick

Besides Trott's performance, which is mentioned in the preceding section, the following instances are recorded of players having performed the hat-trick twice in the same match, Rao doing so in the same innings.

A. Shaw	Nottinghamshire v Gloucestershire at Nottingham	1884
T. J. Matthews	Australia v South Africa at Manchester.....................	1912
C. W. L. Parker	Gloucestershire v Middlesex at Bristol......................	1924
R. O. Jenkins	Worcestershire v Surrey at Worcester.......................	1949
J. S. Rao	Services v Northern Punjab at Amritsar	1963-64
Amin Lakhani	Combined XI v Indians at Multan..........................	1978-79
M. A. Starc	New South Wales v Western Australia at Sydney (Hurstville)..	2017-18

Five Wickets in Six Balls

W. H. Copson	Derbyshire v Warwickshire at Derby	1937
W. A. Henderson	NE Transvaal v Orange Free State at Bloemfontein	1937-38
P. I. Pocock	Surrey v Sussex at Eastbourne	1972
Yasir Arafat	Rawalpindi v Faisalabad at Rawalpindi	2004-05
N. Wagner	Otago v Wellington at Queenstown	2010-11

Yasir Arafat's five wickets were spread across two innings and interrupted only by a no-ball. Wagner was the first to take five wickets in a single over.

Most Hat-Tricks

D. V. P. Wright 7	R. G. Barlow 4	T. G. Matthews 4
T. W. J. Goddard....... 6	Fazl-e-Akbar 4	M. J. Procter 4
C. W. L. Parker 6	A. P. Freeman 4	T. Richardson 4
S. Haigh............... 5	J. T. Hearne 4	F. R. Spofforth......... 4
V. W. C. Jupp 5	J. C. Laker 4	F. S. Trueman 4
A. E. G. Rhodes........ 5	G. A. R. Lock 4	
F. A. Tarrant 5	G. G. Macaulay 4	

Hat-Trick on Debut

There have been **19** instances in first-class cricket. Occurrences since 2000:

S. M. Harwood	Victoria v Tasmania at Melbourne	2002-03
P. Connell	Ireland v Netherlands at Rotterdam	2008
A. Mithun	Karnataka v Uttar Pradesh at Meerut	2009-10
Zohaib Shera	Karachi Whites v National Bank at Karachi	2009-10
R. R. Yadav	Madhya Pradesh v Uttar Pradesh at Indore	2019-20

R. R. Phillips (Border) took a hat-trick in his first over in first-class cricket (v Eastern Province at Port Elizabeth, 1939-40) having previously played in four matches without bowling.

250 WICKETS IN A SEASON

	Season	M	Balls	R	W	5I	10M	Avge
A. P. Freeman	1928	37	11,825	5,489	304	36	15	18.05
A. P. Freeman	1933	35	12,200	4,549	298	40	17	15.26
T. Richardson	1895	31	8,456	4,170	290	36	17	14.37
C. T. B. Turner	1888	36	9,702	3,307	283	30	12	11.68
A. P. Freeman	1931	33	9,708	4,307	276	35	13	15.60
A. P. Freeman	1930	34	11,463	4,632	275	34	15	16.84
T. Richardson	1897	30	8,019	3,945	273	34	13	14.45
A. P. Freeman	1929	34	10,086	4,879	267	29	13	18.27
W. Rhodes	1900	35	9,300	3,606	261	24	7	13.81
J. T. Hearne	1896	35	10,016	3,670	257	34	13	14.28
A. P. Freeman	1932	32	9,455	4,149	253	28	13	16.39
W. Rhodes	1901	37	9,391	3,797	251	25	9	15.12

In four consecutive seasons (1928–1931), A. P. Freeman took 1,122 wickets, and in eight consecutive seasons (1928–1935), 2,090 wickets. In each of these eight seasons he took over 200 wickets.

T. Richardson took 1,005 wickets in four consecutive seasons (1894–1897).

The earliest date by which any bowler has taken 100 in an English season is June 12, achieved by J. T. Hearne in 1896 and C. W. L. Parker in 1931, when A. P. Freeman did it on June 13.

100 WICKETS IN A SEASON MOST TIMES

(Includes overseas tours and seasons)

W. Rhodes 23	C. W. L. Parker 16	G. H. Hirst 15
D. Shackleton 20	R. T. D. Perks 16	A. S. Kennedy 15
A. P. Freeman 17	F. J. Titmus 16	
T. W. J. Goddard 16	J. T. Hearne 15	

D. Shackleton reached 100 wickets in 20 successive seasons – 1949–1968.

Since the reduction of County Championship matches in 1969, D. L. Underwood (five times) and J. K. Lever (four times) are the only bowlers to have reached 100 wickets in a season more than twice. The highest aggregate in a season since 1969 is 134 by M. D. Marshall in 1982.

The most instances of 200 wickets in a season is eight by A. P. Freeman, who did it in eight successive seasons – 1928 to 1935 – including 304 in 1928. C. W. L. Parker did it five times, T. W. J. Goddard four times, and J. T. Hearne, G. A. Lohmann, W. Rhodes, T. Richardson, M. W. Tate and H. Verity three times each.

The last bowler to reach 200 wickets in a season was G. A. R. Lock (212 in 1957).

An expanded and regularly updated online version of the Records can be found at
www.wisdenrecords.com

100 WICKETS IN A SEASON OUTSIDE ENGLAND

W		Season	Country	R	Avge
116	M. W. Tate	1926-27	India/Ceylon	1,599	13.78
113	Kabir Khan	1998-99	Pakistan	1,706	15.09
107	Ijaz Faqih	1985-86	Pakistan	1,719	16.06
106	C. T. B. Turner	1887-88	Australia	1,441	13.59
106	R. Benaud	1957-58	South Africa	2,056	19.39
105	Murtaza Hussain	1995-96	Pakistan	1,882	17.92
104	S. F. Barnes	1913-14	South Africa	1,117	10.74
104	Sajjad Akbar	1989-90	Pakistan	2,328	22.38
103	Abdul Qadir	1982-83	Pakistan	2,367	22.98
101	Zia-ur-Rehman	2017-18	Afghanistan	1,995	19.75

LEADING BOWLERS IN AN ENGLISH SEASON

(Qualification: 10 wickets in 10 innings)

Season	Leading wicket-taker	Wkts	Avge	Top of averages	Wkts	Avge
1946	W. E. Hollies	184	15.60	A. Booth	111	11.61
1947	T. W. J. Goddard	238	17.30	J. C. Clay	65	16.44
1948	J. E. Walsh	174	19.56	J. C. Clay	41	14.17
1949	R. O. Jenkins	183	21.19	T. W. J. Goddard	160	19.18
1950	R. Tattersall	193	13.59	R. Tattersall	193	13.59
1951	R. Appleyard	200	14.14	R. Appleyard	200	14.14
1952	J. H. Wardle	177	19.54	F. S. Trueman	61	13.78
1953	B. Dooland	172	16.58	C. J. Knott	38	13.71
1954	B. Dooland	196	15.48	J. B. Statham	92	14.13
1955	G. A. R. Lock	216	14.49	R. Appleyard	85	13.01
1956	D. J. Shepherd	177	15.36	G. A. R. Lock	155	12.46
1957	G. A. R. Lock	212	12.02	G. A. R. Lock	212	12.02
1958	G. A. R. Lock	170	12.08	H. L. Jackson	143	10.99
1959	D. Shackleton	148	21.55	J. B. Statham	139	15.01
1960	F. S. Trueman	175	13.98	J. B. Statham	135	12.31
1961	J. A. Flavell	171	17.79	J. A. Flavell	171	17.79
1962	D. Shackleton	172	20.15	C. Cook	58	17.13
1963	D. Shackleton	146	16.75	C. C. Griffith	119	12.83
1964	D. Shackleton	142	20.40	J. A. Standen	64	13.00
1965	D. Shackleton	144	16.08	H. J. Rhodes	119	11.04
1966	D. L. Underwood	157	13.80	D. L. Underwood	157	13.80
1967	T. W. Cartwright	147	15.52	D. L. Underwood	136	12.39
1968	R. Illingworth	131	14.36	O. S. Wheatley	82	12.95
1969	R. M. H. Cottam	109	21.04	A. Ward	69	14.82
1970	D. J. Shepherd	106	19.16	Majid Khan	11	18.81
1971	L. R. Gibbs	131	18.89	G. G. Arnold	83	17.12
1972	T. W. Cartwright	98	18.64	I. M. Chappell	10	10.60
	B. Stead	98	20.38			
1973	B. S. Bedi	105	17.94	T. W. Cartwright	89	15.84
1974	A. M. E. Roberts	119	13.62	A. M. E. Roberts	119	13.62
1975	P. G. Lee	112	18.45	A. M. E. Roberts	57	15.80
1976	G. A. Cope	93	24.13	M. A. Holding	55	14.38
1977	M. J. Procter	109	18.04	R. A. Woolmer	19	15.21
1978	D. L. Underwood	110	14.49	D. L. Underwood	110	14.49
1979	D. L. Underwood	106	14.85	J. Garner	55	13.83
	J. K. Lever	106	17.30			
1980	R. D. Jackman	121	15.40	J. Garner	49	13.93
1981	R. J. Hadlee	105	14.89	R. J. Hadlee	105	14.89
1982	M. D. Marshall	134	15.73	R. J. Hadlee	61	14.57
1983	J. K. Lever	106	16.28	Imran Khan	12	7.16
	D. L. Underwood	106	19.28			
1984	R. J. Hadlee	117	14.05	R. J. Hadlee	117	14.05
1985	N. V. Radford	101	24.68	R. M. Ellison	65	17.20

Season	Leading wicket-taker	Wkts	Avge	Top of averages	Wkts	Avge
1986	C. A. Walsh	118	18.17	M. D. Marshall	100	15.08
1987	N. V. Radford	109	20.81	R. J. Hadlee	97	12.64
1988	F. D. Stephenson	125	18.31	M. D. Marshall	42	13.16
1989	D. R. Pringle	94	18.64	T. M. Alderman	70	15.64
	S. L. Watkin	94	25.09			
1990	N. A. Foster	94	26.61	I. R. Bishop	59	19.05
1991	Waqar Younis	113	14.65	Waqar Younis	113	14.65
1992	C. A. Walsh	92	15.96	C. A. Walsh	92	15.96
1993	S. L. Watkin	92	22.80	Wasim Akram	59	19.27
1994	M. M. Patel	90	22.86	C. E. L. Ambrose	77	14.45
1995	A. Kumble	105	20.40	A. A. Donald	89	16.07
1996	C. A. Walsh	85	16.84	C. E. L. Ambrose	43	16.67
1997	A. M. Smith	83	17.63	A. A. Donald	60	15.63
1998	C. A. Walsh	106	17.31	V. J. Wells	36	14.27
1999	A. Sheriyar	92	24.70	Saqlain Mushtaq	58	11.37
2000	G. D. McGrath	80	13.21	C. A. Walsh	40	11.42
2001	R. J. Kirtley	75	23.32	G. D. McGrath	40	15.60
2002	M. J. Saggers	83	21.51	C. P. Schofield	18	18.38
	K. J. Dean	83	23.50			
2003	Mushtaq Ahmed	103	24.65	Shoaib Akhtar	34	17.05
2004	Mushtaq Ahmed	84	27.59	D. S. Lehmann	15	17.40
2005	S. K. Warne	87	22.50	M. Muralitharan	36	15.00
2006	Mushtaq Ahmed	102	19.91	Naved-ul-Hasan	35	16.71
2007	Mushtaq Ahmed	90	25.66	Harbhajan Singh	37	18.54
2008	J. A. Tomlinson	67	24.76	M. Davies	41	14.63
2009	Danish Kaneria	75	23.69	G. Onions	69	19.95
2010	A. R. Adams	68	22.17	J. K. H. Naik	35	17.68
2011	D. D. Masters	93	18.13	T. T. Bresnan	29	17.68
2012	G. Onions	72	14.73	G. Onions	72	14.73
2013	G. Onions	73	18.92	T. A. Copeland	45	18.26
2014	M. H. A. Footitt	84	19.19	G. R. Napier	52	15.63
2015	C. Rushworth	90	20.54	R. J. Sidebottom	43	18.09
2016	G. R. Napier	69	22.30	J. M. Anderson	45	17.00
	J. S. Patel	69	24.02			
2017	J. A. Porter	85	16.74	J. L. Pattinson	32	12.06
2018	O. E. Robinson	81	17.43	O. P. Stone	43	12.30
2019	S. R. Harmer	86	18.15	J. M. Anderson	30	9.40
2020	S. R. Harmer	38	15.86	C. Overton	30	13.43
2021	**L. J. Fletcher**	**66**	**14.90**	**S. J. Cook**	**58**	**14.43**

MOST WICKETS

Dates in italics denote the first half of an overseas season; i.e. *1970* denotes the 1970-71 season.

		Career	M	Balls	R	W	BB	5I	Avge
1	W. Rhodes	1898–1930	1,110	185,742	70,322	4,204	9-24	287	16.72
2	A. P. Freeman	1914–1936	592	154,658	69,577	3,776	10-53	386	18.42
3	C. W. L. Parker	1903–1935	635	157,328	63,819	3,278	10-79	277	19.46
4	J. T. Hearne	1888–1923	639	144,470	54,351	3,061	9-32	255	17.75
5	T. W. J. Goddard	1922–1952	593	142,186	59,116	2,979	10-113	251	19.84
6	A. S. Kennedy	1907–1936	677	150,917	61,035	2,874	10-37	225	21.23
7	D. Shackleton	1948–1969	647	159,001	53,303	2,857	9-30	194	18.65
8	G. A. R. Lock	1946–*1970*	654	150,168	54,709	2,844	10-54	196	19.23
9	F. J. Titmus	1949–1982	792	153,450	63,315	2,830	9-52	168	22.37
10	W. G. Grace	1865–1908	870	124,833	50,980	2,809	10-49	240	18.14
11	M. W. Tate	1912–1937	679	150,449	50,571	2,784	9-71	195	18.16
12	G. H. Hirst	1891–1929	826	123,387	51,371	2,742	9-23	184	18.73
13	C. Blythe	1899–1914	439	103,546	42,094	2,503	10-30	218	16.81

Some works of reference provide career figures which differ from those in this list, owing to the exclusion or inclusion of matches recognised or not recognised as first-class by Wisden, which now accepts the Association of Cricket Statisticians' list of first-class matches.

Current players with 750 wickets

	Career	M	Balls	R	W	BB	5I	Avge
J. M. Anderson.....	2002–2021	269	53,548	25,246	1,025	7-19	52	24.63
T. J. Murtagh	2000–2021	248	43,852	21,915	899	7-82	38	24.37
S. C. J. Broad	2005–2021	240	45,012	22,650	843	8-15	30	26.86
M. D. K. Perera ...	2000–2020	224	42,391	21,454	807	7-71	42	26.58
N. Wagner	2005–2021	184	38,291	20,314	762	7-39	36	26.65

ALL-ROUND RECORDS

REMARKABLE ALL-ROUND MATCHES

V. E. Walker	20*	108	10-74	4-17	England v Surrey at The Oval	1859
W. G. Grace	104		2-60	10-49	MCC v Oxford University at Oxford .	1886
G. Giffen	271		9-96	7-70	South Australia v Victoria at Adelaide	1891-92
B. J. T. Bosanquet	103	100*	3-75	8-53	Middlesex v Sussex at Lord's	1905
G. H. Hirst	111	117*	6-70	5-45	Yorkshire v Somerset at Bath	1906
F. D. Stephenson	111	117	4-105	7-117	Notts v Yorkshire at Nottingham.....	1988

E. M. Grace, for MCC v Gentlemen of Kent in a 12-a-side match at Canterbury in 1862, scored 192* and took 5-77 and 10-69.

HUNDRED AND HAT-TRICK

G. Giffen, Australians v Lancashire at Manchester.............................	1884
*W. E. Roller, Surrey v Sussex at The Oval	1885
W. B. Burns, Worcestershire v Gloucestershire at Worcester.......................	1913
V. W. C. Jupp, Sussex v Essex at Colchester	1921
R. E. S. Wyatt, MCC v Ceylonese at Colombo (Victoria Park)	1926-27
L. N. Constantine, West Indians v Northamptonshire at Northampton	1928
D. E. Davies, Glamorgan v Leicestershire at Leicester	1937
V. M. Merchant, Dr C. R. Pereira's XI v Sir Homi Mehta's XI at Bombay	1946-47
M. J. Procter, Gloucestershire v Essex at Westcliff-on-Sea.......................	1972
M. J. Procter, Gloucestershire v Leicestershire at Bristol	1979
†K. D. James, Hampshire v Indians at Southampton................................	1996
J. E. C. Franklin, Gloucestershire v Derbyshire at Cheltenham....................	2009
Sohag Gazi, Barisal v Khulna at Khulna..	2012-13
Sohag Gazi, Bangladesh v New Zealand at Chittagong	2013-14
†Mahmudullah, Central Zone v North Zone at Savar	2013-14
†K. R. Smuts, Eastern Province v Boland at Paarl	2015-16

* *W. E. Roller is the only player to combine 200 with a hat-trick.*

† *K. D. James, Mahmudullah and K. R. Smuts all combined 100 with four wickets in four balls (Mahmudullah's split between two innings).*

THE DOUBLE

The double was traditionally regarded as 1,000 runs and 100 wickets in an English season. The feat became exceptionally rare after the reduction of County Championship matches in 1969.

Remarkable Seasons

	Season	R	W		Season	R	W
G. H. Hirst	1906	2,385	208	J. H. Parks	1937	3,003	101

1,000 Runs and 100 Wickets

W. Rhodes 16	M. S. Nichols 8	W. G. Grace 7
G. H. Hirst 14	A. E. Relf 8	G. E. Tribe 7
V. W. C. Jupp 10	F. A. Tarrant 8	F. E. Woolley 7
W. E. Astill 9	M. W. Tate .... 8†	
T. E. Bailey 8	F. J. Titmus 8	

†   *M. W. Tate also scored 1,193 runs and took 116 wickets on the 1926-27 MCC tour of India and Ceylon.*

W. G. Grace was the first to achieve the feat in 1874. R. J. Hadlee (1984) and F. D. Stephenson (1988) are the only players to perform the feat since the reduction of County Championship matches in 1969. A complete list of those performing the feat before then may be found on page 202 of the 1982 Wisden. T. E. Bailey (1959) was the last player to achieve 2,000 runs and 100 wickets in a season; M. W. Tate (1925) the last to reach 1,000 runs and 200 wickets. Full lists may be found in Wisdens up to 2003.

Wicketkeeper's Double

The only wicketkeepers to achieve 1,000 runs and 100 dismissals in a season were L. E. G. Ames (1928, 1929 and 1932, when he scored 2,482 runs) and J. T. Murray (1957).

WICKETKEEPING RECORDS

MOST DISMISSALS IN AN INNINGS

9 (8ct, 1st)	Tahir Rashid	Habib Bank v PACO at Gujranwala	1992-93
9 (7ct, 2st)	W. R. James*	Matabeleland v Mashonaland CD at Bulawayo	1995-96
8 (8ct)	A. T. W. Grout	Queensland v Western Australia at Brisbane	1959-60
8 (8ct)†	D. E. East	Essex v Somerset at Taunton.	1985
8 (8ct)	S. A. Marsh‡	Kent v Middlesex at Lord's.	1991
8 (6ct, 2st)	T. J. Zoehrer	Australians v Surrey at The Oval	1993
8 (7ct, 1st)	D. S. Berry	Victoria v South Australia at Melbourne.	1996-97
8 (7ct, 1st)	Y. S. S. Mendis	Bloomfield v Kurunegala Y at Colombo (Bloomfield).	2000-01
8 (7ct, 1st)	S. Nath§	Assam v Tripura at Guwahati	2001-02
8 (8ct)	J. N. Batty¶	Surrey v Kent at The Oval.	2004
8 (8ct)	Golam Mabud	Sylhet v Dhaka at Dhaka.	2005-06
8 (8ct)	A. Z. M. Dyili	Eastern Province v Free State at Port Elizabeth	2009-10
8 (8ct)	D. C. de Boorder	Otago v Wellington at Wellington.	2009-10
8 (8ct)	R. S. Second	Free State v North West at Bloemfontein	2011-12
8 (8ct)	T. L. Tsolekile	South Africa A v Sri Lanka A at Durban	2012
8 (7ct, 1st)	M. A. R. S. Fernando	Chilaw Marians v Colts at Colombo (SSC).	2017-18

There have been 112 further instances of seven dismissals in an innings. R. W. Taylor achieved the feat three times, and G. J. Hopkins, Kamran Akmal, I. Khaleel, S. A. Marsh, K. J. Piper, Shahin Hossain, T. L. Tsolekile and Wasim Bari twice. Khaleel did it twice in the same match. Marsh's and Tsolekile's two instances both included one of eight dismssals – see above. H. Yarnold made six stumpings and one catch in an innings for Worcestershire v Scotland at Dundee in 1951. A fuller list can be found in Wisdens before 2004.

* W. R. James also scored 99 and 99 not out.	† The first eight wickets to fall.
‡ S. A. Marsh also scored 108 not out.	§ On his only first-class appearance.
¶ J. N. Batty also scored 129.	

WICKETKEEPERS' HAT-TRICKS

W. H. Brain, Gloucestershire v Somerset at Cheltenham, 1893 – three stumpings off successive balls from C. L. Townsend.

K. R. Meherhomji, Freelooters v Nizam's State Railway A at Secunderabad, 1931-32 – three catches off successive balls from L. Ramji.

G. O. Dawkes, Derbyshire v Worcestershire at Kidderminster, 1958 – three catches off successive balls from H. L. Jackson.

R. C. Russell, Gloucestershire v Surrey at The Oval, 1986 – three catches off successive balls from C. A. Walsh and D. V. Lawrence (2).

T. Frost, Warwickshire v Surrey at Birmingham, 2003 – three catches off successive balls from G. G. Wagg and N. M. Carter (2).

MOST DISMISSALS IN A MATCH

14 (11ct, 3st)	I. Khaleel	Hyderabad v Assam at Guwahati	2011-12
13 (11ct, 2st)	W. R. James*	Matabeleland v Mashonaland CD at Bulawayo	1995-96
12 (8ct, 4st)	E. Pooley	Surrey v Sussex at The Oval	1868
12 (9ct, 3st)	D. Tallon	Queensland v New South Wales at Sydney	1938-39
12 (9ct, 3st)	H. B. Taber	New South Wales v South Australia at Adelaide	1968-69
12 (12ct)	P. D. McGlashan	Northern Districts v Central Districts at Whangarei	2009-10
12 (11ct, 1st)	T. L. Tsolekile	Lions v Dolphins at Johannesburg	2010-11
12 (12ct)	Kashif Mahmood	Lahore Shalimar v Abbottabad at Abbottabad	2010-11
12 (12ct)	R. S. Second	Free State v North West at Bloemfontein	2011-12

* *W. R. James also scored 99 and 99 not out.*

100 DISMISSALS IN A SEASON

128 (79ct, 49st)	L. E. G. Ames	1929	104 (81ct, 23st)	J. T. Murray	1957
122 (70ct, 52st)	L. E. G. Ames	1928	102 (69ct, 33st)	F. H. Huish	1913
110 (63ct, 47st)	H. Yarnold	1949	102 (95ct, 7st)	J. T. Murray	1960
107 (76ct, 31st)	G. Duckworth	1928	101 (62ct, 39st)	F. H. Huish	1911
107 (96ct, 11st)	J. G. Binks	1960	101 (85ct, 16st)	R. Booth	1960
104 (40ct, 64st)	L. E. G. Ames	1932	100 (90ct, 10st)	R. Booth	1964

L. E. G. Ames achieved the two highest stumping totals in a season: 64 in 1932, and 52 in 1928.

MOST DISMISSALS

Dates in italics denote the first half of an overseas season; i.e. *1997* denotes the 1997-98 season.

		Dis	Career	M	Ct	St
1	R. W. Taylor	1,649	1960–1988	639	1,473	176
2	J. T. Murray	1,527	1952–1975	635	1,268	259
3	H. Strudwick	1,495	1902–1927	674	1,237	258
4	A. P. E. Knott	1,344	1964–1985	511	1,211	133
5	R. C. Russell	1,320	1981–2004	465	1,192	128
6	F. H. Huish	1,311	1895–1914	497	934	377
7	B. Taylor	1,295	1949–1973	572	1,084	211
8	S. J. Rhodes	1,263	1981–2004	440	1,139	124
	D. Hunter	1,263	1888–1909	552	913	350
10	H. R. Butt	1,231	1890–1912	550	954	277

Current Players with 500 Dismissals

		Career	M	Ct	St
622	S. M. Davies	2005–2021	244	588	34
564	J. A. Simpson	2009–2021	173	536	28
562	Sarfraz Ahmed	*2005–2021*	161	508	54
516	T. D. Paine	*2005–2020*	147	494	22
511	J. M. Bairstow	2009–2021	192	487	24

Many of these figures include catches taken in the field.

FIELDING RECORDS

excluding wicketkeepers

MOST CATCHES IN AN INNINGS

7	M. J. Stewart	Surrey v Northamptonshire at Northampton	1957
7	A. S. Brown	Gloucestershire v Nottinghamshire at Nottingham	1966
7	R. Clarke	Warwickshire v Lancashire at Liverpool	2011

MOST CATCHES IN A MATCH

10	W. R. Hammond†	Gloucestershire v Surrey at Cheltenham	1928
9	R. Clarke	Warwickshire v Lancashire at Liverpool	2011
8	W. B. Burns	Worcestershire v Yorkshire at Bradford	1907
8	F. G. Travers	Europeans v Parsees at Bombay	1923-24
8	A. H. Bakewell	Northamptonshire v Essex at Leyton	1928
8	W. R. Hammond	Gloucestershire v Worcestershire at Cheltenham	1932
8	K. J. Grieves	Lancashire v Sussex at Manchester	1951
8	C. A. Milton	Gloucestershire v Sussex at Hove	1952
8	G. A. R. Lock	Surrey v Warwickshire at The Oval	1957
8	J. M. Prodger	Kent v Gloucestershire at Cheltenham	1961
8	P. M. Walker	Glamorgan v Derbyshire at Swansea	1970
8	Masood Anwar	Rawalpindi v Lahore Division at Rawalpindi	1983-84
8	M. C. J. Ball	Gloucestershire v Yorkshire at Cheltenham	1994
8	J. D. Carr	Middlesex v Warwickshire at Birmingham	1995
8	G. A. Hick	Worcestershire v Essex at Chelmsford	2005
8	Naved Yasin	State Bank v Bahawalpur Stags at Bahawalpur	2014-15
8	A. M. Rahane	India v Sri Lanka at Galle	2015-16

† *Hammond also scored a hundred in each innings.*

MOST CATCHES IN A SEASON

78	W. R. Hammond	1928		71	P. J. Sharpe	1962
77	M. J. Stewart	1957		70	J. Tunnicliffe	1901
73	P. M. Walker	1961				

The most catches by a fielder since the reduction of County Championship matches in 1969 is 59 by G. R. J. Roope in 1971.

MOST CATCHES

Dates in italics denote the first half of an overseas season; i.e. *1970* denotes the 1970-71 season.

Ct		Career	M	Ct		Career	M
1,018	F. E. Woolley	1906–1938	978	788	J. G. Langridge	1928–1955	574
876	W. G. Grace	1865–1908	870	765	W. Rhodes	1898–1930	1,110
831	G. A. R. Lock	1946–*1970*	654	760	C. A. Milton	1948–1974	620
820	W. R. Hammond	1920–1951	634	759	E. H. Hendren	1907–1938	833
813	D. B. Close	1949–1986	786	709	G. A. Hick	*1983*–2008	526

Woolley's catches include one as wicketkeeper, Grace's three and Close's one. The most catches by a current player is 391 by R. Clarke in 267 matches between 2002 and 2021.

TEAM RECORDS

HIGHEST INNINGS TOTALS

1,107	Victoria v New South Wales at Melbourne	1926-27
1,059	Victoria v Tasmania at Melbourne	1922-23
952-6 dec	Sri Lanka v India at Colombo (RPS)	1997-98
951-7 dec	Sind v Baluchistan at Karachi.	1973-74
944-6 dec	Hyderabad v Andhra at Secunderabad	1993-94
918	New South Wales v South Australia at Sydney	1900-01
912-8 dec	Holkar v Mysore at Indore	1945-46
912-6 dec†	Tamil Nadu v Goa at Panjim	1988-89
910-6 dec	Railways v Dera Ismail Khan at Lahore.	1964-65
903-7 dec	England v Australia at The Oval.	1938
900-6 dec	Queensland v Victoria at Brisbane	2005-06

† *Tamil Nadu's total of 912-6 dec included 52 penalty runs from their opponents' failure to meet the required bowling rate.*

The highest total in a team's second innings is 770 by New South Wales v South Australia at Adelaide in 1920-21.

HIGHEST FOURTH-INNINGS TOTALS

654-5	England v South Africa at Durban	1938-39
	After being set 696 to win. The match was left drawn on the tenth day.	
604	Maharashtra (*set 959 to win*) v Bombay at Poona.	1948-49
576-8	Trinidad (*set 672 to win*) v Barbados at Port-of-Spain	1945-46
572	New South Wales (*set 593 to win*) v South Australia at Sydney.	1907-08
541-7	West Zone (*won*) v South Zone at Hyderabad	2009-10
529-9	Combined XI (*set 579 to win*) v South Africans at Perth	1963-64
518	Victoria (*set 753 to win*) v Queensland at Brisbane	1926-27
513-9	Central Province (*won*) v Southern Province at Kandy.	2003-04
507-7	Cambridge University (*won*) v MCC and Ground at Lord's.	1896
506-6	South Australia (*won*) v Queensland at Adelaide	1991-92
503-4	South Zone (*won*) v England A at Gurgaon	2003-04
502-6	Middlesex (*won*) v Nottinghamshire at Nottingham.	1925
502-8	Players (*won*) v Gentlemen at Lord's	1900
500-7	South African Universities (*won*) v Western Province at Stellenbosch	1978-79

MOST RUNS IN A DAY (ONE SIDE)

721	Australians (721) v Essex at Southend (1st day).	1948
651	West Indians (651-2) v Leicestershire at Leicester (1st day)	1950
649	New South Wales (649-7) v Otago at Dunedin (2nd day)	1923-24
645	Surrey (645-4) v Hampshire at The Oval (1st day).	1909
644	Oxford U. (644-8) v H. D. G. Leveson Gower's XI at Eastbourne (1st day) . . .	1921
640	Lancashire (640-8) v Sussex at Hove (1st day).	1937
636	Free Foresters (636-7) v Cambridge U. at Cambridge (1st day).	1938
625	Gloucestershire (625-6) v Worcestershire at Dudley (2nd day)	1934

MOST RUNS IN A DAY (BOTH SIDES)

(excluding the above)

685	North (169-8 and 255-7), South (261-8 dec) at Blackpool (2nd day).	1961
666	Surrey (607-4), Northamptonshire (59-2) at Northampton (2nd day).	1920
665	Rest of South Africa (339), Transvaal (326) at Johannesburg (1st day)	1911-12
663	Middlesex (503-4), Leicestershire (160-2) at Leicester (2nd day)	1947
661	Border (201), Griqualand West (460) at Kimberley (1st day).	1920-21
649	Hampshire (570-8), Somerset (79-3) at Taunton (2nd day)	1901

HIGHEST AGGREGATES IN A MATCH

Runs	Wkts		
2,376	37	Maharashtra v Bombay at Poona	1948-49
2,078	40	Bombay v Holkar at Bombay	1944-45
1,981	35	South Africa v England at Durban	1938-39
1,945	18	Canterbury v Wellington at Christchurch	1994-95
1,929	39	New South Wales v South Australia at Sydney	1925-26
1,911	34	New South Wales v Victoria at Sydney	1908-09
1,905	40	Otago v Wellington at Dunedin	1923-24

In Britain

Runs	Wkts		
1,815	28	Somerset v Surrey at Taunton	2002
1,808	20	Sussex v Essex at Hove	1993
1,795	34	Somerset v Northamptonshire at Taunton	2001
1,723	31	England v Australia at Leeds	1948
1,706	23	Hampshire v Warwickshire at Southampton	1997

LOWEST INNINGS TOTALS

6†	The Bs v England at Lord's	1810
12†	Oxford University v MCC and Ground at Oxford	1877
12	Northamptonshire v Gloucestershire at Gloucester	1907
13	Auckland v Canterbury at Auckland	1877-78
13	Nottinghamshire v Yorkshire at Nottingham	1901
14	Surrey v Essex at Chelmsford	1983
15	MCC v Surrey at Lord's	1839
15†	Victoria v MCC at Melbourne	1903-04
15†	Northamptonshire v Yorkshire at Northampton	1908
15	Hampshire v Warwickshire at Birmingham	1922
	Following on, Hampshire scored 521 and won by 155 runs.	
16	MCC and Ground v Surrey at Lord's	1872
16	Derbyshire v Nottinghamshire at Nottingham	1879
16	Surrey v Nottinghamshire at The Oval	1880
16	Warwickshire v Kent at Tonbridge	1913
16	Trinidad v Barbados at Bridgetown	1942-43
16	Border v Natal at East London (first innings)	1959-60
16‡	**Border v KwaZulu-Natal Coastal at Paarl**	**2020-21**
17	Gentlemen of Kent v Gentlemen of England at Lord's	1850
17	Gloucestershire v Australians at Cheltenham	1896
18	The Bs v England at Lord's	1831
18†	Kent v Sussex at Gravesend	1867
18	Tasmania v Victoria at Melbourne	1868-69
18†	Australians v MCC and Ground at Lord's	1896
18	Border v Natal at East London (second innings)	1959-60
18†	Durham MCCU v Durham at Chester-le-Street	2012

† *One man absent.*   ‡ *Two men absent.*

LOWEST TOTALS IN A MATCH

34	(16 and 18) Border v Natal at East London	1959-60
42	(27† and 15†) Northamptonshire v Yorkshire at Northampton	1908

† *Northamptonshire batted one man short in each innings.*

LOWEST AGGREGATE IN A COMPLETED MATCH

Runs	Wkts		
85	11†	Quetta v Rawalpindi at Islamabad...........................	2008-09
105	31	MCC v Australians at Lord's...............................	1878

† *Both teams forfeited their first innings.*

The lowest aggregate in a match in which the losing team was bowled out twice since 1900 is 157 for 22 wickets, Surrey v Worcestershire at The Oval, 1954.

LARGEST VICTORIES

Largest Innings Victories

Inns and 851 runs	Railways (910-6 dec) v Dera Ismail Khan at Lahore...........	1964-65
Inns and 666 runs	Victoria (1,059) v Tasmania at Melbourne	1922-23
Inns and 656 runs	Victoria (1,107) v New South Wales at Melbourne.............	1926-27
Inns and 605 runs	New South Wales (918) v South Australia at Sydney	1900-01
Inns and 579 runs	England (903-7 dec) v Australia at The Oval.................	1938
Inns and 575 runs	Sind (951-7 dec) v Baluchistan at Karachi	1973-74
Inns and 527 runs	New South Wales (713) v South Australia at Adelaide	1908-09
Inns and 517 runs	Australians (675) v Nottinghamshire at Nottingham	1921

Largest Victories by Runs Margin

685 runs	New South Wales (235 and 761-8 dec) v Queensland at Sydney ..	1929-30
675 runs	England (521 and 342-8 dec) v Australia at Brisbane	1928-29
638 runs	New South Wales (304 and 770) v South Australia at Adelaide ...	1920-21
609 runs	Muslim Comm. Bank (575 and 282-0 dec) v WAPDA at Lahore ..	1977-78

Victory Without Losing a Wicket

Lancashire (166-0 dec and 66-0) beat Leicestershire by ten wickets at Manchester......		1956
Karachi A (277-0 dec) beat Sind A by an innings and 77 runs at Karachi		1957-58
Railways (236-0 dec and 16-0) beat Jammu & Kashmir by ten wickets at Srinagar......		1960-61
Karnataka (451-0 dec) beat Kerala by an innings and 186 runs at Chikmagalur.......		1977-78

There have been 32 wins by an innings and 400 runs or more, the most recent being an innings and 425 by Meghalaya v Mizoram and an innings and 405 by Chandigarh v Manipur, both at Kolkata in 2019-20.

There have been 25 wins by 500 runs or more, the most recent being 568 runs by Somerset v Cardiff MCCU at Taunton in 2019.

There have been 34 wins by a team losing only one wicket, the most recent being by Kent v Sussex at Canterbury in 2020.

TIED MATCHES

Since 1948, a tie has been recognised only when the scores are level with all the wickets down in the fourth innings. There have been **41** instances since then, including two Tests (see Test record section); Sussex have featured in five of those, Essex and Kent in four each.

The most recent instances are:

Kalutara PCC v Police at Colombo (Burgher)...................................	2016-17
Guyana v Windward Islands at Providence.....................................	2017-18
Chilaw Marians v Burgher at Katunayake......................................	2017-18
Negombo v Kalutara Town at Gampaha	2017-18
Bloomfield v Army at Colombo (Moors)	2017-18
Somerset v Lancashire at Taunton	2018
Khyber Pakhtunkhwa v Central Punjab at Karachi	**2020-21**

MATCHES COMPLETED ON FIRST DAY

(Since 1946)

Derbyshire v Somerset at Chesterfield, June 11.	1947
Lancashire v Sussex at Manchester, July 12	1950
Surrey v Warwickshire at The Oval, May 16	1953
Somerset v Lancashire at Bath, June 6 (H. F. T. Buse's benefit).	1953
Kent v Worcestershire at Tunbridge Wells, June 15	1960
Griqualand West v Easterns at Kimberley, March 10	2010-11

SHORTEST COMPLETED MATCHES

Balls

121	Quetta (forfeit and 41) v Rawalpindi (forfeit and 44-1) at Islamabad	2008-09
350	Somerset (35 and 44) v Middlesex (86) at Lord's	1899
352	Victoria (82 and 57) v Tasmania (104 and 37-7) at Launceston	1850-51
372	Victoria (80 and 50) v Tasmania (97 and 35-2) at Launceston	1853-54

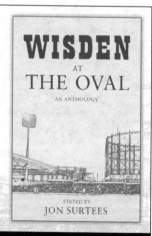

LIST A ONE-DAY RECORDS

List A is a concept intended to provide an approximate equivalent in one-day cricket of first-class status. It was introduced by the Association of Cricket Statisticians and Historians and is now recognised by the ICC, with a separate category for Twenty20 cricket. Further details are available at stats.acscricket.com/ListA/Description.html. List A games comprise:

(a) One-day internationals.
(b) Other international matches (e.g. A-team internationals).
(c) Premier domestic one-day tournaments in Test-playing countries.
(d) Official tourist matches against the main first-class teams (e.g. counties, states and Board XIs).

The following matches are excluded:

(a) Matches originally scheduled as less than 40 overs per side (e.g. Twenty20 games).
(b) World Cup warm-up games.
(c) Tourist matches against teams outside the major domestic competitions (e.g. universities).
(d) Festival games and pre-season friendlies.

This section covers one-day cricket to December 31, 2021. Bold type denotes performances in the calendar year 2021 or, in career figures, players who appeared in List A cricket in that year.

BATTING RECORDS

HIGHEST INDIVIDUAL INNINGS

268	A. D. Brown	Surrey v Glamorgan at The Oval	2002
264	R. G. Sharma	India v Sri Lanka at Kolkata	2014-15
257	D. J. M. Short	Western Australia v Queensland at Sydney	2018-19
248	S. Dhawan	India A v South Africa A at Pretoria	2013
237*	M. J. Guptill	New Zealand v West Indies at Wellington	2014-15
230	**T. M. Head**	**South Australia v Queensland at Adelaide (KRO)**	**2021-22**
229*	B. R. Dunk	Tasmania v Queensland at Sydney	2014-15
227*	**P. P. Shaw**	**Mumbai v Puducherry at Jaipur**	**2020-21**
222*	R. G. Pollock	Eastern Province v Border at East London	1974-75
222	J. M. How	Central Districts v Northern Districts at Hamilton	2012-13
220*	B. M. Duckett	England Lions v Sri Lanka A at Canterbury	2016
219	V. Sehwag	India v West Indies at Indore	2011-12
215	C. H. Gayle	West Indies v Zimbabwe at Canberra	2014-15
212*	S. V. Samson	Kerala v Goa at Alur	2019-20
210*	Fakhar Zaman	Pakistan v Zimbabwe at Bulawayo	2018
209	Abid Ali	Islamabad v Peshawar at Peshawar	2017-18
209	R. G. Sharma	India v Australia at Bangalore	2013-14
208*	R. G. Sharma	India v Sri Lanka at Mohali	2017-18
208*	Soumya Sarkar	Abahani v Sheikh Jamal Dhanmondi at Savar	2018-19
207	Mohammad Ali	Pakistan Customs v DHA at Sialkot	2004-05
206	A. I. Kallicharran	Warwickshire v Oxfordshire at Birmingham	1984
204*	Khalid Latif	Karachi Dolphins v Quetta Bears at Karachi	2008-09
203	A. D. Brown	Surrey v Hampshire at Guildford	1997
203	Y. B. Jaiswal	Mumbai v Jharkhand at Alur	2019-20
202*	A. Barrow	Natal v SA African XI at Durban	1975-76
202*	P. J. Hughes	Australia A v South Africa A at Darwin	2014
202	T. M. Head	South Australia v Western Australia at Sydney	2015-16
202	K. V. Kaushal	Uttarakhand v Sikkim at Nadiad	2018-19
201*	R. S. Bopara	Essex v Leicestershire at Leicester	2008
201	V. J. Wells	Leicestershire v Berkshire at Leicester	1996
200*	S. R. Tendulkar	India v South Africa at Gwalior	2009-10
200	Kamran Akmal	WAPDA v Habib Bank at Hyderabad	2017-18
200	M. B. van Buuren	Gauteng v Western Province at Johannesburg	2018-19

MOST RUNS

	Career	M	I	NO	R	HS	100	Avge
G. A. Gooch............	1973–1997	614	601	48	22,211	198*	44	40.16
G. A. Hick.............	1983–2008	651	630	96	22,059	172*	40	41.30
S. R. Tendulkar	1989–2011	551	538	55	21,999	200*	60	45.54
K. C. Sangakkara.......	1997–2019	529	501	54	19,456	169	39	43.52
I. V. A. Richards	1973–1993	500	466	61	16,995	189*	26	41.96
R. T. Ponting	1992–2013	456	445	53	16,363	164	34	41.74
C. G. Greenidge........	1970–1992	440	436	33	16,349	186*	33	40.56
S. T. Jayasuriya........	1989–2011	557	542	25	16,128	189	31	31.19
A. J. Lamb............	1972–1995	484	463	63	15,658	132*	19	39.14
D. L. Haynes..........	1976–1996	419	416	44	15,651	152*	28	42.07
S. C. Ganguly	1989–2011	437	421	43	15,622	183	31	41.32
K. J. Barnett..........	1979–2005	527	500	54	15,564	136	17	34.89
D. P. M. D. Jayawardene..	1995–2016	546	509	51	15,364	163*	21	33.54
R. Dravid.............	1992–2011	449	416	55	15,271	153	21	42.30
M. G. Bevan	1989–2006	427	385	124	15,103	157*	13	57.86

FASTEST FIFTIES

Balls

12	K. Weeraratne	Ragama v Kurunegala Youth at Colombo (Thurstan) ..	2005-06
13	**N. L. T. C. Perera ...**	**Army v Bloomfield at Panagoda**	**2020-21**
14	R. K. Kleinveldt	Western Province v KwaZulu-Natal at Durban	2010-11
15	Salman Butt.........	National Bank v Lahore Eagles at Lahore	2008-09
16	G. D. Rose	Somerset v Glamorgan at Neath...................	1990
16	A. V. Kale	Maharashtra v Baroda at Vadodara	1994-95
16	A. B. de Villiers......	South Africa v West Indies at Johannesburg	2014-15
16	T. C. Bruce	Central Districts v Canterbury at New Plymouth	2015-16
16	Anwar Ali	Baluchistan v Khyber Pakhtunkhwa at Faisalabad.....	2018
16	**A. A. Sheth ....**	**Baroda v Chhattisgarh at Surat**	**2020-21**
16	**J. L. Smith ....**	**Surrey v Nottinghamshire at Guildford**	**2021**

FASTEST HUNDREDS

Balls

31	A. B. de Villiers	South Africa v West Indies at Johannesburg	2014-15
36	C. J. Anderson	New Zealand v West Indies at Queenstown	2013-14
37	Shahid Afridi	Pakistan v Sri Lanka at Nairobi	1996-97
38	R. Powell............	Jamaica v Leeward Islands at Conaree...............	2019-20
39	D. S. Weerakkody	Sinhalese v Burgher at Colombo (BRC)	2019-20
40	Y. K. Pathan.........	Baroda v Maharashtra at Ahmedabad..............	2009-10
42	**A. Sharma ....**	**Punjab v Madhya Pradesh at Indore**	**2020-21**
43	R. R. Watson	Scotland v Somerset at Edinburgh	2003
44	M. A. Ealham	Kent v Derbyshire at Maidstone...................	1995
44	M. V. Boucher	South Africa v Zimbabwe at Potchefstroom.........	2006-07
44	T. C. Smith..........	Lancashire v Worcestershire at Worcester	2012
44	D. I. Stevens	Kent v Sussex at Canterbury......................	2013

HIGHEST PARTNERSHIP FOR EACH WICKET

367*	for 1st	M. N. van Wyk/C. S. Delport, Dolphins v Knights at Bloemfontein	2014-15
372	for 2nd	C. H. Gayle/M. N. Samuels, West Indies v Zimbabwe at Canberra	2014-15
338	for 3rd	S. V. Samson/S. Baby, Kerala v Goa at Alur	2019-20
276	for 4th	Mominul Haque/A. R. S. Silva, Prime Doleshwar v Abahani at Bogra ..	2013-14
267*	for 5th	Minhazul Abedin/Khaled Mahmud, Bangladeshis v Bahawalpur at Karachi	1997-98
272	for 6th	A. K. Markram/F. Behardien, Titans v Cape Cobras at Cape Town.....	2018-19
215*	for 7th	S. Singh/G. H. Dockrell, Leinster v Northern at Dublin	2018
203	for 8th	Shahid Iqbal/Haaris Ayaz, Karachi Whites v Hyderabad at Karachi	1998-99
155	for 9th	C. M. W. Read/A. J. Harris, Nottinghamshire v Durham at Nottingham ...	2006
128	for 10th	A. Ashish Reddy/M. Ravi Kiran, Hyderabad v Kerala at Secunderabad .	2014-15

BOWLING RECORDS

BEST BOWLING ANALYSES

8-10	S. Nadeem	Jharkhand v Rajasthan at Chennai	2018-19
8-15	R. L. Sanghvi	Delhi v Himachal Pradesh at Una	1997-98
8-19	W. P. U. J. C. Vaas	Sri Lanka v Zimbabwe at Colombo (SSC).	2001-02
8-20*	D. T. Kottehewa	Nondescripts v Ragama at Colombo (Moors)	2007-08
8-21	M. A. Holding	Derbyshire v Sussex at Hove	1988
8-26	K. D. Boyce	Essex v Lancashire at Manchester	1971
8-30	G. D. R. Eranga	Burgher v Army at Colombo (Colts)	2007-08
8-31	D. L. Underwood	Kent v Scotland at Edinburgh	1987
8-38	B. A. Mavuta	Rising Stars v Manicaland Mountaineers at Harare	2017-18
8-40	Yeasin Arafat	Gazi Group Cricketers v Abahani at Fatullah	2017-18
8-43	S. W. Tait	South Australia v Tasmania at Adelaide	2003-04
8-52	K. A. Stoute	West Indies A v Lancashire at Manchester	2010
8-66	S. R. G. Francis	Somerset v Derbyshire at Derby	2004

* Including two hat-tricks.

MOST WICKETS

	Career	M	B	R	W	BB	4I	Avge
Wasim Akram.	1984–2003	594	29,719	19,303	881	5-10	46	21.91
A. A. Donald.	1985–2003	458	22,856	14,942	684	6-15	38	21.84
M. Muralitharan	1991–2010	453	23,734	15,270	682	7-30	29	22.39
Waqar Younis.	1988–2003	412	19,841	15,098	675	7-36	44	22.36
J. K. Lever	1968–1990	481	23,208	13,278	674	5-8	34	19.70
J. E. Emburey	1975–2000	536	26,399	16,811	647	5-23	26	25.98
I. T. Botham	1973–1993	470	22,899	15,264	612	5-27	18	24.94

WICKETKEEPING AND FIELDING RECORDS

MOST DISMISSALS IN AN INNINGS

8	(8 ct)	D. J. S. Taylor	Somerset v Combined Universities at Taunton . . .	1982
8	(5ct, 3st)	S. J. Palframan	Boland v Easterns at Paarl	1997-98
8	(8ct)	D. J. Pipe	Worcestershire v Hertfordshire at Hertford	2001
8	(6ct, 2st)	P. M. Nevill	New South Wales v Cricket Aus XI at Sydney . . .	2017-18

*There have been **16** instances of seven dismissals in an innings, the most recent being **I. P. Kishan** (7ct) for Jharkhand v Madhya Pradesh at Indore in 2020-21.*

MOST CATCHES IN AN INNINGS IN THE FIELD

There have been **16** instances of a fielder taking five catches in an innings. The most recent are:

5	A. R. McBrine	Ireland v Sri Lanka A at Belfast	2014
5	Farhad Hossain	Prime Doleshwar v Sheikh Jamal Dhanmondi at Fatullah . . .	2017-18
5	Zahid Zakhail	Amo v Boost at Kabul.	2018
5	Mominul Haque	Legends of Rupganj v Abahani at Savar.	2018-19

TEAM RECORDS

HIGHEST INNINGS TOTALS

496-4	(50 overs)	Surrey v Gloucestershire at The Oval	2007
481-6	(50 overs)	England v Australia at Nottingham.	2018
458-4	(50 overs)	India A v Leicestershire at Leicester.	2018
457-4	**(50 overs)**	**Mumbai v Puducherry at Jaipur**	**2020-21**
445-8	(50 overs)	Nottinghamshire v Northamptonshire at Nottingham.	2016

444-3	(50 overs)	England v Pakistan at Nottingham	2016
443-9	(50 overs)	Sri Lanka v Netherlands at Amstelveen	2006
439-2	(50 overs)	South Africa v West Indies at Johannesburg	2014-15
438-4	(50 overs)	South Africa v India at Mumbai	2014-15
438-5	(50 overs)	Surrey v Glamorgan at The Oval	2002
438-9	(49.5 overs)	South Africa v Australia at Johannesburg	2005-06
434-4	(50 overs)	Australia v South Africa at Johannesburg	2005-06
434-4	(50 overs)	Jamaica v Trinidad & Tobago at Coolidge	2016-17
433-3	(50 overs)	India A v South Africa A at Pretoria	2013
433-7	(50 overs)	Nottinghamshire v Leicestershire at Nottingham	2019

LOWEST INNINGS TOTALS

18	(14.3 overs)	West Indies Under-19 v Barbados at Blairmont	2007-08
19	(10.5 overs)	Saracens v Colts at Colombo (Colts)	2012-13
23	(19.4 overs)	Middlesex v Yorkshire at Leeds	1974
24	(17.1 overs)	Oman v Scotland at Al Amerat	2018-19
30	(20.4 overs)	Chittagong v Sylhet at Dhaka	2002-03
30	**(19.3 overs)**	**Ace Capital v Nondescripts at Colombo (NCC)**	**2020-21**
31	(13.5 overs)	Border v South Western Districts at East London	2007-08
34	(21.1 overs)	Saurashtra v Mumbai at Mumbai	1999-2000
35	(18 overs)	Zimbabwe v Sri Lanka at Harare	2003-04
35	(20.2 overs)	Cricket Coaching School v Abahani at Fatullah	2013-14
35	(15.3 overs)	Rajasthan v Railways at Nagpur	2014-15
35	(12 overs)	USA v Nepal at Kirtipur	2019-20

LIST A TWENTY20 RECORDS

This section covers Twenty20 cricket (including The Hundred) to December 31, 2021. Bold type denotes performances in the calendar year 2021 or, in career figures, players who appeared in Twenty20 cricket in that year.

BATTING RECORDS

HIGHEST INDIVIDUAL INNINGS

175*	C. H. Gayle	RC Bangalore v Pune Warriors at Bangalore	2012-13
172	A. J. Finch	Australia v Zimbabwe at Harare	2018
162*	H. Masakadza	Mountaineers v Mashonaland Eagles at Bulawayo . . .	2015-16
162*	Hazratullah Zazai	Afghanistan v Ireland at Dehradun	2018-19
161	A. Lyth	Yorkshire v Northamptonshire at Leeds	2017
158*	B. B. McCullum	Kolkata Knight Riders v RC Bangalore at Bangalore	2007-08
158*	B. B. McCullum	Warwickshire v Derbyshire at Birmingham.	2015
156	A. J. Finch	Australia v England at Southampton	2013
153*	L. J. Wright	Sussex v Essex at Chelmsford	2014
152*	G. R. Napier	Essex v Sussex at Chelmsford	2008
151*	C. H. Gayle	Somerset v Kent at Taunton.	2015
150*	Kamran Akmal	Lahore Whites v Islamabad at Rawalpindi	2017-18

MOST RUNS

	Career	M	I	NO	R	HS	100	Avge	SR
C. H. Gayle	2005–2021	453	445	52	14,321	175*	22	36.44	145.44
K. A. Pollard	2006–2021	573	508	148	11,327	104	1	31.46	152.08
Shoaib Malik	2004–2021	461	427	116	11,297	95*	0	36.32	126.73
D. A. Warner	2006–2021	313	312	39	10,308	135*	8	37.75	140.85
V. Kohli	2006–2021	324	307	59	10,204	113	5	41.14	133.28
A. J. Finch	2008–2021	334	329	33	10,057	172	8	33.97	140.93
B. B. McCullum	2004–2018	370	364	33	9,922	158*	7	29.97	136.49
R. G. Sharma	2006–2021	364	351	47	9,779	118	6	32.16	133.92
A. B. de Villiers	2003–2021	340	320	67	9,424	133*	4	37.24	150.13
A. D. Hales.	2009–2021	320	317	25	8,833	116*	5	30.25	145.75
S. R. Watson	2004–2020	343	335	34	8,822	124*	6	29.30	138.31
S. Dhawan	2006–2021	303	300	30	8,774	106*	2	32.49	124.77
S. K. Raina	2006–2021	336	319	50	8,653	126*	4	32.16	137.43
L. J. Wright	2004–2021	336	312	28	8,369	153*	7	29.46	143.15
M. J. Guptill	2005–2021	292	283	24	8,321	120*	4	32.12	131.22

FASTEST FIFTIES

Balls

12	Yuvraj Singh	India v England at Durban	2007-08
12	C. H. Gayle.	Melbourne Ren v Adelaide Str at Melbourne.	2015-16
12	Hazratullah Zazai	Kabul Zwanan v Balkh Legends at Sharjah	2018-19
13	M. E. Trescothick.	Somerset v Hampshire at Taunton	2010
13	M. Ahsan	Austria v Luxembourg at Ilfov	2019

There are 11 instances of 14 balls.

FASTEST HUNDREDS

Balls
30	C. H. Gayle.........	RC Bangalore v Pune Warriors at Bangalore..........	2012-13
32	R. R. Pant.........	Delhi v Himachal Pradesh at Delhi.................	2017-18
33	W. J. Lubbe	North West v Limpopo at Paarl	2018-19
34	A. Symonds	Kent v Middlesex at Maidstone	2004
35	L. P. van der Westhuizen	Namibia v Kenya at Windhoek....................	2011-12
35	D. A. Miller	South Africa v Bangladesh at Potchefstroom	2017-18
35	R. G. Sharma	India v Sri Lanka at Indore......................	2017-18
35	M. J. Guptill	Worcestershire v Northamptonshire at Northampton ...	2018
35	S. Wickramasekara....	Czech Republic v Turkey at Ilfov.................	2019
35	Khushdil Shah	Southern Punjab v Sindh at Rawalpindi.............	2020-21

HIGHEST PARTNERSHIP FOR EACH WICKET

236	for 1st	Hazratullah Zazai/Usman Ghani, Afghanistan v Ireland at Dehradun......	2018-19
229	for 2nd	V. Kohli/A. B. de Villiers, RC Bangalore v Gujarat Lions at Bangalore ...	2015-16
213	for 3rd	S. S. Iyer/S. A. Yadav, Mumbai v Sikkim at Indore	2018-19
202*	for 4th	M. C. Juneja/A. Malik, Gujarat v Kerala at Indore	2012-13
171	for 5th	A. J. Hose/D. R. Mousley, Warwickshire v Northamptonshire at Birmingham	2020
161	for 6th	K. Lewis/A. D. Russell, Jamaica Tallawahs v Trinbago KR at Port-of-Spain .	2018
107*	for 7th	L. Abeyratne/P. S. R. Anurudhha, Colombo v Chilaw Marians at Colombo	2015-16
120	for 8th	Azhar Mahmood/I. Udana, Wayamba v Uva at Colombo (RPS)	2012
132*	**for 9th**	**Saber Zakhil/Saqlain Ali, Belgium v Austria at Waterloo............**	**2021**
63	for 10th	G. D. Elliott/Zulfiqar Babar, Quetta Gladiators v Peshawar Zalmi at Sharjah .	2015-16

BOWLING RECORDS

BEST BOWLING ANALYSES

7-18	C. N. Ackermann	Leicestershire v Warwickshire at Leicester	2019
6-5	A. V. Suppiah	Somerset v Glamorgan at Cardiff......................	2011
6-5	**P. Aho**	**Nigeria v Sierra Leone at Lagos**	**2021-22**
6-6	Shakib Al Hasan	Barbados v Trinidad & Tobago at Bridgetown	2013
6-7	S. L. Malinga	Melbourne Stars v Perth Scorchers at Perth	2012-13
6-7	K. A. Jamieson	Canterbury v Auckland at Auckland	2018-19
6-7	D. L. Chahar	India v Bangladesh at Nagpur.........................	2019-20
6-7	**D. M. Nakrani**	**Uganda v Lesotho at Kigali City**	**2021-22**
6-8	B. A. W. Mendis	Sri Lanka v Zimbabwe at Hambantota...................	2012-13
6-8	A. M. Fernando	Chilaw Marians v Negombo at Colombo (CCC)	2019-20
6-9	P. Fojela	Border v Easterns at East London.....................	2014-15

MOST WICKETS

	Career	M	B	R	W	BB	4I	Avge	ER
D. J. Bravo.............	2005–2021	512	9,865	13,503	553	5-23	13	24.41	8.21
Imran Tahir.............	2005–2021	344	7,367	8,517	435	5-23	13	19.57	6.93
S. P. Narine.............	2010–2021	383	8,736	8,807	425	5-19	13	20.72	6.04
Rashid Khan	2015–2021	296	6,797	7,216	410	5-3	10	17.60	6.36
Shakib Al Hasan	2006–2021	351	7,416	8,438	398	6-6	14	21.20	6.82
S. L. Malinga...........	2004–2019	294	6,484	7,653	389	6-7	15	19.67	7.08
Sohail Tanvir...........	2004–2021	372	7,806	9,687	378	6-14	9	25.62	7.44
Wahab Riaz.............	2004–2021	308	6,545	8,065	370	5-8	6	21.79	7.39
A. D. Russell	2009–2021	392	6,369	8,980	346	5-15	9	25.95	6.74
Shahid Afridi...........	2004–2020	326	6,928	7,788	344	5-7	11	22.63	6.74
K. A. Pollard...........	2006–2021	573	5,435	7,448	300	4-15	7	24.82	8.22

	Career	M	B	R	W	BB	4I	Avge	ER
Mohammad Nabi	*2009–2021*	315	6,122	7,105	294	5-15	8	24.16	6.96
C. H. Morris	*2010–2021*	234	4,962	6,441	290	4-9	9	22.21	7.78
S. R. Patel	*2003–2021*	347	6,249	7,530	289	4-5	3	26.05	7.22
Yasir Arafat	2005–2016	226	4,702	6,344	281	4-5	10	22.57	8.09

WICKETKEEPING AND FIELDING RECORDS

MOST DISMISSALS IN AN INNINGS

7 (7ct) E. F. M. U. Fernando Lankan v Moors at Colombo (Bloomfield) 2005-06

MOST CATCHES IN AN INNINGS IN THE FIELD

5	Manzoor Ilahi	Jammu & Kashmir v Delhi at Delhi	2010-11
5	J. M. Vince	Hampshire v Leeward Islands at North Sound	2010-11
5	J. L. Ontong	Cape Cobras v Knights at Cape Town	2014-15
5	A. K. V. Adikari	Chilaw Marians v Bloomfield at Colombo (SSC).........	2014-15
5	P. G. Fulton	Canterbury v Northern Districts at Hamilton	2015-16
5	M. W. Machan	Sussex v Glamorgan at Hove	2016
5	**Mohammad Nabi**	**Hyderabad Sunrisers v Mumbai Indians at Abu Dhabi ..**	**2021**

TEAM RECORDS

HIGHEST INNINGS TOTALS

278-3	(20 overs)	Afghanistan v Ireland at Dehradun	2018-19
278-4	(20 overs)	Czech Republic v Turkey at Ilfov	2019
267-2	(20 overs)	Trinbago Knight Riders v Jamaica Tallawahs at Kingston	2019
263-3	(20 overs)	Australia v Sri Lanka at Pallekele	2016
263-5	(20 overs)	RC Bangalore v Pune Warriors at Bangalore	2012-13
262-4	(20 overs)	North West v Limpopo at Paarl	2018-19
260-4	(20 overs)	Yorkshire v Northamptonshire at Leeds	2017
260-5	(20 overs)	India v Sri Lanka at Indore	2017-18
260-6	(20 overs)	Sri Lanka v Kenya at Johannesburg.....................	2007-08

LOWEST INNINGS TOTALS

21	(8.3 overs)	Turkey v Czech Republic at Ilfov...........................	2019
26	**(12.4 overs)**	**Lesotho v Uganda at Kigali City**	**2021-22**
28	(11.3 overs)	Turkey v Luxembourg at Ilfov	2019
30	(11.1 overs)	Tripura v Jharkhand at Dhanbad.......................	2009-10
32	(8.5 overs)	Turkey v Austria at Ilfov	2019
37	**(17.2 overs)**	**Panama v Canada at Coolidge**........................	**2021-22**
38	**(10.1 overs)**	**Cameroon v Mozambique at Kigali**	**2021-22**
39	(10.3 overs)	Netherlands v Sri Lanka at Chittagong...................	2013-14

ALL-FORMAT CAREER RECORDS

This section covers combined records in first-class, List A and Twenty20 cricket to December 31, 2021. Bold type denotes a player who appeared in 2021. Daggers denote players who appeared in first-class and List A formats, and double daggers players who appeared in all three; all other players appeared only in first-class cricket.

MOST RUNS

	Career	M	I	NO	R	HS	100	Avge
G. A. Gooch†	1973–2000	1,195	1,591	123	67,057	333	172	45.67
G. A. Hick‡	1983–2008	1,214	1,537	183	64,372	405*	178	47.54
J. B. Hobbs	1905–1934	834	1,325	107	61,760	316*	199	50.70
F. E. Woolley	1906–1938	978	1,530	84	58,959	305*	145	40.77
G. Boycott†	1962–1986	922	1,316	206	58,521	261*	159	52.72
E. H. Hendren	1907–1938	833	1,300	166	57,611	301*	170	50.80
D. L. Amiss†	1960–1987	1,062	1,530	160	55,942	262*	117	40.83
C. P. Mead	1905–1936	814	1,340	185	55,061	280*	153	47.67
W. G. Grace	1865–1908	870	1,478	104	54,211	344	124	39.45
C. G. Greenidge†	1970–1992	963	1,325	108	53,703	273*	125	44.12

MOST WICKETS

	Career	M	B	R	W	BB	5I	Avge
W. Rhodes	1898–1930	1,110	185,742	70,322	4,204	9-24	287	16.72
A. P. Freeman	1914–1936	592	154,658	69,577	3,776	10-53	386	18.42
C. W. L. Parker	1903–1935	635	157,328	63,819	3,278	10-79	277	19.46
J. T. Hearne	1888–1923	639	144,470	54,351	3,061	9-32	255	17.75
D. L. Underwood†	1963–1987	1,089	159,571	61,111	3,037	9-28	161	20.12
F. J. Titmus†	1949–1982	941	180,576	67,396	2,989	9-52	171	22.54
T. W. J. Goddard	1922–1952	593	142,186	59,116	2,979	10-113	251	19.84
D. Shackleton†	1948–1973	684	161,071	54,175	2,898	9-30	194	18.69
A. S. Kennedy	1907–1936	677	150,917	61,035	2,874	10-37	225	21.23
G. A. R. Lock†	1946–1970	662	150,596	54,979	2,854	10-54	196	19.26
W. G. Grace	1865–1908	870	124,833	50,980	2,809	10-49	240	18.14

MOST DISMISSALS

	Dis	Career	M	Ct	St
R. W. Taylor†	2,070	1960–1988	972	1,819	251
S. J. Rhodes‡	1,929	1981–2004	920	1,671	258
R. C. Russell‡	1,885	1981–2004	946	1,658	227
A. P. E. Knott†	1,741	1964–1985	829	1,553	188
J. T. Murray†	1,724	1952–1975	784	1,432	292
Kamran Akmal‡	**1,665**	**1997–2021**	**872**	**1,402**	**263**
C. M. W. Read‡	1,583	1995–2017	801	1,430	153
P. A. Nixon‡	1,549	1989–2011	862	1,360	189
D. L. Bairstow†	1,545	1970–1990	888	1,372	173
A. C. Gilchrist‡	1,498	1992–2013	648	1,356	142

Total dismissals include catches taken when not keeping wicket.

MOST CATCHES IN THE FIELD

Ct		Career	M	Ct		Career	M
1,018	F. E. Woolley	1906–1938	978	1,008	G. A. Hick‡	1983–2008	1,214

Woolley's catches include one as wicketkeeper.

MEN'S TEST RECORDS

This section covers all men's Tests up to January 16, 2022. Bold type denotes performances since January 1, 2021, or, in career figures, players who have appeared in Test cricket since that date.

BATTING RECORDS

HIGHEST INDIVIDUAL INNINGS

400*	B. C. Lara	West Indies v England at St John's	2003-04
380	M. L. Hayden	Australia v Zimbabwe at Perth	2003-04
375	B. C. Lara	West Indies v England at St John's	1993-94
374	D. P. M. D. Jayawardene	Sri Lanka v South Africa at Colombo (SSC)	2006
365*	G. S. Sobers	West Indies v Pakistan at Kingston	1957-58
364	L. Hutton	England v Australia at The Oval	1938
340	S. T. Jayasuriya	Sri Lanka v India at Colombo (RPS)	1997-98
337	Hanif Mohammad	Pakistan v West Indies at Bridgetown	1957-58
336*	W. R. Hammond	England v New Zealand at Auckland	1932-33
335*	D. A. Warner	Australia v Pakistan at Adelaide	2019-20
334*	M. A. Taylor	Australia v Pakistan at Peshawar	1998-99
334	D. G. Bradman	Australia v England at Leeds	1930
333	G. A. Gooch	England v India at Lord's	1990
333	C. H. Gayle	West Indies v Sri Lanka at Galle	2010-11
329*	M. J. Clarke	Australia v India at Sydney	2011-12
329	Inzamam-ul-Haq	Pakistan v New Zealand at Lahore	2002
325	A. Sandham	England v West Indies at Kingston	1929-30
319	V. Sehwag	India v South Africa at Chennai	2007-08
319	K. C. Sangakkara	Sri Lanka v Bangladesh at Chittagong	2013-14
317	C. H. Gayle	West Indies v South Africa at St John's	2004-05
313	Younis Khan	Pakistan v Sri Lanka at Karachi	2008-09
311*	H. M. Amla	South Africa v England at The Oval	2012
311	R. B. Simpson	Australia v England at Manchester	1964
310*	J. H. Edrich	England v New Zealand at Leeds	1965
309	V. Sehwag	India v Pakistan at Multan	2003-04
307	R. M. Cowper	Australia v England at Melbourne	1965-66
304	D. G. Bradman	Australia v England at Leeds	1934
303*	K. K. Nair	India v England at Chennai	2016-17
302*	Azhar Ali	Pakistan v West Indies at Dubai	2016-17
302	L. G. Rowe	West Indies v England at Bridgetown	1973-74
302	B. B. McCullum	New Zealand v India at Wellington	2013-14

There have been 68 further instances of 250 or more runs in a Test innings.

The highest innings for the countries not mentioned above are:

266	D. L. Houghton	Zimbabwe v Sri Lanka at Bulawayo	1994-95
219*	Mushfiqur Rahim	Bangladesh v Zimbabwe at Mirpur	2018-19
200*	**Hashmatullah Shahidi**	**Afghanistan v Zimbabwe at Abu Dhabi**	**2020-21**
118	K. J. O'Brien	Ireland v Pakistan at Malahide	2018

HUNDRED ON TEST DEBUT

C. Bannerman (165*)	Australia v England at Melbourne	1876-77
W. G. Grace (152)	England v Australia at The Oval	1880
H. Graham (107)	Australia v England at Lord's	1893
†K. S. Ranjitsinhji (154*)	England v Australia at Manchester	1896
†P. F. Warner (132*)	England v South Africa at Johannesburg	1898-99
†R. A. Duff (104)	Australia v England at Melbourne	1901-02
§R. E. Foster (287)	England v Australia at Sydney	1903-04
G. Gunn (119)	England v Australia at Sydney	1907-08

†R. J. Hartigan (116)	Australia v England at Adelaide	1907-08
†H. L. Collins (104)	Australia v England at Sydney	1920-21
W. H. Ponsford (110)	Australia v England at Sydney	1924-25
A. A. Jackson (164)	Australia v England at Adelaide	1928-29
†G. A. Headley (176)	West Indies v England at Bridgetown	1929-30
J. E. Mills (117)	New Zealand v England at Wellington	1929-30
Nawab of Pataudi snr (102)	England v Australia at Sydney	1932-33
B. H. Valentine (136)	England v India at Bombay	1933-34
†L. Amarnath (118)	India v England at Bombay	1933-34
†P. A. Gibb (106)	England v South Africa at Johannesburg	1938-39
S. C. Griffith (140)	England v West Indies at Port-of-Spain	1947-48
A. G. Ganteaume (112)	West Indies v England at Port-of-Spain	1947-48
†J. W. Burke (101*)	Australia v England at Adelaide	1950-51
P. B. H. May (138)	England v South Africa at Leeds	1951
R. H. Shodhan (110)	India v Pakistan at Calcutta	1952-53
B. H. Pairaudeau (115)	West Indies v India at Port-of-Spain	1952-53
†O. G. Smith (104)	West Indies v Australia at Kingston	1954-55
A. G. Kripal Singh (100*)	India v New Zealand at Hyderabad	1955-56
C. C. Hunte (142)	West Indies v Pakistan at Bridgetown	1957-58
C. A. Milton (104*)	England v New Zealand at Leeds	1958
†A. A. Baig (112)	India v England at Manchester	1959
Hanumant Singh (105)	India v England at Delhi	1963-64
Khalid Ibadulla (166)	Pakistan v Australia at Karachi	1964-65
B. R. Taylor (105)	New Zealand v India at Calcutta	1964-65
K. D. Walters (155)	Australia v England at Brisbane	1965-66
J. H. Hampshire (107)	England v West Indies at Lord's	1969
†G. R. Viswanath (137)	India v Australia at Kanpur	1969-70
G. S. Chappell (108)	Australia v England at Perth	1970-71
‡§L. G. Rowe (214, 100*)	West Indies v New Zealand at Kingston	1971-72
A. I. Kallicharran (100*)	West Indies v New Zealand at Georgetown	1971-72
R. E. Redmond (107)	New Zealand v Pakistan at Auckland	1972-73
†F. C. Hayes (106*)	England v West Indies at The Oval	1973
†C. G. Greenidge (107)	West Indies v India at Bangalore	1974-75
†L. Baichan (105*)	West Indies v Pakistan at Lahore	1974-75
G. J. Cosier (109)	Australia v West Indies at Melbourne	1975-76
S. Amarnath (124)	India v New Zealand at Auckland	1975-76
Javed Miandad (163)	Pakistan v New Zealand at Lahore	1976-77
†A. B. Williams (100)	West Indies v Australia at Georgetown	1977-78
†D. M. Wellham (103)	Australia v England at The Oval	1981
†Salim Malik (100*)	Pakistan v Sri Lanka at Karachi	1981-82
K. C. Wessels (162)	Australia v England at Brisbane	1982-83
W. B. Phillips (159)	Australia v Pakistan at Perth	1983-84
¶M. Azharuddin (110)	India v England at Calcutta	1984-85
D. S. B. P. Kuruppu (201*)	Sri Lanka v New Zealand at Colombo (CCC)	1986-87
†M. J. Greatbatch (107*)	New Zealand v England at Auckland	1987-88
M. E. Waugh (138)	Australia v England at Adelaide	1990-91
A. C. Hudson (163)	South Africa v West Indies at Bridgetown	1991-92
R. S. Kaluwitharana (132*)	Sri Lanka v Australia at Colombo (SSC)	1992-93
D. L. Houghton (121)	Zimbabwe v India at Harare	1992-93
P. K. Amre (103)	India v South Africa at Durban	1992-93
†G. P. Thorpe (114*)	England v Australia at Nottingham	1993
G. S. Blewett (102*)	Australia v England at Adelaide	1994-95
S. C. Ganguly (131)	India v England at Lord's	1996
†Mohammad Wasim (109*)	Pakistan v New Zealand at Lahore	1996-97
Ali Naqvi (115)	Pakistan v South Africa at Rawalpindi	1997-98
Azhar Mahmood (128*)	Pakistan v South Africa at Rawalpindi	1997-98
M. S. Sinclair (214)	New Zealand v West Indies at Wellington	1999-2000
†Younis Khan (107)	Pakistan v Sri Lanka at Rawalpindi	1999-2000
Aminul Islam (145)	Bangladesh v India at Dhaka	2000-01
†H. Masakadza (119)	Zimbabwe v West Indies at Harare	2001
T. T. Samaraweera (103*)	Sri Lanka v India at Colombo (SSC)	2001

Taufeeq Umar (104)	Pakistan v Bangladesh at Multan	2001-02
†Mohammad Ashraful (114)	Bangladesh v Sri Lanka at Colombo (SSC)	2001-02
V. Sehwag (105)	India v South Africa at Bloemfontein.	2001-02
L. Vincent (104)	New Zealand v Australia at Perth.	2001-02
S. B. Styris (107)	New Zealand v West Indies at St George's	2002
J. A. Rudolph (222*)	South Africa v Bangladesh at Chittagong	2003
‡Yasir Hameed (170, 105).	Pakistan v Bangladesh at Karachi	2003
†D. R. Smith (105*).	West Indies v South Africa at Cape Town	2003-04
A. J. Strauss (112)	England v New Zealand at Lord's	2004
M. J. Clarke (151)	Australia v India at Bangalore	2004-05
†A. N. Cook (104*)	England v India at Nagpur	2005-06
M. J. Prior (126*)	England v West Indies at Lord's	2007
M. J. North (117)	Australia v South Africa at Johannesburg	2008-09
†Fawad Alam (168)	Pakistan v Sri Lanka at Colombo (PSS)	2009
†I. J. L. Trott (119)	England v Australia at The Oval	2009
Umar Akmal (129)	Pakistan v New Zealand at Dunedin	2009-10
†A. B. Barath (104)	West Indies v Australia at Brisbane	2009-10
A. N. Petersen (100)	South Africa v India at Kolkata	2009-10
S. K. Raina (120).	India v Sri Lanka at Colombo (SSC)	2010
K. S. Williamson (131)	New Zealand v India at Ahmedabad	2010-11
†K. A. Edwards (110)	West Indies v India at Roseau	2011
S. E. Marsh (141).	Australia v Sri Lanka at Pallekele	2011-12
Abul Hasan (113).	Bangladesh v West Indies at Khulna	2012-13
†F. du Plessis (110*)	South Africa v Australia at Adelaide	2012-13
H. D. Rutherford (171)	New Zealand v India at Dunedin.	2012-13
S. Dhawan (187)	India v Australia at Mohali.	2012-13
R. G. Sharma (177)	India v West Indies at Kolkata	2013-14
†J. D. S. Neesham (137*)	New Zealand v India at Wellington	2013-14
S. van Zyl (101*).	South Africa v West Indies at Centurion	2014-15
A. C. Voges (130*)	Australia v West Indies at Roseau	2015
S. C. Cook (115)	South Africa v England at Centurion	2015-16
K. K. Jennings (112)	England v India at Mumbai	2016-17
T. A. Blundell (107*)	New Zealand v West Indies at Wellington	2017-18
K. J. O'Brien (118)	Ireland v Pakistan at Malahide	2018
P. P. Shaw (134)	India v West Indies at Rajkot	2018-19
B. T. Foakes (107)	England v Sri Lanka at Galle	2018-19
Abid Ali (109*)	Pakistan v Sri Lanka at Rawalpindi	2019-20
†K. R. Mayers (210*).	**West Indies v Bangladesh at Chittagong**	**2020-21**
†P. Nissanka (103)	**Sri Lanka v West Indies at North Sound**	**2020-21**
D. P. Conway (200)	**New Zealand v England at Lord's**	**2021**
S. S. Iyer (105)	**India v New Zealand at Kanpur**	**2021-22**

† *In his second innings of the match.*

‡ *L. G. Rowe and Yasir Hameed are the only batters to score a hundred in each innings on debut.*

§ *R. E. Foster (287, 19) and L. G. Rowe (214, 100*) are the only batters to score 300 on debut.*

¶ *M. Azharuddin is the only batter to score hundreds in each of his first three Tests.*

L. Amarnath and S. Amarnath were father and son.
Ali Naqvi and Azhar Mahmood achieved the feat in the same innings.
Only Bannerman, Houghton, Aminul Islam and O'Brien scored hundreds in their country's first Test.

TWO SEPARATE HUNDREDS IN A TEST

Triple-Hundred and Hundred in a Test

G. A. Gooch (England)	333 and 123 v India at Lord's	1990
K. C. Sangakkara (Sri Lanka)	319 and 105 v Bangladesh at Chittagong	2013-14

The only instances in first-class cricket. M. A. Taylor (Australia) scored 334 and 92 v Pakistan at Peshawar in 1998-99.*

Double-Hundred and Hundred in a Test

K. D. Walters (Australia)........	242 and 103 v West Indies at Sydney............	1968-69
S. M. Gavaskar (India)........	124 and 220 v West Indies at Port-of-Spain.......	1970-71
†L. G. Rowe (West Indies)........	214 and 100* v New Zealand at Kingston........	1971-72
G. S. Chappell (Australia)........	247* and 133 v New Zealand at Wellington.......	1973-74
B. C. Lara (West Indies)..........	221 and 130 v Sri Lanka at Colombo (SSC)......	2001-02

† *On Test debut.*

Two Hundreds in a Test

There have been **87** instances of a batter scoring two separate hundreds in a Test, including the seven listed above. The most recent was by **U. T. Khawaja for Australia v England at Sydney in 2021-22.**

S. M. Gavaskar (India), R. T. Ponting (Australia) and D. A. Warner (Australia) all achieved the feat three times. C. L. Walcott scored twin hundreds twice in one series, for West Indies v Australia in 1954-55. L. G. Rowe and Yasir Hameed both did it on Test debut.

MOST DOUBLE-HUNDREDS

D. G. Bradman (A)	12	M. S. Atapattu (SL).....	6	A. N. Cook (E)	5
K. C. Sangakkara (SL) ..	11	Javed Miandad (P).....	6	R. Dravid (I)	5
B. C. Lara (WI)	9	R. T. Ponting (A).......	6	**J. E. Root (E)**	**5**
W. R. Hammond (E)....	7	V. Sehwag (I)	6	G. C. Smith (SA).......	5
D. P. M. D. Jayawardene (SL)	7	S. R. Tendulkar (I).....	6		
V. Kohli (I)	**7**	Younis Khan (P)	6		

M. J. Clarke (Australia) scored four double-hundreds in the calendar year 2012.

MOST HUNDREDS

S. R. Tendulkar (I)......	51	A. R. Border (A)	27	M. Azharuddin (I)	22
J. H. Kallis (SA)	45	**V. Kohli (I)**............	**27**	I. R. Bell (E)	22
R. T. Ponting (A).......	41	G. C. Smith (SA).......	27	G. Boycott (E)..........	22
K. C. Sangakkara (SL) ..	38	**S. P. D. Smith (A)**......	**27**	M. C. Cowdrey (E)	22
R. Dravid (I)	36	G. S. Sobers (WI)	26	A. B. de Villiers (SA) ...	22
S. M. Gavaskar (I)......	34	Inzamam-ul-Haq (P) ...	25	W. R. Hammond (E)....	22
D. P. M. D. Jayawardene (SL)	34	G. S. Chappell (A)	24	D. C. Boon (A)	21
B. C. Lara (WI)	34	Mohammad Yousuf (P)..	24	R. N. Harvey (A).......	21
Younis Khan (P)	34	I. V. A. Richards (WI)...	24	G. Kirsten (SA)	21
A. N. Cook (E)	33	**D. A. Warner (A)**......	**24**	A. J. Strauss (E)	21
S. R. Waugh (A)	32	**K. S. Williamson (NZ)**..	**24**	K. F. Barrington (E)	20
S. Chanderpaul (WI) ...	30	Javed Miandad (P)......	23	P. A. de Silva (SL)......	20
M. L. Hayden (A)	30	J. L. Langer (A)........	23	G. A. Gooch (E)	20
D. G. Bradman (A)	29	K. P. Pietersen (E)......	23	M. E. Waugh (A).......	20
H. M. Amla (SA).......	28	**J. E. Root (E)**	**23**		
M. J. Clarke (A)........	28	V. Sehwag (I)	23		

*The most hundreds for Zimbabwe is **9** by A. Flower, the most for Bangladesh is **9** by **Mominul Haque** and **Tamim Iqbal**, the most for Ireland is 1 by K. J. O'Brien, and the most for Afghanistan is 1 by **Asghar Afghan, Hashmatullah Shahidi** and **Rahmat Shah**.*

MOST HUNDREDS AGAINST ONE TEAM

D. G. Bradman...	19	Australia v England	S. R. Tendulkar... 11	India v Australia
S. M. Gavaskar ..	13	India v West Indies	K. C. Sangakkara 10	Sri Lanka v Pakistan
J. B. Hobbs	12	England v Australia	G. S. Sobers..... 10	West Indies v England
S. P. D. Smith ...	**11**	**Australia v England**	S. R. Waugh..... 10	Australia v England

MOST DUCKS

	0s	Inns		0s	Inns
C. A. Walsh (WI)	43	185	H. M. R. K. B. Herath (SL)	23	144
S. C. J. Broad (E)	**39**	**224**	**S. T. Gabriel (WI)**	**22**	**84**
C. S. Martin (NZ)	36	104	M. Morkel (SA)	22	104
G. D. McGrath (A)	35	138	M. S. Atapattu (SL)	22	156
I. Sharma (I)	**34**	**142**	S. R. Waugh (A)	22	260
S. K. Warne (A)	34	199	S. J. Harmison (E/World)	21	86
M. Muralitharan (SL/World)	33	164	M. Ntini (SA)	21	116
J. M. Anderson (E)	**30**	**239**	Waqar Younis (P)	21	120
Zaheer Khan (I)	29	127	M. S. Panesar (E)	20	68
M. Dillon (WI)	26	68	B. S. Bedi (I)	20	101
C. E. L. Ambrose (WI)	26	145	D. L. Vettori (NZ/World)	20	174
Danish Kaneria (P)	25	84	M. A. Atherton (E)	20	212
D. K. Morrison (NZ)	24	71			
B. S. Chandrasekhar (I)	23	80			

CARRYING BAT THROUGH TEST INNINGS

(Figures in brackets show team's total)

A. B. Tancred	26*	(47)	South Africa v England at Cape Town	1888-89
J. E. Barrett	67*	(176)†	Australia v England at Lord's	1890
R. Abel	132*	(307)	England v Australia at Sydney	1891-92
P. F. Warner	132*	(237)†	England v South Africa at Johannesburg	1898-99
W. W. Armstrong	159*	(309)	Australia v South Africa at Johannesburg	1902-03
J. W. Zulch	43*	(103)	South Africa v England at Cape Town	1909-10
W. Bardsley	193*	(383)	Australia v England at Lord's	1926
W. M. Woodfull	30*	(66)§	Australia v England at Brisbane	1928-29
W. M. Woodfull	73*	(193)‡	Australia v England at Adelaide	1932-33
W. A. Brown	206*	(422)	Australia v England at Lord's	1938
L. Hutton	202*	(344)	England v West Indies at The Oval	1950
L. Hutton	156*	(272)	England v Australia at Adelaide	1950-51
Nazar Mohammad¶	124*	(331)	Pakistan v India at Lucknow	1952-53
F. M. M. Worrell	191*	(372)	West Indies v England at Nottingham	1957
T. L. Goddard	56*	(99)	South Africa v Australia at Cape Town	1957-58
D. J. McGlew	127*	(292)	South Africa v New Zealand at Durban	1961-62
C. C. Hunte	60*	(131)	West Indies v Australia at Port-of-Spain	1964-65
G. M. Turner	43*	(131)	New Zealand v England at Lord's	1969
W. M. Lawry	49*	(107)	Australia v India at Delhi	1969-70
W. M. Lawry	60*	(116)‡	Australia v England at Sydney	1970-71
G. M. Turner	223*	(386)	New Zealand v West Indies at Kingston	1971-72
I. R. Redpath	159*	(346)	Australia v New Zealand at Auckland	1973-74
G. Boycott	99*	(215)	England v Australia at Perth	1979-80
S. M. Gavaskar	127*	(286)	India v Pakistan at Faisalabad	1982-83
Mudassar Nazar¶	152*	(323)	Pakistan v India at Lahore	1982-83
S. Wettimuny	63*	(144)	Sri Lanka v New Zealand at Christchurch	1982-83
D. C. Boon	58*	(103)	Australia v New Zealand at Auckland	1985-86
D. L. Haynes	88*	(211)	West Indies v Pakistan at Karachi	1986-87
G. A. Gooch	154*	(252)	England v West Indies at Leeds	1991
D. L. Haynes	75*	(176)	West Indies v England at The Oval	1991
A. J. Stewart	69*	(175)	England v Pakistan at Lord's	1992
D. L. Haynes	143*	(382)	West Indies v Pakistan at Port-of-Spain	1992-93
M. H. Dekker	68*	(187)	Zimbabwe v Pakistan at Rawalpindi	1993-94
M. A. Atherton	94*	(228)	England v New Zealand at Christchurch	1996-97
G. Kirsten	100*	(239)	South Africa v Pakistan at Faisalabad	1997-98
M. A. Taylor	169*	(350)	Australia v South Africa at Adelaide	1997-98
G. W. Flower	156*	(321)	Zimbabwe v Pakistan at Bulawayo	1997-98
Saeed Anwar	188*	(316)	Pakistan v India at Calcutta	1998-99
M. S. Atapattu	216*	(428)	Sri Lanka v Zimbabwe at Bulawayo	1999-2000

R. P. Arnold	104*	(231)	Sri Lanka v Zimbabwe at Harare	1999-2000
Javed Omar	85*	(168)†‡	Bangladesh v Zimbabwe at Bulawayo	2000-01
V. Sehwag	201*	(329)	India v Sri Lanka at Galle	2008
S. M. Katich	131*	(268)	Australia v New Zealand at Brisbane	2008-09
C. H. Gayle	165*	(317)	West Indies v Australia at Adelaide	2009-10
Imran Farhat	117*	(223)	Pakistan v New Zealand at Napier	2009-10
R. Dravid	146*	(300)	India v England at The Oval	2011
T. M. K. Mawoyo	163*	(412)	Zimbabwe v Pakistan at Bulawayo	2011-12
D. A. Warner	123*	(233)	Australia v New Zealand at Hobart	2011-12
C. A. Pujara	145*	(312)	India v Sri Lanka at Colombo (SSC)	2015-16
D. Elgar	118*	(214)	South Africa v England at Durban	2015-16
K. C. Brathwaite	142*	(337)	West Indies v Pakistan at Sharjah	2016-17
A. N. Cook	244*	(491)	England v Australia at Melbourne	2017-18
D. Elgar	86*	(177)	South Africa v India at Johannesburg	2017-18
D. Elgar	141*	(311)	South Africa v Australia at Cape Town	2017-18
F. D. M. Karunaratne	158*	(287)	Sri Lanka v South Africa at Galle	2018
T. W. M. Latham	264*	(578)	New Zealand v Sri Lanka at Wellington	2018-19

† *On debut.*   ‡ *One man absent.*   § *Two men absent.*   ¶ *Father and son.*

T. W. M. Latham (264*) holds the record for the highest score by a player carrying his bat in a Test.
D. L. Haynes and D. Elgar have achieved the feat on three occasions; Haynes also opened the batting and was last man out in each innings for West Indies v New Zealand at Dunedin, 1979-80.
G. M. Turner was the youngest at 22 years 63 days old when he first did it in 1969.

MOST RUNS IN A SERIES

	T	I	NO	R	HS	100	Avge		
D. G. Bradman	5	7	0	974	334	4	139.14	A v E	1930
W. R. Hammond	5	9	1	905	251	4	113.12	E v A	1928-29
M. A. Taylor	6	11	1	839	219	2	83.90	A v E	1989
R. N. Harvey	5	9	0	834	205	4	92.66	A v SA	1952-53
I. V. A. Richards	4	7	0	829	291	3	118.42	WI v E	1976
C. L. Walcott	5	10	0	827	155	5	82.70	WI v A	1954-55
G. S. Sobers	5	8	2	824	365*	3	137.33	WI v P	1957-58
D. G. Bradman	5	9	0	810	270	3	90.00	A v E	1936-37
D. G. Bradman	5	5	1	806	299*	4	201.50	A v SA	1931-32

MOST RUNS IN A CALENDAR YEAR

	T	I	NO	R	HS	100	Avge	Year
Mohammad Yousuf (P)	11	19	1	1,788	202	9	99.33	2006
I. V. A. Richards (WI)	11	19	0	1,710	291	7	90.00	1976
J. E. Root (E)	**15**	**29**	**1**	**1,708**	**228**	**6**	**61.00**	**2021**
G. C. Smith (SA)	15	25	2	1,656	232	6	72.00	2008
M. J. Clarke (A)	11	18	3	1,595	329*	5	106.33	2012
S. R. Tendulkar (I)	14	23	3	1,562	214	7	78.10	2010
S. M. Gavaskar (I)	18	27	1	1,555	221	5	59.80	1979
R. T. Ponting (A)	15	28	5	1,544	207	6	67.13	2005
R. T. Ponting (A)	11	18	3	1,503	257	6	100.20	2003

M. Amarnath reached 1,000 runs in 1983 on May 3, in his ninth Test of the year.
The only case of 1,000 in a year before World War II was C. Hill of Australia: 1,060 in 1902.
M. L. Hayden (Australia) scored 1,000 runs in each year from 2001 to 2005.

MOST RUNS

		T	I	NO	R	HS	100	Avge
1	S. R. Tendulkar (India)	200	329	33	15,921	248*	51	53.78
2	R. T. Ponting (Australia)	168	287	29	13,378	257	41	51.85
3	J. H. Kallis (South Africa/World)	166	280	40	13,289	224	45	55.37
4	R. Dravid (India/World)	164	286	32	13,288	270	36	52.31
5	A. N. Cook (England)	161	291	16	12,472	294	33	45.35

		T	I	NO	R	HS	100	Avge
6	K. C. Sangakkara (Sri Lanka)	134	233	17	12,400	319	38	57.40
7	B. C. Lara (West Indies/World) ..	131	232	6	11,953	400*	34	52.88
8	S. Chanderpaul (West Indies)	164	280	49	11,867	203*	30	51.37
9	D. P. M. D. Jayawardene (SL) ...	149	252	15	11,814	374	34	49.84
10	A. R. Border (Australia)	156	265	44	11,174	205	27	50.56
11	S. R. Waugh (Australia)	168	260	46	10,927	200	32	51.06
12	S. M. Gavaskar (India)	125	214	16	10,122	236*	34	51.12
13	Younis Khan (Pakistan)	118	213	19	10,099	313	34	52.05
14	**J. E. Root (England)**	**114**	**210**	**15**	**9,600**	**254**	**23**	**49.23**
15	H. M. Amla (South Africa)	124	215	16	9,282	311*	28	46.64
16	G. C. Smith (South Africa/Wld) ..	117	205	13	9,265	277	27	48.25
17	G. A. Gooch (England)	118	215	6	8,900	333	20	42.58
18	Javed Miandad (Pakistan)	124	189	21	8,832	280*	23	52.57
19	Inzamam-ul-Haq (Pakistan/World)	120	200	22	8,830	329	25	49.60
20	V. V. S. Laxman (India)	134	225	34	8,781	281	17	45.97
21	A. B. de Villiers (South Africa)..	114	191	18	8,765	278*	22	50.66
22	M. J. Clarke (Australia)	115	198	22	8,643	329*	28	49.10
23	M. L. Hayden (Australia)	103	184	14	8,625	380	30	50.73
24	V. Sehwag (India/World)	104	180	6	8,586	319	23	49.34
25	I. V. A. Richards (West Indies)...	121	182	12	8,540	291	24	50.23
26	A. J. Stewart (England)	133	235	21	8,463	190	15	39.54
27	D. I. Gower (England)...........	117	204	18	8,231	215	18	44.25
28	K. P. Pietersen (England)	104	181	8	8,181	227	23	47.28
29	G. Boycott (England)	108	193	23	8,114	246*	22	47.72
30	G. S. Sobers (West Indies)	93	160	21	8,032	365*	26	57.78
31	M. E. Waugh (Australia)	128	209	17	8,029	153*	20	41.81
32	**V. Kohli (India)**	**99**	**168**	**10**	**7,962**	**254***	**27**	**50.39**
33	**S. P. D. Smith (Australia)**	**82**	**147**	**17**	**7,784**	**239**	**27**	**59.87**
34	M. A. Atherton (England)	115	212	7	7,728	185*	16	37.69
35	I. R. Bell (England)............	118	205	24	7,727	235	22	42.69
36	J. L. Langer (Australia)	105	182	12	7,696	250	23	45.27
37	**L. R. P. L. Taylor (New Zealand)**	**112**	**196**	**24**	**7,683**	**290**	**19**	**44.66**
38	M. C. Cowdrey (England).......	114	188	15	7,624	182	22	44.06
39	**D. A. Warner (Australia)**	**91**	**167**	**7**	**7,584**	**335***	**24**	**47.40**
40	C. G. Greenidge (West Indies) ...	108	185	16	7,558	226	19	44.72
41	Mohammad Yousuf (Pakistan) ...	90	156	12	7,530	223	24	52.29
42	M. A. Taylor (Australia)	104	186	13	7,525	334*	19	43.49
43	C. H. Lloyd (West Indies).......	110	175	14	7,515	242*	19	46.67

MOST RUNS FOR EACH COUNTRY

ENGLAND

A. N. Cook 12,472	G. A. Gooch 8,900	D. I. Gower 8,231
J. E. Root 9,600	A. J. Stewart 8,463	K. P. Pietersen....... 8,181

AUSTRALIA

R. T. Ponting........13,378	S. R. Waugh 10,927	M. L. Hayden 8,625
A. R. Border 11,174	M. J. Clarke.......... 8,643	M. E. Waugh........ 8,029

SOUTH AFRICA

J. H. Kallis†.........13,206	G. C. Smith† 9,253	G. Kirsten 7,289
H. M. Amla 9,282	A. B. de Villiers...... 8,765	H. H. Gibbs 6,167

† *J. H. Kallis also scored 44 and 39* and G. C. Smith 12 and 0 for the World XI v Australia (2005-06 Super Series Test).*

WEST INDIES

B. C. Lara† 11,912	I. V. A. Richards 8,540	C. G. Greenidge...... 7,558
S. Chanderpaul 11,867	G. S. Sobers.......... 8,032	C. H. Lloyd 7,515

†   *B. C. Lara also scored 5 and 36 for the World XI v Australia (2005-06 Super Series Test).*

NEW ZEALAND

L. R. P. L. Taylor.... 7,683	S. P. Fleming........ 7,172	M. D. Crowe 5,444
K. S. Williamson 7,272	B. B. McCullum 6,453	J. G. Wright......... 5,334

INDIA

S. R. Tendulkar 15,921	S. M. Gavaskar 10,122	V. Sehwag† 8,503
R. Dravid† 13,265	V. V. S. Laxman 8,781	**V. Kohli 7,962**

†   *R. Dravid also scored 0 and 23 and V. Sehwag 76 and 7 for the World XI v Australia (2005-06 Super Series Test).*

PAKISTAN

Younis Khan 10,099	Inzamam-ul-Haq† 8,829	**Azhar Ali 6,721**
Javed Miandad....... 8,832	Mohammad Yousuf... 7,530	Salim Malik......... 5,768

†   *Inzamam-ul-Haq also scored 1 and 0 for the World XI v Australia (2005-06 Super Series Test).*

SRI LANKA

K. C. Sangakkara.....12,400	S. T. Jayasuriya 6,973	**A. D. Mathews 6,338**
D. P. M. D. Jayawardene .11,814	P. A. de Silva........ 6,361	M. S. Atapattu 5,502

ZIMBABWE

A. Flower........... 4,794	A. D. R. Campbell.... 2,858	H. Masakadza 2,223
G. W. Flower........ 3,457	**B. R. M. Taylor 2,320**	G. J. Whittall 2,207

BANGLADESH

Mushfiqur Rahim ... 4,873	**Shakib Al Hasan 4,029**	Habibul Bashar 3,026
Tamim Iqbal 4,788	**Mominul Haque..... 3,501**	**Mahmudullah....... 2,914**

IRELAND

No player has scored 1,000 Test runs for Ireland. The highest total is 258, by K. J. O'Brien.

AFGHANISTAN

No player has scored 1,000 Test runs for Afghanistan. The highest total is **440**, by **Asghar Afghan**.

HIGHEST CAREER AVERAGE

(Qualification: 20 innings)

Avge		T	I	NO	R	HS	100
99.94	D. G. Bradman (A)	52	80	10	6,996	334	29
61.87	A. C. Voges (A)	20	31	7	1,485	269*	5
60.97	R. G. Pollock (SA)	23	41	4	2,256	274	7
60.83	G. A. Headley (WI)	22	40	4	2,190	270*	10
60.73	H. Sutcliffe (E)	54	84	9	4,555	194	16
59.87	**S. P. D. Smith (A)**	**82**	**147**	**17**	**7,784**	**239**	**27**
59.23	E. Paynter (E)	20	31	5	1,540	243	4
58.67	K. F. Barrington (E)	82	131	15	6,806	256	20
58.61	E. D. Weekes (WI)	48	81	5	4,455	207	15
58.45	W. R. Hammond (E).	85	140	16	7,249	336*	22
57.78	G. S. Sobers (WI)	93	160	21	8,032	365*	26
57.40	K. C. Sangakkara (SL)	134	233	17	12,400	319	38
56.94	J. B. Hobbs (E)	61	102	7	5,410	211	15
56.92	**M. Labuschagne (A)**	**23**	**40**	**1**	**2,220**	**215**	**6**
56.68	C. L. Walcott (WI)	44	74	7	3,798	220	15
56.67	L. Hutton (E).	79	138	15	6,971	364	19
55.37	J. H. Kallis (SA/World)	166	280	40	13,289	224	45
55.00	E. Tyldesley (E)	14	20	2	990	122	3

S. G. Barnes (A) scored 1,072 runs at 63.05 from 19 innings.

BEST CAREER STRIKE-RATES

(Runs per 100 balls. Qualification: 1,000 runs)

SR		T	I	NO	R	100	Avge
86.97	Shahid Afridi (P)	27	48	1	1,716	5	36.51
83.63	**T. G. Southee (NZ)**	**83**	**117**	**11**	**1,743**	**0**	**16.44**
82.22	V. Sehwag (I).	104	180	6	8,586	23	49.34
81.98	A. C. Gilchrist (A).	96	137	20	5,570	17	47.60
80.73	**C. de Grandhomme (NZ)**	**26**	**39**	**5**	**1,207**	**1**	**35.50**
76.49	G. P. Swann (E).	60	76	14	1,370	0	22.09
72.25	**M. D. K. J. Perera (SL)**	**22**	**41**	**3**	**1,177**	**2**	**30.97**
71.56	**D. A. Warner (A)**	**91**	**167**	**7**	**7,584**	**24**	**47.40**
70.98	Sarfraz Ahmed (P).	49	86	13	2,657	3	36.39
70.93	**Q. de Kock (SA)**	**54**	**91**	**6**	**3,300**	**6**	**38.82**
70.28	M. Muralitharan (SL)	133	164	56	1,261	0	11.67
67.88	D. J. G. Sammy (WI)	38	63	2	1,323	1	21.68
67.48	**R. R. Pant (I)**	**28**	**48**	**4**	**1,735**	**4**	**39.43**
67.39	**M. A. Starc (A)**	**66**	**98**	**22**	**1,751**	**0**	**23.03**
66.94	S. Dhawan (I).	34	58	1	2,315	7	40.61
66.36	**D. P. D. N. Dickwella (SL)**	**45**	**80**	**5**	**2,443**	**0**	**32.57**

Comprehensive data on balls faced has been available only in recent decades, and its introduction varied from country to country. Among earlier players for whom partial data is available, Kapil Dev (India) had a strike-rate of 80.91 and I. V. A. Richards (West Indies) 70.19 in those innings which were fully recorded.

HIGHEST PERCENTAGE OF TEAM'S RUNS OVER TEST CAREER

(Qualification: 20 Tests)

	Tests	Runs	Team Runs	% of Team Runs
D. G. Bradman (Australia)	52	6,996	28,810	24.28
G. A. Headley (West Indies)	22	2,190	10,239	21.38
B. C. Lara (West Indies)	131	11,953	63,328	18.87
M. Labuschagne (Australia)	**23**	**2,220**	**11,886**	**18.67**

	Tests	Runs	Team Runs	% of Team Runs
L. Hutton (England)	79	6,971	38,440	18.13
J. B. Hobbs (England)	61	5,410	30,211	17.90
A. D. Nourse (South Africa)	34	2,960	16,659	17.76
E. D. Weekes (West Indies)	48	4,455	25,667	17.35
B. Mitchell (South Africa)	42	3,471	20,175	17.20
H. Sutcliffe (England)	54	4,555	26,604	17.12
K. C. Sangakkara (Sri Lanka)	134	12,400	72,779	17.03
S. P. D. Smith (Australia)	**82**	**7,784**	**45,844**	**16.97**
B. Sutcliffe (New Zealand)	42	2,727	16,158	16.87

The percentage shows the proportion of a team's runs scored by that player in all Tests in which he played, including team runs in innings in which he did not bat.

FASTEST FIFTIES

Minutes

24	Misbah-ul-Haq	Pakistan v Australia at Abu Dhabi	2014-15
27	Mohammad Ashraful	Bangladesh v India at Mirpur	2007
28	J. T. Brown	England v Australia at Melbourne	1894-95
29	S. A. Durani	India v England at Kanpur	1963-64
30	E. A. V. Williams	West Indies v England at Bridgetown	1947-48
30	B. R. Taylor	New Zealand v West Indies at Auckland	1968-69

The fastest fifties in terms of balls received (where recorded) are:

Balls

21	Misbah-ul-Haq	Pakistan v Australia at Abu Dhabi	2014-15
23	D. A. Warner.	Australia v Pakistan at Sydney	2016-17
24	J. H. Kallis	South Africa v Zimbabwe at Cape Town	2004-05
25	S. Shillingford	West Indies v New Zealand at Kingston	2014
26	Shahid Afridi.	Pakistan v India at Bangalore	2004-05
26	Mohammad Ashraful	Bangladesh v India at Mirpur	2007
26	D. W. Steyn.	South Africa v West Indies at Port Elizabeth .	2014-15

FASTEST HUNDREDS

Minutes

70	J. M. Gregory	Australia v South Africa at Johannesburg. . . .	1921-22
74	Misbah-ul-Haq	Pakistan v Australia at Abu Dhabi	2014-15
75	G. L. Jessop.	England v Australia at The Oval.	1902
78	R. Benaud	Australia v West Indies at Kingston	1954-55
80	J. H. Sinclair	South Africa v Australia at Cape Town	1902-03
81	I. V. A. Richards	West Indies v England at St John's.	1985-86
86	B. R. Taylor	New Zealand v West Indies at Auckland	1968-69

The fastest hundreds in terms of balls received (where recorded) are:

Balls

54	B. B. McCullum	New Zealand v Australia at Christchurch	2015-16
56	I. V. A. Richards	West Indies v England at St John's.	1985-86
56	Misbah-ul-Haq	Pakistan v Australia at Abu Dhabi	2014-15
57	A. C. Gilchrist.	Australia v England at Perth	2006-07
67	J. M. Gregory	Australia v South Africa at Johannesburg. . . .	1921-22
69	S. Chanderpaul	West Indies v Australia at Georgetown	2002-03
69	D. A. Warner.	Australia v India at Perth	2011-12
70	C. H. Gayle.	West Indies v Australia at Perth	2009-10

FASTEST DOUBLE-HUNDREDS

Minutes

214	D. G. Bradman	Australia v England at Leeds	1930
217	N. J. Astle	New Zealand v England at Christchurch.	2001-02
223	S. J. McCabe	Australia v England at Nottingham.	1938
226	V. T. Trumper	Australia v South Africa at Adelaide.	1910-11
234	D. G. Bradman	Australia v England at Lord's	1930
240	W. R. Hammond	England v New Zealand at Auckland	1932-33

The fastest double-hundreds in terms of balls received (where recorded) are:

Balls

153	N. J. Astle	New Zealand v England at Christchurch.	2001-02
163	B. A. Stokes	England v South Africa at Cape Town	2015-16
168	V. Sehwag.	India v Sri Lanka at Mumbai (BS)	2009-10
182	V. Sehwag.	India v Pakistan at Lahore.	2005-06
186	B. B. McCullum	New Zealand v Pakistan at Sharjah.	2014-15
194	V. Sehwag.	India v South Africa at Chennai	2007-08

FASTEST TRIPLE-HUNDREDS

Minutes

288	W. R. Hammond	England v New Zealand at Auckland	1932-33
336	D. G. Bradman	Australia v England at Leeds	1930

The fastest triple-hundred in terms of balls received (where recorded) is:

Balls

278	V. Sehwag.	India v South Africa at Chennai	2007-08

MOST RUNS SCORED OFF AN OVER

28	B. C. Lara (466444).	off R. J. Peterson	WI v SA at Johannesburg .	2003-04
28	G. J. Bailey (462466).	off J. M. Anderson	A v E at Perth	2013-14
28	K. A. Maharaj (444660).	off J. E. Root	SA v E at Port Elizabeth . .	2019-20
	The sixth ball produced four byes.			
27	Shahid Afridi (666621)	off Harbhajan Singh	P v I at Lahore.	2005-06
26	C. D. McMillan (444464) . . .	off Younis Khan	NZ v P at Hamilton.	2000-01
26	B. C. Lara (406664).	off Danish Kaneria	WI v P at Multan.	2006-07
26	M. G. Johnson (446066)	off P. L. Harris	A v SA at Johannesburg . .	2009-10
26	B. B. McCullum (466046). . .	off R. A. S. Lakmal	NZ v SL at Christchurch . .	2014-15
26	H. H. Pandya (446660)	off P. M. Pushpakumara	I v SL at Pallekele.	2017

MOST RUNS IN A DAY

309	D. G. Bradman.	Australia v England at Leeds	1930
295	W. R. Hammond	England v New Zealand at Auckland	1932-33
284	V. Sehwag	India v Sri Lanka at Mumbai	2009-10
273	D. C. S. Compton	England v Pakistan at Nottingham	1954
271	D. G. Bradman.	Australia v England at Leeds	1934

MOST SIXES IN A CAREER

B. B. McCullum (NZ)	107	M. L. Hayden (A)	82
A. C. Gilchrist (A)	100	Misbah-ul-Haq (P)	81
C. H. Gayle (WI)	98	K. P. Pietersen (E)	81
J. H. Kallis (SA/World)	97	M. S. Dhoni (I)	78
V. Sehwag (I/World)	91	**T. G. Southee (NZ)**	**75**
B. C. Lara (WI)	88	R. T. Ponting (A)	73
C. L. Cairns (NZ)	87	C. H. Lloyd (WI)	70
I. V. A. Richards (WI)	84	Younis Khan (P)	70
B. A. Stokes (E)	**83**		
A. Flintoff (E/World)	82		

SLOWEST INDIVIDUAL BATTING

0	in 101 minutes	G. I. Allott, New Zealand v South Africa at Auckland	1998-99
4*	in 110 minutes	Abdul Razzaq, Pakistan v Australia at Melbourne	2004-05
6	in 137 minutes	S. C. J. Broad, England v New Zealand at Auckland	2012-13
9*	in 184 minutes	Arshad Khan, Pakistan v Sri Lanka at Colombo (SSC)	2000
18	in 194 minutes	W. R. Playle, New Zealand v England at Leeds	1958
19*	in 217 minutes	M. D. Crowe, New Zealand v Sri Lanka at Colombo (SSC)	1983-84
25	in 289 minutes	H. M. Amla, South Africa v India at Delhi	2015-16
35	in 332 minutes	C. J. Tavaré, England v India at Madras	1981-82
43	in 354 minutes	A. B. de Villiers, South Africa v India at Delhi	2015-16
60	in 390 minutes	D. N. Sardesai, India v West Indies at Bridgetown	1961-62
62	in 408 minutes	Ramiz Raja, Pakistan v West Indies at Karachi	1986-87
68	in 458 minutes	T. E. Bailey, England v Australia at Brisbane	1958-59
86	in 474 minutes	Shoaib Mohammad, Pakistan v West Indies at Karachi	1990-91
99	in 505 minutes	M. L. Jaisimha, India v Pakistan at Kanpur	1960-61
104	in 529 minutes	S. V. Manjrekar, India v Zimbabwe at Harare	1992-93
105	in 575 minutes	D. J. McGlew, South Africa v Australia at Durban	1957-58
114	in 591 minutes	Mudassar Nazar, Pakistan v England at Lahore	1977-78
120*	in 609 minutes	J. J. Crowe, New Zealand v Sri Lanka at Colombo (CCC)	1986-87
136*	in 675 minutes	S. Chanderpaul, West Indies v India at St John's	2001-02
163	in 720 minutes	Shoaib Mohammad, Pakistan v New Zealand at Wellington	1988-89
201*	in 777 minutes	D. S. B. P. Kuruppu, Sri Lanka v NZ at Colombo (CCC)	1986-87
275	in 878 minutes	G. Kirsten, South Africa v England at Durban	1999-2000
337	in 970 minutes	Hanif Mohammad, Pakistan v West Indies at Bridgetown	1957-58

SLOWEST HUNDREDS

557 minutes	Mudassar Nazar, Pakistan v England at Lahore	1977-78
545 minutes	D. J. McGlew, South Africa v Australia at Durban	1957-58
535 minutes	A. P. Gurusinha, Sri Lanka v Zimbabwe at Harare	1994-95
516 minutes	J. J. Crowe, New Zealand v Sri Lanka at Colombo (CCC)	1986-87
500 minutes	S. V. Manjrekar, India v Zimbabwe at Harare	1992-93
488 minutes	P. E. Richardson, England v South Africa at Johannesburg	1956-57

The slowest hundred for any Test in England is 465 minutes (312 balls) by D. P. Sibley, England v West Indies at Manchester, 2020.

    The slowest double-hundred in a Test was scored in 777 minutes (548 balls) by D. S. B. P. Kuruppu for Sri Lanka v New Zealand at Colombo (CCC), 1986-87, on his debut.

PARTNERSHIPS OVER 400

624	for 3rd	K. C. Sangakkara (287)/ D. P. M. D. Jayawardene (374)	SL v SA	Colombo (SSC)	2006
576	for 2nd	S. T. Jayasuriya (340)/R. S. Mahanama (225)	SL v I	Colombo (RPS)	1997-98
467	for 3rd	A. H. Jones (186)/M. D. Crowe (299)	NZ v SL	Wellington	1990-91
451	for 2nd	W. H. Ponsford (266)/D. G. Bradman (244) . .	A v E	The Oval	1934
451	for 3rd	Mudassar Nazar (231)/Javed Miandad (280*)	P v I	Hyderabad	1982-83
449	for 4th	A. C. Voges (269*)/S. E. Marsh (182).	A v WI	Hobart	2015-16
446	for 2nd	C. C. Hunte (260)/G. S. Sobers (365*)	WI v P	Kingston	1957-58
438	for 2nd	M. S. Atapattu (249)/K. C. Sangakkara (270)	SL v Z	Bulawayo	2003-04
437	for 4th	D. P. M. D. Jayawardene (240)/ T. T. Samaraweera (231)	SL v P	Karachi	2008-09
429*	for 3rd	J. A. Rudolph (222*)/H. H. Dippenaar (177*)	SA v B	Chittagong	2003
415	for 1st	N. D. McKenzie (226)/G. C. Smith (232) . . .	SA v B	Chittagong	2007-08
413	for 1st	M. H. Mankad (231)/Pankaj Roy (173)	I v NZ	Madras	1955-56
411	for 4th	P. B. H. May (285*)/M. C. Cowdrey (154). .	E v WI	Birmingham	1957
410	for 1st	V. Sehwag (254)/R. Dravid (128*)	I v P	Lahore	2005-06
405	for 5th	S. G. Barnes (234)/D. G. Bradman (234). . . .	A v E	Sydney	1946-47

415 runs were added for the third wicket for India v England at Madras in 1981-82 by D. B. Vengsarkar (retired hurt), G. R. Viswanath and Yashpal Sharma. 408 runs were added for the first wicket for India v Bangladesh at Mirpur in 2007 by K. D. Karthik (retired hurt), Wasim Jaffer (retired hurt), R. Dravid and S. R. Tendulkar.

HIGHEST PARTNERSHIPS FOR EACH WICKET

First Wicket

415	N. D. McKenzie (226)/G. C. Smith (232).	SA v B	Chittagong	2007-08
413	M. H. Mankad (231)/Pankaj Roy (173)	I v NZ	Madras	1955-56
410	V. Sehwag (254)/R. Dravid (128*).	I v P	Lahore	2005-06
387	G. M. Turner (259)/T. W. Jarvis (182)	NZ v WI	Georgetown	1971-72
382	W. M. Lawry (210)/R. B. Simpson (201)	A v WI	Bridgetown	1964-65

Second Wicket

576	S. T. Jayasuriya (340)/R. S. Mahanama (225)	SL v I	Colombo (RPS)	1997-98
451	W. H. Ponsford (266)/D. G. Bradman (244).	A v E	The Oval	1934
446	C. C. Hunte (260)/G. S. Sobers (365*)	WI v P	Kingston	1957-58
438	M. S. Atapattu (249)/K. C. Sangakkara (270).	SL v Z	Bulawayo	2003-04
382	L. Hutton (364)/M. Leyland (187)	E v A	The Oval	1938

Third Wicket

624	K. C. Sangakkara (287)/D. P. M. D. Jayawardene (374). .	SL v SA	Colombo (SSC)	2006
467	A. H. Jones (186)/M. D. Crowe (299).	NZ v SL	Wellington	1990-91
451	Mudassar Nazar (231)/Javed Miandad (280*)	P v I	Hyderabad	1982-83
429*	J. A. Rudolph (222*)/H. H. Dippenaar (177*)	SA v B	Chittagong	2003
397	Qasim Omar (206)/Javed Miandad (203*)	P v SL	Faisalabad	1985-86

Fourth Wicket

449	A. C. Voges (269*)/S. E. Marsh (182)	A v WI	Hobart	2015-16
437	D. P. M. D. Jayawardene(240)/T. T. Samaraweera (231) .	SL v P	Karachi	2008-09
411	P. B. H. May (285*)/M. C. Cowdrey (154)	E v WI	Birmingham	1957
399	G. S. Sobers (226)/F. M. M. Worrell (197*).	WI v E	Bridgetown	1959-60
388	W. H. Ponsford (181)/D. G. Bradman (304).	A v E	Leeds	1934

Fifth Wicket

405	S. G. Barnes (234)/D. G. Bradman (234)	A v E	Sydney	1946-47
385	S. R. Waugh (160)/G. S. Blewett (214)	A v SA	Johannesburg	1996-97
376	V. V. S. Laxman (281)/R. Dravid (180)	I v A	Kolkata	2000-01
359	Shakib Al Hasan (217)/Mushfiqur Rahim (159)	B v NZ	Wellington	2016-17
359	Z. Crawley (267)/J. C. Buttler (152)	E v P	Southampton	2020

Sixth Wicket

399	B. A. Stokes (258)/J. M. Bairstow (150*)	E v SA	Cape Town	2015-16
365*	K. S. Williamson (242*)/B-J. Watling (142*)	NZ v SL	Wellington	2014-15
352	B. B. McCullum (302)/B-J. Watling (124)	NZ v I	Wellington	2013-14
351	D. P. M. D. Jayawardene (275)/			
	H. A. P. W. Jayawardene (154*)	SL v I	Ahmedabad	2009-10
346	J. H. Fingleton (136)/D. G. Bradman (270)	A v E	Melbourne	1936-37

Seventh Wicket

347	D. St E. Atkinson (219)/C. C. Depeiza (122)	WI v A	Bridgetown	1954-55
308	Waqar Hassan (189)/Imtiaz Ahmed (209)	P v NZ	Lahore	1955-56
295*	S. O. Dowrich (116*)/J. O. Holder (202*)	WI v E	Bridgetown	2018-19
280	R. G. Sharma (177)/R. Ashwin (124)	I v WI	Kolkata	2013-14
261	B-J. Watling (205)/M. J. Santner (126)	NZ v E	Mt Maunganui	2019-20

Eighth Wicket

332	I. J. L. Trott (184)/S. C. J. Broad (169)	E v P	Lord's	2010
313	Wasim Akram (257*)/Saqlain Mushtaq (79)	P v Z	Sheikhupura	1996-97
256	S. P. Fleming (262)/J. E. C. Franklin (122*)	NZ v SA	Cape Town	2005-06
253	N. J. Astle (156*)/A. C. Parore (110)	NZ v A	Perth	2001-02
246	L. E. G. Ames (137)/G. O. B. Allen (122)	E v NZ	Lord's	1931

Ninth Wicket

195	M. V. Boucher (78)/P. L. Symcox (108)	SA v P	Johannesburg	1997-98
191	**Mahmudullah (150*)/Taskin Ahmed (75)**	**B v Z**	**Harare**	**2021**
190	Asif Iqbal (146)/Intikhab Alam (51)	P v E	The Oval	1967
184	Mahmudullah (76)/Abul Hasan (113)	B v WI	Khulna	2012-13
180	J-P. Duminy (166)/D. W. Steyn (76)	SA v A	Melbourne	2008-09

Tenth Wicket

198	J. E. Root (154*)/J. M. Anderson (81)	E v I	Nottingham	2014
163	P. J. Hughes (81*)/A. C. Agar (98)	A v E	Nottingham	2013
151	B. F. Hastings (110)/R. O. Collinge (68*)	NZ v P	Auckland	1972-73
151	Azhar Mahmood (128*)/Mushtaq Ahmed (59)	P v SA	Rawalpindi	1997-98
143	D. Ramdin (107*)/T. L. Best (95)	WI v E	Birmingham	2012

HIGHEST PARTNERSHIPS FOR EACH COUNTRY

ENGLAND

359	for 1st	L. Hutton (158)/C. Washbrook (195)	v SA	Johannesburg	1948-49
382	for 2nd	L. Hutton (364)/M. Leyland (187)	v A	The Oval	1938
370	for 3rd	W. J. Edrich (189)/D. C. S. Compton (208)	v SA	Lord's	1947
411	for 4th	P. B. H. May (285*)/M. C. Cowdrey (154)	v WI	Birmingham	1957
359	for 5th	Z. Crawley (267)/J. C. Buttler (152)	v P	Southampton	2020
399	for 6th	B. A. Stokes (258)/J. M. Bairstow (150*)	v SA	Cape Town	2015-16
197	for 7th	M. J. K. Smith (96)/J. M. Parks (101*)	v WI	Port-of-Spain	1959-60
332	for 8th	I. J. L. Trott (184)/S. C. J. Broad (169)	v P	Lord's	2010
163*	for 9th	M. C. Cowdrey (128*)/A. C. Smith (69*)	v NZ	Wellington	1962-63
198	for 10th	J. E. Root (154*)/J. M. Anderson (81)	v I	Nottingham	2014

AUSTRALIA

382	for 1st	W. M. Lawry (210)/R. B. Simpson (201)	v WI	Bridgetown	1964-65
451	for 2nd	W. H. Ponsford (266)/D. G. Bradman (244)	v E	The Oval	1934
315	for 3rd	R. T. Ponting (206)/D. S. Lehmann (160)	v WI	Port-of-Spain	2002-03
449	for 4th	A. C. Voges (269*)/S. E. Marsh (182)	v WI	Hobart	2015-16
405	for 5th	S. G. Barnes (234)/D. G. Bradman (234)	v E	Sydney	1946-47
346	for 6th	J. H. Fingleton (136)/D. G. Bradman (270)	v E	Melbourne	1936-37
217	for 7th	K. D. Walters (250)/G. J. Gilmour (101)	v NZ	Christchurch	1976-77
243	for 8th	R. J. Hartigan (116)/C. Hill (160)	v E	Adelaide	1907-08
154	for 9th	S. E. Gregory (201)/J. M. Blackham (74)	v E	Sydney	1894-95
163	for 10th	P. J. Hughes (81*)/A. C. Agar (98)	v E	Nottingham	2013

SOUTH AFRICA

415	for 1st	N. D. McKenzie (226)/G. C. Smith (232)	v B	Chittagong	2007-08
315*	for 2nd	H. H. Gibbs (211*)/J. H. Kallis (148*)	v NZ	Christchurch	1998-99
429*	for 3rd	J. A. Rudolph (222*)/H. H. Dippenaar (177*)	v B	Chittagong	2003
308	for 4th	H. M. Amla (208)/A. B. de Villiers (152)	v WI	Centurion	2014-15
338	for 5th	G. C. Smith (234)/A. B. de Villiers (164)	v P	Dubai	2013-14
271	for 6th	A. G. Prince (162*)/M. V. Boucher (117)	v B	Centurion	2008-09
246	for 7th	D. J. McGlew (255*)/A. R. A. Murray (109)	v NZ	Wellington	1952-53
150	for 8th	{ N. D. McKenzie (103)/S. M. Pollock (111) G. Kirsten (130)/M. Zondeki (59) }	v SL v E	Centurion Leeds	2000-01 2003
195	for 9th	M. V. Boucher (78)/P. L. Symcox (108)	v P	Johannesburg	1997-98
107*	for 10th	A. B. de Villiers (278*)/M. Morkel (35*)	v P	Abu Dhabi	2010-11

WEST INDIES

298	for 1st	C. G. Greenidge (149)/D. L. Haynes (167)	v E	St John's	1989-90
446	for 2nd	C. C. Hunte (260)/G. S. Sobers (365*)	v P	Kingston	1957-58
338	for 3rd	E. D. Weekes (206)/F. M. M. Worrell (167)	v E	Port-of-Spain	1953-54
399	for 4th	G. S. Sobers (226)/F. M. M. Worrell (197*)	v E	Bridgetown	1959-60
322	for 5th†	B. C. Lara (213)/J. C. Adams (94)	v A	Kingston	1998-99
282*	for 6th	B. C. Lara (400*)/R. D. Jacobs (107*)	v E	St John's	2003-04
347	for 7th	D. St E. Atkinson (219)/C. C. Depeiza (122)	v A	Bridgetown	1954-55
212	for 8th	S. O. Dowrich (103)/J. O. Holder (110)	v Z	Bulawayo	2017-18
161	for 9th	C. H. Lloyd (161*)/A. M. E. Roberts (68)	v I	Calcutta	1983-84
143	for 10th	D. Ramdin (107*)/T. L. Best (95)	v E	Birmingham	2012

† *344 runs were added between the fall of the 4th and 5th wickets: P. T. Collins retired hurt when he and Lara had added 22 runs.*

NEW ZEALAND

387	for 1st	G. M. Turner (259)/T. W. Jarvis (182)	v WI	Georgetown	1971-72
297	for 2nd	B. B. McCullum (202)/K. S. Williamson (192)	v P	Sharjah	2014-15
467	for 3rd	A. H. Jones (186)/M. D. Crowe (299)	v SL	Wellington	1990-91
369	**for 4th**	**K. S. Williamson (238)/H. M. Nicholls (157)**	**v P**	**Christchurch**	**2020-21**
222	for 5th	N. J. Astle (141)/C. D. McMillan (142)	v Z	Wellington	2000-01
365*	for 6th	K. S. Williamson (242*)/B-J. Watling (142*) . .	v SL	Wellington	2014-15
261	for 7th	B-J. Watling (205)/M. J. Santner (126)	v E	Mt Maunganui	2019-20
256	for 8th	S. P. Fleming (262)/J. E. C. Franklin (122*) . .	v SA	Cape Town	2005-06
136	for 9th	I. D. S. Smith (173)/M. C. Snedden (22)	v I	Auckland	1989-90
151	for 10th	B. F. Hastings (110)/R. O. Collinge (68*)	v P	Auckland	1972-73

INDIA

413	for 1st	M. H. Mankad (231)/Pankaj Roy (173)	v NZ	Madras	1955-56
370	for 2nd	M. Vijay (167)/C. A. Pujara (204)	v A	Hyderabad	2012-13
336	for 3rd†	V. Sehwag (309)/S. R. Tendulkar (194*)	v P	Multan	2003-04
365	for 4th	V. Kohli (211)/A. M. Rahane (188)	v NZ	Indore	2016-17
376	for 5th	V. V. S. Laxman (281)/R. Dravid (180)	v A	Kolkata	2000-01
298*	for 6th	D. B. Vengsarkar (164*)/R. J. Shastri (121*) . .	v A	Bombay	1986-87
280	for 7th	R. G. Sharma (177)/R. Ashwin (124)	v WI	Kolkata	2013-14
241	for 8th	V. Kohli (235)/J. Yadav (104)	v E	Mumbai	2016-17
149	for 9th	P. G. Joshi (52*)/R. B. Desai (85)	v P	Bombay	1960-61
133	for 10th	S. R. Tendulkar (248*)/Zaheer Khan (75)	v P	Dhaka	2004-05

† *415 runs were scored for India's 3rd wicket v England at Madras in 1981-82, in two partnerships:
D. B. Vengsarkar and G. R. Viswanath put on 99 before Vengsarkar retired hurt, then Viswanath
and Yashpal Sharma added a further 316.*

PAKISTAN

298	for 1st	Aamir Sohail (160)/Ijaz Ahmed snr (151)	v WI	Karachi	1997-98
291	for 2nd	Zaheer Abbas (274)/Mushtaq Mohammad (100)	v E	Birmingham	1971
451	for 3rd	Mudassar Nazar (231)/Javed Miandad (280*) . .	v I	Hyderabad	1982-83
350	for 4th	Mushtaq Mohammad (201)/Asif Iqbal (175) . .	v NZ	Dunedin	1972-73
281	for 5th	Javed Miandad (163)/Asif Iqbal (166)	v NZ	Lahore	1976-77
269	for 6th	Mohammad Yousuf (223)/Kamran Akmal (154)	v E	Lahore	2005-06
308	for 7th	Waqar Hassan (189)/Imtiaz Ahmed (209)	v NZ	Lahore	1955-56
313	for 8th	Wasim Akram (257*)/Saqlain Mushtaq (79) . .	v Z	Sheikhupura	1996-97
190	for 9th	Asif Iqbal (146)/Intikhab Alam (51).	v E	The Oval	1967
151	for 10th	Azhar Mahmood (128*)/Mushtaq Ahmed (59) . .	v SA	Rawalpindi	1997-98

SRI LANKA

335	for 1st	M. S. Atapattu (207*)/S. T. Jayasuriya (188) . .	v P	Kandy	2000
576	for 2nd	S. T. Jayasuriya (340)/R. S. Mahanama (225) .	v I	Colombo (RPS)	1997-98
624	for 3rd	K. C. Sangakkara (287)/ D. P. M. D. Jayawardene (374).	v SA	Colombo (SSC)	2006
437	for 4th	D. P. M. D. Jayawardene (240)/ T. T. Samaraweera (231)	v P	Karachi	2008-09
280	for 5th	T. T. Samaraweera (138)/T. M. Dilshan (168) .	v B	Colombo (PSS)	2005-06
351	for 6th	D. P. M. D. Jayawardene (275)/ H. A. P. W. Jayawardene (154*)	v I	Ahmedabad	2009-10
223*	for 7th	H. A. P. W. Jayawardene (120*)/ W. P. U. J. C. Vaas (100*)	v B	Colombo (SSC)	2007
170	for 8th	D. P. M. D. Jayawardene (237)/ W. P. U. J. C. Vaas (69)	v SA	Galle	2004
124	**for 9th**	**D. M. de Silva (155*)/L. Embuldeniya (39)** . .	**v WI**	**Galle**	**2021-22**
79	for 10th	W. P. U. J. C. Vaas (68*)/M. Muralitharan (43)	v A	Kandy	2003-04

ZIMBABWE

164	for 1st	D. D. Ebrahim (71)/A. D. R. Campbell (103) .	v WI	Bulawayo	2001
160	for 2nd	Sikandar Raza (82)/H. Masakadza (81)	v B	Chittagong	2014-15
194	for 3rd	A. D. R. Campbell (99)/D. L. Houghton (142).	v SL	Harare	1994-95
269	for 4th	G. W. Flower (201*)/A. Flower (156)	v P	Harare	1994-95
277*	for 5th	M. W. Goodwin (166*)/A. Flower (100*)	v P	Bulawayo	1997-98
165	for 6th	D. L. Houghton (121)/A. Flower (59).	v I	Harare	1992-93
154	for 7th	H. H. Streak (83*)/A. M. Blignaut (92)	v WI	Harare	2001
187	**for 8th**	**S. C. Williams (151*)/D. T. Tiripano (95)**. . .	**v Afg**	**Abu Dhabi**	**2020-21**
87	for 9th	P. A. Strang (106*)/B. C. Strang (42).	v P	Sheikhupura	1996-97
97*	for 10th	A. Flower (183*)/H. K. Olonga (11*)	v I	Delhi	2000-01

BANGLADESH

312	for 1st	Tamim Iqbal (206)/Imrul Kayes (150)	v P	Khulna	2014-15
232	for 2nd	Shamsur Rahman (106)/Imrul Kayes (115) . . .	v SL	Chittagong	2013-14
242	**for 3rd**	**Nazmul Hossain (163)/Mominul Haque (127)**	**v SL**	**Pallekele**	**2020-21**
266	for 4th	Mominul Haque (161)/Mushfiqur Rahim (219*)	v Z	Mirpur	2018-19
359	for 5th	Shakib Al Hasan (217)/Mushfiqur Rahim (159)	v NZ	Wellington	2016-17
191	for 6th	Mohammad Ashraful (129*)/			
		Mushfiqur Rahim (80).	v SL	Colombo (PSS)	2007
145	for 7th	Shakib Al Hasan (87)/Mahmudullah (115). . . .	v NZ	Hamilton	2009-10
144*	for 8th	Mushfiqur Rahim (219*)/Mehedi Hasan (68*) .	v Z	Mirpur	2018-19
191	**for 9th**	**Mahmudullah (150*)/Taskin Ahmed (75)**. . .	**v Z**	**Harare**	**2021**
69	for 10th	Mohammad Rafique (65)/Shahadat Hossain (3*)	v A	Chittagong	2005-06

IRELAND

69	for 1st	E. C. Joyce (43)/W. T. S. Porterfield (32).	v P	Malahide	2018
33	for 2nd	P. R. Stirling (14)/A. Balbirnie (82)	v Afg	Dehradun	2018-19
104	for 3rd	A. Balbirnie (82)/J. A. McCollum (39).	v Afg	Dehradun	2018-19
14	for 4th	J. A. McCollum (4)/K. J. O'Brien (12).	v Afg	Dehradun	2018-19
32	for 5th	P. R. Stirling (11)/K. J. O'Brien (118)	v P	Malahide	2018
30	for 6th	K. J. O'Brien (118)/G. C. Wilson (12)	v P	Malahide	2018
114	for 7th	K. J. O'Brien (118)/S. R. Thompson (53).	v P	Malahide	2018
50	for 8th	K. J. O'Brien (118)/T. E. Kane (14)	v P	Malahide	2018
34	for 9th	G. C. Wilson (33*)/W. B. Rankin (17).	v P	Malahide	2018
87	for 10th	G. H. Dockrell (39)/T. J. Murtagh (54*).	v Afg	Dehradun	2018-19

AFGHANISTAN

53	for 1st	Ibrahim Zadran (23)/Javed Ahmadi (62)	v WI	Lucknow	2019-20
139	for 2nd	Ihsanullah Janat (65*)/Rahmat Shah (76).	v Ire	Dehradun	2018-19
130	for 3rd	Rahmat Shah (98)/Hashmatullah Shahidi (61) .	v Ire	Dehradun	2018-19
307	**for 4th**	**Hashmatullah Shahidi (200*)/Asghar**			
		Afghan (164)	**v Z**	**Abu Dhabi**	**2020-21**
117*	**for 5th**	**Hashmatullah Shahidi (200*)/Nasir**			
		Ahmadzai (55*)	**v Z**	**Abu Dhabi**	**2020-21**
81	for 6th	Asghar Afghan (92)/Afsar Zazai (41).	v B	Chittagong	2019-20
34	**for 7th**	**Ibrahim Zadran (76)/Abdul Wasi (9)**.	**v Z**	**Abu Dhabi**	**2020-21**
54	for 8th	Afsar Zazai (32)/Hamza Hotak (34)	v WI	Lucknow	2019-20
31	for 9th	Asghar Afghan (67)/Wafadar Momand (6). . . .	v Ire	Dehradun	2018-19
21	for 10th	Mujeeb Zadran (15)/Wafadar Momand (6*). . .	v I	Bangalore	2018

UNUSUAL DISMISSALS

Handled the Ball

W. R. Endean	South Africa v England at Cape Town..............................	1956-57
A. M. J. Hilditch	Australia v Pakistan at Perth...................................	1978-79
Mohsin Khan	Pakistan v Australia at Karachi.................................	1982-83
D. L. Haynes	West Indies v India at Bombay..................................	1983-84
G. A. Gooch	England v Australia at Manchester...............................	1993
S. R. Waugh	Australia v India at Chennai...................................	2000-01
M. P. Vaughan	England v India at Bangalore...................................	2001-02

Obstructing the Field

L. Hutton	England v South Africa at The Oval.............................	1951

There have been no cases of Hit the Ball Twice or Timed Out in Test cricket.

BOWLING RECORDS

MOST WICKETS IN AN INNINGS

10-53	J. C. Laker............	England v Australia at Manchester.............	1956
10-74	A. Kumble............	India v Pakistan at Delhi.....................	1998-99
10-119	**A. Y. Patel**	**New Zealand v India at Mumbai.............**	**2021-22**
9-28	G. A. Lohmann........	England v South Africa at Johannesburg.........	1895-96
9-37	J. C. Laker...........	England v Australia at Manchester.............	1956
9-51	M. Muralitharan.......	Sri Lanka v Zimbabwe at Kandy	2001-02
9-52	R. J. Hadlee.........	New Zealand v Australia at Brisbane	1985-86
9-56	Abdul Qadir..........	Pakistan v England at Lahore.................	1987-88
9-57	D. E. Malcolm........	England v South Africa at The Oval.	1994
9-65	M. Muralitharan.......	Sri Lanka v England at The Oval	1998
9-69	J. M. Patel	India v Australia at Kanpur...................	1959-60
9-83	Kapil Dev	India v West Indies at Ahmedabad.............	1983-84
9-86	Sarfraz Nawaz	Pakistan v Australia at Melbourne	1978-79
9-95	J. M. Noreiga.........	West Indies v India at Port-of-Spain...........	1970-71
9-102	S. P. Gupte...........	India v West Indies at Kanpur	1958-59
9-103	S. F. Barnes..........	England v South Africa at Johannesburg	1913-14
9-113	H. J. Tayfield........	South Africa v England at Johannesburg	1956-57
9-121	A. A. Mailey	Australia v England at Melbourne	1920-21
9-127	H. M. R. K. B. Herath ...	Sri Lanka v Pakistan at Colombo (SSC)..........	2014
9-129	K. A. Maharaj	South Africa v Sri Lanka at Colombo (SSC)	2018

*There have been **80** instances of eight wickets in a Test innings.*

The best bowling figures for the countries not mentioned above are:

8-39	Taijul Islam	Bangladesh v Zimbabwe at Mirpur	2014-15
8-109	P. A. Strang	Zimbabwe v New Zealand at Bulawayo.........	2000-01
7-137	**Rashid Khan**	**Afghanistan v Zimbabwe at Abu Dhabi.......**	**2020-21**
5-13	T. J. Murtagh..........	Ireland v England at Lord's	2019

OUTSTANDING BOWLING ANALYSES

	O	M	R	W		
J. C. Laker (E)	51.2	23	53	10	v Australia at Manchester.........	1956
A. Kumble (I)	26.3	9	74	10	v Pakistan at Delhi...............	1998-99
A. Y. Patel (NZ)	**47.5**	**12**	**119**	**10**	**v India at Mumbai**	**2021-22**
G. A. Lohmann (E)	14.2	6	28	9	v South Africa at Johannesburg ...	1895-96
J. C. Laker (E)	16.4	4	37	9	v Australia at Manchester.........	1956

	O	M	R	W		
G. A. Lohmann (E)	9.4	5	7	8	v South Africa at Port Elizabeth	1895-96
J. Briggs (E)	14.2	5	11	8	v South Africa at Cape Town	1888-89
S. C. J. Broad (E)	9.3	5	15	8	v Australia at Nottingham.........	2015
S. J. Harmison (E)	12.3	8	12	7	v West Indies at Kingston	2003-04
J. Briggs (E)	19.1	11	17	7	v South Africa at Cape Town	1888-89
M. A. Noble (A)	7.4	2	17	7	v England at Melbourne	1901-02
W. Rhodes (E)	11	3	17	7	v Australia at Birmingham	1902

WICKET WITH FIRST BALL IN TEST CRICKET

	Batter dismissed			
T. P. Horan	W. W. Read	A v E	Sydney	1882-83
A. Coningham	A. C. MacLaren	A v E	Melbourne	1894-95
W. M. Bradley	F. Laver	E v A	Manchester.......	1899
E. G. Arnold	V. T. Trumper	E v A	Sydney	1903-04
A. E. E. Vogler	E. G. Hayes	SA v E	Johannesburg	1905-06
J. N. Crawford	A. E. E. Vogler	E v SA	Johannesburg	1905-06
G. G. Macaulay	G. A. L. Hearne	E v SA	Cape Town	1922-23
M. W. Tate	M. J. Susskind	E v SA	Birmingham	1924
M. Henderson	E. W. Dawson	NZ v E	Christchurch	1929-30
H. D. Smith	E. Paynter	NZ v E	Christchurch	1932-33
T. F. Johnson	W. W. Keeton	WI v E	The Oval........	1939
K. R. Miller	W. A. Hadlee	A v NZ	Wellington	1945-46
R. Howorth	D. V. Dyer	E v SA	The Oval........	1947
Intikhab Alam	C. C. McDonald	P v A......	Karachi	1959-60
R. K. Illingworth	P. V. Simmons	E v WI	Nottingham........	1991
N. M. Kulkarni	M. S. Atapattu	I v SL	Colombo (RPS)	1997-98
M. K. G. C. P. Lakshitha	Mohammad Ashraful	SL v B	Colombo (SSC)	2002
N. M. Lyon	K. C. Sangakkara	A v SL	Galle	2011-12
R. M. S. Eranga	S. R. Watson	SL v A	Colombo (SSC)	2011-12
D. L. Piedt	M. A. Vermeulen	SA v Z	Harare	2014-15
G. C. Viljoen	A. N. Cook	SA v E	Johannesburg	2015-16

HAT-TRICKS

Most Hat-Tricks

S. C. J. Broad	**2**	H. Trumble............	2
T. J. Matthews†	2	Wasim Akram‡	2

† *T. J. Matthews did the hat-trick in each innings of the same match.*
‡ *Wasim Akram did the hat-trick in successive matches.*

Hat-Tricks

There have been **46** hat-tricks in Tests, including the above. Occurrences since 2007:

S. C. J. Broad...........	England v India at Nottingham	2011
Sohag Gazi†	Bangladesh v New Zealand at Chittagong..................	2013-14
S. C. J. Broad...........	England v Sri Lanka at Leeds	2014
H. M. R. K. B. Herath	Sri Lanka v Australia at Galle	2016
M. M. Ali...........	England v South Africa at The Oval.....................	2017
J. J. Bumrah...........	India v West Indies at North Sound.....................	2019
Naseem Shah...........	Pakistan v Bangladesh at Rawalpindi	2019-20
K. A. Maharaj	**South Africa v West Indies at Gros Islet**	**2021**

† *Sohag Gazi also scored 101 not out.*

M. J. C. Allom, P. J. Petherick and D. W. Fleming did the hat-trick on Test debut. D. N. T. Zoysa took one in the second over of a Test (his first three balls); I. K. Pathan in the first over of a Test. Naseem Shah was the youngest to take a Test hat-trick, aged 16 years 359 days.

FOUR WICKETS IN FIVE BALLS

M. J. C. Allom....... England v New Zealand at Christchurch.................... 1929-30
              On debut, in his eighth over: W-WWW
C. M. Old.......... England v Pakistan at Birmingham......................... 1978
              Sequence interrupted by a no-ball: WW-WW
Wasim Akram....... Pakistan v West Indies at Lahore (*WW-WW*) 1990-91

MOST WICKETS IN A TEST

19-90	J. C. Laker............	England v Australia at Manchester............	1956
17-159	S. F. Barnes............	England v South Africa at Johannesburg	1913-14
16-136†	N. D. Hirwani..........	India v West Indies at Madras................	1987-88
16-137†	R. A. L. Massie	Australia v England at Lord's	1972
16-220	M. Muralitharan........	Sri Lanka v England at The Oval	1998

† *On Test debut.*

There have been 18 further instances of 14 or more wickets in a Test match.

The best bowling figures for the countries not mentioned above are:

15-123	R. J. Hadlee	New Zealand v Australia at Brisbane	1985-86
14-116	Imran Khan	Pakistan v Sri Lanka at Lahore...............	1981-82
14-149	M. A. Holding	West Indies v England at The Oval	1976
13-132	M. Ntini	South Africa v West Indies at Port-of-Spain..	2004-05
12-117	Mehedi Hasan...........	Bangladesh v West Indies at Mirpur...........	2018-19
11-104	Rashid Khan............	Afghanistan v Bangladesh at Chittagong	2019-20
11-255	A. G. Huckle	Zimbabwe v New Zealand at Bulawayo........	1997-98
6-65	T. J. Murtagh	Ireland v England at Lord's	2019

MOST BALLS BOWLED IN A TEST

S. Ramadhin (West Indies) sent down 774 balls in 129 overs against England at Birmingham, 1957, the most delivered by any bowler in a Test, beating H. Verity's 766 for England against South Africa at Durban, 1938-39. In this match Ramadhin also bowled the most balls (588) in any first-class innings, since equalled by Arshad Ayub, Hyderabad v Madhya Pradesh at Secunderabad, 1991-92.

MOST WICKETS IN A SERIES

	T	R	W	Avge		
S. F. Barnes	4	536	49	10.93	England v South Africa......	1913-14
J. C. Laker............	5	442	46	9.60	England v Australia.........	1956
C. V. Grimmett	5	642	44	14.59	Australia v South Africa	1935-36
T. M. Alderman........	6	893	42	21.26	Australia v England.........	1981
R. M. Hogg	6	527	41	12.85	Australia v England.........	1978-79
T. M. Alderman........	6	712	41	17.36	Australia v England.........	1989
Imran Khan	6	558	40	13.95	Pakistan v India............	1982-83
S. K. Warne	5	797	40	19.92	Australia v England.........	2005

The most for South Africa is 37 by H. J. Tayfield against England in 1956-57, for West Indies 35 by M. D. Marshall against England in 1988, for India 35 by B. S. Chandrasekhar against England in 1972-73 (all in five Tests), for New Zealand 33 by R. J. Hadlee against Australia in 1985-86, for Sri Lanka 30 by M. Muralitharan against Zimbabwe in 2001-02, for Zimbabwe 22 by H. H. Streak against Pakistan in 1994-95 (all in three Tests), and for Bangladesh 19 by Mehedi Hasan against England in 2016-17 (two Tests).

MOST WICKETS IN A CALENDAR YEAR

	T	R	W	5I	10M	Avge	Year
S. K. Warne (Australia)	15	2,114	96	6	2	22.02	2005
M. Muralitharan (Sri Lanka)	11	1,521	90	9	5	16.89	2006
D. K. Lillee (Australia).	13	1,781	85	5	2	20.95	1981
A. A. Donald (South Africa)	14	1,571	80	7	–	19.63	1998
M. Muralitharan (Sri Lanka)	12	1,699	80	7	4	21.23	2001
J. Garner (West Indies).	15	1,604	77	4	–	20.83	1984
Kapil Dev (India)	18	1,739	75	5	1	23.18	1983
M. Muralitharan (Sri Lanka)	10	1,463	75	7	3	19.50	2000

MOST WICKETS

		T	Balls	R	W	5I	10M	Avge	SR
1	M. Muralitharan (SL/World).	133	44,039	18,180	800	67	22	22.72	55.04
2	S. K. Warne (Australia). . . .	145	40,704	17,995	708	37	10	25.41	57.49
3	J. M. Anderson (England) .	169	36,396	17,014	640	31	3	26.58	56.86
4	A. Kumble (India).	132	40,850	18,355	619	35	8	29.65	65.99
5	G. D. McGrath (Australia). .	124	29,248	12,186	563	29	3	21.64	51.95
6	S. C. J. Broad (England). . .	152	30,575	14,932	537	19	3	27.80	56.93
7	C. A. Walsh (West Indies) . .	132	30,019	12,688	519	22	3	24.44	57.84
8	D. W. Steyn (South Africa). .	93	18,608	10,077	439	26	5	22.95	42.38
9	Kapil Dev (India)	131	27,740	12,867	434	23	2	29.64	63.91
10	H. M. R. K. B. Herath (SL). .	93	25,993	12,157	433	34	9	28.07	60.03
11	R. J. Hadlee (New Zealand) .	86	21,918	9,611	431	36	9	22.29	50.85
12	R. Ashwin (India).	84	22,673	10,485	430	30	7	24.38	52.72
13	S. M. Pollock (South Africa)	108	24,353	9,733	421	16	1	23.11	57.84
14	Harbhajan Singh (India)	103	28,580	13,537	417	25	5	32.46	68.53
15	N. M. Lyon (Australia). . . .	105	26,669	13,193	415	18	3	31.79	64.26
16	Wasim Akram (Pakistan) . . .	104	22,627	9,779	414	25	5	23.62	54.65
17	C. E. L. Ambrose (WI)	98	22,103	8,501	405	22	3	20.99	54.57
18	M. Ntini (South Africa)	101	20,834	11,242	390	18	4	28.82	53.42
19	I. T. Botham (England).	102	21,815	10,878	383	27	4	28.40	56.95
20	D. L. Marshall (West Indies)	81	17,584	7,876	376	22	4	20.94	46.76
21	Waqar Younis (Pakistan) . . .	87	16,224	8,788	373	22	5	23.56	43.49
22	Imran Khan (Pakistan)	88	19,458	8,258	362	23	6	22.81	53.75
22	D. L. Vettori (NZ/World). . .	113	28,814	12,441	362	20	3	34.36	79.59
24	D. K. Lillee (Australia)	70	18,467	8,493	355	23	7	23.92	52.01
24	W. P. U. J. C. Vaas (SL) . . .	111	23,438	10,501	355	12	2	29.58	66.02
26	A. A. Donald (South Africa) .	72	15,519	7,344	330	20	3	22.25	47.02
27	T. G. Southee (New Zealand)	83	18,826	9,297	329	13	1	28.25	57.22
28	R. G. D. Willis (England) . . .	90	17,357	8,190	325	16	–	25.20	53.40
29	M. G. Johnson (Australia). . .	73	16,001	8,891	313	12	3	28.40	51.12
30	I. Sharma (India).	105	19,160	10,078	311	11	1	32.40	61.60
30	Zaheer Khan (India)	92	18,785	10,247	311	11	1	32.94	60.40
32	B. Lee (Australia)	76	16,531	9,554	310	10	–	30.81	53.32
33	M. Morkel (South Africa) . . .	86	16,498	8,550	309	8	0	27.66	53.39
33	L. R. Gibbs (West Indies) . . .	79	27,115	8,989	309	18	2	29.09	87.75
35	F. S. Trueman (England). . . .	67	15,178	6,625	307	17	3	21.57	49.43
36	T. A. Boult (New Zealand) . .	75	16,689	8,254	301	9	1	27.42	55.44

MOST WICKETS FOR EACH COUNTRY

ENGLAND

J. M. Anderson 640	I. T. Botham 383	F. S. Trueman 307
S. C. J. Broad 537	R. G. D. Willis 325	D. L. Underwood 297

AUSTRALIA

S. K. Warne 708	**N. M. Lyon** **415**	M. G. Johnson 313
G. D. McGrath 563	D. K. Lillee 355	B. Lee 310

SOUTH AFRICA

D. W. Steyn 439	M. Ntini 390	M. Morkel 309
S. M. Pollock 421	A. A. Donald 330	J. H. Kallis† 291

† J. H. Kallis also took 0-35 and 1-3 for the World XI v Australia (2005-06 Super Series Test).

WEST INDIES

C. A. Walsh 519	M. D. Marshall 376	J. Garner 259
C. E. L. Ambrose 405	L. R. Gibbs 309	M. A. Holding 249

NEW ZEALAND

R. J. Hadlee 431	**T. G. Southee** **329**	**N. Wagner** **235**
D. L. Vettori† 361	**T. A. Boult** **301**	C. S. Martin 233

† D. L. Vettori also took 1-73 and 0-38 for the World XI v Australia (2005-06 Super Series Test).

INDIA

A. Kumble 619	**R. Ashwin** **430**	**I. Sharma** **311**
Kapil Dev 434	Harbhajan Singh 417	Zaheer Khan 311

PAKISTAN

Wasim Akram 414	Imran Khan 362	Abdul Qadir 236
Waqar Younis 373	Danish Kaneria 261	**Yasir Shah** **235**

SRI LANKA

M. Muralitharan† 795	W. P. U. J. C. Vaas 355	**M. D. K. Perera** **161**
H. M. R. K. B. Herath . .433	**R. A. S. Lakmal** **168**	S. L. Malinga 101

† M. Muralitharan also took 2-102 and 3-55 for the World XI v Australia (2005-06 Super Series Test).

ZIMBABWE

H. H. Streak 216	P. A. Strang 70	A. G. Cremer 57
R. W. Price 80	H. K. Olonga 68	B. C. Strang 56

BANGLADESH

Shakib Al Hasan **215**	**Mehedi Hasan** **119**	Mashrafe bin Mortaza . . . 78
Taijul Islam **144**	Mohammad Rafique 100	Shahadat Hossain 72

IRELAND

T. J. Murtagh 13	S. R. Thompson 10

AFGHANISTAN

Rashid Khan 34	**Hamza Hotak** 16	**Yamin Ahmadzai** 11

BEST CAREER AVERAGES

(Qualification: 75 wickets)

Avge		T	W	Avge		T	W
10.75	G. A. Lohmann (E)	18	112	18.63	C. Blythe (E)	19	100
16.43	S. F. Barnes (E)	27	189	20.39	J. H. Wardle (E)	28	102
16.53	C. T. B. Turner (A)	17	101	20.53	A. K. Davidson (A)	44	186
16.98	R. Peel (E)	20	101	20.94	M. D. Marshall (WI)	81	376
17.75	J. Briggs (E)	33	118	20.97	J. Garner (WI)	58	259
18.41	F. R. Spofforth (A)	18	94	20.99	C. E. L. Ambrose (WI)	98	405
18.56	F. H. Tyson (E)	17	76				

BEST CAREER STRIKE-RATES

(Balls per wicket. Qualification: 75 wickets)

SR		T	W	SR		T	W
34.19	G. A. Lohmann (E)	18	112	45.91	**P. J. Cummins (A)**	38	185
38.75	S. E. Bond (NZ)	18	87	46.76	M. D. Marshall (WI)	81	376
40.77	**K. Rabada (SA)**	**50**	**233**	47.02	A. A. Donald (SA)	72	330
41.65	S. F. Barnes (E)	27	189	**47.75**	**Shaheen Shah Afridi (P)**	**21**	**86**
42.38	D. W. Steyn (SA)	93	439	48.78	Mohammad Asif (P)	23	106
43.49	Waqar Younis (P)	87	373	48.92	J. L. Pattinson (A)	21	81
44.52	F. R. Spofforth (A)	18	94	**49.22**	**M. A. Starc (A)**	**66**	**274**
45.12	J. V. Saunders (A)	14	79	49.32	C. E. H. Croft (WI)	27	125
45.18	J. Briggs (E)	33	118	49.43	F. S. Trueman (E)	67	307
45.42	F. H. Tyson (E)	17	76	**49.82**	**Mohammed Shami (I)**	**57**	**209**
45.46	C. Blythe (E)	19	100				
45.74	Shoaib Akhtar (P)	46	178				

BEST CAREER ECONOMY-RATES

(Runs per six balls. Qualification: 75 wickets)

ER		T	W	ER		T	W
1.64	T. L. Goddard (SA)	41	123	1.94	H. J. Tayfield (SA)	37	170
1.67	R. G. Nadkarni (I)	41	88	1.95	A. L. Valentine (WI)	36	139
1.88	H. Verity (E)	40	144	1.95	F. J. Titmus (E)	53	153
1.88	G. A. Lohmann (E)	18	112	1.97	S. Ramadhin (WI)	43	158
1.89	J. H. Wardle (E)	28	102	1.97	R. Peel (E)	20	101
1.91	R. Illingworth (E)	61	122	1.97	A. K. Davidson (A)	44	186
1.93	C. T. B. Turner (A)	17	101	1.98	L. R. Gibbs (WI)	79	309
1.94	M. W. Tate (E)	39	155				
1.94	W. J. O'Reilly (A)	27	144				

HIGHEST PERCENTAGE OF TEAM'S WICKETS OVER TEST CAREER

(Qualification: 20 Tests)

	Tests	Wkts	Team Wkts	% of Team Wkts
M. Muralitharan (Sri Lanka/World)	133	800	2,070	38.64
S. F. Barnes (England)	27	189	494	38.25
R. J. Hadlee (New Zealand)	86	431	1,255	34.34
C. V. Grimmett (Australia)	37	216	636	33.96
Fazal Mahmood (Pakistan)	34	139	410	33.90
W. J. O'Reilly (Australia)	27	144	446	32.28
S. P. Gupte (India)	36	149	470	31.70

Yasir Shah (Pakistan)	**46**	**235**	**756**	**31.08**
Saeed Ajmal (Pakistan)	35	178	575	30.95
Mohammad Rafique (Bangladesh)	33	100	328	30.48
A. V. Bedser (England)	51	236	777	30.37

Excluding the Super Series Test, Muralitharan took 795 out of 2,050 wickets in his 132 Tests for Sri Lanka, a percentage of 38.78.

The percentage shows the proportion of a team's wickets taken by that player in all Tests in which he played, including team wickets in innings in which he did not bowl.

ALL-ROUND RECORDS

HUNDRED AND FIVE WICKETS IN AN INNINGS

England

A. W. Greig	148	6-164	v West Indies	Bridgetown	1973-74
I. T. Botham	103	5-73	v New Zealand....	Christchurch	1977-78
I. T. Botham	108	8-34	v Pakistan.......	Lord's	1978
I. T. Botham	114	6-58, 7-48	v India	Bombay........	1979-80
I. T. Botham	149*	6-95	v Australia	Leeds..........	1981
I. T. Botham	138	5-59	v New Zealand....	Wellington	1983-84

Australia

C. Kelleway	114	5-33	v South Africa	Manchester	1912
J. M. Gregory	100	7-69	v England........	Melbourne......	1920-21
K. R. Miller	109	6-107	v West Indies	Kingston	1954-55
R. Benaud	100	5-84	v South Africa	Johannesburg ...	1957-58

South Africa

J. H. Sinclair	106	6-26	v England.......	Cape Town	1898-99
G. A. Faulkner	123	5-120	v England.......	Johannesburg ...	1909-10
J. H. Kallis	110	5-90	v West Indies	Cape Town	1998-99
J. H. Kallis	139*	5-21	v Bangladesh	Potchefstroom...	2002-03

West Indies

D. St E. Atkinson	219	5-56	v Australia	Bridgetown	1954-55
O. G. Smith	100	5-90	v India	Delhi	1958-59
G. S. Sobers	104	5-63	v India	Kingston	1961-62
G. S. Sobers	174	5-41	v England.......	Leeds..........	1966
R. L. Chase	137*	5-121	v India	Kingston	2016

New Zealand

B. R. Taylor†	105	5-86	v India	Calcutta........	1964-65

India

M. H. Mankad	184	5-196	v England.......	Lord's	1952
P. R. Umrigar	172*	5-107	v West Indies	Port-of-Spain....	1961-62
R. Ashwin	103	5-156	v West Indies	Mumbai........	2011-12
R. Ashwin	113	7-83	v West Indies	North Sound ...	2016
R. Ashwin	**106**	**5-43**	**v England**	**Chennai**	**2020-21**

Pakistan

Mushtaq Mohammad	201	5-49	v New Zealand....	Dunedin	1972-73
Mushtaq Mohammad	121	5-28	v West Indies	Port-of-Spain....	1976-77
Imran Khan	117	6-98, 5-82	v India	Faisalabad	1982-83
Wasim Akram	123	5-100	v Australia	Adelaide	1989-90

Zimbabwe

P. A. Strang	106*	5-212	v Pakistan........	Sheikhupura	1996-97

Bangladesh

Shakib Al Hasan	144	6-82	v Pakistan	Mirpur	2011-12
Sohag Gazi	101*	6-77‡	v New Zealand	Chittagong	2013-14
Shakib Al Hasan	137	5-80, 5-44	v Zimbabwe	Khulna	2014-15

† *On debut.* ‡ *Including a hat-trick; Sohag Gazi is the only player to score a hundred and take a hat-trick in the same Test.*

HUNDRED AND FIVE DISMISSALS IN AN INNINGS

D. T. Lindsay	182	6ct	SA v A	Johannesburg	1966-67
I. D. S. Smith	113*	4ct, 1st	NZ v E	Auckland	1983-84
S. A. R. Silva	111	5ct	SL v I	Colombo (PSS)	1985-86
A. C. Gilchrist	133	4ct, 1st	A v E	Sydney	2002-03
M. J. Prior	118	5ct	E v A	Sydney	2010-11
A. B. de Villiers	103*	6ct and 5ct	SA v P	Johannesburg	2012-13
M. J. Prior	110*	5ct	E v NZ	Auckland	2012-13
B-J. Watling	124	5ct	NZ v I	Wellington	2013-14
B-J. Watling	142*	4ct, 1st	NZ v SL	Wellington	2014-15
J. M. Bairstow	140	5ct	E v SL	Leeds	2016
J. M. Bairstow	101	5ct	E v NZ	Christchurch	2017-18
B-J. Watling	105*	5ct	NZ v SL	Colombo (PSO)	2019

100 RUNS AND TEN WICKETS IN A TEST

A. K. Davidson	44 80	5-135 6-87 }	A v WI	Brisbane	1960-61
I. T. Botham	114	6-58 7-48 }	E v I	Bombay	1979-80
Imran Khan	117	6-98 5-82 }	P v I	Faisalabad	1982-83
Shakib Al Hasan	137 6	5-80 5-44 }	B v Z	Khulna	2014-15

Wicketkeeper A. B. de Villiers scored 103 and held 11 catches for South Africa against Pakistan at Johannesburg in 2012-13.*

2,000 RUNS AND 200 WICKETS

	Tests	Runs	Wkts	Tests for 1,000/100 Double
R. Ashwin (India)	84	2,844	430	24
R. Benaud (Australia)	63	2,201	248	32
†I. T. Botham (England)	102	5,200	383	21
S. C. J. Broad (England)	152	3,412	537	35
C. L. Cairns (New Zealand)	62	3,320	218	33
A. Flintoff (England/World)	79	3,845	226	43
R. J. Hadlee (New Zealand)	86	3,124	431	28
Harbhajan Singh (India)	103	2,224	417	62
Imran Khan (Pakistan)	88	3,807	362	30
R. A. Jadeja (India)	57	2,195	232	30
M. J. Johnson (Australia)	73	2,065	313	37
†J. H. Kallis (South Africa/World)	166	13,289	292	53
Kapil Dev (India)	131	5,248	434	25
A. Kumble (India)	132	2,506	619	56
S. M. Pollock (South Africa)	108	3,781	421	26
Shakib Al Hasan (Bangladesh)	59	4,029	215	28
†G. S. Sobers (West Indies)	93	8,032	235	48

	Tests	Runs	Wkts	Tests for 1,000/100 Double
W. P. U. J. C. Vaas (Sri Lanka)	111	3,089	355	47
D. L. Vettori (New Zealand/World)	113	4,531	362	47
†S. K. Warne (Australia)	145	3,154	708	58
Wasim Akram (Pakistan)	104	2,898	414	45

H. H. Streak scored 1,990 runs and took 216 wickets in 65 Tests for Zimbabwe.

† *J. H. Kallis also took 200 catches, S. K. Warne 125, I. T. Botham 120 and G. S. Sobers 109. These four and C. L. Hooper (5,762 runs, 114 wickets and 115 catches for West Indies) are the only players to have achieved the treble of 1,000 runs, 100 wickets and 100 catches in Test cricket.*

WICKETKEEPING RECORDS

MOST DISMISSALS IN AN INNINGS

7 (7ct)	Wasim Bari.	Pakistan v New Zealand at Auckland	1978-79
7 (7ct)	R. W. Taylor.	England v India at Bombay	1979-80
7 (7ct)	I. D. S. Smith	New Zealand v Sri Lanka at Hamilton	1990-91
7 (7ct)	R. D. Jacobs.	West Indies v Australia at Melbourne	2000-01

The first instance of seven wicketkeeping dismissals in a Test innings was a joint effort for Pakistan v West Indies at Kingston in 1976-77. Majid Khan made four catches, deputising for the injured wicketkeeper Wasim Bari, who made three more catches on his return.

There have been 32 instances of players making six dismissals in a Test innings, the most recent being Q. de Kock (6ct) for South Africa v England at Centurion in 2019-20.

MOST STUMPINGS IN AN INNINGS

5	K. S. More	India v West Indies at Madras	1987-88

MOST DISMISSALS IN A TEST

11 (11ct)	R. C. Russell.	England v South Africa at Johannesburg . . .	1995-96
11 (11ct)	A. B. de Villiers	South Africa v Pakistan at Johannesburg . . .	2012-13
11 (11ct)	R. R. Pant	India v Australia at Adelaide	2018-19
10 (10ct)	R. W. Taylor.	England v India at Bombay	1979-80
10 (10ct)	A. C. Gilchrist	Australia v New Zealand at Hamilton	1999-2000
10 (10ct)	W. P. Saha	India v South Africa at Cape Town	2017-18
10 (10ct)	Sarfraz Ahmed	Pakistan v South Africa at Johannesburg . . .	2018-19

There have been 26 instances of players making nine dismissals in a Test, the most recent being J. M. Bairstow (9 ct) for England v Sri Lanka at Leeds in 2016. S. A. R. Silva made 18 in two successive Tests for Sri Lanka against India in 1985-86.

The most stumpings in a match is 6 by K. S. More for India v West Indies at Madras in 1987-88.

J. J. Kelly (8ct) for Australia v England in 1901-02 and L. E. G. Ames (6ct, 2st) for England v West Indies in 1933 were the only keepers to make eight dismissals in a Test before World War II.

MOST DISMISSALS IN A SERIES

(Played in 5 Tests unless otherwise stated)

29 (29ct)	B. J. Haddin	Australia v England	2013
28 (28ct)	R. W. Marsh	Australia v England	1982-83
27 (25ct, 2st)	R. C. Russell	England v South Africa	1995-96
27 (25ct, 2st)	I. A. Healy	Australia v England (6 Tests)	1997

S. A. R. Silva made 22 dismissals (21ct, 1st) in three Tests for Sri Lanka v India in 1985-86.

H. Strudwick, with 21 (15ct, 6st) for England v South Africa in 1913-14, was the only wicketkeeper to make as many as 20 dismissals in a series before World War II.

MOST DISMISSALS

			T	*Ct*	*St*
1	M. V. Boucher (South Africa/World)	555	147	532	23
2	A. C. Gilchrist (Australia)	416	96	379	37
3	I. A. Healy (Australia)	395	119	366	29
4	R. W. Marsh (Australia)	355	96	343	12
5	M. S. Dhoni (India)	294	90	256	38
6	B. J. Haddin (Australia)	270	66	262	8
	P. J. L. Dujon (West Indies)	270	79	265	5
8	A. P. E. Knott (England)	269	95	250	19
9	**B-J. Watling (New Zealand)**	**265**	**67**	**257**	**8**
10	M. J. Prior (England)	256	79	243	13
11	A. J. Stewart (England)	241	82	227	14
12	**Q. de Kock (South Africa)**	**232**	**52**	**221**	**11**
13	Wasim Bari (Pakistan)	228	81	201	27
14	R. D. Jacobs (West Indies)	219	65	207	12
	T. G. Evans (England)	219	91	173	46
16	D. Ramdin (West Indies)	217	74	205	12
17	Kamran Akmal (Pakistan)	206	53	184	22
18	A. C. Parore (New Zealand)	201	67	194	7

The record for P. J. L. Dujon excludes two catches taken in two Tests when not keeping wicket; A. J. Stewart's record likewise excludes 36 catches taken in 51 Tests, B-J. Watling's ten in eight Tests and A. C. Parore's three in 11 Tests; Q. de Kock played a further two Tests when not keeping wicket but took no catches.

Excluding the Super Series Test, M. V. Boucher made 553 dismissals (530ct, 23st in 146 Tests) for South Africa, a national record.

W. A. S. Oldfield made 52 stumpings, a Test record, in 54 Tests for Australia; he also took 78 catches.

The most dismissals by a wicketkeeper playing for the countries not mentioned above are:

		T	*Ct*	*St*
K. C. Sangakkara (Sri Lanka)	151	48	131	20
A. Flower (Zimbabwe)	151	55	142	9
Mushfiqur Rahim (Bangladesh)	**113**	**55**	**98**	**15**
Afsar Zazai (Afghanistan)	**10**	**5**	**9**	**1**
G. C. Wilson (Ireland)	6	1	6	0

K. C. Sangakkara's record excludes 51 catches taken in 86 matches when not keeping wicket but includes two catches taken as wicketkeeper in a match where he took over when the designated keeper was injured; A. Flower's record excludes nine catches in eight Tests and Mushfiqur Rahim's nine catches in 23 Tests when not keeping wicket; G. C. Wilson played a further Test in which he did not keep wicket and took no catches.

FIELDING RECORDS

(Excluding wicketkeepers)

MOST CATCHES IN AN INNINGS

5	V. Y. Richardson	Australia v South Africa at Durban	1935-36
5	Yajurvindra Singh	India v England at Bangalore	1976-77
5	M. Azharuddin	India v Pakistan at Karachi	1989-90
5	K. Srikkanth	India v Australia at Perth	1991-92
5	S. P. Fleming	New Zealand v Zimbabwe at Harare	1997-98
5	G. C. Smith	South Africa v Australia at Perth	2012-13
5	D. J. G. Sammy	West Indies v India at Mumbai	2013-14
5	D. M. Bravo	West Indies v Bangladesh at Arnos Vale	2014-15

5	A. M. Rahane................	India v Sri Lanka at Galle.................	2015-16
5	J. Blackwood...............	West Indies v Sri Lanka at Colombo (PSO)....	2015-16
5	S. P. D. Smith..............	Australia v South Africa at Cape Town.......	2017-18
5	B. A. Stokes................	England v South Africa at Cape Town.......	2019-20
5	**H. D. R. L. Thirimanne†.......**	**Sri Lanka v England at Galle**	**2020-21**

† *Thirimanne caught all five off the same bowler, L. Embuldeniya.*

MOST CATCHES IN A TEST

8	A. M. Rahane................	India v Sri Lanka at Galle.................	2015-16
7	G. S. Chappell	Australia v England at Perth...............	1974-75
7	Yajurvindra Singh	India v England at Bangalore..............	1976-77
7	H. P. Tillekeratne............	Sri Lanka v New Zealand at Colombo (SSC) ..	1992-93
7	S. P. Fleming................	New Zealand v Zimbabwe at Harare	1997-98
7	M. L. Hayden...............	Australia v Sri Lanka at Galle	2003-04
7	K. L. Rahul	India v England at Nottingham	2018

*There have been 38 instances of players taking six catches in a Test, the most recent being **M. M. Ali** for England v India at The Oval in 2021, **S. P. D. Smith** for Australia v England at Adelaide in 2021-22 and **T. W. M. Latham** for New Zealand v Bangladesh in 2021-22.*

MOST CATCHES IN A SERIES

(Played in 5 Tests unless otherwise stated)

15	J. M. Gregory...............	Australia v England	1920-21
14	G. S. Chappell	Australia v England (6 Tests)..............	1974-75
14	K. L. Rahul	India v England	2018
13	R. B. Simpson	Australia v South Africa..................	1957-58
13	R. B. Simpson	Australia v West Indies...................	1960-61
13	B. C. Lara..................	West Indies v England (6 Tests)............	1997-98
13	R. Dravid..................	India v Australia (4 Tests)................	2004-05
13	B. C. Lara..................	West Indies v India (4 Tests)	2005-06
13	A. N. Cook.................	England v India	2018

MOST CATCHES

Ct	T		Ct	T	
210	164†	R. Dravid (India/World)	157	104	M. A. Taylor (Australia)
205	149	D. P. M. D. Jayawardene (SL)	156	156	A. R. Border (Australia)
200	166†	J. H. Kallis (SA/World)	**148**	**114**	**J. E. Root (England)**
196	168	R. T. Ponting (Australia)	139	118	Younis Khan (Pakistan)
181	128	M. E. Waugh (Australia)	135	134	V. V. S. Laxman (India)
175	161	A. N. Cook (England)	**134**	**82**	**S. P. D. Smith (Australia)**
171	111	S. P. Fleming (New Zealand)	134	115	M. J. Clarke (Australia)
169	117†	G. C. Smith (SA/World)	128	103	M. L. Hayden (Australia)
164	131†	B. C. Lara (West Indies/World)	125	145	S. K. Warne (Australia)
163	**112**	**L. R. P. L. Taylor (New Zealand)**			

† *Excluding the Super Series Test, Dravid made 209 catches in 163 Tests for India, Kallis 196 in 165 Tests for South Africa, and Lara 164 in 130 Tests for West Indies, all national records. G. C. Smith made 166 catches in 116 Tests for South Africa.*

*The most catches in the field for other countries are Zimbabwe 60 in 60 Tests (A. D. R. Campbell); Bangladesh 38 in 50 Tests (**Mahmudullah**); Ireland 4 in 3 Tests (P. R. Stirling); Afghanistan 6 in 4 Tests (**Ibrahim Zadran**).*

TEAM RECORDS

HIGHEST INNINGS TOTALS

952-6 dec	Sri Lanka v India at Colombo (RPS)	1997-98
903-7 dec	England v Australia at The Oval	1938
849	England v West Indies at Kingston	1929-30
790-3 dec	West Indies v Pakistan at Kingston	1957-58
765-6 dec	Pakistan v Sri Lanka at Karachi	2008-09
760-7 dec	Sri Lanka v India at Ahmedabad	2009-10
759-7 dec	India v England at Chennai	2016-17
758-8 dec	Australia v West Indies at Kingston	1954-55
756-5 dec	Sri Lanka v South Africa at Colombo (SSC)	2006
751-5 dec	West Indies v England at St John's	2003-04

The highest innings totals for the countries not mentioned above are:

715-6 dec	New Zealand v Bangladesh at Hamilton	2018-19
682-6 dec	South Africa v England at Lord's	2003
638	Bangladesh v Sri Lanka at Galle	2012-13
563-9 dec	Zimbabwe v West Indies at Harare	2001
545-4 dec	**Afghanistan v Zimbabwe at Abu Dhabi**	**2020-21**
339	Ireland v Pakistan at Malahide	2018

HIGHEST FOURTH-INNINGS TOTALS

To win

418-7	West Indies (*set 418 to win*) v Australia at St John's	2002-03
414-4	South Africa (*set 414 to win*) v Australia at Perth	2008-09
406-4	India (*set 403 to win*) v West Indies at Port-of-Spain	1975-76
404-3	Australia (*set 404 to win*) v England at Leeds	1948

To tie

347	India v Australia at Madras	1986-87

To draw

654-5	England (*set 696 to win*) v South Africa at Durban	1938-39
450-7	South Africa (*set 458 to win*) v India at Johannesburg	2013-14
429-8	India (*set 438 to win*) v England at The Oval	1979
423-7	South Africa (*set 451 to win*) v England at The Oval	1947

To lose

451	New Zealand (*lost by 98 runs*) v England at Christchurch	2001-02
450	Pakistan (*lost by 39 runs*) v Australia at Brisbane	2016-17
445	India (*lost by 47 runs*) v Australia at Adelaide	1977-78
440	New Zealand (*lost by 38 runs*) v England at Nottingham	1973
431	New Zealand (*lost by 121 runs*) v England at Napier	2007-08

MOST RUNS IN A DAY (BOTH SIDES)

588	England (398-6), India (190-0) at Manchester (2nd day)	1936
522	England (503-2), South Africa (19-0) at Lord's (2nd day)	1924
509	Sri Lanka (509-9) v Bangladesh at Colombo (PSS) (2nd day)	2002
508	England (221-2), South Africa (287-6) at The Oval (3rd day)	1935

MOST RUNS IN A DAY (ONE SIDE)

509	Sri Lanka (509-9) v Bangladesh at Colombo (PSS) (2nd day)	2002
503	England (503-2) v South Africa at Lord's (2nd day)	1924
494	Australia (494-6) v South Africa at Sydney (1st day).....................	1910-11
482	Australia (482-5) v South Africa at Adelaide (1st day)...................	2012-13
475	Australia (475-2) v England at The Oval (1st day)......................	1934

MOST WICKETS IN A DAY

27	England (18-3 to 53 all out and 62) v Australia (60) at Lord's (2nd day)	1888
25	Australia (112 and 48-5) v England (61) at Melbourne (1st day)	1901-02
24	England (69-1 to 145 and 60-5) v Australia (119) at The Oval (2nd day)	1896
24	India (347-6 to 474) v Afghanistan (109 and 103) at Bangalore (2nd day)	2018

HIGHEST AGGREGATES IN A TEST

Runs	Wkts			Days played
1,981	35	South Africa v England at Durban	1938-39	10†
1,815	34	West Indies v England at Kingston.............	1929-30	9‡
1,764	39	Australia v West Indies at Adelaide	1968-69	5
1,753	40	Australia v England at Adelaide	1920-21	6
1,747	25	Australia v India at Sydney...................	2003-04	5
1,723	31	England v Australia at Leeds	1948	5
1,702	28	Pakistan v India at Faisalabad.................	2005-06	5

† *No play on one day.*   ‡ *No play on two days.*

LOWEST INNINGS TOTALS

26	New Zealand v England at Auckland	1954-55
30	South Africa v England at Port Elizabeth	1895-96
30	South Africa v England at Birmingham	1924
35	South Africa v England at Cape Town	1898-99
36	Australia v England at Birmingham	1902
36	South Africa v Australia at Melbourne	1931-32
36†	India v Australia at Adelaide.......................................	2020-21
38	Ireland v England at Lord's..	2019
42	Australia v England at Sydney	1887-88
42	New Zealand v Australia at Wellington	1945-46
42†	India v England at Lord's..	1974
43	South Africa v England at Cape Town	1888-89
43	Bangladesh v West Indies at North Sound	2018
44	Australia v England at The Oval	1896
45	England v Australia at Sydney	1886-87
45	South Africa v Australia at Melbourne	1931-32
45	New Zealand v South Africa at Cape Town	2012-13

† *One man retired or absent hurt.*

The lowest innings totals for the countries not mentioned above are:

47	West Indies v England at Kingston...................................	2003-04
49	Pakistan v South Africa at Johannesburg	2012-13
51	Zimbabwe v New Zealand at Napier	2011-12
71	Sri Lanka v Pakistan at Kandy	1994-95
103	Afghanistan v India at Bangalore	2018

FEWEST RUNS IN A FULL DAY'S PLAY

95	Australia (80), Pakistan (15-2) at Karachi (1st day, 5½ hrs)	1956-57
104	Pakistan (0-0 to 104-5) v Australia at Karachi (4th day, 5½ hrs).	1959-60
106	England (92-2 to 198) v Australia at Brisbane (4th day, 5 hrs).	1958-59
	England were dismissed five minutes before the close of play, leaving no time for Australia to start their second innings.	
111	South Africa (48-2 to 130-6 dec), India (29-1) at Cape Town (5th day, 5½ hrs) . .	1992-93
112	Australia (138-6 to 187), Pakistan (63-1) at Karachi (4th day, 5½ hrs)	1956-57
115	Australia (116-7 to 165 and 66-5 after following on) v Pakistan at Karachi (4th day, 5½ hrs)	1988-89
117	India (117-5) v Australia at Madras (1st day, 5½ hrs)	1956-57
117	New Zealand (6-0 to 123-4) v Sri Lanka at Colombo (SSC) (5th day, 5¾ hrs) .	1983-84

In England

151	England (175-2 to 289), New Zealand (37-7) at Lord's (3rd day, 6 hrs)	1978
158	England (211-2 to 369-9) v South Africa at Manchester (5th day, 6 hrs).	1998
159	Pakistan (208-4 to 350), England (17-1) at Leeds (3rd day, 6 hrs).	1971

LOWEST AGGREGATES IN A COMPLETED TEST

Runs	Wkts			Days played
234	29	Australia v South Africa at Melbourne	1931-32	3†
291	40	England v Australia at Lord's	1888	2
295	28	New Zealand v Australia at Wellington	1945-46	2
309	29	West Indies v England at Bridgetown.	1934-35	3
323	30	England v Australia at Manchester	1888	2

† *No play on one day.*

LARGEST VICTORIES

Largest Innings Victories

Inns & 579 runs	England (903-7 dec) v Australia (201 & 123†) at The Oval	1938
Inns & 360 runs	Australia (652-7 dec) v South Africa (159 & 133) at Johannesburg . .	2001-02
Inns & 336 runs	West Indies (614-5 dec) v India (124 & 154) at Calcutta.	1958-59
Inns & 332 runs	Australia (645) v England (141 & 172) at Brisbane.	1946-47
Inns & 324 runs	Pakistan (643) v New Zealand (73 & 246) at Lahore	2002
Inns & 322 runs	West Indies (660-5 dec) v New Zealand (216 & 122) at Wellington. .	1994-95
Inns & 310 runs	West Indies (536) v Bangladesh (139 & 87) at Dhaka.	2002-03
Inns & 301 runs	New Zealand (495-7 dec) v Zimbabwe (51 & 143) at Napier	2011-12

† *Two men absent in both Australian innings.*

Largest Victories by Runs Margin

675 runs	England (521 & 342-8 dec) v Australia (122 & 66†) at Brisbane.	1928-29
562 runs	Australia (701 & 327) v England (321 & 145‡) at The Oval	1934
530 runs	Australia (328 & 578) v South Africa (205 & 171§) at Melbourne	1910-11
492 runs	South Africa (488 & 344-6 dec) v Australia (221 and 119) at Johannesburg . .	2017-18
491 runs	Australia (381 & 361-5 dec) v Pakistan (179 & 72) at Perth.	2004-05
465 runs	Sri Lanka (384 & 447-6 dec) v Bangladesh (208 and 158) at Chittagong	2008-09
425 runs	West Indies (211 & 411-5 dec) v England (71 & 126) at Manchester	1976
423 runs	New Zealand (178 & 585-4 dec) v Sri Lanka (104 & 236) at Christchurch . . .	2018-19
409 runs	Australia (350 & 460-7 dec) v England (215 & 186) at Lord's.	1948
408 runs	West Indies (328 & 448) v Australia (203 & 165) at Adelaide.	1979-80
405 runs	Australia (566-8 dec & 254-2 dec) v England (312 & 103) at Lord's.	2015

† *One man absent in Australia's first innings; two men absent in their second.*
‡ *Two men absent in England's first innings; one man absent in their second.*
§ *One man absent in South Africa's second innings.*

TIED TESTS

West Indies (453 & 284) v Australia (505 & 232) at Brisbane 1960-61
Australia (574-7 dec & 170-5 dec) v India (397 & 347) at Madras. 1986-87

MOST CONSECUTIVE TEST VICTORIES

16 Australia	1999-2000 to 2000-01		9 South Africa	2001-02 to 2003
16 Australia	2005-06 to 2007-08		8 Australia	1920-21 to 1921
11 West Indies	1983-84 to 1984-85		8 England	2004 to 2004-05
9 Sri Lanka	2001 to 2001-02			

MOST CONSECUTIVE TESTS WITHOUT VICTORY

44 New Zealand	1929-30 to 1955-56		23 New Zealand	1962-63 to 1967-68
34 Bangladesh	2000-01 to 2004-05		22 Pakistan	1958-59 to 1964-65
31 India	1981-82 to 1984-85		21 Sri Lanka	1985-86 to 1992-93
28 South Africa	1935 to 1949-50		20 West Indies	1968-69 to 1972-73
24 India	1932 to 1951-52		20 West Indies	2004-05 to 2007
24 Bangladesh	2004-05 to 2008-09			

WHITEWASHES

Teams winning every game in a series of four Tests or more:

Five-Test Series

Australia beat England	1920-21	West Indies beat England	1985-86
Australia beat South Africa	1931-32	South Africa beat West Indies	1998-99
England beat India	1959	Australia beat West Indies	2000-01
West Indies beat India	1961-62	Australia beat England	2006-07
West Indies beat England	1984	Australia beat England	2013-14

Four-Test Series

Australia beat India	1967-68	England beat India	2011
South Africa beat Australia	1969-70	Australia beat India	2011-12
England beat West Indies	2004	India beat Australia	2012-13

The winning team in each instance was at home, except for West Indies in England, 1984.

PLAYERS

YOUNGEST TEST PLAYERS

Years	Days			
15	124	Mushtaq Mohammad	Pakistan v West Indies at Lahore	1958-59
16	189	Aqib Javed	Pakistan v New Zealand at Wellington	1988-89
16	205	S. R. Tendulkar	India v Pakistan at Karachi	1989-90

The above table should be treated with caution. All birthdates for Bangladesh and Pakistan (after Partition) must be regarded as questionable because of deficiencies in record-keeping. Hasan Raza was claimed to be 14 years 227 days old when he played for Pakistan against Zimbabwe at Faisalabad in 1996-97; this age was rejected by the Pakistan Cricket Board, although no alternative has been offered. Suggestions that Enamul Haque jnr was 16 years 230 days old when he played for Bangladesh against England in Dhaka in 2003-04 have been discounted by well-informed local observers, who believe he was 18.

The youngest Test players for countries not mentioned above are:

17	78	Mujeeb Zadran	Afghanistan v India at Bangalore	2018
17	122	J. E. D. Sealy.	West Indies v England at Bridgetown	1929-30
17	128	Mohammad Sharif	Bangladesh v Zimbabwe at Bulawayo	2000-01
17	189	C. D. U. S. Weerasinghe .	Sri Lanka v India at Colombo (PSS).	1985-86
17	239	I. D. Craig.	Australia v South Africa at Melbourne.	1952-53
17	352	H. Masakadza	Zimbabwe v West Indies at Harare.	2001
18	10	D. L. Vettori	New Zealand v England at Wellington.	1996-97
18	149	D. B. Close.	England v New Zealand at Manchester	1949
18	340	P. R. Adams	South Africa v England at Port Elizabeth	1995-96
23	119	M. R. Adair.	Ireland v England at Lord's	2019

OLDEST PLAYERS ON TEST DEBUT

Years	Days			
49	119	J. Southerton	England v Australia at Melbourne	1876-77
47	284	Miran Bux.	Pakistan v India at Lahore	1954-55
46	253	D. D. Blackie	Australia v England at Sydney	1928-29
46	237	H. Ironmonger	Australia v England at Brisbane	1928-29
42	242	N. Betancourt	West Indies v England at Port-of-Spain	1929-30
41	337	E. R. Wilson	England v Australia at Sydney	1920-21
41	27	R. J. D. Jamshedji.	India v England at Bombay	1933-34
40	345	C. A. Wiles	West Indies v England at Manchester.	1933
40	295	O. Henry	South Africa v India at Durban	1992-93
40	216	S. P. Kinneir	England v Australia at Sydney	1911-12
40	110	H. W. Lee	England v South Africa at Johannesburg	1930-31
40	56	G. W. A. Chubb	South Africa v England at Nottingham.	1951
40	37	C. Ramaswami	India v England at Manchester	1936

The oldest Test player on debut for Ireland was E. C. Joyce, 39 years 231 days,v Pakistan at Malahide, 2018; for New Zealand, H. M. McGirr, 38 years 101 days, v England at Auckland, 1929-30; for Sri Lanka, D. S. de Silva, 39 years 251 days, v England at Colombo (PSS), 1981-82; for Zimbabwe, A. C. Waller, 37 years 84 days, v England at Bulawayo, 1996-97; for Bangladesh, Enamul Haque snr, 35 years 58 days, v Zimbabwe at Harare, 2000-01; for Afghanistan, Mohammad Nabi, 33 years 99 days, v India at Bangalore, 2018. A. J. Traicos was 45 years 154 days old when he made his debut for Zimbabwe (v India at Harare, 1992-93) having played three Tests for South Africa in 1969-70.

OLDEST TEST PLAYERS

(Age on final day of their last Test match)

Years	Days			
52	165	W. Rhodes	England v West Indies at Kingston.	1929-30
50	327	H. Ironmonger.	Australia v England at Sydney	1932-33
50	320	W. G. Grace	England v Australia at Nottingham.	1899
50	303	G. Gunn	England v West Indies at Kingston	1929-30
49	139	J. Southerton	England v Australia at Melbourne	1876-77
47	302	Miran Bux.	Pakistan v India at Peshawar	1954-55
47	249	J. B. Hobbs.	England v Australia at The Oval.	1930
47	87	F. E. Woolley	England v Australia at The Oval.	1934
46	309	D. D. Blackie	Australia v England at Adelaide.	1928-29
46	206	A. W. Nourse	South Africa v England at The Oval.	1924
46	202	H. Strudwick.	England v Australia at The Oval.	1926
46	41	E. H. Hendren	England v West Indies at Kingston.	1934-35
45	304	A. J. Traicos	Zimbabwe v India at Delhi	1992-93
45	245	G. O. B. Allen	England v West Indies at Kingston.	1947-48
45	215	P. Holmes	England v India at Lord's	1932
45	140	D. B. Close.	England v West Indies at Manchester.	1976

MOST TEST APPEARANCES

200	S. R. Tendulkar (India)		134	K. C. Sangakkara (Sri Lanka)
169	**J. M. Anderson (England)**		133	M. Muralitharan (Sri Lanka/World)
168	R. T. Ponting (Australia)		133	A. J. Stewart (England)
168	S. R. Waugh (Australia)		132	A. Kumble (India)
166	J. H. Kallis (South Africa/World)		132	C. A. Walsh (West Indies)
164	S. Chanderpaul (West Indies)		131	Kapil Dev (India)
164	R. Dravid (India/World)		131	B. C. Lara (West Indies/World)
161	A. N. Cook (England)		128	M. E. Waugh (Australia)
156	A. R. Border (Australia)		125	S. M. Gavaskar (India)
152	**S. C. J. Broad (England)**		124	H. M. Amla (South Africa)
149	D. P. M. D. Jayawardene (Sri Lanka)		124	Javed Miandad (Pakistan)
147	M. V. Boucher (South Africa/World)		124	G. D. McGrath (Australia)
145	S. K. Warne (Australia)		121	I. V. A. Richards (West Indies)
134	V. V. S. Laxman (India)		120	Inzamam-ul-Haq (Pakistan/World)

Excluding the Super Series Test, J. H. Kallis has made 165 appearances for South Africa, a national record. The most appearances for New Zealand is 112 by D. L. Vettori; for Bangladesh, 78 by **Mushfiqur Rahim**; *for Zimbabwe, 67 by G. W. Flower; for Afghanistan, 6 by* **Asghar Afghan** *and* **Rahmat Shah**; *and for Ireland, 3 by A. Balbirnie, T. J. Murtagh, K. J. O'Brien, W. T. S. Porterfield, P. R. Stirling and S. R. Thompson.*

MOST CONSECUTIVE TEST APPEARANCES FOR A COUNTRY

159	A. N. Cook (England)	May 2006 to September 2018
153	A. R. Border (Australia)	March 1979 to March 1994
107	M. E. Waugh (Australia)	June 1993 to October 2002
106	S. M. Gavaskar (India)	January 1975 to February 1987
101†	B. B. McCullum (New Zealand)	March 2004 to February 2016
98	A. B. de Villiers (South Africa)	December 2004 to January 2015
96†	A. C. Gilchrist (Australia)	November 1999 to January 2008
93	R. Dravid (India)	June 1996 to December 2005
93	D. P. M. D. Jayawardene (Sri Lanka)	November 2002 to January 2013

The most consecutive Test appearances for the countries not mentioned above (excluding Afghanistan and Ireland) are:

85	G. S. Sobers (West Indies)	April 1955 to April 1972
72	Asad Shafiq (Pakistan)	October 2011 to August 2020
56	A. D. R. Campbell (Zimbabwe)	October 1992 to September 2001
49	Mushfiqur Rahim (Bangladesh)	July 2007 to January 2017

† *Complete Test career.*

Bold type denotes sequence which was still in progress after January 1, 2021.

MOST TESTS AS CAPTAIN

	P	W	L	D		P	W	L	D
G. C. Smith (SA/World)	109	53	29*	27	S. R. Waugh (A)	57	41	9	7
A. R. Border (A)	93	32	22	38†	Misbah-ul-Haq (P)	56	26	19	11
S. P. Fleming (NZ)	80	28	27	25	A. Ranatunga (SL)	56	12	19	25
R. T. Ponting (A)	77	48	16	13	M. A. Atherton (E)	54	13	21	20
C. H. Lloyd (WI)	74	36	12	26	W. J. Cronje (SA)	53	27	11	15
V. Kohli (I)	**68**	**40**	**17**	**11**	M. P. Vaughan (E)	51	26	11	14
J. E. Root (E)	**61**	**27**	**25**	**9**	I. V. A. Richards (WI)	50	27	8	15
M. S. Dhoni (I)	60	27	18	15	M. A. Taylor (A)	50	26	13	11
A. N. Cook (E)	59	24	22	13	A. J. Strauss (E)	50	24	11	15

* *Includes defeat as World XI captain in Super Series Test against Australia.*   † *One tie.*

Most Tests as captain of other countries:

	P	W	L	D
Mushfiqur Rahim (B)	34	7	18	9
A. D. R. Campbell (Z)	21	2	12	7
Asghar Afghan (Afg)	**4**	**2**	**2**	**0**
W. T. S. Porterfield (Ire)	3	0	3	0

A. R. Border captained Australia in 93 consecutive Tests.

W. W. Armstrong (Australia) captained his country in the most Tests without being defeated: ten matches with eight wins and two draws.

Mohammad Ashraful (Bangladesh) captained his country in the most Tests without ever winning: 12 defeats and one draw.

UMPIRES

MOST TESTS

		First Test	Last Test
136	**Aleem Dar (Pakistan)**	**2003-04**	**2020-21**
128	S. A. Bucknor (West Indies)	1988-89	2008-09
108	R. E. Koertzen (South Africa)	1992-93	2010
95	D. J. Harper (Australia)	1998-99	2011
92	D. R. Shepherd (England)	1985	2004-05
84	B. F. Bowden (New Zealand)	1999-2000	2014-15
78	D. B. Hair (Australia)	1991-92	2008
75	**R. J. Tucker (Australia)**	**2009-10**	**2021-22**
74	S. J. A. Taufel (Australia)	2000-01	2012
74	I. J. Gould (England)	2008-09	2018-19
73	S. Venkataraghavan (India)	1992-93	2003-04
72	**R. A. Kettleborough (England)**	**2010-11**	**2021**
71	**H. D. P. K. Dharmasena (Sri Lanka)**	**2010-11**	**2021-22**
70	**M. Erasmus (South Africa)**	**2009-10**	**2021-22**
66	H. D. Bird (England)	1973	1996
62	N. J. Llong (England)	2007-08	2019-20
62	**B. N. J. Oxenford (Australia)**	**2010-11**	**2020-21**
57	S. J. Davis (Australia)	1997-98	2014-15
57	**R. K. Illingworth (England)**	**2012-13**	**2021**
54	**P. R. Reiffel (Australia)**	**2012**	**2021-22**

SUMMARY OF TESTS

1876-77 to January 16, 2022

	Opponents	Tests	E	A	SA	WI	NZ	I	P	SL	Z	B	Ire	Afg	Wld	Tied	Drawn
England	Australia	**356**	110	150	–	–	–	–	–	–	–	–	–	–	–	–	96
	South Africa	**153**	64	–	34	–	–	–	–	–	–	–	–	–	–	–	55
	West Indies	**160**	51	–	–	58	–	–	–	–	–	–	–	–	–	–	51
	New Zealand	**107**	48	–	–	–	12	–	–	–	–	–	–	–	–	–	47
	India	**130**	49	–	–	–	–	31	–	–	–	–	–	–	–	–	50
	Pakistan	**86**	26	–	–	–	–	–	21	–	–	–	–	–	–	–	39
	Sri Lanka	**36**	17	–	–	–	–	–	–	8	–	–	–	–	–	–	11
	Zimbabwe	**6**	3	–	–	–	–	–	–	–	0	–	–	–	–	–	3
	Bangladesh	**10**	9	–	–	–	–	–	–	–	–	1	–	–	–	–	0
	Ireland	**1**	1	–	–	–	–	–	–	–	–	–	0	–	–	–	0
Australia	South Africa	**98**	–	52	26	–	–	–	–	–	–	–	–	–	–	–	20
	West Indies	**116**	–	58	–	32	–	–	–	–	–	–	–	–	–	1	25
	New Zealand	**60**	–	34	–	–	8	–	–	–	–	–	–	–	–	–	18
	India	**102**	–	43	–	–	–	30	–	–	–	–	–	–	–	1	28
	Pakistan	**66**	–	33	–	–	–	–	15	–	–	–	–	–	–	–	18
	Sri Lanka	**31**	–	19	–	–	–	–	–	4	–	–	–	–	–	–	8
	Zimbabwe	**3**	–	3	–	–	–	–	–	–	0	–	–	–	–	–	0
	Bangladesh	**6**	–	5	–	–	–	–	–	–	–	1	–	–	–	–	0
	ICC World XI	**1**	–	1	–	–	–	–	–	–	–	–	–	–	0	–	0
South Africa	West Indies	**30**	–	–	20	3	–	–	–	–	–	–	–	–	–	–	7
	New Zealand	**45**	–	–	25	–	4	–	–	–	–	–	–	–	–	–	16
	India	**42**	–	–	17	–	–	15	–	–	–	–	–	–	–	–	10
	Pakistan	**28**	–	–	15	–	–	–	6	–	–	–	–	–	–	–	7
	Sri Lanka	**31**	–	–	16	–	–	–	–	9	–	–	–	–	–	–	6
	Zimbabwe	**9**	–	–	8	–	–	–	–	–	0	–	–	–	–	–	1
	Bangladesh	**12**	–	–	10	–	–	–	–	–	–	0	–	–	–	–	2
West Indies	New Zealand	**49**	–	–	–	13	17	–	–	–	–	–	–	–	–	–	19
	India	**98**	–	–	–	30	–	22	–	–	–	–	–	–	–	–	46
	Pakistan	**54**	–	–	–	18	–	–	21	–	–	–	–	–	–	–	15
	Sri Lanka	**24**	–	–	–	4	–	–	–	11	–	–	–	–	–	–	9
	Zimbabwe	**10**	–	–	–	7	–	–	–	–	0	–	–	–	–	–	3
	Bangladesh	**18**	–	–	–	12	–	–	–	–	–	4	–	–	–	–	2
	Afghanistan	**1**	–	–	–	1	–	–	–	–	–	–	–	0	–	–	0
New Zealand	India	**62**	–	–	–	–	13	22	–	–	–	–	–	–	–	–	27
	Pakistan	**60**	–	–	–	–	14	–	25	–	–	–	–	–	–	–	21
	Sri Lanka	**36**	–	–	–	–	16	–	–	9	–	–	–	–	–	–	11
	Zimbabwe	**17**	–	–	–	–	11	–	–	–	0	–	–	–	–	–	6
	Bangladesh	**17**	–	–	–	–	13	–	–	–	–	1	–	–	–	–	3
India	Pakistan	**59**	–	–	–	–	–	9	12	–	–	–	–	–	–	–	38
	Sri Lanka	**44**	–	–	–	–	–	20	–	7	–	–	–	–	–	–	17
	Zimbabwe	**11**	–	–	–	–	–	7	–	–	2	–	–	–	–	–	2
	Bangladesh	**11**	–	–	–	–	–	9	–	–	–	0	–	–	–	–	2
	Afghanistan	**1**	–	–	–	–	–	1	–	–	–	–	–	0	–	–	0
Pakistan	Sri Lanka	**55**	–	–	–	–	–	–	20	16	–	–	–	–	–	–	19
	Zimbabwe	**19**	–	–	–	–	–	–	12	–	3	–	–	–	–	–	4
	Bangladesh	**13**	–	–	–	–	–	–	12	–	–	0	–	–	–	–	1
	Ireland	**1**	–	–	–	–	–	–	1	–	–	–	0	–	–	–	0
Sri Lanka	Zimbabwe	**20**	–	–	–	–	–	–	–	14	0	–	–	–	–	–	6
	Bangladesh	**22**	–	–	–	–	–	–	–	17	–	1	–	–	–	–	4
Zimbabwe	Bangladesh	**18**	–	–	–	–	–	–	–	–	7	8	–	–	–	–	3
	Afghanistan	**2**	–	–	–	–	–	–	–	–	1	–	–	1	–	–	0
Bangladesh	Afghanistan	**1**	–	–	–	–	–	–	–	–	–	0	–	1	–	–	0
Ireland	Afghanistan	**1**	–	–	–	–	–	–	–	–	–	–	0	1	–	–	0
		2,449	378	398	171	178	108	166	145	95	13	16	0	3	0	2	776

RESULTS SUMMARY OF TESTS

1876-77 to January 16, 2022 (2,449 matches)

	Tests	Won	Lost	Drawn	Tied	% Won	Toss Won
England	1,045	378	315	352	–	36.17	512
Australia	839†	398†	226	213	2	47.43	423
South Africa	448	171	153	124	–	38.16	211
West Indies	560	178	204	177	1	31.78	292
New Zealand	453	108	177	168	–	23.84	224

India	560	166	173	220	1	29.64	278
Pakistan	441	145	134	162	–	32.87	210
Sri Lanka	299	95	113	91	–	31.77	163
Zimbabwe	115	13	74	28	–	11.30	65
Bangladesh	128	16	95	17	–	12.50	66
Ireland	3	0	3	0	–	0.00	2
Afghanistan	6	3	3	0	–	50.00	3
ICC World XI	1	0	1	0	–	0.00	0

† Includes Super Series Test between Australia and ICC World XI.

ENGLAND v AUSTRALIA

Captains

Season	England	Australia	T	E	A	D
1876-77	James Lillywhite	D. W. Gregory	2	1	1	0
1878-79	Lord Harris	D. W. Gregory	1	0	1	0
1880	Lord Harris	W. L. Murdoch	1	1	0	0
1881-82	A. Shaw	W. L. Murdoch	4	0	2	2
1882	A. N. Hornby	W. L. Murdoch	1	0	1	0

THE ASHES

Captains

Season	England	Australia	T	E	A	D	Held by
1882-83	Hon. Ivo Bligh	W. L. Murdoch	4*	2	2	0	E
1884	Lord Harris[1]	W. L. Murdoch	3	1	0	2	E
1884-85	A. Shrewsbury	T. P. Horan[2]	5	3	2	0	E
1886	A. G. Steel	H. J. H. Scott	3	3	0	0	E
1886-87	A. Shrewsbury	P. S. McDonnell	2	2	0	0	E
1887-88	W. W. Read	P. S. McDonnell	1	1	0	0	E
1888	W. G. Grace[3]	P. S. McDonnell	3	2	1	0	E
1890†	W. G. Grace	W. L. Murdoch	2	2	0	0	E
1891-92	W. G. Grace	J. M. Blackham	3	1	2	0	A
1893	W. G. Grace[4]	J. M. Blackham	3	1	0	2	E
1894-95	A. E. Stoddart	G. Giffen[5]	5	3	2	0	E
1896	W. G. Grace	G. H. S. Trott	3	2	1	0	E
1897-98	A. E. Stoddart[6]	G. H. S. Trott	5	1	4	0	A
1899	A. C. MacLaren[7]	J. Darling	5	0	1	4	A
1901-02	A. C. MacLaren	J. Darling[8]	5	1	4	0	A
1902	A. C. MacLaren	J. Darling	5	1	2	2	A
1903-04	P. F. Warner	M. A. Noble	5	3	2	0	E
1905	Hon. F. S. Jackson	J. Darling	5	2	0	3	E
1907-08	A. O. Jones[9]	M. A. Noble	5	1	4	0	A
1909	A. C. MacLaren	M. A. Noble	5	1	2	2	A
1911-12	J. W. H. T. Douglas	C. Hill	5	4	1	0	E
1912	C. B. Fry	S. E. Gregory	3	1	0	2	E
1920-21	J. W. H. T. Douglas	W. W. Armstrong	5	0	5	0	A
1921	Hon. L. H. Tennyson[10]	W. W. Armstrong	5	0	3	2	A
1924-25	A. E. R. Gilligan	H. L. Collins	5	1	4	0	A
1926	A. W. Carr[11]	H. L. Collins[12]	5	1	0	4	E
1928-29	A. P. F. Chapman[13]	J. Ryder	5	4	1	0	E
1930	A. P. F. Chapman[14]	W. M. Woodfull	5	1	2	2	A
1932-33	D. R. Jardine	W. M. Woodfull	5	4	1	0	E
1934	R. E. S. Wyatt[15]	W. M. Woodfull	5	1	2	2	A
1936-37	G. O. B. Allen	D. G. Bradman	5	2	3	0	A
1938†	W. R. Hammond	D. G. Bradman	4	1	1	2	A
1946-47	W. R. Hammond[16]	D. G. Bradman	5	0	3	2	A
1948	N. W. D. Yardley	D. G. Bradman	5	0	4	1	A
1950-51	F. R. Brown	A. L. Hassett	5	1	4	0	A
1953	L. Hutton	A. L. Hassett	5	1	0	4	E
1954-55	L. Hutton	I. W. Johnson[17]	5	3	1	1	E
1956	P. B. H. May	I. W. Johnson	5	2	1	2	E

Captains

Season	England	Australia	T	E	A	D	Held by
1958-59	P. B. H. May	R. Benaud	5	0	4	1	A
1961	P. B. H. May[18]	R. Benaud[19]	5	1	2	2	A
1962-63	E. R. Dexter	R. Benaud	5	1	1	3	A
1964	E. R. Dexter	R. B. Simpson	5	0	1	4	A
1965-66	M. J. K. Smith	R. B. Simpson[20]	5	1	1	3	A
1968	M. C. Cowdrey[21]	W. M. Lawry[22]	5	1	1	3	A
1970-71†	R. Illingworth	W. M. Lawry[23]	6	2	0	4	E
1972	R. Illingworth	I. M. Chappell	5	2	2	1	E
1974-75	M. H. Denness[24]	I. M. Chappell	6	1	4	1	A
1975	A. W. Greig[25]	I. M. Chappell	4	0	1	3	A
1976-77‡	A. W. Greig	G. S. Chappell	1	0	1	0	—
1977	J. M. Brearley	G. S. Chappell	5	3	0	2	E
1978-79	J. M. Brearley	G. N. Yallop	6	5	1	0	E
1979-80‡	J. M. Brearley	G. S. Chappell	3	0	3	0	—
1980‡	I. T. Botham	G. S. Chappell	1	0	0	1	—
1981	J. M. Brearley[26]	K. J. Hughes	6	3	1	2	E
1982-83	R. G. D. Willis	G. S. Chappell	5	1	2	2	A
1985	D. I. Gower	A. R. Border	6	3	1	2	E
1986-87	M. W. Gatting	A. R. Border	5	2	1	2	E
1987-88‡	M. W. Gatting	A. R. Border	1	0	0	1	—
1989	D. I. Gower	A. R. Border	6	0	4	2	A
1990-91	G. A. Gooch[27]	A. R. Border	5	0	3	2	A
1993	G. A. Gooch[28]	A. R. Border	6	1	4	1	A
1994-95	M. A. Atherton	M. A. Taylor	5	1	3	1	A
1997	M. A. Atherton	M. A. Taylor	6	2	3	1	A
1998-99	A. J. Stewart	M. A. Taylor	5	1	3	1	A
2001	N. Hussain[29]	S. R. Waugh[30]	5	1	4	0	A
2002-03	N. Hussain	S. R. Waugh	5	1	4	0	A
2005	M. P. Vaughan	R. T. Ponting	5	2	1	2	E
2006-07	A. Flintoff	R. T. Ponting	5	0	5	0	A
2009	A. J. Strauss	R. T. Ponting	5	2	1	2	E
2010-11	A. J. Strauss	R. T. Ponting[31]	5	3	1	1	E
2013	A. N. Cook	M. J. Clarke	5	3	0	2	E
2013-14	A. N. Cook	M. J. Clarke	5	0	5	0	A
2015	A. N. Cook	M. J. Clarke	5	3	2	0	E
2017-18	J. E. Root	S. P. D. Smith	5	0	4	1	A
2019	J. E. Root	T. D. Paine	5	2	2	1	A
2021-22	**J. E. Root**	**P. J. Cummins[32]**	**5**	**0**	**4**	**1**	**A**

In Australia			185	57	99	29	
In England			171	53	51	67	
Totals			**356**	**110**	**150**	**96**	

* *The Ashes were awarded in 1882-83 after a series of three matches which England won 2–1. A fourth match was played and this was won by Australia.*

† *The matches at Manchester in 1890 and 1938 and at Melbourne (Third Test) in 1970-71 were abandoned without a ball being bowled and are excluded.*

‡ *The Ashes were not at stake in these series.*

The following deputised for the official touring captain or were appointed by the home authority for only a minor proportion of the series:

[1]A. N. Hornby (First). [2]W. L. Murdoch (First), H. H. Massie (Third), J. M. Blackham (Fourth). [3]A. G. Steel (First). [4]A. E. Stoddart (First). [5]J. M. Blackham (First). [6]A. C. MacLaren (First, Second and Fifth). [7]W. G. Grace (First). [8]H. Trumble (Fourth and Fifth). [9]F. L. Fane (First, Second and Third). [10]J. W. H. T. Douglas (First and Second). [11]A. P. F. Chapman (Fifth). [12]W. Bardsley (Third and Fourth). [13]J. C. White (Fifth). [14]R. E. S. Wyatt (Fifth). [15]C. F. Walters (First). [16]N. W. D. Yardley (Fifth). [17]A. R. Morris (Second). [18]M. C. Cowdrey (First and Second). [19]R. N. Harvey (Second). [20]B. C. Booth (First and Third). [21]T. W. Graveney (Fourth). [22]B. N. Jarman (Fourth) [23]I. M. Chappell (Seventh). [24]J. H. Edrich (Fourth). [25]M. H. Denness (First). [26]I. T. Botham (First and Second). [27]A. J. Lamb (First). [28]M. A. Atherton (Fifth and Sixth). [29]M. A. Atherton (Second and Third). [30]A. C. Gilchrist (Fourth). [31]M. J. Clarke (Fifth). [32]S. P. D. Smith (Second).

HIGHEST INNINGS TOTALS

For England in England: 903-7 dec at The Oval 1938
        in Australia: 644 at Sydney 2010-11

For Australia in England: 729-6 dec at Lord's 1930
        in Australia: 662-9 dec at Perth 2017-18

LOWEST INNINGS TOTALS

For England in England: 52 at The Oval 1948
        in Australia: 45 at Sydney 1886-87

For Australia in England: 36 at Birmingham 1902
        in Australia: 42 at Sydney 1887-88

DOUBLE-HUNDREDS

For England (14)

364	L. Hutton at The Oval	1938	231*	W. R. Hammond at Sydney	1936-37
287	R. E. Foster at Sydney	1903-04	227	K. P. Pietersen at Adelaide	2010-11
256	K. F. Barrington at Manchester	1964	216*	E. Paynter at Nottingham	1938
251	W. R. Hammond at Sydney	1928-29	215	D. I. Gower at Birmingham	1985
244*	A. N. Cook at Melbourne	2017-18	207	N. Hussain at Birmingham	1997
240	W. R. Hammond at Lord's	1938	206	P. D. Collingwood at Adelaide	2006-07
235*	A. N. Cook at Brisbane	2010-11	200	W. R. Hammond at Melbourne	1928-29

For Australia (26)

334	D. G. Bradman at Leeds	1930	232	S. J. McCabe at Nottingham	1938
311	R. B. Simpson at Manchester	1964	225	R. B. Simpson at Adelaide	1965-66
307	R. M. Cowper at Melbourne	1965-66	219	M. A. Taylor at Nottingham	1989
304	D. G. Bradman at Leeds	1934	215	S. P. D. Smith at Lord's	2015
270	D. G. Bradman at Melbourne	1936-37	212	D. G. Bradman at Adelaide	1936-37
266	W. H. Ponsford at The Oval	1934	211	W. L. Murdoch at The Oval	1884
254	D. G. Bradman at Lord's	1930	211	S. P. D. Smith at Manchester	2019
250	J. L. Langer at Melbourne	2002-03	207	K. R. Stackpole at Brisbane	1970-71
244	D. G. Bradman at The Oval	1934	206*	W. A. Brown at Lord's	1938
239	S. P. D. Smith at Perth	2017-18	206	A. R. Morris at Adelaide	1950-51
234	S. G. Barnes at Sydney	1946-47	201*	J. Ryder at Adelaide	1924-25
234	D. G. Bradman at Sydney	1946-47	201	S. E. Gregory at Sydney	1894-95
232	D. G. Bradman at The Oval	1930	200*	A. R. Border at Leeds	1993

INDIVIDUAL HUNDREDS

In total, England have scored **246** hundreds against Australia, and Australia have scored **323** against England. The players with at least five hundreds are as follows:

For England

12: J. B. Hobbs.
 9: D. I. Gower, W. R. Hammond.
 8: H. Sutcliffe.
 7: G. Boycott, J. H. Edrich, M. Leyland.
 5: K. F. Barrington, D. C. S. Compton, A. N. Cook, M. C. Cowdrey, L. Hutton, F. S. Jackson, A. C. MacLaren.

For Australia

19: D. G. Bradman.
11: S. P. D. Smith.
10: S. R. Waugh.
 9: G. S. Chappell.
 8: A. R. Border, A. R. Morris, R. T. Ponting.
 7: D. C. Boon, M. J. Clarke, W. M. Lawry, M. J. Slater.
 6: R. N. Harvey, M. A. Taylor, V. T. Trumper, M. E. Waugh, W. M. Woodfull.
 5: M. L. Hayden, J. L. Langer, C. G. Macartney, W. H. Ponsford.

RECORD PARTNERSHIPS FOR EACH WICKET

For England

323 for 1st	J. B. Hobbs and W. Rhodes at Melbourne......................	1911-12
382 for 2nd†	L. Hutton and M. Leyland at The Oval	1938
262 for 3rd	W. R. Hammond and D. R. Jardine at Adelaide	1928-29
310 for 4th	P. D. Collingwood and K. P. Pietersen at Adelaide...............	2006-07
237 for 5th	D. J. Malan and J. M. Bairstow at Perth	2017-18
215 for 6th	⎰ L. Hutton and J. Hardstaff jnr at The Oval	1938
	⎱ G. Boycott and A. P. E. Knott at Nottingham	1977
143 for 7th	F. E. Woolley and J. Vine at Sydney........................	1911-12
124 for 8th	E. H. Hendren and H. Larwood at Brisbane	1928-29
151 for 9th	W. H. Scotton and W. W. Read at The Oval..................	1884
130 for 10th	R. E. Foster and W. Rhodes at Sydney	1903-04

For Australia

329 for 1st	G. R. Marsh and M. A. Taylor at Nottingham...............	1989
451 for 2nd†	W. H. Ponsford and D. G. Bradman at The Oval	1934
276 for 3rd	D. G. Bradman and A. L. Hassett at Brisbane	1946-47
388 for 4th	W. H. Ponsford and D. G. Bradman at Leeds	1934
405 for 5th‡	S. G. Barnes and D. G. Bradman at Sydney	1946-47
346 for 6th†	J. H. Fingleton and D. G. Bradman at Melbourne.............	1936-37
165 for 7th	C. Hill and H. Trumble at Melbourne	1897-98
243 for 8th†	R. J. Hartigan and C. Hill at Adelaide	1907-08
154 for 9th†	S. E. Gregory and J. M. Blackham at Sydney	1894-95
163 for 10th†	P. J. Hughes and A. C. Agar at Nottingham	2013

† *Record partnership against all countries.*   ‡ *World record.*

MOST RUNS IN A SERIES

England in England .... 732 (average 81.33)	D. I. Gower	1985
England in Australia............ 905 (average 113.12)	W. R. Hammond	1928-29
Australia in England............ 974 (average 139.14)	D. G. Bradman	1930
Australia in Australia .... 810 (average 90.00)	D. G. Bradman	1936-37

MOST WICKETS IN A MATCH

In total, England bowlers have taken ten or more wickets in a match **40** times against Australia, and Australian bowlers have done it **43** times against England. The players with at least 12 in a match are as follows:

For England

19-90 (9-37, 10-53)	J. C. Laker at Manchester	1956
15-104 (7-61, 8-43)	H. Verity at Lord's.................................	1934
15-124 (7-56, 8-68)	W. Rhodes at Melbourne............................	1903-04
14-99 (7-55, 7-44)	A. V. Bedser at Nottingham	1953
14-102 (7-28, 7-74)	W. Bates at Melbourne	1882-83
13-163 (6-42, 7-121)	S. F. Barnes at Melbourne	1901-02
13-244 (7-168, 6-76)	T. Richardson at Manchester.........................	1896

13-256 (5-130, 8-126)	J. C. White at Adelaide	1928-29
12-102 (6-50, 6-52)†	F. Martin at The Oval	1890
12-104 (7-36, 5-68)	G. A. Lohmann at The Oval	1886
12-136 (6-49, 6-87)	J. Briggs at Adelaide	1891-92

There are a further 12 instances of 11 wickets in a match, and 17 instances of ten.

For Australia

16-137 (8-84, 8-53)†	R. A. L. Massie at Lord's	1972
14-90 (7-46, 7-44)	F. R. Spofforth at The Oval	1882
13-77 (7-17, 6-60)	M. A. Noble at Melbourne..............................	1901-02
13-110 (6-48, 7-62)	F. R. Spofforth at Melbourne...........................	1878-79
13-148 (6-97, 7-51)	B. A. Reid at Melbourne	1990-91
13-236 (4-115, 9-121)	A. A. Mailey at Melbourne	1920-21
12-87 (5-44, 7-43)	C. T. B. Turner at Sydney	1887-88
12-89 (6-59, 6-30)	H. Trumble at The Oval.................................	1896
12-107 (5-57, 7-50)	S. C. G. MacGill at Sydney	1998-99
12-173 (8-65, 4-108)	H. Trumble at The Oval.................................	1902
12-175 (5-85, 7-90)†	H. V. Hordern at Sydney	1911-12
12-246 (6-122, 6-124)	S. K. Warne at The Oval	2005

There are a further 13 instances of 11 wickets in a match, and 18 instances of ten.

† *On first appearance in England–Australia Tests.*

A. V. Bedser, J. Briggs, J. C. Laker, T. Richardson, R. M. Hogg, A. A. Mailey, H. Trumble and C. T. B. Turner took ten wickets or more in successive Tests.

MOST WICKETS IN A SERIES

England in England . . . . 46 (average 9.60)	J. C. Laker	1956
England in Australia . . . . . . 38 (average 23.18)	M. W. Tate	1924-25
Australia in England . . . . . . 42 (average 21.26)	T. M. Alderman (6 Tests)	1981
Australia in Australia. . . . . . 41 (average 12.85)	R. M. Hogg (6 Tests)	1978-79

WICKETKEEPING – MOST DISMISSALS

	M	*Ct*	*St*	*Total*
†R. W. Marsh (Australia)	42	141	7	148
I. A. Healy (Australia).	33	123	12	135
A. P. E. Knott (England)	34	97	8	105
A. C. Gilchrist (Australia)	20	89	7	96
†W. A. S. Oldfield (Australia).	38	59	31	90
A. F. A. Lilley (England).	32	65	19	84
B. J. Haddin (Australia)	20	79	1	80
A. J. Stewart (England)	26	76	2	78
A. T. W. Grout (Australia)	22	69	7	76
T. G. Evans (England).	31	64	12	76

† *The number of catches by R. W. Marsh (141) and stumpings by W. A. S. Oldfield (31) are respective records in England–Australia Tests.*

Stewart held a further six catches in seven matches when not keeping wicket.

SCORERS OF OVER 2,500 RUNS

	T	*I*	*NO*	*R*	*HS*	*100*	*Avge*
D. G. Bradman (Australia) .	37	63	7	5,028	334	19	89.78
J. B. Hobbs (England)	41	71	4	3,636	187	12	54.26
A. R. Border (Australia) . . .	47	82	19	3,548	200*	8	56.31
D. I. Gower (England).	42	77	4	3,269	215	9	44.78
S. R. Waugh (Australia) . . .	46	73	18	3,200	177*	10	58.18
S. P. D. Smith (Australia) .	**32**	**56**	**5**	**3,044**	**239**	**11**	**59.68**
G. Boycott (England).	38	71	9	2,945	191	7	47.50
W. R. Hammond (England).	33	58	3	2,852	251	9	51.85

	T	I	NO	R	HS	100	Avge
H. Sutcliffe (England)	27	46	5	2,741	194	8	66.85
C. Hill (Australia)	41	76	1	2,660	188	4	35.46
J. H. Edrich (England)	32	57	3	2,644	175	7	48.96
G. A. Gooch (England)	42	79	0	2,632	196	4	33.31
G. S. Chappell (Australia)	35	65	8	2,619	144	9	45.94

BOWLERS WITH 100 WICKETS

	T	Balls	R	W	5I	10M	Avge
S. K. Warne (Australia)	36	10,757	4,535	195	11	4	23.25
D. K. Lillee (Australia)	29	8,516	3,507	167	11	4	21.00
G. D. McGrath (Australia)	30	7,280	3,286	157	10	0	20.92
I. T. Botham (England)	36	8,479	4,093	148	9	2	27.65
H. Trumble (Australia)	31	7,895	2,945	141	9	3	20.88
S. C. J. Broad (England)	**35**	**7,224**	**3,806**	**131**	**8**	**1**	**29.05**
R. G. D. Willis (England)	35	7,294	3,346	128	7	0	26.14
M. A. Noble (Australia)	39	6,895	2,860	115	9	2	24.86
R. R. Lindwall (Australia)	29	6,728	2,559	114	6	0	22.44
J. M. Anderson (England)	**35**	**7,675**	**3,782**	**112**	**5**	**1**	**33.76**
W. Rhodes (England)	41	5,790	2,616	109	6	1	24.00
S. F. Barnes (England)	20	5,749	2,288	106	12	1	21.58
C. V. Grimmett (Australia)	22	9,224	3,439	106	11	2	32.44
D. L. Underwood (England)	29	8,000	2,770	105	4	2	26.38
A. V. Bedser (England)	21	7,065	2,859	104	7	2	27.49
G. Giffen (Australia)	31	6,391	2,791	103	7	1	27.09
W. J. O'Reilly (Australia)	19	7,864	2,587	102	8	3	25.36
C. T. B. Turner (Australia)	17	5,179	1,670	101	11	2	16.53
R. Peel (England)	20	5,216	1,715	101	5	1	16.98
N. M. Lyon (Australia)	**28**	**6,585**	**2,972**	**101**	**2**	**0**	**29.42**
T. M. Alderman (Australia)	17	4,717	2,117	100	11	1	21.17
J. R. Thomson (Australia)	21	4,951	2,418	100	5	0	24.18

RESULTS ON EACH GROUND

In England

	Matches	England wins	Australia wins	Drawn
The Oval	38	17	7	14
Manchester	30	7	8	15†
Lord's	37	7	15	15
Nottingham	22	6	7	9
Leeds	25	8	9	8
Birmingham	15	6	4	5
Sheffield	1	0	1	0
Cardiff	2	1	0	1
Chester-le-Street	1	1	0	0

† *Excludes two matches abandoned without a ball bowled.*

In Australia

	Matches	England wins	Australia wins	Drawn
Melbourne	57	20	29	8†
Sydney	57	22	27	8
Adelaide	33	9	19	5
Brisbane				
Exhibition Ground	1	1	0	0
Woolloongabba	22	4	13	5
Perth	14	1	10	3
Hobart	1	0	1	0

† *Excludes one match abandoned without a ball bowled.*

ENGLAND v SOUTH AFRICA

	Captains					
Season	*England*	*South Africa*	*T*	*E*	*SA*	*D*
1888-89	C. A. Smith[1]	O. R. Dunell[2]	2	2	0	0
1891-92	W. W. Read	W. H. Milton	1	1	0	0
1895-96	Lord Hawke[3]	E. A. Halliwell[4]	3	3	0	0
1898-99	Lord Hawke	M. Bisset	2	2	0	0
1905-06	P. F. Warner	P. W. Sherwell	5	1	4	0
1907	R. E. Foster	P. W. Sherwell	3	1	0	2
1909-10	H. D. G. Leveson Gower[5]	S. J. Snooke	5	2	3	0
1912	C. B. Fry	F. Mitchell[6]	3	3	0	0
1913-14	J. W. H. T. Douglas	H. W. Taylor	5	4	0	1
1922-23	F. T. Mann	H. W. Taylor	5	2	1	2
1924	A. E. R. Gilligan[7]	H. W. Taylor	5	3	0	2
1927-28	R. T. Stanyforth[8]	H. G. Deane	5	2	2	1
1929	J. C. White[9]	H. G. Deane	5	2	0	3
1930-31	A. P. F. Chapman	H. G. Deane[10]	5	0	1	4
1935	R. E. S. Wyatt	H. F. Wade	5	0	1	4
1938-39	W. R. Hammond	A. Melville	5	1	0	4
1947	N. W. D. Yardley	A. Melville	5	3	0	2
1948-49	F. G. Mann	A. D. Nourse	5	2	0	3
1951	F. R. Brown	A. D. Nourse	5	3	1	1
1955	P. B. H. May	J. E. Cheetham[11]	5	3	2	0
1956-57	P. B. H. May	C. B. van Ryneveld[12]	5	2	2	1
1960	M. C. Cowdrey	D. J. McGlew	5	3	0	2
1964-65	M. J. K. Smith	T. L. Goddard	5	1	0	4
1965	M. J. K. Smith	P. L. van der Merwe	3	0	1	2
1994	M. A. Atherton	K. C. Wessels	3	1	1	1
1995-96	M. A. Atherton	W. J. Cronje	5	0	1	4
1998	A. J. Stewart	W. J. Cronje	5	2	1	2
1999-2000	N. Hussain	W. J. Cronje	5	1	2	2
2003	M. P. Vaughan[13]	G. C. Smith	5	2	2	1

THE BASIL D'OLIVEIRA TROPHY

	Captains						
Season	*England*	*South Africa*	*T*	*E*	*SA*	*D*	*Held by*
2004-05	M. P. Vaughan	G. C. Smith	5	2	1	2	E
2008	M. P. Vaughan[14]	G. C. Smith	4	1	2	1	SA
2009-10	A. J. Strauss	G. C. Smith	4	1	1	2	SA
2012	A. J. Strauss	G. C. Smith	3	0	2	1	SA
2015-16	A. N. Cook	H. M. Amla[15]	4	2	1	1	E
2017	J. E. Root	F. du Plessis[16]	4	3	1	0	E
2019-20	J. E. Root	F. du Plessis	4	3	1	0	E

In South Africa			85	34	20	31
In England			68	30	14	24
Totals			153	64	34	55

The following deputised for the official touring captain or were appointed by the home authority for only a minor proportion of the series:

[1]M. P. Bowden (Second). [2]W. H. Milton (Second). [3]Sir Timothy O'Brien (First). [4]A. R. Richards (Third). [5]F. L. Fane (Fourth and Fifth). [6]L. J. Tancred (Second and Third). [7]J. W. H. T. Douglas (Fourth). [8]G. T. S. Stevens (Fifth). [9]A. W. Carr (Fourth and Fifth). [10]E. P. Nupen (First), H. B. Cameron (Fourth and Fifth). [11]D. J. McGlew (Third and Fourth). [12]D. J. McGlew (Second). [13]N. Hussain (First). [14]K. P. Pietersen (Fourth). [15]A. B. de Villiers (Third and Fourth). [16]D. Elgar (First).

SERIES RECORDS

Highest score	E	258	B. A. Stokes at Cape Town	2015-16
	SA	311*	H. M. Amla at The Oval	2012
Best bowling	E	9-28	G. A. Lohmann at Johannesburg.	1895-96
	SA	9-113	H. J. Tayfield at Johannesburg	1956-57
Highest total	E	654-5	at Durban.	1938-39
	SA	682-6 dec	at Lord's	2003
Lowest total	E	76	at Leeds	1907
	SA {	30	at Port Elizabeth	1895-96
		30	at Birmingham.	1924

ENGLAND v WEST INDIES

			Captains				
Season	England		West Indies	T	E	WI	D
1928	A. P. F. Chapman		R. K. Nunes	3	3	0	0
1929-30	Hon. F. S. G. Calthorpe		E. L. G. Hoad[1]	4	1	1	2
1933	D. R. Jardine[2]		G. C. Grant	3	2	0	1
1934-35	R. E. S. Wyatt		G. C. Grant	4	1	2	1
1939	W. R. Hammond		R. S. Grant	3	1	0	2
1947-48	G. O. B. Allen[3]		J. D. C. Goddard[4]	4	0	2	2
1950	N. W. D. Yardley[5]		J. D. C. Goddard	4	1	3	0
1953-54	L. Hutton		J. B. Stollmeyer	5	2	2	1
1957	P. B. H. May		J. D. C. Goddard	5	3	0	2
1959-60	P. B. H. May[6]		F. C. M. Alexander	5	1	0	4

THE WISDEN TROPHY

			Captains					
Season	England		West Indies	T	E	WI	D	Held by
1963	E. R. Dexter		F. M. M. Worrell	5	1	3	1	WI
1966	M. C. Cowdrey[7]		G. S. Sobers	5	1	3	1	WI
1967-68	M. C. Cowdrey		G. S. Sobers	5	1	0	4	E
1969	R. Illingworth		G. S. Sobers	3	2	0	1	E
1973	R. Illingworth		R. B. Kanhai	3	0	2	1	WI
1973-74	M. H. Denness		R. B. Kanhai	5	1	1	3	WI
1976	A. W. Greig		C. H. Lloyd	5	0	3	2	WI
1980	I. T. Botham		C. H. Lloyd[8]	5	0	1	4	WI
1980-81†	I. T. Botham		C. H. Lloyd	4	0	2	2	WI
1984	D. I. Gower		C. H. Lloyd	5	0	5	0	WI
1985-86	D. I. Gower		I. V. A. Richards	5	0	5	0	WI
1988	J. E. Emburey[9]		I. V. A. Richards	5	0	4	1	WI
1989-90‡	G. A. Gooch[10]		I. V. A. Richards[11]	4	1	2	1	WI
1991	G. A. Gooch		I. V. A. Richards	5	2	2	1	WI
1993-94	M. A. Atherton		R. B. Richardson[12]	5	1	3	1	WI
1995	M. A. Atherton		R. B. Richardson	6	2	2	2	WI
1997-98§	M. A. Atherton		B. C. Lara	6	1	3	2	WI
2000	N. Hussain[13]		J. C. Adams	5	3	1	1	E
2003-04	M. P. Vaughan		B. C. Lara	4	3	0	1	E
2004	M. P. Vaughan		B. C. Lara	4	4	0	0	E
2007	M. P. Vaughan[14]		R. R. Sarwan[15]	4	3	0	1	E
2008-09§	A. J. Strauss		C. H. Gayle	5	0	1	4	WI
2009	A. J. Strauss		C. H. Gayle	2	2	0	0	E
2012	A. J. Strauss		D. J. G. Sammy	3	2	0	1	E
2014-15	A. N. Cook		D. Ramdin	3	1	1	1	E

		Captains					
Season	England	West Indies	T	E	WI	D	Held by
2017	J. E. Root	J. O. Holder	3	2	1	0	E
2018-19	J. E. Root	J. O. Holder[16]	3	1	2	0	WI
2020	J. E. Root[17]	J. O. Holder	3	2	1	0	E

		T	E	WI	D	
	In England.........................	89	36	31	22	
	In West Indies.....................	71	15	27	29	
	Totals	160	51	58	51	

† *The Second Test, at Georgetown, was cancelled owing to political pressure and is excluded.*
‡ *The Second Test, at Georgetown, was abandoned without a ball being bowled and is excluded.*
§ *The First Test at Kingston in 1997-98 and the Second Test at North Sound in 2038-09 were called off on their opening days because of unfit pitches and are shown as draws.*

The following deputised for the official touring captain or were appointed by the home authority for only a minor proportion of the series:

[1]N. Betancourt (Second), M. P. Fernandes (Third), R. K. Nunes (Fourth). [2]R. E. S. Wyatt (Third). [3]K. Cranston (First). [4]G. A. Headley (First), G. E. Gomez (Second). [5]F. R. Brown (Fourth). [6]M. C. Cowdrey (Fourth and Fifth). [7]M. J. K. Smith (First), D. B. Close (Fifth). [8]I. V. A. Richards (Fifth). [9]M. W. Gatting (First), C. S. Cowdrey (Fourth), G. A. Gooch (Fifth). [10]A. J. Lamb (Fourth and Fifth). [11]D. L. Haynes (Third). [12]C. A. Walsh (Fifth). [13]A. J. Stewart (Second). [14]A. J. Strauss (First). [15]D. Ganga (Third and Fourth). [16]K. C. Brathwaite (Third). [17]B. A. Stokes (First).

SERIES RECORDS

Highest score	E	325	A. Sandham at Kingston		1929-30
	WI	400*	B. C. Lara at St John's..................		2003-04
Best bowling	E	8-53	A. R. C. Fraser at Port-of-Spain		1997-98
	WI	8-45	C. E. L. Ambrose at Bridgetown...........		1989-90
Highest total	E	849	at Kingston		1929-30
	WI	751-5 dec	at St John's		2003-04
Lowest total	E	46	at Port-of-Spain.......................		1993-94
	WI	47	at Kingston		2003-04

ENGLAND v NEW ZEALAND

		Captains				
Season	England	New Zealand	T	E	NZ	D
1929-30	A. H. H. Gilligan	T. C. Lowry	4	1	0	3
1931	D. R. Jardine	T. C. Lowry	3	1	0	2
1932-33	D. R. Jardine[1]	M. L. Page	2	0	0	2
1937	R. W. V. Robins	M. L. Page	3	1	0	2
1946-47	W. R. Hammond	W. A. Hadlee	1	0	0	1
1949	F. G. Mann[2]	W. A. Hadlee	4	0	0	4
1950-51	F. R. Brown	W. A. Hadlee	2	1	0	1
1954-55	L. Hutton	G. O. Rabone	2	2	0	0
1958	P. B. H. May	J. R. Reid	5	4	0	1
1958-59	P. B. H. May	J. R. Reid	2	1	0	1
1962-63	E. R. Dexter	J. R. Reid	3	3	0	0
1965	M. J. K. Smith	J. R. Reid	3	3	0	0
1965-66	M. J. K. Smith	B. W. Sinclair[3]	3	0	0	3
1969	R. Illingworth	G. T. Dowling	3	2	0	1
1970-71	R. Illingworth	G. T. Dowling	2	1	0	1
1973	R. Illingworth	B. E. Congdon	3	2	0	1
1974-75	M. H. Denness	B. E. Congdon	2	1	0	1
1977-78	G. Boycott	M. G. Burgess	3	1	1	1
1978	J. M. Brearley	M. G. Burgess	3	3	0	0
1983	R. G. D. Willis	G. P. Howarth	4	3	1	0
1983-84	R. G. D. Willis	G. P. Howarth	3	0	1	2

		Captains					
Season	England		New Zealand	T	E	NZ	D
1986	M. W. Gatting		J. V. Coney	3	0	1	2
1987-88	M. W. Gatting		J. J. Crowe[4]	3	0	0	3
1990	G. A. Gooch		J. G. Wright	3	1	0	2
1991-92	G. A. Gooch		M. D. Crowe	3	2	0	1
1994	M. A. Atherton		K. R. Rutherford	3	1	0	2
1996-97	M. A. Atherton		L. K. Germon[5]	3	2	0	1
1999	N. Hussain[6]		S. P. Fleming	4	1	2	1
2001-02	N. Hussain		S. P. Fleming	3	1	1	1
2004	M. P. Vaughan[7]		S. P. Fleming	3	3	0	0
2007-08	M. P. Vaughan		D. L. Vettori	3	2	1	0
2008	M. P. Vaughan		D. L. Vettori	3	2	0	1
2012-13	A. N. Cook		B. B. McCullum	3	0	0	3
2013	A. N. Cook		B. B. McCullum	2	2	0	0
2015	A. N. Cook		B. B. McCullum	2	1	1	0
2017-18	J. E. Root		K. S. Williamson	2	0	1	1
2019-20	J. E. Root		K. S. Williamson	2	0	1	1
2021	**J. E. Root**		**K. S. Williamson[8]**	**2**	**0**	**1**	**1**
	In New Zealand			51	18	6	27
	In England			**56**	**30**	**6**	**20**
	Totals			**107**	**48**	**12**	**47**

The following deputised for the official touring captain or were appointed by the home authority for only a minor proportion of the series:

[1]R. E. S. Wyatt (Second). [2]F. R. Brown (Third and Fourth). [3]M. E. Chapple (First). [4]J. G. Wright (Third). [5]S. P. Fleming (Third). [6]M. A. Butcher (Third). [7]M. E. Trescothick (First). [8]T. W. M. Latham (Second).

SERIES RECORDS

Highest score	E	336*	W. R. Hammond at Auckland..............	1932-33
	NZ	222	N. J. Astle at Christchurch	2001-02
Best bowling	E	7-32	D. L. Underwood at Lord's................	1969
	NZ	7-74	B. L. Cairns at Leeds.....................	1983
Highest total	E	593-6 dec	at Auckland............................	1974-75
	NZ	615-9 dec	at Mount Maunganui.....................	2019-20
Lowest total	E	58	at Auckland............................	2017-18
	NZ	26	at Auckland............................	1954-55

ENGLAND v INDIA

		Captains					
Season	England		India	T	E	I	D
1932	D. R. Jardine		C. K. Nayudu	1	1	0	0
1933-34	D. R. Jardine		C. K. Nayudu	3	2	0	1
1936	G. O. B. Allen		Maharaj of Vizianagram	3	2	0	1
1946	W. R. Hammond		Nawab of Pataudi snr	3	1	0	2
1951-52	N. D. Howard[1]		V. S. Hazare	5	1	1	3
1952	L. Hutton		V. S. Hazare	4	3	0	1
1959	P. B. H. May[2]		D. K. Gaekwad[3]	5	5	0	0
1961-62	E. R. Dexter		N. J. Contractor	5	0	2	3
1963-64	M. J. K. Smith		Nawab of Pataudi jnr	5	0	0	5
1967	D. B. Close		Nawab of Pataudi jnr	3	3	0	0
1971	R. Illingworth		A. L. Wadekar	3	0	1	2
1972-73	A. R. Lewis		A. L. Wadekar	5	1	2	2
1974	M. H. Denness		A. L. Wadekar	3	3	0	0
1976-77	A. W. Greig		B. S. Bedi	5	3	1	1
1979	J. M. Brearley		S. Venkataraghavan	4	1	0	3
1979-80	J. M. Brearley		G. R. Viswanath	1	1	0	0

Captains

Season	England	India	T	E	I	D
1981-82	K. W. R. Fletcher	S. M. Gavaskar	6	0	1	5
1982	R. G. D. Willis	S. M. Gavaskar	3	1	0	2
1984-85	D. I. Gower	S. M. Gavaskar	5	2	1	2
1986	M. W. Gatting[4]	Kapil Dev	3	0	2	1
1990	G. A. Gooch	M. Azharuddin	3	1	0	2
1992-93	G. A. Gooch[5]	M. Azharuddin	3	0	3	0
1996	M. A. Atherton	M. Azharuddin	3	1	0	2
2001-02	N. Hussain	S. C. Ganguly	3	0	1	2
2002	N. Hussain	S. C. Ganguly	4	1	1	2
2005-06	A. Flintoff	R. Dravid	3	1	1	1
2007	M. P. Vaughan	R. Dravid	3	0	1	2
2008-09	K. P. Pietersen	M. S. Dhoni	2	0	1	1
2011	A. J. Strauss	M. S. Dhoni	4	4	0	0
2012-13	A. N. Cook	M. S. Dhoni	4	2	1	1
2014	A. N. Cook	M. S. Dhoni	5	3	1	1
2016-17	A. N. Cook	V. Kohli	5	0	4	1
2018	J. E. Root	V. Kohli	5	4	1	0
2020-21	**J. E. Root**	**V. Kohli**	**4**	**1**	**3**	**0**
2021†	**J. E. Root**	**V. Kohli**	**4**	**1**	**2**	**1**
	In England...............................		66	35	9	22
	In India...................................		64	14	22	28
	Totals...............................		**130**	**49**	**31**	**50**

*   *Since 1951-52, series in India have been for the De Mello Trophy. Since 2007, series in England have been for the Pataudi Trophy.*
†   *The Fifth Test at Manchester was postponed when India refused to play because of a Covid outbreak, and was rescheduled for Birmingham in 2022.*

The following deputised for the official touring captain or were appointed by the home authority for only a minor proportion of the series:
  [1]D. B. Carr (Fifth). [2]M. C. Cowdrey (Fourth and Fifth). [3]Pankaj Roy (Second). [4]D. I. Gower (First). [5]A. J. Stewart (Second).

The 1932 Indian touring team was led by the Maharaj of Porbandar but he did not play in the Test.

SERIES RECORDS

Highest score	E	333	G. A. Gooch at Lord's......................		1990
	I	303*	K. K. Nair at Chennai		2016-17
Best bowling	E	8-31	F. S. Trueman at Manchester...............		1952
	I	8-55	M. H. Mankad at Madras...................		1951-52
Highest total	E	710-7 dec	at Birmingham...........................		2011
	I	759-7 dec	at Chennai		2016-17
Lowest total	E	**81**	**at Ahmedabad**		**2020-21**
	I	42	at Lord's		1974

ENGLAND v PAKISTAN

Captains

Season	England	Pakistan	T	E	P	D
1954	L. Hutton[1]	A. H. Kardar	4	1	1	2
1961-62	E. R. Dexter	Imtiaz Ahmed	3	1	0	2
1962	E. R. Dexter[2]	Javed Burki	5	4	0	1
1967	D. B. Close	Hanif Mohammad	3	2	0	1
1968-69	M. C. Cowdrey	Saeed Ahmed	3	0	0	3
1971	R. Illingworth	Intikhab Alam	3	1	0	2
1972-73	A. R. Lewis	Majid Khan	3	0	0	3

Captains

Season	England	Pakistan	T	E	P	D
1974	M. H. Denness	Intikhab Alam	3	0	0	3
1977-78	J. M. Brearley[3]	Wasim Bari	3	0	0	3
1978	J. M. Brearley	Wasim Bari	3	2	0	1
1982	R. G. D. Willis[4]	Imran Khan	3	2	1	0
1983-84	R. G. D. Willis[5]	Zaheer Abbas	3	0	1	2
1987	M. W. Gatting	Imran Khan	5	0	1	4
1987-88	M. W. Gatting	Javed Miandad	3	0	1	2
1992	G. A. Gooch	Javed Miandad	5	1	2	2
1996	M. A. Atherton	Wasim Akram	3	0	2	1
2000-01	N. Hussain	Moin Khan	3	1	0	2
2001	N. Hussain[6]	Waqar Younis	2	1	1	0
2005-06	M. P. Vaughan[7]	Inzamam-ul-Haq	3	0	2	1
2006†	A. J. Strauss	Inzamam-ul-Haq	4	3	0	1
2010	A. J. Strauss	Salman Butt	4	3	1	0
2011-12U	A. J. Strauss	Misbah-ul-Haq	3	0	3	0
2015-16U	A. N. Cook	Misbah-ul-Haq	3	0	2	1
2016	A. N. Cook	Misbah-ul-Haq	4	2	2	0
2018	J. E. Root	Sarfraz Ahmed	2	1	1	0
2020	J. E. Root	Azhar Ali	3	1	0	2
	In England		56	24	12	20
	In Pakistan		24	2	4	18
	In United Arab Emirates		6	0	5	1
	Totals		86	26	21	39

† In 2008, the ICC changed the result of the forfeited Oval Test of 2006 from an England win to a draw, in contravention of the Laws of Cricket, only to rescind their decision in January 2009.

U Played in United Arab Emirates.

The following deputised for the official touring captain or were appointed by the home authority for only a minor proportion of the series:
[1]D. S. Sheppard (Second and Third). [2]M. C. Cowdrey (Third). [3]G. Boycott (Third). [4]D. I. Gower (Second). [5]D. I. Gower (Second and Third). [6]A. J. Stewart (Second). [7]M. E. Trescothick (First).

SERIES RECORDS

Highest score	E	278	D. C. S. Compton at Nottingham.............	1954
	P	274	Zaheer Abbas at Birmingham	1971
Best bowling	E	8-34	I. T. Botham at Lord's	1978
	P	9-56	Abdul Qadir at Lahore.....................	1987-88
Highest total	E	598-9 dec	at Abu Dhabi	2015-16
	P	708	at The Oval	1987
Lowest total	E	72	at Abu Dhabi	2011-12
	P	72	at Birmingham...........................	2010

ENGLAND v SRI LANKA

Captains

Season	England	Sri Lanka	T	E	SL	D
1981-82	K. W. R. Fletcher	B. Warnapura	1	1	0	0
1984	D. I. Gower	L. R. D. Mendis	1	0	0	1
1988	G. A. Gooch	R. S. Madugalle	1	1	0	0
1991	G. A. Gooch	P. A. de Silva	1	1	0	0
1992-93	A. J. Stewart	A. Ranatunga	1	0	1	0
1998	A. J. Stewart	A. Ranatunga	1	0	1	0
2000-01	N. Hussain	S. T. Jayasuriya	3	2	1	0
2002	N. Hussain	S. T. Jayasuriya	3	2	0	1

Season	England	Captains	Sri Lanka	T	E	SL	D
2003-04	M. P. Vaughan		H. P. Tillekeratne	3	0	1	2
2006	A. Flintoff		D. P. M. D. Jayawardene	3	1	1	1
2007-08	M. P. Vaughan		D. P. M. D. Jayawardene	3	0	1	2
2011	A. J. Strauss		T. M. Dilshan[1]	3	1	0	2
2011-12	A. J. Strauss		D. P. M. D. Jayawardene	2	1	1	0
2014	A. N. Cook		A. D. Mathews	2	0	1	1
2016	A. N. Cook		A. D. Mathews	3	2	0	1
2018-19	J. E. Root		R. A. S. Lakmal[2]	3	3	0	0
2020-21	**J. E. Root**		**L. D. Chandimal**	**2**	**2**	**0**	**0**
	In England			18	8	3	7
	In Sri Lanka			**18**	**9**	**5**	**4**
	Totals			**36**	**17**	**8**	**11**

The following deputised for the official touring captain or was appointed by the home authority for only a minor proportion of the series:
[1]K. C. Sangakkara (Third). [2]L. D. Chandimal (First).

SERIES RECORDS

Highest score	E	228	J. E. Root at Galle	**2020-21**
	SL	213*	D. P. M. D. Jayawardene at Galle	2007-08
Best bowling	E	7-70	P. A. J. DeFreitas at Lord's	1991
	SL	9-65	M. Muralitharan at The Oval	1998
Highest total	E	575-9 dec	at Lord's..................................	2014
	SL	628-8 dec	at Colombo (SSC)	2003-04
Lowest total	E	81	at Galle..................................	2007-08
	SL	81	at Colombo (SSC)	2000-01

ENGLAND v ZIMBABWE

Season	England	Captains	Zimbabwe	T	E	Z	D
1996-97	M. A. Atherton		A. D. R. Campbell	2	0	0	2
2000	N. Hussain		A. Flower	2	1	0	1
2003	N. Hussain		H. H. Streak	2	2	0	0
	In England			4	3	0	1
	In Zimbabwe			2	0	0	2
	Totals			6	3	0	3

SERIES RECORDS

Highest score	E	137	M. A. Butcher at Lord's	2003
	Z	148*	M. W. Goodwin at Nottingham.................	2000
Best bowling	E	6-33	R. L. Johnson at Chester-le-Street............	2003
	Z	6-87	H. H. Streak at Lord's	2000
Highest total	E	472	at Lord's	2003
	Z	376	at Bulawayo...................................	1996-97
Lowest total	E	147	at Nottingham	2000
	Z	83	at Lord's	2000

ENGLAND v BANGLADESH

		Captains					
Season	*England*	*Bangladesh*	*T*	*E*	*B*	*D*	
2003-04	M. P. Vaughan	Khaled Mahmud	2	2	0	0	
2005	M. P. Vaughan	Habibul Bashar	2	2	0	0	
2009-10	A. N. Cook	Shakib Al Hasan	2	2	0	0	
2010	A. J. Strauss	Shakib Al Hasan	2	2	0	0	
2016-17	A. N. Cook	Mushfiqur Rahim	2	1	1	0	
	In England		4	4	0	0	
	In Bangladesh		6	5	1	0	
	Totals		10	9	1	0	

SERIES RECORDS

Highest score	E	226	I. J. L. Trott at Lord's	2010
	B	108	Tamim Iqbal at Manchester	2010
Best bowling	E	5-35	S. J. Harmison at Dhaka	2003-04
	B	6-77	Mehedi Hasan at Mirpur	2016-17
Highest total	E	599-6 dec	at Chittagong	2009-10
	B	419	at Mirpur	2009-10
Lowest total	E	164	at Mirpur	2016-17
	B	104	at Chester-le-Street	2005

ENGLAND v IRELAND

		Captains					
Season	*England*	*Ireland*	*T*	*E*	*Ire*	*D*	
2019E	J. E. Root	W. T. S. Porterfield	1	1	0	0	
	In England		1	1	0	0	
	Totals		1	1	0	0	

E Played in England.

SERIES RECORDS

Highest score	E	92	M. J. Leach at Lord's	2019
	Ire	55	A. Balbirnie at Lord's	2019
Best bowling	E	6-17	C. R. Woakes at Lord's	2019
	Ire	5-13	T. J. Murtagh at Lord's	2019
Highest total	E	303	at Lord's	2019
	Ire	207	at Lord's	2019
Lowest total	E	85	at Lord's	2019
	Ire	38	at Lord's	2019

AUSTRALIA v SOUTH AFRICA

		Captains					
Season	*Australia*	*South Africa*	*T*	*A*	*SA*	*D*	
1902-03S	J. Darling	H. M. Taberer[1]	3	2	0	1	
1910-11A	C. Hill	P. W. Sherwell	5	4	1	0	
1912E	S. E. Gregory	F. Mitchell[2]	3	2	0	1	
1921-22S	H. L. Collins	H. W. Taylor	3	1	0	2	

Season	Australia	*Captains* South Africa	T	A	SA	D
1931-32*A*	W. M. Woodfull	H. B. Cameron	5	5	0	0
1935-36*S*	V. Y. Richardson	H. F. Wade	5	4	0	1
1949-50*S*	A. L. Hassett	A. D. Nourse	5	4	0	1
1952-53*A*	A. L. Hassett	J. E. Cheetham	5	2	2	1
1957-58*S*	I. D. Craig	C. B. van Ryneveld[3]	5	3	0	2
1963-64*A*	R. B. Simpson[4]	T. L. Goddard	5	1	1	3
1966-67*S*	R. B. Simpson	P. L. van der Merwe	5	1	3	1
1969-70*S*	W. M. Lawry	A. Bacher	4	0	4	0
1993-94*A*	A. R. Border	K. C. Wessels[5]	3	1	1	1
1993-94*S*	A. R. Border	K. C. Wessels	3	1	1	1
1996-97*S*	M. A. Taylor	W. J. Cronje	3	2	1	0
1997-98*A*	M. A. Taylor	W. J. Cronje	3	1	0	2
2001-02*A*	S. R. Waugh	S. M. Pollock	3	3	0	0
2001-02*S*	S. R. Waugh	M. V. Boucher	3	2	1	0
2005-06*A*	R. T. Ponting	G. C. Smith	3	2	0	1
2005-06*S*	R. T. Ponting	G. C. Smith[6]	3	3	0	0
2008-09*A*	R. T. Ponting	G. C. Smith	3	1	2	0
2008-09*S*	R. T. Ponting	G. C. Smith[7]	3	2	1	0
2011-12*S*	M. J. Clarke	G. C. Smith	2	1	1	0
2012-13*A*	M. J. Clarke	G. C. Smith	3	0	1	2
2013-14*S*	M. J. Clarke	G. C. Smith	3	2	1	0
2016-17*A*	S. P. D. Smith	F. du Plessis	3	1	2	0
2017-18*S*	S. P. D. Smith[8]	F. du Plessis	4	1	3	0
	In South Africa.....................		54	29	16	9
	In Australia.........................		41	21	10	10
	In England		3	2	0	1
	Totals		98	52	26	20

S   Played in South Africa.   A   Played in Australia.   E   Played in England.

The following deputised for the official touring captain or were appointed by the home authority for only a minor proportion of the series:

[1]J. H. Anderson (Second), E. A. Halliwell (Third). [2]L. J. Tancred (Third). [3]D. J. McGlew (First). [4]R. Benaud (First). [5]W. J. Cronje (Third). [6]J. H. Kallis (Third). [7]J. H. Kallis (Third). [8]T. D. Paine (Fourth).

SERIES RECORDS

Highest score	A	299*	D. G. Bradman at Adelaide	1931-32
	SA	274	R. G. Pollock at Durban..................	1969-70
Best bowling	A	8-61	M. G. Johnson at Perth	2008-09
	SA	7-23	H. J. Tayfield at Durban.................	1949-50
Highest total	A	652-7 dec	at Johannesburg........................	2001-02
	SA	651	at Cape Town...........................	2008-09
Lowest total	A	47	at Cape Town...........................	2011-12
	SA	36	at Melbourne	1931-32

AUSTRALIA v WEST INDIES

Season	Australia	*Captains* West Indies	T	A	WI	T	D
1930-31*A*	W. M. Woodfull	G. C. Grant	5	4	1	0	0
1951-52*A*	A. L. Hassett[1]	J. D. C. Goddard[2]	5	4	1	0	0
1954-55*W*	I. W. Johnson	D. St E. Atkinson[3]	5	3	0	0	2

THE FRANK WORRELL TROPHY

Season	Australia	*Captains* West Indies	T	A	WI	T	D	Held by
1960-61A	R. Benaud	F. M. M. Worrell	5	2	1	1	1	A
1964-65W	R. B. Simpson	G. S. Sobers	5	1	2	0	2	WI
1968-69A	W. M. Lawry	G. S. Sobers	5	3	1	0	1	A
1972-73W	I. M. Chappell	R. B. Kanhai	5	2	0	0	3	A
1975-76A	G. S. Chappell	C. H. Lloyd	6	5	1	0	0	A
1977-78W	R. B. Simpson	A. I. Kallicharran[4]	5	1	3	0	1	WI
1979-80A	G. S. Chappell	C. H. Lloyd[5]	3	0	2	0	1	WI
1981-82A	G. S. Chappell	C. H. Lloyd	3	1	1	0	1	WI
1983-84W	K. J. Hughes	C. H. Lloyd[6]	5	0	3	0	2	WI
1984-85A	A. R. Border[7]	C. H. Lloyd	5	1	3	0	1	WI
1988-89A	A. R. Border	I. V. A. Richards	5	1	3	0	1	WI
1990-91W	A. R. Border	I. V. A. Richards	5	1	2	0	2	WI
1992-93A	A. R. Border	R. B. Richardson	5	1	2	0	2	WI
1994-95W	M. A. Taylor	R. B. Richardson	4	2	1	0	1	A
1996-97A	M. A. Taylor	C. A. Walsh	5	3	2	0	0	A
1998-99W	S. R. Waugh	B. C. Lara	4	2	2	0	0	A
2000-01A	S. R. Waugh[8]	J. C. Adams	5	5	0	0	0	A
2002-03W	S. R. Waugh	B. C. Lara	4	3	1	0	0	A
2005-06A	R. T. Ponting	S. Chanderpaul	3	3	0	0	0	A
2007-08W	R. T. Ponting	R. R. Sarwan[9]	3	2	0	0	1	A
2009-10A	R. T. Ponting	C. H. Gayle	3	2	0	0	1	A
2011-12W	M. J. Clarke	D. J. G. Sammy	3	2	0	0	1	A
2015W	M. J. Clarke	D. Ramdin	2	2	0	0	0	A
2015-16A	S. P. D. Smith	J. O. Holder	3	2	0	0	1	A
	In Australia		66	37	18	1	10	
	In West Indies		50	21	14	0	15	
	Totals		116	58	32	1	25	

A Played in Australia.   W Played in West Indies.

The following deputised for the official touring captain or were appointed by the home authority for only a minor proportion of the series:
[1]A. R. Morris (Third). [2]J. B. Stollmeyer (Fifth). [3]J. B. Stollmeyer (Second and Third). [4]C. H. Lloyd (First and Second). [5]D. L. Murray (First). [6]I. V. A. Richards (Second). [7]K. J. Hughes (First and Second). [8]A. C. Gilchrist (Third). [9]C. H. Gayle (Third).

SERIES RECORDS

Highest score	A	269*	A. C. Voges at Hobart.....................	2015-16
	WI	277	B. C. Lara at Sydney......................	1992-93
Best bowling	A	8-71	G. D. McKenzie at Melbourne	1968-69
	WI	7-25	C. E. L. Ambrose at Perth	1992-93
Highest total	A	758-8 dec	at Kingston	1954-55
	WI	616	at Adelaide..............................	1968-69
Lowest total	A	76	at Perth.................................	1984-85
	WI	51	at Port-of-Spain	1998-99

AUSTRALIA v NEW ZEALAND

Season	Australia	*Captains* New Zealand	T	A	NZ	D
1945-46N	W. A. Brown	W. A. Hadlee	1	1	0	0
1973-74A	I. M. Chappell	B. E. Congdon	3	2	0	1
1973-74N	I. M. Chappell	B. E. Congdon	3	1	1	1
1976-77N	G. S. Chappell	G. M. Turner	2	1	0	1
1980-81A	G. S. Chappell	G. P. Howarth[1]	3	2	0	1
1981-82N	G. S. Chappell	G. P. Howarth	3	1	1	1

TRANS-TASMAN TROPHY

Season	Australia	Captains	New Zealand	T	A	NZ	D	Held by
1985-86A	A. R. Border		J. V. Coney	3	1	2	0	NZ
1985-86N	A. R. Border		J. V. Coney	3	0	1	2	NZ
1987-88A	A. R. Border		J. J. Crowe	3	1	0	2	A
1989-90A	A. R. Border		J. G. Wright	1	0	0	1	A
1989-90N	A. R. Border		J. G. Wright	1	0	1	0	NZ
1992-93N	A. R. Border		M. D. Crowe	3	1	1	1	NZ
1993-94A	A. R. Border		M. D. Crowe[2]	3	2	0	1	A
1997-98A	M. A. Taylor		S. P. Fleming	3	2	0	1	A
1999-2000N	S. R. Waugh		S. P. Fleming	3	3	0	0	A
2001-02A	S. R. Waugh		S. P. Fleming	3	0	0	3	A
2004-05A	R. T. Ponting		S. P. Fleming	2	2	0	0	A
2004-05N	R. T. Ponting		S. P. Fleming	3	2	0	1	A
2008-09A	R. T. Ponting		D. L. Vettori	2	2	0	0	A
2009-10N	R. T. Ponting		D. L. Vettori	2	2	0	0	A
2011-12A	M. J. Clarke		L. R. P. L. Taylor	2	1	1	0	A
2015-16A	S. P. D. Smith		B. B. McCullum	3	2	0	1	A
2015-16N	S. P. D. Smith		B. B. McCullum	2	2	0	0	A
2019-20A	T. D. Paine		K. S. Williamson[3]	3	3	0	0	A

		T	A	NZ	D
In Australia		34	20	3	11
In New Zealand		26	14	5	7
Totals		60	34	8	18

A   Played in Australia.   N   Played in New Zealand.

The following deputised for the official touring captain: [1]M. G. Burgess (Second). [2]K. R. Rutherford (Second and Third). [3]T. W. M. Latham (Third).

SERIES RECORDS

Highest score	A	253	D. A. Warner at Perth	2015-16
	NZ	290	L. R. P. L. Taylor at Perth	2015-16
Best bowling	A	6-31	S. K. Warne at Hobart	1993-94
	NZ	9-52	R. J. Hadlee at Brisbane	1985-86
Highest total	A	607-6 dec	at Brisbane	1993-94
	NZ	624	at Perth	2015-16
Lowest total	A	103	at Auckland	1985-86
	NZ	42	at Wellington	1945-46

AUSTRALIA v INDIA

Season	Australia	Captains	India	T	A	I	T	D
1947-48A	D. G. Bradman		L. Amarnath	5	4	0	0	1
1956-57I	I. W. Johnson[1]		P. R. Umrigar	3	2	0	0	1
1959-60I	R. Benaud		G. S. Ramchand	5	2	1	0	2
1964-65I	R. B. Simpson		Nawab of Pataudi jnr	3	1	1	0	1
1967-68A	R. B. Simpson[2]		Nawab of Pataudi jnr[3]	4	4	0	0	0
1969-70I	W. M. Lawry		Nawab of Pataudi jnr	5	3	1	0	1
1977-78A	R. B. Simpson		B. S. Bedi	5	3	2	0	0
1979-80I	K. J. Hughes		S. M. Gavaskar	6	0	2	0	4
1980-81A	G. S. Chappell		S. M. Gavaskar	3	1	1	0	1
1985-86A	A. R. Border		Kapil Dev	3	0	0	0	3
1986-87I	A. R. Border		Kapil Dev	3	0	0	1	2
1991-92A	A. R. Border		M. Azharuddin	5	4	0	0	1

THE BORDER–GAVASKAR TROPHY

Season	Australia	Captains India	T	A	I	T	D	Held by
1996-97*I*	M. A. Taylor	S. R. Tendulkar	1	0	1	0	0	I
1997-98*I*	M. A. Taylor	M. Azharuddin	3	1	2	0	0	I
1999-2000*A*	S. R. Waugh	S. R. Tendulkar	3	3	0	0	0	A
2000-01*I*	S. R. Waugh	S. C. Ganguly	3	1	2	0	0	I
2003-04*A*	S. R. Waugh	S. C. Ganguly	4	1	1	0	2	I
2004-05*I*	R. T. Ponting[4]	S. C. Ganguly[5]	4	2	1	0	1	A
2007-08*A*	R. T. Ponting	A. Kumble	4	2	1	0	1	A
2008-09*I*	R. T. Ponting	A. Kumble[6]	4	0	2	0	2	I
2010-11*I*	R. T. Ponting	M. S. Dhoni	2	0	2	0	0	I
2011-12*A*	M. J. Clarke	M. S. Dhoni	4	4	0	0	0	A
2012-13*I*	M. J. Clarke[8]	M. S. Dhoni	4	0	4	0	0	I
2014-15*A*	M. J. Clarke[9]	M. S. Dhoni[10]	4	2	0	0	2	A
2016-17*I*	S. P. D. Smith	V. Kohli[11]	4	1	2	0	1	I
2018-19*A*	T. D. Paine	V. Kohli	4	1	2	0	1	I
2020-21*A*	**T. D. Paine**	**A. M. Rahane[12]**	**4**	**1**	**2**	**0**	**1**	**I**
	In Australia		52	30	9	0	13	
	In India		50	13	21	1	15	
	Totals		**102**	**43**	**30**	**1**	**28**	

A Played in Australia.   *I Played in India.*

The following deputised for the official touring captain or were appointed by the home authority for only a minor proportion of the series:
[1]R. R. Lindwall (Second). [2]W. M. Lawry (Third and Fourth). [3]C. G. Borde (First). [4]A. C. Gilchrist (First, Second and Third). [5]R. Dravid (Third and Fourth). [6]M. S. Dhoni (Second and Fourth). [7]V. Sehwag (Fourth). [8]S. R. Watson (Fourth). [9]S. P. D. Smith (Second, Third and Fourth). [10]V. Kohli (First and Fourth). [11]A. M. Rahane (Fourth). [12]V. Kohli (First).

SERIES RECORDS

Highest score	A	329*	M. J. Clarke at Sydney	2011-12
	I	281	V. V. S. Laxman at Kolkata	2000-01
Best bowling	A	8-50	N. M. Lyon at Bangalore	2016-17
	I	9-69	J. M. Patel at Kanpur	1959-60
Highest total	A	674	at Adelaide	1947-48
	I	705-7 dec	at Sydney	2003-04
Lowest total	A	83	at Melbourne	1980-81
	I	**36**	**at Adelaide**	**2020-21**

AUSTRALIA v PAKISTAN

Season	Australia	Captains Pakistan	T	A	P	D
1956-57*P*	I. W. Johnson	A. H. Kardar	1	0	1	0
1959-60*P*	R. Benaud	Fazal Mahmood[1]	3	2	0	1
1964-65*P*	R. B. Simpson	Hanif Mohammad	1	0	0	1
1964-65*A*	R. B. Simpson	Hanif Mohammad	1	0	0	1
1972-73*A*	I. M. Chappell	Intikhab Alam	3	3	0	0
1976-77*A*	G. S. Chappell	Mushtaq Mohammad	3	1	1	1
1978-79*A*	G. N. Yallop[2]	Mushtaq Mohammad	2	1	1	0
1979-80*P*	G. S. Chappell	Javed Miandad	3	0	1	2
1981-82*A*	G. S. Chappell	Javed Miandad	3	2	1	0
1982-83*P*	K. J. Hughes	Imran Khan	3	0	3	0

		Captains				
Season	Australia	Pakistan	T	A	P	D
1983-84A	K. J. Hughes	Imran Khan[3]	5	2	0	3
1988-89P	A. R. Border	Javed Miandad	3	0	1	2
1989-90A	A. R. Border	Imran Khan	3	1	0	2
1994-95P	M. A. Taylor	Salim Malik	3	0	1	2
1995-96A	M. A. Taylor	Wasim Akram	3	2	1	0
1998-99P	M. A. Taylor	Aamir Sohail	3	1	0	2
1999-2000A	S. R. Waugh	Wasim Akram	3	3	0	0
2002-03S/U	S. R. Waugh	Waqar Younis	3	3	0	0
2004-05A	R. T. Ponting	Inzamam-ul-Haq[4]	3	3	0	0
2009-10A	R. T. Ponting	Mohammad Yousuf	3	3	0	0
2010E	R. T. Ponting	Shahid Afridi[5]	2	1	1	0
2014-15U	M. J. Clarke	Misbah-ul-Haq	2	0	2	0
2016-17A	S. P. D. Smith	Misbah-ul-Haq	3	3	0	0
2018-19U	T. D. Paine	Sarfraz Ahmed	2	0	1	1
2019-20A	T. D. Paine	Azhar Ali	2	2	0	0
	In Pakistan		20	3	7	10
	In Australia		37	26	4	7
	In Sri Lanka		1	1	0	0
	In United Arab Emirates		6	2	3	1
	In England		2	1	1	0
	Totals		66	33	15	18

P   Played in Pakistan.   A   Played in Australia.
S/U   First Test played in Sri Lanka, Second and Third Tests in United Arab Emirates.
U   Played in United Arab Emirates.   E   Played in England.

The following deputised for the official touring captain or were appointed by the home authority for only a minor proportion of the series:
[1]Imtiaz Ahmed (Second). [2]K. J. Hughes (Second). [3]Zaheer Abbas (First, Second and Third). [4]Yousuf Youhana *later known as Mohammad Yousuf* (Second and Third). [5]Salman Butt (Second).

SERIES RECORDS

Highest score	A	335*	D. A. Warner at Adelaide	2019-20
	P	237	Salim Malik at Rawalpindi	1994-95
Best bowling	A	8-24	G. D. McGrath at Perth	2004-05
	P	9-86	Sarfraz Nawaz at Melbourne...............	1978-79
Highest total	A	624-8 dec	at Melbourne	2016-17
	P	624	at Adelaide............................	1983-84
Lowest total	A	80	at Karachi	1956-57
	P	53	at Sharjah..............................	2002-03

AUSTRALIA v SRI LANKA

		Captains				
Season	Australia	Sri Lanka	T	A	SL	D
1982-83S	G. S. Chappell	L. R. D. Mendis	1	1	0	0
1987-88A	A. R. Border	R. S. Madugalle	1	1	0	0
1989-90A	A. R. Border	A. Ranatunga	2	1	0	1
1992-93S	A. R. Border	A. Ranatunga	3	1	0	2
1995-96A	M. A. Taylor	A. Ranatunga[1]	3	3	0	0
1999-2000S	S. R. Waugh	S. T. Jayasuriya	3	0	1	2
2003-04S	R. T. Ponting	H. P. Tillekeratne	3	3	0	0
2004A	R. T. Ponting[2]	M. S. Atapattu	2	1	0	1

THE WARNE–MURALITHARAN TROPHY

		Captains					
Season	*Australia*	*Sri Lanka*	*T*	*A*	*SL*	*D*	*Held by*
2007-08*A*	R. T. Ponting	D. P. M. D. Jayawardene	2	2	0	0	A
2011-12*S*	M. J. Clarke	T. M. Dilshan	3	1	0	2	A
2012-13*A*	M. J. Clarke	D. P. M. D. Jayawardene	3	3	0	0	A
2016*S*	S. P. D. Smith	A. D. Mathews	3	0	3	0	SL
2018-19*A*	T. D. Paine	L. D. Chandimal	2	2	0	0	A
	In Australia.........................		15	13	0	2	
	In Sri Lanka........................		16	6	4	6	
	Totals..............................		31	19	4	8	

A   Played in Australia.   S   Played in Sri Lanka.

The following deputised for the official touring captain or was appointed by the home authority for only a minor proportion of the series:
[1]P. A. de Silva (Third). [2]A. C. Gilchrist (First).

SERIES RECORDS

Highest score	A	219	M. J. Slater at Perth......................	1995-96
	SL	192	K. C. Sangakkara at Hobart...............	2007-08
Best bowling	A	7-39	M. S. Kasprowicz at Darwin..............	2004
	SL	7-64	H. M. R. K. B. Herath at Colombo (SSC).....	2016
Highest total	A	617-5 dec	at Perth...............................	1995-96
	SL	547-8 dec	at Colombo (SSC)......................	1992-93
Lowest total	A	106	at Galle..............................	2016
	SL	97	at Darwin............................	2004

AUSTRALIA v ZIMBABWE

		Captains				
Season	*Australia*	*Zimbabwe*	*T*	*A*	*Z*	*D*
1999-2000*Z*	S. R. Waugh	A. D. R. Campbell	1	1	0	0
2003-04*A*	S. R. Waugh	H. H. Streak	2	2	0	0
	In Australia....................		2	2	0	0
	In Zimbabwe		1	1	0	0
	Totals.........................		3	3	0	0

A   Played in Australia.   Z   Played in Zimbabwe.

SERIES RECORDS

Highest score	A	380	M. L. Hayden at Perth...................	2003-04
	Z	118	S. V. Carlisle at Sydney.................	2003-04
Best bowling	A	6-65	S. M. Katich at Sydney..................	2003-04
	Z	6-121	R. W. Price at Sydney	2003-04
Highest total	A	735-6 dec	at Perth...............................	2003-04
	Z	321	at Perth...............................	2003-04
Lowest total	A	403	at Sydney.............................	2003-04
	Z	194	at Harare	1999-2000

AUSTRALIA v BANGLADESH

Season	Australia	*Captains* Bangladesh	T	A	B	D
2003*A*	S. R. Waugh	Khaled Mahmud	2	2	0	0
2005-06*B*	R. T. Ponting	Habibul Bashar	2	2	0	0
2017-18*B*	S. P. D. Smith	Mushfiqur Rahim	2	1	1	0
	In Australia.		2	2	0	0
	In Bangladesh.		4	3	1	0
	Totals		6	5	1	0

A   Played in Australia.   B   Played in Bangladesh.

SERIES RECORDS

Highest score	A	201*	J. N. Gillespie at Chittagong	2005-06
	B	138	Shahriar Nafees at Fatullah	2005-06
Best bowling	A	8-108	S. C. G. MacGill at Fatullah	2005-06
	B	5-62	Mohammad Rafique at Fatullah.	2005-06
Highest total	A	581-4 dec	at Chittagong	2005-06
	B	427	at Fatullah	2005-06
Lowest total	A	217	at Mirpur	2017-18
	B	97	at Darwin	2003

AUSTRALIA v ICC WORLD XI

Season	Australia	ICC World XI	T	A	ICC	D
2005-06*A*	R. T. Ponting	G. C. Smith	1	1	0	0

A   Played in Australia.

SERIES RECORDS

Highest score	A	111	M. L. Hayden at Sydney	2005-06
	Wld	76	V. Sehwag at Sydney	2005-06
Best bowling	A	5-43	S. C. G. MacGill at Sydney	2005-06
	Wld	4-59	A. Flintoff at Sydney	2005-06
Highest total	A	345	at Sydney	2005-06
	Wld	190	at Sydney	2005-06
Lowest total	A	199	at Sydney	2005-06
	Wld	144	at Sydney	2005-06

SOUTH AFRICA v WEST INDIES

Season	South Africa	*Captains* West Indies	T	SA	WI	D
1991-92*W*	K. C. Wessels	R. B. Richardson	1	0	1	0
1998-99*S*	W. J. Cronje	B. C. Lara	5	5	0	0

SIR VIVIAN RICHARDS TROPHY

		Captains					
Season	*South Africa*	*West Indies*	*T*	*SA*	*WI*	*D*	*Held by*
2000-01*W*	S. M. Pollock	C. L. Hooper	5	2	1	2	SA
2003-04*S*	G. C. Smith	B. C. Lara	4	3	0	1	SA
2004-05*W*	G. C. Smith	S. Chanderpaul	4	2	0	2	SA
2007-08 *S*	G. C. Smith	C. H. Gayle[1]	3	2	1	0	SA
2010*W*	G. C. Smith	C. H. Gayle	3	2	0	1	SA
2014-15*S*	H. M. Amla	D. Ramdin	3	2	0	1	SA
2021*W*	**D. Elgar**	**K. C. Brathwaite**	**2**	**2**	**0**	**0**	**SA**
	In South Africa		15	12	1	2	
	In West Indies		**15**	**8**	**2**	**5**	
	Totals		**30**	**20**	**3**	**7**	

S   Played in South Africa.   W   Played in West Indies.

The following deputised for the official touring captain:
   [1]D. J. Bravo (Third).

SERIES RECORDS

Highest score	SA	208	H. M. Amla at Centurion...................	2014-15
	WI	317	C. H. Gayle at St John's	2004-05
Best bowling	SA	7-37	M. Ntini at Port-of-Spain.................	2004-05
	WI	7-84	F. A. Rose at Durban.....................	1998-99
Highest total	SA	658-9 dec	at Durban............................	2003-04
	WI	747	at St John's	2004-05
Lowest total	SA	141	at Kingston	2000-01
	WI	**97**	**at Gros Islet**	**2021**

SOUTH AFRICA v NEW ZEALAND

		Captains				
Season	*South Africa*	*New Zealand*	*T*	*SA*	*NZ*	*D*
1931-32*N*	H. B. Cameron	M. L. Page	2	2	0	0
1952-53*N*	J. E. Cheetham	W. M. Wallace	2	1	0	1
1953-54*S*	J. E. Cheetham	G. O. Rabone[1]	5	4	0	1
1961-62*S*	D. J. McGlew	J. R. Reid	5	2	2	1
1963-64*N*	T. L. Goddard	J. R. Reid	3	0	0	3
1994-95*S*	W. J. Cronje	K. R. Rutherford	3	2	1	0
1994-95*N*	W. J. Cronje	K. R. Rutherford	1	1	0	0
1998-99*N*	W. J. Cronje	D. J. Nash	3	1	0	2
2000-01*S*	S. M. Pollock	S. P. Fleming	3	2	0	1
2003-04*N*	G. C. Smith	S. P. Fleming	3	1	1	1
2005-06*S*	G. C. Smith	S. P. Fleming	3	2	0	1
2007-08*S*	G. C. Smith	D. L. Vettori	2	2	0	0
2011-12*N*	G. C. Smith	L. R. P. L. Taylor	3	1	0	2
2012-13*S*	G. C. Smith	B. B. McCullum	2	2	0	0
2016*S*	F. du Plessis	K. S. Williamson	2	1	0	1
2016-17*N*	F. du Plessis	K. S. Williamson	3	1	0	2
	In New Zealand		20	8	1	11
	In South Africa....................		25	17	3	5
	Totals		45	25	4	16

N   Played in New Zealand.   S   Played in South Africa.

The following deputised for the official touring captain:
   [1]B. Sutcliffe (Fourth and Fifth).

SERIES RECORDS

Highest score	SA	275*	D. J. Cullinan at Auckland	1998-99
	NZ	262	S. P. Fleming at Cape Town	2005-06
Best bowling	SA	8-53	G. B. Lawrence at Johannesburg.	1961-62
	NZ	6-60	J. R. Reid at Dunedin	1963-64
Highest total	SA	621-5 dec	at Auckland	1998-99
	NZ	595	at Auckland	2003-04
Lowest total	SA	148	at Johannesburg.	1953-54
	NZ	45	at Cape Town	2012-13

SOUTH AFRICA v INDIA

		Captains					
Season	*South Africa*		*India*	*T*	*SA*	*I*	*D*
1992-93S	K. C. Wessels	M. Azharuddin		4	1	0	3
1996-97I	W. J. Cronje	S. R. Tendulkar		3	1	2	0
1996-97S	W. J. Cronje	S. R. Tendulkar		3	2	0	1
1999-2000I	W. J. Cronje	S. R. Tendulkar		2	2	0	0
2001-02S†	S. M. Pollock	S. C. Ganguly		2	1	0	1
2004-05I	G. C. Smith	S. C. Ganguly		2	0	1	1
2006-07S	G. C. Smith	R. Dravid		3	2	1	0
2007-08I	G. C. Smith	A. Kumble[1]		3	1	1	1
2009-10I	G. C. Smith	M. S. Dhoni		2	1	1	0
2010-11S	G. C. Smith	M. S. Dhoni		3	1	1	1
2013-14S	G. C. Smith	M. S. Dhoni		2	1	0	1

THE FREEDOM TROPHY

		Captains						
Season	*South Africa*		*India*	*T*	*SA*	*I*	*D*	*Held by*
2015-16I	H. M. Amla	V. Kohli		4	0	3	1	I
2017-18S	F. du Plessis	V. Kohli		3	2	1	0	SA
2019-20I	F. du Plessis	V. Kohli		3	0	3	0	I
2021-22S	**D. Elgar**	**V. Kohli[2]**		**3**	**2**	**1**	**0**	**SA**
	In South Africa.			**23**	**12**	**4**	**7**	
	In India			19	5	11	3	
	Totals			**42**	**17**	**15**	**10**	

S   Played in South Africa.   I   Played in India.

† *The Third Test at Centurion was stripped of its official status by the ICC after a disciplinary dispute and is excluded.*

The following deputised for the official touring captain or were appointed by the home authority for only a minor proportion of the series:
[1]M. S. Dhoni (Third). [2]K. L. Rahul (Second).

SERIES RECORDS

Highest score	SA	253*	H. M. Amla at Nagpur.	2009-10
	I	319	V. Sehwag at Chennai	2007-08
Best bowling	SA	8-64	L. Klusener at Calcutta	1996-97
	I	**7-61**	**S. N. Thakur at Johannesburg**	**2021-22**
Highest total	SA	620-4 dec	at Centurion	2010-11
	I	643-6 dec	at Kolkata.	2009-10
Lowest total	SA	79	at Nagpur	2015-16
	I	66	at Durban	1996-97

SOUTH AFRICA v PAKISTAN

		Captains					
Season	*South Africa*	*Pakistan*	*T*	*SA*	*P*	*D*	
1994-95*S*	W. J. Cronje	Salim Malik	1	1	0	0	
1997-98*P*	W. J. Cronje	Saeed Anwar	3	1	0	2	
1997-98*S*	W. J. Cronje[1]	Rashid Latif[2]	3	1	1	1	
2002-03*S*	S. M. Pollock	Waqar Younis	2	2	0	0	
2003-04*P*	G. C. Smith	Inzamam-ul-Haq[3]	2	0	1	1	
2006-07*S*	G. C. Smith	Inzamam-ul-Haq	3	2	1	0	
2007-08*P*	G. C. Smith	Shoaib Malik	2	1	0	1	
2010-11*U*	G. C. Smith	Misbah-ul-Haq	2	0	0	2	
2012-13*S*	G. C. Smith	Misbah-ul-Haq	3	3	0	0	
2013-14*U*	G. C. Smith	Misbah-ul-Haq	2	1	1	0	
2018-19*S*	F. du Plessis[4]	Sarfraz Ahmed	3	3	0	0	
2020-21*P*	**Q. de Kock**	**Babar Azam**	**2**	**0**	**2**	**0**	
	In South Africa..................		15	12	2	1	
	In Pakistan		**9**	**2**	**3**	**4**	
	In United Arab Emirates		4	1	1	2	
	Totals..........................		**28**	**15**	**6**	**7**	

S   Played in South Africa.   P   Played in Pakistan.   U   Played in United Arab Emirates.

The following deputised for the official touring captain or were appointed by the home authority for only a minor proportion of the series:
[1]G. Kirsten (First). [2]Aamir Sohail (First and Second). [3]Yousuf Youhana *later known as Mohammad Yousuf* (First). [4]D. Elgar (Third).

SERIES RECORDS

Highest score	SA	278*	A. B. de Villiers at Abu Dhabi	2010-11
	P	146	Khurram Manzoor at Abu Dhabi.............	2013-14
Best bowling	SA	7-29	K. J. Abbott at Centurion	2012-13
	P	6-78	Mushtaq Ahmed at Durban.................	1997-98
		6-78	Waqar Younis at Port Elizabeth	1997-98
Highest total	SA	620-7 dec	at Cape Town	2002-03
	P	456	at Rawalpindi	1997-98
Lowest total	SA	124	at Port Elizabeth	2006-07
	P	49	at Johannesburg.........................	2012-13

SOUTH AFRICA v SRI LANKA

		Captains					
Season	*South Africa*	*Sri Lanka*	*T*	*SA*	*SL*	*D*	
1993-94*SL*	K. C. Wessels	A. Ranatunga	3	1	0	2	
1997-98*SA*	W. J. Cronje	A. Ranatunga	2	2	0	0	
2000*SL*	S. M. Pollock	S. T. Jayasuriya	3	1	1	1	
2000-01*SA*	S. M. Pollock	S. T. Jayasuriya	3	2	0	1	
2002-03*SL*	S. M. Pollock	S. T. Jayasuriya[1]	2	2	0	0	
2004*SL*	G. C. Smith	M. S. Atapattu	2	0	1	1	
2006*SL*	A. G. Prince	D. P. M. D. Jayawardene	2	0	2	0	
2011-12*SA*	G. C. Smith	T. M. Dilshan	3	2	1	0	
2014*SL*	H. M. Amla	A. D. Mathews	2	1	0	1	
2016-17*SA*	F. du Plessis	A. D. Mathews	3	3	0	0	

		Captains					
Season	*South Africa*		*Sri Lanka*	*T*	*SA*	*SL*	*D*
2018*SL*	F. du Plessis		R. A. S. Lakmal	2	0	2	0
2018-19*SA*	F. du Plessis		F. D. M. Karunaratne	2	0	2	0
2020-21*SA*	**Q. de Kock**		**F. D. M. Karunaratne**	**2**	**2**	**0**	**0**
	In South Africa..........................			17	13	3	1
	In Sri Lanka.............................			14	3	6	5
	Totals...................................			31	16	9	6

SA   Played in South Africa.   SL   Played in Sri Lanka.

The following deputised for the official captain:
[1]M. S. Atapattu (Second).

SERIES RECORDS

Highest score	SA	224	J. H. Kallis at Cape Town..................	2011-12
	SL	374	D. P. M. D. Jayawardene at Colombo (SSC)...	2006
Best bowling	SA	9-129	K. A. Maharaj at Colombo (SSC)...........	2018
	SL	7-84	M. Muralitharan at Galle.................	2000
Highest total	SA	**621**	**at Centurion**...........................	**2020-21**
	SL	756-5 dec	at Colombo (SSC)......................	2006
Lowest total	SA	73	at Galle..............................	2018
	SL	95	at Cape Town..........................	2000-01

SOUTH AFRICA v ZIMBABWE

		Captains					
Season	*South Africa*		*Zimbabwe*	*T*	*SA*	*Z*	*D*
1995-96*Z*	W. J. Cronje		A. Flower	1	1	0	0
1999-2000*S*	W. J. Cronje		A. D. R. Campbell	1	1	0	0
1999-2000*Z*	W. J. Cronje		A. Flower	1	1	0	0
2001-02*Z*	S. M. Pollock		H. H. Streak	2	1	0	1
2004-05*S*	G. C. Smith		T. Taibu	2	2	0	0
2014-15*Z*	H. M. Amla		B. R. M. Taylor	1	1	0	0
2017-18*S*	A. B. de Villiers		A. G. Cremer	1	1	0	0
	In Zimbabwe			5	4	0	1
	In South Africa..................			4	4	0	0
	Totals			9	8	0	1

S   Played in South Africa.   Z   Played in Zimbabwe.

SERIES RECORDS

Highest score	SA	220	G. Kirsten at Harare.....................	2001-02
	Z	199*	A. Flower at Harare.....................	2001-02
Best bowling	SA	8-71	A. A. Donald at Harare	1995-96
	Z	5-101	B. C. Strang at Harare	1995-96
Highest total	SA	600-3 dec	at Harare	2001-02
	Z	419-9 dec	at Bulawayo...........................	2001-02
Lowest total	SA	346	at Harare	1995-96
	Z	54	at Cape Town..........................	2004-05

SOUTH AFRICA v BANGLADESH

		Captains				
Season	*South Africa*	*Bangladesh*	*T*	*SA*	*B*	*D*
2002-03S	S. M. Pollock[1]	Khaled Mashud	2	2	0	0
2003B	G. C. Smith	Khaled Mahmud	2	2	0	0
2007-08B	G. C. Smith	Mohammad Ashraful	2	2	0	0
2008-09S	G. C. Smith	Mohammad Ashraful	2	2	0	0
2015B	H. M. Amla	Mushfiqur Rahim	2	0	0	2
2017-18S	F. du Plessis	Mushfiqur Rahim	2	2	0	0
	In South Africa....................		6	6	0	0
	In Bangladesh.....................		6	4	0	2
	Totals		12	10	0	2

S   Played in South Africa.   B   Played in Bangladesh.

The following deputised for the official captain:
  [1]M. V. Boucher (First).

SERIES RECORDS

Highest score	SA	232	G. C. Smith at Chittagong	2007-08
	B	77	Mominul Haque at Potchefstroom..........	2017-18
Best bowling	SA	5-19	M. Ntini at East London	2002-03
	B	6-27	Shahadat Hossain at Mirpur..............	2007-08
Highest total	SA	583-7 dec	at Chittagong	2007-08
	B	326	at Chittagong	2015
Lowest total	SA	170	at Mirpur	2007-08
	B	90	at Potchefstroom	2017-18

WEST INDIES v NEW ZEALAND

		Captains				
Season	*West Indies*	*New Zealand*	*T*	*WI*	*NZ*	*D*
1951-52N	J. D. C. Goddard	B. Sutcliffe	2	1	0	1
1955-56N	D. St E. Atkinson	J. R. Reid[1]	4	3	1	0
1968-69N	G. S. Sobers	G. T. Dowling	3	1	1	1
1971-72W	G. S. Sobers	G. T. Dowling[2]	5	0	0	5
1979-80N	C. H. Lloyd	G. P. Howarth	3	0	1	2
1984-85W	I. V. A. Richards	G. P. Howarth	4	2	0	2
1986-87N	I. V. A. Richards	J. V. Coney	3	1	1	1
1994-95N	C. A. Walsh	K. R. Rutherford	2	1	0	1
1995-96W	C. A. Walsh	L. K. Germon	2	1	0	1
1999-2000N	B. C. Lara	S. P. Fleming	2	0	2	0
2002W	C. L. Hooper	S. P. Fleming	2	0	1	1
2005-06N	S. Chanderpaul	S. P. Fleming	3	0	2	1
2008-09N	C. H. Gayle	D. L. Vettori	2	0	0	2
2012W	D. J. G. Sammy	L. R. P. L. Taylor	2	2	0	0
2013-14N	D. J. G. Sammy	B. B. McCullum	3	0	2	1
2014W	D. Ramdin	B. B. McCullum	3	1	2	0
2017-18N	J. O. Holder[3]	K. S. Williamson	2	0	2	0
2020-21N	J. O. Holder	K. S. Williamson[4]	2	0	2	0
	In New Zealand..................		31	7	14	10
	In West Indies...................		18	6	3	9
	Totals		49	13	17	19

N   Played in New Zealand.   W   Played in West Indies.

The following deputised for the official touring captain or were appointed by the home authority for only a minor proportion of the series:
  [1]H. B. Cave (First). [2]B. E. Congdon (Third, Fourth and Fifth). [3]K. C. Brathwaite (Second). [4]T. W. M. Latham (Second).

SERIES RECORDS

Highest score	WI	258	S. M. Nurse at Christchurch		1968-69
	NZ	259	G. M. Turner at Georgetown		1971-72
Best bowling	WI	7-37	C. A. Walsh at Wellington		1994-95
	NZ	7-27	C. L. Cairns at Hamilton		1999-2000
Highest total	WI	660-5 dec	at Wellington		1994-95
	NZ	609-9 dec	at Dunedin (University)		2013-14
Lowest total	WI	77	at Auckland		1955-56
	NZ	74	at Dunedin		1955-56

WEST INDIES v INDIA

Season	West Indies	*Captains* India	T	WI	I	D
1948-49*I*	J. D. C. Goddard	L. Amarnath	5	1	0	4
1952-53*W*	J. B. Stollmeyer	V. S. Hazare	5	1	0	4
1958-59*I*	F. C. M. Alexander	Ghulam Ahmed[1]	5	3	0	2
1961-62*W*	F. M. M. Worrell	N. J. Contractor[2]	5	5	0	0
1966-67*I*	G. S. Sobers	Nawab of Pataudi jnr	3	2	0	1
1970-71*I*	G. S. Sobers	A. L. Wadekar	5	0	1	4
1974-75*I*	C. H. Lloyd	Nawab of Pataudi jnr[3]	5	3	2	0
1975-76*W*	C. H. Lloyd	B. S. Bedi	4	2	1	1
1978-79*I*	A. I. Kallicharran	S. M. Gavaskar	6	0	1	5
1982-83*W*	C. H. Lloyd	Kapil Dev	5	2	0	3
1983-84*I*	C. H. Lloyd	Kapil Dev	6	3	0	3
1987-88*I*	I. V. A. Richards	D. B. Vengsarkar[4]	4	1	1	2
1988-89*W*	I. V. A. Richards	D. B. Vengsarkar	4	3	0	1
1994-95*I*	C. A. Walsh	M. Azharuddin	3	1	1	1
1996-97*W*	C. A. Walsh[5]	S. R. Tendulkar	5	1	0	4
2001-02*W*	C. L. Hooper	S. C. Ganguly	5	2	1	2
2002-03*I*	C. L. Hooper	S. C. Ganguly	3	0	2	1
2005-06*W*	B. C. Lara	R. Dravid	4	0	1	3
2011*W*	D. J. G. Sammy	M. S. Dhoni	3	0	1	2
2011-12*I*	D. J. G. Sammy	M. S. Dhoni	3	0	2	1
2013-14*I*	D. J. G. Sammy	M. S. Dhoni	2	0	2	0
2016*W*	J. O. Holder	V. Kohli	4	0	2	2
2018-19*I*	J. O. Holder[6]	V. Kohli	2	0	2	0
2019*W*	J. O. Holder	V. Kohli	2	0	2	0
In India			47	14	13	20
In West Indies			51	16	9	26
Totals			98	30	22	46

I Played in India.   *W Played in West Indies.*

The following deputised for the official touring captain or were appointed by the home authority for only a minor proportion of the series:
[1]P. R. Umrigar (First), M. H. Mankad (Fourth), H. R. Adhikari (Fifth). [2]Nawab of Pataudi jnr (Third, Fourth and Fifth). [3]S. Venkataraghavan (Second). [4]R. J. Shastri (Fourth). [5]B. C. Lara (Third). [6]K. C. Brathwaite (First).

SERIES RECORDS

Highest score	WI	256	R. B. Kanhai at Calcutta		1958-59
	I	236*	S. M. Gavaskar at Madras		1983-84
Best bowling	WI	9-95	J. M. Noreiga at Port-of-Spain		1970-71
	I	9-83	Kapil Dev at Ahmedabad		1983-84
Highest total	WI	644-8 dec	at Delhi		1958-59
	I	649-9 dec	at Rajkot		2018-19
Lowest total	WI	100	at North Sound		2019
	I	75	at Delhi		1987-88

WEST INDIES v PAKISTAN

		Captains				
Season	*West Indies*	*Pakistan*	*T*	*WI*	*P*	*D*
1957-58*W*	F. C. M. Alexander	A. H. Kardar	5	3	1	1
1958-59*P*	F. C. M. Alexander	Fazal Mahmood	3	1	2	0
1974-75*P*	C. H. Lloyd	Intikhab Alam	2	0	0	2
1976-77*W*	C. H. Lloyd	Mushtaq Mohammad	5	2	1	2
1980-81*P*	C. H. Lloyd	Javed Miandad	4	1	0	3
1986-87*P*	I. V. A. Richards	Imran Khan	3	1	1	1
1987-88*W*	I. V. A. Richards[1]	Imran Khan	3	1	1	1
1990-91*P*	D. L. Haynes	Imran Khan	3	1	1	1
1992-93*W*	R. B. Richardson	Wasim Akram	3	2	0	1
1997-98*P*	C. A. Walsh	Wasim Akram	3	0	3	0
1999-2000*W*	J. C. Adams	Moin Khan	3	1	0	2
2001-02*U*	C. L. Hooper	Waqar Younis	2	0	2	0
2004-05*W*	S. Chanderpaul	Inzamam-ul-Haq[2]	2	1	1	0
2006-07*P*	B. C. Lara	Inzamam-ul-Haq	3	0	2	1
2010-11*W*	D. J. G. Sammy	Misbah-ul-Haq	2	1	1	0
2016-17*U*	J. O. Holder	Misbah-ul-Haq	3	1	2	0
2016-17*W*	J. O. Holder	Misbah-ul-Haq	3	1	2	0
2021*W*	**K. C. Brathwaite**	**Babar Azam**	**2**	**1**	**1**	**0**
	In West Indies.................		28	13	8	7
	In Pakistan........................		21	4	9	8
	In United Arab Emirates		5	1	4	0
	Totals........................		**54**	**18**	**21**	**15**

P Played in Pakistan.   W Played in West Indies.   U Played in United Arab Emirates.

The following were appointed by the home authority or deputised for the official touring captain for a minor proportion of the series:
[1]C. G. Greenidge (First). [2]Younis Khan (First).

SERIES RECORDS

Highest score	WI	365*	G. S. Sobers at Kingston..................	1957-58
	P	337	Hanif Mohammad at Bridgetown............	1957-58
Best bowling	WI	8-29	C. E. H. Croft at Port-of-Spain..........	1976-77
	P	7-80	Imran Khan at Georgetown................	1987-88
Highest total	WI	790-3 dec	at Kingston	1957-58
	P	657-8 dec	at Bridgetown	1957-58
Lowest total	WI	53	at Faisalabad	1986-87
	P	77	at Lahore	1986-87

WEST INDIES v SRI LANKA

		Captains				
Season	*West Indies*	*Sri Lanka*	*T*	*WI*	*SL*	*D*
1993-94*S*	R. B. Richardson	A. Ranatunga	1	0	0	1
1996-97*W*	C. A. Walsh	A. Ranatunga	2	1	0	1
2001-02*S*	C. L. Hooper	S. T. Jayasuriya	3	0	3	0
2003*W*	B. C. Lara	H. P. Tillekeratne	2	1	0	1
2005*S*	S. Chanderpaul	M. S. Atapattu	2	0	2	0
2007-08*W*	C. H. Gayle	D. P. M. D. Jayawardene	2	1	1	0
2010-11*S*	D. J. G. Sammy	K. C. Sangakkara	3	0	0	3

THE SOBERS–TISSERA TROPHY

		Captains					
Season	West Indies	Sri Lanka	T	WI	SL	D	Held by
2015-16S	J. O. Holder	A. D. Mathews	2	0	2	0	SL
2018W	J. O. Holder	L. D. Chandimal[1]	3	1	1	1	SL
2020-21W	**K. C. Brathwaite**	**F. D. M. Karunaratne**	**2**	**0**	**0**	**2**	**SL**
2021-22S	**K. C. Brathwaite**	**F. D. M. Karunaratne**	**2**	**0**	**2**	**0**	**SL**
	In West Indies..................		**11**	**4**	**2**	**5**	
	In Sri Lanka...................		**13**	**0**	**9**	**4**	
	Totals..........................		**24**	**4**	**11**	**9**	

W   Played in West Indies.   S   Played in Sri Lanka.

The following deputised for the official touring captain:
  [1]R. A. S. Lakmal (Third).

SERIES RECORDS

Highest score	WI	333	C. H. Gayle at Galle	2010-11
	SL	204*	H. P. Tillekeratne at Colombo (SSC)	2001-02
Best bowling	WI	8-62	S. T. Gabriel at Gros Islet	2018
	SL	8-46	M. Muralitharan at Kandy.................	2005
Highest total	WI	580-9 dec	at Galle	2010-11
	SL	627-9 dec	at Colombo (SSC)......................	2001-02
Lowest total	WI	93	at Bridgetown	2018
	SL	150	at Kandy	2005

WEST INDIES v ZIMBABWE

		Captains				
Season	West Indies	Zimbabwe	T	WI	Z	D
1999-2000W	J. C. Adams	A. Flower	2	2	0	0

THE CLIVE LLOYD TROPHY

		Captains					
Season	West Indies	Zimbabwe	T	WI	Z	D	Held by
2001Z	C. L. Hooper	H. H. Streak	2	1	0	1	WI
2003-04Z	B. C. Lara	H. H. Streak	2	1	0	1	WI
2012-13W	D. J. G. Sammy	B. R. M. Taylor	2	2	0	0	WI
2017-18Z	J. O. Holder	A. G. Cremer	2	1	0	1	WI
	In West Indies		4	4	0	0	
	In Zimbabwe		6	3	0	3	
	Totals		10	7	0	3	

W   Played in West Indies.   Z   Played in Zimbabwe.

SERIES RECORDS

Highest score	WI	191	B. C. Lara at Bulawayo.................	2003-04
	Z	147	H. Masakadza at Bulawayo.............	2017-18
Best bowling	WI	6-49	S. Shillingford at Bridgetown.........	2012-13
	Z	6-73	R. W. Price at Harare.................	2003-04
Highest total	WI	559-6 dec	at Bulawayo........................	2001
	Z	563-9 dec	at Harare	2001
Lowest total	WI	128	at Bulawayo........................	2003-04
	Z	63	at Port-of-Spain.....................	1999-2000

WEST INDIES v BANGLADESH

	Captains					
Season	*West Indies*	*Bangladesh*	*T*	*WI*	*B*	*D*
2002-03*B*	R. D. Jacobs	Khaled Mashud	2	2	0	0
2003-04*W*	B. C. Lara	Habibul Bashar	2	1	0	1
2009*W*	F. L. Reifer	Mashrafe bin Mortaza[1]	2	0	2	0
2011-12*B*	D. J. G. Sammy	Mushfiqur Rahim	2	1	0	1
2012-13*B*	D. J. G. Sammy	Mushfiqur Rahim	2	2	0	0
2014-15*W*	D. Ramdin	Mushfiqur Rahim	2	2	0	0
2018*W*	J. O. Holder	Shakib Al Hasan	2	2	0	0
2018-19*B*	K. C. Brathwaite	Shakib Al Hasan	2	0	2	0
2020-21*B*	**K. C. Brathwaite**	**Mominul Haque**	**2**	**2**	**0**	**0**
	In West Indies		8	5	2	1
	In Bangladesh		**10**	**7**	**2**	**1**
	Totals..........................		18	12	4	2

B Played in Bangladesh.   W Played in West Indies.

The following deputised for the official touring captain for a minor proportion of the series:
[1]Shakib Al Hasan (Second).

SERIES RECORDS

Highest score	WI	261*	R. R. Sarwan at Kingston	2003-04
	B	136	Mahmudullah at Mirpur	2018-19
Best bowling	WI	6-3	J. J. C. Lawson at Dhaka.................	2002-03
	B	7-58	Mehedi Hasan at Mirpur	2018-19
Highest total	WI	648-9 dec	at Khulna	2012-13
	B	556	at Mirpur	2012-13
Lowest total	WI	111	at Mirpur	2018-19
	B	43	at North Sound......................	2018

WEST INDIES v AFGHANISTAN

	Captains					
Season	*West Indies*	*Afghanistan*	*T*	*WI*	*Afg*	*D*
2019-20*I*	J. O. Holder	Rashid Khan	1	1	0	0
	In India..........................		1	1	0	0
	Totals..........................		1	1	0	0

I Played in India.

SERIES RECORDS

Highest score	*WI*	111	S. S. J. Brooks at Lucknow		2019-20
	Afg	62	Javed Ahmadi at Lucknow		2019-20
Best bowling	*WI*	7-75	R. R. S. Cornwall at Lucknow		2019-20
	Afg	5-74	Hamza Hotak at Lucknow.		2019-20
Highest total	*WI*	277	at Lucknow		2019-20
	Afg	187	at Lucknow		2019-20
Lowest total	*WI*	277	at Lucknow		2019-20
	Afg	120	at Lucknow		2019-20

NEW ZEALAND v INDIA

		Captains				
Season	*New Zealand*	*India*	*T*	*NZ*	*I*	*D*
1955-56*I*	H. B. Cave	P. R. Umrigar[1]	5	0	2	3
1964-65*I*	J. R. Reid	Nawab of Pataudi jnr	4	0	1	3
1967-68*N*	G. T. Dowling[2]	Nawab of Pataudi jnr	4	1	3	0
1969-70*I*	G. T. Dowling	Nawab of Pataudi jnr	3	1	1	1
1975-76*N*	G. M. Turner	B. S. Bedi[3]	3	1	1	1
1976-77*I*	G. M. Turner	B. S. Bedi	3	0	2	1
1980-81*N*	G. P. Howarth	S. M. Gavaskar	3	1	0	2
1988-89*I*	J. G. Wright	D. B. Vengsarkar	3	1	2	0
1989-90*N*	J. G. Wright	M. Azharuddin	3	1	0	2
1993-94*N*	K. R. Rutherford	M. Azharuddin	1	0	0	1
1995-96*I*	L. K. Germon	M. Azharuddin	3	0	1	2
1998-99*N*†	S. P. Fleming	M. Azharuddin	2	1	0	1
1999-2000*I*	S. P. Fleming	S. R. Tendulkar	3	0	1	2
2002-03*N*	S. P. Fleming	S. C. Ganguly	2	2	0	0
2003-04*I*	S. P. Fleming	S. C. Ganguly[4]	2	0	0	2
2008-09*N*	D. L. Vettori	M. S. Dhoni[5]	3	0	1	2
2010-11*I*	D. L. Vettori	M. S. Dhoni	3	0	1	2
2012-13*I*	L. R. P. L. Taylor	M. S. Dhoni	2	0	2	0
2013-14*N*	B. B. McCullum	M. S. Dhoni	2	1	0	1
2016-17*I*	K. S. Williamson[6]	V. Kohli	3	0	3	0
2019-20*N*	K. S. Williamson	V. Kohli	2	2	0	0
2021*E*‡	**K. S. Williamson**	**V. Kohli**	**1**	**1**	**0**	**0**
2021-22*I*	K. S. Williamson[8]	**V. Kohli**[7]	**2**	**0**	**1**	**1**
	In India		36	2	17	17
	In New Zealand		25	10	5	10
	In England		**1**	**1**	**0**	**0**
	Totals.		62	13	22	27

I   Played in India.   N   Played in New Zealand.   E   Played in England.

†   *The First Test at Dunedin was abandoned without a ball being bowled and is excluded.*

‡   *World Test Championship final.*

The following deputised for the official touring captain or were appointed by the home authority for a minor proportion of the series:
[1]Ghulam Ahmed (First). [2]B. W. Sinclair (First). [3]S. M. Gavaskar (First). [4]R. Dravid (Second). [5]V. Sehwag (Second). [6]L. R. P. L. Taylor (Second). [7]A. M. Rahane (First). [8]T. W. M. Latham (Second).

SERIES RECORDS

Highest score	*NZ*	302	B. B. McCullum at Wellington		2013-14
	I	231	M. H. Mankad at Madras		1955-56
Best bowling	*NZ*	**10-119**	**A. Y. Patel at Mumbai**		**2021-22**
	I	8-72	S. Venkataraghavan at Delhi		1964-65
Highest total	*NZ*	680-8 dec	at Wellington		2013-14
	I	583-7 dec	at Ahmedabad		1999-2000
Lowest total	*NZ*	**62**	**at Mumbai**		**2021-22**
	I	81	at Wellington		1975-76

NEW ZEALAND v PAKISTAN

Season	New Zealand	Captains	Pakistan	T	NZ	P	D
1955-56*P*	H. B. Cave		A. H. Kardar	3	0	2	1
1964-65*N*	J. R. Reid		Hanif Mohammad	3	0	0	3
1964-65*P*	J. R. Reid		Hanif Mohammad	3	0	2	1
1969-70*P*	G. T. Dowling		Intikhab Alam	3	1	0	2
1972-73*N*	B. E. Congdon		Intikhab Alam	3	0	1	2
1976-77*P*	G. M. Turner[1]		Mushtaq Mohammad	3	0	2	1
1978-79*N*	M. G. Burgess		Mushtaq Mohammad	3	0	1	2
1984-85*P*	J. V. Coney		Zaheer Abbas	3	0	2	1
1984-85*N*	G. P. Howarth		Javed Miandad	3	2	0	1
1988-89*N†*	J. G. Wright		Imran Khan	2	0	0	2
1990-91*P*	M. D. Crowe		Javed Miandad	3	0	3	0
1992-93*N*	K. R. Rutherford		Javed Miandad	1	0	1	0
1993-94*N*	K. R. Rutherford		Salim Malik	3	1	2	0
1995-96*N*	L. K. Germon		Wasim Akram	1	0	1	0
1996-97*P*	L. K. Germon		Saeed Anwar	2	1	1	0
2000-01*N*	S. P. Fleming		Moin Khan[2]	3	1	1	1
2002*P‡*	S. P. Fleming		Waqar Younis	1	0	1	0
2003-04*N*	S. P. Fleming		Inzamam-ul-Haq	2	0	1	1
2009-10*N*	D. L. Vettori		Mohammad Yousuf	3	1	1	1
2010-11*N*	D. L. Vettori		Misbah-ul-Haq	2	0	1	1
2014-15*U*	B. B. McCullum		Misbah-ul-Haq	3	1	1	1
2016-17*N*	K. S. Williamson		Misbah-ul-Haq[3]	2	2	0	0
2018-19*U*	K. S. Williamson		Sarfraz Ahmed	3	2	1	0
2020-21*N*	**K. S. Williamson**		**Mohammad Rizwan**	**2**	**2**	**0**	**0**
	In Pakistan			21	2	13	6
	In New Zealand			**33**	**9**	**10**	**14**
	In United Arab Emirates			6	3	2	1
	Totals			**60**	**14**	**25**	**21**

N   Played in New Zealand.   P   Played in Pakistan.   U   Played in United Arab Emirates.

†   *The First Test at Dunedin was abandoned without a ball being bowled and is excluded.*
‡   *The Second Test at Karachi was cancelled owing to civil disturbances.*

The following were appointed by the home authority for only a minor proportion of the series or deputised for the official touring captain:
[1]J. M. Parker (Third). [2]Inzamam-ul-Haq (Third). [3]Azhar Ali (Second).

SERIES RECORDS

Highest score	NZ	**238**	K. S. Williamson at Christchurch	**2020-21**
	P	329	Inzamam-ul-Haq at Lahore	2002
Best bowling	NZ	7-52	C. Pringle at Faisalabad	1990-91
	P	8-41	Yasir Shah at Dubai	2018-19
Highest total	NZ	690	at Sharjah	2014-15
	P	643	at Lahore	2002
Lowest total	NZ	70	at Dacca	1955-56
	P	102	at Faisalabad	1990-91

NEW ZEALAND v SRI LANKA

Season	New Zealand	Captains	Sri Lanka	T	NZ	SL	D
1982-83*N*	G. P. Howarth		D. S. de Silva	2	2	0	0
1983-84*S*	G. P. Howarth		L. R. D. Mendis	3	2	0	1
1986-87*St†*	J. J. Crowe		L. R. D. Mendis	1	0	0	1

		Captains				
Season	New Zealand	Sri Lanka	T	NZ	SL	D
1990-91N	M. D. Crowe[1]	A. Ranatunga	3	0	0	3
1992-93S	M. D. Crowe	A. Ranatunga	2	0	1	1
1994-95N	K. R. Rutherford	A. Ranatunga	2	0	1	1
1996-97N	S. P. Fleming	A. Ranatunga	2	2	0	0
1997-98S	S. P. Fleming	A. Ranatunga	3	1	2	0
2003S	S. P. Fleming	H. P. Tillekeratne	2	0	0	2
2004-05N	S. P. Fleming	M. S. Atapattu	2	1	0	1
2006-07N	S. P. Fleming	D. P. M. D. Jayawardene	2	1	1	0
2009S	D. L. Vettori	K. C. Sangakkara	2	0	2	0
2012-13S	L. R. P. L. Taylor	D. P. M. D. Jayawardene	2	1	1	0
2014-15N	B. B. McCullum	A. D. Mathews	2	2	0	0
2015-16N	B. B. McCullum	A. D. Mathews	2	2	0	0
2018-19N	K. S. Williamson	L. D. Chandimal	2	1	0	1
2019S	K. S. Williamson	F. D. M. Karunaratne	2	1	1	0
	In New Zealand		19	11	2	6
	In Sri Lanka		17	5	7	5
	Totals		36	16	9	11

N   Played in New Zealand.   S   Played in Sri Lanka.

† *The Second and Third Tests were cancelled owing to civil disturbances.*

The following was appointed by the home authority for only a minor proportion of the series:
[1]I. D. S. Smith (Third).

SERIES RECORDS

Highest score	NZ	299	M. D. Crowe at Wellington		1990-91
	SL	267	P. A. de Silva at Wellington		1990-91
Best bowling	NZ	7-130	D. L. Vettori at Wellington		2006-07
	SL	6-43	H. M. R. K. B. Herath at Galle		2012-13
Highest total	NZ	671-4	at Wellington		1990-91
	SL	498	at Napier		2004-05
Lowest total	NZ	102	at Colombo (SSC)		1992-93
	SL	93	at Wellington		1982-83

NEW ZEALAND v ZIMBABWE

		Captains				
Season	New Zealand	Zimbabwe	T	NZ	Z	D
1992-93Z	M. D. Crowe	D. L. Houghton	2	1	0	1
1995-96N	L. K. Germon	A. Flower	2	0	0	2
1997-98Z	S. P. Fleming	A. D. R. Campbell	2	0	0	2
1997-98N	S. P. Fleming	A. D. R. Campbell	2	2	0	0
2000-01Z	S. P. Fleming	H. H. Streak	2	2	0	0
2000-01N	S. P. Fleming	H. H. Streak	1	0	0	1
2005-06Z	S. P. Fleming	T. Taibu	2	2	0	0
2011-12Z	L. R. P. L. Taylor	B. R. M. Taylor	1	1	0	0
2011-12N	L. R. P. L. Taylor	B. R. M. Taylor	1	1	0	0
2016Z	K. S. Williamson	A. G. Cremer	2	2	0	0
	In New Zealand		6	3	0	3
	In Zimbabwe		11	8	0	3
	Totals		17	11	0	6

N   Played in New Zealand.   Z   Played in Zimbabwe.

SERIES RECORDS

Highest score	NZ	173*	L. R. P. L. Taylor at Bulawayo.............	2016
	Z	203*	G. J. Whittall at Bulawayo	1997-98
Best bowling	NZ	6-26	C. S. Martin at Napier...................	2011-12
	Z	8-109	P. A. Strang at Bulawayo	2000-01
Highest total	NZ	582-4 dec	at Bulawayo...........................	2016
	Z	461	at Bulawayo...........................	1997-98
Lowest total	NZ	207	at Harare	1997-98
	Z	51	at Napier	2011-12

NEW ZEALAND v BANGLADESH

		Captains					
Season	*New Zealand*	*Bangladesh*	*T*	*NZ*	*B*	*D*	
2001-02N	S. P. Fleming	Khaled Mashud	2	2	0	0	
2004-05B	S. P. Fleming	Khaled Mashud	2	2	0	0	
2007-08N	D. L. Vettori	Mohammad Ashraful	2	2	0	0	
2008-09B	D. L. Vettori	Mohammad Ashraful	2	1	0	1	
2009-10N	D. L. Vettori	Shakib Al Hasan	1	1	0	0	
2013-14B	B. B. McCullum	Mushfiqur Rahim	2	0	0	2	
2016-17N	K. S. Williamson	Mushfiqur Rahim[1]	2	2	0	0	
2018-19N†	K. S. Williamson	Mahmudullah	2	2	0	0	
2021-22N	**T. W. M. Latham**	**Mominul Haque**	**2**	**1**	**1**	**0**	
	In New Zealand		**11**	**10**	**1**	**0**	
	In Bangladesh.......................		**6**	**3**	**0**	**3**	
	Totals...............................		**17**	**13**	**1**	**3**	

B   Played in Bangladesh.   N   Played in New Zealand.

†   *The Third Test was cancelled owing to a terrorist attack on a nearby mosque.*

The following deputised for the official touring captain for only a minor proportion of the series:
[1]Tamim Iqbal (Second).

SERIES RECORDS

Highest score	NZ	**252**	**T. W. M. Latham at Christchurch.........**	**2021-22**
	B	217	Shakib Al Hasan at Wellington.............	2016-17
Best bowling	NZ	7-53	C. L. Cairns at Hamilton.................	2001-02
	B	7-36	Shakib Al Hasan at Chittagong............	2008-09
Highest total	NZ	715-6 dec	at Hamilton...........................	2018-19
	B	595-8 dec	at Wellington..........................	2016-17
Lowest total	NZ	**169**	**at Mount Maunganui ....**	**2021-22**
	B	108	at Hamilton	2001-02

INDIA v PAKISTAN

		Captains					
Season	*India*	*Pakistan*	*T*	*I*	*P*	*D*	
1952-53I	L. Amarnath	A. H. Kardar	5	2	1	2	
1954-55P	M. H. Mankad	A. H. Kardar	5	0	0	5	
1960-61I	N. J. Contractor	Fazal Mahmood	5	0	0	5	
1978-79P	B. S. Bedi	Mushtaq Mohammad	3	0	2	1	
1979-80I	S. M. Gavaskar[1]	Asif Iqbal	6	2	0	4	
1982-83P	S. M. Gavaskar	Imran Khan	6	0	3	3	
1983-84I	Kapil Dev	Zaheer Abbas	3	0	0	3	
1984-85P	S. M. Gavaskar	Zaheer Abbas	2	0	0	2	
1986-87I	Kapil Dev	Imran Khan	5	0	1	4	
1989-90P	K. Srikkanth	Imran Khan	4	0	0	4	
1998-99I	M. Azharuddin	Wasim Akram	2	1	1	0	

Season	India	Pakistan	T	I	P	D
		Captains				
1998-99*I*†	M. Azharuddin	Wasim Akram	1	0	1	0
2003-04*P*	S. C. Ganguly[2]	Inzamam-ul-Haq	3	2	1	0
2004-05*I*	S. C. Ganguly	Inzamam-ul-Haq	3	1	1	1
2005-06*P*	R. Dravid	Inzamam-ul-Haq[3]	3	0	1	2
2007-08*I*	A. Kumble	Shoaib Malik[4]	3	1	0	2
	In India		33	7	5	21
	In Pakistan		26	2	7	17
	Totals		59	9	12	38

I Played in India.   P Played in Pakistan.

† *This Test was part of the Asian Test Championship and was not counted as part of the preceding bilateral series.*

The following were appointed by the home authority for only a minor proportion of the series or deputised for the official touring captain:
[1]G. R. Viswanath (Sixth). [2]R. Dravid (First and Second). [3]Younis Khan (Third). [4]Younis Khan (Second and Third).

SERIES RECORDS

Highest score	*I*	309	V. Sehwag at Multan	2003-04
	P	280*	Javed Miandad at Hyderabad	1982-83
Best bowling	*I*	10-74	A. Kumble at Delhi	1998-99
	P	8-60	Imran Khan at Karachi	1982-83
Highest total	*I*	675-5 dec	at Multan	2003-04
	P	699-5	at Lahore	1989-90
Lowest total	*I*	106	at Lucknow	1952-53
	P	116	at Bangalore	1986-87

INDIA v SRI LANKA

Season	India	Sri Lanka	T	I	SL	D
		Captains				
1982-83*I*	S. M. Gavaskar	B. Warnapura	1	0	0	1
1985-86*S*	Kapil Dev	L. R. D. Mendis	3	0	1	2
1986-87*I*	Kapil Dev	L. R. D. Mendis	3	2	0	1
1990-91*I*	M. Azharuddin	A. Ranatunga	1	1	0	0
1993-94*S*	M. Azharuddin	A. Ranatunga	3	1	0	2
1993-94*I*	M. Azharuddin	A. Ranatunga	3	3	0	0
1997-98*S*	S. R. Tendulkar	A. Ranatunga	2	0	0	2
1997-98*I*	S. R. Tendulkar	A. Ranatunga	3	0	0	3
1998-99*S*†	M. Azharuddin	A. Ranatunga	1	0	0	1
2001*S*	S. C. Ganguly	S. T. Jayasuriya	3	1	2	0
2005-06*I*	R. Dravid[1]	M. S. Atapattu	3	2	0	1
2008*S*	A. Kumble	D. P. M. D. Jayawardene	3	1	2	0
2009-10*I*	M. S. Dhoni	K. C. Sangakkara	3	2	0	1
2010*S*	M. S. Dhoni	K. C. Sangakkara	3	1	1	1
2015-16*S*	V. Kohli	A. D. Mathews	3	2	1	0
2017*S*	V. Kohli	L. D. Chandimal[2]	3	3	0	0
2017-18*I*	V. Kohli	L. D. Chandimal	3	1	0	2
	In India		20	11	0	9
	In Sri Lanka		24	9	7	8
	Totals		44	20	7	17

I Played in India.   S Played in Sri Lanka.

† *This Test was part of the Asian Test Championship.*

The following were appointed by the home authority for only a minor proportion of the series:
[1]V. Sehwag (Third). [2]H. M. R. K. B. Herath (First).

SERIES RECORDS

Highest score	_I_	293	V. Sehwag at Mumbai (BS)...............	2009-10
	_SL_	340	S. T. Jayasuriya at Colombo (RPS).........	1997-98
Best bowling	_I_	7-51	Maninder Singh at Nagpur	1986-87
	_SL_	8-87	M. Muralitharan at Colombo (SSC)	2001
Highest total	_I_	726-9 dec	at Mumbai (BS).......................	2009-10
	_SL_	952-6 dec	at Colombo (RPS).....................	1997-98
Lowest total	_I_	112	at Galle.............................	2015-16
	_SL_	82	at Chandigarh........................	1990-91

INDIA v ZIMBABWE

		Captains				
Season	_India_	_Zimbabwe_	_T_	_I_	_Z_	_D_
1992-93_Z_	M. Azharuddin	D. L. Houghton	1	0	0	1
1992-93_I_	M. Azharuddin	D. L. Houghton	1	1	0	0
1998-99_Z_	M. Azharuddin	A. D. R. Campbell	1	0	1	0
2000-01_I_	S. C. Ganguly	H. H. Streak	2	1	0	1
2001_Z_	S. C. Ganguly	H. H. Streak	2	1	1	0
2001-02_I_	S. C. Ganguly	S. V. Carlisle	2	2	0	0
2005-06_Z_	S. C. Ganguly	T. Taibu	2	2	0	0
	In India..............		5	4	0	1
	In Zimbabwe		6	3	2	1
	Totals		11	7	2	2

I Played in India.   Z Played in Zimbabwe.

SERIES RECORDS

Highest score	_I_	227	V. G. Kambli at Delhi	1992-93
	_Z_	232*	A. Flower at Nagpur	2000-01
Best bowling	_I_	7-59	I. K. Pathan at Harare.....................	2005-06
	_Z_	6-73	H. H. Streak at Harare	2005-06
Highest total	_I_	609-6 dec	at Nagpur	2000-01
	_Z_	503-6	at Nagpur	2000-01
Lowest total	_I_	173	at Harare...............................	1998-99
	_Z_	146	at Delhi................................	2001-02

INDIA v BANGLADESH

		Captains				
Season	_India_	_Bangladesh_	_T_	_I_	_B_	_D_
2000-01_B_	S. C. Ganguly	Naimur Rahman	1	1	0	0
2004-05_B_	S. C. Ganguly	Habibul Bashar	2	2	0	0
2007_B_	R. Dravid	Habibul Bashar	2	1	0	1
2009-10_B_	M. S. Dhoni[1]	Shakib Al Hasan	2	2	0	0
2015_B_	V. Kohli	Mushfiqur Rahim	1	0	0	1
2016-17_I_	V. Kohli	Mushfiqur Rahim	1	1	0	0
2019-20_I_	V. Kohli	Mominul Haque	2	2	0	0
	In Bangladesh..................		8	6	0	2
	In India........................		3	3	0	0
	Totals		11	9	0	2

B Played in Bangladesh.   I Played in India.

The following deputised for the official touring captain for a minor proportion of the series:
[1]V. Sehwag (First).

SERIES RECORDS

Highest score	*I*	248*	S. R. Tendulkar at Dhaka	2004-05
	B	158*	Mohammad Ashraful at Chittagong	2004-05
Best bowling	*I*	7-87	Zaheer Khan at Mirpur	2009-10
	B	6-132	Naimur Rahman at Dhaka	2000-01
Highest total	*I*	687-6 dec	at Hyderabad	2016-17
	B	400	at Dhaka	2000-01
Lowest total	*I*	243	at Chittagong	2009-10
	B	91	at Dhaka	2000-01

INDIA v AFGHANISTAN

		Captains				
Season	*India*	*Afghanistan*	*T*	*I*	*Afg*	*D*
2018*I*	A. M. Rahane	Asghar Stanikzai†	1	1	0	0
	In India			1	1	0	0
	Totals			1	1	0	0

I Played in India.

† *Later known as Asghar Afghan.*

SERIES RECORDS

Highest score	*I*	107	S. Dhawan at Bangalore	2018
	Afg	36*	Hashmatullah Shahidi at Bangalore	2018
Best bowling	*I*	4-17	R. A. Jadeja at Bangalore	2018
	Afg	3-51	Yamin Ahmadzai at Bangalore	2018
Highest total	*I*	474	at Bangalore	2018
	Afg	109	at Bangalore	2018
Lowest total	*I*	474	at Bangalore	2018
	Afg	103	at Bangalore	2018

PAKISTAN v SRI LANKA

		Captains				
Season	*Pakistan*	*Sri Lanka*	*T*	*P*	*SL*	*D*
1981-82*P*	Javed Miandad	B. Warnapura[1]	3	2	0	1
1985-86*P*	Javed Miandad	L. R. D. Mendis	3	2	0	1
1985-86*S*	Imran Khan	L. R. D. Mendis	3	1	1	1
1991-92*P*	Imran Khan	P. A. de Silva	3	1	0	2
1994-95*S*†	Salim Malik	A. Ranatunga	2	2	0	0
1995-96*P*	Ramiz Raja	A. Ranatunga	3	1	2	0
1996-97*S*	Ramiz Raja	A. Ranatunga	2	0	0	2
1998-99*P*‡	Wasim Akram	H. P. Tillekeratne	1	0	0	1
1998-99*B*‡	Wasim Akram	P. A. de Silva	1	1	0	0
1999-2000*P*	Saeed Anwar[2]	S. T. Jayasuriya	3	1	2	0
2000*S*	Moin Khan	S. T. Jayasuriya	3	2	0	1
2001-02*P*‡	Waqar Younis	S. T. Jayasuriya	1	0	1	0
2004-05*P*	Inzamam-ul-Haq	M. S. Atapattu	2	1	1	0
2005-06*S*	Inzamam-ul-Haq	D. P. M. D. Jayawardene	2	1	0	1
2008-09*P*§	Younis Khan	D. P. M. D. Jayawardene	2	0	0	2
2009*S*	Younis Khan	K. C. Sangakkara	3	0	2	1
2011-12*U*	Misbah-ul-Haq	T. M. Dilshan	3	1	0	2

		Captains				
Season	*Pakistan*	*Sri Lanka*	*T*	*P*	*SL*	*D*
2012*S*	Misbah-ul-Haq[3]	D. P. M. D. Jayawardene	3	0	1	2
2013-14*U*	Misbah-ul-Haq	A. D. Mathews	3	1	1	1
2014*S*	Misbah-ul-Haq	A. D. Mathews	2	0	2	0
2015*S*	Misbah-ul-Haq	A. D. Mathews	3	2	1	0
2017-18*U*	Sarfraz Ahmed	L. D. Chandimal	2	0	2	0
2019-20*P*	Azhar Ali	F. D. M. Karunaratne	2	1	0	1
	In Pakistan		23	9	6	8
	In Sri Lanka		23	8	7	8
	In Bangladesh		1	1	0	0
	In United Arab Emirates		8	2	3	3
	Totals		55	20	16	19

P   Played in Pakistan.   S   Played in Sri Lanka.   B   Played in Bangladesh.
U   Played in United Arab Emirates.

† *One Test was cancelled owing to the threat of civil disturbances following a general election.*
‡ *These Tests were part of the Asian Test Championship.*
§ *The Second Test ended after a terrorist attack on the Sri Lankan team bus on the third day.*

The following deputised for the official touring captain or were appointed by the home authority for only a minor proportion of the series:
[1]L. R. D. Mendis (Second). [2]Moin Khan (Third). [3]Mohammad Hafeez (First).

SERIES RECORDS

Highest score	*P*	313	Younis Khan at Karachi	2008-09
	SL	253	S. T. Jayasuriya at Faisalabad	2004-05
Best bowling	*P*	8-58	Imran Khan at Lahore	1981-82
	SL	9-127	H. M. R. K. B. Herath at Colombo (SSC)	2014
Highest total	*P*	765-6 dec	at Karachi	2008-09
	SL	644-7 dec	at Karachi	2008-09
Lowest total	*P*	90	at Colombo (PSS)	2009
	SL	71	at Kandy	1994-95

PAKISTAN v ZIMBABWE

		Captains				
Season	*Pakistan*	*Zimbabwe*	*T*	*P*	*Z*	*D*
1993-94*P*	Wasim Akram[1]	A. Flower	3	2	0	1
1994-95*Z*	Salim Malik	A. Flower	3	2	1	0
1996-97*P*	Wasim Akram	A. D. R. Campbell	2	1	0	1
1997-98*Z*	Rashid Latif	A. D. R. Campbell	2	1	0	1
1998-99*P*†	Aamir Sohail[2]	A. D. R. Campbell	2	0	1	1
2002-03*Z*	Waqar Younis	A. D. R. Campbell	2	2	0	0
2011-12*Z*	Misbah-ul-Haq	B. R. M. Taylor	1	1	0	0
2013-14*Z*	Misbah-ul-Haq	B. R. M. Taylor[3]	2	1	1	0
2020-21*Z*	**Babar Azam**	**B. R. M. Taylor**	**2**	**2**	**0**	**0**
	In Pakistan		7	3	1	3
	In Zimbabwe		**12**	**9**	**2**	**1**
	Totals		19	12	3	4

P   Played in Pakistan.   Z   Played in Zimbabwe.

† *The Third Test at Faisalabad was abandoned without a ball being bowled and is excluded.*

The following were appointed by the home authority for only a minor proportion of the series:
[1]Waqar Younis (First). [2]Moin Khan (Second). [3]H. Masakadza (First).

SERIES RECORDS

Highest score	P	257*	Wasim Akram at Sheikhupura	1996-97
	Z	201*	G. W. Flower at Harare	1994-95
Best bowling	P	7-66	Saqlain Mushtaq at Bulawayo..............	2002-03
	Z	6-90	H. H. Streak at Harare	1994-95
Highest total	P	553	at Sheikhupura..........................	1996-97
	Z	544-4 dec	at Harare	1994-95
Lowest total	P	103	at Peshawar	1998-99
	Z	120	at Harare	2013-14

PAKISTAN v BANGLADESH

		Captains				
Season	Pakistan	Bangladesh	T	P	B	D
2001-02P†	Waqar Younis	Naimur Rahman	1	1	0	0
2001-02B	Waqar Younis	Khaled Mashud	2	2	0	0
2003-04P	Rashid Latif	Khaled Mahmud	3	3	0	0
2011-12B	Misbah-ul-Haq	Mushfiqur Rahim	2	2	0	0
2014-15B	Misbah-ul-Haq	Mushfiqur Rahim	2	1	0	1
2019-20P‡	Azhar Ali	Mominul Haque	1	1	0	0
2021-22B	**Babar Azam**	**Mominul Haque**	**2**	**2**	**0**	**0**
	In Pakistan		5	5	0	0
	In Bangladesh....................		**8**	**7**	**0**	**1**
	Totals........................		13	12	0	1

P   Played in Pakistan.   B   Played in Bangladesh.

†   *This Test was part of the Asian Test Championship.*
‡   *The Second Test at Karachi was postponed because of the Covid-19 crisis.*

SERIES RECORDS

Highest score	P	226	Azhar Ali at Mirpur	2014-15
	B	206	Tamim Iqbal at Khulna	2014-15
Best bowling	P	**8-42**	**Sajid Khan at Mirpur**	**2021-22**
	B	**7-116**	**Taijul Islam at Chittagong**	**2021-22**
Highest total	P	628	at Khulna	2014-15
	B	555-6	at Khulna	2014-15
Lowest total	P	175	at Multan	2003-04
	B	**87**	**at Mirpur**	**2021-22**

PAKISTAN v IRELAND

		Captains				
Season	Pakistan	Ireland	T	P	Ire	D
2018Ire	Sarfraz Ahmed	W. T. S. Porterfield	1	1	0	0
	In Ireland		1	1	0	0
	Totals..........................		1	1	0	0

Ire   Played in Ireland.

SERIES RECORDS

Highest score	*P*	83	Fahim Ashraf at Malahide	2018
	Ire	118	K. J. O'Brien at Malahide.....................	2018
Best bowling	*P*	5-66	Mohammad Abbas at Malahide	2018
	Ire	4-45	T. J. Murtagh at Malahide......................	2018
Highest total	*P*	310-9 dec	at Malahide..................................	2018
	Ire	339	at Malahide..................................	2018
Lowest total	*Ire*	130	at Malahide..................................	2018

SRI LANKA v ZIMBABWE

		Captains					
Season	*Sri Lanka*		*Zimbabwe*	*T*	*SL*	*Z*	*D*
1994-95Z	A. Ranatunga		A. Flower	3	0	0	3
1996-97S	A. Ranatunga		A. D. R. Campbell	2	2	0	0
1997-98S	A. Ranatunga		A. D. R. Campbell	2	2	0	0
1999-2000Z	S. T. Jayasuriya		A. Flower	3	1	0	2
2001-02S	S. T. Jayasuriya		S. V. Carlisle	3	3	0	0
2003-04Z	M. S. Atapattu		T. Taibu	2	2	0	0
2016-17Z	H. M. R. K. B. Herath		A. G. Cremer	2	2	0	0
2017S	L. D. Chandimal		A. G. Cremer	1	1	0	0
2019-20Z	F. D. M. Karunaratne		S. C. Williams	2	1	0	1
	In Sri Lanka..............................			8	8	0	0
	In Zimbabwe..............................			12	6	0	6
	Totals.................................			20	14	0	6

S Played in Sri Lanka.   Z Played in Zimbabwe.

SERIES RECORDS

Highest score	*SL*	270	K. C. Sangakkara at Bulawayo	2003-04
	Z	266	D. L. Houghton at Bulawayo...............	1994-95
Best bowling	*SL*	9-51	M. Muralitharan at Kandy	2001-02
	Z	7-113	Sikandar Raza at Harare	2019-20
Highest total	*SL*	713-3 dec	at Bulawayo..................................	2003-04
	Z	462-9 dec	at Bulawayo..................................	1994-95
Lowest total	*SL*	218	at Bulawayo..................................	1994-95
	Z	79	at Galle..................................	2001-02

SRI LANKA v BANGLADESH

		Captains					
Season	*Sri Lanka*		*Bangladesh*	*T*	*SL*	*B*	*D*
2001-02S†	S. T. Jayasuriya		Naimur Rahman	1	1	0	0
2002S	S. T. Jayasuriya		Khaled Mashud	2	2	0	0
2005-06S	M. S. Atapattu		Habibul Bashar	2	2	0	0
2005-06B	D. P. M. D. Jayawardene		Habibul Bashar	2	2	0	0
2007S	D. P. M. D. Jayawardene		Mohammad Ashraful	3	3	0	0
2008-09B	D. P. M. D. Jayawardene		Mohammad Ashraful	2	2	0	0
2012-13S	A. D. Mathews		Mushfiqur Rahim	2	1	0	1
2013-14B	A. D. Mathews		Mushfiqur Rahim	2	1	0	1

	Captains					
Season	*Sri Lanka*	*Bangladesh*	*T*	*SL*	*B*	*D*
2016-17*S*	H. M. R. K. B. Herath	Mushfiqur Rahim	2	1	1	0
2017-18*B*	L. D. Chandimal	Mahmudullah	2	1	0	1
2020-21*S*	**F. D. M. Karunaratne**	**Mominul Haque**	**2**	**1**	**0**	**1**
	In Sri Lanka...............................		14	11	1	2
	In Bangladesh		8	6	0	2
	Totals		22	17	1	4

S Played in Sri Lanka.   B Played in Bangladesh.

† *This Test was part of the Asian Test Championship.*

SERIES RECORDS

Highest score	SL	319	K. C. Sangakkara at Chittagong.............	2013-14
	B	200	Mushfiqur Rahim at Galle	2012-13
Best bowling	SL	7-89	H. M. R. K. B. Herath at Colombo (RPS)	2012-13
	B	5-70	Shakib Al Hasan at Mirpur	2008-09
Highest total	SL	730-6 dec	at Mirpur	2013-14
	B	638	at Galle.............................	2012-13
Lowest total	SL	222	at Mirpur	2017-18
	B	62	at Colombo (PSS)	2007

ZIMBABWE v BANGLADESH

	Captains					
Season	*Zimbabwe*	*Bangladesh*	*T*	*Z*	*B*	*D*
2000-01*Z*	H. H. Streak	Naimur Rahman	2	2	0	0
2001-02*B*	B. A. Murphy[1]	Naimur Rahman	2	1	0	1
2003-04*Z*	H. H. Streak	Habibul Bashar	2	1	0	1
2004-05*B*	T. Taibu	Habibul Bashar	2	0	1	1
2011-12*Z*	B. R. M. Taylor	Shakib Al Hasan	1	1	0	0
2012-13*Z*	B. R. M. Taylor	Mushfiqur Rahim	2	1	1	0
2014-15*B*	B. R. M. Taylor	Mushfiqur Rahim	3	0	3	0
2018-19*B*	H. Masakadza	Mahmudullah	2	1	1	0
2019-20*B*	C. R. Ervine	Mominul Haque	1	0	1	0
2021*Z*	**B. R. M. Taylor**	**Mominul Haque**	**1**	**0**	**1**	**0**
	In Zimbabwe..........................		8	5	2	1
	In Bangladesh........................		10	2	6	2
	Totals.............................		18	7	8	3

Z Played in Zimbabwe.   B Played in Bangladesh.

The following deputised for the official touring captain:

[1]S. V. Carlisle (Second).

SERIES RECORDS

Highest score	Z	171	B. R. M. Taylor at Harare	2012-13
	B	219*	Mushfiqur Rahim at Mirpur................	2018-19
Best bowling	Z	6-59	D. T. Hondo at Dhaka....................	2004-05
	B	8-39	Taijul Islam at Mirpur	2014-15
Highest total	Z	542-7 dec	at Chittagong	2001-02
	B	560-6 dec	at Mirpur	2019-20
Lowest total	Z	114	at Mirpur	2014-15
	B	107	at Dhaka.............................	2001-02

ZIMBABWE v AFGHANISTAN

		Captains		T	Zim	Afg	D
Season	Zimbabwe		Afghanistan				
2020-21U	S. C. Williams		Asghar Afghan	2	1	1	0
	In United Arab Emirates............			2	1	1	0
	Totals............................			2	1	1	0

U Played in United Arab Emirates.

SERIES RECORDS

Highest score	Z	151*	S. C. Williams at Abu Dhabi.............	2020-21
	Afg	200*	Hashmatullah Shahidi at Abu Dhabi......	2020-21
Best bowling	Z	4-48	B. Muzarabani at Abu Dhabi............	2020-21
	Afg	7-137	Rashid Khan at Abu Dhabi.............	2020-21
Highest total	Z	365	at Abu Dhabi.........................	2020-21
	Afg	545-4 dec	at Abu Dhabi.........................	2020-21
Lowest total	Z	250	at Abu Dhabi.........................	2020-21
	Afg	131	at Abu Dhabi.........................	2020-21

BANGLADESH v AFGHANISTAN

		Captains		T	B	Afg	D
Season	Bangladesh		Afghanistan				
2019-20B	Shakib Al Hasan		Rashid Khan	1	0	1	0
	In Bangladesh.....................			1	0	1	0
	Totals...........................			1	0	1	0

B Played in Bangladesh.

SERIES RECORDS

Highest score	B	52	Mominul Haque at Chittagong...............	2019-20
	Afg	102	Rahmat Shah at Chittagong	2019-20
Best bowling	B	4-116	Taijul Islam at Chittagong	2019-20
	Afg	6-49	Rashid Khan at Chittagong.................	2019-20
Highest total	B	205	at Chittagong.............................	2019-20
	Afg	342	at Chittagong.............................	2019-20
Lowest total	B	173	at Chittagong.............................	2019-20
	Afg	260	at Chittagong.............................	2019-20

IRELAND v AFGHANISTAN

		Captains		T	Ire	Afg	D
Season	Ireland		Afghanistan				
2018-19I	W. T. S. Porterfield		Asghar Afghan	1	0	1	0
	In India........................			1	0	1	0
	Totals..........................			1	0	1	0

I Played in India.

SERIES RECORDS

Highest score	*Ire*	82	A. Balbirnie at Dehradun	2018-19
	Afg	98	Rahmat Shah at Dehradun....................	2018-19
Best bowling	*Ire*	3-28	S. R. Thompson at Dehradun	2018-19
	Afg	5-82	Rashid Khan at Dehradun	2018-19
Highest total	*Ire*	288	at Dehradun.............................	2018-19
	Afg	314	at Dehradun.............................	2018-19
Lowest total	*Ire*	172	at Dehradun.............................	2018-19
	Afg	314	at Dehradun.............................	2018-19

TEST GROUNDS

in chronological order

	City and Ground	*First Test Match*		*Tests*
1	**Melbourne, Melbourne Cricket Ground**	**March 15, 1877**	A v E	**114**
2	**London, Kennington Oval**	**September 6, 1880**	E v A	**103**
3	**Sydney, Sydney Cricket Ground (No. 1)**	**February 17, 1882**	A v E	**110**
4	Manchester, Old Trafford	July 11, 1884	E v A	82
5	**London, Lord's**	**July 21, 1884**	E v A	**141**
6	**Adelaide, Adelaide Oval**	**December 12, 1884**	A v E	**80**
7	Port Elizabeth, St George's Park	March 12, 1889	SA v E	31
8	**Cape Town, Newlands**	**March 25, 1889**	SA v E	**59**
9	Johannesburg, Old Wanderers	March 2, 1896	SA v E	22
	Now the site of Johannesburg Railway Station.			
10	**Nottingham, Trent Bridge**	**June 1, 1899**	E v A	**64**
11	**Leeds, Headingley**	**June 29, 1899**	E v A	**79**
12	**Birmingham, Edgbaston**	**May 29, 1902**	E v A	**53**
13	Sheffield, Bramall Lane	July 3, 1902	E v A	1
	Sheffield United Football Club have built a stand over the cricket pitch.			
14	Durban, Lord's	January 21, 1910	SA v E	4
	Ground destroyed and built on.			
15	Durban, Kingsmead	January 18, 1923	SA v E	44
16	Brisbane, Exhibition Ground	November 30, 1928	A v E	2
	No longer used for cricket.			
17	Christchurch, Lancaster Park	January 10, 1930	NZ v E	40
	Also known under sponsors' names.			
18	Bridgetown, Kensington Oval	January 11, 1930	WI v E	54
19	Wellington, Basin Reserve	January 24, 1930	NZ v E	65
20	Port-of-Spain, Queen's Park Oval	February 1, 1930	WI v E	61
21	Auckland, Eden Park	February 14, 1930	NZ v E	50
22	Georgetown, Bourda	February 21, 1930	WI v E	30
23	**Kingston, Sabina Park**	**April 3, 1930**	**WI v E**	**54**
24	**Brisbane, Woolloongabba**	**November 27, 1931**	**A v SA**	**64**
25	Bombay, Gymkhana Ground	December 15, 1933	I v E	1
	No longer used for first-class cricket.			
26	Calcutta (*now Kolkata*), Eden Gardens	January 5, 1934	I v E	42
27	**Madras (*now Chennai*),**	**February 10, 1934**	**I v E**	**34**
	Chepauk (Chidambaram Stadium)			
28	Delhi, Feroz Shah Kotla	November 10, 1948	I v WI	34
29	Bombay (*now Mumbai*), Brabourne Stadium	December 9, 1948	I v WI	18
	Rarely used for first-class cricket.			
30	Johannesburg, Ellis Park	December 27, 1948	SA v E	6
	Mainly a football and rugby stadium, no longer used for cricket.			
31	**Kanpur, Green Park (Modi Stadium)**	**January 12, 1952**	**I v E**	**23**
32	Lucknow, University Ground	October 25, 1952	I v P	1
	Ground destroyed, now partly under a river bed.			

	City and Ground	*First Test Match*		*Tests*
33	Dacca (*now Dhaka*),	January 1, 1955	P v I	17
	Dacca (*now Bangabandhu*) Stadium			
	Originally in East Pakistan, now Bangladesh, no longer used for cricket.			
34	Bahawalpur, Dring (*now Bahawal*) Stadium	January 15, 1955	P v I	1
	Still used for first-class cricket.			
35	Lahore, Lawrence Gardens (Bagh-e-Jinnah)	January 29, 1955	P v I	3
	Still used for club and occasional first-class matches.			
36	Peshawar, Services Ground	February 13, 1955	P v I	1
	Superseded by new stadium.			
37	**Karachi, National Stadium**	**February 26, 1955**	**P v I**	**43**
38	Dunedin, Carisbrook	March 11, 1955	NZ v E	10
39	Hyderabad, Fateh Maidan (Lal Bahadur Stadium)	November 19, 1955	I v NZ	3
40	Madras, Corporation Stadium	January 6, 1956	I v NZ	9
	Superseded by rebuilt Chepauk Stadium.			
41	**Johannesburg, Wanderers**	**December 24, 1956**	**SA v E**	**43**
42	Lahore, Gaddafi Stadium	November 21, 1959	P v A	40
43	Rawalpindi, Pindi Club Ground	March 27, 1965	P v NZ	1
	Superseded by new stadium.			
44	Nagpur, Vidarbha CA Ground	October 3, 1969	I v NZ	9
	Superseded by new stadium.			
45	Perth, Western Australian CA Ground	December 11, 1970	A v E	44
	Superseded by new stadium.			
46	Hyderabad, Niaz Stadium	March 16, 1973	P v E	5
47	Bangalore, Karnataka State CA Ground	November 22, 1974	I v WI	23
	(Chinnaswamy Stadium)			
48	**Bombay (*now Mumbai*), Wankhede Stadium**	**January 23, 1975**	**I v WI**	**26**
49	Faisalabad, Iqbal Stadium	October 16, 1978	P v I	24
50	Napier, McLean Park	February 16, 1979	NZ v P	10
51	Multan, Ibn-e-Qasim Bagh Stadium	December 30, 1980	P v WI	1
	Superseded by new stadium.			
52	St John's (Antigua), Recreation Ground	March 27, 1981	WI v E	22
53	Colombo, P. Saravanamuttu Stadium/	February 17, 1982	SL v E	22
	P. Sara Oval			
54	Kandy, Asgiriya Stadium	April 22, 1983	SL v A	21
	Superseded by new stadium at Pallekele.			
55	Jullundur, Burlton Park	September 24, 1983	I v P	1
56	**Ahmedabad, Sardar Patel (Gujarat) Stadium**	**November 12, 1983**	**I v WI**	**14**
	Now known as Narendra Modi Stadium.			
57	Colombo, Sinhalese Sports Club Ground	March 16, 1984	SL v NZ	43
58	Colombo, Colombo Cricket Club Ground	March 24, 1984	SL v NZ	3
59	Sialkot, Jinnah Stadium	October 27, 1985	P v SL	4
60	Cuttack, Barabati Stadium	January 4, 1987	I v SL	2
61	Jaipur, Sawai Mansingh Stadium	February 21, 1987	I v P	1
62	**Hobart, Bellerive Oval**	**December 16, 1989**	**A v SL**	**14**
63	Chandigarh, Sector 16 Stadium	November 23, 1990	I v SL	1
	Superseded by Mohali ground.			
64	Hamilton, Seddon Park	February 22, 1991	NZ v SL	27
	Also known under various sponsors' names.			
65	Gujranwala, Municipal Stadium	December 20, 1991	P v SL	1
66	Colombo, R. Premadasa (Khettarama) Stadium	August 28, 1992	SL v A	9
67	Moratuwa, Tyronne Fernando Stadium	September 8, 1992	SL v A	4
68	**Harare, Harare Sports Club**	**October 18, 1992**	**Z v I**	**39**
69	Bulawayo, Bulawayo Athletic Club	November 1, 1992	Z v NZ	1
	Superseded by Queens Sports Club ground.			
70	Karachi, Defence Stadium	December 1, 1993	P v Z	1
71	**Rawalpindi, Rawalpindi Cricket Stadium**	**December 9, 1993**	**P v Z**	**11**
72	Lucknow, K. D. Singh "Babu" Stadium	January 18, 1994	I v SL	1
73	Bulawayo, Queens Sports Club	October 20, 1994	Z v SL	23
74	Mohali, Punjab Cricket Association Stadium	December 10, 1994	I v WI	13
75	Peshawar, Arbab Niaz Stadium	September 8, 1995	P v SL	6

	City and Ground	First Test Match		Tests
76	**Centurion (*ex Verwoerdburg*), Centurion Park**	**November 16, 1995**	**SA v E**	**27**
77	Sheikhupura, Municipal Stadium	October 17, 1996	P v Z	2
78	St Vincent, Arnos Vale	June 20, 1997	WI v SL	3
79	**Galle, International Stadium**	**June 3, 1998**	**SL v NZ**	**37**
80	Bloemfontein, Springbok Park	October 29, 1999	SA v Z	5
	Also known under various sponsors' names.			
81	Multan, Multan Cricket Stadium	August 29, 2001	P v B	5
82	Chittagong, Chittagong Stadium	November 15, 2001	B v Z	8
	Also known as M. A. Aziz Stadium.			
83	Sharjah, Sharjah Cricket Association Stadium	January 31, 2002	P v WI	9
84	St George's, Grenada, Queen's Park New Stadium	June 28, 2002	WI v NZ	3
85	East London, Buffalo Park	October 18, 2002	SA v B	1
86	Potchefstroom, North West Cricket Stadium	October 25, 2002	SA v B	2
	Now known under sponsor's name.			
87	Chester-le-Street, Riverside Ground	June 5, 2003	E v Z	6
	Also known under sponsor's name.			
88	**Gros Islet, St Lucia, Beausejour Stadium**	**June 20, 2003**	**WI v SL**	**9**
	Now known as Darren Sammy Stadium.			
89	Darwin, Marrara Cricket Ground	July 18, 2003	A v B	2
90	Cairns, Cazaly's Football Park	July 25, 2003	A v B	2
	Also known under sponsor's name.			
91	**Chittagong, Chittagong Divisional Stadium**	**February 28, 2006**	**B v SL**	**21**
	Also known as Bir Shrestha Shahid Ruhul Amin Stadium/Zohur Ahmed Chowdhury Stadium.			
92	Bogra, Shaheed Chandu Stadium	March 8, 2006	B v SL	1
93	Fatullah, Narayanganj Osmani Stadium	April 9, 2006	B v A	2
94	Basseterre, St Kitts, Warner Park	June 22, 2006	WI v I	3
95	**Mirpur (Dhaka), Shere Bangla Natl Stadium**	**May 25, 2007**	**B v I**	**22**
96	Dunedin, University Oval	January 4, 2008	NZ v B	8
97	Providence Stadium, Guyana	March 22, 2008	WI v SL	2
98	**North Sound, Antigua, Sir Vivian Richards Stadium**	**May 30, 2008**	**WI v A**	**10**
99	Nagpur, Vidarbha CA Stadium, Jamtha	November 6, 2008	I v A	6
100	Cardiff, Sophia Gardens	July 8, 2009	E v A	3
101	Hyderabad, Rajiv Gandhi Intl Stadium	November 12, 2010	I v NZ	5
102	Dubai, Dubai Sports City Stadium	November 12, 2010	P v SA	13
103	**Abu Dhabi, Sheikh Zayed Stadium**	**November 20, 2010**	**P v SA**	**15**
104	**Pallekele, Muttiah Muralitharan Stadium**	**December 1, 2010**	**SL v WI**	**9**
105	**Southampton, Rose Bowl**	**June 16, 2011**	**E v SL**	**7**
	Now known under sponsor's name.			
106	Roseau, Dominica, Windsor Park	July 6, 2011	WI v I	5
107	Khulna, Khulna Division Stadium	November 21, 2012	B v WI	3
	Also known as Bir Shrestha Shahid Flight Lt Motiur Rahman/Shaikh Abu Naser Stadium.			
108	**Christchurch, Hagley Oval**	**December 26, 2014**	**NZ v SL**	**9**
109	Indore, Maharani Usharaje Trust Ground	October 8, 2016	I v NZ	2
110	Rajkot, Saurashtra CA Stadium	November 9, 2016	I v E	2
111	Visakhapatnam, Andhra CA-Visakhapatnam DCA Stadium	November 17, 2016	I v E	2
112	Pune (Gahunje), Subrata Roy Sahara Stadium	February 23, 2017	I v A	2
113	Ranchi, Jharkhand State CA Oval Ground	March 16, 2017	I v A	2
114	Dharamsala, Himachal Pradesh CA Stadium	March 25, 2017	I v A	1
115	Malahide (Dublin), The Village	May 11, 2018	Ire v P	1
116	Sylhet, Sylhet Stadium	November 3, 2018	B v Z	1
117	Perth, Optus Stadium	December 14, 2018	A v I	2
118	Canberra, Manuka Oval	February 1, 2019	A v SL	1
119	Dehradun, Rajiv Gandhi Cricket Stadium	March 15, 2019	Afg v Ire	1
120	**Mount Maunganui, Bay Oval**	**November 21, 2019**	**NZ v E**	**3**
121	Lucknow, Ekana Cricket Stadium	November 27, 2019	Afg v WI	1
	Also known as Bharat Ratna Shri Atal Bihari Vajpayee Ekana Cricket Stadium.			

Bold type denotes grounds used for Test cricket since January 1, 2021.

MEN'S ONE-DAY INTERNATIONAL RECORDS

Matches in this section do not have first-class status.

This section covers men's one-day international cricket to December 31, 2021. Bold type denotes performances in the calendar year 2021, or, in career figures, players who appeared in one-day internationals in that year.

SUMMARY OF MEN'S ONE-DAY INTERNATIONALS

1970-71 to December 31, 2021

	Opponents	Matches															Tied	NR
			E	A	SA	WI	NZ	I	P	SL	Z	B	Ire	Afg	Ass	Oth		
England	Australia	152	63	84	–	–	–	–	–	–	–	–	–	–	–	–	2	3
	South Africa	63	28	–	30	–	–	–	–	–	–	–	–	–	–	–	1	4
	West Indies	102	52	–	–	44	–	–	–	–	–	–	–	–	–	–	–	6
	New Zealand	91	42	–	–	–	43	–	–	–	–	–	–	–	–	–	2	4
	India	103	43	–	–	–	–	55	–	–	–	–	–	–	–	–	2	3
	Pakistan	91	56	–	–	–	–	–	32	–	–	–	–	–	–	–	–	3
	Sri Lanka	78	38	–	–	–	–	–	–	36	–	–	–	–	–	–	1	3
	Zimbabwe	30	21	–	–	–	–	–	–	–	8	–	–	–	–	–	–	1
	Bangladesh	21	17	–	–	–	–	–	–	–	–	4	–	–	–	–	–	–
	Ireland	13	10	–	–	–	–	–	–	–	–	–	2	–	–	–	–	1
	Afghanistan	2	2	–	–	–	–	–	–	–	–	–	–	0	–	–	–	–
	Associates	15	13	–	–	–	–	–	–	–	–	–	–	–	1	–	–	1
Australia	South Africa	103	–	48	51	–	–	–	–	–	–	–	–	–	–	–	3	1
	West Indies	143	–	76	–	61	–	–	–	–	–	–	–	–	–	–	3	3
	New Zealand	138	–	92	–	–	39	–	–	–	–	–	–	–	–	–	–	7
	India	143	–	80	–	–	–	53	–	–	–	–	–	–	–	–	–	10
	Pakistan	104	–	68	–	–	–	–	32	–	–	–	–	–	–	–	1	3
	Sri Lanka	97	–	61	–	–	–	–	–	32	–	–	–	–	–	–	–	4
	Zimbabwe	30	–	27	–	–	–	–	–	–	2	–	–	–	–	–	–	1
	Bangladesh	21	–	19	–	–	–	–	–	–	–	1	–	–	–	–	–	1
	Ireland	5	–	4	–	–	–	–	–	–	–	–	0	–	–	–	–	1
	Afghanistan	3	–	3	–	–	–	–	–	–	–	–	–	0	–	–	–	–
	Associates	16	–	16	–	–	–	–	–	–	–	–	–	–	0	–	–	–
	ICC World XI	3	–	3	–	–	–	–	–	–	–	–	–	–	–	0	–	–
South Africa	West Indies	62	–	–	44	15	–	–	–	–	–	–	–	–	–	–	1	2
	New Zealand	71	–	–	41	–	25	–	–	–	–	–	–	–	–	–	–	5
	India	84	–	–	46	–	–	35	–	–	–	–	–	–	–	–	–	3
	Pakistan	82	–	–	51	–	–	–	30	–	–	–	–	–	–	–	–	1
	Sri Lanka	80	–	–	45	–	–	–	–	33	–	–	–	–	–	–	1	1
	Zimbabwe	41	–	–	38	–	–	–	–	–	2	–	–	–	–	–	–	1
	Bangladesh	21	–	–	17	–	–	–	–	–	–	4	–	–	–	–	–	–
	Ireland	8	–	–	6	–	–	–	–	–	–	–	1	–	–	–	–	1
	Afghanistan	1	–	–	1	–	–	–	–	–	–	–	–	0	–	–	–	–
	Associates	19	–	–	18	–	–	–	–	–	–	–	–	–	0	–	–	1
West Indies	New Zealand	65	–	–	–	30	28	–	–	–	–	–	–	–	–	–	–	7
	India	133	–	–	–	63	–	64	–	–	–	–	–	–	–	–	2	4
	Pakistan	134	–	–	–	71	–	–	60	–	–	–	–	–	–	–	3	–
	Sri Lanka	63	–	–	–	31	–	–	–	29	–	–	–	–	–	–	–	3
	Zimbabwe	48	–	–	–	36	–	–	–	–	10	–	–	–	–	–	1	1
	Bangladesh	41	–	–	–	21	–	–	–	–	–	18	–	–	–	–	–	2
	Ireland	12	–	–	–	10	–	–	–	–	–	–	1	–	–	–	–	1
	Afghanistan	9	–	–	–	5	–	–	–	–	–	–	–	3	–	–	–	1
	Associates	19	–	–	–	18	–	–	–	–	–	–	–	–	1	–	–	–
New Zealand	India	110	–	–	–	–	49	55	–	–	–	–	–	–	–	–	1	5
	Pakistan	107	–	–	–	–	48	–	55	–	–	–	–	–	–	–	1	3
	Sri Lanka	99	–	–	–	–	49	–	–	41	–	–	–	–	–	–	1	8
	Zimbabwe	38	–	–	–	–	27	–	–	–	9	–	–	–	–	–	1	1
	Bangladesh	38	–	–	–	–	28	–	–	–	–	10	–	–	–	–	–	–
	Ireland	4	–	–	–	–	4	–	–	–	–	–	0	–	–	–	–	–
	Afghanistan	2	–	–	–	–	2	–	–	–	–	–	–	0	–	–	–	–
	Associates	12	–	–	–	–	12	–	–	–	–	–	–	–	0	–	–	–
India	Pakistan	132	–	–	–	–	–	55	73	–	–	–	–	–	–	–	–	4
	Sri Lanka	162	–	–	–	–	–	93	–	57	–	–	–	–	–	–	1	11
	Zimbabwe	63	–	–	–	–	–	51	–	–	10	–	–	–	–	–	2	–

	Opponents	Matches	E	A	SA	WI	NZ	I	P	SL	Z	B	Ire	Afg	Ass	Oth	Tied	NR
	Bangladesh	36	–	–	–	–	–	30	–	–	–	5	–	–	–	–	–	1
	Ireland	3	–	–	–	–	–	3	–	–	–	–	0	–	–	–	–	–
	Afghanistan	3	–	–	–	–	–	2	–	–	–	–	–	0	–	–	1	–
	Associates	24	–	–	–	–	–	22	–	–	–	–	–	–	2	–	–	–
Pakistan	Sri Lanka	155	–	–	–	–	–	–	92	58	–	–	–	–	–	–	1	4
	Zimbabwe	62	–	–	–	–	–	–	54	–	5	–	–	–	–	–	1	2
	Bangladesh	37	–	–	–	–	–	–	32	–	–	5	–	–	–	–	–	–
	Ireland	7	–	–	–	–	–	–	5	–	–	–	1	–	–	–	1	–
	Afghanistan	4	–	–	–	–	–	–	4	–	–	–	–	0	–	–	–	–
	Associates	21	–	–	–	–	–	–	21	–	–	–	–	–	0	–	–	–
Sri Lanka	Zimbabwe	57	–	–	–	–	–	–	–	44	11	–	–	–	–	–	–	2
	Bangladesh	51	–	–	–	–	–	–	–	40	–	9	–	–	–	–	–	2
	Ireland	4	–	–	–	–	–	–	–	4	–	–	0	–	–	–	–	–
	Afghanistan	4	–	–	–	–	–	–	–	3	–	–	–	1	–	–	–	–
	Associates	17	–	–	–	–	–	–	–	16	–	–	–	–	1	–	–	–
Zimbabwe	Bangladesh	78	–	–	–	–	–	–	–	–	28	50	–	–	–	–	–	–
	Ireland	16	–	–	–	–	–	–	–	–	7	–	7	–	–	–	1	1
	Afghanistan	25	–	–	–	–	–	–	–	–	10	–	–	15	–	–	–	–
	Associates	50	–	–	–	–	–	–	–	–	38	–	–	–	9	–	1	2
Bangladesh	Ireland	10	–	–	–	–	–	–	–	–	–	7	2	–	–	–	–	1
	Afghanistan	8	–	–	–	–	–	–	–	–	–	5	–	3	–	–	–	–
	Associates	26	–	–	–	–	–	–	–	–	–	18	–	–	8	–	–	–
Ireland	Afghanistan	30	–	–	–	–	–	–	–	–	–	–	13	16	–	–	–	1
	Associates	61	–	–	–	–	–	–	–	–	–	–	45	–	12	–	1	3
Afghanistan	Associates	38	–	–	–	–	–	–	–	–	–	–	–	24	13	–	–	1
Associates	Associates	177	–	–	–	–	–	–	–	–	–	–	–	–	171	–	–	6
Asian CC XI	ICC World XI	1	–	–	–	–	–	–	–	–	–	–	–	–	–	1	–	–
	African XI	6	–	–	–	–	–	–	–	–	–	–	–	–	–	5	–	1
		4,338	385	581	388	405	354	518	490	393	140	136	72	62	218	6	37	153

Associate and Affiliate Members of ICC who have played one-day internationals are Bermuda, Canada, East Africa, Hong Kong, Kenya, Namibia, Nepal, Netherlands, Oman, Papua New Guinea, Scotland, United Arab Emirates and USA. Sri Lanka, Zimbabwe, Bangladesh, Afghanistan and Ireland played one-day internationals before gaining Test status; these are not counted as Associate results.

RESULTS SUMMARY OF MEN'S ONE-DAY INTERNATIONALS

1970-71 to December 31, 2021 (4,338 matches)

	Matches	Won	Lost	Tied	No Result	% Won (excl NR)
South Africa	635	388	221	6	20	63.57
Australia	958	581	334	9	34	63.36
India	996	518	428	9	41	54.71
Pakistan	936	490	418	8	20	53.93
England	761	385	339	8	29	53.14
West Indies	831	405	386	10	30	51.18
Afghanistan	129	62	63	1	3	49.60
New Zealand	775	354	375	6	40	48.57
Sri Lanka	867	393	431	5	38	47.70
Ireland	173	72	88	3	10	45.09
Bangladesh	388	136	245	–	7	35.69
Zimbabwe	538	140	379	7	12	27.28
Oman	21	14	6	–	1	70.00
Asian Cricket Council XI	7	4	2	–	1	66.66
Nepal	16	9	7	–	–	56.25
USA	21	9	12	–	–	42.85

	Matches	Won	Lost	Tied	No Result	% Won (excl NR)
Netherlands	**86**	**34**	**47**	**1**	**4**	**42.07**
Scotland	**121**	**46**	**67**	**1**	**7**	**40.78**
Namibia	**16**	**6**	**10**	**–**	**–**	**37.50**
Hong Kong	26	9	16	–	1	36.00
United Arab Emirates	**61**	**18**	**43**	**–**	**–**	**29.50**
Kenya	154	42	107	–	5	28.18
ICC World XI	4	1	3	–	–	25.00
Canada...................	77	17	58	–	2	22.66
Bermuda	35	7	28	–	–	20.00
Papua New Guinea	**35**	**7**	**28**	**–**	**–**	**20.00**
African XI	6	1	4	–	1	20.00
East Africa................	3	–	3	–	–	0.00

Matches abandoned without a ball bowled are not included except (from 2004) where the toss took place, in accordance with an ICC ruling. Such matches, like those called off after play began, are now counted as official internationals in their own right, even when replayed on another day.
In the percentages of matches won, ties are counted as half a win.
Teams which appeared in 2021 are shown in bold.

BATTING RECORDS

HIGHEST INDIVIDUAL INNINGS

264	R. G. Sharma	India v Sri Lanka at Kolkata....................	2014-15
237*	M. J. Guptill	New Zealand v West Indies at Wellington.........	2014-15
219	V. Sehwag	India v West Indies at Indore	2011-12
215	C. H. Gayle	West Indies v Zimbabwe at Canberra.............	2014-15
210*	Fakhar Zaman	Pakistan v Zimbabwe at Bulawayo	2018
209	R. G. Sharma	India v Australia at Bangalore	2013-14
208*	R. G. Sharma	India v Sri Lanka at Mohali	2017-18
200*	S. R. Tendulkar	India v South Africa at Gwalior	2009-10
194*	C. K. Coventry	Zimbabwe v Bangladesh at Bulawayo.............	2009
194	Saeed Anwar	Pakistan v India at Chennai....................	1996-97
193	**Fakhar Zaman**	**Pakistan v South Africa at Johannesburg**	**2020-21**
189*	I. V. A. Richards	West Indies v England at Manchester	1984
189*	M. J. Guptill	New Zealand v England at Southampton...........	2013
189	S. T. Jayasuriya	Sri Lanka v India at Sharjah...................	2000-01
188*	G. Kirsten	South Africa v UAE at Rawalpindi	1995-96
186*	S. R. Tendulkar	India v New Zealand at Hyderabad	1999-2000
185*	S. R. Watson	Australia v Bangladesh at Mirpur...............	2010-11
185	F. du Plessis	South Africa v Sri Lanka at Cape Town...........	2016-17
183*	M. S. Dhoni	India v Sri Lanka at Jaipur	2005-06
183	S. C. Ganguly	India v Sri Lanka at Taunton	1999
183	V. Kohli	India v Pakistan at Mirpur	2011-12
181*	M. L. Hayden	Australia v New Zealand at Hamilton	2006-07
181*	L. R. P. L. Taylor	New Zealand v England at Dunedin (University) ...	2017-18
181	I. V. A. Richards	West Indies v Sri Lanka at Karachi	1987-88
180*	M. J. Guptill	New Zealand v South Africa at Hamilton	2016-17
180	J. J. Roy	England v Australia at Melbourne	2017-18

The highest individual scores for other Test countries are:

177	P. R. Stirling	Ireland v Canada at Toronto....................	2010
176	Liton Das	Bangladesh v Zimbabwe at Sylhet...............	2019-20
131*	Mohammad Shahzad	Afghanistan v Zimbabwe at Sharjah..............	2015-16

MOST HUNDREDS

S. R. Tendulkar (I). 49	Saeed Anwar (P) 20	**M. J. Guptill (NZ)** **16**
V. Kohli (I). **43**	D. P. M. D. Jayawardene	**J. E. Root (E)** **16**
R. T. Ponting (A/World) . 30	(SL/Asia). 19	Mohammad Yousuf (P/As) 15
R. G. Sharma (I) **29**	B. C. Lara (WI/World) . . . 19	V. Sehwag (I/Wld/Asia) . . 15
S. T. Jayasuriya (SL/Asia) 28	D. A. Warner (A). **18**	W. U. Tharanga (SL). . . . 15
H. M. Amla (SA). 27	M. E. Waugh (A). 18	
A. B. de Villiers (SA) . . . 25	**S. Dhawan (I)**. **17**	*Most hundreds for other*
C. H. Gayle (WI/World) . . 25	A. J. Finch (A). 17	*Test countries:*
K. C. Sangakkara (SL) . . 25	D. L. Haynes (WI). 17	**Tamim Iqbal (B)** **14**
T. M. Dilshan (SL) 22	J. H. Kallis (SA/Wld/Af) . 17	**P. R. Stirling (Ire)** **12**
S. C. Ganguly (I/Asia). . . 22	N. J. Astle (NZ) 17	**B. R. M. Taylor (Z)** **11**
H. H. Gibbs (SA). 21	**Q. de Kock (SA)**. **16**	Mohammad Shahzad (Afg) 6
L. R. P. L. Taylor (NZ) . **21**	A. C. Gilchrist (A/World). 16	

Ponting's total includes one for the World XI, the only hundred for a combined team.

MOST RUNS

		M	I	NO	R	HS	100	Avge
1	S. R. Tendulkar (India)	463	452	41	18,426	200*	49	44.83
2	K. C. Sangakkara (SL/Asia/World).	404	380	41	14,234	169	25	41.98
3	R. T. Ponting (Australia/World)	375	365	39	13,704	164	30	42.03
4	S. T. Jayasuriya (Sri Lanka/Asia)	445	433	18	13,430	189	28	32.36
5	D. P. M. D. Jayawardene (SL/Asia)	448	418	39	12,650	144	19	33.37
6	**V. Kohli (India)**	**254**	**245**	**39**	**12,169**	**183**	**43**	**59.07**
7	Inzamam-ul-Haq (Pakistan/Asia)	378	350	53	11,739	137*	10	39.52
8	J. H. Kallis (S. Africa/World/Africa)	328	314	53	11,579	139	17	44.36
9	S. C. Ganguly (India/Asia)	311	300	23	11,363	183	22	41.02
10	R. Dravid (India/World/Asia)	344	318	40	10,889	153	12	39.16
11	M. S. Dhoni (India/Asia).	350	298	85	10,773	183*	10	50.57
12	C. H. Gayle (West Indies/World)	301	294	17	10,480	215	25	37.83
13	B. C. Lara (West Indies/World)	299	289	32	10,405	169	19	40.48
14	T. M. Dilshan (Sri Lanka).	330	303	41	10,290	161*	22	39.27

The leading aggregates for players who have appeared for other Test countries are:

	M	I	NO	R	HS	100	Avge
L. R. P. L. Taylor (New Zealand)	233	217	39	8,581	181*	21	48.20
E. J. G. Morgan (Ireland/England).	246	228	34	7,701	148	14	39.69
Tamim Iqbal (Bangladesh)	219	217	9	7,666	158	14	36.85
A. Flower (Zimbabwe).	213	208	16	6,786	145	4	35.34
Mohammad Nabi (Afghanistan)	127	114	12	2,817	116	1	27.61

Excluding runs for combined teams, the record aggregate for Sri Lanka is 13,975 in 397 matches by K. C. Sangakkara; for Australia, 13,589 in 374 matches by R. T. Ponting; for Pakistan, 11,701 in 375 matches by Inzamam-ul-Haq; for South Africa, 11,550 in 323 matches by J. H. Kallis; for West Indies, 10,425 in 298 matches by C. H. Gayle; for England, 6,957 in 223 matches by E. J. G. Morgan; and for Ireland, 4,982 in 134 matches by P. R. Stirling.

BEST CAREER STRIKE-RATES BY BATTERS

(Runs per 100 balls. Qualification: 1,000 runs)

SR		Position	M	I	R	Avge
130.22	A. D. Russell (WI)	7/8	56	47	1,034	27.21
123.37	G. J. Maxwell (A)	5/6	116	106	3,230	34.36
118.66	**J. C. Buttler (E)**	**6/7**	**148**	**123**	**3,872**	**38.72**
117.00	Shahid Afridi (P/World/Asia)	2/7	398	369	8,064	23.57
116.90	**H. H. Pandya (I)**	**6/7**	**63**	**46**	**1,286**	**32.97**
114.50	L. Ronchi (A/NZ)	7	85	68	1,397	23.67

SR		Position	M	I	R	Avge
112.08	**N. L. T. C. Perera (SL)**	**7/8**	**166**	**133**	**2,338**	**19.98**
108.72	C. J. Anderson (NZ)	6	49	44	1,109	27.72
107.27	**J. J. Roy (E)**	**1**	**98**	**93**	**3,658**	**40.19**
106.39	**S. O. Hetmyer (WI)**	**4/5**	**47**	**44**	**1,447**	**35.29**
105.01	**J. M. Bairstow (E)**	**2/6**	**89**	**81**	**3,498**	**47.91**
104.69	C. Munro (NZ)	2/6	57	53	1,271	24.92
104.33	V. Sehwag (I/World/Asia)	1/2	251	245	8,273	35.05
104.24	J. P. Faulkner (A)	7/8	69	52	1,032	34.40
103.88	**N. Pooran (WI)**	**5**	**31**	**28**	**1,044**	**47.45**
103.27	**Rashid Khan (Afg)**	**8/9**	**74**	**58**	**1,008**	**20.57**
102.18	K. M. Jadhav (I)	6/7	73	52	1,367	42.09
101.29	**M. M. Ali (E)**	**2/7**	**112**	**89**	**1,877**	**25.02**
101.09	A. B. de Villiers (SA/Africa)	4/5	228	218	9,577	53.50
100.83	**D. A. Miller (SA)**	**5/6**	**137**	**118**	**3,367**	**40.56**
100.05	D. J. G. Sammy (WI)	7/8	126	105	1,871	24.94

Position means a batter's most usual position(s) in the batting order.

FASTEST ONE-DAY INTERNATIONAL FIFTIES

Balls

16	A. B. de Villiers......	South Africa v West Indies at Johannesburg	2014-15
17	S. T. Jayasuriya......	Sri Lanka v Pakistan at Singapore	1995-96
17	M. D. K. J. Perera	Sri Lanka v Pakistan at Pallekele	2015
17	M. J. Guptill	New Zealand v Sri Lanka at Christchurch	2015-16
18	S. P. O'Donnell	Australia v Sri Lanka at Sharjah	1989-90
18	Shahid Afridi........	Pakistan v Sri Lanka at Nairobi	1996-97
18	Shahid Afridi........	Pakistan v Netherlands at Colombo (SSC)............	2002
18	G. J. Maxwell	Australia v India at Bangalore	2013-14
18	Shahid Afridi........	Pakistan v Bangladesh at Mirpur	2013-14
18	B. B. McCullum	New Zealand v England at Wellington...............	2014-15
18	A. J. Finch	Australia v Sri Lanka at Dambulla	2016

FASTEST ONE-DAY INTERNATIONAL HUNDREDS

Balls

31	A. B. de Villiers	South Africa v West Indies at Johannesburg	2014-15
36	C. J. Anderson	New Zealand v West Indies at Queenstown..........	2013-14
37	Shahid Afridi........	Pakistan v Sri Lanka at Nairobi	1996-97
44	M. V. Boucher.......	South Africa v Zimbabwe at Potchefstroom	2006-07
45	B. C. Lara	West Indies v Bangladesh at Dhaka	1999-2000
45	Shahid Afridi........	Pakistan v India at Kanpur.......................	2004-05
46	J. D. Ryder	New Zealand v West Indies at Queenstown..........	2013-14
46	J. C. Buttler	England v Pakistan at Dubai	2015-16
48	S. T. Jayasuriya	Sri Lanka v Pakistan at Singapore	1995-96

HIGHEST PARTNERSHIP FOR EACH WICKET

365	for 1st	J. D. Campbell/S. D. Hope.....	WI v Ire	Clontarf	2019
372	for 2nd	C. H. Gayle/M. N. Samuels....	WI v Z	Canberra.............	2014-15
258	for 3rd	D. M. Bravo/D. Ramdin.......	WI v B	Basseterre	2014-15
275*	for 4th	M. Azharuddin/A. Jadeja......	I v Z	Cuttack	1997-98
256*	for 5th	D. A. Miller/J-P. Duminy	SA v Z	Hamilton	2014-15
267*	for 6th	G. D. Elliott/L. Ronchi.......	NZ v SL	Dunedin	2014-15
177	for 7th	J. C. Buttler/A. U. Rashid	E v NZ	Birmingham	2015
138*	for 8th	J. M. Kemp/A. J. Hall	SA v I	Cape Town	2006-07
132	for 9th	A. D. Mathews/S. L. Malinga ..	SL v A	Melbourne	2010-11
106*	for 10th	I. V. A. Richards/M. A. Holding	WI v E	Manchester	1984

BOWLING RECORDS

BEST BOWLING ANALYSES

8-19	W. P. U. J. C. Vaas	Sri Lanka v Zimbabwe at Colombo (SSC)	2001-02
7-12	Shahid Afridi	Pakistan v West Indies at Providence	2013
7-15	G. D. McGrath	Australia v Namibia at Potchefstroom.	2002-03
7-18	Rashid Khan	Afghanistan v West Indies at Gros Islet	2017
7-20	A. J. Bichel	Australia v England at Port Elizabeth	2002-03
7-30	M. Muralitharan	Sri Lanka v India at Sharjah	2000-01
7-33	T. G. Southee	New Zealand v England at Wellington	2014-15
7-34	T. A. Boult	New Zealand v West Indies at Christchurch	2017-18
7-36	Waqar Younis	Pakistan v England at Leeds	2001
7-37	Aqib Javed	Pakistan v India at Sharjah.	1991-92
7-45	Imran Tahir	South Africa v West Indies at Basseterre.	2016
7-51	W. W. Davis	West Indies v Australia at Leeds	1983

The best analyses for other Test countries are:

6-4	S. T. R. Binny	India v Bangladesh at Mirpur	2014
6-19	H. K. Olonga	Zimbabwe v England at Cape Town	1999-2000
6-26	Mashrafe bin Mortaza	Bangladesh v Kenya at Nairobi	2006
6-26	Rubel Hossain	Bangladesh v New Zealand at Mirpur.	2013-14
6-31	P. D. Collingwood	England v Bangladesh at Nottingham	2005
6-55	P. R. Stirling	Ireland v Afghanistan at Greater Noida.	2016-17

HAT-TRICKS

Four Wickets in Four Balls

S. L. Malinga	Sri Lanka v South Africa at Providence.	2006-07

Four Wickets in Five Balls

Saqlain Mushtaq	Pakistan v Zimbabwe at Peshawar.	1996-97
A. U. Rashid	England v West Indies at St George's	2018-19

Most Hat-Tricks

S. L. Malinga (SL)	3	Saqlain Mushtaq (P).	2	Wasim Akram (P)	2
T. A. Boult (NZ)	**2**	W. P. U. J. C. Vaas† (SL)	2	**K. Yadav (I)**	**2**

† *W. P. U. J. C. Vaas took the second of his two hat-tricks, for Sri Lanka v Bangladesh at Pietermaritzburg in 2002-03, with the first three balls of the match.*

Hat-Tricks

There have been **49** hat-tricks in one-day internationals, including the above. Those since 2017-18:

K. Yadav	India v Australia at Kolkata	2017-18
D. S. M. Kumara	Sri Lanka v Bangladesh at Mirpur	2017-18
Imran Tahir	South Africa v Zimbabwe at Bloemfontein	2018-19
T. A. Boult	New Zealand v Pakistan at Abu Dhabi.	2018-19
Mohammed Shami	India v Afghanistan at Southampton	2019
T. A. Boult	New Zealand v Australia at Lord's.	2019
K. Yadav	India v West Indies at Visakhapatnam	2019-20

MOST WICKETS

		M	Balls	R	W	BB	4I	Avge
1	M. Muralitharan (SL/World/Asia).	350	18,811	12,326	534	7-30	25	23.08
2	Wasim Akram (Pakistan).	356	18,186	11,812	502	5-15	23	23.52
3	Waqar Younis (Pakistan).	262	12,698	9,919	416	7-36	27	23.84
4	W. P. U. J. C. Vaas (SL/Asia)	322	15,775	11,014	400	8-19	13	27.53

		M	Balls	R	W	BB	4I	Avge
5	Shahid Afridi (Pakistan/World/Asia) ...	398	17,670	13,635	395	7-12	13	34.51
6	S. M. Pollock (SA/World/Africa)	303	15,712	9,631	393	6-35	17	24.50
7	G. D. McGrath (Australia/World)	250	12,970	8,391	381	7-15	16	22.02
8	B. Lee (Australia)	221	11,185	8,877	380	5-22	23	23.36
9	S. L. Malinga (Sri Lanka)	226	10,936	9,760	338	6-38	19	28.87
10	A. Kumble (India/Asia).	271	14,496	10,412	337	6-12	10	30.89
11	S. T. Jayasuriya (Sri Lanka/Asia)	445	14,874	11,871	323	6-29	12	36.75
12	J. Srinath (India)	229	11,935	8,847	315	5-23	10	28.08
13	D. L. Vettori (New Zealand/World)	295	14,060	9,674	305	5-7	10	31.71
14	S. K. Warne (Australia/World)	194	10,642	7,541	293	5-33	13	25.73
15	Saqlain Mushtaq (Pakistan).	169	8,770	6,275	288	5-20	17	21.78
	A. B. Agarkar (India).	191	9,484	8,021	288	6-42	12	27.85
17	Zaheer Khan (India/Asia)	200	10,097	8,301	282	5-42	8	29.43
18	**Shakib Al Hasan (Bangladesh)**.	**215**	**11,003**	**8,155**	**277**	**5-29**	**12**	**29.44**
19	J. H. Kallis (S. Africa/World/Africa). ...	328	10,750	8,680	273	5-30	4	31.79
20	A. A. Donald (South Africa).	164	8,561	5,926	272	6-23	13	21.78
21	Mashrafe bin Mortaza (Bang/Asia)	220	10,922	8,893	270	6-26	8	32.93
22	J. M. Anderson (England)	194	9,584	7,861	269	5-23	13	29.22
	Abdul Razzaq (Pakistan/Asia).	265	10,941	8,564	269	6-35	11	31.83
	Harbhajan Singh (India/Asia)	236	12,479	8,973	269	5-31	5	33.35
25	M. Ntini (South Africa/World)	173	8,687	6,559	266	6-22	12	24.65
26	Shakib Al Hasan (Bangladesh)	206	10,517	7,857	260	5-29	10	30.21
27	Kapil Dev (India).	225	11,202	6,945	253	5-43	4	27.45

The leading aggregates for players who have appeared for other Test countries are:

	M	Balls	R	W	BB	4I	Avge
H. H. Streak (Zimbabwe)	189	9,468	7,129	239	5-32	8	29.82
C. A. Walsh (West Indies)	205	10,882	6,918	227	5-1	7	30.47
Rashid Khan (Afghanistan)	**74**	**3,732**	**2,601**	**140**	**7-18**	**9**	**18.57**
K. J. O'Brien (Ireland)	153	4,296	3,727	114	4-13	5	32.69

Excluding wickets taken for combined teams, the record for Sri Lanka is 523 in 343 matches by M. Muralitharan; for South Africa, 387 in 294 matches by S. M. Pollock; for Australia, 380 in 249 matches by G. D. McGrath; for India, 334 in 269 matches by A. Kumble; for New Zealand, 297 in 291 matches by D. L. Vettori; and for Zimbabwe, 237 in 187 matches by H. H. Streak.

BEST CAREER STRIKE-RATES BY BOWLERS

(Balls per wicket. Qualification: 1,500 balls)

SR		M	W
26.14	**M. A. Starc (A)**	**99**	**195**
26.34	**Mustafizur Rahman (B)**	**68**	**127**
26.65	**Rashid Khan (Afg)**	**74**	**140**
27.22	S. W. Tait (A).	35	62
27.32	Mohammed Shami (I).	79	148
27.32	B. A. W. Mendis (SL).	87	152
28.34	L. H. Ferguson (NZ)	37	69
28.48	M. J. McClenaghan (NZ)	48	82
28.72	R. N. ten Doeschate (Netherlands)	33	55

BEST CAREER ECONOMY-RATES

(Runs conceded per six balls. Qualification: 50 wickets)

ER		M	W
3.09	J. Garner (WI).	98	146
3.28	R. G. D. Willis (E)	64	80
3.30	R. J. Hadlee (NZ)	115	158
3.32	M. A. Holding (WI)	102	142
3.40	A. M. E. Roberts (WI)	56	87
3.48	C. E. L. Ambrose (WI).	176	225

WICKETKEEPING AND FIELDING RECORDS

MOST DISMISSALS IN AN INNINGS

6 (6ct)	A. C. Gilchrist......	Australia v South Africa at Cape Town	1999-2000
6 (6ct)	A. J. Stewart	England v Zimbabwe at Manchester.........	2000
6 (5ct, 1st)	R. D. Jacobs	West Indies v Sri Lanka at Colombo (RPS)	2001-02
6 (5ct, 1st)	A. C. Gilchrist......	Australia v England at Sydney...........	2002-03
6 (6ct)	A. C. Gilchrist......	Australia v Namibia at Potchefstroom........	2002-03
6 (6ct)	A. C. Gilchrist......	Australia v Sri Lanka at Colombo (RPS)	2003-04
6 (6ct)	M. V. Boucher......	South Africa v Pakistan at Cape Town	2006-07
6 (5ct, 1st)	M. S. Dhoni........	India v England at Leeds...................	2007
6 (6ct)	A. C. Gilchrist......	Australia v India at Vadodara	2007-08
6 (5ct, 1st)	A. C. Gilchrist......	Australia v India at Sydney...............	2007-08
6 (6ct)	M. J. Prior	England v South Africa at Nottingham.......	2008
6 (6ct)	J. C. Buttler.......	England v South Africa at The Oval.........	2013
6 (6ct)	M. H. Cross........	Scotland v Canada at Christchurch	2013-14
6 (5ct, 1st)	Q. de Kock	S. Africa v N. Zealand at Mount Maunganui ...	2014-15
6 (6ct)	Sarfraz Ahmed	Pakistan v South Africa at Auckland.........	2014-15

MOST DISMISSALS

			M	Ct	St
1	482	K. C. Sangakkara (Sri Lanka/World/Asia)................	360	384	98
2	472	A. C. Gilchrist (Australia/World).................	282	417	55
3	444	M. S. Dhoni (India/Asia)	350	321	123
4	424	M. V. Boucher (South Africa/Africa).................	294	402	22
5	287	Moin Khan (Pakistan)	219	214	73
6	242	B. B. McCullum (New Zealand)	185	227	15
7	234	I. A. Healy (Australia)	168	195	39
8	**233**	**Mushfiqur Rahim (Bangladesh)**	**213**	**187**	**46**
9	220	Rashid Latif (Pakistan).........................	166	182	38
10	**213**	**J. C. Buttler (England)**...........................	**147**	**181**	**32**
11	206	R. S. Kaluwitharana (Sri Lanka)	186	131	75
12	204	P. J. L. Dujon (West Indies)........................	169	183	21

The leading aggregates for players who have appeared for other Test countries are:

165	A. Flower (Zimbabwe)........................	186	133	32
96	N. J. O'Brien (Ireland).....................	80	82	14
88	Mohammad Shahzad (Afghanistan)..........	83	63	25

Excluding dismissals for combined teams, the most for Sri Lanka is 473 (378ct, 95st) in 353 matches by K. C. Sangakkara; for Australia, 470 (416ct, 54st) in 281 matches by A. C. Gilchrist; for India, 438 (318ct, 120st) in 347 matches by M. S. Dhoni; and for South Africa, 415 (394ct, 21st) in 289 matches by M. V. Boucher.

K. C. Sangakkara's list excludes 19 catches taken in 44 one-day internationals when not keeping wicket; M. V. Boucher's record excludes one in one; B. B. McCullum's excludes 35 in 75; Mushfiqur Rahim's two in 14; R. S. Kaluwitharana's one in three; A. Flower's eight in 27; N. J. O'Brien's eight in 23; and Mohammad Shahzad's one in one. A. C. Gilchrist played five one-day internationals and J. C. Buttler one without keeping wicket, but they made no catches in those games. R. Dravid (India) made 210 dismissals (196ct, 14st) in 344 one-day internationals but only 86 (72ct, 14st) in 74 as wicketkeeper (including one where he took over during the match).

MOST CATCHES IN AN INNINGS IN THE FIELD

5	J. N. Rhodes..............	South Africa v West Indies at Bombay	1993-94

*There have been **40** instances of four catches in an innings.*

MOST CATCHES

Ct	M		Ct	M	
218	448	D. P. M. D. Jayawardene (SL/Asia)	127	273	A. R. Border (Australia)
160	375	R. T. Ponting (Australia/World)	127	398	Shahid Afridi (Pak/World/Asia)
156	334	M. Azharuddin (India)			
140	463	S. R. Tendulkar (India)			*Most catches for other Test countries:*
139	**233**	**L. R. P. L. Taylor (New Zealand)**	124	301	C. H. Gayle (WI/World)
133	280	S. P. Fleming (New Zealand/World)	108	197	P. D. Collingwood (England)
132	**254**	**V. Kohli (India)**	86	221	G. W. Flower (Zimbabwe)
131	328	J. H. Kallis (SA/World/Africa)	**69**	**200**	**Mahmudullah (Bangladesh)**
130	262	Younis Khan (Pakistan)	**67**	**153**	**K. J. O'Brien (Ireland)**
130	350	M. Muralitharan (SL/World/Asia)	**56**	**127**	**Mohammad Nabi (Afghanistan)**

Excluding catches taken for combined teams, the record aggregate for Sri Lanka is 213 in 442 matches by D. P. M. D. Jayawardene; for Australia, 158 in 374 by R. T. Ponting; for New Zealand, 132 in 279 by S. P. Fleming; for South Africa, 131 in 323 by J. H. Kallis; and for West Indies, 123 in 298 by C. H. Gayle.

Younis Khan's record excludes five catches made in three one-day internationals as wicketkeeper.

TEAM RECORDS

HIGHEST INNINGS TOTALS

481-6	(50 overs)	England v Australia at Nottingham....................	2018
444-3	(50 overs)	England v Pakistan at Nottingham	2016
443-9	(50 overs)	Sri Lanka v Netherlands at Amstelveen	2006
439-2	(50 overs)	South Africa v West Indies at Johannesburg..........	2014-15
438-4	(50 overs)	South Africa v India at Mumbai	2015-16
438-9	(49.5 overs)	South Africa v Australia at Johannesburg............	2005-06
434-4	(50 overs)	Australia v South Africa at Johannesburg............	2005-06
418-5	(50 overs)	South Africa v Zimbabwe at Potchefstroom	2006-07
418-5	(50 overs)	India v West Indies at Indore.......................	2011-12
418-6	(50 overs)	England v West Indies at St George's................	2018-19
417-6	(50 overs)	Australia v Afghanistan at Perth....................	2014-15
414-7	(50 overs)	India v Sri Lanka at Rajkot	2009-10
413-5	(50 overs)	India v Bermuda at Port-of-Spain	2006-07
411-4	(50 overs)	South Africa v Ireland at Canberra	2014-15
411-8	(50 overs)	Sri Lanka v India at Rajkot	2009-10
408-5	(50 overs)	South Africa v West Indies at Sydney................	2014-15
408-9	(50 overs)	England v New Zealand at Birmingham	2015
404-5	(50 overs)	India v Sri Lanka at Kolkata	2014-15
402-2	(50 overs)	New Zealand v Ireland at Aberdeen	2008
401-3	(50 overs)	India v South Africa at Gwalior	2009-10

The highest totals by other Test countries are:

399-1	(50 overs)	Pakistan v Zimbabwe at Bulawayo....................	2018
389	(48 overs)	West Indies v England at St George's................	2018-19
351-7	(50 overs)	Zimbabwe v Kenya at Mombasa	2008-09
338	(50 overs)	Afghanistan v Ireland at Greater Noida.............	2016-17
333-8	(50 overs)	Bangladesh v Australia at Nottingham	2019
331-6	(50 overs)	Ireland v Scotland at Dubai	2017-18
331-8	(50 overs)	Ireland v Zimbabwe at Hobart.......................	2014-15

HIGHEST TOTALS BATTING SECOND

438-9	(49.5 overs)	South Africa v Australia at Johannesburg (*Won by 1 wicket*) ..	2005-06
411-8	(50 overs)	Sri Lanka v India at Rajkot (*Lost by 3 runs*)	2009-10
389	(48 overs)	West Indies v England at St George's (*Lost by 29 runs*)	2018-19

372-6	(49.2 overs)	South Africa v Australia at Durban (*Won by 4 wickets*)	2016-17
366-8	(50 overs)	England v India at Cuttack (*Lost by 15 runs*)	2016-17
365-9	(45 overs)	England v New Zealand at The Oval (*Lost by 13 runs DLS*)...	2015
365	(48.5 overs)	England v Scotland at Edinburgh (*Lost by 6 runs*)	2018
364-4	(48.4 overs)	England v West Indies at Bridgetown (*Won by 6 wickets*)	2018-19
362-1	(43.3 overs)	India v Australia at Jaipur (*Won by 9 wickets*)	2013-14
361-7	(50 overs)	Pakistan v England at Southampton (*Lost by 12 runs*)	2019

HIGHEST MATCH AGGREGATES

872-13	(99.5 overs)	South Africa v Australia at Johannesburg	2005-06
825-15	(100 overs)	India v Sri Lanka at Rajkot	2009-10
807-16	(98 overs)	West Indies v England at St George's	2018-19
763-14	(96 overs)	England v New Zealand at The Oval	2015
747-14	(100 overs)	India v England at Cuttack	2016-17
743-12	(99.2 overs)	South Australia v Australia at Durban	2016-17
736-15	(98.5 overs)	Scotland v England at Edinburgh	2018
734-10	(100 overs)	England v Pakistan at Southampton	2019
730-9	(100 overs)	South Africa v West Indies at Johannesburg	2014-15
727-13	(100 overs)	Australia v India at Sydney	2020-21
726-14	(95.1 overs)	New Zealand v India at Christchurch	2008-09
724-12	(98.4 overs)	West Indies v England at Bridgetown	2018-19

LOWEST INNINGS TOTALS

35	(18 overs)	Zimbabwe v Sri Lanka at Harare	2003-04
35	(12 overs)	USA v Nepal at Kirtipur	2019-20
36	(18.4 overs)	Canada v Sri Lanka at Paarl	2002-03
38	(15.4 overs)	Zimbabwe v Sri Lanka at Colombo (SSC)	2001-02
43	(19.5 overs)	Pakistan v West Indies at Cape Town	1992-93
43	(20.1 overs)	Sri Lanka v South Africa at Paarl	2011-12
44	(24.5 overs)	Zimbabwe v Bangladesh at Chittagong	2009-10
45	(40.3 overs)	Canada v England at Manchester	1979
45	(14 overs)	Namibia v Australia at Potchefstroom	2002-03

The lowest totals by other Test countries are:

54	(26.3 overs)	India v Sri Lanka at Sharjah	2000-01
54	(23.2 overs)	West Indies v South Africa at Cape Town	2003-04
58	(18.5 overs)	Bangladesh v West Indies at Mirpur	2010-11
58	(17.4 overs)	Bangladesh v India at Mirpur	2014
58	(16.1 overs)	Afghanistan v Zimbabwe at Sharjah	2015-16
64	(35.5 overs)	New Zealand v Pakistan at Sharjah	1985-86
69	(28 overs)	South Africa v Australia at Sydney	1993-94
70	(25.2 overs)	Australia v England at Birmingham	1977
70	(26.3 overs)	Australia v New Zealand at Adelaide	1985-86
77	(27.4 overs)	Ireland v Sri Lanka at St George's	2006-07
86	(32.4 overs)	England v Australia at Manchester	2001

LARGEST VICTORIES

290 runs	New Zealand (402-2 in 50 overs) v Ireland (112 in 28.4 ov) at Aberdeen	2008
275 runs	Australia (417-6 in 50 overs) v Afghanistan (142 in 37.3 overs) at Perth	2014-15
272 runs	South Africa (399-6 in 50 overs) v Zimbabwe (127 in 29 overs) at Benoni	2010-11
258 runs	South Africa (301-8 in 50 overs) v Sri Lanka (43 in 20.1 overs) at Paarl	2011-12
257 runs	India (413-5 in 50 overs) v Bermuda (156 in 43.1 overs) at Port-of-Spain	2006-07

257 runs	South Africa (408-5 in 50 overs) v West Indies (151 in 33.1 overs) at Sydney	2014-15
256 runs	Australia (301-6 in 50 overs) v Namibia (45 in 14 overs) at Potchefstroom	2002-03
256 runs	India (374-4 in 50 overs) v Hong Kong (118 in 36.5 overs) at Karachi	2008
255 runs	Pakistan (337-6 in 47 overs) v Ireland (82 in 23.4 overs) at Dublin	2016

There have been 55 instances of victory by ten wickets.

TIED MATCHES

There have been 37 tied one-day internationals. West Indies have tied ten matches; Bangladesh are the only Test country never to have tied. The most recent ties are:

South Africa (230-6 in 31 overs) v West Indies (190-6 in 26.1 overs) at Cardiff (D/L)	2013
Ireland (268-5 in 50 overs) v Netherlands (268-9 in 50 overs) at Amstelveen	2013
Pakistan (229-6 in 50 overs) v West Indies (229-9 in 50 overs) at Gros Islet	2013
Pakistan (266-5 in 47 overs) v Ireland (275-5 in 47 overs) at Dublin (D/L)	2013
New Zealand (314 in 50 overs) v India (314-9 in 50 overs) at Auckland	2013-14
Sri Lanka (286-9 in 50 overs) v England (286-8 in 50 overs) at Nottingham	2016
Zimbabwe (257 in 50 overs) v West Indies (257-8 in 50 overs) at Bulawayo	2016-17
Zimbabwe (210 in 46.4 overs) v Scotland (210 in 49.1 overs) at Bulawayo	2017-18
Afghanistan (252-8 in 50 overs) v India (252 in 49.5 overs) at Dubai	2018-19
India (321-6 in 50 overs) v West Indies (321-7 in 50 overs) at Visakhapatnam	2018-19

In the 2019 World Cup final at Lord's, New Zealand scored 241-8 and England 241, but England won the match on boundary count after a super over was also tied. Similarly at Rawalpindi in 2020-21, Zimbabwe won in a super over after they scored 278-6 and Pakistan 278-9.

OTHER RECORDS

MOST APPEARANCES

463	S. R. Tendulkar (I)		330	T. M. Dilshan (SL)	
448	D. P. M. D. Jayawardene (SL/Asia)		328	J. H. Kallis (SA/World/Africa)	
445	S. T. Jayasuriya (SL/Asia)		325	S. R. Waugh (A)	
404	K. C. Sangakkara (SL/World/Asia)		322	W. P. U. J. C. Vaas (SL/Asia)	
398	Shahid Afridi (P/World/Asia)		311	S. C. Ganguly (I/Asia)	
378	Inzamam-ul-Haq (P/Asia)		308	P. A. de Silva (SL)	
375	R. T. Ponting (A/World)		304	Yuvraj Singh (I/Asia)	
356	Wasim Akram (P)		303	S. M. Pollock (SA/World/Africa)	
350	M. S. Dhoni (I/Asia)		301	C. H. Gayle (WI/World)	
350	M. Muralitharan (SL/World/Asia)		300	T. M. Dilshan (SL)	
344	R. Dravid (I/World/Asia)				
334	M. Azharuddin (I)				

*Excluding appearances for combined teams, the record for Sri Lanka is 441 by S. T. Jayasuriya; for Pakistan, 393 by Shahid Afridi; for Australia, 374 by R. T. Ponting; for South Africa, 323 by J. H. Kallis; for West Indies, 298 by C. H. Gayle; for New Zealand, 291 by D. L. Vettori; for Bangladesh, 227 by **Mushfiqur Rahim**; for England, 223 by **E. J. G. Morgan**; for Zimbabwe, 221 by G. W. Flower; for Ireland, 153 by **K. J. O'Brien**; and for Afghanistan, 127 by **Mohammad Nabi**.*

MOST MATCHES AS CAPTAIN

	P	W	L	T	NR		P	W	L	T	NR
R. T. Ponting (A/World)	230	165	51	2	12	S. C. Ganguly (I/Asia)	147	76	66	0	5
S. P. Fleming (NZ)	218	98	106	1	13	Imran Khan (P)	139	75	59	1	4
M. S. Dhoni (I)	200	110	74	5	11	W. J. Cronje (SA)	138	99	35	1	3
A. Ranatunga (SL)	193	89	95	1	8	D. P. M. D.					
A. R. Border (A)	178	107	67	1	3	Jayawardene (SL/As)	129	71	49	1	8
M. Azharuddin (I)	174	90	76	2	6	B. C. Lara (WI)	125	59	59	1	7
G. C. Smith (SA/Af)	150	92	51	1	6	**E. J. G. Morgan (Eng)**	124	74	40	2	8

MEN'S WORLD CUP FINALS

1975	WEST INDIES (291-8) beat Australia (274) by 17 runs	Lord's
1979	WEST INDIES (286-9) beat England (194) by 92 runs	Lord's
1983	INDIA (183) beat West Indies (140) by 43 runs.....................	Lord's
1987	AUSTRALIA (253-5) beat England (246-8) by seven runs	Calcutta
1992	PAKISTAN (249-6) beat England (227) by 22 runs...................	Melbourne
1996	SRI LANKA (245-3) beat Australia (241-7) by seven wickets	Lahore
1999	AUSTRALIA (133-2) beat Pakistan (132) by eight wickets.............	Lord's
2003	AUSTRALIA (359-2) beat India (234) by 125 runs...................	Johannesburg
2007	AUSTRALIA (281-4) beat Sri Lanka (215-8) by 53 runs (D/L method)	Bridgetown
2011	INDIA (277-4) beat Sri Lanka (274-6) by six wickets	Mumbai
2015	AUSTRALIA (186-3) beat New Zealand (183) by seven wickets	Melbourne
2019	ENGLAND (241) beat New Zealand (241-8) on boundary count after a super over	Lord's

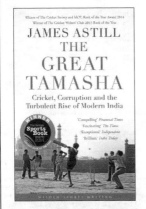

MEN'S TWENTY20 INTERNATIONAL RECORDS

Matches in this section do not have first-class status.

This section covers men's Twenty20 international cricket to December 31, 2021. Bold type denotes performances in the calendar year 2021, or, in career figures, players who appeared in Twenty20 internationals in that year. The ICC extended official international status to Associate Twenty20 matches from the start of 2019.

RESULTS SUMMARY OF MEN'S TWENTY20 INTERNATIONALS

2004-05 to December 31, 2021 (1,452 matches)

	Matches	Won	Lost	Tied	No Result	% Won (excl NR)
Afghanistan	89	60	29*	–	–	67.41
India	153	98‡	51	–	4	65.77
Pakistan	189	118*	66†	–	5	64.13
South Africa	147	86*	60	–	1	58.90
England	143	77†	61	–	5	55.79
Australia	153	79	71†	–	3	52.66
New Zealand	160	80†	76§	–	4	51.28
Sri Lanka	148	68*	78*	–	2	46.57
West Indies	152	65†	78*	–	9	45.45
Ireland	114	48*	58	1	7	45.32
Bangladesh	123	43	78	–	2	35.53
Zimbabwe	96	26†	70	–	–	27.08
Namibia	30	21	9	–	–	70.00
Qatar	26	18†	8	–	–	69.23
Uganda	29	19	9	–	1	67.85
Germany	26	16	10	–	–	61.53
Papua New Guinea	31	17	13	–	1	56.66
Nepal	39	20	18	–	1	52.63
Netherlands	83	41	38*	1	3	51.87
United Arab Emirates	53	26	26	–	1	50.00
Malaysia	28	13	13	1	1	50.00
Canada	37	17	19†	–	1	47.22
Scotland	78	34	40	1	3	46.00
Oman	39	17	21	–	1	44.73
Kenya	51	22	28	–	1	44.00
Malta	25	10	13	1	1	43.75
Hong Kong	44	16	28	–	–	36.36
Nigeria	27	8	19	–	–	29.62

*   *Includes one game settled by a tie-break.*   †   *Includes two settled by a tie-break.*
‡   *Includes three settled by a tie-break.*   §   *Includes six settled by a tie-break.*
Most ties were decided by bowling contests or super overs.

Matches abandoned without a ball bowled are not included except where the toss took place, when they are shown as no result. In the percentages of matches won, ties are counted as half a win.
   Teams which appeared in 2021 are shown in bold.

A further 60 teams have played men's Twenty20 internationals, as follows: **Romania** (P17 W15 L2); **Isle of Man** (P5 W4 L1); **Spain** (P14 W11 L3); **Malawi** (P13 W9 L3 NR1); **Portugal** (P8 W6 L2); **Switzerland** (P4 W3 L1); **Tanzania** (P10 W7 L3); **Jersey** (P23 W16 L7); **Austria** (P12 W8 L4); **Cyprus** (P6 W4 L2); **Argentina** (P11 W7 L4); **Italy** (P14 W8 L5 NR1); **USA** (P16 W9 L6 NR1); **Belgium** (P15 W9 L6); Singapore (P15 W8 L7); **Bahrain** (P12 W7 L5); **Ghana** (P15 W8 L7); **Saudi Arabia** (P12 W6 L6); **Greece** (P7 W3 L3 NR1); **Hungary** (P4 W2 L2); Peru (P4 W2 L2); **Kuwait** (P19 W9 L10); **Rwanda** (P11 W5 L6); **Czechia** (P18 W8 L10); **Belize** (P9 W4 L5); **Luxembourg** (P16 W7 L9); **Sweden** (P7 W3 L4); **Bermuda** (P21 W8 L12 NR1); **Denmark** (P18 W6 L10 NR2); Mexico (P8 W3 L5); **Vanuatu** (P14 W5 L9); **Guernsey** (P10 W3 L6 NR1); **Finland** (P9 W3 L6); **Panama** (P9 W3 L6); **Bahamas** (P6 W2 L4); **Seychelles** (P6 W2 L4); Philippines (P4 W1 L2 NR1); **Bulgaria** (P22 W6 L14 NR2); **Sierra Leone** (P10 W3 L7);

Botswana (P11 W3 L8); Brazil (P4 W1 L3); Chile (P4 W1 L3); **France (P4 W1 L3);** Samoa (P4 W1 L3); World XI (P4 W1 L3); **Mozambique (P11 W2 L8 NR1);** Norway (P10 W2 L8); eSwatini **(P6 W1 L5);** Thailand (P8 W1 L7); **Maldives (P18 W2 L15 NR1);** Gibraltar (P13 W1 L11 T1); Cayman Islands (P6 L6); **Estonia (P6 L6); Lesotho (P6 L6); Serbia (P6 L6); Cameroon (P4 L4);** Turkey (P4 L4); Costa Rica (P3 L3); Iran (P3 L3); Bhutan (P2 L2).

BATTING RECORDS

HIGHEST INDIVIDUAL INNINGS

172	A. J. Finch	Australia v Zimbabwe at Harare......................	2018
162*	Hazratullah Zazai	Afghanistan v Ireland at Dehradun....................	2018-19
156	A. J. Finch	Australia v England at Southampton...................	2013
145*	G. J. Maxwell	Australia v Sri Lanka at Pallekele....................	2016
133*	**M. P. O'Dowd**	**Netherlands v Malaysia at Kirtipur**	**2021**
127*	H. G. Munsey	Scotland v Netherlands at Malahide...................	2019
125*	E. Lewis	West Indies v India at Kingston......................	2017
125*	Shaheryar Butt	Belgium v Czechia at Walferdange....................	2020
124*	S. R. Watson	Australia v India at Sydney.........................	2015-16
124	K. J. O'Brien	Ireland v Hong Kong at Al Amerat....................	2019-20
123	B. B. McCullum	New Zealand v Bangladesh at Pallekele...............	2012-13
122	Babar Hayat	Hong Kong v Oman at Fatullah......................	2015-16
122	**Babar Azam**	**Pakistan v South Africa at Centurion**	**2020-21**
119	F. du Plessis	South Africa v West Indies at Johannesburg...........	2014-15
118*	Mohammad Shahzad	Afghanistan v Zimbabwe at Sharjah..................	2015-16
118	R. G. Sharma	India v Sri Lanka at Indore.........................	2017-18
117*	R. E. Levi	South Africa v New Zealand at Hamilton...............	2011-12
117*	Shaiman Anwar	United Arab Emirates v Papua New Guinea at Abu Dhabi ..	2016-17
117	C. H. Gayle	West Indies v South Africa at Johannesburg............	2007-08
116*	B. B. McCullum	New Zealand v Australia at Christchurch...............	2009-10
116*	A. D. Hales	England v Sri Lanka at Chittagong....................	2013-14
115*	**P. R. Stirling**	**Ireland v Zimbabwe at Bready**	**2021**

MOST RUNS

		M	I	NO	R	HS	100	Avge	SR
1	**M. J. Guptill (New Zealand)**	112	108	7	3,299	105	2	32.66	136.71
2	V. Kohli (India)	95	87	25	3,227	94*	0	52.04	137.90
3	R. G. Sharma (India)	119	111	15	3,197	118	4	33.30	140.28
4	Babar Azam (Pakistan)	73	68	10	2,620	122	1	45.17	129.12
5	A. J. Finch (Australia)	83	83	10	2,608	172	2	35.72	148.01
6	**P. R. Stirling (Ireland)**	94	93	8	2,606	115*	1	30.65	136.51
7	D. A. Warner (Australia)	88	88	10	2,554	100*	1	32.74	140.48
8	Mohammad Hafeez (Pakistan)	119	108	13	2,514	99*	0	26.46	122.03
9	Shoaib Malik (Pakistan/World)	124	111	33	2,435	75	0	31.21	125.38
10	E. J. G. Morgan (England)	113	104	20	2,428	91	0	28.90	137.64
11	{ J. C. Buttler (England)	88	80	18	2,140	101*	1	34.51	141.16
	{ B. B. McCullum (New Zealand)	71	70	10	2,140	123	2	35.66	136.21
13	K. S. Williamson (New Zealand)	74	72	10	2,021	95	0	32.59	123.98
14	Mohammad Shahzad (Afghanistan) ..	70	70	3	2,015	118*	1	30.07	133.62
15	K. J. O'Brien (Ireland)	110	103	10	1,973	124	1	21.21	130.92
16	Mahmudullah (Bangladesh)	113	105	23	1,971	64*	0	24.03	117.88
17	J-P. Duminy (South Africa)	81	75	25	1,934	96*	0	38.68	126.24
18	L. R. P. L. Taylor (New Zealand)	102	94	21	1,909	63	0	26.15	122.37
19	**C. H. Gayle (West Indies)**	79	75	7	1,899	117	2	27.92	137.50
20	Shakib Al Hasan (Bangladesh)	94	93	10	1,894	84	0	22.81	120.48
21	T. M. Dilshan (Sri Lanka)	80	79	12	1,889	104*	1	28.19	120.47
22	**G. J. Maxwell (Australia)**	79	72	12	1,844	145*	3	30.73	155.74
23	**K. L. Rahul (India)**	56	52	7	1,831	110*	2	40.68	142.49

		M	I	NO	R	HS	100	Avge	SR
24	Q. de Kock (South Africa)	61	61	7	1,827	79*	0	33.83	135.03
25	D. A. Miller (South Africa)	95	83	27	1,786	101*	1	31.89	140.62
26	S. Dhawan (India)	68	66	3	1,759	92	0	27.92	126.36
27	Tamim Iqbal (Bangladesh)	78	78	5	1,758	103*	1	24.08	116.96
28	C. Munro (New Zealand)	65	62	7	1,724	109*	3	31.34	156.44

The record aggregate for Zimbabwe is 1,662 in 66 matches by H. Masakadza.

FASTEST TWENTY20 INTERNATIONAL FIFTIES

Balls

12	Yuvraj Singh	India v England at Durban	2007-08
13	Mirza Ahsan	Austria v Luxembourg at Ilfov	2019
14	C. Munro	New Zealand v Sri Lanka at Auckland	2015-16
14	**R. Satheesan**	**Romania v Serbia at Sofia**	**2021**
15	Faisal Khan	Saudi Arabia v Kuwait at Al Amerat	2018-19
16	S. D. Hope	West Indies v Bangladesh at Sylhet	2018-19
16	**M. Akayezu**	**Rwanda v Ghana at Kigali.**	**2021**
16	**K. Nassoro**	**Tanzania v Cameroon at Kigali.**	**2021-22**
17	P. R. Stirling	Ireland v Afghanistan at Dubai	2011-12
17	S. J. Myburgh	Netherlands v Ireland at Sylhet	2013-14
17	C. H. Gayle	West Indies v South Africa at Cape Town	2014-15
17	Q. de Kock	South Africa v England at Durban	2019-20
17	T. H. David	Singapore v Malaysia at Bangkok	2019-20
17	**L. S. Livingstone**	**England v Pakistan at Nottingham**	**2021**
17	**H. S. Gericke**	**Malta v Gibraltar at Valletta.**	**2021-22**

FASTEST TWENTY20 INTERNATIONAL HUNDREDS

Balls

35	D. A. Miller	South Africa v Bangladesh at Potchefstroom	2017-18
35	R. G. Sharma	India v Sri Lanka at Indore	2017-18
35	S. Wickramasekara . . .	Czechia v Turkey at Ilfov	2019
39	S. Periyalwar	Romania v Turkey at Ilfov	2019
41	H. G. Munsey	Scotland v Netherlands at Malahide	2019
42	Hazratullah Zazai	Afghanistan v Ireland at Dehradun	2018-19
42	Shaheryar Butt	Belgium v Czechia at Walferdange	2020
42	**L. S. Livingstone**	**England v Pakistan at Nottingham**	**2021**
43	J. P. Kotze	Namibia v Botswana at Windhoek	2019
45	R. E. Levi	South Africa v New Zealand at Hamilton	2011-12
46	F. du Plessis	South Africa v West Indies at Johannesburg	2014-15
46	K. L. Rahul	India v West Indies at Lauderhill	2016
46	G. D. Phillips	New Zealand v West Indies at Mount Maunganui	2020-21
46	**F. Damiao Couana** . . .	**Mozambique v Cameroon at Kigali**	**2021-22**

HIGHEST PARTNERSHIP FOR EACH WICKET

236	for 1st	Hazratullah Zazai/Usman Ghani .	Afg v Ire	Dehradun	2018-19
167*	for 2nd	J. C. Buttler/D. J. Malan	E v SA	Cape Town	2020-21
184	for 3rd	D. P. Conway/G. D. Phillips	NZ v WI	Mt Maunganui . . .	2020-21
166*	**for 4th**	**B. Arora/V. P. Thamotharam** . .	**Malta v Gibr**	**Albergaria**	**2021**
119*	for 5th	Shoaib Malik/Misbah-ul-Haq	P v A	Johannesburg	2007-08
101*	for 6th	C. L. White/M. E. K. Hussey	A v SL	Bridgetown	2010
92	**for 7th**	**M. P. Stoinis/D. R. Sams**	**A v NZ**	**Dunedin**	**2020-21**
80	for 8th	P. L. Mommsen/S. M. Sharif	Scot v Neth	Edinburgh	2015
132*	**for 9th**	**Saber Zakhil/Saqlain Ali**	**Belg v Austria**	**Waterloo**	**2021**
62*	**for 10th**	**K. Ahir/N. Ahir**	**Panama v Arg**	**North Sound**	**2021-22**

BOWLING RECORDS

BEST BOWLING ANALYSES

6-5	**P. Aho**	**Nigeria v Sierra Leone at Lagos**	**2021-22**
6-7	D. L. Chahar	India v Bangladesh at Nagpur	2019-20
6-7	**D. M. Nakrani**	**Uganda v Lesotho at Kigali City**	**2021-22**
6-8	B. A. W. Mendis	Sri Lanka v Zimbabwe at Hambantota	2012-13
6-16	B. A. W. Mendis	Sri Lanka v Australia at Pallekele.	2011-12
6-18	**H. Fennell**	**Argentina v Panama at North Sound**	**2021-22**
6-24	**J. N. Frylinck**	**Namibia v United Arab Emirates at Dubai**	**2021-22**
6-25	Y. S. Chahal	India v England at Bangalore	2016-17
6-30	**A. C. Agar**	**Australia v New Zealand at Wellington**	**2020-21**
5-3	H. M. R. K. B. Herath	Sri Lanka v New Zealand at Chittagong.	2013-14
5-3	Rashid Khan	Afghanistan v Ireland at Greater Noida	2016-17
5-4	P. Arrighi	Argentina v Brazil at Lima	2019-20
5-4	Khizar Hayat	Malaysia v Hong Kong at Kuala Lumpur.	2019-20
5-5	**Aqib Iqbal**	**Austria v Belgium at Waterloo**	**2021**
5-6	Umar Gul	Pakistan v New Zealand at The Oval	2009
5-6	Umar Gul	Pakistan v South Africa at Centurion	2012-13
5-6	S. L. Malinga	Sri Lanka v New Zealand at Pallekele	2019
5-6	A. Nanda	Luxembourg v Turkey at Ilfov	2019
5-8	**D. M. Nakrani**	**Uganda v Seychelles at Kigali City**	**2021-22**
5-9	C. Viljoen	Namibia v Botswana at Kampala	2019
5-9	**K. S. Bagabena**	**Ghana v Seychelles at Kigali**	**2021-22**

HAT-TRICKS

Four Wickets in Four Balls

Rashid Khan	Afghanistan v Ireland at Dehradun.	2018-19
S. L. Malinga	Sri Lanka v New Zealand at Pallekele	2019
C. Campher	**Ireland v Netherlands at Abu Dhabi.**	**2021-22**

Four Wickets in Five Balls

T. G. Southee	New Zealand v Pakistan at Auckland.	2010-11
D. A. Blignaut	**Germany v Italy at Almeria.**	**2021-22**

Hat-Tricks

There have been **21** hat-tricks in Twenty20 internationals, including the above; S. L. Malinga has taken two. The most recent are:

A. Dananjaya	**Sri Lanka v West Indies at Coolidge.**	**2020-21**
N. T. Ellis	**Australia v Bangladesh at Mirpur**	**2021**
E. A. Otieno	**Kenya v Uganda at Entebbe**	**2021-22**
C. Campher	**Ireland v Netherlands at Abu Dhabi.**	**2021-22**
D. A. Blignaut	**Germany v Italy at Almeria.**	**2021-22**
D. M. Nakrani	**Uganda v Seychelles at Kigali**	**2021-22**
P. W. H. de Silva	**Sri Lanka v South Africa at Sharjah**	**2021-22**
K. Rabada	**South Africa v England at Sharjah**	**2021-22**

MOST WICKETS

		M	B	R	W	BB	4I	Avge	ER
1	**Shakib Al Hasan (Bangladesh)**	94	2,085	2,316	117	5-20	6	19.79	6.66
2	**T. G. Southee (New Zealand)**	92	1,997	2,729	111	5-18	2	24.58	8.19
3	S. L. Malinga (Sri Lanka).	84	1,799	2,225	107	5-6	3	20.79	7.42
4	**Rashid Khan (Afghanistan/World)**. .	56	1,268	1,312	103	5-3	6	12.73	6.20

		M	B	R	W	BB	4I	Avge	ER
5	Shahid Afridi (Pakistan/World)	99	2,168	2,396	98	4-11	3	24.44	6.63
6	**Mustafizur Rahman (Bangladesh)** . .	61	1,318	1,678	86	5-22	4	19.51	7.63
7	{ Umar Gul (Pakistan).	60	1,203	1,443	85	5-6	6	16.97	7.19
	{ Saeed Ajmal (Pakistan).	64	1,430	1,516	85	4-19	4	17.83	6.36
9	I. S. Sodhi (New Zealand)	66	1,359	1,824	83	3-18	2	21.97	8.05
10	C. J. Jordan (England).	71	1,481	2,114	79	4-6	2	26.75	8.56
11	D. J. Bravo (West Indies).	91	1,505	2,036	78	4-28	3	26.10	8.11
12	G. H. Dockrell (Ireland).	86	1,382	1,642	76	4-20	1	21.60	7.12
13	A. U. Rashid (England)	68	1,400	1,725	74	4-2	2	23.31	7.39
14	{ **Shadab Khan (Pakistan)**	64	1,341	1,591	73	4-14	2	21.79	7.11
	{ **Mohammad Nabi (Afghanistan)**	86	1,690	2,041	73	4-10	3	27.95	7.24
16	{ B. A. W. Mendis (Sri Lanka).	39	885	952	66	6-8	5	14.42	6.45
	{ J. J. Bumrah (India).	55	1,187	1,290	66	3-11	0	19.54	6.52
	{ M. J. Santner (New Zealand)	62	1,250	1,515	66	4-11	2	22.95	7.27
	{ K. M. D. N. Kulasekara (Sri Lanka). .	58	1,231	1,530	66	4-31	2	23.18	7.45
20	{ A. Zampa.	57	1,211	1,374	65	5-19	1	21.13	6.80
	{ S. C. J. Broad (England).	56	1,173	1,491	65	4-24	1	22.93	7.62
22	{ D. W. Steyn (South Africa)	47	1,015	1,175	64	4-9	2	18.35	6.94
	{ **Y. S. Chahal (India)**	50	1,173	1,620	64	6-25	3	25.31	8.28
24	Imran Tahir (South Africa/World)	38	845	948	63	5-23	4	15.04	6.73
25	T. A. Boult (New Zealand)	44	993	1,345	62	4-34	1	21.69	8.12
26	{ R. Ashwin (India)	51	1,146	1,298	61	4-8	2	21.27	6.79
	{ **Mohammad Hafeez (Pakistan)**	119	1,261	1,388	61	4-10	1	22.75	6.60
	{ S. M. Sharif (Scotland).	53	1,087	1,470	61	4-24	2	24.09	8.11
29	{ **Hasan Ali (Pakistan)**	48	979	1,359	60	4-18	1	22.65	8.32
	{ M. A. Starc (Australia).	48	1,086	1,361	60	3-11	0	22.68	7.51

The leading aggregates for other Test countries are:

	A. G. Cremer (Zimbabwe)	29	570	660	35	3-11	0	18.85	6.94

*Excluding the World XI, the record aggregate for Pakistan is 97 in 98 matches by Shahid Afridi and for Afghanistan 101 in 54 matches by **Rashid Khan**.*

WICKETKEEPING AND FIELDING RECORDS

MOST DISMISSALS IN AN INNINGS

5 (3ct, 2st)	Mohammad Shahzad	Afghanistan v Oman at Abu Dhabi	2015-16
5 (5ct)	M. S. Dhoni	India v England at Bristol.	2018
5 (2ct, 3st)	I. A. Karim	Kenya v Ghana at Kampala	2019
5 (5ct)	K. Doriga	Papua New Guinea v Vanuata at Apia.	2019
5 (5ct)	**I. A. Karim**	**Kenya v Uganda at Kigali City**	**2021-22**

MOST DISMISSALS

			M	Ct	St
1	91	M. S. Dhoni (India)	98	57	34
2	64	Q. de Kock (South Africa).	59	49	15
3	63	D. Ramdin (West Indies).	71	43	20
4	61	Mushfiqur Rahim (Bangladesh).	82	32	29
5	60	Kamran Akmal (Pakistan)	53	28	32
6	**58**	**Mohammad Shahzad (Afghanistan)**.	69	30	28
7	**48**	J. C. Buttler (England).	72	38	10
8	**46**	Sarfraz Ahmed (Pakistan).	61	36	10
9	{ **45**	**M. H. Cross (Scotland)**.	51	31	14
	{ 45	K. C. Sangakkara (Sri Lanka)	56	25	20

Mushfiqur Rahim's record excludes ten catches in 17 matches when not keeping wicket, and Buttler's one catch in 16 matches. Kamran Akmal played five matches, de Kock and Cross two each and Mohammad Shahzad one in which they did not keep wicket or take a catch.

MOST CATCHES IN AN INNINGS IN THE FIELD

There have been **14** instances of four catches in an innings. The most recent are:

4	D. A. Miller	South Africa v Pakistan at Cape Town		2018-19
4	J. W. Jenner	Jersey v Guernsey at Castel		2019
4	L. Siaka	Papua New Guinea v Vanuatu at Apia		2019
4	C. S. MacLeod	Scotland v Ireland at Malahide		2019
4	T. H. David	Singapore v Scotland v Dubai		2019
4	C. de Grandhomme	New Zealand v England at Wellington		2019-20
4	P. Sarraf	Nepal v Malaysia at Bangkok		2019-20
4	**M. G. Erasmus**	**Namibia v United Arab Emirates at Dubai**		**2021-22**

MOST CATCHES

Ct	M		Ct	M	
69	94	**D. A. Miller (South Africa/World)**	45	119	R. G. Sharma (India)
64	112	M. J. Guptill (New Zealand)	44	52	A. B. de Villiers (South Africa)
50	124	Shoaib Malik (Pakistan/World)	44	91	D. J. Bravo (West Indies)
47	86	Mohammad Nabi (Afghanistan)	42	78	S. K. Raina (India)
47	88	D. A. Warner (Australia)	42	86	G. H. Dockrell (Ireland)
47	92	T. G. Southee (New Zealand)	42	95	V. Kohli (India)
46	102	L. R. P. L. Taylor (New Zealand)	42	113	Mahmudullah (Bangladesh)
46	113	E. J. G. Morgan (England)	40	110	K. J. O'Brien (Ireland)

D. A. Miller's record excludes 2 dismissals (1ct, 1st) in one match when keeping wicket and A. B. de Villiers's excludes 28 (21ct, 7st) in 26 matches.

TEAM RECORDS

HIGHEST INNINGS TOTALS

278-3	(20 overs)	Afghanistan v Ireland at Dehradun	2018-19
278-4	(20 overs)	Czechia v Turkey at Ilfov	2019
263-3	(20 overs)	Australia v Sri Lanka at Pallekele	2016
260-5	(20 overs)	India v Sri Lanka at Indore	2017-18
260-6	(20 overs)	Sri Lanka v Kenya at Johannesburg	2007-08
252-3	(20 overs)	Scotland v Netherlands at Malahide	2019
248-6	(20 overs)	Australia v England at Southampton	2013
245-1	**(20 overs)**	**Canada v Panama at Coolidge**	**2021-22**
245-5	(18.5 overs)	Australia v New Zealand at Auckland	2017-18
245-6	(20 overs)	West Indies v India at Lauderhill	2016
244-4	(20 overs)	India v West Indies at Lauderhill	2016
243-5	(20 overs)	New Zealand v West Indies at Mount Maunganui	2017-18
243-6	(20 overs)	New Zealand v Australia at Auckland	2017-18
242-6	**(20 overs)**	**Tanzania v Mozambique at Kigali**	**2021-22**
241-3	(20 overs)	England v New Zealand at Napier	2019-20
241-6	(20 overs)	South Africa v England at Centurion	2009-10
240-3	(20 overs)	Namibia v Botswana at Windhoek	2019
240-3	(20 overs)	India v West Indies at Mumbai	2019-20
240-5	**(20 overs)**	**Tanzania v Cameroon at Kigali**	**2021-22**

LOWEST INNINGS TOTALS

21	(8.3 overs)	Turkey v Czechia at Ilfov	2019
26	**(12.4 overs)**	**Lesotho v Uganda at Kigali City**	**2021-22**
28	(11.3 overs)	Turkey v Luxembourg at Ilfov	2019
32	(8.5 overs)	Turkey v Austria at Ilfov	2019
37	**(17.2 overs)**	**Panama v Canada at Coolidge**	**2021-22**
38	**(10.1 overs)**	**Cameroon v Mozambique at Kigali**	**2021-22**
39	(10.3 overs)	Netherlands v Sri Lanka at Chittagong	2013-14

44	(10 overs)	**Netherlands v Sri Lanka at Sharjah**............................	**2021-22**
45	(11.5 overs)	West Indies v England at Basseterre.......................	2018-19
46	(12.1 overs)	Botswana v Namibia at Windhoek...........................	2019
50	**(13 overs)**	**Malta v Belgium at Valletta**............................	**2021**
51	**(16 overs)**	**Cameroon v Botswana at Kigali**.........................	**2021-22**
52	(15.2 overs)	Serbia v Greece at Corfu	2019-20
53	(14.3 overs)	Nepal v Ireland at Belfast................................	2015
53	(16 overs)	Germany v Italy at Utrecht................................	2019
53	(13 overs)	Turkey v Romania at Ilfov................................	2019
55	**(16 overs)**	**Sierra Leone v Nigeria at Lagos**.........................	**2021-22**
55	**(14.2 overs)**	**West Indies v England at Dubai**.........................	**2021-22**

OTHER RECORDS

MOST APPEARANCES

124	Shoaib Malik (Pakistan/World)		102	L. R. P. L. Taylor (New Zealand)
119	Mohammad Hafeez (Pakistan)		**99**	**Mushfiqur Rahim (Bangladesh)**
119	R. G. Sharma (India)		99	Shahid Afridi (Pakistan/World)
113	Mahmudullah (Bangladesh)		98	M. S. Dhoni (India)
113	E. J. G. Morgan (England)		**95**	**V. Kohli (India)**
112	M. J. Guptill (New Zealand)		**95**	**D. A. Miller (South Africa/World)**
110	K. J. O'Brien (Ireland)			

MEN'S TWENTY20 WORLD CUP FINALS

2007-08	INDIA (157-5) beat Pakistan (152) by five runs....................	Johannesburg
2009	PAKISTAN (139-2) beat Sri Lanka (138-6) by eight wickets	Lord's
2010	ENGLAND (148-3) beat Australia (147-6) by seven wickets	Bridgetown
2012-13	WEST INDIES (137-6) beat Sri Lanka (101) by 36 runs.............	Colombo (RPS)
2013-14	SRI LANKA (134-4) beat India (130-4) by six wickets..............	Mirpur
2015-16	WEST INDIES (161-6) beat England (155-9) by four wickets	Kolkata
2021-22	**AUSTRALIA (173-2) beat New Zealand (172-4) by eight wickets ...**	**Dubai**

MISCELLANEOUS RECORDS

LARGE ATTENDANCES

Test Series

943,000	Australia v England (5 Tests)	1936-37

In England

549,650	England v Australia (5 Tests)	1953

Test Matches

†‡465,000	India v Pakistan, Calcutta	1998-99
350,534	Australia v England, Melbourne (Third Test)	1936-37

Attendance at India v England at Calcutta in 1981-82 may have exceeded 350,000.

In England

158,000+	England v Australia, Leeds	1948
140,111	England v India, Lord's....................................	2011
137,915	England v Australia, Lord's................................	1953

Test Match Day

‡100,000	India v Pakistan, Calcutta (first four days).................	1998-99
91,112	Australia v England, Melbourne (Fourth Test, first day).......	2013-14
90,800	Australia v West Indies, Melbourne (Fifth Test, second day)......	1960-61
89,155	Australia v England, Melbourne (Fourth Test, first day).........	2006-07

Other First-Class Matches in England

93,000	England v Australia, Lord's (Fourth Victory Match, 3 days)	1945
80,000+	Surrey v Yorkshire, The Oval (3 days)	1906
78,792	Yorkshire v Lancashire, Leeds (3 days).....................	1904
76,617	Lancashire v Yorkshire, Manchester (3 days)	1926

One-Day Internationals

‡100,000	India v South Africa, Calcutta............................	1993-94
‡100,000	India v West Indies, Calcutta.............................	1993-94
‡100,000	India v West Indies, Calcutta.............................	1994-95
‡100,000	India v Sri Lanka, Calcutta (World Cup semi-final)	1995-96
‡100,000	India v Australia, Kolkata	2003-04
93,013	Australia v New Zealand, Melbourne (World Cup final)	2014-15
‡90,000	India v Pakistan, Calcutta	1986-87
‡90,000	India v South Africa, Calcutta............................	1991-92
87,182	England v Pakistan, Melbourne (World Cup final)	1991-92
86,133	Australia v West Indies, Melbourne	1983-84

Twenty20 International

84,041	Australia v India, Melbourne..............................	2007-08

Women's International

86,174	Australia v India, Melbourne (Twenty20 World Cup final)	2019-20

† *Estimated.*
‡ *No official attendance figures were issued for these games, but capacity at Calcutta (now Kolkata) is believed to have reached 100,000 following rebuilding in 1993.*

LORD'S CRICKET GROUND

Lord's and the Marylebone Cricket Club were founded in London in 1787. The Club has enjoyed an uninterrupted career since that date, but there have been three grounds known as Lord's. The first (1787–1810) was situated where Dorset Square now is; the second (1809–13), at North Bank, had to be abandoned owing to the cutting of the Regent's Canal; and the third, opened in 1814, is the present one at St John's Wood. It was not until 1866 that the freehold of Lord's was secured by MCC. The present pavilion was erected in 1890 at a cost of £21,000.

MINOR CRICKET

HIGHEST INDIVIDUAL SCORES

1,009*	P. P. Dhanawade, K. C. Gandhi English School v Arya Gurukul at Kalyan	2015-16
	Dhanawade faced 327 balls in 6 hours 36 minutes and hit 129 fours and 59 sixes	
628*	A. E. J. Collins, Clark's House v North Town at Clifton College..............	1899
	Junior house match. He batted 6 hours 50 minutes spread over four afternoons	
566	C. J. Eady, Break-o'-Day v Wellington at Hobart	1901-02
556*	P. Moliya, Mohinder Lal Amarnath C Ac U14 v Yogi C Ac U14 at Vadodara...	2018-19
546	P. P. Shaw, Rizvi Springfield School v St Francis D'Assisi School at Mumbai ...	2013-14
515	D. R. Havewalla, B. B. and C. I. Railways v St Xavier's at Bombay	1933-34
506*	J. C. Sharp, Melbourne GS v Geelong College at Melbourne	1914-15
502*	M. Chamanlal, Mohindra Coll., Patiala v Government Coll., Rupar at Patiala ...	1956-57
498	Arman Jaffer, Rizvi Springfield School v IES Raja Shivaji School at Mumbai....	2010-11
490	S. Dadswell, North West University v Potchefstroom at Potchefstroom	2017-18
486*	S. Sankruth Sriram, JSS Intl School U16 v Hebron School U16 at Ootacamund .	2014-15
485	A. E. Stoddart, Hampstead v Stoics at Hampstead..........................	1886
475*	Mohammad Iqbal, Muslim Model HS v Government HS, Sialkot at Gujranwala.	1958-59
473	Arman Jaffer, Rizvi Springfield School v IES VN Sule School at Mumbai......	2012-13
466*	G. T. S. Stevens, Beta v Lambda (Univ Coll School house match) at Neasden...	1919
	Stevens scored his 466 and took 14 wickets on one day	
461*	Ali Zorain Khan, Nagpur Cricket Academy v Reshimbagh Gymkhana at Nagpur	2010-11
459	J. A. Prout, Wesley College v Geelong College at Geelong	1908-09
451*	V. H. Zol, Maharashtra Under-19 v Assam Under-19 at Nasik	2011-12

The highest score in a Minor County match is 323* by F. E. Lacey for Hampshire v Norfolk at Southampton in 1887; the highest in the Minor Counties Championship is 282 by E. Garnett for Berkshire v Wiltshire at Reading in 1908.

HIGHEST PARTNERSHIPS

721* for 1st	B. Manoj Kumar and M. S. Tumbi, St Peter's High School v St Philip's High School at Secunderabad.	2006-07
664* for 3rd	V. G. Kambli and S. R. Tendulkar, Sharadashram Vidyamandir School v St Xavier's High School at Bombay..............................	1987-88

Manoj Kumar and Tumbi reportedly scored 721 in 40 overs in an Under-13 inter-school match; they hit 103 fours between them, but no sixes. Their opponents were all out for 21 in seven overs. Kambli was 16 years old, Tendulkar 14. Tendulkar made his Test debut 21 months later.

MOST WICKETS WITH CONSECUTIVE BALLS

There are **two** recorded instances of a bowler taking nine wickets with consecutive balls. Both came in school games: Paul Hugo, for Smithfield School v Aliwal North at Smithfield, South Africa, in 1930-31, and Stephen Fleming (not the future Test captain), for Marlborough College A v Bohally School at Blenheim, New Zealand, in 1967-68. There are five further reported instances of eight wickets in eight balls, the most recent by Mike Walters for the Royal Army Educational Corps v Joint Air Transport Establishment at Beaconsfield in 1979.

TEN WICKETS FOR NO RUNS

There are **30** recorded instances of a bowler taking all ten wickets in an innings for no runs, the most recent Akash Choudhary, for Disha Cricket Academy v Pearl Academy in the Late Bahwer Singh T20 Tournament in Jaipur 2017-18. When Jennings Tune did it, for the Yorkshire club Cliffe v Eastrington at Cliffe in 1922, all ten of his victims were bowled.

NOUGHT ALL OUT

In minor matches, this is more common than might be imagined. The historian Peter Wynne-Thomas says the first recorded example was in Norfolk, where an Eleven of Fakenham, Walsingham and Hempton were dismissed for nought by an Eleven of Litcham, Dunham and Brisley in July 1815.

MOST DISMISSALS IN AN INNINGS

The only reported instance of a wicketkeeper being involved in all ten dismissals in an innings was by Welihinda Badalge Bennett. Details are disputed, but some sources state that it was for Mahinda College against Richmond College in Ceylon (now Sri Lanka) in 1952-53, and his feat comprised six catches and four stumpings (or vice versa). There are three other known instances of nine dismissals in the same innings, one of which – by H. W. P. Middleton for Priory v Mitre in a Repton School house match in 1930 – may have included eight stumpings. Young Rangers' innings against Bohran Gymkhana in Karachi in 1969-70 included nine run-outs.

The widespread nature – and differing levels of supervision – of minor cricket matches mean that record claims have to be treated with caution. Additions and corrections to the above records for minor cricket will only be considered for inclusion in Wisden if they are corroborated by independent evidence of the achievement.

Research: Steven Lynch

RECORD HIT

The Rev. W. Fellows, while at practice on the Christ Church ground at Oxford in 1856, reportedly drove a ball bowled by Charles Rogers 175 yards from hit to pitch; it is claimed that the feat was matched by J. W. Erskine in a match at Galle in 1902.

BIGGEST HIT AT LORD'S

The only known instance of a batter hitting a ball over the present pavilion at Lord's occurred when A. E. Trott, appearing for MCC against Australians on July 31, August 1, 2, 1899, drove M. A. Noble so far and high that the ball struck a chimney pot and fell behind the building.

THROWING THE CRICKET BALL

140 yards 2 feet	Robert Percival, on the Durham Sands racecourse, Co. Durham .	c1882
140 yards 9 inches . . .	Ross Mackenzie, at Toronto	1872
140 yards	"King Billy" the Aborigine, at Clermont, Queensland	1872

Extensive research by David Rayvern Allen has shown that these traditional records are probably authentic, if not necessarily wholly accurate. Modern competitions have failed to produce similar distances although Ian Pont, the Essex all-rounder who also played baseball, was reported to have thrown 138 yards in Cape Town in 1981. There have been speculative reports attributing throws of 150 yards or more to figures as diverse as the South African Test player Colin Bland, the Latvian javelin thrower Jānis Lūsis, who won a gold medal for the Soviet Union in the 1968 Olympics, and the British sprinter Charley Ransome. The definitive record is still awaited.

COUNTY CHAMPIONSHIP

MOST APPEARANCES

762	W. Rhodes	Yorkshire	1898–1930
707	F. E. Woolley	Kent	1906–1938
668	C. P. Mead	Hampshire	1906–1936
617	N. Gifford	Worcestershire (484), Warwickshire (133)	1960–1988
611	W. G. Quaife	Warwickshire	1895–1928
601	G. H. Hirst	Yorkshire	1891–1921

MOST CONSECUTIVE APPEARANCES

423	K. G. Suttle	Sussex	1954–1969
412	J. G. Binks	Yorkshire	1955–1969

J. Vine made 417 consecutive appearances for Sussex in all first-class matches (399 of them in the Championship) between July 1900 and September 1914.

J. G. Binks did not miss a Championship match for Yorkshire between making his debut in June 1955 and retiring at the end of the 1969 season.

UMPIRES

MOST COUNTY CHAMPIONSHIP APPEARANCES

570	T. W. Spencer	1950–1980	517	H. G. Baldwin	1932–1962
531	F. Chester	1922–1955	511	A. G. T. Whitehead	1970–2005
523	D. J. Constant	1969–2006			

MOST SEASONS ON ENGLISH FIRST-CLASS LIST

38	D. J. Constant	1969–2006	27	J. W. Holder	1983–2009
36	A. G. T. Whitehead	1970–2005	27	J. Moss	1899–1929
31	K. E. Palmer	1972–2002	26	W. A. J. West	1896–1925
31	T. W. Spencer	1950–1980	25	H. G. Baldwin	1932–1962
30	R. Julian	1972–2001	25	A. Jepson	1960–1984
30	P. B. Wight	1966–1995	25	J. G. Langridge	1956–1980
29	H. D. Bird	1970–1998	25	B. J. Meyer	1973–1997
28	F. Chester	1922–1955	25	D. R. Shepherd	1981–2005
28	B. Leadbeater	1981–2008			
28	R. Palmer	1980–2007			
27	B. Dudleston	1984–2010			

WOMEN'S TEST RECORDS

This section covers all women's Tests to December 31, 2021.

RESULTS SUMMARY OF WOMEN'S TESTS

1934-35 to December 31, 2021 (141 matches)

	Tests	Won	Lost	Drawn	% Won	Toss Won
Ireland.................	1	1	0	0	100.00	0
Sri Lanka	1	1	0	0	100.00	1
Australia	75	20	10	45	26.66	28
England	96	20	14	62	20.83	56
India....................	37	5	5	27	13.51	19
South Africa	12	1	5	6	8.33	6
New Zealand.............	45	2	10	33	4.44	19
Netherlands..............	1	0	1	0	0.00	1
Pakistan	3	0	2	1	0.00	1
West Indies.............	11	0	3	8	0.00	10

Teams which appeared in 2021 are shown in bold.

BATTING RECORDS

HIGHEST INDIVIDUAL INNINGS

242	Kiran Baluch.............	Pakistan v West Indies at Karachi.............	2003-04
214	M. D. Raj	India v England at Taunton...................	2002
213*	E. A. Perry	Australia v England at North Sydney	2017-18
209*	K. L. Rolton	Australia v England at Leeds.............	2001
204	K. E. Flavell	New Zealand v England at Scarborough.......	1996
204	M. A. J. Goszko	Australia v England at Shenley..............	2001
200	J. Broadbent	Australia v England at Guildford	1998

MOST RUNS

		T	I	NO	R	HS	100	Avge
1	J. A. Brittin (England)...........	27	44	5	1,935	167	5	49.61
2	C. M. Edwards (England)	23	43	4	1,676	117	4	44.10
3	R. Heyhoe Flint (England)	22	38	3	1,594	179	3	45.54
4	D. A. Hockley (New Zealand)....	19	29	4	1,301	126*	4	52.04
5	C. A. Hodges (England)	18	31	2	1,164	158*	2	40.13
6	S. Agarwal (India).............	13	23	1	1,110	190	4	50.45
7	E. Bakewell (England)..........	12	22	4	1,078	124	4	59.88
8	S. C. Taylor (England)	15	27	2	1,030	177	4	41.20
9	M. E. Maclagan (England)	14	25	1	1,007	119	2	41.95
10	K. L. Rolton (Australia)	14	22	4	1,002	209*	2	55.66

HIGHEST PARTNERSHIP FOR EACH WICKET

241	for 1st	Kiran Baluch/Sajjida Shah	P v WI	Karachi	2003-04
275	for 2nd	M. D. Thirush Kamini/P. G. Raut ..	I v SA	Mysore	2014-15
309	for 3rd	L. A. Reeler/D. A. Annetts........	A v E	Collingham	1987
253	for 4th	K. L. Rolton/L. C. Broadfoot	A v E	Leeds........	2001
138	for 5th	J. Logtenberg/C. van der Westhuizen	SA v E	Shenley	2003
229	for 6th	J. M. Fields/R. L. Haynes.........	A v E	Worcester	2009
157	for 7th	M. D. Raj/J. N. Goswami.........	I v E	Taunton.......	2002
181	for 8th	S. J. Griffiths/D. L. Wilson........	A v NZ	Auckland (CP) .	1989-90
107	for 9th	B. A. Botha/M. Payne	SA v NZ	Cape Town	1971-72
119	for 10th	S. Nitschke/C. R. Smith	A v E	Hove	2005

BOWLING RECORDS

BEST BOWLING ANALYSES

8-53	N. David	India v England at Jamshedpur	1995-96
7-6	M. B. Duggan	England v Australia at Melbourne	1957-58
7-7	E. R. Wilson	Australia v England at Melbourne	1957-58
7-10	M. E. Maclagan	England v Australia at Brisbane	1934-35
7-18	A. Palmer	Australia v England at Brisbane	1934-35
7-24	L. Johnston	Australia v New Zealand at Melbourne	1971-72
7-34	G. E. McConway	England v India at Worcester	1986
7-41	J. A. Burley	New Zealand v England at The Oval	1966

MOST WICKETS IN A MATCH

13-226	Shaiza Khan	Pakistan v West Indies at Karachi	2003-04

MOST WICKETS

		T	Balls	R	W	BB	5I	10M	Avge	SR
1	M. B. Duggan (England)	17	3,734	1,039	77	7-6	5	0	13.49	48.49
2	E. R. Wilson (Australia)	11	2,885	803	68	7-7	4	2	11.80	42.42
3	D. F. Edulji (India)	20	5,188	1,624	63	6-64	1	0	25.77	82.34
4	M. E. Maclagan (England)	14	3,432	935	60	7-10	3	0	15.58	57.20
	C. L. Fitzpatrick (Australia)	13	3,603	1,147	60	5-29	2	0	19.11	60.05
	S. Kulkarni (India)	19	3,320	1,647	60	6-99	5	0	27.45	55.33
7	R. H. Thompson (Australia)	16	4,304	1,040	57	5-33	1	0	18.24	75.50
8	J. Lord (New Zealand)	15	3,108	1,049	55	6-119	4	1	19.07	56.50
9	E. Bakewell (England)	12	2,698	831	50	7-61	3	1	16.62	53.96

WICKETKEEPING RECORDS

SIX DISMISSALS IN AN INNINGS

8 (6ct, 2st)	L. Nye	England v New Zealand at New Plymouth	1991-92
6 (2ct, 4st)	B. A. Brentnall	New Zealand v South Africa at Johannesburg	1971-72

MOST DISMISSALS IN A CAREER

		T	Ct	St
58	C. Matthews (Australia)	20	46	12
43	J. Smit (England)	21	39	4
36	S. A. Hodges (England)	11	19	17
28	B. A. Brentnall (New Zealand)	10	16	12

TEAM RECORDS

HIGHEST INNINGS TOTALS

569-6 dec	Australia v England at Guildford	1998
525	Australia v India at Ahmedabad	1983-84
517-8	New Zealand v England at Scarborough	1996
503-5 dec	England v New Zealand at Christchurch	1934-35

LOWEST INNINGS TOTALS

35	England v Australia at Melbourne	1957-58
38	Australia v England at Melbourne	1957-58
44	New Zealand v England at Christchurch	1934-35
47	Australia v England at Brisbane	1934-35

WOMEN'S ONE-DAY INTERNATIONAL RECORDS

This section covers women's one-day international cricket to December 31, 2021. Bold type denotes performances in the calendar year 2021 or, in career figures, players who appeared in that year.

RESULTS SUMMARY OF WOMEN'S ONE-DAY INTERNATIONALS

1973 to December 31, 2021 (1,231 matches)

	Matches	Won	Lost	Tied	No Result	% Won (excl NR)
Australia	**338**	**266**	**64**	**2**	**6**	**80.12**
England	**359**	**212**	**134**	**2**	**11**	**60.91**
India	**283**	**154**	**124**	**1**	**4**	**55.19**
South Africa	**209**	**108**	**90***	**3**	**8**	**53.73**
New Zealand	**352**	**172**	**172**	**2**	**6**	**49.71**
West Indies	**191**	**88***	**97**	**1**	**5**	**47.31**
Sri Lanka	167	56	106	–	5	34.56
Trinidad & Tobago	6	2	4	–	–	33.33
Bangladesh	**42**	**13**	**27**	**–**	**2**	**32.50**
Pakistan	**178**	**51**	**123**	**1**	**3**	**29.14**
Ireland	**153**	**42**	**105**	**–**	**6**	**28.57**
Jamaica	5	1	4	–	–	20.00
Netherlands	101	19	81	–	1	19.00
Denmark	33	6	27	–	–	18.18
International XI	18	3	14	–	1	17.64
Young England	6	1	5	–	–	16.66
Scotland	8	1	7	–	–	12.50
Zimbabwe	**8**	**1**	**7**	**–**	**–**	**12.50**
Japan	5	0	5	–	–	0.00

* *Includes one settled by a super over.*

Matches abandoned without a ball bowled are not included except where the toss took place, when they are shown as no result. In the percentages of matches won, ties are counted as half a win.

Teams which appeared in 2021 are shown in bold.

BATTING RECORDS

HIGHEST INDIVIDUAL INNINGS

232*	A. C. Kerr	New Zealand v Ireland at Dublin	2018
229*	B. J. Clark	Australia v Denmark at Mumbai	1997-98
188	D. B. Sharma	India v Ireland at Potchefstroom	2017
178*	A. M. C. Jayangani	Sri Lanka v Australia at Bristol	2017
173*	C. M. Edwards	England v Ireland at Pune	1997-98
171*	H. Kaur	India v Australia at Derby	2017
171	S. R. Taylor	West Indies v Sri Lanka at Mumbai	2012-13
168*	T. T. Beaumont	England v Pakistan at Taunton	2016
168	S. W. Bates	New Zealand v Pakistan at Sydney	2008-09
157	R. H. Priest	New Zealand v Sri Lanka at Lincoln	2015-16
156*	L. M. Keightley	Australia v Pakistan at Melbourne	1996-97
156*	S. C. Taylor	England v India at Lord's	2006
154*	K. L. Rolton	Australia v Sri Lanka at Christchurch	2000-01
153*	J. Logtenberg	South Africa v Netherlands at Deventer	2007
152*	M. M. Lanning	Australia v Australia at Bristol	2017
151	K. L. Rolton	Australia v Ireland at Dublin	2005
151	S. W. Bates	New Zealand v Ireland at Dublin	2018

MOST RUNS

		M	I	NO	R	HS	100	Avge
1	M. D. Raj (India)	220	199	55	7,391	125*	7	51.32
2	C. M. Edwards (England)	191	180	23	5,992	173*	9	38.16
3	S. R. Taylor (West Indies) ...	134	130	18	5,103	171	7	45.56
4	B. J. Clark (Australia)	118	114	12	4,844	229*	5	47.49
5	K. L. Rolton (Australia)......	141	132	32	4,814	154*	8	48.14
6	S. W. Bates (New Zealand)	130	124	12	4,605	168	10	41.11
7	A. E. Satterthwaite (NZ) ...	133	127	17	4,298	137*	7	39.07
8	S. C. Taylor (England).......	126	120	18	4,101	156*	8	40.20
9	D. A. Hockley (New Zealand) ..	118	115	18	4,066	117	4	41.91
10	S. J. Taylor (England)	126	119	13	4,056	147	7	38.26
11	M. M. Lanning (Australia) ..	88	88	13	3,984	152*	14	53.12
12	M. du Preez (South Africa) ..	142	129	23	3,554	116*	2	33.52

FASTEST ONE-DAY INTERNATIONAL FIFTIES

Balls			
20	D. J. S. Dottin	West Indies v Sri Lanka at Mumbai	2012-13
22	N. R. Sciver...........	England v Pakistan at Worcester................	2016
23	M. M. Lanning	Australia v New Zealand at Sydney	2012-13

FASTEST ONE-DAY INTERNATIONAL HUNDREDS

Balls			
45	M. M. Lanning	Australia v New Zealand at Sydney	2012-13
57	K. L. Rolton...........	Australia v South Africa at Lincoln............	2000-01
59	S. F. M. Devine	New Zealand v Ireland at Dublin	2018

HIGHEST PARTNERSHIP FOR EACH WICKET

320	for 1st	D. B. Sharma/P. G. Raut	I v Ire	Potchefstroom	2017
295	for 2nd	A. C. Kerr/L. M. Kasperek.....	NZ v Ire	Clontarf	2018
244	for 3rd	K. L. Rolton/L. C. Sthalekar ...	A v Ire	Dublin (Sandymount).	2005
224*	for 4th	J. Logtenberg/M. du Preez....	SA v Neth	Deventer	2007
188*	for 5th	S. C. Taylor/J. Smit	E v SL	Lincoln...........	2000-01
142	for 6th	S. E. Luus/C. L. Tryon.......	SA v Ire	Dublin (Merrion)	2016
104*	for 7th	{ S. J. Tsukigawa/N. J. Browne .	NZ v E	Chennai	2006-07
104		{ N. R. Sciver/D. Hazell	E v SL	Colombo (RPS)	2016-17
88	for 8th	N. N. D. de Silva/ O. U. Ranasinghe..........	SL v E	Hambantota	2018-19
73	for 9th	L. R. F. Askew/I. T. Guha	E v NZ	Chennai	2006-07
76	for 10th	A. J. Blackwell/K. M. Beams. .	A v I	Derby.............	2017

† *110 runs were scored for West Indies' 7th wicket v Sri Lanka at Dambulla in 2012-13, in two partnerships: S. A. Campbelle and A. Mohammed put on 34 before Mohammed retired hurt, then Campbelle and S. C. Selman added a further 76.*

BOWLING RECORDS

BEST BOWLING ANALYSES

7-4	Sajjida Shah............	Pakistan v Japan at Amsterdam.................	2003
7-8	J. M. Chamberlain......	England v Denmark at Haarlem	1991
7-14	A. Mohammed..........	West Indies v Pakistan at Mirpur	2011-12
7-22	E. A. Perry.............	Australia v England at Canterbury	2019
7-24	S. Nitschke.............	Australia v England at Kidderminster...........	2005
6-10	J. Lord.................	New Zealand v India at Auckland	1981-82
6-10	M. Maben	India v Sri Lanka at Kandy	2003-04
6-10	S. Ismail...............	South Africa v Netherlands at Savar	2011-12

HAT-TRICKS

Four Wickets in Five Balls

D. van Niekerk   South Africa v West Indies at Basseterre   2012-13

Hat-Tricks

There have been **11** hat-tricks in one-day internationals, all by different bowlers. The most recent:

M. M. Klaas	South Africa v Pakistan at Potchefstroom	2019
M. Schutt	Australia v West Indies at North Sound	2019-20

MOST WICKETS

		M	Balls	R	W	BB	4I	Avge
1	**J. N. Goswami (India)**	**192**	**9,387**	**5,182**	**240**	**6-31**	**9**	**21.59**
2	C. L. Fitzpatrick (Australia)	109	6,017	3,023	180	5-14	11	16.79
3	**A. Mohammed (West Indies)**	**134**	**5,966**	**3,458**	**171**	**7-14**	**13**	**20.22**
4	**K. H. Brunt (England)**	**130**	**6,344**	**3,712**	**160**	**5-18**	**8**	**23.20**
5	**S. Ismail (South Africa)**	**110**	**5,348**	**3,261**	**154**	**6-10**	**5**	**21.17**
6	**E. A. Perry (Australia)**	**118**	**5,230**	**3,827**	**152**	**7-22**	**4**	**25.17**
7	Sana Mir (Pakistan)	120	5,942	3,665	151	5-32	8	24.27
8	**S. R. Taylor (West Indies)**	**134**	**5,501**	**3,167**	**148**	**4-17**	**5**	**21.39**
9	L. C. Sthalekar (Australia)	125	5,965	3,646	146	5-35	2	24.97
10	N. L. David (India)	97	4,892	2,305	141	5-20	6	16.34
11	**D. van Niekerk (South Africa)** . . .	**107**	**4,576**	**2,642**	**138**	**5-17**	**8**	**19.14**
12	J. L. Gunn (England)	144	5,906	3,822	136	5-22	6	28.10
13	**M. Kapp (South Africa)**	**118**	**5,229**	**3,200**	**134**	**4-14**	**4**	**23.88**

WICKETKEEPING AND FIELDING RECORDS

MOST DISMISSALS IN AN INNINGS

6 (4ct, 2st)	S. L. Illingworth	New Zealand v Australia at Beckenham	1993
6 (1ct, 5st)	V. Kalpana	India v Denmark at Slough	1993
6 (2ct, 4st)	Batool Fatima	Pakistan v West Indies at Karachi	2003-04
6 (4ct, 2st)	Batool Fatima	Pakistan v Sri Lanka at Colombo (PSO)	2010-11

MOST DISMISSALS

			M	Ct	St
1	**164**	**T. Chetty (South Africa)**	**117**	**115**	**49**
2	136	S. J. Taylor (England)	118	85	51
3	133	R. J. Rolls (New Zealand)	101	90	43
4	114	J. Smit (England)	108	69	45
5	103	M. R. Aguilleira (West Indies)	104	76	27
6	99	J. C. Price (Australia)	83	69	30
7	97	Batool Fatima (Pakistan)	68	51	46
8	93	R. H. Priest (New Zealand)	86	72	21
9	81	A. Jain (India)	61	30	51

T. Chetty's total excludes two catches in two matches, S. J. Taylor's and M. R. Aguilleira's each exclude two in eight matches and Batool Fatima's three in 15 while not keeping wicket; J. C. Price's excludes one taken in the field after giving up the gloves mid-game. R. J. Rolls did not keep wicket in three matches and J. Smit in one; neither took any catches in these games.

MOST CATCHES IN AN INNINGS IN THE FIELD

4	Z. J. Goss	Australia v New Zealand at Adelaide		1995-96
4	J. L. Gunn	England v New Zealand at Lincoln		2014-15
4	Nahida Khan	Pakistan v Sri Lanka at Dambulla		2017-18

MOST CATCHES

Ct	M		Ct	M	
67	130	**S. W. Bates (New Zealand)**	55	144	**A. J. Blackwell (Australia)**
65	192	**J. N. Goswami (India)**	52	126	**L. S. Greenway (England)**
60	134	**S. R. Taylor (West Indies)**	52	191	**C. M. Edwards (England)**
58	220	**M. D. Raj (India)**	51	133	**A. E. Satterthwaite (NZ)**
56	107	**D. van Niekerk (South Africa)**			

TEAM RECORDS

HIGHEST INNINGS TOTALS

491-4	New Zealand v Ireland at Dublin	2018
455-5	New Zealand v Pakistan at Christchurch	1996-97
440-3	New Zealand v Ireland at Dublin	2018
418	New Zealand v Ireland at Dublin	2018
412-3	Australia v Denmark at Mumbai	1997-98
397-4	Australia v Pakistan at Melbourne	1996-97
378-5	England v Pakistan at Worcester	2016
377-7	England v Pakistan at Leicester	2017
376-2	England v Pakistan at Vijayawada	1997-98
375-5	Netherlands v Japan at Schiedam	2003

LOWEST INNINGS TOTALS

22	Netherlands v West Indies at Deventer	2008
23	Pakistan v Australia at Melbourne	1996-97
24	Scotland v England at Reading	2001
26	India v New Zealand as St Saviour	2002
27	Pakistan v Australia at Hyderabad (India)	1997-98
28	Japan v Pakistan at Amsterdam	2003
29	Netherlands v Australia at Perth	1988-89

LARGEST VICTORIES

408 runs	New Zealand (455-5 in 50 overs) v Pakistan (47 in 23 overs) at Christchurch	1996-97
374 runs	Australia (397-4 in 50 overs) v Pakistan (23 in 24.1 overs) at Melbourne	1996-97
363 runs	Australia (412-3 in 50 overs) v Denmark (49 in 25.5 overs) at Mumbai	1997-98

*There have been **37** instances of victory by ten wickets.*

TIED MATCHES

New Zealand (147-9 in 60 overs) v England (147-8 in 60 overs) at Auckland	1991-92
England (167-8 in 60 overs) v Australia (167 in 60 overs) at Christchurch	1981-82
New Zealand (176-9 in 50 overs) v India (176 in 49.1 overs) at Indore	1997-98
South Africa (180-6 in 50 overs) v West Indies (180-8 in 50 overs) at Cape Town	2009-10
Australia (242 in 49.5 overs) v South Africa (242 in 50 overs) at Coffs Harbour	2016-17
South Africa (265-6 in 50 overs) v Pakistan (265-9 in 50 overs) at Benoni	2019

OTHER RECORDS

MOST APPEARANCES

220	**M. D. Raj (I)**	133	A. E. Satterthwaite (NZ)
192	**J. N. Goswami (I)**	131	D. J. S. Dottin (WI)
191	C. M. Edwards (E)	130	S. W. Bates (NZ)
144	A. J. Blackwell (A)	**130**	**K. H. Brunt (E)**
144	J. L. Gunn (E)	127	A. Chopra (I)
142	**M. du Preez (SA)**	126	L. S. Greenway (E)
141	K. L. Rolton (A)	126	S. C. Taylor (E)
134	S. J. McGlashan (NZ)	126	S. J. Taylor (E)
134	**A. Mohammed (WI)**	125	N. J. Browne (NZ)
134	**S. R. Taylor (WI)**	125	L. C. Sthalekar (A)

WOMEN'S WORLD CUP WINNERS

1973	England	1993	England	2008-09	England
1977-78	Australia	1997-98	Australia	2012-13	Australia
1981-82	Australia	2000-01	New Zealand	2017	England
1988-89	Australia	2004-05	Australia		

WOMEN'S TWENTY20 INTERNATIONAL RECORDS

This section covers women's Twenty20 international cricket to December 31, 2021. Bold type denotes performances in the calendar year 2021 or, in career figures, players who appeared in that year. The ICC extended official international status to Associate Twenty20 matches from June 2018.

RESULTS SUMMARY OF WOMEN'S TWENTY20 INTERNATIONALS

2004 to December 31, 2021 (1,013 matches)

	Matches	Won	Lost	No Result	% Won (excl NR)
Zimbabwe	24	**22**	2	–	91.66
England	155	**112***	42†	1	72.72
Australia	147	**98†**	47*	2	67.58
New Zealand	136	**78***	56*	2	58.20
West Indies	141	**78§**	60*	3	56.52
India	132	**69**	60	3	53.48
South Africa	120	**54**	63	3	46.15
Pakistan	123	**48**	73‡	2	39.66
Bangladesh	75	**27**	48	–	36.00
Ireland	82	**28**	53	1	34.56
Sri Lanka	100	**24**	72	4	25.00
Thailand	42	**27**	14	1	65.85
Namibia	37	**24**	13	–	64.86
Scotland	28	**18***	10	–	64.28
Uganda	25	**13**	12	–	52.00
Rwanda	31	**15**	16	–	48.38
Malaysia	29	**11**	18	–	37.93
Nigeria	24	**9**	15	–	37.50
Botswana	25	**7**	18	–	28.00
Netherlands	39	**8**	29†	2	21.62

*   *Includes one settled by a tie-break.* †   *Includes two settled by a tie-break.*
‡   *Includes three settled by a tie-break.* §   *Includes four settled by a tie-break.*
Most ties were decided by super overs, apart from one bowling contest between Australia and New Zealand.

Matches abandoned without a ball bowled are not included except where the toss took place, when they are shown as no result. In the percentages of matches won, ties are counted as half a win.
  Teams which appeared in 2021 are shown in bold.

A further 46 teams have played women's Twenty20 internationals, as follows: Guernsey (P1 W1); **Sweden (P1 W1); Brazil (P16 W14 L2);** Samoa (P12 W10 L2); Belize (P6 W5 L1); **Tanzania (P17 W14 L3); Nepal (P22 W17 L5); Germany (P22 W15 L7); United Arab Emirates (P21 W14 L7);** Indonesia (P17 W11 L6); **USA (P14 W9 L5);** Papua New Guinea (P22 W14 L8); **Kenya (P17 W10 L7);** Jersey (P7 W4 L3); **Hong Kong (P20 W11 L9);** China (P16 W8 L8); Vanuatu (P12 W6 L6); Malawi (P13 W6 L7); Chile (P9 W4 L5); Japan (P9 W4 L5); **Austria (P19 W8 L11);** Myanmar (P11 W4 L6 NR1); **Italy (P5 W2 L3); Sierra Leone (P13 W5 L8); France (P15 W5 L10); Canada (P9 W3 L6);** Oman (P9 W3 L6); Mexico (P10 W3 L7); **Mozambique (P22 W6 L16); Argentina (P11 W3 L8);** Kuwait (P16 W3 L13); Singapore (P12 W2 L9 NR1); **Norway (P7 W1 L6); Qatar (P7 W1 L6);** South Korea (P7 W1 L6); Costa Rica (P8 W1 L7); **Bhutan (P9 W1 L8);** Fiji (P12 L12); Lesotho (P6 L6); Mali (P6 L6); **eSwatini (P5 L5); Cameroon (P4 L4);** Peru (P4 L4); Philippines (P4 L4); **Belgium (P3 L3);** Maldives (P3 L3).

BATTING RECORDS

HIGHEST INDIVIDUAL INNINGS

148*	A. J. Healy	Australia v Sri Lanka at Sydney	2019-20
133*	M. M. Lanning	Australia v England at Chelmsford	2019
127*	**F. O. Kibasu**	**Tanzania v eSwatini at Gaborone**	**2021**
126*	S. L. Kalis	Netherlands v Germany at La Manga	2019
126	M. M. Lanning	Australia v Ireland at Sylhet	2013-14
124*	S. W. Bates	New Zealand v South Africa at Taunton	2018
124	D. N. Wyatt	England v India at Mumbai (BS)	2017-18
117*	B. L. Mooney	Australia v England at Canberra	2017-18
116*	S. A. Fritz	South Africa v Netherlands at Potchefstroom	2010-11
116	T. T. Beaumont	England v South Africa at Taunton	2018
116	P. Alako	Uganda v Mali at Kigali	2019

MOST RUNS

		M	I	NO	R	HS	100	Avge	SR
1	S. W. Bates (New Zealand)	125	122	9	3,344	124*	1	29.59	110.18
2	S. R. Taylor (West Indies)	111	109	23	3,121	90	0	36.29	
3	M. M. Lanning (Australia)	113	106	23	2,943	133*	2	35.45	115.23
4	D. J. S. Dottin (West Indies)	124	122	20	2,681	112*	2	26.28	
5	C. M. Edwards (England)	95	93	14	2,605	92*	0	32.97	106.93
6	S. F. M. Devine (New Zealand)	101	98	12	2,561	105	1	29.77	123.60
7	M. D. Raj (India)	89	84	21	2,364	97*	0	37.52	
8	H. Kaur (India)	120	108	21	2,307	103	1	26.51	
9	Bismah Maroof (Pakistan)	108	101	21	2,202	70*	0	27.52	92.40
10	S. J. Taylor (England)	90	87	12	2,177	77	0	29.02	110.67
11	A. J. Healy (Australia)	121	105	17	2,129	148*	1	24.19	129.97

Balls and strike-rates are not available for all matches.

FASTEST TWENTY20 INTERNATIONAL FIFTIES

Balls			
18	S. F. M. Devine	New Zealand v India at Bangalore	2015
20	Nida Dar	Pakistan v South Africa at Benoni	2019

FASTEST TWENTY20 INTERNATIONAL HUNDREDS

Balls			
38	D. J. S. Dottin	West Indies v South Africa at Basseterre	2010
49	H. Kaur	India v New Zealand at Providence	2018-19

HIGHEST PARTNERSHIP FOR EACH WICKET

257	for 1st	Y. Anggraeni/K. W. Prastini .	Indonesia v Philippines	Dasmarinas	2019-20
227	for 2nd	P. Alako/R. Musamali	Uganda v Mali	Kigali	2019
236*	for 3rd	Nigar Sultana/Farzana Haque.	Bangladesh v Maldives	Pokhara ...	2019-20
147*	for 4th	K. L. Rolton/A. J. Blackwell .	Australia v England	Taunton ...	2005
119*	for 5th	M. M. Lanning/R. L. Haynes .	Australia v New Zealand	N Sydney . .	2018-19
135*	**for 6th**	**G. Ishimwe/A. Ikuzwe**	**Rwanda v eSwatini**	**Gaborone** . .	**2021**
72	for 7th	M. I. Pascal/N. N. Saidi	Tanzania v Uganda	Kigali	2019
53	for 8th	I. C. Chuma/A. Monjane	Mozambique v Malawi	Blantyre ...	2019-20
67*	for 9th	D. Foerster/A. van Schoor ...	Namibia v Botswana	Windhoek..	2018-19
44	for 10th	W. M. Delgado/A. J. A. Campos	Costa Rica v Belize	San Jose ...	2019-20

BOWLING RECORDS

BEST BOWLING ANALYSES

7-3	F. C. J. Overdijk	**Netherlands v France at La Manga**	**2021**
6-0	A. Chand	Nepal v Maldives at Pokhara.	2019
6-3	Mas Elysa	Malaysia v China at Bangkok	2018-19
6-3	**S. Mosweu**	**Botswana v Mozambique at Gaborone**	**2021**
6-8	B. Mpedi	Botswana v Lesotho at Gaborone	2018
6-8	N. Thapa	Nepal v Hong Kong at Bangkok	2018-19
6-10	Zon Lin	Myanmar v Indonesia at Bangkok	2018-19
6-11	**E. Mbofana**	**Zimbabwe v eSwatini at Gaborone**	**2021**
6-16	**S. B. Wetoto**	**Kenya v Namibia at Kigali**	**2021**
6-17	A. E. Satterthwaite.......	New Zealand v England at Taunton	2007
5-0	N. N. Saidi	Tanzania v Mali at Kigali	2019
5-1	A. Doddaballapur	Germany v Austria at Seebarn.	2020
5-3	C. R. Seneviratne........	United Arab Emirates v Kuwait at Bangkok	2018-19
5-3	**M. J. McColl**	**Scotland v France at La Manga**	**2021**
5-4	C. Sutthiruang	Thailand v Indonesia at Bangkok	2018-19
5-5	D. J. S. Dottin	West Indies v Bangladesh at Providence.	2018-19
5-5	I. D. A. D. A. Laksmi	Indonesia v Philippines at Dasmarinas	2019-20

HAT-TRICKS

There have been **18** hat-tricks in Twenty20 internationals, two by C. Aweko. The most recent:

A. Bierswich	Germany v Austria at Seebarn	2020
A. Doddaballapur	Germany v Austria at Seebarn (*four wickets in four balls*)......	2020
C. Aweko	**Uganda v Cameroon at Gaborone**......................	**2021**
S. R. Taylor	**West Indies v Pakistan at North Sound**	**2021**
L. Cardoso	**Brazil v Canada at Naucalpan**	**2021-22**

MOST WICKETS

		M	B	R	W	BB	4I	Avge	ER
1	A. Mohammed (West Indies)........	117	2,373	2,206	125	5-10	7	17.64	5.57
2	E. A. Perry (Australia)............	126	2,285	2,237	115	4-12	4	19.45	5.87
3	S. Ismail (South Africa)	98	2,063	1,990	110	5-12	2	18.09	5.78
4	Nida Dar (Pakistan)	108	2,084	1,871	103	5-21	2	18.16	5.38
5	A. Shrubsole (England)	79	1,598	1,587	102	5-11	3	15.55	5.95
6	P. Yadav (India)	71	1,536	1,461	98	4-9	3	14.90	5.70
	S. R. Taylor (West Indies)	111	1,736	1,639	98	4-12	2	16.72	5.66
	K. H. Brunt (England)	94	2,027	1,864	98	3-6	0	19.02	5.51
9	S. F. M. Devine (New Zealand)	101	1,620	1,712	97	4-22	1	17.64	6.34
10	M. Schutt (Australia)	73	1,461	1,474	96	4-18	3	15.35	6.05
11	Sana Mir (Pakistan)	106	2,246	2,066	89	4-13	4	23.21	5.51
12	D. Hazell (England)	85	1,905	1,764	85	4-12	1	20.75	5.55

WICKETKEEPING AND FIELDING RECORDS

MOST DISMISSALS IN AN INNINGS

5 (1ct, 4st)	Kycia A. Knight......	West Indies v Sri Lanka at Colombo (RPS)	2012-13
5 (1ct, 4st)	Batool Fatima	Pakistan v Ireland at Dublin	2013
5 (1ct, 4st)	Batool Fatima	Pakistan v Ireland at Dublin (semi-final)........	2013
5 (3ct, 2st)	B. M. Bezuidenhout...	New Zealand v Ireland at Dublin	2018
5 (1ct, 4st)	S. J. Bryce	Scotland v Netherlands at Arbroath.............	2019

MOST DISMISSALS

			M	Ct	St
1	96	**A. J. Healy (Australia)**............................	**106**	**44**	**52**
2	74	S. J. Taylor (England).............................	88	23	51
3	73	R. H. Priest (New Zealand)........................	74	41	32
4	70	M. R. Aguilleira (West Indies).....................	85	36	34
5	67	T. Bhatia (India).................................	50	23	44
6	66	**T. Chetty (South Africa)**........................	**79**	**39**	**27**
7	50	Batool Fatima (Pakistan)...........................	45	11	39
	50	**K. J. Martin (New Zealand)**......................	**57**	**25**	**25**

A. J. Healy's record excludes two catches in 15 matches, M. R. Aguilleira's excludes two in ten and K. J. Martin's six in 37 while not keeping wicket. S. J. Taylor did not keep wicket in two matches and R. H. Priest in one; neither took any catches in these games.

MOST CATCHES IN AN INNINGS IN THE FIELD

4	L. S. Greenway	England v New Zealand at Chelmsford.................	2010
4	V. Krishnamurthy	India v Australia at Providence.....................	2018-19
4	**R. M. A. M. Avery** ...	**Brazil v Canada at Naucalpan**	**2021-22**

MOST CATCHES

Ct	M		Ct	M	
66	**125**	**S. W. Bates (New Zealand)**	47	120	H. Kaur (India)
58	104	J. L. Gunn (England)	44	89	N. R. Sciver (England)
54	85	L. S. Greenway (England)	41	113	M. M. Lanning (Australia)

TEAM RECORDS

HIGHEST INNINGS TOTALS

314-2	Uganda v Mali at Kigali....................................	2019
285-1	Tanzania v Mali at Kigali..................................	2019
260-1	Indonesia v Philippines at Dasmarinas......................	2019-20
255-2	Bangladesh v Maldives at Pokhara..........................	2019-20
250-3	England v South Africa at Taunton	2018
246-1	Rwanda v Mali at Kigali	2019
226-2	Australia v Sri Lanka at Sydney	2019-20
226-3	Australia v England at Chelmsford..........................	2019
217-2	Indonesia v Philippines at Dasmarinas	2019-20
217-4	Australia v Sri Lanka at Sydney	2019-20
216-1	New Zealand v South Africa at Taunton	2018
213-4	Ireland v Netherlands at Deventer	2019
210-5	Namibia v Lesotho at Gaborone	2018

LOWEST INNINGS TOTALS

6	Mali v Rwanda at Kigali..	2019
6	Maldives v Bangladesh at Pokhara..................................	2019-20
8	Maldives v Nepal at Pokhara.......................................	2019-20
10	Mali v Uganda at Kigali..	2019
11	Mali v Tanzania at Kigali..	2019
12	**Argentina v Brazil at Naucalpan**...............................	**2021-22**
14	China v United Arab Emirates at Bangkok...........................	2018-19
15	Philippines v Indonesia at Dasmarinas.............................	2019-20
16	Maldives v Nepal at Pokhara.......................................	2019-20
17†	Mali v Tanzania at Kigali..	2019
17	**Mozambique v Rwanda at Gabarone**.............................	**2021**
17	**eSwatini v Zimbabwe at Gabarone**.............................	**2021**
18†	Mexico v Brazil at Bogota..	2018-19
19	**eSwatini v Rwanda at Gaborone**...............................	**2021**

† *One woman absent.*

LARGEST VICTORIES

304 runs	Uganda (314-2 in 20 overs) v Mali (10 in 11.1 overs) at Kigali..........	2019
268 runs	Tanzania (285-1 in 20 overs) v Mali (17 in 12.5 overs) at Kigali..........	2019
256 runs	**Tanzania (279-2 in 20 overs) v eSwatini (23 in 11.5 overs) at Gaborone** .	**2021**
249 runs	Bangladesh (255-2 in 20 overs) v Maldives (6 in 12.1 overs) at Pokhara ...	2019-20

*There have been **40** instances of victory by ten wickets.*

OTHER RECORDS

MOST APPEARANCES

126	E. A. Perry (A)		111	S. R. Taylor (WI)
125	S. W. Bates (NZ)		108	Bismah Maroof (P)
124	D. J. S. Dottin (WI)		**108**	**M. Du Preez (SA)**
122	D. N. Wyatt (E)		**108**	**Nida Dar (P)**
121	A. J. Healy (A)		107	S. A. Campbelle (WI)
120	H. Kaur (I)		106	Sana Mir (P)
117	A. Mohammed (WI)		**105**	**Javeria Khan (P)**
113	M. M. Lanning (A)		104	J. L. Gunn (E)
111	A. E. Satterthwaite (NZ)		**101**	**S. F. M. Devine (NZ)**

WOMEN'S TWENTY20 WORLD CUP WINNERS

2009	England	2013-14	Australia	2019-20	Australia
2010	Australia	2015-16	West Indies		
2012-13	Australia	2018-19	Australia		

BIRTHS AND DEATHS

TEST CRICKETERS (MEN)

Full list from 1876-77 to January 16, 2022

In the Test career column, dates in italics indicate seasons embracing two different years (i.e. non-English seasons). In these cases, only the first year is given, e.g. *1876* for 1876-77. Some non-English series taking place outside the host country's normal season are dated by a single year.

The Test career figures are complete up to January 16, 2022; the one-day international and Twenty20 international totals up to December 31, 2021. Career figures are for one national team only; those players who have appeared for more than one Test team are listed on page 1442, and for more than one one-day international or Twenty20 international team on page 1446.

The forename by which a player is known is underlined if it is not his first name.

Family relationships are indicated by superscript numbers; where the relationship is not immediately apparent from a shared name, see the notes at the end of this section. (*CY 1889*) signifies that the player was a Wisden Cricketer of the Year in the 1889 Almanack. O/T signifies number of one-day and Twenty20 internationals played.

[1] *Father and son(s).*   [2] *Brothers.*   [3] *Grandfather, father and son.*
[4] *Grandfather and grandson.*   [5] *Great-grandfather and great-grandson.*
† *Excludes matches for another Test team.*   ‡ *Excludes matches for another ODI or T20I team.*
§ *Includes the Super Series Test for Australia v the ICC World XI in 2005-06.*

ENGLAND (699 players)

	Born	Died	Tests	Test Career	O/T
Abel Robert (*CY 1890*)	30.11.1857	10.12.1936	13	1888–1902	
Absolom Charles Alfred	7.6.1846	30.7.1889	1	*1878*	
Adams Christopher John (*CY 2004*)	6.5.1970		5	*1999*	5
Afzaal Usman.	9.6.1977		3	2001	
Agnew Jonathan Philip MBE (*CY 1988*)	4.4.1960		3	1984–1985	3
Ali Kabir	24.11.1980		1	2003	14
Ali Moeen Munir (*CY 2015*).	18.6.1987		64	2014–2021	112/44
Allen David Arthur	29.10.1935	24.5.2014	39	*1959–1966*	
Allen *Sir* George Oswald Browning ("Gubby"). .	31.7.1902	29.11.1989	25	1930–*1947*	
Allom Maurice James Carrick.	23.3.1906	8.4.1995	5	*1929–1930*	
Allott Paul John Walter	14.9.1956		13	1981–1985	13
Ambrose Timothy Raymond	1.12.1982		11	2007–*2008*	5/1
Ames Leslie Ethelbert George CBE (*CY 1929*). . .	3.12.1905	27.2.1990	47	1929–*1938*	
Amiss Dennis Leslie MBE (*CY 1975*).	7.4.1943		50	1966–1977	18
Anderson James Michael OBE (*CY 2009*).	30.7.1982		169	2003–*2021*	194/19
Andrew Keith Vincent.	15.12.1929	27.12.2010	2	*1954–1963*	
Ansari Zafar Shahaan	10.12.1991		3	*2016*	1
Appleyard Robert MBE (*CY 1952*).	27.6.1924	17.3.2015	9	1954–1956	
Archer Alfred German	6.12.1871	15.7.1935	1	*1898*	
Archer Jofra Chioke (*CY 2020*)	1.4.1995		13	2019–*2020*	17/12
Armitage Thomas.	25.4.1848	21.9.1922	2	*1876*	
Arnold Edward George	7.11.1876	25.10.1942	10	*1903*–1907	
Arnold Geoffrey Graham (*CY 1972*)	3.9.1944		34	1967–1975	14
Arnold John.	30.11.1907	4.4.1984	1	1931	
Astill William *Ewart* (*CY 1933*)	1.3.1888	10.2.1948	9	*1927–1929*	
Atherton Michael Andrew OBE (*CY 1991*)	23.3.1968		115	1989–2001	54
Athey Charles *William* Jeffrey	27.9.1957		23	1980–1988	31
Attewell William (*CY 1892*).	12.6.1861	11.6.1927	10	*1884–1891*	
Bailey Robert John	28.10.1963		4	1988–*1989*	4
Bailey Trevor Edward CBE (*CY 1950*)	3.12.1923	10.2.2011	61	1949–*1958*	
[1] **Bairstow** David Leslie.	1.9.1951	5.1.1998	4	*1979–1980*	21
[1] **Bairstow** Jonathan Marc (*CY 2016*).	26.9.1989		80	2012–*2021*	89/63

	Born	Died	Tests	Test Career	O/T
Bakewell Alfred Harry (*CY 1934*)	2.11.1908	23.1.1983	6	1931–1935	
Balderstone John <u>Christopher</u>	16.11.1940	6.3.2000	2	1976	
Ball Jacob Timothy	14.3.1991		4	2016–*2017*	18/2
Ballance Gary Simon (*CY 2015*)	22.11.1989		23	*2013*–2017	16
Barber Robert William (*CY 1967*)	26.9.1935		28	1960–1968	
Barber Wilfred	18.4.1901	10.9.1968	2	1935	
Barlow Graham Derek	26.3.1950		3	*1976–1977*	6
Barlow Richard Gorton	28.5.1851	31.7.1919	17	*1881–1886*	
Barnes Sydney Francis (*CY 1910*)	19.4.1873	26.12.1967	27	*1901–1913*	
Barnes William (*CY 1890*)	27.5.1852	24.3.1899	21	1880–1890	
Barnett Charles John (*CY 1937*)	3.7.1910	28.5.1993	20	1933–1948	
Barnett Kim John (*CY 1989*)	17.7.1960		4	1988–1989	1
Barratt Fred	12.4.1894	29.1.1947	5	1929–*1929*	
Barrington Kenneth Frank (*CY 1960*)	24.11.1930	14.3.1981	82	1955–1968	
Barton Victor Alexander	6.10.1867	23.3.1906	1	*1891*	
Bates Willie	19.11.1855	8.1.1900	15	*1881–1886*	
Batty Gareth Jon	13.10.1977		9	2003–2016	10/1
Bean George	7.3.1864	16.3.1923	3	*1891*	
Bedser *Sir* Alec Victor CBE (*CY 1947*)	4.7.1918	4.4.2010	51	1946–1955	
Bell Ian Ronald MBE (*CY 2008*)	11.4.1982		118	2004–*2015*	161/8
Benjamin Joseph Emmanuel	2.2.1961	8.3.2021	1	1994	2
Benson Mark Richard	6.7.1958		1	1986	1
Berry Robert	29.1.1926	2.12.2006	2	1950	
Bess Dominic Mark	22.7.1997		14	2018–*2020*	
Bicknell Martin Paul (*CY 2001*)	14.1.1969		4	1993–2003	7
Billings Samuel William	15.6.1991		1	2021	25/32
Binks James Graham (*CY 1969*)	5.10.1935		2	1963	
Bird Morice Carlos	25.3.1888	9.12.1933	10	*1909–1913*	
Birkenshaw Jack MBE	13.11.1940		5	*1972–1973*	
Blackwell Ian David	10.6.1978		1	*2005*	34
Blakey Richard John	15.1.1967		2	1992	3
Bligh *Hon.* Ivo Francis Walter	13.3.1859	10.4.1927	4	*1882*	
Blythe Colin (*CY 1904*)	30.5.1879	8.11.1917	19	*1901–1909*	
Board John Henry	23.2.1867	15.4.1924	6	*1898–1905*	
Bolus John <u>Brian</u>	31.1.1934	6.5.2020	7	*1963–1963*	
Booth Major William (*CY 1914*)	10.12.1886	1.7.1916	2	*1913*	
Bopara Ravinder Singh	4.5.1985		13	2007–2012	120/38
Borthwick Scott George	19.4.1990		1	*2013*	2/1
Bosanquet Bernard James Tindal (*CY 1905*) . . .	13.10.1877	12.10.1936	7	*1903–1905*	
Botham *Lord* [Ian Terence] OBE (*CY 1978*) . . .	24.11.1955		102	1977–1992	116
Bowden Montague Parker	1.11.1865	19.2.1892	2	*1888*	
Bowes William Eric (*CY 1932*)	25.7.1908	4.9.1987	15	1932–1946	
Bowley Edward Henry (*CY 1930*)	6.6.1890	9.7.1974	5	1929–1929	
Boycott *Sir* Geoffrey OBE (*CY 1965*)	21.10.1940		108	1964–*1981*	36
Bracey James Robert	3.5.1997		2	2021	
Bradley Walter Morris	2.1.1875	19.6.1944	2	1899	
Braund Leonard Charles (*CY 1902*)	18.10.1875	23.12.1955	23	*1901–1907*	
Brearley John <u>Michael</u> OBE (*CY 1977*)	28.4.1942		39	1976–1981	25
Brearley Walter (*CY 1909*)	11.3.1876	30.1.1937	4	1905–1912	
Brennan Donald Vincent	10.2.1920	9.1.1985	2	1951	
Bresnan Timothy Thomas (*CY 2012*)	28.2.1985		23	2009–*2013*	85/34
Briggs John (*CY 1889*)	3.10.1862	11.1.1902	33	*1884–1899*	
¹**Broad** Brian <u>Christopher</u>	29.9.1957		25	1984–1989	34
¹**Broad** Stuart Christopher John MBE (*CY 2010*) . . .	24.6.1986		152	*2007–2021*	121/56
Brockwell William (*CY 1895*)	21.1.1865	30.6.1935	7	1893–1899	
Bromley-Davenport Hugh Richard	18.8.1870	23.5.1954	4	*1895–1898*	
Brookes Dennis (*CY 1957*)	29.10.1915	9.3.2006	1	*1947*	
Brown Alan	17.10.1935		2	1961	
Brown David John	30.1.1942		26	1965–1969	
Brown Frederick Richard MBE (*CY 1933*)	16.12.1910	24.7.1991	22	1931–1953	

	Born	Died	Tests	Test Career	O/T
Brown George	6.10.1887	3.12.1964	7	1921–1922	
Brown John Thomas (*CY 1895*)	20.8.1869	4.11.1904	8	1894–1899	
Brown Simon John Emmerson	29.6.1969		1	1996	
Buckenham Claude Percival	16.1.1876	23.2.1937	4	1909	
Burns Rory Joseph (*CY 2019*)	26.8.1990		32	2018–2021	
[1] **Butcher** Alan Raymond (*CY 1991*)	7.1.1954		1	1979	1
[1] **Butcher** Mark Alan	23.8.1972		71	1997–2004	
Butcher Roland Orlando	14.10.1953		3	1981	3
Butler Harold James	12.3.1913	17.7.1991	2	1947–1947	
Butt Henry Rigden	27.12.1865	21.12.1928	3	1895	
Buttler Joseph Charles MBE (*CY 2019*)	8.9.1990		57	2014–2021	148/88
Caddick Andrew Richard (*CY 2001*)	21.11.1968		62	1993–2002	54
Calthorpe Hon. Frederick Somerset Gough-	27.5.1892	19.11.1935	4	1929	
Capel David John	6.2.1963	2.9.2020	15	1987–1989	23
Carberry Michael Alexander	29.9.1980		6	2009–2013	6/1
Carr Arthur William (*CY 1923*)	21.5.1893	7.2.1963	11	1922–1929	
Carr Donald Bryce OBE (*CY 1960*)	28.12.1926	12.6.2016	2	1951	
Carr Douglas Ward (*CY 1910*)	17.3.1872	23.3.1950	1	1909	
Cartwright Thomas William MBE	22.7.1935	30.4.2007	5	1964–1965	
Chapman Arthur <u>Percy</u> Frank (*CY 1919*)	3.9.1900	16.9.1961	26	1924–1930	
Charlwood Henry Rupert James	19.12.1846	6.6.1888	2	1876	
Chatterton William	27.12.1861	19.3.1913	1	1891	
Childs John Henry (*CY 1987*)	15.8.1951		2	1988	
Christopherson Stanley	11.11.1861	6.4.1949	1	1884	
Clark Edward Winchester	9.8.1902	28.4.1982	8	1929–1934	
Clarke Rikki	29.9.1981		2	2003	20
Clay John Charles	18.3.1898	11.8.1973	1	1935	
Close Dennis <u>Brian</u> CBE (*CY 1964*)	24.2.1931	14.9.2015	22	1949–1976	3
Coldwell Leonard John	10.1.1933	6.8.1996	7	1962–1964	
Collingwood Paul David MBE (*CY 2007*)	26.5.1976		68	2003–2010	197/35‡
[4] **Compton** Denis Charles Scott CBE (*CY 1939*) . . .	23.5.1918	23.4.1997	78	1937–1956	
[4] **Compton** Nicholas Richard Denis (*CY 2013*)	26.6.1983		16	2012–2016	
Cook *Sir* Alastair Nathan CBE (*CY 2012*)	25.12.1984		161	2005–2018	92/4
Cook Cecil ("Sam")	23.8.1921	5.9.1996	1	1947	
Cook Geoffrey	9.10.1951		7	1981–1982	6
Cook Nicholas Grant Billson	17.6.1956		15	1983–1989	3
Cope Geoffrey Alan	23.2.1947		3	1977	2
Copson William Henry (*CY 1937*)	27.4.1908	13.9.1971	3	1939–1947	
Cork Dominic Gerald (*CY 1996*)	7.8.1971		37	1995–2002	32
Cornford Walter Latter	25.12.1900	6.2.1964	4	1929	
Cottam Robert Michael Henry	16.10.1944		4	1968–1972	
Coventry Hon. Charles John	26.2.1867	2.6.1929	2	1888	
Cowans Norman George	17.4.1961		19	1982–1985	23
[1] **Cowdrey** Christopher Stuart	20.10.1957		6	1984–1988	3
[1] **Cowdrey** *Lord* [Michael Colin] CBE (*CY 1956*) . . .	24.12.1932	4.12.2000	114	1954–1974	1
Coxon Alexander	18.1.1916	22.1.2006	1	1948	
Crane Mason Sidney	18.02.1997		1	2017	0/2
Cranston James	9.1.1859	10.12.1904	1	1890	
Cranston Kenneth	20.10.1917	8.1.2007	8	1947–1948	
Crapp John Frederick	14.10.1912	13.2.1981	7	1948–1948	
Crawford John Neville (*CY 1907*)	1.12.1886	2.5.1963	12	1905–1907	
Crawley John Paul	21.9.1971		37	1994–2002	13
Crawley Zak (*CY 2021*)	3.2.1998		18	2019–2021	3
Croft Robert Damien Bale MBE	25.5.1970		21	1996–2001	50
[2] **Curran** Samuel Matthew (*CY 2019*)	3.6.1998		24	2018–2021	11/16
[2] **Curran** Thomas Kevin	12.03.1995		2	2017	28/30
Curtis Timothy Stephen	15.1.1960		5	1988–1989	
Cuttell Willis Robert (*CY 1898*)	13.9.1863	9.12.1929	2	1898	
Dawson Edward William	13.2.1904	4.6.1979	5	1927–1929	
Dawson Liam Andrew	1.3.1990		3	2016–2017	3/6

	Born	Died	Tests	Test Career	O/T
Dawson Richard Kevin James.	4.8.1980		7	*2001–2002*	
Dean Harry	13.8.1884	12.3.1957	3	1912	
DeFreitas Phillip Anthony Jason (*CY 1992*).	18.2.1966		44	*1986–1995*	103
Denly Joseph Liam	16.3.1986		15	*2018–2020*	16/13
Denness Michael Henry OBE (*CY 1975*).	1.12.1940	19.4.2013	28	1969–1975	12
Denton David (*CY 1906*)	4.7.1874	16.2.1950	11	1905–1909	
Dewes John Gordon.	11.10.1926	12.5.2015	5	*1948–1950*	
Dexter Edward Ralph CBE (*CY 1961*).	15.5.1935	25.8.2021	62	1958–1968	
Dilley Graham Roy	18.5.1959	5.10.2011	41	*1979–1989*	36
Dipper Alfred Ernest.	9.11.1885	7.11.1945	1	1921	
Doggart George Hubert Graham OBE.	18.7.1925	16.2.2018	2	1950	
D'Oliveira Basil Lewis CBE (*CY 1967*).	4.10.1931	18.11.2011	44	1966–1972	4
Dollery Horace Edgar ("Tom") (*CY 1952*).	14.10.1914	20.1.1987	4	*1947–1950*	
Dolphin Arthur.	24.12.1885	23.10.1942	1	*1920*	
Douglas John William Henry Tyler (*CY 1915*). . .	3.9.1882	19.12.1930	23	*1911–1924*	
Downton Paul Rupert	4.4.1957		30	*1980–1988*	28
Druce Norman Frank (*CY 1898*).	1.1.1875	27.10.1954	5	*1897*	
Ducat Andrew (*CY 1920*).	16.2.1886	23.7.1942	1	1921	
Duckett Ben Matthew (*CY 2017*).	17.10.1994		4	*2016*	3/1
Duckworth George (*CY 1929*).	9.5.1901	5.1.1966	24	1924–1936	
Duleepsinhji Kumar Shri (*CY 1930*).	13.6.1905	5.12.1959	12	1929–1931	
Durston Frederick John.	11.7.1893	8.4.1965	1	1921	
Ealham Mark Alan	27.8.1969		8	1996–1998	64
Edmonds Philippe-Henri	8.3.1951		51	1975–1987	29
Edrich John Hugh MBE (*CY 1966*).	21.6.1937	23.12.2020	77	1963–1976	7
Edrich William John (*CY 1940*)	26.3.1916	24.4.1986	39	*1938–1954*	
Elliott Harry.	2.11.1891	2.2.1976	4	*1927–1933*	
Ellison Richard Mark (*CY 1986*).	21.9.1959		11	1984–1986	14
Emburey John Ernest (*CY 1984*).	20.8.1952		64	1978–1995	61
Emmett George Malcolm	2.12.1912	18.12.1976	1	1948	
Emmett Thomas.	3.9.1841	29.6.1904	7	*1876–1881*	
Evans Alfred John.	1.5.1889	18.9.1960	1	1921	
Evans Thomas Godfrey CBE (*CY 1951*).	18.8.1920	3.5.1999	91	1946–1959	
Fagg Arthur Edward	18.6.1915	13.9.1977	5	1936–1939	
Fairbrother Neil Harvey	9.9.1963		10	1987–1992	75
Fane Frederick Luther.	27.4.1875	27.11.1960	14	1905–1909	
Farnes Kenneth (*CY 1939*).	8.7.1911	20.10.1941	15	*1934–1938*	
Farrimond William	23.5.1903	15.11.1979	4	*1930–1935*	
Fender Percy George Herbert (*CY 1915*).	22.8.1892	15.6.1985	13	1920–1929	
Ferris John James.	21.5.1867	17.11.1900	1†	*1891*	
Fielder Arthur (*CY 1907*).	19.7.1877	30.8.1949	6	*1903–1907*	
Finn Steven Thomas	4.4.1989		36	*2009–2016*	69/21
Fishlock Laurence Barnard (*CY 1947*).	2.1.1907	25.6.1986	4	1936–1946	
Flavell John Alfred (*CY 1965*).	15.5.1929	25.2.2004	4	1961–1964	
Fletcher Keith William Robert OBE (*CY 1974*). .	20.5.1944		59	1968–*1981*	24
Flintoff Andrew MBE (*CY 2004*).	6.12.1977		78†	1998–2009	138‡/7
Flowers Wilfred.	7.12.1856	1.11.1926	8	*1884–1893*	
Foakes Benjamin Thomas	15.2.1993		8	*2018–2020*	1/1
Ford Francis Gilbertson Justice.	14.12.1866	7.2.1940	5	*1894*	
Foster Frank Rowbotham (*CY 1912*).	31.1.1889	3.5.1958	11	*1911–1912*	
Foster James Savin	15.4.1980		7	*2001–2002*	11/5
Foster Neil Alan (*CY 1988*).	6.5.1962		29	1983–1993	48
Foster Reginald Erskine ("Tip") (*CY 1900*). . . .	16.4.1878	13.5.1914	8	*1903–1907*	
Fothergill Arnold James	26.8.1854	1.8.1932	2	*1888*	
Fowler Graeme.	20.4.1957		21	1982–*1984*	26
Fraser Angus Robert Charles MBE (*CY 1996*). . .	8.8.1965		46	1989–*1998*	42
Freeman Alfred Percy ("Tich") (*CY 1923*).	17.5.1888	28.1.1965	12	*1924–1929*	
French Bruce Nicholas	13.8.1959		16	1986–*1987*	13
Fry Charles Burgess (*CY 1895*).	25.4.1872	7.9.1956	26	*1895–1912*	
Gallian Jason Edward Riche.	25.6.1971		3	*1995–1995*	

	Born	Died	Tests	Test Career	O/T
Gatting Michael William OBE (*CY 1984*)	6.6.1957		79	*1977–1994*	92
Gay Leslie Hewitt	24.3.1871	1.11.1949	1	*1894*	
Geary George (*CY 1927*)	9.7.1893	6.3.1981	14	*1924–1934*	
Gibb Paul Antony	11.7.1913	7.12.1977	8	*1938–1946*	
Giddins Edward Simon Hunter	20.7.1971		4	*1999–2000*	
Gifford Norman MBE (*CY 1975*)	30.3.1940		15	*1964–1973*	2
Giles Ashley Fraser MBE (*CY 2005*)	19.3.1973		54	*1998–2006*	62
[2] **Gilligan** Arthur Edward Robert (*CY 1924*)	23.12.1894	5.9.1976	11	*1922–1924*	
[2] **Gilligan** Alfred Herbert Harold	29.6.1896	5.5.1978	4	*1929*	
Gimblett Harold (*CY 1953*)	19.10.1914	30.3.1978	3	*1936–1939*	
Gladwin Clifford	3.4.1916	9.4.1988	8	*1947–1949*	
Goddard Thomas William John (*CY 1938*)	1.10.1900	22.5.1966	8	*1930–1939*	
Gooch Graham Alan OBE (*CY 1980*)	23.7.1953		118	*1975–1994*	125
Gough Darren MBE (*CY 1999*)	18.9.1970		58	*1994–2003*	158‡/2
Gover Alfred Richard MBE (*CY 1937*)	29.2.1908	7.10.2001	4	*1936–1946*	
Gower David Ivon OBE (*CY 1979*)	1.4.1957		117	*1978–1992*	114
[2] **Grace** Edward Mills	28.11.1841	20.5.1911	1	*1880*	
[2] **Grace** George Frederick	13.12.1850	22.9.1880	1	*1880*	
[2] **Grace** William Gilbert (*CY 1896*)	18.7.1848	23.10.1915	22	*1880–1899*	
Graveney Thomas William OBE (*CY 1953*)	16.6.1927	3.11.2015	79	*1951–1969*	
Greenhough Thomas	9.11.1931	15.9.2009	4	*1959–1960*	
Greenwood Andrew	20.8.1847	12.2.1889	2	*1876*	
[2] **Greig** Anthony William (*CY 1975*)	6.10.1946	29.12.2012	58	*1972–1977*	22
[2] **Greig** Ian Alexander	8.12.1955		2	*1982*	
Grieve Basil Arthur Firebrace	28.5.1864	19.11.1917	2	*1888*	
Griffith Stewart Cathie CBE ("Billy")	16.6.1914	7.4.1993	3	*1947–1948*	
Gunn George (*CY 1914*)	13.6.1879	29.6.1958	15	*1907–1929*	
[2] **Gunn** John Richmond (*CY 1904*)	19.7.1876	21.8.1963	6	*1901–1905*	
Gunn William (*CY 1890*)	4.12.1858	29.1.1921	11	*1886–1899*	
Habib Aftab	7.2.1972		2	*1999*	
Haig Nigel Esmé	12.12.1887	27.10.1966	5	*1921–1929*	
Haigh Schofield (*CY 1901*)	19.3.1871	27.2.1921	11	*1898–1912*	
Hales Alexander Daniel	3.1.1989		11	*2015–2016*	70/60
Hallows Charles (*CY 1928*)	4.4.1895	10.11.1972	2	*1921–1928*	
Hameed Haseeb	17.1.1997		10	*2016–2021*	
Hamilton Gavin Mark	16.9.1974		1	*1999*	0‡
Hammond Walter Reginald (*CY 1928*)	19.6.1903	1.7.1965	85	*1927–1946*	
Hampshire John Harry	10.2.1941	1.3.2017	8	*1969–1975*	3
Hardinge Harold Thomas William ("Wally") (*CY 1915*)	25.2.1886	8.5.1965	1	*1921*	
[1] **Hardstaff** Joseph snr	9.11.1882	2.4.1947	5	*1907*	
[1] **Hardstaff** Joseph jnr (*CY 1938*)	3.7.1911	1.1.1990	23	*1935–1948*	
Harmison Stephen James MBE (*CY 2005*)	23.10.1978		62†	*2002–2009*	58/2
Harris Lord [George Robert Canning]	3.2.1851	24.3.1932	4	*1878–1884*	
Hartley John Cabourn	15.11.1874	8.3.1963	2	*1905*	
Hawke Lord [Martin Bladen] (*CY 1909*)	16.8.1860	10.10.1938	5	*1895–1898*	
Hayes Ernest George (*CY 1907*)	6.11.1876	2.12.1953	5	*1909–1912*	
Hayes Frank Charles	6.12.1946		9	*1973–1976*	6
Hayward Thomas Walter (*CY 1895*)	29.3.1871	19.7.1939	35	*1895–1909*	
[3] **Headley** Dean Warren	27.1.1970		15	*1997–1999*	13
[2] **Hearne** Alec (*CY 1894*)	22.7.1863	16.5.1952	1	*1891*	
[1, 2] **Hearne** Frank	23.11.1858	14.7.1949	2†	*1888*	
[2] **Hearne** George Gibbons	7.7.1856	13.2.1932	1	*1891*	
Hearne John Thomas (*CY 1892*)	3.5.1867	17.4.1944	12	*1891–1899*	
Hearne John William (*CY 1912*)	11.2.1891	14.9.1965	24	*1911–1926*	
Hegg Warren Kevin	23.2.1968		2	*1998*	
Hemmings Edward Ernest	20.2.1949		16	*1982–1990*	33
Hendren Elias Henry ("Patsy") (*CY 1920*)	5.2.1889	4.10.1962	51	*1920–1934*	
Hendrick Michael (*CY 1978*)	22.10.1948	26.7.2021	30	*1974–1981*	22
Heseltine Christopher	26.11.1869	13.6.1944	2	*1895*	
Hick Graeme Ashley MBE (*CY 1987*)	23.5.1966		65	*1991–2000*	120

	Born	Died	Tests	Test Career	O/T
Higgs Kenneth (*CY 1968*).	14.1.1937	7.9.2016	15	1965–1968	
Hill Allen.	14.11.1843	28.8.1910	2	*1876*	
Hill Arthur James Ledger.	26.7.1871	6.9.1950	3	*1895*	
Hilton Malcolm Jameson (*CY 1957*).	2.8.1928	8.7.1990	4	1950–*1951*	
Hirst George Herbert (*CY 1901*).	7.9.1871	10.5.1954	24	1897–1909	
Hitch John William (*CY 1914*).	7.5.1886	7.7.1965	7	*1911*–1921	
Hobbs *Sir* John Berry (*CY 1909*).	16.12.1882	21.12.1963	61	1907–1930	
Hobbs Robin Nicholas Stuart	8.5.1942		7	1967–1971	
Hoggard Matthew James MBE (*CY 2006*).	31.12.1976		67	2000–2007	26
Hollies William Eric (*CY 1955*).	5.6.1912	16.4.1981	13	1934–1950	
² **Hollioake** Adam John (*CY 2003*).	5.9.1971		4	1997–*1997*	35
² **Hollioake** Benjamin Caine (*CY 1999*).	11.11.1977	23.3.2002	2	1997–1998	20
Holmes Errol Reginald Thorold (*CY 1936*).	21.8.1905	16.8.1960	5	1934–1935	
Holmes Percy (*CY 1920*).	25.11.1886	3.9.1971	7	1921–1932	
Hone Leland.	30.1.1853	31.12.1896	1	*1878*	
Hopwood John Leonard.	30.10.1903	15.6.1985	2	*1934*	
Hornby Albert Neilson ("Monkey").	10.2.1847	17.12.1925	3	1878–1884	
Horton Martin John.	21.4.1934	3.4.2011	2	*1959*	
Howard Nigel David.	18.5.1925	31.5.1979	4	*1951*	
Howell Henry.	29.11.1890	9.7.1932	5	1920–1924	
Howorth Richard	26.4.1909	2.4.1980	5	1947–*1947*	
Humphries Joseph	19.5.1876	7.5.1946	3	*1907*	
Hunter Joseph	3.8.1855	4.1.1891	5	*1884*	
Hussain Nasser OBE (*CY 2003*).	28.3.1968		96	1989–2004	88
Hutchings Kenneth Lotherington (*CY 1907*). . . .	7.12.1882	3.9.1916	7	1907–1909	
¹ **Hutton** *Sir* Leonard (*CY 1938*).	23.6.1916	6.9.1990	79	1937–*1954*	
¹ **Hutton** Richard Anthony	6.9.1942		5	1971	
Iddon John.	8.1.1902	17.4.1946	5	1934–1935	
Igglesden Alan Paul	8.10.1964	1.11.2021	3	1989–*1993*	4
Ikin John Thomas	7.3.1918	15.9.1984	18	1946–1955	
Illingworth Raymond CBE (*CY 1960*)	8.6.1932	25.12.2021	61	1958–1973	3
Illingworth Richard Keith	23.8.1963		9	1991–*1995*	25
Ilott Mark Christopher.	27.8.1970		5	1993–*1995*	
Insole Douglas John CBE (*CY 1956*).	18.4.1926	5.8.2017	9	1950–1957	
Irani Ronald Charles.	26.10.1971		3	1996–1999	31
Jackman Robin David (*CY 1981*).	13.8.1945	25.12.2020	4	1980–1982	15
Jackson *Sir* Francis Stanley (*CY 1894*).	21.11.1870	9.3.1947	20	1893–1905	
Jackson Herbert Leslie (*CY 1959*).	5.4.1921	25.4.2007	2	1949–1961	
James Stephen Peter	7.9.1967		2	1998	
Jameson John Alexander MBE	30.6.1941		4	1971–*1973*	3
Jardine Douglas Robert (*CY 1928*).	23.10.1900	18.6.1958	22	1928–*1933*	
Jarvis Paul William.	29.6.1965		9	1987–1992	16
Jenkins Roland Oliver (*CY 1950*).	24.11.1918	22.7.1995	9	1948–1952	
Jennings Keaton Kent	19.6.1992		17	2016–2018	
Jessop Gilbert Laird (*CY 1898*).	19.5.1874	11.5.1955	18	1899–1912	
Johnson Richard Leonard	29.12.1974		3	2003–*2003*	10
Jones Arthur Owen	16.8.1872	21.12.1914	12	1899–1909	
Jones Geraint Owen MBE	14.7.1976		34	2003–2006	49‡/2
¹ **Jones** Ivor Jeffrey	10.12.1941		15	1963–1967	
¹ **Jones** Simon Philip MBE (*CY 2006*).	25.12.1978		18	2002–2005	8
Jordan Christopher James	4.10.1988		8	2014–*2014*	34/71
Jupp Henry	19.11.1841	8.4.1889	2	*1876*	
Jupp Vallance William Crisp (*CY 1928*).	27.3.1891	9.7.1960	8	1921–1928	
Keeton William Walter (*CY 1940*).	30.4.1905	10.10.1980	2	1934–1939	
Kennedy Alexander Stuart (*CY 1933*)	24.1.1891	15.11.1959	5	*1922*	
Kenyon Donald	15.5.1924	12.11.1996	8	1951–1955	
Kerrigan Simon Christopher	10.5.1989		1	2013	
Key Robert William Trevor (*CY 2005*).	12.5.1979		15	2002–*2004*	5/1
Khan Amjad	14.10.1980		1	*2008*	0/1‡
Killick *Rev.* Edgar Thomas.	9.5.1907	18.5.1953	2	1929	

	Born	Died	Tests	Test Career	O/T
Kilner Roy (*CY 1924*)	17.10.1890	5.4.1928	9	*1924–1926*	
King John Herbert.	16.4.1871	18.11.1946	1	*1909*	
Kinneir Septimus Paul (*CY 1912*)	13.5.1871	16.10.1928	1	*1911*	
Kirtley Robert James.	10.1.1975		4	*2003–2003*	11/1
Knight Albert Ernest (*CY 1904*)	8.10.1872	25.4.1946	3	*1903*	
Knight Barry Rolfe	18.2.1938		29	*1961–1969*	
Knight Donald John (*CY 1915*)	12.5.1894	5.1.1960	2	*1921*	
Knight Nicholas Verity	28.11.1969		17	*1995–2001*	100
Knott Alan Philip Eric MBE (*CY 1970*).	9.4.1946		95	*1967–1981*	20
Knox Neville Alexander (*CY 1907*).	10.10.1884	3.3.1935	2	*1907*	
Laker James Charles (*CY 1952*).	9.2.1922	23.4.1986	46	*1947–1958*	
Lamb Allan Joseph (*CY 1981*)	20.6.1954		79	*1982–1992*	122
Langridge James (*CY 1932*).	10.7.1906	10.9.1966	8	*1933–1946*	
Larkins Wayne	22.11.1953		13	*1979–1990*	25
Larter John David Frederick	24.4.1940		10	*1962–1965*	
Larwood Harold MBE (*CY 1927*).	14.11.1904	22.7.1995	21	*1926–1932*	
Lathwell Mark Nicholas	26.12.1971		2	*1993*	
Lawrence David Valentine ("Syd").	28.1.1964		5	*1988–1991*	1
Lawrence Daniel William	12.7.1997		8	*2020–2021*	
Leach Matthew Jack	22.6.1991		19	*2017–2021*	
Leadbeater Edric	15.8.1927	17.4.2011	2	*1951*	
Lee Henry William	26.10.1890	21.4.1981	1	*1930*	
Lees Walter Scott (*CY 1906*).	25.12.1875	10.9.1924	5	*1905*	
Legge Geoffrey Bevington	26.1.1903	21.11.1940	5	*1927–1929*	
Leslie Charles Frederick Henry	8.12.1861	12.2.1921	4	*1882*	
Lever John Kenneth MBE (*CY 1979*)	24.2.1949		21	*1976–1986*	22
Lever Peter	17.9.1940		17	*1970–1975*	10
Leveson Gower *Sir* Henry Dudley Gresham. . . .	8.5.1873	1.2.1954	3	*1909*	
Levett William Howard Vincent ("Hopper"). . . .	25.1.1908	1.12.1995	1	*1933*	
Lewis Anthony Robert CBE.	6.7.1938		9	*1972–1973*	
Lewis Clairmonte Christopher	14.2.1968		32	*1990–1996*	53
Lewis Jonathan.	26.8.1975		1	*2006*	13/2
Leyland Maurice (*CY 1929*).	20.7.1900	1.1.1967	41	*1928–1938*	
Lilley Arthur Frederick Augustus ("Dick") (*CY 1897*)	28.11.1866	17.11.1929	35	*1896–1909*	
Lillywhite James.	23.2.1842	25.10.1929	2	*1876*	
Lloyd David.	18.3.1947		9	*1974–1974*	8
Lloyd Timothy Andrew	5.11.1956		1	*1984*	3
Loader Peter James (*CY 1958*)	25.10.1929	15.3.2011	13	*1954–1958*	
Lock Graham Anthony Richard (*CY 1954*). . . .	5.7.1929	30.3.1995	49	*1952–1967*	
Lockwood William Henry (*CY 1899*)	25.3.1868	26.4.1932	12	*1893–1902*	
Lohmann George Alfred (*CY 1889*)	2.6.1865	1.12.1901	18	*1886–1896*	
Lowson Frank Anderson	1.7.1925	8.9.1984	7	*1951–1955*	
Lucas Alfred Perry	20.2.1857	12.10.1923	5	*1878–1884*	
Luckhurst Brian William (*CY 1971*)	5.2.1939	1.3.2005	21	*1970–1974*	3
Lyth Adam (*CY 2015*).	25.9.1987		7	*2015*	
Lyttelton *Hon.* Alfred	7.2.1857	5.7.1913	4	*1880–1884*	
Macaulay George Gibson (*CY 1924*).	7.12.1897	13.12.1940	8	*1922–1933*	
MacBryan John Crawford William (*CY 1925*) . .	22.7.1892	14.7.1983	1	*1924*	
McCague Martin John.	24.5.1969		3	*1993–1994*	
McConnon James Edward	21.6.1922	26.1.2003	2	*1954*	
McGahey Charles Percy (*CY 1902*).	12.2.1871	10.1.1935	2	*1901*	
McGrath Anthony	6.10.1975		4	*2003*	14
MacGregor Gregor (*CY 1891*).	31.8.1869	20.8.1919	8	*1890–1893*	
McIntyre Arthur John William (*CY 1958*)	14.5.1918	26.12.2009	3	*1950–1955*	
MacKinnon Francis Alexander.	9.4.1848	27.2.1947	1	*1878*	
MacLaren Archibald Campbell (*CY 1895*). . . .	1.12.1871	17.11.1944	35	*1894–1909*	
McMaster Joseph Emile Patrick	16.3.1861	7.6.1929	1	*1888*	
Maddy Darren Lee	23.5.1974		3	*1999–1999*	8/4
Mahmood Sajid Iqbal	21.12.1981		8	*2006–2006*	26/4
Makepeace Joseph William Henry	22.8.1881	19.12.1952	4	*1920*	

	Born	Died	Tests	Test Career	O/T
Malan Dawid Johannes	03.09.1987		22	2017–*2021*	6/36
Malcolm Devon Eugene (*CY 1995*)	22.2.1963		40	1989–1997	10
Mallender Neil Alan	13.8.1961		2	1992	
¹ **Mann** Francis George CBE	6.9.1917	8.8.2001	7	1948–1949	
¹ **Mann** Francis Thomas	3.3.1888	6.10.1964	5	*1922*	
Marks Victor James	25.6.1955		6	1982–*1983*	34
Marriott Charles Stowell ("Father")	14.9.1895	13.10.1966	1	1933	
Martin Frederick (*CY 1892*)	12.10.1861	13.12.1921	2	1890–*1891*	
Martin John William	16.2.1917	4.1.1987	1	1947	
Martin Peter James	15.11.1968		8	1995–1997	20
Mason John Richard (*CY 1898*)	26.3.1874	15.10.1958	5	1897	
Matthews Austin David George	3.5.1904	29.7.1977	1	1937	
May Peter Barker Howard CBE (*CY 1952*)	31.12.1929	27.12.1994	66	1951–1961	
Maynard Matthew Peter (*CY 1998*)	21.3.1966		4	1988–*1993*	14
Mead Charles Philip (*CY 1912*)	9.3.1887	26.3.1958	17	1911–*1928*	
Mead Walter (*CY 1904*)	1.4.1868	18.3.1954	1	1899	
Midwinter William Evans	19.6.1851	3.12.1890	4†	*1881*	
Milburn Colin ("Ollie") (*CY 1967*)	23.10.1941	28.2.1990	9	1966–*1968*	
Miller Audley Montague	19.10.1869	26.6.1959	1	1895	
Miller Geoffrey OBE	8.9.1952		34	1976–1984	25
Milligan Frank William	19.3.1870	31.3.1900	2	1898	
Millman Geoffrey	2.10.1934	6.4.2005	6	1961–1962	
Milton Clement Arthur (*CY 1959*)	10.3.1928	25.4.2007	6	1958–1959	
Mitchell Arthur	13.9.1902	25.12.1976	6	1933–1936	
Mitchell Frank (*CY 1902*)	13.8.1872	11.10.1935	2†	*1898*	
Mitchell Thomas Bignall	4.9.1902	27.1.1996	5	1932–1935	
Mitchell-Innes Norman Stewart ("Mandy")	7.9.1914	28.12.2006	1	1935	
Mold Arthur Webb (*CY 1892*)	27.5.1863	29.4.1921	3	1893	
Moon Leonard James	9.2.1878	23.11.1916	4	*1905*	
Morgan Eoin Joseph Gerard CBE (*CY 2011*)	10.9.1986		16	2010–*2011*	223‡/113
Morley Frederick	16.12.1850	28.9.1884	4	1880–*1882*	
Morris Hugh	5.10.1963		3	1991	
Morris John Edward	1.4.1964		3	1990	8
Mortimore John Brian	14.5.1933	13.2.2014	9	1958–1964	
Moss Alan Edward	14.11.1930	12.3.2019	9	1953–1960	
Moxon Martyn Douglas (*CY 1993*)	4.5.1960		10	1986–1989	8
Mullally Alan David	12.7.1969		19	1996–2001	50
Munton Timothy Alan (*CY 1995*)	30.7.1965		2	1992	
Murdoch William Lloyd	18.10.1854	18.2.1911	1†	*1891*	
Murray John Thomas MBE (*CY 1967*)	1.4.1935	24.7.2018	21	1961–1967	
Newham William	12.12.1860	26.6.1944	1	1887	
Newport Philip John	11.10.1962		3	1988–*1990*	
Nichols Morris Stanley (*CY 1934*)	6.10.1900	26.1.1961	14	1929–1939	
Oakman Alan Stanley Myles	20.4.1930	6.9.2018	2	1956	
O'Brien *Sir* Timothy Carew	5.11.1861	9.12.1948	5	1884–*1895*	
O'Connor Jack	6.11.1897	22.2.1977	4	1929–*1929*	
Old Christopher Middleton (*CY 1979*)	22.12.1948		46	1972–1981	32
Oldfield Norman	5.5.1911	19.4.1996	1	1939	
Onions Graham (*CY 2010*)	9.9.1982		9	2009–2012	4
Ormond James	20.8.1977		2	2001–*2001*	
Overton Craig	10.4.1994		6	2017–*2021*	4
Padgett Douglas Ernest Vernon	20.7.1934		2	1960	
Paine George Alfred Edward (*CY 1935*)	11.6.1908	30.3.1978	4	*1934*	
Palairet Lionel Charles Hamilton (*CY 1893*)	27.5.1870	27.3.1933	2	1902	
Palmer Charles Henry CBE	15.5.1919	31.3.2005	1	1953	
Palmer Kenneth Ernest MBE	22.4.1937		1	1964	
Panesar Mudhsuden Singh ("Monty") (*CY 2007*) .	25.4.1982		50	2005–2013	26/1
Parfitt Peter Howard (*CY 1963*)	8.12.1936		37	1961–1972	
Parker Charles Warrington Leonard (*CY 1923*) . .	14.10.1882	11.7.1959	1	1921	
Parker Paul William Giles	15.1.1956		1	1981	

	Born	Died	Tests	Test Career	O/T
Parkhouse William <u>Gilbert</u> Anthony	12.10.1925	10.8.2000	7	1950–1959	
Parkin Cecil Harry (*CY 1924*)	18.2.1886	15.6.1943	10	1920–1924	
¹ **Parks** James Horace (*CY 1938*).	12.5.1903	21.11.1980	1	1937	
¹ **Parks** James Michael (*CY 1968*)	21.10.1931		46	1954–*1967*	
¹ **Pataudi** Iftikhar Ali Khan, Nawab of (*CY 1932*) . .	16.3.1910	5.1.1952	3†	1932–1934	
Patel Minal Mahesh	7.7.1970		2	1996	
Patel Samit Rohit	30.11.1984		6	2011–*2015*	36/18
² **Pattinson** Darren John.	2.8.1979		1	2008	
Paynter Edward (*CY 1938*)	5.11.1901	5.2.1979	20	1931–1939	
Peate Edmund	2.3.1855	11.3.1900	9	1881–1886	
Peebles Ian Alexander Ross (*CY 1931*)	20.1.1908	27.2.1980	13	1927–1931	
Peel Robert (*CY 1889*).	12.2.1857	12.8.1941	20	1884–1896	
Penn Frank.	7.3.1851	26.12.1916	1	1880	
Perks Reginald Thomas David	4.10.1911	22.11.1977	2	1938–1939	
Philipson Hylton	8.6.1866	4.12.1935	5	1891–1894	
Pietersen Kevin Peter MBE (*CY 2006*)	27.6.1980		104	2005–*2013*	134‡/37
Pigott Anthony Charles Shackleton	4.6.1958		1	1983	
Pilling Richard (*CY 1891*)	11.8.1855	28.3.1891	8	1881–1888	
Place Winston	7.12.1914	25.1.2002	3	1947	
Plunkett Liam Edward	6.4.1985		13	2005–2014	89/22
Pocock Patrick Ian	24.9.1946		25	1967–*1984*	1
Pollard Richard	19.6.1912	16.12.1985	4	1946–1948	
Poole Cyril John	13.3.1921	11.2.1996	3	1951	
Pope George Henry	27.1.1911	29.10.1993	1	1947	
Pope Oliver John Douglas	2.1.1998		23	2018–*2021*	
Pougher Arthur <u>Dick</u>.	19.4.1865	20.5.1926	1	1891	
Price John Sidney Ernest	22.7.1937		15	1963–1972	
Price Wilfred <u>Frederick</u> Frank	25.4.1902	13.1.1969	1	1938	
Prideaux Roger Malcolm.	31.7.1939		3	1968–*1968*	
Pringle Derek Raymond	18.9.1958		30	1982–1992	44
Prior Matthew James (*CY 2010*).	26.2.1982		79	2007–2014	68/10
Pullar Geoffrey (*CY 1960*).	1.8.1935	26.12.2014	28	1959–1962	
Quaife William George (*CY 1902*)	17.3.1872	13.10.1951	7	1899–*1901*	
Radford Neal Victor (*CY 1986*)	7.6.1957		3	1986–1987	6
Radley Clive Thornton MBE (*CY 1979*)	13.5.1944		8	1977–*1978*	4
Ramprakash Mark Ravin MBE (*CY 2007*)	5.9.1969		52	1991–*2001*	18
Randall Derek William (*CY 1980*)	24.2.1951		47	1976–*1984*	49
Ranjitsinhji Kumar Shri (*CY 1897*)	10.9.1872	2.4.1933	15	1896–1902	
Rankin William <u>Boyd</u>	5.7.1984		1†	2013	7‡/2‡
Rashid Adil Usman	17.2.1988		19	2015–2018	112/68
Read Christopher Mark Wells (*CY 2011*)	10.8.1978		15	1999–*2006*	36/1
Read Holcombe Douglas ("Hopper").	28.1.1910	5.1.2000	1	1935	
Read John <u>Maurice</u> (*CY 1890*)	9.2.1859	17.2.1929	17	1882–1893	
Read Walter William (*CY 1893*)	23.11.1855	6.1.1907	18	1882–1893	
Reeve Dermot Alexander OBE (*CY 1996*)	2.4.1963		3	1991	29
Relf Albert Edward (*CY 1914*)	26.6.1874	26.3.1937	13	1903–*1913*	
Rhodes Harold James	22.7.1936		2	1959	
Rhodes Steven John (*CY 1995*).	17.6.1964		11	1994–*1994*	9
Rhodes Wilfred (*CY 1899*).	29.10.1877	8.7.1973	58	1899–*1929*	
Richards Clifton James ("Jack").	10.8.1958		8	1986–1988	22
² **Richardson** Derek Walter ("Dick").	3.11.1934		1	1957	
² **Richardson** Peter Edward (*CY 1957*).	4.7.1931	16.2.2017	34	1956–1963	
Richardson Thomas (*CY 1897*)	11.8.1870	2.7.1912	14	1893–*1897*	
Richmond Thomas Leonard	23.6.1890	29.12.1957	1	1921	
Ridgway Frederick	10.8.1923	26.9.2015	5	1951	
Robertson John David Benbow (*CY 1948*).	22.2.1917	12.10.1996	11	1947–*1951*	
Robins Robert <u>Walter</u> Vivian (*CY 1930*)	3.6.1906	12.12.1968	19	1929–1937	
Robinson Oliver Edward (*CY 2022*)	1.12.1993		9	2021–*2021*	
Robinson Robert <u>Timothy</u> (*CY 1986*)	21.11.1958		29	1984–1989	26
Robson Samuel David	1.7.1989		7	2014	

	Born	Died	Tests	Test Career	O/T
Roland-Jones Tobias Skelton.	29.01.1988		4	2017	1
Roope Graham Richard James	12.7.1946	26.11.2006	21	1972–1978	8
Root Charles <u>Frederick</u>	16.4.1890	20.1.1954	3	1926	
Root Joseph Edward MBE *(CY 2014)*	30.12.1990		114	2012–2021	152/32
Rose Brian Charles *(CY 1980)*.	4.6.1950		9	1977–1980	2
Roy Jason Jonathan	21.7.1990		5	2019	98/53
Royle Vernon Peter Fanshawe Archer	29.1.1854	21.5.1929	1	1878	
Rumsey Frederick Edward.	4.12.1935		5	1964–1965	
Russell Albert Charles ("Jack") *(CY 1923)* . .	7.10.1887	23.3.1961	10	1920–1922	
Russell Robert Charles ("Jack") *(CY 1990)*.	15.8.1963		54	1988–1997	40
Russell William <u>Eric</u>	3.7.1936		10	1961–1967	
Saggers Martin John	23.5.1972		3	2003–2004	
Salisbury Ian David Kenneth *(CY 1993)*	21.11.1970		15	1992–2000	4
Sandham Andrew *(CY 1923)*.	6.7.1890	20.4.1982	14	1921–1929	
Schofield Christopher Paul.	6.10.1978		2	2000	0/4
Schultz Sandford Spence	29.8.1857	18.12.1937	1	1878	
Scotton William Henry	15.1.1856	9.7.1893	15	1881–1886	
Selby John	1.7.1849	11.3.1894	6	1876–1881	
Selvey Michael Walter William.	25.4.1948		3	1976–1976	
Shackleton Derek *(CY 1959)*.	12.8.1924	28.9.2007	7	1950–1963	
Shah Owais Alam	22.10.1978		6	2005–2008	71/17
Shahzad Ajmal	27.7.1985		1	2010	11/3
Sharp John.	15.2.1878	28.1.1938	3	1909	
Sharpe John William *(CY 1892)*	9.12.1866	19.6.1936	3	1890–1891	
Sharpe Philip John *(CY 1963)*.	27.12.1936	19.5.2014	12	1963–1969	
Shaw Alfred	29.8.1842	16.1.1907	7	1876–1881	
Sheppard *Rt Rev. Lord* [David Stuart] *(CY 1953)* .	6.3.1929	5.3.2005	22	1950–1962	
Sherwin Mordecai *(CY 1891)*.	26.2.1851	3.7.1910	3	1886–1888	
Shrewsbury Arthur *(CY 1890)*	11.4.1856	19.5.1903	23	1881–1893	
Shuter John	9.2.1855	5.7.1920	1	1888	
Shuttleworth Kenneth.	13.11.1944		5	1970–1971	
Sibley Dominic Peter *(CY 2021)*	5.9.1995		22	2019–2021	
[1] **Sidebottom** Arnold	1.4.1954		1	1985	
[1] **Sidebottom** Ryan Jay *(CY 2008)*.	15.1.1978		22	2001–2009	25/18
Silverwood Christopher Eric Wilfred.	5.3.1975		6	1996–2002	7
Simpson Reginald Thomas *(CY 1950)*	27.2.1920	24.11.2013	27	1948–1954	
Simpson-Hayward George Hayward Thomas . . .	7.6.1875	2.10.1936	5	1909	
Sims James Morton	13.5.1903	27.4.1973	4	1935–1936	
Sinfield Reginald Albert.	24.12.1900	17.3.1988	1	1938	
Slack Wilfred Norris	12.12.1954	15.1.1989	3	1985–1986	2
Smailes Thomas <u>Francis</u>	27.3.1910	1.12.1970	1	1946	
Small Gladstone Cleophas	18.10.1961		17	1986–1990	53
Smith Alan Christopher CBE.	25.10.1936		6	1962	
Smith Andrew <u>Michael</u>	1.10.1967		1	1997	
Smith *Sir* Charles <u>Aubrey</u>	21.7.1863	20.12.1948	1	1888	
Smith Cedric Ivan <u>James</u> *(CY 1935)*	25.8.1906	8.2.1979	5	1934–1937	
[2] **Smith** Christopher Lyall *(CY 1984)*	15.10.1958		8	1983–1986	4
Smith Denis *(CY 1935)*	24.1.1907	12.9.1979	2	1935	
Smith David Mark	9.1.1956		2	1985	2
Smith David Robert	5.10.1934	17.12.2003	5	1961	
Smith Donald Victor	14.6.1923	10.1.2021	3	1957	
Smith Edward Thomas	19.7.1977		3	2003	
Smith Ernest James ("Tiger").	6.2.1886	31.8.1979	11	1911–1913	
Smith Harry	21.5.1891	12.11.1937	1	1928	
Smith Michael John Knight OBE *(CY 1960)*	30.6.1933		50	1958–1972	
[2] **Smith** Robin Arnold *(CY 1990)*.	13.9.1963		62	1988–1995	71
Smith Thomas <u>Peter</u> Bromley *(CY 1947)*	30.10.1908	4.8.1967	4	1946–1946	
Smithson Gerald Arthur.	1.11.1926	6.9.1970	2	1947	
Snow John Augustine *(CY 1973)*.	13.10.1941		49	1965–1976	9
Southerton James.	16.11.1827	16.6.1880	2	1876	

	Born	Died	Tests	Test Career	O/T
Spooner Reginald Herbert (CY 1905)	21.10.1880	2.10.1961	10	1905–1912	
Spooner Richard Thompson	30.12.1919	20.12.1997	7	1951–1955	
Stanyforth Ronald Thomas	30.5.1892	20.2.1964	4	1927	
Staples Samuel James (CY 1929)	18.9.1892	4.6.1950	3	1927	
Statham John **Brian** CBE (CY 1955)...........	17.6.1930	10.6.2000	70	1950–1965	
Steel Allan Gibson	24.9.1858	15.6.1914	13	1880–1888	
Steele David Stanley OBE (CY 1976)	29.9.1941		8	1975–1976	1
Stephenson John Patrick	14.3.1965		1	1989	
Stevens Greville Thomas Scott (CY 1918)	7.1.1901	19.9.1970	10	1922–1929	
Stevenson Graham Barry	16.12.1955	21.1.2014	2	1979–1980	4
[1] **Stewart** Alec James OBE (CY 1993)............	8.4.1963		133	1989–2003	170
[1] **Stewart** Michael James OBE (CY 1958)	16.9.1932		8	1962–1963	
Stoddart Andrew Ernest (CY 1893)..........	11.3.1863	3.4.1915	16	1887–1897	
Stokes Benjamin Andrew OBE (CY 2016).......	4.6.1991		76	2013–2021	101/34
Stone Oliver Peter.............	9.10.1993		3	2019–2021	4
Stoneman Mark Daniel	26.06.1987		11	2017–2018	
Storer William (CY 1899)	25.1.1867	28.2.1912	6	1897–1899	
Strauss *Sir* Andrew John OBE (CY 2005)	2.3.1977		100	2004–2012	127/4
Street George Benjamin.	6.12.1889	24.4.1924	1	1922	
Strudwick Herbert (CY 1912).	28.1.1880	14.2.1970	28	1909–1926	
[2] **Studd** Charles Thomas.	2.12.1860	16.7.1931	5	1882–1882	
[2] **Studd** George Brown.	20.10.1859	13.2.1945	4	1882	
Subba Row Raman CBE (CY 1961)	29.1.1932		13	1958–1961	
Such Peter Mark	12.6.1964		11	1993–1999	
Sugg Frank Howe (CY 1890)	11.1.1862	29.5.1933	2	1888	
Sutcliffe Herbert (CY 1920)	24.11.1894	22.1.1978	54	1924–1935	
Swann Graeme Peter (CY 2010)	24.3.1979		60	2008–2013	79/39
Swetman Roy.	25.10.1933		11	1958–1959	
[1] **Tate** Frederick William	24.7.1867	24.2.1943	1	1902	
[1] **Tate** Maurice William (CY 1924)	30.5.1895	18.5.1956	39	1924–1935	
Tattersall Roy	17.8.1922	9.12.2011	16	1950–1954	
Tavaré Christopher James	27.10.1954		31	1980–1989	29
Taylor Jonathan **Paul**.	8.8.1964		2	1992–1994	1
Taylor James William Arthur	6.1.1990		7	2012–2015	27
Taylor Kenneth	21.8.1935		3	1959–1964	
Taylor Leslie Brian.	25.10.1953		2	1985	2
Taylor Robert William MBE (CY 1977)	17.7.1941		57	1970–1983	27
Tennyson *Lord* Lionel Hallam (CY 1914).	7.11.1889	6.6.1951	9	1913–1921	
Terry Vivian **Paul**.	14.1.1959		2	1984	
Thomas John **Gregory**.	12.8.1960		5	1985–1986	3
Thompson George Joseph (CY 1906)	27.10.1877	3.3.1943	6	1909–1909	
Thomson Norman **Ian**	23.1.1929	1.8.2021	5	1964	
Thorpe Graham Paul MBE (CY 1998).	1.8.1969		100	1993–2005	82
Titmus Frederick John MBE (CY 1963).	24.11.1932	23.3.2011	53	1955–1974	2
Tolchard Roger William	15.6.1946		4	1976	1
Townsend Charles Lucas (CY 1899)	7.11.1876	17.10.1958	2	1899	
[1] **Townsend** David Charles Humphery.	20.4.1912	27.1.1997	3	1934	
Townsend Leslie Fletcher (CY 1934).	8.6.1903	17.2.1993	4	1929–1933	
Tredwell James Cullum	27.2.1982		2	2009–2014	45/17
[4] **Tremlett** Christopher Timothy	2.9.1981		12	2007–2013	15/1
[4] **Tremlett** Maurice Fletcher.	5.7.1923	30.7.1984	3	1947	
Trescothick Marcus Edward MBE (CY 2005)	25.12.1975		76	2000–2006	123/3
[2] **Trott** Albert Edwin (CY 1899)	6.2.1873	30.7.1914	2†	1898	
Trott Ian **Jonathan** Leonard (CY 2011).	22.4.1981		52	2009–2014	68/7
Trueman Frederick Sewards OBE (CY 1953).	6.2.1931	1.7.2006	67	1952–1965	
Tudor Alex Jeremy.	23.10.1977		10	1998–2002	3
Tufnell Neville Charsley	13.6.1887	3.8.1951	1	1909	
Tufnell Philip Clive Roderick.	29.4.1966		42	1990–2001	20
Turnbull Maurice Joseph Lawson (CY 1931)....	16.3.1906	5.8.1944	9	1929–1936	
[2] **Tyldesley** [George] **Ernest** (CY 1920)	5.2.1889	5.5.1962	14	1921–1928	

	Born	Died	Tests	Test Career	O/T
[2]**Tyldesley** John Thomas (*CY 1902*)	22.11.1873	27.11.1930	31	1898–1909	
Tyldesley Richard Knowles (*CY 1925*)	11.3.1897	17.9.1943	7	1924–1930	
Tylecote Edward Ferdinando Sutton	23.6.1849	15.3.1938	6	1882–1886	
Tyler Edwin James	13.10.1864	25.1.1917	1	1895	
Tyson Frank Holmes (*CY 1956*)	6.6.1930	27.9.2015	17	1954–1958	
Udal Shaun David	18.3.1969		4	2005	11
Ulyett George	21.10.1851	18.6.1898	25	1876–1890	
Underwood Derek Leslie MBE (*CY 1969*)	8.6.1945		86	1966–*1981*	26
Valentine Bryan Herbert	17.1.1908	2.2.1983	7	1933–1938	
Vaughan Michael Paul OBE (*CY 2003*)	29.10.1974		82	1999–2008	86/2
Verity Hedley (*CY 1932*)	18.5.1905	31.7.1943	40	1931–1939	
Vernon George Frederick	20.6.1856	10.8.1902	1	1882	
Vince James Michael	14.3.1991		13	2016–*2017*	19/12
Vine Joseph (*CY 1906*)	15.5.1875	25.4.1946	2	1911	
Voce William (*CY 1933*)	8.8.1909	6.6.1984	27	1929–1946	
Waddington Abraham	4.2.1893	28.10.1959	2	1920	
Wainwright Edward (*CY 1894*)	8.4.1865	28.10.1919	5	1893–1897	
Walker Peter Michael	17.2.1936	4.4.2020	3	1960	
Walters Cyril Frederick (*CY 1934*)	28.8.1905	23.12.1992	11	1933–1934	
Ward Alan	10.8.1947		5	1969–1976	
Ward Albert (*CY 1890*)	21.11.1865	6.1.1939	7	1893–*1894*	
Ward Ian James	30.9.1972		5	2001	
Wardle John Henry (*CY 1954*)	8.1.1923	23.7.1985	28	1947–1957	
Warner *Sir* Pelham Francis (*CY 1904*)	2.10.1873	30.1.1963	15	1898–1912	
Warr John James	16.7.1927	9.5.2016	2	1950	
Warren Arnold	2.4.1875	3.9.1951	1	1905	
Washbrook Cyril CBE (*CY 1947*)	6.12.1914	27.4.1999	37	1937–1956	
Watkin Steven Llewellyn (*CY 1994*)	15.9.1964		3	1991–1993	4
Watkins Albert John ("Allan")	21.4.1922	3.8.2011	15	1948–1952	
Watkinson Michael	1.8.1961		4	1995–*1995*	1
Watson Willie (*CY 1954*)	7.3.1920	24.4.2004	23	1951–*1958*	
Webbe Alexander Josiah	16.1.1855	19.2.1941	1	1878	
Wellard Arthur William (*CY 1936*)	8.4.1902	31.12.1980	2	1937–1938	
Wells Alan Peter	2.10.1961		1	1995	1
Westley Thomas	13.03.1989		5	2017	
Wharton Alan	30.4.1923	26.8.1993	1	1949	
Whitaker John James (*CY 1987*)	5.5.1962		1	1986	2
White Craig	16.12.1969		30	1994–*2002*	51
White David William ("Butch")	14.12.1935	1.8.2008	2	1961	
White John Cornish (*CY 1929*)	19.2.1891	2.5.1961	15	1921–*1930*	
Whysall William Wilfrid (*CY 1925*)	31.10.1887	11.11.1930	4	1924–1930	
Wilkinson Leonard Litton	5.11.1916	3.9.2002	3	1938	
Willey Peter	6.12.1949		26	1976–1986	26
Williams Neil FitzGerald	2.7.1962	27.3.2006	1	1990	
Willis Robert George Dylan MBE (*CY 1978*)	30.5.1949	4.12.2019	90	1970–1984	64
[2]**Wilson** Clement Eustace Macro	15.5.1875	8.2.1944	2	1898	
Wilson Donald	7.8.1937	21.7.2012	6	1963–*1970*	
[2]**Wilson** Evelyn Rockley	25.3.1879	21.7.1957	1	1920	
Woakes Christopher Roger (*CY 2017*)	2.3.1989		42	2013–*2021*	106/16
Wood Arthur (*CY 1939*)	25.8.1898	1.4.1973	4	1938–1939	
Wood Barry	26.12.1942		12	1972–1978	13
Wood George Edward Charles	22.8.1893	18.3.1971	3	1924	
Wood Henry (*CY 1891*)	14.12.1853	30.4.1919	4	1888–*1891*	
Wood Mark Andrew	11.1.1990		25	2015–*2021*	57/19
Wood Reginald	7.3.1860	6.1.1915	1	1886	
Woods Samuel Moses James (*CY 1889*)	13.4.1867	30.4.1931	3†	1895	
Woolley Frank Edward (*CY 1911*)	27.5.1887	18.10.1978	64	1909–1934	
Woolmer Robert Andrew (*CY 1976*)	14.5.1948	18.3.2007	19	1975–1981	6
Worthington Thomas Stanley (*CY 1937*)	21.8.1905	31.8.1973	9	1929–1936	
Wright Charles William	27.5.1863	10.1.1936	3	1895	

	Born	Died	Tests	Test Career	O/T
Wright Douglas Vivian Parson (*CY 1940*)	21.8.1914	13.11.1998	34	*1938–1950*	
Wyatt Robert Elliott Storey (*CY 1930*)	2.5.1901	20.4.1995	40	*1927–1936*	
Wynyard Edward George	1.4.1861	30.10.1936	3	*1896–1905*	
Yardley Norman Walter Dransfield (*CY 1948*)	19.3.1915	3.10.1989	20	*1938–1950*	
Young Harding Isaac ("Sailor")	5.2.1876	12.12.1964	2	*1899*	
Young John Albert	14.10.1912	5.2.1993	8	*1947–1949*	
Young Richard Alfred	16.9.1885	1.7.1968	2	*1907*	

AUSTRALIA (463 players)

	Born	Died	Tests	Test Career	O/T
a'Beckett Edward Lambert	11.8.1907	2.6.1989	4	*1928–1931*	
Agar Ashton Charles	14.10.1993		4	*2013–2017*	15/40
Alderman Terence Michael (*CY 1982*)	12.6.1956		41	*1981–1990*	65
Alexander George	22.4.1851	6.11.1930	2	*1880–1884*	
Alexander Harry Houston	9.6.1905	15.4.1993	1	*1932*	
Allan Francis Erskine	2.12.1849	9.2.1917	1	*1878*	
Allan Peter John	31.12.1935		1	*1965*	
Allen Reginald Charles	2.7.1858	2.5.1952	1	*1886*	
Andrews Thomas James Edwin	26.8.1890	28.1.1970	16	*1921–1926*	
Angel Jo	22.4.1968		4	*1992–1994*	3
[2] **Archer** Kenneth Alan	17.1.1928		5	*1950–1951*	
[2] **Archer** Ronald Graham	25.10.1933	27.5.2007	19	*1952–1956*	
Armstrong Warwick Windridge (*CY 1903*)	22.5.1879	13.7.1947	50	*1901–1921*	
Badcock Clayvel Lindsay ("Jack")	10.4.1914	13.12.1982	7	*1936–1938*	
Bailey George John	7.9.1982		5	*2013*	90/29‡
Bancroft Cameron Timothy	19.11.1992		10	*2017–2019*	0/1
[2] **Bannerman** Alexander Chalmers	21.3.1854	19.9.1924	28	*1878–1893*	
[2] **Bannerman** Charles	23.7.1851	20.8.1930	3	*1876–1878*	
Bardsley Warren (*CY 1910*)	6.12.1882	20.1.1954	41	*1909–1926*	
Barnes Sidney George	5.6.1916	16.12.1973	13	*1938–1948*	
Barnett Benjamin Arthur	23.3.1908	29.6.1979	4	*1938*	
Barrett John Edward	15.10.1866	6.2.1916	2	*1890*	
Beard Graeme Robert	19.8.1950		3	*1979*	2
Beer Michael Anthony	9.6.1984		2	*2010–2011*	
[2] **Benaud** John	11.5.1944		3	*1972*	
[2] **Benaud** Richard OBE (*CY 1962*)	6.10.1930	10.4.2015	63	*1951–1963*	
Bennett Murray John	6.10.1956		3	*1984–1985*	8
Bevan Michael Gwyl	8.5.1970		18	*1994–1997*	232
Bichel Andrew John	27.8.1970		19	*1996–2003*	67
Bird Jackson Munro	11.12.1986		9	*2012–2017*	
Blackham John McCarthy (*CY 1891*)	11.5.1854	28.12.1932	35	*1876–1894*	
Blackie Donald Dearness	5.4.1882	18.4.1955	3	*1928*	
Blewett Gregory Scott	28.10.1971		46	*1994–1999*	32
Boland Scott Michael	11.4.1989		3	*2021*	14/3
Bollinger Douglas Erwin	24.7.1981		12	*2008–2010*	39/9
Bonnor George John	25.2.1855	27.6.1912	17	*1880–1888*	
Boon David Clarence MBE (*CY 1994*)	29.12.1960		107	*1984–1995*	181
Booth Brian Charles MBE	19.10.1933		29	*1961–1965*	
Border Allan Robert (*CY 1982*)	27.7.1955		156	*1978–1993*	273
Boyle Henry Frederick	10.12.1847	21.11.1907	12	*1878–1884*	
Bracken Nathan Wade	12.9.1977		5	*2003–2005*	116/19
Bradman Sir Donald George AC (*CY 1931*)	27.8.1908	25.2.2001	52	*1928–1948*	
Bright Raymond James	13.7.1954		25	*1977–1986*	11
Bromley Ernest Harvey	2.9.1912	1.2.1967	2	*1932–1934*	
Brown William Alfred (*CY 1939*)	31.7.1912	16.3.2008	22	*1934–1948*	
Bruce William	22.5.1864	3.8.1925	14	*1884–1894*	
Burge Peter John Parnell (*CY 1965*)	17.5.1932	5.10.2001	42	*1954–1965*	
Burke James Wallace (*CY 1957*)	12.6.1930	2.2.1979	24	*1950–1958*	

	Born	Died	Tests	Test Career	O/T
Burn Edwin James **Kenneth** (K. E.)	17.9.1862	20.7.1956	2	*1890*	
Burns Joseph Antony	6.9.1989		23	*2014–2020*	6
Burton Frederick John	2.11.1865	25.8.1929	2	*1886–1887*	
Callaway Sydney Thomas	6.2.1868	25.11.1923	3	*1891–1894*	
Callen Ian Wayne	2.5.1955		1	*1977*	5
Campbell Gregory Dale	10.3.1964		4	*1989–1989*	12
Carey Alex Tyson	27.8.1991		5	*2021*	45/38
Carkeek William ("Barlow")	17.10.1878	20.2.1937	6	*1912*	
Carlson Phillip Henry	8.8.1951		2	*1978*	4
Carter Hanson	15.3.1878	8.6.1948	28	*1907–1921*	
Cartwright Hilton William Raymond	14.2.1992		2	*2016–2017*	2
Casson Beau	7.12.1982		1	*2007*	
[2,4] **Chappell** Gregory Stephen MBE (*CY 1973*)	7.8.1948		87	*1970–1983*	74
[2,4] **Chappell** Ian Michael (*CY 1976*)	26.9.1943		75	*1964–1979*	16
[2,4] **Chappell** Trevor Martin	21.10.1952		3	*1981*	20
Charlton Percie Chater	9.4.1867	30.9.1954	2	*1890*	
Chipperfield Arthur Gordon	17.11.1905	29.7.1987	14	*1934–1938*	
Clark Stuart Rupert	28.9.1975		24	*2005–2009*	39/9
Clark Wayne Maxwell	19.9.1953		10	*1977–1978*	2
Clarke Michael John (*CY 2010*)	2.4.1981		115§	*2004–2015*	245/34
Colley David John	15.3.1947		3	*1972*	1
Collins Herbert Leslie	21.1.1888	28.5.1959	19	*1920–1926*	
Coningham Arthur	14.7.1863	13.6.1939	1	*1894*	
Connolly Alan Norman	29.6.1939		29	*1963–1970*	1
Cook Simon Hewitt	29.1.1972		1	*1997*	
Cooper Bransby Beauchamp	15.3.1844	7.8.1914	1	*1876*	
[5] **Cooper** William Henry	11.9.1849	5.4.1939	2	*1881–1884*	
Copeland Trent Aaron	14.3.1986		3	*2011*	
Corling Grahame Edward	13.7.1941		5	*1964*	
Cosier Gary John	25.4.1953		18	*1975–1978*	9
Cottam John Thomas	5.9.1867	30.1.1897	1	*1886*	
Cotter Albert ("Tibby")	3.12.1883	31.10.1917	21	*1903–1911*	
Coulthard George	1.8.1856	22.10.1883	1	*1881*	
Cowan Edward James McKenzie	16.6.1982		18	*2011–2013*	
Cowper Robert Maskew	5.10.1940		27	*1964–1968*	
Craig Ian David	12.6.1935	16.11.2014	11	*1952–1957*	
Crawford William Patrick Anthony	3.8.1933	21.1.2009	4	*1956–1956*	
Cullen Daniel James	10.4.1984		1	*2005*	5
Cummins Patrick James (*CY 2020*)	8.5.1993		38	*2011–2021*	69/37
Dale Adam Craig	30.12.1968		2	*1997–1998*	30
Darling Joseph (*CY 1900*)	21.11.1870	2.1.1946	34	*1894–1905*	
Darling Leonard Stuart	14.8.1909	24.6.1992	12	*1932–1936*	
Darling Warrick Maxwell	1.5.1957		14	*1977–1979*	18
Davidson Alan Keith MBE (*CY 1962*)	14.6.1929	30.10.2021	44	*1953–1962*	
Davis Ian Charles	25.6.1953		15	*1973–1977*	3
Davis Simon Peter	8.11.1959			*1985*	39
De Courcy James Harry	18.4.1927	20.6.2000	3	*1953*	
Dell Anthony Ross	6.8.1945		2	*1970–1973*	
Dodemaide Anthony Ian Christopher	5.10.1963		10	*1987–1992*	24
Doherty Xavier John	22.12.1982		4	*2010–2012*	60/11
Donnan Henry	12.11.1864	13.8.1956	5	*1891–1896*	
Doolan Alexander James	29.11.1985		4	*2013–2014*	
Dooland Bruce (*CY 1955*)	1.11.1923	8.9.1980	3	*1946–1947*	
Duff Reginald Alexander	17.8.1878	13.12.1911	22	*1901–1905*	
Duncan John Ross Frederick	25.3.1944		1	*1970*	
Dyer Gregory Charles	16.3.1959		6	*1986–1987*	23
Dymock Geoffrey	21.7.1945		21	*1973–1979*	15
Dyson John	11.6.1954		30	*1977–1984*	29
Eady Charles John	29.10.1870	20.12.1945	2	*1896–1901*	
Eastwood Kenneth Humphrey	23.11.1935		1	*1970*	

	Born	Died	Tests	Test Career	O/T
Ebeling Hans Irvine	1.1.1905	12.1.1980	1	1934	
Edwards John Dunlop	12.6.1860	31.7.1911	3	1888	
Edwards Ross	1.12.1942		20	1972–1975	9
Edwards Walter John	23.12.1949		3	1974	1
Elliott Matthew Thomas Gray (*CY 1998*)	28.9.1971		21	1996–2004	1
Emery Philip Allen	25.6.1964		1	1994	1
Emery Sidney Hand	15.10.1885	7.1.1967	4	1912	
Evans Edwin	26.3.1849	2.7.1921	6	1881–1886	
Fairfax Alan George	16.6.1906	17.5.1955	10	1928–1930	
Faulkner James Peter	29.4.1990		1	2013	69/24
Favell Leslie Ernest MBE	6.10.1929	14.6.1987	19	1954–1960	
Ferguson Callum James	21.11.1984		1	2016	30/3
Ferris John James (*CY 1889*)	21.5.1867	17.11.1900	8†	1886–1890	
Finch Aaron James	17.11.1986		5	2018	132/83
Fingleton John Henry Webb OBE	28.4.1908	22.11.1981	18	1931–1938	
Fleetwood-Smith Leslie O'Brien ("Chuck")	30.3.1908	16.3.1971	10	1935–1938	
Fleming Damien William	24.4.1970		20	1994–2000	88
Francis Bruce Colin	18.2.1948		3	1972	
Freeman Eric Walter	13.7.1944	14.12.2020	11	1967–1969	
Freer Frederick Alfred William	4.12.1915	2.11.1998	1	1946	
Gannon John Bryant ("Sam")	8.2.1947	5.2.2021	3	1977	
Garrett Thomas William	26.7.1858	6.8.1943	19	1876–1887	
Gaunt Ronald Arthur	26.2.1934	30.3.2012	3	1957–1963	
Gehrs Donald Raeburn <u>Algernon</u>	29.11.1880	25.6.1953	6	1903–1910	
George Peter Robert	16.10.1986		1	2010	
³ **Giffen** George (*CY 1894*)	27.3.1859	29.11.1927	31	1881–1896	
² **Giffen** Walter Frank	20.9.1861	28.6.1949	3	1886–1891	
Gilbert David Robert	29.12.1960		9	1985–1986	14
Gilchrist Adam Craig (*CY 2002*)	14.11.1971		96§	1999–2007	286‡/13
Gillespie Jason Neil (*CY 2002*)	19.4.1975		71	1996–2005	97/1
Gilmour Gary John	26.6.1951	10.6.2014	15	1973–1976	5
Gleeson John William	14.3.1938	8.10.2016	29	1967–1972	
Graham Henry	22.11.1870	7.2.1911	6	1893–1896	
Green Cameron David	3.6.1999		9	2020–2021	1
Gregory David William	15.4.1845	4.8.1919	3	1876–1878	
¹,² **Gregory** Edward James	29.5.1839	22.4.1899	1	1876	
Gregory Jack Morrison (*CY 1922*)	14.8.1895	7.8.1973	24	1920–1928	
Gregory Ross Gerald	28.2.1916	10.6.1942	2	1936	
¹ **Gregory** Sydney Edward (*CY 1897*)	14.4.1870	31.7.1929	58	1890–1912	
Grimmett Clarence Victor (*CY 1931*)	25.12.1891	2.5.1980	37	1924–1935	
Groube Thomas Underwood	2.9.1857	5.8.1927	1	1880	
Grout Arthur Theodore <u>Wallace</u>	30.3.1927	9.11.1968	51	1957–1965	
Guest Colin Ernest John	7.10.1937	8.12.2018	1	1962	
Haddin Bradley James	23.10.1977		66	2007–2015	126/34
Hamence Ronald Arthur	25.11.1915	24.3.2010	3	1946–1947	
Hammond Jeffrey Roy	19.4.1950		5	1972	1
Handscomb Peter Stephen Patrick	26.4.1991		16	2016–2018	22/2
Harris Marcus Sinclair	21.7.1992		14	2018–2021	
Harris Ryan James (*CY 2014*)	11.10.1979		27	2009–2014	21/3
Harry John	1.8.1857	27.10.1919	1	1894	
Hartigan Roger Joseph	12.12.1879	7.6.1958	2	1907	
Hartkopf Albert Ernst Victor	28.12.1889	20.5.1968	1	1924	
² **Harvey** Mervyn Roye	29.4.1918	18.3.1995	1	1946	
² **Harvey** Robert <u>Neil</u> MBE (*CY 1954*)	8.10.1928		79	1947–1962	
Hassett Arthur <u>Lindsay</u> MBE (*CY 1949*)	28.8.1913	16.6.1993	43	1938–1953	
Hastings John Wayne	4.11.1985		1	2012	29/9
Hauritz Nathan Michael	18.10.1981		17	2004–2010	58/3
Hawke Neil James Napier	27.6.1939	25.12.2000	27	1962–1968	
Hayden Matthew Lawrence (*CY 2003*)	29.10.1971		103§	1993–2008	160‡/9
Hazlewood Josh Reginald	8.1.1991		56	2014–2021	56/24

	Born	Died	Tests	Test Career	O/T
Hazlitt Gervys Rignold	4.9.1888	30.10.1915	9	*1907–1912*	
Head Travis Michael	29.12.1993		23	*2018–2021*	42/16
Healy Ian Andrew (*CY 1994*)	30.4.1964		119	*1988–1999*	168
Hendry Hunter Scott Thomas Laurie ("Stork") . . .	24.5.1895	16.12.1988	11	*1921–1928*	
Henriques Moises Constantino	1.2.1987		4	*2012–2016*	16/24
Hibbert Paul Anthony	23.7.1952	27.11.2008	1	*1977*	
Higgs James Donald	11.7.1950		22	*1977–1980*	
Hilditch Andrew Mark Jefferson	20.5.1956		18	*1978–1985*	8
Hilfenhaus Benjamin William	15.3.1983		27	*2008–2012*	25/7
Hill Clement (*CY 1900*)	18.3.1877	5.9.1945	49	*1896–1911*	
Hill John Charles	25.6.1923	11.8.1974	3	*1953–1954*	
Hoare Desmond Edward	19.10.1934		1	*1960*	
Hodge Bradley John	29.12.1974		6	*2005–2007*	25/15
Hodges John Robart	11.8.1855	d unknown	2	*1876*	
Hogan Tom George	23.9.1956		7	*1982–1983*	16
Hogg George Bradley	6.2.1971		7	*1996–2007*	123/15
Hogg Rodney Malcolm	5.3.1951		38	*1978–1984*	71
Hohns Trevor Victor	23.1.1954		7	*1988–1989*	
Hole Graeme Blake	6.1.1931	14.2.1990	18	*1950–1954*	
Holland Jonathan Mark	29.5.1987		4	*2016–2018*	
Holland Robert George	19.10.1946	17.9.2017	11	*1984–1985*	2
Hookes David William	3.5.1955	19.1.2004	23	*1976–1985*	39
Hopkins Albert John Young	3.5.1874	25.4.1931	20	*1901–1909*	
Horan Thomas Patrick	8.3.1854	16.4.1916	15	*1876–1884*	
Hordern Herbert Vivian MBE	10.2.1883	17.6.1938	7	*1910–1911*	
Hornibrook Percival Mitchell	27.7.1899	25.8.1976	6	*1928–1930*	
Howell William Peter	29.12.1869	14.7.1940	18	*1897–1903*	
Hughes Kimberley John (*CY 1981*)	26.1.1954		70	*1977–1984*	97
Hughes Mervyn Gregory (*CY 1994*)	23.11.1961		53	*1985–1993*	33
Hughes Phillip Joel	30.11.1988	27.11.2014	26	*2008–2013*	25/1
Hunt William Alfred	26.8.1908	30.12.1983	1	*1931*	
Hurst Alan George	15.7.1950		12	*1973–1979*	8
Hurwood Alexander	17.6.1902	26.9.1982	2	*1930*	
Hussey Michael Edward Killeen	27.5.1975		79	*2005–2012*	185/38
Inverarity Robert John	31.1.1944		6	*1968–1972*	
Iredale Francis Adams	19.6.1867	15.4.1926	14	*1894–1899*	
Ironmonger Herbert	7.4.1882	31.5.1971	14	*1928–1932*	
Iverson John Brian	27.7.1915	24.10.1973	5	*1950*	
Jackson Archibald Alexander	5.9.1909	16.2.1933	8	*1928–1930*	
Jaques Philip Anthony	3.5.1979		11	*2005–2007*	6
Jarman Barrington Noel	17.2.1936	17.7.2020	19	*1959–1968*	
Jarvis Arthur Harwood	19.10.1860	15.11.1933	11	*1884–1894*	
Jenner Terrence James	8.9.1944	24.5.2011	9	*1970–1975*	1
Jennings Claude Burrows	5.6.1884	20.6.1950	6	*1912*	
Johnson Ian William Geddes CBE	8.12.1917	9.10.1998	45	*1945–1956*	
Johnson Leonard Joseph	18.3.1919	20.4.1977	1	*1947*	
Johnson Mitchell Guy	2.11.1981		73	*2007–2015*	153/30
Johnston William Arras (*CY 1949*)	26.2.1922	25.5.2007	40	*1947–1954*	
Jones Dean Mervyn (*CY 1990*)	24.3.1961	24.9.2020	52	*1983–1992*	164
Jones Ernest	30.9.1869	23.11.1943	19	*1894–1902*	
Jones Samuel Percy	1.8.1861	14.7.1951	12	*1881–1887*	
Joslin Leslie Ronald	13.12.1947		1	*1967*	
Julian Brendon Paul	10.8.1970		7	*1993–1995*	25
Kasprowicz Michael Scott	10.2.1972		38	*1996–2005*	43/2
Katich Simon Mathew	21.8.1975		56§	*2001–2010*	45/3
Kelleway Charles	25.4.1886	16.11.1944	26	*1910–1928*	
Kelly James Joseph (*CY 1903*)	10.5.1867	14.8.1938	36	*1896–1905*	
Kelly Thomas Joseph Dart	3.5.1844	20.7.1893	2	*1876–1878*	
Kendall Thomas Kingston	24.8.1851	17.8.1924	2	*1876*	

	Born	Died	Tests	Test Career	O/T
Kent Martin Francis	23.11.1953		3	1981	5
Kerr Robert Byers	16.6.1961		2	1985	4
Khawaja Usman Tariq	18.12.1986		46	2010–2021	40/9
Kippax Alan Falconer	25.5.1897	5.9.1972	22	1924–1934	
Kline Lindsay Francis	29.9.1934	2.10.2015	13	1957–1960	
Krejza Jason John	14.1.1983		2	2008	8
Labuschagne Marnus (CY 2020)	22.6.1994		23	2018–2021	13
Laird Bruce Malcolm	21.11.1950		21	1979–1982	23
Langer Justin Lee (CY 2001)	21.11.1970		105§	1992–2006	8
Langley Gilbert Roche Andrews (CY 1957)	14.9.1919	14.5.2001	26	1951–1956	
Laughlin Trevor John	30.1.1951		3	1977–1978	6
Laver Frank Jonas	7.12.1869	24.9.1919	15	1899–1909	
Law Stuart Grant (CY 1998)	18.10.1968		1	1995	54
Lawry William Morris (CY 1962)	11.2.1937		67	1961–1970	1
Lawson Geoffrey Francis	7.12.1957		46	1980–1989	79
Lee Brett (CY 2006)	8.11.1976		76§	1999–2008	221/25
Lee Philip Keith	15.9.1904	9.8.1980	2	1931–1932	
Lehmann Darren Scott (CY 2001)	5.2.1970		27	1997–2004	117
Lillee Dennis Keith MBE (CY 1973)	18.7.1949		70	1970–1983	63
Lindwall Raymond Russell MBE (CY 1949)	3.10.1921	23.6.1996	61	1945–1959	
Love Hampden Stanley Bray	10.8.1895	22.7.1969	1	1932	
Love Martin Lloyd	30.3.1974		5	2002–2003	
Loxton Samuel John Everett OBE	29.3.1921	3.12.2011	12	1947–1950	
Lyon Nathan Michael	20.11.1987		105	2011–2021	29/2
Lyons John James	21.5.1863	21.7.1927	14	1886–1897	
McAlister Peter Alexander	11.7.1869	10.5.1938	8	1903–1909	
Macartney Charles George (CY 1922)	27.6.1886	9.9.1958	35	1907–1926	
McCabe Stanley Joseph (CY 1935)	16.7.1910	25.8.1968	39	1930–1938	
McCool Colin Leslie	9.12.1916	5.4.1986	14	1945–1949	
McCormick Ernest Leslie	16.5.1906	28.6.1991	12	1935–1938	
McCosker Richard Bede (CY 1976)	11.12.1946		25	1974–1979	14
McDermott Craig John (CY 1986)	14.4.1965		71	1984–1995	138
McDonald Andrew Barry	15.6.1981		4	2008	
McDonald Colin Campbell	17.11.1928	8.1.2021	47	1951–1961	
McDonald Edgar Arthur (CY 1922)	6.1.1891	22.7.1937	11	1920–1921	
McDonnell Percy Stanislaus	13.11.1858	24.9.1896	19	1880–1888	
McGain Bryce Edward	25.3.1972		1	2008	
MacGill Stuart Charles Glyndwr	25.2.1971		44§	1997–2007	3
McGrath Glenn Donald (CY 1998)	9.2.1970		124§	1993–2006	249‡/2
McIlwraith John	7.9.1857	5.7.1938	1	1886	
McIntyre Peter Edward	27.4.1966		2	1994–1996	
McKay Clinton James	22.2.1983		1	2009	59/6
Mackay Kenneth Donald MBE	24.10.1925	13.6.1982	37	1956–1962	
McKenzie Graham Douglas (CY 1965)	24.6.1941		60	1961–1970	1
McKibbin Thomas Robert	10.12.1870	15.12.1939	5	1894–1897	
McLaren John William	22.12.1886	17.11.1921	1	1911	
Maclean John Alexander	27.4.1946		4	1978	2
[2] **McLeod** Charles Edward	24.10.1869	26.11.1918	17	1894–1905	
[2] **McLeod** Robert William	19.1.1868	14.6.1907	6	1891–1893	
McShane Patrick George	18.4.1858	11.12.1903	3	1884–1887	
Maddinson Nicolas James	21.12.1991		3	2016	0/6
Maddocks Leonard Victor	24.5.1926	27.8.2016	7	1954–1956	
Maguire John Norman	15.9.1956		3	1983	23
Mailey Arthur Alfred	3.1.1886	31.12.1967	21	1920–1926	
Mallett Ashley Alexander	13.7.1945	29.10.2021	38	1968–1980	9
Malone Michael Francis	9.10.1950		1	1977	10
Mann Anthony Longford	8.11.1945	15.11.2019	4	1977	
Manou Graham Allan	23.4.1979		1	2009	4
Marr Alfred Percy	28.3.1862	15.3.1940	1	1884	

	Born	Died	Tests	Test Career	O/T
[1] **Marsh** Geoffrey Robert	31.12.1958		50	*1985–1991*	117
[1,2] **Marsh** Mitchell Ross.	20.10.1991		32	*2014–2019*	63/36
Marsh Rodney William MBE (*CY 1982*).	4.11.1947		96	*1970–1983*	92
[1,2] **Marsh** Shaun Edward	9.7.1983		38	*2011–2018*	73/15
Martin John Wesley	28.7.1931	16.7.1992	8	*1960–1966*	
Martyn Damien Richard (*CY 2002*).	21.10.1971		67	*1992–2006*	208/4
Massie Hugh Hamon	11.4.1854	12.10.1938	9	*1881–1884*	
Massie Robert Arnold Lockyer (*CY 1973*)	14.4.1947		6	*1972–1972*	3
Matthews Christopher Darrell	22.9.1962		3	*1986–1988*	
Matthews Gregory Richard John	15.12.1959		33	*1983–1992*	59
Matthews Thomas James.	3.4.1884	14.10.1943	8	*1911–1912*	
Maxwell Glenn James	14.10.1988		7	*2012–2017*	116/79
May Timothy Brian Alexander	26.1.1962		24	*1987–1994*	47
Mayne Edgar Richard	2.7.1882	26.10.1961	4	*1912–1921*	
Mayne Lawrence Charles.	23.1.1942		6	*1964–1969*	
Meckiff Ian	6.1.1935		18	*1957–1963*	
Mennie Joe Matthew	24.12.1988		1	*2016*	2
Meuleman Kenneth Douglas	5.9.1923	10.9.2004	1	*1945*	
Midwinter William Evans	19.6.1851	3.12.1890	8†	*1876–1886*	
Miller Colin Reid	6.2.1964		18	*1998–2000*	
Miller Keith Ross MBE (*CY 1954*).	28.11.1919	11.10.2004	55	*1945–1956*	
Minnett Roy Baldwin	13.6.1886	21.10.1955	9	*1911–1912*	
Misson Francis Michael	19.11.1938		5	*1960–1961*	
Moody Thomas Masson (*CY 2000*)	2.10.1965		8	*1989–1992*	76
Mooney John	24.7.1917	1.7.1999	7	*1950–1951*	
Morris Arthur Robert MBE (*CY 1949*)	19.1.1922	22.8.2015	46	*1946–1955*	
Morris Samuel	22.6.1855	20.9.1931	1	*1884*	
Moses Henry	13.2.1858	7.12.1938	6	*1886–1894*	
Moss Jeffrey Kenneth	29.6.1947		1	*1978*	1
Moule William Henry	31.1.1858	24.8.1939	1	*1880*	
Muller Scott Andrew.	11.7.1971		2	*1999*	
Murdoch William Lloyd	18.10.1854	18.2.1911	18†	*1876–1890*	
Musgrove Henry Alfred.	27.11.1858	2.11.1931	1	*1884*	
Nagel Lisle Ernest	6.3.1905	23.11.1971	1	*1932*	
Nash Laurence John	2.5.1910	24.7.1986	2	*1931–1936*	
Neser Michael Gertges.	29.3.1990		1	*2021*	2
Nevill Peter Michael	13.10.1985		17	*2015–2016*	0/9
Nicholson Matthew James	2.10.1974		1	*1998*	
Nitschke Homesdale Carl ("Jack") . .	14.4.1905	29.9.1982	2	*1931*	
Noble Montague Alfred (*CY 1900*)	28.1.1873	22.6.1940	42	*1897–1909*	
Noblet Geffery	14.9.1916	16.8.2006	3	*1949–1952*	
North Marcus James	28.7.1979		21	*2008–2010*	2/1
Nothling Otto Ernest	1.8.1900	26.9.1965	1	*1928*	
O'Brien Leo Patrick Joseph	2.7.1907	13.3.1997	5	*1932–1936*	
O'Connor John Denis Alphonsus	9.9.1875	23.8.1941	4	*1907–1909*	
O'Donnell Simon Patrick.	26.1.1963		6	*1985–1985*	87
Ogilvie Alan David	3.6.1951		5	*1977*	
O'Keefe Stephen Norman John.	9.12.1984		9	*2014–2017*	0/7
O'Keeffe Kerry James.	25.11.1949		24	*1970–1977*	2
Oldfield William Albert Stanley MBE (*CY 1927*) . .	9.9.1894	10.8.1976	54	*1920–1936*	
O'Neill Norman Clifford Louis (*CY 1962*)	19.2.1937	3.3.2008	42	*1958–1964*	
O'Reilly William Joseph OBE (*CY 1935*)	20.12.1905	6.10.1992	27	*1931–1945*	
Oxenham Ronald Keven	28.7.1891	16.8.1939	7	*1928–1931*	
Paine Timothy David.	8.12.1984		35	*2010–2020*	35/10‡
Palmer George Eugene	22.2.1859	22.8.1910	17	*1880–1886*	
Park Roy Lindsay	30.7.1892	23.1.1947	1	*1920*	
Pascoe Leonard Stephen	13.2.1950		14	*1977–1981*	29
Patterson Kurtis Robert.	5.4.1993		2	*2018*	
[2] **Pattinson** James Lee	3.5.1990		21	*2011–2019*	15/4

	Born	Died	Tests	Test Career	O/T
Pellew Clarence Everard ("Nip").	21.9.1893	9.5.1981	10	1920–1921	
Phillips Wayne Bentley	1.3.1958		27	1983–1985	48
Phillips Wayne Norman.	7.11.1962		1	1991	
Philpott Peter Ian	21.11.1934	31.10.2021	8	1964–1965	
Ponsford William Harold MBE (*CY 1935*).	19.10.1900	6.4.1991	29	1924–1934	
Ponting Ricky Thomas (*CY 2006*).	19.12.1974		168§	1995–2012	374‡/17
Pope Roland James.	18.2.1864	27.7.1952	1	1884	
Pucovski William Jan	2.2.1998		1	2020	
Quiney Robert John	20.8.1982		2	2012	
Rackemann Carl Gray.	3.6.1960		12	1982–1990	52
Ransford Vernon Seymour (*CY 1910*).	20.3.1885	19.3.1958	20	1907–1911	
Redpath Ian Ritchie MBE.	11.5.1941		66	1963–1975	5
Reedman John Cole	9.10.1865	29.3.1924	1	1894	
Reid Bruce Anthony	14.3.1963		27	1985–1992	61
Reiffel Paul Ronald.	19.4.1966		35	1991–1997	92
Renneberg David Alexander	23.9.1942		8	1966–1967	
Renshaw Matthew Thomas	28.3.1996		11	2016–2017	
Richardson Arthur John	24.7.1888	23.12.1973	9	1924–1926	
Richardson Jhye Avon	20.9.1996		3	2018–2021	13/14
[4] **Richardson** Victor York OBE	7.9.1894	30.10.1969	19	1924–1935	
Rigg Keith Edward	21.5.1906	28.2.1995	8	1930–1936	
Ring Douglas Thomas.	14.10.1918	23.6.2003	13	1947–1953	
Ritchie Gregory Michael	23.1.1960		30	1982–1986	44
Rixon Stephen John.	25.2.1954		13	1977–1984	6
Robertson Gavin Ron	28.5.1966		4	1997–1998	13
Robertson William Roderick	6.10.1861	24.6.1938	1	1884	
Robinson Richard Daryl	8.6.1946		3	1977	2
Robinson Rayford Harold	26.3.1914	10.8.1965	1	1936	
Rogers Christopher John Llewellyn (*CY 2014*)	31.8.1977		25	2007–2015	
Rorke Gordon Frederick	27.6.1938		4	1958–1959	
Rutherford John Walter	25.9.1929		1	1956	
Ryder John	8.8.1889	3.4.1977	20	1920–1928	
Saggers Ronald Arthur	15.5.1917	17.3.1987	6	1948–1949	
Saunders John Victor	21.3.1876	21.12.1927	14	1901–1907	
Sayers Chadd James	31.8.1987		1	2017	
Scott Henry James Herbert.	26.12.1858	23.9.1910	8	1884–1886	
Sellers Reginald Hugh Durning.	20.8.1940		1	1964	
[5] **Sheahan** Andrew _Paul_.	30.9.1946		31	1967–1973	3
Shepherd Barry Kenneth	23.4.1937	17.9.2001	9	1962–1964	
Siddle Peter Matthew.	25.11.1984		67	2008–2019	20/2
Sievers Morris William	13.4.1912	10.5.1968	3	1936	
Simpson Robert Baddeley (*CY 1965*).	3.2.1936		62	1957–1977	2
Sincock David John.	1.2.1942		3	1964–1965	
Slater Keith Nichol.	12.3.1936		1	1958	
Slater Michael Jonathon	21.2.1970		74	1993–2001	42
Sleep Peter Raymond.	4.5.1957		14	1978–1989	
Slight James.	20.10.1855	9.12.1930	1	1880	
Smith David Bertram Miller.	14.9.1884	29.7.1963	2	1912	
Smith Steven Barry	18.10.1961		3	1983	28
Smith Steven Peter Devereux (*CY 2016*)	2.6.1989		82	2010–2021	128/52
Spofforth Frederick Robert	9.9.1853	4.6.1926	18	1876–1886	
Stackpole Keith Raymond MBE (*CY 1973*).	10.7.1940		43	1965–1973	6
Starc Mitchell Aaron.	30.1.1990		66	2011–2021	99/48
Stevens Gavin Byron.	29.2.1932		4	1959	
Symonds Andrew	9.6.1975		26	2003–2008	198/14
Taber Hedley _Brian_	29.4.1940		16	1966–1969	
Tait Shaun William.	22.2.1983		3	2005–2007	35/21
Tallon Donald (*CY 1949*).	17.2.1916	7.9.1984	21	1945–1953	

	Born	Died	Tests	Test Career	O/T
Taylor John Morris.	10.10.1895	12.5.1971	20	1920–1926	
Taylor Mark Anthony (*CY 1990*)	27.10.1964		104	1988–1998	113
Taylor Peter Laurence.	22.8.1956		13	1986–1991	83
Thomas Grahame.	21.3.1938		8	1964–1965	
Thoms George Ronald.	22.3.1927	29.8.2003	1	1951	
Thomson Alan Lloyd ("Froggy")	2.12.1945		4	1970	1
Thomson Jeffrey Robert.	16.8.1950		51	1972–1985	50
Thomson Nathaniel Frampton Davis	29.5.1839	2.9.1896	2	1876	
Thurlow Hugh Motley ("Pud").	10.1.1903	3.12.1975	1	1931	
Toohey Peter Michael	20.4.1954		15	1977–1979	5
Toshack Ernest Raymond Herbert.	8.12.1914	11.5.2003	12	1945–1948	
Travers Joseph Patrick Francis.	10.1.1871	15.9.1942	1	1901	
Tribe George Edward (*CY 1955*).	4.10.1920	5.4.2009	3	1946	
²**Trott** Albert Edwin (*CY 1899*)	6.2.1873	30.7.1914	3†	1894	
²**Trott** George Henry Stevens (*CY 1894*).	5.8.1866	10.11.1917	24	1888–1897	
²**Trumble** Hugh (*CY 1897*)	12.5.1867	14.8.1938	32	1890–1903	
²**Trumble** John William.	16.9.1863	17.8.1944	7	1884–1886	
Trumper Victor Thomas (*CY 1903*).	2.11.1877	28.6.1915	48	1899–1911	
Turner Alan.	23.7.1950		14	1975–1976	6
Turner Charles Thomas Biass (*CY 1889*).	16.11.1862	1.1.1944	17	1886–1894	
Veivers Thomas Robert	6.4.1937		21	1963–1966	
Veletta Michael Robert John	30.10.1963		8	1987–1989	20
Voges Adam Charles.	4.10.1979		20	2015–2016	31/7
Wade Matthew Scott.	26.12.1987		36	2011–2020	97/55
Waite Mervyn George.	7.1.1911	16.12.1985	2	1938	
Walker Maxwell Henry Norman.	12.9.1948	28.9.2016	34	1972–1977	17
Wall Thomas Welbourn ("Tim").	13.5.1904	26.3.1981	18	1928–1934	
Walters Francis Henry.	9.2.1860	1.6.1922	1	1884	
Walters Kevin Douglas MBE	21.12.1945		74	1965–1980	28
Ward Francis Anthony	23.2.1906	25.3.1974	4	1936–1938	
Warne Shane Keith (*CY 1994*).	13.9.1969		145§	1991–2006	193‡
Warner David Andrew	27.10.1986		91	2011–2021	128/88
Watkins John Russell	16.4.1943		1	1972	
Watson Graeme Donald.	8.3.1945	24.4.2020	5	1966–1972	2
Watson Shane Robert	17.6.1981		59§	2004–2015	190/58
Watson William James.	31.1.1931	29.12.2018	4	1954	
²**Waugh** Mark Edward (*CY 1991*).	2.6.1965		128	1990–2002	244
²**Waugh** Stephen Rodger (*CY 1989*)	2.6.1965		168	1985–2003	325
Wellham Dirk Macdonald	13.3.1959		6	1981–1986	17
Wessels Kepler Christoffel (*CY 1995*).	14.9.1957		24†	1982–1985	54‡
Whatmore Davenell Frederick	16.3.1954		7	1978–1979	1
White Cameron Leon	18.8.1983		4	2008	91/47
Whitney Michael Roy	24.2.1959		12	1981–1992	38
Whitty William James.	15.8.1886	30.1.1974	14	1909–1912	
Wiener Julien Mark	1.5.1955		6	1979	7
Williams Brad Andrew	20.11.1974		4	2003	25
Wilson John William.	20.8.1921	13.10.1985	1	1956	
Wilson Paul	12.1.1972		1	1997	11
Wood Graeme Malcolm.	6.11.1956		59	1977–1988	83
Woodcock Ashley James.	27.2.1947		1	1973	1
Woodfull William Maldon OBE (*CY 1927*)	22.8.1897	11.8.1965	35	1926–1934	
Woods Samuel Moses James (*CY 1889*).	13.4.1867	30.4.1931	3†	1888	
Woolley Roger Douglas	16.9.1954		2	1982–1983	4
Worrall John	20.6.1860	17.11.1937	11	1884–1899	
Wright Kevin John	27.12.1953		10	1978–1979	5
Yallop Graham Neil	7.10.1952		39	1975–1984	30
Yardley Bruce	5.9.1947	27.3.2019	33	1977–1982	7
Young Shaun	13.6.1970		1	1997	
Zoehrer Timothy Joseph	25.9.1961		10	1985–1986	22

SOUTH AFRICA (349 players)

	Born	Died	Tests	Test Career	O/T
Abbott Kyle John	18.6.1987		11	*2012–2016*	28/21
Ackerman Hylton Deon	14.2.1973		4	*1997*	
Adams Paul Regan	20.1.1977		45	*1995–2003*	24
Adcock Neil Amwin Treharne (*CY 1961*)	8.3.1931	6.1.2013	26	*1953–1961*	
Amla Hashim Mahomed (*CY 2013*)	31.3.1983		124	*2004–2018*	181/41‡
Anderson James Henry	26.4.1874	11.3.1926	1	*1902*	
Ashley William Hare	10.2.1863	14.7.1930	1	*1888*	
Bacher Aron ("Ali")	24.5.1942		12	*1965–1969*	
Bacher Adam Marc	29.10.1973		19	*1996–1999*	13
Balaskas Xenophon Constantine	15.10.1910	12.5.1994	9	*1930–1938*	
Barlow Edgar John	12.8.1940	30.12.2005	30	*1961–1969*	
Baumgartner Harold Vane	17.11.1883	8.4.1938	1	*1913*	
Bavuma Temba	17.5.1990		47	*2014–2021*	13/21
Beaumont Rolland	4.2.1884	25.5.1958	5	*1912–1913*	
Begbie Denis Warburton	12.12.1914	10.3.2009	5	*1948–1949*	
Bell Alexander John	15.4.1906	1.8.1985	16	*1929–1935*	
Bisset *Sir* Murray	14.4.1876	24.10.1931	3	*1898–1909*	
Bissett George Finlay	5.11.1905	14.11.1965	4	*1927*	
Blanckenberg James Manuel	31.12.1893	d unknown	18	*1913–1924*	
Bland Kenneth Colin (*CY 1966*)	5.4.1938	14.4.2018	21	*1961–1966*	
Bock Ernest George	17.9.1908	5.9.1961	1	*1935*	
Boje Nico	20.3.1973		43	*1999–2006*	113‡/1
Bond Gerald Edward ("Boysie")	5.4.1909	27.8.1965	1	*1938*	
Bosch Tertius	14.3.1966	14.2.2000	1	*1991*	2
Botha Johan	2.5.1982		5	*2005–2010*	76‡/40
Botten James Thomas ("Jackie")	21.6.1938	14.5.2006	3	*1965*	
Boucher Mark Verdon (*CY 2009*)	3.12.1976		146†	*1997–2011*	290‡/25
Brann William Henry	4.4.1899	22.9.1953	3	*1922*	
Briscoe Arthur Wellesley ("Dooley")	6.2.1911	22.4.1941	2	*1935–1938*	
Bromfield Harry Dudley	26.6.1932	27.12.2020	9	*1961–1965*	
Brown Lennox Sidney	24.11.1910	1.9.1983	2	*1931*	
Burger Christopher George de Villiers	12.7.1935	5.6.2014	2	*1957*	
Burke Sydney Frank	11.3.1934	3.4.2017	2	*1961–1964*	
Buys Isaac Daniel	4.2.1895	d unknown	1	*1922*	
Cameron Horace Brakenridge ("Jock") (*CY 1936*)	5.7.1905	2.11.1935	26	*1927–1935*	39/12
Campbell Thomas	9.2.1882	5.10.1924	5	*1909–1912*	
Carlstein Peter Rudolph	28.10.1938		8	*1957–1963*	
Carter Claude Padget	23.4.1881	8.11.1952	10	*1912–1924*	
Catterall Robert Hector (*CY 1925*)	10.7.1900	3.1.1961	24	*1922–1930*	
Chapman Horace William	30.6.1890	1.12.1941	2	*1913–1921*	
Cheetham John Erskine	26.5.1920	21.8.1980	24	*1948–1955*	
Chevalier Grahame Anton	9.3.1937	14.11.2017	1	*1969*	
Christy James Alexander Joseph	12.12.1904	1.2.1971	10	*1929–1931*	
Chubb Geoffrey Walter Ashton	12.4.1911	28.8.1982	5	*1951*	
Cochran John Alexander Kennedy	15.7.1909	15.6.1987	1	*1930*	
Coen Stanley Keppel ("Shunter")	14.10.1902	29.1.1967	2	*1927*	
Commaille John McIllwaine Moore ("Mick")	21.2.1883	28.7.1956	12	*1909–1927*	
Commins John Brian	19.2.1965		3	*1994*	
Conyngham Dalton Parry ("Conky")	10.5.1897	7.7.1979	1	*1922*	
Cook Frederick James	1870	30.11.1915	1	*1895*	
¹ **Cook** Stephen Craig	29.11.1982		11	*2015–2016*	
¹ **Cook** Stephen James (*CY 1990*)	31.7.1953		3	*1992–1993*	4
Cooper Alfred Henry Cecil	2.9.1893	18.7.1963	1	*1913*	
Cox Joseph Lovell	28.6.1886	4.7.1971	3	*1913*	
Cripps Godfrey	19.10.1865	27.7.1943	1	*1891*	
Crisp Robert James	28.5.1911	2.3.1994	9	*1935–1935*	
Cronje Wessel Johannes ("Hansie")	25.9.1969	1.6.2002	68	*1991–1999*	188
Cullinan Daryll John	4.3.1967		70	*1992–2000*	138

	Born	Died	Tests	Test Career	O/T
Curnow Sydney Harry.	16.12.1907	28.7.1986	7	*1930–1931*	
Dalton Eric Londesbrough	2.12.1906	3.6.1981	15	*1929–1938*	
Davies Eric Quail	26.8.1909	11.11.1976	5	*1935–1938*	
Dawson Alan Charles	27.11.1969		2	2003	19
Dawson Oswald Charles	1.9.1919	22.12.2008	9	*1947–1948*	
Deane Hubert Gouvaine ("Nummy").	21.7.1895	21.10.1939	17	*1924–1930*	
de Bruyn Theunis Booysen	8.10.1992		12	2016–2019	0/2
de Bruyn Zander.	5.7.1975		3	2004	
de Kock Quinton	17.12.1992		54	*2013–2021*	124/61
de Lange Marchant.	13.10.1990		2	2011	4/6
de Villiers Abraham Benjamin	17.2.1984		114	*2004–2017*	223‡/78
de Villiers Petrus Stephanus ("Fanie").	13.10.1964		18	*1993–1997*	83
de Wet Friedel.	26.6.1980		2	2009	
Dippenaar Hendrik Human ("Boeta").	14.6.1977		38	*1999–2006*	101‡/1
Dixon Cecil Donovan ("Dickie").	12.2.1891	9.9.1969	1	*1913*	
Donald Allan Anthony (*CY 1992*).	20.10.1966		72	*1991–2001*	164
Dower Robert Reid.	4.6.1876	16.9.1964	1	*1898*	
Draper Ronald George	24.12.1926		2	*1949*	
Duckworth Christopher Anthony Russell.	22.3.1933	16.5.2014	2	*1956*	
Dumbrill Richard	19.11.1938		5	*1965–1966*	
Duminy Jacobus Petrus	16.12.1897	31.1.1980	3	*1927–1929*	
Duminy Jean-Paul.	14.4.1984		46	2008–2017	199/81
Dunell Owen Robert	15.7.1856	21.10.1929	1	*1888*	
du Plessis Francois ("Faf").	13.7.1984		69	*2012–2020*	143/47‡
du Preez John Harcourt	14.11.1942	8.4.2020	2	*1966*	
du Toit Jacobus Francois ("Vlooi").	2.4.1869	10.7.1909	1	*1891*	
Dyer Dennis Victor.	2.5.1914	16.6.1990	3	*1947*	
Eksteen Clive Edward.	2.12.1966		7	*1993–1999*	6
Elgar Dean	11.6.1987		72	*2012–2021*	8
Elgie Michael Kelsey ("Kim")	6.3.1933		3	*1961*	
Elworthy Steven MBE	23.2.1965		4	*1998–2002*	39
Endean William Russell	31.5.1924	28.6.2003	28	*1951–1957*	
Farrer William Stephen ("Buster").	8.12.1936		6	*1961–1963*	
Faulkner George Aubrey.	17.12.1881	10.9.1930	25	*1905–1924*	
Fellows-Smith Jonathan Payn ("Pom-Pom").	3.2.1932	28.9.2013	4	*1960*	
Fichardt Charles Gustav	20.3.1870	30.5.1923	2	*1891–1895*	
Finlason Charles Edward.	19.2.1860	31.7.1917	1	*1888*	
Floquet Claude Eugene	23.11.1882	22.11.1963	1	*1909*	
Francis Howard Henry	26.5.1868	7.1.1936	2	*1898*	
Francois Cyril Matthew ("Froggy")	20.6.1897	26.5.1944	5	*1922*	
Frank Charles Newton	27.1.1891	25.12.1961	3	*1921*	
Frank William Hughes Bowker	23.11.1872	16.2.1945	1	*1895*	
Fuller Edward Russell Henry	2.8.1931	19.7.2008	7	*1952–1957*	
Fullerton George Murray.	8.12.1922	19.11.2002	7	*1947–1951*	
Funston Kenneth James.	3.12.1925	15.4.2005	18	*1952–1957*	
Gamsy Dennis	17.2.1940		2	*1969*	
Gibbs Herschelle Herman	23.2.1974		90	*1996–2007*	248/23
Gleeson Robert Anthony	10.12.1872	27.9.1919	1	*1895*	
Glover George Keyworth.	13.5.1870	15.11.1938	1	*1895*	
Goddard Trevor Leslie.	1.8.1931	25.11.2016	41	*1955–1969*	
Gordon Norman ("Mobil")	6.8.1911	2.9.2014	5	*1938*	
Graham Robert	16.9.1877	21.4.1946	2	*1898*	
Grieveson Ronald Eustace	24.8.1909	24.7.1998	2	*1938*	
Griffin Geoffrey Merton	12.6.1939	16.11.2006	2	*1960*	
Hall Alfred Ewart	23.1.1896	1.1.1964	7	*1922–1930*	
Hall Andrew James	31.7.1975		21	*2001–2006*	88/2
Hall Glen Gordon	24.5.1938	26.6.1987	1	*1964*	
Halliwell Ernest Austin (*CY 1905*)	7.9.1864	2.10.1919	8	*1891–1902*	
Halse Clive Gray	28.2.1935	28.5.2002	3	*1963*	
Hamza Mogammad Zubayr	19.6.1995		5	2018–2019	1

	Born	Died	Tests	Test Career	O/T
[2] **Hands** Philip Albert Myburgh ("Pam")	18.3.1890	27.4.1951	7	*1913–1924*	
[2] **Hands** Reginald Harry Myburgh	26.7.1888	20.4.1918	1	*1913*	
Hanley Martin Andrew	10.11.1918	2.6.2000	1	*1948*	
Harmer Simon Ross (*CY 2020*)	10.2.1989		5	*2014–2015*	
Harris Paul Lee	2.11.1978		37	*2006–2010*	3
Harris Terence <u>Anthony</u>	27.8.1916	7.3.1993	3	*1947–1948*	
Hartigan Gerald Patrick Desmond	30.12.1884	7.1.1955	5	*1912–1913*	
Harvey Robert Lyon	14.9.1911	20.7.2000	2	*1935*	
Hathorn Christopher <u>Maitland</u> Howard	7.4.1878	17.5.1920	12	*1902–1910*	
Hayward Mornantau ("Nantie")	6.3.1977		16	*1999–2004*	21
[1, 2] **Hearne** Frank	23.11.1858	14.7.1949	4†	*1891–1895*	
[1] **Hearne** George Alfred Lawrence	27.3.1888	13.11.1978	3	*1922–1924*	
Heine Peter Samuel	28.6.1928	4.2.2005	14	*1955–1961*	
Henderson Claude William	14.6.1972		7	*2001–2002*	4
Hendricks Beuran Eric	8.6.1990		1	*2019*	8/19
Henry Omar	23.1.1952		3	*1992*	3
Hime Charles Frederick William	24.10.1869	6.12.1940	1	*1895*	
Hudson Andrew Charles	17.3.1965		35	*1991–1997*	89
Hutchinson Philip	25.1.1862	30.9.1925	2	*1888*	
Imran Tahir	27.3.1979		20	*2011–2015*	107/35‡
Ironside David Ernest James	2.5.1925	21.8.2005	3	*1953*	
Irvine Brian <u>Lee</u>	9.3.1944		4	*1969*	
Jack Steven Douglas	4.8.1970		2	*1994*	2
Jansen Marco	1.5.2000		3	*2021*	
Johnson Clement Lecky	31.3.1871	31.5.1908	1	*1895*	
Kallis Jacques Henry (*CY 2013*)	16.10.1975		165†	*1995–2013*	323‡/25
Keith Headley James	25.10.1927	17.11.1997	8	*1952–1956*	
Kemp Justin Miles	2.10.1977		4	*2000–2005*	79‡/8
Kempis Gustav Adolph	4.8.1865	19.5.1890	1	*1888*	
Khan Imraan	27.4.1984		1	*2008*	
[2] **Kirsten** Gary (*CY 2004*)	23.11.1967		101	*1993–2003*	185
[2] **Kirsten** Peter Noel	14.5.1955		12	*1991–1994*	40
Klaasen Heinrich	30.7.1991		1	*2019*	24/28
Kleinveldt Rory Keith	15.3.1983		4	*2012*	10/6
Klusener Lance (*CY 2000*)	4.9.1971		49	*1996–2004*	171
Kotze Johannes Jacobus ("Kodgee")	7.8.1879	7.7.1931	3	*1902–1907*	
Kuhn Heino Gunther	1.4.1984		4	*2017*	0/7
Kuiper Adrian Paul	24.8.1959		1	*1991*	25
Kuys Frederick	21.3.1870	12.9.1953	1	*1898*	
Lance Herbert Roy ("Tiger")	6.6.1940	10.11.2010	13	*1961–1969*	
Langeveldt Charl Kenneth	17.12.1974		6	*2004–2005*	72/9
Langton Arthur Chudleigh Beaumont ("Chud")	2.3.1912	27.11.1942	15	*1935–1938*	
Lawrence Godfrey Bernard	31.3.1932		5	*1961*	
le Roux Frederick Louis	5.2.1882	22.9.1963	1	*1913*	
Lewis Percy Tyson ("Plum")	2.10.1884	30.1.1976	1	*1913*	
Liebenberg Gerhardus Frederick Johannes	7.4.1972		5	*1997–1998*	4
Linde George Fredrik	4.12.1991		3	*2019–2020*	2/14
[1] **Lindsay** Denis Thomson	4.9.1939	30.11.2005	19	*1963–1969*	
[1] **Lindsay** John Dixon	8.9.1908	31.8.1990	3	*1947*	
Lindsay Nevil Vernon	30.7.1886	2.2.1976	1	*1921*	
Ling William Victor Stone	3.10.1891	26.9.1960	6	*1921–1922*	
Llewellyn Charles Bennett ("Buck") (*CY 1911*)	29.9.1876	7.6.1964	15	*1895–1912*	
Lundie Eric Balfour ("Bill")	15.3.1888	12.9.1917	1	*1913*	
Macaulay Michael John	19.4.1939		1	*1964*	
McCarthy Cuan Neil	24.3.1929	14.8.2000	15	*1948–1951*	
McGlew Derrick John ("Jackie") (*CY 1956*)	11.3.1929	9.6.1998	34	*1951–1961*	
McKenzie Neil Douglas (*CY 2009*)	24.11.1975		58	*2000–2008*	64/2
McKinnon Atholl Henry	20.8.1932	2.12.1983	8	*1960–1966*	
McLaren Ryan	9.2.1983		2	*2009–2013*	54/12
McLean Roy Alastair (*CY 1961*)	9.7.1930	26.8.2007	40	*1951–1964*	

	Born	Died	Tests	Test Career	O/T
McMillan Brian Mervin.	22.12.1963		38	*1992–1998*	78
McMillan Quintin.	23.6.1904	3.7.1948	13	*1929–1931*	
Maharaj Keshav Athmanand	7.2.1990		39	*2016–2021*	15/8
Malan Pieter Jacobus	13.8.1989		3	*2019*	
Mann Norman Bertram Fleetwood ("Tufty") . .	28.12.1920	31.7.1952	19	*1947–1951*	
Mansell Percy Neville Frank MBE	16.3.1920	9.5.1995	13	*1951–1955*	
Markham Lawrence Anderson ("Fish").	12.9.1924	5.8.2000	1	*1948*	
Markram Aiden Kyle	4.10.1994		29	*2017–2021*	34/20
Marx Waldemar Frederick Eric	4.7.1895	2.6.1974	3	*1921*	
Matthews Craig Russell.	15.2.1965		18	*1992–1995*	56
Meintjes Douglas James	9.6.1890	17.7.1979	2	*1922*	
Melle Michael George	3.6.1930	28.12.2003	7	*1949–1952*	
Melville Alan (*CY 1948*)	19.5.1910	18.4.1983	11	*1938–1948*	
Middleton James ("Bonnor")	30.9.1865	23.12.1913	6	*1895–1902*	
Mills Charles	26.11.1866	d unknown	1	*1891*	
Milton *Sir* William Henry	3.12.1854	6.3.1930	3	*1888–1891*	
Mitchell Bruce (*CY 1936*)	8.1.1909	2.7.1995	42	*1929–1948*	
Mitchell Frank (*CY 1902*)	13.8.1872	11.10.1935	3†	*1912*	
Morkel Denijs Paul Beck	25.1.1906	6.10.1980	16	*1927–1931*	
[2] Morkel Johannes Albertus	10.6.1981		1	*2008*	56‡/50
[2] Morkel Morne	6.10.1984		86	*2006–2017*	114‡/41‡
Morris Christopher Henry	30.4.1987		4	*2015–2017*	42/23
Mulder Peter Wiaan Adriaan	19.2.1998		7	*2018–2021*	12/5
Murray Anton Ronald Andrew.	30.4.1922	17.4.1995	10	*1952–1953*	
Muthusamy Senuran.	22.2.1994		2	*2019*	
Nel Andre	15.7.1977		36	*2001–2008*	79/2
Nel John Desmond	10.7.1928	13.1.2018	6	*1949–1957*	
Newberry Claude	1.11889	1.8.1916	4	*1913*	
Newson Edward Serrurier ("Bob") OBE . . .	2.12.1910	24.4.1988	3	*1930–1938*	
Ngam Mfuneko	29.1.1979		3	*2000*	
Ngidi Lungisani True-man	29.03.1996		13	*2017–2021*	29/23
Nicholson Frank ("Nipper")	17.9.1909	30.7.1982	4	*1935*	
Nicolson John Fairless William.	19.7.1899	13.12.1935	3	*1927*	
Nortje Anrich Arno	16.11.1993		12	*2019–2021*	12/16
Norton Norman Ogilvie ("Pompey").	11.5.1881	25.6.1968	1	*1909*	
[1] Nourse Arthur Dudley (*CY 1948*)	12.11.1910	14.8.1981	34	*1935–1951*	
[1] Nourse Arthur William ("Dave")	25.1.1879	8.7.1948	45	*1902–1924*	
Ntini Makhaya	6.7.1977		101	*1997–2009*	172‡/10
Nupen Eiulf Peter ("Buster")	1.1.1902	29.1.1977	17	*1921–1935*	
Ochse Arthur Edward ("Okey")	11.3.1870	11.4.1918	2	*1888*	
Ochse Arthur Lennox	11.10.1898	5.5.1949	3	*1927–1929*	
O'Linn Sidney ("Micky")	5.5.1927	11.12.2016	7	*1960–1961*	
Olivier Duanne.	9.5.1992		12	*2016–2021*	2
Ontong Justin Lee.	4.1.1980		2	*2001–2004*	27‡/14
Owen-Smith Harold Geoffrey ("Tuppy") (*CY 1930*)	18.2.1909	28.2.1990	5	*1929*	
Palm Archibald William	8.6.1901	17.8.1966	1	*1927*	
Parker George Macdonald.	27.5.1899	1.5.1969	2	*1924*	
Parkin Durant Clifford ("Dante")	20.2.1871	20.3.1936	1	*1891*	
Parnell Wayne Dillon	30.7.1989		6	*2009–2017*	66/40
Partridge Joseph Titus	9.12.1932	6.6.1988	11	*1963–1964*	
Paterson Dane	4.4.1989		2	*2019*	4/8
Pearse Charles Ormerod Cato.	10.10.1884	28.5.1953	3	*1910*	
Pegler Sydney James.	28.7.1888	10.9.1972	16	*1909–1924*	
Petersen Alviro Nathan	25.11.1980		36	*2009–2014*	21/2
Petersen Keegan Darryl.	8.8.1993		5	*2021–2021*	
Peterson Robin John	4.8.1979		15	*2003–2013*	79/21
Phehlukwayo Andile Lucky.	3.3.1996		4	*2017*	68/35
Philander Vernon Darryl.	24.6.1985		64	*2011–2019*	30/7
Piedt Dane Lee-Roy	6.3.1990		9	*2014–2019*	
[2] Pithey Anthony John	17.7.1933	17.11.2006	17	*1956–1964*	

	Born	Died	Tests	Test Career	O/T
[2]**Pithey** David Bartlett	4.10.1936	21.1.2018	8	*1963–1966*	
Plimsoll Jack Bruce	27.10.1917	11.11.1999	1	*1947*	
[1,2]**Pollock** Peter Maclean (*CY 1966*)	30.6.1941		28	*1961–1969*	
[2]**Pollock** Robert *Graeme* (*CY 1966*)	27.2.1944		23	*1963–1969*	
[1]**Pollock** Shaun Maclean (*CY 2003*)	16.7.1973		108	*1995–2007*	294‡/12
Poore Robert Montagu (*CY 1900*)	20.3.1866	14.7.1938	3	*1895*	
Pothecary James Edward	6.12.1933	11.5.2016	3	*1960*	
Powell Albert William	18.7.1873	11.9.1948	1	*1898*	
Pretorius Dewald	6.12.1977		4	*2001–2003*	
Pretorius Dwaine	29.3.1989		3	*2019*	22/22
Prince Ashwell Gavin	28.5.1977		66	*2001–2011*	49‡/1
Prince Charles Frederick Henry	11.9.1874	2.2.1949	1	*1898*	
Pringle Meyrick Wayne	22.6.1966		4	*1991–1995*	17
Procter Michael John (*CY 1970*)	15.9.1946		7	*1966–1969*	
Promnitz Henry Louis Ernest	23.2.1904	7.9.1983	2	*1927*	
Quinn Neville Anthony	21.2.1908	5.8.1934	12	*1929–1931*	
Rabada Kagiso	25.5.1995		50	*2015–2021*	82/40
Reid Norman	26.12.1890	6.6.1947	1	*1921*	
Rhodes Jonathan Neil (*CY 1999*)	27.7.1969		52	*1992–2000*	245
[2]**Richards** Alfred Renfrew	14.12.1867	9.1.1904	1	*1895*	
Richards Barry Anderson (*CY 1969*)	21.7.1945		4	*1969*	
[2]**Richards** William Henry Matthews ("Dicky")	26.3.1861	4.1.1903	1	*1888*	
Richardson David John	16.9.1959		42	*1991–1997*	122
Robertson John Benjamin	5.6.1906	5.7.1985	3	*1935*	
Rose-Innes Albert	16.2.1868	22.11.1946	2	*1888*	
Routledge Thomas William	6.6.1867	9.5.1927	4	*1891–1895*	
[2]**Rowan** Athol Matthew Burchell	7.2.1921	22.2.1998	15	*1947–1951*	
[2]**Rowan** Eric Alfred Burchell (*CY 1952*)	20.7.1909	30.4.1993	26	*1935–1951*	
Rowe George Alexander	15.6.1874	8.1.1950	5	*1895–1902*	
Rudolph Jacobus Andries	4.5.1981		48	*2003–2012*	43‡/1
Rushmere Mark Weir	7.1.1965		1	*1991*	4
Samuelson Sivert Vause	21.11.1883	18.11.1958	1	*1909*	
Schultz Brett Nolan	26.8.1970		9	*1992–1997*	1
Schwarz Reginald Oscar (*CY 1908*)	4.5.1875	18.11.1918	20	*1905–1912*	
Seccull Arthur William	14.9.1868	20.7.1945	1	*1895*	
Seymour Michael Arthur ("Kelly")	5.6.1936	18.2.2019	7	*1963–1969*	
Shalders William Alfred	10.2.1880	19.3.1917	12	*1898–1907*	
Shamsi Tabraiz	18.2.1990		2	*2016–2021*	31/47
Shepstone George Harold	9.4.1876	3.7.1940	2	*1895–1898*	
Sherwell Percy William	17.8.1880	17.4.1948	13	*1905–1910*	
Siedle Ivan Julian ("Jack")	11.1.1903	24.8.1982	18	*1927–1935*	
Sinclair James Hugh	16.10.1876	23.2.1913	25	*1895–1910*	
Sipamla Lubabalo *Lutho*	12.5.1998		2	*2020*	5/9
Smith Charles James Edward	25.12.1872	27.3.1947	3	*1902*	
Smith Frederick William	31.3.1861	17.4.1914	3	*1888–1895*	
Smith Graeme Craig (*CY 2004*)	1.2.1981		116§	*2001–2013*	196‡/33
Smith Vivian *Ian*	23.2.1925	25.8.2015	9	*1947–1957*	
Snell Richard Peter	12.9.1968		5	*1991–1994*	42
[2]**Snooke** Stanley de la Courtte	11.11.1878	6.4.1959	1	*1907*	
[2]**Snooke** Sibley John ("Tip")	1.2.1881	14.8.1966	26	*1905–1922*	
Solomon William Rodger Thomson	23.4.1872	13.7.1964	1	*1898*	
Stewart Robert Burnard	3.9.1856	12.9.1913	1	*1888*	
Steyn Dale Willem (*CY 2013*)	27.6.1983		93	*2004–2018*	123‡/47
Steyn Philippus Jeremia *Rudolf*	30.6.1967		3	*1994*	1
Stricker Louis Anthony	26.5.1884	5.2.1960	13	*1909–1912*	
Strydom Pieter Coenraad	10.6.1969		2	*1999*	10
Susskind Manfred John	8.6.1891	9.7.1957	5	*1924*	
Symcox Patrick Leonard	14.4.1960		20	*1993–1998*	80
Taberer Henry Melville	7.10.1870	5.6.1932	1	*1902*	
[2]**Tancred** Augustus *Bernard*	20.8.1865	23.11.1911	2	*1888*	

	Born	Died	Tests	Test Career	O/T
[2] **Tancred** Louis Joseph	7.10.1876	28.7.1934	14	*1902–1913*	
[2] **Tancred** Vincent Maximillian	7.7.1875	3.6.1904	1	*1898*	
[2] **Tapscott** George Lancelot ("Dusty")	7.11.1889	13.12.1940	1	*1913*	
[2] **Tapscott** Lionel Eric ("Doodles")	18.3.1894	7.7.1934	2	*1922*	
Tayfield Hugh Joseph ("Toey") (*CY 1956*)	30.1.1929	24.2.1994	37	*1949– 1960*	
Taylor Alistair Innes ("Scotch")	25.7.1925	7.2.2004	1	*1956*	
[2] **Taylor** Daniel	9.1.1887	24.1.1957	2	*1913*	
[2] **Taylor** Herbert Wilfred (*CY 1925*)	5.5.1889	8.2.1973	42	*1912–1931*	
Terbrugge David John	31.1.1977		4	*1998–2003*	4
Theunissen Nicolaas Hendrik Christiaan de Jong .	4.5.1867	9.11.1929	1	*1888*	
Thornton George	24.12.1867	31.1.1939	1	*1902*	
Tomlinson Denis Stanley	4.9.1910	11.7.1993	1	*1935*	
Traicos Athanasios John	17.5.1947		3†	*1969*	0‡
Trimborn Patrick Henry Joseph	18.5.1940		4	*1966–1969*	
Tsolekile Thami Lungisa	9.10.1980		3	*2004*	
Tsotsobe Lonwabo Lennox	7.3.1984		5	*2010–2010*	61/23
[1] **Tuckett** Lindsay Richard ("Len")	19.4.1885	6.4.1963	1	*1913*	
[1] **Tuckett** Lindsay Thomas Delville	6.2.1919	5.9.2016	9	*1947–1948*	
Twentyman-Jones Percy Sydney	13.9.1876	8.3.1954	1	*1902*	
van der Bijl Pieter Gerhard Vincent	21.10.1907	16.2.1973	5	*1938*	
van der Dussen Hendrik Erasmus ("Rassie")	7.2.1989		13	*2019–2021*	29/34
van der Merwe Edward Alexander	9.11.1903	26.2.1971	2	*1929–1935*	
van der Merwe Peter Laurence	14.3.1937	23.1.2013	15	*1963–1966*	
van Jaarsveld Martin	18.6.1974		9	*2002–2004*	11
van Ryneveld Clive Berrange	19.3.1928	29.1.2018	19	*1951–1957*	
van Zyl Stiaan	19.9.1987		12	*2014–2016*	
Varnals George Derek	24.7.1935	9.9.2019	3	*1964*	
Verreynne Kyle	12.5.1997		4	*2021–2021*	9
Vilas Dane James	10.6.1985		6	*2015–2015*	0/1
Viljoen G. C. ("Hardus")	6.3.1989		1	*2015*	
Viljoen Kenneth George	14.5.1910	21.1.1974	27	*1930–1948*	
Vincent Cyril Leverton	16.2.1902	24.8.1968	25	*1927–1935*	
Vintcent Charles Henry	2.9.1866	28.9.1943	3	*1888–1891*	
Vogler Albert Edward Ernest (*CY 1908*)	28.11.1876	9.8.1946	15	*1905–1910*	
[2] **Wade** Herbert Frederick	14.9.1905	23.11.1980	10	*1935–1935*	
[2] **Wade** Walter Wareham ("Billy")	18.6.1914	31.5.2003	11	*1938–1949*	
Waite John Henry Bickford	19.1.1930	22.6.2011	50	*1951–1964*	
Walter Kenneth Alexander	5.11.1939	13.9.2003	2	*1961*	
Ward Thomas Alfred	2.8.1887	16.2.1936	23	*1912–1924*	
Watkins John Cecil	10.4.1923	3.9.2021	15	*1949–1956*	
Wesley Colin ("Tich")	5.9.1937		3	*1960*	
Wessels Kepler Christoffel (*CY 1995*)	14.9.1957		16†	*1991–1994*	55‡
Westcott Richard John	19.9.1927	16.1.2013	5	*1953–1957*	
White Gordon Charles	5.2.1882	17.10.1918	17	*1905–1912*	
Willoughby Charl Myles	3.12.1974		2	*2003*	3
Willoughby Joseph Thomas	7.11.1874	11.3.1952	2	*1895*	
Wimble Clarence Skelton	9.11.1863	28.1.1930	1	*1891*	
Winslow Paul Lyndhurst	21.5.1929	24.5.2011	5	*1949–1955*	
Wynne Owen Edgar	1.6.1919	13.7.1975	6	*1948–1949*	
Zondeki Monde	25.7.1982		6	*2003–2008*	11‡/1
Zulch Johan Wilhelm	20.1.1886	19.5.1924	16	*1909–1921*	

WEST INDIES (327 players)

	Born	Died	Tests	Test Career	O/T
Achong Ellis Edgar	16.2.1904	30.8.1986	6	*1929–1934*	
Adams James Clive	9.1.1968		54	*1991–2000*	127
Alexander Franz Copeland Murray ("Gerry")	2.11.1928	16.4.2011	25	*1957–1960*	
Ali Imtiaz	28.7.1954		1	*1975*	
Ali Inshan	25.9.1949	24.6.1995	12	*1970–1976*	

	Born	Died	Tests	Test Career	O/T
Allan David Walter	5.11.1937		5	*1961–1966*	
Allen Ian Basil Alston	6.10.1965		2	*1991*	
Ambris Sunil Walford	23.3.1993		6	*2017–2018*	16
Ambrose *Sir* Curtly Elconn Lynwall (*CY 1992*)	21.9.1963		98	*1987–2000*	176
Arthurton Keith Lloyd Thomas	21.2.1965		33	*1988–1995*	105
Asgarali Nyron Sultan	28.12.1920	5.11.2006	2	*1957*	
[2] **Atkinson** Denis St Eval	9.8.1926	9.11.2001	22	*1948–1957*	
[2] **Atkinson** Eric St Eval	6.11.1927	29.5.1998	8	*1957–1958*	
Austin Richard Arkwright	5.9.1954	7.2.2015	2	*1977*	1
Austin Ryan Anthony	15.11.1981		2	*2009*	
Bacchus Sheik Faoud Ahamul Fasiel	31.1.1954		19	*1977–1981*	29
Baichan Leonard	12.5.1946		3	*1974–1975*	
Baker Lionel Sionne	6.9.1984		4	*2008–2009*	10/3
Banks Omari Ahmed Clemente	17.7.1982		10	*2002–2005*	5
Baptiste Eldine Ashworth Elderfield	12.3.1960		10	*1983–1989*	43
Barath Adrian Boris	14.4.1990		15	*2009–2012*	14/2
Barrett Arthur George	4.4.1944	6.3.2018	6	*1970–1974*	
Barrow Ivanhoe Mordecai	16.1.1911	2.4.1979	11	*1929–1939*	
Bartlett Edward Lawson	10.3.1906	21.12.1976	5	*1928–1930*	
Baugh Carlton Seymour	23.6.1982		21	*2002–2011*	47/3
Benjamin Kenneth Charlie Griffith	8.4.1967		26	*1991–1997*	26
Benjamin Winston Keithroy Matthew	31.12.1964		21	*1987–1994*	85
Benn Sulieman Jamaal	22.7.1981		26	*2007–2014*	47/24
Bernard David Eddison	19.7.1981		3	*2002–2009*	20/1
Bess Brandon Jeremy	13.12.1987		1	*2010*	
Best Carlisle Alonza	14.5.1959		8	*1985–1990*	24
Best Tino la Bertram	26.8.1981		25	*2002–2013*	26/6
Betancourt Nelson	4.6.1887	12.10.1947	1	*1929*	
Binns Alfred Phillip	24.7.1929	29.12.2017	5	*1952–1955*	
Birkett Lionel Sydney	14.4.1905	16.1.1998	4	*1930*	
Bishoo Devendra	6.11.1985		36	*2010–2018*	42/7
Bishop Ian Raphael	24.10.1967		43	*1988–1997*	84
Black Marlon Ian	7.6.1975		6	*2000–2001*	5
Blackwood Jermaine	20.11.1991		43	*2014–2021*	2
Bonner Nkrumah Eljego	23.1.1989		9	*2020–2021*	3/2
Boyce Keith David (*CY 1974*)	11.10.1943	11.10.1996	21	*1970–1975*	8
Bradshaw Ian David Russell	9.7.1974		5	*2005*	62/1
Brathwaite Carlos Ricardo	18.7.1988		3	*2015–2016*	44/41
Brathwaite Kraigg Clairmonte	1.12.1992		74	*2010–2021*	10
[2] **Bravo** Dwayne John	7.10.1983		40	*2004–2010*	164/91
[2] **Bravo** Darren Michael	6.2.1989		56	*2010–2020*	119/22
Breese Gareth Rohan	9.1.1976		1	*2002*	
Brooks Shamarh Shaqad Joshua	1.10.1988		8	*2019–2020*	0/3
Browne Courtney Oswald	7.12.1970		20	*1994–2004*	46
Browne Cyril Rutherford	8.10.1890	12.1.1964	4	*1928–1929*	
Butcher Basil Fitzherbert (*CY 1970*)	3.9.1933	16.12.2019	44	*1958–1969*	
Butler Lennox Stephen	9.2.1929	1.9.2009	1	*1954*	
Butts Clyde Godfrey	8.7.1957		7	*1984–1987*	
Bynoe Michael Robin	23.2.1941		4	*1958–1966*	
Camacho George Stephen	15.10.1945	2.10.2015	11	*1967–1970*	
[2] **Cameron** Francis James	22.6.1923	10.6.1994	5	*1948*	
[2] **Cameron** John Hemsley	8.4.1914	13.2.2000	2	*1939*	
Campbell John Dillon	21.9.1993		15	*2018–2020*	6/2
Campbell Sherwin Legay	1.11.1970		52	*1994–2001*	90
Carew George McDonald	4.6.1910	9.12.1974	4	*1934–1948*	
Carew Michael Conrad ("Joey")	15.9.1937	8.1.2011	19	*1963–1971*	
Challenor George	28.6.1888	30.7.1947	3	*1928*	
Chanderpaul Shivnarine (*CY 2008*)	16.8.1974		164	*1993–2014*	268/22
Chandrika Rajindra	8.8.1989		5	*2015–2016*	
Chang Herbert Samuel	2.7.1952		1	*1978*	

	Born	Died	Tests	Test Career	O/T
Chase Roston Lamar	22.3.1992		43	2016–2021	30/3
Chattergoon Sewnarine.	3.4.1981		4	2007–2008	18
[2] **Christiani** Cyril Marcel	28.10.1913	4.4.1938	4	1934	
[2] **Christiani** Robert Julian	19.7.1920	4.1.2005	22	1947–1953	
Clarke Carlos *Bertram* OBE	7.4.1918	14.10.1993	3	1939	
Clarke Sylvester Theophilus	11.12.1954	4.12.1999	11	1977–1981	10
[2] **Collins** Pedro Tyrone	12.8.1976		32	1998–2005	30
Collymore Corey Dalanelo	21.12.1977		30	1998–2007	84
Constantine *Lord* [Learie Nicholas] MBE (*CY 1940*).	21.9.1901	1.7.1971	18	1928–1939	
Cornwall Rahkeem Rashawn Shane	1.2.1993		9	2019–2021	
Cottrell Sheldon Shane	19.8.1989		2	2013–2014	38/34
Croft Colin Everton Hunte	15.3.1953		27	1976–1981	19
Cuffy Cameron Eustace	8.2.1970		15	1994–2002	41
Cummins Anderson Cleophas	7.5.1966		5	1992–1994	63‡
Cummins Miguel Lamar	5.9.1990		14	2016–2019	11
Da Costa Oscar Constantine	11.9.1907	1.10.1936	5	1929–1934	
Daniel Wayne Wendell	16.1.1956		10	1975–1983	18
Da Silva Joshua	19.6.1998		11	2020–2021	2
[2] **Davis** Bryan Allan.	2.5.1940		4	1964	
[2] **Davis** Charles Allan.	1.1.1944		15	1968–1972	
Davis Winston Walter	18.9.1958		15	1982–1987	35
de Caires Francis Ignatius	12.5.1909	2.2.1959	3	1929	
Deonarine Narsingh	16.8.1983		18	2004–2013	31/8
Depeiaza Cyril *Clairmonte*.	10.10.1928	10.11.1995	5	1954–1955	
Dewdney David *Thomas*	23.10.1933		9	1954–1957	
Dhanraj Rajindra	6.2.1969		4	1994–1995	6
Dillon Mervyn	5.6.1974		38	1996–2003	108
Dowe Uton George	29.3.1949		4	1970–1972	
Dowlin Travis Montague	24.2.1977		6	2009–2010	11/2
Dowrich Shane Omari	30.10.1991		35	2015–2020	1
Drakes Vasbert Conniel.	5.8.1969		12	2002–2003	34
Dujon Peter *Jeffrey* Leroy (*CY 1989*). . . .	28.5.1956		81	1981–1991	169
[2] **Edwards** Fidel Henderson	6.2.1982		55	2003–2012	50/26
Edwards Kirk Anton.	3.11.1984		17	2011–*2014*	16
Edwards Richard Martin	3.6.1940		5	1968	
Ferguson Wilfred	14.12.1917	23.2.1961	8	1947–1953	
Fernandes Maurius Pacheco	12.8.1897	8.5.1981	2	1928–*1929*	
Findlay Thaddeus *Michael* MBE	19.10.1943		10	1969–1972	
Foster Maurice Linton Churchill.	9.5.1943		14	1969–1977	2
Francis George Nathaniel	11.12.1897	12.1.1942	10	1928–1933	
Frederick Michael Campbell	6.5.1927	18.6.2014	1	1953	
Fredericks Roy Clifton (*CY 1974*)	11.11.1942	5.9.2000	59	1968–1976	12
Fudadin Assad Badyr	1.8.1985		3	2012	
Fuller Richard Livingston	30.1.1913	3.5.1987	1	1934	
Furlonge Hammond Allan	19.6.1934		3	1954–1955	
Gabriel Shannon Terry	28.4.1988		56	2012–2021	25/2
Ganga Daren	14.1.1979		48	1998–2007	35/1
Ganteaume Andrew Gordon	22.1.1921	17.2.2016	1	1947	
Garner Joel MBE (*CY 1980*).	16.12.1952		58	1976–1986	98
Garrick Leon Vivian.	11.11.1976		1	2000	3
Gaskin Berkeley Bertram McGarrell	21.3.1908	2.5.1979	2	1947	
Gayle Christopher Henry	21.9.1979		103	1999–2014	298/79
Gibbs Glendon Lionel	27.12.1925	21.2.1979	1	1954	
Gibbs Lancelot Richard (*CY 1972*)	29.9.1934		79	1957–1975	3
Gibson Ottis Delroy (*CY 2008*).	16.3.1969		2	1995–*1998*	15
Gilchrist Roy	28.6.1934	18.7.2001	13	1957–1958	
Gladstone Morais George	14.1.1901	19.5.1978	1	1929	
Goddard John Douglas Claude OBE	21.4.1919	26.8.1987	27	1947–1957	
Gomes Hilary Angelo ("Larry") (*CY 1985*).	13.7.1953		60	1976–1986	83
Gomez Gerald Ethridge	10.10.1919	6.8.1996	29	1939–*1953*	

	Born	Died	Tests	Test Career	O/T
[2]**Grant** George Copeland ("Jackie")	9.5.1907	26.10.1978	12	*1930–1934*	
[2]**Grant** Rolph Stewart.	15.12.1909	18.10.1977	7	*1934–1939*	
Gray Anthony Hollis.	23.5.1963		5	*1986*	25
Greenidge Alvin Ethelbert	20.8.1956		6	*1977–1978*	1
Greenidge *Sir* Cuthbert <u>Gordon</u> MBE (*CY 1977*) . .	1.5.1951		108	*1974–1990*	128
Greenidge Geoffrey Alan	26.5.1948		5	*1971–1972*	
Grell Mervyn George	18.12.1899	11.1.1976	1	*1929*	
Griffith Adrian Frank Gordon.	19.11.1971		14	*1996–2000*	9
Griffith *Sir* Charles Christopher (*CY 1964*).	14.12.1938		28	*1959–1968*	
Griffith Herman Clarence	1.12.1893	18.3.1980	13	*1928–1933*	
Guillen Simpson Clairmonte ("Sammy") . .	24.9.1924	2.3.2013	5†	*1951*	
Hall *Sir* Wesley Winfield	12.9.1937		48	*1958–1968*	
Hamilton Jahmar Neville.	22.9.1990		1	*2019*	1
Harper Roger Andrew	17.3.1963		25	*1983–1993*	105
Haynes Desmond Leo (*CY 1991*)	15.2.1956		116	*1977–1993*	238
[3]**Headley** George Alphonso (*CY 1934*).	30.5.1909	30.11.1983	22	*1929–1953*	
[3]**Headley** Ronald George Alphonso	29.6.1939		2	*1973*	1
Hendriks John Leslie	21.12.1933		20	*1961–1969*	
Hetmyer Shimron Odilon	26.12.1996		16	*2016–2019*	47/42
Hinds Ryan O'Neal	17.2.1981		15	*2001–2009*	14
Hinds Wavell Wayne	7.9.1976		45	*1999–2005*	119/5
Hoad Edward Lisle Goldsworthy	29.1.1896	5.3.1986	4	*1928–1933*	
Holder Chemar Keron	3.3.1998		1	*2020*	1
Holder Jason Omar (*CY 2021*)	5.11.1991		53	*2014–2021*	121/30
Holder Roland Irwin Christopher	22.12.1967		11	*1996–1998*	37
Holder Vanburn Alonzo	10.10.1945		40	*1969–1978*	12
Holding Michael Anthony (*CY 1977*)	16.2.1954		60	*1975–1986*	102
Holford David Anthony Jerome	16.4.1940		24	*1966–1976*	
Holt John Kenneth Constantine.	12.8.1923	3.6.1997	17	*1953–1958*	
Hooper Carl Llewellyn	15.12.1966		102	*1987–2002*	227
[2]**Hope** Kyle Antonio	20.11.1988		5	*2017–2017*	7
[2]**Hope** Shai Diego (*CY 2018*)	10.11.1993		38	*2014–2021*	83/15
Howard Anthony Bourne.	27.8.1946		1	*1971*	
Hunte *Sir* Conrad Cleophas (*CY 1964*).	9.5.1932	3.12.1999	44	*1957–1966*	
Hunte Errol Ashton Clairmore	3.10.1905	26.6.1967	3	*1929*	
Hylton Leslie George	29.3.1905	17.5.1955	6	*1934–1939*	
Jacobs Ridley Detamore	26.11.1967		65	*1998–2004*	147
Jaggernauth Amit Sheldon	16.11.1983		1	*2007*	
Johnson Hophnie Hobah Hines.	13.7.1910	24.6.1987	3	*1947–1950*	
Johnson Leon Rayon.	8.8.1987		9	*2014–2016*	6
Johnson Tyrell Fabian	10.1.1917	5.4.1985	1	*1939*	
Jones Charles Ernest Llewellyn	3.11.1902	10.12.1959	4	*1929–1934*	
Jones Prior Erskine Waverley.	6.6.1917	21.11.1991	9	*1947–1951*	
Joseph Alzarri Shaheim	20.11.1996		17	*2016–2021*	37
Joseph David Rolston Emmanuel	15.11.1969		4	*1998*	
Joseph Sylvester Cleofoster	5.9.1978		5	*2004–2007*	13
Julien Bernard Denis.	13.3.1950		24	*1973–1976*	12
Jumadeen Raphick Rasif.	12.4.1948		12	*1971–1978*	
Kallicharran Alvin Isaac BEM (*CY 1983*).	21.3.1949		66	*1971–1980*	31
Kanhai Rohan Bholalall (*CY 1964*).	26.12.1935		79	*1957–1973*	7
Kentish Esmond Seymour Maurice	21.11.1916	10.6.2011	2	*1947–1953*	
King Collis Llewellyn	11.6.1951		9	*1976–1980*	18
King Frank McDonald.	14.12.1926	23.12.1990	14	*1952–1955*	
King Lester Anthony.	27.2.1939	9.7.1998	2	*1961–1967*	
King Reon Dane	6.10.1975		19	*1998–2004*	50
Lambert Clayton Benjamin	10.2.1962		5	*1991–1998*	11‡
Lara Brian Charles (*CY 1995*)	2.5.1969		130†	*1990–2006*	295‡
Lashley Patrick Douglas ("Peter").	11.2.1937		4	*1960–1966*	
Lawson Jermaine Jay Charles.	13.1.1982		13	*2002–2005*	13
Legall Ralph Archibald	1.12.1925	2003	4	*1952*	

	Born	Died	Tests	Test Career	O/T
Lewis Desmond Michael	21.2.1946	25.3.2018	3	1970	
Lewis Rawl Nicholas	5.9.1974		5	1997–2007	28/1
Lewis Sherman Hakim	21.10.1995		2	2018	
Lloyd *Sir* Clive Hubert CBE (*CY 1971*)	31.8.1944		110	1966–1984	87
Logie Augustine Lawrence	28.9.1960		52	1982–1991	158
McGarrell Neil Christopher	12.7.1972		4	2000–2001	17
McLean Nixon Alexei McNamara	20.7.1973		19	1997–2000	45
McMorris Easton Dudley Ashton St John	4.4.1935	1.2.2022	13	1957–1966	
McWatt Clifford Aubrey	1.2.1922	20.7.1997	6	1953–1954	
Madray Ivan Samuel	2.7.1934	23.4.2009	2	1957	
Marshall Malcolm Denzil (*CY 1983*)	18.4.1958	4.11.1999	81	1978–1991	136
²**Marshall** Norman Edgar	27.2.1924	11.8.2007	1	1954	
²**Marshall** Roy Edwin (*CY 1959*)	25.4.1930	27.10.1992	4	1951	
Marshall Xavier Melbourne	27.3.1986		7	2005–2008	24‡/6‡
Martin Frank Reginald	12.10.1893	23.11.1967	9	1928–1930	
Martindale Emmanuel Alfred	25.11.1909	17.3.1972	10	1933–1939	
Mattis Everton Hugh	11.4.1957		4	1980	2
Mayers Kyle Rico	8.9.1992		10	2020–2021	3/2
Mendonca Ivor Leon	13.7.1934	14.6.2014	2	1961	
Merry Cyril Arthur	20.1.1911	19.4.1964	2	1933	
Miller Nikita O'Neil	16.5.1982		1	2009	50/9
Miller Roy Samuel	24.12.1924	21.8.2014	1	1952	
Mohammed Dave	8.10.1979		5	2003–2006	7
Moodie George Horatio	26.11.1915	8.6.2002	1	1934	
Morton Runako Shakur	22.7.1978	4.3.2012	15	2005–2007	56/7
Moseley Ezra Alphonsa	5.1.1958	6.2.2021	2	1989	9
Moseley Sheyne Akeel Richard	11.4.1994		2	2020	
¹**Murray** David Anthony	29.5.1950		19	1977–1981	10
Murray Deryck Lance	20.5.1943		62	1963–1980	26
Murray Junior Randalph	20.1.1968		33	1992–2001	55
Nagamootoo Mahendra Veeren	9.10.1975		5	2000–2002	24
Nanan Rangy	29.5.1953	23.3.2016	1	1980	
Narine Sunil Philip	26.5.1988		6	2012–2013	65/51
Nash Brendan Paul	14.12.1977		21	2008–2011	9
Neblett James Montague	13.11.1901	28.3.1959	1	1934	
Noreiga Jack Mollinson	15.4.1936	8.8.2003	4	1970	
Nunes Robert Karl	7.6.1894	23.7.1958	4	1928–1929	
Nurse Seymour MacDonald (*CY 1967*)	10.11.1933	6.5.2019	29	1959–1968	
Padmore Albert Leroy	17.12.1946		2	1975–1976	
Pagon Donovan Jomo	13.9.1982		2	2004	
Pairaudeau Bruce Hamilton	14.4.1931		13	1952–1957	
Parchment Brenton Anthony	24.6.1982		2	2007	7/1
Parry Derick Recaldo	22.12.1954		12	1977–1979	6
Pascal Nelon Troy	25.4.1987		2	2010–2010	1
Passailaigue Charles Clarence	4.8.1901	7.1.1972	1	1929	
Patterson Balfour Patrick	15.9.1961		28	1985–1992	59
Paul Keemo Mandela Angus	21.2.1998		3	2018–2018	19/20
Payne Thelston Rodney O'Neale	13.2.1957		1	1985	7
Permaul Veerasammy	11.8.1989		7	2012–2021	7/1
Perry Nehemiah Odolphus	16.6.1968		4	1998–1999	21
Peters Keon Kenroy	24.2.1982		1	2014	
Phillip Norbert	12.6.1948		9	1977–1978	1
Phillips Omar Jamel	12.10.1986		2	2009	
Pierre Lancelot Richard	5.6.1921	14.4.1989	1	1947	
Powell Daren Brentlyle	15.4.1978		37	2002–2008	55/5
Powell Kieran Omar Akeem	6.3.1990		44	2011–2021	46/1
Powell Ricardo Lloyd	16.12.1978		2	1999–2003	109
Rae Allan Fitzroy	30.9.1922	27.2.2005	15	1948–1952	
Ragoonath Suruj	22.3.1968		2	1998	
Ramadhin Sonny (*CY 1951*)	1.5.1929		43	1950–1960	

	Born	Died	Tests	Test Career	O/T
Ramdass Ryan Rakesh	3.7.1983		1	*2005*	1
Ramdin Denesh	13.3.1985		74	*2005–2015*	139/71
Ramnarine Dinanath.	4.6.1975		12	*1997–2001*	4
Rampaul Ravindranath	15.10.1984		18	*2009–2012*	92/27
Reifer Floyd Lamonte	23.7.1972		6	*1996–2009*	8/1
Reifer Raymon Anton	11.5.1991		1	*2017*	5
Richards Dale Maurice	16.7.1976		3	*2009–2010*	8/1
Richards Sir Isaac <u>Vivian</u> Alexander (*CY 1977*) . .	7.3.1952		121	*1974–1991*	187
Richardson Sir Richard Benjamin (*CY 1992*)	12.1.1962		86	*1983–1995*	224
Rickards Kenneth Roy	22.8.1923	21.8.1995	2	*1947–1951*	
Roach Clifford Archibald.	13.3.1904	16.4.1988	16	*1928–1934*	
Roach Kemar Andre Jamal.	30.6.1988		68	*2009–2021*	92/11
Roberts Sir Anderson Montgomery Everton CBE (*CY 1975*)	29.1.1951		47	*1973–1983*	56
Roberts Alphonso Theodore.	18.9.1937	24.7.1996	1	*1955*	
Roberts Lincoln Abraham	4.9.1974		1	*1998*	
Rodriguez William Vicente	25.6.1934		5	*1961–1967*	
Rose Franklyn Albert.	1.2.1972		19	*1996–2000*	27
Rowe Lawrence George.	8.1.1949		30	*1971–1979*	11
Russell Andre Dwayne	29.4.1988		1	*2010*	56/67
²**St Hill** Edwin Lloyd	9.3.1904	21.5.1957	2	*1929*	
²**St Hill** Wilton H	6.7.1893	d unknown	3	*1928–1929*	
Sammy Daren Julius Garvey	20.12.1983		38	*2007–2013*	126/66‡
²**Samuels** Marlon Nathaniel (*CY 2013*)	5.1.1981		71	*2000–2016*	207/67
²**Samuels** Robert George	13.3.1971		6	*1995–1996*	8
Sanford Adam	12.7.1975		11	*2001–2003*	
Sarwan Ramnaresh Ronnie	23.6.1980		87	*1999–2011*	181/18
Scarlett Reginald Osmond	15.8.1934	14.8.2019	3	*1959*	
¹**Scott** Alfred Homer Patrick	29.7.1934		1	*1952*	
¹**Scott** Oscar Charles ("Tommy")	14.8.1892	15.6.1961	8	*1928–1930*	
Seales Jayden Nigel Tristan	10.9.2001		4	*2021*	
Sealey Benjamin James	12.8.1899	12.9.1963	1	*1933*	
Sealy James Edward <u>Derrick</u>.	11.9.1912	3.1.1982	11	*1929–1939*	
Shepherd John Neil (*CY 1979*).	9.11.1943		5	*1969–1970*	
Shillingford Grayson Cleophas.	25.9.1944	23.12.2009	7	*1969–1971*	
Shillingford Irvine Theodore	18.4.1944		4	*1976–1977*	2
Shillingford Shane	22.2.1983		16	*2010–2014*	
Shivnarine Sewdatt.	13.5.1952		8	*1977–1978*	1
Simmons Lendl Mark Platter	25.1.1985		8	*2008–2011*	68/68
Simmons Philip Verant (*CY 1997*)	18.4.1963		26	*1987–1997*	143
Singh Charran Kamkaran	27.11.1935	19.11.2015	2	*1959*	
Singh Vishaul Anthony	12.1.1989		3	*2016*	
Small Joseph Archer..	3.11.1892	26.4.1958	3	*1928–1929*	
Small Milton Aster	12.2.1964		2	*1983–1984*	2
Smith Cameron Wilberforce.	29.7.1933		5	*1960–1961*	
Smith Dwayne Romel	12.4.1983		10	*2003–2005*	105/33
Smith Devon Sheldon	21.10.1981		43	*2002–2018*	47/6
Smith O'Neil Gordon ("Collie") (*CY 1958*) . . .	5.5.1933	9.9.1959	26	*1954–1958*	
Sobers Sir Garfield St Aubrun (*CY 1964*) . . .	28.7.1936		93	*1953–1973*	1
Solomon Joseph Stanislaus.	26.8.1930		27	*1958–1964*	
Solozano Jeremy Len	5.10.1995		1	*2021*	
Stayers Sven Conrad ("Charlie").	9.6.1937	6.1.2005	4	*1961*	
²**Stollmeyer** Jeffrey Baxter	11.3.1921	10.9.1989	32	*1939–1954*	
²**Stollmeyer** Victor Humphrey.	24.1.1916	21.9.1999	1	*1939*	
Stuart Colin Ellsworth Laurie.	28.9.1973		6	*2000–2001*	5
Taylor Jerome Everton	22.6.1984		46	*2003–2015*	90/30
Taylor Jaswick Ossie	3.1.1932	13.11.1999	3	*1957–1958*	
Thompson Patterson Ian Chesterfield	26.9.1971		2	*1995–1996*	2
Tonge Gavin Courtney.	13.2.1983		1	*2009*	5/1
Trim John	25.1.1915	12.11.1960	4	*1947–1951*	

	Born	Died	Tests	Test Career	O/T
Valentine Alfred Louis (*CY 1951*).	28.4.1930	11.5.2004	36	*1950–1961*	
Valentine Vincent Adolphus	4.4.1908	6.7.1972	2	*1933*	
Walcott *Sir* Clyde Leopold (*CY 1958*)	17.1.1926	26.8.2006	44	*1947–1959*	
Walcott Leslie Arthur	18.1.1894	27.2.1984	1	*1929*	
Wallace Philo Alphonso	2.8.1970		7	*1997–1998*	33
Walsh Courtney Andrew (*CY 1987*)	30.10.1962		132	*1984–2000*	205
Walton Chadwick Antonio Kirkpatrick	3.7.1985		2	*2009*	9/19
Warrican Jomel Andrel.	20.5.1992		13	*2015–2021*	
Washington Dwight Marlon	5.3.1983		1	*2004*	
Watson Chester Donald.	1.7.1938		7	*1959–1961*	
[1] **Weekes** *Sir* Everton de Courcy (*CY 1951*)	26.2.1925	1.7.2020	48	*1947–1957*	
Weekes Kenneth Hunnell.	24.1.1912	9.2.1998	2	*1939*	
White Anthony Wilbur	20.11.1938		2	*1964*	
Wight Claude Vibart.	28.7.1902	4.10.1969	2	*1928–1929*	
Wight George Leslie.	28.5.1929	4.1.2004	1	*1952*	
Wiles Charles Archibald	11.8.1892	4.11.1957	1	*1933*	
Willett Elquemedo Tonito	1.5.1953		5	*1972–1974*	
Williams Alvadon Basil.	21.11.1949	25.10.2015	7	*1977–1978*	
Williams Courtney David	4.11.1963		11	*1991–1997*	36
Williams Ernest Albert Vivian ("Foffie").	10.4.1914	13.4.1997	4	*1939–1947*	
Williams Stuart Clayton.	12.8.1969		31	*1993–2001*	57
Wishart Kenneth Leslie.	28.11.1908	18.10.1972	1	*1934*	
Worrell *Sir* Frank Mortimer Maglinne (*CY 1951*) .	1.8.1924	13.3.1967	51	*1947–1963*	

NEW ZEALAND (282 players)

	Born	Died	Tests	Test Career	O/T
Adams Andre Ryan.	17.7.1975		1	*2001*	42/4
Alabaster John Chaloner	11.7.1930		21	*1955–1971*	
Allcott Cyril Francis Walter	7.10.1896	19.11.1973	6	*1929–1931*	
Allott Geoffrey Ian	24.12.1971		10	*1995–1999*	31
Anderson Corey James	13.12.1990		13	*2013–2015*	49/31
[1] **Anderson** Robert Wickham	2.10.1948		9	*1976–1978*	2
[1] **Anderson** William McDougall	8.10.1919	21.12.1979	1	*1945*	
Andrews Bryan	4.4.1945		2	*1973*	
Arnel Brent John	3.1.1979		6	*2009–2011*	
Astle Nathan John	15.9.1971		81	*1995–2006*	223/4
Astle Todd Duncan	24.9.1986		5	*2012–2019*	9/5
Badcock Frederick Theodore ("Ted")	9.8.1897	19.9.1982	7	*1929–1932*	
Barber Richard Trevor	3.6.1925	7.8.2015	1	*1955*	
Bartlett Gary Alex	3.2.1941		10	*1961–1967*	
Barton Paul Thomas	9.10.1935		7	*1961–1962*	
Beard Donald Derek	14.1.1920	15.7.1982	4	*1951–1955*	
Beck John Edward Francis	1.8.1934	23.4.2000	8	*1953–1955*	
Bell Matthew David.	25.2.1977		18	*1998–2007*	7
Bell William.	5.9.1934	23.7.2002	2	*1953*	
Bennett Hamish Kyle	22.2.1987		1	*2010*	19/11
Bilby Grahame Paul	7.5.1941		2	*1965*	
Blain Tony Elston	17.2.1962		11	*1986–1993*	38
Blair Robert William.	23.6.1932		19	*1952–1963*	
Blundell Thomas Ackland	1.9.1990		15	*2017–2021*	2/7
Blunt Roger Charles (*CY 1928*).	3.11.1900	22.6.1966	9	*1929–1931*	
Bolton Bruce Alfred	31.5.1935		2	*1958*	
Bond Shane Edward	7.6.1975		18	*2001–2009*	82/20
Boock Stephen Lewis	20.9.1951		30	*1977–1988*	14
Boult Trent Alexander.	22.7.1989		75	*2011–2021*	93/44
[1,2] **Bracewell** Brendon Paul	14.9.1959		6	*1978–1984*	1
[1] **Bracewell** Douglas Alexander John.	28.9.1990		27	*2011–2016*	19/20
[2] **Bracewell** John Garry	15.4.1958		41	*1980–1990*	53
[1] **Bradburn** Grant Eric	26.5.1966		7	*1990–2000*	11

	Born	Died	Tests	Test Career	O/T
[1] **Bradburn** Wynne Pennell	24.11.1938	25.9.2008	2	1963	
Broom Neil Trevor	20.11.1983		2	2016	39/11
Brown Vaughan Raymond	3.11.1959		2	1985	3
Brownlie Dean Graham	30.7.1984		14	2011–2013	16/5
Burgess Mark Gordon	17.7.1944		50	1967–1980	26
Burke Cecil	27.3.1914	4.8.1997	1	1945	
Burtt Thomas Browning	22.1.1915	24.5.1988	10	1946–1952	
Butler Ian Gareth	24.11.1981		8	2001–2004	26/19
[1] **Butterfield** Leonard Arthur	29.8.1913	5.7.1999	1	1945	
[1] **Cairns** Bernard Lance	10.10.1949		43	1973–1985	78
[1] **Cairns** Christopher Lance (CY 2000)	13.6.1970		62	1989–2004	214‡/2
Cameron Francis James MBE	1.6.1932		19	1961–1965	
Cave Henry Butler	10.10.1922	15.9.1989	19	1949–1958	
Chapple Murray Ernest	25.7.1930	31.7.1985	14	1952–1965	
Chatfield Ewen John MBE	3.7.1950		43	1974–1988	114
Cleverley Donald Charles	23.12.1909	16.2.2004	2	1931–1945	
Collinge Richard Owen	2.4.1946		35	1964–1978	15
Colquhoun Ian Alexander	8.6.1924	26.2.2005	2	1954	
Coney Jeremy Vernon MBE (CY 1984)	21.6.1952		52	1973–1986	88
Congdon Bevan Ernest OBE (CY 1974)	11.2.1938	10.2.2018	61	1964–1978	11
Conway Devon Philip (CY 2022)	8.7.1991		5	2021–2021	3/20
Cowie John OBE	30.3.1912	3.6.1994	9	1937–1949	
Craig Mark Donald	23.3.1987		15	2014–2016	
Cresswell George Fenwick	22.3.1915	10.1.1966	3	1949–1950	
Cromb Ian Burns	25.6.1905	6.3.1984	5	1931–1931	
[2] **Crowe** Jeffrey John	14.9.1958		39	1982–1989	75
[2] **Crowe** Martin David MBE (CY 1985)	22.9.1962	3.3.2016	77	1981–1995	143
Cumming Craig Derek	31.8.1975		11	2004–2007	13
Cunis Robert Smith	5.1.1941	9.8.2008	20	1963–1971	
D'Arcy John William	23.4.1936		5	1958	
Davis Heath Te-Ihi-O-Te-Rangi	30.11.1971		5	1994–1997	11
de Grandhomme Colin	22.7.1986		26	2016–2021	42/41
de Groen Richard Paul	5.8.1962		5	1993–1994	12
Dempster Charles Stewart (CY 1932)	15.11.1903	14.2.1974	10	1929–1932	
Dempster Eric William MBE	25.1.1925	15.8.2011	5	1952–1953	
Dick Arthur Edward	10.10.1936		17	1961–1965	
Dickinson George Ritchie	11.3.1903	17.3.1978	3	1929–1931	
Donnelly Martin Paterson (CY 1948)	17.10.1917	22.10.1999	7	1937–1949	
Doull Simon Blair	6.8.1969		32	1992–1999	42
Dowling Graham Thorne OBE	4.3.1937		39	1961–1971	
Drum Christopher James	10.7.1974		5	2000–2001	5
Dunning John Angus	6.2.1903	24.6.1971	4	1932–1937	
Edgar Bruce Adrian	23.11.1956		39	1978–1986	64
Edwards Graham Neil ("Jock")	27.5.1955	6.4.2020	8	1976–1980	6
Elliott Grant David	21.3.1979		5	2007–2009	83/16‡
Emery Raymond William George	28.3.1915	18.12.1982	2	1951	
Ferguson Lachlan Hammond ("Lockie")	13.6.1991		1	2019	37/15
Fisher Frederick Eric	28.7.1924	19.6.1996	1	1952	
Fleming Stephen Paul	1.4.1973		111	1993–2007	279‡/5
Flynn Daniel Raymond	16.4.1985		24	2008–2012	20/5
Foley Henry	28.1.1906	16.10.1948	1	1929	
Franklin James Edward Charles	7.11.1980		31	2000–2012	110/38
Franklin Trevor John	15.3.1962		21	1983–1990	3
Freeman Douglas Linford	8.9.1914	31.5.1994	2	1932	
Fulton Peter Gordon	1.2.1979		23	2005–2014	49/12
Gallichan Norman	3.6.1906	25.3.1969	1	1937	
Gedye Sidney Graham	2.5.1929	10.8.2014	4	1963–1964	
Germon Lee Kenneth	4.11.1968		12	1995–1996	37
Gillespie Mark Raymond	17.10.1979		5	2007–2011	32/11
Gillespie Stuart Ross	2.3.1957		1	1985	19

	Born	Died	Tests	Test Career	O/T
Gray Evan John	18.11.1954		10	1983–1988	10
Greatbatch Mark John	11.12.1963		41	1987–1996	84
Guillen Simpson Clairmonte ("Sammy")	24.9.1924	2.3.2013	3†	1955	
Guptill Martin James.	30.9.1986		47	2008–2016	186/112
Guy John William.	29.8.1934		12	1955–1961	
¹·² **Hadlee** Dayle Robert.	6.1.1948		26	1969–1977	11
¹·² **Hadlee** *Sir* Richard John (*CY 1982*).	3.7.1951		86	1972–1990	115
¹ **Hadlee** Walter Arnold CBE.	4.6.1915	29.9.2006	11	1937–1950	
Harford Noel Sherwin.	30.8.1930	30.3.1981	8	1955–1958	
Harford Roy Ivan.	30.5.1936		3	1967	
¹ **Harris** Chris Zinzan	20.11.1969		23	1992–2002	250
¹ **Harris** Parke Gerald Zinzan	18.7.1927	1.12.1991	9	1955–1964	
Harris Roger Meredith	27.7.1933		2	1958	
² **Hart** Matthew Norman	16.5.1972		14	1993–1995	13
² **Hart** Robert Garry.	2.12.1974		11	2002–2003	2
Hartland Blair Robert.	22.10.1966		9	1991–1994	16
Haslam Mark James	26.9.1972		4	1992–1995	1
Hastings Brian Frederick	23.3.1940		31	1968–1975	11
Hayes John Arthur	11.1.1927	25.12.2007	15	1950–1958	
Henderson Matthew	2.8.1895	17.6.1970	1	1929	
Henry Matthew James.	14.12.1991		14	2015–2021	55/6
Hopkins Gareth James.	24.11.1976		4	2008–2010	25/10
² **Horne** Matthew Jeffery	5.12.1970		35	1996–2003	50
² **Horne** Philip Andrew	21.1.1960		4	1986–1990	4
Hough Kenneth William	24.10.1928	20.9.2009	2	1958	
How Jamie Michael.	19.5.1981		19	2005–2008	41/5
² **Howarth** Geoffrey Philip OBE.	29.3.1951		47	1974–1984	70
² **Howarth** Hedley John	25.12.1943	7.11.2008	30	1969–1976	9
Ingram Peter John	25.10.1978		2	2009	8/3
James Kenneth Cecil.	12.3.1904	21.8.1976	11	1929–1932	
Jamieson Kyle Alex	30.12.1994		12	2019–2021	5/8
Jarvis Terrence Wayne	29.7.1944		13	1964–1972	
Jones Andrew Howard.	9.5.1959		39	1986–1994	87
Jones Richard Andrew.	22.10.1973		1	2003	5
Kennedy Robert John	3.6.1972		4	1995	7
Kerr John Lambert	28.12.1910	27.5.2007	7	1931–1937	
Kuggeleijn Christopher Mary	10.5.1956		2	1988	16
Larsen Gavin Rolf	27.9.1962		8	1994–1995	121
¹ **Latham** Rodney Terry.	12.6.1961		4	1991–1992	33
¹ **Latham** Thomas William Maxwell	2.4.1992		63	2013–2021	102/18
Lees Warren Kenneth MBE	19.3.1952		21	1976–1983	31
Leggat Ian Bruce	7.6.1930		1	1953	
Leggat John Gordon	27.5.1926	9.3.1973	9	1951–1955	
Lissette Allen Fisher	6.11.1919	24.1.1973	2	1955	
Loveridge Greg Riaka	15.1.1975		1	1995	
Lowry Thomas Coleman	17.2.1898	20.7.1976	7	1929–1931	
McCullum Brendon Barrie (*CY 2016*)	27.9.1981		101	2003–2015	260/71
McEwan Paul Ernest.	19.12.1953		4	1979–1984	17
MacGibbon Anthony Roy	28.8.1924	6.4.2010	26	1950–1958	
McGirr Herbert Mendelson	5.11.1891	14.4.1964	2	1929	
McGregor Spencer Noel	18.12.1931	21.11.2007	25	1954–1964	
McIntosh Timothy Gavin	4.12.1979		17	2008–2010	
McKay Andrew John	17.4.1980		1	2010	19/2
McLeod Edwin George	14.10.1900	14.9.1989	1	1929	
McMahon Trevor George	8.11.1929		5	1955	
McMillan Craig Douglas	13.9.1976		55	1997–2004	197/8
McRae Donald Alexander Noel	25.12.1912	10.8.1986	1	1945	
² **Marshall** Hamish John Hamilton	15.2.1979		13	2000–2005	66/3
² **Marshall** James Andrew Hamilton	15.2.1979		7	2004–2008	10/3
Martin Bruce Philip	25.4.1980		5	2012–2013	

	Born	Died	Tests	Test Career	O/T
Martin Christopher Stewart	10.12.1974		71	2000–2012	20/6
Mason Michael James	27.8.1974		1	2003	26/3
Matheson Alexander Malcolm	27.2.1906	31.12.1985	2	1929–1931	
Meale Trevor	11.11.1928	21.5.2010	2	1958	
Merritt William Edward	18.8.1908	9.6.1977	6	1929–1931	
Meuli Edgar Milton.	20.2.1926	15.4.2007	1	1952	
Milburn Barry Douglas	24.11.1943		3	1968	
Miller Lawrence Somerville Martin.	31.3.1923	17.12.1996	13	1952–1958	
Mills John Ernest	3.9.1905	11.12.1972	7	1929–1932	
Mills Kyle David	15.3.1979		19	2004–2008	170/42
Mitchell Daryl Joseph	20.5.1991		7	2019–2021	3/25
Moir Alexander McKenzie.	17.7.1919	17.6.2000	17	1950–1958	
Moloney Denis Andrew Robert ("Sonny") . . .	11.8.1910	15.7.1942	3	1937	
Mooney Francis Leonard Hugh.	26.5.1921	8.3.2004	14	1949–1953	
Morgan Ross Winston.	12.2.1941		20	1964–1971	
Morrison Bruce Donald.	17.12.1933		1	1962	
Morrison Daniel Kyle.	3.2.1966		48	1987–1996	96
Morrison John Francis MacLean	27.8.1947		17	1973–1981	18
Motz Richard Charles (*CY 1966*).	12.1.1940	29.4.2007	32	1961–1969	
Munro Colin	11.3.1987		1	2012	57/65
Murray Bruce Alexander Grenfell	18.9.1940		13	1967–1970	
Murray Darrin James	4.9.1967		8	1994	1
Nash Dion Joseph	20.11.1971		32	1992–2001	81
Neesham James Douglas Sheehan	17.9.1990		12	2013–2016	66/38
Newman *Sir* Jack	3.7.1902	23.9.1996	3	1931–1932	
Nicholls Henry Michael	15.11.1991		44	2015–2021	52/10
Nicol Robert James	28.5.1983		2	2011	22/21
O'Brien Iain Edward.	10.7.1976		22	2004–2009	10/4
O'Connor Shayne Barry	15.11.1973		19	1997–2001	38
Oram Jacob David Philip.	28.7.1978		33	2002–2009	160/36
O'Sullivan David Robert.	16.11.1944		11	1972–1976	3
Overton Guy William Fitzroy.	8.6.1919	7.9.1993	3	1953	
Owens Michael Barry	11.11.1969		8	1992–1994	1
Page Milford Laurenson ("Curly")	8.5.1902	13.2.1987	14	1929–1937	
Papps Michael Hugh William.	2.7.1979		8	2003–2007	6
²**Parker** John Morton	21.2.1951		36	1972–1980	24
³**Parker** Norman <u>Murray</u>.	28.8.1948		3	1976	1
Parore Adam Craig.	23.1.1971		78	1990–2001	179
Patel Ajaz Yunus	21.10.1988		11	2018–2021	0/7
Patel Dipak Narshibhai	25.10.1958		37	1986–1996	75
Patel Jeetan Shashi (*CY 2015*).	7.5.1980		24	2005–2016	43/11
Petherick Peter James	25.9.1942	7.6.2015	6	1976	
Petrie Eric Charlton	22.5.1927	14.8.2004	14	1955–1965	
Phillips Glenn Dominic	6.12.1996		1	2019	0/35
Playle William Rodger.	1.12.1938	27.2.2019	8	1958–1962	
Pocock Blair Andrew	18.6.1971		15	1993–1997	
Pollard Victor	7.9.1945		32	1964–1973	3
Poore Matt Beresford	1.6.1930	11.6.2020	14	1952–1955	
Priest Mark Wellings	12.8.1961		3	1990–1997	18
Pringle Christopher.	26.1.1968		14	1990–1994	64
Puna Narotam ("Tom")	28.10.1929	7.6.1996	3	1965	
Rabone Geoffrey Osborne	6.11.1921	19.1.2006	12	1949–1954	
Raval Jeet Ashokbhai	22.5.1988		24	2016–2019	
Ravindra Rachin	18.11.1999		3	2021	0/6
¹**Redmond** Aaron James	23.9.1979		8	2008–2013	6/7
¹**Redmond** Rodney Ernest.	29.12.1944		1	1972	2
Reid John Fulton.	3.3.1956	28.12.2020	19	1978–1985	25
Reid John Richard OBE (*CY 1959*).	3.6.1928	14.10.2020	58	1949–1965	
Richardson Mark Hunter.	11.6.1971		38	2000–2004	4
Roberts Andrew Duncan Glenn	6.5.1947	26.10.1989	7	1975–1976	1

	Born	Died	Tests	Test Career	O/T
Roberts Albert William	20.8.1909	13.5.1978	5	*1929–1937*	
Robertson Gary Keith	15.7.1960		1	*1985*	10
Ronchi Luke	23.4.1981		4	*2015–2016*	81‡/29‡
Rowe Charles <u>Gordon</u>	30.6.1915	9.6.1995	1	*1945*	
[1] **Rutherford** Hamish Duncan	27.4.1989		16	*2012–2014*	4/8
[1] **Rutherford** Kenneth Robert	26.10.1965		56	*1984–1994*	121
Ryder Jesse Daniel	6.8.1984		18	*2008–2011*	48/22
Santner Mitchell Josef	5.2.1992		24	*2015–2021*	75/62
Scott Roy Hamilton	6.3.1917		1	*1946*	
Scott Verdun John	31.7.1916	2.8.1980	10	*1945–1951*	
Sewell David Graham	20.10.1977		1	*1997*	
Shrimpton Michael John Froud	23.6.1940	13.6.2015	10	*1962–1973*	
Sinclair Barry Whitley	23.10.1936		21	*1962–1967*	
Sinclair Ian McKay	1.6.1933	25.8.2019	2	*1955*	
Sinclair Mathew Stuart	9.11.1975		33	*1999–2009*	54/2
Smith Frank Brunton	13.3.1922	6.7.1997	4	*1946–1951*	
Smith Horace <u>Dennis</u>	8.1.1913	25.1.1986	1	*1932*	
Smith Ian David Stockley MBE	28.2.1957		63	*1980–1991*	98
Snedden Colin Alexander	7.1.1918	23.4.2011	1	*1946*	
Snedden Martin Colin	23.11.1958		25	*1980–1990*	93
Sodhi Inderbir Singh ("Ish")	31.10.1992		17	*2013–2018*	33/66
Somerville William Edgar Richard	9.8.1984		6	*2018–2021*	
Southee Timothy Grant	11.12.1988		83	*2007–2021*	143/92
Sparling John Trevor	24.7.1938		11	*1958–1963*	
Spearman Craig Murray	4.7.1972		19	*1995–2000*	51
Stead Gary Raymond	9.1.1972		5	*1998–1999*	
Stirling Derek Alexander	5.10.1961		6	*1984–1986*	6
Styris Scott Bernard	10.7.1975		29	*2002–2007*	188/31
Su'a Murphy Logo	7.11.1966		13	*1991–1994*	12
Sutcliffe Bert MBE (*CY 1950*)	17.11.1923	20.4.2001	42	*1946–1965*	
Taylor Bruce Richard	12.7.1943	6.2.2021	30	*1964–1973*	2
Taylor Donald Dougald	2.3.1923	5.12.1980	3	*1946–1955*	
Taylor Luteru <u>Ross</u> Poutoa Lote	8.3.1984		112	*2007–2021*	233/102
Thomson Keith	26.2.1941		2	*1967*	
Thomson Shane Alexander	27.1.1969		19	*1989–1995*	56
Tindill Eric William Thomas	18.12.1910	1.8.2010	5	*1937–1946*	
Troup Gary Bertram	3.10.1952		15	*1976–1985*	22
Truscott Peter Bennetts	14.8.1941		1	*1964*	
Tuffey Daryl Raymond	11.6.1978		26	*1999–2009*	94/3
Turner Glenn Maitland (*CY 1971*)	26.5.1947		41	*1968–1982*	41
Twose Roger Graham	17.4.1968		16	*1995–1999*	87
Vance Robert Howard	31.3.1955		4	*1987–1989*	8
van Wyk Cornelius Francois <u>Kruger</u>	7.2.1980		9	*2011–2012*	
Vaughan Justin Thomas Caldwell	30.8.1967		6	*1992–1996*	18
Vettori Daniel Luca	27.1.1979		112†	*1996–2014*	291‡/34
Vincent Lou	11.11.1978		23	*2001–2007*	102/9
[1] **Vivian** Graham Ellery	28.2.1946		5	*1964–1971*	
[1] **Vivian** Henry <u>Gifford</u>	4.11.1912	12.8.1983	7	*1931–1937*	1
Wadsworth Kenneth John	30.11.1946	19.8.1976	33	*1969–1975*	13
Wagner Neil	13.3.1986		56	*2012–2021*	
Walker Brooke Graeme Keith	25.3.1977		5	*2000–2002*	11
Wallace Walter <u>Mervyn</u>	19.12.1916	21.3.2008	13	*1937–1952*	
Walmsley Kerry Peter	23.8.1973		3	*1994–2000*	2
Ward John Thomas	11.3.1937	12.1.2021	8	*1963–1967*	
Watling Bradley-John	9.7.1985		75	*2009–2021*	28/5
Watson William	31.8.1965		15	*1986–1993*	61
Watt Leslie	17.9.1924	15.11.1996	1	*1954*	
Webb Murray George	22.6.1947		3	*1970–1973*	
Webb Peter Neil	14.7.1957		2	*1979*	5
Weir Gordon <u>Lindsay</u>	2.6.1908	31.10.2003	11	*1929–1937*	

	Born	Died	Tests	Test Career	O/T
White David John	26.6.1961		2	1990	3
Whitelaw Paul Erskine	10.2.1910	28.8.1988	2	1932	
Williamson Kane Stuart (*CY 2016*)	8.8.1990		86	2010–2021	151/74
Wiseman Paul John	4.5.1970		25	1997–2004	15
Wright John Geoffrey MBE	5.7.1954		82	1977–1992	149
Young Bryan Andrew	3.11.1964		35	1993–1998	74
Young Reece Alan	15.9.1979		5	2010–2011	
Young William Alexander	22.11.1992		7	2020–2021	2/8
Yuile Bryan William	29.10.1941		17	1962–1969	

INDIA (303 players)

	Born	Died	Tests	Test Career	O/T
Aaron Varun Raymond	29.10.1989		9	2011–2015	9
Abid Ali Syed	9.9.1941		29	1967–1974	5
Adhikari Hemchandra Ramachandra	31.7.1919	25.10.2003	21	1947–1958	
Agarkar Ajit Bhalchandra	4.12.1977		26	1998–2005	191/4
Agarwal Mayank Anurag	16.2.1991		19	2018–2021	5
[2] **Amar Singh** Ladha	4.12.1910	21.5.1940	7	1932–1936	
[1,2] **Amarnath** Mohinder (*CY 1984*)	24.9.1950		69	1969–1987	85
[1] **Amarnath** Nanik ("Lala")	11.9.1911	5.8.2000	24	1933–1952	
[1,2] **Amarnath** Surinder	30.12.1948		10	1975–1978	3
Amir Elahi	1.9.1908	28.12.1980	1†	1947	
Amre Pravin Kalyan	14.8.1968		11	1992–1993	37
Ankola Salil Ashok	1.3.1968		1	1989	20
[2] **Apte** Arvindrao Laxmanrao	24.10.1934		1	1959	
[2] **Apte** Madhavrao Laxmanrao	5.10.1932	23.9.2019	7	1952	
Arshad Ayub	2.8.1958		13	1987–1989	32
Arun Bharathi	14.12.1962		2	1986	4
Arun Lal	1.8.1955		16	1982–1988	13
Ashwin Ravichandran	17.9.1986		84	2011–2021	111/51
Azad Kirtivardhan	2.1.1959		7	1980–1983	25
Azharuddin Mohammad (*CY 1991*)	8.2.1963		99	1984–1999	334
Badani Hemang Kamal	14.11.1976		4	2001	40
Badrinath Subramaniam	30.8.1980		2	2009	7/1
Bahutule Sairaj Vasant	6.1.1973		2	2000–2001	8
Baig Abbas Ali	19.3.1939		10	1959–1966	
Balaji Lakshmipathy	27.9.1981		8	2003–2004	30/5
Banerjee Sudangsu Abinash	1.11.1917	14.9.1992	1	1948	
Banerjee Sarodindu Nath ("Shute")	3.10.1911	14.10.1980	1	1948	
Banerjee Subroto Tara	13.2.1969		1	1991	6
Bangar Sanjay Bapusaheb	11.10.1972		12	2001–2002	15
Baqa Jilani Mohammad	20.7.1911	2.7.1941	1	1936	
Bedi Bishan Singh	25.9.1946		67	1966–1979	10
Bhandari Prakash	27.11.1935		3	1954–1956	
Bharadwaj Raghvendrarao Vijay	15.8.1975		3	1999	10
Bhat Adwai Raghuram	16.4.1958		2	1983	
Bhuvneshwar Kumar	5.2.1990		21	2012–2017	119/55
[1] **Binny** Roger Michael Humphrey	19.7.1955		27	1979–1986	72
[1] **Binny** Stuart Terence Roger	3.6.1984		6	2014–2015	14/3
Borde Chandrakant Gulabrao	21.7.1934		55	1958–1969	
Bumrah Jasprit Jasbirsingh (*CY 2022*)	6.12.1993		27	2017–2021	67/55
Chandrasekhar Bhagwat Subramanya (*CY 1972*)	17.5.1945		58	1963–1979	1
Chauhan Chetandra Pratap Singh	21.7.1947	16.8.2020	40	1969–1980	7
Chauhan Rajesh Kumar	19.12.1966		21	1992–1997	35
Chawla Piyush Pramod	24.12.1988		3	2005–2012	25/7
Chopra Aakash	19.9.1977		10	2003–2004	
Chopra Nikhil	26.12.1973		1	1999	39
Chowdhury Nirode Ranjan	23.5.1923	14.12.1979	2	1948–1951	
Colah Sorabji Hormasji Munchersha	22.9.1902	11.9.1950	2	1932–1933	

	Born	Died	Tests	Test Career	O/T
Contractor Nariman Jamshedji	7.3.1934		31	*1955–1961*	
Dahiya Vijay	10.5.1973		2	*2000*	19
Dani Hemchandra Tukaram	24.5.1933	19.12.1999	1	*1952*	
Das Shiv Sunder	5.11.1977		23	*2000–2001*	4
Dasgupta Deep	7.6.1977		8	*2001*	5
Desai Ramakant Bhikaji	20.6.1939	27.4.1998	28	*1958–1967*	
Dhawan Shikhar (*CY 2014*)	5.12.1985		34	*2012–2018*	145/68
Dhoni Mahendra Singh	7.7.1981		90	*2005–2014*	347‡/98
Dighe Sameer Sudhakar	8.10.1968		6	*2000–2001*	23
Dilawar Hussain	19.3.1907	26.8.1967	3	*1933–1936*	
Divecha Ramesh Vithaldas	18.10.1927	11.2.2003	5	*1951–1952*	
Doshi Dilip Rasiklal	22.12.1947		33	*1979–1983*	15
Dravid Rahul (*CY 2000*)	11.1.1973		163†	*1996–2011*	340‡/1
Durani Salim Aziz	11.12.1934		29	*1959–1972*	
Engineer Farokh Maneksha	25.2.1938		46	*1961–1974*	5
Gadkari Chandrasekhar Vaman	3.2.1928	11.1.1998	6	*1952–1954*	
¹**Gaekwad** Anshuman Dattajirao	23.9.1952		40	*1974–1984*	15
¹**Gaekwad** Dattajirao Krishnarao	27.10.1928		11	*1952–1960*	
Gaekwad Hiralal Ghasulal	29.8.1923	2.1.2003	1	*1952*	
Gambhir Gautam	14.10.1981		58	*2004–2016*	147/37
Gandhi Devang Jayant	6.9.1971		4	*1999*	3
Gandotra Ashok	24.11.1948		2	*1969*	
Ganesh Doddanarasiah	30.6.1973		4	*1996*	1
Ganguly Sourav Chandidas	8.7.1972		113	*1996–2008*	308‡
Gavaskar Sunil Manohar (*CY 1980*) . . .	10.7.1949		125	*1970–1986*	108
Ghavri Karsan Devjibhai	28.2.1951		39	*1974–1980*	19
Ghorpade Jayasinghrao Mansinghrao . . .	2.10.1930	29.3.1978	8	*1952–1959*	
Ghulam Ahmed	4.7.1922	28.10.1998	22	*1948–1958*	
Gill Shubman	8.9.1999		10	*2020–2021*	3
Gopalan Morappakam Joysam	6.6.1909	21.12.2003	1	*1933*	
Gopinath Coimbatarao Doraikannu	1.3.1930		8	*1951–1959*	
Guard Ghulam Mustafa	12.12.1925	13.3.1978	2	*1958–1959*	
Guha Subrata	31.1.1946	5.11.2003	4	*1967–1969*	
Gul Mahomed	15.10.1921	8.5.1992	8†	*1946–1952*	
²**Gupte** Balkrishna Pandharinath	30.8.1934	5.7.2005	3	*1960–1964*	
²**Gupte** Subhashchandra Pandharinath ("Fergie") . .	11.12.1929	31.5.2002	36	*1951–1961*	
Gursharan Singh	8.3.1963		1	*1989*	1
Hafeez Abdul (see Kardar)					
Hanumant Singh	29.3.1939	29.11.2006	14	*1963–1969*	
Harbhajan Singh	3.7.1980		103	*1997–2015*	234‡/28
Hardikar Manohar Shankar	8.2.1936	4.2.1995	2	*1958*	
Harvinder Singh	23.12.1977		3	*1997–2001*	16
Hazare Vijay Samuel	11.3.1915	18.12.2004	30	*1946–1952*	
Hindlekar Dattaram Dharmaji	1.1.1909	30.3.1949	4	*1936–1946*	
Hirwani Narendra Deepchand	18.10.1968		17	*1987–1996*	18
Ibrahim Khanmohammad Cassumbhoy . . .	26.1.1919	12.11.2007	4	*1948*	
Indrajitsinhji Kumar Shri	15.6.1937	12.3.1973	4	*1964–1969*	
Irani Jamshed Khudadad	18.8.1923	25.2.1982	2	*1947*	
Iyer Shreyas Santosh	6.12.1994		2	*2021*	22/32
Jadeja Ajaysinhji	1.2.1971		15	*1992–1999*	196
Jadeja Ravindrasinh Anirudhsinh	6.12.1988		57	*2012–2021*	168/55
³**Jahangir Khan** Mohammad	1.2.1910	23.7.1988	4	*1932–1936*	
Jai Laxmidas Purshottamdas	1.4.1902	29.1.1968	1	*1933*	
Jaisimha Motganhalli Laxmanarsu	3.3.1939	6.7.1999	39	*1959–1971*	
Jamshedji Rustomji Jamshedji Dorabji . .	18.11.1892	5.4.1976	1	*1933*	
Jayantilal Hirji Kenia	13.1.1948		1	*1970*	
Johnson David Jude	16.10.1971		2	*1996*	
Joshi Padmanabh Govind	27.10.1926	8.1.1987	12	*1951–1960*	
Joshi Sunil Bandacharya	6.6.1970		15	*1996–2000*	69
Kaif Mohammad	1.12.1980		13	*1999–2005*	125

	Born	Died	Tests	Test Career	O/T
Kambli Vinod Ganpat	18.1.1972		17	*1992–1995*	104
[1] **Kanitkar** Hrishikesh Hemant	14.11.1974		2	*1999*	34
[1] **Kanitkar** Hemant Shamsunder	8.12.1942	9.6.2015	2	*1974*	
Kapil Dev (*CY 1983*)	6.1.1959		131	*1978–1993*	225
Kapoor Aashish Rakesh	25.3.1971		4	*1994–1996*	17
Kardar Abdul Hafeez	17.1.1925	21.4.1996	3†	*1946*	
Karim Syed Saba	14.11.1967		1	*2000*	34
Karthik Krishankumar Dinesh	1.6.1985		26	*2004–2018*	94/31‡
Kartik Murali	11.9.1976		8	*1999–2004*	37/1
Kenny Ramnath Baburao	29.9.1930	21.11.1985	5	*1958–1959*	
Kirmani Syed Mujtaba Hussein	29.12.1949		88	*1975–1985*	49
Kishenchand Gogumal	14.4.1925	16.4.1997	5	*1947–1952*	
Kohli Virat (*CY 2019*)	5.11.1988		99	*2011–2021*	254/95
[2] **Kripal Singh** Amritsar Govindsingh	6.8.1933	22.7.1987	14	*1955–1964*	
Krishnamurthy Pochiah	12.7.1947	28.1.1999	5	*1970*	1
Kulkarni Nilesh Moreshwar	3.4.1973		3	*1997–2000*	10
Kulkarni Rajiv Ramesh	25.9.1962		3	*1986*	10
Kulkarni Umesh Narayan	7.3.1942		4	*1967*	
Kumar Praveen	2.10.1986		6	*2011*	68/10
Kumar Vaman Viswanath	22.6.1935		2	*1960–1961*	
Kumble Anil (*CY 1996*)	17.10.1970		132	*1990–2008*	269‡
Kunderan Budhisagar Krishnappa	2.10.1939	23.6.2006	18	*1959–1967*	
Kuruvilla Abey	8.8.1968		10	*1996–1997*	25
Lall Singh	16.12.1909	19.11.1985	1	*1932*	
Lamba Raman	2.1.1960	22.2.1998	4	*1986–1987*	32
Laxman Vangipurappu Venkata Sai (*CY 2002*)	1.11.1974		134	*1996–2011*	86
Madan Lal	20.3.1951		39	*1974–1986*	67
Maka Ebrahim Suleman	5.3.1922	7.9.1994	2	*1952*	
Malhotra Ashok Omprakash	26.1.1957		7	*1981–1984*	20
Maninder Singh	13.6.1965		35	*1982–1992*	59
[1] **Manjrekar** Sanjay Vijay	12.7.1965		37	*1987–1996*	74
[1] **Manjrekar** Vijay Laxman	26.9.1931	18.10.1983	55	*1951–1964*	
[1] **Mankad** Ashok Vinoo	12.10.1946	1.8.2008	22	*1969–1977*	1
[1] **Mankad** Mulvantrai Himmatlal ("Vinoo") (*CY 1947*)	12.4.1917	21.8.1978	44	*1946–1958*	
Mantri Madhav Krishnaji	1.9.1921	23.5.2014	4	*1951–1954*	
Meherhomji Khershedji Rustomji	9.8.1911	10.2.1982	1	*1936*	
Mehra Vijay Laxman	12.3.1938	25.8.2006	8	*1955–1963*	
Merchant Vijay Madhavji (*CY 1937*)	12.10.1911	27.10.1987	10	*1933–1951*	
Mhambrey Paras Laxmikant	20.6.1972		2	*1996*	3
[2] **Milkha Singh** Amritsar Govindsingh	31.12.1941	10.11.2017	4	*1959–1961*	
Mishra Amit	24.11.1982		22	*2008–2016*	36/10
Mithun Abhimanyu	25.10.1989		4	*2010–2011*	5
Modi Rustomji Sheryar	11.11.1924	17.5.1996	10	*1946–1952*	
Mohammed Shami	3.9.1990		57	*2013–2021*	79/17
Mohanty Debasis Sarbeswar	20.7.1976		2	*1997*	45
Mongia Nayan Ramlal	19.12.1969		44	*1993–2000*	140
More Kiran Shankar	4.9.1962		49	*1986–1993*	94
Muddiah Venkatappa Musandra	8.6.1929	1.10.2009	2	*1959–1960*	
Mukund Abhinav	6.1.1990		7	*2011–2017*	
Mushtaq Ali Syed	17.12.1914	18.6.2005	11	*1933–1951*	
Nadeem Shahbaz	12.8.1989		2	*2019–2020*	
Nadkarni Rameshchandra Gangaram ("Bapu")	4.4.1933	17.1.2020	41	*1955–1967*	
Naik Sudhir Sakharam	21.2.1945		3	*1974–1974*	2
Nair Karun Kaladharan	6.12.1991		6	*2016*	2
Naoomal Jeoomal	17.4.1904	28.7.1980	3	*1932–1933*	
Narasimha Rao Modireddy Venkateshwar	11.8.1954		4	*1978–1979*	
Natarajan Thangarasu	27.5.1991		1	*2020*	2/4
Navle Janardan Gyanoba	7.12.1902	7.9.1979	2	*1932–1933*	
Nayak Surendra Vithal	20.10.1954		2	*1982*	4
[2] **Nayudu** Cottari Kanakaiya (*CY 1933*)	31.10.1895	14.11.1967	7	*1932–1936*	

	Born	Died	Tests	Test Career	O/T
[2]**Nayudu** Cottari Subbanna	18.4.1914	22.11.2002	11	*1933–1951*	
[2]**Nazir Ali** Syed	8.6.1906	18.2.1975	2	*1932–1933*	
Nehra Ashish	29.4.1979		17	*1998–2003*	117‡/27
Nissar Mohammad	1.8.1910	11.3.1963	6	*1932–1936*	
Nyalchand Sukhlal Shah	14.9.1915	3.1.1997	1	*1952*	
Ojha Naman Vijaykumar	20.7.1983		1	*2015*	1/2
Ojha Pragyan Prayish	5.9.1986		24	*2009–2013*	18/6
Pai Ajit Manohar	28.4.1945		1	*1969*	
Palia Phiroze Edulji	5.9.1910	9.9.1981	2	*1932–1936*	
Pandit Chandrakant Sitaram	30.9.1961		5	*1986–1991*	36
Pandya Hardik Himanshu	11.10.1993		11	*2017–2018*	63/54
Pankaj Singh	6.5.1985		2	*2014*	1
Pant Rishabh Rajendra	4.10.1997		28	*2018–2021*	18/41
Parkar Ghulam Ahmed	25.10.1955		1	*1982*	10
Parkar Ramnath Dhondu	31.10.1946	11.8.1999	2	*1972*	
Parsana Dhiraj Devshibhai	2.12.1947		2	*1978*	
Patankar Chandrakant Trimbak	24.11.1930		1	*1955*	
[1]**Pataudi** Iftikhar Ali Khan, Nawab of (*CY 1932*) . .	16.3.1910	5.1.1952	3†	*1946*	
[1]**Pataudi** Mansur Ali Khan, Nawab of (*CY 1968*) . .	5.1.1941	22.9.2011	46	*1961–1974*	
Patel Akshar Rajeshbhai	20.1.1994		5	*2020–2021*	38/15
Patel Brijesh Pursuram	24.11.1952		21	*1974–1977*	10
Patel Jasubhai Motibhai	26.11.1924	12.12.1992	7	*1954–1959*	
Patel Munaf Musa	12.7.1983		13	*2005–2011*	70/3
Patel Parthiv Ajay	9.3.1985		25	*2002–2017*	38/2
Patel Rashid Ghulam Mohammad	1.6.1964		1	*1988*	1
Pathan Irfan Khan	27.10.1984		29	*2003–2007*	120/24
Patiala Maharajah of (Yadavendra Singh)	17.1.1913	17.6.1974	1	*1933*	
Patil Sandeep Madhusudan	18.8.1956		29	*1979–1984*	45
Patil Sadashiv Raoji	10.10.1933	15.9.2020	1	*1955*	
Phadkar Dattatraya Gajanan	10.12.1925	17.3.1985	31	*1947–1958*	
Powar Ramesh Rajaram	20.5.1978		2	*2007*	31
Prabhakar Manoj	15.4.1963		39	*1984–1995*	130
Prasad Bapu Krishnarao Venkatesh	5.8.1969		33	*1996–2001*	161
Prasad Mannava Sri Kanth	24.4.1975		6	*1999*	17
Prasanna Erapalli Anatharao Srinivas	22.5.1940		49	*1961–1978*	
Pujara Cheteshwar Arvind	25.1.1988		95	*2010–2021*	5
Punjabi Pananmal Hotchand	20.9.1921	4.10.2011	5	*1954*	
Rahane Ajinkya Madhukar	6.6.1988		82	*2012–2021*	90/20
Rahul Kannur Lokesh	18.4.1992		43	*2014–2021*	38/56
Rai Singh Kanwar	24.2.1922	12.11.1993	1	*1947*	
Raina Suresh Kumar	27.11.1986		18	*2010–2014*	226/78
Rajinder Pal	18.11.1937	9.5.2018	1	*1963*	
Rajindernath Vijay	7.1.1928	22.11.1989	1	*1952*	
Rajput Lalchand Sitaram	18.12.1961		2	*1985*	4
Raju Sagi Lakshmi Venkatapathy	9.7.1969		28	*1989–2000*	53
Raman Woorkeri Venkat	23.5.1965		11	*1987–1996*	27
Ramaswami Cotar	16.6.1896	1.1990	2	*1936*	
Ramchand Gulabrai Sipahimalani	26.7.1927	8.9.2003	33	*1952–1959*	
Ramesh Sadagoppan	16.10.1975		19	*1998–2001*	24
[2]**Ramji** Ladha	10.2.1900	20.12.1948	1	*1933*	
Rangachari Commandur Rajagopalachari	14.4.1916	9.10.1993	4	*1947–1948*	
Rangnekar Khanderao Moreshwar	27.6.1917	11.10.1984	3	*1947*	
Ranjane Vasant Baburao	22.7.1937	22.12.2011	7	*1958–1964*	
Rathore Vikram	26.3.1969		6	*1996–1996*	7
Ratra Ajay	13.12.1981		6	*2001–2002*	12
Razdan Vivek	25.8.1969		2	*1989*	3
Reddy Bharath	12.11.1954		4	*1979*	3
Rege Madhusudan Ramachandra	18.3.1924	16.12.2013	1	*1948*	
Roy Ambar	5.6.1945	19.9.1997	4	*1969*	
[1]**Roy** Pankaj	31.5.1928	4.2.2001	43	*1951–1960*	

	Born	Died	Tests	Test Career	O/T
¹ **Roy** Pranab	10.2.1957		2	*1981*	
Saha Wriddhiman Prasanta.	24.10.1984		40	*2009–2021*	9
Saini Navdeep	23.11.1992		2	*2020*	8/11
Sandhu Balwinder Singh	3.8.1956		8	*1982–1983*	22
Sanghvi Rahul Laxman	3.9.1974		1	*2000*	10
Sarandeep Singh	21.10.1979		3	*2000–2001*	5
Sardesai Dilip Narayan	8.8.1940	2.7.2007	30	*1961–1972*	
Sarwate Chandrasekhar Trimbak	22.7.1920	23.12.2003	9	*1946–1951*	
Saxena Ramesh Chandra	20.9.1944	16.8.2011	1	*1967*	
Sehwag Virender	20.10.1978		103†	*2001–2012*	241‡/19
Sekhar Thirumalai Ananthapillai	28.3.1956		2	*1982*	4
Sen Probir Kumar ("Khokhan")	31.5.1926	27.1.1970	14	*1947–1952*	
Sengupta Apoorva Kumar	3.8.1939	14.9.2013	1	*1958*	
Sharma Ajay Kumar.	3.4.1964		1	*1987*	31
Sharma Chetan	3.1.1966		23	*1984–1988*	65
Sharma Gopal	3.8.1960		5	*1984–1990*	11
Sharma Ishant	2.9.1988		105	*2007–2021*	80/14
Sharma Karan Vinod	23.10.1987		1	*2014*	2/1
Sharma Parthasarathy Harishchandra	5.1.1948	20.10.2010	5	*1974–1976*	2
Sharma Rohit Gurunath (*CY 2022*)	30.4.1987		43	*2013–2021*	227/119
Sharma Sanjeev Kumar.	25.8.1965		2	*1988–1990*	23
Shastri Ravishankar Jayadritha.	27.5.1962		80	*1980–1992*	150
Shaw Prithvi Pankaj	9.11.1999		5	*2018–2020*	6/1
Shinde Sadashiv Ganpatrao	18.8.1923	22.6.1955	7	*1946–1952*	
Shodhan Roshan Harshadlal ("Deepak")	18.10.1928	16.5.2016	3	*1952*	
Shukla Rakesh Chandra.	4.2.1948	29.6.2019	1	*1982*	
Siddiqui Iqbal Rashid	26.12.1974		1	*2001*	
Sidhu Navjot Singh	20.10.1963		51	*1983–1998*	136
Singh Rabindra Ramanarayan ("Robin") . . .	14.9.1963		1	*1998*	136
Singh Robin	1.1.1970		1	*1998*	
Singh Rudra Pratap	6.12.1985		14	*2005–2011*	58/10
Singh Vikram Rajvir	17.9.1984		5	*2005–2007*	2
Siraj Mohammed	13.3.1994		12	*2020–2021*	1/4
Sivaramakrishnan Laxman	31.12.1965		9	*1982–1985*	16
Sohoni Sriranga Wasudev	5.3.1918	19.5.1993	4	*1946–1951*	
Solkar Eknath Dhondu	18.3.1948	26.6.2005	27	*1969–1976*	7
Sood Man Mohan	6.7.1939	19.1.2020	1	*1959*	
Sreesanth Shanthakumaran	6.2.1983		27	*2005–2011*	53/10
Srikkanth Krishnamachari.	21.12.1959		43	*1981–1991*	146
Srinath Javagal.	31.8.1969		67	*1991–2002*	229
Srinivasan Thirumalai Echambadi	26.10.1950	6.12.2010	1	*1980*	2
Subramanya Venkataraman	16.7.1936		9	*1964–1967*	
Sunderam Gundibail Rama	29.3.1930	20.6.2010	2	*1955*	
Surendranath Raman	4.1.1937	5.5.2012	11	*1958–1960*	
Surti Rusi Framroze	25.5.1936	13.1.2013	26	*1960–1969*	
Swamy Venkatraman Narayan	23.5.1924	1.5.1983	1	*1955*	
Tamhane Narendra Shankar.	4.8.1931	19.3.2002	21	*1954–1960*	
Tarapore Keki Khurshedji.	17.12.1910	15.6.1986	1	*1948*	
Tendulkar Sachin Ramesh (*CY 1997*)	24.4.1973		200	*1989–2013*	463/1
Thakur Shardul Narendra	16.10.1991		7	*2018–2021*	15/24
Umrigar Pahlanji Ratanji ("Polly").	28.3.1926	7.11.2006	59	*1948–1961*	
Unadkat Jaydev Dipakbhai	18.10.1991		1	*2010*	7/10
Vengsarkar Dilip Balwant (*CY 1987*)	6.4.1956		116	*1975–1991*	129
Venkataraghavan Srinivasaraghavan	21.4.1945		57	*1964–1983*	15
Venkataramana Margashayam	24.4.1966		1	*1988*	1
Vihari Gade Hanuma	13.10.1993		13	*2018–2021*	
Vijay Murali.	1.4.1984		61	*2008–2018*	17/9
Vinay Kumar Ranganath.	12.2.1984		1	*2011*	31/9
Viswanath Gundappa Rangnath	12.2.1949		91	*1969–1982*	25
Viswanath Sadanand.	29.11.1962		3	*1985*	22

	Born	Died	Tests	Test Career	O/T
Vizianagram Maharajkumar of (*Sir* Vijaya Anand)	28.12.1905	2.12.1965	3	1936	
Wadekar Ajit Laxman.	1.4.1941	15.8.2018	37	*1966–1974*	2
Washington Sundar M. S.	5.10.1999		4	*2020*	1/31
Wasim Jaffer.	16.2.1978		31	*1999–2007*	2
Wassan Atul Satish.	23.3.1968		4	*1989–1990*	9
[1,2] **Wazir Ali** Syed.	15.9.1903	17.6.1950	7	*1932–1936*	
Yadav Jayant.	22.1.1990		5	*2016–2021*	1
Yadav Kuldeep.	14.12.1994		7	*2016–2020*	65/23
Yadav Nandlal <u>Shivlal</u>.	26.1.1957		35	*1979–1986*	7
Yadav Umeshkumar Tilak	25.10.1987		52	*2011–2021*	75/7
Yadav Vijay.	14.3.1967		1	*1992*	19
Yajurvindra Singh	1.8.1952		4	*1976–1979*	
Yashpal Sharma	11.8.1954	13.7.2021	37	*1979–1983*	42
[1] **Yograj Singh**	25.3.1958		1	*1980*	6
Yohannan Tinu	18.2.1979		3	*2001–2002*	3
[1] **Yuvraj Singh**	12.12.1981		40	*2003–2012*	301‡/58
Zaheer Khan (*CY 2008*)	7.10.1978		92	*2000–2013*	194‡/17

PAKISTAN (246 players)

	Born	Died	Tests	Test Career	O/T
Aamer Malik.	3.1.1963		14	*1987–1994*	24
Aamir Nazir.	2.1.1971		6	*1992–1995*	9
Aamir Sohail.	14.9.1966		47	*1992–1999*	156
Abdul Kadir.	10.5.1944	12.3.2002	4	*1964*	
Abdul Qadir.	15.9.1955	6.9.2019	67	*1977–1990*	104
Abdul Razzaq	2.12.1979		46	*1999–2006*	261‡/32
Abdullah Shafiq	20.11.1999		2	*2021*	0/3
Abdur Rauf	9.12.1978		3	*2009–2009*	4/1
Abdur Rehman	1.3.1980		22	*2007–2014*	31/8
Abid Ali	16.10.1987		16	*2019–2021*	6
[2] **Adnan Akmal**	13.3.1985		21	*2010–2013*	5
Afaq Hussain.	31.12.1939		2	*1961–1964*	
Aftab Baloch	1.4.1953	24.1.2022	2	*1969–1974*	
Aftab Gul	31.3.1946		6	*1968–1971*	
Agha Saadat Ali	21.6.1929	25.10.1995	1	*1955*	
Agha Zahid	7.1.1953		1	*1974*	
Ahmed Shehzad.	23.11.1991		13	*2013–2016*	81/59
Aizaz Cheema	5.9.1979		7	*2011–2012*	14/5
Akram Raza	22.11.1964		9	*1989–1994*	49
Ali Hussain Rizvi	6.1.1974		1	*1997*	
Ali Naqvi	19.3.1977		5	*1997*	
Alim-ud-Din.	15.12.1930	12.7.2012	25	*1954–1962*	
Amir Elahi	1.9.1908	28.12.1980	5†	*1952*	
Anil Dalpat	20.9.1963		9	*1983–1984*	15
Anwar Hussain	16.7.1920	9.10.2002	4	*1952*	
Anwar Khan	24.12.1955		1	*1978*	
Aqib Javed	5.8.1972		22	*1988–1998*	163
Arif Butt	17.5.1944	10.7.2007	3	*1964*	
Arshad Khan	22.3.1971		9	*1997–2004*	58
Asad Shafiq	28.1.1986		77	*2010–2020*	60/10
Ashfaq Ahmed.	6.6.1973		1	*1993*	3
Ashraf Ali	22.4.1958		8	*1981–1987*	16
Asif Iqbal (*CY 1968*).	6.6.1943		58	*1964–1979*	10
Asif Masood	23.1.1946		16	*1968–1976*	7
Asif Mujtaba	4.11.1967		25	*1986–1996*	66
Asim Kamal	31.5.1976		12	*2003–2005*	
Ata-ur-Rehman	28.3.1975		13	*1992–1996*	30
Atif Rauf	3.3.1964		1	*1993*	
Atiq-uz-Zaman	20.7.1975		1	*1999*	3

	Born	Died	Tests	Test Career	O/T
Azam Khan	1.3.1969		1	*1996*	6
Azeem Hafeez	29.7.1963		18	*1983–1984*	15
Azhar Ali	19.2.1985		91	*2010–2021*	53
Azhar Khan	7.9.1955		1	*1979*	
Azhar Mahmood	28.2.1975		21	*1997–2001*	143
² Azmat Rana	3.11.1951	30.5.2015	1	*1979*	2
Babar Azam	15.10.1994		37	*2016–2021*	83/73
Basit Ali	13.12.1970		19	*1992–1995*	50
³ Bazid Khan	25.3.1981		1	*2004*	5
Bilal Asif	24.9.1985		5	*2018*	3
Bilawal Bhatti	17.9.1991		2	*2013*	10/9
Danish Kaneria	16.12.1980		61	*2000–2010*	18
D'Souza Antao	17.1.1939		6	*1958–1962*	
Ehsan Adil	15.3.1993		3	*2012–2015*	6
Ehtesham-ud-Din	4.9.1950		5	*1979–1982*	
Fahim Ashraf	16.1.1994		13	*2018–2021*	31/42
Faisal Iqbal	30.12.1981		26	*2000–2009*	18
Fakhar Zaman	10.4.1990		3	*2018*	53/64
Farhan Adil	25.9.1977		1	*2003*	
Farooq Hamid	3.3.1945		1	*1964*	
Farrukh Zaman	2.4.1956		1	*1976*	
Fawad Alam	8.10.1985		15	*2009–2021*	38/24
Fazal Mahmood (*CY 1955*)	18.2.1927	30.5.2005	34	*1952–1962*	
Fazl-e-Akbar	20.10.1980		5	*1997–2003*	2
Ghazali Mohammad Ebrahim Zainuddin	15.6.1924	26.4.2003	2	*1954*	
Ghulam Abbas	1.5.1947		1	*1967*	
Gul Mohomed	15.10.1921	8.5.1992	1†	*1956*	
¹,² Hanif Mohammad (*CY 1968*)	21.12.1934	11.8.2016	55	*1952–1969*	
Haris Sohail	9.1.1989		16	*2017–2020*	42/14
Haroon Rashid	25.3.1953		23	*1976–1982*	12
Hasan Ali	7.2.1994		17	*2016–2021*	57/48
Hasan Raza	11.3.1982		7	*1996–2005*	16
Haseeb Ahsan	15.7.1939	8.3.2013	12	*1957–1961*	
² Humayun Farhat	24.1.1981		1	*2000*	5
Ibadulla Khalid ("Billy")	20.12.1935		4	*1964–1967*	
Iftikhar Ahmed	3.9.1990		3	*2016–2019*	7/17
Iftikhar Anjum	1.12.1980		1	*2005*	62/2
Ijaz Ahmed snr	20.9.1968		60	*1986–2000*	250
Ijaz Ahmed jnr	2.2.1969		2	*1995*	2
Ijaz Butt	10.3.1938		8	*1958–1962*	
Ijaz Faqih	24.3.1956		5	*1980–1987*	27
Imam-ul-Haq	12.12.1995		11	*2018–2019*	46/2
Imran Butt	27.12.1995		6	*2020–2021*	
² Imran Farhat	20.5.1982		40	*2000–2012*	58/7
Imran Khan (*CY 1983*)	25.11.1952		88	*1971–1991*	175
Mohammad Imran Khan	15.7.1987		10	*2014–2019*	
Imran Nazir	16.12.1981		8	*1998–2002*	79/25
Imtiaz Ahmed	5.1.1928	31.12.2016	41	*1952–1962*	
Intikhab Alam	28.12.1941		47	*1959–1976*	
Inzamam-ul-Haq	3.3.1970		119†	*1992–2007*	375‡/1
Iqbal Qasim	6.8.1953		50	*1976–1988*	15
Irfan Fazil	2.11.1981		1	*1999*	1
Israr Ali	1.5.1927	1.2.2016	4	*1952–1959*	
Jalal-ud-Din	12.6.1959		6	*1982–1985*	8
Javed Akhtar	21.11.1940	8.7.2016	1	*1962*	
Javed Burki	8.5.1938		25	*1960–1969*	
Javed Miandad (*CY 1982*)	12.6.1957		124	*1976–1993*	233
Junaid Khan	24.12.1989		22	*2011–2015*	76/9
Kabir Khan	12.4.1974		4	*1994*	10
² Kamran Akmal	13.1.1982		53	*2002–2010*	157/58

	Born	Died	Tests	Test Career	O/T
Kardar Abdul Hafeez	17.1.1925	21.4.1996	23†	*1952–1957*	
Khalid Hassan	14.7.1937	3.12.2013	1	*1954*	
¹ **Khalid Wazir**	27.4.1936	27.6.2020	2	*1954*	
Khan Mohammad	1.1.1928	4.7.2009	13	*1952–1957*	
Khurram Manzoor	10.6.1986		16	*2008–2014*	7/3
Liaqat Ali	21.5.1955		5	*1974–1978*	3
Mahmood Hussain	2.4.1932	25.12.1992	27	*1952–1962*	
³ **Majid** Jahangir **Khan** (*CY 1970*) . . .	28.9.1946		63	*1964–1982*	23
Mansoor Akhtar	25.12.1957		19	*1980–1989*	41
² **Manzoor Elahi**	15.4.1963		6	*1984–1994*	54
Maqsood Ahmed	26.3.1925	4.1.1999	16	*1952–1955*	
Masood Anwar	12.12.1967		1	*1990*	
Mathias Wallis	4.2.1935	1.9.1994	21	*1955–1962*	
Mir Hamza	10.9.1992		1	*2018*	
Miran Bux	20.4.1907	8.2.1991	2	*1954*	
Misbah-ul-Haq (*CY 2017*)	28.5.1974		75	*2000–2016*	162/39
Mohammad Abbas	10.3.1990		25	*2016–2021*	3
Mohammad Akram	10.9.1974		9	*1995–2000*	23
Mohammad Amir (formerly Mohammad Aamer)	13.4.1992		36	*2009–2018*	61/50
Mohammad Asif	20.12.1982		23	*2004–2010*	35‡/11
Mohammad Aslam Khokhar	5.1.1920	22.1.2011	1	*1954*	
Mohammad Ayub	13.9.1979		1	*2012*	
Mohammad Farooq	8.4.1938		7	*1960–1964*	
Mohammad Hafeez	17.10.1980		55	*2003–2018*	218/119
Mohammad Hussain	8.10.1976		2	*1996–1998*	14
Mohammad Ilyas	19.3.1946		10	*1964–1968*	
Mohammad Irfan	6.6.1982		4	*2012–2013*	60/22
Mohammad Khalil	11.11.1982		2	*2004*	3
Mohammad Munaf	2.11.1935	28.1.2020	4	*1959–1961*	
Mohammad Nawaz	21.3.1994		3	*2016*	16/30
Mohammad Nazir	8.3.1946		14	*1969–1983*	4
Mohammad Ramzan	25.12.1970		1	*1997*	
Mohammad Rizwan (*CY 2021*)	1.6.1992		19	*2016–2021*	41/55
Mohammad Salman	7.8.1981		2	*2010*	7/1
Mohammad Sami	24.2.1981		36	*2000–2012*	87/13
Mohammad Talha	15.10.1988		4	*2008–2014*	3
Mohammad Wasim	8.8.1977		18	*1996–2000*	25
Mohammad Yousuf (*CY 2007*)					
(formerly Yousuf Youhana)	27.8.1974		90	*1997–2010*	281‡/3
Mohammad Zahid	2.8.1976		5	*1996–2002*	11
Mohsin Kamal	16.6.1963		9	*1983–1994*	19
Mohsin Khan	15.3.1955		48	*1977–1986*	75
² **Moin Khan**	23.9.1971		69	*1990–2004*	219
¹ **Mudassar Nazar**	6.4.1956		76	*1976–1988*	122
Mufasir-ul-Haq	16.8.1944	27.7.1983	1	*1964*	
Munir Malik	10.7.1934	30.11.2012	3	*1959–1962*	
Musa Khan	20.8.2000		1	*2019*	2/2
Mushtaq Ahmed (*CY 1997*)	28.6.1970		52	*1989–2003*	144
² **Mushtaq Mohammad** (*CY 1963*) . . .	22.11.1943		57	*1958–1978*	10
Nadeem Abbasi	15.4.1964		3	*1989*	
Nadeem Ghauri	12.10.1962		1	*1989*	6
² **Nadeem Khan**	10.12.1969		2	*1992–1998*	2
Naseem Shah	15.2.2003		9	*2019–2020*	
Nasim-ul-Ghani	14.5.1941		29	*1957–1972*	1
Nasir Jamshed	6.12.1989		2	*2012*	48/18
Nauman Ali	7.10.1986		7	*2020–2021*	
Naushad Ali	1.10.1943		6	*1964*	
Naved Anjum	27.7.1963		2	*1989–1990*	13
Naved Ashraf	4.9.1974		2	*1998–1999*	
Naved Latif	21.2.1976		1	*2001*	11

	Born	Died	Tests	Test Career	O/T
Naved-ul-Hasan.	28.2.1978		9	2004–2006	74/4
¹ Nazar Mohammad.	5.3.1921	12.7.1996	5	1952	
Niaz Ahmed.	11.11.1945	12.4.2000	2	1967–1968	
² Pervez Sajjad.	30.8.1942		19	1964–1972	
Qaiser Abbas.	7.5.1982		1	2000	
Qasim Omar.	9.2.1957		26	1983–1986	31
Rahat Ali.	12.9.1988		21	2012–2018	14
² Ramiz Raja.	14.8.1962		57	1983–1996	198
Rashid Khan.	15.12.1959		4	1981–1984	29
Rashid Latif.	14.10.1968		37	1992–2003	166
Rehman Sheikh Fazalur.	11.6.1935		1	1957	
² Riaz Afridi.	21.1.1985		1	2004	
Rizwan-uz-Zaman.	4.9.1961		11	1981–1988	3
³ Sadiq Mohammad.	3.5.1945		41	1969–1980	19
² Saeed Ahmed.	1.10.1937		41	1957–1972	
Saeed Ajmal.	14.10.1977		35	2009–2014	113/64
Saeed Anwar (CY 1997).	6.9.1968		55	1990–2001	247
Sajid Khan.	3.9.1993		4	2020–2021	
Salah-ud-Din.	14.2.1947		5	1964–1969	
Saleem Jaffer.	19.11.1962		14	1986–1991	39
Salim Altaf.	19.4.1944		21	1967–1978	6
² Salim Elahi.	21.11.1976		13	1995–2002	48
Salim Malik (CY 1988).	16.4.1963		103	1981–1998	283
Salim Yousuf.	7.12.1959		32	1981–1990	86
Salman Butt.	7.10.1984		33	2003–2010	78/24
Sami Aslam.	12.12.1995		13	2014–2017	4
Saqlain Mushtaq (CY 2000).	29.12.1976		49	1995–2003	169
Sarfraz Ahmed.	22.5.1987		49	2009–2018	117/61
Sarfraz Nawaz.	1.12.1948		55	1968–1983	45
Shabbir Ahmed.	21.4.1976		10	2003–2005	32/1
Shadab Kabir.	12.11.1977		5	1996–2001	3
Shadab Khan.	4.10.1998		6	2016–2020	48/64
Shafiq Ahmed.	28.3.1949		6	1974–1980	3
² Shafqat Rana.	10.8.1943		5	1964–1969	
³ Shaheen Shah Afridi.	6.4.2000		21	2018–2021	28/39
Shahid Afridi.	1.3.1980		27	1998–2010	393‡/98‡
Shahid Israr.	1.3.1950	29.4.2013	1	1976	
Shahid Mahboob.	25.8.1962		1	1989	10
Shahid Mahmood.	17.3.1939	13.12.2020	1	1962	
Shahid Nazir.	4.12.1977		15	1996–2006	17
Shahid Saeed.	6.1.1966		1	1989	10
Shakeel Ahmed snr.	12.2.1966		1	1998	
Shakeel Ahmed jnr.	12.11.1971		3	1992–1994	2
Shan Masood.	14.10.1989		25	2013–2020	5
Sharjeel Khan.	14.8.1989		1	2016	25/21
Sharpe Duncan Albert.	3.8.1937		3	1959	
Shoaib Akhtar.	13.8.1975		46	1997–2007	158‡/15
Shoaib Malik.	1.2.1982		35	2001–2015	287/123‡
¹ Shoaib Mohammad.	8.1.1961		45	1983–1995	63
Shuja-ud-Din Butt.	10.4.1930	7.2.2006	19	1954–1961	
Sikander Bakht.	25.8.1957		26	1976–1982	27
Sohail Khan.	6.3.1984		9	2008–2016	13/5
Sohail Tanvir.	12.12.1984		2	2007	62/57
Tabish Khan.	12.12.1984		1	2020	
Tahir Naqqash.	6.6.1959		15	1981–1984	40
Talat Ali Malik.	29.5.1950		10	1972–1978	
Tanvir Ahmed.	20.12.1978		5	2010–2012	2/1
Taslim Arif.	1.5.1954	13.3.2008	6	1979–1980	2
Taufeeq Umar.	20.6.1981		44	2001–2014	22
Tauseef Ahmed.	10.5.1958		34	1979–1993	70

	Born	Died	Tests	Test Career	O/T
[2]Umar Akmal	26.5.1990		16	2009–2011	121/84
Umar Amin	16.10.1989		4	2010	16/14
Umar Gul	14.4.1984		47	2003–2012	130/60
Usman Salahuddin	2.12.1990		1	2018	2
Usman Shinwari	1.5.1994		1	2019	17/16
Wahab Riaz	28.6.1985		27	2010–2018	91/36
Wajahatullah Wasti	11.11.1974		6	1998–1999	15
[2]Waqar Hasan	12.9.1932	10.2.2020	21	1952–1959	
Waqar Younis (CY 1992)	16.11.1971		87	1989–2002	262
Wasim Akram (CY 1993)	3.6.1966		104	1984–2001	356
Wasim Bari	23.3.1948		81	1967–1983	51
[2]Wasim Raja	3.7.1952	23.8.2006	57	1972–1984	54
[2]Wazir Mohammad	22.12.1929		20	1952–1959	
Yasir Ali	15.10.1985		1	2003	
Yasir Arafat	12.3.1982		3	2007–2008	11/13
Yasir Hameed	28.2.1978		25	2003–2010	56
Yasir Shah	2.5.1986		46	2014–2021	25/2
[2]Younis Ahmed	20.10.1947		4	1969–1986	2
Younis Khan (CY 2017)	29.11.1977		118	1999–2016	265/25
Yousuf Youhana (see Mohammad Yousuf)					
Zafar Gohar	1.2.1995		1	2020	1
Zaheer Abbas (CY 1972)	24.7.1947		78	1969–1985	62
Zahid Fazal	10.11.1973		9	1990–1995	9
[2]Zahoor Elahi	1.3.1971		2	1996	14
Zakir Khan	3.4.1963		2	1985–1989	17
Zulfiqar Ahmed	22.11.1926	3.10.2008	9	1952–1956	
Zulfiqar Babar	10.12.1978		15	2013–2016	5/7
Zulqarnain	25.5.1962		3	1985	16
Zulqarnain Haider	23.4.1986		1	2010	4/3

SRI LANKA (157 players)

	Born	Died	Tests	Test Career	O/T
Ahangama Franklyn Saliya	14.9.1959		3	1985	1
Amalean Kaushik Naginda	7.4.1965		2	1985–1987	8
Amerasinghe Amerasinghe Mudalige Jayantha Gamini	2.2.1954		2	1983	
Amerasinghe Merenna Koralage Don Ishara	5.3.1978		1	2007	8
Anurasiri Sangarange Don	25.2.1966		18	1985–1997	45
Arnold Russel Premakumaran	25.10.1973		44	1996–2004	180/1
Asalanka Kariyawasam Indipalage Charith	29.6.1997		1	2021	8/9
Atapattu Marvan Samson	22.11.1970		90	1990–2007	268/2
Bandara Herath Mudiyanselage Charitha Malinga	31.12.1979		8	1997–2005	31/4
Bandaratilleke Mapa Rallage Chandima Niroshan	16.5.1975		7	1997–2001	3
Chameera Pathira Vasan Dushmantha	11.1.1992		12	2015–2021	37/39
Chandana Umagiliya Durage Upul	7.5.1972		16	1998–2004	147
Chandimal Lokuge Dinesh	18.11.1989		64	2011–2021	150/61
Dananjaya Akila (Mahamarakkala Kurukulasooriya Patabendige Akila Dananjaya Perera)	4.10.1993		6	2017–2019	39/31
Dassanayake Pubudu Bathiya	11.7.1970		11	1993–1994	16
de Alwis Ronald Guy	15.2.1959	12.1.2013	11	1982–1987	31
de Mel Ashantha Lakdasa Francis	9.5.1959		17	1981–1986	57
de Saram Samantha Indika	2.9.1973		4	1999	15/1
de Silva Ashley Matthew	3.12.1963		3	1992–1993	4
de Silva Dhananjaya Maduranga	6.9.1991		38	2016–2021	56/23
de Silva Dandeniyage Somachandra	11.6.1942		12	1981–1984	41
de Silva Ellawalakanakanamge Asoka Ranjit	28.3.1956		10	1985–1990	28
de Silva Ginigalgodage Ramba Ajit	12.12.1952		4	1981–1982	6
de Silva Karunakalage Sajeewa Chanaka	11.1.1971		8	1996–1998	38
de Silva Pinnaduwage Aravinda (CY 1996)	17.10.1965		93	1984–2002	308

	Born	Died	Tests	Test Career	O/T
de Silva Pinnaduwage <u>Wanindu Hasaranga</u>	29.7.1997		4	*2020*	29/33
de Silva Sanjeewa Kumara <u>Lanka</u>	29.7.1975		3	*1997*	11
de Silva Weddikkara Ruwan <u>Sujeewa</u>	7.10.1979		3	*2002–2007*	
Dharmasena Handunnettige Deepthi Priyantha Kumar	24.4.1971		31	*1993–2003*	141
Dias Roy Luke	18.10.1952		20	*1981–1986*	58
Dickwella Dickwella Patabandige Dilantha <u>Niroshan</u>	23.6.1993		45	*2014–2020*	53/28
Dilshan Tillekeratne Mudiyanselage	14.10.1976		87	*1999–2012*	330/80
Dunusinghe Chamara Iroshan.	19.10.1970		5	*1994–1995*	1
Embuldeniya Lasith	20.10.1996		13	*2018–2021*	
Eranga Ranaweera Mudiyanselage <u>Shaminda</u>....	23.6.1986		19	*2011–2016*	19/3
Fernando Asitha Madusanka	31.7.1997		3	*2020*	4
Fernando Aththachchi <u>Nuwan Pradeep</u> Roshan ..	19.10.1986		28	*2011–2017*	47/16
Fernando Bodiyabaduge <u>Oshada</u> Piumal	15.4.1992		13	*2018–2021*	8/7
Fernando Congenige Randhi <u>Dilhara</u>	19.7.1979		40	*2000–2012*	146‡/18
Fernando Ellekutige Rufus Nemesion <u>Susil</u>	19.12.1955		5	*1982–1983*	7
Fernando Kandana Arachchige <u>Dinusha</u> Manoj ..	10.8.1979		2	*2003*	1
Fernando Kandage <u>Hasantha</u> Ruwan Kumara....	14.10.1979		2	*2002*	7
Fernando Muthuthanthrige <u>Vishwa</u> Thilina	18.9.1991		14	*2016–2020*	8/1
Fernando Thudellage <u>Charitha</u> Buddhika.......	22.8.1980		9	*2001–2002*	17
Gallage Indika Sanjeewa	22.11.1975		1	*1999*	3
Gamage Panagamuwa <u>Lahiru</u> Sampath	5.4.1988		5	*2017–2018*	9
Goonatillake Hettiarachige <u>Mahes</u>	16.8.1952		5	*1981–1982*	6
Gunaratne Downdegedara <u>Asela</u> Sampath	8.1.1986		6	*2016–2017*	31/12
Gunasekera Yohan.	8.11.1957		2	*1982*	3
Gunathilleke Mashtayage <u>Dhanushka</u>	17.03.1991		8	*2017–2018*	44/30
Gunawardene Dihan <u>Avishka</u>	26.5.1977		6	*1998–2005*	61
Guneratne Roshan Punyajith Wijesinghe.	26.1.1962	21.7.2005	1	*1982*	
Gurusinha Asanka Pradeep	16.9.1966		41	*1985–1996*	147
Hathurusinghe Upul <u>Chandika</u>.	13.9.1968		26	*1990–1998*	35
Herath Herath Mudiyanselage <u>Rangana</u> Keerthi Bandara	19.3.1978		93	*1999–2018*	71/17
Hettiarachchi Dinuka Sulaksana	15.7.1976		1	*2000*	
Jayasekera Rohan Stanley Amarasiriwardene ...	7.12.1957		1	*1981*	2
Jayasundera Madurawelage Don <u>Udara</u> Supeksha	3.1.1991		2	*2015*	
Jayasuriya Sanath Teran (*CY 1997*)	30.6.1969		110	*1990–2007*	441‡/31
Jayawardene Denagamage Proboth <u>Mahela</u> de Silva (*CY 2007*)	27.5.1977		149	*1997–2014*	443‡/55
Jayawardene Hewasandatchige Asiri <u>Prasanna</u> Wishvanath.	9.10.1979		58	*2000–2014*	6
Jayawickrama Perumapperuma Arachchige Kaveesha <u>Praveen</u>	30.9.1998		3	*2020–2021*	5/1
Jeganathan Sridharan	11.7.1951	14.5.1996	2	*1982*	5
John Vinothen Bede	27.5.1960		6	*1982–1984*	45
Jurangpathy Baba <u>Roshan</u>.	25.6.1967		2	*1985–1986*	
Kalavitigoda Shantha	23.12.1977		1	*2004*	
Kalpage Ruwan Senani	19.2.1970		11	*1993–1998*	86
Kaluhalamulla H. K. S. R. (*see* Randiv, Suraj)					
[2] **Kaluperuma** Lalith Wasantha Silva	25.6.1949		2	*1981*	4
[2] **Kaluperuma** Sanath Mohan Silva.	22.10.1961		4	*1983–1987*	2
Kaluwitharana Romesh Shantha	24.11.1969		49	*1992–2004*	189
Kapugedera Chamara Kantha	24.2.1987		8	*2006–2009*	102/43
Karunaratne Chamika	29.5.1996		1	*2018*	10/14
Karunaratne Frank <u>Dimuth</u> Madushanka	28.4.1988		74	*2012–2021*	34
Kaushal Paskuwal Handi <u>Tharindu</u>	5.3.1993		7	*2014–2015*	1
Kulasekara Chamith <u>Kosala</u> Bandara	15.7.1985		1	*2011*	4
Kulasekara Kulasekara Mudiyanselage Dinesh <u>Nuwan</u>	22.7.1982		21	*2004–2014*	184/58
Kumara Chandradasa Brahmammana Ralalage <u>Lahiru</u> Sudesh........................	13.2.1997		23	*2016–2020*	13/14
Kuruppu Don Sardha <u>Brendon</u> Priyantha.	5.1.1962		4	*1986–1991*	54

	Born	Died	Tests	Test Career	O/T
Kuruppuarachchi Ajith *Kosala*	1.11.1964		2	*1985–1986*	
Labrooy Graeme Fredrick	7.6.1964		9	*1986–1990*	44
Lakmal Ranasinghe Arachchige *Suranga*	10.3.1987		68	*2010–2021*	86/11
Lakshitha Materba Kanatha <u>Gamage</u> Chamila Premanath.	4.1.1979		2	*2002–2002*	7
Liyanage Dulip Kapila	6.6.1972		9	*1992–2001*	16
Lokuarachchi Kaushal Samaraweera	20.5.1982		4	*2003–2003*	21/2
Madugalle Ranjan Senerath	22.4.1959		21	*1981–1988*	63
Madurasinghe Madurasinghe Arachchige Wijayasiri <u>Ranjith</u>	30.1.1961		3	1988–1992	12
Mahanama Roshan Siriwardene	31.5.1966		52	*1985–1997*	213
Maharoof Mohamed *Farveez*	7.9.1984		22	*2003–2011*	109/8
Malinga Separamadu *Lasith*	28.8.1983		30	*2004–2010*	226/84
Mathews Angelo Davis *(CY 2015)*	2.6.1987		92	*2009–2021*	218/78
Mendis Balapuwaduge <u>Ajantha</u> Winslo	11.3.1985		19	2008–2014	87/39
Mendis Balapuwaduge <u>Kusal</u> Gimhan	2.2.1995		47	*2015–2020*	79/29
Mendis Louis Rohan *Duleep*	25.8.1952		24	*1981–1988*	79
Mirando Magina *Thilan Thushara*.	1.3.1981		10	*2003–2010*	38/6
Mubarak Jehan	10.1.1981		13	*2002–2015*	40/16
Muralitharan Muttiah *(CY 1999)*	17.4.1972		132†	*1992–2010*	343½/12
Nawaz Mohamed *Naveed*	20.9.1973		1	2002	3
Nissanka Pathum (<u>Pathum Nissanka</u> Silva).	18.5.1998		6	*2020–2021*	9/12
Nissanka Ratnayake Arachchige <u>Prabath</u>	25.10.1980		4	2003	23
Paranavitana Nishad *Tharanga*	15.4.1982		32	*2008–2012*	
Perera Anhettige Suresh Asanka.	16.2.1978		3	1998–2001	20
Perera Mahawaduge <u>Dilruwan</u> Kamalaneth	22.7.1982		43	*2013–2020*	13/3
Perera Mathurage Don <u>Kusal</u> Janith	17.8.1990		22	*2015–2020*	107/60
Perera M. K. P. A. D. (*see* Dananjaya, Akila)					
Perera Narangoda Liyanaarachchilage <u>Tissara</u> Chirantha	3.4.1989		6	2011–2012	166/80‡
Perera Panagodage Don <u>Ruchira</u> Laksiri	6.4.1977		8	1998–2002	19/2
Prasad Kariyawasam Tirana Gamage <u>Dammika</u> . .	30.5.1983		25	*2008–2015*	24/1
Prasanna Seekkuge	27.6.1985		1	*2011*	40/20
Pushpakumara Karuppiahyage <u>Ravindra</u>	21.7.1975		23	*1994–2001*	31
Pushpakumara Paulage <u>Malinda</u>	24.3.1987		4	*2017–2018*	2
Rajitha Chandrasekara Arachchile <u>Kasun</u>	1.6.1993		9	2018–2020	10/10
Ramanayake Champaka Priyadarshana Hewage .	8.1.1965		18	*1987–1993*	62
Ramyakumara <u>Wijekoon</u> Mudiyanselage *Gayan* .	21.12.1976		2	2005	0/3
Ranasinghe Anura Nandana.	13.10.1956	9.11.1998	2	*1981–1982*	9
Ranasinghe <u>Minod</u> Bhanuka	29.4.1995		1	*2020*	6/5
² **Ranatunga** Arjuna *(CY 1999)*.	1.12.1963		93	*1981–2000*	269
² **Ranatunga** Dammika	12.10.1962		2	1989	4
² **Ranatunga** Sanjeeva	25.4.1969		9	*1994–1996*	13
Randiv Suraj (Hewa Kaluhalamullage <u>Suraj</u> Randiv Kaluhalamulla; formerly M. M. M. Suraj)	30.1.1985		12	*2010–2012*	31/7
Ratnayake Rumesh Joseph	2.1.1964		23	*1982–1991*	70
Ratnayake Joseph <u>Ravindran</u>	2.5.1960		22	*1981–1989*	78
Samarasekera Maitipage <u>Athula</u> Rohitha	5.8.1961		4	*1988–1991*	39
² **Samaraweera** Dulip Prasanna	12.2.1972		7	*1993–1994*	5
² **Samaraweera** Thilan Thusara	22.9.1976		81	*2001–2012*	53
Samarawickrama Wedagedara <u>Sadeera</u> Rashen .	30.8.1995		4	*2017*	7/9
Sandakan Paththamperuma Arachchige Don Lakshan Rangika	10.6.1991		11	*2016–2018*	31/20
Sangakkara Kumar Chokshanada *(CY 2012)*	27.10.1977		134	*2000–2015*	397½/56
Senanayake Charith Panduka	19.12.1962		3	1990	7
Senanayake Senanayake Mudiyanselage <u>Sachithra</u> Madhushanka	9.2.1985		1	*2013*	49/24
Shanaka Madagamagamage <u>Dasun</u>.	9.9.1991		6	2016–2020	34/57
Silva Athege <u>Roshen</u> Shivanka	17.11.1988		12	*2017–2018*	
Silva Jayan *Kaushal*.	27.5.1986		39	*2011–2018*	
Silva Kelaniyage *Jayantha*	2.6.1973		7	*1995–1997*	1

	Born	Died	Tests	Test Career	O/T
Silva Lindamlilage Prageeth <u>Chamara</u>	14.12.1979		11	*2006–2007*	75/16
Silva P. N. (*see* Nissanka, Pathum)					
Silva Sampathawaduge <u>Amal</u> Rohitha	12.12.1960		9	*1982–1988*	20
Siriwardene Tissa Appuhamilage <u>Milinda</u> . .	4.12.1985		5	*2015–2016*	27/22
Tharanga Warushavithana <u>Upul</u>	2.2.1985		31	*2005–2017*	234‡/26
Thirimanne Hettige Don Rumesh <u>Lahiru</u> . . .	8.9.1989		42	*2011–2020*	127/26
Tillekeratne Hashan Prasantha.	14.7.1967		83	*1989–2003*	200
Udawatte Mahela Lakmal	19.7.1986		2	2018	9/8
Upashantha Kalutarage <u>Eric</u> Amila.	10.6.1972		2	*1998–2002*	12
Vaas Warnakulasuriya Patabendige Ushantha					
Joseph <u>Chaminda</u>.	27.1.1974		111	*1994–2009*	321‡/6
Vandort Michael Graydon	19.11.1980		20	*2001–2008*	1
Vithanage Kasun Disi <u>Kithuruwan</u>	26.2.1991		10	*2012–2015*	6/3
Wanigamuni <u>Ramesh</u> Tarinda <u>Mendis</u>.	7.7.1995		4	*2020–2021*	3/2
Warnapura Bandula.	1.3.1953	18.10.2021	4	*1981–1982*	12
Warnapura Shalith <u>Malinda</u>	26.5.1979		14	*2007–2009*	3
Warnaweera Kahakatchchi Patabandige <u>Jayananda</u> . .	23.11.1960		10	*1985–1994*	6
Weerasinghe Colombage Don Udesh <u>Sanjeewa</u> . .	1.3.1968		1	*1985*	
Welagedara Uda Walawwe Mahim Bandaralage					
<u>Chanaka</u> Asanka	20.3.1981		21	*2007–2014*	10/2
² **Wettimuny** Mithra de Silva	11.6.1951	20.1.2019	2	*1982*	1
² **Wettimuny** Sidath (*CY 1985*).	12.8.1956		23	*1981–1986*	35
Wickremasinghe Anguppulige <u>Gamini</u> Dayantha .	27.12.1965		3	*1989–1992*	4
Wickremasinghe Gallage <u>Pramodya</u>	14.8.1971		40	*1991–2000*	134
Wijegunawardene Kapila Indaka Weerakkody . .	23.11.1964		2	*1991–1991*	26
Wijesuriya Roger Gerard Christopher Ediriweera .	18.2.1960		4	*1981–1985*	8
Wijetunge Piyal Kashyapa.	6.8.1971		1	1993	
Zoysa Demuni <u>Nuwan</u> Tharanga.	13.5.1978		30	*1996–2004*	9

ZIMBABWE (120 players)

	Born	Died	Tests	Test Career	O/T
Arnott Kevin John	8.3.1961		4	*1992*	13
Blignaut Arnoldus Mauritius ("Andy")	1.8.1978		19	*2000–2005*	54/1
Brain David Hayden	4.10.1964		9	*1992–1994*	23
Brandes Eddo André.	5.3.1963		10	*1992–1999*	59
Brent Gary Bazil.	13.1.1976		4	*1999–2001*	70/3
Briant Gavin Aubrey.	11.4.1969		1	*1992*	5
Bruk-Jackson Glen Keith	25.4.1969		2	*1993*	1
Burl Ryan Ponsonby	15.4.1994		3	*2017–2020*	21/34
Burmester Mark Greville	24.1.1968		3	*1992*	8
Butchart Iain Peter	9.5.1960		1	*1994*	20
Campbell Alistair Douglas Ross	23.9.1972		60	*1992–2002*	188
Carlisle Stuart Vance.	10.5.1972		37	*1994–2005*	111
Chakabva Regis Wiriranai.	20.9.1987		22	*2011–2021*	47/26
Chari Brian Bara	14.2.1992		7	*2014–2018*	14/3
Chatara Tendai Larry	28.2.1991		9	*2012–2018*	73/30
Chibhabha Chamunorwa Justice	6.9.1986		3	*2016–2017*	107/36
Chigumbura Elton	14.3.1986		14	*2003–2014*	210‡/57
Chinouya Michael Tawanda.	9.6.1986		2	*2016*	2
Chisoro Tendai Sam	12.2.1988		3	*2017–2020*	21/14
Coventry Charles Kevin	8.3.1983		2	*2005*	39/13
Cremer Alexander <u>Graeme</u>	19.9.1986		19	*2004–2017*	96/29
Crocker Gary John	16.5.1962		3	*1992*	6
Dabengwa Keith Mbusi.	17.8.1980		2	*2005*	37/8
Dekker Mark Hamilton	5.12.1969		14	*1993–1996*	23
Duffin Terrence	20.3.1982		2	*2005*	23
Ebrahim Dion Digby	7.8.1980		29	*2000–2005*	82
² **Ervine** Craig Richard.	19.8.1985		18	*2011–2019*	99/34
² **Ervine** Sean Michael.	6.12.1982		5	*2003–2003*	42

	Born	Died	Tests	Test Career	O/T
Evans Craig Neil.	29.11.1969		3	1996–2003	53
Ewing Gavin Mackie.	21.1.1981		3	2003–2005	7
Ferreira Neil Robert.	3.6.1979		1	2005	
[2] **Flower** Andrew OBE (*CY 2002*).	28.4.1968		63	1992–2002	213
[2] **Flower** Grant William	20.12.1970		67	1992–2003	221
Friend Travis John	7.1.1981		13	2001–2003	51
Goodwin Murray William	11.12.1972		19	1997–2000	71
Gripper Trevor Raymond	28.12.1975		20	1999–2003	8
Hondo Douglas Tafadzwa	7.7.1979		9	2001–2004	56
Houghton David Laud.	23.6.1957		22	1992–1997	63
Huckle Adam George	21.9.1971		8	1997–1998	19
James Wayne Robert.	27.8.1965		4	1993–1994	11
[1] **Jarvis** Kyle Malcolm.	16.2.1989		13	2011–2019	49/22
[1] **Jarvis** Malcolm Peter.	6.12.1955		5	1992–1994	12
Johnson Neil Clarkson	24.1.1970		13	1998–2000	48
Jongwe Luke Mafuwa	6.2.1995		1	2020	28/22
Kaia Roy.	10.10.1991		3	2020–2021	1
Kaitano Takudzwanashe	15.6.1993		1	2021	
Kamungozi Tafadzwa Paul	8.6.1987		1	2014	14/1
Kasuza Kevin Tatenda.	20.6.1993		7	2019–2020	
Lamb Gregory Arthur	4.3.1980		1	2011	15/5
Lock Alan Charles Ingram	10.9.1962		1	1995	8
Madhevere Wessly Nyasha	4.9.2000		2	2020	12/21
Madondo Trevor Nyasha.	22.11.1976	11.6.2001	3	1997–2000	13
Mahwire Ngonidzashe Blessing	31.7.1982		10	2002–2005	23
Maregwede Alester.	5.8.1981		2	2003	11
Marillier Douglas Anthony	24.4.1978		5	2000–2001	48
Maruma Timycen Hlahla	19.4.1988		4	2012–2021	22/13
[2] **Masakadza** Hamilton	9.8.1983		38	2001–2018	209/66
[2] **Masakadza** Shingirai Winston	4.9.1986		5	2011–2014	16/7
[2] **Masakadza** Wellington Pedzisai	4.10.1993		1	2018	20/28
Masvaure Prince Spencer	7.10.1988		8	2016–2020	2
Matambanadzo Everton Zvikomborero.	13.4.1976		3	1996–1999	7
Matsikenyeri Stuart	3.5.1983		8	2003–2004	113/10
Mavuta Brandon Anesu.	4.3.1997		2	2018	7/5
Mawoyo Tinotenda Mbiri Kanayi	8.1.1986		11	2011–2016	7
Mbangwa Mpumelelo ("Pommie").	26.6.1976		15	1996–2000	29
Meth Keegan Orry	8.2.1988		2	2012	11/2
Mire Solomon Farai	21.8.1989		2	2017	47/9
Moor Peter Joseph	2.2.1991		8	2016–2018	49/21
Mpofu Christopher Bobby	27.11.1985		15	2004–2017	84/32
Mudzinganyama Brian Simbarashe . . .	9.4.1999		1	2019	
Mumba Carl Tapfuma.	6.5.1995		3	2016–2019	7/2
Mupariwa Tawanda	16.4.1985		1	2003	40/4
Murphy Brian Andrew	1.12.1976		11	1999–2001	31
Musakanda Tarisai Kenneth	31.10.1994		5	2017–2020	15/12
Mushangwe Natsai	9.2.1991		2	2014	6/5
Mutendera David Travolta	25.1.1979		1	2000	9
Mutizwa Forster.	24.8.1985		1	2011	17/3
Mutombodzi Confidence Tinotenda	21.12.1990		1	2019	14/15
Mutumbami Richmond.	11.6.1989		6	2012–2014	36/27
Muzarabani Blessing	2.10.1996		6	2017–2021	27/21
Mwayenga Waddington.	20.6.1984		1	2005	3
Myers Dion Nephy	21.3.2002		1	2021	4/8
Ncube Njabulo	14.10.1989		1	2011	1
Ndlovu Ainsley.	26.1.1996		2	2019	2/3
Ngarava Richard	28.12.1997		3	2020–2021	17/18
Nkala Mluleki Luke	1.4.1981		10	2000–2004	50/1
Nyauchi Victor Munyaradzi.	8.7.1992		6	2019–2021	
Nyumbu John Curtis.	1.3.1983		3	2014–2016	19/2
Olonga Henry Khaaba.	3.7.1976		30	1994–2002	50

	Born	Died	Tests	Test Career	O/T
Panyangara Tinashe	21.10.1985		9	*2003–2014*	65/14
Peall Stephen Guy	2.9.1969		4	*1993–1994*	21
Price Raymond William	12.6.1976		22	*1999–2012*	102/16
Pycroft Andrew John	6.6.1956		3	*1992*	20
Ranchod Ujesh	17.5.1969		1	*1992*	3
² **Rennie** Gavin James	12.1.1976		23	*1997–2001*	40
² **Rennie** John Alexander	29.7.1970		4	*1993–1997*	44
Rogers Barney Guy	20.8.1982		4	*2004*	15
Shah Ali Hassimshah	7.8.1959		3	*1992–1996*	28
Shumba Milton	19.10.2000		3	*2020–2021*	1/12
Sibanda Vusimuzi	10.10.1983		14	*2003–2014*	125‡/26
Sikandar Raza	24.4.1986		17	*2013–2020*	108/42
² **Strang** Bryan Colin	9.6.1972		26	*1994–2001*	49
² **Strang** Paul Andrew	28.7.1970		24	*1994–2001*	95
Streak Heath Hilton	16.3.1974		65	*1993–2005*	187‡
Taibu Tatenda	14.5.1983		28	*2001–2011*	149‡/17
Taylor Brendan Ross Murray	6.2.1986		34	*2003–2021*	205/45
Tiripano Donald Tatenda	17.3.1988		15	*2014–2021*	36/17
Traicos Athanasios John	17.5.1947		4†	*1992*	27
Tshuma Charlton Kirsh	19.4.1993		1	*2019*	2/1
Utseya Prosper	26.3.1985		4	*2003–2013*	164/35
Vermeulen Mark Andrew	2.3.1979		9	*2002–2014*	43
Viljoen Dirk Peter	11.3.1977		2	*1997–2000*	53
Vitori Brian Vitalis	22.2.1990		4	*2011–2013*	24/11
¹ **Waller** Andrew Christopher	25.9.1959		2	*1996*	39
¹ **Waller** Malcolm Noel	28.9.1984		14	*2011–2017*	79/32
Watambwa Brighton Tonderai	9.6.1977		6	*2000–2001*	
Whittall Andrew Richard	28.3.1973		10	*1996–1999*	63
Whittall Guy James	5.9.1972		46	*1993–2002*	147
Williams Sean Colin	26.9.1986		14	*2012–2020*	139/50
Wishart Craig Brian	9.1.1974		27	*1995–2005*	90

BANGLADESH (100 players)

	Born	Died	Tests	Test Career	O/T
Abdur Razzak	15.6.1982		13	*2005–2017*	153/34
Abu Jayed	2.8.1993		13	*2018–2021*	2/3
Abul Hasan	5.8.1992		3	*2012*	7/5
Aftab Ahmed	10.11.1985		16	*2004–2009*	85/11
Akram Khan	1.11.1968		8	*2000–2003*	44
Al-Amin Hossain	1.1.1990		7	*2013–2019*	15/31
Al Sahariar	23.4.1978		15	*2000–2003*	29
Alamgir Kabir	10.1.1981		3	*2002–2003*	
Alok Kapali	1.1.1984		17	*2002–2005*	69/7
Aminul Islam	2.2.1968		13	*2000–2002*	39
Anamul Haque	16.12.1992		4	*2012–2014*	38/13
Anwar Hossain Monir	31.12.1981		3	*2003–2005*	1
Anwar Hossain Piju	10.12.1983		1	*2002*	1
Ariful Haque	18.11.1992		2	*2018*	1/9
Bikash Ranjan Das	14.7.1982		1	*2000*	
Ebadat Hossain	7.1.1994		12	*2018–2021*	
Ehsanul Haque	1.12.1979		1	*2002*	6
Elias Sunny	2.8.1986		4	*2011–2012*	4/7
Enamul Haque snr.	27.2.1966		10	*2000–2003*	29
Enamul Haque jnr.	5.12.1986		15	*2003–2012*	10
Fahim Muntasir	1.11.1980		3	*2001–2002*	3
Faisal Hossain	26.10.1978		1	*2003*	6
Habibul Bashar	17.8.1972		50	*2000–2007*	111
Hannan Sarkar	1.12.1982		17	*2002–2004*	20
Hasibul Hossain	3.6.1977		5	*2000–2001*	32
Imrul Kayes	2.2.1987		39	*2008–2019*	78/14

	Born	Died	Tests	Test Career	O/T
Jahurul Islam	12.12.1986		7	*2009–2012*	14/3
Javed Omar Belim.	25.11.1976		40	*2000–2007*	59
Jubair Hossain	12.9.1995		6	*2014–2015*	3/1
Junaid Siddique	30.10.1987		19	*2007–2012*	54/7
Kamrul Islam	10.12.1991		7	*2016–2018*	
Khaled Ahmed	20.9.1992		3	*2018–2021*	
Khaled Mahmud	26.7.1971		12	*2001–2003*	77
Khaled Mashud	8.2.1976		44	*2000–2007*	126
Liton Das	13.10.1994		29	*2015–2021*	47/46
Mahbubul Alam	1.12.1983		4	*2008*	5
Mahmudul Hasan	13.11.2000		2	*2021*	
Mahmudullah	4.2.1986		50	*2009–2021*	200/113
Manjural Islam	7.11.1979		17	*2000–2003*	34
Manjural Islam Rana	4.5.1984	16.3.2007	6	*2003–2004*	25
Marshall Ayub	5.12.1988		3	*2013*	
Mashrafe bin Mortaza	5.10.1983		36	*2001–2009*	218‡/54
Mehedi Hasan Miraz	25.10.1997		31	*2016–2021*	52/13
Mehrab Hossain snr.	22.9.1978		9	*2000–2003*	18
Mehrab Hossain jnr..	8.7.1987		7	*2007–2008*	18/2
Mithun Ali	3.2.1990		10	*2018–2020*	34/17
Mohammad Ashraful	9.9.1984		61	*2001–2012*	175‡/23
Mohammad Naim	22.8.1999		1	*2021*	2/32
Mohammad Rafique	5.9.1970		33	*2000–2007*	123‡/1
Mohammad Salim	15.10.1981		2	*2003*	1
Mohammad Shahid	1.11.1988		5	*2014–2015*	1
Mohammad Sharif	12.12.1983		10	*2000–2007*	9
Mominul Haque	29.9.1991		49	*2012–2021*	28/6
Mosaddek Hossain	10.12.1995		3	*2016–2019*	40/16
Mushfiqur Rahim	1.9.1988		78	*2005–2021*	227/99
Mushfiqur Rahman	1.1.1980		10	*2000–2004*	28
Mustafizur Rahman	6.9.1995		14	*2015–2020*	68/61
Naeem Islam	31.12.1986		8	*2008–2012*	59/10
[2]**Nafis Iqbal**	31.1.1985		11	*2004–2005*	16
Naimur Rahman	19.9.1974		8	*2000–2002*	29
Nasir Hossain	30.11.1991		19	*2011–2017*	65/31
Nayeem Hasan	2.12.2000		7	*2018–2020*	
Nazimuddin	1.10.1985		3	*2011–2012*	11/7
Nazmul Hossain	5.10.1987		2	*2004–2011*	38/4
Nazmul Hossain Shanto	25.5.1998		13	*2016–2021*	8/6
Nazmul Islam	21.3.1991		1	*2018*	5/13
Nurul Hasan	21.11.1993		5	*2016–2021*	3/30
Rafiqul Islam	7.11.1977		1	*2002*	1
Rajin Saleh	20.11.1983		24	*2003–2008*	43
Raqibul Hasan	8.10.1987		9	*2008–2011*	55/5
Robiul Islam	20.10.1986		9	*2010–2014*	3/1
Rubel Hossain	1.1.1990		27	*2009–2019*	104/28
Sabbir Rahman	20.8.1991		11	*2016–2017*	66/44
Saif Hasan	30.10.1998		6	*2019–2021*	0/2
Sajidul Islam	18.1.1988		3	*2007–2012*	0/1
Sanjamul Islam	17.1.1990		1	*2017*	3
Sanwar Hossain	5.8.1973		9	*2001–2003*	27
Shadman Islam	18.5.1995		12	*2018–2021*	
Shafiul Islam	6.10.1989		11	*2009–2017*	60/20
Shahadat Hossain	7.8.1986		38	*2005–2014*	51/6
Shahriar Hossain	1.6.1976		3	*2000–2003*	20
Shahriar Nafees	1.5.1985		24	*2005–2012*	75/1
Shakib Al Hasan	24.3.1987		59	*2007–2021*	215/94
Shamsur Rahman	5.6.1988		6	*2013–2014*	10/9
Shoriful Islam	3.6.2001		3	*2020–2021*	4/17
Shuvagata Hom	11.11.1986		8	*2014–2016*	4/5
Sohag Gazi	5.8.1991		10	*2012–2013*	20/10

	Born	Died	Tests	Test Career	O/T
Soumya Sarkar	25.2.1993		16	*2014–2020*	61/66
Subashis Roy	28.11.1988		4	*2016–2017*	1
Suhrawadi Shuvo	21.11.1988		1	*2011*	17/1
Syed Rasel	3.7.1984		6	*2005–2007*	52/8
Taijul Islam	7.2.1992		35	*2014–2021*	9/2
Talha Jubair	10.12.1985		7	*2002–2004*	6
[2] **Tamim Iqbal** (*CY 2011*)	20.3.1989		64	*2007–2020*	219/74‡
Tapash Baisya	25.12.1982		21	*2002–2005*	56
Tareq Aziz	4.9.1983		3	*2003–2004*	10
Taskin Ahmed	3.4.1995		10	*2016–2021*	42/33
Tushar Imran	10.12.1983		5	*2002–2007*	41
Yasir Ali	6.3.1996		3	*2021*	
Ziaur Rahman	2.12.1986		1	*2012*	13/14

IRELAND (17 players)

	Born	Died	Tests	Test Career	O/T
Adair Mark Richard	27.3.1996		1	*2019*	21/31
Balbirnie Andrew	28.12.1990		3	*2018–2019*	84/59
Cameron-Dow James	18.5.1990		1	*2018*	4
Dockrell George Henry	22.7.1992		1	*2018*	96/86
Joyce Edmund Christopher	22.9.1978		1	*2018*	61‡/16‡
Kane Tyrone Edward	8.7.1994		1	*2018*	0/7
McBrine Andrew Robert	30.4.1993		2	*2018–2019*	62/20
McCollum James Alexander	1.8.1995		2	*2018–2019*	10
Murtagh Timothy James	2.8.1981		3	*2018–2019*	58/14
[2] **O'Brien** Kevin Joseph	4.3.1984		3	*2018–2019*	153/110
[2] **O'Brien** Niall John	8.11.1981		1	*2018*	103/30
Porterfield William Thomas Stuart	6.9.1984		3	*2018–2019*	145/61
Poynter Stuart William	18.10.1990		1	*2018*	21/25
Rankin William Boyd	5.7.1984		2†	*2018–2019*	68‡/48‡
Stirling Paul Robert	3.9.1990		3	*2018–2019*	134/94
Thompson Stuart Robert	15.8.1991		3	*2018–2019*	20/41
Wilson Gary Craig	5.2.1986		2	*2018–2019*	105/81

AFGHANISTAN (24 players)

	Born	Died	Tests	Test Career	O/T
Abdul Malik	11.3.1998		1	*2020*	
Abdul Wasi	6.7.2002		1	*2020*	
Afsar Zazai	10.8.1993		5	*2018–2020*	17/1
Asghar Afghan Stanikzai	27.2.1987		6	*2018–2020*	114/75
Hamza Hotak	15.8.1991		3	*2019–2020*	31/33
Hashmatullah Shahidi	4.11.1994		5	*2018–2020*	41/4
Ibrahim Zadran	12.12.2001		4	*2019–2020*	1/3
Ihsanullah Janat	28.12.1997		3	*2018–2019*	16
Ikram Alikhil	29.9.2000		1	*2018*	12
Javed Ahmadi	2.1.1992		3	*2018–2019*	47/3
Mohammad Nabi	7.3.1985		3	*2018–2019*	127/86
Mohammad Shahzad	15.7.1991		2	*2018–2018*	84/70
Mujeeb Ur Rahman Zadran	28.3.2001		1	*2018*	43/22
Munir Ahmad	1.2.1996		1	*2020*	
Nasir Ahmadzai	21.12.1993		2	*2019–2020*	16
Qais Ahmad	15.8.2000		1	*2019*	0/1
Rahmat Shah	6.7.1993		6	*2018–2020*	76
Rashid Khan	20.9.1998		5	*2018–2020*	74/55‡
Sayed Shirzad	1.10.1994		1	*2020*	2/4
Shahidullah	6.2.1999		1	*2020*	
Wafadar Momand	1.2.2000		2	*2018–2018*	
Waqar Salamkheil	2.10.2001		1	*2018*	
Yamin Ahmadzai	25.7.1992		5	*2018–2020*	4/2
Zahir Khan	20.12.1998		3	*2019–2020*	1

Notes

*Family relationships in the above lists are indicated by superscript numbers; the following list
contains only those players whose relationship is not apparent from a shared name.*

In one Test, A. and G. G. Hearne played for England; their brother, F. Hearne, for South Africa.

The Waughs and New Zealand's Marshalls are the only instance of men's Test-playing twins.

Adnan Akmal: brother of Kamran and Umar Akmal.

Amar Singh, L.: brother of L. Ramji.

Azmat Rana: brother of Shafqat Rana.

Bazid Khan (Pakistan): son of Majid Khan (Pakistan) and grandson of M. Jahangir Khan (India).

Bravo, D. J. and D. M.: half-brothers.

Chappell, G. S., I. M. and T. M.: grandsons of V. Y. Richardson.

Collins, P. T.: half-brother of F. H. Edwards.

Cooper, W. H.: great-grandfather of A. P. Sheahan.

Edwards, F. H.: half-brother of P. T. Collins.

Hanif Mohammad: brother of Mushtaq, Sadiq and Wazir Mohammad; father of Shoaib Mohammad.

Headley, D. W. (England): son of R. G. A. and grandson of G. A. Headley (both West Indies).

Hearne, F. (England and South Africa): father of G. A. L. Hearne (South Africa).

Jahangir Khan, M. (India): father of Majid Khan and grandfather of Bazid Khan (both Pakistan).

Kamran Akmal: brother of Adnan and Umar Akmal.

Khalid Wazir (Pakistan): son of S. Wazir Ali (India).

Kirsten, G. and P. N.: half-brothers.

Majid Khan (Pakistan): son of M. Jahangir Khan (India) and father of Bazid Khan (Pakistan).

Manzoor Elahi: brother of Salim and Zahoor Elahi.

Moin Khan: brother of Nadeem Khan.

Mudassar Nazar: son of Nazar Mohammad.

Murray, D. A.: son of E. D. Weekes.

Mushtaq Mohammad: brother of Hanif, Sadiq and Wazir Mohammad.

Nadeem Khan: brother of Moin Khan.

Nafis Iqbal: brother of Tamim Iqbal.

Nazar Mohammad: father of Mudassar Nazar.

Nazir Ali, S.: brother of S. Wazir Ali.

Pattinson, D. J. (England): brother of J. L. Pattinson (Australia).

Pervez Sajjad: brother of Waqar Hasan.

Ramiz Raja: brother of Wasim Raja.

Ramji, L.: brother of L. Amar Singh.

Riaz Afridi: brother of Shaheen Shah Afridi.

Richardson, V. Y.: grandfather of G. S., I. M. and T. M. Chappell.

Sadiq Mohammad: brother of Hanif, Mushtaq and Wazir Mohammad.

Saeed Ahmed: brother of Younis Ahmed.

Salim Elahi: brother of Manzoor and Zahoor Elahi.

Shafqat Rana: brother of Azmat Rana.

Shaheen Shah Afridi: brother of Riaz Afridi.

Sheahan, A. P.: great-grandson of W. H. Cooper.

Shoaib Mohammad: son of Hanif Mohammad.

Tamim Iqbal: brother of Nafis Iqbal.

Umar Akmal: brother of Adnan and Kamran Akmal.

Waqar Hasan: brother of Pervez Sajjad.

Wasim Raja: brother of Ramiz Raja.

Wazir Ali, S. (India): brother of S. Nazir Ali (India) and father of Khalid Wazir (Pakistan).

Wazir Mohammad: brother of Hanif, Mushtaq and Sadiq Mohammad.

Weekes, E. D.: father of D. A. Murray.

Yograj Singh: father of Yuvraj Singh.

Younis Ahmed: brother of Saeed Ahmed.

Yuvraj Singh: son of Yograj Singh.

Zahoor Elahi: brother of Manzoor and Salim Elahi.

Teams are listed only where relatives played for different sides.

PLAYERS APPEARING FOR MORE THAN ONE MEN'S TEST TEAM

Fifteen cricketers have appeared for two countries in Test matches, namely:

Amir Elahi (India 1, Pakistan 5)
J. J. Ferris (Australia 8, England 1)
S. C. Guillen (West Indies 5, New Zealand 3)
Gul Mahomed (India 8, Pakistan 1)
F. Hearne (England 2, South Africa 4)
A. H. Kardar (India 3, Pakistan 23)
W. E. Midwinter (England 4, Australia 8)
F. Mitchell (England 2, South Africa 3)

W. L. Murdoch (Australia 18, England 1)
Nawab of Pataudi snr (England 3, India 3)
W. B. Rankin (England 1, Ireland 2)
A. J. Traicos (South Africa 3, Zimbabwe 4)
A. E. Trott (Australia 3, England 2)
K. C. Wessels (Australia 24, South Africa 16)
S. M. J. Woods (Australia 3, England 3)

Rankin also played seven one-day internationals and two Twenty20 internationals for England and 68 ODIs and 48 T20Is for Ireland; Wessels played 54 ODIs for Australia and 55 for South Africa.

The following players appeared for the ICC World XI against Australia in the Super Series Test in 2005-06: M. V. Boucher, R. Dravid, A. Flintoff, S. J. Harmison, Inzamam-ul-Haq, J. H. Kallis, B. C. Lara, M. Muralitharan, V. Sehwag, G. C. Smith, D. L. Vettori.

In 1970, England played five first-class matches against the Rest of the World after the cancellation of South Africa's tour. Players were awarded England caps, but the matches are no longer considered to have Test status. Alan Jones (born 4.11.1938) made his only appearance for England in this series, scoring 5 and 0; he did not bowl and took no catches; the ECB awarded him his England cap in 2020.

CONCUSSION SUBSTITUTES

From 2019, Test regulations provided for a full playing substitute to replace a player suffering from concussion. The following substitutions have been made:

Original player	*Concussion substitute*		
S. P. D. Smith	M. Labuschagne	Australia v England at Lord's	2019
D. M. Bravo	J. Blackwood	West Indies v India at Kingston	2019
D. Elgar	T. B. de Bruyn	South Africa v India at Ranchi	2019-20
Liton Das	Mehedi Hasan	Bangladesh v India at Kolkata	2019-20
Nayeem Hasan	Taijul Islam	Bangladesh v India at Kolkata	2019-20
K. T. Kasuza	B. S. Mudzinganyama	Zimbabwe v Sri Lanka (1st Test) at Harare . . .	2019-20
K. T. Kasuza	T. H. Maruma	Zimbabwe v Sri Lanka (2nd Test) at Harare . .	2019-20
N. E. Bonner	K. O. A. Powell	West Indies v South Africa at Gros Islet	2021
J. L. Solozano	S. D. Hope	West Indies v Sri Lanka at Galle	2021-22
Yasir Ali	Nurul Hasan	Bangladesh v Pakistan at Chittagong	2021-22

Y. S. Chahal was a concussion substitute for R. A. Jadeja in a T20 international for India v Australia at Canberra in 2020-21, Mohammad Saifuddin for Taskin Ahmed in an ODI for Bangladesh v Sri Lanka at Mirpur in 2021, and A. R. McBrine for N. A. Rock in an ODI for Ireland v West Indies at Kingston in 2021-22. Uniquely, B. S. Mudzinganyama made his Test debut as a concussion substitute.

ONE-DAY AND TWENTY20 INTERNATIONAL CRICKETERS (MEN)

The following players had appeared for Test-playing countries in one-day internationals or Twenty20 internationals by December 31, 2021, but had not represented their countries in Test matches by January 16, 2022. (Numbers in brackets signify number of ODIs for each player: where a second number appears, e.g. (5/1), it signifies the number of T20Is for that player.)

By January 2022, South Africa's D. A. Miller (137 ODIs/95 T20Is, including three for the World XI) was the most experienced international player never to have appeared in Test cricket. R. G. Sharma (India) held the record for most international appearances before making his Test debut, with 108 ODIs and 36 T20Is. S. Badree (West Indies) had played a record 52 T20Is (including two for the World XI) without a Test or ODI appearance.

England

M. W. Alleyne (10), I. D. Austin (9), T. Banton (6/9), D. R. Briggs (1/7), A. D. Brown (16), D. R. Brown (9), P. R. Brown (0/4), B. A. Carse (3), G. Chapple (1), J. W. M. Dalrymple (27/3), S. M. Davies (8/5), J. W. Dernbach (24/34), M. V. Fleming (11), P. J. Franks (1), I. J. Gould (18), A. P. Grayson (2), L. Gregory (3/9), H. F. Gurney (10/2), G. W. Humpage (3), T. E. Jesty (10), E. C. Joyce (17/2), C. Kieswetter (46/25), L. S. Livingstone (3/14), G. D. Lloyd (6), A. G. R. Loudon (1), J. D. Love (3), M. B. Loye (7), M. J. Lumb (3/27), M. A. Lynch (3), S. Mahmood (7/9), A. D. Mascarenhas (20/14), S. C. Meaker (2/2), T. S. Mills (0/8), P. Mustard (10/2), P. A. Nixon (19/1), M. W. Parkinson (5/4), S. D. Parry (2/5), P. D. Salt (3), J. A. Simpson (3), M. J. Smith (5), N. M. K. Smith (7), J. N. Snape (10/1), V. S. Solanki (51/3), R. J. W. Topley (13/6), J. O. Troughton (6), C. M. Wells (2), V. J. Wells (9), A. G. Wharf (13), D. J. Willey (52/32), L. J. Wright (50/51), M. H. Yardy (28/14).

D. R. Brown also played 16 ODIs for Scotland, J. W. Dernbach six T20Is for Italy, and E. C. Joyce one Test, 61 ODIs and 16 T20Is for Ireland.

Australia

S. A. Abbott (2/7), W. A. Agar (2), J. P. Behrendorff (11/9), T. R. Birt (0/4), G. A. Bishop (2), C. J. Boyce (0/7), R. J. Campbell (2), D. T. Christian (20/23), M. J. Cosgrove (3), N. M. Coulter-Nile (32/28), B. C. J. Cutting (4/4), M. J. Di Venuto (9), B. R. Dorey (4), B. R. Dunk (0/5), N. T. Ellis (0/2), Fawad Ahmed (2/2), P. J. Forrest (15), B. Geeves (2/1), S. F. Graf (11), I. J. Harvey (73), S. M. Harwood (1/3), S. D. Heazlett (1), J. R. Hopes (84/12), D. J. Hussey (69/39), M. Klinger (0/3), B. Laughlin (5/3), S. Lee (45), M. L. Lewis (7/2), C. A. Lynn (4/18), R. J. McCurdy (11), B. R. McDermott (2/17), K. H. MacLeay (16), J. P. Maher (26), R. P. Meredith (1/5), J. M. Muirhead (0/5), D. P. Nannes (1/15), A. A. Noffke (1/2), J. S. Paris (2), J. R. Philippe (3/10), L. A. Pomersbach (0/1), G. D. Porter (2), N. J. Reardon (0/2), K. W. Richardson (25/26), B. J. Rohrer (0/1), L. Ronchi (4/3), D. R. Sams (0/4), G. S. Sandhu (2), D. J. M. Short (8/23), J. D. Siddons (1), B. Stanlake (7/19), M. P. Stoinis (45/35), A. M. Stuart (3), M. J. Swepson (0/7), C. P. Tremain (4), G. S. Trimble (2), A. J. Turner (9/18), A. J. Tye (7/32), J. D. Wildermuth (0/2), D. J. Worrall (3), B. E. Young (6), A. Zampa (64/57), A. K. Zesers (2).

R. J. Campbell also played three T20Is for Hong Kong, D. P. Nannes two T20Is for the Netherlands, and L. Ronchi four Tests, 72 ODIs and 26 T20Is for New Zealand.

South Africa

Y. A. Abdulla (0/2), S. Abrahams (1), F. Behardien (59/38), D. M. Benkenstein (23), G. H. Bodi (2/1), L. E. Bosman (13/14), R. E. Bryson (7), D. J. Callaghan (29), G. L. Cloete (0/2), D. N. Crookes (32), C. J. Dala (2/10), H. Davids (2/9), D. M. Dupavillon (2), B. C. Fortuin (1/13), R. Frylinck (0/3), T. Henderson (0/1), R. R. Hendricks (24/40), C. A. Ingram (31/9), C. Jonker (2/2), J. C. Kent (2), L. J. Koen (5), G. J-P. Kruger (3/1), E. Leie (0/2), R. E. Levi (0/13), J. Louw (3/2), W. J. Lubbe (0/2), S. S. B. Magala (1/4), J. N. Malan (11/11), D. A. Miller (137/92), M. Mosehle (0/7), P. V. Mpitsang (2), S. J. Palframan (7), A. M. Phangiso (21/16), N. Pothas (3), A. Q. Puttick (1), S. Qeshile (0/2), C. E. B. Rice (3), M. J. R. Rindel (22), R. R. Rossouw (36/15), D. B. Rundle (2), T. G. Shaw (9), M. Shezi (1), E. O. Simons (23), J. T. Smuts (6/13), G. J. Snyman (0/1), E. L. R. Stewart (6), G. A. Stuurmaan (0/1), R. Telemachus (37/3), J. Theron (4/9), A. C. Thomas (0/1), T. Tshabalala (4), P. J. van Biljon (0/10), R. E. van der Merwe (13/13), J. J. van der Wath (10/8), V. B. van Jaarsveld (2/3), M. N. van Wyk (17/8), C. J. P. G. van Zyl (2), D. Wiese (6/20), H. S. Williams (7), L. B. Williams (1/6), M. Yachad (1), K. Zondo (6).

J. Theron also played nine ODIs and four T20Is for USA, R. E. van der Merwe three ODIs and 33 T20Is for the Netherlands, and D. Wiese 11 T20Is for Namibia.

West Indies

F. A. Allen (17/28), H. A. G. Anthony (3), S. Badree (0/50), C. D. Barnwell (0/6), M. C. Bascombe (0/1), R. R. Beaton (2), D. Brown (3), B. St A. Browne (4), P. A. Browne (5), H. R. Bryan (15), D. C. Butler (5/1), J. L. Carter (33), J. Charles (48/34), D. O. Christian (4), R. T. Crandon (1), D. C. Drakes (0/3), R. R. Emrit (2/4), S. E. Findlay (9/2), A. D. S. Fletcher (25/45), R. S. Gabriel (11), K. J. Harding (1), K. C. Haynes (8), C. Hemraj (6), A. J. Hosein (9/13), R. O. Hurley (9), D. P. Hyatt (9/5), K. C. B. Jeremy (6), B. A. King (4/14), E. Lewis (57/50), A. M. McCarthy (2/1), O. C. McCoy (2/13), A. Martin (9/1), G. E. Mathurin (0/3), J. N. Mohammed (36/9), G. Motie (0/1), A. R. Nurse (54/13), K. Y. Ottley (2), W. K. D. Perkins (0/1), A. Phillip (1), K. A. Pierre (3/10), K. A. Pollard (119/93), N. Pooran (31/49), R. Powell (37/33), M. R. Pydanna (1), A. C. L. Richards (1/1),

S. E. Rutherford (0/6), K. Santokie (0/12), K. F. Semple (7), R. Shepherd (7/9), K. Sinclair (0/6), O. F. Smith (0/5), D. C. Thomas (21/4), O. R. Thomas (20/20), C. M. Tuckett (1), H. R. Walsh (12/22), K. O. K. Williams (8/26), L. R. Williams (15).

H. R. Walsh also played one ODI and eight T20Is for USA.

New Zealand

G. W. Aldridge (2/1), F. H. Allen (0/6), M. D. Bailey (1), M. D. Bates (2/3), B. R. Blair (14), T. C. Bruce (0/17), C. E. Bulfin (4), T. K. Canning (4), M. S. Chapman (4/14), P. G. Coman (3), A. P. Devcich (12/4), B. J. Diamanti (1/1), M. W. Douglas (6), J. A. Duffy (0/4), A. M. Ellis (15/5), L. H. Ferguson (19/2), B. G. Hadlee (2), L. J. Hamilton (2), R. T. Hart (1), R. L. Hayes (1), R. M. Hira (0/15), P. A. Hitchcock (14/1), L. G. Howell (12), A. K. Kitchen (0/5), S. C. Kuggeleijn (2/18), M. J. McClenaghan (48/28), C. E. McConchie (0/5), N. L. McCullum (84/63), P. D. McGlashan (4/11), B. J. McKechnie (14), E. B. McSweeney (16), A. W. Mathieson (1), J. P. Millmow (5), A. F. Milne (40/31), T. S. Nethula (5), C. J. Nevin (37), A. J. Penn (5), R. G. Petrie (12), G. D. Phillips (0/11), S. H. A. Rance (2/8), R. B. Reid (9), S. J. Roberts (2), B. V. Sears (0/2), T. L. Seifert (3/40), S. L. Stewart (4), L. W. Stott (1), G. P. Sulzberger (3), A. R. Tait (5), E. P. Thompson (1/1), B. M. Tickner (0/8), M. D. J. Walker (3), R. J. Webb (3), B. M. Wheeler (6/6), J. W. Wilson (6), W. A. Wisneski (3), L. J. Woodcock (4/3), G. H. Worker (10/2).

M. S. Chapman also played 2 ODIs and 19 T20Is for Hong Kong.

India

K. K. Ahmed (11/14), S. Aravind (0/1), P. Awana (0/2), A. C. Bedade (13), A. Bhandari (2), Bhupinder Singh snr (2), G. Bose (1), Y. S. Chahal (56/50), D. L. Chahar (5/17), R. D. Chahar (1/6), V. V. Chakravarthy (0/6), V. B. Chandrasekhar (7), U. Chatterjee (3), N. A. David (4), P. Dharmani (1), R. Dhawan (3/1), A. B. Dinda (13/9), S. R. Dube (1/13), F. Y. Fazal (1), R. D. Gaikwad (0/2), R. S. Gavaskar (1), R. S. Ghai (6), M. S. Gony (2), K. Gowtham (1), Gurkeerat Singh (3), V. R. Iyer (0/3), K. M. Jadhav (73/9), Joginder Sharma (4/4), A. V. Kale (1), S. Kaul (3/3), S. C. Khanna (10), G. K. Khoda (2), A. R. Khurasiya (12), I. P. Kishan (2/5), P. M. Krishna (3), D. S. Kulkarni (12/2), T. Kumaran (3), Mandeep Singh (0/3), M. Markande (0/1), J. J. Martin (10), D. Mongia (57/1), S. P. Mukherjee (3), A. M. Nayar (3), P. Negi (0/1), D. B. Padikkal (0/2), G. K. Pandey (2), M. K. Pandey (29/39), K. H. Pandya (5/19), J. V. Paranjpe (4), Parvez Rasool (1/1), A. K. Patel (8), H. V. Patel (0/2), Y. K. Pathan (57/22), N. Rana (1/2), Randhir Singh (2), S. S. Raul (2), A. T. Rayudu (55/6), C. Sakariya (1/2), A. M. Salvi (4), S. V. Samson (1/10), S. Sandeep Warrier (0/1), V. Shankar (12/9), M. Sharma (26/8), R. Sharma (4/2), S. Sharma (0/2), L. R. Shukla (3), R. P. Singh (2), R. S. Sodhi (18), S. Somasunder (2), B. B. Sran (6/2), S. Sriram (3), Sudhakar Rao (1), M. K. Tiwary (12/3), S. S. Tiwary (3), S. Tyagi (4/1), R. V. Uthappa (46/13), P. S. Vaidya (4), Y. Venugopal Rao (16), Jai P. Yadav (12), S. A. Yadav (3/11).

Pakistan

Aamer Hameed (2), Aamer Hanif (5), Aamer Yamin (4/2), Ahsan Ali (0/2), Akhtar Sarfraz (4), Anwar Ali (22/16), Arshad Iqbal (0/1), Arshad Pervez (3), Asad Ali (4/2), Asif Ali (20/38), Asif Mahmood (2), Awais Zia (0/5), Azam Khan (0/3), Danish Aziz (2/2), Faisal Athar (1), Ghulam Ali (3), Haafiz Shahid (3), Haider Ali (2/21), Hammad Azam (11/5), Haris Rauf (8/34), Hasan Jamil (6), Hussain Talat (1/18), Imad Wasim (55/58), Imran Abbas (2), Imran Khan jnr (0/3), Iqbal Sikandar (4), Irfan Bhatti (1), Javed Qadir (1), Junaid Zia (1), Kamran Hussain (2), Kashif Raza (1), Khalid Latif (5/13), Khushdil Shah (1/12), Mahmood Hamid (1), Mansoor Amjad (1/1), Mansoor Rana (2), Manzoor Akhtar (7), Maqsood Rana (1), Masood Iqbal (1), Mohammad Hasnain (8/18), Mohammad Wasim (0/10), Moin-ul-Atiq (5), Mujahid Jamshed (4), Mukhtar Ahmed (0/6), Naeem Ahmed (1), Naeem Ashraf (2), Najaf Shah (1), Naseer Malik (3), Nauman Anwar (0/1), Naumanullah (1), Parvez Mir (3), Rafatullah Mohmand (0/3), Rameez Raja (0/2), Raza Hasan (1/10), Rizwan Ahmed (1), Rumman Raees (9/8), Saad Ali (2), Saad Nasim (3/3), Saadat Ali (8), Saeed Azad (4), Sahibzada Farhan (0/3), Sajid Ali (13), Sajjad Akbar (2), Salim Pervez (1), Samiullah Khan (2), Saud Shakil (3/0), Shahid Anwar (1), Shahnawaz Dhani (0/2), Shahzaib Hasan (3/10), Shakeel Ansar (0/2), Shakil Khan (1), Shoaib Khan (0/1), Sohaib Maqsood (29/26), Sohail Fazal (2), Tanvir Mehdi (1), Usman Qadir (1/17), Usman Shinwari (9/13), Waqas Maqsood (0/1), Wasim Haider (3), Zafar Iqbal (8), Zahid Ahmed (2), Zahid Mahmood (0/1).

Sri Lanka
M. A. Aponso (9/3), J. R. M. W. S. Bandara (0/8), K. M. C. Bandara (1/1), K. N. A. Bandara (5/4), J. W. H. D. Boteju (2), D. L. S. de Silva (2), G. N. de Silva (4), P. C. de Silva (7/2), S. N. T. de Silva (0/3), L. H. D. Dilhara (9/2), E. R. Fernando (3), K. B. U. Fernando (4/6), T. L. Fernando (1), U. N. K. Fernando (4), W. I. A. Fernando (26/30), J. C. Gamage (4), W. C. A. Ganegama (4), F. R. M. Goonatilleke (1), P. W. Gunaratne (23), A. A. W. Gunawardene (1), P. D. Heyn (2), W. S. Jayantha (17), P. S. Jayaprakashdaran (1), C. U. Jayasinghe (0/5), S. A. Jayasinghe (2), G. S. N. F. G. Jayasuriya (12/18), N. G. R. P. Jayasuriya (2), S. H. T. Kandamby (39/5), S. H. U. Karnain (19), H. G. J. M. Kulatunga (0/2), D. S. M. Kumara (1/2), P. A. D. Lakshan (1), L. D. Madushanka (4/3), B. M. A. J. Mendis (58/22), C. Mendis (1), P. H. K. D. Mendis (4/5), A. M. N. Munasinghe (5), E. M. D. Y. Munaweera (2/13), H. G. D. Nayanakantha (3), A. R. M. Opatha (5), S. P. Pasqual (2), S. S. Pathirana (18/5), A. K. Perera (6/6), K. G. Perera (1), P. A. R. P. Perera (2/3), H. S. M. Pieris (3), S. M. A. Priyanjan (23/3), M. Pushpakumara (3/1), P. B. B. Rajapaksa (5/18), R. L. B. Rambukwella (0/2), S. K. Ranasinghe (4), N. Ranatunga (2), N. L. K. Ratnayake (2), R. J. M. G. M. Rupasinghe (0/2), A. P. B. Tennekoon (4), M. M. Theekshana (1/10), M. H. Tissera (3), I. Udana (21/35), J. D. F. Vandersay (12/10), D. M. Vonhagt (1), A. P. Weerakkody (1), D. S. Weerakkody (3), S. Weerakoon (2), K. Weeraratne (15/5), S. R. D. Wettimuny (3), R. P. A. H. Wickremaratne (3).

Zimbabwe
R. D. Brown (7), K. M. Curran (11), S. G. Davies (4), K. G. Duers (6), E. A. Essop-Adam (1), Faraz Akram (0/2), D. A. G. Fletcher (6), T. N. Garwe (1), J. G. Heron (6), R. S. Higgins (11), V. R. Hogg (2), A. J. Ireland (26/1), D. Jakiel (0/2), I. Kaia (0/1), T. S. Kamunhukamwe (7/8), F. Kasteni (3), A. J. Mackay (3), N. Madziva (12/15), G. C. Martin (5), T. R. Marumani (3/11), W. T. Mashinge (0/2), M. A. Meman (1), T. V. Mufambisi (6), T. T. Munyonga (0/5), R. C. Murray (5), C. T. Mutombodzi (11/5), T. Muzarabani (8/9), I. A. Nicolson (2), G. A. Paterson (10), G. E. Peckover (3), E. C. Rainsford (39/2), P. W. E. Rawson (10), H. P. Rinke (18), L. N. Roche (3), R. W. Sims (3), G. M. Strydom (12), C. Zhuwao (9/7).
    G. M. Strydom also played 6 T20Is for Cayman Islands.

Bangladesh
Abu Haider (2/13), Afif Hossain (7/39), Ahmed Kamal (1), Alam Talukdar (2), Aminul Islam (Bhola) (1), Aminul Islam (Biplob) (0/10), Anisur Rahman (2), Arafat Sunny (16/10), Ather Ali Khan (19), Azhar Hussain (7), Dhiman Ghosh (14/1), Dolar Mahmud (7), Farhad Reza (34/13), Faruq Ahmed (7), Fazle Mahmud (2), Gazi Ashraf (7), Ghulam Faruq (5), Ghulam Nausher (9), Hafizur Rahman (2), Harunur Rashid (2), Hasan Mahmud (7/1), Jahangir Alam (3), Jahangir Badshah (5), Jamaluddin Ahmed (1), Mafizur Rahman (1), Mahbubur Rahman (1), Mazharul Haque (1), Mehedi Hasan snr (3/29), Minhazul Abedin (27), Mohammad Saifuddin (29/29), Moniruzzaman (2), Morshed Ali Khan (3), Mosharraf Hossain (5), Mukhtar Ali (0/1), Nadif Chowdhury (0/3), Nasir Ahmed (7), Nasum Ahmed (0/18), Nazmus Sadat (0/1), Neeyamur Rashid (2), Nurul Abedin (4), Rafiqul Alam (2), Raqibul Hasan snr (2), Rony Talukdar (0/1), Saiful Islam (2), Sajjad Ahmed (2), Samiur Rahman (2), Saqlain Sajib (0/1), Shafiuddin Ahmed (11), Shahidul Islam (0/1), Shahidur Rahman (2), Shamim Hossain (0/10), Shariful Haq (1), Sheikh Salahuddin (6), Tanveer Haider (2), Wahidul Gani (1), Zahid Razzak (3), Zakir Hasan (0/1), Zakir Hassan (2).

Ireland
J. Anderson (8/4), A. C. Botha (42/14), J. P. Bray (15/2), S. A. Britton (1), C. Campher (10/9), K. E. D. Carroll (6), P. K. D. Chase (25/12), P. Connell (13/9), A. R. Cusack (59/37), D. C. A. Delany (0/8), G. J. Delany (9/29), P. S. Eaglestone (1/1), M. J. Fourie (7), S. C. Getkate (4/25), P. J. Gillespie (5), R. S. Haire (2), J. D. Hall (3), D. T. Johnston (67/30), N. G. Jones (14/5), D. I. Joyce (3), G. E. Kidd (6/1), D. Langford-Smith (22), J. B. Little (16/27), W. K. McCallan (39/9), R. D. McCann (8/3), G. J. McCarter (1/3), B. J. McCarthy (38/17), W. T. McClintock (0/5), J. F. Mooney (64/27), P. J. K. Mooney (4), E. J. G. Morgan (23), J. Mulder (4/8), A. D. Poynter (19/19), D. A. Rankin (0/2), E. J. Richardson (2), N. A. Rock (0/13), J. N. K. Shannon (1/8), S. Singh (33/39), M. C. Sorensen (13/26), R. Strydom (9/4), H. T. Tector (17/28), S. P. Terry (5/1), G. J. Thompson (3/10), L. J. Tucker (25/22), A. van der Merwe (6), R. M. West (10/5), R. K. Whelan (2), A. R. White (61/18), B. C. White (0/9), C. A. Young (30/42).
    E. J. G. Morgan also played 16 Tests, 223 ODIs and 113 T20Is for England.

Afghanistan
Abdullah Mazari (2), Aftab Alam (27/12), Ahmed Shah (1), Azmatullah Omarzai (1), Dawlat Ahmadzai (3/2), Dawlat Zadran (82/34), Fareed Ahmad (5/16), Fazal Haque (0/1), Fazal Niazai (0/1), Gulbadeen Naib (68/53), Hamid Hassan (38/25), Hasti Gul (2), Hazratullah Zazai (16/20), Izatullah Dawlatzai (5/4), Karim Janat (1/32), Karim Sadiq (24/36), Khaliq Dad (6), Mirwais Ashraf (46/25), Mohibullah Paak (2), Najeeb Tarakai (1/12), Najibullah Zadran (70/68), Nasim Baras (0/3), Naveen-ul-Haq (7/13), Nawroz Mangal (49/32), Noor Ali Zadran (51/20), Noor-ul-Haq (2), Raees Ahmadzai (5/8), Rahmanullah Gurbaz (3/18), Rokhan Barakzai (1/3), Samiullah Shenwari (84/64), Shabir Noori (10/1), Shafiqullah Shinwari (24/46), Shapoor Zadran (44/36), Sharafuddin Ashraf (17/10), Usman Ghani (15/23), Zakiullah (1), Zamir Khan (0/1), Ziaur Rahman (0/1).

Izatullah Dawlatzai also played 12 T20Is for Germany.

PLAYERS APPEARING FOR MORE THAN ONE MEN'S ONE-DAY/TWENTY20 INTERNATIONAL TEAM

The following players have played ODIs for the **African XI** in addition to their national side:

N. Boje (2), L. E. Bosman (1), J. Botha (2), M. V. Boucher (5), E. Chigumbura (3), A. B. de Villiers (5), H. H. Dippenaar (6), J. H. Kallis (2), J. M. Kemp (6), J. A. Morkel (2), M. Morkel (3), T. M. Odoyo (5), P. J. Ongondo (1), J. L. Ontong (1), S. M. Pollock (5), A. G. Prince (3), J. A. Rudolph (2), V. Sibanda (3), G. C. Smith (1), D. W. Steyn (3), H. H. Streak (1), T. Taibu (1), S. O. Tikolo (4), M. Zondeki (2). (Odoyo, Ongondo and Tikolo played for Kenya, who do not have Test status.)

The following players have played ODIs for the **Asian Cricket Council XI** in addition to their national side:

Abdul Razzaq (4), M. S. Dhoni (3), R. Dravid (1), C. R. D. Fernando (1), S. C. Ganguly (3), Harbhajan Singh (2), Inzamam-ul-Haq (3), S. T. Jayasuriya (4), D. P. M. D. Jayawardene (5), A. Kumble (2), Mashrafe bin Mortaza (2), Mohammad Ashraful (2), Mohammad Asif (3), Mohammad Rafique (2), Mohammad Yousuf (7), M. Muralitharan (2), A. Nehra (3), K. C. Sangakkara (4), V. Sehwag (3), Shahid Afridi (3), Shoaib Akhtar (3), W. U. Tharanga (1), W. P. U. J. C. Vaas (1), Yuvraj Singh (3), Zaheer Khan (6).

The following players have played ODIs for an **ICC World XI** in addition to their national side:

C. L. Cairns (1), R. Dravid (3), S. P. Fleming (1), A. Flintoff (3), C. H. Gayle (3), A. C. Gilchrist (1), D. Gough (1), M. L. Hayden (1), J. H. Kallis (3), B. C. Lara (4), G. D. McGrath (1), M. Muralitharan (3), M. Ntini (1), K. P. Pietersen (2), S. M. Pollock (3), R. T. Ponting (1), K. C. Sangakkara (3), V. Sehwag (3), Shahid Afridi (2), Shoaib Akhtar (2), D. L. Vettori (4), S. K. Warne (1).

The following players have played T20Is for a **World XI** in addition to their national side:

H. M. Amla (3), S. Badree (2), G. J. Bailey (1), S. W. Billings (1), P. D. Collingwood (1), B. C. J. Cutting (1), F. du Plessis (1), G. D. Elliott (1), Imran Tahir (3), K. D. Karthik (1), S. Lamichhane (1), M. J. McClenaghan (1), D. A. Miller (3), T. S. Mills (1), M. Morkel (3), T. D. Paine (2), N. L. T. C. Perera (1), Rashid Khan (1), L. Ronchi (1), D. J. G. Sammy (2), Shahid Afridi (1), Shoaib Malik (1), Tamim Iqbal (4).

K. C. Wessels played Tests and ODIs for both Australia and South Africa. **D. R. Brown** played ODIs for England plus ODIs and T20Is for Scotland. **C. B. Lambert** played Tests and ODIs for West Indies and one ODI for USA. **E. C. Joyce** played ODIs and T20Is for England and all three formats for Ireland; **E. J. G. Morgan** ODIs for Ireland and all three formats for England; and **W. B. Rankin** all three formats for Ireland and England. **A. C. Cummins** played Tests and ODIs for West Indies and ODIs for Canada. **G. M. Hamilton** played Tests for England and ODIs for Scotland. **D. P. Nannes** played ODIs and T20Is for Australia and T20Is for the Netherlands. **L. Ronchi** played ODIs and T20Is for Australia and all three formats for New Zealand. **G. O. Jones** played all three formats for England and ODIs for Papua New Guinea. **R. E. van der Merwe** played ODIs and T20Is for South Africa and the Netherlands. **R. J. Campbell** played ODIs and T20Is for Australia and T20Is for Hong Kong. **M. S. Chapman** played ODIs and T20Is for Hong Kong and New Zealand. **Izatullah Dawlatzai** played ODIs and T20Is for Afghanistan and T20Is for Germany. **X. M. Marshall** played all three formats for West Indies and ODIs and T20Is for USA. **G. M. Strydom** played ODIs for Zimbabwe and T20Is for Cayman Islands. **J. Theron** played ODIs and T20Is for South Africa and

ODIs for USA. **H. R. Walsh** played ODIs and T20Is for both USA and West Indies. **A. Khan** played Tests and T20Is for England and T20Is for Denmark. **J. W. Dernbach** played ODIs and T20Is for England and T20Is for Italy. **D. Wiese** played ODIs and T20Is for South Africa and T20Is for Namibia. **A. R. Berenger** played ODIs for UAE and T20Is for Qatar.

ELITE TEST UMPIRES

The following umpires were on the ICC's elite panel in February 2022, apart from Oxenford, who retired in April 2021. The figures for Tests, one-day internationals and Twenty20 internationals and the Test Career dates refer to matches in which they have officiated as on-field umpires (excluding abandoned games). The totals of Tests are complete up to January 16, 2022, the totals of one-day internationals and Twenty20 internationals up to December 31, 2021.

	Country	Born	Tests	Test Career	ODIs	T20Is
Aleem Dar	P	6.6.1968	136	*2003–2020*	211	60
Dharmasena Handunnettige Deepthi						
Priyantha Kumar	SL	24.4.1971	71	*2010–2021*	111	33
Erasmus Marais	SA	27.2.1964	70*	*2009–2021*	99	35
Gaffaney Christopher Blair	NZ	30.11.1975	39	*2014–2021*	71	35
Gough Michael Andrew	E	18.12.1979	24	*2016–2021*	65	17
Illingworth Richard Keith	E	23.8.1963	57*	*2012–2021*	71	21
Kettleborough Richard Allan	E	15.3.1973	72	*2010–2021*	92	30
Menon Nitin Narendra	I	2.11.1983	9	*2019–2021*	27	24
Oxenford Bruce Nicholas James	A	5.3.1960	62	*2010–2020*	97	20
Reiffel Paul Ronald	A	19.4.1966	54	*2012–2021*	71	21
Tucker Rodney James	A	28.8.1964	75	*2009–2021*	85	43
Wilson Joel Sheldon	WI	30.12.1966	25	2015–2021	72	37

* *Includes one Test where he took over mid-match.*

BIRTHS AND DEATHS

OTHER CRICKETING NOTABLES

The following list shows the births and deaths of cricketers, and people associated with cricket, who have *not* played in men's Test matches.

Criteria for inclusion All non-Test players who have either (1) scored 20,000 first-class runs, or (2) taken 1,500 first-class wickets, or (3) achieved 750 dismissals, or (4) reached both 15,000 runs and 750 wickets. Also included are (5) the leading players who flourished before the start of Test cricket, (6) Wisden Cricketers of the Year who did not play Test cricket, and (7) others of merit or interest.

Names Where players were normally known by a name other than their first, this is underlined.

Teams Where only one team are listed, this is normally the one for which the player made most first-class appearances. Additional teams are listed only if the player appeared for them in more than 20 first-class matches, or if they are especially relevant to their career. School and university teams are not given unless especially relevant (e.g. for the schoolboys chosen as wartime Cricketers of the Year in the 1918 and 1919 *Wisdens*).

		Born	Died
Adams Percy Webster	Cheltenham College; *CY 1919*	5.9.1900	28.9.1962
Aird Ronald MC	Hampshire; sec. MCC 1953–62, pres. MCC 1968–69	4.5.1902	16.8.1986
Aislabie Benjamin	Surrey, secretary of MCC 1822–42	14.1.1774	2.6.1842
Alcock Charles William	Secretary of Surrey 1872–1907	2.12.1842	26.2.1907
Editor, Cricket magazine, 1882–1907. Captain of Wanderers and England football teams.			
Aleem Dar	Umpire in a record 136 Tests by January 2022	6.6.1968	
Allardice Geoffrey John	Victoria; chief executive of ICC 2021–	7.5.1967	
Alley William Edward	NSW, Somerset; Test umpire; *CY 1962*	3.2.1919	26.11.2004
Alleyne Mark Wayne	Gloucestershire; *CY 2001*	23.5.1968	
Altham Harry Surtees CBE	Surrey, Hants; historian; pres. MCC 1959–60	30.11.1888	11.3.1965
Arlott Leslie Thomas <u>John</u> OBE	Broadcaster and writer	25.2.1914	14.12.1991
Arthur John <u>Michael</u>	Griq. W, OFS; coach SA 2005–10, Australia 2011–13, Pakistan 2016–19, SL 2019–21	17.5.1968	
Ashdown William Henry	Kent	27.12.1898	15.9.1979
The only player to appear in English first-class cricket before and after the two world wars.			
Ash Eileen (*née* Whelan)	England women	30.10.1911	3.12.2021
The longest-lived international cricketer, at 110 years 34 days.			
Ashley-Cooper Frederick Samuel	Historian	22.3.1877	31.1.1932
Ashton *Sir* Hubert KBE MC Cam U, Essex; pres. MCC 1960–61; *CY 1922*		13.2.1898	17.6.1979
Austin *Sir* Harold Bruce Gardiner	Barbados	15.7.1877	27.7.1943
Austin Ian David	Lancashire; *CY 1999*	30.5.1966	
Azeem Rafiq	Yorkshire	27.2.1991	
Bailey Jack Arthur	Essex; secretary of MCC 1974–87	22.6.1930	12.7.2018
Bainbridge Philip	Gloucestershire, Durham; *CY 1986*	16.4.1958	
Bakewell Enid (*née* Turton) MBE	England women	16.12.1940	
Bannister John David	Warwickshire; writer and broadcaster	23.8.1930	23.1.2016
Barclay Gregor John	ICC chair 2020–	19.9.1961	
Barker Gordon	Essex	6.7.1931	10.2.2006
Bartlett Hugh Tryon	Sussex; *CY 1939*	7.10.1914	26.6.1988
Bates Suzannah Wilson	New Zealand women	16.9.1987	
Bayliss Trevor Harley OBE	NSW; coach SL 2007–11, England 2015–19	21.12.1962	
Beauclerk *Rev. Lord* Frederick	Middlesex, Surrey, MCC	8.5.1773	22.4.1850
Beaumont Tamsin Tilley MBE	England women; *CY 2019*	11.3.1991	
Beldam George William	Middlesex; photographer	1.5.1868	23.11.1937
Beldham William ("Silver Billy")	Hambledon, Surrey	5.2.1766	26.2.1862
Beloff Michael Jacob QC	Head of ICC Code of Conduct Commission	18.4.1942	
Benkenstein Dale Martin	KwaZulu-Natal, Durham; *CY 2009*	9.6.1974	
Berry Anthony <u>Scyld</u> Ivens	Editor of *Wisden* 2008–11	28.4.1954	
Berry Leslie George	Leicestershire	28.4.1906	5.2.1985
Bird Harold Dennis ("Dickie") OBE	Yorkshire, Leics; umpire in 66 Tests	19.4.1933	
Blofeld Henry Calthorpe OBE	Cambridge Univ; broadcaster	23.9.1939	

		Born	Died
Bond John David	Lancashire; *CY 1971*	6.5.1932	11.7.2019
Booth Roy	Yorkshire, Worcestershire	1.10.1926	24.9.2018
Bowden Brent Fraser ("Billy")	Umpire in 84 Tests	11.4.1963	
Bowley Frederick Lloyd	Worcestershire	9.11.1873	31.5.1943
Bradshaw Keith	Tasmania; secretary/chief executive MCC 2006–11	2.10.1963	8.11.2021
Brewer Derek Michael	Secretary/chief executive MCC 2012–17	2.4.1958	
Briers Nigel Edwin	Leicestershire; *CY 1993*	15.1.1955	
Brittin Janette Ann MBE	England women	4.7.1959	11.9.2017
Brookes Wilfrid H.	Editor of *Wisden* 1936–39	5.12.1894	28.5.1955
Brunt Katherine Helen	England women	2.7.1985	
Bryan John Lindsay	Kent; *CY 1922*	26.5.1896	23.4.1985
Buchanan John Marshall	Queensland; coach Australia 1999–2007	5.4.1953	
Bucknor Stephen Anthony	Umpire in 128 Tests	31.5.1946	
Bull Frederick George	Essex; *CY 1898*	2.4.1875	16.9.1910
Buller John Sydney MBE	Worcestershire; Test umpire	23.8.1909	7.8.1970
Burnup Cuthbert James	Kent; *CY 1903*	21.11.1875	5.4.1960
Caine Charles Stewart	Editor of *Wisden* 1926–33	28.10.1861	15.4.1933
Calder Harry Lawton	Cranleigh School; *CY 1918*	24.1.1901	15.9.1995
Cardus *Sir* John Frederick Neville	Writer	2.4.1888	27.2.1975
Chalke Stephen Robert	Writer	5.6.1948	
Chapple Glen	Lancashire; *CY 2012*	23.1.1974	
Chester Frank	Worcestershire; Test umpire	20.1.1895	8.4.1957
Stood in 48 Tests between 1924 and 1955, a record that lasted until 1992.			
Clark Belinda Jane	Australia women	10.9.1970	
Clark David Graham	Kent; president MCC 1977–78	27.1.1919	8.10.2013
Clarke Charles Giles CBE	Chairman ECB, 2007–15, pres. ECB, 2015–18	29.5.1953	
Clarke William	Nottinghamshire; founded the All-England XI	24.12.1798	25.8.1856
Collier David Gordon OBE	Chief executive of ECB, 2005–14	22.4.1955	
Collins Arthur Edward Jeune	Clifton College	18.8.1885	11.11.1914
Made 628* in a house match in 1899, the highest score in any cricket until 2016.			
Conan Doyle *Dr Sir* Arthur Ignatius	MCC	22.5.1859	7.7.1930
Creator of Sherlock Holmes; his only victim in first-class cricket was W. G. Grace.			
Connor Clare Joanne CBE	England women; administrator; MCC pres. 2021-22	1.9.1976	
Constant David John	Kent, Leics; first-class umpire 1969–2006	9.11.1941	
Cook Thomas Edwin Reed	Sussex	5.1.1901	15.1.1950
Cox George jnr	Sussex	23.8.1911	30.3.1985
Cox George snr	Sussex	29.11.1873	24.3.1949
Cozier Winston Anthony Lloyd	Broadcaster and writer	10.7.1940	11.5.2016
Dalmiya Jagmohan	Pres. BCCI 2001–04, 2015, pres. ICC 1997–2000	30.5.1940	20.9.2015
Davies Emrys	Glamorgan; Test umpire	27.6.1904	10.11.1975
Davison Brian Fettes	Rhodesia, Leics, Tasmania, Gloucestershire	21.12.1946	
Dawkes George Owen	Leicestershire, Derbyshire	19.7.1920	10.8.2006
Day Arthur Percival	Kent; *CY 1910*	10.4.1885	22.1.1969
de Lisle Timothy John March Phillipps	Editor of *Wisden* 2003	25.6.1962	
Dennett Edward George	Gloucestershire	27.4.1880	14.9.1937
Deutrom Warren Robert	Chief executive, Cricket Ireland 2006–	13.1.1970	
Dhanawade Pranav Prashant	K. C. Gandhi English School	13.5.2000	
Made the highest score in any cricket, 1,009*, in a school match in Mumbai in January 2016.			
Di Venuto Michael James	Tasmania, Derbys, Durham; coach	12.12.1973	
Domingo Russell Craig	Coach South Africa 2013–17, Bangladesh 2019–	30.8.1974	
Eagar Edward Patrick	Photographer	9.3.1944	
Eddings Earl Robert	Chairman of Cricket Australia 2018–21	10.12.1967	
Edwards Charlotte Marie CBE	England women; *CY 2014*	17.12.1979	
Ehsan Mani	President ICC 2003–06; Chairman PCB 2018–21	23.3.1945	
Engel Matthew Lewis	Editor of *Wisden* 1993–2000, 2004–07	11.6.1951	
Farbrace Paul	Kent, Middx; coach SL 2014; asst coach Eng. 2014–19	7.7.1967	
"Felix" (Nicholas Wanostrocht)	Kent, Surrey, All-England	4.10.1804	3.9.1876
Batsman, artist, author (Felix on the Bat) and inventor of the Catapulta bowling machine.			
Ferguson William Henry BEM	Scorer	6.6.1880	22.9.1957
Scorer and baggage-master for five Test teams on 43 tours over 52 years, and "never lost a bag".			

		Born	Died
Findlay William	Oxford U., Lancs; sec. MCC 1926–36	22.6.1880	19.6.1953
Firth John D'Ewes Evelyn	Winchester College; *CY 1918*	21.2.1900	21.9.1957
Fitzpatrick Cathryn Lorraine	Australia women	4.3.1968	
Fletcher Duncan Andrew Gwynne OBE	Zimbabwe; coach England	27.9.1948	
	1999–2007, India 2011–15		
Foot David George	Writer	24.4.1929	25.5.2021
Ford Graham Xavier	Natal B; coach SA 1999–2002, SL 2012–14,	16.11.1960	
	2016–17, Ireland 2017–21		
Foster Henry Knollys	Worcestershire; *CY 1911*	30.10.1873	23.6.1950
Frindall William Howard MBE	Statistician	3.3.1939	30.1.2009
Frith David Edward John	Writer	16.3.1937	
Gibbons Harold Harry Ian Haywood	Worcestershire	8.10.1904	16.2.1973
Gibson Clement Herbert	Eton, Cam. U., Sussex, Argentina; *CY 1918*	23.8.1900	31.12.1976
Gibson Norman <u>Alan</u> Stanley	Writer	28.5.1923	10.4.1997
Gore Adrian Clements	Eton College; *CY 1919*	14.5.1900	7.6.1990
Gould Ian James	Middlesex, Sussex, England; Test umpire	19.8.1957	
Grace *Mrs* Martha	Mother and cricketing mentor of WG	18.7.1812	25.7.1884
Grace William Gilbert jnr	Gloucestershire; son of WG	6.7.1874	2.3.1905
Graveney David Anthony	Gloucestershire, Somerset, Durham	2.1.1953	
Chairman of England selectors 1997–2008.			
Graves Colin James CBE	Chairman of ECB, 2015–20	22.1.1948	
Gray James Roy	Hampshire	19.5.1926	31.10.2016
Gray Malcolm Alexander	President of ICC 2000–03	30.5.1940	
Green David Michael	Lancashire, Gloucestershire; *CY 1969*	10.11.1939	19.3.2016
Grieves Kenneth James	New South Wales, Lancashire	27.8.1925	3.1.1992
Griffith Mike Grenville	Sussex, Camb. Univ; president MCC 2012–13	25.11.1943	
Guha Isa Tara	England women; broadcaster	21.5.1985	
Haigh Gideon Clifford Jeffrey Davidson	Writer	29.12.1965	
Hair Darrell Bruce	Umpire in 78 Tests	30.9.1952	
Hall Louis	Yorkshire; *CY 1890*	1.11.1852	19.11.1915
Hallam Albert William	Lancashire, Nottinghamshire; *CY 1908*	12.11.1869	24.7.1940
Hallam Maurice Raymond	Leicestershire	10.9.1931	1.1.2000
Hallows James	Lancashire; *CY 1905*	14.11.1873	20.5.1910
Hamilton Duncan	Writer	24.12.1958	
Harper Daryl John	Umpire in 95 Tests	23.10.1951	
Harrison Tom William	Derbyshire; chief executive of ECB 2015–	11.12.1971	
Hartley Alfred	Lancashire; *CY 1911*	11.4.1879	9.10.1918
Harvey Ian Joseph	Victoria, Gloucestershire; *CY 2004*	10.4.1972	
Hedges Lionel Paget	Tonbridge School, Kent, Glos; *CY 1919*	13.7.1900	12.1.1933
Henderson Robert	Surrey; *CY 1890*	30.3.1865	28.1.1931
Hesson Michael James	Coach New Zealand 2012–18	30.10.1974	
Hewett Herbert Tremenheere	Somerset; *CY 1893*	25.5.1864	4.3.1921
Heyhoe Flint *Baroness* [Rachael] OBE	England women	11.6.1939	18.1.2017
Hide Mary Edith ("Molly")	England women	24.10.1913	10.9.1995
Hodson Richard <u>Phillip</u>	Cambridge Univ; president MCC 2011–12	26.4.1951	
Horton Henry	Hampshire	18.4.1923	2.11.1998
Howard Cecil <u>Geoffrey</u>	Middlesex; administrator	14.2.1909	8.11.2002
Hughes David Paul	Lancashire; *CY 1988*	13.5.1947	
Huish Frederick Henry	Kent	15.11.1869	16.3.1957
Humpage Geoffrey William	Warwickshire; *CY 1985*	24.4.1954	
Hunter David	Yorkshire	23.2.1860	11.1.1927
Ingleby-Mackenzie Alexander <u>Colin</u> David OBE	Hants; pres. MCC 1996–98	15.9.1933	9.3.2006
Iremonger James	Nottinghamshire; *CY 1903*	5.3.1876	25.3.1956
Isaac Alan Raymond	Chair NZC 2008–10; president ICC 2012–14	20.1.1952	
Jackson Victor Edward	NSW, Leicestershire	25.10.1916	30.1.1965
James Cyril Lionel Robert ("Nello")	Writer	4.1.1901	31.5.1989
Jesty Trevor Edward	Hants, Griq. W., Surrey, Lancs; umpire; *CY 1983*	2.6.1948	
Johnson Paul	Nottinghamshire	24.4.1965	
Johnston Brian Alexander CBE MC	Broadcaster	24.6.1912	5.1.1994

		Born	Died
Jones Alan MBE	Glamorgan; *CY 1978*	4.11.1938	

Played once for England, against Rest of World in 1970, regarded at the time as a Test match.

Keightley Lisa Maree	Aust women; coach Australian women 2019–	26.8.1971	
Kerr Amelia Charlotte	New Zealand women	13.10.2000	

Hit 232*, the highest score in women's ODIs, against Ireland in 2018, aged 17.

Kilburn James Maurice	Writer	8.7.1909	28.8.1993
King John Barton	Philadelphia	19.10.1873	17.10.1965

"Beyond question the greatest all-round cricketer produced by America" – Wisden.

Knight Heather Clare OBE	England women; *CY 2018*	26.12.1990	
Knight Roger David Verdon OBE	Surrey, Glos, Sussex; sec. MCC 1994–2005, pres. MCC 2015–16	6.9.1946	
Knight W. H.	Editor of *Wisden* 1864–79	29.11.1812	16.8.1879
Koertzen Rudolf Eric	Umpire in 108 Tests	26.3.1949	
Lacey *Sir* Francis Eden	Hants; secretary of MCC 1898–1926	19.10.1859	26.5.1946
Lamb Timothy Michael	Middx, Northants; ECB chief exec. 1997–2004	24.3.1953	
Langridge John George MBE	Sussex; Test umpire; *CY 1950*	10.2.1910	27.6.1999
Lanning Meghann Moira	Australia women	25.3.1992	
Lavender Guy William	Secretary/chief executive MCC 2017–	8.7.1967	
Lee Peter Granville	Northamptonshire, Lancashire; *CY 1976*	27.8.1945	
Lillywhite Frederick William	Sussex	13.6.1792	21.8.1854
Long Arnold	Surrey, Sussex	18.12.1940	
Lord Thomas	Middlesex; founder of Lord's	23.11.1755	13.1.1832
Lorgat Haroon	Chief executive of ICC 2008–12	26.5.1960	
Lovett Ian Nicholas	President of ECB 2018–	6.9.1944	
Lyon Beverley Hamilton	Gloucestershire; *CY 1931*	19.1.1902	22.6.1970
McEwan Kenneth Scott	Eastern Province, Essex; *CY 1978*	16.7.1952	
McGilvray Alan David MBE	NSW; broadcaster	6.12.1909	17.7.1996
Maclagan Myrtle Ethel	England women	2.4.1911	11.3.1993
MacLaurin *Lord* [Ian Charter]	Chair of ECB 1997–2002, pres. MCC 2017–18	30.3.1937	
Mandhana Smriti Shriniwas	India women	18.7.1996	
Manners John Errol DSC	Hampshire	25.9.1914	7.3.2020

Believed to be the longest-lived first-class cricketer, at 105 years 164 days.

Manohar Shashank Vyankatesh	Pres. BCCI 2008–11, 2015–16; ICC chair 2015–20	29.9.1957	
Marlar Robin Geoffrey	Sussex; writer; pres. MCC 2005–06	2.1.1931	
Marshal Alan	Surrey; *CY 1909*	12.6.1883	23.7.1915
Martin-Jenkins Christopher Dennis Alexander MBE	Writer; broadcaster; pres. MCC 2010–11	20.1.1945	1.1.2013
Maxwell James Edward	Commentator	28.7.1950	
Mendis Gehan Dixon	Sussex, Lancashire	20.4.1955	
Mercer John	Sussex, Glamorgan; coach and scorer; *CY 1927*	22.4.1893	31.8.1987
Meyer Rollo *John* Oliver OBE	Somerset	15.3.1905	9.3.1991
Miller David Andrew	232 ODIs/T20Is for South Africa and World XI	10.6.1989	
Modi Lalit Kumar	Chairman, Indian Premier League 2008–10	29.11.1963	
Moles Andrew James Warwicks; coach NZ 2008–09, Afg 2014–15, 2019		12.2.1961	
Mooney Bethany Louise	Australia women	14.1.1994	
Moores Peter	Sussex; coach England 2007–09, 2014–15	18.12.1962	
Moorhouse Geoffrey	Writer	29.11.1931	26.11.2009
Morgan Derek Clifton	Derbyshire	26.2.1929	4.11.2017
Morgan Frederick *David* OBE	Chair ECB 2003–07, pres. ICC 2008–10, pres. MCC 2014–15	6.10.1937	
Mynn Alfred	Kent, All-England	19.1.1807	1.11.1861
Neale Phillip Anthony OBE	Worcestershire; England manager; *CY 1989*	5.6.1954	
Newman John Alfred	Hampshire	12.11.1884	21.12.1973
Newstead John Thomas	Yorkshire; *CY 1909*	8.9.1877	25.3.1952
Nicholas Mark Charles Jefford	Hampshire; broadcaster	29.9.1957	
Nicholls Ronald Bernard	Gloucestershire	4.12.1933	21.7.1994
Nixon Paul Andrew	Leicestershire, Kent	21.10.1970	
Nyren John	Hants; author of *The Young Cricketer's Tutor*, 1833	15.12.1764	28.6.1837

	Born	Died
Nyren Richard Hants; Landlord Bat & Ball, Broadhalfpenny Down	1734	25.4.1797
Ontong Rodney Craig Border, Glamorgan, N. Transvaal	9.9.1955	
Ormrod Joseph *Alan* Worcestershire, Lancashire	22.12.1942	
Pardon Charles Frederick Editor of *Wisden* 1887–90	28.3.1850	18.4.1890
Pardon Sydney Herbert Editor of *Wisden* 1891–1925	23.9.1855	20.11.1925
Parks Henry William Sussex	18.7.1906	7.5.1984
Parr George Notts, captain/manager of All-England XI	22.5.1826	23.6.1891
Partridge Norman Ernest Malvern College, Warwickshire; *CY 1919*	10.8.1900	10.3.1982
Patel *Lord* [Kamlesh Kumar] of Bradford OBE Chair of Yorkshire 2021–	28.9 1960	
Pawar Sharadchandra Govindrao Pres. BCCI 2005–08, ICC 2010–12	12.12.1940	
Payton Wilfred Richard Daniel Nottinghamshire	13.2.1882	2.5.1943
Pearce Thomas Neill Essex; administrator	3.11.1905	10.4.1994
Pearson Frederick Worcestershire	23.9.1880	10.11.1963
Perrin Percival Albert ("Peter") Essex; *CY 1905*	26.5.1876	20.11.1945
Perry Ellyse Alexandra Australia women; *CY 2020*	3.11.1990	
Pilch Fuller Norfolk, Kent	17.3.1804	1.5.1870
"The best batsman that has ever yet appeared" – Arthur Haygarth, 1862.		
Pollard Kieron Adrian Trinidad & Tobago; 212 ODIs/T20Is for WI	12.5.1987	
Porter James Alexander Essex; *CY 2018*	25.5.1993	
Preston Hubert Editor of *Wisden* 1944–51	16.12.1868	6.8.1960
Preston Norman MBE Editor of *Wisden* 1952–80	18.3.1903	6.3.1980
Pritchard Thomas Leslie Wellington, Warwickshire, Kent	10.3.1917	22.8.2017
Pybus Richard Alexander Coach Pak 1999–2003, Bang 2012, WI 2019	5.7.1964	
Rainford-Brent Ebony-Jewel England women; broadcaster and coach 31.12.1983		
Cora-Lee Camellia Rosamond		
Rait Kerr *Col.* Rowan Scrope Europeans; sec. MCC 1936–52	13.4.1891	2.4.1961
Raj Mithali Dorai India women	3.12.1982	
Reeves William Essex; Test umpire	22.1.1875	22.3.1944
Rheinberg Netta MBE England women; writer and administrator 24.10.1911		18.6.2006
Rice Clive Edward Butler Transvaal, Nottinghamshire; *CY 1981*	23.7.1949	28.7.2015
Richardson Alan Warwicks, Middx, Worcs; *CY 2012*	6.5.1975	
Roberts Kevin Joseph NSW; CEO Cricket Australia 2018–20	25.7.1972	
Robertson-Glasgow Raymond Charles Somerset; writer	15.7.1901	4.3.1965
Robins Derrick Harold Warwickshire; tour promoter	27.6.1914	3.5.2004
Robinson Mark Andrew OBE Northants, Yorkshire, Sussex; coach	23.11.1966	
Robinson Raymond John Writer	8.7.1905	6.7.1982
Roebuck Peter Michael Somerset; writer; *CY 1988*	6.3.1956	12.11.2011
Rotherham Gerard Alexander Rugby School, Warwickshire; *CY 1918*	28.5.1899	31.1.1985
Sainsbury Peter James Hampshire; *CY 1974*	13.6.1934	12.7.2014
Samson Andrew William Statistician	17.2.1964	
Sawhney Manu Chief executive of ICC 2019–21	1.11.1966	
Sciver Natalie Ruth England women; *CY 2018*	20.8.1992	
Scott Stanley Winckworth Middlesex; *CY 1893*	24.3.1854	8.12.1933
Sellers Arthur <u>Brian</u> MBE Yorkshire; *CY 1940*	5.3.1907	20.2.1981
Seymour James Kent	25.10.1879	30.9.1930
Shepherd David Robert MBE Gloucestershire; umpire in 92 Tests	27.12.1940	27.10.2009
Shepherd Donald John Glamorgan; *CY 1970*	12.8.1927	18.8.2017
Shrubsole Anya MBE England women; *CY 2018*	7.12.1991	
Silk Dennis Raoul Whitehall CBE Somerset; pres. MCC 1992–94	8.10.1931	19.6.2019
Simmons Jack MBE Lancashire, Tasmania; *CY 1985*	28.3.1941	
Skelding Alexander Leics; first-class umpire 1931–58	5.9.1886	17.4.1960
Smith Sydney Gordon Northamptonshire; *CY 1915*	15.1.1881	25.10.1963
Smith William Charles ("Razor") Surrey; *CY 1911*	4.10.1877	15.7.1946
Solanki Vikram Singh Worcestershire, Surrey, England	1.4.1976	
Southerton Sydney James Editor of *Wisden* 1934–35	7.7.1874	12.3.1935
Speed Malcolm Walter Chief executive of ICC 2001–08	14.9.1948	
Spencer Thomas William OBE Kent; Test umpire	22.3.1914	1.11.1995
Srinivasan Narayanaswami Pres. BCCI 2011–14; ICC chair 2014–15	3.1.1945	
Stephenson Franklyn Dacosta Nottinghamshire, Sussex; *CY 1989*	8.4.1959	
Stephenson Harold William Somerset	18.7.1920	23.4.2008

		Born	Died
Stephenson Heathfield Harman	Surrey, All-England	3.5.1832	17.12.1896

Captained first English team to Australia, 1861-62; umpired first Test in England, 1880.

		Born	Died
Stephenson *Lt.-Col.* John Robin CBE	Secretary of MCC 1987–93	25.2.1931	2.6.2003
Stevens Darren Ian	Leicestershire, Kent; *CY 2021*	30.4.1976	
Studd *Sir* John Edward Kynaston	Middlesex	26.7.1858	14.1.1944

Lord Mayor of London 1928–29; president of MCC 1930.

		Born	Died
Surridge Walter Stuart	Surrey; *CY 1953*	3.9.1917	13.4.1992
Sutherland James Alexander	Victoria; CEO Cricket Australia 2001–18	14.7.1965	
Suttle Kenneth George	Sussex	25.8.1928	25.3.2005
Swanton Ernest William ("Jim") CBE	Middlesex; writer	11.2.1907	22.1.2000
Tarrant Francis Alfred	Victoria, Middlesex; *CY 1908*	11.12.1880	29.1.1951
Taufel Simon James Arnold	Umpire in 74 Tests	21.1.1971	
Taylor Brian ("Tonker")	Essex; *CY 1972*	19.6.1932	12.6.2017
Taylor Samantha Claire MBE	England women; *CY 2009*	25.9.1975	
Taylor Stafanie Roxann	West Indies women	11.6.1991	
Taylor Tom Launcelot	Yorkshire; *CY 1901*	25.5.1878	16.3.1960
Thornton Charles Inglis ("Buns")	Middlesex	20.3.1850	10.12.1929
Timms John Edward	Northamptonshire	3.11.1906	18.5.1980
Todd Leslie John	Kent	19.6.1907	20.8.1967
Tunnicliffe John	Yorkshire; *CY 1901*	26.8.1866	11.7.1948
Turner Francis Michael MBE	Leicestershire; administrator	8.8.1934	21.7.2015
Turner Robert Julian	Somerset	25.11.1967	
Ufton Derek Gilbert	Kent	31.5.1928	27.3.2021
van der Bijl Vintcent Adriaan Pieter	Natal, Middx, Transvaal; *CY 1981*	19.3.1948	
van Niekerk Dane	South Africa women; *CY 2022*	14.5.1993	
Virgin Roy Thomas	Somerset, Northamptonshire; *CY 1971*	26.8.1939	
Ward William	Hampshire	24.7.1787	30.6.1849

Scorer of the first recorded double-century: 278 for MCC v Norfolk, 1820.

		Born	Died
Wass Thomas George	Nottinghamshire; *CY 1908*	26.12.1873	27.10.1953
Watmore Ian Charles	Chair of ECB, 2020–21	5.7.1958	
Watson Frank	Lancashire	17.9.1898	1.2.1976
Webber Roy	Statistician	23.7.1914	14.11.1962
Weigall Gerald John Villiers	Kent; coach	19.10.1870	17.5.1944
West George H.	Editor of *Wisden* 1880–86	1851	6.10.1896
Wheatley Oswald Stephen CBE	Warwickshire, Glamorgan; *CY 1969*	28.5.1935	
Whitaker Edgar Haddon OBE	Editor of *Wisden* 1940–43	30.8.1908	5.1.1982
Wight Peter Bernard	Somerset; umpire	25.6.1930	31.12.2015
Wilson Elizabeth Rebecca ("Betty")	Australia women	21.11.1921	22.1.2010
Wilson John Victor	Yorkshire; *CY 1961*	17.1.1921	5.6.2008
Wisden John	Sussex	5.9.1826	5.4.1884

"The Little Wonder"; founder of Wisden Cricketers' Almanack, *1864.*

		Born	Died
Wood Cecil John Burditt	Leicestershire	21.11.1875	5.6.1960
Woodcock John Charles OBE	Writer; editor of *Wisden* 1981–86	7.8.1926	18.7.2021
Wooller Wilfred	Glamorgan	20.11.1912	10.3.1997
Wright Graeme Alexander	Editor of *Wisden* 1987–92, 2001–02	23.4.1943	
Wright Levi George	Derbyshire; *CY 1906*	15.1.1862	11.1.1953
Wright Luke James	Leicestershire, Sussex, England	7.3.1985	
Wynne-Thomas Peter	Statistician, historian and archivist	30.7.1934	15.7.2021
Young Douglas Martin	Worcestershire, Gloucestershire	15.4.1924	18.6.1993

CRICKETERS OF THE YEAR, 1889–2021

| 1889 | *Six Great Bowlers of the Year:* J. Briggs, J. J. Ferris, G. A. Lohmann, R. Peel, C. T. B. Turner, S. M. J. Woods. |

1889   *Six Great Bowlers of the Year:* J. Briggs, J. J. Ferris, G. A. Lohmann, R. Peel, C. T. B. Turner, S. M. J. Woods.

1890   *Nine Great Batsmen of the Year:* R. Abel, W. Barnes, W. Gunn, L. Hall, R. Henderson, J. M. Read, A. Shrewsbury, F. H. Sugg, A. Ward.

1891   *Five Great Wicketkeepers:* J. M. Blackham, G. MacGregor, R. Pilling, M. Sherwin, H. Wood.

1892   *Five Great Bowlers:* W. Attewell, J. T. Hearne, F. Martin, A. W. Mold, J. W. Sharpe.

1893   *Five Batsmen of the Year:* H. T. Hewett, L. C. H. Palairet, W. W. Read, S. W. Scott, A. E. Stoddart.

1894   *Five All-Round Cricketers:* G. Giffen, A. Hearne, F. S. Jackson, G. H. S. Trott, E. Wainwright.

1895   *Five Young Batsmen of the Season:* W. Brockwell, J. T. Brown, C. B. Fry, T. W. Hayward, A. C. MacLaren.

1896   W. G. Grace.

1897   *Five Cricketers of the Season:* S. E. Gregory, A. A. Lilley, K. S. Ranjitsinhji, T. Richardson, H. Trumble.

1898   *Five Cricketers of the Year:* F. G. Bull, W. R. Cuttell, N. F. Druce, G. L. Jessop, J. R. Mason.

1899   *Five Great Players of the Season:* W. H. Lockwood, W. Rhodes, W. Storer, C. L. Townsend, A. E. Trott.

1900   *Five Cricketers of the Season:* J. Darling, C. Hill, A. O. Jones, M. A. Noble, Major R. M. Poore.

1901   *Mr R. E. Foster and Four Yorkshiremen:* R. E. Foster, S. Haigh, G. H. Hirst, T. L. Taylor, J. Tunnicliffe.

1902   L. C. Braund, C. P. McGahey, F. Mitchell, W. G. Quaife, J. T. Tyldesley.

1903   W. W. Armstrong, C. J. Burnup, J. Iremonger, J. J. Kelly, V. T. Trumper.

1904   C. Blythe, J. Gunn, A. E. Knight, W. Mead, P. F. Warner.

1905   B. J. T. Bosanquet, E. A. Halliwell, J. Hallows, P. A. Perrin, R. H. Spooner.

1906   D. Denton, W. S. Lees, G. J. Thompson, J. Vine, L. G. Wright.

1907   J. N. Crawford, A. Fielder, E. G. Hayes, K. L. Hutchings, N. A. Knox.

1908   A. W. Hallam, R. O. Schwarz, F. A. Tarrant, A. E. E. Vogler, T. G. Wass.

1909   *Lord Hawke and Four Cricketers of the Year:* J. B. Hobbs, A. Marshal, J. T. Newstead.

1910   W. Bardsley, S. F. Barnes, D. W. Carr, A. P. Day, V. S. Ransford.

1911   H. K. Foster, A. Hartley, C. B. Llewellyn, W. C. Smith, F. E. Woolley.

1912   *Five Members of MCC's team in Australia:* F. R. Foster, J. W. Hearne, S. P. Kinneir, C. P. Mead, H. Strudwick.

1913   *Special Portrait:* John Wisden.

1914   M. W. Booth, G. Gunn, J. W. Hitch, A. E. Relf, Hon. L. H. Tennyson.

1915   J. W. H. T. Douglas, P. G. H. Fender, H. T. W. Hardinge, D. J. Knight, S. G. Smith.

1916–17   *No portraits appeared.*

1918   *School Bowlers of the Year:* H. L. Calder, J. D. E. Firth, C. H. Gibson, G. A. Rotherham, G. T. S. Stevens.

1919   *Five Public School Cricketers of the Year:* P. W. Adams, A. P. F. Chapman, A. C. Gore, L. P. Hedges, N. E. Partridge.

1920   *Five Batsmen of the Year:* A. Ducat, E. H. Hendren, P. Holmes, H. Sutcliffe, E. Tyldesley.

1921   *Special Portrait:* P. F. Warner.

1922   H. Ashton, J. L. Bryan, J. M. Gregory, C. G. Macartney, E. A. McDonald.

1923   A. W. Carr, A. P. Freeman, C. W. L. Parker, A. C. Russell, A. Sandham.

1924   *Five Bowlers of the Year:* A. E. R. Gilligan, R. Kilner, G. G. Macaulay, C. H. Parkin, M. W. Tate.

1925   R. H. Catterall, J. C. W. MacBryan, H. W. Taylor, R. K. Tyldesley, W. W. Whysall.

1926   *Special Portrait:* J. B. Hobbs.

1927   G. Geary, H. Larwood, J. Mercer, W. A. Oldfield, W. M. Woodfull.

1928   R. C. Blunt, C. Hallows, W. R. Hammond, D. R. Jardine, V. W. C. Jupp.

1929   L. E. G. Ames, G. Duckworth, M. Leyland, S. J. Staples, J. C. White.

1930   E. H. Bowley, K. S. Duleepsinhji, H. G. Owen-Smith, R. W. V. Robins, R. E. S. Wyatt.

1931   D. G. Bradman, C. V. Grimmett, B. H. Lyon, I. A. R. Peebles, M. J. Turnbull.

1932   W. E. Bowes, S. S. Dempster, James Langridge, Nawab of Pataudi snr, H. Verity.

1933   W. E. Astill, F. R. Brown, A. S. Kennedy, C. K. Nayudu, W. Voce.

1934   A. H. Bakewell, G. A. Headley, M. S. Nichols, L. F. Townsend, C. F. Walters.

1935   S. J. McCabe, W. J. O'Reilly, G. A. E. Paine, W. H. Ponsford, C. I. J. Smith.

1936   H. B. Cameron, E. R. T. Holmes, B. Mitchell, D. Smith, A. W. Wellard.
1937   C. J. Barnett, W. H. Copson, A. R. Gover, V. M. Merchant, T. S. Worthington.
1938   T. W. J. Goddard, J. Hardstaff jnr, L. Hutton, J. H. Parks, E. Paynter.
1939   H. T. Bartlett, W. A. Brown, D. C. S. Compton, K. Farnes, A. Wood.
1940   L. N. Constantine, W. J. Edrich, W. W. Keeton, A. B. Sellers, D. V. P. Wright.
1941–46 No portraits appeared.
1947   A. V. Bedser, L. B. Fishlock, V. (M. H.) Mankad, T. P. B. Smith, C. Washbrook.
1948   M. P. Donnelly, A. Melville, A. D. Nourse, J. D. Robertson, N. W. D. Yardley.
1949   A. L. Hassett, W. A. Johnston, R. R. Lindwall, A. R. Morris, D. Tallon.
1950   T. E. Bailey, R. O. Jenkins, John Langridge, R. T. Simpson, B. Sutcliffe.
1951   T. G. Evans, S. Ramadhin, A. L. Valentine, E. D. Weekes, F. M. M. Worrell.
1952   R. Appleyard, H. E. Dollery, J. C. Laker, P. B. H. May, E. A. B. Rowan.
1953   H. Gimblett, T. W. Graveney, D. S. Sheppard, W. S. Surridge, F. S. Trueman.
1954   R. N. Harvey, G. A. R. Lock, K. R. Miller, J. H. Wardle, W. Watson.
1955   B. Dooland, Fazal Mahmood, W. E. Hollies, J. B. Statham, G. E. Tribe.
1956   M. C. Cowdrey, D. J. Insole, D. J. McGlew, H. J. Tayfield, F. H. Tyson.
1957   D. Brookes, J. W. Burke, M. J. Hilton, G. R. A. Langley, P. E. Richardson.
1958   P. J. Loader, A. J. McIntyre, O. G. Smith, M. J. Stewart, C. L. Walcott.
1959   H. L. Jackson, R. E. Marshall, C. A. Milton, J. R. Reid, D. Shackleton.
1960   K. F. Barrington, D. B. Carr, R. Illingworth, G. Pullar, M. J. K. Smith.
1961   N. A. T. Adcock, E. R. Dexter, R. A. McLean, R. Subba Row, J. V. Wilson.
1962   W. E. Alley, R. Benaud, A. K. Davidson, W. M. Lawry, N. C. O'Neill.
1963   D. Kenyon, Mushtaq Mohammad, P. H. Parfitt, P. J. Sharpe, F. J. Titmus.
1964   D. B. Close, C. C. Griffith, C. C. Hunte, R. B. Kanhai, G. S. Sobers.
1965   G. Boycott, P. J. Burge, J. A. Flavell, G. D. McKenzie, R. B. Simpson.
1966   K. C. Bland, J. H. Edrich, R. C. Motz, P. M. Pollock, R. G. Pollock.
1967   R. W. Barber, B. L. D'Oliveira, C. Milburn, J. T. Murray, S. M. Nurse.
1968   Asif Iqbal, Hanif Mohammad, K. Higgs, J. M. Parks, Nawab of Pataudi jnr.
1969   J. G. Binks, D. M. Green, B. A. Richards, D. L. Underwood, O. S. Wheatley.
1970   B. F. Butcher, A. P. E. Knott, Majid Khan, M. J. Procter, D. J. Shepherd.
1971   J. D. Bond, C. H. Lloyd, B. W. Luckhurst, G. M. Turner, R. T. Virgin.
1972   G. G. Arnold, B. S. Chandrasekhar, L. R. Gibbs, B. Taylor, Zaheer Abbas.
1973   G. S. Chappell, D. K. Lillee, R. A. L. Massie, J. A. Snow, K. R. Stackpole.
1974   K. D. Boyce, B. E. Congdon, K. W. R. Fletcher, R. C. Fredericks, P. J. Sainsbury.
1975   D. L. Amiss, M. H. Denness, N. Gifford, A. W. Greig, A. M. E. Roberts.
1976   I. M. Chappell, P. G. Lee, R. B. McCosker, D. S. Steele, R. A. Woolmer.
1977   J. M. Brearley, C. G. Greenidge, M. A. Holding, I. V. A. Richards, R. W. Taylor.
1978   I. T. Botham, M. Hendrick, A. Jones, K. S. McEwan, R. G. D. Willis.
1979   D. I. Gower, J. K. Lever, C. M. Old, C. T. Radley, J. N. Shepherd.
1980   J. Garner, S. M. Gavaskar, G. A. Gooch, D. W. Randall, R. C. Rose.
1981   K. J. Hughes, R. D. Jackman, A. J. Lamb, C. E. B. Rice, V. A. P. van der Bijl.
1982   T. M. Alderman, A. R. Border, R. J. Hadlee, Javed Miandad, R. W. Marsh.
1983   Imran Khan, T. E. Jesty, A. I. Kallicharran, Kapil Dev, M. D. Marshall.
1984   M. Amarnath, J. V. Coney, J. E. Emburey, M. W. Gatting, C. L. Smith.
1985   M. D. Crowe, H. A. Gomes, G. W. Humpage, J. Simmons, S. Wettimuny.
1986   P. Bainbridge, R. M. Ellison, C. J. McDermott, N. V. Radford, R. T. Robinson.
1987   J. H. Childs, G. A. Hick, D. B. Vengsarkar, C. A. Walsh, J. J. Whitaker.
1988   J. P. Agnew, N. A. Foster, D. P. Hughes, P. M. Roebuck, Salim Malik.
1989   K. J. Barnett, P. J. L. Dujon, P. A. Neale, F. D. Stephenson, S. R. Waugh.
1990   S. J. Cook, D. M. Jones, R. C. Russell, R. A. Smith, M. A. Taylor.
1991   M. A. Atherton, M. Azharuddin, A. R. Butcher, D. L. Haynes, M. E. Waugh.
1992   C. E. L. Ambrose, P. A. J. DeFreitas, A. A. Donald, R. B. Richardson, Waqar Younis.
1993   N. E. Briers, M. D. Moxon, I. D. K. Salisbury, A. J. Stewart, Wasim Akram.
1994   D. C. Boon, I. A. Healy, M. G. Hughes, S. K. Warne, J. L. Watkin.
1995   B. C. Lara, D. E. Malcolm, T. A. Munton, S. J. Rhodes, K. C. Wessels.
1996   D. G. Cork, P. A. de Silva, A. R. C. Fraser, A. Kumble, D. A. Reeve.
1997   S. T. Jayasuriya, Mushtaq Ahmed, Saeed Anwar, P. V. Simmons, S. R. Tendulkar.
1998   M. T. G. Elliott, S. G. Law, G. D. McGrath, M. P. Maynard, G. P. Thorpe.
1999   I. D. Austin, D. Gough, M. Muralitharan, A. Ranatunga, J. N. Rhodes.
2000   C. L. Cairns, R. Dravid, L. Klusener, T. M. Moody, Saqlain Mushtaq.

Cricketers of the Century D. G. Bradman, G. S. Sobers, J. B. Hobbs, S. K. Warne, I. V. A. Richards.

2001	M. W. Alleyne, M. P. Bicknell, A. R. Caddick, J. L. Langer, D. S. Lehmann.
2002	A. Flower, A. C. Gilchrist, J. N. Gillespie, V. V. S. Laxman, D. R. Martyn.
2003	M. L. Hayden, A. J. Hollioake, N. Hussain, S. M. Pollock, M. P. Vaughan.
2004	C. J. Adams, A. Flintoff, I. J. Harvey, G. Kirsten, G. C. Smith.
2005	A. F. Giles, S. J. Harmison, R. W. T. Key, A. J. Strauss, M. E. Trescothick.
2006	M. J. Hoggard, S. P. Jones, B. Lee, K. P. Pietersen, R. T. Ponting.
2007	P. D. Collingwood, D. P. M. D. Jayawardene, Mohammad Yousuf, M. S. Panesar, M. R. Ramprakash.
2008	I. R. Bell, S. Chanderpaul, O. D. Gibson, R. J. Sidebottom, Zaheer Khan.
2009	J. M. Anderson, D. M. Benkenstein, M. V. Boucher, N. D. McKenzie, S. C. Taylor.
2010	S. C. J. Broad, M. J. Clarke, G. Onions, M. J. Prior, G. P. Swann.
2011	E. J. G. Morgan, C. M. W. Read, Tamim Iqbal, I. J. L. Trott.
2012	T. T. Bresnan, G. Chapple, A. N. Cook, A. Richardson, K. C. Sangakkara.
2013	H. M. Amla, N. R. D. Compton, J. H. Kallis, M. N. Samuels, D. W. Steyn.
2014	S. Dhawan, C. M. Edwards, R. J. Harris, C. J. L. Rogers, J. E. Root.
2015	M. M. Ali, G. S. Ballance, A. Lyth, A. D. Mathews, J. S. Patel.
2016	J. M. Bairstow, B. B. McCullum, S. P. D. Smith, B. A. Stokes, K. S. Williamson.
2017	B. M. Duckett, Misbah-ul-Haq, T. S. Roland-Jones, C. R. Woakes, Younis Khan.
2018	S. D. Hope, H. C. Knight, J. A. Porter, N. R. Sciver, A. Shrubsole.
2019	T. T. Beaumont, R. J. Burns, J. C. Buttler, S. M. Curran, V. Kohli.
2020	J. C. Archer, P. J. Cummins, S. R. Harmer, M. Labuschagne, E. A. Perry.
2021	Z. Crawley, J. O. Holder, Mohammad Rizwan, D. P. Sibley, D. I. Stevens.
2022	**J. J. Bumrah, D. P. Conway, O. E. Robinson, R. G. Sharma, D. van Niekerk.**

From 2001 to 2003 the award was made on the basis of all cricket round the world, not just the English season. This ended in 2004 with the start of Wisden's Leading Cricketer in the World award. Sanath Jayasuriya was chosen in 1997 for his influence on the English season, stemming from the 1996 World Cup. In 2011, only four were named, after the Lord's spot-fixing scandal made one selection unsustainable.

CRICKETERS OF THE YEAR: AN ANALYSIS

The special portrait of John Wisden in 1913 marked the 50th anniversary of his retirement – and the 50th edition of the Almanack. Wisden died in 1884. The special portraits of P. F. Warner in 1921 and J. B. Hobbs in 1926 followed their earlier selection as a Cricketer of the Year in 1904 and 1909 respectively. These portraits, and the Cricketers of the Century in 2000, are excluded from the analysis below. The latest five players bring the number chosen since 1889 to 615. They come from 44 different teams, as follows:

Australians	75	Sussex	23	Cambridge Univ	10	Cranleigh School	1
Surrey	52	Somerset	21	Durham	8	Malvern College	1
Yorkshire	47	Indians	18	Leicestershire	8	Oval Invincibles	1
Lancashire	35	Gloucestershire	17	Oxford Univ	7	Rugby School	1
Kent	30	Worcestershire	17	Sri Lankans	7	Southern Brave	1
Middlesex	30	Hampshire	16	England Women	6	Staffordshire	1
Nottinghamshire	29	Northamptonshire	15	Eton College	2	Tonbridge School	1
South Africans	28	Pakistanis	15	Australia Women	1	Univ College School	1
West Indians	28	Derbyshire	13	Bangladeshis	1	Uppingham School	1
Warwickshire	27	Glamorgan	13	Berkshire	1	Winchester College	1
Essex	26	New Zealanders	11	Cheltenham College	1	Zimbabweans	1

Schoolboys were chosen in 1918 and 1919, because first-class cricket had been suspended during the war. The total number of sides comes to 649 because 34 players appeared for more than one side (excluding England men) in the year for which they were chosen.

Types of Player

Of the 615 Cricketers of the Year, 304 are best classified as batters, 167 as bowlers, 103 as all-rounders and 41 as wicketkeepers or wicketkeeper-batsmen.

Research: Robert Brooke

PART NINE

The Almanack

OFFICIAL BODIES

INTERNATIONAL CRICKET COUNCIL

The ICC are world cricket's governing body. They are responsible for managing the playing conditions and Code of Conduct for international fixtures, expanding the game and organising the major tournaments, including World Cups. Their mission statement says the ICC "will lead by providing a world-class environment for international cricket, delivering major events across three formats, providing targeted support to members and promoting the global game".

Twelve national governing bodies are currently Full Members of the ICC; full membership qualifies a nation (or geographic area) to play official Test matches. A candidate for full membership must meet a number of playing and administrative criteria, after which elevation is decided by a vote among existing Full Members. The former categories of associate and affiliate membership merged in 2017; there are currently 94 Associate Members.

The ICC were founded in 1909 as the Imperial Cricket Conference by three Foundation Members: England, Australia and South Africa. Other countries (or geographic areas) became Full Members, and thus acquired Test status, as follows: India, New Zealand and West Indies in 1926, Pakistan in 1952, Sri Lanka in 1981, Zimbabwe in 1992, Bangladesh in 2000, and Afghanistan and Ireland in 2017. South Africa ceased to be a member on leaving the Commonwealth in 1961, but were re-elected as a Full Member in 1991.

In 1965, "Imperial" was replaced by "International", and countries from outside the Commonwealth were elected for the first time. The first Associate Members were Ceylon (later Sri Lanka), Fiji and the USA. Foundation Members retained a veto over all resolutions. In 1989, the renamed International Cricket Council (rather than "Conference") adopted revised rules, aimed at producing an organisation which could make a larger number of binding decisions, rather than simply make recommendations to national governing bodies. In 1993, the Council, previously administered by MCC, gained their own secretariat and chief executive. The category of Foundation Member was abolished.

In 1997, the Council became an incorporated body, with an executive board, and a president instead of a chairman. The ICC remained at Lord's, with a commercial base in Monaco, until August 2005, when after 96 years they moved to Dubai in the United Arab Emirates, which offered organisational and tax advantages.

In 2014, the ICC board approved a new structure, under which they were led by a chair again, while India, Australia and England took permanent places on key committees. But in 2016 the special privileges given to these three were dismantled and, in early 2017, the board agreed to revise the constitution on more egalitarian lines.

Officers

Chair: G. J. Barclay. *Deputy Chair:* I. Khwaja. *Chief Executive:* G. J. Allardice.

Committee Chairs – Chief Executives' Committee: G. J. Allardice. *Men's Cricket:* S. C. Ganguly. *Women's Cricket:* C. J. Connor. *Finance and Commercial Affairs:* TBC. *Audit:* Y. Narayan. *Development:* I. Khwaja. *Nominations Committee:* G. J. Barclay. *Code of Conduct Commission:* M. J. Beloff QC. *Disputes Resolution Committee:* M. J. Beloff QC. *Membership:* R. A. McCollum *Medical Advisory:* Dr P. Harcourt. *Independent Anti-Corruption Oversight:* D. Howman. *HR & Remuneration:* R. O. Skerritt. *Anti-Corruption Unit Chair:* Sir Ronnie Flanagan. *ICC Ethics Officer:* P. Nicholson.

ICC Board: The chair and chief executive sit on the board *ex officio*. They are joined by I. K. Nooyi (independent female director), M. Darlow (England), R. J. Freudenstein (Australia), S. C. Ganguly (India), I. Khwaja (Singapore), R. A. McCollum (Ireland), T. Mukuhlani (Zimbabwe), L. Naidoo (South Africa), Nazmul Hassan (Bangladesh), Ramiz Raja (Pakistan), A. S. S. Silva (Sri Lanka), R. O. Skerritt (West Indies), M. C. Snedden (New Zealand), N. Speight (Bermuda), M. Vallipuram (Malaysia). There was no Afghanistan representative at the start of 2022.

Chief Executives' Committee: The chief executive, chair and the chairs of the cricket and women's committees sit on this committee *ex officio*. They are joined by the chief executives of the 12 Full Member boards and three Associate Member boards: R. Bajwa (Canada), S. Damodar (Botswana), A. M. de Silva (Sri Lanka), W. R. Deutrom (Ireland), Faisal Hasnain (Pakistan), J. M. Grave (West Indies), T. W. Harrison (England), N. Hockley (Australia), G. Makoni (Zimbabwe), P. Moseki (South Africa), Nizam Uddin Chowdhury (Bangladesh), J. Shah (India), M. Usmani (UAE), D. J. White (New Zealand). There was no Afghanistan representative at the start of 2022.

Chief Financial Officer: A. Khanna. *Chief Commercial Officer:* A. Dahiya. *General Counsel/ Company Secretary:* J. Hall. *General Manager – Cricket:* TBC. *General Manager – Integrity Unit:* A. J. Marshall. *General Manager – Marketing & Communications:* C. Furlong. *General Manager – Development:* W. Glenwright. *Head of Events:* C. M. B. Tetley. *Head of Internal Audit:* Muhammad Ali. *Senior Manager Broadcast/Executive Producer – ICC TV:* A. Ramachandran. *Vice-President – Media Rights:* S. Manoharan.

Membership

Full Members (12)   Afghanistan, Australia, Bangladesh, England, India, Ireland, New Zealand, Pakistan, South Africa, Sri Lanka, West Indies and Zimbabwe.

Associate Members* (94)

Africa (18)   Botswana (2005), Cameroon (2007), eSwatini (formerly Swaziland) (2007), Gambia (2002), Ghana (2002), Kenya (1981), Lesotho (2001), Malawi (2003), Mali (2005), Mozambique (2003), Namibia (1992), Nigeria (2002), Rwanda (2003), St Helena (2001), Seychelles (2010), Sierra Leone (2002), Tanzania (2001), Uganda (1998).

Americas (16)   Argentina (1974), Bahamas (1987), Belize (1997), Bermuda (1966), Brazil (2002), Canada (1968), Cayman Islands (2002), Chile (2002), Costa Rica (2002), Falkland Islands (2007), Mexico (2004), Panama (2002), Peru (2007), Suriname (2002), Turks & Caicos Islands (2002), USA (1965/2019).

Asia (18)   Bahrain (2001), Bhutan (2001), China (2004), Hong Kong (1969), Iran (2003), Kuwait (2005), Malaysia (1967), Maldives (2001), Mongolia (2021), Myanmar (2006), Nepal (1996), Oman (2000), Qatar (1999), Saudi Arabia (2003), Singapore (1974), Tajikistan (2021), Thailand (2005), United Arab Emirates (1990).

East Asia Pacific (9)   Cook Islands (2000), Fiji (1965), Indonesia (2001), Japan (2005), Papua New Guinea (1973), Philippines (2000), Samoa (2000), South Korea (2001), Vanuatu (1995).

Europe (33)   Austria (1992), Belgium (2005), Bulgaria (2008), Croatia (2001), Cyprus (1999), Czechia (2000), Denmark (1966), Estonia (2008), Finland (2000), France (1998), Germany (1999), Gibraltar (1969), Greece (1995), Guernsey (2005), Hungary (2012), Isle of Man (2004), Israel (1974), Italy (1995), Jersey (2007), Luxembourg (1998), Malta (1998), Netherlands (1966), Norway (2000), Portugal (1996), Romania (2013), Russia (2012), Scotland (1994), Serbia (2015), Slovenia (2005), Spain (1992), Sweden (1997), Switzerland (1985/2021), Turkey (2008).

* Year of election shown in parentheses. Switzerland (1985) were removed in 2012 (but returned in 2021); Cuba (2002) and Tonga (2000) in 2013; Brunei (1992) in 2014; the USA in 2017, though a new USA body were admitted in 2019; Morocco (1999) in 2019; and Zambia in 2021. Russia were suspended in 2021.

Full Members are the governing bodies for cricket of a country recognised by the ICC, or nations associated for cricket purposes, or a geographical area, from which representative teams are qualified to play official Test matches.

Associate Members are the governing bodies for cricket of a country recognised by the ICC, or countries associated for cricket purposes, or a geographical area, which does not qualify as a Full Member, but where cricket is firmly established and organised.

Addresses

ICC Street 69, Dubai Sports City, Sh Mohammed Bin Zayed Road, PO Box 500 070, Dubai, United Arab Emirates (+971 4382 8800; www.icc-cricket.com; enquiry@icc-cricket.com; Twitter: @ICC).

Afghanistan Afghanistan Cricket Board, Kabul International Cricket Stadium, Kabul Nandari, District 8, Kabul (+93 78 813 3144; www.cricket.af; info@afghancricket.af; @ACBofficials).

Australia Cricket Australia, 60 Jolimont Street, Jolimont, Victoria 3002 (+61 3 9653 9999; www.cricketaustralia.com.au; public.enquiries@cricket.com.au; @CricketAus).

Bangladesh Bangladesh Cricket Board, Sher-e-Bangla National Cricket Stadium, Mirpur, Dhaka 1216 (+880 2 803 1001; www.tigercricket.com.bd; info@tigercricket.com.bd; @BCBtigers).

England England and Wales Cricket Board (see below).

India Board of Control for Cricket in India, Cricket Centre, 4th Floor, Wankhede Stadium, D Road, Churchgate, Mumbai 400 020 (+91 22 2289 8800; www.bcci.tv; office@bcci.tv; @BCCI).

Ireland Cricket Ireland, 15c Kinsealy Business Park, Kinsealy, Co Dublin K36 YH61 (+353 1 894 7914; www.cricketireland.ie; info@cricketireland.ie; @CricketIreland).

New Zealand New Zealand Cricket, PO Box 8353, Level 4, 8 Nugent Street, Grafton, Auckland 1023 (+64 9 393 9700; www.nzc.nz; info@nzc.nz; @Blackcaps).

Pakistan Pakistan Cricket Board, Gaddafi Stadium, Ferozpur Road, Lahore 54600 (+92 42 3571 7231; www.pcb.com.pk; inquiry@pcb.com.pk; @TheRealPCB).

South Africa Cricket South Africa, PO Box 55009 Northlands 2116; 86, 5th & Glenhove St, Melrose Estate, Johannesburg (+27 11 880 2810; www.cricket.co.za; info@cricket.co.za; @OfficialCSA).

Sri Lanka Sri Lanka Cricket, 35 Maitland Place, Colombo 07000 (+94 112 681 601; www.srilankacricket.lk; info@srilankacricket.lk; @OfficialSLC).

West Indies West Indies Cricket Board, PO Box 616 W, Factory Road, St John's, Antigua (+1 268 481 2450; www.windiescricket.com; cwi@cricketwestindies.org; @windiescricket).

Zimbabwe Zimbabwe Cricket, PO Box 2739, Josiah Tongogara Avenue/Fifth Street, Harare (+263 4 788 090; www.zimcricket.org; info@zimcricket.org; @ZimCricketv).

Associate Members' addresses may be found on the ICC website, www.icc-cricket.com.

ENGLAND AND WALES CRICKET BOARD

The England and Wales Cricket Board (ECB) are responsible for the administration of all cricket – professional and recreational – in England and Wales. In 1997, they took over the functions of the Cricket Council, the Test and County Cricket Board and the National Cricket Association, which had run the game since 1968. In 2005, a streamlined constitution replaced a management board of 18 with a 12-strong board of directors, three appointed by the first-class counties, two by the county boards. In 2010, this expanded to 14, and added the ECB's first women directors. After a governance review, it returned to 12, including four independent non-executive directors, in 2018.

Officers

President: I. N. Lovett. *Interim Chair:* B. J. O'Brien. *Chief Executive Officer:* T. W. Harrison.

Board of Directors: Baroness Amos, K. Bickerstaffe, M. Darlow, A. P. Dickinson, T. W. Harrison, R. M. Kalifa, B. J. O'Brien, L. C. Pearson, S. A. Smith, B. D. H. Trenowden, J. H. Wood.

Committee Chairs – Anti-Corruption: M. Darlow. *Finance, Audit & Risk:* A. P. Dickinson. *Environmental, Social & Governance:* B. D. H. Trenowden. *Cricket:* Sir Andrew Strauss. *Discipline:* T. J. G. O'Gorman. *Recreational Assembly:* J. H. Wood. *Regulatory:* N. I. Coward. *Remuneration:* B. J. O'Brien.

Chief Operating Officer: D. J. Mahoney. *Chief Financial Officer:* S. A. Smith. *Chief Commercial Officer:* T. Singh. *Chief Diversity & Communications Officer:* K. Miller. *Managing Director, County Cricket:* N. Snowball. *Managing Director, The Hundred:* S. Patel. *Managing Director, England Men's Cricket (Interim):* Sir Andrew Strauss. *Managing Director, England Women's Cricket:* C. J. Connor. *People & Culture Director:* C. F. Dale.

ECB: Lord's Ground, London NW8 8QZ (020 7432 1200; www.ecb.co.uk; feedback@ecb.co.uk; Twitter @ECB_cricket).

THE MARYLEBONE CRICKET CLUB

The Marylebone Cricket Club evolved out of the White Conduit Club in 1787, when Thomas Lord laid out his first ground in Dorset Square. Their members revised the Laws in 1788 and gradually took responsibility for cricket throughout the world. However, they relinquished control of the game in the UK in 1968, and the International Cricket Council finally established their own secretariat in 1993. MCC still own Lord's, and remain the guardian of the Laws. They call themselves "a private club with a public function", and aim to support cricket everywhere, especially at grassroots level and in countries where the game is least developed.

Patron: HER MAJESTY THE QUEEN

Officers

President: 2021–22 – C. J. Connor. *Club Chairman:* B. N. Carnegie-Brown. *Treasurer:* A. B. Elgood. *Trustees:* M. V. Fleming, R. S. Leigh, J. S. Varley. *Hon. Life Vice-Presidents:* C. A. Fry, M. G. Griffith, A. R. Lewis, Sir Oliver Popplewell, O. H. J. Stocken, M. O. C. Sturt.

Chief Executive and Secretary: G. W. Lavender. *Assistant Secretaries – Cricket:* J. Cox. *Estates:* R. J. Ebdon. *Finance:* A. D. Cameron. *Commercial:* A. N. Muggleton. *Legal:* H. A. Roper-Curzon. *Membership:* M. H. Choudhury.

MCC Committee: R. Q. Cake, A. R. C. Fraser, N. J. C. Gandon, V. K. Griffiths, C. M. Gupte, W. J. House, G. W. Jones, N. M. Peters. The president, club chair, treasurer and committee chairs are also on the committee.

Committee Chairs – Cricket: S. C. Taylor. *Estates:* A. J. Johnston. *Finance:* A. B. Elgood. *Heritage and Collections:* J. O. D. Orders. *Membership and General Purposes:* Sir Ian Magee. *World Cricket:* M. W. Gatting.

MCC: Lord's Ground, London NW8 8QN (020 7616 8500; www.lords.org; reception@mcc.org.uk; Twitter@MCCOfficial. Tickets 020 7432 1000; ticketing@mcc.org.uk).

PROFESSIONAL CRICKETERS' ASSOCIATION

The Professional Cricketers' Association were formed in 1967 (as the Cricketers' Association) to be the collective voice of first-class professional players, and enhance and protect their interests. During the 1970s, they succeeded in establishing pension schemes and a minimum wage. In recent years, their strong commercial operations and greater funding from the ECB have increased their services to current and past players, including education, legal and financial help. In 2011, these services were extended to England's women cricketers.

President: C. M. Edwards. *Chair:* J. A. R. Harris. *Vice-chairs:* A. K. Dal and H. C. Knight. *President – Professional Cricketers' Trust:* D. A. Graveney. *Non-Executive Chair:* J. R. Metherell. *Non-Executive Directors:* I. T. Guha, P. G. Read, S. N. White. *Chief Executive:* R. K. Lynch. *Director of Member Services:* I. J. Thomas. *Director of Cricket Operations:* D. K. H. Mitchell. *Director of Finance:* P. Garrett. *Head of Cricket Operations:* R. Hudson. *Head of Player Rights and Women's Cricket:* E. M. Reid. *Player Rights Manager:* E. Caldwell. *Membership Services Manager:* A. Prosser. *Commercial Manager:* A. Phipps. *Head of Fundraising:* K. Ford. *Head of Communications:* L. Reynolds.

PCA: *London Office* – The Bedser Stand, The Oval, Kennington, London SE11 5SS (0207 449 4228; www.thepca.co.uk; communications@thepca.co.uk; Twitter @PCA). *Birmingham Office* – Box 108–9, R. E. S. Wyatt Stand, Edgbaston Stadium, Birmingham B5 7QU.

CRIME AND PUNISHMENT

ICC Code of Conduct – Breaches and Penalties in 2020-21 to 2021-22

T. G. Southee New Zealand v Australia, Third T20I at Wellington
Shouted at umpire after batter survived on umpire's call. Reprimand/1 demerit pt – J. J. Crowe

M. D. Gunathilleke Sri Lanka v West Indies, Third ODI at Coolidge
Inappropriate language on dismissing N. Pooran. Reprimand/1 demerit pt – R. B. Richardson

K. A. Jamieson New Zealand v Bangladesh, Second ODI at Christchurch
Inappropriate language to umpire after DRS appeal rejected. 15% fine/1 demerit pt – J. J. Crowe

S. S. B. Magala South Africa v Pakistan, Fourth T20I at Centurion
Knocked bails off stumps while walking back to his mark. Reprimand/1 demerit pt – A. J. Pycroft

B. R. M. Taylor Zimbabwe v Pakistan, Second Test at Harare
Indicated thigh pad when given out caught behind. Reprimand/1 demerit pt – A. J. Pycroft

Tamim Iqbal Bangladesh v Sri Lanka, Third ODI at Mirpur
Inappropriate language after unsuccessful review. 15% fine/1 demerit pt – Neeyamur Rashid

B. Muzarabani Zimbabwe v Bangladesh, Only Test at Harare
Inappropriate physical contact with Taskin Ahmed. 15% fine/1 demerit pt – A. J. Pycroft

Taskin Ahmed Bangladesh v Zimbabwe, Only Test at Harare
Inappropriate physical contact with B. Muzarabani. 15% fine/1 demerit pt – A. J. Pycroft

J. B. Little Ireland v South Africa, Third ODI at Malahide
Inappropriate physical contact with Q. de Kock. 15% fine/1 demerit pt – K. Gallagher

M. R. Adair Ireland v South Africa, Third ODI at Malahide
Audible obscenity when hit for four. Reprimand/1 demerit pt – K. Gallagher

H. T. Tector Ireland v South Africa, Third ODI at Malahide
Audible obscenity after asking for DRS too late. Reprimand/1 demerit pt – K. Gallagher

T. Bavuma South Africa v Ireland, First T20I at Malahide
Audible obscenity when given out caught behind. Reprimand/1 demerit pt – K. Gallagher

Shoriful Islam Bangladesh v Australia, Third T20I at Mirpur
Provocative celebration on dismissing M. R. Marsh. Reprimand/1 demerit pt – Neeyamur Rashid

J. N. T. Seales West Indies v Pakistan, First Test at Kingston
Inappropriate verbal send-off on dismissing Hasan Ali. Reprimand/1 demerit pt – R. B. Richardson

K. L. Rahul India v England, Fourth Test at The Oval
Dissent when given out caught behind on DRS. 15% fine/1 demerit pt – B. C. Broad

S. E. Luus South Africa v West Indies, First women's ODI at Coolidge
Showed umpire her bat when given lbw. Reprimand/1 demerit pt – R. D. King

C. B. R. L. S. Kumara Sri Lanka v Bangladesh, men's T20 World Cup at Sharjah
Provocative behaviour on dismissing Liton Das. 25% fine/1 demerit pt – J. Srinath

Liton Das Bangladesh v Sri Lanka, men's T20 World Cup at Sharjah
Aggressive reaction after dismissal by C. B. R. L. S. Kumara. 15% fine/1 demerit pt – J. Srinath

Hasan Ali Pakistan v Bangladesh, First T20I at Mirpur
Inappropriate send-off on dismissing Nurul Hasan. Reprimand/1 demerit pt – Neeyamur Rashid

Shaheen Shah Afridi Pakistan v Bangladesh, Second T20I at Mirpur
Threw ball at Afif Hossain, knocking him to the ground. 15% fine/1 demerit pt – Neeyamur Rashid

T. M. Head Australia v England, First Test at Brisbane
Audible obscenity when beaten while facing B. A. Stokes. 15% fine/1 demerit pt – D. C. Boon

Twenty-one further breaches took place in Associate Member internationals during this period.

Under ICC regulations on minor over-rate offences, captains and players are fined 20% of their match fee for every over their side fail to bowl in the allotted time. There were 16 instances in Full Member men's internationals and four in Full Member women's internationals reported in this edition of Wisden:

V. Kohli/India v England, 2nd T20I at Ahmedabad, 20% – J. Srinath

F. D. M. Karunaratne/SL v WI, 3rd ODI at Coolidge, Antigua, 40% – R. B. Richardson
Sri Lanka were also fined two points in the World Cup Super League.

E. J. G. Morgan/England v India, 4th T20I at Ahmedabad, 20% – J. Srinath

V. Kohli/India v England, 5th ODI at Ahmedabad, 40% – J. Srinath

T. Bavuma/South Africa v Pakistan, 1st ODI at Centurion, 20% – A. J. Pycroft
South Africa were also fined one point in the World Cup Super League.

H. Klaasen/South Africa v Pakistan, 1st T20I at Johannesburg, 20% – A. J. Pycroft

J. E. Root/England v New Zealand, 1st Test at Lord's, 40% – B. C. Broad

K. C. Brathwaite/West Indies v South Africa, 2nd Test at Gros Islet, 60% – R. B. Richardson
West Indies were also fined six points in the World Test Championship.

H. Kaur/India v England, 2nd women's T20I at Hove, 20% – P. Whitticase

S. R. Taylor/West Indies v Pakistan, 5th women's ODI at Coolidge, 20% – R. D. King

Javeria Khan/Pakistan v West Indies, 5th women's ODI at Coolidge, 40% – R. D. King

M. D. Shanaka/Sri Lanka v India, 2nd ODI at Colombo (RPS), 20% – R. S. Madugalle
Sri Lanka were also fined one point in the World Cup Super League.

V. Kohli/India v England, 1st Test at Nottingham, 40% – B. C. Broad
India were also fined two points in the World Test Championship.

J. E. Root/England v India, 1st Test at Nottingham, 40% – B. C. Broad
England were also fined two points in the World Test Championship.

M. D. Raj/India v Australia, 2nd women's ODI at Mackay, 80% – R. W. Stratford

Mahmudullah/Bangladesh v Pakistan, 1st T20I at Mirpur, 20% – Neeyamur Rashid

J. E. Root/England v Australia, 1st Test at Brisbane, 100% – D. C. Boon
England were also fined eight points in the World Test Championship.

V. Kohli/India v South Africa, 1st Test at Centurion, 20% – A. J. Pycroft
India were also fined one point in the World Test Championship.

T. Bavuma/South Africa v India, 2nd ODI at Centurion, 20% – A. J. Pycroft

K. L. Rahul/India v South Africa, 3rd ODI at Centurion, 40% – A. J. Pycroft

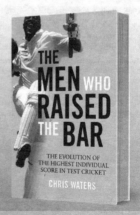

INTERNATIONAL UMPIRES' PANELS

In 1993, the ICC formed an international umpires' panel, containing at least two officials from each Full Member. A third-country umpire from this panel stood with a home umpire in every Test from 1994 onwards. In 2002, an elite panel was appointed: two elite umpires – both independent – were to stand in all Tests, and at least one in every ODI, where one home umpire was allowed. (During the pandemic, local umpires were used.) A supporting panel of international umpires was created to provide cover at peak times in the Test schedule, second umpires in one-day internationals, and third umpires to give rulings from TV replays. There is also a panel of development umpires, mostly drawn from Associate Members but also including several female umpires from Full Members. The panels are sponsored by Emirates Airlines.

The elite panel at the start of 2022: Aleem Dar (P), H. D. P. K. Dharmasena (SL), M. Erasmus (SA), C. B. Gaffaney (NZ), M. A. Gough (E), R. K. Illingworth (E), R. A. Kettleborough (E), N. N. Menon (I), P. R. Reiffel (A), R. J. Tucker (A), J. S. Wilson (WI).

The international panel: G. A. Abood (A), Ahmed Shah Durrani (Afg), Ahmed Shah Pakteen (Afg), Ahsan Raza (P), K. N. Ananthapadmanabhan (I), Asif Yaqoob (P), Bismillah Shinwari (Afg), R. E. Black (Ire), G. O. Brathwaite (WI), C. M. Brown (NZ), M. Burns (E), I. Chabi (Z), A. K. Chowdhury (I), S. A. J. Craig (A), N. Duguid (WI), Gazi Sohel (B), S. George (SA), P. A. Gustard (WI), S. B. Haig (NZ), L. E. Hannibal (SL), M. Hawthorne (Ire), A. T. Holdstock (SA), Izatullah Safi (Afg), P. B. Jele (SA), W. R. Knights (NZ), J. Madanagopal (I), Masudur Rahman (B), D. J. Millns (E), F. Mutizwa (Z), A. J. Neill (Ire), S. J. Nogajski (A), A. Paleker (SA), R. S. A. Palliyaguruge (SL), C. Phiri (Z), R. M. P. J. Rambukwella (SL), Rashid Riaz (P), L. S. Reifer (WI), P. A. Reynolds (Ire), L. Rusere (Z), M. J. Saggers (E), Sharfuddoula (B), V. K. Sharma (I), Shozab Raza (P), Tanvir Ahmed (B), A. G. Wharf (E), P. Wilson (A), R. R. Wimalasiri (SL).

ICC development panel: L. Agenbag (SA), Akbar Ali (UAE), V. R. Angara (Botswana), S. N. Bandekar (USA), N. R. Bathi (Netherlands), E. Carrington (Bermuda), K. D. Cotton (NZ), R. D'Mello (Kenya), H. Grewal (Canada), D. A. Haggo (Scotland), Harikrishna Pillai (Oman), R. Hassan (Italy), Iftikhar Ali (UAE), M. Jameson (Germany), N. Janani (I), J. Jensen (Denmark), V. K. Jha (Nepal), A. Kapa (PNG), H. E. Kearns (Jersey), J. A. Lindo (USA), A. W. Louw (Namibia), D. H. McLean (Scotland), A. R. Maddela (Canada), V. P. Mallela (USA), R. G. Milne (Scotland), P. M. Musoke (Uganda), L. Oala (PNG), D. Odhiambo (Kenya), B. Olewale (PNG), I. O. Oyieko (Kenya), C. A. Polosak (A), B. B. Pradhan (Nepal), S. S. Prasad (Singapore), Rahul Asher (Oman), A. K. Rana (Thailand), V. G. Rathi (I), S. Redfern (E), Rizwan Akram (Netherlands), F. T. Samura (Sierra Leone), C. Schumacher (Namibia), E. Sheridan (A), Shiju Sam (UAE), Shivani Mishra (Qatar), D. N. Subedi (Nepal), S. Subramanian (Indonesia), Tabarak Dar (Hong Kong), C. H. Thorburn (Namibia), A. van der Dries (Netherlands), R. V. Venkatesh (Hong Kong), Vinod Babu (Oman), K. Viswanadan (Malaysia), M. V. Waldron (Ire), J. M. Williams (WI).

ICC REFEREES' PANEL

In 1991, the ICC formed a panel of referees to enforce their Code of Conduct for Tests and one-day internationals, and to support the umpires in upholding the game's conduct. In 2002, the ICC launched an elite panel, on full-time contracts, for all international cricket, sponsored by Emirates Airlines. At the start of 2022, it consisted of D. C. Boon (A), B. C. Broad (E), J. J. Crowe (NZ), R. S. Madugalle (SL), A. J. Pycroft (Z), R. B. Richardson (WI), J. Srinath (I).

A further panel of international referees consisted of Akhtar Ahmad (B), Ali Naqvi (P), G. A. V. Baxter (NZ), S. R. Bernard (A), O. Chirombe (Z), E. T. Dube (Z), S. A. Fritz (SA), K. Gallagher (Ire), Hamim Talwar (Afg), D. O. Hayles (WI), R. E. Hayward (NZ), D. T. Jukes (E), R. D. King (WI), G. F. Labrooy (SL), W. C. Labrooy (SL), G. S. Lakshmi (I), G. McCrea (Ire), Mohammad Javed (P), V. Narayanan Kutty (I), M. Nayyar (I), Neeyamur Rashid (B), W. M. Noon (E), G. H. Pienaar (SA), R. W. Stratford (A), S. Wadvalla (SA), P. Whitticase (E), Zarab Shah Zaheer (Afg).

ENGLISH UMPIRES FOR 2021

Professional team   R. J. Bailey, N. L. Bainton, P. K. Baldwin, I. D. Blackwell, M. Burns, N. G. B. Cook, B. J. Debenham, M. A. Gough, A. C. Harris, P. J. Hartley, Hassan Adnan, R. K. Illingworth, R. A. Kettleborough, N. J. Llong, G. D. Lloyd, T. Lungley, N. A. Mallender, J. D. Middlebrook, D. J. Millns, Naeem Ashraf, M. Newell, S. J. O'Shaughnessy, P. R. Pollard, N. Pratt, S. Redfern, R. T. Robinson, M. J. Saggers, J. D. Shantry, S. Shanmugam, B. V. Taylor, R. J. Warren, C. M. Watts, A. G. Wharf, R. A. White.

National panel for Second XI and National Counties games S. Beswick, P. Brown, T. Caldicott, G. I. Callaway, D. Daniels, A. Davies, C. Dunn, R. G. Eagleton, C. W. Evans, J. Farrell, J. P. Flatley, B. Gates, D. J. Gower, D. Gregory, I. L. Herbert, N. Hewitt, A. Hicks, S. Hollingshead, C. Johnson, M. Johnson, D. Jones, W. Jones, H. E. Kearns, I. P. Laurence, S. E. Lavis, S. Lilley, K. A. Little, A. Lunn, G. W. Marshall, R. P. Medland, B. Morris, P. Mustard, J. K. H. Naik, P. D. Nicholls, N. Oddy, R. Parker, R. Patel, D. N. Pedley, B. J. Peverall, N. J. Piper, J. Pitcher, J. P. Prince, M. A. Qureshi, I. G. Rich, S. Richardson, S. J. Ross, A. Seymour, B. M. Shafayat, P. J. Sparshott, J. C. Tredwell, D. R. Turl, C. J. Viljoen, D. M. Warburton, I. G. Warne, M. Waseem, M. D. Watton, A. J. Wheeler, S. Widdup, P. Witney.

THE DUCKWORTH/LEWIS/STERN METHOD

In 1997, the ECB's one-day competitions adopted a new method to revise targets in interrupted games, devised by Frank Duckworth of the Royal Statistical Society and Tony Lewis of the University of the West of England. The method was gradually taken up by other countries and, in 1999, the ICC decided to incorporate it into the standard playing conditions for one-day internationals.

The system aims to preserve any advantage that one team have established before the interruption. It uses the idea that teams have two resources from which they make runs – an allocated number of overs, and ten wickets. It also takes into account when the interruption occurs, because of the different scoring-rates typical of different stages of an innings. Traditional run-rate calculations relied only on the overs available, and ignored wickets lost.

It uses one table with 50 rows, covering matches of up to 50 overs, and ten columns, from nought to nine wickets down. Each figure gives the percentage of the total runs that would, on average, be scored with a certain number of overs left and wickets lost. If a match is shortened before it begins, to, say, 33 overs a side, the figure for 33 overs and ten wickets remaining would be the starting point.

If overs are lost, the table is used to calculate the percentage of runs the team would be expected to score in those missing overs. This is obtained by reading the figure for the number of overs left, and wickets down, when play stops, and subtracting the figure for the number of overs left when it resumes. If the delay comes between innings, and the second team's allocation of overs is reduced, then their target is obtained by calculating the appropriate percentage for the reduced number of overs with all ten wickets standing. For instance, if the second team's innings halves from 50 overs to 25, the table shows that they still have 66.5% of their resources left, so have to beat two-thirds of the first team's total, rather than half. If the first innings is complete and the second innings interrupted or prematurely terminated, the score to beat is reduced by the percentage of the innings lost.

The version known as the "Professional Edition" was introduced into one-day internationals from 2003, and subsequently into most national one-day competitions. Using a more advanced mathematical formula (it is entirely computerised), it adjusts the tables to allow for the different scoring-rates that emerge in matches with above-average first-innings scores. In 2014, analysis by Steven Stern, an Australian professor of data science, indicated further modification was needed; Stern, based at Bond University in Queensland, became responsible for the method after Duckworth and Lewis retired. The Duckworth/Lewis/Stern method is now used in all one-day and Twenty20 internationals, as well as most national competitions (including The Hundred, with its five-ball format). The original "Standard Edition" is used where computers are unavailable, and at lower levels of the game.

The system also covers first-innings interruptions, multiple interruptions and innings ended by rain. The tables are revised slightly every two years, taking account of changing scoring-rates; the average total in a 50-over international is now 259 (slightly down from 263 – the first time the average has decreased, after a steady rise from 225 in 1999).

In the World Cup semi-final between South Africa and New Zealand at Auckland in March 2015, South Africa were 216 for three from 38 overs when seven overs were lost to rain; after the innings resumed, they finished on 281. With three wickets down, the lost overs constituted 14.85% of South Africa's scoring resources, meaning they used only 85.15%. By contrast, New Zealand's 43-over chase constituted 90% of the resources of a full innings. Their revised target was determined by multiplying South Africa's total, 281, by 90% divided by 85.15% and adding one run: 281 x (90/85.15) + 1 = 298. New Zealand scored 299 for six in 42.5 overs to win, with a six off the penultimate delivery. Had South Africa been two down at the interruption, the lost overs would have constituted a higher percentage of their scoring resources; the revised target would have been 301, and New Zealand would have needed two more runs off the final ball.

A similar system, usually known as the VJD method, is used in some domestic matches in India. It was devised by V. Jayadevan, a civil engineer from Kerala.

POWERPLAYS

In one-day and Twenty20 internationals, two semi-circles of 30-yard (27.43 metres) radius are drawn on the field behind each set of stumps, joined by straight lines parallel to the pitch.

At the instant of delivery in the first ten overs of an uninterrupted one-day international innings (the first six overs in a Twenty20 international), only two fielders may be positioned outside this fielding restriction area. During the next 30 overs, no more than four fielders may be stationed outside the area; and in the final ten overs, no more than five. (In Twenty20 internationals, no more than five may be positioned outside the area for the last 14 overs.) In matches affected by the weather, the number of overs in each powerplay stage is reduced in proportion to the overall reduction of overs.

COVID REGULATIONS FOR RECREATIONAL CRICKET IN 2021

When recreational cricket recommenced in England and Wales in April 2021, it was subject to the same Covid precautionary regulations as applied in 2020. These included:

- All matches limited to a maximum of 30 participants, including coaches and officials.
- Players to adhere to government social-distancing guidance, except in the following limited circumstances during competitive play in England only, where 1m+ is permitted: 1) wicketkeepers standing up to the stumps and 2) distance between slip fielders.
- No sweat or saliva to be applied to the ball.
- A hygiene break must take place every six overs or 20 minutes, whichever is sooner; the ball is to be cleaned with an antimicrobial wipe, and all participants' hands cleaned using a sanitiser. This routine should also be followed at the start of any drinks break, or the close of an innings.
- The responsibility for sanitising the ball during the match lies with the fielding captain. Umpires should refrain from any contact with the ball, which should be returned to the base of the stumps at breaks and wickets.
- Batters should sanitise their bat when leaving the field of play, and wicketkeepers their gloves.
- Players should not hand any personal items to the umpire. Only the umpires should replace the bails, if dislodged.
- Batters to run in distinct lines to ensure they are not within 2m of the bowler or the other batter. Lines should be marked on the square on either side of the wicket.
- Social distancing to be maintained at all times, including during wicket celebrations, drinks breaks and tactical discussions.
- Sharing of the ball to be minimised, e.g. it should go straight from wicketkeeper to bowler, instead of via fielders.
- Clubs to outline socially distanced areas for teams, officials and spectators.
- Players to bring their own food and drink; bottles should not be shared.
- Players to arrive, and return home, in kit.
- Changing-rooms to be closed, except for necessary use by disabled people, for emergency requirements and toilet access – all subject to risk assessment, occupancy limits, suitable ventilation, and frequent and effective cleaning.
- Spectators not permitted, except carers for people with disabilities, adults needed to supervise under-18s in a safeguarding role, or patrons attending the venue for hospitality, as permitted by the government. (In 2020, spectators were allowed to gather in groups of six. They were not allowed to touch the ball if it crossed the boundary.)

From May 17, the following changes were made:

- Changing-rooms to reopen, subject to social-distancing rules and capacity limits being observed.
- Clubs to serve teas, if done safely and in compliance with government guidance on hospitality settings.
- Spectators permitted, subject to social-distancing and legal-gathering size limits (this did not apply in Wales until June 7).

From July 19 in England, and from **August 7** in Wales, the social-distancing rules and group-size restrictions no longer applied. Most on-field adaptations ceased to be mandated, except that the ECB discouraged sweat or saliva being applied to the ball, and in Wales (though not in England) sanitisation breaks remained recommended.

MEETINGS AND DECISIONS IN 2021

ECB SPONSORSHIP DEALS

On January 12, the ECB announced that LV= General Insurance would sponsor men's and women's Test cricket in England and Wales, and the County Championship, from 2021 to 2023. LV previously sponsored the County Championship from 2002 to 2015 (for the first four years this was under the name Frizzell).

MCC WORLD CRICKET COMMITTEE

The MCC world cricket committee met in February via conference call – their first meeting since August 2019, after those in 2020 were postponed because of the Covid-19 pandemic.

They heard that MCC were to hold a global consultation on the Law on short-pitched deliveries, given recent research on concussion. It should consider the balance between bat and ball; whether concussion was different from other injuries; changes in particular sectors, eg junior cricket; and whether lower-order batters should have further protection. The committee were unanimous that short-pitched bowling is a core part of the game, particularly at the elite level, but discussed how to mitigate the risk of injury.

The committee debated the use of "umpire's call" for lbw verdicts via the Decision Review System. Some felt the watching public found it confusing that the result could be out or not out depending on the on-field umpire's original decision, and argued it would be simpler if the third umpire disregarded that. They would retain the "hitting zone" of the stumps (which had to be hit by at least 50% of the ball for it to be out), and felt that, if umpire's call was dropped, each team should have only one unsuccessful review, or the relevant review should be lost irrespective of its outcome. Other committee members believed supporters did understand umpire's call, and it was important to retain the human element of the on-field umpire's decision, including the traditional benefit of the doubt.

More widely, the committee felt the ICC should provide the same DRS technology for all international cricket, rather than rely on the host broadcasters. The third umpire should look at replays from a neutral perspective, rather than looking for evidence to overturn the on-field decision. The soft-signal system seemed to work well for catches within the 30-yard fielding circle, but catches near the boundary often left the umpires unsighted; for these, the committee proposed that on-field umpires could give an "unsighted" instruction to the third umpire.

In 2020, MCC had supported interim changes to playing regulations ahead of the England v West Indies Test series, including a ban on applying saliva to the ball because of Covid-19; similar changes had been introduced for domestic and recreational cricket. The committee had been monitoring the application of sweat without saliva; there had been fears that prohibiting saliva might make conditions too friendly to batters. While there was support for permanently prohibiting saliva, some felt it would be premature, and it might be allowable in a post-Covid world. The regulation should remain for the present, with its impact monitored. A Law change would have the dual benefit of being more hygienic, and eliminating the grey area of players using sweets and chewing gum to make their saliva more sugary.

Another result of the pandemic had been the use of home umpires in Tests. So far, the umpiring had appeared good, with very few accusations of bias, and DRS available to correct mistakes. The committee recommended further use of home umpires in internationals, saving travel and expense; the best umpires should be able to officiate anywhere. A balance, such as one home umpire and one neutral umpire, was also recommended, ensuring umpires could improve their skills by officiating overseas. The neutrality of the third umpire and referee was also deemed important. The committee supported exploring the viability of specialist third umpires at a central location, rather than based at the ground.

They were pleased by the advent of the World Test Championship, due to reach its first final in June; they had backed such a tournament for years. They would suggest improvements for the second cycle to the ICC cricket committee, such as a simplified points system, a clear window for the fixtures, and marketing the tournament to make it easier for supporters to understand.

The committee heard that a disproportionate amount of international women's cricket had been cancelled during the pandemic. Some countries were yet to play any international cricket since the outbreak of Covid-19, and some could not afford to play, given the increased costs of staging matches and touring, and the inconvenience of lengthy spells in quarantine.

INDEPENDENT COMMISSION FOR EQUITY IN CRICKET

On March 3, the ECB appointed Cindy Butts to establish and chair the independent Commission for Equity in Cricket, which was to examine issues of race and equity. Butts, formerly deputy chair of the Metropolitan Police Authority and commissioner at the Criminal Cases Review Commission, and currently on the House of Lords conduct committee and the Speaker's committee for the Independent Parliamentary Standards Authority, was to work with the ECB Board, and especially senior independent director Brenda Trenowden, to finalise the commission's terms of reference and appoint independent commissioners. (Four commissioners were announced in July: they were former England and Surrey player Zafar Ansari, now a barrister; Sir Brendan Barber, former general secretary of the TUC; Dr Michael Collins, associate professor of modern British history at University College, London; and Michelle Moore, a former athlete now on the Sport England talent inclusion advisory board.) The commission were to gather and assess the evidence of inequalities and discrimination of all forms within cricket and identify the actions needed to tackle them. A call for evidence began in November, with an anonymous online survey offering everyone involved in cricket a chance to give their views on the game's culture.

The ECB reported in April that they were implementing an anti-discrimination code of conduct across the professional game, as well as the recreational leagues and clubs under their jurisdiction.

ICC WOMEN'S TOURNAMENTS

On March 8, the ICC announced plans to expand women's cricket over the next decade. The World Cup would expand from eight teams in 2022 and 2025 to ten in 2029; the T20 World Cup would expand from ten teams in 2024 to 12 in the three editions from 2026 to 2030; and there would be a T20 Champions Cup for six teams in 2027 and 2031.

WORLD TEST CHAMPIONSHIP FINAL

On March 10, the ICC announced that the inaugural World Test Championship final, due to be played by India and New Zealand in June, would be staged in a biosecure bubble at the Rose Bowl in Southampton, rather than at Lord's as originally planned. The decision was taken by the ICC Board after discussing a range of options with the ECB to minimise the potential impact of Covid, and was based on the ECB's experience of delivering a full summer of international cricket in 2020. The venue provided world-class playing and training facilities, while on-site accommodation reduced the risk of infection. Should the UK government's phased easing of lockdown measures proceed as planned, a limited number of fans would be allowed to watch the final.

ICC BOARD AND COMMITTEE MEETINGS

On April 1, a series of ICC board and committee meetings concluded, conducted by virtual conference calls.

Several recommendations from the cricket committee were approved. They said the system of "umpire's call" should remain; the principle underpinning DRS was to correct clear errors in the game while preserving the umpire's role as the decision-maker on the field, bearing in mind the element of prediction involved in technology. But they recommended three changes to DRS and third umpire protocols: for lbw reviews, the height margin of the wicket zone should be lifted to the top of the stumps, to ensure the same margin around the stumps for both height and width; players should be able to ask the umpire whether a genuine attempt had been made to play the ball before deciding to review an lbw decision; and the third umpire should check a replay of any short run called, to correct any error before the next ball.

The Covid regulations introduced in 2020 to allow international cricket to resume should continue. These were the flexibility to be able to appoint home umpires where neutrals were previously required; an additional DRS review per team per innings in all formats; the ban on using saliva to polish the ball; and the availability of Covid replacement players in Tests.

The committee noted the excellent performances by home umpires over the past nine months but encouraged the more widespread appointment of neutral elite panel umpires when circumstances allowed. The recent introduction of replacement players for concussion and Covid prompted a discussion on the more general use of replacements; to better understand the implications, the definition of a first-class match would be changed to allow the unqualified use of replacement players.

Two changes in women's ODI playing conditions were approved: the discretionary five-over batting powerplay was removed, and all tied matches would be decided by a super over. It was decided that Test and ODI status should be permanently awarded to all Full Member women's teams, and all matches at the Birmingham 2022 Commonwealth Games should be classified as women's T20 Internationals. It was agreed to postpone the inaugural women's Under-19 World Cup, due to be held in Bangladesh at the end of the year, to January 2023, as the pandemic had significantly affected Under-19 programmes in many countries. Similarly, to allow teams the best possible preparation, the global qualifier for the women's World Cup 2022 was postponed until December 2021.

The board received an update on preparations for the men's T20 World Cup, due to be held in India later in 2021, including discussions with the Indian government on tax arrangements and visa guarantees.

Teams would be allowed to take up to seven additional players and/or support staff to accompany the squad of 23 to ICC events where a period of quarantine was required and/or teams were accommodated in a biosecure bubble.

The board agreed to set up a Member Support Fund, with $5m available in grants to support the playing of international cricket. Funding would be made through a "co-payment" contribution, with a maximum grant of 50%.

Mel Jones (Australia) and Catherine Campbell (New Zealand) were appointed as the Full Member representatives on the women's committee.

ICC FUTURE LEADERS PROGRAMME

On April 19, the ICC launched their "100% Cricket" future leaders programme, to support female talent across administration, coaching and officiating, broadcast and journalism, address the low percentage of women in leadership positions in global cricket, and build a pipeline of new female leaders. Aspiring leaders in junior-to-middle-management positions of any ICC Member or ICC themselves were encouraged to apply, and those taking part would be matched with a mentor to support their development and unlock their potential, acting as a confidential sounding-board and providing advice, guidance and connections. The programme would last for six months and include a workshop with former Australian captain Belinda Clark.

In June, the ICC reported that 40 women from 29 countries had been selected for the programme, and would be mentored in two batches over the coming year.

ENGLAND SELECTION SYSTEM

On April 20, the ECB announced a restructure of the selection system for men's international teams, developed by Ashley Giles, the managing director of England men's cricket. The role of national selector, held by Ed Smith since 2018, was abolished, and the head coach, Chris Silverwood, was given overall responsibility for squad selections, working with the Test and white-ball captains, Joe Root and Eoin Morgan, on selecting the final playing XI. There would be input from the England men's performance director, Mo Bobat, and James Taylor, whose job title changed from England selector to head scout, and coaches aligned to the men's international teams would feed into the process.

SUPER 1s DISABILITY CRICKET PROGRAMME

On April 29, the ECB announced a £2m partnership with the Lord's Taverners to expand the Super 1s disability cricket programme to all 39 English counties by 2024. The programme, already established in 20 counties and Scotland, and delivered through county cricket boards, aims to give young people with a disability the chance to play regular competitive cricket, improving their physical and mental well-being, and allowing them to make friends and gain confidence and independence. The partnership would also fund the development of table cricket, currently played by over 8,800 people in 357 schools, to give those with more limiting disabilities a chance to engage in the game.

ECB ANNUAL GENERAL MEETING

The ECB AGM on May 11 ratified the appointment of Baroness Valerie Amos as an independent non-executive director, replacing Delia Bushell. A former cabinet minister and leader of the House of Lords, and current Master of University College in Oxford, Amos had been a passionate cricket fan since she was a child in Guyana.

The ECB also published their annual review and financial statements, covering a year in which the pandemic caused significant disruption, but cricket became the first sport to resume international fixtures. Across the game, including the ECB and first-class counties, losses in 2020 amounted to more than £100m. In the year ended January 31, when revenue had been projected to increase significantly, turnover was £207m, a fall of £21m compared with the previous year, and the loss on ordinary activities before taxation was £16m, compared with a profit of £6.5m. Staging international cricket, albeit behind closed doors, and taking swift action to reduce costs – by stopping some planned investment, staff furlough and pay reductions from April to October, and a redundancy programme which cut the staff from 389 to 331 – had avoided the worst-case financial scenarios and enabled the ECB to provide emergency assistance to the cricket network, although revenue was further impacted by postponing The Hundred and the costs of staging biosecure cricket. It was also the first year of the new County Partnership Agreement, with increased distributions to the network and stakeholders.

MCC ANNUAL GENERAL MEETING

The 234th AGM of the Marylebone Cricket Club was held online on May 12, with voting remaining open to members over the following five days. Though president Kumar Sangakkara was able to address the meeting from his home in Sri Lanka, club chair Gerald Corbett presided.

Bruce Carnegie-Brown, the chair of Lloyd's of London, was approved to succeed Corbett in October 2021, when Clare Connor would become president, as announced at the 2020 AGM. Mike Gatting was re-appointed chair of the world cricket committee, John Varley was confirmed as a trustee and Andrew Lowenthal as deputy chair of the new nominations committee.

Members approved an increase in entrance fees, and changes to the club rules to facilitate greater use of technology in holding general meetings and communicating with the membership. They also voted to suspend their normal rights of entry to Lord's for the 2021 cricket season, because of the continuing Covid.

Membership on December 31, 2020, totalled 24,254, made up of 17,910 full members, 5,648 associate members, 366 honorary members, 208 senior members and 122 out-match members. There were 12,211 candidates awaiting election to full membership; 549 vacancies arose in 2020.

ICC MEN'S TOURNAMENTS

On June 1, the ICC confirmed their schedule of men's events from 2024 to 2031.

The men's World Cup would expand from ten teams in 2023 to 14 in 2027 and 2031: two groups of seven, followed by a Super Six, semis and a final. The men's T20 World Cup would expand from 16 in 2021 and 2022 to 20 in the four editions from 2024 to 2030: four groups of five, followed by a Super Eight, semis and a final. There would also be an eight-team men's Champions Trophy in 2025 and 2029, with two groups of four, semis and a final.

The board approved the process for determining the hosts for all events in the next cycle: the hosts for the men's events would be decided in September, and the process for the women's and Under-19 events would commence in November.

They also asked management to focus planning efforts for the 2021 men's T20 World Cup, originally due to be held in India, on staging the event in the United Arab Emirates and perhaps another venue in the Middle East; a final decision on whether to move the tournament would be taken later in the month.

MEN'S T20 WORLD CUP RELOCATED

On June 29, the ICC confirmed that the men's T20 World Cup in October and November would be staged in the UAE and Oman, because of the uncertainty around a serious Covid situation in India, and the difficulty of staging a biosecure event there. The BCCI would remain the official hosts.

ICC CHIEF EXECUTIVE

On July 8, the ICC announced that chief executive Manu Sawhney was leaving the organisation with immediate effect, after two years in the post. Sawhney had been suspended in March pending a disciplinary hearing, after a cultural review carried out by PricewaterhouseCoopers alleged he had bullied staff and taken decisions without properly consulting the board.

Geoff Allardice acted as chief executive from March to November, when he was appointed to the role permanently. Allardice, who played for Victoria in the early 1990s, had previously served as the ICC's general manager for cricket for eight years.

ICC ANNUAL GENERAL MEETING

The ICC held their AGM virtually on July 18. Three new Associate Members were admitted: Mongolia, Tajikistan and Switzerland, bringing the total number of ICC Members to 106, including 94 Associates. Switzerland had previously been a member from 1985 to 2012, when the Swiss Cricket Association were expelled, and now returned under a new governing body, Cricket Switzerland. Zambia, whose membership was suspended in 2019, were expelled because of continuing non-compliance with membership criteria, and Russia were suspended for similar reasons, and instructed to demonstrate compliance by the 2022 AGM.

Three Associate representatives were elected to the chief executives' committee for the next two years: Sumod Damodar (Botswana), who had already served one term, Rashpal Bajwa (Canada) and Mubashshir Usmani (UAE).

The ICC convened a working group led by ECB chair Ian Watmore and including USA Cricket chair Paraag Marathe to lead a bid for cricket's inclusion in the Olympic Games at Los Angeles in 2028, Brisbane in 2032, and beyond.

ECB CHAIR

On October 7, the ECB announced that chair Ian Watmore was standing down with immediate effect, only 13 months after assuming the job. He stated that the pandemic had made a dramatic difference to the demands of the role. His deputy, Barry O'Brien, stepped up as interim chair while the board began the process to appoint a new leader.

ENGLAND MEN'S PLAYER CONTRACTS

On October 8, the ECB announced a new structure for England men's central contracts, developed in consultation with the players, the Team England Player Partnership and the Professional Cricketers' Association. Since 2016, they had awarded separate contracts for Test and white-ball cricket, but the list was now being combined, given the likelihood of players featuring across formats in the coming year. Players on central contracts have their salaries paid in full by the ECB.

Twenty central contracts were awarded to run for 12 months from October 1. They went to Moeen Ali, James Anderson, Jofra Archer, Jonny Bairstow, Stuart Broad, Rory Burns, Jos Buttler, Zak Crawley, Sam Curran, Jack Leach, Dawid Malan, Eoin Morgan, Ollie Pope, Adil Rashid, Ollie Robinson, Joe Root, Jason Roy, Ben Stokes, Chris Woakes and Mark Wood. Increment contracts were awarded to Dom Bess, Tom Curran, Chris Jordan and Liam Livingstone. Saqib Mahmood, Craig Overton and Olly Stone retained pace bowling development contracts.

Leach and Malan (who were previously on increment contracts) and Robinson received central contracts for the first time, and Livingstone received his first increment contract; Tom Curran, who had had a white-ball contract, returned to incremental status. Dom Sibley, previously on a Test contract, dropped off the list.

COUNTY CHAMPIONSHIP IN 2022

On October 14, the ECB confirmed that the chairs of the 18 first-class counties had voted to restore the County Championship to a two-division format from 2022, after the pandemic had forced its replacement by a shortened competition in 2020, followed by a seeded group structure in 2021. The alternative of continuing the group structure for one more season was rejected, with the counties preferring to return immediately to the format originally due to begin in 2020: a first division of ten and a second division of eight (replacing the 2019 divisions of eight and ten), with all teams playing 14 matches. The counties would be assigned to divisions on the basis of their results in 2019, rather than those in the latest tournament.

ECB WOMEN'S CONTRACTS

On October 29, the ECB announced that each of the eight regional women's teams would have an additional, sixth, professional contract for 2022; with Lancashire funding one extra contract for Thunder, and Yorkshire two for Northern Diamonds, this would increase the number of professional players in the women's regional structure from 41 to 51. Including the players centrally contracted to England, there were now 67 professional women cricketers in England and Wales. In November, Tash Farrant regained an England central contract.

ECB ACTION AGAINST YORKSHIRE

On November 11, the ECB issued a statement on Yorkshire CCC's handling of Azeem Rafiq's allegations of racism, which they said was wholly unacceptable and causing serious damage to cricket's reputation, as well as raising serious questions regarding Yorkshire's governance and management.

The ECB announced that Yorkshire would be suspended from hosting international or major matches at Headingley until the club had clearly demonstrated they could meet the standards expected of an international venue, ECB member and first-class county. A review of the club's governance would consider whether the existing arrangements were fit for purpose. The regulatory processes into the allegations brought by Rafiq would ultimately be determined by an independent tribunal (the Cricket Disciplinary Commission). In the meantime, Yorkshire's Gary Ballance was suspended indefinitely from selection for England (though the ECB conceded that he had not been selected since 2017).

ICC BOARD

On November 17, the ICC Board met in Dubai – their first face-to-face meeting in over two years. They set up a working group to review the status of the Afghanistan Cricket Board, and cricket in Afghanistan, after the Taliban regained control of the government. The ICC chair, Greg Barclay, said they would continue to support the ACB in developing men's and women's cricket, and hoped the popularity of the men's national team would enable cricket to influence positive change.

The board approved the continuation of the World Test Championship in its current form of a nine-team league over two years culminating in a final between the top two teams. With the men's World Cup expanding to 14 teams in 2027, the board accepted a recommendation from the chief executives' committee that the ten leading teams in the ODI rankings at a fixed date should qualify automatically, with the remaining four determined via a global qualifier.

BCCI chair Sourav Ganguly was appointed chair of the men's cricket committee after Anil Kumble – another former Indian Test captain – stepped down, having served nine years, the maximum permitted.

The board approved the award of first-class and List A status to women's cricket, to align with the men's game, which would also be applied retrospectively. The women's committee were renamed the women's cricket committee, assuming decision-making responsibility for women's cricket and reporting directly to the chief executives' committee. Johnny Grave, chief executive of Cricket West Indies, was appointed to the women's committee.

The ICC also announced that 11 Full Members (all except Afghanistan) and three Associates (the USA, Namibia and Scotland) would host eight men's tournaments between 2023 and 2031.

ACTION PLAN ON RACISM AND DISCRIMINATION

On November 26, following a meeting at The Oval a week earlier, the ECB, MCC, the PCA, NCCA and the first-class counties, women's regional hosts and recreational county cricket network unveiled their plan to tackle racism and promote inclusion and diversity at all levels of the game.

The initial aims included:

Understanding and educating more

- Adopting a standardised approach to reporting, investigating and responding to complaints, allegations and whistle-blowing.
- Full promotion of the aims of the independent Commission for Equity in Cricket.
- Equity, diversity and inclusion (EDI) training for staff, volunteers, recreational club officials, umpires, directors and coaches.

Addressing dressing-room culture

- A review of dressing-room culture in all men's and women's professional teams, domestic and international.
- A redesigned programme of player and coach education, addressing gaps identified through the review.

Removing barriers in talent pathways

- Aiding progress into professional teams of people from diverse backgrounds (especially South Asian, Black and less privileged youngsters) through talent identification and scouting, education and diversity of coaches and targeted support programmes for players from diverse or underprivileged backgrounds.

Creating welcoming environments for all

- A review, ahead of the 2022 season, into the detection, enforcement and sanctions against discriminatory and abusive crowd behaviour at professional cricket grounds.
- Plans (tailored to local communities) to ensure professional cricket venues are welcoming to all, including accessible seating, food and beverage catering to all faiths and cultures, and facilities such as multi-faith rooms and alcohol-free zones.
- Upgraded education in recreational cricket to ensure players, volunteers and coaches understand and champion inclusion and diversity in the game.

Publishing localised EDI action plans within six months

In addition to publishing their own EDI action plan, the ECB promised to work with their members to create (or revise) their own localised version within six months, to include:

- A commitment to best-practice governance with targets for board diversity (30% female, locally representative ethnicity by April 2022) and plans to increase diversity across the wider organisation.
- Fairer recruitment processes, including anonymised recruitment tools for senior roles, open appointment processes, and the use of balanced and diverse panels to assess interviews.
- Every senior executive across the game to have personal EDI objectives as part of their annual performance targets.

The ECB committed to providing additional resources and to take further steps, including a review of governance and regulation; £25m strategic funding over five years; the formation of a new anti-discrimination unit; EDI minimum standards for all venues; a link between funding and EDI minimum standards, withholding central distributions where necessary; and collaboration with Sport England to help achieve increased diversity on boards.

DATES IN CRICKET HISTORY

c. 1550	Evidence of cricket being played in Guildford, Surrey.
1610	Reference to "cricketing" between Weald & Upland and North Downs near Chevening, Kent.
1611	Randle Cotgrave's French–English dictionary translates the French word "crosse" as a cricket staff.
	Two youths fined for playing cricket at Sidlesham, Sussex.
1624	Jasper Vinall becomes first man known to be killed playing cricket: hit by a bat while trying to catch the ball – at Horsted Green, Sussex.
1676	First reference to cricket being played abroad, by British residents in Aleppo, Syria.
1694	Two shillings and sixpence paid for a "wagger" (wager) on a match at Lewes.
1697	First reference to "a great match" with 11 players a side for 50 guineas, in Sussex.
1700	Cricket match announced on Clapham Common.
1709	First recorded inter-county match: Kent v Surrey.
1710	First reference to cricket at Cambridge University.
1727	Articles of Agreement written governing the conduct of matches between the teams of the Duke of Richmond and Mr Brodrick of Peperharow, Surrey.
1729	Date of earliest surviving bat, belonging to John Chitty, now in the Oval pavilion.
1730	First recorded match at the Artillery Ground, off City Road, central London, still the cricketing home of the Honourable Artillery Company.
1744	Kent beat All-England by one wicket at the Artillery Ground.
	First known version of the Laws of Cricket, issued by the London Club, formalising the pitch as 22 yards long.
c. 1767	Foundation of the Hambledon Club in Hampshire, the leading club in England for the next 30 years.
1769	First recorded century, by John Minshull for Duke of Dorset's XI v Wrotham.
1771	Width of bat limited to 4 1/4 inches, which it has remained ever since.
1774	Lbw law devised.
1776	Earliest known scorecards, at the Vine Club, Sevenoaks, Kent.
1780	The first six-seamed cricket ball, manufactured by Dukes of Penshurst, Kent.
1787	First match at Thomas Lord's first ground, Dorset Square, Marylebone – White Conduit Club v Middlesex.
	Formation of Marylebone Cricket Club by members of the White Conduit Club.
1788	First revision of the Laws of Cricket by MCC.
1794	First recorded inter-school match: Charterhouse v Westminster.
1795	First recorded case of a dismissal "leg before wicket".
1806	First Gentlemen v Players match at Lord's.
1807	First mention of "straight-armed" (i.e. roundarm) bowling: by John Willes of Kent.
1809	Thomas Lord's second ground opened, at North Bank, St John's Wood.
1811	First recorded women's county match: Surrey v Hampshire at Ball's Pond, London.
1814	Lord's third ground opened on its present site, also in St John's Wood.
1827	First Oxford v Cambridge match, at Lord's: a draw.
1828	MCC authorise the bowler to raise his hand level with the elbow.
1833	John Nyren publishes *Young Cricketer's Tutor* and *The Cricketers of My Time*.

1836 First North v South match, for years regarded as the principal fixture of the season.

c. **1836** Batting pads invented.

1841 General Lord Hill, commander-in-chief of the British Army, orders that a cricket ground be made an adjunct of every military barracks.

1844 First official international match: Canada v United States.

1845 First match played at The Oval.

1846 The All-England XI, organised by William Clarke, begin playing matches, often against odds, throughout the country.

1849 First Yorkshire v Lancashire match.

c. **1850** Wicketkeeping gloves first used.

1850 John Wisden bowls all ten batsmen in an innings for North v South.

1853 First mention of a champion county: Nottinghamshire.

1858 First recorded instance of a hat being awarded to a bowler taking wickets with three consecutive balls.

1859 First touring team to leave England, captained by George Parr, draws enthusiastic crowds in the US and Canada.

1864 "Overhand bowling" authorised by MCC.
John Wisden's *The Cricketer's Almanack* first published.

1868 Team of Australian Aboriginals tour England.

1873 W. G. Grace becomes the first player to record 1,000 runs and 100 wickets in a season.
First regulations restricting county qualifications, regarded by some as the official start of the County Championship.

1877 First Test match: Australia beat England by 45 runs in Melbourne.

1880 First Test in England: a five-wicket win against Australia at The Oval.

1882 Following England's first defeat by Australia in England, an "obituary notice" to English cricket in the *Sporting Times* leads to the tradition of the Ashes.

1889 Work begins on present Lord's Pavilion.
South Africa's first Test match.
Declarations first authorised, but only on the third day, or in a one-day match.

1890 County Championship officially constituted.

1895 W. G. Grace scores 1,000 runs in May, and reaches his 100th hundred.

1899 A. E. J. Collins scores 628 not out in a junior house match at Clifton College, the highest recorded individual score in any game – until 2016.
Selectors choose England team for home Tests, instead of host club issuing invitations.

1900 In England, six-ball over becomes the norm, instead of five.

1909 Imperial Cricket Conference (ICC – now the International Cricket Council) set up, with England, Australia and South Africa the original members.

1910 Six runs given for any hit over the boundary, instead of only for a hit out of the ground.

1912 First and only triangular Test series played in England, involving England, Australia and South Africa.

1915 W. G. Grace dies, aged 67.

1926 Victoria score 1,107 v New South Wales at Melbourne, still a first-class record.

1928 West Indies' first Test match.
A. P. Freeman of Kent and England becomes the only player to take more than 300 first-class wickets in a season: 304.

1930 New Zealand's first Test match.
Donald Bradman's first tour of England: he scores 974 runs in five Tests, still a record for any series.

1931   Stumps made higher (28 inches not 27) and wider (nine inches not eight – this was optional until 1947).

1932   India's first Test match.
Hedley Verity of Yorkshire takes ten wickets for ten runs v Nottinghamshire, the best innings analysis in first-class cricket.

1932-33   The Bodyline tour of Australia in which England bowl at batsmen's bodies with a packed leg-side field to neutralise Bradman's scoring.

1934   Jack Hobbs retires, with 199 centuries and 61,760 runs, both records.
First women's Test: Australia v England at Brisbane.

1935   MCC condemn and outlaw Bodyline.

1947   Denis Compton (Middlesex and England) hits a record 3,816 runs in an English season.

1948   First five-day Tests in England.
Bradman concludes Test career with a second-ball duck at The Oval and an average of 99.94 – four runs would have made it 100.

1952   Pakistan's first Test match.

1953   England regain the Ashes after a 19-year gap, the longest ever.

1956   Jim Laker of England takes 19 wickets for 90 v Australia at Manchester, the best match analysis in first-class cricket.

1960   First tied Test: Australia v West Indies at Brisbane.

1963   Distinction between amateurs and professionals abolished in English cricket.
The first major one-day tournament begins in England: the Gillette Cup.

1968   Garry Sobers becomes the first to hit six sixes in an over, for Nottinghamshire against Glamorgan at Swansea.

1969   Limited-over Sunday league inaugurated for first-class counties.

1970   Proposed South African tour of England cancelled; South Africa excluded from international cricket because of their government's apartheid policies.

1971   First one-day international: Australia beat England at Melbourne by five wickets.

1973   First women's World Cup: England are the winners.

1975   First men's World Cup: West Indies beat Australia in final at Lord's.

1976   First women's match at Lord's: England beat Australia by eight wickets.

1977   Centenary Test at Melbourne, with identical result to the first match: Australia beat England by 45 runs.
Australian media tycoon Kerry Packer signs 51 of the world's leading players in defiance of the cricketing authorities.

1978   Graham Yallop of Australia is the first batsman to wear a protective helmet in a Test.

1979   Packer and official cricket agree peace deal.

1981   England beat Australia in Leeds Test after following on, with bookmakers offering odds of 500-1 against them winning.

1982   Sri Lanka's first Test match.

1991   South Africa return, with a one-day international in India.

1992   Zimbabwe's first Test match.
Durham become first county since Glamorgan in 1921 to attain first-class status.

1993   The ICC cease to be administered by MCC, becoming an independent organisation.

1994   Brian Lara becomes the first player to pass 500 in a first-class innings: 501 not out for Warwickshire v Durham.

2000   South Africa's captain Hansie Cronje banned from cricket for life after admitting receiving bribes from bookmakers in match-fixing scandal.
Bangladesh's first Test match.
County Championship split into two divisions, with promotion and relegation.

2001   Sir Donald Bradman dies, aged 92.

2003   First Twenty20 game played, in England.

2004   Lara is the first to score 400 in a Test innings, for West Indies v England in Antigua.

2005   England regain the Ashes after 16 years.

2006   Pakistan become first team to forfeit a Test, for refusing to resume at The Oval.
Shane Warne becomes the first man to take 700 Test wickets.

2007   Australia complete 5–0 Ashes whitewash for the first time since 1920-21.
Australia win the World Cup for the third time running.
India beat Pakistan in the final of the inaugural World Twenty20.

2008   Indian Premier League of 20-over matches launched.
Sachin Tendulkar becomes the leading scorer in Tests, passing Lara.

2009   Terrorists in Lahore attack buses containing Sri Lankan team and match officials.

2010   Tendulkar scores the first double-century in a one-day international, against South
Africa; later in the year, he scores his 50th Test century.
Muttiah Muralitharan retires from Test cricket, after taking his 800th wicket.
England's men win the World T20, their first global title.
Pakistan bowl three deliberate no-balls in Lord's Test against England; the ICC ban
the three players responsible.

2011   India become the first team to win the World Cup on home soil.
Salman Butt, Mohammad Asif and Mohammad Amir are given custodial sentences of
between six and 30 months for their part in the Lord's spot-fix.

2012   Tendulkar scores his 100th international century, in an ODI against Bangladesh.

2013   150th edition of *Wisden Cricketers' Almanack*.
Tendulkar retires after his 200th Test match, with a record 15,921 runs.

2014   Australia complete only the third 5–0 Ashes whitewash.
India's Rohit Sharma hits 264 in one-day international against Sri Lanka at Kolkata.
Australian batsman Phillip Hughes, 25, dies after being hit on the neck by a bouncer.

2015   Australia win World Cup for fifth time, beating New Zealand in final at Melbourne.

2016   Pranav Dhanawade, 15, makes 1,009 not out – the highest recorded individual score in
any match – in a school game in Mumbai.
Brendon McCullum hits Test cricket's fastest hundred, from 54 balls, in his final match,
for New Zealand against Australia at Christchurch.

2017   England women beat India by nine runs to win the World Cup at Lord's.
England play their first day/night home Test, against West Indies at Edgbaston.

2018   Three Australians are banned after sandpaper used on the ball in a Test in South Africa.
Afghanistan and Ireland's men play their first Test matches.
Alastair Cook retires after 161 Tests, 12,472 runs and 33 centuries.

2019   England's men win their first 50-over World Cup, after super over against New Zealand.
England (362-9) complete their record run-chase to win Ashes Test, at Leeds.

2020   The coronavirus pandemic forces most cricket behind closed doors.
County Championship suspended; replaced by Bob Willis Trophy.
James Anderson reaches 600 Test wickets; Stuart Broad passes 500.

2021   New Zealand beat India at Southampton in the final of the first World Test Championship.
The ECB launch The Hundred – their new 100-ball competition – for men and women.
James Anderson takes his 1,000th first-class wicket.

ANNIVERSARIES IN 2022–23

Compiled by Steven Lynch

2022

Apr 17 Muttiah Muralitharan (Sri Lanka) born, 1972.
Unorthodox off-spinner who leads the wicket-takers in Tests (800) and ODIs (534).

Apr 25 C. B. Fry (Sussex and England) born, 1872.
Multi-talented sportsman; first to score six successive first-class hundreds.

Jun 21 Jim McConnon (Glamorgan and England) born, 1922.
Off-spinner with 136 wickets in 1951, his first full season; he toured Australia in 1954-55.

Jun 24 Hampshire take on England on Broadhalfpenny Down, Hambledon, 1772.
This game is now recognised as the first first-class match.

Jun 26 Bob Massie (Australia) completes debut haul of 16 wickets at Lord's, 1972.
Swinging the ball hugely, Massie claimed 16 for 137 to ensure victory in his first Test.

Jul 7 Ghulam Ahmed (India) born, 1922.
Off-spinner who took 68 wickets in 22 Tests, captaining in three.

Jul 8 Sourav Ganguly (India) born, 1972.
Elegant left-hander who scored 7,212 runs in 113 Tests, captaining in 49.

Aug 5 Aqib Javed (Pakistan) born, 1972.
Precocious seamer who took 7-37 in an ODI against India in 1991-92.

Aug 16 Arthur Jones (Nottinghamshire and England) born, 1872.
Prolific county batsman who captained in two Ashes Tests in 1907-08.

Aug 17 George Collins (Kent) takes all ten Nottinghamshire wickets, 1922.
Medium-pacer Collins claimed 10-65 as the prolific Tich Freeman finished wicketless.

Aug 17 Roy Tattersall (Lancashire and England) born, 1922.
Off-spinner: first Cricket Writers' Young Player of the Year, after 193 wickets in 1950.

Aug 23 Mark Butcher (Surrey and England) born, 1972.
Left-hander whose superb 173* won the Ashes Test at Headingley in 2001.

Sep 1 Tich Freeman (Kent and England) takes 17 wickets in match, 1922.
Leg-spinner Freeman took 9-11 and 8-56 as Sussex were skittled for 47 and 126 at Hove.

Sep 5 Alan Kippax (New South Wales and Australia) dies aged 75, 1972.
Elegant batsman: 22 Tests, and shared a first-class tenth-wicket record stand of 307.

Sep 10 K. S. Ranjitsinhji (Sussex and England) born, 1872.
Indian prince who was one of the most glamorous figures of cricket's Golden Age.

Sep 17 Denis Compton and Bill Edrich conclude their golden summer, 1947.
Respective totals of 3,816 and 3,539 first-class runs both broke the old seasonal record.

Sep 21 Tom Armitage (Yorkshire and England) dies aged 74, 1922.
All-rounder, and occasional lob bowler; played in the first Test, at Melbourne in 1876-77.

Sep 30 Allan Rae (Jamaica and West Indies) born, 1922.
Opener for the strong West Indian team in England in 1950; later an administrator.

Oct 10 Harry Cave (New Zealand) born, 1922.
Popular seamer who played 19 Tests, captaining in nine.

Nov 10 Charles Hallows (Lancashire and England) dies aged 77, 1972.
Stylish left-hander who reached 1,000 runs before the end of May in 1928.

Nov 22 Marvan Atapattu (Sri Lanka) born, 1972.
Opener who overcame a horror start to finish with 5,502 Test runs, and 8,529 in ODIs.

Dec 24 Jane Smit (England) born, 1972.
Polished wicketkeeper who played in the World Cup final win at Lord's in 1993.

2023

Jan 8   Johnny Wardle (Yorkshire and England) born, 1923.
              Brilliant if controversial slow left-armer: 1,846 first-class wickets at 18.97.

Jan 11   Rahul Dravid (India) born, 1973.
              Rock-solid batsman who piled up 13,288 runs in 164 Tests, and 10,889 in ODIs.

Jan 28   Monty Noble (New South Wales and Australia) born, 1873.
              Great all-rounder: 1,997 runs and 121 wickets in Tests, captaining in three Ashes series.

Feb 5   Bill Ponsford (Victoria and Australia) scores 429, 1923.
              Victoria racked up 1,059 at the MCG, the highest first-class total at the time.

Feb 6   Albert Trott (Australia and England) born, 1873.
              Ultimately tragic figure who took 8-43 on Test debut for Australia in 1894-95.

Feb 19   Rodney Redmond (New Zealand) scores 107 and 56 on Test debut, 1973.
              Despite a stunning debut against Pakistan, he never played another Test.

Feb 20   Charles "Jack" Russell (England) scores two centuries in a Test at Durban, 1923.
              Essex opener Russell was the first to do so for England; he never played another Test.

Mar 10   Mary Duggan (England) dies aged 47, 1973.
              All-rounder who captained England in Australia and New Zealand in 1957-58.

Mar 19   Ashley Giles (Warwickshire and England) born, 1973.
              Left-arm spinner who took 143 wickets in 54 Tests; later an administrator.

Apr 1   Stephen Fleming (New Zealand) born, 1973.
              Elegant left-hander who scored 7,172 runs in 111 Tests, 80 as captain.

Apr 2   Pelham "Plum" Warner (Middlesex and England) born, 1873.
              Test batsman, captain, administrator – and founder of The Cricketer *magazine.*

Apr 19   Sydney Barnes (Warwickshire and England) born, 1873.
              Often cited as the greatest bowler of all: 189 wickets at 16 in just 27 Tests.

Apr 24   Sachin Tendulkar (India) born, 1973.
              Batting genius who made 100 international centuries, 51 in his 200 Tests.

FIFTY YEARS AGO

Wisden Cricketers' Almanack 1973

FIVE CRICKETERS OF THE YEAR: JOHN SNOW, by Basil Easterbrook   Man is born to trouble as the sparks fly upwards, and John Augustine Snow, poet, thinker, introvert, would surely be one of the last to disagree with the proverb. Assaulted on the boundary edge of a great Test arena, dropped by his county for lack of effort, stood in a corner by England's selectors for barging over an Indian Test batsman at Lord's, and while all this was swirling around him, writing and getting published a volume of poems – controversy, thy name was Snow, in the early 1970s. Popular imagination likes its fast bowlers to be ale-swilling extroverts, but this enigmatic cricketer refuses to be typed… Reading, music, painting, poetry are as necessary to him as food and fresh air… He owes his inclusion in one of the most coveted sections of this Almanack to none of these things. He is here on naked merit, which first played a major part in bringing the Ashes back home to England after an absence of 12 years and then helped keep them here last summer. A haul of 55 wickets in two series against Australia is his passport to cricket immortality.

A WORLD TEAM IN AUSTRALIA, 1971-72, by T. L. Goodman   The 1971-72 visit by a World Team for a tour including 12 first-class matches, with five representative matches against Australia, came in place of the proposed tour by a South African team. The Springboks' visit… was cancelled by the Australian Board of Control, following sustained political and moral pressures… The Rest of the World, a multinational team chosen by the Australian authorities, did include two South African Test players, the brothers P. M. and R. G. Pollock… The most distinguished innings of the season came from the captain, G. S. Sobers, 35, when in Melbourne at the New Year he scored 254 runs against Australia. It was an unforgettable display, combining such elegance of strokeplay, power and aggression that the crowds responded ecstatically… It was majestic batting… Sir Donald Bradman said of this innings: "I believe Gary Sobers's innings was probably the best ever seen in Australia. The people who saw Sobers have enjoyed one of the historic events of cricket; they were privileged to have such an experience."

SUSSEX v SURREY, AT EASTBOURNE, AUGUST 12, 14, 15, 1972   Drawn… Everything that really mattered happened on the last day… Prideaux, the individual star, hit 106 not out, the last 50 coming in an hour, and he was again in sparkling form as Sussex tried to get 205 in two and a quarter hours. He reached within three of another hundred before he was removed in the midst of a remarkable spell of bowling by Pocock. The Surrey off-spinner took seven wickets for four runs in his last two overs, leaving Sussex three runs short of their target with one wicket left. The scorebook recorded his, and the game's final over, as WWW1W1(W), with a second run attempted off the last ball leading to the dismissal of Joshi.

NOTES BY THE EDITOR [Norman Preston]   The latest move by the Test and County Cricket Board against slow over-rates is to impose fines on those counties which fall below 18.5 overs an hour. Counties may face fines of £500 and, looking at the figures for 1972, one finds that only Hampshire and Leicestershire would have escaped. Sides which better 19.5 overs an hour will share the kitty, but none qualified in 1972. I very much dislike the idea of imposing fines. To use cricket's own phrase, "It isn't cricket", and I am afraid the authorities might be held to ridicule if a county wins the Championship by exceedingly good cricket, but its over-rate does not fall into line and it is heavily fined. Moreover, is it fair on our own bowlers, when apparently nothing will be done to compel a touring team to attain the same high rate?… I reckoned Australia averaged 15.5 overs an hour in the Tests last summer.

OBITUARY: HALLOWS, CHARLES, the cricketer who refused to grow old, died suddenly at his Bolton home on November 10, 1972, and the fact that he was aged 77 must have surprised all but the older generation of Lancashire cricket followers. They remembered Hallows as a stylish left-hander who in 1928 hit 1,000 runs in May... and scored more than 20,000 runs for his county between 1914 and 1932... yet played only twice in Test matches for England. A member of the Lancashire side which won the County Championship three years in succession, in 1926, '27 and '28, Hallows... spanned two world wars in his cricketing career and, when he retired from the first-class game at the age of 37... he earned the unique distinction of holding professional posts in leagues in England, Scotland, Ireland and Wales... His weight never varied from the day he first took guard to the last. His hair showed only a faint tinge of grey, and the spirit of the man was remarkable. Yet he was within a month of celebrating his golden wedding when he returned from the local library, sat in front of the fire and passed away, complaining only that he was a little short of breath.

AUSTRALIANS IN ENGLAND, 1972, by Norman Preston In many respects, the Australian team to visit England... surpassed themselves, even if they did not regain the Ashes. It must be remembered that for three years Australian cricket in the international scene had been at a low level. They had surrendered the Ashes to Ray Illingworth's team in 1970-71, and the previous season they had been overwhelmed in all four Tests they played in South Africa... Dennis Lillee was the real find of the tour. He first surprised the England batsmen by taking six wickets for 66 in the second innings of the First Test at Old Trafford, but Australia were put out for 142 and 152 and the England players dispersed happy in the thought that they were the masters. Then came the Lord's Test, where Lillee unloosened the top-notchers, and Bob Massie, on his Test debut, swept through the rest with the staggering analysis of 16 wickets for 137. So, by the end of June, Australia were on level terms and brimful of confidence. Bowlers win matches, and in Lillee and Massie they possessed such a combination, for Lillee by sheer speed and bounce, and Massie with skilful control of length allied to prodigious swing, mainly away from the right-hander, were largely responsible for the disappointing batting displays by England... Lillee and Massie helped themselves to 54 of the 83 wickets England lost in the Tests.

WEST INDIES v NEW ZEALAND, FIRST TEST, AT KINGSTON, FEBRUARY 16, 17, 18, 19, 21, 1972 Drawn. An astonishing innings of 223 not out by Turner saved New Zealand from an overwhelming defeat which had seemed a certainty since just before lunch on the third day when New Zealand were 108 for five in reply to West Indies' 508 for four declared. Turner was then helped in a sixth-wicket stand of 220 by Wadsworth, whose previous highest Test score had been 21. Statistically, Turner was overshadowed by Rowe, who in his first Test made 214 and 100 not out, becoming the first batsman ever to score two separate hundreds in his first Test match. Rowe continued where he had left off for Jamaica against the New Zealanders. His was a phenomenal performance and he did not appear to have any technical weaknesses... Rowe is a stockily built right-hander who is a more compact batsman than most instinctive West Indian strokeplayers, in that he seldom plays with his bat far from his pad. In the final analysis, West Indies had only themselves to blame for not winning, as Turner was badly dropped by Carew at extra cover off Gibbs when he had made 47... When the last day began, Rowe was 67 not out, and Sobers probably delayed his declaration to allow him to reach his second hundred. Even so, New Zealand had an anxious afternoon. Holford removed Dowling and Turner immediately after lunch, and only a fighting hundred by Burgess enabled them to survive an amazing game of cricket.

ESSEX v GLOUCESTERSHIRE, AT WESTCLIFF, JULY 15, 17, 18, 1972 Gloucestershire won by 107 runs... Nearly all the honours of the match went to Procter for a fine all-round feat. Twice he rescued Gloucestershire from impending danger, scoring an aggregate of 153 runs, and he took eight wickets for 73. Most excitement came on the last day when

Essex went in to get 245 to win. Any hope they may have possessed disappeared when Procter, bowling round the wicket at a great pace, dismissed the first four batsmen in 27 balls for eight runs. He performed the hat-trick when disposing of Edmeades, Ward and Boyce. Making the ball rear from the hard pitch, Procter caused the temporary retirement through injury of Taylor and Turner. Fletcher alone played him with any assurance.

WARWICKSHIRE IN 1972 Warwickshire, after being beaten on a technicality by Surrey the previous year, won the County Championship for the third time in their history... In addition, they reached the final of the Gillette Cup, the semi-final of the new Benson and Hedges League Cup, and only in the John Player League did their performance fall below par. They won by a margin of 36 points, and six of their nine victories were achieved the hard way, by bowling the opposition out twice. Their total of victories was two more than any other county, and they were the only unbeaten team – although... the season began on a very unpropitious note when, in the very first match, the county were defeated by Oxford University... Success was sealed in the penultimate match against Derbyshire, and the captain made true his promise of a champagne and kippers breakfast on the morning of the first day of the final match.

Compiled by Christopher Lane

ONE HUNDRED YEARS AGO

Wisden Cricketers' Almanack 1923

WARWICKSHIRE v HAMPSHIRE, AT BIRMINGHAM, JUNE 14–16, 1922   This was the sensational match of the whole season, at Birmingham or anywhere else, Hampshire actually winning by 155 runs after being out for a total of 15. That their astounding failure in the first innings was just one of the accidents of cricket, and not due in any way to the condition of the ground, was proved by their getting 521 when they followed on. The victory, taken as a whole, must surely be without precedent in first-class cricket. Hampshire looked in a hopeless position when the sixth wicket in their second innings went down at 186, but Shirley helped Brown to put on 85 runs, and then, with Livsey in after McIntyre had failed, the score was carried to 451.

YORKSHIRE IN 1922   Yorkshire won the Championship handsomely last summer… Of their 30 county matches they won 19 and lost only two, and in the nine games left drawn they gained points on the first innings six times… They simply slaughtered the weakest of their opponents… in no match, perhaps, did they look a better side than when beating Middlesex at Lord's in June. They declared with seven wickets down and yet won by an innings and 21 runs, their batting, bowling and fielding reaching an equally high standard. Playing nearly every day, they were extraordinarily consistent… They had only one bad match and that, curiously enough, came just after their triumph at Lord's. Against Notts at Sheffield, their batting, without any adequate excuse, failed in both innings, and their bowling, for once, proved quite ineffective. The result was that Notts won by an innings and 75 runs… Yorkshire were very good at every point, but their main strengths lay in the excellence and variety of their bowling… Though Rhodes had the satisfaction of heading the averages, he was not in reality quite such a bowling force on the side as Macaulay, Roy Kilner or Waddington… Still, he bowled uncommonly well, with all the accuracy, if not the spin, of his early days. He was, as in many other seasons, a great all-round man in the XI… Sutcliffe, after two rather disappointing seasons, came into his own, fulfilling all the hopes inspired in 1919, when he stepped into the XI for the first time and met with such startling success. All going well, he should be one of our Test match batsmen in the immediate future.

MCC IN 1922   The Memorial to Dr W. G. Grace shall take the form of a gateway with handsome iron gates, at the members' entrance, to be adapted to harmonise with certain improvements at that entrance. Originally intended to be erected exclusively by MCC it was afterwards determined… to accept donations up to a moiety of the cost, in the belief that cricket clubs and admirers of the late Dr Grace would like to be associated with it. A tender has been accepted amounting to £2,268.

NOTES BY THE EDITOR [Sydney Pardon]   Following the excitement and bitter disappointments of 1921, we had a comparatively uneventful season, but with better weather there would have been no cause for complaint. I am afraid some of the smaller counties suffered severely, but speaking generally the game held its own in quite a wonderful way in the face of adverse conditions. To some of us… the recollection of England having lost eight Test matches in succession was a perpetual nightmare, but despondency affected only the old. It may have been due to the fact that Hobbs was back in the field, getting hundreds in his inimitable way, but I think English cricket as a whole was appreciably better than in 1921. I do not cherish any illusion that, even with Hobbs to help us, we could have beaten the great Australian XI on a hard wicket… we lacked a new Barnes, a new Frank Foster. Bowlers of that class appear at long intervals without the slightest warning; they cannot be made. When one or two of them come forward – the hour is overdue – English cricket may regain its old supremacy.

FIVE CRICKETERS OF THE YEAR: ANDREW SANDHAM Sandham describes himself as a self-taught batsman, having imbibed all his ideas of correct play from watching Tom Hayward at The Oval. He certainly could not have chosen a better model. In two respects he recalls Hayward vividly – the beautiful straightness of his bat and his remarkable power of forcing the ball away off his legs. His play off his legs is indeed his most distinctive gift and… as an out-field it would not be easy to find his superior. Those of us who year after year see more than half our cricket at The Oval need not apologise for being enthusiastic about his work at long-on and deep third man. He is untiring and seldom indeed does the ball beat him if there is any possibility of crossing it. Though not over fond of cricket statistics I wish there were some means of calculating the number of runs he saves in a season.

GLAMORGAN IN 1922 There was assuredly really nothing in Glamorgan cricket last year to shake one's conviction as to the county's promotion to the first-class in 1921 having been altogether premature. Without in any way wishing to discourage ambition, one cannot get away from the patent fact that the Glamorgan team were first-class only in name. The record was even more disheartening than in the previous year, as out of 22 county matches, 18 were lost, the only set-off against this series of disasters being a surprising victory, late in the season, over Somerset by 117 runs.

J. T. TYLDESLEY AND D. DENTON IN THE CRICKET FIELD, by Major R. O. Edwards When asked by the Editor to give John Tyldesley's record in the pages of *Wisden*, it seemed appropriate to couple with the great Lancashire cricketer his famous counterpart in the Yorkshire ranks – David Denton… Each was a joy to the critics from the first. Tyldesley and Denton belonged to a school of professional batsmen all too rare in these days of the two-shouldered stance. They made a point of going for the bowling. Each will live in cricket history as essentially a brilliant batsman, with Tyldesley by far the more dependable. Their position on the batting order was the same – first wicket down, and their cricket a source of unmixed delight. Both showed a partiality for off-side play. Tyldesley revelled in the cut (he even jumped back and cut Armstrong in 1905), and Denton specialised in the drive… Denton was perhaps the luckiest great batsmen that ever lived (vide Sammy Woods), but he took risks, and never counted the cost. It was his nature… It was said that Denton never missed a catch in the deep until his 12th season – then he dropped two in one afternoon, and one renowned Yorkshire comrade wept… Small in stature, modest in demeanour, these two were good cricketers and good fellows – an honour to the game.

SUSSEX v KENT, AT BRIGHTON, AUGUST 30–SEPTEMBER 1, 1922 Sussex wound up their season in dismal fashion, Kent beating them in an innings with 23 runs to spare. Beyond everything else, the bowling of Freeman stood out by itself. In the whole match he took 17 wickets for 67 runs – an astounding performance, much as rain had affected the pitch. His nine wickets for 11 runs in the first innings was altogether out of the common even among the many feats of bowlers getting rid of nine or ten men in one innings.

DERBYSHIRE v WARWICKSHIRE, AT DERBY, JUNE 3, 5, 1922 Weak batting again brought about Derbyshire's defeat, Warwickshire winning easily on the second afternoon by ten wickets… Warwickshire lost four men for 84 on the Saturday, but W. G. Quaife mastered the bowling on Monday and was the one batsman in the match to be seen to much advantage. At the wickets four and a half hours, he did not make a mistake until after completing his hundred. At one time, the two Quaifes were opposed by the two Bestwicks. For father and son to be batting against bowlers similarly related was a remarkable incident – regarded as unique in county cricket.

Compiled by Christopher Lane

ONE HUNDRED AND FIFTY YEARS AGO

Wisden Cricketers' Almanack 1873

THE MARYLEBONE CLUB IN 1872   The 86th Season of the MCC was commenced on May 6, at Lord's, and concluded on September 6, at Aberdeen. It was a season to remember for its frequent and furious storms; for the extraordinary contrasts in the cricket played on the old ground; for the largest innings by Cambridge and Mr Yardley that were ever made in the Inter-Universities' matches; for the brilliant and unprecedentedly large attendances on the first days of the Oxford v Cambridge contest, and that "fashionable match of the season" – Harrow v Eton; for the introduction on the ground of the conveniently useful Travelling Telegraph Trap; for the erection of the Clock for the convenience of visitors, and a warning to umpires and cricketers to henceforth "keep true time"; for Mr Grace being twice out in MCC matches for "that beastly 0"; *for his being first man in and taking his bat out for 170 in another match*;...its being the season wherein Notts and Yorkshire first played the rest of England; and for the increase in the number of matches played by the Club, and consequent increase of encouragement to the game throughout the country given by MCC... Mr W. G. Grace, the monarch of all MCC (and other batsmen), notwithstanding the wet and slow wickets that prevailed in the early part of last season, again contributed very largely to the Club's success on several occasions, for out of the gross total of 1,556 runs made for MCC in the 15 innings Mr Grace played for the Club, he made 528, or more than one third; his MCC average for 1872 being 40.8 runs per innings.

ENGLAND v NOTTS AND YORKSHIRE, AT LORD'S, JULY 8–9, 1872   "Mr Grace first: the rest nowhere." Such was the brief emphatic verdict pronounced by an old cricketer on the wonderful innings played by the great batsman in this match. This record requires a more extended notice of this extraordinary "bit of batting", and to the best of the compiler's ability it shall have one. The match was one of the novelties of the MCC season... but the weather was dull, cold and wet... [At 225 for five] Roger Iddison went on with lobs, and with the first six of these he had three wickets... Of course, Roger was jubilant at such success – what bowler would not be? But his next batch of lobs was tremendously thrashed by Mr Grace... Mr Grace was first man in... and when the innings was up with the total 290 – 283 from the bat, Mr Grace had scored 170, or 57 more than his ten colleagues had collectively contributed... What a splendid, magnificent driving display this 170 of the great batsman's was, and how lustily and long he was cheered by those that were present.

PREFACE   John Wisden & Co., in again thankfully acknowledging the annual increasing support awarded to the Cricketers' Almanack, beg to inform the cricketing community that, notwithstanding the Cricket at Prince's and The Visit of the Twelve to Canada and America necessitated an enlargement by 36 pages of this year's edition, their little Record of The Full Scores, etc, of the season's important matches, *is not increased in price.*

ETON v HARROW, AT LORD'S, JULY 12–13, 1872   Never before was congregated on Lord's Ground so numerous and brilliant a company as that which on the 12th of last July crushed and crowded on to that famous cricket arena to witness the first day's play in this, "the fashionable match of the season". Every seat in the spacious Grand Stand had been secured several days prior to the match... On "the day before the battle commenced", so extensive a use had been made of members' privileges in regard to standing room for *their* carriages, and so numerous had been the applications from non-members for space for *their* vehicles, that every available foot of the old ground set apart for carriage standing was secured... The crush at the gates on the first day was great and lasting beyond all precedent... and for hours the "clack, clack" of the turnstiles resounded as rapidly and as regularly as the men in the two boxes could take the admission shillings… Friday was a superb day for cricket and other outdoor pleasures, and when about 5.30 that afternoon the Prince and Princess of Wales and Prince Arthur came on the ground, the scene at old Lord's was indeed "splendid"… Stand, drags, and carriages were all made bright and glorious by a crowd and wealth of brilliantly attired, beauteous women, such as can be seen nowhere out of grumbling but glorious Old England.

SUSSEX v KENT, AT BRIGHTON, AUGUST 12–13, 1872 The Kent manager had brought the Canterbury ground bowler, Geo. Shaw of Notts, to play in their XI, but the Sussex authorities very properly, firmly and successfully objected to his playing against them as a Kent man in 1872, so Fryer played and Shaw umpired… The second innings of Kent was only remarkable for Bennett being out for "Handling the Ball"; Southerton bowled to Bennett, who played the ball, which fell inside the top of his pad; there it stuck despite the efforts to shake it out made by Bennett, who then took it out and threw it on the ground, consequently he was out.

MCC AND GROUND v SURREY, AT LORD'S, MAY 14, 1872 This was the most remarkable match of the MCC season. Seven MCC wickets, including the crack's [W. G. Grace], being got rid of before a run was scored. Eight noughts were booked in that innings of MCC's, whose XI were out in three quarters of an hour for a total of 16 runs. Nineteen was the highest score made in the match, which was commenced at 12.10 and concluded at 6.40; the whole number of runs made in the match being 175… Incessant rain from dawn to dusk on the 13th (the day set to commence the match) necessitated a postponement until the following day, when on dead, deceitful playing wickets, and in a queer light for batting, Mr W. Grace and John Smith commenced (!) MCC's marvellous little innings of 16 runs… At 1.10, the Surrey innings was commenced; at 2.30 it was concluded for 49 runs, made from 46 overs (less one ball). At 3.05, the second innings of MCC was commenced… but at 5.30, the innings was over for 71 runs, made from 77 overs (less one ball). At 5.45, Jupp and R. Humphrey commenced Surrey's second innings, and at 6.40 the county had won by five wickets; but if Captain Beecher had not missed R. Humphrey when he had scored only three runs, and Mr Howell when he had scored but two, the probability was the match would have been a very close affair.

ALL THE 20 WICKETS Mr C. Absolon – an old and liberal supporter of Metropolitan cricket and cricketers – was the grey-haired hero of this very successful bowling feat, having a hand in the downfall of all the 20 wickets; he bowled ten, two hit wicket, six were caught from his bowling, and he caught out the remaining two. The match made famous by this bowling of Mr Absolon's was Wood Green v United Willesden, played at Wood Green, July 21, 1872. Wood Green won by an innings and 45 runs.

QUALIFICATIONS FOR A COUNTY CRICKETER A meeting, as influential in composition as it was important in its results, was held last December (1872), in London, to settle the vexed question of what in future should form the qualifications of a county cricketer. With the very important exception of Nottinghamshire, all the cricketing counties of England were represented… [The resolutions were:]

That no player, either amateur or professional, play for more than one county during the same season…

Every player, gentleman or professional, born in one county and residing in another, shall be free to choose, at the commencement of each season, which county he will play for, and shall then during that year play for that county only, and that such intention be publicly notified…

That a bona fide residence of three years be considered for the future a residential qualification for any professional cricketer, accepting the existing qualifications.

NOTTINGHAMSHIRE v SURREY, AT NOTTINGHAM, JULY 11, 12, 1872 On the Friday… the light was bad and gradually grew worse, a storm evidently brewing all round, but they played on until the score reached 180 runs; then (3.30) play was stopped by one of the most terrific outbursts of lightning, thunder, hail, rain and wind witnessed for many years in the Midlands. One account stated: "In two minutes after the storm commenced every tent but the printers' was blown down, the water lay in pools all over the ground, the flagpole was broken in twain, and many trees were dismantled." Another account recorded: "That four tents were blown down, the trees struck with lightning, and a greater portion of the ground submerged in water… The storm was truly alarming, and will make this match a remarkable event in cricket annals." A third local account thought it: "The most violent storm ever witnessed in the district. To say it rained would be ridiculous; it poured in torrents, and not only flooded the ground, but, with the assistance of the wind and lightning, tore down the refreshment and ladies' booths as though they were mere shreds of paper." Of course there was no more play on that stormy Friday, and as rain set in again at 11am on the Saturday and continued to fall until one o'clock "the match was quashed".

THE MARYLEBONE CLUB IN 1872 The 85th anniversary meeting of the members of The Marylebone Club was held at Lord's Ground on Wednesday, May 1, when a ballot took place and the unprecedentedly large number of 90 *new members were elected*. Dinner was served in the new Tavern at 7.30 the same day, the president, The Right Hon. the Earl of Clarendon, in the chair. What took place after the removal of the cloth will be best told by the following graphic report taken from *Bell's Life in London*: "After dinner the usual loyal toasts were given, and cordially responded to, the president making special allusion to the late illness of HRH the Prince of Wales [later Edward VII], who, as patron of the MCC, had enlisted the sympathies and anxieties of the members during that trying period, his lordship adding that though uninitiated in the mysteries of medicine, he could recommend with confidence to HRH's medical advisers, as a thorough restoration, a gentle dose of cricket, to be taken weekly at Lord's."

THE FIRST ELEVEN OF MCC AND GROUND v THE NEXT TWENTY, AT LORD'S, MAY 9, 1872 This was an experimental match, wherein wickets were used one inch higher, one inch wider, and somewhat thicker than the orthodox 27 by 8. Rylott was the only bowler who hit the big (and ugly) wickets in the Eleven's innings, but Alfred Shaw bowled eight of "The next Twenty"… So piercingly cold and rheumatically strong did the wind blow, that when, at 5.10, Alfred Shaw had so summarily settled the tail of The Twenty, it was wisely resolved to play no more in such weather, so, to the gratifying comfort of all, the big sticks were forthwith pulled up.

Compiled by Christopher Lane

HONOURS AND AWARDS IN 2021-22

In 2021-22, the following were decorated for their services to cricket:

Queen's Birthday Honours, 2021: W. K. Craig (Eglinton CC; services to cricket and the community) BEM; C. Edwards (England Learning Disability Team; services to learning disabilities cricket) BEM; I. D. Nairn (England Physical Disability Team; services to physical disabilities cricket) MBE; E-J. C-L. C. R. Rainford-Brent (England Women, broadcaster and coach; services to cricket and charity) MBE.

Queen's Birthday Honours (Australia), 2021: A. S. Connolly (services to cricket in New South Wales) OAM; C. S. Dempsey (services to cricket in New South Wales) OAM; R. McKenzie (services to cricket and the community of Rye in Victoria) OAM; A. D. Owen (services to cricket in New South Wales) OAM.

Queen's Birthday Honours (New Zealand), 2021: G. A. A. Baker (services to cricket at the community in Wellington) QSM.

Khel Ratna Award (India), 2021: M. D. Raj (Railways and India Women).

Arjuna Award (India), 2021: S. Dhawan (Delhi and India).

New Year's Honours, 2022: P. J. Colbourne (Bath CC; services to young people through cricket and charity) BEM; I. C. Crawford (Gloucestershire, president of Bristol Youth Cricket League; services to sport and the community) BEM; Q. M. Khan (Hamro Foundation; services to cricket and charity) MBE.

Australia Day Honours, 2022: R. G. Cairney (services to cricket in Adelaide) OAM; A. I. C. Dodemaide (Victoria and Australia; services to cricket and sports administration) OAM; W. E. Franks (services to cricket and sports history) OAM; D. J. Kelly (services to cricket and education in Geelong) OAM; R. A. Martin (services to cricket in NSW) OAM; M. Vergano (services to sports administration in ACT) OAM; B. G. Wood (services to cricket in Hornsby, Ku-ring-gai & Hills, NSW) OAM; John Wylie (former chair of MCG Trust; services in the sporting, cultural, philanthropic and business sectors) AC.

ICC AWARDS

The International Cricket Council's annual awards were announced in January 2022.

Men's Cricketer of the Year (Sir Garfield Sobers Trophy)	**Shaheen Shah Afridi** (Pakistan)
Women's Cricketer of the Year (Rachael Heyhoe Flint Trophy)	**Smriti Mandhana** (India)
Men's Test Cricketer of the Year	**Joe Root** (England)
Men's ODI Cricketer of the Year	**Babar Azam** (Pakistan)
Women's ODI Cricketer of the Year	**Lizelle Lee** (South Africa)
Men's T20I Cricketer of the Year	**Mohammad Rizwan** (Pakistan)
Women's T20I Cricketer of the Year	**Tammy Beaumont** (England)
Emerging Men's Cricketer of the Year	**Janneman Malan** (South Africa)
Emerging Women's Cricketer of the Year	**Fatima Sana** (Pakistan)
Men's Associate Cricketer of the Year	**Zeeshan Maqsood** (Oman)
Women's Associate Cricketer of the Year	**Andrea-Mae Zepeda** (Austria)
Umpire of the Year (David Shepherd Trophy)	**Marais Erasmus** (South Africa)
Spirit of Cricket Award	**Daryl Mitchell** (New Zealand)†

† *For refusing to take a single in the T20 World Cup semi-final with England when he felt he had impeded the bowler.*

The ICC selected three men's world XIs and two women's world XIs from the previous 12 months:

	Men's Test team		*Men's ODI team*		*Men's T20I team*
1	Dimuth Karunaratne (SL)	1	Paul Stirling (Ire)	1	Jos Buttler (E)
2	Rohit Sharma (I)	2	Janneman Malan (SA)	2	Mohammad Rizwan (P)
3	Marnus Labuschagne (A)	3	*Babar Azam (P)	3	*Babar Azam (P)
4	Joe Root (E)	4	Fakhar Zaman (P)	4	Aiden Markram (SA)
5	*Kane Williamson (NZ)	5	Rassie van der Dussen (SA)	5	Mitchell Marsh (A)
6	Fawad Alam (P)	6	Shakib Al Hasan (B)	6	David Miller (SA)
7	†Rishabh Pant (I)	7	†Mushfiqur Rahim (B)	7	W. Hasaranga de Silva (SL)
8	Ravichandran Ashwin (I)	8	W. Hasaranga de Silva (SL)	8	Tabraiz Shamsi (SA)
9	Kyle Jamieson (NZ)	9	Mustafizur Rahman (B)	9	Josh Hazlewood (A)
10	Hasan Ali (P)	10	Simi Singh (Ire)	10	Mustafizur Rahman (B)
11	Shaheen Shah Afridi (P)	11	Dushmantha Chameera (SL)	11	Shaheen Shah Afridi (P)

ICC CRICKET HALL OF FAME

The ICC Cricket Hall of Fame was launched in 2009 in association with the Federation of International Cricketers' Associations to recognise legends of the game. In the first year, 60 members were inducted: 55 from the earlier FICA Hall of Fame, plus five players elected in October 2009 by a voting academy made up of the ICC president, 11 ICC member representatives, a FICA representative, a women's cricket representative, ten journalists, a statistician, and all living members of the Hall of Fame. Candidates must have retired from international cricket at least five years ago.

In June 2021, to mark the inaugural World Test Championship final, the ICC added ten members, two from each of five eras: *Pre-1918* – G. A. Faulkner (South Africa) and M. A. Noble (Australia); *1918–1945* – Lord Constantine (West Indies) and S. J. McCabe (Australia); *1946–1970* – E. R. Dexter (England) and M. H. Mankad (India); *1971–1995* – D. L. Haynes (West Indies) and R. G. D. Willis (England); *1996–2015* – A. Flower (Zimbabwe) and K. C. Sangakkara (Sri Lanka). In November 2021, ahead of the T20 World Cup final, they added J. A. Brittin (England), D. P. M. D. Jayawardene (Sri Lanka) and S. M. Pollock (South Africa). This brought the total to 106.

ICC DEVELOPMENT AWARDS

The International Cricket Council announced the global winners of their 2020 Development Awards for Associate Members in April 2021. **Cricket Argentina** won the Development Initiative of the Year, after they established 17 coaching, umpiring and scoring courses in Spanish, and then moved them online during the pandemic; this resulted in 257 new coaches. The 100% Cricket Female Initiative of the Year went to **Cricket Brazil**, after they gave professional central contracts to 14 members of the women's national team. **Vanuatu Cricket Association** won the Digital Fan Engagement of the Year: in the early days of the pandemic, when sport across the world had ground to a halt, they live-streamed their Women's T20 Grand Final and the Vanuatu T10 Blast to over 16m people. And the Cricket 4 Good Social Impact Initiative of the Year was claimed by the **Uganda Cricket Association**, who supported 1,500 players, coaches, umpires and school teachers during the pandemic with food, soap, financial aid, psychological support and online courses on financial literacy.

ALLAN BORDER MEDAL

Steve Smith won his third Allan Border Medal, for the best Australian men's international player of the previous 12 months, in February 2021. He was also named One-day International Player of the Year after a run of form against India, split across away and home series at opposite ends of the year, that included 98 followed by three successive centuries. **Pat Cummins** was Test Player of the Year, and **Ashton Agar** Twenty20 International Player of the Year. Smith claimed the Allan Border Medal after earning 126 votes from team-mates, umpires and journalists, 12 ahead of Cummins. The award has also been won by Glenn McGrath, Steve Waugh, Matthew Hayden, Adam Gilchrist, Ricky Ponting (four times), Michael Clarke (four times), Brett Lee, Shane Watson (twice), Mitchell Johnson, David Warner (three times) and Cummins. **Beth Mooney** won the Belinda Clark Award for the leading woman player, with 60 votes, two ahead of Meg Lanning; she was also named Twenty20 International Player of the Year, while **Rachael Haynes** won the One-Day International award. **Shaun Marsh** of Western Australia retained his title as Men's Domestic Player of the Year, and Victoria's **Will Sutherland** was the Bradman Young Cricketer of the Year. **Elyse Villani** of Victoria and Melbourne Stars was Women's Domestic Player of the Year, and **Hannah Darlington** (NSW and Sydney Thunder) was the Betty Wilson Young Cricketer of the Year. New South Wales seamer **Josh Lalor** won the Community Champion award, for his role in setting up the Reflect Forward campaign against racism in cricket.

CRICKET SOUTH AFRICA AWARDS

Pace bowler **Anrich Nortje** was named Men's Cricketer of the Year, Test Cricketer of the Year and Fans' Player of the Year at the CSA awards, staged online in May 2021; he also shared the Players' Player award with **Aiden Markram**. **Rassie van der Dussen** was the Men's ODI Cricketer of the Year and **Tabraiz Shamsi** Men's T20I Cricketer of the Year, while **George Linde** was International Newcomer of the Year (won a year earlier by Nortje). The CSA Delivery of the Year was bowled by **Wiaan Mulder**, when he had Kusal Mendis caught by van der Dussen in the Second Test against Sri Lanka in January.

Another fast bowler, **Shabnim Ismail**, won three of the four women's awards: Women's Cricketer of the Year, T20I Cricketer of the Year (for the third year running) and Players' Player; **Lizelle Lee** was the Women's ODI Cricketer of the Year and also won the Streetwise Award for her 132* against India in March.

In the domestic awards, **Markram** (Titans) was the Four-Day Domestic Series Cricketer of the Season, and his team-mate **Neil Brand** was the Domestic Newcomer of the Season. Dolphins picked up five awards: newly-retired **Robbie Frylinck** was One-Day Cup Cricketer of the Season, **Keshav Maharaj** was SACA Most Valuable Player and Domestic Players' Player, **Ottniel Baartman** won the inaugural Makhaya Ntini Power of Cricket Award (intended to highlight cricket's ability to change lives), and **Imraan Khan** was Coach of the Season. **Sisanda Magala** (Lions) was T20 Challenge Cricketer of the Season. **Adrian Holdstock** was Umpire of the Year again, while **Lubabalu Gcuma** was the Umpires' Umpire. **Warriors** retained the Fair Play Award.

NEW ZEALAND CRICKET AWARDS

New Zealand captain **Kane Williamson** won the Sir Richard Hadlee Medal for Player of the Year at the NZC awards in April 2021. He was also named Test Player of the Year, and collected the Redpath Cup for first-class batting. **Devon Conway** was the Men's ODI Player and T20I Player of the Year, while **Amy Satterthwaite** won the Women's ODI award and **Amelia Kerr** the T20I equivalent. Both Domestic Player of the Year awards went to Canterbury, with **Daryl Mitchell** claiming the men's award and **Frankie Mackay** the women's, while **Kerr** and **Finn Allen**, both Wellington, were the Domestic T20 Players of the Year. **Kyle Jamieson** (Auckland) won the Winsor Cup for first-class bowling. **Kate Ebrahim** won the Ruth Martin Cup for women's domestic batting, and **Sarah Asmussen** the Phil Blackler Cup for women's domestic bowling; both played for Canterbury, who had won the 20-over and 50-over competitions. Former Test player **Jeff Crowe**, now an ICC referee, won the Bert Sutcliffe Medal for Outstanding Services to Cricket.

PROFESSIONAL CRICKETERS' ASSOCIATION AWARDS

The following awards were announced between August and October. Eve Jones, who had never won an England cap, was the first female domestic professional to be named Women's Player of the Year.

Cinch PCA Men's Player of the Year	**Joe Root** (England, Yorkshire and Trent Rockets)
Cinch PCA Women's Player of the Year	**Eve Jones** (Central Sparks and Birmingham Phoenix)
Cinch PCA Men's Young Player of the Year	**Harry Brook** (Yorkshire and Northern Superchargers)
Cinch PCA Women's Young Player of the Year	**Alice Capsey** (South East Stars and Oval Invincibles)
Test Player of the Summer	**Joe Root**
Royal London Men's ODI Player of the Summer	**Saqib Mahmood**
Royal London Women's ODI Player of the Summer	**Heather Knight**
Vitality Men's IT20 Player of the Summer	**Liam Livingstone**
Vitality Women's IT20 Player of the Summer	**Nat Sciver**
County Championship Player of the Year	**Luke Fletcher** (Nottinghamshire)
Royal London Cup Player of the Year	**Scott Borthwick** (Durham)
Rachael Heyhoe Flint Trophy Player of the Year	**Kathryn Bryce** (Lightning)

Vitality Blast Player of the Year	**Samit Patel** (Nottinghamshire)
Charlotte Edwards Cup Player of the Year	**Eve Jones** (Central Sparks)
Men's Hundred PCA MVP	**Liam Livingstone** (Birmingham Phoenix)
Women's Hundred PCA MVP	**Dane van Niekerk** (Oval Invincibles)
Men's Domestic Overall MVP	**Simon Harmer** (Essex)
Women's Domestic Overall MVP	**Eve Jones** (Central Sparks and Birmingham Phoenix)

Men's Team of the Year: Jake Libby, Tom Haines, †Ricardo Vasconcelos, David Bedingham, Harry Brook, Matt Critchley, Darren Stevens, *Simon Harmer, Craig Overton, Luke Fletcher, Sam Cook.

Women's Team of the Year: *Eve Jones, Georgia Adams, Emma Lamb, Alice Capsey, Sophie Luff, Bryony Smith, †Abbey Freeborn, Kate Cross, Emily Arlott, Linsey Smith, Lauren Bell.

WALTER LAWRENCE TROPHY

Liam Livingstone of Lancashire won the Walter Lawrence Trophy for the fastest century in 2021 – and, unusually, he did it in an international. His 42-ball hundred against Pakistan at Trent Bridge was England's fastest in T20 internationals, beating 48 balls by Dawid Malan. The last man to receive the trophy for an England performance was Geoffrey Boycott, whose 157 at The Oval in 1970 was judged "the most meritorious" innings of England's series against The Rest of the World, rather than the fastest (he took 222 balls to reach 100). Since 2008, the Trophy has been available for innings in all senior cricket in England; traditionally, it was reserved for the fastest first-class hundred (in 2021, Darren Stevens's 67-ball century for Kent at Leicester). The women's award, which goes to the highest individual score of the season, was won by **Amy Jones** of Central Sparks for her 163* against Western Storm at Birmingham in the Rachael Heyhoe Flint Trophy. The MCCU Universities Award, suspended in 2020 because of the Covid-19 crisis, was won by **Jack Timby**, who scored a run-a-ball 152 for Leeds/Bradford UCCE against Loughborough. Livingstone and Jones each won £2,500, Timby won £500, and all three received a special medallion.

CRICKET WRITERS' CLUB AWARDS

The Cricket Writers' Club announced their annual awards in October 2021. Members voted **Harry Brook** Young Cricketer of the Year (sponsored by NV Play) for a breakthrough season in which he scored 797 Championship runs, was the fourth-highest run-scorer in the Vitality Blast with 486 at 69, and the ninth-highest in the Men's Hundred, despite playing only five matches. The LV= Insurance County Championship Player of the Year was **Luke Fletcher** of Nottinghamshire, the season's leading first-class wicket-taker with 66 at 14. The JM Finn Women's Cricketer of the Year was **Sophia Dunkley**, who scored 74 not out against India when she became the first black woman to play Test cricket for England, and followed up with an unbeaten 73 in her first one-day international innings. Later, her 244 runs in the Women's Hundred steered Southern Brave to the final. A new award for the Emerging Women's Cricketer of the Year (sponsored by Sumaridge Estate Wines) went to **Alice Capsey**, the 17-year-old all-rounder who won two titles – the Women's Hundred with Oval Invincibles and the Charlotte Edwards Cup with South East Stars. The Lord's Taverners Disability Cricketer of the Year was **Alex Jervis** from Yorkshire, who not only played for Yorkshire Tykes in the D40 league, but coached them and raised funds for kit and training facilities with a sponsored bike ride. The Peter Smith Memorial Award "for services to the presentation of cricket to the public" went to **Michael Holding**, described as an icon of the game as a player and a broadcaster, and praised for opening eyes and ears with his searing words on racism. The Derek Hodgson Cricket Book Award was won by **Nick Greenslade** for *The Thin White Line: The Inside Story of Cricket's Greatest Scandal*, his account of the spot-fixing scandal of 2010.

A list of Young Cricketers from 1950 to 2004 appears in Wisden 2005, page 995. *A list of Peter Smith Award winners from 1992 to 2004 appears in* Wisden 2005, page 745.

SECOND XI PLAYER OF THE YEAR

The Association of Cricket Statisticians and Historians named Nottinghamshire all-rounder **Joey Evison** as the Les Hatton Second XI Player of the Year for 2021. Evison was the leading wicket-taker in the Second XI Championship, with 35 at 15, including seven for 25 against Leicestershire in their last match; he made 513 runs at 51, with a highest score of 152 against Warwickshire. He also scored 251 in ten games in the Second XI Twenty20 tournament.

GROUNDS MANAGERS OF THE YEAR

The ECB Grounds Manager of the Year was **Matt Merchant**, who won the award for his four-day pitches at Old Trafford for the third time; **Neil Godrich** (Derby) and **Scott Hawkins** (Taunton) were runners-up, with commendations for Gary Barwell (Edgbaston), Lee Fortis (The Oval) and Ben Gibson (Hove). The one-day award went to **Adrian Llong** at Canterbury, who had won the outground award at Beckenham in 2018. Hawkins was also runner-up in this category, while Barwell, Vic Demain (Chester-le-Street), Karl McDermott (Lord's) and Andy Ward (Leicester) were commended. **Christian Brain** of Cheltenham won the award for the best outground; Ben Harris was commended for Clifton Park in York and Alex Kegg for Chester Boughton Hall in Cheshire. A retrospective recognition award was made to **Simon Lee**, for the first of the three Test pitches he prepared at Southampton in the Covid-hit season of 2020 – his first year with Hampshire after moving from Taunton. (No other grounds awards were made for 2020.)

WOMBWELL CRICKET LOVERS' SOCIETY AWARDS

George Spofforth Cricketer of the Year	**Joe Root** (Yorkshire/England)
Women's Cricketer of the Year	**Heather Knight** (England)
Brian Sellers Captain of the Year	**Will Rhodes** (Warwickshire)
C. B. Fry Young Cricketer of the Year	**Harry Brook** (Yorkshire)
Arthur Wood Wicketkeeper of the Year	**Tom Moores** (Nottinghamshire)
Learie Constantine Fielder of the Year	**Adam Lyth** (Yorkshire)
Denis Compton Memorial Award for Flair	**Liam Livingstone** (Lancashire/England)
Denzil Batchelor Award for Services to English Cricket	**Phil Neale** (former England operations manager)
Dr Leslie Taylor Award (best Roses performance)	**Keaton Jennings** (Lancashire)
Les Bailey Most Promising Young Yorkshire Player	**George Hill and Jemimah Rodrigues***
Ted Umbers Award – Services to Yorkshire Cricket	**John Potter** (Yorkshire scorer)
J. M. Kilburn Cricket Writer of the Year	**Mick Pope**
Jack Fingleton Cricket Commentator of the Year	**Ebony Rainford-Brent**

* Jemimah Rodrigues appeared for Northern Superchargers.

SJA BRITISH SPORTS JOURNALISM AWARDS

The Sports Journalists' Association awards were announced in March. **Sky Sports'** piece on Black Lives Matter, broadcast on the opening day of the England v West Indies Test series in July 2020, won the award for the Television/Digital Live Event Coverage of the Year. **Michael Holding** was Sports Pundit of the Year, with Ebony Rainford-Brent, who appeared with him in the Sky Sports item, taking the bronze award. **Jonathan Liew** of *The Guardian* was named Sports Writer of the Year, and his colleague **Andy Bull** Sports Feature Writer of the Year. **Nick Hoult** of *The Daily Telegraph* was Cricket Journalist of the Year, ahead of Mike Atherton and Ali Martin; Atherton was also runner-up for Sports Columnist of the Year.

Sky Sports' Black Lives Matter broadcast also won the Royal Television Society's Sports Programme Award, and a BAFTA (British Academy of Film and Television) award in the sport category.

ECB COUNTY JOURNALISM AWARDS

The ECB announced the winners of the tenth annual County Cricket Journalism Awards for the coverage of domestic cricket in March 2021. **Adam Collins** was named the Christopher Martin-Jenkins Domestic Cricket Broadcaster of the Year, for his live-stream commentary, with Dave Fletcher and Richard Rae commended. The Christopher Martin-Jenkins Young Journalist of the Year was **Nick Friend** of *The Cricketer*, ahead of Taha Hashim and Matt Roller. The award for Outstanding Online Coverage of Domestic Cricket went to **thecricketer.com** for the third time running, with BBC Sport commended. The *Gloucestershire Echo and Gloucester Citizen* won the award for Outstanding Newspaper Coverage; they were also one of the runners-up, alongside *The Yorkshire Post* and Stoke's *Sentinel*, for the Regional Newspaper of the Year, won by the *Liverpool Echo*.

ECB GRASSROOTS CRICKET AWARDS

The ECB announced their Grassroots Cricket Awards (previously known as the OSCAs) to volunteers from recreational cricket in September.

Connecting Communities **Des O'Dell** (Southwick, Sussex)
Formed the Adur Cricket Cluster Group: six clubs co-operating to promote inclusion and participation by sharing projects and facilities, and developing junior and women's cricket.

Inspired to Play **Shana Thomas** (Ynystawe, Wales)
Has made Ynystawe one of the leading Welsh clubs for women's cricket through the All Stars and Dynamos programmes, and launched the Sporting Memories Club to tackle loneliness for over-55s.

Rising Star **Oliver Sebire-Harris** (Hurstpierpoint, Sussex)
Part of the Young Leaders scheme, he coached Hurstpierpoint's junior teams, as well as scoring, umpiring and organising a charity match for Alzheimer's UK and the Ruth Strauss Foundation.

Rising Star **Mollie Rathbone** (Wedgwood, Staffordshire)
Recognised for her part in running junior cricket sessions, helping at summer camps and on women and girls' days, and progressing her coaching skills.

Unsung Hero **Don Winspear** (Knaresborough, Yorkshire)
Chaired Knaresborough CC for 35 years until standing down in 2021.

Growing the Game **David and Lucy Lyle** (Malden Wanderers, Surrey)
Increased junior registrations at Malden from 190 to 282 over three years, and started women's cricket at the club, which now plays in 19 leagues, up from nine in 2019.

Lifetime Achiever **Tom Haworth** (Longridge, Lancashire)
Served Longridge CC since 1949 as player, captain, coach, manager, chair and president.

Cricket Innovators **Luke Brooksby** (Illingworth St Mary's, Yorkshire)
Ran a trial of Frogbox live-streaming Halifax League matches and creating highlights packages and clips for members and social media; input club scorecards since 1884 on play-cricket.com.

Game Changer **Harry Boyle** (Horwich RMI, Lancashire)
Despite a difficult childhood dealing with cerebral palsy, every week he helps the coaches run the All Stars sessions for children and inspires the whole club with his commitment and enthusiasm.

CRICKET COMMUNITY CHAMPION AWARD

MCC and *The Cricketer* introduced a new award in 2017 recognising individuals working to build, maintain and support the game at grassroots level. The fourth winner – after a hiatus in 2020 – was **Caroline Carter** of Hatherley and Reddings CC in Gloucestershire, who has greatly expanded the club's youth section since 2013 by providing inclusive and accessible cricket for all age groups and abilities, helped volunteers become fully qualified coaches, and introduced an interclub indoor tournament. She was invited to ring the bell at Lord's before England's second one-day international with Pakistan in July.

Clare Adams, MCC

Long-service reward: for its 158th edition, Wisden becomes the first recipient of the Stephen Fay Award; with Prudence Fay are Lawrence Booth and Hugh Chevallier. For an obituary of Stephen Fay, see *Wisden 2021*, p 246.

ACS STATISTICIAN OF THE YEAR

In March 2022, the Association of Cricket Statisticians and Historians awarded the Brooke-Lambert Statistician of the Year trophy to **Julian Lawton Smith**, for his work on the Minor Counties project, which established and published full scorecards for the Minor Counties Championship from 1895 to 1914, along with averages, county records and biographical information.

CRICKET SOCIETY AWARDS

Most Promising Young Male Cricketer	**Tom Haines** (Sussex)
Most Promising Young Female Cricketer	**Charlie Dean** (Hants and London Spirit)
The Howard Milton Award for Cricket Scholarship	**Ramachandra Guha**
(in association with the British Society of Sports History)	
The Cricket Society and MCC Book of the Year Award	**The Unforgiven** by Ashley Gray (Pitch)
The Stephen Fay Award	**Wisden Cricketers' Almanack 2021**
(for services to cricket publishing)	
The Perry-Lewis/Kershaw Memorial Trophy	**Stuart Cosstick**
(for contribution to the Cricket Society XI)	

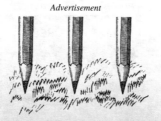

2022 FIXTURES

Test	Test match
RLODI	Royal London one-day international
VT20I	Vitality T20 international
W Test	Women's Test match
RLWODI	Royal London women's one-day international
VWT20I	Vitality women's T20 international
LV=CC D1/2	LV= County Championship Division 1/2
Men's/women's 100	The Hundred
RLC	Royal London Cup
VB T20	Vitality Blast
RHFT	Rachael Heyhoe Flint Trophy (50-over)
CEC T20	Charlotte Edwards Cup (T20)
NC	National Counties (50-over)
Univs	University matches (not first-class)
⚲	Day/night or floodlit game

Tue Mar 22–Thu 24 Univs	Nottinghamshire	v Loughboro UCCE	Nottingham
Wed Mar 23–Fri 25 Univs	Durham UCCE	v Durham	Durham
	Oxford UCCE	v Worcestershire	Oxford
Mon Mar 28–Wed Wed 30	Hampshire	v Loughboro UCCE	Southampton
	Leicestershire	v Leeds/Brad UCCE	Leicester
	Northamptonshire	v Cardiff UCCE	Northampton
	Sussex	v Durham UCCE	Hove
Sat Apr 2–Mon 4 Univs	Glamorgan	v Cardiff UCCE	Cardiff
	Gloucestershire	v Exeter U	Bristol
	Leeds/Brad UCCE	v Yorkshire	Weetwood
	Loughboro UCCE	v Lancashire	Loughborough
	Oxford UCCE	v Derbyshire	Oxford
	Worcestershire	v Durham UCCE	Kidderminster
Thu Apr 7–Sun 10 LV=CC D1	Essex	v Kent	Chelmsford
	Hampshire	v Somerset	Southampton
	Northamptonshire	v Gloucestershire	Northampton
	Warwickshire	v Surrey	Birmingham
LV=CC D2	Glamorgan	v Durham	Cardiff
	Leicestershire	v Worcestershire	Leicester
	Middlesex	v Derbyshire	Lord's
	Sussex	v Nottinghamshire	Hove
Thu Apr 14–Sun 17 LV=CC D1	Gloucestershire	v Yorkshire	Bristol
	Kent	v Lancashire	Canterbury
	Somerset	v Essex	Taunton
	Surrey	v Hampshire	The Oval
LV=CC D2	Derbyshire	v Sussex	Derby
	Durham	v Leicestershire	Chester-le-Street
	Nottinghamshire	v Glamorgan	Nottingham
Thu Apr 21–Sun 24 LV=CC D1	Kent	v Hampshire	Canterbury
	Lancashire	v Gloucestershire	Manchester
	Northamptonshire	v Yorkshire	Northampton
	Surrey	v Somerset	The Oval
	Warwickshire	v Essex	Birmingham
LV=CC D2	Durham	v Nottinghamshire	Chester-le-Street
	Glamorgan	v Middlesex	Cardiff
	Leicestershire	v Derbyshire	Leicester
	Worcestershire	v Sussex	Worcester

Thu Apr 28– Sun May 1	LV=CC D1	Essex	v Northamptonshire	Chelmsford
		Gloucestershire	v Surrey	Bristol
		Hampshire	v Lancashire	Southampton
		Somerset	v Warwickshire	Taunton
		Yorkshire	v Kent	Leeds
	LV=CC D2	Derbyshire	v Glamorgan	Derby
		Middlesex	v Leicestershire	Lord's
		Nottinghamshire	v Worcestershire	Nottingham
		Sussex	v Durham	Hove
Thu May 5–Sun 8	LV=CC D1	Essex	v Yorkshire	Chelmsford
		Hampshire	v Gloucestershire	Southampton
		Lancashire	v Warwickshire	Manchester
		Surrey	v Northamptonshire	The Oval
	LV=CC D2	Glamorgan	v Leicestershire	Cardiff
		Sussex	v Middlesex	Hove
		Worcestershire	v Durham	Worcester
Thu May 12–Sun 15	LV=CC D1	Gloucestershire	v Somerset	Bristol
		Kent	v Surrey	Beckenham
		Warwickshire	v Northamptonshire	Birmingham
		Yorkshire	v Lancashire	Leeds
	LV=CC D2	Derbyshire	v Worcestershire	Derby
		Durham	v Glamorgan	Chester-le-Street
		Leicestershire	v Sussex	Leicester
		Middlesex	v Nottinghamshire	Lord's
Sat May 14	CEC T20	L'boro Lightning	v N Diamonds	Loughborough
		S Vipers	v Thunder	Hove
		Sunrisers	v SE Stars	Chelmsford
		W Storm	v Central Sparks	Cardiff
Sun May 15	Univ (o-d)	Cambridge U	v Oxford U	Arundel
Wed May 18	CEC T20	S Vipers	v L'boro Lightning	Southampton
		SE Stars	v Central Sparks	Guildford
		Sunrisers	v W Storm	Chelmsford ♀
		Thunder	v N Diamonds	Sale
Thu May 19–Sun 22	LV=CC D1	Lancashire	v Essex	Manchester
		Northamptonshire	v Kent	Northampton
		Somerset	v Hampshire	Taunton
		Yorkshire	v Warwickshire	Leeds
	LV=CC D2	Middlesex	v Durham	Lord's
		Nottinghamshire	v Derbyshire	Nottingham
		Worcestershire	v Leicestershire	Worcester
Fri May 20–Mon 23	Tour	Sussex	v New Zealand	Hove
Sat May 21	CEC T20	Central Sparks	v Sunrisers	Birmingham
		L'boro Lightning	v Thunder	Leicester
		N Diamonds	v S Vipers	TBC
		SE Stars	v W Storm	Beckenham
Wed May 25	VB T20	Kent	v Somerset	Canterbury ♀
		Yorkshire	v Worcestershire	Leeds ♀
Thu May 26	VB T20	Leicestershire	v Durham	Leicester ♀
		Middlesex	v Gloucestershire	Radlett
		Sussex	v Glamorgan	Hove ♀
		Warwickshire	v Northamptonshire	Birmingham ♀
Thu May 26–Sun 29	Tour	FCC Select XI	v New Zealand	Chelmsford

Fri May 27	VB T20	Derbyshire	v Warwickshire	Derby	♀
		Gloucestershire	v Sussex	Bristol	♀
		Hampshire	v Middlesex	Southampton	♀
		Kent	v Essex	Canterbury	♀
		Lancashire	v Yorkshire	Manchester	♀
		Northamptonshire	v Durham	Northampton	♀
		Nottinghamshire	v Worcestershire	Nottingham	♀
		Surrey	v Glamorgan	The Oval	♀
Sat May 28	VB T20	Leicestershire	v Derbyshire	Leicester	
Sun May 29	VB T20	Lancashire	v Worcestershire	Manchester	
		Middlesex	v Glamorgan	Radlett	
		Nottinghamshire	v Northamptonshire	Nottingham	
		Somerset	v Essex	Taunton	
		Sussex	v Kent	Hove	
		Warwickshire	v Durham	Birmingham	
		Yorkshire	v Leicestershire	Leeds	
	CEC T20	Central Sparks	v SE Stars	Birmingham	
		L'boro Lightning	v S Vipers	Nottingham	
		N Diamonds	v Thunder	Leeds	
		W Storm	v Sunrisers	Taunton	
Mon May 30	VB T20	Hampshire	v Somerset	Southampton	♀
Tue May 31	VB T20	Essex	v Hampshire	Chelmsford	♀
		Nottinghamshire	v Lancashire	Nottingham	♀
		Surrey	v Gloucestershire	The Oval	♀
		Yorkshire	v Derbyshire	Leeds	♀
Wed Jun 1	VB T20	Durham	v Worcestershire	Chester-le-Street	♀
		Gloucestershire	v Kent	Bristol	♀
		Lancashire	v Derbyshire	Manchester	♀
		Northamptonshire	v Leicestershire	Northampton	♀
		Somerset	v Sussex	Taunton	♀
	CEC T20	N Diamonds	v L'boro Lightning	Chester-le-Street	
		Sunrisers	v Central Sparks	Northampton	
		Thunder	v S Vipers	Manchester	
		W Storm	v SE Stars	Bristol	
Thu Jun 2–Mon 6	First Test	**ENGLAND**	**v NEW ZEALAND**	**Lord's**	
Thu Jun 2	VB T20	Glamorgan	v Essex	Cardiff	♀
		Surrey	v Hampshire	The Oval	♀
		Warwickshire	v Leicestershire	Birmingham	♀
Fri Jun 3	VB T20	Derbyshire	v Nottinghamshire	Derby	♀
		Gloucestershire	v Essex	Bristol	♀
		Kent	v Surrey	Canterbury	♀
		Lancashire	v Northamptonshire	Manchester	♀
		Somerset	v Glamorgan	Taunton	♀
		Sussex	v Middlesex	Hove	♀
		Worcestershire	v Warwickshire	Worcester	
		Yorkshire	v Durham	Leeds	♀
	CEC T20	Thunder	v L'boro Lightning	Manchester	
Sat Jun 4	VB T20	Hampshire	v Sussex	Southampton	♀
	CEC T20	Central Sparks	v W Storm	Worcester	
		S Vipers	v N Diamonds	Southampton	
Sun Jun 5	VB T20	Durham	v Northamptonshire	Chester-le-Street	
		Glamorgan	v Surrey	Cardiff	
		Kent	v Middlesex	Canterbury	
		Warwickshire	v Nottinghamshire	Birmingham	
		Worcestershire	v Leicestershire	Worcester	
	CEC T20	SE Stars	v Sunrisers	Guildford	

Mon Jun 6	VB T20	Yorkshire	v Nottinghamshire	Leeds	♀
Tue Jun 7	VB T20	Essex	v Kent	Chelmsford	♀
		Glamorgan	v Gloucestershire	Cardiff	♀
		Leicestershire	v Lancashire	Leicester	♀
		Middlesex	v Hampshire	Radlett	
		Northamptonshire	v Derbyshire	Northampton	♀
Wed Jun 8	VB T20	Durham	v Warwickshire	Chester-le-Street	♀
		Surrey	v Sussex	The Oval	♀
		Yorkshire	v Lancashire	Leeds	♀
Thu Jun 9	VB T20	Derbyshire	v Leicestershire	Derby	♀
		Gloucestershire	v Somerset	Bristol	♀
		Hampshire	v Essex	Southampton	♀
		Middlesex	v Surrey	Lord's	♀
		Northamptonshire	v Worcestershire	Northampton	♀
Fri Jun 10–Tue 14	Second Test	**ENGLAND**	**v NEW ZEALAND**	**Nottingham**	
Fri Jun 10	VB T20	Durham	v Lancashire	Chester-le-Street	♀
		Essex	v Middlesex	Chelmsford	♀
		Glamorgan	v Hampshire	Cardiff	♀
		Leicestershire	v Nottinghamshire	Leicester	♀
		Somerset	v Kent	Taunton	♀
		Sussex	v Gloucestershire	Hove	♀
		Warwickshire	v Yorkshire	Birmingham	♀
		Worcestershire	v Derbyshire	Worcester	
Sat Jun 11	CEC T20	**Finals day**		Northampton	
Sun Jun 12–Wed 15	LV=CC D1	Hampshire	v Yorkshire	Southampton	
		Kent	v Gloucestershire	Canterbury	
		Somerset	v Surrey	Taunton	
		Warwickshire	v Lancashire	Birmingham	
	LV=CC D2	Derbyshire	v Middlesex	Chesterfield	
		Durham	v Worcestershire	Chester-le-Street	
		Glamorgan	v Sussex	Cardiff	
		Leicestershire	v Nottinghamshire	Leicester	
Fri Jun 17	ODI	**NETHERLANDS**	**v ENGLAND**	**Amstelveen**	
	VB T20	Durham	v Yorkshire	Chester-le-Street	♀
		Essex	v Sussex	Chelmsford	♀
		Hampshire	v Kent	Southampton	♀
		Leicestershire	v Worcestershire	Leicester	♀
		Northamptonshire	v Lancashire	Northampton	♀
		Nottinghamshire	v Warwickshire	Nottingham	♀
		Somerset	v Gloucestershire	Taunton	♀
		Surrey	v Middlesex	The Oval	♀
Sat Jun 18	VB T20	Derbyshire	v Yorkshire	Chesterfield	
		Gloucestershire	v Glamorgan	Bristol	
		Worcestershire	v Northamptonshire	Worcester	
Sun Jun 19	ODI	**NETHERLANDS**	**v ENGLAND**	**Amstelveen**	
	VB T20	Durham	v Leicestershire	Chester-le-Street	
		Essex	v Somerset	Chelmsford	
		Glamorgan	v Sussex	Cardiff	
		Hampshire	v Surrey	Southampton	
		Lancashire	v Nottinghamshire	Blackpool	
		Middlesex	v Kent	Lord's	
		Warwickshire	v Derbyshire	Birmingham	
Tue Jun 21	VB T20	Derbyshire	v Northamptonshire	Derby	♀
		Glamorgan	v Middlesex	Cardiff	♀
		Kent	v Gloucestershire	Canterbury	♀
		Nottinghamshire	v Leicestershire	Nottingham	♀
		Surrey	v Somerset	The Oval	♀

Date	Comp	Home		Away	Venue	
Wed Jun 22	ODI	**NETHERLANDS**	v	**ENGLAND**	**Amstelveen**	
	VB T20	Northamptonshire	v	Warwickshire	Northampton	♀
Thu Jun 23–Mon 27	**Third Test**	**ENGLAND**	v	**NEW ZEALAND**	**Leeds**	
Thu Jun 23	VB T20	Lancashire	v	Durham	Blackpool	
		Middlesex	v	Essex	Lord's	♀
		Nottinghamshire	v	Derbyshire	Nottingham	♀
		Somerset	v	Hampshire	Taunton	♀
		Sussex	v	Surrey	Hove	♀
		Worcestershire	v	Yorkshire	Worcester	
Fri Jun 24	VB T20	Derbyshire	v	Lancashire	Derby	♀
		Durham	v	Nottinghamshire	Chester-le-Street	♀
		Essex	v	Surrey	Chelmsford	♀
		Glamorgan	v	Somerset	Cardiff	♀
		Gloucestershire	v	Hampshire	Bristol	♀
		Kent	v	Sussex	Canterbury	♀
		Northamptonshire	v	Yorkshire	Northampton	♀
		Warwickshire	v	Worcestershire	Birmingham	♀
Fri Jun 24–Mon 27	Tour	Leicestershire	v	India	Leicester	
Sun Jun 26–Wed 29	LV=CC D1	Essex	v	Hampshire	Chelmsford	
		Gloucestershire	v	Lancashire	Bristol	
		Northamptonshire	v	Warwickshire	Northampton	
		Surrey	v	Kent	The Oval	
	LV=CC D2	Nottinghamshire	v	Middlesex	Nottingham	
		Sussex	v	Derbyshire	Hove	
		Worcestershire	v	Glamorgan	Worcester	
Mon Jun 27–Thu 30	W Test	**ENGLAND WOMEN**	v	**S AFRICA WOMEN**	**Taunton**	
Mon Jun 27	Univ (T20)	Cambridge U	v	Oxford U	Lord's	
	W Univ (T20)	Cambridge U	v	Oxford U	Lord's	
Tue Jun 28	Univ (T20)	Cambridge U	v	Oxford U	Arundel	
Fri Jul 1–Tue 5	**Fifth Test**	**ENGLAND**	v	**INDIA**	**Birmingham**	
Fri Jul 1	VB T20	Hampshire	v	Gloucestershire	Southampton	♀
		Leicestershire	v	Northamptonshire	Leicester	♀
		Middlesex	v	Somerset	Lord's	♀
		Nottinghamshire	v	Durham	Nottingham	♀
		Surrey	v	Kent	The Oval	♀
		Sussex	v	Essex	Hove	♀
		Worcestershire	v	Lancashire	Worcester	
		Yorkshire	v	Warwickshire	Leeds	♀
Sat Jul 2	VB T20	Essex	v	Glamorgan	Chelmsford	♀
	RHFT	Central Sparks	v	S Vipers	Edgbaston (CSG)	
		L'boro Lightning	v	W Storm	Loughborough	
		SE Stars	v	Sunrisers	Guildford	
Sun Jul 3	VB T20	Derbyshire	v	Durham	Derby	♀
		Gloucestershire	v	Middlesex	Bristol	♀
		Kent	v	Glamorgan	Canterbury	♀
		Lancashire	v	Warwickshire	Manchester	♀
		Leicestershire	v	Yorkshire	Leicester	♀
		Somerset	v	Surrey	Taunton	♀
		Sussex	v	Hampshire	Hove	♀
		Worcestershire	v	Nottinghamshire	Worcester	
	RHFT	Thunder	v	N Diamonds	Sale	
Mon Jul 4–Thu 7	Univ	Oxford U	v	Cambridge U	Oxford	
Wed Jul 6	VB T20	**Quarter-final**				♀

Thu Jul 7	VT20I	**ENGLAND**	**v INDIA**	**Southampton**	♀
Fri Jul 8	VB T20	**Quarter-finals**			♀
Sat Jul 9	VT20I	**ENGLAND**	**v INDIA**	**Birmingham**	
	VB T20	**Quarter-final**			♀
	RHFT	L'boro Lightning	v Thunder	Loughborough	
		N Diamonds	v Sunrisers	Leeds	
		S Vipers	v SE Stars	Hove	
		W Storm	v Central Sparks	Bristol	
Sun Jul 10	VT20I	**ENGLAND**	**v INDIA**	**Nottingham**	
Mon Jul 11	RLWODI	**ENGLAND WOMEN**	**v S AFRICA WOMEN**	**Northampton**	♀
Mon Jul 11–Thu 14	LV=CC D1	Essex	v Gloucestershire	Chelmsford	
		Hampshire	v Warwickshire	Southampton	
		Kent	v Northamptonshire	Canterbury	
		Lancashire	v Somerset	Southport	
		Yorkshire	v Surrey	Scarborough	
	LV=CC D2	Durham	v Derbyshire	Chester-le-Street	
		Glamorgan	v Nottinghamshire	TBC	
		Middlesex	v Worcestershire	Northwood	
		Sussex	v Leicestershire	Hove	
Tue Jul 12	RLODI	**ENGLAND**	**v INDIA**	**The Oval**	♀
	Tour	England Lions	v South Africa	Taunton	
Thu Jul 14	RLODI	**ENGLAND**	**v INDIA**	**Lord's**	♀
	Tour	England Lions	v South Africa	Worcester	
Fri Jul 15	RLWODI	**ENGLAND WOMEN**	**v S AFRICA WOMEN**	**Bristol**	♀
Sat Jul 16	VB T20	**Finals day**		Birmingham	
	RHFT	Central Sparks	v N Diamonds	Worcester	
		L'boro Lightning	v S Vipers	Derby	
		Sunrisers	v W Storm	Chelmsford	
		Thunder	v SE Stars	Southport	
Sun Jul 17	RLODI	**ENGLAND**	**v INDIA**	**Manchester**	
Mon Jul 18	RLWODI	**ENGLAND WOMEN**	**v S AFRICA WOMEN**	**Leicester**	♀
Tue Jul 19	RLODI	**ENGLAND**	**v SOUTH AFRICA**	**Chester-le-Street**	♀
Tue Jul 19–Fri 22	LV=CC D1	Gloucestershire	v Hampshire	Cheltenham	
		Northamptonshire	v Lancashire	Northampton	
		Somerset	v Yorkshire	Taunton	
		Surrey	v Essex	The Oval	
		Warwickshire	v Kent	Birmingham	
	LV=CC D2	Derbyshire	v Nottinghamshire	Derby	
		Middlesex	v Sussex	Lord's	
Wed Jul 20–Sat 23	LV=CC D2	Leicestershire	v Glamorgan	Leicester	
Thu Jul 21	VWT20I	**ENGLAND WOMEN**	**v S AFRICA WOMEN**	**Chelmsford**	♀
Fri Jul 22	RLODI	**ENGLAND**	**v SOUTH AFRICA**	**Manchester**	♀
Sat Jul 23	VWT20I	**ENGLAND WOMEN**	**v S AFRICA WOMEN**	**Worcester**	
	RHFT	N Diamonds	v L'boro Lightning	Chester-le-Street	
		S Vipers	v Sunrisers	Southampton	
		Thunder	v Central Sparks	Manchester	
		W Storm	v SE Stars	Cheltenham	
Sun Jul 24	RLODI	**ENGLAND**	**v SOUTH AFRICA**	**Leeds**	
Mon Jul 25	VWT20I	**ENGLAND WOMEN**	**v S AFRICA WOMEN**	**Derby**	♀

Mon Jul 25–Thu 28	**LV=CC D1**	Essex	v Somerset	Chelmsford
		Gloucestershire	v Northamptonshire	Cheltenham
		Lancashire	v Kent	Manchester
		Surrey	v Warwickshire	The Oval
		Yorkshire	v Hampshire	Scarborough
	LV=CC D2	Durham	v Middlesex	Chester-le-Street
		Worcestershire	v Derbyshire	Worcester
Tue Jul 26–Fri 29	**LV=CC D2**	Nottinghamshire	v Sussex	Nottingham
Wed Jul 27	**VT20I**	**ENGLAND**	**v SOUTH AFRICA**	**Bristol** ♀
Thu Jul 28	**VT20I**	**ENGLAND**	**v SOUTH AFRICA**	**Cardiff** ♀
Sun Jul 31	**VT20I**	**ENGLAND**	**v SOUTH AFRICA**	**Southampton**
	NC	Bedfordshire	v Northamptonshire	
		Berkshire	v Middlesex	
		Buckinghamshire	v Surrey	
		Cambridgeshire	v Essex	
		Cheshire	v Warwickshire	
		Cornwall	v Somerset	
		Cumberland	v Lancashire	
		Dorset	v Hampshire	
		Herefordshire	v Worcestershire	
		Lincolnshire	v Durham	
		Norfolk	v Nottinghamshire	
		Northumberland	v Yorkshire	
		Oxfordshire	v Sussex	
		Shropshire	v Derbyshire	
		Staffordshire	v Leicestershire	
		Suffolk	v Kent	
		Wales MC	v Glamorgan	
		Wiltshire	v Gloucestershire	
Tue Aug 2	**RLC**	Derbyshire	v Glamorgan	Derby
		Gloucestershire	v Warwickshire	Cheltenham
		Lancashire	v Essex	Sedbergh
		Nottinghamshire	v Sussex	Nottingham
		Surrey	v Leicestershire	Guildford
		Worcestershire	v Kent	Worcester
		Yorkshire	v Northamptonshire	York
	NC	Devon	v Somerset	
		Hertfordshire	v Middlesex	
Wed Aug 3	**Men's 100**	Southern B	v Welsh F	Southampton ♀
Thu Aug 4	**Men's 100**	Oval I	v London S	The Oval ♀
	RLC	Durham	v Surrey	Chester-le-Street
		Glamorgan	v Kent	
		Middlesex	v Leicestershire	Radlett
		Somerset	v Nottinghamshire	Taunton
		Yorkshire	v Lancashire	York
Fri Aug 5	**Men's 100**	Manchester O	v Northern S	Manchester ♀
	RLC	Essex	v Derbyshire	Chelmsford ♀
		Hampshire	v Worcestershire	Southampton
		Sussex	v Gloucestershire	Hove
Sat Aug 6	**Men's 100**	Trent R	v Birmingham P	Nottingham
Sun Aug 7	**Men's 100**	Welsh F	v Oval I	Cardiff
	RLC	Durham	v Middlesex	Chester-le-Street
		Gloucestershire	v Somerset	Bristol
		Kent	v Hampshire	Beckenham
		Lancashire	v Derbyshire	Manchester
		Northamptonshire	v Essex	Northampton
		Surrey	v Warwickshire	The Oval
		Sussex	v Leicestershire	Hove
		Yorkshire	v Worcestershire	Scarborough

Mon Aug 8	Men's 100	London S	v Manchester O	Lord's	♀
Tue Aug 9	Men's 100	Northern S	v Trent R	Leeds	♀
	RLC	Hampshire	v Northamptonshire	Southampton	
Tue Aug 9–Fri 12	Tour	FCC Select XI	v South Africa	Canterbury	
Wed Aug 10	Men's 100	Birmingham P	v Southern B	Birmingham	♀
	RLC	Glamorgan	v Yorkshire	TBC	
		Gloucestershire	v Nottinghamshire	Bristol	
		Lancashire	v Worcestershire	Manchester	
		Middlesex	v Surrey	Radlett	
		Somerset	v Durham	Taunton	
Thu Aug 11	Men's 100	Oval I	v Northern S	The Oval	
	Women's 100	Oval I	v Northern S	The Oval	♀
	RLC	Essex	v Kent	Chelmsford	♀
Fri Aug 12	Women's 100	Southern B	v London S	Southampton	
	Men's 100	Southern B	v London S	Southampton	♀
	RLC	Derbyshire	v Hampshire	Derby	
		Durham	v Gloucestershire	Chester-le-Street	
		Leicestershire	v Somerset	Leicester	
		Northamptonshire	v Glamorgan	Northampton	
		Nottinghamshire	v Middlesex	Grantham	
		Warwickshire	v Sussex	Birmingham	
Sat Aug 13	Women's 100	Manchester O	v Trent R	Manchester	
	Men's 100	Manchester O	v Trent R	Manchester	
	Women's 100	Welsh F	v Birmingham P	Cardiff	
	Men's 100	Welsh F	v Birmingham P	Cardiff	♀
Sun Aug 14	Women's 100	Northern S	v London S	Leeds	
	Men's 100	Northern S	v London S	Leeds	
	Women's 100	Oval I	v Southern B	The Oval	
	Men's 100	Oval I	v Southern B	The Oval	♀
	RLC	Essex	v Glamorgan	Chelmsford	
		Hampshire	v Lancashire	Southampton	
		Kent	v Northamptonshire	Canterbury	
		Leicestershire	v Warwickshire	Leicester	
		Nottinghamshire	v Durham	Grantham	
		Somerset	v Middlesex	Taunton	
		Sussex	v Surrey	Hove	
		Worcestershire	v Derbyshire	Worcester	
Mon Aug 15	Women's 100	Birmingham P	v Trent R	Birmingham	
	Men's 100	Birmingham P	v Trent R	Birmingham	♀
Tue Aug 16	Women's 100	Manchester O	v Welsh F	Manchester	
	Men's 100	Manchester O	v Welsh F	Manchester	♀
Wed Aug 17–Sun 21	First Test	**ENGLAND**	**v SOUTH AFRICA**	**Lord's**	
Wed Aug 17	Women's 100	Trent R	v Oval I	Nottingham	
	Men's 100	Trent R	v Oval I	Nottingham	♀
	RLC	Derbyshire	v Kent	Derby	
		Durham	v Sussex	Chester-le-Street	
		Essex	v Yorkshire	Chelmsford	
		Glamorgan	v Lancashire	Neath	
		Gloucestershire	v Leicestershire	Bristol	
		Northamptonshire	v Worcestershire	Northampton	
		Surrey	v Somerset	The Oval	
		Warwickshire	v Nottinghamshire	Birmingham	
Thu Aug 18	Women's 100	Southern B	v Manchester O	Southampton	
	Men's 100	Southern B	v Manchester O	Southampton	♀

Date	Competition	Match	Venue	
Fri Aug 19	Women's 100	Birmingham P v Northern S	Birmingham	
	Men's 100	Birmingham P v Northern S	Birmingham	♀
	RLC	Glamorgan v Hampshire	Neath	
		Kent v Yorkshire	Canterbury	
		Lancashire v Northamptonshire	Manchester	
		Middlesex v Warwickshire	Radlett	
		Somerset v Sussex	Taunton	♀
		Surrey v Gloucestershire	The Oval	
		Worcestershire v Essex	Worcester	
Sat Aug 20	Women's 100	Trent R v London S	Nottingham	
	Men's 100	Trent R v London S	Nottingham	♀
	RLC	Leicestershire v Nottinghamshire	Leicester	♀
Sun Aug 21	Women's 100	Northern S v Manchester O	Leeds	
	Men's 100	Northern S v Manchester O	Leeds	♀
	RLC	Derbyshire v Yorkshire	Chesterfield	
		Hampshire v Essex	Southampton	
		Middlesex v Gloucestershire	Radlett	
		Warwickshire v Durham	Birmingham	
Mon Aug 22	Women's 100	Welsh F v Southern B	Cardiff	
	Men's 100	Welsh F v Southern B	Cardiff	♀
Tue Aug 23	Women's 100	Oval I v Birmingham P	The Oval	
	Men's 100	Oval I v Birmingham P	The Oval	♀
	RLC	Kent v Lancashire	Canterbury	
		Leicestershire v Durham	Leicester	
		Northamptonshire v Derbyshire	Northampton	
		Nottinghamshire v Surrey	Sookholme	
		Sussex v Middlesex	Hove	
		Warwickshire v Somerset	Birmingham	
		Worcestershire v Glamorgan	Worcester	
		Yorkshire v Hampshire	Scarborough	
Wed Aug 24	Women's 100	London S v Welsh F	Lord's	
	Men's 100	London S v Welsh F	Lord's	♀
Thu Aug 25–Mon 29	Second Test	ENGLAND v SOUTH AFRICA	Manchester	
Thu Aug 25	Women's 100	Southern B v Trent R	Southampton	
	Men's 100	Southern B v Trent R	Southampton	♀
Fri Aug 26	Men's 100	Welsh F v Northern S	Cardiff	
	Women's 100	Welsh F v Northern S	Cardiff	♀
	RLC	Quarter-finals		
Sat Aug 27	Women's 100	London S v Oval I	Lord's	
	Men's 100	London S v Oval I	Lord's	♀
Sun Aug 28	Women's 100	Birmingham P v Manchester O	Birmingham	
	Men's 100	Birmingham P v Manchester O	Birmingham	♀
Mon Aug 29	Men's 100	Trent R v Welsh F	Nottingham	
	Women's 100	Trent R v Welsh F	Nottingham	♀
Tue Aug 30	Men's 100	London S v Birmingham P	Lord's	
	Women's 100	London S v Birmingham P	Lord's	♀
	RLC	Semi-finals		
Wed Aug 31	Men's 100	Manchester O v Oval I	Manchester	
	Women's 100	Manchester O v Oval I	Manchester	♀
	Women's 100	Northern S v Southern B	Leeds	
	Men's 100	Northern S v Southern B	Leeds	
Fri Sep 2	Women's 100	Eliminator	Southampton	
	Men's 100	Eliminator	Southampton	♀
Sat Sep 3	Women's 100	Final	Lord's	
	Men's 100	Final	Lord's	♀

Mon Sep 5–Thu 8	LV=CC D1	Hampshire	v Northamptonshire	Southampton
		Kent	v Essex	Canterbury
		Lancashire	v Yorkshire	Manchester
		Somerset	v Gloucestershire	Taunton
	LV=CC D2	Derbyshire	v Durham	Derby
		Glamorgan	v Worcestershire	Cardiff
		Nottinghamshire	v Leicestershire	Nottingham
Thu Sep 8–Mon 12	Third Test	**ENGLAND**	**v SOUTH AFRICA**	**The Oval**
Fri Sep 9	RHFT	Central Sparks	v L'boro Lightning	Worcester
		S Vipers	v W Storm	Hove
		SE Stars	v N Diamonds	Beckenham
		Sunrisers	v Thunder	Northampton
Sat Sep 10	VWT20I	**ENGLAND WOMEN**	**v INDIA WOMEN**	**Chester-le-Street** ♀
Sun Sep 11	RHFT	S Vipers	v Thunder	Southampton
		SE Stars	v Central Sparks	Beckenham
		Sunrisers	v L'boro Lightning	Chelmsford
		W Storm	v N Diamonds	Taunton
Mon Sep 12–Thu 15	LV=CC D1	Northamptonshire	v Surrey	Northampton
		Warwickshire	v Somerset	Birmingham
		Yorkshire	v Essex	Leeds
	LV=CC D2	Leicestershire	v Durham	Leicester
		Middlesex	v Glamorgan	Lord's
		Sussex	v Worcestershire	Hove
Tue Sep 13	VWT20I	**ENGLAND WOMEN**	**v INDIA WOMEN**	**Derby** ♀
Thu Sep 15	VTW20I	**ENGLAND WOMEN**	**v INDIA WOMEN**	**Bristol** ♀
Sat Sep 17	RLC	**Final**		Nottingham
	RHFT	Central Sparks	v Sunrisers	Worcester
		L'boro Lightning	v SE Stars	Leicester
		N Diamonds	v S Vipers	Leeds
		Thunder	v W Storm	Manchester
		National Club Championship final		Lord's
Sun Sep 18	RLWODI	**ENGLAND WOMEN**	**v INDIA WOMEN**	**Hove**
		Village Cup final		Lord's
Tue Sep 20–Fri 23	LV=CC D1	Essex	v Lancashire	Chelmsford
		Gloucestershire	v Warwickshire	Bristol
		Hampshire	v Kent	Southampton
		Somerset	v Northamptonshire	Taunton
		Surrey	v Yorkshire	The Oval
	LV=CC D2	Durham	v Sussex	Chester-le-Street
		Glamorgan	v Derbyshire	Cardiff
		Leicestershire	v Middlesex	Leicester
		Worcestershire	v Nottinghamshire	Worcester
Wed Sep 21	RLWODI	**ENGLAND WOMEN**	**v INDIA WOMEN**	**Canterbury** ♀
	RHFT	**Play-off**		
Sat Sep 24	RLWODI	**ENGLAND WOMEN**	**v INDIA WOMEN**	**Lord's**
Sun Sep 25	RHFT	**Final**		Lord's
Mon Sep 26–Thu 29	LV=CC D1	Kent	v Somerset	Canterbury
		Lancashire	v Surrey	Manchester
		Northamptonshire	v Essex	Northampton
		Warwickshire	v Hampshire	Birmingham
		Yorkshire	v Gloucestershire	Leeds
	LV=CC D2	Derbyshire	v Leicestershire	Derby
		Nottinghamshire	v Durham	Nottingham
		Sussex	v Glamorgan	Hove
		Worcestershire	v Middlesex	Worcester

CRICKET TRADE DIRECTORY

BOOKSELLERS

CHRISTOPHER SAUNDERS, Kingston House, High Street, Newnham-on-Severn, Glos GL14 1BB. Tel: 01594 516030; email: chris@cricket-books.com; website: cricket-books.com. Office/bookroom open by appointment. Second-hand/antiquarian cricket books and memorabilia bought and sold. Regular catalogues issued containing selections from over 12,000 items in stock.

GRACE BOOKS AND CARDS (Ted Kirwan), Donkey Cart Cottage, Main Street, Bruntingthorpe, Lutterworth, Leics LE17 5QE. Tel: 0116 247 8417; email: ted@gracecricketana.co.uk. Second-hand and antiquarian cricket books, *Wisdens*, autographed material and cricket ephemera of all kinds. Now also modern postcards of current international cricketers.

JOHN JEFFERS, The Old Mill, Aylesbury Road, Wing, Leighton Buzzard LU7 0PG. Tel: 01296 688543; e-mail: edgwarerover@live.co.uk. *Wisden* specialist. Immediate decision and top settlement for purchase of *Wisden* collections. Why wait for the next auction? Why pay the auctioneer's commission anyway?

J. W. McKENZIE, 12 Stoneleigh Park Road, Ewell, Epsom, Surrey KT19 0QT. Tel: 020 8393 7700; email: mckenziecricket@btconnect.com; website: mckenzie-cricket.co.uk. Old cricket books and memorabilia specialist since 1971. Free catalogues issued regularly. Large shop premises open 9–4.30 Monday–Friday. Thirty minutes from London Waterloo. Please phone before visiting.

KEN PIESSE CRICKET BOOKS, PO Box 868, Mt Eliza, Victoria 3930, Australia. Tel: (+61) 419 549 458; email: kenpiesse@ozemail.com.au; website: cricketbooks.com.au. Australian cricket's internet specialists. Publishers of quality limited-edition biographies: Turner, Collins, Duff, McDonald, Ironmonger, Loxton, Potter and *Fifteen Minutes of Fame*, Australia's 70 One-Test Wonders.

ROGER PAGE, 10 Ekari Court, Yallambie, Victoria 3085, Australia. Tel: (+61) 3 9435 6332; email: rpcricketbooks@iprimus.com.au; website: rpcricketbooks.com. Australia's only full-time dealer in new and second-hand cricket books. Distributor of overseas cricket annuals and magazines. Agent for the Association of Cricket Statisticians and the Cricket Memorabilia Society.

ST MARY'S BOOKS & PRINTS, 9 St Mary's Hill, Stamford, Lincolnshire PE9 2DP. Tel: 01780 763033; email: info@stmarysbooks.com; website: stmarysbooks.com. Dealers in *Wisdens*, second-hand and rare cricket books, and *Vanity Fair* prints. Book-search service offered.

THE SOMERSET BADGER, River House, Porters Hatch, Meare, Glastonbury, Somerset BA6 9SW. Tel: 0791 232 2620; email: thesomersetbadger@outook.com; website: tinyurl.com/thesomersetbadger. We specialise in buying and selling post-war *Wisdens*. Viewing and valuation by appointment; over 500 editions in stock, and 90% in VGC or better.

SPORTSPAGES, 7 Finns Business Park, Mill Lane, Farnham, Surrey GU10 5HP. Tel: 01252 851040; email: info@sportspages.com; website: sportspages.com. Large stock of *Wisdens*, fine sports books and sports memorabilia. Books and sports memorabilia also purchased. Visitors welcome to browse by appointment.

TIM BEDDOW, 66 Oak Road, Oldbury, West Midlands B68 0BD. Tel: 0121 421 7117 or 07956 456112; email: wisden1864@hotmail.com. Wanted: any items of sporting memorabilia. Cricket, football, boxing, motor racing, TT, F1, stock cars, speedway, ice hockey, rugby, golf, horse racing, athletics and *all* other sports. Top prices paid for vintage items.

WILLIAM H. ROBERTS, Long Low, 27 Gernhill Avenue, Fixby, Huddersfield, West Yorkshire HD2 2HR. Tel: 01484 654463; email: william@roberts-cricket.co.uk; website: williamroberts-cricket.com. Second-hand/antiquarian cricket books, *Wisdens*, autographs and memorabilia bought and sold.

WISDEN DIRECT: wisdenalmanack.com/books. *Wisden Cricketers' Almanacks* since 2019 (plus 1864–78 and 1916–19 reprints) and other Wisden publications, all at discounted prices.

WISDEN REPRINTS, email: wisdenauction@cridler.com; website: wisdenauction.com. Limited-edition Willows *Wisden* reprints still available for various years at wisdenauction.com. Second-hand *Wisdens* also sold (see WisdenAuction entry in Auctioneers section).

WISDENWORLD.COM, Tel: 01480 819272 or 07966 513171; email: bill.wisden@gmail.com; website: wisdenworld.com. A unique and friendly service; quality *Wisdens* bought and sold at fair prices, along with free advice on the value of your collection. The world's largest *Wisden*-only seller; licensed by Wisden.

AUCTIONEERS

GRAHAM BUDD AUCTIONS, PO Box 47519, London N14 6XD. Tel: 020 8366 2525; website: grahambuddauctions.co.uk. Specialist auctioneer of sporting memorabilia.

KNIGHTS AUCTIONEERS, Norfolk. Tel: 01263 768488; email: tim@knights.co.uk; website: knights.co.uk. Respected auctioneers, specialising in cricket memorabilia and *Wisden Cricketers' Almanacks*, established in 1993. Three major cricket and sporting memorabilia auctions per year, including specialist *Wisden* sale day in each auction. Entries invited.

MULLOCK'S SPECIALIST AUCTIONEERS, The Old Shippon, Wall under Heywood, Church Stretton, Shropshire SY6 7DS. Tel: 01694 771771; email: info@mullocksauctions.co.uk; website: mullocksauctions.co.uk. For worldwide exposure, contact a leading sporting auction specialist. Regular cricket sales are held throughout the year and are fully illustrated on our website.

WISDENAUCTION.COM. Tel: 0800 7 999 501; email: wisdenauction@cridler.com; website: wisdenauction.com. A specially designed auction website for buying and selling *Wisdens*. List your spares today and bid live for that missing year. Every original edition for sale, including all hardbacks. Built by collectors for collectors, with the best descriptions on the internet.

CRICKET DATABASES

CRICKET ARCHIVE: cricketarchive.com. The most comprehensive searchable database on the internet with scorecards of all first-class, List A, pro T20 and major women's matches, as well as a wealth of league and friendly matches. The database currently has more than 1.25m players and over 700,000 full and partial scorecards.

CRICVIZ: cricviz.com; email: marketing@cricviz.com. CricViz is the largest cricket database, providing predictive modelling and analytics to broadcasters, teams and media clients.

CSW DATABASE FOR PCs. Contact Ric Finlay, email: ricf@netspace.net.au; website: tastats.com.au. Men's and women's internationals; major T20 leagues; domestic cricket in Australia, NZ, South Africa and England. Full scorecards and 2,500 searches. Suitable for professionals and hobbyists alike.

WISDEN RECORDS: wisdenrecords.com. Up-to-date and in-depth cricket records from *Wisden*.

CRICKET COLLECTING, MEMORABILIA AND MUSEUMS

BRADMAN FOUNDATION AND MUSEUM, St Jude Street, NSW 2576, Australia. Tel: (+61) 4862 1247; email: store@bradman.com.au; website: internationalcrickethall.com. Whether you are a cricket fan or just interested in learning more about one of the world's most popular sports, the Bradman Museum is an exciting and interactive experience for the whole family.

CRICKET MEMORABILIA SOCIETY. See entry in Cricket Societies section.

LORD'S MUSEUM & GROUND TOURS, Lord's Cricket Ground, St John's Wood, London NW8 8QN. Tel: 020 7616 8595; email: tours@mcc.org.uk; website: lords.org/tours. A tour of Lord's provides a fascinating behind-the-scenes insight into the world's most famous cricket ground. See the original Ashes urn, plus an outstanding collection of art, memorabilia and much more.

WILLOW STAMPS, 10 Mentmore Close, Harrow, Middlesex HA3 0EA. Tel: 020 8907 4200; email: willowstamps@gmail.com. Standing-order service for new cricket-stamp issues.

WISDEN COLLECTORS' CLUB. Tel: 01480 819272 or 07966 513171; email: bill.wisden@gmail.com; website: wisdencollectorsclub.co.uk. Free and completely impartial advice on *Wisdens*. We also offer *Wisdens* and other cricket books to our members, usually at no charge except postage. Quarterly newsletter, discounts on publications, and a great website. Licensed by Wisden.

WISDENS.ORG. Tel: 07793 060706; email: wisdens@cridler.com; website: wisdens.org; Twitter: @Wisdens. The unofficial *Wisden* collectors' website. Valuations, guide, discussion forum, all free to use. *Wisden* prices updated constantly. We also buy and sell *Wisdens* for our members. Email us for free advice about absolutely anything to do with collecting *Wisdens*.

CRICKET EQUIPMENT

ACUMEN BOOKS, Pennyfields, New Road, Bignall End, Stoke-on-Trent ST7 8QF. Tel: 07956 239801; email: wca@acumenbooks.co.uk; website: acumenbooks.co.uk. Specialist for umpires, scorers, officials, etc. MCC Lawbooks, Tom Smith, other textbooks, Duckworth/Lewis, scorebooks, trousers, over & run counters, gauges, bails (heavy, Hi-Vis and tethered), etc.

BOLA MANUFACTURING LTD, Ravenscourt Road, Patchway, Bristol, BS34 6PL. Tel: 0117 924 3569; email: info@bola.co.uk; website: bola.co.uk. Manufacturer of bowling machines and ball-throwing machines for all sports. Machines for professional and all recreational levels for sale to the UK and overseas.

CHASE CRICKET, Dummer Down Farm, Basingstoke, Hampshire RG25 2AR. Tel: 01256 397499; email: info@chasecricket.co.uk; website: chasecricket.co.uk. Chase Cricket specialises in handmade bats and hi-tech soft goods. Established 1996. "Support British Manufacturing."

CRICKET SOCIETIES

CRICKET MEMORABILIA SOCIETY, Hon. Secretary: Steve Cashmore, 4 Bluebell Close, Cheltenham, Glos GL53 0FF. Email: cmscricket87@outlook.com; website: cricketmemorabilia.org. To promote and support the collection and appreciation of all cricket memorabilia. Four meetings annually at first-class grounds, with a minimum of two auctions. Meetings attended by former Test players. Regular members' magazine. Research and valuations undertaken.

THE CRICKET SOCIETIES' ASSOCIATION, Secretary: Mike Hitchings, 34 Derwent Drive, Mitton, Tewkesbury GL20 8BB. Tel: 07979 464715; email: mikehitchings@aol.com; website: cricketsocietiesassociation.com. For cricket lovers in the winter – join a local society and enjoy speaker evenings with fellow enthusiasts for the summer game.

THE CRICKET SOCIETY, c/o the Membership Secretary, Matthew Stevenson. Email: matthewstevenson@cricketsociety.com; website: cricketsociety.com. A worldwide society which promotes cricket through its awards, publications, regular meetings, lunches and special events.

CRICKET TOUR OPERATORS

GULLIVERS SPORTS TRAVEL, Ground Floor, Ashvale 2, Ashchurch Business Centre, Alexandra Way, Tewkesbury, Glos GL20 8NB. Tel: 01684 879221; email: gullivers@gulliverstravel.co.uk; website: gulliverstravel.co.uk. The UK's longest-established cricket tour operator offers a great choice of supporter packages to all of England's away fixtures.

PITCHES AND GROUND EQUIPMENT

HUCK NETS (UK) LTD, Gore Cross Business Park, Corbin Way, Bradpole, Bridport, Dorset DT6 3UX. Tel: 01308 425100; email: sales@huckcricket.co.uk; website: huckcricket.co.uk. Alongside manufacturing our unique knotless high-quality polypropylene cricket netting, we offer the complete portfolio of ground and club equipment necessary for cricket clubs of all levels.

NOTTS SPORT, Bridge Farm, Holt Lane, Ashby Magna, Leics LE17 5NJ. Tel: 01455 883730; email: info@nottssports.com; website: nottssports.com. With various ECB-approved pitch systems, Notts Sport, the world's leading supplier of artificial grass pitch systems for coaching, practice and matchplay, can provide a solution tailored to suit individual needs and budgets.

ERRATA

Wisden 1926	II, Page 455	There were 221 hundreds in 1925: 176 in the Championship, 45 in other matches. The list omits J. R. Gunn, 166 for Nottinghamshire v Hampshire at Southampton, and M. C. Parry, 124 for Ireland v Scotland at Dublin.
Wisden 1927	II, Page 503	There were 296 hundreds in 1926: 232 in the Championship, 35 others and 29 by the tourists (the list on page 58 includes six which were not first-class).
Wisden 1928	II, Page 445	Ireland v Scotland at College Park took place on July 9, 11 and 12.
	II, Page 502	The list of hundreds omits J. Kerr, 136 for Scotland v Ireland at Dublin.
Wisden 1931	II, Page 689	F. I. de Caires's highest score in the Representative Matches (ie Tests) was 80.
Wisden 1940	Page 304	W. R. Hammond hit six Championship hundreds; the seventh was in a Test.
Wisden 1947	Page 110	D. C. S. Compton's 103 was for The Rest v An England XI, and C. Washbrook's 120 was for An England XI v The Rest (not Lancs v Leics, the same week).
	Page 112	J. F. Crapp's 102 for Gloucestershire v Essex was at Brentford, not Bristol.
	Page 114	B. P. King's 145 was for Lancashire v Gloucestershire at Gloucester, not v Oxford University at Oxford.
	Page 115	P. Vaulkhard's 264 was for Derbyshire v Nottinghamshire, not vice versa. The list omits F. M. Quinn's 140 for Ireland v Scotland at Greenock, which brings the total number of hundreds to 258 (191 in the Championship, 46 others and 21 by the tourists).
	Page 273	J. F. Crapp's best Championship score was 117, not 121 (which was v Oxford).
Wisden 1949	Page 197	There were 303 hundreds in 1948; the list omits 164* by W. J. Edrich for the All England XI v Glamorgan at Cardiff.
	Page 202	A. J. Watkins's 111* for Glamorgan v South of England was at Swansea.
Wisden 1950	Page 199	The 354 hundreds in 1949 were made up of 251 in the Championship, 74 others and 29 by the tourists.
	Page 308	F. H. Vigar hit three Championship hundreds, not two.
Wisden 1952	Page 204	The 310 hundreds in 1951 were made up of 233 in the Championship, 61 others and 16 by the tourists.
	Page 206	M. C. Cowdrey's 106 for Gentlemen v Players was at Scarborough, not Hastings.
Wisden 1957	Page 219	The 189 hundreds in 1956 were made up of 117 in the Championship, 55 others and 17 by the tourists.
	Page 622	Yorkshire played 35 first-class matches, including 11 wins.
Wisden 1959	Page 73	The list of hundreds in each English season from 1935 to 1958 should be corrected in the following years (Total–Championship–Other–Tourists): 1939 261–216–31–14; 1946 258–191–46–21; 1948 303–207–49–47; 1949 354–251–74–29; 1951 310–233–61–16; 1956 189–117–55–17.
Wisden 1962	Page 920	Iftikhar Bokhari retired hurt after his 203 for Lahore v Punjab University, which means that he led the Ayub Trophy averages with 357 at 178.50, ahead of A. H. Kardar's 127 for once out and Maqsood Ahmed, who averaged 80.00 not 86.00.
Wisden 1963	Page 305	There were 20 first-class hundreds against the Pakistan touring team in 1962, including 119 by P. B. H. May for Surrey at The Oval and 228* by R. E. Marshall for Hampshire at Bournemouth.
Wisden 1966	Page 267	The 149 hundreds in the 1965 season included 103 in the Championship, 30 others and 16 for the tourists.
	Page 417	Hampshire played 31 first-class matches, including 21 draws.
	Page 571	Sussex played 32 first-class matches, including 17 draws.
Wisden 1969	Page 279	There were 174 hundreds in the 1968 season, made up of 123 in the Championship, 38 others and 13 for the tourists.
	Page 587	Sussex played 31 first-class matches, including three wins.

Wisden 1970	Page 288	M. J. K. Smith's 148 for D. H. Robins's XI was against Oxford University not West Indies.
Wisden 1971	Page 101	Peter May was 25 years 160 days old when he first led England in 1955 – 185 days younger than Percy Chapman in 1926. At that time, May was the fifth-youngest man to captain England, after Monty Bowden and Ivo Bligh (both 23) in the 1880s, and Donald Carr and David Sheppard (both 25), who deputised for the official captains.
	Page 287	The 234 hundreds in 1970 were made up of 192 in the Championship and 42 in other first-class matches.
Wisden 1973	Page 899	Garry Sobers reached 139 not out for the World XI on January 3, not May 3.
Wisden 1974	Page 320	In the Second Test against New Zealand, the second-innings partnership between Fletcher and Illingworth was for the fifth wicket, not the sixth.
Wisden 1976	Page 118	In the list of M. J. K. Smith's career hundreds, his 148 for D. H. Robins's XI was against Oxford University not West Indies.
Wisden 2020	Pages 616 and 621	Contrary to the erratum published last year, Middlesex's matches against Oxford MCCU and Gloucestershire at Northwood were played on the same ground at Merchant Taylors' School.
	Page 957	D. R. Briggs was registered with Sussex, not Hampshire, when he toured India with England Lions in 2018-19.
	Page 1049	In the table of cheapest Test five-fors, Philander took 5-7 in 2012-13 not 1912-13.
Wisden 2021	Page 131	J. E. Raphael attended Merchant Taylors' School before it moved to Northwood; in 1901 it was situated near Charterhouse Square. P. D. Johnson did the double of 1,000 runs and 50 wickets in a school season in successive years; he combined 1,061 runs with 75 wickets in 1968.
	Page 256	The Lodge School is in St John, Barbados, not Bridgetown. Michael Frederick won a Test cap in 1953-54.
	Page 267	Douglas Morgan toured New Zealand, not South Africa, with the British Lions in 1977.
	Page 335	Preston McSween appeared for Barbados in 2016-17, but was born in Grenada and subsequently played for Windward Islands.
	Page 428	In Durham's first innings, Lees was run out by Vilas and Davies, not Tattersall.
	Page 564	Henry George Munsey, who scored 32 for Hampshire, is known as George.
	Page 567	In the tie on August 29, it was Kent who needed five off the last over.
	Page 722	Michael Snedden was New Zealand's first fourth-generation first-class cricketer, not the first in the world.
	Page 733	The only ODI between Pakistan and Bangladesh, originally scheduled for April 3, was moved to April 1 before being cancelled because of the pandemic.
	Page 755	The Perera playing for Sri Lanka in the Second Test v South Africa was Kusal.
	Page 902	Perry's WBBL career total was 2,612 runs not 612, and Mooney's 2,576 not 576.
	Page 1206	Greg Blewett was born on October 28, 1971 – a day before Matthew Hayden.

A list of Errata in Wisden *since 1920 may be found at https://www.bloomsbury.com/uk/special-interest/wisden/errata/.*

CHARITIES IN 2021

ARUNDEL CASTLE CRICKET FOUNDATION has helped more than 30,000 disadvantaged youngsters, many with special educational needs and disabilities, mainly from inner-city areas, to benefit from sporting and educational activities at Arundel over the past 30 years. Director: Tim Shutt, Arundel Park, High Street, Arundel BN18 9LH; 07766 733152; tim@arundelcastlecricket.co.uk; www.arundelcastlecricketfoundation.co.uk.

THE BUNBURY CRICKET CLUB has raised over £17m for national charities, schools' cricket and worthwhile causes since 1987. A total of 1,960 boys have appeared in the Bunbury Festival; 1,046 have gone on to play first-class cricket, and 119 for England. The 35th ECB David English Bunbury Festival will be staged at the ECB Performance Centre at Loughborough from July 31– August 6. The Bunburys also presented the only two Under-15 World Cups (1996 and 2000), while this year sees the 15th match between the Bunbury English Schools Cricket XI and MCC Schools, at Lord's. Contact: Dr David English CBE, 1 Highwood Cottages, Nan Clark's Lane, London NW7 4HJ; davidenglishbunbury@gmail.com; www.bunburycricket.co.uk.

CAPITAL KIDS CRICKET, which is celebrating its 33rd anniversary, aims to improve the physical, social and emotional development of young people in all abilities, including refugee children. It is a fully inclusive organisation providing sporting and social opportunities in the more deprived areas of Greater London, and organises activities in state schools, hospitals, community centres, local parks, refugee camps and residential centres away from London: the Spirit of Cricket is at the heart of what we do. Around 10,000 young people are involved every year. Chairman: Haydn Turner; haydn.turner@yahoo.co.uk. Chief executive: Shahidul Alam Ratan; 07748 114811; shahidul.alam@ckc.london; www.ckc.london.

CHANCE TO SHINE is a national children's charity on a mission to spread the power of cricket throughout schools and communities. Since launching in 2005, Chance to Shine has reached over five million children across more than 17,000 state schools. Contact: The Kia Oval, London SE11 5SW; 020 7735 2881; www.chancetoshine.org.

THE CHANGE FOUNDATION is an award-winning UK-based charity that uses cricket and other sports to create transformational change in the lives of marginalised and vulnerable young people. The charity has been designing sport-for-development initiatives for 41 years, and has worked in 39 countries with a range of partners, including the ICC and UNICEF. We pioneered disability cricket, setting up and running the England Blind cricket team. Our cricket centre in the London Borough of Sutton was built – with the help of our president, Phil Tufnell – to cater for cricketers with a disability, and is home to many projects, including our new "walking cricket" programme. Chief executive: Andy Sellins, The Cricket Centre, Plough Lane, Wallington SM6 8JQ; 020 8669 2177; office@changefdn.org.uk; www.thechangefoundation.org.uk.

CRICKET BUILDS HOPE, formerly the Rwanda Cricket Stadium Foundation, successfully completed efforts in 2017 to raise £1m to build a new cricket facility in Rwanda's capital, Kigali. The charity now plans more cricketing projects. Partnership head: Jon Surtees, The Kia Oval, London SE11 5SS; 020 7820 5780.

THE CRICKET SOCIETY TRUST helps to deliver opportunities for young people to learn about and play cricket. It currently supports the Arundel Castle Cricket Foundation, the MCC Foundation, and the Fred Trueman Schools Cricket League, as well as other programmes. President: Isabelle Duncan. Chairman: Ronald Paterson, 3 Orlando Road, London SW4 0LE; 07710 989004; www.cricketsocietytrust.org.uk.

THE DICKIE BIRD FOUNDATION, set up by the former umpire in 2004, helps financially disadvantaged young people under 18 to participate in the sport of their choice. Grants are made towards the cost of equipment and clothing. Trustee: Ted Cowley, 3 The Tower, Tower Drive, Pool-in-Wharfedale, Otley LS21 1NQ; 07503 641457; www.thedickiebirdfoundation.co.uk.

THE ENGLAND AND WALES CRICKET TRUST was established in 2005 to aid community participation in cricket, with a fund for interest-free loans to amateur clubs. In its last financial year it spent £19.65m on charitable activities – primarily grants to cricket charities and amateur clubs, and to county boards to support their programmes. Contact: ECB, Lord's, London NW8 8QN; 020 7432 1200; feedback@ecb.co.uk.

FIELDS IN TRUST is a UK charity that actively maintains parks and green spaces by protecting them in perpetuity. Green spaces are good, do good, and need to be protected for good. Almost 3,000 spaces have been protected since our foundation in 1925. Chief executive: Helen Griffiths, 36 Woodstock Grove, London W12 8LE; 020 7427 2110; www.fieldsintrust.org.

THE HORNSBY PROFESSIONAL CRICKETERS' FUND supports former professional cricketers "in necessitous circumstances", or their dependants, through regular financial help or one-off grants towards healthcare or similar essential needs. Where appropriate, it works closely with the PCA and a player's former county. The Trust was established in 1928 from a bequest from the estate of J. H. J. Hornsby (Middlesex, MCC and the Gentlemen), augmented more recently by a bequest from Sir Alec and Eric Bedser, and a merger with the Walter Hammond Memorial Fund. Secretary: Stephen Coverdale, 1 Court Cottages, Overstone Park, Overstone, Northampton NN6 0AP; 01604 643070.

THE JOHNNERS TRUST, in memory of former commentator Brian Johnston, supports cricket for the blind, and aims to ease the financial worries of talented young cricketers through scholarships. Trust administrator: Richard Anstey, 178 Manor Drive North, Worcester Park KT4 7RU; raganstey@btinternet.com; www.johnners.com/brian-johnston-johnners-trust.

LAMBETH FOOD BANK TRUST is the official domestic charity partner of Surrey CCC and The Kia Oval. The Trust raises money for food banks across the London Borough of Lambeth. Partnership head: Jon Surtees, The Kia Oval, London SE11 5SS; 020 7820 5780; www.kiaoval.com.

THE LEARNING FOR A BETTER WORLD (LBW) TRUST, established in 2006, provides tertiary education to disadvantaged students in the cricket-playing countries of the developing world. In 2021, it assisted over 1,800 students in India, Nepal, Uganda, Afghanistan, Sri Lanka, South Africa, Kenya, Tanzania and Indonesia. Chairman: David Vaux, GPO Box 3029, Sydney, NSW 2000, Australia; www.lbwtrust.com.au.

THE LORD'S TAVERNERS is the UK's leading youth cricket and disability sports charity. Its cricket programmes (Wickets, Super Ones, Table Cricket and Sports Kit Recycling) break down barriers and empower disadvantaged and disabled young people to fulfil their potential and build links between communities. Contact: The Lord's Taverners, 90 Chancery Lane, London WC2A 1EU; 020 7025 0000; contact@lordstaverners.org; www.lordstaverners.org.

THE MARYLEBONE CRICKET CLUB FOUNDATION runs 74 Cricket Hubs across the UK, supporting promising players from disadvantaged and under-represented groups through free coaching and match play. Overseas, it champions Nepal's ambition to be a top cricketing nation, delivering cricket to thousands of young people and training coaches. It supports cricket programmes for Syrian refugees in Lebanon, and for township schools in South Africa. Contact: MCC Foundation, Lord's, London NW8 8QN; 020 7616 8529; info@mccfoundation.org.uk; www.lords.org/mccfoundation.

THE PRIMARY CLUB provides sporting facilities for the blind and partially sighted. Membership is nominally restricted to those dismissed first ball in any form of cricket; almost 10,000 belong. In total, the club has raised £4m, helped by sales of its tie, popularised by *Test Match Special*. Secretary: Chris Larlham, PO Box 12121, Saffron Walden CB10 2ZF; 01799 586507; www.primaryclub.org.

THE PRINCE'S TRUST supports 11–30-year-olds who are struggling at school or unemployed. Founded by HRH The Prince of Wales in 1976, the charity has helped more than one million young people to date. The Trust's programmes use a variety of activities, including cricket, to engage young people and give them the skills and confidence they need to change their lives. Contact: The Prince's Trust, 8 Glade Path, London SE1 8EG; 0800 842842, or text "call me" on 07983 385418; www.princes-trust.org.uk.

THE PROFESSIONAL CRICKETERS' TRUST was created to support the lifelong health and wellbeing of PCA members and their immediate families. We look out for players throughout their active careers and long afterwards, funding life-changing medical assistance, crisis helplines and educational programmes in England and Wales. Director of member services: Ian Thomas, PCA, The Kia Oval, London SE11 5SS; 07920 575578; www.thepca.co.uk.

THE TOM MAYNARD TRUST, formed in 2012 after Tom's death, covers two main areas: helping aspiring young professionals with education projects, currently across six sports; and providing grants to help with travel, kit, coaching, training and education. From 2014 to 2018, the charity also ran an academy in Spain for young county cricketers. Contact: Mike Fatkin, 67a Radnor Road, Cardiff CF5 1RA; www.tommaynardtrust.com.

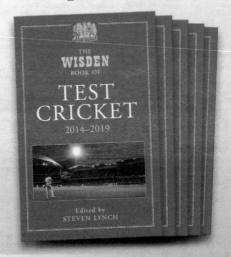

CHRONICLE OF 2021

And now, the rest of the news…

COMPILED BY MATTHEW ENGEL   CARTOONS BY NICK NEWMAN

THE SUNDAY TIMES   January 3
James Anderson was not given a knighthood in the 2021 New Year's Honours list for fear he would be sledged by rough Australians in the Ashes series later in the year, according to Whitehall sources. He would have become the fourth English cricketing knight in two years, after 11 in the previous 95.

SYDNEY MORNING HERALD   January 8
Melbourne club cricketer Jan Pucovski was bracing himself for the number 460 being tattooed on his body after his son Will, just picked for Australia, held him to a promise he had made when he was ten. "I'm sure you appreciate we say a lot of really dumb things to our kids when they're nine or ten, which you hope they'll forget, or will never come true," said Jan on Channel Seven. "We had a conversation one day about tattoos, and I wasn't a big fan." However, he agreed to have his son's number inscribed if ever he made the Test team. When he did, Will said: "Dad, work out where it's going." Jan replied: "It might be on the ankle."

WIGAN TODAY   January 29
Vandals broke into a container at Atherton CC near Wigan, and dragged out 20 inscribed memorial benches before setting them alight.

THE CRICKETER January 29

Sidmouth CC, the Devon club whose beautiful seafront ground has long had safety concerns, is to penalise sixes hit on to the esplanade. They will now incur a five-run deduction, though the rule will only apply in friendlies.

THE LIVE, NAGPUR February 7

Tennis-ball cricket has now been included in the official list of games whose best exponents can receive preferential treatment for Indian government jobs. Being a "meritorious sportsperson" is considered a plus for candidates.

WISDEN.COM February 10

A study by Liverpool School of Tropical Medicine has found that white cricket balls are likelier to spread Covid than red. Although the risk of becoming ill from an item of sports equipment is considered much less than originally thought, the synthetic grease used to finish a red ball is apparently safer than the nitrocellulose on the white. In June 2020, prime minister Boris Johnson described a cricket ball as "a natural vector of disease".

SUNDAY OBSERVER, SRI LANKA February 21

A Sri Lankan cricket squad has been founded, comprised entirely of sets of twins.

NEW ZEALAND HERALD March 1

Ronnie Hira, who played 15 Twenty20 internationals for New Zealand in 2012 and 2013, hit a 12-ball half-century for North Shore against Takapuna in a Hedley Howarth Championship two-day game; he also gained match figures of 14 for 78 with his left-arm spin.

NATIONAL HERALD, INDIA   March 3

Salauddin Abbasi won the match award at a tournament in Bhopal. The prize was a five-litre can of petrol.

THE STAR, SHEFFIELD   March 4

Sheffield, which has lost at 18 least cricket pitches in recent years, is to have its first new ground for nearly two decades. The city council have agreed it will become the new home of Norton Woodseats CC.

SKY TV   March 10

Former Leicestershire cricketer and Test umpire Barry Dudleston spoke to Sky News after losing £70,000 in a financial scam promoted by an unregulated foreign-exchange platform called OFC Markets. "I don't think I'm going to get the money back, and I don't think anybody is going to feel sorry for me," he said. "But I do believe that, if it can be put into the public domain, it might help others not to get caught." Dudleston formerly ran a successful travel company.

SYDNEY MORNING HERALD   March 12

The University of New South Wales is launching a three-year course leading to an MBA in cricket administration. The brainchild of the Australian players' union, it hopes to persuade the best and brightest to remain in the game after their career ends. The course features traditional business-oriented units, plus modules on marketing, fan engagement, governance, the media, sports law – and a unit based on the Indian Premier League that includes a trip to India to observe it first-hand.

BBC   March 16/17

Council officials vetoed a plan to name a new road in Accrington after one of the town's favourite sons, the cricketer, coach, umpire and commentator David Lloyd. They insisted that policy decreed roads should not be named after the living. Bumble Avenue was suggested as a compromise. However, it was pointed out that the runner Ron Hill and his wife, May, had both had roads named after them in their lifetime, and the decision was overturned by Hyndburn council leader Miles Parkinson. The road is on a new estate close to the town's football and cricket grounds, both close to Lloyd's heart. Parkinson said Lloyd had "put Accrington on the map internationally".

THE TRIBUNE, CHANDIGARH   April 4

Having just been caught for 49, batsman Sanjay Paliya walked over to the fielder, Sachin Parashar, and bashed him with his bat. Parashar was said to be critically ill in hospital in Gwalior, Madhya Pradesh. Paliya had disappeared.

THE GUARDIAN   April 10

After the death of Prince Philip, several of the BBC's county cricket commentators continued their work, unaware they had been taken off air as a sign of national mourning. The death was announced just after midday, but no one told the commentary teams, and some blithely talked to themselves until the lunch interval.

MAIL ONLINE   April 16

Club cricketers described as "impractical" an ECB suggestion that they should stop play for 70 minutes during Prince Philip's funeral on Saturday afternoon, following an edict handed down to county players. Under Covid rules, changing-rooms and bars were closed, leaving players no choice but to sit alone in their cars, or outside. "ECB: how out of touch can you be? What is to be gained by club cricketers sitting outside their closed clubhouses, gazing into the middle distance for an hour?" responded Aylsham St Giles CC, Norfolk. Many leagues observed a minute's silence, then played on.

MAIL ONLINE April 16

In an incident caught on video, a batsman in Ghaziabad, India, smashed a ball straight into a bowler's head. The bowler, who was not named, slumped to the ground unconscious, and rumours circulated that he had died. However, he issued a video message from hospital, saying: "Rest, all is fine." It was thought he might suffer some damage to his hearing.

NVPLAY.COM April 18

Southern Vipers all-rounder Tara Norris contrived to be out for nought three times in a single day, having faced two balls. Norris, a key member of the Vipers' team who won the premier English women's trophy in 2020, was taking part in a pre-season practice day, including two games between the Vipers and their Academy. Opening in the first game, played under Twenty20 rules, she was bowled first ball. In the second, played under Hundred rules, she was run out without facing. It being a practice day, she was allowed to bat again at No. 10 (though the scorecard refers to her as Player AA, which may have been a kindness). This time, she was lbw to her first delivery.

BLACKPOOL GAZETTE April 18

Two generations of Flintoffs failed to save St Annes from defeat by Morecambe in their opening Northern Premier League match of the season. Fifteen-year-old Corey had been picked on merit; it was thought it might help if his father, Andrew, 43, gave him moral support seven years after his last game for the club. However, hopes of their batting together were dashed: Corey, at No. 6, was out for two; dad, in next, went for three – but Corey did get an early breakthrough with the ball. Morecambe won by four wickets.

BBC April 24

Twelve-year-old Owen Forbes, making his senior debut for Allendale CC, Northumberland, won the match by taking the last four Mitford wickets in four balls. He had been out first ball and taken nought for 21 before the drama began. "It was kind of crazy," said Owen, who models his game on Stuart Broad.

DAWN, KARACHI   April 28

A teenager was shot dead on the field after an argument with opponents in Swabi, near Pakistan's border with Afghanistan.

ECB PRESS RELEASE   April 28

The England and Wales Cricket Board, the Professional Cricketers' Association plus the 18 first-class counties, and eight women's regional teams have agreed to take part in a football-inspired social media boycott over the May bank holiday to protest against online abuse. Tom Harrison, the ECB chief executive, said they were "sending a message" – by not sending messages.

DAVIDJOHNLANG.COM/BENAUDTRIO.COM   April

Composer David John Lang's new work *The Tied Test*, a four-movement tribute to a famous match, is due to be performed in Adelaide and Melbourne by the Benaud Trio on piano, violin and cello. The group say they regard "cricket's avuncular figurehead" as their inspiration.

THE SUNDAY TELEGRAPH   May 2

The high-walled compound in Abbottabad, Pakistan, used by 9/11 mastermind Osama bin Laden as his hideout until he was killed by US forces in 2011, has been razed, and is now being used by local boys to play cricket.

CORNWALL LIVE   May 4

The match between Launceston and Menheniot/Looe CC was abandoned after an alleged assault on an umpire.

NORTHERN ECHO   May 8

In Yorkshire, Tom Stead of Thornton-le-Moor CC took ten for 43 against Markington. This was only the fifth ten-for in the 127-year history of the Nidderdale League.

THE GUARDIAN/ESPNCRICINFO   May 10/11

Scientists have suggested that bamboo could be an alternative to willow for cricket bats. Dr Darshil Shah of Cambridge University, himself a cricketer, says bamboo is cheaper, faster-growing, more widely cultivated, more sustainable and less wasteful. Trials showed a bat made from strips of bamboo also had a bigger sweet spot, further down the blade. MCC, guardians of the laws, said its use would be in breach of the game's current Law 5 which specifies wooden bats – bamboo is a grass. The lamination used in the prototypes would also be illegal in senior cricket. But they welcomed the initiative and the search for alternatives.

KEIGHLEY NEWS   May 11

In the Halifax League Parish Cup, Southowram dismissed Augustinians for six, thought to be the lowest score in the competition's history. This was in reply to 272 for five. There were nine ducks, one four and two extras. Neil Johnson had figures of seven for four and Ashley Johnson three for none.

VIMPSATTHECREASE.COM   May 12

Eighteen-year-old Tom Prest embarked on an innings of 303 not out in Hampshire's Second XI Championship match against Sussex – immediately after his geography A-level. On a day that began with an essay on water pollution, he arrived just in time to strap on his pads after Sussex were dismissed. By the close, he was 111 not out, and next day completed Hampshire's first triple-century in the competition.

FELSTED.ORG   May 15

The boys and girls of Felsted School, Essex, tied their Twenty20 matches on the same afternoon on adjacent pitches. The boys were playing Brentwood School, both scoring 149, while the girls took on Free Foresters, and both made 128.

CRICTRACKER   May 21

In a T10 match, Aritharan Vaseekaran hit six sixes in an over for Bayer Uerdingen Boosters against Köln Challengers; this was presumably the first instance in Germany.

BBC RADIO LINCOLNSHIRE   May 24

Arran Brindle, the former England international, shared a match-winning stand of 143 with her 12-year-old son, Harry, for Owmby Trojans in the third division of the Lincoln & District League. Harry had already taken four for 27 to help bowl out Nettleham Academy for 141, and they knocked off the runs for a ten-wicket win – mum scoring 94 and son 32. Arran was not too distressed to miss a century: she had made a more important one against Australia to save a Test at Hove in 2005. She was, though, mighty proud of Harry.

NEWSWIRE, SRI LANKA   May 25

Children playing cricket on a playground in Mirihana, outside Colombo, were spotted by a police drone, and admonished for breaching lockdown rules.

NEWS POST LEADER, SUNDERLAND   May 25

Ten year-old Lennon Harmison, nephew of the so-far more famous Steve, achieved his first hat-trick for Ashington Under-13 against Tynemouth. He was helped by catches from two other Harmisons: Charlie, Steve's son, and Ava, another cousin.

JERSEY EVENING POST   May 28

Fifteen-year-old left-arm spinner Louis Kelly took hat-tricks in his first two senior matches, for Old Victorians in Jersey.

AHMEDABAD MIRROR   June 7

A 12-year-old boy was killed in the suburb of Thaltej, when he fell on a spiked gate while retrieving a cricket ball from a temple compound.

THE IMPARTIAL REPORTER, ENNISKILLEN   June 11/18

Enniskillen CC in County Fermanagh have come back to life after a 28-year slumber. Kenny Maxwell, a team member in 1993, opened the batting against Lurgan Victoria in the re-formed club's opening match.

IT'S THE VILLAGE CRICKET PEOPLE

EDGBASTON.COM June 18
What was said to be the first ever match between two LGBTQ+ teams took place at Weoley Hill CC, when the well-established London-based Graces scored a 38-run win over the newly formed Birmingham Unicorns. Further teams are now being organised in Leeds, Manchester and Bath.

BBC June 21
In the Huntingdonshire County League, Buckden Second XI were bowled out for two by Falcons CC. Captain Joel Kirschner pointed out that they had 15 players unavailable, only nine in their team – one of whom was 30 overs late due to work – and no recognised batsmen. Kirschner did not expect to threaten a target of 261, but had hoped to get closer. There were no runs off the bat, just a bye and a wide. "Therapy will begin this week for those involved," said the Buckden Twitter feed.

YORKSHIRE EVENING POST June 22
Taxi driver Asif Ali lost a day's work awaiting the repair man after smashing his own rear windscreen with a six into the car park in a Halifax League cup tie. "It felt great coming off the bat," he said.

ESPNCRICINFO June 28
Anshula Rao of the Madhya Pradesh women's team has been banned for four years for taking anabolic steroids.

CRICTRACKER June 29
Ten years after being banned and jailed for his role in match-fixing, former Pakistan Test captain Salman Butt enrolled on a course run by the Pakistan board to train umpires and match referees.

THE SCARBOROUGH NEWS July 1
Duncombe Park CC in Yorkshire were banned from playing at their long-established home ground until they erected a net – at a cost of £12,750 – to protect people in a new housing development.

CRICTRACKER July 4

Subodh Bhati, an all-rounder for Delhi, scored a double-century in a T20 club game for a Delhi XI against Simba. He hit 17 sixes and 205 from 79 balls in a total of 256. He reportedly reached 200 in a T20 match in Goa in 2018.

BBC July 16

Needing 35 off the last over to beat Cregagh in a Twenty20 final in Northern Ireland, John Glass of Ballymena went from 51 to 87 in the grand manner – six sixes – to secure victory.

THE NEWS, PAKISTAN July 16

Pakistani activist Malala Yousafzai, who in 2014 became the youngest winner of the Nobel Peace Prize, has spoken about her annoyance at playing cricket as a child. "Boys would throw a slower ball to me, assuming girls were afraid to hit a fast ball," she recalled – so she told them to bowl at her as if she were a boy. Malala was shot in the face in 2012 by a gunman as revenge for her campaign for female education. She is now in the UK, married to Asser Malik, a manager for the Pakistan Cricket Board, and has an Oxford degree.

MANCHESTER EVENING NEWS July 19

Left-arm swing bowler Mudassar Bashir had figures of 7.5–4–8–10 for Stalybridge in a Second XI match at Hollingworth in the Derbyshire & Cheshire League. Hollingworth quickly wrapped up an eight-wicket victory.

THE TRIBUNE, CHANDIGARH July 19

To mark the 50th anniversary of the Indian victory over Pakistan (at war, not cricket) in 1971, their army organised a tournament (at cricket, not war) at the base of Siachen Glacier in the Himalayas, the site of the decisive Indian victory in the Battle of Turtuk. Eight teams of local youngsters took part.

KENT MESSENGER July 19

A charity cricket day at Mote Park, Maidstone, ended in a free-for-all, when a shirtless man appeared from the crowd and started lashing out with a bat. Four people were reported injured. The T10 tournament was primarily to raise funds for those needing medical treatment in Pakistan.

THE TIMES/PLAYCRICKET.COM   July 22/August 8

Rob Franks of Parley CC, Dorset, has returned to playing club cricket much as he did before a series of medical issues concluded in 2018 with his left leg being amputated above the knee. He was able to play again on an ordinary artificial leg three months after the operation, but needed a runner to bat and had to field in the slips. Following a crowdfunding campaign (backed by Mike Atherton), he was able to afford a £12,500 blade, which transformed his cricket – and his life. In June, captaining the Second XI, he took four for 44 against Winton, and finished the season as the team's top wicket-taker.

MANCHESTER EVENING NEWS   July 26

Phil Jones's proposal to his girlfriend, Jill Boosie, in the Old Trafford stands at the Twenty20 international against Pakistan was shown on TV with a caption saying "Decision Pending", before – to general delight – Jill said yes. The couple were particularly anxious to trace a kind stranger in the neighbouring seat to ask him to be their best man. "He really made that special moment even better with his reaction," Phil said.

INDIAN EXPRESS   July 26

Two cricketers died at Noida, Uttar Pradesh, while trying to retrieve a ball from a sewage tank. Police said they were overcome by toxic fumes, and suffocated.

JOONDALUP TIMES   July 28

One of the few aluminium cricket bats ever made has vanished after a celebrity charity match at the governor of Western Australia's official home in Perth. Its owner, Bradley Skipworth, had lent it to organisers for promotional purposes, but it disappeared. Dennis Lillee infamously used one of the bats for four balls (and three runs) in the 1979-80 Test against England at Perth, before England captain Mike Brearley complained; non-wooden bats were swiftly outlawed. It is not clear if Lillee ever used this particular bat, thought to be worth about $A10,000 (£5,000). "It's a family heirloom," said Skipworth. "It has a lot of sentimental value. I don't care about the dollar value whatsoever."

ABC NEWS (AUSTRALIA)   July 30

Brody Price of Kalgoorlie posted pictures of himself in cricket gear, including wicketkeeping gloves, ready to catch his imminent child as it emerged in the hospital delivery room. His daughter, Hadley, was born safely in the customary manner; nonetheless, the pictures went viral.

INDIAN EXPRESS   August 1

The BCCI have warned that overseas players joining the new Kashmir Cricket League, a T20 tournament promoted by the Pakistan board, will be barred from cricket-related work in India. The disputed territory of Kashmir is split between Pakistan, India and China. The former South African player Herschelle Gibbs, who had signed for one of the six teams, Overseas Warriors, accused India of promoting their political agenda. Monty Panesar withdrew in response to the threats.

WORCESTER NEWS   August 5

Worcestershire CCC were one of 191 companies named in a government report for paying below the national minimum wage. The club said there was a technical error affecting two employees which was corrected as soon as they were told about it.

THE WEEK, INDIA   August 8

The Indian Premier League team Chennai Super Kings awarded one crore rupees (£100,000) to Neeraj Chopra, after he claimed independent India's first Olympic athletics gold medal, in the javelin, at Tokyo. They also created a special 8758 jersey to mark his winning throw of 87.58 metres.

TEAMUSA.ORG/YAHOO.COM   August

Rai Benjamin, son of the former West Indian fast bowler, Winston, won silver in the Olympic 400 metres hurdles, competing for the US. He broke the previous world record, but narrowly lost to Karsten Warholm of Norway. In Bangladesh, Australian players broke off from training to watch Brandon Starc, brother of fast bowler Mitchell, finish fifth in the high jump.

CRICTRACKER   August 15

Eighteen-year-old Ajay Gill walked 800 miles from his home in Haryana to M. S. Dhoni's home in Ranchi in the hope of ten minutes with the great man. Told that Dhoni was preparing for the IPL and would not be home for three months, Gill said he would wait, but a local businessman bought him a plane ticket to Delhi and persuaded him to come back another time.

YORKSHIRE EVENING POST   August 19

An 86-year-old umpire from Leeds has had a shoulder replacement operation to enable him to get back on the field. Keith Dibb was made a life member of the Dales Council League for services to umpiring in 2010, and was desperate to carry on. Surgeon Roger Hackney says Dibb has pain-free movement, and added: "Most importantly for him, he can signal a six."

DAILY MAIL/FINANCIAL TIMES   August 23

After the prime minister made him a trade envoy to Australia, Lord Botham of Ravensworth (formerly known as Ian) received a torrid welcome on social media. "Who next?" asked one Twitter user. "Ross Kemp as defence secretary? Jim Davidson to the UN? Cast of *Emmerdale* to Agriculture?" International trade secretary Liz Truss said Botham would "bat for British business Down Under". A *Financial Times* reader noted that Botham was currently importing Australian wine to Britain with his name on the label.

NORTHERN ECHO   August 26

Father and son John and Andrew Gedye put on 236 for the second wicket, playing for Aldbrough St John Second XI against Middleton Tyas in the Darlington and District League. Both scored centuries: John 124, Andrew 111.

OPINDIA.COM   August 26
Immediately after the militantly Islamist Taliban regained control of
Afghanistan, a team called Taliban Cricket Club entered a tournament in
Jaisalmer, Rajasthan, a part of India with sensitive interfaith relations.
Organisers apologised, and expelled the team after their first match.

MANCHESTER EVENING NEWS/BIRMINGHAM LIVE   Sep 5/Oct 28
Sixes Cricket Club, a gastropub concept already established in London, which
offers nets with automated bowling machines, along with food and drink, has
now spread to Manchester and Birmingham.

INDIAN EXPRESS   September 6
Police in Gurgaon, near Delhi, arrested three people for conning an aspiring
cricketer out of ten lakh rupees (£10,000) by promising him a place in top-
class teams.

DAILY TELEGRAPH   September 6
Weeks after being airlifted out of Afghanistan, a group of refugees were welcomed
to Buckinghamshire with a game of cricket. About 200 Afghans, whose
breadwinners had worked for either the British army or embassy, have been
temporarily billeted, pending permanent resettlement, around Newport Pagnell.
The game, organised by the town's cricket club and Baptist church, ended with a
two that tied the game, hit by a 17-year-old who declined gloves and pads,
thinking a cricket ball a unthreatening weapon compared to their recent worries.

INDIAN EXPRESS   September 7
In Bihar, two rival political factions have selected separate Under-19 teams to
represent the state in the Vinoo Mankad Trophy.

YORKSHIRE POST   September 11
Actor Samuel West, who plays grumpy vet Siegfried Farnon in the Channel 5
remake of *All Creatures Great and Small*, tore his Achilles tendon attempting a
quick single while filming a village cricket scene at Studley Royal, North Yorkshire.

BBC/THE TIMES   September 11/12

The Colin Milburnesque Australian tenor Stuart Skelton gave the traditional rousing rendition of "Rule Britannia" at the Last Night of the Proms wearing cricket whites. His outfit was topped by a Baggy Green cap; he waved a bat vigorously, and sandpapered a ball. Bryn Terfel had set a precedent at a previous Last Night by wearing Welsh rugby kit.

FREE PRESS, MUMBAI   September 22

The Taliban regime in Afghanistan have banned broadcasts of the IPL, apparently because of dancing girls and female spectators.

THE SUNDAY TELEGRAPH   October 1

The Lord's Taverners, the charity bound up with cricket since it began over a drink in the old Lord's Tavern in 1950, have faced mass resignations after they decided to disband their largely autonomous female fundraising arm, the Lady Taverners, founded in 1987, and merge the two groups. The charity said the aim was to promote "diversity and inclusion". Objectors claim the decision was made without consultation, and resented the loss of their own regional presidents and committees. They have set up their own organisation called Phoenix, and will arrange events for causes of their own choosing, rather than simply the Taverners' aim of "giving young people a sporting chance". The Surrey president, Diana Moran, will remain a Taverner, but said: "I miss my county and the branch members and all the fun I have had raising money and awareness."

FOX CRICKET/SDCC.WA.CRICKET.COM.AU   October 10

Sam Harrison of Sorrento–Duncraig CC in Perth hit *eight* sixes in one of the most spectacular overs of all time. Because Nathan Bennett of Kingsley–Woodvale bowled two no-balls, his over cost 50, and Harrison's score soared from 31 to 79. There was one of the 40 overs remaining, but Harrison was not on strike. His partner took a single off the first ball, giving Harrison his chance; he then walloped 46661, to finish on 102 not out from 53. Bennett somewhat redeemed himself by making 28 as an opener in a brave but unavailing reply to 276 for six. Sorrento–Duncraig won the North Suburban Community Association D-Grade game by 82 runs.

NEW ZEALAND HERALD/WAIRARAPA TIMES-AGE Nov 1/3
Cricket became a very long game when Post Office Hotel, Wairarapa, played Manawatu in New Zealand. The pitch was marked as 25yds 5in (22.99m), not the traditional 22yds (20.12m), a fact noticed by the Wairarapa opening bowler after two balls, but – despite regular complaints – the umpires refused to concede the point for 12 overs. Two who had no complaints were the Manawatu batsmen: they serenely put on 50 before the umpires called a halt, and the creases were re-marked. Masterton Council, who are responsible for the ground in Queen Elizabeth Park, apologised; a "visiting groundsman" was blamed, along with the umpires. Wairarapa were further disadvantaged by the energy they wasted, and they lost the two-day game by an innings.

DAILY MAIL November 23
A guest at the Conservative Party's annual winter party (formerly known as the Black and White Ball) paid £35,000 at an auction for the chance to play cricket with the chancellor of the exchequer, Rishi Sunak. Tickets for the event cost more than £1,000 a head.

ESPNCRICINFO December 8
Two Sri Lanka Cricket groundstaff at the Sooriyawewa Stadium in Hambantota have died in what is believed to have been an elephant attack, the board confirmed. They were cycling home after work, and their bodies were found close to the stadium, but several hundred metres apart. Such incidents are not

uncommon in up-country Sri Lanka, and four people were killed in 2020 in the Hambantota area. The problem has increased since the end of the civil war in 2009, as cities have expanded into previously war-ravaged areas, where humans – though not elephants – had feared to tread.

THE SUNDAY TIMES   December 12

Ray Dagg, suddenly famous after being revealed as the 19-year-old constable who shut down the Beatles' last concert, says he was only on the spot because he was a cricketer. In 1969, PC Dagg was sent from the nearest police station, West End Central, to the rooftop in Savile Row where the group's performance had prompted complaints. West End Central was regarded as *the* posting for a young copper; Dagg was a left-arm quick for a police team, where he had become friends with the inspector in charge of placements.

GULF NEWS   December 12

Left-arm spinner Harshit Seth, 15, took six wickets in an over for Dubai Starlets against a touring Hyderabad Hawks Academy team from Pakistan. He took eight wickets as the Hawks were all out for 44. However, in another game between the teams, he went wicketless.

KENT ONLINE   December 15

Upchurch CC in Kent have installed less saleable blue astroturf in their nets after the green variety was ripped up by thieves and wheeled away. They are also installing "impenetrable" metal cages and locks. Total cost: £70,000.

GISBORNE HERALD   December 16

Timoti Weir of OBR Cricket Club in Poverty Bay, New Zealand, has been banned for life after threatening to kill a player-umpire in a match against the High School Old Boys. He had breached regulations twice before.

THE YORKSHIRE POST   December 30

Letters written by W. G. Grace and his older brother Edward in 1896 and 1897 have been discovered in a Bristol farmhouse. Sent by the brothers to Lord Edward Somerset, they mention hunting – and cricket. In one, WG writes: "It was in the hope you would have been in the ground to have seen us running after the Yorkshire hits. We have a poor lot playing but still ought to have made more runs." (Gloucestershire lost to Yorkshire by ten wickets.) The story appeared two days after England went 3–0 down in the Ashes.

This is the 28th year of the Chronicle. Highlights of the first 25 have been published in *WHAT Did You Say Stopped Play?* (John Wisden).

Contributions from readers are always welcome. Items must have been previously published in print or online. Please send weblinks/cuttings to hugh.chevallier@wisdenalmanack.com, or post them to Matthew Engel at Fair Oak, Bacton, Herefordshire HR2 0AT.

INDEX OF TEST MATCHES

Four earlier men's Test series in 2020-21 – New Zealand v West Indies, Australia v India, New Zealand v Pakistan and South Africa v Sri Lanka – appeared in *Wisden 2021*. WTC signifies that a series formed part of the World Test Championship.

MEN'S TEST MATCHES

1536

INDEX OF UNUSUAL OCCURRENCES

INDEX OF ADVERTISEMENTS

PART TITLES

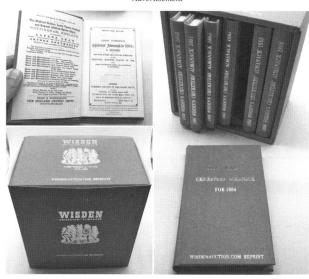